Chronicle of AMERICA

Editorial director: Clifton Daniel

Editor-in-chief: John W. Kirshon

Associate editor: Ralph Berens

Writers/researchers: Tom Anderson, Benton Boggs, Susan Breen, Kevin Delaney, Sean Dolan, Robert Dyer (Midwest), Edward Edelson, Philip Farber, Robert Fleming, James Forsht, John Goolrick, Esther Gottfried, Arthur Holch, Catherine Hulbert, Marjorie Hunter (Washington, D.C.), Pamela Ivinski, Marguerite Jones, Iris Kelso (New Orleans), Charles King (Canada), Jennifer Kingson (Northeast), Nicholas Lee (Northwest), Perry Leopard, Stephen Levi (Alaska), John Mariani, Susan Merrill, Roberta Oster, Edward Queen, Linda Rae, Noel Rae, Angela Read, Karen Rohan, Paige Rosenberg, Marianne Ruuth (Los Angeles), Don Schanche (Southeast), Julie Siler (Chicago), Burt Solomon, Sam Tanenhaus, William Teague (Southwest), James Tuite, Charles Turner (Hawaii), Jiri Weiss (San Francisco), Kenneth Weinstock

Editorial research: Tod Olson (Managing editor), Vincent DeSomma (Editor), Alice J. Vollaro (Index), Kristie Simco

Picture research: Erik Migdail (Editor), Catherine Seignouret, Steven T. Taylor Peter Dervis (The Bettmann Archive)

Historical consultant: Alan Brinkley, Professor of History, The Graduate Center of the City University of New York

Production: Christine Remonte (Manager), Ginny DePaso (Assistant manager), Emmanuelle Berenger, Martine Colliot, Marie Dautet, Maud Escalona, Nadège Guy

Computer systems: Catherine Legrand (Manager), Dominique Klutz (Software), Pascal Wauters de Besterfeld

Created and produced by Jacques Legrand

Acknowledgments

The publishers would like to thank The Granger Collection, New York, for its special contribution to *Chronicle of America*.

We also express our gratitude to the following institutions for their assistance: The Bettmann Archive; The Estate of J.L.G. Ferris; National Gallery of Art; Architect of the Capitol; Smithsonian Institution; International Museum of Photography at George Eastman House; John Carter Brown Library; Library of Congress; National Archives; Pierpont Morgan Library; New York Public Library.

Published in 1995 by
Dorling Kindersley Publishing, Inc.
95 Madison Avenue
New York, NY 10016
10 9 8 7 6 5 4 3 2 1

ISBN 0-7894-0124-X
A catalog record is available from the Library of Congress.

Printed in Belgium by
Brepols

Chronicle *of* America

DORLING KINDERSLEY
LONDON • NEW YORK • STUTTGART • MOSCOW

"As we stand at the edge of the 21st Century, let us begin anew with energy and hope ... and let us work until our work is done"

The American generation molded by a glorious victory in the most destructive war of all time has yielded to a new generation emotionally scarred by the most futile conflict that had ever engaged the energies of a powerful but agonized and divided nation: World War II, the good war, versus Vietnam, the wasted one.

In the national election on November 3, 1992, the 42nd (and third youngest) American President was chosen. Only 46 years old, he was the first President born after the Second World War. Everybody called him Bill until he was sworn in on January 20, 1993, as William Jefferson Clinton. A Democrat, he replaced George Herbert Walker Bush, who only two years before had been the most popular of all Presidents in public opinion polls. Thus ended the 12-year reign of the Republicans in the White House.

What a climax and what a contrast – the unseating of an aristocrat by a product of the new American meritocracy! He had been six times Governor of Arkansas, serving a total of nearly twelve years, and was married to one of the cleverest among the emerging professional women of America, Hillary Rodham Clinton. She was given an office in the executive wing of the White House and put in charge of a committee to plan a national health care system.

What are Bill Clinton's other priorities, problems and prospects? He crisply addressed these questions in a 14-minute speech on the Capitol steps in Washington after taking the oath of office. Among other things, he delivered this message:

Today, a generation raised in the shadows of the Cold War assumes new responsibilities in a world warmed by the sunshine of freedom, but threatened still by ancient hatreds and new plagues ...

We have drifted, and that drifting has eroded our resources, fractured our economy, and shaken our confidence.

Our democracy must be not only the envy of the world but the engine of our own renewal. There is nothing wrong with America that cannot be cured by what is right with America.

To renew America we must be bold ... We must do what America does best: offer more opportunity to all and demand more responsibility from all. It is time to break the bad habit of expecting something for nothing, from our government or from each other.

To renew America, we must revitalize our democracy ... Let us give this capital back to the people to whom it belongs.

To renew America, we must meet challenges abroad as well as at home. There is no longer a clear division between what is foreign and what is domestic ...

Now, we must do the work the season demands ... But no President, no Congress, no government, can undertake this mission alone. My fellow Americans, you, too, must play your part in our renewal.

I challenge a new generation of young Americans to a season of service ... We need each other. And we must care for one another.

And so, my fellow Americans, as we stand at the edge of the 21st Century, let us begin anew with energy and hope, with faith and discipline, and let us work until our work is done.

William J. Clinton

A New World B.C.-1606

Even before the arrival of the first Europeans, the continents we know as the Americas were peopled by immigrants. Human beings were not native to the Western Hemisphere. They had to find it. For humans, at least, the Americas were indeed what the first, bewildered European explorers called them four centuries ago: a New World.

The story of America, therefore, is different from the story of any other part of the world. It is a story less of evolution and development than of discovery and exploration. It is the story of escapes from old civilizations and of the creation of new ones. And it is, beginning with the arrival of Europeans in the late 15th century, the story of a brutal collision between two civilizations, a collision that left one civilization decimated and another precariously enthroned.

Relatively little is known about the first humans who settled in the Americas. The earliest arrivals, it seems likely, were hunters, members of Siberian tribes who crossed the Bering land bridge into what is now Alaska beginning perhaps 30,000 to 40,000 years ago. They were nomadic peoples, almost certainly unaware they were leaving Asia; and they moved restlessly through the new continent, as they had moved through the old, seeking better game and better land. Little by little, over many centuries, they fanned out across the two continents, reaching the southern tip of South America perhaps as early as 8,000 B.C. By the time Christopher Columbus first sighted the New World in 1492, perhaps 12 million people lived in the Americas (all but two million in Mexico, the Caribbean, and the lands to the south). By then, most were no longer nomadic hunters, but sedentary farmers, clustered in hundreds, perhaps thousands of small societies, speaking many languages and dialects.

Among these societies were several great civilizations whose accomplishments rivaled, and in some respects exceeded, those of Europe and Asia. In what is now Peru, the Incas established a vast empire of some six million people with a sophisticated political system and an extensive network of paved roads. In Mexico, the Mayas of the Yucatan created another powerful empire, with a written language, a calendar, a numerical system and advanced agricultural techniques. In the late 13th century, they were surpassed by the Aztecs, who established control over most of central and southern Mexico and who built a great capital city – Tenochtitlan, on the site of modern-day Mexico City – whose 100,000 people made it as large as the greatest cities of Europe.

Despite their many achievements, these civilizations retained characteristics that would encourage the Europeans who first encountered them to dismiss them as backward and primitive. That was in part because of the incomprehension and condescension with which Westerners have traditionally viewed cultures different from their own. But it was also because of particular characteristics of the American societies.

For one thing, the first Americans still lacked many of the technologies that Europeans and Asians considered basic tools of civilization. The Incas, for example, had no written language. And by the time of Columbus, no American society had yet discovered the wheel. Many Americans also embraced religions that were, by European standards, not only exotic but savage. The Aztecs practiced human sacrifice on a massive scale; Tenochtitlan contained pyramids as large as those of ancient Egypt filled with the remains of hundreds of thousands of victims.

And while the greatest civilizations of the Americas were great indeed, most societies in the New World were relatively simple. North of Mexico, in the lands that now constitute the United States and Canada, there was nothing to match the empires of the Aztecs and the Incas – no great cities, no large armies, no advanced political systems. North Americans lived in relatively small and scattered communities. They subsisted on agriculture, hunting and fishing, and they engaged in little trade. In some areas of North America – the Southwest and parts of the Mississippi Valley – there were elaborate irrigation systems and well-established agricultural communities. In other areas, tribes retained something of the nomadic character of their ancestors of many centuries before. They lived as wandering hunters or engaged in forms of agriculture that required them to abandon their settlements and move to new lands every few years.

◄ *"Columbus on the Island of Hispaniola" (1728), colored etching, Spanish.*

The arrival of Europeans in the New World at the end of the 15th century opened a new era in the history of the Americas. For the native peoples, the collision of cultures was cataclysmic – an era of death and destruction perhaps unprecedented in human history. The original Americans did, it is true, gain some things of value from the Europeans: horses, which had been unknown in the New World since the Ice Age; new crops and livestock (sugar, bananas, cattle, pigs and sheep); new technologies. But these modest benefits were insignificant compared to the horrendous costs to the natives of their contact with the strangers from the east.

Even many Europeans were appalled at the callousness and violence with which their countrymen treated the native populations. For from the beginning, most white immigrants considered the natives (or, as they called them, Indians) either obstacles to be destroyed or instruments of their own purposes, to be enslaved and exploited. Hundreds and thousands of natives died in military encounters with greedy, ambitious and at times frightened immigrants. The 16th-century conquistadores of Spain, the most daring and brutal of the invaders, set out deliberately to destroy the civilizations they encountered. They destroyed cities, razed temples, burned records and documents, and murdered Indian leaders. They conquered the Inca and Aztec empires and extinguished the vital aspects of their existence. They disrupted and dispersed other societies, driving the peoples into restless exile or capturing them and putting them to work in the service of the conquerors.

But the military consequences of the European arrival were much less significant than the biological ones. For the explorers and settlers brought with them to America deadly diseases to which Indian societies were tragically vulnerable: influenza, typhus, measles and smallpox. Europeans had by then developed at least some immunity to these infections, but the natives had no such defense. Some groups fared better than others; many of the tribes of North America, who had much later and much less intimate contact with Europeans, escaped the worst epidemics. But in others areas – for example, the Caribbean islands that Columbus first visited – the native populations were virtually extinguished by plagues. Hispaniola, where Columbus established a small colony in the 1490's, saw its civilization decline from perhaps one million to about 500 people in a few decades. In other parts of South and Central America, as much as 95 percent of the native populations died within a century as a result of European diseases. It may have been the greatest demographic catastrophe in the history of mankind.

For the Europeans themselves, the encounter with the New World was also difficult. The first explorations and settlements were perilous enterprises, fatal to most and rewarding to few. Here and there, explorers and settlers managed to establish successful colonies and even flourishing towns. More often, however, the new colonies became places of starvation, violence and death.

By the middle of the 16th century, European settlers had established secure and profitable footholds in the New World. And by the end of the century, the Spanish and Portuguese had together established there one of the largest and richest empires in the history of the world – a realm that extended from Mexico, Florida, and other parts of North America, southward across the Caribbean, and into the farthest reaches of the vast continent to the south.

Reports of riches and opportunities in America, some accurate and some wildly and romantically exaggerated, began to spread throughout Europe. In response to them, men and women from many lands – not only Spain and Portugal, but France, Holland, England and others – began to dream of beginning new lives in the New World. These were people of courage and vision, ambition and greed; people enchanted by the promise of an unknown land or driven by a desire to escape the lands they knew; people willing to leave behind everything familiar, comfortable and predictable and seek a future in a strange and often hostile New World. From their imaginings and their struggles emerged the beginnings of a great new civilization.

Prehistory: Asians cross land bridge to new world

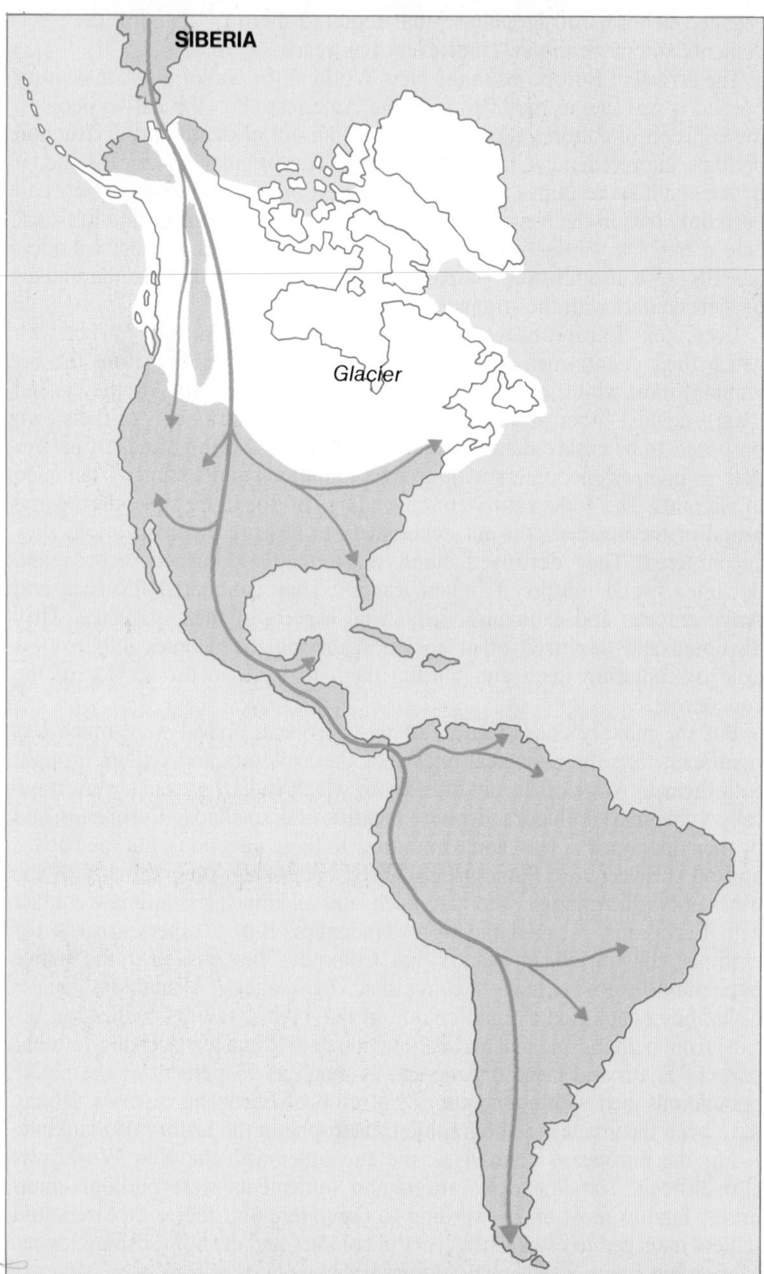

"The Moose Chase" (1888) by George de Forest Brush.

[North America] 40,000-8,000 B.C.

With the arrival of two closely related tribal groups, the Aleuts and the Inuits [Eskimos], the long period of immigration that has brought uncounted numbers of people to new lands from Asia appears to have come to an end.

Unlike their predecessors, who kept moving, the newest arrivals seem to have decided to put down roots close to their point of arrival. The Inuits, though rapidly pushing their way across to the east, are remaining in the northernmost region of the land mass, an area that is less barren than it might seem but capable of sustaining only a very light population. The Aleuts have taken up residence on the extreme northwest coast and in the chain of scattered islands that stretches out toward the Asian continent, sites that are characterized by cold, damp, fog, rocky soil and very few trees.

The fact that these two tribes have chosen such relatively inhospitable regions is an indication that there is no room for them to the south. If that is so, and if they remain where they are, blocking the entrance to the new land mass, then it can be assumed that the long wave of immigration is over.

Although it is difficult to say just when this population shift began, there can be little doubt that it would not have taken place – or at least not on the same scale – had it not been for the extreme cold of the recent glaciation. One effect of this was that vast quantities of water were drawn up from the oceans and deposited as snow on the bitterly cold northern regions of the earth. The snow compacted to form huge long-lasting mountains of ice, up to two miles high; and as the process continued, the level of the oceans fell. Between the two areas a land bridge appeared – not just a narrow isthmus, but a broad stretch of fertile land several hundred miles wide.

When the first settlers came, they could not have known they were leaving Asia. Probably they were just following a migrating herd of caribou or other game. They took their time, living for generations on the low-lying isthmus, moving on only when they had to.

No one can tell for certain when the first settlers to arrive in this new land mass left the isthmus. Some believe it was about 40,000 B.C.; others say 8,000 B.C.

Once in the new land, they kept moving. Some might have gone south along the shoreline, but even with the lower sea levels the coast was still rocky and pitted with steep fjords. More likely, they passed through a narrow gap between the two great ice sheets.

Once past the ice, there was nothing and no one to stop them. Moving in small groups, as hunters do, and bringing their dogs with them, they fanned out across the northern and southern regions.

The newcomers came from various places in Asia, but all were Mongoloids. Their hair was black and straight, their skin a reddish-brown, their eyes dark. They had prominent cheekbones and very little hair on their bodies. They varied greatly in height and build, and in the shape of their noses and heads. They spoke a wide variety of languages. They were the first human beings to live here.

Some of the animals they found in the northern regions would have been familiar: the camel and the horse, which originated here and had migrated in the opposite direction, to the Eurasian land mass. Moose, elephants, caribou and bison had, by contrast, migrated to the east. Other game were the woolly mammoth and the musk ox, the mastodon, giant beaver, giant sloths, bears, saber-toothed tigers and giant armadillos.

To hunt them, the newcomers used spears tipped with stones chiseled to a very sharp point. Tied to a shaft by strips of leather or sinew, the stones could pierce the toughest hide. However, knowing how to make a fire, either from a flintstone or by rubbing two pieces of wood together, was probably the most vital skill the newcomers brought with them.

They also found an abundance of fruit, nuts, berries and seeds, particularly as they moved south toward more temperate areas. Fishing, too, was an important source of food, and many tribes have chosen to settle near rivers or on the coast for this reason.

Receding glacier carves out great lakes

The Chippewa inhabited the Great Lakes region, living off the plentiful supply of fish and creating pictographs of animals like the one above.

[Mid-America] 13,000-9,000 B.C.

Five huge freshwater lakes, covering a total of more than 95,000 square miles, have been formed in the middle section of the northern region of this great new land mass as the northern ice cap continues to melt. Connected to each other by straits, rivers and falls, the lakes drain west to east, then into a river that carries their waters out to sea.

The bottoms of the lakes [Huron, Ontario, Michigan, Erie, Superior] are well below sea level. The sites of the lakes were originally stream valleys. As the vast mountains of ice built up, these valleys were widened and deepened by the pressure above and the action of the glaciers that formed in them. Now that the ice has melted, the earth has risen, but the gouges remain deep enough to contain a vast amount of water, most of it glacial run-off.

4,000 B.C.: Culture of pottery develops

Natives of the Southwest [Mimbres Valley, New Mexico] were master potters.

[North America] 4,000 B.C.

With very few exceptions, most notably the Arctic, the production and use of pottery has spread far and wide thoughout all regions. This is not surprising since pottery makes it much easier to cook, and to store food and water.

The main drawback of pottery is its fragility, which makes it unsuitable for nomadic people. Most pots and bowls are made by building up coils of clay that are scraped smooth before being fired over hot stones. In many areas, the pottery is then elaborately decorated.

The end of an era: Big game extinct

[North America] 8,000 B.C.

For some time now, the megafauna, the "big game" that were such a distinctive feature of this land mass, and whose pursuit may well have lured the first settlers to press onward, have been dwindling in number. Now they seem to have disappeared entirely. The mastodon, the woolly mammoth, the giant ground sloth, camels, horses, tapirs and giant armadillos all appear to have become extinct.

Why? One obvious reason is that as the ice age has been drawing to a close, and the climate becomes warmer and dryer, the kind of food needed by these large animals has been disappearing. But perhaps over-killing by hunters is just as much to blame. The fluted flint points attached to spears have proven themselves lethal weapons. There have also been numerous instances of mass-killings, when whole herds have been stampeded over cliffs or into narrow gullies, there to be butchered.

Plenty of game still remains, but the disappearance of the larger species, along with the increasingly warmer climate, will inevitably bring profound changes in the way people live.

People settle down to cultivate maize

[Mississippi Basin] 1,000 B.C.

A new strain of maize [corn] recently introduced from the south [Mexico] seems destined to have a profound influence on the way of life of people here. Unlike earlier forms of maize, which need at least 200 frost-free days to mature, the new breed, a hardy eight-row variety, can flourish in a growing season of only 120 days.

Maize, which is unknown outside this land mass, is extremely adaptable to different growing conditions; a strain that is resistant to drought has already been introduced into the arid lands in the Southwest [New Mexico]. It is highly nutritious and, when combined with beans, the two plants are sufficient to maintain human life.

Cultivation of maize means that it will no longer be necessary for people to range so far in their search for food, either by hunting or gathering. These pursuits will of course continue, but the amount of wandering may be restricted.

Population will probably also increase, since areas that cultivate the "three sisters" – maize, beans and squash – will be able to sustain many more people than those given over to hunting only.

Spearheads show early evidence of man

To hunt their prey of moose, caribou, bison, mastodon, bear and other big game, people in the new world used spears tipped with such stone material as chert, chalcedony or obsidian. Chiseled to a very sharp point, they were formidable weapons in the hands of skilled hunters. Found with animal bones throughout the land mass, the spearheads indicate human habitation for at least 11,000 years. [Spearheads found in a cave in Clovis, New Mexico, in 1932 appear to have been used from around 9,500 B.C. to 8,500 B.C.]

Northwesterners blessed with wealth

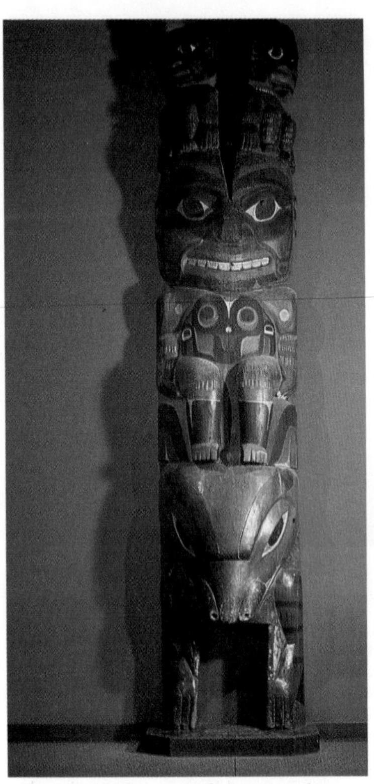
An intricately carved totem pole.

Northwest coast

Thanks to an abundant supply of fish, especially salmon, and a climate that is kept temperate by warming ocean currents and air masses, this is one of the most prosperous and densely populated regions of the new world. Giant cedar trees provide ample supplies of wood for dugout canoes and large houses. Mountain goats supply wool for clothes and blankets.

Life here centers on the village, rather than on the tribe, and settlements are generally large and permanent. Elaborate ceremonialism is becoming another distinctive feature of the region's culture. Intricately carved and brightly colored totem poles are to be seen in an increasing number of the villages, their purpose being either heraldic, historical or mortuary. Also becoming more common is the practice of making public displays of wealth and rank by extravagant giving of gifts, in ceremonies that are called "potlatches."

Few people inhabit vast, open plains

Western plains

Despite their enormous expanse and apparent fertility, the open plains seem able to support only a very small population. Much of the soil is unsuited for simple methods of cultivation, and water is scarce, except near the rivers. Certainly, there is an abundance of game. Bison, pronghorn antelope, white-tailed deer, elk and bear abound. The people who hunt them, however, are handicapped by inadequate means. Since the domestic horse died out several thousand years ago, there are no animals that might be used as mounts, so all hunting must be done on foot. Another problem is that the only projectile in use is the flintstone-tipped spear. Even with the help of a thrower that gives added impetus, this weapon is ill-suited to the pursuit of swift-moving game. Only communal hunts, when several groups combine to stampede a herd over a cliff, are able to produce substantial kills.

A Sioux leader and his family live on the plains.

Pueblo peoples live in cliffside dwellings

Southwest, 1050

In a radical switch of architectural style and location, the Anasazi people living in this largely arid region have moved from their above-ground adobe houses on top of the mesas to an elaborate complex of dwellings built into the overhang of a massive cliff. Access to the new buildings, which number about 500, is extremely difficult, and the site itself seems to have been chosen for defensive purposes.

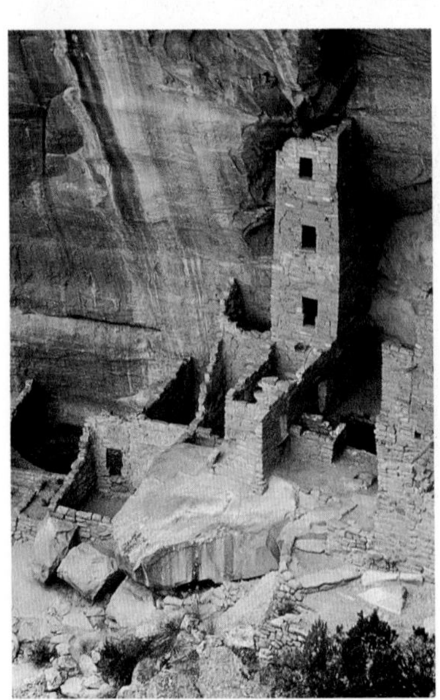
At Mesa Verde, the Anasazi people built huge pueblos, naturally sheltered by towering cliffs.

The new buildings, which are built on several levels and so closely together as to be mostly contiguous, contain numerous underground rooms for ceremonial purposes. Walls are made of cut stone and are extremely thick, as they have to bear a tremendous weight. Doors and windows are small, the lower rooms being reached by a ladder through the ceiling.

All this is a great change for the Anasazi. Originally, most of them lived in pit houses, then shifted to above-ground buildings of stone, or pole and adobe; but these have now been abandoned.

Apart from this recent move, the Anasazi continue to live much as before. They are master weavers, and rely greatly on baskets woven from yucca leaves for storage, carrying and cooking. They have also developed a very fine style of decorative pottery, much of it in their distinctive black-on-white or red-on-white patterns.

Arctic inhabitants survive barren area

Arctic

Despite the hostile conditions of this region, whose hazards include polar bears as well as extreme cold, the Inuits [Eskimos] who have settled here continue to flourish.

Physically adapting to the bitter cold, they have developed solid torsos and short extremities to prevent loss of body heat. They get their food by catching fish and birds, and, when the herds migrate north during the summer months, hunting caribou; but for the most part they live off sea mammals, especially walrus, seal and whale, which also provide them with oil for the lamps that give them heat and light. They have developed sophisticated hunting equipment, including kayaks and harpoons, as well as snow knives for building igloos. They have also become master storytellers, no doubt to while away the long winter nights, and almost all their tools are finely decorated.

Natives of Far West gather their food

Far West

Until relatively recently, this great low-lying basin, which is hemmed in between the central and coastal mountain ranges, was filled with a vast freshwater sea, formed by run-off from the melting ice cap. But as the climate has continued to warm up, the water has evaporated, leaving only brackish lakes, marshlands and deserts.

As a consequence, opportunities for hunting game such as bison are rare, and the people who live here have to depend primarily on a diet of seeds, insects, rabbits, rodents and waterfowl. But even these are often insufficient, and many people migrate annually to the mountain slopes where they gather pine nuts, which can then be stored for use in the winter.

Those who live on the higher plateaus to the north are better off, because there is an abundant supply of salmon in the rivers and game on the grasslands.

Ancient mariners in a new wilderness?

[North America]

Myths and legends abound among the tribes that have settled here. Common among them are intriguing stories of men with pale skins and strange folkways, and of visitors from across the ocean that lies to the east. These legends are not to be dismissed lightly. True, there is no tribe of white-skinned hunters out on the plains, but there do exist, especially along the eastern seaboard, numerous objects whose presence can apparently be explained only by the existence of such visitors. Stone tablets and megaliths, bearing inscriptions that appear to be in a variety of indecipherable languages, can often be found in the woodlands of the Northeast. Who made them? Certainly not the local people. The same is true of the urns, giant stone phalluses, pyramid mounds, inscribed monoliths, calendar circles and temple observatories scattered throughout the land. Are these the work of an earlier race of inhabitants? Or of visitors who came and then departed, or merged with the tribes already here? Probably not until the inscriptions have been deciphered will the answer be known for sure.

Hopewell chiefs build great burial mounds

[Middle America]

In an astonishing display of lavish expenditure on the dead, an entire native culture appears to be devoting the major part of its energies and wealth to the erection of massive burial mounds for its tribal leaders. Measuring over 30 yards at their base, and over 15 yards in height, many of these mounds are surrounded by huge earthwork enclosures that sometimes exceed 500 yards in length.

Inside the mounds, buried along with the dead chiefs, are the most precious objects the Hopewell can obtain. Some, such as the finely made ceramic pots and figurines, or the elaborately-carved pipe bowls for smoking dried leaves, are made locally, and solely for the purpose of being placed in the graves. Others are brought in from distant places, the product of a huge trading network – turtle shells and shark teeth [from the Gulf coast], silver and gold nuggets [from Ontario], copper for axes, beads and breastplates [from Michigan], sheets of mica for cutouts of serpents, bird talons and human hands [from Appalachia]. The Hopewell culture, [which is centered in the Scioto River Valley], has spread across the plains, and well into the woodlands of the East.

The Serpent Mound, built by the Hopewell, snakes its way for 1,330 feet through the woods [of Ohio]. It is the most extensive of the region's effigy mounds.

Toolmakers abound in Northeast woods

Northeast woodlands

A distinct culture has been developing among the tribes that have settled in this region of lakes, rivers and deciduous woods. One of its features is a steady, if rather slow, development in the quality and variety of the tools and implements that are being produced. Some of these, such as copper awls and needles, and polished stone forms, are for burial purposes, but most of them are of a functional nature, for this is an area that produces few surpluses.

Since the people here live mostly by hunting, they have concentrated their skills on their weapons. Perforators, knives, scrapers and spearheads made of chipped flint are now often ground and polished, as are plummets and axes.

In areas near the lakes where there is an abundance of copper, this metal has been employed for making implements and tools, while to the east slate has been widely used for knives and projectile points. Trade between the two areas has resulted in an interchange of these products.

Fishing is also an important part of the economy of this region, and there have been significant developments in making nets, fishhooks and sinkers.

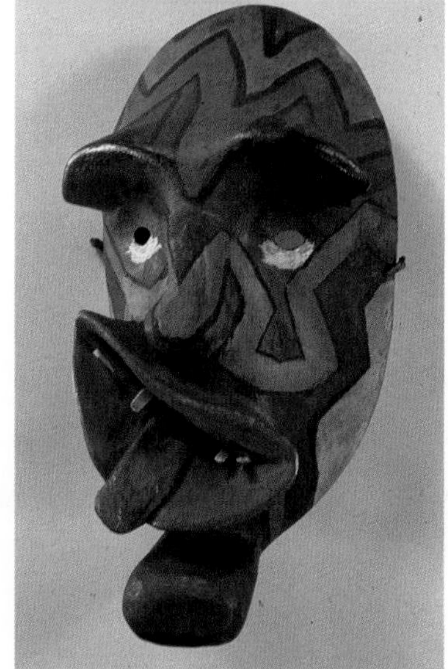

Ritual Iroquois "false face" mask.

Small game sustains Southeast natives

Southeast

A graphic example of how settlers can not merely survive, but live well, by exploiting every possible source of food that is available, is provided by the Muskogean-speaking tribes of this area.

In addition to hunting deer and bear, they go after smaller game such as raccoons, rabbits and squirrels. They catch and devour reptiles, snails and turkeys, use nets to catch fish, and collect oysters, clams and freshwater mussels.

Gathering is an important method of providing food. Hickory nuts, pecans, plums and other fruits and nuts are collected routinely, as are acorns and tubers. Sunflower, goosefoot, knotweed and other plants are also sought, the seeds being stored in dry underground pits in the villages. And as the people here join the general trend to more settled forms of horticulture, there have been regular harvests of maize, pumpkins, beans, millet and, of course, dried leaves for smoking.

The result of all this activity is a culture that, while certainly not rich, has managed to achieve and maintain a fair level of prosperity. The size of the population has been growing steadily, and there has even been enough of a surplus to afford some imports – mica from the mountains to the north, for one. A substantial number of mounds and earthworks have also been built.

Carved wooden feline figurines of the Calusa, one of the three main tribes of the Southeastern region.

▷

Leif Eriksson returns from Vinland

"Leif Eriksson Discovers America, A.D. 1,000" (1936) by Per Krohg.

Sod huts at L'Anse aux Meadows, Newfoundland, are Leif's or Karlsefni's.

Greenland, 1004

Leif Eriksson, gone a year from his coastal home, is back with tales of a new land he calls Vinland.

Like his father, Erik the Red, a Norwegian who happened upon Greenland in 980 while exiled from Iceland, Leif is easily seduced by the unknown. Rarely unprepared, however, he obtained both ship and course from Bjarni Herjulfsson, a Norwegian trader who made regular winter trips to see his father in Iceland. Herjulfsson arrived in 985 to find his father gone to Greenland. Driven by filial longing, Bjarni set out again. Blown off course to the southwest, he sighted three new lands before finally joining his father. Not for 18 years, when forest land began to dwindle, did anyone set out to solve Bjarni's mystery.

Heading southwest, Leif "found first the land that Bjarni had found last." He named it Helluland, or Land of Flat Rocks. Next, he saw a flat and wooded shore, naming it Markland, or Forestland. Pressing on to the southwest, he sailed between an island and a "cape jutting out to the north." Turning inland into a shallow river, Leif and his crew decided to winter near a lake at the river's source. Salmon were in abundance; cattle fed on grass unharmed by frost, and on the shortest day of the year, the sun was visible at breakfast and at dinner. Feasting on grapes, Leif called the land Vinland, or Wineland.

Leif Christianizes all except father

Greenland, 1001

When Erik the Red returned to Iceland in 984 to tell of the new land he found while exiled for murder, he successfully converted quite a few farmers into adventurers, artfully referring to the icy wasteland as "Greenland." Almost two decades later, the wasteland colonized, Erik's son is hard at work teaching the farmers about Jesus Christ.

Recently back from Norway a rather reluctant missionary, Leif Eriksson had told King Olaf Tryggvasson that Greenlanders would be difficult converts. He was no doubt thinking of his father. Leif captivated old Erik with tales of sexual conquest in exotic Atlantic islands, but Jesus is a topic the father could not stand. Erik is a rugged, devout man, who prides himself on a red beard like that of Thor, god of thunder. To Erik, Jesus is weak and effeminate, and emasculates those who pray to him.

Thor's defender, however, is outnumbered. Greenlanders are drawn to the new faith. Of course, the Norwegian King has threatened to halt trading voyages to heathen lands. But Leif deserves credit as well. His brothers, Thorvald and Thorstein, converted. And Erik's wife, Thjodhild, has built a church, though "not too near the house." Erik is as stubborn as ever, and rumor has it that he is weathering a sexual embargo imposed by his wife.

Europe's plunderers: raiders, traders

"Never before did I see men with more perfect bodies, tall as date palms, with coppery fair hair," said one Arab who met men from the Northern lands on a trading voyage. Setting out from Denmark in boats with fearsome dragon heads affixed to their bows, the Vikings made their presence felt from the Dnieper River in the east to new places across the Atlantic.

Countless raiding voyages took place between 800 and 1050. Norsemen controlled much of the British Isles from 886 to 954. By 900, they had settled Iceland, by 986, Greenland and by 1013, Vinland. They failed to take Paris in 986, but a settlement on the Seine evolved into the Duchy of Normandy. Dragon ships attacked Lisbon in 844 and sailed to North Africa. In the east, Norse Varangian tribes, or Rus, went to the Dnieper Valley in the ninth century.

Aggression leads to a thriving trade and plunder. Vikings grow up in a cult of strength that finds boys trying to best each other in athletics, and pre-teens killing serfs to display their military prowess. Strong women rule the home, while men keep concubines and feud with other clans.

First European child is born in new world

Greenland, 1015

The latest expedition to Vinland, the first attempt at permanent settlement there, has returned with the new land's first human export, a child called Snorro. The voyage began four years ago, at the urging of Gudrid, widow of one of Erik the Red's sons. In the ships of her new husband, Thorfinn Karlsefni, a merchant from Iceland, 160 settlers set off with only a vague course to start a new life in Leif's cabins.

Their first landfall they called Straumfjord. It was there that Snorro was born. But grapes and frost-free pastures were not to be found. In spring, they left to settle at Hop [Tidal Lake], where they began to trade with the natives, or Skraelings (Screechers). Peace was short-lived. During one visit, a bull broke loose, and in the chaos, a settler killed one of the Skraelings. Soon they returned, "swarthy men" with "large eyes and broad cheekbones." Driven off, the settlers were saved only by Freydis, Erik the Red's illegitimate daughter. At the rear, she turned, "pulled her breast from under her dress and slapped her sword on it," thus scaring off the natives.

Sailing north, the settlers wintered at Straumfjord. But food was scarce and the men began making life miserable for their wives. Rife with dissension, the crew headed home. Snorro was only 3 years old.

Norse brothers venture forth and die

"Norsemen on the Coast of America," a 19th-century engraving.

Greenland, 1008

Four years after Leif Eriksson's pioneer voyage to Vinland, both of his brothers have been defeated in the search for his promised land to the southwest. A few months after Leif returned, his father, Erik the Red, discoverer of Greenland, died, leaving Thorstein, the eldest son, to head the farm and Thorvald, next in line, to explore the new frontier.

Wintering at Leif's cabins, Thorvald's crew found the most striking discovery yet, a structure for grain storage built by human hands. In spring, wary with the knowledge that they were not alone, Thorvald led his men up the coast to a tree-laden promontory on which he decided to make his home. On the beach, they stumbled across nine natives, letting only one escape the ax. The weary crew then slept, only to be awakened by natives attacking from skin boats. Before retreating, the dark men left Thorvald dead with an arrow under his arm.

Upon the crew's return, Erik's youngest son was distressed to find his brother had been buried in Vinland. Though named for Thor, god of thunder, Thorstein was now a Christian, and wanted a holy resting place for Erik. With his wife, Gudrid, he left in the spring on an ill-fated voyage. "All summer long they were storm driven over the sea and they had no notion of where they were going." It was all they could do to get back to Greenland by winter. Thorstein died when disease broke out among the crew.

Marco Polo journeys overland to Orient

Shang-tu, China, Summer 1275

Traveling over blistering deserts and treacherous mountain passes, and among many different peoples, the Venetian explorer Marco Polo has reached the Far East. The Emperor Kublai Khan greeted Marco, his father, Niccolo, and his uncle Maffeo at the summer capital of the Mongol Empire. The Polos presented holy oils and papal letters to the Chinese leader.

The arduous trip was a return journey for the elder Polos, who had established relations with Kublai Khan in 1265 when they were the first Europeans to visit China. The Khan, a Confucian scholar, became intrigued with his guests. As the brothers left China for Venice, he asked that they act as his ambassadors to the Pope and requested the Vatican to dispatch 100 intelligent Europeans to Mongolia so he might learn about the Christian religion. Upon their return to Italy, Niccolo and Maffeo found that Pope Clement IV had died. They waited two years for a successor to be selected. Unable to wait any longer, they departed for the Orient in 1271 without the 100 men, but with young Marco. The teenager has been documenting the trip, as well as courting many princesses along the way.

Sailing south on the Mediterranean, the travelers stopped in Acre, Palestine. There, a papal legate gave them letters for the Great Khan and the expedition continued overland to China. Now, the Polos are with their gracious host. Europe awaits their return, hoping the cultural chasm between East and West may soon be bridged.

Marco Polo and party present the Pope's letters at the court of Kublai Khan.

Leif's sister axes all women on trip

Greenland, 1015

Greenland is abuzz with a scandalous tale of murder in Vinland. Threatening torture, Leif Eriksson has extracted indictments of his sister Freydis from three adventurers returning from her voyage to the new land. Gone only a winter, she had reappeared laden with cargo, yet unencumbered by the two Icelandic brothers who were her partners on the trip. Freydis, it appears, in a fit of greed, goaded her husband into murdering the brothers and their men. And when chivalry inhibited her soldiers, Freydis axed the five remaining women herself.

Interest of Vikings in exploring wanes

Norway, 1354

Reports from Iceland that Norsemen have deserted their homes in western Greenland have prompted Paul Knutsson to set out in search of the missing settlers. The climate there had been getting colder for a century, and many believe they joined with the nomadic natives of the icy northern lands to the west. Hopes of settling Vinland appear to have been abandoned, although Greenlanders have made regular trips west to hunt black bears. Erik Gnupsson, an Icelandic bishop traveling in 1121, is perhaps the last Norseman to have visited Vinland.

Ancient Sagas support Norse adventures

The Vikings left little imprint on America, offering to posterity their own oral history as the primary evidence of early settlement in the new world. Though time eroded physical remains, Vinland tales endured around the frontier fires of Greenland and Iceland. And when settlers attained parchment and quill pens, they recorded the lore. In the mid-1600's, a proud Icelandic farmer on Flatey [Flat Island] showed an old book to a visiting bishop, who sent it to the royal library in Copenhagen. Its section on Vinland deals with the voyages of Erik and his brothers, and probably comes from stories told in Greenland. Another manuscript, apparently originating in Iceland in the early 1300's, focuses on the voyages of Thorfinn Karlsefni. Not until 1837 were the Sagas translated and published, alerting thousands to the possibility that America had been an outpost for Norsemen. There may be traces of the Vikings [in Rhode Island, Maine and Minnesota], but the only indisputable physical evidence lies in Newfoundland, at L'Anse aux Meadows. Buried on a grassy coastal terrace is a tiny array of sod huts, big enough for 150 Vikings.

Portuguese settle islands in Atlantic

Lisbon, 1440

When Diego de Senill laughed off horror stories of dangerous waters in 1427 and sailed to discover the Azores Islands, he found no traces of humans. Under orders from the crown, colonists are starting to settle a small series of islands situated 800 miles east of Portugal. Their fertile soil promises to bring agricultural riches to the King's empire. It is felt that conditions may be suitable for growing sugar. The nearby Madeira Islands, discovered by Prince Henry's sailors in 1418 when a storm forced them off course, have already been colonized. Henry sent some grapes from Crete with the Madeira settlers; since then, vineyards have been cultivated. Some believe that the islands are going to prove strategic for future explorations.

Henry dies, a prince among navigators

Prince Henry the Navigator.

Portugal, Nov. 13, 1460

Under the leadership of Prince Henry, Portugal has established itself as the great power in sea navigation. The man who declined the crown of Portugal to study maps and the stars and to teach others the ways of the sea has died. While never embarking on a maritime exploration of his own, Prince Henry sponsored expeditions that resulted in the discovery of many new lands. He also developed the advanced-style caravel, improved the science of cartography and enhanced sea trade, including commerce beyond Morocco.

In 1418, he began to promote ocean voyages along the coast of Africa. Under his auspices, explorers discovered the Madeira and Azores Islands. Perhaps his biggest achievement came in 1434 when he persuaded Gil Eanes to defy tales of evil sea creatures and sail beyond the Cape of Bojador. This inspired Portugal's sailors to venture further down the coast to Cape Verde and Sierra Leone, returning with gold and slaves. The one dream Prince Henry left unrealized is the discovery of a sea route to India.

Columbus presents his case to Isabella

Cordoba, Spain, May 1, 1486

Christopher Columbus, intent on discovering a western route to the Indies, finally received the opportunity today to unveil his ambitious plan to Spain's Queen Isabella. During an audience at the Alcazar, Columbus used all his charm and enthusiasm in an attempt to persuade the Spanish monarch to sponsor the expedition. She seemed impressed by his spirit and determination but rejected the idea for the time being. All is not lost, however, because Isabella established a special commission under the direction of a trusted adviser to study Columbus's project further.

The arrangement of today's meeting was something of a coup for the 35-year-old seaman from Genoa, Italy. He is certain that a westerly route across the Atlantic leads to the land of the spices, but he has many detractors who say he is little more than a dreamer. Two years ago, the King of Portugal rejected Columbus's plea to sponsor the voyage, and a royal commission branded the idea as "vain, simply founded on imagination." In despair, Columbus obtained passage on a small ship from Portugal to Spain with his son, Diego. Short of funds, they were forced to walk to a Franciscan priory, where the former sea captain persuaded the monks to care for his son while he set off to appeal to the Queen. During the past few months, it has been rumored that the charming seaman has been living in Cordoba with a peasant girl (→Aug. 3, 1492).

Sebastiano del Piombo's Columbus.

Printing press promises broad changes

Mainz, Germany, 1455

After long years of experiment, Johannes Gutenberg, a craftsman and inventor, has succeeded in developing a printing press that uses movable type. The device allows different manuscripts to be reproduced with the same materials, simply by rearrangement of the type.

Europeans find themselves confronted for the first time with the realistic prospect of spreading the fruits of civilization far and wide. Already, those close to the seat of power speak of circulating laws farther afield and with greater accuracy than ever before. Controlling the content of printed material, however, may prove to be an intractable problem. Even as paupers may soon be reading Petrarch and Chaucer, so too may they expose themselves to more subversive ideas. As yet there is no problem: The first book to come off Gutenberg's press is a Bible.

Mainz, Duchy of Franconia, 1455. *The first book with mechanical, movable type to come off Johannes Gutenberg's press is The Holy Bible.*

Spanish monarchs display new power

Madrid, 1491

Following the marriage of Ferdinand and Isabella in 1469, the two realms of Spain were united under a centralized government. This move away from medieval disunity was the beginning of the rapidly expanding empire that now holds power in the western Mediterranean. From this seat of strength, Ferdinand and Isabella have begun a program of exploration destined to give their country a dominant position in European affairs.

Part of this program has involved formation of a special commission led by Hernando de Talavera to examine a proposal made by the Italian explorer Christopher Columbus concerning an expedition to find a route across the Atlantic Ocean to the riches of the Indies. The commission has spent several years in deliberation, and in the meantime, Columbus has been receiving a retaining fee of 12,000 maravedis per year, which is standard payment for a seaman. Should this expedition be approved, it could serve to further expand the sea power of Spain, which has already consolidated the Balearic Islands, Sardinia, Naples, Corsica and Sicily.

Monsters that lurk at the world's edge

Columbus sailing through uncharted waters, surrounded by unknown perils, without map or previous experience; the ocean appears a foreboding obstacle.

Portugal, 1491

The world beyond the ocean seas offers both riches and peril to those bold enough to board a ship and sail off into the unknown. Some say that the coast of Africa is a "green sea of darkness" full of monsters. At the Equator, men allegedly turn black for the rest of their lives. And in the frozen wastelands to the north, Judas is supposedly awaiting men at the mouth of hell.

But others are lured by tales of wealth in distant Edens to overlook the danger. St. Brendan, an Irish monk of the sixth century who endured a seven-year voyage, may have found a mysterious, sweetly perfumed Promised Land of the Saints, according to the widely read *Navigato.* In Antilia, land of the Seven Cities, which supposedly lies west of the Azores, grains of gold are said to mix with sand on soft beaches. And tales of gold-roofed houses and other luxuries can still be heard two centuries after Marco Polo's adventures in Asia.

According to Paolo Toscanelli, Pierre d'Ailly's *Imago Mundi* and even Aristotle, Asia is not far west. D'Ailly's most optimistic figures place Japan about 3,500 miles off the coast of Portugal.

Dias discovers the Cape of Good Hope

Lisbon, May 1488

Sailing to the bottom of the African continent, the Portuguese explorer Bartolomeu Dias has discovered and named the Cape of Good Hope. Going where no man went before, Dias verified that there is a sea route to India via the tip of Africa. The commercial potential has excited the sailing community.

On assignment from King John II, Dias set sail on the Sao Cristovao from here last August. The King spared no expense for this mission, commissioning some of Portugal's finest sailors to accompany Dias, including Joao Infante on the San Pantaleao.

Heavy storms hit the fleet in January, pushing it away from the African coast, into unknown regions of the South Atlantic. But Dias guided the boats north and east. On February 3, he sighted land and realized it was the east coast of the continent, that the flotilla had unwittingly rounded the cape. Dias then turned back, satisfied the expedition had realized a dream of the late navigator Prince Henry: to find a Europe-Asia seaway. On the return voyage, he went ashore and erected a stone pillar, claiming the land for Portugal (→ May 1500).

Tribes and languages by the hundreds

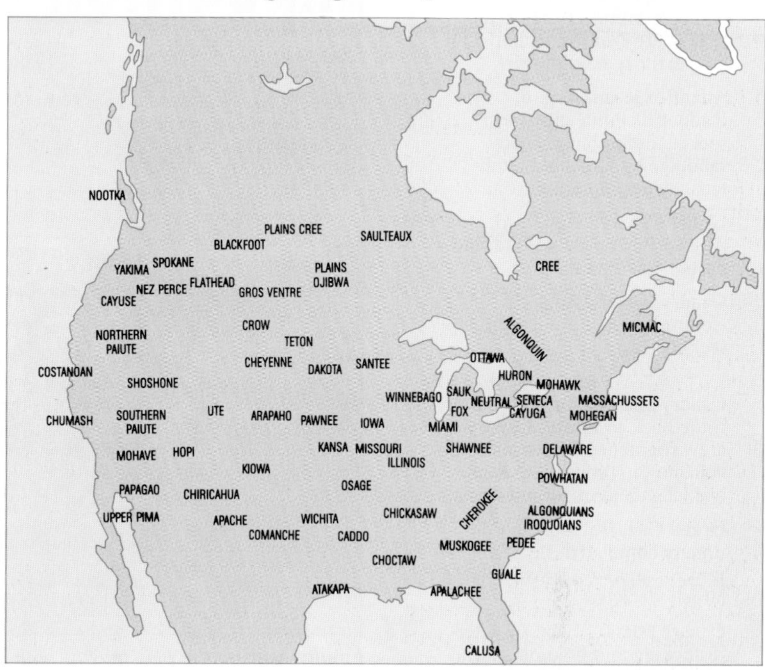

A portrait of ethnological diversity: There are hundreds of tribal groups speaking hundreds of languages in the northern part of the New World.

[North America] 1490

The new world is a crazy quilt of Indian tribes and languages. Because the people who came over from Asia have kept no records, and have no written languages, it is almost impossible to guess at their population and linguistic diversity.

It is reasonable to suppose, however, that there are about 240 tribal entities and 300 languages. The native population is probably close to 1,500,000, with about 850,000 people living in the deep forests, plains and swamps of the central part of the northern region.

Although there is tremendous diversity in their languages, customs and cultures, they have much in common physically. Their hair is usually straight, long and black, their skin reddish brown, their eyes dark and their body hair scant. The inhabitants commonly have high, prominent cheekbones and proportionately large faces.

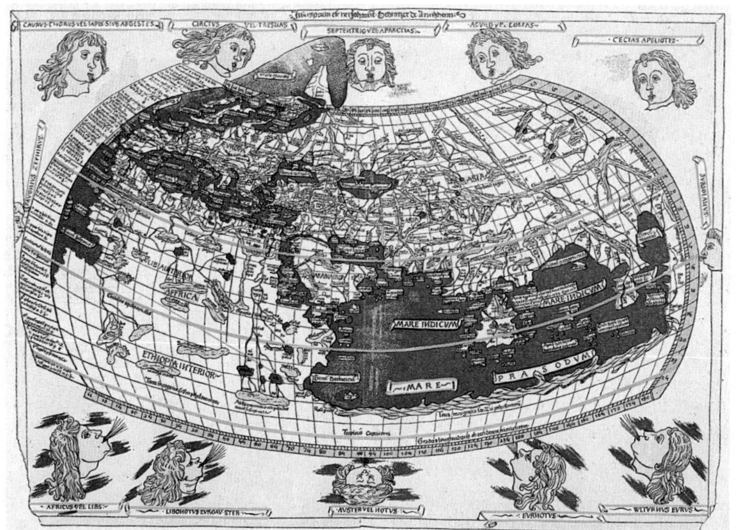

Europe, 1482. *The world according to Ptolemy: The great Greek astronomer, propounder of geocentricity, drew on the work of Hipparchus, Strabo and Marinus of Tyre to create his world map. Little has been done to elaborate on his version of the globe since the second century A.D.*

1492

Spain, Apr. 30. Columbus is named admiral of the ocean sea, viceroy and governor of any territory he discovers.

Atlantic Ocean, Aug. 6. Rudder of Pinta slips from socket; Columbus suspects sabotage by Cristobal Quintero, owner of caravel.

Grand Canary, Aug. 9. Martin Alonso Pinzon puts Pinta into harbor for repairs.

Canary Islands, Aug. 12. Columbus reaches Gomera, seeking ship to replace the damaged Pinta.

Canary Islands, Aug. 24. En route back to Grand Canary, crew frightened by eruption of volcano on Tenerife; Columbus tells them of Mount Etna.

Grand Canary, Aug. 31. All repairs completed, fleet sails for Gomera with provisions largely depleted.

Canary Islands, Sept. 6. After restocking and holding special service of thanksgiving on Gomera, Columbus and crew sail westward.

Atlantic Ocean, Sept. 8. Fleet loses sight of land; to buoy hopes of crew, Columbus deliberately underestimates distance from Spain.

Atlantic, Sept. 15. Meteorite drops 15 miles from fleet, seen as bad omen by crew.

Atlantic, Sept. 18. Martin Alonso insists he sighted land to north; Columbus rejects appeals for change of course.

Atlantic, Oct. 3. Columbus calculates distance traveled at 2,379 miles.

Atlantic, Oct. 11. Crew of Pinta spots reeds, plants, stick that seems carved by man; Columbus sights light to west.

Guanahani, Oct. 12. Columbus goes ashore, unfurling royal banner and naming island San Salvador; natives, naked and friendly, bring gifts.

San Salvador, Oct. 14. Finding gold nose rings among natives, Columbus sails south in search of wealthy kingdom.

Caribbean Sea, Oct. 21. Columbus anchors off island he calls Isabella, killing a serpent with lances and collecting aloe.

Caribbean, Oct. 28. Columbus arrives in Cuba, surmising that it is Japan.

Caribbean, Dec. 6. After exploring islands in search of gold, Columbus lands on island similar to Castile, naming it Hispaniola.

Expedition leaves Spain, sails west

Finally bearing the blessings of both church and state, Christopher Columbus and his crew prepare to set sail on their long-awaited journey to the Indies.

Palos, Spain, Aug. 3, 1492

As dawn broke over this community today and the chant of Franciscan monks rose from a nearby priory, 40-year-old Christopher Columbus set sail on his long-awaited journey. He is in command of three small ships as he heads west into uncharted waters, but he is convinced that God is with him and that he will bring glory and riches back to Spain. The rising tide swept the expedition down the Rio Tinto toward the Atlantic and the unknown. Before leaving, Columbus said he has learned from the mistakes of previous explorers. At all costs, he will avoid the treacherous winds and high seas of the North Atlantic by setting his course south toward the Canary Islands and then west to the Indies.

Columbus captains the largest of the ships, the 85-foot Santa Maria. Its sides are brightly painted and the flag of Queen Isabella flies majestically over the main deck. The 69-foot Pinta is under the command of Martin Alonso Pinzon, a member of one of the top maritime families in Palos. The smallest of the caravels is named Santa Clara after the saint, but the crew has nicknamed it the Nina. Almost all of the crew members have been recruited in Palos, and most of them are Spaniards. Three of the sailors were set free from a prison, where they had been serving time for helping a murderer escape.

This proud and promising expedition seemed doomed until recently. The special commission established by Queen Isabella reported that the Columbus plan seemed "uncertain and impossible to any educated person." The Queen herself was more receptive, but her attention has been distracted until recently by the war with the Moors. She found time to meet Columbus again in January, but by this time he had increased his demands. He wanted the title of admiral as well as a 10 percent share of any trade resulting from the explorations for himself and his heirs. The Queen rejected the demands at first but relented when an adviser persuaded her that a title for Columbus would cost her nothing and that 10 percent of nothing would not put a dent in the royal coffers either.

Dejected Columbus finally sights land

October 12, 1492. *Columbus and the crew of the Santa Maria, though alerted to the sighting of land by the Pinta's cannon shot at 2 in the morning, find themselves overwhelmed by their first glimpse of land.*

Santa Maria crew threatens mutiny

Atlantic Ocean, Oct. 10, 1492

The crew of the Santa Maria, desperate and fearful, acted against their captain today, and Columbus's long journey of hope and adventure was nearly swamped by mutiny. Columbus reckons he has already sailed over 2,400 miles, but many of his men fear they are in the midst of a journey to nowhere. They complain of rancid water and boring food. The captain of the Pinta has been arguing for several days that they should alter course, but Columbus refused to relent until a flock of birds flew by to the southwest. The sighting of the birds eased tensions on board, and in his log Columbus commented that he "cheered the men as best he could."

Columbus, seeking India, lands on distant shore

San Salvador, Oct. 12, 1492

Surviving five weeks of uncertainty and false hopes, Admiral Christopher Columbus and his restless crew have finally reached land. Hopeful that he has found the coveted western passage to the Indies, the admiral knelt and took possession of the area for Ferdinand and Isabella, King and Queen of Spain. Giving thanks to the Lord for a safe passage, he named the island San Salvador [Bahamas].

Soon after the midday landfall, the island's natives began to appear on the beach, completely naked. To Columbus they seem to be a "very well-built people, with handsome bodies and very fine faces, though their appearance is marred somewhat by very broad heads and foreheads." Much to the relief of the crew, they seem to be a peaceable lot, ignorant of weaponry save for small wooden spears. One even cut himself when examining the admiral's sword at the wrong end.

Numerous gifts have been exchanged. The natives offer such trifles as parrots, balls of cotton thread and dried leaves, which, as much as can be surmised, they like to ignite in order to inhale the fumes. For now, the crew is under orders to treat the people with care. Says Columbus: "I know that they are a people who can be made free and converted to our Holy Faith more by love than by force."

Peace is welcomed by the sailors, who have weathered a journey fraught with disillusionment. From the moment they watched Hierro, the westernmost island of the Canaries, recede over the horizon on September 9, their hopes rose with every possible sign of land. In the second week, a swamp of sargasso weeds threatened to slow the caravels; many insisted it meant land lay nearby. Soon, every flock of birds was hailed as a harbinger of the journey's end.

By October 6, the little fleet had covered more than the 2,000 nautical miles estimated from Gomera in the Canaries to Japan. Only the admiral's deliberately shortened estimates of the distance traveled kept the crew at bay, until 2 a.m. on Friday, October 12 – none too soon – the cry came from the Pinta, "Tierra, tierra."

Columbus lands at San Salvador, taking "possession ... by public proclamation and with unfurled banners."

Weary crew settles at hospitable harbor

Hispaniola, Dec. 27, 1492

Admiral Christopher Columbus has lost his ship, but he believes his destiny is guided by God, and he is convinced he has finally found the Indies. After more than two months, sailing from island to island, the admiral has found a hospitable harbor and ordered his men to build fortifications. He calls the island La Isla Espanola [Hispaniola], and the fort is to be named Navidad, or Town of the Nativity, in honor of Christmas Day, when the Santa Maria was shattered on a reef. Planks from the battered ship will be used to build the fort.

The islanders are gentle, showing respect for the sailors and hoping they will win defenders against enemies. The crew, in turn, expects to find caches of gold hidden in the jungle. Columbus and his men marvel at the exotic lives of the natives. They grow yellow vegetables that sprout in kernels on hard stalks; and from the ground they harvest a kind of orange potato. Some natives suck smoke from burning sticks they call tobacos. Columbus writes of "the fair and sweet smell of flowers or trees from this land, the sweetest in the world." The natives, he says, "invite you to share anything that they possess and show as much love as if their hearts went with it." They will, the admiral thinks, make diligent laborers.

Asia has not been found, but Columbus refuses to give up hope. On the island of Colba [Cuba], natives maintained there was gold at an inland city called Cubanacan. Thinking they were referring to Kublai Khan of China, Columbus sent a search party into the jungle. Instead of an imperial city, there was a tiny group of thatched huts. Despite the disappointments, he still believes he can convince Queen Isabella he has found a new route to the Indies (→March 15, 1493).

"Columbus Bearing Christ to the New World" (1500), from a world map by Juan de la Cosa. A western route to Asia, if more than a fantasy, would allow Christians to bypass Muslim traders in exploiting the riches of the East, and open up new roads to missionaries seeking to combat Islam's broad expansion since the eighth century.

1493 (1493-1499)

Rome, May 4, 1493. Pope Alexander VI issues Inter Caetera II, granting to Spain all lands west of line running 100 leagues west of the Cape Verde Islands (→ June 7, 1494).

Cadiz, Spain, Sept. 9, 1493. Christopher Columbus, with 17 ships and 1,200 men, sails on second voyage (→ Nov. 4).

Caribbean, Nov. 4, 1493. Columbus reaches Leeward Islands and Puerto Rico (→ Jan. 2, 1494).

Hispaniola, Jan. 2, 1494. Columbus founds Isabella, second colony (→ May 5).

Hispaniola, 1495. Columbus imposes gold tax on natives 14 years of age and older (→ March 10, 1496).

Hispaniola, March 10, 1496. After establishing city of Santo Domingo, Columbus departs for Spain, leaving brother in command (→ June 11).

England, March 5, 1497. John Cabot gets patent from King Henry VII to gain land for England; crown to get 20 percent of profits in return for trade monopoly (→ June 24).

North Atlantic, June 24, 1497. Cabot sights land [near Cape Breton], claiming it and land to south [Maine] for King Henry (→ May 1498).

Africa, Nov. 22, 1497. Vasco da Gama rounds Cape of Good Hope on voyage from Lisbon to India (→ May 23, 1498).

Bristol, England, May 1498. Cabot leaves on second voyage, seeking Japan and Spice Islands via Newfoundland (→ July 1498).

India, May 23, 1498. Da Gama reaches Calicut, opening sea route to India (→ Sept. 9, 1499).

Madeira, Spain, June 7, 1498. Columbus leaves for Santo Domingo (→ Aug. 1).

South Atlantic, Aug. 1, 1498. Columbus is first European to sight mainland coast, naming land Ile Sancta (→ 31).

Santo Domingo, Aug. 31, 1498. Columbus arrives, hoping to recover from arthritis; he finds island in disarray (→ Sept. 1499).

South Atlantic, June 27, 1499. Amerigo Vespucci, on Spanish-financed trip, sights coast south of Cape Cassipore (→ May 13, 1501).

DEATH

1499. John Cabot (Giovanni Caboto), Italian explorer, at sea (*1450).

Admiral reports to the court: No monsters

Columbus and Indians fascinate Spain's King Ferdinand and Queen Isabella.

Barcelona, Apr. 20, 1493

Amidst shouts, applause and banners waving in the air, Christopher Columbus entered the court of King Ferdinand and Queen Isabella today, hiding neither his joy nor his pride. For more than an hour, the sovereigns besieged the Italian-born seaman with questions.

Two months ago, on February 15, taking shelter in the Azores, he reviewed his report about the residents of the Indies, whom he calls "Indians." "In their islands," he wrote, "I have found no monstrosities. Although they are well-built people of handsome stature, they are wonderfully timorous. They believe very firmly that I, with these ships and people, came from the sky – and this does not result from their being ignorant, for they are of a very keen intelligence."

During most of the crossing, the crews of the Pinta and Nina faced gale winds that Columbus said "seemed to raise the ship into the air." After the men landed in the Azores, they faced new troubles. The Portuguese captain of the island settlement was certain they were returning from a raiding party in West Africa. He threw them into jail and did not release them until he realized their story of adventure was too incredible not to be true.

Pope allows Spain lands west of islands

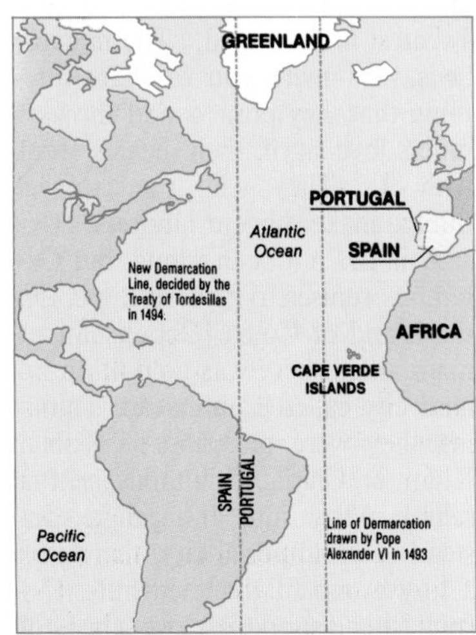

The Treaty of Tordesillas between Spain and Portugal gives the latter nation only a small edge of new land.

Rome, June 7, 1494

In April of 1493, a Latin version of a letter by Christopher Columbus describing his voyage to the west was published in Rome for the benefit of Pope Alexander VI. Acting in accord with European public law, the Spanish sovereigns needed to have the Pope declare that the discoveries of Columbus are outside the area previously given to Portugal. On May 4, 1493, the Pope drew a line of demarcation 100 leagues (about 250 miles) west of the Azores, giving all undiscovered lands west of that line to Spain. Now, after a protest from Portugal, Spain has agreed to move the line to a position 370 leagues west of the Cape Verde Islands.

"Indians" brought over for first time

Palos, Spain, March 15, 1493

More than seven months after his voyage began, Christopher Columbus has returned to the Spanish port where his expedition began. He is eager to tell his story, and he believes that gold artifacts he has brought back are proof that he reached the Indies. He is also accompanied by living proof: a group of natives, whom in a letter to Lord Raphael Sanchez, a patron, he called "Indians." The King of Portugal saw them 10 days ago. Royal advisers suggested they were Africans, but the King said that was impossible. He also realized that he made a mistake when he refused to be the explorer's patron (→ Apr. 20).

"Fairest island that eyes have beheld"

Santa Gloria, May 5, 1494

Christopher Columbus, still in search of treasures for the Spanish empire, dropped anchor off a new island today and named it Santa Gloria [Jamaica]. More than 60 natives attacked his vessels with bows and arrows from their dugout canoes, but Columbus scared them off with a cannon shot. The admiral thinks that this island may be the jewel in his crown, "the fairest island that eyes have beheld."

Since September, when Columbus left Spain in glory on this second expedition, he has discovered more than 60 islands and named many of them for Spain: Dominica, Santa Maria de Guadalupe, Santa Maria de Monserrate and Santa Maria la Antigua. On an island he named Santa Cruz [Saint Croix], savages armed with arrows killed one of his men. When Columbus returned to Navidad [Hispaniola] to inspect his first settlement, he discovered a tragedy. All his men had been killed by natives who were enraged over the settlers' greed for gold and women. Columbus set up a trading post on the island and called it Isabella after his patron, the Queen. His primary mission is to convert the natives, but he is also charged with finding gold for the royal treasury. So far, however, he has found little that glitters (→ 1495).

Cabot claims Atlantic lands for England

Cabot off coast of Newfoundland.

Bristol, England, July 1498
Vast coastal areas of Vinland and of the mainland to the south and west have been claimed on behalf of King Henry VII of England by the Genoa-born explorer John Cabot (Giovanni Caboto). Following the northerly route used by Norsemen 500 years ago, Cabot left Bristol in May with five ships and 200 men. This was his second expedition. Last year, after sighting land on June 24, he reported finding vast fisheries off Vinland.

This Cabot expedition is sailing under letters patent granted by the King to possess lands "unknown to all Christians" and the explorer is also hoping to discover a northwest route to the Orient. His present whereabouts are unknown (→ 1499).

Columbus disconsolate after second trip

Bay of Cadiz, Spain, June 11, 1496
The second voyage by Christopher Columbus ended today, and he has a great deal of explaining to do. He left 33 months ago with new titles, 17 ships and more volunteers than he needed. He has returned with little gold and a crew that is exhausted and sick. Isabella, his new town in Hispaniola, was meant to be a center of trade and religious conversion. Instead, it has become a symbol of murder and despair.

Hundreds of natives died after they were seized to be traded as slaves. Hundreds more were killed when Columbus marched on the interior of the island to look for the gold that remains elusive. The admiral, disconsolate at not finding China, has become ill and nervous. He coughs a lot, he complains that his bones ache, and he is filled with anguish because many view his expedition as a failure. The King and Queen are tempted to abandon Columbus, but they are unlikely to do so because England and Portugal are set to sponsor their own voyages of discovery (→ June 7, 1498).

The opening of all-sea routes from Europe around the Cape of Good Hope and across the Atlantic has led to more trade and a need for larger ships.

Vasco da Gama opens sea route to India

Lisbon, Sept. 9, 1499
The citizens of Lisbon are celebrating the triumphal return of Vasco da Gama today. The explorer has completed his two-year journey around the Cape of Good Hope to India, bringing back spices, gems and silks to King Manuel. The voyage was the first of its kind, opening a sea trade route between Europe and the subcontinent. The three-ship fleet encountered hostile Muslim merchants, blustery winds at the tip of Africa and an outbreak of scurvy that killed so many men that da Gama, lacking crewmen, burned one of the ships. But the other two vessels completed the trip, paving the way for commercial exchanges between the two cultures. Appropriately, Bartolomeu Dias, the man who discovered the Cape of Good Hope, accompanied da Gama as far as the Cape Verde Islands.

Da Gama arriving in India.

Monk is the first to describe tobacco

Europe, 1496
Christopher Columbus and his crew discovered many oddities during their voyage to the Indies. Among the strangest is a "bewitching vegetable" that the natives use in a unusual way – they smoke it.

According to Romano Pane, a monk who accompanied Columbus, the leafy vegetable is dried, and put in a pipe shaped like a slingshot called a "tabaco." The Indians then insert two ends of the pipe in their nostrils, light the leaf and inhale. Exhaling makes the smokers look like small dragons.

When Columbus landed on San Salvador on October 12, several Arawak Indians gave him some of the leaves as a gift. The following month, when he sailed to Cuba, two of his officers went ashore and observed "many people who were going to their villages, women and men, with a firebrand in hand, and herbs to drink the smoke thereof."

The leaf can also be chewed or rolled in the shape of a candle and smoked, but this can make one light-headed if used too much. The Indians use it in many of their ceremonies and venerate it because they believe it has health-giving properties.

Hispaniola revolt is finally suppressed

Hispaniola, Sept. 1499
The third voyage of Christopher Columbus has been filled with exciting new discoveries, but his ambitious plans of colonization remain threatened by open revolt over his poor administration of the Isabella colony. Detractors say he has been cruel to both the Spanish settlers and the natives, and has even withheld food and supplies from those who have displeased him. Columbus did achieve a truce with the rebel leader Francisco Roldan, and he gave immunity to all the rebels. They remain displeased, however, and reports of the dissension have traveled back to Spain. The King and Queen have ordered a knight of the military order of Calatrava, Francisco de Bobadilla, to sail to Isabella and investigate the charges against Columbus.

This third expedition is ending as badly as it began. The prestige of the admiral is dropping, and so is the number of volunteer sailors. Many crewmen are released prisoners. Despite the problems, Columbus has managed to claim more islands for Spain. He believes that for the first time he has set foot on the mainland, at a place called Paria [Venezuela] (→ Dec. 12, 1500).

1500 (1500-1509)

South Atlantic, Apr. 23, 1500. Portuguese explorer Pedro Alvarez Cabral reaches new coastal area [Brazil].

Southern Africa, May 1500. Bartolomeu Dias, on Cabral expedition, is lost off Cape of Good Hope.

Greenland, June 1500. Portuguese explorer Gaspar Corte-Real charts east coast of Greenland.

Portugal, May 13, 1501. Amerigo Vespucci, this time under Portuguese flag, sets sail for western lands (→1502).

Spain, 1501. King Ferdinand issues directives to colonial Governor Nicolas de Ovando, setting up system of tribute and labor for natives.

Lisbon, 1501. Some 50 natives, sent by Corte-Real [from south of Cape Breton], arrive to be sold into slavery.

Cadiz, Spain, May 11, 1502. Columbus leaves on his fourth [and last] voyage (→Nov. 7, 1504).

London, Dec. 9, 1502. Henry VII grants patent to Anglo-Portuguese group called "Company of Adventures to the New World" (→Aug. 1505).

Lisbon, 1502. Amerigo Vespucci, upon return from second trip, writes to Lorenzo de Piero Francesco de Medici that land he visited is a new continent, distinct from India (→Apr. 25, 1507).

Mexico, 1502. Montezuma II becomes Aztec chief (→1518).

Bristol, England, 1502. The Gabriel, belonging to Hugh Elyot, returns (under Cabot patent) with 180 pounds worth of fish, inaugurating Newfoundland as fishery (→1504).

Spain, 1503. House of Trade organized to control New World trade.

Spain, Nov. 7, 1504. Columbus returns from last voyage (→May 20, 1506).

England, Aug. 1505. Joao Gonsalves and Francisco Fernandes rewarded for bringing bobcats and parrots back from mainland in North Atlantic.

Cuba, 1508. Spain's Sebastian de Ocampo sails around Cuba, proving it is an island.

Rome, 1508. Papal bull "Universae ecclesiae regni" grants Spain right to appoint church officials in New World.

America, 1508. Sebastian Cabot reaches large bay in North Atlantic [Hudson Bay] in search of Northwest Passage.

America gets its name from Vespucci

Amerigo Vespucci imagines denizens of the deep en route to New World.

Martin Waldseemuller's is the first map to display the New World as distinct from Asia. He also names the new land "America ... after its discoverer, Americus," or Amerigo Vespucci. Amerigo means "rich in wheat" in Italian.

St.-Die, Lorraine, Apr. 25, 1507

A revealing new map by a young geography professor displays the New World as a distinct continent between Europe and Asia, and names the land America. The man who made the map, Martin Waldseemuller, took at face value Amerigo Vespucci's claim to have found the mainland in 1497, a year before Columbus. "The fourth part of the globe," he writes, "... since Americus discovered it, may be called Land of Americus, or America."

Until Vespucci's recent circulation of his self-congratulatory narratives, his claim to fame was his relationship to Simonetta Vespucci, the voluptuous model for the Botticelli "Birth of Venus." Suddenly he is a famed navigator. His published letters narrate three voyages as if no one else was aboard. The first left in 1499 (a year after Columbus's third voyage), though Vespucci dates it 1497. It was a brutal raid up the coast to Santo Domingo, where a revolt against Columbus was underway. Its highlight was the discovery of an Indian city built on water, which got the name Little Venice, or Venezuela. The second and third journeys, led by Goncalo Coelho, charted Brazil's coast. A southern post, founded January 1, 1502, was called Rio de Janeiro.

But Vespucci's talents seem to be more for propaganda than for navigation. Columbia might be a more appropriate name (→1538).

Columbus is sent home in chains

Hero to villain: Columbus in chains.

Seville, Spain, Dec. 12, 1500

Christopher Columbus, the greatest explorer Spain has ever known, looks more like a common criminal. He was put in chains and returned to Spain from Hispaniola after the Queen's commissioner, Francisco de Bobadilla, arrived in the Isabella colony and found the bodies of seven Spaniards hanging in the square. Columbus says he was forced to act harshly because of a rebellion against the Queen. "By divine will," he wrote, "I have placed under the sovereignty of the King and Queen our lords an Other World, whereby Spain, which was reckoned poor, is become the richest of countries" (→May 11, 1502).

Spanish novel coins name "California"

Madrid, 1509

Count Ordones de Montalvo has published a sequel to the *Amandis Cycle* that is as popular as his earlier work. The new book, *Las Sergas de Esplandian*, is a romantic novel about pagan forces fighting for and occupying Constantinople. During the battle, the pagans are helped by Califia, a warrior queen who comes from a place "at the right hand of the Indies, an island named California," which abounds in gold, precious metals and fabulous beasts called griffins. Because of this book, the myth of California is spreading widely (→1533).

Spain exploits Indian labor in New World

American Indians, chosen by the Spanish to serve as slaves on an estate in the encomienda system.

Hispaniola, 1508.
Spanish explorers have found gold to be in short supply on this little island. Manpower, however, is not, though it is dwindling under the burden of European demands. In 1495, desperate to repay backers, Columbus seized 1,500 Arawak Indians. But of the 500 sent to Spain, 200 died en route. And pious people bridled at the idea of infusing the Spanish society with primitive slaves. So, to raise revenue, Columbus imposed a gold tax, placing a copper necklace on those who pay. Those found without a necklace often have their hands cut off. Others work as slaves in exchange for Spanish protection under the system known as encomienda. Of 250,000 natives, there are only 60,000 left (→1510).

Columbus dies, believing he found Asia

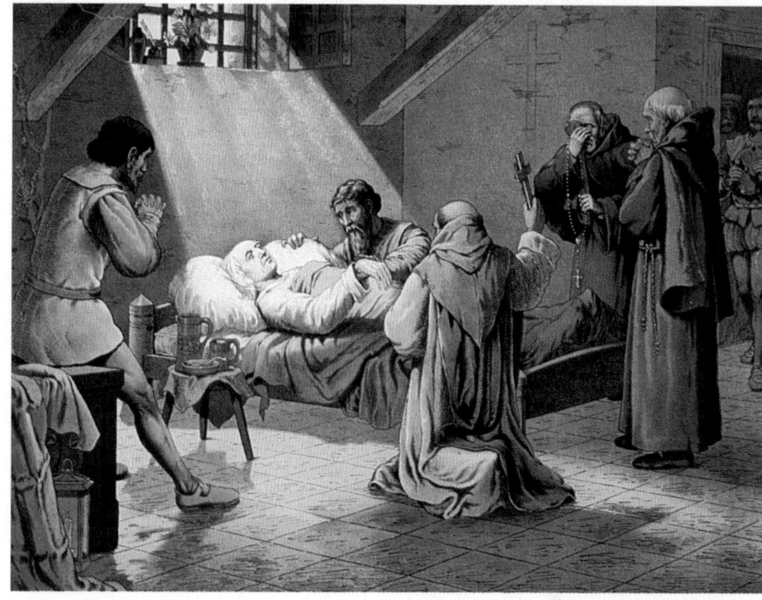

Christopher Columbus receives last rites on his deathbed in Valladolid, Spain.

Valladolid, Spain, May 20, 1506
Christopher Columbus, his spirit broken, died today in the country that launched his great adventures. He was 54. "Into thy hands, Oh Lord, I commend my spirit," Columbus mumbled before he passed away. On his deathbed, he remained faithful to his Lord, but he felt Spain's King had betrayed him.

The Genoa-born admiral signed his final will and testament yesterday and left most of his property to his son, Diego. Columbus was still hoping that Diego would inherit the titles he had won after his first voyage. He also hoped that Diego would eventually win the claims he still has against the crown. After his patron, Queen Isabella, died, Columbus believed that he was being cheated of money he was promised before the first expedition. The original agreement guaranteed Columbus 10 percent of all income from trade with lands he discovered. The King offered to give him a large estate if he would drop his claims, but the proud Columbus refused. He died believing that he had found the Indies, but his fourth voyage was far from satisfying. He never found China, he was refused shelter by the authorities on Hispaniola and he was marooned on Jamaica for more than a year.

Sugar cane brought to America by Spain

Hispaniola, 1508
Following the lead of the Portuguese, who planted sugar cane in Madeira, the Cape Verde Islands and the Canary Islands by 1503, and of Columbus, who brought the plant to the West Indies on hls second voyage, the Spanish have switched from unsuccessful mineral mining here to profitable sugar cane plantings, using native slaves for the work. Sugar shows great promise for cultivation in the Indies.

Europeans exploit New World fishery

Newfoundland, 1504
Since 1502, when Hugh Elyot returned to Bristol with 180 pounds worth of fish, European ships have been exploiting the rich waters of this rugged coastline. This year, French fishermen from Normandy have joined the British and the Portuguese in mining these waters. And since the forays of John Cabot down the mainland coast, the British have kept up sporadic trade with the natives of the New World.

Seven Indians stir up debate in France

Normandy, 1509
When Thomas Aubert returned to port after a long trip across the Atlantic to the Newfoundand fishery, his ship was carrying more than just fish. The seven Indians brought back by Aubert are a topic of debate across all of France. Tales of a race of strange savages in the New World reached here via Spain and Portugal, but never before had one of their kind set foot in Northern Europe. In Paris, one can hear radical speculations as to whether the natives might be a noble and pristine race, uncorrupted by the influence of civilization.

Puerto Rico is prize of Ponce de Leon

Puerto Rico, 1509
Juan Ponce de Leon, a romantic exile who traveled with Columbus in 1493, has seized this craggy tropical island for Spain. With pious speed and efficiency, reluctant natives have been annihilated or enslaved. The conquistador credits his success to his canine companion, Bercerillo. The dog allegedly can discern a friendly native from a treacherous one at a glance, earning himself a one-and-a-half share of all booty. Ponce de Leon was appointed Governor of the island without the consent of Don Diego Columbus, Governor of Hispaniola.

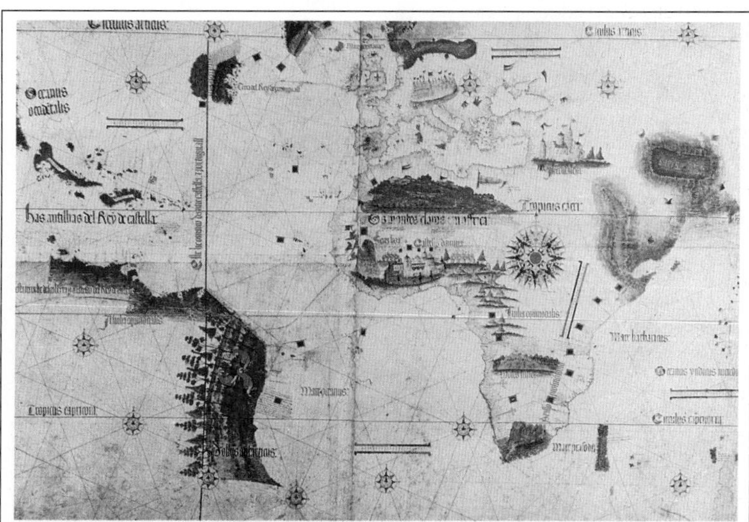

1502. *The Cantino chart is the earliest Portuguese map to show New World discoveries. Also this year, Amerigo Vespucci wrote to Lorenzo de Piero Francesco de Medici that the land he visited is a new continent, not Asia.*

1510 (1510-1519)

Seville, 1510. "La Casa de Contratacion" sanctions importation of Negro slaves, from Africa to America (→ 1511).

North America, 1510. Exploration of east coast is proceeding north [to Charleston].

Caribbean, 1511. Spanish take Cuba by force.

Cuba, 1511. Hatuay, an Indian about to be burned at stake for refusing conversion, asks if there are Spaniards in heaven; when told yes, he refuses salvation, saying: "I will not go to a place where I may meet with one of that accursed race!" (→ Dec. 27, 1512).

Spain, Dec. 27, 1512. Laws of Burgos passed, giving New World natives legal protection against abuse, authorizing Negro slavery (→ 1514).

Spain, 1514. "Requerimiento" orders New World natives to convert under threat of enslavement or death (→ 1516).

Atlantic, 1515. Spaniard Juan de Bermudez finds archipelago, naming it the Bermudas.

Cuba, 1515. Spanish found city of Havana.

Spain, Feb. 23, 1516. Carlos I ascends throne upon death of King Ferdinand.

Hispaniola, 1516. Bananas brought from Spain are first in New World.

Panama, 1516. Ponciaco, son of Balboa's chief Indian aide, demands, "What is the matter with you Christian men, that you esteem a little bit of gold so much more than your own peace of mind?" (→ 1518).

Mexico, Sept. 1517. Spanish explorer Francisco Hernandez de Cordoba discovers Yucatan Peninsula.

Mexico, 1518. Spanish explorer Juan de Grijalva, while exploring region, is told of Aztec empire (→ March 25, 1519).

Mexico, March 25, 1519. Hernando Cortez, entering province of Tabasco, defeats Tabascan Indians (→ Nov. 9, 1519).

Mexico, 1519. Negroes here are first to harvest wheat in New World.

DEATHS

Spain, Feb. 22, 1512. Amerigo Vespucci, Italian explorer (*March 1454).

Panama, Jan. 1519. Vasco Nunez de Balboa, Spanish explorer, beheaded by his successor (*1475).

De Leon claims Florida for Spain

Florida, Apr. 8, 1513

Juan Ponce de Leon, whose quest for a fabled Fountain of Youth remains unsuccessful, has discovered and claimed for the Spanish King a new land he has named Florida.

De Leon, former Governor of Puerto Rico, reached the territory on Easter Sunday after a 36-day sail toward the northwest. During his voyage, he stopped at several islands and sampled their waters, but the white-haired explorer failed to find the legendary fountain that is said to restore youthful vigor.

Details of the de Leon landing in Florida – believed to be an island – are not available. It is, however, the custom of Spanish explorers to clasp their national flag in one hand, take a sword in the other, claim the land in the King's name and offer a prayer. De Leon named the new territory for its abundance of flowers and also for this season's religious holiday, Pasqua de Flores.

De Leon outfitted three ships for the voyage after he was granted a patent from the King more than a year ago. He was authorized to explore the island of Bimini and govern it. While de Leon had planned to make the trip a year earlier, he was delayed because of the need to subdue an Indian disturbance in Puerto Rico.

A native of San Servas, Spain, de Leon sailed with Christopher Columbus in 1493 on the Italian explorer's second voyage to the New World. He served on Hispaniola and explored Puerto Rico in 1508. He was named Governor of Puerto Rico the next year, but was later removed from office as the result of a political dispute (→ Feb. 20, 1521).

Juan Ponce de Leon and his men sample the waters of Florida, hoping for instant rejuvenation.

Africans are sent to New Spain as slaves

Spain, 1518

Seeking to quiet Dominican protests over Indian slavery, King Carlos I has granted an "asiento de Negros," the first European monopoly for the importation of African slaves to the Indies. The Dominican conscience awoke in 1511 on Hispaniola following Fray Antonio de Montesinos's fiery sermon opposing the encomienda system of enslavement. Bartolome de Las Casas, who in 1510 became the first priest ordained in the New World, has since taken up the cause. Two years after his ordination, he witnessed a "pacification" mission in Cuba. Led by Captain Panfilo de Narvaez, it turned into a massacre: "There was a river of blood, as if a multitude of cows had been slaughtered." Two years later, Las Casas gave up his encomienda and went to Spain to seek abolition of the system. To meet labor needs, Las Casas turned to the Africans, who have proven stoic under adverse conditions in southern Iberia and the Canary Islands. Negroes have been going to the Indies since 1502. It is hoped that mass importation will relieve the labor burden borne by Indians, who appear open to the sway of Christian morality (→ 1519).

Bartolome de Las Casas.

Americas seen as two new continents

Europe, 1513.

Cartographers and geographers in Europe now agree that the newly discovered western lands are not in fact Asia. A new edition of Ptolemy's *Geography*, an authoritative source since its revival in 1405, displays the land mass as two continents, situated between Europe and Asia. Columbus was misled by the Romans' 1,400-year-old calculations, which underestimated the circumference of the earth.

Copernicus: Earth rotates around Sun

Frombork, Poland, 1514

Nicolas Copernicus, an astronomer who returned to his native Poland after long studies in Italy, has determined that the accepted belief placing the earth at the center of the universe is wrong. His planetary studies have convinced him the earth circles the sun, contrary to the Ptolemaic theory taught for 1,400 years. Copernicus is said to be writing a book on his theory but is hesitant about publishing it for fear that his new ideas will be branded heresy.

Nicolas Copernicus of Poland.

"Utopia" foresees ideal American life

Europe, 1516

The New World promises to be a humanist haven, according to Sir Thomas More, the English lawyer, statesmen and thinker. His book *Utopia* (Greek for no place) describes an imaginary American island that boasts public education, freedom of religion, equal rights for women and other farsighted measures. A more realistic account of the New World became available this year in a new installment of *De Orbe Novo Decades (Decades of the New World)*, by the Italian historian Pietro Martire d'Anghiera. He has mapped the careers of Columbus, Cortez, Magellan and other explorers and has documented their deeds in an unsparing analysis of exploration and conquest in America.

Balboa sees the Pacific from isthmus

Darien, Sept. 25, 1513

Vasco Nunez de Balboa today became the first European to sight the South Sea from the New World. Crossing a narrow isthmus from Darien on the Caribbean Sea, Balboa and his men traversed 45 miles of heavy jungle to the highest mountain peak that overlooked the South Sea. He clambered alone to the top of the peak where he prayed; he then called for his men to join him in viewing what they called the Pacific Ocean. Balboa's party was made up of 190 Spaniards and several hundred Indian slaves who were serving him as attendants and bearers. Armed with swords, crossbows and arquebuses and led by a pack of bloodhounds, the expedition was attacked by hostile Indians, who were defeated in a bloody onslaught. According to witnesses, the Spaniards' big swords "hewed from one an arme, from another a legge and a buttocke, from another a shoulder, and the neck from the bodie at one stroke" (→1519).

Balboa is the first European to view the Pacific on its American shore.

Magellan leaves to sail around world

Seville, Spain, Sept. 20, 1519

The Armada de Molucca, a fleet of five ships commanded by Ferdinand Magellan, has set sail on a voyage to cross the Pacific Ocean and circumnavigate the globe. Magellan, Portuguese by birth, is sailing under the authority of Spain, in spite of opposition from his native land. The fleet had been anchored at Sanlucar de Barrameda, near Seville, where the crew was trying to replace the rancid food it ended up with after being cheated by "land sharks" (→Nov. 28, 1520).

Magellan with the tools of his trade.

Martin Luther calls for church reform

Wittenberg, Saxony, Oct. 31, 1517

The Augustinian monk Martin Luther posted a series of debating propositions on the door of the Wittenberg Cathedral today. These 95 Theses are a strong attack on the sale of indulgences granting forgiveness of sins. The theses, written in strident language, attack the entire basis of the sales, rejecting the ability of the Pope to grant remission of sins without penance. This harsh attack on a very lucrative business for princes and the Pope is not likely to go unnoticed (→1520).

Luther, conscience of the church.

Cortez is received by Emperor of Aztecs

Mexico, Nov. 1519

After a long trek through the jungle, Hernando Cortez and his 500 Spanish soldiers, heads held high, marched into Mexico City and finally met the ruler of the Aztecs. Emperor Montezuma exercises a command over his subjects more absolute than any European king. The Emperor was carried in an elaborate litter and his people swept the ground before him while carefully avoiding his gaze. Exotic plumage adorning his dress gave every motion an inimitable grandeur.

The Spanish responded with care when Montezuma addressed them as gods returning from the land of the rising sun. Taking advantage of their special status, the troops explored the thriving city of 300,000 inhabitants. Tens of thousands attend a market where goose quills are filled with gold dust and sold. Montezuma, who is about 40 years old, says he "loves pleasure and song" and amuses himself watching games and drinking vast quantities of a liquid called "chocolatl." Made from cacao, it is said to give him great power over women.

The cordiality between the Aztecs and Spaniards, however, was superficial. While the Spanish were approaching his capital, Montezuma sent gifts with pleas to them to stay away. "Like monkeys," his envoys reported, the Spanish "seized upon the gold. They stuffed themselves with it, and starved for it, and lusted for it like pigs."

Days after their arrival, relations collapsed as the Aztec ruler led a tour of his temples. Revolted by sacrificial practices, the Spanish insisted that a cross be erected. Montezuma replied, "If I had thought you would insult my gods, I would not have shown them to you." After reports of Indian attacks on his rear guard, Cortez has imprisoned the Aztec ruler in his own city (→May 20, 1520).

Montezuma II, adorned with gold.

1520 (1520-1529)

Mexico, May 20, 1520. Hernando Cortez defeats Panfilo de Narvaez, sent by Spain to punish him for insubordination (→Aug. 13, 1521).

Pacific Ocean, Nov. 28, 1520. Ferdinand Magellan reaches the Pacific Ocean (→Sept. 6, 1522).

Rome, 1520. Pope Leo X declares Martin Luther a heretic.

Spain, 1520. Chocolate from Mexico introduced.

Puerto Rico, Feb. 20, 1521. Juan Ponce de Leon sets out for Florida with about 200 prospective colonists (→July 1521).

Florida, June 1521. Spanish explorers Pedro de Quexo and Francisco Gordillo enter river they name Jordan [Santee River; they are first Europeans to visit Carolinas] (→1525).

Florida, July 1521. Ponce de Leon wounded by natives; discouraged settlers leave.

Atlantic, 1523. French privateers, armed by Jean Ango of Dieppe, ambush Spanish fleet carrying Aztec treasures.

Mexico, May 1524. Twelve Franciscan friars of Observantine Order greeted by Cortez.

Panama, Nov. 1524. Francisco Pizarro leaves on first expedition to Peru (→Aug. 29, 1533).

Florida, 1525. Pedro de Quexo, sent by Lucas Vasquez de Ayllon, surveys coast north of Bay of the Mother of God [Chesapeake Bay] (→Nov. 1526).

Spain, 1525. Pietro Martire d'Anghiera writes, in *De Orbe Novo*, that a ship could travel from Lucayos [Bahamas] to Hispaniola "without compass or chart, guiding itself solely by the trail of dead Indians who had been thrown from the ships" (→1538).

Spain, June 1527. Panfilo de Narvaez, with five ships and 600 men, sets out to explore and settle lands between Florida and Mexico (→Apr. 14, 1528).

Caribbean, Nov. 19, 1527. British ship Mary Guilford, after exploring North Atlantic coast, reaches West Indies; sister ship Samson lost.

Florida, Apr. 14, 1528. Spanish conquistador Panfilo de Narvaez lands [at Tampa Bay] with 400 colonists (→Nov. 6).

DEATH

Cochin, India, Dec. 24, 1524. Vasco da Gama, Portuguese navigator (*c.1460).

Verrazano finds great bay and river

Verrazano's ship splits the horizon, an unlikely sight for coastal natives.

Northeast America, Apr. 17, 1524

In his journey along the shore of the new land, the explorer Giovanni Verrazano has discovered "a very pleasant place, situated amongst certain little steep hills; from amidst the hills there ran down into the sea a great stream of water, which within the mouth was very deep, and from the sea to the mouth of same, with the tide, which we found to rise eight feet, any great vessel laden may pass up [New York harbor]."

Sailing under the flag of France, Verrazano departed with a four-ship fleet. In the autumn of 1523, two of the vessels were lost in a storm. Following a stop for repairs at an English port, the remaining ships sailed south, making a successful raid off the coast of Spain. One of the ships was then assigned to take the booty back to France and Verrazano continued on to the New World in the single remaining ship, La Dauphine.

He first sighted land on March 1, 1524, a long strip beyond which could be seen open water [the Outer Banks of North Carolina]. Verrazano then sailed south for 150 to 200 miles, and north again, seeking a passage to what he believed was the Pacific Ocean. The northern part of the voyage brought him to the bay and river, where he spent a day exploring in a small boat. He observed that the country was inhabited by people "clad with feathers . . . of divers colors."

Spanish force meets disaster in Southeast

Gulf of Mexico, Nov. 6, 1528

For the natives of one tiny island off the mainland coast [Galveston Island], the new sun has revealed an unusual sight: A band of emaciated white men lie naked on the beach, not far from death. Their tale is of a brutal ordeal in a strange land.

"Cabeza de Vaca" of Narvaez expedition, by Frederick Remington.

Only seven months ago they were 300 strong. Their treasurer was Cabeza de Vaca, and their leader was Panfilo de Narvaez, who, though dreaming of empire as they hit the Florida coast, was eager, but incapable of making successful decisions. After finding traces of gold, he split his party, sending the ships to the River of Palms [Rio Grande], while taking a land force to find the allegedly rich city of Apalachen [near Tallahassee].

Pressing on through "vast forests with astonishingly high trees," they found only tiny villages with naked Indians, meagerly fed on corn. Because supplies were running low, it soon appeared that they "could leave this terrible land only by dying." After 16 days of labor without tools, the 260 survivors set out on makeshift boats with shirts for sails and stones for ballast. Worn out from bailing and half-crazed from drinking salt water, only one boatload made it ashore, far from the safety of New Spain. Narvaez himself was lost at sea (→Sept. 1534).

Europe invaded by American disease

Lisbon, 1521

The New World, advertised as a fount of riches and eternal youth, appears to have passed on to the Old World the most hideous of diseases [syphilis]. According to Dr. Ruy Diaz de Isla, who is a specialist in the illness, Columbus's crew was rewarded for its efforts with a veritable epidemic that is now spreading rapidly across Europe. The disease produces open sores and fever, and it can result in blindness and often death. It appears to be transmitted through the sexual act.

Called "bubas" by the Spanish, it is said to be common among natives of the New World. Some people even claim that most Indians have had the disease. Bartolome de Las Casas, a priest in New Spain, reports it has been infecting native communities longer than anyone can remember. But Dr. Diaz de Isla says it now affects one in three Europeans, perhaps as a form of repayment for the harsh conditions of encomienda in New Spain (→1530).

Magellan killed; expedition is completed

Vittoria is the only ship to survive Magellan crew's three-year ordeal.

Spain, Sept. 6, 1522

The Magellan expedition to circumnavigate the globe has returned to Spain, without Magellan. Only one of the five ships that made up the Armada de Molucca was able to complete the historic journey, bearing a ragged crew of 18 Spanish sailors and four West Indian islanders picked up en route. The group, under Juan Sebastian de Elcano, bore tales of discovery, mutiny, warfare and the death of their leader, Ferdinand Magellan.

According to the account of Pigafetta, a sailor, the great explorer met his end during a battle on an island in the Pacific [Philippines] on April 27 last year. Asked for military aid by one island chief who was fighting another, Magellan sailed with three longboats against the Lapu Lapu tribe. Approaching the beach, some Spanish sailors were massacred. Magellan tried to land anyway. Further enraged, the natives attacked and Magellan died covering the retreat of his men.

Cortes completes conquest of the Aztecs

Cortes's conquistadors battle the Aztecs, fierce defenders of their sacred city.

Mexico, Aug. 13, 1521

Its streets thick with the smell of death, the Aztec capital of Tenotchitlan has finally succumbed to Hernando Cortez. A year ago, lust for power began to catch up with Cortes. Cuban Governor Velasquez sent troops to try to subdue the insubordinate conquistador. In May 1520, Cortes left Tenotchitlan to march to the coast and defeat Panfilo de Narvaez's Cuban force. He returned to find his garrison besieged by angry Mexicans, anxious to eject the impudent Spanish and free their ruler, Montezuma. But the ruler died in the revolt, and the Spanish retreated. Returning with almost 150,000 men, mostly Indians hostile to the Aztecs, Cortes besieged the capital on May 26, 1521. Spaniards who survived the Aztec ritual sacrifice of hundreds of captives, were there to celebrate the city's fall and the capture of the new emperor, Cuauhtemoc. The men were left to their own devices. No Mexican was safe.

First of European settlements fails

Hispaniola, Nov. 1526

Settlers from a failed Florida colony organized by Lucas Vasquez de Ayllon are returning to Hispaniola without their leader, who died October 18. Survivors of the ill-fated colony, called San Miguel de Gualdalupe, said Ayllon was among the many who succumbed to the cold and lack of food as winter approached. Ayllon had set sail July 26 with several hundred settlers, Negro slaves and three Dominican friars. They arrived far to the north of other expeditions and lost one ship near the mouth of a river [Savannah]. They moved south and tried to set up an encampment in a flat, marshy area. Despite an abundance of fish, many people grew too weak to obtain food.

Gomes sails whole coast from Florida

Portugal, Aug. 21, 1525

After a year on the high seas, the expedition of Estavao Gomes put into port today. He was met by cartographer Diego Ribeiro, eager for new data on the lay of the western lands. Gomes, it appears, sailed the whole coast, from Florida to the northern reaches, without finding a clear waterway through to Asia. Toward the north, he charted a long cape, jutting west and then north like a crooked finger [Cape Cod]. Sailing north into a river he calls the Santa Maria [Penobscot], he captured a number of natives, 58 of whom are still alive after the journey. They will be placed under royal guardianship and baptized, perhaps to be trained for use as interpreters at a later date.

Aztec drawing of the Spanish conquest, from the Lienzo de Tlaxcala canvas.

1530 (1530-1539)

South America, 1530. Brazil colonized by Portuguese.

Italy, 1530. Girolamo Fracastoro applies name of syphilis to disease Spanish call bubas.

Spain, 1532. Government orders all fleets to New World to transport livestock and crops.

Mexico, 1533. Cortes, following King Carlos V's directive to "Explore. Find gold. Find the island of Queen Califia," sends warriors north (→1535).

England, 1533. Parliament passes legislation making Church of England an independent national church, free of Rome; King Henry VIII is free to marry Anne Boleyn.

Canada, July 24, 1534. Jacques Cartier, under patronage of French King Francis I, reaches mouth of River of Canada [St. Lawrence River] (→Sept. 5).

Southwest, Sept. 1534. Cabeza de Vaca, Estevanico (a slave) and two other survivors of Narvaez expedition escape after six years of Indian captivity (→July 24, 1536).

Normandy, Sept. 5, 1534. Cartier returns with furs after exploring Prince Edward Island, Chaleur Bay and Gaspe Bay (→May 19, 1535).

Brittany, May 19, 1535. Cartier, inspired by stories of wealthy kingdom of Saguenay, sets out on second trip to North America (→Aug. 13).

Canada, Aug. 13, 1535. Cartier told by two Indian youths that Canada is derived from Huron-Iroquois kanata, meaning village or settlement (→Sept. 7).

Canada, Sept. 7, 1535. Cartier reaches Stadacona [Quebec] (→Oct. 2).

Canada, Oct. 2, 1535. Cartier lands at Hochelaga [Montreal] (→July 16, 1536).

Hispaniola, 1537. Pope Paul III declares that Indians are not to be enslaved (→1549).

Mexico, March 7, 1539. Father Marcos, with Negro slave Estevanico, leads scouting party north [to New Mexico] in search of fabled Seven Cities of Cibola (→June 1539).

Florida, June 4, 1539. Hernando de Soto finds Juan Ortiz, survivor of Narvaez voyage, living with Indians (→Sept. 15).

Florida, Sept. 15, 1539. De Soto clashes with Timucuas in Battle of Lakes (→Aug. 1540).

Mexico City, 1539. First viceroy of Mexico, Antonio de Mendoza, establishes first printing press in the New World.

Cartier claims vast region in north

"Jacques Cartier's Landing" by Thomas Hart Benton.

St. Malo, France, July 16, 1536

Jacques Cartier, the noted navigator and explorer, has returned home after claiming Stadacona [Quebec], Hochelaga [Montreal] and the River of Canada [St. Lawrence River] region for France. This was Cartier's second voyage of exploration to North America and his first penetration of the river that he hopes will become an axis of French power in the New World.

With him on his return to St. Malo, Cartier brought as a captive the Iroquois chief, Donnaconna, whose two sons he had claimed as hostages on his first voyage two years earlier. The voyage of 1534, with two vessels and 61 men, had been commissioned by King Francis I to search for gold and to seek out a passage to Asia. It took Cartier as far as Newfoundland and the north coast of the gulf of the River of Canada, but the entrance to the river eluded him. He found it with the assistance of Indian guides on his second voyage, with three ships and a crew of 110, last year.

Members of the second expedition spent a bitter winter with their ships locked in the ice at Stadacona, where they lost 25 men to scurvy before they finally headed for home in May (→May 1542).

No griffins or gold, just California

La Paz, Santa Cruz, 1535

Hernando Cortes had listened to such tales many times, stories of a warrior queen named Califia and an island of griffins, one rich with pearls and gold. But Cortes did not expect to find griffins and gold. He was a realist and he wanted the territory for his King because his King had told him to acquire it. This he did, placing on the shore of what he believes is an island [Baja California] some 100 colonists and 30 horses. Since the expedition landed on the feast day of the cross, Cortes named the bay Santa Cruz. And because it was peaceful, he named the town La Paz. The Indians here relate promising tales of mighty kingdoms to the north, with lakes of quicksilver and rivers that flow with gold.

Great comet stirs fears, superstitions

Ingolstadt, Bohemia, 1531

A bright comet [Halley's] that appeared in the sky early in August is being observed here by Peter Apian, astronomer to the Austrian Emperor. Apian has tracked it as it has moved from the constellation Leo through Virgo to Libra. On clear nights, crowds of the superstitious gather in streets and fields to view the comet, whose color seems to vary from red to yellow. Old men are reminded of the comet that appeared 75 years ago, in 1456, and was described as "terrible, trailing after it a tail that covered two celestial signs." It is also compared to the spectacular long-tailed comet of 1301, a depiction of which the Florentine painter Giotto included in his fresco "Adoration of the Magi," as the Star of Bethlehem.

De Vaca back after years with Indians

Mexico City, July 24, 1536

Four stragglers, brought in by a slaving party, are being received with skepticism after claiming to be part of Panfilo de Narvaez's 1527 expedition to the north. But their story seems too bizarre to be a lie. Cabeza de Vaca, a Moor called Estevanico and two others claim to have survived slavery and starvation, while 80 of their compatriots succumbed to cannibalism and disease. After six years' living naked and following seasonal foods as bearers for the Indians, they escaped. Posing as shamans, they crossed the country, curing sick Indians and attracting a fawning crowd of thousands, all looking for enlightenment from the "children of the sun." The south seacoast, they report, has "the best and all the most opulent countries."

Ex-slave slain seeking 7 golden cities

Estevanico, in command in the desert, surveys the rugged new landscape.

Mexico, June 1539

Estevanico is reported to be dead. A veteran of Cabeza de Vaca's exploration of northern New Spain, Estevanico was searching at the time of his death for the so-called Seven Golden Cities of Cibola, the legendary but elusive Indian cities of riches. A former slave who became a respected explorer, Estevanico was a North African Moor attached to the service of Fray Marcos, a Christian friar who has traveled throughout northern Mexico with Francisco Vasquez de Coronado. After Estevanico's murder by the Zuni Indians, Marcos found the Golden Cities. From a distance, they did reflect a golden hue; upon closer inspection, the Zuni villages yielded no gold, and the inhabitants lived in extreme poverty. While serving with de Vaca, Estevanico was the first man of Old World blood to traverse this vast, uncharted region.

European woman arrives with de Soto

Florida, May 30, 1539

The famous Spanish explorer Hernando de Soto landed some 600 troops on the west coast of Florida today with a single mission: to find gold. De Soto sailed nine days ago from Cuba with a flotilla of nine ships. In addition to the troops, he brought along a pack of bloodhounds and the first European woman in Florida. The landing party was attacked by a band of Indians who were soon driven off by reinforcements from the ship.

De Soto rose to prominence as a soldier with the Pizarro expedition to Peru in 1524. At the age of 21, he left home to seek adventure in the New World and to restore the de Soto family's failing fortunes. He succeeded beyond his wildest dreams. In Panama, he joined the troops with Pizarro and helped capture the Inca capital of Cuzco and King Atahualpa. Pizarro rewarded his courage and de Soto returned to Spain with more than a million dollars worth of gold and silver.

But de Soto grew restless at home and decided to return to the Americas to search for new treasures. Rather then compete with the conquistadors in Peru, he decided to explore the vast unknown region of Florida, which Cabeza de Vaca had described as a land of gold. King Carlos V of Spain supported these plans and made de Soto Governor of Cuba as well as any area that he discovered in Florida. De Soto landed in Havana in 1538 and spent a year marshaling his forces before he set off for Florida (→June 4).

De Soto and his huge party prepare to set up camp on the coast of Florida.

Calvin, King Henry in Protestant revolt

Geneva, 1536

A wave of religious reform is sweeping Europe, and at its crest sit a poor French scholar and the King of England. Several years ago, John Calvin converted to Protestantism, which seeks to purge the Catholic Church of worldly sins. The publication of *Institutes of the Christian Religion* this year makes him one of the faith's primary theologians.

Three years ago in London, King Henry VIII embraced Protestantism for reasons of his own. His wife of two decades, Catherine of Aragon, had borne him no heirs. But Pope Clement VII, reluctant to help Henry discard the aunt of Emperor Charles V, refused an annulment. So, with the help of chief minister Thomas Cromwell, the King broke with his wife and also with Rome.

Maps begin using the name America

Cleves, Westphalia, 1538

Maps published by the great cartographer Gerardus Mercator use the word America to refer to the new lands discovered by Christopher Columbus. Although it is widely accepted, the name is based on an error by Martin Waldseemuller, who in 1507 published the first map showing North and South America separated from Asia. The mapmaker believed the new lands should be named after Amerigo Vespucci, the Florentine voyager, because he "discovered a fourth part of the world." In fact, Vespucci was only a junior officer on ships that made trips to Brazil and he wrote a book on the country. The book's editor erroneously described Vespucci as the ship's captain, a mistake that gave him immortality.

Despite ransom, Pizarro kills Inca chief

Peru, Aug. 29, 1533

Despite his having paid a $15 million ransom for his freedom, the Inca Chief Atahualpa was executed today by order of Governor Francisco Pizarro. Atahualpa, a great leader, was believed to be a major obstacle to the conquest of Peru and the chief's death opens the way to Spanish control of the area. Captured by deceptive means and convicted of plotting an insurrection against the Spanish, Atahualpa said before he died, "Your own God, as you tell me, was put to death by the very men he created. But my God still looks down upon his children." Pizarro will leave next week for the Indian capital of Cuzco.

Atahualpa, despite ransom payment, is about to be burned at the stake.

1540 (1540-1549)

Mexico, Feb. 1540. Francisco Vasquez de Coronado leaves for Cibola with 400 Spaniards (287 soldiers) and 1,000 Indian "allies" (→ July 7).

Southwest, July 7, 1540. Coronado conquers Indian pueblo, thinking it is one of Seven Cities of Cibola (→ March 1541).

Southwest, Aug. 1540. Spaniard Hernando de Alvarado forges up Rio Grande to Indian village of Taos.

Southeast, Aug. 1540. De Soto, at Coosa [Alabama], encounters Temple Mound Indian culture (→ Oct. 19).

Southeast, Oct. 19, 1540. De Soto set upon by Choctaws at Mabila [Mobile]; 18 killed, 170 injured, supplies destroyed; de Soto claims 2,800 Indians killed (→ May 8, 1541).

Southeast, 1540. Priests accompanying de Soto conduct first recorded baptism in New World, of an Indian guide.

Tiguex, March 1541. Spanish suppress native rebellion after siege of pueblos (→ Apr. 1542).

Southeast, May 8, 1541. De Soto and party reach large river [south of Memphis], naming it Rio de Espiritu Santo [Mississippi] (→ Sept. 10, 1542).

Quebec, May 1542. Jacques Cartier leaves for France; relations with Indians in decline.

Southwest, Sept. 28, 1542. Spanish explorer Juan Rodriguez Cabrillo enters harbor [San Diego] on Pacific Coast. [He is first European in California] (→ Apr. 14, 1543).

Europe, 1542. Earliest picture of corn, or maize, appears in botany tract, *De historia stirpium,* by Leonhard Fuchs.

Southwest, 1543. Oil found first time in region [Texas] by Spaniard Luis de Moscoso.

Mexico, 1545. Spanish gain control over Maya (→ 1697).

DEATHS

Southeast, May 21, 1542. Hernando de Soto, Spanish explorer, buried in Mississippi River (*1496).

Eisleben, Feb. 18, 1546. Martin Luther, leader of Protestant Reformation in Germany (*Nov. 10, 1483).

Panama, Jan. 28, 1596. Sir Francis Drake, British navigator and admiral (*c.1541).

Spain, Dec. 2, 1547. Hernando Cortes, Spanish conqueror of Mexico (*1485).

De Soto discovers big, muddy river

Mexico, Sept. 10, 1542

A remnant of Hernando de Soto's expedition has landed in Mexico after a long journey that proved fatal to its commander, who discovered a big, muddy river [the Mississippi] on May 8, 1541, before he died on May 21.

A mere 332 remain of the 600 who set out from Spain with de Soto to conquer Florida and search for gold in April 1538. They found no gold, but they did find a big river several hundred miles inland. It was on the banks of that river that de Soto died of a fever.

The survivors told a harrowing tale of a hard trek across the continent and sporadic battles with the natives they had tried to enslave. The well-armed company had set forth from the coast with many cavaliers, a contingent of clergy and a herd of pigs for provisions. They bore handcuffs, iron neck collars and chains to hold captives.

De Soto set a hostile tone with the natives from the start, sending armed men to capture some of them while he was at the coast. In May 1540, at Cofitachequi on the Savannah River, they met a tribe led by a woman. She befriended de Soto, but he later took her hostage. In July, after wandering westward, de Soto's band took prisoners in the villages of Coste and Coosa [Alabama].

Some three months later, they encountered Chief Tuscaloosa, whom de Soto also imprisoned. The chief, a tall, proud man, managed to arrange an ambush in which more than 20 Spaniards and as many as 2,000 natives were slain, including Tuscaloosa's son.

De Soto and his men pressed on, generally to the west, through the land of the Cherokee and Chickasaw tribes, to the banks of a wide, muddy river in May 1541. They spent a year exploring the country west of that river, which de Soto named Rio de Espiritu Santo, and reached the slopes of a great mountain chain before turning back.

The commander was buried in the mud at the river's bottom. His companions then built seven boats with forced labor. They ate the last of their livestock, floated south and landed in Mexico, where the Viceroy welcomed them.

William H. Powell's "Discovery of the Mississippi," displaying cannon and cross, depicts the double-edged thrust of the Spanish foray into the New World.

Natives are no match for Spanish technology, fueled by a hot lust for gold.

De Soto is buried in the mud at the bottom of the great river. With him lie the romantic adventurer's dreams of finding gold and jewels in a strange land.

Spanish explorer finds Grand Canyon

Mexico, Dec. 1540

One of General Francisco de Coronado's officers, Captain Lopez de Cardenas, reports that he has come upon a deep and vast canyon in the far north of Mexico. A leading member of General Coronado's expedition that was assigned to conduct a search for the Seven Cities of Gold, Cardenas also discovered a great reddish-colored waterway to which he has given the name Colorado River. Although Cardenas has not come across a shred of evidence concerning the legendary golden cities, the captain evidently was the first European to view and to enter the awesome chasm to which he has given the appropriate name of Grand Canyon.

Horses introduced into North America

Mexico, Winter 1540

Governor General Francisco de Coronado left Compostela, New Galicia, in February, at the head of one of the largest exploration parties ever authorized by the King. The entourage includes 230 mounted cavalrymen, 1,000 horses – said to be the first on the continent – and 600 pack animals to carry the equipment needed on a long mission. His mission: to explore uncharted areas north of the settled parts of upper New Spain and to find the Golden Cities of Cibola.

Dominican priest killed by Indians

Tampa, Florida, June 26, 1549

Luis Cancer de Barbastro, a Dominican monk and a veteran of missionary activity in Guatemala, was killed by the Indians today. Fray Cancer, who had been looking for three companions captured by natives several days earlier, was clubbed to death by the natives as he prayed. The deaths make Fray Cancer and his companions the first martyrs of the faith in the province of Florida. It seems that the warlike Indians of this province are unlikely to be converted easily.

Coronado, seeks gold, finds pueblo

Mexico, Apr. 1542

General Francisco Vasquez de Coronado has returned to Mexico after failing to find in the North American interior either the fabled Seven Cities of Cibola or another legendary land of fabulous riches called Quivira.

After hearing the tales of the wealthy Seven Cities of Cibola, Coronado left Compostela, New Galicia, in February 1540 in order to determine whether the legends were true. With an army of 300 men and an experienced guide named Melchor Diaz, Coronado traveled due north for five months. He arrived at the site of the reputed City of Gold in July and found not a rich Cibola but a poor Indian village named Zuni. The Indians tried to resist but were no match for the Spaniards, and were quickly and violently defeated.

Afterward, Coronado heard of Quivira from a captive Indian called the Turk because of the turbanlike headdress he wore. Coronado and his men, with the Turk as a guide, marched north to a windswept spot on the plains [Kansas]. They found Indians living in huts with roofs of straw. When questioned, the Turk admitted he had misled the Spaniards out of hatred, hoping they would die of cold and hunger. On Coronado's orders, the Turk was choked to death.

"Coronado's March" (1898), from an illustration by Frederick Remington. Although the explorer found no riches, a new area is open to the Spanish.

Natives' bondage barred by King

New Spain, 1549

Labor relations between colonists and natives are now a pawn in the struggle of the Spanish crown to assert royal power over the colonies. A system called encomienda gives settlers in New Spain the right to impose commodity and labor taxes on the Indians. Politically and economically, encomienda is the engine that drives colonial society. He who controls encomienda controls the colonies.

In 1542, explaining the move in humanitarian terms, Carlos V enacted the New Laws for the Indies, barring new grants of encomienda. Throughout the colonies, the powerful backers of the system rebelled. The Mexican Viceroy refused to announce the legislation. By 1546, the crown reconsidered, repealing the New Laws. But the King will not give up; he has barred the exaction of labor as tribute. Colonists may soon have to regulate themselves to preserve the work force. Brutality is decimating the native population of the Indies. And disease and overwork threaten Indians on the continent (→1552).

Ferrelo enters harbor; Cabrillo sails coast

Mexico, Apr. 14, 1543

A Christian Levantine, Bartoleme Ferrelo, returned to Puerto de Navidad today after discovering and exploring a large bay area [San Francisco]. He took over command of the fleet after the death in January of Captain Juan Rodriguez Cabrillo, who had explored the western coast from lower California to the north for 1,000 miles [Oregon]. On their voyage of more than nine months, Cabrillo and Ferrelo discovered other bays [San Diego] on the western coast as well as islands [Catalina].

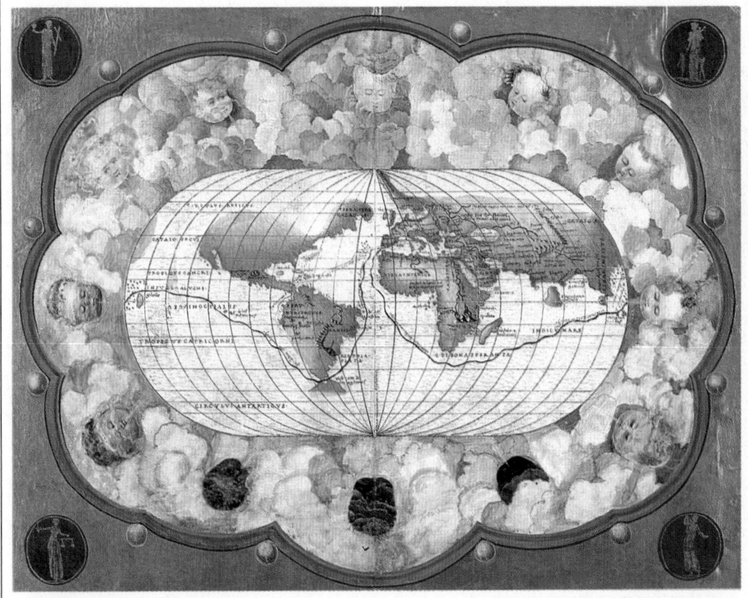

Spain, 1543. *Commissioned by Emperor Carlos V as a gift for his son Philip, a map by Battista Agnese shows the Spanish treasure fleet's route.*

1550 (1550-1559)

Spain, 1550. Spanish explorers describe great wooden temple mounds, built by Indians in southeastern North America.

Florida, 1550. Spanish bring first beef cattle to North America.

New Spain, 1551. Law decrees that Negroes, free or slave, may not take Indian mistresses or carry firearms; punishments include whipping, cutting off ears and imprisonment.

Europe, 1551. Sir Thomas More's *Utopia* translated from Latin into English.

Cuba, 1555. French sack Spanish settlement at Havana.

Newfoundland, 1555. Basque privateering fleet led by Captain Juan de Erauso and Perez de Hoa raids French fort at St. John's fishery, capturing it for Spanish (→1557).

South America, 1555. Vice Admiral Durand de Villegagnon founds French colony at Rio de Janeiro.

Mexico City, 1556. *Ordinary of the Mass* is first book with music printed in New World.

Newfoundland, 1557. French revive St. John's fishery with help of armed escort.

Europe, 1558. Indian shown smoking long, fat cigar in drawing in Andre Thevet's *Les Singularites de la France.*

Vera Cruz, Mexico, June 11, 1559. Don Tristan de Luna y Arellano sails for Florida with party of 1,500, intending to settle on gulf coast (→Aug. 14).

Florida, Aug. 14, 1559. De Luna enters bay on gulf coast [Pensacola] (→1559).

Florida, 1559. De Luna founds settlement [on Mobile Bay] (→July 9, 1561).

Europe, 1559. Peace of Cateau-Cambrais halts conflict between France and Spain.

Italy, 1550's. Ramusio's *Delle Navigationi e Viaggi* is first narrative of North American voyages widely circulated in Europe.

DEATHS

Mexico, Sept. 22, 1554. Francisco Vasquez de Coronado, Spanish explorer of American Southwest (*c.1510).

St. Malo, Normandy, Sept. 1, 1557. Jacques Cartier, French explorer of St. Lawrence Valley (*1491).

London, 1557. Sebastian Cabot, British explorer of North Atlantic; may have reached Hudson Bay (*c.1482).

New book details cruelty toward natives

The natives take revenge: In a Theodor de Bry woodcut, "Indi Hispanis aurum sitientibus," Indians pour molten gold down the throat of a captured Spaniard.

Seville, Spain, 1552

New evidence backs the claim made by the historian Pietro Martire d'Anghiera that a boat could travel from the Bahamas to Hispaniola "without compass or chart, guiding itself solely by the trail of dead Indians who had been thrown from ships." The new evidence appears in *Brief Relations of the Destruction of the Indies,* a stinging attack on colonial practices in the New World written by Bartolome de Las Casas, a member of the Dominican Order of Friars. He is best known for drafting Spain's New Laws (1542-43), which call for the eventual abolition of encomienda – the colonial system of enslaving natives to conquistadors. Lately, the system has crept back into favor, and the Las Casas book is a plea for its end.

The author writes from first-hand experience. The son of a merchant who traveled on Columbus's second voyage to the New World, Las Casas joined Spain's 1502 expedition to the West Indies. There he was so appalled by the cruelty Spanish troops showed toward natives that he began the campaign for reform that became his life's work. After entering the Dominican order in 1523, Las Casas sought to convert Indians to Christianity and to improve their status in the eyes of their conquerors. His efforts have earned him the title "protector of the Indians" (→Sept. 23, 1595)

Queen Mary dies; burned Protestants

London, Nov. 17, 1558

Queen Mary, daughter of Henry VIII and Katherine of Aragon, died at 42 today after a five-year reign most notable for the restoration of Catholicism as the official state religion and for brutal persecution of Protestant "heretics."

Prominent among her approximately 300 victims were the former Archbishop of Canterbury, Thomas Cranmer, and Bishops Latimer, Ridley and Hooper. Large crowds witnessed their executions, which were often gruesome affairs, the slow burning of the wood prolonging the victims' agony. Such scenes were largely unprecedented in England and have done much to win sympathy for the Protestant cause.

Denounced by Scottish preacher John Knox as "a wicked Jezebel," the Queen is already becoming known as "Bloody Mary."

Bloody Mary, Queen of England.

Europe enjoys tobacco: Who brought it?

First cigar in print.

Europe

Tobacco, the leafy herb from the New World, is being hailed as a miracle medicine, but there is a dispute over who first imported it to Europe. Andre Thevet, a Franciscan, says he brought tobacco seeds back from a trip to Brazil in 1555. But Jean Nicot, French Ambassador to Portugal, denies this and says he has been given seeds by a New World sailor.

After one of Nicot's servants claimed that an ulcer he had was cured by a tobacco poultice, Nicot sent some seeds to the Queen of France. Many European noblemen now claim it as a cure for everything from the pox to dental problems. Some have suggested naming the active ingredient in tobacco nicotine, in honor of Nicot.

Spain, Sept. 23, 1561. King Philip II issues cedula, ordering halt to colonizing efforts in Florida (→ June 29, 1565).

Florida, May 1, 1562. Jean Ribault and 150 French Huguenots land on coast, naming waterway River of May [St. Johns River] (→ 1563).

Hispaniola, 1562. Briton John Hawkins arrives with illegal shipment of Negro slaves.

England, 1563. Ribault visits English court early in year with *The Whole and True Discoverye of Terra Florida*, first account of Florida published in English (→ June 22, 1564).

Europe, 1563. Term "Puritan" applied to British Protestants who want to purify the church.

Florida, June 22, 1564. Rene de Goulaine de Laudonniere lands at Matanzas Inlet to set up Fort Caroline on River of May (→ May 1565).

Spain, June 29, 1565. Admiral Pedro Menendez de Aviles leaves on mission to break up French colony in Florida, knowing French reinforcements are on the way (→ Aug. 28).

Florida, Aug. 28, 1565. Ribault and reinforcements arrive at Fort Caroline, long overdue (→ Sept. 13).

Florida, Aug. 28, 1565. Pedro Menendez de Aviles enters harbor, naming it San Augustin [St. Augustine] (→ Sept. 8).

Florida, Sept. 13, 1565. Ribault beset by devastating storm en route to attack Spanish at St. Augustine (→ 20).

Florida, Sept. 20, 1565. Menendez, marching to Fort Caroline, wipes out French force, killing 132 in first hour (→ Oct. 1565).

Florida, Nov. 1565. Menendez, after renaming French fort San Mateo, builds forts along Indian River with 500 Negro slaves (→ May 1566).

St. Augustine, May 1566. Spanish fend off Indian attack, but lose supplies and most of fort to fire (→ March 2, 1568).

Spain, Oct. 1566. Expedition, launched at Santa Elena, home after exploration of new coastal region [Chesapeake Bay].

Florida, 1566. First Jesuit missionaries arrive (→ 1569).

Santa Elena, March 2, 1568. Pardo returns from second expedition to West with corn for settlers, having charted route to river [Mississippi] (→ June 1570).

French venture into Spanish Florida

Florida, 1563

The French have constructed a settlement here on land that Captain Jean Ribault describes as "the fairest, fruitfullest and pleasantest of all the worlds." Ribault and 150 men left France on February 8 of last year, hoping to stake out a French Huguenot colony in this Spanish territory. On May 1, 1562, sailing into what Ribault named the River of May [St. Johns River], he and his crew continued along the coast and anchored at a bluff on the south bank, Port Royal [Parris Island, South Carolina], where they began the settlement of Charlesfort.

Before returning to France, Ribault placed Captain La Pierria in charge of the colony with 30 men, hoping that they would become acquainted with the region while he was pressing for more financial support from those back home.

Food, however, was scarce and the angry, famished men revolted against La Pierria. They elected a Captain Barre in his place, and with the help of local Indians, Barre and the men constructed a small vessel for their return to France.

Unfortunately, they did not have enough food to get them through the journey, and with no other resources, the desperate sailors resorted to cannibalism. Perhaps because of this diet, they were able to persevere until their rescue by an English privateer. The survivors have returned to France with the gruesome details (→ June 22, 1564).

Captain Ribault's landing party is met by Indians at the River of May. Engraving (1591) by Theodor de Bry after Jacques Le Moyne de Morgues.

French try again at Florida settlement

Florida, May 1565

Rene de Goulaine de Laudonniere, now serving as Lieutenant of Florida, is in charge of a new post at the River of May, where a lack of food has led to mutinies and a kidnapping. Laudonniere, 300 men and four women constructed the settlement, Fort Caroline, last year. But troubles started almost immediately, since the chances of finding gold or even enough food proved to be miniscule. Reports came in last fall that two mutinies had occurred. In September, one band of dissatisfied men seized a French privateer's vessel hoping for better profits raiding Spanish ships in the West Indies. November brought another uprising, with Laudonniere captured and imprisoned by his own men. But he overpowered the crew and subsequently executed four of its leaders. This month, in a desperate move, Laudonniere attacked one of the villages of the Utina tribe. He is holding its chief for ransom, hoping that the Indians will pay him with a supply of corn (→ Aug. 28).

Spanish give up on colony at Pensacola

Hispaniola, July 9, 1561

Another effort to colonize Florida has failed, with the return of Angel de Villafane and the remnants of the 1559 expedition of Tristan de Luna y Arellano. The group had attempted to establish a colony at Pensacola Bay. De Luna sailed for Florida with a party of 1,500. Many grew ill while he was exploring and fighting the natives. The Viceroy of Mexico, dissatisfied with de Luna's leadership, replaced him with de Villafane, but he gave up after an unsuccessful attempt to move to the Atlantic coast.

Athore, a Florida Indian chief, shows Laudonniere a column erected by his predecessor, Ribault. Watercolor (1564) by Jacques Le Moyne de Morgues.

Menendez and colonists establish St. Augustine

St. Augustine, Sept. 8, 1565

After an inconsequential battle with French Huguenot settlers at Fort Caroline, Admiral Pedro Menendez de Aviles sailed south, returning to the harbor of St. Augustine, Florida, today. Two companies of infantry were sent ashore and proceeded to create a defensive position around a house that was supplied to them by the natives. Menendez has also gone ashore.

Menendez first entered the harbor August 28, and, celebrating the feast day of Saint Augustine with a High Mass, gave the site its current name. The activities of the Spaniards have been closely observed by the natives, who have been treated to a banquet by Menendez.

The new Spanish settlement at St. Augustine has raised many important issues. Most definitely it suggests that King Philip II of Spain looks upon Florida as a Spanish territory worthy of the attention of so distinguished a personage as Menendez. The wealth flowing into Spain from the colonies of the New World could be attacked easily from the French bases in Florida. The Spanish have had their share of experience with piracy in the region. Religion also plays a major role in these fears. Most of the French settlers now at Fort Caroline are Huguenots who have broken away from the Catholic Church. As such, they are in the eyes of the Spanish monarch not only foreign invaders but heretics as well. If the altercation between Admiral Menendez and the French is any indication, the chance of new outbreaks of violence is great.

Meanwhile, the Spaniards are rejoicing in their new settlement and hoping that it will last longer than their previous attempts at colonization of the region (→ Nov. 1565).

Admiral Pedro Menendez de Aviles supervises the building of St. Augustine.

Spanish wipe out French settlement; all but a few slaughtered

Florida, Oct. 1565

A Spanish army has slaughtered hundreds at the French Fort Caroline, sparing only a few Catholics and some women and children. Under Admiral Pedro Menendez de Aviles, the Spanish showed little mercy, hacking the men to pieces with swords and daggers. Some were even promised clemency, one survivor said, and then massacred.

Captain Jean Ribault of France, who founded the settlement on May 1, 1562, was among the dead, apparently captured by Menendez and executed. As Menendez wrote in a letter to his King on October 15, "I had Juan Ribao and all the rest put to the knife, considering it to be necessary to the service of God and your majesty." Menendez has wiped out the first non-Spanish colony near Mexico, one of Protestants, and in Spain's eyes heretics.

Surveying at the mouth of the River of May [St. Johns River], Menendez spotted four French ships and fired a warning. But because of approaching storms, he retreated temporarily. Ribault, who had just returned from France to discover the fort near extinction, had found out about the enemy vessels and took many of his ships with him to fight at sea. Later in the battle, 200 of Ribault's men were shipwrecked in a hurricane south of St. Augustine. The Spanish captured and massacred virtually all of them, giving the area the name of Matanzas, Spanish for slaughter.

Some 240 women, children, servants and sick men were left in the garrison, with a few soldiers. On September 20, the Menendez force marched overland through the swamps to strike. They killed 132 people in the first hour. Menendez had the survivors hanged under a placard citing the reason for the battle: "I do this not as to Frenchmen, but as to Lutherans [Huguenots]" (→ May 3, 1568).

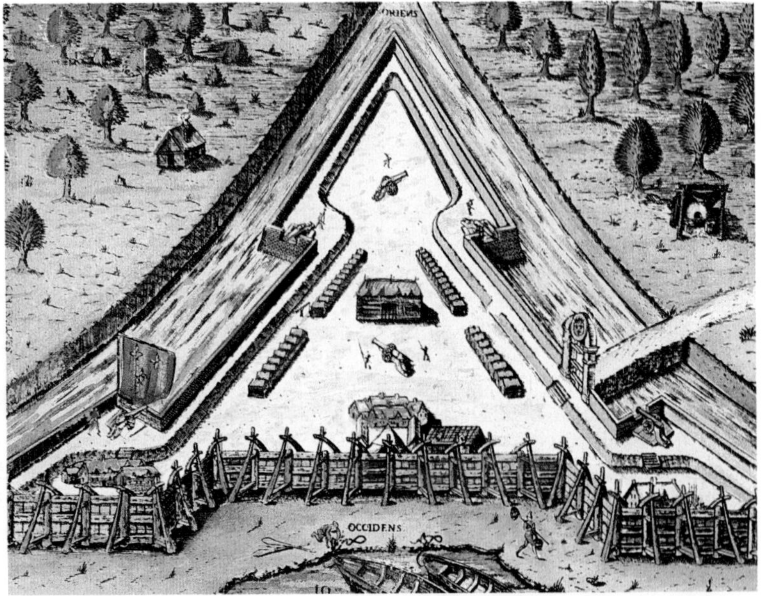

Fort Caroline, failed bulwark against the onslaught of Menendez and the zeal of the Spanish. Engraving (1591) by de Bry after Jacques Le Moyne.

Billiards in America

St. Augustine, Florida, 1565

Spanish settlers are playing a new game in which the players try to hit a little ball into a table pouch with a stick. The game is said to have evolved as an indoor version of lawn bowls. Some credit the French, who call the ball a bille, as in billiard, with popularizing the game. Others trace it to England.

More Jesuits land

Florida, 1569

The missionaries of the Society of Jesus are continuing their activities in all of New Spain despite an inauspicious beginning in the New World. Of the first three Jesuits to arrive in Florida in 1566, one was killed by Indians and the others were forced to return to Havana after the captain of their ship failed to locate St. Augustine. The martyrdom of Father Martinez spurred the order's activities and 12 more Jesuits arrived in the colony in June 1568. Presently, the missionaries are working among the Indians in Florida, Guale [Georgia] and Orista [South Carolina], hoping to establish permanent missions among the Indians (→ Feb. 1571).

Spanish attack Hawkins, angering Britain

Hawkins, slave trader and privateer.

London, Oct. 1568

News that the popular John Hawkins narrowly escaped capture at the hands of an attacking Spanish fleet in the West Indies has provoked an angry reaction in England, resulting in a state of undeclared war.

The 36-year-old Hawkins has been a pioneer in the highly profitable business of shipping slaves from the west coast of Africa and selling them in the Spanish West Indies, despite a ban by the Madrid government. When trapped by the Spanish fleet in San Juan de Ulua this month, Hawkins was on his third slaving voyage since 1562. Commanding one of the three English ships that escaped the Spanish fleet was Hawkins's kinsman, Francis Drake. Two other ships were lost in the attack. Adding to the annoyance of the British crown is the fact that Queen Elizabeth, while officially disapproving of the slave trade, has herself been an investor in the Hawkins ventures.

In addition to pioneering the slave trade, Hawkins is credited with having introduced the sweet potato to Britain from America four years ago, and tobacco in 1565, when he brought a shipload back with him from Florida.

Indian views France

France, 1562

The writer Montaigne, talking to an Indian about Europe, found the native wondering why "half the people had enough comforts, while the other half were emaciated by poverty" and "how the needy half could bear such injustice," and "why they did not seize them by the throat and burn down their houses."

Mercator's map

Cleves, Westphalia, 1569

A map that could greatly aid explorers has been published by Gerardus Mercator. A cylindrical projection, it shows all lines of longitude as parallel. Although it distorts the size of land masses in the far north and south, it simplifies navigation by showing a constant compass direction as a straight line.

Revenge: French burn down Spanish fort

Florida, May 3, 1568

Angered by the brutal onslaught of Spanish troops at Fort Caroline, a French force has burned the San Mateo fort and massacred hundreds of Spaniards. Led by a Catholic soldier, Dominique de Gourgues, a strong and determined body of French soldiers landed on Cumberland Island earlier this year, assembling the help of the Tacatacuru Indians. On April 12, the French and Indians began their operation with all-out frontal and rear attacks against the northern post of San Mateo. They swiftly overpowered 60 Spaniards: most were slaughtered immediately, with the rest held for a later execution.

In a second battle, some of the Spanish managed to escape. But on April 13, Gourgues, with an even stronger force of Indians, mounted an assault on the main garrison. Those who did not flee or were not immediately killed, were assembled and bluntly told they were being executed in revenge for the massacre at Fort Caroline. Gourgues hanged the men beneath a placard: "Not as to Spaniards, but as to Traitors, Robbers and Murderers."

After the French raided the fort, an explosion in a storage room set the structure afire. Gourgues led a final celebration, demolishing the garrison and its blockhouses. Satisfied that he had accomplished his mission of revenge, Gourgues left for France today (→ Dec. 1576).

Widening horizons: Navigating the seas

Navigators in the Northern Hemisphere use the North Star to determine their latitude. Not until the mid-15th century, when Prince Henry's voyages took the Portuguese below the equator, did seamen begin using solar indicators.

Portsmouth, England, 1560

The British navy is building more ships on the pattern of Henry VIII's Henri Grace a Dieu, nicknamed the "Great Harry," the first four-masted vessel launched in Britain and a symbol of a revolution in shipbuilding and navigation begun by Portugal and Spain that has taken Europeans around the world. This century has seen the development of the carrack, with its towering poop deck, and of the slimmer, more maneuverable galleon, which has sails that can make use of favorable winds. In navigation, the cross-staff has replaced the ancient astrolabe as a way to determine latitudes at sea by measuring the altitude of heavenly bodies. The need now is a way to measure longitude. It can be done with an accurate clock, but no such timepiece is available.

"The Student of Navigation" (1556), a woodcut from Martin Cortes's "Breve Compendio de la Sphera," Seville. Shortly after the 12th-century invention of the compass, seamen began looking to marine charts as guides.

1570 (1570-1579)

Florida, June 1570. Las Alas cuts garrisons to bare minimum to avoid starvation; he returns to Spain with 120 settlers (→Apr. 1577).

Mexico, 1571. Spanish install Inquisition tribunal here (→1578).

Seville, Spain, 1571. Dr. Nicolas Monardes publishes book lauding medicinal value of tobacco, making him a widely cited authority.

Europe, 1572. Woodcuts of bananas and other American fruit trees seen for first time in Girolamo Benzoni's *Historia del Mundi Nuovo*.

Florida, 1573. Franciscans begin to replace Jesuits.

Spain, 1573. New Laws of the Indies bar territorial conquest without explicit royal sanction.

Canada, June 1576. Martin Frobisher sails up east coast in first British search for the fabled Northwest Passage (→Oct. 15, 1577).

Florida, Dec. 1576. Nicolas Strozzi, in command of French privateer wrecked north of Santa Elena, tells Indians he is enemy of Spain and builds fort (→Apr. 1578).

Mexico, 1576. Epidemic kills nearly 40% of Indians in New Spain.

Florida, July 1577. Pedro Menendez Marques arrives in St. Augustine to take over as Governor and rebuild Santa Elena, destroyed by Indians (→1587).

Bristol, England, Oct. 15, 1577. Frobisher returns with 200 tons of ore [mistakenly believed to be gold] after second voyage (→1578).

Florida, Apr. 1578. Menendez Marques burns Indian village at Cocopay, trading prisoners for Frenchmen previously taken by Indians (→Aug. 1579).

South America, Dec. 5, 1578. Sir Francis Drake, after sailing through Strait of Magellan, raids Valparaiso (→July 26, 1579).

Florida, Aug. 1579. Menendez Marques attacks Cusabo tribe, killing some 40 Frenchmen from Nicolas Strozzi's party now scattered among Indians (→July 17, 1580).

DEATH

Santander, Spain, Sept. 7, 1574. Pedro Menendez de Aviles, who founded St. Augustine, the first city in North America (*Feb. 15, 1519).

Drake, circling globe, finds huge bay

Drake's Bay, July 26, 1579

Francis Drake, the English explorer, has discovered a major bay on the coast of California [San Francisco Bay]. Drake had left Portsmouth, England, in 1577 to harass Spanish shipping along the Pacific coast. After having captured several galleons that were carrying cargoes of gold and silver worth millions of pounds, he directed his ship, the Golden Hind, into a huge natural bay so it could undergo repairs. On June 17, naming "the fair and good bay" Drake's Bay, he claimed the entire territory for Queen Elizabeth and called it New Albion because with its white cliffs and a summertime coolness, it reminded him of England.

After they came ashore, Drake and the crew were greeted by friendly natives who lived in a nearby village. His men ventured inland and reported sighting herds of deer that numbered in the thousands. The crew took fish and fowl, picked up samples of the local seeds such as acorns, and hunted for wild game. During the next week, Drake conducted Protestant services, the first in the New World, aboard the Golden Hind.

Since the vessel had been at sea for a year and half, battling the elements as well as the Spanish men-of-war, it was desperately in need of refitting. And the weary crew was just as desperately in need of time to rest. Consequently, Drake stayed on in the bay for a month. He is due to set sail for England today by way of a "northeast passage" that he thinks cuts across the New World to the Atlantic. Since the Spanish are still searching the seas off Mexico for him, this seems a wise decision (→Sept. 26, 1580).

Drake, scourge of Spanish shipping.

Indians destroy Spanish Florida outpost

Spain, Apr. 1577

The Governor of Florida, ruler of a swampy, infertile land guarded jealously by its native population, has returned home only to face a warrant for his arrest. It appears that Hernando de Miranda, shaken by Indian wars, took 6,000 ducats from a garrison chest before fleeing his post earlier this year.

Miranda first went to Florida last year. Finding the colonists of Santa Elena trapped on a barren island [Parris Island], he ordered military leader Alonso de Solis to get tough with Indians on the mainland. After raiding the village of Oristan in July, Solis and 26 of his men were killed by Cusabo warriors. A siege followed at Santa Elena, and the 287 colonists had to be evacuated. With the loss of its northern settlement and its leader, Florida's prospects look grim (→July 1577).

Paris, 1570. *Abraham Ortelius, a Flemish cartographer, has produced this year a unique book, collecting maps of the world under a single cover. Above is his rendering of the New World, incorporating the latest of findings.*

Indians kill group of Spanish Jesuits

Virginia, Feb. 2, 1571.

The Jesuit mission here [Virginia] met a tragic end this morning; all eight missionaries to the colony were murdered by Indians who pretended to be their friends. This scheme was planned by Don Luis, an Indian who had converted to Christianity, taken a Spanish name and been a guest at the court of King Philip II of Spain.

In 1570, Don Luis left Spain and traveled to Havana. There he met Fathers Quiros and Segura, who planned a journey to a large bay area to the north [Chesapeake Bay]. Don Luis said that he would like to travel with them and serve as both preacher and translator. Six other Jesuits and a boy named Alonso sailed with them; they went ashore at Axacan on September 10.

Initially, Don Luis helped the Jesuits obtain food and acted as interpreter. But as winter approached, he began living with the Indians while the Jesuits were forced to grub for roots and herbs. This morning, Don Luis instructed several Indians to ask the Jesuits for their hatchets so they could chop wood. Given the tools, the Indians fell on the unarmed Jesuits and killed them. Only the life of the boy, Alonso, was spared (→1573).

Briton pursues search for northwest route

Milford Haven, England, 1578
British mariner Martin Frobisher has come back empty-handed from his third expedition to North America in search of gold and a passage to India through the northern ice. His flotilla of 15 vessels made a landing at Kodlunarn Island in Warwick's Sound, where crew members excavated tons of ore that later proved worthless.

In spite of the disappointments, the three Frobisher expeditions added immeasurably to the knowledge of the northern islands that Queen Elizabeth has christened Meta Incognita and over which the explorer claimed sovereignty in the name of the Queen.

Last year, on Frobisher's second voyage, the three ships under his command carried as provisions oatmeal, hardtack, flour, pickled beef and pork, dried peas, codfish, butter, cheese, rice, honey and vinegar, as well as eight tuns of beer. All three vessels returned safely after a stormy Atlantic crossing. On the first expedition in 1576, with a company of skilled craftsmen and miners, Frobisher came upon a strait [Hudson Strait] at the head of a great bay [Frobisher Bay], but he turned back. Plans for a permanent settlement were dropped and the fleet sailed for England.

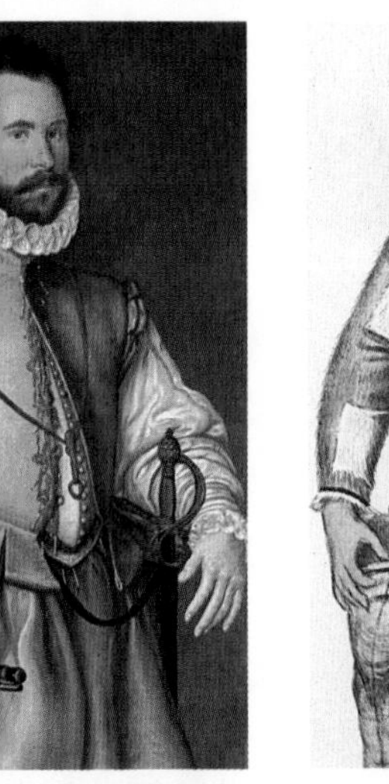

"Sir Martin Frobisher" by C. Ketel.

An Eskimo mother by John White.

One of Frobisher's exploratory boats is beset by ice and Eskimo bowmen.

Iroquois form peace league of five tribes

Northeast America, 1570
Deganawida, a divine leader, was greatly distressed at the wars that had brought so much unhappiness to his people. So he and his disciple, Hiawatha, a Mohawk chief and shaman, decided that they would found a league of Indian tribes in order to meet peacefully and settle their differences.

This is the legend that the Iroquois relate around their fires about the birth of an Indian alliance among the Cayuga, Oneida, Seneca, Mohawk and Onondaga tribes. The league is not a loose confederation of tribes but rather an extension of Iroquois social organization, which has its foundation in the smallest unit of tribal life, known as the "fireside." A fireside is made up of a mother and her children, and it is part of a larger group that is called an "ohwachira," or a group of related families whose lineage can be traced through the mothers. Two or more ohwachiras make up a clan, and various clans form a tribe or a nation. Authority stems from the ohwachiras, the heads of which must always be women. The women choose the male delegates to the clan or tribal councils that get together every summer.

Grasset's "Iroquois Warrior" (1787).

Spain executes first American heretics

Mexico City, 1578
The Holy Office of the Inquisition has found itself busy in New Spain since its official inception in 1571. The primary focus of its activities has been the English and French who were shipwrecked on or settled in the colony. Most of these men have been influenced by Lutheranism. The greatest of the autos-da-fe held so far was in Mexico City on February 28, 1574. At this event, which witnesses claim was equal to the one at Valladolid in 1559, 60 people were scourged and sent to the galleys, seven imprisoned, and two Englishmen and an Irishman were burned for heresy. While 36 were punished for Lutheranism, others suffered for having committed bigamy, sorcery and blasphemy and for asserting that fornication between the unmarried was not a sin.

Although in the three executions held since then only one man has been burned, for Lutheranism in 1575, it seems the Inquisition is not moribund. The recent trial of two so-called Judaizers attests to that.

Europe and America swap food products

Europe, 1576
Trade between the colonies and Europe has resulted in a wide range of new foods for both regions. Europeans have successfully cultivated sugar cane in the Americas, and have introduced such fruits and vegetables as bananas, limes, lemons, oranges, olives, cabbages and lettuce in the New World. The Spanish brought cows to Florida in 1550, and cattle are being raised for beef and hogs for pork. But the Americas themselves have offered up a bounty of new, sometimes unusual foods, including the popular animal feed, Indian corn. The Spanish and Portuguese have begun to cultivate American peanuts in Asia, and England has been enjoying pineapples since their importation began 22 years ago. Spices like redhot chile peppers and flavorings like vanilla and chocolate have become quite fashionable, but tomatoes are believed to be poisonous and are cultivated only for animals. The Spanish have also been propagating sweet potatoes at home, but the white potato is still a curiosity.

1580 (1580-1589)

Florida, July 17, 1580. French vessel under Gilberto Gil, inquiring about Nicolas Strozzi at mouth of St. Johns, is trapped and destroyed by Spanish.

Plymouth, England, Sept. 26, 1580. Drake ends voyage around globe (→ June 18, 1586).

New Mexico, Aug. 21, 1581. Francisco Chamuscado, leading voyage to Pueblo area, claims it for Spain, with name San Felipe del Nuevo Mexico.

Florida, Jan. 1581. Spanish quell Indian uprising.

Europe, 1582. Richard Hakluyt's book *Divers Voyages* gives English-speaking world a view of American discoveries.

St. John's, Newfoundland, Aug. 5, 1583. Sir Humphrey Gilbert, with royal patent, annexes area for Britain.

Atlantic, Sept. 1583. Gilbert, on ship bound for England, cries out, "We are as near to heaven by sea as by land"; later, he drowns in a storm.

East Coast, July 13, 1584. Raleigh expedition puts into shore [at Oregon Inlet, North Carolina], claiming area for England (→ Jan. 25, 1585).

England, Jan. 25, 1585. Raleigh is knighted, shortly after renaming North American region "Virginia," in honor of virgin Queen (→ July 27).

Virginia, July 27, 1585. Raleigh's second expedition of 108 colonists, led by Sir Richard Grenville, reaches Roanoke Island (→ May 1586).

Virginia, May 1586. Ralph Lane, military leader, heads off Indian attack, killing chief Wingina (→ Aug. 1586).

Virginia, Aug. 1586. Grenville reaches Roanoke to find Lane gone; he leaves only 15-18 settlers and continues privateering (→ Aug. 18, 1587).

Florida, 1587. Spanish evacuate Santa Elena early in year (→ Sept. 23, 1595).

Virginia, Aug. 27, 1587. John White, after arriving at Roanoke on July 22, sails for Europe for supplies, leaving his 177 colonists behind (→ June 1588).

Virginia, June 1588. Spaniard Vincente Gonzalez explores area, finding trace of colony (→ July 1589).

Spain, July 1589. Menendez Marques persuades Spanish authorities to agree to plan to sail from Havana to Virginia and destroy British settlement (→ Aug. 17, 1590).

Raleigh calls new discovery Virginia

Virginia, July 4, 1584.

Sailors equipped by Walter Raleigh landed here today and took possession of this entire coastline for England. Raleigh, who remained in England, has the permission of Queen Elizabeth to name the area, some 1,800 nautical miles long, Virginia, after "the virgin queene." Commanders Arthur Barlow and Phillip Amadas left England with their expedition in April, and had crossed the Atlantic by June 10. They stopped at Puerto Rico and Florida before heading north. Barlow commands Raleigh's 50-ton Dorothy. Amadas who is to act as admiral of a new colony, is aboard the Tiger.

Chief Wingina, his brother Granganimeo and Indians from Roanoke Island, have sent the English presents of meat and fish, as well as maize, squash, walnuts and gourds.

Trading has been established with the Indians, who have "leather, coral and diverse kinds of dyes, very excellent." The Indians here use the word "wampum" to describe many articles used in trade.

Barlow said he visited a village on the northern tip of Roanoke Island [North Carolina] "where they were entertained with all love and kindness, and with as much bounty, after their manner, as they could possibly devise. We found the people most gentle, loving and faithful, void of all guile and treason, and such as lived after the manner of the Golden Age" (→ 13).

Sir Walter Raleigh and son.

Elizabeth I, the virgin Queen.

"The Arrival of the Englishmen in Virginia" (1590) by Theodor de Bry.

Calendar changed

Rome, Feb. 1582

Easter had moved 10 days away from its proper date and it was decided that something would have to be done. After great deliberation and consultations, what was decided by the astronomers of Pope Gregory XIII, therefore, was to bring the vernal equinox back to March 21 by removing 10 days, those between October 5 and October 15 of this year. Also as a result of their discussions, the astronomers decided to adopt a more accurate length of the year, that is, 365.2422 days. This count differs from the Julian calendar adopted in 46 B.C. by 0.0078 of a day.

Sir Francis Drake, knighted (above) in 1581, saved Captain Lane at Roanoke. In 1585, Raleigh was also knighted for his service to the Queen of England.

British wreck Spanish Armada, show new power

London, Sept. 15, 1588

The so-called "Invincible Armada" sent by Catholic King Philip of Spain to overthrow Protestant Queen Elizabeth of England has been handed a crushing defeat. Of the 130 ships that set out from Lisbon in May, barely half are straggling back toward home port. The rest have been destroyed in running battles up the English Channel, by fire ships sent in among the fleet when anchored off Calais and in a closely fought encounter off Gravelines, France, on July 29. Many ships that escaped were destroyed by fierce storms as they tried to return home by sailing round the northern tip of Scotland and past the west coast of Ireland.

Preparations for the Armada began in 1586, but they were dealt a stunning blow last year when Sir Francis Drake "singed the beard of the King of Spain" by attacking Cadiz and destroying scores of vessels. When it was finally ready to sail, the fleet's command was given to the Duke of Medina Sidonia, scion of one of Spain's most illustrious families, but totally without naval experience. His orders were to rendezvous with the Duke of Parma in Spanish-held Flanders, and convoy his army to England.

The English fleet was commanded by Lord Howard of Effingham, with Drake as second in command.

The Armada carries Spain's imperial ambitions up the English Channel.

Drake sacks Spanish American colonies

Roanoke, June 18, 1586

Sir Francis Drake, who six years ago became the first Englishman to circumnavigate the world, sailed from Roanoke Island today, his course set for England. This brings to an end a voyage that began on September 14 of last year when he sailed from Plymouth with a fleet of 29 ships and some 2,300 men.

His first target was Vigo, where he looted the cathedral as well as the city. After attacking and burning Santiago in the Cape Verde Islands, he reached the West Indies at Christmas, and on New Year's Day made a surprise attack on the heavily fortified city of San Domingo in Hispaniola. The city fell quickly and the Governor was forced to ransom it, for 25,000 ducats.

Seven weeks later, Drake sailed into the harbor of Cartagena on the Spanish Main and captured it with a land and sea attack. After plundering the city, he ransomed it for 110,000 ducats, then left the area and headed north. Before reaching Roanoke, where he took aboard Sir Ralph Lane and the surviving settlers, he burned the Spanish city of St. Augustine on June 7.

The boldness of these attacks is certain to arouse the wrath of the Spanish, to whom Drake is already known as El Draque – the Dragon.

First English child is born in America

Roanoke, Aug. 18, 1587

Glad tidings from Sir Walter Raleigh's settlement: the first English child is born in the New World. The daughter of Ananias and Ellinor Dare is named Virginia in honor both of the Queen and the fledgling colony. By way of a good omen, the birth is sorely needed, since previous attempts to settle the windswept isle have ended in mysterious failure. Two years ago, Sir Richard Grenville left 108 colonists here to seek gold and other riches. Neglecting to bring proper means of getting food, they began to starve. After they demanded that the Indians feed them, the natives set upon them with wooden knives. When Sir Francis Drake's vessel passed in June 1586, they gladly sailed with it.

Days later, a supply ship from Grenville dropped anchor, and 15 men remained ashore. Yet in May, when Captain John White returned with Ananias Dare and the hundred-odd members of the new party, no sign of the 15 was found. Unlike their predecessors, the latest colonists are a God-fearing people, and in recent weeks converted a friendly Indian, Manteo, to Christianity. If they can convert all his brethren, then they and Britain's New World may yet prosper (→27).

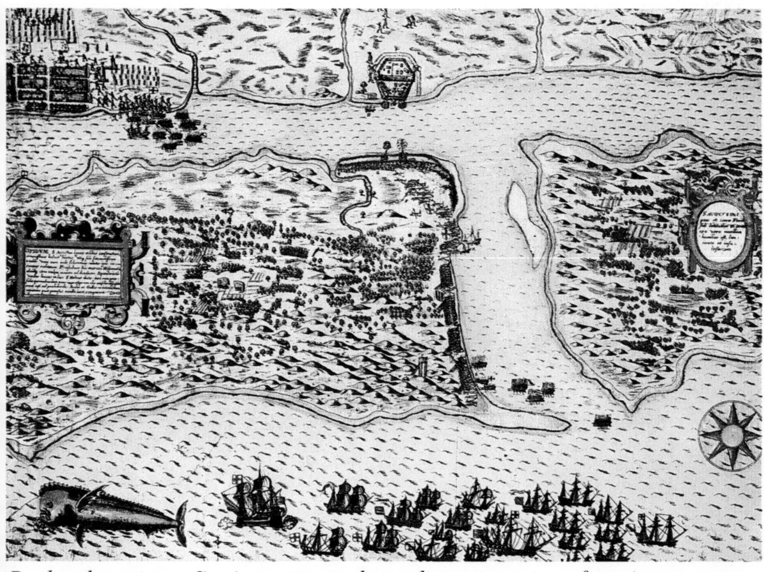

Drake closes in on St. Augustine in the earliest engraving of an American city.

Tiny Virginia Dare, the colony's portent of hope, is baptized at Roanoke.

1590 (1590-1599)

Mexico, July 27, 1590. Castana de Sosa sets out from Nueva Leon with 150 settlers in unauthorized effort to establish mining town in New Mexico (→Aug. 1591).

Mexico, Aug. 1591. De Sosa, arrested in New Mexico, is brought back to face disobedience charges.

Pacific Northwest, 1592. Juan de Fuca claims to have traveled through Northwest Passage to North Sea.

Central Plains, 1593. Entire Spanish expedition under Francisco de Levya Bonilla and Antonio Gutierez de Humana killed by Indians [in Kansas] while searching for "gold mines of Tindan."

Florida, 1594. Father Baltasar Lopez holds mass baptism of 80 Indians to encourage 13 new friars.

Southeast, Sept. 23, 1595. Spain divides region into mission provinces, in belief that conversion of Indians is preferable to conquest (→1596).

Mexico, Jan. 1596. Sebastian Rodriguez Cermeno returns after 22-month sea voyage up Pacific coast.

Florida, 1596. An estimated 1,500 natives converted by Spanish Franciscan priests in past two years (→1599).

Northeast, 1597. Simon Ferdinando, Portuguese navigator working for English crown, lands on coast [Maine] looking for treasure; he leaves frustrated.

England, 1597. Parliament passes act allowing deportation of convicted criminals to colonies.

Mexico, Jan. 8, 1598. Don Juan de Onate, with some 500 colonists, heads for New Mexico (→Dec. 24, 1599).

France, 1598. Marquis de la Roche leaves 40 convicts to colonize Sable Island [off Nova Scotia] (→1603).

DEATHS

Atlantic, 1591. Sir Richard Grenville, founder of Roanoke Island colony, killed in battle with Spanish off Azores (*c.1541).

Flanders, Dec. 2, 1594. Gerardus Mercator, Flemish cartographer and geographer (*March 5, 1512).

England, Jan. 27, 1596. Sir Francis Drake, British naval leader and privateer; circumnavigated the globe in 1577-80 (*1546).

Roanoke's English colony abandoned

John White arrives in August 1590 to find no trace of the settlers he left three years ago, save the word "Croatoan" carved in the doorpost of the palisade.

Roanoke, Virginia, Aug. 17, 1590

John White, the Governor of Roanoke Island [North Carolina], has returned to America only to find the settlement abandoned. After anchoring his two ships, Hopewell and Moonlight, within sight of where the colonists had been, White and his men arrived at the fort with supplies and casks of fresh water only to find the houses dismantled and the villagers gone. Among the missing settlers are White's daughter and his granddaughter, Virginia Dare.

On one of the entrance posts to the palisade was carved the word "Croatoan" and nearby was a tree with the letters "Cro" carved in "fair Roman letters." These carvings were evidently used to indicate a link between the departure of the settlers and the Croatan Indians, but the full meaning is not known.

In the abandoned fort, White's men came upon large guns that had been left with the colonists. All of the smaller weapons, equipment and supplies had been removed. Evidently, the colonists left only the equipment that was too heavy to carry and there is every indication that they left in an orderly fashion. It is believed that the colonists followed the Indians under Chief Manteo to the native village called Croatan where Manteo was born and which would be safer than the original settlement site. White intended to set sail immediately for Croatan, but a lost anchor, bad weather and dwindling supplies forced him to abandon the search until the spring (→March 1602).

Spanish expedition seizes New Mexico

San Gabriel, Dec. 24, 1599

Governor Juan de Onate announced today from this territorial capital that for all practical purposes the subjugation of New Mexico was complete. The struggle to conquer this territory was long and bitter. Onate originally invaded the country from his base, Chihuahua, last year. With a force of some 500 soldiers, servants and Spanish settlers, he was determined to acquire for the King a vast land, a land that was richer and "greater than New Spain" itself. But the area that he explored was not at all aglitter with the gold and silver he had heard of, and the task was arduous. He met fierce resistance from the Indians in his "war by blood and fire." Onate was a harsh general. When one Indian village resisted, he ordered that a foot be cut off every man over 25 years of age and every man in the pueblo give him 25 years of "personal service." After this show of resolve and brutality, the Indians surrendered to the Spanish forces (→Nov. 24, 1601).

Indians at war again, despite conversions

Florida, 1599

The number of martyred priests and lay brothers in Florida is rising steadily as marauding Indians continue to ravage coastal missions. The latest victims are two Franciscans, Father Pedro de Corpa and Father Blas Rodriguez of the Tolomato mission. Father de Corpa precipitated the crisis by reprimanding an Indian chief, Don Juanillo, for having more than one wife. The Franciscans also tried to prevent Don Juanillo from exercising his rights as chief in his village. The chief left the village and recruited followers from seven tribes in the area. After killing the priests, they went on to Guale [Saint Catherine's Island] and murdered another priest and a lay brother. It is expected that Governor Mendez de Canzo will call out troops to crush the uprising (→Nov. 5, 1600).

De Bry (1591) captures the chaos confronting the Spanish posts in Florida.

Edict of Nantes gives Huguenots freedom

King Henry IV of France.

Nantes, France, Apr. 13, 1598

An end to the religious wars that have plagued France for the last quarter century now seems in sight. King Henry IV has promulgated an edict in this Brittany port town that grants his Protestant subjects a large measure of religious freedom.

Under the terms of the edict, Huguenots, as French Protestants are generally called, are to have full freedom of conscience and the right to hold public worship in any place where they have held it in the last 25 years. Important nobles may hold services in their own homes. All civil rights, including the right to hold public office, attend schools and colleges, inherit property and conduct trade, are guaranteed by the edict, which also allows for special courts composed of Protestant and Catholic judges to settle disputes. Lastly, the Huguenots will be allowed to keep a number of important strongholds, among them La Rochelle, as "places de surete," with the cost of garrisoning them to be covered by the King.

Although the edict also intends to put a halt to the spread of Protestantism, opposition is expected from Pope Clement VIII and the Catholic clergy. Other critics are complaining that the terms of the edict are so generous that they may create a state within the state (→Oct. 18, 1685).

New laws to curb Protestant Separatists

London, 1593

Stringent new legislation aimed at curbing religious dissenters was passed during the recent session of Parliament. Under the new laws, Protestant Separatists who establish self-governing congregations outside the Church of England are to be punished by prison terms as well as fines. In the view of Queen Elizabeth and her Privy Council, only such stern measures can counter the growth of the Separatist movement. Since, by the Act of Supremacy of 1559, the Queen is the Supreme Governor of the Church of England, any threat to the Anglican Church is also to be seen as a challenge to the power of the monarchy. The move to suppress Protestant dissenters has been expected since the Catholic threat was eliminated with the defeat of the Spanish Armada (→May 1, 1609).

First plays offered

New Spain, July 11, 1598

America cannot yet claim any home-grown playwrights, but theater is catching on among Spanish colonists, who for the second time will be entertained by actors. Tonight, a troupe is presenting *Moros y los Christianos (Moors and Christians)*, by an anonymous playwright. Its sober title suggests that this work will contrast starkly with the very first theatrical performance in North America, a comedy staged on April 30 [near El Paso], about an expedition of soldiers.

An American wheel

Southwest, 1596

Invented in pre-historic times, the wheel has played a major role in the progress of Old World civilization. During the last century, the Hungarians developed the coach and almost all Europeans have used it. Now, thanks to the Spanish conquistadors, the New World has seen its first wheeled vehicle – a wagon, quite similar to that of the German farm cart. It is currently being used to haul travel supplies as the Spanish continue to explore and settle the region.

Europeans view first images of America

This engraving depicts Florida natives peacefully plumbing the prodigious Florida rivers for gold, very little of which has yet found its way to Europe.

Fruit of the New World Eden is not to be procured without danger. Well acquainted with the requisites of survival, Florida Indians kill alligators.

London, 1591

There are pictures of monstrous reptiles called alligators, and of savages with tattoos all over their bodies. There are scenes of terrible executions and barbarous rites. Europeans are seeing the New World for the first time, and they can't get enough of it. The publication of the second in a series of *Voyages* by Theodor de Bry is a huge success. The new book features engravings of Florida Indians based upon the paintings of the French artist Jacques Le Moyne de Morgues, who lived with the French Huguenots at Fort Caroline until it was destroyed by the Spanish in 1565.

Le Moyne, one of the few survivors, found refuge on the Levriere bound for France, but he was shipwrecked off the coast of Wales. The painter made his way to London, where he married and became a servant to Sir Walter Raleigh. Le Moyne's work did not receive wide attention until he died and his widow sold all of it to the Flemish engraver de Bry, who lives in London and who saw its commercial potential.

Vivid drawings of Indian culture by John White

England, 1593.

Strange and stunning images of the New World, drawn by John White, the late Governor of the Roanoke colony, can be found in a recent edition of Thomas Harriot's *A Brief and True Report of the New Found Land of Virginia.* White first traveled to Virginia in April of 1585 on an expedition sponsored by Sir Walter Raleigh. He spent a full year at the Roanoke colony, sketching plant, animal and human life before the settlement was abandoned in June of the following year. White lost his daughter and his granddaughter in a second attempt at settlement. After searching in vain for them, he retired to a home in Ireland. He died there this year after writing his own account of the final voyage to Virginia.

Algonquin life as seen by White.

Fishing off the coast of Virginia.

A native American male . . .

and a female, drawn by John White.

The alligator, a treacherous reptile found nowhere in Europe, inhabits the swamps and lakes of Florida, waiting to prey upon any creature that crosses its path. It is perhaps related to the beast Columbus referred to when he reported slaying a "serpent" during his premiere voyage to the New World.

The flora and fauna of Virginia are certain to generate as much interest as do the human inhabitants. The terrapin is one of many beasts that the Indians treat with reverence, taking care to use every part of each one slaughtered.

Unashamed of their nakedness, natives enact one of many idolatrous dances.

Artist with Drake depicts far side of the world

Nombre de Dios, nestled on the Caribbean coast of the Panama isthmus, is a major link in the flow of gold and other treasures from New Spain to Europe. Mined in the southern lands, the gold arrives at a port on the Pacific coast [Panama City] and are carried overland before making the long ocean voyage.

Europe, 1590's

A new collection of 200 images depicting the New World, entitled *The Natural History of the Indies*, is sure to appeal to those interested in life overseas. The illustrations show a wide array of flora and fauna as well as scenes of contact between Europeans and the natives of the Caribbean. The captions, written in French, describe economic and social conditions. The manuscript has been linked to an unknown artist accompanying Sir Francis Drake, who is mentioned twice by name in the text.

Native courtship: A suitor bearing gifts calls to prove his skill as a provider.

The treasures of New Spain: A foundry melts and refines silver. The Spanish add dead dogs and yellow stones called "tuf" to this precious witches' brew in order to help the molten silver flow freely. At left, an Indian stokes the fire; at right, a worker maintains the flow of silver into bullion molds.

New World wealth at its source: African slaves mine, wash and dry gold over a fire, then present it as tribute to their Spanish overseer. Africans, initially brought to the New World to quiet Dominican protests over the treatment of American Indians, often die tragically in rock slides and tropical storms.

1600 (1600-1606)

Spain, Nov. 5, 1600. King Philip III notifies Cuban Governor Pedro de Valdes of his reservations about missionary and military efforts in Florida.

San Gabriel, New Mexico, Nov. 24, 1601. Mexican Gov. Onate returns, after six month search for fabled Quivira [in Kansas], to find colony nearly deserted (→ Aug. 1607).

England, March 1602. Raleigh sends final party in search of Roanoke settlers (→ July 29, 1603).

Pacific Coast, Dec. 14, 1602. Sebastian Vizcaino, leading attempt to link up with Onate, directs expedition into bay [Monterey] (→ March 21, 1603).

France, March 15, 1603. Samuel de Champlain leaves with Sieur de Monts on first voyage to New World (→ June 1604).

Mexico, March 21, 1603. The San Diego, one of Vizcaino's ships, returns with first full account of Pacific coast.

Virginia, July 29, 1603. Bartholomew Gilbert killed by Indians during search for Roanoke colonists (→ Sept. 1605).

Northeast, Aug. 1603. Martin Pring leaves for Bristol after profitable two-month trading venture [near Provincetown or Plymouth].

Northeast, June 1604. Pierre du Guast, Sieur de Monts, founds first French colony in region, on St. Croix River [Maine] (→ July 20, 1605).

London, 1604. King James I calls smoking "vile and stinking," "dangerous."

England, July 17, 1605. George Weymouth returns from Northeast coast [Maine] with glowing reports of barley and pea cultivation.

London, Sept. 1605. *Eastward Ho*, by Ben Jonson and others, published, satirizing promotion of Virginia and belief that Roanoke colonists are still alive.

St. Augustine, Florida, March 1606. Juan de la Cabezade de Altimirano is first Bishop to visit North America.

Port Royal, Acadia, Nov. 14, 1606. French performance of *La Theatre de Neptune en la Nouvelle France* is one of first plays staged in New World.

England, Dec. 20, 1606. London Company dispatches Sarah Constant, Discovery and Goodspeed, led by Captain Christopher Newport, to Virginia (→ Apr. 26, 1607).

Briton at Cape Cod, Martha's Vineyard

Gosnold and his men open trade with friendly natives on the new shores.

Northeast, June 16, 1602

Captain Bartholomew Gosnold has decided to give up his colonizing efforts and return to England. But on May 15, he became the first Englishman to go ashore on the Northeast mainland of America.

Gosnold had set sail on March 26 from Falmouth aboard the Concord, with the goal of starting a colony. He plied strange waters for weeks before coming to a place he called Savage Rock, where eight naked Indians boarded his vessel and drew a map of the coast. Gosnold continued south, encountering a hooked land spit that he had interpreted as an island from the Indians' map. Gosnold called the region Cape Cod, after the fish he found there. He then came upon a vine-covered island, and he named it Martha's Vineyard in honor of his daughter. His last stop before he came ashore here [New Bedford], where Indians gave him tobacco, furs and turtles, was an island that he named for his sister, Elizabeth, and there he and the natives feasted on codfish with English mustard. But that proved too pungent for Gosnold's guests.

Spanish make rum from sugar cane

Barbados, 1600

A new spirit [rum] is being produced by the Spanish from sugar cane. By refining the sugar by-product molasses, a high-alcohol liquor can be made cheaply. Its color is deep brown, its taste unique, and its production should easily fit in with the slave farm system of the Indies plantations, which are rich in sugar cane. Although much of the natlve work force has been used up, the Spanish can readily bring in slaves from Africa to work the plantations, turn the sugar cane into molasses and then turn the molasses into this new spirit.

Penal colony fails; 11 survivors found

Sable Island, New France, 1603

At first it seemed that the small penal colony established by the Marquis de La Roche was going to be self-sufficient. Fifty minor criminals and their guards had been sending sealskins and oil back to France. Gardens were established. No word was received last year and when, in June of this year, Captain Chefdhostel returned, he found that all the guards had been killed, that the prisoners had turned on each other and, by the time help arrived, only 11 men were alive. The penal colony has since been abandoned.

King James I vows to fight Puritans

London, Jan. 1604

Declaring that "I will make them conform themselves or I will harry them out of the land," King James dashed the hopes of Puritan clergymen that the newly ascended ruler would reform the Church of England along lines proposed in last year's Millenary Petition. Advocating a change in the episcopal system of church government, reform of the Prayer Book and abolition of such "popish" rituals as wearing surplices, using rings in marriage services and bowing at the name of Jesus Christ, the petition, called Millenary because it was endorsed by a thousand clergymen, prompted James to call the conference at the royal palace of Hampton Court early this month.

Since the King is known to be sympathetic to many aspects of Calvinism, Puritans had hoped that he would give them a favorable hearing. But during his 16 years as King of Scotland, James had become convinced that the presbyterian form of church government undermines royal authority. "A Scottish presbytery agreeth as well with monarchy as God with the Devil," he said. "Then Jack, Tom, Will and Dick shall meet and at their pleasure censure me and my council." Or, as he put it more succinctly, "No Bishop, no King." The King has, however, authorized a new translation of the Bible.

King James I, fulfilling his inherited role as Defender of the Faith.

European diseases decimating Indians

Due to the onslaught of Europeans, American Indians face a grim future.

North and South America, 1605

Disease has spread among the Indian populations like ripples in a giant pond. Epidemics of diseases such as smallpox, measles, dysentery, typhoid, tuberculosis and other European maladies are initiated at contact points along the coasts of both continents and then spread inland by trade and by warfare, destroying millions of native inhabitants, sometimes before they have as much as set eyes on the white man. Initial calculations regarding Indian populations failed to take this fact into consideration, so figures were probably considerably lower than they should have been. In addition to disease, slave catchers and fur traders have introduced alcohol, and that alone has disrupted and in many cases destroyed entire societies. Population losses among the Indians in New Spain are believed to be running as high as 90 percent.

Conquistador armies, composed of adventurers seeking loot, have penetrated deep into the heartland of both continents, laying waste to cultures along their paths. But even their lethal weapons are not as devastating as the spread of disease.

Horses change culture of Plains Indians

When introduced in Mexico, the beasts were thought to be gods by the Aztecs.

North American Plains, 1600

Life in this expansive region may never be the same. The Spaniards tried to keep horses out of the hands of the Indians, but they were unsuccessful. The natives stole them and bred them and initiated other Indians to the advantages of riding and hunting on horseback.

Apaches and Utes of the Southwest territories were the first to raid Spanish settlements there, and in doing so, have been able to capture hundreds of horses and sell or trade them to other Indian tribes in the North. Large herds of horses have also been captured by the Pueblo Indians, who have revolted against their Spanish masters. As the white men have gradually advanced into Indian territory, guns and horses have been disseminated through intertribal trade and warfare, until Indians of every tribe and nation in the West may soon have them. Some Indian bands have made permanent migrations to new areas of the Plains in search of horses.

Champlain ranges widely over Northeast

Cape Cod, July 20, 1605

The French cartographer and explorer Samuel de Champlain has reached Cape Cod on his second voyage of discovery in search of an ideal location for French settlement in the New World.

Last year, he and a small group of French colonists, led by the Sieur de Monts and the Sieur de Pontgrave, endured a bitter winter on St. Croix Island, at the mouth of the St. Croix River, where severe shortages of firewood and fresh water caused hardships. Scurvy killed nearly half of the colonists and the others survived on a diet of salt meat and a few vegetables. On Christmas Day of 1604, the hardy group marked the religious observance of Christ's birth for the first time in northeastern America.

Samuel de Champlain, the son of a naval captain, showed great talents for navigation and draftsmanship. At 38, he is fulfilling his early promise, mapping large parts of the Northeastern coast and extending French influence throughout the region.

On Champlain's initial visit to North America in 1603, he sailed up the St. Lawrence and Saguenay Rivers and on his return to France published *Des Sauvages,* the first account of the area since Jacques Cartier's explorations 70 years earlier. Last year, Champlain crossed the Atlantic Ocean again with the Sieur de Monts and was assigned to explore the coastline to the south of the two established French settlements, at St. Croix and Port Royal.

Last September, Champlain sailed up the Penobscot River in search of the mythic kingdom of Norumbega, where natives, clad in expensive furs, gold and pearls, were said to live in fabulous mansions of silver and crystal. But he discovered no precious metals, no magnificent city, nothing (→ Sept. 28, 1607).

Dragon from Samuel de Champlain's "Brief Discours" (1601). Champlain has dispelled hopes of finding Norumbega, a luxurious mythic kingdom.

1620

Conceived in Liberty 1607-1763

European adventurers (and the Africans they forcibly imported to serve them) had been creating settlements and building new societies in America for nearly a century before there were any serious efforts to colonize the lands that today constitute the United States. The Spanish and Portuguese, masters of the southern part of the New World, showed relatively little interest in the lands above Mexico. It was the English who looked at this North American wilderness and dreamed of a great empire. Late in the 16th century, they began to create it, conceiving in the process new communities that they hoped would be free of the problems found in England and where they could live their lives in liberty.

The first English contact with the New World came only five years after Columbus reached America. In 1497, John Cabot (like Columbus, a native of Genoa) crossed the Atlantic under the patronage of Henry VII and landed on the Northeastern coast of North America. Other Englishmen followed and claimed dominion over the lands they surveyed. But for many decades, the English made no serious efforts to establish colonies there.

That changed in the last decades of the 16th century, in part because of a single event. For many years, the Spanish presence in the New World, and the Spanish navy's control of the Atlantic Ocean, had discouraged English interest in America. But in 1588, the great Spanish Armada was defeated (and largely destroyed) as it attempted to invade England. In a single stroke, the English navy put an end to Spain's domination of the Atlantic and opened the way to exploration and settlement in America.

But colonization was also a result of conditions within England itself, which was in the age of Elizabeth not only a venturesome society but also a troubled one – both economically and religiously. The troubles emerged in part from a harsh transformation of the economy. In response to the increasing worldwide demand for wool, English landowners were converting more and more of their fields into pastures for sheep. Not only did this reduce the food supply, it also pushed many of the serfs and tenants who had once tilled the farms off the land and created a large floating population, which the domestic economy could not absorb. At the same time, English merchant capitalists were developing a thriving overseas trade. As European markets became saturated (or collapsed), they began looking for new outlets. By the late 16th century, therefore, interest in colonizing North America was growing – both because such colonies might help alleviate poverty and unemployment by siphoning off the surplus population and because they might create new markets for English goods.

These economic incentives coincided with powerful religious ones. The 16th century was the age of the Protestant Reformation in Europe; and in England, the spirit of the Reformation helped create a population of religious dissenters, influenced by the teachings of John Calvin and others, who rejected both the traditional teachings of the Catholic Church and the newer orthodoxy of the Church of England (which had been established by Henry VIII in 1529). These dissenters sought to "purify" the church of corruption; and they were known, therefore, as Puritans. By the beginning of the 17th century, as persecution of religious nonconformists increased, many began looking outside England for places of refuge.

Part of the attraction of America, therefore, was its contrast to England itself. It was a place, many English came to believe, where civilization could start over, where great wealth could be found and where a perfect society could be created free of the flaws and inequities of the Old World. People who felt superfluous in England thought they could become essential, and successful, in America. People who considered themselves dissenters and outsiders at home felt they could build communities in the wilderness where their own ideas could prevail. The New World was appealing, in short, precicely because it was new.

The pioneers of English colonization – Sir Humphrey Gilbert and his half-brother Sir Walter Raleigh pre-eminent among them – had tried for nearly 30 years in the late 16th century to establish a permanent settlement in America. The failure of their efforts had temporarily dampened enthusiasm for any further such efforts. But the lure of the New World was too strong to be suppressed for long. By the early 17th century, other companies were ready to pick up where Gilbert and Raleigh had left off.

In 1607, one such company established what would become the first permanent English settlement in America, at Jamestown, on the coast of what is now the state of Virginia. Its early history was at least as disastrous as that of its predecessors. For 17 years, one wave of settlers after another attempted to make Jamestown a stable and profitable place. Every effort failed. The colony became, instead, a place of discord, violence, misery and death. More than 80 percent of those who settled in Jamestown died within a few years of their arrival. Yet somehow, Jamestown itself survived to become the nucleus of what eventually developed into a flourishing new society in Virginia.

The second English settlement took root 13 years later, when a group of Puritan Separatists established a small colony at Plymouth, on the coast of what is now Massachusetts. Ten years later, in 1630, another, larger group of Puritans established the Massachusetts Bay Colony at Boston. And within a decade, English settlement was spreading throughout New England.

Other English settlements soon followed: through the expansion of the original colonies into neighboring lands; through the establishment of new settlements in Maryland, the Carolinas, and Pennsylvania; through the British conquest of the Dutch possessions in New York and New Jersey. By the end of the 17th century, England had established a string of settlements from northern New England to southern Carolina. In 1724, it stretched its realm farther south by establishing the colony of Georgia.

From the beginning, the societies of the colonies were very different from one another. The differences were sharpest between the settlements in New England and those in the Tidewater. In Virginia and Maryland, the character of settlement was shaped by the discovery of tobacco, which became a valuable export crop. Because of their success, settlers avoided developing a substantial merchant class. Instead, they created large estates and imported a servile work force – at first mainly white indentured servants from England, but later, from 1619 on, mostly African slaves. In New England, where the land was less fertile, farming remained mostly a family enterprise devoted to growing food rather than staple crops. At the same time, the Northern colonies began to develop a substantial merchant community and an important commercial life centered in its thriving port cities.

Despite the many differences, there were also similarities between the Southern and Northern regions. All the English colonies, unlike those of Spain and Portugal, were designed to be "transplantations" of English society to the New World (hence the term "plantation," which was used to describe both Jamestown and Plymouth). The colonists made no serious efforts to blend English civilization with that of the Indians. They tried, instead, to isolate themselves from the natives and to create enclosed communities. When such efforts failed, as they almost always did, the settlers seldom tried to conciliate the Indians; they attempted, instead, to defeat them, destroy them or drive them away. The Spanish and Portuguese had considered themselves colonial "rulers," imposing new forms on an existing society. The English, by contrast, saw themselves as creators of communities that would be entirely their own. Therefore, the native population basically was an obstacle to be overcome, not a resource to be exploited.

The Northern and Southern colonies were alike, too, in their very loose relationship to the crown (which for a time took little interest in them). All were responsible not to the English government, but to private companies or individual proprietors. All became accustomed very quickly to thinking of themselves as relatively independent communities. And all began from the start, sometimes without realizing it, to develop political and social institutions that were quite different from those they had left behind in England. However much the settlers might try to re-create English habits and customs in America, life in the New World forced them to adjust constantly to conditions for which their experiences had not prepared them. Out of those adjustments came the beginnings of a distinctive American civilization.

◀ *"Liberty's Pulpit" by Jean Leon Gerome Ferris, American history painter.*

1607

Virginia, Apr. 26. Three London Company vessels arrive off Virginia coast (→May 24).

England, May 1. The Gift of God, funded by Sir Ferdinando Gorges and commanded by George Popham, leaves on voyage to North America (→June 1).

England, June 1. Outfitted by Gorges, the Mary and John leaves for North America (→Aug. 7).

Jamestown, June 15. Colonists finish building James Fort, to defend against Spanish and Indian attacks.

France, July 17. Sieur de Monts's trade monopoly [in Maine] is revoked.

Northeast, Aug. 7. Two Plymouth Company ships reach coast [north of Monhegan, Maine] (→14).

Northeast, Aug. 14. Popham expedition reaches Sagadahoc River and prepares to settle.

New Mexico, August. Juan de Onate resigns as first Spanish Governor here, notifying Viceroy of New Spain that colony will be abandoned if reinforcements do not arrive by June of 1608 (→Dec. 1610).

Jamestown, Sept. 10. Edward M. Wingfield ousted as first President of colony; he is replaced by John Ratcliffe.

France, Sept. 28. Samuel de Champlain and colonists return, ending settlement at Port Royal (→July 3, 1608).

Jamestown, September. Living on sturgeon and sea crabs in summer, colonists have in four months buried 50 people, lost to disease or starvation.

Scrooby, England, November. Ecclesiastical Commission of York undertakes investigation of Separatist group led by William Brewster, William Bradford and John Robinson (→May 1, 1609).

Jamestown, Dec. 10. John Smith heads up Chickahominy River in search of food (→29).

Northeast. First ship built [in New England] is christened the Virginia, at Popham's colony at mouth of Kennebec River.

England. *On the Value of the Colonies to England*, written by either Richard Hakluyt or Sir John Popham, is published.

DEATH

England, June 10. Sir John Popham, sponsor of colony [in Maine] (*c.1531).

British set up colony at Jamestown

Captain Newport and fellow colonists arrive on the shores of Virginia, debarking on a "fruitful and delightsome" island at the mouth of the James River.

Colonists go to work felling trees for shelter and unloading what supplies remain after the five-month journey. Of the 144 colonists who left England, only 105 survived to build new homes on the swampy island they call Jamestown.

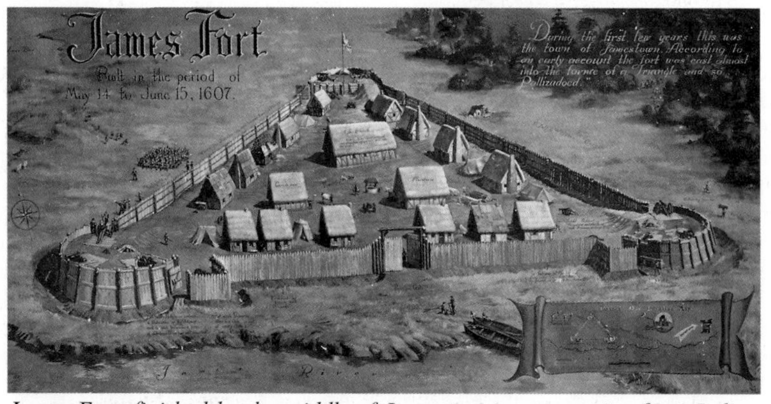

James Fort, finished by the middle of June, promises protection from Indian attacks. The Powhatans and other tribes, who had been friendly, arriving at the gates with gifts of corn and meat, are becoming more and more hostile.

Jamestown, Virginia, May 24, 1607

With a flourish of trumpets, 105 men under the leadership of Captain Christopher Newport have established the colony called Jamestown at the mouth of the James River on the Virginia coast.

The Reverend Robert Hunt offered a prayer, and the settlers immediately went to work unloading supplies from three ships that lay offshore. The ships were the Susan Constant, the Godspeed and the Discovery. They left England last December with 144 colonists, including several "gentlemen," a blacksmith, a carpenter, a barber, a minister and a number of bricklayers and soldiers. Of those who embarked, no fewer than 39 men died during the crossing. Captain Newport arrived with a steel box given to him by the London Company, which is underwriting the venture. The box contains the royal council's instructions for governing the colony. This information was read aloud to all the members of the colony following landfall.

The company's instructions, given by way of advice, were aimed at averting the mistakes made at Roanoke Island, where all of the colonists have been lost, evidently to Indian attacks or disease. Having arrived at the mouth of the James River over a month ago, the council that rules this fledgling colony, about 30 miles from the ocean, opted for a spit of land jutting into the James River. The site is low and swampy with brackish water, but it is extremely defendable from both the land or sea, which is an absolute prerequisite for the colony's safety, according to the members of the ruling body. The settlers have been divided into three groups: one to build a fort and erect cabins within the palisade, another to clear the ground of trees and brush that surround the fort, and a third to explore the river upstream for a possible passage to the Far East.

Planners have described the colony as a "factory-fort" and it is hoped that this concept will make the settlement self-sustaining on a permanent basis. The Indians, under the leadership of Powhatan, were at first friendly to the colonists, but recently they have become increasingly suspicious.

First treason in colonies at Jamestown

Jamestown, Dec. 1607

George Kendall, a member of the Royal Council that rules the colony at Jamestown, has been found guilty of treason and shot. Kendall was accused of spying for the Spanish government. Discord and misunderstanding have plagued the council, and the colony, from the outset, but this incident is the most acrimonious and disturbing to date.

Kendall was one of the original seven councilors elected by royal decree and receiving their power directly from King James's Council in London. The other members are Edward Maria Wingfield, Christopher Newport, Bartholomew Gosnold, John Ratcliff, John Martin and Captain John Smith. The opposition to Kendall was led by Captain Smith, who has assumed at least partial leadership of a colony that is torn by strife and inner divisions. Smith is both loved and hated among the members, but the evidence amassed against Kendall seems clear cut.

Kendall, like Ratcliff, must have had notable connections back in London to be named to the council. However, his name is tainted because of his continued connection with the Roman Catholic Church. Kendall evidently paid lip service to the Anglican Church without having severed his ties with the Catholic faith. Wingfield hopes the execution will put an end to "mortall hatred and intestinal garboile."

Smith wins first American jury trial

Jamestown, Sept. 1607

Captain John Smith has been exonerated of all charges of conspiracy to mutiny and awarded 200 pounds in damages in the first jury trial in America. This same jury has found Edward Maria Wingfield guilty of libel against Smith. Evidently there has been some acrimony between Smith and Wingfield since the colonists left England, and they were reported to have had a violent disagreement at the deathbed of Captain Bartholomew Gosnold. Wingfield charged Smith was a liar and said that he had "begged in Ireland like a rogue, without a lycence," adding, "To such I would not my name be a companyon."

Smith, trained fighting the Turks.

Captain sails with cargo he calls gold

England, July 1607

After safely establishing the first settlers in Jamestown, Captain Christopher Newport set sail on June 22 for England, arriving here this month with metal ore he believed to be gold. This information caused great excitement among those who invested in the new colony. Their hopes for quick enrichment were dashed, however, when it was shown that the initial analysis of the ore had been faulty. In spite of their disappointment, most investors agreed with Sir Thomas Roe, who believes there is a sound basis for "the honor and profit to our nation to make provincial to us [this] land."

Settlers sow crops

Jamestown, June 3, 1607

Hungry settlers here have begun to plant crops. They are attempting to grow oranges, cotton, potatoes and melons, all of which are experimental. Grains such as wheat and barley would have been planted; the lateness of the season, however, has prevented this. It is believed that the result may be severe problems in the coming winter, because provisions are in short supply and a return ship from England is not expected at least until early 1609.

Pocahontas saves John Smith from death

Young Pocahontas lays her head upon Smith's, saving him from execution.

Jamestown, Dec. 29, 1607

Tonight an Indian princess saved Captain John Smith from murder. Since August, more than half of the original Jamestown settlers have died of hunger. Three weeks ago, Captain Smith and a handful of others headed up the Chickahominy River to trade beads and metal hatchets for corn from local tribes. About 25 miles up river, they came to a sandy bank. Smith entered the woods by himself and there he was quickly seized by several warriors, who led him to the royal hunting ground of Wahunsacock. He, who also calls himself Powhatan to symbolize his power, rules the Powhatans and other tribes over an area of some 8,500 square miles.

After days of captivity, Smith was taken to a large hut and placed upon two stones. Powhatan's men raised their clubs ominously above him; then Pocahontas, a girl of but 10 or 11 years, rushed forward and lay her head upon Smith's. The chief then spared him. Perhaps she can urge Powhatan to show Jamestown mercy as well (→Jan. 1608).

John Smith's "Map of Virginia" offers detailed locations of Indian villages and tribal regions. Powhatan, who captured the Jamestown leader and is preparing to release him, rules over an area of some 8,500 square miles.

1608 (1608-1614)

Jamestown, Jan. 1608. Christopher Newport returns same day as John Smith to find 73 of 105 settlers dead.

London, Aug. 13, 1608. John Smith's *A True Relation of Such Occurrences and Accidents of Noate as Hath Hapned in Virginia Since the First Planting of That Collony* is submitted, first book from colonies.

Jamestown, Dec. 1608. Newport leaves again, taking first cargo of commodities; it includes pitch, soap, tar, lumber, iron, glass products.

London, June 2, 1609. Virginia gets new charter, extending borders from "sea to sea."

Bermuda, July 25, 1609. Hurricane hits fleet headed for Jamestown; ship carrying Sir Thomas Gates and Sir Thomas Dale runs aground.

Canada, July 30, 1609. Champlain, sailing up Richelieu River, reaches lake [Champlain] (→July 28, 1615).

England, 1609. Richard Hakluyt's *Virginia Richly Valued* is published.

Jamestown, May 24, 1610. Sir Thomas Gates institutes "Laws Divine Morall and Martial," harsh civil code (→Feb. 13, 1611).

Jamestown, June 10, 1610. Baron De la Warr arrives as Governor with settlers.

Canada, Aug. 3, 1610. Henry Hudson enters great bay [Hudson's Bay] (→June 23, 1611).

Jamestown, 1610. Church attendance made compulsory.

Jamestown, May 1611. Game of bowls is first such recorded recreational activity in British colonies.

England, Dec. 13, 1611. "Dale Code" comprises two years of harsh legislation passed by Dale and others in Virginia.

Manhattan, 1612. Dutch send ships, Tiger and Fortune, to trade with Indians on Hudson's River; huts built [at 45 Broadway] (→Oct. 1, 1614).

Virginia, 1613. Governor Dale rents three acres to each colonist, abandoning unsuccessful collectivism.

Amsterdam, Oct. 1, 1614. Adriaen Block returns with maps of Manhattan coast (→Apr. 1624).

DEATH

June 23, 1611. Henry Hudson, English navigator, set adrift by crew, not heard from again.

Champlain founds Quebec colony

Champlain Habitation at Quebec.

Quebec, July 3, 1608

Samuel de Champlain, the noted French geographer and explorer, has formally asserted his country's authority over Quebec as the capital of New France. The site of the new colony, which was formerly known by its Iroquois name of Stadacona, was discovered three-quarters of a century ago by Jacques Cartier, the famous navigator.

Champlain first visited the area in 1603, entering the St. Lawrence River with an expedition under the command of Francois Grave du Pont. When Champlain returned to France, he published an account of his experiences called *Des Sauvages.* Later, he sailed with other expeditions to France's Acadian colonies, conducting exploratory journeys and producing accurate maps of areas along the Atlantic coast that ranged as far south as Cape Cod.

The decision to locate in Quebec was finally made on the basis of the advantages that it offers to the French in controlling the fur trade.

Although Cartier had made contact with the natives on his earlier visits and taken the Iroquois chief Donnaconna back to France with him as a hostage, no permanent French settlement was founded before Champlain's arrival. By this time, the Algonquins had taken over the territory from the Iroquois. Champlain built a wide trading network with the Montagnais along the St. Lawrence River and with the Hurons along the great lakes. The Montagnais were enemies of the Iroquois, who had settled south of one of the lakes [Lake Ontario].

While merchant traders might prefer to concentrate on the fur business, Champlain apparently plans to extend French control over the whole region (→July 30, 1609).

Samuel de Champlain (center), the founder of Quebec, helps friendly Algonquin Indians defeat an Iroquois war party on the banks of a large lake.

Spanish set up Santa Fe; New Mexico Governor builds palace

The Palace of the Governors houses the Spanish administration of New Mexico. [Today, it is the oldest surviving public building in the United States.]

Santa Fe, Dec. 1610

Governor Pedro de Peralta announced this month that this small Indian village is going to be the new capital of the province of New Mexico. The first provincial capital was established at San Gabriel in 1599 by Governor Juan de Onate. But because of the proximity of hostile Indians, Peralta has decided that Santa Fe, situated 25 miles to the south in the foothills of the Sangre de Cristo Mountains, would be more secure in its vital role as the seat of Spanish governmental territory. As for the governor's palace, Peralta says that he has not constructed it in the traditional European style but in accordance with Indian architecture and using indigenous building materials such as the sun-dried clay that is called adobe.

Hudson sails ship up great Northeast river

Manhattan, Sept. 13, 1609
In his second attempt to locate a passage to China, the English navigator Henry Hudson today sailed his ship, the Half-Moon, up the wide-mouthed river [Hudson River] near Manhattan island far enough to determine that the waters do not lead to the Orient. It is a great disappointment for Hudson, who was promised 800 guilders by the Dutch East India Company if his voyage proved successful.

But the trip has not been in vain. Hudson, who left Amsterdam with a crew of 20 on April 6, reports that the uncharted river is full of fish and that the reception by Indians who live along the banks was mixed. Some were quite eager to trade furs and beaver skins for some red gowns that the sailors had brought, and one offered Hudson some very tasty dried currants. Elsewhere, some of the tribes were hostile and one crew member, John Coleman, was killed by an arrow. By far the friendliest natives have been those of the heavily forested island of Manhattan, where the entire population turned out to welcome Hudson and his crew, and where the least timid Indians were given their first taste of rum (→Aug. 3, 1610).

Pocahontas seized, baptized, weds Rolfe

Jamestown, Virginia, Apr. 5, 1614
The small church of Jamestown, graced as always with displays of wildflowers, is the scene of an event offering hope for all Virginia. Pocahontas, daughter of King Powhatan, has wed the farmer John Rolfe. Powhatan refused to attend the ceremony, but intimated that he approved the union and would cease the attacks on Jamestown that have been going on since the settlement began. While the marriage is based on true affection, Pocahontas, now named Rebecca, did not enter the Jamestown community of her own volition. Last year, Samuel Argall, an ambitious ship's captain, lured her onto his craft and held her captive, hoping to ransom the freedom of some Jamestown men whom Powhatan held prisoner. He was successful; however, many in the colony were ashamed of the sorry usage of the young woman, who had brought them corn and game in the grim years of 1608 and 1609. Still, Pocahontas was treated well and took daily lessons in the Bible. Last April, at 17, she was baptized in her new faith. Rolfe, who last month shipped his first cargo of tobacco to England, may spend his profits on her (→March 21, 1617).

J.L.G. Ferris's "Hudson the Dreamer." In 1609, Hudson's orders from the Dutch East India Company were to find a northeast passage; only by disobeying orders and sailing west did he find the wide-mouthed Hudson River.

J.L.G. Ferris's "The Abduction of Pocahontas." Seized by Captain Samuel Argall, the Indian princess is made aware that she must learn the ways of her British captors, the heralds of civilization in the wilderness of America.

English Separatists settle in Holland

Leyden, Holland, May 1, 1609
Following a brief sojourn in Amsterdam, a group of religious Separatists originally from Scrooby, Nottinghamshire, have settled in this small Dutch town. Among them are the Rev. John Robinson, and William Bradford and William Brewster. Persecuted for their nonconformist practices, the group first tried to leave England two years ago, but they succeded only on their third attempt. In 1606, a like-minded group from nearby Gainsborough also decided to migrate to Holland, attracted by the country's reputation for religious tolerance of Protestant sects (→July 22, 1620).

Jamestown colony faces starving time

Jamestown, Winter 1609-10
Winter has brought unrelieved horror to the colonists here. Forced to stay in their palisaded fort by hostile Indians who have sensed their vulnerability, survivors still weak from the previous winter's hardships are dying by the score. Livestock that were penned outside the fort and intended for winter use have been slaughtered or stolen by the savages. "So lamentable is our scarcity," reports one colonist, "that we are constrained to eat dogs, cats, rats, snakes, toadstools, horsehides and what not." One man was put to death for having eaten his wife's body.

"Baptism of Pocahontas" by John G. Chapman. Pocahontas's sister sits next to a small child; her brother, Nantequaus, stands behind them; the Rev. Alexander Whiteaker performs rite; John Rolfe stands behind Pocahontas.

1615 (1615-1619)

New France, July 28, 1615. Champlain, on seventh voyage, finds lake [Huron], opening easier route inland for fur traders (→Jan. 20, 1616).

Quebec, 1615. Franciscans arrive to start missionary work.

New France, Jan. 20, 1616. Wounded in battle with Iroquois, Champlain arrives to winter in Huron village.

Virginia, 1616. Population is 351: 205 officials and workers on company land; 81 tenants, 65 women and children.

North America, 1616. Briton William Baffin sails into large bay while searching for Northwest Passage.

Virginia, May 1617. Rolfe returns from England with new Deputy Governor Samuel Argall; settlers have nearly deserted Jamestown to grow tobacco in hinterlands (→1619).

Virginia, Dec. 23, 1617. Penal colony is set up by British crown to house exiled convicts.

Hudson's River, 1617. Dutch traders abandon Fort Nassau settlement, stockaded post at Castle Island set up in 1614.

New England, 1617. Smallpox epidemic, probably transmitted by 1615 slaving expedition, reduces native population from 10,000 to 1,000 (→Apr. 1618).

Virginia, Nov. 18, 1618. Argall recalled for crop failure and open criticism of Virginia Company officials; Sir George Yardley named new Governor.

Virginia, 1618. Governor decrees that those who miss church will be jailed "lying neck and heels in the Corps of Gard ye night following and be a slave ye week following."

Jamestown, 1618. Colonists begin to raise wheat (→Sept. 1619).

Virginia, 1618. Headright laws offer 50 acres per colonist to each investor who pays cost of Trans-Atlantic passage.

Virginia, Sept. 1619. Colonists harvest crop large enough to prevent starvation.

Virginia, 1619. Some 1,200 new settlers this year send population over 3,000; they are "choice men, born and bred up to labour and industry," plus 90 women and 100 London slum children.

DEATH

England, June 7, 1618. Lord De la Warr, first governor of Virginia (*July 9, 1577).

First legislature created in America

Governor George Yardley presides over new House of Burgesses in Jamestown.

Jamestown, Aug. 14, 1619

The first general assembly in the New World has adjourned after meeting in a little church beside the James River – under miserable conditions. The weather was unbearably hot, and of the 30 men present, several were taken ill and one died. Nevertheless, the body of men, called "burgesses," was a able to pass many laws as well as a half dozen revisions of what is called the "Greate Charter."

The assembly would most likely never have met but for the progressive influence of Sir Edwin Sandys, son of the Archbishop of York and a leader of the House of Commons. He has championed popular rights and the abolition of feudal tenures. His views have antagonized powerful members of the nobility.

Delegates to the newly created House of Burgesses are to be elected by the inhabitants of the colony, or the "freemen," a term that includes the "indentured servants." The plantations were represented by 22 burgesses, two each from 11 districts. The assembly also included a six-member governor's council and a speaker, John Pory.

Laws curb gambling, drinking, idleness

Jamestown, Aug. 14, 1619

The first general assembly in Virginia has passed a series of laws that restrict individual behavior. In only six days, the burgesses have approved stern enactments against gambling, drunkenness, immorality, idleness and "excess in apparell." All colonists are required to attend two divine services held every Sunday, and they must bring along "their pieces, swords, powder and shot." Laws were also passed that govern the distribution of land and that prohibit the settlers from planting mulberry trees, grapes and hemp. In addition, the burgesses enacted a measure that requires each city, borough or plantation to educate the Indian children.

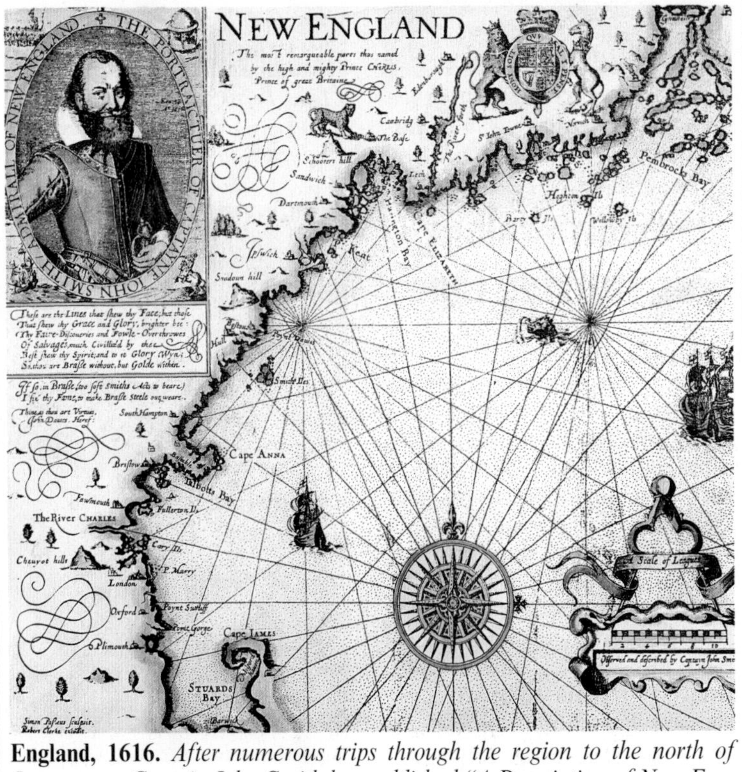

England, 1616. *After numerous trips through the region to the north of Jamestown, Captain John Smith has published "A Description of New England," providing a detailed map and suggesting the new name for the land.*

Colony is saved by tobacco, No. 1 crop

Jamestown, 1619

This English colony in Virginia, which was almost destroyed by disease and bad weather, has been saved by a vegetable, tobacco. Captain John Rolfe decided that the colony needed a cash crop to survive. Taking advantage of the new European penchant for tobacco, he convinced his fellows to dedicate their spare time and land to raising the crop, first planted here in 1612. The new mild blend of seed that Rolfe brought from the West Indies has proved such a popular export that many residents have taken to growing the leaf in the streets of Jamestown. This year, the colonists raised 20,000 pounds of tobacco.

King James of England has denounced tobacco as "dangerous to the Lungs," but such noblemen as Sir Walter Raleigh have so popularized smoking, it may be a tough habit to break (→June 29, 1620).

Dutch ship brings 20 Africans to be sold

Dutch traders display their human wares. Illustration by Howard Pyle.

Jamestown, Aug. 20, 1619

"There came in a Dutch man-of-warre that sold us 20 negars," reports settler John Rolfe. Welcomed by the English colonists as a useful addition to the labor force, these Africans, the first to be brought to the settlement, are indentured servants who will be free after a term of service. Most indentured servants, in return for their passage to America, have agreed to serve for a period of five years. When that time is completed, they may buy land and, in general, act as full citizens of Jamestown, although many end up being tenant farmers, working fields along the James River. It is not known whether the African immigrants have freely consented to these terms.

Of these 20 newly arrived immigrants, 15 have been purchased to serve for Sir George Yardley, the Governor of Virginia. Yardley is owner of the 1,000-acre Flowerdew Hundred plantation.

Since one of the goals of the Jamestown colony is to make full use of the resources of the land, and to turn a profit for the colony as quickly as possible, it is believed that the 20 Africans will be given extremely hard work to do during their term of indenture. Their arrival is part of a great influx of settlers, many coming in as servants to help exploit the riches of the new land. It will, therefore, be no surprise if more Africans are transported to the colony.

An introduction to a bleak future.

Women arrive, assuring colony's growth

Often the women immigrants were convicts in England. To the loneliest of male colonists, however, their past pales in importance next to their gender.

Jamestown, Aug. 1619

To the joy of the men of Jamestown, the Virginia Company has sent 90 well-chaperoned spinsters, of an age warranted to be called "young maidens," to the colony. Although the first woman arrived in 1609, this sizable influx may help to assure the colony's growth.

The women come of their own free will, but not freely; each bachelor who weds one has to pay the company 120 pounds of tobacco to defray the cost of her passage. The company arranged the importation to assuage the men, who have gone without female companionship.

There is also a financial advantage in adding the women. By assuming domestic chores, they will free men for more hours in the fields. In fact, last month the House of Burgesses considered but rejected a proposal that would have given wives a share in land "because in a plantation it is not known whether man or woman be the most necessary." Certainly it is more economical for the colony to grow by means of that domestic product, children, than the imported one, adult men, who may find tedious chores are worth nothing more than a swift trip back to England.

Pocahontas, rage of Britain, dies there

Gravesend, Eng., March 21, 1617

The celebrated Indian princess Pocahontas was buried here today,

Pocahontas, also known as Rebecca.

an untimely end to her sojourn in England. Rebecca (her Christian name) came to London last April, supported on a stipend from the Virginia Company. Major figures from the worlds of art and commerce sought her out, among them the playwright Ben Jonson and the explorer Captain John Smith, who had not seen her in nearly 10 years. The high point of her visit was attendance at Jonson's *Twelfth Night* masque, seated with the King and Queen. Sadly, few noted her declining health, and her death, from smallpox, seemed to come quickly. Her entourage of 10 Indians (there had been 12, but two died here), will return home without her, hopefully escaping the smallpox epidemic decimating the tribes there.

Smallpox epidemic stuns New England

New England, Apr. 1618

An epidemic of smallpox is raging throughout New England and is spreading down the coast as far as Virginia. Indian tribes from the Penobscot River [in Maine] to Narragansett Bay [in Rhode Island] have been hardest hit, losing as much as 90 percent of their population. The disease may have originally been transmitted from a slaving expedition three years ago. At its present rate, the epidemic could wipe out the remaining Indians in the area in a few years. One of its latest victims is Powhatan, the proud chief in Virginia whose daughter, Pocahontas, died of the same disease just last year.

Raleigh beheaded on treason charge

London, Oct. 29, 1618

Sir Walter Raleigh, poet, explorer, scientist and a once-favored courtier to Queen Elizabeth, has been beheaded at Westminster Palace. In 1603, Raleigh and others were accused of plotting to overthrow King James. Raleigh was convicted on the testimony of Lord Cobham. After a last-minute reprieve from the death sentence, he was held in the Tower, where he lingered until October 28, when he was taken to the gatehouse of the palace. There he was writing poetry on the eve of his execution. Raleigh's last words were to his executioner. "What dost thou fear?" he asked. "Strike man, strike!"

1620

Virginia, Jan. 31. Leaders of colony write to Virginia Company, asking for more orphaned apprentices for employment (→ 1627).

London, Feb. 20. Clothmaker John Peirce and ironmonger Thomas Weston gain New World patent from Virginia Company.

London, June 29. Crown bans tobacco growing in England, giving the Virginia Company monopoly in exchange for tax of one shilling per pound (→ July 1621).

Netherlands, July 22. Leyden group [Pilgrims] leaves for England on the Speedwell, under leadership of William Brewster (→ Aug. 1620).

Bermuda, Aug. 1. Second assembly in New World convenes for first time, one year after Virginia's House of Burgesses.

England, August. The Rev. John Robinson writes letter of instruction and encouragement to Pilgrims before their voyage (→ Sept. 16).

Atlantic Ocean, Nov. 9. Pilgrims and fellow settlers sight land at Cape Cod (→ 11).

Cape Cod Bay, Nov. 11. After journey to find mouth of Hudson's River is aborted by bad weather, Pilgrims put into cape harbor (→ 21).

England, Nov. 13. Plymouth Company gets charter for Council for New England (→ Dec. 30, 1622).

Cape Cod, Dec. 8. Third exploring party drives off Indian attack with muskets (→ 11).

Plymouth, Dec. 11. Scouting party lands, finding cornfields and little running brooks, indicating an auspicious site (→ Dec. 1620).

Plymouth, Dec. 26. Governor Bradford writes, "no man rested all that day," while colony is busy building houses; he does, however, procure beer for Pilgrims (→ June 1, 1621).

Plymouth. Congregational Church is founded by 102 Pilgrim Separatists under William Bradford, William Brewster and Edward Winslow.

Virginia. First public library founded at site of proposed college in Henrico; books donated by English landowners.

Virginia. Public school for Negroes and Indians is established.

Virginia. Over 1,000 colonists die in epidemic.

Separatists set out for New World

Robert Weir's "Embarkation of the Pilgrims." Brewster leads them in prayer.

Plymouth, England, Sept. 16, 1620

A determined band of 35 religious dissenters set sail for Virginia today in the Mayflower, jubilant at the prospect of practicing their unorthodox brand of worship in the New World. Accompanied by 66 non-Puritans, the Separatists, led by William Bradford and William Brewster, have rejected the Anglican Church's official interpretation of the Bible in favor of their own reading, and they have obtained an 80,000-acre land grant from the Virginia Company complete with fishing rights, permission to trade with neighboring Indians and a degree of latitude in self-government.

Most of these passengers are Londoners, although some of them are from a Separatist group that migrated to Holland a decade ago in the hope of escaping further persecution. Many of the group that had moved to Holland returned to England to make this trip but were unable to do so because a second vessel that had been made ready for them, the Speedwell, was deemed unseaworthy for the arduous crosssing. The excess passengers and some who had second thoughts returned to London on the Speedwell, while its sister ship left for America with whole families aboard.

The Mayflower, once used to transport barrels of wine from Bordeaux to London, is now laden with enough beds, tables and chairs to furnish 19 cottages, plus family pets, goats and poultry, and a generous supply of dried ox tongues, spices, turnips and oatmeal. Living quarters for each passenger on the ship are no larger than a single bed, but there is some room for one's personal belongings. William Mullins, for instance, took 126 pairs of shoes and 13 pairs of boots, while Captain Miles Standish took a few books with him, including a volume of Caesar, a history of the world and a history of Turkey (→ Nov. 9).

The Mayflower approaches the coast.

Fearing rebellion, leaders draft Mayflower Compact aboard ship

"The Mayflower Compact" by J.L.G. Ferris. Setting up "just and equal laws."

Near Cape Cod, Nov. 21, 1620

The leaders of the Mayflower expedition, grouchy and weary after two months at sea, assembled in the ship's main cabin today and prepared a social compact designed to bolster unity. The Mayflower Compact, signed by all 41 household heads aboard, establishes a civil body politic for the new colony that will set up "just and equal laws" based on church covenants. The document is meant to silence the rebellious murmurings of those passengers on board who are angry at having reached a place not granted to them by charter. Dropping all quarrels, the men agreed on a plan to explore the shore and elected John Carver, a merchant, to serve as their Governor (→ Dec. 8).

Low on beer, Mayflower lands in Massachusetts

After sending out several scouting parties, the Pilgrims land at Plymouth.

"The Beginning of New England," after a painting by Clyde O. DeLand.

New Plymouth, Dec. 1620

The passengers on the Mayflower, weary and diseased after six weeks on the choppy Atlantic Ocean, have anchored their boat in the shallow harbor here and rejoiced on the beach at having found a suitable site for a settlement. The decision to land came not a moment too soon, since most of the passengers are sick or dying of poor nutrition, and the healthy ones have been carrying the infirm to resting spots on shore with a glad eye toward garnering for themselves the boat's remaining stock of beer.

The Mayflower first reached this harbor December 11, when 16 men rowed off in a shallop, explored the land, and deemed it fit. The site, which has been named New Plymouth after the Pilgrims' port of departure, boasts a tall hill suitable for erecting a fort, a brook with clear water and clearances in the trees perfect for building homes.

But the site is far from ideal. The harbor is uncomfortably shallow and the soil is fairly depleted from earlier growths of corn. The colonists are also nervous that the Indians who cultivated corn and cleared land here will return and want the site back.

Further tempering the colonists' excitement over touching down in the New World is news of the death of William Bradford's wife, Dorothy, who fell overboard and drowned while the shallop party was on its mission. The mood on the ship has also been solemn because of the cold weather, which is hampering attempts to hunt and fish for food and killing vegetation that the Pilgrims had hoped to store as food for winter.

After anchoring, the passengers began hauling their furniture, tools and other belongings by boat to the shore, a mile and a half away, and constructing a makeshift shelter for storage. Since tomorrow is the Sabbath, when such arduous work is forbidden, they are trying to make haste. The women began the arduous task of washing clothes, fetid from the cramped trip, and the children and dogs have been exercising their legs on the sand. Some of the men are mapping out building lots, measuring eight feet by 49 feet. Others are mulling over what form of government should be put in place in the colony.

The travelers, numbering 101 including crew, left the English town of Plymouth September 16, having spent the previous few days in that town eating and drinking joyously with friends and relatives. Some had to leave relatives behind in England, including Bradford, who left his son. Stephen Hopkins of London brought the largest family, a wife and four children, including one born at sea named Oceanus. Deaths on board included that of the servant William Butten, whom everyone mourned, and a profane sailor, infamous for his angry threats to throw seasick passengers overboard. To the sorrow of no one, he suddenly took ill and died. A third death seemed imminent when John Howland was thrown overboard in a fierce mid-Atlantic storm, but the strong youth grabbed onto the ship and was fished out with a boat hook.

The effect of foul weather on people occupying berths of three feet by six feet has been harrowing. A few men threatened mutiny after learning that the ship was headed nowhere near Virginia, for which the company had chartered it. Some men asked to turn back, and others vowed they would not follow the government that was to be set up on shore. But the grumblers have turned cheerful since the signing of a compact last month, binding passengers into a civic body, and since the arrival on land.

After weighing anchor, Captain Miles Standish led a team of men, armed with swords and muskets, along the seashore. Here they encountered Indians, who fled from them, and tasted their first New England water. The men came upon an Indian grave, which they covered reverently with soil, before stumbling on a rich cache of Indian corn. Filling their pockets, the Pilgrims vowed to repay the favor to the Indians, and continued exploring until they found what would become New Plymouth. Meanwhile, at the ship, Susannah White gave birth to a son, Peregrine, the first male English child born on American soil (→26).

"Landing of the Pilgrims at Plymouth" by Nathaniel Currier.

1621 (1621-1624)

Plymouth, June 1, 1621. Living outside Virginia (area of original patent), Pilgrims get new patent, legalizing settlement here.

Netherlands, June 3, 1621. Dutch West India Company established with New World monopoly and colonization rights.

Plymouth, June 1621. Andrew Weston and 50 settlers land to found fishing and trading post at Wessagusset (→Apr. 1623).

Virginia, July 1621. Sir Edwin Sandys tells colonists King has criticized raising of tobacco in colonies; settlers refuse to diversify (→1624).

England, Oct. 21, 1621. Privy Council orders all exports from colonies to have customs paid in England.

Plymouth, Dec. 25, 1621. Governor Bradford halts card playing by newcomers.

Falling Creek, Virginia, 1621. First ironworks in colonies is constructed.

England, Dec. 30, 1622. Council for New England names Robert Gorges lieutenant general of New England, deeding him 300 square miles on Boston Bay (→1624).

Wessagusset, Plymouth, Apr. 1623. Settlers saved from extinction by Miles Standish.

Plymouth, Sept. 10, 1623. Lumber and furs in first cargo sent to England, on ship commanded by William Pierce.

Virginia, March 5, 1624. Class-based legislation passed, exempting upper classes from punishment by whipping.

Plymouth, March 1624. First cattle in colony brought from England by Edward Winslow.

Jamestown, May 24, 1624. Charter revoked after years of unprofitable operation; Virginia becomes royal colony.

Plymouth, 1624. Accused of Anglican bias, John Lyford, Puritan minister sent by English sponsors, is banished from colony.

Virginia, 1624. General Assembly rules each borough should round up a number of Indian children to be educated in religion and civilization.

Rome, 1624. Pope Urban VIII, angered by tobacco from New World, pledges to excommunicate snuff users (→Nov. 1627).

New England, 1624. Robert Gorges leaves for England [ending pre-Massachusetts attempts to settle New England].

Squanto helps with farming practices

Plymouth Colony, Apr. 1621

After a difficult winter in which many settlers died, help has appeared in the form of a tall, English-speaking Indian named Tisquantum, called Squanto by the Pilgrims. Squanto is giving the colonists desperately needed lessons in how to fish, how to plant crops and how to find other sources of food.

In 1605, Squanto accompanied Weymouth to England, where he learned English and British customs. He went back to America with John Smith's mapping expedition in 1614, but was captured by Captain Thomas Hunt and sold to be a slave in Spain. Making his way to England, he was able to return to America again in 1619 (→1625).

Squanto teaches settlers how to plant corn, in a drawing by C.W. Jefferys.

First thanksgiving feast

"The First Thanksgiving" by J.L.G. Ferris. New feast for the New World.

Plymouth Colony, Autumn 1621

After a winter of terrible deprivation and many deaths from disease, the Pilgrims of this colony have celebrated their survival at an autumn harvest feast in order to give thanks to God. Governor William Bradford decreed a celebration sometime between September 21 and November 9 in which the settlers would gather with the Indians who had helped them to get through their first year.

This first feast of thanksgiving celebrated the successful harvest of the native corn crop, which came in great abundance (the European wheat has failed to grow well). The honored guests included Chief Massasoit of the Wampanoag tribe and 99 of his braves. Whlle the Governor had sent out four of his own men to hunt fowl, providing plenty of meat for at least a week, Massasoit's men brought five deer to the feast, as well as a novelty called "popped corn." The celebration may have gone on for as long as nine days, and it was a feast of generous proportions, featuring the bounty of the region, including oysters, eel, corn bread, goose, venison, watercress, leeks, plums, berries, and, probably, that native wild bird, the turkey.

One observer at the celebration said of the colonists' guests: "We have found the Indians very faithful in their covenant of peace with us, very loving and ready to pleasure us. We often go to them, and they often come to us."

Indian chief signs treaty with colonists, aided by Squanto

Plymouth Colony, March 22, 1621

The Pilgrims have made peace with the Indians who attacked them on the first day in the New World. In the severe first winter of the colony, the Pilgrims were visited by the English-speaking natives Squanto and Samoset, with whom they have become friends. Samoset has now brought Massasoit, the chief of his tribe, the Wampanoags, and a peace treaty has been signed. The Wampanoags had initially distrusted the settlers because several of their people had been carried off by an English slaver in 1614.

Massasoit, chief of the Wampanoags, is treated to a rousing British welcome.

Indians murder 350 settlers in Virginia

Jamestown, March 22, 1622

An eight-year peace has been shattered by an Indian attack that left 350 settlers dead. Chief Opechencanough had recently signed a peace treaty and declared that "the sky would fall" before he would break it. Trusting his word, colonists took Indians into their homes, let them use their boats and went about unarmed. But at 8 this morning, families at breakfast and farmers in the fields were struck down throughout the James River area. Jamestown, the main settlement, was spared by the warning of Chanco, an Indian who had converted to Christianity and who felt that Richard James, with whom he lived, had "used him like a son."

Spanish lose prize galleon in storm

Havana, Sept. 5, 1622

A hurricane has overrun a Spanish fleet bound from Havana to Cadiz and sunk the prize galleon Atocha. A six-week delay in departure put the fleet right in the middle of hurricane season. On the second day out, a violent storm scattered the ships over a 50-mile radius and drove them north toward the Florida Keys. As the passengers prayed below deck, a huge wave dashed the Atocha against a coral reel and the ship sank beneath the waves. Five men were rescued the next morning, but 260 passengers were drowned and 200 million pesos were buried with the Atocha under 50 feet of water (→July 21, 1985).

January 21, 1621. *The Pilgrims gather to give thanks for a safe passage and to inaugurate the Common House, a church and their first public building. Services are welcomed by the 35 devout Separatists. Many in the party, "profane fellows" according to William Bradford, were not to be found.*

New Hampshire is vast landed estate

New Hampshire, Spring 1623

With dreams of founding a hereditary principality, Captain John Mason of Hampshire, England, has established the territory of New Hampshire from land granted to him by King James I. The land is now a dense forest that is inhabited by wild animals and Indians, but Mason intends to people it with tenant farmers and venturesome aristocrats like himself. Captain Mason has sent his men to carve two settlements out of the coastal forests, where fish and waterfowl are reported to be in abundance.

Another settlement in New Netherland

New Netherland, Apr. 1624

To strengthen its trading post at Fort Nassau, the Dutch West India Company has sent a group led by Captain Cornelius Jacobsen May to establish Fort Orange [Albany] on Hudson's River. The colonists are Walloons, French-speaking Calvinist refugees from the low countries caught in the middle of a struggle between Spain and Holland. Thirty Walloon families left Amsterdam in March on the New Netherland. They live aboard ship while building huts of bark and plant grain (→June 1, 1625).

The Pilgrims worship from 8 to 12 on Sunday, and again in the afternoon.

First Negro is born

Jamestown, 1624

This year, the first Negro child to be born in the American colonies, William Tucker, was baptized. Tucker is a child of Africans who were sold to the British colony in 1619 as indentured servants. These Africans, brought to work on the plantations of the settlers, were expected to serve out a term of indenture before being freed. It is not known whether the child will be expected to work as a servant or a free man, but he will be welcomed as an addition to the laborers harvesting the riches of the new land.

Jury trial instituted

Plymouth, Dec. 13, 1623

The Plymouth colonists today established the system of trial by 12-man jury in the American colonies. This procedure requires that jurors be selected from good and lawful men "according to the commendable custom of England." The 12-man jury was instituted by King Henry II in the late 1100's to replace trial by combat or torture, which the defendant had to survive to be proved innocent. Trial by jury applies to all civil and criminal matters and requires a unanimous decision for a guilty verdict.

April 5, 1621. *Mayflower departs; the Pilgrims must fend for themselves.*

1625 (1625-1629)

England, March 27, 1625. Charles I becomes King upon death of King James I.

New Amsterdam, June 1, 1625. Family of Jan Joris Raphaelje has first Dutch child born in America (→ Sept. 1626).

Plymouth, 1625. For first time, colony has "corn sufficient, and some to spare for others."

Plymouth, Nov. 15, 1626. Pilgrims buy out their London investors for 1,800 pounds.

Europe, March 1627. War breaks out between England and France (→ July 20, 1629).

Canada, Apr. 25, 1627. Control of New France passes to Company of New France (The Hundred Associates); it gains fur monopoly and land from Florida to Arctic.

Newfoundland, July 23, 1627. Sir George Calvert arrives to develop 1622 land grant.

England, Nov. 1627. King Charles I, referring to tobacco trade, says Virginia is "wholly built upon smoke" (→ 1627).

Virginia, 1627. Tobacco exports total 500,000 pounds, up from 18,000 in 1617 (→ Feb. 1, 1633).

New Amsterdam, Apr. 7, 1628. Jonas Michaelius arrives as first Dutch Reformed minister in colonies.

Naumkeag [Salem], Sept. 8, 1628. John Endecott, sailing for New England Company, arrives with colonists; he serves as Governor (→ March 4, 1629).

Virginia, Oct. 1628. Lord Baltimore arrives to form colony; being Catholic, he refuses Anglican oaths (→ March 25, 1634).

France, 1628. Royal decree bars Protestants from settling in New France, sending Huguenots to English colonies (→ 1685).

England, March 4, 1629. New England Company changed into Massachusetts Bay Company by new charter, freeing it from conflicts with Council for New England (→ Apr. 25).

London, March 10, 1629. King Charles I dissolves Parliament (→ Aug. 20, 1642).

England, Apr. 25, 1629. Massachusetts Bay Company sends fleet to New World (→ Aug. 6).

Netherlands, June 7, 1629. States General allows Dutch West India Company to grant patroonships to those bringing 50 settlers to colonies in America (→ Sept. 10).

Manhattan bought for $24 by Dutch

Manhattan, Sept. 1626

Following negotiations, a Dutch group led by Peter Minuit agreed to pay the Canarsee Indians the value of 60 guilders, or $24, in beads and trinkets for the 22-square-mile island of Manhattan. The Canarsees were reportedly not interested in being paid in gold or silver.

Last year, the Dutch settled New Amsterdam at the tip of Manhattan Island. Willem Verhulst, who had been sent over by the Dutch West India Company to establish the first farms and a fort, has since been accused of mismanagement. He was replaced by Minuit, who arrived in May on the ship Sea-Mew and who will be responsible for the entire settlement.

In a letter to the government in The Hague, a delegate of the States General in the West India Company reported that women on the island are bearing children and that this year's harvest was a bountiful success. The first child born in the Dutch settlement was to the family of Jan Joris Raphaelje. More are certain to be on their way.

Minuit, who came over to gather the 200 Dutch scattered along the rivers of the region [Hudson, Delaware and Connecticut] to protect them from attacks by the Indians, has expressed the view that, because of its deep bays and abundant farming soil, Manhattan seemed to be an excellent choice for both the fort and the farms.

Minuit buys Manhattan from Indians, after a painting by Alfred Fredericks.

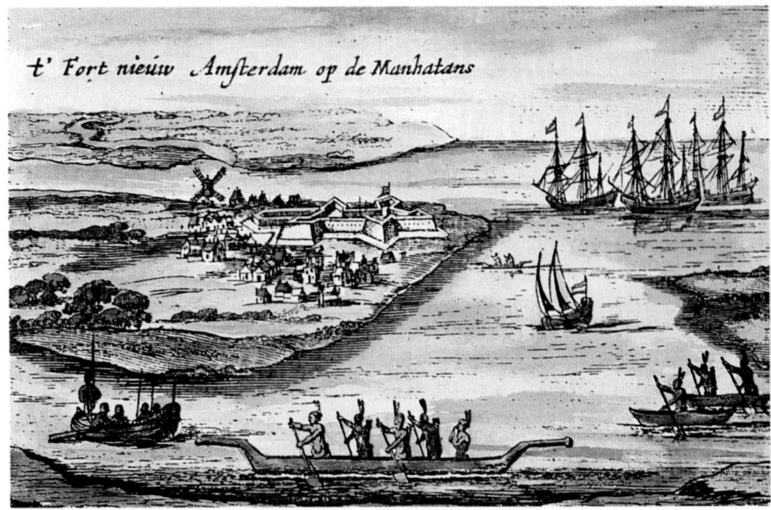

Hartgers' view of the fledgling settlement at New Amsterdam (c.1626-1628).

Guns and goodwill traded with natives

Dover, New Hampshire, 1628

The enterprising spirit of the American settler has found a new outlet: gun-running. Indians in Dover are now hunting with rifles. Selling firearms to the natives is forbidden, but profit has a way of eluding law at the edges of civilization. Even without guns, Indians tend to survive better than the colonists. A Virginia settler wrote of the winter of 1625, "winde, rayne, froste, and snow caused us to keepe Christmas among the savages where we were never more merry, nor fed on more plenty of good Oysters, Fish, Flesh, Wilde fowl and good bread."

1,500 kidnapped children imported

Virginia, 1627

More than 1,500 children who were kidnapped from the streets of London arrived in Virginia this year, many to seek work as servants. This practice has its origins in a policy adopted by King James I. In 1619, James decided that orphans had a better chance of finding a home and employment in the colonies and 50 were soon shipped to Virginia. Criminals saw an opportunity to exploit the situation and have stolen children throughout London. One kidnapper has been drawn and quartered, but the traffic in children has not stopped.

Dutch establish a patroon system

New Netherland, Sept. 10, 1629

The Dutch West India Company has put into effect a plan to colonize its holdings in the New World. Land and titles are being given away by the concern. A candidate who can round up 50 potential settlers and pay for their passage to New Netherland will be awarded a huge estate and be called a patroon. The award provides all the privileges of a feudal land baron, including that of jurisdiction over civil and criminal matters. The immigrants must agree to live and work on these estates in conditions of near servitude (→ Dec. 1646).

Quebec surrenders

Quebec, July 20, 1629

The controversial British adventurer Sir David Kirke has seized power in Quebec from the destitute French administration of Samuel de Champlain. The once-proud fortress surrendered without a shot having been fired.

Kirke, the son of a wealthy London merchant, had been commissioned by King Charles I to drive the French settlers from Quebec. He did so by first ransacking the supply base that the French had established at Tadoussac, 30 miles down river, and then conquering a French fleet of supply vessels that were off the Gaspe Peninsula. When Kirke returned to Quebec a year later, the starving settlers readily yielded to his command, and Champlain is heading back to his homeland (→ March 29, 1632).

Cambridge accord

Cambridge, England, Aug. 26, 1629

Twelve wealthy and influential Puritans who have been flirting with the idea of immigrating to the colonies met here today in the town where many of them had been to college and signed a compact. They agreed to depart for the New World next March as long as the plantation they establish be governed in America, not by English overseers. The idea that a new settlement have its headquarters in New England is considered daring even among the 12 men, many of whom are members of the Massachusetts Bay Company, but the company's directors have agreed to renounce authority in favor of those who would risk their lives founding a colony. One who signed the accord, John Winthrop, has been tentatively selected Governor (→ March 29, 1630).

Salem and non-Separatist church founded

Salem, Aug. 6, 1629

Filled with joy and optimism, the leaders of this farming and fishing town, founded last September by Governor John Endecott, today framed a covenant for their new church, the first in the colonies that has not repudiated the Church of England. They have rejected the Separatist movement in favor of a highly inclusive form of worship in which the people of the town "covenant with the Lord, and one with another." Residents agree that the chief function of the church here is going to be that of strengthening the town's sense of community rather than overloading worshipers with doctrine. One pastor of the new church, the Rev. Francis Higginson, who arrived in Salem along with 300 new settlers in June, has written to some of his Puritan colleagues in London defending the brand of worship in Salem and stating that the beauty of this region's untouched wilderness will bring about a moral environment (→ 26).

Gov. John Endecott, Salem pioneer.

Irish Catholics flee

Virginia, 1629

More and more Irish immigrants have been turning up as servants in the homes of the first families of Virginia. These immigrants have been fleeing worsening English oppression in their homeland and are settling in Maryland and the Carolinas as well as in Virginia. Many of the colonists, however, appear alarmed about the increasing number of Catholics entering their colonies and may soon take steps to restrict this Irish immigration.

Dane Jonas Bronk buys Indian land

New Amsterdam, 1629

Jonas Bronk, a Danish immigrant, has bought some 500 acres of land north of New Amsterdam from local Indians. Bronk plans to develop the area between the Harlem and the Aquahung Rivers by leasing plots to farmers to raise tobacco and maize. They will be allowed to keep their crops, but must return the land at the end of three years. Bronk brings a large family, a herd of cattle and a sizable library with him. Some local residents have already begun calling the Aquahung the Bronk's [Bronx] River in his honor.

Governor opposes May Day drinking, dancing and "frisking"

Plymouth, June 1628

Governor William Bradford does not like celebrations, and when he sees one begin, he stops it immediately. One Christmas, he found settlers "in the street at play, openly," so he cut their pleasure short and swore that as long as he ruled the colony "nothing hath been attempted that way, at least openly." It was with some dismay, therefore, that he discovered May Day festivities, led by Thomas Morton, going full tilt at Mare Mount. As Bradford wrote: "They set up a May Pole, drinking and dancing aboute it many days together, inviting the Indean women for their consorts, dancing and frisking together like so many fairies or furies rather . . ." Bradford sent Miles Standish, who finally put a stop to the revels.

The Puritans have tried hard to get rid of the old folkways of the colonists, who used to enjoy many holidays, such as Candlemas, St. Valentine's Day, Shrove Tuesday and Whitsunweek. The celebration of these holidays, however, has been discouraged and now, except for Easter week, there are only four holidays left, those marking the seasons: Lady's Day [Annunciation Day] on March 25, Midsummer Day on June 24, Michelmas on September 29 and Christmas Day on December 25 (→ Jan. 19, 1633).

Squanto leads Miles Standish and his warriors to root out evil at Mare Mount.

Standish watches as Indians and colonists join in revels steeped in paganism.

1630 (1630-1634)

Southampton, England, March 29, 1630. John Winthrop, Governor of Massachusetts, sails with first of 11 ships, carrying 700 passengers (→June 12).

Plymouth, Sept. 30, 1630. John Billington hanged for murder in first colonial execution.

Boston, Oct. 29, 1630. First General Court rules governor to be chosen by assistants only.

Massachusetts, Nov. 9, 1630. First ferry route in colonies opens from Boston to Charlestown on Charles River.

Virginia, 1630. Middle Plantation [Williamsburg] started between York and James Rivers (→1699).

Maryland, 1631. William Claiborne, Virginia colonist, sets up trading post on Kent Island [first European settlement in Maryland] (→Apr. 4, 1638).

New Amsterdam, Winter 1632. Governor Peter Minuit sets up first public brewery.

New Netherland, March 19, 1632. Governor Minuit recalled for granting excessive trading privileges to patroons.

France, March 29, 1632. England returns Acadia to France in Treaty of St. Germain-en-Laye.

Smithfield, Virginia, 1632. St. Luke's Church built [oldest English colonial church still standing].

London, Jan. 19, 1633. Privy Council, after hearing testimony from people abused by Massachusetts authorities, upholds colony's right to exist (→July 23, 1637).

Virginia, Feb. 1, 1633. Tobacco laws are codified, limiting production to reduce dependence on single-crop economy.

New Netherland, June 8, 1633. Dutch open post at Fort Good Hope [Hartford] (→May 31, 1638).

Massachusetts, Oct. 8, 1633. Dorchester organizes first town government.

Virginia, 1633. Benjamin Harrison arrives from England to settle on James River. [Descendants include William Henry Harrison, ninth U.S. President; Benjamin Harrison, 23rd U.S. President.]

Boston, March 4, 1634. First tavern opened by Samuel Cole.

DEATH

London, June 21, 1631. John Smith, Jamestown leader (*1579).

Massachusetts Bay Colony founded

John Winthrop is rowed ashore at Salem to ascend his "City upon a Hill."

Naumkeag, Mass., June 12, 1630

The flagship of the Massachusetts Bay Company, the Arbella, has docked here [Salem] in Cape Ann and the passengers have gleefully clambered ashore to enjoy the crisp spring air and pick fresh strawberries. John Winthrop, who brought the company charter with him on board, immediately took over as Governor of the colony.

The new arrivals lent great cheer to colonists in the area who had seen 80 die over the winter and are themselves suffering from lack of corn and bread. The Arbella is the first of 11 ships sent from Southampton, bearing 700 passengers, 40 cows and 60 horses in all.

A deeply religious people on a holy quest, the Puritans prepared thoroughly for their voyage. They had planned to leave in March to allow for a spring planting, and lime juice was aboard each of the 11 ships to prevent scurvy. Nonetheless, the journey proved arduous and the newcomers have little to offer the old residents except an optimism born of the conviction that God smiles on their venture.

Naumkeag, it appears, may not be to the Puritans' liking and they shall soon set about the task of finding a place to settle. The new spot must befit a mission so blessed, for as Governor Winthrop told his fellow Puritans, ". . . we shall be like a City upon a Hill; the eyes of all people are on us."

Colony is proclaimed "a City upon a Hill"

Naumkeag, Mass., June 12, 1630

"The Lord will make our name a praise and glory," predicts John Winthrop, Governor of Massachusetts, "so that men shall say of succeeding plantations: 'The Lord make it like that of New England.' For we must consider that we shall be like a City upon a Hill; the eyes of all people are on us."

To the settlers of Virginia, America is a potential fount of riches. To the Puritans it is a Promised Land. As their name suggests, the colonists arriving today believe their mission is to purify their lives in accord with the word of the Lord. They consider themselves a chosen people, the spiritual heirs of the people of Israel. "He has taken us to be His own," says Winthrop.

Winthrop, "spiritual aristocrat."

Winthrop spent much of the voyage ruminating on his reasons for leaving England. The result, a sermon he calls *A Model of Christian Charity,* is also a plan for behavior in the New World; for along with their divine privileges come special responsibilities. According to Winthrop, the Lord is telling the Puritans, "just as He told the people of Israel, 'You only have I known of all the families of the Earth; therefore will I punish you for your transgressions.' " What most people "only profess as a truth," Winthrop insists, "we must bring into familiar and constant practice." The task is thus set forth for Winthrop's flock. And, as the only self-governing colony in America, Massachusetts has the means to succeed or fail on its own.

Shawmut renamed Boston, gets church

Boston, Sept. 7, 1630

Governor John Winthrop and his assistants passed a resolution today, declaring "that Trimontaine," on the Shawmut peninsula, "shall be called Boston" from now on. The decision to rename the area and place the seat of government here came after Winthrop paid a visit to the reclusive clergyman William Blackstone, who lived with 180 books in a garden in Trimontaine, across the river from Winthrop's settlement in Charlestown.

Winthrop had already established the settlement's first church, which was Puritan but non-Separatist and Congregational, three months ago in Charlestown, but he agreed to move the church and the frame of the home he was building there to the Shawmut peninsula, which the Indians had named "living fountain" after a spring that Blackstone pointed out. The name "Boston" was chosen to honor Lady Arbella and Isaac Johnson, settlers with Winthrop who both came from the English town of Boston.

Indians wipe out a new Dutch settlement

In more peaceful times, settlers maintained a thriving trade with the Indians.

Swanadael, Dec. 6, 1632

A minor theft has led to the the massacre of this entire colony of Swanadael in New Netherland. In the fall, an Indian chief stole a tin sign with the coat of arms of Holland printed on it to make a pipe. Settlers reported the theft to another Indian tribe that retaliated by severing the chief's head and presenting it to the colonists. Members of the chief's tribe later approached the settlers in a friendly manner, then slew everyone in the colony. Only one of the settlers managed to escape to a nearby colony.

First white man explores Northwest area

Northwest, 1634

French explorer Jean Nicolet, wrapped in a Chinese robe, crossed a Great Lake [Lake Michigan] and entered what he thought was the Orient. Instead, he found the wilds of the Northwest [Wisconsin]. Nicolet became the first white man to set foot in the area and the Winnebago Indians were friendly. The tribe told Nicolet, the first European to study Indian languages, of "a great water." Believing it could be the ocean route to China, he went west to explore the great river [Mississippi]. No closer to China than ever, a disappointed Nicolet returned to his Quebec base.

Midwestern natives greet the French in E.W. Deming's "Landfall of Nicolet."

Catholics found colony

A first in British America: A priest celebrates a Roman Catholic mass.

Maryland, March 25, 1634

George Calvert's dream of founding a Catholic enclave in the English colonies has become a reality with the landing of 128 Catholic settlers on Saint Clement Island in Maryland. Calvert had been the principal secretary to King James I of England, but he left the government after he declared his conversion to Roman Catholicism. Calvert later persuaded King James to grant him a new colony north of Virginia that would be dedicated to religious freedom. Calvert was awarded the title of Lord Baltimore, but he died before he was able to sign the deed to the colony.

His son Cecil commissioned two ships, the Ark and the Dove, to sail for the new land. Yesterday, the two vessels sailed up the Potomac River and landed on Saint Clement Island. Today, two Jesuit priests who accompanied the colonists erected a large cross and celebrated the first Catholic mass in this part of the world. Cecil Calvert is staying in England to fight anti-papist feelings against the new colony and he has appointed his brother Leonard to govern in his stead.

Boston builds first American vessel

Boston, Aug. 1631

Cheering crowds in Boston harbor celebrated the first launching of an American-built sailing ship this month and the new 30-ton sloop, the Blessing of the Bay, sailed out to sea amid a rising tide of optimism. Many Bostonians believe that this could be the beginning of a prosperous new industry for the area. The availabilty of inexpensive American lumber, making it possible to construct boats at about half the price of those in England, is the major reason for the high hopes. Last November, the first ferry route in the colonies was opened, linking Boston to Charlestown by way of the Charles River (→ May 20, 1644).

French explorer is eaten by Indians

Ontario, 1633

Etienne Brule was the first of a new kind of trader, the "coureur de bois," the rover in the woods who lives and travels and hunts among the Indians and becomes virtually a citizen of both worlds, that of the white man and of the red man. But the Huron Indians whom he lived among turned against him, killed him and ate him. It is not known whether they cooked him first. Brule migrated to New France in 1608 and was probably the first European to explore the region of the north and, with Samuel de Champlain, to discover the Great Lakes in 1615 [Ontario] and 1622 [Superior].

1635 (1635-1639)

Maryland, 1635. Algonquin chief responds to imposition of English law on Indians: "Since you are strangers here, you should rather conform to the customs of our country."

Salem, Massachusetts, 1635. Samuel Lincoln arrives from Norfolk, England. [He is ancestor of Abraham Lincoln, 16th U.S. President.]

Providence, June 1636. Roger Williams founds new colony here on land purchased from Indians (→ 1638).

New Netherland, October 5, 1636. Dutch grant first patents on Long Island.

Plymouth, Oct. 5, 1636. Fundamentals of Plymouth install representative government, as expansion hinders travel to General Court.

Maine, 1636. Richmond Island fishermen boycott jobs [possibly first strike in colonies].

London, July 23, 1637. After court battle prosecuted by Thomas Morton, King hands over Massachusetts to Sir Ferdinando Gorges (→ Apr. 1638).

Boston, March 13, 1638. Ancient and Honorable Artillery Company, one of first military units in colonies, is chartered.

London, Apr. 1638. After Gorges fails to serve warrant on Massachusetts, Land Commission sends letter demanding surrender of charter; Winthrop refuses (→ June 25, 1640).

London, Apr. 4, 1638. After naval clashes with Virginia, Claiborne gets ruling that Kent Island is part of Maryland.

Salem, 1638. Captain William Pierce sails to the West Indies to exchange Indian slaves for Negro slaves and goods.

Braintree, Massachusetts, 1638. Henry Adams arrives from Somerset, England. [Descendants include John Adams, second U.S. President; John Quincy Adams, sixth U.S. President.]

Massachusetts, Sept. 4, 1639. General Court enacts law against drinking toasts.

Virginia, Nov. 1639. Privy Council, tired of conflict between Governor and council, ousts Governor John Harvey.

DEATHS

Quebec, Dec. 25, 1635. Samuel de Champlain, father of New France (*c.1567).

Atlantic, June 1638. Peter Minuit, in shipwreck en route from Delaware River to Sweden (*1580).

Freedom is aim of Williams colony

Roger Williams, a pariah among his own people, is welcomed by the natives.

Providence, Autumn 1638

Declaring that "forced worship stinks in God's nostrils," the Puritan pastor Roger Williams has invited political dissenters of every stripe to join him in establishing a free-wheeling colony on the riverfront here. So far, the minister's offer has been taken up by 20 families, all delighted to be able to worship as they please. The colonists have agreed that they will be governed by majority rule and by Williams's tenet that no one can be compelled to attend church or to honor the Sabbath.

Williams, who had served as pastor at churches in Salem and Plymouth, was convicted of heresy in 1636 and was banished from Massachusetts Bay for his belief that church and state should be separate. Leaving his sick wife and children behind, he wandered south through snowy woods and came upon a tribe of Indians with whom he became friends. In June 1636, the Indians gave him land to start his settlement. Williams then asked that all "persons distressed of conscience" join him and live under a covenant he drafted that mandated religious liberty. This fall, Williams founded a Baptist church, the first of its denomination in the colonies. At least 10 colonists have joined the church, having rejected the validity of their baptism by the Church of England (→ March 24, 1644).

Settlers destroy an Indian village of 500, ending Pequot War

Puritan forces shoot and kill 500 Pequot Indian men, women and children.

Connecticut, June 5, 1637

The pale light of dawn discloses the blood-stained snow and the smoldering remains of a Pequot encampment. The Pequot will threaten no more. During the night, combined forces from Plymouth, Massachusetts, and Connecticut militia, with several hundred Narragansett and Niantic Indian allies, surprised and slaughtered 500 Pequot in their fort. Setting fire to the village, the colonists clubbed or shot to death all the Pequot who had not burned. This, the third battle between settlers of the Connecticut River area and the Pequot, is almost sure to win the war for the English.

The Pequot were once dominant in this area. Yet, this battle shows the strength and tactics of the settlers. The English population has been growing recently. While the Dutch and English contest rights over the area, the movement of several tribes, including the Housatonic Mohegan, into Pequot land also set off disputes. The shores of the area are lucrative because the shells and beads used as wampum are collected and created here.

Neither the Dutch nor English would aid the Mohegans, and the Pequots grew arrogant. In January 1634, skipper John Stone and seven companions were murdered on the Connecticut River. The assailants were said to be Pequots. Two years later, a New England trader, John Oldham, was killed at Block Island. That incident prompted John Endecott, the Massachusetts Governor, to send three fighting vessels to the area where the Narragansett village was raised in retribution.

Returning to the mainland, the men sought John Stone's killers among the Pequot. Since no culprits were found, the village was burned and blood was shed. By May 1637, the Pequot had struck back, attacking Wethersfield, Connecticut, killing nine and abducting two residents. A small force of militia fought a Pequot band last month. But it lacked superiority so the stage was set for last night's show of force (→ May 19, 1643).

First constitution is adopted in colonies

Hartford, Conn., Jan. 24, 1639

Representatives from three Connecticut towns have banded together to write the Fundamental Orders, the first constitution in the New World. The document makes the radical claim that "the foundation of authority is in the free consent of the people." And it makes no mention of allegiance to the British crown. Written by men from the towns of Hartford, Windsor and Wethersfield, the constitution establishes a general assembly, the office of governor and the right to tax. It also guarantees the political rights of freemen – except, of course, those who are given to scandalous behavior.

100 Puritans migrate to Connecticut

Hartford, Conn., May 31, 1638

Thomas Hooker, a Congregationalist minister who rejects the autocratic rule of the Puritans in Boston, arrived here with 100 settlers this morning and gave a sermon in which he claimed that authority rests in the people's consent.

He echoes the sentiments of others who have come to Connecticut seeking self-determination. Early in April, the Rev. John Davenport led a congregation of devout Puritans out of Boston, a city they find ever more corrupted, and brought them to Quinnipiac, a lush region they call a "new haven." Davenport's settlement may eventually flourish more than neighboring Saybrook or Wethersfield, for Davenport brings wealthy and learned merchants, among them Theophilus Eaton and David Yale.

Thomas Hooker delivers his sermon.

Regarding commerce, Quinnipiac is ideally situated between the trading centers of Massachusetts Bay and New Amsterdam. Regarding religion, it is well distant from Winthrop's colony, where the non-Puritan ideas of Antinomians are still viewed with sympathy. Therefore, the future holds promise; the present brings misery. The Quinnipiac settlers live in damp cellars while waiting to raise homes of timber. To buoy spirits, Davenport reads aloud from John Mather's *Discourse About Civil Government in a New Plantation Whose Design Is Religion* (→Jan. 24, 1639).

First colonial press prints freedom oath

Cambridge, Mass., Jan. 1639

The first publication has come off a colonial press. It is *Oath of a Free-Man,* a broadside that lambastes the vow of allegiance colonists must swear to the English crown. The "oath" is a triumph for Stephen Daye, who came to New England in 1638 with no knowledge of typography – his employer perished on their voyage from England. Daye next offers *An Almanak for the Year of Our Lord, 1639, Calculated for New England,* by shipmaster William Pierce, who says it may lure people to America.

Stephen Daye's font of wisdom, a "common press" imported from the mother country to Cambridge.

College founded in 1636 named Harvard

Boston, March 3, 1639

The college founded three years ago near the Charles River in Newetowne, has been named Harvard to honor the man who gave it half his fortune. The Rev. John Harvard, a Presbyterian who came to the colonies one year ago, willed 780 pounds sterling and his 400-volume library to the college. Newetowne has also been renamed Cambridge to honor the university that Harvard attended in England.

The college was founded by the Puritans of the Massachusetts Bay Colony who landed at Plymouth 19 years ago. They hope that Harvard will succeed in training ministers who will help perpetuate their religious beliefs. As one of the founders wrote: "After God had carried us safe to New-England, and wee had builded our houses, provided necessaries for our livli-hood, rear'd convenient places for God's worship and settled the Civill Government; One of the next things we longed for, and looked after was to advance Learning and Perpetuate it to Posterity . . ."

Rough Indian game

Iroquois Territory [Ontario], 1636

A Jesuit missionary, Jan de Brebeuf, reported to his superiors in this territory [Thunder Bay] that he saw Indians playing a game in which they propelled a ball with an odd-looking stick. A rawhide bag was attached to the end of the stick, which resembled a bishop's crozier, called a crosse [lacrosse] in French. He said rival teams seemed more intent on crippling each other with the sticks until the forces were reduced to reasonable size. Then they concentrated on scoring.

Puritans expel radical Anne Hutchinson, who founds new colony

Pocasset, Mass., March 7, 1638

A new settlement is springing up here [Portsmouth, Rhode Island] as a direct result of the Antinomian controversy, which many feared was going to tear the colony apart. Anne Hutchinson, William Coddington and John Coggeshall are a few of the leaders of a band of dissidents who have either been banished by the Puritans or have decided to depart because of their religious differences. Coddington has purchased the large island of Aquidneck, which lies between Narragansett Bay and the Sakonnet River, and he is planning to build on the northern end of the island. The colonists have agreed that no one in this new settlement is going to have to endure religious persecution.

Mrs. Hutchinson, banished from Massachusetts on November 17, has been called a "perfectionist." She believes the Holy Spirit dwells in every person. Representative of the Antinomians, she denies there is a need to provide any evidence of good works or sanctification other than the realization of Christ in oneself. She contends that one is a Christian not by works, but by virtue of the inner spirit that prevails within oneself. The Puritan leaders, on the other hand, maintain that churchgoing, good works, obedience, family exercises, diligence in calling and reverence toward ministers are among the necessary duties of a Christian (→May 1, 1639).

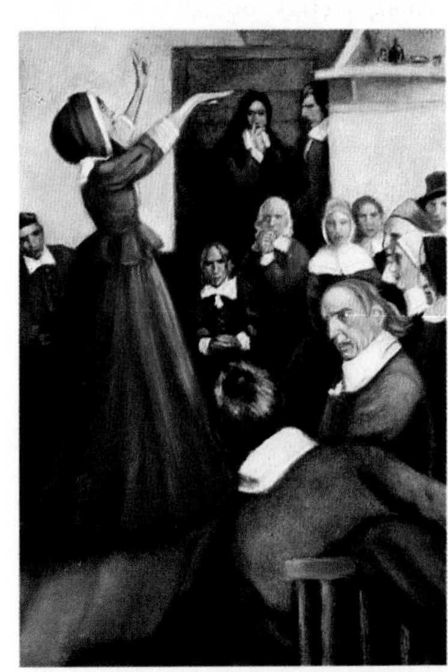

Mrs. Hutchinson preached in Boston.

New Sweden is set up on Delaware

"The Landing of the Swedes and Finns" by Stanley Arthur.

Fort Christina, May 1638

The name New Sweden to describe the new colony on the Delaware River is something of a misnomer since the backbone of the settlement is Finnish. And it is led by three angry Dutchmen, the most prominent of whom is Peter Minuit, who bought Manhattan from the Indians. When accused by the Dutch West India Company of having sown discord and misappropriated funds, Minuit and two others approached Willem Usselinx of Antwerp, who had proposed a plan for religious refugees as early as 1623. Minuit joined the Swedish West Indian Company, and sufficient funds were raised. The enterprise has the backing of Queen Christina, who believes that Delaware is the perfect place for the hordes of Finns who have been migrating to Sweden, where they are accused of destroying the forests.

In March of 1638, the Key of Calmar and the Griffin, both flying the Swedish ensign, dropped anchor just above Cape Henlopen, with cargoes of Swedish deportees and minor criminals, as well as the forest-loving Finns and a few Dutch. The Finns have brought to America a type of house that may be uniquely suited to the frontier: the one-story log cabin, which is caulked with fire-hardened clay inside and out, and is warmed by huge clay-plastered chimneys. Also imported is the huge log "bastu," a steam bathhouse common in Sweden (→ May 31, 1654).

Newport is founded as a farm colony

Newport, May 1, 1639

William Coddington and his supporters have landed on the southern tip of Aquidneck Island [Rhode Island] to lay out the plantation of Newport. Coddington, a former associate of Mrs. Anne Hutchinson, a critic of Puritanism, was ousted last month as chief magistrate of Hutchinson's community of Pocassett [Portsmouth], on the north side of the island. Though outmanuevered by rivals embracing English law, Coddington has shown he does not remain idle long. A shrewd, powerful leader and a firm believer in religious freedom, he seems likely to suceed in the Newport venture. Corn, tobacco and pigs do well here and the site commands approaches to Providence and Pocassett. But can Newport compete with these colonies? And if so, will it stay independent of Massachusetts and Plymouth?

A peace compact is signed in Exeter

Exeter, N.H., July 14, 1639

Establishing peace and security in the wilderness, the Rev. John Wheelwright, founder of Exeter, New Hampshire, and 36 male settlers signed a pact outlining a system of local government. Modeled on the Mayflower Compact, the Exeter Compact lets the men manage their civic affairs for the common good, until another government is formed in the region. The agreement marks one of the first institutions of independent government in New England north of Massachusetts. The area has been eyed for annexation by Massachusetts since the death of the Council for New England colonizer John Mason in 1635. Wheelwright, formerly a Boston and Braintree clergyman, was banished from Massachusetts last year for "kindling" the population with seditious Antinomian teachings.

Puritans assail drink and vanity

Plymouth, Massachusetts, 1639

Raging from their pulpits, Puritan ministers are determined that this new colony, which they say is like "a City upon a Hill," shall be free of sins and abominations before God. The General Court of Massachusetts has enacted a law against drinking toasts, declaring that "the common custom of drinking to one another is a mere useless ceremony and draweth on the abominable practice of drinking healths." The court has also passed measures that govern the clothing of men, who have been censured for going about in "immoderate great breeches." The ministers and the lawmakers are particularly concerned about the current fashions in England that are quickly being brought to the colony. These include broad shoulderbands, capes, double ruffles and silk roses that are worn on the shoes as adornments.

1640 (1640-1644)

Maine, June 25, 1640. Thomas Gorges sets up provincial court at York to govern in face of Massachusetts expansionism (→ June 29, 1652).

Plymouth, March 2, 1641. Bradford, after getting patent from Council for New England, deeds colony to freemen.

Massachusetts, June 2, 1641. First patent in colonies, for a salt-making process, is given to Samuel Winslow.

New Hampshire, June 14, 1641. Four towns placed under jurisdiction of Massachusetts.

Maryland, 1641. Andrew Monroe arrives from Scotland. [Descendants include James Monroe, 5th U.S. President.]

New Netherland, Feb. 25, 1642. Dutch slaughter lower Hudson Valley Indians, who are seeking refuge from Mohawk attacks (→ March 1644).

Massachusetts, June 14, 1642. First compulsory school law goes into effect.

Lynn, Massachusetts, 1642. Briton Joseph Jencks arrives to set up iron and brass works.

New Netherland, Sept. 1643. Indians kill Anne Hutchinson (*1591) and family [in Eastchester].

New Haven, Nov. 6, 1643. General Court, with deputies from Stamford, Guilford and Milford, adopt Frame of Government with legal system based on Mosaic Law.

Boston, 1643. First restaurant or "cook's shop" opened by Goody Armitage.

Rowley, Massachusetts, 1643. First American textile factory established.

New Netherland, March 1644. Public thanksgiving declared to mark killing of 500 Indians (→ Oct. 1644).

Virginia, March 18, 1644. Opechancanough Indians launch uprising (→ Oct. 1644).

London, March 24, 1644. Roger Williams, pressed by New England Confederation, gains charter for Rhode Island.

Massachusetts, May 20, 1644. Shipbuilding guild formed.

Massachusetts, Nov. 29, 1644. General Court issues call for pastors to learn Indian dialects to aid in conversions (→ Oct. 28, 1646).

Rhode Island, 1644. Roger Williams writes *The Bloudy Tenent of Persecution for Cause of Conscience*; book is burned publicly in London (→ 1657).

Missionary colony set in New France

New France, May 17, 1641

With the objective of bringing Christianity to the native Indian population that the explorers of New France have encountered, a Roman Catholic missionary settlement has been established by the Societe Notre-Dame de Montreal. This new Catholic colony will be under the governorship of Paul de Chomedey de Maisonneuve. The colony, which will be called Ville-Marie [Montreal], will be protected by a fort that is to serve as a defense against the possibility of attacks by the Iroquois Indians, who have shown hostility to other explorers and settlement attempts in New France. The missionary settlement will contain a hospital, a chapel and, at the outset, accommodations for about 70 people.

Puritan Parliament versus King

Nottingham, Engl., Aug. 20, 1642

King Charles I raised his standard here today, bringing the country to the verge of civil war. The long-simmering feud between those who support the "divine right of kings" to rule absolutely and those who advocate the supremacy of Parliament came to a head last month when, following his failed attempt to arrest John Pym, John Hampden and other leaders of the opposition, the King was forced to leave London.

Profound religious differences have added to the bitterness of the conflict, with most members of Parliament backing the Puritans while the King and his party have fully backed the High Church policies of Archbishop William Laud, which he has enforced vigorously (→ Jan. 30, 1649).

At Nottingham, King Charles I declares war on Puritan parliamentarians.

Hundreds slaughtered in Indian conflicts

Virginia, Oct. 1644

European settlers in Virginia and along the Hudson remain vigilant, although wars with the Indians over territory and trade are waning. Over 350 English farmers south of the James River were killed by warriors of Opechancanough four months ago. But counterattacks by William Berkeley and Acting Governor Richard Kemp crushed Indian resistance, ending 37 years of violence. Along the Hudson, Dutch expansion and threats from the furtrading, rifle-toting Mohawks halted the Algonquins. Seeking refuge near New Amsterdam [New York City], 120 Algonquins were massacred by the Dutch, in revenge for earlier murders. Eleven Algonquin tribes united, causing mayhem between the Housatonic and Raritan Rivers. And war ended when 150 Dutch killed 700 Indian fighters near Stamford, Connecticut, eight months ago (→ Aug. 9, 1645).

New England unites

Plymouth, Mass., May 19, 1643

The river towns of Connecticut, Plymouth and New Haven have signed a constitution for "the Confederation of the United Colonies of New England" in response to the Pequot War with the Indians. Some towns initially feared dominance by the Bay Colony and refused to sign the document, but they finally gave in to their fears of danger from the Dutch and French, as well as the Indians (→ Oct. 29, 1684).

Immigration ebbing

Plymouth, Mass., 1643

Improved conditions in England are slowing the steady stream of colonists who have flocked to New England during the past 12 years. As many as 20,000 settlers came to Massachusetts, but only 5,000 were Puritans. Many colonial problems have arisen, mostly around conflicts between Puritans and non-Puritans. Still, towns keep emerging. In 1631, there were 11 on Massachusetts Bay. Now there are 21.

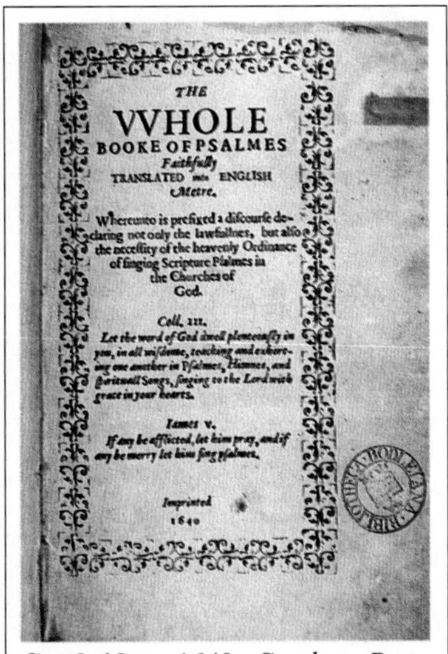

THE
VVHOLE
BOOKE OF PSALMES
Faithfully
TRANSLATED into ENGLISH
Metre.
Whereunto is prefixed a discourse declaring not only the lawfullnes, but also the necessity of the heavenly Ordinance of singing Scripture Psalmes in the Churches of God.

Coll. III.
Let the word of God dwell plenteously in you, in all wisdome, teaching and exhorting one another in Psalmes, Himnes, and spirituall Songs, singing to the Lord with grace in your hearts.

Iames V.
If any be afflicted, let him pray, and if any be merry let him sing psalmes.

Imprinted
1640

Cambridge, 1640. *Stephen Daye prints the first real book in America, "The Bay Psalm Book."*

Adulterers branded

Plymouth, Mass., Dec. 1641

A man and a woman, the letters "AD" on their clothes plainly in view, have been severely whipped at the public post. Likewise, two years ago a woman was whipped, then dragged through the streets wearing letters on her left sleeve. She was told that if she removed the badge, her face would be burned with a hot iron. Adultery persists in the colony, perhaps, as some argue, through the influence of immigrants from the Middle and Southern colonies. Whatever has led them into sin, these adulterers must be glad the law of 1632 has been overturned: that measure punished adultery with death.

The Delaware River Valley is now the site of New Sweden, displaying dwellings of the most curious construction: The cabins of notched, layered logs are apparently a mainstay of peasant life in Finland.

1645 (1645-1649)

New Netherland, Aug. 9, 1645. Settlers gain peace with Indians after intervention of Mohawks.

Boston, Aug. 30, 1645. New England Confederation makes peace with Narragansetts.

Massachusetts, March 3, 1646. Joseph Jencks gets patent for water-powered mill engine.

New Netherland, July 28, 1646. Willem Kieft ousted as Governor after Indian war.

New Netherland, Oct. 18, 1646. Indians kill Jesuit missionary Isaac Joques and Hurons' convert Jean Laland.

Virginia, Oct. 1646. Chief Necotowance agrees to acknowledge that Indian lands are held courtesy of British crown, ending two-and-a-half-year war.

Virginia, 1646. Colony's first law for education of poor provides for sending out poor children as apprentices.

Massachusetts, 1646. *The Day-Breaking if not the Sun-Rising of the Gospell with the Indians in New-England* written by the Rev. John Eliot.

Massachusetts, May 26, 1647. Law bars Catholic priests from colony; penalty is banishment, or death for second offense.

Massachusetts, 1647. Trade with Canaries, Madeiras and Spain begins to help colony out of economic depression.

Cambridge, Mass., Aug. 15, 1648. Cambridge Platform adopted, establishing Congregational religious polity and backing Westminster Assembly.

Maryland, 1648. Richard Bennett leads 400-600 Virginians to form Puritan outpost of Providence [Annapolis].

New Netherland, 1648. Jan Claes Maertenszen van Rosenvelt arrives from the Netherlands. [Descendants include Theodore, 26th U.S. President; Franklin Delano, 32nd President.

London, July 19, 1649. Society for Propagating the Gospel in New England incorporated by Parliament after John Eliot's success at converting Indians (→ 1653).

New Netherland, 1649. Iroquois defeat Hurons, disperse Neutrals, Eries (→ 1650).

DEATH

Massachusetts, March 26, 1649. John Winthrop, first Governor of Massachusetts Bay Colony (*Jan. 12, 1588).

Stuyvesant feuds with own tax board

New Amsterdam, Dec. 1647

In a move to silence growing demands for limited self-government, Peter Stuyvesant, director general of New Netherland, jailed Adrian van der Donck, a local burgher and leader of the Board of Nine Men. The Nine Men, an advisory group, and Stuyvesant have disagreed over taxes and representation since the authoritarian director arrived in New Amsterdam seven months ago. The colony is nearly bankrupt and it is facing collapse in the wake of last year's Algonquin war unless funds are found soon.

Stuyvesant lost leg fighting Portugal.

King Charles beheaded

Charles insisted, until the end, that he had been divinely chosen to govern.

London, Jan. 30, 1649

Condemned after a brief trial as a "tyrant, traitor, murderer and public enemy" and sentenced to die "by the severing of his head from his body," Charles I was beheaded today in a heavily guarded execution that took place just outside the banquet hall of Whitehall Palace.

The day was bitterly cold as the doomed King, appearing calm and dignified, stepped through the specially enlarged window that gave on to the scaffold where two masked executioners awaited him. Closely formed ranks of soldiers armed with pikes and halberds kept back the large crowd and prevented the King from addressing them. But among those who stood nearby was William Juxon, Bishop of London, who stated that the King died "a Christian according to the profession of the Church of England" and was going from "a corruptible to an incorruptible crown."

After laying his head on the block, he stretched out his hands as a sign that he was ready, and the ax fell. "At the instant whereof," said a witness, "there was such a grone by the thousands then present as I never heard before."

Holding up the severed head, one of the executioners then uttered the traditional cry, "Behold the head of a traitor!" Before the crowd was dispersed by the troops, many of the men and women dipped their handkerchiefs in King Charles's blood. In England, the divine right of kings is dead (→ Dec. 1653).

John Eliot holds first Protestant service for Indians in colonies

The Rev. John Eliot and guest, Father Druillettes, speak of spiritual matters by the fire, while natives who have been brought to God listen intently.

Nonantum, Mass., Oct. 28, 1646

For the first time, Indians can hear about the gospel in their own language. The Rev. John Eliot, who studied at Jesus College, Cambridge, England, preached to the Algonquins in their own tongue in the wigwam of Waban, a chieftain who lives about five miles from Boston. He used as his text, Ezekiel 37:9, which is the story of Ezekiel's vision of the dry bones. He recited the catechism to the Indian children and had them repeat the answers. Eliot also read the 10 Commandments and explained each of them. He has been studying Indian languages since 1632 and is a scholar of both Hebrew and Greek (→ July 19, 1649).

Maryland grants all Christians equality

Maryland, Apr. 21, 1649

The Maryland Provincial Assembly has adopted a law granting legal equality to all who profess Jesus Christ to be the son of God. "An Act Concerning Religion" was a compromise between the Roman Catholic proprietor, Lord Baltimore, and the Puritan-dominated assembly. It is expected to go far toward easing the religious tensions that have troubled the colony during England's Civil War and the recent revolt in Maryland.

The act explicitly states that no one "professing to believe in Jesus Christ shall henceforth be in any ways troubled . . . for or in respect of his or her religion nor in the free exercise thereof within this province nor any way be compelled to the belief or exercise of any religion against his will." While the legislation does contain provisions requiring that those who "deny Our Saviour Jesus Christ to be the Son of God" be punished, it also contains provisions calling for the punishment of those people who criticize others for their religious beliefs.

Among the proscribed behaviors is that of speaking reproachfully toward others by calling them Lutheran, Calvinist, papist, Jesuit, Brownist, Roundhead, Antinomian or popish priest (→ Oct. 20, 1654).

First woman lawyer is denied the ballot

Maryland, Jan. 21, 1648

Miss Margaret Brent, the first woman lawyer in the colonies, has been denied a vote in the Maryland Assembly. Executor of the estate of former Governor Leonard Calvert, Miss Brent protested today's assembly proceedings and implied that they were unlawfully conducted without her: all owners of land should be represented, and she is one of the wealthiest. Since her arrival in St. Mary's Parish 10 years ago, the attorney has ousted Irish fugitives from the colony and assigned land grants to new settlers.

Woman guilty of witchcraft to hang

Plymouth, Mass., May 13, 1648

Miss Margaret Jones of Charlestown, indicted and found guilty of witchcraft, is to be hanged by the neck. The Plymouth Court found that Miss Jones has a "malignant touch," causing pain or vomiting in those she approaches. She has administered physics – she says they were harmless aniseed or liquors – yet those people who used them and were already ill drew nearer to death. Members of the colony have been assured that Miss Jones will be watched day and night until the sentence is carried out.

Leaders deplore frivolities trade brings

A most righteous Puritan leader lectures on the immorality of winter sports.

Cambridge, Massachusetts, 1648

Orthodox Puritans are determined that the prosperous trading in the colony not be permitted to undermine their holy experiment. Greater trade with the Old World, as well as with the Wine Islands (Madeira, the Azores, and Canaries) is bringing in raucous sailors, gaudy clothing and the baubles of life. The leaders in New England, as well as in the Chesapeake Colonies, fear that their traditional religious ways will be undermined.

But there is the other side. In an effort to gain greater freedom, the merchants of the Commonwealth, led by a young scientist named Dr. Robert Child, supported a "Remonstrance and Petition" to the General Court in 1646 demanding that "civil liberty and freedom be forthwith granted to all truly English." The court not only turned down their petition as scandalous, but also fined the petitioners and threw two of them in jail. This year, a synod called the Cambridge Platform of Church Discipline explicitly granted the colonies the authority to "enforce in matters of godliness." Furthermore, the synod declared the right to vote should be taken away from those who "shall walk incorrigibly or obstinately in any corrupt way of their own."

These measures are part of a pattern that seems to be an attempt by older leaders to counter the corruptive influences of modern or English ways. The General Court of Massachusetts has even gone so far as to ban amusements "such as the shovelboard in houses of common entertainment whereby much precious time is spent unfruitfully."

Patroonships fail

New Netherland, Dec. 1646

The Dutch West India Company's experiment in colonization, the patroon system, failed this year. The company had offered huge tracts of land in New Netherland and feudal powers to those willing to pay the passage for 50 settlers who would agree to work on the estates. But the company then undermined the system by failing to support the patroons. The deeper flaw in the plan, however, lay in a misjudgment of the character of the Dutch. They are a freedom-loving people and had little interest in migrating to the colonies to sell themselves into a condition of servitude.

First slaving ships sent from America

Boston, 1645

The profitable but unpleasant trade of slaving has become an American industry with ships now frequently leaving Boston harbor for raids along the West African coast. There, natives are captured or purchased by the Americans and taken to Barbados, where they are traded for salt, tobacco, sugar and wine. These valuable commodities are sold in Boston at a huge profit. In fact, the profits have been so great as to encourage the continuance and growth of this trade in the North American ports. The market in Barbados ships slaves to colonies throughout the Americas.

More books written

New England, 1649

Clerics are writing away, spurred by the success of Thomas Shepard's *Sincere Convert* (1641). Roger Williams's *The Bloudy Tenent of Persecution for the Cause of Conscience,* a defense of free thought (1644), is answered by *The Bloudy Tenent Washed and Made White in the Bloude of the Lamb* (1647), by John Cotton, also author of *The Keyes of the Kingdom of Heaven* (1644), and, for young people, *Spiritual Milk for Boston Babes in Either England* (1645). Calvinist Thomas Hooker pierces sinners' hearts with *Survey of the Summe of Church Discipline* (1648).

For conversation not fit for gentle company, or simply to discuss intimate matters in crowded rooms, discreet companions might do well to direct their communications through a whispering rod.

1650 (1650-1654)

Hartford, Sept. 29, 1650. New Netherland Governor Peter Stuyvesant signs border pact with New England Confederation, recognizing English claims to much of Long Island, Connecticut.

Michigan, 1650. French Jesuits abandon last of Huron missions after Iroquois raids destroy Huron Nation.

New Amsterdam, 1650. Jan Aertsen Vanderbilt arrives from der Bilt, Holland. [Descendants include industrialists Cornelius and William Henry Vanderbilt.]

Massachusetts, Oct. 14, 1651. Laws passed forbidding poor to adopt excessive dress.

Boston, Dec. 25, 1651. General Court levies five-shilling fine for anyone "observing any such day as Christmas."

Virginia, 1651. Anthony Johnson, free Negro, imports five servants, forms Negro community on Pungoteague River.

Virginia, March 12, 1652. Loyalist Governor Sir William Berkeley submits to warships sent by Parliament (→Apr. 30).

Virginia, Apr. 30, 1652. Assembly, in consultation with British commissioners, names provisional government to be headed by Richard Bennett.

Rhode Island, May 18, 1652. Slavery banned for first time in colonies [law never enforced].

Barbados, 1652. Governor complains of shortages due to parliamentary ban on foreign trade with colonies.

New Amsterdam, Dec. 14, 1653. Governor Stuyvesant tells colony's first representative assembly, "We derive our authority from God and the Company, not from a few ignorant subjects."

London, Dec. 1653. Puritan Oliver Cromwell becomes lord protector (→May 29, 1660).

Massachusetts, 1653. The Rev. John Eliot publishes *Catechism in the Indian Language*, first book printed in Indian tongue.

King and Queen County, Virginia, 1653. John Madison Sr. arrives from Gloucester, England. [Descendants include James Madison, 4th President.]

Massachusetts, May 3, 1654. First toll bridge licensed to Richard Thurley, at Newbury River; a charge for animals; free for humans.

Boston, 1654. Joseph Jencks commissioned to build first fire engine in America.

Swedish invaders seize major Dutch fort

Fort New Amsterdam in 1651, just prior to the outbreak of hostilities.

Delaware River, May 31, 1654

Some 20 to 30 Swedish soldiers swiftly and almost effortlessly took over the Dutch Fort Casimir while Dutch Commander Bikker stood by, according to some at the fort.

After Dutch mediators met on board the Swedish ship Orn with the new Governor Rysingh, they reported to Bikker that if they did not surrender "we should soon see his bullets." Bikker said that he was unsuspecting and that he welcomed the Swedes "as friends." However, Adriaen van Tienthoven, the clerk of Fort Casimir's court, suggested that Bikker may have given in too quickly. Responding to the request of his soldiers that they defend the fort, Bikker said "What can I do? There is no powder."

When Rysingh landed on May 20 with 350 settlers, he found only 18 families left in the Swedish Fort Christina, while 50 Dutch families were settled downriver at the prospering Fort Casimir. The Indians had sold the land just below the Swedish fort in 1651 to the Dutch, but they they had refused to negotiate any sales to the Swedes.

When Queen Christina of Sweden appointed Rysingh the Governor of New Sweden last year, she promised that he would receive as much land in the new country as he and 30 to 40 peasants could cultivate (→Sept. 1655).

Baptists arrested; one publicly whipped

Boston, July 1651

Dr. John Clarke and Obediah Holmes, two members of the Baptist sect, which this city's religious leaders consider a prejudiced and ignorant one, were arrested in Lynn this month for holding an unauthorized religious meeting. The two Baptists, who reject infant baptism and the standing order of the colony, were holding a service in someone's home when the sheriff arrested them. Clarke, a friend and colleague of Roger Williams in Rhode Island, which proper Bostonians regard as a sewer of filth, was imprisoned. But the Baptist minister from Newport was later freed without punishment. Holmes was whipped in the streets of Boston. The Governor, John Endecott, hopes that such punishment will serve to deter encroachment from the neighboring colony by people he finds schismatic and disruptive.

Whipping of Baptist pariah Holmes.

Trade monopoly is imposed by London

London, Oct. 9, 1651

In a move designed to break the Dutch hold on the carrying trade, Parliament has passed a Navigation Act that greatly favors England's shipping. Under the terms of the new legislation, all goods brought into England or its colonies from countries outside Europe must be carried in ships owned by Englishmen or colonials. Further, at least half of the crews of these ships must be of English nationality. Imports into England or its colonies from any part of Europe must be carried either in English or colonial vessels, or vessels belonging to the country in which the imported goods were made. Most of the commodities that are produced in the colonies are to be shipped to England only.

Although the new law does no more than re-state principles that have long been in existence, it is certain to arouse the anger of Dutch shipping interests. The recent increase in the strength of the English navy, and its successes under Admiral Blake, make it seem likely that the new legislation will be rigorously enforced. If that is indeed what happens, then a war with Holland is considered likely.

Passage of the act is attributed to the influence of commercial and shipping interests that favor protectionist measures (→May 20, 1657).

London, 1651. *Pilgrim father Edward Winslow, depicted above by Robert Walker, returned to England in 1646 to defend Massachusetts in court. [The painting is the only existing likeness of a Mayflower Pilgrim.]*

Maryland is taken over by Puritans

St. Marys, Oct. 20, 1654

At one time, Maryland was regarded as "the only colony where Roman Catholics are entitled to the rights of man." An assembly dominated by Puritans, however, recently arrived from Virginia, and has replaced the Act Concerning Religion, which made such toleration possible, and replaced it with a law taken word for word from the Cromwellian Instrument of Government. This new law states that "none who profess and exercise the popish religion . . . can be protected in this province." Now the Puritans are seen as adopting in Maryland the intolerant spirit they are said to be fostering in Massachusetts.

English establish Albemarle colony

Albemarle Sound, July 1653

Virginians, dissatisfied with conditions in the Chesapeake Bay area, have bequn to trickle into this territory, first as pioneers and explorers, and finally as families seeking to start a permanent colony. Sparse settlements of plantations are situated between the Pasquotank and Chowan Rivers, which flow into the north shore of Albemarle Sound. The planters have an uncertain land tenure because no patents were granted and no quitrents [rents] were paid by those who worked the land and now are claiming it.

For Iroquois, a respite from the warpath

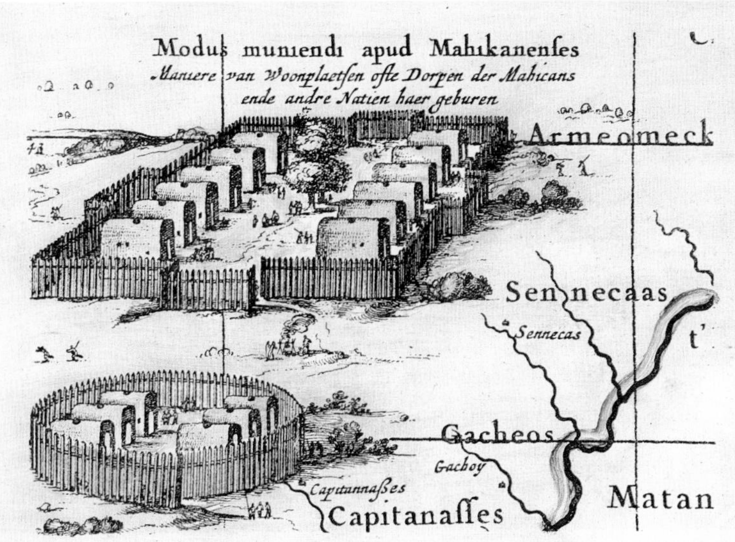

Iroquois village, from Nicolas Visscher's map in "Novum Belgium" (1655).

New France, Nov. 5, 1653

A peace treaty that has been signed by the Iroquois League and the French may put an end to years of warfare between Indian tribes and the colonials. Since prehistoric times, the Iroquois have been waging war against neighboring tribes, including the Hurons, Erie, Neutrals and Andastes.

The Iroquois were among the first North Americans to obtain firearms and, between 1648 and 1650, they destroyed the greater part of the Huron population. The Hurons, first visited by the French under Champlain in 1615, numbered nearly 30,000 people. Huron towns were destroyed and most of the population killed or enslaved. Survivors of the massacres sought refuge with the French or moved west. In 1651, the Iroquois League turned its attention to the Neutral Nation along the northern shore of a Great Lake [Erie], again destroying a large part of the population. The alliance of surviving Hurons and Neutrals with the French led the Iroquois to join forces with the British in an effort to erode the power of New France. Through this alliance, the Iroquois had much success, but, somewhat overextended, they are now making peace.

Since the organization of the Iroquois League in the last century, the government has been called "the great peace." The league itself has no authority to wage war, this being the prerogative of war chiefs elected by warriors of the tribes.

First Jew arrives; 23 others follow

New Amsterdam, Sept. 7, 1654

A group of 23 Sephardic Jews reached here today aboard the St. Charles, a French armed vessel. Their arrival follows an order giving the 5,000 Jews of Recife, Brazil, three months to leave. That order came after the Portuguese seized control of the territory from the Dutch in January. Jacob Barsimon, the first Jew to settle in New Amsterdam, landed on August 22, possibly sent by the Jewish community in Recife to start a colony. On the day the 23 Jews arrived, a suit was filed by the captain of the St. Charles for the rest of the 1,600 guilders he claims the Jews owed him for the trip (→ Apr. 26, 1655).

Massachusetts says it is independent

Plymouth, June 29, 1652

Under Puritan leadership, which is convinced of its divine mission, the Massachusetts colony has defied Parliament and declared itself to be a self-governing independent commonwealth. The colony, after more than three decades of development, has extended its power and influence as far as Kennebec, Maine, and New Hampshire. The colony's origins trace back to the New England Company, which became the Massachusetts Bay Company when it was presented with its charter in 1629 (→ Apr. 21, 1664).

Boston, June 1652. *A mint is producing the first American coin, the pine-tree shilling, despite the fact that Britain forbids colonial coinage.*

Allegorical view of America, from Frankfurt, depicts barely tamed serpents and savages inhabiting a land that is still a fantasy to most Europeans.

1655 (1655-1659)

Maryland, March 25, 1655. Puritans jail Governor Stone after military victory over Catholic forces (→ 1658).

New Amsterdam, Apr. 26, 1655. Dutch West India Company rules Jews must be allowed to stay in colony.

Caribbean, May 10, 1655. British seize Jamaica from Spanish.

Boston, May 23, 1655. Joseph Jencks gets commission to build engine "for the more speedy cutting of grass."

America, 1655. Women's illiteracy rate in Massachusetts is 50 percent; in New Netherland, 60; in Virginia, 75.

Virginia, March 10, 1656. Suffrage extended to all freemen, regardless of faith.

Virginia, March 10, 1656. Plan calls for seizing Indian children until conversion, giving chiefs a cow for every eight wolves' heads brought in, to teach them about private property.

Boston, July 1656. First Quakers to enter colony, Mary Fisher and Ann Austin, are met with strip searches, jail and banishment (→ Oct. 27, 1659).

New Haven, July 23, 1656. Colony adopts Code of 1656, outlining fundamental body of law. [It is only colony in New England to reject trial by jury.]

New Netherland, Sept. 6, 1656. Mohawks ask Dutch to stop selling rum to Indians.

Patuxent, Maryland, Sept. 22, 1656. First all-woman jury in colonies acquits Judith Catchpole of murdering her unborn child.

Westmoreland County, Virginia, 1656. Colonel John Washington arrives from Essex, England. [Descendants include George Washington, first U.S. President.]

Cambridge, 1656. Harvard accepts Copernican theory.

Rhode Island, May 20, 1657. Colony is third to defy British trade ban with Dutch (→ Oct. 1, 1660).

Maine, July 13, 1658. Massachusetts takes over Casco Bay [Falmouth], completing annexation of Maine lands.

New Netherland, Apr. 21, 1657. Dutch reorganize Fort Casimir as New Amstel.

New Amsterdam, Aug. 12, 1658. Ratelwacht, the first police force in colony, is formed.

Quakers hanged for resisting banishment

A trail of shame: Quakers are tied to a cart and whipped through Boston.

Boston, October 27, 1659

Two men of the Quaker sect, which Boston's authorities regard as pestilential and disruptive, were hanged today on Boston Common. William Robinson and Marmaduke Stevenson, along with Mary Dyer, were led from their cells under a 200-man guard. The guard, with drums and colors, and armed with halberds, guns, swords and pikes, were under orders to prevent the Quakers from haranguing the crowd. Each time they began to speak, the drummers played loudly to prevent their being heard.

The three have been repeatedly transported from the colony, the last time under penalty of death should they return. However, they showed their disregard for the city fathers by returning again. The authorities, carrying out their previous threat, sent the Quakers to the gallows. Following the executions of Robinson and Stevenson, Dyer was led to the gallows. She was blindfolded and the noose was placed around her neck. Before the sentence could be carried out, however, her son interceded on her behalf. As a result, she is once again to be transported out of the colony, never, the authorities hope, to return. The bodies of her two compatriots were thrown into a pit as an example to any who might consider religious dissent (→ June 1, 1660).

Boston, 1657. *Residents congregate in the port city's first town house to discuss public matters, while stern Puritan justice is dispensed outside.*

Dutch expedition captures two forts

Delaware River, Sept., 1655

Swedish rule in America appears to have come to an abrupt end. The Dutch, in their continuing war with New Sweden, have seized the Swedish Fort Christina and retaken Fort Casimir, allowing the Dutch West India Company to sell Fort Casimir to New Amsterdam. General Peter Stuyvesant's New Amsterdam army of 317 men overpowered the Swedes at Fort Casimir and moved up river in seven ships to Fort Christina, where Stuyvesant played a waiting game with its 30 remaining soldiers. After 10 days, New Sweden Governor Rysingh capitulated (→ Apr. 21, 1657).

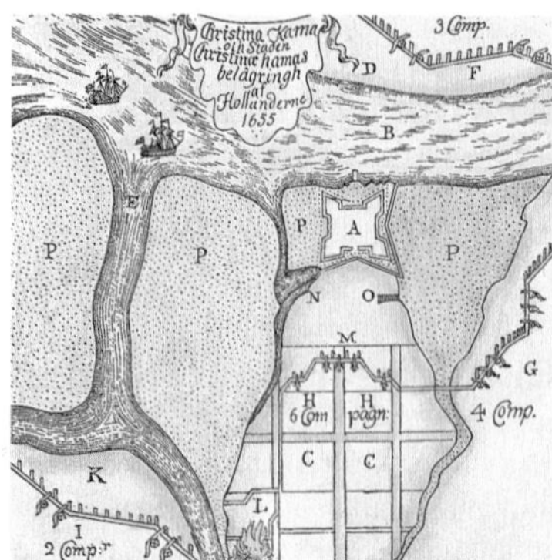

Plan for the siege of Fort Christina.

Puritans ease rules for infant baptism

Massachusetts Bay Colony, 1657

In response to a growing crisis in the colony, a Connecticut-Massachusetts ministerial council has advocated changing the rules on infant baptism. The decreasing number of church members able to baptize their children because of the parents' lack of an experience of regeneration has caused a steady decline in both church members and in voting population. The compromise that the council worked out, called the Half-Way Covenant, will allow baptized church members who agree with the doctrine of faith and do not lead scandalous lives to take on the church covenant before the church. They may then bring in their children to be baptized. These members, however, will continue to be excluded from voting on church affairs.

French group is exploring Northern Plains

Radisson and Chouart find hospitality on the frozen Plains, by C.W. Jefferys.

Montreal, Aug. 1658

French explorer and fur trader Medard Chouart, Sieur des Groseilliers, and his brother-in-law Pierre Esprit Radisson have left their homes in Trois-Rivieres, New France, on the lower St. Lawrence River with a party of 31 other Frenchmen to explore the southern shores of Lake Superior and the Northern Plains region south and west of the lake. They hope to establish trade relations with the Indians in the area, and it is hoped that their rumored failure to obtain a government trading license from French authorities will not cause them any problems. Prior to this expedition, the two men made several exploratory forays into the country surrounding the lakes.

King restores Catholic control in Maryland

Maryland, 1658

The continuing conflict between the Lord Proprietor and a rebellious Puritan population has ended with the restoration of power to Lord Baltimore. The three-year rebel rule saw a marked drop in Roman Catholic religious activity in the colony due to both legal proscription and personal harassment. Protestants who came here quickly overwhelmed all other groups. This numerical predominance gave rise to a rebellion in 1655 that overthrew the Lord Proprietor's appointed Governor and produced an elected assembly dominated by Puritans. Among this assembly's first acts was the repeal of the Toleration Act, which guaranteed that no person professing the divinity of Jesus would be molested for his religion. Through the intervention of the King, power has been restored to the proprietor and the Toleration Act has been restored (→ Nov. 1660).

Williams builds case for religious liberty

Rhode Island, 1657

The colony here is fast becoming a haven for dissenting Puritans, prompting orthodox churchmen to refer to it as a "moral sewer," but this is not stopping Roger Williams from continuing his struggle for religious toleration and liberty.

In January of 1655, Williams wrote a letter to the town of Providence, explaining his ideas about toleration by comparing a commonwealth to a ship at sea with a variety of faiths represented.

In 1644, Williams published *The Bloudy Tenent of Persecution for the Cause of Conscience Discussed*, in which he argued against the involvement of secular authorities in religious affairs. This involvement, he wrote, not only sullies religion but also is unnecessary for secular government. His ideas found expression in the 1647 document organizing the colony's government. This states: "And otherwise than thus, what is herein forbidden, all men may walk as their consciences persuade them, every one in the name of his God" (→ July 8, 1663).

Bradford dies after serving thirty years

Plymouth, May 21, 1657

William Bradford wrote his will in the morning and in the evening the great leader of the Massachusetts colony was dead. His legacy was considerable. In 1620, he was aboard ship when the Mayflower Compact was devised and framed. Bradford played a large part in creating that historic agreement. He also helped put Plymouth on a firm economic footing and was unanimously chosen to be Governor in 1621, and re-elected every year after that for 30 years. Bradford kept a journal, which has proven an invaluable source of rich detail about the first permanent colony in New England. A self-taught man, Bradford persisted in pushing ideas such as the franchise and the town meeting, which became integral parts of colonial government.

New laws curb scolding, meddling, drinking, pulling the goose

New Amsterdam, Jan. 25, 1658

Governor Peter Stuyvesant has prohibited tennis during the time of divine services, and the sport of "pulling the goose" has been banned by the Dutch. Their neighbors in Massachusetts have gone even further. Listed among the crimes for which colonists there were punished in 1655 and 1656 were: eavesdropping, scolding, neglect of work, meddling, delivering naughty speeches, profane dancing, killing, making love without the congregation's consent, uncharitableness to a poor man in distress, bad grinding at a mill, carelessness in dealing with fire, drinking, tobacco (smoking), playing cards, selling strong water by small measure, pulling hair and pushing one's wife.

Dancing has become so prevalent in the colonies that the Puritans, the Dutch and the Quakers have all failed in their efforts to suppress it. Scriptural authority for such suppression has been cited and the example of David is mentioned by those who want it prohibited. In Massachusetts, the Westminster Assembly has expressly prohibited "lascivious dancing," which it has described as wanton and unseemly. At the same time, the Puritans are of the belief that all "bawdy ballads" and music in general are "useless frivolity."

In New Amsterdam, the burgomasters have banned a game called "kolven" [a forerunner of golf].

Sins exposed in the pillory for all to see: The victim's conscience is laid open to the edifying influence of physical pain and public embarrassment.

1660 (1660-1664)

Virginia, March 13, 1660. Statute limits tax on sale of slaves [first law indicating slavery is institutionalized].

London, May 29, 1660. King Charles II enthroned, restoring Stuart monarchy.

London, Oct. 1, 1660. Crown strengthens Navigation Acts (→ Sept. 12, 1662).

Maryland, Nov. 1660. Assembly replaces Governor Josias Fendall with Philip Calvert, returning control to initial proprietors.

America, 1660. Passaconaway, Narragansett sachem, makes deathbed speech: ". . . be careful how you quarrel with the English. Although you may do them much harm, yet assuredly you will all be destroyed and rooted off the earth if you do."

Rhode Island, 1661. Quakers hold first annual meeting (→ 1709).

England, Sept. 12, 1662. Governor Berkeley, in England seeking revision of Navigation Acts, gets final denial of appeal (→ July 27, 1663).

England, July 8, 1663. Crown grants Rhode Island charter guaranteeing freedom of worship (→ May 13, 1665).

New Netherland, 1663. Laurens Duyts sentenced to be flogged and have his right ear cut off for selling his wife.

England, Apr. 21, 1664. Richard Nicolls named head of commission to investigate colonial disputes and discipline Massachusetts (→ July 23).

Boston, May 27, 1664. Increase Mather becomes minister of Boston's Second Church.

New Jersey, June 24, 1664. Area between Hudson, Delaware Rivers named New Jersey in honor of new proprietor, Sir George Carteret, who was Governor of Isle of Jersey (→ Aug. 1665).

New Netherland, July 1664. Dongan Treaty makes Iroquois subjects of English King.

Massachusetts, July 23, 1664. Wealthy non-church members get right to vote (→ June 7, 1677).

Carolina, Nov. 1664. Proprietors split northern part of colony into counties of Albemarle and Clarendon.

New Netherland, 1664. Horse racing becomes first organized sport in America, as Governor Nicolls establishes Newmarket course at Hempstead Plains, Long Island (→ 1668).

Dutch meekly yield colony to British

New Amsterdam, Sept. 5, 1664

Following several days of tense negotiation and the eminent threat of seizure by force, the Dutch settlement of New Amsterdam has surrendered, without firing a shot, to the British forces surrounding this little town at the tip of Manhattan. The British move, ordered by King Charles II, took New Netherland by surprise; the Dutch defenses included only 20 cannon and 250 soldiers and militia, while the British fleet here boasts 120 guns and 500 veteran troops.

Dutch Governor Peter Stuyvesant sought to rally his small detachment to defend the colony, but crowds of townspeople thronged the street begging Stuyvesant to avoid bloodshed and destruction. The Governor allowed his closest advisers to lead him away from the walls of the fort as burning matchsticks were poised above the cannons. "Let it be so," the old general said, "I would rather be carried to my grave."

The English commander, Colonel Richard Nicolls, writing from his flagship, assured the protection of life and property, and rights of direct trade with Holland. His restraint and tact have given rise to speculation that he is an uncommonly considerate leader. Winning New Netherland gives the British control of North American ports from Virginia to Massachusetts, and eases enforcement of the English Navigation Act (→ Feb. 2, 1665).

Stuyvesant is of little comfort to his subjects, as depicted by J.L.G. Ferris.

King gives Dutch lands to Duke of York

London, March 22, 1664

King Charles has granted large tracts of land in North America to his brother James, Duke of York. The royal order gives James "all the land from the west side of Connecticutte River to the east side of De la Ware Bay" with "power and Authority of Government and Command in or over the Inhabitants of the said Territories or Islands." Much of this land has been claimed by the Dutch, although English farmers in the area outnumber the Dutch by more than two to one. James had convinced Charles II to assist a conquest of New Netherland after a report described the loss of trade to English merchants due to the Dutch colony. While the action will no doubt worsen relations between the British and the Dutch, Charles says the area "did belong to England heretofore, but the Dutch drove our people out of it" (→ Sept. 5).

Winthrop honored

London, May 3, 1662

John Winthrop the Younger, son of the first Governor of Massachusetts, has been honored by being named a fellow in the Royal Society, England's oldest scientific society. Through it, he gained access to the King, who has granted him a new charter uniting the colonies of Connecticut and New Haven, and setting a boundary with Massachusetts. He migrated to Boston in 1631, served on the governor's council and helped found Aqawan [Ipswich], Massachusetts, in 1633. He was Governor of Connecticut in 1635, in 1657-58 and is again in that post (→ Jan. 1, 1665).

Fear of witchcraft widespread in colonies

A witch trial, by Howard Pyle.

America, 1663

If one is to judge by court records, the struggle to build viable communities in America appears to be under steady attack by witchery. In Connecticut alone, 10 offenders have been hanged for "familiarity with the Devil." In one account, the fatal crime was an utterance to the effect that "Christ was a Bastard and she could prove it by scripture." And witch hunts are not just the province of Puritan New England. Once, in Catholic Maryland, a "little old woman" was slain in order to calm a storm. Her corpse was cast into the sea, but failed to soothe the waters. Ironically, Rhode Island, criticized for excessive religious license, has escaped the witches' grasp (→ Oct. 1692).

Nobles get Carolinas

London. March 24, 1663

Charles II, one of the most popular kings in the history of Britain, has decided to reward those supporters who played principal roles in preparing the way for the restoration by granting them an immense area of land. The land is called "Carolina" and it is situated between the Virginia colony and Spain's Florida territory.

The most prominent of the eight men being awarded the vast grant is General George Monk, the Duke of Albemarle, whose armed forces kept the peace in London during the period in 1660 when plans were afoot to place Charles on the throne of England.

Other notables among the fortunate eight are the Earl of Clarendon, Sir George Carteret, Lord Ashley and Sir John Colleton. Of this group, the most important figure from a practical point of view is the young and aggressive Lord Ashley, who, with the assistance of his secretary, the philosopher John Locke, has come up with a form of government that many political observers consider to be the most unusual and reactionary of all colonial systems ever devised. Their concept, which goes by the name "The Fundamental Constitution of Carolina," will grant nobility to any person in a position to purchase more than 3,000 acres of land. A baronetcy can be obtained with such a purchase; the wealthy individual who has enough money to buy 12,000 acres will be granted a title and for 20,000 the purchaser can earn the right to be called landgrave, a title that originated in the German nobility.

Quaker is hanged for re-entering colony

Marching to the beat of a solemn drum, Mary Dyer goes to her death.

Boston, June 1, 1660

Mary Dyer, after sorely and repeatedly trying the patience of the commonwealth of Massachusetts, was hanged today. Dyer, who escaped the noose last year through her son's intervention, once again violated the directive of the authorities by re-entering the colony to spread the doctrines of Quakerism. What the authorities regarded as her rebellious disobedience forced their hand in the end. She showed neither remorse nor contrition when she spoke after her sentencing. The court, unconvinced of her claimed mission from God, ordered her execution (→ 1661).

Children of mixed marriage face slavery

Maryland, Sept. 1664

In the latest of a series of laws dealing with slaves, Maryland has proclaimed the marriage of English women to Negro slaves a disgrace to the nation and has ruled that any children from such a marriage be given over to slavery. Virginia enacted the first law acknowledging slavery as an institution in 1660, citing an impost on tobacco grown with the help of slaves imported by foreigners. The next year, a Virginia law assumed that some Negroes had to serve for life. Earlier, Negroes were held for periods of indenture, as many white servants were. A Maryland law says baptism does not affect the status of a slave, thus barring any judicial decisions freeing a slave on baptism.

Eliot, "Apostle to the Indians," establishes a church for them

Natick, Massachusetts, 1661

The first church for Indians was formed in this "praying town" last year following English custom by the Rev. John Eliot, "Apostle to the Indians." He would not allow the Indians to become church members until they had "come up into civil Cohabitation, Government and Labor." Fifteen years ago, he held the first service at the wigwam of an Algonquin chief. This year, he published the first Bible in the colonies: the New Testament in the Algonquin language (→ Aug. 22, 1670).

Prophet in the wilderness: Rev. John Eliot preaches to a native congregation.

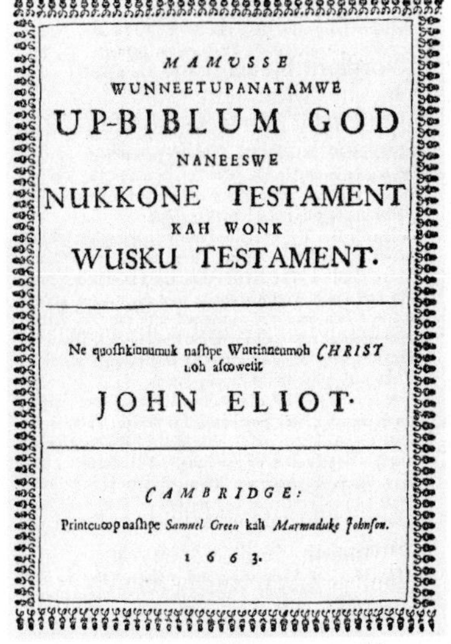

MAMUSSE
WUNNEETUPANATAMWE
UP-BIBLUM GOD
NANEESWE
NUKKONE TESTAMENT
KAH WONK
WUSKU TESTAMENT.

Ne quoshkinnumuk nashpe Wuttinneumoh CHRIST
noh asoowesit
JOHN ELIOT.

CAMBRIDGE:
Printeuoop nashpe Samuel Green kah Marmaduke Johnson.
1663.

Eliot's Algonquin-language Bible.

Trade in colonies is further restricted

London, July 27, 1663

Parliament has passed a second Navigation Act, requiring all goods for the colonies to travel in British ships from British ports. Some items must be traded only within the empire. Extending the 1651 act, the law aims to make England and its colonies less dependent on foreign goods. By ruling that wool, sugar, cotton and tobacco only be consumed within the empire, it is hoped self-sufficiency will ensue. But the act lacks teeth, so smugglers flourish (→ May 3, 1665).

1665 (1665-1669)

Connecticut, Jan. 1, 1665. New Haven submits to rule by Connecticut.

England, Jan. 7, 1665. Carolina proprietors draft Concessions and Agreements, outlining government of province (→ Aug. 17, 1669)).

New England, May 3, 1665. Rhode Island agrees to comply with royal commission sent to enforce Navigation Acts and gain aid against Dutch (→ 1673).

Rhode Island, May 13, 1665. Statute offers freemanship with no specifically Christian requirements, thus effectively enfranchising Jews.

America, 1665. France has only about 3,500 settlers in New World, compared with 75,000 English colonists.

New Jersey, 1666. Governor Philip Carteret lures settlers from New Haven with land grants; colonists form settlements on model of New England towns.

Williamsburg, Virginia, Sept. 23, 1667. New law bars slaves from obtaining freedom by converting to Christianity.

England, 1667. William Penn experiences sudden conversion to Quakerism (→ Feb. 14, 1675).

Carolina, 1667. Barbadian colony on Cape Fear River abandoned in summer, a year after population swelled to 800.

New England, March 24, 1668. Governor Edmund Andros takes personal control of colonial militias to quiet unrest.

Massachusetts, May 27, 1668. Thomas Gold, William Turner and John Farnum are first Baptists exiled from colony.

Maine, July 6, 1668. Convention at York accepts rule by Massachusetts, voting to send deputies to General Court.

Northern Plains, 1668. Father Jacques Marquette establishes settlement [Sault Sainte Marie, first permanent colony in Michigan].

England, Aug. 17, 1669. Three ships under Joseph West sail for Carolina via Barbados, funded by Carolina proprietors in their first sign of willingness to absorb costs of settlement (→ March 1, 1670).

Midwest, 1669. Rene Robert Cavalier, Sieur de La Salle, explores region [probably first white explorer in Ohio].

Plymouth, 1669. Colony founds first recorded Sunday school.

New Amsterdam is renamed New York

New York City, Feb. 2, 1665

Richard Nicolls, the Governor of the New Amsterdam province since the takeover from the Dutch last year, has renamed the area after its new proprietor, the Duke of York. Last September, Dutch General Peter Stuyvesant signed papers surrendering New Amsterdam. King Charles II, in a letter to his sister in Paris, wrote, "You will have heard of our taking New Amsterdam, which lies by New England. 'Tis a place of great importance. It did belong to England heretofore, but the Dutch, by degrees, drove our people away . . . but we have got the better of it" (→ July 21, 1667).

Freedom granted to all New York sects

Hempstead, L.I., March 11, 1665

Deputies of New York's Dutch and English towns have approved the colony's new legal code. Among other elements of the law is an article guaranteeing all Protestants the right to continue their religious observances unhindered. This principle, restating a provision in the articles of surrender of New Netherland to the British, can only be welcome in a colony of myriad Protestant sects.

Pirate vessel frees Spaniards' prisoner

St. Augustine, Florida, 1668

In a daring attack on this Spanish colony, the buccaneer Robert Searles freed Henry Woodward, an English pioneer in the Carolinas. Woodward, who was born on the island of Barbados, joined the Carolina settlement that was started at Cape Fear in 1664. Two years later, he accompanied Robert Sandford, secretary of Clarendon County, on a voyage of exploration to Port Royal. Woodward remained there so that he could learn the Indian language. Shortly after, the Spaniards arrived and they promptly carried him off to Florida. There he professed Catholicism and was appointed the official surgeon.

New Jersey is founded

George Carteret, ex-Governor of Isle of Jersey, goes ashore in his new domain.

Elizabethtown, N.J., Aug. 1665

The English, having taken over New Netherland from the Dutch with a naval expedition that did not fire a shot, have proceeded to create a new colony with a stroke of the quill. In July of 1664, the Duke of York granted the area between the Hudson River and the Delaware to two of his favorites, John Lord Berkeley and Sir George Carteret. The area is to be known as Nova Caesarea, or New Jersey, in honor of the island in the English Channel where, in 1650, Carteret, as Governor, had sheltered the duke from Puritan England. The new proprietors have commissioned 26-year-old Philip Carteret, a cousin of Sir George, to serve as the first English Governor of New Jersey. Patents have been issued by the Duke of York's deputy governor in New York, Richard Nicolls, to Elizabethtown and Monmouth, providing for the foundation of New Jersey towns according to the model that is being used in New England.

First trophy given for American horse race

Long Island, March 25, 1668

There is now a reward for racing horses, started here three years ago. Captain Sylvester Salisbury, an English officer, has been given a large silver bowl for the victory of his horse at the Newmarket race course at Hempstead Plains. It is the first trophy awarded for an American sporting event.

This silver porringer by Pieter van Inburg, presented to the winner of the horse race at the Newmarket course at Hempstead Plains, is America's first sports trophy. [It is also the oldest authentic piece of colonial silver.]

Peace treaty gives Dutch lands to British

Breda, Holland, July 21, 1667

The Peace of Breda has ended the second Anglo-Dutch War with a treaty confirming Britain's hold on the former Dutch colony of New Netherland, now New York, in exchange for Surinam and the island of Poleron near the Moluccas.

The conquest of New Netherland (New York) by English forces in the summer of 1664 along with increasing competition between England and the Dutch led the two powers to war in December 1664. In the two and a half years since they occupied New York, the English administration of Colonel Richard Nicolls has been viewed as conciliatory and kind. Though many place names were changed or anglicized, Nicolls, at first, maintained the Dutch municipal and civil officers, even letting them name successors. Property of the Dutch West India Company, however, was confiscated during the recent war, as was that of inhabitants who did not pledge an oath of allegiance to the British crown. By 1665, The Duke's Law, civil and criminal measures based on codes of the New England settlements, was ratified by representatives of five Dutch towns and 13 English towns around New York. The Duke's Law established elections of overseers and constables for each of the towns, organized the courts and militia, and assured freedom of conscience (→Nov. 10, 1674).

British colonial policy chief is dismissed

London, Aug. 30, 1667

Edward Hyde, first Earl of Clarendon, has been dismissed as Lord Chancellor by Charles II. Clarendon has been the chief architect of colonial policy since the Restoration, and in this capacity he supported measures to set the colonies against one another and to weaken Massachusetts in particular. Clarendon was also one of the eight lord proprietors of Carolina who granted the original charter in 1663, and he served as a member of the General Council for Foreign Plantations.

Although he favored a strong crown against too much colonial influence, he was a staunch supporter of religious freedom, and he granted freedom of conscience to all the settlers in Carolina. He also instructed the Governors of Virginia and Jamaica that they should not molest nonconformists.

Clarendon's power began eroding this June after the Dutch fleet burned Britain's ships as they lay at anchor in the Medway in southeastern England. Public opinion blamed him for this, the worst disaster in recent British naval history. On July 21, the Peace of Breda was concluded and Clarendon was regarded as having played the most important role in drafting the terms of an ignominious treaty. On the day the document was signed, a mob cut down the trees in front of his house and set up a gibbet.

An earlier Dutch surrender to the Spanish at Breda was depicted by Velazquez.

"The Fall of Clarendon," from an engraving by Frederick Bacon.

"Bare and Cubb" put on trial for frivolity

Accomack, Virginia, Dec. 1665

It was a lively session at the Accomack County Court this year as actors Cornelius Watkinson, Philip Howard and William Darby reprised their roles in *Ye Bare and Ye Cubb*, the first dramatic work ever staged in the English-speaking colonies.

A translation of a French playlet written in 1606, *Bare and Cubb* had its premiere in the colonies August 27 on the Accomack Peninsula. The performance so incensed Edward Martin, a local citizen, that he reported the actors to the King's attorney, John Fawsett, who charged the trio of thespians with "excessive frivolity." On November 16, the actors made their first appearance in the courtroom, and were ordered to return for the December session in "the habiliments which they acted in, and [to] give a draught of such verses or other speeches and passages which were then acted by them." The costumed players ran through their parts – to the evident pleasure of the court, which not only dismissed the charges but also decreed that the plaintiff must foot the cost of the suit.

Colonization pushes deeper into the West

Northwest, 1669

Exploration of the American continent continues as religious missionaries and adventurers chart new territory in the west.

On Chequamegon Bay [in Wisconsin], a Jesuit priest, Father Claude Allouez, has established the first permanent mission, named La Pointe, near a trading post that was organized by Pierre Radisson and his brother-in-law, Medard Chouart, Sieur des Groseilliers.

To the east, at Sault Ste. Marie, two Jesuit missionaries, Fathers Jacques Marquette and Claude Dablon, have set up the first permanent settlement [in Michigan].

Rene Robert Cavelier, Sieur de La Salle, has established friendly relations with the Iroquois and become the first white explorer of new lands [Ohio] south of Lake Erie.

Meanwhile, the Virginia Assembly has granted a permit to John Lederer, a German adventurer and friend of Governor William Berkeley, to explore westward, and he has made three journeys [into the Blue Ridge Mountains of Kentucky and] through the passes in the western region of Virginia.

1670 (1670-1674)

England, March 1, 1670. Carolina proprietors replace Concessions and Agreements with Fundamental Constitutions, written by John Locke (→Apr. 1670).

Carolina, Apr. 1670. Joseph West leads party away from the Spanish at St. Helena Sound to found Charleston at Albemarle Point (→Aug. 11, 1691).

Spain, July 18, 1670. England and Spain sign Treaty of Madrid, recognizing occupation as basis for settling boundary disputes in New World.

[Martha's Vineyard,] Aug. 22, 1670. John Eliot and John Cotton found Indian church with educated Indians Hiacoomes and Tackanash as pastor and teacher.

Virginia, Oct. 13, 1670. Slavery banned for Negroes who arrive in colonies as Christians (→Nov. 10, 1682).

Maryland, Dec. 18, 1670. Suffrage restricted to wealthy.

Massachusetts, 1670. Woodcut of Richard Mather is first portrait engraving in colonies.

Virginia, 1670. Sir William Berkeley estimates 2,000 Negroes and 6,000 white servants in overall population of 40,000.

New Jersey, 1670. Attempts at collecting quitrents spark rebellion (→June 13, 1674).

Carolina, Sept. 1671. New Governor Joseph West calls first assembly.

Boston, May 15, 1672. General Court passes first copyright law in colonies.

Carolina, 1672. Charleston population, as a result of immigration from Barbados, reaches 400.

Plymouth, 1673. John Winslow elected as first native-born Governor of American colony.

St. Augustine, Florida, 1674. Bishop Gabriel Diaz Vara Calderon ordains seven priests [first Catholic ordinations in present-day United States].

Rensselaerwyck, New Netherland, 1674. Maria van Rensselaer becomes administrator of colony after husband's death.

Virginia, 1674. Englishman William Byrd arrives. [Descendants include explorer Richard Byrd and Senators Harry and Robert Byrd.]

DEATH

New York City, Feb. 1672. Peter Stuyvesant, New Netherland Governor (*1610).

French pair explore "Mississippi" basin

Joliet and Father Marquette paddle their way down the vast muddy river.

Montreal, Dec. 4, 1674

The fur trader Louis Joliet and Jesuit Father Jacques Marquette have returned from an epic four-month, 2,500-mile journey on the great river that flows south through the center of the continent, a river the Indians call the "Mississippi." Little was known of this river until now, but the explorers were told it empties into the Gulf of Mexico, where the Spanish have outposts.

The journey began last May when the explorers left from the Strait of Mackinac and canoed down the Fox and Wisconsin Rivers to the Mississippi. They floated south for hundreds of miles, passing a large muddy river they call the "Pekitanoui," entering from the west. Continuing south, they found another large river entering from the west where they met the Quapaw Indians and learned from them the Mississippi's destination.

Having achieved the expedition's major goal, the explorers returned to New France. Marquette's trip was delayed by illness, but he has recovered and has established a mission at the southern tip of a Great Lake [Michigan]. Joliet lost his maps and charts when his canoe overturned in the Lachine Rapids not far from Montreal, but he was able to redraw some from memory.

Quakers' founder ends American tour

Rhode Island, 1674

George Fox, founder of the Society of Friends, has ended his tour of America. From his arrival in North Carolina in 1671 to his departure last year, the visit has produced a quickening of Quaker activity across the colonies. Fox, who was accompanied by several leading English Quakers, spent much time preaching and speaking of his sect's doctrines. The crowds were surprisingly large for such a persecuted group. In Rhode Island, Fox was even entertained by the Governor. And this year in west Jersey, a new Quaker colony was established.

Fox: no stranger to Anglican jails.

French annex vast area of Western lands

Sault Ste. Marie, June 14, 1671

At a ceremony here today, Simon Francois Daumont, Sieur de St. Lusson, in the name of King Louis XIV of France, formally claimed possession of Sault Sainte Marie, Lakes Huron and Superior, Caientoton [Manitoulin] Island and "all other countries, streams, lakes and rivers contiguous and adjacent, as well discovered as to be discovered which are bounded on one side by the seas of the North and of the West, and on the other side by the South Sea, and in all their length and breadth."

The ceremony, in which a French flag was held and St. Lusson proclaimed possession of the Western lands three times, was the idea of Jean Talon, Canada's "great intendant," who has long dreamed of expanding the French empire into mid-continental North America. A record of the proceedings was drawn up and signed by 19 witnesses. It was then attached with the French arms to a tree, while Father Claude Jean Allouez, a Jesuit, addressed the Indians who had been invited to attend.

The St. Lusson document does not take into account the previous claims to the territory that were made by the Spanish and the English, and English exploration of the area continues. Backed by an English syndicate that is headed by Prince Rupert, Pierre Radisson and Medard Chouart, Sieur des Grosseilliers, are now exploring Hudson Bay.

Slaving monopoly

London, Sept. 27, 1672

A new corporation, called the Royal African Company, has been granted a charter with monopoly slave rights under the English flag, covering an area from Sallee on the coast of Morocco down to the Cape of Good Hope. The corporation is supported by recently raised capital of more than 100,000 pounds. Royal African has announced that it will place great stress on promptness of sale, and that if those interested would contract to receive whole cargoes, then any slave between 12 and 40 years of age "able to go over the ship's side unaided" would be supplied for 15 pounds per head in Barbados, for 16 pounds in Nevis, 17 pounds in Jamaica and 18 pounds in Virginia.

Mail delivered by Boston Post Road

Boston, Jan. 1, 1673

Regular mounted mail service has begun between New York and Boston, costing nine pence for the delivery of a letter. The mail is delivered by what is called a "Post Road" because men and horses are posted at intervals. Last year, Governor Lovelace of New York attempted to set up a monthly post to Boston. He issued a notice stating that anyone "disposed to send letters" should bring them to his office, where they would be locked up until it was time to send them. Lovelace also wrote to the Governor of Connecticut, asking him to support his efforts and saying that he should "discourse with some able woodmen to make out the best and most facile way for a post which in process of tyme would be the King's best highway."

Dutch recapture New York; quickly lose it

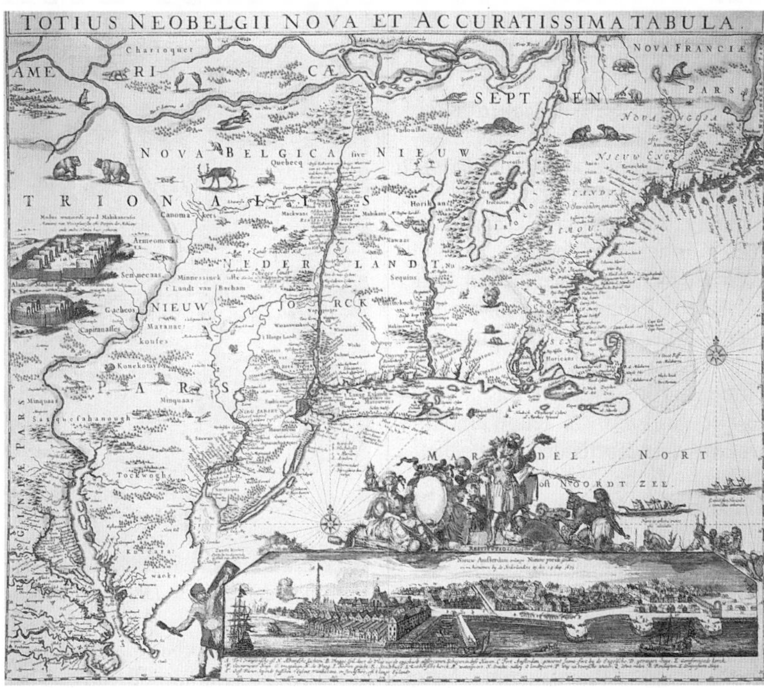

Hugo Allard's "New and Exact Map of All New Netherland" (1673).

New York City, Nov. 10, 1674

Nine months after conclusion of the third Anglo-Dutch War, the British flag has replaced the Dutch over the fort at Manhattan and Sir Edmund Andros, deputy to James, Duke of York, has become Governor of the colony. By the Treaty of Westminster, all Dutch-held areas have returned to British control.

The war of England and France against Holland crossed the ocean when 23 Dutch ships under Cornelius Evertsen with 1,600 soldiers arrived in New York harbor on August 7, 1672. Reversing the scene of eight years earlier, the 80 soldiers at Fort James exchanged a feeble volley with the large fleet. By August 9, the Dutch had regained the town. Other towns were occupied, and the colony renamed New Orange, though five English towns on Long Island resisted the Dutch by allying with Connecticut and the New England Confederacy.

The war was costly to French and English allies of the Duke of York, who lost much property. However, after the war, the Royal Charter, which gave the land to James, was reissued exactly as it was granted in 1650. The problem is that King Charles has given away segments of the land, and treaties were promulgated changing many boundaries. How will Governor John Winthrop of Connecticut and the Carterets, proprietors of New Jersey, take this?

One more attempt to collect customs

London, 1673

Colonial merchants have developed a lively trade selling products outside the British empire for huge profits and now Parliament is putting a stop to it. With passage of the Plantation Duty Act, Britain will, for the first time, impose duties on any ship carrying certain products, such as sugar, cotton and tobacco, between colonial ports. Because merchants had been able to transport these items between the colonies without having to pay duty, they often shipped their products to another colonial port, labeled them as something else, and then shipped them to a foreign port. To deal with the growing practice, the British have enacted legislation to appoint colonial customs commissioners and give naval officers authority to enforce the act (→June 7, 1677).

Another picture by New England limner

Boston, 1674

As time begins to civilize the rough wilderness of New England, prominent citizens are deeming it fashionable to commission their portraits from local painters. These limners (from the British "illuminers") must generally make their living from another craft. Their art echoes the Tudor style, now waning in England. *Mrs. Freake and Baby Mary* (1674) is a particularly fine example.

"Mrs. Freake and Baby Mary."

New areas explored west of Virginia

Virginia, Sept. 11, 1673

James Needham is just back from a four-month expedition to the region west of Virginia [Tennessee] and describes it as mountainous, with many rich valleys and fordable rivers. He is the first Englishman to penetrate the area and was accompanied by an indentured servant named Gabriel Arthur and nine Indians. They followed a series of buffalo paths and Indian trails, and crossed a river that Needham described as "half a mile broad and all sandy bottoms."

Revolt over rents

New Jersey, June 13, 1674

Governor Philip Carteret is back in New Jersey, determined to collect rents that are long past due. The quitrents were levied on land that was initially offered free to settlers to foster development of the new colony. Payments came due in 1670, and rampant defaults resulted. In 1672, colonists in Elizabethport formed their own assembly and elected Carteret's son James as its president. The revolt is the first of its kind in the British colonies.

Long Island. *Hunting for sustenance and sport occupies the time of many colonists. Game includes deer, bear, fox, skunk, pigeons, cranes and ducks.*

1675 (1675-1679)

West Jersey, Feb. 14, 1675. Edward Byllinge transfers land rights to William Penn (→ March 13, 1677).

Massachusetts, May 3, 1675. Puritans begin locking church doors to keep congregation inside until end of sermons.

New England, June 20, 1675. King Philip, chief of Wampanoags, launches attack on Swansea in retaliation for execution of three Indians accused of murder (→ Nov. 19).

Rhode Island, Nov. 19, 1675. Josiah Winslow leads troops in assault on Narragansett fort; 300 women and children killed (→ Aug. 28, 1676).

Massachusetts, 1675. General Court blames Indian attacks on sins of people, including "manifest pride openly appearing amongst us in that long hair, like women's hair, is worn by some men."

Cambridge, 1675. Cotton Mather enters Harvard at age 12.

New England, May 2, 1676. Mary Rowaldson, captured in Indian raid on Lancaster, is ransomed (→ 1682).

Virginia, Apr. 27, 1677. Colonel Jeffreys takes command from Governor Berkeley, halting executions of Nathaniel Bacon's men, now totaling 23 (→ May 10, 1680).

London, June 7, 1677. Edward Randolph brings broad indictment of Massachusetts before Lords of Trade (→ Oct. 10).

Boston, Oct. 10, 1677. General Court accepts Navigation Acts to avoid total breach with London (→ May 16, 1678).

Henrico County, Virginia, 1677. Thomas Jefferson arrives from England. [Descendants include Thomas Jefferson, third U.S. President.]

London, May 16, 1678. Lords of Trade seek legal action against Massachusetts after reading clause in declaration of October 1677: "the lawes of England are bounded within the fower seas, and doe not reach America" (→ Apr. 10, 1696).

London, July 10, 1679. In attack on Massachusetts, crown makes New Hampshire a royal colony (→ Sept. 1680).

DEATHS

Northern Plains, 1675. Father Jacques Marquette, French explorer (*June 1, 1637).

England, July 9, 1677. Sir William Berkeley, colonial Governor (*1606).

Indians rise against British settlers

Massachusetts, Aug. 28, 1676

Metacom, chief sachem of the Wampanoags who is called King Philip by the British, has been killed by soldiers at Mount Hope, his original home. Metacom's remaining warriors have escaped to the Northern wilderness, leaving New England at peace after a year of vicious fighting marked by torture and betrayal on both sides.

Metacom was in hiding at Mount Hope, but his location was leaked to the British by a fellow Indian whom he had offended. Canochet, sachem of the Narragansett, was ambushed and captured earlier in the year. Pequot warriors, allied with the English, shot him and sent his head to the colonists at Hartford as a token of friendship. With the death of these two chiefs, and the dispersal of their warriors, New England is once more considered secure. At one point in the autumn of 1675, it looked as though King Philip and his allies would drive the colonists into the sea.

The origins of the war are in dispute. Prior to 1675, there was only one major conflict with the Indians in New England; the brief and savage Pequot conflict of 1637. The probable underlying cause of the recent fighting is the incompatibility of Indian life with that of the colonists. Missionaries had only mixed success in converting the Algonquin tribes to Christianity. This was due, in part, to the resistance of the tribal sachems, who regarded religion as something that undermined their authority. Earlier in the century such missionaries as John Eliot, John Cotton and Richard Bourne had met with considerable success. However, the number of converted Indians had never totaled more than a quarter of the Indian population in the region, which numbered over 10,000.

Wampanoags attack Deerfield.

Indian King Philip is slain.

La Salle sees new trade vistas in north central region

Michigan, Dec. 1679

French explorer Rene Robert Cavelier, Sieur de La Salle, is traveling through a region in the north central part of the continent [Indiana]. Last year, he and his chaplain, Father Louis Hennepin, a Franciscan Recollect friar, reached a great falls at Niagara. These areas were never seen before by Europeans.

La Salle first came to Canada in 1667 to help with the development of a seigniory near Montreal. In 1672, when Count Frontenac was appointed the Governor of New France, La Salle was given the opportunity to exploit the wealth that he suspected could be obtained by means of trade with the Indians. He was given royal approval for his plans, and a patent of nobility.

The explorer has had a small sailing vessel, the Griffon, constructed above Niagara, a fort that he has established this year. He sailed the Griffon to Green Bay, then sent it back to Niagara laden with furs. He continued his journey by canoe, heading southward to the mouth of the St. Joseph River, and there he has been awaiting the return of the Griffon. However, the vessel seems to have disappeared (→ Apr. 9, 1682).

Father Hennepin, a French Franciscan friar, may be the first white man to see Niagara Falls.

Pirate arrested, but knighted for exploits

London, 1675

In a stunning reversal of fortune, Henry Morgan, who returned to England three years ago in disgrace, has been knighted by King Charles II and taken up residence in Jamaica, where he is now serving as lieutenant governor.

The dramatic turnabout is nothing new in the stormy career of this buccaneer. He was born in Glamorgan, Wales, went to America as a young man and by 1666 was commanding a ship in the fleet led by the privateer Edward Mansfield. Morgan took part in the raids on Cuba, Nicaragua and along the coasts of Central and South America. When Mansfield was killed, Morgan took his place.

In 1668, he was commissioned by Sir Thomas Modyford, the Governor of Jamaica, to ascertain whether Spanish forces were planning to attack English possessions. After Morgan confirmed that they were, he exceeded his orders by sailing to Portobelo in Panama, capturing the city and sacking it.

Three years ago, Morgan again attacked Spanish possessions, this time in Venezuela, where he sacked Maracaibo. Last year, he crossed the Isthmus of Panama and captured Panama City. The city was plundered and then destroyed by fire. Since peace had by then been negotiated between England and Spain, the attack could not be condoned, and Morgan, along with Sir Thomas Modyford, was ordered to return to London.

Now that he has been restored to royal favor, however, Morgan has the chance to make good in Jamaica.

Henry Morgan's Knights of the Double Cross, as depicted by J.L.G. Ferris.

Bacon's harsh rebellion

Berkeley (left) and Bacon, eye to eye.

Yorktown, Virginia, Oct. 26, 1676

Succumbing to a severe attack of the "bloody flux," Nathaniel Bacon, the leader of the armed insurrection that has plunged this colony into turmoil, died while preparing to make a last stand against the forces of Governor William Berkeley. With Bacon's death, the uprising, sparked by the Governor's refusal to support Bacon's raids on the Indians, will likely collapse.

Well-connected and wealthy, Bacon arrived in Virginia three years ago and at the age of 28 was appointed to the governor's council. Soon after, he took command of a militia force that conducted a reprisal attack against neighboring Indians. The exploit made him a hero and he soon became leader of a movement in opposition to Governor Berkeley, who was resisting westward expansion. Discontent was widespread, caused by high taxes and weakness in defense of the frontiers against the Indians.

Bacon defied the Governor, denouncing him and his "clique" as "sponges" who "sucked up the Publik Treasure." He marched on Jamestown, but the Governor fled to the Eastern Shore, and proclaimed Bacon and his supporters traitors and rebels.

While Bacon had managed to take over control of much of Virginia, he was unable to maintain his position. Although many people dislike the Governor, not many have been willing to take part in a rebellion against the representative of the King (→Apr. 27, 1677).

First coffeehouse is licensed in Boston

Boston, 1676

A new fashion from London is catching on, the drinking of bitter, stimulating beverages called coffee and chocolate, and it has led to the spread of "chocolate houses" and "coffeehouses." Six years ago, Dorothy Jones, a Boston taverner, first advertised "cuchaletto," a drink made from ground, roasted South American beans. This year, Boston licensed its first coffeehouse.

An Indian lament

Nova Scotia, 1676

As the white man pushes farther and farther into the forests that once belonged to the Indian, the native culture is being eroded, even destroyed. One chief responded to French criticism of Indian ways by saying that ". . . we are very content with the little we have . . . if France, as you say, is a little terrestrial paradise, are you wise to leave it?" Once, in a bitter mood, Okanion, who is the chief of the Delawares, told a critical British colonist that strong drink was causing the destruction of his people.

New Jersey divided

Bergen, N.J., March 13, 1677

The proprietors of New Jersey have attempted to settle a disagreement among themselves by signing a "quintipartite deed." This document attempts to clarify a bewildering series of acrimonious and contradictory land claims by drawing a line down the underpopulated middle of the colony, thus creating an East New Jersey and a West New Jersey. Sir George Carteret is to retain the eastern part while the western portion is intended to come under the control of several Quakers (→Feb. 1, 1681).

Awash in newsprint, colonists digest reports from abroad as coffee grows cold.

1680 (1680-1684)

Virginia, May 10, 1680. Thomas Lord Culpeper takes over as Governor with royal instructions to punish burgesses who opposed King's 1677 inquiry.

New York, May 1680. Jury clears East Jersey Governor Philip Carteret of ruling illegally (→ June 2).

New Jersey, June 2, 1680. New Netherland Governor Andros, determined to control province, attends East Jersey assembly and dissolves it.

New Mexico, Aug. 13, 1680. Spanish driven out of Santa Fe by Indians under Chief Pope; state of war exists (→ 1693).

New England, Sept. 1680. Royal commission separates New Hampshire from Massachusetts, sets up government.

Virginia, 1680. John Banister compiles catalogue of flora, first study of American plants.

Maryland, 1680. Facing starvation, colonists reluctantly begin eating oysters.

London, Feb. 1, 1681. William Penn and 11 associates buy title to East Jersey after death of Sir George Carteret in 1680 (→ Dec. 1682).

Virginia, Aug. 1682. Militia suppresses last of tobacco rioters calling for plan to cut production and raise prices.

Virginia, Nov. 10, 1682. Law of 1670, which freed Christian Negroes arriving in America, is repealed.

New England, 1682. Mary Rowlandson writes narrative of her Indian captivity.

Yselta, New Spain, 1682. Settlement [first in Texas] is started by Spanish fleeing New Mexican Pueblo revolt (→ 1690).

New England, 1682. Josiah Franklin, a nonconformist, flees England to settle here. [He is Ben Franklin's father].

Sylvania, Oct. 6, 1683. Germantown settled by Mennonites under Francis Daniel Pastorius and Johann Kelpius (→ Feb. 18, 1688).

New York, Nov. 1683. First British assembly enacts Charter of Liberties, barring taxation without consent.

France, Apr. 14, 1684. Sieur de La Salle is named Governor of Louisiana (→ Jan. 20, 1685).

DEATH

Rhode Island, March 1683. Roger Williams, founder of Rhode Island (*1603).

William Penn founds Quaker colony

Penn is greeted by Indians and fellow Quakers upon arrival, by J.L.G. Ferris.

Pennsylvania, Dec. 1682

Since the arrival of the proprietor in October, much work has been done in organizing the governmental and economic structure of the new colony. William Penn, son of the late admiral and a convert to Quakerism, received the land from Charles II in lieu of 16,000 pounds owed the family by the King. Penn, who sees the colony as a refuge for his co-religionists, has been adamant in his insistence on religious tolerance in the colony. This is no surprise considering the persecution under which he and his fellow Quakers have suffered both in England and America. To prevent such persecution, Penn has seen to it that the principle of tolerance was written into the Great Law of the colony, passed on December 12, and bolstered by the assembly in a bill requiring freedom of conscience passed on December 17.

Much work has been done to improve the colony. A surveyor sent by the proprietor has begun laying out a new city, to be called Philadelphia. The colony is to be governed by an elected assembly under the proprietor. Land is to be offered to the immigrant at a reasonable price, although payment of a quitrent, the rent payable to the proprietor for a commutation of services, is to be required.

Penn and Indians sign brotherhood pact

Shackamaxon, June 23, 1683

A major step toward continued peace and prosperity in the colony of Pennsylvania took place today with the signing of a treaty of peace and brotherhood between the proprietor and the Indians. Penn has always tried to maintain good relations with the natives and he has insisted that all land be purchased from them prior to settlement. Also, the pacifism of the Quakers has led them to search out peaceful ways of settling disputes while their scruples have prevented them from engaging others to battle for them. This treaty and the good model of the propietor and his co-religionists should help spare the Pennsylvanians from the massacres that are plaguing colonists in other regions of America.

"Penn's Peace Treaty With the Indians" (1771) by Benjamin West.

Penn plans his city with brotherly love

Philadelphia, Sept. 1682

If ever a man intended to create a city by himself, it is William Penn. He has named the city in advance – Philadelphia – chosen the site for it, devised a street plan and will distribute the house lots himself.

Working closely with his surveyor general, Thomas Holme, Penn has combed through several plans to arrive at an urban design that is both original and beautiful. He wants his city to be a place of refuge for the persecuted as well as a meeting place for Indians. In short, he wants his Philadelphia, or "city of brotherly love," to be unlike any other city in the New World or Old World.

The plan shows a rectangular grid of about 1,200 acres, which is going to make it the largest city in the colonies if all the lots are taken up by what the Quaker leader labels "first purchasers." Each lot is large enough for a garden and an orchard, thus achieving a bucolic aspect for a city in keeping with Penn's peaceful dreams.

Culpeper cleared of treason charges

London, Nov. 20, 1680

"Culpeper's Rebellion" ended today, and with it has come the end of the first popular uprising in America. John Culpeper, a customs officer from South Carolina, has been found not guilty of treason, by the Court of the King's Bench, in Westminster. Culpeper was one of the leaders who opposed the proprietary government in its efforts to enforce British trade laws. When Governor Thomas Miller arrested George Durant, head of the "Popular Party," Culpeper and others seized the Governor and jailed him in a log house. Miller escaped to England and told the Privy Council about these activities. The insurgents sent Culpeper to defend them before the British government. During the legal battle in this branch of the High Court of Justice, Miller accused Culpeper of treason.

La Salle travels length of Mississippi

"La Salle Claiming Louisiana for France" (1847) by George Catlin.

Mouth of Mississippi, Apr. 9, 1682

Robert Cavelier, Sieur de La Salle, along with his companion, Henri de Tonti, and a large party of Frenchmen and Indians, arrived here yesterday after a four-month journey from Fort Miami on the southwestern tip of Lake Michigan. The group floated down the Illinois River in canoes in the dead of winter to its junction with the Mississippi, and then proceeded to this place, thus realizing a long-held dream of both La Salle and Tonti.

Today, La Salle, in the presence of those who accompanied him, erected a cross, fired off a volley of musket shots and formally claimed possession of the entire Mississippi Valley for France. He has named the country "Louisiana" in honor of his King, Louis XIV.

Today's ceremony brought La Salle one step closer to his goal of founding an empire for France in the West, though he knows he will not be able to establish a permanent French post now because he lacks manpower. But he is talking of going back to France to win royal support for an expeditionary force that could return here to build a fortified coastal port and launch an invasion of the Spanish province of Mexico (→Apr. 14, 1684).

Court ends New England Confederation

London, Oct. 29, 1684

The High Court of Chancery has handed down a decree abrogating the Charter of Massachusetts, and with it the Confederation of New England. The confederation was created in 1643 to counteract a lack of cooperation and coordination in the Pequot War, when the Indians almost pushed the disorganized colonists into the sea. Since then, the loose union of New England colonies has weakened. The conquest of New Netherland in 1664 removed one of the hostile neighbors necessitating the union, and the crown's resumption of control of foreign affairs, after the Restoration of the monarchy in 1660 under Charles II, further undermined the group.

French friar finds falls during captivity

Montreal, 1680

Father Louis Hennepin, a Recollect friar who accompanied Sieur de La Salle on his first voyage to the Illinois country, was recently rescued by Daniel Greysolon, Sieur Duluth, from captivity among the Sioux Indians along the Illinois River. Father Hennepin says he was seized on April 11, and that while captive he saw a most impressive falls on the Mississippi River. He named it St. Anthony's Falls in honor of his patron saint, who he feels helped him survive his tribulations. The Indians starved and taunted him, but apparently spared his life because they feared he could summon supernatural powers with his compass and chalice.

Cambridge, Massachusetts, 1682. *Harvard Hall, completed this year, will soon house some of the colonies' most promising young men of letters.*

Father Hennepin and a scout look out over the falls near the junction of the Mississippi and the Minnesota Rivers. Hennepin, a Recollect friar, came to Canada from Flanders in 1679, and went out West with La Salle last year.

1685 (1685-1689)

New Spain, Jan. 20, 1685. La Salle establishes headquarters on Gulf coast (→ March 19, 1687).

England, Feb. 6, 1685. Duke of York inherits British crown as James II upon death of Charles II.

England, Oct. 17, 1685. Lords of Trade nullify Lord Baltimore's claim to Delaware Bay region, validating William Penn's claim (→ Apr. 1691).

Massachusetts, May 1686. Provisional council takes over as first royal government here (→ Dec. 20).

Virginia, Sept. 9, 1686. Maryland ex-Governor George Talbot, convicted of murdering customs collector, has death sentence commuted.

Carolina, Sept. 1686. Stuart's Town is destroyed in Spanish attack.

Boston, Dec. 20, 1686. Sir Edmund Andros arrives to form Dominion of New England, royal plan to unite colonies (→ 21).

Boston, Dec. 21, 1686. Governor Andros orders Old South Meeting House opened to Anglicans (→ Aug. 1687).

South, 1686. Frenchman Henri de Tonti founds Arkansas Post, first permanent European settlement in area.

Southwest, March 13, 1687. Father Eusebio Kino, Italian-born, Austrian-trained Jesuit, begins missionary work.

Boston, Aug. 1687. King James's Declaration of Indulgence published, freeing dissenters from penalties for nonconformity (→ Oct. 27, 1687).

Chester County, Pennsylvania, 1687. George Harlan arrives from Down, Ireland. [Descendants include Supreme Court Justices John Marshall Harlan and John Marshall Harlan II.]

New England, Aug. 10, 1688. The Rev. Increase Mather leaves for England to press complaints against Governor Andros (→ Apr. 19, 1689).

Massachusetts, May 24, 1689. Colonial leaders re-establish government by old charter.

Maryland, Aug. 22, 1689. New assembly, called by Protestant rebels, meets to petition crown to take over colony (→ June 27, 1691).

Philadelphia, 1689. William Penn Charter School, free to the needy, is founded; first in colonies to teach such practical subjects as science and inventions.

William and Mary become co-rulers

London, Feb. 13, 1689

The constitutional crisis that has brought England to the brink of anarchy ended today with the proclamation that Prince William of Orange and his wife, Mary, the older daughter of James II, are to become joint sovereigns of this nation. Prince William alone is to be responsible for the administration of the kingdom; at the same time, he will continue as the Stadtholder of Holland.

The proclamation follows weeks of intensive maneuvering between the rival Whig and Tory parties in the recently elected parliamentary convention. The Tory party, in a vain attempt to re-assert the principle of the divine hereditary right of kings in the wake of the flight by Catholic King James II last year, first proposed a regency in James's name, then suggested that Mary alone be the sovereign. Both attempts foundered when William refused to act as regent, and Mary refused to reign alone.

Since William is the grandson of Charles I and Mary is the older daughter of James II, the principle of hereditary monarchy remains, but it does so in a greatly weakened form, since the claims of James and his recently born son have been set aside. The power of the Parliament to decide who shall rule has thus clearly triumphed over the Tory doctrine of the divine right of kings. Similarly, the doctrine of non-resistance to the crown has been invalidated by recent events.

Legislation protecting the rights of the people and confirming the power of their elected representatives in Parliament is expected to be introduced shortly, now that the question of who is to govern has been resolved.

A major change in English foreign policy is now inevitable, since the new monarchs will replace the present alliance with the French by one with the Dutch.

New sovereigns William and Mary.

A dejected James II receives word of the landing of William, Prince of Orange.

Armed uprising deposes hated Governor

Boston, Apr. 19, 1689

Emboldened by news of William and Mary's victory in England, the residents of Boston have ousted Governor Edmund Andros and effectively broken up the Dominion of New England. The Governor was fighting Indians in Maine when word of the Glorious Revolution reached the colonies. When his militia mutinied, Andros chased them back to Boston, only to find the city in revolt. As of today, Sir Edmund is in flight, the colonists are in control of the fort and Ex-Governor Simon Bradstreet has been restored to power. For the rebels, this day has been a long time in coming. Fiercely independent, Massachusetts did not adjust well to crown rule. Imposition of quitrents, restriction of town meetings and taxation without consent have been constant sources of friction for three years (→ May 24).

Andros and his spirited subjects.

American knighted

London, June 28, 1687

William Phips, the 36-year-old American-born commander of the expedition that recently returned to England with a vast haul of sunken Spanish treasure, has been knighted by King James II. It is now four years since Phips, a former ship's carpenter who was born in Woolwich, Maine, set out on his first treasure-seeking voyage. The following year, he heard about a Spanish vessel, the Concepcion, which had been wrecked off the coast of Hispaniola more than 40 years ago. A syndicate of English aristocrats put up the money for Phips's third voyage, and he returned with some 300,000 pounds' worth of silver. Phips has also been appointed provost marshal at Boston.

Charter Oak Incident: The villain is foiled

Captain Joseph Wadsworth hides the charter in the hollow of a white oak.

Hartford, October 27, 1687

Connecticut's free spirit endures in the heart of an old oak tree tonight. Sir Edmund Andros, Governor of the Dominion of New England, arrived here yesterday to assert the authority of the crown, and this evening the colony's assembly joined him in the meetinghouse to surrender – reluctantly – the Connecticut charter. But when the paper was spread upon a table, the candles blew out. Light returned – the document did not. Andros may govern, but the charter, safe within a hollow tree before the home of the Honorable Samuel Wyllys, remains the same (→Aug. 10, 1688).

French Protestants lose their freedoms

South Carolina, Oct. 18, 1685

The decision by Louis XIV, King of France, to revoke the Edict of Nantes this year is expected to spur a major migration of French Huguenots to South Carolina. This edict, established in 1598 by Henry IV, guaranteed religious freedom to Protestants in the mostly Catholic France. But Louis XIV has encouraged persecution of Protestants ever since he came to the throne in 1643. As a result, many of the Protestants have already departed for Holland and England.

Meanwhile, seeking to attract additional settlers to their struggling colony, the proprietors of South Carolina, John Archdale and the Earl of Craven, have published 10 pamphlets and distributed them to French Huguenots in the last three years. The proprietors guarantee freedom of religion and the right of the Huguenots to tax their own church members. Some Huguenots migrated here as early as 1670, but the first large group arrived about a decade later when 45 landed at Oyster Point and were given several parcels of land. The Huguenots are a hard-working and highly skilled people, and the colony's proprietors are hoping that this trickle of immigrants will soon turn into a steady stream.

Mennonites oppose slavery in America

Germantown, Penn., Feb. 18, 1688

The Mennonites are a radical Protestant sect whose members first settled at Germantown, near Philadelphia, in 1683. After their regular monthly meeting, held at the home of Rigert Worrels, they issued a statement condemning slavery. This is the first time any religious group in the colonies has condemned the rapid growth in what the Mennonites call the "traffic of mensbody." Many reasons were given for their condemnation, but primarily it is a matter of liberty: "Now, though they are black, we cannot conceive there is more liberty to have them slaves as it is to have the other white ones." The Mennonites also see slavery as theft and evoke a principle they call "liberty of body," which they say is everyman's due except those who have done evil. The German sect is also critical of its Quaker neighbors, who it says handles men like cattle.

The Mennonites evolved out of the Anabaptist movement of the 16th century, although their name derives from Menno Simons, a Dutch priest who joined the movement in 1536. The sect's stand on slavery is consistent with its views opposing militarism and in favor of nonconformity. From a theological standpoint, the Mennonites were influenced by Pietism, a Lutheran-based movement that emphasized personal religious belief.

Rebel takes New York, ousting old regime

Heartened by news of James II's fall, New Yorkers sign Leisler's declaration.

New York City, Oct. 14, 1689

The Glorious Revolution in England that ousted King James II has had major repercussions on this side of the Atlantic. In a recent uprising in Boston, William and Mary, the new King and Queen, were proclaimed the sovereigns of the colony and the Governor, Sir Edmund Andros, was imprisoned.

Alarmed by the events in Boston, Lieutenant Governor Nicholson, Andros's deputy for New York, called together an informal body consisting of three councilors of the dominion, Nicholas Bayard, Stephen van Courtlandt and Frederick Philipse, as well as city fathers and officers of the militia. In spite of public sentiment in favor of William and Mary, this council announced its support for James II. During an evening of drinking, Nicholson touched off a popular revolt when he idly threatened to burn New York City. A local militia captain, the German-born Jacob Leisler, stepped forward to lead the rebellion and to set up a provisional government. Six counties of New York and one of New Jersey elected delegates who hailed William and Mary and appointed Leisler as acting governor of the province on June 22 of this year.

Busy quelling Jacobite rebellions in Scotland and Ireland, William and Mary did not make any decisions concerning America until July 30, when they issued a proclamation stating that Nicholson was to have power, or in his absence whoever was in power. Nicholson is en route to England to meet with the sovereigns, and Leisler holds power. In Albany, a rival government has been elected to oppose Leisler's regime (→May 26, 1691).

La Salle is killed in Gulf coast mutiny

Fort St. Louis, March 19, 1687

Robert Cavelier, Sieur de La Salle, intrepid explorer of the Mississippi River, has been murdered by his own men while searching for the mouth of the Mississippi along the coast of the Gulf of Mexico. Word of the tragedy was brought to La Salle's old friend Henri de Tonti by Henri Joutel, who was with La Salle when he was murdered and who barely escaped himself.

According to Joutel, the expedition was plagued by disaster from the beginning and La Salle was unable to find the Mississippi's mouth by sea. Finally, he and a small party of men went ashore at Matagorda Bay to continue the search by land, but after a fruitless march of nearly 200 miles through coastal swampland the men became desperate, turned on La Salle and shot him.

La Salle seized by his own men.

1690 (1690-1694)

New France, May 11, 1690. Massachusetts troops seize Port Royal as King William's War spreads (→Aug. 1690).

Albany, Aug. 1690. Shortages force Fitz-John Randolph to halt march on Montreal (→Oct. 23, 1694).

America, Sept. 25, 1690. *Publick Occurences,* published by Benjamin Harris, is first newspaper printed in colonies; suppressed after first issue.

Pennsylvania, Sept. 29, 1690. Printer William Bradford and papermaker William Rittenhouse lease 20 acres for first paper mill in colonies.

Boston, Dec. 1690. Assembly issues first paper money in colonies to pay troops returning from Quebec.

New Spain, 1690. Spanish drive 200 head of cattle to San Francisco de los Tejas [probably first in Texas] (→1716).

Pennsylvania, Apr. 1691. Lower counties [Delaware] get independent legislature (→1704).

Maryland, June 27, 1691. Proprietor Lord Baltimore deprived of power; Sir Lionel Copley becomes first royal Governor (→May 10, 1692).

New England, Oct. 17, 1691. Maine and Plymouth incorporated within Massachusetts by new charter providing for property rather than religious voting qualifications.

Virginia, 1691. Statute bars slaveowners from freeing Negroes unless they pay freedman's way out of colony.

Maryland, May 10, 1692. Anglicanism designated official religion in colony (→1696).

New York, June 1692. Iroquois reply to English offer of ammunition but no guns, "We return you thanks for the powder and lead given us, but what shall we do without guns, throw them at the enemy?"

Pennsylvania, Oct. 1692. Governorship awarded to Colonel Benjamin Fletcher by crown suspicious of Penn's Quaker pacifism (→Aug. 20, 1694).

Cambridge, 1692. Increase Mather receives America's first divinity degree, from Harvard.

Portsmouth, New Hampshire, May 1, 1693. Intercolonial postal service begins.

New Mexico, 1693. Governor Ponce de Leon completes reconquest for Spanish.

Pennsylvania, Aug. 20, 1694. British reinstate William Penn as Governor (→Nov. 30, 1699).

20 in Salem executed for witchcraft

A woman is disrobed, her nakedness apparently revealing evidence of witchery.

Puritan justice: Divine, or perhaps Satanic, intervention at a Salem trial.

Those condemned to preserve purity in Salem are led off to the gallows.

Salem, Massachusetts, Oct. 1692

Like a child awakening from a convulsion, the people of Massachusetts slowly find themselves conscious of their terrifying deeds. Since March, 20 men and women have been executed for witchcraft; 19 were hanged, and one man, stubbornly silent about his actions, was pressed to death by a stone. Most of these "witches" were once respected parents and grandparents. A deputy constable was among the number, as was a minister. All those who have been killed professed to be innocent, while all those who have confessed have been spared. And the accused are many: more than 50 people from Salem and nearby towns crowd the dank prison awaiting trial. But to their good fortune, the people of the colony have begun to rouse themselves to sanity. They see that without intervention, the condemnations may condemn all.

In December of last year, Salem was quiet, and the home of the Rev. Samuel Parris was as quiet as any. Betty Parris, age 9, and her cousin, 11-year-old Abigail Adams, relieved the tedium of their housebound tasks by talking with the family slave, Tituba, a woman of uncertain years raised in the West Indies. In January, the girls and some of their friends, ranging in age from 12 to 20, began to be taken with fits, writhing on the floor, contorting themselves and screaming when the Lord's name was spoken. Doctors examined them and found no illness within their ken.

"Who torments you?" members of the families pleaded to know. "Tituba," the girls said.

In March, preliminary hearings were held. While Tituba never invoked Satan's name, she did confess to be his servant, muttering of rats, cats and a book of black magic signed by nine in Salem. The girls shrieked the names of two of the signers, and the witch hunt began.

"Spectral evidence," which is supernatural visions of the accused performing wicked acts, has condemned the guilty. Yet since September 22, when five were hanged on Gallows Hill, an uneasy suspicion grows that there exists less supernatural evil in Salem than simple mortal cruelty (→Apr. 1, 1693).

Americans besiege Quebec, but in vain

Indians allied with French launch reprisal raids against American colonials.

Quebec, Oct. 23, 1694

American colonial forces have failed in an attempt to seize Quebec, the capital of New France. Their two-week siege ended with the withdrawal of the invaders by ship to their home base in Boston.

Under the command of Sir William Phips, an American-born adventurer, 2,200 Massachusetts militiamen laid siege to the capital with a fleet of 32 ships. However, Phips's call for surrender met this response from the French Governor, the Count of Frontenac: "I have no reply . . . other than from the mouths of my cannons and muskets." Three days later, sickness and cold forced the invading Americans to withdraw.

Cotton Mather rationalizes witchery trials

Boston, Apr. 1, 1693

The Rev. Cotton Mather's first child, a four-day-old son, has died. The neighbors blame bowels that were impaired in the womb – but Mather suspects witchcraft. The minister's *Wonders of the Invisible World,* published last October, explains his beliefs in spectral phenomena and his approval of the recent Salem trials. The work has become, as Mather concedes, a "reviled book," yet he feels compelled to act "in direct opposition to the devil." And as he reminded the public before one hanging in Salem, Satan may fool us by seeming an angel of light (→Jan. 15, 1697).

The Wonders of the Invisible World:

Being an Account of the

TRYALS

OF

Several Witches,

Lately Excuted in

NEW-ENGLAND:

And of several remarkable Curiosities therein Occurring.

Together with,

I. Observations upon the Nature, the Number, and the Operations of the Devils.

II. A short Narrative of a late outrage committed by a knot of Witches in *Swede-Land*, very much resembling, and so far explaining, that under which *New-England* has laboured.

III. Some Councels directing a due Improvement of the Terrible things lately done by the unusual and amazing Range of *Evil-Spirits* in *New-England*.

IV. A brief Discourse upon those *Temptations* which are the more ordinary Devices of Satan.

By COTTON MATHER.

Published by the Special Command of his EXCELLENCY the Govenour of the Province of the *Massachusetts-Bay* in *New-England*.

Printed first, at *Bostun* in *New-England*; and Reprinted at *London*, for *John Dunton*, at the *Raven* in the *Poultry*. 1693.

Title page of Mather's apologia.

College in Virginia

Williamsburg, Feb. 8, 1693

The Rev. James Blair, the Scottish rector of Varina, has succeeded in obtaining a royal charter for a college, to be called William and Mary, which will prepare students for the ministry. Blair met resistance to the idea in London. When he approached Sir Edward Seymour, lord of the Treasury, saying that more souls would be saved because of the new school, Sir Edward responded, "Souls? Damn your souls! Make tobacco." Blair has been an important figure in Virginia's politics for more than 50 years. He is going to be president of William and Mary.

Two are hanged for treason in New York

New York City, May 26, 1691

The loyalty of Jacob Leisler to William and Mary has led to his conviction for treason and his execution for the crime, in spite of the fact that a Governor appointed by William and Mary presided over the trial. Leisler, a local militia captain, led a popular uprising and took power following the revolution in England that replaced James II with William of Orange. Lieutenant Governor Nicholson, acting governor of New York, was a supporter of James II and therefore fell out of popularity.

During his reign, Leisler led the colonies of Massachusetts, Plymouth, Connecticut and New York in an offensive against Canada, whose forces had been raiding New England frontiers. A smallpox epidemic contributed to the failure of the Leisler expedition.

In January of this year, Henry Sloughter arrived to assume the governorship of New York by authority of William and Mary. Prior to Sloughter's arrival, Leisler actively opposed a group of redcoats, choosing to wait for Sloughter to relinquish the government. Sloughter has chosen to regard Leisler's refusal to yield as treason. Leisler and his son-in-law were hanged and then dismembered.

Carolinas are divided into two colonies

Charleston, S.C., Aug. 11, 1691

After many years of unrest and internal bickering, the proprietors of the two Carolinas and the Palatine Court in England have created two provinces, establishing in law what already exists in fact. Phillip Ludwell has been named the Governor of both provinces with power to name a deputy for the northern colony of Albemarle, which is also known as North Carolina.

Bitterly divided by factions consisting of Quakers, Anglicans and Anabaptists, the colony has been in almost constant turmoil since 1676. Matters were made even worse by the appointment of Seth Sothell as Governor. During his six-year tenure, Sothell managed to undo much of what the proprietors had accomplished toward re-establishing peace. He was accused by the colonists of having disregarded the "Fundamental Constitutions of Carolina," as well as of arbitrary conduct of his duties in unjustly imprisoning some of the colony's wealthiest men. When news of the difficulties reached the proprietors back in England, they suspended Sothell, whose main function had been to prevent this sort of turmoil (→May 9, 1712).

Seth Sothell and his followers taking over in Charleston in 1690.

1695 (1695-1699)

Rhode Island, May 6, 1696. Bicameral legislature opens.

London, 1696. Parliament revokes law making Anglicanism official faith in Maryland (→ May 1715).

America, 1696. First grapefruit cultivated from mutant form of Polynesian pomelo tree.

London, Feb. 8, 1697. William Penn, appearing before Board of Trade, proposes intercolonial congress, to be headed by president appointed by crown.

England, Apr. 1697. Crown warns private colonies they may lose charters for failure to enforce Navigation Acts, fight piracy and contribute to colonial defense (→ March 26, 1701).

Massachusetts, Oct. 1697. Terms of punishment under new law against atheists include whipping and boring through tongue with hot iron.

New York, 1697. First paid colonial firemen appointed.

New York City, 1697. Trinity Church is founded.

Baja California, 1697. Spanish Jesuits found mission at Loreta [first in California].

Central America, 1697. Last vestiges of Mayan civilization wrecked by Spanish.

Connecticut, 1698. Bicameral legislature instituted.

America, 1698. *Bay Psalm Book* revised to include 13 tunes, becoming first book with music printed in colonies.

Casco Bay, Maine, Jan. 1, 1699. Abenaki Indians and Massachusetts colonists sign treaty, ending conflict in New England.

Pennsylvania, Nov. 30, 1699. William Penn returns as Governor after 15 years in England.

Virginia, 1699. Government moved from recently burned-out Jamestown to Middle Plantation [Williamsburg] (→ 1705).

America, 1699. Some 4,500 convicts have arrived from England since 1655 to avoid death penalty.

Philadelphia, 1699. First clearly reported yellow fever epidemic in colonies kills one-sixth of population.

Boston, 1699. Brattle Street Church is first Puritan church to allow communion without public confession of faith.

Virginia and Maryland, 1699. Colonies restrict Irish Catholic immigration.

Captain Kidd is seized on piracy charges

Captain Kidd, a barbarian at sea, but the picture of civility on land.

New York City, July 6, 1699

Captain William Kidd has been charged with piracy on the high seas. A legitimate English naval hero who served the King well during the war with France, Kidd was granted a royal commission four years ago to seek out and capture pirates wherever he found them. But since the lure of plunder apparently was greater than the benefits of His Majesty's service, the captain himself turned into a fierce buccaneer and has been waylaying ships, their crews and cargoes from the Red Sea to the Americas. Now he has turned himself in to authorities in New York, where he was arrested and faces a variety of piracy and murder charges (→ May 23, 1701).

War ends; colonial status quo is restored

Ryswick, Holland, Sept. 30, 1697

Peace has finally been restored among the European powers by a treaty to end the War of the Grand Alliance, also called King William's War. The pact returns to Britain the territories on Hudson Bay that were seized by France's colonial forces. The French retain their Acadian colony, but control of Newfoundland is ceded to Britain. The pact requires that King Louis XIV of France accept William III as rightful King of England and to withdraw support from the exiled King James II. Signing the treaty are Britain, Spain, the Netherlands and the Holy Roman Empire on one side, and France on the other.

Puritans seek forgiveness for witch hunt

Massachusetts, Jan. 15, 1697

The citizens of Massachusetts have spent a day of fasting and repentance, recalling the 1692 witch trials and their tacit roles in them. Judge Samuel Sewall, who had presided over many of the sad proceedings, attended church this morning and offered a bill of confession, admitting "the blame and shame." Some former jurors signed a document that read in part, "We fear we have been instrumental with others, though ignorantly and unwillingly, to bring upon ourselves the guilt of innocent blood." The community begged forgiveness of the families of the 20 who died. But there were few apologies for those who escaped the noose, many of whom have since fled the colony. Some erstwhile accusers, like young Ann Putnam, were silent today. And Tituba, the West Indian who wove the first tales of black magic that wrapped Salem in a web of fear, remains somewhere in slavery, possibly weaving more.

New act enlarges powers of customs

London, Apr. 10, 1696

Parliament has passed a far-ranging Navigation Act to tighten its control over colonial trade. Among other things, the act gives provincial customs commissioners powers similar to those in England, expanding the authority of colonial naval officers, confining trade to ships owned and manned by Englishmen, and voiding colonial laws that contradict the Navigation Act. To manage colonial commerce better, a Board of Trade replaces the Lords of Trade. The board is authorized to rule whether colonial laws violate parliamentary acts or common law, or work against the empire's interests (→ Apr. 1697).

200 French begin settling Louisiana

Louisiana, March 2, 1699

France has now taken a clear lead in the three-nation race to occupy Louisiana on North America's Southern coast. Earlier this year, two Canadian explorers, the Le Moyne brothers, established a fort and a settlement of 200 people at Biloxi on the Gulf of Mexico. Pierre Le Moyne, Sieur d'Iberville, led the expedition. Today, the 38-year-old Iberville and 17-year-old Jean Baptiste Le Moyne, Sieur de Bienville, found a red stick marking an Indian hunting ground and named the area "Baton Rouge." The events put the French ahead of Spain and England in the race to develop the strategic region.

Merchants prosper

New York City, 1695

The economy of the colonies is rapidly expanding, with exports expected to exceed 200,000 pounds sterling this year. Trade is, however, evenly balanced, since about the same amount of goods will be imported from the mother country. The biggest problem for the merchants has been a shortage of money. In an attempt to help solve this problem, several newly created land banks started to issue paper currency in 1690.

Early American architecture shows various styles

A classic New England "salt box" house on Cape Cod, Massachusetts.

Green Spring Plantation, built near Jamestown in 1642. By B. Latrobe.

An early American church.

A typical American kitchen, in a house in Malden, Massachusetts, in 1695.

Adam Thoroughgood House in Virginia Beach, Va., built c. 1680.

Philipsburg Manor, in North Tarrytown, New York, built in the 1690's.

Captain John Turner (Seven Gables) House in Salem, Mass., built in 1668.

1700 (1700-1704)

Boston, June 17, 1700. Assembly, sparked by fear of Stuart revival, orders all Roman Catholic priests to leave colony in three months.

Rhode Island, 1700. Yearly meeting of General or Six Principle Baptists founded, first Baptist association in colonies.

Boston, 1700. First commercial distillery opened to make rum.

Pennsylvania, 1700. Assembly passes law banning "stage-plays, masks, revels" and "rude and riotous sports."

Salem, 1700. John Cabot arrives from Isle of Jersey. [Descendants include Samuel Cabot, judge; and Henry B. Cabot, lawyer and statesman.]

London, March 26, 1701. Board of Trade proposes placing all colonies under jurisdiction of crown (→ 1706).

Saybrook, Connecticut, Oct. 16, 1701. The Rev. John Pierpont gains charter to establish Collegiate School [Yale University] under auspices of Congregational Church (→ Sept. 10, 1718).

Pennsylvania, Nov. 8, 1701. Charter of Liberties, colony's first constitution, calls for unicameral legislature with assembly given consent role only in setting of laws.

Philadelphia, 1701. John Davis arrives from Wales. [Descendants include Jefferson Davis, President of Confederacy.]

London, March 8, 1702. Queen Anne takes throne upon King William's death (→ May 4).

New Jersey, Apr. 26, 1702. Crown seizes government from proprietors of East and West, uniting both under royal rule.

Europe, May 4, 1702. Grand Alliance declares war on France to stall union of Spain and France (→ Aug. 29, 1704).

London, 1702. Cotton Mather publishes *Magnalia Christi Americana, or The Ecclesiastical History of New England.*

Massachusetts, 1702. Cotton Mather forms Society for Suppression of Disorders, to monitor swearing and blasphemy.

Florida, 1702. Governor James Moore of Carolina invades mid-Florida, forcing Christianized Indians and Spanish to abandon Apalachee missions.

Maryland, Sept. 28, 1704. Statute gives ministers right to impose divorce on unholy couples.

Colonial population stands at 275,000

Boston, 1700

Colonial towns continue their rapid expansion, but the areas of growth appear to differ widely. The city of Boston has probably lost population, or stayed about the same, over the last decade, while the population of Charlestown has doubled from about 1,000 people in 1690. During the same period, New York City grew from 3,900 to approximately 5,000. Most of the colonists, however, are living in small towns and on farms rather than in the cities, which now account for only about 8 percent of the total population. Negro slaves continue to pour into the colonies, especially the South. The total slave population in America is reported to be approximately 25,000.

Queen Anne's War spreads to America

Newfoundland, Aug. 29, 1704

After a desultory 12-day engagement, the English settlement at Bonavista, on Newfoundland's east coast, has been taken by a combined French and Indian force. The loss is not considered serious, and was preceded by two successful expeditions to the north by Colonel Benjamin Church: last month's raid against the Abenaki supply base at Beaubassin and the earlier attack on Minas, in Acadia. These actions are American extensions of the Queen Anne's War with the French in Europe. The reverse at Bonavista is on a much smaller scale than the brutal assault on Deerfield, Massachusetts, on February 29 of this year, when 49 settlers were massacred, more than 100 taken prisoner, and the town destroyed by fire.

"Queen Anne" by Michael Dahl.

Boston has become principal slave port

Boston, 1700

Although there are only about a thousand slaves in all of New England, the port of Boston has become the most important center of the slave business. Ships laden with food and commodities leave Boston for the West Indies, where the goods are traded for rum. The ships then travel to Africa, where the rum is used to buy slaves. Shipped to the West Indies, the slaves are sold and the ships return to Boston. The West Indian slave market then supplies the colonies with slaves.

Recently, Judge Samuel Sewall of Massachusetts has attempted to stem the slave trade by imposing a heavy tax on it, but his efforts have not been successful.

Slaves on a British tobacco label.

Harvard head ousted; reform pledged

Cambridge, Mass., Dec. 1701

In a struggle between conservatives and liberals over the appropriate curriculum for Harvard College, the reformists seem to have scored a clear victory. Having served for 15 years as president of the school, which was conceived primarily as a theological institute to train future clergymen, the famed preacher Increase Mather resigned this month. The new president, John Leverett, has wide support from the more progressive, reformist elements who want to see Harvard adopt a broad liberal arts curriculum that will rival Oxford and Cambridge Universities.

French trappers explore middle America

Great Lakes, 1700

During the past century, demand for beaver pelts has driven the French to explore the Great Lakes region, and penetrate the interior of the American continent. In 1615, Samuel de Champlain blazed the way, leading an expedition into Georgian bay, the huge arm of Lake Huron. In 1634, Jean Nicolet, a Champlain agent, crossed Lake Huron to Lake Michigan and explored its western shores. By the middle of the century, fur traders Pierre Radisson and Medard Chouart, Sieur des Groseilliers, had found Lake Superior and began trading with the Sioux. Since then, trappers have further explored the interior, using the Great Lakes as a route to bring their highly valued pelts to market.

A French fur trapper, ready for another colonial winter, prepares to go exploring on snowshoes.

Newspaper founded and issued weekly

Boston, Apr. 24, 1704

John Campbell, an astute and prudent Scotsman who is postmaster of Boston, has begun publication of a regular, weekly newspaper called the *Boston News-Letter*. Campbell, 51, developed a thriving business as a bookseller and printer of casual and occasional news on a "half-sheet" called *Letters of Intelligence* that has been extremely popular. The format and content of the newspaper is similar to that of the *London Gazette*, and the new publication is two-thirds filled with items that have been gleaned from the English paper. The other third is made up of brief articles about deaths, sermons, ship arrivals and departures, storms and activities in the courts (→Jan. 19, 1708).

A baronial manor rises in Scarsdale

Westchester, March 21, 1701

Caleb Heathcote, the epitome of the English gentleman and staunch promoter of the Church of England, has bought a huge tract of land in Westchester County, which he will call the Manor of Scarsdale. The deed describes the purchase as "the Three Great Patents of Central Westchester" and it consists of some 70,000 acres. Heathcote came to America in 1691 and made his home in New York City, where he became mayor. He moved to Westchester County when his bride-to-be decided to marry his brother Gilbert, a former lord mayor of London. The Scarsdale manor is named after the Hundred of Scarsdale in Derbyshire, where Caleb Heathcote was born.

Anti-slave tract: "The Selling of Joseph"

Boston, June 24, 1700

Judge Samuel Sewall, known to New Englanders as the only judge who publicly renounced his participation in the Salem witchcraft trials of the 1690's, has taken another bold stand by writing a three-page tract, *The Selling of Joseph*, the first outright appeal for the abolition of slavery to appear in America. The pamphlet makes a religious argument that draws a strong parallel between the enforced servitude of African natives and the Old Testament story of Joseph, whose brothers sold him into slavery for 20 pieces of silver.

"There is no proportion between Twenty Pieces of Silver," Sewall's tract asserts, "and LIBERTY." He adds, "Joseph was rightfully, no more a Slave to his Brethren, than they were to him, and they had no more Authority to Sell him than they had to Slay him." Sewall is personally handing out copies of his tract.

Judge Sewall, a man of conscience.

Captain Kidd hanged for piracy, murder

London, May 23, 1701

Captain William Kidd, previously found guilty on all counts of piracy, robbery on the high seas and murder, was hanged at Execution Dock today. To the end, he maintained his innocence. Kidd said he had had no intention of turning pirate and had always been a loyal servant of the King. He argued that "I am the innocentest person of them all, only I have been sworn against by perjured persons." But because of the strength of the evidence that he was a most willing buccaneer, his pleas were rejected. Kidd's body was hung in chains, in public view, on the Thames River.

Cadillac establishes French fort at Detroit

Michigan, July 24, 1701

Leading a band of 50 soldiers, 50 artisans and traders and two priests, Sieur Antoine de La Mothe Cadillac has traveled down the St. Clair River and erected Fort Pontchartrain to guard the route for those who will follow to settle the Mississippi Valley. Cadillac has named the settlement La Ville d'Etroit [Detroit], French for the city of the strait. In a report appealing to the government ministers back in France, Cadillac wrote: "This country, so temperate, so fertile, and so beautiful that it may justly be called the earthly paradise of North America deserves all the care of the King."

Fashions are set by French in 1704

New York City, 1704

French influence in American fashions has become quite apparent this year. A very popular ensemble for ladies features a cherry-colored gown and petticoat with a short "working" apron, accompanied by a necklace of immoderate length with both ends trailing down to the girdle. The well-tailored gentleman may be wearing a French "campaign" wig that features long, full curls hanging down toward the front of the face. If this gentleman has little or no natural hair, a bit of horse hair is used to create a realistic, attractive wig that is appropriate for any social occasion. He also can be seen wearing blue or scarlet stockings and these are held up by velvet garters that should be fastened just below the knee.

New England Christians called to work

Boston, 1701

The true Christian, while looking constantly to heaven, must never fail to keep his feet firmly planted on the earth. Such is the argument of the Rev. Cotton Mather, whose most popular sermon has appeared in print under the title *A Christian at His Calling.*

Mather argues that devotion to work is a necessary expression of one's devotion to Jesus. Comparing the journey through life to a boat ride, he warns all navigators, "If he mind but one of his callings, be it which it will, he pulls the oar, but on one side of the boat, and will make but a poor dispatch to the shore of eternal blessedness." "A man slothful in business," adds the noted Massachusetts minister, "is not a man serving the Lord."

Thus, to draw nearer to salvation, he says, a Christian must pursue his calling with industry, discretion, honesty, contentment and piety. "A poor man, that minds the business of his calling and weaves a thread of holiness into all his business, may arrive to some of the highest glories in heaven at the last." What of those for whom work is drudgery? "Yea," he says, "but hath not the God of heaven cast you into that business?"

Mather's exhortations to industry are echoed in churches all over New England. And if one is to judge by the rapid rise of tradesmen in their myriad businesses in the austere Puritan towns, the inhabitants appear to be listening.

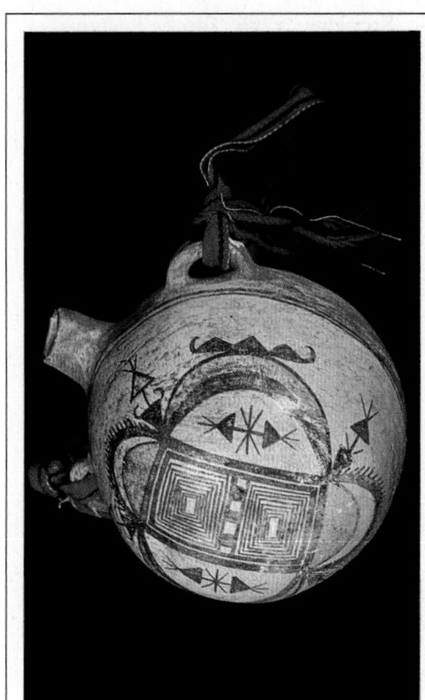

As Europeans explore more and more of the American continent, they are acquiring beautiful Indian artifacts, such as this Hopi water jug used by natives in the arid Southwestern region.

1705 (1705-1709)

Massachusetts, 1705. Statute bars marriage between whites and Negroes.

Philadelphia, March 1706. First presbytery in colonies established by the Rev. Francis Makemie, Irishman who immigrated in 1683 (→ Oct. 14, 1708).

South Carolina, Nov. 30, 1706. Anglicanism becomes established religion.

Yorktown, Virginia, 1706. First major customshouse in colonies is established (→ 1711).

Western America, 1706. Juan de Uribarri claims vast area [Colorado] for Spain.

Philadelphia, 1707. Mechanics form guild to protest unfair competition from Negro slaves.

Canada, 1707. British expedition tries to capture French colony of Acadia [Nova Scotia, New Brunswick, Prince Edward Island] (→ Dec. 21, 1708).

America, 1707. John Williams publishes best-seller, *The Redeemed Captive,* a narrative of life with Indians.

Boston, Jan. 19, 1708. *Boston News-Letter* carries the first illustration printed in a colonial newspaper.

Newfoundland, Dec. 21, 1708. French forces seize control of eastern shore after winning a victory at St. Johns (→ Apr. 1709).

Pennsylvania, 1708. William Penn, to get out of debt in England, mortgages province to trustees.

America, 1708. James Logan introduces Newton's *Principia* into colonies.

Connecticut, 1709. First mining charter in colonies granted to copper mine in Simsbury; the ore is to be exported to England.

Boston, Apr. 1709. Samuel Vetch arrives back in the colonies (with Francis Nicholson), charged by Board of Trade with the task of raising a colonial force for proposed invasion of Canada (→ Oct. 1709).

Boston, Oct. 1709. News arrives in the colonies that the invasion of Canada has been canceled (→ June 25, 1711).

Philadelphia, 1709. Quakers establish first colonial center for the treatment of mental illness.

DEATH

America, June 10, 1705. Michael Wigglesworth, poet (*Oct. 18, 1631).

England and Scotland are formally united

London, March 6, 1707

A new country, Great Britain, was created today by the Act of Union between England and Scotland. Although the two countries have been sharing the same monarch since 1603, when James VI of Scotland succeeded Queen Elizabeth and became James I of England as well, they had remained separate in all other respects.

Scotland's Parliament and Privy Council will cease to exist; instead, Scotland will send members to the House of Commons and House of Lords in London. The country will keep its distinctive legal system and, most importantly, will not be expected to receive the Anglican Church as its official religion. This will continue to be Presbyterianism, and church government will remain in the hands of the General Assembly. Edinburgh will remain the Scottish capital.

Scotland will also gain access to markets in England and its colonies – an important advantage in light of the recent collapse of the Darien Scheme to set up the colony of New Caledonia in Panama.

The benefit to the English will be political rather than economic, basically a lessening of the threat of a Jacobite uprising in a country where so many of the people still nurse very strong feelings of loyalty to the House of Stuart

New capitol finished at Williamsburg

Williamsburg, Virginia, 1705

Colonists in America might be accused of engaging in radical politics, but they are conservative when it comes to architecture. The recently completed capitol at Williamsburg is a reflection of that fact. Begun in 1701 and completed this year, the building is probably the design of Sir Christopher Wren or of his pupil James Gibbs. The colonists have rejected futuristic and ponderous experiments of the Palladian school, popular in Europe, in favor of the simplicity and elegance of the school of Wren.

Neither Wren nor Gibbs has ever paid a visit to the colonies, but this has not prevented their influence from being felt. Gibbs is the author of a number of pattern books and builders handbooks that express the ideas of his teacher. The City Hall of New York, which was completed in 1699, is also believed to be from a design by Wren. It is quite similar in appearance to the capitol in Virginia, whose former seat of government was Jamestown. When a fire virtually destroyed that community in 1698, the burgesses of the colony decided that they would shift the government to Williamsburg, until then a health resort.

An elegant carriage deposits callers at the Governor's Williamsburg mansion.

Slaves considered as "real estate"

Planters rest while their slaves labor.

Virginia, Oct. 23, 1705

A new slavery act states that all imported servants shall remain in lifelong bondage, except those who had been Christian in their native country or who had been free in a Christian country. This, in effect, limits lifelong slavery to Negroes and covers nearly all Negroes in the colony. The current legislation also restricts the movements of Negroes within the colony and strictly forbids marriage between whites and Negroes. In addition, the laws now consider all "Negro, mulatto and Indian slaves" as "real estate" and not as chattels. Also, Negroes, mulattos and Indians are now forbidden to hold any civil or military office.

Albuquerque built

Mexico, Apr. 23, 1706

The Governor of New Mexico, Francisco Cuervo y Valdes, writes that he has founded a new town to serve as the administrative center for the lower Rio Grande area. Albuquerque, as he calls it, in honor of the Duke of Albuquerque, Viceroy of New Spain, already has 252 inhabitants. It also has a church, and government buildings are now being constructed. The Governor calls the town "a good place as regards land, water, pasture and firewood." The expenses of establishing the new town were borne entirely by the citizens themselves. Albuquerque has been given the patron saint of the Indies, San Francisco Xavier.

Connecticut's churches are reorganized

New Haven, Oct. 14, 1708

The assembly enacted into law today the Saybrook Platform. It was the work of delegates meeting last month in Saybrook by order of the General Court. Their charge was to develop a doctrinal and organizational order for the colony's congregations. Doctrinally, the platform adopted the Savoy Declaration as approved by the English independents in 1658. By doing this, the colony followed the lead of its brethren in Massachusetts, who issued a declaration along similar lines in 1680.

A major difference with Massachusetts is the organizational structure outlined in the document. Individual congregations will be organized into county consociations empowered to enforce discipline and orthodoxy among the member churches. This system, which the ministers of Massachusetts, including both Increase and Cotton Mather, have wanted but have failed to achieve, should help overcome the laxness that has marked the religious life of the colony. Ministers are going to be organized into ministerial associations that will regularize ordinations and adjudicate any conflicts that may arise between ministers and their congregations. A general association of ministers will oversee the churches of the commonwealth (→ 1729).

Quakers gain more religious tolerance

Boston, 1709

The establishment of a meetinghouse of the Society of Friends in the city of Boston represents the gains that the Quakers have made in the last 50 years. From their strongholds in Pennsylvania, West Jersey and Rhode Island, they have had an increasing impact upon the region. That they have been quietly tolerated in Massachusetts for some years is well known, but a public building is a different matter. While some of the increase in tolerance is the result of a greater degree of restraint in their religious activities, the major part is no doubt a result of the Toleration Act promulgated in 1689 by King William and Queen Mary and the change in the colony's charter that turned it into a royal colony in 1684.

Through the years, Quakers have offered hardy resistance to religious persecution. Their defiance of restrictive laws after the Restoration of 1660 influenced the passage of the Toleration Act. Quakers threaten entrenched religious hierarchies because they believe in none at all. God is said to speak directly to each individual without the help of clergy. Quaker services have no clear leader, and all decisions must be unanimous. Meetings are often silent, a sort of group meditation devoted to experiencing the "Inward Light." Those who "quaked" in revelation gave the group its name.

Counterfeiting calls for harsh penalties

Boston, 1705

As disputes between the royal government and the provincial legislature continue over control of the quantity of paper currency in circulation, counterfeiting has captured the attention of all involved parties. In May of 1704, there were 25,500 pounds in bills circulating, and when the first counterfeiting case was uncovered in July, legislation was passed criminalizing the act. Thomas Odell was sentenced to a year in prison for masterminding the operation. James Mar barely escaped the hangman's noose in New York for the same crime.

Ezekiel Cheever: master educator

Boston, Aug. 21, 1708

Ezekiel Cheever, New England's most beloved and respected schoolmaster, died today at the age of 83. Born in London, he came to America in 1637 and spent his life here teaching. For the last 38 years, he was at the Boston Latin School. However, Cheever's teaching talent was not limited by the classroom. He is also well known for having written the first Latin textbook published in America, *Accidence, a Short Introduction to the Latin Tongue*. The Rev. Cotton Mather will deliver the funeral oration.

Cotton Mather foresees Christian revival

Boston, 1706

Printer B. Green has brought out a new tract by the Rev. Cotton Mather, co-minister of the Second Church here and a prolific author whose works include *Memorable Providences, Relating to Witchcrafts* (1689), a defense of the verdicts reached at the Salem witch trials, and *Magnalia Christi Americana* (1702), a criticism of the method used in the trials. Mather's most recent pamphlet is a call for a return to old-fashioned Puritanism. Titled *The Good Old Way or, Christianity Described From the Glorious Lustre of It, Appearing In the Lives of the Primitive Christians*, Mather's polemic rues the "decay of Christianity" and argues that religious purity will return in a new age of sobriety, righteousness and piety. The capstone of his plan is "Conversion," which he calls "the Foundation of Godliness" and the "Beginning of Wisdom." He tells worshipers to "Glorify that Almighty Spirit of Grace, who wrought such Great Things in the Primitive Christians."

Mather (1727) by Peter Pelham.

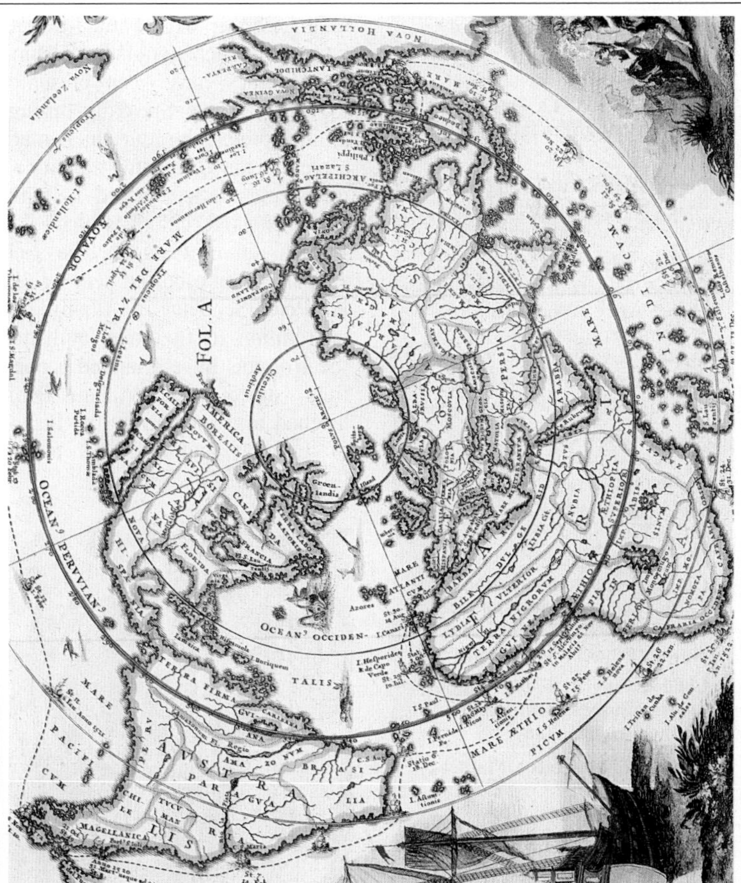

New Spain, 1705. *Since the earliest explorations by the Spanish of the Pacific coast of America, it has been assumed that the land called California – named for a mythical warrior queen named Califia – is an island, separated from the mainland by water, as depicted in the map above. This year, however, a new map has been published, showing once and for all that Baja (lower) California is a peninsula attached to Alta (upper) California and that California itself is part of the American continent.*

1710 (1710-1714)

Virginia, June 21, 1710. Newly appointed Governor Alexander Spotswood arrives, bearing instructions to introduce right of habeas corpus in colony.

Louisiana, 1710. French move settlement from Biloxi [to present-day Mobile].

Carolina, 1710. New Bern [second town in North Carolina] settled by 650 Swiss and German colonists (→Sept. 22, 1711).

Boston, June 25, 1711. As 64 British ships arrive, carrying 5,000 troops and 6,000 seamen, preparations begin for advance on Canada (→Aug. 23).

Carolina, Sept. 22, 1711. Indians upset by new wave of settlement attack colonists on Roanoke and Chowan Rivers, launching Tuscarora War (→March 23, 1713).

London, 1711. Parliament bans cutting of trees by American colonists; all timber reserved for Royal Navy (→1720).

Carolina, May 9, 1712. Separation into North and South officially completed; Edward Hyde becomes first Governor of North Carolina.

Detroit, May 1712. Outagamie and Mascoutin Indians attack settlement.

Pennsylvania, June 7, 1712. Assembly bars importation of slaves into colony.

Europe, March 26, 1713. Britain, as part of settlement in Queen Anne's War, gains Assiento, contract allowing South Sea Company to bring 4,800 Negro slaves per year into Spanish colonies.

Virginia, Nov. 5, 1713. Tobacco inspection act adopted in attempt to raise quality of exports and reduce quantity to drive price up (→Nov. 12, 1717).

Gloucester, Massachusetts, 1713. First schooner, uniquely American ship, designed and built by Andrew Robinson.

London, Aug. 1, 1714. King George I ascends throne upon death of Queen Anne.

Boston, 1714. Cotton Mather gives sermon favoring Copernicus's heliocentric model of universe.

Central Plains, 1714. French explorer Etienne Veniard, Sieur de Bourgmont, on journey up Missouri River, notes Otoe Indian name for tributary [Platte River] is "Nebraska."

Virginia, 1714. Governor Alexander Spotswood opens iron works on Rapidan River.

Indian chiefs taken on tour of London

Chief of the Maquas in London.

London, July 1710

Wearing their feather headdresses, matchcoat wraps and full warpaint, four sachems of the Iroquois Confederacy have been presented to Queen Anne. Speaking through an interpreter, the four chiefs made a plea to the Queen for military reinforcements that would help the New England colonists drive the French out of Canada. The sachems are being escorted here by Major Peter Schuyler of Albany, and in addition to the royal audience, the Iroquois have attended a cockfight, dined with William Penn, listened to a sermon by the Bishop of London and attended a performance of *Macbeth*.

Tee Yee Ho Gahow, Mohawk Chief of the Six Nations (1710).

Canadian invasion fails

Quebec, Aug. 23, 1711

Devastated by the wrecking of eight ships with the loss of nearly 1,000 lives during a storm in the Gulf of St. Lawrence, a major British naval assault on Quebec has been abandoned. The dead include 35 women and a number of drummer boys who accompanied the invading force. The disaster is being called the "magnificent fiasco."

The British expedition, made up of nine ships in all, left Boston July 30 under the command of Admiral Sir Hovenden Walker. It appeared doomed from the start. A shortage of provisions and the inadequate seamanship of the admiral were contributing factors.

According to accounts of the disaster, the British flotilla got lost in fog off Egg Island in the gulf and heavy winds blew eight of the nine ships onto the rocks. By the time a French force had arrived in Quebec from Montreal to meet the attackers, the British survivors had departed. Admiral Walker escaped.

In Quebec, Father de la Columbiere repeated a sermon he delivered some 20 years earlier on the defeat of Sir William Phips's expedition, ascribing Quebec's deliverance to the intervention of the Virgin Mary on France's side. The Church of Notre Dame de la Victoire in Quebec's Lower Town has been renamed Notre Dame des Victoires, which may result in linking the Walker and Phips expeditions forever as historic failures (→Apr. 11, 1713).

Stroke fells William Penn; wife in charge

Philadelphia, 1712

William Penn, the British Quaker who founded the colony of Pennsylvania, suffered a stroke this year and his recovery does not seem likely. His wife, Hannah, is taking over the duties of governing the colony. Penn, the son of a British admiral, Sir William Penn, attended Oxford University and had a promising political career ahead of him before he decided to become a Quaker in 1667. He was later jailed several times for his vigorous support of religious freedom.

In 1680, King Charles II gave Penn a huge tract of land west of the Delaware, between New York and Maryland, in lieu of a debt owed to Penn's father. Penn invited Quakers throughout the world to the colony and thousands have poured in from Wales, England, Germany and Holland. He has honored every treaty he made with the Indians and they have never attacked his colony. He has penned 100 works, including *No Cross, No Crown*, in which he wrote, "True Godliness doesn't turn men out of the world, it excites their endeavors to mend it" (→July 30, 1718)

"On the Road to Penn's Manor," early Pennsylvania, depicted by J.L.G. Ferris.

Militia crushes an uprising by slaves

New York City, July 4, 1712

After one of the first recorded slave uprisings in North America, 12 slaves have been executed for their part in the revolt, and six committed suicide before they were brought to the gallows. The renegade slaves had killed nine whites before the militia was called in to quell the violence and to arrest the revolutionaries. Although some New York and New England merchants have major interests in the slave trade, and are largely responsible for supplying the rest of the colonies with Africans, the number of slaves actually held in the northeastern part of America remains small, and such violent incidents are apparently rare. Most of the slaves imported to America are owned by settlers in the colonies of Virginia and South Carolina.

One unfortunate result of the uprising is the closing of the Catechism School for Negroes at Trinity Church in New York City. It was founded by a Frenchman, Elias Neau, in 1704 for the purpose of religious education. Slave owners are suspicious of his work, fearing that education will inspire revolt.

Tuscaroras wage a bloody war in South

The Tuscaroras track fugitive settlers through the North Carolina woods. Europeans in the area enjoyed general peace with the natives until the arrival in 1710 of several hundred Swiss and German colonists who settled New Bern.

North Carolina, March 23, 1713

Troops from both Carolinas, under the command of Colonel John Barnwell, have captured Fort Nohucke, the Tuscarora base near New Bern, and forced the Indians there to negotiate a treaty. The war began in 1711 when a force of Tuscaroras and other Indians fell on a settlement near Trent with devastating effect. As the Indians continued the slaughter, vast stretches of the countryside were depopulated, plantations destroyed and colonists massacred. The colony's trade was also hard hit because there has been no grain or pork to provide for incoming ships. And the treasury is reported to be thousands of pounds in debt for wages owed to soldiers, as well as for ammunition and provisions.

Bookstore reaches even to Barbados

Philadelphia, 1714

A new bookstore here, The Sign of the Bible, is filling orders for religious publications placed by customers who live as far away as Barbados. The bookstore's growing reputation is a coup for its 28-year-old entrepreneur, Andrew Bradford, who returned to his native city two years ago after spending his youth in New York, where his father, William Bradford, was appointed the crown's official printer. In addition to selling religious publications, such as blank books, pamphlets and rebound Bibles, The Sign of the Bible serves as a general store where customers can buy such items as whalebone, beaver hats, lamp black and Spanish snuff.

Anglicanism leads to Carolina revolt

Charleston, March 1711

The fiery Thomas Cary, Anglican deputy for North Carolina, who was impeached by the General Assembly, has escaped from the provost marshal, and now he vows to lead a campaign to overthrow the government of the two Carolina colonies in Charleston. For a decade Cary has opposed both Quakers and Puritans who are resisting the movement to establish the Anglican Church as an official religion (→1715).

Music, suppressed by Puritans, gaining popularity in America

Boston, 1713

The King's Chapel of the Anglican Church has received an organ, the first of its kind to be installed in America, from Thomas Brattle. Interest in music appears to be picking up in the colonies despite the Puritans, who have long fulminated against it and have even tried to have it banned outright. But the Puritans are being pushed back. The first singing-instruction book written in the colonies, *A Very Plain and Easy Introduction to the Whole Art of Singing Psalm Tunes*, was published last year.

Musical activity in the English colonies is generally of three kinds – singing in the churches (mostly Anglican), formal concerts presented on the European model (but only in the cities), and informal music-making of a basically simple type.

"The Anthem America*" by J.L.G. Ferris. Despite any anthems Europeans might sing about the New World, musical revelry has been scarce in the drawing rooms of Puritan New England. In 1713, King's Chapel of Boston's Anglican Church acquired an organ from Thomas Brattle. The Puritans, however, ban music from houses of worship for religious reasons.*

War ends; British win French lands

Utrecht, Holland, Apr. 11, 1713

The war between Britain and France has formally ended with the signing here of a treaty that confirms British possession of many colonies conquered during the last 12 years. Among them are Acadia, which is to be renamed Nova Scotia; Newfoundland, and the Hudson Bay Territory. At the same time, talks between England and Spain are nearing completion, with some moves to open Spanish America to British trade expected, along with confirmation of British ownership of Gibraltar and Minorca.

1715 (1715-1719)

South Carolina, Apr. 15, 1715. Yamassee Indians, goaded by Spanish agitation, kill hundreds of English settlers.

Maryland, May 1715. Charter of 1632 restored to Baltimores upon death of Leonard Calvert, who had, after his own conversion, raised his son, Charles, in Church of England.

North Carolina, 1715. Third Vestry Act establishes Anglican Church after first two attempts vetoed by proprietors.

Louisiana, 1715. Louis St. Denis establishes fort [at site of modern Natchitoches and first permanent European settlement in colony].

Louisiana, June 6, 1716. First slaves are brought to French territory, in ships owned by Company of the West.

Boston, 1716. First lighthouse built in colonies, to guard harbor.

New Spain, 1716. Spanish settlers found colony of Nacogdoches [first permanent European settlement in Texas] (→ May 1, 1718).

Middle Plantation, Virginia, 1716. First theater in colonies is opened.

Virginia, Nov. 12, 1717. Tobacco inspection act of 1713 is repealed by proclamation.

America, 1717. Colonial ships, now allowed to trade in West Indies, begin bringing back cheap French molasses, used to distill rum in New England.

Boston, 1717. Cotton Mather begins a school for Negroes and Indians.

Northampton, Massachusetts, 1718. Solomon Stoddard, Puritan clergyman, extends covenant to anyone willing to accept it; orthodox ministers aggravated by democratization.

South Carolina, Nov. 1719. Colonists overthrow British proprietors (→ May 29, 1721).

Natchez, Mississippi, Nov. 29, 1719. Natchez Indians kill or capture all settlers in Fort Rosalie.

Boston, 1719. Eliakim Hutchison presents first street light in America, a single lantern.

Philadelphia, 1719. American Mercury periodical founded by Andrew Bradford.

DEATH

Pennsylvania, July 30, 1718. William Penn, Quaker founder of Pennsylvania (*Oct. 14, 1644).

Dreaded Blackbeard killed and beheaded

"The Capture of the Pirate Blackbeard" by J.L.G. Ferris.

Virginia, Nov. 22, 1718

The scourge of the Atlantic Ocean and the Caribbean Sea, "Captain" Edward Teach, popularly known as "Blackbeard," is no more. He was killed and his body mutilated by a member of the Royal Navy, Lieutenant Maynard, who engaged the notorious pirate off the coast of Virginia today.

Teach got his nickname because of his immense beard, full to his eyes, twisted into curls and tied with ribbons. When doing battle, he customarily stuck lighted matches in his hat, which gave his bearded face the appearance of the devil himself. A murderer and a rapist, he was the husband of 14 wives, whom he shared with his crew. When slain, Blackbeard had 25 wounds, including five inflicted by the pistols of Lieutenant Maynard and his men.

The government of Virginia had offered a bounty of 100 pounds for the capture of Blackbeard. When confronted by Lieutenant Maynard, Teach is reported to have said, "Damnation seize my soul if I give you quarter or take any from you." The brave Lieutenant Maynard told the pirate that he expected no quarter from him, nor would he give any. Both men held firm. After Maynard had killed Teach, he cut off his head and mounted it on his ship's mast.

"Knights" promote westward expansion

Governor Spotswood and his knights.

Williamsburg, Virginia, Sept. 1716

Beset by rattlesnakes, hornets, bears and measles but fortified with an ample supply of alcoholic beverages, the "Knights of the Golden Horseshoe," led by Governor Alexander Spotswood, returned safely after four weeks in the wilderness. The expedition covered 438 miles, reaching Shenandoah Mountain 13 miles north of Swift Run. When they got to the summit, the men toasted the King's health in champagne, the princess in burgundy and the rest of the royal family in claret, firing a volley with each toast. Governor Spotswood then gave every "knight" a golden horseshoe to remember the event.

Mother Goose sings tunes to grandson

Boston, Dec. 1719

Mother Goose's Melodies for Children has become a best-seller in the American colonies this year. This collection of rhymes was inspired by one "Mrs. Goose," the mother-in-law of the publisher Thomas Fleet of Boston. According to local rumor, he issued the collecton of rhymes in honor of – or to avenge himself for – her endless and somewhat unmusical chanting of these catchy but rather mindless poems to his infant son. Regardless of the motives for its publication, this popular book can be purchased from Fleet's publishing house on Pudding Lane. The price is two coppers.

College named for benefactor, Yale

New Haven, Sept. 10, 1718

The trustees of the Collegiate School, established in 1701 and moved here from Saybrook in 1716, have voted to rename it Yale College. Elihu Yale, a merchant, has been the most generous donor to the institution, founded by conservative Congregationalists unhappy with the religious liberalism they think prevails at Harvard. Students have plenty of studies to preoccupy them. They rise at 6 and follow morning prayers with Bible readings. Then come lessons in Greek, Hebrew, Latin, logic, mathematics, physics and metaphysics. With this curriculum, it is unlikely that the school will become, as Elihu Yale fears, an "academy of dissenters."

Yale, donor of 562 pounds sterling.

Promoter bringing Germans to Louisiana

Louisiana, Dec. 1719

A new kind of immigrant began arriving in Louisiana this month. The latest arrivals are industrious German farmers fleeing the turmoil after the wars of Louis XIV and seeking land of their own. The Company of the West, which had sought only French settlers before, began recruiting German peasants in the hope that they would increase food production in the colony. Many earlier settlers were convicts and others who had no interest in farming. The colony has been forced to import food from France. John Law, head of the Company of the West, said, "These are just the kind of colonists we need." The company has promised to provide the settlers with land and supplies. Many of the immigrants complain about the tropical climate and others charge that the company has not kept its promises on the supplies. Some settlers have been put to work on Law's lands. Others are farming along the Mississippi north of New Orleans.

John Law, of Company of the West.

Most of the settlers are from the Rhineland, but others are from German-speaking cantons in Switzerland. The first Germans arrived at Ship Island near Biloxi in November. Thousands of the prospective immigrants had been ailing and succumbed while awaiting the voyage or aboard ship (→ Oct. 1720).

Gentleman pirate is captured and hanged

South Carolina, Dec. 10, 1718

A most unlikely pirate, Major Stede Bonnet, was hanged today. Somewhat of a romantic adventurer, Bonnet was a gentleman from the West Indies and had a considerable family fortune and an outstanding education. Once a man of excellent reputation but a poor seaman, he decided for some unknown reason that he would lead the life of a buccaneer.

He embarked on his brief but flamboyant career in piracy last year. Commanding a sloop of 10 guns and 70 men, he raided in the Caribbean, the Carolinas and off the coast of New England. Besides capturing dozens of cargoes and maiming numerous sailors, Bonnet killed at least 18 seamen. In September, Bonnet boldly declared that if the Governor should send any forces to attempt to capture him, he would "burn and destroy all ships or vessels going in or coming out of South Carolina."

Colonel William Rhet of South Carolina, with two sloops, was sent to capture Bonnet. After a fierce fight on September 27, the gallant colonel and his men forced the buccaneer to surrender. When charged with murder and piracy, Bonnet pleaded not guilty. But English justice being swift and sure, the gentleman pirate met his maker today at the gallows.

Stede Bonnet, scourge of the seas.

Settlement named

New Orleans, Nov. 1718

Governor Bienville has founded a new settlement at the mouth of the Mississippi River and named it New Orleans. The settlement was named in honor of the Regent of France, Philippe, Duke of Orleans. Bienville has instructed his engineering staff to lay out streets for the town, although there are now only 68 inhabitants. Bienville is hoping to make New Orleans the capital of Louisiana, replacing the Gulf Coast town of Biloxi.

New frontier posts

New Spain, May 1, 1718

Two new outposts have been set up by the Spanish on the frontier where the San Antonio and San Pedro Rivers meet [Texas]. One, a new town to be called San Antonio de Bexar, was founded by Martin de Alarcon. The other, a small church being built about two gunshots from the town, is called the mission of San Antonio de Valero. It was founded by Fray Antonio de San Buenaventura.

Sperm whales: A new age for Nantucket's whaling industry

Nantucket, Massachusetts, 1715

In 1712, after being blown far off shore by a terrible storm, Christopher Hussey happened upon a school of sperm whales. The captain brought one into port, the first sperm whale ever killed in New England, and thus began a new age for Nantucket's whaling industry.

Nantucket became involved in whaling after it was settled when a small whale entered its harbor and stayed for three days. The townsfolk devised a plan to kill it with harpoons that they would make specifically for that purpose. Successful in their effort, they turned whaling into a new business.

At that time, efforts were confined to coastline whaling, because the whales were abundant off Nantucket. A lookout would first spot a whale blowing, which indicated the size of the whale and its potential oil yield. Shallops were sent out in the whale's direction and the most skilled harpooner would throw from the prow, trying to strike forward on the whale's body. The wounded whale would submerge, leashed to the shallop by hawsers attached to the harpoon. Often the whale would drag the shallop out to sea, and sometimes a boat under water. If a whale was killed, it would be towed to shore to test its oil, with sperm whales producing the highest quality. Now, three years after the first sperm whale capture, Nantucket has a fleet of six 30-ton sloops that can cruise six weeks at a time.

Bear is harpooned on right, but new focus is on harpooning whales.

1720 (1720-1724)

Central Plains, Aug.13, 1720. Pawnees kill Pedro de Vilasur's party, sent [to Platte Valley] to investigate rumors of French settlement.

North America, 1720. Population of British colonies now at 474,000; Boston is largest city at 12,000; Philadelphia has 10,000, and New York 7,000.

Philadelphia, May 25, 1721. John Copson establishes first marine and fire insurance company in colonies.

South Carolina, May 29, 1721. Francis Nicholson, already Governor or Deputy Governor of three other colonies, is appointed Governor of South Carolina by the crown, transforming province officially into royal colony.

Montreal, 1721. Jesuit priest reports Algonquin lacrosse games lasting three days, with hundreds of players to a side.

Maryland, 1721. Swedish artist Gustavus Hesselius receives first art commission in colonies, to paint *The Last Supper* as altarpiece for a church.

Cambridge, Jan. 24, 1722. Edward Wigglesworth named to fill Thomas Hollis chair at Harvard College, becoming first divinity professor in colonies.

Cambridge, 1722. Judah Monis, first Jew to get college degree in colonies, is baptized a Christian and begins teaching Hebrew at Harvard.

Williamsburg, Virginia, 1723. Brafferton Hall, endowed by English scientist Robert Boyle, is built at William and Mary College to house the first permanent Indian school in colonies.

Pennsylvania, 1723. Alexander Mack organizes Dunkers, sect distinguished by pacifism, triple immersion, agape feasts.

Somerset County, New Jersey, 1723. Johann Peter Rockefeller arrives from Germany. [Descendants include John D. Rockefeller, industrialist; Nelson Rockefeller, U.S. Vice President and New York Governor.]

Louisiana, 1724. Black Code makes it legal for slaveowners to cut off runaways' ears, hamstring and brand them; also bars Jews and Catholics from colony.

DEATH

Boston, Aug. 23, 1723. Increase Mather, Puritan theologian, father of Cotton Mather (*June 21, 1639).

Doctor uses African smallpox inoculation

Boston, May 1, 1721

The recent outbreak of smallpox in the Boston area has caused many deaths, some bold experimentation and a good deal of debate. The epidemic has produced 5,889 known cases of the contagious disease and at least 844 deaths.

Dr. Zabdiel Boylston of Boston has been experimenting with a new method of preventing the disease. His experiments come as the result of prompting by the Rev. Cotton Mather, who learned of the method of developing a resistance to the disease by inoculation from his African slave Onesimus. The slave had described to Mather how African tribesmen would develop immunities to smallpox after having been deliberately infected with a dose of the disease. At Mather's urging, Dr. Boylston first inoculated his son Thomas and two slaves. As the epidemic continued, Boylston inoculated 240 more people. All but six of those who underwent the treatment survived. Mather has urged widespread use of the inoculation treatment, but his appeal has been largely ignored.

Actually, the practice of inoculation has come under sharp criticism from Dr. William Douglass, who charges that Doctor Boylston's use of the treatment has caused a further spread of the disease.

Smallpox is characterized by high fever, large pustules on the skin and permanent scarring.

Investors ruined by Mississippi scheme

Paris, Oct. 1720

It began when the Regent of France, Philip of Orleans, met a Scotsman named John Law at a casino. It ended in a financial panic that has touched all of Europe. Law persuaded the Regent of France to give Law's Company of the West control of the vast Louisiana territory. He promised investors riches from the gold, silver and diamond mines along the Mississippi. Investors stampeded to the scheme, called "Le Mississippi." By the time the bubble burst this month, the town of New Orleans had been founded and colonized, but Law and his investors had been ruined.

French send prostitutes to New Orleans

Women of ill repute embark from Le Havre, after painting by Edouard Delort.

New Orleans, 1721

The shortage of women for colonists to marry has been relieved this year with the arrival of a group of females taken from a house of correction in France. Some of them are prostitutes. Others are orphans who were kept in the Salpetriere in France. When the ship carrying the females arrived at Ship Island near Biloxi earlier this year, woman-hungry men paddled to the island in pirogues to greet them. Some of the women were married by a secular priest in Biloxi shortly after their arrival. The remaining women were parceled out to French settlements such as New Orleans, Mobile and Biloxi.

The Company of the Indies, the John Law concern that was formerly known as the Company of the West, has continued to bring prostitutes, murderers, thieves and other undesirables to the Louisiana colony despite protests from Governor Bienville. Some have been put on board vessels in chains. Male colonists, however, keep demanding wives. Although Bienville has complained about the sending of convicts to the colony, he has repeatedly asked for wives for his colonists, particularly the Canadian soldiers here. In one of his letters, he pleaded, "Send me wives for my Canadians. They are running in the woods after Indian girls."

New Franklin venue

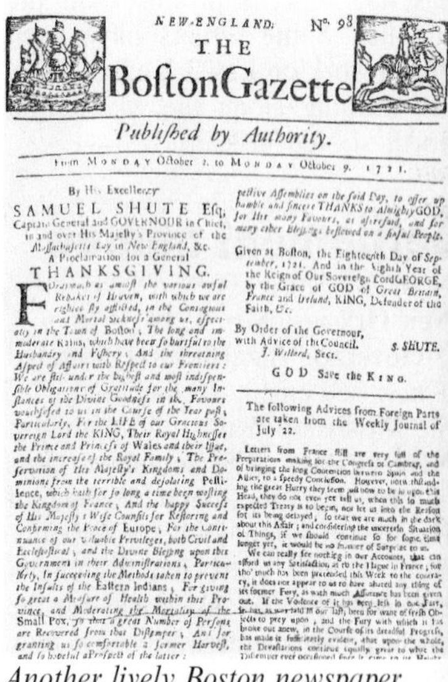

NEW-ENGLAND. No. 98

THE Boston Gazette

Published by Authority.

From MONDAY October 2. to MONDAY October 9. 1721.

By His Excellency SAMUEL SHUTE Esq; Captain General and GOVERNOUR in Chief, in and over His Majesty's Province of the *Massachusetts Bay in New England*, &c.

A Proclamation for a General THANKSGIVING.

FOrasmuch as amidst the various awful Rebukes of Heaven, with which we are righteously afflicted, in the Contagious and Mortal Sickness among us, especially in the Town of Boston; The long and immoderate Rains, which have been so hurtful to the Husbandry and Fishery; And the threatning Aspect of Affairs with Respect to our Frontiers: We are still under the highest and most indispensible Obligations of Gratitude for the many Instances of the Divine Goodness in the Favours vouchsafed to us in the Course of the Year past; Particularly, For the LIFE of our Gracious Sovereign Lord the KING, Their Royal Highnesses the Prince and Princess of Wales and their Issue, and the increase of the Royal Family; The Preservation of His Majesty's Kingdoms and Dominions from the terrible and desolating Pestilence, which hath for so long a time been wasting the Kingdom of France; And the happy Success of His Majesty's Wise Counsils for Restoring and Confirming the Peace of Europe; For the Continuance of our valuable Privileges, both Civil and Ecclesiastical; and the Divine Blessing upon their Government in their Administrations; Particularly, In succeeding the Methods taken to prevent the Insults of the Eastern Indians; For giving so great a Measure of Health within this Province, and Moderating the Mortality of the Small Pox, [illegible] a great Number of Persons are Recovered from that Distemper; And for granting us so comfortable a former Harvest, and so hopeful a Prospect of the latter: [illegible] respective Assemblies on the said Day, to offer up humble and sincere THANKS to Almighty GOD, for His many Favours, as aforesaid, and for many other Blessings bestowed on a sinful People.

Given at Boston, the Eighteenth Day of September, 1721. And in the Eighth Year of the Reign of Our Sovereign Lord GEORGE, by the Grace of GOD of Great Britain, France and Ireland, KING, Defender of the Faith, &c.

By Order of the Governour, with Advice of the Council. J. Willard, Secr. S. SHUTE.

GOD Save the KING.

The following Advices from Foreign Parts are taken from the Weekly Journal of July 22.

Letters from France still are very full of the Preparations making for the Congress of Cambray, and of bringing the long Contention between Spain and the Allies, to a speedy Conclusion. However, notwithstanding the great Hurry they seem just now to be in upon this Head, they do not even yet tell us, when this so much expected Treaty is to begin, nor let us into the Reason for its being delayed, so that we are much in the dark about this Affair; and considering the uncertain Situation of Things, if we should continue so for some time longer yet, it would be no Matter of Surprize to us.

We can really see nothing in our Accounts, that can afford us any Satisfaction, as to the Plague in France; for tho' much has been pretended this Week to the contrary, it does not appear to us to have abated any thing of its former Fury, as with much Assurance has been given out. If the Violence of it has been less in one Part, it has, as we told in our last, been for want of fresh Objects to prey upon, and the Fury with which it has broke out anew, in the Course of its dreadful Progress, has made it sufficiently evident, that upon the whole, the Devastations continue equally great to what the Distemper ever occasioned [illegible]

Another lively Boston newspaper.

Philadelphia, Oct. 1723

Benjamin Franklin, 17-year-old former publisher of the *New England Courant*, an irreverent weekly, moved here early this month. Franklin left Boston after a long quarrel, culminating in fisticuffs, with his older half-brother, James, former publisher of the *Courant*. Benjamin succeeded his brother when the latter was imprisoned and then was forced to stop publishing because of his repeated criticism of the royal Governor. The satirical essays of the younger Franklin, written under the pseudonym Silence Dogood, were a delight to the readers, and the paper thrived under his stewardship.

hree of Yale clergy ecome Anglicans

ew Haven, Oct. 23, 1722

The colony was shocked today y the news that three of its most istinguished divines have taken or-ers in the Church of England. The hree are Timothy Cutler, late rec-or of Yale College; Daniel Brown, he tutor in the college, and Samuel ohnson. On September 13, they net with several Congregational ninisters to discuss their problems. The colloquy, which was called by he Governor after the three admit-ed their doubts to the trustees, ailed to convince them of their er-ors. The three men sailed short-y afterward for England, where hey were ordained.

How to sing psalms

oston, 1721

Three books recently published ere point up a growing disagree-nent over the right way to sing salms. The books are *The Rea-onableness of Regular Singing or, Singing by Note*, by the Rev. Thom-s Symmes, *An Introduction to the Singing of PsalmTunes*, by the Rev. ohn Tufts, and *The Grounds and Rules of Musick Explained*, by the Rev. Thomas Walter, the first mus-cal book printed in America that as bar lines. Each defends tradi-ional note-reading against the rise f "lining-out," or the singing of a ine by ear after it has first been ung by a "presenter."

Triangular trade is thriving, from molasses to rum to slaves

Boston, 1720

American ingenuity has developed a clever way of redressing the unfavorable balance of trade with England. In New England, it is known as "three-cornered trade," "the round about" or, most commonly, "triangular trade." The method works like this: New Englanders need a lot of what Britain manufactures, such as hardware, furniture, guns, farm tools and textiles. But the colonists are forbidden by English law to sell their surpluses, such as fish and meats in English markets. To get around this, a ship will leave Boston or Philadelphia carrying tobacco or lumber to Lisbon or Cadiz, exchange the cargo for European goods, and these are traded, in turn, for molasses, sugar and silver in the West Indies.

There are many variations on this pattern. A brigantine, for instance, will leave Newport with a cargo of rum and iron, sail to Africa and trade that cargo for slaves, then transport the slaves to Barbados, where they are exchanged for molasses and sugar, then proceed home. The triangular trade in slaves has soared since Parliament rescinded the monopoly once held by the Royal African Company. The colonists have also become more competitive with European countries; New England rum, for example, has nearly displaced French brandy.

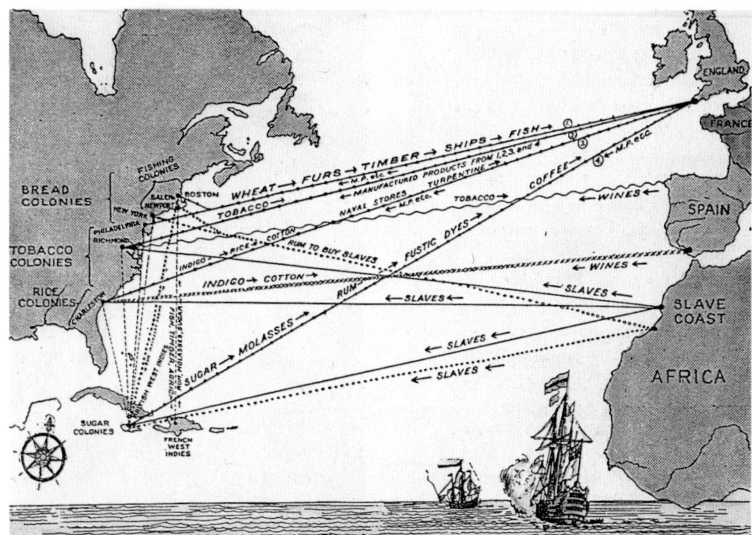

Triangular route of trade: bringing prosperity despite British restrictions.

Indians massacred in war between French and English settlers

Norridgewock, Me., Aug. 23, 1724

Captain Jeremiah Moultan and 80 men attacked the Abnaki Indian village here, and the Indians who fled were slaughtered as they crossed the Kennebec River. Seven chiefs and the Jesuit missionary Sebastian Rasles were killed in the fight but the English lost only two men and one Mohawk Indian ally.

The battle caps a series of conflicts along the border between English and French settlers begun by the French governors of Canada to obstruct English designs on the area. The French encouraged the Abnaki Indians to strike at colonial settlements along the border. The Americans replied with raids that wiped out Jesuit missions on the Kennebec, sending the Indians deep into the forest.

The series of battles has acquired the name "Dummer's War" after Acting Governor William Dummer of Massachusetts, the region in dispute.

London, 1722. *Minted in England by William Wood, the Rosa Americana two-pence copper coin has gained only light circulation in the colonies.*

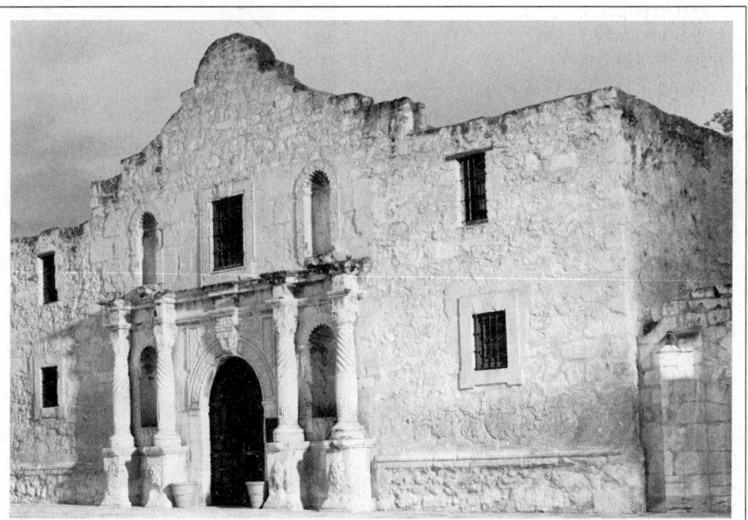

New Spain, 1722. *Priests at the church [The Alamo] at the mission of San Antonio de Valero are seeking converts among Coahuiltecan Indians.*

1725 (1725-1729)

Williamsburg, Virginia, 1725. First Church of Colored Baptists established.

New York City, 1725. William Bradford founds *New York Gazette,* first newspaper in city.

Neshaminy, Pennsylvania, 1726. William Tennent, Presbyterian minister from Ireland, founds Log College, emphasizing revivalism.

Virginia, 1726. Morgan Morgan of Delaware builds a cabin in Berkeley County [becoming first white man to settle in West Virginia].

New Orleans, Aug. 6, 1727. French Ursuline nuns arrive to set up first Catholic charitable institutions in America [an orphanage, a girl's school and a hospital].

Northern Plains, 1727. Sieur de La Perriere and Jesuits found Fort Beauharnois on Lake Pepin [first mission in Minnesota].

Philadelphia, 1727. Christ Church, modeled after classical Greek architecture, completed.

Philadelphia, 1728. John Bartram opens first botanical garden in colonies.

Boston, 1728. City bans horses and carriages on Boston Common, turning park into fashionable setting for late-afternoon promenades.

Northampton, Connecticut, Feb. 11, 1729. Jonathan Edwards takes over church after death of his grandfather Solomon Stoddard.

North Carolina, May 25, 1729. Province becomes a royal colony.

Philadelphia, 1729. Mob breaks into mayor's garden and destroys plants to protest deteriorating economic conditions.

Boston, 1729. Old South Meeting House is built by master mason Joshua Blanchard to replace initial 1670 building.

Philadelphia, 1729. American Presbyterians adopt their first constitution.

Philadelphia, 1729. Benjamin Franklin buys year-old *Universal Instructor in All Arts and Sciences and Pennsylvania Gazette,* and continues it as *Pennsylvania Gazette*.

DEATH

Massachusetts, Feb. 13, 1728. Cotton Mather, Puritan theologian, scientist and prolific writer (*Feb. 12, 1663).

George I of England dies; George II reigns

George I, by Sir Godfrey Kneller.

George II, by Charles Jervas.

London, June 12, 1727

Following the news that King George I died yesterday in Hanover at the age of 67, his son, George Augustus, has been proclaimed King. He will reign as George II.

There is little evidence of public grief at the passing of the King. Boorish and unable to speak a word of English, he was more interested in the affairs of his native Hanover, of which he was Elector, than he was in English activities. He succeeded Queen Anne in August 1714 as a result of the Act of Settlement of 1701, which kept Roman Catholics from the throne.

The King's lack of interest in English affairs, except if they could be influenced for the benefit of Hanover, has greatly increased the power amassed by his ministers, notably Sir Robert Walpole, who has developed his position into that of Prime Minister.

The King's wife, Sophia Dorothea, whom he divorced for adultery in 1694, died last year after spending 32 years confined to a castle in northern Germany. Her son was forbidden to visit her.

The new King was born in Herrenhausen, Hanover, on October 30, 1683. He is married to Caroline of Anspach and they have three sons and five daughters.

Rhode Island, 1729. *John Smibert came here with British philosopher George Berkeley, hoping to teach at his Indian school. Instead, he has become a painter; above is his "Dean George Berkeley and His Entourage."*

Indian scalps sold in New Hampshire

Pigwacket, N.H., May 8, 1725

Captain John Lovewell, an Indi- an hunter, and his men paraded 1[illegible] scalps atop poles in Dover las[illegible] February. They left town 1,00[illegible] pounds richer, the first men t[illegible] capitalize on the 100-pounds-per scalp bounty that has been offere[illegible] by England. Yesterday, Lovewel[illegible] led another hunt for Pigwacket Indians near Ossippe Lake. But thi[illegible] time, Chief Paugus and his warrior[illegible] surprised them. Outnumbering th[illegible] frontiersmen nearly two to one, th[illegible] Indians surrounded the Lovewel[illegible] encampment and avenged the scalpings. After a brutal encounter Lovewell, many of his men as wel[illegible] as Chief Paugus were dead in a se[illegible] of blood.

Ben Franklin starts a philosophy club

Philadelphia, June 1729

Two months ago, an anonymou[illegible] essay titled *A Modest Enquiry int[illegible] the Nature and Necessity of a Pape[illegible] Currency* was published. The essay it turns out, was written b[illegible] Benjamin Franklin and endorse[illegible] by his philosophy club, the Junto This "cry among the people fo[illegible] more paper money," as Frankli[illegible] puts it, is one of the many project[illegible] the group has explored.

The Junto was formed two year[illegible] ago by Franklin for "the sincer[illegible] enquiry after truth," based on [illegible] model by the Rev. Cotton Mathe[illegible] and on various drinking clubs tha[illegible] Franklin is known to attend. Eac[illegible] of the members – all astute cit[illegible] men – writes an essay for discussion on such topics as morals, politics or philosophy. He calls it th[illegible] colony's best philosophy school.

The club's main rule bars the us[illegible] of dogmatic remarks. Members fee[illegible] this provision fosters open-minde[illegible] debate. Franklin says the law prevents members from "disgustin[illegible] each other." One requirement fo[illegible] membership is an affirmative answer to the question: Do you lov[illegible] mankind in general?

Word is out that the Junto's civic-minded goals include creation o[illegible] a system for easy access to book[illegible] and a volunteer team to fight fires.

Anglo-Spanish War spreads to America

Florida, March 9, 1728

In yet another flare-up of the ong-simmering rivalry between English and Spanish settlements on he American continent, a party of Carolinians has attacked a Yamassee village near St. Augustine, Florida. Since the Yamassees, once friendly to the English colonists, have recently become allies of the Spanish, the attack is being construed as an extension of the recent outbreak in Europe of war between Spain and England.

This is by no means the first time that St. Augustine, a major port that was founded by Pedro Menendez de Aviles in 1565, has been the target of an English attack. The city was sacked and then burned by Sir Francis Drake in 1586 and again by Captain John Davis in 1665. In this century, it was attacked, though not successfully, by Carolinians in 1702, in the early days of Queen Anne's War.

Further outbreaks of fighting between the English and Spanish colonists in the region can be expected, although it is not likely that there will be any major battles.

This applies to Europe, too. Although the Spanish siege of Gibraltar continues, in clear violation of the Treaty of Utrecht, no alliances between the other major powers have been drawn up, and the conflict is not expected to spread.

"Casket girls" sent from France to wed

New Orleans, 1728

The young women take daily walks through the city while the men gather in the streets to admire them. But they are chaperoned by Ursuline nuns. These women, mostly in their teens, are the first females of good character sent from France to marry colonists. They are called "casket girls" or the "filles a la cassette," because they arrived carrying small chests containing their trousseaus. In previous years, most of those transported to marry the colonists were prostitutes and the homeless. The newly arrived women are from middle class families and have been educated, according to their sponsors. French authorities say the previous female immigrants must be replaced by respectable wives and mothers if the colony is going to be able to grow and become an asset to France.

Natchez Indians kill nearly 300 French

An increasingly familiar sight on the frontier: Indians in war council.

Natchez, Nov. 28, 1729

A bloody massacre took place at Fort Rosalie today. Natchez Indians killed most of the 300 French soldiers and settlers at the fort and took the surviving women and children to be sold as slaves.

The massacre was the most vicious attack in the history of the Louisiana colony. It was triggered by the demand of a Canadian military captain that the Natchez give up their sacred burial ground and temple. Captain Chepard planned to use the site of the cemetery and temple as part of a plantation.

Today, the Indians had no sooner entered the fort and its grounds than they quickly opened fire, mowing down everyone in sight, setlers as well as soldiers. Captain Chepard was put to death on the orders of the Sun Chief, leader of the Natchez. He summoned his aide Snake, who proceeded to club Captain Chepard to death.

Relations between French settlers and Indians in this area have been hostile ever since the fort was constructed in 1716 (→Dec. 1730).

A true way to do songs of the Lord

New Haven, 1728

Regular Singing Defended, by the Rev. Nathaniel Chauncey, is the most recent of a spate of books inspired by New England's psalm-singing controversy. It attempts to prove that "regular singing" (by note) is "the only TRUE WAY of Singing the SONGS of the LORD; by Arguments both from Reason and Scripture." At issue is the practice of "lining-out," which is being increasingly embraced by country congregations. Since most country folk can't read music, they can sing only after a "presenter" has first sung a particular line, or "lined-it" out. Unencumbered by any printed notes, the singers take great liberties with their response, embellishing the music to suit their own tastes – and giving the traditionalists something to cluck about.

Maryland town named Baltimore in honor of founding family

Annapolis, Maryland, Aug. 8, 1729

Landholders Daniel and Charles Carroll have united with other leading tobacco growers to ask the assembly to establish a town on the north side of the Patapsco River above Chesapeake Bay. The town will be named Baltimore in honor of the Lords Baltimore, Barons of England. George Calvert, the first Baron, was active in the Virginia Company as well as in the founding of Maryland. It was he who procured a royal charter for the colony under the name "Avalon." At one point, Baltimore was prohibited from bringing colonists to the Chesapeake Bay region because he and his followers were Roman Catholic. Later, however, a new "cession" was obtained from the crown and the Catholics were permitted to emigrate. The colony was actually established on June 20, 1692, by a son of Baltimore, Cecil Calvert, the second Baron.

The third Baron, proprietor as of 1675, was Charles Calvert. Anti-Catholic feeling was strong in England and America during his life, and he was forced to defend himself against the hostility of the Protestant majority as well as the encroachments of William Penn, the Quaker, to the north.

Maryland's new port city is named after the Calvert family's Irish estate.

1730 (1730-1734)

Newport, Rhode Island, 1730. George Berkeley, Irish-born philosopher and Anglican bishop who recently arrived in colonies, founds Literary and Philosophical Society.

America, 1730. Daniel Cox becomes first appointed grand master of Masons in America.

America, 1730. Total population in British colonies reaches 655,000; Boston has 13,000; New York, 8,500; Philadelphia, 8,500, and Charleston, 4,000.

Pennsylvania, 1730. Ben Franklin publishes *Ephrata Hymnbook*, with tunes of Johann Conrad Beissel, and *A Witch Trial at Mount Holly*, satirizing superstition of witchcraft.

Louisiana, Jan. 23, 1731. John Law, ruined by bursting of "Mississippi Bubble" in 1720, gives up Company of the West charter; trade rights pass to French crown.

Boston, Dec. 30, 1731. Newspaper records *A Concert of Music on Sundry Instruments*, run by Peter Pelham, engraver, dancing master, keeper of boarding school and tobacco retailer [First known concert in colonies].

Philadelphia, Feb. 26, 1732. Mass celebrated for first time at St. Joseph's, only public Catholic church in colonies.

Philadelphia, May 1732. *Philadelphia Zeitung*, first foreign-language newspaper in British colonies, is published by Ben Franklin.

New York City, Dec. 6, 1732. Farquhar's play *The Recruiting Officer* performed in first theater in city; Governor's barber plays leading role.

Philadelphia, 1732. Quakers found first known publicly funded almshouse in colonies.

New York City, Dec. 17, 1733. Peter Zenger's *New York Weekly Journal*, founded last month, prints article criticizing Governor Cosby (→Nov. 11, 1734).

America, 1733. New York City and Philadelphia are struck by first major influenza epidemic in colonies.

Philadelphia, 1734. Ben Franklin, in *Poor Richard's Almanac*, observes, "Where there's marriage without love, there will be love without marriage."

Midwest, 1734. French families settle on Wabash River at Vincennes [first permanent settlement in Indiana].

Oglethorpe arrives with 130 settlers

Charleston, S.C., Jan. 13, 1733

Thirty-five families arrived in Charleston harbor today to found a unique colony in America. Led by James Edward Oglethorpe, a member of Parliament, the colonists include many people released from debtor's prison. Oglethorpe, a leader in prison reform, promoted the colony to help "the industrious yet unfortunate poor." He plans to call the colony Georgia in honor or King George II.

Leading citizens in England and many churches collected money to help found the colony. There are 130 settlers. Besides the English, there are German and Swiss Protestants fleeing persecution. Oglethorpe said he will select a site along the Savannah River on the coast south of Charleston.

Unlike many immigrants, these colonists had a pleasant two-month voyage. They said that their boat was crowded, but that they had plenty of food and plenty of beer. Oglethorpe said the settlers will be given land, seeds and tools. He hopes they will be able to produce silk and wine for the export trade. The settlers will grow mulberry trees providing leaves for silkworms to eat. Colonists will not be allowed to own slaves, and the use of rum is going to be prohibited.

Oglethorpe, an Oxford-educated member of Parliament, arrives in America.

In Oglethorpe's vision, Georgia is a haven in which the poor can build anew.

Religious revival starts in Massachusetts

Northampton, Massachusetts, 1734

There are reports out of the wilderness that a religious renewal is occurring in Northampton. Under the pastorship of the Rev. Jonathan Edwards, grandson of the late Solomon Stoddard, there appears to be a refreshening of religious interest and activity. From these reports, it seems that Edwards is following in the footsteps of his grandfather, who presided over several religious freshenings in the colony's backwoods. Edwards states that the revival had its beginnings last year when the young people began to improve their manner while at religious services and became increasingly heedful of pastoral advice. This attitude spread throughout the population and a sermon dealing with "justification by faith alone," along with the conversion of a woman of questionable morals, seems to have increased their religious concern (→Aug. 1739).

Edwards, Puritan rationalist.

French seize chief of Natchez Indians

Louisiana, Dec. 1730

Troops led by Governor Etienne de Perier have captured the Sun Chief of the Natchez Indians in a battle north of Fort Rosalie. The attack on the Indians' new encampment was in retribution for last year's massacre at Fort Rosalie. Several hundred Natchez women and children and some warriors were captured and enslaved along with the chieftain. Hundreds of Indian fighters escaped, however. The Perier forces included regular soldiers, militia and Choctaw Indians, rivals of the Natchez. The Perier troops attacked Fort Rosalie in February, but the Natchez held out in the fort for three weeks before escaping across the Mississippi River to another encampment.

ditor imprisoned for libeling Governor

ew York City, Nov. 11, 1734

Peter Zenger, publisher of the *ew York Weekly Journal*, was ar-ested today on a warrant for sedi-ous libel. The warrant was issued y the executive council of the royal iovernor, William Cosby, after a rand jury refused to issue an in-ictment. Zenger is accused of libel-ng the Governor himself, and at ssue is the freedom of a newspaper o criticize an official. Zenger, a ierman-born printer, is a former pprentice and partner of William Bradford, the first printer in the ity and publisher of the pro-gov-rnment paper *New York Weekly iazette*. Zenger's journal is fi-nanced with the help of lawyer ames Alexander and other sup-orters of Lewis Morris. Zenger rinted reports backing the Morris eform plans. It is believed that a tory on a recent assembly election n Eastchester provoked the Gov-rnor. Recently, Lewis Morris was fired by Cosby from his post as Chief Justice. James de Lancy, his successor, is expected to make jus-tice painful for Zenger and Morris's supporters (→Aug. 5, 1735).

Zenger's journal burned on Wall St.

Big success for "Poor Richard's Almanac"

Philadelphia, Oct. 1732

The inaugural issue of *Poor Richard's Almanac* this month has captured the public's fancy; the first print run sold out. Readers enlightened by the wisdom of the almanac's putative publisher, the indigent scholar Richard Saunders, and amused by the carping of his wife, Bridget, will be surprised to learn that the almanac is actually the handiwork of Benjamin Franklin, editor of the *Pennsylvania Gazette*. In his new almanac, Franklin freely spices his forecasts with moral instruction. Indeed, the pithy maxims that accompany his meteorological predictions are the pamphlet's most distinctive feature. "Poor Richard" holds that thrift and industry lead to wealth and virtue, and though the destitute and lackadaisical Saunders hardly practices what he preaches, readers are thoroughly entertained by the advice he is offering them.

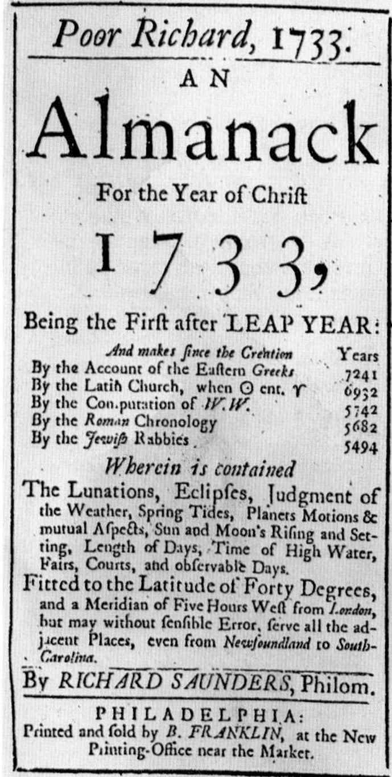

Poor Richard, 1733.

AN

Almanack

For the Year of Chrift

1733,

Being the Firft after LEAP YEAR:

And makes fince the Creation	Years
By the Account of the Eaftern *Greeks*	7241
By the Latin Church, when ☉ ent. ♈	6932
By the Computation of *W.W.*	5742
By the *Roman* Chronology	5682
By the *Jewifh* Rabbies	5494

Wherein is contained

The Lunations, Eclipfes, Judgment of the Weather, Spring Tides, Planets Motions & mutual Afpects, Sun and Moon's Rifing and Setting, Length of Days, Time of High Water, Fairs, Courts, and obfervable Days.

Fitted to the Latitude of Forty Degrees, and a Meridian of Five Hours Weft from *London*, but may without fenfible Error, ferve all the adjacent Places, even from *Newfoundland* to *South-Carolina*.

By *RICHARD SAUNDERS*, Philom.

PHILADELPHIA:

Printed and fold by *B. FRANKLIN*, at the New Printing-Office near the Market.

Title page of Franklin's almanac.

irst stagecoach line opens in New Jersey

ew Jersey, March 1732

An advertisement in *Mercury* ignals that the wheels of progress re spinning in New Jersey. It says: Gentlemen, Merchants, Trades-nen and Travellers, Solomon Smith and James Moore keepth two tage wagons intending to go from Burlington to Amboy and back." This marks the start of the first regularly scheduled public stage-coach line. The line links two port cities, since passengers can travel by boat from Amboy to New York and from Burlington to Philadelphia. Some citizens feel the eight-mile-per-hour speed of the coaches makes them a hazard on the roads.

Manhattan lot to become a bowling green

New York City, 1732

The vacant lot just north of the fort is about to be turned into a green for the enjoyment of nine-pin bowling. Residents of lower Broadway's mansions are planning to transform this "dirty spot" into one suitable for the popular Dutch game. Inhabitants of the area such as John Chambers, John Bayard and Peter Jay have leased the spot from the city for the sum of one peppercorn per year. Legend has it that the lot is on the site where Peter Minuit struck the deal that gave the Dutch Manhattan. From 1638 to 1647, it was the site of the hog and cow market in the Markveldt. Later, it was a parade ground for Dutch militiamen. In recent years, the expanse has not been maintained, to the annoyance of its neighbors. The residents say this will be the city's first park.

aws restrict trade to protect the British

1 hat maker, hampered by London.

London, 1732

Responding to pressure from the British hat makers and other interest groups, Parliament has passed a law that prohibits the export of American-made hats to England. The legislation also attempts to limit local production by allowing colonial hat makers to have no more than two apprentices. To the British, the act is a reasonable response to the unfair advantage enjoyed by American hat makers, who are close to an abundant supply of beaver fur, essential for making felt. To the colonists, the law is seen as yet another example of the unfair operation of the so-called mercantile system, which all too often seems to work to the advantage of the mother country only (→1750).

Rich pick Newport

Newport, Rhode Island, Dec. 1730

As the year draws to a close, Newport finds itself a bustling port of more than 4,500 residents. Some families – the Champlins, the Vernons and the Wantons – are particularly well off. The source of their good fortune? The slave trade. For a decade or more, the business has been growing steadily. Ships that average 100 tons sail to West Africa, acquire 75 to 150 slaves (low numbers limit the spread of disease), transport the slaves to the West Indies and sell them there for rum. The ship owners then sell their cargo of rum to thirsty New Englanders for a handsome profit.

"De Peyster Boy With a Deer" (1730) by an unknown artist. Also in 1730, John Smibert, known in Boston, showed his paintings publicly, a first in the colonies.

1735 (1735-1739)

Charleston, South Carolina, Feb. 18, 1735. *Flora, or Hob in the Well* is first known opera performed in colonies.

Georgia, 1735. Colonists establish town of Augusta, a trading post on the Savannah River.

New York, 1735. John van Zandt cleared after whipping slave to death; coroner's jury rules: "Correction given by the master was not the cause of his death, but that it was by the visitation of God."

Boston, 1735. First colonial medical society founded.

Upper Louisiana, 1735. St. Genevieve established on Mississippi River [oldest permanent settlement in Missouri].

New York City, Jan. 1736. Karl Theodor Pachelbel, son of renowned composer-organist, gives harpsichord recital at Todd's Tavern, becoming first notable European musician to perform in colonies.

Virginia, 1736. William Byrd II, in a remark directed at Puritan hypocrisy, charges that "the Saints of New England" import so many Negroes into Virginia that "the Colony will some time or other be Confirmed by the name of New Guinea."

Boston, March 17, 1737. Charitable Irish Society holds first municipal (as opposed to purely religious) celebration of St. Patrick's Day.

Simsbury, Connecticut, 1737. John Higley mints first copper coins in colonies, inscribed with words "I am good copper" and "Value me as you will."

New York City, 1737. Jews are denied right to vote in assembly elections.

Cambridge, 1738. Isaac Greenwood, one of first colonial science teachers, ends his career at Harvard; he is succeeded by John Winthrop, now the most important scientist in America next to Ben Franklin.

Northern Plains, 1738. Pierre de la Verendrye visits Mandan Indians [on Missouri River, becoming first white man to enter North Dakota] (→ March 30, 1743).

Louisiana, 1739. Governor Bienville and 1,200 French troops force the Chickasaw Indians to agree to permanent peace treaty.

Philadelphia, 1739. Ben Franklin writes in *Poor Richard's Almanac,* "He that falls in love with himself will have no rivals."

Wesley arrives to preach Methodism

Georgia, Feb. 1737

The Rev. John Wesley arrived in the colony this month to take over the position of chaplain. The colony, which has been without a chaplain for the past few months, cannot but welcome this event. Wesley, along with his brother, Charles, was one of the more active members in Oxford's Holy Club, the purpose of which was an improvement in the Church of England through a more rigid attention to the sacraments. Wesley is well known for the punctiliousness of his approach to religion, an approach that is called Methodism.

Wesley (1766) by Nathaniel Hone.

Press freedom upheld

Standing up for freedom of the press: Andrew Hamilton defends Zenger.

New York City, Aug. 5, 1735

The printer Peter Zenger has been released from prison after a jury found him not guilty of seditious libel against Governor William Cosby. Zenger had been in jail for nearly 10 months after opening the columns of his *New York Weekly Journal* to Lewis Morris's criticism of Cosby, who took Zenger to court for false and scandalous libel. The government tried hard to keep Zenger in jail: Chief Justice James de Lancy disbarred several lawyers to prevent Zenger from getting legal help. Andrew Hamilton, a veteran Philadelphia lawyer, led the defense. He persuaded the jury that it, not the judges, should decide the question of truth in the case, not simply the fact of printing. Hamilton presented the radical defense that the articles told the truth and that truth should be a defense against libel. Hamilton argued that the "cause of English liberty is at stake," not merely the liberty of a poor printer. He used Zenger as a symbol of the right to criticize government, saying that nature and the laws of our country have given us as a right "the liberty of exposing and opposing arbitrary power . . . by speaking and writing the truth."

George Whitefield spreads Great Awakening along East Coast

Philadelphia, Aug. 1739

The itinerant preacher and colleague of the Wesley brothers, the Rev. George Whitefield, has been active in his preaching along the Atlantic seaboard. While the purpose of Whitefield's tour is to raise money for the orphanage in Bethesda, Georgia, the result has been to increase the religious feelings of many. This is the second trip to the colonies by the minister and the first since he was ordained. His speaking abilities would be the envy of any actor, and his pamphlets are already quite popular. Still, he is not without his detractors. Some condemn the irregular nature of his meetings, many held outdoors and without the permission of local pastors. Whitefield also attracts opposition because of his frequent attacks on what he terms "unconverted ministers," whom he blames for the religious failings of the people. Whitefield's followers are hoping the recent trip, which brought him to Philadelphia from Savannah and is to take him to New York, will soon be followed by one into the provinces of New England (→ 1743).

Whitefield, of the Wesley brothers' Oxford Holy Club, spreads the Word.

Britain vs. Spain in War of Jenkins' Ear

London, Oct. 1739

With the wry comment, "They now ring the bells, but they will soon wring their hands," Sir Robert Walpole has been reluctantly swept along by the tide of bellicose fervor that has carried this country into war with Spain.

Contributing to the war fever was the appearance, on March 17 of last year, of Captain Jenkins before the House of Commons. Jenkins, master of the Rebecca, told how his ship had been boarded in the West Indies eight years ago by Spanish coast guards, who cut off one of his ears. Although few doubt that Jenkins was a smuggler, and violating the Asiento Contract, which limits English trade with the Spanish colonies to one ship a year, he was given a more than sympathetic hearing by the House. His response, when asked what he was thinking when he was about to have his ear cut off – "I committed my soul to God and my cause to my Country" – was particularly well received.

Causes of a more serious nature underlie the conflict. Fear of seeing Europe dominated by an alliance between France and Spain is one, and territorial conflict in America is another. As for these disputes, Spain is known to resent the recent founding by General James Oglethorpe of the colony of Georgia, which it regards as a threat to its own settlements in Florida.

First Moravian collective in Savannah

Indians hear the Moravian gospel, after a painting by Christian Schussele.

Savannah, Georgia, Apr. 6, 1735

The first group of Moravians invited by General James Oglethorpe to settle in the colony arrived today. It is expected that they will leave their ship within the next day or two. The Moravians, or Unitas Fratrum as they call themselves, are a religious body that dates its founding to the time of Jan Hus in the 15th century. The Moravians are widely admired for their piety and simplicity of life. They have suffered much persecution at the hands of Catholics, who nearly exterminated the movement in its homeland of Moravia and Bohemia. The group was reconstituted through the efforts of Christian David and it owes its current good fortune to the power and authority of Count Nikolaus von Zinzendorf, who protected the Moravians on his estates in Saxony.

The present group of 10 males under the leadership of Augustus Gottlieb Spangenberg, John Toltschig and Anton Siefert arrived in January of this year in London and was widely and well received. The Moravians sailed from England in February and are to take up residence on land that was allocated to them by the trustees. From there, it is anticipated that they will start religious work among the Indians. It is being widely assumed that they will improve the atmosphere of a colony that is already dedicated to piety and good works (→ 1741).

Slaves revolt; many die

Human bondage breeds revolt.

Charleston, S.C., Sept. 9, 1739

A series of slave revolts has jolted South Carolina, leaving dozens dead at Charleston, Stono River and Berkeley County. Local people charge that the rebellions were incited by Spanish missionaries who created among the slaves a false expectation of delivery from bondage.

The Charleston insurrection began when a group of Negroes set out for St. Augustine and freedom, killing all whites they met on the way. They were quickly surrounded and the entire group was massacred. The death toll is 21 whites and 44 Negroes. A similar revolt occurred near the Stono River when a slave named Cato led a large group of Negroes against whites. Before the Stono Rebellion could be put down, 30 whites and a larger number of Negroes were dead. Yet another revolt took place in Berkeley County at St. John's Parish.

A 1715 census showed that of all the colonies South Carolina had the second largest number of slaves, after Virginia, and the largest percentage of Negroes in the population, up to 60 percent. South Carolina has had serious problems with so-called Maroons, escaped slaves, and has offered large rewards for their capture. Many slaves have sought to reach Spanish lands because of a 1733 Spanish decree stating that escaped slaves from the North will be considered free (→ Jan. 1740).

Hundreds of gloves given away at funeral

Boston, Feb. 22, 1738

In the ostentatious sorrow so much in style of late, the noted merchant Peter Faneuil arranged a lavish funeral cortege today for his lamented uncle Andrew Faneuil. The procession was led by the coffin, richly encased and drawn by two black horses. More than 1,000 mourners followed, and many were given gloves to suit the occasion. Since 1721, the general court has repeatedly issued laws prohibiting "extraordinary" funeral expenses, fearing that the poor will emulate the rich in funeral displays.

French explorers trek across Great Plains

Colorado, Spring 1739

After an exhausting nine-month, journey of 2,000 miles across the Great Plains, Pierre and Paul Mallet and their party have arrived in New Orleans. These hardy French explorers left their outpost on the Missouri River earlier this spring. From there, the adventurers traveled northward up the Missouri, then to the west on the Platte River across the vast, unknown area that the Spanish gave the name Great Plains. After a few rugged months that were filled with dangerous Indian encounters, droughts and snowstorms, the Mallet brothers arrived at the Spanish outpost of Santa Fe. After the French explorers were reprovisioned, they followed the Canadian River eastward to its end at the Arkansas River, then headed down the Mississippi River and into New Orleans.

While the Mallet expedition was on the westernmost headwaters of the Platte, it discovered a mighty range of high, rugged mountains that the Indians call the Rockies. Since this great chain does not appear on any of the current charts or maps, it is likely that the Mallets were the first Europeans to come upon it.

1740 (1740-1744)

Charleston, Jan. 1740. Some 50 slaves hanged after exposure of insurrection plans.

Florida, Jan. 1740. Governor Oglethorpe, taking advantage of protection from friendly Indians, invades Florida, capturing Forts Picolata and San Francisco de Pupo (→ March 1743).

New Jersey, July 30, 1740. Caspar Wistar opens a glass factory with Belgian glassblowers.

Charleston, Nov. 18, 1740. Fire destroys half of city.

Europe, Dec. 16, 1740. Frederick II of Prussia invades Silesia, launching war on the continent.

London, 1740. Parliament passes law allowing naturalization of immigrants to American colonies seven years after arrival; Quakers and Jews exempt from standard oaths.

South Carolina, 1740. Assembly bans teaching slaves to write or hiring them as scribes.

Philadelphia, March 1741. *American Magazine*, founded by Andrew Bradford, discontinued after two-month run as first magazine in colonies.

America, May 1741. Presbyterians split into "New Side" (favoring revivalism) and "Old Side" (favoring doctrinal orthodoxy) (→ 1758).

Bethlehem, Pennsylvania, 1741. Moravians arrive to set up collectivist settlement under Gottlieb Spangenberg (→ 1742).

Boston, Sept. 24, 1742. Faneuil Hall, designed by John Smibert and built by French Huguenots, is opened.

Philadelphia, Nov. 25, 1742. Lutheran pastor Henry Melchior Muhlenberg arrives from Germany (→ Aug. 26, 1748).

Northern Plains, March 30, 1743. Francois and Louis-Joseph de la Verendrye bury an inscribed lead plate [at Fort Pierre, South Dakota], claiming area for France.

New Jersey, 1743. John Woolman, itinerant Quaker clergyman, begins preaching about evils of slavery.

Boston, 1743. Congregationalist Charles Chauncy gives sermon *Seasonable thoughts on the State of Religion in New England,* stressing rationalism over passions of revivalism (→ July 8, 1743).

Lancaster, Pennsylvania, 1744. Iroquois League grants land in Ohio Valley – also claimed by French – to English colonies.

Survivors sail for home

Bering's death on Commander Island, as depicted by C.J.L. Portman.

Alaska, Aug. 9, 1742

Just a year after a member of their crew first set foot in America, the last 31 members of Vitus Bering's expedition began a desperate bid for survival today on a raft made of timbers from their marooned ship, the St. Peter. Since Bering died December 8, Lieutenant Sven Waxel has led them. If the winds hold, Waxel says they may reach Petropavlovsk, Siberia, in 30 days. If they do, the furs they have are sure to interest the promysleniki (Russian entrepreneurs).

Georg Wilhelm Steller, a German naturalist, was the first man to set foot on this land east of Siberia [Alaska]. At his urging, a small crew went ashore on Kayak Island and stayed long enough for Steller to make a few scientific observations. Studying a large jay that had been shot, Steller noted that it was exactly like the jay found on the Atlantic coast of America. Said Steller: "This bird proved to me that we were really in America!" Although Steller could see what he thought was the mainland, Bering refused to stop for fuller exploration.

Bering, a Danish navigator in the service of Russia, discovered the strait off Siberia in 1728. Last year he had two ships built at Petropavlovsk in Kamchatka, explored islands off Alaska and discovered the Aleutian chain. Bad weather forced the crew ashore and Bering, already suffering from scurvy, succumbed.

Philadelphia, 1741. *Builders are finishing the State House [Independence Hall], designed by lawyer Andrew Hamilton, for the colony's government.*

Suspected of arson, 29 slaves executed

New York City, Dec. 31, 1741

A series of suspicious fires has occurred across New York City this year, and many people have linked the arson to Negro slaves, who, it is alleged, were aiming to take control of the city. As a result, 11 Negroes have been burned at the stake and 18 hanged. Four poor whites were also implicated in the crimes and hanged. Now a prosecutor in the case, Daniel Horsemanden, has revealed his conclusion: There was, in fact, no conspiracy. The relations between whites and Negroes in the New York colony have been very tense in recent years. It is estimated that Negroes now make up a fifth of the colony's total population.

Burning slaves at the stake.

An orchestral first

Bethlehem, Pennsylvania, 1742

Moravians who settled in their new Pennsylvania community here last year have lost no time in founding an orchestra, the first in the colonies. This year, one of their first presentations was Handel's *Messiah.* Music comes naturally to the German musicians and has a vital role in the Moravian religion. The sect's leader, Count Nikolaus von Zinzendorf, responsible for their having immigrated to America, has been visiting Moravian settlements in Pennsylvania since last year, trying to unite German Protestant churches (→ May 4, 1746).

Scotch-Irish join in flood of immigration

Georgia Governor James Oglethorpe, in Highland dress, greets Scottish settlers in New Inverness, Georgia.

Philadelphia, 1741

The flow of Scotch-Irish immigrants to the American colonies is starting to look like an exodus, and the renewal of religious persecution in the Irish province of Ulster is probably the cause. Increasingly, Ulster Presbyterians are looking to the colonies as a refuge, and immigration will probably exceed 10,000 a year before this decade is out. The term Scotch-Irish is rather ambiguous. It refers to descendants of Presbyterians from lowland Scotland who were said to have been settled in Northern Ireland in the 17th century to safeguard English Protestant interests there.

"Sinners in the Hands of an Angry God"

Enfield, Connecticut, July 8, 1741

During a visit here, the celebrated minister Jonathan Edwards delivered a most eloquent and engrossing sermon today. The discourse, surprisingly out of character for Edwards, for he rarely delivers imprecatory sermons, was titled *Sinners in the Hands of an Angry God.* The text, Deuteronomy 32:35, reads: "Their foot shall slide in due time."

In the sermon, Edwards explains that we are always in danger of sliding into destruction because of our wicked and evil nature. He says all that preserves us is the mere pleasure of God. But evil men are not to be preserved from their deserved punishment forever, he warns. Divine justice demands that punishment be meted out. Divine power means that there shall be nothing to prevent execution of the sentence. Man can do nothing to avoid the punishment. Divine mercy, the minister argues, has provided a way of salvation.

Mercy resides solely in the promises given in Christ, in the covenant of grace. But they are available only to those who take up the covenant. And here lies the aim of the Edwards sermon, to awaken hearers to the awareness that they must be truly converted to be part of that covenant of grace (→ June 22, 1750).

Oglethorpe strikes Spanish in Florida

Savannah, Georgia, March 1743

General James Oglethorpe, commander of the armed forces in Georgia and South Carolina, has returned from what appears to have been a final, and anticlimactic, sortie against the Spanish in Florida.

With a force of Highland troops, Oglethorpe ventured to the gates of St. Augustine, but the Spanish refused to fight. The response contrasted with their behavior nine months ago when more than 2,000 Spanish soldiers descended upon St. Simons Island.

An English force no greater than a fourth their size thrashed the Spanish soundly at the Battle of Bloody Marsh. Oglethorpe's men killed or captured more than 200 Spaniards as they made their way down a narrow road linking Fort St. Simons and Fort Frederica. The battle, one small skirmish in three years of war between England and Spain, capped 10 years of tension between England's southernmost colony and the Spanish in Florida. In 1739, the Spaniards killed two Highlanders at Amelia Island and in 1740 Oglethorpe retaliated by harassing the Spanish at St. John's River and seizing Forts Picolata and San Francisco de Pupo. He besieged St. Augustine, but Spanish ships broke through with supplies.

At 37, versatile Franklin retires in favor of scientific pursuits

Philadelphia, Jan. 1743

Benjamin Franklin has sold his newspaper, the *Pennsylvania Gazette*; *Poor Richard's Almanac*, the most popular such compilation in the colonies, and the rest of his lucrative printing enterprises to his partner, David Hall, who joined him a year ago. Franklin will continue his affiliation with the business, which will bear the name Franklin and Hall, and it is expected that he will contribute editorial guidance to the *Gazette* as well as articles to *Poor Richard's Almanac.* Although he is currently busy with plans to establish Pennsylvania's first college, Franklin intends to spend the bulk of his time pursuing scientific interests, particularly the study of electricity.

Franklin came to Philadelphia 20 years ago, following a brief stint as the editor of his brother James's newspaper, the *New England Courant.*. He worked in the hire of local printers before he achieved success as the printer-editor of the *Pennsylvania Gazette* in 1729. Greater fame and fortune were to come three years later when he wrote and published his almanac. Its witty, aphoristic inducements to virtue made it an immediate success; its yearly circulation has reached the unprecedented number of 10,000 readers. Two years ago, his *General Magazine and Historical Chronicle* failed after a six-month run. But last year, a pamphlet by Franklin, *Plain Truth*, which told of the city's vulnerability to attack by an outside power, persuaded Philadelphians to raise and outfit their first militia, and it was Franklin's idea to use a lottery to raise the money necessary to support the battery that currently guards the harbor.

Franklin has long been interested in scientific matters. The Franklin stove, which he developed six years ago as a modification of an existing German design, has warmed many colonial homes. And this year, he founded the American Philosophical Society, which is dedicated to the study of botany, chemistry, anthropology, medicine, mathematics and related disciplines.

Although his wit, intellect and popularity obviously qualify him to hold high public office, Franklin has consistently discouraged supporters who have urged him to run for the state assembly, saying that he prefers to devote his time to science.

THE
GENERAL MAGAZINE,
AND
Historical Chronicle,
For all the *British* Plantations in *America.*
[To be Continued Monthly.]

JANUARY, 1741.

ICH DIEN

VOL. I.

PHILADELPHIA:

Franklin's bookshop, by Ferris.

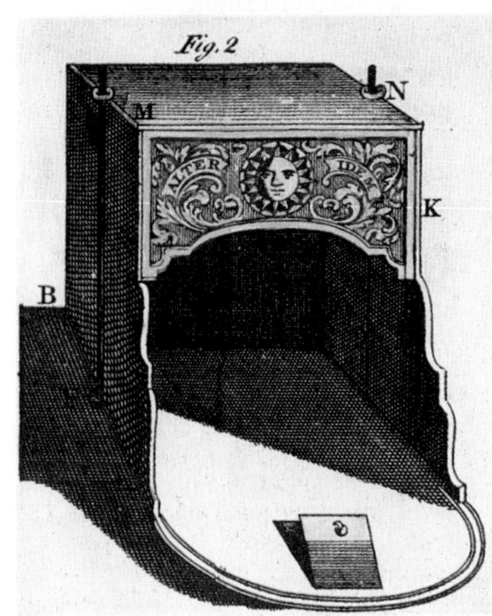

Design for the Franklin stove.

1745 (1745-1749)

Maine, Aug. 1745. French and Indians carry out series of raids on English settlements, launching King George's War.

America, 1745. French philosopher Montesquieu's writings appear in colonial periodicals.

Elizabethtown, New Jersey, Oct. 22, 1746. College of New Jersey founded by splinter group of Presbyterians (→ 1756).

Philadelphia, Sept. 29, 1747. Four ministers and 27 elders convene to organize German Reformed Church.

Boston, 1747. Jonathan Mayhew, now West Church pastor, is one of first New England clergymen to dispute doctrine of Trinity and preach Arminianism (belief in free will, salvation by works) (→ Jan. 30, 1750).

New York City, 1747. New York Bar Association is first legal society in colonies, founded to protect against hostility of Lieutenant Governor Cadwallader Colden.

Ohio Valley, Oct. 20, 1748. Ohio Company expedition under Hugh Parker and Thomas Cresap reaches Ohio territory (→ May 19, 1749).

Boston, 1748. Prayer *Now I Lay Me Down to Sleep* first appears in *New England Primer.*

New Hampshire, Jan. 1, 1749. Governor Wentworth grants land (also claimed by New York) for town of Bennington [Vermont] (→ Oct. 1763).

Ohio Valley, May 19, 1749. Ohio Company gains royal charter and 500,000 acres along upper Ohio (→ July 12).

Ohio Valley, July 12, 1749. Virginia, defying crown, grants 800,000 acres to Ohio and Loyal Companies (→ 1749).

Philadelphia, Aug. 1749. Due to city ban on theater, Thomas Kean and Walter Murray are ousted for performing play *Cato* (→ March 5, 1750).

Philadelphia, Nov. 13, 1749. Following lead of Ben Franklin's pamphlet, city's leaders found institution of higher education [University of Pennsylvania] (→ May 3, 1765).

Nova Scotia, 1749. Some 2,500 settlers, sent by Lord Halifax to consolidate British hold on region, found town of Halifax (→ June 19, 1755).

Ohio Valley, 1749. Pierre Joseph de Celeron sails down river, planting lead plates at tributaries to assert French claims to area (→ March 1751).

British win fort with 9,000 cannonballs

New Englanders swarm ashore at Cape Breton Island in Canada in 1745.

Cape Breton Island, June 16, 1745

After a siege that lasted more than six weeks, during which some 9,000 cannonballs were hurled at the French defenders, Fort Louisbourg has fallen to the British colonial forces from New England. The British victory may well foretell the destruction of the French presence in the maritime provinces.

The invading expedition sailed from Boston harbor on March 24 and was joined at Canso by smaller groups from New Hampshire and Connecticut along with a British naval squadron from the West Indies. Most of the members of the invading force had little or no training. They included a number of students from Harvard College and a 70-year-old Puritan preacher by the name of Sam Moody.

The main body of the fleet anchored off Louisbourg on April 30 in preparation for the onslaught. The fortress was defended by a French force of 500 regular soldiers and 1,400 militiamen. After the surrender, Commodore Peter Warren, the British naval commander, was named the first British Governor of Cape Breton Island (→ 1749).

2-million-acre tract is sold by N.H. man

New Hampshire, 1746

John Mason has just sold a huge tract of land that was in his family for five generations: two million acres of New Hampshire. The land was granted to his great-great-grandfather, Captain John Mason, a London merchant, in 1629. Jurisdiction over the region has been in dispute ever since. Massachusetts ignored the grant and claimed the area from 1641 to 1679. It became a royal colony in 1680 and was under the rule of governors appointed by the crown. The new owners are a group of businessmen from Portsmouth whose intent is to establish many new towns in the region.

1st Lutheran synod

Philadelphia, Aug. 26, 1748

A meeting of Lutheran ministers to consecrate St. Michael's Church ended today with the formation of the first Lutheran synod in the colonies. Six pastors, led by Henry Melchior Muhlenberg, agreed on a book of common worship and to the formation of a synodical organization. A second meeting of the synod called the United Congregations is scheduled for next year in Lancaster.

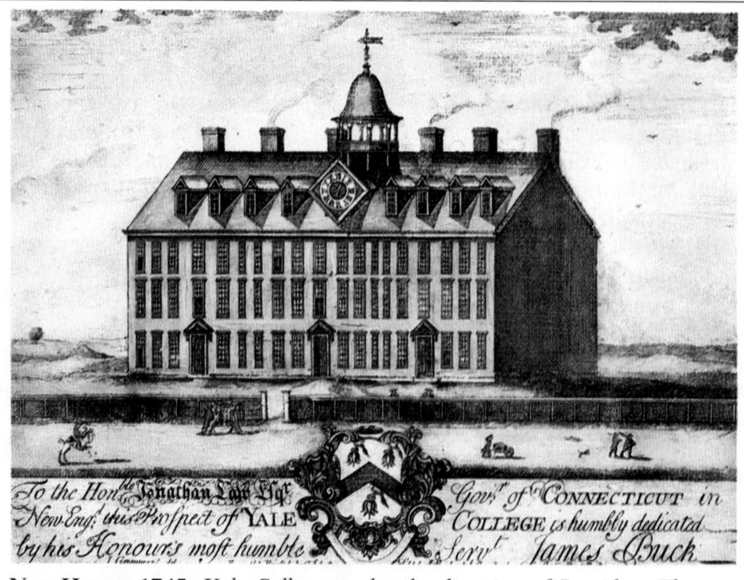

New Haven, 1745. *Yale College, under the direction of President Thomas Clap, has some strict new regulations and a new charter. An applicant must now, among other things, recite Virgil and the Greek Testament, write in Latin and "bring sufficient testimony of his blameless and inoffensive life."*

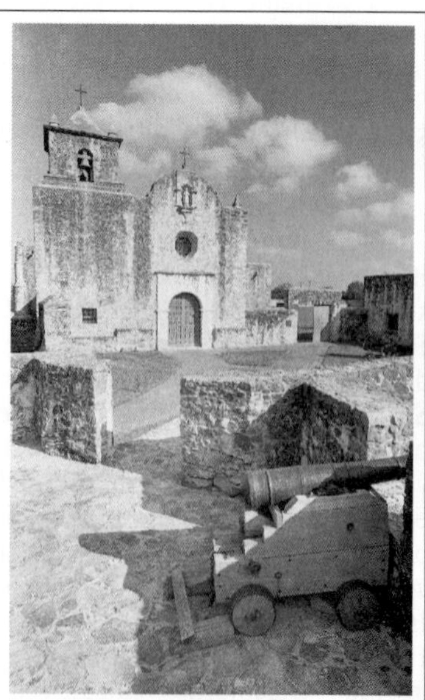

New Spain, 1749. *Presidio La Bahia has been built in Coahuila y Tejas [Texas] to defend the Spanish border against the French.*

G. Washington becomes county surveyor

Young Washington, well schooled in mathematics, surveys land in Virginia.

Williamsburg, Va., July 31, 1749

George Washington, who is only 16 years old, has been made surveyor for the new county of Culpeper. He presented his credentials, from the College of William and Mary, to the court and was directed to take four oaths of office. First he was told to swear allegiance to the King, next to disclaim all allegiance to the issue of James II, then he took the "test oath" of non-belief in transubstantiation and finally he took the special oath of surveyor. Once he had been "sufficiently sworn," Washington exercised his new authority by surveying a 400-acre tract of land in Culpeper for a Richmond landowner, Richard Barnes. The fee paid to the new surveyor was 2 pounds, 3 shillings.

Washington will also copy deeds for a fee. The young Virginian lives on the 2,500-acre estate of Mount Vernon with an older half-brother who suffers from poor health. Washington first turned to surveying under the guidance of Lord Fairfax, a bachelor who owns some five million acres of land in the northern part of Virginia and the Shenandoah Valley (→July 1752).

First settlement made west of Alleghenies

A lone frontiersman treks through a stream to hide his tracks from natives.

Western Virginia, 1749

Jacob Marlin and Stephen Sewell have established Marlinton, the first settlement west of the Allegheny Mountains. The two New Englanders, who reached the area while on a hunting trip, have said it is divided by deep valleys with rich bottom lands. Though still on speaking terms, Marlin and Sewell have religious differences, leading Sewell to seek a new residence: a hollow tree not far from the shelter the two built together.

Governor Spotswood of Virginia traveled to the eastern side of the Alleghenies in 1716 and has encouraged pioneers to migrate there ever since. Morgan Morgan of Delaware built the first cabin at Bunker Hill in 1726. Soon afterward, immigrants from Wales, Scotland and Germany began to trickle into the area. The Indians resisted this intrusion into their hunting grounds and the settlers built Fort Henry, Fort Lee, and Fort Randolph after they were attacked several times.

Despite Indian resistance, rough terrain and crude living conditions, Americans seem determined to move the frontier ever westward.

Boarding school for girls is established

Bethlehem, Penn., May 4, 1746

The Unitas Fratrum, or Moravian collectivist community, has established a boarding school for girls here. The school, in English called the Moravian Women's Seminary (most members of the sect still speak German exclusively), is to serve as a major educational center for the Moravian sect. The school, which is reported to be the first of its kind in British America, is a major step in female education in the colonies. Despite the fact that the Moravians are a tight-knit group living in communities with shared meals and goods, the school will not be limited to believers, but will be available to all who are interested in attending (→1762).

Advice to lovelorn by Ben Franklin

Philadelphia, Dec. 1746

Philadelphia's favorite polymath, Benjamin Franklin, is now diverting his mighty intellect toward affairs of the heart. In the past year, he has written and published essays entitled *Advice to a Young Man on Choosing a Mistress* and *Reflections on Courtship and Marriage*. Franklin's thoughts on such subjects are much earthier than the readers might expect from the author of the Poor Richard maxims. "As in the Dark all Cats are grey, the Pleasure of Corporal Enjoyment with an old woman is at least equal and frequently superior," he recently advised a friend, "every Knack being by practice capable of improvement."

Colonial fashions are simple but elegant

At mid-century in America, men's dress consists of an outer frock coat, an inner jacket fronted with rich embroidery, knee breeches, silk stockings, buckled shoes and a tricornered hat. Women's dress is less exaggerated than in Europe; hoop petticoats provide shape, but are also considered sinful.

1750 (1750-1753)

Boston, Jan. 30, 1750. The Rev. Jonathan Mayhew delivers sermon *Discourse Concerning Unlimited Submission,* attacking divine right of kings and ecclesiastical absolutism.

New York City, March 5, 1750. London's Murray-Kean Company of Comedians begins staging plays in building on Nassau Street, owned by Rip Van Dam (→ Dec. 1752).

Kentucky, Apr. 1750. Dr. Thomas Walker, dispatched by Loyal Company of Virginia, leads expedition through Cumberland Gap to explore mountains [in eastern Kentucky].

America, 1750. Slaves imported to colonies over last 35 years at annual rate of 2,500.

Virginia, 1750. First colonial bituminous coal mine opens.

Pennsylvania, 1750. Jacob Yoder invents flatboat.

Western Frontier, March 1751. Christopher Gist of Maryland, an agent of Ohio Company, crosses Muskingum-Miami areas [into Kentucky Valley] (→ June 13, 1752).

London, 1751. Parliament bars new land banks in colonies, prohibiting paper money except in times of war.

Georgia, 1751. Popularly elected assembly begins meeting in colony.

Virginia, June 13, 1752. Colony signs Treaty of Logstown with Delaware and Iroquois Indians, gaining land south of Ohio River for Ohio Company (→ July 1752).

Georgia, July 4, 1752. Crown takes over colony upon last meeting of trustees.

Ohio River Valley, July 1752. French overrun English trading post of Pickawillany in effort to re-establish control over region (→ Dec. 12, 1753).

Southwest, 1752. Spanish presidio (fort) built on Santa Cruz River at Tubac [first European settlement in Arizona].

Onondaga, New York, Sept. 10, 1753. Sir William Johnson, British head of Indian affairs in North, hears grievances of Mohawk chief King Hendrick: "We are so hemmed in by you . . . if we find a bear in a tree, there will immediately appear an owner of the land to claim the property and hinder us from killing it, by which we live."

Philadelphia, 1753. Ben Franklin and William Hunter chosen to manage British-run postal service in America.

Repaired Liberty Bell tolls for all to hear

Ferris's "The Liberty Bell's First Note" depicts the bell as yet not cracked.

Philadelphia, Aug. 28, 1753

The great bell has finally tolled for all to hear, convening the Pennsylvania State Assembly exactly as it was first intended to. But there was one ominous slip between cup and lip, and the debut of the bell was anything but auspicious. It was ordered in November 1751 by the Pennsylvania Assembly to occupy a special niche on the second story of its new State House.

It was cast by the Whitechapel Bell Foundry in England for 100 pounds sterling, amd was modeled after the "Great Tom" bell that hangs in Westminster Abbey. Its voyage to the colonies was smooth enough and it was thought to be in good condition when it arrived in Philadelphia in September. The trouble began when it was tested. With the very first stroke of the clapper, the mighty bell cracked.

At first, the assembly planned to return it to England for repairs. But after the captain of the ship refused the consignment, it was recast in its new home town by Charles Stow Jr. and John Pass, with results that were admired by all at its official inauguration yesterday at the State House. It is hoped it will not crack again. The bell measures 12 feet around the rim and weighs 2,080 pounds. One part of the inscription contains a quotation from Leviticus 25:10, saying: "Proclaim Liberty throughout all the land unto all the inhabitants thereof."

Virginia, July 1752. *The estate of Mount Vernon has entered the possession of George Washington, 20, upon the death of his half-brother Lawrence this month. The family has owned the estate on the Potomac since 1690.*

Colonial population exceeds one million

New York City, 1750

For the first time since the colonies were established, their population has passed the one-million mark. The main factor is the immigration that has occurred since 1660. Another factor is the wealth of new land that makes the necessities of life relatively easy to come by, thus leading to early marriages in an overwhelmingly agricultural populace. A third factor is the wide dispersal of the settlements. This keeps down the toll from contagious diseases, the kind that have decimated the densely populated cities of Europe. Over the last century, the rise in population has averaged 37.3 percent per decade.

New York theater presents classics

New York City, Dec. 1752

This year, the English actor Lewis Hallam and his troupe of 10 presented Shakespeare's *Merchant of Venice* and other classics to a somewhat indifferent public. The great Thomas Kean, who came here in 1750 to perform *Richard III,* won far more approbation. Yet even Kean and his company were forced to work at odd jobs to earn their keep. Actually, the theater can thank the clergy for its survival: Because ministers rail at its indecency, the curious masses attend.

Gregorian calendar adopted by Britain

London, 1752

The British government decided to switch to the new Gregorian calendar after the annual error in the old Julian calendar had mounted to 11 days. There has been much public confusion about the change and demonstrators have demanded that the crown "give us back our 11 days." Despite the advantages of the new calendar, which corrects the annual error of over 11 minutes in the Julian calendar, adoption has been slow. France and Spain began using the new style in 1582; Sweden still uses the old calendar.

Franklin discovers electricity in lightning

Renaissance man Franklin tries his hand at experimental science. From the 1876 lithograph, "Benjamin Franklin's Experiment," by Currier and Ives.

Philadelphia, June 1752

After flying a kite in a thunderstorm and performing other experiments, Benjamin Franklin, postmaster and printer, has concluded that lightning and electricity are identical. Franklin has published his studies in a book, *Experiments and Observations on Electricity*, and in it he describes electricity as "an Element diffused among, and attracted by other matter, particularly by Water and Metals." He believes electricity to be a sort of fluid and that it can flow from an object that contains too much of it to another that contains too little.

In addition to its theoretical importance, Franklin's discovery may have a practical use. He proposes to protect buildings from lightning by erecting pointed metal rods atop them to conduct the lightning harmlessly into the ground.

England restricts colonial iron mills

London, 1750

Prompted by its trading difficulties with Sweden, where Britain obtained most of its bar iron for manufacturing in the past, Parliament has approved an Iron Act aimed at encouraging other sources. Hoping to spur the colonies to supply British manufacturers with iron while at the same time restricting their iron-finishing industry, the law allows colonial iron to enter Britain duty free under certain conditions. However, the influence of English manufacturers led Parliament to place restrictive clauses in the law that forbid the construction of new steel furnaces and finishing mills in the colonies (→ Apr. 5, 1764).

Jonathan Edwards is ousted by church

Northampton, Mass., June 22, 1750

Nearly a year of conflict in the church here has ended with the dismissal of its celebrated minister, Jonathan Edwards. The dispute had its roots in Edwards's insistence on a profession of "sanctifying grace" for admission to full church communion. His opponents felt that "a competency of knowledge" and a "blameless life" were sufficient. A council of delegates from nearby churches voted 10 to 9 for a separation between the church and its minister. The council exonerated Edwards's character and proclaimed him "eminently qualified" to lead a church that agrees with his principles.

Franklin says slavery is not cost-effective

Philadelphia, 1753

Benjamin Franklin, recently appointed postmaster general for the colonies, believes slavery is poor economic policy. He argues the point in *Observations Concerning the Increase of Mankind and the Peopling of Countries*, a detailed analysis, published this summer, comparing the use of slave labor in the colonies with the wage-labor system now prevalent in Britain. On a subject of comparable interest to American settlers, Franklin has written that all attempts at educating Indians are doomed to failure because the Indians are wild by heritage and predilection.

Thoroughbred horse displays superiority

Baltimore, Maryland, 1752

The sport of horse racing appears to be stirring some lively interest among the gentry in these parts. Recently, Colonel Tasker transported a horse from Great Britain to Maryland and accomplished a notable success with her. He entered the horse, Selima by name, in a race against Tyrol, owned by Colonel Boyd. Selima, a daughter of Godolphin's Arabian, outran Colonel Boyd's Tyrol. It has been two decades since the first blooded English stallion was imported to the American continent. That first colonial thoroughbred was a horse named Bully Rock.

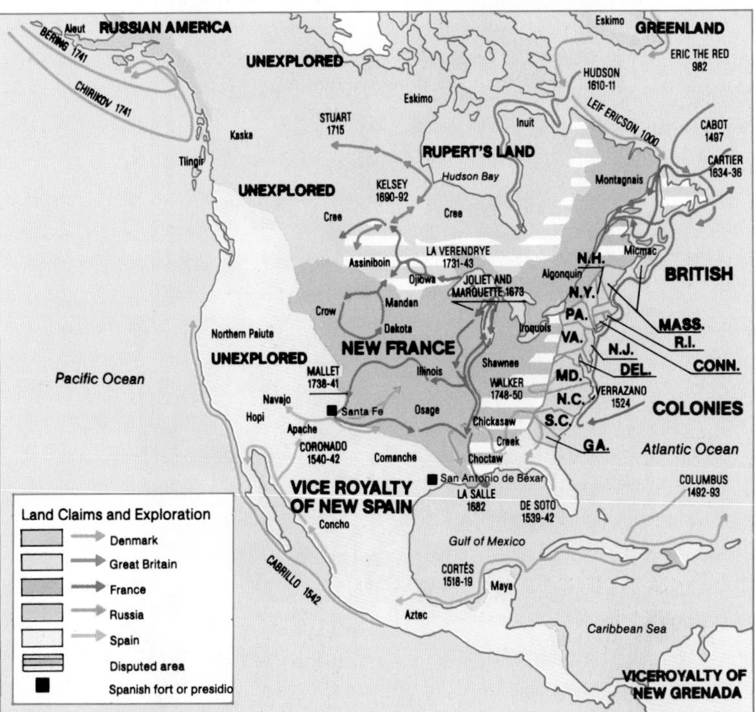

1753. *Describing British ambitions in America, Bishop George Berkeley wrote, "Westward the course of empire takes its way." Now, with Britain demanding French evacuation of the Ohio River Valley, is war inevitable?*

Washington gives an ultimatum to French

Ohio River Valley, Dec. 12, 1753

Major George Washington, adjutant of Virginia, has delivered an ultimatum to Captain Legardeur de St. Pierre de Repentigny, commander of the French forces at Fort Le Boeuf, 20 miles south of Lake Erie near the Allegheny River. Washington, 21, was accompanied on his mission by a frontiersman and guide, Christopher Gist; a Dutch interpreter, Jacob an Braam; several Virginians, and an Indian sachem named Half King, who hates the French because he says they boiled and ate his father.

The letter from Lieutenant Governor Robert Dinwiddie that Washington delivered to the French commander reiterates England's claim to the entire Ohio River Valley. Upon receiving the demand, St. Pierre suggested that they go to Quebec to present the letter to the Governor of Canada. Washington declined (→ Jan. 1754).

Durable, elegant furniture graces colonial homes

Beautifully decorated blanket chest from Berks County, Pennsylvania, 1778.

Sturdy, black walnut and tulip desk on frame from Philadelphia, 1750.

American Howe high chest made of mahogany, pine, poplar and cedar, c.1775.

Room from the John Hewlett House, Long Island, New York, c.1700-60.

Room from the Arnold Elzey House, Somerset County, Maryland, c.1730-60.

An original American interior style in the making

American silver coffee pot, elegant, ornamental, but also useful, c.1753.

Painted walnut plank chair made by Pennsylvania German craftsman, 1770.

Mahogany, wool and linen firescreen from N.Y., with needlework dated 1766.

Solid black walnut and pine dressing table from Connecticut, 1740-60.

1754 (1754-1755)

Virginia, Jan. 1754. George Washington returns from scouting of French forts in Ohio Valley, telling Governor Dinwiddie force is required to remove them (→Apr. 17).

Ohio River Valley, Apr. 17, 1754. French seize site of British fort at fork of Allegheny and Monongahela (→May 28).

Ohio River Valley, May 28, 1754. Washington, en route to French Fort Duquesne with 150 men, encounters French reconnaissance party and defeats it [opening shots of French and Indian War] (→July 3).

Lebanon, Connecticut, 1754. School for Indians founded by the Rev. Eleazar Wheelock [Dartmouth College] (→1769).

New York City, 1754. King's College is chartered under regulations that bar religious discrimination [Columbia University] (→1770).

America, 1754. Jonathan Edwards writes *A Careful and Strict Enquiry into the Modern Prevailing Notions of Freedom of the Will,* elaborating Calvinist notion of predestination.

Nova Scotia, June 19, 1755. Colonels Robert Monckton and John Winslow lead force of 2,000 New Englanders and a few British soldiers in taking Fort Beausejour (→Nov. 30).

Ohio Valley, July 9, 1755. French rout British in Battle of the Wilderness (→13).

Virginia, July 31, 1755. The Rev. Samuel Davis preaches: "I may point out to the public that heroic youth, Colonel Washington, whom I cannot but hope Providence has hitherto preserved in so signal a manner, for some important service to his country" (→Nov. 25, 1758).

New York, Sept. 8, 1755. William Johnson, building Fort William Henry with 3,500 colonials and 400 Indians, defeats Baron Dieskau in Battle of Lake George (→Oct. 24).

Virginia, Autumn 1755. Washington appointed commander-in-chief of Virginia.

New France, Oct. 24, 1755. Massachusetts Governor William Shirley abandons march on Fort Niagara, leaving 700 men at Oswego (→Jan. 16, 1756).

America, 1755. First regular ship passenger service between England and colonies begins.

Boston, 1755. Minister claims lightning rods used here caused earthquake in Portugal.

France, England at war in America

Ohio River Valley, July 3, 1754

With many men killed or wounded, many more drunk with rum intended for the Indians and with everyone wet, exhausted and surrounded by a superior force, Lieutenant Colonel George Washington has surrendered to Coulon de Villiers, the commander of the French forces at Great Meadows, where Fort Necessity is situated. The English, rather than being treated as prisoners of war, will be permitted to return to Virginia with their guns and ammunition.

This expedition started April 2, 1754, when Washington set out from Alexandria, Virginia, with about 160 men. He marched to the Cumberland, where he learned that the French had anticipated his blow and had occupied the unfinished British fort situated at the confluence of the Allegheny and Monongahela Rivers, renaming it Fort Duquesne [Pittsburgh]. The Indians of the area offered their support to Washington and many braves joined the Virginians. Having come within 40 miles of the French forces, Washington surprised a detachment of French soldiers, killing their commander and nine men, while taking the rest prisoner.

Col. George Washington, by Peale.

Washington's success was short-lived because his attack precipitated a full-fledged assault by the French forces, who outnumbered his men by about 700 to 350. He was forced to retreat to Fort Necessity, whose construction was a military disaster because it lay in a water-filled creek bottom, commanded on three sides by forested elevations from which the enemy could fire. Following a fierce day-long struggle, with heavy casualties suffered by both sides, Washington decided that his only option was to negotiate.

Only further fighting, however, will determine whether the upper Ohio Valley will be British, and thus fair game for the traders and settlers of Virginia and Pennsylvania, or French, adding to their empire in Canada and the Northwest. Both the French and British see the region as a stepping stone to control over the heart of North America. And the battle at Great Meadows is only the latest episode in an ongoing European struggle for control of overseas possessions. With King William's War (1689-1697), Queen Anne's War (1702-1713) and King George's War (1744-1748), France and Britain have rarely been at peace in the last 70 years (→July 9, 1755).

Colonists and Iroquois chiefs approve Franklin's plan for union

Albany, New York, July 10, 1754

Colonial delegates and chiefs of the six Iroquois Nations have conferred and approved a plan for union based on the ideas of Benjamin Franklin, one of the delegates from Pennsylvania. The idea of a colonial union was instigated by the British government so that it could conciliate the Indians and manage their affairs. The Indians received many gifts and promises, and the old alliances between them and the colonists were renewed. But at the conclusion of the conference, the Iroquois chiefs appeared to be only half satisfied. There has been a great deal of dissatisfaction among the Iroquois ever since the removal of William Johnson, a representative of the crown who not only spoke several languages of the Indians but also knew their affairs and had their interests at heart.

Philadelphia, May 9, 1754. *Benjamin Franklin appears to have found a new medium for expressing political opinions. This cartoon, the first on this side of the Atlantic, appeals for a union of Britain's 13 colonies.*

A more positive note was sounded at the meeting when delegates discussed Franklin's plan for a general union of the colonies. The plan calls for a "voluntary union" under a central government, with each of the colonies retaining its separate existence and assembly. The new government would be administered by a president general to be appointed by the crown and a general council of delegates from the colonial assemblies.

Exclusive control of Indian affairs would go to the central government, which would regulate Indian trade, purchase Indian land for the crown, construct forts and raise troops and pay them.

Man who never saw a clock builds one

Maryland, Dec. 1754

A young Negro named Benjamin Banneker has constructed the first clock built entirely in America. Although the 23-year-old Banneker had never before seen a clock, his device functions perfectly, striking the hour with great accuracy. Banneker is the son of free parents who own a prosperous farm outside Baltimore. He was taught to read at an early age by his grandmother, who came to America from England as an indentured servant. Benjamin studied at a local school and he has proven himself adept at all kinds of mechanical things.

Benjamin Banneker, 23, is a free Negro farmer, self-educated in astronomy by watching the stars, and in mathematics by reading borrowed books. His clock keeps precise time.

"Yankee Doodle" written by Briton

America, 1755

Some new words have been set to an old English song known variously as *Lucy Locket*, *Nancy Dawson* and *Kitty Fisher*. The song was introduced in the colonies several years ago by an English fife player. The new words are also said to be by an Englishman – Dr. Richard Shuckburg, an army surgeon. The words aren't friendly to colonial ways. They mention a man named "Yankee Doodle," who comes to town on a pony, sticks a feather in his cap and "calls it macaroni," an allusion to the fancy dress that the French are wearing (→ 1776).

Washington commands British forces

Ohio River Valley, July 13, 1755

French forces, knowing that they were about to be surrounded, left Fort Duquesne four days ago and ambushed a force of British and colonial troops under the command of Major General Edward Braddock, wounding him fatally and routing his forces. The Battle of the Wilderness took place seven miles south of Fort Duquesne at a ford of the Monongahela River. Today, Braddock died, and leadership of the British forces has fallen to Colonel George Washington, 23.

The Sieur de Contrecoeur, who commands the French, ordered Captain Daniel Beaujou to lead the daring attack made by about 650 Indians, 100 French and 100 Canadians. The French as well as the Indians fought Indian style, hiding behind bushes and rocks, but the British chose to defend themselves in the European fashion, dressing ranks when they came under attack. This made them excellent targets. Of the approximately 1,500 colonial and British troops, 977 have been killed or wounded, including 63 officers and eight women. The French casualties were very light. The presence of the women is rather an indication of the overconfidence of the British, who had actually expected that the French would blow up Fort Duquesne when they arrived.

Because of the carnage among the officers, due to a great extent to the brightness of their uniforms, leadership on the battlefield and during the retreat fell on the shoulders of Colonel George Washington, General Braddock's aide-de-camp. Washington had two horses shot from under him and had four bullet holes in his clothes, yet he came away unscathed. When it was clear that the battle was lost, he rode back to the rear guard of Braddock's army to bring reinforcements to the front, but by then the British had been completely routed.

The Virginians who accompanied General Braddock fought back the longest and hardest, but they sustained such casualties that a defense became impossible. When one British officer cried, "Stand and fight," there came a Virginian reply: "We would fight if we could see anybody to fight with" (→ 31).

Ambushed, Braddock's men fall dead to the beat of a lone drummer boy.

The wounded general is carried off in Alonzo Chappel's "Braddock's Defeat."

French expelled from Acadia flee to South

Maryland, Nov. 30, 1755

Some 900 French Acadians, expelled by the British from Nova Scotia, have arrived here to begin a new life. They are lucky to have made it safely. Last month, two ships evacuating about 1,200 of the refugees sank in an Atlantic storm. No survivors were reported. The British gave the expulsion order, covering some 6,000 or 7,000 settlers, after the Acadians refused to take an oath of allegiance to the British crown.

At its inception in 1603, Nova Scotia, called Acadia by the French, extended down the North American coast from Cape Breton to the lower Hudson River, heavily encroaching on land claimed by the British. After a century of contention, the area was ceded to Britain by the Treaty of Utrecht in 1713. Since then, the British have regarded the Acadians with suspicion. And with the onset of the war in America, their presence has apparently become intolerable.

Most of the Acadians have been sent to England or relocated in Britain's American colonies. In addition to those expelled, some 2,000 Acadian refugees scattered voluntarily in small groups through other sections of the maritime areas, or sought sanctuary with other French settlers in neighboring areas of Quebec (→ 1764).

1756 (1756-1758)

America, Jan. 9, 1756. Voicing belief that land fraud is major cause of conflict with Indians, Peter Wraxhall, secretary to Indian commissioner, advises clearance be required for all land transfers (→ Oct. 13, 1761).

Europe, Jan. 16, 1756. England and Prussia sign anti-French pact, spreading French and Indian War to Europe (→ May 11).

New France, May 11, 1756. Louis Joseph Marquis de Montcalm arrives with reinforcements (→ July 23).

America, July 23, 1756. John Campbell, Earl of Loudon, arrives to take command of British forces (→ Aug. 31).

Northeast, 1756. Stagecoach line opens, covering Philadelphia to New York in three days, traveling 18 hours a day.

Philadelphia, 1756. Regiment and Artillery Company of Philadelphia parades under command of Ben Franklin.

Virginia, 1756. Negro population, 40 percent of total, is 120,156, up from 23,000 in 1715.

London, July 27, 1757. Ben Franklin arrives as agent for Pennsylvania Assembly.

Fort Louisbourg, Sept. 24, 1757. British fleet under Rear Admiral Francis Holborne destroyed attempting to trap French in harbor (→ Dec. 30).

America, Dec. 30, 1757. General James Abercromby arrives to replace Lord Loudon (→ July 8, 1758).

London, 1757. Iron Act revised to let colonies export iron to England duty free.

Philadelphia, 1757. New street lights, designed by Ben Franklin, burn whale oil.

North America, Sept. 18, 1758. Abercromby, after defeat at Ticonderoga, replaced by General Amherst (→ June 27, 1759).

Philadelphia, 1758. Quaker annual meeting bars slave traders.

Sandy Creek, North Carolina, 1758. Churches organized by Shubal Stearns form Sandy Creek Baptist Association.

America, 1758. "Old Side" and "New Side" Presbyterians heal schism.

DEATH

New Jersey, March 22, 1758. Jonathan Edwards, Puritan theologian, dies before becoming new president of College of New Jersey (*Oct. 5, 1703).

British seize French fort

Braddock's loss avenged, Washington raises the British flag at Fort Duquesne.

Fort Duquesne, Nov. 25, 1758

Fort Duquesne [Pittsburgh], long the center of French territorial and trading control of the upper Ohio River Valley, was taken over today by General John Forbes's 6,500-man force at the end of an expedition that provided the British with a major victory in the French and Indian War.

The severely ailing general directed the campaign from mid-September onward by means of letters of instruction to his colonels, including George Washington, John Armstrong and Henry Bouquet.

Despite intense opposition from Washington and other Virginians, Bouquet insisted on building a road across the rugged wilderness of western Pennsylvania for use in the expedition. Frequent rains made the road-building effort extremely difficult and hampered communication. But the desperate situation of the French at Fort Duquesne – their Indian allies had deserted them and communication with Canada was cut by Colonel John Bradstreet's campaign against Fort Frontenac – convinced General Forbes that his men should move onward.

When the British arrived, they found only the smoking remains of an abandoned fort, which they renamed Fort Pitt (→ Feb. 10, 1763).

British fort taken; Indians kill 1,000

New York, Aug. 31, 1756

In a series of bitter engagements, French forces under the command of the Marquis de Montcalm have opposed British forces in the New York area. At Fort William Henry, the British defender, Colonel Monro, was so hopelessly outnumbered that he quickly surrendered while he still had about 2,400 men. Although Montcalm pledged safe conduct, some 1,000 British soldiers died in an attack by France's Indian allies. Pressing on, Montcalm also overran Fort Oswego on August 14, ousting General Webb from the Mohawk Valley. The French are now poised at Fort Ticonderoga with 5,000 troops (→ Sept. 24, 1757).

Emigration forced on some servants

Wurttemberg, Germany, 1756

The only opportunity that awaits many immigrants to the land of America – even those with white skin – is that of enslavement, says a German observer. In his *Journey to America,* Gottlieb Mittelberger deplores the fate of thousands of Europe's poor, induced by threats and promises to go into debt in order to make the trans-Atlantic passage. Those who survive the voyage, he writes, are sold "like so many head of cattle." Families are often broken up. The less fortunate work up to 10 years to pay their debt, learning quickly "that stumps of oak trees are in America certainly as hard as in Germany."

Princeton now site of Jersey college

Princeton, New Jersey, 1756

Authorities have decided to move the College of New Jersey from Newark to Princeton in order to make it accessible to the New York-to-Philadelphia stagecoach line. The college has grown remarkably since its humble beginnings 10 years ago in the Elizabeth, New Jersey, home of its founder, the Rev. Jonathan Dickinson. The growth of his school parallels the expansion of his pro-revival or "New Side" faction of the Presbyterian Church, which split from the "Old Side" in 1741. The Rev. Aaron Burr has become the college's second president.

Pitt to map policy for war in America

London, June 29, 1757

Following the collapse of the Henry Fox ministry, King George II has named William Pitt and the Duke of Newcastle to form a new administration. Newcastle will take charge of the political side of things from the House of Lords, while Pitt, who becomes the secretary of state, will be responsible for foreign affairs and the running of the war against the French and the Austrians. Just two months ago, opposition from King George II resulted in Pitt's dismissal as secretary of state in the administration of the Duke of Devonshire. Pitt needs to win some decisive battles soon.

Pitt, committed to turning the tide in the war against the French.

French defeat British

Montcalm (center) doffs his hat to his troops after battle at Ticonderoga.

Ticonderoga, July 8, 1758

British forces were driven off with heavy casualties today when they tried to capture the French bastion here, known as Fort Carillon. Reports said that 464 of the 15,000-man attack force were killed, 1,115 wounded and 19 are still missing. The losses on the French side were minimal – 106 killed and 266 wounded.

The heavily outnumbered defenders were led by the Marquis of Montcalm, who came to North America two years ago as commander of the French forces in the field. The assault forces were under the direction of the British commander-in-chief, James Abercromby, a career officer.

Although the British assault was indeed a surprise, Abercromby's strategy was fatally flawed. The commander was forced to retreat because he had attacked from the wrong direction. His monumental blunder had the effect of halting the advance of the British on Montreal, forcing his armies to adopt a defensive position on Lake George instead and creating consternation among his soldiers. This stone fort between Lakes Champlain and George was built by the French three years ago as an outpost of Fort Saint Frederic (→26).

British take Louisbourg

Tightening the noose: British ships lay siege to French fortress of Louisbourg.

Cape Breton Island, July 26, 1758

The British flag flew over the French fortress of Louisbourg once more today after a two-week siege ended with the surrender of its defenders. The winning British commander was General James Wolfe.

Fort Louisbourg had previously been captured by British forces in 1745, but it was returned to the French three years later under the Treaty of Aix-la-Chapelle. In 1756, Britain renewed hostilities, at the start of a war that began in North America but has spread to Europe – with no end in sight.

On May 28 of this year, a British fleet of 157 ships with 27,000 men sailed from Halifax to recapture the French fortress. It arrived in front of Louisbourg five days later and began the siege. The commander of the French, Augustin Boschenry de Drucour, held out courageously with a much smaller fighting force, some 3,500 soldiers and 4,000 sailors and militia, but he was forced to capitulate after a seven-week struggle.

French losses were heavy, including 11 warships, eight of which were sunk and three captured by the British. Nevertheless, by holding up the British advance, the French did manage to protect their colony of Quebec (→ Sept. 18, 1758).

"Early to bed, early to rise . . ." et cetera

Philadepphia, 1758

"Early to bed and early to rise, makes a man healthy, wealthy and wise," asserts Ben Franklin. This year, he published *The Way to Wealth* in the fictional guise of "Father Abraham." It reprints many of the proverbs that have delighted readers of *Poor Richard's Almanac* for 26 years. *The Way to Wealth* has made this year's almanac the most popular yet (selling more than the usual 10,000 copies), but it marks Franklin's swan song as publisher. He was sent to London last year as an agent for the Pennsylvania Assembly, and from now on he will channel his talents into politics and science.

March 13, 1758. *Rogers' Rangers, a band of sturdy frontiersmen led by Major Robert Rogers, are proving the value of light infantry. Today, however, they lost 130 men in the Battle of Snowshoes. Painting by Ferris.*

Latest gossip: Maid weds the Governor

Portsmouth, N.H., 1756

Tongues are wagging over the news that Benning Wentworth, the royal colonial Governor here for the last 15 years, has married his maid, Martha Hilton. The Governor, recently a widower, is best known for his practice of riding through Portsmouth in a gilded chariot while wrapped in a cloak of crimson velvet. Wentworth has infuriated his many relatives with his choice of a bride, who, of course, will eventually inherit his vast fortune along with his nearby seaside estate, Wentworth Hall. Witnesses say that even the rector expressed a reluctance to marry such a modest woman to the Governor.

1759 (1759-1760)

Pennsylvania, May 31, 1759. Law bans stage plays; penalty is 50-pound fine.

St. Lawrence River, June 27, 1759. British General Wolfe arrives at Ile d'Orleans, linking with Rear Admiral Durell for advance up river (→July 25).

New France, July 25, 1759. Brigadier General John Prideaux leads 2,000 British regulars to victory over French at Fort Niagara; he is killed in battle (→26).

Quebec, July 27, 1759. French fail to burn British fleet, led up St. Lawrence by Rear Admiral Charles Saunders in June (→31).

New France, July 31, 1759. Fort Saint Frederic blown up by French in face of British attack on Crown Point (→Sept. 18).

London, Aug. 10, 1759. Privy Council, responding to objections of clergy, reverses Virginia Act of 1755 allowing clergy to be paid in currency rather than tobacco.

Philadelphia, Dec. 13, 1759. Michael Hillegas opens first music store in America.

South Carolina, Dec. 26, 1759. Cherokees agree to treaty with Governor Lyttleton requiring surrender of Indians guilty of raiding settlements between spring 1758 and September 1759 (→Jan. 19, 1760).

Philadelphia, Dec. 28, 1759. American Company performs *Hamlet*, closing six-month stay on Society Hill.

Philadelphia, 1759. Presbyterian Ministers Fund, first recorded life insurance firm in colonies, is established.

America, 1759. *My Days Have Been So Wonderous Free,* first secular song by native-born American, written by Francis Hopkinson.

South Carolina, Jan. 19, 1760. Cherokees attack Fort Prince George in attempt to free negotiators held by Governor Lyttleton (→Feb. 16).

South Carolina, Feb. 16, 1760. Cherokee hostages at Fort Prince George slain in revenge as Indians attack frontier settlements (→Aug. 10).

Quebec, Apr. 28, 1760. French, besieging Quebec, defeat British under General James Murray in second battle on Plains of Abraham; British retreat into city (→Sept. 8).

Western Frontier, 1760. Daniel Boone commissioned to scout sites for settlements [in Tennessee].

French flee Ticonderoga

Ticonderoga, July 26, 1759

Outnumbered French defenders blew up Fort Carillon and fled before an attacking British force today. The defeat may represent a death-blow to French hopes of stopping the British conquest.

The French garrison commander, Francois-Charles de Bourlamaque, was acting under orders from the Marquis de Montcalm to keep his corps of 3,000 troops intact and to keep them between the enemy and Montreal. His instructions were to withdraw slowly, avoiding losses, and to abandon Forts Carillon and Saint Frederic successively as each of them was threatened by British encirclement. The French strategy was to fall back to positions at Ile aux Noix that could be defended more easily and block the British advance on Montreal.

Bourlamaque carried out his assignment, pulling out of Carillon when the British forces under General Jeffrey Amherst made their appearance. He left a rear guard to light the fuses and blow up the fort. But in the disorder that followed, 20 of his soldiers were left behind, sleeping off a drunken binge.

The French forces are now on their way to Fort Saint Frederic. If they carry out their orders successfully, the two principal French fortresses that have held up the advance of the British will fall into enemy hands without a shot even being fired (→27).

Regiment of Black Watch soldiers at Ticonderoga. Painting by J.L.G. Ferris.

Cherokee Indians battle British in South

Fort Loudoun, S.C. Aug. 10, 1760

The garrison of Fort Loudoun was overrun three days ago by Cherokees after it was forced by starvation to surrender. The commander, Captain Raymond Devere, and many others were killed and scalped. The rest are prisoners. The surrendering soldiers had thought they were to be led out of Cherokee territory. Instead, they were abandoned, then ambushed by attackers who hid in nearby tall grass.

The incident is the latest in a series of clashes over the last decade. The Cherokees, spurred on by the French and angered by the heavyhanded treatment of the English, have grown increasingly bitter toward the English. In 1756, a starving band of Cherokees was slaughtered by British settlers in Virginia. The Cherokees retaliated by killing settler families in Virginia and the Carolinas. South Carolina Governor Lyttleton responded by imprisoning a group of warriors who had been negotiating a treaty at Fort Prince George on the Savannah River. That led to another Cherokee raid, which led to the slaying of the Cherokee prisoners (→1761).

George III is new British King

George III, ruler of an empire at 22.

London, Oct. 26, 1760

Felled by a stroke, George II died yesterday at Kensington Palace at the age of 77. He is succeeded by his grandson, George, who became Prince of Wales nine years ago following the death of his father, Frederick. The new King, who is 22 years old and has yet to marry, is the first Hanoverian monarch to have been born in England. Educated largely by his mother, the former Princess Augusta of Saxe-Coburg-Altenburg, along with his tutor, Lord Bute, the new King is considered widely popular. Following the admonition of his mother, "George, be King!" the monarch is expected to take an active role in the running of the country.

January 6, 1759. *George Washington weds widow Martha Custis. Painting by J.L.G. Ferris.*

British capture Quebec; rival generals both killed

Quebec, Sept. 18, 1759

This capital of New France has surrendered to British troops following a brief but fierce battle in which the commanders of both sides were killed. The British now stand in firm control of the French bastion in the New World.

The dead leaders were General James Wolfe, who commanded the British forces, and the Marquis de Montcalm, who was in charge of the French defenders. Wolfe died on the battlefield on the 13th; Montcalm succumbed a day later.

The Battle of the Plains of Abraham is probably the most consequential of the many that have been fought by the rival British and French armies in the conquest of New France. Yet it lasted no more than 10 minutes, and its result may have been due as much to the mistakes of the two generals as to the valor of their forces.

Wolfe and his troops had been advancing up the Gulf of St. Lawrence for more than a year, destroying small French settlements along the way. His force arrived at Quebec toward the end of June in a flotilla of 168 ships carrying 30,000 men. The British first landed on the south shore of the Ile d'Orleans. Two days later, more went ashore at Point Levis, across the river from Quebec. On July 12, British guns began firing from the south shore heights, and Quebec was soon in flames.

By last month, the fortress was in ruins. More than 500 houses had been destroyed, others were struck by cannonballs and not a single building escaped damage. Despite the destruction, however, a British attempt to land on the shore below Quebec on July 31 was driven off with heavy losses. Finally, early this month, the British fleet moved upstream to Cap Rouge, and before dawn on September 13, Wolfe landed his main force at l'Anse au Foulon [Wolfe's Cove]. The British scaled the cliffs by following a creek bed and took up positions on the Plains of Abraham just west of Quebec in the morning.

General Wolfe's forces arrive in 168 ships on the south shore of the Ile d'Orleans, ready to do battle with the French on the Plains of Abraham.

"Since I have conquered, I will die in peace," General James Wolfe said as he lay wounded in Quebec. "The Death of Wolfe" (1771) by Benjamin West.

It was at this point that Montcalm made his fatal mistake. He ordered his poorly trained and ill-equipped troops into an attack on the British lines. When the French came within 40 feet of them, the British opened fire and charged. The French fled in confusion and the battle was over.

During the brief clash, Wolfe was shot three times. "Now God be praised," he reportedly said as he lay dying. "Since I have conquered, I will die in peace." Montcalm succumbed inside his ruined fortress, which remained in the hands of the French for four more days. Yesterday, the Duke de Levis took command of the main body of French troops west of Quebec and ordered a withdrawal to Montreal. The Quebec commander and his forces surrendered today and the British troops are preparing to enter the city tomorrow. British Brigadier James Murray summed up the cost of the conquest with these words: "We were surprised into a victory which cost the conquered very little indeed" (→ Apr. 28, 1760).

386,000 slaves

London, 1760

Since the revolution of 1688, and the abolition of a monopoly in 1697, the slave trade has been booming. Private traders are sending more than 8,000 slaves a year to the Southern colonies, and the Royal African Company, which remains competitive despite serious financial problems, has delivered them at an annual rate of 2,500. In all, there are 386,000 slaves in the colonies, with 299,000 of them in the South. About 33 percent of Georgia's population are slaves.

Amherst receives surrender of Montreal

Montreal, Sept. 8, 1760

Governor Pierre Francois de Rigaud today surrendered Montreal to British forces massed outside the city. Thus ended the last encounter between British and French forces on the mainland of North America. The surrender of the French was accepted by the British commander, General Jeffrey Amherst.

The collapse of New France had been a long time coming, although it had been regarded as inevitable. The British were advancing on the city from three directions with a force of more than 17,000 men, while the French were defending Montreal with only 2,000.

Yesterday, when the British approached, they were met by country people, men and women, presenting pitchers of milk and water to the soldiers and expressing concern that they had no better drinks to offer the conquerors. In the end, with no relief for the beleaguered French forces expected from the homeland, Montreal peacefully opened its gates to the advancing enemy troops (→ Feb. 10, 1763).

Rogers takes Detroit

Detroit, Nov. 29, 1760

Accompanied by a force of about 200 Royal Rangers, Major Robert Rogers took possession of Detroit for Britain today. After having reached the mouth of the Detroit River, Major Rogers sent an emissary to inform Captain Francois-Marie Picote, Sieur de Belestre, that the rangers were approaching. At first, Belestre refused to believe that Canada had fallen. But when the captain saw a letter from Governor Vaudreuil, he surrendered to Rogers peacefully.

1761 (1761-1762)

London, May 22, 1761. Board of Trade loses power to nominate colonial officials.

Detroit, Sept. 9, 1761. British, in talks with Indians, refuse to lower prices on traded goods as well as supply Indians with ammunition.

Northern Plains, Oct. 1761. Capt. Henry Balfour and force of British and colonial troops build Fort Edward Augustus [on site of Green Bay].

England, Dec. 2, 1761. Lord Egremont, secretary of state for Southern Department, bars land grants in Indian territory without royal approval (→ Sept. 2, 1763).

London, Dec. 9, 1761. British crown gets right to final approval of colonial judgeship appointments.

Southeast, 1761. Under pressure from English Colonel Grant, Cherokee Indians end raids on frontier settlements.

Newport, Rhode Island, 1761. Describing plays as "moral dialogues" to evade law against theater, American Company begins a run in New England.

Virginia, 1761. Governor Spotswood journeys west to convince Virginians to settle frontier.

Portsmouth, New England, 1761. Englishman John Stavers opens stagecoach service between Portsmouth and Boston [first public transportation in New Hampshire].

Spain, Jan. 2, 1762. Anticipating attack in colonies, France declares war on Spain (→ Aug. 12).

Caribbean, Feb. 15, 1762. British seize Martinique, major French base in lesser Antilles.

Cuba, Aug. 12, 1762. British capture Cuba from Spain after two-month siege (→ Oct. 5).

Philippines, Oct. 5, 1762. British seize Manila (→ Nov. 3).

Salisbury, Connecticut, 1762. Ironworks and blast furnace set up by Ethan Allen.

New York, 1762. Influential members of Dutch Reformed Church petition for services in English, prompting defection of some conservative members to Church of England.

Florida, 1762. Appointed Botanist Royal in America by crown, John Bartram studies indigenous flora and fauna.

Boston, 1762. James Otis's *A Vindication of the Conduct of the House of Representatives* elaborates colonial rights.

France gives all Western lands to Spain

France, Nov. 3, 1762

In an effort to compensate Spain for some of the staggering losses that it has suffered during the Seven Years War, France has ceded all its claims to lands west of the Mississippi – the territory that is generally known as Upper Louisiana.

Spain, which for the last three years has been ruled by the reform-minded Carlos III, was dragged into the war in 1761 as a result of the Third Family Compact, which, like earlier family compacts, made its foreign policy subservient to the interests of France. Since joining the war, the Spaniards have lost Cuba, Florida, Minorca and the Philippines to the British.

The cession of Upper Louisiana is the main clause of the supposedly secret treaty between Spain and France that has just been signed here at Fontainebleau, a royal palace surrounded by hunting preserves 37 miles south of Paris.

Skeptics may be of the opinion that in ceding this territory France is not giving up all that much, since following its defeat in Canada and the loss of all its fortified outposts in the West it is in no position to maintain any possessions in North America anyway. But the pact, like the negotiations currently being conducted at Hubertusburg in Saxony between the Austrians and Prussians, is undoubtedly going to help clear the way for the final settlement of the war.

British colonies are a symphony of sound

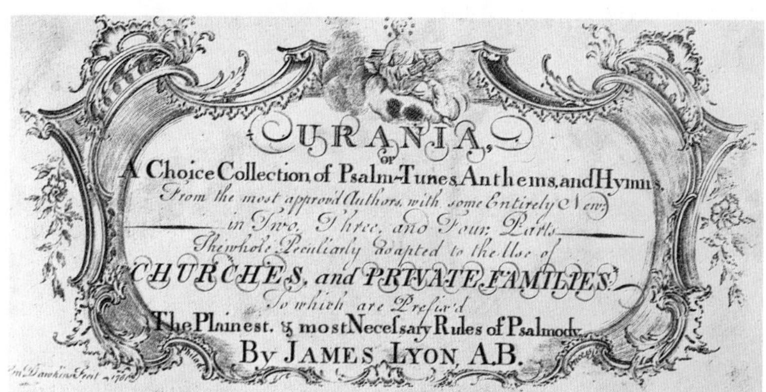

URANIA,
or
A Choice Collection of Psalm-Tunes, Anthems, and Hymns,
From the most approv'd Authors, with some Entirely New;
in Two, Three, and Four, Parts.
The whole Peculiarly Adapted to the Use of
CHURCHES, and PRIVATE FAMILIES:
To which are Prefix'd
The Plainest & most Necessary Rules of Psalmody.
By JAMES LYON, A.B.

Rev. James Lyon's "Urania," a collection of hymns, was published in 1761.

New York City, May 3, 1762

In Charleston this year, citizens founded the St. Cecilia Society, while in Stoughton, Massachusetts, they formed Ye Olde Musical Society, the first such groups in America. In New England, folks are humming *Springfield Mountain*, and even the versatile Ben Franklin has turned his hand to music.

According to Britain's *Bristol Journal*, "The celebrated Glassychord invented by Mr. Franklin, . . . has greatly improved the musical glasses and formed them into a compleat instrument." Previously, the glasses were bowls partly filled with water and their rims were stroked with a moist finger. Last year, Franklin arranged the bowls on a horizontal rod in a box placed before the performer. The moistened bowls are rotated by a foot pedal and the player's hands rub them to produce a sound. Also called the "glass harmonica," it is becoming a big hit in Europe.

Franklin, who plays the harp and guitar, is one of several noted gentlemen amateur musicians. Thomas Jefferson often plays violin duets with Patrick Henry. In Philadelphia, Judge Francis Hopkinson plays the organ and harpsichord, while Gov. John Penn, a violinist, arranges chamber music programs.

For 20 years, the American Company has traveled the Atlantic seaboard, performing such works as *The Beggar's Opera, The Mock Doctor, The Devil to Pay, Love in a Village,* and *No Song, No Supper.* Today, the manager of the company placed an advertisement offering "a reward to whoever can discover the person who was so very rude as to throw eggs from the gallery upon the stage . . ."

British try to halt migration west

Bouquet in council with the Indians.

Fort Pitt, Oct. 13, 1761

Colonel Henry Bouquet, commander of Fort Pitt, is worried. He cannot see how the Indians could be treated more abysmally. And yet, they have shown great patience. But he fears their forbearance will not last forever as white settlers continue to pour into Western lands supposedly owned solely by them. This ownership was established by the 1758 Treaty of Easton. With 12 extremely strategic forts in British control, the 43-year-old commander is aware that he cannot stem the tide, he can only repeatedly issue warnings – which are routinely ignored (→ Dec. 2, 1761).

American cookbook

London, 1761

An English publisher has turned out an indispensable guide for the American homemaker. It is called *The Colonial Housewife; or, Accomplished Gentlewoman's Companion*, which covers "every article which can add to the knowledge of the housewife." Compiled by Mrs. E. Smith, the *Companion* offers the housewife more than 700 recipes, including such New World dishes as West Indian turtle and roast turkey (dressed "the genteel way"), along with selected repasts from France, the Netherlands, Spain, Italy and elsewhere. The author has also provided the readers with a collection of more than 300 home remedies for ailments that range from cancer to dropsy.

Moravians call off communal experiment

Bethlehem, Pennsylvania, 1762

After 21 years, the Moravians of Bethlehem have decided to end their experiment in communal living. Seventy-four members of this much-persecuted Christian sect migrated to Pennsylvania in 1741 in search of religious freedom. In the year that followed, they decided that they would pool their resources under a plan called the *General Economy* to help carve a community out of the wilderness. Rather than build a separate house for each of the families, they decided that the congregation would be divided into "choirs," such as "Single Brethren" and "Single Sisters," and to lodge them in dormitories. Jobs were assigned by the group and money and property were held communally. In return, members were given bed and board, and their children received a free education.

But the ingredients that made the experiment a success at first carried the seeds of its demise. As the economy prospered, members began to feel that the communal agreement was becoming a barrier to further progress. Tradesmen wanted to start their own businesses. Families wanted to build their own houses and move out of the dormitories. As a result of these pressures, the Moravians have now decided to abandon the *General Economy* in favor of a living arrangement that is going to provide individuals with greater freedom.

An aristocrat and a slave are painted

Maryland, 1761

The painter John Hesselius, who only recently settled in Anne Arundel County, Maryland, has already successfully captured the aristocratic ambiance of the colony. In his latest work, *Charles Calvert and Colored Slave*, a richly attired boy of about 5 is shown accompanied by his Negro slave in a composition that is probably derived from English prints. Hesselius, son of the Swedish-born artist Gustave Hesselius, captures our interest by juxtaposing these two very disparate denizens of the genteel Southern society.

They're the same age but worlds apart: John Hesselius's "Charles Calvert and Colored Slave" (1761).

Fraunces purchases house for a tavern

New York City, 1762

Samuel Fraunces has purchased a building that was once the home of the powerful loyalist merchant Stephen De Lancey and turned it into the Queen's Head Tavern. The mansion was constructed by Colonel Van Cortlandt in 1719; the De Lanceys moved out of it in 1757 when most of their property was confiscated as a result of their pro-British politics. Fraunces, a renowned innkeeper from the West Indies who is often called "Black Sam," bought the building earlier this year and came to America to supervise the renovation work.

An actor's life . . .

Providence, R.I., May 3, 1761

The actor's life at David Douglass's Histrionic Academy is not an easy one. A mob, mostly composed of religious groups from the area, was aroused to such a frenzy of hostility today that a prominent citizen trained a cannon on them and had to threaten to fire before the mob dispersed. The troupe was performing in a play by William Shakespeare. Douglass has tried to avoid confrontation with religious groups by presenting his plays as "moral dialogues," but so far with limited success. He founded his acting troupe in 1758.

Lawyer slams British search warrants

Boston, Feb. 24, 1761

James Otis, a lawyer who represents the merchants of Boston, has denounced writs of assistance in the Massachusetts Superior Court and has urged Parliament to declare them null and void and contrary to the British constitution. The writs are general warrants that grant British customs officers the right to search private property without stating their grounds for suspicion. These English officials have been directed by Prime Minister William Pitt to seize all cargoes they suspect are going to the French. America's wartime trade with the French and the Dutch has appalled Pitt, who is of the opinion that the French would have had to sue for peace had they been deprived of their colonial trade.

The merchants have contested the writs because under British law they are renewable up to six months after the death of a monarch. King George II died in October of 1760 and if Parliament gets them successfully reinstated, they will be valid until the death of George III, who is only 22 years old.

Otis leaves Town Hall to an ovation.

Kitchen is the center of American life

New England

The center of life for the American colonist is not the church or the parlor; it is the kitchen, with its huge stone fireplace. In the other rooms, the rafters may be bare and the floor made of raw boards. But in the kitchen, there is room enough near the hearth for finishing chores, and for children to play and watch their mothers cook in big iron pots. On the hearth's back-bar are hooks of varied lengths called trammels, hakes, pot-claws, potclips and pot crooks. There are also lugpoles, job-crokes, recons, gallows-balke and gallows-crooks. On these, hang pots and kettles.

In kettles on the fire are hasty puddings and cornmeal porridge, while corn dumplings are baked on the side. If the colonist travels, he takes with him nocake, or Indian corn, which is corn parched in ashes and carried in a leathern bag.

In the kitchen, colonial women maintain a thriving domestic industry.

1763

Philadelphia, Feb. 13. Discontented frontiersmen, popularly known as the Paxton Boys, march to provincial council and submit list of grievances (→ Dec. 27).

Northwest, May 7. British discover plan to seize Detroit, orchestrated by Ottawa Chief Pontiac; betrayed, Pontiac chooses all-out war on British garrisons west of Niagara (→ 16).

Northwest, May 16. British garrison of Fort Sandusky, on Western frontier, is destroyed by Ottawa forces under Chief Pontiac (→ 27).

Northwest, May 27. British at Fort Ouiatenon defeated by Indian forces under Chief Pontiac (→ June 2).

Northwest, June 2. Fort Michilimackinac overrun by Chief Pontiac after Indians disguise intentions by staging lacrosse game outside fort (→ July 13).

Northwest, July 31. Chief Pontiac turns back British attack led by Major Gladwin in Battle of Bloody Ridge (→ Nov. 1763).

London, Sept. 2. Lord Shelburne replaced by Lord Hillsborough in effort to avoid further conflict with Indians angered over British settlement of Western territories (→ Oct. 7).

America, Sept. 9. George Washington's Mississippi Company requests 2.5 million acres of land at fork of Ohio and Mississippi Rivers in plan to repay militia for service in French and Indian War.

Louisiana, Sept. 24. Jesuits are expelled from colony; their property is confiscated.

Charleston, South Carolina, Oct. 29. Chimney sweeps form first organization of Negro workers, refusing to work until city raises price charged for their labor.

Pennsylvania, December. George Croghan, Indian commissioner's agent, and two Pennsylvania merchant firms organize Suffering Traders group in attempt to gain compensation for damage done by Indian raids.

Lancaster, Pennsylvania. Inventor Henry Williams conducts unsuccessful test of steam-powered boat.

London. American artist Benjamin West arrives and introduces into English painting the Neoclassical style.

America. Quaker reformer John Woolman prints *A Plea for the Poor.*

France cedes all of Canada to Britain

Paris, Feb. 10

The removal of France as a power in North America has been confirmed with the signing here of a treaty that brings the French and Indian War to a conclusion. Although the islands of Guadeloupe and Martinique in the West Indies and St. Pierre and Miquelon at the entrance to the Gulf of St. Lawrence have been returned to the French, they have lost all of their possessions on the continent.

The treaty thus confirms the actual situation following the long run of British military successes during the war. These began in July 1758, when Louisbourg was captured and razed by General Amherst and Admiral Boscawen. Later that year, Fort Frontenac and Fort Duquesne were taken by the British. Ticonderoga was recaptured in July 1759, and General Wolfe's decisive victory over General Montcalm on the Plains of Abraham took place in September of that year. With the surrender of Montreal to General Amherst on September 8, 1760, the conquest of Canada by Britain was completed.

Britain will soon have to decide what concessions it should offer the French-Canadian settlers who now find themselves reluctant subjects of King George III. A conciliatory policy that will allow these settlers to keep their Catholic religion as well as their own legal and educational systems is expected.

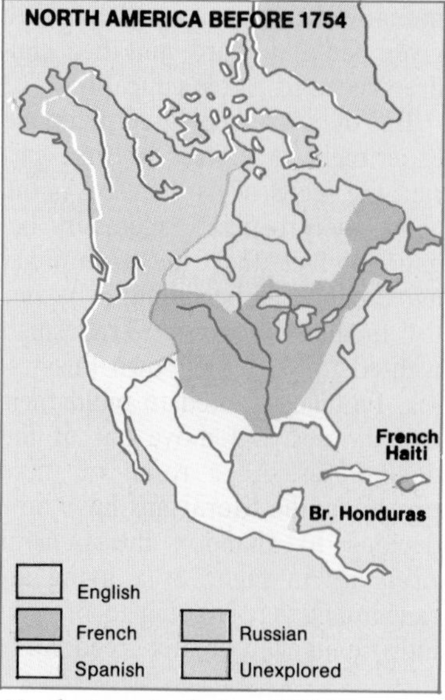

North America before 1754.

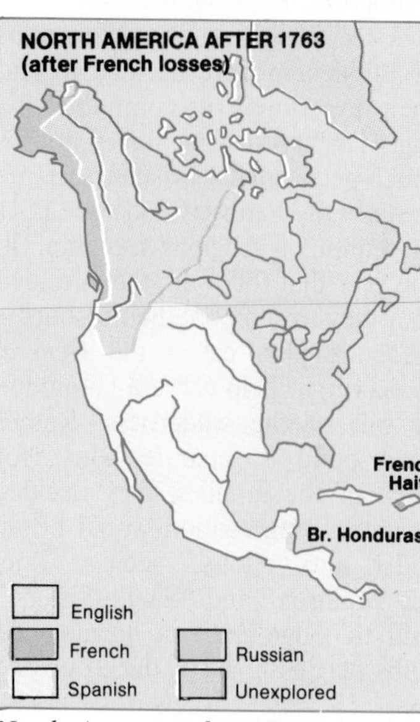

North America after 1763.

After three attempts to seize the city, the British finally occupy Quebec.

Mason and Dixon drawing a border

Philadelphia

If all of Pennsylvania's grievances are ruled justified, Maryland will be reduced to a mere strip of land. If all of Maryland's desires are granted, then Philadelphia will be in Maryland. In order that these rather absurd situations be avoided, two English surveyors, Charles Mason and Jeremiah Dixon, have begun to survey a boundary line between the two colonies. Many of the acute disputes over boundaries can be traced to the grant and charter obtained by William Penn in 1681, which included many indefinite and some impossible clauses.

"Paxton Boys" kill Indians in 2 raids

Philadelphia, Dec. 27

The Paxton Boys, a band of Scotch-Irish Presbyterians from the town of Paxton on the Susquehanna River, attacked a Moravian mission for Indians in Lancaster County today, killing several Delaware there. The attack was the second by the Paxtons this month. On December 14, some 50 Paxton Boys rode into the town of Conestoga, where they killed six Indians, supposedly in revenge for atrocities committed by Indians during Pontiac's war, one that never involved eastern Pennsylvania.

In February, an armed Paxton band rode into Philadelphia with a list of grievances to present to Governor John Penn. Many Philadelphians have rallied to defend the city against the Paxtons and to protect its Moravian Indian converts as well. They fear these "rioters," as missionary John Heckewelder calls them, may harm more Indians.

It is the belief of the Paxton Boys that Indians are descended from Canaanites, who, by God's commandments, are to be cut off the face of the earth; that is, destroyed. Many Philadelphians suspect that the band's real aim is to overthrow the government. It was Benjamin Franklin's idea to persuade the visitors that the odds were against them and that they ought to just go back home.

Proclamation bans colonies in West

London, Oct. 7

Winning the French and Indian War has left the British with a unique problem: what to do with all the land they have acquired by treaty and default. This May, they placed the problem in the hands of the Board of Trade, which until last month was headed by the Earl of Shelburne. A dedicated servant of the crown, Shelburne came up with an answer: simply ban settlers in the entire region west of the Appalachian Mountains.

To this end, the King has signed a proclamation preventing permanent settlement in the region and creates, as well, the crown colonies of East and West Florida and Canada. All colonial claims west of a line that runs the length of the Appalachian Mountains, from Canada to Florida, have been annulled. Britain intends to put its army to work patrolling the borders of this huge area, keeping the settlers out and the Indians in. Only traders who are licensed by the crown will be permitted to proceed past the demarcation line. The Shelburne proposals were ignored until Indians, under Pontiac, laid siege to the British at their fort in Detroit (→Apr. 17, 1766).

Pontiac ravages British

Pontiac raises a tomahawk in a gesture of defiance against the British.

Fort Niagara, November

Ottawa Chief Pontiac has lifted his six-month siege of Fort Detroit after learning that the French would not provide the expected support for his rebellion against the British in the Great Lakes region.

The ravages of Pontiac and his allies, the Delaware, Potawatomie, Chippewa, Huron, Shawnee, Seneca and Mingo, began in May and left a path of death and destruction among the forts and settlements along the frontier. After the attack on Fort Detroit in early May, the British garrisons of Sandusky, Saint Joseph, Miami and Ouiatenon fell in rapid succession. In June, Fort Sault Ste. Marie on the St. Mary's River was burned, and British troops at Fort Michilimackinac were overrun and murdered by the Chippewa. Forts Venango, Le Boeuf and Presque Isle fell to the Seneca in mid-June. Fort Pitt at the fork of the Ohio River, however, successfully resisted an attack by the Delaware late in June.

The only other fort in the Great Lakes region to escape destruction is Fort Niagara, which supplied much of the support for the defense of Fort Detroit. But this support was not without cost. Pontiac constantly harassed supply ships and reinforcements, inflicting heavy casualties on the troops of Captain James Dalyell at the Battle of Bloody Run late in July, and destroying a supply train at Devil's Hole on the Niagara River in September. The only significant defeat of the Indians during the rebellion came in August, when Col. Henry Bouquet's troops on their way to relieve the garrison at Fort Pitt, repulsed an attack near Bushy Run. Though the rebellion has lost much support, a renewal of the attacks in the spring is feared (→Nov. 1764).

Killing Indians by smallpox proposed

Fort Niagara, July 13

Informed sources say General Jeffrey Amherst, British commander of colonial forces on the Great Lakes frontier, recently wrote a vice commander, Colonel Henry Bouquet, advising him to try to inoculate Chief Pontiac's rebellious Indians with smallpox by means of infected blankets. The questionable ethics of this form of warfare have caused alarm in some quarters, and Colonel Bouquet is said to have advised General Amherst that the tactic could backfire by spreading the feared disease among British soldiers and citizens. Others, however, are supporting the proposal (→31).

Amherst: proposes blanket solution.

Northern area is named Verd-mont

Verd-mont, October

Amid the wilderness of an area that is claimed by two colonies, the Rev. Richard Peters stood before a gathering of hardy residents and called the land "Verd-mont," a name that he said was "worthy of the Athenians and ancient Spartans." The name, which means "green mountain," is still not official, because the land is not autonomous and until now has served mostly as a route for French and Indian incursions from Canada into Massachusetts. What's more, colonial authorities are still squabbling over whether the Governor of New Hampshire, Benning Wentworth, really has the authority to make land grants in the region, because New York also has a claim to ownership here (→July 20, 1764).

Sephardic Jews open splendid synagogue

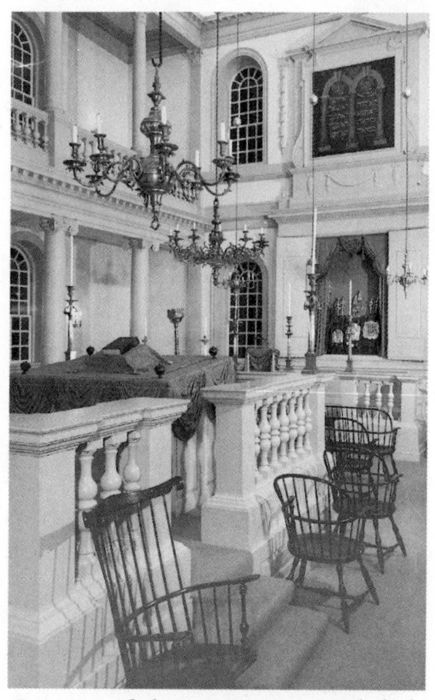

Interior of the synagogue, with light from its chandeliers, proclaims a Judaism practiced openly and freely.

Newport, Dec. 2

The city of Newport was captivated today by the opening ceremonies for the Touro Synagogue, the first major center of Jewish culture in America. The 20 Sephardic Jewish families who make up the Congregation Jeshuat Israel chose a small lot on Griffin Street as the site for their synagogue. Money was collected from other Sephardic groups in Jamaica and Surinam, and in London and Amsterdam to cover the cost of putting up this magnificent structure. The building was designed by Peter Harrison, a local and renowned architect, who asked no fee for his participation, which was exclusively the creation of the plans. Although Harrison relied principally on classic architectural elements, the building is set at an angle of 30 degrees to the street so the synagogue's ark faces east.

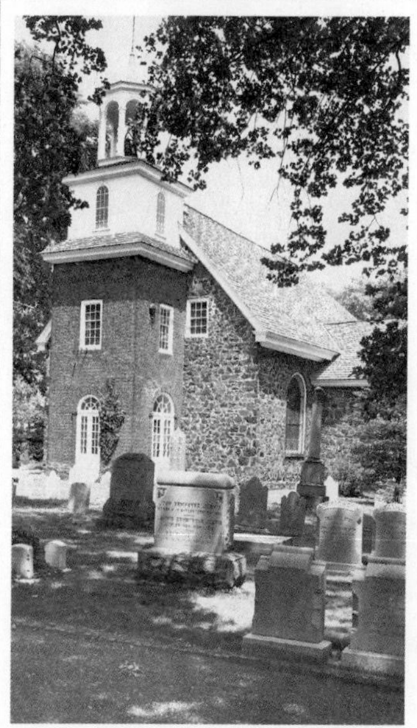

America is a land of religious liberty. "Gloria Dei," or Old Swedes' Church, dedicated in 1700, is the oldest house of worship in Philadelphia. [It is still in use today].

DOODLE
Pub.by
Ryder

Harvest of Freedom 1764-1788

The American Revolution was the most important event in the history of the United States. Not only did it transform the English colonies in America into a free, independent nation that would eventually become the richest and most powerful in the world, it also did much to determine what kind of nation it would be. The Revolution was, therefore, more than simply a rebellion against English rule and a long, difficult war. It was a process of national self-definition. In the course of the Revolution, Americans decided what principles they would embrace, how they would be governed and how they would relate to each other. They also decided, if only by inaction, what problems they would avoid and leave for future generations to solve.

Few Americans would have predicted even in the early 1760's that in a little more than a decade their society would be moving toward independence. Most colonists valued their membership in the British Empire and saw no reason to challenge it. The imperial system offered many benefits and few costs. It tied the American colonies into a system of international trade. It offered them military protection. It gave them a stable political system. And it asked almost nothing in return. The colonies were, on the whole, left alone to run their affairs as they liked. Even the British laws designed to regulate external trade were administered so casually that American merchants had little difficulty circumventing them.

But the apparent stability of the imperial relationship in the early 1760's obscured some potentially disruptive realities. Ever since the beginning of English settlement in America, the colonies had been developing – culturally, intellectually and politically – into societies very different from the English world they were ostensibly re-creating. As long as the British left the Americans alone, it was possible to overlook these fundamental differences. But with the end of the French and Indian (or, as Europeans knew it, Seven Years) War in 1763, the colonial relationship changed. For the first time in 50 years, England was genuinely at peace and was able to turn its attention to the organization of its empire. At the same time, Britain found itself burdened with enormous debts from the many years of fighting. In addition, the end of the war had given England dominion over vast new lands in the New World that had once belonged to the French. For all these reasons, the government of the new King, George III, who had assumed the throne in 1760, felt both entitled to and obliged to expand its involvement in the colonies.

Americans, in the meantime, had grown so accustomed to managing their own affairs that they had come to consider such freedom their right. And the victorious war for empire in which they had played an important role had given them a heightened sense of their own importance and hardened their assumptions about their political autonomy. The colonial assemblies, which officials in London considered minor local bodies subordinate to Parliament, were to Americans centers of great authority, with rights and privileges that even Parliament could not abridge. The power of taxation, which the British believed lay ultimately with them, the Americans considered an inalienable local prerogative. On these, and on many other issues, the British and the Americans were operating under very different assumptions. And the result was a series of events that, more rapidly than anyone would have predicted, ended British rule in much of America.

For more than a decade after the end of the French and Indian War, the imperial relationship was beset by a series of steadily escalating tensions. In 1765, there was the Stamp Act crisis, the first effort by the British government to impose a direct tax on the Americans. This offensive statute brought the colonies to the brink of revolt before Parliament repealed it. Two years later, the Townshend Acts, another effort by the crown to raise revenue from the colonies, sparked more resistance, which culminated three years later in a bloody clash between British troops and American protesters – an event that became known as the Boston Massacre. Then, in 1773, after several years of relative calm, Parliament passed the Tea Act, which gave the struggling British East India Company special privileges in the American market and enraged colonists who considered the law another infringement on their rights. The act spurred an American boycott of tea (and the famous Boston Tea Party of December 1773) – resistance that prompted Parliament to pass a series of laws designed to punish resisters in Massachusetts by stripping the colony of much local authority.

◄ *"The Spirit of '76" (1874), Archibald M. Willard's symbol of the Revolution.*

These Intolerable Acts, as they were known in the colonies, finally brought to a head grievances that had been accumulating for years. The laws appeared to confirm what many Americans had long believed: that the British government had become hopelessly corrupt; that a conspiracy had been hatched to rob them of their liberties; that the colonies must take a united stand against tyranny.

A Continental Congress, with representatives from 12 of the 13 colonies, met to coordinate colonial resistance. And in Massachusetts, the target of the Intolerable Acts, colonists began to store arms and to train "Minutemen" (volunteers ready to fight at a minute's notice), to oppose the English by force, if necessary. In April 1775, British troops attempted to arrest the rebel leaders and seize an illegal supply of arms in Concord. The result was the battles of Lexington and Concord – the first hostilities of the War of Independence.

The shots fired in Massachusetts were neither the first nor the last steps along the road to the creation of an independent nation. Although hostilities between the Americans and the British quickly escalated, many colonists continued for over a year to believe that they were fighting not for freedom, but for their rightful place in the British Empire. Gradually, however, that came to seem too small a goal for which to pay so high a price. By the summer of 1776, sentiment for independence had gained wide popular favor. And on July 4 of that year, the Continental Congress, meeting in Philadelphia, proclaimed the existence of a new nation: the United States of America.

To make that nation a reality, the American people had to fight a long and difficult war against the greatest military power in the world, a war that few outside observers believed they could win. The fighting continued for more than six years, and the American cause at times seemed on the verge of collapse. But a series of British blunders and a succession of dramatic American successes gradually turned the tide. In 1781, the principal British army in America surrendered at Yorktown. Two years later, a peace treaty confirmed the existence of the new nation.

At the same time that they were fighting the war, Americans were designing a political system. Early in 1776, even before the Declaration of Independence, Americans in several colonies were beginning to create written constitutions. And over the next several years – in a burst of political creativity with few precedents in history – one after another of the new states formed governments for themselves that expressed the principles for which they believed they were fighting. Americans were slower to agree on the form of their national government. At first, most thought the central government should remain relatively weak, that each state should be something close to a sovereign nation. Such assumptions helped produce the Articles of Confederation of 1777 and the first government of the United States. But the confederation failed to satisfy those who hoped for an effective central mechanism. Unpopular during the war because of its apparent ineffectuality, it failed in peacetime as well to provide the stability and coherence that many Americans believed their society required. By the late 1780's, there was substantial sentiment for change.

Serious discussions about the construction of a new political system began in 1786. And in 1787, the nation finally created for itself what the individual states had produced years before: a written constitution and a government consisting of three independent branches. The American Constitution was not without flaws. Delegates could not agree on how to handle the most potentially divisive issue facing the new nation: slavery. So they left the question unresolved, to plague future generations. But on balance, the creation of the Constitution was a remarkable achievement. In the space of a few hot summer weeks in Philadelphia, a remarkable group of men wrote a document that, two centuries later, would survive as the basis of one of the oldest and stablest governments in the world.

1764

Pennsylvania, Feb. 14. James Davenport gets patent for machinery designed to spin and card wool.

Virginia, Apr. 10. General Court orders England to give back pay to the Rev. James Maury, ruling crown had broken compact with subject by paying him in currency rather than agreed upon quantity of tobacco.

Presque Isle, Lake Michigan, Apr. 12. Colonel John Bradstreet gains treaty with certain rebellious Indian tribes, Ottawa Chief Pontiac's not among them.

London, Apr. 19. Parliament passes Currency Act, third Grenville law, which bans colonies from printing paper money (→ May 14).

Boston, May 14. *Boston Evening Post* comes out in support of colonial effort to oppose British trade regulations (→ 24).

Boston, May 24. Speaking at a town meeting, lawyer James Otis raises issue of "taxation without representation" and calls for a united colonial protest against Grenville measures (→ July 23).

New England, July 20. Land west of Connecticut River and north of Massachusetts [Vermont] is annexed to New York colony by royal order.

Boston, July 23. James Otis publishes *The Rights of the British Colonies Asserted and Proved,* a polemic criticizing the Sugar Act for taxing colonies without representation (→ Aug.).

Boston, August. City merchants organize boycott of luxury imports from England, inaugurating policy of non-importation (→ Sept.).

Providence, Rhode Island, Dec. 22. Governor Stephen Hopkins, with assent of assembly, publishes *The Rights of the Colonies Examined* in *Providence Gazette*.

New York. Prussian ironmonger Peter Hasenclever establishes ironworks.

Boston. Samuel Adams refuses to allow a slave, offered as a present to his wife, into his house except as a free woman.

Boston. *The Administration of the Colonies*, by Thomas Pownall, proposes program that would bind colonies to England.

Boston. *Collection of the Best Psalm Tunes* is compiled by Josiah Flagg.

British set sugar tax

London, Apr. 5

For the first time, Parliament today enacted a law specifically aimed at raising revenue from the colonists. Burdened by the cost of keeping troops in America, a vast debt resulting from the war with France and heavy taxes at home, Parliament has approved the American Revenue Act, or the Sugar Act.

While an extension of last year's Molasses Act, the measure is far-reaching. It cuts the duty on foreign molasses from sixpence a gallon to three, raises duties on foreign refined sugar, increases the export bounty on British refined sugar and tells colonists they no longer may import French wine or foreign rum.

What Parliament really is doing is granting British planters a monopoly in the American sugar market. The act makes smuggling of foreign sugar unprofitable and goes after the widespread and illicit colonial trading in foreign molasses.

Accustomed to paying a sum of roughly a penny to a penny and a half a gallon on foreign molasses, the American colonists are outraged at the prospect of now having to pay twice as much (→ 19).

The act threatens a thriving trade with West Indies plantations like this one.

Angry Americans rally against Sugar Act

Boston, September

At a town meeting here May 24, James Otis denounced "taxation without representation" and called for the colonies to unite in protest against Brtain's new tax measures. To promote his argument, Otis has published *The Rights of the British Colonies Asserted and Proved.*

Some of Boston's merchants object to the Sugar Act for a different reason, however. They oppose the measure on the grounds that sugar and molasses are an integral part of the slave trade and that they therefore should be regarded as "vital commerce."

In protest, the merchants have organized a boycott of imported luxury goods from England, including lace and ruffles, thus launching a policy of non-importation. The mechanics of the city have also joined the protest by agreeing not to buy any leather work clothes made outside of Massachusetts. Mechanics in New York followed suit this month (→ June 8, 1765).

Otis, volatile partisan of the colonies.

French trading post to start at St. Louis

Chouteau, by Joseph C. Barlow.

Fort de Chartres, February

Auguste Chouteau, the remarkable 14-year-old assistant of Pierre Laclede, recently led a group of workmen from here to begin clearing a site chosen earlier by Laclede for a new French trading post on the west bank of the Mississippi River not far below the mouth of the Missouri. The purpose of the post, which will be called St. Louis, is to establish a strong French presence in the area to counter the British influence. Laclede, representing the New Orleans firm of Maxent, Laclede, believes the post might eventually become a big city because of its fortunate location.

Catherine orders Alaska exploration

St. Petersburg, Russia

Catherine II has ordered another exploration of Alaska (the territory across from Siberia), and Russian entrepreneurs, the promysleniki, are excited because it is sure to produce more high-quality furs such as those brought back by the ill-fated Bering expedition. Also certain to please the promysleniki is the great Catherine's decision to drop the yasaki, the fur tax, because the Aleuts, the natives there, do not grasp the concept of taxes.

Times have been good for the traders. For decades, the fur industry has been booming. Trade with the Aleuts has grown every year for the last 20. And now discussions are under way about the establishment of a permanent colony in this new land to the east.

Expelled Acadians arriving in Louisiana

New Orleans, Apr. 4

Four families of French-speaking Acadians deported from Canada arrived in New Orleans today from New York City. The 20 Acadians are the first to reach Louisiana. They had lived on the East Coast since 1755, when the British expelled them for refusing to take an oath of loyalty to England. The Acadians say their French ancestors had lived on a peninsula on the eastern coast of Canada since 1605.

Recounting the events as if they had happened yesterday, the new arrivals tell a heartbreaking story of their expulsion from Canada. The men were first imprisoned in a church and forced to give up their guns. Then English troops herded them onto ships, often separating families. Leaving hastily, the Acadians lost, in addition to their land and homes, almost all their belongings. The ships took large numbers of them to ports on the Atlantic. Many died aboard ship and two vessels sank with hundreds aboard. Some Acadians were sent to England, then to France. In all, 7,000 people were deported. The Acadians say some of their friends found their way back to Canada.

The families arriving here say that they decided to come to Louisiana after learning that the area was settled by French and that most of its citizens are Catholic. They hope to settle along the bayous of southern Louisiana. Most are farmers and many are skilled fishermen and trappers.

Pontiac allies surrender

Pontiac's warriors besiege Fort Detroit. Illustration by Frederick Remington.

Fort Niagara, November

One of the largest and most impressive gatherings of Indians in North America was held at Fort Niagara in July when more than 2,000 representatives of the Indian tribes lately allied with the rebellious Ottawa Chief Pontiac came to participate in peace negotiations conducted by Sir William Johnson. Also present were 1,200 troops under Colonel John Bradstreet's command, sent from Albany to impress the Indians with the strength and resolve of the British government to end the rebellion. Observers on the scene noted that many of the Indians are suffering from a lack of food and other supplies, and seem as weary of the war as the British.

Wasson, principal chief of the Chippewas and the ranking chief present, set the tone for the conference with a speech professing humble submission to the will of the British. Negotiations then continued for several weeks with representatives of each tribe present.

Conspicuous by their absence in the early meetings were the Seneca, Delaware and Shawnee, as well as Pontiac himself. Later, however, Johnson convinced the Seneca to attend the conference; and last month, the Delaware and Shawnee came in following Colonel Henry Bouquet's meeting with them on the upper Muskingum River. There is still no evidence that Pontiac or his small band of Ottawa followers want to enter the peace talks. Captain Thomas Morris, who met with Pontiac while on a mission from General Bradstreet to Fort de Chartres, reports Pontiac made it clear he still considers the English his enemies and has no intention of surrendering (→ July 24, 1766).

Acadians leaving Canada in 1755 after refusing to swear allegiance to Britain.

Baptist college in Rhode Island opens

Providence, Rhode Island

Although sometimes associated with anti-intellectualism, the ecstatic religious revival known as the Great Awakening has led to the formation of several new colleges in the colonies. The latest, founded by the Baptists, is the College of Rhode Island [Brown University] in Providence. Elsewhere, the evangelical movement inspired by the Rev. George Whitefield has been responsible for interrupting college classes and promoting scenes of mass religious ecstasy, with people shrieking and rolling about on the floor.

Wild orange groves found in Florida

Florida

In order to discourage westward migration, which might move settlers beyond the reach of commerce with Britain, King George III has instituted policies to promote the settlement of sparsely populated areas on the eastern seaboard. Two years ago, George sent the Botanist Royal in America, farmer John Bartram, to explore Florida and to study the indigenous flora and fauna. He now reports the discovery of wild orange groves in this region, some of them up to 40 miles long. Few Europeans now inhabit this area.

The Connecticut Courant.

MONDAY, October 29, 1764. (Number 00.)

HARTFORD: Printed by Thomas Green, at the Heart and Crown, near the North-Meeting-Houfe.

Hartford, October 29th, 1764.

December. *A new weekly extols the virtue of printing, "for hereby the greatest Geniuses of all Ages . . . live and speak for the Benefit of future Generations." [As the Hartford Courant, it is the oldest paper in the nation.]*

1765

Philadelphia, May 3. College of Philadelphia offers first professional medical training.

Boston, June 8. Massachusetts Assembly invites other assemblies to send delegates to New York City in October for an intercolonial meeting on the Stamp Act (→Aug. 15).

Upper Louisiana, July 17. St. Ange de Bellerive surrenders Fort de Chartres to British, moves capital to St. Louis, maintaining control over government.

Boston, Aug. 15. Threats of violence force Andrew Oliver, stamp agent, to quit (→25).

Boston, Aug. 25. Mob burns lieutenant governor's house following Johathan Mayhew's sermon, *Ye Have Been Called Unto Liberty* (→26).

Boston, Aug. 31. Governor Francis Bernard writes account of Stamp Act riots and sends it to Earl of Halifax (→Oct. 7).

America, August. John Adams writes, in *Dissertation on the Canon and the Feudal Law,* "The preservation of the means of knowledge among the lowest ranks is of more importance to the public than all the property of all the rich men in the country."

New York City, Oct. 7. Stamp Act Congress convenes with delegates from Maryland, South Carolina, Massachusetts, Delaware, New Jersey, Rhode Island, Pennsylvania, New York and Connecticut (→25).

New York City, Oct. 31. Non-importation plan joined by 200 merchants vowing not to buy British goods until Stamp and Sugar Acts repealed (→Nov. 1).

Philadelphia, November. More than 400 merchants join non-importation movement.

New York City, Dec. 13. General Thomas Gage, commander of British forces in colonies, asks New York Assembly to provide housing and supplies for his troops under Quartering Act (→Jan. 1766).

North Carolina. Establishment Act passed as addendum to 1715 Vestry Act, making Anglicanism official religion.

Massachusetts. John Harmon makes first chocolate in North America at Dorchester Lower Mills on Neponset River.

London. Major Robert Rogers proposes to make an overland search for Northwest Passage, using the name "Ouragon" [Oregon] in letter to King George III.

Another hated law: The Stamp Act

London, Nov. 1

The highly controversial Stamp Act finally took effect today, but it may be many months before the Parliament collects even a penny from the colonies. The act was passed March 22 with very little dissent, but in the intervening months significant opposition developed across the Atlantic. Riots erupted in New York City and an effigy of the Prime Minister was hanged from a liberty pole in Boston and later moved to the public gallows. Bells rang and patriots pledged that they would not comply with the first direct tax imposed by Parliament on the colonies.

The legislation was designed to raise money in the colonies to help support British troops stationed there. The treasury is still running a high deficit in the wake of the French and Indian War, and leaders of Parliament thought it only right that the colonies should pay for their own defense. Similar taxes have been used with great success in England for years. The legislation calls for revenues to be collected from stamps affixed to different sorts of printed matter, including newspapers, pamphlets and almanacs; most legal documents, such as mortgages, deeds and licenses, and other items, like dice and playing cards. Although Parliament expected little opposition, the legislation attempted to make the tax more acceptable by appointing certain colonists as tax agents and paying them 300 pounds a year.

The chief sponsor of the Stamp Act was Prime Minister George Grenville. He recently had a falling out with King George III and was forced to resign. During debate in the House of Commons, Grenville refused to heed the warnings of Colonel Isaac Barre, a strong supporter of the colonists. The colonel noted that earlier acts of Parliament, specifically the Molasses and Sugar Acts, had "made the blood of those sons of liberty boil within them," and he predicted the Stamp Act would create even more dissent. Events have proved Barre right. At first, the colonists pleaded poverty in the post-war depression. Now they are raising larger, legal issues, and claim England has no right to tax them (→Jan. 14, 1766).

In Boston, a city that is quickly turning into a hotbed of agitation against British rule, patriots burn stamps to protest the Stamp Act.

A Tory stamp agent is strung up by the seat of his pants on a liberty pole, while protesters prepare to tar and feather another agent of the crown.

During a series of protests orchestrated by Boston's Sons of Liberty, colonists ransack the house of Thomas Hutchinson, Massachusetts lieutenant governor.

At the root of it all: One of the stamps that have placed an indelible imprint on British-American relations.

"The Pennsylvania Journal & Advertiser" sardonically suggested affixing this stamp to all imported goods.

Patrick Henry: "If this be treason . . ."

Williamsburg, Virginia, May 30

Patrick Henry, a self-educated lawyer and fiery orator, tasted victory today as the Virginia House of Burgesses adopted most of his seven resolutions condemning efforts by Parliament to tax the colonies. At the height of the debate yesterday, Henry was interrupted by the speaker and branded a traitor after he exclaimed, "Caesar had his Brutus, Charles the First his Cromwell, and George the Third may profit by their example." As cries of "Treason!" filled the chamber, Henry glared at the speaker, rose even taller on his feet and retorted without hesitation, "If this be treason, make the most of it."

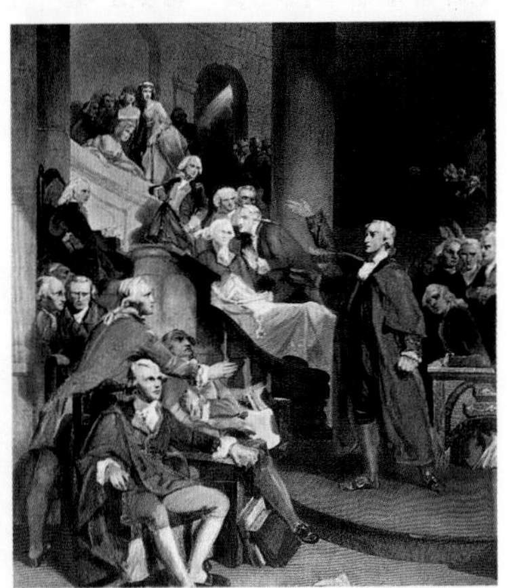

Patrick Henry defends his seven proposals before the House of Burgesses.

The 29-year-old Henry is serving his first term in the House. He made a name for himself two years ago in court as he defended efforts to reduce the size of the stipends paid to the Anglican clergy. After a spirited argument, the jury sided with Henry and agreed to pay a minister the salary of one penny.

British troop quartering act takes effect

London, March 24

Parliament is again attempting to force the reluctant colonies to help support the troops in America. The latest legislation, taking effect today, is called the Quartering Act. It requires the colonies to provide shelter and food to British soldiers and their horses. General Thomas Gage, commander-in-chief of British soldiers in America, requested the legislation after many colonists refused to offer his men any services. Earlier legislation, the Mutiny Act, contained a clause for quartering troops in private homes. The colonists generally contended that the law did not apply to them. They also objected to the soldiers sleeping in their own bedrooms. The new Quartering Act is more specific and says the troops should be provided with barracks. Colonial leaders are opposed nonetheless. They resent the intrusion of soldiers into their private lives. They also believe that compliance with the law would acknowledge the right of Parliament to tax them. The law is to be in effect for two years (→Dec. 13).

J.S. Copley paints "Boy With a Squirrel"

Boston

In his latest work, *Boy With a Squirrel*, John Singleton Copley proves himself to be an American painter with an international vision. Copley's sensitive portrait of his 16-year-old half-brother and artistic apprentice, Henry Pelham, reveals a technical mastery that rivals his English contemporaries while rendering a distinctly colonial spirit. Among artists in America, Copley is now without peer. The Boston painter's level of achievement may soon be compared with those in England, for he plans to send his new portrait to be exhibited at the Society of Artists in London.

"Boy With a Squirrel" by Copley, an American artist without peer.

Stamp Act Congress petitions for repeal

New York City, Oct. 25

From Virginia to Massachusetts, Parliament's effort to tax the colonies through the Stamp Act has provoked spirited oratory and violence. The reaction was more moderate in New York today as the Stamp Act Congress adopted a series of resolutions and adjourned after meeting for more than two weeks. A formal Declaration of Rights and Grievances states that Parliament has no right to impose taxes on the colonies since they are not represented in Parliament.

In England, efforts have also been mounted to repeal the controversial measure. Former Prime Minister William Pitt says the act was a mistake, and many merchants agree. Their business with the colonies has declined dramatically. The chief sponsor of the act, former Prime Minister Grenville, believes, however, that it could be enforced with military support.

John Dickinson, the Pennsylvania politician, wrote most of the colonists' declaration. James Otis, the Massachusetts patriot, backed the resolutions but denounced what he called the "treason" of Patrick Henry and urged "dutiful and loyal addresses to His Majesty" (→31).

Sons of Liberty active in colonial towns

Boston, Aug. 26

A mob burned and sacked the magnificent home of the Massachusetts lieutenant governor, Thomas Hutchinson, last night. The attackers were enraged by Hutchinson's strong support of the widely despised Stamp Act. It is believed that the mob has links to a fast-growing band of patriots who call themselves the Sons of Liberty. The loosely organized group has chapters in many of the colonies, but one of the strongest is active right here in Boston. Its leader is a firebrand by the name of Sam Adams, 43, a man who seems to have finally found his calling in life.

Until now, Adams has failed at almost everything. He abandoned the study of law after graduating from Harvard in 1740 and then lost the 1,000 pounds he borrowed from his father to start a new business. He later squandered a large inheritance and was an abysmal failure as a tax collector. Recently, he turned to politics and drafted several key documents promoting the cause of the patriots in the Massachusetts legislature. Adams, who speaks venomously of the Stamp Act, believes that the minds of oppressed people "will be irritated as long as they have any sense of honor, liberty and virtue." Despite his growing reputation as an agitator, Adams did not invent the name "Sons of Liberty." It was first used in a speech in Parliament by Colonel Isaac Barre, a strong supporter of the colonists' cause (→31).

Great Britain dismembered: A French depiction of the American conflict portrays England and its American colonies as mutual prisoners in a sort of war of attrition that the mother country is clearly losing. Still embittered by the loss of their American territory two years ago in the Treaty of Paris, the French delight in England's recent troubles overseas.

1766

London, Jan. 14. Parliament convenes; Grenville leads fight for Stamp Act; William Pitt leads fight against (→ 17).

London, Jan. 17. English merchants testify against Stamp Act before Parliament, complaining that colonial non-importation movement is ruining businesses (→ Feb. 11).

New York City, January. Assembly refuses General Thomas Gage's demand for full quarters and supplies for British troops (→ Dec. 19).

Northampton, Virginia, Feb. 11. Court declares Stamp Act unconstitutional (→ 13).

London, Feb. 13. Ben Franklin, representing Pennsylvania, tells Parliament that Stamp Act is undue hardship on colonies and may cause revolution (→ March 18).

London, March 18. King approves repeal of Stamp Act; Declaratory Act is passed as measure to save face, declaring Parliament's right to legislate affairs of colonies "in all cases whatsoever" (→ Apr. 26).

London, Apr. 17. Auditor general of North America Cholmondely asserts that Proclamation of 1763 leaves pre-existing grants in West intact, prompting struggle for legitimacy of land claims (→ Nov. 5, 1768).

London, Aug. 8. Order in council curbs power of Board of Trade, channeling colonial correspondence through secretary of state.

London, Nov. 1. Parliament revises 1764 trade acts, lowering molasses and sugar duties, but requiring colonial exports to Northern Europe to pass through English ports (→ Jan. 1767).

London, August. Charles Townshend becomes chancellor of the Exchequer as Lord Chatham's ministry takes over.

Louisiana. Benjamin Cutbird voyages to Mississippi River, exploring beyond frontier to New Orleans to sell furs.

New Jersey. Flying Machine stagecoach cuts 90-mile trip from Camden to Jersey City to two days.

London. Robert Rogers's *Ponteach, or, The Savages of America* is first published play about American Indians.

Boston. *Sixteen Anthems* compiled by Josiah Flagg.

Philadelphia. Gloucester Fox Hunting Club, first hunting club in America, is founded.

Gen. Gage closes New York Assembly

New York City, Dec. 19

The New York Assembly, its resolve stiffened following the bloody clash between patriots and British citizens, still refuses to comply with the controversial Quartering Act. In retribution, General Thomas Gage, the commander-in-chief of British forces, today ordered all activities of the assembly suspended.

The tension in New York escalated August 10 when the Sons of Liberty leader Isaac Sears was injured in a fight with the British. Supporters of the crown believe Sears is little more than a mob leader. To the Americans, who call him "King," Sears is a hero. He was hurt in a struggle that began after British soldiers tore down a liberty pole. The troops were protesting the assembly's refusal to enforce the Quartering Act.

Since the Stamp Act was passed last year, General Gage has pulled most of his troops in from the Western outposts and stationed many of them in New York to quell the angry protests. At the general's request, Governor Henry Moore formally asked the assembly last year to provide for the troops under the provisions of the Quartering Act. He has repeated the request on several occasions, but the assembly has turned him down on the grounds that it does not have the financial resources (→ June 6, 1767).

British drop Stamp Act

British engraving depicts the funeral procession of "Miss Americ-Stamp."

Boston, Apr. 26

Throughout the colonies, bells rang, flags fluttered and patriots cheered as word spread that Parliament had repealed the hated Stamp Act. Describing the scene, colonial leader John Adams wrote: "The Liberty Tree was adorned all day with banners and illuminated in the evening, till the boughs could hold no more. The whole town was splendidly illuminated. The Common was covered with multitudes. Rockets blazed in every quarter."

The House of Commons took the lead in repealing the act on March 4. The vote was 250-122. To a great extent, members were swayed by the testimony of merchants who complained about the precipitous drop in exports to the colonies. The Prime Minister, Lord Rockingham, was told by one merchant: "Our trade is hurt; what the devil have you been doing? We don't pretend to understand your policies on American matters, but our trade is hurt; pray remedy it, and plague you if you don't."

Ben Franklin, the statesman from Pennsylvania, aided the colonial cause by saying the colonies were not averse to all taxes. Lord Mansfield was not convinced. He said repeal amounted to "giving up the total legislature of this kingdom . . . and will put us in the position of being dictated to by the Americans . . . What then," he wondered, "will become of us?" (→ Nov. 1).

Boys study classics, aim for college; girls learn domestic skills

America

In New England, education for boys is compulsory; in the South, it is generally not. Across the colonies, however, girls are well tutored – by their mothers – in domestic skills, learning to preserve and prepare foods, to make clothing using a spinning wheel or loom and to manage details of a home or plantation. In New England, both boys and girls may attend a dame school, one where the young learn the alphabet; at 7 or 8, a boy goes to grammar school to learn Latin and Greek (or get a paddling if he does not). A well-born lad of 15 may hope for college. A girl that age may hope one day to wed him.

In the schoolroom, a teacher keeps order under the threat of the rod.

ranklin invents bifocal spectacles

Philadelphia

Printer, inventor and leading itizen Benjamin Franklin has add-d to his already long list of inventions and contributions to American and European society with the levelopment of a new type of spectacles that he calls the bifocal. The new spectacles combine the advantages of regular glasses and eading glasses by fitting one type of lens in the upper part of the rame and another type in the lower o that the wearer of spectacles can asily change activities without aving to change glasses. Truly, Franklin is a man of vision.

Franklin (1766) by David Martin.

Colonies get first theater for drama

Philadelphia

This year has seen the construction of the Southwark Theater, the first edifice in the colonies built expressly for the staging of drama. David Douglass, entrepreneur and actor, designed and raised funds for the two-and-a-half-story building of brick and wood. It stands outside the city limits, no doubt to operate beyond earshot of local ministers. The inaugural presentation at Southwark was *Katharine and Petruchio*, which is adapted from Shakespeare's *Taming of the Shrew*. A wise choice, it appeals to all social classes.

Pontiac rebellion is ended by treaty

Fort Ontario, July 24

Chief Pontiac, who three years ago sparked a rebellion against the British among the Indian tribes of the Great Lakes region, concluded the final chapter in that rebellion today by signing a treaty of peace and amity with Sir William Johnson, superintendent of Indian affairs, at Fort Ontario. Much of the credit for persuading the Ottawa chief to end his rebellion goes to diplomat George Croghan and his interpreter, Albert Fraser, who met with Pontiac last summer at Kaskaskia and prepared the way for the treaty (→Apr. 20, 1769).

Spanish Governor arrives in Louisiana

New Orleans, March 5

The colony of Louisiana at last has a Spanish Governor, but he may face opposition before he settles into office. Antonio de Ulloa, named Spain's first Governor of Louisiana, arrived in the city today with 80 soldiers, a small force for a vast colony. Opposition to Spanish rule is reportedly smoldering. Although France transferred most of the colony to Spain in 1762, until now the Spanish have not made any move to take control. Ulloa is rather well known in Europe as a scholar, but he is lacking in ad-administrative experience.

Cricket, anyone?

New York City

New Yorkers are fond of games and gaming. An advertisement by the firm of James Rivington says he imports shuttlecocks, the battledores used to bat them, cricket balls, pellets and racquets for tennis, fives, and backgammon. Since the early part of the century, cricket has become increasingly popular in all the outposts of the British Empire. But this popularity has drawn considerable criticism from the pulpit because the fans usually bet very heavily on the outcome of the matches.

With war over, colonial trade is booming

Philadelphia

With the French and Indian War over, trade between England and the colonies is expanding at a quick pace. Americans are exporting a growing volume of sheep, pork, cattle, beef and hogs to English markets.

The Delaware and Schuylkill Rivers form a highway through the rich farmlands of Pennsylvania and have made Philadelphia the hub of an agricultural empire. It has become America's richest city, the envy of New York and Boston. Last year, more ships cleared Philadelphia, "than the city of Bristol, and I believe, any other port in Britain except London and Liverpool," said one resident, adding, "We shall begin to be the wonder of the world and soon rival considerable states in Europe."

In the Middle Atlantic colonies, the value of wheat products exceeds 770,000 pounds sterling; oats, peas, corn and beans total 52,000 pounds sterling, and the colonies have turned out meat products valued at 81,000 pounds this year alone.

Mighty ships in the harbor of Philadelphia, now America's richest city.

Frontiersman finds bones of mastodon

Ohio River

Frontiersman George Croghan, on a mission to make peace with the Indians in the Illinois region, made an unusual discovery about a mile and a half east of the Ohio River. There he found the bones of one or more prehistoric animals, most likely a mastodon, an elephant-like beast that once roamed North America. Croghan was sent to the region to make sure the Indians of the area, who are led by Chief Pontiac, will be friendly enough to allow British settlement in lands recently taken from the French. Croghan is traveling with two boatloads of gifts to be presented to the Indians.

Church establishes New Jersey college

New Brunswick, N.J., Nov. 10

In recent years, partly in response to the religious revival known as the Great Awakening, the leaders of several churches in America have founded colleges to sustain their traditions while teaching useful techniques of science. Here in New Jersey, the Dutch Reformed Church has established Queen's College [Rutgers University] to provide for "the education of youth in the learned languages, liberal and useful arts and sciences, and especially in divinity, preparing them for the ministry and other good offices." The start of such schools has encouraged religious tolerance.

1767

London, January. Charles Townshend, chancellor of the Exchequer and acting head of government during Lord Chatham's illness, opposes distinction between external and internal taxes, proposing revenue plan that would bypass colonial legislatures (→Feb. 27).

Burlington, New Jersey, Feb. 22. Quakers hold annual meeting; of 60 leaders in attendance, 25 are women.

London, Feb. 27. New admiralty courts, set up by Townshend Acts, to allow final legal appeal to take place in colonies, rather than England (→June 15).

Philadelphia, Apr. 20. First performance of Andrew Barton's *The Disappointment, or, the Force of Credulity* is canceled for fear its satirizing of England and Philadelphia would cause controversy. [It is only American ballad opera written before Revolution.]

Philadelphia, Apr. 24. Thomas Godfrey's *Prince of Parthia* is first professionally performed American play.

New York City, June 6. Assembly, in reversal, allots 3,000 pounds for quartering of British troops in hope Parliament will revoke ban on legislature (→Dec. 31, 1768).

London, June 15. First Townshend Act passed, suspending New York Assembly until it complies with Quartering Act (→29).

London, June 29. Second and third Townshend Acts passed, imposing new external taxes to support independent civil establishment, previously paid through colonial legislatures (→July 1).

London, July 1. Fourth Townshend Act passed, repealing inland duties on tea in England and allowing export free of British taxes (→Sept. 4).

London, Sept. 4. Charles Townshend dies; he is replaced by Lord North (→Nov. 20).

Boston, Oct. 28. Non-importation revived in anticipation of Townshend taxes (→Dec. 2).

Providence, Rhode Island, Dec. 2. Strict non-importation agreement signed (→29).

Boston, Dec. 21. *Boston Chronicle*, supporting Tory cause, publishes first issue.

New York City, Dec. 29. Committee named at meeting to develop means of asserting economic independence from England (→Feb. 11, 1768).

British set new taxes

London, Nov. 20

Their author died September 4, but the Townshend Acts have gone into effect, placing new taxes on articles imported by the American colonies. Piloting the act through the Parliament was the crowning achievement in Charles Townshend's 18-year political career.

Townshend died, but his laws live on.

Townshend so often changed positions through so many governments that many people called him "the Weathercock." But he was an able politician and, as chancellor of the Exchequer, thought he had a solution to the problem of raising taxes in the colonies, as well as a way to bring the recalcitrant New York Assembly to heel.

Why not place duties on such small and innocuous items as lead, glass, paints, paper and tea, Townshend asked. For one thing, this would be an external tax, therefore less likely to raise a fuss in the colonies. It is the internal taxes that the Americans seem to get into a lather about. The tax on tea did not seem to matter much anyway, since tea from the Netherlands is so openly smuggled into the major ports that it could hardly be called smuggling at all. Perhaps the tax on the other items would be shrugged off as well. But taxes have to be raised somewhere, and it is the general feeling in the British government that the Americans are the most obvious candidates.

When Parliament reconvened last November, in the midst of riots and insurrections over the price of grain, it cut the land tax of four shillings to three shillings, depriving the crown of about 500,000 pounds in annual revenue. The need to replace this revenue by funds from some other source forced the chancellor to consider taxing the colonists. Several other solutions were debated before the present proposals were approved June 29. One was to open the Mediterranean trade to American merchants, thus broadening the tax base; another was to place a levy on all goods in vessels that enter colonial ports. Townshend considered the American distinction between external and internal taxes ridiculous. "If we have a right to impose one," he said, "we have the other" (→Dec. 2).

The artisans of Boston, now laboring under the weight of even heavier taxation.

Lawyer's letters examine trade acts

Philadelphia, Nov. 5

In taverns and libraries, men' faces grow red – sometimes wit rage, at other times in hearty ap proval – as they read a series o letters by Pennsylvania farmer an lawyer John Dickinson. Other pub lications pick them up and they ca be read in a pamphlet in England.

Dickinson argues that nothing i new and that nothing is going t change: The colonies are at th mercy of the British. He write persuasively that Parliament doe not have the right to tax the colc nies, that the Townshend Acts ar blatantly unconstitutional and tha colonial assemblies can now be dis missed at the pleasure of the crow following the precedent that was se by Townshend's suspension of th New York legislature.

Dickinson comments furthe that if the Parliament across th ocean has the authority to orde colonists to furnish a single articl of clothing for British troops, wha is to prevent it from orderin Americans to furnish everything Colonists will soon be asked to pro vide clothes, arms and "every ne cessary." How, asks the lawyer, i this more tolerable than the Stamp Act? Somewhat ominously, Dick inson closes one letter by statin simply, "Small things grow great b concord." Although he asserts tha he is a man who hates anythin inflammatory, his readers may per haps see him otherwise (→20).

Permanent theater opens in New York

New York City

Thespian David Douglass ha built a theater on John Street mod eled on his Southwark Theater ir Philadelphia. Its walls are painted in ochre and skim-milk hues, and seating ranges from pit to gallery tc boxes. The first professionally acted American play, Thomas Godfrey's *Prince of Parthia*, which began a run in Philadelphia in April, is likely to make its way to John Street soon. The existence of the two playhouses may suggest public approval, but many people still call them "synagogues of Satan."

Boone goes beyond the Appalachians

Rowan County, N.C., December

Daniel Boone, famed marksman and hunter, left in early autumn to seek a way west over the mountains. With Squire and William Hill of Florida, he crossed the Blue Ridge and traveled to the headwaters of the Big Sandy by following the Holston and Clinch Rivers. Boone is convinced the Big Sandy must flow into the Ohio, which is the passage to the territory that the Indians call Ken-ta-ke [Kentucky]. At their camp, Boone told of how his men were "ketched by a snowstorm" and forced to stay the winter (→June 7, 1769).

Irish politician is boss in New Spain

Coahuila y Tejas, Summer

Hugo O'Conor, reputedly the first Irishman to settle here [Texas], has become interim Governor of this Mexican province. O'Conor, who has such flaming red hair that the Indians call him the "Red Captain," was formerly Spain's inspector general of the Provincias Internas. He arrived last year to investigate political and personal squabbles between the incumbent Governor, Angel de Martos y Navarrete, and an old rival, Rafael Martinez Pacheco. O'Conor's appointment, it is hoped, will restore order in the turbulent province.

Colonial economy emerges despite curbs

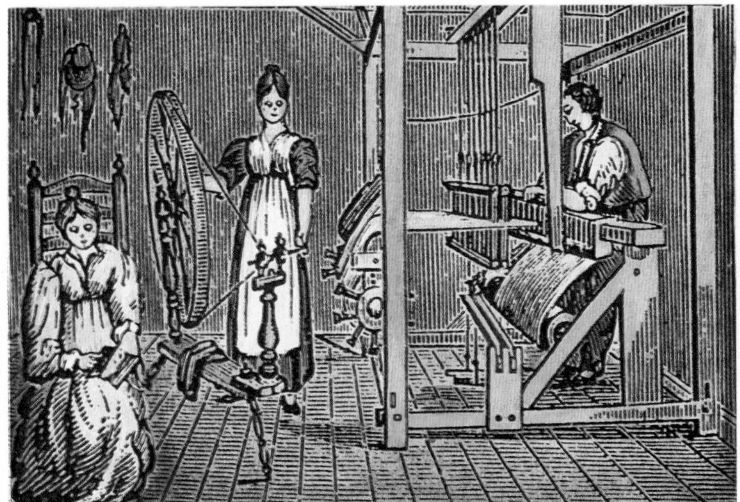

The cottage industry of carding, spinning and weaving wool into cloth.

America

"The only use of American colonies or West Indies islands is the monopoly of their consumption and the carriage of their produce." The sentiments of British statesman Lord Sheffield are echoed in the halls of policy thoughout London. But under the restrictive blanket of British mercantilism, a distinctly American economy is awakening.

The South's fertile tidewater makes it the ideal colonial region, naturally endowed to produce staples for export. In Virginia, the cash crop is tobacco; in the Carolinas and Georgia, rice and indigo. Although small farmers cannot compete with huge plantations, trade is mainly profitable. But dependency on a single crop has drawbacks. Soil exhaustion pushes settlers ever westward in search of new land. And the region remains dependent on England and the Northern colonies for manufactures.

Happy to oblige, New England and the middle colonies are developing thriving village industries. Most manufacture still takes place in the home. But production of bar iron in New Jersey and Pennsylvania now rivals England in quantity. Bounties on naval stores help spark forest industries in New England. And a surplus of wood allows shipbuilders to work at half the cost of their European competitors. All in all, the colonies prosper.

Device depicts how the planets rotate

Philadelphia

The astronomer David Rittenhouse has constructed a fascinating device that will help educate Americans about astronomy. Called an orrery, it is a detailed model of the solar system showing the relative positions and movements of the planets. As the device is operated, models of the planets swing around a central sun, timed with wheels and gears to reflect planetary observations. It is hoped that the invention can eventually be enlarged in such a way that many people can watch this re-creation of planetary rotation in some kind of a "planetarium."

Jesuits ordered out of Spanish colonies

Southwest

The Jesuit priests who brought Christianity to the Indians of the Southwest have been expelled from the Spanish provinces in the New World. Jealous of their influence, European political leaders have already banned the "Black Robes," as the Indians call them, in all French and Portuguese colonies. The Jesuits first visited the Southwest in the early 1600's and have ministered to six Indian tribes. Father Eusebio Kino founded 24 missions. The more tractable Franciscans have acceded to a request that they take over the Jesuit missions.

John Singleton Copley's "Portrait of Rebecca Boylston" (1767). Copley drew praise last year when he exhibited his work in London.

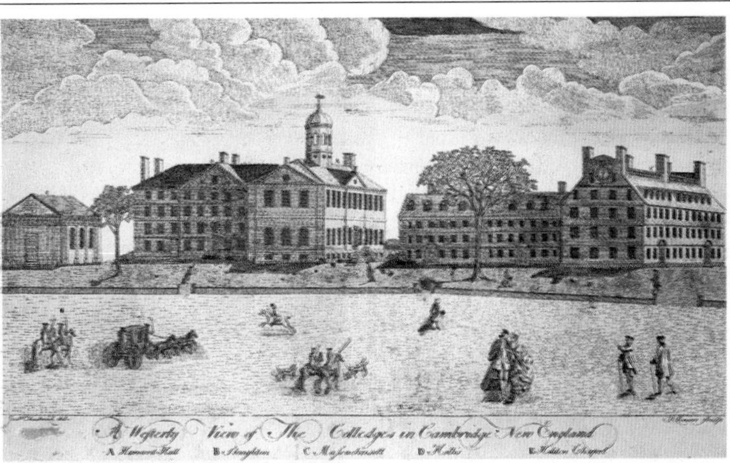

Paul Revere's engraving of Harvard College, the nation's oldest and most respected educational institution. Revere, son of a Huguenot refugee named De Revoire, is distinguishing himself in Boston as a fine silversmith. He also dabbles in surgical instruments and spectacles as well as dentistry.

Map of the rapidly expanding city of New York, as surveyed by Lieutenant Bernard Ratzer.

1768

London, Jan. 20. Lord Hillsborough, is named both secretary of state and president of Board of Trade, further centralizing colonial administration.

Boston, February. Harassed by colonial agitators, customs agents ask British government for military protection.

New York City, Apr. 5. Chamber of Commerce holds founding meeting.

London, Apr. 22. Hillsborough sends off order instructing colonial governors to block assemblies from endorsing Sam Adams's circular letter (→ Sept.).

America, April. With Connecticut, New Jersey and New Hampshire already supporting Adams's circular letter, Virginia issues letter promoting Massachusetts's stance (→ July 1).

Boston, May 17. Responding to customs commissioners' request for protection, British frigate Romney arrives in harbor armed with 50 guns (→ June 15.).

Boston, July 1. Governor Bernard dissolves General Court day after assembly votes to defy his order to rescind Adams's letter (→ Aug. 27).

New Smyrna, East Florida, Aug. 19. Dr. Alexander Trumbull leads Minorcan colonists into rebellion against poor working conditions.

New York City, Aug. 27. Merchants agree to stop importing British goods after Nov. 1 until Townshend Acts are repealed (→ Sept. 5).

Princeton, New Jersey, August. The Rev. John Witherspoon arrives from Scotland to become president of College of New Jersey.

New York, Sept. 5. Tradesmen agree to boycott businesses not complying with non-importation policy (→ Sept. 13).

Virginia, Oct. 14. Treaty of Hard Labor, negotiated with Cherokee Indians, moves Virginia border farther west.

New York City, Oct. 30. Wesley Chapel, first Methodist church in colonies, dedicated.

New York City, Dec. 31. Assembly refuses to renew financial support for upkeep of British troops (→ Dec. 16, 1769).

Philadelphia. Benjamin Franklin studies effects of lead poisoning.

Boston. Foundry for manufacturing printer's type established by a Mr. Michaelson.

Sam Adams issues call for united action

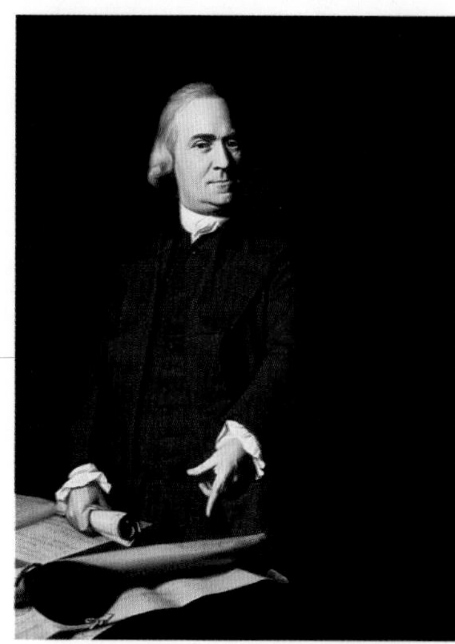

Sam Adams (c.1772) by Copley.

Boston, Feb. 11

Caustic, disheveled and palsied, Samuel Adams has been a whirlwind of activity ever since Parliament's passing of the Townshend Acts. After receiving his handiwork from the printers, Messrs. Edes and Gill, Adams took it straight to the Massachusetts Assembly. There his words were probably toned down a bit by his more conservative friends. But his circular letter, as it has come to be called because it is to circulate widely, has passed easily, and that's one more barb in the side of the British as far as Adams is concerned. In so many words, it informs the other colonial state assemblies that Massachusetts considers Parliament's new legislation a violation of the principle of no taxation without representation. The Adams letter also declares that colonial representation in London is a physical impossibility. In many ways, this letter resembles a series called the Farmer's Letters, written by the lawyer John Dickinson and, like them, it is moderate enough in tone and ends by calling for united action on the part of the colonists.

The mildness of the letter Adams submitted is due in part to the efforts of his friend James Otis, who is viewed as a moderating influence on him. In the past, Adams has not been overly scrupulous in his attacks on British authorities and policies. In many letters and essays, he has described British measures and officials in the most odious of terms. Adams is the first American leader to deny the authority of Parliament over the colonies, and it is thought that American independence is his long-range political goal. In this respect, he differs from other colonial leaders, whose reaction to the Townshend Acts has been primarily one of moderation. At a town meeting in Boston last September, a majority of the participants simply called for the promotion of colonial manufactures (→ Apr. 22).

Colonists import Madeira illegally

Boston, June 15

The customs declaration for John Hancock's ship Liberty, arriving from Madeira with a full cargo of wine, listed only a few kegs of wine, so the customs official decided to inspect below, where, much to his dismay, he was nailed up in a cabin by the crew. When he was later released, he reported the incident to Benjamin Hallowell, comptroller of customs, who had the Liberty seized by His Majesty's frigate Romney. This so enraged the Bostonians that they stoned both ships, forcing British officials to take refuge in Castle William in the harbor.

John Hancock (1765) by Copley.

Legislators get Revere bowl for resistance

Boston, Sept. 13

Lord Hillsborough, the newly appointed crown secretary for the colonies, today ordered the Massachusetts Assembly to rescind a circular letter drafted by Sam Adams and James Otis that was critical of the Townshend Acts. The assembly refused to rescind the letter that is circulating to the other state assemblies by a 92-17 vote, and Boston's Sons of Liberty lost no time in making the assembly decision a matter for patriotic celebration.

They ordered a commemorative punch bowl from the silversmith Paul Revere, who engraved it with the "Immortal 92," "No. 45," "No General Warrants" and other symbols of liberty. To Jack Wilkes, a sympathizer attempting to retain a seat in Parliament to which he had been elected, they sent two turtles, one weighing 45 pounds, and the other 47, "making in the whole 92 pounds, which is the Massachusetts patriotic number!!" (→ 28).

Paul Revere (1768) by Copley.

Business spirit in colonies is thriving

New York City

British authorities, who strain to keep their American offspring dependent on the mother country, are dismayed at the rapid growth of their children. General Thomas Gage, commander of British forces in North America, found manufacture thriving during a recent trip to Philadelphia. In a letter to the Earl of Shelburne, he warns that discharged British soldiers crowd "into the towns to work at trades, and help to supply the inhabitants with necessaries, which should be imported from the mother country." In New York, home to the British command, prominent citizens have formed the first American Chamber of Commerce "to promote and extend just and lawful commerce."

British troops debark to face rebels

British warships crowd Boston harbor, from a 1770 engraving by Paul Revere.

Boston, Oct. 1

With flags flying, drums beating and fifes playing, two regiments of infantry, the 14th and the 29th, marched up King Street today on the way to their quarters following disembarkation at the Long Wharf. Under the command of Lieutenant Colonel Dalrymple, the regiments arrived in the harbor from Halifax three days ago, escorted by men-of-war of the Royal Navy. Two other regiments, the 64th and 65th, have been ordered to Boston by Lord Hillsborough, secretary of state for the colonies. The operation was supervised by Major General Thomas Gage, commander-in-chief of Britain's forces, who came up to Boston from New York City only a short while back.

After a dispute with the governor's council about finding quarters for the troops, most of them are temporarily being billeted in the courthouse and in Faneuil Hall, with others pitching camp on the Common. There is space in the barracks at Castle William, but the authorities, intent on making a show of force, want to station the troops in the town rather than at the fort.

Despite rumors that the Sons of Liberty planned to rouse the country and actively resist the troops, the disembarkation has taken place peacefully. As expected, the soldiers have been warmly welcomed by British officials and Tory sympathizers, who hope that their presence will restore order to the colony which, in their opinion, has been hovering on the brink of anarchy. To General Gage, their presence is the result of the "Treasonable and desperate Resolves" of the opposition leaders. To the patriots, the redcoats are, of course, a provocation. But even to many moderates, billeting troops on a civilian population in a time of peace is an infringement of traditional liberties. The tension between a hostile civilian population and a military force that is made up of "brutal and licentious soldiery," the patriots say, is obviously great (→ May 13, 1769).

Armed British troops parade Union Jack through the streets of Boston.

West rebels against Carolina Easterners

Anson County, North Carolina

They are known as "Regulators" and, while their origins are shrouded in mystery, they certainly stem from the backwoods, the hill country of North and South Carolina. The first Regulators were probably formed after Christmas 1755, when a party of settlers, with Daniel Boone among their leaders, set out from the Moravian settlements to attack a band of robbers. But today's Regulators are after a different kind of robber. They are after those who would corrupt colonial government and give unfair representation to the tidewater aristocracy at the expense of the liberty-loving, free-spirited hill folk.

If their principal grievance is corruption in government, then second on their list would be the tax system that favors the tidewater aristocrats. Ever since 1765, petitions, resolutions and formal protests from the West have poured into the General Assembly, but these have gone unheeded. Now the Regulators want to take, by force, what has been denied them by law. They have become, in effect, an unofficial government where no real government exists.

They are opposed by North Carolina's colonial Governor, William Tryon, who wants to disband the group by force (→ Jan. 15, 1771).

Colonists acquire more Indian lands

Albany, New York, Nov. 5

Northern Indian Commissioner Sir William Johnson has signed a treaty with the Iroquois at Fort Stanwix to acquire much of the land between the Tennessee and Ohio Rivers for future settlement. Colonists have made similar treaties with Creek Indians in Georgia and Florida, and with Cherokees at Hard Labor Creek. Following the Royal Proclamation of 1763, which forbade the purchasing of land from Indians, there has been a hue and cry among the Western settlers for more land to be opened to whites, and an increasing number of settlers have been flowing into the territories of the Indians (→ Apr. 1769).

First patriotic song printed in America

Boston, July 18

The Gazette has published a song by John Dickinson of Pennsylvania entitled *In Freedom We're Born*. The first patriotic song printed in the colonies, it opens with the stirring words, "Come join hand in hand, brave Americans all, and rouse your bold hearts at fair Liberty's call. No tyrannous acts shall suppress your just claim nor stain with dishonor America's claim." The "tyranny" refers to the Townshend Acts, which have angered many Americans and led to the boycott of British products. Dickinson, a lawyer, rejects British taxation, but he hopes for a peaceful outcome to this vexing problem.

Boston up in arms over tax policies

Boston, Sept. 28

Resistance to Britain's tax policies is now focused in Boston. At Faneuil Hall today, delegates from 96 towns compiled a list of grievances against Britain. At a town meeting two weeks ago, citizens resolved that they have the right to arm themselves, and they asked Massachusetts Governor Bernard to call the General Court into session. The Governor refused, however, claiming that he needed permission from England. Now the patriots' resolutions are being printed. The principal demand of the colonists is that the King be allowed to rule only if he has the consent of the governed (→ Oct. 1).

Creole rebels chase Spanish Governor

New Orleans, Oct. 28

As many as 1,000 armed rebels roamed the city's streets today as the Spanish Governor, Antonio de Ulloa, sought refuge on a ship anchored in the river. Germans and Acadians have joined French Creoles in a revolt that began yesterday. Some of the city's principal businessmen are leading it and the superior council has called for Ulloa's expulsion. The causes include the fact that many citizens are loyal to France and there have been economic losses under Spanish rule. An immediate cause was a new law requiring that all wine be imported from Spain. Many in the mob today were drunk (→ Aug. 17, 1769).

1769

Suffolk, Virginia, Jan. 10. Boats begin to sail monthly to New York and Charleston, linking Northern and Southern postal systems at midpoint.

Pittsburgh, April. Hordes line up at office seeking to buy land in Western territories opened up by new Indian treaties (→ Apr. 9, 1772).

London, May 13. Board of Trade, due to non-importation movement, tells colonial governors it is considering revising Townshend Acts (→ 18).

Williamsburg, Virginia, May 18. Delegates to House of Burgessess, dissolved yesterday by Governor Botetourt, meet at Raleigh Tavern to enact Virginia Association, banning importation of goods from England pending repeal of Townshend Acts (→ July 22).

Charleston, S.C., July 22. South Carolina joins in Virginia's embargo, pending repeal of Townshend Acts (→ Nov. 7).

New Orleans, Aug. 17. Alexander O'Reilly arrives with 2,000 soldiers to re-establish Spanish rule.

California, Nov. 1. Sergeant Jose de Ortega, pathfinder in Gaspar de Portola's expedition, discovers entrance to large bay [San Francisco].

New York City, Dec. 16. Alexander McDougall, day after assembly voted 2,000 pounds for upkeep of British troops, blasts legislators in *To the Betrayed Inhabitants of the City and Colony of New York* (→ Jan. 17, 1770).

America, Dec. 27. George Grenville, Lord Hertford, Thomas Walpole and Samuel Wharton, under auspices of Grand Ohio Company, gain 20-million-acre royal grant in Treaty of Stanwix.

America. Imports from Britain drop from 2,157,218 pounds in 1768 to 1,336,122 pounds in 1769, primarily due to non-importation movement.

Cambridge. Harvard accepts idea that reptiles in America were descended from Noah's animals.

Philadelphia. Ben Franklin reorganizes American Philosophical Society and charts Gulf Stream.

Mannheim, Pennsylvania. Henry William Stiegel opens glass factory in German tradition.

Western Frontier. William Bean settles on Boone's Creek [first European to settle in Tennessee].

Spaniards begin to settle California

Junipero Serra and the Portola party survey site of San Diego de Alcala.

Bringing God to the wilderness.

San Diego, July 16

With the establishment today of the Mission San Diego de Alcala by Father Junipero Serra, Spain has given the European world indisputable proof of its intention to make California a bastion of Spanish authority and influence on the West Coast of North America. Although Spain has long claimed and indeed has occupied this area for more than a century, its policy of establishing permanent missions and settlements is expected to give a new credibility to its desired hegemony in the American West.

The establishment of the Mission San Diego represents the culmination of a plan, developed last year by the King's visitor general, Jose de Galvez, to send out four parties – two by sea and two by land – from the west coast of Mexico to a rendezvous at the port of San Diego. Under the command of Don Gaspar de Portola and accompanied by a few Franciscans headed by Serra, the hardy band of soldiers, sailors and churchmen traveled some 2,000 miles overland and by sea, battling Indians and scurvy all the way. The expedition, which left Mexico on January 9, arrived in San Diego two weeks ago.

Situated on a peaceful bay, San Diego is covered by grassy plains. The churchmen say that fresh water and good land abound, which should enable the settlers to produce an abundance of grain, fruits and vegetables. They have also noted plenty of deer, antelope and rabbits. The local Indians seem to be friendly enough, and receptive to Christian conversion.

The mission's founder, the 55 year-old Father Serra, was born on the Mediterranean island of Majorca. He took his orders in the Franciscan brotherhood in 1731, then was a teacher of philosophy at the College of San Fernando for a number of years. Coming to the New World, Serra worked as a missionary in the Northern provinces of New Spain for almost two decades.

In a letter to Mexico, Serra has warned prospective settlers they may "suffer many real privations." Distance and "the presence of pagans" cut off communication with civilization. But men of the cloth, he says, expect hardship in the service of God. And the heathen natives "have cost incomparably more to Lord Jesus Christ" (→ Sept. 1771).

Franciscan Father Junipero Serra.

Spanish bring wheat, wine and oranges

San Diego, Autumn

In a desperate attempt to prevent widespread malnutrition and even starvation among both Indians and Spanish Franciscans who live in and around the new mission at San Diego, Spanish religious authorities have begun importing such necessities as wheat, wine, grapes, olives and oranges in the hope that they can be grown locally.

San Diego itself is a green, fertile area. Grapevines and asparagus are plentiful. The Indians eat deer and antelope and catch sardines, tuna and sole in the adjacent ocean.

The areas to the north and south of San Diego, however, are not so bountiful. Most Spaniards eat a meal that typically might consist of figs, a small portion of meat and tortillas. This usually is accompanied by atole, a watery porridge made of corn and wheat.

Currently, the missionaries are extremely dependent on foodstuffs that are shipped from the west coast of northern Mexico. Successful local production of wine, citrus fruits and grain would greatly improve the chances of the mission's achieving permanency.

ꟷaniel Boone crosses the Cumberland Gap

'Daniel Boone Coming Through Cumberland Gap" (1851) by George Caleb ʒingham. Boone, born and bred a Quaker, leads his wife and daughter.

ʞentucky, June 7

Daniel Boone has led a group of killed woodsmen and adventurers hrough the Cumberland Gap into he fabled territory west of the Blue ʀidge Mountains. Boone, who is rom North Carolina, first ventured nto the region two years ago. But t was John Findley, an explorer ınd itinerant peddler, who first nade the routes known. The eastːrnmost of the trails followed by ʙoone's party were used only reːently by Cherokee braves in atːacks on frontier settlements.

Colonists who are intent on pushing westward see themselves as the envoys of civilization. The natives merely call them invaders. Long ago the Iroquois named the region "Ken-ta-ke," or "great meadow." They consider it paradise and they consider it theirs, reserved for Indians by the Great Father, away from the persistent encroachment of the white man. Residents of the Eastern seaboard, however, see it as Britain's next territory, and they intend to make it that in spite of the fact that the crown has acknowledged Cherokee ownership of the Kentucky heartland (→Apr. 1771).

Pontiac is killed by Indian; British blamed

Cahokia, Apr. 20

The Ottawa Chief Pontiac, leader of the rebellion against the British in 1763, was murdered today as he left a store in Cahokia where he had come to do some trading. His murderer is believed to be a Peoria Indian named Black Dog, who witnesses say struck Pontiac from behind with a club and then stabbed him. The murderer escaped and rumors are rampant about the motive for the killing. Some observers believe that Pontiac had been alienated from his own people for several years because of the apparent reversal of his attitude toward the British after signing a treaty with them three years ago. Others note that several tribes feared or were jealous of the Ottawa chief's reputation. But there are those who believe that the British themselves still saw him as a threat and therefore had him assassinated.

Chief Pontiac meets an abrupt end.

Connecticut, Pennsylvania fight over land

Pennsylvania, December

Men from Pennsylvania and Connecticut recently took aim at each other because of a boundary dispute that is almost a century old. Connecticut's original land grant extended all the way to the Pacific Ocean. But in 1681, King Charles II gave William Penn territory that overlapped this claim. The dispute was quiescent until 1754, when the Susquehanna Company was formed in Connecticut to send pioneers to an area northwest of Philadelphia. Thousands settled there over the next decade, and last year, the company made plans to establish five towns in the area. Forty men from Connecticut moved into Kingston, the first of these towns, last February. Pennsylvanians took action against the supposed intruders and fired off a barrage of writs and warrants. This month, Pennsylvanians brought a cannon into town to back up their claims.

ɪndian school becomes Dartmouth College

The Rev. Wheelock at the founding.

Lebanon, Connecticut

Out of the religious fervor of the Great Awakening inspired by the fiery preacher George Whitefield, another college has been born. This institute, renamed Dartmouth College this year, was founded here by the Rev. Eleazar Wheelock about 20 years ago to educate Indians. Of the present 28 students, 10 are Indians. Now under charter from the British crown, the college is operated by a board of trustees and is beginning to expand its enrollment. Most colleges begun in recent years have been founded by churches to stimulate and sustain the revival enthusiasm created by the Great Awakening. Though starting from those roots, Dartmouth is expected to move toward a more universal scope (→1771).

Support is growing for non-importation

North Carolina, Nov. 7

The non-importation movement, which began in New England, has taken hold in the South. North Carolina today joined South Carolina in adopting the Virginia Association's ban on trade with Britain pending repeal of the Townshend Act taxes. The plan was proposed in May by George Washington. In Maryland, delegates to a June convention voted not to buy imported wares, to lend all encouragement to domestic manufacturers and to boycott merchants who fail to comply. Newspapers are calling on women to abandon the use of "luxurious and enervating" tea. In Boston and Providence, lists of banned items are circulating (→March 5, 1770).

Jefferson proposes law to free slaves

Virginia

Recently elected to the House of Burgesses, scientist and freethinker Thomas Jefferson has, in his first legislative effort, introduced a measure calling for the emancipation of the slaves. The proposal, not very popular, was ultimately rejected. Another act was passed, however, that exempts free-born Negroes from "the payment of any public county or parish levies." This comes as the result of a petition brought to Virginia's legislature by free Negroes and mulattoes asking that their wives and daughters be exempt from taxation, which they called burdensome and derogatory to the rights of free-born subjects. The petition met with approval.

1770

New York City, Jan. 17. British soldiers cut down colonists' liberty pole (→ 19).

New York City, Jan. 19. Alexander McDougall leads Sons of Liberty, armed with swords and clubs, into skirmish with British troops on Golden Hill; several men seriously wounded in clash over British demands for compliance with Quartering Act (→ Feb. 8).

New York City, Feb. 8. McDougall is arrested for publication of broadside condemning colonial authorities for quartering British troops (→ Apr. 29).

New York City, Apr. 29. McDougall is released on bail after pleading not guilty to charges stemming from anti-royalist broadside.→

Northeast, May. Merchants of Newport, Providence and Albany agree to drop non-importation curb in light of repeal of Townshend Acts (→ Sept. 12).

Boston, Aug. 7. Isaiah Thomas and Zechariah Fowle publish the *Massachusetts Spy*, hoping to reach those not interested in traditional newspapers.

Philadelphia, Sept. 12. Merchants decide to resume importation of goods formerly taxed by Townshend Acts (→ July 1771).

Virginia, Oct. 18. Treaty with Cherokees, renegotiated by Indian commissioner Colonel John Stuart, extends Virginia's land by 9,000 square miles.

America, Nov. 11. General Gage writes letter to Lord Hillsborough, advising the closing of the frontier, since expansion in the West would weaken ties to England.

Virginia. George Washington signs resolution banning importation of slaves as part of non-importation agreement.

New York City. King's College [Columbia] awards colonies' first two doctorates of medicine (→ 1784).

Boston. William Billings publishes *The New England Psalm Singer, or, American Chorister,* a collection of 126 of his own compositions.→

Williamsburg, Virginia. The Public Hospital for Persons of Insane and Disordered Minds, first mental institution in America, opens.

Virginia. Using classical Greek and Roman models, Thomas Jefferson designs and builds home at Monticello.

British fire on enraged Boston mob

Boston, March 5

Insults quickly turned into violence tonight, and by the time the shooting had stopped, three patriots were dead. Two others were critically wounded and near death after a battle with British soldiers. Six other men were wounded, but they will apparently survive.

The trouble began when a young barber named Edward Garrick accused a soldier of the 29th Regiment of striking his head with a gun. Captain Thomas Preston mustered a small group of soldiers to assist the sentry, but they were all attacked by a mob led by a mulatto named Crispus Attucks. Sticks, oyster shells and snowballs were thrown as the mob dared the British troops to fire and people shouted: "Come on, you bloodybacks [redcoats], you lobster scoundrels, fire if you dare, God damn you, fire and be damned, we know you dare not." It is not clear whether Preston himself ordered the soldiers to fire, but a short while later Attucks and the other men lay dead in the street.

Several clashes have occurred between colonists and the British soldiers since they were dispatched from Halifax two years ago, presumably to keep the peace. Their presence has only made Boston more tense. Although they were not involved, the British were blamed for the death of a boy two weeks ago. Christopher Snider was killed in a fight outside the home of a merchant who refused to stop importing goods from Britain (→ Dec. 12).

With an eye for the dramatic, Paul Revere has captured the Boston battle for posterity. Only months after the shooting, prints of his engraving are to be found all over the colony. The print's bloody foreground and Revere's addition of the words "Butcher's Hall" over the Customs House lend credence to those who are calling the incident a "massacre." Revere, however, may not be solely responsible for the propaganda masterpiece. Revere's brother-in-law, Henry Pelham, accuses the silversmith of duplicating his work. Christian Remick, a mariner and an artist, probably did the coloring. Whatever the case, the prints are stirring up anti-British sentiment throughout Massachusetts and if matters continue to grow violent, Revere's services may be valued highly.

Crispus Attucks, a mulatto, lies dying among the Boston patriots felled by British muskets. Attucks led the crowd that challenged the troops and was the first to fall.

Colonial lawyers defend British "killers"

Boston, Dec. 12

The last of the trials resulting from the so-called March Massacre has ended, and the verdicts have outraged radical patriots. Captain Thomas Preston, eight soldiers and four Customs House workers were accused of shooting five patriots to death. All were cleared of murder charges. Two soldiers were found guilty of manslaughter, but were spared prison terms. Their hands were branded in punishment.

The defense of the British was led by John Adams and Josiah Quincy Jr., both of Massachusetts. Adams, a cousin of Sam Adams, the radical patriot, opposes many of Britain's policies in America, but he has distanced himself from Sam's activities. In taking this case, Adams is said to have argued that even the British soldiery is entitled to the best available defense. He was also critical of the politicking that took place outside the courtroom when he said, "The law is deaf, deaf as an adder, to the clamors of the populace." Adams described one of the victims, Crispus Attucks, as a man "whose very look was enough to terrify any person" and he held that the Preston men acted legally when the firing erupted (→ March 5, 1772).

Sons of Liberty attack British in New York

New York City, Apr. 29

Patriot leader Alexander McDougall has been released on bail after pleading not guilty to charges of contempt. He was jailed in January after leading fellow Sons of Liberty, armed with swords and clubs, into a skirmish with British troops on Golden Hill. Several participants on both sides were seriously wounded. Only two days earlier, the colonists' liberty pole had succumbed to an assault by the British.

The charges against McDougall stem from a broadside he wrote attacking the New York Assembly for allocating funds to shelter British soldiers. He accused the assembly of "betraying the common cause of liberty," and denounced a delegate for conspiring with Acting Governor Cadwallader Colden "to secure to them the sovereign lordship of this colony." The broadside is addressed "To the Betrayed Inhabitants of the City and Colony of New York" and is signed "A Son of Liberty." Tensions between soldiers and patriots have been rising all year. The colonists resent the Quartering Act and abhor the fact that British soldiers supplement their income by taking jobs from Americans (→ Apr. 27, 1771).

British end duties on all imports but tea

London, Apr. 12

One month after British troops fired into a mob in Boston, Parliament has taken action that may ease repercussions from the grim event, repealing all the Townshend duties except the tea tax. The new government of Lord North, who became Prime Minister on January 31, said it was keeping the duty on tea "as a mark of the supremacy of Parliament, and as a declaration of their right to govern the colonies." Many members of Parliament believe the tax on tea should also be abandoned because it is going to cause further trouble, but Lord North wishes it to remain as a symbol of the power of Parliament. Radical colonists will probably continue their non-importation protests until Parliament relents and repeals the duty on tea. Many colonial merchants are beginning to import British goods again because their stocks are dwindling (→ May).

Portrait of the new Prime Minister, Lord North, by Nathaniel Dance.

Benjamin West, an American in London

London

Americans are proud of Benjamin West, a native of Philadelphia, though he has chosen London as his home. West's historical paintings, fine examples of the Neoclassical style he learned in Italy, have attracted the attention of King George III. And the painter himself appears to be attracting American artists to England in droves. In the past five years, Henry Benbridge, Matthew Pratt and Charles Willson Peale have worked at West's studio. West arrived in 1763, patronized by Philadelphia merchants, one of whom has written, "It is a pity such a genius should be cramped for the want of cash." Just this year, West painted his self-portrait (→ 1771).

West's self-portrait. The artist is thriving as an expatriate in London.

Quakers establish school for Negroes

Quaker Benezet is an ex-Huguenot.

Philadelphia, June 28

Anthony Benezet and his fellow Quakers opened a school for Negroes here today with Moses Patterson as the teacher. This is one of the first such schools in America and it comes as no surprise that it was organized by the Quakers, who have been quite outspoken about the rights of Negroes.

The first school for Negroes in America was started by the Rev. Cotton Mather, when he arranged night classes for Negroes and Indians in 1717. Another school for Negroes was opened in South Carolina by Anglican missionary Samuel Thomas in 1744. Slave owners have long considered it dangerous to educate Negroes, fearing that they may gain the knowledge that will enable them to revolt. This attitude is frequently disguised with the claim that it is impossible to educate Negroes because they are incapable of learning.

Jefferson advocates freedom of religion

Virginia

Thomas Jefferson is in the forefront of a movement intent on establishing freedom of religion and opinion as basic rights of all Americans. The first signs were the legislature's decision to grant absolute religious toleration to dissenters and to suspend tax-supported salaries for ministers. The suspension was made permanent this year, and the assembly has also published Jefferson's Bill for Establishing Religious Freedom. This strongly worded bill seems to test the public's reaction to a new mood of tolerance. As Jefferson writes, "the opinions of men are not the object of civil government, nor under its jurisdiction." Although the bill has yet to win approval, the atmosphere in the colonies indicates change.

Revere's frontispiece for William Billings's "New England Psalm Singer."

1771

North Carolina, Jan. 15. Prompted by three-year-old frontier revolt, assembly passes "Bloody Act," making rioting a treasonable crime (→ May 17).

New York City, Apr. 27. Alexander McDougall is released from prison.

North Carolina, April. Hunting expedition, led by Daniel Boone and sponsored by Judge Richard Henderson, returns from West [after exploring Licking, Kentucky, and Green and Cumberland River Valleys].

North Carolina, May 17. James Few, leader of Regulator rebels, executed on battlefield at Alamance Creek.→

North Carolina, June 17. Twelve members of Regulators found guilty of treason. [Six eventually executed, while rest, plus 6,500 residents of the Piedmont, are forced to swear oath of allegiance.]

Virginia, July. Colony is last to resume importing British goods following repeal of Townshend Acts.

Birmingham, England, Aug. 17. Scientist Joseph Priestley discovers that oxygen is released from growing plants.

Pennsylvania, August. Proprietors try to oust Connecticut settlers from Wyoming Valley and fail.

Princeton, New Jersey, September. Aaron Burr graduates from college here at age 15.

Connecticut. Legislature forbids slave trade.

New Hampshire. Colony divided into five counties in order to govern effectively after surge in settlement; town meeting still primary form of government.

Pennsylvania. Benjamin Franklin begins work on autobiography, intended for his son William.

America. American Philosophical Society begins publication of its journal *Transactions*.

England. Benjamin West shatters standards of conventional art in such historical paintings as *The Death of Wolfe* and *Penn's Peace Treaty With the Indians.*

Hanover, New Hampshire. Dartmouth College, after relocating here from Connecticut in 1770, graduates first four students, including John Wheelock, son of college president; each graduate receives land for a farm.

Carolina Governor suppresses rebels

The Regulators stop a shipment of gunpowder sent by Governor William Tryon.

Alamance Creek, N.C., May 17

Governor William Tryon has finally gotten his way, putting down a stiff-necked group called the Regulators, who have been in rebellion against the Eastern elite here since 1764. The Governor, a soldier by profession, led 1,200 well-trained troops to the neighborhood of Alamance Creek and defeated a loosely organized mob of about 2,000 Regulators. Before firing on the rebels, the Governor gave them an ultimatum to lay down their arms. When they refused, the Governor fired the first shot of the battle, killing an unarmed negotiator. With the battle joined, the Regulators took refuge behind rocks and trees before His Majesty's forces, fighting from formation, won the day (→ June 17).

Spanish found three California missions

California, September

The Franciscans have founded three more permanent missions. On June 3, 1770, the Carmel Mission was set up on the Monterey Peninsula by Father Serra. Last July, he began the San Antonio de Padua mission in the Los Robles Valley of the Santa Lucia Mountains. This month, he founded Mission San Gabriel Arcangel north of San Diego (→ Sept. 1, 1772).

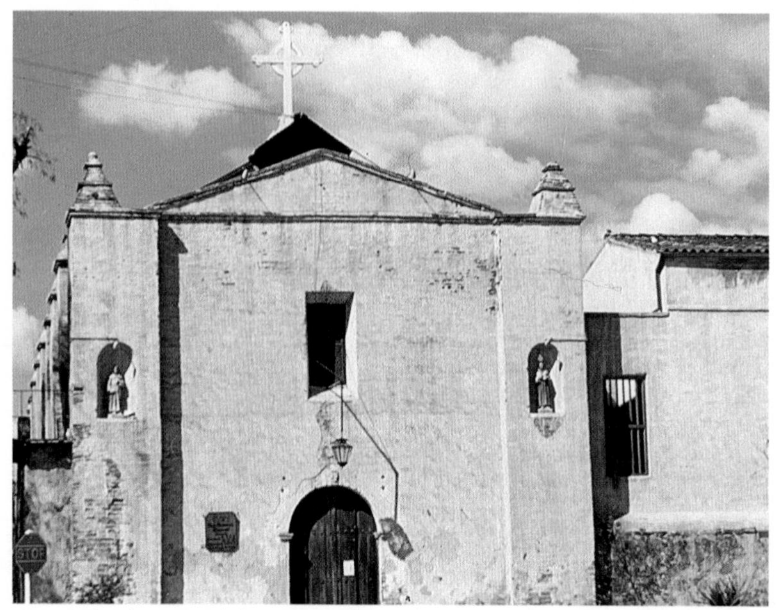

San Gabriel Arcangel, latest in a chain of missions set up by Father Serra.

Peace spurs a boom in New Hampshire

New Hampshire

It is now eight years since the French and Indian War ended, and this colony's population has swollen rapidly, with land speculation reaching an all-time high. Farmers who had often stayed indoors because of the threat of Indian attacks are now able to clear their lands, while settlers have penetrated the White Mountains, an area that hostile Indians once made uninhabitable. The growth has led Governor Benning Wentworth to divide the colony into five counties, all of which have been named after his friends back in England.

Umbrellas mocked, called effeminate

Philadelphia

When Londoners first saw umbrellas early in the century, there was pandemonium. Philanthropist and world traveler James Hanway first used one and all the sedan porters and public coachmen stopped what they were doing to watch. Now the umbrella has made it to Philadelphia. The newspapers have ridiculed it as being effeminate. Doctors, however, claim that the umbrella can benefit your health by preventing epilepsy, shading sore eyes, keeping off fevers and serving as a curative against vertigo.

Concert in Boston presents classics

Boston, May 17

Josiah Flagg is offering a concert today of "vocal and instrumental musick accompanied by French Horns, Hautboys, etc." The announcement says the program includes Johann Christoph Bach's *Third Symphony*, Handel's *Overture to Ptolemy*, the Stamitz *Organ Concerto*, an Abel duetto, Ricci's *Periodical Symphony*, a new hunting song by Morgan along with works by Stanley, Harington and Schwindl. This English and European mixture typifies the fare of music concerts being patronized by the more cultivated folk.

1772

Boston, March 5. Leading radical Joseph Warren speaks on anniversary of Boston Massacre to arouse anti-British sentiments (→ June 13).

California, March 20. Captain Pedro Fages and his men explore central region [San Francisco Bay and San Joaquin and Sacramento Valleys].

Boston, March. Mercy Otis Warren's first play, poking fun at British, is published in *Massachusetts Spy*.

Pennsylvania, Apr. 9. George Croghan, trader and frontiersman, gets amended Camden-Yorke opinion from British attorney general; in one interpretation, it allows purchase of Indian lands without approval of crown.

Boston, June 13. Governor Thomas Hutchinson announces he will henceforth receive salary from crown (→ Sept.).

England, June 22. In Somerset case, Lord Mansfield rules against slavery on English soil.

England, July. Crisis in British banking system causes reduction of credit in colonies; as merchants begin selling off inventories, financial panic ensues.

Mexico, Aug. 22. Provinces of northern Mexico [including Texas] are separated under new authority as Provincias Internas.

California, Sept. 1. Mission San Luis Obispo de Tolosa founded (→ July 1773).

Boston, September. Massachusetts judges begin receiving salary from crown, giving judiciary further independence from General Court (→ Oct. 28).

Boston, Oct. 28. Despite opposition from John Hancock, Sam Adams calls town meeting to discuss threats to self-rule posed by crown (→ Nov. 20).

London. Benjamin Franklin, agent for Massachusetts Assembly, acquires letters sent to colonial administration in London, from Massachusetts Governor Thomas Hutchinson, misrepresenting situation in colonies (→ June 1773).

Western Frontier. John Sevier of Virginia and James Robertson of North Carolina found Watauga Association to govern area ceded to England by Six Nations of the Iroquois [east Tennessee]; first local independent government in American colonies (→ Nov. 19, 1776).

Mexico. San Antonio becomes capital of northern province of New Spain.

British customs boat grounded, burned

Colonists row silently back to shore, the burning Gaspee in the background.

Providence, Rhode Island, June 10

In an act of defiance certain to infuriate British authorities, patriots led by Abraham Whipple seized and destroyed the revenue cutter Gaspee last night after it ran aground on a sandbar at Namquit Point near Providence. Lieutenant William Dudingston, the Gaspee commander, was put ashore with his crew before the ship was burned to the waterline today. Unpopular for having behaved, as patriots put it, in a manner "more imperious and haughty than the Grand Turk himself," Dudingston led a drive to end smuggling in Narragansett Bay (→ March 12, 1773).

Slaves dying en route; importation drops

America

Figures obtained from slave ships indicate that an increasing number of slaves are dying en route to America from Africa. This is believed to be the result of overcrowding, lack of hygiene and generally poor care provided by the slave traders. Meanwhile, the average number of slaves imported to the colonies each year has dropped to 1,700, due in part to growing opposition to the trade.

The African slave coast: Where slavers once made provisions for the welfare of their cargo, they now tend to use every inch of space for human bodies.

Boston radicals set up new committee

Boston, Nov. 20

The radicals in Boston have a new grievance to add to their list and they have a new way of airing their grievances. This June, Governor Thomas Hutchinson announced that he would begin receiving his salary from the crown, which effectively cuts him off from any dependence upon the Massachusetts Assembly. Furthermore, the crown has announced that it will pay the salaries of the judges of the Superior Court.

In response to these actions, Boston citizens called a town meeting and on November 2, under the guidance of James Otis and Samuel Adams, formed a committee of correspondence for the purpose of communicating and publishing news of any infringements of colonists' rights by the crown.

In its first report, issued today, the committee presented three papers – by Sam Adams, Dr. Benjamin Church and Joseph Warren. All three deal with grievances of Massachusetts citizens against Britain. Dr. Church's paper calls upon other towns to form similar committees of correspondence and not "to doze or sit supinely indifferent on the brink of destruction."

Hutchinson has described the committee of correspondence as "the foulest, subtlest and most venomous serpent ever issued from the egg of sedition" (→ May 10, 1773).

Charles Willson Peale's life-sized portrait of George Washington as a 40-year-old member of the Virginia militia, finished this year.

1773

Charleston, Jan. 12. First museum in America founded.

Boston, Jan. 27. The Dartmouth arrives in Boston harbor, first of three ships bound for Boston bearing tea.

Boston, March 5. John Adams writes in his diary, "The rich are seldom remarkable for modesty, ingenuity, or humanity. Their wealth has rather a tendency to make them penurious and selfish."

London, June. Crown disbands commission appointed to hunt perpetrators in burning of the cutter Gaspee.

Boston, June. Ignoring Franklin's protests, Sam Adams and others go before assembly to read letters of Governor Hutchinson, sent to him by Franklin (→ Dec. 25).

Philadelphia, July 14. Methodists hold first annual conference.

California, July. Viceroy Antonio Bucareli issues Reglamento, providing government for Alta California.

Boston, Sept. 27. Sam Adams writes in *Boston Gazette* of need to organize congress of American states with a bill of rights (→ May 17, 1774).

England, September. Parliament gives East India Co. right to ship 500,000 pounds of tea to specified American merchants (→ Oct. 13).

Philadelphia, Oct. 13. Mass meeting protests tax on tea and East India Company's monopoly on tea trade; committee named to seek ouster of consignees scheduled to receive East India tea (→ Nov. 30).

Philadelphia, Nov. 10. *Gazette* advertisement protests that theater is an affront to decent citizens, describing players as "vagrants and sturdy beggars."

Charleston, South Carolina, Dec. 3. Colonists force all tea consignees to resign day after arrival of tea-bearing vessel from London (→ 16).

Boston, Dec. 25. Assembly, after exposure of Hutchinson letters, petitions Parliament to oust Governor Hutchinson and provincial secretary, Andrew Oliver (→ Jan. 31, 1774).

New Haven. Ezra Stiles, Yale president, and Congregational clergyman Samuel Hopkins propose sending free Negroes to colonize West Africa.

Newport. First Jewish sermon printed in America is preached by Rabbi Haym Carregal.

London passes Tea Act; keeps import tax

London, May 10

King George assented today to the latest plan from Parliament to keep the troubled East India Tea Company afloat. The Tea Act permits the deficit-plagued company to export tea directly to the colonies. As fashioned by the Prime Minister, Lord North, the act retains the Townshend Act duty of threepence a pound on tea. North insists, however, that the colonists will not object to the tax because subsidies granted to the East India Company will make its tea cheaper than the tea smuggled into the colonies from other European countries. Members of Parliament, many of whom have large financial interests in the company, voted approval of the Tea Act with little debate over the political consequences.

William Dowdeswell, a former chancellor of the Exchequer and supporter of the Americans, is not convinced by the government's arguments. "I tell the Noble Lord now if he don't take off the duty they won't take the tea," Dowdeswell argued without much success. Figures from the colonies support his thinking. When the non-importation agreements went into effect, the imports of British tea dropped 60 percent to 200,000 pounds a year. It is estimated that a million pounds of tea are being smuggled into the colonies every year (→ Sept.).

Virginia establishes patriots' committee

Virginia, March 12

Word of the Gaspee Affair has greatly alarmed members of the House of Burgesses, which met today and created a committee to improve communications with the Northern colonies. Patrick Henry and Thomas Jefferson, who are both members of this committee of correspondence, say the new British threat to put patriots on trial in England is very dangerous. The King has ordered trials for the men who set the cutter Gaspee on fire in Rhode Island. The vessel had been searching for colonists who refuse to pay customs duties (→ June).

Ben Franklin: How to shrink an empire

London, September

Benjamin Franklin, enraged at England's move to tax all tea imported by the colonies, offers some satirical advice to the crown in *Rules By Which A Great Empire May Be Reduced To A Small One: Presented to a Late Minister When He Entered Upon His Administration*, which has run in several English papers. The proposal likens the empire to a "great cake, easily diminished at the edges" and it satirically advises the crown to rid itself of colonists by honing policies to be sure "they do not enjoy the same common rights [and] the same privileges in commerce, and that they are governed by severer laws."

Corsets spoil view of "snowy bosoms"

Philadelphia, Jan. 5

A Miss Sarah Eves notes in her diary that the family doctor failed to arrive for an appointment today. The poor man, she writes, "thought his clothes were not good enough ... therefore he delays his visit until he gets fitted up in the Macaronia taste, I suppose." A Macaroni, of course, is a regular fop who wears his waistcoat exceedingly short and his hair exceedingly high. Macaronis are seen this year with big bunches of flowers at the breast. Ladies, too, are wearing blooms there, which, combined with high corsets, mar the view of their "snowy bosoms," leaving more and more to a gentleman's imagination.

Patriots sing about "Revolutionary Tea"

There was an old lady lived over the sea,
And she was an Island Queen;
Her daughter lived off in a new country,
With an ocean of water between,
The old lady's pockets were full of gold,
And never contented was she,
So she called on her daughter to pay her a tax
Of three pence a pound on her tea
Of three pence a pound on her tea

The tea was conveyed to the daughter's door,
All down by the ocean's side;
And the bouncing girl poured out every pound
In the dark and boiling tide.
And then she called out to the Island Queen,
"Oh mother, dear mother," quoth she,
Your tea you may have when 'tis steeped enough,
But never a tax from me

Book of poetry by Negro maid issued

Frontispiece to Wheatley's "Poems."

London, Sept. 1

Phillis Wheatley, the 20-year-old Boston slave whose poetry has amazed New England's literati, has now conquered London with her *Poems on Various Subjects, Religious and Moral*, published by Archibald Bell, a British printer after the book was rejected by American houses. The maid, who came to London last June for a long literary tour, began writing poetry at the age of 12, five years after a slave ship brought her to the Boston household of John and Susannah Wheatley, now her agents. She first tasted fame in 1771, when her elegy for a British evangelist captivated colonial readers.

olonists to resist ritish tea imports

oston, Nov. 30

An angry crowd gathered again oday at the Old South Meeting-ouse to demand that the Dart-outh and its cargo of tea be sent ack to England. The tea ship has een anchored off Boston harbor or two days. Francis Rotch, one of ne ship's owners, promised the rowd of 2,500 patriots that the)artmouth would return to Lon-on without unloading its cargo.

Opposition to the Tea Act has een building steadily in the colo-ies since the legislation was ap-roved in May. Because of the con-using nature of the act, it was not lear at first that the duty on tea vas in fact being retained. A letter rom London printed in the *Penn-ylvania Journal* last month helped nd the confusion. An American vrote that the Tea Act, if enforced, "will for ever after be pleaded as recedent for every imposition the arliament of Great Britain shall hink proper to saddle us with.")ther newspapers were quick to pread similar messages through-ut the colonies.

At a meeting in Philadelphia last nonth, a resolution was passed ondemning the act as an assault "upon the liberties of America vhich every American was in duty ound to oppose." A committee of orrespondence in Massachusetts rged committees in other colonies ot to import British tea. Yester-lay, the Sons of Liberty met in New York and agreed to embargo all axed tea from Britain (→ Dec. 3).

A 15-shilling banknote, issued by the Pennsylvania Assembly.

Patriots fling tea into Boston harbor

Boston, Dec. 16

Shortly after 6 o'clock tonight, the doors of the Old South Meetinghouse burst open and a thousand patriots ran toward the three British ships anchored in the harbor. Many of the colonists shouted chilling war cries. Some were disguised as Indians. They ran down Milk Street, turned down Hutchinson Street and ran straight to Griffin's Wharf. Armed with axes and pistols, the patriots climbed aboard the Dartmouth and chopped open all the tea chests, then hurled the tea into the harbor, where it piled up in the low tide like haystacks. A short while later, they attacked the Eleanor and the Beaver. By 9 o'clock, all three ships had been stripped of their hated cargo, and the jubilant crowd began to disperse. Most of the patriots vowed they would never pay British taxes, and they boasted of winning a great victory. While it is to early to know how England will respond to this brazen assault on its authority, one patriot leader, Josiah Quincy Jr., predicted that the night no one in Boston will ever forget would lead "to the most trying and terrific struggle this country ever saw."

"Steeping" tea in Boston harbor: A "war party" carries out its act of defiance.

John Adams, who supported the action despite his moderate views, also saw the dumping of the tea as an event of great consequence. "The people should never rise," he said, "without doing something to be remembered, something notable and striking. This destruction of the tea is so bold, so daring, so firm, intrepid and inflexible, and it must have so important consequences, and so lasting, that I can't but consider it an epoch in history."

An unconfirmed report spread in Boston tonight that John Hancock was a leader of the raiding party. The report was discounted by several observers who doubted that a man of Hancock's stature would participate in such an event. All of the raiders were careful to conceal their identities, covering themselves with blankets and coloring their faces with bronze paint. Describing their Indian disguises, witness John Andrews said the patriots were "cloath'd in blankets with the heads muffled, and copper color'd countenances, being each arm'd with a hatchet or axe, and pair of pistols, nor was their dialect different from which I conceive these geniuses to speak, as their jargon was unintelligible to all but themselves."

At a mass meeting earlier in the day, the patriots afforded one of the ship owners, Francis Rotch, an opportunity to return to London. When they ordered him to leave Boston with his cargo, however, he answered, "Gentlemen, I cannot. It is wholly impracticable. It would cause my ruin." Under pressure, he rode his horse to Milton Hill and asked Governor Hutchinson for an exemption from the customs duties, but the Governor refused. When Rotch returned to the meetinghouse, at least 7,000 people were jammed inside. Many more mingled outside in the damp chill. Shortly after Rotch gave the Governor's answer, one man shouted, "Who knows how tea will mingle with salt water?" While one man screamed for mob action and another shouted, "Boston harbor is a teapot tonight," Samuel Adams rose to his feet. Usually a fiery orator, he now seemed to be resigned and spoke in a low voice. "This meeting can do nothing more to save the country," Adams said.

None of the British sailors on the ships was injured, and the attackers took care to destroy only the tea on board. The rest of the cargo was left intact. Their mission completed, the patriots stepped back onto the wharf and carefully removed their shoes so that any tea leaves that had slipped inside could also be dumped into the harbor to await high tide (→ March 31, 1774).

Some 340 chests of tea were dumped by patriots disguised as Indians.

Colonists, Negro and white, look on as the ships are relieved of their cargo.

1774

London, Jan. 31. Privy Council, in hearings on Hutchinson letters, fires Ben Franklin as postmaster general for America (→ March 30).

America, January. *Royal American Magazine* founded, first in colonies to use frequent illustrations (→ June).

Boston, March 30. Governor Hutchinson dissolves General Court before it can try Andrew Oliver on charges he accepted salary from crown.

London, March 31. Parliament passes Boston Port Bill, closing harbor until Massachusetts pays duties and damages owed for Boston tea party (→ May 12).

Boston, May 12. Residents vote to resume non-importation action to fight Port Bill (→ 13).

Boston, May 13. General Thomas Gage, British commander-in-chief in colonies, leads four regiments into city and replaces Thomas Hutchinson as Governor (→ May 20).

Providence, Rhode Island, May 17. Residents are first in colonies to urge intercolonial congress (→ 27).

London, May 20. Parliament passes Quebec Act, enlarging boundaries of Quebec to include French-speaking settlements [in Ohio and Illinois].

Williamsburg, Virginia, May 27. House of Burgesses, officially dissolved yesterday, convenes in Raleigh Tavern, drafts resolution calling for annual intercolonial congress (→ Oct. 26).

London, June 2. Parliament reactivates Quartering Act of 1765, requiring that all colonies provide housing for British troops (→ 17).

Philadelphia, Oct. 4. Congress passes anti-theater act to "discourage every species of extravagance and dissipation, especially horse-racing, and all kinds of gaming . . ."

St. Andrew's Parish, Georgia, Dec. Slave revolt results in deaths of four whites; slave leaders burned to death.

Massachusetts. Plymouth Rock is mentioned publicly for first time in official ceremony marking 154th anniversary of Pilgrims' landing.

Western Frontier. James Harrod leads a party of Pennsylvania traders up Kentucky River to found Harrodsburg at head of Salt River [first European settlement in Kentucky].

Defiant Continental Congress meets

Philadelphia, Oct. 26.

A widely attended congress of colonial leaders adjourned today after criticizing British infuence in North America and affirming the colonies' right to "life, liberty and property." Delegates from 12 colonies convened at Carpenter's Hall on September 5. Georgia's popular royal governor persuaded the colony's leaders not to participate.

The delegates vary widely in their politics and the degree of their loyalty to England. The Suffolk Resolves, proposed by Massachusetts radicals and adopted September 17, call for defiance of the Coercive Acts, tax resistance and the arming of a militia. But just 11 days later, a Pennsylvania plan calling for union with Britain went down by only one vote. The most significant vote came on October 14, when delegates passed the Declarations and Resolves, a sweeping condemnation of British interference in American internal affairs. Its 10 resolutions grant colonial assemblies the right to enact legislation and taxes.

Of the 56 delegates, half were lawyers, the rest largely merchants, planters or otherwise men of accomplishment. Despite their differences, all the congressmen have expressed a point of view that sounds increasingly American. As Patrick Henry has stated, "The distinctions between New Englanders and Virginians are no more. I am not a Virginian, but an American."

George Washington, Richard Henry Lee and Patrick Henry by Clyde Deland.

Washington signs anti-slavery text

Virginia, Dec. 1

George Washington today signed the Fairfax Resolves, which bar the importation of slaves and threaten to put a halt to all colonial exports to England. The influential landowner George Mason is the author of the document, which pledges America's loyalty to Britain. But the resolutions stipulate that exports are to end within the month unless the King faces up to the grievances of the colonists. Washington, although he owns slaves, agreed to the sections that call for an end to the "wicked, cruel and unnatural trade."

British Coercive Acts seek to curb colonies

London, May 20

His Majesty's government today announced a series of measures designed to punish the American colonists for their increasingly belligerent and anti-British behavior. The so-called Coercive Acts close the port of Boston and take away much of the power of the Massachusetts legislature. This power will be turned over to the colony's royal governor. Also, from now on, juries will be selected by the local sheriffs (not by the people), and henceforth, a town meeting can be called into session only by the governor, who will also set and otherwise determine its agenda. Another provision of the legislation states that if any royal official serving in the American colonies is sued for carrying out his official duties, the trial of that representative of the crown will be removed from the "unfriendly" colony to England (where he can get a more favorable hearing). There is also a provision in the Coercive Acts that establishes a permanent government for the province of Canada. While this part of the legislation has nothing to do with the American colonies, it is regarded as another attempt by the crown to interfere with colonial self-government. How are Americans going to respond to these strict measures? They certainly will not be taken lightly (→ June 2).

Patriots ruin three British tea cargoes

Annapolis, Maryland, Oct. 19

Inspired by the tea party in Boston last year, the patriots of Annapolis have burned the Peggy Stewart, a British vessel with a full cargo of tea. New Yorkers, more faithful to the original model, dressed as Indians in April in order to brew their own batch of British tea in the East River. Virginia too has had its tea party. Angered by the tax on their favorite drink, the colonies are simply refusing to take delivery. After Parliament repealed the Stamp Act, it hoped to assert its right to tax Americans by dropping the price of tea so low that it would be irresistible. Even with the threepence tax, British tea is cheaper than the illegal import many merchants are selling. But so far, Americans are not buying (→ Dec. 14).

Anti-tax actions are continuing.

Colonies ponder political combine

Boston, June 17

Twelve days after the committee of correspondence drafted the non-importation pact known as the Solemn League and Covenant, the Massachusetts House of Representatives has issued a call for a congress of committees from all the colonies to meet in Philadelphia early in September. Standing alone, individual colonies have little impact on the colossal British economy. A well-enforced continental boycott, however, could move British merchants to pressure Parliament into repealing the Coercive Acts (→ Sept. 6).

Arsenal captured in first military move

Portsmouth, N.H., Dec. 14

Warned by Paul Revere of British plans to station troops here, John Sullivan along with some 400 men of the local militia has captured Fort William and Mary and seized gunpowder, weapons and other military stores. No lives were lost, but this does not diminish the gravity of the incident: For the first time, colonists have resorted to direct military action against the forces of the crown. The 34-year-old Sullivan, a lawyer, recently attended the Continental Congress in Philadelphia (→ Feb. 9, 1775).

Colonists mobilize; Gage holds at Boston

Boston, Sept. 6

General Thomas Gage, who is in charge of the British forces that are garrisoned in Boston, was stunned by the quick and efficient mobilization of almost 40,000 colonial militia from the 50-mile area surrounding Boston after rumors circulated that the British had burned the city. The British force of 3,000 men there would be easily overwhelmed by the larger American force, so General Gage quickly ordered that entrenchments be dug on Boston Neck, a narrow strip of land that provides the only access to the city. This strip can easily be defended by a small force, and Gage has ordered a full regiment placed there, with field guns in support.

The general's explanation of his action, which he claimed was an attempt to prevent desertions, reflects the growing tension between colonial and British factions. The Americans reject the Gage explanation, just as the British reject the American claim that their military exercises are a response to their fear of a war with the French. The selectmen of Boston have protested Gage's actions and sent him a letter requesting that he abandon his fortifications. He has declined, asserting that his primary responsibility of defending the inhabitants of Boston made the measures he has taken necessary (→ Oct. 19).

General Gage hears pleas for leniency from a delegation of children.

Numerous anti-British pamphlets appear

America

The colonists' mounting discontent with recent measures enacted by Parliament has produced a rash of publications critical of British rule here. In his pamphlet *Considerations on the Nature and Extent of the Legislative Authority of the British Parliament*, James Wilson, a Philadelphia attorney, argues that because the colonists are not represented in the mother country's legislature they owe allegiance only to the monarchy, not to Parliament. Thomas Jefferson, a Virginia planter and lawyer, is even more forthright. In *A Summary View of the Rights of British America*, he cites the lengthy history of British infringement on the colonists' rights – "which nature has given to every man" – to free trade and self-government. Jefferson demands that King George III remedy these injustices and asserts that the monarch's "felicity and future fame" may hinge on his compliance.

The most surprising of the recent polemics may be *A Full Vindication of the Measures of Congress from the Calumnies of Their Enemies*. Its content has occasioned less comment than the identity of its author, Alexander Hamilton, a 17-year-old King's College student. Readers had supposed the anonymous polemic to be the work of an established writer.

Boston, June. *Paul Revere lampoons the British in a cartoon in the new "Royal American Magazine," the first colonial publication to use frequent illustrations. It portrays British officials forcing America to swallow a bitter draft of tea. Also this year, Thomas Jefferson, in "A Summary View of the Rights of British America," wrote: "Force cannot give right."*

1775

South Carolina, Jan. 11. First Jewish elected official in colonies, Francis Salvador, seated in provincial congress.

London, Feb. 9. Parliament declares Massachusetts to be in state of rebellion (→21).

America, Feb. 22. American Manufactory of Woolens, Linens and Cottons is first joint stock manufacturing firm in colonies.

Philadelphia, February. Thomas Paine, who arrived last year from England, at urging of Ben Franklin, founds *Pennsylvania Magazine* (→1776).

Sycamore Shoals, Kentucky, March 15. Transylvania Land Company gains treaty with Cherokees, obtaining all land south of Ohio River, north of Cumberland River and west of Appalachians, in exchange for $10,000 in goods.

Boston, Apr. 14. General Gage gets orders from Lord Dartmouth to use force to implement Coercive Acts and halt colonial military buildup (→19).

Philadelphia, Apr. 14. Ben Franklin and Dr. Benjamin Rush form Society for the Relief of Free Negroes Unlawfully Held in Bondage, first colonial group formed to combat slavery.

Massachusetts, June 12. General Gage, imposing martial law, proclaims all armed colonists traitors and offers pardons to those who swear allegiance to crown (→17).

London, Aug. 23. King George III, rejecting peace offer, declares colonies in open rebellion against crown (→Dec. 6).

Philadelphia, Oct. 13. Congress bars Negroes from Continental Army.

Virginia, Nov. 17. Governor Dunmore offers freedom to slaves who will join loyalist army, thus losing support of most planters (→Dec. 31).

Philadelphia, Nov. 29. To open contact with friends abroad, Congress forms five-man committee of secret correspondence (→March 3, 1776).

Philadelphia, Dec. 3. Lieutenant John Paul Jones raises Congress Colors or Grand Union flag, official banner.→

Massachusetts, Dec. 31. Fearing response to Lord Dunmore's offer to slaves, George Washington orders recruiting officers to accept free Negroes in army (→Autumn, 1782).

British attack arsenal, alert Minutemen

New England families now face separation as the militia is called to duty.

Boston, Feb. 26

The detachment of troops sent by General Thomas Gage to Salem to seize weapons and military supplies stored there by defiant colonists has just returned to Boston, empty-handed. In fact, the principal result of the expedition seems to have been to alert the Minutemen (volunteers ready to fight at a minute's notice) to increased vigilance.

The failure of the sortie brings home the difficult situation facing General Gage, who was recently appointed Governor and Captain-General of Massachusetts Bay. With several regiments now garrisoned in the city and ships of the Royal Navy anchored in the harbor, he is in firm control of Boston itself; but he has virtually no authority outside it. Government of the rest of the province is in the hands of a provincial congress that has been meeting at Concord under the presidency of John Hancock.

Expecting that Gage will make a major move in the spring, the committee of safety has spent much of the winter building up the militia and gathering supplies, mostly at Concord (→Apr. 14).

Parliament urges amity with America

London, March 22

In a major speech to the House of Commons, Edmund Burke urged the government to reverse its present colonial policy of coercion and to adopt one of reconciliation. "The use of force alone is but temporary," he said. "It may subdue for the moment; but it does not remove the necessity of subduing again: and a nation is not governed which is perpetually to be conquered." Such arguments, however, are unlikely to persuade Lord North, who controls a solid majority of votes and might also have resented Burke's pointed comment, "Magnanimity in politics is not seldom the truest wisdom; and a great empire and little minds go ill together" (→Aug. 23).

Edmund Burke by Joshua Reynolds.

Massachusetts plans contingent defense

This cartoon, popular in England, shows Tories taunting Bostonians imprisoned in a liberty tree. But now, patriots will have their own defense.

Cambridge, Feb. 21

Acting swiftly to prepare for the colony's defense, the committee of public safety has just voted to buy military supplies for an army of 15,000 men. Though the militia totals over four times that number, the committee has decided on a system of volunteer regiments whose ranks are to be filled with the pick of the militia. While these regiments are being organized, field officers are to set up Minuteman companies of 50 men each. Articles of war to ensure proper discipline in the "army of . . . defense" are being drawn up. Generals Preble, Thomas, Heath and Pomeroy have been confirmed in their ranks, and Artemas Ward has been named commander-in-chief (→26).

"A time to fight," so pastor joins up

Woodstock, Virginia

The Rev. John Peter Muhlenberg concluded his farewell sermon with a dramatic and patriotic flourish. First, Pastor Muhlenberg told his congregation: "There is a time to pray and a time to fight. This is the time to fight." Then he cast off his clerical gown, revealing the uniform of an officer in the militia. Muhlenberg is both a Lutheran and an Episcopal minister. In 1774, he was elected to the House of Burgesses, many of whose members belong to the radical Revolutionary Party. Pastor Muhlenberg chose Ecclesiastes 3 as his text, which says that there is a time to kill and a time to heal.

ritain restrains olonies' trading

ndon, Apr. 13

Continuing his policy of trying to erce the colonies into submission, rd North has extended the New ngland Restraining Act to South arolina, Virginia, Pennsylvania, aryland and New Jersey.

The act, which won the King's proval only two weeks ago, fords the designated colonies to trade th any countries other than Britn and Ireland, and bans American shermen from the banks off Nova otia and Newfoundland.

The extension of the law, which as originally aimed at the New ngland colonies only, is clearly tended to punish the others for ving joined the Colonial Associan, the name generally being giv- to the non-importation and nonnsumption agreements that were proved by the Continental Conress last year.

Merchants in Britain have aleady suffered severe losses as a sult of the association, but they e known to prefer a policy of coniation rather than of coercion.

"Give me liberty, or give me death!"

Richmond, Virginia, March 23

A political firebrand here has declared a private war against Britain, thus inflaming the passions of fellow Virginians. The lawyer Patrick Henry, 39, has been in the House of Burgesses since May 1765. In that very month and year, he offered a series of resolutions, the last of which held that only the General Assembly "had any right or power to impose or lay any taxation on the people here." At that time, his heated words were cooled by his compeers; not so today.

Standing before the second revolutionary convention, Henry explained, first in even tones and then in breathless, explosive speech, why the colony must raise a militia and do battle: "Our brethren are already in the field. Why stand we here idle? What is it that gentlemen wish? What would they have? Is life so dear, or peace so sweet, as to be purchased at the price of chains and slavery? Forbid it, Almighty God! I know not what course others may take, but as for me, give me liberty, or give me death!"

The clarion call of a revolutionary: Patrick Henry offers his clear choice.

ohn Adams responds to Tory viewpoint

oston, Feb. 6

John Adams, back from the Conental Congress in Philadelphia, as added his voice to the debate ver the colonies' relationship with ngland. Answering Tory lawyer aniel Leonard's letters to the *azette*, Adams stops short of a ll for independence. In the absence of colonial representation, he contends, Parliament's authority should be limited to trade issues. "Metaphysicians and politicians may dispute forever," says Adams, "but they will never find any other moral principle or foundation of rule or obedience than the consent of governors and governed."

minent lawyer John Adams.

Iron output mounts

America

Industry continues to expand. Miners are digging enough iron ore out of the ground to place America seventh in world production. The flour mills of Maryland, Pennsylvania and Delaware are considered among the best in the world. Manufacturing is flourishing; the colonies are even slicing off a share of Mother England's reign in the global export of small manufactured goods. However, a severe shortage of gunpowder and labor has slowed production in the critical American armaments industry.

Boone cuts Wilderness Road, founds town

Fort Boone, Kentucky, Apr. 1

At the urging of frontiersman Daniel Boone and the Transylvania Land Company, land-hungry Virginians and North Carolinians have started to build the town of Boonesborough here. Boone, who found his way through the Cumberland Gap six years ago, led some 30 woodchoppers, cutting a forest path called the "Wilderness Road." Started on March 9 near Longisland, North Carolina, the road blazes a trail through the Allegheny Mountains for 250 miles before it ends at Otter Creek, near a bend in the Kentucky River. Now that there is a passable route through the mountains, these settlers are hoping that they will be followed by many more, and that they will found a 14th colony.

This is the dream of Richard Henderson, a North Carolina lawyer and aristocrat. He befriended Boone, whose debts have made him no stranger to the courtroom. Together, they have obtained more than 20 million acres of land from Cherokee chiefs, plying them with money, firearms and rum at the treaty grounds of Sycamore Shoals. The Governors of Virginia and North Carolina have declared the purchases illegal, describing the colonists as an "infamous company of land pyrates" (→June 1, 1792).

Daniel Boone on the frontier.

▷

Revere's ride warns: "The British are coming"

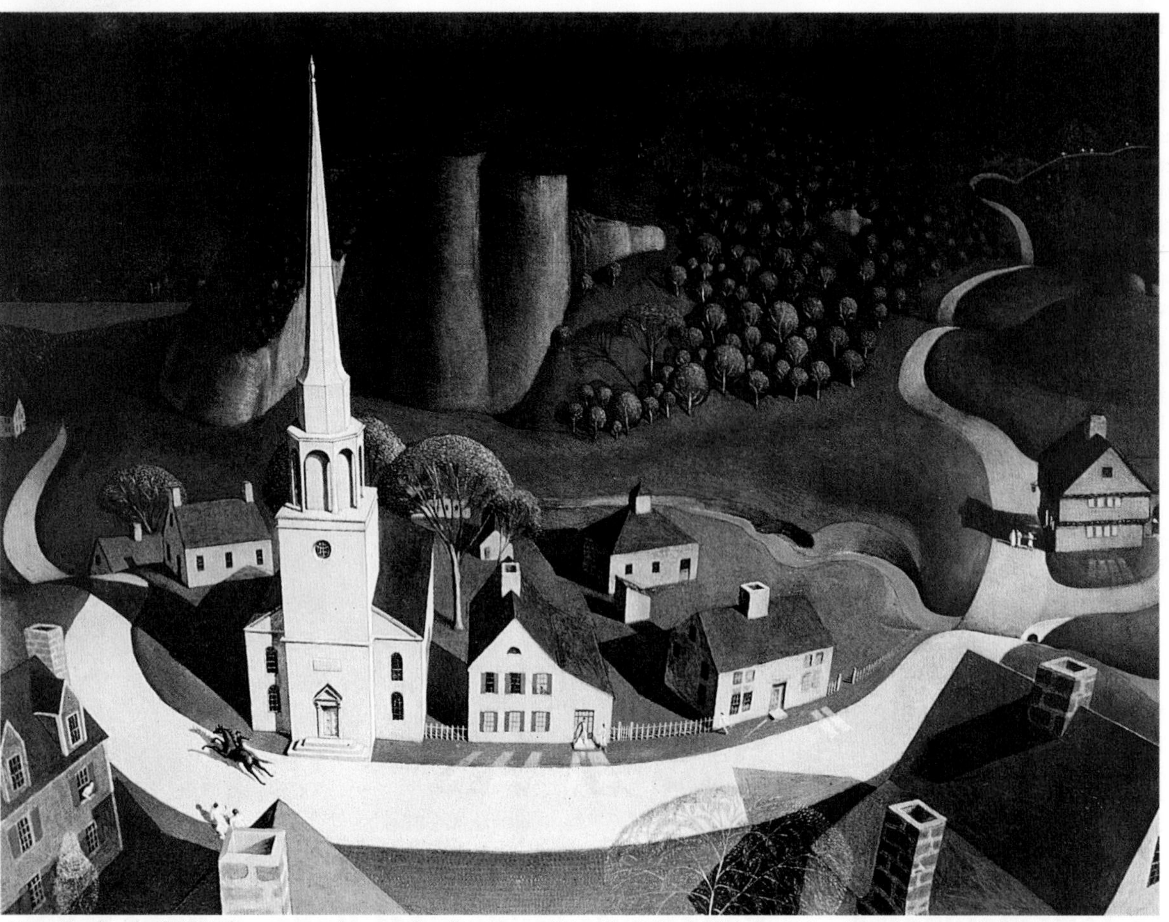

New England of 1775 becomes a fantasy land in Grant Wood's "The Midnight Ride of Paul Revere" (1931).

Lexington, Massachusetts, Apr. 19

Near the hour of 2 in the morning, the Rev. Jonas Clark heard a rap on his front door. He was not awakened; he had been up all night with his guests, Samuel Adams and John Hancock. They recognized the knock at once, and opened the door to reveal a man in spurs and riding boots, spattered with mud. Paul Revere had walked from a mile outside Lexington to tell them he had failed – he had been stopped, his horse was gone, he never got to Concord. Yet his friends voiced no disappointment: They led him to the warm fire, and assured him in hurried whispers that he had indeed spread the word that "The British are coming." Patriots were ready.

On the afternoon of the 18th, a Tuesday, Paul Revere was in his shop in Boston. He may have been designing a sugar bowl, engraving a tea tray or extricating a troublesome tooth from a patient. Revere is a silversmith, a dentist and a Son of Liberty. For nearly a decade, he has spent his evenings in secret activities, but his allegiance has been clearly known since 1770, when he signed his name to an engraving depicting the first British massacre. He is a man more of action than words, an artisan and a member of the Masons. Yet he counts among his friends men of a higher class, the lawyers John Adams and James Otis, and the businessman John Hancock. The cause unites them.

On this afternoon, a stable boy came to Revere and told him he had heard that this very evening General Gage would dispatch 800 troops to Concord. There they would raid the munitions stored by the provincial congress, rendering the Massachusetts militia impotent. The news was not so fearful: Revere and his allies had made contingency plans, drawn up over drafts at the Green Dragon tavern and perfected at the home of the radical Dr. Joseph Warren. They agreed that if the attack came by land, a lantern would be hung in the tower of Christ's Church to warn patriots miles off; if the approach was by sea, two lanterns would be lit. Then a few men would ride from Boston to alert Concord nearly 20 miles away.

At sunset, the sexton at Christ's Church ascended the tower and hung a single lantern. Revere saw it and saw British troops assembling on the Boston Common. At 10 o'clock, a messenger came from Doctor Warren: Revere must ride to Lexington. William Dawes, a cordwainer and fellow Son of Liberty, had been sent on already. If either could make it as far as Concord, God be with them. Revere ran to the north part of Boston and met with his friends Joshua Bentley and Tom Richardson. They had agreed to row him across the Charles River to Charlestown, on the first leg of his journey. As they lowered the boat in the water, they feared crews on British ships would hear them. One man said that a lady friend lived nearby; he gave a whistle below her window and entreated for a bit of cloth. She tossed him down a part of her petticoat, which they shredded and wrapped around the oars. Quietly, they rowed across.

Revere then hurried to the home of his friend Colonel Conant, where he was told that British officers had been seen on the roads to both Cambridge and Concord. Conant gave Revere the finest horse in Charlestown and wished him an earnest Godspeed. Revere dug his spurs into his horse's sides and rode at a fierce gallop due north. It was 11 o'clock by now, and the moon cast dark shadows. After just a few miles, Revere spied two British officers by a tree at the side of the road. They told him to halt, and when he did not, one gave chase. Revere's steed plunged off the road into the fields. The officer tried to follow, but his well-fed horse stumbled into a clay pond and was mired there. Revere turned back to the road and reached the town of Medford, roused the captain of the Minutemen there and rode on. To every home he passed, he called the alarm. West he rode to Menotomy, then north to Lexington. Exhausted, he reached the home of the minister Jonas Clark. "The Regulars are out!" he shouted. Clark and Adams brought Revere inside, and after half an hour, a weary William Dawes, too, arrived.

The two then headed for Concord, and after a short while heard hoofbeats behind them. Prepared for the worst, they turned to find a fellow patriot, Dr. Samuel Prescott. He joined them, and they pressed on. Then, half way to Concord, while Dawes and Prescott stopped at a home, four British soldiers surrounded Revere. He called to his friends: Prescott swung his horse about and forced it over a stone wall – he escaped and, it is hoped, reached Concord. Dawes, too, escaped, but on foot. The British drew their swords. One officer, a major, clapped a pistol to Revere's head and demanded to know what he was about. Boldly, Revere told them. The major ordered Revere to follow them to their camp, most likely to face a swift trial. But after a mile, when a faraway Minuteman's gun was heard, the major knew that the battle mattered more than its messenger. He seized Revere's horse and left the patriot to walk alone to the moonlit but restless town of Lexington.

Redcoats lose battles at Lexington and Concord

Boston, Apr. 19

Nearly 2,000 weary and dispirited British redcoats straggled back into Boston tonight, surprised by the ferocious response of the colonial minutemen in Lexington and Concord earlier in the day. The two sides disagree about who fired the first shot as dawn broke on the common in Lexington, but both realize that the shouting has finally ended and a real war has begun.

John Adams, the moderate colonist, called the fighting today "the most shocking (event) New England ever beheld." He worried that "the fight was between those whose parents but a few generations ago were brothers," adding, "I shudder at the thought, and there is no knowing where our calamities will end." The radicals do not share Adams's concerns. His cousin Sam, upon hearing the first crackle of gunfire in Lexington, cheered. "What a glorious morning this is," he said, "I mean for America."

Before the battle was even joined in Concord, jubilant couriers were racing to the other colonies with word of the brave response. They carried a message from the Boston committee of safety addressed to "All Friends of American Liberty."

Sixteen companies of redcoats, divided equally between infantry and grenadiers, set off from Boston late last night under the command of the aging and obese Colonel Francis Smith. Their secret mission was to destroy the colonists' armaments and supplies stored on a farm in Concord. But the patriots were aware of their mission long before the redcoats crossed the river and landed at Lechmere's Point [East Cambridge]. Paul Revere, William Dawes and Samuel Prescott had all spread word of the advance. When the redcoats arrived in Lexington, they were met by a small contingent of Minutemen. "Don't fire unless fired upon!" shouted Captain John Parker, the patriots' leader. He also reportedly said, "But if they want a war, let it begin here." Realizing they were outnumbered by the hundreds of British troops, the Minutemen began to disperse. "Lay down your arms, damn you," a British officer shouted. "Why don't you lay down your arms?" Suddenly a shot rang out and then both sides opened fire. The Americans lost eight men. One of the casualties was Parker's cousin Jonas, who was mortally wounded by a redcoat wielding a bayonet. British casualties were light.

The British met their match a few hours later when they marched six more miles to Concord looking for the rebel supplies. The minutemen, true to their name, had mustered early. "Before sunrise, there was, I believe, 150 of us and more," said Corporal Amos Barrett. The patriots had also managed to spirit away most of their battle supplies, and they evacuated Concord before the redcoats arrived. From a hilltop, they watched in anger as the British ransacked their community.

At North Bridge, several hundred colonists battled three companies of redcoats. Three of the British soldiers were killed, and most of them were unable to return fire because they were grouped in a very narrow line after crossing the bridge. "The weight of their fire was such that we were obliged to give way," a British soldier recalled, "then run with the greatest precipitance." The redcoats, who said the Minutemen had committed atrocities, retreated to the center of town and spent two hours trying to reorganize. The delay was deadly. Hundreds of patriots rushed to the Lexington road, where they hid behind walls, hedges and trees. When the badly organized redcoats began their retreat, they were ambushed by snipers. "The numbers of the patriots were increasing from all parts," said Lieutenant John Barker, "while ours were reducing by deaths, wounds and fatigue. We were totally surrounded with such an incessant fire as it is impossible to conceive. Our ammunition was likewise near expended."

The British suffered more than an affront to their pride today. Their casualties were listed at 73 dead and 200 wounded or missing. The Americans say 49 of their men were killed, 39 were wounded and five are reported missing.

"Thus ended this expedition, which from beginning to end was ill planned and ill executed," said Lt. Barker of Britain (→ June 12).

Action at Lexington. Engraving after a painting by Alonzo Chappel.

American patriots drive off a group of redcoats at Concord's North Bridge.

Lexington: at point-blank range.

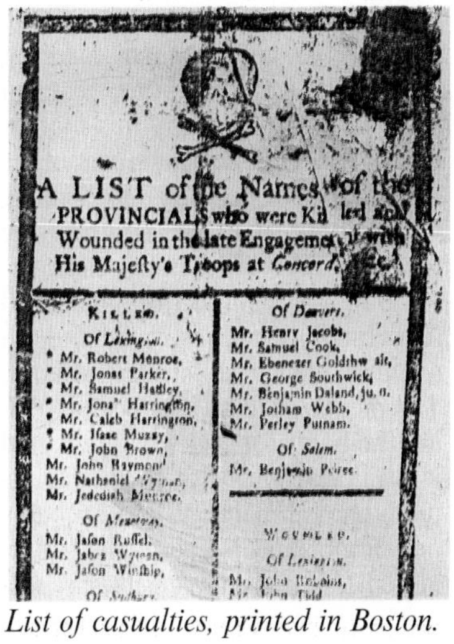

A LIST of the Names of the PROVINCIALS who were Killed and Wounded in the late Engagement with His Majesty's Troops at Concord, &c.

KILLED.

Of Lexington.
* Mr. Robert Monroe,
* Mr. Jonas Parker,
* Mr. Samuel Hadley,
* Mr. Jona. Harrington,
* Mr. Caleb Harrington,
* Mr. Isaac Muzzy,
* Mr. John Brown,

Mr. John Raymond,
Mr. Nathaniel Wyman,
Mr. Jedediah Munroe.

Of Menotomy.
Mr. Jason Russel,
Mr. Jabez Wyman,
Mr. Jason Winship,

Of Danvers.
Mr. Henry Jacobs,
Mr. Samuel Cook,
Mr. Ebenezer Goldthwait,
Mr. George Southwick,
Mr. Benjamin Daland, jun.
Mr. Jotham Webb,
Mr. Perley Putnam.

Of Salem.
Mr. Benjamin Peirce.

WOUNDED.

Of Lexington.
Mr. John Robbins,

List of casualties, printed in Boston.

Washington takes command of army

"George Washington on a White Charger" (early 19th c.), artist unknown.

Boston, June 26

George Washington of Virginia arrived in Boston today to assume command of the Continental Army. Creation of this army was authorized last month by the Second Continental Congress. John Adams of Massachusetts presented the unanimous resolution that appointed Washington commanding general on June 15. Congress also voted to raise six companies of infantry from the Middle Atlantic and Southern colonies, and they will join with colonial forces currently stationed in and around Boston.

Washington apparently is none too pleased with this army. While most of his troops are from New England, the Southern general has described these Yankees as "an exceedingly nasty and dirty people," who seem to think of little else but money. Although other officers find the men competent enough, some reveal that the troops are poorly disciplined, do not follow orders well and often do not refer to their superior officers by their proper titles. Nevertheless, the ragged army proved quite successful last week in its encounter with British regulars at the battle of Bunker Hill, just outside Boston. On that occasion, the scrappy colonials inflicted more than a thousand casualties on the redcoats. Still, Washington's task of building a hardened fighting force is not going to be easily accomplished (→ July 3).

British send over 3 more generals

Boston, May 25

After repeated pleas to Londo for top-level military assistance British General Thomas Gage Governor of Massachusetts, toda welcomed the arrival of General Sir William Howe, Sir Henry Clin ton and John Burgoyne. Gage, wh has felt that the colonial resistanc was getting beyond his control an that "civil government is near it end," plans to concentrate on hi role as civilian governor and to tur over the military command of a British forces in North America t Howe, the senior general.

N.C. county first to claim independence

North Carolina, May 20

Mecklenburg today became th first county in America to declar its independence from Britain. Th safety committee of Mecklenburg formed to carry out the will of th Continental Congress, took thi radical step in response to th British attack on colonists in Lex ington and Concord, Massachu setts, last month. The committe called for the election of militar officers, declared all colonial con stitutions void and said that an person who accepted an office from the crown was an "enemy to hi country."

British arsenal is captured at Ticonderoga

Fort Ticonderoga, N.Y., May 10

In a victory that was more comic than heroic, an irregular force of Americans captured this fort on Lake Champlain. Early this month, Ethan Allen led 200 members of his Green Mountain Boys to Hand's Cove, about two miles south of the fort. At the same time, Benedict Arnold, who had no troops, headed for Hand's Cove as well, and on arriving declared himself leader. The men argued as they began loading the boats for a dawn attack, and it is unclear which of them was actually in command. It was probably not important because the dilapidated fort was indefensible.

The members of the garrison, which consisted of two officers, 40 men and 24 women and children, were surprised in their beds. Allen caught Lieutenant Jocelyn Feltham standing sleepily with his breeches still in hand. "Come out of there, you damned old rat" said Allen. "By what authority are you acting?" asked Feltham. "In the name of the Great Jehovah and the Continental Congress," bellowed Allen. Presumably, Feltham was suitably impressed by these twin deities and surrendered immediately. Two days later, the garrison at Crown Point was also captured. There were no British or American casualties reported in either of these engagements (→ Dec. 31).

With his Green Mountain Boys assembled in the background, Ethan Alle demands the surrender of Fort Ticonderoga by its British commander.

$2 million in bills to finance the war

Philadelphia, June 22

The Second Continental Congress today resolved to issue paper currency of a "sum not exceeding 2,000,000 Spanish milled dollars" in bills of credit to help finance the war. Congress also decided that the "12 Confederated Colonies" (Georgia is not officially represented) would pledge themselves to redeem the bills in proportion to their populations within seven years. Recognizing that the sum would not be enough, John Adams wrote, "We must, I suppose, vote to issue a great deal more" (→Oct. 3, 1776).

British schooner seized in Maine

Machias, Maine, June 12

In the first naval action of the war, the British schooner Margaretta, commanded by Midshipman Moore, has been boarded and captured by a group of local patriots under the command of Jeremiah O'Brien. The action follows a dispute between local citizens and officers of two supply ships from Boston. After seizing one of the ships, O'Brien and his men pursued the fleeing Margaretta, shot the man at the wheel and, though suffering nine casualties from hand grenades hurled by Moore, boarded her with clubbed muskets.

Revolution's start causes London stir

London, May 29

The first news regarding the battles of Lexington and Concord has created a stir in London coffeehouses and in the press. In the *London Evening Post* it was reported that "the prevailing toast in every company of true Englishmen is Victory to the Americans . . ." The initial accounts of the battles were hastily prepared by American patriots and the news has put them in a most favorable light. While there have not been any outbursts of political feeling against the Americans, the public reaction here has varied.

British win fierce fight at Bunker Hill

Charlestown, Mass., June 17

A fierce, day-long battle for control of this vital peninsula ended late this afternoon, and both patriots and redcoats agreed that the day belonged to the British. Their operation around Bunker Hill was most costly, however. The British lost 1,000 men, triple the number of American casualties, and the patriots proved again that the redcoats are not invincible. As they did at Lexington and Concord, the Americans exhibited a voracious taste for battle and an intelligence network that pries free most British secrets.

Frustrated by the siege of Boston and embarrassed by the inability of his regulars to dislodge a rag-tag band of farmers and merchants, General Gage resolved several days ago to turn the tables by seizing the peninsula here and Dorchester Heights. Within a few hours, the Americans had learned about his secret plans. Last night, several American regiments got through Charlestown Neck, crawled in the dark across Bunker Hill and began to construct a fortification on the somewhat lower Breed's Hill. Angered by the patriots' action, Gage called a council of war and approved a frontal assault on the peninsula. Foolishly, it turns out, he rejected General Clinton's idea of sending several other regiments behind the patriots' lines to cut off an eventual retreat. Supported by several warships as well as cannon fire from Copp's Hill in Boston, 1,500 British soldiers landed at Morton's Hill and struck at the new fortification. General Burgoyne called it "one of the greatest scenes of war that can be conceived," but the British generals were also humbled as they advanced. They believed, said Burgoyne, that "a defeat was a final loss to the British Empire in America."

On Breed's Hill, the Americans dug in. "Don't fire until you see the whites of their eyes," one commander ordered. The first two British assaults failed, and the redcoats were unable to seize the fortification until reinforcements arrived. But on the third British assault, the Americans were overwhelmed and forced to retreat toward nearby Bunker Hill. A short while later, that also fell (→26).

"Attack on Bunker Hill With the Burning of Charlestown" (1873), anonymous.

The battle rages: Newly reinforced by troops from overseas, General Gage moved on Charlestown Heights with 11 regiments and a train of artillery.

John Trumbull's poignant rendering of "The Battle of Bunker Hill" (1785).

"Olive Branch" spurned by King George

King George III of England.

Philadelphia, December 6

Declaring that in spite of his rejection of its overtures, it still has no intention of denying the King's sovereignty, Congress has brought to a close the matter of the Olive Branch Petition. Originally proposed and drafted by John Dickinson of Pennsylvania, the petition was adopted by the Second Congress on July 5. A key passage stated: "Attached to your Majesty's person, family and government with all the devotion that principles and affection can inspire, connected with Great Britain by the strongest ties that can unite societies, and deploring every event that tends in any degree to weaken them, we solemnly assure your Majesty, that we not only most ardently desire the former harmony between her and these colonies may be restored, but that a concord may be established between them upon so firm a basis as to perpetuate its blessings uninterrupted by any future dissensions to succeeding generations."

The petition called on the King to put an end to the war, repeal the Coercive Acts and bring about a "happy and permanent reconciliation." However, the colonial agents in London could not persuade Lord Dartmouth to present the congressional petition to King George III, who was known to be unwilling to receive it, and whose real reply came on August 23, when he declared that the colonies were in open rebellion against the crown.

17,000-man mob displeases Washington

Boston, July 3

General George Washington of Mount Vernon, Virginia, took formal command of the Continental Army at Cambridge today. After a journey of 10 days from Philadelphia, he arrived June 26 to find that his "army" of 17,000 men was more of a ragtag mob than a disciplined fighting force.

When Washington assumed command, his army had not had sufficient training to perform a traditional pass-in-review for its new chief. No one, enlisted man or officer, seems to be able to give or take orders. Some observers have even questioned whether the predominantly New England army will ever take orders from a Southerner. And to make matters worse, fewer than 12,000 of the general's men are healthy enough for active service. The lack of properly constructed privies has caused many deaths and greatly contributed to the generally wretched sanitary conditions that plague the area. The army's severe shortage of gunpowder, rifles, clothing and food only confirms what many local observers view as a hopeless military position.

Washington himself apparently does not have high hopes of military success. As he told his friend and fellow Virginian Patrick Henry last week, "From the day I enter upon the command of the American armies, I date my fall and the ruin of my reputation" (→Jan. 1, 1776).

Untrained troops attempt to pass in review before General Washington.

Post Office set up; Franklin to run it

Philadelphia, July 26

The Continental Congress created its own postal system today. It chose the experienced Benjamin Franklin as the first postmaster general and will pay him $1,000 a year. Franklin was deputy postmasster general under the British.

Ben Franklin by Joseph S. Duplessis.

Georgia 13th colony to join Congress

Philadelphia, Sept. 12

The Second Continental Congress, which has been in session since May, today welcomed the representatives from the colony of Georgia. With the arrival of the Georgians, the Congress now includes members from all 13 colonies as it desperately seeks a peaceful solution to the growing British-American crisis. As Lord North's plan for a reconciliation with the colonies was being rejected, the Congress took up the task of self-government. It has set up a board of commissioners to negotiate with the Indians and is now making plans for the establishment of a postal system, a foreign office and a navy. At the same time, Thomas Jefferson has prepared a proposal to the King in which the Virginian rejects the idea of independence, yet argues that the Americans have no intention of living like slaves under the British government. Is there to be war or reconciliation?

Editorial by Paine is attack on slavery

Philadelphia, Oct. 18

The Pennsylvania Journal this day bears an editorial that urges the public to enact "continental legislation which shall put a stop to . . . Negroes for sale." The essay is signed "Humanus"; while it may be the first abolitionist letter from "Humanus," it is not the first from Thomas Paine, the former Englishman who writes in local papers under the names "Aesop," "Atlanticus" and now, apparently, "Humanus." Since March, Paine, who migrated to Philadelphia only last year, has attacked dueling, bad marriages and disrespect of women.

Perilous times spur literary production

America

The widening breach between America and England is causing intense literary debate. Essays such as *A Calm Address to Our American Colonies* by the Methodist evangelist John Wesley and plays such as *The Americans Aroused* by Jonathan Sewall support the British, but works backing the colonists' fight for independence, such as John Trumbull's satirical verses *M'Fingal*, Mercy Otis's dramatic lampoon *The Group* and Phillip Freneau's poems *General Gage's Confession* and *General Gage's Soliloquy*, have been better received here.

Colonial navy formed

Philadelphia, Dec. 3

The Continental Congress of the United Colonies of North America has issued orders that a fleet be fitted out, in Delaware Bay, to challenge the might of the most powerful navy in the world. The commander of this tiny new fleet is Esek Hopkins. His flagship is the Alfred, formerly a solid Philadelphia merchantman that was called the Black Prince. Commodore Hopkins was piped aboard by green-coated marines. After the commodore read his orders, the flag was raised by his first lieutenant, John Paul Jones. This new banner, called the Grand Union flag or Congress Colors, is made up of British crosses in the upper left hand corner, on a field consisting of 13 alternating red and white stripes.

Toward the end of this year, the Congress passed much of the legislation that was required to organize a navy. John Adams and a naval committee are responsible for the *Rules for the Regulation of the Navy of the United Colonies*, which is based upon British regulations. Last month the naval committee purchased four merchant vessels that have since been converted to men-of-war.

While the organization of a navy was being ponderously discussed in Philadelphia, General George Washington, commander-in-chief of the Continental Army, watched in frustration as the British army received a steady supply of reinforcements and materiel by sea.

On September 2, orders were delivered to Nicholas Broughton, an officer in Colonel John Glover's "Web-footed Marblehead Regiment," made up of sailors and fishermen, to "proceed on board the Schooner Hannah, at Beverly, lately fitted out & equipp'd with Arms, Ammunition and Provisions at the Continental Expence . . . and to cruise against such vessels as may be found on the high seas and elsewhere." Three days later, he took to sea and captured an unarmed ship named Unity. That vessel turned out to be an American ship that had earlier been captured by the British.

Lieutenant John Paul Jones (painting by Charles Willson Peale) raised the Congress Colors, the new colonial flag, for the first time on Dec. 3.

800 Indians burn San Diego mission

San Francisco, Dec. 24

Indians wiped out the mission at San Diego last month, it was learned today. A violent uprising by the Indians resulted in the burning of every building in the Spanish coastal enclave. A force of more than 800 attacked the Franciscan mission and killed almost all of its inhabitants. including Father Luis Juame, the leading priest. A Castilian corporal named Rocha is credited with having finally driven off the tribesmen as a result of his deadly musket fire. Spanish church authorities say that the mission is going to be rebuilt.

Britain's Gage says it is time for war

Boston, Oct. 15

While keeping the peace in Boston, General Thomas Gage is urging his masters in England to wage war. In a letter to the Earl of Dartmouth, he said peace was no longer possible, especially if the treasonous leaders were arrested in either England or America. Gage told Dartmouth, who is secretary for the colonies, that he should have 20,000 men, including cavalry, field artillery and picked German troops. He also said the government should suspend the punitive Coercive Acts and ask that emissaries from Massachusetts be invited to talks in London.

Attack on Quebec fails

Montgomery dies leading the assault on Quebec. Painting by John Trumbull.

Quebec, Dec. 31

American troops suffered a disastrous defeat today when they attempted to capture Quebec, the last British foothold in North America.

In the fierce fighting, General Richard Montgomery, the American commander who had seized Montreal in November, was killed and his second in command, General Benedict Arnold, was wounded. In addition, some 100 Americans were killed or wounded, with 300 more taken prisoner by the British defenders.

The defeat was a stunning turnabout for the American invasion force that took Fort Ticonderoga from the British in May and began its march to the north in August under the command of General Philip Schuyler. When Schuyler fell ill, Montgomery took over and led his troops via Lake Champlain and the Richelieu River to the St. Lawrence. The British Governor-General, Sir Guy Carleton, surrendered Montreal to the invaders on November 11 and American troops entered the city a day later. This left all of Canada under American occupation except for Quebec city.

The victory at Ticonderoga was the key to the Americans' advance because it allowed them to move north along the Richelieu. By June, Carleton was forced to declare martial law and call out volunteers to augment the 800 troops under his command. The mixed force was no match for the numerically superior Americans. Carleton then pulled his forces out of Montreal and withdrew to Quebec, which he reached on November 19.

General Arnold, meanwhile, arrived at Levis, across the St. Lawrence River from Quebec, on November 8 after an arduous two-month trek through uncharted land along the Kennebec, Dead and Chaudiere Rivers. Only 700 of the 1,100 men he started with finished the journey. They crossed the river five days later and took up positions on the Plains of Abraham, but soon after they moved upriver to Pointe aux Trembles to wait for reinforcements from Montreal. When they were joined by 300 troops under Montgomery, they laid siege to the capital on December 5. But after a two-day battle, yesterday and today, the Americans abandoned the attack (→ May 6, 1776).

Arnold, wounded in the debacle.

1776

Massachusetts, Jan. 23. General Court, urged by Continental Congress, calls for ousting of royal Governor (→24).

Cambridge, Massachusetts, Jan. 24. Colonel Henry Knox arrives with armaments captured by Ethan Allen at Fort Ticonderoga and transported over land (→March 26).

North Carolina, Feb. 27. Colonial forces take 900 prisoners in defeating Scottish loyalists at Moore's Creek Bridge [near Wilmington] (→May 10).

Philadelphia, March, 3. In effort to open channel for foreign aid, Congress names Silas Deane agent to France (→May 2).

Philadelphia, March, 14. Congress votes policy of disarming all loyalists.

Philadelphia, Apr. 6. Congress opens ports to trade with all nations except Britain.

Philadelphia, Apr. 9. Congress calls for end to slave trade.

Canada, May 6. Fresh troops reinforce Sir Guy Carleton, enabling him to pursue retreating American army (→June 7).

Philadelphia, May 26. John Adams, in letter to James Sullivan, writes: "The balance of power in a society accompanies the balance of property in land."

Canada, July 5. General Benedict Arnold ends Montreal siege to prepare for defense of Lake Champlain (→Nov. 3).

Far West, Aug. 5. Spanish explorer Padre Francisco Escalante reaches San Juan River and founds town of Nuestra Sonoro las Nieves [first settlement in Colorado].

America, Aug. 10. Franklin, Jefferson, John Adams propose "E Pluribus Unum" as nation's motto (→Sept. 9).

New York, Sept. 11. Franklin, Adams and Rutledge meet British on Long Island; peace talks founder on Howe's insistence that Congress revoke Declaration of Independence (→21).

California, Nov. 11. Father Junipero Serra formally founds Mission San Juan Capistrano.

North Carolina, Nov. 19. Colony annexes Watauga, renaming it Washington County.

France, Dec. 4. Ben Franklin arrives in France to negotiate treaty.

East Coast. Roadways now extend from Boston to Savannah; none is hard-surfaced.

"Common Sense" by Thomas Paine

Philadelphia

The flames of rebellion are being fanned by an immigrant from England. He is Thomas Paine, whose pamphlet *Common Sense*, published January 10 by Robert Bell of Third Street, Philadelphia, exhorts the colonies to sever all ties to the mother country. Paine, the editor of *Pennsylvania Magazine* since arriving on these shores in 1774, makes the boldest case yet for the American claim to complete autonomy, going so far as to propose establishment of a government that is based on equal representation for all of the 13 colonies.

The outspoken Paine not only rejects the idea of a truce, he also impugns the morality of those people who are in favor of it. "If you say you can still pass (England's) offenses over, then I ask, has your house been burned? Has your property been destroyed before your face? Are your wife and children destitute of a bed to lie on or bread to live on? Have you lost a parent or child by their hands, and yourself the ruined and wretched survivor? If you have not, and can still shake hands with the murderers, then are you unworthy the name of husband, father, friend, or a lover, and whatever may be your rank and title in life, you have the heart of a coward and the spirit of a sycophant."

Common Sense has stirred the passions of prominent colonists. George Washington, appointed last June to command the Continental Army, lauded the Paine pamphlet in a letter sent on January 31 to his military colleague Joseph Reed, saying, "A few more of such flaming arguments, as were exhibited at Falmouth [Portland, Maine] and Norfolk (towns burned by the British), added to the sound doctrine and unanswerable reasoning contained in . . . *Common Sense* will not leave numbers at a loss to decide upon the propriety of separation."

Not everyone, however, finds Paine's reasoning "unanswerable." The Rev. William Smith of Pennsylvania has robustly met Paine's challenge to "show a single advantage that this continent can reap by being connected with Great Britain." In his open letters to the people of Pennsylvania, published in March, Smith, better known by his pen name, Cato, asserts that what Paine terms "common sense" is actually "nonsense."

Smith takes strong exception to the assertion in Paine's pamphlet that the colonies should look for assistance from foreign powers, such as France or Spain, and he argues that the rebellious Americans should continue to stand alone against England "till Great Britain is convinced, as she must soon be, of her fatal policy, and open her arms to reconciliation, upon the permanent and sure footing of mutual interests and safety."

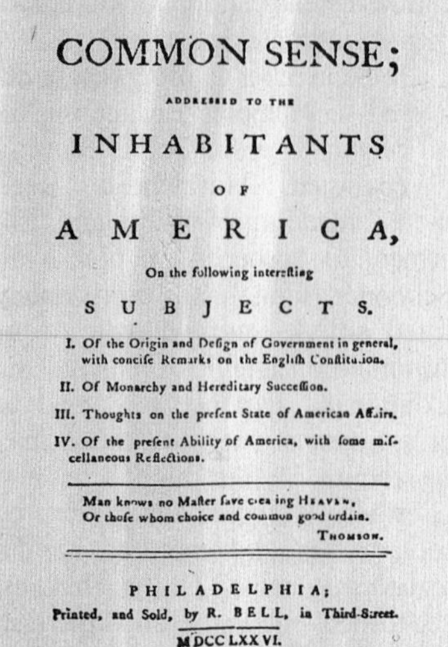

COMMON SENSE;

ADDRESSED TO THE

INHABITANTS

OF

AMERICA,

On the following intereſting

SUBJECTS.

I. Of the Origin and Deſign of Government in general, with conciſe Remarks on the Engliſh Conſtitution.

II. Of Monarchy and Hereditary Succeſſion.

III. Thoughts on the preſent State of American Affairs.

IV. Of the preſent Ability of America, with ſome miſcellaneous Reflections.

Man knows no Maſter ſave creating Heaven,
Or thoſe whom choice and common good ordain.

THOMSON.

PHILADELPHIA;
Printed, and Sold, by R. BELL, in Third-Street.
MDCCLXXVI.

Thomas Paine's title page and . . .

the author himself, by J.W. Jarvis.

The Pine Tree flag of Massachusetts, flown at Bunker Hill last year, is giving way to the Congress Colors or Grand Union flag.

247 colonists reach San Francisco area

Monterey, California, March 28

A party of 247 Spaniards arrived today at an estuary that they call San Francisco, which is situated some distance to the north of here. Led by the noted expedition leader Luis Anza, the group includes farmers, soldiers, churchmen and servants. One friar, Pedro Font, states that he has never seen such "safe and spacious waters with their commanding heights. A city built here might rival any seaport in Europe for splendor and security." Authorities say that two sites are being reserved for missions (→Sept. 17).

Washington lauds Negro woman poet

Cambridge, Massachusetts, Feb. 28

General Washington has written to a Negro poet, Phillis Wheatley, inviting her to visit him at his headquarters in Cambridge. His letter came in response to a poem Wheatley wrote in praise of the general. Washington mentioned her "elegant lines" and "poetical talent," adding that ". . . I shall be happy to see a person favored by the muses, and to whom nature has been so liberal and beneficent in her dispensations." The poet is a slave and housemaid owned by John Wheatley of Boston.

Grand Union flag unfurled over Boston

Boston, Jan. 1

In a recent speech, King George III called on the colonial troops in America to lay down their arms. The American forces surrounding Boston responded today by burning copies of the King's speech and raising their new flag. It has 13 alternating horizontal red and white stripes and a blue field in the upper left-hand corner bearing the crosses of St. George and St. Andrew. The bars represent the colonies and the crosses symbolize their hope of remaining attached to Britain.

Authorized by the Continental Congress, the flag is called the Congress Colors. General Washington, who refers to it as the Grand Union flag, has noted that the inclusion of the crosses had led the British to mistake the intentions of the colonists.

"Behold!" said Washington, "it was received in Boston as a token of the deep impression the speech had made on us . . . By this time I presume they think it strange that we have not made a formal surrender of our lines."

But the colonial siege of British troops is now in its seventh month and shows no sign of wavering. The American troops came from the many colonies in response to the British attack on Lexington and Concord last spring and they now number some 15,000. Washington was made the commander-in-chief by the Continental Congress on June 15 and rode out to join his forces in July (→23).

The Congress Colors or Grand Union, raised over Prospect Hill, is the first true national flag in America. The 13 alternating stripes represent the colonies and the crosses symbolize the hope of remaining attached to Britain.

British evacuate Boston

Howe's men destroy the fortifications of Boston before sailing to Halifax.

Boston, March 26

After an unexplained delay of more than a week, a British fleet of 125 transports and warships has left Boston harbor bound for Halifax, Nova Scotia. Aboard are General Sir William Howe, some 9,000 officers and men, and more than 1,000 loyalists and their families. The British fleet left the harbor unmolested in return for a promise by General Howe that the city would not be burned.

The immediate cause of the withdrawal was the capture and fortification of Dorchester Heights by General John Thomas and 2,000 soldiers of the Continental Army on the night of March 4. Once taken, the heights were reinforced with cannons and mortars captured last year at Ticonderoga and recently brought here on sleds over 300 miles of rough and frozen terrain by Henry Knox, General Washington's chief of artillery. The British, who had inexplicably failed to secure the heights, were faced with the choice of attempting to drive the Americans off, and in doing so risking an even bloodier repetition of Bunker Hill, or abandoning the town. A counterattack was planned, but it was canceled due to bad weather and the decision to evacuate was approved by a full military council.

The decision to leave Boston is not surprising since it is of small strategic value to the British, who have been unable to venture beyond the city itself. After regrouping in Halifax, they are expected to head for New York and make that city their center of operations (→May).

Shakers, devout sect, found first colony

Niskayuna, New York, September

A new religious group on the American scene has established a settlement near Niskayuna [Watervliet]. This group, officially named the United Society of Believers in Christ's Second Coming and popularly called "Shakers," has very distinctive ideas regarding the beliefs and activities of its members. The society was founded in England by Ann Lee, whose followers call her Mother, and several of the adherents came to these shores with her in 1774.

Among the most distinctive characteristics of the Shakers are the rejection of marriage and of all carnal desires, the holding of goods in common, and religious services that include dancing and much singing. The Shakers practice many of the activities associated with the primitive church, such as prophesying and speaking in tongues. During their services, they wait for the spirit to descend upon them. After it does so, they often break into jerking and twitching motions, which gives them their nickname. A sturdy sect, the Shakers have chosen a rugged location for a settlement.

Washington basks in success, watching British ships leave Boston harbor.

Jefferson's independence draft presented

Philadelphia, June 28

The Second Continental Congress took a momentous step forward today in the effort to separate the colonies from Britain permanently. A committee headed by Thomas Jefferson of Virginia presented a draft document that would sever ties with London and establish the independence of the colonies. The document's language, for the most part drafted by Jefferson, is majestic. "We hold these truths to be sacred and undeniable," he wrote, "that all men are created equal and independent, that from that equal creation they derive rights inherent and inalienable, among which are the preservation of life and liberty and the pursuit of happiness."

Many delegates were impressed by the document, but they do not all favor independence. As John Adams of Massachusetts said to a close friend: "It is now universally acknowledged that we are and must be independent. But still, objections are made to a declaration of it. It is said that such a declaration will arouse and unite Great Britain." Adams realizes that delegates from New England and the South are strong supporters of the declaration, but the Middle States, New York in particular, still favor a strong association with Britain. Adams was greatly cheered by the recent vote in the Virginia House of Burgesses in favor of independence. Virginia delegate Richard Henry Lee, speaking of the vote in an address to the Congress, said the 13 colonies "are and of right ought to be free and independent states."

Jefferson was joined on the committee by Adams, Benjamin Franklin, Robert Livingston and Roger Sherman. Adams and Franklin are seeking minor changes, but the inspirational language is Jefferson's. The Virginian has rarely been an effective speaker, but his writing skills are superlative (→ July 4).

Franklin, Adams and Jefferson labor over the Declaration of Independence. Jefferson prepared the draft; Franklin and Adams suggested revisions.

Washington goes to defense of New York

New York City, May

Since General Howe's army and 1,000 loyalists left Boston harbor in March, the strategic focus of the American rebellion has become New York City. General George Washington is determined to defend the city in spite of the many potential difficulties involved. Having moved his army here from Boston, he is now faced with splitting it up in order to defend New York's many vulnerable points, includin Long Island, which is a sprawlin region that many military expert consider to be indefensible becaus it is so big. Washington has place Charles Lee in charge of construc ing a series of fortifications througl out the area, as well as barricadin key streets. In addition, a hug chain is to be forged that will b stretched across the Hudson Rive at West Point (→ June 29).

Americans pursued in retreat from Quebec

Quebec, June 7

Retreating American forces attempted a counterattack today but were defeated by a fresh British force under the command of Sir Guy Carleton. The Americans, led by General John Sullivan, now appear to be in full flight after their ill-fated attempt to drive the English out of Quebec.

Sullivan took charge of the invasion forces only five days ago afte the smallpox death of General Joh Thomas. Thomas had taken ove just a month before from Genera David Wooster, who in turn re placed General Benedict Arnold i April. Arnold, who took over afte General Richard Montgomery die in the attack on Quebec in Decem ber, was relieved of his comman and sent to Montreal (→ July 5).

North Carolina first to end British ties

North Carolina, May 10

North Carolina today became the first colony to declare its independence from Britain. In a unanimous vote, the provincial government at Halifax went a step further and encouraged the 12 other colonies to do the same. The attack against colonists at Moore's Creek Bridge last February was the catalyst that spurred them to revolution. John Penn, who was a delegate to th Continental Congress, wrote tha "recent events in the colony hav wholly changed the disposition o the inhabitants who are friends o liberty; all regard for the King an the nation of Britain is gone. A to tal separation is what they want." Penn also observed that in man counties "there was not one dis senting vote" on the issue.

France offers help to American cause

Paris, May 2

In a major gesture of support for the American cause, Louis XVI, the young King of France, has offered one million livres in military and financial aid. Muskets, powder, blankets and uniforms, all desperately needed by the Continental Army, will be bought and shipped through a fictitious company, Roderigue Hortalez et Cie., managed by the playwright turned secret agent Caron de Beaumarchais. In another gesture of support, the French will allow their ports to be used by American ships (→ May 1, 1777).

Dying captain says "Don't give up ship"

Boston, May 19

The British were vexed that a American named James Mugford had the temerity to sail a capture vessel, the Hope, loaded with mili tary supplies, right under thei noses in broad daylight. Mugford did, and got away with it, but whe his ship ran aground, the British had an opportunity for revenge During the British attack, Mugford received "a fatal ball." But he ex horted his men: "Don't give up th ship, you will beat them off." The Americans succeeded in repelling the boarding party.

Virginia enacts first state constitution

The Virginia constitutional convention debates George Mason's bill of rights.

Virginia, June 29

Virginia today declared itself an independent commonwealth and became the first colony to enact its own state constitution. The document was written by George Mason, a strong believer in decentralized government. The constitution provides that a governor will be elected annually and that he will have no power of veto over the State Senate or House of Representatives. Mason also included a strong bill of rights in the constitution, guaranteeing trial by jury, freedom of the press and freedom of religion.

British fail in South Carolina island attack

Charleston, S.C., June 28

South Carolina is safe. Defenders of the colony, led by Generals William Moultrie and Charles Lee, fought off a flurry of British sea attacks with a little luck and a lot of fortitude. A powerful British fleet, under Sir Peter Parker, had waited all month to launch today's offensive. But bad weather as well as poor scouting held up the assault. The delay enabled the army on Sullivan's Island to prepare a defense. British cannons fired relentlessly at General Moultrie's island fort. But the walls of the fort, which Lee had feared were not strong enough, withstood the pummeling. Tonight, the bloodied British were retreating in defeat.

Sergeant William Jasper replaces a flag during the British attack on Sullivan's Island at the entrance to the harbor of Charleston, South Carolina.

New York faces invasion

New York City, June 29

The greatest military buildup ever seen on this side of the Atlantic continues as the British concentrate their forces for the capture of New York, the second largest city in the colonies, after Philadelphia.

General Washington, who arrived here with the bulk of his army in April after the successful siege of Boston and now commands a force of some 18,000 men, has done his best to fortify the town and its environs. A strong position has been established on Brooklyn Heights, and batteries have been set up on either side of the Narrows to deny entry to the British fleet. In addition, fortified positions have been prepared on the northern tip of Manhattan Island and on either side of the Hudson River.

Britain's General Howe, who arrived in advance of his fleet on June 25, will have at his disposition some 30 men-of-war, under the command of his brother, Lord Howe, and a land force of at least 25,000 men, all of them trained regulars. Further reinforcements are expected when Admiral Sir Peter Parker and General Clinton arrive from Charleston. Thousands of Hessians are also on their way (→ July 9).

Invasion by sea. "British Ships on the Hudson" by C.T. Warren.

Kentucky settlers plan for defense

Harrodsburg, Kentucky, June 6

Dissatisfied with the rule of the Transylvania Company, which had purchased the land, and under frequent attack by Indians, who are often helped by the British, the settlers of Kentucky were called together today by a young Virginian named George Rogers Clark to discuss their defense. They chose delegates to go to Williamsburg to petition Virginia to annex the Kentucky settlements. The move should help assure Virginia's political control of the West and may be the start of a campaign by Clark to capture Britain's Northwest outposts.

Continental Navy attacks in Bahamas

Nasssau, Bahamas, March 4

Commodore Esek Hopkins, in command of the first fleet of the new Continental Navy, arrived at Nassau in the Bahamas yesterday in an attempt to seize a large cache of powder known to be stored there. Captain Samual Nicholas led a force of 270 marines ashore and they met with no opposition. The islanders thought that the marines were Spaniards. The Governor of Nassau had been warned that the American fleet was coming and managed to dispose of the powder. However, the marines did capture 71 cannons.

Congress approves declaration of Independence

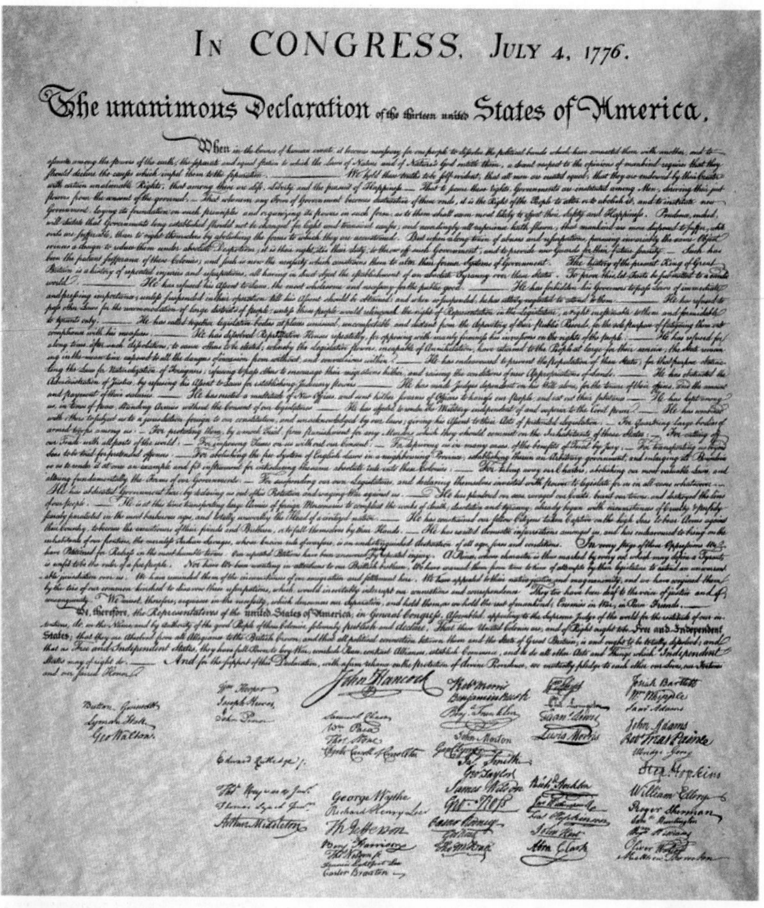

IN CONGRESS, JULY 4, 1776.

The unanimous Declaration of the thirteen united States of America,

Philadelphia, July 4

Three days of spirited debate ended today as the Continental Congress approved Thomas Jefferson's Declaration of Independence from Great Britain. Of the 13 colonies, 12 voted to approve the impressive document. New York abstained. From this time forward, the colonies will be known as "free and independent states," as Jefferson wrote. "They are absolved from all allegiance to the British crown, and . . . all political connection between them, and the state of Great Britain is . . . dissolved."

Debate on the declaration began Tuesday, a day John Adams described as "the most memorable epoch in the history of America." He called the document the greatest "ever debated." Despite his enthusiasm, he failed at first to gain the support of Delaware, New York, Pennsylvania and South Carolina. Jefferson criticized delegates who favored retention of ties with Britain and he rejected "the pusillanimous idea that we had friends in England worth keeping." The resistance of South Carolina softened when the Congress agreed to strike a clause "reprobating the enslaving (of) the inhabitants of Africa." Certain Northern delegates were also relieved when the anti-slavery language was removed. The arrival of a new delegate from Delaware also helped to break the deadlock.

Adams was delighted, but somewhat restrained, when the final vote was taken. "You will think me transported with enthusiasm, but I am not," he wrote to his wife, Abigail. "I am well aware of the toil, and blood, and treasure, that it will cost us to maintain this declaration and support and defend these States. Yet, through all the gloom, I can see the ravishing light and glory. I can see that the end is more than worth all the means."

Adams predicted the first day of debate will be forever celebrated in America. "It ought to be commemorated as the day of deliverance, by solemn acts of devotion to God Almighty," he wrote. "It ought to be solemnized with pomp and parade, with shows, games, sports, guns, bells, bonfires and illuminations, from one end of this continent to the other, from this time forward, forevermore" (→Aug. 2).

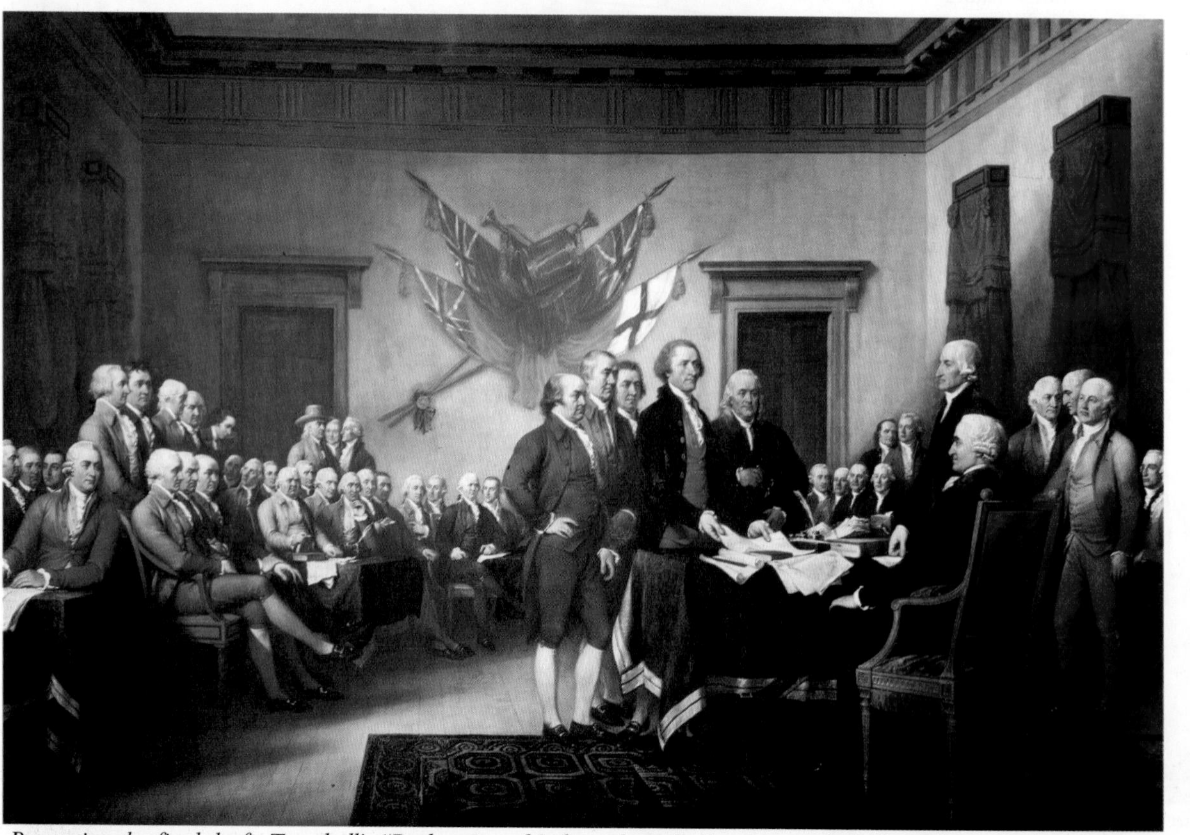

Presenting the final draft. Trumbull's "Declaration of Independence in Congress at the Independence Hall" (1797).

Congress delegates sign declaration

Philadelphia, August 2

Delegates to the Continental Congress began affixing their signatures to the Declaration of Independence today. The president of the Congress, John Hancock, scrawled his name boldly across the document. "There," he said, "I guess King George will be able to read that." Hancock has been one of the most strident enemies of the crown and was excluded from an amnesty offer last year because his offenses were "of too flagitious a nature." Ben Franklin reflected a concern of the Congress when he wryly told Hancock, "Yes, we must, indeed, all hang together, or, most assuredly, we shall all hang separately." The King believes all signers of the declaration are guilty of treason. For security reasons, their names are not being made public. It is believed that 56 delegates will sign the document (→Sept. 9).

Declaration of Independence

When, in the course of human events, it becomes necessary for one people to dissolve the political bands which have connected them with another, and to assume, among the powers of the earth, the separate and equal station to which the laws of nature and of nature's God entitle them, a decent respect to the opinions of mankind requires that they should declare the causes which impel them to the separation.

We hold these truths to be self-evident, that all men are created equal, that they are endowed by their Creator with certain unalienable rights, that among these are life, liberty, and the pursuit of happiness. That, to secure these rights, governments are instituted among men, deriving their just powers from the consent of the governed. That, whenever any form of government becomes destructive of these ends, it is the right of the people to alter or to abolish it, and to institute new government, laying its foundation on such principles, and organizing its powers in such form, as to them shall seem most likely to effect their safety and happiness.

Prudence, indeed, will dictate that governments long established should not be changed for light and transient causes; and, accordingly, all experience has shown, that mankind are more disposed to suffer, while evils are sufferable, than to right themselves by abolishing the forms to which they are accustomed.

But, when a long train of abuses and usurpations, pursuing invariably the same object, evinces a design to reduce them under absolute despotism, it is their right, it is their duty, to throw off such government, and to provide new guards for their future security. Such has been the patient sufferance of these colonies, and such is now the necessity which constrains them to alter their former systems of government. The history of the present King of Great Britain is a history of repeated injuries and usurpations, all having in direct object the establishment of an absolute tyranny over these states. To prove this, let facts be submitted to a candid world.

He has refused his assent to laws the most wholesome and necessary for the public good.

He has forbidden his governors to pass laws of immediate and pressing importance, unless suspended in their operation till his assent should be obtained; and when so suspended, he has utterly neglected to attend to them.

He has refused to pass other laws for the accommodation of large districts of people, unless those people would relinquish the right of representation in the legislature; a right inestimable to them and formidable to tyrants only.

He has called together legislative bodies at places unusual, uncomfortable, and distant from the depository of their public records, for the sole purpose of fatiguing them into compliance with his measures.

He has dissolved representative houses repeatedly, for opposing, with manly firmness, his invasions on the rights of the people.

He has refused for a long time, after such dissolutions, to cause others to be elected; whereby the legislative powers, incapable of annihilation, have returned to the people at large for their exercise; the state remaining in the meantime exposed to all the dangers of invasion from without, and convulsions within.

He has endeavored to prevent the population of these states; for that purpose obstructing the laws for naturalization of foreigners; refusing to pass others to encourage their migrations hither, and raising the conditions of new appropriations of lands.

He has obstructed the administration of justice, by refusing his assent to laws for establishing judiciary powers.

He has made judges dependent on his will alone, for the tenure of their offices, and the amount and payment of their salaries.

He has erected a multitude of new offices, and sent hither swarms of officers to harass our people, and eat out their substance.

He has kept among us, in times of peace, standing armies, without the consent of our legislatures.

He has affected to render the military independent of and superior to the civil power.

He has combined with others to subject us to a jurisdiction foreign to our constitution, and unacknowledged by our laws; giving his assent to their acts of pretended legislation:

For quartering large bodies of armed troops among us;

For protecting them, by a mock trial, from punishment for any murders which they should commit on the inhabitants of these states;

For cutting off our trade with all parts of the world;

For imposing taxes on us without our consent;

For depriving us, in many cases, of the benefits of trial by jury;

For transporting us beyond seas to be tried for pretended offenses;

For abolishing the free system of English laws in a neighboring province, establishing therein an arbitrary government, and enlarging its boundaries, so as to render it at once an example and fit instrument for introducing the same absolute rule into these colonies;

For taking away our charters, abolishing our most valuable laws, and altering fundamentally the forms of our governments;

For suspending our own legislatures, and declaring themselves invested with power to legislate for us in all cases whatsoever.

He has abdicated government here, by declaring us out of his protection, and waging war against us.

He has plundered our seas, ravaged our coasts, burnt our towns, and destroyed the lives of our people.

He is at this time transporting large armies of foreign mercenaries to complete the works of death, desolation, and tyranny, already begun with circumstances of cruelty and perfidy scarcely paralleled in the most barbarous ages, and totally unworthy the head of a civilized nation.

He has constrained our fellow citizens, taken captive on the high seas, to bear arms against their country, to become the executioners of their friends and brethren, or to fall themselves by their hands.

He has excited domestic insurrections amongst us, and has endeavored to bring on the inhabitants of our frontiers, the merciless Indian savages, whose known rule of warfare is an undistinguished destruction of all ages, sexes, and conditions.

In every stage of these oppressions, we have petitioned for redress, in the most humble terms. Our repeated petitions have been answered only by repeated injury. A prince, whose character is thus marked by every act which may define a tyrant, is unfit to be the ruler of a free people.

Nor have we been wanting in attentions to our British brethren. We have warned them from time to time of attempts by their legislature to extend an unwarrantable jurisdiction over us. We have reminded them of the circumstances of our emigration and settlement here. We have appealed to their native justice and magnanimity, and we have conjured them by the ties of our common kindred, to disavow these usurpations, which would inevitably interrupt our connections and correspondence. They too have been deaf to the voice of justice and of consanguinity. We must, therefore, acquiesce in the necessity, which denounces our separation, and hold them, as we hold the rest of mankind, enemies in war, in peace friends.

We, therefore, the representatives of the United States of America, in General Congress assembled, appealing to the Supreme Judge of the world for the rectitude of our intentions, do, in the name, and by authority of the good people of these colonies, solemnly publish and declare, that these United Colonies are, and of right ought to be free and independent states; that they are absolved from all allegiance to the British Crown, and that all political connection between them and the state of Great Britain is and ought to be totally dissolved; and that, as free and independent states, they have full power to levy war, conclude peace, contract alliances, establish commerce, and to do all other acts and things which independent states may of right do.

And for the support of this declaration, with a firm reliance on the protection of Divine Providence, we mutually pledge to each other our lives, our fortunes, and our sacred honor.

New Yorkers pull down statue of King

New York City, July 10

A crowd of Continental soldiers and New York patriots pulled down a gilt equestrian statue of King George III last night as they celebrated the signing of the Declaration of Independence in Philadelphia. After the document was read to the assembled troops here at 6 p.m., the Continental soldiers roared three cheers and, upon being dismissed, joined the New Yorkers in a round of rejoicing.

The statue has been the laughing stock of New York because its sculptor, Wilton of London, failed to put stirrups on the horse that the King is riding. This gave rise to a saying among the soldiers: "The tyrant ought to ride a hard-trotting horse without stirrups."

Lieutenant Isaac Bangs of the Massachusetts militia reported the events of the evening in this way: "Last night the statue on the Bowling Green representing George Guelph, alias George Rex, was pulled down by the populace. In it were 4,000 pounds of lead, and a man undertook to take 10 ounces of gold from the supefices (surface) as both man and horse were covered with gold leaf; the lead we hear is to be run up into musket balls for the use of Yankees, when it is hoped that the emanations from the leaden George will make deep impressions in the bodies of some of his redcoated and Tory subjects."

Although the Continentals in the field are sometimes plagued by a shortage of gunpowder, one would never have known it here. Salutes were fired and bonfires lit, and throughout the day and the evening church bells tolled. Meanwhile, in the harbor, the great British fleet lies quietly at anchor (→Aug. 30).

Dethroning the monarch. Detail of a painting (1854) by William Walcutt.

United States becomes new nation's name

Philadelphia, September 9

The Continental Congress passed a resolution today changing the name of the nation from the United Colonies to the United States. The alteration seems to give at least a symbolic victory to opponents of a strong central government by including the more autonomous word "states" in the title. Almost all congressional members agreed that "united" must be retained.

In August, Benjamin Franklin, Thomas Jefferson and John Adams were appointed by Congress to research and select a motto and work on designs for the seal of the nation. The committee selected "E Pluribus Unum" as the national motto. It is Latin for "From many, one," that is, one nation made of many states. While a vote on the selection is pending, it is believed the motto will eventually appear on currency.

Declaration evokes diverse reaction

Vienna, Aug. 30

Reaction to the American Declaration of Independence is as diverse abroad as it is in England. Empress Maria Theresa of Austria wrote to King George III expressing a "hearty desire to see the restoration of obedience and tranquillity in every quarter of your dominion." Long articles on the declaration have been appearing in newspapers, and some, such as the *Altonaischer Mercurius*, the German-language paper of Denmark, printed the entire document. The Dutch welcomed the rebellion, but reaction is most divided in England itself. When John Horne Tooke, a radical, collected funds for the relief of widows and children of American patriots "murdered" at Lexington, he was jailed.

Mission dedicated at San Francisco

San Francisco, Sept. 17

The Spanish mission in this small presidio has been consecrated as San Francisco, in honor of Saint Francis, patron of the Franciscan order that has built several missions along the California coast. Today's event was well attended by churchmen and soldiers as well as sailors from the Spanish ship San Carlos. The mission was adorned with banners and wall hangings that were taken from the vessel. In addition, the ship's carpenter built two tables of carved wood to serve as the altars. Beef was served in liberal portions to all the celebrants. The little presidio here is made up of only two groups of log huts. One of them houses the military commander and the other consists of a warehouse and the church.

Declaration is read to Washington's army

New York, July 9.

The troops of General Washington heard the Declaration of Independence today and their fellow citizens heated the city's streets with feverish celebration. After the reading, mobs of New Yorkers smashed windows of loyalists and toppled a statue of George III. The first Governor of New York, William Clinton, authorized endorsement of the declaration, granting the document unanimous support among the colonies. Yesterday, the first public reading of the declaration took place in Philadelphia. The event was politically timed to reinforce support among radical statesmen who had gathered to pick delegates to the state convention.

After a painting by Howard Pyle.

The night the Turtle took on the Eagle

New York City, Sept. 7

A daring attack on a British warship by a one-man American submarine failed tonight, but it may open a new era in naval warfare. The submarine Turtle was invented by David Bushnell, a student at Yale. Built of wood, it is powered by propellers cranked by its operator. Tonight's attack was made on the warship Eagle, anchored in New York harbor, which was to have been blown up by a charge of gunpowder that would be attached to the British vessel by a screw device. Piloting the Turtle, army Sergeant Ezra Lee approached the Eagle underwater without being detected. But several efforts to attach the gunpowder charge to the ship failed because Lee could not pierce the copper sheathing on its hull. Lee released the gunpowder, which exploded harmlessly, then pedaled away safely. Nevertheless, this attack is the first offensive use of a submarine in naval history.

British are victorious on Long Island

Americans try to hold the line against advancing redcoats on Long Island.

New York City, Aug. 30

Outnumbered, outgunned and outmaneuvered, American forces have suffered a serious defeat at the hands of the British army in the Battle of Long Island. American losses, in prisoners and casualties, exceed 2,000, while British losses are under 400. Three American generals have been taken prisoner. Long Island has been abandoned and few military observers believe that General Washington is going to be able to maintain his hold on New York much longer.

But there is no need for the Americans to despair. Thanks to the failure of General Sir William Howe to push home his advantage at the end of the fighting on August 27, the Americans were able to regroup in their fortified positions on Brooklyn Heights, and from there they have been transported across the East River in an evacuation supervised by General Washington himself. So the army, although it was defeated and badly mauled, has by no means been destroyed.

Moreover, despite the incompetence of Generals John Sullivan and Rufus Putnam, American soldiers and officers fought well. This is the first major battle in which they have had to face a superior force of disciplined and professional soldiers. The fighting spirit shown by the American troops indicates that though the battle has been lost, the war will continue (→ Sept. 11).

Retreating Washington fights off pursuers

Harlem Heights, N.Y., Sept. 21

Fully occupied with battling yesterday's disastrous fire, which destroyed some 500 buildings in New York, British forces commanded by General Howe have eased off on their pursuit of General Washington, who remains entrenched in his fortified position here at the northern tip of Manhattan Island. Five days ago, in "a brisk little skirmish," as Washington has described it, American forces halted the advance guard of the British, who had occupied New York City on September 15. The fact that this time American soldiers stood their ground and fought hard has given the Continental Army's morale a much-needed boost (→ Oct. 28).

Hale regrets having but one life to lose

New York City, Sept. 22

Nathan Hale's career as an American spy was a tragic short-lived debacle. It began earlier this month when Hale, a Yale graduate who was a Connecticut schoolmaster, volunteered to penetrate the British forces that were occupying New York and to bring back information. He was to go alone, making the mission particularly dangerous from the outset. On September 12, Hale set out on his mission from Harlem Heights. He had no prior training and only a vague set of orders. Captured nine days later by the British, he was hanged without a trial. Hale's last words were: "I only regret that I have but one life to lose for my country."

General Washington watches the city burn after the Battle of Harlem Heights.

His spirit unbroken, Nathan Hale is led off to his execution by the British.

"Yankee Doodle" popular in America

YANKEE DOODLE, or (as now Christened by the SAINTS of New England) THE LEXINGTON MARCH

First sheet music of the song, 1775.

United States

The tables are being turned on the British in more than one way. *Yankee Doodle*, the song that they have so mockingly directed against Americans, is now being lustily sung by the targets of their derision, including the soldiers of General Washington. The tune has been attributed to a British fifer, and the music is highly popular with the British army's bands. As for the words, everyone seems to have a different version. And while we know what "Yankee" refers to, the "Doodle" is anyone's guess. One thing *is* certain: the British are no longer calling the tune.

Howe wins White Plains

White Plains, N.Y., Oct. 28

Despite rugged natural defenses that favored the Americans, British forces under General Howe have dislodged General Washington's Continental Army and forced it to retreat. Howe had outflanked the Americans on Harlem Heights 10 days earlier, forcing Washington to retreat to a defensible position just north of White Plains. The stone walls, gullies, small hills and valleys that abound in the area gave Washington an excellent defensive position, but there were fatal flaws in his strategy. First, his army was too small for the long lines he tried to defend. Also, he failed to take into consideration a prominence named Chatterton's Hill. When General Howe occupied this hill, Washington's entire right flank was exposed to enemy fire. Fortunately, the terrain was so rough that the American forces could pull back their flank, hold the center and retreat without suffering any serious damage. When Howe added four or five batteries of artillery to blast the Americans out of their lines, General Washington was obliged to start moving his troops to the small village of North Castle (→ Dec. 26).

Smith's "Wealth of Nations" published

London, March 9

Inquiry into the Nature and Causes of the Wealth of Nations, an exhaustive treatise on political economy, was published today. Its author, Adam Smith, a retired professor of philosophy at Oxford and Glasgow, advocates an economic system that allows the individual to pursue his own self-interest, free of excessive governmental restraint. The professor's thesis is sure to find favor with American readers, as is his proposal that the colonies be represented in Parliament and his daring prediction that America is destined to become "one of the foremost nations of the world."

West's "Colonel Guy Johnson."

Congress approves $5 million war loan

The Continental dollar is the first coinage of the United States of America.

Philadelphia, Oct. 3

In an effort to halt the rapid depreciation of the young nation's paper currency, the Congress of the United States has arranged to borrow $5 million on a long-term basis and authorized its agents to borrow up to two million pounds from France.

With meager financial resources and without the ability to tax, Congress had begun printing paper money, or bills of credit, to finance the war. Yet, as more and more bills were issued, the amount of paper money in circulation grew faster than the supply of coins and goods backing it, thus lowering the paper money's worth.

The currency's plummeting value had devastating economic and social consequences. Morale among the young soldiers of the Continental Army suffered mightily as their pay shrunk relative to their buying power, and merchants found that it did not pay to keep merchandise on their shelves.

To avoid issuing more bills of credit yet still be able to raise money, Congress came up with a plan to sell certificates, which were to be sold at loan offices throughout the states in denominations ranging from $300 to $1,000. They would yield 4 percent interest, and were to be paid after three years. The sponsors of the plan hoped they would be bought by wealthy citizens with paper currency, thus reducing the total number of Continental bills in circulation (→ Nov. 29, 1779).

Paine: "Times that try men's souls"

Philadelphia, Dec. 19

In the wake of repeated thrashings by the redcoats, a rallying cry has been sounded by Thomas Paine, now shouldering a musket under the command of General Nathanael Greene. By day a participant in the army's November retreat from Fort Lee, New Jersey, to Newark, by night Paine has taken up his true weapon, the pen, and fired off *Crisis*, published today in the *Pennsylvania Journal*. "These are the times that try men's souls," Paine's message begins. "Tyranny, like hell, is not easily conquered," it warns. "The harder the conflict, the more glorious the triumph."

Arnold's makeshift fleet loses battle

Lake Champlain, N.Y., Nov. 3

General Sir Guy Carleton has defeated Benedict Arnold's fleet and turned Lake Champlain into King George's swimming hole. Ticonderoga, however, is safe. The makeshift American navy, thrown together in less than three months, engaged the British on October 11. After falling back on Crown Point with heavy casualties, Arnold burned the fort and retreated to Ticonderoga. But his naval heroics have delayed the British enough to drive them back into Canada for the winter (→ June 17, 1777).

Dutch first to salute the American flag

Dutch West Indies, Nov. 16

Cannon fire from tiny Fort Orange in the harbor of the Dutch island of St. Eustatius is the first official voice of recognition for the new American republic. The Andrea Doria, flying the flag of the Continental Congress, sailed into the harbor to pick up military supplies and to deliver a copy of the Declaration of Independence to Governor Johannes de Graaff, who is also commander of the garrison. When the American vessel fired its cannon in a ritual salute, the Governor issued orders that the Dutch guns return the fire, hailing the new American nation for the first time since its independence.

Washington stuns Hessian fighters

Trenton, New Jersey, Dec. 26

American bravery and determination, contrasting sharply with the indifference and arrogance of the Hessian mercenaries, led to a stunning victory for the patriots here this morning. A division of 2,400 Americans, their bodies virtually frozen and their feet wrapped in blood-stained rags, managed to get across the Delaware River in small boats during the night and routed 1,200 Hessians in an hour and a half. For Commander-in-Chief Washington, it was a brilliant victory and sweet revenge. Two weeks ago, he retreated across the river in the opposite direction, pursued by Lord Cornwallis's 12 regiments.

Washington reassured his men as they braved the sleet and powerful current. "I have never seen Washington so determined as he is now," wrote Colonel Fitzgerald in his diary. "He stands on the bank of the river, wrapped in his cloak, superintending the landing of his troops." Fitzgerald said that the Americans were "ready to suffer any hardship and die rather than give up their liberty."

Washington's men crossed the Delaware nine miles above Trenton. Two other columns, commanded by General Ewing and Colonel Cadwalader, were trapped in the ice to the south. Washington was on his own. He had guessed correctly that the Hessians would still be in bed, recovering from their Christmas drinking parties. Their commander, Johann Rall, was sound asleep, snoring and dead drunk. He had already dismissed intelligence reports that Washington might attack. "Let them come," he said. "We will go at them with the bayonet." But the Hessian bayonets were inadequate, their musket fire ineffective. The Americans routed one outpost after another, and the belated efforts of Rall to retreat were halted by the quick response of the patriots. Rall and 100 other Hessians were killed; 900 were taken prisoner. American casualties were light, but Washington had to delay a march on Brunswick and Princeton because of the problems of his other columns (→ Jan. 3, 1777).

Delaware River, December 25. *With disaster looming, General Washington has taken a desperate chance and crossed the Delaware to launch a surprise attack on the Hessian quarters at Trenton. With morale falling as fast as the temperature, and enlistments rapidly expiring, the commander had little choice. Painting is "Washington Crossing the Delaware" (1851) by Emanuel Leutze. [Fellow artist Worthington Whittredge posed as Washington.]*

1777

California, Jan. 12. Santa Clara Mission founded.

America, January. Washington is authorized to inoculate entire army against smallpox.

Philadelphia, March 12. Congress reconvenes here after Washington's victories in New Jersey (→ Aug. 3).

Philadelphia, May 1-9. Arthur Lee, Ralph Izard and William Lee appointed to represent colonies in Europe (→ Feb. 6, 1778).

South Carolina, May 19. Treaty of DeWitts Corner cedes Cherokee land in South Carolina to colonists (→ July 20).

Philadelphia, June 14. John Paul Jones named captain of Ranger with orders to raid British towns (→ Apr. 24, 1778).

Canada, June 17. General Burgoyne heads south, planning to cut colonies in half along Hudson Valley then link up with Howe in New York City (→ July 7).

North Carolina, July, 20. Treaty of Longisland cedes Overhill Cherokee Indian lands east of Blue Ridge Mountains and Nolichucky River.

New York, July 30. George Clinton becomes state's first Governor.

New York, Aug. 3. Howe deserts New York City for drive on Philadelphia; Burgoyne presses towards Albany anyway (→ Sept. 11).

Philadelphia, Sept. 19. Congress, fearing approach of Howe, flees to Lancaster, Pennsylvania (→ 21).

Philadelphia, Sept. 25. Irishman Thomas Conway blames Commander Lord Stirling for poor direction of war (→ Dec. 23).

Philadelphia, Sept. 26. British General Howe occupies Philadelphia (→ Oct. 4).

Pennsylvania, Nov. 20. Americans evacuate Fort Mercer (just below Philadelphia); Delaware River undefended against British.

California, November. San Jose established as first non-religious settlement in California.

America, December. David Bushnell, inventor of one-man submarine, the Turtle, creates minefield of gunpowder kegs to harass British.

America, December. First English-language American edition of the *New Testament* is published (→ 1782).

British troops routed at Princeton

General Washington's surprise. "The Battle of Princeton" by Mercer.

Washington: "It's a fine fox chase, my boys!" Painting by Alonzo Chappel.

Princeton, New Jersey, Jan. 3

The tall, portly Lord Cornwallis vowed that he would "bag the fox" in the morning. After all, Washington and his men were dug in on the ridge behind Assunpink Creek. Where could they possibly go?

The answer came in an act as daring as the crossing of the Delaware on Christmas night. Under cover of darkness, Washington and his men stole silently away. They muffled the wheels of their cannons with cloth, and a detail stayed behind to create a lot of clanging and banging, producing a mock army that the British could hear.

At sunrise, English troops from Princeton, under way to reinforce Cornwallis at Trenton, were taken by complete surprise when they saw 350 Virginians, under the command of General Hugh Mercer, bearing down on their left flank. British Colonel Charles Mawhood opened up with his artillery and ordered a bayonet charge that threw back the Americans and mortally wounded General Mercer. At that moment, Washington rode up and, fearing a rout, re-formed the Virginia forces himself. He led the troops to within 30 yards of the redcoats, where volleys were exchanged. Finally, the thin red line broke and a jubilant Washington exclaimed, "It's a fine fox chase, my boys!" and led his men in pursuit of the British across the smoke-shrouded battlefield. In 45 minutes of fighting, British losses numbered 275 to 400 men; 40 Americans were killed and 100 wounded (→ March 12).

Vermont proclaims an independent state

Windsor, Vermont, July 8

While the British forces under General Burgoyne, having recaptured Fort Ticonderoga and Crown Point, continue their drive south toward Albany, the people of this state have found time to provide themselves with a new constitution. The document is the work of a convention that has been meeting here since July 2, and provides for a unicameral general assembly, a governor who is to be elected annually, a ban on slavery, and universal manhood suffrage qualified only by the requirement that a citizen must take the so-called Freeman's Oath to vote "without fear or favor of any person." It also provides for a school in each town and a grammar school in each county.

The state declared itself a free, independent republic on January 15. The name it chose was New Connecticut, but it was changed to Vermont on June 4. Meanwhile, the war continues. Yesterday, a rearguard action was fought at Hubbarton by the Green Mountain Boys, delaying Burgoyne's advance and giving the American army time to regroup (→ March 4, 1791).

Navy chief is fired after taking Nassau

Philadelphia, Jan. 2

Is Esek Hopkins a hero, an incompetent or just disobedient? The Continental Congress sent the navy's first commodore and a six-ship fleet down the American east coast to destroy two flotillas of English boats. Instead, he sailed to Nassau in the Bahamas, took the British-ruled town and seized 88 cannons. On his return trip, he captured two British ships, but he was defeated in another battle. Congress has fired Hopkins for failing to obey orders.

Girl rider alerts patriots to British attack

Sybil Ludington, at 16 filling Paul Revere's shoes, calls the militia to arms.

Fredericksburg, N.Y. Apr. 26

Early this evening, a messenger came to the house of Colonel Ludington and broke the news that General William Tryon's troops were raiding a supply center in Danbury, Connecticut. Only 200 patriots were stationed at the center, and the number of British reported to be burning and looting the town was estimated at 2,000. Ludington commands a small patriot militia unit, and as a leader, he was the man to notify. But Danbury lies 35 miles east, across the border between the colonies, and Ludington was not sure he could summon enough men to the Ludington mill yard in time.

Then, his 16-year-old daughter, Sybil, said she could do it. Ignoring warnings that the way might be imperiled by British patrols, spies and the thieves who work in both peace and wartime, she leaped on her father's favorite horse, Star, and set off. She rode south to Carmel, then to Lake Mahopac, Tompkins Corners and Farmers Mills. "Muster at Colonel Ludington's mill!" Sybil told the farmers. "The British are raiding Danbury!" She rode as far as Pecksville, 40 miles off, before turning back. She may not have rescued Danbury, but the patriots are ready for the next British move.

A silk velvet dress for society affairs in areas untouched by war.

American soldier dressed in one of the rare uniforms of the time.

Outnumbered patriots yield Ticonderoga

Ticonderoga, N.Y., July 7

A poorly supplied Continental Army force has given up Fort Ticonderoga and is fleeing today before the advancing British forces under Major General John Burgoyne.

The huge fortress complex on Lake Champlain, originally built by the French, spans the southern end of the lake and requires a garrison of 10,000 men. The American force, commanded by Major General Arthur St. Clair, consisted of only about 3,500 and they were poorly clothed, barely armed and often diseased and malnourished. The Burgoyne attack force involved about 7,500 men and a sizable flotilla that included the warship Thunderer. About 3,000 of the troops accompanying the English are Germans.

Earlier in the week, Burgoyne's flotilla anchored just out of range of the Continental cannons and began to study the battleground. It did not take long for the British to find the weak link in the complex, nearby Sugar Loaf Mountain, which, unfortified, overlooks Ticonderoga. On July 5, Burgoyne ordered two 12-pound guns mounted on the crest of Sugar Loaf.

When St. Clair realized that defeat was imminent, he decided to preserve his force by an evacuation under cover of darkness. Baggage, artillery and stores went first, by boat, and the bulk of the Continental soldiers fled eastward across the footbridge that spans Lake Champlain. American efforts to maintain secrecy failed and the St. Clair troops barely escaped, with the redcoats in hot pursuit (→27).

St. Clair, after C.W. Peale.

Burgoyne (1767) by J. Reynolds.

British troops accused of lust, brutality

Philadelphia, Apr. 18

A committee appointed by the Continental Congress issued its report today on the conduct of British troops. Among the crimes they are accused of committing are "lust and brutality in abusing women," ravishing females from the age of 10 to 70. The British are also charged with looting homes for their own gain and wantonly setting fire to civilians' homes. While facts may support these statements, Congress must sift through many reports of sheer propaganda. It is now common knowledge that the tales Samuel Adams related about the battles of Lexington and Concord, which told of women being dragged from their beds and made to run naked through the streets, were pure lies. On the whole, the British troops suffer from the same sins that plague the Coninental Army: drunkenness (soldiers' wives smuggle cheap New England rum to them), desertion (colonists welcome deserters as though they were prodigal sons) and disease (smallpox first spread among them in Boston in 1774). Perhaps the only problem unique to the British is love: A few of the soldiers are married to loyalist women, whose patriot relatives ward off impending arguments by hanging a large sign that reads "No Tory talk here!" over the home mantlepiece.

Congress ordains Stars and Stripes flag

The Stars and Stripes: A banner day for the United States of America.

Philadelphia, June 14

The Continental Congress has designated: "That the flag of the 13 United States be 13 stripes, alternate red and white; that the union be 13 stars, white in a blue field, representing a new constellation." Congress explained the color symbolism: "White signifies Purity and Innocence; Red, Hardiness and Valor; Blue signifies Vigilance, Perseverance and Justice." But recent history indicates that the colors carry deeper political meaning. In 1775, a congressional committee said the design of a flag should represent autonomy without disenfranchising England. The red stripes were to signify unity against oppression, the blue and the crosses to represent a continued union with England. The English crosses have been dropped, but a vestige of blue remains.

Lafayette, French nobleman, volunteers

Philadelphia, July 31

The Continental Army now has a new major general: Marie Joseph Paul Yves Roch Gilbert du Motier, Marquis de Lafayette.

Marie Joseph Paul Yves Roch Gilbert du Motier, Marquis de Lafayette.

Declaring "It is especially in the hour of danger that I wish to share your fortune," the young nobleman arrived in America last month on a ship that he bought and equipped entirely at his own expense. Although he is only 20 years old, Lafayette is not without military experience, having spent five years in the French army. A man of high ideals and great charm, the marquis is married to Adrienne d'Ayen, of the Noailles family, and they have one daughter.

Congress, having had to deal with a surfeit of Europeans wanting commissions, was at first doubtful about taking on the young Frenchman. But it was won over when he announced, "After the sacrifices I have made, I have the right to exact two favors: one is to serve at my own expense, the other is to serve at first as a volunteer." The commission granted to him carries no command, and it is up to Washington to decide how the marquis is to be employed (→July 12, 1780).

Americans are besieged in Fort Stanwix

Mohawk Valley, N.Y., Aug. 6

With ingenuity and dash, Continental forces seem to be withstanding a siege by British troops under General Barry St. Leger. The general's forces, consisting of 750 British and German troops, as well as 1,000 Indians, have been advancing down the Mohawk Valley from Oswego to rendezvous at Albany with British troops under the command of General Burgoyne. St. Leger's route led him over the Grand Portage trail, where he would find the presumably vacant Fort Stanwix. What he did not know was that Americans under the command of Colonel Gansevoort had recently occupied the fort. On August 3, the British came upon the Americans at the fort and the siege was on. But the Americans had just been supplied with arms and reinforcements and were able to hold off the British.

Continental militia under General Nicholas Herkimer set out to relieve Gansevoort's men, bringing along 800 men and many supply-laden oxcarts. Learning of the approaching reinforcements, St. Leger led most of his siege force out to ambush Herkimer. Though Herkimer was badly wounded in the initial attack, his brilliant strategy sent the British fleeing to their camp, where they met with another surprise: Troops from Fort Stanwix had raided the camp and left it in shambles.

Burgoyne advances down the Hudson

New York City, Aug. 3

King George III of England and his secretary of state for the colonies, Lord George Germain, have never been noted for their keen minds or for their military strategy. Recently, the King and Germain somehow approved two diametrically opposite and uncoordinated methods of attack against the Continental Army. One of the plans, submitted by General Howe, entails a vast march by British troops from New York against Philadelphia, capital of the revolutionaries. The other plan, submitted by General Burgoyne, consists of a march from Canada to Albany. Each general assumed that he would have the support of the other.

Burgoyne, after scoring a sweeping victory at Fort Ticonderoga, continued his advance down the Hudson, with Continental troops under St. Clair and Schuyler abandoning Fort Edward and fleeing before him. Even though Burgoyne learned that Howe has left New York and was on his way south to Philadelphia, rather than north to support him, he continues to press on toward Albany, probably expecting more victories of the kind that he has grown accustomed to.

Burgoyne, who is often called "Gentleman Johnny," is known for the unusual respect he shows for his troops as well as for a certain rashness in his strategy (→16).

Burgoyne's Indians slay Jane McCrea

Albany, New York, July 27

On their march from Canada to Albany, the Indians traveling with General John Burgoyne have made a mistake for which the British may ultimately pay a stiff price. The Iroquois warriors who march alongside British regulars and German mercenaries have been indiscriminate in their killing of Americans. News that the Indians murdered a settler named Jane McCrea has galvanized some of the colonists into action, sending army enrollments soaring and providing fresh troops to fight Burgoyne (→Aug. 3).

Detail of "The Death of Jane McCrea" (1804) by John Vanderlyn.

Wayne is surprised by pre-dawn raid

Paoli, Pennsylvania, Sept. 21

The forces of General Howe have the Americans on the run as the British advance toward their objective: capturing the seat of the Continental Congress at Philadelphia. The latest in a series of setbacks for the Americans came in the early hours this morning when the brigade of General Anthony Wayne was routed in a surprise bayonet attack by the troops of General Charles Grey, under the command of General Howe.

Howe is the tactician and commanding officer of one of two major British offensives. The other main English force is en route from Canada to Albany, and is being led by General John Burgoyne. Each of these generals originally expected the aid of the other in his efforts, but the forces have become widely separated. Some consider this a major weakness in the British campaign.

Anthony Wayne was, before the Revolution, a tanner and surveyor from Chester County, Pennsylvania. Awarded the rank of brigadier general this year, he recently commanded the Pennsylvania Line under General Washington at the battle of Brandywine. Because of a reconnaissance error, the American force was pushed back at Brandywine, and it was Wayne who helped the retreat by delaying the Hessians. But after the Paoli rout, Wayne may face trial for negligence (→26).

U.S. militia triumphs at Bennington

Bennington, Vermont, Aug. 16

British General John Burgoyne needed food and pack horses so he decided to raid Bennington, where he knew he could get them. In the sardonic words of one American, "He gave them a German marching band to help preserve secrecy." German band or not, General John Stark knew the British were coming and he rounded up all the militiamen he could find from the Vermont and New Hampshire countryside. The result was a force that was about twice the size of Lieutenant Colonel Baum's 600 German mercenaries. The Yankees were desperately short of ammunition, and scoured the surrounding area for plates and spoons that could be melted into musket balls.

Because General Stark's men were wearing white badges on their caps, Baum assumed they were troops loyal to Britain. By the time he discovered his mistake, he was surrounded and his contingent of Indians had fled. The Germans fought bravely, but they were overwhelmed by the more numerous Americans, who carried a new flag consisting of 13 stars and a field of alternating red and white stripes. Now sensing victory, General Stark did manage to reform the militia in time to fend off British reinforcements under Lieutenant Colonel von Breyman. The British lost 900 men, half of them regulars. American losses were light (→Sept. 19).

The Bennington flag. Before the battle, General Stark told his men, "Tonight, the American flag floats from yonder hill or Molly Stark sleeps a widow."

General Stark, on horseback, directs traffic around the battleground.

Washington thrown back at Brandywine

Chadd's Ford, Penn., Sept. 11

Poor reconnaissance lost a battle for General Washington today.

Back on July 23, when General Howe's redcoats boarded ships and left New York, Washington believed the move might be a feint and that Howe would return and join up with the troops of Burgoyne, who are progressing down the Hudson. Nevertheless, Washington sent his troops into central New Jersey where they would be effective in defending Philadelphia, if such was Howe's objective. That Howe did indeed plan to attack the Continental capital became clear when his ships arrived in Chesapeake Bay last month. Washington was able to move about 15,000 men into place between Wilmington and Philadelphia by September 1. He selected Brandywine Creek as a defensive position in the belief that, based on reports from Pennsylvania officers, there were no fords for 12 miles north of his position. A good reconnaissance party would have told him the Great Valley Road crossed the Brandywine just to the north.

After a diversionary attack across the creek early today, Howe moved his main force across the Great Valley Road. Washington, unable to defend his position, pulled back, losing approximately 1,000 men. The British, though on the offensive, lost 576 (→19).

Americans check Burgoyne near Saratoga

Saratoga, New York, Sept. 19

As General Burgoyne's troops advance from Canada on their way to Albany, support of the British is thinning steadily and the resistance to them is growing. Receiving no help from the troops of General Howe, who have headed south to attack Philadelphia, Burgoyne nevertheless presses on toward his objective. On September 13, he led his troops across a bridge of boats to the west bank of the Hudson River, effectively cutting him off from his already thin Canadian supply line. To get through to Albany, Burgoyne must take on the entrenched forces of General Horatio Gates at Bemis Heights near Saratoga.

Today, at Freeman's Farm, about a mile north of the American fortifications, Burgoyne's troops confronted the Americans and their progress was checked. The riflemen of General Daniel Morgan and the troops commanded by Benedict Arnold engaged the British in a confused firefight on the 15-acre farm. While the riflemen were most successful in picking off Burgoyne's artillery gunners, Arnold's men were unable to capture the guns. After a full day of battle, both sides retired.

British losses were put at 600 men, American at 350. Through all the fighting, Burgoyne has gained no ground and has lost valuable men and supplies (→Oct. 7).

Washington suffers Germantown defeat

Germantown, Penn., Oct. 4

Fog and an overcomplicated plan of attack led to the defeat of Continental forces under General Washington here today.

It was at Germantown that General Howe's forces set up a base after they occupied Philadelphia on September 26. Since British forces were split between those occupying Philadelphia and those at the camp here, Washington felt that with his knowledge of the region and his superior numbers the Continentals could defeat the British at Germantown. But his attempt to coordinate four columns in a surprise pre-dawn attack was foiled when a thick layer of fog delayed deployment and put the main attack force, under General Greene, an hour behind the rest of the men. Two American divisions, blinded by the fog, fired on each other. Though the size of the attack surprised the British, they were able to repulse it. There were more than a thousand American casualties (→ Dec. 25).

Benedict Arnold is wounded in attack

Bemis Heights, N.Y., Oct. 7

The British army, under General John Burgoyne, has again been halted in its southward advance by the American army commanded by General Horatio Gates and his brilliant subordinate, Benedict Arnold, who was wounded today.

At the second Battle of Freeman's Farm, after General Burgoyne had dispatched 1,500 troops to reconnoiter General Gates's position at Bemis Heights, the two armies clashed. Suffering more than 400 casualties in less than an hour and inflicting only slight losses, the British troops began to fall back. Arnold pursued them to their entrenched camp, leading a bold charge that left him wounded.

Before the battle, General Arnold had been temporarily relieved of his command because of his quarreling with Gates. Nevertheless, he stayed with his troops, and his courageous actions on the battlefield today should help him regain his position in the army (→ Oct. 17).

Burgoyne loses his army at Saratoga

Relinquishing the sword. "The Surrender of Burgoyne at Saratoga" (1817-1821) by John Trumbull.

Saratoga, New York, Oct. 17

General John Burgoyne's four-month effort to drive a wedge between American forces in New England and the Middle States collapsed today. Outwitted and outnumbered, Burgoyne surrendered to General Horatio Gates. "The fortunes of war, General Gates, has made me your prisoner," General Burgoyne said. "I shall always be ready," Gates replied graciously, "to bear testimony that it has not been through any fault of your Excellency." Commander-in-Chief Washington said the victory surpassed "our most sanguine expectations," and American officers were heard speculating that the success of Gates might mean that he will replace Washington. Speaking in the privacy of his tent, Gates was jubilant. "If old England is not by this lesson taught humility," he said, "then she is an obstinate old slut, bent upon her ruin."

Burgoyne's surrender could represent a turning point in this war, but the significance of his defeat was lost in the ceremony at Saratoga today. Apparently concerned that British reinforcements under General Clinton were rushing to help Burgoyne, Gates gave him extraordinary privileges. The less sophisticated observer might have concluded that Burgoyne, not Gates, was the victor. The British general's dress and bearing were more elegant, and he seemed to tower over Gates, who stared at him through thick spectacles. Gates had originally demanded an unconditional surrender, but Burgoyne asked for and got a "convention" rather than a "capitulation."

Burgoyne was also allowed to write the terms of the Saratoga Convention. It allowed all of the British soldiers to march out of their camp with full honors. Their arms were surrendered and "piled by word of command of their own officers." The British will also be granted "free passage" back home "on condition of not serving again in North America during the present contest." Burgoyne believes that this arrangement will not hamper his country's war effort in the least. In a letter to George Sackville Germain, the British secretary of state for the American colonies, Burgoyne says, "I call it saving the army, because if sent home, the State is thereby enabled to send forth the troops now destined for her internal defense."

The Burgoyne letter may make good reading back home, but his troops were fully aware of the indignity of the situation. Seven of their generals have been captured in recent days. So have 300 other officers. In all, nearly 6,000 soldiers have been forced to lay down their arms and more than 1,400 are dead. In his journal, Lieutenant William Digby of the Shropshire Regiment reflected on the moment. The men marched, he said, "with drums beating and the honor of war, but the drums seem to have lost their inspiring sound, and though we beat the *Grenadiers March*, which not long before was so animating, yet then it seemed by its last effort, as if almost ashamed to be heard on such an occasion." When the British marched through two columns of Americans, their instruments fell silent and the patriots began playing a light piece of music to ease tensions. According to one report, they were playing *Yankee Doodle*. Generals Gates and Burgoyne emerged from a tent and watched in silence. Burgoyne handed Gates his sword, and Gates solemnly returned it.

Congress offers Articles of Confederation

York, Pennsylvania, Nov. 15

Long debated and often altered, the Articles of Confederation have finally been completed. The Continental Congress finished revision of the document, considered a national constitution, and sent it to the states for ratification, which must be unanimous.

John Dickinson of Delaware drafted the "Articles of Confederation and Perpetual Union" in July to consolidate power in the colonies. But radicals vehemently opposed provisions that would create strong central rule. Thomas Burke has been one of the loudest detractors. He warns that hiding behind a mask of war emergency are seekers of power trying to impose a centralized government. Because of such opposition, the constitution has been changed to forge a "firm league of friendship" that allows the states to keep "sovereignty, freedom and independence." It says that two to seven delegates from each state shall make up Congress.

Prevailing despite the winds of dissent is a document that does, in fact, empower a national legislature, Congress. While it grants sovereignty to the states, the constitution does not permit a state to create an army without congressional approval. Moreover, Congress will have the power to set foreign policy and declare war (→March 2, 1781).

Valley Forge: A cold, bleak Christmas

"Washington at Valley Forge," an idealized version, artist unknown.

Valley Forge, Penn., Dec. 25

"No meat! No meat!" Those defiant words echoed through the hills of Valley Forge a few days ago. Now it is deathly still at the winter headquarters of Washington's army. Christmas dinner, little more than flour and scraps of beef, is over. The men lie on the damp ground in the open air or in makeshift tents and huts, too weak from cold and hunger to know the difference between waking and sleeping. If a British regiment suddenly appeared at the camp, these men might even be grateful to be taken prisoner.

Valley Forge is neither a valley (merely a series of small hills) nor a forge – although an iron works once stood here. It is simply a bleak terrain 18 miles northwest of Philadelphia. Washington would have preferred to have his troops in the warm homes of Lancaster and York, yet these towns would be vulnerable to surprise operations by General Howe's army. Philadelphia, bursting with refugees from nearby villages, has no room for the soldiers. Besides, as early as last summer, Congress had fixed its sights on Valley Forge, hiding thousands of barrels of flour, horseshoes, tools and other necessities there – goods that the British subsequently discovered and removed. Half of the troops at Valley Forge are without blankets and a third are without shoes, stockings or breeches. Washington has written Congress a warning that unless there are new supplies of food and clothing, the army must "starve, dissolve or disperse" (→Feb. 23, 1778).

Two young officers given promotions

United States

Two young patriots, just a year apart in age, have earned the rank of lieutenant colonel, though General Washington favors one and not the other. Aaron Burr, 21, antagonized his commander during a brief stay in the official household last year. Sent to General Putnam, Burr made good at Long Island and was promoted in July. Alexander Hamilton, 22, also gained the general's approval. Desirous of military glory, Hamilton impressed Washington with his writing skills instead. The chief has made the young man his personal secretary.

Conspiracy against Washington fails

United States, Dec. 23

A plot to overthrow General George Washington as head of the army has been thwarted and its chief instigator shot. General Thomas Conway took advantage of Washington's recent military setbacks to suggest that he is incompetent and should be replaced by General Horatio Gates. Several high-ranking congressional officials and military officers were among supporters of the Conway plan. The plot was abandoned after Washington boldly confronted the conspirators and one of the general's aides wounded Conway gravely in a duel.

November 15. *The lower Delaware belongs to the British with the fall of Fort Mifflin; 300 American survivors escaped after six days of bombing.*

The spoils of war. While American troops suffer in the cold at Valley Forge, Howe and the British enjoy the comforts of Philadelphia. By J.L.G. Ferris.

1778

Philadelphia, Jan. 5. Four killed in a mine attack on the Delaware River.

Paris, Feb. 6. French-American treaties permit U.S. to conquer Canada and Bermuda; France allowed to take British West Indies (→ May 4).

Lower Blue Licks, Feb. 7. Shawnee Indians capture Daniel Boone (→ June 20).

London, March 16. Commons passes Lord North's plan to offer concessions to the colonists, forms British peace commission, hoping to forestall treaties with France (→ Apr. 22).

York, Pennsylvania, Apr. 22. Congress passes resolution branding as traitors all who come to terms with British peace commission (→ Aug. 26).

Mississippi River Basin, May 15. George Rogers Clark, in campaign to clear West of forces hostile to Revolution, captures Kaskaskia [near East St. Louis, Illinois] (→ July 4).

Philadelphia, June 18. British General Henry Clinton evacuates 13,000 troops from Philadelphia (→ 19).

Valley Forge, Pennsylavania, June 19. Washington breaks camp; General Charles Lee pursues British evacuating Philadelphia (→ 28).

America, June. Headquarters Secret Service set up, commanded by Aaron Burr (→ 8).

America, July 4. Lee suspended by court-martial for disobedient retreat at Monmouth (→ 30).

New York, July 8. Washington sets up headquarters at West Point (→ 30).

New York, July 11. French commander Comte d'Estaing anchors fleet off New York harbor (→ 29).

English Channel, July 27. British and French navies clash for first time in war off the coast of Brittany.

Newport, Rhode Island, July 29. Admiral d'Estaing's fleet arrives after invasion of New York is abandoned when French ships prove unmanageable (→ Aug. 29).

Philadelphia, Aug. 26. George Johnstone resigns from British peace commission after trying to bribe congressmen (→ Oct. 27).

Georgia, Dec. 29. British Lieutenant Colonel Archibald Campbell captures Savannah; 1,000 militia under Howe are overrun (→ Jan. 29, 1779).

Von Steuben to drill colonial troops

Von Steuben (c.1786) by Ralph Earl.

Valley Forge, Penn., Feb. 23

A Prussian soldier who does not speak a word of English presented himself to General Washington today and explained through an interpreter that he was volunteering to train the general's men. Washington may consider this offer propitious news; or he may not consider it good tidings at all. Officers from armies all over the world have come to his camp and made similar offers – and in the same breath demanded pay and a lofty rank for their "volunteer" efforts. Even the foreigners who have attained recognition for their leadership, such as Count Pulaski, fail to receive Washington's complete confidence. Yet this robust, 47-year-old soldier from Hohenzollern-Hechingen may prove to be different.

Friedrich Wilhelm Augustin, Baron von Steuben, is a former captain of the general staff in the service of King Frederick. He presents himself as a former lieutenant general (perhaps at the advice of his American friends, Benjamin Franklin among them). Whatever his actual title, he has not seen any kind of military duty in 14 years. Still, Congress, which sent von Steuben to Washington's headquarters, feels he can bring the colonial army the same disciplined military training that has made Prussia the envy of Europe. Steuben will see that there are constant inspections; even if the men are wrapped in rags, they will conduct themselves as if they were in full military dress. They will learn to march – not in disorderly array, nor with exaggerated strides, but in an easy and natural step, paced between slow and swift. They will be drilled in the use of their rifles until they are able to load and fire them in their sleep. And there will be only 10 words of command that they must obey, because the fewer the commands, the faster those commands can be followed.

A week ago, Washington wrote to Congress warning that his army faced collapse unless "vigorous and effectual measures are pursued to prevent it." He pointed to the desperate need for food and clothes: some men are naked beneath the blankets that they wrap about themselves, and no one has eaten meat since February 9. But if the body can take strength from the spirit, the efforts of von Steuben may help keep the men alive (→ June 18).

Some 2,500 men have succumbed to disease and an unusually harsh winter.

France and America agree on alliance

York, Pennsylvania, May 4

Two treaties, one of amity and commerce, the other of alliance, that were negotiated by Benjamin Franklin and others in Paris earlier this year have been ratified by Congress. Despite doubts expressed by Thomas Paine and John Adams about the dangers of foreign entanglements, and the reluctance of others to become allies of a Catholic country, the need for military aid against Britain has proved decisive. The amount of assistance has not been specified, but it will most likely be substantial; it is in the interest of the French to do all they can to weaken their traditional enemy, the British (→ July 11).

TRAITÉ
D'AMITIÉ ET DE COMMERCE,
CONCLU
ENTRE LE ROI
ET
LES ÉTATS-UNIS
DE
L'AMÉRIQUE SEPTENTRIONALE.

Le 6 Février 1778.

LOUIS, par la grace de Dieu, Roi de France et de Navarre : A tous ceux qui ces présentes Lettres verront ; SALUT. Comme notre cher et bien amé le sieur CONRAD-ALEXANDRE GERARD, Syndic royal de la ville de Strasbourg et Secrétaire de notre Conseil d'État, auroit, en vertu des pleins-pouvoirs que nous lui avions donnés à cet effet, conclu, arrêté et signé le 6 Février de la présente année 1778, avec les sieurs BENJAMIN FRANKLIN, SILAS DEANE et ARTHUR LEE, Députés du Congrès général des États-unis de l'Amérique septentrionale, également munis de pleins-pouvoirs, en bonne forme, un Traité d'Amitié et de Commerce, dont la teneur s'ensuit :

LE ROI TRÈS-CHRÉTIEN et les TREIZE ÉTATS-UNIS de l'Amérique septentrionale ; savoir, New-Hampshire, la baie de Massachusset, Rhode-Island, Connecticut, New-York, New-Jersey, Pensylvanie, les Comtés de New-Castle, de Kent et de Sussex sur la Delaware, Maryland, Virginie, Caroline septentrionale, Caroline méridionale et Georgie, voulant établir d'une manière équitable et permanente, les règles qui devront être suivies relativement à la correspondance et au commerce que les deux Parties desirent d'établir entre leurs pays, États et sujets respectifs ; Sa Majesté Très-Chrétienne et lesdits États-unis ont jugé ne pouvoir mieux atteindre à ce but, qu'en prenant pour base de leur arrangement l'égalité et la réciprocité la plus parfaite, et en observant d'éviter toutes les préférences onéreuses, source de discussions, d'embarras et de mécontentemens ; de laisser à chaque Partie la liberté de faire, relativement au

A

First page of the French-American treaty of friendship and commerce.

Americans pillage loyalist property

Manchac, Louisiana, Feb. 23

Captain James Willing and his American expeditionary force continued their attacks against Tory-owned properties along the Mississippi today. The Americans raided plantations on the Mississippi and the Amite Rivers. In Natchez last week, Willing's troops arrested English citizens and seized slaves and other property. Willing claims to have the authority to seize English properties, but those affected are planning to lodge a protest.

ritish escape after Battle of Monmouth

Washington at Battle of Monmouth" by Alonzo Chappel.

Monmouth, New Jersey, June 28

After a desperate winter at Valley Forge, General Washington's army has broken out and engaged General Clinton's British troops in New Jersey. The British had evacuated Philadelphia, which they call the "rebel capital," and were heading for New York to prevent the landing of a French fleet. Washington's troops followed in hot pursuit, with General Charles Lee commanding an advance corps that caught up with the British at Monmouth. From tangled reports, it seems that Lee, far from pressing an early advantage, actually ordered a retreat. Thus encouraged, Clinton counterattacked until Washington's arrival lifted morale and the Americans gave better than they got. Unfortunately, during the night, the British slipped away to the coast and boarded ships for New York. Still, the Americans can claim some sort of victory, thanks in no small part to Major General von Steuben's recent reorganization of the army. He has broken it up into battalions of 200 men, which have proved more flexible than the previous groups of 500 (→ July 4).

Woman helps soldiers in Monmouth fight

Monmouth, New Jersey, June 28

Today a woman by the name of Mary Hays helped her husband, an enlisted gunner, fire cannons during battle. While she reached for a cartridge, a cannon ball fired by the enemy passed between her ankles and tore away the fringe of her petticoat. She was overheard to say she was glad that the aim was not high enough to carry *her* away. Mary Hays is just one of many women aiding the patriot forces. "Molly Pitchers" they are called, fetching water to slake the thirst of the fighting men – or to swab the cannons after each firing. And there have been casualties among these women. In November 1776, during the defense of Fort Washington, Margaret Corbin, attending a small cannon, was severely wounded by grapeshot. Physicians fear that she will be an invalid for life.

Mary Hays, in full dress, expands the idea of "All men are created equal."

Peace mission to America ends in failure

New York City, Oct. 27

Their mission a total failure, Lord Carlisle and other peace commissioners set sail for London today.

The departure of the commissioners ends a futile attempt by Lord North's government to head off the alliance between France and the United States by offering what, until recently, would have been considered generous terms. While the commissioners had been authorized to offer an armistice, repeal of the Coercive Acts and reconsideration of Parliament's claim to regulate American trade, they had not been allowed to agree to "open and avowed independence."

As a result, Congress refused even to meet with them, declaring that it would not consider any peace proposals until "the King of Great Britain shall demonstrate a sincere disposition for that purpose. The only solid proof of this disposition will be an explicit acknowledgement of the independence of these states, or the withdrawing of his fleet and armies."

Thus rebuffed, Lord Carlisle, who has been described as "a young man of pleasure and fashion, fond of dress and gaming," made an effort to bypass the Congress with a Manifesto and Proclamation threatening the American people with "condign punishment" if the war against Britain continued. Just as offensive and ineffective were the attempts by George Johnstone, another of the commissioners, to bribe members of Congress to support their mission.

The peace mission quickly turned into a farce. An American political cartoon portrays the commissioners pleading on their knees to an uninterested America.

Boone flees Indians and foils a raid

Boonesborough, Kentucky, June 20

The settlers couldn't believe their eyes. Daniel Boone, barefoot, wearing ragged Indian leggings and sporting a scalp lock, had returned home after covering 160 miles of Indian country and wilderness, on foot, in less than four days. In January, Boone and 27 other men were captured by Chief Black Fish and his Shawnee braves at a salt lick some 40 miles north of Boonesborough. Boone, who had been adopted by Black Fish, escaped in time to warn the colonists that the Indians were planning a raid.

Warship captured by John Paul Jones

Carrickfergus, Scotland, Apr. 24

Boldly carrying the war home to the British – indeed to the very town where he was born 31 years ago – Captain John Paul Jones has followed up his daring raid on the west coast port of Whitehaven, where he burned several ships lying at anchor, with the capture of the 20-gun British warship Drake. The captured vessel, along with 200 prisoners, has been sent to the French port of Brest. Jones's ship, the Ranger, is the first navy vessel to fly the recently authorized flag of the United States (→ Sept. 23, 1779). ▷

Captain Cook brings civilization to Pacific

Cook (detail, 1776) by John Webber.

Sandwich Islands, Jan. 19

Captain James Cook, 17 days out of Christmas Island on his second Pacific voyage, brought Western civilization to these islands [Hawaii] today, naming them for his benefactor, the Earl of Sandwich. The islanders were awed by the tall, handsome Briton, who they thought was their god Lono and they feared to board his ship, the Resolution. Once they did, however, they excitedly examined and touched everything. Of special interest were objects of iron, which seems precious in their existence.

The Resolution's navigator said it was apparent that no other Europeans had visited the islands, despite the claims of explorers such as the Portuguese Vasco da Gama.

The natives bear a striking resemblance to the people Cook saw on his Tahiti voyage. Their gestures and singing are also similar to those of the Tahitians, as is a penchant for petty theft. In addition to warnings to protect against thefts, Cook instructed the crew not to fraternize with the women, who are most comely (→ June).

Cook discovers Alaskan anchorage

Alaska, June

Captain James Cook, in search of a water route from the Pacific to the Atlantic, has reported good anchorage at the entrance to what he believed to be the fabled Northwest Passage in Russian America. Proceeding up an arm of water, however, his ship Resolution became lodged on a sandbar as the tide went out. When the tide came in, Cook had to "turn again," and come out of this bottleneck. Cook has named the waterway Turnagain Arm. This is Cook's third voyage of discovery for the Earl of Sandwich, first lord of the Admiralty. Cook has named the Sandwich Islands [Hawaii] in his honor and rumor has it the earl is planning to name a major inlet in Russian America after the Admiralty's famed explorer (→ Feb. 14, 1779).

Howe yields British command to Clinton

Clinton, after a Trumbull painting.

Philadelphia, May 8

In a move that surprised many, General Lord Howe, commander-in-chief of the North American British army, has resigned. General Sir Henry Clinton is to replace him.

Howe appeared to have done well enough, capturing New York and beating Washington at White Plains, Germantown and Brandywine. Last winter, he occupied Philadelphia, where he apparently had quite a time with the ladies. On the negative side, his inadequate support of General John Burgoyne's battle near Albany led to the latter's humiliating surrender at Saratoga. This was not taken well by the government in Britain, which also criticized Howe for not having moved out of Philadelphia to confront Washington's depleted forces at nearby Valley Forge.

Clark clearing West of America's enemies

Mississippi River Basin, July 4

With fewer than 200 men, George Rogers Clark, a militia leader from Harrodsburg, Kentucky, today captured the British outpost at Kaskaskia on the Mississippi River.

Last fall, Clark had proposed to the Virginia authorities that a campaign be waged to clear the West of British, loyalist and Indian forces that are hostile to the American Revolution. Under the command of the British administrator, Lieutenant Governor Henry Hamilton, nicknamed the "hair-buyer" because he was said to purchase enemy scalps from the Indians," these forces had increased their attacks against American forts and isolated settlements after Virginia created Kentucky County. Indeed, by the time that Clark devised his plan, only four of the forts had withstood these raids by the British.

Clark, concluding that he could end the attacks only by going on the offensive, took his men to the Ohio River, sailed down it almost to the Mississippi, and then moved northwestward in Illinois to Kaskaskia, where he forced the British to surrender the fort (→ Feb. 25, 1779).

Ben Franklin named minister to France

Philadelphia, Sept. 14

There seems to be no end to the list of Ben Franklin's accomplishments. Famous in America as a writer and inventor, he was sent to France in 1776 to work toward an alliance in the war against Britain. This February, a two-part treaty of amity and defensive alliance was signed by Franklin's commission and France's King. Now Congress, recognizing his diplomatic worth, has named Franklin the minister to France (→ March 10, 1785).

An imperious George Rogers Clark forces British to surrender at Kaskaskia.

Franklin at the court of Louis XVI.

British General Lord Howe.

Washington heads south of West Point

White Plains, New York, July 30
George Washington, after defeating the British at Monmouth and establishing strategic headquarters at West Point, crossed the Hudson River and has taken up positions in White Plains. Washington broke his winter encampment at Valley Forge, Pennsylvania on June 19 in pursuit of the British forces heading for New York, and assisted General Charles Lee in defeating General Henry Clinton's army at Monmouth, New Jersey. By July 8, he had stationed forces at West Point, anticipating the arrival of the British in New York. West Point is high above the shore of the Hudson River, and is therefore a strategic position to hold. Now Washington has taken his troops south and established positions in White Plains (→June 1, 1779).

French fleet to join fight

Newport, Rhode Island, Aug. 29
The critical American need for French naval support against powerful British forces was clearly demonstrated today. The Americans, under General John Sullivan, attacked the nearby English army garrison and inflicted more than 250 casualties. But they suffered approximately the same number. If Sullivan had enjoyed a strong French naval presence, observers believe, his attack would have been decisive. The skirmish, however, proved to be a costly draw.

Admiral d'Estaing's fleet arrived off Sandy Hook last month, but when the British fortified the Narrows at New York he decided not to force a passage. Instead, his fleet sailed to Newport. While Comte d'Estaing was trying to intercept British reinforcements there, his ships were damaged by a storm and had to put into Boston for repairs. Nevertheless, the participation of the French fleet in the war could prove to be of considerable help to the Americans (→July 4, 1779).

Admiral d'Estaing by Freiselhein.

Settlers massacred after surrendering

Cherry Valley, N.Y., Nov. 11
In the latest attack planned by Sir John Johnson and Guy Johnson, 40 surrendering settlers were massacred after the village of Cherry Valley was taken by loyalist John Butler's Rangers and his Indian allies. The Indians were led by Mohawk Chief Joseph Brant, long an Anglophile. After attending Moor's Charity School for Indians in Lebanon, Connecticut, Brant was a missionary's interpreter, converted to the Anglican Church and helped translate religious works into Mohawk. In 1774, Guy Johnson, head of Indian affairs, made Brant his secretary and sent him to England, where he was presented at court, feted by Boswell and painted by Romney. Brant's defenders say the massacre was the fault of the Indians, not the chief (→Aug. 29, 1779).

200 scalped; farms afire in Pennsylvania

Pennsylvania, July 3
In a kind of civil war between Americans loyal to the British and those who aren't, loyalist Major John Butler and his Indian allies all but wiped out a settlement of farmers in the Wyoming Valley. The farmers were led by Colonel Zebulon Butler, who was home on leave from the Continental Army. Colonel Butler, no relation to Major Butler, gathered some 300 men, mostly boys and old men. Far outnumbered, the farmers battled bravely before succumbing to the Indians. The wounded men were slain viciously, 16 by a half-breed named Queen Esther. The victims were scalped, farms burned and 60 men lived to surrender (→Nov. 11).

Americans are slaughtered by Tory and Indian raiders at Battle of Wyoming. Major John Butler, Sir John and Guy Johnson and the English-educated Chief Joseph Brant rallied four Indian Nations into an alliance with England.

"Battle of Kegs," revolutionary poem

Philadelphia
The talented Francis Hopkinson has scored again with his poem *The Battle of the Kegs*, which everyone is quoting, and his song *Toast to Washington* is just as popular. Active in government, the Philadelphian is no mean author and musician. His poem deals with the incident this year in which David Bushnell launched some of his floating kegs filled with explosives in an attempt to blow up British warships. Although none of the ships was hit, one explosion killed four sailors, and the alarmed British began shooting at every floating thing in sight. Another song now popular is *Let Tyrants Shake*, by the Bostonian composer William Billings.

John Singleton Copley's "Watson and the Shark" (1778) portrays Brook Watson, a friend of the artist who, as a boy, lost his leg to a shark.

1779

Georgia, January 29. Augusta falls to British Colonel Campbell.

Illinois, March 26. Illinois and Wabash Company is formed; new company seeks to establish towns and develop trade in region.

Virginia, May 10. British capture and burn Portsmouth and Norfolk.

Fluvanna County, Virginia, May 18. Southern Conference of the Methodist Societies demands separation from the Anglican Church.

New York, June 1. Clinton, leading 6,000 men up Hudson River from New York, seizes American ports of Stony Point and Verplanck Point (→July 15).

Virginia, June 1. Thomas Jefferson elected colonial Governor; he is the progressive faction's unchallenged leader.

Spain, June 21. Spain declares war on France over Gibraltar, refuses to recognize American independence.

South Carolina, June 29. General Augustine Prevost, having failed to take Charleston, marches to Savannah following an attack by American General Benjamin Lincoln at Stony Ferry.

Caribbean, July 4. French Admiral d'Estaing disables four British ships at the Battle of Grenada (→Sept. 15).

Bedford, New York, July 11. Only one house remains standing after British burn town.

New York, July 15. American General Anthony Wayne takes 700 prisoners in bayonet attack on British fort at Stony Point (→July 26).

New York, July 26. French Colonel Francois Louis Teisseidre de Fleury is first foreigner awarded an American decoration, a silver medallion (→Aug. 19).

Newtown, New York, Aug. 29. Generals Sullivan and James Clinton defeat loyalist and Indian forces, halting raids on frontier settlements of New York and Pennsylvania.

Georgia, Sept. 15. Admiral D'Estaing, having returned to American coast, begins siege of Savannah (→Oct. 28).

New York City, Dec. 26. British General Clinton leaves for drive on Charleston with 8,000 men.

America. Jonathan Carver first to use the word "Oregon" in print (→Feb. 1, 1780).

Clark lures Indians away, captures fort

Wading in bitter-cold water en route to Vincennes. Painting by F.C. Yohn.

Vincennes, Illinois, Feb. 25

George Rogers Clark and his band of fighters recaptured the fort at Vincennes today, causing Lieutenant Governor Henry Hamilton to surrender. Last July, the Virginia militia leader and his men floated down the Ohio River, crossed the wilderness to take the British fort at Kaskaskia, then seized the British outpost at Vincennes by surprise. Clark began incorporating the area into Virginia, but on December 17, Hamilton, with 500 soldiers and Indians, won back Vincennes. Clark's men returned, lured away Hamilton's Indian allies and forced the British administrator to surrender.

Daring Wayne bayonet attack wins fort

New York, Aug. 19

In a daring attack last month that has earned him the nickname "Mad Anthony," General Anthony Wayne led a hand-picked brigade of 1,300 men through the fortifications of British-held Stony Point. After moving in silently, his forces used axes to break through the walls and set up a bayonet attack. Stony Point, originally an American fort, was seized by General Clinton in May, giving the British control of King's Ferry crossing on the Hudson. Down river today, Major Harry Lee drove the British from Paulus Hook, their last outpost in New Jersey (→Dec. 26).

General Wayne leads the charge on the British garrison at Stony Point.

Colonists routed in Maine naval battle

Castine, Maine, Aug. 15

Disaster has overtaken the Massachusetts expeditionary force sent to recapture this town from the British. Although the land forces, consisting of some 900 militiamen commanded by General Lovell, made a successful landing on July 25, the naval forces were taken completely by surprise when a strong British squadron, led by the 64-gun Raisonable, appeared in Penobscot Bay. Rather than stay and fight, the American Captain Saltonstall and his 19 armed vessels fled upriver where two ships surrendered after light resistance and the rest were burned by their crews.

Freedom of religion draft is proposed

Williamsburg, Virginia, June

Governor Thomas Jefferson, the author of the *Declaration of Independence*, has proposed a bill in the colony's House of Burgesses to establish religious freedom in Virginia. The bill, offered this month, would amount to a complete disestablishment of religion and would remove all laws circumscribing religious belief. It is now languishing before the assembly and is not likely to be passed this year. Many citizens have been shocked by the forthright nature of the bill, condemning the Governor as though he were the Antichrist himself (→Jan. 16, 1786).

Shelby's raid beats Chickamauga tribe

Tennessee, April

Americans continue to retaliate against those Indian tribes that have sided with the British. Most recently, Colonel Evan Shelby, at the head of a force of 2,000 men from Virginia and North Carolina, beat the Chickamaugas in a battle at their villages near Chattanooga. Welsh by birth and now a Virginian, Shelby is an experienced Indian fighter. After leading attacks against the Cherokees in 1776, he was made a colonel in the militia of his home county, Washington.

John Paul Jones defiant: "I have not yet begun to fight"

England, Sept. 23

After reportedly answering a British demand that he strike his colors with the ringing phrase, "I have not yet begun to fight," the American Captain John Paul Jones scored a stunning victory against superior odds in a duel at Flamborough Head off the east coast of England.

On the British side was the Serapis, a newly built double-decker with 54 guns commanded by the seasoned Captain Pearson. The American ship was the Bonhomme Richard, an old French vessel formerly called the Duc de Duras. After refitting the ship, Jones rechristened it in honor of his patron, Benjamin Franklin, Le Bonhomme Richard being a French translation of Poor Richard, the character of the Franklin almanac.

The Serapis was convoying a fleet of English merchantmen when it came upon the Bonhomme Richard, which was marauding off the mouth of the River Humber. Although the Serapis outgunned his ship, Jones quickly closed for battle and managed to grapple the ships together. The duel lasted well into the night, ending only when the British, with 49 dead and 68 wounded, surrendered.

American losses were even greater – 150 killed or wounded of a crew of 300. The Bonhomme Richard was so badly damaged that it had to be abandoned and the vessel sank not long after the battle.

John Paul Jones in action. "The Ship That Sunk in Victory" by J.L.G. Ferris.

French fleet fails to rescue Savannah

Savannah, Georgia, Oct. 28

The French fleet that came to rescue Savannah from the English sailed away today, leaving most of coastal Georgia in British hands. Comte Henri d'Estaing, the fleet's commander, is recovering from wounds suffered in an attack he led on October 9. Some 800 allied troops died in battle, including Casimir Pulaski, the Polish cavalry leader. The British lost only 155 men, but D'Estaing's bombing seriously damaged the town. The count brought his forces to Savannah at the request of South Carolina Governor John Rutledge. The British captured the city in December. Augusta fell to the British in January.

Pulaski, martyr to the U.S. cause.

Cook slain on return to Pacific islands

Sandwich Islands, Feb. 14

An attempt to recover a pair of stolen tongs caused a riot at Kealakekua Bay [Hawaii] today, resulting in the death of Captain James Cook. Several marines and natives also were killed in the massacre, after the natives said that Cook violated their laws by trying to take their King hostage. An aide on the Discovery said a pair of tongs from his ship's armory had been stolen and Cook ordered a party ashore to recover them and halt the mounting thefts. Finally, Cook ordered the King taken hostage. On seeing him seized, the natives rioted and gunfire erupted. When Cook shot a native, he was clubbed, stabbed and stripped of his flesh. Later, his bare bones were recovered and buried at sea.

Natives of the Sandwich Islands [Hawaii] make an offering before Cook and his men. The captain was killed during a struggle over the theft of a pair of tongs, but his explorations have forever altered maps of the Pacific.

War cost in paper money: 242 million

Philadelphia, Nov. 29

The Continental Congress has issued the last paper money of the war, bringing the total to nearly $242 million since June of 1775.

To finance the war, Congress had authorized the printing of greater and greater amounts of paper money. This year alone, $140 million was authorized – more than twice the amount of the previous year. Meanwhile, the states had also started printing paper money, putting almost $210 million into circulation, and counterfeit currency was rampant. As a result, the Continental currency began to depreciate, and the phrase "not worth a Continental" became popular. A dollar in coin that could be exchanged for eight in paper early this year is now exchanged for 38 1/2.

"Our finances are in such a condition," wrote Cornelius Harnett to Thomas Burke in late 1777, "that unless the States agree immediately, to tax as high as the people can possibly bear, the credit of our money must be ruined" (→ March 18, 1780).

Spanish take Baton Rouge from English

Louisiana, Sept. 21, 1779

An English fort at Baton Rouge fell to Spanish troops today after a few hours of bombardment. Not a single member of the Spanish army was wounded. The English also relinquished Fort Panmure at Natchez. Louisiana Governor Bernardo de Galvez announced that 375 English soldiers had been taken prisoner. The successful attack on the fort at Baton Rouge was the first major battle since the Spaniards declared war on England on June 21. Instead of waiting for the British to attack New Orleans, Galvez took the war to the enemy.

1780

Philadelphia, Jan. 15. Congress establishes court of appeals.

New York, Feb. 1. Colony cedes all Western lands to Congress (→ Oct. 10).

South Carolina, Feb. 1. General Henry Clinton arrives off coast of Charleston with fleet carrying 8,000 troops (→ Apr. 8).

North Carolina, Feb. 28. Fort Nashborough [renamed Nashville in 1782] established on Cumberland River to protect Appalachian region from Indian raids.

Russia, Feb. 28. Catherine II declares all belligerents open to attack by Russian navy in attempt to protect neutral shipping.

Philadelphia, March 18. Congress passes Forty-to-One Act, offering redemption of paper money at one-fortieth of face value (→ May 26, 1781).

South Carolina, Apr. 8. Clinton sends fleet past Fort Moultrie and into harbor, initiating attack on Charleston (→ May 12).

United States, May. Benedict Arnold secretly opens negotiations with British (→ July 12).

Boston, May 4. American Academy of Arts and Sciences founded.

Waxhaw, South Carolina, May 29. Regiment from Virginia destroyed by British cavalry under Colonel Sir Banastre Tarleton (→ Nov.).

Charleston, South Carolina, June 5. Clinton sets out for New York; Cornwallis stays here to defend city (→ Aug. 16).

America, July 12. Arnold informs British Major John Andre he wishes to plan "disposal" of West Point after taking command (→ Aug. 5).

New York, Aug. 5. Arnold takes command of West Point (→ Oct. 2).

Philadelphia, Oct. 10. Congress calls upon more states to cede Western lands to allow incorporation into union (→ Jan. 2, 1781).

Philadelphia, Dec. 19. Congress names Francis Dana minister to Russia.

Massachusetts. Free Negroes petition Massachusetts General Court for relief from taxes because they are denied citizenship.

South Carolina. Law grants slave to each volunteer in army as incentive to join up.

Charleston is lost: Major U.S. defeat

Charleston, S.C., May 12

American forces surrendered today to General Sir Henry Clinton. In what has been called a "Saratoga in reverse," 5,000 troops under General Benjamin Lincoln gave up in total defeat. The Americans also lost four ships and an arsenal of desperately needed munitions. In turn, the victory was cheap for the British; they suffered fewer than 260 casualties.

General Clinton began operations in February, when he sent his fleet and 8,000 regular soldiers against the patriots who garrisoned Fort Moultrie, a colonial bastion situated in Charleston harbor. Clinton's invasion began on a sour note. While crossing the Atlantic, one Royal Navy transport was dismasted by a fierce storm and drifted, with its war cargo, to St. Ives, in Cornwall. But Clinton persevered and turned disaster into victory.

Clinton's invasion seems to represent a new British strategy. Many American experts feel the British do not have enough troops in the North to defeat Washington, and therefore decided to invade the South, where they assume loyalists will give them the critical support needed for final victory in America. Meanwhile, this disastrous loss, called "Saratoga in reverse" because of the terrible effect that the Saratoga defeat had on the British, has devastated American morale and demonstrates that triumph in this war will not come easily (→ June 5).

Waiting for the fall: Charleston, S.C., seen from behind British lines.

Greene wins battle, moves to higher post

Philadelphia, Oct. 14

General Nathanael Greene today was appointed to succeed General Horatio Gates as commander of the Southern Department of the Continental Army. General Greene, a Vermonter who has long been a supporter of General Washington, inflicted a thrashing on the British forces at Springfield, Massachusetts, earlier this year.

Nathanael Greene by C.W. Peale.

Many Americans believe that Greene is one of the most underrated of the corps of American generals who have been leading this Revolution. He is considered to be a man of creativity and imagination, and one who has not been afraid to divide his limited forces. Nor has he been reluctant to retreat when the occasion warranted it.

When word of his appointment reached General Greene, he wrote to his wife, "What I have been dreading has come to pass. His Excellency George Washington has appointed me to the command of the Southern Army. This is so foreign from my wishes that I am distressed exceedingly; especially as I have just received your letter of the 2nd of this month where you describe my soul into the deepest distress. How unfriendly war is to domestic happiness."

It is going to be a difficult war to pursue; when Greene took over command today at Charlottesville, Virginia, the army was lacking in virtually every item that is needed to conduct a campaign.

Arnold found guilty and is reprimanded

Philadelphia, Apr. 6

General Washington mildly reprimanded Major General Benedict Arnold today, carrying out the sentence of last December's court-martial. Washington called on Arnold to "exhibit anew those noble qualities which have placed you on the list of our most valued commanders," and pledged to provide Arnold "with opportunities of regaining the esteem of your country." The executive council of Pennsylvania accused Arnold of having used his position as military commander of Philadelphia for his own gain and asked Congress to replace him. Arnold resigned his command and asked to be court-martialed, in order to clear his name. But the court found him guilty of some of the charges, including having issued a pass for a ship to enter a closed harbor. Critics revived accusations that in the Quebec invasion, he "plundered Montreal"; Congress has yet to settle Arnold's accounts from that campaign (→ May).

5,500 French troops arrive in Newport

Newport, Rhode Island, July 12

Thanks are due to the persuasive owers of the Marquis de Lafayette. Vhile on a mission back to France ist year, the young nobleman made strong personal plea on behalf f the American cause to Louis (VI. Partly as a result of that ffort, a substantial French expedi- onary force landed here yesterday. 'he troops, numbering about 5,500, re seasoned professionals and in- lude some of France's most famous egiments. They are commanded by ne 55-year-old Comte de Rocham- eau, a lieutenant general with ex- ensive military experience gained uring the War of the Austrian Suc- ession and the Seven Years War.

It is known that General Washington had intended to use the French force in a combined attack on New York, which was lost to the British after the Battle of Long Island. But this plan will almost certainly have to be postponed because a large British fleet, commanded by Admirals Arbuthnot and Rodney, arrived today, hot on the heels of the French, and has effectively blockaded Newport.

What happens next will thus depend to a considerable extent on whether the French are able to send a naval force powerful enough to wrest control of the seas from the British. America's navy, though it has had its successes, is still far too small to hope to succeed in such an undertaking (→ May 21, 1781).

Var drums by Nicholas Hoffmann.

French infantrymen by Hoffmann.

James Baker buys a chocolate factory

Dorchester, Massachusetts

It has been 15 years since John Hannan built the first American hocolate mill here. Now the highly espected Dr. James Baker has pur- hased the mill on the Neponset River and plans to sell chocolate all ver Massachusetts. He says the lark brown cocoa product is benefi- ial to the health and that because is so nutritious it is especially elpful to long-distance travelers who are not able to obtain meals reg- larly. The French have long in- ulged in chocolate, mixing mashed ocoa beans with sugar and arrow- oot. Some less reputable producers dd red earth to their product.

Pennsylvania first with ban on slavery

Philadelphia, March 1

The Pennsylvania legislature today passed a bill to abolish slavery. But the law, written by Thomas Paine, George Bryan and Charles Willson Peale, does not extend as far as the framers desired; it gives freedom to the offspring of existing slaves only when they reach the age of 28. Regardless, it is the first such ban. Paine advocates freedom for Negroes as a basic "right of man." He endorses the assertion of his radical Massachusetts colleague William Gordon that, "a black, tawny or reddish skin in not so unfavorable a hue to the genuine son of liberty as a Tory complexion."

Cornwallis repels assault; De Kalb slain

"Death of General De Kalb at the Battle of Camden," after a Chappel painting.

Camden, S.C., Aug. 16

A numerically superior American army of 3,500, under General Horatio Gates was routed during an advance on Camden today when inexperienced militiamen fled before a British bayonet charge. General Gates himself rode off ahead of his panicked men. The Americans were attacked by a force of 2,400 British commanded by General Lord Cornwallis. At the sight of the British blades, the militiamen ran, leaving the fight to German Baron Johann De Kalb's regulars. All but 60 of the men were killed or captured and De Kalb was mortally wounded (→ March 15, 1781).

Frontiersmen beat loyalists, stall attack

Philadelphia, October

Word has arrived that the Continental Army, consisting mainly of frontiersmen, scored a major victory in North Carolina over British regulars and their loyalist allies on October 7. Troops fighting under the English commander, Major Ferguson, are estimated to have suffered 1,000 casualties at the Battle of King's Mountain. General Cornwallis, the British commander, has stated that his invasion of North Carolina was "necessary" for victory in America. The survivors have pulled back to Winnsboro, where they are under constant attack by American guerrilla forces.

Defeat of the British at the Batttle of King's Mountain in North Carolina.

Arnold betrays U.S.; Andre hanged

Arnold gets Andre to hide papers in his stocking. Painting by C.F. Blauvelt.

Major Andre, in civilian clothes, caught. After painting by Asher Durand.

Just before being hanged as a spy on October 2, Andre said, "Witness to the world that I die like a man."

Arnold's wife, Peggy, who has been said to harbor loyalist sympathies, faints when told of his treason.

Tappan, New York, Oct. 2

General Benedict Arnold, whose heroic actions have been responsible for many of the Continental Army's victories during the war, has attempted to sell the plans of West Point to the British. Papers detailing the number of troops and the placement of fortifications around the Hudson River garrison were discovered in the possession of Major John Andre, the adjutant general under Sir Henry Clinton, leader of the British forces. Arnold, who received notice of Andre's capture just hours before General Washington arrived at West Point, fled on his official barge to the British man-of-war Vulture, which was anchored in the Hudson. Andre was captured on September 23 near Tarrytown by three men, described by some as former militiamen and by others as highwaymen, who discovered the treasonous papers concealed in Andre's stockings.

According to Andre's statement before a hastily summoned court of inquiry, he came ashore from the Vulture on September 21 to meet with Arnold, at the request of Clinton. Andre was unable to return to the man-of-war, which was under bombardment from the shore, and he was forced to make his way on land in an attempt to reach British-occcupied territory. He admitted to the court that he was not traveling under a flag of truce. On September 29, the court found that Andre was a spy. And today, he was hanged.

The motive behind Arnold's betrayal remains the great puzzle of this case. Arnold fought brilliantly against the British during many of the campaigns of the war, and he still suffers from wounds received at the Battle of Freeman's Farm during the fighting at Saratoga. However, Arnold is known for his extravagant manner of living. He was reprimanded earlier this year by General Washington for having violated regulations while commander of Philadelphia to raise money for his own use. Clinton reportedly offered Arnold 20,000 pounds for the surrender of West Point. In addition, Arnold was greatly insulted three years ago when Congress promoted five officers to general over him.

Sheet music leads to more serenading

Philadelphia

As more sheet music is being printed and sold, more cultivated ladies and gentlemen are gathering in their parlors for an evening of serenading. And if you don't know the words, you can always buy a "songster." Such a book is small enough to fit in your pocket and contains the lyrics to many of today's songs. And more instruments are being made, too. While the harpsichord remains the preferred choice, the new pianofortes have been making inroads since 1775, when John Behrent placed an advertisement here offering "an extraordinary instrument, by the name of the pianoforte, in mahogany in the manner of a harpsichord."

Ladies ride in races

Long Island, New York

Three days of horse racing at the track in Hempstead Plains included an event for women riders. There was also a Gentlemen's Purse and a Ladies' Subscription event. The races were held at the Newmarket course, named for the town in England. A local minister wrote that "toward the middle of the island lyeth a plain 16 miles long and 4 broad where you will find neither stick nor stone to hinder the horses' heels or endanger them in their races."

Swords and sabers, traditional companions to musket warfare.

Troops near revolt quieted by others

Morristown, New Jersey, May 25

Two Connecticut regiments on the verge of revolt over lack of food and pay have been subdued by Pennsylvania troops. Rations, cut after the March currency deflation, amount to a bit of rice and meat but no bread or flour. The two regiments of armed Connecticut soldiers walked away from the Morristown camp after demanding full rations and payment of their wages. However, officers acted swiftly, ordering a group of Pennsylvania soldiers to surround the regiments. Some of the Pennsylvanians were reported to have sympathized with the angry men and considered joining them, but officers quelled the potential rebellion (→Jan. 7, 1781).

Iroquois defeated

Mohawk Valley, N.Y., Autumn

The Iroquois, who have occupied the valleys of the Mohawk River in central New York for generations, have been dealt an overwhelming defeat by the troops of General John Sullivan. In slightly more than a month late this summer, the Sullivan forces destroyed their vast community – homes, barns, storehouses and cultivation. However, most of the Iroquois managed to escape. General George Washington reportedly ordered the assault to discourage attacks by the Indians.

Tarleton's cavalry in search of Swamp Fox

Tarleton calls his adversary . . .

Francis Marion, the Swamp Fox.

South Carolina, November

Sir Banastre Tarleton, known as the Butcher to Americans, has set out in search of the elusive Francis Marion, whom he calls the Swamp Fox. "As for this damned old fox," Tarleton has said of the man who for years has been outwitting the British with guerrilla tactics, "the devil himself could not catch him."

For the third time in recent months, American forces were devastated on August 18 by Tarleton and his cavalry in the continuing battle for South Carolina. Tarleton destroyed Thomas Sumter's guerrilla force at Fishing Creek. Sumter and his men had just captured Fort Carey on August 15. The victory is said to open the way for a British invasion of the area.

On August 16, Tarleton's cavalry defeated 900 Continentals dispatched to South Carolina by General Washington and under the leadership of General De Kalb, who was killed in the battle.

And last May 27, Tarleton was sent after Colonel Abraham Buford's Third Regiment of Virginia Continentals, who were retreating toward Salisbury. In two days, he met up with them at Waxhaw, and defeated Buford's force. Tarleton is said to have had his men massacre the survivors (→Jan. 17, 1781).

State constitution calls all men equal

Massachusetts, June 15

The state ratified its constitution today with a declaration of rights that emphatically states, "All men are born free and equal." Drafted by John Adams, his cousin Sam, and James Bowdoin, the constitution nevertheless requires a high property-value qualification for voting. Candidates for office must also own property. These conservative clauses, advocated by John Adams and Bowdoin, angered many residents. The radical Joseph Hawley voiced bitter opposition, arguing that the propertyless would not be represented. Despite the protests, the state became the first to draft and ratify a constitution through the democratic process.

British-Dutch war

London, Dec. 20

Angered by continued Dutch support for the rebellious American colonies, Britain has once again gone to war with its traditional maritime rival. Although earlier this year the Dutch refused to recognize American independence, their relations with England have been bad for some time. The Dutch resent the British practice of stopping and searching neutral ships at sea, while the British are angry with the Dutch for allowing privateers to use their ports.

A Dutch cartoon displays England's misery in symbolic detail. Britain, in the form of a cow, stands helplessly while the American Congress saws off her horns. The Netherlands gleefully milks her while France and Spain wait to be fed. In the background, a British warship, rudderless and stripped of its guns, has run aground at Philadelphia while American militiamen sleep. At right, the royal British lion lies prostrate, oblivious to the monkey on its back and the Briton in mourning, praying for her rejuvenation.

Louis XVI (left) presents John Paul Jones with a gold-hilted sword and makes the naval hero a chevalier of France. Painting by J.L.G. Ferris.

1781

Virginia, Jan. 2. Colony cedes Western lands to Congress, removing obstacle to Maryland's ratification of Articles of Confederation (→ March 2).

Philadelphia, March 2. Congress's new name is The United States in Congress Assembled.

North Carolina, Apr. 25. General Cornwallis leaves Wilmington with 1,500 men, planning to eliminate Virginia as American supply base.→

United States, Apr. 30. Alexander Hamilton writes to Robert Morris: "A national debt, if not excessive, will be to us a national blessing."

Monticello, April. Thomas Jefferson escapes British raid (→ Dec. 12).

Florida, May 9. British surrender Pensacola to Spanish, giving up West Florida (→ 10).

Wethersfield, Connecticut, May 21. Washington meets with French General Comte de Rochambeau (→ Aug. 26).

Philadelphia, May 26. Congress approves national bank, Morris's first proposal since becoming superintendent of finance (→ Dec. 31).

Philadelphia, June 11. John Adams named sole peace negotiator; commission includes Franklin, John Jay, Jefferson, and Henry Laurens (→ July).

Williamsburg, Virginia, July 20. Slaves rebel, burning buildings, including capitol.

United States, July. John Adams rejects European plan to hold peace conference at which delegates would represent states separately (→ Feb. 27, 1782).

Philadelphia, Aug. 10. Robert R. Livingston named secretary for foreign affairs (→ Dec. 1783).

New York, Aug. 26. Washington, intent upon attacking Cornwallis in Virginia, crosses Hudson and heads South (→ Sept. 28).

Virginia, Sept. 28. Washington and Rochambeau begin siege of Yorktown (→ 30).

Yorktown, Virginia, Sept. 30. General Cornwallis, recoiling under initial attack, abandons outer defenses (→ Oct. 19).

Netherlands, Nov. 5. United States is granted large loan by The Netherlands.

United States. George Washington asserts, "Laws made by common consent must not be trampled on by individuals."

Army veterans mutiny; demands are met

General Anthony Wayne tries to reason with mutinous troops in New Jersey.

Morristown, New Jersey, Jan. 7

The mutiny by veterans of the Pennsylvania regiment has been ended peacefully, with the rebellious troops receiving a pardon, payment and a hearing concerning their period of enlistment.

The mutiny began after a group of the veterans learned that new recruits were being offered their pay in coin. Some of the veterans had not received any payments for a year. Some 1,500 veterans paraded around the camp at Morristown, randomly firing shots, one of which hit a captain in the head, killing him almost instantly. Although sergeants were able to restore order, a small army marched off to Princeton with a cannon and supplies.

Following negotiations led by the president of the Pennsylvania Executive Council, Joseph Reed, the demands of the mutineers were met, including a hearing for those soldiers who have fulfilled their three years of service.

Army officers acknowledged that the mutineers had conducted themselves admirably, maintained a reasonable degree of order and always made it clear that they would continue to fight the British, regardless of their mutiny (→ 27).

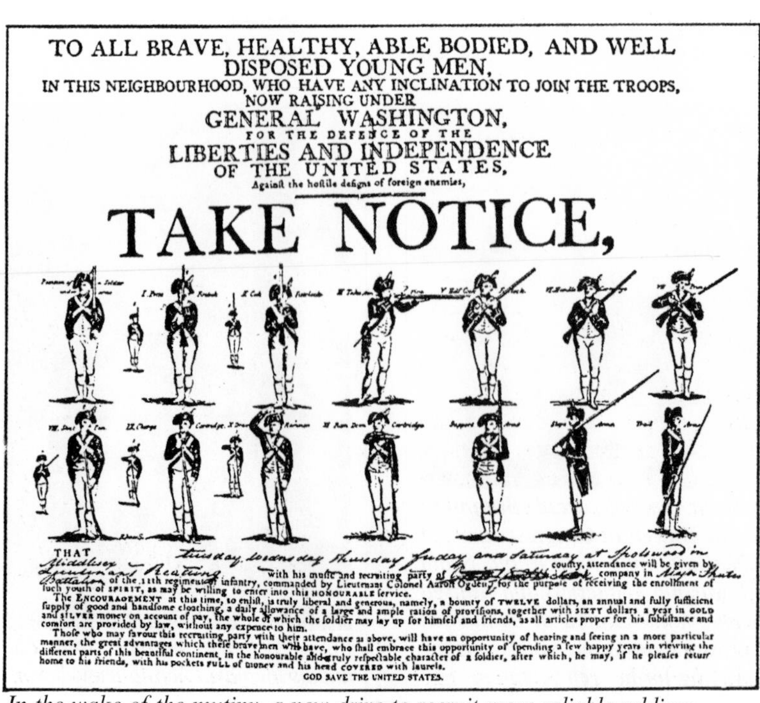

TO ALL BRAVE, HEALTHY, ABLE BODIED, AND WELL DISPOSED YOUNG MEN,
IN THIS NEIGHBOURHOOD, WHO HAVE ANY INCLINATION TO JOIN THE TROOPS,
NOW RAISING UNDER
GENERAL WASHINGTON,
FOR THE DEFENCE OF THE
LIBERTIES AND INDEPENDENCE
OF THE UNITED STATES,
Against the hostile designs of foreign enemies,

TAKE NOTICE,

THAT tuesday, wednesday, thursday, friday and saturday at Spotswood in Middlesex county, attendance will be given by Lieutenant Reading with his music and recruiting party of [illegible] company in Major Shute's Battalion of the 11th regiment of infantry, commanded by Lieutenant Colonel Aaron Ogden, for the purpose of receiving the enrollment of such youth of SPIRIT, as may be willing to enter into this HONOURABLE service.

The ENCOURAGEMENT at this time, to enlist, is truly liberal and generous, namely, a bounty of TWELVE dollars, an annual and fully sufficient supply of good and handsome cloathing, a daily allowance of a large and ample ration of provisions, together with SIXTY dollars a year in GOLD and SILVER money on account of pay, the whole of which the soldier may lay up for himself and friends, as all articles proper for his subsistance and comfort are provided by law, without any expence to him.

Those who may favour this recruiting party with their attendance as above, will have an opportunity of hearing and seeing in a more particular manner, the great advantages which these brave men will have, who shall embrace this opportunity of spending a few happy years in viewing the different parts of this beautiful continent, in the honourable and truly respectable character of a soldier, after which, he may, if he pleases return home to his friends, with his pockets FULL of money and his head COVERED with laurels.

GOD SAVE THE UNITED STATES.

In the wake of the mutiny, a new drive to recruit more reliable soldiers.

Shaker leader stirs opposition on tour

New England

Mother Ann Lee, founder of the Shakers, has aroused intense opposition during her missionary travels in this region. Many are appalled by the Shakers' religious doctrines. Others have been enraged by the claims of some members that Mother Ann is God in a female incarnation (she rejects the claims). More dangerous to her than the angry critics have been attacks by ruffians and blackguards who inhabit local taverns. Their assaults on religious believers know no limits. Mother Ann's preachings against the flesh have made her a particular target for their violence.

"Americanisms"

Philadelphia

Americans are hatching a unique form of English, John Witherspoon writes in "The Druid," an essay published in the *Pennsylvania Journal*. He admires the native idiom, but feels "errors in grammar, improprieties and vulgarisms" are polluting common speech. He has also come up with the word "Americanisms" to refer to redundancies such as "fellow countrymen" and odd locutions such as "I was quite mad" (for "angry").

Two executions end New Jersey mutiny

Pompton, New Jersey, Jan. 27

Following Washington's order to crush the rebellion by whatever means are necessary, General Robert Howe had two leaders of a New Jersey mutiny shot by a firing squad made up of fellow mutineers today. Spurred by the Pennsylvania army's revolt over rations and pay earlier this month, the New Jersey soldiers had left their camp for Trenton to seek relief. Hearing that the state assembly had passed laws to provide aid, the mutineers requested and were granted a pardon contingent on their return to duty. But many, still discontent, were disobeying orders when Howe and his men paid a surprise visit to the Pompton camp (→ June 13, 1783).

arleton is finally defeated at Cowpens

;eneral Morgan's encirclement of Tarleton was a brilliant tactical feat.

:owpens, S.C., Jan. 17

The scourge of American forces 1 South Carolina, Sir Banastre 'arleton, was defeated by General)aniel Morgan in the fields and orests of Cowpens today. A few lays before the battle, General 'ornwallis learned that the Ameri-an forces had been split. Morgan ad been sent on a western sweep, eaving the rest of the American outhern Army with General Na-hanael Greene. Tarleton pursued vith 1,100 men, about equal to Morgan's forces. Chasing the rebels had been one of Tarleton's most successful strategies. But this time the fox was waiting for the hounds. Morgan's men took up four positions around the battle site, and, in a brilliant tactical display, feigned retreat to draw the British into a great envelopment. When the British moved in, 110 were killed, and 830 captured. Only a handful were able to flee, including Tarleton. The American casualties were 12 men killed and 61 wounded.

Cornwallis wins Guilford, losses are heavy

Guilford, N.C., March 15

In the end, it was General Nathanael Greene and the American army that gave up the field and fled in retreat from the Battle at the Guilford Courthouse, but that fact alone does not adequately describe the day. It was a day that was three weeks in the making, while Greene and his men maneuvered around the area staging small attacks and never taking up a position. This was a constant source of frustration to General Cornwallis, who commands the Southern British Army.

On March 11, Greene's strength was bolstered to 4,300 men and, although most of these men had never before been in battle, the decision was made to challenge the British openly. The challenge was made by taking up position at the Guilford Courthouse, and anticipating the inevitable British attack. Cornwallis, it would seem, had been waiting for this opportunity for weeks, and knew beforehand that his men would be outnumbered by at least three to one.

Greene chose tactics in his battle plan similar to those of General Daniel Morgan when he devastated Sir Banastre Tarleton at Cowpens in January. He established three lines centering around Salisbury Road, which leads through a valley and some woodland to the courthouse, where Greene had his headquarters during the battle. Cornwallis and his men were stationed 12 miles to the south, and he must have begun the trek to the courthouse hours before sunrise, confident that the experience of his men would overwhelm the American amateurs regardless of their number.

American cavalry at Guilford.

Technically, Cornwallis won the day. By mid-afternoon, Greene was in retreat, and the redcoats had the field. However, Cornwallis led 1,900 men into battle, and lost 738, with 184 killed. In contrast, General Greene began the day with 4,300 men and lost 312, with 78 fatalities (→Apr. 25).

Campaign to retake South Carolina fails

:amden, South Carolina, Apr. 25

Lord Rawdon's British forces de-eated General Nathanael Greene t Hobkirk's Hill today and sent his rmy retreating into the woods. American losses are estimated at !66 casualties, including 18 killed, nd British losses are put at about he same, or slightly more.

The battle began late this morn-ng, when Rawdon attacked Ameri-an positions around the hill and aught Greene's men off guard. As he battle developed, Greene made n unsuccessful attempt to envelop he British forces and was nearly ncircled by the second British line. While the Americans conducted a ninor retreat in order to regroup, he British suddenly struck and sent he American army running.

General Greene had arrived at Iobkirk's Hill on April 19 and was waiting for reinforcements to help take Camden from the British. The rest of the American Southern Army was occupied keeping Colonel John Watson and his 500 redcoats from rejoining Rawdon's forces at Camden. Two days earlier, Greene had moved from his position on the hill to assure that Watson's men would not get through. He returned to the hill when he learned that Watson had been stopped.

Rumor has it Rawdon was informed of American movements by a deserter. Luckily for the Americans and unbeknownst to Rawdon or his informer, the big guns arrived with Virginia's artillerymen before the attack. Greene thus averted disastrous defeat and the loss of the Southern campaign. Afterwards, he said, "We fight, get beat, rise and fight again" (→Sept. 8).

Propaganda war continues, the pen struggling to prove its might against the sword. A British call to arms lampoons the Americans and their allies.

Articles of Confederation in effect after Maryland's ratification

John Dickinson, drafted articles.

Philadelphia, March 2

A disgusted politician once remarked: "Maryland has seldom done anything in good grace. She's always been a forward hussy." Again the state delayed while her politicians and private interests bickered. But at last, Maryland has ratified the Articles of Confederation, the last state in the union to do so. As a result, yesterday Congress proclaimed the articles in effect.

The state, controlled by land speculators, had been blocking ratification because of a dispute with Virginia. The latter held land claims to Western areas. Maryland's leaders sought a congressional pledge that the lands would be nationalized, giving speculators hope of getting control of the disputed property. Chevalier de La Luzerne, a lobbyist for ratification, persuaded Maryland's senators that Congress would acknowledge the claims if they ratified the articles. He also eased security worries, pledging that the articles would assure protection against British naval raids from Chesapeake Bay.

Under provisions of the articles, drafted by John Dickinson, there is a "perpetual union" between the states, which, however, remain sovereign, retaining every right not expressly ceded to the central government. The document also gives Congress the power to control national and international affairs.

Today, Congress officially becomes: The United States in Congress Assembled (→ Jan. 24, 1785).

Spanish settlement named Los Angeles

Los Angeles, Sept. 4

The tiny village near San Gabriel has been named Los Angeles by the local Spanish authorities. It was originally settled by a group of 46 men and women. Of these, just two were of Spanish descent, while the rest were either Indians or mulattoes. Los Angeles, unlike most of the towns in Spanish California, is a secular community and it has no resident Catholic monks or friars. The people of the settlement are totally dependent on several nearby missions for their religious needs. The new community is to be ruled by Governor Felipe de Neve. He, in turn, will be under Viceroy Martin de Mayorga.

Battle cuts British hold on South Carolina

Eutaw Springs, S.C., Sept. 8

General Nathanael Greene has once again lost the field in retreat while inflicting serious damage on the British Southern Army. With a force of 2,200 men, Greene attacked the British camp here, taking Lieutenant Colonel Alexander Stewart by suprise. When Stewart learned of the attack, he sent troops out to meet the approaching American army. As the battle progressed, the British were driven back into their camp, and finally took position in a brick house near Eutaw Creek. From this secured base, the British rallied, forcing the Americans to retreat from the field. Although the brick house was a crucial element in the British victory, American soldiers were said to have been significantly distracted by the supplies they came upon in the British camp.

Some 375 American casualties were reported by General Greene, including 139 men killed, 17 of them officers. Stewart is said to have lost 693 men, including 85 killed and about 600 missing or wounded.

The battle was well fought by both sides, but it is clear that Greene has struck a devastating blow to Britain's Southern Army, even in defeat.

General Greene, on white horse, directs the strategic victory at Eutaw Springs.

British relinquish all of West Florida

Pensacola, West Florida, May 10

British forces surrendered Pensacola to the troops of Bernardo de Galvez today, placing all of West Florida in Spanish hands. The formal surrender came after a two-and-a-half-month siege of the English garrison. Many in the garrison were Indians. Greatly outnumbering the British, Galvez had 2,600 men and a fleet of ships from Havana. He seized Mobile last year. West Florida includes all of the lands east of the Mississippi with the exception of New Orleans.

Jefferson is cleared

Virginia, Dec. 12

Thomas Jefferson was exonerated today of charges that as Governor he failed to provide military preparation in Virginia. A state assembly committee investigated Jefferson because of an incident this year. The Governor and his guests, including some legislators, were ambushed at Jefferson's home, Monticello. A British raid startled the party, but all escaped uninjured. Political foes of the Governor felt he was not prepared for such a crisis and accused him of cowardice. Jefferson beat the charges convincingly, but his foes keep circulating rumors that he is a coward.

Minister of finance plans central bank

Philadelphia, Dec. 31

Robert Morris, America's minister of finance, today announced plans to establish a central or national bank. The bank, which is designed to bring economic stability to the nation, would be created by Congress and headed by a manager appointed by it. To be called the Bank of North America, it will provide the means "of saving the liberties, lives, and property of the virtuous part of America," Morris explained. While leading men such as George Washington and Alexander Hamilton support the bank, there is much opposition among states' rights advocates (→ May 28, 1784).

Morris, financier of the Revolution.

3ritish surrender to United States at Yorktown

ast act of the drama. The Americans (right) and the French flank the leading actors in John Trumbull's "Surrender of Cornwallis at Yorktown" (1820).

orktown, Virginia, Oct. 19
British and German troops, ıgered and dejected by defeat, arched sullenly out of their en- ımpment in Yorktown early this ternoon. Quite appropriately, a ınd was playing a tune entitled *he World Turned Upside Down.* he victory of Commander-in- hief George Washington could ery well mean the end of the war.)h God!" exclaimed Prime Min- ter Lord North when he heard the ews. "It is all over."

The royal troops under the com- and of General Lord Cornwallis ere forced to march through two ılumns of French and American ıldiers. Cornwallis had issued ost of his men flashy new uni- rms, but the bright colors failed dispel their gloom. Some ap- eared to be drunk, and most of the ritish were "disorderly and unsoldierly," in the words of one American. "Their step was irregular, and their ranks frequently broken." When ordered to surrender their weapons, many of them started "throwing their arms on the pile with violence, as if determined to render them useless." The victorious Americans, wearing tattered uniforms, "exhibited an erect soldierly air, and every countenance beamed with satisfaction and joy."

The victory by Washington added to his reputation as a military genius, and stories from Yorktown can only enhance his reputation. Today, his admirers noted, Washington dictated the terms of surrender, even though he knew British reinforcements were on the way.

Washington's original intention was to attack the forces of General Sir Henry Clinton at New York. He abandoned the plan after realizing he was badly outnumbered. Upon learning that French warships under the command of Comte Francois de Grasse were sailing from the West Indies for the Chesapeake – to prevent a British escape by sea – Washington outsmarted Clinton and rushed to Virginia.

Cornwallis abandoned his outer defenses with scarcely a fight on September 30. The Americans solidified their position by digging trenches and moving in heavy guns. Their mortar and artillery fire was devastatingly accurate. One British officer spoke fearfully of "the noise and thundering of the cannon and the distressing cries of the wounded." British resistance was surprisingly weak. "The enemy seems embarrassed and confused," an American colonel said. "Their fire seems feeble." As British defenses crumbled, the Americans and French, accompanied by the Marquis de Lafayette, mounted an assault on two major enemy fortifications. The French crashed over the top of one redoubt within half an hour. The Americans, "advancing with drums beating and loud huzzas," seized the other earthwork later. Cornwallis realized the cause was lost. Last night, he tried to retreat across the river to Gloucester. A storm made the crossing impossible.

This morning, pleading illness, Cornwallis sent General O'Hara to surrender. O'Hara offered his sword to Comte de Rochambeau, commander of the French forces, who directed him to Washington, who in turn directed him to General Lincoln, who had been humiliated by the British at the Battle of Charleston. Lincoln accepted the sword (→ Jan. 5, 1782).

1782

North Carolina, Jan. 5. Putting into effect their plan to withdraw from all American cities, British forces begin by evacuating Wilmington.

London, Feb. 27. Parliament repudiates Lord North's ministry, voting to abandon further prosecution of American war (→March 5).

London, March 5. Parliament passes bill authorizing crown to seek peace with United States (→Nov. 10).

America, July 4. Alexander Hamilton, writing as "The Continentalist," advocates a strong central government.

America, Aug. 7. Badge of Military Merit, known as Purple Heart, established by George Washington.

Bryan Station, Kentucky, Aug. 15. British and Indians launch major attack on Americans.

Virginia, Sept. 6. Thomas Jefferson's wife, Martha, dies, [pushing him back into public service] (→June 1783).

Philadelphia, Oct. 18. Congressional legislation gives government postal monopoly.

London, Nov. 10. King George III remarks: "I cannot conclude without mentioning how sensibly I feel the dismemberment of America from this empire . . ." (→30).

Philadelphia, November. Alexander Hamilton enters Continental Congress.

Philadelphia, Dec. 30. Congressionally appointed court awards Wyoming Valley to Pennsylvania, not Connecticut.

Philadelphia. First parochial school started by St. Mary's Church.

Philadelphia. Robert Aitken publishes first complete English Bible printed in U.S.

United States. As their fears mount, loyalists begin to leave the country, most heading for Canada (→Dec. 31, 1783).

Virginia. Legislature makes it legal for any man "to emancipate and set free his slaves."

New England. Use of the scarlet letter "A" to identify adulterers is discontinued.

United States. Thomas Jefferson writes in his *Notes on Virginia* of the British Empire: "The sun of her glory is fast descending to the horizon."

London. Crevecoeur's *Letters from an American Farmer* asks: "What is an American, this new man?"→

Peace accord drawn up

"American Commissioners of the Peace Negotiations . . ." Benjamin West did not finish this painting because British negotiators refused to pose for it.

Paris, Nov. 30

Following several months of negotiations, a preliminary agreement has been drawn up here that, if ratified by both parties, will bring the war between Britain and the United States to an end.

The most notable clause is, of course, British recognition of American independence – a fact that was acknowledged back in September when the British negotiator, Richard Oswald, received from London specific authorization to treat with "the 13 United States." No less unexpected, particularly in light of Parliament's resolution of February 27 that the war should no longer be prosecuted, is the clause providing for the withdrawal of British troops.

Other provisions fix the boundary between the United States and Canada, and confirm the right of New Englanders to use the fishing banks off the coasts of Newfoundland and Labrador. There are also clauses that provide protection for those Americans still loyal to Britain, and for the recovery of debts that have been outstanding since the beginning of the war.

The generally favorable nature of the terms can be attributed both to the desire of the Shelburne government to end the war promptly, and to the skill of the American negotiators, Benjamin Franklin, John Jay and John Adams. As for King George III, he has remarked: "I should be miserable indeed if I did not feel that no blame . . . can be laid at my door" (→Jan. 20, 1783).

Secretary of Congress Charles Thomson's rendering of the Great Seal of the United States.

Last battle of war is fought in Ohio

Ohio, Nov. 10

George Rogers Clark avenged a bloody summer defeat today by devastating the British-backed Shawnee Indians. Clark led about 1,000 Kentucky riflemen to the Ohio territory town of Chillicothe, where the frontiersmen fired unremittingly on the Indians and destroyed their food supply. Last August, at Bryan Station, Kentucky, British agents Alexander McKee and William Caldwell raided the Kentuckians. The frontiersmen gathered forces, pursued the enemy, then engaged them in a vicious clash that took 80 American lives. More men would have been lost had Colonel Daniel Boone not alerted them to danger from the rear. But Clark retaliated today in what appears to have been the war's last land battle.

Clark, after a J.W. Jarvis painting.

French troops leave; U.S. ties strained

Boston, Dec. 24

As the first French troops to return home began embarking here today, hopes were expressed that feelings of warmth and friendship will replace the chill that has recently developed in French-American diplomatic relations.

The rift, if it can be called that, stems from French resentment at being excluded from the peace negotiations recently concluded in Paris between American and British diplomats. Congress had instructed its commissioners to work closely with the French Foreign Ministry. Benjamin Franklin was willing to comply, but John Jay, who suspected the French of wanting to reward Spain with American territory east of the Mississippi, insisted on dealing independently. In this he was supported by John Adams.

Since the conclusion of the negotiations, however, a tactful message sent by the diplomatic Franklin has done much to smooth some ruffled French feathers.

Holland recognizes U.S. independence

The Hague, Netherlands, Oct. 8

John Adams, minister plenipotentiary to The Netherlands and one of the peace commissioners now working in Europe, today signed a treaty of friendship and commerce with the Dutch. The accord follows months of negotiations here and caps two earlier successes.

In April, the Dutch agreed to formally recognize the United States. And in June, Adams obtained from Dutch bankers a $2 million loan that he had worked on for two years. With this loan, Holland has given the United States an important measure of financial independence to match its political independence. The loan also points up the close trading partnership that developed with the Dutch during the war.

Village is destroyed by Seneca Indians

Hannastown, Penn., July 13

This frontier village is in ashes after an attack by a force of 100 Senecas and 60 Canadian Rangers under the command of Chief Guyasuta. The attackers, who sailed down the Allegheny River in canoes, were spotted in the woods. Some 60 villagers retreated to a stockade and tried to defend it, but they had only nine working rifles. The Senecas set the town afire and by dawn they had vanished.

Joseph Brant, British ally, has renounced war and is now in Canada. Portrait by Gilbert Stuart.

Swamp Fox has staged his last ambush

The Swamp Fox, in his own habitat, invites a British general to share his meal.

South Carolina, December

Francis Marion has disbanded his troops, praising them for their contributions and ending his tenure as a war leader famous for his best weapon – the surprise attack. Marion, known in the field as the Swamp Fox for his tactic of ambushing from the marshes in the South, never operated with a force of more than 70 men, and sometimes with as few as 20.

A small, quiet man of Huguenot descent, Marion could be quick and relentless. After organized resistance against the British in South Carolina ended, Marion and his men took part in skirmishes at such places as Great Savannah, Blue Savannah, Tearcoat Swamp, Black Mingo and Halfway Swamp. Legend has it that the Swamp Fox and his men never camped more than two nights in the same place.

Nathanael Greene, writing Marion about his fortitude in the South, observed: "Certain it is no man has a better claim to the public thanks or is more generally admired than you are . . . Surrounded on every side with a superior force, hunted from every quarter with veteran troops, you have found means to elude all their attempts, and to keep alive the expiring hopes of an oppressed militia."

Revolution: up to 10,000 Negroes fought

Virginia, Autumn

Thomas Jefferson recently urged the Virginia legislature to permit slaveholders to free their slaves. He and others who favor such a release say that moral arguments aside, there is a sound, practical reason for their position. Since the Revolution began, they say, free Negroes have performed brilliantly for the colonial cause. Since 1775, it has been estimated that up to 10,000 Negroes have served either in the Continental Army or in the colonial militias. For the most part, the slaves joined the army to obtain their liberty.

In fact, in one Connecticut regiment, many of the Negroes adopted names quite fitting to their struggle. A review of the regimental rolls showed 48 Negroes with names such as Pomp and Jeffrey Liberty as well as Dick, Prinnis, Cuff, Ned and Jube Freedom.

The majority of the former slaves served as privates in the army or as seamen in the navy. A substantial number, say those who favor their being freed, saw heavy combat, and most fought with courage and determination. Interestingly, Negro sailors are said to enjoy greater equality than the former slaves in the army (→ June 13, 1783).

Book asks, "What Is an American?"

London

Praise for America comes from the author Hector St. John Crevecoeur, a French nobleman who ran a farm in New York for years before returning in 1780 to France, where he has been writing about life in America. A London firm has just released 12 of his essays under the title *Letters From an American Farmer, Describing Certain Provincial Situations, Manners, and Customs, and Conveying Some Idea of the State of the People of North America*. In the third of his essays, *What Is an American?*, Crevecoeur says the new nation - "the most perfect society existing in the world" – is unique for its blend of people "melted into a new race of men, whose labors and posterity will one day cause great changes in the world."

Two more missions

San Diego, California, Apr. 21

Spain's Franciscan Order established two additional missions in California this week. The mission of San Buenaventura was founded by Father Junipero Serra, while Governor Felipe de Neve sponsored the mission at Santa Barbara. Both missions are situated near the Santa Barbara Channel, about halfway between San Diego to the south and San Francisco to the north.

"The Skater," Gilbert Stuart's latest, has won praise in London.

1783

Europe, Jan. 20. Preliminary articles of peace are signed, ending hostilities between Spain and Britain and France and Britain (→Feb. 4).

Spain, Feb. 3. Spain recognizes U.S. independence. [Sweden and Denmark follow suit later in month.]

London, Feb. 4. England officially proclaims end to hostilities in America (→Apr. 11).

Newburgh, New York, March 15. Washington meets rebellious officers, promising redress of grievances (→June 17).

Philadelphia, Apr. 11. After receiving copy of provisional treaty on March 13, Congress proclaims formal end to hostilities with Britain (→Sept. 3).

Alabama, Apr. 15. Alabama becomes part of United States as British relinquish all territory east of Mississippi except Florida.

Saratoga, New York, June 13. "The Black Regiment" is disbanded.

Virginia, June. Jefferson elected delegate to Congress.

United States, September. Benjamin Franklin, writing to Josiah Quincy: "May we never see another war! For in my opinion there never was a good war or a bad peace."

New York City, Nov. 25. Last British troops leave docks of New York City; Generals Washington, Clinton enter city (→Dec. 23).

United States, December. Robert R. Livingston resigns as secretary for foreign affairs (→May 7, 1784).

New York City. Alexander Hamilton opens law practice at 58 Wall Street.

Woodbury, Connecticut. Dr. Samuel Seabury elected first Epscopal bishop in America.

United States. Between 1702 and 1783, Society for the Propagation of the Gospel in Foreign Parts has founded 340 missions in colonies.

Florida. *East Florida Gazette*, first newspaper here, prints "extra" to announce British defeat in Revolution.

Maryland. State prohibits slave trade, by now banned in all Northern states.

United States. Lafayette proposes to Washington they buy an estate with freed Negroes as tenants to show feasibility of emancipation; Washington praises idea [Lafayette later carries it out alone].

About 100,000 Tories emigrate from U.S.

Starting over: Tories draw lots for land in Canada. Drawing by C.W. Jefferys.

New York City, Dec. 31

Although no precise record of their numbers has been kept, it is estimated that up to 100,000 loyalists will have left America by the end of this year. Some, such as those who left for Halifax with Lord Howe's fleet when he evacuated Boston in March 1776, have been gone for years. Others left during the course of the war. But it is only in the last few months that the mass departure has taken place.

A few have gone to England, but the vast majority have settled in Nova Scotia and other parts of Canada, where land grants are being made available. The Bahamas and other parts of the West Indies have also received large numbers.

Apart from such obvious cases as members of the Anglican clergy and former royal officials, loyalists belong to no particular group or class, and include back-country farmers as well as lawyers, merchants and great landowners. In New York, New Jersey, Georgia and Pennsylvania, they probably constituted a majority of the population. During the Revolution, most of them did no more than sympathize with the British; but those who took an active part in the fighting, enlisting in such regiments as Butler's Tory Rangers or the Tarleton British Legion, have little choice but to leave.

Rebellious officers promised redress

Newburgh, New York, June 17

Army officers, previously denie payment by Congress, have finall been assured of compensation. I discussions with their fellow officers at General Washington's cam here after being refused their pay the veterans suggested they meet t respond to the "coldness and seve ity" displayed by Congress. Washington denounced the officers' re bellious tactics, but he promised t help settle their grievances. Th next week Congress voted to giv officers five years' back pay. Las month, Congress also promised fu loughs, but much of the army gav up waiting and headed home. Washington wrote to Congress today i the hope of obtaining public lan for the veterans.

American English speller is published

Goshen, New York

Americans no longer must co form to the rules favored by Britis spelling books. Noah Webster, 25-year-old Yale graduate who no teaches school here in Goshen, ha just released *The American-Spe ling Book*, the first volume of th projected work *A Grammatical In stitute of the English Languag* The illustrated Webster speller i meant for American classrooms. I opening sentence declares: "N man may put off the law of God.'

First daily paper in America is born

Philadelphia, May 30

For the first time, Americans can keep up with events on a daily basis, thanks to Benjamin Towne, publisher of the *Pennsylvania Evening Post*, who has converted the newspaper from a thrice-weekly into a daily. The *Post* was born on January 24, 1775, when Towne started it in opposition to the Tory *Ledger*. Since then, Towne has had a history of switching allegiances. When the redcoats seized Philadelphia, he became a royalist. When they left, he resumed his Whig sympathies.

Negro woman was serving as soldier

Boston, October

Robert Shirtliffe was discharged from a Massachusetts regiment this month. There would be nothing unusual about such a release except for the fact that "Robert" is actually a Negro woman named Deborah Sampson. She served in the Continental Army for three years and was wounded by both sword and gun. General Washington discharged her with kind words and sent her enough money to "bear her expenses to some place where she might find a home."

Father Serra makes first American wine

California, Autumn

The Spanish Franciscan pries Junipero Serra, founder of severa California missions over the las decade, has succeeded in makin good wine from cuttings brough over from Spain and planted at th San Juan Capistrano mission. Th cuttings are said to have been sen to California aboard the San An tonio in 1778 and produced the first harvest last year. This success ful propagation of a European var etal grape may mean a promisin future for wine-making in the Wes

Treaty of Paris signed, formally ends 8-year war

Paris, Sept. 3

Following conclusion of a preliminary accord between the Dutch and British, the way has been cleared for today's ceremony at which representatives of the United States, England, Spain, France and The Netherlands will sign a series of treaties formally ending the war.

Known collectively as the Treaty of Paris, the various documents do no more than confirm the provisional agreements already reached over the last year in a series of bilateral negotiations. Thus it has already been agreed between Britain and Spain that the Bahamas and Gibraltar will be returned to Britain, and East and West Florida are to go to Spain. Spanish rule over all lands west of the Mississippi River and south of the 31st parallel has also been agreed upon by all parties, which leaves Spain in control of by far the greatest amount of territory on the continent of North America.

By contrast, France, whose aid to the United States was so vital in winning the war, gets very little – some minor possessions in the West Indies and the prospect of access to available American markets. But apart from the satisfaction of seeing their traditional enemy, England, defeated, the French have little to show in return for the vast debts the war has forced upon them.

The treaty confirms the agreement between the United States and Britain that was signed here last November 30 and ratified by Congress on April 15. Its terms are generally considered to be extremely favorable to the Americans. Although the claim of the United States to Canada has been rejected, the decision about the boundary between the two countries is sure to please most Americans. This will now run from the source of the St. Croix River north to "the highlands" and then along the 45th parallel to the St. Lawrence. From that point, a line is drawn midway through the St. Lawrence and the Great Lakes to the northwest corner of the Lake of the Woods, and from there "due west" to the source of the Mississippi River.

The new boundary thus hands over to the United States the vast territory west of the Ohio River. It is a region that has become the center of the fur trade, and therefore its cession is certain to provoke angry outcries among the traders and trappers of Canada.

The treatment of those loyal to the crown and their property is another topic likely to cause continuing complaint. Although Congress has promised to "earnestly recommend" to states that loyalists be allowed to sue for the return of confiscated property, this clause is likely to have little effect. But there have been no confiscations since hostilities came to an end, and although many loyalists are still expected to leave, the vast majority of them are undoubtedly going to stay where they are and make their own peace (→Apr. 8, 1784).

Signing of the Treaty of Paris is announced in the Jardin des Tuileries.

Taking leave of army, Washington retires

Annapolis, Maryland, Dec. 23

Appearing before the Confederation Congress today, General Washington gave the nation official notice of his retirement as commanding general of the Continental Army. The ceremony before Congress was awash in tears, according to some of those who were present.

Earlier in the month, Washington bid farewell at a private gathering of officers at Fraunces Tavern in New York. At that gathering, Washington, with tears in his eyes, embraced each man, then silently strode out of the room. Now, after nine years of military service, he can look forward to spending the remainder of his life on the family plantation at Mount Vernon.

He leaves a legacy similar to that of Caesar and Hannibal. Yet he has shown none of their pomposity. According to a French officer who had served with him, "He is a foe to ostentation and to vainglory ... He does not seem to estimate himself at his true worth." But then, many have forgotten that he was not really a soldier by profession. It was fate that propelled him into that role, which he played with classic success. Now, with the coming of peace and American independence, he can return to his preferred life, that of a gentleman farmer.

After his speech before Congress today, George Washington went home to Mount Vernon, where there were candles in the windows, and where his wife, Martha, awaited him in the doorway.

New York, December. *American warships fire a last salute to their wartime commander-in-chief as he leaves New York. Painting by C.M. Cooke.*

"General Washington Resigning His Commission" (1824) by John Trumbull.

1784

New York City, Feb. 22. Captain John Green sails for China on Empress of China, marking start of trade with East (→ May 1785).

England, Apr. 8. Canadian Governor General Haldimand receives word that British troops will remain on Great Lakes until Americans honor Treaty of Paris (→ Feb. 28, 1786).

United States, May 7. John Jay named secretary for foreign affairs.

Annapolis, Maryland, May 28. Congress replaces position of Treasury superintendent with Treasury Board, made up of Samuel Osgood and Walter Livingston (→ July).

Annapolis, Maryland, July. Arthur Lee is third commissioner of Treasury Board (→ Sept. 1786).

China, Aug. 30. Captain John Green reaches Canton.

United States, Sept. 1. Washington begins tour of West to assess feasibility of land development.

Philadelphia, Sept. 21. *Packet and Daily*, first successful daily publication in America, puts out first issue.

United States. Economic depression begins.

Litchfield, Connecticut. Judge Tapping Reeve opens first law school, the Litchfield Law School.

Clarkville, Michigan. First American settlement established on north bank of Ohio River.

United States. Ethan Allen publishes *Reason, the Only Oracle of Man*; first anti-Christian book published in America.

United States. Alexander Hamilton writes series of newspaper articles, under pseudonym of "Phocion," defending fair treatment of Tories.

Philadelphia. English painter Robert Edge Pine arrives with cast of Venus de Milo statue; it is kept in a case because of its nudity.

DEATHS

Monterey, California. Franciscan Father Junipero Serra, founded nine missions in West (*Dec. 24, 1713).

United States Phillis Wheatley, African-born slave-turned-poet, first published at 14 (*1753).

War aide Kosciusko returns to Poland

Philadelphia

General Thaddeus Kosciusko, the military engineer who provided invaluable assistance in several campaigns of the Revolution, has returned to his native Poland. After the war, Congress, in appreciation of his help, made Kosciusko an American citizen and gave him the rank of brigadier general in the United States Army. Kosciusko, trained in military academies in Warsaw and Paris, came to America to join the fight for independence. In 1777, his assistance to General Horatio Gates was a key factor in the success of the Battle of Saratoga. During two years working on the West Point fortifications, Kosciusko became engineering corps chief. He then served under General Nathanael Greene in the Southern campaign, and organized a blockade of Charleston, South Carolina.

Brigadier General Kosciusko.

Lafayette and Washington at Mt. Vernon

The war's postmortem at Mount Vernon. After a painting by Thomas Rossiter.

Mount Vernon, Virginia, December

Conditions are gradually returning to normal following the autumn visit of the Marquis de Lafayette. A French general of the highest caliber, Lafayette spent several days on the plantation of former General Washington, with whom he served during some of the hardest years of the Revolutionary War. The nobleman from France originally enlisted to fight the English; he never claimed to have joined the struggle for any other reason. However, during the war, he developed a respect for the revolutionary ideals of liberty and freedom. And by war's end, he had become a full-fledged advocate of the Declaration of Independence as penned by Jefferson and pursued by Washington.

Lafayette was so closely connected to the French court that when he came to America and was made a major general in the Continental Army, the English issued an official diplomatic protest. Only 20 years old at the time, Lafayette served General Washington in some of the war's most crucial campaigns. One can only speculate as to what these old friends may have discussed here at Mount Vernon, but the visit is almost certain to have further cemented the French-American alliance of 1778.

Ben prefers turkey as the national bird

Philadelphia, Jan. 26

Benjamin Franklin declared today that he is irrevocably opposed to the adoption of the American bald eagle as the symbolic national bird of the United States. Instead, Franklin proposed that the turkey have the honor. Franklin said that the eagle "is a bird of bad moral character . . . and often very lousy. The turkey is a much more respectable bird, and withal a true original native of America."

Madison advocates church-state division

Virginia, Dec. 24

A pamphlet by James Madison entitled *Remonstrances Against Religious Assessments* was issued today in which he not only argues against a system where all Protestant teachers of religion receive financial support from the government, but also against any state support for religion.

The arguments are brilliant and well written, as one has come to expect of Madison. Most important is his argument that religion cannot be coerced, that it inheres within the human conscience. One cannot be forced to believe something, he says, just because another tells him to; one's obligations to the "Governor of the Universe" precede one's obligations to civil society. As Madison argues, "no man's right (in religion) is abridged by the institution of Civil Society and that Religion is wholly exempt from its cognizance." Madison thus arrays himself against such men as Patrick Henry and Richard Henry Lee. The debate on this issue seems to get livelier all the time.

Congress to create 10 states in West

Annapolis, Maryland, Apr. 23

If all goes according to Thomas Jefferson's plan, the Western territories will soon have names like Cherronesus, Michigania, Saratoga and Polypotamia. Today's Congressional Land Ordinance, which was drafted by Jefferson, names 10 new states to be created from the land ceded to the government by New York, Connecticut and, most recently, Virginia. But it provides for a grand total of 16 after other Southern states have similarly ceded their Western claims. The vast new frontier ranges from Florida to Canada and from Pennsylvania to the Mississippi River. New states would be rectangular units divided along lines of latitude and longitude. Jefferson also proposed that slavery be banned in the Northwest after 1800, but this was narrowly defeated in Congress (→May 20, 1785).

Journal out to win women readers

Boston, May

American women can now enjoy a journal written, in part, for them. Editors Job Weeden and William Barrett have put out the first issue of *Gentlemen and Ladies' Country Magazine*. The inaugural number offers *Advice to a Young Lady Concerning Marriage*, along with other useful tips. The journal hopes to spur a lively correspondence from all its readers, but especially from those wielding "the Female Pen."

King's College to reopen as Columbia

New York City

King's College, named for King George II, is to reopen as Columbia College. The school was founded in 1754 on a grant from the King, and its first president, the Rev. Samuel Johnson, held classes in the Trinity Church schoolhouse. His successor, Myles Cooper, expanded the college, adding a medical school and hospital. Cooper, an ardent loyalist, closed the school when the rebellion began and fled to England.

State of Frankland formed near Carolina

Frontier living: A homestead in west North Carolina, now called Frankland.

Frankland, Dec. 14

Since last June, when North Carolina passed a resolution ceding its Western territories to Congress, three Western counties decided that they would create their own state. The new state, called Frankland, is an attempt by residents of the area to govern themselves and to exert control over their land and how it is apportioned. John Sevier is serving as the Governor. Frankland has petitioned Congress to recognize the region as a state under a temporary government. However, the North Carolina Assembly was displeased by Frankland's divisive action and today revoked the June resolution before Congress could accept the cession (→Nov. 28, 1785).

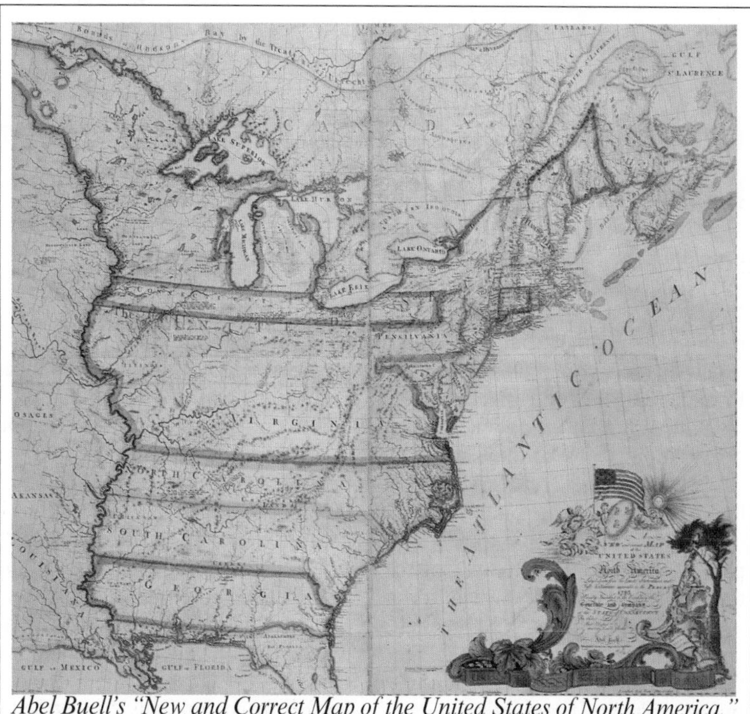

Abel Buell's "New and Correct Map of the United States of North America."

Moving experience for congressmen

New Jersey, December

In what may have been an attempt not to wear out its welcome, Congress has met in Philadelphia, Princeton, Annapolis and Trenton, all in a little over a year, and now it will head for New York before it settles on a spot on the Delaware River. After leaving Philadelphia in the face of angry army mutineers demanding payment, Congress made its home in Princeton last year from June through November, although many representatives found the town provincial and often did not show up for sessions. Annapolis was the next capital, through this August. While sitting in Trenton, Congress appointed a commission to establish a federal district on land on the Delaware River. During the interim, Congress will meet in its last capital this year, New York (→Jan. 11, 1785).

Methodists sever ties with Anglicans

Baltimore, Maryland, Dec. 27

At a conference over the Christmas holidays here, the Methodists in the United States succeeded in completely separating themselves from the Church of England. The bishops of the Methodist Episcopal Church, Thomas Coke and Francis Asbury, were consecrated and the conference adopted a form of discipline, liturgy and articles of faith that John Wesley developed for the American church.

Russia founds first colony in Alaska

St. Petersburg, Autumn

The Russian government has announced that it is establishing its first colony in North America. The first settlers were sent to the small island of Kodiak in September. Kodiak, situated in the Gulf of Alaska and only a few miles from the Aleutian Islands, has been inhabited by many huge bears but only a small group of Eskimos. American diplomats have yet to determine why the Russians have started the colony.

1785

New York City, Jan. 11. Congress convenes in nation's temporary capital (→Sept. 13, 1788).

New York City, Jan. 24. James Madison of Virginia named to head committee designed to persuade states to give up power to central government (→July 11).

New York City, Feb. 24. Congress names John Adams minister to Britain.

New York City, March 8. Henry Knox is named to fill post of secretary of war.

United States, June 17. Thomas Jefferson writes to James Monroe about United States: "its soul, its climate, its equality, its liberty, laws, people, and manners. My God! how little do my countrymen know what precious blessings they are in possession of, and which no other people on earth enjoy!"

United States, July 26. Jefferson proposes coinage system based on Spanish milled dollar.

United States, Aug. 7. James Madison writes to James Monroe on trade systems: "A perfect system is the system which would be my choice."

United States, Sept. 17. Constitutional Convention approves three clauses protesting slavery.

Philadelphia. The Act for the Prevention of Vice and Immorality outlaws theater and opera in city.

New York. State makes slavery illegal.

Virginia. Primogeniture abolished, due to efforts of Thomas Jefferson.

Virginia. Little River Turnpike is built; first such roadway in United States.

Pennsylvania. Legislature challenges legitimacy of Bank of North America.

Kentucky. First lawsuit against Daniel Boone begins over allegedly forged land tract entries.

London. Minister John Adams to King George III, "I must avow to your Majesty I have no attachment but to my own country."

Falmouth, Maine. First newspaper in Maine, *Falmouth Gazette*, established for expressed purpose of promoting separation from Massachusetts.

East Dorset, Vermont. Isaac Underhill digs nation's first marble quarry.

Jefferson takes Franklin's post in France

New York City, March 10

Following last month's decision to name John Adams minister to Britain, Congress today made another diplomatic appointment of critical importance: Thomas Jefferson is to replace Benjamin Franklin as minister to France.

Though the difficulties facing Adams in London are formidable, Jefferson has perhaps the greater challenge, for he is to replace a man who has won a unique place in the hearts of people in a nation where he has lived for the last seven years. Admired for the simplicity of his dress (his coonskin cap became his trademark) amid the pomp of the court of Louis XVI, Franklin was as warmly welcomed by philosophers as by the ladies, with whom he was very popular.

During the American Revolution, he worked tirelessly on his country's behalf, constantly prodding France into outright support for the American cause. "Our firm connection with France," he has said, "gives us weight with England, and respect throughout Europe." Jefferson shares this view, so there will be no change in policy; but Jefferson will not find it easy to escape Franklin's shadow.

Benjamin Franklin returns home to Philadelphia a hero for his part in negotiating France's decisive entry into the war. Painting by J.L.G. Ferris.

Stronger central regime is proposed

Boston, July 11

Politicians in Massachussetts formally added their voices today to the growing consensus that there is not much unity in the United States of America. The legislature recommended a new national convention to strengthen the central authority in the country. The Articles of Confederation are widely viewed as meaningless, and actions of the Congress are generally ignored. Many members do not even show up for meetings.

Supporters of a stronger central government say the biggest weakness of the Congress is its inability to levy taxes. In the words of Alexander Hamilton, "Government without revenue cannot subsist. That Government implies trust, and every government must be trusted so far as it is necessary to enable it to attain the ends for which it is instituted." Hamilton's critics point out, however, that it was a dispute over taxation by a powerful central government that led to the war with Britain.

Since independence, the states have lost their favored trading status with Britain. They have also put up barriers restricting trade with each other. Earlier this year, during a meeting at the home of George Washington, Virginia and Maryland took steps to drop barriers and promote trade (→Feb. 15, 1786).

Frankland's name becomes Franklin

Franklin, Nov. 28

The independent state just west of North Carolina is still seeking admission to the union, but it now has a new name – Franklin instead of Frankland. This year the government of Franklin expanded its territory, adding most of the Cherokee lands through the Treaty of Dumpling. Congress has not only turned down Franklin's petition to become part of the union but today signed the Treaty of Hopewell, which turns most of the Franklin land, including its capital, Greenville, back to the Cherokees. North Carolina continues to resist Franklin's request for independence (→Oct. 1788).

Most popular opera is "Poor Soldier"

New York City, December

The American Company, just back from Jamaica, has scored a big hit with *The Poor Soldier*. In fact, the opera's run of 18 performances at the John Street Theater has set a new record. The work is of a potpourri nature, a collection of today's popular tunes. But one of them, *A Rose Tree*, has become a great favorite. The troupe went into exile after Congress passed the Anti-Theater Act in 1774. With the passage this year of a similar measure by the city of Philadelphia, the only two places where theater performances are any longer legal are New York and Maryland.

Negro is pastor of white congregation

Torrington, Connecticut

Lemuel Haynes, born to an African father and a white mother, has become America's first Negro minister to a white congregation. Haynes wrote sermons at an early age, but halted his preparation for the ministry to follow Paul Revere's call to arms. After fighting at Lexington, and with Ethan Allen, he made his mark as an impassioned preacher. A parishioner recently insulted Haynes by coming to church with his hat on. Minutes into the sermon, he was so moved he "thought him the whitest man he ever saw." The hat came off, and its owner is now a man of prayer.

Land law divides U.S. into townships

United States, May 20

Gone are the days of land claims marked out by stakes and stones – at least federal ones. Congress today passed a Basic Land Ordinance regarding the "Territory Northwest of the River Ohio." The act aims at an orderly development of the land by means of scientific surveying, with boundaries based on latitude and longitude. The main unit will be the township, a rectangular area six miles square and divided into 36 lots of 640 acres each. The ordinance also provides that the sale of one lot in each township shall pay for the maintenance of public schools. A similar proposal would have used the income of a second lot to support the majority religion of white males. It was defeated. The minimum purchase is one lot. The price, $640, will prevent many individuals from buying any land (→ July 13, 1787).

Boston-New York coach trip takes 6 days

Commissions from Congress to carry mail promise a lift to stagecoach travel.

Boston

"Climb up and tuck yourself in for the long and dusty trail," is a common greeting for the stagecoach traveler. Weddale Stage Lines is now providing coach service between Boston and New York City. When a passenger boards a coach, he or she should be prepared for six days of bumpy roads along postal routes. The coaches are on the road for about 19 hours a day, stopping at inns at night. Some passengers have complained that the drivers often drink too much whiskey during the grueling trip.

A miller develops an "assembly line"

Philadelphia, Autumn

Oliver Evans of Delaware seems to have come upon a new and perhaps revolutionary method of harnessing the new water-and-steam-powered industrial technologies. Evans proposes the virtual substitution of machine power for human labor. He has instituted what he calls the "assembly line" or automatic production in place of the traditional manual processes of production at his flour mill in the tiny town of Redclay Creek, Pennsylvania. Evans has mechanized the complex craft of the miller by building a plant in which the grain is moved from the point of its unloading through its processing into finished flour by means of a number of conveyors in a continuous production line that requires no human intervention. The new idea will ease the workers' load and cut production costs, but it will mean fewer jobs.

Ship returns from China with rich cargo

New York City, May

Americans have joined Europeans in taking advantage of the lucrative China trade. Captain John Green's merchant ship, the Empress of China, has returned from Canton with a cargo of tea and silk as well as many unfamiliar goods. Green left New York 15 months ago with a varied cargo to trade with the Chinese. The Portuguese have been trading in China since the 16th century, and the Dutch, French and British are currently active there. In 1757, the Chinese, wary of the increasing influence of foreigners, restricted outside trade to the port of Canton.

A decorated ceramic bowl, only one of the boundless treasures of the Orient.

U.S. hydrogen balloon traverses channel

London, Jan. 7

The American balloonist Dr. John Jeffries today successfully flew his hydrogen-filled craft across the English Channel to the French mainland. Taking off from Dover on the eastern coast of England, Jeffries, a physician in the British army, made the 20-mile journey with the French balloon pioneer Jean Pierre Blanchard. The latter gained world renown last year when he made a solo flight from Paris to Meudon, a few miles southwest of the French capital. The journey by Jeffries and Blanchard was the first crossing of the channel by a balloon.

Harbingers of good will? Bringing Britain and France closer together.

1786

New York City, Feb. 15. Congress hears report calling for increased federal power (→ June 27).

New Jersey, Feb. 20. New Jersey challenges Congress, refusing to pay requisition.

London, Feb. 22. Tripoli demands 200,000 pounds for protection of American shipping (→ July 11).

London, Feb. 28. British tell John Adams they will not leave bases in U.S. until British creditors are repaid by American debtors (→ Nov. 19, 1794).

New Haven, May. First musical periodical published, *American Musical Magazine*.

United States, June 27. John Jay writes letter to George Washington, expressing disfavor with the way America is governed (→ Aug. 1).

United States, Aug. 1. Washington writes back to John Jay, agreeing that American system of government is in crisis (→ Sept. 14).

New York City, Aug. 8. Coinage system proposed by Jefferson adopted by Congress.

Hatfield, Massachusetts, Aug. 25. Delegates from 50 towns meet to discuss tax system, lawyers, high cost of justice, legislature and paper money (→ Sept. 20).

New Hampshire, Sept. 20. Legislature besieged by armed protesters demanding issuance of paper money (→ 26).

Springfield, Massachusetts, Sept. 26. Some 500 protesters under Daniel Shays force state Supreme Court to adjourn (→ Oct. 20).

Virginia, September. States meet for convention on economic issues (→ Jan. 14, 1790).

Cambridge, Massachusetts, Oct. 20. Samuel Williams organizes first astronomical field expedition, to Penobscot Bay in Maine.

New York City, Oct. 20. Congress authorizes General Henry Knox to raise 1,340 troops in order to suppress Shays' Rebellion (→ Dec. 26).

United States. Washington makes first serious effort to breed jackasses in U.S.

Maryland. Congress meets in Annapolis for six months, through September.

Kentucky. Daniel Boone elected legislator of territory.

Virginia. Jefferson fails to gain approval from legislature for an education bill.

New constitution sought

Annapolis State House was site of the sparsely attended convention that adjourned after endorsing Hamilton's call for a new meeting in Philadelphia.

Annapolis, Sept. 14

Alexander Hamilton, undeterred by the lack of enthusiasm in most states for a stronger central government, submitted today a revised draft resolution that calls for a new constitution to be written in Philadelphia next May. His document criticizes "important defects" in the present system and "the embarrassments which characterise the present State of our national affairs." The document was approved unanimously by a special commission in Annapolis, but the small panel has limited authority. Only 12 delegates, representing five states, bothered to attend. There were no delegates from New England or the South (→ Feb. 21, 1787).

Slaveholder Washington favors abolition

Mount Vernon, Va., Sept. 9

The tide is rising for the abolition of slavery. While most Southerners cling to the belief that enslaving Negroes is quite natural, some are calling for an end to the practice. One Virginian, George Washington, a slaveholder himself, has expressed a desire to see legislation ending slavery. Washington wrote to Robert Morris: "There is not a man living who wishes more sincerely than I do to see a plan adopted for the abolition of slavery. But there is only one proper way and effectual mode by which it can be accomplished, and that is by legislative authority." This is quite an about-face for a man who in 1779 opposed a plan to give Negro soldiers freedom lest it encourage the emancipation of all slaves.

Washington, back in civilian life, discusses the plantation with a foreman.

Depression: States issue paper money

Georgia, August

Hard times in the state of Georgi[a] have forced the issuance of pape[r] money to combat the depressio[n] that has followed the Revolution[.] Some legal authorities say that th[e] money will be ruled illegal once [a] federal constitution is adopted, bu[t] the state's authorities insist tha[t] they have no alternative. Georgi[a] has now become the seventh stat[e] to issue its own paper money. Th[e] state's legislature has already bee[n] forced to levy taxes on the people[.] In 1783, it placed a tax of 25 cent[s] on each 100 acres of land, town lo[t] or slave (→ Aug. 25).

Peale displays art and science at home

"The Artist in His Museum," sel[f-]portrait by Charles Willson Peale.

Philadelphia, July 19

From famous portraits to mam[-]moth bones to moving pictures[:] Famed Philadelphia artist Charle[s] Willson Peale announced yesterda[y] that he is augmenting his exhibitio[n] of portraits and the demonstratio[n] of a system that makes pictures ap[-]pear to move with a "Repositor[y] for Natural Curiosities." On vie[w] at Peale's home and in a buildin[g] behind the State House will be [a] broad range of artifacts, includin[g] exotic plant and animal specimens[,] fossils and minerals, as well as th[e] portraits of Revolutionary heroes[.] Peale says his aim is "to please an[d] entertain the public."

U.S. pays Morocco to end pirate raids

Morocco, July 11

Morocco has agreed to stop attacking American ships, for a payment of $10,000. Although this is a positive step toward ensuring safe passage for United States merchant ships in the Mediterranean, the other Barbary States – Algiers, Tunis and Tripoli – still pose a threat. The small North African states are home to the Barbary pirates, who prey on ships in the area. The countries that want to continue trading there, such as Britain, have found it easier to pay the pirates to leave their ships alone than to fight them.

Religious freedom is voted in Virginia

Virginia, Jan. 16

Seven years after Thomas Jefferson introduced the first version, the Virginia legislature has adopted the Ordinance of Religious Freedom. The bill, introduced by James Madison, functionally disestablishes the Anglican Church. It also guarantees that no person will be molested for religious beliefs. While the bill seemed radical when it was introduced in 1779, attitudes have shifted since then. Following failure of the bill calling for religious assessments in 1784, opinion has begun to favor this measure. Its supporters constitute an odd coalition. Madison and Jefferson have allied with Baptists and Presbyterians of the Western part of the state – who were quite successful in bringing their views before the legislature.

Daniel Shays leads farmers' revolt

The rebels occupy a courthouse.

Springfield, Mass., Dec. 26

Some 1,200 farmers, armed with pitchforks and staffs, marched on the arsenal here today to protest what they termed "intolerable conditions." At the head of the insurgents, who this fall forced the state Supreme Court to adjourn, was Daniel Shays. He is a veteran of the Revolutionary War, having served "with distinction" as a captain in a Massachusetts regiment. A resident of Pelham, Shays agreed only reluctantly to be chairman of the committee of farmers. He has been described as a "poor man," a man who is unable to raise the $12 needed to pay his own debts. The demands of the farmers range from various forms of tax and debt relief to an end to imprisonment for debt to more paper money.

Discontent among the farmers escalated in July when the commerce-focused Massachusetts legislature failed to act on petitions from the debt-ridden families that were facing foreclosure on their farms and homes. Some of the states have assisted farmers and other debtors by issuing them scrip and making it legal tender for taxes and for other obligations and by enacting laws that postpone debt and mortgage collections during times of crisis.

However, in Massachusetts, the legislature is dominated by the maritime counties with little interest in agricultural difficulties, so relief measures that managed to win approval in the lower house were defeated when they came before the senate. Court judgments for delinquent debts and overdue taxes are often enforced in this state by the seizure of farms, livestock and household goods. In 1785, in the town of Worcester alone, 92 debtors were given prison sentences.

When protest meetings proved futile, the farmers took stronger steps – arming, staging county-level conventions to air grievances and preventing courts from sitting in hopes of halting further judgments for debt. John Hancock's successor as Governor, a tough merchant named James Bowdoin, acted very swiftly. He issued a proclamation to prevent unlawful assembly and called out the militia to defend the courthouse and federal arsenal (→Jan. 25, 1787).

A state divided: Fight between a Shays rebel and a government supporter.

New York sees Shakespeare and Sheridan

New York City

The American Company made theater history here recently with the first American performance of Shakespeare's *Hamlet*. It followed up with seven nights of Sheridan's *School for Scandal*, which had its premiere in England nine years ago. Another treat for those who fancy the theater is publication in New Haven of the *American Musical Magazine*, the first journal of its kind. While Philadelphia has prohibited theater, musical performances are going strong. In a concert there to benefit the sick and poor, the Urania Society gathered the most staggering force yet heard in the land – a chorus of 230 and an orchestra of 50. And in Boston, the nation's most published composer, William Billings, has come out with his fifth book, *The Suffolk Harmony*. Of special note are *Jordan*, a hymn, and *Anthem for Easter*, which is already catching on.

Strike is advertised

Philadelphia, June 2

Members of the Typography Society today announced in the *Pennsylvania Mercury and Universal Advertiser* that they are on strike. They refuse to work for less than $6 a day. It is the first time strikers in this country have advertised such an action. A union benefit was held at the home of Henry Myers to gain support for the 26 strikers. Myers believes that the publisher will yield to the workers' demands.

A spaghetti-maker

Virginia

Thomas Jefferson, minister to France, has been collecting European objects and instruments to bring home to the United States. His emissary, William Short, has returned from Italy with a macaroni machine. However, it produces unfamiliarly thin strands of macaroni (the Italians call it *spaghette*, or "little strings") from a flour-and-water dough instead of the larger, tubular macaroni Jefferson knows.

1787

Springfield, Massachusetts, Jan. 25. Daniel Shays leads 1,200 in attack on arsenal (→ March).

New York City, Feb. 21. Congress endorses move to revise Articles of Confederation (→ May).

Philadelphia, May. Dr. Benjamin Rush speaks in support of Constitutional Convention, giving added credibility to its work.

Philadelphia, June 18. Hamilton proposes strong federal government and popularly elected House of Representatives (→ 19).

Philadelphia, June 19. Constitutional Convention votes 7-3 to use Virginia Plan as model for national government (→ July 16).

Paris, July 14. Thomas Jefferson, in a letter to Edward Rutledge, writes of slavery: "This abomination must have an end. And there is a superior bench in Heaven reserved for those who hasten it."

Philadelphia, July 16. Congress accepts Connecticut Compromise: proportional representation in lower house and equal representation in Senate (→ July).

Philadelphia, September. Hamilton writes: "Take mankind in general, they are vicious, [thus] their passions may be operated upon."

Philadelphia, September. James Madison, "Father of the Constitution," synthesizes various points of contention at Constitutional Convention.

New York City, Oct. 27. First of Federalist Papers, all signed "Publius," published; a collaborative effort by Hamilton, Madison and Jay.

New York City, Nov. 22. Madison's Federalist Paper on constitutional political theory appears in *New York Daily Advertiser*.

Boston, Nov. 26. Essay, anonymously published, condemns Constitution's framers as self-interested aristocrats.

Philadelphia. August Tench Coxe hails abundance of goods available to Americans.

Beverly, Massachusetts. First cotton factory in New England established.

Philadelphia. James Madison, in debate at Constitutional Convention, asserts: "A standing army is one of the greatest mischiefs that can possibly happen."

Shays' rebellion fails

Petersham, Massachusetts, March

Shays' rebellion is over. What began on a high note last December, when insurgent farmers led by Daniel Shays marched on the Springfield arsenal after forcing the state Supreme Court to adjourn, has ended in total collapse.

Shays, a former captain in the Revolutionary War and the reluctant leader of the farmers' uprising against the commercial interests, has been indicted for treason. Facing a death sentence in Massachusetts, he has fled to Vermont.

The rebellion crumbled after 1,100 men led by Shays decided to attack the arsenal on January 1. They were met by militia forces under the command of Major General William Shepherd. The farmers, armed only with pitchforks and staffs, broke and ran after one volley was fired by Shepherd's artillery. After several minor skirmishes, General Benjamin Lincoln's militia pursued the insurgents through the winter snows to Petersham. And there, on February 4, the farmers were defeated. General Lincoln's troops took many prisoners including 14 of the rebel leaders, who have received death sentences.

The farmers have been desperate. Farm produce has been a glut on the market, taxes in Massachusetts are higher than in other regions and the farmers lack the political power to obtain relief. Although they have been totally defeated militarily, the farmers have now scored a kind of political victory because they have created a public awareness. Informed observers note that the rebellion has focused attention on the plight of the farmers and is likely to reap a harvest of legislation that will ease their problems.

Outside the arsenal at Springfield.

The measures that would be of help would include the elimination of direct taxation, the lowering of court fees and the exempting of household goods and workmen's tools from seizure to satisfy debts.

In the long run, the uprising may aid the advocates of a strong federal government. Conservatives point to the rebels as evidence that an excess of democracy leads to anarchy. George Washington was left to wonder whether "mankind, when left to themselves, are unfit for their own government" (→ June 13, 1788).

The United States gold doubloon by Ephraim Brasher, 1787. Financial matters will be a major topic at the Constitutional Convention. As yet, the government has no power to tax and seems incapable of paying debts.

Jefferson favors a revolt now and the

Paris, November 13

Unlike most American leaders Thomas Jefferson, minister to France, has lauded Shays' Rebellion. In a letter to Colonel William Stevens Smith, Jefferson wrote "God forbid we should ever be 20 years without such a rebellion .. The tree of liberty must be refreshed from time to time with the blood of patriots and tyrants." And last January 30, he wrote, in a note to his friend James Madison, "I hold it, that a little rebellion, now and then, is a good thing and as necessary in the political world as storms in the physical."

Jefferson, in Paris, has professed support for the Massachusetts rebels. Painting (1791) by C.W. Peale.

Totally free press urged by Jefferson

Paris

From abroad, Thomas Jefferson continues to comment on domestic issues, underscoring his support of a free press. "Our liberty depends on the freedom of the press, and that cannot be limited without being lost," he said in a letter to Colonel Edward Carrington this winter. In a second letter to Carrington, he wrote: "Were it left to me to decide whether we should have a government without newspapers, or newspapers without government I should not hesitate a moment to prefer the latter."

Convention shown the first steamboat

Delaware River, Aug. 11

Delegates to the Constitutional Convention were given a demonstration of a new invention today. John Fitch displayed his steam-powered boat. Fitch has harnessed James Watt's steam engine to turn six paddles, which move the boat at about three miles an hour. Chains attached to ratchet wheels convert the reciprocating motion of the steam piston rod. Fitch hopes he will be able to find financial backers so that he can step up the speed and efficiency. He claims the steamboat can change the complexion of transportation in the country.

Fitch motors his steamboat across the Delaware, carrying the American flag and members of Congress. The boat travels three miles per hour.

Shakers starting revival movement

New Lebanon, N.Y., Dec. 20

With the establishment of a community here, the Shakers are starting to experience a revival of sorts. Under the Rev. Joseph Meacham, they have tried to reduce irregularities in worship and behavior. Meacham assumed leadership upon the death of the Rev. Joseph Whittaker, who succeeded Mother Ann Lee. Meacham wants to develop an organized and growing movement by insuring that members truly give their "hands to work and hearts to God," as Mother Ann said they should.

Constitutional Convention convened

Philadelphia, July

Step by step, the convention meeting at the State House is reaching agreement on a Constitution that will serve as a legal framework for life in the United States. The meeting began 11 days behind schedule, Rhode Island is still not represented and the discussion has been frequently animated and even divisive. But the delegates are carving out a compromise that gives greater power to the central government and attempts to bridge the differences between the large states and the smaller ones.

The most controversial spokesman at the convention has undoubtedly been Alexander Hamilton, the New York lawyer and banker who favors a strong central government. At one point, he walked out in anger after fellow delegates had accused him of trying to set up an American monarchy. Hamilton also proposes a reduction in the powers of the chief executive, who would in turn appoint an executive in each state. Many delegates agree the present Congress has been impotent, but they were shocked when Hamilton said, "The people are gradually ripening in their opinion of government. They begin to be tired of an excess of democracy."

James Madison, the brilliant theorist from Virginia, concurred with Hamilton that govenment power should be divided into three separate branches. He is calling for a "national executive," a judiciary department with a "national supremacy" and a new Congress that is elected in proportion to the population of the states. Madison believes that the Congress should have two houses, a large one that is elected for a short term and a smaller one elected for a longer term. After the smaller states objected that the plan would reduce their authority in Congress, Dr. Johnson of Connecticut offered an alternative proposal. His "Connecticut Compromise" accepts Madison's idea of proportional representation in the lower house. In the other chamber each state would have an equal number of delegates. "In one branch the people ought to be represented," Johnson told the convention. "In the other, the states" (→Sept. 17).

Washington presides over the convention. Painting by Junius B. Stearns.

Congress approves a colony in Northwest

Philadelphia, July 13

Congress has passed a Northwest Ordinance in response to a petition by New Englanders who want to found a colony in that region. The act establishes government guidelines and says that the land may be developed into at least three but no more than five states. A colony can become a state once it has 60,000 free inhabitants. The new ordinance has a New England tone. It provides for religious freedom and the fair treatment of Indians, and it calls for English standards of liberty. It prohibits slavery and declares that "religion, morality and knowledge being necessary to good government and the happiness of mankind, schools and the means of education shall forever be encouraged."

Three to five states may eventually be created out of the Northwest Territory.

Constitutional Convention Proceedings

The following are highlights only of the Constitutional Convention:

May 25. Seven states have a quorum of delegates; business of convention begins 11 days late.

May 25. Robert Morris, in name of ailing Benjamin Franklin, nominates George Washington chairman; passes unanimously.

May 29. Edmund Randolph presents James Madison's bicameral plan of government, known as Virginia Plan; Charles Pinckney proposes alternative.

May 30. Convention resolves itself into committee of the whole, giving it greater speed and flexibility.

May 30. Committee supports three-branch government: legislative, judiciary and executive.

May 31. Four proposals – bicameral legislature, a popularly elected first house, second house not elected by first, and bill origination in both houses – adopted for debate.

June 2. Executive term is temporarily set at seven years.

June 4. Committee of the whole prefers single executive with veto power to be overridden by two-thirds of legislature.

June 7. John Dickinson proposes second house chosen by state legislatures; passes in committee.

June 12. Committee majority opts for three-year House term, federal salary for its members and 30-year age requirement for Senate.

June 13. After proposing Senate authority to appoint federal judges, committee reports to convention.

June 15. William Paterson, in convention, proposes unicameral plan of government, signaling small states' discontentment.

June 20. Convention seeks "Government of the United States"; Articles of Confederation abandoned.

June 21. Convention, considering committee proposals, approves of bicameral national legislature and popular election to first house.

June 22. Age requirement of 25 for House members adopted; salaries are not to be paid by the states.

June 25. Convention agrees to recommendation of Senate age requirement of 30, and empowers state legislatures to elect senators.

June 26. Delegates set Senate term at six years, forbid senators from holding other offices while serving.

June 28. Franklin, citing convention's slow progress, proposes a prayer at beginning of sessions; accepted without vote.

June 29. Resolved: Each state will not have equal voting power in lower house.

July 5. Connecticut Compromise, aimed at settling legislative representation issue, proposed.

July 12. Delegates accept James Madison's plan to set House representation according to each state's white population plus three-fifths its Negro population.

July 16. States are granted equal votes in Senate; Connecticut Compromise saves convention.

July 18. Convention agrees to executive veto power, two-thirds legislative override and a supreme judicial tribunal.

July 20. Executive to be determined by 25 electors, allocation based upon state populations; executive impeachment debate starts.

July 23. Delegates require state and federal officers to swear allegiance to national government.

"Every word of the Constitution," said James Madison, its architect, "decides a question between power and liberty." Portrait (1815) by Gilbert Stuart.

July 26. Convention recesses, ordering committee of detail, of which James Madison is a member, to draft a preliminary Constitution.

Aug. 6. Convention reconvenes; committee of detail distributes printed copies of work to delegates.

Aug. 7. Final debate begins on proposed Constitution; move by Gouverneur Morris to restrict voting to landowners defeated.

Aug. 8. Convention sets House term at two years.

Aug. 9. Delegates agree on six-year Senate term and require nine years of U.S. residency for Senate service.

Aug. 14. Convention approves fixed salary for congressmen, with members determining amount.

Aug. 16. Congress given right to tax, coin money, regulate interstate and overseas commerce; this is favorable to Northern states.

Aug. 17. Convention amends and passes provision on making war.

Aug. 20. Treason defined, based largely upon British statute law.

Aug. 22. Issue of slavery threatens to split convention; committee on the slave trade seeks compromise.

Aug. 23. Provision passes making all congressional acts, treaties pursuant to Constitution supreme law.

Aug. 25. Ban on slave trade – but only after 1808 – adopted in concession to Southern states; federal commerce regulation retained; compromise saves convention.

Aug. 28. Citizens granted universal rights regardless of state residency.

Aug. 30. Convention allows for amendment of Constitution provided two-thirds of states approve.

Sept. 6. President's term set at four years; failure to attain electoral college majority requires House vote.

Sept. 7. Provision passes requiring President to be 35 years of age and a natural-born citizen.

Convention approves United States Constitution

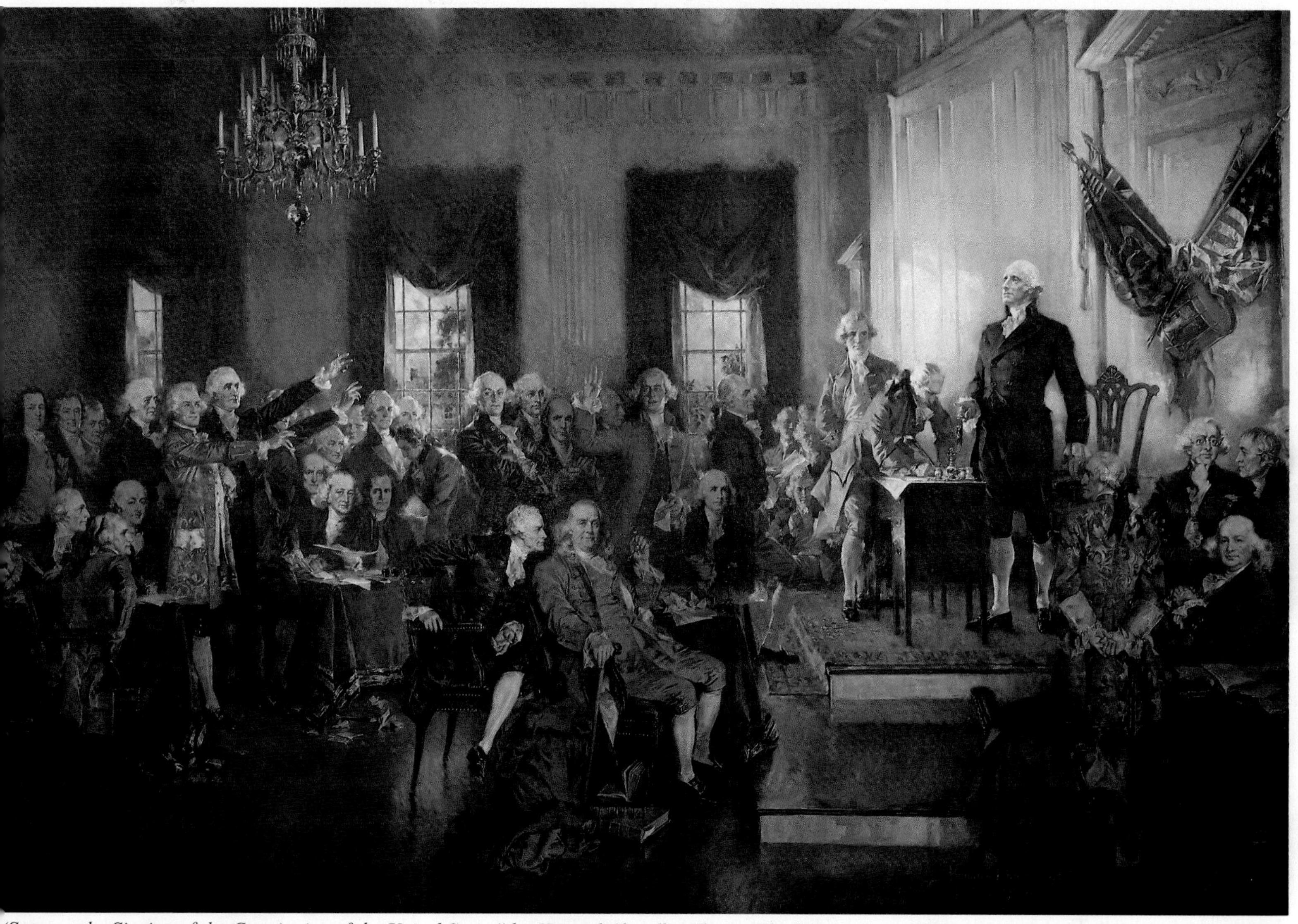

'Scene at the Signing of the Constitution of the United States" by Howard Chandler Christy. The framers forge "the supreme law of the land."

Philadelphia, Sept. 17

After weeks of occasionally tumultuous debate, a Constitution for the United States of America was approved today. Thirty-nine delegates, representing 12 of the 13 states, signed the stirring revolutionary document two days after the committee of style had approved the final wording. One of the committee's last decisions was to omit names of individual states from the document because it is not clear whether it will be ratified unanimously. After today's session, George Washington, who presided over the convention, said the delegates "adjourned to the City Tavern, dined together and took a cordial leave of each other."

Alexander Hamilton admitted that no delegate's ideas were "more remote" from the final document than his own, but he conceded graciously that the convention had taken the appropriate steps to avoid "anarchy and convulsion." Benjamin Franklin also admitted he had reservations about the Constitution, but he said, "The older I grow, the more apt I am to doubt my own judgment and pay more respect to the judgment of others."

The Constitution is described as "the supreme law of the land," but it is not totally clear who will enforce it. Power will be given to a new federal judicial system, led by a Supreme Court. On the matter of the executive branch, the delegates argued for days about the process of electing a president. Should the decision be made by the people directly, by the states or by the Congress? Ultimately it was decided that the president will be elected by electors chosen by the states.

The framers of the Constitution state quite clearly that its purpose is "to form a more perfect Union, establish Justice, insure domestic Tranquility, provide for the common defense, promote the general Welfare, and secure the blessings of Liberty to ourselves and our Posterity." Most delegates point out, however, that the real purpose of the Constitution is to regulate commerce between the states. The Northern states are generally content with the final formula, but Southern delegates fear they will suffer a competitive disadvantage. As Charles Pinckney of South Carolina put it, "The Southern states are the minority in both houses" of Congress. In one of his most brilliant speeches, James Madison urged Southerners not to be shortsighted. "As we are laying the foundation for a great empire," Madison said, "we ought to take a permanent view of the subject. " Madison's argument carried the day.

The Southerners did manage to prevail in one of the most emotional debates of the session, the argument over the abolition of slavery. Many delegates consider the practice hideous, but the convention delayed a move to outlaw it. George Mason of Virginia broke ranks with his fellow Southerners when he argued, "The poor despise labor when performed by slaves . . . Every master of slaves is born a petty tyrant. They bring the judgment of heaven upon a country" (→July 2, 1788).

The Constitution of the United States of America

Preamble

We the people of the United States, in order to form a more perfect Union, establish justice, insure domestic tranquility, provide for the common defense, promote the general welfare, and secure the blessings of liberty to ourselves and our posterity, do ordain and establish this Constitution for the United States of America.

Article I

Section 1. All legislative powers herein granted shall be vested in a Congress of the United States, which shall consist of a Senate and House of Representatives.

Section 2. The House of Representatives shall be composed of members chosen every second year by the people of the several states, and the electors in each state shall have the qualifications requisite for electors of the most numerous branch of the state legislature.

No person shall be a representative who shall not have attained to the age of twenty-five years, and been seven years a citizen of the United States, and who shall not, when elected, be an inhabitant of that state in which be shall be chosen.

Representatives and direct taxes shall be apportioned among the several states which may be included within this Union, according to their respective numbers, which shall be determined by adding to the whole number of free persons, including those bound to service for a term of years, and excluding Indians not taxed, three-fifths of all other persons. The actual enumeration shall be made within three years after the first meeting of the Congress of the United States, and within every subsequent term of ten years, in such manner as they shall by law direct. The number of representatives shall not exceed one for every thirty thousand, but each state shall have at least one representative; and until such enumeration shall be made, the state of New Hampshire shall be entitled to choose three, Massachusetts eight, Rhode Island and Providence Plantations one, Connecticut five, New York six, New Jersey four, Pennsylvania eight, Delaware one, Maryland six, Virginia ten, North Carolina five, South Carolina five, and Georgia three.

When vacancies happen in the representation from any state, the executive authority thereof shall issue writs of election to fill such vacancies.

The House of Representatives shall choose their speaker and other officers; and shall have the sole power of impeachment.

Section 3. The Senate of the United States shall be composed of two Senators from each state, chosen by the legislature thereof, for six years; and each Senator shall have one vote.

Immediately after they shall be assembled in consequence of the first election, they shall be divided as equally as may be into three classes. The seats of the Senators of the first class shall be vacated at the expiration of the second year, of the second class at the expiration of the fourth year, and of the third class at the expiration of the sixth year, so that one-third may be chosen every second year; and if vacancies happen by resignation, of otherwise, during the recess of the legislature of any state, the executive thereof may make temporary appointments until the next meeting of the legislature, which shall then fill such vacancies.

No person shall be a Senator who shall not have attained to the age of thirty years, and been nine years a citizen of the United States, and who shall not, when elected, be an inhabitant of that state for which he shall be chosen.

The Vice President of the United States shall be President of the Senate, but shall have no vote, unless they be equally divided.

The Senate shall choose their other officers and also a President pro tempore, in the absence of the Vice President, or when he shall exercise the office of President of the United States.

The Senate shall have the sole power to try all impeachments. When sitting for that purpose, they shall be on oath or affirmation. When the President of the United States is tried, the Chief Justice shall preside: And no person shall be convicted without the concurrence of two-thirds of the members present.

Judgment in cases of impeachment shall not extend further than to removal from office, and disqualification to hold and enjoy any office of honor, trust, or profit under the United States; but the party convicted shall nevertheless be liable and subject to indictment, trial, judgment, and punishment according to law.

Section 4. The times, places, and manner of holding elections for Senators and Representatives shall be prescribed in each state by the legislature thereof; but the Congress may at any time by law make or alter such regulations, except as to the places of choosing Senators.

The Congress shall assemble at least once in every year, and such meeting shall be on the first Monday in December, unless they shall by law appoint a different day.

Section 5. Each House shall be the judge of the elections, returns, and qualifications of its own members, and a majority of each shall constitute a quorum to do business; but a smaller number may adjourn from day to day, and may be authorized to compel the attendance of absent members, in such manner and under such penalties as each house may provide.

Each House may determine the rules of its proceedings, punish its members for disorderly behavior, and, with the concurrence of two-thirds, expel a member.

Each House shall keep a journal of its proceedings and from time to time publish the same, excepting such parts as may in their judgment require secrecy; and the yeas and nays of the members of either House on any question shall, at the desire of one-fifth of those present, be entered on the journal.

Neither House, during the session of Congress, shall, without the consent of the other, adjourn for more than three days, nor to any other place than that in which the two Houses shall be sitting.

Section 6. The Senators and Representatives shall receive a compensation for their services, to be ascertained by law, and paid out of the Treasury of the United States. They shall in all cases, except treason, felony, and breach of the peace, be privileged from arrest during their attendance at the session of their respective Houses, and in going to and returning from the same; and for any speech or debate in either House, they shall not be questioned in any other place.

No Senator or Representative shall, during the time for which he was elected, be appointed to any civil office under the authority of the United States, which shall have been created, or the emoluments whereof shall have been increased during such time; and no person holding any office under the United States, shall be a member of either House during his continuance in office.

Section 7. All bills for raising revenue shall originate in the House of Representatives; but the Senate may propose or concur with amendments as on other bills.

Every bill which shall have passed the House of Representatives and the Senate shall, before it become a law, be presented to the President of the United States; if he approve he shall sign it, but if not, he shall return it, with his objections, to that House in which it shall have originated, who shall enter the objections at large on their journal, and proceed to reconsider it. If, after such reconsideration, two-thirds of that House shall agree to pass the bill, it shall be sent, together with the objections, to the other House, by which it shall likewise be reconsidered, and, if approved by two-thirds of that House, it shall become a law. But in all such cases the votes of both Houses shall be determined by yeas and nays, and the names of the persons voting for and against the bill shall be entered on the journal of each House respectively. If any bill shall not be returned by the President within ten days (Sundays excepted) after it shall have been presented to him, the same shall be a law, in like manner as if he had signed it, unless the Congress by their adjournment prevent its return, in which case it shall not be a law.

Every order, resolution, or vote to which the concurrence of the Senate and House of Representatives may be necessary (except on a question of adjournment) shall be presented to the President of the United States; and before the same shall take effect, shall be approved by him, or being disapproved by him, shall be repassed by two-thirds of e Senate and House of Representatives, accord-g to the rules and limitations prescribed in the ase of a bill.

Section 8. The Congress shall have power to lay nd collect taxes, duties, imposts, and excises, to ay the debts and provide for the common defense nd general welfare of the United States; but ll duties, imposts and excises shall be uniform roughout the United States;

To borrow money on the credit of the United tates;

To regulate commerce with foreign nations, and mong the several states, and with the Indian ibes;

To establish a uniform rule of naturalization nd uniform laws on the subject of bankruptcies roughout the United States;

To coin money, regulate the value thereof, and f foreign coin, and fix the standard of weights and easures;

To provide for the punishment of counterfeiting e securities and current coin of the United tates;

To establish post offices and post roads;

To promote the progress of science and useful rts, by securing for limited times to authors and nventors the exclusive right to their respective writ-ngs and discoveries;

To constitute tribunals inferior to the Supreme Court;

To define and punish piracies and felonies com-nitted on the high seas, and offenses against the aw of nations;

To declare war, grant letters of marque and re-risal, and make rules concerning captures on land nd water;

To raise and support armies, but no appropri-tion of money to that use shall be for a longer term han two years;

To provide and maintain a navy;

To make rules for the government and regu-ation of the land and naval forces;

To provide for calling forth the militia to execute he laws of the Union, suppress insurrections, and epel invasions;

To provide for organizing, arming, and disci-lining the militia, and for governing such part of hem as may be employed in the service of the United States, reserving to the states respectively he appointment of the officers, and the authority f training the militia according to the discipline rescribed by Congress;

To exercise exclusive legislation in all cases what-oever, over such district (not exceeding ten miles quare) as may, by cession of particular states and he acceptance of Congress, become the seat of the overnment of the United States, and to exercise ike authority over all places purchased by the con-ent of the legislature of the state in which the same hall be, for the erection of forts, magazines, ar-enals, dockyards, and other needful buildings;

And to make all laws which shall be necessary nd proper for carrying into execution the fore-oing powers and all other powers vested by this Constitution in the government of the United States, or in any department or officer therof.

Section 9. The migration or importation of such persons as any of the states now existing shall think proper to admit shall not be prohibited by the Congress prior to the year 1808, but a tax or duty may be imposed on such importation, not exceeding ten dollars for each person.

The privilege of the writ of habeas corpus shall not be suspended, unless, when in cases of rebellion or invasion, the public safety may require it.

No bill of attainder or ex post facto law shall be passed.

No capitation, or other direct, tax shall be laid, unless in proportion to the census or enumeration hereinbefore directed to be taken. No tax or duty shall be laid on articles exported from any state.

No preference shall be given by any regulation of commerce or revenue to the ports of one state over those of another; nor shall vessels bound to, or from, one state be obliged to enter, clear, or pay duties in another.

No money shall be drawn from the Treasury but in consequence of appropriations made by law; and a regular statement and account of the receipts and expenditures of all public money shall be published from time to time.

No title of nobility shall be granted by the United States; and no person holding any office of profit or trust under them shall, without the consent of the Congress, accept of any present, emolument, office, or title, of any kind whatever, from any king, prince, or foreign state.

Section 10. No state shall enter into any treaty, alliance, or confederation; grant letters of marque and reprisal; coin money; emit bills of credit; make anything but gold and silver coin a tender in payment of debts; pass any bill of attainder, ex post facto law, or law impairing the obligation of contracts, or grant any title of nobility.

No state shall, without the consent of the Congress, lay any imposts or duties on imports or exports, except what may be absolutely necessary for executing its inspection laws; and the net produce of all duties and imposts, laid by any state on imports or exports, shall be for the use of the Treasury of the United States; and all such laws shall be subject to the revision and control of the Congress.

No state shall, without the consent of Congress, lay any duty of tonnage; keep troops or ships of war in time of peace; enter into any agreement or compact with another state or with a foreign power, or engage in war, unless actually invaded, or in such imminent danger as will not admit of delay.

Article II

Section 1. The executive power shall be vested in a President of the United States of America. He shall hold his office during the term of four years, and, together with the Vice President, chosen for the same term, be elected as follows:

Each state shall appoint, in such manner as the legislature thereof may direct, a number of electors, equal to the whole number of Senators and Representatives to which the state may be entitled in the Congress; but no Senator or Representative, or person holding an office of trust or profit under the United States, shall be appointed an elector.

The electors shall meet in their respective states and vote by ballot for two persons, of whom one at least shall not be an inhabitant of the same state with themselves. And they shall make a list of all the persons voted for, and, of the number of votes for each; which list they shall sign and certify, and transmit sealed to the seat of the government of the United States, directed to the President of the Senate. The President of the Senate shall, in the presence of the Senate and House of Representatives, open all the certificates, and the votes shall then be counted. The person having the greatest number of votes shall be the President, if such number be a majority of the whole number of electors appointed; and if there be more than one who have such majority, and have an equal number of votes, then the House of Representatives shall immediately choose by ballot one of them for President; and if no person have a majority, then from the five highest on the list the said House shall in like manner choose the President. But in choosing the President, the votes shall be taken by states, the representation from each state having one vote; a quorum for this purpose shall consist of a member or members from two-thirds of the states, and a majority of all the states shall be necessary to a choice. In every case, after the choice of the President, the person having the greatest number of votes of the electors shall be the Vice President. But if there should remain two or more who have equal votes, the Senate shall choose from them by ballot the vice-president. The Congress may determine the time of choosing the electors and the day on which they shall give their votes; which day shall be the same throughout the United States.

No person except a natural-born citizen, or a citizen of the United States, at the time of the adoption of this Constitution, shall be eligible to the office of President; neither shall any person be eligible to that office who shall not have attained to the age of thirty-five years, and been fourteen years a resident within the United States.

In case of the removal of the President from office, or of his death, resignation, or inability to discharge the powers and duties of the said office, the same shall devolve on the Vice President, and the Congress may by law provide for the case of removal, death, resignation, or inability, both of the President and Vice President, declaring what officer shall then act as President; and such officer shall act accordingly, until the disability be removed, or a President shall be elected.

The President shall, at stated times, receive for his services a compensation, which shall neither be increased nor diminished during the period for which he shall have been elected; and he shall not receive within that period any other emolument from the United States or any of them.

Before he enter on the execution of his office, he shall take the following oath or affirmation: "I do solemnly swear (or affirm) that I will faithfully execute the office of President of the United States, and will, to the best of my ability, preserve, protect, and defend the Constitution of the United States."

Section 2. The President shall be Commander-in-Chief of the Army and Navy of the United States, and of the militia of the several states when called into the actual service of the United States; he may require the opinion, in writing, of the principal officer in each of the executive departments upon any subject relating to the duties of their respective offices; and he shall have power to grant reprieves and pardons for offenses against the United States, except in cases of impeachment.

He shall have power, by and with the advice and consent of the Senate, to make treaties, provided two-thirds of the Senators present concur; and he shall nominate, and by and with the advice and consent of the Senate, shall appoint ambassadors, other public ministers and consuls, judges of the Supreme Court, and all other officers of the United States, whose appointments are not herein otherwise provided for, and which shall be established by law; but the Congress may by law vest the appointment of such inferior officers, as they think proper, in the President alone, in the courts of law, or in the heads of departments.

The President shall have power to fill up all vacancies that may happen during the recess of the Senate, by granting commissions which shall expire at the end of their next session.

Section 3. He shall from time to time give to the Congress information of the state of the Union, and recommend to their consideration such measures as he shall judge necessary and expedient; he may, on extraordinary occasions, convene both Houses, or either of them, and in case of disagreement between them with respect to the time of adjournment, he may adjourn them to such time as he shall think proper; he shall receive ambassadors and other public ministers; he shall take care that the laws be faithfully executed; and shall commission all the officers of the United States.

Section 4. The President, Vice President, and all civil officers of the United States shall be removed from office on impeachment for, and conviction of, treason, bribery, or other high crimes and misdemeanors.

Article III

Section 1. The judicial power of the United States shall be vested in one Supreme Court, and in such inferior courts as the Congress may from time to time ordain and establish. The judges, both of the Supreme and inferior courts, shall hold their offices during good behavior, and shall, at stated times, receive for their services a compensation which shall not be diminished during their continuance in office.

Section 2. The judicial power shall extend to all cases, in law and equity, arising under this Constitution, the laws of the United States, and treaties made, or which shall be made, under their authority; to all cases affecting ambassadors, other public ministers and consuls; to all cases of admiralty and maritime jurisdiction; to controversies to which the United States shall be a party; to controversies between two or more states; between a state and citizens of another state; between citizens of different states; between citizens of the same state claiming lands under grants of different states; and between a state, or the citizens thereof, and foreign states, citizens, or subjects.

In all cases affecting ambassadors, other public ministers, and consuls, and those in which a state shall be party, the Supreme Court shall have original jurisdiction. In all the other cases beforementioned, the Supreme Court shall have appellate jurisdiction, both as to law and fact, with such exceptions, and under such regulations, as the Congress shall make.

The trial of all crimes, except in cases of impeachment, shall be by jury; and such trial shall be held in the state where the said crimes shall have been committed; but when not committed within any state, the trial shall be at such place or places as the Congress may by law have directed.

Section 3. Treason against the United States shall consist only in levying war against them, or in adhering to their enemies, giving them aid and comfort. No person shall be convicted of treason unless on the testimony of two witnesses to the same overt act, or on confession in open court.

The Congress shall have power to declare the punishment of treason, but no attainder of treason shall work corruption of blood or forfeiture except during the life of the person attainted.

Article IV

Section 1. Full faith and credit shall be given in each state to the public acts, records, and judicial proceeding of every other state. And the Congress may by general laws prescribe the manner in which such acts, records, and proceedings shall be proved, and the effect thereof.

Section 2. The citizens of each state shall be entitled to all privileges and immunities of citizens in the several states.

A person charged in any state with treason, felony, or other crime, who shall flee from justice and be found in another state, shall, on demand of the executive authority of the state from which he fled, be delivered up to be removed to the state having jurisdiction of the crime.

No person held to service or labor in one state under the laws thereof, escaping into another, shall, in consequence of any law or regulation therein, be discharged from such service or labor, but shall be delivered up on claim of the party to whom such service or labor may be due.

Section 3. New states may be admitted by the Congress into this Union; but no new state shall be formed or erected within the jurisdiction of any other state; nor any state be formed by the junction of two or more states, or parts of states, without the consent of the legislatures of the states concerned as well as of the Congress.

The Congress shall have power to dispose of and make all needful rules and regulations respecting the territory or other property belonging to the United States; and nothing in this Constitution shall be so construed as to prejudice any claims of the United States, or of any particular State.

Section 4. The United States shall guarantee to every state in this Union a republican form of government, and shall protect each of them against invasion; and, on application of the legislature, or of the executive (when the legislature cannot be convened), against domestic violence.

Article V

The Congress, whenever two-thirds of both Houses shall deem it necessary, shall propose amendments to this Constitution, or, on the application of the legislatures of two-thirds of the several states, shall call a convention for proposing amendments, which, in either case, shall be valid, to all intents and purposes, as part of this Constitution, when ratified by the legislatures of three-fourths of the several states, or by conventions in three-fourths thereof, as the one or the other mode of ratification may be proposed by the Congress; provided that no amendment which may be made prior to the year one thousand eight hundred and eight shall in any manner affect the first and fourth clauses in the Ninth Section of the First Article; and that no state, without its consent, shall be deprived of its equal suffrage in the Senate.

Article VI

All debts contracted and engagements entered into, before the adoption of this Constitution, shall be as valid against the United States under this Constitution, as under the Confederation.

This Constitution, and the laws of the United States which shall be made in pursuance thereof; and all treaties made, or which shall be made, under the authority of the United States, shall be the supreme law of the land; and the judges in every state shall be bound thereby, anything in the constitution or laws of any state to the contrary notwithstanding.

The Senators and Representatives before mentioned, and the members of the several state legislatures, and all executive and judicial officers, both of the United States and of the several states, shall be bound by oath or affirmation to support this Constitution; but no religious test shall ever be required as a qualification to any office or public trust under the United States.

Article VII

The ratification of the conventions of nine states shall be sufficient for the establishment of this Constitution between the states so ratifying the same.

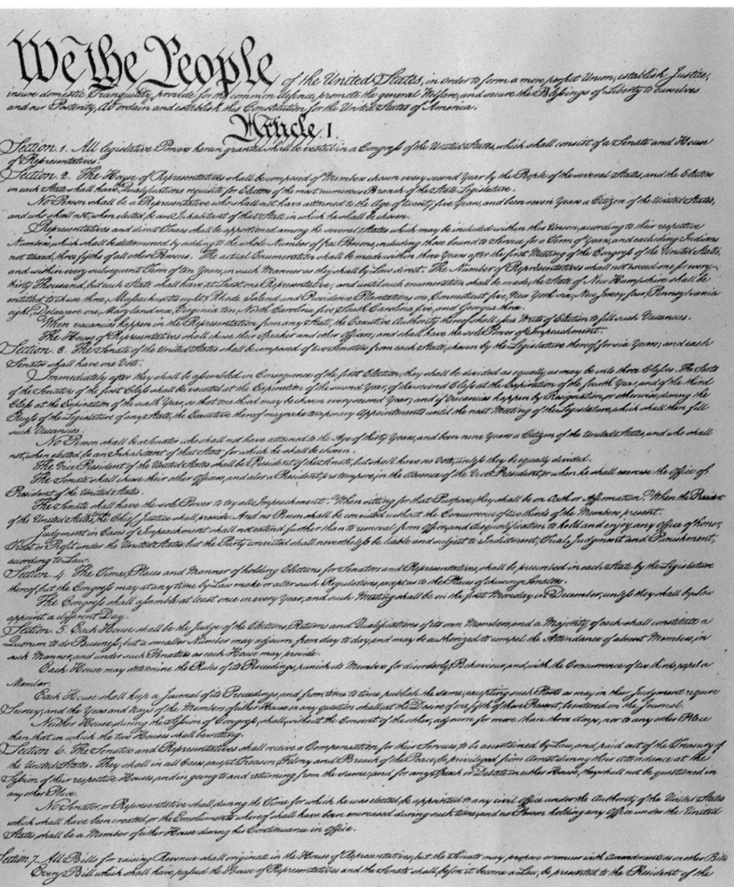

We the People of the United States, in Order to form a more perfect Union, establish Justice, insure domestic Tranquility, provide for the common defence, promote the general Welfare, and secure the Blessings of Liberty to ourselves and our Posterity, do ordain and establish this Constitution for the United States of America.

Article I.

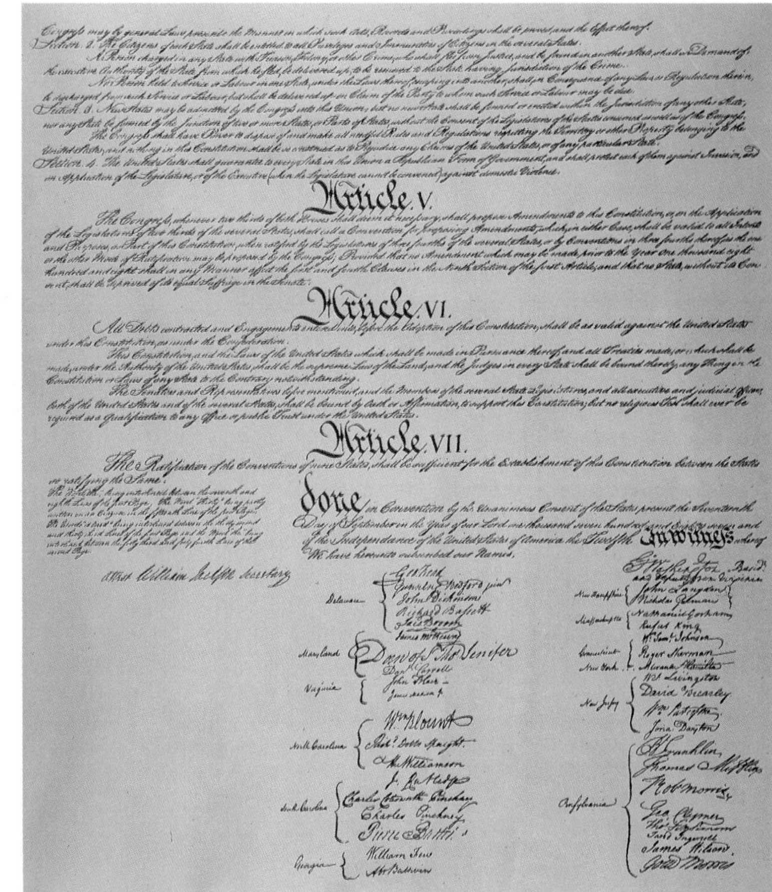

Article V.

Article VI.

Article VII.

done in Convention by the Unanimous Consent of the States present the Seventeenth Day of September in the Year of our Lord one thousand seven hundred and Eighty seven and of the Independance of the United States of America the Twelfth In witness whereof We have hereunto subscribed our Names,

ouverneur Morris, Penn. delegate.

The State House [Independence Hall], site of Constitutional Convention.

Charles Pinckney, S.C. delegate.

Framers inspired by Locke, Montesquieu

Philadelphia

The framers of the Constitution may be, as some say, inaugurating a "new age"; their ideas, however, are anything but new. Debaters in the State House lend weight to their arguments by citing the history of ancient Greece and the political theories of John Locke and Montesquieu. The more radical delegates point to Athens as a model of democracy, a society built on republican virtue in which all citizens were committed to public service.

While the Greeks believed that the people must rule, they had no provision for protecting the rights of minorities. It is for that latter purpose, according to British philosopher Locke, that governments exist in the first place. Locke's contribution to the document is his belief that life, property, and freedom of thought, speech and worship are man's inalienable rights. Montesquieu, a French philosopher, offers the institutional means for protecting those rights. In *The Spirit of the Laws,* he said the three functions of government – executive, legislative and judicial – must be entrusted to three separate entities.

hn Locke, British philosopher.

Baron de Montesquieu of France.

1788

Savannah, Georgia, Jan. 20. Andrew Bryan ordained as first pastor of First African Baptist Church.

Boston, March 26. Petition from freed Negroes protesting violent exportation of Negroes from Boston to Martinique prompts assembly to declare slave trade illegal.

United States, May 27. In letter to Edward Carrington, Jefferson writes, "The natural progress of things is for liberty to yield and government to gain ground."

Massachusetts, June 13. Daniel Shays, leader of 1787 rebellion, pardoned.

Virginia, June 25. Virginia ratifies Constitution by vote of 89-79, attaching proposed 20-article bill of rights (→ 26).

Portsmouth, N.H., June 26. Large crowds witness parade in celebration of adoption of Constitution (→ July 2).

United States, Aug. 16. Eighty-fifth and final *Federalist Paper* published.

Northwest Territory, Aug. 17. Land speculator John Cleve Symmes and group from New Jersey establish town of Losantiville [Cincinnati].

Oregon Territory, August. North West America, first ship built in Northwest, launched by Captain Meares at Clayoquot.

United States, Oct. 26. Washington, in letter to Benjamin Lincoln, hopes presidency "may not fall on me" (→ Apr. 4, 1789).

New York City, Nov. 1. Congress under Articles of Confederation officially adjourns.

Maryland, Dec. 23. Site ceded to Congress as site for future federal capital (→ Dec. 1789).

United States. Alexander Hamilton asserts that "Constitutions should consist only of general provisions; the reason is that they must necessarily be permanent, and that they cannot calculate for the possible change of things."

Andover, Massachusetts. Phillips Academy, first chartered academy in America, founded by Samuel and John Phillips.

Worcester, Massachusetts. William Perry's first American edition of *The Royal Standard English Dictionary* published.

Newbury, Massachusetts. Nicolas Pike publishes *A New and Complete Arithmetic Composed for the Citizen of the United States.*

Constitution ratified and takes effect

Philadelphia, July 2

A new era in American law and politics dawned today when the president of Congress formally announced that the much-debated Constitution is now in effect. Seven months ago, Delaware became the first state to ratify it. The required total of nine was reached with the ratification in New Hampshire 10 days ago. Approval by Virginia followed quickly.

When the ratification debate began, the small states were the most vocal opponents; but they fell into line. They were apparently persuaded that their equal representation in the Senate would offset the imbalance in the House of Representatives. Many state legislatures opposed the Constitution, but they were bypassed in the process by the use of special ratifying conventions.

Revealed in the heated debate of recent months are major divisions in the country that are not to be smoothed over simply by ratification. In Pennsylvania, for example, many anti-Federalists are farmers who spoke acidly of their opponents' commercial interests. "They expect to be the managers of this Constitution, and get all the power and all the money into their own hands," said the anti-Federalist Amos Singletary, "and then they will swallow up all of us little folks like the great Leviathan" (→ Aug. 2).

New York, encouraged by Hamilton, finally celebrates ratification on July 26.

Bill of Rights proposed for Constitution

Hillsborough, N.C., Aug. 2

Federalist hopes for unanimous ratification of the Constitution faded today as North Carolina refused to approve it. The delegates insisted that a second Constitutional Convention be called to draw up a bill of rights and consider a series of amendments. Many of the delegates voting today are self-sufficient frontiersmen who think their rights in such matters as practicing religion and bearing arms will be violated by creating a new federal government.

One anti-Federalist leader, William Goudy, warned that a bill of rights was necessary to prevent tyranny. "We know that private interest governs mankind generally," he said. "Power belongs originally to the people, but if rulers be not well guarded, that power may be usurped from them." And in Virginia, one of the greatest supporters of individual rights, Patrick Henry, is still attacking the Federalist model. He calls it "a great consolidated government, destroying the rights of the states" (→ Sept. 25, 1789).

Strong central U.S. government or not? That is the question

New York City

A fierce debate is raging across the 13 states over the new Constitution. The strongest argument of the anti-Federalists is that the document takes too much power from the states and gives it to a central authority. Their great weakness is that they offer no sound alternative.

One of the most vocal opponents is Richard Henry Lee of Virginia. In his *Letters From the Federal Farmer to the Republican*, Lee argues that the "change now proposed is a transfer of power from the many to the few." James Winthrop of Massachusetts agrees. In a series of letters signed "Agrippa," he says the transfer of power from the states to the federal system will create a permanent aristocracy. George Mason, author of Virginia's Declaration of Rights, claims that his document will be rendered useless by the Constitution. And in Baltimore, Luther Martin predicts that the federal form of government will eventually become too expensive.

A series of tracts called *The Federalist Papers*, printed in newspapers here from May 1787 to August 1788, attempts to answer the critics. Alexander Hamilton, James Madison and John Jay argue that their plan is federal and not national, leaving more than enough power to the states. They insist that the Constitution derives its authority from the states and that the power of the people, represented by the House, is balanced by the power of the states in the Senate.

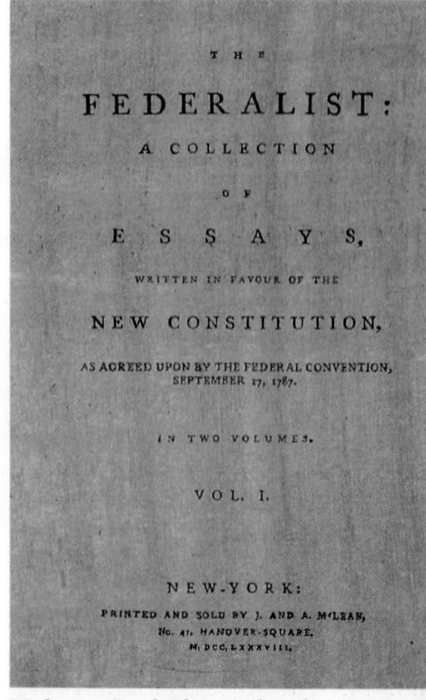
THE
FEDERALIST:
A COLLECTION
OF
ESSAYS,
WRITTEN IN FAVOUR OF THE
NEW CONSTITUTION,
AS AGREED UPON BY THE FEDERAL CONVENTION, SEPTEMBER 17, 1787.
IN TWO VOLUMES.
VOL. I.
NEW-YORK:
PRINTED AND SOLD BY J. AND A. M'LEAN,
No. 41, HANOVER-SQUARE,
M,DCC,LXXXVIII.

Volume I of The Federalist Papers.

North Carolina recovers state of Franklin

North Carolina, October

After four years of a tumultuous existence, the maverick separatist state of Franklin, named after Ben Franklin, has come to an end. In February, some North Carolina officers, hoping to regain control of the land, seized the slaves of Franklin Governor John Sevier after the state neglected to pay its taxes. A small battle followed in which Sevier and his forces stormed the home of North Carolina officer John Tipton. The Franklinites, however, were defeated and North Carolina took over the beleaguered region.

Franklin had led a troubled life since it first broke away from North Carolina in 1784. Aside from being unable to win recognition for the state either from Congress or North Carolina, Franklin's Governor opposed the desire of the people for a democratic state constitution. In addition, Sevier, disillusioned with the American government's reconciliatory policy toward the Indians, sought the protection of Spain while he tried to expand the borders of Franklin past Muscle Shoals and down the Tennessee River. In return, Sevier said that he would pledge his allegiance to Spain.

It was not until this month that Sevier was captured, after North Carolina ordered his arrest on a charge of high treason. Although threatened with a trial, Sevier was bailed out of jail and has been granted a pardon by the state.

The state of North Carolina has regained control over its Western frontier.

New Orleans fire turns city into inferno

The community bands together in crisis. Volunteer firemen operate a pump while neighbors laboriously transport water from the nearest pond.

New Orleans, March 21

A fierce fire that started when a votive candle fell on a lace curtain destroyed almost the entire city today. Governor Don Esteban de Miro said that 856 buildings burned down, including the St. Louis Cathedral, the Cabildo and the Presbytere. The blaze started in a home on Chartres Street and rapidly turned the city into an inferno. Don Andres Almonester y Roxas, the richest man in the colony, has announced that he will rebuild the cathedral as well as two government buildings.

Quadroon balls were center of social life

New Orleans

New Orleans has enjoyed an active social life, where beautiful free women of color, carefully trained as courtesans, meet young planters and rich businessmen looking for mistresses. At quadroon balls, the women dress in lavish gowns while their mothers keep a watchful eye on their dancing partners. Before approving an "arrangement", the mother insists on a house for the daughter and often a legacy. The women, most of Spanish or French and African heritage, are of such light complexion that a law requires them to wear kerchiefs or chignons to identify them as colored.

Body-nabbing tale sets off riot in N.Y.

New York, Apr. 13

"Bring out your doctors!" the mob yelled outside a city jail. The crowd was out for the hides of physicians put in jail for their own protection after rumors of body-snatching had angered residents. All the city's doctors were suspected after some boys said they saw an arm dangling from a corpse in a medical laboratory. The simmering anger turned to rage today and many people were hurt in the riot, including Governor George Clinton, Mayor James Duane and Alexander Hamilton. Order was restored by nightfall.

New York chosen as federal capital

New York, Sept. 13

Congress made it official today: New York City is the capital of the nation. Actually, the city has been the federal government's home since January 11, 1785, when Congress convened here. The French architect Pierre L'Enfant reworked a big room in City Hall to handle congressional meetings. There is talk of converting the building into a federal hall to house Congress. L'Enfant is likely to be commissioned to refurbish it and to find a home for the man who is chosen the nation's leader (→ Dec. 23).

Nation overcomes economic decline

New York City, December

Stimulated by a rise in commodity prices and an increase in international trade, the American economy is experiencing a period of prosperity unknown since the war. The South was the first to recover, with heavy exports of tobacco, rice, indigo and naval stores to France and even Britain, the former enemy. Shipbuilding in New England has been slower to recover, but the North has developed by opening new banks and factories and establishing routes of trade with Europe, the Indies and the Orient.

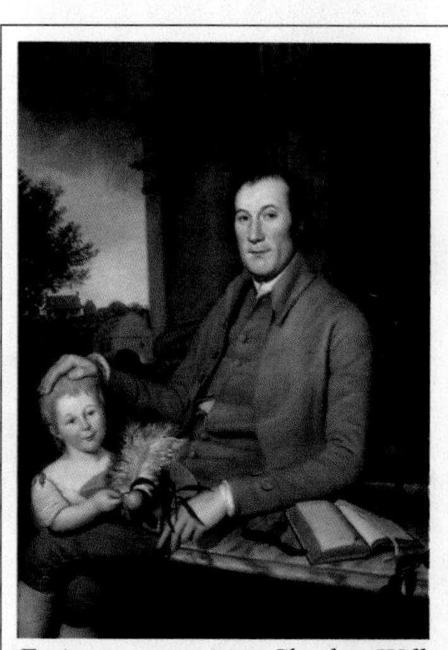

Eminent portraitist Charles Willson Peale's rendering of William Smith and his grandson (1788).

CAPTIS·AVT·

A Perfect Union? 1789-1849

The ratification of the Constitution and the launching of the federal government in 1789 completed the first phase of the building of a new nation in America. The independence of the United States was now secure and could not again be seriously threatened. A political system was now in place that would last for more than two centuries with only modest changes.

But 1789 was also the beginning of the task of creating a nation. For the next half century (and many decades beyond), Americans struggled to define themselves politically, economically, socially and culturally, to find the common bonds that would permit a large, growing and heterogeneous society to live together under one government. For a time, almost everything was open to question: Should the federal government be strong or weak? Should the nation promote manufacturing or should it seek to preserve the essentially agrarian character of its society? Should America remain a small, coastal nation or should it strive to expand its boundaries into the vast and underpopulated lands in the West? Should the United States play an active role in world affairs or should the New World insulate itself from the intrigues and conflicts of the Old? Above all, perhaps, should a democracy based on the inalienable rights of individuals tolerate the existence of human slavery in its midst or should the institution be limited and ultimately abolished?

During the first decades of American independence, national debate centered largely on the nature of the new federal government. Although the founders had envisioned a political system free of political parties, identifiable factions quickly emerged, expressing distinctive views of the nation's future. The Federalists, who looked to Alexander Hamilton for guidance and leadership, envisioned a strong central government dominated by an enlightened elite and promoting economic growth and industrial development. The Republicans, whose patron saint was Thomas Jefferson, favored an agrarian society, states' rights and the supremacy of the "common man." The debate between these two factions (few yet considered them actual "parties") dominated American politics in its first decades and culminated in a bitter presidential campaign between Jefferson and John Adams in 1800. So important did Americans consider the issues in the campaign that Jefferson's victory was widely described as "the revolution of 1800."

In fact, the victory of Jefferson proved much less revolutionary than some had hoped and others had feared. For over the next two decades, the Republican Party gradually absorbed some of the Federalists' ideas, and the Federalist Party gradually faded into obscurity. Perhaps most strikingly, the Republicans – who had long argued for a small, simple, agrarian republic – presided over the greatest single addition to the territory of the United States in the nation's history: the Louisiana Purchase, which more than doubled the national domain.

The most serious challenge to face the United States in the first decades of the new century proved to be from abroad: a prolonged struggle with Britain that culminated in the War of 1812. The United States drifted into war slowly and haltingly, without ever galvanizing public opinion behind it. There was, therefore, widespread domestic opposition to it throughout. More important, American forces experienced a series of humiliating defeats, indluding the British capture and burning of Washington, D.C. There were, to be sure, a number of decisive American victories as well. But the war concluded with a treaty that fell far short of the nation's war aims. The conflict ended in what was, at best, a draw.

By 1820, with the early political struggles and the inconclusive war with Britain apparently resolved, the United States seemed poised for an era of unity and tranquility. Indeed, factional passions had by then subsided to the point that Americans talked of an "era of good feeling," in which no serious political divisions remained. But the illusion of tranquility was not to last for long. In politics, the next two decades saw the emergence of formal parties, a series of bitterly contested elections and the re-emergence of fundamental debates about the nature of government and the direction in which the nation should develop. The election of Andrew Jackson to the presidency in 1828, like the election of Jefferson in 1800, was the result of deep political divisions that continued to produce controversy for decades to come.

But it was less political disagreement than social and economic change that destroyed the illusion of unity and stability in mid-19th century America. For the nation was in those years experiencing remarkable growth and development as it greatly expanded in population, in territory and in the extent and complexity of its economic life.

By 1850, the United States was a nation of more than 23 million people, eight times as many as in 1789. It was a nation whose territory had expanded – through the Louisiana Purchase, the accession of Florida and Texas, and the controversial Mexican War – to make it one of the largest countries in the world. And it was a nation whose economy was transforming itself with startling speed. Agriculture in both the North and the South grew dramatically, making America a leading international producer of staple crops. Commerce expanded rapidly both at home and overseas. And the beginnings of the Industrial Revolution made manufacturing a major element of the nation's economy, if not yet as dominant as it would later become.

Alongside this territorial, demographic and economic growth came a rise in nationalism. Americans in the first half of the 19th century developed a deep reverence for the memory of the Revolution, for the Constitution and its framers, and for what they considered the distinctive virtues and special destiny of their society. As if to symbolize this sense of national mission, Americans made much of the events of a single day: July 4, 1826, the 50th anniversary of the signing of the Declaration of Independence. On that day, Thomas Jefferson and John Adams – both heroes of the Revolution, both former presidents, both beloved symbols of the nation's supposedly divine origins – died within a few hours of each other at their homes in Virginia and Massachusetts. To many Americans, the timing of their passing seemed to confirm that theirs was a nation specially graced by God.

But the dramatic growth and development of American society in these years was not simply a result of Providence. Nor was it just a result of the energy and resourcefulness of the American people, as important as that energy and resourcefulness had been. It was also a result of ruthless exploitation – of land, of resources and most troublingly of people. Again and again, Indian tribes were driven from their lands to make room for the inexorable westward expansion of white society. Through a series of traumatic displacements, virtually all the tribes of Eastern North America were relocated to new "Indian territories" in the West, from which they would be displaced again in future decades.

In the North, industrialization progressed in part through the exploitation of industrial workers – some native-born Americans, some immigrants, but all confronted with the task of making the harsh adjustment from agrarian to urban-industrial life. And probably most significant for the future of the nation, social and economic life in the American South rested on the exploitation of men and women of African descent: the black slaves who provided a labor force for the growing of rice, tobacco and above all cotton. In other nations of the world, slavery was declining and even disappearing in these years. Despite the outlawing of slave importation in 1808, the economic importance of slavery in the South was growing. The nation would be forced to confront the contradiction that it had tried for years to ignore: the tolerance of a labor system that permitted neither freedom nor mobility by a country that professed commitment to these ideals.

That the issue of slavery might become not only a difficult moral question but also a threat to national unity first became clear in 1820, when a bitter dispute broke out over the terms by which the territory of Missouri would be admitted to the union as a state. That controversy ended in compromise, but it suggested how the rapid expansion of the nation might make it impossible for the issue to remain dormant for long. Thomas Jefferson had compared the Missouri crisis to a "fire bell in the night." In the decades to come, that bell would ring again and again, warning of tensions and divisions that would eventually sunder the union.

◀ *Revolutionary leaders at the Constitutional Convention by J.L.G. Ferris.*

1789

Washington

United States, Feb. 2. Madison elected to Congress over friendly rival James Monroe.

New York City, March 4. First Congress under new Constitution convenes, but is short of quorum.

Mount Vernon, Virginia, Apr. 14. Charles Thomson, secretary of Congress, informs Washington of his election to presidency (→ 30).

New York City, May 7. First inaugural ball held.

United States, May 15. Washington to James Madison: "As the first of everything, in our situation, will serve to establish a precedent, it is devoutly wished on my part, that these precedents may be fixed on true principles."

New York City, June 1. First act passed in new Congress sets procedure for administering oaths of public office.

New York City, July 27. Department of Foreign Affairs first executive agency created under new Constitution.

Virginia, December. Assembly cedes Potomac River land, including Alexandria, for national capital (→ March 9, 1791).

New York City. German-born fur trader John Jacob Astor buys his first piece of real estate, on Bowery.

Connecticut. Temperance group of 200 farmers in Litchfield County vows to abstain from alcohol during farming season.

United States. Vice President John Adams remarks, "My country has in its wisdom contrived for me the most insignificant office that ever the invention of man contrived or his imagination conceived."

Honolulu. U.S. ship Columbia arrives via Cape Horn; first American ship to visit Sandwich Islands [Hawaii] and circle globe (→ Aug. 10, 1790).

Louisiana. French aristocrats, fleeing French Revolution, arrive, settling in St. Martinville.

New York City. *A Survey of the Roads of the United States*, by Christopher Colles, published; nation's first road maps.

United States. Scotsman Adam Smith's *The Wealth of Nations*, seminal work of laissez-faire economic theory, published in United States.

Washington takes oath as President

Hail to the chief. Washington arrives in splendor at New York's Battery.

New York City, Apr. 30

George Washington took the oath of office as President of the United States today before a joint session of Congress. Swearing to "preserve, protect and defend the Constitution," the new chief executive becomes the first President under the new federal Constitution adopted by the states in the past year.

Washington was unanimously selected by the members of the Electoral College only two weeks ago. After certifying his election, the college dispatched Charles Thomson, the secretary of Congress, to Mount Vernon to inform General Washington officially of his selection. Although the new President has huge landholdings in Virginia, he is reputed to be somewhat "cash-poor." Indeed, there are rumors that he was forced to borrow money to pay the expenses of his trip to the inauguration. Regardless of his financial condition, he is obviously much beloved and remembered if one is to judge by the way well-wishers surrounded his coach all the way from Mount Vernon to New York City.

The new President took his oath wearing a simple, American-made worsted suit and white silk stockings, along with his old army dress sword. Some of those who witnessed the ceremony described Washington as looking tired and gaunt, and one said that "time had made havoc" with his face. He was also depicted as "grave almost to the point of sadness." Senator William Maclay of Pennsylvania in depicting the scene said Washington "was agitated and embarrassed more than he ever was by the leveled cannon or pointed musket. He trembled, and several times could scarce make out to read (his address), though it must be supposed he had often read it before."

Washington's address was read in the Senate chamber, but he was publicly inaugurated at Federal Hall. Engraving (1790) by Amos Doolittle.

President Washington's inaugural speech, however, was both simple and powerful. Fisher Ames, a legislator who has served Washington for years, said, "It seemed to me an allegory in which virtue was personified." Those present in Federal Hall at the corner of Broad and Wall Streets were witnessing the end of one American era and the beginning of another.

Washington forms governmental Cabinet

New York City

George Washington took office as the nation's first President on April 30 and has been putting together a governmental Cabinet since then. On July 27, the Department of Foreign Affairs became the first executive agency. President Washington chose Thomas Jefferson to head it. After Benjamin Franklin, who is weak with age, and John Adams, who is Vice President, Jefferson is the most experienced American in dealing with foreign lands. Recently, Jefferson returned from France and expressed a desire to go back to Paris, but he said that if the President needed his services, he would accept the appointment.

Washington's Cabinet (left to right): Henry Knox, Thomas Jefferson, Edmund Randolph, Alexander Hamilton and Washington himself.

The War Department was created August 7 and Henry Knox was named Secretary of War. He will be in charge of the army, which has about 840 men. The Treasury Department was formed September 2, and Washington turned to Alexander Hamilton, the nation's most knowledgeable man on finance, to head it. Edmund Randolph will serve as Attorney General.

The issue of the right of removal of Cabinet members has been resolved, with Congress deciding to give the President the power to remove those officers he appoints.

Army is authorized by new Congress

New York City, Sept. 29

Congress voted today to create the United States Army. The new force will be made up of 1,000 enlisted men and officers, all of whom will be considered "regulars" with specified terms of service, pay schedules and uniforms. America has had no "standing" or professional military force since General Washington disbanded the Continental Army almost seven years ago. The new army will consist of men already on hand, and will be augmented as vacancies occur. The army's civilian head will be former General Henry Knox, now Secretary of War.

Bastille is stormed by Parisian rebels

Paris, July 14

In a dramatic blow to the authority of the French monarchy, a Paris mob today attacked and captured the Bastille, a grim state prison and fortress that commands one of the gates to the city. Although only seven prisoners, none of them political, were found and released, the citadel has long been a symbol of arbitrary royal power, since it was here that many victims of the infamous lettres de cachet that sanctioned imprisonment without trial, including Voltaire, were held, in some cases for years (→ Feb. 2, 1793).

Amos Doolittle's commemoration of the Constitution lists all 13 states, their population and number of delegates to Congress.

Congress creates federal judiciary

New York City, Sept. 24

Congress passed the Federal Judiciary Act today, creating three circuit courts, 13 district courts and a Supreme Court. The act enhances the concept of a system of checks and balances within the government. Congress has been busy in recent months. In June, it enacted legislation setting procedures for the oaths of public office. On July 4, it passed the First Tariff Act, setting taxes on certain imports and giving tax breaks on goods imported on American ships. And on July 20, the Tonnage Act was passed, imposing a 50-cents-per-ton tax on foreign ships sailing into American ports.

Georgetown is first Catholic college

Georgetown, Maryland, Jan. 23

The first Roman Catholic college in the United States, the Academy of Georgetown, was dedicated here today. The school, a personal project of Father John Carroll, superior of the United States Catholic Mission, received major impetus in 1786 when the Roman Catholic clergy of the country voted to build such an institution. Georgetown is to serve both as a college and a seminary for the training of Roman Catholic clergymen. The academy should begin to accept students within three years.

A Tammany Society formed in New York

New York City, May 12

A collection of anti-Federalists have reorganized themselves into a fraternal order they call the Tammany Society of Columbian Order. Originally, it was satirically named the Society of Saint Tammany after Chief Tammany, a Delaware Indian who greeted William Penn in 1682. The chief has become a legend, posthumously endowed with the attributes of Hercules and Alfred the Great. While Tammany's ostensible purpose is social, some believe the society of tradesmen and laborers has political goals in mind.

Congress offers 12 constitutional changes

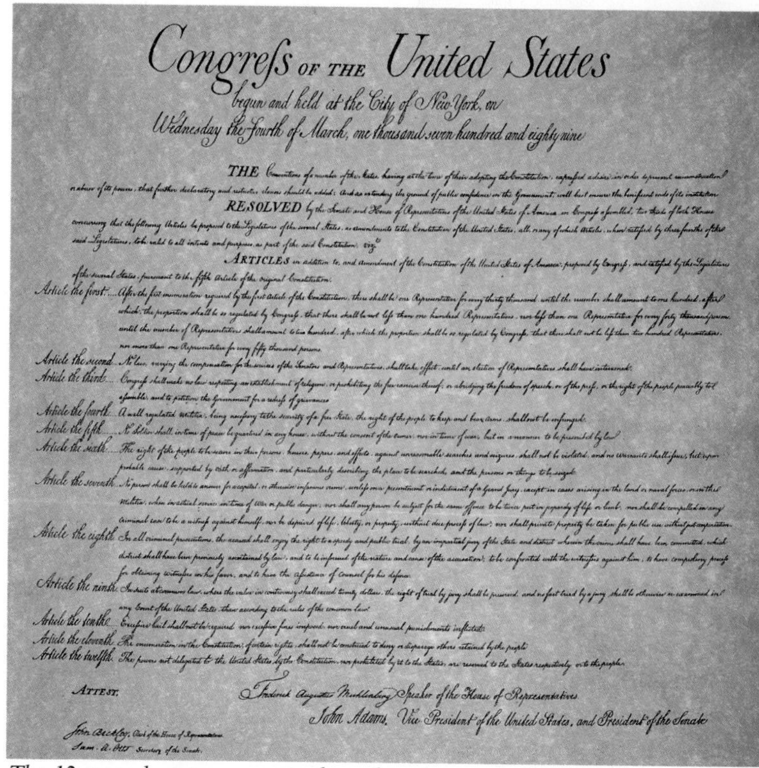
Congress of the United States
begun and held at the City of New-York, on
Wednesday the Fourth of March, one thousand seven hundred and eighty nine

The 12 amendments as promised, ready to be sent to the states for ratification.

New York City, Sept. 25

The new Congress took action today to ease the fears and suspicions over the powers of the federal government. It offered a series of 12 amendments [Bill of Rights] to the Constitution that incorporate many of the changes demanded by anti-Federalists. For the most part, they delineate rights reserved specifically for individuals and the states, and are based on George Mason's Virginia bill of rights of 1776. In discussions with Thomas Jefferson last year, James Madison agreed that they were necessary and acted to turn them into federal law. He rejected appeals for a second Constitutional Convention and decided instead to seek approval by Congress. It was announced today that the required two-thirds in each house had agreed. Now it is up to the states to ratify the amendments. Approval by three-quarters of them is necessary (→ Dec. 15, 1791).

New whiskey made in Bourbon County

Virginia

Residents of Bourbon County, Virginia [Kentucky], now favor native Indian corn as the principal base for distilled spirits. First distilled in 1746, the whiskey, which is made from 65 to 70 percent corn, has taken on a distinctive, regional flavor that seems to have much to do with the water that flows over the region's limestone rock, and the use of charred oak barrels. No one is sure how the use of charred barrels came about, but some say the Rev. Elijah Craig is responsible for creating this American spirit.

Seduction feared in 1st American novel

Philadelphia

The Power of Sympathy, or The Triumph of Nature, by William Hill Brown, is the first novel published in America. The purpose of this tragic tale, the author writes, is to "expose the dangerous Consequences of Seduction" and to promote "the Advantages of Female Education." Also this year, in *Dissertations on the English Language*, written at the urging of Benjamin Franklin, Noah Webster has outlined an American idiom wholly free of the British tongue and anchored in republican principles.

1790

Washington

New York City, Jan. 14. Treasury Secretary Hamilton reports foreign debt of $12 million, domestic debt of $40 million; proposes allowing creditors to redeem securities at face value (→Aug. 4).

New York City, Feb. 11. Congress hears first formal petition for abolition of slavery from Society of Friends, or Quakers.

New York City, Apr. 4. Revenue Marine Service created by Congress to stop smugglers.

Philadelphia, May 25. Universalists Dr. Benjamin Rush and the Rev. Elhanan Winchester forge anti-Trinitarian doctrine.

New York City, May 31. First Copyright Act signed by Washington, protecting plays, books and maps for 14 years.

Connecticut, June 30. *Connecticut Journal* advertises exhibition of two Arabian camels, "the greatest natural Curiosity ever exhibited to the Public on this Continent."

New York City, July 31. Samuel Hopkins receives first U.S. patent, for "process for making pot and pearl ashes."

Philadelphia, Dec. 14. Hamilton calls for Bank of United States in second address to House on public credit (→Feb. 25, 1791).

Philadelphia. Mathew Carey prints first Catholic Bible in United States.

Philadelphia. To celebrate commerce, High Street is renamed Market Street.

Maine. Work begins on lighthouse ordered by Washington.

New York City. Trinity Church, burned during Revolution, rededicated, with Washington in attendance.

United States. Phrase "Not worth a continental" refers to value of currency issued by Congress at end of Revolution.

Pennsylvania. Last 500 Amish leave Europe, ending migration begun in 1727.

United States. Naturalization law states only "free white" persons may become citizens.

Sandwich Islands [Hawaii]. Pineapples are introduced to the islands from South America.

Census counts 4,000,000 Americans

New York, Aug. 1

The first census taken in the United States shows a population of 3,929,625. The count was taken under a constitutional provision that an enumeration of the population "be made within three years after the first meeting of the Congress of the United States and within every subsequent term of 10 years." It thus will be the first modern census to be repeated at regular intervals.

The results of the census, published in a 56-page volume, will be used to give each state a number of representatives in the House that is proportionate to its population. According to the Constitution, each slave will count as three-fifths of a person for the apportionment of representatives. The census counted 697,642 slaves and 59,557 free Negroes among the inhabitants of the United States.

The most populous state is Virginia, with 820,000 inhabitants. Massachusetts, Pennsylvania and North Carolina have about 400,000 each. South Carolina, New Jersey, Connecticut and New Hampshire have 200,000 each and Delaware, Rhode Island and Georgia have under 100,000 each. The tally shows vast population growth since colonial days; a 1726 census counted only 32,442 inhabitants in New Jersey, while New Hampshire had 52,700 residents in 1767. Exact comparisons are not possible because some states never took censuses.

The largest city is Philadelphia, with a population of 42,000. New York has 33,000 residents, Charleston 16,000 and Baltimore 13,000.

The census shows a nation made up of many ethnic groups. The largest is British, followed by 400,000 Irish-Americans, many of them Catholics who came to the United States to escape harsh treatment by Protestants. There are 260,000 Scots, some of whose ancestors were sent to America for crimes or for opposing the established church. The census listed 2,000 Jews.

Members of some ethnic groups are concentrated in certain states. A third of Pennsylvanians are of German origin and New York has 80,000 people of Dutch descent. But the 19,000 Swedes and 9,000 French Canadians are scattered through several Northern states.

America in its infancy: a patchwork quilt of colors, creeds and nationalities.

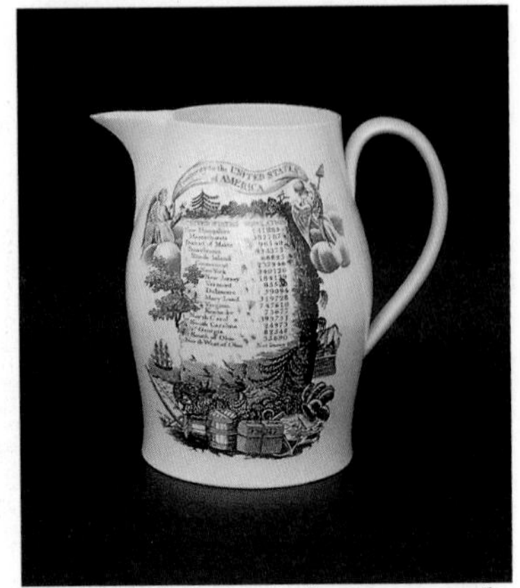

Token of good will from across the Atlantic. A British pitcher features a transfer print of the census with population figures for each state.

Federal funding of states' debts enacted

New York, Aug. 4

Under a bill signed today by President Washington, the federal government assumes responsibility for the debts of the individual states, estimated to total as much as $25 million. Federal funding of the debts of the states is the last step in an ambitious program laid out by Secretary of the Treasury Alexander Hamilton to establish sound credit for the nation. Securities already have been issued to redeem the $50 million in debt contracted by the Continental Congress to fight the war and found the nation.

Funding of the old debts on Hamilton's terms was bitterly opposed by many in Congress. Much of the debt consisted of scrip that was issued to soldiers, farmers and producers at times when the Continental Congress lacked ready cash to pay them. Many original creditors have sold their debts to professional dealers for a few cents on the dollar. James Madison, among others, proposed that only the original holders of debt be paid in full, with speculators and dealers getting just partial payment. But Hamilton argued that only full payment to present holders of the debt would induce the business and financial community to trust future bonds issued by the United States. Hamilton's argument prevailed with Congress; the bill became law today (→Dec. 14).

Franklin dies; funeral is largest in U.S.

Philadelphia, Apr. 21

In the largest public gathering the United States has ever seen, 20,000 people today mourned the passing of a great public servant here. They had also come to pay their respects to an author, who wrote *Poor Richard's Almanac*, and at the same time they were paying homage to the inventor of the life-saving lightning rod. Benjamin Franklin, who died at the age of 84 on April 17, was all these things and more, a man who merged an almost self-centered fascination for new ideas with Puritan aims to benefit the common good. And age was no barrier to realizing these goals; just last month, he was active in the Pennsylvania Abolition Society, writing a satire on slaveholders (equating them with Muslims who enslave Christians).

Franklin's life was not unblemished: He was known to look the other way when a friend was profiteering; he had an illegitimate son (whom he raised under his own roof), and he dallied with many women while ambassador to France (in his 70's). This extraordinary man was extraordinarily human.

Ben Franklin (1789) by C.W. Peale.

First cotton mill in United States opens

Pawtucket, Rhode Island, Dec. 21

The first cotton mill in the United States was opened here today by Samuel Slater, who brought with him from England the secret of the latest textile machinery. The mill has 250 spindles, which are powered by water and operated by children aged 4 to 10. The mill's opening is a direct result of financial incentives offered by the United States for the introduction of textile manufacturing equipment that will enable the country to become independent of foreign sources of supply.

In England, Slater learned the textile industry as an apprentice to Jedediah Strutt, partner of Richard Arkwright. It was Arkwright who inaugurated the modern textile factory system by his invention of the water frame for spinning cotton into yarn. His new technology, introduced in 1773, established cotton-cloth manufacture as the leading industry in northern England. The next year, Parliament passed an act forbidding the exportation of drawings of any machine used in textile manufacture or the emigration of textile workers, under heavy penalties. The aim was to avoid the loss of the profitable American market. But Americans offered bounties to promote a native textile industry.

Slater secretly memorized the details of the machinery used by Arkwright and other British textile manufacturers. He evaded the rule against emigration and came to the United States only last year, at the age of 21, carrying his knowledge with him and claiming the bounty. The Rhode Island firm of Almy and Brown provided the financial backing he needed, and the new mill was quickly built and put into operation. Slater plans to build more mills, taking advantage of the abundant sources of water power that are available in New England to meet the rapidly growing demand for cotton cloth.

Slater, new arrival from England.

Pacific volcano kills soldiers and families

Kau, Sandwich Islands, Aug. 15

The volcano Kilauea erupted today, engulfing dozens of families in hot, deadly lava. The warrior Keoua was leading his troops and their families back from battling the forces of Kamehameha when the volcano erupted. Keoua and his rear guard were spared, but many others were not. Men, women and children were found cast in hardened lava, some with their noses joined, which is the [Hawaiian] islanders way of showing affection.

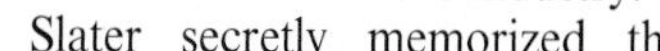

U.S. ship completes trip around world

Boston, Aug. 10

The ship Columbia returned to Boston today after a three-year voyage that made it the first American vessel to sail around the world. It was in 1787 that the Columbia, commanded by Robert Gray, sailed for Vancouver Island to trade its cargo of iron tools, looking glasses and trinkets to the Indians for otter furs. After spending the winter on the northwest coast, Gray headed for Canton, where he exchanged the furs for Chinese tea, porcelain and silk. He returned to the United States via Europe, thus circumnavigating the globe. The voyage was so profitable that Boston merchants already are talking of others and of a regular China trade. Plans for the Columbia's next trip include exploration of the Pacific coast.

First U.S. bishop is consecrated

Dorsetshire, England, Aug. 15

Father John Carroll was consecrated as the first Roman Catholic Bishop of the United States today at a ceremony in the Lulworth Castle Chapel here. A Jesuit from Maryland who studied in Europe, Bishop Carroll has been serving as the superior of the U.S. mission. He was chosen by his country's priests as their episcopal candidate last year and the election was recognized by Pope Pius VI in the bull *Ex Hac Apostolicae*. Bishop Carroll, who is related to signers of the Declaration of Independence and Constitution, has favored creation of an American Roman Catholicism. He urged the appointment of a bishop ordinary for the United States and argued for the bishop's selection by the clergy rather than by a "foreign tribunal."

The cotton mill in Pawtucket is operated by 4- to 10-year-old boys.

1791

Washington

Philadelphia, Jan. 28. Congress hears Hamilton's report on establishment of national mint (→ Apr. 2, 1792).

Potomac River, March 30. Washington selects site for capital encompassing Alexandria and Georgetown (→ Apr. 15).

Boston, March. *The Death Song of an Indian Chief*, first orchestral score printed in United States, published in *The Massachusetts Magazine*.

England, March. First section of Thomas Paine's *The Rights of Man* published (→ Jan. 1792).

Potomac River, Apr. 15. Government holds official ceremony marking choice of 70-square-mile site for federal district (→ Oct. 13, 1792).

Louisiana, June 12. Group of slaves, inspired by recent revolt in Haiti, rebel against Spanish.

Baltimore, Maryland, June. French Suplicans found St. Mary's, first Roman Catholic seminary in United States. [One hundred priests arrive during French Revolution].

Philadelphia, July 4. Subscription drive launched by Bank of United States in effort to raise capital (→ Dec. 12).

Monterey, California, Sept. 13. First American, John Groeham, reaches California; dies same day.

United States, October. George Hammond, first British minister to U.S., arrives.

Philadelphia, Dec. 12. Bank of United States opens main office (→ Feb. 20, 1811).

California. Father Fermin Francisco de Lasuen helps found four missions: Santa Cruz, Santa Barbara, La Soledad and La Purisma Concepcion.

Massachusetts. Scholar Jeremy Belknap establishes Massachusetts Historical Society, first of its kind in United States.

Pennsylvania. Deposits of anthracite coal discovered.

New Orleans. Nation's first successful sugar refinery opens.

United States. First macadam road, turnpike between Lancaster and Philadelphia, finished.

United States. John Adams publishes *Discourses of Davila*, advocating rule by elite in order to deter demagoguery.

States vote Bill of Rights into effect

Virginia, Dec. 15

Virginia today became the 10th state to approve the first amendments to the Constitution. Three-quarters of the states have now ratified the 10 amendments and that means they are the law of the land. The amendments, known collectively as the Bill of Rights, provide guarantees for the preservation of state and individual liberties that many anti-Federalists believe were insufficiently protected by the Constitution.

Their adoption is generally regarded as James Madison's finest hour, for it was Madison who drafted the language and argued that the amendments be considered by the new Congress and the states rather than by a second Constitutional Convention. It is also not without significance that Virginia provided the 10th vote required for ratification. Many of the most stirring speeches in the revolutionary movement were made in this state. Patrick Henry will long be remembered for his rhetoric – against both the British and the Federalists.

Originally, there were 12 amendments, but several states rejected the two that would have set up new formulas for the election of Congress and the reimbursement of its members. The first eight amendments all guarantee the rights of individuals. The first is perhaps the most wide-ranging, since it prohibits Congress from infringing upon the free exercise of religion, the freedom of speech or the press, the right to assemble peaceably and the right "to petition the Government for a redress of grievances." The following two amendments guarantee the rights to bear arms and to refuse shelter to soldiers. The central five amendments all guarantee legal rights, including protection "against unreasonable searches and seizures" and the "right to a speedy and public trial." No person shall be held prisoner for a capital crime without indictment and "the right of trial by jury shall be preserved." The ninth and tenth amendments are general guarantees of the rights of individuals and the states.

The Spirit of '76 endures.

President signs bill creating Bank of U.S.

Philadelphia, Feb. 25

The President today signed a bill creating the Bank of the United States despite bitter opposition by many landowners, who feel it will be used by financial interests to oppress them. Washington acted primarily on the urging of Alexander Hamilton, overriding the protests of Thomas Jefferson. The bill makes the bank the depository for government funds and authorizes it to establish branches and to issue currency. It will have 25 directors, five appointed by the President, the rest by its stockholders. Hamilton proposed establishment of the bank as a method of providing capital for new industry and of insuring a sound money supply (→ July 4).

First Bank of U.S., Philadelphia. Engraving (1799) by William Birch & Son.

Frenchman chosen to lay out capital

Maryland, March 9

Major Pierre Charles L'Enfant arrived here today to make sketches for the nation's capital, the Federal City. L'Enfant, a French engineer and veteran of the Revolution, has designed many buildings in New York. President Washington chose the major, calling him "the artist of the American Revolution."

L'Enfant actually petitioned for the assignment in a 1789 letter to Washington. At the time, a capital site had not yet been determined. There were two popular choices, on the Delaware River near the falls above Trenton and the Potomac River location finally chosen on the Maryland-Virginia border.

The decision results from a compromise between Alexander Hamilton, James Madison and Thomas Jefferson. The Virginians agreed to support Hamilton's financial policies if he would support their plan to build a capital on the Potomac.

It is believed that L'Enfant will design a spectacular Parisian-style city, complete with monuments, parks and wide avenues (→ 30).

'ermont admitted ·o union, as No. 14

'ermont, March 4

Vermont's lucky number is 14. 'or 14 years, the region thrived as n independent republic, and today : becomes the 14th state. It is the irst state formed since the ratifica-ıon of the United States Constitu-ion (which it accepted on January 0), and the first to have a no-slav-ry clause in its state constitution. Aany of Vermont's 85,000 inhab-ıants desired statehood years ago, ut there had been a major obstacle n their path: New York. A long-tanding territorial dispute ended ast year when New York was paid 30,000 for the acreage in question.

Ohio Indians beat St. Clair's troops

Northwest Territory, Nov. 4

Word was received today of the lisastrous defeat of U.S. troops un-ler Major General Arthur St. Clair n a branch of the Wabash River y a combined force of Ohio In-lians led by the Miami Chief Little Turtle. According to survivors, at east two-thirds of their original orce of about 1,200 men were slain n the fighting, which began at ıbout sunrise and lasted nearly two ours. The Indians, though inferior n numbers, were well organized nd seasoned warriors, while the Americans were poorly trained, aw militiamen (→Aug. 20, 1794).

ackson is married, causing a scandal

Nashville, Tennessee, Autumn

Tennessee's state prosecutor, An-lrew Jackson, has married Mrs. Rachel Robards in spite of reports hat she and Lewis Robards are not egally divorced. In face of the scan-lal over the cohabitation of Jackson nd his bride, the 24-year-old prose-cutor says he was under a misim-pression. He thought the divorce hat Robards, a Kentucky land-owner, sought after the marriage ıad become final. Mrs. Jackson eems shy and retiring, in contrast o her hotheaded new husband, who has been in countless brawls.

Fine furnishings for a free people

Finely crafted, walnut cradle from Cantwell's Bridge, Delaware, 1800.

Mahogany breakfast table, made by John Townsend of Newport, R.I., 1780.

United States

As the spirit of freedom permeates society, more Americans fill their homes with furnishings of a distinctively American style. London still supplies the South with furniture, but the craftsmen of Newport, Philadelphia, Boston and New York City are thriving.

Three styles have dominated the century: Baroque, Rococo and Neoclassical. By 1725, cabinetmakers focused on comfort. Upholstered chairs and sofas displayed Baroque ornamentation in Queen Anne's reign. This entailed the cabriole support, shaped after an animal's leg and terminating in a claw-and-ball or paw foot.

By 1760, craftsmen were adopting Thomas Chippendale's *Gentleman and Cabinet Maker's Director* (1754) as their Rococo guide. Free ornament was in fashion. In Newport, John Townsend decorated block-front cabinets with wood grain rather than carvings. In Philadelphia, Benjamin Randolph fashioned a linear style in contrast to the more sturdy British lines.

Now, craftsmen are turning to classical models. Inspired by archeology in Greece and Italy, Duncan Phyfe leads in creating small, simple rectangular designs with light wood finishes. His manuals are George Hepplewhite's *Cabinet-Maker and Upholsterer's Guide* (1788) and Thomas Sheraton's *Cabinet-Maker and Upholsterer's Drawing Book*, published this year.

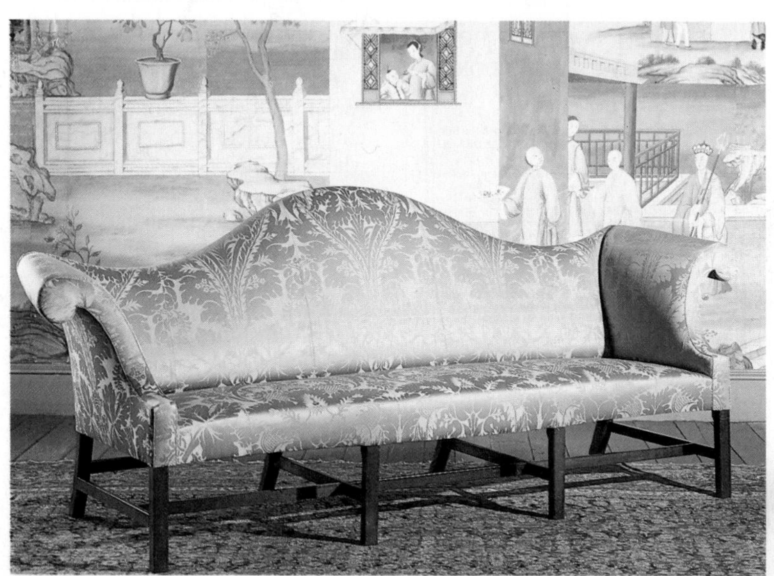

Mahogany sofa, richly upholstered in gold silk, from New York, 1780.

"Fanback" Windsor chair, 1790.

1792

Washington

Philadelphia, Jan. 12. Federalist Thomas Pinckney appointed first U.S. minister to Britain.

United States, January. Second part of Paine's *Rights of Man* argues that power rests with democratic majority (→ Sept. 13).

Philadelphia, Feb. 21. Congress passes Presidential Succession Act; president pro tempore of Senate, speaker of House follow vice president in line of command.

Philadelphia, Apr. 2. Congress passes Coinage Act, setting up national mint here.

United States, Apr. 24. Negroes appear for first time on American stage, in *The Yorker's Stratagem, or Banana's Wedding*, by J. Robinson.

England, Sept. 13. William Blake warns Thomas Paine his views endanger his life (→ 19).

New York, Sept. 21. First performance of James Hewitt's *Battle of Trenton* played; contains *Yankee Doodle* and *Washington's March.*

United States, Oct. 11. Antoine Blanc founds first Negro Catholic sisterhood.

New York City, Oct. 12. Society of St. Tammany marks first Columbus Day.

Territory of Columbia, Oct. 13. Cornerstone laid for Presidential Palace [White House].

Boston. During smallpox epidemic, 8,000 volunteer for inoculation.

Alaska. Russian Orthodox Church begins missionary work under Sitka bishop (→ 1794).

Pennsylvania. Pennsylvania buys land on Lake Erie, gaining access to lake.

Rhode Island. Legislature appoints panel to study condition of unemployed ex-slaves who fought in Revolution.

United States. Hamilton writes of Jefferson, a man of "profound ambition and violent passions."

Denmark. Nation becomes first in West to abolish slavery.

Bellows Falls, Vermont. Colonel Ewel Hale completes first important wooden truss bridge in United States.

London. Mary Wollstonecraft's *A Vindication of the Rights of Women* published, prompting debate about woman's role in American society.

24 in N.Y. organize a stock exchange

New York, May 17

A group of 24 merchants and brokers met here today to set up the city's first stock exchange. They plan to do most of their trading outdoors, under a buttonwood tree situated in front of the building at 68 Wall Street. Under today's agreement, the 24 founders will give each other preference in their negotiations and will charge commissions while acting as brokers for other people. To start, they will trade government securities only, but they plan to expand to stocks of banks and insurance companies.

The stock exchange in New York could prove a formidable rival for the nation's only other exchange, established last year in Philadelphia. While the latter has the advantage of being the nation's leading city in both domestic and foreign trade, the pace of growth indicates that New York could overtake it before long. When it comes to financial dealings, the United States is not far behind Britain. It was just 19 years ago that British stock dealers moved into their own building.

Almanac by Negro

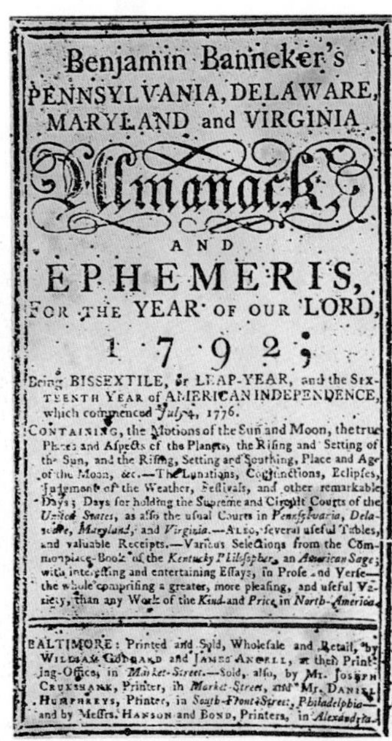

Benjamin Banneker's
PENNSYLVANIA, DELAWARE, MARYLAND and VIRGINIA
Almanack
AND
EPHEMERIS,
FOR THE YEAR OF OUR LORD
1792;
Being BISSEXTILE, or LEAP-YEAR, and the SIXTEENTH YEAR of AMERICAN INDEPENDENCE, which commenced July 4, 1776.
CONTAINING, the Motions of the Sun and Moon, the true Places and Aſpects of the Planets, the Riſing and Setting of the Sun, and the Riſing, Setting and Southing, Place and Age of the Moon, &c.—The Lunations, Conjunctions, Eclipſes, Judgment of the Weather, Feſtivals, and other remarkable Days; Days for holding the Supreme and Circuit Courts of the *United States*, as alſo the uſual Courts in *Pennſylvania, Delaware, Maryland*, and *Virginia*.—ALSO, ſeveral uſeful Tables, and valuable Receipts.—Various Selections from the Commonplace-Book of the *Kentucky Philoſopher*, an *American Sage*; with intereſting and entertaining Eſſays, in Proſe and Verſe—the whole compriſing a greater, more pleaſing, and uſeful Variety, than any Work of the *Kind* and *Price* in *North-America*.
BALTIMORE: Printed and Sold, Wholeſale and Retail, by WILLIAM GODDARD and JAMES ANGELL, at their Printing-Office, in *Market-Street*.—Sold, alſo, by Mr. JOSEPH CRUKSHANK, Printer, in *Market-Street*, and Mr. DANIEL HUMPHREYS, Printer, in *South-Front-Street, Philadelphia*—and by Meſſrs. HANSON and BOND, Printers, in *Alexandria*.

Benjamin Banneker, a free Negro and self-taught astronomer, has put out his second almanac. He sent the first to Thomas Jefferson with a plea to end slavery.

Jefferson feuds with Hamilton over policy

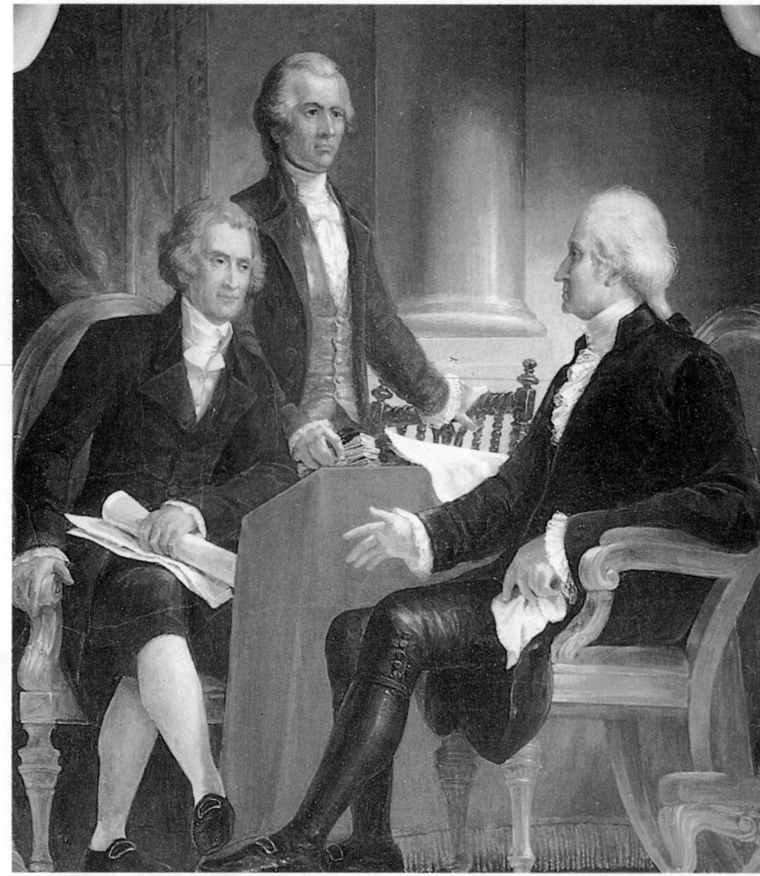

Jefferson and Hamilton consulting with Washington. By Constantino Brumidi

Philadelphia, December

President Washington, disturbed by the escalating battle between his Secretaries of State and the Treasury, is urging both men to bury the hatchet. He asked Treasury Secretary Alexander Hamilton "for mutual forebearances and temporising yieldings on all sides," and warned Secretary of State Thomas Jefferson that the public feud threatens the stability of the government.

The main point of contention between the two statesmen is the extent of federal power. Hamilton, whose Bank of the United States was incorporated last year, seeks to expand the powers of the executive and use the federal government to develop American industry. Jefferson believes the secretary has violated the Constitution and endangered the republic by assuming powers that are the province of the states.

For months, Jefferson has tried to have Hamilton dismissed, but he has decided against exposing new evidence of Hamilton's unsavory conduct. Jefferson learned of Hamilton's affair with Maria Reynolds, the wife of a man who has allegedly been swindling the Treasury. Hamilton is reported to have offered James Reynolds $1,000 to keep the liaison secret. Jefferson's discovery has confirmed his suspicions that Hamilton is playing fast and loose with Treasury funds. Earlier, Jefferson wrote that "the credit and fate of the nation seem to hang on the desperate throws and plunges of gambling scoundrels." The Secretary of State believes the Treasury chief has been giving away secrets to his banker friends, who, he says, are getting rich at the expense of the poor and the uninformed.

The enmity between the two which began during the Constitutional Convention, deepened as they became rivals to succeed Washington. Jefferson convinced a friend to mount a series of attacks in the *National Gazette* that called Hamilton a Tory and portrayed Jefferson as a "colossus of liberty." An enraged Hamilton said the attack reminded him "of the Fable of the Viper which stung to death the Countryman, the genial warmth of whose bosom had reanimated its frozen carcass" (→ Dec. 31, 1793).

Whiskey tax stirs Pennsylvania protest

Philadelphia, Sept. 29

Despite widespread protest in the West and South, President Washington said today that he plans strict enforcement of the whiskey tax in the excise law enacted last year. This announcement was prompted by the recent Pittsburgh convention of delegates from Pennsylvania's four Western counties at which Republican leader Albert Gallatin chaired a committee that drafted resolutions opposing the tax and outlining ways to circumvent it. Protests have been equally loud in central North Carolina where, as in western Pennsylvania and other parts of the West and South, whiskey is one of the chief transportable and barterable products. The government has received many reports of defiance directed at government representatives seeking to inspect distilleries (→Nov. 1794).

Washington re-elected President of U.S.

Philadelphia, Dec. 5

George Washington, running virtually unopposed, has been unanimously re-elected President of the United States. His fellow Federalist, John Adams, the incumbent Vice President, came in second in the electoral vote and was thus also re-elected to his post.

Washington had been expected to announce that he was not going to seek a second term. But because of the current conflict involving the two primary members of his Cabinet, Thomas Jefferson and Alexander Hamilton, both of whom want to be Washington's successor, the President decided that the republic would best be served if he continued in office until the political situation cooled. It seems that growing French-American differences also had a part in persuading Washington to seek a second term.

British and Americans explore Northwest

Oregon Territory

Exploration of the Northwest is in full swing and one big reason was the discovery by the British Captain James Cook back in 1778 that Indians here are willing to sell sea otters for a few pence that the Chinese will buy for $100 each.

So interest in the area boomed and explorers followed. The American Captain Robert Gray, exploring the region on his way to China, came upon a major tributary that he named after his ship, the Columbia, as well as a harbor on the coast that his men named after the captain.

Captain George Vancouver of the British navy saw the river now named the Columbia on an earlier voyage, but he failed to explore it. What he did do was survey the region's coastline. Among other things, Captain Vancouver circled an island he has named after himself, and sailed on a sound he has named after the officer who first sighted it, Peter Puget. Vancouver has since sent in Lieutenant William Broughton to survey the Columbia. Other discoveries of interest in the region included Mount Hood, south of the Columbia, and Mount Baker.

Women line up to vote in New Jersey. Under English rule, a few colonies, most notably New York, allowed suffrage to women of property. But since independence only New Jersey's women have retained the right to vote.

Kentucky becomes union's 15th state

Lexington, Kentucky, June 5

After eight years of debate, Kentucky has been admitted to the union as the 15th state. It was formed from the western district of Virginia. The government was organized today in Lexington with frontier hero Isaac Shelby as Governor.

The constitution, the first devised for a frontier state, is considered important as a precedent-setting document. Its bill of rights copies the Pennsylvania constitution of 1790, and the body of the document is conservative. Neither the governor nor the senators will be directly elected by the people, slavery is permitted and membership in the legislature is denied to ministers of the gospel. On the other hand, provisions for unrestricted white male suffrage, representation based on population and not on county units, and nullification of primogeniture rights reflect the democratizing influences of the frontier.

Paine visits France after British threat

Paris, Sept. 19

Another hero's welcome greeted Tom Paine as he arrived in the French capital today less than a week after fleeing England, where he faces treason charges for views expressed in *The Rights of Man*, a defense of the current uprising in France. Two weeks ago, while Paine was still in London, he was elected to the French national convention, which sent a deputy to fetch him. Paine stayed put, preferring to answer the treason charges. But he was persuaded to flee by his supporters, one of whom, the poet William Blake, warned, "You must not go home, or you are a dead man." Paine reluctantly set off for Dover, slipping through customs 20 minutes before the order for his arrest reached there. When Paine's boat docked at Calais, cannons fired a salute, onlookers cheered, and the refugee strode through the streets to cries of "Vive Thomas Paine!"

New plan for the capital city unveiled

October 13. *In the nation's new capital, on the banks of the Potomac, workers have laid the cornerstone of the Presidential Palace. Andrew Ellicott's map (above) shows Pierre L'Enfant's design for the city, adopted by Congress this year. The French architect's innovative plan calls for broad avenues radiating out from public buildings. L'Enfant, however, has been dismissed after objecting to the public sale of city lots (→Sept. 18, 1793).*

1793

Washington

Philadelphia, Feb. 18. Supreme Court rules in Chisholm v. Georgia that a citizen of one state may sue a different state in federal court.

Philadelphia, Feb. 28. Nine resolutions submitted in House against Hamilton's policies.

Charleston, South Carolina, Apr. 8. Citizen Edmond Charles Genet, French minister to United States, arrives seeking American support for French war effort (→22).

Philadelphia, Apr. 22 Washington issues Neutrality Proclamation; U.S. at peace with Britain, France (→28).

Philadelphia, Apr. 22. Washington attends performance of John Bill Ricketts's popular circus.

United States, Apr. 28. Jefferson on relations with France: "An injured friend is the bitterest of foes" (→May 18).

Philadelphia, May 18. Citizen Genet receives cool reception from Washington; President is determined to maintain American neutrality (→Aug. 2).

Baltimore, May 25. Father Stephen Theodore Budin becomes first Catholic priest ordained in the United States.

Monticello, Virginia. Jefferson designs classic American plow, but does not patent it.

Spring Mill, Pennsylvania. Pennsylvania Vine Company plants first commercial grapevines in United States.

Philadelphia. Mederic Louis Moreau de Saint-Mery, intrigued by odd and even house-numbering method, brings system back to Europe.

Oregon Territory. Sir Alexander MacKenzie becomes first white man to cross N. American continent; canoes down Bella Coola River to Pacific.

New York City. Noah Webster founds city's first daily newspaper, *American Minerva.*

Philadelphia. Andrew Law's *Musical Primer* attacks native composition as "harsh."

United States. Poem supporting French Revolution, *On the Anniversary of the Storming of the Bastille*, by Philip Freneau, published.

United States. *A Word of Remembrance and Caution to the Rich*, by the Rev. John Woolman, calls for abolition of slavery and other reforms.

Eli Whitney's cotton gin expands farming

Whitney's gin promises prosperity even in the less fertile Southern piedmont.

New Haven, Conn., Oct. 28

Eli Whitney, a Massachusetts-born inventor, has filed a patent application for a device that removes seeds from cotton quickly and cheaply. The machine, the cotton gin, should vastly increase the amount of land devoted to growing cotton in the South, because the cost of removing seeds has been a major impediment for farmers.

The gin works on short-staple cotton, which is easily grown in many areas and is greatly desired by English mills. Plantation owners generally have produced long-staple cotton because it has easily removable seeds. However, it can only be grown near the coast. By expanding the area suitable for cotton, the gin will increase the demand for plantation slave labor.

Whitney developed the gin on the South Carolina plantation of Catherine Greene, widow of the Revolutionary War hero, General Nathanael Greene. It is a series of rollers, bristles and hooks that strain out the seeds and it is simple enough for any worker to operate. Whitney will build the gins at a factory in New Haven and charge growers 40 percent of their crops to clean the cotton (→March 14, 1794).

Philadelphia, March 4. *Washington's second inaugural by J.L.G. Ferris.*

Jefferson bows out as State Secretary

Monticello, Virginia, Dec. 31

Thomas Jefferson will begin the new year far from the political fray and the government that he helped establish. President Washington attempted to change his mind, but the Secretary of State insisted that the time has finally come to retire from public life. "The motion of my blood no longer keeps time with the tumult of the world," Jefferson told his confidant, James Madison. Jefferson has been greatly dispirited since his adversary, Treasury Secretary Alexander Hamilton, successfully defended himself in Congress against charges of impropriety. The feud between Jefferson and Hamilton was one of the major factors in Washington's decision to seek a second term as President.

Jefferson (1791) by C.W. Peale.

President sees first U.S. balloon flight

Philadelphia, Jan. 9

Up and away went the inflated balloon of Jean-Pierre Francois Blanchard today as an excited crowd, including an impressed President Washington looked on. The Frenchman's air-tight, helium-filled bag soared to a height of 5,812 feet on this, the first free flight of a balloon in America. The French developed the balloon and were the first to send men aloft in one, when Jean-Francois Pilatre de Rozier and Francois Laurent sailed above Paris in 1783; peasants were so alarmed at the sight that they set upon it with pitchforks.

Cabinet asks recall of France's Genet

Philadelphia, Aug. 2

The brief but remarkable American episode in the diplomatic career of Edmond Charles Edouard Genet, famous as Citizen Genet, has ended with a Cabinet resolution asking France to recall him at once.

Wildly popular with Americans who support the French Revolution, Citizen Genet, who arrived in Charleston April 8, lost no time in issuing letters of marque to American privateers so they could attack ships of France's enemies, and in trying to raise regiments to strike at Spanish possessions in Florida and Mississippi. Told to desist, he demanded a special session of Congress to hear his case, and threatened to appeal to Americans if this were denied (→ June 5, 1794).

Fugitive Slave Law

Philadelphia, Feb. 12

The Federal Fugitive Law passed this year has come to be known as the Fugitive Slave Law. Intended to provide for the extradition of criminals from one state to another, the law allows slave owners to seize a runaway in another state. By taking the fugitive slave before a magistrate, the master can acquire authority to take the slave back to bondage. The law also forbids harboring a fugitive slave or preventing his arrest (→ Jan. 30, 1797).

France kills King, goes to war with Europe

Revenge of the masses. Louis XVI, deposed and renamed Citizen Capet, is guillotined in Place de la Revolution. His fate was sealed when leaders of the new republic found evidence of his intrigues in a secret cabinet in the Tuileries.

Paris, Feb. 2

Following the execution of King Louis XVI by guillotine on January 21, the revolutionary government of France now finds itself at war with Britain, The Netherlands and Spain. As it has also been at war with Austria, Prussia and Sardinia since last April, France is now in a state of armed conflict with almost the whole of Europe.

What will the United States do? Secretary of State Thomas Jefferson, a Francophile who until recently was the American minister here, is known to favor the revolutionary cause. While deploring its excesses, he has described it as "the most sacred cause that ever man was engaged in," and has stated that "the liberty of the whole earth" depends on its success. Those who agree with him can also point to the treaty of alliance of 1778, which obligates the United States to come to France's assistance.

By contrast, Alexander Hamilton and other Federalists are afraid of French radicalism spreading to other countries, and look to Britain as a bulwark of conservatism.

The final decision about which course to follow lies, of course, with President Washington (→ Apr. 8).

4,044 die of fever in Philadelphia

Philadelphia, August

In the worst health disaster ever to strike an American city, nearly 24,000 of this city's residents have been infected with yellow fever. The death toll is reported to be 4,044. Symptoms of the disease, which is usually associated with tropical regions, include a sudden high fever, prostration, jaundice and hemorrhaging. Science has yet to determine how this often-fatal affliction is spread. However, Dr. Benjamin Rush, the Philadelphian who founded the nation's first medical college, has expressed the belief that Negroes are immune to it. Therefore, during the epidemic, Dr. Rush has been recruiting many Negroes to help care for those who are struck down by the fever.

Slaves burn Albany

Albany, New York, Nov. 25

The fears of some have turned to reality as Negro slaves in Albany set fires that caused damage totaling a quarter of a million dollars. Three men and two women are now being held, awaiting execution for the crime of arson. Fear of Negro uprisings has been fairly widespread recently. In August, the Virginia cities of Richmond, Powhatan and Elizabeth City sent requests to their Governor for arms to quell rumored and actual rebellions.

The copper "chain" cent is one of the first issues to be cast at the United States Mint established last year in Philadelphia.

Washington, D.C., September 18. *In a ceremony replete with Masonic ritual, President Washington lays the cornerstone for the Capitol. Stephen Hallet, who won the initial architectural competition, is directing the project. But he is under instructions to use a more artistic design submitted after the original deadline by William Thornton. Rumor has it that Hallet intends to substitute his own plan. A mural by Allen Cox (→ Nov. 17, 1800).*

Gilbert Stuart, upon returning to New York from London this year, completed his understated portrait of Mrs. Richard Yates.

1794

Washington

New York, March 3. James Hewitt writes music for opera *Tammany* or *The Indian Chief.*

United States, March 14. Eli Whitney granted patent for cotton gin (→ 1795).

United States, March 22. Congress forbids slave trade to foreign ports, fearing spread of Haitian slave revolt.

Philadelphia, March 27. United States Navy authorized by Congress.

Pennsylvania, Apr. 24. Legislature passes revised criminal code, eliminating death penalty except for murder.

New Jersey, May 6. First steam engine built in United States by John Hewett at Belleville waterworks.

United States, May. James Madison asks Aaron Burr for formal introduction to Dolley Payne Todd.

Philadelphia, June 5. Fleeing persecution in England, scientist Joseph Priestley arrives.

Philadelphia. American Convention of Abolition Societies founded, condemning slavery and legal restrictions on free Negroes.

United States. Charles Willson Peale establishes first privately run museum of natural history in United States.

United States. Powdering of men's hair out of fashion; black ribbon in back retained.

New York City. Elihu Palmer organizes Deistical Society supporting French Revolution and republican religion called the cult of the Supreme Being.

Kayak Island, Alaska. Holy Synod of Russian Orthodox Church sends 10 missionary monks to Alaska (→ 1795).

New York City. Tontine Coffee House first serves soda water; first modern hotel, City Hotel, opens.

United States. National arsenal established in Springfield, Massachusetts, Harpers Ferry, Virginia; Springfield musket made official U.S. weapon.

Alaska. First vessel built in Alaska at Voskresensk [Resurrection Bay.]

Philadelphia. Susanna Haswell Rowson's *Charlotte Temple* published, first best-seller in United States.

Whiskey rebels give in

Perils of the tax collector: tarring and feathering during the rebellion.

Philadelphia, November

After three months of disregard for the law, threats and near-insurrection, the so-called "whiskey rebels" have laid down their arms. In what had become the gravest test of its ability to enforce the laws of the land, the federal government has apparently emerged victorious.

The uprising began in June when farmers in western Pennsylvania and throughout the Appalachians refused to pay the federal excise tax on whiskey. The farmers, whose primary crop is grain and whose cheapest way of marketing it is in the form of whiskey, argued that the tax was unfair and excessively high – about 25 percent of the going price for a quart of whiskey. In addition, the farmers said that because of the shortage of hard currency, whiskey often proved to be the only practical medium of exchange. The government, in turn, contended that the tax was equitable and a legitimate source of desperately needed revenue.

After giving the rebellious farmers two firm warnings that the government would not tolerate their lawlessness, Commander-in-Chief Washington personally took the field with a force of 12,500 militiamen. When the farmers realized their predicament, they dispersed, and the once-formidable uprising simply melted away (→ May 1795).

Riding to the hounds. "The End of the Hunt" by an anonymous artist.

Negro Episcopalian forms congregation

Philadelphia, July

The African Protestant Episcopal Church of St. Thomas held the first service in its new building this month. Construction started last year, with the help of many local dignitaries. The congregation was founded because of the ill-treatment Negroes suffered at St. George's Methodist Church. Many Negroes, including the Rev. Absalom Jones and the Rev. Richard Allen, left the church as a result. In 1791, Allen and Jones started two Negro congregations, Methodist and Episcopalian respectively. The latter takes its place among the nation's Negro churches, such as Allen's Bethel Church here and the First African Baptist Church in Charleston.

Philadelphia Pastor Absalom Jones (1810) by Raphaelle Peale.

U.S. adopts neutral position in conflict

Philadelphia, June 5

President Washington's policy set forth in last year's Neutrality Proclamation, of avoiding alliance with either party in the war between revolutionary France and Britain and its allies, has now been confirmed by an act of Congress. American ports are closed to all foreign warships and to domestic vessels that are being fitted out for service against one of the belligerents; and American citizens are barred from serving in any foreign army in a war against a nation with which the United States is at peace (→ Nov. 19).

Wayne ends Indian war in Northwest

Battle of Fallen Timbers. "Mad Anthony" Wayne's legion, outnumbered two to one, hunts down Indians' Northwest Confederation along Maumee River.

Northwest Territory, Aug. 20

The colorful and brilliant Revolutionary General "Mad Anthony" Wayne, with a well-trained army of nearly 3,000 men, has broken the back of Indian resistance in the Ohio country with the decisive defeat of an Indian force of about 2,000 at Fallen Timbers on the Maumee River, under the very noses of the British at Fort Miami. The Indian force, made up of Shawnee, Miami, Delaware and Potawatami warriors led by the Shawnee Chief Blue Jacket, had expected British help, but it did not materialize. General Wayne, acting on the counsel of his chief spy, William Wells, delayed his attack for three days. During that time, the resolve of the Indians weakened and about a third of them left their positions among the fallen trees to return to Fort Miami. When Wayne finally attacked, the Indians were easily routed. The defeat is expected to end the Indian threat in the Northwest Territory (→Aug. 10, 1795).

Shoemakers form first trade union

Philadelphia, May 1

The shoemakers of Philadelphia proudly announced today that they have formed the Federal Society of Journeymen Cordwainers, the first trade union in the country. The cordwainers, or shoemakers, like many other workers, had previously used a mutual aid society for protection during illnesses and for aid to widows and orphans. But a spokesman for the union said a stronger organization was needed to defend the men against the employers, who set up their own league five years ago. The shoemakers say the employers created the league to cut workers' wages. The union plans to concentrate its efforts on fighting for higher wages, although no strike has yet been planned (→1799).

Writings of women have more impact

Philadelphia, June 30

Mrs. Susanna Haswell Rowson appeared tonight in the opening performance of *Slaves in Algiers*, a theatrical drama she wrote herself. It has been a banner year for Mrs. Rowson; besides her current stage appearance, her 1791 novel, *Charlotte Temple, a Tale of Truth*, about a schoolgirl deserted by a British officer, was recently reprinted here to wide acclaim. Another author of some repute is Mrs. Sarah Morton; her poem *Ouabi, or the Virtues of Nature*, an American Indian tale, was published in 1790 and remains popular. And a work by an Englishwoman, Mary Wollstonecraft, *Vindication of the Rights of Woman*, has been finding its way into American girls' schools.

British to quit Northwest under Jay treaty

Philadelphia, Nov. 19

The government announced today the signing of a treaty with Britain negotiated by the American Chief Justice John Jay and the British Foreign Secretary, Lord Grenville. The accord will settle several serious Anglo-American diplomatic disputes that had been threatening to precipitate hostilities. One key provision is Britain's agreement to withdraw support of the Indians and evacuate its posts in the Northwest Territory by June 1, 1796. Other important provisions relate to settling American damage claims against Britain and the payment of debts incurred by the United States. The treaty was signed despite widespread opposition here, and a lively debate is expected before it is ratified (→March 1795).

Chief Justice John Jay, a reluctant patriot in the 1770's, negotiated treaty. Portrait by Gilbert Stuart.

Boston relaxes ban; theaters very lively

Boston, February

Boston is back on stage. After repeal of the city's Anti-Theater Act, showman Charles Stuart Foster wasted no time in raising the curtain on *The Farmer* at the Federal Street Theater this month. The production was Boston's first legal theatrical program since 1750.

The long absence hasn't changed American audiences. They still love to sidetrack a show with their own impromptu – even menacing – activities. That is why Boston musicians took out an advertisement to "entreat a generous people from throwing stones, apples, etc., into the orchestra" so that while the players "eat the bread of industry in a free country, it may not be tinctured with the poison of humiliation."

There is a new theatrical mood in Philadelphia, where the composer-conductor-impresario Alexander Reinagle recently led the country's best orchestra in Samuel Arnold's *The Castle of Andalusia* at the gala opening of the Chestnut Theater. Reinagle was a major force in getting the new theater built. It is modeled on the Theater Royal in Bath, England.

Philadelphia is now also home to the versatile English composer Benjamin Carr, whose *Federal Overture* had its successful premiere there. It parades a loosely woven medley of popular tunes, including *Yankee Doodle*, *The Marseillaise*, and *Oh, Dear, What Can the Matter Be*.

Eager crowds attended the opening of Philadelphia's new theater in February.

1795

Washington

Philadelphia, Jan. 29. Naturalization Act passed by Congress, mandating five-year residency for citizenship.

Philadelphia, March. Terms of Jay Treaty made public, sparking fierce debate (→June 24).

New Orleans, April. Cabildo is built as seat of Spanish colonial government.

New York City, May 8. Congress creates Post Office Department.

United States, May. Two of 200 "Whiskey Boys" arrested for 1794 rebellion are convicted of treason [later pardoned].

Philadelphia, June 24. Jay Treaty ratified by Senate after long debate (→July 22).

Northwest Territory, July 19. Connecticut Land Company and its agent Moses Cleaveland buy Western Reserve on Lake Erie.

United States, July 22. Hamilton publishes *Camillus* papers supporting Jay Treaty (→Dec.).

United States, Oct. 9. Writing to Patrick Henry, Washington asserts, "My ardent desire is . . . to keep the United States free from political connections with every other country, to see them independent of all and under the influence of none."

Boston. Wooden-railed tramway built; first primitive railroad in United States.

London. American Robert Fulton patents first power shovel for excavating canals.

United States. Congress regulates trade with Indians by establishing system of factors.

Philadelphia. Richard Allen ordained as first black deacon in American Methodism.

United States. In letter to Tenche Coxe, Jefferson explains, "The ball of liberty is not so well in motion that it will roll around the globe."

Kodiak, Alaska. First Russian Orthodox Church established here (→1799).

New Orleans. Rivermen from Kentucky and other states begin arriving in New Orleans aboard flatboats; they are known to Creoles as "Kaintucks."

United States. Wilderness Road opens to wagon traffic.

Treaty stirs debate; key officials resign

Republicans burn Jay in effigy.

Philadelphia, December

The debate over ratification of the Jay Treaty is continuing to have serious repercussions. The treaty, intended to settle the diplomatic disputes with Britain, was signed August 14 by President Washington. Republicans in the House, however, consider it a sellout. On August 19, Secretary of State Edmund Randolph resigned after he was accused of having conspired with the French to block ratification of the treaty. This was followed by the resignation of Chief Justice John Jay, principal U.S. negotiator of the treaty, who decided to return to his political career as Governor of New York. President Washington's nomination of John Rutledge to fill the court vacancy that was created by Jay's resignation was then rejected by the Senate because Rutledge has acknowledged his opposition to adoption of the treaty.

A significant aspect of the affair may well have been the precedent set by President Washington in exerting his executive prerogative to sign the treaty despite its failure to win approval in the House, which is not required according to the Constitution (→Feb. 15, 1796).

Gilbert Stuart paints Washington portrait

Philadelphia

The United States can boast an image of George Washington that is as strong as the President himself now that Gilbert Stuart has completed his portrait of the nation's leader. In March, Stuart made good use of the rare opportunity to paint Washington from life, for those who know the President find the likeness convincing. And the painting is more than a portrait; it is an icon for the nation. The formal pose and patrician air of the depiction give Washington a nobility that derives from Stuart's European training. But the lack of ostentation in Washington's dress and the somber execution of the work reflect the democracy in which the painting was conceived. Stuart has already received requests for new versions.

Sitting for posterity. "The Painter and the President" by J.L.G. Ferris.

Hamilton quits job but keeps influence

Fiscal wizard Hamilton, caught in a storm over his support for England. Portrait (1806) by John Trumbull.

Philadelphia, December

Alexander Hamilton's resignation as Treasury Secretary during the furor over the Jay Treaty with Britain has not reduced his influence in the adminstration of President Washington. Hamilton wrote the speech that the President delivered to Congress this month urging approval of the controversial treaty to settle land and trade differences. The ratification battle has exacerbated the deep divisions between the Republicans and Hamilton's Federalists. The Republicans think the treaty is far too generous to the British, but Hamilton insists that it bestows great economic benefits on the United States. He also says it keeps America at peace during the war between Britain and France.

Nation of drinkers

Philadelphia

Drinking spirits has become very much an American pastime, and the availability of beer, cider, rum, wine, gin, and rye and bourbon whiskey has made the consumption of alcoholic beverages very much a family affair and one of the rewards of hard work. Americans drink far more than the English; rough estimates indicate that annually an American over 15 years old drinks 34 gallons of beer and cider, five gallons of distilled spirits and nearly a gallon of wine. The morals and values of the American communities, however, apparently keep public drunkenness under control.

Whitney cotton gin is copied by slave

Fort Adams, Mississippi

The slave had only a crude drawing and an oral description of the cotton gin that Eli Whitney invented. But from those "bare bones" he built machinery for a cotton gin that does the job. Like Whitney's, this cotton gin separates the fibers from their seeds. The slave, a skilled mechanic whose name has not been disclosed, is owned by Daniel Clark of Fort Adams [Wilkinson County], who introduced the gin to this area. Cotton growers are flocking to it. The gin that Whitney introduced in 1793 has been revolutionizing the production of cotton.

U.S. pays $1 million to ransom sailors

Philadelphia, Sept. 5

Angry and humiliated, but left with no other choices, Congress has agreed to pay the Bey of Algiers a sum equal to $992,463 for protection of American shipping in the Mediterranean and for the ransom of 115 sailors, including some who have been held captive for 10 years. Part of the payment is to be in the form of warships and naval stores, the rest in cash. Congress has been paying tribute to some of the Barbary potentates since 1784. Distasteful though this is, the United States is simply following the example of the maritime powers of Europe, including France and Britain (→Nov. 4, 1796).

Indians yield land after Wayne victory

Fort Greenville, Ohio, Aug. 10

General Anthony Wayne today completed long negotiations with representatives of the Delaware, Shawnee, Wyandot, Miami and other Indian tribes that were lately at war with the United States but soundly defeated by "Mad Anthony" at the Battle of Fallen Timbers last year. A treaty was signed here August 3, followed by councils that ended today. It provides for the cession of large amounts of land in the eastern part of the Northwest Territory and sets a definite boundary between Indian and white lands, thus opening the territory to settlement (→May 18, 1796).

Negro has romantic role in new play

New York City, May 22

For the first time in American theatrical history, a Negro has been given a romantic role and is not playing the comic servant. The play involved, by James Murdock, is called *The Triumph of Love*, and it features a Negro actor in the role of Sambo, a secondary romantic character. Until this production, the only theatrical roles that have ever been assigned to Negroes were those of bumbling and shiftless servants, a stereotypical image of the African slaves that would not be threatening to a public that has grown accustomed to the Negroes' holding only subordinate positions.

Treaty gives U.S. use of Mississippi

Spain, Oct. 27

Americans today won the right to ship goods down the Mississippi River through the port of New Orleans without paying duty to the Spanish government. The right was granted in the Treaty of San Lorenzo, which is expected to ease the long-standing friction over trading. It also sets 31 degrees latitude [now the northern boundary of the state of Louisiana east of the Mississippi] as the dividing line between the United States and Spanish territory. The U.S. minister to Britain, Thomas Pinckney, negotiated the treaty at San Lorenzo del Escorial, near Madrid (→Apr. 7, 1798).

Slave revolt fails; 25 slain, 23 hang

Pointe Coupee, Louisiana, April

A slave insurrection plot was foiled in a delta area north of New Orleans recently when word of it leaked out. Authorities killed 25 slaves on the spot, and 23 were hanged on a riverboat trip. The plot allegedly was hatched by a band of white men trying to overthrow the Spanish rulers. Punishment for the slaves was swift and bloody. After killing 25 here, the officials placed 23 others, in chains, on a boat and floated them down the Mississippi River. At each landing, one slave was hanged. Their heads were left on poles from Pointe Coupee to New Orleans. The white plotters were banished from the colony.

From Peale's easel, triumph in illusion

Peale's masterly "trompe l'œil."

Philadelphia, May 1

Watch your step at the Columbianum's art exhibition or you may find yourself walking into a Charles Willson Peale painting instead of a stairway. A tour de force of illusionistic painting, *The Staircase Group* is installed in a doorway above an actual step, as if one could climb the stairs along with the young Peales, Raphaelle and Titian.

May 1. *Congress has added two stars and stripes to the American flag in honor of Vermont and Kentucky, the 14th and 15th states (→July 4, 1818).*

Philadelphia. *The half eagle, designed by Robert Scot and struck at the United States Mint, is the nation's first official coin made of gold.*

1796

Washington

Paris, Feb. 15. French inform envoy James Monroe that Jay Treaty voids all French-American treaties (→29).

Philadelphia, Feb. 29. Washington declares Jay Treaty in effect; U.S. and France on brink of war (→Nov. 15).

Tennessee, February. Andrew Jackson as delegate to state convention opposes inclusion of "God" in state constitution.

Philadelphia, March 8. Supreme Court backs 1794 carriage tax, upholding constitutionality of a congressional act for first time (→Apr. 22).

Philadelphia, May 18. Land Act passed by Congress, opening Northwest Territory land for sale to public (→Spring).

Northwest Territory, July 11. U.S. Captain Moses Porter occupies fort at Detroit after British withdraw under terms of Jay Treaty (→May 7, 1800).

Boston, Aug. 17. African Society formed to aid Negroes.

Paris, Nov. 15. French minister Adat announces breaking of diplomatic ties between France and U.S. (→Dec.).

Tennessee, November. Andrew Jackson chosen as state's first delegate to Congress.

Philadelphia. Scientists conduct first experiments with gas illumination.

Philadelphia. Rep. Albert Gallatin fights to create House Committee of Ways and Means.

Philadelphia. Joseph Priestley, English scientist, establishes Unitarian church here.

United States. Philosopher Constantin François de Chassebœuf expelled, charged with spying for France.

Charlotte, North Carolina. Grand jury accuses Quakers of inciting slave unrest and arson.

United States. Jefferson, in letter to Edward Rutledge, writes, "No man will ever bring out of the Presidency the reputation which carries him into it."

Virginia. New criminal code in state eliminates death penalty for several types of crimes, signaling national trend away from capital punishment.

New Orleans. Spanish Governor Carondelet establishes first police force and system of street lighting here.

Tennessee becomes 16th state in U.S.

Tennessee, June 1

The Southwest Territory today became the state of Tennessee, the 16th in the nation. After a census that was taken last year showed the population of the territory had passed the figure required for statehood, 60,000 residents, a constitutional convention was assembled in the capital of the territory, Knoxville, and it put together Tennessee's first constitution. As a slaveholding state, however, it will be allowed only one delegate in Congress. The decision to set this limit was reached when Federalists, who predicted a Republican leaning in the state, expressed their reluctance to grant it admission. John Sevier, who served as Governor of the defunct state of Franklin, has been chosen to become the first Governor of Tennessee.

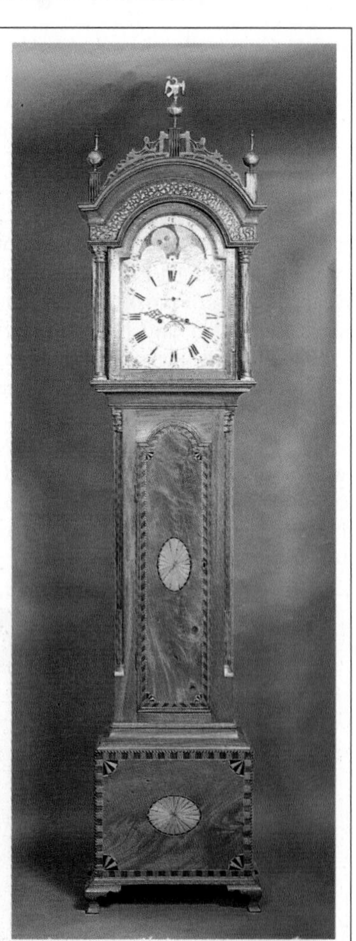

This mahogany tall-case clock, made in 1796 by Ichabod Sanford with works by Caleb Wheaton, is eight feet high and belongs to Luther Metcalf of Massachusetts.

France severs links with United States

Paris, December

Still smarting from last year's ratification of the Jay Treaty between the United States and Britain, the French government has refused to receive Charles Cotesworth Pinckney, who recently arrived here to replace James Monroe as American minister. The snub was not unexpected since Monsieur Adat, the Directory's minister to the United States, announced on November 15 that diplomatic ties between the two countries would be severed.

The aggressive stance of France is attributable to its chagrin at the U.S. decision to follow a policy of strict neutrality in the present conflict with England, rather than join on the French side. Added to this is a restored feeling of confidence in Paris following a string of victories in Italy achieved by General Napoleon Bonaparte (→May 15, 1797).

Speculators active in Northwest land sale

Northwest Territory, Spring

Since the passage of the Land Act by the federal government at Philadelphia in May, speculators have been busy buying up large blocks of acreage in the Northwest Territory. The lands are being sold at public auction to the highest bidders at or above a minimum price of $2 per acre. But the smallest unit that can be bought is 640 acres. Because of the high minimum that has been set, the number of potential buyers is restricted. As a result, many people have criticized the act for discouraging purchases by the kind of ordinary settlers that the territory needs.

Court expands power to review legislation

Philadelphia, Apr. 22

The United States Supreme Court has extended its power to adjudicate the law of the land. Today, it ruled that all international agreements negotiated and ratified under the authority of the Constitution are federal law. The decision gives precedence to federal law over conflicting state laws.

On March 8, the high court upheld the constitutionality of a congressional act for the first time. The case, Hylton v. United States, was brought before the court through the tenacity of Alexander Hamilton. In 1794, Congress levied a tax on carriages. Hylton refused to pay $16 in taxes on his vehicle, claiming the law was unconstitutional. Former Secretary of Treasury Hamilton sought to enforce payment and receive an upholding of the tax law. After Hamilton's skillful presentation before the court, the justices ruled that Hylton must submit payment. More importantly, the court has widened its jurisdiction; how far its power extends is open to debate (→Feb. 24, 1803).

Cleaveland lays out new city, and leaves

Northwest Territory, Sept. 30

General Moses Cleaveland, a director of the Connecticut Land Company, which bought three million acres of the so-called Western Reserve from the State of Connecticut a year ago, has spent the summer surveying the country with some 50 men and recently laid out a city on the high ground where the Cuyahoga River empties into Lake Erie. Streets have been plotted around a 10-acre common and several log houses have been erected. Cleaveland, a lawyer from Canterbury, Connecticut, proposed that the new city be called Cuyahoga, but his men overruled him and named it after him, though they misspelled his name Cleveland on the documents describing the city.

General Cleaveland, who owns more than $32,000 worth of shares in the Connecticut Land Company, is intent on protecting his investment. Before returning to his home in Canterbury, he contracted with 41 of the men who accompanied him to recruit 40 families to settle in the area in the next three years, helping to build them houses and clear land for farms (→July 4, 1805).

John Adams is to become new President

Adams (1826) by Gilbert Stuart.

Philadelphia, Dec. 7

After a bitter campaign, John Adams has defeated Thomas Jefferson for the presidency. The Vice President won 71 electoral votes, while Jefferson got 68. And as the Constitution provides, Jefferson will become the next Vice President. The Federalist Party, torn between the Adams and Hamilton factions, was accused of being too sympathetic to England. In turn, the Jeffersonian Republicans were charged with being overly Francophile. Now political observers are wondering whether these two political enemies can effectively work together in the same administration. Throughout the campaign, President Washington has maintained his neutrality, saying only that the wisdom and strength of republican government would be confirmed at the ballot box (→March 4, 1797).

Washington delivers presidential farewell

Philadelphia, Sept. 17

President Washington issued his official report and farewell address to the American people today. After having served the nation in war and peace for more than two decades, Washington has arranged to have this last political will and testament published in principal newspapers throughout the country.

The farewell address is primarily concerned with one of his greatest fears: the rise of political parties. According to the President, "the spirit of party" aggravates sectional tensions in the country and encourages the rule of minorities and of dangerous demagogues. With eloquence, he issues a warning to the citizenry against "a small but artful, enterprising minority" of politicians whose ambitions and ploys can be fatal to the union. The antidote to such factionalism, he says, is a union of the people, a spiritual union that will transcend party, state or section.

The President also attacks those who would takes sides in the current conflicts among the European powers. With great force, he argues for a complete and lasting neutrality in these wars as well as in the inevitable future ones. The key to American security, happiness and prosperity in the coming years, Washington warns the citizens of his young country, is the avoidance of "permanent alliances with any portion of the foreign world."

Dubuque wins land, opens lead mine

Prairie du Chien [Wisconsin]

The enterprising French-Canadian Julien Dubuque, who came to the Northwest 10 years ago and developed a lead mine near the Sac and Fox Indian village on Catfish Creek across the Mississippi in Spanish Upper Louisiana, has won a private land grant from the Spanish. Earlier, the Indians gave him the land as a mark of their respect and affection, but Dubuque asked the Spanish government to approve his claim and grant him the area in fee simple, or ownership without limitation. Dubuque's men built cabins, a trading post and smelting furnaces nearby [Dubuque, Iowa].

Tribute is paid to Barbary pirates

Tripoli, Nov. 4

In an agreement that resembles the one signed last year with the Bey of Algiers, the United States today agreed to pay a yearly tribute to the Pasha of Tripoli, whose corsairs have been ravaging American mercantile shipping in the Mediterranean. With virtually no navy at its command, and separated by the Atlantic from the Barbary coast strongholds, the U.S. government now has no choice but to submit to the demands of the pirate rulers, whose ships dominate the region. A similar agreement has been in effect with the Sultan of Morocco since 1787 (→Aug. 28, 1797).

Joseph Jefferson stars on New York stage

New York City, Dec. 20

This has been a busy theatrical season, from the long-awaited New York debut of the celebrated English actor Joseph Jefferson in February to the opening yesterday of Victor Pellisier's opera *Edwina and Angelina* here.

Jefferson, who appeared here as Squire Richard in *The Provoked Husband*, made his American debut last year in Boston, where he was acclaimed in *The Surrender of Calais*. April in Boston saw the mounting of *The Archers*, an opera with music by Benjamin Carr and libretto by that energetic literateur William Dunlap. Viewers were sympathetic to a plot based on William Tell's struggle for freedom. Of special note was *Why, Huntress, Why?* sung to a woman who pleads for the right to fight alongside the men.

One of the nation's most popular songs this year was written by the English organist-composer George K. Jackson, who no sooner was settled in Virginia than he penned the romantic *One Kind Kiss*.

In matters literary, the year was marked by the first American printing of Shakespeare's plays.

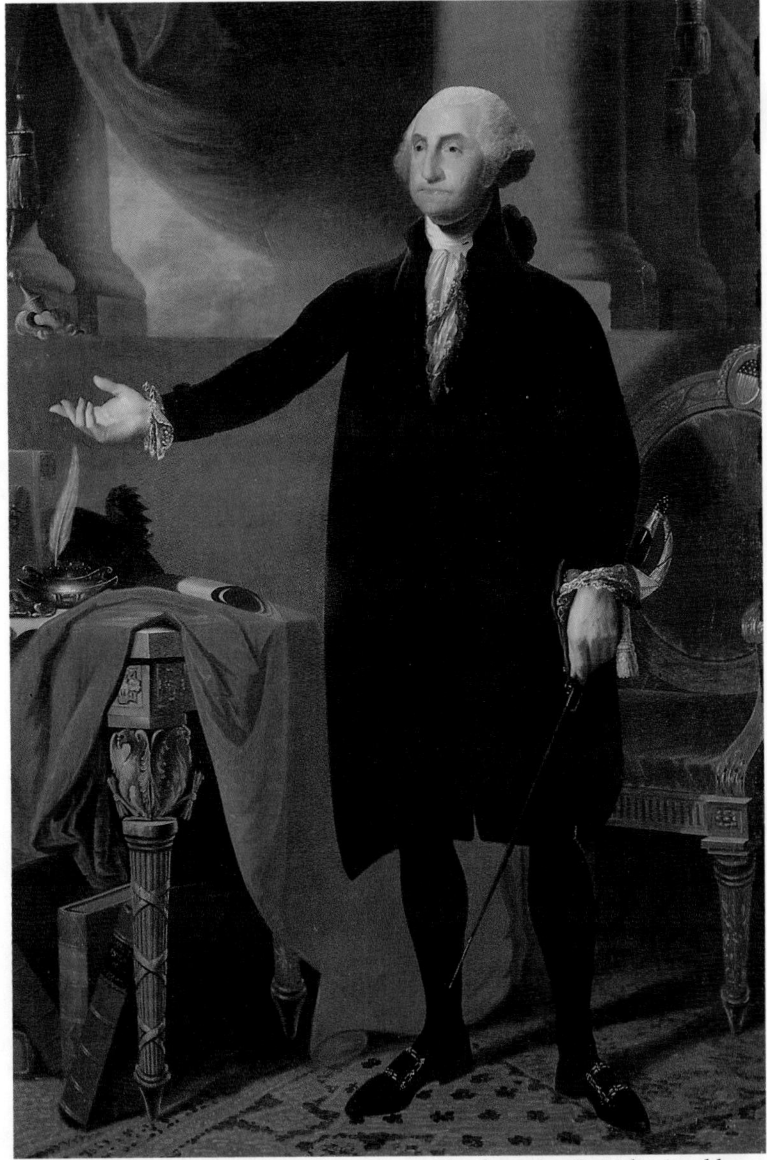
Washington, as rendered by Gilbert Stuart. The departing President's address, like so many others during his tenure, was prepared by Alexander Hamilton.

1797

Adams

Pittsburgh, Feb. 8. First coal-fueled glass factory established.

United States, Feb. 17. Cast of *Bunker Hill*, by John Daly Burk, thrills audiences by realistically re-enacting battle on stage.

Philadelphia, March 4. John Adams inaugurated President, Thomas Jefferson Vice President; Washington's Cabinet retained.

United States, May 10. The United States, first ship in new navy, launched under command of John Barry (→ Oct. 21).

Philadelphia, May 15. President Adams calls Congress into first special session, hoping to resolve crisis with France (→ 31).

Philadelphia, May 31. Adams appoints three-man commission, composed of Charles C. Pinckney, Elbridge Gerry and John Marshall, to negotiate a settlement with France (→ June 24).

Philadelphia, June 24. Congress orders 80,000-man militia readied to undertake defense in case of war with France (→ Oct. 18).

Mediterranean Sea, Aug. 28. United States agrees to pay tribute to Tunis in effort to halt Mediterranean piracy (→ Jan. 10, 1800).

United States. Eli Terry receives first American patent for a clock (→ 1803).

Philadelphia. Tower and tunnel network to draw water from Schuylkill River is first American attempt to create central water supply system.

New York. Samuel Morey builds steamboat with side paddle wheels.

Virginia. In his will, George Washington writes: "Upon the decease of my wife, it is my will and desire that all slaves whom I hold in my own right shall receive their freedom."

Boston. The Rev. Jedidiah Morse publishes *The American Gazetteer*, generally considered to be country's first gazetteer.

Philadelphia. Dr. James Woodhouse's booklet on experimental chemistry is nation's first such text.

United States. Country's first medical journal, *Medical Repository*, founded by Samuel Latham Mitchell.

United States, Constellation and Constitution built for new navy

The 44-gun Constitution, shown at left during its launching in Boston in October, is one of the navy's largest ships at 1,576 tons. And its imposing hull of bent, hard oak timbers is an innovation in naval technology.

Boston, Oct. 21

The fledgling United States Navy was bolstered today by another man-of-war when the Constitution slid down into Boston harbor. Built at Hart's shipyard mostly of oak and cedar, the ship has 44 guns and cost $302,718. It is called Old Ironsides because its hard oak timbers were not steamed into place in the usual manner but bent into place. This leaves the wood harder. The 1,576-ton frigate became the third completed this year of six ordered by Congress in 1794. The first was the Constitution's sister ship, the 44-gun United States, launched May 10 under the command of John Barry. The 36-gun Constellation followed on September 7.

The reasons for the flurry of activity have to do with recent pirate raids on American vessels off North Africa's Barbary Coast, recent problems with France, and the lack of American privateers. During the war, most American sea battles were fought by privately owned ships. With peacetime, the United States joined the European movement to ban privateers as the need for any navy at all vanished. This changed, first with the Barbary pirates, then with the war between France and England. When French privateers began seizing ships in the West Indies last year to halt American trade with the British, a full-fledged navy became doubly important. And if the new ships need more help, there is talk of turning to privateers again (→ May 3, 1798).

Southwest gets San Xavier del Bac church

Arizona, Autumn

A church has been built and consecrated at the old San Xavier del Bac mission in the far northwestern province of Mexico [Tucson]. San Xavier was founded in 1700 by Father Eusebio Kino, a Spanish Franciscan friar. The Tyrolean-born Kino reached Sonora Province in 1687 and devoted his life to establishing a string of Catholic missions in this region. An explorer, Father Kino developed maps that have added to Spain's knowledge. The new church, built in the classic Spanish colonial style, is an appropriate monument to the man many call "the father of Arizona."

San Xavier del Bac, a house of God, fortified against all intruders.

Group set up to aid widowed mothers

New York City, November

Finding that churches do not have the means to assist all the needy, a group of 15 Protestant women, led by Mrs. Isabella Graham, have formed a Society for the Relief of Poor Widows With Small Children. The women will try to keep the fatherless families they encounter fed, clothed and sheltered. While their aims appear virtuous, the women have critics who question the morality of their conspicuous acts. But other New Yorkers, citing the growing division between rich and poor, have applauded the efforts by Mrs. Graham and her companions to narrow the difference. These Protestant women feel they must have some expression of their religious upbringing, and acts of charity seem a natural outlet.

Farmers suspicious of cast-iron plow

Philadelphia, June 26

Although science and technology have been making great strides in the United States, the changes may be coming too fast for some. In New Jersey, inventor Charles Newbold has received a patent for a cast-iron plow, but many farmers are suspicious of the potentially labor-saving device, fearing that iron will poison the soil. Other recent advances include the country's first published text on chemistry, by Dr. James Woodhouse of Philadelphia, a patent for an inexpensive clock to Eli Terry, a centralized water system for Philadelphia, and in New York, a paddle-wheel steamboat developed by Samuel Morey.

Freed slaves plead to retain liberty

North Carolina, Jan. 30

Four Negro slaves who fled to the North have petitioned Congress, protesting a state law that requires illegally freed slaves to be returned to their masters. Their petition, the first ever submitted by American Negroes, was rejected. The slaves, manumitted by Quaker masters, had asked Congress to consider "our relief as a people." Quakers, who strongly oppose the institution of slavery, have made a practice of buying and freeing slaves.

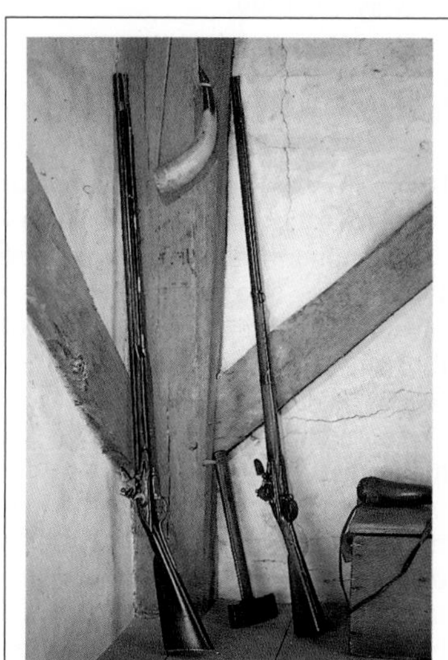

The frontiersman's best friends: powder horn and flintlock rifles, one French-made and one U.S.

New trading post in the Northwest

Montreal

Charles Chaboillez, a member of the aggressive North West Company of Montreal, has established a new strategically located fur trading post known as Pembina in the Northern Plains country at the junction of the Red and Pembina Rivers. The valley of the Red River south of this point has belonged to the Hudson's Bay Company by charter up to this time, but the North West Company is challenging its rival's exclusive right to the fur trade in that region. The North West Company has been a force to reckon with in the British North for 20 years, and may yet become a challenge to American traders.

View of Revolution by loyalist printed

New York City

Although America has survived its separation from England and created what could well be a stable government, doubts about independence linger in some quarters, especially among those who view political rebellion as an inherently sinful act. One critical voice belongs to Jonathan Bucher, whose *A View of the Causes and Consequences of the American Revolution*, a collection of loyalist sermons, has outraged many readers this year.

Trumbull preserves history in paintings

United States

On the advice of Thomas Jefferson, the Connecticut-born painter John Trumbull has devoted his artistic career to the portrayal of formative events in American history. Foremost among the scenes he has been preparing for engravers since 1786 is his *Declaration of Independence in Congress at the Independence Hall*, finished this year. Trumbull has splendid qualifications as a patriot as well as an artist: He is the son of the first governor of his home state and served as an aide to George Washington during the Revolution.

French ask bribe from U.S. peace envoys

The French Directory, as a five-headed monster, greedily approaches American envoys Gerry, Pinckney and Marshall. Responding to the demand for a bribe, Pinckney said, "Millions for defense, sir, but not one cent for tribute."

Paris, Oct. 18

After being forced to wait for two weeks without being received by the Directory's Foreign Minister, the three-man American peace commission, consisting of Elbridge Gerry, Charles Pinckney and John Marshall, has been subjected to one of the most brazen proposals ever made to a diplomatic mission. As a condition for even discussing the issues that have brought the two countries to the brink of war, three representatives of the French, referred to by the Americans as Messrs. X, Y and Z, have demanded a loan of $10 million to their government, and an outright bribe of $250,000 for the Foreign Minister. He, of course, is Charles Maurice de Talleyrand, a consummate diplomat who also enjoys a well-deserved reputation for corruption.

The first hint that a bribe would be required was made by Talleyrand's friend, Madame de Villette. Further negotiations were carried on with Jean Conrad Hottinguer and Lucien Hauteval, both Swiss, and a Hamburg-based American banker named Bellamy – the X, Y and Z referred to in dispatches.

Responding to the demand for a bribe, Pinckney is reported to have said, "Millions for defense, sir, but not one cent for tribute." Another version of his words runs, "No, no, not a sixpence" (→Jan. 17, 1798).

"The Christmas Coach" by J.L.G. Ferris. Holiday travel, even in the East, requires the protection of a rifleman and any friendly and willing Indian.

1798

Adams

Paris, Jan. 17. John Marshall issues formal rejection of French attempts to elicit bribes in exchange for negotiations (→Apr. 3).

New York City, April. John Daly Burk's *Female Patriotism, or the Death of Joan d'Arc*, staged at Park Theater, celebrating spirit of liberty.

Philadelphia, May 3. Congress establishes Department of Navy in preparation for war (→July 11).

Philadelphia, May 28. Adams authorized by Congress to raise volunteer army of 10,000 for three years and seize menacing French ships (→Nov. 20).

Philadelphia, June 6. Congress ends imprisonment of debtors.

Philadelphia, July 7. George Washington appointed commander-in-chief of United States Army.

United States, Aug. 8. Secretary of Navy bars Negroes from naval service.

Philadelphia, Sept. 12. Newspaper editor Benjamin Franklin Bache, grandson of Benjamin Franklin, arrested under Sedition Act for "libeling" President Adams (→Nov. 16).

Kentucky, Nov. 16. Legislature adopts Kentucky Resolutions, reserving states' right to override federal powers not referred to by U.S. Constitution (→Dec. 24).

United States, Dec. 14. David Wilkinson obtains patent for screw threading machine.

United States. Adams to Washington as France poses war: "We must have your name. There will be more efficacy in it than in many an army."

Philadelphia. A Frenchman opens first pasta factory in United States.

Pennsylvania. John "Johnny Appleseed" Chapman plants his first apple seed nursery (→Autumn, 1800).

Kentucky. Daniel Boone receives grant of 850 acres from Spanish government in Femme Osage district of Louisiana (→Sept. 1799).

United States. Robert Fulton builds a four-man submarine, the Nautilus.

United States. Joseph Hopkinson publishes patriotic poem, *Hail Columbia.*

War threat prompts protective laws

Philadelphia, July 11

In response to growing hysteria regarding the so-called "XYZ affair," in which the French attempted diplomatic intimidation of America, and the undeclared naval war between the United States and France, Congress today passed the Sedition Act. The last of four pieces of legislation aimed at curbing dissent against the administration and preventing internal subversion, the act subjects any American citizen to a fine and/or imprisonment for obstructing the implementation of federal law, or for publishing malicious or false writings against Congress, the president or the government.

Congress already approved three measures that have a similar intent. The Naturalization Act, passed June 18, extends to 14 years, from five, the period of residence that is required for citizenship. The Alien Friends Act, passed June 25, gives the president the authority to deport any alien who is suspected of treasonable intent. And the Alien Enemies Act, passed five days ago, gives the president the power to arrest any citizen of a foreign nation in time of war, and to deport him.

The Republicans have roundly denounced the measures as unconstitutional and gross violations of the freedoms of speech and press. Although President Adams apparently supports the laws, the inspiration for them comes from the Federalist-controlled Congress, a hotbed of Francophobia (→Sept. 12).

The controversial Alien and Sedition Acts are raising tempers in Congress.

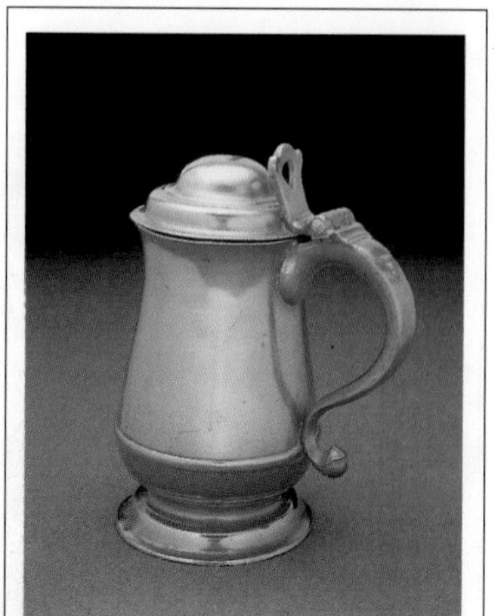

Tavernware: Pewter quart tankard made by William Will, a member of Philadelphia's thriving community of artisans.

Virginia objects to Alien and Sedition Acts

Williamsburg, Virginia, Dec. 24

The Virginia legislature today adopted James Madison's resolution that the powers of the federal government must be curbed. Madison's so-called "Virginia Resolution," along with Thomas Jefferson's "Kentucky Resolution" introduced last month, are specifically designed to give the states the authority to declare null and void the controversial Alien and Sedition Acts, recently passed by the federal government. According to Madison and Jefferson, the states created the union in the hope of receiving good laws. If the states get beneficial and benevolent laws, the legislators say, then the states are constrained to obey them. If, on the other hand, they are not given good and wise laws, then the states have no obligation to observe them.

Most observers feel the Alien and Sedition Acts are dangerous to American liberties. And many feel that the Virginia and Kentucky Resolutions are equally dangerous. Will they lead to the riddance of the detestable laws – or to the dissolution of the union? Former President Washington is said to oppose this latest expression of "states' rights" (→May 13, 1799).

U.S. ends treaty with France, stops trade

Guadeloupe, Nov. 20

Full-scale war with France came a step closer today with the report of the capture off Guadeloupe of the American schooner Retaliation. Many believe that it is now only a matter of time before war between the two countries is declared.

If that should happen, the United States is far better prepared than it was a year ago. Riding the tide of anti-French feeling, Congress has suspended trade with France and, by a vote taken on July 7 of last year, repudiated the 1778 treaty of alliance. Money has been voted to create a Navy Department and to accelerate the shipbuilding program begun in response to the actions of the Barbary corsairs against American shipping in the Mediterranean. Funds have also been voted for a substantial increase in the size of the army, now back in command of former President Washington.

Although Alexander Hamilton and other "High Federalists" are pushing for an outright declaration of war against France, President Adams is known to be reluctant to go that far. Diplomatic signals from France indicate Foreign Minister Talleyrand also would prefer to see differences between the nations settled by diplomacy rather than war (→Feb. 9, 1799).

Standardized parts in guns foreseen

New Haven, Connecticut

Eli Whitney, inventor of the cotton gin, has told the government he can supply 10,000 muskets with parts that are interchangeable. Instead of using the conventional method in which a skilled workman makes an entire musket, Whitney plans to employ machine tools that allow unskilled workmen to produce large numbers of standardized parts, any one of which will fit a musket of this design. Whitney says his new system of production will allow him to supply the 10,000 muskets within two years, much faster than possible with the conventional method. It is said that the government will offer him a contract soon.

Congress creates U.S. Marine Corps

United States, July 11

Congress today called for the creation of a Marine Corps. This action followed by only two months the authorization of a Navy Department. Both of these official acts were de facto, since peacetime marine recruiting got under way last year, as did the construction of six frigates. Both official moves have the same intention, that of deterring piracy by the French in the West Indies and marauding by Moorish privateers along the northern shore of Africa, the infamous Barbary Coast. Both of the new groups are actually extensions of colonial branches mustered during the Revolutionary War.

Ex-Spanish area now Mississippi Territory

Philadelphia, Apr. 7

Congress today established the Mississippi Territory from a thin rectangle of land that is near the Gulf of Mexico. This land, which is north of the 31st parallel, was ceded to the United States by the Spanish under the Treaty of San Lorenzo in 1795. The territory stretches from the Mississippi River eastward all the way to the Chatahoochee River [including the southern part, although not the coastal area, of present Mississippi and Alabama]. The land just north of the Mississippi Territory remains under the control of the Indians.

President John Adams has appointed Winthrop Sargent, a native of Massachusetts, to be Governor of the new territory, and the capital is to be at Natchez, which was evacuated by the Spanish earlier this year. But the President's appointment of Sargent is expected to run into vigorous opposition because of his Federalist connections.

In preparing the treaty, William Dunbar, a wealthy planter and scientist from Natchez, surveyed the territory for the Spanish and Andrew Ellicott, who had served as America's surveyor-general, represented the United States.

Adams exposes French bribe offer

Philadelphia, Apr. 3

Taking advantage of the political opportunities offered by last year's "XYZ affair" in which bribes were sought from American envoys by three representatives of Talleyrand, X, Y and Z, President Adams has sent Congress the peace commissioners' dispatches exposing the French attempts at intimidating the United States. The reaction is one of outrage and indignation. And Adams is being hailed as a national hero. His wife, Abigail, said, "The Jacobins in the Senate and House were struck dumb" (→May 28).

U.S. citizens cannot sue another state

Philadelphia, Jan. 8

The judicial system agreed upon by Congress in 1789 has proved generally adequate, but the constitutional provision allowing citizens of one state to sue another state, Congress says, does not work. Today, the 11th Amendment to the Constitution was ratified, stating that "The judicial power of the United States shall not be construed to extend to any suit in law or equity, commenced or prosecuted against one of the United States, by citizens of another State, or by citizens of any foreign State."

Cartoonists leap into the political fray

Philadelphia

The framers of the Constitution believe the public welfare should always stand above party politics. As Federalists and Republicans, however, they do not seem to be heeding their own advice. And the cartoonists have taken sides. At right, a Federalist cartoon depicts Republican Thomas Jefferson (or perhaps Tom Paine) making a pact with the devil to destroy the federal government. Below, a drawing from 1793 depicts Hamilton's Republican opponents as anarchists and hypocrites. At bottom, the devil and the British lion urge Federalist editor William Cobbett ("Peter Porcupine") to libel Republicans.

"Mad Tom in a Rage" attacks the pillars of government.

Ridiculing Hamilton's opponents: "A Peep into the Anti-Federal Club."

1799

Adams

Bethlehem, Pennsylvania, Feb. 7. John Fries, tax rebellion leader, arrested for treason.

Philadelphia, Feb. 23. First federal quarantine act voted by Congress, offering federal aid for local quarantine enforcement.

United States, Apr. 1. Editor Charles Brockden Brown publishes first quarterly review in United States, *American Review and Literary Journal*.

United States, May 13. Madison to Jefferson: "Perhaps it is a universal truth that the loss of liberty at home is to be charged to provisions against danger, real or pretended, from abroad" (→ Nov. 22).

Philadelphia, Dec. 12. Sixth Congress convenes; [last to hold Federalist majority.]

Cambridge, Massachusetts. Benjamin Waterhouse devises first American vaccination against smallpox.

Alaska. Russian American Company establishes headquarters in Sitka, Alaska (→ 1809).

Philadelphia. In first organized labor action in United States, Federal Society of Cordwainers (shoemakers) wins nine-day strike; term "scab" (strike-breaker) used for first time (→ May 25, 1805).

Arkansas. Census records only 368 people living in Arkansas Territory.

New York. State passes gradual emancipation act.

Southhampton County, Virginia. Slaves rebel, killing two whites; four to 10 Negroes executed.

Louisiana. Authorities arrest Bailey E. Chaney, Baptist minister, for conducting services near Baton Rouge.

Kentucky. Second state constitution adopted; state officers subject to direct election.

Bering Strait. Joasaph Bolotov drowns on way to Alaska following his consecration as first Russian Orthodox bishop to New World.

New York City. Gracie Mansion constructed; [acquired for mayor's residence in 1924].

Boston. Johann Christian Gottlieb Graupner plays in blackface in performance of *Oroonoko*, one of earliest Negro minstrel shows.

U.S. Navy victory: French frigate seized

The U.S. Navy roams the seas. Giving chase, the Constellation at full sail bears down on the Insurgente off the coast of Nevis in the West Indies.

Nevis, West Indies, Feb. 9

The first clear-cut victory for the newly formed United States Navy was scored off this island today by the recently commissioned frigate Constellation in a duel with the French ship Insurgente. After a sharp engagement fought in winds that rose to gale force, the Insurgente was forced to strike its colors, and a prize crew under the command of Lieutenant John Rodgers and Midshipman David Porter are bringing the vessel and 173 prisoners into St. Kitts.

Commanding the Constellation was Captain Thomas Truxtun, the man whose activities as a privateer in the War of Independence caused General Washington to comment that he was worth a regiment. The Constellation is one of a fleet of five ships patrolling the seas near St. Kitts to protect American shipping against French raiders.

After sighting the Insurgente off Nevis, Truxtun overhauled it in a squall that carried away the French ship's maintop. During the battle, the enemy fired at the Constellation rigging but to no avail, then tried to grapple. Avoiding this, Captain Truxtun maneuvered ahead and raked the enemy ship with fire from his 40 guns. After fighting that lasted less than an hour, during which the casualties of the French were 29 dead and 41 wounded, they surrendered. American losses were three men wounded (→ Feb. 1, 1800).

French coup hands power to Bonaparte

Paris, Nov. 10

In a coup d'etat engineered by veteran politician Abbe Sieyes, the Directory has been overthrown and replaced by a three-man Consulate made up of Sieyes, Roger Ducos and Napoleon Bonaparte, who recently returned to France from military campaigns in Egypt and Syria. General Bonaparte also has the title of first consul. The coup nearly failed when the general lost his nerve in a confrontation with the Council of 500. But his brother Lucien saved the day with a bold harangue to the troops. Today is the 18th of Brumaire, the revolutionary calendar's second month, which gets its name from the mist at this time of year (→ Dec. 2, 1804).

Napoleon, back from a failed invasion of Syria, will rule France as part of a triumvirate of consuls.

Postal service, the sole link to civilization in some parts of the West, is expanding as fast as the frontier it serves. Mail carriers now travel on 16,000 miles of postal roads, a six-fold increase over the last 10 years. The intrepid postmen, who began to appear on a full-time basis in 1794, are paid by the piece, generally two cents per letter.

Personal diplomacy denied to citizens

Philadelphia, Jan. 30

Responding to a peace-seeking effort by Dr. George Logan, Congress has passed legislation that prohibits private citizens from negotiating international affairs with foreign governments. At the height of tensions between the United States and France last year, Dr. Logan, a Quaker, visited leaders of the French Directory in Paris in the hope of averting an all-out war between the two countries. He suggested that an embargo on American shipping in France played into British hands. The American government feared that actions such as Logan's might conflict with official foreign policy and has therefore ruled such efforts treasonable.

First products from Japan arrive in U.S.

Boston, May

Captain James Devereaux landed in Boston harbor this month not only with coffee and spices from the Dutch East Indies, but also the first products imported from Japan. Last year, after sailing his chartered ship, the Franklin, to the East Indies to pick up a cargo of Java coffee, Devereaux accepted a lucrative offer to continue on a trade run to Nagasaki. On the island of Deshima in the Nagasaki harbor, Captain Devereaux unloaded his cotton items, sugar, tin, elephant teeth, pepper and cloves in exchange for Japanese mats, lacquered goods and pans. He is not planning to sell the items but to use them for his own business.

New Hampshire backs Alien, Sedition Acts

Kentucky, Nov. 22

The nature of the union and indeed the basic meaning of the Constitution are again being questioned. New Hampshire adopted a resolution June 15 vigorously supporting the Alien and Sedition Acts and rebutting the Virginia and Kentucky Resolutions of Thomas Jefferson and James Madison stressing the need for states' rights. Today, Jefferson rose to the attack on the powers claimed by the federal government with a second Kentucky Resolution. In this one, he again claimed that since the states created the union they had the right to "oppose in a constitutional manner" all present and future violations of the Constitution. So the question remains: Who rules this nation, the states or the federal government?

Second Street, Philadelphia. *Fear of the city's dominance in trade and finance will result in the shifting of the capital to Washington next year.*

Washington, dying words: "'tis well"

Philadelphia, Dec. 26

Eulogizing George Washington, General Henry "Light Horse Harry" Lee today pronounced the late President "first in war, first in peace, first in the hearts of his countrymen." The eloquence is strengthened by truth: Washington led the Continental Army to victory in war; he was its first President for two terms in a time of relative peace, and upon his death December 14, the nation mourned the greatest friend it has ever known. Yet Washington had been reluctant to serve as President, calling himself more fit for overseeing the planting of fruit trees on his estate at Mount Vernon. Once in office, he was somewhat aloof; he saw no visitor without an invitation, he would not shake hands in greeting. He did not seem one of the common people; but the people respected the dignity he brought his office.

On the eve of December 13, when his severe ague made it difficult for him to speak, he bid his wife, Martha, procure his last will and testament from its hiding place. He told her it directed for her care and later for the freeing of the slaves who worked their estate. With his affairs in order, he told his physician, "I die hard, but I am not afraid to go." His last words were " 'tis well."

Washington idealized. A memorial from Philadelphia (c.1800).

Washington was captured on canvas by Gilbert Stuart three years ago.

Daniel Boone heads for Spanish region

Kentucky, September

Plagued by lawsuits and having lost all his land claims in Kentucky, Daniel Boone, the old pioneer, and a large group of his family and friends left Kentucky today for the Spanish lands west of the Mississippi in the Missouri River country. His wife and children will make the journey in a 60-foot canoe that Boone carved out of a yellow poplar this summer. The 65-year-old Boone will go by land with his sons-in-law, William Hays and Flanders Callaway, and several others, driving their cattle and pack horses. Asked why he was leaving, the famous frontiersman did not mention the endless legal battles over his Kentucky lands, simply saying he felt a need for more "elbow room."

Loyalists drifting back from Canada

United States

Many of the British loyalists who fled to Nova Scotia and other Canadian areas after the Revolutionary War have been making their way back to the United States over the last few years. The reasons most frequently mentioned by these men, women and even children for their return are homesickness, family ties and rough conditions in Canada. Many of the loyalists lost their property in the United States when anti-loyalist legislation was passed after the war. Subsequently, the British government helped them migrate to Canada and the West Indies by buying them property and offering financial aid. Approximately 40,000 loyalists had moved to Canada to remain under the British flag.

1800

Adams

Philadelphia, Jan. 2. Free Negroes present petition to Congress opposing slavery.

Philadelphia, Jan. 10. Treaty with Tunis, negotiated in 1797, ratified by Congress (→ Oct. 19).

High Seas, Feb. 1. Constellation clashes with French vessel La Vengeance (→ Sept. 30).

Philadelphia, Apr. 4. Federal Bankruptcy Act passes Congress, provides merchants and traders protection from debtors (→ Dec. 19, 1803).

Richmond, Virginia, Aug. 30. Gabriel Prosser leads more than 1,000 slaves in revolt (→ Oct. 30).

New York, September. Cayuga Bridge, spanning Cayuga Lake and Montezuma Swamp, completed; 1 1/8 miles long, it allows passage for two wagons simultaneously.

Charleston, South Carolina. First canal in United States completed, from Santee River to Charleston harbor.

New York City. Sailors' strike broken with arrest of leader for disturbing peace and inciting to riot; demand of $4 raise denied.

Philadelphia. William Young makes shoes designed specifically for right and left feet.

Ohio River Valley. Gouging is a popular sport on frontier; long thumbnails are used to gouge eyes of opponents.

Central Plains. Blackbird, chief of Omaha Indians, dies and is buried astride his favorite horse on west side of Missouri River.

Virginia. Virginia tobacco warehouse auctioning begun.

Kentucky. State experiences a religious revival of such magnitude that it is referred to as the "Great Revival."

Newport, Rhode Island. Pierre Samuel du Pont de Nemours journeys from France to United States. [He is originator of du Pont family dynasty.]

Worcester, Massachusetts. Isaiah Thomas is nation's foremost publisher, with 400 titles since end of Revolution.

United States. *Hymns and Odes Composed on the Death of General George Washington,* with contributions by Thomas Paine and Charles Brockden Brown, published.

United States capital now is Washington

Capitol of the United States at Washington, D.C. (c.1800) by William Birch.

Washington, D.C., Nov. 17

Congress opened its first session in this new capital of Washington, District of Columbia, today. While most of the district is swamp and farmland, and there is little in the way of lodgings for members of Congress, construction of homes, shops and taverns is under way. The city's population is 8,144.

Over the last few months, the 137 members of the congressional clerical staff have been moving in from their homes in Philadelphia. But President John Adams's administration may have only a few weeks in the new city before a new administration under Thomas Jefferson and the Republicans takes over.

Adams, the first President to occupy the Presidential Palace [White House], found the plaster on the walls of the unfinished building still damp when he arrived. But he expressed his hopes for the future of the house and for the people who will ocupy it in a letter to his wife, Abigail, who was in New York City. "I pray Heaven to bestow the best of blessings on this house and all that shall hereafter inhabit it," the President wrote. "May none but wise and honest men ever rule under this roof."

New census shows total of 5.3 million

Washington, D.C.

This year's census puts the nation's population at 5.3 million, an increase of more than 30 percent in a decade. Virginia remains the most populous state, with 807,557 inhabitants, but both Pennsylvania (602,365, up from 434,373) and New York (589,051, up from 340,120) are gaining rapidly. The fastest-growing states are Tennessee and Kentucky, which have nearly tripled in population since 1790. Ohio, not counted in the last census, has a population of 45,365. Other new entries on the census rolls include Alabama, with a population of 1,250, and Mississippi, with 7,600. There are about one million Negroes in the country.

French prince ends his exile above bar

Philadelphia, January

After five years living in a one-room flat above a bar here, Prince Louis Philippe is going home. Although poor, he moved in the best circles and once asked for the hand of Sen. William Bingham's daughter. He was rejected by the senator on the ground that if he became King of France he would be too good for Miss Bingham; if he did not, he would not be good enough.

Algiers ruler humiliates U.S. sea captain

The Bey of Algiers and Bainbridge.

Algiers, Oct. 19

More bad news from the Barbary Shore today. The American ship George Washington has been humiliated at Algiers, where the ship was anchored to pay the yearly tribute as insurance against piracy. The Ottoman governor, the Bey, ordered Captain William Bainbridge to carry not only gifts to the Turkish sultan in Constantinople but also an Algerian emissary. To add insult to injury, he was ordered to fly the Ottoman flag until he left the harbor. It has been American and European policy to make payments to Barbary states to guarantee the safe passage of ships. But this humiliation has sparked talk in Washington of reprisals (→ May 14, 1801).

Northwest Territory cut into two parts

Philadelphia, May 7

Congress divided the Northwest Territory into two parts today, with the border between them running north from the junction of the Ohio and Kentucky Rivers. The western part will be known as the Indiana Territory and will be governed by William Henry Harrison in Vincennes. The eastern half will retain the name Northwest Territory, with its capital at Chillicothe. The territorial split was necessary because of the rise in population since the Treaty of Greenville five years ago reduced the fear of Indian raids. The Northwest Territory was founded in 1787 (→ Nov. 29, 1802).

Louisiana returned to France by Spain

France, Oct. 1

King Carlos IV of Spain is reported to have signed a secret treaty with Napoleon returning the Louisiana Territory to France. The territory has been under the rule of Spain since 1763. Informed sources say Napoleon has agreed to establish a kingdom in Italy for Carlos's son-in law, the Duke of Parma. There are reports that not only is President Thomas Jefferson aware of the agreement but also that he has expressed alarm about it because he looks upon the French as a potentially dangerous enemy. The American minister in Paris, Robert Livingston, is said to be seeking details of this reported Treaty of San Ildefonso (→Apr. 19, 1802).

U.S.-French treaty will end naval war

Paris, Sept. 30

The undeclared but bloody naval war with France that has been waged mostly in the West Indies ended today with the signing here of a convention known as the Treaty of Morfontaine. France will lift its embargo on American ships, cancel all letters of marque, which authorized privateering, and respect neutral ships and property. The United States will return captured warships but not captured privateers. The American negotiators, led by William Vans Murray, along with Oliver Ellsworth and William Davie, met with a friendly reception from Foreign Minister Talleyrand, who had already signaled his desire to stop the drift into open war.

Johnny Appleseed spreads the good Word

Pennsylvania, Autumn

It's apple picking time, and farmers are gathering their Jonathans and pippins. Trees of the McIntosh, the new strain from Ontario, are not yet bearing fruit here. But the farmers are thankful to nature – and to Johnny Appleseed. Johnny, born John Chapman 26 years ago in Leominster, Massachusetts, passed through these farmlands three years ago, planting young apple trees. That wasn't all he spread. He also spread the gospel of his faith, Swedenborgianism. His religion, which gives credence to only certain chapters of the Bible, has not taken root as well as his trees. Only Baltimore has a sizable Swedenborgian church. Still, as Johnny roams westward, he will continue to spread both the Word and the seed.

Chapman is a follower of Emanuel Swedenborg, a mystic who taught that all reality is filled with the spirit.

Nation has 50 libraries, 80,000 books

Philadelphia, Apr. 24

Congress passed a resolution today calling for the establishment of a Library of Congress. It is a natural step for the nation to take. According to a federal census that has just been completed, the country now has 50 lending libraries containing more than 80,000 volumes.

What works belong in the proposed Library of Congress? That remains to be discussed in full. Certainly the country will want to preserve the papers of the late Benjamin Franklin (who started Philadelphia's first library in 1731). The letters of Presidents Washington and Adams would also be desirable. And it is believed that the book collection of Thomas Jefferson is so extensive that it could constitute a library in itself. Whatever the eventual contents of the Library of Congress, its existence will signal a pride of American heritage. The building will be erected in the District of Columbia, where Congress meets after November (→Jan. 29, 1802).

The library (dedicated to Ben Franklin) on Fifth Street, Philadelphia. Surgeon's Hall is in background. Engraving (1799) by William Birch & Son.

1,000 slaves revolt; leaders are hanged

Richmond, Virginia, Oct. 30

Gabriel Prosser, his family and some 25 other Negroes were hanged today for having planned a slave revolt. That revolt, Governor James Monroe said, "embraced most of the slaves in this city and the neighborhood."

Prosser, his wife and two brothers, from Henrico County, had organized the slaves outside Richmond, where they fashioned bayonets, bullets and swords. Their objective was to seize Richmond's arsenals and kill all whites except Methodists, Frenchmen and Quakers, thus ending slavery in Virginia.

On August 30, Prosser gathered more than 1,000 slaves for the attack. But they disbanded after discovering that an essential bridge had been ruined by a storm the night before. Two slaves then betrayed the rebellion to the Governor, who called out the military. After the trial of the slaves, the state ordered monetary compensation for their owners.

Who will be next President of U.S.?

Philadelphia, Dec. 3

Preliminary reports indicate that Thomas Jefferson will be the next President. Although ballots will not be officially counted until February, it seems that Jefferson and his Republicans have won the public's trust. In his campaign, he expressed his commitment to democracy, a defense buildup and a continuing attack on the Federalists' Alien and Sedition Acts. Pennsylvania was a critical state in the battle between Jefferson and John Adams. Jefferson has said that if he can win there, "We can defy the universe." And, he might add, gain the presidency in the process (→March 4, 1801).

London, 1800. *"An Emblem of America." After a quarter of a century, has Britain come to terms with American independence?*

1801

Jefferson

Petersburg, Virginia, January. Governor James Monroe warned of slave unrest; stockpiles arms in response.

United States, Feb. 11. William Dunlap's play *Abaellino, the Great Bandit* opens, [beginning 25-year run.]

Washington, D.C., Feb. 27. Congress assumes jurisdiction over District of Columbia.

United States, March 21. Jefferson, in letter to Joseph Priestley, writes, "We can no longer say there is nothing new under the sun. For this whole chapter in the history of man is new."

Paris, Apr. 21. Eleuthere Irenee du Pont files articles of incorporation (→June 19, 1802).

Tripoli, May 14. Pasha Yusuf Karamanli declares war on United States (→Aug. 1).

Brest, France, August. Robert Fulton completes second submarine, Nautilus.

Washington, D.C., Dec. 7. Seventh Congress convenes under Democratic-Republican majority in both houses for first time.

Washington, D.C., Dec. 8. President Jefferson, expressing dislike for ceremony, gives first address to Congress in writing.

England. American Benjamin Thompson appoints scientists Humphry Davy and Michael Faraday to positions in Royal Institution.

Boston. Paul Revere first in United States to produce cold, rolled copper.

New York City. Black members withdraw from John Street Methodist Church to found Zion Church.

United States. Congregationalists and Presbyterians adopt Plan of Union.

Milton, Massachusetts. Josiah Bent produces cold water crackers, claiming they help digestion.

New Haven, Connecticut. Yale President Timothy Dwight leads religious revival.

Washington, D.C. Court system installed for capital.

Louisiana. Louisiana slave trade reopens and flourishes.

Philadelphia. *The Easy Instructor* published, introducing "shape" musical notation; it is used to teach music to frontier folk.

Jefferson, Burr tie: Jefferson is chosen

Jefferson by Thomas Sully.

Burr: settling for second place.

Washington, D.C., March 4

In a history-making decision, the House of Representatives has chosen Thomas Jefferson to be the next President, while naming Aaron Burr Vice President. The House was called upon to select the nation's two highest officials when the two Republican candidates, Jefferson and Burr, received the same number of votes in the Electoral College. According to the Constitution, presidential electors do not specify their preference for their choice of candidates for either president or vice president. Rather, the candidate with a majority of electoral votes becomes president, while the man with the next highest number of votes automatically becomes vice president.

Many Federalists in Congress preferred Burr and would have chosen him over Jefferson. However, most sided with Alexander Hamilton, who advised them to vote for the Virginian because he, as Hamilton put it, at least "had some pretension to character." Apparently the House members took Hamilton's advice to heart and chose his old adversary.

In the new President's inauguration address today, he praised democratic ideas and promised "peace, commerce, and honest friendship with all nations – entangling alliances with none" (→Dec. 9, 1803).

John Marshall gets Chief Justice post

Washington, D.C., Feb. 4

John Marshall took the oath of office today, replacing Oliver Ellsworth as Chief Justice. He was appointed last month in one of President John Adams's last major executive acts. The choice is vital to the Federalists, who are losing control of the executive and legislative branches of government. Marshall was a lieutenant in the Revolution, a Virginia legislator and a United States representative before serving as Adams's Secretary of State. He is expected to base his decisions on the idea that the Constitution prevails over all other laws.

Marshall, lame-duck appointment.

Once richest man is out of debt prison

Philadelphia, Aug. 26

Once the richest man in America, Robert Morris is out of debtor's prison – free but ruined. At his peak, Morris financed the Revolution on credit. He cornered the tobacco market and controlled a vast empire in land, banking and shipping. But that empire collapsed when the Bank of England failed in 1797, crushing the Atlantic trade and Morris's credit. In a locked mansion, he held out for months. But he finally went to Prune Street Jail, where his friend, George Washington, paid him a visit. But even Washington could not get him out. That took an act of Congress – the Bankruptcy Act of 1800.

Hamilton and Jay publish N.Y. Post

New York City, Nov. 16

A new paper hit the streets of New York today. The *New York Evening Post*, published by Alexander Hamilton and John Jay, covers a wide range of topics, but is intended to carry a Federalist edge. The *Post* had its start at the end of the New York gubernatorial election. Hamilton's candidate, Stephen Van Rensselaer, lost to George Clinton, and Hamilton links the failure of the Federalist campaign to the lack of an influential newspaper. The *Post* will get support and funds from loyal Federalists and editorial direction from William Coleman. Ironically, Coleman was once a law partner of Hamilton's foe, Aaron Burr.

Congress enlarges system of courts

Washington, D.C., March 3

The Republicans are seething. The passage last month of the Judiciary Act provided for creation of 16 circuit courts. Tonight, John Adams acted in the last hours of his presidency, appointing what are being called "midnight judges" to fill the posts. Couple that with Adams's selection of John Marshall to be Chief Justice of the Supreme Court and one can sense the fury of President-elect Jefferson and his fellow Republicans. Senator James Gunn has referred to the appointees as "scoundrels placed on the seat of justice." The act also reduces the number of high court justices from six to five (→Apr. 29, 1802).

Mastodon bones uncovered in New York

Newburgh, New York, Aug. 21

Public excitement is rising as the hunt for bones of the extinct mastodon, called the "carnivorous elephant of the North," heads for a new site. Farmers in the nearby Shawangunk Mountains who have been unearthing the bones for years are being enlisted in the search by Charles Willson Peale. The noted portrait painter hopes to be the first man to assemble a complete skeleton, demonstrating the frightening appearance of the mammoth beast that once roamed North America with, as Peale describes it, "the ferocity and agility of the tiger, the terror of the forest and of man!" Peale devised a unique man-powered treadmill to drain the bogs where the fossils lie. He has made it clear that he plans to move the bones to Philadelphia and put them together in all their massive splendor with the help of the vertebrate paleontologist Dr. Caspar Wistar for display in Peale's Museum at Independence Hall, solving at last the momentous mystery: "What did the behemoth look like?"

The importance of the discovery is indicated by the encouragement and material support the project has received from President Thomas Jefferson, who, incidentally, received a 1,000-pound "mammoth cheese" as a gift honoring his election. The giant fossil has also inspired a Philadelphia baker to produce a "mammoth bread" and a Washington "mammoth eater" to consume 42 eggs in 10 minutes.

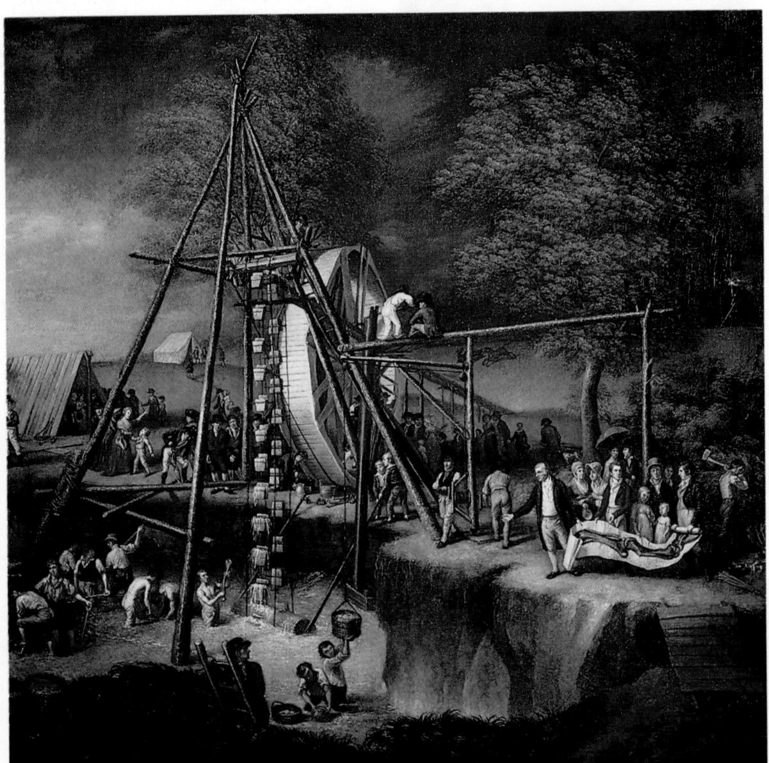

A monster unearthed. "Exhuming the Mastodon" by Charles Willson Peale.

Frontiersmen devise own entertainment

Western Frontier

The rugged life on the Western frontier has spawned distinctive forms of recreation. Many one-eyed frontiersmen are victims of the brutal sport of wrestling, Western style, in which eye-gouging with thumbnails grown especially long for that purpose is not uncommon. This and other tests of rude frontier skills, such as shooting, knife throwing and log-rolling may be accompanied by outrageous bragging. Tamer entertainments may have a utilitarian role, such as house-raising, cornshucking and quilting. Dancing to the strains of a backwoods fiddle is popular and religion also offers a respite from frontier hardships in the form of protracted meetings.

Pirates at war with U.S.

Lieutenant Sterett and schooner Enterprise are attacked by Tripolitan pirates.

Malta, Aug. 1

After a sharply fought engagement that lasted three hours and cost the enemy 20 killed and 30 wounded, the American schooner Enterprise has captured the 14-gun Barbary corsair Tripoli. Since Lieutenant Andrew Sterett's instructions do not allow him to take prizes, the American commander ordered the guns of the captured ship to be heaved over the side and its masts cut down. In this sorry state, the Tripoli has been allowed to return home, where a grim fate doubtless awaits the unfortunate captain at the hands of the Pasha Yusuf Karamanli, a ruler noted for his fondness for inflicting punishment. For his part, Sterett, who lost not a man in the fight, continued on his way to Malta to take on water for the rest of the fleet.

It is now 10 weeks since the Pasha, enraged at not receiving extra tribute, declared war on the United States by the traditional method of sending a group of soldiers to the American consulate in Tripoli and having them chop down the flagpole. Unfortunately for him, this action happened to coincide with the final readying of Commodore Richard Dale's squadron, which then set sail for the Mediterranean June 2 and has been blockading Tripoli since July 17.

James Cathcart, who remains as U.S. envoy to Tripoli, is trying to persuade the Pasha to reduce his demands, which were for a quarter-million-dollar payment and an annual tribute of $20,000. Some payment will be necessary, but the Americans consider such demands excessive (→ Feb. 6, 1802).

Philadelphians get an aqueduct system

Philadelphia

Philadelphia residents can now drink water delivered through a system of aqueducts powered by that miracle of modern technology, the steam engine. The first "atmospheric engine" used in America was one installed in a New Jersey copper mine in 1755; it was of the type invented by the Englishman Thomas Newcomen, in 1712. In 1774, New York City built a similar steam engine to power its waterworks.

The family that paints together: "Rubens Peale With a Geranium" (1801) by Rembrandt Peale.

1802

Jefferson

United States, Jan. 8. Commission rules that United States owes $2,664,000 to British citizens in settlement of Revolutionary War claims.

Washington, D.C., Jan. 29. John James Beckley, ex-clerk of House, named first Librarian of Congress.

Washington, D.C., Feb. 6. Congress authorizes arming of merchant ships to ward off attacks by Tripoli (→ Sept. 5, 1804).

Europe, March 27. France, England, Spain and The Netherlands sign Treaty of Amiens; ends war in Europe and lifts restraints on U.S. shipping.

Washington, D.C., Apr. 6. All excise duties, including whiskey tax, are repealed by Congress.

Mississippi, Apr. 24. Georgia legislature cedes land involved in Yazoo land fraud of 1795 to federal government.

Washington, D.C., May 3. Congress incorporates federal capital as a city; President to appoint a mayor.

West Point, New York, July 4. United States Military Academy officially opens.

United States, Aug. 11. United States and Spain resolve to refer all disputes between two nations to special commission.

Washington, D.C., Oct. 2. United States Patent Office established as bureau of Department of State.

Louisiana, Oct. 16. Breaking 1795 Treaty of San Lorenzo, Spain closes New Orleans to U.S. cargo (→ Apr. 19, 1803).

New York City. American Academy of Arts established; funded through sale of stock.

Waterbury, Connecticut. Abel Porter & Company opens first brass mill run on horsepower.

Hawaii. Chinese build islands' first sugar mill.

New York. Screw-driven steamboat built by John Stevens.

United States. Colonel David Humphreys, U.S. minister to Spain, brings back 100 Merino sheep, improving quality of American wool.

Washington, D.C., April *Catalogue of Books, Maps, and Charts, Belonging to the Library of the Two Houses of Congress* published.

U.S. wary of Napoleon's role in America

Washington, D.C., Apr. 19

Since the retrocession of Louisiana from Spain to France by the secret treaty of October 1, 1800, fears have been growing here that Napoleon Bonaparte will attempt to re-establish a major French presence on the North American continent. With Europe at peace following the Treaty of Amiens, the French have been able to dispatch a large military force to Haiti to suppress the revolt led by Toussaint L'Ouverture. Once that has been achieved, the French army could easily be shipped across to New Orleans and from there take military possession of Louisiana.

Should that happen, westward expansion by Americans would be stopped. More immediately, the right of transit in New Orleans guaranteed to American traders by the Treaty of San Lorenzo would be seriously endangered. Writing to Robert Livingston, U.S. minister in Paris, President Jefferson commented: "The day that France takes New Orleans . . . we must marry ourselves to the British fleet and nation." In the meantime, Livingston is to broach the question of Americans buying territory on the lower Mississippi (→ Dec. 20, 1803).

Livingston, minister to France.

Jefferson continues to cut central power

Washington, D.C., Dec. 6

President Thomas Jefferson, in his annual address to Congress today, restated his plan to streamline the federal government. In the view of most Republicans, the nation is too large to be governed effectively from the banks of the Potomac. The states, Jefferson says, must be "independent as to everything within themselves, and united as to everything respecting foreign nations." The federal government, overfed by the Federalists, should shrink to fill its proper role, he said, "a few plain duties to be performed by a few servants." Under the wholly visible hand of Treasury Secretary Albert Gallatin, meanwhile, the administration has limited its own duties. In April, the Republican-dominated Congress lifted all excise taxes, including the levy on spirits, which is widely held responsible for the Whiskey Rebellion of 1794.

Slave uprisings plague South; slavery curbed in Northern states

United States

All states north of the Mason-Dixon Line have now passed anti-slavery laws or laws calling for gradual emancipation, except for New Jersey. This creates an official and well-delineated division of the nation into Northern free states and Southern slave states.

While Northerners seem to have come to terms with their Negroes, the South still seems to be boiling with slave uprisings and conspiracies. In North Carolina, at least six counties have reported slave conspiracies recently, including a plot in May led by the outlaw Tom Cooper that resulted in as many as 15 slaves being executed.

Virginia has also been the scene of many insurrections. Alleged conspiracies in Richmond, Williamsburg, Brunswick, Norfolk, Princess Anne, Hanover County, Halifax and elsewhere have resulted in the banishing, flogging or hanging of a large number of slaves. Some white men, as well as Negroes, were reported to be involved in the revolutionary plot in Halifax.

Paris. *Benjamin West has taken Paris by storm. Art connoisseurs visit Le Salon daily to stare breathlessly at the colorful, passionate melodrama of "Death on the Pale Horse," completed earlier this year by West in London.*

Congress restores Supreme Court seat

Washington, D.C., Apr. 29

Legislative revenge. That's what the Republicans gained today when they repealed the Judiciary Act of 1801. That act, reducing the Supreme Court by one seat and creating new courts, was passed by lame-duck Federalists. President Adams filled the new courts with Federalists. Republican John Randolph called this judiciary "a hospital for decaying politicians." Today's move restores the sixth high court seat and gives the justices jurisdiction over the 16 circuit courts.

West Point site of military academy

West Point, New York, March 16

Congress passed an act today establishing an official United States Military Academy, to be situated at the fort of West Point on the Hudson. Although former President George Washington first suggested the idea several years ago, no action was taken until last year, when a corps of veteran engineers and artillerymen was transferred to West Point for the purpose of training officer candidates. Official opening of the academy has been scheduled for July 4 (→ July 4).

Martha Washington, first First Lady, dies

Mount Vernon, May 22

Martha Dandridge Custis Washington, the nation's first First Lady, has died at the age of 70. She was a young widow when she first met Washington, and he won not just her hand but her 17,000-acre farm as well. Mrs. Washington spent the long winters of the Revolution by her husband's side, and during his presidency, she served as a gracious hostess. Yet the role was not always to her liking. During that period when she was First Lady, she wrote a relative in Virginia, "I live a very dull life . . . I am more like a state prisoner than anything else."

First Lady, after Peale and Stuart.

Du Pont prepares to make gunpowder

Wilmington, Delaware, June 19

Eluthere Irenee du Pont arrived at his new home along Brandywine Creek with his family today to supervise construction of his modern gunpowder plant based on designs made available by France to help break the British gunpowder monopoly. The plans are said to provide maximum safety. Du Pont, who paid for the land but cannot own it because he is not a citizen, chose Delaware at the urging of Peter Bauduy, a rich planter who fled from Haiti's slave revolt and yellow fever epidemic. The labor for the plant will be provided by other French refugees.

Eleuthere Irenee du Pont, refugee from the French Revolution. Painting by Rembrandt Peale.

Future state of Ohio writes constitution

The courthouse at Chillicothe, birthplace of Ohio's new constitution.

Washington, D.C., Nov. 29

After an unsuccessful last-ditch effort by the territorial Governor Arthur St. Clair to block Ohio's bid for statehood at the constitutional convention held in Chillicothe over the past three weeks, President Thomas Jefferson announced today that St. Clair would be removed from office and that the constitution drafted by Republican delegates would be approved. These actions were the culmination of a bitter battle over Ohio statehood between Federalist political forces led by St. Clair and Jeffersonian Republicans led by Thomas Worthington, a wealthy liberal from Chillicothe.

St. Clair, who was named Governor of the Northwest Territory soon after its formation in 1787, grew increasingly unpopular over the years because of his overbearing manner and his autocratic administrative policies. He made numerous attempts to block the move toward statehood, and it was only through the diligence of Worthington and his supporters that Governor St. Clair was defeated.

The new constitution incorporates provisions of the Ordinance of 1787 that forbids slavery and it outlines a governmental structure intended to inhibit the kind of dictatorial power assumed by St. Clair. The legislature of the new state will choose all the officials except the governor, and will have supreme authority over the executive, judicial and legislative branches of government. The governor, himself, will have few important duties (→ March 1, 1803).

Treachery does not pay, bandit learns

Washington, Mississippi

Little Wiley Harpe, the terror of Natchez Trace, rode into town with a fellow criminal's head, expecting to collect a reward. Instead, Little Wiley found himself charged with another murder and sentenced to be hanged. Harpe killed Sam Mason, the leader of a band of robbers and murderers. He brought the head into town plastered in blue clay. After Harpe was identified in another crime, he was sentenced to be hanged. Harpe and his older brother, the late Big Harpe, developed their reputations for brutal murders while they were terrorizing travelers on the Natchez Trace.

Citizenship rules are changing again

Washington, D.C., Apr. 14

The laws dealing with naturalization have been subject to political vicissitudes. In 1795, under President Washington, the required length of residency before an alien could become a citizen was set by Congress at five years. But the predominance of the Federalists, and their fears of political intrusion by foreign powers, changed the law in 1798. They passed legislation requiring aliens to live in the United States for 14 years before being naturalized. Today, the Republicans altered the law again, returning the length of residency to five years.

1803

Jefferson

New York City, Feb. 4. *The Voice of Nature*, by America's first professional playwright, William Dunlap, opens; considered first U.S. melodrama.

Louisiana, Apr. 19. Spain reopens New Orleans to American merchants.

United States, May. Architect Benjamin Henry Latrobe addresses American Philosophical Society, intimating that steam engine has no future.

Boston, Sept. 29. City's first Catholic church dedicated.

Washington, D.C., Dec. 19. Congress repeals Bankruptcy Act of 1800.

Maryland. First icebox patented by farmer Thomas Moore.

London. British Passenger Act, aimed at curbing overcrowding on immigrant ships, actually raises prices, restricting passage from British Isles.

Salisbury, Connecticut. First tax-funded public library in nation founded.

South Carolina. State legislature opens slave trade from South America and West Indies.

Honolulu. Richard Cleveland and William Shaler introduce first horses to Hawaiian Islands.

Boston. Canal completed connecting Merrimac River with Concord River and flowing into Boston harbor.

New Ipswich, New Hampshire. First cotton-goods factory in New Hampshire built, powered by Souhegan River.

Louisiana. Lorenzo Dow, a Methodist evangelist who also sells patent medicine, attracts crowds with fiery oratory.

Philadelphia. First professional American novelist Charles Brockden Brown founds *Literary Magazine and American Register.*

Philadelphia. Magazine *Portfolio* charges $5 for a year's subscription.

Loudon County, Virginia. John Alexander Binns publishes *A Treatise on Practical Farming*, advocating crop rotation, deep plowing and fertilization.

United States. *Letters of a British Spy*, by William Wirt, published, first anonymously, in newspaper, as best-selling book later in year.

Lewis and Clark set out to explore West

Lewis, aquatint after Saint-Memin.

Clark (1832) by George Catlin.

Pittsburgh, Aug. 31

Captain Meriwether Lewis, the 29-year-old former private secretary and aide-de-camp to President Thomas Jefferson, left Pittsburgh today with a small party of men and his large Newfoundland dog, Scammon, on the first leg of what is rumored to be a major government exploration of the Far Western country. The group will travel by river in a keelboat called the Discovery, designed and built in Pittsburgh to Lewis's specifications. It will stop at Louisville to take on 33-year-old Captain William Clark, an old friend of Lewis's, who will be co-leader of the expedition. From there, the party will proceed to St. Louis to make the final preparations for the journey.

Although the reports are still sketchy, it is believed that Lewis is under orders to look for a passage through the Western mountains to the Pacific Ocean. Some observers, question the advisability of sending a government-sponsored expedition into country still under Spanish jurisdiction. On the other hand, rumors abound that the whole of Louisiana is being ceded back to France and that American representatives may be negotiating with the French over possession of all or part of the territory. If this is the case, the expedition is of even more significance (→ May 21, 1804).

High court cancels an act of Congress

Washington, D.C., Feb. 24

Chief Justice Marshall has written that the Constitution is the law of the land, and the Supreme Court has applied the principle of judicial review of Congress for the first time by declaring a federal law unconstitutional. Today's ruling made Marbury v. Madison a historic case.

William Marbury, one of President Adams's "midnight judges" (named the night his term ended) had been refused his commission by Secretary of State James Madison. To gain his appointment, he petitioned the Supreme Court, which ruled that he had a right to his office. However, the high court also overturned the Judicial Act of 1789, and thus asserted its authority to be the final arbiter of the Constitution (→ March 16, 1810).

Separate votes set for President, V.P.

Washington, D.C., Dec. 9

Congress has passed the 12th Amendment, requiring electors to vote for president and vice president separately. It ends the tradition of the runner-up in a presidential race becoming vice president and prevents the possibility of an accidental deadlock. The reform was motivated by the 1800 election, when Thomas Jefferson defeated Aaron Burr after a tie forced the House of Representatives to cast the deciding vote (→ Dec. 5, 1804).

11 houses burned in N.Y. Negro riot

New York, September

The courts have convicted 20 Negroes of arson in connection with the burning of 11 houses in New York City. A plan drafted by the rioting Negroes is reported to have called for burning the entire city. The arrest of some Negroes incited others and even wider rioting ensued for several days before the violence could be brought under control. The riot parallels one in York, Pennsylvania, where Negroes burned about a dozen buildings.

Ohio joins union as the 17th state

Chillicothe, March 1

Republican leaders are celebrating here today after learning that Ohio has been admitted as the 17th state in the union and the first to be carved out of the Northwest Territory despite efforts by Federalists to block the bid for statehood. The state's constitution becomes the first in the union to forbid slavery by law, and the new state legislature, which will convene here in a few days, has been given extraordinary powers (→ March 26, 1804).

Napoleon's brother weds Baltimore girl

Baltimore, Dec. 24

Jerome Bonaparte, the youngest brother of Napoleon and a naval commander of the French fleet, has wed Elizabeth Patterson of Baltimore. Both the bride and groom are 18 years old. The couple were first acquainted through the bride's father, William Patterson, a shipbuilder and one of the wealthiest men in America. For the ceremony, the bridegroom wore purple satin and diamond buckles. The bride wore a shockingly brief gown.

U.S. doubles size; buys Louisiana for $15 million

New Orleans, Dec. 20

The French tricolor was lowered in New Orleans today and the Stars and Stripes raised in its place, thus symbolizing the transfer of the Louisiana Territory from France to the United States. In what has been one of the largest peaceful cessions of territory in history, the United States acquired a vast segment of the North American continent for the minuscule sum of $15 million. In one fell swoop, the territory of the United States of America was virtually doubled.

Spain originally claimed this vast and largely unexplored land that stretches from Canada to the Gulf of Mexico. In 1801, the Spaniards ceded the territory to France. This caused grave concerns in Washington, because whoever controlled the territory also controlled the port of New Orleans and the entrance to the Gulf of Mexico. Fortunately for the United States, France, which had suffered the loss of thousands of troops in the Caribbean as the result of slave revolts and tropical disease on the island of Santo Domingo, was starting to lose interest in maintaining a strategic presence in either the gulf or on the North American continent. Realizing that Napoleon might be persuaded to part with Louisiana, President Jefferson sent fellow Virginian James Monroe to ask the Emperor whether he would agree to sell the territory to the United States, and if so, under what conditions. Reaching Paris in April, Monroe directly posed the question to the French. He was startled to hear that they would be willing – almost eager – to sell not only the port of New Orleans, but also the entire Louisiana Territory for 60,000 francs, with 20,000 francs more thrown in for the alleged American damages against France in the undeclared naval war of 1798.

Monroe and his party of diplomats were flabbergasted at both the graciousness and generosity of the French. The Americans had not been authorized by the President to conclude a purchase. But because they knew such a bargain could not be rejected, they accepted the offer, signed the cession document and sent it to Jefferson on April 30.

When the report of the amazing French offer – and the American response – reached the nation's capital, a great political and constitutional debate ensued. Many Federalists opposed what one called "a miserable calamitous business," the doubling of the size of the United States. These Congressmen feared that the country would be so large and unwieldy that it would literally be ungovernable and therefore disintegrate. Other Federalists were unhappy with the provision that made American citizens of the territory's French and Spanish residents. The Republicans themselves held grave constitutional reservations about the acquisition. Even Jefferson believed that such a vast territorial acquisition could not be carried out except through a constitutional amendment, and that therefore he had exceeded his legal authority as chief executive.

Nevertheless, Jefferson adopted a pragmatic position on the Louisiana affair. He strongly believed that, constitutional questions aside, he had to accept Napoleon's offer for two reasons. First, Napoleon's time in office might be limited and the offer withdrawn. Second, France could decide to expand and reinforce its holdings in Louisiana if the United States did not buy it. Such an expansion of French power would point a knife at America's throat. Consequently, as the President has said, "The laws of self-preservation overrule the laws of obligations." Therefore, Jefferson was determined to proceed at full speed to take advantage of the geat opportunity.

The President submitted the cession, or Louisiana Purchase Treaty as it is more popularly known, to the Senate on October 20. By then, doubts had waned and enthusiasm was mounting. The treaty received overwhelming bipartisan support and won approval by a vote of 24 to 7. On October 31, a special postal rider left Washington for New Orleans with the official instructions and documents that were necessary to carry out the historic transfer. He was received by the United States Commissioners C.C. Claiborne and General James Wilkinson, who took legal possession of the Louisiana Territory on behalf of the United States (→ Feb. 20, 1811).

The Stars and Stripes hoisted over the city of New Orleans to replace the French tricolor, raised only 20 days ago. Painting by Thor de Thulstrup.

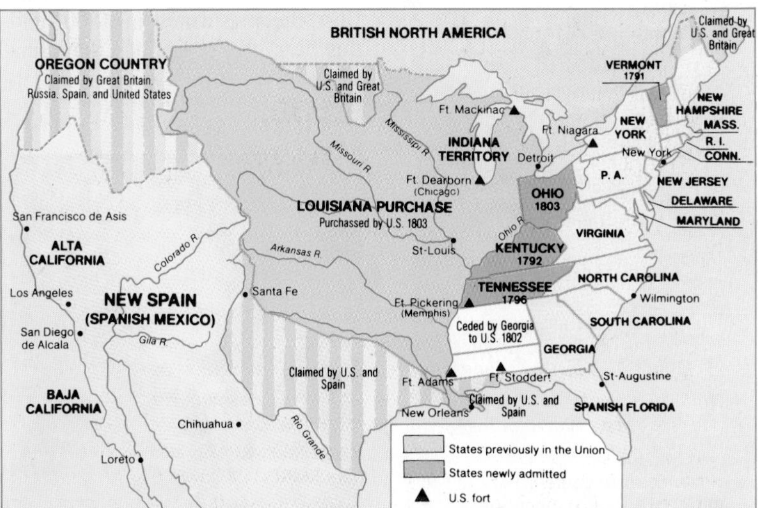

The Louisiana Purchase, a 909,000-square-mile region sold by France to American diplomats for $15 million, has been called "the greatest real estate deal in history." French Foreign Minister Talleyrand called it simply "a noble bargain." In either case, the United States is twice as big as it was before.

1804

Jefferson

United States, Feb. 1. Jefferson writes to French economist Jean Baptiste Say of his hopes for a productive agrarian society in United States.

Western Frontier, May 21. Lewis and Clark arrive at the home of Daniel Boone (→ Oct. 27).

Washington, D.C., October. Modeled after British, first local agricultural fair held.

United States, Nov. 23. John Quincy Adams writes of Jefferson: "His genius is of the old French school. It conceives better than it combines."

Paris, Dec. 2. Napoleon Bonaparte, snatching crown from Pope's hands, proclaims himself Emperor of France (→ Apr. 11, 1814).

Philadelphia. Thomas Moore inherits Joseph Priestley's chemical laboratory.

California. First California orange grove planted, at San Gabriel Mission.

Atlantic. France and England renew hostilities, prompting British to resume harassing American shipping (→ July 23, 1805).

Tennessee. Andrew Jackson and wife inaugurate The Hermitage as a three-room cabin north of Nashville.

United States. Two inventors get patent for galluses, or suspenders.

Marietta, Ohio. "Coonskin Library" founded when Ohio River merchants trade coonskins for books with Boston merchants.

Alabama. Ephraim Kirby becomes first judge in Louisiana Territory.

Columbia, Pennsylvania. Freed slave Stephen Smith's mother follows him north, to be protected by Stephen's buyer [Underground Railroad begins.]

Providence, Rhode Island. Rhode Island College renamed Brown University after benefactor Nicholas Brown.

Honolulu. Epidemic, possibly of cholera or bubonic plague, kills thousands of Hawaiians.

United States. John Marshall publishes first volume of his *Life of George Washington.*

Boston. Booksellers bring out important joint publication, *The Catalogue of All the Books Printed in the United States.*

Hamilton killed in duel

Hamilton, whose son also died in a duel, is felled by a bullet from Burr's gun.

Weehawken, New Jersey, July 12

Former Treasury Secretary Alexander Hamilton has died a most painful death of wounds suffered yesterday in a duel with a political opponent, Aaron Burr. Burr, who survived the duel unscathed, has not yet extended sympathy to Hamilton's grieving family and seems to have secluded himself. Hamilton's fellow statesmen, however, have expressed dismay over his untimely death. Acquaintances find it inconceivable that Hamilton would willingly indulge in dueling, a practice he publicly deplored after an "affaire d'honneur" claimed the life of his son Philip three years ago. Yet Hamilton helped to deny Burr the presidency in 1800, and this year his accusations that Burr was a traitor probably cost the latter the governorship of New York.

Hamilton by John Trumbull.

Burr challenged Hamilton to a duel.

Hamilton was born January 11, 1757, on the West Indian island of Nevis. After attending King's College in New York, he threw himself into the cause of the patriots, writing incendiary pamphlets and drilling with the local militia. By the age of 20, he was aide-de-camp to General Washington. Following the war, Hamilton was elected New York delegate to the Continental Congress. He founded the Society for Promoting the Manumission of Slaves, served in the New York Assembly and was appointed secretary of the Treasury. In 1798, he was named inspector general of the army. Resigning the position in 1800, he opened a law practice.

These positions hardly suggest Hamilton's immense influence on government policy. He opposed the weak Articles of Confederation and fought for the Constitution, which he ironically called "that frail and worthless fabric." He outlined a plan for a national bank and a system of internal and external taxation. If the public did not accept all his innovations, the distrust was mutual; Hamilton wanted a government run by the educated few.

Of his many enemies, Burr was foremost. Hamilton felt Burr truly wished to "subvert the republican system of the country." Yet moments before the duel on the banks of the Hudson River, Hamilton told his second he would not aim at Burr, but fire into the air.

Jefferson in again; Clinton beats King

Washington, D.C., Dec. 5

By a surprisingly large majority, the Electoral College today elected Thomas Jefferson to a second term as President. He gained 162 votes to only 14 for his Federalist opponent, Charles Cotesworth Pinckney. George Clinton defeated Rufus King for the vice presidency. This presidential election is the first since passage in September of the 12th Amendment, which calls for each of the presidential electors to vote separately for president and vice president. This change prevents any repetition of an intra-party tie vote, which happened in the last election, when it was left to the House of Representatives to decide who would be the next president.

Justice investigated in high court feud

Washington, D.C., March 12

Supreme Court Justice Samuel Chase is being investigated for bias in the sedition trial of a publisher and, many say, for his criticism of President Jefferson. But most observers say Congress lacks the votes to remove him. Another judge, John Pickering, was ousted today for behavior unbecoming a magistrate. He was impeached because of illegal decisions, intoxication and profanity (→ March 1, 1805).

Smallholders get better land deal

Washington, March 26

Congress today passed a significant amendment to the Harrison Land Law of 1800 regulating the sale of public lands in the West. The amended law should stimulate settlement in the Ohio country because it cuts the minimum acreage a person must buy from 320 to 160 acres, trims the price per acre from \$2 to \$1.64, and permits an extension of payments over a 10-year period. These changes should enable ordinary settlers to get land directly from the government instead of having to pay inflated prices to speculators.

ewis and Clark at upper Missouri River

landan villages, Oct. 27

Despite a near-fatal encounter ith a group of Sioux Indians near e Teton River about a month ago, e expedition launched by Cap- ins Meriwether Lewis and Wil- am Clark from St. Charles in May as now reached the villages of the iendly Mandan Indians and the en are preparing to spend their rst winter in the wilderness.

Except for the tense encounter ith the Sioux and the treacherous ondition of the Missouri River, the xpedition has met remarkably few ifficulties so far, and much of value has been learned about the flora, fauna and Indian tribes of the upper Missouri River country. Lewis and Clark have proven skilled negotiators at councils with the Mandans, Missouris and Otoes, as well as with the Ree or Arikara.

Only three members of the expedition have deserted, and after a few floggings for breaches of discipline, the rest have buckled down to the task before them, and performed admirably. The only casualty has been Sergeant Charles Floyd, who died from the effects of a violent colic (→Apr. 26, 1805).

Many slaves held for arson and rebellion

ichmond, Virginia

Numerous arrests of slaves have een made in Georgia, South Car- lina and Virginia for arson and nsurrection. Twenty have been ex- cuted for poisoning whites. One aptured slave reportedly said: "I ave nothing more to offer [in my efense] than what George Wash- ngton would have had to offer had he been taken by the British and put to trial by them. I have adventured my life in endeavoring to obtain the liberty of my countrymen, and am willing to sacrifice to their cause: and I beg as a favor, that I may be immediately led to execution ... You have predetermined to shed my blood, why then this mockery of a trial?" (→May 1, 1805).

Haitians flee to U.S. during freedom fight

Port-au-Prince, Haiti, Jan. 1

Despite the surrender last year of he French army and today's proc- amation of independence by Gen- ral Jean-Jacques Dessalines, no nd is yet in sight to the civil strife hat has engulfed this country since Toussaint L'Ouverture began the slave revolt in 1791. Fearing for their lives, thousands of creoles and French-born whites have fled to the United States, particularly to Philadelphia, but their prospects of being able to return are slim.

Philadelphia. *Despite a cumbersome name, a new steam-powered vehicle manages to propel itself across land and water, a unique feat for a wheeled contraption. It is the creation of Oliver Evans, who calls it the Orukter Amphibolos. Evans invented the high-pressure steam engine (1790) on his vehicle, as well as an automated production line for grinding grain (1784).*

U.S. fleet batters Tripoli

Burning of the frigate Philadelphia.

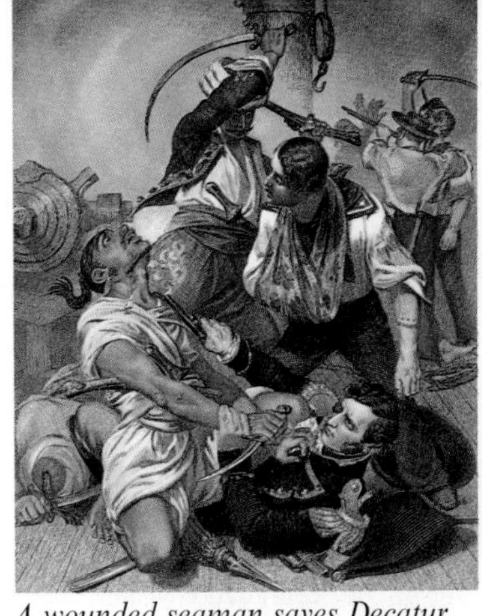

A wounded seaman saves Decatur.

Tripoli, Sept. 5

Acting on his conviction that the Barbary potentates are "a deep designing artfull treacherous sett of Villains" who will respond only to a strong show of force, Commodore Edward Preble has just completed the fifth general attack on the fortifications and town of the Pasha's capital. The final blow was to have been last night's detonation among the enemy's fleet of the ketch Intrepid, which had been converted into an "infernal" – a fire ship loaded with a large quantity of gunpowder. But though moving under cover of darkness, the ship was sighted by enemy gunners and blown up, with the loss of its crew of 13, including Captain Somers and Lieutenants Israel and Wadsworth.

Ironically, it was the Intrepid that, on February 16, carried Lieutenant Stephen Decatur and his crew on their night raid into the same harbor, where they set fire to the captured frigate Philadelphia, an exploit that Admiral Lord Nelson himself has called "the most bold and daring act of the age."

But though the 36-gun Philadelphia was thus denied to the Tripolitans, Captain William Bainbridge and his crew of 306 remain prisoners. It was to gain their release, and to force the Pasha to agree to peace terms, that the 43-year-old Commodore Preble arrived here at the end of July aboard the 44-gun Constitution, along with three brigantines of 16 guns, three schooners of 12 guns, six gunboats and two mortar-boats. Confronting him was a fleet of about equal strength as well as massive fortifications and batteries armed with 115 heavy guns. Since the Pasha has an army of 25,000, Preble has had no choice but to confine the fighting to the sea (→June 4, 1805).

Commodore Preble's fleet bombs Tripoli. Lithograph (1846) by N. Currier.

1805

Jefferson

New Orleans, Feb. 17. New Orleans incorporated as a city.

Washington, D.C., March 1. Samuel Chase reoccupies Supreme Court seat as Senate cancels impeachment proceedings.

Western Wilderness, Apr. 26. Lewis and Clark reach mouth of Yellowstone River (→Nov. 7).

Virginia, May 1. State law requires all slaves freed hereafter to leave state.

Philadelphia, May 25. Leaders of Federal Society of Journeyman Cordwainers seized for conspiracy in first employer court action against strikers (→July 12, 1810).

Ohio, July 4. Final treaty arranged with Indians for purchase of Cleveland.

London, July 23. British invoke Rule of 1756, justifying seizure of American ships in neutral ports (→May 16, 1806).

Louisiana, July 25. Aaron Burr visits New Orleans as he allegedly develops plans to establish a separate country with New Orleans as its capital (→Sept.).

Washington, D.C., Dec. 4. President Jefferson addresses Congress in belligerent tones, apparently to frighten Spain.

Philadelphia. First covered bridge in United States built over Schuylkill River.

Paris. Robert Fulton successfully tests first torpedo.

Philadelphia. Pennsylvania Academy of Fine Art founded by painter Charles Willson Peale.

United States. Rembrandt Peale paints portrait of Thomas Jefferson.

New England. Frederick Tudor ships ice to French island of Martinique, both as ballast and as export item.

Virginia. State general assembly sends resolution to United States government, asking that Negroes be settled in parts of Louisiana Purchase.

Staten Island. Cornelius Vanderbilt ends his last year of formal education at age 11.

United States. Elizabeth Ann Seton [future saint] converts to Roman Catholicism.

United States. First herd of corn-fed cattle guided to East from Ohio River Valley.

Pasha of Tripoli signs treaty ending war

Tripoli, June 4

Threatened by the guns of the American squadron patrolling outside his harbor, and with his rebel brother Hamet installed by American-backed forces in the eastern city of Derna, Yusuf Karamanli, the Pasha of Tripoli has signed a treaty with the United States, agreeing to terms that clearly reflect his reduced circumstances. In return for a payment of $60,000, Captain Bainbridge and the 306 crew members of the captured Philadelphia will be released. But there is to be no payment for the treaty itself; nor will there be any future tribute. The United States has agreed to remove its forces from Derna, and to try to persuade Hamet Karamanli to withdraw.

This undertaking will certainly be opposed by William Eaton, former American consul at Tunis and self-appointed general, who has been the driving force behind an overland expedition. After enlisting Hamet's support in Cairo last fall, "General" Eaton went to Alexandria where he recruited a motley army of 400 men, mostly Arabs and Greeks, but also including Midshipman Peck and Lieutenant O'Bannon with seven marines. With this force, he marched 600 miles across the desert and reached Derna late in April. Joined there by the Argus and Hornet, his men stormed the town, which they still hold despite repeated counterattacks. Hamet, however, has no choice but to agree to withdraw since his wife and children remain in Tripoli, at the mercy of his brother (→March 3, 1815).

Aaron Burr on mysterious Southern trip

New Orleans, September

Former Vice President Aaron Burr's voyage down the Mississippi River has created widespread curiosity about his intentions. Some believe that he may replace W.C.C. Claiborne as Governor of the Territory of Orleans, although that seems unlikely. Others have raised questions about Burr's loyalty to the government in Washington, alleging that he has approached the British for help in a plan to separate some of the Western states from the nation. Burr's friendship with General James Wilkinson, the new Governor of the Louisiana Territory, who himself took part in a scheme just after the Revolution to form a separate country from territory in the Southwest, lends a degree of credence to these charges. Other rumors have linked Burr to a plot to invade Mexico (→July 20, 1806).

Aaron Burr, out West, reviews a makeshift contingent of adventurers.

Jefferson proposes lighter tax load

Jefferson (1800) by R. Peale.

Washington, D.C., March 4

In his second inaugural address President Jefferson emphasized his past and present concern with domestic affairs – particularly the sensitive issue of taxes. The speech, which was delivered in a half-filled Senate chamber today, proposed that Federalist-inspired internal taxes be completely eliminated. Jefferson argued that the revenue lost by such a step can more than be made up through the assessment of luxury taxes. In a direct appeal to the working classes, the President observed that "it may be the pleasure and pride of an American to ask, what farmer, what mechanic, what laborer, ever sees a tax-gatherer of the United States."

N.Y. Negro boxer is famed in England

Staten Island, New York

Bill Richmond, a Negro servant in the employ of Lord Percy, a British general who was stationed in New York in the colonial era, was able to improve his lot by boxing British soldiers. He defeated all rivals, and when Lord Percy returned to England in 1777, the general took Richmond back with him. In England, the "Black Terror," as Richmond became known, kept winning until he was knocked out this year by the claimaint to the British title, Tom Cribb, in 1 hour, 30 minutes.

Congress sets up 3 separate territories

Detroit, July 1

Residents here have cause to celebrate. Congress has made Michigan and Indiana separate territories. This move seems to spell the end of nearly 10 years of congressional boundary manipulation in the Northwest Territory. During this decade the Michigan country was first divided between the Northwest Territory and the Indiana Territory, and then attached to the Indiana Territory when Ohio was admitted as a state in 1803. Michigan's capital will be at Detroit, with General William Hull the territory's first Governor. Also this year, on March 3, the Territory of Louisiana was created, independent of Indiana Territory (→ Apr. 29, 1809).

Pennsylvania gets utopian settlement

Butler County, Penn., Feb. 15

Some 600 German immigrants today agreed to give their worldly goods to a community that promises to meet all their needs in return. The group, led by George Rapp, a 48-year-old prophet who says the millennium is almost upon us, is building a town, Harmonie, on land bought here in western Pennsylvania. The German group left Wurttemberg to escape persecution by a Lutheran Church that accused their leader Rapp of losing sight of true Christian principles.

Negro wins $691.25 in damages in suit

Kentucky

In the case of Thompson v. Wilmot, a court has awarded a Negro $691.25 in damages. The Negro was taken from Maryland to Kentucky, supposedly to serve for a limited time. However, he was kept captive beyond the time appointed for his freedom and brought suit against his owner. The decision has been appealed by the former master. Kentucky was admitted to the union as a slave state in 1792. However, its constitution does not deny suffrage to free Negroes.

Lewis and Clark sight Pacific at last

"Lewis and Clark on the Lower Columbia" (1905) by Charles Russell. The Indians of the Columbia River, short and bowlegged according to Clark, live on roots and fish. They gave the explorers their first taste of Pacific salmon.

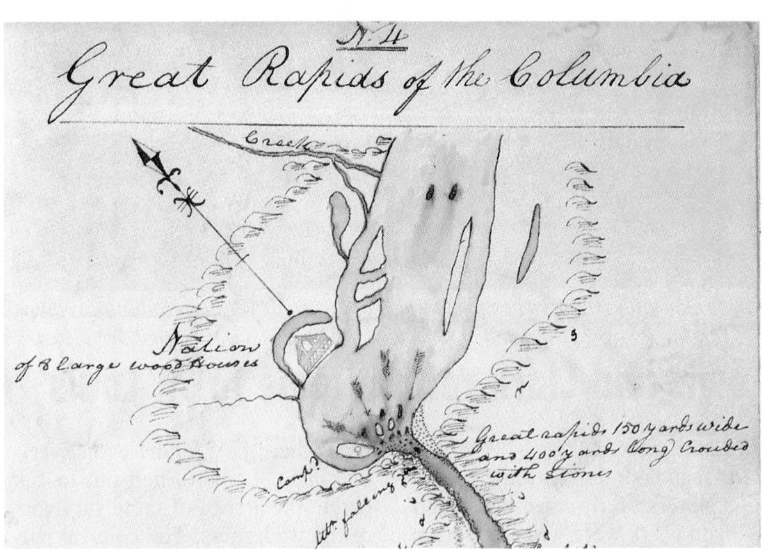

In his detailed journal, Clark sketched a map of the Columbia River Rapids.

Indian guide Sacajawea has proved an invaluable asset. Painting by C. Russell.

Columbia River, Nov. 7

After a perilous journey of 18 months and nearly 4,000 miles, the Lewis and Clark expedition has finally reached its objective, the Pacific Ocean, opening what many hope will be a new era of westward expansion for the United States.

The group that completed the grueling final leg of the trek to the mouth of the Columbia River is made up of Captains Meriwether Lewis and William Clark; Clark's hardy Negro companion, York; George Drouillard, Lewis's valued scout and hunter; the interpreter, Toussaint Charbonneau; his Shoshone squaw, Sacajawea, who has carried their infant son, Jean Baptiste, the entire way, and a 26-man military detachment.

This Corps of Discovery left Fort Mandan on the upper Missouri River on April 7 in six canoes and two large pirogues. The keel boat that took the group to the Mandan villages was sent back downriver under the command of Corporal Warfington loaded with plant, mineral and animal specimens collected on the first leg of the journey. These will be delivered for scientific study.

Near the end of April, the expedition passed the mouth of the Yellowstone River, and a month later caught its first sight of the Rocky Mountains. By mid-June, the group reached the awesome Great Falls of the Missouri, and, after a long portage, set out again by water. It came to the three upper forks of the Missouri on July 27, taking a needed rest and giving Clark a chance to recover from illness and exhaustion.

By mid-August, the expedition had crossed the continental divide and encountered the Shoshone or Snake Indians, parent tribe of Charbonneau's squaw, Sacajawea, a guide, and, with her help, struck a deal for 30 horses to begin the difficult trek through the Bitterroot Mountains. On October 1, the party once more took to the handhewn canoes and headed down the Clearwater and Snake Rivers to the Columbia. For nearly three weeks, the team fought treacherous rapids and harassing thefts by the Chinook Indians, but at last it reached its goal. After a long winter's rest, the explorers will be heading for home in the spring (→ Aug. 3, 1806).

1806

Jefferson

St. Louis, Apr. 30. Lieutenant Zebulon M. Pike returns from northern expedition thinking Minnesota is source of Mississippi River (→Nov. 15).

London, May 16. Charles James Fox, British Foreign Minister, imposes naval blockade on European coast, from Brest to mouth of Elbe River (→Aug. 27).

New York City, May 19. One school adopts cost-saving Lancastrian teaching system, employing student teachers.

Ohio River, July 20. Aaron Burr and Irishman Harman Blennerhasset meet on Blennerhassett's Island to prepare military expedition aimed at annexing land in Southwest (→Nov. 27).

Montana, Aug. 3. Clark reaches mouth of Yellowstone River and is followed by Lewis three days later (→Sept. 23).

London, Aug. 27. American negotiators James Monroe and William Pinkney open talks with Lord Holland on naval hostilities (→Dec. 31).

Washington, D.C., Oct. 21. Congress passes legislation providing for a military organizational structure.

Washington, D.C., Dec. 12. President Thomas Jefferson appeals to Congress for a ban on slave trade (→March 2, 1807).

Rhode Island. David Melville attempts construction of gas street lighting for Newport.

New York. John Stevens launches first steam-powered ferry, crossing Hudson River at three miles per hour.

Washington, D.C. United States Mint ordered to halt production of silver dollar.

Louisiana Territory. John Colter, and two others, quit Lewis and Clark's expedition to return to Montana.

Washington, D.C. Schools open with taxes levied for their support and a $5 quarterly charge to wealthy families.

Louisiana Territory. Daniel Boone's sons, Nathan and Daniel Morgan, start manufacturing salt at Boone's Lick salt spring.

United States. *Exhuming the Mastodon* painted by Charles Willson Peale, depicting discovery of a mastodon skeleton in upstate New York.

Pike discovers 18,000-foot peak

Colorado, Nov. 15

An Army explorer, Lieutenant Zebulon M. Pike, discovered a peak over 18,000 feet high today. The mountain, which Pike likened to a "small blue cloud," was so rugged that he and several of his men were unable to reach the top.

This summer, General James Wilkinson ordered Pike, a professional soldier, to explore the headwaters of the Arkansas and Red Rivers in the newly acquired Louisiana Territory. Accordingly, he left St. Louis on July 15 with a party of 22 men. Heading westward across a vast expanse of African-like "sandy deserts," he ventured up the Arkansas River, an area heavily populated by Indians, and on to what the Indians call the "Rocky Mountains," where Pike and his men came upon the peak. The lieutenant, a seasoned explorer who has scouted the Mississippi River region northward into Minnesota, will continue his search for the headwaters of the Red River.

Pike's expedition approaches the foothills of the great Western mountain range.

Lewis and Clark return home to St. Louis

St. Louis, Sept. 23

At high noon today, those intrepid explorers Meriwether Lewis and William Clark were welcomed back from their incredible 7,000-mile odyssey to the Pacific Ocean that began here 28 months ago. Everyone in St. Louis turned out to celebrate the arrival of these survivors of the wilderness. The colorful party accompanying the explorers included the Mandan Chief Big White and his squaw, Yellow Corn, who will soon travel with Lewis to Washington to visit President Jefferson before returning to their people on the upper Missouri.

The remarkable story of this epic journey is only beginning to unfold, but Captain Lewis's accounts of just a few of the adventures since leaving Fort Clatsop on the Pacific have whetted the appetites of those who heard them. Among the more exciting of the stories are those about the arduous passage through the Bitterroot Mountains, the narrow escape of Lewis and his men from the Piegan or Blackfoot Indians and the mysterious wounding of Lewis during an otherwise routine hunt not far from the Mandan villages.

One of the many drawings from Lewis and Clark's journals.

First missionary society is organized

Williamstown, Mass., August

A group of Williams College students, led by Samuel J. Mills Jr., have formed the first organization for the promotion of foreign missions to which they have all dedicated themselves. This group, "The Brethren," had its roots in a series of prayer meetings at Williams, including one reportedly held in a haystack while waiting for a storm to subside.

Jackson, wounded, kills man in duel

Logan County, Kentucky, May 30

Former Tennessee Senator Andrew Jackson shot to death a Nashville resident, Charles Dickinson, in a duel today. Jackson himself was hit in the chest before he delivered the fatal shot; if Jackson lives, he will have his heavy, loose-fitting coat to thank for impeding the bullet. The duel arose over insults that pertained to a gambling debt, not, as many believe, calumny regarding the legitimacy of Jackson's 15-year marriage.

Russians get rights to trade in America

San Francisco, Apr. 5

In the past, Spanish authorities here have been wary of selling food and supplies to Russian-American colonists who come down from Alaska in search of such provisions. Now, in an abrupt turnaround, the Spanish government has agreed to sell supplies to these colonists. The Russians' representative, Nikolai Rezanov, has been in San Francisco for months trying to negotiate a sale. Spanish officials deny that the reason for the sudden reversal of policy was Rezanov's recent engagement to Dona Maria de la Concepcion Arguello, the daughter of San Francisco's commander. Regardless of the reason for the change, the sale of food and other critical supplies to the Russians in New Archangel assures the colony that it will not face the kind of famine this year that it has experienced in past winters.

Jefferson warns of military adventure

Washington, D.C., Nov. 27

President Jefferson today warned citizens not to take part in a plot to invade Spanish territory. Groups advocating separation of the Western states from Spain hope to provoke a war in an effort to claim more Western territory. Former Vice President Aaron Burr has twice been brought before a Kentucky federal grand jury on charges of involvement in Western separatist plots, but he was cleared both times (→ June 24, 1807).

Trotter gets record

New York City, June 5

A trotter has raced a mile in less than three minutes for the first time. The gelding, named Yankee, covered the distance in 2:59 at a race course in Harlem. Nothing is known about Yankee's breeding, but trotting fans are excited over a feat that they had long considered to be impossible.

British may end harassment of U.S. ships

British ships accost an American vessel. The Senate, in February, condemned British acts as "unprovoked aggression," but relations have improved of late.

London, Dec. 31

Hopes for a substantial improvement in relations with Britain have risen with the signing here of a treaty intended to halt British harassment of American ships. The treaty follows President Jefferson's suspension earlier in the month of the anti-British Non-Importation Act. But Europe is again at war, Foreign Secretary Charles James Fox has declared the coast from Brest to the mouth of the Elbe to be under blockade, and Napoleon, by his Berlin Decrees of November 21, has declared the same of Britain. So it remains to be seen whether the Royal Navy will stop seizing American ships and impressing their crews (→ Jan. 7, 1807).

Sparks will seek Red River's source

Oklahoma, June 2

Captain Richard Sparks, commander of the Second Infantry and one of the senior officers of the Freeman Expedition, left camp today to search for the source of the Red River, northwest of Natchitoches in the Louisiana Territory. Sparks and Thomas Freeman, a noted astronomer and frontiersman, were appointed by President Jefferson to explore and map this unknown area. Their party of 40 left Natchez in mid-April (→ 1811).

Bigger cotton crops

Mississippi

Amazing results are being reported from the use of a new cotton seed on the Petit Gulf Plantation here. The yield is extraordinarily large and the bolls do not rot. One story has it that Walter Burling of Natchez, envoy to Mexico, brought the seeds into the United States stuffed in dolls.

Noah Webster publishes new dictionary

New York City

Noah Webster, whose recent writings have argued for a unique American language, distinct from that spoken in England, takes a more conservative stand in his latest publication, *A Compendious Dictionary of the English Language*. This work, though it lists 5,000 words not included in any British collection, faults other lexicographers, even the great Samuel Johnson, for polluting the language with Latinate locutions – such as "opiniatry" – offensive to "any man of correct taste."

Webster and his "Compendious Dictionary." Lithograph by Root and Tinker.

Cherry tree grafted on to Washington lore

Philadelphia

George Washington's honesty had a precocious start, according to the fifth edition of *The Life and Memorable Actions of George Washington*. Author Mason Locke Weems, quondam minister and book peddler, conveniently finds new lore for each edition. Parson Weems now writes that when Washington was 6 years old, he cut down an English cherry tree with a hatchet he received as a gift. Questioned by his father, George confessed with the words, "I can't tell a lie, Pa; you know I can't tell a lie."

Little George told the whole truth to his father, according to Parson Weems.

1807

Jefferson

London, Jan. 7. Responding to Napoleon's Berlin Decree, a British council order closes coastal waters of France and its allies to all commercial shipping (→ June 22).

United States, Jan. 13. Thomas Jefferson, in a letter to John Dickinson, asserts that presidency "brings nothing but unceasing drudgery and daily loss of friends."

Washington, D.C., Feb. 10. Congress authorizes agency under Treasury Department to conduct survey of nation's coastline.

England, March 25. British Parliament abolishes slave trade.

Richmond, Virginia, June 24. Federal Circuit Court indicts Aaron Burr for treason, though he is arrested on a misdemeanor charge (→ Aug. 3).

Richmond, Virginia, Aug. 3. Treason proceedings begin against Aaron Burr (→ Sept. 1).

New York City, Aug. 21. Clermont, 150-foot paddle-wheel steamboat, returns from Albany after 32-hour round-trip (→ Sept. 4).

Washington, D.C., Oct. 26. Tenth Congress convenes with Democratic-Republicans dominating 28-6 in Senate and 118-24 in House.

Boston. Boston Atheneum established as intellectual club, library and natural history museum.

New York. Chemist Benjamin Silliman bottles and markets carbonated water.

New York. Lutheran Ministerium of New York changes its official language from German to English.

Wyoming. John Colter is first white American in Wyoming.

Montana. Manuel Lisa builds first fur-trading post here, at mouth of Bighorn River.

Philadelphia. The Rev. John Gloucester organizes First African Presbyterian Church.

Northern Plains. First white child in area born at Pembina.

Connecticut. Seth Thomas and Eli Terry begin large-scale production of clocks with interchangeable parts.

New England. *Life of Washington* by Aaron Bancroft.

Fulton steamboat starts commercial trips

Fulton's 150-foot riverboat. His first was tested in 1803 on Seine near Paris.

New York, Sept. 4

Fitch tried it with paddles, Rumsey with hydraulics. But it took the paddle wheels designed by the painter Robert Fulton to make the steam-powered boat a commercial success. In spite of the apprehensions of some of the passengers and spectators on the shore, the Clermont, powered by an imported Boulton and Watt steam engine, chugged and churned its way up the Hudson River toward Albany today on its first commercial voyage. In August, the 150-foot vessel, traveling at five miles per hour, completed a test journey on the same route in 32 hours, with 40 adventurous passengers on board.

Fulton, the son of a farmer, previously achieved a quiet fame as an artist, painting portraits of such luminaries as Benjamin Franklin. In 1787, he went to England to study art and to exhibit his paintings at the Royal Academy. But his efforts brought him little wealth and in 1793 he moved to France, where he turned his attention to engineering. By 1800, Fulton had completed his first engineering project, a submarine named the Nautilus. The little vessel was used in an attack on British ships in the English Channel, remaining under water for more than six hours. The Nautilus, however, was detected by the British, who were able to move their ships out of its range.

Fulton, a skilled painter as well.

Shortly after, Fulton met and formed a partnership with Robert Livingston, the American ambassador to France. Livingston had previously worked on developing a steamboat with John Stevens and held a monopoly on steam travel along the Hudson. Although Livingston and Stevens constructed a few workable boats, they were never able to produce an efficient commercial design. With Livingston's assistance, Fulton set up a 66-foot tank of water to experiment in, testing models that used paddles, endless chains and water wheels before he finally decided on the side paddle wheels.

The fears of some about steam travel were typified by a warning given by a friend of one passenger on today's voyage: "John, will thee risk thy life in such a concern? I tell thee she is the most fearful wild fowl living, and thy father ought to restrain thee" (→ 1811).

Importing of slaves barred by Congress

Washington, D.C., March 2

At the insistence of President Jefferson, Congress has passed a law that prohibits the importation of slaves from Africa, effective next January 1. A person knowingly purchasing an illegally imported slave will be fined $800. Equipping a ship for the slave trade will result in a fine of $20,000. States may dispose of such illegally imported Negroes as they see fit. Jefferson has long been known as a critic of slavery and attempted to introduce anti-slavery statements in his first draft of the Declaration of Independence and into Virginia legislation (→ Jan. 1, 1808).

U.S. eating habits decried by visitors

New York City

Although the average American is eating bountifully, some French visitors find his sense of taste and eating habits wanting. Constantin Francois de Chasseboeuf, Count of Volney, has decried the amount of lard, butter, salt pork, greasy puddings, coffee and tea Americans consume. And Francois Jean Marquis de Chastellux, in his *Travels in North America*, says the days pass "in heaping indigestions upon one another," noting that Americans' consumption of spirits completes "the ruin of the nervous system."

The Whimsies of Launcelot Longstuff

New York, Jan. 24

New York literati are sure to be buzzing about a pamphlet called *Salmagundi; or the Whim-Whams and Opinions of Launcelot Longstuff, Esq., and Others* that was issued here today. A miscellany of whimsical essays and poems lampooning the city's social and political life, the pamphlet was the idea of several well-born young Federalists who style themselves the "Nine Worthies of Cockloft Hall." Contributors to *Salmagundi* include the brothers William and Washington Irving and James Kirke Paulding.

ritish fire on U.S. ship, remove four men

'aptured sailors of the Chesapeake are marched before its fallen flag.

orfolk, Virginia, June 22

Outraged demands for retaliation ave greeted the news brought to ort today by Captain James Barn of the Chesapeake that his ip was intercepted, attacked, oarded and searched while on the gh seas by a vessel belonging the Royal Navy. Four crew memers were removed by the boarding arty and 21 were killed or woundd when the British ship Leopard pened fire on the Chesapeake after s commander had refused to allow to be boarded. Totally unprepared r such a sudden onslaught, Captain Barron had no choice but to come about and submit to the humiliating and illegal treatment.

While impressment of seamen from American merchant ships is bad enough, many will feel that extending such an offense to ships of the navy is intolerable. And the speciousness of the claim by the British that they are merely recapturing their own nationals who have deserted their service is glaringly revealed by the fact that David Martin, one of the four taken from the Chesapeake, is a Negro who was born in Massachusetts (→ Dec. 22).

'ribe attacks chief who visited Jefferson

t. Louis, September

Word has been received here of n Arikara Indian attack on the fficial party that was returning the Mandan chief, Big White, and his ntourage to their villages on the pper Missouri River after a visit to resident Jefferson in Washington.

Early reports tell of the killing f at least three soldiers in the ofcial party, which was led by Engn Nathaniel Pryor, a former nember of the Lewis and Clark exedition. Several men were woundd, including the interpreter for Chief Big White, Rene Jusseaume. Luckily, neither Big White nor his wife and child were harmed and they will probably be returned to St. Louis. It may be remembered that they were with Lewis and Clark last year as emissaries of the friendly upper Missouri River Indians.

The trader Pierre Chouteau and 23 of his men were in Pryor's party when it was attacked, and there are reports that the volatile St. Louis trader Manuel Lisa, who preceded Pryor's party upriver, may have agitated the Arikaras to attack so as to discourage Chouteau's efforts to establish trade with the Mandans.

Congress bars trading with all nations

Washington, D.C., Dec. 22

Responding to pressure from the President to act quickly, the House yesterday passed the Embargo Act, only four days after receiving it from the Senate; the new law takes effect today. Unlike the Non-Importation Act, which banned a long list of British goods, the Embargo Act puts a complete halt to all trading, not only with Britain and France, but with the whole world. No American ship may sail to any foreign port, and all exports from the United States, whether by land or sea, are prohibited.

President Jefferson believes that these economic sanctions will have such a drastic effect on the British, and on the French as well, that they will be forced to rescind their various orders-in-council and decrees against neutral trade, and stop their harassment of American shipping. There is much uncertainty about whether the Embargo Act will have the desired effect, but one thing is certain: Those intimately involved in these matters – ship owners, merchants, sailors and producers of exported goods – view the act with dismay (→Apr. 17, 1808).

Jefferson, with quill-pen sword, is satirized over his efforts to keep peace.

Aaron Burr is indicted, tried, acquitted

Richmond, Virginia, Sept. 1

A jury acquitted former Vice President Aaron Burr of treason today. Burr was initially only accused of preparing an expedition against Spanish territory, but testimony before a grand jury by General James Wilkinson resulted in a charge of treason as well. Chief Justice John Marshall, presiding in the Circuit Court of the district of Virginia, ruled that Burr could be found guilty of treason, defined by the Constitution as "levying war" against the United States, only if it could be proved that he actually participated in an "overt act." Though the prosecution failed to prove this to the jury's satisfaction, public opinion is still strongly aginst Burr.

The wildest testimony against Burr accused him of scheming to overthrow the federal government in order to set up a dictatorship and, if that plan could not be carried out, of planning to declare an independent nation in the West, with New Orleans as its capital and himself as ruler. More credible testimony established that Burr, with financial help from Harman Blennerhasset, an Irish expatriate and proponent of Western separatism, had readied a group of colonists to settle an area in the Bastrop grant, near Spanish territory [northeastern Louisiana], and a naval commander testified that Burr approached him about leading a force against Mexico. Burr also tried unsuccessfully to get British financial aid for his Western plans. The most damaging testimony concerning Burr's motives came from his former friend, General Wilkinson, who barely escaped being named in the treason indictment.

The trial of Aaron Burr.

1808

Jefferson

United States, Jan. 1. Law banning slave trade goes into effect, though it is widely ignored (→March 3, 1819).

United States, Jan. 23. James Madison nominated as Republican presidential candidate over rival James Monroe (→Dec. 7).

Louisiana Territory, July. St. Louis incorporated and first elections are held.

United States, Sept. 27. John Adams, in letter to Benjamin Rush, writes, "But you know that commerce, luxury and avarice have destroyed every republican government."

United States, October. In a letter to W.C.C. Claiborn, Thomas Jefferson writes that United States "must . . . exclude all European influence from this hemisphere."

United States. Daniel Pettibone invents a stove for heating.

New York City. Physician John Stearns describes effects of an ergot-based medication in easing labor pains.

Andover, Massachusetts. Congregationalists under the Rev. Jedediah Morse found Andover Seminary, in an effort to counter Harvard's growing liberalism.

Arkansas. U.S. government moves Cherokee Indians, who had clashed with settlers in Tennessee, to Arkansas.

Alabama. First Baptist church in state built near Huntsville.

Washington, D.C. Court declares Negroes can be witnesses in all court cases.

United States. Canal built along Potomac River is first in nation with water locks.

Iowa. Fort Madison, first military post in region, set up.

Louisiana. First public schools in Louisiana founded, in Pointe Coupee parish.

Indiana. Two dozen members of United Society of the Believers in Christ's Second Appearing, known as Shakers, form a colony.

Baltimore. John Elihu Hall's *American Law Journal* starts publication, probably first such periodical in Untied States.

Philadelphia. Alexander Wilson, first ornithologist in America, publishes first volume of *American Ornithology.*

Madison elected; Clinton is V.P. again

James Madison of Virginia.

George Clinton of New York.

Washington, D.C., Dec. 7

James Madison, President Thomas Jefferson's Secretary of State and his hand-picked successor, has won election as President in a bitter though lopsided contest. From newspaper tabulation of their affiliations, electors who are meeting today in the various states are believed to have cast more than 120 votes for the Republican Madison and fewer than 50 votes for his chief opponent, the Federalist Charles Cotesworth Pinckney of South Carolina. Couriers are now en route to Washington with the exact totals. The vice presidency has been won with similar strength by the incumbent New Yorker, George Clinton, who has trailed badly in his simultaneous run for the presidency.

Thus, when the new administration takes over here, the same Vice President will be in office, and the same official hostess will be presiding socially. The wife of the new President, Dolley Madison, has been serving the outgoing President Jefferson, a widower, in the capacity of hostess for the last eight years, earning wide fame for the magnificence of her entertaining and her statuesque presence. She stands 5 feet 9 inches to her husband's 5 feet 4. Only the President will be new to this scene (→March 4, 1809).

U.S. racing loses 2 famous stallions

Virginia

Two great stallions that provided the foundation for racing in America, Diomed and Messenger, are dead. Diomed, winner of the first English Derby in 1780, died after 10 years on the breeding farms of Virginia. Messenger achieved some success as a thoroughbred in England, but realized fame as a sire of trotting horses in America. Diomed produced, among others, a speedy racer named Peacemaker, who set a record in a two-mile heat. Messenger was imported here in 1788 and, while he sired some running horses, he made his reputation producing sons and daughters that proved superior in trotter breeding. Their progeny far surpassed all others in speed and quality.

Congressmen turn from debate to due

Washington, D.C.

The war of words between Fede alists and Republicans was punct ated by the sound of pistol fire thi year. George Washington Camp bell, a Jeffersonian Republica from Tennessee, has won the firs duel fought between two Congress men. His unfortunate opponen New York Federalist Barent Ga denier, had charged that Congres was too heavily influenced b French radicals. Campbell re sponded with a personal insul drawing the challenge from Ga denier. The Federalist is now nurs ing a painful wound to the body His honor, however, is intact.

Hard coal is burned

Wilkes-Barre, Penn., Feb. 11

In an experiment using an open grate hearth in his home today Judge Jesse Fell successfull burned anthracite coal for the firs time. A common mineral here, an thracite is a hard, shiny form o coal with less volatile substance than the commonly used softer bi tuminous. The discovery that an thracite can burn may open a nev resource for heating purposes an to operate steam engines.

Proper dress for ladies. Benjamin Rush's advice to a young woman on the eve of her marriage: "You will be well received in all companies only in proportion as you are inoffensive, polite and agreeable to everybody."

Astor's fur monopoly to expand in West

John Jacob Astor raids the West to feed the fashion passions of the East.

New York City, Apr. 6

The New York State Legislature passed an act today to incorporate John Jacob Astor's newest enterprise, the American Fur Company. The venture is Astor's attempt to establish a competitive American company in an industry that has so far been dominated by foreigners. At present, three-fourths of the furs purchased in the United States are supplied by two Canadian firms, the North West Company and the Michilmackinac Company, and more than $400,000 worth of these furs are trapped each year in United States territories. Shifting the business to American hands, Astor claims, will lower prices for consumers and increase tax revenues for the government.

According to the charter, the initial stock issue may not exceed $1 million for the first two years. After that, however, it may be increased to $2 million. Stock will be offered at $500 a share, and Astor has announced that he plans to invest $100,000 of his own money in the corporation. If the venture is successful, he will also consider expanding beyond the Mississippi.

It is expected that Astor will receive official approval of his project from the federal government, to which he presented his plan several months ago. The establishment of American trading posts in the territories would mesh well with the President's program of westward expansion by encouraging a peaceful fur trade with the Indians, as well as the growth of American settlements (→June 23, 1810).

Napoleon plans to seize American vessels

Bayonne, France, Apr. 17

Going one better than Britain, whose shipowners have been rubbing their hands in glee at the virtual monopoly of the carrying trade handed to them by President Jefferson's embargo policy, Emperor Napoleon has ordered the confiscation of every American ship putting in at a French port. His justification for this order is that he will simply be helping the United States government enforce its new policy.

Although most American merchant ships are presently confined to home ports or to coastal trading, a number of them were outside American waters when the embargo was imposed, and have remained there, or have since managed to slip away. It is these vessels that are the targets of the Emperor's order, which applies as much to French possessions in the West Indies as to mainland France.

His order is known as the Bayonne Decree, named after this town in the Pyrenees, where Napoleon is meeting with King Ferdinand VII of Spain, whom he intends to replace as monarch with his brother, Joseph Bonaparte.

The Emperor's seizure order is bound to be a disappointment to President Jefferson, who had been looking for some expression of gratitude from the French, since, although the embargo applies to all countries, it was obviously aimed primarily at Britain (→Aug. 9, 1809).

Osage pact may solve Cherokee problem

Fort Osage, Nov. 10

A government treaty with the Osage Indians signed here today may open the way to relocating the Cherokees in the Southwest Territory east of the Mississippi River, thus solving a long-standing problem in this troubled area.

The Osage have agree to cede all their lands east of a line drawn south from Fort Osage to the Arkansas River. These lands are bounded on the east by the Mississippi River, and on the south and north by the Arkansas and Missouri Rivers. Because these lands will become available and because President Jefferson was given authority in the Louisiana Purchase Act of 1804 to exchange Indian lands east of the Mississippi for government lands west of the river it will now be possible to move the Cherokees (and potentially other Indians), thus easing the conflict over land rights.

For more than 20 years now, white settlers have been infringing on Cherokee land in the Southwest. The result: violence on both sides. The Hopewell Treaty of 1785 and the Holston Treaty of 1791 tried to resolve the problems, but for the most part they failed. If the Cherokees can be persuaded to exchange lands with the government, the problem may be solved. Some of the Cherokees have already agreed and will soon be moving (→Dec. 1838).

Drama is the first with Indian theme

Philadelphia, Apr. 6

Spectators at the Theater Philadelphia witnessed a unique event tonight as Mrs. Wilmot, in the role of Pocahontas, led a troupe of local thespians in *The Indian Princess, or La Belle Sauvage*, by James N. Barker. The author says that his three-act opus, billed as an "operatic melo-drame," with a score by John Bray, draws heavily on the *Generall Historie of Virginia, New England, and the Summer Isles*, written by Captain John Smith, the renowned English adventurer, in 1624.

Enemies of alcohol form first society

Moreau, New York, Apr. 14

A meeting of some 25 men was held last night at the Mawney Tavern in the town of Moreau in order to form a Temperate Society. The meeting was called by Dr. Billy J. Clark, who claimed, "We shall become a community of drunkards unless something is done to arrest the progress of intemperance." Colonel Sidney Berry was elected chairman, and a committee of five was appointed to draw up by-laws for the next meeting, which will be held on April 20 (→Feb. 13, 1826).

Osage Indians perform their scalp dance. Painting by John Mix Stanley.

1809

Madison

Washington, D.C., Feb. 20. Supreme Court rules that Pennsylvania may not nullify federal court cases, affecting federal-state relations.

Virginia, Feb. 25. Thomas Jefferson qualifies earlier contention of Negroes' inferiority in letter to French Roman Catholic priest Henri Gregoire.

Washington, D.C., March 4. James Madison inaugurated as nation's fourth President, with George Clinton as Vice President.

Washington, D.C., June 27. John Quincy Adams appointed United States minister to Russia.

New York City, July 5. Abyssinian Baptist Church organized.

Indiana Territory, Sept. 30. Indians sign Treaty of Fort Wayne with Governor William Henry Harrison, ceding three parcels of land on Wabash River to United States (→1810).

Massachusetts. Abel Stowel designs and builds country's first screw-cutting machine.

United States. Jefferson, as President, invented dumbwaiter, an improved plow, a pedometer and a machine for beating hemp into fiber.

Boston. Boston Crown Glass Company, producer of superior glass, incorporates, freeing itself from paying taxes.

Louisiana. Court rules that slave marriages have no civil effect until couples are freed.

Maryland. Although state law facilitates manumission, children of freed slaves remain captive unless freed by owner.

Boston. The *Boston Patriot* reports John Adams as saying, "Had I been chosen President again, I am certain I could not have lived another year."

London. Painter Thomas Sully studies under Benjamin West.

United States. Royall Tyler's satire *The Yankey in London* published.

United States. William Maclure's *Observations on the Geology of the United States*, containing first geological survey map of U.S., published.

DEATH

New Rochelle, New York, June 8. Thomas Paine, revolutionary writer (*Jan. 29, 1737).

Embargo on trade with Britain reinstated

Virginia's tobacco ports will hum again with trade bound for Europe.

Washington, D.C., Aug. 9
The on-again, off-again course of economic sanctions against European powers that violate American rights as neutrals continues with today's announcement by President Madison that he is reinstating the embargo on trade with Britain. The action comes as a response to the refusal by the British Foreign Secretary, George Canning, to revoke the orders-in-council that have been used to justify British harassment of American shipping.

Though the embargo is widely unpopular among Americans, having led some New England states to talk of seceding, many felt the President had to do something to protest Canning's repudiation of the assurances given last April by David Erskine, the ambassador to the United States, that the offending orders would be withdrawn. Because the United States lacks a strong navy, its only course of action seems to be economic retaliation. Selective retaliation is a far cry from the total embargo that caused hardship in much of the nation and led to such repressive measures as Britain's Enforcement Act (→Nov. 2, 1810).

Haitian refugees flood into New Orleans

New Orleans
Thousands of refugees from the revolution in Haiti are pouring into New Orleans after having been driven out of Cuba. Nearly 6,000 have joined earlier refugees here this year. Some are talented professionals, artists and craftsmen. Most of them left Haiti for Cuba in 1791 to escape the bloody uprising against French rule. Many are rich property owners who arrived here with their slaves. Others are Negro free men and women. Both slaves and free men of color revolted in the former French colony, which became the second independent republic in the New World. One troupe of immigrant actors opened the city's first theater. An earlier refugee, James Pitot, became the mayor of New Orleans in 1805.

Washington Irving pokes fun at New York

Irving and Diedrich Knickerbocker.

Philadelphia, Dec. 6
Inskeep and Bradford have just released *A History of New York, From the Beginning of the World to the End of the Dutch Dynasty*, ostensibly the work of Diedrich Knickerbocker, a "small elderly gentleman, dressed in an old black coat and cocked hat," whose misadventures have lately been reported in local papers. Knickerbocker was actually invented by 26-year-old Washington Irving, who is also the author of the *History*, a mock scholarly tome that burlesques Jeffersonian democracy, academic pedantry and all pretense, ancient or modern.

Wild birds banded by young Audubon

Pittsburgh, Spring
With simple experiments, young naturalist is proving tha migratory birds return to the plac where they were hatched. Joh James Audubon, the illegitimat son of a French sea captain wh fought at the Battle of Yorktowr attached a silver thread to the leg

Audubon at work by Henry V. Poor

of young pewee birds nesting at th entrance of a cave at his father' farm. And he has seen some of th banded birds return the next year Audubon, who was sent to Americ by his father to learn English, self discipline and a trade, has insteac spent most of his time observin and drawing birds, especiall pewees. Seeing a female pewee la an egg, Audubon said, "filled m mind with the same wonder that feel when I search the heavens fo the meaning of all I see" (→1813).

"Samuel Eels," anonymous. As art grows in popularity, American amateur painters abound.

llinois is granted erritorial status

askaskia, Illinois Terr., Apr. 29

Congress, in the face of growing ensions with the British on the Northern frontier and rising agitaon among the Indians of the Ohio ountry, has approved territorial tatus for the Illinois region. The ndian agitation in the Ohio country reportedly tied to the activities of he Shawnee Chief Tecumseh and is visionary brother, The Prophet.

The territory will embrace the hole western part of the Indiana erritory, from Vincennes north to he British Canadian border, with he territorial capital here at Kasaskia on the Mississippi River. rontier statesman Ninian Edwards as been appointed territorial Govrnor. Although settlement in the ew territory is still sparse, prinarily along the Mississippi, Illiois, Rock and Wisconsin Rivers, he strategic importance of the Illiois country is becoming increasingy obvious to authorities (→ July 2).

Tecumseh to resist loss of Indian lands

Western Territories, July 2

The government of the Western Territories announced today that the famous Shawnee Indian Chief Tecumseh and his brother, The Prophet, have launched a campaign to unite the estimated 10,000 Indians who live in this vast area west of the Mississippi River. The object of this confederation of tribes is to put an end to the American expansion into their lands. The major grievance of the Indians is that they feel defenseless against the many white criminals to be found in the area, men who prey on them, sell them illegal whiskey and take their land. They argue that over the past seven years, more than 30 million acres of their territory have been appropriated by unscrupulous, land-hungry Americans.

Tecumseh and his brother preach a type of "Indian Puritanism" that calls for racial separatism, a monklike ascetism and full Indian independence. These Indians are militantly anti-white and they worship the warrior ideal. General William Henry Harrison, Governor of the Western Territories, believes that they are little more than British agents. He fears that the Shawnee community of Prophet's Town, built on the Tippecanoe River in Indiana last year, will rapidly develop into a center for widespread and violent Indian depredations against Americans (→ Sept. 30).

Tecumseh, Shawnee defender.

Phoenix is the first seaworthy steamer

New York City, June

The Phoenix, a steamboat built by Colonel John Stevens, has completed the first ocean voyage by a steam-powered vessel. Stevens has built several steamboats, originally in partnership with Robert Livingston. But none was commercially feasible. Livingston, while remaining on friendly terms with Stevens, dissolved their partnership and entered into a new business relationship with Robert Fulton. With the success of their boat, the Clermont, in 1807, Fulton and Livingston hold a monopoly on travel along the Hudson River. Although there have been renewed discussions of a partnership with Stevens, he is as yet unable to sail his boats on the Hudson. He has, therefore, sent his Phoenix, the most seaworthy steamboat ever built, on an ocean voyage to Chesapeake Bay, where it will begin commercial trade between Philadelphia and Trenton.

Catholic nun forms an American order

mmitsburg, Maryland, June

Elizabeth Seton, the well-known onvert to Catholicism and founder f St. Joseph's Academy in Baltinore, has formed a religious order ased upon the rule of the Sisters of Charity of St. Vincent de Paul. This rder (as yet to be named) was ounded at the urging of Father William DuBourg and with the blesing of Bishop John Carroll and is he first Catholic religious order to e organized in the United States. The order is expected to apply for ecognition by the Holy See soon.

Indian encampment, target of future white expansion. Painting by Paul Kane.

Dissident organizes new Christian sect

Washington, Penn., Aug. 17

Thomas Campbell, former minister of the Associate, or Seceder Presbyterian Church, and a likeminded set of people today formed the Christian Association of Washington. Beyond its abhorrence of the divisions within Christendom, this group's central tenet is a rejection of all statements of organization or belief that do not appear in the Bible. As its members have described it, "Where Scriptures speak, we speak; where the Scriptures are silent we are silent."

Doctor succeeds with ovarian operation

Danville, Kentucky, Dec. 25

Mrs. Crawford of Greentown had a Christmas gift today, but not the kind she had anticipated. Mrs. Crawford had believed herself to be expecting twins, and thought she would have delivered them by now. But today, Dr. Ephraim McDowell removed instead a 20-pound tumor from her abdomen. Dr. McDowell predicts a complete recovery and foresees Mrs. Crawford's being up and about in less than a month. He has previously performed ovariotomies 12 times, with but one fatality. A modest man, the 38-year-old, Virginia-born surgeon has been slow to publicize these feats. McDowell has also performed several successful operations for stones in the bladder, using the lateral perineal incision.

25 Russian settlements in North America

New Archangel, Alaska

There will be great cause to celebrate this year, officials of the Russian American colony here say. In addition to the New Archangel area, there are 24 colonies scattered down the northern Pacific coast and into California. Though there has been trouble with the Spanish in California before, colonial leaders feel there is no longer any need to worry about conflicts with the Spanish military. Napoleon Bonaparte conquered Spain last year, installing his brother Joseph as King. So Spain will be more concerned about European affairs than with what the Russians are doing in California. Authorities deny it, but the rumor is the Russian American Company wants to set up colonies as far south as San Francisco (→ Sept. 4, 1821).

1810

Madison

United States, June 23. Pacific Fur Company founded by John Jacob Astor in effort to expand fur empire to Pacific Coast.

Georgetown, D.C., July 4. *The Agricultural Museum* begins publication; nation's first agricultural magazine.

New York City, July 12. Journeymen Cordwainers go on trial for conspiracy to use strike in order to gain wage increase.

Spanish West Florida, Sept. 26. American settlers seize fort at Baton Rouge, declaring a republic from New Orleans to Pearl River (→Oct. 27).

United States, Dec. 17. John Quincy Adams writes, "It is the law of nature between master and servant that the servant shall spoil or plunder the master."

United States. Bermuda grass first grown in United States.

United States. Legislators in Maryland, Kentucky and Tennessee support movement toward freeing of slaves.

Schenectady, New York. Lotteries held with up to $100,000 in prize money.

New York. State law requires slave owners to teach slave children to read Bible.

United States. Congressional law excludes Negroes from carrying mail.

New York. Cornelius Vanderbilt, age 16, begins ferry service between New York and Staten Island; $100 advance secures business.

Goshen, Connecticut. Cooperative dairying initiated.

United States. Frenchman Nicolas Appert refines food-canning process.

Lexington, Kentucky. First Western theater season launched.

Indiana. Shawnee Chief Tecumseh leads region's Indians in battle (→Nov. 8, 1811).

Massachusetts. Newburyport Bridge built over Merrimac River; [best known suspension bridge of 19th century].

United States. Rembrandt Peale paints portrait of Robert Fulton.

Worcester, Massachusetts. Isaiah Thomas publishes *The History of Printing in America.*

Kamehameha of Honolulu unifies islands

King Kamehameha the Great.

Honolulu, Spring

King Kamehameha the Great has ended years of frustration by finally winning obeisance from the last island monarch, King Kaumualii of Kauai, without bloodshed.

In swearing allegiance to the 6-foot 6-inch Kamehameha, Kaumualii joined other island kings conquered by the man that Lieuenant James King of Captain Cook's expedition described as having "as savage a looking face as I ever saw."

But Kamehameha was not fierce in his meeting with Kaumualii, allowing the Kauai regent to retain control over his kingdom for the rest of his life. At their meeting off Honolulu, aboard the British ship O'Cain under the command of his friend, Nathan Winship, Kamehameha was adorned in a brilliant yellow cloak and helmet of rare mamo bird feathers. Kaumualii was resplendent in a gold-braided red cloak presented to him on behalf of England's King George IV by Captain George Vancouver.

Among the courtiers attending Kamehameha were his Prime Minister, Kalanimoku (better known as Billy Pitt, after Britain's Prime Minister), and the former British seaman Isaac Davis, now called Aikake, supreme commander of Kamehameha's forces on Oahu.

English seamanship proved invaluable in Kamehameha's earlier battles to win the islands of Maui, Hawaii and Molokai. Aikake and John Young, another expatriate, taught Kamehameha's warriors how to use cannons and sail the heavy ships. Cannons were widely used in Kamehameha's victory over King Kalanikupule in Oahu, where hundreds of the beaten warriors leaped to their deaths over a 2,000-foot precipice.

Conquest of the island of Kauai was the most difficult for Kamehameha. He tried to invade Kaumualii's domain in 1796, only to have his fleet shattered by a storm in the Kauai Channel. It took 13 years for Kamehameha to rebuild his fleet, though it emerged as an even more impressive armada, with over 40 warships, plus countless canoes.

Peace had finally come, without firing a shot or throwing a spear.

The Clermont steams past West Point on a journey up the Hudson. Its inventor, Robert Fulton, owns monopoly rights to steamboat travel on the river. French lithograph (c.1810) is only known contemporary view of ship.

Third census in U.S. records 7,239,881

Washington, D.C.

The population of the United States jumped 36.4 percent in the last decade, according to the third census. The number of inhabitants in the United States and its territories rose to 7,239,881, from 5,308,483 counted in 1800. Of the new total, 1,191,364 are slaves, up from 481,746 a decade earlier. Non-white free persons, counted for the first time, number 186,446. The door-to-door census conducted by marshals and aides took 11 months to complete and cost $178,444.67. Congress had stipulated a five-month count. The first effort to tally the manufacturing capacity has only just begun.

Boston musicians found Philharmonic

Boston

Boston's first family of music is bringing beautiful sound to a city still reluctant to indulge in frivolous arts. Johann Gottlieb Graupner, who first played in a Prussian army band, is host to Boston's 12-member Philharmonic Society on Saturdays at Graupner's Hall. Partly social, it often attracts a big audience. Graupner's wife, Catherine Comerford Hillier, an English opera star, often sings, and he shifts between clarinet, oboe, double bass, flute and piano.

Society to combat ruff-scruff clergy

Hartford, Connecticut, Jan. 17

The *Courant* today published an article on public worship, deploring intemperance both before and behind the pulpit, Sabbath-breaking and sleeping in the pews. Earlier this month, the Rev. Lyman Beecher voiced similar complaints and called for a Connecticut Moral Society based on such societies in parts of Maryland, Massachusetts and Pennsylvania. Beecher and his followers are particularly angered by what they call the "ruff-scruff" clergy who are tolerant of ostentatious dress, dueling, dancing, stage theatrics and waxwork shows.

Boone comes home to pay his debts

Maysville, Kentucky

Daniel Boone has come home to Kentucky and cleared his name of the debts he amassed some 24 years ago. Boone was a prominent Kentucky legislator and fell into debt when it was discovered that he owned a great deal of land for which he had filed incorrectly. In the actions that followed, he lost all his land and property, and he moved to Point Pleasant [West Virginia], where he later was elected the legislative delegate to Kanawha County. Now, having paid off all his debts, he is rumored to be left without a cent. While the process has been painfully expensive, Boone says it has ultimately been very satisfying.

Boone, after a painting by Harding.

More than cattle at this livestock show

Pittsfield, Massachusetts, Sept. 1

If you look out your window here and see a cow, blame Elkanah Watson, because it is he who arranged for the parade and livestock show, not to mention a band, due today. The 52-year-old Watson first gained attention two years ago when he bought a breeding pair of Merino sheep and displayed them in Pittsfield's common. But America has yet to see a livestock show the likes of today's festivities. Watson has gathered together neighbors and other farmers and, not least of all, a plow that is drawn by a fantastic team of 69 oxen.

U.S. will trade with France, not Britain

Washington, D.C., Nov. 2

Assured that orders closing European ports to American ships have been revoked, President Madison is reviving trade with France. In doing so, he is applying the Macon Bill that renewed trade with Britain and France but pledged to the first power recognizing neutral rights the reward of America ending trade with its enemy. This bill was passed anticipating expiration of the Non-Intercourse Act that pledged to renew trade with France or Britain, whichever ended curbs on U.S. trade first. For now, trade with Britain will not be resumed. Despite French assurances, questions remain on the fate of seized ships (→May 1, 1811).

Madison to annex western W. Florida

Washington, D.C., Oct. 27

President James Madison today issued an order claiming the western part of West Florida for the United States and sent troops to the region to enforce his claim. The President's order follows a rebellion in which settlers in the area captured its capital, Baton Rouge, from the Spanish and established their own republic. The area is east of the Mississippi River and north of Lake Pontchartrain [Louisiana] (→Jan. 15, 1811).

For first time, court overturns state law

Washington, D.C., March 16

The Supreme Court, establishing itself more and more as a powerful arm of government, has overturned a state law for the first time. In the case of Fletcher v. Peck, the court validated a Georgia land sale to the Yazoo Land Company. An act of the Georgia legislature in 1795 made the sale invalid because the previous legislature had been bribed to approve the sale. Chief Justice John Marshall wrote that the buyers of the land are entitled to it, despite the corrupt action of the lawmakers, and that the Georgia legislation is unconstitutional in that it impaired the obligation of a contract.

U.S. ex-slave boxes for the world title

London, Dec. 10

Tom Molineaux, a slave who won his freedom by beating a neighborhood bully, has became the first American boxer to fight for a world championship. As the unofficial American champ, he went to England, where he was knocked out in the 33rd round by the world title holder, Tom Cribb. It was found that Molineaux had fractured his skull in the 31st round. In a return bout, Cribb broke Molineaux's jaw, winning in the 11th round this time.

Dolley Madison's ice cream a la mode

Rembrandt Peale painting of Dolley Madison, who was the White House hostess for widower Jefferson, too.

Washington, D.C.

Ice cream is in fashion now that Dolley Madison serves it at state dinners. "Mrs. Madison always entertains with Grace and Charm," notes a visitor, "but last night there was a sparkle in her eye that set astir an Air of Expectancy among her guests. When finally the brilliant Assemblage, America's best, entered the dining room, they beheld a Table set with French china and English silver, laden with good things to eat, and in the Centre high on a silver platter, a large shining dome of pink Ice Cream." The passion is not new. Some say Washington spent $200 on ice cream in the hot 1790 summer.

The Puritan passion for order. An anonymous rendering of a New England village in the early 1800's.

1811

Monroe

Washington, D.C., Jan. 15. Congress, in secret session, authorizes plans to annex Spanish East Florida (→May 14, 1812).

West Coast, Feb. 2. Russian settlers land at Bodega Bay, founding Fort Ross.

Washington, D.C., Feb. 20. Vice President George Clinton breaks tie in Senate, voting down bill to recharter Bank of United States (→March 4).

Louisiana, Feb. 20. President Madison signs bill proposing Louisiana for statehood (→Jan. 22, 1812).

Washington, D.C., Apr. 2. President Madison names political foe James Monroe Secretary of State.

Sandy Hook, New York, May 1. Americans are impressed as British frigate Guerriere overtakes American brig Spitfire (→16).

United States, Aug. 28. John Adams writes in a letter to Dr. Benjamin Rush, "The government of the United States of America is not in any sense founded on the Christian religion . . ."

Washington, D.C., Nov. 1. United States informs British it will settle for damages in Little Belt ship incident if Britain will revoke retribution orders (→March 14, 1812).

Washington, D.C., Nov. 4. The 12th Congress convenes; Republicans dominated by new breed of nationalistic, expansion-oriented "war hawks."

Canada. Scottish philanthropist Lord Selkirk founds agricultural settlement on Red River.

New York City. John Stevens starts world's first steamboat ferry, from Hoboken to New York, challenging Robert Livingston's monopoly on steamboat travel in New York.

United States. Construction begins on National Road, the first major federal highway project.

Cabarrus County, North Carolina. Fugitive slave community attacked by whites seeking to recover or destroy them; two Negroes killed, one wounded.

United States. Washington Allston paints *The Poor Author and the Rich Bookseller*.

United States. *The Maternal Physician* published; an important baby-care book.

American warship attacks British; 9 slain

British impress American sailors.

Cape Charles, Virginia, May 16

Mindful of his instructions "to vindicate the injured honor of our Navy, and revive the drooping spirit of the nation," Commodore John Rodgers of the warship President today conducted a brief but sharp night-time engagement with the British sloop Little Belt. The British toll was nine dead and 23 wounded; only one American was hurt. The action lasted 15 minutes and each captain said the other fired first.

The sloop, when first sighted, was mistaken for the British frigate Guerriere, whose crew had recently boarded an American ship and impressed a seaman named John Diggio, of Maine. In giving chase, Commodore Rodgers intended to reclaim the unfortunate Diggio; since the British would certainly have refused to comply, a major sea duel would have resulted. But even though the Guerriere turned out to be half the size of the President, Rodgers is already being hailed as a national hero (→Nov. 1).

"Ograbme, the American Snapping Turtle," enforcing the trade embargo.

Slaves killed in rebellion; heads shown

New Orleans, Jan. 10

A rebellion of more than 400 slaves that began two days ago has forced many white residents of the parishes of St. Charles and St. John the Baptist to flee to safety in New Orleans. The rebellion began at the plantation of Major Andry when slaves armed with cane knives, axes, clubs and a few guns killed Andry's son and marched on to other plantations, destroying them and killing at least one other white. The rebellion was led by Charles Deslondes, a free mulatto from Haiti; the other rebels were said to be local slaves. Yesterday, the insurrection was opposed by a group of planters led by Major Andry, who pursued the slaves and caught and executed many. Today, the militia and state troops were called out, surrounding the remaining rebels. In all, 66 slaves were killed; their heads were strung up along the road from New Orleans to Andry's plantation.

In another incident involving slaves, white forces were sent to annihilate a fugitive slave community in Cabarrus County, North Carolina. At least two slaves were killed and the others were captured.

Astor expedition reaches Northwest

Fort Astoria, Oregon, May 18

After a grueling nine-month trip around the tip of South America, Captain Thorne has guided an expedition of the Pacific Fur Company into the Columbia River. Sent by fur magnate John Jacob Astor, they plan to open a trading post and call it Astoria. Despite sickness and signs of Indian hostility, the small party has begun building a fort of logs and earth. Fort Astoria is the latest attempt by Astor to best the North West Fur Company and monopolize the fur trade with the Far East. Another party of "Astorians," led by William Price Hunt, is making its way from St. Louis to the Pacific Northwest via the Lewis and Clark trail.

Steamboat makes first trip on Ohio

Louisville, Kentucky, Oct. 20

The New Orleans, a steamboat built by Robert Fulton and Nicholas Roosevelt, arrived here from Pittsburgh today after a 700-mile trip along the Ohio River, the first voyage of a steam-powered vessel on westward waters. The boat took 14 days to navigate the course, overcoming a flood, an earthquake and an Indian attack. No passengers were aboard because none would risk the trip. Fulton is famous for his Clermont, the first commercial steamboat. It sailed the Hudson in 1807 (→Jan. 12, 1812).

Crew events draw crowds in New York

New York City

Rowing has caught on in a big way here. In the first publicized race, between two four-oared barges from New Jersey to New York, the Knickerbocker overcame a rough sea to defeat the Invincible. And in another event, a crowd of 60,000 turned out to watch the American Star outrow the British Hussar in a race from Bedloe's Island to Hoboken. The American Star won by 400 yards and its skipper won a $1,000 side bet.

Congressional vote closes Bank of U.S.

Washington, D.C., March 4

The Bank of the United States, a point of contention between Federalists and Republicans for 20 years, has closed its doors. Vice President Clinton sounded the death knell two weeks ago, breaking a Senate tie with a vote against its recharter. Since 1791, the bank has provided the young republic with a federal fiscal agent, a source of paper money and a safe repository for public funds. It is testimony to its success that many Republicans who fought the bank 20 years ago backed it this time. But "Old Republicans," still consider it an unlawful use of federal power. Others fear it is controlled by Britons, who own two-thirds of the stock (→ Jan. 20, 1815).

Catastrophic quake along Mississippi

Mississippi Valley, Dec. 16

The earth burst, spewing water, sand and tar to the height of trees. Rivers boiled. Lakes were formed within an hour, while old ones were drained. The topography of whole counties changed in a day. These were the effects of the earthquake that struck the Mississippi Valley today. It was the most severe quake in the history of the valley. The village of New Madrid [Missouri] is virtually destroyed and serious damage has been reported as far south as the Arkansas district and the Mississippi Territory.

John Hall invents breech-loading rifle

New York City, December

John H. Hall has invented a firearm that is a substantial improvement over the musket. Hall's gun is a breech-loading carbine that is lightweight, and easier and quicker to load than existing guns. The new rifle is manufactured by a method that employs interchangeable parts for the guns. In 1798, Eli Whitney, after securing a government contract, first began the revolutionary process of building muskets with interchangeable parts.

Harrison routs Indians at Tippecanoe

Indiana Territory, Nov. 8

Travelers report that General William Henry Harrison defeated a huge number of Shawnee Indians yesterday at the Battle of Tippecanoe in the Indiana Territory. Earlier today, General Harrison and his army warded off a ferocious counterattack and responded by wiping out the main Indian community at Prophet's Town, near the Tippecanoe River. The encounter was by far the most significant of Indian-American conflicts since 1791. In that bloody clash, which also took place in the Northwest Territories, the army of General St. Clair was destroyed.

Yesterday's battle is the culmination of a growing hostility between the white settlers and the Indians who live in the vast reaches of the Northwest Territories. American towns with about 25,000 settlers have grown up along the major road in the Indiana Territory, which is commonly called the "Buffalo Trace" and is situated between the Ohio and the Vincennes Rivers. Because of this tremendous influx, the conflict at Tippecanoe was inevitable. Indian resistance to the American migration was accelerated by Harrison's attempts to expand the American frontier in the Northwest Territories. In February of 1803, President Jefferson ordered the general to consolidate all land westward to the Mississippi.

After consummation of the Louisiana Purchase, Harrison, under pressure from the government in Washington, continued to capture and pacify former Indian lands in the area. In a number of treaties betweeen 1803 and 1809, the general bought, "stole" and received presents of a total of 30 million acres of land north of the Ohio River – land that the Indians, particularly the Shawnees, had always considered to be their birthright. Perhaps it was inevitable then that the great Shawnee Chief Tecumseh and his brother, The Prophet, would lead their people in a last great stand against the Americans.

These Indian leaders had created a confederacy of tribes with the aim of stopping American expansion. They argued for an Indian united front and regarded any individual chief's sale of land to the Americans to be invalid. Tensions reached the breaking point after Harrison imposed military pressure on chiefs to continue land sales to the whites.

Fearing a pre-emptive attack by the Indians, the white settlers in Indiana voted to have Harrison's army attack the major Indian encampment at Tippecanoe Creek. His troops set out on their mission on September 26, but yesterday they came under attack by Tecumseh's massed warriors. The chief is said to have promised them immunity from the white man's bullets, but the inevitable happened. The Harrison forces killed several dozen braves, routed the rest and burned Prophet's Town (→ June 3, 1812).

General Harrison, back on his horse after turning to a career in politics.

Surprised at first by the Shawnee assault, Harrison's force of some 800 men rallied and began to use their superior firepower to a distinct advantage.

General Harrison directs the devastating counterattack on the Shawnee leaders Tecumseh and The Prophet. Lithograph (1889) by Kurz and Allison.

1812

Madison

Louisiana, Jan. 22. Admitted to union as slave state; first state constitution allowing Negroes to enlist in militia (→Apr. 4).

Washington, D.C., March 14. To finance military preparations, Congress passes an $11 million bond issue (→Apr. 1).

Washington, D.C., Apr. 1. Congress passes, upon President Madison's urging, a 60-day trade embargo on all foreign nations (→June 16).

Canada, June 3. British Governor George Prevost, in anticipation of war with United States, invites Shawnee Chief Tecumseh to conference (→July 22, 1814).

London, June 16. To fight economic decline, British Prime Minister Lord Castlereagh repeals orders affecting neutral shipping.

Ohio, July 1. British gain valuable military information by intercepting General William Hull's baggage (→Aug. 16).

Connecticut, July 2. Governor John Cotton vows to withhold state's contribution to war (→Aug. 5).

Lake Erie, Oct. 9. British ships Detroit and Caledonia captured in surprise raid by U.S. Lieutenant Elliott (→Jan. 22, 1813).

Canada, Oct. 13. General Stephen Van Rensselaer captures Queenstown Heights from British (→16).

Indiana. Indian fight occurs near Peru; [last in territory].

Worcester, Massachusetts. Isaiah Thomas, premier publisher in United States, founds American Antiquarian Society to preserve historical record.

Concord, Massachusetts. William Monroe produces first lead pencils in United States.

Wyoming. First known cabin in Wyoming built by Robert Stuart near Bessemer Bend.

Maryland. State university sets up first law faculty in U.S.

Illinois Territory. Legislature forbids immigration of free Negroes and requires registration of those within territory.

United States. Benjamin Rush's *Medical Inquiries and Observations Upon the Diseases of the Mind* published; first study of mental illness in United States.

United States at war with Britain

Washington, D.C., June 19

The war cloud that has loomed over the United States for several years has finally burst, resulting in a declaration of war against England. The "war hawks" in Congress, mainly legislators from the South and the West, carried the vote by 79 to 49 in the House of Representatives and by 19 to 13 in the Senate. Speeches by President Madison and members of Congress make it clear that the principal cause of the war is continued British harassment of American shipping and the impressment of American sailors.

Impressment may be the most explosive issue. Because of harsh conditions below deck on British ships, sailors have, for years, sought the first opportunity to desert, usually in an American port. The sailors often find both better conditions and higher wages aboard American merchantmen. In an attempt to reverse this trend, the British started to seize the deserters aboard American vessels, and angered the United States by impressing some 2,500 American seamen as well.

Since President Jefferson's administration, Americans have tried with both diplomatic and economic measures to prevent a war, but the French and the British, engaged in a conflict on land and sea for control of Europe, have insisted that the United States stop trading with the other, and both have ignored America's cries of "free trade and sailors rights" by commandeering American vessels. War fever has been mounting steadily since 1807, when the British frigate Leopard attacked the Chesapeake, killing or wounding 21 men and impressing four.

As the likelihood of a war kept growing, Congress has been frantically trying to prepare a nation that is not ready. It has authorized a vast bond issue to finance the war as well as a 100,000-man militia that will serve for six months.

The U.S. military, ready for battle.

At present, there are only about 6,000 men in the regular American army, while the navy consists of 16 to 20 ships with about 4,000 men (→Aug. 19).

Gerrymandering is named after Governor

Boston, February

The Governor of Massachusetts, it appears, has inadvertently given birth to a new political animal. In a move to ensure a Republican legislative majority, Governor Elbridge Gerry, on February 11, signed a law dividing the state into new senatorial districts. Federalist voters, not so inadvertently, were lumped into a few districts, restricting the number of senators they can send to Boston. A stroke of political brilliance, this act has challenged Federalists across the state to match wits with the Republican Governor. Editor Benjamin Russell, imaginative and partisan, gave the new technique a name. One of the districts, he thought, looks like a salamander. Why not give it wings, claws and a head with sharp teeth and a forked tongue? Then call it a "Gerrymander." Gerry is not flattered. He has gained his legislative majority, but, considering the backlash, has he sealed his political fate?

The plan and its architect. One cartoonist depicted Governor Gerry's plan for redistricting as a new kind of political monster called the "Gerrymander."

Louisiana becomes a state, the 18th

New Orleans, Apr. 30

The Territory of Orleans, by an Act of Congress, today became the 18th state to join the union. It is to be called Louisiana, and it is the first state to be created out of the vast province that was acquired from Napoleon Bonaparte in the Louisiana Purchase of 1803.

New Orleans, which is currently the fifth largest city in the United States, will be the capital. Congress approved the state's new constitution, which declares slavery legal, but allows Negroes to enlist in the militia. The constitution was adopted by a constitutional convention that met in New Orleans last year. Under this constitution, the governor will serve a four-year term, but he will not be permitted to succeed himself. The constitution also created a bicameral legislature, a House of Representatives and a Senate.

Governor W.C.C. Claiborne, who has served as territorial Governor of Mississippi as well as Governor of the Territory of Orleans, is expected to run for election as Governor of the new state.

Two states rule out participation in war

Boston, Aug. 5

The states of Massachusetts and Connecticut in Federalist New England have told the federal government that they will not fight. When the Governor of Massachusetts, Caleb Strong, learned of the declaration of war against Britain, he proclaimed a day of fasting to mourn over a war "against the nation from which we are descended." In Connecticut, acting Governor John Cotton Smith stated that the American declaration of war was unconstitutional because there has been no invasion of the United States. Major General Henry Dearborn, the officer in charge of defending New England, has met inertia and hostility in Boston (→Dec. 15, 1814).

Spanish lose a part of Florida to U.S.

Washington, D.C., May 14

Congress today agreed that Spanish West Florida shall become part of the Mississippi Territory and the nation. The action, annexing the land between the Pearl and Perdido Rivers, is a further step in the growing domination of Florida by the United States. In 1810, settlers in another part of West Florida seized Baton Rouge, which became the Territory of Orleans, and, in April was named the State of Louisiana. Earlier this year, American settlers in eastern Florida declared independence from Spain, but the Spanish ended that rebellion. President Madison and the Republicans have long claimed that Florida should be part of the nation (→Apr. 15, 1813).

Americans lose Detroit

Fort Detroit, Michigan, Aug. 16

General William Hull has not only failed to defeat the British at Detroit with bombastic language, but he has also managed to lose his luggage and the fort as well. Hull, who is both the Governor of Michigan and the military commander of the area, left Dayton, Ohio, on May 25 with a force of 1,500 Ohio militiamen and 400 regulars on a mission aimed at driving the British back into Canada. But he put his plan of campaign and his muster rolls on a schooner that promptly fell into the hands of the British. Lieutenant General Isaac Brock, the British commander, with 730 redcoat regulars and 600 Indians, captured Fort Detroit without a fight. Hull's principal activity at the time of the engagement seems to have been that of writing and issuing proclamations. The purpose of this attack on the fort was to serve as one prong of a pincers that was aimed at knocking Canada out of the war (→Oct. 9).

Hull relinquishes his sword.

Dutch (misnamed) pour into Pennsylvania

Pennsylvania

German immigrants in search of religious freedom are pouring into Pennsylvania. This immigration is made up of two distinct groups: the "church people," such as Lutherans and Moravians, and the "plain people," including the Amish and Mennonites. The groups have been lumped together under the term "Pennsylvania Dutch," a misnomer that derives from the word "Deutsch" for German. The plain people have isolated themselves from the surrounding communities and believe in unusual religious practices such as the shunning of errant church members. The church people are not so insular. Both groups are made up of hardworking farmers who find that the limestone soil of Pennsylvania is quite similar to that of their homeland. Many of them have constructed solid stone houses and barns, and their agricultural abilities are turning this "Dutch country" into the granary of Pennsylvania.

Americans routed as Canada drive fails

Queenstown, Ontario, Oct. 16

British forces defeated the disorganized Americans again today in a battle at this Canadian village below Niagara Falls. While British casualties included only 17 killed, one of them was their commander, General Isaac Brock. The Americans lost 350 killed or wounded, and 900 were captured. The Americans had tried an amphibious assault across the Niagara River. This might have succeeded in capturing Fort George and holding the heights, but when the militia saw wounded Americans being ferried across the river it refused to cross and help the regular army. For the Americans, this defeat means the second pincer of a movement aimed at driving Canada out of the war has also failed (→Nov. 23).

Handiwork of the German newcomers: The 34th Psalm by George Geistweite.

Mississippi getting riverboat service

New Orleans, Jan. 12

Weathering a birth and an earthquake, the steamboat New Orleans has arrived in the city it is named for. Its four-month journey is the first ever made under steam power on the Mississippi. Nicholas Roosevelt, his wife, their dog Tiger and, half-way through the trip, their newborn baby were the ship's only passengers. An earthquake, however, uprooted residents who had to be turned away as they sought refuge on the boat. Funded by statesman Robert Livingston and designed by Robert Fulton, the boat has yet to prove it can negotiate the upriver return (→Aug. 23, 1818).

"Daniel Lamotte," by Thomas Sully, who, at 29, is the most elegant portraitist in Philadelphia.

Constitution wins at sea

The Constitution and the Guerriere. Engraving by Cornelius Tiebout.

Boston, Aug. 19

With towering masts carrying an acre of white canvas and protected by copper sheathing made by the patriot Paul Revere, the warship Constitution scored a major victory for the fledgling United States Navy today by blowing the British frigate Guerriere out of the water. Under the command of Captain Isaac Hull, the American frigate, rated 44 guns but carrying 55, was out searching for British warships off the St. Lawrence waterway when it encountered the 38-gun Guerriere, which was commanded by Captain James R. Dacres. Both ships ran before the wind for almost an hour until the Constitution finally closed upon its prey. There followed an exchange of fire from the guns and, although the rigging of the Constitution was badly damaged, the mizzenmast of the Guerriere fell into the starboard quarter.

In the haze of timber smoke and black powder, each ship swung round while marines from both sides reaped a steady and deadly harvest. The vessels continued to fire at close range and, although the Guerriere's guns were served faster, those on the Constitution were deadlier. When the Guerriere finally tore free of the tangle, its masts were blown away and the guns on its main deck were dipping into the sea. The Guerriere struck its colors with 15 men killed and 63 wounded. The toll aboard the Constitution was seven killed and seven wounded. The British vessel was so badly damaged that it was burned in the water (→ Dec. 29).

The Constitution victorious.

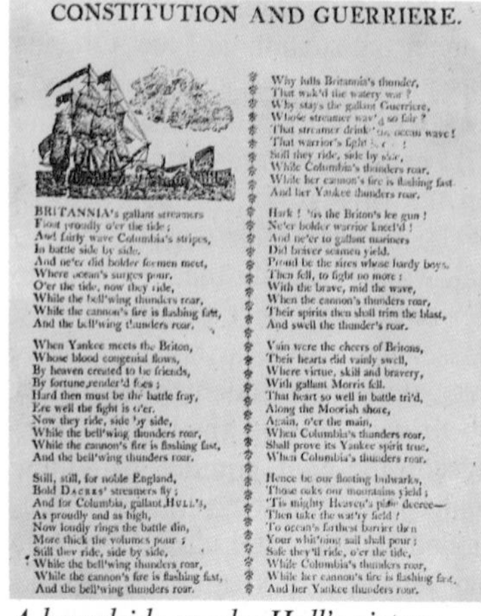

CONSTITUTION AND GUERRIERE.

BRITANNIA'S gallant streamers
Float proudly o'er the tide;
And fairly wave Columbia's stripes,
In battle side by side.
And ne'er did bolder foemen meet,
Where ocean's surges pour,
O'er the tide, now they ride,
While the bell'wing thunders roar,
While the cannon's fire is flashing fast,
And the bell'wing thunders roar.

When Yankee meets the Briton,
Whose blood congenial flows,
By heaven created to be friends,
By fortune render'd foes;
Hard then must be the battle fray,
Ere well the fight is o'er.
Now they ride, side by side,
While the bell'wing thunders roar,
While the cannon's fire is flashing fast,
And the bell'wing thunders roar.

Still, still, for noble England,
Bold DACRES' streamers fly;
And for Columbia, gallant HULL'S,
As proudly and as high,
Now loudly rings the battle din,
More thick the volumes pour;
Still they ride, side by side,
While the bell'wing thunders roar,
While the cannon's fire is flashing fast,
And the bell'wing thunders roar.

Why lulls Britannia's thunder,
That wak'd the watery war?
Why stays the gallant Guerriere,
Whose streamer wav'd so fair?
That streamer drink's the ocean wave!
That warrior's fight [illegible]!
Still they ride, side by side,
While Columbia's thunders roar,
While her cannon's fire is flashing fast
And her Yankee thunders roar.

Hark! 'tis the Briton's lee gun!
Ne'er bolder warrior kneel'd!
And ne'er to gallant mariners
Did braver seamen yield.
Proud be the sires whose hardy boys
Then fell, to fight no more:
With the brave, mid the wave,
When the cannon's thunders roar,
Their spirits then shall trim the blast,
And swell the thunder's roar.

Vain were the cheers of Britons,
Their hearts did vainly swell,
Where virtue, skill and bravery,
With gallant Morris fell.
That heart so well in battle tri'd,
Along the Moorish shore,
Again, o'er the main,
When Columbia's thunders roar,
Shall prove its Yankee spirit true,
When Columbia's thunders roar.

Hence be our floating bulwarks,
Those oaks our mountains yield;
'Tis mighty Heaven's plain decree—
Then take the wat'ry field!
To ocean's farthest barrier then
Your whit'ning sail shall pour;
Safe they'll ride, o'er the tide,
While Columbia's thunders roar,
While her cannon's fire is flashing fast,
And her Yankee thunders roar.

A broadside marks Hull's victory.

U.S. setback in Canada

Montreal, Nov. 23

An American army, under Major General Henry Dearborn, has managed to take both sides in a battle, defeat itself and save the British in Montreal the trouble of repulsing an invasion. Dearborn intended to invade Canada with a force of about 5,000 men. Simultaneously, Brigadier General Alexander Smyth would conduct a campaign against the British farther west by crossing the Niagara River. Disease whittled away at Dearborn's army and, when the general got to the Canadian border, about two-thirds of his force refused to cross. Colonel Zebulon Pike was not content to begin an invasion and end it without a battle, so he asked for permission to march on Montreal with about 600 regulars. Meanwhile, some 400 New York militiamen crossed the St. Lawrence by another route and occupied a blockhouse at La Cole Mill, which had been abandoned by the British.

At dawn, the column, under Pike, marched up and, not knowing the fort was occupied by Americans, attacked. Two American columns fought until about 50 casualties were inflicted and the error was discovered. This battle so deflated the invasion zeal of the American forces that they retired to Plattsburg, New York, and went into winter quarters (→ Jan. 22, 1813).

Royal Navy is humbled by American ships

Constitution, fresh from victory over the Guerriere, engages the Java off Brazil.

New London, Conn., Dec. 29

At the beginning of the war, anyone suggesting that the puny American navy, consisting of 16 vessels, could shame the most powerful navy in the world, would have been considered foolish. But this is what has happened. The Constitution, under Isaac Hull, sank the frigate Guerriere. The frigate United States, under Stephen Decatur, defeated and captured the Macedonian. On a second cruise under a new captain, William Bainbridge, the Constitution destroyed the Java. On a smaller scale, the American sloop Wasp defeated the British gun brig Frolic in a 16-minute battle.

These American victories are not a fluke but the result of several key factors. The most important is the single-ship strategy that is matching the more-heavily armed American vessels against a weaker enemy. This was the case in each of these engagements. American captains do not sail in squadrons; they seek out and engage the enemy on a ship-to-ship basis. The Americans have proven themselves better sailors and better shots. In each of these encounters, British ships were riddled while the Americans were hardly touched (→ Feb. 24, 1813).

s peace efforts falter, Czar offers help

The Russian bear mediates between a broken John Bull and a coy Columbia.

Washington, D.C., Oct. 27

In the midst of war, diplomatic channels have been busy with peace proposals that have either failed or that seem likely to fail.

Last summer, after war had been declared, the British Admiralty instructed its new commander in American waters, Sir John Borlase Warren, "to endeavor to re-establish Peace & Amity" between the two countries. After reading the commander's peace proposal, Secretary of State James Monroe made it clear that before negotiations could begin, American neutrality must be respected. In London, Jonathan Russell, the American charge, made an effort to discuss the Royal Navy's kidnapping practice with Viscount Castlereagh, the Foreign Secretary, and has twice been rebuffed. Russell had proposed that the British abandon blockades and impressment, and offer reparations for shipping losses. In return, the U.S. would stop naturalizing British seamen.

Meanwhile, in September, a diplomatic channel was opened in Russia by Count Rumiantzov, the Czar's Foreign Minister. He has made an offer of his court's mediation to John Quincy Adams, minister to Russia, who has reportedly encouraged this effort. In London, however, the Russian initiative has met with a polite refusal. The British chill is probably a result of Russia's habit of showing its preference toward neutrals in their disputes with belligerent countries such as Britain and France (→Nov. 11, 1813).

Philadelphia. *"Fourth of July in Centre Square" by John Krimmel.*

President Madison wins a second term

Washington, D.C., Dec. 2

James Madison was re-elected President today, defeating De Witt Clinton, a Federalist from New York. The electoral vote was 128 for Madison to 89 for Clinton. Madison, a 61-year-old Virginian, won his first term in 1808 after having served as Secretary of State in the Cabinet of Thomas Jefferson, whom he succeeded in the White House. Both are Democratic-Republicans. In the race for the vice presidency, Elbridge Gerry, a 68-year-old Democratic-Republican from Massachusetts, won by a vote of 131 to 86, over Jared Ingersoll, a Federalist. Democratic-Republicans control Congress, but Federalists made gains (→March 4, 1813).

Madison, after a Gilbert Stuart.

Louisiana lands are Missouri Territory

Arkansas, June 4

President James Madison today approved an Act of Congress that names the lands in the Louisiana Purchase north of the 33rd parallel the Territory of Missouri. This territory will include the District of Arkansas and all other Louisiana Purchase lands with the exception of the former Territory of Orleans, which has become the State of Louisiana. The Louisiana region was admitted to the union back in April. The Missouri territory is being divided into five counties: St. Louis, St. Charles, St. Genevieve, Cape Girardeau and New Madrid.

American history, cock-and-bull style

New York City

The history of the United States *is* a laughing matter to judge from *The Diverting History of John Bull and Brother Jonathan*, by one Hector Bull-us. A three-century romp, it starts with a religious debate between John Bull (the English Church) and his youngest son, Brother Jonathan (the Puritans). This cock-and-bull tale may remind us of another comic jape, Washington Irving's *History of New York*. In fact, Hector Bull-us is the pen name of 34-year-old James Kirk Paulding, who teamed with Irving on a journal called *Salmagundi*.

Earthquake levels California mission

San Juan Capistrano, Calif., Dec. 8

An earthquake today leveled the Mission San Juan Capistrano, a favorite of American traders seeking provisions. The mission had a reputation for flouting a Spanish law curbing contact with foreigners. The building, with its lofty tower and five stone archways, was designed by the Mexican Isidoro Aguilar. It was started in 1797 and finished in 1803. San Juan was a key link in the chain of California missions, so many fear its loss may slow the area's development.

An American desk and bookcase, based on a design by Thomas Sheraton, circa 1812.

1813

Madison

Washington, D.C, March 4. James Madison inaugurated for second term as President; Elbridge Gerry as Vice President.

United States, April. Special express mail delivers military dispatches during war.

Washington, DC, May 24. The 13th Congress convenes with Republican majorities in both House and Senate.

St. Michaels, Maryland, Aug. 9. First blackout in U.S. history engineered by commanding officer of county militia to confuse British ships.

Philadelphia, Sept. 4. *Religious Remembrancer,* first religious weekly, begins publication.

Mississippi Valley, Nov. 3. General John Coffee destroys Indian village of Tallushatchee in retaliation for Creek attack on Fort Mims (→ Dec. 23).

West Florida, Nov. 9. Andrew Jackson, upon raising militia of 2,000 men, kills over 500 Indians in attack on village of Talladega.

Chrysler's Farm, Canada, Nov. 11. 2,000 troops under General John Parke Boyd suffer crushing defeat by 700 British troops led by Colonel J.W. Morrison (→ Dec. 30).

London, Nov. 16. British announce blockade of Long Island Sound, leaving only New England coast open to shipping.

Washington, D.C, Dec. 17. Embargo banning trade with Britain in effect, aimed at New England merchants who have been supplying British in Canada (→ Apr. 14, 1814).

United States. Captain Perry, complaining about Negro reinforcements, is told by Commodore Chauncey: "I have yet to learn that the color of the skin . . . can affect a man's qualifications or usefulness."

Washington, D.C. Circuit Court rules that a free-born mulatto is competent to testify against a white person.

North Andover, Massachusetts. Nathaniel Stevens starts woolen broadcloth mill; first to produce and market flannels.

United States. John Krimmel paints *Interior of an American Inn* and *The Quilting Party*.

United States. *Boston Daily Advertiser* begins publication with Nathan Hale as editor.

British and Indians rebuff Michigan drive

Frenchtown, Michigan, Jan. 22

American troops on the northwest frontier who have been planning a drive on Detroit were dealt a devastating blow today by British forces under Major General Henry Procter. The British, with about 6,000 regulars and militia and several hundred Indians, surprised a force of 1,000 Kentuckians, surrounded them and almost wiped them out. The undisciplined Kentuckians, known for their individual fighting skills, failed to follow even the rudiments of military discipline and did not post pickets or issue ammunition. The British and Indians camped within five miles of the Americans, who did not even send out patrols. Moreover, the British had cannons and the Americans did not.

The Kentuckians were camped in the village of Frenchtown on the Raisin River and the British force trapped them with their backs to the water. As soon as the Americans found out that they were surrounded, they began to fight fiercely. But it was far too late: they were outflanked, out-gunned, out-manned and out-led. Reports on casualties disagree, but several hundred Kentuckians were taken prisoner, and between 100 and 400 were killed. British losses were light (→ Apr. 27).

Outgunned Americans sink British sloop

U.S. cartoon shows John Bull stung in agony by the Wasp and the Hornet.

Guiana, Feb. 24

The British sloop Peacock, with 20 guns, was cruising on the northern coast of South America when it spotted an unknown vessel flying British colors off the mouth of the Demerara River. The ships circled each other until Captain James Lawrence of the 18-gun sloop Hornet decided that he had gained the weather gauge and hoisted his true colors, the Stars and Stripes. After having played cat and mouse for two hours, the ships bore down on each other and exchanged broadsides at short range. The commander of the British ship, Lieutenant William Peake, attempted to cross his enemy's stern, but the Hornet turned, caught him and started shooting him to pieces. Against a flaming sunset, the Peacock was destroyed, but its masts still stood. Lieutenant Peake was killed in the fighting. As the British struck the vessel's colors, a prize crew from the American ship went on board to claim it. The Peacock went down so rapidly that a number of sailors, Americans as well as Britons, were trapped below and drowned. The Hornet suffered a few casualties, and its rigging was shot up, but other damage was slight (→ June 1).

Spanish surrender city without a fight

Mobile, Mississippi Terr., Apr. 15

Major General James Wilkinson and a force of 600 men seized the city of Mobile today without firing a shot, but they are believed to have acted against the wishes of the government. Wilkinson's troop landed three miles below the fort that guards the city and later anchored five gunboats nearby. Far outnumbered, the Spanish commander surrendered. Officials in Washington report that Wilkinson had been ordered to steer clear of the Spanish city, but that the order had not reached him (→ Nov. 7, 1814).

Lafitte's pirates ignore official ban

New Orleans, March 15

Although Governor W.C.C. Claiborne has put a price on the head of Jean Lafitte, the pirate and slave dealer has publicly defied the Governor. When Claiborne offered a $500 reward for the capture of Lafitte, the pirate put up posters offering a reward for the Governor's capture. Lafitte moved back into the city, wined and dined merchants and publicly announced more illegal slave sales. Lafitte and his brother, Pierre, head a band of smugglers who operate from an island near Barataria Bay, preying on vessels in the Gulf of Mexico. Little is known about the early life of these French pirate brothers, but Jean Lafitte is gaining a reputation for hospitality, gentlemanly manners – and ruthlessness.

Pigeon flock takes three days to pass

Louisville, Kentucky

A flock of passenger pigeons so vast that it darkened the sky and took three days to pass was reported by the naturalist John James Audubon. A similar flock in 1810 was measured at 250 miles long. The migratory passenger pigeon, one of this area's most numerous birds, is shot for food and as a pest; as it darkens the sky, such a flock can also whiten the ground (→ 1827).

U.S. victory in Canada

York, Canada, Apr. 27

The American army has finally achieved a success in the Northwest, but it has cost the life of the man who produced the victory. General Zebulon Pike was killed when his troops captured York, the seat of government in Ontario, and the retreating British blew up the main magazine rather than let it fall into American hands. Some 300 other Americans were killed or wounded in the explosion.

The invasion of York was the plan of Major General Henry Dearborn, who believed that control of Lake Ontario could be achieved by capturing York rather than the better-defended Kingston. The Americans, 1,700 strong, crossed Lake Ontario on April 24 in spite of bad weather. The British commander, Major General Roger Sheaffe, could do little to defend the town with only 700 regulars and about 100 Indians. An effective bombardment enabled the Americans to advance into York with small losses and it might have been a bloodless victory if not for the carnage that was caused by the exploding magazine. Angry Americans retaliated by burning many public buildings, including the Parliament (→ May 27).

Winfield Scott forces British out of 3 forts

On the Northern front: Scott leads a charge through the gates of Fort George.

Fort George, Ontario, May 27

Led by a gigantic, angry Colonel Winfield Scott, the Americans have dislodged the British from three forts and are now in control of Lake Ontario. The battle was planned by the ailing and indecisive Major General Henry Dearborn, who had 16 warships and 7,000 men to accomplish his goal of securing Lake Ontario for the Americans. The British had only 1,800 regulars to defend not only the three forts but the entire Niagara frontier.

The Americans were successful in the amphibious assault largely thanks to Commodore Oliver Hazard Perry, who on several occasions prevented assault craft from going astray or landing in the wrong place. Once ashore, the Americans were spearheaded by the 6-foot 5-inch Colonel Scott and the green-clad sharpshooters under Benjamin Forsyth. The British and Canadian militia were protected by a 12-foot-high embankment that the Americans stormed. The forces clashed at the crest and terrible carnage ensued. After the battle, the American surgeon James Mann counted 400 dead in an area of just 200 yards by 15 yards.

As a result of the fall of Fort George, the British realized that Fort Niagara and Fort Erie were in an untenable position and both have been abandoned (→ Nov. 11).

Dying captain: "Don't give up the ship"

Fatally wounded, Captain Lawrence is carried below by crew members.

Boston, June 1

In a classic naval battle involving frigates of identical strength today, the British emerged victorious. The 38-gun British frigate Shammon, under Captain Phillip Broke, issued a formal challenge to the American frigate Chesapeake, also 38 guns, but its Captain James Lawrence was already under sail. The weather was good, the sea calm, and the ships met almost head-on before they exchanged extremely destructive broadsides. Captain Lawrence was wounded and as he was being carried below to die, he pleaded with his men: "Don't give up the ship." While it was the Americans who were defeated, the casualties were heavy on both sides.

Harrison breaks 10-day siege of Ohio fort

Fort Meigs, Ohio, May 9

General William Henry Harrison has broken the 10-day siege of Fort Meigs, but it cost the Americans dearly in loss of life and prisoners taken. The British, under Major General Henry Procter, had made life miserable for the Americans with cannon and mortar fire. When 1,200 reinforcements arrived, the Americans attacked the besiegers, taking British positions and spiking the guns that had tormented them. But Procter counterattacked, taking 500 men prisoner and killing 150 (→ Aug. 2).

Harrison's men, under siege, defend Fort Meigs from British and Indians.

Carnage heavy on both sides in Creek war

Massacre at Fort Mims. Only 36 of the 533 residents survived the attack.

Mississippi Territory, Dec. 23

General Ferdinand Claiborne's forces took Escanachaha, the so-called "Holy City" of the Creek nation today, driving even higher the death toll in the Indian war. Claiborne's troops, including the Third Infantry and a volunteer unit, killed 30 Indians near the Coosa and Tallapoosa Rivers, with only one American reported lost. Chief Red Eagle, also known as Billy Weatherford, escaped dramatically by riding off a high bluff and into deep water.

The clash was the latest in a series of battles that have been costly to both sides in the Creek lands of the Mississippi Territory [Alabama]. The conflict began in August when 100 of Red Eagle's men massacred 517 of the 533 settlers at Fort Mims on Lake Tensa. In November, General John Coffee retaliated in an attack on Tallushatchee, killing all 186 male adults and seizing 84 women and children. The frontiersman Davy Crockett, a member of the force, said, "We shot them like dogs." General Andrew Jackson struck later in November against hostile Creeks near the friendly village of Talladega. He said he was out to cause as much destruction as at Tallushatchee. He killed 290 Indians and lost 17 of his own men (→ Aug. 9, 1814).

Americans beat off British at Sandusky

Fort Stephenson, Ohio, Aug. 2

Against all odds, against orders and against a superior force of British regulars, Major George Croghan, aged 21, fought off an attack on Fort Stephenson [Sandusky] today and lost only one man in the clash. The British had probed the Americans at Fort Meigs, but it seemed too strong, so they moved down the Maumee River to take Fort Stephenson. They didn't figure on Major Croghan. Arriving at the fort, Major General Henry Procter warned the defenders that unless they surrendered he could not guarantee their safety with the Indians. This worked at Detroit. It did not work here. The redcoats struck, were beaten off, and paid with 100 casualties (→ Sept. 10).

Sloop is lost after capturing 27 ships

London, Aug. 14

After terrorizing ships in the English Channel for months, and causing great consternation along the coasts of Britain, the career of the American sloop Argus, 16 guns, was brought to an end today by the British sloop Pelican, 18 guns. Some shame has been cast on the American crew because it struck its colors before being boarded. In the midst of the engagement, U.S. Captain William Henry Allen's leg was shot off and he was taken to London. He is not expected to live. The American vessel, which has captured 27 ships, was faster than the Pelican and it could have escaped, but it chose to fight and fought poorly. The shooting of the crew was inaccurate (→ March 28, 1814).

Harrison hits enemy evacuating Detroit

Moravian Town, Canada, Oct. 5

The British retreat from Fort Detroit has turned into a fiasco, a rout and finally a defeat. Against the violent objections of Shawnee Chief Tecumseh, who was later killed in the battle, the British, under Major General Henry Procter, gathered their forces and Indian allies when they heard that their fleet had been lost on Lake Erie. Procter had intended to make a stand on the heights of the Moravian Town, but General William Henry Harrison and the Americans caught him before he could get there. Procter had only about 1,000 men and a single six-pound cannon, and he was facing an army of 3,000 Americans, including Richard M. Johnson's mounted Kentucky infantry. The Kentuckians headed for the British center, capturing the lone cannon there before it could fire a shot. Most of the British fired only one shot before they fled to the north. The Indians fought harder, but the Kentuckians had an easy day of it, with only three men wounded and none killed.

Craps is big gamble in New Orleans

New Orleans

The nation's port of entry for Europe's most tempting amusements has admitted a game of dice called "crabs" or "craps." It derives from the French game hazard and seems to have been imported eight years ago by Bernard Xavier Philippe de Marigny, a once-wealthy playboy who has not profited by his gift to America. But there are profits to be had. Louisiana legalized gambling last year. And New Orleans's transient population of merchants and sailors make it a fertile haven for the professional sharper.

"Uncle Sam" first used in newspaper

Troy, New York, Sept. 7

Those who regard the phrase "United States government" as too dry or too much of a mouthful may want to substitute the sobriquet "Uncle Sam," which appeared for the first time today in an editorial in the *Troy Post*, an upstate New York daily newspaper. No one is certain how the expression originated, but people here say that it combines two references – one to the "U.S." that is stamped on all government property, the other to a local army supply inspector, one "Uncle Sam" Wilson.

Tecumseh falls at the Battle of the Thames. His loss deprives the Shawnee Indians of their leader in fighting the encroachment of American settlement.

Perry: "Enemy is ours" on Lake Erie

Lake Erie, Sept. 10

Commander Oliver Hazard Perry sat down on a dismounted cannon aboard the frigate Niagara today and, with his round hat serving as a table, scrawled out the following message to Major General William Henry Harrison on the back of an envelope: "We have met the enemy and they are ours. Two ships, two brigs, one schooner. Yours, etc. O.H. Perry." It was the first time in history that an entire British fleet has been defeated and captured virtually intact.

The Battle of Lake Erie began at noon on a glorious late summer's day when an American lookout, anchored at Put-in Bay, sighted British masts on the horizon. The British, under the command of Captain Robert Heriot Barclay, had sailed to meet the enemy even though their vessels were outnumbered and outgunned. They were also out of food. In spite of the host of problems, the British had a strategy. At close range, the vessels were at a disadvantage. But there were long guns on the Detroit and the Queen Charlotte that would wreak terrible damage on the Americans if they stayed at a distance. For a while, the two ships were able to do this and the Detroit battered the American flagship Lawrence. Survivors tell of terrible carnage on all the decks. One gunner, David Bunnel, recalled seeing a shot rip open a pot of peas that spilled all over the deck. A pig had squirmed loose and was eating them even though both its hind legs had been shot off.

The Lawrence finally struck its colors, but all the boats on the Detroit had been smashed and it could not be boarded. Perry got into a small boat and was rowed to the Niagara, where he took command and continued the fight.

The British might have won the battle, but the two ships, the Detroit and Queen Charlotte, became entangled and were rendered almost useless. The Niagara cut directly through the British line and shot up both ships. The masts of the Detroit were completely shot away and the mizzen of the Queen Charlotte had dropped into the water when Captain Barclay struck his colors at about 3 p.m. (→Oct. 5).

Perry directs the action from a rowboat. His flagship, the Lawrence, met British fire alone before his squadron could close. When the brig was paralyzed, Perry rowed to the Niagara under heavy fire. From there, he broke British lines and crippled two warships. "Perry's Victory on Lake Erie" by W.H. Powell.

Cartoonist's war. Above: Brother Jonathan forces a draft of Oliver Hazard Perry on John Bull. Below: John Bull making ships to send to the lakes.

British seem ready for peace talks

London, Nov. 11

Having blunted several diplomatic initiatives from Washington and St. Petersburg, the British government finally seems ready to discuss negotiations toward ending the conflict in America. Viscount Castlereagh, the Foreign Secretary, has transmitted a note to Secretary of State James Monroe apprising him of Britain's willingness to talk. The British seem to have all the advantages because they are uncommitted to either a date or terms. If Napoleon is defeated in Europe, as now seems likely, the Duke of Wellington's army will be freed to bring great pressure on the Americans. The British also seem to be responding to pressure from the court of the Czar in St. Petersburg.

British foil second invasion of Canada

Buffalo, New York, Dec. 30

The year is drawing to an end and with it American plans for invading Canada. The Americans have tried for 18 months and they have failed.

What brought about the disastrous conclusion of the latest American effort was the ill-advised burning of Newark, Ontario, which was the work of Brigadier General George McClure who, by all accounts, is not much of a soldier. A former miller and carpenter, he had only 70 regulars to defend Newark against what he believed was an advancing horde of British. There was no horde, but he set the town afire anyway, and this did not set well with Lieutenant General Gordon Drummond, who assumed control of upper Canada in mid-December. Drummond decided to attack Fort Niagara immediately with 550 regulars under Lieutenant Colonel John Murry. On a bitterly cold morning, the lieutenant advanced on the fort, learned the password to the huge gate from a captured sentry and, in the battle that ensued, killed 65 Americans and captured 350. The final humiliation came at month's end when the British advanced on Buffalo and avenged the arson by burning 333 buildings (→May 1, 1814).

1814

Madison

Washington, D.C., Jan. 27. Congress authorizes army of 62,733 men.

Valparaiso, March 28. U.S. frigate Essex, under command of Captain David Porter, captured by British, after attacking 40 enemy ships (→Apr. 29).

Plattsburg, New York, May 1. U.S. General Wade Hampton, ousted for incompetence in Montreal campaign, replaced by Major General George Izard (→July 5).

Washington, D.C., Aug. 27. President Madison and much of Cabinet return to capital (→Sept. 14).

Baltimore, Sept. 14. Force of 13,000 regulars and militia under General Samuel Smith hold off three-day British attack on Baltimore.→

Jamaica, Nov. 26. Some 7,500 British soldiers sail on 50 ships to attack New Orleans (→Dec. 13).

New Orleans, Dec. 13. Major General Andrew Jackson proclaims martial law as British disembark at Lake Borgne, 40 miles east of New Orleans (→23).

Hartford, Connecticut, Dec. 15. Convention of five New England states' anti-war delegations meets to discuss states' rights (→Jan. 5, 1815).

Waltham, Massachusetts. Francis Cabot Lowell establishes first factory with automated cotton weaving and spinning machines in same building.

United States. First circular saw in United States made by Benjamin Cummings.

Philadelphia. The Rev. Richard Allen organizes African Methodist Episcopal Church.

Oregon Territory. A ship arriving from California brings first livestock to territory.

Oregon Territory. Jane Barnes, first white woman to reach Pacific Northwest, arrives at Fort George.

United States. Andrew Jackson explains to Creek Chief Big Warrior, "The great body of the Creek chiefs and warriors did not respect the power of the United States – they thought we were an insignificant nation . . . we bleed our enemies in such cases to give them their senses."

Battle of Horseshoe Bend ends Creek War

Creek Chief Billy Weatherford surrenders to Jackson at Horseshoe Bend.

Fort Jackson, Miss. Terr., Aug. 9

General Andrew Jackson signed a treaty with the Creek Indians today, obtaining 23 million acres of land for the United States. The pact, a direct result of the March 27 Battle of Horseshoe Bend on the Tallapoosa River, ends the year-long Creek War. The Creeks, who had been allied with the British in the larger conflict, signed away half of their lands in Georgia and the Mississippi Territory. Jackson said the beaten Creeks were so hungry that they ate discarded corn from the ground.

Congress ends embargo on British trade

Washington, D.C., Apr. 14

Starvation, smuggling and cutting off one's nose to spite one's face are the reasons for today's repeal of the Embargo and Non-Importation Acts. Both the House and the Senate voted for nullification of the legislation of 1813 that banned trade with England. Earlier this year, Congress acted to modify the rigid laws to ease the pain from famine endured by the citizens on Nantucket Island in particular. Since passage of the embargo laws, smugglers have profited and American manufacturing has suffered.

The bloody death of the embargo, at the hand of President Madison.

Napoleon's ouster may affect U.S. war

Paris, Apr. 11

In a short, emotional ceremony at his palace in Fontainebleau, Napoleon abdicated the French throne today. In a low voice, the Emperor wondered what will become of France. He closed with words that will undoubtedly appear in history books for generations: "I have done what I could." Now many military strategists wonder what effect the freeing of 14,000 of the Duke of Wellington's men will have. It is rumored that this force will be sent to America, where war with the British is raging. No one doubts the balance of military power may be tipped in Britain's favor with the use of Wellington's men.

American fort built and then is seized

Prairie du Chien [Wisconsin]

Just one month after the first American flag was raised over Fort Shelby near here, the British have captured the post in the only military confrontation to date between the British and Americans in this part of the Northwest Territory. The fort, erected by an American expedition that had traveled up the Mississippi from St. Louis, quickly became the target of British Major William McKay, who seized it with a force of English soldiers, French settlers and Indians from this area.

Washington lauded in Jefferson letter

Monticello, Virginia, Jan. 2

In repose, Thomas Jefferson has written some kind words of the Father of our Country in a letter to Dr. Walter Jones. "His mind was great and powerful," writes Jefferson of George Washington, "without being of the first order . . . little aided by invention or imagination, but sure in conclusion." His judgment was prudent and his integrity pure, says Jefferson, who displays striking reverence for a man with whom he rarely agreed. "He was, indeed, in every sense of the words, a wise, a good, and a great man."

Outnumbered Americans win over British

Scott's infantrymen advance shoulder to shoulder into fire at Chippewa.

Chippewa, Canada, July 5

British Major General Phineas Riall launched an all-out attack against an inferior force of Americans under Major General Jacob Brown today and was repulsed. A raging fever was partly to blame.

General Riall's problems began with the commander of the 100th Regiment, Lord Tweeddale, an eccentric giant of a man who was suffering a violent fit of ague. The marquis told Riall that he was "in the cold fit of the disease" but expected a hot fit soon. As a result, Riall postponed the attack for an hour, allowing Brigadier General Winfield Scott just enough time to get his brigade in order.

General Scott faced the Royal Scots under Lieutenant Colonel John Gordon, and the 100th Regiment under the ailing marquis. When Riall saw the Americans dressed in homespun gray, he cried, "Why it's nothing but a body of Buffalo militia." He was wrong, and when his forces tried to advance against the Americans through the three-foot-high grass, they were met with canister and cold steel. Both of the British regiments now came to a standstill. As the American force fixed bayonets, the British line crumbled and the Americans held the field. The day was theirs (→25).

Canada is scene of terribly bloody battle

In five hours, there were 860 American casualties, including 174 killed.

Lundy's Lane, Canada, July 25

Under a waning moon, British and American armies fought to a chaotic standstill here today in one of the bloodiest battles of the war. The Americans, who were camped across the Niagara River from Fort Schlosser, thought that they were about to be attacked by a superior British force. The British, however, were massed at Lundy's Lane, which is the main route between Niagara Falls and Lake Ontario.

The ever-bellicose Brigadier General Winfield Scott decided to attack immediately. The British held the heights, a knoll above Lundy's Lane, the site of a red Presbyterian church flanked by a cemetery. By the time General Scott ordered the charge, it was nearly dark and difficult to distinguish between friend and foe. In the gloom, the Americans captured Major General Phineas Riall and his entire staff.

The actual fighting for the knoll was bedlam. British and American soldiers were intermingled in a brutal contest: swinging musket butts, comrades mistaken for enemies. The carnage was terrible. At about 11 o'clock, with the moon down, both sides called it a night. American casualties, put at 860, included 174 killed. The British toll was 84 killed and 559 wounded (→Nov. 5).

American ships win several sea battles

Havana, Cuba, Apr. 29

The war on the high seas has become a back-and-forth affair. The American sloop Peacock evaded the British blockade last month and, commanded by Lewis Warrington, escaped to the Carribean where it seized the British brig Epervier, carrying $100,000 in silver and gold. The frigate Essex, under the command of Captain David Porter, headed for the South Pacific where it captured more than 40 British vessels, until a squadron under the British Captain Hillyar captured him in turn. Battling the Cherub and the Phoebe, Porter suffered 120 casualties (→Oct. 29).

United States. *"Ariadne Asleep on the Island of Naxos" is considered in such poor taste that it has almost ruined artist John Vanderlyn's career.*

Five tribes agree to join war on British

Ohio, July 22

Choosing what appears to be the lesser of evils, five native tribes in Ohio have made peace with the United States and agreed to declare war on the British. The tribes involved are the Shawnees, Delawares, Senecas, Wyandots and Miamis. Spurned by England after supporting it during the Revolution, the Indians of the old Northwest appear finally to have given up hope for British aid against American expansion. Nonetheless, in upcoming peace talks at Ghent, the British may revive proposals for an Indian buffer state between the U.S. and Canada (→Dec. 11, 1816).

British burn down Washington, D.C.

Dolley Madison carries the Declaration of Independence to safety.

Washington, D.C., Aug. 25

This town is a ghostly theater tonight: The House of Representatives, the President's House, the Library of Congress and other landmarks of the young republic are a charred backdrop to a tragic, inconceivable play. In two days, the British have burned down much of the capital and forced President James Madison to flee. He is rumored to be somewhere west of the Potomac. The First Lady, Dolley Madison, safe in the home of a Virginian friend, watched from afar as Washington burned, and bitterly imagined the British enjoying the roast ham and wines that she had ordered prepared for serving in the President's House – food to celebrate a victory she was certain would go to the Americans. Yet she has rescued two treasures that the British shall never win: Gilbert Stuart's life-size portrait of George Washington and the original Declaration of Independence.

On August 19, some 4,000 British troops, fresh from war in France, arrived in Benedict, Maryland, 40 miles southeast of Washington. General Robert Ross might have led them to Baltimore or Alexandria; capture of either city would have been a major victory for the British. But the destruction of Washington – though it is a town of just 8,000 inhabitants, half of them freed slaves – could cripple the spirit of the nation. With this intent, Ross ordered his men to march. The air was stifling, the heat intense; more than 60 redcoats succumbed to exhaustion or sunstroke. The men feared no other enemy, for no militiamen appeared.

It was not until this morning, when the British reached the outskirts of Washington, that American forces assembled across the Potomac's Bladensburg Bridge. Why had the militia delayed? Why were they so few in number? The Commander-in-Chief, President Madison, seemed overly confident, riding leisurely among the ranks. He would have strayed into firing range if soldiers had not warned him in time. General William Henry Winder, next in command, seemed to suffer from the other extreme: He had no confidence at all; he *looked* frightened.

"Even if it rains militia, we go on!" General Ross exclaimed as the British stormed the bridge. Congreve rockets hurtled after them; the air was bombarded with sound; red flares filled the sky. "Comets! They're shooting comets!" shouted militiamen as they scattered in disarray. Just 500 men stood their ground – and that was something they had not done before. They were the marines who served under Commander Joshua Barney. They had hauled their ships' guns to Bladensburg when they learned that it would be the site of the crucial battle. They fought bravely, but in vain. Scores were killed; Barney was wounded and taken prisoner. The British then marched into the captive city and set it afire (→Aug. 27).

The battle rages on the waters of the Potomac, illuminated by flames from the Capitol, the President's House and the rest of the beleaguered capital.

A British engraving depicts an orderly regiment of redcoats surveying the scene from across the Potomac as Washington, D.C., is thrown into chaos.

British fleet routed on Lake Champlain

Lake Champlain, Sept. 11

Superior seamanship gave the Americans a victory over the British and control of Lake Champlain today. The British fleet had a slight advantage in long guns, and its flagship, the 36-gun frigate Confiance was the largest on the lake. But it had just been launched and Captain George Downie knew that it was ill prepared. The Americans were led by Captain Thomas Macdonough, a hero of the attack on Tripoli, who commanded the 26-gun Saratoga. He waited for the British in Plattsburg Bay and was well prepared. The British were not, and were shot to pieces after having been outmaneuvered. Downie died in the battle and the Confiance and three other ships surrendered (→Dec. 24).

On leaving Canada, Americans raze fort

Fort Erie, Nov. 5

The Americans have decided to abandon the Niagara frontier to the British and ordered Brigadier General George Izard to blow up Fort Erie today. The American high command feared the British would overrun General Izard's position with some 10,000 reinforcements from Europe, veterans of the war against Napoleon. In addition, at Kingston early last month the British navy launched the Lawrence, a warship of oceanic size that carried 110 guns. General Izard said that this move had "defeated all the objects of the operation by land in this quarter."

Izard detached about 900 men, under Brigadier General Daniel Bissell, to burn gristmills and to harass the British food supply. This was accomplished, but it cost Bissell 67 casualties. The Americans were also lacking in food supplies, while the British were getting plenty of beef from New England. General Izard said that cattle, "like herds of buffaloes pass through the forest making paths for themselves." He said he did not have the manpower to stretch a cordon of troops to stop this traffic, but he suggested that the St. Lawrence River line be cut somewhere else (→Dec. 24).

Jackson captures city, defying orders

Pensacola, West Florida, Nov. 7

Major General Andrew Jackson, disobeying direct orders from the Secretary of War, attacked and captured Pensacola today, defeating the Spanish and driving out a British force. His army of 3,000 to 4,000 arrived at the small town yesterday and overran it, meeting little resistance. The Spanish Governor had sought and received British assistance, but forbade his allies to attack until the American forces were actually in sight. Secretary of War James Monroe had ordered Jackson to do nothing to provoke a war with Spain. But Jackson replied that he must attack, to end the Indian war and foreign influence in the area. He expects to leave soon for New Orleans (→ Dec. 26, 1817).

Old Hickory halts British in Louisiana

New Orleans, Dec. 23

An American army under Major General Andrew Jackson halted an uncertain British probe toward New Orleans today. The British left Jamaica on November 26 and, after a leisurely trip, landed in Louisiana December 8. The Americans did not know whether the British target was Mobile or New Orleans. But "Old Hickory" Jackson was sure it was New Orleans and gathered his dispersed forces to defend it.

Admiral Alexander Cochran, in overall command of the British forces, did not know how to get to the city. One of his officers said it seemed impossible to reach unless "assisted by the aerial flight of the bird of prey or astride the alligator's scaly back." Such discouraging words notwithstanding, Cochran selected a route across Lake Borgne because it was easy to navigate and chose a landing place believed to be just below the city. But the British had not anticipated what Jackson might do. What he did was strike the advancing column with a force of 2,000 men, a motley assortment that included Jean Lafitte, free Negroes and militiamen from several states. The British were stopped in the dark, giving the Americans precious time (→ Jan. 8, 1815).

Lawyer writes: "O say can you see"

Baltimore, Maryland, Sept. 14

At daybreak, the defenders of the city of Baltimore were exultant to discover British land forces in full retreat. At the same time, the defenders of Fort McHenry, stationed at the mouth of the harbor, rejoiced to see the ships of the British fleet heading out to sea. Three Americans, Francis Scott Key, an attorney, and two companions, disembarked from one of those very ships. Detained aboard the Minden, they had watched the all-night bombardment of the fort, and this morning they hailed the immense American flag – 42 by 30 feet – that still waved over Fort McHenry.

The attack began on September 12. General Robert Ross, who left the city of Washington smoldering behind him, had brought his 4,000 men ashore near North Point at the mouth of the Patapsco River. They were halted by a series of deep trenches that the Baltimoreans had dug. Heavy fighting ensued, and before Ross was fatally wounded, he called for the reinforcement of the British fleet. Admiral Sir George Cockburn sent his ships upriver to pass before Fort McHenry, which houses a battery of 57 guns, a furnace for heating cannon balls and 1,000 men under the command of Major George Armistead.

Yesterday morning, while the British fleet was yet out of cannon reach, Key, a 33-year-old Virginian, rowed out to the Minden. A friend, Dr. William Beanes, was aboard: The physician had been accused of spying and was taken prisoner after the burning of Washington. With President Madison's approval, Key and a friend named Colonel John Skinner, hoped to negotiate Beanes's release. The British agreed to talk, and the Minden ran up a flag of truce. The Americans and British officers had a congenial dinner; the release would be arranged, but only after an imminent attack on Fort McHenry was concluded. So the Americans were in a sense prisoners, their fates tied to the outcome of the battle. They stood on deck and peered into the night and a blackness that was lit and relit by the flames of red Congreve rockets and the fiery explosion of bombs. The men strained to see the star-spangled banner, often hidden by drifting smoke. And as they stood there, Key wrote on the back of an old envelope a few poetic lines in praise of the free and the brave that serve as the basis for a stirring hymn:

O say can you see, by the dawn's early light,
What so proudly we hail'd at the twilight's last gleaming.
Whose broad stripes and bright stars through the perilous fight,
O'er the ramparts we watched were so gallantly streaming?
And the rockets' red glare, the bombs bursting in air,
Gave proof through the night that our flag was still there.
O say does that star-spangled banner yet wave
O'er the land of the free, and the home of the brave? (→ Dec. 24).

Key, a Federalist, had little interest in Madison's fight against Britain.

Key watched the bombing from captivity on a British ship. Finding his captors "illiberal, ignorant and vulgar," he was moved despite his dislike for the war.

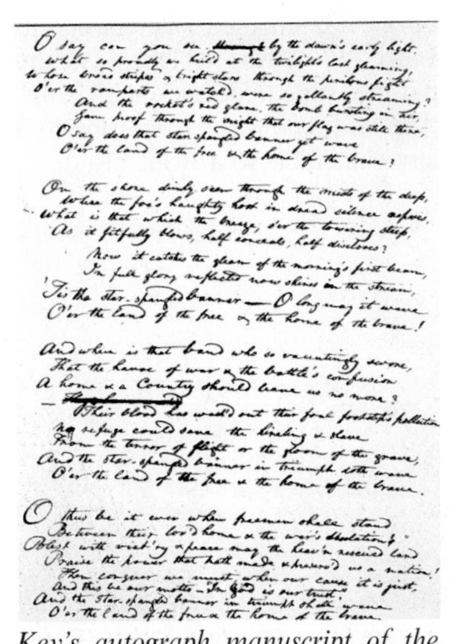

Key's autograph manuscript of the poem, initially printed as a handbill.

"Star Spangled Banner." Front page of the first edition printed with music.

▷

1812 war ends in treaty

Lord Gambier and John Adams shake hands at Ghent. Painting by Forestier.

Ghent, Belgium, Dec. 24

While other diplomats were deciding the fate of Europe at talks in Vienna, American and British negotiators here were finally getting around to ending a war that nobody wanted. In 1809, President Madison sent John Quincy Adams to Russia and, for a while, it seemed possible that the Czar might be able to broker a peace. But this effort failed because England would have nothing to do with the effort. Adams was joined in Europe by Albert Gallatin, Henry Clay, James Bayard and Jonathan Russell, and they began the negotiations with English commissioners that resulted in the signing of the treaty today. The agreement made no mention of neutral rights, especially of seamen, one of the chief reasons for the United States having gone to war. American expansionist sentiment was better served, however, with the territory seized by Britain along the Canadian border being ceded to the United States (→Feb. 11, 1815).

First steam-powered warship is launched

New York City, Oct. 29

It's heavily armed and it protects New York. The "it" is the world's first steam-engined warship, a 38-ton vessel with a paddle wheel tucked between twin hulls, where it is safe from enemy fire. Designer Robert Fulton wanted to call it "Demologos," or Voice of the People, and officials preferred "Pyremon" or Vomiting Fire. It wound up the Fulton I. Mobile enough to ward off attack, it has a steam-pumped hose to defuse enemy guns. And its firepower is reassuring to a city vulnerable to a British raid.

With a salutary blast of steam, the Fulton I heads out of New York harbor.

Jefferson's library bought by Congress

Washington, D.C., Oct. 21

At 71, Thomas Jefferson continues to share his vast knowledge with his countrymen. Upon learning that marauding British troops had razed the congressional library during the war, the former President promptly offered to replace the lost volumes with 7,000 of his own, part of the splendid collection that graces his mansion in Monticello, Virginia. The collection includes treatises in ancient and modern languages on agriculture, mathematics and philosophy, and it features rare volumes obtained from the finest dealers in the world. Congress has just approved a payment of $23,950 to Jefferson, who, according to rumors, is seriously in debt.

Book traces Lewis and Clark's trek

Philadelphia

Armchair travelers can join a thrilling journey by picking up a copy of *The History of the Expedition of Captains Lewis and Clark.* Explorer Meriwether Lewis was to have written it, but in 1809, when the despondent 35-year-old Lewis died mysteriously, either murdered or a suicide, on a trip to Washington, editors Paul Allen and Nicholas Biddle took over, using Lewis's notes and those of his partner, William Clark. The volume, with a preface by Thomas Jefferson, traces the 1803-6 trek to find "the courses and source of the Missouri" and a waterway to the Pacific Ocean.

Country stores a hit

Homer, New York

. Country stores are becoming popular centers of trade and gossip all around the United States. At places like Jedediah Barber's newly opened Great Western Store here, farmers sell their surplus grain to the store owners and they in turn ship it to the cities at a profit. These stores also carry hardware for the farmers and fabrics for their wives. Many people stop by to discuss planting and politics, and some just drop in for a game of checkers.

1815

Madison

Washington, D.C., Jan. 20. President Madison vetoes bill calling for second national bank, saying it would create a weak institution (→Apr. 10, 1816).

United States, Feb. 11. News of the Treaty of Ghent finally reaches Americans, one month after Battle of New Orleans (→Apr. 10, 1817).

Washington, D.C., March 3. Angered by resumption of piracy in Mediterranean, Congress authorizes hostilities against Bey of Algiers (→June 30).

Washington, D.C., March 3. Trade reciprocity with all nations authorized by Congress.

Boston, May. Historian Jared Sparks publishes first issue of *North American Review,* designed to raise standards of American literature.

Algiers, June 30. Bey of Algiers agrees to cease piracy and release American prisoners, after Stephen Decatur threatens to bomb Algiers (→Aug. 5).

Baltimore, July 4. Cornerstone of first monument to George Washington laid; designed by leading architect Robert Mills.

Troy, New York. James cookstove patented, replacing open-hearth stove.

New Orleans. Artists flocking to city to paint portraits of wealthy Creoles and plantation owners.

Massachusetts. Large number of Congregationalist churches and pastors are becoming Unitarian.

Western Virginia. First natural gas in United States discovered at Charlestown.

United States. Thomas Jefferson writes merchant-financier Thomas Leiper, "The less we do with the amities or enmities of Europe, the better."

Pennsylvania. Some of Napoleon Bonaparte's relatives migrate and settle in Pennsylvania and Baltimore.

California. First recorded Chinese man in California comes to Monterey as a cook for Spanish Governor.

United States. Gilbert Stuart paints portraits of John Adams, Mrs. John Adams, Thomas Jefferson, James Madison.

British suffer defeat at New Orleans

Andrew Jackson by Alonzo Chappel.

New Orleans, Jan. 8

A veteran British army was repulsed while attempting a massive frontal attack on American positions in New Orleans today. The British assembled some 8,000 regulars for the assault, most of them veterans of the Peninsular Campaign in Europe. They were led by Major General Sir Edward Pakenham, Wellington's brother-in-law, who fought gallantly at Salamanca. Defending the city were 5,000 troops under Major General Andrew Jackson, former commander of the Tennessee militia. Jackson assembled a ragtag army of regulars, militiamen, civilian volunteers, the pirates of Barataria Bay and free Negro troops called the Battalion of the Free Men of Color.

The American command chose to defend a strip of land that an invading army would need to cross, a choice that now seems perfect. An advancing army had the Mississippi on its left and an impenetrable cypress swamp on its right. The American site was constructed along the axis of a canal running at right angles to any line of advance. The troops dug a ditch along the canal, filled it with water and set guns behind it. A battery was placed along the river to prevent the British from turning the American flank. Behind these obstacles, the Americans erected a high fortification.

The British launched their frontal assault on the fortified line this morning with inevitable results. The Americans massed musket and artillery fire on a narrow front that decimated the British column. After the first wave was repulsed, General Pakenham tried to rally his troops and was killed in the charge. The main column, under the command of Major General Samuel Gibbs, advanced directly at the Americans, who sat shielded by cotton bales while their fife-and-drummers played *Yankee Doodle Dandy*. American grape and ball resulted in great destruction. The column was stopped twice and reformed. General Gibbs was killed close to the American line.

The British were more successful with an attack on unfinished American fortifications across the Mississippi. The American troops there were driven off after having spiked their guns. The British might have turned the entire engagement at this point, but they failed to follow up. Reinforcements that were rushed in by Jackson shored up the American defenses and, with most of the general officers of the British army dead, it was in no mood to press on with the attack. British casualties totaled more than 2,000 while the toll for the defending Americans came to 45.

Before this battle, the British intended to occupy New Orleans and use the city as a bargaining chip in the peace negotiations. Now, however, they have been forced to head for the West Indies (→Feb. 11).

At point blank range. On the banks of the Mississippi, Jackson and his men defend the bulwarks with rifles and artillery. Lithograph by Kurz and Allison.

The battlefield. Pakenham, the overconfident British general who led the assault, lies dying in the foreground. British casualties quickly soared to more than 2,000 and 500 captured. American casualties included 45 dead.

Pirate Lafitte helps Jackson win battle

New Orleans, Jan. 8

In General Andrew Jackson's successful defense of New Orleans, he has received assistance from an unexpected quarter – the pirates at Barataria Bay, who were led by the colorful Jean Lafitte. The buccaneer and his two brothers, Pierre and Dominique, rule over a small kingdom of robbers and smugglers at Barataria, some 60 miles southwest of New Orleans. They have grown rich by means of privateering and smuggling and continue in power because they have been able to buy off some of the most powerful citizens in the region (→Jan. 1817).

Jean Lafitte, American partisan.

Treaty news late; sea war goes on

Cape of Good Hope, March 23

Because there is no way to communicate with ships at sea, the war continues despite the signing of the Treaty of Ghent on Christmas eve in Belgium. Off the coast of Portugal, the American frigate Constitution captured the British sloops Levant and Cyane and 70 men were killed or maimed in the battle. Off the cape here, the American sloop Hornet encountered the British brig Penguin. After a brief but bitter engagement, in which a third of the Penguin's crew was killed or wounded, the vessel had to haul down its colors.

Federalists issue a call for states' rights

William Charles cartoon: New England ready to fall into King George's arms.

Hartford, Connecticut, Jan. 5

Secret meetings held at the State House for 20 days ended today with the issuance of a report that is liable to be branded treasonous. Federalists representing Connecticut, Massachusetts and Rhode Island, as well as unofficial delegates from New Hampshire and Vermont, excoriated President Madison's governmental policies and demanded several changes in the United States Constitution. They insist on seven amendments, which include limiting the President to one term, denying any state the opportunity of supplying two consecutive presidents, apportioning tax duties and representatives according to population and requiring a two-thirds vote of Congress for admission of a new state and on declaring war.

The Hartford Convention is clearly a product of the times. The war with the British has nearly ruined the seagoing economy of New England, and the region particularly objects to the use of militia in the national effort; the Hartford delegates feel that the militias exist for local defense, not for the stratagems of the national government, which, the convention claims, may try to "erect a military despotism out of the ruins." Despite these opinions, secession is not suggested. As the Massachusetts delegate Harrison Gray Otis put it, "a severance of the Union . . . can be justified only by absolute necessity."

Indian who started a new faith dies

Onondaga, New York, Aug. 10

Ga-ne-o-di-yo (Handsome Lake), who founded Gai'wiio or the Longhouse religion among the Seneca Indians, died on the reservation here today at the age of 75. The religion is really more of a restorationist movement, preaching a return to old Seneca values and beliefs as well as abstinence from the alcoholic beverages that Handsome Lake saw destroying tribal and family life. The Seneca leader began his movement in 1800 after he had a vision in which four angels commanded him to preach against intemperance and to urge a return to the faith and values of their fathers.

Catholic cathedral to be nation's first

Baltimore, Maryland

After a delay caused by the war with Britain, construction has resumed here on the Cathedral of the Assumption, the nation's first. Designed in neoclassical style by Benjamin H. Latrobe, it was begun in July 1806, when the cornerstone was laid by Bishop John Carroll. The monumental structure is built of local granite and owes much to the vision of Bishop Carroll and his support of Latrobe, especially in light of the animosity stirred up by the architect's demanding ways. The bishop has made it a personal duty to see that the cathedral is constructed as designed (→ 1821).

Barbary Pirates neutralized by Decatur

Tripoli, Aug. 5

The marauding along the Barbary Shore is now a thing of the past thanks to the salvos, both diplomatic and real, fired by the naval hero Stephen Decatur. During his June encounter with the Algerian fleet, in which Admiral Hammida was killed, Captain Decatur seized two ships, most prominently the 44-gun flagship Mashouda. Decatur engaged the pirates only six months after the Treaty of Ghent ended America's conflict with the British. It will be recalled that the United States fought that war for "free trade and sailors' rights."

Decatur's actions followed a congressional resolve to enforce the same principle in the Mediterranean, especially in view of the Algerian Bey's demands for an ever higher tribute. The treaty served by Decatur included a dose of the Bey's own medicine – accept it or see Algiers bombed. The United States will no longer pay tributes, all American prisoners are to be released and all Christian slaves who fled the Bey's realm to the safety of American ships are to be emancipated. The Bey of Tripoli has now agreed to similarly tough terms, including freedom of the seas in the Mediterranean as well as an end to piracy and to payments for American vessels that are seized in the waters off Tunisia (→ Aug. 1816).

Limit of 10,000 put on United States Army

Washington, D.C., March 3

The executive and congressional arms of government have been bargaining over the military. President Madison and Secretary of State Monroe sought a 20,000-man peacetime army. Worried over the $5 million a year such a force requires, the House countered with a proposal of 6,000. After much haggling, a 10,000-limit was set, including two major generals and four brigadier generals. Last month, Congress ordered the sale of the navy's gunboat flotilla and the docking of the Great Lakes warships as a result of a peace arrangements with the British that required such reductions.

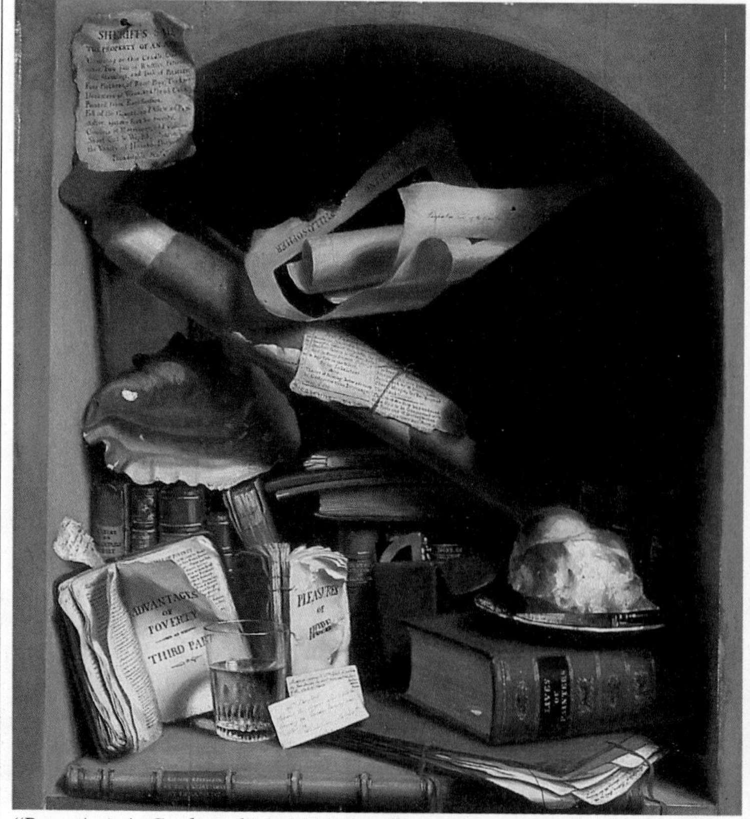

"Poor Artist's Cupboard" (c.1815) by Washington artist Charles Bird King.

1816

Madison

United States, Jan. 1. Public debt rises to $127 million.

California, Jan. 15. Thomas Doak becomes first American settler in California, near Santa Barbara.

Maine, May 20. Citizens of Maine vote to secede from Massachusetts, but state legislature dismisses them as "childish and irresponsible."

Baltimore, June. Rembrandt Peale uses coal gas to light his museum, encouraging lighting of whole city with coal gas.

Alabama, Sept. 14. Chickasaws surrender their claims to land south of Tennessee (→Oct. 19, 1818).

Boston, Dec. 13. Provident Institution for Savings chartered as first savings bank in United States.

Washington, D.C., Dec. 28. Robert Finley, Presbyterian clergyman, establishes American Colonization Society, aimed at recolonizing American Negroes in Africa (→Jan. 1817).

United States. Race horse Timoleon sets one-mile record of 1:47.

United States. American Bible Society organized.

United States. Coast Survey agency, under Treasury Department, begins survey of American coast.

Florida. Region becomes a refuge for runaway slaves.

Spotsylvania, Pennsylvania. "Boxley's Conspiracy" betrayed; 30 slaves are arrested and six hanged; George Boxley flees [and is never recaptured].→

Wilmington, Delaware. A school and library for Negroes established.

United States. Jacob Hyer beats Tom Beasley in a bare-knuckle fight, proclaiming himself "America's first champion."

Cape Cod, Massachusetts. Commercial cranberry cultivation begins when Henry Hall notices sand blown onto bogs makes for heartier cranberries.

United States. *The Culprit Fay*, a long poem, written by Joseph Rodman Drake.

United States. John Pickering's *A Vocabulary of Words and Phrases Peculiar to the United States*, published.

Monroe elected; Republicans get stronger

Monroe, after a John Vanderlyn.

Washington, D.C., Dec. 4

James Monroe was elected President of the United States today, continuing the hold of the Democratic-Republican Party on the nation's highest office. The 58-year-old Virginian won the electoral votes of 16 states, far outdistancing the Federalist Rufus King of New York, who won three states. Monroe takes office in March, succeeding his friend and fellow party member, James "Jemmy" Madison, whom he serves as Secretary of State. His Vice President is to be Daniel D. Tompkins, a Democratic-Republican (→July 12, 1817).

Decatur toasts U.S. "right or wrong"

Virginia, August

Drinks were downed, tributes paid and salutes rendered at the banquet held earlier this month for Commodore Stephen Decatur. He had just returned from his successful mission on the Barbary Coast. Pirates from Tripoli, Algiers and Tunis had been raiding American ships until Decatur forced a halt to it. At the banquet, he toasted America: "Our country! In her intercourse with foreign nations may she always be in the right; but our country right or wrong!"

U.S. Bank created

Washington, D.C., Apr. 10

In an effort to check the wild fluctuations of currency issued by hundreds of state banks, Congress today chartered a second national bank to serve as a regulator. Of the bank's capital of $35 million, $28 million is going to be raised by public subscription (→Feb. 8, 1817).

270 slaves slain in siege of stronghold

Fort Apalachicola, Florida, July 27

The slave stronghold at Apalachicola was destroyed today and 270 fugitives were killed after a 10-day siege by American troops. Most of the slaves in the fort were killed when their powder exploded. There were about 40 survivors. Apalachicola, abandoned by the British, had been occupied by runaways who used it as a base from which to attack slaveholders. In another slave uprising this year, George Boxley of Virginia plotted to free the slaves in Spotsylvania. He was betrayed, but he escaped and remains at large. Six of the slave conspirators were hanged.

Year of no summer

New England, August

Intense cold is destroying crops both here and in parts of the South. Livestock are dying. In Vermont, it has snowed this month and last, and a foot fell in June. Some farmers are heading west and south, and those who remain are already calling this "The Starvation Year."

Astor dominates fur trade below Canada

Northern Plains

An act of Congress excluding foreigners from the fur trade has enabled John Jacob Astor's American Fur Company to gain control of the trade south of the Canadian border. Astor, who began life as a poor German immigrant, founded his fur company in 1808. Three years later, his firm and two Canadian fur producers, the North West Company and the Michilimackinac Company, agreed to operate in the Great Lakes region as one. The legislation that has been approved by Congress, which many say was Astor-inspired, helped him to buy out his partners at a low price.

Indiana 19th state

Indiana, Dec. 11

The Indiana Territory, with some 80,000 inhabitants, was admitted as the 19th state in the union today. The state's constitution, drafted in June, outlawed slavery and established the state capital at Corydon. An event crucial to Indiana's effort to become a state was the Battle of Tippecanoe five years ago between confederated Indian tribes under Tecumseh and American forces under General William Henry Harrison. Harrison's victory resulted in a decision by the Indians to sell their land and move beyond the Mississippi River (→Dec. 3, 1818).

A lone fur trapper, slogging through a frontier creek. By Frederic Remington.

1817

Monroe

United States, January. Free Negroes gather to protest American Colonization Society's efforts to "exile us from the land of our nativity" (→Apr. 7)

Washington, D.C., Feb. 8. Congress passes plan to devote $1.5 million from Bank of United States to public works program (→Jan. 1822).

Albany, New York, March 15. New York State Legislature authorizes $7 million for building of Erie Canal, linking Albany and Buffalo.

Gloucester, Massachusetts, Aug. 18. Accounts of a sea serpent off coast lead to an inquiry by Linnaean Society of Boston; it is reported to be 70 to 100 feet long.

United States, September. *North American Review* prints *Thanatopsis*, by William Cullen Bryant, earning him praise.

United States, Nov. 25. Jefferson, in a letter to author-educator George Ticknor, writes, "Knowledge is power . . . knowledge is safety . . . knowledge is happiness."

Washington, D.C., Dec. 2. President Monroe gives first annual address to Congress, saying federal works programs are within bounds of Constitution.

Wilmington, Delaware. Thomas Gilpin produces first machine-made paper in nation.

Kentucky. Henry Clay imports first Hereford cow into U.S.

New Hampshire. Congregationalism disestablished.

United States. William Cobbett, English journalist-reformer, notes widespread literacy of Americans over their European counterparts.

Pennsylvania. Plumstock Rolling Mill produces rolled iron.

Tennessee. Returning to home state, frontiersman Davy Crockett is appointed local magistrate, relying on "natural-born sense."

Texas. First Methodist minister, possibly first Protestant, arrives in Red River area.

California. San Rafael Arcangel Mission founded.

Cambridge, Massachusetts. Harvard opens law school.

Boston. Handel and Haydn Society gives first complete performance of *Messiah*.

Monroe hailed for "era of good feeling"

Boston, July 12

In what appeared to be a bid for peaceful coexistence, the *Columbian Sentinel* of Boston, the nation's leading Federalist Party newspaper, hailed James Monroe's presidency for ushering in what it called an "era of good feeling." In the article, appearing at a time when the new President was on a tour of the North, Benjamin Russell expressed the wish that the nearly defunct Federalist Party should be treated as though earlier differences had never existed.

President Monroe, a member of the Democratic-Republican Party, was elected a year ago, defeating Rufus King, a New York Federalist, and took office in March. While there have been no conflicts during his brief tenure, such as the War of 1812 during that of his predecessor and fellow Virginian, James Madison, no one can know at this point how tranquil Monroe's administration will be, either domestically or in the realm of foreign affairs. Thus, the article in the *Sentinel* is viewed by many readers as little more than an effort to heal past differences between the two parties. Indeed, President Monroe made a peace gesture of his own in the spring by naming John Quincy Adams, son of a Federalist President and himself once a nominal Federalist, to be his Secretary of State (→Dec. 6, 1820).

The eagle drinks from Liberty's chalice (early 19th century), anonymous.

Naval treaty limits British, U.S. units

Washington, D.C., Apr. 10

The Senate today approved an agreement with Britain setting limits on naval forces on the Great Lakes. The accord, which is not a formal treaty, was worked out between Charles Bagot of Britain and Richard Rush, acting secretary of state. Each nation is to have no more than one single-gun ship of 100 tons on each lake, and has agreed not to build other warships to be placed in these waters. The accord reflects the desire of President Monroe and Lord Castlereagh to "smooth all asperities between the two nations" (→Oct. 20, 1818).

Pardoned, Lafitte resumes his piracy

Mexico, January

President Monroe has pardoned the infamous Jean Lafitte for helping the United States in the war with Britain. The French buccaneer was forgiven his trespasses because of his sterling performance against the British on the high seas. Some of Lafitte's men fought for Andrew Jackson at New Orleans and Lafitte provided flints for Jackson's troops. Critics say Lafitte "always seemed willing to help the cause of liberty for the proper price," but others call him a hero. With his pardon, but with Britain's price still on his head, he has moved to Texas and resumed his old profession. Sailors beware!

Alabama is carved out of Mississippi

Alabama Territory, March 3

Alabama is now a separate territory with its own seat of government and the prospect of becoming a state. Congress voted its approval of the step today. Two days ago, it split the Mississippi Territory into two regions. The western half is to become the State of Mississippi. The eastern half is the new Territory of Alabama. The seat of government is to be at Fort St. Stephens. William Wyatt Bibb, a Senator from Georgia, is expected to become Governor (→Dec. 10).

Seminole War begins with raids on border

Two Seminole chiefs, towering over their captors, are seized in Florida.

Fort Scott, Georgia, Dec. 26

General Andrew Jackson was ordered today to do anything necessary to subdue Seminole Indians along the West Florida border. Jackson, who replaces General Edmund Gaines, is known for his aim of ending not only Indian but also Spanish influence in Florida. By giving Jackson command, President Monroe may have signaled a tougher policy. The conflict began escalating last year when the Seminoles refused to leave lands between Georgia and Florida. U.S. troops wiped out the Seminoles at Fowltown, and the Indians retaliated by massacring a boatload of soldiers, women and children on the Apalachicola River (→Nov. 28, 1818).

Erie Canal to link Great Lakes and Atlantic

Rome, New York, July 4

With great pomp and ceremony, Governor De Witt Clinton broke ground today for a canal that will connect the Great Lakes with New York harbor and the Atlantic. The third major canal project to be undertaken in the nation, the Erie Canal is the first entirely designed by American engineers and will be some 350 miles long. Earlier American canals, near Charleston, South Carolina, and Boston, were not so ambitious, measuring only about 20 miles long, and were designed by British engineers (→Oct. 22, 1819).

Mississippi, with slaves, 20th state

Natchez, Mississippi, Dec. 10

Mississippi became the 20th state in the union today with Natchez as its capital. The area is the western half of the Mississippi Territory, now split between the states of Mississippi and Alabama. The admission of Mississippi as a state where slavery is legal gives the nation 10 slave states and 10 states that prohibit slavery. Mississippi's new constitution allows only white male property owners to vote. The convention met in July at a Methodist church in Washington, a few miles from Natchez. Presiding was David Holmes, who many think is destined to become Governor.

Slaves in Maryland riot, attack whites

St. Mary's County, Md., April 7

In a series of apparently spontaneous outbursts, some 200 Negro slaves attacked whites with sticks and brickbats today, injuring several. The riots were finally halted by police and patrols that were called in to restore peace. It is not known whether the riots here were related to recent gatherings held in many cities to protest plans by the American Colonization Society to return Negroes to Africa. Negroes at a gathering in Philadelphia made it clear they would fight any attempt to exile them from America, their native land (→Feb. 6, 1820).

Calhoun the hawk is Secretary of War

John C. Calhoun of South Carolina (c.1825) by Charles Bird King.

Washington, D.C., Oct. 8

Senator John C. Calhoun of South Carolina, never one to run from a fight, has appropriately been named Secretary of War by President Monroe. Formerly Speaker of the House, the elegant Calhoun was the most eloquent of a group in the 12th Congress called the "war hawks," and his rousing speech of 1812 seeking a declaration of war against Britain put him in the national eye (the real author, kept secret at that time, was Monroe). The young firebrand Calhoun got the war he wanted and seemed to carry it all by himself as he beat the drum for national conscription and better armed forces. His backers hold that America's sorry showing in the war makes his desire to improve the military all the more urgent.

Russians banished by King in Honolulu

Honolulu

Russian fur traders who abused the hospitality of the Hawaiian Islands for more than a dozen years have felt the wrath of King Kamehameha, who has banished them forever. The Russians, who used Honolulu as a re-provisioning and recreational port, outraged the King by trying to build a fort here. When he ordered construction halted, the Russians moved to Kauai, where they tried to put up another fort. That was too much for Kamehameha. He had the traders ousted.

Kentucky rings with sound of Beethoven

Louisville, Kentucky

The hills of Kentucky are ringing with the sounds of Beethoven, at least near Louisville. The Bohemian musician Anthony Heinrich recently conducted a Beethoven symphony here, reportedly the first performance of a Beethoven symphony anywhere in America. The number of the symphony was not noted, but it was noted that Heinrich had found players equal to the task. Heinrich is a composer, too, and has written some music inspired by the American landscape.

Gallaudet establishes first school for deaf

Hartford, Connecticut, Apr. 15

An American minister, Thomas Hopkins Gallaudet, and Laurent Clerc, a deaf Frenchman, have opened the first American school for the deaf. The American Asylum will instruct children and teachers of the deaf. Its methodology is not yet certain: While Clerc is experienced in a French method of hand signs he learned at the Paris Institute, Gallaudet and most Americans are more familiar with one based on English speech. The men hope to develop a sign-language system, which could conceivably be more efficient than speaking.

Gallaudet, trained in Paris.

1818

Monroe

New Haven, Connecticut, Jan. 1. Professor Benjamin Silliman of Yale founds *American Journal of Science and Arts.*

Alabama, Jan. 19. First session of territorial assembly held at St. Stephens.

Massachusetts, Feb. 13. John Adams writes that the American Revolution "was effected before the war commenced. The revolution was in the minds and hearts of the people."

Washington, D.C., March 18. Congress passes Pension Act, offering pensions for veterans of Revolutionary War.

Missouri River, October. Cantonment Martin, first U.S. military post in region [Kansas], established on Isle au Vache.

Monterey, California, Nov 22. City captured and looted by Hippolyte de Bouchard.

Newark, New Jersey. Seth Boyden starts first production of patent leather.

Alabama. St. Stephens Steamboat Company founded; Alabama is first ship to steam from St. Stephens to Mobile.

Alabama. First pig iron made in Alabama Territory smelted near Russellville.

New Hampshire. Legislature sets floor of $13.34 for debtor's prison, the exact amount owed by Revolutionary War hero Captain Mason Bresser.

Philadelphia. Free Negroes organize Pennsylvania Augustine Society, "for the education of people of color."

Oregon Territory. Walla Walla trading post built, becoming a vital link in fur trade.

United States. Scots introduce curling and golf to United States.

Northern Plains. First church and school opened in present-day North Dakota.

Connecticut. Congregationalism disestablished.

Minnesota. Settlers of Red River Valley see their crops destroyed by grasshoppers.

West Point, New York. Gouverneur Kemble establishes a foundry for cannons and projectiles.

New Orleans. The Orleans Theater, rebuilt after a fire, opens with opera companies from Paris.

Seminole War is ended by Jackson attack

Andrew Jackson by Ralph Earl.

Washington, D.C., Nov. 28

Secretary of State John Quincy Adams today defended General Andrew Jackson's controversial, unauthorized war against the Spanish in Florida and said that if Spain cannot rule the colony it should cede it to the United States.

He told Spanish Minister Don Luis de Onis that officially Jackson was acting against the Seminoles, not the Spanish, when he took the Spanish forts at Pensacola and St. Marks earlier this year. Jackson's actions caused an international firestorm and a crisis for the Monroe administration. The irate Spanish minister wanted Jackson punished severely and the captured Spanish cities returned. But Adams told de Onis that if Spain cannot control the Indians, the Americans should assume control of Florida. He also said Monroe "will neither inflict punishment nor pass a censure" on General Jackson. The general, however, still faces a congressional inquiry into the campaign.

Jackson, known as "Old Hickory" for his unyielding manner, says that he was, indeed, authorized to push against Spanish elements in Florida when he was ordered to suppress Seminole aggression along the Florida-Georgia border. He noted that he wrote to Monroe late last year, promising to seize all of Florida from Spain "in 60 days." Monroe insists that he knew nothing of the letter, but Jackson says that the President authorized his plan indirectly, through Congressman J. Rhea of Tennessee.

Jackson launched his campaign from Fort Scott, Georgia, with 1,000 men. He received reinforcements from the Tennessee militia and friendly Indians. They made a brutal sweep against the Seminoles and pushed south. On April 7, they took St. Marks without firing a shot, and executed two Creek chiefs. They also arrested Alexander Arbuthnot, a 70-year-old Scotsman who infuriated Jackson by showing sympathy for the Seminoles. Arbuthnot and a renegade English soldier, Robert Armbrister, were executed for having helped the Seminoles. After seizing St. Marks, Jackson captured a Seminole stronghold in central Florida. The next month he headed for Pensacola, captured it after overcoming minor resistance, and set up a military government (→ Feb. 8, 1819).

Jackson the butcher. Cartoon satirizing the general's ruthless frontier tactics.

Ship begins regular Atlantic crossings

New York City, Jan. 5

"Damn the weather, we're sailing on schedule." With that bold proclamation, the James Monroe made maritime history at 10 a.m. sharp today as the sturdy ship left New York harbor bound for Liverpool. The sailing marked the start of the Black Ball Line, the first regularly scheduled trans-Atlantic service. Until now, Europe-bound ships were often stymied by inclement weather. But the Black Ball Line is determined to take on nature and defy it in order to establish a dependable line. As the ship sailed off, some observers speculated that a new era had begun, one that would give New York a corner on European trade.

President's House is now White House

Washington, D.C., Jan. 1

President James Monroe and his wife, Elizabeth, threw open the doors of the President's House today and held a public reception. Visitors were calling the place the White House, because of its new coat of paint, and many found it more handsome now than before it was burned by the British in 1814. The First Lady has bought French Empire furniture for the oval Blue Room and she has fully redecorated the East Room, the chamber where Abigail Adams once hung out her laundry (→ 1819).

Chickasaw, Quapaw lands ceded to U.S.

Tennessee, Oct. 19

The Chickasaw Indians sold all their lands north of the southern boundary of Tennessee for $300,000 in a treaty completed today. The money will be provided over a period of 15 years. This major cession follows one by the Quapaw Indians of holdings in Arkansas. The Chickasaws in 1721 owned vast territories in eight Southern states. Since that time, they have given up 20 million acres, keeping smaller tracts in Georgia, Alabama, Tennessee and North Carolina.

Steamboat service begins on Great Lakes

Walk-in-the-Water on Lake Erie. Modern miracles with the power of steam.

Black Rock, New York, Aug. 23

When an Indian saw Robert Fulton's steamboat Clermont, he called it "Walk-in-the-Water." The term intrigued steamboat builder Robert McQueen, who gave his new craft the name. Today, the pioneer ship Walk-in-the-Water left its port near Buffalo, establishing the first steamship service on the Great Lakes. Carrying 29 passengers, the ship chugged into Lake Erie, destined for Detroit.

Those aboard paid a high fare, $24 for the 44-hour trip, to help offset the construction price of $50,000. The owners also had to pay the Livingston-Fulton monopoly a high fee for the right to traverse the lakes. A special wharf was constructed in Detroit to accommodate the 338-ton steamer. And a cannon has been placed on deck to announce its arrival. Merchants feel that the lakes' trade potential justifies the expenses (→ Sept. 1819).

49th parallel is western Canadian border

London, Oct. 20

Four years after the end of hostilities along the Canadian-American border, Britain and the United States have settled on the 49th parallel as the international boundary from Lake of the Woods west to the Rocky Mountains. American negotiators wanted the line extended to the Pacific, but the British, seeking to protect the fur trade, proposed the Columbia River as the boundary. Eventually, negotiators compromised on joint occupation of the Oregon territory.

Eastward to the Atlantic, the boundary will remain exactly as it was established back in 1783, running through the Great Lakes and the St. Lawrence River to the 45th parallel, skirting New England and continuing to the ocean.

Jefferson deplores religious intolerance

Monticello, Virginia, May 28

In a letter to Mordecai Noah, a lawyer, playwright and journalist of Portuguese-Jewish ancestry, former President Thomas Jefferson has set forth his opinions on religious intolerance. Jefferson points to the laws of the United States as applying "the only antidote to the vice, protecting our religious as they do our civil rights, by putting all men on an equal footing." He feels there is still more to be done. "For although we are free by the law," he writes, "we are not so in practice; public opinion erects itself into an inquisition, and exercises its office with as much fanaticism as fans the flames of an auto-da-fe. The prejudice still scowling on your section of our religion, although the elder one, cannot be unfelt by yourselves."

Cumberland Road draws settlers to West

Wheeling, Virginia

Bullwhips are cracking and stagecoach bugles are blaring as Americans surge ahead on a new road into the West – the Cumberland Road or National Highway, which has been completed from Baltimore to Wheeling. Formerly a path fit only for horses or shank's mare, the trail carried a trickle of pioneers into the Western territories during the Revolution. But nowadays, thousands of immigrants are turning this trickle into a torrent. Unable to find property or satisfying work in the East, many people are loading their families onto stagecoaches and Conestoga wagons and heading west, toward the promise of cheap land and a new beginning.

"Lady with a Harp" (1818), by Philadelphia portraitist Thomas Sully. Model is Eliza Ridgely.

Illinois 21st state; will include Chicago

Kaskaskia, Illinois, Dec. 3

With its capital at Kaskaskia, Illinois became the 21st state in the union today. The boundaries of the state were determined by the Enabling Act that was approved by Congress earlier in the year. The northern region of the territory was ceded to Michigan, and Lake Michigan bounds its eastern edge. In disregard of the Northwest Ordinance, the northeastern boundary of the state will include the village of Chicago. Slavery, which is still practiced by some of the French villages in this region, will not be permitted under the state's new constitution.

5 stars added to flag; 13 stripes remain

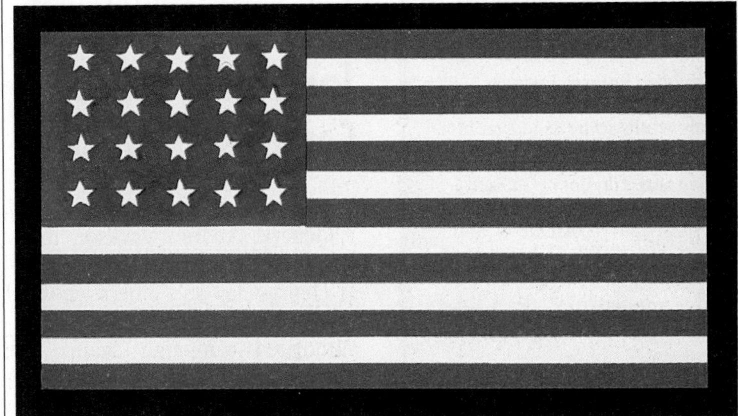

Washington, D.C., July 4. *The American flag flies with five more stars than its predecessor. To avoid exorbitant cloth demands, however, Congress has limited the number of stripes to 13, one for each of the original states. The new stars are for Ohio, Tennessee, Louisiana, Indiana and Mississippi.*

1819

Monroe

Washington, D.C., March 3. In attempt to block slave smuggling, Congress offers $50 reward to informants, and authorizes President to return illegal slaves to Africa (→May 15, 1820).

Missouri Territory, Apr. 23. *The Missouri Intelligencer,* first newspaper west of St. Louis, established at Franklin.

Boston, June 19. Massachusetts agrees to allow District of Maine to petition for statehood.

United States, July 4. A 21st star is added to flag for Illinois.

United States, Sept. 1. Jethro Wood granted patent for a plow with interchangeable parts.

Rome, New York, Oct. 22. First boat to travel Erie Canal makes its way to Utica, New York (→Oct. 27, 1822).

Washington, D.C., Dec. 6. Democratic-Republicans strengthen majority in Congress, dominating House 156-27 and Senate 35-7.

Vermont. John Conant invents an improved stove.

Tennessee. General Jackson is first steamboat to arrive in Nashville.

Washington, D.C. Reconstruction of White House and Capitol, burned in War of 1812, completed.

Washington, D.C. Congress approves $10,000 for education of Indians.

Philadelphia. Building, designed by Benjamin H. Latrobe for Second Bank of United States, completed.

Boston. William Underwood founds nation's first successful food canning business.

Virginia. Jefferson writes, "Advertisements contain the only truths to be relied on in a newspaper."

Missouri Territory. Chester Harding paints only known representation of Daniel Boone from life, at Boone homestead in St. Charles County.

United States. John W. Jarvis paints portrait of Andrew Jackson.

Utica, New York. Thomas Hastings publishes popular collection of hymns, including tune for *Toplady* [*Rock of Ages*].

Honolulu mourns King Kamehameha

Kamehameha II, known to be open to the influence of mainlanders.

Honolulu, May 8

Kamehameha the Great, Conqueror of the Islands and first chief of a united Hawaiian people, died today. Death came at his palace, where relatives, courtiers and soothsayers gathered two days ago when an ominous red tide appeared in Honolulu harbor. The 71-year-old monarch's crown passes to his son, Lilohilo, who becomes Kamehameha II. Dowager Queen Kaahumanu shares the throne. As word of the death spread among the people, there was frenzied activity – the knocking out of teeth, the burning of homes, assaults on women and strangers, and other mourning procedures customary with the death of a chief (→July 14, 1823).

Jackson is spared Congress's censure

Washington, D.C., Feb. 8

General Andrew Jackson today won total victory over House Speaker Henry Clay and others who had tried to censure him for his unauthorized campaign against the Spanish in Florida. Following a 28-day hearing, the longest on record, the House voted 107 to 63 to reject a resolution of censure. It also turned down five other resolutions that expressed its disapproval of the general's behavior (→22).

Depression touched off by financial panic

United States

A financial panic sweeping the United States has triggered one of the worst economic depressions in the country's history. As one observer put it: "Nothing is to be seen but a boundless expanse of desolation! Wealth is impoverished, enterprise checked, commerce at a stand, the currency depreciated."

Confronted with reckless practices on the part of many state banks, a case of runaway depreciation and rampant speculation following the War of 1812, the Second Bank of the United States called for the immediate repayment of loans in hard currency. Such a move, the authorities hoped, would compel the state banks to resume payment in gold and silver coin and would drive the depreciated state bank notes out of circulation.

But many of the state banks, unable to meet their obligations, have suspended coin payments, and a large number have failed. The Second Bank of the United States, which was almost forced to declare bankruptcy itself, underwent a congressional investigation for alleged mismanagement and has been reorganized by the institution's new president, Langdon Cheves.

Meanwhile, prices for basic goods have plunged. Cotton has dropped by 50 percent in a year. And foreclosures are common.

In Kentucky, many of the older banks, as well as the 40 new independent ones chartered a year ago, were plunged into bankruptcy. The collapse of the state banking system and the failure of the "Forty Thieves" as the independents were called, led to impassioned pleas for relief that led to a political struggle known as the "relief wars."

Steamboats now ply mid-America rivers

Missouri River, September

The Western Engineer achieved a first this month in the continuing effort to harness the Missouri River. It became the first steamboat to voyage up the river to Council Bluffs. The "crew" included some of America's leading artists and scientists.

The Missouri River expedition, led by Major Stephen H. Long and sponsored by Secretary of War John C. Calhoun, has commissioned five steamboats to survey the Missouri. The first, the Independence, traveled 200 miles upstream as far as Franklin in May, unloading sugar, flour and whiskey. Three of the ships, carrying much of the 1,100-man force, were not built for this tortuous river and did not get far.

But the Western Engineer, which is shaped like a dragon and whose raised "head" snorts steam, draws only 20 inches of water and so has been able to push through, advancing at about three miles an hour.

The botanist Dr. William Baldwin, the landscape painter and ornithologist Samuel Seymour and the geologist Augustus Edward Jessup are aboard. Each time the boat lands, the artists and scientists go ashore to sketch the prairie and collect specimens (→Apr. 23, 1838).

Major Stephen Long meets with the Pawnees on his voyage up the Missouri.

Two court decisions limit states' powers

Chief Justice Marshall by Brooke.

Washington, D.C., March 6

Chief Justice John Marshall ruled today that a state law taxing branches of the Bank of the United States is illegal. He asserted that "implied powers" within the Constitution grant the Supreme Court authority to strike down the statute, that the decision abides by "the letter and spirit of the Constitution."

The case, McCulloch v. Maryland, was brought before the court after a cashier of a Baltimore branch of the national bank refused to pay a tax. Local bankers and Maryland politicians had collaborated to create legislation requiring the tax, some say with the aim of forcing the national bank out of business. The court ruled that if the state law won legitimacy, states would have the right "to tax the mail, [and] tax the mint . . . which would defeat all ends of the (federal) government."

States' rights suffered another blow February 2, when the court decided the Dartmouth College v. Woodward case. The state of New Hampshire had passed a law revoking the charter granted to the trustees of Dartmouth College in the colonial era. After hearing an eloquent argument for Dartmouth by a young lawyer and graduate of the school, Daniel Webster, the court ruled against the state and confirmed the sanctity of private contracts from federal or state usurpation. Marshall wrote that the state law had intended "to convert a literary institution . . . under the control of private literary men, into a machine entirely subservient to the will of the government."

Alabama in union as a slave state

Huntsville, Alabama, Dec. 14

Alabama became the 22nd state in the union today as President James Monroe signed a congressional statehood act. The measure put into force the constitution that was adopted during a convention held here in July. Huntsville will be the capital of the new state. Former territorial Governor William Wyatt Bibb has been named the state Governor. Although the constitution has a bill of rights, it is not applicable to Negroes because the constitution recognizes slavery. No opposition to this constitution was voiced in Congress. The slavery provision in the Alabama constitution is much the same as those in force in all the Southern states as well as in some of the states in the North.

Channing defends Unitarian beliefs

Channing, at odds with Calvinism's unbending view of human nature.

Baltimore, Maryland, May 5

The Rev. William Ellery Channing departed from custom in his sermon at Jared Spark's ordination today and spoke to the values and meanings of Unitarianism rather than the duties of a minister. Channing argued that Unitarianism is not only scriptural but is also truer than Trinitarianism. The minister held that the doctrine of the Trinity "acknowledges in words" what it "subverts in practice," namely the unity of God. Channing called for a critical analysis of scripture: "It is because scripture is authoritative for belief that it demands close scrutiny. To do otherwise, risks failing to correctly understand God and the ministry of Jesus."

Americans acquire all of Spanish Florida

Washington, D.C., Feb. 22

All of Spanish Florida is now officially under American authority, according to a treaty signed today with Spain. The accord between Secretary of State John Quincy Adams and Spanish Minister Don Luis de Onis also settles larger issues relating to American control of Spanish claims in the West.

Under treaty terms, the United States is assuming $5 million in claims against Spain. The Spanish, in turn, are ceding all territories east of the Mississippi River, regions known as East and West Florida.

The treaty was signed just two weeks after Congress declined to censure General Andrew Jackson for his unauthorized military conquest of the Spanish settlements in Florida last year.

The United States has long been claiming Florida as its own, and conflicts have periodically surfaced between the two nations over the Florida territories. Americans have been plagued by Florida Indian raids, and the Southern states have rankled over runaway slave strongholds that the Spanish permitted to develop. The treaty ends more than 300 years of Spanish domination of Florida (→Apr. 15, 1821).

Savannah crosses Atlantic in 27 days

Liverpool, England, June 20

Captain Moses Rogers sailed the Savannah into Liverpool today, the first steamer to cross the Atlantic. As onlookers watched the ship leave Savannah, Georgia, 27 days ago, some were calling her "the steam coffin." While the ship needed wind power to complete its journey, Rogers still made the critics eat their words. Last month, the Independence became the first steamboat to traverse the lower Missouri River.

Florida, site of the continent's first European settlements. In exchange, for the area, the U.S. has renounced claims to Texas and canceled Spain's debt.

Odd Fellows come to United States

Baltimore, Maryland

At the behest of Thomas Wildey, the initiated are entering into Odd Fellowship in America. The Independent Order of Odd Fellows, a secret society, traces its roots to 1745. But others claim it began six years ago in Manchester, England, when part of the United Order tired of too much drinking and created its own group. It has grown popular quickly because of generous benefits for orphans, widows and the ill.

1820

Monroe

Washington, D.C., Jan. 23. House authorizes Maine's admission to union as a free state (→March 15).

United States, February. Military refuses to accept Negroes.

Honolulu, March 30. First American missionaries arrive from New England aboard brig Thadeus.

Roanoke, Virginia, Apr. 12. Term "doughface" popularized by John Randolph, for Northern Congressmen easily molded into Southern sympathizers.

Rocky Mountains, July 15. Edwin James, member of Stephen Long's expedition, scales Pike's Peak [unsuccessfully attempting to rename it for himself].

Portland, Nov. 17. Longfellow publishes his first poem, *The Battle of Lovell's Pond*, in *Portland Maine Gazette.*

Hitchcockville, Connecticut. Lambert Hitchcock opens a chair factory.

New York and New Hampshire. First state-supported libraries established.

United States. General Synod of Lutheran Churches formed.

Washington, D.C. White property owners granted permission to vote for city mayor.

Washington, D.C. Ithiel Town granted a patent for Town lattice truss, revolutionizing bridge construction.

Arkansas. Comet is first steamboat on Arkansas River.

Maine. State constitution gives suffrage and school privileges to all, regardless of race.

Arkansas. Government treaties with Cherokee Indians give tribe large areas in western Arkansas; whites intrude only to be expelled by government.

California. More than 20,000 Indian slaves now live in California missions.

New York. *U.S. Pharmacopoeia*, government-approved list of medical drugs, established by Lyman Spalding.

United States. Sir Walter Scott's *Ivanhoe* is published here [and sells 2.5 million copies].

DEATH

Missouri Territory, Sept. 26. Daniel Boone, legendary frontiersman (*Nov. 2, 1734).

Missouri Compromise is passed

Washington, D.C., March 15

Congress reached a compromise on the issue of slavery today by admitting Maine as a free state and Missouri as a slave state. The debate on the question of slavery was so rancorous, so vindictive that Thomas Jefferson said it seemed to him "like a fire bell in the night."

A great number of Americans feel that if the nation's leaders are not able to come up with some solution to the problem of slavery, it may well tear the country apart. As of last year, the numbers were even, the same number of slave states as free states. But the application of Maine for statehood upset that balance. A solution was to emerge. It came in the form of an agreement effected by Senator Jesse B. Thomas of Illinois, who seized the opportunity provided by Maine's application to frame the compromise measure. He proposed, as an amendment to the Missouri statehood bill, that Maine be admitted as a free state, Missouri as a slave state, and that slavery be prohibited north of 36 degrees 30 minutes in the Louisiana Purchase area.

The question of Missouri's admission to the union has proved to be the most important political issue not only in Washington, but also across the entire country, for the last three years. There are constitutional debates wherever leaders gather, and the disputes between regions are growing more bitter by the day, so much so that many politicians foresee the possibility of open hostilities, even war.

The growth of Missouri and other parts of the West has led to a struggle between North and South over who will finally control the nation's destiny (→Aug. 10, 1821).

Seedbed of tragedy. Forced march to slave markets on the African coast.

Free Negroes sail to colony in Africa

New York City, Feb. 6

A ship christened the Mayflower of Liberia left New York harbor today for Sierra Leone in West Africa with 86 free Negroes aboard. Sierra Leone is the home of a colony of freed slaves, founded about 30 years ago by British abolitionists.

The "colonization" of Africa by free Negroes from America has been a hotly debated issue in recent years. In 1816, the American Colonization Society was founded, including members such as Francis Scott Key and Henry Clay, to "rid our country of a useless and pernicious, if not dangerous, portion of its population," meaning free Negroes. The Negroes themselves have been divided on the migration issue. In 1788, the Negro Union of Newport, Rhode Island, called for an exodus of Negroes to Africa, but it was opposed by the Philadelphia Free African Society. In 1816, Negroes gathered in many major cities to protest the idea of colonization, which would amount to exile from their native land (→1822).

Slave trade classed as piracy by Congress

Washington, D.C., May 15

Congress has taken steps toward designating the slave trade a form of piracy, thus threatening slave importers with the kind of penalties meted out to pirates, including death. The move involves negotiations with Britain and other countries, hopefully to produce a treaty that would authorize the seizure of slave ships along the coasts of Africa, America and the West Indies. A law passed in 1808 made the importation of slaves from Africa illegal and imposing heavy fines on those who knowingly trafficked in illegally imported slaves. This law has been widely violated. Slavery is still legal and practiced in most of the Southern states.

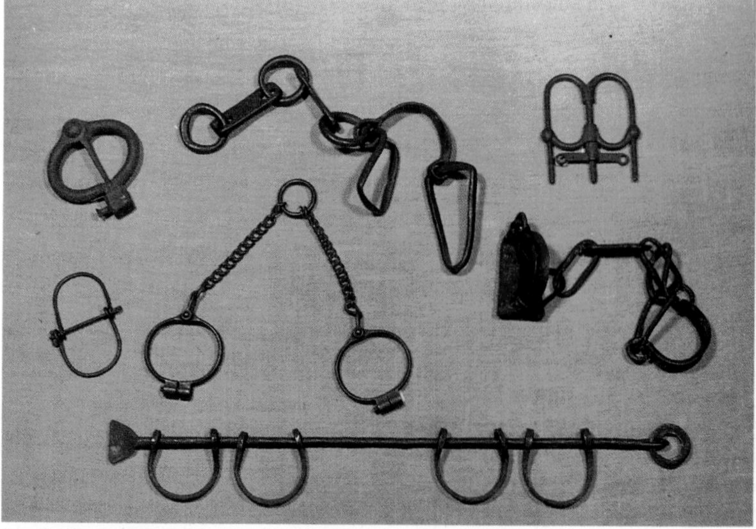

Trade in the instruments of oppression has supported many a blacksmith.

Monroe re-elected, with Tompkins V.P.

Washington, D.C., Dec. 6

President James Monroe won a landslide re-election victory today, garnering an astounding 231 electoral votes to just one cast for his opponent, Secretary of State John Quincy Adams. Vice President Daniel D. Tompkins was also re-elected. Both the President and Vice President are Democratic-Republicans. Adams, once a nominal Federalist, ran as an independent. The Federalist Party has continued to lose strength in recent years.

President Monroe, 62, won his first term in 1816, succeeding a fellow Virginia member of the Democratic-Republican Party, James Madison. In fact, four of the first five Presidents were Virginians, including Washington and Jefferson.

A major issue facing the Monroe administration in its second term is whether to admit Missouri into the union as a slave state, a move opposed by Northerners in Congress (→March 5, 1821).

Land prices cut; speculators profit

Washington, D.C., March 9

Congress passed the Land Act of 1820 today, paving the way for westward expansion – expansion, that is, for rich land speculators.

The legislation reduces the minimum price for property from $2 an acre to $1.25 and limits tracts of land to 80 acres. But settlers are denied credit. Since laws were enacted in 1800 that established property credit, pioneers of the Western frontier domesticated the raw land. However, many purchasers under the credit system failed to make profits and have defaulted on their obligations. The federal Treasury has been forced to pay the losses. The new law will prevent such delinquencies.

Lawmakers believe the act will speed the cultivation of fertile soils in the West to supplement the weak harvests of New England farms and for the sale of crops to European markets. Settlers see the law only as an enhancement to the rich.

Nation at 10 million; New York, 124,000

"Horizon of the New World," a quaint view of the new looking toward the old.

New York City

The population of the United States is 9,638,453, according to the nation's fourth census. This figure includes all inhabitants except Indians, who do not pay taxes. New York is the largest city with 124,000, and Philadelphia ranks second with 113,000. Since the last census, 10 years ago, the country has admitted five more states, for a total of 22. Over the decade, the population has grown by approximately 30 percent. It is estimated that 72 percent of the Americans who work are in agriculture, and 90 percent of the Negro population of almost 1.8 million are slaves. The first census was taken in 1790, and the population at that time came to 3,929,214. The survey has since become a far more detailed affair, including information regarding manufacturers, an addition that was arranged by Secretary of State John Quincy Adams.

Washington Irving's "Sketch-book" out

New York City, September

Good news for devotees of America's most acclaimed author. The newest string of fanciful tales by Washington Irving, *Rip Van Winkle, The Legend of Sleepy Hollow*, and others, which caused a sensation when they first appeared in the *Evening Post* and other New York papers in May, have now been brought out in a volume entitled *The Sketch-book.* The 36-year-old author, who has been living in Europe since May 1815, is reportedly overwhelmed by the enthusiastic response to his latest work. In a recent letter from London, Irving expressed his reaction: "I feel almost appalled by such success, and fearful that it cannot be real."

Twenty years later. "The Return of Rip Van Winkle" (1849) by J. Quidor.

Democracy in dress: Long pants for men

Summer

Trousers appear to have permanently supplanted breeches as the garb of men's choice. For centuries, the French peasantry wore the rather shapeless "pantalons"; since they came to power with the French Revolution three decades ago, their sympathizers in America have expressed their support with every trousered step they take. Knee-length breeches are seen only on older gentlemen who are set in their ways. Yet how many dandies standing in the heat of the noonday sun in their democratically correct full-length pants do not envy their elders in light, aristocratic breeches?

Revolutionary long pants from France. The shape of things to come.

1821

Monroe

Mexico, Jan. 17. Mexico issues grant to Moses Austin to settle 300 families in Texas (→Autumn, 1822).

Washington, D.C., March 3. Supreme Court's ruling in Cohens v. Virginia reaffirms federal courts' right to overrule state court decisions.

Washington, D.C., March 5. James Monroe and Daniel Tompkins inaugurated for second term; Cabinet remains the same.

Washington, D.C., Apr. 15. President Monroe names General Andrew Jackson Governor of Florida region (→July 17).

Boston, Oct. 18. Music book by Lowell Mason, including hymn *Nearer my God to thee*, published; [it goes through 22 editions, sells over 50,000 copies and earns $30,000].

Fredonia, New York. Nation's first natural gas well tapped.

Columbus, Mississippi. First public school in state, Franklin Academy, opens.

Alabama. A patrol system established to prevent escape of slaves.

United States. Thomas Jefferson and James Madison, while supporting cause of emancipation, argue that persistent prejudices would make multiracial coexistence impossible.

Maine. State law declares mixed marriages void.

Texas. Samuel Isaaks, first recorded Jewish settler in Texas, arrives with Stephen F. Austin.

Baltimore. Cathedral of the Assumption, nation's first, is consecrated.

United States. Hudson's Bay Company and North West Company merge.

New York. The African Company, first all-Negro acting troupe, begins performing classics and popular melodramas.

United States. Samuel Lovett Waldo completes portrait *Major General Andrew Jackson*.

Mt. Pleasant, Ohio. One of first abolition journals, *The Genius of Universal Emancipation*, issued by Quaker Benjamin Lundy.

United States. James Fenimore Cooper's *The Spy* published.

United States. Magazine *Saturday Evening Post* founded.

Russia claims northwestern Pacific coast

St. Petersburg, Russia, Sept. 4

Declaring that Russian influence extends as far south as Oregon, Czar Alexander announced today that Alaskan waters are closed to all foreigners. This will immediately hit Yankee whalers, who traditionally fish these waters. The Czar's declaration may also create a diplomatic incident, since part of the area the Czar claims is now being disputed by both the United States and Britain. By signing a piece of paper, the Czar has moved the Russian American Company's boundary from 55 degrees north to 51 degrees. Insiders see this as a bid by the Czar to profit from the company's position in America. The Russian government reissued the company's charter, which expired two years ago, and there are indications the Czar will expand his exploration program (→July 24, 1822).

Rugged pioneer shows way to Santa Fe

Franklin, Missouri, November

William Becknell, a famed Indian fighter and veteran of the War of 1812, left here last month in search of a trade route to Santa Fe, Mexico. He got there, but the trip wasn't easy. During the first encampment, 20 of the expedition's horses, frightened by night-roaming buffalo, scattered across the prairie and had to be rounded up the next day. Later, two of Becknell's men were seized by Osage warriors, stripped of their horses, guns and clothing, and "barbarously whipped." Becknell now offers a warning to other venturesome pioneers: Keep a strict guard against Indians when crossing Osage territory. And for other Missourians who might set out to do business in Spanish-held Santa Fe, he has this advice: "Take goods of excellent quality and unfaded colors."

Compromise gives Missouri statehood

Springfield, Missouri, Aug. 10

Missouri's legislature today declared its acceptance of the final phase of a compromise, "by a solemn public act," thus ending more than three years of political struggle over the question of Negro slavery in the westward expansion of the United States. The first phase of the Missouri Compromise, as it has become known, did not end the acrimonious debate, and a second compromise was found by the House of Representatives over a clause in Missouri's constitution that concerned free Negroes. The sectional rivalry generated by Missouri's admission to statehood has become a reality, and the slave-owning minority, in the South, has succeeded in maintaining the concept that its property interests are synonymous with the welfare of the region. The final phase of the compromise was accepted by the Senate on February 28 (→May 26, 1836).

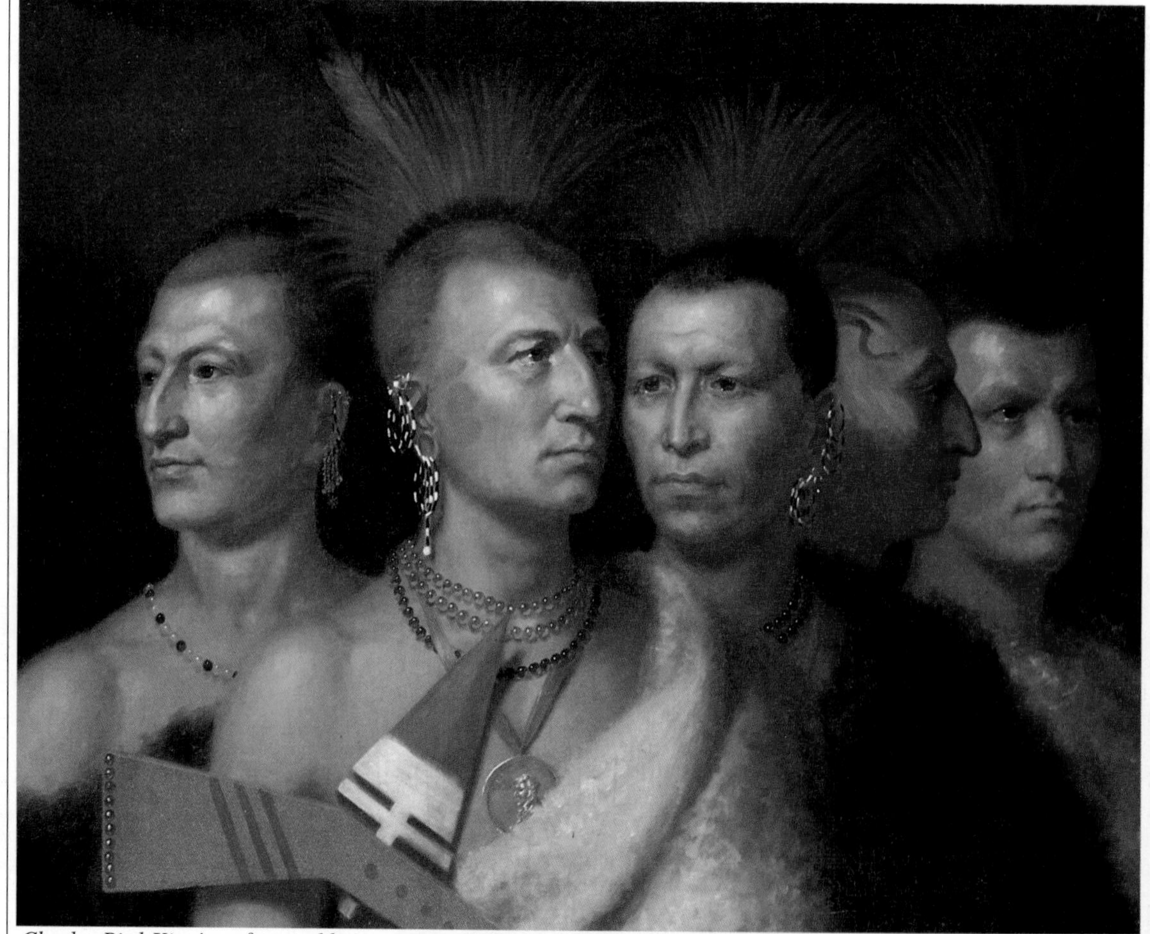

Charles Bird King's unforgettable masterpiece "Young Omaha, War Eagle, Little Missouri, and Pawnees" (1821).

86-symbol Cherokee alphabet is invented

Sequoyah with his new "syllabary."

Oklahoma, Winter

Linguistic experts report that a Cherokee Indian named Sequoyah has developed an 86-letter alphabet that promises to help unlock the mysteries of native American languages. The erudite Sequoyah borrowed many symbols from an English grammar book, then created other "marks" as they were needed. His alphabet enables virtually anyone who can speak Cherokee, once he has learned the sight and sound of the 86 characters and symbols, to read and write the difficult language. Cherokee is an Iroquoian tongue, spoken in Tennessee primarily, and in Georgia and elsewhere in the South. It is closely related to other languages in this family, which includes Mohawk, Oneida and Seneca-Cayuga.

While not much has been learned of Sequoyah's life, it is said that he is a hunter, a trader and a silversmith. He was apparently born in Tuskegee, Tennessee, probably between 1760 and 1765. Because his Indian name is translated as "Hog's Foot" and it is an old custom among the Cherokees to name their people after physical characteristics, there is speculation that Sequoyah has a clubfoot that leaves a hoof-like print in the ground.

Crockett, killer of bears, elected to office

Tennessee, 1821

The Tennessee Legislature need fear no marauding bears: Davy Crockett has been sworn into office as a state legislator.

The 34-year-old Crockett is perhaps best known for his boast that, after settling in the western Tennessee wilderness, he killed 105 bears in seven months. He is also a distinguished soldier, having fought under General Andrew Jackson in the Creek War. Crockett comes to the legislature after serving as a justice of the peace in 1817 and earning the rank of colonel in the Tennessee militia the following year.

A native of Greene County in eastern Tennessee, Crockett is the son of a tavern keeper. His father is reported to have hired him out to the wealthier backwoodsmen of the region. As a result, the young Crockett had little formal schooling – anywhere from five days to 100 days in all, depending on who is telling the story. But Crockett, whose lack of education seems to have a special appeal to his similarly unschooled constituents, actually capitalizes on his homespun character. He once said that he regarded proper spelling as "contrary to nature." He is twice married, his first wife having died in 1815.

Davy Crockett, master of the homespun yarn, was elected despite his total lack of formal education.

Chouteau opens trading post in Missouri

Chouteau's Landing, Missouri

French fur traders, led by Francois Chouteau, have established a trading post here at the junction of the Kansas and Missouri Rivers. The Chouteau family intends to build fur trading posts all along the river so that the furs can be shipped south, but there are a host of problems. From Grand River to Kaw, the Missouri River is rough on navigators. It is full of shallows, narrow chutes, snags and bars, bends and eddies, drifts of logs, even "traveling islands." Lewis and Clark, who previously examined the region during their Louisiana Purchase expedition, had many problems here. But the rewards are probably worth the risks. The country abounds in resources, in game, in fruit such as apples, papaws and mulberries.

Emma Willard founds academy for women

Troy, New York, Autumn

Mrs. Emma Willard, an instructor of young women, has accepted students to Troy Female Seminary, the second college for women to be established in the United States. The first was her own Waterford Academy, which opened in Waterford, New York, two years ago and closed quickly due to a lack of promised state aid. Mrs. Willard has no intention of making her college a mere charm school: She will have a curriculum that stresses mathematics, history and philosophy. Raised in Berlin, Connecticut, the 34-year-old Mrs. Willard became cognizant of geometry and economics the only way she knew how, by reading over the shoulder of a nephew who was enrolled at Middlebury College in Vermont.

Phrenology gaining popularity in U.S.

Kentucky

If you live in Kentucky, you ought to have your head examined. So says the phrenologist Charles Taylor Caldwell, who is gaining fame as an "American Spurzheim," a reference to Johann Kaspar Spurzheim, a German founder of phrenology. The new "science" holds that a person's psychological traits can be determined by feeling 37 "organs" on the skull. Caldwell boned up on phrenology during an expedition sponsored by Kentucky's Transylvania University.

Jackson takes over Florida from Spain

Pensacola, Florida, July 17

Andrew Jackson, scourge of the Spanish and the Seminoles, rode triumphantly into Pensacola today for the third time in his career – this time to receive the territory from Spain and to take office as Governor. In a ceremony this morning, Governor Callava officially gave control to Jackson and released Floridians from their allegiance to Spain. Jackson, who is known as "Old Hickory," gave up his general's commission in May to accept the presidential appointment.

The 1821 gold half-eagle, part of a national coinage system based on the Spanish model. In July, $5 million went to Spain in return for Florida.

1822

Monroe

Philadelphia, January. Nicholas Biddle replaces Langdon Cheves as president of Bank of United States (→ Dec. 8, 1829).

Nashville, January. *Nashville Gazette* endorses Andrew Jackson for President, sparking West's interest in presidential politics (→ July 20).

Philadelphia, April. Meeting of trustees of St. Mary's Catholic Church results in rioting between supporters of two different priests.

California, April. Spanish flag lowered throughout California (→ Nov. 29).

Washington, D.C., May 4. Congress allots President Monroe $100,000 to open diplomatic missions in independent Latin American nations (→ Nov.).

South Carolina, July. State restricts movement of free Negroes, including temporary jailing of Negro seaman on shore leave.

New York, Oct. 27. Rochester and Albany are linked as 280-mile section of Erie Canal opens (→ Oct. 25, 1825).

Vienna, November. Holy Alliance of Austria, France, Prussia and Russia pledge support to Spain in her attempt to recover lost colonies in New World (→ Dec. 12).

United States. William Church invents mechanical typesetter.

New Haven, Connecticut. College officials prohibit playing a form of football at Yale.

United States. Congress abolishes factor system for regulating Indian trade.

United States. John Jacob Astor organizes a Western department of his American Fur Company as his operations extend westward.

Philadelphia. Philadelphia College of Pharmacy, first of its kind, established.

New York City. During yellow fever epidemic, thousands flee north to rural Greenwich Village.

Massachusetts. Water-powered cotton mills begin operation.

United States. Romantic treatment of Indians becomes popular in American literature.

Philadelphia. Economist and publisher Mathew Carey publishes pro-tariff *Essays on Political Economy*.

U.S. recognizing Latin American states

Simon Bolivar, known as "The Liberator," led Colombia to independence from Spain three years ago.

In Mexico, Augustin de Iturbide, a royalist until two years ago, is the most unlikely of revolutionaries.

Washington, D.C., Dec. 12

Mexico's new revolutionary government, headed by Augustin de Iturbide, was granted formal recognition today. This initiative is the latest American effort to aid the rebellions of the Latin American colonies against Spain. The Monroe administration asked Congress for $100,000 in March to set up diplomatic missions in the newly independent Latin countries. In June, President Monroe extended diplomatic recognition to Gran Colombia. He also recommended the eventual recognition of Argentina, Chile and Peru. The recognition by the United States is the first accorded to any of these revolutionary governments by a major power. However, Washington promises no financial or military assistance to the new countries. Diplomatic experts argue that such help would be necessary if the European powers should attempt to recover the former colonies – which appears to be a real possibility (→ Jan. 23, 1823).

Tennessee wants Jackson for President

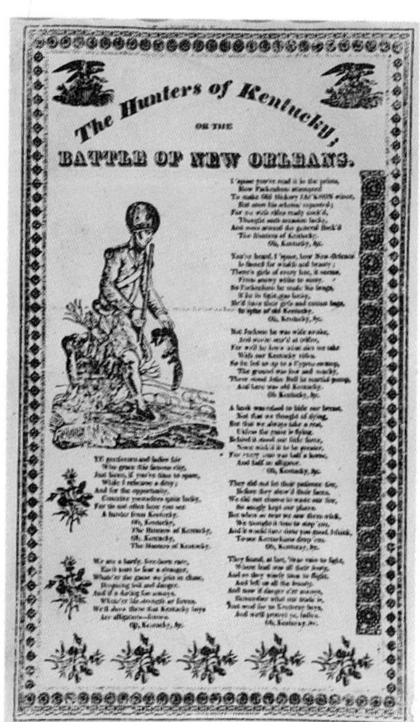

The Hunters of Kentucky, or the Battle of New Orleans.

A celebration of Jackson's greatest military victory. His army career may be his biggest political asset.

Nashville, Tennessee, July 20

In a radical departure from tradition, the Tennessee Legislature today nominated Andrew Jackson, a favorite son, to run for President. The move resulted from the efforts of a small group of faithful followers who saw the death of the Federalist Party as an opportunity for their candidate to gain office. It was these friends who successfully maneuvered the legislature into the formal nomination of their hero. Jackson is best known for his exploits while a major general of the Tennessee militia, a position he held when the War of 1812 broke out. Jackson offered his services to the federal government, and he was given a command in the field. In January of 1815, Jackson led a force against a British army that was in the process of invading New Orleans and scored a resounding victory.

California now part of a free Mexico

Monterey, California, Nov. 29

It's official! Mexico became a republic today, and the repercussions of independence from Spain are already being felt here. Luis Antonio Arguello, head of the port of San Francisco, is the new Governor of California, which became part of Mexico after Spanish settlement began in 1769. Symbolically, Arguello is replacing the word "imperial" with "nacional" on papers, dropping the title "don" for "ciudad" or citizen, and removing the motto "God and liberty" from letters. Now the Governor is forming a six-man legislative unit of pueblos and presidio district aides.

Austin establishes settlement in Texas

New Orleans, Autumn

Stephen F. Austin has established the first American settlement in the Mexican territory of Texas. Austin, formerly a member of the legislature in Missouri, inherited some 200,000 acres from his father, Moses, in Texas. Mexico is permitting Austin to arrange for a group of settlers to form a community along the San Antonio River. He says he expects many land-hungry frontiersmen to take up lands in the new domain (→ Dec. 20, 1835).

Austin, in his father's footsteps.

Free Negro hanged for plotting revolt

Charleston, South Carolina, July 2

With the betrayal of an elaborate plot for a slave uprising, conspiracy leader Denmark Vesey was hanged today, along with 34 other revolutionaries. Vesey, a former slave who purchased his freedom with money won in a lottery, organized a revolution based on a system of cells, with only cell leaders having knowledge of the full plot. The city and military installations of Charleston were to be seized and whites were to be eradicated. In spite of the plotters' secrecy and careful planning, authorities learned of the revolt, set for July 16, and arrested Vesey and 130 other Negroes.

Liberia colony is started by freed slaves

Exodus. A boatload of freed slaves arrives in the harbor of Monrovia.

Cape Mesurado, Liberia

The American Colonization Society has purchased a site here in West Africa to establish a colony of free Negroes from America. The society appointed a Congregationalist minister, the Rev. Jehudi Ashmun, as the head of the colony and he is responsible for the survival of the immigrants. In its first year, the colony, dubbed Monrovia, has been beset with fever and attacks by Africans. This wave of colonists in Liberia was preceded last year by a Norfolk, Virginia, group called the First Baptist Church of Monrovia. There has been a British settlement of former slaves in the region for more than 30 years.

Colonization of West Africa by free Negroes from the United States has been a popular and controversial issue for several years. In 1809, Thomas Jefferson advocated the removal of Negroes from white society, for the purpose of preserving what he called the purity of the white race. In 1816, the American Colonization Society was founded to facilitate the removal of what some considered to be an undesirable element, free Negroes. The early proclamations of this group were met with widespread protests from Negroes in most of the major cities. The idea of colonization has been opposed by many Negroes and some abolitionist groups who support emancipation and education of Negroes and feel they must be treated as native citizens in the land of their birth (→ 1833).

Cumberland Road toll bill is vetoed

Washington, D.C., May 4

President Monroe today vetoed the Cumberland Road Toll Bill, a measure to provide federal funds to repair the nation's first federal highway. In his message to Congress, the President argued that the Constitution prohibits heavy federal involvement in such public works. Congress authorized the Cumberland Road, also called the National Road, in 1806 to stretch from Cumberland, Maryland, through parts of Pennsylvania and Virginia to a point on the Ohio River. Construction began in 1811, but work was halted during the War of 1812. The first section was completed in 1818.

America warns Czar of military force

Washington D.C., July 24

President Monroe sent a sharp warning to Czar Alexander today that the Russians must not establish a physical presence on the Pacific Coast in an area claimed as American territory and that any steps to do so would be met by force. The United States and Britain have vigorously resisted the Russian policy of barring foreign ships from coming within 100 miles of land Russia claims. This policy has hurt the fur trade and caused legal problems in areas disputed by Britain, the U.S. and Russia (→ Apr. 17, 1824).

Control of fur trade in Rockies sought

St. Louis, Missouri, March 22

William Henry Ashley, a former lieutenant governor and general in the state militia, is advertising for mountain men to travel to the source of the Missouri River and develop the fur trade. Ashley, and his partner, Andrew Henry, will face many problems, including the hostile Blackfoot Indians, who are experts at horse stealing and will do anything to keep white men out of their territory. Missourians and other Americans in the fur trade consider the Rocky Mountains as an area of tremendous potential.

Wounded man is a medical showcase

Mackinac, Michigan, June 6

Struck by an accidental shotgun blast, a French-Canadian fur trader named Alexis St. Martin has become the subject of an important medical study. The wound in St. Martin's side has healed, but it has left a small hole into the stomach of the otherwise healthy man. An Army surgeon, Dr. William Beaumont, has begun observations of the actions of St. Martin's stomach and of the fluids inside it. This is the first study that has ever been conducted with a functioning digestive system.

"The Old House of Representatives" by Samuel F.B. Morse, who has written of his desire "to rival the genius of a Raphael, a Michelangelo or a Titian."

Bread and cheese and culture in N.Y.

New York City

Once a week, the brightest intellectual lights of New York can all be found in one room sharing a simple Bread and Cheese Lunch, which also happens to be the humble name of an elite club whose members include the painter-scientist Samuel F.B. Morse, the poet William Cullen Bryant and the jurist James Kent. The group's founder, a newcomer to the city, is James Fenimore Cooper, 33, author of *The Spy*, a novel published last year that has gone through several printings and won praise from British critics.

1823

Monroe

Washington, D.C., February. Supreme Court rules in Green v. Biddle that a contract between two states is as valid as one between private parties.

Boston, Apr. 13. After hearing a program of Anthony Heinrich's music, a critic hails him as "the first regular or general American composer . . ."

New Orleans, May 8. Gas lights are used to illuminate a theatrical production at American Theater.

Boston, Nov. 5. Father William Taylor becomes first Roman Catholic priest to deliver invocation at opening session of Massachusetts General Court.

Troy, New York, Dec. 23. *Troy Sentinel* publishes poem entitled *A Visit from St. Nicholas* [*Twas the Night Before Chistmas*], without name or permission of Clement Clarke Moore [who publishes it himself in 1847].

United States. Samuel Pennock granted a patent for a revolving hay rake.

Mississippi. State law prohibits gatherings of more than five Negroes and prohibits teaching them to read and write.

New York. Seeking to apply Bible to daily life, Brigham Young joins Methodists.

Wyoming. Term "great desert" used to describe Wyoming by Dr. Edwin James, chronicler of Stephen Long's expedition.

Concord, Vermont. Samuel R. Hall establishes nation's first teachers' school.

North Dakota. Stephen Long's survey expedition designates a point north of Pembina as official boundary between United States and Canada.

Washington, D.C. Congress passes legislation requiring federal regulation of all mail sent by steamer.

Europe. Lord Byron devotes seven stanzas to Daniel Boone in *Don Juan*, giving Boone posthumous international fame.

United States. American Tract Society founded to publish religious and moral magazines and pamphlets.

United States. *The Pioneer*, first of *Leatherstocking Tales*, and *The Pilot*, his first sea novel, are published by James Fenimore Cooper.

Smith says angel discloses hidden book

"Moroni's Appearance to Joseph Smith" (1869-70) by Carl Christensen.

Palmyra, New York, Sept. 21

Joseph Smith says that the angel Moroni appeared to him, telling him the location of a hidden religious book made of gold leaves. He says that the book, which is supposed to be buried in this area, tells the story of the lost tribes of Israel and their life in present-day America. It also supposedly tells of the true nature of a Christian Church that is in need of restoration. Along with the book, he says, is buried a giant breastplate, and attached to it are two magic stones that provide one with the ability to interpret the book, written as it is in some unkown ancient script.

The 18-year-old Smith has been the subject of much ridicule in the past. Even in this region of overheated religious passions and activities, Smith has been an oddity. An ardently religious child much given to dreaming, he claimed three years ago that he beheld a vision of the Father and the Son. He said he approached them to ask which of myriad religious sects was true and which he should join. He claims that the vision informed him that none were true and that he should not join any of them, but should wait, instead, for the messenger of God. After word of this alleged vision was made public, the entire Smith family became the target of abuse and persecution. His latest revelation may just increase the hostility (→Sept. 22, 1827).

Latest in fashion is the spencer, a long-sleeved jacket fitted to a high waistline just below the bust.

Argentina and Chile recognized by U.S.

Washington, D.C., Jan. 23

The United States today gave formal recognition to Argentina and Chile. The South American colonies had been in a state of revolt against their Spanish masters for years. Today's American diplomatic initiative offically recognizes the successful revolutions and goes far in welcoming the nations to the world community of independent republics. Many observers, however, believe Spain and other European monarchies will attempt to recover the lost colonies by force. How the U.S. would respond to such a move is unclear (→Nov. 7).

Hawaiian rulers die on visit to England

London, July 14

Both King Kamehameha II and Queen Kamamalu of the Hawaiian Islands have succumbed to measles, physicians announced today. Their deaths leave the islands with a 9-year-old ruler, Prince Kauikeaouli, who was designated heir to the throne before the fateful voyage. Since Dowager Queen Kaahumanu had been named Regent pro tem, she will reign until Kauikeaouli reaches the age of 18. Before the royal couple sailed from Honolulu last November to visit King George IV, courtiers had advised them not to go because the kahunas had foreseen their never returning (→1824).

Sour mash distilling started in Kentucky

Kentucky

A new way of distilling Kentucky corn whiskey has made this American spirit – called "bourbon" after the county from which it comes – even better. A Scotsman, Dr. James C. Crow, has started "sour mashing," a process in which corn meal is first scalded with the thin, spent "beer" (the working yeast) left over from the last batch in the still. The whiskey gains a special flavor and character, not really sour but faintly sweet. Crow's distillery and product are showing the way in the industry.

U.S. croons "Home, Sweet Home," too

United States, Autumn

Americans are humming a new tune, "Home, Sweet Home." Written by Sir Henry Bishop, it took London by storm not long ago, and now the music is selling like hotcakes here. In fact, it may soon edge out "There's Nothing True but Heav'n." Composed in 1816 by Oliver Shaw, America's top songwriter, "Heav'n" rarely leaves a dry eye in the house. After several printings, it has earned Shaw $1,000. In Boston, where music can be taken quite seriously, the Bohemian Anthony Heinrich is being hailed as "the Beethoven of America."

Monroe Doctrine: No more colonizing in Americas

Washington, D.C., Dec. 2

In his annual message to Congress today, President James Monroe announced a major change in the foreign policy of the United States. No longer, President Monroe said, would the United States permit the European monarchies the privilege of interfering in the affairs of the nations of the Western Hemisphere. In addition, Monroe put the Old World on notice that the era of colonization in the New World is over. At the same time, he gave assurances to those on the other side of the Atlantic that the United States would not interfere in the affairs of Europe.

The President's so-called Monroe Doctrine came about primarily because of the increasing threat of intervention by the Holy Alliance in the newly formed Latin American republics. Last year, the members of the alliance, Russia, Prussia, Austria and France, promised Spain that they would help it recover its former Latin American colonies. To counter this possibility, Monroe and Secretary of State John Quincy Adams devised the doctrine and worded it in such a way that, in effect, the national interests of Britain would parallel those of the United States. Thus, if any or all the members of the Holy Alliance actually invades one of the Latin American countries – and the British are dead set against the strengthening of any Holy Alliance member at its expense – the invading nation will have to deal with the awesome Royal Navy. While the American military and naval forces are not strong enough to effectively resist a European intervention in this hemisphere, those of the British are more than equal to the task. Consequently, the threat of British military involvement should effectively deter any future meddling or actual intervention by the Holy Alliance – or others, for that matter, in the Western Hemisphere. The British will support the Monroe Doctrine, and the United States will enjoy the welcome prospect of peace in the Western Hemisphere, at minimal cost or risk.

Clyde O. De Land's "Birth of the Monroe Doctrine" (1912). Secretary of State Adams sits at far left. War Secretary Calhoun sits third from the right. President Monroe, who still wears old-fashioned knee breeches, stands.

Britain grew alarmed earlier this year when an attack by the Holy Alliance on the former Spanish colonies in America seemed imminent. In August, British Foreign Secretary George Canning proposed that an Anglo-American alliance be created. President Monroe rejected the idea because he believed that such a relationship would be dominated by the British and that America's policies could be manipulated by them. Last month, Secretary of State John Quincy Adams laid the offer to rest. As the secretary argued, "It would be more candid as well as dignified to avow our principles explicitly than to come in as a cockboat in the wake of the British man-of-war."

While it is President Monroe whose name has been attached to this new strategy, insiders say the policy's true inspiration is Secretary Adams. He has long argued that the United States must fulfill its destiny by becoming a major player on the world stage (→ Aug. 4, 1824).

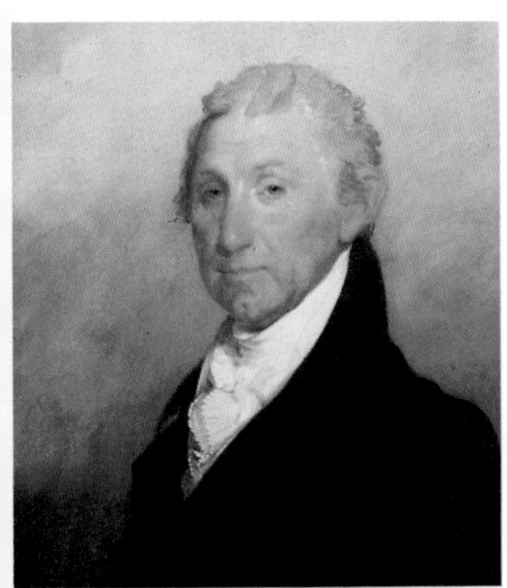

President James Monroe by Gilbert Stuart. A new era for America?

Adams spurns British help in New World

Washington D.C., Nov. 7

Secretary of State John Quincy Adams rejected out of hand today an offer by the British to ally themselves with the United States in a joint effort to thwart possible Holy Alliance intervention in Latin America. Adams's decision was tough. Former Presidents Madison and Jefferson both recommended that he accept British Foreign Secretary George Canning's offer unequivocably. Madison recently wrote Adams, saying, "My own impression is that we ought to meet the proposal of the British govt." Jefferson argued that "with her on our side we need not fear the whole world." Nevertheless, Adams turned down the British offer. The secretary, a fervent continentalist and neomercantilist, believes that Britain is not only a powerful economic rival, but that it could also be a formidable military adversary again. So Adams's advice to President Monroe is now official United States policy (→ Dec. 2).

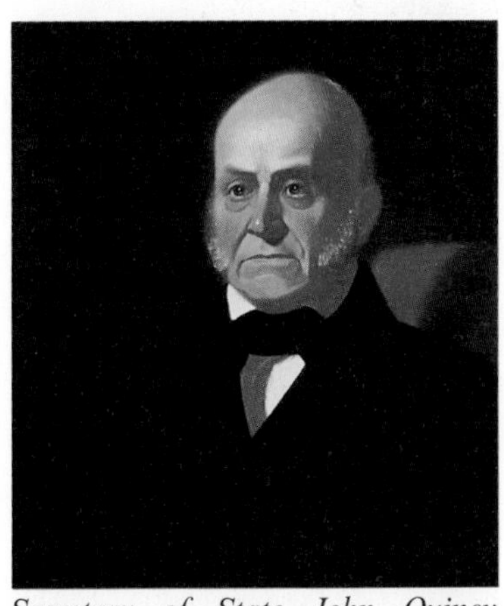

Secretary of State John Quincy Adams (c.1844) by G.C. Bingham.

1824

Monroe

Washington, D.C., Feb. 10. Congress passes General Survey Bill empowering president to direct surveys for canals and roads for national purposes.

Washington, D.C., March 2. Chief Justice John Marshall, in Gibbons v. Ogden, rules that only federal government has control over interstate trade.

Washington, D.C., May 24. President Monroe signs bill directing U.S. Army Corps of Engineers to build harbors, dams and other civil projects.

Philadelphia, May 25. American Sunday School Union formed to organize and further Sunday School activities across nation.

Washington, D.C., June 17. Bureau of Indian Affairs is established under the War Department.

United States, October. The *Workingman's Gazette* founded as one of first labor papers in United States.

Pawtucket, Rhode Island. Female weavers wage first recorded strike involving women employees in United States.

Missouri. State law enables slaves to sue for freedom.

Ohio. Assembly urges colonization of slaves after emancipation.

United States. German immigrants introduce gymnastics to American people.

Honolulu. Dowager Queen Kaahumanu becomes Regent, ruling Hawaiian Islands until her brother, Kauikeaouli, is old enough to assume throne.

Central Plains. Senator Daniel Webster describes Kansas as a worthless area.

Oklahoma. U.S. Army's westernmost outpost is named Fort Gibson.

California. Constitution of United Mexican States adopted, giving California territorial status.

Illinois. State proposal to establish slavery defeated.

Louisiana. Philanthropist Julien Poydras bequeaths $30,000 each to West Baton Rouge and Pointe Coupee parishes to be divided among every bride as a dowry.

United States. *Tales of a Traveller*, a book of Gothic stories by Washington Irving, published.

Treaty limits Russian claims to 54-40 line

Washington D.C., Apr. 17

The United States and the Czar finally settled their border dispute today. It started when Alexander moved the Russian American Company's southern boundary from 55 degrees north to 51 degrees north. The United States and Britain were already squabbling over the area and Russia's entry as a claimant made negotiations even harder.

Additionally, Russia's refusal to let foreigners into its colony created a host of problems. On land, the fur trade was hit because previously open trapping areas were closed. At sea, an arbitrary border of almost 100 miles was set as a buffer for the Russian company, letting Russians harvest the sea but not Americans or English. Also, passage into the Bering Sea from the Pacific through the Aleutian Islands was restricted.

But these problems are now history. Today's treaty sets the border at 54 degrees 40 minutes north. Further, American ships can operate within the 100-mile limit and enter all rivers in Russian territory that empty into the Pacific.

The Czar may have yielded because of Russian weakness in Europe, but experts feel the real reason is the Monroe Doctrine, which tells the Old World it may not start new colonies or expand old ones in the New World, thus blocking Russian expansion. With the expected backing of Britain's navy, America speaks from a position of strength.

Traders led West via Rockies' South Pass

Rocky Mountains, Winter

Word has come from the Jedediah Smith party that it has crossed the continental divide near the Idaho country. According to reliable reports, the group of fur traders must have gone through the South Pass. That pass was first discovered in 1812, but its actual location has long been forgotten. The 24-year-old Smith is considered to be a real "mountain man" even though he is originally from New York. Friends say that Smith was given a book about the Lewis and Clark expedition 10 years ago and that he has been "Westering" ever since. He gained his first experience in the West three years ago when he was a member of Major Henry's Yellowstone expedition. During that journey, Smith was attacked by a savage grizzly bear, lost an ear and was almost killed.

Smith and his party spent much of this winter at a friendly Indian village in the Rockies. From a deerskin and sand map furnished by the Crow Indians, he was instructed on how to get to the South Pass and across the Rockies. By the end of February, his party struck out for the pass, and at last report, had successfully managed what seems to be the only viable route across the divide. Other fur traders report that Smith and his men are now headed toward the Sweetwater country at the southern extreme of the Wind River mountain range.

Spending the winter with friendly Indians. Painting by Frederic Remington.

Congress enacts protective tariffs

Clay (1821) by Charles Bird King.

Washington, D.C., May 22

After an impassioned appeal by the lawyer-statesman Henry Clay, Congress today approved by a narrow margin the Tariff Act of 1824. The protectionist measure was supported by grain, wool and manufacturing states and opposed by shipping, fishing and other farm states. The Tariff Act is at the heart of Clay's "American System," a plan that includes protective tariffs, internal improvements and a central banking system. Clay has argued that his system would defend industries from competition and lessen the nation's dependence on foreign goods (→ Feb. 28, 1827).

Whites convicted of killing Indians

Fall Creek, Indiana, March 22

The trial of four white men charged with brutally murdering nine Indians ended today with a guilty verdict from a white jury. The four men will be the first whites ever executed in the United States for killing Indians. The nine Indians – men, women and children – were actually murdered by five men. Four of them were swiftly captured, but one has not been apprehended. At the trial, in a crowded courtroom, the prosecution followed a two-pronged strategy, appealing to the jurors' respect for the equality of all men under the law and playing on their fear of revenge by other Indians in the region.

Lafayette arrives for year-long tour

Lafayette, "hero of two worlds." Painting (1825) by Charles B. King.

New York, Aug. 14

Accompanied by his son Georges Washington Lafayette, his secretary and his valet, the Marquis de Lafayette arrived off Staten Island today for what promises to be a triumphal year-long tour as the guest of the nation. While artillery from shore batteries and warships moored in the harbor thundered salvos in his honor, Vice President Tompkins, the city's leading citizens and many old comrades-in-arms boarded the packet ship to greet the 67-year-old marquis. Hundreds of boats decked with colorful flags and pennants surrounded the ship while crowds lined the shore to welcome "home" the man they call the "hero of two worlds" (→Apr. 10, 1825)

Trapper finds big salt lake in West

Western Frontier, December

Word is that one of General William Ashley's scouts has discovered a huge salt lake west of the Rocky Mountains. Ashley, a well-known explorer, recently led an expedition into the forbidding region where the Green and the Bear Rivers flow. Jim Bridger, a veteran fur trapper and a leader in Ashley's scout corps, was reputed to be the discoverer of this previously unreported lake [Great Salt Lake, Utah]. Bridger is a tough man. As one of the trappers who knows him observed, he had "little fear of God, and none of the devil."

A Reform Judaism society is founded

Charleston, S.C., November

About 20 members of Congregation Beth Elohim here in Charleston have organized the Reformed Society of Israelites, the first organization of Reform Judaism in America. The members are from a group of 47 who petitioned for changes in the religious services, desiring "to follow the reformation which has been recently adopted by our brethren in Holland, Germany, and Prussia." Changes sought included a weekly sermon and the use of English for most prayers. Rejection of the petition led some of the petition's signers to set up the new society along Reform lines.

Whites riot because Negroes are hired

Providence, Rhode Island, October

The "Hard Scrabble" district of this town has been virtually destroyed by a mob of more than 400 whites who rioted and attacked Negro residents in a protest against their employment. The district has become home to increasing numbers of Negroes, who are moving in from the waterfront area. Four white men have been arrested and tried for their parts in the violence. Although two of the men were found guilty, they have been released on a technicality.

Empire of Brazil recognized by U.S.

Washington, D.C., Aug. 4

The United States gave formal diplomatic recognition to the newly independent Latin American nation of Brazil today. Dom Pedro, about 24 years old and son of the Portuguese royal family, is the Emperor of this former Portuguese colony. He has established what most observers consider a liberal constitution. Having gained American recognition of his empire, the next step for Don Pedro seems to be recognition by England, which will probably support him, if for no other reason than to thwart its old European enemies (→Dec. 25, 1825).

House to rule on close presidential vote

Washington, D.C., Dec. 1

The most bitterly fought presidential election in the history of the nation remains unresolved today, with no candidate having won a majority of the electoral vote. The outcome must now be decided in the House of Representatives, with each state, whether large or small, entitled to one vote.

While failing to win a majority, Andrew Jackson of Tennessee, a war hero, led with 99 votes, trailed by Secretary of State John Quincy Adams of Massachusetts, with 84; Secretary of the Treasury W.H. Crawford of Georgia, with 41, and Henry Clay of Kentucky, a leading member of Congress, with 37.

The 57-year-old Jackson, a former member of the House and now a Senator, drew his main support from states populated for the most part by Southern small planters, upland farmers and back-country residents. He was a major general in the War of 1812 and victor in the Battle of New Orleans.

Adams, also 57, is the son of the nation's second President, John Adams, and held a number of top diplomatic posts, including minister at the Hague, St. Petersburg and London. He also served in the Senate, as a Federalist, but, like others in this year's race, ran with no party label. President Monroe, who leaves office next spring, did not indicate any preference by way of a successor (→Feb. 9, 1825).

Path to the Capitol, and the presidency. Painting by Charles Burton.

Washington, D.C. *Severely damaged by the British in 1814, the area around the capital has undergone gradual recovery. Still, unable to tax federal property, the local government struggles to provide public services.*

1825

Adams

Washington, D.C., February. On the urging of John C. Calhoun, President Monroe begins policy of relocating Eastern Indians to Western frontier.

Maine, June 12. Conference of timberland operators proposes committee to conduct campaign promoting hard woods production.

New England, July 19. Discontented liberals in Congregational Church, inspired by 1819 sermon of William Ellery Channing, establish American Unitarian Association.

New York City, Nov. 4. Samuel F.B. Morse and other disgruntled members of Academy of Arts establish New York Drawing Association.

United States, Dec. 25. United States signs commercial treaty with Central American Federation, composed of five Central American nations.

United States. Homeopathy introduced into American medical practice.

United States. Gunsmith Henry Deringer designs small, single-bore pistol.

New York. Thomas Tredgold publishes first treatise on railroad engineering.

Hoboken, New Jersey. John Stevens invents steam locomotive for use on railroad lines (→May 13, 1826).

Washington, D.C. Fire in Library of Congress, second in less than 15 years, causes extensive loss and damage.

Sandwich, Massachusetts. Deming Jarves inaugurates large-scale production of mechanically pressed glass.

Tennessee. Nashoba, colony for freed slaves, founded.

Colorado. Fur traders Kit Carson and Jim Bridger penetrate interior and set up posts.

Texas. First known Scots settle in Texas.

New York City. Thomas Kensett takes out patent for first tin can in America, though invented in England by Bryan Donkin.

United States. Nation's schools begin adopting John Pierpont's *Readers*.

United States. Comprehensive American guidebook, *The American Traveller* by Daniel Hewett, published.

Adams wins presidency in House election

Adams, "minority President."

Washington, D.C., Feb. 9

John Quincy Adams was elected President today, ending an impasse of nearly two months over choosing a new chief of state. While he trailed Senator Andrew Jackson in the regular electoral count, the 57-year-old Adams, with Henry Clay's help, won a bare majority on the first ballot in the House of Representatives, with 13 votes to Jackson's seven, and Treasury Secretary W.H. Crawford's four.

The tense vote, with each state entitled to a single ballot, came on a cold and snowy winter's day, ending what the nation viewed as the murkiest campaign in its history.

While Adams, the Secretary of State under the departing Monroe, had vowed not to stoop to politicking or deals, he succumbed to the presidential lure by tacitly promising to make Clay his own Secretary of State. Clay, a Kentucky Congressman who trailed the field in the December electoral tally, when the failure of any candidate to win a majority necessitated the House vote, readily agreed. Jackson reacted angrily, saying of Clay: "The Judas of the West has closed the contract and will receive 30 pieces of silver" (→March 30, 1826).

As new Congress meets, old party expires

Washington, D.C., Dec. 12

As the new Congress convened today, one fact became startlingly clear: The Federalist Party is dead. Once dominant in the early days of the republic, the party of John Adams and John Jay, of Alexander Hamilton and John Marshall had been fatally ill for some years. And now, in the new administration of John Quincy Adams, son of one of its founders, the old party has expired. Instead, the rival Democratic-Republican Party has split into two factions in Congress, with the Adams group now in the majority.

The Federalists first emerged as a power base in the final years of the Washington administration and they succeeded in electing a President, John Adams. But when the party failed to expand beyond New England, it lost touch with a growing America and was unable to produce leaders well versed in the art of political compromise.

New utopian colony buys Indiana home

Scottish industrialist Robert Owen. Painting by Mary Ann Knight.

Harmony, Indiana, Jan. 3

Harmony is blossoming in Posey County, Indiana, where Robert Owen bought 20,000 acres of land on the Wabash River for $125,000 from George Rapp today. Rapp began the Harmony Society in 1814, and when he brought his group to Indiana to live a celibate communal life, he named the town Harmony. Owen, 54, is changing the name to New Harmony. A well-spoken industrialist from Scotland with radical ideas for social change, Owen will put those ideas into practice with all who accept his free invitation to live in New Harmony, sharing the work and property of the community. Rapp will move his Harmony Society to Pennsylvania, where it began. One difference between the projects is that Owen's is a secular endeavor, and Rapp's has a religious base (→March 29, 1827).

Charlottesville. *Chartered in 1819 at the urging of Thomas Jefferson, the University of Virginia has now opened its doors. Jefferson, who designed the buildings, wants students to play a large role in governing the school.*

New York, Nov. 29. *"Barber of Seville" at the Park Theater.*

Perkins lays out Akron on canal site

Akron, Ohio, Sept. 6

General Simon Perkins, a man who once owned so much land that he paid one-seventh of all the real estate taxes collected by the state of Ohio, has laid out the town of Akron at the highest point of the projected Ohio and Erie Canal. It was 21 years ago that General Perkins paid a little over $4 for 1,000 acres of what appeared to be worthless land. Over the two decades, he did almost nothing about his investment, that is until he realized that the canal from Cleveland would be coming through his property. Seizing an opportunity, next to the canal's first lock he laid out a town and named it Akron, Greek for "city on the hill."

Lafayette, on tour, showered with gifts

New Orleans, Apr. 10

Continuing his triumphal tour of America, the Marquis de Lafayette arrived here today to be greeted by cheering crowds, ringing bells, parades, speeches, balls and reunions. The marquis has been showered with gifts, and great care is being taken to see that he is put to no expense, for it is well known that the marquis impoverished himself while helping America win its freedom. Congress made substantial, if belated, amends in January by voting him the sum of $200,000 and a Florida township of 24,000 acres.

Douglas fir named for Scot botanist

Oregon

In two years in America, David Douglas has identified more than 200 species unknown in Europe. The Scottish botanists's most impressive find is a coniferous evergreen bearing his name: Douglas fir. Supporting wilderness whenever it comes up against commerce, he has made few friends here. Hudson's Bay Company people at Fort Vancouver recall his comment that the company had no officer "with a soul above that of a beaver skin."

Erie Canal, East-West link, finished

The joining of the waters. A part of Lake Erie is united with the ocean.

New York, Oct. 25

The Erie Canal, linking Lake Erie with New York City via the Hudson River, was completed today, and newly elected Governor De Witt Clinton, who has been pushing for this project for over 15 years, is the man behind its creation. The 363-mile-long canal incorporates 83 locks, which allow ships to travel across unequal water levels by closing off sections of the canal and changing the level.

The idea for the canal may have been a result of President Jefferson's suggestion in 1805 that surplus federal revenue be utilized to renovate the country's road and canal systems. Lake Erie was chosen as a potential site by James Geddes, who was sent to survey the area in 1809. But persuading Congress to authorize the project was a long and difficult struggle. Clinton first attempted to get approval for funds in 1810, when he formed a commission with Senator Jonas Platt and Thomas Eddy. Although this first effort was poorly planned, rejection only temporarily halted progress on the canal. In 1815, Clinton put together a petition and gave Congress detailed accounts on construction and benefits of the canal. And on April 17, 1816, funds were approved and legislation was passed to get construction under way.

Clinton served as both Governor of New York and as acting leader of the new canal commission during most of the canal's construction. However, political strife led to his retiring from government in 1823 and the next year he was taken off the canal commission. But Clinton's supporters rallied to overcome opposition and he was reelected Governor in time to see the canal's completion.

Indians in South and Missouri sign treaties ceding their lands

Indian Springs, Georgia, December

Creek chiefs, under the control of William MacIntosh, who is in the pay of the Georgia Indian Commissioners, have signed a treaty that cedes all of the remaining Creek land to the state of Georgia. MacIntosh is opposed by a large number of Creek chiefs who argue that the treaty with Georgia is in violation of the tribe's custom and law, which provides the death sentence for any Creek who sells land without the consent of the entire Nation. In this case, the consent has been withheld by a majority of Creeks, but the chiefs who signed were given large bribes. In the past, tribal leaders accepted treaties that provided for the eventual subdivision of their lands and removal to the West.

Grand Council at Prairie du Chien. United States reserves the right to make "an amicable and final adjustment" of boundaries. Painting by J.O. Lewis.

White squatters and land speculators have swarmed into Georgia and Alabama, where they have stripped the Indians of their land by fraud, liquor or force. Many of the Indians who were once prosperous have been forced to take to the woods and swamps, divested of all their possessions and driven from their homes.

Meanwhile, up in the Northwest, talks under the supervision of the federal government have ended at Prairie du Chien [Wisconsin] between the Chippewa, Iowa, Potawatomi, Sauk and Fox tribes, who have agreed upon a border accord that aims to put an end to intertribal conflict over land claims. And in Missouri, the Big and Little Osage and the Kansas Indians have ceded all their remaining territory to the federal government.

1826

Adams

Georgia, Jan. 24. Creek Indians sign Treaty of Washington, offering smaller piece of land to United States than originally agreed upon.

Washington, D.C., March 30. John Randolph, in Senate debate, accuses John Quincy Adams and Henry Clay of "corrupt bargaining" to win Adams presidency (→Apr. 8).

Washington, D.C., Apr. 26. United States signs treaty of friendship, commerce and navigation with Denmark.

Washington, D.C., May 2. Diplomatic recognition extended to republic of Peru.

Boston, Aug. 2. Daniel Webster, in Faneuil Hall, gives moving eulogy for John Adams and Thomas Jefferson.

Batavia, New York, Sept. 12. Former Freemason William Morgan disappears mysteriously after disclosing order's secrets.

Waltham, Massachusetts, Oct. 26. Ralph Waldo Emerson delivers first sermon as ordained minister.

San Francisco, Nov. 11. San Francisco Bay mapped by Captain Frederick Beechey of British navy.

New York City. Tenor Manuel del Popolo Vincente Garcia rents Park Theater in attempt to start permanent Italian opera company here.

Boston. Alexander Parris lays out Quincy Market, using individual granite slabs rather than blocks and mortar.

Tennessee. Davy Crockett elected to United States Congress.

Maine. John Russworm is first Negro to graduate from an American college.

Hartford. Samuel and David Collins begin production of standardized axes and machetes.

Honolulu. Crew of Dolphin, first American warship to visit Honolulu, storms Governor's house after he bans native women from boarding ships.

New York City. Poet William Cullen Bryant becomes editor of *New York Evening Post*.

United States. Publication begins of major four-volume legal work by noted jurist James Kent, *Commentaries on American Law*.

Randolph, Clay duel over "corrupt" deal

Randolph, an anti-Federalist, who claims descent from Pocahontas.

Clay, under fire for "bargain and sale." Portrait by George Healy.

Washington, D.C., Apr. 8

Neither man was hurt in today's keenly awaited duel between Secretary of State Henry Clay and Senator John Randolph of Virginia. Clay pierced Randolph's coat, but Randolph purposely fired into the air; both men walked away unscathed. The duel is an extension of the bitter election in which the House gave the presidency to John Quincy Adams, after Andrew Jackson won the most popular and electoral votes but not a majority. Today's duel follows last week's charge by Randolph on the Senate floor that Clay struck a "corrupt bargain" when he supported Adams in return for appointment as Secretary of State.

Jed Smith crosses Southwest to the coast

San Diego, California, Nov. 27

The first Americans to cross the Southwestern part of the continent arrived in San Diego today. Their leader, who is already a legend among the mountain men and the fur trappers of the West, is the 25-year-old Jedediah Smith, whose expedition of 16 men trekked from the basin of the Great Salt Lake up the Colorado River, over the western slopes of the southern Rocky Mountains, through the Mojave Desert, then on to the Mission San Gabriel in California. Smith and his party started out from their camp near the Great Salt Lake on or about August 22.

The great frontier. Crossing an unknown and seemingly endless desert.

New steam wagon travels at 12 mph

Hoboken, New Jersey, May 13

Colonel John Stevens has made his most emphatic, if not outright clamorous argument in favor of steam-powered railways. The feisty 76-year-old veteran of the Revolution built the nation's first "steam wagon" in back of his estate here, and the contraption is astonishing onlookers and even a few daring passengers as it clangs and rattles around a small circular track at up to 12 miles per hour. The old firebrand has long exhorted the merits of steam power to a skeptical public, but now fewer people laugh when he speaks of a day when railways will carry tons of cargo and hundreds of people across the nation (→Oct. 7).

Horses pull wagons on first railroad

Quincy, Massachusetts, Oct. 7

It was a struggle at first, but once under way a single horse managed to pull a 16-ton slab of stone with seeming ease today at the opening of Gridley Bryant's "Granite Railway." Inspired by England's railways, Bryant's venture, the first of its kind in America, will speed construction of the Bunker Hill Monument, at a cost of $50,000. The load, supported by three wagons rolling on hardwood tracks, was moved downhill for three miles, from the quarry here to the Neponset Wharf. The slabs will go by barge across Boston harbor to the construction site (→Aug. 8, 1829).

Boston men form temperance society

Boston, Feb. 13

It could be last call at pubs across the nation if the new American Society for the Promotion of Temperance has its way. Citing divine inspiration for a mandate of abstinence, 16 Protestant evangelists today signed a charter establishing the all-male society, whose members are pledged to preach against the evils of alcohol. Support for temperance has been building since the first such society was formed in 1808.

Cooper's new book "Last of Mohicans"

Boston, Feb. 4

Clad in his trademark deerskin leggings, Natty Bumppo, the fictional rifleman whose bravery and knowledge of the great north woods delighted readers of James Fenimore Cooper's *The Pioneers*, returns in the author's new romance of the wilds, *The Last of the Mohicans*, which was published today. Bumppo, who was known as Deerslayer in the earlier volume, is called Hawkeye in this saga, but he is still clever, modest, solitary, taciturn, a crack shot, and the consummate woodsman, a quintessential hero of the distinctively American literature that Cooper is creating.

The Last of the Mohicans, like

THE

LAST OF THE MOHICANS.

BY

JAMES FENIMORE COOPER.

NEW YORK:

D. APPLETON AND COMPANY, PUBLISHERS.

The Pioneers, is a story of the frontier set in America's recent past. During the French and Indian siege of the British fort at Lake George in 1757, Hawkeye and two Indian friends, Chingachook and Uncas – the last descendants of the once-powerful Mohican tribe – become responsible for the welfare of Cora and Alice Munro, two unwilling refugees from civilization. Through the perfidy of Magua, a treacherous Iroquois, the lives of the two girls are endangered, and Hawkeye must come to their rescue. Tragedy ensues, but readers will be gratified to know that at novel's end Bumppo returns to his beloved wilderness, ready to venture forth again at his skilled creator's behest.

Founding fathers Jefferson and Adams die on Independence Day

Jefferson. An engraving by Tiebout.

Quincy, Massachusetts, July 4

Today, on the 50th anniversary of the signing of the Declaration of Independence, John Adams and Thomas Jefferson have passed away. Adams, aged 90, died tonight at his boyhood home in Quincy. Jefferson, aged 83, died a few hours earlier at his Virginia home, Monticello. If Jefferson seems to have been the more powerful leader, perhaps it is only because Adams promoted his own powers poorly. He defied partisan politics and removed himself from inner circles, trusting he would be placed in high offices simply because he merited them. While Vice President under Washington, Adams should by rights have led the Federalists. Yet he left the task to Alexander Hamilton. And his presidency lasted but one term, partly because he failed to publicize successes such as his negotiated peace with France.

Erstwhile rivals, in recent years Adams and Jefferson would often write to each other. Adams put it this way: "You and I ought not to die before we have explained ourselves to each other."

But who can explain the paradoxes of Jefferson? He could be very informal; while President, he often received diplomats in his carpet slippers. He could be oddly restrained; at his wife's funeral, he shed not a tear but watched the men turn the soil of her grave and calculated how long it would take them to turn an acre. He was a sophisticated intellectual, yet he hoped for a nation of simple, yeoman farmers. He negotiated far-ranging commercial treaties with foreign nations, but was often in personal debt. Jefferson moved for the abolition of slavery, yet he kept under his roof for 40 years a mulatto slave named Sally Hemings who, rumors say, bore him children. And he acted boldly as President, as in buying Louisiana, yet he said he felt a president's powers should be limited.

Jefferson and Adams are gone at once, and perhaps it is a sign of divine favor, of God's blessing on the Revolution and the men who made it. Just before he died, Jefferson asked, "Is it the Fourth?" Only hours later, John Adams's last words were: "Thomas Jefferson still lives" (→Aug 2).

Monticello, Jefferson's home for half a century. Painting by Reynard.

Scottish woman starts Southern commune

Nashville, Tennessee, March 3

Shovels and spades broke ground today on a few acres west of here. Overseeing the proceedings, the revolutionary social reformer Fanny Wright rejoiced that her model town, which she calls Nashoba, is becoming a reality. Nashoba will be home to freed slaves who can work together in a communal setting, raising for mutual benefit staples such as wheat and corn.

Yet the only seeds sown thus far are those of controversy, for the people of neighboring communities eye Nashoba with suspicion. Whoever heard of a settlement deliberately mixing Negroes and whites? Rumors circulate of free love between the races. And the greatest source of scandal is Miss Wright herself, a wealthy, Scottish-born radical who has made a name for herself in the United States with shocking stage plays and a frank volume entitled *Views of Society and Manners in America*.

Miss Wright, tall and handsome, 30 years old and unwed, has denounced marriage and other social institutions. In spite of her strong views, she has many friends (including the Marquis de Lafayette) who have pledged support for Nashoba.

Professor shows way to better body

Cambridge, Massachusetts

An outspoken German professor, hoping to upgrade the physical condition of American students, has introduced a program of physical education and gymnastics at Harvard College, where he teaches. Charles Follen, a radical so fiery in his student days in Germany that he was accused of an assassination attempt, was ordered out of Switzerland and migrated to America last year. In addition to teaching German and law, he also gives lessons in the new art of gymnastics.

1827

Adams

Washington, D.C., Feb. 2. Supreme Court rules that state militias may be mobilized in national interest only by president.

Washington, D.C., Feb. 28. Vice President John C. Calhoun breaks tie in Senate, rejecting protectionist tariff bill on wool (→ July 2).

United States, March 5. John Quincy Adams writes of presidency, "I can scarcely conceive a more harassing, wearying, teasing condition of existence . . ."

New York City, March 16. First Negro newspaper, *Freedom's Journal,* published by John Russworm and Samuel Cornish.

Columbia, South Carolina, July 2. Thomas Cooper, president of South Carolina College, says that protective tariffs favor Northern industry over agricultural South (→ 30).

New York, July 4. Slavery is officially abolished in state, and 10,000 slaves are freed.

Boston, July 23. First swimming school in nation opened.

Raynham, Massachusetts, Oct. 17. Methodist Salome Lincoln, first American woman to conduct public lecture tour, begins it at church.

Washington, D.C., Dec. 13. The 20th Congress convenes, with Jacksonian majority in both House and Senate.

Tennessee. Sam Houston, exhibiting great charm and dignity, elected Governor.

Arizona. Mission period ends as Franciscans are banished.

Louisiana. Legislature approves $10,000 gift for family of Thomas Jefferson, who died in debt.

United States. John Hill Hewitt's *The Minstrel's Return from the War* is first hit song by native American.

Boston. Edgar Allen Poe's first book of poetry, *Tamerlane and Other Poems,* published.

United States. German refugee philosopher Francis Lieber begins work on 13-volume *Encyclopedia Americana.*

United States. Friedrich List's, *Outlines of American Political Economy* published.

Massachusetts. Sarah Hale publishes *Northwood,* first American anti-slavery novel.

Indians go to war to drive out lead miners

Prairie du Chien, Michigan Terr.

Prompt and vigorous action by the Governor of this territory, Lewis Cass, a 45-year-old veteran of the War of 1812, has put an end to the so-called Winnebago War with the loss of only a few lives. Backing the Governor and local militia were regular army troops stationed at Fort Howard, in Green Bay [Wisconsin], under the command of Major William Whistler. Chief Red Bird, leader of the uprising, was captured and is being held prisoner.

At the root of the trouble is the continued intrusion by whites into tribal lands, especially in the Galena area, which is rich in lead deposits. The price of lead has soared in recent years, attracting a steady influx of miners, some of whom have decided to settle in the region. More immediate causes of trouble were tied to the murders of two white farming families last year by the Winnebagos, followed this June by an incident in which a group of white boatmen kidnapped and raped seven Indian women.

Red Bird, burdened with the task of defending the ancestral lands.

With tariff rejected, issue splits nation

Harrisburg, Pennsylvania, July 30

After an anti-tariff rally in Columbia, South Carolina, 100 delegates from 13 states met here to urge a tariff rise. A bill seeking an increase lost in February as Vice President Calhoun cast a tie-breaking vote against it. The issue is splitting America on economic and regional lines. The North wants tariff protection; the South opposes high prices. South Carolina College head Thomas Cooper has asked "Is it worth our while to continue this union of States, where the North demands to be our master and we are required to be their tributaries?" (→ Jan. 31, 1828).

First saw mill in Pacific Northwest opens

Fort Vancouver, Pacific Northwest

Local residents have just received a lesson in economics. Since the California demand for lumber has increased, there has been a corresponding rise in the price of lumber. Currently, for example, 1,000 board feet will bring $40 to $50 in San Francisco. What this means to the Pacific Northwest is that there is a market for its wood if the timber here can be milled. To take advantage of this rise in lumber's value, Dr. John McLoughlin of the Hudson's Bay Company has supervised contruction of the Northwest's first sawmill. It is five miles from town on a swift-moving river and will employ 28 Kanaka Indians as cutters. McLoughlin expects to turn a profit soon, but he has even greater long-run hopes. If the market keeps growing, he says, within a decade the mill may turn out 2,400 board feet a day.

"Angel" aids Smith in translating book

Palmyra, New York, Sept. 22

After a four-year wait, Joseph Smith says he has been instructed to take the mysterious book of golden pages from its hiding place in Palmyra where he says he dug it up. With the book, Smith says, is a golden breastplate connected to a pair of stones that enable the wearer to translate the otherwise indecipherable script. With the stones and the aid of an angel, Smith says, he was able to translate part of a book that tells the story of the lost tribes of Israel (→ Apr. 6, 1830).

Dixon opens first lead pencil factory

Salem, Massachusetts

A 28-year-old inventor, Joseph Dixon, has opened the first lead pencil factory in the United States. Dixon, who is largely self-educated, is quite skilled at chemistry and has made several inventions based on the use of graphite. His factory will also produce a graphite-based stove polish and will provide the inventor and manufacturer with a laboratory to continue his experiments with graphite crucibles, which may have uses in the pottery and metal industries. Dixon began his experiments with graphite while still in his teens.

Edinburgh, Scotland. *French-American ornithologist John James Audubon has brought his paintings here and printed them as "Birds of America."*

New Harmony folds; Owen out $125,000

Lakeside idyll, an empty shell once filled with dreams of freedom and equality.

New Harmony, Indiana, March 29

The New Harmony community officially disbanded today, costing Robert Owen, its founder, a tremendous sum of money, at least equivalent to the $125,000 he paid for the land in 1825. Owen began his radical project in communal living two years ago when he posted invitations to join his community on the Wabash River at no cost other than participation in the society's functions. All the work and the property in New Harmony was to be shared, and members of the group were to have equal status.

The 56-year-old Owen came to America to attempt to establish his ideas for social change because these ideas were not widely accepted in his native Scotland. Hovever, New Harmony was beset with difficulties from the outset. Many of those who responded to Owen's invitation to all people except Negroes wanted nothing more than a free place to live, and had no interest in involving themselves in the work of a communal society.

In the Hall of New Harmony, on April 27, 1825, Owen's speech welcomed all comers to "an enlightened social system which shall gradually unite all interests into one, and remove all causes for conflicts between indiviuals." Yesterday, the *New Harmony Gazette* declared the community of equals disbanded because of the rising discordance in New Harmony.

Jim Bowie's knife kills major in duel

Vidalia, Louisiana, Sept. 19

Using a fearsome new knife, Jim Bowie killed Major Morris Wright in a duel on a sandbar in the Mississippi River today. Spectators from Natchez watched from the bluffs across the river as the battle raged. Before he was knifed, the major had wounded Bowie with his sword. Bowie's knife is of tempered steel with a handle and blade so balanced that it can be thrown as well as used for stabbing. Some claim Bowie's brother, Resin, developed it, but others say the inventor was James Black, a blacksmith on Resin Bowie's plantation.

Anarchist sets up not-for-profit store

Cincinnati, May

In a country based on a capitalist economy, a new store opened by 29-year-old Josiah Warren is unique. Warren, regarded as the founder of philosophical anarchism in the United States, has opened a shop that intends to make no profit. Called an "equity" store, the business will trade goods for an equivalent amount of labor, with what the goods cost Warren determining the limit of what he charges for them. Warren's political philosophy, to which the store is linked, advocates a society based on "the sovereignty of the individual."

Mardi Gras comes to New Orleans

New Orleans, February

Some students just home from Paris have introduced a Mardi Gras (Shrove Tuesday) custom. They donned costumes and threw flowers at onlookers in the streets.

Of course, New Orleans has had masked balls celebrating the pre-Lenten season since colonial times. They are believed to have started in the administration of Pierre-Cavagnal de Rigaud, Marquis de Vaudreuil, who became Governor in 1743. A sophisticate from France, Vaudreuil was known for his state dinners, card parties and balls.

The French are said to have originated the celebration of Mardi Gras with the pre-Lenten festival that is held before the 40-day fast. Shrove Tuesday is the last day before the period of penance that starts on Ash Wednesday.

By donning masks and parading in the streets the students may have started a tradition in this city where all forms of celebration are welcomed.

New York buzzing over risque ballet

New York City, Feb. 7

Some thought it scandalous, others sensational, but virtually everyone packed into the Bowery Theater agreed that Madame Francisquay Hutin's dance performance was unlike anything they had seen before. In her American debut, the voluptuous young French ballerina bounded onto the stage draped in a semitransparent garment scarcely covering her calves and executed a dazzling series of pirouettes. Although her performance was clocked at under three minutes, the display of so much leg was enough to redden the cheeks of many in the audience and prompt the ladies in the lower tier of box seats to file out of the theater.

The ballerina has been described as "une jeune and jolie personne of distinguished reputation" and her solo in *La Bergere Coquette* (The Flirtatious Shepherdess) had been eagerly awaited. Not everyone was chagrined by the performance – in fact, she repeated her shocking act in response to calls for an encore.

Pennsylvania. *Embroidered linen sampler made in the craft shop of one of the many talented and industrious German immigrants to the region.*

1828

Adams

Washington, D.C., Jan. 31. Jacksonians introduce doomed protectionist bill, designed to make President Adams appear anti-protectionist (→ May 19).

Oklahoma, Feb. 21. *Cherokee Phoenix* published; first Indian-language newspaper.

Washington, D.C., Apr. 28. Senate ratifies agreement with Mexico, designating Sabine River as common boundary.

Washington, D.C., May 24. Reciprocity Act passes Congress, calling for elimination of discriminatory duties on goods imported from reciprocating nations (→ July 14, 1832).

Oregon Territory, June. First party to travel overland from California reaches Pacific Northwest, only to be slaughtered by Indians (→ July 14).

Baltimore, July 4. Charles Carroll, only surviving signer of Declaration of Independence, attends ground-breaking ceremony for Baltimore and Ohio Railroad.

New York, Oct. 16. Delaware and Hudson Canal begins transporting anthracite coal from Pennsylvania to Eastern industrial centers.

Washington, D.C., October. Will of James Smithson bequeaths funds for national institution of learning [Smithsonian] (→ 1846).

Albany, New York. Joseph Henry invents insulation for electric wire.

Paterson, New Jersey. First recorded factory strike prompts first suppression of labor violence by militia.→

United States. Postmaster General rules that Negroes may carry mail only if supervised by a white man.

New Orleans. Jews, free to live in Louisiana with repeal of Black Code, form Gates of Mercy congregation.

New York City. New York Drawing Association renamed National Academy of Design.

United States. Nathaniel Hawthorne's first novel, *Fanshawe*, published anonymously.

Boston. Journalist Sarah Josepha Hale becomes editor of new publication, *Ladies Magazine*.

Spain. Washington Irving writes *History of the Life and Voyages of Christopher Columbus.*

Congress okays "Tariff of Abominations"

Spinning cotton cloth, one of the products heavily protected in the new bill.

Washington, D.C., May 19

After approval by the House on April 23, and the Senate six days ago, the tariff bill was signed into law today by President Adams. Labeled the "Tariff of Abominations" by its opponents, it imposes high duties on a wide range of manufactured products, most notably glass, textiles and ironware.

The law is the result of complicated political maneuvering. Hoping to discredit President Adams in the coming election, congressional supporters of Andrew Jackson introduced a bill with tariff rates so high they felt confident it would be rejected not only by anti-protectionist Southerners, but also by moderates from other regions.

But the maneuver went awry. Although the bill contained many features the New Englanders disliked, such as a high tax on imported raw wool and items needed for shipbuilding, they found the main provisions so favorable to manufacturing that they pushed hard for the measure and, with some assistance from the Western states, succeeded in passing it. As Senator Daniel Webster, one of the bill's supporters, said, "Its enemies spiced it with whatever they thought would help render it distasteful; its friends took it, drugged as it was" (→ 24).

Webster publishes weighty dictionary

Amherst, Massachusetts, Apr. 21

A Dictionary of the English Language, compiled by the grammarian and editor Noah Webster, was published today. The twovolume work, which contains some 38,000 entries and is the result of 20 years' labor by Webster, is the first lexicon to treat distinctly American pronunciation and usage. *Webster's Spelling Book* is generally considered to be the definitive guide to American spelling and it is used in almost every classroom in the country; his dictionary is expected to prove no less authoritative a source of reference.

Famed portraitist Gilbert Stuart dies

Boston, July 9

Gilbert Stuart, brilliant painter of American leaders, is dead at 73. Born in Rhode Island, Stuart worked with Benjamin West in England and achieved his earliest success at London's Royal Academy exhibition in 1782 with *The Skater*. He may never have put his brush to American subjects had his taste for high living and his difficulties in completing commissions not forced him to flee from creditors, first to Ireland, then to the United States. Stuart made his name – and his living – with his portraits of George Washington, whom he first painted in 1795. As charming as he was gifted, Stuart was able to put his illustrious sitters, among them Jefferson and Madison, at ease. However, he was unable to overcome lifelong financial woes and too frequently resorted to copying his popular Washington portraits to make ends meet.

The master's self-portrait.

First labor paper

Philadelphia, July 21

The *Mechanics' Free Press*, the first wage-earners' newspaper, celebrated its first half year of publication this month. Last year, skilled laborers organized the Mechanics' Union of Trade Associations. With January's publication, the union achieved one of its aims: to create a paper of labor news. Today's issue reports on the violence between striking textile workers and the militia in Paterson, New Jersey. The strike was called to protest management's changing of the dinner hour from noon to 1 p.m. The militia was sent in to end the strike – and succeeded. This is the first time the national militia has been used for strike control. Although the workers lost the strike, the noon dinner hour is expected to be reinstated.

ˈmith explorers ˈcalped in Oregon

ˈregon Country, July 14

Reports have arrived here that ˈe famous American mountain ˈan Jedediah Smith and his expe-ˈitionary force were the victims of savage attack by Indians today ˈear the Sacramento River in Cal-ˈornia. Some sources say 15 men ˈere killed, while others put the toll ˈ 18. In any case, the disaster sug-ˈests that Smith's party was virtual-ˈ wiped out. In the fierce hand-to-ˈand fighting, most of the men were ˈomahawked and scalped. Smith ˈanaged to escape, fleeing into the ˈoods. Now he is reportedly fit and ˈeady for his next foray.

ˈlackface Jim Crow ˈn minstrel show

ˈouisville, Kentucky

A new form of entertainment was ˈorn this year on a Louisville stage ˈhen Thomas Dartmouth "Daddy" ˈice, a comedian from New York, ˈerformed a song-and-dance act ˈith his face painted black to look ˈke a Negro. Rice portrayed a cha-ˈacter named "Jim Crow," based on ˈ stable boy who lived behind Rice's ˈheater. The character relies on a ˈtereotype of Negroes as hapless, ˈgnorant and foolish, and its popu-ˈarity indicates it may become a fix-ˈure in this type of performance, ˈhich Rice calls a minstrel show.

ˈhomas Dartmouth "Daddy" Rice ˈn blackface as "Jim Crow." Litho-ˈraph songsheet cover (c.1835).

Jackson is President after tough race

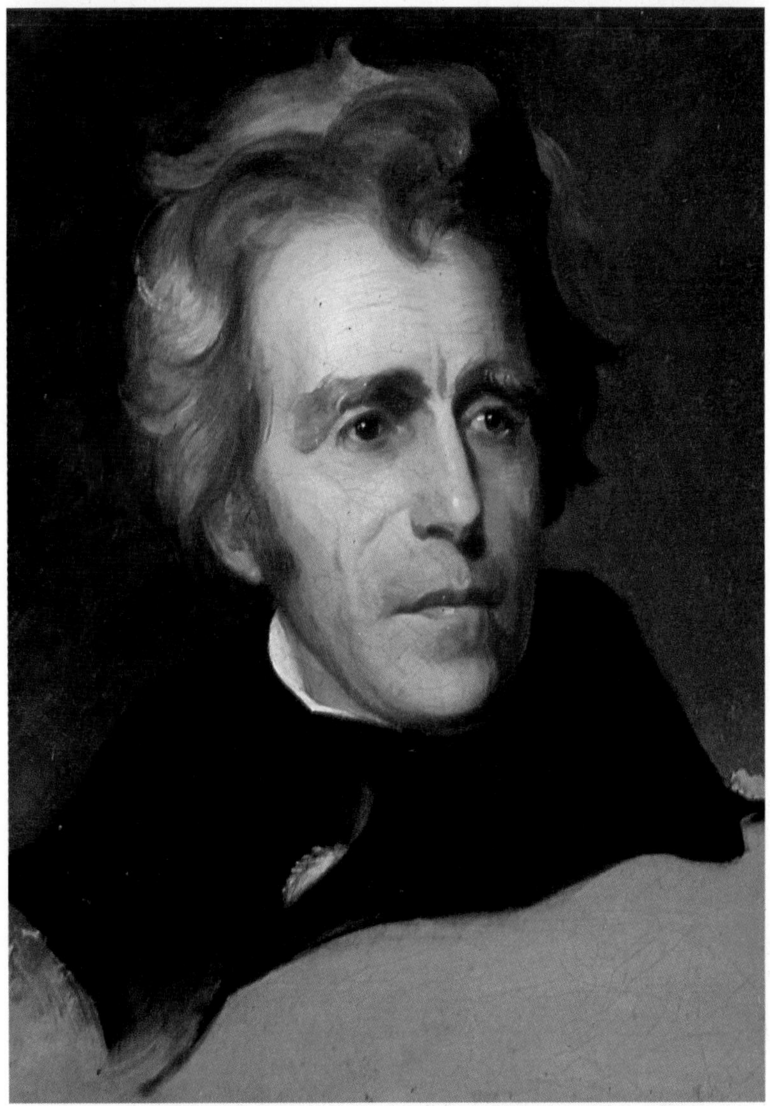

Jackson, at 61 the nation's seventh President. Painting (1845) by Sully.

Washington, D.C., Dec. 3

Backed by the fledgling Democratic Party, Andrew Jackson was elected President of the United States today, defeating his long-time rival and sitting President, John Quincy Adams. Jackson, a former senator from Tennessee and hero of the Battle of New Orleans, polled 187 electoral votes to 89 for Adams, the son of a former President.

While neither man campaigned formally, their backers turned the election into perhaps the most vicious yet. Jackson forces pictured Adams as an aristocrat with European leanings, a man whose purchase of a billiard table for the White House was proof of his dissipated tastes. The Adams forces, in turn, accused Jackson of spending his time in such pursuits as horse racing, gambling and cock-fighting.

Just four years earlier, Adams won the presidency over Jackson by picking up the support of Henry Clay after an electoral-vote deadlock in which no candidate ran on a party ticket. This time, Jackson ran with the support of the newly fashioned Democratic Party, which Martin Van Buren and others had pulled together from the remnants of the old Democratic-Republican Party. It is largely a coalition of planters in the South and laborers in the North. Adams ran as a National Republican and found most of his support in the Northeast (→March 4, 1829).

Cherokee agree to cede traditional lands

Washington, D.C., Dec. 20

The government announced today that the Cherokee Indians have decided to cede their traditional lands in the Arkansas Territory to the United States and to migrate voluntarily to lands west of the Mississippi River, which is known as Indian Territory. This peaceful group of Cherokees has lived in Arkansas for years. Many American citizens have moved into the region in the past decade, however, and Indian-white conflicts have been increasing in both number and violence. President Jackson has long urged the removal of the Indians to the region west of the Mississippi and out of the path of the advancing settlers. Jackson has always believed that removal is the wisest policy, holding that otherwise, the Indians would face annihilation.

The Cherokees in Georgia are facing a similar and growing problem because American settlers are looking covetously at their tribal lands. The President is probably going to have to deal with this situation soon. Jackson, at least, indicates some concern for the wellbeing and fate of the Indians. His rival, Senator Henry Clay, has said it is impossible to civilize those he calls inferior "savages" and he feels that "their disappearance from the human family would be no great loss to the world" (→Dec., 1838).

Hoowaunneka, or Little Elk, a Winnebago Indian warrior from the Northwest. Painting (1828) by Charles Bird King.

1829

Jackson

United States, Jan. 18. Anti-slavery pamphlet, *Walker's Appeal*, widely distributed, calls upon slaves to revolt.

Boston, March 2. Dr. John Dix Fisher incorporates New England Asylum for the Blind, first such school in nation.

New York harbor, June 4. The steam-engined warship Fulton I explodes.

Mount Vernon, Va., July 23. Village resident William A. Burt receives patent for a typographer, or typewriter.

Baltimore, August. *American Turf Register and Sporting Magazine,* first of its kind, founded by John Stuart Skinner.

Mexico City, Sept. 15. Guerrero Decree issued, abolishing slavery in Texas and throughout Mexico (→ Dec. 2).

Louisiana, Oct. 7. Governor Derbigny killed in runaway carriage accident.

Chesapeake Bay, Oct. 17. Canal opens, spanning 14 miles between Chesapeake Bay and Delaware River.

New York, Nov. 7. Ebenezer Ford, president of Carpenters' Union and candidate for New York State Assembly, becomes first labor union member elected to public office in United States.

New York, Nov. 13. Sam Patch dies attempting to dive 125 feet into Genessee Falls.

Mexico, Dec. 2. President Guerrero, revising decree, exempts Texas from Mexican prohibition of slavery.

Greenfield, Massachusetts. Fellenberg Manual Labor Institution founded; first recorded manual labor training school in United States.

United States. Deborah and Susan Tripp, ages 3 and 5 years, weigh 124 and 205 pounds respectively.

Pierre's Hole, Idaho. At congregation site for traders, Rocky Mountain Fur Company establishes rendezvous for fur trading with Indians.

Texas. First Sunday School in state established at Sealy by Baptist Thomas J. Pilgrim.

New York. Robert E. Lee graduates, second in his class, from West Point.

United States. G.A. Shrycock produces paper from straw.

Unruly Jacksonians mob White House as President takes over

Triumph of the common man. Jackson on his way to the nation's capital.

"The President's Levee" (1829) by Robert Cruikshank. One Republican noted the scene was "like the inundation of the northern barbarians into Rome, save that the tumultous tide came in from a different point of the compass."

"Quelling the riot in the Kitchen Cabinet." Many think the President's personal advisers, such as Amos Kendall, Francis Preston Blair, A.J. Donelson and Martin Van Buren, exercise more influence than his regular Cabinet.

Washington, D.C., March 4

People of every color, age, size and shape mobbed the first floor of the White House this afternoon to celebrate the inauguration of "their" President, Andrew Jackson. Shortly after noon, having ended his inaugural speech on the East Portico of the Capitol building, Jackson, in somber black (he is mourning the recent death of his wife), mounted a white horse and rode up the unpaved Pennsylvania Avenue. An adoring crowd of some 20,000 followed. A few hundred people surged into the White House after him. So many tried to touch the lean, pale man that officials had to form a human wall to keep him from being crushed. Many visitors just climbed wherever they could, some in muddy boots on damask chairs, to get a closer look. Others broke thousands of dollars worth of china as they lunged for drinks of orange punch and liquor.

The inauguration ritual was calmer. Jackson spoke for just 10 minutes: He skirted the issues of tariffs and the national bank, but he did call for "a just and liberal policy" toward the Indians and an "invigoration of the public morals."

Last month Jackson swore to oust from office all men appointed "against the will of the people or (those who) are incompetent." Still, his critics note that Jackson's best friend, John Eaton, has been named Secretary of War even though he has had no war experience.

"Kitchen Cabinet" to advise Jackson

Washington, D.C., Apr. 15

Turning away from his official Cabinet, President Jackson has begun seeking advice on crucial matters from men more in tune with his political views. Critics have dubbed the advisers Jackson's "Kitchen Cabinet," a group described by one disgruntled member of the official Cabinet as "an influence at Washington unknown to the Constitution and to the country." The new advisers include two newsmen: Francis Preston Blair, editor of the *Washington Globe*, and Amos Kendall, a Yankee who made his journalistic mark in Kentucky.

B.&O. opens first passenger railroad

Precarious perches for a few trusting passengers on the Baltimore and Ohio.

Baltimore, Maryland, Dec. 22

The Erie Canal may have given New York a jump commercially, but Baltimore is envisioning its own link to the Western states. The Baltimore and Ohio Railroad began carrying passengers today from the western edge of the city to Ellicott's Mills, the first completed 13-mile stretch of a railway that may one day run 300 miles, clear across the Alleghenies to the Ohio River. A horse can pull 10 times its normal load on the railway, and carriages roll over iron-strap tracks at up to 12 miles per hour. But some on the B.&O. foresee new forms of locomotion, either with sail power or the steam-driven engines now gaining favor in England (→1830).

English steam locomotive makes trial run

The seven-ton Stourbridge Lion, a triumph for engine but not for track.

Honesdale, Pennsylvania, Aug. 8

As onlookers cheered and cannons boomed, Horatio Allen set out today to test his English-built steam locomotive, the Stourbridge Lion. With its emblazoned red lion's head and mass of sputtering valves and joints, the behemoth was an awesome sight, but many feared its seven-ton weight would crush the hemlock-and-iron track built here by the Delaware and Hudson Company. Undaunted, Allen lurched forward at a confident 10 miles per hour for three miles, then returned to the great acclaim of the crowd. Despite its impressive showing, the locomotive will not run again until the railway, designed for horses, is reinforced (→Dec. 22).

Hotel features water closets and forks

Boston, Oct. 16

The Tremont, an elegant new hotel here, is the object of great curiosity, not only for its 170 bedrooms, vast dining room and marble floors, but also for its imported indoor water closets that set a new standard for public accommodations. Used in the grand 200-seat dining room instead of the two-tined forks found in America are four-tined forks, which Europeans hold in their left hand (this necessitates moving the fork from the left to the right hand).

Sam Houston plans liberation of Texas

Arkansas

Sam Houston, who lived with the Cherokees when he ran away from home as a boy, has resigned his job as an Indian agent and returned to the tribe seeking comfort from a recent divorce. The former Tennessee Governor is said to have designs on the Mexican province of Texas. In October, a U.S. envoy seeking to buy the land was recalled at the request of Mexico. Houston thinks he can incite Americans in Texas to revolt (→Dec. 20, 1835).

Jackson questions legitimacy of bank

Washington, D.C., Dec. 8

President Andrew Jackson has expressed fears about the future of the national banking system in his annual message to Congress. The President questioned the constitutionality of the Second Bank of the United States and charged that the bank, which is in control of the country's money and credit supply, has "failed in the great end of establishing a uniform and sound currency." Known to believe that the bank worked against his election, Jackson called for substantial changes in its charter, scheduled to expire in 1836 (→Jan. 9, 1832).

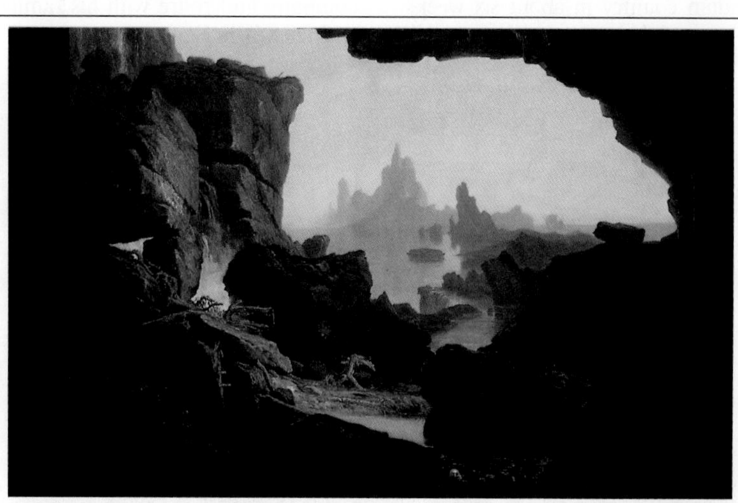

"Subsiding of the Waters of the Deluge" (1829) by Thomas Cole. One of America's most promising painters, Cole spent his early 20's as an itinerant portraitist. Four years ago, at 25, struck by the beauty of the Hudson Valley, he settled in New York on a bluff overlooking the Catskill Mountains.

Antipodean feats dazzle New Yorkers

New York City, Sept. 14

He may not be remembered as the finest showman of the era, but he may be remembered. Billed as Peters the Antipodean and presented by Henry James Hackett, he performed feats of strength and dexterity that astounded the crowd at the Bowery Theater tonight. He walked across a tightrope. He walked upside down on the ceiling. And he heaved 16 men and 10 wagon wheels off the ground. Meanwhile, his wife and daughter also appeared in this spectacle, walking on tightropes as well as dancing.

1830

Jackson

Washington, D.C., Jan. 18. In debate on land sale, Missouri Senator Thomas Hart Benton accuses Northeastern states of slowing Western growth (→27).

Harrisburg, Pennsylvania, Feb. 11. Series of cockfights draws large crowds.

Washington, D.C., Apr. 13. President Jackson, in toast at celebration of Jefferson's birthday, says on the issue of nullification, "Our Federal Union – it must be preserved!" Vice President Calhoun replies, "The Union – next to our liberty, the most dear!" (→Dec. 10, 1832).

Washington, D.C., May 29. Squatters are protected by Preemption Act, offering 160 acres at $1.25 each to settlers who have cultivated public land for 12 months.

Philadelphia, Sept. 11. Anti-Masonics hold convention, giving movement political status.

Washington, D.C., Oct. 5. Following diplomatic negotiations, President Jackson opens trade with British West Indies.

Liverpool, England, Nov. 26. American Robert Stevens invents T-rail railroad track while visiting England.

United States, December. Robert Dale Owen's *Moral Physiology* published; nation's first book on birth control.

United States. There are 73 miles of railroad track and 1,277 miles of canals in nation.

Fort Dearborn, Illinois. Town of Chicago planned.

United States. John Nepomuk Maelzel arrives from Europe, attracting large crowds with demonstrations of his mechanical chess player and automatic trumpeter.

New England. Town ball, a sport based on English rounders, is popular.

Utah. Fierce rivalries between companies break out for control of fur trade in Utah.

Keokuk, Iowa. Benjamin Jennings opens first log schoolhouse.

United States. Cotillion, a medley of five or six separate dances, is popular.

New Orleans. As Louisiana prospers, many plantation owners along Mississippi River and bayous build opulent mansions.

"Liberty and union, now and forever"

Daniel Webster by Chester Harding.

Washington, D.C., Jan. 27

The Senate was galvanized today by the ringing conclusion of Daniel Webster – "Liberty and union, now and forever" – in his marathon states' rights debate with Robert Y. Hayne of South Carolina.

Starting as a discussion about the sale of Western lands, the contest began 10 days ago when Senator Hayne declared: "The very life of our system is the independence of the states." In reply, the 58-year-old New Hampshire Senator Webster declared: "I go for the Constitution as it is, and for the union as it is. It is, sir, the people's Constitution, the people's government, made for the people, made by the people, and answerable to the people." The 38-year-old Hayne then held the Senate spellbound as he argued that the rights of the states give them the power to nullify acts of the federal government, and even to secede if they so choose. The Dartmouth-educated Webster concluded today with his ringing affirmation of that "sentiment dear to every true American heart – liberty and union, now and forever, one and inseparable."

First covered wagons cross the Rockies

Western Frontier, Autumn

The first wagon train to cross the Rocky Mountains reached the Upper Wind River this summer. Led by Jedediah Strong Smith and his partner in the Rocky Mountain Fur Company, William Sublette, the covered wagons left the western reaches of the Missouri River and made the 500-mile journey through Indian country in about six weeks. The explorers report that heavily loaded wagons and even milk cows can safely – and rather easily – cross the prairies and the Rockies (through the South Pass), and go on to the Pacific Ocean. Smith, who is probably the most famous "mountain man" in the country, has told his associates that this is going to be his last trip. He is planning to sell his large interests in the fur company and retire with his family and friends in St. Louis.

"Rocky Mountains: Emigrants Crossing the Plains" (1866). Currier & Ives.

Population nearing the 13-million mark

United States

The latest census has recorded the population of the United States at 12,866,020, an overall increase of more than 3 million people. That includes 150,000 immigrants who arrived since since the last census a decade ago. California is now inhabited by 4,000 Americans, Alabama is said to have over 300,000, and Tennessee's population has grown to 681,000 residents. The nation's population now includes 6,000 Jews. The census further reports that there are 3,777 free Negro citizens in the United States who own slaves. Questions about manufacturing, introduced by John Quincy Adams in the last census, were not included this year.

Temperance leader advocates dieting

Philadelphia

While most Americans are indulging in a rich diet, the Rev. Sylvester Graham of the Pennsylvania Temperance Society is gaining wide attention by urging them to abstain from red meat, shellfish, eggs, milk, pepper, mustard and alcohol. He preaches that such foods cause everything from moral dissipation to insanity. Instead, Graham cites the virtues of fruit, vegetables and whole wheat bread, "natural foods" he says the Creator designed as fit for the human physiology.

Smith starts church and publishes book

Fayette, New York, Apr. 6

Joseph Smith today founded the Church of Jesus Christ of the Latter-Day Saints. Claiming to have had visions from age 14, he has also published a book this year allegedly detailing the history of America's original inhabitants. Smith says this *Book of Mormon* is a translation of a book of golden pages given to him by an angel. The church now has six members They believe Smith is a prophet, and claim that God has told their leader all other churches are in error (→Jan. 1831).

'team powers American-built locomotives

'om Thumb motors ahead before faltering in its race for control of the rails.

'nited States

As Peter Cooper started his ex-erimental steam locomotive, the 'om Thumb, on the return stretch f the B.&O.'s 13-mile railway on ıe western edge of Baltimore on eptember 18, he was met with a hallenge from a carriage hitched n a parallel track to the railway's vast power of steam is now seen as railroading's future. Impressed by the coal-burning Tom Thumb, the B.&O. expects to harness steam for its planned expansion.

Already, the West Point Foundry has begun manufacturing locomotives, and an American, Robert Stevens, has invented a solid-iron rail

'he native-born Best Friend of Charleston, South Carolina's technical marvel.

egular source of energy, a power-ılly muscled gelding. The New 'ork inventor-industrialist, who uilt the Tom Thumb himself to how his faith in steam power over orses, needed no prodding, and he two vied at a breakneck pace. But just when the engine began to ase ahead, a pulley snapped and its ival galloped to victory.

But the carriage driver could not ave reveled for long, because the to support the heavier machines. The first West Point engine, the Best Friend of Charleston, has begun passenger service for the South Carolina Canal and Railroad Company. With Horatio Allen as engineer, it made its first run on Christmas, hauling three carriages filled with dignitaries, as crowds roared, cannons boomed and bands played. Americans may be learning to love these contraptions (→ Jan. 12, 1853).

Washington, D.C. *The White House, designed by Irish-born James Hoban. The North Portico, the work of Benjamin Latrobe, was added last year.*

Removal Act exiles Indian tribes to West

Washington, D.C., May 28

Indian tribes are likely to be swept west of the Mississippi under the Indian Removal Act signed into law today by President Andrew Jackson. Passage of the legislation was accompanied by some of the most acrimonious debate ever heard in Congress, with critics claiming the blll was inhuman while proponents said it was the only way to save Indians from extinction.

Under the law, Indians will receive perpetual title to Western lands, along with financial assistance and a government guarantee of security. Although the act does not mandate the surrender of Eastern lands, it is certain to speed the pace of resettlement, which has been escalating since the War of 1812. Passage of the bill was a triumph for Jackson, a staunch nationalist who has made no secret of his desire to drive the Indians west. After taking office last year, the President urged the Creek tribe to cede its land and head west, noting, "Your white brothers will . . . have no claim to the land and you can live upon it, you and all your children, as long as the grass grows or the water runs, in peace and plenty. It will be yours for ever" (→ June 20, 1834)

British crew raises Union Jack at Astoria

Fort Astoria, Oregon, Dec. 13

History was made today when Captain Black, a British naval officer aboard the Racoon, landed here and took charge of Fort Astoria. With four soldiers and four sailors, Black raised the Union Jack, broke a bottle of Madeira on the flagpole and declared the post Fort George. Three rounds were fired and the fort was officially British. More importantly, its taking signals the end of John Jacob Astor's venture, the Pacific Fur Company. Inside sources say the buyout was not a good deal for Astor. He will get $58,000 for the company, but it is clear that he sold under duress.

In God's country. Astoria, nestled at the mouth of the Columbia River.

Lady's Book for the fashionable female

Philadelphia

Elegance has a new spokesman in Louis Godey, who has started a magazine he calls *Lady's Book.* It instructs women in etiquette and home economics. But its pages are only the stuff of dreams for women who work at mills like Cabot Lowell's in Massachusetts. There, young workers from the countryside, 90 percent of them female, live in supervised boarding houses and work long hours. These women long to lead lives like the women featured in Godey's *Lady's Book*.

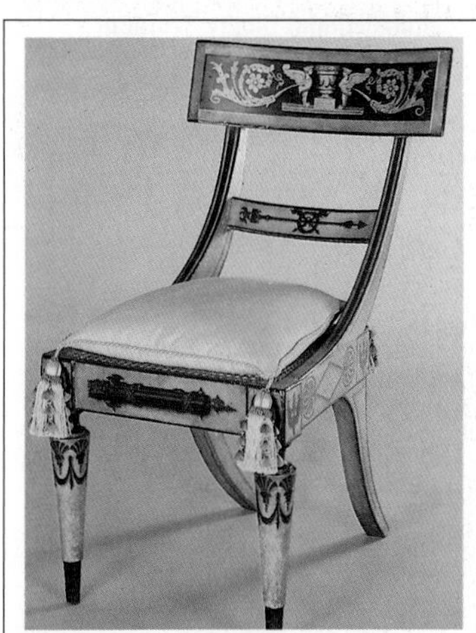

Painted wood, side chair made in the currently popular American Empire style, c.1815-1830.

1831

Jackson

Washington, D.C., January. Free Negroes are whipped and imprisoned for picking up copies of *The Liberator.*

Raleigh, North Carolina, June 21. Statue of George Washington destroyed by fire.

Salem, Massachusetts, Aug. 10. William Driver, captain of the vessel Charles Daggett, coins phrase "Old Glory" when presented with an American flag.

United States, August. Baptist minister William Miller begins preaching in public on Christ's imminent return to earth [marks beginning of Adventist movement] (→ Oct. 22, 1844).

Washington, D.C., Dec. 5. Former President John Quincy Adams joins House of Representatives as member from Massachusetts.

Washington, D.C., Dec. 12. John Quincy Adams introduces 15 petitions calling for ban on slavery in District of Columbia.

United States. Cowcatcher invented for locomotive use.

Albany, New York. First electric motor and first telegraph invented by Joseph Henry.

New York City. Gramercy Park established to attract wealthy residents; one of few private parks in United States.

Salmon River, Idaho. Kit Carson leads group of Rocky Mountain Fur Company traders wintering on shores; four traders killed by Indians.

Montana. Missionaries arrive among Nez Perce and Flathead Indians [beginning of Christianization of natives].

Philadelphia. Negro women form Female Literary Society.

Key West, Florida. Sixteen Cubans, first known in United States, work in cigar factory.

New Haven, Connecticut. Trumbull Gallery at Yale established.

New York City. Rossini's *La Cenerentola* offered as *Cinderella*; [becomes era's most popular musical production.]

New York City. Edgar Allan Poe, dismissed from West Point for "gross neglect of duty" and "disobedience of orders," publishes *Poems.*

Boston. *Legends of New England* by John Greenleaf Whittier published.

Feuding wives bring on Cabinet shake-up

Washington, D.C., May

President Jackson has put an end to the "petticoat war" here with a sweeping purge of his Cabinet. The move leaves an unprecedented vacuum, but ends a long-simmering feud. The scandal began when other Cabinet wives refused to socialize with the 29-year-old ex-barmaid bride of Secretary of War John Eaton. She is the former Margaret "Peggy" O'Neale Timberlake and her navy husband is rumored to have committed suicide because of her romance with Eaton. President Jackson championed her cause, and official Washington took sides, entwining the "petticoat war" with politics. Secretary of State Martin Van Buren has led Mrs. Eaton's cause. Vice President Calhoun and his wife led her detractors. The President's strong defense of the ostracized bride is linked to the time when he and his wife, Rachel, were denounced for having married before completion of a divorce that had ended Rachel's previous marriage. Many said that the campaign of villification hastened her death.

De Witt Clinton steams up Hudson Valley

The De Witt Clinton, namesake of New York's industrious Governor.

Albany, New York, Aug. 9

A great celebration and some misadventure marked the first run of the Mohawk & Hudson's new locomotive, the De Witt Clinton, today. Thousands from here to Schenectady watched as the iron horse jounced riders on its bumpy route and even ignited some hats with hot cinders. But railroads are spreading, with a new one, the Pontchartrain, as far west as New Orleans.

Phoenix Line "safety coach," traveling from Washington to Philadelphia in five days, shuttles the nation's luminaries from the capital of politics to the capital of finance. It may soon be racing the railroads for survival.

Delmonico's opens for business in N.Y.

New York City

Two Swiss cafe owners, John and Peter Delmonico, have opened a European-style dining room that New Yorkers have taken to calling a "restaurant." Derived from Parisian models, Delmonico's, at 23-25 William Street, offers patrons a chance to order all kinds of food – from vegetables and salads to ice cream and pastries – from a menu rather than the custom of eating whatever is presented.

Clay is nominated to oppose Jackson

Baltimore, Maryland, Dec. 12

The Whig Party nominated Henry Clay of Kentucky as it presidential candidate at the national convention today. The party declared it would do everything in its power to "deprecate the reelection of Andrew Jackson." John Sargeant of Pennsylvania won the vice presidential nomination. Clay, a former speaker of the House and Secretary of State, is a bitter rival of Jackson. He has vigorously opposed Jackson's aggressive policies against Indians and the President's terse dismissals of government officials. A fierce campaign is likely.

In September, the Anti-Masonic Party held its first national nominating convention, selecting William Wirt of Maryland for president and Pennsylvania's Amos Ellmaker for vice president (→ Dec. 5, 1832).

Mormons in Ohio in search of Zion

Kirtland, Ohio, January

To escape persecution and obey a claimed revelation from God, Joseph Smith has led 70 followers, called Mormons, from their home in New York to the wilderness of Ohio. They have joined an earlier group near Kirtland, where they plan to build a new Zion. The Mormons are hoping that their doctrines will not stir the animosity here they did in New York, and they will be able to live in peace with their neighbors (→ May 10, 1839).

Garrison founds radical abolitionist paper

Boston, Jan. 1

The abolitionist editor William Lloyd Garrison rang in the new year today with a stinging denunciation of the American institution of slavery. In the first edition of *The Liberator*, his new journal, Garrison calls for complete and immediate emancipation of all the nation's slaves. In his opening editorial, Garrison promises that he will be an unyielding advocate on this issue, saying: "I am in earnest – I will not equivocate – I will not excuse – I will not retreat a single inch – *and I will be heard*" (→ Jan.).

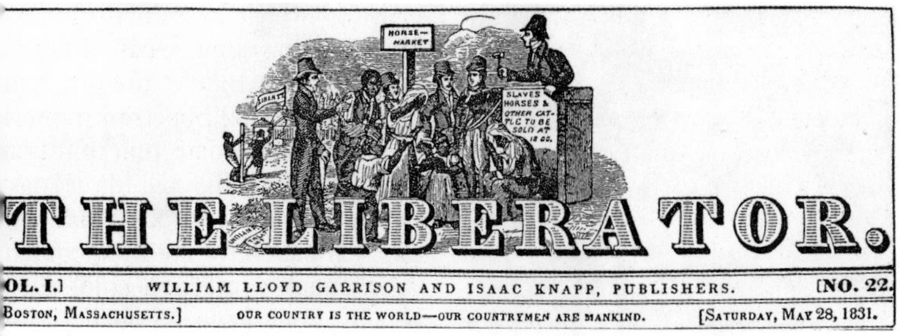
HORSE-MARKET
THE LIBERATOR.
VOL. I.] WILLIAM LLOYD GARRISON AND ISAAC KNAPP, PUBLISHERS. [NO. 22.
BOSTON, MASSACHUSETTS.] OUR COUNTRY IS THE WORLD—OUR COUNTRYMEN ARE MANKIND. [SATURDAY, MAY 28, 1831.

Garrison: "I do not wish to think, or speak, or write, with moderation."

People of Color hold first annual meeting

Philadelphia, June 11

For the past five days, delegates from five states met at the Wesleyan Church on Lombard Street here for the first Annual Convention of the People of Color, the first such convention ever for free Negroes. The delegates resolved to study the conditions of free Negroes, discuss the possibility of settlement in Canada, develop further annual conventions, oppose the policies of the American Colonization Society for migration to Africa and approve the raising of funds for a New Haven industrial college, provided that at least one Negro was on the board of trustees.

In the last few years, several other organizations for free Negroes have been established. These now include the New York Philomathean Society and the Female Literary Society for Negro Women here in Philadelphia.

Samuel Francis Smith, a theology student, has written a poem to go with a tune whose melody happens to be the British national anthem. He calls it *America:*

My country, 'tis of thee,
Sweet land of liberty,
Of thee I sing;
Land where my fathers died,
Land of the pilgrims' pride,
From every mountainside
Let freedom ring.
My native country, thee,
Land of the noble free –
Thy name I love;
I love thy rocks and rills,
Thy woods and templed hills;
My heart with rapture thrills,
Like that above ...
Our fathers' God, to Thee,
Author of liberty,
To Thee we sing;
Long may our land be bright
With freedom's holy light;
Protect us by thy might,
Great God, our King.

High court rules Indians cannot sue

Washington, D.C., March 18

There's gold in Georgia. But, it's on Cherokee Indian land and the tribe wants to guard its property from intrusion by gold prospectors. The Cherokees filed a suit to protect their land, but today the Supreme Court decided to disallow that suit. In the case of Cherokee Nation v. Georgia, Chief Justice John Marshall ruled that the tribe is a "domestic dependent" nation, "a distinct political society . . . capable of managing its own affairs." But because the Indians are not bound by the laws of the Constitution, the court asserted, they do not have the right to sue. At the time that this decision was handed down, the Mississippi Choctaws began their move west, in compliance with government orders.

Nat Turner leads revolt

Nat Turner, a religious mystic, preaches rebellion to fellow slave fugitives.

Jerusalem, Virginia, Nov. 11

Nat Turner, a literate slave and radical preacher, was hanged today for the crime of organizing and leading a slave revolt that resulted in the deaths of more than 50 whites.

In August, Turner, along with his chief disciples, Hark Travis, Nelson Williams, Henry Porter and Samuel Francis, incited a group of about 30 slaves from Southhampton County in the Virginia tidewater, to kill whites. Whites in the county responded to the insurrection by forming a force of some 3,000 armed men to pursue the Negro rebels. With the militia, and regular troops and sailors from nearby bases, they killed many of the rebels, but they also killed many Negroes whose only connection with the rebels was the color of their skin. Nat Turner managed to escape and remained at large until his recent capture.

During his time as a fugitive, Turner wrote an autobiography, *The Confessions of Nat Turner*, which was edited by Thomas R. Gray and published in Baltimore.

Captured, Turner leaves the forest at the end of Benjamin Phipps's gun.

1832

Jackson

New England, Jan. 6. New England Anti-Slavery Society is founded.

Washington, D.C., Jan. 9. Bank of the United States, fearing mounting criticism of its policies, applies to Congress for charter extension (→ July 10).

Washington, D.C., March 3. Supreme Court rules in Worcester v. Georgia that federal government, not states, has jurisdiction over Indian territories.

Seekonk, Massachusetts, Apr. 1. Robert the Hermit, colorful figure in American lore, dies at his hermitage, ending long life of slavery and suffering.

South Texas, June 26. Battle of Velasco waged, probably first case of bloodshed between Texans and Mexicans (→ Apr. 3, 1833).

New York City, June. Some 4,000 die in cholera epidemic.

Washington, D.C., July 10. President Jackson vetoes bill to extend charter of Bank of United States (→ 13).

Lake Itasca, Minnesota, July 13. Led by Henry Schoolcraft, expedition discovers source of Mississippi River.

Washington, D.C., July 14. New tariff prolongs duties on textiles and iron (→ Dec. 10).

Michigan Territory. Chief Black Hawk defeated at Battle of Bad Axe (→ Sept. 21).

Philadelphia, Nov. 26. Old Ironsides locomotive, built by Mathias Baldwin, makes first run.

Washington, D.C., Dec. 14. Jackson writes, "Can anyone of common sense believe the absurdity that a a state has a right to secede and destroy this union and the liberty of our country with it, or nullify the laws of the union; then is our Constitution a rope of sand; under such I would not live."

Western Frontier. Oregon Trail, from Independence, Missouri, through Snake and Platte River valleys, to mouth of Columbia River, becomes main route to West.

Texas. Committees on safety and correspondence, similar to those of pre-Revolutionary period, established as protest against Mexican government.

New Orleans. Cholera and yellow fever cause 5,000 deaths.

Black Hawk defeated, Keokuk cedes land

Sauk and Fox women and children retreat along the Mississippi at Bad Axe.

Michigan Territory, Sept. 21

In the wake of last month's crushing defeat of Chief Black Hawk at the Battle – some call it the Massacre – of Bad Axe, the rival Sauk chief, Keokuk, has signed an agreement giving up his tribe's claims to lands east of the Mississippi. In doing so, he confirms the Treaty of 1804 that was negotiated by General William Henry Harrison but was later rejected by Black Hawk as a fraud on his people.

The Sauk chief, whose Indian name is Ma-ka-tai-me-she-kia-disk, surrendered to authorities on August 27, along with White Cloud, who is also called the Winnebago Prophet.

In two years of fighting, the Sauk leader and his 300 warriors scored some successes, but the odds were against them: regulars under General Henry Atkinson, state militia under General Whiteside, the armed ship Warrior and hostile Sioux. Cornered while trying to cross the river at Bad Axe, 300 Indians, many of them women and children, were shot down.

Jackson beats back bid to extend bank

Washington, D.C., July 13

As expected, the Senate failed to come up with the two-thirds majority required to override President Jackson's veto of the bill to renew the charter of the Second Bank of the United States. Although the charter, which was first granted in 1816, has four more years to run, Nicholas Biddle, the president of the bank, had hoped to renew it well before the date of expiration. When vetoing the bill three days ago, Jackson declared: "Many of our rich men have not been content with equal protection and equal benefits, but have besought us to make them richer by an act of Congress" (→ June 1, 1833).

Easy life is making rich women flabby

United States

Too many women are living sedentary lives and would be healthier if they did more housework, according to the *Journal of Health*. Piano lessons, needlework and reading leave wealthy women less robust than the "females in the middling classes," it reported. As for men, several experts believe that stress is a growing problem. One said that nervous maladies were "already a formidable national evil," adding that stress could result in memory loss, timidity and jealousy.

Catlin, on journey up Missouri River, depicts lives of Indians

Catlin, a Pennsylvania native, painted "St. Louis From the River" on his trip up the Missouri this year.

St. Louis, October

The artist George Catlin has returned with sensational and sometimes shocking illustrations of Indian life along the Missouri River. In March, Catlin set out on a voyage of more than 2,000 miles upriver to remote Fort Union with trappers from the American Fur Company on the steamboat Yellowstone. The artist befriended the Sioux and Mandan tribes, whose colorful figures, villages and ceremonies he depicted in paint. His temerity was richly rewarded by permission to document the Mandans' gruesome but sacred Okee-pa torture ritual.

"Buffalo Bull's Back Fat, Head Chief, Blood Tribe" (1832), Catlin's stunning portrait of a Blackfoot.

Jackson re-elected despite sectional fight

Jackson, lampooned as an autocrat.

Washington, D.C., Dec. 5

Despite new sectional conflicts, President Jackson was re-elected today, piling up 219 electoral votes to 49 for his chief rival, Henry Clay. Chosen Vice President was Martin Van Buren of New York.

Both Jackson and Van Buren are Democrats, while Clay ran on the National Republican ticket. The election marked the first time that the Anti-Masonic Party, which began organizing four years ago, sponsored a candidate, William Wirt, who polled just seven votes. The splinter party opposes members of the Masonic Order because it considers the order a secret society that threatens public institutions.

The year just ending marked two dramatic developments: One, the Democrats chose their nominees in a national convention for the first time, and two, South Carolina, chafing under protective tariffs, sought to nullify such federal laws in that state. What shaped up as a major challenge to the authority of the federal government was skirted when the politicians achieved a compromise on the tariff issue.

President responds to secession threat

Washington, D.C., Dec. 10

Continuing his firm opposition to any move to break up the union, President Jackson has issued a Proclamation to the People of South Carolina in which he denounces nullification, the right of a state to nullify federal laws, as "an impractical absurdity" and declares that "disunion by armed force is treason." Jackson acknowledges that there may be justified complaints because of the Tariff Acts of 1828 and of this July, but adds: "The wisdom of man never yet contrived a system of taxation that would operate with perfect equality."

Jackson has not responded to South Carolina's nullification resolution of November 24 with just words. Ships sailed to Charleston, forts have been reinforced and General Winfield Scott commands troops there (→March 18, 1833).

Friction increasing as slave prices rise

Virginia

Recent advances in agriculture and industry have increased the demand for slaves in the Southern states, with a corresponding rise in price of nearly 25 percent. This increase in demand and value has created a growing antagonism toward anti-slavery sentiments in the North and South. Free Negroes have also become targets of hostility. Here in Virginia, all meetings of free Negroes for teaching, reading and writing have been classified as "unlawful assembly." Those convicted of such crimes may receive up to 20 lashes, and whites caught teaching slaves can be fined. In spite of such laws in the South, Negroes in several Northern cities have formed literary societies. A Negro was admitted by Wesleyan University in Connecticut, but protests have forced him to leave.

"To the victor belong the spoils"

Washington, D.C., Jan. 21

President Jackson calls his practice of rewarding political supporters with government jobs "reform." But the Jackson camp's own William Marcy of New York proudly defended it in different terms in the Senate today. He put it this way: "To the victor belong the spoils of the enemy."

Jackson atop a pig. Thomas Nast satirizes the Civil Service spoils system.

Embittered Englishwoman writes attack on American manners

London, March 19

The first copy of *The Domestic Manners of the Americans* came out today, and many Americans hope it purports to be a novel. It does not.

The book, by Mrs. Frances Trollope, mother of the famous author Anthony Trollope, recounts the Englishwoman's travels in America between December 1827 and last summer. Her experience may best be summed up by her observation that she had gone to America with high hopes, but "before I had half completed my tour I was quite cured. Were I an English legislator, instead of sending (a seditionist) to the Tower, I would send her to make a tour of the United States."

Mrs. Trollope, traveling with a son and two daughters – her barrister husband, Thomas, remained in England – first arrived in New Orleans. She was dismayed to see dispossessed Indians and slaves in the land of liberty. She noted sadly that Creole girls, some three-quarters white, were legally unable to marry. On the other hand, she had no appreciation for the familiarity of hired help; she frowned with disapproval as one servant girl called her son "honey."

Moving west to Cincinnati, Mrs. Trollope's family settled into a hotel. Finding little in the local shops that interested them, they bought dried beef and brown sugar candy and proceeded to eat in their room. Mrs. Trollope says that the landlord promptly knocked upon their door and demanded they eat at the common table downstairs. "What is good enough for our folks is good enough for yours," he exclaimed roughly. Mrs. Trollope then tried to explain that she was unaccustomed to American ways. "Our manners are very good manners," the landlord told her, "and we do not wish any changes from England."

Nor books, either.

American cartoon poking fun at the Trollopes and artist Auguste Hervieu.

1833

Jackson

San Felipe de Austin, Texas, Apr. 3. American settlers adjourn three-day meeting; they agree to make Texas independent of Mexico.

Oberlin, Ohio, May. Oberlin Collegiate Institute chartered, becoming nation's first coeducational college (→Oct. 30, 1838).

Washington, D.C., June 1. President Jackson makes Cabinet changes, hoping to gain support for his position on Bank of United States (→Sept. 26).

Cambridge, Massachusetts, August. John Quincy Adams refuses to confer an honorary Harvard degree on Andrew Jackson, claiming he is "a barbarian who cannot write a sentence of grammar and can hardly spell his own name."

California, Aug. 17. Mexico orders all missions in territory to drop their religious affiliation.

Hamburg, South Carolina, September. South Carolina Railroad is world's longest at 136 miles.

United States, Dec. 31. Obed Hussey granted patent for a horse-drawn grain reaper (→June 21, 1834).

United States. Samuel Colt develops revolver (→1835).

Philadelphia. Thomas Dyott institutes system of paternalism at Kensington Glass Works, imposing strict moral codes on workers.

New York City. George Fibbleton invents shaving machine – but it hurts.

Haverford, Pennsylvania. Society of Friends founds first Quaker College in U.S., School Association of Haverford.

Washington, D.C. Treasury building burns.

New York City. Phoenix Society maintains a library and job bank and urges fellow Negroes to attend school.

United States. James Madison becomes president of American Colonization Society, advocating emigration of free Negroes.

Honolulu. Kauikeaouli becomes King after reaching legal age, crowned Kamehameha III.

New York City. Tyrone Power, famous Irish actor, makes debut.

Jackson slays the Bank

Big Bank Battle: General Jackson slaying the hydra-headed monster.

Washington, D.C., Sept. 26

The "Big Bank War" switched from talk to action today when President Jackson carried out his threat to withdraw federal funds from the Second Bank of the United States.

After ordering his Treasury Secretary, William John Duane, to reorganize the bank, and firing him for refusing to do so, the President has found a replacement eager to go along. Three days after moving to the Treasury from the Justice Department, Roger Taney carried out the President's order and shifted funds to the Girard Bank of Philadephia. Called a "pet bank" by Jackson's opponents, the Girard is the first of many state banks expected to receive additional transfers soon, until the Second Bank is left without government deposits.

Today's move is the latest in a series of blows to the bank that President Jackson calls a "hydra-headed monster" and a "threat to our liberty." The popular President, known as the "Hero of the Battle of New Orleans," has applied all his battlefield skills to his conflict with a bank that he regards as a creature of his political enemies in Congress. Jackson has told his confidants that the bank is trying to kill him, but he is going to kill the bank instead (→March 28, 1834).

South Carolina row with Jackson eases

Charleston, S.C., March 18

In a final gesture of defiance against "King Jackson," South Carolina's convention has passed an ordinance nullifying the Force Act that the President signed into law on March 2 to put force behind the new tariff. However, since Jackson at the same time signed the Henry Clay compromise Tariff Act, which removes many Southern grievances, and since the South Carolina convention has now voted to revoke its Ordinance of Nullification, it is hoped that the crisis is over. While civil war has been avoided, the question of secession has not been settled definitively. Jackson himself has predicted that "the next pretext will be the Negro, or slavery question."

Minister introduces the potato in Idaho

Idaho

The potato, a native South American tuber vegetable that has become a staple of the poor in Ireland and increasingly popular in the United States, has been planted in the Idaho territory of the Oregon country. Credited with introducing the vegetable here is the Rev. Henry R. Spaulding, a Presbyterian minister and missionary to the Indians, who believes the cold climate ideal for propagation of the vegetable.

Europeans study Indians along Missouri

Karl Bodmer's "Fighting Chief."

St. Louis, Spring

Less than a year after the American artist George Catlin completed his excursion into Indian country along the Missouri River, the German naturalist Prince Maximilian has embarked upon an ambitious expedition into the same region. The learned aristocrat brings with him the talented Swiss painter Karl Bodmer, who is adding to the visual archive of Indian culture started by Catlin. Maximilian and Bodmer began their trip on the Yellowstone, the same steamboat that carried Catlin, and they are using maps copied from the Lewis and Clark expedition of 1804-06.

Parting of church and state complete

Massachusetts

There is no longer an established church in any state. Massachusetts, the last holdout, finally removed the last vestige of religious establishment from state law. The tax to support the church, like a religious test for political office shed nine years ago, is gone. The laws stayed here longest primarily because the established Congregationalists were early, strong backers of the Revolution. In the effort to keep religion's position, Congregationalists held that town churches and town meetings had made New England unique.

Anti-slavery group excludes women

Philadelphia, December

Although there are actually three Negroes on the executive committee of the newly formed American Anti-Slavery Society, women of both races have been excluded. Upon discovering this, a group of Philadelphia women led by Lucretia Mott have formed the Female Anti-Slavery Society to to do the same work as the all-male group. Most abolitionist efforts have been white-dominated, largely because whites have the political and economic power needed to produce results; but the American Anti-Slavery Society includes among its founders such esteemed Negroes as the young and wealthy Robert Purvis, the Boston reformer James Barbadoes and the dentist James McCrummell.

Court frees states from Bill of Rights

Washington, D.C., Feb. 16

States are not bound by the Bill of Rights, according to today's Supreme Court decision in Barron v. Baltimore. Baltimore officials had built sidewalks, leaving deposits in plaintiff Barron's wharf area that disrupted shipping. Citing a Fifth Amendment clause that bars public usurpation of private property without just compensation, Barron sued. The court ruled the Bill of Rights applies only to federal jurisdiction.

Texans seeking end of rule by Mexico

Texas, Apr. 3

Texans meeting at San Felipe de Austin announced today that they were planning to lead Texas out of the Mexican confederacy. The head of the Texas delegation, Stephen F. Austin, and other members of the secession group put together a constitution based on that of the United States. Austin himself did not really approve of this secession effort, particularly since no Mexican government officials were present. Nevertheless, he said he would carry the Texas independence proposals to Mexico City.

First penny paper published in New York

THE SUN.

Number 1.] NEW YORK, TUESDAY, SEPTEMBER 3, 1833. [Price One Penny.

The Sun, offering the news "at a price within the means of every one."

New York City, Sept. 1

Murders! Suicides! Accidents! Read all about it! New York City has a paper for you and the price is right: one cent.

Benjamin Day, a former publisher and failing New York printer, has founded and distributed the first penny paper, the *New York Sun*. The four-page newspaper covers subjects Day thinks New Yorkers want to read about. Devoid of the usual political articles and editorials, the paper offers human-interest news, sensational accounts of crime and horror, and police-court news with a humorous bent. Day says he will utilize the "London plan" of selling papers to newsboys, who then sell them to the readers. The publisher has abolished credit; If people want to read, they must fork over a penny. Because of the *Sun's* low price, he plans to sell a lot of advertising. Publishers of "serious" papers doubt that this one will survive, but Day feels there's a market for a penny daily (→Aug. 25, 1835).

"Connecticut Sea Captain" (1833) by Isaac Sheffield. The stalwart ship's captain is New England's answer to the Western frontiersman. Many fishermen have left for more fertile waters in the Northern Pacific, but the image of the independent, industrious seafarer remains alive in the region's art.

New city is plotted on Missouri River

Missouri, Autumn

Earlier this year, John McCoy, a noted surveyor, plotted several sections of land that lie on both sides of the Missouri River just south of its junction with the Platte River and a few miles from Shawnee Mission. McCoy was hired by a group of businessmen who want to lay out a city that will be able to compete successfully with such older river towns as St. Louis and Cincinnati for the lucrative trade between the East and the developing West. The town, which has tentatively been given the name Westport [Kansas City] could also prove valuable to the army because military units based there would be able to make the thousand-mile trip to newly built Fort Laramie in 38 days.

John Deere makes first steel plow

Grand Detour, Illinois

A young Illinois inventor has come up with a tool that promises to open the vast lands of the West to agriculture. He is 29-year-old John Deere and he has developed a plow with a steel blade and polished moldboard that can cut and turn the dense soils of the West without clogging. Previous plows used in American agriculture, most based on a design by Thomas Jefferson, are suited to the lighter soils of the East.

"The night stars fell on Alabama"

Alabama, Nov. 13

A brilliant display of shooting stars has been observed up and down North America, but the people of Alabama were treated to the most spectacular part of the meteor shower. It is estimated that observers here could see more than 10,000 of the flashing lights in a single hour. A meteor display called the Leonid Shower is seen every year at this time, but tonight's "show" was by far the greatest ever recorded. It is believed that the observations of this shower will provide important clues to the origins of meteors.

1834

Jackson

New York City, May 6. James Gordon Bennett publishes *New York Tribune*; pledges to print news according to its importance not its sensation value (→May 6, 1835).

Washington, D.C., June 24. Senate refuses to confirm Roger B. Taney's nomination as secretary of Treasury.

New York City, June 28. Shortly after Harlem Railroad's first run, engine explodes; seen by some as a divine sign dooming trains.

Washington, D.C., June 30. Department of Indian Affairs established to administer Indian land west of Mississippi River.

New York City, July 4. Annual Convention of People of Color sets July 4th as day of prayer and contemplation of Negro condition.

England, Aug. 1. Slavery abolished throughout British Empire.

United States, Oct. 14. Henry Blair is first Negro to receive a patent; he develops a corn harvester.

Washington, D.C., Dec. 12. President Jackson demands reprisals for French failure to meet reparations payments for claims issuing from Napoleonic Wars.

Canterbury, Connecticut. Private school shut after Prudence Crandall is jailed for admitting black girls to school.

United States. Norwegian violinist Ole Broneman Bull concludes that the American people prefer the Negro's fiddle to his violin.

Wyoming. William Sublette and Robert Campbell open first permanent trading post at Fort Laramie.

New Orleans. Rioting erupts after news is announced that French Quarter resident Madame Lalaurie has been torturing her slaves.

United States. Minstrel team of Farrell and Dixon become popular for such songs as *Zip Coon*, sung to melody of *Turkey in the Straw*.

United States. Samuel F.B. Morse publishes *Foreign Conspiracy Against the Liberties of the United States*, claiming presence of a monarchical-papal conspiracy to overthrow government of the United States.

Cyrus McCormick's grain reaper patented

Washington, D.C., June 21

Cyrus Hall McCormick of Virginia was awarded a patent today for an automatic grain-reaping machine that is expected to bring great economic benefits to American farmers and consumers. If it is successful, the McCormick reaper will eliminate the need for hiring large numbers of laborers for harvesting, thus reducing the cost of producing food.

McCormick, self-taught tinkerer.

McCormick's father, Robert, is a farmer who previously worked as a blacksmith and dabbled in inventing. The elder McCormick tried for many years to develop a successful reaper but never managed it. As a boy, Cyrus spent more time in the workshop on his father's farm in Rockbridge County, Virginia, than in school. Three years ago, Cyrus, then 22, made the first working model of his reaper, using parts available on the farm. Its essential components were a reel to gather grain, a vibrating blade to cut it and a platform on which the cut grain is collected. Resembling a two-wheeled chariot, the original reaper revealed a major flaw when it was tested on a neighbor's farm. Its clatter was so loud that the horses drawing it had to be restrained from bolting. The young inventor proceeded to improve the reaper and lessen its effect on the horses.

McCormick says that he has no immediate plans to manufacture and market the reaper because his major interest now is running an iron foundry established by his father. However, he continues to improve the reaper, with an eye toward bringing it into production when opportunity allows. Farmers who have seen the reaper say they would be interested in buying it to reduce their reliance on high-priced seasonal labor.

Its first test was at Steele's Tavern, Virginia, in 1831. Painting by N.C. Wyeth.

Clay leads Senate censure of Jackson

Washington, D.C., March 28

The latest battle in the "Big Bank War" was won today by the foes of the seemingly unbeatable President Jackson. Led by Henry Clay, the Senate voted 26 to 20 to censure the President for his withdrawal of government funds from the Second Bank of the United States without Congressional approval. Clay, the 57-year-old Kentuckian who has branded President Jackson a tyrant and who ran a poor second against him in the last election, wrote the resolution. It declares that "the President, in the late executive proceedings in relation to the public revenue, has assumed upon himself authority and power not conferred by the Constitution and laws, but in derogation of both."

Earlier in the bank fight, the President transferred government funds to so-called "pet banks," and vetoed a bill to recharter the Second Bank. Now that Clay has attacked, all eyes are on the former general they call "Old Hickory" and how he will counterattack (→June 24).

Anti-Jackson party is named "Whig"

Washington, D.C., Apr. 14

President Jackson's opponents have made it official. From now on, they are the "Whigs." The name was adopted formally today following a Senate speech in which Henry Clay gave his blessing to a term that has been used informally here for the last two years, and in England for much longer.

The term's popularity can be traced to a New York newspaper cartoon depicting President Jackson as "King Andrew," dressed in royal finery and wearing a crown. Just as England's Whigs question the power of royalty, America's Whigs question the President's power. They include Senators Henry Clay and Daniel Webster, as well as supporters of former Vice President John Calhoun and his campaign for the right of states to nullify federal laws. Opponents of the President's war against the Second Bank of the United States are also prominent among the Whigs.

Race riots terrorize N.Y. and Philadelphia

Philadelphia, October

Riots that destroyed 31 houses and two churches in the city's Negro section this summer have been condemned by a town meeting at which citizens voted in favor of reimbursements for damage done by white mobs. The riots began when nearly 500 whites entered an amusement area in the Negro quarter and attempted to drive the residents out of town. A free-for-all broke out and the whites were eventually chased from the neighborhood. But they regrouped and returned the next night, beating Negroes and destroying their homes and personal property. On the third night of violence, a posse led by the mayor and sheriff dispersed the rioters. It is believed that the riot was begun by unemployed whites who were upset by the hiring of Negroes. Although the town meeting condemned the riots, it also condemned the noise coming out of Negro churches and recommended that Negroes behave inoffensively and unobtrusively while on the streets or whenever assembling.

Similar riots occurred in New York in July, raging for eight days and ending only after many buildings were destroyed. It is believed that the New York riots were set off by a clash at a large anti-slavery meeting that was supposed to have been solemn in nature.

Troops called out in canal labor riots

Washington, D.C., Jan. 29

President Jackson today ordered Secretary of War Louis Cass to halt rioting by Irish immigrant workers on the Chesapeake and Ohio Canal. Jackson, who is of Scotch-Irish descent, is the first President to use federal troops in a labor dispute.

Anti-Catholic riot destroys convent

Charlestown, Mass., Aug. 11

Newspaper reports that falsely charged a woman was being held against her will at the Ursuline convent led to rioting tonight that destroyed the convent and its school. Fortunately, none of the children or the nuns were injured in the attack.

Most of West becomes "Indian Country"

George Catlin's "Keokuk on Horseback" (1834). Keokuk gave up his lands in 1832, but the Cherokees, Seminoles and Creeks are resisting relocation.

Washington, D.C., June 20

Congress today passed a law that makes "Indian Country" of all territory west of the Mississippi River other than in the states of Missouri and Louisiana and in the Arkansas Territory. It was three years ago that President Jackson asked Congress to set aside "an ample district west of the Mississippi" for the permanent residence of the Indians. The "aborigines" can learn the "arts of civilization," the President said, and thus "attest to the humanity and justice of this government" (→ 30).

"Baseball" rules like those for rounders

New York City

A book published five years ago in England about the sport of rounders has now been put out in America and it cites the same rules for "Base, or Goal Ball." The game of rounders is played on a square field with four stones up to 20 yards apart as the boundaries. If the "striker" hits the ball, he runs the bases clockwise. If he misses the ball on three swings, he is declared out (→ 1839).

Coinage Act creates a shortage of silver

Washington, D.C., June 28

The Second Coinage Act, changing the ratio of silver to gold, has now become law. Under the previous ratio, gold coins were overvalued and, as a consequence, were being hoarded. By lessening the coins' gold content, their value has been reduced so that the silver-gold ratio now stands at 16 to 1. But silver is now overvalued and is rapidly disappearing from circulation.

Competition mounts in American fur trade

St. Louis, Missouri, Autumn

Businessmen here are expecting the competition in the highly lucrative fur trade to become even more intense as a result of the recent announcement that Pierre Chouteau Jr. has bought the western division of John Jacob Astor's American Fur Company. Since the 1780's, Astor's company has dominated the Northwestern fur trade and, in fact, it has made him America's first millionaire. Recently, however, the company's position has declined because of the emergence of many competitors, particularly the Rocky Mountain Fur Company and the British fur trading firms of Hudson's Bay Company and the Northwest Company, both of which have been the dominant enterprises in that area since the 1780's.

Chouteau, a member of one of the leading families in St. Louis and a top manager of the Astor empire, is considered to be an excellent administrator. Under his leadership, the new firm's future seems assured. He is said to have bought the western division for the small fortune of $250,000. The fur businesss is both rich and huge. But insiders are wondering whether it is big enough for all these powerful players.

The United States quarter eagle has less gold content and is less valuable.

1835

Jackson

Washington, D.C., January. Congress allocates surplus revenue as government makes final payment on national debt.

Washington, D.C., March 3. Congress authorizes new federal mints in Louisiana, North Carolina and Georgia.

Maine, Apr. 3. *Maine Farmer* reports growing problem with drunk stagecoach drivers.

Paris, Apr. 25. France authorizes payment of American claims for damages incurred during Napoleonic Wars.

United States, June 5. Fifth National Negro Convention supports removal of words "African" and "colored" from Negro vernacular.

United States, August. American Anti-Slavery Society distributes 75,000 anti-slavery tracts through mail to South, inciting slave owners.

New York City, Aug. 25. *New York Sun* publishes article suggesting that vegetation grows on moon, gaining national recognition for paper.

Boston, Oct. 21. William Lloyd Garrison led through streets with rope around his neck after pro-slavery mob attacks meeting of Female Anti-Slavery Society.

Florida, November. Second Seminole War begins as Chief Osceola leads Indian resistance to scheduled relocation to West (→Dec. 28).

Troy, New York, Nov. 23. Henry Burden patents machine for production of horseshoes.

Harrisburg, Pennsylvania, Dec. 16. Anti-Masonic Party holds convention, nominating General William Henry Harrison of Ohio for president.

North Carolina. Region acquires nickname "Rip Van Winkle State" because of its provincialism.

Central Plains. The Rev. Jotham Meeker publishes first newspaper in Kansas, *Shawnee Sun,* for Shawnee Indians in their language.

Boston. Unitarian minister William Ellery Channing preaches abolition in pamphlet called *Slavery*.

United States. Lyman Beecher's *Plea for the West* expresses view that the West is vital to American prosperity and must be saved from barbarism and Roman Catholicism.

Assassin fails in attempt to kill President

A narrow escape at the Capitol. Picture drawn from a sketch by a witness.

Washington, D.C., Jan. 30

President Jackson survived an assassination attempt in the Capitol rotunda today. Armed with two pistols, Richard Lawrence was only six feet away from the President when he pulled the triggers. But both weapons misfired. Lawrence, who is a house painter, had gone around telling people he was the rightful heir to the English throne.

Although this is the first time any one has attempted to kill an American President, Andrew Jackson is no stranger to close calls in gunplay. As a matter of fact, he carried two bullets in his body at the time he took office. One, fired in a fight more than 20 years ago, was removed from the President's arm in 1832. A second, still resting near the President's heart, was fired in 1806 by Charles Dickinson in a duel over insults about a gambling debt. After being struck by the bullet, Jackson killed Dickson with a shot that was deliberately aimed at the groin.

Colt patents gun with revolving chamber

Hartford, Connecticut

Samuel Colt has patented a handgun that fires up to six shots in rapid succession. The 21-year-old inventor calls the weapon a revolver because it uses a cartridge cylinder that revolves to bring each bullet under the hammer. Colt carved the first model of his revolver out of wood while serving as a seaman on a merchant ship after running away from home at the age of 16. He plans to produce the gun in a factory here and hopes to interest the military. He thinks he has a good case since the revolver will greatly increase the firepower of infantrymen, who must now reload after each shot.

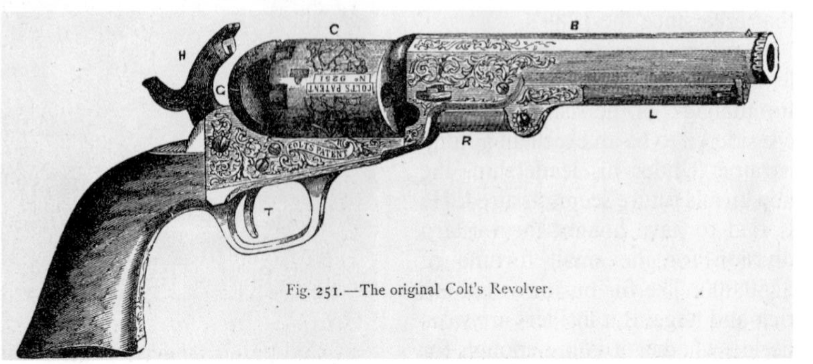

The Colt's chamber rotates into place simply by pulling the hammer or trigger.

Liberty Bell cracks tolling for Marshall

Philadelphia, July 8

The death knell that sounded today for Chief Justice John Marshall dealt a fatal blow to the Liberty Bell as well, cracking it and silencing the symbolic voice of American freedom. The Liberty Bell was cast in England and recast twice in the United States, then installed in the State House (now Independence Hall), before the Revolution. The bell rang to commemorate significant events in American history, including the first reading of the Declaration of Independence, in spite of the Philadelphians who petitioned to have it muted in 1772. Though it may never ring true again, the Liberty Bell remains a symbol of American democracy.

Indian site becomes town of Milwaukee

Milwaukee, March 17

Long a meeting place for Indians, the settlement of Milwaukee on the western shore of Lake Michigan in the Michigan Territory was incorporated as a town today. Situated at the confluence of the Menominee, Milwaukee and Kinnickinnic Rivers, it was visited by Father Zenobius of La Salle's expedition in 1679. Jacques Vieau, another Frenchman, started a fur-trading post here in 1795. His son-in-law, Solomon Juneau, arrived in 1818 and is called the town's founder. Most other settlers are from New England and New York.

New Orleans gets steam streetcars

New Orleans, December

Residents are riding steam-driven streetcars on the New Orleans and Carrollton Railroad for the first time as the line puts its horses out to pasture. Cars run on St. Charles Avenue from Canal Street to the suburb of Carrollton. This is also the year the curtain went up on the new St. Charles Theater. Seating 4,000 and glittering under gaslight chandeliers, it has been called "the most beautiful theater in America."

Texas revolution erupts

President Santa Ana, who is known as the Hero of Tampico for his military feats against Spain in 1829.

Goliad, Texas, Dec. 20

The long-simmering conflict between Mexico and Americans in Texas has finally erupted into full-scale civil war and revolution. Leaders of the secession movement today issued their declaration of independence from the dictatorship of Mexican President Santa Ana and officially proclaimed the creation of the Republic of Texas.

For more than a year, the Texans have been in constant preparation for this momentous day. On October 2, the first significant battle between the Texan and Mexican armies took place on the Guadalupe River near Gonzales. This fight erupted when Mexican soldiers came to retrieve a cannon that they had given the Texans for protection against Indian attacks. When the Mexicans tried to repossess it, the Texans unfurled a battle flag that said, "Come and get it!" The Mexicans didn't. Then the Texans created a navy as well as the Texas Rangers, and named Sam Houston, former Tennessee Governor, to head an army (→Feb. 12, 1836).

Seminoles on warpath to halt relocation

Florida, Dec. 28

Major Francis L. Dade and 108 soldiers were massacred by Seminole Indians near Fort Brooke today and Indian agent Wiley Thompson was killed near Fort King. The Dade massacre was the bloodiest incident since the Seminoles began efforts earlier this year to block their ouster from Florida.

Under two recent treaties, the Indians were to give up their lands here and move west by January 1. The Seminoles' settlements center around the Everglades, but stretch from Silver Springs to the southern tip of Florida. Pressure to remove the Indians has been building because white settlers want to take over more of their lands in the former Spanish province.

Chief Osceola is leading the Indians with the help of Negroes, some slaves of the Indians and others runaways from Georgia, who have encouraged Indian resistance because they fear enslavement elsewhere (→Oct. 21, 1837).

Bennett launches non-party Herald

New York City, May 6

Another penny paper has hit the streets of the city: The *New York Herald*. But unlike some of its predecessors, the *Herald* will not carry sensational stories or cater to political parties. Publisher James Gordon Bennett says he intends to present the news with "industry, good taste, brevity, variety, point and piquancy." Last year, Bennett founded the *New York Tribune* with the same goals in mind.

"Locofocos" score Tammany victory

New York City, Oct. 29

Let there be light – and there was light. Thus arose the "Locofocos," a dissident group of Democrats who seized control of a nominating convention in New York's Tammany Hall tonight. Seeking to quell an uprising, conservative Democratic leaders doused the gas lights, leaving the hall dark. Using friction matches, known as locofocos, the insurgents lit 50 candles and proceeded to elect their slate of candidates.

"Skating Scene" (c.1835) by J. Toole. The romantic movement turned the artist's eye toward nature and the vastness of America's landscape.

"Bargaining for a Horse" (1835) by W.S. Mount. No longer impelled to treat subjects of antique grandeur, modern painters look to the simple.

"Ichabod Crane and the Headless Horseman" (1835) by J. Wilgus was inspired by Washington Irving's story, "The Legend of Sleepy Hollow."

1836

Jackson

Caracas, Venezuela, Jan. 20. United States and Venezuela complete treaty of peace, amity, commerce and navigation.

Texas, Feb. 12. St. Augustine's committees of vigilance and safety solicit donations from American women to raise a "ladies battalion" (→ March 6).

Pennsylvania, March 1. Bank of United States officially becomes Bank of United States of Pennsylvania under recently issued state charter.

United States, March 23. U.S. Mint produces first coins on Franklin Beale's steam press.

Texas, March 27. Mexican army commits infamous Goliad Massacre of Texas army (→ Apr. 21).

Washington, D.C., June 28. Hiram Moore and J. Hascall get patent for grain combine.

Texas, September. Referendum here calls for annexation by the United States (→ Oct. 22).

Boston. American Temperance Union organized on platform of total abstinence.

United States. Louis Napoleon takes refuge in United States after coup fails in Strasbourg.

New York City. New York Women's Anti-Slavery Society bars Negroes from membership.

United States. Edgar Allan Poe, 27, marries his cousin, 13.

Arctic Ocean. Thomas Simpson, of Hudson's Bay Company, discovers oil deposits along North Slope.

United States. India rubber boom fails as all rubber products melt in sun.

Louisiana. New Orleans divided into three municipalities, one in French Quarter, other two above Canal Street.

New Orleans. Two Creoles, Lieutenant Shamburg and Adolph Cuvillier, fight duel on horseback with lances.

United States. Oliver Wendell Holmes's *Poems* published.

Boston. William A. Alcott's etiquette book, *The Young Woman's Guide*, published.

DEATH

Montpelier, Virginia. James Madison, 4th President, "Father of the Constitution" (*March 16, 1751).

Alamo falls; all 187 defenders killed

Santa Ana's troops rush the Alamo, heavily outnumbering its defenders.

Americans fiercely defend the walls in spite of the futility of their task.

San Antonio, Texas, March 6

The Alamo, defended by 187 Texans who have been besieged by up to 5,000 regular Mexican forces, has been captured. Reports indicate that no prisoners were taken, and all Texan combatants were killed.

The struggle began February 26, when General Santa Ana led his huge Mexican force into San Antonio to put down the Texas rebellion. On the same day, Colonels William B. Travis of South Carolina and James Bowie of Tennessee and their Texas forces retreated to the Alamo, an old Spanish mission, to make their stand against Santa Ana's advancing infantry.

General Sam Houston ordered that Travis and Bowie abandon their defenseless position, but they refused. When Santa Ana asked the Texans to surrender unconditionally, they answered with a defiant cannon shot. The Mexican general then ran up the red flag, the traditional military symbol that the Mexican army would offer no quarter to the Alamo defenders.

For 12 days, the Mexican forces bombarded the fortress with intense artillery fire, reducing the old mission to a ruin. Early this morning, the massed Mexican infantry began its frontal attack on the Alamo. Reporters say that the beleaguered defenders inflicted more than a thousand casualties on the Mexicans, but within an hour, all the Texans were dead.

Colonel Travis, who had sworn to "Victory or death," lay where he had fallen, rifle in hand, next to a cannon. And Colonel Bowie, who had won fame from his exploits with the Bowie knife, was bayoneted to death on his cot, where he had been confined with pneumonia.

The body of the legendary frontiersman, Colonel Davy Crockett, who had arrived in Texas only a couple of weeks earlier, was found mutilated, surrounded by his companions from Tennessee.

Once Santa Ana had overrun the Alamo, he ordered that the bodies of the 187 defenders be piled up like cordwood and burned. He reportedly spared the lives of some 30 Texan noncombatants. To the Mexican general, the Alamo had become a symbol of Texan defiance and he succeeded in wiping it out. To the Texans, it has also become a symbol – one of liberty and independence. Throughout San Antonio today everyone was saying "Remember the Alamo" (→ 13).

The fight turns to hand-to-hand combat. "Battle of the Alamo" by F.C. Yohn.

A woman survivor tells story of Alamo

Gonzales, Texas, March 13

Susanna Dickinson, the wife of a blacksmith, gave General Sam Houston her eyewitness account of the fall of the Alamo tonight. Mrs. Dickinson was sheltered at the former mission while her husband and 186 other men defended it against thousands of Mexican soldiers under General Santa Ana. For 12 days, Mrs. Dickinson says, the Alamo was under siege. At dawn on March 6, the Mexicans sounded the "deguello," the bugle call that means "Fire and death." Mrs. Dickinson and the other women went to the sacristy while every last man fought to the death. Days later, she was taken to Santa Ana, who bid her tell the Texans that fighting is hopeless (→ March 27).

Texans seize Santa Ana

Wounded General Houston receives Santa Ana. Engraving by Norman Price.

Texas, Apr. 21

The Texas army, commanded by General Sam Houston, launched a surprise attack on Mexico's forces earlier today, routed them and took General Santa Ana prisoner. The brief but decisive clash took place on the banks of the San Jacinto River, situated near the southern coast and Galveston Bay. Santa Ana is the commander who ordered the destruction of the Alamo last month with the death of all 187 Texan defenders. Three weeks ago, he captured 300 Texas soldiers at Goliad and executed all of them by firing squad. Since then, the self-styled "Napoleon of the West" has been pursued by the entire Texas army, bent on revenge. When Santa Ana was captured, he was reportedly enjoying the company of his lover, Jenny. After he yielded to his captors without resistance, Santa Ana was forced to sign documents that surrendered all the Mexican forces that were under his command, and to acknowledge the independence of Texas. The losses of the Texans in the San Jacinto battle were light, with Houston suffering only an ankle wound (→ Sept).

Houston is 1st President

Texas, Oct. 22

General Sam Houston was sworn in last week as the first President of the new Republic of Texas. Houston is orginally from Tennessee, where he served as Governor. A colorful character, he lived with the Indians for several years after leaving the Tennessee governor's mansion. While with the Indians in Arkansas, he took a squaw for his bride and some say he drank about a barrel of whiskey a day. His Indian friends called him "The Raven."

Later, Houston migrated to Texas and during its revolution, he was commanding general of the army. His defeat of Mexican General Santa Ana has won independence for Texas. In the election, where his principal opponent was Stephen F. Austin, Houston received about 80 percent of the 6,000 votes cast.

Houston is an old frontier friend of President Andrew Jackson. Since the President has long been an advocate and a supporter of the Texans' cause, observers here believe that it is only a matter of time before Jackson can persuade Congress that Texas should be admitted to the union (→ March 3, 1837).

Houston enters his capital city.

Arkansas in union as a slave state

Little Rock, Arkansas, June 15

After a long wait, Arkansas became the 25th state to join the union today. President Andrew Jackson signed the act granting statehood to Arkansas. The statehood bill was introduced three years ago by Arkansas Senator Ambrose H. Sevier, but admission was held up because its constitution states that slavery is permitted. Free-state senators delayed approval of the admission until another free state, Michigan, could be added to the union. When Michigan is admitted next year, the nation will have 13 free states and 13 slave states. Sevier argued that statehood was imperative because of the large number of settlers who have been pouring into the region from the East (→ Jan. 26, 1837).

Wisconsin created as a new territory

Washington, D.C., Apr. 20

Marking a further step in westward expansion, Congress today separated the western part of the Michigan Territory and formed a new territory to be known as Wisconsin. The temporary seat of government will be Belmont, and Henry Dodge, a veteran of the Black Hawk War, will be Governor. Although the region became part of the United States in 1783, the British did not withdraw until after the War of 1812 and it was not till 1816 that the American presence was established with the construction of Fort Howard at Green Bay and Fort Crawford at Prairie du Chien. The number of white settlers has grown rapidly since Black Hawk's defeat and now totals some 12,000.

House Southerners gag slavery debates

Washington, D.C., May 26

As anti-slavery sentiments across the country grow, Congress has chosen to respond by not responding. A resolution was passed today stating that Congress has no authority over state slavery laws. Just yesterday, John Quincy Adams, representing the Plymouth District in Massachusetts, said in Congress that although petitioners against slavery had a right to be heard, state slavery laws were not within the jurisdiction of Congress except in case of war. He said "the war powers of Congress would extend to interference with the institution of slavery in every way." The resolution, apparently a reaction to Adams's remarks, insures a "gag" on petitions to Congress about state slavery laws (→ June 15).

Rebels in California proclaim freedom

Monterey, California, Nov. 3

Isaac Graham, a somewhat unsavory American fur trader and hunter, wrote a new page in the history of California today, declaring its freedom from Mexico. Leaving his whiskey distillery, he, 50 Mexican renegades and over 100 Californians under Jose Castro took over the capitol here. No one was hurt and only one shot was fired. But that was said to have been a cannon ball that hit the home of Governor Gutierrez, who surrendered. Shipped off to Mexico, he was the third governor to leave in disgrace.

"Chee-Ah-Ka-Tchee, wife of Not-To-Way" by George Catlin. Catlin's first glimpse of Indians, in the 1820's, convinced him of the grace and beauty of nature.

Van Buren elected; Senate to name V.P.

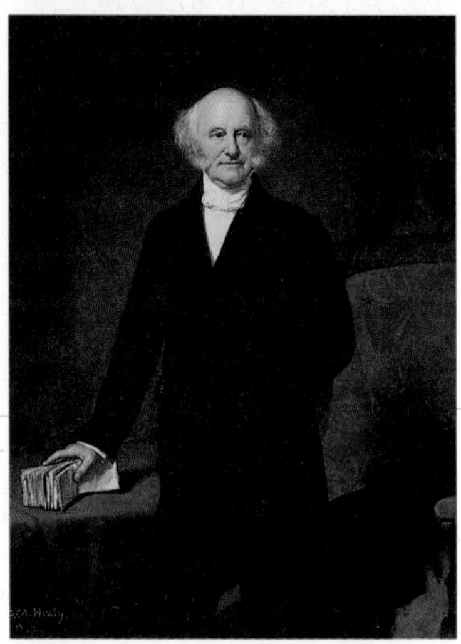

Van Buren, the politically adept "little magician," by G.P.A. Healy.

Washington, D.C., Dec. 7

Vice President Martin Van Buren of New York, the "little magician" of the Democratic Party, was elected President today, defeating William Henry Harrison and three others. Van Buren won 170 electoral votes to just 73 cast for Harrison, a Whig. Among others defeated was Daniel Webster, also a Whig. While Van Buren won handily, pledging support to the policies of the departing President Andrew Jackson, his running mate on the Democratic ticket did not fare so well. Colonel Richard M. Johnson of Kentucky failed to attract a majority and the election of a vice president therefore is now to be decided by the Senate (→March 4, 1837).

First white women to go out West arrive

Marcus Whitman and his party stop to give thanks at the South Pass.

Oregon Country, Sept. 1

When two Protestant missionaries, the Revs. Marcus Whitman and H.H. Spalding, arrived at the junction of the Columbia and Snake Rivers here today, they were accompanied by their wives, Narcissa and Eliza. They are the first white women to have traveled overland to this destination. In doing so, they also brought the first wagons west of Fort Laramie. Whitman and Spalding have been sent to Oregon by the American Home Mission Society to establish a mission for the local Indians in the hope that they can be converted.

The trip has not been an easy one, especially for Mrs. Spalding. She suffered terribly, having been run over by a runaway mule team and thrown from her horse after it stumbled into a wasps' nest. On the latter occasion, her foot was caught in the stirrup and she was dragged quite a distance across the prairie.

The appearance of the two women on July 6 at the fur rendezvous caused a great stir among both Indians and white trappers. Nasty rumors have also accompanied the group. Spalding supposedly once proposed to the present Mrs. Whitman, who spurned his offer, and their situation seems to be uncomfortable for all (→Nov. 29, 1847).

Transcendentalists hold first meeting

Boston, Sept. 19

The Transcendental Club met for the first time today in the home of the Rev. George Ripley of the Purchase Street Unitarian Church. Attending were Ralph Waldo Emerson, the poet-essayist, Bronson Alcott, educator-philosopher, and Orestes Brownson, writer. On October 3, the topic will be "American Genius, the Causes Which Hinder Its Growth, Giving Us No First Rate Productions" (→Aug. 31, 1837)

Americans worship "almighty dollar"

New York City, November

A rampant materialism is abroad in the land, says Washington Irving, America's best-known man of letters, in a recent article in *Knickerbocker* magazine. According to Irving, a trenchant social observer whose *History of New York* and *The Sketch-book* have earned him international recognition, Americans have turned "the almighty dollar" into a "great object of universal devotion throughout our land."

"Farmers Nooning" (1836) by William Sidney Mount of rural Long Island.

Country now has 30 traveling circuses

United States

With the help of a growing railroad system, traveling circuses are cropping up all across the country. Some 30 of these circuses, which in their way try to be educational institutions, are bringing entertainment to many previously isolated areas by setting up "portable barns" that are large enough for the shows and private enough to keep out non-paying spectators. Round tents have replaced the 10-foot canvas walls used in earlier days. At the same time, the circuses have merged menageries and acrobatic companies with equestrian performances. One of the most innovative of the impresarios is P.T. Barnum.

McGuffey scores a hit with "Reader"

Cincinnati, Ohio

Most American schoolchildren will soon be learning their ABC's from a new primer if the early success of the first two editions of William Holmes McGuffey's readers are any indication. McGuffey, a prominent educator who is president of Cincinnati College, believes that it is as important to mold the character of a young student as it is to shape his or her mind. The popular new texts, which are being referred to as "eclectic readers," combine instructive axioms and proverbs, the fundamentals of grammar and selections from the finest British literature – Shakespeare, Byron, Scott and Shelley.

1837

Van Buren

New Orleans, Jan. 25. The *Picayune* newspaper begins publication, selling for small coin called a "picayune."

New York City, Feb. 12. Unemployed workers destroy flour warehouses, protesting high rents and high food prices.

Washington, D.C., February. Congress receives petition from 56 British authors seeking American copyright protection.

Washington, D.C., March 3. President Jackson, on last day in office, recognizes Lone Star Republic of Texas (→ Aug. 25).

Washington, D.C., March 3. Congress passes act raising number of Supreme Court justices from seven to nine.

Washington, D.C., March 4. Democrat Martin Van Buren sworn in as nation's eighth President, Richard M. Johnson as Vice President.

Florida, Oct. 21. Under flag of truce at peace talks, American troops seize Seminole Chief Osceola (→ Dec. 25).

Cincinnati, Oct. 31. William Procter and James Gamble join in partnership with capital investment of $7,192.24.

Winthrop, Massachusetts, Dec. 29. Hiram Avery and John Avery Pitts granted patent for combined thresher and fanning mill.

Florida. Negro John Horse is one of three leaders of Seminole Indian forces that defeat U.S. troops at Battle of Okeechobee.

United States. Plows using steel blade instead of cast iron manufactured by John Deere.

Baltimore, Maryland. Recent arrival William Knabe begins manufacturing pianos.

United States. American Peace Society begins active opposition to all forms of war.

Philadelphia. American Moral Reform Society holds first convention.

Lapwai, Idaho. Indian children are beneficiaries of first school in Idaho.

United States. *A Manual of Politeness for Both Sexes* is published.

Philadelphia. Publication of economic nationalist Henry C. Carey's *Principles of Political Economy.*

Financial panic in U.S.

Washington, D.C., Oct. 12

In a move to stem the financial panic that is sweeping the country, Congress today authorized the issue of $10 million in short-term government notes. Another measure, to create an independent federal Treasury, is still with the House.

While opinions differ about who is responsible for the panic, some of its immediate causes are clear enough. The 10-year boom in business, industry, banking, transportation and Western land has led to extensive borrowing, fueled by the recent demise of the conservative Bank of the United States. The order that government land should be paid for in coin has caused large amounts of hard money to be withdrawn from circulation. Last year the wheat crop failed. Brokers in New York and growers in the South have been hit by a 50 percent drop in the price of cotton. The failure of three banks in England along with a downturn in business in Europe have resulted in many overseas bankers calling in their short-term American loans.

As a result, banks have been failing all over the country and unemployment has soared. The high cost of flour has caused riots in New York. The poorhouses are full, and as winter comes vast numbers of people are having to turn to private charity for food and fuel.

Texans' annexation request is rejected

Washington, D.C., Aug. 25

The United States Government officially notified the leaders of the Republic of Texas today that their bid for admission to the United States has been rejected. The Senate voted down the Texas statehood bill by a vote of 35 to 16 last month. While most Southern senators voted for Texas statehood, anti-slavery Whigs blocked the effort. Former President Jackson is furious at the action of the Senate. He called the Whigs "traitors to the best interest of our country." But given his determination to get Texas into the union, the admission issue is far from settled (→ Sept. 29, 1839).

Jackson leaves office with $90 in pocket

Tennessee, March 17

His days of glory behind him, Andrew Jackson returned to his home, the Hermitage, here today lamenting that he left Washington "with barely $90 in my pocket." But the old soldier and war hero who served as the President for eight years left his nation a legacy far richer – and to some critics, more controversial.

His legacy, Jacksonian Democracy, is based on the belief that there is a deep conflict between the haves and have-nots, the business community on the one hand and the farmers and laborers on the other. Jacksonians sought to reign in the power of capitalist groups. In one dramatic move that was characteristic of his years in office, Jackson vetoed a bill to recharter the Bank of United States, calling the bank a monopoly that is designed to make "rich men . . . richer by act of Congress." He forced removal of federal deposits and put them in smaller banks. Jackson may have summed up his thinking best in his farewell address, pleading for loyalty to the union and condemning the monopolies.

The Great Cheese Levee. Thanks to this rush of hungry visitors, the President got very little of a 1,400-pound cheese sent to him by admirers in New York.

New Mexico revolt put down by troops

New Mexico, Sept. 12

The revolt that broke out here on August 25 has been crushed by the Mexican army. It erupted after the government imposed higher taxes and ordered other basic changes that the residents feel are against their best interests. Some of the American settlers say that the actions of the government and the counteractions of the rebels, as in most Latin revolutions, are so complex that the situation is virtually incomprehensible (→ Dec. 25, 1846).

"Shot heard round the world" is sung

Concord, Massachusetts, July 4

Today is the anniversary of the Revolutionary War battle here 62 years ago and all Concord turned out to mark it. A battlefield monument was unveiled and residents sang a hymn set to a new poem by the local clergyman Ralph Waldo Emerson. His much-praised ode began with these stirring lines:

By the rude bridge that arched
the flood
Their flag to April's breeze
unfurled
Here once the embattled farmers
stood
And fired the shot heard round
the world . . .

▷

Seminole chief seized; U.S. wins a battle

Chief Osceola, seized by American troops under a flag of truce.

Florida, Dec. 25

General Zachary Taylor's forces routed Seminole Indian fighters at Lake Okeechobee today, but the price was high: 27 officers killed and more than 100 men wounded. The Seminoles lost only 14 men. The battle began when the army charged the Indians in a swamp and were met by deadly fire. But in a three-hour struggle, Taylor's force of more than 1,000 men drove the Indians from the field.

This reverse for the Seminoles follows the capture of the charismatic Chief Osceola in October. Osceola and a group of warriors, including Chief Wild Cat, came to St. Augustine to discuss a plan for peace. They assembled under a white flag of truce, but they were ordered imprisoned by General Thomas Sidney Jessup, who had earlier initiated efforts to end this Second Seminole War. Sidney's seizure of Indians in this way has been criticized as a dishonorable act, but his defenders say the Indians had been told they would only be heard under terms of surrender (→Autumn, 1842).

Tecumseh's twin, Shawnee Prophet, dies

Argentina, Kansas, November

Tenskwatawa, the famed "Shawnee Prophet," died today at the age of 69 in this Wyandotte County town. His name means "a door to be opened," but ever since he prophesied the solar eclipse of 1806, he has been reknowned as the "Prophet." He spent much of his life working with his twin brother, Tecumseh, in an effort to unite the Shawnee people against encroachment by white settlers of Indian lands. Tecumseh, who died in 1813, was a famous Shawnee chief and warrior, remembered as a brave and honorable man. The Shawnee chief believed deeply in the intrinsic right of all Indians to maintain their lands, and that all restrictions on those lands were the impositions of white men and therefore invalid. Tenskwatawa joined his brother's crusade in 1808, and he added his spiritual teaching to Tecumseh's revolutionary teaching. The culmination of their attempts to create solidarity among the Shawnee was at the Battle of Tippecanoe in 1811, but the Indian confederacy was defeated.

Tenskwatawa, "Shawnee Prophet."

Sioux cede lands, opening vast area

Northern Plains, Autumn

Word has arrived at outposts here that the fierce Sioux Indians have agreed to give up their traditional lands east of the Mississippi River to the United States government. This tribe, which lives mostly on the Great Plains, has held the land for aeons. But in the face of white settlers, the Indians apparently feel they can best maintain their tribal existence by moving westward. The government is now preparing to deal with a huge land rush.

Mount Holyoke, a school for women

South Hadley, Mass., Nov. 8

It was the first day of classes and some 80 young women strode into Mount Holyoke Female Seminary today. Educator Mary Lyon almost single-handedly raised the funds required for the new school, although many in society consider education an improper activity for a woman. Miss Lyon persuaded benefactors that education can enrich a woman's life, making her a better wife, mother and homemaker.

15,000 Indians in 3 tribes die of smallpox

"Bull Dance, Mandan Okipa Ceremony" (c.1835-39) by George Catlin.

North Dakota, August

Another devastating smallpox epidemic has swept through the Indian communities on the Missouri River, almost annihilating the Mandan, Hidatsa and Arikara tribes. A steamboat representing the American Fur Company that came up the river in June is thought to have been the origin of the epidemic that has taken 15,000 lives. In the three months since, the Mandan tribe has been reduced from 2,000 people to fewer than 100. Chief Mato Tope died on July 30, having starved himself after he saw his wives and children die horrible deaths.

Emerson envisions a new U.S. society

Cambridge, Mass., Aug. 31

"Each age must write its own books," said Ralph Waldo Emerson, 34-year-old essayist and former pastor of the Second Church of Boston, speaking to an audience spellbound by his princely cadences at Harvard University's Phi Beta Kappa Society today. In his speech on *The American Scholar*, he called for a society led by the best thinkers, who must combine knowledge of European culture with a study of nature and men (→Apr. 1841).

Book alerts women to dangers of riding

United States

Donald Walker's new book, *Exercise for Ladies*, advises women against horseback riding because it deforms the lower part of the body that performs womanly duties. Another popular work, *Dr. Combes's Principles of Physiology*, seemingly advocates the opposite, and stresses outdoor activity as well as frequent use of soap and water. But some women say they prefer a pale "indoor" complexion to a ruddy one.

Abolitionist editor slain defending press

The rage of the mob. Lovejoy's press is besieged by armed belligerents.

Boston, Dec. 8

A call for an end to slavery in America was delivered in a public speech today by one of Boston's leading citizens, the lawyer Wendell Phillips, a 36-year-old graduate of Harvard College and Harvard Law School and the son of John Phillips, Boston's first mayor. In a fiery oration entitled "The Murder of Lovejoy," delivered at Faneuil Hall, where citizens had gathered to protest the death of the abolitionist editor Elijah Parish Lovejoy, Phillips repudiated his traditional upbringing by casting his lot with the nation's slave population and eulogizing Lovejoy, the crusading editor martyred by a mob in Alton, Illinois, on November 7, after he refused to stop publishing his anti-slavery newspaper.

Lovejoy, who died at the age of 35, had stared down many attempts to silence his abolitionist views. A native of Maine, he became editor of the *St. Louis Observer*, an anti-slavery paper in 1833, but his views enraged residents, who threatened him with bodily harm. Lovejoy fled across the Mississippi River and a few miles up the shore on the Illinois side to Alton, where he continued to publish the *Observer* and to agitate for the abolition of slavery. In spite of repeated assaults by the pro-slavery forces, Lovejoy persisted, even after his press had been hurled into the river by his enemies on two occasions. Then, on November 7, his office was stormed by a mob. When the editor tried to protect his press with his body, he was shot to death.

"View on the Catskill, Early Autumn" (1837) by Thomas Cole. This rich, poetic masterwork is modeled after the westward view along Cole's favorite evening walk, Catskill Creek, the mountains and the sunset.

Non-slave Michigan 26th state in union

Detroit, Michigan, Jan. 26

Three years after the territorial legislature first petitioned Congress for permission to form a state, Michigan has joined the union. The delay was due, first to the need to hold a convention, draw up a constitution and have it ratified by the electorate, and second to a boundary dispute with Ohio, over the 470-square-mile Toledo Strip, a dispute that was resolved in Michigan's favor. A third cause of the delay involved the objection of Southern senators to the candidacy of another free state unless a slave state were also admitted. This objection was dealt with last year when Arkansas, with a population barely able to meet the minimum of 50,000 needed for statehood, joined the union (→Aug. 10, 1846).

Morse asks patent for his telegraph

New York City, Sept. 4

The well-known painter Samuel F.B. Morse is seeking a patent on a device capable of transmitting messages almost instantly over long distances. Called a telegraph, the device sends electrical impulses through wires. By using long and short impulses, the signals may be used to send words and sentences. A number of individuals have proposed such a device, which is based on the latest discoveries in magnetism and electricity, but Morse is the first to demonstrate a working model of a telegraph. To put the telegraph to practical use, Morse must arrange to have wires strung over long distances, so that messages can be sent from city to city. He is now seeking government and private financing (→1838).

"St. Nicholas" (c.1837) by Robert W. Weir. A gentle, somewhat unworldly man, Weir studied for four years in Rome and Florence, but his talent is for illustrations and literary subjects, not history in the classical style.

1838

Van Buren

South Manchester, Connecticut, March 31. First commercially successful silk mill in United States opens.

Central Plains, July 4. Territory of Iowa established and Robert Lucas appointed first Governor.

Washington, D.C., July 7. Rail lines designated as postal routes by act of Congress.

Hampton Roads, Virginia, Aug. 18. Lieutenant Charles Wilkes begins scientific fact-finding tour of Pacific Ocean and South Seas; first federally funded expedition (→ Jan. 19, 1840).

Baltimore, Sept. 3. Considered no more than "real estate," Frederick Douglass escapes from slavery.

Washington, D.C., November. Failing to court political support, President Martin Van Buren loses control of House and Senate in mid-term elections.

Washington, D.C., Dec. 3. Ohio Whig Representative Joshua Giddings becomes first abolitionist in Congress.

New York City. Walter Hunt withdraws patent request for improved sewing machine, fearing negative impact upon employment.

New York City. Women enjoy hoop-rolling on the Parade Grounds.

South Braintree, Massachusetts. Hollingsworth brothers start production of manila paper.

Oklahoma. U.S. Army engineers clear Red River, opening waterway to steamboats.

United States. 1838 marks third year of race riots and lynchings across nation.

Missouri. As result of "wildcat banking," Mormon leader Joseph Smith settles at a site he calls the Garden of Eden.

Missouri. "Mormon Wars" erupt as Mormons are driven from Missouri into Illinois.

Boston. Boston introduces music studies into city school system; first in U.S. to do so.

United States. James Fenimore Cooper turns to social criticism in *The American Democrat.*

Boston. William Ellery Channing's *Self Culture* published; self-improvement offered as alternative to strict Calvinism.

Act that hurt supply of coins is repealed

Washington, D.C., May 21

The Specie Circular promulgated by President Jackson early last year requiring that all purchases of government land be made in hard currency was repealed today. The measure has been widely blamed for worsening the economic crisis by removing large sums of coinage from circulation. A similar bill of repeal was passed on March 1 of last year but was "pocket-vetoed" by President Jackson, who left office two days later.

Rebels in Canada laying down arms

Niagara River, Jan. 13

In what may have been the continent's shortest war, Canadian rebels laid down their arms today, 13 days after it started. In a war so brief it is called an affair – the Caroline Affair, after an arms supply ship the Canadians destroyed – the rebels quit the fight when they learned that General Winfield Scott had taken charge of the American border force. Without arms from the U.S. side, the rebels could not win (→ March 25, 1839).

Morse devises code for new telegraph

New York City

Samuel Morse, inventor of the electric telegraph, has developed a code that makes it possible to send messages quickly over long distances. The Morse code uses a system of dots and dashes to represent letters of the alphabet. A is represented by a dot and a dash, B by a dash and three dots, and so on. He is trying to persuade Congress to finance construction of a telegraph line between two cities, but has not succeeded (→ June 20, 1841).

"The Trail of Tears": 18,000 Cherokees driven from homelands

Missouri, December

The forced removal of the Cherokees, mainly from Georgia, to the Indian Territory west of the Mississippi, is about to be completed. The removal process began October 1, and is expected to be concluded in early spring. The United States Army is conducting the transfer operation under General Winfield Scott. The forced removal policy has been roundly denounced by most humanists and constitutional experts. While the Supreme Court has essentially ruled that the Indians had the legal right to remain at their ancestral homes in Georgia, President Jackson did not feel that way. After hearing former Chief Justice John Marshall's verdict, he reputedly said, "He has made his decision; now let him enforce it." Whereupon Jackson ordered the army to move the Indians out of Georgia. Reliable witnesses say that as many as 18,000 Indians are being sent through the summer heat, droughts and winter snows to the Indian country. They also say that many of the Indians are dying of starvation, heat-induced diseases and exposure from the cold. An epidemic of smallpox is also reportedly decimating their ranks.

General Scott has announced that he intends to conduct this operation with as little bloodshed and hardship as possible. The Indians, however, have already termed this long journey "The Trail of Tears." The Cherokees were herded into 645 wagons and are being guarded by soldiers at bayonet point. At the moment, they are crossing Missouri on their way west.

"The Trail of Tears" by R. Lindneux. The long, forced march of a people uprooted from their sacred land.

British steamships start Atlantic service

The 1,320-ton Great Western leaving on a gray day in Bristol harbor.

New York City, Apr. 23

The British steamer Great Western whistled into port on its first trans-Atlantic trip today, completing the journey in 16 days. Expected tomorrow is the steamer Sirius, which left Bristol, England, on the same day as the Great Western. The ships average about 10 knots per hour. Although steam drives them, sails are also used. The two packet liners, carrying both freight and passengers, are inaugurating British trans-Atlantic service.

While American ships have made the voyage before, this showing of British steam power indicates that American shipping will face stiff competition. The Royal Admiralty lauded Isambard Brunel, builder of the Great Western, and others responsible for the successful journey, and is expected to arrange government financing for the lines.

British engineers are now working on ways to convert from wood-generated steam to coal-generated steam. The introduction of British service to America is likely to motivate American nautical innovation.

Tocqueville's views on U.S. in English

New York City

"Americans are so enamored of equality that they would rather be equal in slavery than unequal in freedom." This is one of many bold assertions scattered through the pages of *Democracy in America*, which has just been published in English after having caused an international sensation when it first appeared in French three years ago. The author, Alexis de Tocqueville, a 33-year-old nobleman, has drawn on first-hand observations made during a stay in America that lasted from May 1831 to February 1832. He analyzes American goverment, economics, art and customs in two penetrating volumes.

The book has some kind words for its subject. Tocqueville lauds the generosity, know-how and gumption of Americans. And he offers a prediction guaranteed to warm the hearts of American readers. Someday, the author claims, the United States will surpass the leading European countries and become one of the most powerful nations on earth. What nation will emerge as its rival? His answer, Russia, has already left many experts shaking their heads.

Tocqueville by T. Chasseriau.

Oberlin is accepting women as students

Oberlin, Ohio, Oct. 30

With this year's class, Oberlin College becomes the nation's first institution of higher learning to admit women to its college programs on an equal basis with men. Oberlin had previously had boys and girls together in its primary and secondary programs and older girls studied in its female seminary. When the four women who entered today applied last spring, the authorities saw no reason not to admit qualified applicants simply because of their sex. Oberlin, by admitting these women, continues its policy of openness. It was also the first to admit qualified Negroes to college.

House of abolition burned by arsonists

Philadelphia, May 7

The new meeting house of the Philadelphia Female Anti-Slavery Society was set afire by supporters of slavery tonight. Some arsonists also headed for the home of abolitionist Lucretia Mott, but a friend supplied them with misleading directions, and the mob eventually dispersed. Mrs. Mott, a 45-year-old Quaker minister, intends to continue her anti-slavery activities with the help of fellow abolitionists such as Sarah and Angelina Grimke of South Carolina. The Anti-Slavery Convention of American Women, which was interrupted by the fire, may reconvene elsewhere.

Underground Railroad helps slaves flee

Philadelphia

The abolitionist Robert Purvis has been named president of the now formally established Underground Railroad. This network of private homes and establishments has long been at work helping slaves to escape and protecting fugitive Negroes from the violence of their pursuers. Southern slave owners put their losses at over $200,000 a year from slaves who flee across the Mason-Dixon line. Efforts to help slaves escape began with the Quakers in the late 1700's, and a system has now evolved into a map of organized and tightly structured rest stops and hiding places on the trek north. Slaves who are caught by their masters face terrible beatings, sometimes death. Also, escape to the North is no guarantee of freedom or safety. Under the 1793 Fugitive Slave Law, fugitives will be returned to their masters even when found in states that do not allow slavery; whites who help runaways face fines (→Sept. 18, 1850).

$150 REWARD

RANAWAY from the subscriber, on the night of the 2d instant, a negro man, who calls himself *Henry May*, about 22 years old, 5 feet 6 or 8 inches high, ordinary color, rather chunky built, bushy head, and has it divided mostly on one side, and keeps it very nicely combed; has been raised in the house, and is a first rate dining-room servant, and was in a tavern in Louisville for 18 months. I expect he is now in Louisville trying to make his escape to a free state, (in all probability to Cincinnati, Ohio.) Perhaps he may try to get employment on a steamboat. He is a good cook, and is handy in any capacity as a house servant. Had on when he left, a dark cassinett coatee, and dark striped cassinett pantaloons, new—he had other clothing. I will give $50 reward if taken in Louisvill; 100 dollars if taken one hundred miles from Louisville in this State, and 150 dollars if taken out of this State, and delivered to me, or secured in any jail so that I can get him again.

WILLIAM BURKE.

Bardstown, Ky., September 3d, 1838.

Advertisement in a Kentucky paper offers $50-150 for the return of a runaway.

1839

Van Buren

Mauch Chunk, Pennsylvania, Jan. 12. Anthracite coal first used in iron smelting process.

Washington, D.C., Feb. 20. By act of Congress, dueling is banned in District of Columbia.

Washington, D.C., March 3. Congress allocates $1,000 to Patent Office for seed distribution, agricultural statistical research and agricultural experimentation.

Texas, June. Steamship Zavala commissioned into Texas navy.

Texas, Sept. 29. France recognizes Texas as sovereign nation (→Jan. 19, 1840).

Warsaw, New York, Nov. 13. Abolitionist Liberty Party nominates James G. Birney for president, Thomas Earle for vice president.

Idaho, Nov. 17. Chief Timothy, Indian leader who embraced Christianity, is baptised.

Harrisburg, Pennsylvania, Dec. 4. Whigs nominate William Henry Harrison over controversial Henry Clay.

United States. Power loom for weaving two-ply carpets developed by Erastus B. Bigelow.

United States. Corn planter capable of sowing two rows at once, invented by D.S. Rockwell.

Mississippi. For first time in United States, women are given legal control over their property.

Washington, D.C. Wheat is gaining in importance as a cash crop, as American farmers sell more than 84 million bushels.

Philadelphia. Joseph Saxton makes daguerrotype which he calls *Old Arsenal and Cupola of the Old Philadelphia High School.*

United States. Longellow's *Voices of the Night*, first book of poems, published.

United States. Daniel Pierce's novel *The Green Mountain Boys* is best-seller.

New York City. *The Pathfinder* by James Fenimore Cooper is published.

New York City. *Hunts' Merchants' Magazine*, first business periodical in United States, published.

By luck, Goodyear invents rubber-making

Rubber, Goodyear's surprise.

New Haven, Connecticut

A new way to treat rubber so that it remains flexible but does not melt in hot weather has been developed by Charles Goodyear, a 39-year-old New Haven man. The discovery was made by accident, after eight years of experimentation with rubber. Goodyear had already patented a way of treating rubber with nitric acid to make it less sticky, but the treatment was not as successful as he had hoped.

The discovery occurred while Goodyear was working with rubber that had been mixed with sulfur and white lead, and accidentally dropped the mixture on his stove. When he scraped the charred substance off the stove, he found it was still flexible, did not become rigid in the cold and did not soften when heated again. In a series of experiments that followed, Goodyear found that heating sulfur-treated rubber to 212 degrees Fahrenheit produced the best result.

He expects greatly expanded use of rubber for raincoats and other waterproof clothing, in the household and in other applications, and he plans to start large-scale production of the product. But Goodyear faces a major challenge in competition from those who have appropriated the technique. A long series of court fights has been forecast.

Morse makes 1st photographs in America

New York City, December

New Yorkers are flocking to have their portraits made by a technique that captures camera images on copper plates. The technique, developed in France by Louis Jacques Mande Daguerre, was introduced here by two New Yorkers, John W. Draper and Samuel F.B. Morse, the latter better known as a painter and inventor of the telegraph.

"Les Boulevards de Paris," made early this year by Louis Jacques Mande Daguerre of France. In a daguerrotype such as this one, the image seen is actually reversed.

A daguerrotype, as the picture is called, is made by coating a copper plate with silver and exposing it to iodine fumes to make it light-sensitive. The plate is placed in a camera, and the person whose portrait is being made holds a pose for several minutes while the plate is exposed. The image is developed by treating the plate first with mercury and then hyposulfite of soda. The result is a true-to-life image that rivals those of the best portrait painters.

Daguerre, a professional scene painter, developed the technique in collaboration with an amateur inventor, Joseph Nicephore Niepce, who died before the method was perfected. Daguerre sold all rights to the French government earlier this year and published full details of the process in a booklet that at once became a best-seller. Draper and Morse, apparently the first Americans to use the process, made their first daguerrotype in September, just one month after announcement of the process. Their success is leading others to set up daguerrotype studios in a number of cities.

Doubleday writes rules for baseball

Cooperstown, New York

Abner Doubleday, a 20-year-old West Point cadet, has assigned himself the task of taking some of the chaos out of the increasingly popular sport of baseball. Doubleday, reportedly dismayed by the sight of dozens of boys running aimlessly over the field, colliding in their efforts to catch a batted ball and trying to put out runners by hitting them with the ball, has mapped out a field with 11 players in set positions. Cynics call Doubleday's role in developing the game minimal, insisting that this American sport is just an offshoot of the English game of rounders, and that this year Doubleday did not even visit Cooperstown, which many call the home of baseball (→June 19, 1846).

Poe tales run from eerie to grotesque

Philadelphia

The spooky world of Edgar Allan Poe, 30, grows stranger with publication of his first book of stories, *Tales of the Grotesque and Arabesque*, which includes one about *Berenice*, whose heroine suffers epileptic trances, and *Ligeia*, which explores madness, death and reincarnation. Last year, he published his first novel, *The Narrative of Arthur Gordon Pym, of Nantucket*.

American desk and bookcase, 1836-50, made of rosewood and silkwood in the now fashionable Gothic Revival style, which is also coming to dominate architecture.

Aroostook War with Canada finally ended

Washington, D.C., March 25

After a year and a half of skirmishes, the Aroostook War is over. Total casualties: one American.

The war began as a border spat between Maine and New Brunswick. When the Americans won the Revolutionary War, the treaty recognizing their claims was not based on valid geographic data. As a result, both Maine and New Brunswick claimed the Aroostook Valley. Fighting erupted as lumbermen of both sides sought the same trees. All truce efforts failed, including arbitration by the Dutch King.

The situation worsened as Canadian rebels, backed by American sympathizers, set up an outpost on Navy Island in the Niagara River. Canadian forces attacked, crossing the river into the United States to burn a supply boat. One American soldier died in the raid. The rebels held out for two weeks but were overpowered by their government.

But this did not end the Maine-New Brunswick dispute. For 18 months, marauders have been active on both sides of the Niagara. Last month, Canadian authorities arrested Rufus McIntire, a land agent for the State of Maine, starting another round of conflict.

To end this sorry episode, President Van Buren sent General Winfield Scott to bring calm to the area and create a climate for negotiations with New Brunswick. Today, the talks succeeded (→ Aug. 9, 1842).

Mormon headquarters is moved to Illinois

Nauvoo, Illinois, May 10

As a result of heated and unrelenting hostility experienced in the state of Missouri, Joseph Smith has led his band of followers to the Commerce Purchase in the state of Illinois. Life in Missouri had become far too dangerous for the Mormons, especially after an attack last October that left 17 Mormons dead and many injured. Some of the leading citizens of Illinois offered the Mormons refuge in their state because they were appalled by their treatment in Missouri. Here in the settlement that he has named Nauvoo, Smith hopes to find some peace after his persecution and imprisonmemt in Missouri and his previous troubles in the East (→ July 12, 1843).

Joseph Smith by Adrian Lamb.

Clay: To be right or to be president

Washington D.C., Feb. 7

Whig Henry Clay, himself a slave owner, gave a speech denouncing abolitionists today, clearly trying to distance himself from the growing anti-slavery movement in the Whig Party. Clay says a sudden freeing of slaves might stir up racial wars across the land. He says he is not worried about how voicing these opinions will affect his presidential campaign: "I trust the sentiments and opinions are correct; I had rather be right than be president."

Iowa and Missouri clash in Honey War

Iowa Territory, December

Out in a land that romantics say knows no boundaries, a battle is raging over the border dividing Iowa and Missouri. Militia from the two states are at a standoff in Van Buren County, the area in dispute. Its residents, abhorring slavery, have arrested a Missouri tax collector. Missouri militiamen responded by felling three prized "bee trees." The conflict, dubbed the Honey War, will most likely be referred to Congress (→ Feb. 1849).

Africans held after slave revolt at sea

Connecticut, August

A battered Spanish slave ship has arrived off the coast of Connecticut with 53 Africans in command. According to the two surviving crew members, the Amistad was headed from one Cuban port to another when the slaves on board rebelled. Led by a Mendi tribesman named Cinque, they killed the captain and nearly all of the crew, leaving only two alive to sail north. Spain is expected to demand extradition of the rebels (→ March 9, 1841).

"Two Years Before Mast" is published

New York City

It's a unique "pilgrim's progress" that is described by Richard Henry Dana Jr., who at the age of 19 quit Harvard's ivied walls for residence in the foc's'le of the brig Pilgrim when it sailed for California on August 31, 1834. The 150-day voyage is vividly related in Dana's first book, *Two Years Before the Mast*, issued by Harper's. The 25-year-old Dana, who now has a Harvard law degree, wrote a legal article, *Cruelty to Seamen*, last year.

Male moralists often warn women of the age never to imitate "the fluttering votaries of that capricious dame called Fashion." Nonetheless, wardrobes of the wealthy change with the seasons. Waistlines are dropping, and growing ever narrower thanks to the tyranny of the corset. Pastel bonnets stretch skyward, replacing the low hats of an earlier day. And men are hardly immune to vanity. The sporting dandy distinguishes himself with a tapered waistline to match his lady friend's and a high hat to top it off.

"The Peaceable Kingdom" (c.1839) by Edward Hicks. A devout Quaker, Hicks has given voice to the pacifist vision of the lion lying with the lamb.

1840

Van Buren

Antarctica, Jan. 19. Charles Wilkes's expedition comes within sight of Antarctica (→June 10, 1842).

Texas, Jan. 19. Austin chosen as site for Texas capital (→June 19, 1841).

Washington, D.C., March 31. President Martin Van Buren issues executive order establishing 10-hour day on government work projects.

California, April. All 47 foreign trappers are imprisoned.

Wisconsin, June. Three Welshmen produce first ale made in Milwaukee.

Washington, D.C., Dec. 13. British Minister to United States, Henry Stephen Fox, demands release of Canadian deputy sheriff Alexander McLeod, arrested in New York as accomplice in Amos Durfee's 1837 murder (→26).

Washington, D.C., Dec. 26. Secretary of State John Forsyth tells British Minister Fox that New York State courts must decide fate of Alexander McLeod (→Oct. 12, 1841).

United States. Cotillions now dominated by recently introduced waltz.

Toronto, Canada. New York club, first U.S. team to take part in international cricket match, defeats Toronto.

Baltimore. First rabbi in United States, Abraham Rice, installed here.

Baltimore. Washington Temperance Society founded by rehabilitated alcoholics.

Baltimore. Baltimore College of Dental Surgery, first dental school in nation, is founded.

England. Brigham Young conducts speaking tour in order to advertise Mormon Church.

Mississippi. Blacks outnumber whites as cotton crop expands.

United States. Approximately 93 percent of Northern free Negroes are disenfranchised.

Tampa Bay, Florida. Grapefruit introduced by Don Philippe of Spain.

Missouri. Last antelope seen in Missouri.

Washington, D.C. *An Essay on a Congress of Nations* by William Ladd advocates an international court and system of international law.

"Tippecanoe and Tyler, Too" win

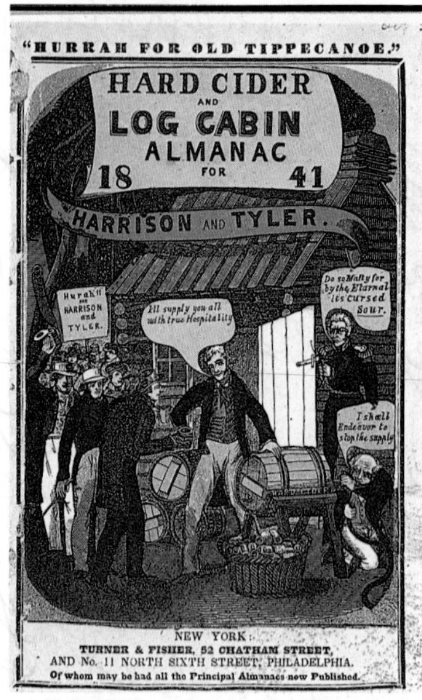

Almanac cover promoting Harrison.

Washington, D.C., Dec. 2

William Henry Harrison, the hero of the Battle of Tippecanoe, was elected President of the United States today. A wealthy Whig, Harrison won the hearts of America's voters with his "Log Cabin and Hard Cider" campaign.

For Harrison and his running mate, John Tyler, a twosome hailed as "Tippecanoe and Tyler, Too" during the campaign, it was a solid victory over a former foe, the outgoing President Martin Van Buren, who just four years earlier defeated Harrison in the contest for chief executive. Today, Harrison polled 234 electoral votes to just 60 for Van Buren, almost the reverse of the 170-73 electoral victory that Van Buren scored in 1836.

It was only by happenstance that Harrison stumbled on what was to become the major theme of his campaign. One of his detractors observed early in the campaign that if someone gave Harrison a supply of hard cider, a small pension and his choice of how to spend his time, the old warrior would sit happily by his log cabin for the rest of his days. The Harrison forces worked this to their advantage by having him run his campaign from a log cabin built atop a wagon bed to which was attached a barrel of hard cider, thus emphasizing his close links to the common man. The people loved it, guzzling cider at campaign stops, stroking coonskins attached to the wagon and dancing in the streets. The country rang with log cabin songs, hard-cider ditties, marches, quicksteps and lots of dance tunes. It turned into the liveliest campaign in the nation's history and Van Buren and his advisers could not stem the exodus of many previously loyal Democrats from their party.

Harrison, at 67 the oldest man ever elected President, was born in Virginia and joined the army as a young man. He was a war hero long before entering politics, famed as "Old Tippecanoe" after he routed Tecumseh's warriors in 1811 at Tippecanoe in the Indiana Territory. Two years later, Harrison won a key victory over the Indians at what was called the Battle of the Thames, where Tecumseh was killed.

Despite his image as a common man, Harrison lives in a mansion on a big estate. He served in the House from 1816-19 and the Senate from 1825-28. Tyler, too, has served in Congress (→Apr. 4, 1841).

"Log Cabin and Hard Cider" hospitality. Harrison greets a war veteran.

"O.K." in vogue

United States

Are folks more optimistic these days? It seems that everybody is finding everything O.K., even if they're not sure what O.K. stands for. Did it start with President Andrew Jackson's signing his papers "Oll Korrect"? Is it from the Choctaw Indian word "hoke," meaning "it is so"? Is it an Americanized Scottish "och aye"? Wherever it originated, O.K. is O.K. by Americans.

Daguerrotype studios opening in America

New York City

The number of daguerrotype studios here continues to multiply as the portrait-making technique imported from France becomes ever more popular. Although the subject must sit immobile for minutes on end, this inconvenience does not seem to be inhibiting the boom. Dozens of studios have opened or are planned. One daguerrian artist, Matthew Brady, is planning a Gallery of Illustrious Americans.

Experimentation with daguerrotypes is producing new methods and images. Some artists are turning wagons into portable studios and plan to travel from town to town making portraits. In Boston, Samuel Bemis made a daguerrotype of King's Chapel this year. It required an exposure of nearly an hour. In New York, John William Draper captured images of the moon. Now improvements are being made to cut the exposure time for portraits.

Washington statue, in toga, stirs furor

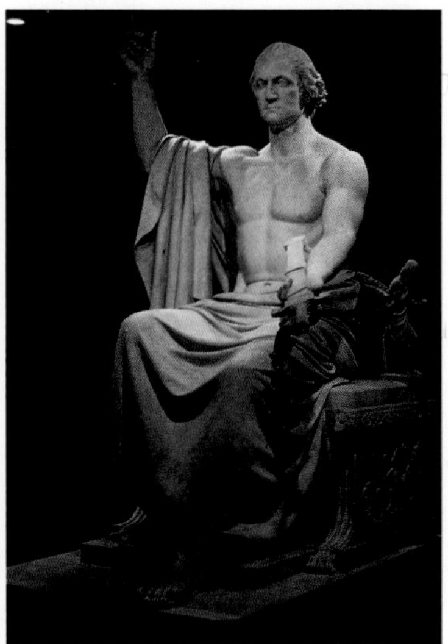

The Father of His Country, bare-chested and wearing sandals.

United States

Many American citizens are outraged to learn that a barely clad statue of George Washington has been completed by Horatio Greenough, the expatriate sculptor who lives in Italy. He has depicted Washington in the manner of a classical figure, draped in Roman toga and wearing sandals. Although Greenough designed his monument after a renowned statue of Zeus from antiquity, Americans would prefer to see the first President attired in full Revolutionary uniform. Perhaps offended citizens should be thankful that Greenough did not take as his model the nude statue of Napoleon (→ 1842).

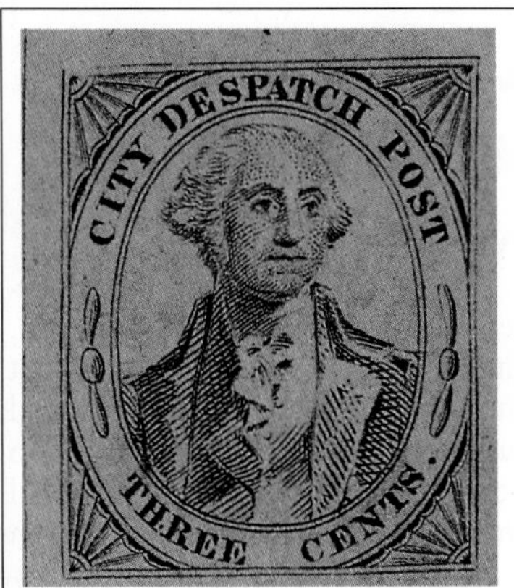

May 6. *Hoping to collect prepayment for all mail, the Post Office has issued stamps to be affixed to letters. The system is the brainchild of Rowland Hill of England.*

17 million people; new land a magnet

Washington, D.C.

The nation's population grew by nearly a third in the past decade, to just over 17 million, the latest census shows. Some 600,000 immigrants contributed to the growth, with the opening of new lands a major factor. Missouri nearly tripled its population, to 383,000, in the past decade, while Indiana and Alabama nearly doubled the number of inhabitants. New York remains the most populous state, up 500,000 to 2.4 million. Only one state, Virginia, lost population. New states included in the census were Wisconsin, with 31,000 inhabitants, and Iowa, with 43,000. The United States has 2,818 miles of railroad and 3,326 miles of canals, with 69 percent of workers in agriculture.

Swiss found town called "Pig's Eye"

Northern Plains, May 6

A group of Swiss immigrants squatting at Fort Snelling were expelled by order of the Secretary of War. Today they found themselves a site nearby along the Mississippi River where they plan to establish a village. They are naming it "Pig's Eye" [St Paul] in honor of Pierre Parant, who led them in the search for a suitable site and who helped lay the first claim on the area. Parant is affectionately nicknamed "Pig's Eye."

Uncouth Vanderbilt snubs high society

Staten Island, New York

Cornelius Vanderbilt, who has money but no manners, turns up his nose at New York high society (which in turn has given him the cold shoulder) and remains with his family at his $27,000 Staten Island mansion. The 45-year-old Vanderbilt has already compiled a fortune, building several large steamers noted for luxurious accommodations and low fares. Despite Vanderbilt's success, le beau monde looks down on the man's tobacco-chewing and use of profanity.

Anti-slavery meeting: U.S. women barred

"Anti-Slavery Convention at London" (1841) by Benjamin Robert Haydon.

London, June 12

American abolitionist Wendell Phillips made the first motion at the World Anti-Slavery Convention today, calling for a complete list of the delegates, including "all persons bearing credentials from any anti-slavery society." The word "person" was very carefully chosen, for Phillips realized that a rejection of the women delegates from the American party was imminent. The presence of women in the abolition movement has spurred a great deal of controversy in the United States, sundering the Anti-Slavery Society there. And now that controversy, like a stubborn stowaway, has crossed the Atlantic Ocean to be reckoned with on another shore.

The American women delegates, who include Mrs. Elizabeth Cady Stanton, Mrs. Lucretia Mott and Phillips's wife, Ann, observed decorum and did not address the mixed audience; and when Phillips's pleas were vehemently rejected, the women were escorted to the curtained gallery. The official delegates then proceeded with the discussion of their abolitionist strategies.

Most of the men are in favor of methods for achieving emancipation swiftly, as based on the influential pamphlet *Immediate and Gradual Abolition*, which was written by a woman, Mrs. Elizabeth Heyrick, a British abolitionist.

"Quilting Party," anonymous, a colorful creation of American folk culture.

1841

Harrison

Fairhaven, England, Jan. 3. Herman Melville boards whaler Auschnet, bound for South Seas; [voyage inspires *Moby-Dick.*]

New York City, February. *New York Tribune* issued under editorship of new owner Horace Greeley.

United States, April. Edgar Allan Poe's *The Murders in the Rue Morgue* introduces detective story genre.

Texas, May. Sam Houston creates Port of Houston to enhance seaborne commerce.

Texas, June 19. Group of Texas soldiers embarks on Sante Fe Expedition to claim part of Spanish-controlled New Mexico for Texas (→Sept. 18, 1842).

New York City, June 20. Samuel F.B. Morse patents telegraph (→May 24, 1844).

United States, Aug. 19. Uniform national bankruptcy law enacted, allowing for voluntary declaration of bankruptcy.

Cincinnati, Aug. 29. Street fighting turns into five-day anti-Negro riot.

New York City, Oct. 29. Bishop John Joseph Hughes publicly urges state support of parochial schools.

Massachusetts, Dec. 24. Henry David Thoreau writes in his journal of his desire to "go soon and live by the pond" (→July 1, 1845)

West Virginia. Natural gas used as industrial fuel for first time.

Connellsville, Pennsylvania. Industrial coke produced for first time.

Tarentum, Pennsylvania. Samuel M. Kier peddles oil from father's salt wells as cure for numerous ills.

South Carolina. State law forbids Negro and white cotton mill workers from looking out of same window.

Oberlin, Ohio. Three Americans are first women in the world to earn bona fide A.B. degrees.

California. John Sutter buys Fort Ross, ending Russian presence in California.

Missouri. Last great concentration of elk seen.

Philadelphia. Edgar Allan Poe becomes associate editor of new *Graham's Magazine*.

Harrison dies after inaugural in cold

Under gray skies, throngs filled the capital's streets for the inaugural parade.

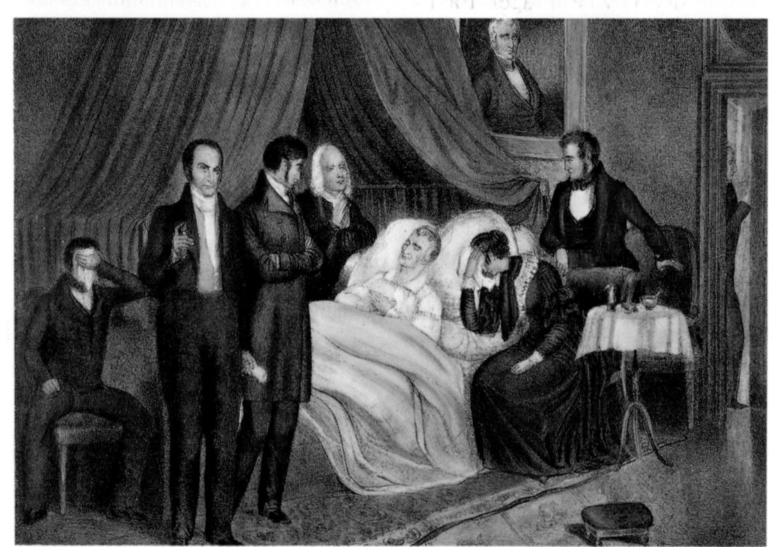

Intimates of the President collect around his deathbed, by Nathaniel Currier.

Washington, D.C., Apr. 4

President Harrison is dead.

Beloved by many Americans as "Old Tippecanoe," the 68-year-old Virginian died today, just 31 days after taking office. It is expected that he will be succeeded by his fellow Whig, Vice President John Tyler, although the Constitution is not explicit on a line of succession in the event of a President's death. The oldest man ever elected President, Harrison is the first to die in office. Funeral plans are under way.

The President's brief tenure was marked by ill health stemming from a bout of pneumonia that set in shortly after Inauguration Day. On that day, despite the chill of early March, Harrison had shunned both overcoat and hat as he rode horseback to the site just outside the Capitol where he delivered an address that lasted nearly two hours. In the speech, Harrison said, "We admit of no government by divine right, believing that so far as power is concerned the Beneficent Creator has made no distinction amongst men." Later that night, he attended three inaugural balls.

Harrison won the presidency last year in a campaign that had twin slogans: "Tippecanoe and Tyler, Too," a reference to his victory over the Indians, and "Log Cabin and Hard Cider," a theme Harrison's supporters used to picture their candidate as having close links to the common man, despite the fact that he was a wealthy landowner who lived in a mansion (→9).

Tyler now officially Harrison's successor

Washington, D.C., Apr. 9

Congress made it official today: John Tyler is the nation's President, not just acting President. The 51-year-old son of Virginia's tobacco-growing aristocracy was sworn into office three days ago, following the death of President William Henry Harrison. But some people questioned whether he was anything more than acting President, for the Constitution is not explicit on the line of succession should a president die. Determined to have full control of the office, he appealed to Congress, which passed resolutions that declared him President.

Tyler (1864) by Alexander Healy.

Court frees slaves who seized ship

Washington, D.C., March 9

Accepting the arguments of defense counsel John Quincy Adams, the Supreme Court ruled today that the African mutineer Cinque and his 52 fellow slaves be freed. Two years ago, the Africans had seized the Spanish slave ship on which they were prisoners, killing the captain and most of the crew. Spain had been requesting extradition. But Cinque and the others plan to steer clear of Europe. Instead, they will appear publicly to raise money for their return to Africa.

Brook Farm set up as a cooperative

Roxbury, Massachusetts, April

On a 2,000-acre farm in West Roxbury, George Ripley and 20 others are seeking the good life at the new Brook Farm Institute of Agriculture and Education. Ripley, a Transcendentalist, developed his views on communal living at Harvard College and later at Harvard Divinity School. The community will encourage freedom of expression in an atmosphere of sharing and growth. The 39-year-old Ripley will lead the community insofar as it is his philosophy on which the structure is based. Education and agriculture are the keystones of this innovative experiment.

First Oregon Trail wagons cross Rockies

Oxen pulling the load, a wagon train negotiates the rugged Western trails.

Sacramento, California, November

The first covered wagon train to cross the Rocky Mountains over the recently opened Oregon Trail arrived in Sacramento this month. The leader of the expedition is 25-year-old John Bidwell, who says he is from Missouri. Bidwell organized a group called the Western Emigration Society back home and more than 500 would-be adventurers signed on to make the journey. But after hearing about the severe hardships that they would encounter along the trail and because local shopkeepers began an anti-California campaign to keep their customers at home, most of them abandoned the dangerous project. Bidwell left from Sapling Grove, Kansas, in the spring with a party of 69 adults and children (→Dec. 1845).

Bill for Fiscal Bank is vetoed by Tyler

Washington, D.C., Aug. 16

President Tyler vetoed the Fiscal Bank bill today, heightening the tensions already growing between him and Congress. Three months ago, the powerful Whig Senator Henry Clay offered a fiscal reform plan that called for a new national bank, a tariff hike and the distribution of public land sales to the states. To make way for the Clay plan, the old treasury was abolished and a bill to create a Fiscal Bank of the United States was passed to replace it. Tyler vetoed the bill on constitutional grounds and the Clay forces in the Senate are said to lack the votes to override a veto (→Aug. 30, 1842).

Canadian acquitted in 1837 murder

Utica, New York, Oct. 12

A former Canadian militiaman was acquitted today of a murder charge resulting from the sinking of the American steamship Caroline in the Niagara River in December of 1837. The incident brought Britain and the United States close to war. Three years after the event, Alexander McLeod was accused of killing Amos Durfee because he had boasted about it in a tavern. But at McLeod's trial, British Lieutenant Elmsley admitted responsibilbility in the American crewman's death.

Godey's Lady's Book says tight sleeves are in, showing "the beautiful contour of a lady's arm."

Texas "Pig War"

Austin, Texas, April

The French government has severed diplomatic relations with the Republic of Texas because a local jury has refused to find a hotel keeper in Austin guilty of having slaughtered the personal pigs of the French minister here.

Emerson, Cooper, Longfellow and Lowell all publish new works

Boston

Some of the brightest stars in the literary galaxy are glowing this year. Henry Wadsworth Longfellow, 34, has released his second book of poetry, *Ballads and Other Poems*, which includes *The Village Blacksmith*, *The Wreck of the Hesperus* and other such gems. One fresh new voice from New England, James Russell Lowell, 22, uses delightful cadences in his first collection, *A Year's Life*. And the dean of the country's novelists, James Fenimore Cooper, 52, has put together another pleasing yarn, *The Deerslayer*, for his series of *Leatherstocking Tales*.

The presses have not turned out just poetry and fiction. Indeed, one important book makes its impact visually, because it offers 300 engravings. They are all by George Catlin, 45, whose two-volume work, *The Manners, Customs and Condition of the North American Indian*, describes his eight years among the many exotic tribes who inhabit the vast region bounded by the Yellowstone River and Florida.

Possibly the most remarkable book of all bears the simple title *Essays, First Series* by Ralph Waldo Emerson, the 38-year-old messenger of radical ideas. The book's mind-stretching pieces include *Circles*, *The Over-Soul*, *History* and nine other entries, all of them written in the author's brilliant prose style. One essay in particular is bursting with insight. Called *Self-Reliance*, it is the author's bold plea for nonconformism and it contains this pithy maxim: "In every work of genius we recognize our own rejected thoughts; they come back with a certain alienated majesty." Emerson chides his readers for being "afraid of truth, afraid of fortune, afraid of death, and afraid of each other," and reminds them "to be great is to be misunderstood," especially in a society that "is in conspiracy against the manhood of every one of its members." Calling on all Americans to embark on a quest for truth, Emerson brings *Self-Reliance* to its conclusion with this strong admonition: "Nothing can bring you peace but the triumph of principles."

Emerson, Transcendental thinker.

1842

Tyler

Fairmont, Pennsylvania, Jan. 2. First wire suspension bridge opens across Schuylkill River.

Washington, D.C., March 1. Supreme Court rules in Prigg v. Commonwealth of Pennsylvania that owners may recover fugitive slaves, but states need not assist them.

Massachusetts, March 3. State law bars children under 12 from working more than 10 hours a day in factories.

Jefferson, Georgia, March 30. Dr. Crawford Long is first to use anesthetic, ether, to kill pain during non-dental operation (→ 1844).

New York City, Apr. 12. Mutual Life Insurance Company of New York, first of its kind, chartered.

Wyoming, May 2. Expedition under John C. Fremont leaves to explore Rocky Mountains (→ Aug).

Washington, D.C., June 25. Reapportionment Act passed, mandating that House members be elected by district.

Honolulu, August. French warship under Captain S. Mallett arrives, demanding broad powers for islands' Catholics.

Texas, Sept. 18. Mexican army commits "Dawson Massacre" during invasion (→ Oct. 21).

Washington, D.C. Horatio Greenough's barely clad statue of George Washington is unveiled at Capitol, causing further American outrage.

Buffalo, New York. Nation's first grain elevator built.

United States. Milk shipped by rail for first time.

New York City. Morse lays first successful underwater telegraph cable between Governors Island and Castle Garden.

Baltimore. First explicitly reformed Jewish congregation, Temple Har Sinai, founded in United States.

Wyoming. John C. Fremont, leading expedition, names Fremont Peak.

Raleigh, North Carolina. After having described being tarred and feathered to New York antislavery convention, free Negro Allen Jones is dragged from his home and whipped.

New Hampshire. Settlement of Indian Stream Republic founded, beginning of independent republic of 160,000 acres.

Fremont and Kit Carson explore Far West

Fremont's party, carrying the flag westward, camps in front of Fort Laramie.

Washington, D.C., August

News has arrived that Lieutenant John C. Fremont of the Army Topographical Corps has successfully completed the first major American scientific expedition into the Rocky Mountains. Fremont, the son-in-law of Senator Thomas Hart Benton of Missouri, took part in several earlier explorations of the Plains, but this is his first major attempt to penetrate the mountain region.

Fremont and his party left Wyoming on May 2, stopped in St. Louis May 22 for supplies and a guide, and began their march to the mountains on June 10. From St. Louis they followed the Oregon Trail across the Plains and the Platte River, then due west to the Rocky Mountains. They reached their first objective, St. Vrain's Fort, between Santa Fe and Fort Laramie, on July 10. Between the South Pass and the Wind River Mountains in Wyoming, Fremont and his men discovered an extraordinarily high peak, and witnesses say the lieutenant and four of his men climbed it. On reaching the top, they planted a special American flag, prepared just for such an occasion. After this historic moment, the expedition immediately began the long journey back to St. Louis and civilization.

One of the principal reasons for the tremendous success of the Fremont expedition is the expertise of his guide, Christopher "Kit" Carson. Lieutenant Fremont, with obvious affection and respect, has described this experienced "mountain man" and fur trapper as "one of the finest horsemen" that he has ever seen. The 30-year-old Carson is said to be quiet and unassuming, and, according to the expedition leader, possessed of "a steady blue eye and frank speech."

Not a man to rest on his laurels, Fremont is now planning a second expedition to the Rockies (→ 1843).

This flag was raised atop the Wind River chain's highest peak on August 15.

Californian seeks onions, strikes gold

Los Angeles, Nov. 22

While scrounging about in search of gold, Francisco Lopez got hungry. So he plunged his sheaf knife into the ground in search of some wild onions. Lopez came up with an onion – and more. In the onion's roots, he found gold dust, and that has touched off a small gold rush in San Feliciano Canyon. Today, Abel Stearns, a trader, sent 20 ounces of the placer to the Mint in Philadelphia for assay. While experts say this field is "played out," there may be gold nearby (→ March 15, 1848).

Second war with Seminoles is over

Florida, Autumn

The so-called Second Seminole War has finally ended. This struggle, which pitted the United States Army against the Seminole Indians and their runaway Negro slave allies under Chief Osceola, began five years ago when the Indians refused to be moved west of the Mississippi River. Rejecting Andrew Jackson's Indian removal policy, they launched a vicious war that cost the American government over $20 million. Of the 10,000 soldiers who fought in this conflict, 1,500 died in action. Despite victory, such losses are probably both bitter and ironic for the former President, who once boasted that with 50 women, he "could whip every Indian that had ever crossed the Suwannee."

First champagne in America produced

Cincinnati, Ohio

Ohio is fast becoming the most important state in the union for the production of wines made from native grapes like Catawba, a red grape named after the Indian tribe. One of the vineyard pioneers in Ohio is Nicholas Longworth, who has been producing wines in nearby Tusculum since 1823. Now Longworth has come up with America's first "champagne" – called Sparkling Catawba, and it is already selling well in the East.

Mexican troops invade; massacre Texans

Texas, Oct. 21

The recent bloody Mexican invasion of Texas has created havoc and confusion across the region. Mexican military forces under General Woll struck at San Antonio in July. His 1,200 soldiers were ruthless in killing many of the Texas defenders and they also seized many prisoners, including such civilians as the town's most prominent judge. This attack, now called the "Dawson Massacre," and the fear of further Mexican military onslaughts has resulted in moving the Texas seat of government from Austin to Washington-on-the-Brazo.

But punitive activity is already under way. Two months ago, Colonel Charles Warfield and a cavalry force headed toward Santa Fe to avenge the attack (→ Feb. 11, 1843).

Tyler finally signs tariff after two vetoes

Washington D.C., Aug. 30

After two vetoes, President Tyler has finally signed the Tariff Act, a measure that raises duties on foreign goods. Known as the Whig Tariff, the act returned duties to their 1832 level. The new measure supersedes Senator Henry Clay's compromise tariff of 1832, which provided for the gradual reduction of all duties that were above 20 percent. President Tyler vetoed an earlier version of the current bill because it would have nullified a law halting the practice of passing on surplus revenues to the states when tariffs rose above 20 percent. The bill he signed ended the distribution of revenues to states when tariffs rise above a certain level.

Wilkes odyssey: a 90,000-mile trip

New York City, June 10

He's back! After four years and more than 90,000 miles in the Pacific Ocean, Charles Wilkes today returned to New York harbor, where his odyssey began. Wilkes has had a remarkable career with the United States Navy. Ten years ago, he surveyed Narragansett Bay, then was promoted to head the division of charts. Over the past four years, the Wilkes Expedition visited a variety of ports in the South Pacific and Australia, and surveyed the Antarctic coast. Returning via Hawaii and the American West Coast, the Wilkes party visited John Sutter in California and it is rumored that Wilkes will confirm the discovery of small amounts of gold on the American River in California. As for Wilkes, he says he plans to write about the expedition's travels.

Crusader Dickens pays a visit to U.S.

Cleveland, Ohio, Apr. 25

Charles Dickens, the marvel of British letters who at the age of 30 has already penned three acclaimed novels – *The Pickwick Papers* (1837), *Oliver Twist* (1838), and *Nicholas Nickleby* (1839) – arrived here today on the latest stop of his American tour. He and his wife landed in New York in January and on February 14 were feted at the Box Ball, a gala named for the author's nom de plume and held at the Park Theater. The city's toniest citizens paid $10 a head to attend. Dickens, famed for his crusading attacks on London slum conditions, spoke well of the American scene, but he has already embraced two new causes. He is urging international copyright laws to prevent the pirating of authors' works and he has denounced slavery.

Barnum takes over the American Museum

New York City, Jan 1

The dog named Apollo that plays dominoes and the midget named Caroline Clark who plays solitaire will no doubt continue to be a vital part of the American Museum. However, the house of exhibition situated on lower Broadway, which reopened this morning under new management, is expected to put an even greater emphasis on curiosities. The new proprietor, Phineas T. Barnum, is a 31-year-old Connecticut showman who once presented Joice Heth, a former Negro slave who said that she had nursed the infant George Washington a century ago. After she died, an autopsy suggested she was less than 80. "I never knew," Barnum swore.

U.S. and Britain settle issues over Canada

Washington, D.C., Aug. 9

The United States and Britain reached agreement today on several outstanding issues concerning the borders of British North America. The Ashburton-Webster Treaty, named for Britain's Lord Ashburton and the American Secretary of State Daniel Webster, gave 5,000 square miles of disputed territory on the Maine border to the Canadian province of New Brunswick, and some 7,000 square miles to Maine. It also provided for mapping and marking the boundary, made minor changes on the northern borders of Vermont and New York, and settled for the first time the Canadian-American boundary from Lake Huron to Lake of the Woods.

P.T. Barnum's American Museum at Broadway and Ann Street in New York City. The exhibits include living curiosities as well as relics of the past.

"The Bashful Cousin" (1842) by F.W. Edmonds, painter and bank clerk.

1843

Tyler

Texas, Feb. 11. Twenty-five soldiers executed by Mexican army (→ Aug. 23).

Honolulu, Feb. 25. British flag raised over Hawaiian Islands (→ July 26).

Independence, Missouri. Some 1,000 pioneers leave for Oregon, [beginning of huge westward migration.]

London, June. American delegates arrive to participate in World Peace Conference.

Buffalo, New York, Aug. 22. Henry Highland Garnet calls for slave revolt at National Convention of Colored Men.

Mexico, Aug. 23. Mexican President Santa Ana warns that annexation of Texas by U.S. would be considered an act of war (→ Oct. 16).

Texas, Sept. 29. Major peace treaty signed between Edward Terrant and George Terrell and nine Indian tribes at Bird's Fort in North Texas.

Honolulu. United States installs George Brown as commissioner, refusing to recognize islands' independence.

Vermont. State legislature attempts to block enforcement of Fugitive Slave Act of 1793, which authorized owners to recover runaway slaves.

United States. Benjamin Babbitt starts production of soap powder, [later known as Babbitt's Best Soap.]

Tennessee. Nashville becomes permanent state capital.

Washington, D.C. United States and Britain agree to joint patrol of Africa's west coast in effort to intercept slave-trading vessels.

West Point, New York. Ulysses Grant graduates from academy with no special honors, ranking in middle of his class.

Washington, D.C. Congress budgets $30,000 for construction of trial telegraph line from Washington to Baltimore.

New York City. B'nai B'rith Society founded.

Missisippi River Valley. Yellow fever sweeps Mississippi Valley, killing 13,000.

Colorado. John C. Fremont, guided by Kit Carson, explores Colorado and Rocky Mountains on way to California.

Dorothea Dix publishes appeal for insane

Massachusetts, January

Miss Dorothea Dix, a former teacher from Hampden, Maine, has published *Memorial to the Legislature of Massachusetts.* The document, which she recently presented to the legislature, is an indictment of the treatment of the insane in the state's jails and almshouses. According to Miss Dix, the places are more like "cages, closets, cellars, stalls and pens," and the inmates are "chained, naked" and "beaten with rods." There are currently only eight insane asylums in the whole country, and as Miss Dix's research shows, they are often in deplorable condition.

Dix, champion of the mentally ill.

Elias Howe invents a new sewing machine

Howe, Massachusetts machinist.

Boston

Elias Howe, a 21-year-old textile machinist, has invented an automatic sewing machine of a completely new design. He spent five years developing the machine while at work in a Cambridge cotton machinery factory. His idea is to use two threads, with stitches made by a shuttle. Early reaction to Howe's machine has not been good, some critics saying it is too complicated and others saying it will throw thousands out of work. Earlier, a mob of workers in France wrecked a sewing machine plant. Howe says his machine will save women from drudgery. He will seek financial aid in England (→ Aug. 12, 1851).

Sojourner Truth, a freed slave, on tour

Brooklyn, Long Island, June 1

This morning, a tall, stately Negro woman crossed into Brooklyn from Manhattan, carrying in her hands her only possessions – a few clothes in a pillowcase and a basket of food. She calls herself Sojourner Truth, though her original name was Isabella Van Wagener, and she has lately been a housekeeper for a minister. Deeply religious, she offers her services as a speaker at camp meetings around the country so that she can spread the Word of the Gospel. Miss Truth is also eager to speak against slavery, having been a slave for most of her 46 years and having seen most of her 13 children sold into bondage.

Sojourner Truth, preacher of justice.

America loses two of its great artists

New York City, November

The United States has lost two of its greatest artistic talents with the recent deaths of Washington Allston and John Trumbull. Allston, a Harvard-educated native of South Carolina, is recognized as the most accomplished Romantic painter in America. Although he was best known for landscapes tinged with mystery and reverie, his passion was the never-completed *Belshazzar's Feast.* Trumbull, a soldier in the Revolutionary War and son of Jonathan Trumbull, the first Governor of Connecticut, favored the historical genre and recorded in paint many of the events that shaped the country's birth.

Allston, self-portrait (1805).

Eternal happiness goal of board game

New York City

Sometimes happiness comes with just a roll of the dice, particularly if you play a game called *Eternal Happiness.* The W. & S.B. Ives Company created this board game and is planning others. In *Eternal Happiness*, players move small pegs on a wooden playing board as directed by the numbers that come up when the dice are rolled. Players must avoid certain spaces that represent financial ruin and imprisonment in order to achieve love, spiritual enrichment (the game was invented by a minister's daughter) and the ultimate goal: eternal happiness.

Briton's brief reign in Hawaii is ended

Honolulu, July 26

British Rear Admiral Richard Thomas today ended five months of autocratic rule and mistreatment of Islanders by the hotheaded Lord George Paulet, who forced King Kamehameha III to cede the Hawaiian Islands to England. During Paulet's reign, efforts of American missionaries to introduce Christian restraints were subverted, and fornication, heavy drinking and general hell-raising were rampant. Talks between royalists and court adviser Gerrit Judd, a missionary-physician who came here in 1828, led to a plea to the British Foreign Office, and the admiral's visit that terminated the illegal possession.

U.S. seeks to annex Texas; Houston wary

Washington, D.C., Oct. 16

Secretary of State Abel Upshur today informed Isaac Van Zandt, the Texas minister to the United States, that the American government would like to begin annexation negotiations with the Republic of Texas as soon as possible. Such an annexation has long been a politically volatile subject, with most Southerners and Westerners in favor of statehood for Texas, while most Easterners and Northerners bitterly oppose admission.

The question is doubly critical because the Mexican President Santa Ana has announced that annexation of Texas will be considered an act of war against his country. President Sam Houston of Texas, while fervently in favor of eventual annexation, is said to oppose opening negotiations on statehood at this time. He believes that Texas must have the continued support of England during these turbulent days. Because he knows that annexation discussions will require much time, he fears England might withdraw its support and leave Texas in a terrible predicament, vulnerable to a Mexican invasion with no diplomatic or military assistance from either England or the United States. Such a situation could prove fatal to the survival of Texas as either a state or a republic. In the meantime, President Houston is beset by the Mexican threat of reconquest, the uncertain attitude of the English and the indecisive policy of the United States (→March 22, 1844).

Smith asserts God called for polygamy

Nauvoo, Illinois, July 12

Mormon leader Joseph Smith declared today that he had received a revelation from God that plural marriage should be restored. Since the Mormons are the new Israel, he said he was told, they should return to the ways of the patriarchs by resuming polygamy. Rumors of plural wives and reports of seduction have already marred Smith's reputation. Further, a Mormon stance that is viewed as self-righteous, not to mention a degree of business acumen among members, has resulted in hostility, if not hatred among non-Mormons in the region. Smith's new "revelation" can only worsen the friction (→Feb. 15, 1844).

Utopian societies founded in Jersey

Red Bank, New Jersey

Small communal societies based on the philosophy of Associationism are springing up in New Jersey. Associationism is the creation of Albert Brisbane, 39, a charismatic writer and educator. Brisbane preaches the pragmatic application of the concepts formulated by the French writer Charles Fourier. Applying these ideas means reinstilling self-respect into the simple and necessary work of any society. Brisbane writes for New Jersey newspapers.

Washington, D.C., March. *John Quincy Adams sits for the camera of Philip Haas. At 75, "Old Man Eloquent" is the first President ever captured on a daguerreotype. He has been out of the White House for 14 years now, but his intense gaze still captivates Washington's political elite. Back in public service, he is devoting his congressional career to raising a consistent and forceful voice against slavery as a moral evil.*

Term "millionaire" is increasingly used

United States

Do you have a million dollars? Not many Americans are worth that much. If you are, call yourself a "millionaire." That was the term used in reports on the death of Henri Lorillard, the tobacco producer, banker and landlord. American innovation is increasing the number of rich people. Exports have gone up from $74 million in 1830 to $150 million this year. Many of those contributing to this growth are becoming millionaires.

Nativist party aims to bar immigrants

New York, June

They are called Nativists, members of a new splinter political party that has been organized here by those who oppose the recent influx of immigrants, primarily the Irish and other Roman Catholics. By forming coalitions with the Whigs, the Nativists, whose formal name is the American Republican Party, are seeking to push for legislation that will stem immigration and deny those not born in the United States the right to vote or to hold public office. There are indications that the new movement may spread to other Northern states.

Grisly tales by Poe, master of macabre

United States

Edgar Allan Poe, the 34-year-old master of the macabre, has just issued three grisly tales. *The Pit and the Pendulum* is a chilling story of torture and terror told by a prisoner of the Spanish Inquisition. In *The Tell-Tale Heart*, a crazed murderer is betrayed by his own sense of guilt; Poe's first-person narration lets the reader share in the killer's psychotic delusions. *The Murders in the Rue Morgue* introduces one C. Auguste Dupin, a reclusive Parisian who uses his exceptional powers of "ratiocination" to solve an outbreak of brutal slayings.

1844

Tyler

Nauvoo, Illinois, Feb. 15. Mormon leader Joseph Smith becomes candidate for President of United States (→ June 27).

Richmond, Virginia, March 22. *Richmond Enquirer* publishes letter by Andrew Jackson advocating annexation of Texas (→ Apr. 12).

Washington, D.C., Apr. 12. United States and Texas sign annexation treaty negotiated by John C. Calhoun (→ June 8).

Missouri, Apr. 25. Dr. John Sappington publishes, *Theory and Treatment of Fevers,* advocating quinine treatment of malaria for the first time.

Philadelphia, May, 8. Violence erupts between native-born Protestants and immigrant Catholics.

China, July 3. Treaty of Wanghiya, first between China and United States, gives latter use of five Chinese ports for commerce and confers legal rights on Americans living in China.

St. Louis, Missouri, Aug. 7. John Charles Fremont returns from westward expedition and publishes popular account of journey.

Nauvoo, Illinois, Aug. 8. Brigham Young chosen to succeed Joseph Smith as head of Mormon Church (→ 1846).

Iron Hills, Minnesota, Sept. 15. William A. Burt discovers Mesabi iron mines.

New Mexico, September. Government orders all ports of entry closed to all trade.

Washington, D.C., Dec. 3. President Tyler, in fourth annual address, asks Congress for annexation of Texas (→ March 28, 1845).

Philadelphia, Pennsylvania. Stephen Foster publishes first song, *Open Thy Lattice, Love.*

New York City. The New York Hotel offers first private bath in an American hotel.

Cincinnati. Negroes form Knights and Daughters of Tabor, dedicated to eradication of slavery by any means.

Oregon Country. Amos L. Lovejoy, conceiving new town, clears and plots first few blocks of Portland.

New York City. Photographer Mathew Brady establishes daguerrotype studio.

Morse wires, "What hath God wrought!"

Morse's telegraph key. A handy device, wrought by the miracle of science.

Washington, D.C., May 24

Sitting at a desk in this city today, the inventor Samuel F.B. Morse tapped out the message, "What hath God wrought!" by telegraph to a friend 40 miles away in Baltimore. It was the first telegraph message ever transmitted between two cities. What's more, it was the culmination of many years of work by Morse, who barely persuaded Congress to appropriate the $30,000 needed to establish a telegraph line between the cities. Morse, a noted painter and pioneer in photography, thus has earned new acclaim.

But praise for Morse is mixed with criticism by those who challenge his claim to a patent on the telegraph. Legal challenges are being planned not only by Morse's business partners but also by rival inventors who say Morse merely used ideas that others originated. One of the greatest challenges is by Joseph Henry, acclaimed as America's foremost scientist, who says he freely shared his knowledge of electrical apparatus with Morse but has been given neither credit for helping invent the telegraph nor a share of the profits that Morse will reap. The legal battle over Morse's patent claim may go on for years.

Even Morse's critics, however, acknowledge his bulldog tenacity in obtaining financial support for the telegraph. And everyone envisions a nation bound closer together by a web of telegraph wires (→ 1848).

Oregon Country. *As the revival spirit grows, so do calls for temperance. Oregon's provisional government has banned the sale of "ardent spirits." Lithograph is "The Bible and Temperance" by Nathaniel Currier.*

Baptists split up over slavery issue

Montgomery, Alabama, December

Alabama's Baptist Convention has called for a meeting of all Southern Baptists to discuss forming their own association now that the Northern-controlled Baptist Foreign Mission Board has declared slaveholding a bar to appointment as a missionary. This issue has been a problem for Baptists and much has been done to avoid facing it. The Southerners seemed committed to forcing the decision, and the Northerners appeared willing to let them. The Foreign Mission Board's ban on slave-holders as missionaries is the act for which many had been waiting.

Report of a balloon flight to U.S. false

New York City, Apr. 13

Readers of the *New York Sun* were astonished to learn today of the first airborne crossing of the Atlantic, but the report has proved to be as full of hot air as the balloon Victoria, which supposedly carried eight Englishmen from Wales to South Carolina. Soon after reporters rushed to interview the intrepid aerialists, the story was exposed as a hoax. Its perpetrator, author and critic Edgar Allan Poe, 35, has been known for a fanciful if not particularly buoyant imagination.

German introduces lager in Milwaukee

Milwaukee, Wisconsin, April

A new beer called "lager" has been brought to America by German immigrants. It is brewed and aged longer, using a different method of fermentation and is much lighter in color and alcoholic content than most of the beers produced in America. This lager was first brewed by John Wagner in Philadelphia two years ago and has caught on fast. Now Jacob Best Sr., a German beer maker, has extended the brewing of lager to Milwaukee, Wisconsin, where he and his four sons have established the Best Brewery at Chestnut Street Hill.

Polk elected on motto "54-40 or Fight"

Campaign poster by Currier.

Washington, D.C., Dec. 4

James K. Polk, with "54-40 or Fight," as his slogan, was elected President today, defeating his Whig rival, Senator Henry Clay. Polk, a Democrat, won 170 electoral votes to 105 for Clay. Polk's running mate, George M. Dallas, was elected Vice President. Polk, a leading supporter of Presidents Jackson and Van Buren during his years in Congress, had held the posts of Speaker of the House and Governor of Tennessee. In his campaign for the presidency, he rallied the voters by pledging to fight for a treaty setting the Oregon Country's northern border at 54 degrees 40 minutes latitude, a move that Britain opposed (→June 15, 1846).

Mob kills Joseph Smith and his brother

Carthage, Illinois, June 27

A mob of 200 men burst into the jail at Carthage tonight and murdered Joseph Smith, the Mormon leader, and his brother Hyrum. The two had been jailed for destroying the press and offices of the rival Mormon newspaper the *Expositor*, which opposed polygamy. The Mormons resisted the arrest and the militia was called. The Governor assured Smith's safety if he would give up, but this proved illusory. When it appeared that the Smiths would be freed, the mob formed, saying that as "law could not reach them, powder and shot should." The mob overran the guards, killing the Smiths and wounding two of their friends (→Aug. 8).

The murder of Joseph Smith.

Foes of slavery thwart Texas annexation

Washington, D.C., June 8

The United States Senate today overwhelmingly rejected the Texas annexation treaty. In a contest that pitted the supporters of slavery against foes of the system, a coalition of Democrats and Whigs from the North and East voted down the controversial measure resoundingly. Veteran observers had predicted a much closer vote.

In March, former President Andrew Jackson came out publicly for immediate annexation. President John Tyler also advocated it. And the author of the annexation treaty, Secretary of State John C. Calhoun, has been its most vocal supporter. But the pro-slavery contingent from the South was effectively countered by the large number of anti-slavery legislators, who refuse to approve admission of another slave state into the union. Henry Clay and Martin Van Buren, who are both presidential candidates, announced their firm opposition to the treaty. Clay asserted that "annexation and war with Mexico were identical" with the dissolution of the union. So while the Texas question has been put aside, it continues to fester, ready to erupt again at any time (→Dec. 3).

Second Coming fails; prophet discredited

United States, Oct. 22

As the day passed and the Second Coming of Christ failed to materialize, one could only hope that William Miller and his prophecies would sink into oblivion. Miller, a former Baptist minister, had won over many with his mesmerizing style. There are reports that when the day for the great event arrived, many believers gathered on hills clad in white sheets to greet their Lord. Others gave away their property. Some assembled in cemeteries. There are even hints of sexual debauchery resulting from the mass hysteria. Now that the time has passed, the disenchanted are sheepishly heading home with the hope that friends and family will forget.

Tragedy and romance on Potomac cruise

New York City, June 26

President John Tyler and Julia Gardiner married here today after a romance that grew out of tragedy. The navy was displaying its new frigate Princeton on a cruise down the Potomac February 28, when one of the 12-inch guns blew up. Killed were two Tyler Cabinet officials, Secretary of State Abel Upshur and Navy Secretary Thomas Gimner, and N.Y. State Senator Gardiner. The senator's daughter Julia had met Tyler on this cruise.

Tragedy aboard the frigate Princeton. Lithograph by Nathaniel Currier.

Anesthesia used in birth and dentistry

Boston

Reports of painless surgery, dentistry and childbirth through the use of inhaled gases are circulating in the medical community. Horace Wells, a Vermont dentist, has had one of his teeth extracted without pain after inhaling nitrous oxide, a gas whose unusual properties were noted nearly half a century ago. Crawford W. Long, a physician in Georgia, is said to have removed a tumor from a patient after rendering him senseless with ether and to have used the same method to deliver a child. But many doctors doubt such reports (→Jan. 24, 1848).

Ship tycoon starts N.Y. Yachting Club

New York City, July 30

Steamship magnate John Cox Stevens and eight well-to-do companions met today aboard Stevens's yacht Gimcrack, which was anchored in New York harbor, and formed the New York Yachting Club. Stevens, owner of a catamaran and a 56-foot yacht, was elected the club's commodore. The members, who have nine yachts among them, plan to hold regular regattas. Hopefully, they will have more success than the first American yachting society, the Boston Boat Club, which started in 1834 and failed in the economic panic of 1837.

1845

Polk

Washington, D.C., Jan. 23. Congress designates Tuesday after first Monday in November as day of presidential elections.

New York City, Jan. 29. Edgar Allan Poe's *The Raven* published in New York Evening Mirror.

Washington, D.C., March 3. Congress overrides presidential veto for first time, blocking payment for ships ordered by President Tyler.

Washington, D.C., March 4. Democrat James Polk, 11th president, says in his inaugural speech: "In truth, though I occupy a very high position, I am the hardest working man in this country."

Mexico, March 28. Relations with United States are severed (→ July 4).

Missouri, May. John C. Fremont sets out on third expedition to the West.

Philadelphia, June 4. *Leonora* premieres at Chestnut Street Theater; first opera by an American, William Henry Fry, to reach stage.

Massachusetts, July 1. Henry David Thoreau takes up residence at Walden Pond (→ 1846).

Texas, July 4. Texas convention announces acceptance of annexation by United States (→ Dec. 29).

New York City, Sept. 23. Knickerbocker Base Ball Club formed (→ June 19, 1846).

Annapolis, Maryland, Oct. 10. Naval school opens at Fort Severn; [becomes U.S. Naval Academy after 1850.]

Missouri. Dr. William Keil sets up utopian communistic Bethel settlement in Shelby County.

Boston. First written examinations in American elementary schools given.

United States. *Scientific American* magazine founded by Alfred Beach.

New Orleans. *Les Cenelles*, a collection of love poems by Negro writers, published; first anthology of Negro verse in America.

DEATH

Nashville, Tennessee, June 8. Andrew Jackson, general and 7th U.S. President (*March 17, 1767).

Westward expansion proclaimed America's "Manifest Destiny"

Conquering the frontier. "Westward the Course of Empire Takes Its Way" by German-born Emanuel Leutze.

Washington, D.C., July

A strange mixture of exhilaration and foreboding seems to be permeating the atmosphere in the capital this summer. The general feeling is that, for good or bad, the nation is preparing to enter a new phase in its evolutionary history. And this new era appears to be one that is founded on extreme nationalism, and perhaps even militarism.

Many observers interpret President James K. Polk's recent landslide election as a mandate for acquisition of Spanish California, the British-controlled Oregon Country, the annexation of Texas and even a preemptive war with Mexico. Before Texas had accepted annexation terms, Polk offered the republic United States military protection as a state. Accordingly, he sent General Zachary Taylor and his army to the Rio Grande in a major show of force. And perhaps not so coincidentally, earlier this month, John L. O'Sullivan, editor of the *United States Magazine and Democratic Review*, wrote an influential article in which he lambasted the nation's weak posture toward Mexico on the Texas issue. Going further, O'Sullivan argued the notion of what he called "Manifest Destiny," the belief that it is the will of God that the United States should expand into and control the entire North American continent. It is "our Manifest Destiny," he wrote, "to overspread the continent allotted by Providence for the free development of our yearly multiplying millions."

Margaret Fuller's new book urges women to be independent

New York City, Feb. 15

A review of Miss Margaret Fuller's revolutionary new book *Woman in the Nineteenth Century* appeared today in the *Broadway Journal*. The review was quite favorable; but perhaps this is because the reviewer, using the signature LMC, is Mrs. Lydia Maria Child, a woman and fellow Transcendentalist. Miss Fuller's book reviews the history of women and reaches the conclusion that they should now seek careers and fulfillment outside of marital duties. She writes, "I have urged on woman independence of man, not that I do not think the sexes mutually needed by one another, but because in woman this fact has led to excessive devotion, which has cooled love, degraded marriage and prevented either sex from being what it should be to itself or the other . . . That her hand may be given with dignity, she must be able to stand alone."

For about three years, Miss Fuller served as editor of the *Dial*, a small newspaper based in Concord, Massachusetts, that furthers Transcendentalist ideas – those ideas based on intuitive or spiritual knowledge rather than on information received from the five senses.

Margaret Fuller, Transcendentalist.

Over 5,000 travel on the Oregon Trail

Missouri, December
Reliable estimates indicate that more than 5,000 pioneers have traveled the Oregon Trail within the past 12 months (including one man so tall that he wore his spurs on the calves of his legs). Traveling in trains of eight to 10 wagons, the pioneers usually jump off at Independence, Missouri, follow the lengthy Missouri River westward, then leave the trail when they reach the Willamette Valley on the Columbia River in Oregon.

The recent publication of John C. Fermont's detailed description of his explorations in the Rockies and along the trail has been a significant stimulant to migration. President Polk's apparent determination to obtain sole ownership of the Oregon Country (which the British also claim) by either peaceful negotiations or military means has also been a factor in the growing westward movement.

Ex-slave, harassed at home, emigrates

Liverpool, England, Aug. 28
Was this Negro really a slave? That is a question regularly asked by those who hear the eloquent Frederick Douglass speak on the anti-slavery campaign. To silence his disbelievers, he has published his autobiography, *Narrative of the Life of Frederick Douglass*, a revealing account of his horrendous treatment as a Baltimore slave. Reactions to the book put him in danger of re-enslavement, so friends persuaded Douglass to migrate to England, where he arrived today.

His trip on the steamer Cambria was not without perils. Douglass was not allowed cabin accommodations, raising the anger of many abolitionists aboard. Through their efforts, he was given a cabin and he asked to lecture. One speech so incited some passengers that they threatened to throw him overboard. Only the intervention of the captain saved Douglass.

The abolitionist leader is expected to meet with English intellectuals, gathering support for the emancipation of American Negroes.

Slave state Florida, free Iowa in union

Washington, D.C., March 3
Florida joined the union as a slave state today, the last day of President John Tyler's term in office. As one of the President's final acts, he put his signature on a congressional act that grants statehood to Florida and Iowa. The two new states, one slave and the other free, were admitted at the same time by Congress under the principle of balanced representation between slave and free states.

Florida has been under territorial rule since the region was acquired from Spain in 1821. It has undergone severe hardship during the past decade, much of it related to the seven years of war against the Seminoles that cost thousands of lives and millions of dollars. A financial crisis in 1837 sent many residents into destitution. Despite these problems, Florida has managed to double its population, now at 58,000 (→Dec. 28, 1846).

Texas annexed to union

Washington, D.C., Dec. 29
The Republic of Texas is no more! After a whirlwind of diplomatic activity, Texas has joined the union as the 28th state. The sequence of events began in March, when President Polk signed the congressional joint resolution of annexation. Texas agreed to the terms of the resolution on July 4. Then, last month, President Polk sent John Slidell to Mexico City to negotiate a financial settlement covering the costs of annexing the former Mexican province and also to bargain for the eventual purchase of New Mexico and California.

Slidell was also ordered to try to smooth still-simmering American-Mexican relations and to help "restore those ancient relations of peace and good will which formerly existed between the governments and citizens of the sister republics." Given the current atmosphere of hostility, this task is not going to be easy. The peaceful acquisition of Texas, however, may signify a new, positive relationship between the two nations (→Feb. 19, 1846).

Texas term "maverick" becomes popular

Texas, August
Samuel A. Maverick, a pioneer Texas cattleman, has unwittingly added his name to the American vocabulary. The San Antonio man has habitually left the calves in his herds unbranded. So unbranded calves, cows and steers in general have been labeled in the language of cowboys as "mavericks." By extension, any lone dissenter who takes a stand independent of his or her associates has become known as a maverick – not a member of the herd. It's a term that seems to be catching on.

"Fur Traders Descending the Missouri" (1845) by George Caleb Bingham, who has just returned to his Missouri home after working in Washington. Like many other American painters, he is drawn to the landscapes of the frontier.

1846

Polk

California Province,, Jan. 1. Of approximately 35,000 inhabitants, 500 are American traders.

Texas, Feb. 19. Authority formally transferred from Republic of Texas to United States government (→ May 9).

Texas, February. Sam Houston and Thomas Jefferson Rusk elected as state's first United States senators.

California, July 5. American rebels choose John C. Fremont to lead "Republic of California" (→ 7).

Washington, D.C., Sept. 10. Elias Howe granted patent for sewing machine with eye-pointed needle.

California, Nov. 22. General Zachary Taylor, after taking Monterey, receives notice from War Department nullifying truce with Mexico.

Philadelphia. Richard Hoe designs and produces first rotary printing press.

Boston. Eastern Exchange Hotel is first public building heated by steam.

Louisiana. Slave on Oak Alley plantation develops method of trunk grafting; first instance of scientific pecan cultivation in Louisiana, possibly in world.

Washington, D.C.. Construction begins on Smithsonian Institution (→ May 1, 1847).

Albany, New York. American Missionary Association formed.

Oregon Country. Applegate Trail opened, providing access to Oregon from California.

Illinois. Mormons begin trek westward [to Utah] (→ July 24, 1847).

Hartford, Connecticut. Samuel Colt receives government contract to mass-produce revolvers for Mexican War.

New Orleans. Receiving news by Pony Express, *New Orleans Picayune* is first newspaper to report war with Mexico.

United States. Panoramas become popular form of entertainment; huge picture scenes are mounted on rollers and moved past viewers.

United States. *Mince Pie for the Million*, book of tall tales about frontier life, issued.

United States. Herman Melville's first novel, *Typee*, published.

The U.S. has declared war on Mexico

Washington, D.C., May 13

After two decades of bickering and turmoil, perhaps the inevitable has happened. At the request of President Polk and by means of a congressional joint resolution, the United States has formally declared war on Mexico. According to the President, Mexico initiated the war when its cavalry forces attacked American troops on territory south of the Nueces River in Texas, which both the United States and Mexico claim. Some diplomats say that Polk has always sought war with Mexico, and that the attack on the American troops simply gave him the pretext he needed. Inside sources say that the night before the Mexican attack, Polk was already preparing a message asking for a war declaration. The conflict will be a popular cause for the Texans, Southerners and Westerners who have sought it so long and for all those who say it is the "Manifest Destiny" of the United States to dominate the continent.

Nonetheless, many diplomats and politicians doubt the wisdom of Polk's war. Former President John Quincy Adams, for example, condemned the declaration, calling the conflict "a most unrighteous war." Senator John C. Calhoun, fearing this will be a war of aggression, abstained from voting on the war resolution (→ Nov. 16).

Polk (1858) by G.P.A. Healy.

Americans win two battles after minor skirmish with Mexicans

At Palo Alto, American cavalry was backed up by devastating heavy artillery.

General Taylor's forces roll over the Mexican army at Resaca de la Palma.

Mexico, May 9

Even though war has not been declared, full-scale hostilities between the United States and Mexico have broken out. Reports indicate that the United States Army, after one setback, has scored two resounding victories. The army, commanded by General Zachary Taylor (whom his men affectionately call "Old Rough and Ready"), was ordered to the Rio Grande River in March by President Polk. With Taylor came more than 4,000 soldiers, or half the nation's forces.

On April 12, a patrol of 63 American dragoons were assaulted by 1,600 Mexican soldiers. The Americans suffered heavy casualties and the survivors surrendered.

The Mexicans, under General Arista, crossed the Rio Grande on the Texas coast with 6,000 men to attack 2,200 soldiers marching with General Taylor. But yesterday, Taylor surprised the Mexicans at the village of Palo Alto. The general told his infantry that their "main dependence must be the bayonet." In the fierce battle that followed, Arista's forces were routed. And earlier today, at the Battle of Resaca de la Palma a few miles farther south, the scene was much the same, an American victory. After a massive cavalry charge led by Captain May of the American dragoons, the Mexicans panicked and stampeded in wild retreat. Army sources put U.S. casualties at about 200 (→ 13).

U.S. flag over California

John C. Fremont, chosen by rebels to lead the "Republic of California," raises the Bear Flag at Monterey. On July 7, it was replaced with the U.S. flag.

California, July 7

The Stars and Stripes now fly over this former Mexican province. Commodore John D. Sloat, commander of the United States Navy's Pacific Squadron, sailed into Monterey today, raised the American flag and assumed his post of military Governor. The events are the culmination of four months of American intrigue and intervention. In March, Captain John C. Fremont of the army attempted to claim California for the United States but failed. Last month, an American settler, William Ide, led a rebellion in Sonoma and declared California's independence from Mexico. This "Bear Flag Revolt" (named for the grizzly on the rebel flag) was followed last week by the arrival in Sonoma of Fremont, whom the residents declared head of the "Republic of California."

In the meantime, President Polk has ordered the Army of the West, several thousand soldiers led by General Stephen Kearny, to proceed to California. Their mission is said to be the conquest of all the Mexican territory west of Fort Leavenworth to the Pacific. Mexico has apparently lost California – and perhaps more – forever (→ Dec. 6).

Fremont by William S. Jewett.

Mexican revolt in California put down

California, Dec. 6

General Stephen Kearny and a small force of American soldiers defeated a band of insurgent pro-Mexico Californians at San Pascual today. The rebels, well-armed and mounted on stolen horses, had terrorized American settlers throughout Southern California for months. This battle effectively ends the revolt that broke out in September, but the victory was costly, with 18 American soldiers killed. General Kearny was seriously wounded, but an army spokesman says that he is expected to make a full and rapid recovery (→ Jan. 13, 1847).

British give up Oregon

"Ridiculous Exhibition; or, Yankee-Noodle Putting His Head into the British Lion's Mouth," an English view of the dispute over Oregon's border.

Washington, D.C., June 15

After years of squabbling that led to the brink of war, Britain finally agreed today to end the joint occupation of the Oregon Country. President Polk, who had been advised that "the only way to treat John Bull was to look him straight in the eye," apparently did just that – and it worked. Polk had insisted that the just claim of the United States in Oregon extended to the 54'40" line, south of the Alaska boundary. Britain refused to accept this notion. As the possibility of war over the issue became real, a diplomatic compromise appeared increasingly attactive to both parties.

The Oregon Treaty gives the United States all the territory west of the Rocky Mountains south of the 49th parallel. The document was signed today by Secretary of State James Buchanan and the British representative, Lord Packenham, and its terms are expected to raise few objections when the Senate takes it up (→ Aug. 14, 1848).

U.S. victory assures New Mexico conquest

New Mexico, Dec. 25

After a three-day march across the desert without water or rest, Colonel S.W. Doniphan and his battalion of 863 infantrymen and cavalrymen defeated a force of about 1,200 Mexican soldiers near Las Cruces today. According to witnesses, the Mexicans – elegantly clad in red coats, white belts and brass helmets – ordered Colonel Doniphan's weary troops to surrender or "charge and be damned." The colonel refused the order and calmly walked among his soldiers as they knelt and fired. When the smoke had cleared, 100 Mexican soldiers were dead; the rest had fled in panic. Doniphan's victory near Las Cruces has virtually completed the conquest of New Mexico by the United States.

U.S. takes over at Santa Fe.

Taylor seizes two cities

U.S. troops in Saltillo pose for one of the first war daguerreotypes.

Mexico, Nov. 16
General Zachary Taylor seized Saltillo today in the second major triumph of the fall campaign for "Old Rough and Ready." On September 24, General Taylor's troops defeated a large Mexican force at Monterey. There, Taylor was outnumbered two to one and had no heavy artillery. But his soldiers made up with bravado what they lacked in firepower. Viewing a reinforced bastion, Lieutenant Jefferson Davis of Mississippi excitedly exclaimed, "If I had 50 men with knives, I could take that fort!" After the battle, which involved a total of about 14,000 men, the Mexicans marched out of the city, while the victorious American army band played *Yankee Doodle*. And so the trend continued at Saltillo. Taylor's reputation was so great and the Mexicans' fear of him so real that he captured the town without having to fire a shot (→Feb. 23, 1847).

U.S. granted rights in Panama isthmus

Panama, Dec. 12
The United States and New Granada [Colombia] today signed an agreement that granted the United States transit rights on the narrow isthmus of Panama between the Atlantic and Pacific Oceans. Under the Mallarino-Bidlack Treaty, the United States guarantees Colombian dominance of the isthmus, and gets Panamanian transit rights. The pact may speed development of a canal across Panama. Washington has weighed the idea since at least 1826, when Secretary of State Henry Clay sent aides to the Bolivarian Congress. Panama has been part of New Granada since 1821, the year Panama declared independence from Spain (→Apr. 19, 1850).

Iowa, a free state, 29th to join union

Washington, D.C., Dec. 28
After disagreements with Congress over boundaries, Iowa was admitted today as the non-slave 29th state in the union. The territory was established eight years ago [including parts of Minnesota, and North and South Dakota] and when it sought non-slave statehood, it faced stiff Southern opposition. But with Florida's admission as a slave state, the way was cleared. Iowa's size has been set at 56,000 square miles. Earlier, the clamor for statehood resulted in the drafting of a constitution that proscribed low salaries, limited debt and regulated banks. The boundary fight led to the drafting of a second charter, this one farm-oriented.

Some voices raised against Mexican War

United States, December
In February, Thomas Corwin addressed the Senate and denounced the impending war with Mexico. "If I were a Mexican," he said, "I would tell you, 'Have you not enough room in your country to bury your dead men? If you come into mine, I will greet you with bloody hands and welcome you to hospitable graves.'" His warning went unheeded as America rushed into war. But since then, opposition to it has reached a fever pitch.

Whigs and abolitionists, most from the Northern states, argue that the eight-month-old war was contrived by Southern slave owners to acquire Texas as another slave state. Unitarian and Congregational ministers deplore the violence. And a poet from Concord, Massachusetts, named Henry David Thoreau spent a night in jail last July as a protest against the use of his taxes to benefit the war.

Christmas gift: Beans to starving children

Sierra Mountains, Dec. 25
"Children, eat slowly, for this one day you can have all you wish." That was what Mrs. James Reed told her family today as they enjoyed their Christmas dinner: some beans, a few dried apples, a scrap of bacon and a little tripe. It was a true feast, for the Reed family, camped by Truckee Lake in the Eastern Sierras, is slowly starving to death. Mrs. Reed had hidden this special cache of food; tomorrow the Reeds resume their diet of boiled animal hides. Friends in nearby cabins are worse off; half mad, they are eating the flesh of the dead.

The tragedy began in April in Springfield, Illinois. James Reed and his family decided to join 31 friends in a move to California, where they had heard the land was rich and fertile. They loaded their wagons and headed west. On July 20, they reached Fort Bridger on the south side of the Great Salt Lake. Reed and a few others were anxious to shorten the journey, and when George Donner, a strong-willed member of the party, said that he could lead them through the Hastings Cut-off, a shortcut of 200 miles, they took the chance. They became hopelessly lost. Tempers flared, and Reed knifed another man in an argument. He was banished, while his family stayed with the Donner party. On October 31, mired in waist-high snows, they camped by Truckee Lake. Half have died of hunger and exposure, and no help is expected.

"Volunteers for Texas." Cartoon lampoons the American war effort.

Surgery performed with use of ether

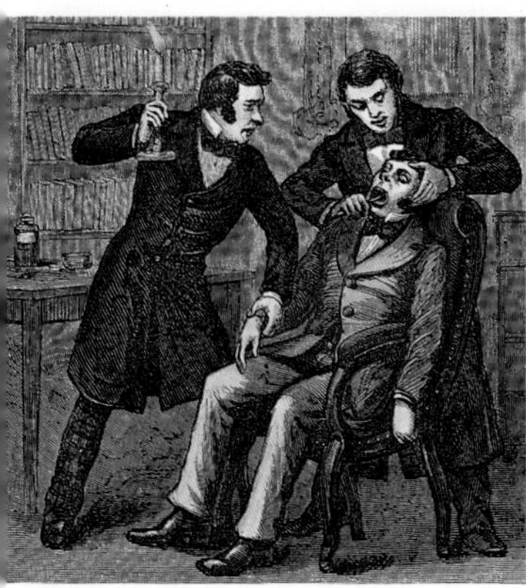

Morton at work. Painless dentistry?

Boston, Oct. 16

Dr. William T.G. Morton provided convincing proof today that painless surgery is possible. Dr. Morton, a dentist and student at Harvard Medical School, used ether gas to render a patient unconscious so that a facial tumor could be removed in a historic operation at Massachusetts General Hospital. "Gentlemen, this is no humbug," exclaimed the doctor who performed the surgery. Those who saw the operation hailed Dr. Morton as a benefactor of mankind. He plans to patent the method and demonstrate it widely.

No slavery ban for ex-Mexican lands

Washington, D.C., Aug. 10

The Senate adjourned today without acting on the Wilmot Proviso, which would ban slavery in the new Mexican lands. The ban amendment to a bill requested by President Polk for the appropriation of $2 million to acquire Mexican territories was proposed by Pennsylvania Democrat David Wilmot. It borrows the wording of the Northwest Ordinance of 1787, which states "that neither slavery nor involuntary servitude shall exist . . . in the said territory."

The House adopted the application of this provision to the Mexican area. But today, Senator Louis Cass, Michigan Democrat and supporter of the South, proposed that settlers be allowed to decide the slavery issue for themselves. Southerners embraced the plan and killed the proviso (→March 10, 1849).

Mormon converts migrating to U.S.

Nauvoo, Illinois

Less than nine years since the first Mormon missionaries arrived on European shores and only six years since Brigham Young made a preaching tour of England, converts have begun to flock to the Mormon city of Nauvoo on the banks of the Mississippi. More than 4,000 Mormons from England, Ireland and Wales have joined their American brethren. Here in Nauvoo, Smith plans a new holy city for his co-religionists. But the immigrants face a test. Theirs is not only a new environment but one that is menaced by violent hostility among non-Mormons (→July 24, 1847).

Ice cream freezer

New Jersey

Americans' love of ice cream should soon become an everday affair thanks to a new hand-cranked ice cream freezer for home use. With some ice, rock salt and a little muscle, anyone can now make ice cream. The portable, hand-cranked ice cream freezer was invented here by Nancy Johnson.

New baseball: Knickerbockers are routed

"The American National Game of Baseball" (1866) by Currier and Ives.

Hoboken, New Jersey, June 19

This was baseball as no one has seen it before. A club made up mostly of volunteer firemen from Manhattan, named the Knickerbockers, was routed by another amateur team by the embarrassing score of 23 to 1. The winners, who were simply called the New York Nine, romped to victory on the Elysian Fields under a new set of rules prepared by Alexander J. Cartwright, who also designed the diamond-shaped playing field.

Cartwright, a bank teller who organized the Knickerbocker team, set the canvas bases 90 feet apart and decided that only nine men could play on each side. The pitcher threw from 45 feet out, and he tried to let the batsmen hit his underhand throws. The score was lopsided because a lot of the better Knickerbocker players did not choose to travel across the Hudson River all the way to Hoboken.

Failure of potato crop sends thousands of poor Irish to America

Ireland

"There's a curse on ould green Ireland," a poor peasant told her children before fleeing the decimated land, "but we'll get out." Indeed, when last year's potato blight returned this year with such vengeance as to turn a promising harvest black and rotten overnight, it seemed to be an act of divine retribution. Ireland depends almost entirely on the potato, and the malignant fungus has left a country that one observer called a land of "famished and ghastly skeletons." England, meanwhile, imports Ireland's healthy grain crop.

Emigration, which has risen since 1820 because of overpopulation and evictions, is now an exodus due to disease and hunger. Last year's emigration was 75,000, but that was dwarfed by the 106,000 this year. Most migrants go to America in fever-ridden "coffin ships." Unlike earlier waves of Ulster Protestants or Scotch-Irish, who settled on farms, Southern Catholics are jamming the ghettos of Eastern cities, only to battle against poverty and bigotry.

Irish peasants, starved off the land, storm the gate of a city workhouse.

1847

Polk

California, January. Mormon battalion, 300 recruits from Utah, arrives too late to fight in war with Mexico.

California, Jan. 19. John C. Fremont becomes first Governor of California (→ May 31).

Oregon City, Feb 1. Webster's *Speller,* abridged edition, is first book published in Oregon.

Washington, D.C., March 3. Congress authorizes adoption of gas lights on Capitol grounds.

Mexico, March 9. In first large-scale U.S. amphibious military operation, General Winfield Scott lands thousands of troops on beaches south of Vera Cruz (→ 29).

Baltimore, Maryland., Apr. 26. Samuel F.B. Morse forms first telegraph firm, Magnetic Telegraph Company; operating on Baltimore-Washington line.

Washington, D.C., May 1. Smithsonian Institution dedicated, with Princeton physicist Joseph Henry as first secretary.

Philadelphia, May 7. American Medical Association founded under leadership of Dr. Nathan Smith Davis.

Honolulu, Sept. 11. First theater in Hawaiian Islands, the Thespian, opens.

Boston, Dec. 3. Ex-slave Frederick Douglass begins publication of a newspaper, *North Star.*

Nebraska, Dec. 5. Brigham Young elected president of Mormon Church, at Winter Quarters.

Washington, D.C., Dec. 6. Illinois Republican Abraham Lincoln joins House of Representatives.

Salem, Massachusetts. First steam-powered cotton mill opens.

Washington, D.C. Compulsory education is established.

New York City. Astor Place Opera House, largest to date, seats 1,500; opening production is Verdi's *Ernani.*

United States. Negro Freemasons form National Grand Lodge of Negroes.

Easton, Pennsylvania. Cheaply produced tin cans enable widespread distribution and sale of such foodstuffs as tomatoes.

Mexico loses California

California, Jan. 13

Army Captain John C. Fremont accepted the final surrender of the pro-Mexico resisters in California today, ending 25 years of Mexican rule and bringing the western campaign of the Mexican War to a successful conclusion.

It was thought that General Stephen Kearny's defeat of the holdouts last month at the Battle of San Pascual had ended hostilities in California. But the pro-Mexico forces once again rallied under the command of Captain Jose Flores and captured Los Angeles. The Mexican troops, 450 strong, were attacked last week by Commodore David Stockton's American force of 400 sailors and marines, augmented by General Kearny's dragoons. With the massed troops shouting: "New Orleans!" – it was the anniversary of Andrew Jackson's defeat of the British in 1815 – the Americans charged the Mexicans and decimated them. In the meantime, the "California Battalion" under the command of Captain Fremont, arrived and joined up with the Stockton-Kearny forces.

The resulting Treaty of Cahuenga allows the Mexicans honor in their defeat. More importantly, the treaty makes California the territory of the United States (→ 19).

The Volunteer State does itself proud

Tennessee

The people of Tennessee will volunteer to fight – in fact, they'll even pay good money for the chance. Some 30,000 Tennesseans have volunteered to do battle with the Mexicans on behalf of Texas independence, more than 10 times the 2,800 the federal government requested. Some of the would-be soldiers are reported to be offering as much as $250 for a chance to fight in Mexico. The situation confirms Tennessee as the "Volunteer State," a nickname that it received after sending eager volunteer soldiers to fight in the Creek Indian War 35 years ago.

Taylor's troops vanquish Santa Ana's 15,000 in northern Mexico

Mexican cavalry almost overran the American artillery at Buena Vista.

General Taylor's officers relax at camp after the Battle of Buena Vista.

Mexico, Feb. 23

The battle of Buena Vista ended today with a smashing victory for the Americans. Outnumbered by more than three to one, General Zachary Taylor's troops routed General Santa Ana's Mexican army and sent it scurrying south to safety.

Santa Ana launched his winter campaign last month, ordering his force of 15,000 men north toward Taylor's encampment at the sleepy village of Buena Vista. As the Mexicans neared the American lines to attempt a flanking movement, Taylor's band stirred his men with the strains of *Hail Columbia* and other patriotic songs. When Santa Ana ordered Taylor to surrender, "Old Rough and Ready" answered with a massed volley of canister and grapeshot that tore through the advancing infantry. "Double shot your guns and give them hell!" he calmly ordered. Even though the American cavalry and infantry under Captain Braxton Bragg repulsed the first Mexican charge, Taylor found himself virtually surrounded. Nevertheless, Captain William Tecumseh Sherman's expert artillerymen smashed each Mexican advance, while the Indiana and Mississippi regiments, with their bayonets and Bowie knives, slashed at the enemy cavalrymen as they were pulled from their horses. Santa Ana lost 1,800 men, Taylor 700. Experts believe that the American victory signifies the end of the war in northern Mexico (→ March 9).

;cott occupies Vera Cruz

·eneral Scott (left, on horseback) orchestrates the siege, by Currier and Ives.

Iexico, March 29

General Winfield Scott and his ·oops have taken possession of the Iexican stronghold at Vera Cruz. 'he general announced today that ffective enemy opposition has been rushed and that his forces are in rm control of the city.

Scott, the United States Army's upreme commander, is a giant of man at six feet five inches and 250 ounds, and he is nicknamed "Old 'uss and Feathers" because of his ısistence that his men maintain a pit-and-polish appearance. In this ampaign, Scott led an armada of 00 warships and support craft that ransported 10,000 soldiers and maines to the shores of Vera Cruz on he Gulf of Mexico. In what was alled the world's largest amphibi·us operation, he moved his huge force ashore without the loss of a single life. After a reconaissance patrol revealed that the city was surrounded by fortifications that were virtually impregnable to conventional infantry or cavalry attack, Scott opted for an artillery bombardment to level the fortresses and reinforced bunkers. He brought ashore a dozen 8-inch and 24- and 32-pound naval guns – the most powerful artillery anywhere. With these, he literally ground the defenses to dust. After only a minimal fight, the Mexicans surrendered.

American losses were put at 82 killed and wounded. Enemy casualties were about the same, but unfortunately they included a group of women and children who were in a church that collapsed while the bombardment occurred (→ Apr. 18).

U.S. wins brutal battle

General Santa Ana flees Cerro Gordo. Some 200 of his officers were seized.

Mexico, Apr. 18

American forces defeated a large Mexican army under President Santa Ana at Cerro Gordo today in one of the bloodiest battles of the war. The 8,500 Americans, commanded by General Winfield Scott, met General Santa Ana's 12,000-man army in the rough mountains on the road from Vera Cruz to Mexico City. According to American military sources, the Mexican general had command of the best-trained and experienced soldiers that ever faced American troops. Santa Ana's choice of a battle site was superb. He placed his massed artillery on high cliffs that overlooked the only road available for Scott's passage. Lieutenant Ulysses S. Grant and Captain Robert E. Lee of the American army called the cliffs "unscalable" and ravines "impassable." Santa Ana said the land was so rough that not even a rabbit could get through.

General Scott saw that a frontal attack on the Mexican forces, who held the "high ground," would be suicidal. So he sent troops experienced in the New England mountains to carve footpaths up the steep slopes on both sides of the cliffs. Once on top, there was a vicious hand-to-hand struggle. The Mexicans were finally forced from the summit, and the Americans raised the Stars and Stripes. United States losses were put at 400 dead and wounded. Casualties were about the same among the Mexicans, but more than 3,000 of them were captured by the Americans. When last seen, Santa Ana was in fast retreat, minus his wooden leg (→ Oct. 12).

Music of the plantation, as heard in the minstrel shows, now printed in a collection of Negro melodies.

Washington, D.C., July 1. *Following a directive by Congress, passed in March, the Post Office has issued the nation's first government-sponsored postage stamps. The Franklin is worth 5 cents, and the Washington 10.*

A British cartoon depicts a dissolute Brother Jonathan, making a mockery of the Land of Liberty.

Mexico City is captured; war is effectively ended

Molino del Rey on the 8th: Scott ousts 12,000 Mexicans from a gun foundry.

Chapultepec on the 13th: The last hill outside Mexico City is taken by storm.

Mexico City on the 16th: General Scott's troops march into town uncontested. A series of tough battles fought on the six-month march to the Mexican capital has whittled the Scott force from 10,000 at the outset to only about 6,500.

Mexico City, Oct. 12

With the victorious entry of General Joseph Lane and his battle-tested Americans into Puebla today, the Mexican War is over. General Santa Ana turned over his battered command to an underling and has vanished. While the events at Puebla, situated near Mexico City, signify the end of hostilities, the real and definitive conclusion to this long and hard war actually took place on September 16, when the sizable army of General Winfield Scott, after a long series of battles, finally captured and secured this capital of Mexico.

The road from Vera Cruz to Cerro Gordo and on to Mexico City proved costly to "Old Fuss and Feathers" Scott and his American army. The advance toward the capital began in early April after the occupation of Vera Cruz. The savage battles of Contreras and Churubusco and the many skirmishes before and after cost 1,000 American lives. At the same time, Santa Ana was losing more than one-third of his army.

Scott's forces, beating off attacks from both guerrillas and the regular Mexican army over a 300-mile trek, finally stood before the gates of Mexico City at the end of August.

General Santa Ana defended the Mexican capital with at least 25,000 troops (including a battalion of 200 American deserters) and hundreds of cannons. Against him, marched 6,500 men, what remained of Scott's army of 10,000. Santa Ana's strategy was one of defense. His troops were concentrated at the capital with General Alvarez's men outside the city to attack Scott's rear guard.

When the Duke of Wellington in England heard of the strategic brilliance of the Mexican general's plan, he reportedly said, "Scott is lost. He cannot capture the city and he cannot fall back upon his base." Obviously, Scott hadn't heard the Duke's grim prediction. The bombardment of Chapultepec, Mexico City's military fortress, began September 12 and lasted all day. The cannonade was followed by an infantry assault by the troops of General Gideon Pillow and General David Twiggs, followed by General John Quitman's division. Between the devastating artillery barrage and the savage infantry charges, Santa Ana's army caved in. On September 14, the Mexican dictator declared the capital an open city and retreated with the remnants of his army to the suburb of Guadalupe-Hidalgo. Later that day, the American flag went up over the National Palace, and Scott, in full dress uniform, reviewed the soldiers and marines who had taken "the Halls of Montezuma."

The smoke of war is hardly lifted, but already rumors are reaching here that General Scott, rapidly emerging as a popular national hero, is being seriously considered for the next presidential candidate of the Whig Party (→Aug. 2, 1848).

PLUCKED:
THE MEXICAN EAGLE BEFORE THE WAR!
THE MEXICAN EAGLE AFTER THE WAR!

Manifest Destiny on the march. Defeat of Mexico by the colossus of the North

Power in California and the fight for it

California, May 31

Ever since the United States took over California, there has been an almost comic struggle between the huge egos of Captain John C. Fremont and General Stephen Kearny over the governorship. Fremont believes he should be governor because Commodore David Stockton appointed him as such. Kearny cites War Department orders giving him the job. Meanwhile, Kearny is having Fremont court-martialed and kicked out of the army, and has now named Colonel R.B. May to be governor (→ Jan. 31, 1848).

James Smith makes tasty cough drops

Poughkeepsie, N.Y., Apr. 19

A local restaurant operator, James Smith, has concocted a new brew in his kitchen that has won instant popularity here. Congealed into hard candy drops, the secret formula, Smith claims, is a soothing remedy for sore throats. A lot of locals may be feigning coughs, it seems, because Smith's drops are as tasty as they are medicinal; they come in two flavors: wild cherry and black licorice. Perhaps it is the pronunciation of "Poughkeepsie" which has made such medicine necessary in the first place.

Woman to get prize for comet discovery

Nantucket, Massachusetts, Oct. 1

Peering through a telescope last night, Miss Maria Mitchell, daughter of an amateur astronomer, spotted a previously unknown comet. This discovery will earn her a gold medal that the King of Denmark recently offered for the first identification of a new comet. Miss Mitchell is 29 years old and a librarian at the Nantucket Atheneum. Her father, William Mitchell, encouraged her study of mathematics and the stars and approves of her independent spirit. Self-reliance is a must for the women of Nantucket, whose seafaring men are often gone for months on end.

Mormons settle on Great Salt Lake

Brigham Young, Mormon pioneer.

Great Salt Lake, Utah, July 24

After many tribulations, a Mormon party led by Brigham Young arrived in the Utah territory today and here they plan to build a settlement where they can find the peace that has so far eluded them. Having been driven from one home to another, the Mormon leaders hope that this location is remote enough to afford them sanctuary.

The present company pulled out of Nauvoo, Illinois, in February of last year. When it reached Council Bluffs, Iowa, a Captain Allen of the United States Army showed up and requested 500 volunteers to fight in the war against Mexico. The Mormons quickly favored this request and a Mormon battalion was organized. Its departure left only a small colony – mostly women, children and the elderly – to spend the long, cold winter on the Great Plains.

When spring arrived, the Mormons proceeded west again. They endured many privations on their journey of more than a thousand miles, finally reaching Utah earlier this month. Here on the shores of the Great Salt Lake, Brigham Young has declared that they will build their new settlement, which is to be called the State of Deseret.

Young: "This is the right place."

The Mormon elders are already planning to encourage their brethren to join them here, including the remnant that was driven from Nauvoo in September (→ Dec. 5).

Indians massacre 14 at Oregon mission

Oregon Country, Nov. 29

Violent clashes between Indians and whites continued as the Cayuse massacred 14 members of an Oregon mission today. The Waiilatpu Mission was built in 1843 by Marcus Whitman on orders from the American Board of Commissioners for Foreign Missions. His group, known as the Walla Walla settlement, drifted away from the intention of teaching the Cayuse how to farm and build houses, and became entangled in land disputes. These escalated to violence when Indians died in a measles epidemic. Cayuse traditionally kill doctors who fail to cure their patients. All the missionaries, including Whitman, 45, were killed (→ June 3, 1850).

"Oh Susannah"

Cincinnati

Stephen Foster has accepted $100 for a new song entitled *Oh Susannah*. Foster, 21, has written music since boyhood. His tunes ring with a Negro sound from church meetings he attended with a servant and from Negro laborers at the Pittsburgh warehouse where he was a bookkeeper last year.

Taylor: War hero in the presidency?

New Orleans, Dec. 3

General Zachary Taylor, hero of the Mexican War, returned to the country today to a resounding welcome. Rumors abound that the general wishes to ride his military glory to victory in next year's presidential election. Taylor claims he doesn't "care a fig about the office." But in a January letter to New York's *Morning Express*, he criticized the Polk administration for lax prosecution of the war. Taylor, who grew up on the Kentucky frontier, is strongly pro-slavery, believing "the South must throw ourselves on the Constitution and . . . appeal to the sword, if necessary" (→ Nov. 7, 1848)

"Evangeline," epic poem by Longfellow

Cambridge, Massachusetts

Henry Wadsworth Longfellow, the gentle New England bard, has spun an American myth in his latest work, the epic romance *Evangeline, A Tale of Acadie*. The long poem describes the fate of its tragic heroine, the Acadian (Nova Scotian) lass Evangeline, who spends years searching for her lost lover, uniting with him, at long last, in death. The 40-year-old Longfellow has taken a time-worn subject – a doomed romantic affair – and theme – endless longing redeemed by eternal love – and breathed new life into them by drawing on recent history and by setting his tale in the spectacular, isolated wilderness of the North American continent.

"Evangeline" by J.L.G. Ferris.

Washington, D.C., Jan. 12. Abraham Lincoln, opposing Mexican War, advances right of "any people . . . to shake off existing government and form a new one."

California, Jan. 24. Gold is discovered (→ March 15).

New York City, Jan. 24. Under influence of chloroform, anesthetic pioneer Horace Wells arrested; [commits suicide in jail.]

United States, Jan. 31. John C. Fremont, found guilty of mutiny, disobedience and prejudicial conduct for usurping power in California, court-martialed and dimissed from army (→ Sept. 9, 1850).

Mexico, Feb. 18. General Scott relinquishes command of American army here.

California, March 15. First story of gold discovery, printed in San Francisco newspaper, [but goes largely unnoticed] (→ Dec. 5).

Chicago, Apr. 24. Chicago Board of Trade, nation's first futures exchange, opens for trading in agricultural products.

United States, April. To serve growing population in West, Pacific Mail Steamship Company is established.

Buffalo, New York, Aug. 9. Free Soil Party, a coalition of anti-slavery groups, nominates Martin Van Buren for president, Charles Frances Adams for vice president.

New York City, Aug. 10. Walter Hunt patents bullet with own explosive charge.

Oregon Territory, Aug. 14. Oregon Territory organized.

Washington, D.C., Every state east of Mississippi River, except Florida, now has telegraph (→ Apr. 6, 1852).

Brussels, Belgium. International congress, called by American pacifist Elihu Burritt, agrees to support international court of arbitration.

Bangor, Maine. First commercially manufactured chewing gum in United States produced by John B. Curtis.

Washington, D.C. Building of Washington Monument begins.

Boston. Patrick Kennedy, from Dunganstown, Ireland, arrives; [descendants include President John F. Kennedy and Senators Robert F. and Edward M. Kennedy.]

Treaty gives U.S. vast Mexican lands

Vera Cruz, Mexico, Aug. 2

With the war behind them, the weary soldiers of "Old Fuss and Feathers," General Winfield Scott, embarked on navy transports today bound for home and a hero's welcome. The Mexican War has been costly. In three years, almost 13,000 Americans have died, either in combat or from disease, while 4,000 more were wounded. But the nation comes away from the war with about 33 percent more territory than it started with. Under the Treaty of Guadalupe-Hidalgo that was signed February 2, the Mexicans ceded the provinces and territories of Texas, New Mexico, California and other significant parts of the Southwest. In return, the United States agreed to pay Mexico $15 million outright and to assume some $3.25 million in American claims against the republic.

While Generals Zachary Taylor and Scott have been the military heroes of this war, the civilian who crowned their martial successes with a brilliant diplomatic coup has turned out to be Nicholas P. Trist, the chief clerk of the State Department. The surprise-hero Trist, by birth a "Virginia gentleman," is married to a granddaughter of Thomas Jefferson. As the war was nearing an end and President Polk realized that it would not be proper for as distinguished a diplomat as Secretary of State James Buchanan to have to follow the army around Mexico waiting for the right moment to conclude a treaty, he chose the obscure but faithful Trist for the job. Trist set out for Mexico to join Scott's army in May of last year. His orders were to negotiate a treaty officially concluding the war on terms that would be most favorable to the United States.

Finding Scott's army at Vera Cruz, he immediately fell out with the commanding general. At one point, he called Scott the "greatest imbecile that I have ever had anything to do with." But they wound up becoming fast friends.

In Washington, it was a different story. As the months passed with Trist unable to conclude a peace treaty, Polk grew more and more frustrated. Finally, he ordered Trist back to the capital; but the diplomat ignored his Commander-in-Chief's directive. Instead, he went with Scott through the war's last, decisive battles. With the Mexicans fearing that the Americans wanted all of their country as the spoils of war, they decided to sit down and negotiate seriously with Trist. He did not demand the entire nation of Mexico, but he did manage to get the most prosperous and valuable third of the land. President Polk proclaimed the landmark treaty in effect on July 4.

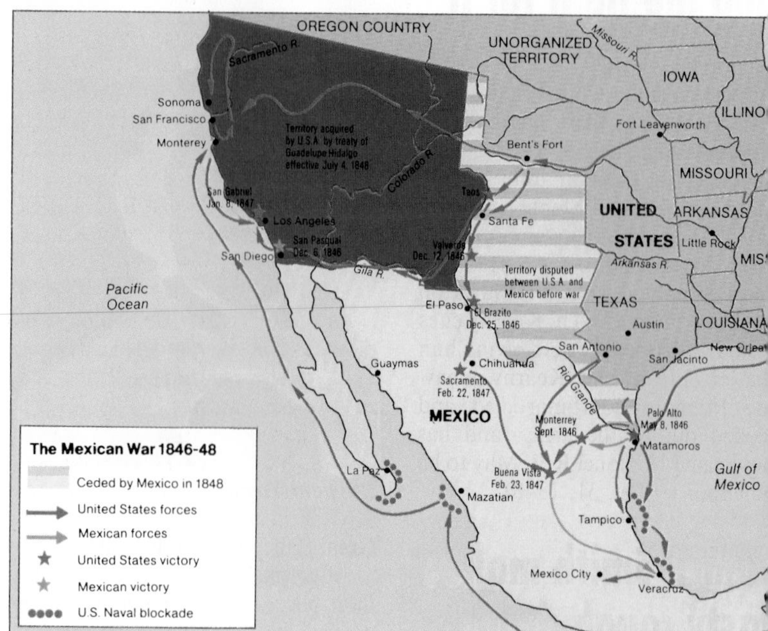

The Mexican War was costly, but the United States emerges 33 percent larger.

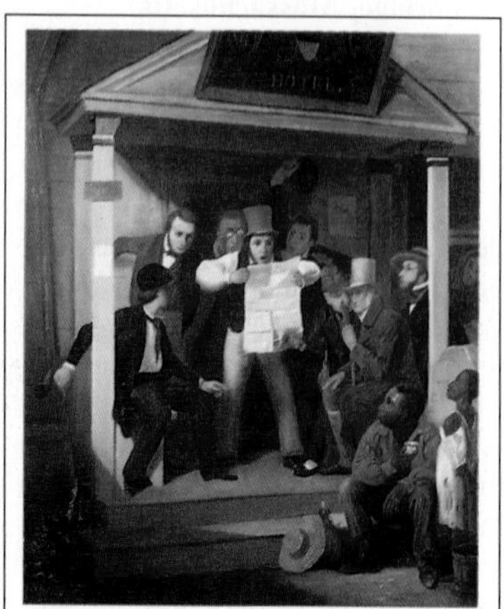

Victory on the front pages. "War News from Mexico" (1848) by Richard Caton Woodville.

Taylor elected; all states vote same day

Washington, D.C., Nov. 7

Zachary Taylor, who won the nickname "Old Rough and Ready" during his long military career, was elected President today. The 64-year-old Whig candidate beat Democrat Lewis Cass and former President Martin Van Buren, who ran on the anti-slavery Free Soil ticket. It was the first time that all the states voted on the same day and the first time Taylor, a career soldier, sought office. Taylor ran less than 150,000 votes ahead of Cass in the popular vote, but he carried such large states as New York and Pennsylvania for a clear electoral victory, 163 to 127. The new Vice President is Millard Fillmore of New York.

Taylor, the 12th President. Painting attributed to James Lambdin.

Women rally for rights

Seneca Falls, New York, July 19

"We hold these truths to be self-evident: that all men and women are created equal ... " So began a startling manifesto read aloud to 300 women and 40 men who met today at a Wesleyan church in this small upstate town. Mrs. Elizabeth Cady Stanton, who was the major force behind the recent New York Married Women's Property Act, and Mrs. Lucretia Mott, the famed abolitionist, recognized the need for a women's rights forum and organized the unprecedented convention, publicizing it through an advertisement in the *Seneca County Courier*.

The women knew that if the convention were to have any substance, it must revolve around a firm platform; and to warrant attention, it must be bold. Therefore, they reworded the original document of 1776 to become a Declaration of Sentiments. Mrs. Stanton, who addressed the assembly in a voice that wavered at first but grew strong, read a list of wrongs: Woman has no voice in laws; she cannot keep the wages she earns; divorce and separation laws are to the benefit of men; women have no vote; colleges are closed to women; church affairs usually exclude them; man has tried to "destroy her confidence in her own powers, to lessen her self-respect and make her willing to lead a dependent and abject life."

Mrs. Stanton and her followers admit that they expect "misconception, misrepresentation and ridicule," but will press on. Among those objecting are Mrs. Stanton's husband, who so strongly opposes the concept of women voting that he has abruptly left town.

Elizabeth Cady Stanton speaks at Seneca Falls. The resolves adopted at the meeting offer a revision of the Declaration of Independence: "We hold these truths to be self-evident: that all men and women are created equal."

Gold found in California

The site of James Marshall's fortuitous find: Sutter's sawmill at Coloma, on the south fork of the American River, will rarely be this tranquil again.

San Francisco, Dec. 5

Now that President Polk has confirmed that there's "gold in them thar hills," the rush is on.

Actually, tales of California gold are not new. Six years ago, a rancher near Los Angeles found gold dust in the roots of an onion he dug up for lunch. At about the same time, a herder stumbled on some gold.

The incident that ignited the new interest was the discovery of gold on the American River at Coloma, 50 miles from Sacramento. A New Jersey mechanic, James Marshall, who was building a sawmill for John Sutter, made the initial find. Oddly enough, when press reports of gold first appeared in San Francisco on March 15, no one was excited. Even a message sent East about the find drew little attention. But interest built, causing shockwaves around the world, with Basques, Croats and Chinese all rushing here.

What did pique American interest was really a publicity stunt. Sam Brennan, head of San Francisco's Mormon community and a grocer who stood to profit from a boom, started a rush by riding down the streets shouting "Gold! Gold on the American River!" He did what the press could not. The *New York Herald* picked up the story and the rest is history (→ Dec. 31, 1849).

Seagulls gobble up swarms of crickets

Great Salt Lake, Utah, May

Mormon farmers have been saved from disaster by a huge flock of seagulls that devoured swarms of crickets that were ravaging their fields. These crickets, which some say resemble a cross between a spider and a buffalo, had poured down from the mountains and were leaving the crops "as if touched with an acid, or burnt by fire." Efforts to get rid of them were futile, but what human action could not do, the Mormon farmers said, divine response to prayer achieved. The pests are gone and the Mormons may come up with a crop after all.

Industrial utopia founded at Oneida

Oneida, New York, March 1

Practice may make perfect, but the idea of practicing "Perfectionism" here is raising social questions. John Humphrey Noyes's family arrived in this near-wilderness between Syracuse and Utica today to form a cooperative communal society called "Perfectionist." Focusing on noncompetitive industrial economics and total equality, the 37-year-old Noyes has often been the focus of controversy over his belief in polygamy. This caused problems for his Putney group in Connecticut, and many of Oneida's members were in the Putney experiment.

Detail of Edward Hicks's "The Cornell Farm" (1848). A sign painter by trade and a Quaker by faith, Hicks seeks to represent simple country life in his art. He is known to fellow Quakers as a preacher and, imbued with their austere outlook on life, he often fears that art offends religion.

1849

Taylor

United States, January. *The Lily* is published by Amelia Bloomer, advocating temperance, women's rights and popularization of women's pants known as "bloomers."

Washington, D.C., February. Supreme Court, finding for Iowa, accepts Sullivan Line as boundary with Missouri.

Washington, D.C., March 3. Congress authorizes gold dollar and $20 double eagle.

Missouri, March 10. State legislature supports "popular sovereignty," seeking to exclude Congress from deciding slavery issue in territories (→ Sept. 20, 1850).

New York City, Apr. 10. Walter Hunt patents safety pin.

San Francisco, Apr. 12. First mail service from West to East Coast completed over "Ocean Route" via Panama.

California, July 5. "Pretty Juanita," convicted of knife murder, is first person hanged in mountain camps during gold rush.

Maryland, July. Harriet Tubman escapes from slavery.

Wheeling, Virginia, Nov. 14. Longest suspension bridge in world opens across Ohio River.

San Francisco, Dec. 24. First major fire in San Francisco destroys 50 houses.

United States. James Davis introduces Angora goats from Turkey to American farmers.

Roxbury, Massachusetts. American Horloge Company begins operation as first successful American watch manufacturer.

Geneva, New York. Elizabeth Blackwell, upon graduation from Geneva College, is first woman in United States to receive a medical degree (→ Nov. 4).

Utah. Mormons organize Perpetual Emigrating Company to help poor converts migrate to Utah.

San Francisco. First commercial sourdough bakery, the French Bakery, opens during Gold Rush.

California. Sacramento settled on part of Sutter's grant.

Rochester, New York. Margaret and Kate Fox introduce Spiritualism, sparking interest in seances and afterlife.

Gold rush 49ers flock to California

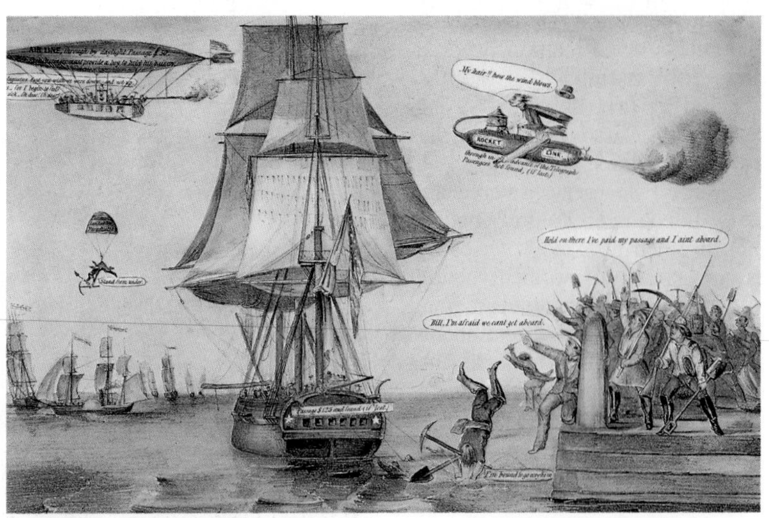

Gold fever strikes. Cartoon pokes fun at "The Way They Go to California."

A hungry prospector pans for gold in a California creek. Eight times heavier than sand, the valuable flakes sink while water washes out the rest.

The 1849 gold dollar. Prospectors on the frontier, where nuggets serve as currency, do not need the U.S. Mint to turn their gold into money.

Rugged miners fill in for the opposite sex during a night of dancing and general revelry near the mother lode. The boom towns of California are transient and anarchic, ruled by grass-roots democracy or frontier vigilantism. Women, and thus families, have not yet found their niche on the gold frontier.

California, Dec. 31

It's been just over a year since President Polk announced the discovery of gold in California, and already the face of the world has changed forever. In terms of people alone, it is said that more than 80,000 have headed west.

The continent's once wide open, unexplored heartland is now crisscrossed with trails. Out West, there are paths through Kansas, Idaho and Utah. In the Southwest, thousands follow the Gila River toward California, and in Texas there are reports of 49ers crossing the Panhandle and unintentionally decimating the Comanches with cholera.

In the Deep South, Forts Smith and Van Buren have become starting points for many prospectors. But the largest surge has been by ship, with the first, appropriately the California, arriving on February 28. Americans pour into California, some via the tip of South America. Others take clippers to Panama, crossing the isthmus by train, then reboarding ships in the Pacific. Some 10,000 Australians had no problem getting to California. But residents wish they did. Some of the Aussies, in gangs called "Sydney Ducks," blatantly break the law.

San Francisco has changed dramatically. It now has a bakery, which specializes in a bread that has become synonymous with the prospectors: sourdough. The city also has a new newspaper, *Alta California*, featuring humorous pieces by clever writers.

There are also quick profits. Take Henderson Lewelling, in from Oregon with a load of apples. He sold them all, at $5 apiece, to miners hungry for fresh fruit. Lewelling is sure to be back with more apples.

There is so much gold that Congress approved a gold dollar and a $20 "double eagle." Oregon, also seeing an influx of California gold – plus its own strike at Gold Hill – is minting $5 and $10 coins called "Beaver Money."

But there is violence, too, in the gold fields. A woman known as "Pretty Juanita" was hanged for stabbing to death a man who had insulted her. Justice in the camps is sure and quick. At her hanging, as the rope pulled tight, Juanita gave a laugh and a farewell salute.

.0 die in riots tied to feud between actors

›reat Riot at the Astor Place Opera House" by Nathaniel Currier.

ew York City, May 10

Long-simmering anti-British sen- ments flared into a riot outside the stor Place Opera House tonight, aving at least 20 dead. Over 10,000 ›ople, many from Irish gangs, sur- unded the theater presenting the ritish tragedian William Charles Macready, who is feuding with Edwin Forrest, the popular American actor now appearing at a nearby theater. The Astor Place mob turned uglier as the night wore on, chanting "Down with the English hog," hurling stones and charging the militia, who eventually opened fire.

ssociated Press set up to distribute news

ew York City, Jan. 11

Today marks the official start of e Associated Press, a cooperative enture organized to distribute tel- graphic news to the daily press. he idea for such an agency was uilt around the efforts of James Vebb of the *New York Courier* in 1827. He was the first man to collect news and sell it to newspapers. Last year, Henry Raymond expanded on Webb's work by arranging to sell news of Boston to a group of New York publishers. He signed the contact letter "Associated Press," and the agency was born.

dgar Allan Poe dies, deranged and poor

oe, tormented chronicler of the ma- ıbre with a life as dark as his fiction.

Baltimore, Maryland, Oct. 7

In an ending as horrible as anything in his morbid and fantastic fiction, Edgar Allan Poe died today at the age of 40, four days after he was found drunk and delirious in front of a saloon here. It is believed that the celebrated author, whose weakness for alcohol and other addictive substances had long played havoc with his personal and professional life, was waylaid by thugs in the employ of a candidate for local office, plied with liquor and forced to vote repeatedly in the municipal elections. In spite of Poe's considerable talent, his vices had rendered him destitute during his final years.

Thoreau is sailed for refusing to pay tax

Concord, Massachusetts, December

Prison is the rightful place for an honest man. So argues the philosopher and poet Henry David Thoreau in his most recent essay, *Civil Disobedience*. Thoreau's honesty is attested to by his recent one-day stay in the jail here for refusing to pay a poll tax. Payment, the anchorite of Walden Pond argues, would constitute complicity in the crimes of the government – slavery, persecution of the Indians and the war with Mexico. "I quietly declare war with the State," the philosopher writes, and he invites his readers to join him.

Thoreau, rebel of conscience.

Lincoln against slavery; Calhoun for it

Washington, D.C., Jan. 22

South Carolina Senator John C. Calhoun of South Carolina blasted abolitionist Northerners today in response to anti-slavery legislation proposed earlier this month by Representative Abraham Lincoln of Illinois. Calhoun said: "To destroy the existing relation between the free and servile races in the South would lead to consequences unparalleled in history." He said a change would only come as a result of Northern might "against the resistance of the Southern." Lincoln is planning to introduce a bill that would free the children born of slave mothers in the District of Columbia. Lincoln did not take part in the debate that followed his proposal.

Lincoln, in an 1846 daguerreotype.

First woman doctor blinded in one eye

Paris, Nov. 4

Dr. Elizabeth Blackwell, the first female physician to graduate from an American school of medicine, has suffered eye damage that may impede her hopes of becoming a surgeon. While she was on duty at the hospital La Maternite, she was hit in the eye by a spray of acid from an accident nearby. The 28-year-old Dr. Blackwell was born in Bristol, England, and was brought up in New York City and Cincinnati, Ohio. Defying public ridicule, she went to Geneva Medical School in Geneva, New York, and was graduated earlier this year.

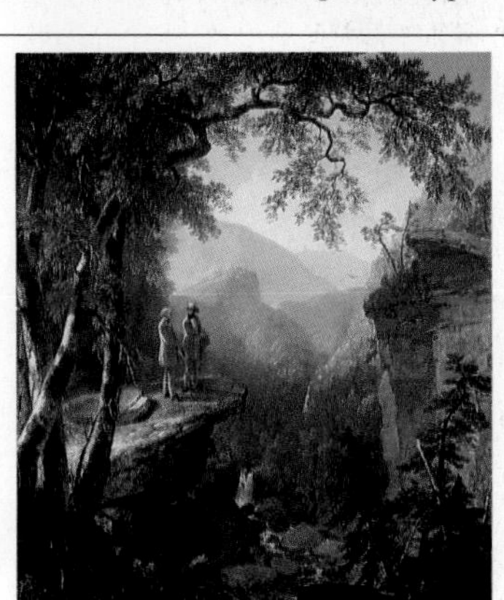

Asher Durand's "Kindred Spirits" (1849) is a romantic tribute to nature and to the artist Thomas Cole, who died last year. It depicts Cole and the poet William Cullen Bryant on a picturesque cliff in the Catskills, gazing at a brook.

A house divided 1850-1877

The election of Abraham Lincoln to the presidency was a heavy blow to ıose Southerners who hoped for a peaceful resolution of the nation's ectional conflicts. A Northern Republican, Lincoln represented a party ommitted since its origins to preventing any extension of slavery. And hile Lincoln himself at first had no intention of attacking slavery where existed, the Republicans did have the support of most abolitionists, who anted to eliminate the institution entirely, everywhere, and at once. To the outh, therefore, the Republican victory was the triumph of a man and a arty deeply hostile to its interests. In the past, national leaders had at-mpted to bridge the gap between North and South by appealing across egional lines to a common national interest. Now, opinion in both sections ad hardened to the point where compromise seemed impossible. One of incoln's prophecies seemed to be borne out. "A house divided against self," he had warned in a debate in 1858, "cannot stand."

It was not at first clear, however, that the solution of the sectional crisis ould be war. As the Southern states began to secede from the union late 1860, many people in both regions assumed, and hoped, that the North ould let them go in peace. Others believed secession was a temporary crisis nd would soon resolve itself if only cool heads could prevail. Even in id-April 1861, when forces of the new Confederate States of America pened fire on Fort Sumter (the last military installation in the South still nder the control of the United States government), people on both sides ssumed that any armed conflict would be brief and limited.

Instead, it became the bloodiest conflict in the nation's history. More than 00,000 Americans died in the Civil War, more Americans than died in all f the country's 20th-century conflicts combined. Large areas of the South vere utterly ruined, physically and economically. It was the first American var to employ devastating new military technologies that made massive laughter an integral part of armed conflict. It was the first American war o mobilize virtually the entire population and the first that employed (in he North, at least) the resources of an industrial economy.

In retrospect, the vastly superior resources of the North – the larger opulation, the greater industrial capacity, the sounder finances, the better stablished government – made its triumph seem virtually inevitable. In fact, owever, for at least two years, there was substantial doubt as to who would vin the conflict. Southern forces, thanks in part to a group of remarkably ifted generals, scored a series of major victories early in the war that left he Northern armies reeling and the Northern public restive. There were everal points at which, had Northern popular opinion been allowed to revail, the war might have ended on terms favorable to the Confederacy. Abraham Lincoln, however, refused to waver in his commitment to sus-aining the union, no matter what the cost.

In the middle of 1863, his patience was rewarded. During the first three ays of July, the greatest battle of the war was fought at Gettysburg, Pennsylvania, and ended in a major Northern victory. And on July 4, the own of Vicksburg, Mississippi, surrendered to troops under the command of Ulysses S. Grant, giving the North complete control of the Mississippi River and effectively cutting the Confederacy in half. Important battles emained to be fought, and substantial political challenges continued to hreaten the Northern war effort. But the tide of battle had shifted decis-vely, and over the next two years the North's superior manpower and irepower gradually wore down the Confederate resistance. By the spring of 1865, most of the Confederate military forces had been decimated. And on April 9, 1865, at Appomattox Courthouse, Virginia, Robert E. Lee urrendered the major remaining Confederate army to Ulysses S. Grant. Nine days later, General Joseph Johnston surrendered other Southern forces o William Tecumseh Sherman near Durham, North Carolina. The Civil War had come to an end.

But the issues that had caused the war, and the problems that the war tself had created, were not easy to resolve. The complete elimination of lavery, which many Republicans had not advocated before the war, became during the conflict a central Northern war aim. On January 1, 1863, President Lincoln issued the Emancipation Proclamation, decreeing the end of slavery in all areas of the union still in rebellion. The 13th Amendment to the Constitution, passed by Congress in early 1865 and ratified a few months later, finally brought legalized slavery to an end.

Eliminating slavery, however, was only the first step in resolving the nation's problems. For more than a decade, an era known as Reconstruction, residents of both regions struggled to find a way to live together peacefully while also addressing the needs of the newly emancipated slaves. They succeeded in the former task, but largely failed in the latter.

Perhaps no period in American history has produced so much controversy as Reconstruction. White Southerners considered it a vicious and destructive time – a period of unscrupulous politics, when vindictive Northerners set out to inflict humiliation and revenge on a prostrate South. According to them, the natural leaders of Southern society were removed or barred from office, replaced by outsiders and incompetents – "carpetbaggers," "scalawags" and their Negro allies – with no political support among the mass of the white population. These new leaders, white Southerners maintained, presided over an era of political corruption, fiscal extravagance and social radicalism. When, in 1877, the last of the Reconstruction governments fell and were replaced with new regimes dominated by conservative white Southerners, the residents of the former Confederate states rejoiced, saying that their region had been "redeemed" and that the long nightmare of Northern tyranny had at last come to an end.

Many Northerners saw Reconstruction very differently. To them, it was the only way to prevent unrepentant Southerners from rebuilding their antebellum society in only slightly altered form. Northerners were strengthened in this belief by the efforts of white Southerners in late 1865 and 1866 – through a series of draconian laws known as the "Black Codes" – to reduce the newly freed slaves to a new form of bondage almost indistinguishable from slavery. Reconstruction, Northerners argued, was a reasonable response to Southern intransigence. It was also a humane response to the plight of the former slaves, providing them with legal protections, education, and at times even land. At the same time, white Northerners had only limited taste for the task of remaking Southern society. And as the task proved more difficult than many of them imagined, most began to retreat from their commitment to social change. Long before the final "compromise" that formally ended Reconstruction in 1877, Northerners had acquiesced in the return to power of conservative Southern leaders and had abandoned most of their efforts to assist the emancipated slaves to achieve equality. To many white Northerners, therefore, the end of Reconstruction came as something of a relief. It marked the restoration of a more "normal" relationship between the sections of the country.

To black Americans, in both the South and the North, Reconstruction was significant for other reasons. To them, it was the first systematic effort in the history of the United States to provide them with the basic rights of citizenship. The 14th Amendment to the Constitution guaranteed them equal treatment under the law. The 15th Amendment promised them the right to vote. And the Reconstruction governments, they believed, would ensure that those rights would be protected. The withdrawal of federal support for black efforts in the South consigned the former slaves to a new form of political and economic bondage. Most blacks became sharecroppers and tenant farmers for white landowners, consigned to a system of debt peonage that left them economically enslaved. In the meantime, white Southern leaders began a process that by the end of the century would strip black citizens of many of their rights (including the right to vote) and would produce a system of legalized segregation which, while very different from slavery, guaranteed the survival of white supremacy.

The Civil War and Reconstruction had provided blacks with at least some level of liberty, a considerable accomplishment. But it had not made them fully free. The nation's racial problem, which had done so much to produce the Civil War, was left unresolved – to plague and at times to inspire future generations of Americans.

◀ *"Abraham Lincoln at Independence Hall" by Jean Leon Gerome Ferris.*

1850

Fillmore

Washington, D.C., Feb. 22. Congress approves purchase of George Washington's *Farewell Address* manuscript.

Milwaukee, Wisconsin, March 4. Mob destroys State Senator John B. Smith's home in retaliation for his tax legislation on whiskey and beer.

Washington, D.C., Apr. 19. Clayton-Bulwer Treaty, between United States and Britain, pledges both to protective role in Central America and insures neutrality of prospective Panama Isthmus canal.

New York City, Apr. 27. Steamship Atlantic launched by Collins Line in attempt to compete with Britain's Cunard Line (→Aug. 21).

Oregon City, June 3. Five Cayuse Indians hanged for Whitman Massacre; state's first capital punishment victims.

New York City, June 27. Edwin Booth makes acting debut in *The Iron Chest* at age of 16.

London, Aug. 21. Collins Line steamer Pacific sets trans-Atlantic speed record of 10 days, four and one-half hours.

Washington, D.C., Sept. 20. Federal land grant, first of kind, obtained for railroad between Chicago and Mobile.

Washington, D.C., Sept. 28. Congress bans flogging in merchant marine and navy.

St. Louis. "Sold down the river" becomes colloquialism as slaves believe plantations in North are better than those down Mississippi River.

Philadelphia. For first time, women employed as shopkeepers.

Rochester, New York. Attending anti-slavery meeting, Susan B. Anthony meets Frederick Douglass and Elizabeth Cady Stanton for first time.

Ohio. Largest meat-packing center in United States, Cincinnati earns nickname "Porkopolis."

New Orleans. Cast-iron "lacework" becomes style for balconies of courtyard houses in French Quarter.

New York City. *Daguerrian Journal*, devoted to "daguerrian and photogenic" art, issued.

New York City. Mathew Brady publishes *Gallery of Illustrious Americans.*

Congress adopts slavery compromise

Clay, "The Great Compromiser." Painting (1843) by John Neagle.

Washington, D.C., Sept. 20

After months of bitter sectional struggle and the threat of a civil war, a bundle of legislative bills that have become known collectively as the Compromise of 1850 has been signed into law by President Millard Fillmore. The great conflicts over the admission of California as a state and the extension of slavery are settled for now, and the union has been preserved.

Senator Henry Clay originally introduced his Omnibus Compromise Bill in January. Designed to pacify both North and South, the bill contained five provisions: immediate admission of California as a free state; organization of the other areas taken from Mexico into the territories of New Mexico and Utah without any restriction on slavery; the assumption of the Texas national debt by the federal government; abolition of the slave trade in Washington, and the passage of a strong new fugitive slave law.

Speaking in opposition to the bill was Senator John C. Calhoun, who died on March 31. And when Clay became ill this summer and retired, his leadership of those forces pressing for the Compromise was taken over by Senator Stephen A. Douglas of Illinois. The Compromise was finally completed earlier today when the last of the provisions was signed by President Fillmore (→ May 26, 1854).

Calhoun: "Cease the agitation of the slave question." Painting by Healy.

Runaway slaves subject to federal law

Washington, D.C., Sept. 18

President Fillmore today signed into law the controversial Fugitive Slave Bill. A provision of the Compromise of 1850, the legislation calls for federal jurisdiction over runaway slaves and for the prompt return of the Negroes to their Southern owners. The law also denies the fugitive slaves a trial by jury or the right to testify in their own behalf. Any white man who attempts to help a slave escape his owner will now be subject to a heavy fine and/or imprisonment. The federal commissioner who awards an escaped slave to his owner receives $10; if he does not return the slave, he receives $5. It's a slaveholder's dream law, but it is expected to be opposed in the North (→ Feb. 15, 1851).

The escape of a slave, Henry Brown, from Richmond to Philadelphia in a crate.

California becomes 31st state in union

Washington, D.C., Sept. 9

By act of Congress and the signature of the President, California has become the 31st state in the union. The state's admission concludes a month of hot debate in Congress by the pro- and anti-slavery forces. The bill finally passed the Senate by a vote of 34 to 18, and by a 3-to-1 ratio in the House earlier yesterday. Since then, the capital has been witnessing an unprecedented orgy of bonfires, processions, serenades, speeches, suppers, cannon salutes – but mostly of drinking. In fact, the word seems to have been passed around Washington that it is the duty of every patriot to get howling drunk. Even now, wild crowds are wobbling about with many people tipsily shouting, "The union is saved!" Other crowds have been concentrating in front of the residences of their heroes, Senators Daniel Webster and Stephen A. Douglas, to offer their congratulations on the California bill. A veteran of the Washington scene remarked: "One thing is certain: every face I meet is happy."

Jenny Lind arrives, welcomed by fans

New York City, Sept. 12

America's musical spirit took wings last night as Jenny Lind, "the Swedish Nightingale," made her long-awaited debut at the jam-packed Castle Garden. Although some wondered whether her voice could live up to her reputation, a crowd of about 40,000 – one of the largest ever to greet a steamship – turned out and deluged the Song Bird with a shower of flowers. The purity of Lind's voice last night dispelled all doubt as she offered songs by Bellini, Rossini, Weber, Meyerbeer and, as an encore, Stephen Foster. Promoter P.T. Barnum is nurturing his Nightingale with a fee of $1,000 for each of 150 concerts.

Barnum introducing Lind to Ossian Dodge (l.), who paid $625 for ticket.

Fillmore succeeds Taylor

Washington, D.C., July 10

Millard Fillmore was sworn into office today as President of the United States while the country mourned the death yesterday of President Zachary Taylor, the second of the country's chief executives to die in office. The first was William Henry Harrison in 1841. President Taylor, a 65-year-old native of Virginia, died in the White House after suffering a coronary thrombosis. He had served just one year and 126 days of his term. The new President, a 50-year-old New Yorker, took his oath of office in a simple ceremony at the Capitol. A Whig, like his predecessor, he had served as a member of the House of Representatives for four terms.

Fillmore, conservative Whig. Painting (1847) by James Bogle.

"Scarlet Letter" is an instant best-seller

New York City

The season's biggest star is the 46-year-old Nathaniel Hawthorne, known for his tales of Puritan life, the milieu he explores in *The Scarlett Letter*, a tale of adultery set in 17th-century Boston. The book has sold 4,000 copies in 10 days.

As the century reaches its midpoint, publishers are reaching deep into their pockets to satisfy authors. *Harper's Monthly*, a New York-based publication edited by Henry J. Raymond, promises to "bring the unbounded treasures of periodical literature" to the American public. So far, the treasures have been British: Charles Dickens, George Eliot and William Makepeace Thackeray head the list of serialized imports. Not that Americans are having trouble getting published. Herman Melville, 31, has issued his fifth book, *White-Jacket*, a novel based on the author's stint on the man-of-war United States. Ralph Waldo Emerson's new essay collection, *Representative Man*, includes lectures that the sage delivered at home (Boston) and abroad (London and Manchester). And a new voice belongs to the Negro poet Daniel Payne, author of *Pleasures and Other Miscellaneous Poems*.

Nation's population up a third in decade

Washington, D.C.

Americans are moving from the farm to the city in unprecedented numbers, and the nation's population continues to soar, according to the 1850 census. As immigrants pour in from Europe, the United States now counts 23.2 million residents, a gain of more than a third in 10 years. And while there were 10 farm dwellers for every urban resident in 1840, the rural-urban ratio has now dropped to five to one. The total population of New York, Boston, Philadelphia and Baltimore has tripled in the past 30 years.

Many city residents are immigrants, encouraged to make a new start in America by trans-Atlantic fares as low as $10. But many of the newcomers are living in wretched conditions. In New York alone, 18,456 people inhabit cellars, unable to afford permanent homes.

At the same time, Americans continue to move into virgin territory. Tennessee has become the fifth most populous state with more than a million people, while New York continues in the lead with just over three million. The census lists 92,957 people in California, 12,093 in Oregon, 212,592 in Texas and 11,380 in Utah. None of these were listed in the 1840 census. Of the large states, the fastest growing are Mississippi, with 605,000 people, and Missouri with 682,000, both nearly double the 1840 total. Wisconsin grew almost tenfold, to 305,391.

National rally held on women's rights

Worcester, Massachusetts, Oct. 23

A thousand people from 11 states have gathered to discuss women's rights. The opening statement at the meeting was written by Mrs. Elizabeth Cady Stanton of Seneca Falls, New York, who regretted that she could not be present; she is at home expecting her fourth child. Delegates include Miss Lucy Stone, a graduate of Oberlin College, and Dr. Harriot Hunt, a self-styled and self-educated physician. Participants voted to organize a committee of civil and political functions, an education committee and others.

"Soames Harbor, Maine" (c.1850) by Fitz Hugh Lane. A lithographer in Boston for 20 years, Lane has just returned to Gloucester to paint the sea.

Hutchinsons, famed singers, disbanded

Washington, D.C.

The nation's most famous troubadours, the Hutchinson Family, are calling it a day. Sister Abby is marrying, leaving brothers Judson, Asa and John to go it alone. Thus ends a phenomenal 10-year run that took the quartet in a widening gyre of fame from their native New Hampshire to a tour of England and a White House dinner with their most famous fan, President John Tyler. In recent years, their songs turned political, and many of their rallies in support of abolition ended inharmoniously, some in rioting.

1851

Fillmore

Oregon Territory, Jan. 23. New city incorporated, and flip of coin decides to name it after Portland, Maine, not Boston, Massachusetts.

Honolulu, Feb. 1. French commissioner Emile Perrin demands islands' homage to France, but yields when monarchy receives U.S. protection.

California, February. Quartz discovery in Amador County begins quartz mining boom.

California, March 25. Yosemite Valley discovered by Major James Savage while pursuing band of Indians.

Milwaukee, Wisconsin, Apr. 6. Catholic mob prevents excommunicated priest, Edward Leahy, from speaking; [becomes known as "Leahy Riot."]

Washington, D.C., Apr. 25. President Fillmore calls revolutionary expeditions to Cuba "palpable violations" of U.S. neutrality (→Sept. 1).

New York City, May 3. *Gleason's Pictorial Drawing-Room Companion,* nation's first illustrated weekly, issued.

Florida, May 6. Dr. John Gorrie patents artificial ice-making machine; developed to cool rooms of feverish patients.

New York, May 14. Nation's longest rail line opens from New York City to Lake Erie.

Akron, Ohio, May 29. Second Women's Rights Convention hears freed slave Sojourner Truth give speech (→1852).

Washington, D.C., June 5. Anti-slavery paper *National Era* begins serializing *Uncle Tom's Cabin,* by Harriet Beecher Stowe (→1852).

Iowa, July 23. Sioux sign Treaty of Traverse des Sioux, ceding all lands in Iowa and most in Minnesota to United States government.

New York City. Horace Greeley's *New York Tribune* carries serialized version of Karl Marx's *Revolution and Counter-Revolution.*

San Francisco. Organization intended to serve interests of Chinese-Americans founded.

Cleveland, Ohio. Young Men's Christian Association founded as result of informal prayer meetings by young men.

New York City. Nathaniel Hawthorne's *The House of the Seven Gables* published.

Spanish garrote Lopez for Cuban revolt

Havana, Cuba, Sept. 1

Spanish authorities have garroted General Narciso Lopez for his role as leader of a filibustering expedition to Cuba. The failed insurrection was manned mostly by Americans, and the quick execution of "the gallant 51" captured members of the Lopez invasion force triggered rioting in New Orleans and Key West and prompted less-violent protests in several other American cities. The Venezuelan-born Lopez had made previous attempts to incite rebellion in the Spanish colony, most recently last year.

The status of Cuba has proved a divisive issue in the United States. Support for annexation of the Spanish possession has been strong in the Southern states, which want to expand slave territory. And supporters of slavery are afraid that Spain might decide to free Cuba's large slave population, creating unrest among Negroes in the United States. Spain's refusal in 1848 to consider an American offer to purchase Cuba has closed such an option for now, but the island's strategic location on the shipping routes to the Pacific and California means Cuba will continue to be an important subject (→Jan. 5, 1852).

N.Y. to San Francisco by clipper in 89 days

Flying Cloud, under full sail, on the high seas. Lithograph by Buttersworth.

San Francisco, Aug. 31

The clipper Flying Cloud, commanded by 37-year-old Captain Josiah P. Creesy, set a record today as it completed a voyage from New York to San Francisco in 89 days 21 hours. The 225-foot, 1,783-ton ship averaged 227 miles a day on its 5,912-mile journey around Cape Horn. "It is a truly national triumph," said the *New York Commercial* of the achievement. The wooden clipper, a vessel that is built for speed rather than for capacity, was developed in 1850 because of the growing demands of the California trade. So far this year, 31 of these ships have been launched, boasting such stormy names as Typhoon and Tornado.

Douglass splits from Garrison on abolition

New York City

In a speech before the annual convention of the American Anti-Slavery Society, the Negro leader Frederick Douglass made it clear that he opposed the dissolution of the union and favored political action to end slavery. This was a departure in tactics and strategy from those of William Lloyd Garrison, a prominent abolitionist whose ideas have set policy in the anti-slavery movement. Douglass declared that the Constitution implied the eventual end of slavery, and that a split in the union would leave slaves at the mercy of Southern slave owners. He also predicted that pro- and anti-slavery factions would eventually come to violence.

New sewing device patented by Singer

Singer gives a demonstration.

Washington, D.C., Aug. 12

A patent has been awarded to Isaac Merritt Singer for his new sewing machine. A previous patent had been granted to Elias Howe in 1846 for a machine that was quite similar. Since the patents are apparently conflicting, it is expected that Singer and Howe will come to an agreement permitting both to make sewing machines.

Negroes storm jail, free fugitive slave

Boston, Feb. 15

An angry mob of free Negroes stormed a jail here today and released a slave named Shadrach, who had been arrested under the new federal Fugitive Slave Law, valid even in free states. To claim a runaway, a master need only show an affidavit proving ownership. Bounties are often paid for runaways.

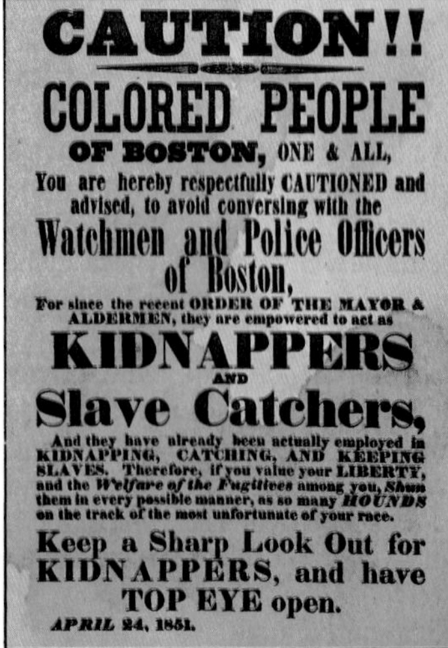

otato famine adds o Irish migration

oston

"Poor Ireland's done." The call hoes across a blighted, starving nd as vast numbers turn to their e remaining hope, America. This ar's total of 250,000 immigrants, e highest yet, means that since the lack" harvest of 1845 over a miln Irish have arrived. New York, oston, Philadelphia and Baltiore are now one-quarter Irish, th most living in slums described "the permanent abode of fever." ut these are determined Irish, cking to their adage that the only ace in Ireland where a man can ake his fortune is America.

oule's advice: Go Vest, young man

erre Haute, Indiana

The words "Go West, young an, go West" have quickly caught n with Americans, most likely beuse they capture the spirit of e nation. What's more, if asked, any Americans will tell you they now where the expression origined. They will say the words came om the pen of Horace Greeley, the ominent journalist and founder of e *New York Tribune*. Not so. In uth, the advice first appeared in n editorial that John L. Soule rote earlier this year in the *Terre aute Express*. And poor Horace reeley, while he has indeed traved in the West and been impressed y it, vigorously disclaims authorip of the now-famous advice.

Yacht America wins cup in British race

Cowes, England, Aug. 22

A United States yacht has stunned the sailing world with a triumph over Britain's best. The America, designed more on clipper-ship lines than the traditional cod's head and mackerel tail configuration, captured the 100-guinea cup of the Royal Yacht Squadron by winning the 60-mile race around the Isle of Wight. Because the America won the prize, it has been dubbed the America's Cup. Queen Victoria, on hearing America had won, asked an attendant who had finished second. "Madam," he said, "there is, alas, no second place."

New conquest for Lola Montez: America!

New York City, Dec. 29

The play is called *Betley, the Tyrolean*, but it's all Lola Montez, the Courtesan. By any other name – she was born Marie Dolores Eliza Rosanna Gilbert – the actress-dancer is a rare beauty of an Irish rose, and her American debut proved it. The play in which she is appearing is little more than an excuse for the ravishing Miss Montez to capitalize on her highly publicized European conquests: in public, the theater; in private, Franz Liszt and King Ludwig II of Bavaria, among others. Let the critics prattle about her shallow notoriety. The men in last night's audience are probably still rubbing their eyes.

Montez, dancer and adventuress.

Herman Melville's "Moby-Dick" issued

"The Sperm Whale in a Flurry" by Currier and Ives. Melville, whose father died when he was 12, spent five years at sea as a young man. In 1841, he embarked on a whaling ship, only to desert in a South Sea island port.

New York City

The prolific Herman Melvile has produced his most ambitious book yet. *Moby-Dick; or, The Whale* is many things at once. First, it is a yarn that features such memorable characters as Queequeg, a Polynesian prince and nonpareil harpoonist, and Captain Ahab, a pegleg who leads the crew of the Pequod on a mad maritime chase in pursuit of a white whale. The book is also an encyclopedic treatment of whaling, full of bizarre and obscure facts. Finally, it is a brooding exploration of man's doomed search for meaning.

Indeed a whale of an effort is required to fathom the mysteries of Melville's dense prose, and the book's sales have not been encouraging. But some critics have been lavish in their praise. The *Morning Courier and New York Enquirer* declares that the 32-year-old author "writes with the gust of true genius," and *Harper's Monthly* asserts that the novel "surpasses" all of Melville's previous books. Meanwhile, the press in Britain has been showering the author and his work with compliments. For example, the periodical *John Bull* raved about the novel, citing Melville's many "flashes of truth ... which sparkle on the surface of the foaming sea of thought."

Foster's latest hit is "Swanee River"

New York City, Aug. 26

The sheet music says that *Old Folks at Home*, also known as *Swanee River*, was written by E.P. Christy. But don't let that fool you. This year's runaway hit bears the indelible mark of Stephen Foster, whose previous "Negro" songs, turned out for Christy's Minstrels, include *Oh, Susanna*, in 1847, and *Camptown Races*, published earlier this year. Foster, aged 25, has been composing songs since he was a boy. A few years ago, he signed an unusual and prestigious publishing contract that will guarantee him two cents a copy for each song sold instead of the customary outright price, such as the $15 that Christy paid him for *Swanee River*.

Women's fashions reflect new wealth

United States

The prosperity of the nation is worn on the backs of its women. As the economy grows, men's fortunes increase. And where else should they drape their new-found wealth but on the shoulders of the women they love? Ladies of high society are wearing dresses of velvet and silk. The basque, a bodice with a short skirt or tails under the waistline, is popular. Colorful India muslins are also in style, as are straw hats.

1852

Fillmore

Washington, D.C., Jan. 5. Announcing release of Americans captured by the Spanish in Cuba, President Fillmore urges Congress to vote indemnity payments for damage done in New Orleans anti-Spanish riots (→June 2, 1854).

Chicago, Feb. 20. First non-stop train from East arrives on Michigan Southern Railway.

Albany, New York, Apr. 6. Albany newspaper is first to use term "telegram" in reference to telegraphic communication.

New York City, June 6. Knickerbockers don first uniforms in baseball.

Baltimore, June 5. Democrats end national convention, nominating Franklin Pierce of New Hampshire for president on 49th ballot (→Nov. 2).

New York City, October. The Rev. Thomas Gallaudet founds St. Ann's Church for the deaf.

Boston. Pharmaceutical firm distills coal oil from coal tar, discovering that it will burn in lamps.

Boston. Congregationalists repudiate Plan of Union with Presbyterians.

United States. Matrimonial agencies are becoming increasingly popular, advertising "cheap wives for poor and deserving young men."

Lake Pend Oreille, Idaho. French Canadians discover gold.

United States. Negro physician Martin R. Delaney calls for establishment of Negro "Promised Land" in Central or South America.

West Point, New York. Robert E. Lee appointed superintendent of academy and befriends cadets James Whistler and Jeb Stuart.

Utah. Mormons announce plural marriage as facet of their faith.

Colorado. William Bent blows up his "Fort Bent" when United States government refuses to meet his price for it.

Indiana. State legislators authorize vigilante societies to arrest horse thieves.

Hartford, Connecticut. The Rev. Arthur Coxe denounces Nathaniel Hawthorne's *The Scarlet Letter* as a "brokerage of lust."

"Uncle Tom's Cabin" published; sells 300,000, made into play

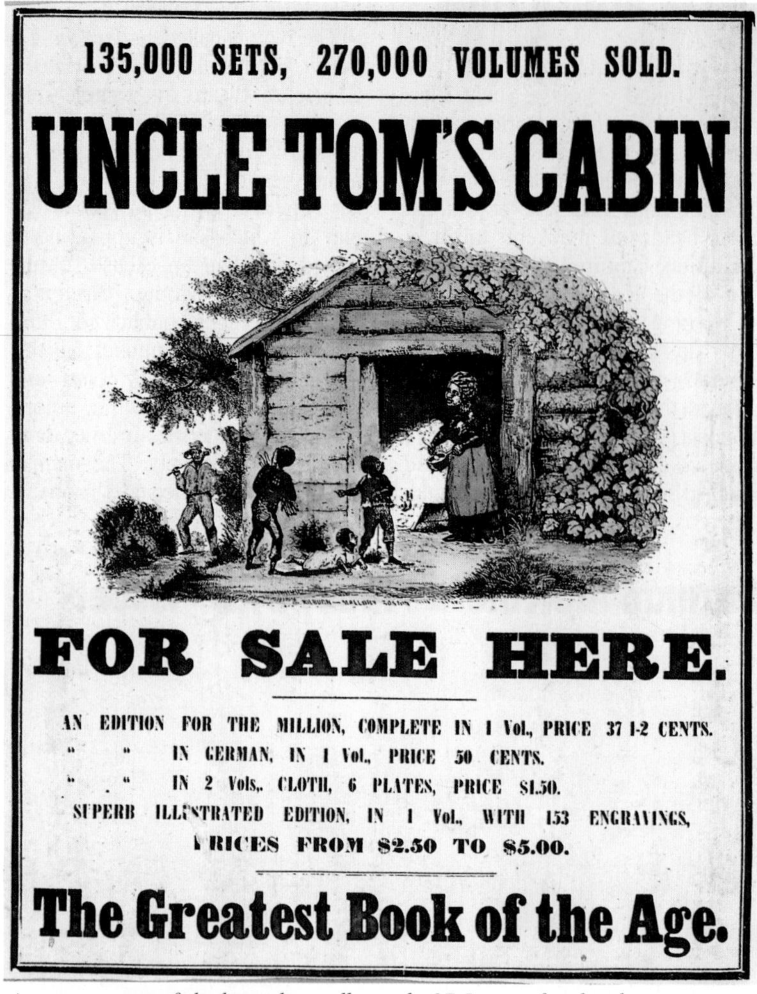

Announcement of the latest best-seller; only 37.5 cents for the cheapest copy.

New York City

The anti-slavery movement h found its most effective spoke woman in a novice novelist, Ha riet Beecher Stowe, the 39-year-o daughter of Calvinist thinker L man Beecher and the wife of h disciple C.E. Stowe. Mrs. Stow who now lives in Maine, has stirre up a storm of controversy with *U cle Tom's Cabin, or, Life Amon the Lowly*, the tragic tale of a d vout and selfless slave who rescu a white child, but then is sold to sadistic master, Simon Legree. L gree is so unhinged by Tom's Chri tian virtue and quiet fortitude th he has the slave flogged to death.

The story first appeared serial in the journal *National Era*, and th completed volume, published c August 23, has sold 300,000 copie a record for American novels. O September 27, a month after th book's publication, a theatrical ve sion was presented in Troy, Ne York, without Mrs. Stowe's co sent by George Aiken, who als starred in it. The show ran fo months before moving to the N tional Theater here, and it has bee a triumph. Advocates of slaver shaken by the furor, have issued defense of their cause in a collectio of essays, *The Pro-Slavery Arg ment* (→March 15, 1853).

Phillips: "Vigilance is price of liberty"

Boston, Jan. 28

Speaking before the Massachusetts Anti-Slavery Society, Wendell Phillips asserted that "Eternal vigilance is the price of liberty." Phillips is a universal reformer, concerned with the rights of women, factory workers, Indians, prisoners and slaves. He is best known for his eloquence as an abolitionist. An associate of American Anti-Slavery Society president William Lloyd Garrison, Phillips maintains that the Constitution is a pro-slavery document and, therefore, he refuses to vote or run for public office. In the last few years, the 40-year-old Phillips has become well known on the lecture circuit, and he has made it known that abolition, and moral agitation in general, have become his profession.

Douglass: Should Negro observe July 4?

Rochester, New York, July 4

In a public address, Negro abolitionist Frederick Douglass today questioned whether people of his race should celebrate Independence Day, since Negroes are held as slaves in many parts of the country and have never benefited from the document that freed the colonies from British rule. Although the Declaration of Independence originally contained a section denouncing slavery, it was edited before its approval so as not to offend those signers who held slaves.

The 35-year-old Douglass is widely known as an orator, journalist and abolitionist. He was born a slave and kept as a house servant in Baltimore, where he learned to read and write. In September 1838, disguised as a sailor, he escaped to New York, where he became active in the anti-slavery movement. He has published a book, *Narrative of the Li of Frederick Douglass*, and has le tured widely in the United State England and Ireland, not only o slavery but also on women's rights.

Douglass (1844) by E. Hammond.

Sojourner Truth is hailed for speech

Cleveland, Ohio

"Ain't I a woman?" These words follow Sojourner Truth everywhere in her crusade to rid this state of its persecution of Negroes and women. Spoken last year at the Akron Women's Rights Convention, her words link the two causes in a way that may bring their advocates closer together. "I could work as much and eat as much as any man," cried the former slave, "and bear the lash as well. And ain't I a woman?" Delegates feared a colored speaker might discredit their cause, but Truth gains acceptance daily.

Order reorganized to oppose Catholics

New York City

The Order of the Star Spangled Banner, founded in 1849 by Charles Allen as a fraternal society dedicated to the preservation of the Constitution, has been reorganized by James W. Barker into a secret society that is dedicated to restricting immigration and opposed to what is seen as the increasing influence of Catholicism in the United States. All of its members are sworn to withhold information about the order and have pledged to respond to questions about it with the phrase "I know nothing" (→ June 17, 1854).

Pierce roundly defeats Scott for President

Washington, D.C., Nov. 2

Franklin Pierce won a landslide victory for President of the United States today, swamping his Whig opponent, General Winfield Scott. Pierce, a 47-year-old Democrat from New Hampshire, carried 27 states with 254 electoral votes to just four states and 42 electoral votes for General Scott, a native of New Jersey. William Rufus De Vane King, a Democrat, was elected Vice President. The President-elect, a general in the Mexican War, had been chosen on the 49th ballot at the Democratic convention, breaking a deadlock over the slavery issue (→ March 4, 1853).

Pierce (1853) by G.P.A. Healy.

Yale, Harvard hold first rowing meet

Lake Winnepesaukee, N.H., Aug. 2

The sport of rowing is gaining steadily in popularity among New England colleges, and Yale and Harvard have taken their friendly rivalry to the waters here for what is believed to be the first intercollegiate meeting in any sport. The Eli crew began rowing a decade ago, using a canoe. The Crimson crew has been rowing since 1845. The sport has also attracted the interest of the students at Amherst, Bowdoin, Brown and Massachusetts Agricultural.

King Ranch created in Southern Texas

Texas, Autumn

Richard King, a 27-year-old former steamboat pilot and a veteran of the Seminole War, has established what many South Texans regard as the largest ranch in the state. Situated between San Antonio and the Gulf Coast, the King Ranch covers more than 75,000 acres on what was once the Spanish land grant of Santa Gertrudis. An ambitious man, King says he plans to buy and raise enough cattle to cover the range from the Nueces River to the Rio Grande.

Webster and Clay, old rivals, are dead

Marshfield, Massachusetts, Oct. 24

Daniel Webster is dead at 70, four months after Henry Clay, 75, who died June 29. The two had been rivals for the presidency, which eluded both. Kentuckian Clay and New Englander Webster often clashed, but they agreed that union was more important than the slavery issue. The silver-tongued Webster was famous for his call for "union now and forever" in 1830. Clay, "the Great Compromiser," had a key role in the Missouri Compromise and the one in 1850.

Brown paper bags made by machine

West Dennis, Massachusetts

Anyone who has ever gone shopping and had to lug home his or her purchases in a variety of baskets and containers is going to appreciate a new product that has come on the market. It is a paper bag and it is fabricated from a stiff brown paper that is strong enough to hold almost any items a shopper might wish to carry home. The bags are the invention of Luther C. Crowell of West Dennis, and a machine to fold and seal them has been patented by Francis Wolle.

"The Speculator" (c.1852) by Francis William Edmonds of New York.

"Miners in the Sierra" (c.1852) by Nahl and Wenderoth of San Francisco.

1853

Pierce

Oregon Territory, Jan. 12. Willamette University chartered; first university west of Rockies.

Washington, D.C., Feb. 21. Coinage Act of 1853 passes Congress, cutting quantity of silver in coins under one dollar and authorizing gold $3 pieces.

Sacramento, California, Feb. 25. City chosen to be state capital.

Washington, D.C., March 4. Reciting inaugural speech from memory, Franklin Pierce is sworn in as 14th President.

Washington, D.C., March 7. After resigning Senate seat in 1851 to protest Compromise of 1850, Jefferson Davis is named Secretary of War.

New York City, March 15. *Uncle Tom's Cabin* opens at Purdy Theater, with separate viewing area for "respectable" Negroes.

New York City, June. Mathew Brady opens Broadway daguerrotype studio; $2.50 to $4.50 for portrait.

Rochester, New York, July 6. Delegates from several states form National Council of Colored People, to encourage vocational training of Negroes.

Oregon Territory, Sept. 10. Table Rock Treaty concluded; Indians agree to transfer land to settlers for $60,000, [but payment is never made].

New York City. Heinrich Steinweg, better known as Henry Steinway, opens piano factory.

Wisconsin. Norwegian immigrants found Norwegian Evangelical Church of America.

San Francisco. Kong Chow Temple constructed; first Buddhist temple in nation.

United States. Fire at Harper's publishers destroys plates for Herman Melville's *Moby-Dick* and most of remaining copies.

New Orleans. Yellow fever epidemic kills 11,000 people.

New York. John Roebling finishes building Niagara suspension bridge.

Indiana. Wabash Canal, 459 miles long, is completed.

United States. *United States Review* predicts that in 50 years "machinery will perform all work . . . The only tasks of the human race will be to make love, study and be happy."

Amelia's bloomers create a sensation

"The Bloomer Costume" by Currier.

Hartford, Connecticut, July 4

As everyone knows, women do not have "legs"; the word is simply too indelicate to utter in public. The reader should be reminded of this fact before being informed that Mrs. Amelia Jenks Bloomer, a publisher and an advocate of women's rights, delivered a Fourth of July address today while dressed in a pair of Turkish-style pantaloons draped loosely over her limbs. A bodice and a short skirt completed the curious outfit. In spite of the jeers of onlookers, some friends of Mrs. Bloomer have followed suit, among them Mrs. Elizabeth Cady Stanton and Miss Lucy Stone.

Levi Strauss sells brown jeans to miners

San Francisco

A Bavarian dry goods dealer named Levi Strauss is doing a brisk business fashioning and selling a kind of heavyweight trousers to the gold prospectors here. The jeans, as they are sometimes called, being made of the durable twilled cotton cloth known in France as "genes," are loose fitting with plenty of pockets. Miners need these pockets to keep their tools accessible. The pants are also very strong. In fact, when Strauss came to San Francisco three years ago, he intended to sell the same material for tents; not finding a market for them, he converted the fabric into trousers. Usually, the cloth is brown, but Strauss has been experimenting with indigo dye, a cheaper coloring that perhaps some of the less successful miners might appreciate.

Strauss is not the only San Francisco merchant catering to the newly found, wealthy clientele. Businesses are thriving selling jewelry and fine men's and women's clothes. Some enterprises are a little more out of the ordinary. A man named David Robison came to town in 1849 planning to pan for gold like everyone else. It happened that he sailed by way of Panama and picked up some green bananas there. When he saw how quickly they sold in San Francisco, he decided to be a greengrocer, and since then he has been quite successful selling rare tropical fruits. And an Italian named Domingo Ghirardelli has been offering richly flavored chocolates that are said to be worth their weight in – well, silver at least.

Jeans made with plenty of pockets to please the productive workingman.

Chinatown emerges out of Gold Rush

San Francisco

The Gold Rush is encouraging a flood of immigration from China. Between 1820 and 1849, only 43 Chinese came to America. But last year alone, more than 18,000 Chinese, all but 17 of them men, poured in through San Francisco. About 25,000 Chinese, who only rarely adopt American dress and customs, now occupy an area in the heart of the city along Dupont Street [Grant Avenue]. "They seem to have driven out everything and everybody else," laments the daily newspaper *Alta California*.

The first Chinese restaurants opened in late 1848 and they are growing popular. Other Chinese businesses, which started a few years later, offer cut-rate prices on many items. The Chinese have organized into six societies, each representing a homeland region. Each society has its own officials and interpreter. They make up Chinatown's de facto government. Last year an insidious and secret structure known as the "tong" moved in. The Hip Yee Tong, the best known, has been smuggling in "daughters of joy" (prostitutes). Overall, resentment against the Chinese is on the increase.

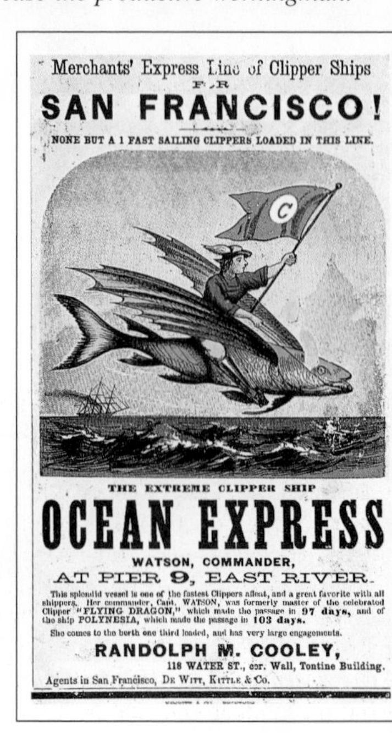

Large Mexico tract bought by Gadsden

Mexico, City, Dec. 30

At his inauguration, President Pierce said his administration "will not be controlled by any timid forebodings of evil from expansion." And it hasn't been. His emissary, James Gadsden, a railroad president from South Carolina, said today that Mexico had agreed to the sale of 29,640 square miles of its northern territory on the 32nd parallel, along the Gila River, and west of New Mexico. The price was $10 million. The area was sought so that all of the strategic overland trail to California and the route of the proposed southern transcontinental railroad will be on American soil. In addition, rumors indicate vast gold and silver deposits in the area.

First potato chips made in Saratoga

Saratoga, New York

Fried potatoes have long been popular in America, but a new variation has come in vogue since its accidental creation at Moon's Lake Lodge here. It seems a customer at this exclusive resort (some say it was Cornelius Vanderbilt) ordered chef George Crum to make him thin fried potatoes. Out of spite, Crum sliced them paper thin and fried them – to the delight of his customers. Thus were "Saratoga chips" invented.

Frenchman leading monster concerts

New York City, Aug. 29

The dazzling French conductor Louis Antoine Jullien is now beating his own drum at the Castle Garden – the celebrated Monster Drum. But then, everything about these "monster concerts for the masses" is immense. The orchestra is the largest – and best – ever heard; the drum and ophicleide (it's a brass wind instrument) are the biggest ever built. As for Jullien himself, his jeweled baton is borne to him on a silken pillow and he beats time with white kid gloves. After each piece, he recuperates in a red plush chair near the podium.

Baltimore and Ohio are finally linked

Wheeling, [West] Virginia, Jan. 12

After 25 years of struggle, the B.&O. Railroad realized its dream of a link between Baltimore and the banks of the Ohio River today when one of its trains completed the 379-mile journey to the bustling steamboat center of Wheeling. To cover steep Allegheny grades, the line will use giant engines like the 10-wheelers designed by Samuel Hayes. At the same time, 10 lines have consolidated as the New York Central Railroad, under Erastus Corning. And Congress is preparing for a transcontinental railroad. In March, it granted $150,000 for a study of five routes to the Far West. Governor Isaac Stevens of Washington, an engineer, heads the study.

First Negro novel, on Jefferson slave

London

William Wells Brown continues to get under people's skin. In the past, the former slave, who is in his mid-30's, has published poems calling for abolition. His latest work, the first novel ever penned by an American Negro, is a shocker. *Clotelle; or, the President's Daughter* describes the plight of a mulatto born into the household of Thomas Jefferson. No wonder Brown turned to a British publisher.

Walker filibusters invade Mexico area

Baja California, Nov. 3

William Walker and an armed expedition landed at La Paz in the Mexican state of Lower California today to "colonize" the area. Walker, a lawyer and editor turned swashbuckling filibuster, declared the state an independent republic and himself its president. His army left San Francisco last month on the brig Carolina, claiming Mexican residents had asked protection from Apache Indians. But the brigade will be on its own as officials in San Francisco say they do not approve of the action and will not send supplies (→Jan. 18, 1854).

Perry arrives in Japan

Yedo Bay, Japan, July 14

Commodore Matthew Calbraith Perry, overcoming initial Japanese resistance, has met with representatives of the Emperor of Japan. Perry, arrived here [Tokyo Bay] last week with four men-of-war and refused to comply with Japanese demands that he move on to Nagasaki, the site of a small Dutch trading post and the only port open to foreigners. The sight of Perry's well-armed force, which includes the frigates Mississippi and Susquehanna, evidently convinced Japan's rulers that they could not force the Americans to leave.

Commodore Perry presented a letter from former President Millard Fillmore, who sent Perry on this mission to the Orient last year, requesting that the Japanese provide protection for American sailors shipwrecked in Japan, open additional ports to foreign trade and make available coaling stations for the American steamships that ply the routes between the west coast of the United States and China.

Japan has not always been closed to visitors from the outside world. In the 16th century, Portuguese traders and Jesuit missionaries were welcomed, but by the mid-17th century, Japan had turned to a policy of seclusion. The recent example of China, which was forced to open many ports, first to the ships of the British and then to those of other Western powers after being easily defeated in the Opium War of 1842, has no doubt made the Japanese even more wary of foreigners' intentions. Other Occidental powers have tried to make contact with Japan in an effort to end the country's isolation, but without success (→March 31, 1854).

Perry, depicted in a Japanese print.

The multi-colored invasion of overseas merchants. Foreign steamships motor into Nagasaki harbor, as portrayed in a Japanese "Bai-oban" print (c.1850).

1854

Pierce

Chester, Pennsylvania, Jan. 1. First Negro college chartered as Ashmun Institute [Lincoln University].

Mexico, Jan. 18. William Walker proclaims Mexican state of Sonora part of his "Republic of Lower California."

Havana, Cuba, Feb. 28. Spanish officials seize U.S. merchant ship Black Warrior, confiscating cargo and fining captain for improper documentation (→March 3, 1855).

Kanagawa, Japan, March 31. Commodore Perry signs Treaty of Kanagawa, opening ports of Shimoda and Hakodate to American trade.

Washington, D.C., March 31. United States and England sign Reciprocity Treaty, agreeing on North American fishing rights and abolishing certain import duties.

Washington, D.C., Apr. 4. Secretary of State William Marcy asks David Gregg, envoy in Honolulu, to learn if U.S. annexation would be acceptable to King Kamehameha III.

New York City, May 6. Cyrus Field granted 50-year monopoly on trans-Atlantic cable industry.

Wisconsin, July 17. Supreme Court declares Fugitive Slave Law inapplicable in case of fugitive slave Joshua Glover, freed from jail by abolitionist mob and helped to Canada.

Washington, D.C., Oct. 31. Nation's 128 woman postal workers are only female workers making as much as their male counterparts.

San Francisco. Flying Cloud clipper, built by Donald McKay, sets sailing record for Boston-to-San Francisco run in 89 days, eight hours.

Philadelphia. Dentist Mahlon Loomis patents kaolin (ceramic) process for producing false teeth.

Texas. Knights of the Golden Circle organized as secret society dedicated to preservation of slave system.

United States. More than 80,000 Mexicans have become American residents as a result of U.S. expansion.

New York City. *Ten Nights in a Barroom and What I Saw There* by Timothy S. Arthur is best-seller.

Smith and Wesson invent a revolver

Boston

A new kind of revolver has been developed by two local gunsmiths, Horace Smith and Daniel Wesson. Like the Colt revolver, the Smith and Wesson has a revolving cylinder that contains the bullets. But the new revolver uses a more efficient mechanism for turning the cylinder, which allows for fast firing. Smith and Wesson are working to improve their weapon so that it can use cartridges made of metal instead of the usual paper cartridges.

Kansas, Nebraska free to choose slavery

Washington, D.C., May 26

Congress today passed the Kansas-Nebraska Act, allowing settlers of the newly created territories of Kansas and Nebraska to chose between free soil and slavery. The bill, which was accompanied by an amendment repealing the Missouri Compromise of 1820, has touched off a violent and bloody struggle between pro-slavery and abolitionist forces.

After three months of bitter debate, the Senate passed the bill at 1:10 a.m. by a vote of 37 to 14. Three days earlier, the House passed it by a vote of 113 to 110. Sponsored by Illinois Senator Stephen Douglas, the act established the doctrine of congressional nonintervention in the territories. The repeal of the Missouri Compromise, which had prohibited slavery north of the southern boundary line of Missouri, now allows slaveholders to move into new territories. In protest, anti-slavery advocates today threatened to disobey the Fugitive Slave Law, and a Boston mob attacked a courthouse in a failed attempt to free a fugitive named Anthony Burns (→Dec. 15, 1855).

Fastest U.S. trotter is Flora Temple

Kalamazoo, Michigan

They said that Flora Temple would never amount to anything and now she is the fastest trotting horse in the country. The mare, who was bought for a song, has grown faster as she grows older and at the age of 14 has set a mile record of 2:19 3/4. Little was expected of Flora Temple after she was foaled on the farm of Samuel Welsh in Oneida, New York. In fact, she was passed from hand to hand at cheap prices until the age of 4, when Jonathan Vielee bought her for $175. It was then that the durable mare began to show real speed on the road, hitched to a four-wheel wagon. After hitting a mark of 2:36, she was sold for a whopping $4,000.

Safety hoist lives up to its name

New York City, May

Thirty feet over a gasping crowd at the Crystal Palace this month, Elisha Graves Otis proved he has invented a lift that will carry passengers safely. Rising on a square platform, the Vermont-born inventor kept his audience busy by explaining the lifting device. Suddenly, at the apex, he drew a knife and cut the suspending cable. As observers shuddered, clamps shot out, grabbed the guard rails and held the lift in mid-air. Otis calls the creation a "safety hoist," and hopes the demonstration will boost sales in his Yonkers, New York, outlet. In the new iron-framed buildings of James Bogardus, Otis's hoist could extend urban life skyward.

U.S. seeks Cuba after ship is seized

Washington, D.C., June 2

Secretary of State William Marcy received notice today that Spain has refused indemnity for the February seizure of an American merchant ship in Havana. The note accuses the United States of using the incident as a "pretext for exciting estrangement." The Black Warrior, detained on a technicality, will be fined $6,000. Its seizure indicates growing Spanish anger over filibustering expeditions and talk of Cuban annexation. Marcy has ordered Pierre Soule, minister to Spain to "detach that island from the Spanish dominion." Soule is authorized to offer $130 million for Cuba. If refused Marcy may consider military options (→March 3, 1855).

Stephen Foster, composer for minstrel shows, has a hit in "Jeanie With the Light Brown Hair."

"Boston Harbor, Sunset" (1850-55) by Fitz Hugh Lane. A romantic realist in genre, Lane has devoted himself to capturing the moods of New England's coastline area. A precise attention to detail and outline tends to balance Lane's exploration of broad, suffusing shades of light.

Know-Nothing Party has annual meeting

Cartoon attacks the Irish and the Germans for allegedly subverting elections.

New York City, June 17

A splinter political group once known as Nativists met again this week under the name of the Order of the Star Spangled Banner. But to many, the name actually is the Know-Nothing Party, a group that appeals to an unfortunate, common prejudice against immigrants and Roman Catholics.

The Know-Nothing tag has been applied because members, when asked by curious onlookers outside their meeting place, what went on inside are wont to reply curtly: "I know nothing about it."

The *Cleveland Plain Dealer* recently poked fun at the new splinter party by writing: "When one Know-Nothing wishes to recognize another, he closes one eye, makes an O with his thumb and forefinger and places his nose through it – which, interpreted, reads eye-nose-O, I know nothing."

The party first surfaced five years ago to protest the large influx of immigrants, most of them Irish. The Nativists, or Know-Nothings, wanted to stem immigration and to retain control in the hands of those whose families had lived in the United States for at least 50 years. The Know-Nothings' platform would, in addition to depriving newcomers of voting rights and the right to hold office, ban such rights for Roman Catholics as well.

Henry David Thoreau's "Walden" issued

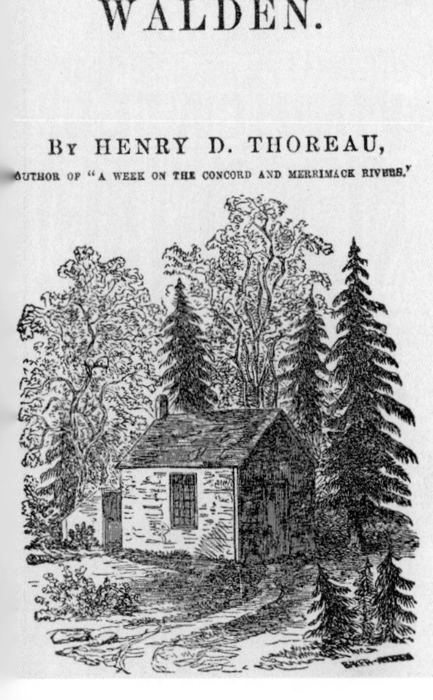
WALDEN.

BY HENRY D. THOREAU,

AUTHOR OF "A WEEK ON THE CONCORD AND MERRIMACK RIVERS."

Concord, Massachusetts

On July 4, 1845, while his countrymen celebrated Independence Day, Henry David Thoreau began two years of solitary living in a one-room hut he built at Walden Pond near his hometown here. This experiment in self-reliance – Thoreau ate only what grew wild or what he planted himself – is described in *Walden, or Life in the Woods.* "The mass of men lead lives of quiet desperation," says the 37-year-old recluse. "From the desperate city you go to the desperate country . . . But it is a characteristic of wisdom not to do desperate things." Thoreau's holiday was briefly interrupted when he was jailed for refusing to pay taxes that supported the Mexican War, which he opposed.

Slavery issue leads to Republican Party

Ripon, Wisconsin, July

United in their opposition to slavery, a group of Whigs, Free-Soil Democrats and Liberty Party men gathered at a schoolhouse here on February 28 to discuss what actions they would take if the Kansas-Nebraska Act should pass. The group, which had been called together by a local lawyer, Alvan E. Bovay, resolved that if it should pass, they would form a new party. Bovay suggested they call it "Republican," after the party of Thomas Jefferson, who was seen as an opponent of slavery, a champion of the concept of a nation of small landholders and a radical opponent of the established aristocracy.

Now, five months later, after the passage of the Kansas-Nebraska Act, which allows settlers of the newly created territories to chose between free soil and slavery, a Republican state convention is being held in Jackson, Michigan. Republican delegates are also meeting in Madison to begin organizing the party in Wisconsin. The Republicans, whose opposition to slavery and aristocracy is coupled with their support for new railroads, free homesteads and the opening of the Western lands by free labor, are intent on gaining power on both the state and federal government levels. The time seems right for the new party.

Lincoln calls for emancipation of slaves

Peoria, Illinois, Oct. 16

Abraham Lincoln today condemned the Kansas-Nebraska Act and called for the gradual emancipation of Southern slaves. "I have no predjudice against the Southern people," declared Lincoln, a lawyer and politician whose reputation had been largely confined to Illinois until now. "I surely will not blame them for not doing what I should not know how to do myself." The former member of the House also declared: "No man is good enough to govern another man without that other's consent."

Baronet leads 6,000-mile hunt for buffalo

Fort Leavenworth, Spring

Buffalo herds on the Great Plains are in trouble. Sir George Gore, a British baronet of Irish descent, has begun a 6,000-mile hunting expedition and they are the principal target. The hunters, with 75 rifles, 12 shotguns, 50 riding horses, packs of dogs and 27 wagons of supplies, will spend three years hunting the buffalo and other game. The Plains are now safer for hunting as a result of a treaty with the Sioux, who had been constantly battling the whites.

Shooting buffalo for sport. "The Buffalo Hunt" (1862) by Currier and Ives.

1855

Pierce

New York City, Feb. 6. Anti-Slavery Society hears Ralph Waldo Emerson estimate that $200 million would be enough to buy every slave's freedom.

Washington, D.C., March 3. Congress agrees to Secretary of War Jefferson Davis's plan to import Egyptian camels to Southwest at cost of $30,000.

Massachusetts, Apr. 28. Segregation banned in all schools.

New York City, May 9. Brownhelm County, Ohio, clerk John Mercer Langston, first Negro elected to public office in United States, addresses American Anti-Slavery Society.

Kansas, August. John Brown joins his sons and becomes leader of local militia (→Aug. 30, 1856).

Seattle, Washington, Sept. 28. Puget Sound Anti-Chinese Congress decides to frighten Chinese into leaving state; [many do depart] (→Nov. 3).

Tacoma, Washington, Nov. 3. Led by mayor, sheriff and deputies, a mob travels through Chinese district, throwing Chinese out of town (→9).

Tacoma, Washington, Nov. 9. U.S. troops arrive to arrest residents who were involved in expulsion of Chinese.

California. First lighthouse on Pacific Ocean is built off coast of San Diego.

Newtown Creek, New York. Dr. Abraham Gesner makes kerosene from raw petroleum; promotes it as patent medicine.

Watertown, Wisconsin. First kindergarten in United States, though German-speaking, founded by Mrs. Carl Schurz.

Salt Lake City. Brigham Young proclaims that a single drop of Negro blood renders a man unfit to enter Mormon priesthood.

United States. American Telegraph Co. formed to transmit messages in Eastern states.

United States. Frank Leslie's *Illustrated Newspaper* begun.

New York City. In seven years since its printing, Stephen Foster's *Camptown Races* has earned him only $101.25.

New York City. *My Bondage, My Freedom* published by ex-slave and abolitionist Frederick Douglass.

Kansas Territory has two governments

Vigilante "justice." "Border ruffians" head for free-soil territory as their Law and Order Party, organized in November, pushes for slavery in Kansas.

Kansas Territory, Dec. 15

Kansas has two governments now that the territory's anti-slavery settlers have adopted their own constitution. Ever since the passage last year of the Kansas-Nebraska Act, which allowed settlers of newly created territories to choose between free soil and slavery, a violent struggle has raged between pro- and anti-slavery forces, and it does not seem to be winding down.

A pro-slavery territorial governor was appointed in June of 1854, followed by the election of a pro-slavery territorial delegate. In March, a pro-slavery legislature was also elected – but only after 6,300 ballots were cast for the territory's 3,000 voters. The fraudulent election was the work of 5,000 "border ruffians" from neighboring Missouri, who also incited violence near Lawrence last month.

After the territorial governor refused to declare the election a fraud and the pro-slavery legislature passed laws penalizing anti-slavery agitation, free-soil settlers declared that the pro-slavery legislature was illegal and asked that the territory be admitted to the union as a free state. And today, they adopted a constitution outlawing slavery and planned to elect their own governor and legislature (→May 4, 1856).

"The Lackawanna Valley" (1855) by George Inness. A restless, religious man who has visited Europe twice, Inness shows great promise at age 30.

Aides want Cuba wrested from Spain

Washington, D.C., March 3

A public outcry has forced Congress to publish the so-called Ostend Manifesto, which outlines proposed American policy on Cuba. The memorandum, prepared by James Buchanan, John Y. Mason and Pierre Soule, the American ministers to Britain, France and Spain respectively, suggests "wresting" Cuba from Spain if an agreement to buy the island cannot be reached. Secretary of State William L. Marcy has repudiated the ministers' suggestion, but the Pierce administration has been unable to stem the criticism the document provoked. Free-soilers have condemned the recommendations of the three diplomats, all pro-slavery Democrats, as a plan to expand slave territory.

Strawberry fever leads to shortcake

United States

The passion Americans have for wild strawberries in every conceivable form has led to a kind of "strawberry fever" across the country. The latest reason – or excuse – for eating more strawberries is a confection that has been named "strawberry shortcake." A combination of a biscuit-like pastry with fresh strawberries and whipped cream on top, it is quickly becoming an American summer dessert.

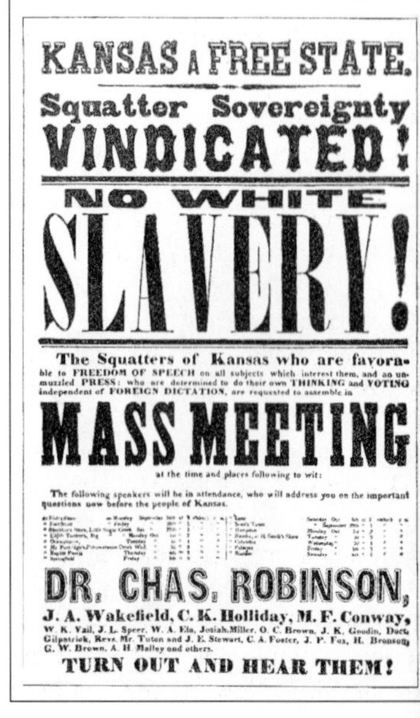

rohibition gaining nomentum in U.S.

'or the strong-willed only: membership in the Sons of Temperance.

ew York City, July 4

Drink it if you've got it, because s of today it is illegal to manuacture or sell alcoholic beverages n New York State. The prohibition novement is gaining support across ne nation, and 13 states now have anning laws. New York is followng the example Maine set in 1851. he American Society for the Pronotion of Temperence has been argely responsible for shaping ublic opinion, fighting the use of lcohol since 1826. New York City Mayor Fernando Wood, a foe of the aw, has told police to use discreion, that while it is illegal to sell lcohol it is not illegal to drink it.

Walker names self Nicaragua's leader

Nicaragua, Dec. 8

President Franklin Pierce today condemned Willliam Walker, the "gray-eyed man of destiny," who declared himself dictator of Nicaragua in September. The charismatic Walker seized power as Nicaragua was embroiled in a bloody civil war. Walker says that Patricio Rivas and his liberal faction had asked his military help. So Walker and his army, the "Immortal 56," sailed from San Francisco last spring to join the fight. He now seems capable of holding power. Many abolitionists think Southerners are supporting Walker as part of a plan to extend slavery. But actually, he is being financed by Cornelius Vanderbilt's Accessory Transit Company (→ Dec. 2, 1856).

Catholics victims of riots by nativists

Louisville, Kentucky, Aug. 6

Mobs of angry nativists backing the Know-Nothing Party in today's elections rioted through the streets, burning buildings and killing Irish and German immigrants. Earlier, a Mr. Burge, American, was beaten up at the polls by a few men thought to be Irish, and later, shots were reportedly fired at American passers-by from buildings housing Irish and German immigrants. The mob killed 20 people.

Railroad traverses Isthmus of Panama

Panama

Responding to a spiraling demand for better travel connections, America's railroad planners are growing bolder, in Panama to ease the path to California, and in the North to smooth the way to Canada. Spurred by the gold-rush traffic, W.H. Aspinwall's Panama Railroad conquered 47 miles of jungle and swamp to link the Atlantic and Pacific on January 28. Built at a staggering cost of $150,000 per mile, it turns the New York-San Francisco trip of 19,000 miles via Cape Horn into a five-week jaunt. In the North is the awesomely beautiful bridge John Roebling has built over the Niagara Gorge. On March 8, a 23-ton locomotive, the London, crossed the steel-cable span to Canada.

Whitman must pay to print "Leaves"

Brooklyn, New York

If you want something to be done right, you do it yourself. So says the eccentric Brooklyn journalist Walt Whitman, who footed the bill for *Leaves of Grass*, a book of 12 poems – his first – that he hired legal printers James and Thomas Rome to produce in their shop on Cranberry Street here. Whitman himself set 10 pages of type, of the total of 95, and read the galleys in the office of the Romes.

Longfellow writes poem on Hiawatha

Hiawatha is wed. Currier and Ives.

Cambridge, Massachusetts

Henry Wadsworth Longfellow mythologizes native lore in *The Song of Hiawatha*, a narrative poem that combines heady scholarship with rustic and simple storytellling. The learning of the 48-year-old Harvard professor informs the poem's meter, which is borrowed from an ancient Finnish model. The story is pure homespun. It tells of a young Ojibway Indian, Hiawatha, raised on the shore of Lake Superior. The young warrior learns to converse with birds and beasts and to traverse a mile in a single stride. He also foretells the arrival of the white man. His adventures include a contest with the evil Pearl Feather and betrothal to the beautiful Minnehaha, who dies when famine destroys Hiawatha's peaceful reign.

astle Garden welcomes new immigrants

New York City

Five years ago, Castle Garden, ne of the city's finest theaters, inroduced opera singer Jenny Lind, he "Swedish Nightingale," to New York's high society. Today it initiates another kind of visitor into a lifferent milieu. On its stage sit lesks staffed by officials of the New York State Commission of Emigraion. In its lobby are rooms for medcal exams. As of this year, the recast theater is the nation's first officiai port of entry for immigrants.

A massive round structure with tone walls three feet thick, the Garlen was initially built as Fort Clinon in 1807. Now, at the southern tip of Manhattan, it accepts immigrants in droves, 95 percent of them from Ireland, England or Germany.

New arrivals spend about six hours registering and taking medical exams. If all is in order, they cross a wooden gangplank to Manhattan, where they meet a host of hustlers. Women may be taken to boarding houses that turn out to be brothels. Men can enter a bar for a drink and wake up on a boat bound for the Barbary Coast. In the absence of government aid, immigrants help their own through private groups like the Irish Emigrant Society, the German Society and the Hebrew Benevolent Society.

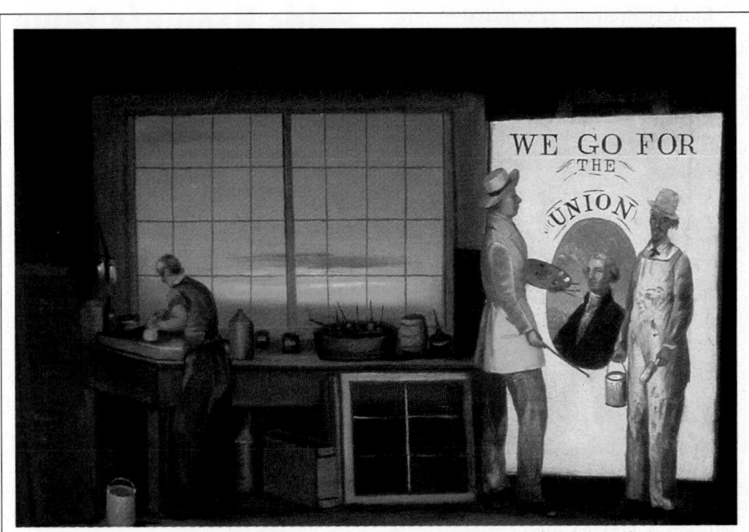

At a poster shop somewhere up North, artisans work through sunset in support of the union. Painting is "We Go for the Union." Anonymous.

1856

Pierce

Oregon Territory, Feb. 22. Indians kill father and sons while holding mother and daughter captive; Geisel Family Massacre enrages settlers.

California, Feb. 22. First railroad in state links Sacramento and Folsom.

Boston, March 26. Operation of first steam trains in New England begins.

United States, Apr. 1. Western Union Telegraph formed to handle Western telegraphic communication.

Texas, Apr. 29. First camels purchased by U.S. Army for experimental duty in Texas arrive (→June 16, 1857).

San Francisco, May 15. Politician James Casey lynched after murdering James King, crusading reformist editor.

Kansas Territory, May 21. Lawrence looted and sacked by pro-slavery forces; one man killed (→Aug. 30).

Bloomington, Illinois, May 29. In a speech, Abraham Lincoln says, "You can fool some of the people all of the time, and all of the people some of the time, but you can't fool all of the people all of the time."

Boston, May. Emulating large European music festivals, first American festival consists of a chorus of 600 and an orchestra of 78.

Cincinnati, June 6. Democrats end week-long national convention, nominating James Buchanan for president and John C. Breckinridge for vice president (→Nov. 4).

Illinois, Sept. 21. Illinois Central Railroad completed between Chicago and Cairo; longest in country with 700 miles of track.

Chicago. Railroad companies employ telegraph to aid engineers and operators.

Terre Haute, Indiana. T.T. Woodruff patents three-tiered berth railroad car; Andrew Carnegie is principal investor.

Richmond, Virginia. Editorial in *Examiner* is first to warn that fundamental social and economic differences between North and South may lead to civil conflict.

New York City. Freeman Hunt, author of *Wealth and Worth,* predicts that business will become a form of culture.

Abolitionists kill 5 pro-slave settlers

Kansas Territory, May 4

Four days after a pro-slavery pillage of Lawrence, abolitionists have murdered five settlers in the escalating border war between Kansas and Missouri. The five pro-slavery settlers, who lived at Dutch Henry's Crossing on Pottawatomie Creek, were slashed with sabers, their heads and bodies mutilated. Pro-slavery gangs, who promise immediate retaliation, have accused the abolitionist John Brown and his family of the murders. Brown moved here to join the fight to keep Kansas from being admitted to the union as a slave state (→21).

John Brown, crusader in Kansas.

Pro-slavery band raids Brown's town

Kansas Territory, Aug. 30

The stronghold of the abolitionist John Brown, Osawatomie, was attacked today by a gang of 300 pro-slavery men. The onslaught came just five days after a proclamation by the new pro-slavery Governor, Daniel Woodson, declared Kansas to be in a state of open insurrection. Guerrilla warfare between pro-slavery and free-state gangs is raging throughout the territory, with heavy casualties on both sides as well as property losses. In the battle at Osawatomie, Brown and 40 free-staters, though outnumbered, conducted a successful defense and drove off the attackers (→March 9, 1857).

Senator beaten after anti-slavery speech

The club is mightier than the voice. Sumner under attack on the Senate floo

Washington, D.C., May 22

Charles Sumner of Massachusetts was severely beaten at his Senate desk today. The outspoken 55-year-old abolitionist was bloodied, then battered unconscious by Representative Preston Brooks of South Carolina. Brooks, using his walking stick as a club, beat Sumner to avenge the honor of his uncle, a pro-slavery senator whom Sumner had denounced in a fiery speech three days ago. Senator Sumner compared South Carolina's Senator Andrew Butler to a "chivalrous knight" who had chosen as a mistress the "harlot Slavery" and he charged that his opponent was preparing to "conduct the state of South Carolina out of the union."

Sumner had never met his assail ant before Brooks strode up to hi desk, called his name and declare that he had read the speech "twic over carefully," branding it a "libe on South Carolina, and Mr. Butler who is a relative of mine." The he swung his stick – the 6-foo 4-inch Sumner was pinned unde his desk – drew blood and struck him repeatedly. Before his speech Sumner's opponents had brande him a "sneaking, sinuous, snakelik poltroon" and urged his expulsion The incident was part of a debate o the war over the future of Kansas pitting pro-slavery forces agains abolitionists (→Dec. 5, 1859).

"Sleighing in New York." Though beset by yellow fever, financial instability and horse traffic congestion, New York City is a fine example of American urban life, the seat of the stock exchange and the nation's entertainment capital, where such fabulous diversions as the Barnum Museum are located.

Buchanan wins presidency on fourth try

Buchanan, photo by Mathew Brady.

Fremont, 1st Republican candidate.

Washington, D.C., Nov. 4

James Buchanan proved today that political persistence pays off as he was elected President of the United States, topping a field that included former President Millard Fillmore of New York and John C. Fremont of California. Buchanan, a 65-year-old Pennsylvanian, carried 19 states with 174 electoral votes, but he did not win a majority of the popular vote. Representative John C. Breckinridge of Kentucky was elected Vice President.

This year's race marked Buchanan's fourth run for the presidency. A former member of the Senate and House and one-time chairman of the Senate Foreign Affairs Committee, he sought the Democratic nomination for president in 1844, again in 1848 and yet again in 1852 before succeeding today.

This year, the regular parties and splinter groups vied strenuously for the top spot. Fillmore was picked by the American (Know-Nothing) Party and the Whigs endorsed him. Fremont won the nomination of both the Northern American (anti-slavery) Party and Republican Party.

A key to Buchanan's win may have been the plank advocating annexation of Cuba, which the South favors. Buchanan carried 14 proslavery states and five free states; Fremont won 11 free states, and Fillmore one (→ March 4, 1857).

Central Americans fight to eject Walker

Granada, Nicaragua, Dec. 2

Leaving a taunting sign that reads, "Here was Granada," over the smoking ruins of this 300-year-old city, William Walker has saved his men from a combined force of Central American troops. But Walker, a short, slight, stoic man whose tempermant belies the melodrama of his life, has little more than taunts left at his disposal.

When he set up his puppet government last year, Walker at least impressed some of the Nicaraguan people as a man of action. General Corral, the man he deposed, was made Secretary of War. When Walker caught Corral conspiring with other Central American leaders to take back Nicaragua, he executed the beloved patriot. In July, Walker "elected" himself President and held a gala inaugural in Granada. But ceremony would not create the substance of authority.

A Costa Rican invasion in the spring left his troops ravaged by battle and disease. And after breaking a contract with financial backer Cornelius Vanderbilt, Walker found himself cut off from new recruits by Vanderbilt's shipping line.

The destruction of Granada was an act of desperation. Holed up in Rivas with his dying adventurers, Walker can only wonder if disease or the Central American army will find him first (→ Dec. 29, 1857).

William Walker tries to impose discipline on his motley assortment of recruits.

Seattle, January. *Here at the last frontier outpost, Indian warriors are fighting for their lives and their land. Two whites died in the latest battle of the Yakima War. The Indians were driven off and martial law declared, but many whites had to flee to the Decatur, anchored in Puget Sound.*

Schlitz is a brewer; Borden makes milk

Milwaukee, Wisconsin, July

Upon the death of August Krug, Joseph Schlitz, Krug's bookkeeper, has taken over the operation of the August Krug brewery, married Krug's widow and is running the enterprise with the help of Krug's nephews, August, Henry Alfred and Edward Uihlein. Meanwhile, Gail Borden has been awarded a patent for a milk-condensing process. Six years earlier, he had won a medal at the London Exposition for developing a one-pound meat biscuit which contained the nutrients of 5 pounds of meat and 10 pounds of flour. Borden was the first American food producer to win such a prize.

Only U.S. monarch victim of assassin

Beaver Island, Lake Michigan

James Jesse Strang, seer, revelator, prophet and self-proclaimed king of Beaver Island, has proved himself mortal. His death at the hands of an assassin leaves his 5,000 followers leaderless, for the dying king refused to appoint a successor. The small, red-bearded ruler, expelled from the Mormon Church after failing in an attempt to succeed Joseph Smith as its leader, brought his flock to this island in 1847. He impressed the members of his secret society by translating the *The Book of the Law of the Lord* (using spectacles he said an angel gave him). In return, they twice elected him to the Michigan legislature.

Where cotton is king and the slave is his subject

The South

As the patchwork quilt that is the union grows into maturity, and as its seam splits slowly and painfully along the Mason-Dixon Line, the two halves seem barely part of the same fabric. To the planter aristocracy, a British journalist has observed, "New England and the kindred states (are) the birthplace of impurity of mind among men and of unchastity in women." Their "valor and manhood have been swallowed up in ... the marts of dishonest commerce." The gentleman of the South, by contrast, fancies himself a chivalrous knight with a morality based on human values rather than the marketplace. Or as one Natchez resident put it, "The Northerner loves to make money, the Southerner to spend it."

But it is the way the Southerner makes his money that truly sets him apart from the Bostonian. Slavery, the South's "peculiar institution," as apologists call it, forms the foundation of Southern society and plantation prosperity. Since the first Negroes arrived in 1619, planters have seen little conflict between slavery and their code of honor. "Civilizing" the African is viewed as a noble service; and slaves are seen as children in an extended family.

The domestic slave market transfers thousands yearly to the most fertile lands.

But if family is the norm in plantation life, some patriarchs stretch the meaning of the dictum "spare the rod and spoil the child." One master is known to put slaves in a barrel with nails driven into it, then roll them down a hill. Another puts salt and pepper in lash wounds and blisters them by a fire, then allows a cat to claw the sores until they bleed. Even the paternalistic master has little respect for the Negro family. Negro women may endure submission in the beds of their white masters. And healthy men may be farmed out to another plantation. Rations are limited to what will keep slaves working during 80-hour weeks in the fields. Children often eat from a trough to simplify cleaning up after meals.

Along with its ruthlessness, the slave system is an iron ball and chain to the Southern economy. The vast amounts of capital invested in buying and feeding a labor force leaves little to devote to machinery. So while the North grows by leaps and bounds because of labor-saving techniques, the South prospers only by grinding out more hours from its overworked slaves. Soil depletion also takes its toll on the once-fertile tidewater. And as settlement pushes west, Eastern planters see a golden opportunity to sell slaves in order to raise capital.

But Northerners every day grow more committed to free soil in the new territories. So the seam splits ever wider. And the South grows restless. Each slave revolt and each Northern abolition rally reminds the slave society that it sits atop a powder keg. Slaveholders comprise only 25 percent of the population. The rest are half slaves and half poor whites, some of whom resent the planters' control over the region's politics. Somewhere under the surface, even those who attest loudest to the Negro's "childlike docility" understand that a people can only tolerate brutality for so long. And as North and South diverge in culture, their conflict grows more irreconcilable. In the words of George Fitzhugh, a Southern intellectual, "One set of ideas will govern and control after awhile the civilized world. Slavery will everywhere be abolished or everywhere be reinstituted."

"A Cotton Plantation on the Mississippi" by Currier and Ives. "King Cotton" is enthroned in the South by the enforced labor of Negro slaves from Africa.

Wheels of industry propel economy in the North

The North

When the visionary French writer Alexis de Tocqueville came to the United States in 1831, he marveled at the fervent ardor with which Americans "pursue their own welfare." He was speaking of Northerners. The Kentuckian, Tocqueville thought, was covetous of money "much less than pleasure or excitement." But the Ohioan was "tormented by wealth." And in the 25 years since the Frenchman's visit, torment has often seemed the tenor of the times north of the Mason-Dixon Line, and wealth the object.

While the South picks cotton, the North turns it into fabric. And textile mills are only part of an industrialization process that has lifted manufactures from 17 to 32 percent of the nation's output in 20 years. A web of railroads has opened vast new markets; total track mileage now approaches 30,000, up from 9,000 just six years ago. Transportation rates have fallen to 6 percent of their level in 1815. And the railroads themselves are big business, pulling iron, lumber and coal industries along in their tracks. Pennsylvania, at the heart of a vast coalfield that is estimated to be 12 times larger than Europe's, fuels a boom that nearly rivals England's. Pittsburgh has become, proudly, the "Birmingham of America."

Shaping the raw materials of the South in a New England textile mill.

Farm life may be the main target of this revolution. Railroad men are eager to load their cars with corn and wheat, so farmers produce more and more for the market. And the market grows daily; innovations like the steel plow and the horse-drawn reaper have increased food production 400 to 500 percent in the last 50 years, while the farm population has risen only 300 percent. Those no longer needed on the farm now live in cities and buy the corn they used to harvest.

In the mills of Massachusetts, the coalfields of Pennsylvania and the railroad yards of Chicago, the new laborers form a class rivaling the slaves of the South in numbers, and often in condition as well. The 12-hour day is normal in the mills of the Northeast, and many of the sufferers are children of 10 or less. The "lords of the loom," some say, are more evil than the "lords of the lash." After a recent industrial accident, one observer mused, "It becomes us to prate about the horrors of slavery. What Southern capitalist trifles with the lives of his operatives as do our philanthropes of the North?" Tocqueville himself labeled the "manufacturing aristocracy" as "one of the harshest that ever existed in the world."

A veiled war between the classes besieges America's cities. The wealthy in New York carry guns; Philadelphia is plagued by labor riots. The pious fear that erosion of life on the land will wear away moral values. But the relentless pressure of the factory machine offers a new discipline. Drunkenness and indolence are not just sins against God; they are wrenches in the cogs of production. The cycles of boom and bust add to the turmoil. There was a severe panic in 1854, but the years since have revived confidence. During the worst of times, America has found one source of consolation – land. A seemingly endless supply feeds the ballooning cities and at the same time absorbs their overflow to keep the urban bubble from bursting. But as the territories ease pressure from Northern cities, the slavery issue in the West causes a friction with the South that may rend the bonds of union.

Lowell, Massachusetts, archetype of a New England mill town, where man and machine meld, causing one observer to call workers "moral machinery."

1857

Buchanan

Washington, D.C., Feb. 21. Congress passes legislation barring use of foreign coins in United States.

Washington, D.C., March 3. Congress appropriates $70,000 to assist trans-Atlantic cable financed by Cyrus Field.

United States, May 26. Dred Scott freed by his new owner (→ Dec. 31).

United States, June 27. *Scientific American* cites threat to whale population, as increased literacy rate heightens demand for lamp oil.

Oregon Territory, July 1. Henry Pittock and three others reach top of Mount Hood.

Washington, D.C., July 13. Alfred Cumming officially replaces Brigham Young as Governor of Utah, with authority to use federal troops to enforce national law (→ Oct. 4).

Valentia Bay, Ireland, Aug. 14. Ships from United States and Britain assemble to begin laying first trans-Atlantic cable (→ Sept. 2, 1858).

New York City. First passenger elevator, invented by Elisha Otis, installed in Haughwout Department Store.

Moline, Illinois. John Deere is producing 10,000 steel plows a year.

Chicago. Baseball ruling sets length of game at nine innings.

New York City. Cooper Union founded by Peter Cooper, providing education for working class.

Michigan. Thomas Edison founds chemistry lab at home, marking all bottles "poison," to amusement of friends.

Arizona. Edward Beale blazes wagon trail from Fort Defiance to Colorado, using camels as pack animals (→ June 16).

United States. American cities reportedly have highest death rates in world, due, in large part, to tuberculosis.

San Diego, California. Introduction of Italian honeybees begins honey industry here.

New York City. Lithographers Nathaniel Currier and James Merritt Ives establish their own imprint.

Charleston, S.C. Hinton Rower Helper, in *The Impending Crisis of the South,* argues that slavery ultimately impoverishes whites in South.

Scott case voids Missouri Compromise

Washington, D.C., March 9

The Supreme Court has decided the Dred Scott case, ruling that a Negro descended from slaves is not a citizen and that the Missouri Compromise is unconstitutional. The decision, handed down three days ago, has outraged the North and excited the South. Its ramifications may be as far-reaching as any case since Marbury v. Madison.

The case centers around Scott, a slave from Missouri who was taken by his owner to the free state of Illinois, the Minnesota Territory and back to Missouri. Having tasted freedom up North, Scott sued for permanent freedom. Missouri's Supreme Court and a federal Circuit Court both ruled against Scott. But, on appeal, and with prodding from Southern politicians in search of an all-encompassing ruling for states' rights to own slaves, the Supreme Court heard the case.

Scott, an "article of merchandise."

Chief Justice Roger Taney stated in his majority opinion that no Negro born as a slave has citizenship. Furthermore, he said that with the adoption of the Constitution in 1787, Negroes were considered "so far inferior that they had no rights which the white man was bound to respect." But he went further, ruling that the Constitution specifically grants states the right to own slaves and that no act of Congress can remove those rights in the states or in new territories, and that therefore, the Missouri Compromise is unconstitutional.

While the decision was by a 7-2 vote, five of those in the majority wrote separate opinions. In dissent, Justice Benjamin Curtis wrote that the ruling was worthless, that the "judicial power transcends the limits of authority of the court."

The Northern press has been bombastic. The *New York Tribune* wrote that the court "has draggled and polluted its garments in the filth of pro-slavery politics." But the South has rejoiced. The *Enquirer* stated: "Abolitionism has been staggered and stunned" (→ May 26)

U.S. marshals arrest Walker in Nicaragua

Washington, D.C., Dec. 29

William Walker, the former renegade leader of Nicaragua, was arrested by United States federal marshals and reprimanded today, but not jailed for his unbridled exploits. His saga took many twists in a struggle for control over Nicaragua.

Forced to flee Granada by Central American troops irate over his dictatorial reign, Walker and his men regrouped. But a fatal error wrecked his military comeback. He crossed his financial backer, Cornelius Vanderbilt, owner of the Accessory Transit Company. Vanderbilt therefore not only refused to rearm him, but also sent a private army against him. Ironically, Walker was routed in the city of Rivas, named for the man he deposed.

Back in the United States, Walker found himself faced with arrest in New Orleans. But he escaped and returned to Nicaragua in an attempt to regain power. He failed miserably and the marshals had him extradited here (→ Dec. 1, 1858).

The America's Cup has come to New York. Deeded to the city's yacht club, the trophy is now up for challenges from other yacht clubs, American and foreign. Painting is "New York Club Regatta, II" (1857) by Fitz Hugh Lane.

Cavalry is sending camels to California

Texas, June 16

The army reports that camels, imported a year ago from the Middle East, are being sent to California. Known for their ability to survive on very little water, the camels have been serving as beasts of burden with the United States Second Cavalry in the deserts and dry mountains of far West Texas. The soldiers here say they will not miss the smelly, cantankerous critters.

Disunion meeting firm on separation

Worcester, Massachusetts, Jan. 15

"No union with slaveholders" was the often repeated slogan at the Disunion Convention, a gathering of those who favor a split between the Southern slave states and the slave-free states of the North. The main speaker at the convention, William Lloyd Garrison, a founder of the New England Anti-Slavery Society, is a moral agitator famous for uncompromising integrity and for such dramatic gestures as burning a copy of the Constitution.

eriodicals thrive; imes trims name

oston

The rage for periodicals shows o signs of cooling. Boston literati ave banded together to launch the *tlantic Monthly*, whose editor, ames Russell Lowell, is planning) carry pieces by Ralph Waldo :merson, Harriet Beecher Stowe nd others. Meanwhile, British au-iors Charles Dickens and Wilkie :ollins are contributing to the illus-·ated *Harper's Weekly*. Very few eaders noticed that *The New York)aily Times* is now *The New York 'imes*. What's in a name?

'rom "Cart War," he Texas Rangers

\ustin, Texas, Nov. 14

Faced with a sharp increase in iolence and bloodshed, Governor :lisha M. Pease today called on he Texas legislature to author-ze a special force of Rangers to elp end the so-called "Cart War.")riginally a disagreement between Texan and Mexican teamsters in San Antonio concerning a matter so rivial that no one seems to re-member what it was, the dispute has pread throughout central Texas. The conflict has now become down-ight nasty, with kidnappings, beat-ngs and even murders becoming almost commonplace.

German immigrants tap U.S. beer trade

St. Louis, Missouri

Displaced Germans in the Unit-ed States are turning their national pastime into profit. Eberhard An-ieuser, following the lead of coun-trymen in Milwaukee and else-where, has added a small brewery to his soap business. Adolphus Busch, who arrived this year from Hesse, Germany, has a brewers' supply firm. In Milwaukee, St. Louis's sister city of beer, Joseph Schlitz is rapidly expanding the brewery he took over upon August Krug's death last year. And Freder-ick Miller is prospering with the Menominee Valley Brewery, ac-quired in 1855 from Charles Best.

Buchanan stresses tolerance of slavery

Washington, D.C., March 4

The inaugural address of James Buchanan, sworn in today as the 15th President of the United States, continued the theme of his "Save the union" campaign platform, stressing tolerance of slavery for the purpose of keeping the states united. This platform defeated the anti-slavery platform of John Fremont by a fair margin. Buchanan said: "The great object of my administration will be to arrest . . . the agitation of the slavery question" in the North "and to destroy sectional parties."

120 killed in Utah; U.S. troops sent in

Utah Territory, Oct. 4

The Mormon conflict with the army keeps getting worse. President Buchanan sent troops to Utah in May. Last month, the Mormons killed 120 immigrants who had fought off Mormons and Indians for days. The Mormons reportedly penetrated the immigrants' site by waving a truce flag and posing as rescuers. Only the 17 children were spared. The Mormons say the immigrants were hostile and were tied to the death of their leader, Joseph Smith. Today, the Nauvoo Legion hit a supply unit, leaving the army low on provisions (→ Apr. 6, 1858).

4,932 firms fail in panic

Panicked investors rush to pull their money out of the Seaman's Savings Bank.

New York City

The failure of the New York branch of the Ohio Life Insurance and Trust Company on August 24 set off a financial panic here that has spread across the nation. Most of the city's banks were forced to suspend specie payments, and the branch office's parent company went under, with huge liabilities to Eastern institutions. Many of the Western railroads have plunged into bankruptcy, as have a number of other speculative enterprises. The panic, which was caused by over-speculation in railroad securities and real estate, has led to the failure of 4,932 companies nationwide.

Battle over slavery persisting in Kansas

Kansas Territory, Dec. 31

A "constitution with slavery" passed by referendum today after anti-slavery settlers refused to participate. The vote was the result of a convention in Lecompton two months ago where pro-slavery delegates – recognizing that a pro-slavery constitution was certain to be rejected if it was put to a fair vote – agreed to submit only a special article on slavery to voters. Yet whether settlers voted for or against the article, the constitution would still protect slaveholders' rights in the territory. Anti-slavery groups thus boycotted the vote (→ Jan. 4, 1858).

"Niagara" (1857) by Frederick E. Church. A true naturalist, Church was born in rationalist New Haven, but lives amid the beauty of New York's Catskill Mountains. He is inspired by the writings of German scientist Alexander von Humbolt, who believes that, in the civilized world, art and science "infuse their spirit into one another."

1858

Buchanan

Washington, D.C., Apr. 6. President Buchanan, in demanding that Mormons obey federal law, accuses them of "levying war against the United States" (→June 26).

Rosalia, Washington, May 17. U.S. soldiers suffer a humiliating defeat by Nez Perce and Spokan Indians.

Titusville, Pennsylvania, May. Colonel E.L. Drake begins drilling for oil, using technique of driving iron pipe into well (→Aug. 28, 1859).

Memphis, Tennessee, June 13. Steamship Pennsylvania explodes on Mississippi River, killing 160 people.

Springfield, Illinois, June 16. Republican Abraham Lincoln, upon receiving Senate nomination, proclaims, "A house divided against itself cannot stand" (→Oct. 15).

Utah Territory, June 26. Colonel Johnston's federal troops march into Salt Lake City, finding it mostly empty as Mormons move south.

New York City, July 20. Admission charged to baseball game for first time; New York All-Stars defeat Brooklyn.

Kansas Territory Aug. 2. State constitution rejected in popular vote, 11,812 to 1,926; Kansas fails to gain admission to union (→Jan. 29, 1861).

Massachusetts, Oct. 16. Henry Wadsworth Longfellow publishes *The Courtship of Miles Standish*, narrative poem about romance among Pilgrims.

New York City. In his popular *The Unwelcomed Child; or the Crime of an Undesigned and Undesired Maternity*, H.C. Wright openly examines birth control.

Washington, D.C. Lewis Mill issued patent for a lawn mowing machine.

Washington, D.C. Charles Wesley March receives patent for bundling harvester.

New York City. Steel pens are placed on the market.

New York City. Ladies Christian Association [YWCA] founded.

Haddonfield, New Jersey. First dinosaur skeleton excavated in United States.

Brooklyn, New York. Edward R. Squibb founds pharmaceutical company.

Lincoln faces Douglas in seven debates in race for the Senate

Galesburg, Illinois, Oct. 15

Abraham Lincoln and Stephen A. Douglas, adversaries in the Illinois race for the U.S. Senate, today wound up a series of seven debates that began two months ago.

The Lincoln-Douglas Debates, as they have became known, attracted a wide audience not only in their home state of Illinois but also beyond the borders. The idea of a series of debates had come from Lincoln in a letter to Douglas: "Will it be agreeable to you to make an arrangement for you and myself to divide time and address the same audiences during the present canvass?" Douglas reluctantly agreed.

The two proved a study in contrasts, the towering 6-foot 4-inch Lincoln with his high-pitched voice, and the 5-foot 4-inch Douglas with his resonant tones.

In his opening speech, Douglas attacked Lincoln's doctrine of a "house divided," a reference to the speech Lincoln made at the convention when he was nominated. In that speech, Lincoln had addressed the issue of slavery, saying, "A house divided against itself cannot stand . . . I believe this government cannot endure, permanently half slave and half free."

Douglas predicted in that opening debate that the Lincoln stand on the slavery issue would bring about Negro equality. Instead, Douglas advocated that settlers in each territory be allowed to decide whether or not to have slavery. Lincoln promptly dubbed this as "squatter sovereignty" and argued that all men had the right to "life, liberty and the pursuit of happiness." Not so, Douglas replied, arguing that the fate of the Negro was not so important as the principle of democratic government. By today' final debate, Lincoln had reduce the argument to the moral questio of whether slavery was right o wrong (→Jan. 5, 1859).

Lincoln speaks; Douglas listens.

Two gold finds are made in Colorado

Colorado, Autumn

John Beck and William Russell, both miners from Georgia, report that they have found gold in two locations in central Colorado, on the east slope of the Rocky Mountains along the south fork of the Platte River. It is not clear whether these "finds" are of the truly rich, veined variety or are the more limited "gulch" or "surface washings." But Beck and Russell do believe most of the gold is situated in the Cherry Creek area.

The 1858 $3 gold piece. A coin to be hoarded in defense against rapid cycles of boom and bust.

Stagecoach covers long route in 20 days

Los Angeles, California, Oct. 7

A stagecoach owned by the Overland Mail Company arrived here today, only 20 days after its departure from St. Louis over the longest stage route in the world. The stagecoach, which carried no more than five passengers along the way, included a correspondent of the *New York Herald*, along with some letter mail. It ran day and night, non-stop, over 2,600 miles of deserts, plains and hostile Comanche Indian territory.

Leaving St. Louis, it set out on a southwesterly course to Fort Smith, Arkansas, across Texas to Sherman, over the plains of Wes Texas to El Paso, then struck a course due westward across Nev Mexico Territory and Fort Yuma to Los Angeles. The company uses the big Concord coaches that are drawn by teams of four or six horses o mules that can sometimes trave more than 100 miles in 24 hours i the terrain is flat. Overland Mail i owned primarily by John Butter field and William G. Fargo, along with five other investors. Today, the record-breaking stagecoach is to head north on the final leg of the journey, to San Francisco.

The stagecoach, traveling in the ever-growing shadow of the locomotive.

Minnesota becomes union's 32nd state

Washington, D.C., May 11

Congress today admitted Minnesota to the union as a free state. Settled by people from the Eastern states and immigrants from Ireland, Germany, England and Canada, many of the state's settlers strongly oppose slavery. Yet, Minnesota has other problems to worry about, having experienced rampant speculation in land prices since 1855. Huge tracts of prairie, purchased for $1.25 an acre, were sold as "improved" property for four times as much in a matter of days. When the Panic of 1857 struck, the speculation bubble burst. Many pioneers turned their attention away from get-quick-rich schemes and toward serious farming. By spring, the territory's cultivated land had more than doubled.

Constitution fails in new Kansas vote

Kansas Territory, Jan. 4

Voters here overwhelmingly rejected a "constitution with slavery" today, reversing a pro-slavery vote taken three weeks ago. Arguing that the vote scheduled for December 21 on the Lecompton constitution would not be fair, the Free State Party last month convinced acting Governor Frederick P. Stanton to convene the territorial legislature before the vote took place. The legislature met and called for a second vote, which would permit voting for or against the entire constitution, versus voting on a special article on slavery only. In the second vote, held today, 10,226 out of 10,338 Kansans rejected the pro-slavery constitution. The U.S. Congress is expected to take up the matter (→Aug. 2).

Trans-Atlantic cable service breaks down

London, Sept. 2

The first trans-Atlantic telegraph cable, which went into operation only 28 days ago, ceased to operate today. Its failure is believed to be the result of a break somewhere in its 3,000-mile mile length, and officials do not know whether the break can be repaired. The cable was largely the work of Cyrus W. Field, the American financier. The 48-year-old Field, who made his first fortune in the paper business, founded the New York, Newfoundland and London Telegraph Company in the United States and helped organize a similar company in England, arranging for both American and British ships to lay the cable, which runs from the United States to England via Newfoundland. Field insists the setback is only temporary. He has a charter giving him exclusive rights to put telegraph cables on the coast of Newfoundland and says the companies he organized will lay another cable if efforts to repair the existing one are unsuccessful.

Sheet music cover celebrating cable.

Mason jars devised for home canning

New York City

A jar that makes it possible for any housewife to preserve food for extended periods has been patented by John L. Mason. The Mason jar utilizes a rubber seal and a screw top to prevent deterioration of food once it is cooked. This invention is one of several this year that promise to make life easier for workers, farmers and homeowners. Others include the steel-nibbed pen, a lawn-mowing machine and a harvester that ties grain into bundles.

Ignoring Buchanan, Walker sails again

Mobile, Alabama, Dec. 1

William Walker incurred President Buchanan's wrath earlier this year with his exploits in Nicaragua. The President told the Senate that relations with Central America would be fractured if Walker continued his interference; he also ordered Walker to stay home. Despite this, Walker called for the "Americanizing" of Central America and sailed for Nicaragua. A shipwreck off British Honduras today thwarted his efforts (→Sept. 12, 1860).

Peace treaty signed with Oregon tribes

Oregon Territory, Sept. 24

Coeur d'Alene, Spokan and other Indian tribes have signed a treaty with Colonel George Wright ending a war the Yakima Indians began in 1855. Many chiefs were taken prisoner and 900 of the Indians' horses were destroyed September 5 after the tribe attacked Wright's men. Coeur d'Alene Chief Vincent had to give up those who staged an attack earlier this year, return seized property and make peace with the Nez Perce tribe.

First billiard champ racks them all up

Detroit, Michigan, Apr. 12

Mike Phelan has become the first billiard champion of the United States. In a winner-take-all contest, he defeated John Seereiter and won $10,000. The men played four-ball caroms, in which a carom on one of two object balls counts as one point and a carom on three object balls is worth two points. Phelan has been responsible for many improvements in the billiard table and has pioneered the use of the combination cushion.

Bank failures and secession talk seem to be driving more and more people every day to seek comfort in the moral certainties of the revival meeting.

The iron steamship Great Eastern, behemoth of the industrial age, dwarfs a cluster of rowboats off New England. Lithograph by Currier and Ives.

1859

Buchanan

Springfield, Illinois, Jan. 5. Stephen A. Douglas wins second term in Senate, defeating Abraham Lincoln.

Texas, Feb. 23. Governor Hardin R. Runnels issues proclamation instructing Texans to avoid hostilities against Indians.

Mississippi River, Apr. 9. Samuel Clemens becomes licensed riverboat pilot on Mississippi River.

Springfield, Illinois, April. Abraham Lincoln, in letter to editor T.J. Pickett, confides, "I must, in candor, say I do not consider myself fit for the Presidency."

Vicksburg, Mississippi, May 9-19. Southern Commercial Convention meets to call for reinstitution of legal slave trade.

Utah Territory, July 2. Mail service established to Salt Lake City by stagecoach.

Colorado, September. Voters reject proposed constitution for "State of Jefferson."

Massachusetts, Oct. 30. Henry David Thoreau speaks out on behalf of John Brown.

Colorado, Nov. 16. "Claim jumpers" lay waste to St. Charles, renaming it "Denver" after first Governor of Kansas Territory, James Denver.

Washington, D.C., Dec. 5. Charles Sumner of Massachusetts resumes Senate duties after recovery from beating by Representative Preston Brooks of South Carolina.

Salem, Massachusetts. Moses Gerrish Farmer demonstrates his electric incandescent lighting with two lamps powered by wet-cell battery with platinum filaments.

Mount Vernon, Virginia. George Washington's home dedicated as national monument.

Cambridge, Massachusetts. Massachusetts Institute of Technology founded.

Mississippi. Legislature resolves to secede from union immediately if a Republican is elected president.

Ohio. John D. Rockefeller helps Negro buy his wife out of slavery.

Chicago. Approximately 2,000 daguerrotype studios have opened across the nation.

World's first oil well dug

Titusville, Pennsylvania, Aug. 28

Oil began flowing today from a well drilled by Edwin L. Drake on property owned by the Pennsylvania Rock Oil Company. It is the first such well to be drilled anywhere in the world. The firm has been in the business of collecting oil that seeped out of the ground and selling it for medicinal purposes, but Drake plans to produce it in much greater quantities for possible use in heating and for illumination.

The 49-year-old Drake, born in New York City, conceived the idea of drilling for oil while working as a railroad conductor. He bought stock in Rock Oil and persuaded the company to lease some of its land for drilling, using techniques developed to drill salt wells. His drill struck oil at a depth of 69 feet, and the oil is flowing steadily. Drake's effort is being watched by businessmen and landowners in this part of northern Pennsylvania, and some plan to lease land and use his drilling method to sink other wells in the hope that oil can become the basis of a new industry.

Drake (in top hat) and his gusher.

Large silver lode unearthed in West

Nevada, June

News that a rich deposit of silver has been discovered in this state has brought miners and fortune hunters pouring in. Already a boom town named Virginia City has sprung up. The vein of silver was discovered on a piece of property owned by Henry Tomkins Paige Comstock, but it is believed to extend well beyond the boundaries of the Comstock land. While the amount of wealth contained in the Comstock lode has not been assessed, there is speculation that it may run to tens or even hundreds of millions of dollars. There has been talk of establishing a mint in Carson City to coin the Comstock silver. Many of those now rushing to Virginia City are miners who failed to make their fortunes in the California gold rush that started a decade ago.

"Pike's Peak or bust" is gold rush slogan

Colorado, December

The "Pike's Peak or bust" phenomenon is reaching epidemic proportions. Since gold was discovered in Boulder Canyon on January 15, the "rush" that ensued has brought an estimated 100,000 would-be miners from all parts of the United States to the slopes of the Rocky Mountains. Some experts say that fully half of this number have given up or died along the way.

A favorite jumping-off place for the miners is Fort Leavenworth, where there are many enterprises with such names as the Pike's Peak Hotel, Pike's Peak Ranch, Pike's Peak Outfits and the Pike's Peak Lunch. As one local citizen observed, "Around here, it's Pike's Peak almost everything!"

Although most of these adventurers come by horse-drawn wagons, others try the "wind wagon," a carriage-like contraption that is powered by sails. One gold-seeker came by means of a sled that was pulled by a team of dogs.

Mining the mountains in search of a fortune. Lithograph by Currier & Ives.

Gold dust will buy copy of new paper

Colorado, Apr. 23

The Colorado Territory's first newspaper, the *Rocky Mountain News*, costs 25 cents per copy, payable in either cash or gold dust. With so many people either rich or flat broke, is the sum reasonable, too high or too low? Monetary values are topsy turvy. While some folks have become wealthy, other would-be argonauts are leaving with signs saying, "Pike's Peak Be Damned!"

The 1859 $20 gold eagle, product of a U.S. Mint that now has a bigger gold supply than ever before.

Prosperity and gold luring immigrants

United States

Whether drawn by the rush for gold or the simple promise of steady wages, a massive wave of immigrants, 2.5 million of them, has entered the United States this decade. Nearly a million were from German states, mostly farmers fleeing disastrous harvests, craftsmen escaping industrialization and revolutionaries seeking asylum. In addition, gold in the West enticed 66,000 Chinese, while a depression sent 86,000 Canadians south.

Hardships for immigrants are severe, yet most groups are gaining an economic foothold, such as European Jews in the New York garment industry. Most immigrants try to preserve something of their heritage: The 40,000 Swiss, for example, have their own German-language newspaper, *Helvetia*.

John Brown hangs for Harpers Ferry

John Brown the colossus stands astride the violent symbols of a country rapidly descending into chaos.

Charleston, [West] Virginia, Dec. 2

John Brown was hanged here today, four blocks from the courthouse where he had been found guilty of treason, murder and conspiring with slaves to create an insurrection at nearby Harpers Ferry. On Brown's way to the gallows, he handed his jailer a note that predicted more bloodshed. It said: "I, John Brown, am now quite certain that the crimes of this guilty land will never be purged away but with blood. I had, as I now-think, vainly flattered myself that without very much bloodshed it might be done."

Brown had been held in jail here since he was captured by a force of United States Marines under the command of Captain Robert E. Lee after the failure of his plan to seize the arsenal at Harpers Ferry and turn the town into a base for an uprising by the slaves and a free-Negro mountain stronghold. All through his trial, Brown had a single answer when asked about his motives. He said he wanted to free slaves and that God had given him this mission.

John Brown was born in Connecticut 59 years ago. He became obsessed with the freeing of the slaves when well past 50. Then he and five sons joined the fight to keep Kansas free, and his friends say Brown turned into "an old man" overnight. Virginia's Governor received 17 affidavits calling Brown insane. But the abolitionist won praise during his trial from thinkers such as Henry David Thoreau, who compared him to "the best of those who stood at Concord, Lexington and Bunker Hill." Just before the execution, Henry Wadsworth Longfellow wrote, "They are leading old John Brown to execution. This is sowing the wind to reap the whirlwind, which will soon come" (→ Dec. 3, 1860).

Minstrel tune about "Dixie" composed

New York City, Apr. 4

Bryant's Minstrels are parading a new tune *Dixie's Land*, written by the Irish-American Dan Emmett. Described as a "plantation song and dance," it recalls other such "Negro" songs with its sentimental evocation of life "back home" in the opening words, "I wish I was in the land of cotton." Emmett is the first person known to use the name Dixie.

Oregon 33rd state; slavery is ruled out

Washington, D.C., Feb. 14

Oregon, a territory of some 94,560 square miles, was admitted to the union as a free state today. Congressional advocates of admission argued that the territory has more than 93,000 white residents, enough to warrant a representative in the House. Republicans sought to delay admission because Oregon would add two Democrats to the Senate. They argued (unsuccessfully) that if Kansas, a state that would add two Republicans, was kept out, so should one adding two Democrats.

Susan B. Anthony vs. white males

New York City, May 12

"Where, under our Declaration of Independence, does the Saxon man get his power to deprive all women and Negroes of their inalienable rights?" Miss Susan B. Anthony asked this rhetorical question today at the Ninth National Women's Rights Convention. Miss Anthony, on the national committee of the Anti-Slavery Society, speaks increasingly on women's issues. The society has employed her as an agent in the field and is paying her $10 a week plus expenses.

U.S. chess champ checkmates Europe

Paris

A 22-year-old chess player from New Orleans has won the plaudits of experts with his surprising victories over Europe's established champions. Paul Morphy's triumph over the master Anderssen, the last and greatest of an era, signaled a revolutionary change in the chess world. Morphy fascinates women of society and was the only chess hero to be borne on the shoulders of citizens in the streets of Paris. Cheers or no, in the tradition of chess masters, young Morphy is a moody fellow.

Latest in baseball is interschool game

Pittsfield, Massachusetts, July 1

The game of baseball has moved up from an intramural to an interschool activity on college campuses. This afternoon, Williams and Amherst Colleges came together in a contest that lasted 26 rounds here. With 65 runs constituting a game, Amherst breezed through this first intercollegiate contest, 66 to 32. There were 13 players on each side and the rules provided that a man could be retired only on a caught fly ball. These rules differ sharply from the accepted amateur code.

1860

Buchanan

New York City, Feb. 27. Mathew Brady takes Abraham Lincoln's portrait [later claims it won presidency].

United States, May. Indian disturbances interrupt Pony Express services for month (→ Oct. 24, 1861).

Washington, D.C., June 20. President Buchanan vetoes Homestead Bill, which calls for federal land grants to Western settlers.

Oregon, Sept. 13. Five of 44 pioneers, attacked by Indians west of Fort Hall, resort to cannibalism while starving in wilderness.

Groton, Connecticut, Sept. 17. Fire destroys Commonwealth, great steamship.

New Orleans, Nov. 19. Adelina Patti, nation's foremost opera star, makes French Opera House debut.

Florida, November. State legislature appropriates $100,000 for troops after Lincoln's election.

Washington, D.C., Dec. 8. Georgia's Howell Cobb resigns as Secretary of Treasury.

Washington, D.C., Dec. 20. Senate names Committee of Thirteen to seek ways of preserving union; members include Stephen A. Douglas and Jefferson Davis.

Boston. Press condemns labor strikes as "revolution."

United States. Olympia Brown becomes first woman to study theology alongside men.

Washington, D.C. Department of Education survey finds over half of nation's 321 high schools are situated in Massachusetts, New York and Ohio.

Charleston, South Carolina. As state prepares to secede, James L. Petigru, directing someone to local insane asylum, states, "The whole state is one vast insane asylum."

Kansas Territory. Severe drought leads to exodus of 30,000 settlers from Kansas.

Charleston, S.C. Cotton production exceeds two billion pounds a year.

West Point, New York. Explosive shells begin to replace cannon balls.

South Carolina. Henry Timrod, dubbed "poet laureate of the South," publishes *Poems.*

Pony Express makes 11-day run to West

En route to California, the Pony Express service easily outdistances the laborious advance that is being made by the transcontinental telegraph cable.

Sacramento, California, Apr. 13

A thin dust cloud rising in the distance inspired a wave of elation here today as hundreds gathered to hail the first Pony Express delivery. Minutes later, young Tom Hamilton received a rousing welcome as he galloped furiously into town bearing a satchel with 49 letters and three newspapers that left St. Joseph, Missouri, just 11 days ago.

The relentless run across 1,966 miles of desolate prairie, rugged mountains and desert wastes was organized by William H. Russell and Alexander Majors of the Central Overland California & Pike's Peak Express Service Company in just 65 days. They bought 500 fine horses, then put out a notice calling for "skinny, expert riders willing to risk death daily." The horsemen race each animal at great speed for about 12 miles, then dismount and leap atop a rested horse at each of 119 stations along the trail. Most of these consist of a well, a stable and a stout-hearted stationmaster.

To the joyous Californians, who shouted "Hurrah for the Central Route" today, the 11-day pace is an astounding improvement over the eight-week wagon convoys. But the brave riders, who vow "the mail must get through" despite all kinds of dangers, ranging from hostile Indians on the prairie to storms in the mountains, may only be a temporary link as the West comes into its own. Just before young Billy Richardson mounted to ride out of St. Joseph this month on the first leg of the trail to California, Majors himself proclaimed that "someday a tireless iron horse must make the long overland journey" (→ May).

Lampooning the frontier. "Flax Scutching Bee" (c.1860) by Linton Park.

Firing squad death for William Walker

Trujillo, Honduras, Sept. 12

Smirking with revenge, members of a Honduras firing squad executed William Walker today. As his limp body fell, a saga of one man's tenacious, lustful quest for power ended, on the road to Nicaragua, where he was determined to regain control. Walker landed in Honduras, swiftly seized a British customhouse, then tried to push into Nicaragua by land. But a British captain, Norvell Salmon, captured him and turned him over to General Mariano Alvarez. Walker was then tried and sentenced. For many Americans, Walker's death swept away an adventurer, a hero of the headlines. For Central Americans, the execution helped avenge the hundreds he killed during his ruthless Nicaraguan reign.

Walker prepares to die.

English-speaking kindergarten opens

Boston

It's a garden of children, where young ideas grow. That was the view of Friedrich Froebel, a German educator who, believing that teaching infants is the first step toward society's reform, founded the first kindergarten. German-speaking women have established schools based on his theories, and now a Boston Transcendentalist, Miss Elizabeth Peabody, is teaching the nation's first privately owned English-speaking kindergarten.

Lincoln nominated by Republican Party

Full house in Chicago, where the Republicans chose Lincoln over Seward.

Chicago, May 16

As a nearby cannon boomed to mark the occasion, Abraham Lincoln was declared the Republican presidential nominee today, defeating New York abolitionist William Seward on the third ballot at the party's national convention here. Hannibal Hamlin of Maine was nominated for vice president. It was a major victory for the towering lawyer from Springfield, Illinois, a man who once served in the House of Representatives but who tasted defeat when he lost a Senate race two years ago to the Democrat Stephen S. Douglas, after their famous debates.

Lincoln had expressed his own doubts about his fitness to be president a year ago in a letter to Thomas J. Pickett, editor of the *Rock Island Register*. He wrote: "I must, in candor, say I do not think I am fit for the presidency." Yet, in the months that followed, he made speaking tours, urging abolition of slavery in the territories (→ June 28).

Democrats split; two to run for president

Baltimore, Maryland, June 28

Hopelessly split over the issue of slavery, the Democratic Party has now become two separate political entities, thus clouding the outlook for victory by either faction.

The problem became a crushing reality early last month, when most of the Southern delegates walked out of the Democratic National Convention in Charleston, South Carolina, after failing to win a plank in the platform to assure federal protection of slavery in the territories. The convention then adjourned, having failed to achieve a two-thirds majority for any presidential nominee.

Earlier this month, Northern Democrats regrouped their splintered forces here and proceeded to nominate Senator Stephen A. Douglas, the "Little Giant" from Illinois, for president and Herschel V. John of Georgia for vice president.

Buoyed by defections of still more Southern Democrats from the regular party, delegates from eight states in the South met here this week and named their own slate: John C. Breckinridge of Kentucky for president and Joseph Lane of Oregon for vice president.

The Democratic slates will face strong opposition in the November election. Last month, Republicans chose Abraham Lincoln, a lanky Illinois lawyer, as their nominee for president, and Hannibal Hamlin of Maine for vice president (→ Nov. 6).

First big factory accident kills 77 workers

Lawrence, Massachusetts

An inquiry into the terrible accident at Pemberton Mill on January 10 has concluded that "defective pillars .. were the primary cause of the disaster." Some 670 workers, mostly female and many no older than 12, were buried when the huge textile factory building collapsed on January 10. A total of 77 people died under piles of wood and brick and tons of steel from the heavy carding and weaving machines. Never has American industry seen such a disaster. Little in the way of compensation has been offered to the families of the victims, and current legal precedent provides them with little recourse. As one observer noted, "Society has no avenging gibbet for the respectable millionaire homicide."

Shoemakers out; Lincoln defends strike

New Haven, Connecticut, March 6

In a campaign speech, Abraham Lincoln today backed the right to strike, the first presidential candidate to do so. With thousands of Massachusetts shoemakers out, the Republican leader said he is "glad to see that a system of labor prevails in New England .. where laborers can strike when they want to."

Some 800 women shoemakers join parade of strikers in Lynn, Massachusetts.

Nation's population reaches 31 million

Washington, D.C.

America's population has grown to 31.4 million, the latest census shows. New York remains the most populous state, with nearly 3.9 million inhabitants. Pennsylvania is second with 2.9 million. More than 58 percent of Americans work on farms, the census reports, but signs of growing industrialization include 30,000 miles of railroad tracks. Cotton remains king in the South, with a crop of more than a million tons a year. Immigrants continue to pour into the country, with Italians concentrating in California, French in Louisiana and Jews in New York. Negroes are concentrated in the South. Nearly a third of the 600,000 residents of Texas are black, and the percentage is even higher in other Southern states. There are 4 million slaves in the United States.

☞ THE QUESTION

IF LINCOLN

will be elected or not, is one which interests all parties, North and South. Whether he

IS ELECTED

or not, the people of

SOUTH CAROLINA

(whose rights have been for a number of years trampled upon) have the advantage of supplying themselves with CLOTHING, at the well-known CAROLINA CLOTHING DEPOT, 261 King-street, at such prices as

WILL LEAD

them to be satisfied that the reputation of this Establishment has been

BOLDLY

and fearlessly maintained

FOR A

number of years, supplying its

SOUTHERN

Customers with all the Latest Styles, and at as low prices as any Clothing House *in the present*

CONFEDERACY

of all the States.

Thankful for the liberal patronage extended, the Proprietors desire merely to inform their customers and the public generally, that their present STOCK OF CLOTHING IS COMPLETE in all its departments, and are now prepared to offer Goods on the most reasonable and satis factory terms. A call is therefore solicited by

OTTOLENGUIS, WILLIS & BARRETT,

November 5 — 261 King-street.

Lincoln ekes out presidential victory

On the day of his address at Cooper Union February 27, Lincoln stopped at Mathew Brady's New York studio to pose for this picture. Brady believes its circulation is largely responsible for Lincoln's narrow victory.

Washington, D.C., Nov. 6

Despite his own gloomy forecast, Abraham Lincoln of Illinois was elected President of the United States today, topping a political career that has known both victory and defeat. While failing to win a majority of the popular vote, the 51-year-old lawyer carried 18 states with 180 of the total 303 electoral votes. Elected Vice President is Hannibal Hamlin of Maine.

Lincoln, who rarely shows emotion, left the cheering throngs on the streets of Springfield to rush home and excitedly tell his wife: "Mary, Mary, we are elected."

This year's campaign had stirred political forces both in the South and the North, as the debate over extending slavery into the territories got hotter. In his race, Lincoln, a Republican, faced a divided Democratic Party with two sets of candidates: his old foe and debate rival, Senator Stephen A. Douglas of Illinois, on the Northern ticket and John C. Breckinridge of Kentucky on the Southern. Douglas carried just one state, Missouri, and its 12 electoral votes, despite running second to Lincoln in the popular vote. Breckinridge won 11 states, all in the South, with 72 electoral votes. A third man in the race, John Bell of Tennessee, the Constitutional Union Party's candidate, took three states and 39 electoral votes.

During the campaign, Southerners had warned that the Cotton Belt states would secede if Lincoln, "that Black Republican," were elected. Lincoln also was opposed by many in the business community, as his old friend, Horace Greeley, editor of the *New York Tribune*, noted in several articles.

For Lincoln and Douglas, this was a rematch, with a reverse result. In 1858, after their series of debates, Douglas beat Lincoln to win Senate re-election (→ Dec. 20).

Winchester's rifle is now in production

New Haven

A fast-firing rifle developed by the Volcanic Repeating Arms Company is now in production at its factory here. The rifle was developed by Oliver F. Winchester, a 49-year-old shirt manufacturer who has gone into the business of guns and ammunition. Winchester's rifle uses improved versions of mechanisms originated by several other inventors. In particular, Winchester has the help of B.T. Henry, inventor of the widely used Henry repeating rifle. The new weapon is one of several new rifles that are loaded through the breech, rather than the muzzle, allowing the rifleman to fire rounds much faster and with greater accuracy over longer distances than previously possible. Winchester rifles are being purchased by the government and put into service as fast as possible to replace the muzzle-loaders used by most soldiers.

Slave ship is seized

Key West, Florida, Apr. 30

The Spanish began trading slaves to the New World in 1517. Today, nearly 350 years later, a galleon sailed into Key West, in the custody of the American navy's Mohawk. Since 1808, the United States has held the slave trade illegal. In 1820, slavers were ruled pirates, subject to search and seizure. With the growth of sectional hostility, American warships have grown ever more vigilant.

Slave deck of the Wildfire, a ship seized by the Mohawk off the coast of Cuba and brought to Key West.

Mob disrupts John Brown memorial rally

Boston, Dec. 3

A martyr to some, a madman to others, radical abolitionist John Brown remains a source of controversy a year after his execution for treason, conspiracy and murder. A rally, organized by abolitionist Frederick Douglass, of those who thought that Brown's raid on Harpers Ferry, Virginia, was justified clashed today with a mob that obviously agreed with the court that sentenced him to death on December 2, 1859. In the summer of 1859, John Brown and his "army of emancipation" set up headquarters in Maryland, in preparation for an attack on the United States arsenal at Harpers Ferry. On October 16, they crossed the Potomac and seized the town. Local militia and federal troops under the command of Robert E. Lee responded, killing 10 raiders and capturing Brown.

Frederick Douglass stands his ground while police help the mob to disperse his supporters. Meanwhile, in the nation's capital, President Buchanan told Congress the union "can never be cemented by the blood of its citizens."

Novels for a dime

New York City

Good stories may not be a dime a dozen, but how about a dime a piece? That's the price of *Maleska: The Indian Wife of the White Hunter*, the potboiler by Ann Sophia Stephens, whose previous tales include several works of historical fiction. Readers have applauded her product by purchasing 300,000 copies – a mountain of dimes that adds up to a heap of dollars.

"Boston as the Eagle and the Wild Goose see it," says O.W. Holmes of the first U.S. aerial photograph.

uchanan waffles on secession issue

Vashington, D.C., Dec. 3

In his final State of the Union message to Congress, President Buchanan said today that states have no legal right to secede from the union but that the federal government has no legal power to stop them. The President's somber message, in his waning days in office, comes at a time when there are loud rumblings from the pro-slave states of the South and even threats of resignation within his own Cabinet.

In his message, Buchanan said the danger must be looked squarely in the face, that "Secession is neither more nor less than revolution." He suggested that "our union rests upon public opinion and can never be cemented by the blood of its citizens shed in civil war."

In his nearly four years in office, the President has tried to please both pro-slave and anti-slave states and has ended up pleasing neither.

A 36-round battle

Farnborough, England, Apr. 17

John C. Heenan, the Benicia Boy, got more than he bargained for when the American champion challenged Tom Sayers, the English pugilist, for the world boxing title. The 2 hour 6 minute bout ended in the 36th round as toughs broke into the ring. Spectators say they did so when Sayers, who is smaller at 154 pounds, was about to be knocked out. The bout was called a draw.

South Carolina secedes from union

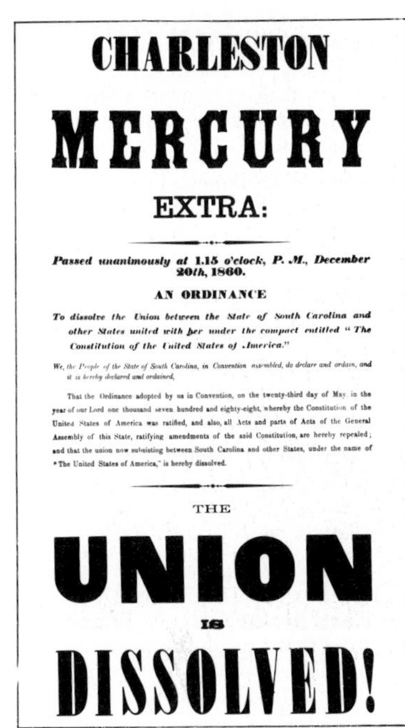

CHARLESTON

MERCURY

EXTRA:

Passed unanimously at 1.15 o'clock, P. M., December 20th, 1860.

AN ORDINANCE

To dissolve the Union between the State of South Carolina and other States united with her under the compact entitled "The Constitution of the United States of America."

We, the People of the State of South Carolina, in Convention assembled, do declare and ordain, and it is hereby declared and ordained,

That the Ordinance adopted by us in Convention, on the twenty-third day of May, in the year of our Lord one thousand seven hundred and eighty-eight, whereby the Constitution of the United States of America was ratified, and also, all Acts and parts of Acts of the General Assembly of this State, ratifying amendments of the said Constitution, are hereby repealed; and that the union now subsisting between South Carolina and other States, under the name of "The United States of America," is hereby dissolved.

THE

UNION

IS

DISSOLVED!

The nation splits. A states' rights flag is paraded through the streets of Columbia, S.C., following a special convention's unanimous vote to secede from the union. At right, banner headlines announce the radical move in Charleston, where advocates of states' rights raised a Palmetto flag only a day after the Lincoln election.

Charleston, S.C., Dec. 20

As crowds milled about outside, South Carolina political leaders met in St. Andrew's Hall on Meeting Street today and, in just 22 minutes, voted to secede from the union.

"We, the people of South Carolina, in convention assembled, do declare and ordain ... that the union now subsisting between South Carolina and other states under the name of the United States of America is hereby dissolved."

Word rapidly spread that the state, which became part of the union in 1788, had now voted to leave it, the first state in the pro-slavery Cotton Belt to do so. Cannons roared at the Citadel. Bells chimed in the church steeples. The crowds cheered in approval and marched through the city.

South Carolina's move was not unexpected, although the outgoing President Buchanan had sought through much of his term to heal the breach that had been developing over the slavery issue. Just a few weeks ago, the President declared that the states have no legal right to secede. However, in an attempt to appease the angry Southerners, he had refused to reinforce federal troops at nearby Fort Moultrie. Buchanan's stand had resulted in the resignation of his Secretary of State, Lewis Cass.

Fanning the flames of a potential secession by the Cotton Belt states was the election last month of Abraham Lincoln, an Illinois Republican and an outspoken foe of slavery. His victory was aided by a split over the slavery issue in the Democratic Party (→31).

Federal troops now hold only Fort Sumter

Charleston, S.C., Dec. 31

With war seemingly imminent, the federal government has lost control of all its installations in this strategic city except Fort Sumter, a massive brick and concrete fortress rising 40 feet above high water on an island in the harbor.

Within days after South Carolina seceded from the union on December 20, Major Robert Anderson secretly moved his 73 soldiers from Charleston's Fort Moultrie to Fort Sumter. Angry South Carolina leaders demanded he return the troops to Fort Moultrie, but Major Anderson refused. The South Carolina militia then took control of Moultrie and other federal installations in the city, including the customhouse, the post office and Castle Pinckney. South Carolina's troops now occupy Fort Moultrie.

The state's leaders have been in Washington for days demanding that President Buchanan order the troops withdrawn from Fort Sumter. While refusing to meet the delegation, the President has put in writing that Fort Sumter will remain in federal hands. Meanwhile, Secretary of War John Floyd quit over Buchanan's refusal to withdraw the troops (→Apr. 14, 1861).

"A Ride for Liberty: The Fugitive Slaves" (c.1860) by Eastman Johnson.

1861

Lincoln

Washington, D.C., Jan. 21. Mississippi Senator Jefferson Davis delivers farewell address to Senate after his state secedes from union.

Springfield, Illinois, Feb. 11. Abraham Lincoln gives "farewell address" before leaving for Washington.

South Carolina, Apr. 20. Thaddeus S.C. Lowe, attempting to display value of balloons, makes record journey, flying 900 miles from Cincinnati to South Carolina.

Montgomery, Alabama, May 6. Confederate Congress, in session since April 29, declares war on United States (→June 8).

Washington, D.C., May 27. Chief Justice Roger B. Taney rules that Lincoln's suspension of habeas corpus is unconstitutional (→Dec. 1, 1865).

California, May 27. State sides with union when news of Civil War reaches California.

Tennessee, June 8. Volunteer State is 11th and last to secede.→

Washington, D.C., July 22. Senate passes Crittenden Resolution, stating war's main purpose as preservation of union, not abolition of slavery (→Sept. 2).

Washington, D.C. July. Mathew Brady and team of 20 aides begin photographic record of Civil War.

Washington, D.C., Aug. 16. President Lincoln bars all commerce with Confederacy (→Nov. 7).

Washington, D.C., Sept. 2. President Lincoln rescinds General Fremont's decree freeing Missouri's slaves, and transfers Fremont (→March 6, 1862).

West Virginia, Oct. 24. State created as majority of citizens vote in favor of secession from Virginia (→June 20, 1863).

New Haven, Connecticut. Yale University grants first American Ph.D's.

Lititz, Pennsylvania. First commercial pretzel factory founded by Julius Sturgis and Ambrose Rauch.

California. California's first oil well is drilled near Eureka.

New York City. Antonio "Tony" Pastor opens his vaudeville theater on Broadway.

One by one, states join Confederacy

Davis, Lincoln's adversary in the South. Photo by Mathew Brady.

Tennessee, June 8

Voters endorsed Tennessee's secession from the union today, making it the 11th state to join the Confederacy, though the state remains sharply divided. Sentiment in east Tennessee counties is strongly pro-union. Jefferson Davis, the acting president of the Confederacy, now heads a government of four border states and seven Deep South states. Fiery South Carolina led the way last December 20, shortly after Abraham Lincoln was elected President. Mississippi followed this January 9. Twelve days later, Davis resigned from the United States Senate, predicting a war "the like of which men have not seen." By early March, five other Deep South states had seceded: Florida on January 10, Alabama on January 11, Georgia on January 19, Louisiana on January 26, and Texas on March 2. There was opposition in every state, but it was silenced by those called "fire-eaters" who were bent on secession. Virginia, the mother commonwealth, reluctantly seceded on April 17. It was joined by Arkansas on May 6 and North Carolina on May 20. Tennessee made the Confederacy complete with its vote today.

Davis, a native of Mississippi and a West Pointer, is a former Secretary of War. He was elected acting president of the Confederacy at a convention in Montgomery, Alabama, in February. Alexander H Stephens of Georgia was named the provisional vice president. The Confederate capital was moved from Montgomery to Richmond, Virginia, last month (→Apr. 15).

Montgomery: "Inauguration of Jefferson Davis." Painting by Massalon.

Lincoln, in inaugural address, puts stress on union, not slavery

Washington, D.C., March 3

As soldiers with fixed bayonets watched from rooftops and along the Capitol plaza, Abraham Lincoln was sworn in today as President of the United States, a nation that is already divided by the secession of seven Southern states.

The tall, 52-year-old Illinois lawyer, sporting a newly grown beard, arrived in Washington by secret train 10 days ago, heavily guarded because of assassination threats.

As he stood on the east portico of the Capitol today to take his oath, he sought to reassure the nation of survival, saying, "The union of these states is perpetual ... No state upon its own mere motion, can get out of the union."

Then, determined to hold out his hand to the Southerners not in the crowd here, he said: "I am loath to close. We are not enemies, but friends. We must not be enemies. Though passion may have strained, it must not break the bonds of affection. The mystic chords of memory stretching from every battlefield and patriot grave, to every living heart and hearthstone, all over this broad land, will yet swell the chorus of union, when again touched, as surely they will be, by the better angels of our nature."

Earlier in the day, Lincoln and his wife, Mary, emerged from the Willard Hotel, where they have been staying, for the ride to the Capitol in President Buchanan's carriage. A few drops of rain had fallen, but just enough to settle the dust along the Pennsylvania Avenue parade route (→Apr. 15).

Lincoln, at his inaugural, said that work on the Capitol dome, a symbol of union, must go on despite conflict.

The burdens of leadership in a time of crisis. President Lincoln sits for a portrait by George P.A. Healy.

Fort Sumter is bombarded, yields to Southerners

Charleston, S.C., Apr. 14

Following a bombardment lasting more than two days, the 73-man United States garrison, led by Major Robert Anderson, has surrendered to General Pierre Beauregard, commander of the Provisional Forces of the Confederate States of America. For several months in both the North and the South, all eyes have been watching the new island fort in Charleston harbor and its beleaguered commander. President Jefferson Davis, the leader of the new Confederate government, had insisted that the federal fort belonged to the fledgling Confederacy. President Lincoln, whose election platform swore to keep, possess and defend all property of the United States, disagreed, but he did not want his stand to lead to civil war, particularly not to the Union's firing of the first shot.

The drama centered around the ability of Major Anderson to feed his troops. A supply ship had already been turned away when it was fired on. President Lincoln had shown great political acumen when he informed Davis that he intended to resupply Anderson with food and water, but no military supplies. Davis could fire on the supply ship, thus precipitating war, or he could not fire, and lose face in front of the South Carolina firebrands who ardently desire war. Either way, Lincoln won, politically if not morally. Davis ordered General Beauregard, in command of 7,000 men who completely surrounded the fort, to ask for Anderson's surrender. Failing that, the general was under orders to "reduce the fort as you see fit."

The garrison had enough supplies to last only until April 15, and a supply ship was under way when three Confederate officers landed at the fort on April 11. There they asked for Anderson's surrender. When the major refused, the Confederate captain informed him that: "by authority ... of the Provisional Forces of the Confederate States, we have the honor to notify you that (Beauregard) will open the fire of his batteries on Fort Sumter in one hour from this time." It was then 3:20 a.m., April 12. At 4:30 a.m., there was a flash of light and a huge mortar shell traced its thin red line into the early morning air, exploding directly over the fort and the Stars and Stripes, which rippled in the breeze blown in from the ocean. Within minutes, hundreds of howitzers and mortars surrounding the fort were blazing and the fort was encircled by a ring of fire. Major Anderson did not call muster until daylight, at which time his tiny band of men began to return fire.

After two days, Anderson surrendered. He and his men were allowed to leave with the federal supply ship. There were no casualties on either side, although the fort sustained a lot of damage (→15).

"Bombardment of Fort Sumter, Charleston Harbor" (1861) by Currier & Ives.

Union troops in the fort scramble to defend against Confederate cannon fire.

Lincoln declares an insurrection, not war

Washington, D.C., Apr. 15

Carefully avoiding use of the word "war," President Lincoln today declared a state of "insurrection" as he issued an appeal for 75,000 volunteers for three months of military service. His call for troops came only a day after the fall of Fort Sumter into the hands of the Confederate militia.

The imposing fortress, the last federal installation in Charleston, had been under siege by Southern troops since shortly after South Carolina seceded from the Union on December 20. Since then, six other states have seceded: Florida, Mississippi, Alabama, Louisiana, Georgia and Texas.

In his proclamation today, the President called for volunteers to suppress what he called "combinations" in the seven Southern states "too powerful to be suppressed by the ordinary course of judicial proceedings." He called for "all loyal citizens" to defend "the Union and to redress wrongs already long enough endured."

Fort Sumter, with 73 soldiers under the command of Major Robert Anderson, had run out of food and ammunition in recent days as the shelling by Southern militiamen followed. Yesterday, after they surrendered, Union troops set sail for New York while Confederate forces moved into the fort (→May 6).

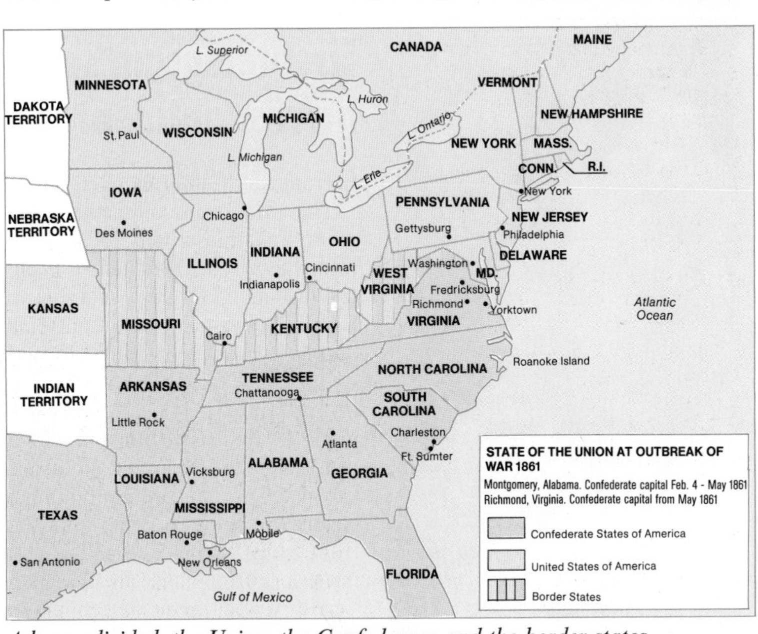

A house divided: the Union, the Confederacy and the border states.

North now blockading South's ports

Port Royal, South Carolina, Nov. 7

Naval cannons pounded Confederate troops into submission here today, the second major victory for the Union blockade in little more than two months. After shells fell into the fort "as fast as a horse's feet beat the ground in a gallop," as one participant described the scene, the rebel forces abandoned the fort. Their casualties were 10 killed and 20 wounded. Union casualties were six killed and 20 wounded.

Although the attack was a joint land-sea operation, it is generally conceded that the victory was won by the naval artillery.

The military expedition was strikingly similar to the Union naval victory on August 28, in which Flag Officer Silas H. Stringham and Major General Benjamin Butler were able to seize Forts Clark and Hatteras on the Carolina coast.

The string of victories is expected to strengthen the Union's blockade, which got under way on April 19. The operation has already illustrated the importance of sea warfare, and it is likely to continue doing so as the war wears on.

The Union now has 90 ships listed in military service, but many are not ready yet. To upgrade naval technology, the War Department has contracted with a Missouri engineer to construct seven of the new "ironclad" gunboats that some believe are going to render the wooden warship obsolete.

Ships bound for Southern ports are pirates in the eyes of Union admirals. "Confederate Blockade Runner and Union Man-o-War" (1861) by F. Mullen.

Blockade takes effect: "King Cotton Bound, or the Modern Prometheus."

Baltimore mob kills four Union soldiers

Baltimore, Maryland, Apr. 19

An angry mob attacked the Sixth Massachusetts Regiment passing through here on its way to Washington today, resulting in the death of four soldiers and the wounding of 36. Twelve Baltimore residents were also killed. Hostile crowds of Southern sympathizers blocked the right of way of the 800-man force, pelting the soldiers with stones and shouting curses at them. No one knows who fired first, but a full-scale riot was the result.

Kansas is now 34th state, slavery-free

Washington, D.C., Jan. 29

After a protracted struggle over the issue of slavery, Kansas today joined the union as a free state. In 1858, President Buchanan, acting under the influence of his powerful Southern Cabinet, had recommended that Congress accept a pro-slavery constitution that the territory's voters had rejected earlier that year. The House voted to resubmit it to a popular vote. Once again, it was rejected. A new constitution, framed by the opponents of slavery, was prepared at Wyandotte in the fall of 1859. A majority of the territory's settlers accepted it. Kansas thus became the nation's 34th state.

Three territories created in the West

Washington, D.C., Feb. 28

Congress today authorized the creation of two new organized territories in the West, Colorado and Nevada. Last month, Congress created the Territory of Dakota. The entities admitted today consist mainly of lands that were taken from Mexico. William Gilpin has been named territorial Governor of Colorado. Now the big question that everybody is asking is: Are these new territories going to be pro- or anti-slavery?

Behind the scenes: Women fitting Confederate soldiers for their uniforms. Painting by Sheppard.

First telegram sent across continent

Sacramento, California, Oct. 24

The first transcontinental telegram was transmitted today, sent from this city to President Lincoln in Washington by Stephen Johnson Field, chief justice of the California Supreme Court. It will be followed by a message from the mayor of San Francisco to the mayor of New York City. The effort to build a coast-to-coast telegraph line has been made urgent by the outbreak of the Civil War. Crews working from both directions met to join lines at Fort Bridger in the Utah Territory. The cost of sending a message is $6 for every 10 words.

Dorothea Dix made nursing supervisor

Washington, D.C., June 10

The Surgeon General has appointed Miss Dorothea Dix, the noted mental health reformer, to be the superintendent of women nurses. Miss Dix has just returned from England, where she coordinated efforts to improve facilities for the insane. Miss Dix can count on many women to assist her in the new endeavor; among them is a 39-year-old former teacher and Patent Office employee named Miss Clara Barton, who in April collected supplies to send to the men of the Sixth Massachusetts Regiment after it met with heavy casualties.

Those who are left behind to wonder about fate of loved ones. "Letting Him Go" by J.L.G. Ferris.

First income tax is voted to aid war

Washington, D.C., Aug. 5

In an effort to finance the Civil War, President Lincoln today signed into law the first nationwide income tax, making citizens with incomes above $800 a year subject to a 3 percent annual tax. Up until now, the government relied mostly on borrowing to support the effort. And it collected only $1 in taxes for every $8.52 that it borrowed. The Confederacy, meanwhile, has been even more handicapped in raising revenue to finance the war. Taxation is unpopular in those states, too; the population is sparse, and there is a limited market for Confederate bonds (→ Feb. 25, 1863).

Seesaw fighting points to long war

Washington, D.C., Nov. 7

The seesaw nature of this war is exemplified by three recent battles. General Robert E. Lee suffered a defeat at Cheat Mountain September 13 when his forces attempted to gain control of western Virginia. On October 21, Union General Edward Baker's forces were beaten by Confederates at Ball's Bluff on the banks of the Potomac. And today, General Ulysses S. Grant won a limited victory at Belmont, Missouri, on the Mississippi River.

Jackson is hero at battle of Bull Run

Manassas, Virginia, July 21

The first thrust by Union forces toward the new Confederate capital of Richmond has been repulsed. The retreat became a rout, with sightseers and congressmen fleeing along with the troops. A Union army of 34,000 men, mainly raw recruits under Brigadier General Irvin McDowell, met a Confederate army led by General Pierre Beauregard that was waiting behind a small creek called Bull Run, three miles from Centreville, Virginia. Both commanders knew their untried soldiers would have difficulty with surprises, so they moved their armies cautiously. McDowell tried to attack the Confederate left flank but moved too slowly to turn it. Regiments went into battle piecemeal, and at first it looked as though the Union forces would win. The Confederates rallied behind Thomas Jackson's brigade of Virginians, who stood fast. Seeing the Virginians' brave stand, General Barnard Bee cried, "Look, there is Jackson standing like a stone wall," a catchy description of the general. Moments later, Bee was fatally wounded, but the Southerners held. They soon began getting fresh reinforcements, and these brigades simply punched the battle-weakened Union line. At first, the Federal retreat was orderly. But it soon was transformed into a rout that did not stop until the troops had returned to Washington.

Confederate soldiers busy building fortifications at Manassas, Virginia.

Some of Major General McDowell's 28,500 Federal troops run into a stone wall of Confederate forces while trying to envelope General Beauregard's left.

Lee and McClellan opposing generals

Southerner on a white horse: General Robert E. Lee of Virginia.

Richmond, Virginia, Nov. 1

Some of the generals now facing each other in the Union and Conferate armies have had similar careers. Both Generals George McClellan and Robert E. Lee are military engineers out of West Point. But the similarities between these two end there. McClellan, 35, and known as "Little Mac," is popular, outspoken and flamboyant. Named to command Union forces today by President Lincoln, he has called Lee, who was promoted to General and military adviser to Confederate President Jefferson Davis June 14, "cautious and weak." The unassuming Lee, 52, fought with distinction in Mexico (→ June 2, 1862).

Wilson's Creek, Missouri, August 10. *In a dying effort, General Nathaniel Lyon saved Missouri for the Union. Lithograph (1893) by Kurz & Allison.*

1862

Lincoln

Green Point, N.Y., Jan. 30. Ironclad warship Monitor, designed by John Ericsson, launched (→ March 9).

North Carolina, Feb. 8. Roanoke Island captured by General Ambrose Burnside, giving Union forces a base from which to invade North Carolina.

Richmond, Virginia, Feb. 22. Jefferson Davis elected President of the Confederacy.

Washington, D.C., March 6. President Lincoln asks Congress to offer aid to any state promising gradual abolition of slavery (→ Apr. 4).

Washington, D.C., Apr. 4. At Lincoln's proposal, slaves in capital are freed, compensated with up to $300 and encouraged to move to Haiti or Liberia (→ June 19).

Georgia, Apr. 11. Rifle-bore cannons used for first time in Union victory over Confederacy, at Fort Pulaski.

Charleston, S.C., May 13. Negro pilot Robert Smalls commandeers Confederate steamer Planter and presents it to Union navy.

Virginia, May 14. General McClellan takes Union troops to White House, Virginia, 20 miles from Richmond (→ June 1).

Virginia, June 2. General Robert E. Lee assumes command of Confederate Armies of Northern Virginia.

Washington, D.C., June 5. United States recognizes Liberia and Haiti, first Negro nations it has recognized.

Washington, D.C., June 19. President Lincoln signs bill outlawing slavery in territories but not states (→ Aug. 22).

Richmond, Virginia. Confederate army constructs balloon using silk dresses.

United States. John D. Rockefeller invests $4,000 in his first oil refinery.

Washington, D.C. U.S. Department of Agriculture set up.

Virginia City, Nevada. Samuel Clemens becomes a reporter, using pen name Mark Twain.

DEATH

Concord, Mass., May 6. Henry David Thoreau, essayist and poet (*July 12, 1817).

Monitor and Merrimack fight to draw

Exercise in futility. The two ironclads batter each other's impenetrable hulls. "Engagement Between the Monitor and Merrimack" (1891) by J.G. Tanner.

Hampton Roads, Virginia, March 9

War on the open seas will never be the same following the battle, inconclusive though it was, between two ironclad warships, the Monitor and the Merrimack. The two behemoths, unwieldy as floating barns, faced each other in the shallow bay between Fort Monroe and Norfolk, Virginia. The Merrimack, renamed the Virginia by the Confederacy, was the first vessel to be refitted with iron plates. It had been scuttled the previous spring when the Navy Yard at Norfolk was abandoned. The Confederates raised it and completely covered its 275-foot sides with an iron superstructure. They refitted it with 10 new powerful guns and gave it a huge cast-iron beak at the bow. The skipper is Captain Franklin Buchanan, formerly of the United States Navy.

On March 8, the Confederate vessel made mincemeat of three of the Union's most powerful ships, sinking the Minnesota, Cumberland and Congress, with much loss of life. The Merrimack suffered only slight damage, with iron shot rolling off like water from an oilcloth.

Today, Union hopes were raised by the Monitor, which carries only a single armored turret with two 11-inch guns. If the Merrimack looks like a half-submerged barn, as witnesses say, then the Monitor looks like a tin can on a shingle. Lieutenant John Worden, the skipper of the Monitor, immediately took his ship into battle with the Merrimack. The ironclads exchanged fire all morning, at near point-blank range, but neither side seemed to have gained an advantage before the engagement was over.

Grant wins Kentucky forts, gets promoted

Fort Donelson, Kentucky, Feb. 15

In the Union's first key land victory of the war, Brigadier General Ulysses S. Grant took Fort Donelson on the Cumberland River today and was promoted to major general. With 17,000 men, the 39-year-old Grant took Fort Henry a week ago. At Fort Donelson, after his troops and a gunboat flotilla outmaneuvered its defenders, Grant forced Brigadier General Simon Buckner into an "unconditional and immediate surrender" (→ Apr. 7).

Grant leads a Union force to Fort Donelson. Lithograph by Currier & Ives.

McClellan removed as General-in-Chief

Washington, D.C., March 11

General George McClellan's inability to move any faster than molasses in winter has caused President Lincoln to remove him as General-in-Chief of all United States forces and leave that post vacant. McClellan remains in charge of the Army of the Potomac.

Lincoln's problems with his faltering high command began with McClellan's failure to move his army to Centreville, Virginia, and attack the Confederates who were camped there. McClellan's failure to do so was not without certain elements of farce. For one thing, he had ordered special boats to provide supplies for his army, but no one bothered to measure the canal locks and the boats were inches too wide. Later, McClellan planned to march on to Richmond via Annapolis. But cynics would have seen that as a retreat because the army would have had to head north and east rather than south (→ May 14).

Grant holds fast at Battle of Shiloh

Shiloh, Tennessee, Apr. 7

A Confederate army led by General Albert Sidney Johnston has pounded at Union forces led by General Ulysses S. Grant for over 36 hours, but failed to dislodge him from his lines. Johnston, and about 40,000 Confederate troops, attacked Grant, with an equal force of men, near Pittsburg Landing, on the Tennessee River. Grant's forces were encamped on an east-west line, running at right angles to the river, which anchored his left.

The Confederate forces attacked from the south, coming up from Corinth, along roads that had been made muddy by the cold spring rains. The Johnston plan was for a swift movement to catch General Grant's troops napping, but his untried soldiers proceeded too slowly for that, and the Yankees were waiting for him when he attacked. The battle was a two-day slugfest of piecemeal clashes between small units, much like the encounter at Bull Run, but it was a longer and bloodier engagement. The most intensive fighting took place in the Union's center, along a little country lane renamed the "Hornet's Nest." About 2,200 Union soldiers were taken prisoner here when the Confederates captured the lane.

Both armies remained in place after the battle, the Union having lost approximately 13,000 men; the Confederates 10,000. Perhaps the most significant loss for the Confederates was that of General Johnston, who was killed during the first day of the fighting.

The Battle of Shiloh. Death in the mud of Tennessee at point-blank range.

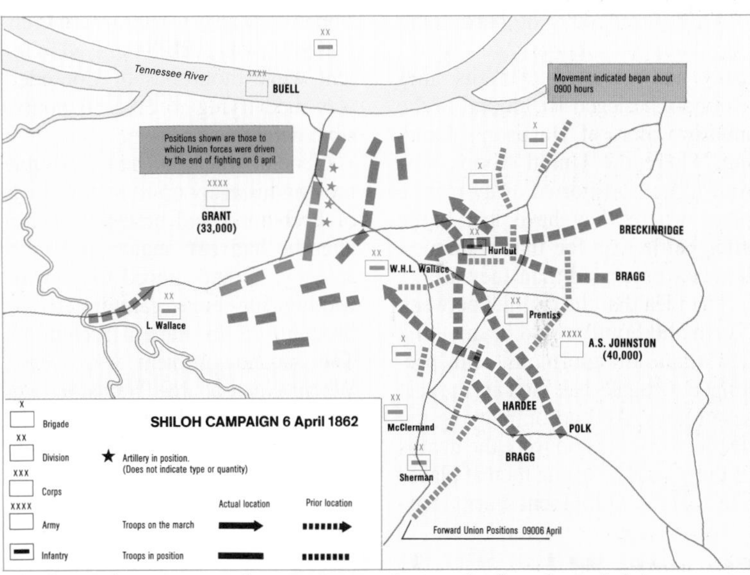

The Confederate army's hasty advance during the first day's fighting.

"The Battle Hymn of the Republic"

Mine eyes have seen the glory of the coming of the Lord;
He is trampling out the vintage where the grapes of wrath are stored;
He hath loosed the fateful lightning of his terrible swift sword;
His truth is marching on.
Glory, glory, hallelujah,
Glory, glory, hallelujah,
Glory, glory, hallelujah,
His truth is marching on.
I have seen Him in the watch-fires of a hundred circling camps;
They have builded Him an altar in the evening dews and damps;
I can read His righteous sentence by the dim and flaring lamps;
His day is marching on.

In the beauty of the lilies Christ was born across the sea,
With a glory in His bosom that transfigures you and me;
As He died to make men holy, let us die to make men free,
While God is marching on.

Federal authority outlaws polygamy

Washington, D.C., July 8

President Lincoln today signed the Morrill Anti-Bigamy Law prohibiting polygamy in the territories. The law is primarily aimed at the Mormons in Utah and many provisions affect only them. It annuls several acts of the Utah legislature, including the incorporation of the Mormon Church and its authority to regulate and to perform marriages. The law also limits the amount of property any religious association in the territory can own.

ashville is first tate capital to fall

ashington, D.C., Apr. 15

Nashville, the first Confederate apital to fall to Union forces, apitulated on February 25. But the var is far from over. Since Nashille, the war has spread throughut the South and into the Western erritories. And the results have een mixed. Confederate forces von the battles of Val Verde and ucson in the New Mexico Teriory in February. Last month, Jnion troops defeated an Indianed Confederate force at the Battle f Elkhorn Tavern in Indian Teriory. Three weeks ago, regular Jnion troops and volunteers topped a Confederate force at the Battle of Glorieta Pass in New Mexico. And the territorial wars rind on. Reports received this eveing indicate that Northern troops arlier today defeated Southern orces at Peralta, New Mexico.

incoln's third son, Willie, is dead at 11

Washington, D.C., Feb. 20

"Well, Nicolay, my boy is gone - he is actually gone!" President Lincoln uttered these words to his secretary, John Nicolay, before he burst into tears and walked out of he room. William Wallace Lincoln, 11, the President's third son, had died after a cold developed into an intreatable fever. Mrs. Lincoln and Willie's brothers Robert Todd and Tad grieve with the President.

"Lincoln and Son Tad" by Courter.

Lee halts Union army near Richmond

Killed: Private Edwin E. Jennison.

Manning the guns during the vicious fighting of the Battle of the Seven Days.

Richmond, Virginia, July 2

After seven days of hard fighting, General George McClellan's army has retreated from its lines around a besieged Richmond to the muddy waters of Harrison's Landing, where the Union troops now wait to be transported away from a place where they have lost battle after battle to a foe that is unquestionably better led than they are.

The idea that the conflict between North and South would be anything less than an enormous and prolonged struggle has died in the last seven days. And accompanying the death of this illusion were the deaths of thousands of young men at places like Gaines Mill, Trent Farm, Savage Station and finally the bloody slopes of Malvern Hill, where General Stonewall Jackson prayed in his tent while thousands of Confederates died trying to take an impossible defensive position.

General McClellan had no trouble moving his army up to the outskirts of Richmond and besieging it, but later he had two major problems. Initially, he had moved too slowly, waiting for huge cannons to be brought up to flatten Richmond. The second problem was worse. When General Joe Johnston was severely wounded on May 31, the command of his army went to Robert E. Lee, who was not slow and, rather than wait for McClellan's big guns, moved rapidly and decisively, forcing McClellan back to the James River, in a series of savage battles that has demoralized the Army of the Potomac. President Lincoln intends to have a long talk with McClellan regarding the general's caution (→ Aug. 30).

New Orleans taken by Farragut's fleet

New Orleans, Apr. 25

New Orleans residents stood o the banks of the Mississippi Rive and watched today as Admiral Da vid Farragut's Union vessels saile into the harbor. The fleet now hold the largest seaport. in the South.

Warships and schooners, they a rode high on a swollen river, thei guns trained menacingly on the city They met no armed resistance. Th city's militia had been sent north t avoid bombardment of the city.

On April 18, Farragut's nav had sailed through a barrage of fir from two forts downriver of Nev Orleans. "Capture or be captured," the stern old admiral told his aides

The city's authorities had be lieved that the forts would repel an invasion. On April 24, the Unio fleet easily defeated a hastily as sembled fleet of riverboats sent ou to oppose them. Occupation troop under the command of Genera Benjamin Butler accompanied th Union navy and they are now pre pared to take over the city.

Reinforcements aid Union at Seven Pines

Richmond, Virginia, June 1

General Joe Johnston would have caught George McClellan, whose army was split by the flooded Chickahominy River, had he moved fast enough at Seven Pines. But, as one Southern soldier said, "He didn't have no luck." McClellan escaped with a severe pounding and a close call. The casualties were high, with the Confederates losing 5,000 me and the Union 6,000. Johnston trie to take advantage of the flooding which stopped McClellan from cross ing the river and keeping his army together, but the Southerner move too slowly. His men had to fight an trudge through waist-high water The time lost allowed reinforcements to reach McClellan (→ July 2).

Stuart's Ride wreaks havoc on McClellan

Stuart rides to encircle McClellan.

White House, Virginia, June 15

Brigadier General James Ewell Brown (Jeb) Stuart looks like the stuff legends are made of. He wears an ostrich feather in his hat and a gray cape lined with scarlet, and he travels with a banjo player who keeps him entertained. But he is also a competent and aggressive leader of light horse who, with 1,200 of his cavalrymen, rode completely around General George McClellan's army, which is besieging Richmond. "Stuart's Ride," behind the Union lines, resulted in four days of great military adventure of the sort that he and his men love: surprising Yankees and stealing their military supplies.

Hand-to-hand combat at Seven Pines. Lithograph by Currier and Ives.

Government grants homesteaders land

Washington, D.C., May 20

President Lincoln signed the Homestead Act today, granting tracts of land at minimal cost to settlers of the West. Missouri Senator Thomas Hart Benton is chiefly responsible for the legislation. He lobbied hard for liberal land policies before the outbreak of the war and his debating skill and compromise diplomacy were instrumental in finally gaining approval for the act, though he failed to win the exact terms he wanted. Citizens are now allowed to buy up to 160 acres of the hundreds of thousands of acres of public property available at a cost of $1.25 per acre, providing they settle the land for five years. The law may cut speculation (→ Jan. 1, 1863).

States given land to set up colleges

Washington, D.C., July 2

President Lincoln today signed the Morrill Land-Grant College Act, providing 30,000 acres of land to each state to establish colleges devoted to agriculture, engineering and military science. While the act is named for Representative Justin Morrill of Vermont, credit is also given to Jonathan Turner of Illinois College, who for years promoted the bill with impassioned appeals.

Union Pacific will build line to West

Washington, D.C., July 1

Although the nation staggers under the weight of divisiveness, President Lincoln insured a new bond with the Far West today by signing the Pacific Railroad Act. It incorporates the Union Pacific Company, which will begin the epic task of building a railroad across the Plains and over the Rockies to link with California's Central Pacific, which will expand eastward, surmounting the rugged Sierras. Congress has offered public land rights and up to $48,000 a mile. Said a lawmaker: "You cannot hold this continent together without rapid communication across it" (→ May 10, 1869).

South wins again, at second Bull Run

Manassas, Virginia, Aug. 30

The inability of Union field commanders to coordinate their attack has led to another defeat for the weary Army of the Potomac. Major General John Pope had a good offensive plan and good soldiers to execute it. He could have smashed the Confederate right flank but, for some reason, General Horace Porter, who commanded a corps of 30,000 men, simply halted on his way to the Confederate flank, sat down and didn't get up again. The Confederate army was drawn up along a line running due south from Sudley Church, roughly parallel to the position held by the army at the first battle of Bull Run, but a little further east. General Pope used the famous Stone House, which was in the middle of the earlier battle, as his headquarters. Stonewall Jackson's corps was in front of the Federal right and General A.P. Hill's famous "light division" was on Jackson's flank when a Federal corps, under the command of General Franz Sigel, struck it with all it had. The Union followed this assault by sending in veterans under Generals Philip Kearny and Joseph Hooker and assaulting the Confederate center again and again, almost succeeding, but never quite able to break the Jackson and Hill line. While Porter was equivocating, the Union army beat the Confederate inner defensive line back on itself, but still the Confederates held, in a battle that involved fierce hand-to-hand fighting. In the interim, General James Longstreet's corps, on the Confederate right, was also not being used to good effect. Had his forces been in action, they might well have enabled General Lee to rout the Federals completely. And when Longstreet finally did attack, Pope had already pulled back (→ Sept. 13).

Company C of the 41st New York Infantry awaits action at Bull Run.

Lincoln's main war aim: Save the Union

Washington, D.C., Aug. 22

Questioned about the purpose of the war by the *New York Tribune* editor Horace Greeley, President Lincoln said, "My paramount object in this struggle is to save the Union, and not either to save or destroy slavery. If I could save the Union without freeing any slaves I would do it; if I could save it by freeing all the slaves, I would do it, and if I could do it by freeing some and leaving others alone, I would do that" (→ Sept. 22).

Sioux kill over 400 in Minnesota revolt

St. Paul, Minnesota, Dec. 26

An Indian uprising has taken the lives of over 400 whites along the Minnesota River. The Santee tribe, recently relocated to a reservation near St. Paul, found itself surrounded by hostile white settlers and without the annuities that the government had pledged. The impoverished Santees, led by Chief Little Crow, attacked white settlements from August 18 to 23. New Ulm was devastated and had to be evacuated. General Sibley defeated the Santees at Wood Lake on Sept. 23, and 38 Indians who surrendered were hanged today in the largest mass execution in American history.

Virginia, September 15. *Union troops march to defend Harpers Ferry from attack by General Stonewall Jackson. Despite their effort, the garrison was doomed. Trapped on low ground, 12,000 men surrendered at the first sound of Confederate artillery. Colonel Benjamin Davis, however, led 1,300 cavalrymen through Confederate lines in a daring escape last night. Jackson has already left for Antietam to reinforce General Robert E. Lee (→ 18).*

Battle of Antietam ends in stalemate

McClellan's Army of the Potomac engages the forces of the Confederacy.

The President meets with his generals after the battle. Lincoln and McClellan, in uneasy alliance, face each other. Photograph by Alexander Gardner.

Sharpsburg, Maryland., Sept. 18

Having come back to lead the Union army after General John Pope's retirement, General George McClellan had a very good chance to smash the Confederate Army of Northern Virginia at Antietam today, but indecision allowed General Robert E. Lee to turn apparent defeat into a stalemate.

When Lee invaded Maryland, he used the vast South Mountain to screen his army, and McClellan would not have known where he was except for a fluke; a Confederate officer lost his campaign orders and two Union soldiers found them. So McClellan knew where Lee was going. But he took his time getting there, and, when he arrived, he simply parked his army for an entire day. It is not known why Lee chose to fight rather than retreat, since he was vastly outnumbered, and he had the Potomac behind him. Had McClellan broken his lines, Lee's entire army could have been taken. But McClellan attacked with his army corps in a series of jabs rather than all at once, and Lee's veterans drove back the Yankees time after time. The armies fought from dawn to dusk and, in the heaviest losses of the war, 23,500 men were killed in the cornfields, the woodlots and a country road known as "bloody lane." One Union soldier said: "No tongue can tell, no mind can see, no pen portray the horrible sights I witnessed this morning" (→Nov. 5).

Open-hearth steel furnace is installed

New York City

Quality steel will become widely available as the first open-hearth furnace goes into operation. This new method of producing steel was invented in 1856 by a German, Friedrich Siemens. Using an efficient technique of recirculating gases through the furnace, the hearth can achieve higher temperatures, make use of scrap steel and pig iron, remove impurities and produce steel with a desired carbon content. The amount of carbon in steel determines the hardness and smoothness of the finished product. Availability of this kind of steel will reap enormous benefits in the production of all kinds of tools.

Dissatisfied Lincoln removes McClellan

Washington, D.C., Nov. 5

President Lincoln has fired General George McClellan from his job as commander of the Army of the Potomac and turned over the job to General Ambrose E. Burnside. The main reason for the President's decision seems to have been McClellan's unwillingness to do battle. In addition, McClellan has made many enemies, some of them in Lincoln's Cabinet. The stalemate at Antietam was probably the last straw for Lincoln (→Dec. 13).

Bloodiest single day on the battlefield

Antietam, September 17. *Failing to bury their differences, the North and South are left with the task of burying their dead. With 12,410 Federals and 11,172 rebels lost, no day has brought greater tragedy to America.*

Washington, D.C., September 22. *President Lincoln has released a proclamation that will, if signed next year, free all slaves. As advised by Secretary of State Seward at a July Cabinet meeting (above), the President held up the announcement until after the Antietam battle (→Jan. 1, 1863).*

Gatling patents gun with rotating barrel

Indianapolis, Indiana, Nov. 4

A gun that fires hundreds of rounds a minute by using a cluster of rotating barrels was patented today by Richard J. Gatling, a 44-year-old inventor best known for his automatic wheat-planting machine. Gatling says the sight of wounded men returning from battle prompted him to invent the gun, with the hope of making war so terrible that nations would turn away from it. The Gatling gun is cranked by hand, with each barrel firing its cartridge in turn. The first models were destroyed in a fire and production is limited, so the Gatling gun is not expected to be widely used in the Civil War that is now raging.

"Fighting Parson" wars on secession

Philadelphia

William Gannaway Brownlow, the "Fighting Parson," has made headlines again. He first came to attention when, as a preacher and newspaper editor in Tennessee, he denounced the Civil War and sided with the North. First he was hit with a jail sentence and then he was driven from the South. Since then Brownlow has been cheering on the Union. Now, at the age of 57, he has written *Sketches of the Rise, Progress, and Decline of Secession*, a best-seller that is warming many Northern hearts at a time when optimism is in short supply.

Burnside meets disaster pursuing Lee

Fredericksburg, Virginia, Dec. 13

When General Ambrose E. Burnside asked the Army of the Potomac to do the militarily impossible, the result was disastrous. Burnside tried to dislodge General Robert E. Lee's army from an almost impregnable ridge called Marye's Heights behind Fredericksburg. His soldiers did their duty – trying to take the heights, by the use of two columns in a frontal assault, one on the Confederate left, another on the right. In spite of the odds, the Burnside plan almost succeeded as the Union forces of General George Meade got through the Confederate lines at a most unexpected place, the southern tip, defended by the soldiers of General Stonewall Jackson. For some unknown reason, there was an undefended gap in General Jackson's position. Some 4,500 of General Meade's troops attacked that spot, and it began to crumble. But Meade received no support and Jackson responded rapidly with a powerful counterattack. As a result, any possibility of a breakthrough by the Union forces quickly disappeared.

As Lee was watching the doomed Union assault on his position, he commented to General James Longstreet: "It is well that war is so terrible – we should grow too fond of it." During the battle, the town of Fredericksburg was destroyed. As he looked at the scene of desolation, shrouded in a cold white fog, Confederate General Jeb Stuart described it as "the saddest sight I ever saw" (→Jan. 26, 1863).

Under fire, Mathew Brady took this first photo of the U.S. Army in combat.

Dealing with disaster: Behind Union lines at Fredericksburg, Virginia.

Corinth, Mississippi, October 4. *General Rosecrans has won Corinth for the Union, but he let Confederate General Earl Van Dorn slip away again.*

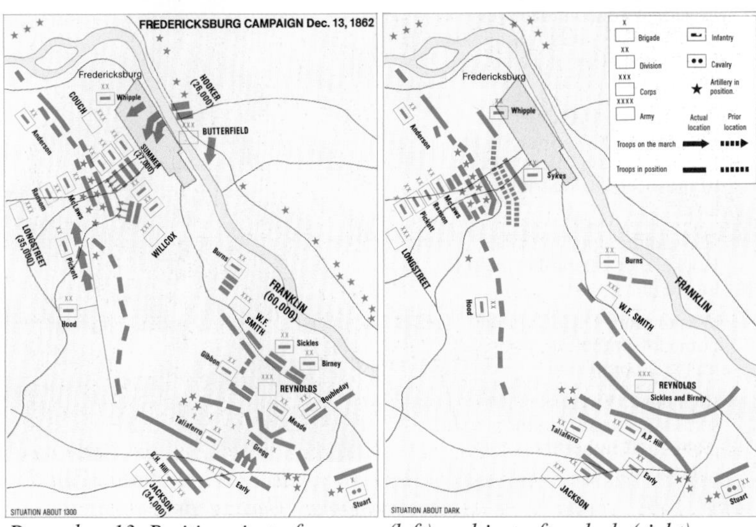

December 13: Positions just after noon (left) and just after dark (right).

1863

Lincoln

Murfreesboro, Tennessee, Jan. 3. Union army led by General Rosecrans halts attack by General Bragg's Confederates.

Virginia, Jan. 7. *Richmond Enquirer* refers to Emancipation Proclamation as a "startling political crime" and a "most stupid political blunder" (→ Apr. 8, 1864).

Washington, D.C., Feb. 2. Congress allocates $3,000 to buy and distribute cotton and tobacco seeds in the Union states.

Kansas, March 3. Congress provides for removal of all Indians from state.

Richmond, Virginia, Apr. 2. Police and militia called upon to halt looting of shops during bread riot.

South Carolina, Apr. 7. Union Rear Admiral Francis DuPont fails in attempt to take Charleston harbor with nine ironclad warships.

Washington, D.C., Apr. 13. William Bullock granted patent for continuous-roll printing press; first to print on both sides of sheet.

Richmond, Virginia, May 1. Confederate Congress permits enslavement or execution of captured Negro Union soldiers.

Baton Rouge, Louisiana, May 3. Colonel Benjamin Grierson completes two-week raid through Mississippi as diversion for Grant's Vicksburg campaign (→ July 4).

Fredericksburg, Virginia, June 3. Setting out with 75,000 Confederate troops, General Robert E. Lee begins second invasion of Union territory (→ July 3).

Washington, D.C., Oct. 3. President Lincoln declares last Thursday in November as national holiday of Thanksgiving.

Washington, D.C., Dec. 8. Proclamation of Amnesty and Reconstruction offers pardon to most rebels swearing oath of loyalty.

Cleveland, Ohio. John D. Rockefeller establishes petroleum refinery.

Washington, D.C. Capitol dome, a symbol of national unity, is completed.

Richmond, Virginia. Jefferson Davis urges Southerners to plant food rather than cotton and tobacco.

North orders first draft

Still seeking volunteers. Union army recruiting station at City Hall, New York.

Washington, D.C., March 3

With today's signing of the Conscription Act, President Lincoln can, by executive order, compel American citizens to report for duty in the Civil War – unless they can buy their way out instead.

The law empowers the War Department to draft males of 20 to 46, for the Union army. However, for a fee of $300, one's military obligation can be waived. This provision is expected to raise needed revenue for the war effort; on the other hand, critics contend that it gives unfair advantage to the rich. It is no doubt going to stir angry sentiments among the poor.

Congress initiated the resolution because of the drop in enrollment of volunteers and the high rate of desertions. Last year, each side lost about 10 percent of its ranks to desertion. Worse, there is a new breed of soldier: the bounty jumper. Undesirables (some observers call them "plain thieves and vagabonds") enlist, take the army's cash bounty, desert as soon as possible, change names and find another regiment to pull the trick again and again. One soldier admitted having "jumped" 32 times before he was arrested and sent to jail (→ July 17).

After mudmarch, Lincoln ousts Burnside

Commander of the Army of the Potomac, General Burnside is famous for his whiskers or "sideburns."

Washington, D.C., Jan. 26

President Lincoln has removed General Ambrose Burnside from command of the Army of the Potomac and replaced him with General Joseph Hooker, who is nicknamed "Fighting Joe" and who commanded the Grand Central Division of the army until today. After Burnside's stinging defeat at the hands of General Lee at Fredericksburg, he became completely ineffectual as a leader, to the point that his army literally got stuck in the muds of the last week's torrential rains. Many members of the officer corps, including his own friends, and the general staff, were unhappy with Burnside's so-called mudmarch, and Hooker let it be known, on many an occasion, he would like to have Burnside's job (→ May 6).

1st homestead site made in Nebraska

Nebraska Territory, Jan. 1

Daniel Freeman knows a good deal when he sees one. He has become the first settler to take advantage of the Homestead Act by establishing a farm on government property. Freeman, a former Union soldier, claimed a tract at Cub Creek in Gage County, Nebraska. Under the provisions of the 1861 legislation, he must farm the land five years for it to become his property. Nebraska reported a population of nearly 29,000 in 1860. But the Homestead Act is expected to boost its population considerably as more pioneers follow Freeman's example.

35-inch Tom Thumb takes 32-inch bride

New York Ciy, Feb. 10

It was no small affair today when Charles S. Stratton, better known as General Tom Thumb, and Miss Lavinia Warren were married at Grace Church. Thumb is 35 inches tall and 25 years old; Miss Warren is 32 inches tall and 20 years old. All 29 inches of George McNutt, better known as Commodore Nutt, served as Tom's best man. There were 2,000 guests at the ceremony, including, showman P.T. Barnum, who brought along a music box as a wedding present.

Banking system set up to finance war

Washington, D.C., Feb. 25

Congress today created a national banking system to help finance the war and provide a stable national currency. Under the new law, banks will be encouraged to secure their charters from the federal government. These national banks will be required to have as much as one-third of their capital invested in government bonds. They can then obtain bank notes for up to 90 percent of the value of those bonds. If the banks fail, the federal government can sell the bonds and use the proceeds to redeem the notes.

Emancipation Proclamation is signed by Lincoln

Vashington, D.C., Jan. 1

Fulfilling a pledge made last Sep-ember, President Abraham Lin-oln has signed the Emancipation Proclamation, freeing all slaves in Confederate states and radically al-ering the nature of the war. "The Constitution as it is; the Union as was," though still the slogan of Northern Democrats, seems ever nore distant from reality. For the ecree, Lincoln says, turns the war nto one of "subjugation." The Old outh must be "destroyed and re-laced by new propositions and deas," the President says.

Last night, abolitionists gathered o celebrate the demise of the old rder. In Boston, free Negroes be-an a candlelight vigil at dusk. People of both races filled church-s to sing and pray, sharing the ju-ilation of one Negro minister who roclaimed, "God Almighty's New Year will make the United States he land of freedom!" In Washing-on today, a multitude gathered out-ide the *Evening Star* office awaiting copy of the proclamation. The President watched and waved from window of the White House.

The decree actually frees no one et. In loyal states, the President does not have the constitutional au-hority to abolish slavery; in the Confederate states, he does not have he power. According to one British ewspaper, the act is "like a China-nan beating his two swords togeth-r to frighten his enemy." But the decree heralds new resolve on the part of the administration. And its importance was not lost on the abo-litionists. William Lloyd Garrison, who had compared Lincoln to "a wet rag," now lauds his "act of immense historical significance." Frederick Douglass, also tired of Lincoln's balancing act, had called him "the miserable tool of traitors and rebels." Now, Douglass says, "We shout for joy that we live to recall this righeous moment."

Speculation persisted until today on whether the President would ac-tually sign the document. The pre-liminary proclamation of Septem-ber 22 nearly wrecked Lincoln's political base for the election. Dele-gates to Pennsylvania's Democratic convention were told that the "par-ty of fanaticism" would free "two or three million semi-savages" to "overrun the North and enter into competition with the white laboring masses," mixing with "their sons and daughters." But the Repub-licans, allaying white fear with a plan to colonize freed slaves over-seas, held a majority in the House and added five seats in the Senate.

The proclamation's moral force may guide the administration and millions of Negroes in the war-torn South through the horror of the months ahead. Last month Lincoln told Congress: "The fiery trial through which we pass, will light us down, in honor or dishonor, to the latest generation ... In giving freedom to the slave, we assure free-dom to the free" (→7).

Lady Liberty rides through the capital, her torch held aloft, in A.A. Lamb's "Emancipation Proclamation" (1863).

First Negro regiment organized for Union

Power in the barrel of a gun. Infantry corporal poses with pocket revolver.

Boston, Jan. 26

One of the worst nightmares of the South, armed Negroes fighting for the Union, has materialized. Abolitionists empowered by the Emancipation Proclamation have been authorized to recruit for two regiments, the 54th and the 55th Massachusetts. Negro units already exist in South Carolina, Louisiana and Kansas, where the first Negro war casualties occurred in October. But the Massachusetts units are the first officially recognized. Freder-ick Douglass hopes more will be formed. Now, he says, "there is no power on earth which can deny that (the Negro) has earned the right to citizenship" (→May 1).

Freed Negroes at a Northern dock. In the South, the proclamation has only the power to give hope, not freedom, though it may encourage slaves to rebel. ▷

Lee mauls Hooker; Jackson wounded

The fall of Stonewall. Officers at Chancellorsville attend to General Jackson, mistakenly wounded on May 2 by North Carolinians. By Kurz and Allison.

Surveying the damage. A Confederate wagon lies in ruins on Marye's Heights, its bearers dead at its side. Photograph by Mathew Brady.

Chancellorsville, Virginia, May 6

It is a hallowed military dictum that a general should never divide his forces in the face of the enemy, but Robert E. Lee did it, not once but three times and, in the process, completely routed the Army of the Potomac under its new commander, General "Fighting Joe" Hooker. This happened as twilight was falling and, as one Union soldier put it, "Darkness was upon us, and Jackson was on us and fear was on us."

In a way, Lee stole Hooker's plan, which was to divide *his* army and bring a corps behind Lee's defensive position at Fredericksburg. But Lee found out what was going on through his able cavalry commander, General Jeb Stuart, and came up with his own plan to flank Hooker's army with General Stonewall Jackson's corps. Lee left one corps at Fredericksburg, placed another corps in front of General Hooker, and sent Jackson around behind the Federal right flank, which he accomplished with crushing force, completely routing the German mercenaries that the other soldiers referred to as "those Dutchmen."

While this was happening, Jackson got out in front of his own troops, looking into the darkness for a road that his men could follow. Soldiers from a North Carolina regiment mistakenly fired on him, wounding him severely. If General Lee ever loses Jackson, he would be losing his best general (→ 10).

Worst cavalry clash of war is a standoff

Brandy Station, Virginia, June 9

Perhaps, as one Confederate soldier said, Jeb Stuart's troops were all "worried out" from the grand reviews that they had been staging. For whatever reason, the Confederates did not do well against Major General Alfred Pleasonton and his eight brigades of blue-coated cavalry, who took them by surprise and almost surrounded them. It was a cavalry battle in the classic manner, with head-on charges, emptied saddles, rebel yells and breakneck riding. And when it was all over, 1,500 men were dead and the Southerners held the field. But their pride had been shaken.

West Virginia joins union as 35th state

Wheeling, West Virginia, June 20

West Virginia's admission to the union as the 35th state was approved today by President Lincoln. With Wheeling as its capital, the new state grew out of internal conflicts in Virginia that predate, but were exacerbated by, the Civil War. Since the 1700's, the frontiersmen and farmers of the western region have resented political and economic domination by the rich planters of the east. Some had wanted to call the new state Kanawha, for the valley of that name. West Virginia will be required to abolish slavery gradually.

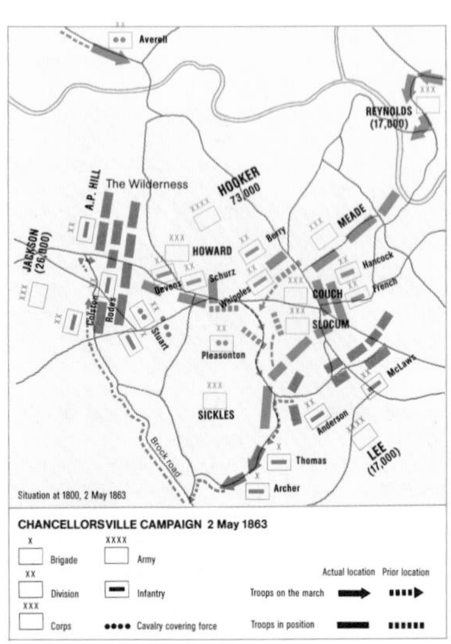

The campaign at Chancellorsville: positions as of 6 p.m. on May 2.

Stonewall Jackson, a Confederate hero for his many tactical victories.

Stonewall Jackson, hero of South, dies

Guiney Station, Virginia, May 10

The best tactical commander that General Lee had, Thomas Jonathan "Stonewall" Jackson, died today at the age of 39. He died of wounds he received at the battle of Chancellorsville four days ago. Though his left arm was amputated successfully, pneumonia set in and he fell into a coma in a little cottage where his surgeons had moved him. He came out of his delirium and said he "wanted to cross the river and rest under the shade of those trees." Then he died (→ June 3).

800 Negroes freed by Harriet Tubman

South Carolina, June 2

Mrs. Harriet Tubman, the former slave whom other slaves call "Moses" because of her efforts to free them, led a group of Negro soldiers up the Combahee River today. Familiar with the territory, she brought her troops to plantations undetected; they set fire to the mansions and liberated an estimated 800 slaves. Mrs. Tubman helps Union General David Hunter by performing duties ranging from the menial – she has been cook and laundress – to the magnitudinous.

Desperate Gettysburg battle forces Lee's retreat

Gettysburg, Pennsylvania, July 3

After three days of the bloodiest fighting of the war, the Army of the Potomac has finally scored a decisive victory against its tormentor, the formidable Robert E. Lee and his Army of Northern Virginia.

Today, the third day, saw the worst fighting as General Lee sent 14,000 men, under General George Pickett, against the Federal center, where they were repulsed with terrible carnage. Only half of Pickett's men returned to their lines after the charge. The attack on the Union center was preceded by the biggest artillery duel of the war; Lee had concentrated 150 cannons in front of his army and, at 3 p.m., all of them began firing. Union soldiers responded with all their cannons and, for a while, 200 guns were firing at once. Both lines were obscured by vast clouds of gunsmoke, shot and shell. And at the center of the cloud, men, caissons and horses were being blown to bits.

Some 20 minutes after the guns stopped firing, the divisions under Pickett formed a battle line a mile wide. It may have been the most spectacular sight in the history of warfare. The Confederate army began its advance, red battle flags snapping in the wind and the hot July sun flashing on thousands of swords and bayonets. The Southerners had nearly a mile of open fields to cross to get at the Federals, and the bluecoats simply tore them to shreds. A few hundred men reached the Union lines, but they were killed or captured. General Lewis Armisted died at the high-water mark with his hand on a Union cannon. As the beaten and wounded men returned to the Confederate lines, Lee, astride his horse Traveler, kept repeating, "It's all my fault, it's all my fault."

Major General George Meade had command of the Army of the Potomac for only a few days when he began to look for Lee's army, which invaded Pennsylvania last month. Lee began concentrating his forces near the closest crossroads, at Gettysburg.

In a way, it all began with shoes. Confederate General Heth had been told that there were shoes for sale at Gettysburg, and his men needed shoes. He asked General Ambrose Hill if there was any reason that he couldn't get those shoes. Hill replied, "None in the world."

On July 1, the Federals had the worst of it, being forced back on some hills and a long ridge south of the town. The following day, Lee pounded at the Union army on both flanks and especially at the far left, which was anchored by two small hills called Little and Big Round Top. Terrible struggles ensued at the Peach Orchard, the Wheatfield and Devil's Den. But the Union generals, especially Meade, did not panic, and made the right decisions, delivering reinforcements where they were needed. Southern casualties came to 20,000 men and the North lost some 23,000 during the three days of the battle (→ Nov. 20).

General Meade in charge, the Army of the Potomac does battle at Gettysburg.

In desperation, Southern troops storm the Union lines in Pickett's Charge.

Gettysburg, Pennsylvania, July 4. *The aftermath: "A Harvest of Death." Photo by Timothy O'Sullivan captures Confederate dead at Gettysburg.*

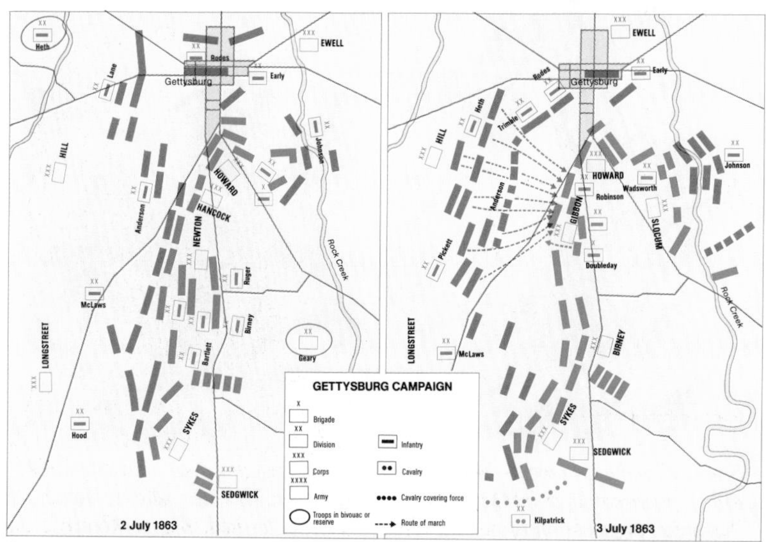

Positions on evening of July 2 (left) and Pickett's charge, July 3 (right).

Grant wins Vicksburg, splitting South

Admiral David Porter's ironclad warships keep withering gunfire trained on the Confederate garrison at Vicksburg. His gunboats Queen of the West and Indianola menaced Confederate shipping on the Mississippi with a series of daring runs past the Vicksburg batteries in February and March. Confederate warships later seized the Queen and destroyed the Indianola.

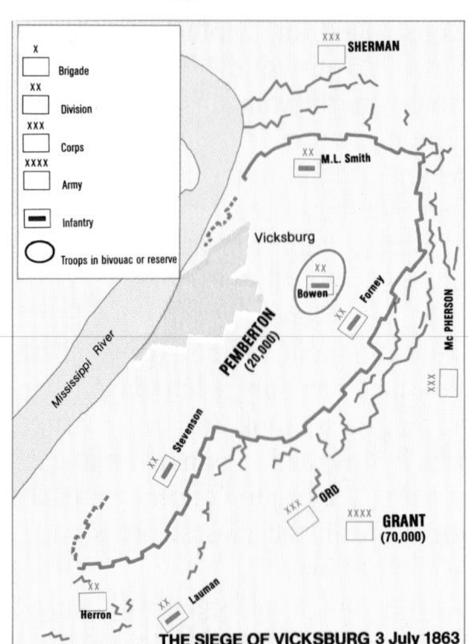

The siege of Vicksburg. By July 3, the city was surrounded.

Vicksburg, Mississippi, July 4

Confederate forces under General Joseph Pemberton today surrendered unconditionally to Ulysses S. Grant, commanding general of the Federal armies that have besieged Vicksburg since May. The Southern defeat is catastrophic. With Union forces now in possession of this strategic town on the Mississippi River, the Confederacy is effectively split in two. Long dependent on Louisiana, Texas and the trans-Mississippi west for supplies, equipment and men for its eastern armies, the Confederacy is effectively cut off from these invaluable resources, while Union forces now have absolute control of the north-south waterway that traverses Dixie.

Grant had originally planned to attack Vicksburg, the last Confederate stronghold on the Mississippi, from a position north of the city, But because of the difficult terrain, bayous and swamps, he decided to move his men south of the town, along the west bank of the river. In the bold move of April 30, he ferried his huge army across the Mississippi and cut the vital railroad line that linked the powerful Confederate army under General Joseph Johnston at Jackson with Pemberton's forces at Vicksburg. On May 16, Grant soundly defeated Pemberton at the battle of Champion's Hill and drove the remaining Confederate forces into Vicksburg. Then, on May 22, he tried two massive frontal assaults against the Southern forces there, but he turned back after suffering severe losses. Grant next besieged Vicksburg and battered the city with his heavy guns. Pemberton, with his troops low on food and ammunition and with all hopes of relief by Johnston dashed, appealed to Grant for terms of surrender. But the Union general turned down his plea yesterday, saying that he would accept nothing less than unconditional surrender (→Nov. 25).

Leader of Morgan's Raiders is captured

New Lisbon, Ohio, July 26

Union forces have finally corraled John Hunt Morgan and his marauding cavalrymen, ending a 24-day rampage through Indiana and Ohio. His Raiders captured 6,000, escaped from 14,000 regulars, destroyed 34 bridges and dozens of rail lines. A Kentucky gentleman, Morgan is never caught less than impeccably dressed or mounted, even in battle. His exploits are legend. Union jails force recalcitrant prisoners to sit astride a tall saw horse called "Morgan's Mule." The horseman's activities in July of last year led President Lincoln to remark, "They are having a stampede in Kentucky" (→Nov. 28).

Troops retaliate for Minnesota killings

Whitestone Hill, N.D., Sept. 3

General Alfred Sully and 2,000 men under his command killed 200 Sioux Indian men, women and children as they fled from their camp near Maple Creek today. The attack was said to be in retaliation for the Santee Sioux raids in Minnesota last year. The Santee had been denied government annuities, and many white settlers died in ensuing attacks. Sully took 156 prisoners and destroyed the Indian camp.

Snakes in the Midwest. Many Northern Republicans fear that their war effort is threatened by Midwestern Democrats who are said to favor a "vigorous prosecution of peace." They are often termed "Copperheads."

Quantrill's Raiders strike at Kansas town

Lawrence, Kansas, Aug. 21

The band of pro-Confederates known as Quantrill's Raiders struck again today. At dawn, some 450 mounted guerrillas descended on the peaceful town of Lawrence. Racing wildly through the streets, the raiders looted stores and pistol-whipped any residents who happened to get in their way. As Quantrill yelled, "Kill, kill, Lawrence must be cleansed," his band murdered every man in the two squads of Negro Federal troopers stationed here. When Quantrill heard that a regular Union cavalry force was approaching, he and his band rode out of town and made their escape. But by then, the raiders had killed some 150 residents.

William Clarke Quantrill, who once was an Ohio schoolteacher, is known for his pro-slavery sentiments. Some insiders say he relies heavily on the advice of two of his lieutenants, Frank and Jesse James, and on a couple of men known simply as the Younger Brothers. Many who know him say that ever since Quantrill was expelled from Lawrence before the war because of his activities there, he had sworn vengeance on the town and its citizens. Last year he promised that any "bushwackers" who joined him in his attack on Lawrence would get "more revenge and more money there than anywhere else." Local townsmen are wondering where Quantrill is likely to strike next.

Negro troops attack fort; one wins medal

Fort Wagner is stormed by the 54th Massachusetts (Colored) Regiment.

Charleston, S.C., July 18

Badly wounded twice during the attack, Sergeant William H. Carney of Company C, 54th Massachusetts Colored Infantry, has earned the Congressional Medal of Honor for his bravery in leading troops in the Battle of Fort Wagner. Early in the assault, the standard-bearer for the Union troops was killed; Sergeant Carney picked up the fallen flag and spurred his company on.

Negro troops have only been a part of Union forces since January 1, when the Emancipation Proclamation announced that Negro volunteers would be accepted. Although most Negroes who volunteer for service are placed in the federalized United States Colored Troops, the 54th Massachusetts Colored Infantry, which led the attack on Fort Wagner, is a separate regiment. Standards for admitting Negroes to the army are very high and Negro troops already have a reputation for bravery and exemplary service. As General Ullman has remarked, "They are far more earnest than we ... They know the deep stake they have in the issue ... "

Anti-draft riots hit N.Y.

New York City, July 17

To the cry of "rich man's war, poor man's fight," a virulent anti-draft demonstration erupted into four days of mass terror here this week, as deep-rooted racial and class hatred ignited in rioting, lynchings and arson. "The bloody week" may have cost 1,000 lives.

Tension began to mount Monday morning, July 13, as about 4,000 men marched to the draft drawing. The angry men were mostly poor Irish laborers embittered by the Conscription Act's clause allowing the well-to-do to buy their way out of military service. Many also fear the war will send an influx of Negroes north to threaten their jobs. When the first names were drawn, the crowd surged forward and police opened fire.

First the draft building was set afire; then the furious crowd went hunting for more targets. As it grew larger, separate factions split off, looting, burning mansions and seizing guns. The Brooks Brothers store and the pro-war *Tribune* were ransacked. At night, lynch mobs terrorized Negro sections and the Colored Orphan Asylum was set afire.

On Tuesday and Wednesday, as many as 70,000 people may have been swept into the spiraling "carnival of violence," as one observer called it. Order was restored yesterday, but not until five regiments from Gettysburg had moved in with cannons and Gatling guns.

Looting an East Side drugstore.

Fires of hatred: hanging a Negro.

Great Coat, for Union men.

Writing home: A drummer boy finds a moment of repose in the field.

Overcoat, Confederate cavalry.

Union troops repulsed

Bragg crosses Chickamauga Creek to do battle with Rosecrans's army.

Chickamauga, Georgia, Sept. 20

"A mad, irregular battle" is how one Federal officer described it, "very much resembling guerrilla warfare on a vast scale." It could also have been described as a brawl. The Union got the worst of it, being hammered for two days by General Braxton Bragg's army in the rock and scrub and sandy hills of northern Georgia. Major General William Rosecrans blundered in a manner typical of the Union generals: winning the battle in your head before the battle ever begins. "Old Rosey" thought that he was chasing General Bragg's army into Georgia just as Bragg was getting ready to smash into the divided Union army. Rosecrans would have been destroyed, but the Confederates, for once, failed to act fast, and he had time to get his forces together just as they were attacked. On September 19, he was struck by the soldiers of General Nathan Bedford Forrest's cavalry, who fought dismounted as infantrymen. The armies battled on until twilight and, in the morning, the Confederates attacked once again, pounding at the Union's center, which was under the command of General George H. Thomas. He refused to run and now he is being called "the Rock of Chickamauga." Nevertheless, in the end he had no choice but to retreat.

Grant wins in Tennessee

Hooker storms Lookout Mountain in the "battle above the clouds."

Chattanooga, Tennessee, Nov. 25

With a magnificent charge that no one ordered, and that was compared to General Pickett's charge with different results, General Ulysses S. Grant's Army of the Cumberland drove the Confederates from the high ground above Chattanooga today. Grant and his generals looked on with amazement as the troops in the center of his line, who were only supposed to advance and put pressure on the Confederates, seemed to be pulled along by their own momentum until the Southern line was swept away. Now Grant found himself holding all of Missionary Ridge, a position that had appeared to be impregnable. Some of the best soldiers in the Confederacy ran when the Yankees got "too far into our innards," as one Southerner put it.

The assault was magnificent: There were four divisions in a line two miles wide, with dressed ranks and battle flags held aloft as they advanced. All this took place in a natural amphitheater created by Lookout Valley, where everyone on both sides could see what was taking place. After the battle was over, the Union troops celebrated atop the ridge. Waving captured Confederate flags, the bluecoats stood astride the cannons of the enemy that should have blown them to bits, but hadn't (→Apr. 4, 1864).

Morgan and six others break out of prison

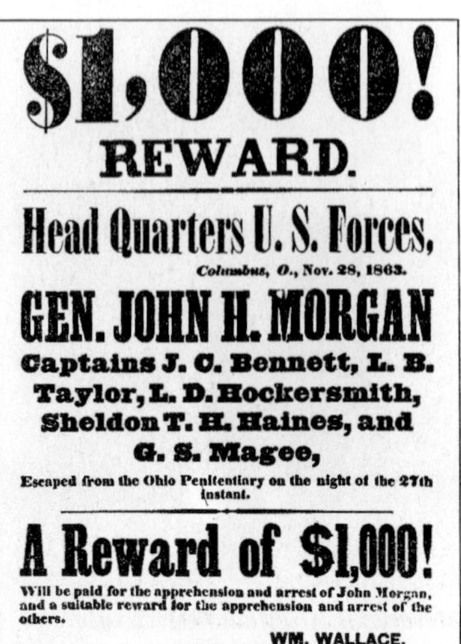
$1,000!

REWARD.

Head Quarters U. S. Forces,

Columbus, O., Nov. 28, 1863.

GEN. JOHN H. MORGAN

Captains J. C. Bennett, L. B. Taylor, L. D. Hockersmith, Sheldon T. H. Haines, and G. S. Magee,

Escaped from the Ohio Penitentiary on the night of the 27th instant.

A Reward of $1,000!

Will be paid for the apprehension and arrest of John Morgan, and a suitable reward for the apprehension and arrest of the others.

WM. WALLACE,
Colonel 15th O. V. I. Commanding.

Columbus, Ohio, Nov. 28

Last night, in a daring escape, Confederate General John Hunt Morgan and six of his men fled for the South after tunneling their way out of the Ohio State Penitentiary. Hunt spent the summer raiding towns in Kentucky, Ohio and Indiana, finally surrendering to Federal forces in Salineville, Ohio, on July 26. Approximately 2,400 Confederate troops were killed or captured by the Union as a result. Prisson officials feel that the men escaped using only knives and spoons to dig through their cell floors, allowing them access to an underground air chamber.

Sherman's men force Bragg into retreat at Missionary Ridge, Chattanooga.

On hallowed ground, Lincoln's Gettysburg Address

Gettysburg, Pennsylvania, Nov. 20

Looking out over a battlefield still strewn with the carcasses of horses shot more than four months ago, President Abraham Lincoln dedicated a cemetery for the nation's neglected war dead yesterday. He spoke, according to a report in *Harper's Weekly,* "from the heart to the heart." Indeed, Lincoln has suffered in sympathy with his divided nation. En route to Gettysburg, he confronted a man who had lost his son in battle there. "When I think of the sacrifices of life yet to be offered," the President reflected, "and the heart and homes yet to be desolated before this dreadful war is over, my heart is like lead within me, and I feel at times like hiding in deep darkness." This deep personal grief animated Lincoln's remarks at Gettysburg. Words can do little to stop the casualties that mount daily. Nonetheless, the crowd of 15,000 on Cemetery Hill strained to hear some consolation.

"Fourscore and seven years ago," Lincoln began in his high-pitched monotone, "our fathers brought forth .. a new nation, conceived in liberty and dedicated to the proposition that all men are created equal. Now we are engaged in a great civil war, testing whether that nation – or any nation, so conceived and so dedicated – can long endure." Lincoln exuded reverence for the soldiers who died at Gettysburg five months ago. In the ambiguous language of political oratory, he appeared to declare the aim of their struggle to be the abolition of slavery. "These dead shall not have died in vain," he concluded, "that this nation, under God, shall have a new birth of freedom, and that government of the people, by the people, for the people, shall not perish from the earth."

The moment passed, the listeners strangely unresponsive, the applause formal and restrained. Perhaps they were numbed by the two-hour oration of the eminent politician, scholar and lecturer Edward Everett, who preceded Lincoln. The President himself worried to an aide, "It is a flat failure and the people are disappointed." But around the nation, the oracles of public opinion have responded in a highly partisan fashion. The *Chicago Times* called the speech "silly, flat and dishwatery," and accused Lincoln of bending history by insisting that the soldiers gave their lives for "a new birth of freedom." A newspaper in Richmond, Virginia, railed against the President for suggesting that thousands have died for "an abstraction." Indeed, in invoking the Declaration of Independence, President Lincoln not only called upon the symbols of nationalism, but also elevated the war to a moral level. In the end, the judgment of the *Chicago Tribune* may come closest to the truth. The President's remarks, it predicts, "will live among the annals of man."

Gettysburg: Lincoln eulogizes the dead, martyrs to "a new birth of freedom."

Gettysburg Address

Fourscore and seven years ago, our fathers brought forth on this continent a new nation, conceived in liberty and dedicated to the proposition that all men are created equal. Now we are engaged in a great civil war, testing whether that nation – or any nation, so conceived and so dedicated – can long endure. We are met on a great battlefield of that war. We have come to dedicate a portion of that field as the final resting place for those who here gave their lives that that nation might live. It is altogether fitting and proper that we should do this. But in a larger sense, we cannot dedicate, we cannot consecrate, we cannot hallow, this ground. The brave men, living and dead, who struggled here, have consecrated it, far above our power to add or to detract. The world will very little note nor long remember what we say here; but it can never forget what they did here. It is for us, the living, rather, to be dedicated, here, to the unfinished work that they have thus far so nobly carried on. It is rather for us to be here dedicated to the great task remaining before us; that from these honored dead we take increased devotion to that cause for which they gave the last full measure of devotion; that we here highly resolve that these dead shall not have died in vain; that this nation, under God, shall have a new birth of freedom, and that government of the people, by the people, for the people, shall not perish from the earth.

Since the Emancipation Proclamation, slaves liberated by Union armies are legally free. "Lincoln and the Contrabands" by J.L.G. Ferris.

1864

Lincoln

Mississippi, Jan. 14. Union General William Tecumseh Sherman seizes Meridian, destroying everything in his path (→June 27).

Charleston, Illinois, March 28. 100 Copperheads attack furloughed Union soldiers, killing five.

Washington, D.C., Apr. 8. Senate approves 13th Amendment by vote of 38 to 6 (→Jan. 31, 1865).

Washington, D.C., Apr. 22. In attempt to cut off South's dwindling manpower supply, General Grant orders halt to all prisoner exchanges (→Aug.)

Richmond, Apr. 30. President Davis's 5-year-old son Joe dies after fall in Confederate White House.

Cleveland, Ohio, May 31. Radical Republicans, unhappy with Lincoln's moderate stance on slavery, nominate General John C. Fremont for president (→June 7).

Washington, D.C., June 4. Government passes act guaranteeing each immigrant a 12-month employment contract.

United States, June 28. Fugitive Slave Laws repealed.

Boise, Idaho, Aug. 4. Merchants begin closing shops on Sundays, giving frontier town a more staid appearance.

Washington, D.C., Aug. 23. Abraham Lincoln considers electoral defeat "exceedingly probable" (→Sept. 17).

Cleveland, Ohio, Sept. 17. John C. Fremont withdraws bid for presidency, in effort to assure a unified Republican ticket (→Nov. 8).

Washington, D.C., Dec. 6. President Lincoln names Salmon P. Chase, ex-Treasury Secretary, fifth Chief Justice of Supreme Court.

Washington, D.C., Dec. 28. Law enacted, forbidding racial discrimination in hiring of letter carriers.

Georgia. Thousands of Union prisoners die of disease, starvation and exposure in overcrowded Andersonville Prison (→Nov. 10, 1865).

Oklahoma. Confederate Indian Cavalry Brigade led by Brigadier General Stand Watie, only Indian general of war.

Colorado. Gold rush dries up as many lodes run out.

Grant and Lee clash at Wilderness

Wilderness, Virginia, May 6

General Grant's hopes of striking decisively at General Lee's army have been dashed during two days of savage fighting in the thick undergrowth of the Wilderness.

Hampered by darkness and blinded by the smoke from thousands of rifles, soldiers on both sides fired wildly. The musket fire ignited the dry, dense brush in a dozen places. Many of the wounded suffered agonizing deaths as the forests burned. Grant and Lee are both claiming victory, but the Federals lost more than 17,000 men. Lee, who was outnumbered two to one, had about 8,000 casualties.

The Army of the Potomac, under the command of George "Snapping Turtle" Meade, crossed the Rapidan River on May 4. Lee lay in wait until the Federals were across yesterday, then struck in the undergrowth. Two of his corps attacked from the west near Wilderness Tavern. They dented the Federals' line, but were later forced to retreat and erect new defenses. This morning, the Confederates were pushed back to Lee's headquarters. He attempted to lead his men into battle, but he fell back when they shoute "Go back, General Lee, go back! Nevertheless, as the day progres ed, the Confederates made gains both ends of the front (→11).

Fierce Battle of the Wilderness in Virginia. Lithograph by Kurz & Allison.

Grant, taking over Federal forces, plans all-out drive to end war

Culpeper, Virgina, Apr. 4

Lieutenant General Ulysses S. Grant, who may rival President Lincoln in popularity, is planning a consolidated strike against Confederate forces in an all-out effort to win the war. As soon as he received his commission to command Union forces today, Grant increased the size of the Army of the Potomac in an effort to defeat General Lee in Virginia. The commander of the army, General George Meade, offered to step down, but Grant ordered him to stay on. "It is men who wait to be selected," Grant said, "and not those who seek, from whom we may always expect the most efficient service." Grant placed General William Tecumse Sherman in charge of forces in th West. According to Grant, he ha carte blanche from Lincoln, wh stated that "he had never professe to be a military man or to kno how campaigns should be conduc ed" (→May 6).

General Grant. Photo by Brady.

Foster, a beloved songwriter, dies poor

New York City, Jan. 13

America's greatest songwriter, Stephen Foster, died in Bellevue Hospital today at 37. The life that produced many of the nation's best-loved songs – and more than 200 in all – was marked early on by phenomenal success and a happy marriage. But Foster couldn't handle money and he always seemed in need of quick cash. In 1857, he sold all future song rights for about $1,900. His marriage fell apart; he started to drink heavily and his health ebbed. A native of Pittsburgh, Foster spent his final years in a hotel on the Bowery, where he wrote to the very end of his life. One of his last songs, and one of his most popular, was "Beautiful Dreamer."

Cover of an 1858 song sheet.

Armies clash 5 days at Spotsylvania

Apex of Lee's V-shaped defense fends off Union troops. Painting by Thulstrup.

Spotsylvania, Virginia, May 11

As night fell on this once-tranquil community, exhausted soldiers on both sides crept back to their camps. Many wounded have been left to die between the lines of battle. Over five days, the struggle for control of the crossroads in front of the courthouse here has turned into what may be the bloodiest battle of the war. Yet neither side can claim victory outright. General Grant's forces have suffered more casualties by far, but General Lee may find it harder to replace his fallen heroes. Grant shows no intention of falling back. In a letter to General Henry W. Halleck, he wrote, "I propose to fight it out on this line if it takes all summer."

The race for the crossroads began in earnest the night of May 7. The Federals approached from the north of the Po River. Lee, who had anticipated the maneuver, ordered his men to march to the courthouse on the southern bank of the Po. Despite the bruising the Federals took in the Wilderness, their spirits were said to be "of the highest pitch of animation." The Union forces lost the race to the crossroads, however, and the battle became more difficult as each day went by. The Confederates are still outnumbered, but they are determined not to lose on their home turf (→ June 3).

Lincoln to call up 500,000 more men

Washington, D.C., August

President Lincoln issued a decree in February to obtain more soldiers. Today, the Confederacy, suffering a dire shortage of men, declared it would begin drafting men between the ages of 17 and 50. The Union's call for 500,000 troops follows last October's draft of 300,000 men.

The President signed the first conscription law in March 1863, with an exemption clause that allowed men to buy their way out of military duty. The poor saw this as unfair and riots erupted. Last month, racial tension in New York City exploded. Impoverished Irishmen showed their contempt for the draft and its exemption system by staging a bloody assault against Negroes, believing that they were responsible for the war. Some people felt that the draft was counterproductive. For example, General Henry Halleck remarked, "It takes more soldiers to enforce it than we get from its enforcement."

Tensions were eased as the Union acted to reduce exemptions. The manpower needs of the Union are expected to be met (→ Jan. 11, 1865).

The endless consumption of human lives. "Trooper Meditating Beside a Grave" by Winslow Homer.

Southern sub sinks with ship it torpedoed

Charleston, S.C., Feb. 17

In what is considered the first "successful" attack by a submarine warship, the Confederate sub H.L. Hunley has destroyed the Union's Housatonic. But the attack spelled disaster for the crew of the Hunley as well because the submarine became lodged in the hole made by its spar torpedo and the Confederate ship also was lost.

Submarine warfare seems a desperate attempt by the Confederates to develop a secret weapon that might give them an advantage over the better-equipped Union navy. Ultimately, the project has cost the Confederates more lives than it has cost the Union. Originally christened the Pioneer, the Southern submersible, based on earlier vessels developed by the steamboat inventor Robert Fulton, sank with a test crew and its builder, H.L. Hunley, killing everyone aboard. The craft was raised, rechristened the Hunley and tried four more times. Each time, the entire crew drowned. The sixth trip, attacking the Housatonic, was therefore a relative success.

Deadly submarine Hunley. Painting (1863) by Conrad Wise Chapman.

Confederates seize fort, slay Negroes

Fort Pillow, Tennessee, Apr. 13

Confederate troops slaughtered 238 Negro soldiers along with dozens of white soldiers, and even women and children yesterday and today at Fort Pillow in what is emerging as one of the war's worst atrocities.

Survivors said that most of the 262 Negro soldiers in the Sixth Heavy Artillery were killed, many of them as they were begging for mercy after surrendering. Three-quarters of the 557-man force, including white troops of the 13th Tennessee Union Cavalry, were reportedly wiped out.

The massacre began after Confederate Major General Nathan B. Forrest called a truce and demanded that the fort surrender. While his white flag flew, his troops crept in. When his demand was rejected by Federal forces, the Confederate troops took over the fort, shouting, "No quarter!"

Witnesses said that the Union troops surrendered, but were shot or bayonetted as rapidly as they gave up. The slaughter went on until dark and resumed this morning.

Lee halts bloody assault

Cold Harbor, Virginia, June 3

General Grant had hoped to overwhelm General Lee today in a final battle for Virginia, but his men knew better. And they were right. Thousands of Federal soldiers were killed in a matter of minutes, and Lee remains entrenched in fortifications just six miles from the Confederate capital of Richmond. For the past month, Grant has made dogged progress in his war against Lee, but today was not his finest hour. Said one Confederate general, "This is not war, this is murder."

For the past few days, the opposing armies have been skirmishing along a seven-mile front from the Totopotomy Creek to the Chickahominy River. Grant, unable to break through the center of the Confederate line, was also stymied as he tried to maneuver around Lee's right flank. He was reluctant to move any farther to the southeast for fear of becoming trapped in swampland. Yesterday afternoon, Grant decided that a frontal assault on Lee's forces was the only option. The attack was delayed until dawn today because of objections that it would be suicidal. As the Federals jumped out of their trenches, many had written their names on slips of paper pinned to their backs so their families could be informed of their deaths. One Union soldier was so certain he would die that the last entry in his diary read, "June 3. Cold Harbor. I was killed" (→21).

Collecting remains at Cold Harbor. "This is not war, this is murder."

Union victory off France

The Alabama and the Kearsarge do battle in the English Channel.

Cherbourg, France, June 19

After a sharp fight that lasted a little over an hour, the warship Alabama, the best-known of the Confederate raiders, has been sunk by the Kearsarge, commanded by Captain John Ancrum Winslow.

The Kearsarge, a two-engine sloop commissioned two years ago, was at anchor in the Scheldt River in the Netherlands when Captain Winslow heard that the Alabama had put into Cherbourg for repairs. Setting sail at once, he arrived here five days ago and sent a challenge to Captain Raphael Semmes of the Alabama, inviting him to come out and fight. The challenge was accepted and a crowd of 15,000 spectators, many of them arriving on special excursion trains from Paris, gathered to watch the duel from the cliffs.

After the battle, Captain Semmes and 40 other survivors were rescued by an English yacht anchored nearby, and all but 10 of the other crewmen were picked up by local French boats or by the Kearsarge.

The Alabama was constructed in Liverpool and though its officers were Confederates, most of the crew were English. During its two years of service, the Alabama inflicted tremendous damage, capturing and destroying well over 60 American merchantmen.

Montana Territory taken out of Idaho

Bannock, Montana, May 26

Residents of this remote area are celebrating their new status as a territory of the United States. Carved out of the northeastern section of the old Idaho Territory, Montana has chosen little Bannock as its capital and Sidney Edgerton as its first Governor. Whether the settlers here are pro-Confederate or pro-Union, they will have to abide by and pay allegiance to the law of the United States. As with Dakota, Colorado and all the territories created thus far during the war, the federal government insists that its rule be paramount – with no exceptions.

Republicans choose Lincoln once again

Washington, D.C., June 7

Republicans, meeting in Baltimore for the first time, today nominated President Lincoln for a second term and chose Andrew Johnson of Tennessee as his running mate. The Lincoln nomination, at what Republicans called their National Union convention, comes at a time when the nation is still engaged in a bloody Civil War, and there had been rumors that the party might turn to General Ulysses S. Grant as its nominee. However, what Grant support there might have been vanished after his loss of 7,000 men in the clash with Confederates at Cold Harbor (→Aug. 23).

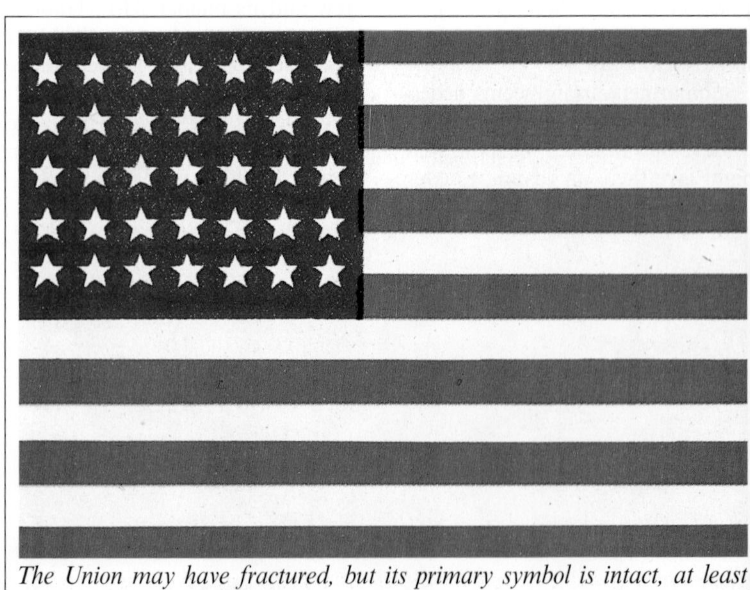

The Union may have fractured, but its primary symbol is intact, at least in the North. President Lincoln and Unionists, with hope and tenacity, still fly a 35-star flag that includes a star for each of the 11 Confederate states.

Sherman's march halted

Armies clash in Battle of Kennesaw Mountain. Lithograph by Kurz & Allison.

Marietta, Georgia, June 27

General William Tecumseh Sherman's march through Georgia was stopped in its tracks on the slopes of Kennesaw Mountain today. Confederate forces, after days of fighting, turned back the Union army, inflicting heavy casualties. Confederate General Joseph E. Johnston placed the Federal loss in killed and wounded at 6,000. Sherman put his loss at 2,500. Sherman learned General Ulysses S. Grant's lesson at Cold Harbor three weeks ago – that well dug-in Confederate forces are impervious to frontal attack. Union forces fought bravely. One Confederate soldier said they seemed to "take death as coolly as if they were automatic or wooden men." Among the Union dead were Colonel Daniel McCook, one of Ohio's "fighting McCooks." He was the fourth member of the family to be killed in action.

Sherman had acknowledged that Johnston's dug-in position was "as dangerous to assault as a permanent fort." But he decided to make a fight of it. The dead piled up on the mountainside. One night, the armies called a truce to bury their dead. Soldiers from the two armies worked side by side, using boards from hardtack boxes as headstones for fallen comrades (→Nov. 16).

Yanks fail at Petersburg

Petersburg, Virginia, June 21

Exhausted Federal soldiers tumbled back into their trenches tonight, and their leaders were at a loss to explain why the badly outnumbered Confederates were still holding Petersburg. General Grant ordered a halt to the assaults and said, "I shall try to give the army a few days' rest, which they now stand much in need of." His dispirited soldiers seem even more humiliated than they were after the standoff at Cold Harbor.

Grant's strategy here was to seize Petersburg and use it as the "back door" to invade Richmond from the south. The effort began in promising fashion on June 15, when General W.F. "Baldy" Smith crossed the James River on a hastily constructed pontoon bridge. Within hours, Smith's men were breaching the Dimmock Line, the 10-mile-long stretch of forts and fieldworks that serve as the outer defenses of Petersburg. The advantage clearly lay with the Federals, but they failed to seize it. Instead of pushing on to Petersburg, Smith decided to await the arrival of three more Union corps. The delay was costly. Confederate reinforcements rushed to the breach, and then General Pierre Beauregard ordered his men to pull back to an impregnable line of defense closer to the city. For a while, the back door to Richmond was ajar, but it has been slammed shut in Grant's face (→Apr. 5, 1865).

Photographer Mathew Brady was at Petersburg during the battle.

The sounds of battle. A regimental fife and drum corps poses for Mathew Brady's camera. Their refrains are as much a part of the dissonance of the American Civil War as the percussive sounds of cannon and rifle fire.

Maximilian named Emperor of Mexico

Mexico City, June 10

Backed by the conservative and clerical Junta de Notables, and by a large French army, the 32-year-old Austrian Archduke Ferdinand Maximilian Joseph has been proclaimed Emperor of Mexico. The new ruler, who recently arrived here with his wife, Carlotta, is known to favor liberal reforms and had insisted that the offer of the throne be endorsed by a plebiscite. But many believe that had the plebiscite been carried out fairly it would have endorsed the republican regime of President Benito Juarez, who is currently holding out in Paso del Norte (→June 19, 1867).

Federal income tax is increased again

Washington, D.C., June 30

Earning money in America is becoming an expensive proposition. A floor amendment in Congress today raised the maximum Federal Income Tax to 10 percent if one earns over $10,000 a year. This second Internal Revenue Act comes in the face of a national debt well over $1.5 billion. There is now a 5 percent tax on income between $600 and $10,000 per year. Rep. Justin Morrill, a founder of the Republican Party and head of the House tax subcommittee, led the futile fight against the increase. The first Federal Income Tax was established in 1861 at 3 percent.

Sherman takes Atlanta, burns city, marches to sea

Sherman: "Atlanta is ours and fairly won." Lithograph by Kurz & Allison.

The ruin of Atlanta. Retreating General Hood burned arms caches and other supplies before Sherman's arrival. What he left standing, Sherman destroyed.

Atlanta, Nov. 16

Atlanta lay in smoldering ruins today as General William Tecumseh Sherman and his troops evacuated the city and headed eastward toward the Atlantic. After months of shelling and nearby battles, Atlanta became an inferno yesterday. Sherman was determined that this industrial and railroad center would no longer serve as a major supply center for the Confederacy.

The massive destruction began when troops destroyed a railroad roundhouse, piled the railroad depot high with wagons, tents and bedding and put the torch to them. The blaze at the railroad square spawned a firestorm. A foundry, an oil refinery, the Atlanta Hotel, theaters, stores, the fire stations and jail went up in flames. By nightfall, flames towered hundreds of feet in the air. All that remained were about 400 houses and a few larger buildings, most of them churches.

Sherman left the city early this morning, riding erectly as usual on his favorite mount, Sam, and smoking his ever-present cigar. In this city, the eccentric general is considered a "beast." Some newspaper reporters have said he is insane. But he is an idol to his troops and considered a brilliant military strategist. He has said the most humane way to end the war would be to end the South's power to resist.

The battle for Atlanta started in earnest July 20, when Confederate General John B. Hood attacked Sherman's forces at Peachtree Creek, north of the city. Confederate President Jefferson Davis had named Hood to replace General Joseph E. Johnston in Atlanta. Savage battles were fought outside the city, with probably the bloodiest fighting around Ezra Church. But Sherman's much larger forces soon approached the city from three sides and cut Hood's supply lines. On September 2, the Hood army retreated and General Sherman took over the city. He ordered residents to evacuate. Hood protested, but Sherman told him, "You might as well appeal against the thunderstorm as against the terrible hardships of war." More than any Southern city, Atlanta has come to know those hardships as Sherman continues his march (→ Dec. 24).

General Sherman. Photo by Brady.

Sherman marches through Georgia, cutting a swath of destruction. His 68,000 troops are living off the land and burning what they cannot carry.

Sherman's Yule gift to Lincoln: Savannah

Savannah, Georgia, Dec. 24

Elated by his army's capture of Savannah, General William Tecumseh Sherman fired off a telegram to President Lincoln today. "I beg to present you as a Christmas gift the city of Savannah," he wrote. The gift was accompanied, he said, by "150 heavy guns and plenty of ammunition, also about 25,000 bales of cotton." The guns and cotton were captured when the Union troops stormed Fort McAllister, the key to capture of the seaport, in the late afternoon of December 13. The assault lasted only 15 minutes. The United States flag went up over the fort at 5 p.m. Torpedoes buried in the ground surrounding the fort killed many Northerners.

Sherman armed Confederate prisoners with picks and spades and forced them to march in close formation around the fort. They could walk through the torpedoes or dig them up. "I could hardly help laughing at their stepping so gingerly along the road," said Sherman.

Confederate General William S. Hardee managed to get his 9,000 troops out of the city. They escaped over a makeshift bridge crossing the wide Savannah River. Hardee had been ordered to withdraw to avoid destruction of Savannah, the only city Sherman has spared.

;outherners enter Nashington briefly

Vashington, D.C., July 12

Confederate troops achieved a :unning psychological victory to-ay before withdrawing from the uter limits of the Union capital. 'hey advanced within shooting dis-ance of Fort Stevens and even sent ullets whizzing over the head of resident Lincoln, who had come › watch the advance of General ubal Early. "Old Jube" never oc-upied the city, but he did give ;eneral Grant a scare. Even a navy fficial admitted the episode was rather humiliating." In the past ıonth, Early has cleared the Shen-ndoah of Union forces and forced ;rant to rush thousands of men orth from Richmond (→Oct. 22).

'arragut shouts lefiance at Mobile

Aobile, Alabama, Aug. 5

Shouting "Damn the torpedoes – ull speed ahead," Admiral David ;. Farragut took Mobile Bay for he Union today. Farragut's fleet teamed through a harbor that had een mined with torpedoes and ained command of the port. His ousing cry came after one of his varships had been destroyed by . torpedo. The rest of the battle ine hesitated, but Farragut ordered hem "full speed ahead." The ad-niral's victory closes the port to rms shipments and other trade.

Admiral David G. Farragut (left).

Union forces ruin Nashville defenses

Nashville, Tennessee, Dec. 16

The impetuous and unpredictable General John B. Hood finally met his match over the last two days outside Nashville. His soldiers, exhausted by the zigzag march north from Atlanta and numbed by ice and storms, were soundly defeated by Union forces under the command of General George Thomas. Hood had 35,000 men when he left Atlanta at the beginning of September. By today, half of his Confederate soldiers were dead and the Federals were in firm control all along the western front.

Thomas had been under intense pressure for 10 days from General Grant to attack Hood. On December 11, Grant telegraphed angrily: "Let there be no further delay." When Thomas hesitated because of an ice storm, Grant set off for Nashville to take personal command of Federal forces. Thomas acted before Grant arrived, and his caution is being credited for the victory.

Hood's goal when he left Atlanta was to draw Federal forces away from General Sherman. When Sherman refused to bite, Hood unrealistically set out to defeat the Federals in Tennessee and Kentucky and then join Lee in Virginia.

Battle of Nashville, decisive Southern defeat. Lithograph by Kurz & Allison.

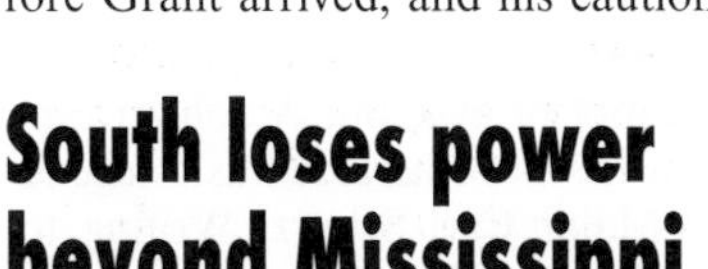

South loses power beyond Mississippi

Westport, Missouri, Oct. 23

Confederate forces under General Sterling Price were soundly defeated today in the biggest engagement yet on the western front. Samuel Curtis, the Union's commanding general in Kansas, moved into the area last night and set up a line along Brush Creek. Price, who was also being squeezed to the rear, could have retreated to the south, but he elected instead to attack Curtis. The Federals won the day and sent the Confederates scurrying.

Price crossed from Arkansas into Missouri a month ago with 12,000 men. He lost 1,500 of them in a vicious battle at Pilot Knob on September 27. Price then began to advance toward St. Louis, but he changed his mind when he learned that Federals under Andrew Jackson Smith had arrived there first. Price then turned to the west and achieved a string of small victories as he took Hermann and Boonville. State militiamen tried to stop him, but they were too disorganized. Price became more confident as the days went by, but confidence alone was an insufficient weapon today.

Confederates swept out of Shenandoah

Cedar Creek, Virginia, Oct. 22

Three months after his daring foray into Washington, the tables have been turned on Jubal Early. His Confederate forces were soundly defeated by General Sheridan. The Southerners had only half the number of casualties, but they have now been swept from the Shenandoah Valley. Sheridan received a congratulatory telegram from President Lincoln. "With great pleasure, I tender to you and your brave army the thanks of the nation and my own personal admiration and gratitude for the month's operations," Lincoln wrote. Sheridan's success began last month, when he defeated Early at Winchester. His victories have boosted Northern morale and are helping Union politicians at the polls (→Nov. 25).

General Sheridan rallies to turn disaster into triumph at Cedar Creek.

President Lincoln elected to second term

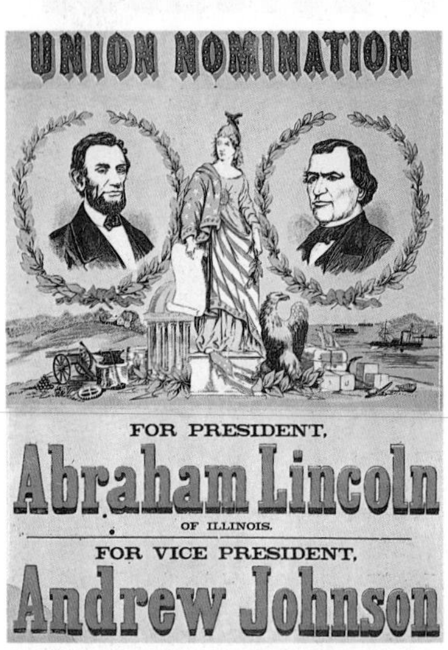

UNION NOMINATION
FOR PRESIDENT,
Abraham Lincoln
OF ILLINOIS.
FOR VICE PRESIDENT,
Andrew Johnson

For Union: Lincoln and Johnson.

Washington, D.C., Nov. 8

President Lincoln was re-elected today, soundly defeating General George B. McClellan, the man he relieved of his army command earlier in the war. President Lincoln carried 22 states with 212 electoral votes while McClellan won just Delaware, Kentucky and New Jersey to claim 21 electoral votes. The popular vote, however, was much closer: 2,330,552 for Lincoln; 1,835,985 for McClellan. Andrew Johnson of Tennessee was elected Vice President on Lincoln's ticket.

President Lincoln was noticeably relieved by the outcome. Often, in recent months, he had expressed concern over a possible defeat. At one point in his campaign, he mused that it is not wise to swap horses while crossing a stream, adding: "I am not so poor a horse that they might not make a botch of it in trying to swap."

Until mid-September, President Lincoln found himself campaigning against not one but two generals. In addition to General McClellan, the candidate of the Democratic Party, the Radical Republicans had selected General John Charles Fremont as their candidate. In September, Fremont quit and swung his support to Lincoln. Yet, even today, despite recent Union army victories, Lincoln expressed some fear that he might lose (→ March 4, 1865).

"Lincoln, the rail-splitter" by Ferris.

Nevada becomes 36th state in union

Washington, D.C., Oct. 31

The former Territory of Nevada was no sooner officially accepted as the 36th state in the union today than many political observers were discussing the implications of its quick admission. Because at this point the presidential election next month still appears to be a toss-up, Washington insiders believe it is more than a coincidence that Nevada has been admitted at this particular moment. Cynical observers will tell you that President Lincoln is in need of Nevada's votes – and any marginal states he can land – for re-election.

James brothers tied to Centralia killings

Centralia, Missouri, Sept. 27

Pro-Confederate guerrillas under "Bloody Bill" Anderson attacked and robbed the Centralia railroad station today. When they finally rode out of town, at least 24 people lay dead. It is reported that the murderous band included the James brothers, Frank and Jesse. It is not known whether the Anderson group is connected with Quantrill's Raiders, who sacked and burned Lawrence, Kansas, last year. But observers say it is likely that the James brothers are associated with, perhaps working hand in hand with both groups.

Abe Lincoln viewed as man for the ages

Washington, D.C., Oct. 12

Many love him as a man of honor and purpose. Others despise him as the root of evil. But Abraham Lincoln has been heralded as a legend by Major Carl Schurz. Writing to the lawyer Theodore Petrasch, he said: "I will make a prophecy that will perhaps sound strange at the moment. In 50 years, perhaps sooner, Lincoln's name will stand written on the honor roll of the American Republic next to that of Washington, and there it will remain."

First curve ball by a pitcher noted

Brooklyn, New York

Scientists tut-tutted the report that a pitcher was able to throw a baseball that curved on its way to home plate. An optical illusion, they said. Yet, those who saw William "Candy" Cummings pitch against the Atlantics say that the Brooklyn Stars hurler put a curve on the ball. The "curve" took on extra importance coming six years after the rulebook added the "called strike" – a pitch in the strike zone that the batter does not swing at.

Attempt to burn New York City fails

New York City, Nov. 25

Confederate agents set 19 fires here this evening in an apparent attempt to spread a conflagration in revenge for the Shenandoah Valley campaign. The arsonists struck most of the city's major hotels, including the Astor House, the Everett and New England House, as well as the Barnum Museum and river wharfs. The raiders used improperly mixed phosphorous incendiaries, however, and only the Barnum Museum burned with any intensity. All the fires were doused by midnight, with no injuries reported. But some people fear such acts may become common as the Confederate battlefield position grows more desperate.

Thoughts about war by Bryant, Whittier

Boston

Not surprisingly, the Civil War that has rent this nation for the better part of three years now has provided grist for many a poet's mill. William Cullen Bryant, America's best-loved bard, has written a volume called *Thirty Poems*, many of which express his belief in the justness of the Union's cause. John Greenleaf Whittier, a longtime activist for abolition, is another popular poet whose muse has often served his political ideals. Whittier's new volume, *In War Time and Other Poems*, sings the praises of Barbara Frietchie, a Maryland housewife, along with other heroes and heroines of the conflict.

Paris. *Isolated from the tempest at home, James McNeill Whistler has painted "Little White Girl: Symphony in White, II" (1864).*

A moment of repose. Removed from the terror of the battlefield, Mathew Brady captures a Civil War belle for posterity.

Faces that shaped the fate of a divided nation

George B. McClellan, Union General-in-Chief, Nov. 1861-Nov. 1862.

Joseph "Fighting Joe" Hooker, led Army of Potomac Jan.-June 1863.

George Meade, commander of Army of Potomac, June 1863-April 1865.

Ulysses S. Grant, Union General-in-Chief, March 1864-April 1865.

Nurse Clara Barton, "angel of the battlefield," through Brady's lens.

"Ulysses S. Grant and his Generals" (1865) by O.P.H. Balling. Union generals included William T. Sherman, Philip Sheridan and George Thomas.

Mathew Brady braved gunfire to chronicle the war on daguerreotype.

Pierre Gustave Toutant Beauregard, General in the Confederate army.

James Ewell Brown "Jeb" Stuart, Confederate cavalry officer.

Joseph Eggleston Johnston, General in the Confederate army.

Robert E. Lee, General-in-Chief of Confederate forces. Photo by Brady.

1865

Lincoln

Richmond, Virginia, Jan. 11. General Robert E. Lee declares it necessary for South to impress Negro slaves as soldiers (→ March 3).

Washington, D.C., Jan. 31. House passes 13th Amendment, calling for ban on slavery (→ March 17).

Richmond, Jan. 31. Robert E. Lee appointed general-in-chief of Confederate forces.

Washington, D.C., Feb. 17. Senate cancels all Confederate debts owed to Union.

North Carolina, Feb. 22. Last open Confederate port, Wilmington, falls to Union under General John Schofield.

Washington, D.C., March 2. Lincoln rejects General Lee's plea for peace talks, demands unconditional surrender.

Washington, D.C., March 11. President Lincoln issues amnesty order for all deserters who return within 60 days.

Richmond, March 13. President Davis signs bill allowing slaves to serve in army in exchange for freedom.

Washington, D.C., March 17. Lincoln tells Indiana troops, "Whenever I hear anyone arguing for slavery, I feel a strong impulse to see it tried on him personally" (→ Dec. 18).

Georgia, May 10. Jefferson Davis, his wife and other Confederate leaders captured near Irwinville, bringing official end of Confederate government (→ 22).

White's Ranch, Texas, May 13. Last recorded death of war is that of Sergeant Crocker, of all-Negro unit.

Washington, D.C., June 23. President Andrew Johnson ends blockade of South.

Washington, D.C., Dec. 1. Johnson restores writ of habeas corpus, freedom from arbitrary arrest, suspended by Lincoln at outset of war.

United States. Food cans made of thinner steel precipitate invention of can opener.

New York City. Benjamin Altman opens dry goods store.

Washington, D.C. Wartime inflation enlarges national money supply to more than $1 billion (→ March 18, 1869).

New York City. *Hans Brinker*, by Mary Mapes Dodge, published.

Richmond occupied by Union troops

Remnants of rebellion: the gutted buildings of Richmond. Photo by Brady.

Southern women in mourning move silently through the ruins of Richmond.

Union soldiers stand guard, watching Southern children play amid the rubble.

Richmond, Virginia, Apr. 5

The victorious Union army, with bands loudly playing *The Girl I Left Behind Me* and *Dixie*, marched into this capital of the Confederacy two days ago. Today, the city is still a smoldering ruin.

As regiments of Negro soldiers entered the city, crowds of former slaves came out to greet them, cheering wildly. The first troops to enter Richmond were combat patrols, followed almost immediately by fire brigades, which went about saving as much of the burning city as they could.

This morning, President Lincoln came to Richmond accompanied by his son, Tad, who clutched his hand as they walked through the streets. Lincoln walked to the Confederate White House where General Weitzel, in charge of the Union troops in this area, has his headquarters. When Negro citizens recognized the President, cheering erupted. One large Negro woman kept crying "glory, glory, glory." At the house, Lincoln, who looked pale and worn out, sat down in Jefferson Davis's chair and the Union troops broke into a loud hurrah.

The beginning of the end for the Confederacy came with the Union assault on Five Forks, south of Petersburg, Virginia, on March 29. General Grant had 50,000 men poised on Hatcher's Run, the extreme left of his line. Aware of the danger to his right, Lee instructed General George Pickett to "hold Five Forks at all hazards," but Pickett could not contain the pressure of Grant's massive assault, and his line collapsed. Cavalry troops, under General Phil Sheridan, who spearheaded the attack, took more than 5,000 prisoners. Lee attempted to bolster his crumbling right by taking three brigades from his center, already stretched thin to the point of non-existence. At dawn on April 1, Wright's Sixth Corps attacked the Confederate trenches and lost some 2,000 men in a confused assault. The attack succeeded, and the Union army broke through to the Appomattox River.

The long siege of Petersburg was over, and Richmond lay ahead, almost completely undefended. And now, the capital of the Confederacy has fallen, too (→9).

Lee surrenders to Grant in meeting at Appomattox

With the stroke of a pen, a somber General Lee ends the war, signing the surrender at Appomattox under Grant's terms. Painting by Thomas Lovell.

Appomattox, Virginia, Apr. 9

General Robert E. Lee met with General Ulysses S. Grant at Appomattox Courthouse today and surrendered the Army of Northern Virginia, thus effectively ending the American Civil War.

Following the fall of Richmond, Lee and his army fought their way west with hopes of reaching Lynchburg and its railroad, which could have transported the army south to unite with General Johnston in North Carolina. On April 8, however, Lee found his way blocked by General Phil Sheridan and his cavalry and 50,000 men under General Meade. Behind him were Grant and another large, well-fed Union army. Lee's 27,000 men were entirely surrounded and starving.

It was time to end the war, so he sent a note to Grant requesting terms. Grant told him that unconditional surrender was the only option. When he was ready to sign the surrender, Lee told an aide, "There is nothing left for me to do but go and see Grant, and I would rather die a thousand deaths."

Lee and Grant met in the front parlor of the brick house of Wilmer McLean, who had moved to Appomattox from Manassas Junction after a shell passed through his house during the first Battle of Bull Run. Lee arrived at the house first and was seated when Grant came in. Lee rose, a resplendent figure in his dress gray uniform, to shake hands with Grant, dressed in a rumpled military tunic with mud-spattered trousers that were stuffed into muddy boots.

Grant allowed Lee's men to keep their small arms and horses and to be paroled without punishment as long as they did not take up arms against the North again. Lee appreciated the generous terms. After the surrender was signed, Grant asked Lee if he would permit him to send rations to the starving Confederate troops, and Lee gratefully accepted.

The surrender took about three hours and at 4 p.m. Lee was free to go. After bowing slightly to the men in the room, Lee walked out to the porch to wait for his horse. He drew on his gauntlets and struck his fist repeatedly into his hand as he stared across the valley at the army he had just surrendered.

After four bloody years and half a million deaths, the American Civil War was over (→May 10).

Lincoln sworn in with malice toward none

Washington, D.C., March 4

Against a somber sky and the finished dome of the Capitol, Abraham Lincoln was sworn in today as President of a still-divided nation for a second term of office.

The 56-year-old Lincoln "looked badly and felt badly – apparently more depressed than I have seen him since he became President," said his friend Joshua Speed. As Lincoln moved to the speaker's platform, the sun broke through the clouds for a moment, and then vanished behind the clouds once again.

The President delivered his speech in a high, almost broken voice. He said that no one could have expected the cause of the war to cease before the conflict itself had ceased, but that slavery, nevertheless, had perished.

He continued by saying that if it were God's will, the country must see this war through to its conclusion, "with malice toward none; with charity for all ... to do all which may achieve a just, and a lasting peace, among ourselves, and with all nations" (→Apr. 15). ▷

Ravages of the Civil War: Half of nation in tatters

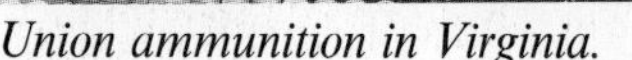

Union ammunition in Virginia.

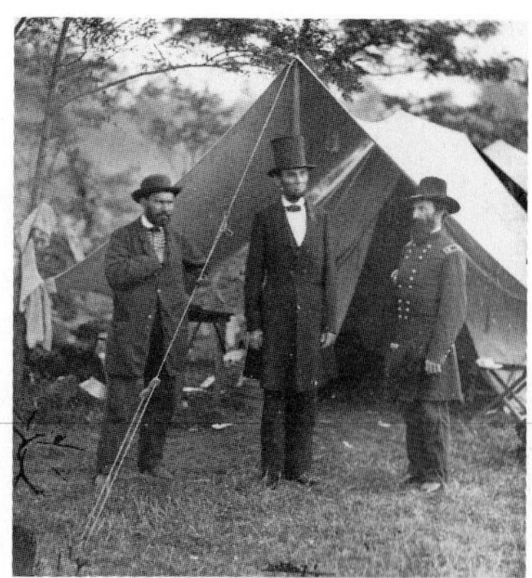

President Lincoln at the front.

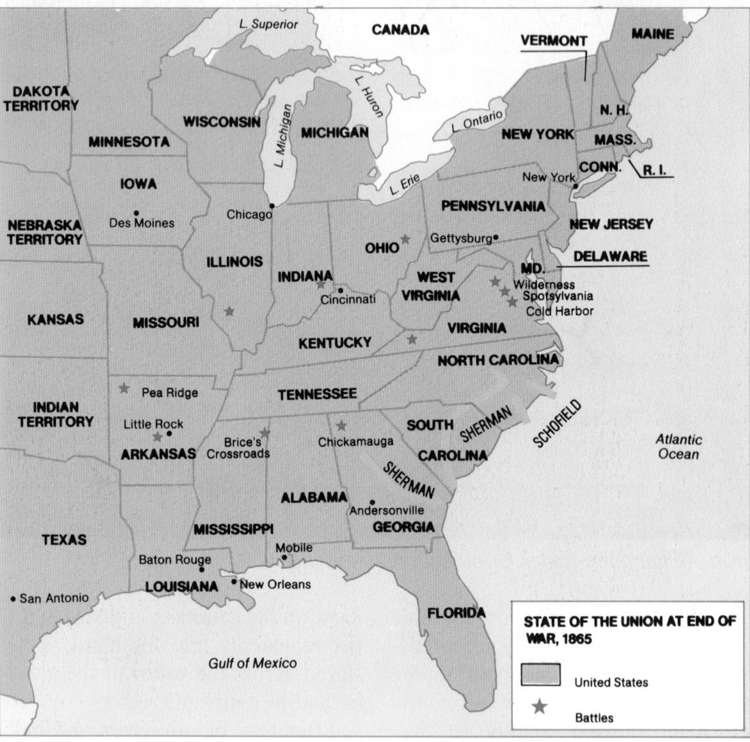

The Union restored. Sites of the war's major battles are identified.

Washington, D.C.

After four long years, the Civil War has left American society with deep scars that may perhaps never be healed. The war has "carried mourning to almost every home," President Lincoln has said, until "it can almost be said that 'the heavens are hung in black.'"

No indisputable figures exist, but it is believed the fighting claimed 360,000 Union and 258,000 Confederate casualties. Even the heroes were scarred by their accomplishments. By 1864, General Ulysses S. Grant's war of attrition had earned him the name "butcher." In the words of a Confederate general who helped inflict 12,000 casualties on Grant's army at Cold Harbor, "This is not war, this is murder."

The North may have paid dearly in human life, but the South has been ravaged to its core. Huge land areas are laid waste and two-thirds of the livestock have been killed. Capital resources are depleted and railroads destroyed. One-quarter of the white male population is dead or maimed and slaves worth $2 billion have been liberated.

The Union blockade, launched during the first months of war, strangled a Southern economy that was highly dependent on manufacturing imports. It was 1863 before the industrially infant South could supply its own munitions. Farmers shifted from cotton to food staples when war broke out, but without adequate rails for transportation, troops went hungry anyway. A soldiers' $11 monthly pay was hardly enough when a cabbage cost $1.25 and boots $200 a pair. Families of soldiers, left without male labor or support from Jefferson Davis's government, often persuaded their men to desert. As early as 1862, a determined anti-war movement had developed in the upcountry among slaveless smallholders who saw no reason to fight a war for the survival of the plantation system.

Many in the North, by contrast, prospered from the war. Aided by protective tariffs and volumes of paper money, large-scale industry has grown fat. Telegraph and railway construction were sped up to meet the need for communications on the battlefield. But the war has distributed its spoils unevenly. Working people saw a 60 percent rise in wages from 1861 to 1865, while the cost of living doubled. Strikes were ineffective, often degenerating into race riots when employers used Negro strikebreakers. Meanwhile, profiteers struck it rich on war contracts, and not all of them honestly. The name of a poor quality wool sold by some manufacturers has been applied to a class of ignoble businessmen, the "shoddy rich."

So it is in war, bemoans President Lincoln, when "every foul bird comes abroad and every dirty reptile rises up to add crime to confusion." Writing to a woman in Boston who lost five sons in the war, however, the President hoped pride would overcome "the grief that must be yours to have laid so costly a sacrifice on the altar of freedom."

In the trenches of Petersburg, Union soldiers await the surrender of Richmond.

In the path of battle: a family flees the war. Photograph by Mathew Brady.

"So costly a sacrifice on the altar of freedom"

Dressed for the chill of winter battle. Captain George Hillyer of Company C of the Ninth Georgia Infantry.

Union troops lay dead at Devil's Run, overwhelmed by a Confederate charge on the second day at Gettysburg. By the third day, more than 50,000 soldiers, Union and Confederate, were killed or wounded in the war's bloodiest battle.

Confederate Major George Duffey. The question remains, to what extent are the rebels to be punished?

A legacy of shattered limbs and broken lives. The Northern wounded at Fredericksburg, in a photo by Brady.

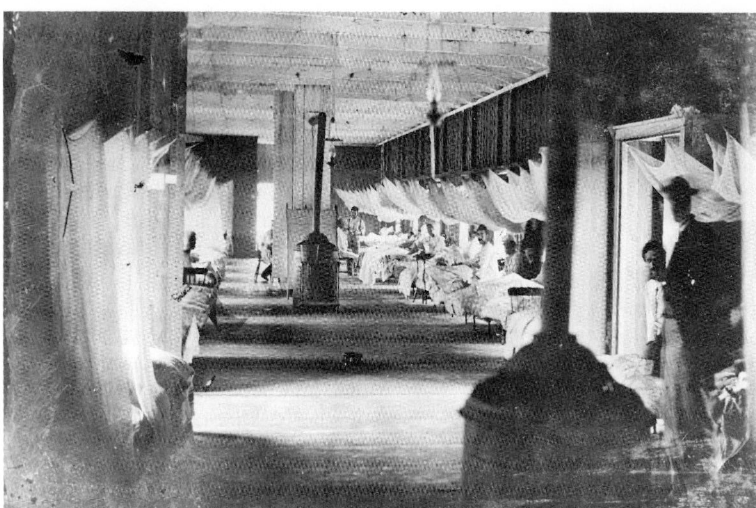

Mosquito netting hangs above the heads of the wounded in a military hospital. In the field, according to Walt Whitman, patients often lay "on the ground, lucky if their blankets are spread on layers of pine or hemlock twigs."

Union soldier in a Zouave uniform awaits attention amid the cold remains of an army encampment.

William Brown, Southern captain.

Wounded soldiers in the aftermath of Fredericksburg. Photo by Brady.

Union private, young and unknown.

President Lincoln shot attending Ford's Theater

Booth commits the fatal deed at Ford's Theater as Mrs. Lincoln and guests watch in horror. Right after firing his pistol, the assassin lept from the balcony and onto the stage, shouting "Sic semper tyrannis! The South is avenged."

Abraham Lincoln, the "Illinois rail-splitter," (1809-1865) saw his beloved nation torn asunder. Divided by war and shocked by the President's murder, the United States is now uniting in grief. Photograph by Mathew Brady.

Washington, D.C., Apr. 15

A freezing drizzle enveloped Washington this morning as the dreaded announcement was made. President Lincoln, the target of an assassin's bullet, died at 7:22. Secretary of State William Seward, who was stabbed several times in a separate incident, is in critical condition. Vice President Andrew Johnson has assumed the powers of the presidency. A massive manhunt has been mounted to find the killer, who is believed to be John Wilkes Booth, a 26-year-old actor. The nation, long divided by war, is now uniting in grief. Outside the White House, a crowd gathered to mourn. Many of the people were Negroes. One cried out, "If death can come to him, what will happen to us?"

The President was shot last night while he sat in a rocking chair next to his wife in a box at Ford's Theater during a performance of the play *Our American Cousin*. Many newspapers are refraining from publishing the assassin's name this morning, but it is acknowledged that authorities are looking for Booth, an emotional actor who holds exalted notions about the South. Secretary of War Edwin Stanton believes that Booth is only one player in a conspiracy, and he warned an associate that hundreds of terrorists may be on the loose. Stanton has ordered round-the-clock guards placed outside the homes of Cabinet members and high officials. He says they may be the next victims of what he believes is a Confederate plot.

Lincoln died in the home of William Petersen at 453 Tenth Street. The tailor's house is situated near the theater. This morning, Mrs. Lincoln emerged from the residence, her face streaked with tears as she pointed at the theater. "Oh, that dreadful house," she shouted, "that dreadful house."

Booth entered the theater at 9:30 last night after calling out for someone to care for his horse. He tried to cross behind the set, but was told to use the underground passage if he wished to reach the other side of the stage. He did so and apparently emerged briefly into an alley outside the theater. Shortly after 10, he re-entered the theater, took the steps up to the dress circle and walked to Box 7. The President was inside, but no one attempted to stop Booth. At 10:15, he opened the door, walked the four feet to the President's chair and shot him in the back of the head with a single bullet from his Derringer. The weapon was later recovered. Most of the audience was laughing at the action on the stage, and few people heard the shot. Major Henry Rathbone, who had been invited by Mrs. Lincoln to sit in the box, saw the blue cloud of smoke rising from the President's chair. He realized that Lincoln had been shot and rushed toward Booth. Booth slashed the major's arm, crawled over the front of the box and jumped down to the stage. "Sic semper tyrannis! ("Thus always to tyrants!") The South is avenged," Booth yelled. And then he hobbled across the stage with what appeared to be a twisted ankle, went out the door, mounted his horse with some difficulty and headed for Ninth Street and Pennsylvania Avenue.

A young doctor, Charles Leale, rushed to the President's box and told Mrs. Lincoln that he would help her husband. But a short while later, he informed another physician, "His wound is mortal. It is impossible for him to recover."

The assassination was apparently well planned, but it was a closely guarded secret. Booth, who is the son of the well-known actor Junius Brutus Booth, did refer indirectly to his odious plan while at a bar earlier in the evening when a man yelled out, "You'll never be the actor your father was." Booth smiled and replied, "When I leave the stage, I will be the most famous man in America" (→Apr. 27).

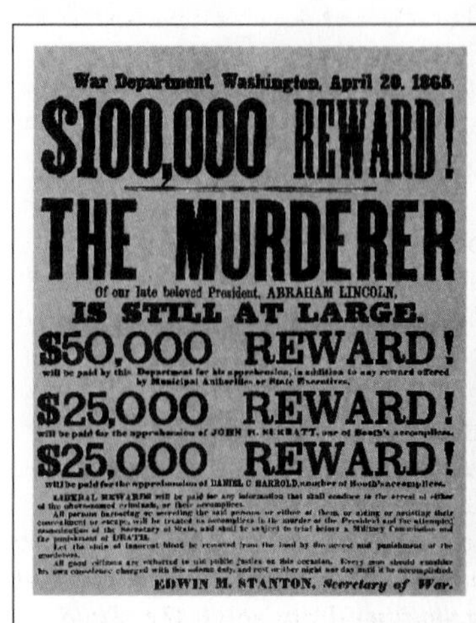

War Department, Washington, April 20, 1865.

$100,000 REWARD!

THE MURDERER

Of our late beloved President, ABRAHAM LINCOLN,

IS STILL AT LARGE.

$50,000 REWARD!

$25,000 REWARD!

$25,000 REWARD!

EDWIN M. STANTON, Secretary of War.

President Johnson faces difficulties

Washington, D.C., May 2

President Johnson faces extraordinary difficulties in the days ahead as he tries to reunite the badly fractured country. The divisions over reconstruction have been exacerbated by the assassination of President Lincoln, and Northerners are insisting upon revenge. Johnson publicly implicated Jefferson Davis today in the deadly conspiracy and offered a $100,000 reward for the arrest of the former Confederate president.

Shortly after Johnson, a Democrat, was sworn in on April 15, a leader of the radical wing of Lincoln's Republican Party pledged to support him. "Johnson, we have faith in you," Senator Benjamin Wade said. "By the gods, there will be no more trouble in running the government." Wade may be overly optimistic. Johnson, a Southerner and former slaveholder, is mistrusted by both sides. He also lacks Lincoln's popularity and ability to compromise. With the future of the country in doubt, many observers wonder whether Lincoln himself would have been up to the task.

Booth caught and killed

Final curtain for John Wilkes Booth.

Port Royal, Virginia, Apr. 27

John Wilkes Booth, the accused assassin of President Lincoln, was shot dead in a barn near this small town by federal cavalrymen early this morning. Another conspirator, David Herold, was taken into custody. The federal force, commanded by Lieutenant L.B. Baker and Colonel E.J. Conger, say they tried to take Booth alive. But the actor, who had vowed earlier that he had "too great a soul to die like a criminal," refused to surrender. Booth pleaded for fairness in the last minutes of his life and asked the soldiers to drop back and fight like men. When they refused, he yelled out, "Well then, my brave boys, prepare a stretcher for me." The soldiers set the barn on fire. A few moments passed, then a shot rang out. Five hours later, at 7, Booth died of the wound. Coincidentally, it was noted, Booth died at the same hour as Lincoln.

For 10 days, Booth managed to avoid thousands of Union soldiers and police officers as he fled from Washington to Maryland and then over to Virginia. Two days ago, he crossed the Rappahannock River and went into hiding on Richard Garrett's farm. "After being hunted like a dog through swamps, woods, and last night chased by gunboats ..." the dramatic actor wrote in his diary, "I am here in despair. And why? For doing what Brutus was honored for" (→ May 4).

Southern struggle effectively ended

New Orleans, May 25

Seven weeks after the surrender of General Lee at Appomattox, the last of the Southern holdouts formally ended their hostilities against the North today. In a low-key ceremony, General Kirby Smith surrendered to General Edward Canby here. Earlier in the month, the last sizable contingent of Confederates east of the Mississippi, commanded by General Richard Taylor, surrendered to Canby in Alabama.

Hostilities between the two sides continued after Appomattox, partly because of communication problems, but also because of simmering resentments. True believers of the Southern cause were offended when the Confederate Secretary of War, John Breckinridge, approved the terms of the general surrender that had been reached by Generals Sherman and Johnston. The agreement suggested that the status of governments in the Southern states would be reassessed by the Union, and it provided little inducement for many Confederate soldiers to lay down their arms.

1,450 soldiers are killed in boat blast

Memphis, Tennessee, Apr. 7

An estimated 1,600 people were killed early this morning, including 1,450 Union soldiers just released from Confederate prisoner-of-war camps, in a boiler explosion aboard the steamer Sultana on the Mississippi River.

As many as 600 survivors of the flaming wreck were rescued from the water by vessels in the vicinity that rushed to the scene. But many women and children were too weak to remain afloat, and drowned.

The $80,000 sidewheeler steamed out of Memphis around midnight, after unloading a cargo of sugar. It had traveled seven miles when the boilers exploded, hurling the pilothouse and part of the cabin high into the air. The parts fell upon the deck, burying many passengers in the flaming debris. Those who could, threw themselves in the water. The river was so wide at that point, that many could not reach the shore.

Lincoln has martyr's burial in Springfield

Springfield, Illinois, May 4

President Lincoln was laid to rest today in the city where he was married and started his legal career. After lying in state for two weeks at the White House, Lincoln's body was brought home by a special train that passed thousands of mourners. Throughout his life, Lincoln was seen as a simple man of the prairie, the rail-splitter called "Honest Abe." In his death, he is being called a martyr, a binder of wounds and a savior of the union. It is likely, however, that the preservation of the union will be more difficult now that Lincoln has gone to his grave (→ July 8).

The New York procession was described as "imposing, sad and sorrowful."

Davis is captured, dressed as woman

Fort Monroe, Virginia, May 22

Jefferson Davis, former president of the defeated Confederacy, was incarcerated here today. It is not clear yet when or if he will be tried. President Johnson offered a $100,000 reward at the beginning of the month for Davis's capture on charges connected to the assassination of President Lincoln. Other officials, however, do not believe that Davis was involved.

Davis was disguised as a woman when he was captured near Irwinville, Georgia, on May 10. His wife and other members of the government were also taken into custody.

Davis was a military leader and politician after graduation from West Point, but his detractors say he failed at both when he headed the Confederacy. General Pierre Beauregard says the South was nibbled away, not crushed, "because its executive head never gathered and wielded its great strength" (→ 25).

Eight are convicted in President's assassination; four hanged

Justice by the rope: Mary E. Surratt, Lewis T. Paine, David E. Herold and George A. Atzerodt hang as conspirators in the murder of President Lincoln.

Washington, D.C., July 8

Four of the conspirators convicted in the assassination of President Lincoln were hanged today. Mary E. Surratt, Lewis T. Paine and David E. Herold and George A. Atzerodt all walked to the gallows. It was Paine who stabbed Secretary William Seward. Herold was with John Wilkes Booth when he was shot. Mrs. Surratt's daughter Anna tried but failed to see President Johnson today to win her a reprieve.

Three other conspirators, Samuel Arnold, Samuel Mudd and Michael O'Laughlin, are serving life terms in prison. Edward Spangler was given a six-year sentence. They are all imprisoned at the penitentiary in Albany, New York.

President Johnson and General Grant were both reported to have been targets of the original plot, which was hatched in Mrs. Surratt's boarding house. A larger number of conspirators was originally involved, but some of them apparently dropped out when Booth decided to assassinate Lincoln rather than to kidnap him.

Nearly three months have passed since the assassination, and wild rumors about it abound. Some people even suggest that Booth is still on the loose and that it was another man who was gunned down in the barn in Virginia.

Freedmen's Bureau to aid freed slaves

Songs for the freedman.

Washington, D.C., December

Through the Freedmen's Bureau, the War Department is now spending millions of dollars on jobs and medical treatment for the emancipated slaves. Another state bureau was just set up in Texas, but other states are fighting the federal government's efforts to assist the Negroes. Mississippi has begun enacting laws to restrict the slaves' activities. Federal agents have fanned out through the South to find jobs and homes for the Negroes, give them food and help build them hospitals. Abolitionists applaud the efforts of the bureau, but they believe that Congress is not acting firmly enough to force Southern landowners to renounce slavery.

Brutal Andersonville prison chief hanged

Andersonville, Georgia, Nov. 10

The commandant of the Confederacy's most notorious prison paid with his life today for the atrocities committed at the institution. Captain Henry Wirz, head of the Andersonville prison, went to the gallows and became the first Confederate official to be executed for activities during the war. Thousands of Union soldiers died in the prison, many from starvation. What little food was produced nearby went to the battlefront, and conditions inside the overcrowded and unsanitary Andersonville facility were appalling. Union prisoners were moved to the prison last year when they became too much of a drain on supplies in Richmond. Captain James Moore led the Union search of the prison earlier this year.

Yale patents lock

Shelburne Falls, Massachusetts

Linus Yale Jr. has patented an improved version of the cylinder lock, a device he first developed in 1861. Using a system of tumblers and a notched key, Yale's invention is dependable, pick-resistant and easily mass-produced. It has an advantage over the combination lock, which cannot thwart a robber who solves the combinations.

Winslow Homer's "Prisoners From the Front" (1866). During the Civil War, Union troops captured 220,000 prisoners, not including Confederate armies that surrendered at war's end. Confederates captured 210,000 prisoners. Some 26,000 Southerners and 22,000 Northerners died in prison camps.

From Mark Twain's pen: "Jumping Frog"

New York City, Nov. 18

With the long Civil War over and the shock of President Lincoln's assassination wearing off, many Americans have been looking for lighthearted fare in their newspapers. Such readers should turn to today's *New York Saturday Press* and a story by one Mark Twain entitled *The Celebrated Jumping Frog of Calaveras County*, a tall tale about the exploits of an athletic amphibian set in a roisterous California mining town. Twain is the nom de plume of Samuel Clemens, a 30-year-old Missouri journalist with a past as colorful as the wide-open West that he portrays.

The author rides his jumping frog.

Reconstruction era is starting in South

Washington, D.C., Dec. 14

Congressman Thaddeus Stevens, the outspoken and uncompromising Republican abolitionist from Pennsylvania, was named today to head the Committee on Reconstruction in the House. Many Republicans feel that President Johnson is acting too quickly in allowing Southern states to rejoin the union. They also see their majority in the Congress threatened by Democrats from the South. Despite the opposition of radical Republicans, Johnson has offered amnesty to most Confederate citizens who swear allegiance to the union. The President has also paroled several political leaders in the South and lifted the blockade of Southern ports.

Lee vows allegiance

Lexington, Virginia, Oct. 2

General Robert E. Lee, commander of the defeated Confederate army and the newly named president of Washington College, today swore his allegiance to the union. He also pledged to support the emancipation of the slaves. This may help President Johnson's policy of Reconstruction, but it is not clear yet whether other Confederate leaders are going to fall in line.

Amendment frees slaves

All men are created equal. "Allegory of Freedom" by an unknown artist.

Washington, D.C., Dec. 18

After years of division and bloodshed, slavery is now illegal in America. Secretary of State William Seward announced today that the 13th Amendment is a part of the Constitution. It states that "neither slavery nor involuntary servitude . . . shall exist" and that Congress can enforce the law. The fight for Negro freedom spanned generations, but the legislative battle began in January of last year, when Senator John Henderson proposed the amendment. Congress passed it amid pandemonium in January, pushing it onto the states for ratification. President Lincoln had said that no state could expect legitimate status in the union without ratification, forcing Southern states to acquiesce. Today, Seward got the required certifications of 27 states (→ Feb. 19, 1866).

Anti-Negro Klan organized in South

Pulaski, Tennessee, December

A secret society formed this year in central Tennessee, with members riding at night in hooded white robes, has alarmed some observers, who fear it may be used against the freed Negroes. Although reports are sketchy, because the group maintains strict secrecy, it appears that the Ku Klux Klan was established in the spring by six former Confederate soldiers in a Pulaski law office. The name is taken from the Greek word "kuklos," or circle. The founders are said to assert that the KKK is a harmless fraternity, but some believe that the organization has been formed to resist Reconstruction in the former Confederate states (→ 1866).

Stockyards opened

Chicago, Dec. 25

Chicago Union Stockyards began operations today, accepting a shipment of 761 pigs from the Burlington Railroad. The growth of Chicago's population and economy during the Civil War and the recent development of the railroads in recent years has made this a primary terminal. Its proximity to the prairies makes it an ideal site for an agricultural business center.

Washington, D.C. *With the completed Capitol dome hovering in the background, returning troops parade through the capital of all the 36 states.*

"Aurora Borealis," (1865) by Frederick Church, offers a kind of glorious allegory for the dawn of a rejuvenated nation. Its ethereal realism owes inspiration to the belief of the German scientist Alexander von Humboldt that a painter ought to "resolve beneath his touch the great enchantment of nature." Church, along with his colleagues in the naturalist movement, finds spirituality in the detailed scientific study of the beauties of nature.

1866

Johnson

New York City, Jan. 2. Elizabeth Cady Stanton submits petition to Congress, protesting exclusionary language of 14th Amendment (→ Aug.).

Idaho, Feb. 10. Governor Lyon absconds with territorial treasury of $41,062.

Washington, D.C., Feb. 12. First formal observance of Lincoln's birthday takes place at Capitol, with President Johnson in attendance.

Washington, D.C., Feb. 19. President Johnson vetoes extension of Freedmen's Bureau, saying freed slaves should advance by "their own merits and exertions" (→ Feb. 22).

Mobile, Alabama, February. Mardi Gras celebrations, oldest in the country, resume after wartime suspension.

New York City, Apr. 1. Western Union gains telegraph monopoly by absorbing U.S. Telegraph Company.

Washington, D.C., June 16. The 14th Amendment guaranteeing equal rights up for ratification after congressional passage (→ March 27, 1867).

Washington, D.C., July 28. Congress passes law legalizing use of metric measurements.

New Orleans, July 30. Some 200 killed or wounded as race riot erupts at political rally.

New York City, Oct. 10. Elizabeth Cady Stanton receives 24 votes in bid for congressional seat (→ Jan. 1, 1868).

Atlanta, December. Legislature approves hiring of convicts by private firms, beginning chain-gang system.

Pithole, Pennsylvania. First oil pipeline in nation completed, connecting Pithole oil fields with railroad five miles away.

New Orleans. First Greek Orthodox parish in United States organized.

Texas. Bars and saloons ordered closed on Sundays.

Cape Cod, Mass. Price of sperm oil creates demand for petroleum products.

Southwestern United States. Charles Goodnight and Oliver Loving blaze the Goodnight-Loving cattle trail.

United States. Mrs. F.G. Pankhurst's temperance song, *Father's a Drunkard and Mother is Dead*, is popular.

President officially declares end of war

Johnson stumping for Democrats on the rails, Washington to Chicago.

Washington, D.C., Aug. 20

It may come as a surprise to only a few to know that the Civil War is over. In a proclamation today, President Johnson made it official, declaring that the "insurrection" was finally ended and that "peace, order, tranquillity and civil authority now exist in and throughout the whole of the United States."

The President had issued a somewhat similar proclamation last April, declaring the war at an end everywhere except Texas, where sporadic jousting was continuing between Union troops and pro-slavery forces. While skirmishes are still erupting in that state, the President made it clear today that his proclamation declaring an end to the war included Texas.

Except for minor clashes, the war actually ended April 9 of last year when the Confederate forces surrendered at Appomattox Courthouse, five days before President Lincoln was assassinated. Less than a month later, a proclamation by President Johnson stated that the war "may be regarded at an end."

Ku Klux Klan spreads throughout South

Tennessee, Autumn

The head of the Ku Klux Klan reports that the organization has received an enthusiastic welcome from Tennessee to Texas and across the old Confederacy. Former General Nathan B. Forrest, one of Robert E. Lee's foremost cavalrymen during the war, founded the Klan last year in the town of Pulaski. While Forrest says the Klan is nothing more than a congenial club of former Confederate veterans, many government officials argue that the group is committed to the denial of Negro rights.

Deadly visitors in the night. Klansmen attack a family in the South.

Act makes Negroes citizens of U.S.

Washington, D.C., Apr. 6

With the passage of the Civil Rights Act by Congress, Negroes and "all persons born in the U.S. and not subject to any foreign powers, excluding Indians not taxed," have become citizens of the United States. This gives persons "of every race and color" all privileges to make contracts, hold property and testify in court. Citizens are also subject to all laws, punishments and penalties. Although President Johnson vetoed the act, the Senate was able to override his veto (→ June 16).

Jubilation outside House chambers.

Amendment terms disturb suffragist

New York City, August

Mrs. Elizabeth Cady Stanton is running for Congress in New York's Eighth District. Never mind that this suffragist cannot even vote for herself: The gesture protests a proposed draft of the 14th Amendment. This draft, which would acknowledge the citizenship of Negro Americans and imply their right to vote, uses the word "male" – a word that has never yet appeared in the Constitution. Without the presence of the word, women could legally demand suffrage. The amendment, which was passed by both houses of Congress on June 16, has yet to be ratified by the states. In the meantime, Mrs. Stanton is writing to her would-be electors, promising "free speech, free press, free men and free trade" (→ Oct. 10).

Whites riot, battle Negroes in Memphis

On the morning of May 2, white gunmen hold Memphis under siege.

Memphis, Tennessee, May 4

Whites rioted in Memphis at the start of the month, leaving 46 dead and many Negro schools and churches burned. The riots during the first three days of May are thought to have been a response to tough post-war government measures that have angered whites.

Witnesses said a white mob, assisted by Memphis policemen, began a drunken campaign of violence against the Negro population. One victim, whose husband served in the Northern army, said she was attacked in her home while other rioters ransacked it hunting for her husband's savings from his war service.

Major General George Stoneman, commander of the Department of Tennessee, has been criticized by some because he delayed taking stern countermeasures for three days, until matters had gotten entirely out of hand.

The sheriff first asked Stoneman to use his forces the day the riot erupted. But Stoneman replied that he would prefer his small force of 150 men to be used only in case of dire necessity. Not until yesterday, when the leading white and Negro citizens pleaded with Stoneman, did he issue orders forbidding crowds to assemble and post guards to enforce the order. Military forces are looking into the affair, and a congressional group will also investigate.

American ship starts mail service to China

San Francisco, Dec. 31

At noon tomorrow, the red paddle wheels of the steamship Colorado will splash into San Francisco Bay on the Pacific Mail's first voyage to China. The 340-foot, 3,728-ton craft's black wooden hull and brass are shined up for the occasion. The steamer is due to stop in Yokohama, Japan, by January 24.

Tonight, 250 businessmen and dignitaries, including three Chinese, attended the "Grand China Mail Dinner" presided over by Governor Frederick F. Low. The Pacific Mail company is building four new steamers, at a cost of more than $1 million, each to provide monthly service to China under contract to the postmaster general. The four 4,000-ton ships are each over 360 feet long and are powered with engines rated at 1,500 horsepower. Masts and sails are mere auxiliaries.

The Great Republic, launched in November on Long Island, is designed with quarters for 250 cabin passengers and 1,200 in steerage. It carries up to 2,800 tons of cargo. The woodwork is of black walnut, the furniture upholstered with silk. Peach blossom, lavender, pea-green and purple are the chief colors used with ornamental work in gold. Each of the Pacific Mail's steamers is fitted with five 20-pound cannons and two 30-pound guns to protect it from pirates.

The clipper ship Great Republic on the high seas. Lithograph by Currier.

Sheridan reports 100 million buffalo in one part of West

Plains Indians have always depended on the buffalo for their very survival.

Kansas

General Philip H. Sheridan, commander of the army's forces in the trans-Mississippi West, says there are at least 100 million buffalo from Fort Dodge, Kansas, to the Indian Territory. Ten years ago, Colonel Grenville Dodge reported he had seen columns of bison 50 miles wide and 10 miles long, almost blackening the earth. Sheridan and General William Tecumseh Sherman, his superior, feel the buffalo must be exterminated. Their theory is: Kill off the bison and the Plains Indians will have no way to hold on to their way of life. Kill the buffalo, Sheridan says, and you kill the Indians.

New York cheers its first "leg show"

New York City, Sept. 23

Ever since *The Black Crook* opened on September 12 at Niblo's Garden, burlesque has taken Broadway by storm. Classic burlesque, long popular in Europe, is generally a musical stage show meant to make fun of the serious and make melodrama from the mundane. A typical performance will have three acts, ranging from gaudy comic sketches to serious musical solos. The finale is invariably a dance with revealing costume. *The Black Crook*, New York's first "leg show," has catapulted burlesque to the forefront of the season. Complaints about nudity have forced the closing of a few shows. ▷

Injured Mary Baker Patterson cures self

Mary Baker Patterson, who says she was healed by the power of faith, had spinal ills till she "rediscovered" the medical methods of Jesus.

Lynn, Massachusetts, Feb. 5

Mrs. Mary Baker Patterson appears to have made a miraculous recovery from injuries sustained in a fall. Mrs. Patterson, a lecturer on the theories of the late Phineas Quimby that illness exists only in the mind, now seems to be proof of those beliefs. Mrs. Patterson, always a sickly woman, was "cured" by Quimby in 1862. Her fall on the ice last Thursday seemed to end this cure. But she astounded her doctor, who thought she would be bedridden for months, by getting up yesterday, just three days after her accident. She attributes this to reading Matthew 9:2, where Jesus heals a man stricken with palsy.

Forts are going up to protect Westerners

Texas

With the Civil War's conclusion, the Western frontier has become wilder and more dangerous than ever. Because of a constant threat from Indians, a string of forts has been built that stretches from the Dakotas to the Texas border. As some army veterans say: "Building forts in Indian country demoralizes them more than anything, except money and whiskey."

Accordingly, a thin blue line of cavalry-manned installations has been estalished on the Western frontier to protect the advancing edge of civilization from the Indians. From Fort Laramie in Wyoming and Fort Reno on the Powder River, to Fort Riley in Kansas, to Fort Apache in Arizona, and to the military posts in Texas, the men wearing the "Yellow Ribbon" have become the first line of defense.

A typical army fort that has been built in the West since the war is Fort Richardson in Jacksboro, Texas. Every day, Sixth Cavalry troops will have to face the Comanches and Arapahoes – among the world's best light cavalry – who descend from the hills of the Indian Territory and the plains of West Texas. For what reward? Is it the pleasure of a gutsy song like *Forty Miles a Day on Beans and Hay* – or is it pride and patriotism?

Texas, January 4. *Fort Richardson set up to fight Indians in West Texas.*

Sioux ambush and kill 80 near Idaho fort

Idaho Territory, Dec. 21

Striking back at white encroachment on lands that have been reserved for them by treaty, a war party of Oglala Sioux led by Chief Red Cloud today ambushed and wiped out a military force of 80 men stationed at Fort Phil Kearny.

The fort, which was recently constructed on Piney Creek near the Powder River to protect the Bozeman Trail to the Western goldfields, had already been a target of Sioux hostilities when word arrived that a pack train bringing wood and other supplies had been attacked. Captain William Fetterman, a veteran of the Civil War twice breveted for bravery, was sent to assist the pack train but was specifically ordered not to cross a range of hills called Lodge Trail Ridge. However, when Captain Fetterman sighted a small party of mounted Sioux warriors, he immediately set off in pursuit, crossed the Lodge Trail Ridge and then found that he had been lured into an ambush by a much larger force of Sioux that was led by Chief High Backbone. Not a single member of Captain Fetterman's party has survived (→ Nov. 6, 1868).

Red Cloud, chief of Oglala Sioux.

American Equal Rights Association formed

New York City, May 10

At the first post-war meeting of the National Women's Rights Convention, a unanimous vote confirmed the organization of the American Equal Rights Association. Numbering about 100, the group seeks to unite other radical organizations striving for suffrage for women and blacks. Lucretia Mott will be president, and Elizabeth Stanton as vice president will assume most of the actual responsibilities. Both women have long been dedicated advocates of women's rights and the abolition of slavery. Women's suffrage, first proposed by Stanton at the first Women's Rights Convention in Seneca Falls in 1848, has become a focal point of the group's active struggle. Lucretia Mott, 73, organized the Anti-Slavery Society in 1833, and has served as the president of the female Anti-Slavery Society in Philadelphia.

Freedman's dream: 40 acres and mule

Washington, D.C., Feb. 22

With the hope that Congress will grant them land, recently freed Negroes have popularized the slogan "Forty acres and a mule." Though such aid seems unlikely, much as many indigent freedmen may need it, the Freedmen's Bureau has procured legal aid for Negroes and food and land for schools and other institutional purposes. The bureau exists despite continued opposition by President Johnson, who feels former slaves should get by through "their own merits" (→ Apr. 6).

Ezra Cornell getting university started

Ithaca, New York

Businessman-legislator Ezra Cornell has taken charge of his latest project, funding Cornell University here. Cornell, 59, made his fortune in 1855, when he organized the Western Union Telegraph Company and devised a way to put telegraph wires on poles. He has been a state senator since 1863 and spent two years in the state assembly before that. In 1865, he convinced New York State to use land obtained through the Morrill Land Grant Act for the new university.

60,000 from locals unite in national union

Baltimore, Maryland, Aug. 20

Union leaders, in response to growing dangers in mills, mines and other workplaces, have united to form the National Labor Union. Its aim is to develop safeguards and guidelines to help workers. The national union includes some 60,000 workers from local unions and was created when the National Labor Congress met here two days ago with 77 delegates from 13 states. Delegates issued an "Address to the Workmen Throughout the Country," saying that the first goal "to accomplish before we can hope for any great results is a thorough organization of labor."

Cholera kills 50,000; 2,000 New Yorkers

New York City

The latest outbreak of the dreaded cholera, after taking 90,000 lives in Russia, has spread across Europe and into the United States, where it has taken 50,000 lives this year. The highly contagious disease can kill within hours of the first symptoms, and it is believed to be spread by unsanitary conditions. In New York, where the disease has killed 2,000 people this year, a Metropolitan Board of Health was created on February 26 to enforce a clean-up in tenements and streets and to screen immigrant ships.

Refrigerated rails

Detroit

A refrigerated freight car has been built here by J. B. Sutherland, who says it can be used to ship fresh fruit and vegetables from one end of the country to the other. The car is cooled by passing air through containers of ice at each end. Another inventor, Parker Earle of Illinois, plans to ship fresh, ice-cooled strawberries by rail and says that he will charge customers $2 a quart.

New art museum

Paris, July 4

Inspired no doubt by the proximity of the Louvre, home to many of the world's great art treasures, John Jay today proclaimed his intention of founding a National Institution and Gallery of Art [Metropolitan Museum] in New York City. Jay, who is a grandson of the first Chief Justice, was promised support by prominent New Yorkers attending the July 4th luncheon.

Book of photos depicts Civil War horrors

Ruins of Richmond, Va., April 1865, by Alexander Gardner. The photographer began working for Mathew Brady in 1856, but went out on his own in 1863.

Washington, D.C.

The devastation of the Civil War can now be experienced with startling realism in the safety of one's own home thanks to the publication of *Gardner's Sketch Book of the War*. The Scottish-born photographer Alexander Gardner took his journalistic skills and photographic talents to the battlefields, where he often prepared and developed plates in a specially equipped horse-drawn darkroom. Although many of the 100 photographs in the *Sketch Book* document picturesque historical sites, melancholy ruins and prominent figures such as President Lincoln, the volume is punctuated with appalling scenes of military carnage. Particularly ghastly are pictures such as *Harvest of Death*, which depicts a field littered with the bodies of soldiers like so many broken stalks of corn, their faces frozen in open-mouthed anguish. Gardner's pictures show the inhumanity of civil strife with an immediacy far more compelling than the prints that until now served as journalistic illustration of the war.

Romantic painters of the Hudson River

Hudson River Valley, New York

In the last 40 years, a distinctive American school of landscape painting has grown up around the natural beauty of New York's Hudson River Valley. Such artists as Thomas Cole, Asher Durand, John F. Kensett and Samuel Colman have depicted the untrammeled wilderness of the area with obvious reverence. Though some have studied in Europe, all have a fierce pride in the American landscape and in their own romantic style. Many of their colleagues have brought a similar spirit to other landscapes. Thomas Moran and Albert Bierstadt depict the beauty of vast stretches of the West, while Frederick Church revels in the mystical side of nature.

"Storm King on the Hudson" (1866) by Samuel Colman, a picturesque rendering of the Catskill Mountains in pastel hues. Although he developed his skills during travels abroad in the early 1860's, Colman owes a great debt to his teacher Asher Durand, who was one of the first painters to explore the American landscape.

1867

Johnson

Wyoming, January. Reinforcements against Indian attacks reach Fort Phil Kearny, but they fail to keep open the Bozeman Trail.

Panama, Feb. 25. First survey conducted for a canal linking Atlantic and Pacific Oceans.

Washington, D.C., March 2. Congress repeals excise taxes and taxes on income under $1,000.

Fort Monroe, Va., March 13. "Caged eagle" Jefferson Davis released from prison on $100,000 bail, pending trial (→ May 11).

Alabama, March 27. Military rule imposed after Alabama refuses to ratify 14th Amendment (→ July 28, 1868).

Tennessee, March 29. *Pulaski Citizen* carries first known expose of Ku Klux Klan, in an article called "Invisible Empire of the South."

Utah, Aug. 20. Anson Mills patents army cartridge belt.

Oregon, August. First white woman climbs Mount Hood.

Helena, Montana, Sept. 16. "Chinese Mary," killed for her gold, is first Asian to be burned to death by whites.

New York City, Dec. 2. Charles Dickens, giving readings of his own works, draws large crowds.

San Francisco. Andrew Hallidie invents cable car (→ Oct. 1, 1873).

New York City. Phrase "Now is the time for all good men to come to the aid of their party" used to test typewriters.

New York City. Nation's first tenement-house laws enacted as slums begin to develop.

Charleston, S.C. George Peabody Fund started with a gift of $3.5 million to further education throughout South.

Washington, D.C. In an unprecedented act, Congress invalidates all acts of Montana Territory's second and third legislative sessions.

Salt Lake City, Utah. Mormon Tabernacle completed.

San Francisco. Strike for better pay by 2,000 Chinese working on Central Pacific Railroad fails.

United States. *Slave songs of the United States*, first book of Negro spirituals, is published.

U.S. purchases Alaska for $7 million

Secretary Seward shown being duped into the purchase of a frozen wasteland.

Washington D.C., Apr. 9

It was a close shave. The former Russian colony of Alaska is now a territory of the United States, but it became so with but a single congressional vote to spare. After an impassioned, three-hour speech by Senator Charles Sumner of Massachusetts, the vote to transfer Alaska from Russian hands to the United States was approved by a vote of 27 to 12 with six legislators absent. The total in favor of buying was one vote more than the two-thirds that is required for ratification.

The administration's campaign to win support for the purchase of Alaska has been one of the more bitter of the post-war era. For years, the Secretary of the Interior, William Seward, has been urging Congress to approve the acquisition of this vast acreage in the Far North. But the response has been strongly negative with both members of Congress and the nation's journalists laughingly referring to the country's new territory as "Walrussia," "Seward's Icebox," "Polaria," "Seward's Folly" and "Icebergia."

Even with approval of the purchase of the territory for $7.2 million, which comes to two cents an acre, there is still criticism. Many citizens express the feeling that the purchase by the United States of an "utterly useless" land of "perpetual snow" was an investment that only the insane would make. But its supporters are confident that this territory is some day going to be one of the nation's greatest resources.

First-hand reports from Alaska confirm Seward's belief that this is a rich, promising region. The United States Minister to Russia, Cassius M. Clay, has echoed Seward's sentiments. In a letter from Russia, Clay has written that Alaska's mines, waters, furs and fisheries are of "untold value" and that the territory was worth seven times what the government is paying the Russians for it. He said that future generations will wonder "that we ever got it at all."

"The 9:45 Accommodation, Stratford, Connecticut" (1867) by Edward L. Henry of the Pennsylvania Academy.

First Alger story is "Ragged Dick"

From rags to riches in America.

New York City, January

At a price that even those most in need of his gospel can afford – a dime – schoolmaster Horatio Alger, a former Unitarian minister, offers the first of what he envisions as a long series of inspirational novels. *Ragged Dick* is the story of an orphaned and destitute Manhattan bootblack who through the application of such time-honored virtues as thrift and perseverance travels from rags to riches. The Alger theme is sure to win him scores of readers in this era of unrivaled economic growth in the Northeast.

2 colleges founded to help ex-slaves

Augusta, Georgia, March 2

Before the Civil War, it was illegal in most places to teach slaves to read and write. Now, two schools have been opened to give Negroes a chance at a college education. Morehouse College here has three teachers and 37 students, who were all slaves. Howard University in Washington, D.C., named for General Oliver Otis Howard, a Civil War hero who helped get the school started, is temporarily holding classes in abandoned railway cars because of a lack of space. Both of the schools offer degrees in education and divinity to help make teachers and preachers out of former slaves.

Nebraska becomes nation's 37th state

Nebraska, March 1

Nebraska, the land that one explorer called "the Great American Desert," has become the 37th state in the union. In 1820, Major Stephen Long of the United States Army led an expedition to this region and declared it "wholly unfit for farming." Farmers disagreed. Drawn by the promise of free land under the Homestead Act of 1862, thousands flocked to these prairies and began building sod houses. Settlers from the East Coast and Europe caused the population to surge from 28,000 in 1860 to more than 100,000 today. Nebraskans voted for statehood last year, but their effort was blocked by President Andrew Johnson's veto. Johnson is in danger of impeachment and he feared that Republican representatives from Nebraska would tip the scales against him. Today, Congress overrode his veto.

Carnegie, Pullman form sleeper firm

Chicago

Andrew Carnegie and George M. Pullman have merged their railroad sleeping-car companies to form the Pullman Palace Car Corporation, which will have a near monopoly in the field. Pullman will serve as president of the company. Its headquarters now are in Chicago, but Pullman has plans to build a new city to house his employees and factory.

Although Carnegie is best known as a rising figure in the steel industry, he has been involved in sleeping car production for many years. Pullman, however, has had a dominating position since he built his first sleeper, the Pioneer, in 1863. It had an ingenious arrangement of folding upper berths and seat cushions that are extended to form lower berths. Pullman cars now are used by all American railroads. Rather than selling them, Pullman retains control by leasing the cars.

Emerson, after 30 years, at Harvard

Cambridge, Massachusetts

A different sort of homecoming was celebrated on the Harvard campus recently when the flinty apostle of self-reliance, Ralph Waldo Emerson, lectured there. Some 30 years ago an address by Emerson at the Harvard Divinity School so angered faculty and students alike with its calls for the primacy of intuitive, personal spiritual experience over structured religion that all formal contact between America's foremost educational institution and its leading intellectual light was severed. During the intervening years Emerson's poems and essays such as *Nature*, *The Transcendentalist* and *The American Scholar* have cemented his reputation as the father of the literary and philosophical movement that is known as Transcendentalism. He is also well know as an activist in the cause of abolition.

Texas longhorns sent up Chisholm Trail to Abilene and then East

Abilene, Kansas, Sept. 5

The little railroad town of Abilene is going wild today following the first shipment of 35,000 Texas longhorn cattle to markets back East. All day long, Southern cattle drovers and Northern beef dealers have been toasting each others' health and the staggering profits to come at a party thrown by the Illinois meat dealer-turned-Abilene-entrepreneur, Joseph M. McCoy.

What has become known as "the long drive" is the brainchild of Texas cattlemen and Yankee businessmen. After the Civil War ended two years ago, cattle-rich Texans realized cows that cost them $3 or $4 a head could be sold in the North at $40 a head. The problem was how to get them north. McCoy, at the same time, knew that a fortune awaited anyone who could control the place where Southern sellers and Northern buyers could meet advantageously. In a brilliant game of deductive reasoning, he figured that the perfect spot was at the end of the railroad, in Kansas. Consequently, he obtained a contract with the Hannibal and St. Joe Railroad for cattle shipped to the meat-packing houses in Chicago.

He then arranged for Texas cattlemen to drive their animals over the 1,000 miles from South Texas to Abilene. He also decided on Abilene because "the country was entirely unsettled, well watered, and offered excellent grass." Accordingly, he built stockholding pens, chutes, barns and even a hotel to house the migrant cowhands.

This autumn, more than 35,000 cattle are passing through sleepy little Abilene, where there is so little to do that the saloon keeper spends his spare time raising prairie dogs he then tries to sell to the occasional tourists who happen to venture through the village.

The cattle are driven to Abilene over the Chisholm Trail, which gets its start in South Texas, then winds its way north to Dallas and on to the stock pens that are found at the railhead here in town.

A herd of Texas cattle cross a stream by moonlight en route to Kansas.

Reconstruction is enforced in South

Freedmen cast their first votes.

Washington, D.C., July 19

With the passage by Congress today of the third Reconstruction Act, the machinery is now in place to impose drastic social and political reforms on the states of the defeated Confederacy. The new act, which authorizes military governors to decide on voter eligibility, comes on the heels of earlier laws that divided the South, except for Tennessee, into five regions; placed a major general in charge of each region and empowered these governors to organize constitutional conventions, remove local officials, impose martial law and require the states to pass laws that guarantee Negro freedmen the right to vote.

The new policy is in marked contrast to the softer approach that was favored by President Lincoln and largely continued by President Johnson. For civil rule to be restored, only 10 percent of voters had to swear allegiance to the union, and the new state governments were required to do no more than ratify the 13th Amendment, repudiate their war debts and annul secession ordinances. Many senior officials not covered by the amnesty were then pardoned by President Johnson and returned to office in state and congressional elections.

Already angered by such leniency, the Republicans were outraged by so-called Black Codes passed by most Southern legislatures. These laws, which severely restricted the civil rights of the freedmen, were seen as little more than a bid to restore slavery by another name. Riots in Memphis and New Orleans in which white mobs killed hundreds of Negroes added to the sense of moral outrage in the North and the belief that the war had been fought in vain. The last straw was the refusal by Southern states to adopt the 14th Amendment, which protects civil rights of freedmen.

The radical Republicans won sweeping victories in both houses in last year's elections, preparing the way for passage of the Reconstruction acts (→March 11, 1868).

Back into slavery? Forcing a freedman in Florida to pay his debt for vagrancy.

Man walks 1,326 miles for $10,000

Chicago

Edward P. Weston is $10,000 richer and holds a new world's record, but it may be a few days before he goes out on the town to celebrate. The 28-year-old Weston is weary, having just finished a 26-day walk that brought him 1,326 miles from Portland, Maine, to Chicago, Illinois, on a bet. In 1861, a 10-day walk took Weston from Boston to Washington, D.C., a 478-mile trek. Previously, he held a job as a circus drummer, but he decided that it was not his calling when he was struck by lightning.

"Caged eagle" is released from jail

Richmond, Virginia, May 11

Former Confederate President Jefferson Davis walked out of a federal courtroom a free man today after two years in prison. He still faces charges of treason and involvement in the assassination of President Lincoln. Northern newspapers campaigning for Davis's release and criticizing his harsh treatment in jail called him "the caged eagle." The haggard but dignified leader, in a black suit and green gloves, appeared in the Customs House courtroom that had been his office in the war. His wife, Varina, worked for Davis's release by writing pleas to notable Northerners.

Carpetbaggers profit from Reconstruction

Austin, Texas, July

The removal of Texas Governor James W. Throckmorton and his replacement by the Republican Elisha M. Pease marks yet another step in the growing power of the carpetbaggers over state and local governments in the former Confederacy. Like the "scalawags" (native white Southerners who are cooperating in the Reconstruction programs) and the "satraps" (the major generals commanding the five regions into which the South has been divided), the "carpetbaggers" – so named because they are said to arrive from the North with such few possessions that they can all be fitted into satchels made of carpeting material – are despised and resented by the white Southerners, who believe that their principal motive in coming down to these states is to enrich themselves by dishonest means.

But that is only part of the picture. With the vast majority of whites boycotting the constitutional conventions, a political vacuum has been created, and the scalawags and carpetbaggers filling it have been pushing hard for progressive laws; moreover, it is clearly in their interest to see to it that Negro freedmen are given full political rights and encouraged to exercise them (→19).

Louisiana Knights

Franklin, Louisiana, May 22

A secret society aimed at preserving white supremacy and opposing "carpetbag rule" was formed at Franklin last night. It is called the Knights of the White Camelia. Alcibiade DeBlanc is the Grand Commander. DeBlanc said the white camelia was chosen as the symbol of the organization because of the "purity of its beautiful whiteness," DeBlanc said the St. Mary Parish organization was in no way connected with the Ku Klux Klan formed in Pulaski, Tennessee, in 1865, although the two societies may have similar goals. Knights units will be called "circles."

Davis, after his term in jail.

ouse unit asks to mpeach Johnson

Vashington, D.C., Nov. 20

Charging "high crimes and mis-lemeanors," the House Judiciary Committee has voted 5 to 4 to ecommend impeachment proceed-ngs against President Johnson. If he measure is approved by the ull House, the President will then be tried by the Senate.

Most of the alleged crimes stem rom Johnson's action in order-ng Secretary of War Edwin Stanton o resign. In doing so, the Presi-lent violated the Tenure of Office Act passed in March of last year, which requires Senate approval for emovals as well as appointments. Johnson believes the law to be un-constitutional, but he has not been able to obtain a ruling from the Supreme Court (→ May 26, 1868).

Britain makes Canada a dominion

London, March 29

A stroke of the pen gave Canada self-governing status as a dominion under the British crown today. Parliament enacted the British North America Act, providing for the union of its former colonies of New Brunswick and Nova Scotia with Quebec and Ontario, which had been joined earlier as the Province of Canada East and West. Two of Britain's other colonies in the Atlantic region, Newfoundland and Prince Edward Island, were participants in the confederation talks but chose to remain separate. The largely uninhabited territory west of the Great Lakes similarly was not included. Ottawa was chosen as the capital of the new dominion and Sir John A. Macdonald was appointed its first Prime Minister.

Pressure from the British government as well as threatening gestures from the United States have led to the signing of the British North America Act.

Ruthless captures 1st Belmont Stakes

New York, June 19

Ruthless was the victor today in the first running of the Belmont Stakes at the race course on Long Island and took the winner's share of the $1,850 purse. The Ruthless jockey was J. Gilpatrick, carrying only 107 pounds, as he triumphed over DeCoursey. Rivoli finished third.

First white settlers arrive in Cheyenne

Cheyenne, Wyoming, July 12

With territorial status reported likely to be approved within two weeks, the first permanent, non-Indian settlers have arrived in the village of Cheyenne. A party of six men and three women took up residence here three days ago. And a realtor, James Whitehead, is offering house lots (→ July 25, 1868).

Midway annexed as Pacific coaling station

Midway Islands, Pacific, Aug. 28

In marked contrast to the acquisition earlier this year of the vast and icy territory of Alaska, two tiny sun-drenched islands have also become part of the United States. Situated some 1,300 miles northwest of Honolulu, the uninhabited Midway Islands were discovered only eight years ago by Captain N.C. Brooks. In the opinion of Captain William Reynolds, the officer who annexed them, they have great potential value as coaling stations for naval and commercial shipping. The steamship, which can carry four times the cargo of the square-rigger, is rapidly taking over the carrying trade; and while most of the trans-Atlantic shipping is now in the hands of British concerns, an American-owned steamship company, the Pacific Mail Line, is flourishing.

Grange set up to aid farm recovery

Washington, D.C., Dec. 4

A new organization called the National Grange has been formed to help farmers in the wake of the Civil War. Oliver Kelley, a government clerk who recently toured the South for the Bureau of Agriculture, was struck by the devastation of the war and the lack of organization among farmers. So Kelley and six associates have formed the National Grange of the Patrons of Animal Husbandry. The purpose of their organization is to disseminate information and train farmers in new techniques. Local chapters are to be called granges and the regional allegiances of old will be discouraged (→ Apr. 13, 1869).

Vanderbilt captures N.Y. Central control

New York City, December

"Law! What do I care about law," Cornelius Vanderbilt once said in his drive for industrial might. The 73-year-old steamship and rail baron has now seized control of the New York Central Railroad by outmaneuvering rival stockholders. Meanwhile, railroad builders take on vast rivers and hills. Andrew Hallidie is planning underground cables to pull cars up San Francisco hills while Charles Harvey opened an elevated railway over Ninth Avenue in New York. John Eads' radical steel-arch bridge will cross the Mississippi at St. Louis and John Roebling's graceful steel-cable design has spanned the Ohio at Cincinnati.

Queretaro, Mexico, June 19. *The four-year reign of Maximilian has ended with the execution of the Emperor by the forces of the new liberal President Benito Juarez. "Death of Maximilian" is by Edouard Manet.*

1868

Johnson

Washington, D.C., Jan. 16. Detroit fish dealer William Davis granted patent for his refrigerated railroad car.

Chicago, May 21. Ulysses S. Grant nominated by Republicans for president (→ July 9).

Washington, D.C., May 25. Omnibus Act reinstates congressional delegations of six Southern states, leaving only Texas without representation in Congress.

Washington, D.C., May 25. Congress mandates eight-hour day for government employees.

United States, May 30. Decoration Day celebrated for first time.

Boston, May. First Triennial Festival held, with "first truly satisfactory performance in this country" of Beethoven's 9th.

Wisconsin, June 23. Milwaukee residents C.C. Scholes, Carlos Glidden and Samuel Soule receive patent for typewriter.→

New York City, July 9. Democratic Party nominates Horatio Seymour for president and Francis P. Blair for vice president (→ Nov. 3).

Moline, Illinois, Aug. 5. John and Charles Deere incorporate their firm as Deere & Company.

Boston, Oct. 13. While working for Western Union, Thomas A Edison receives invention papers for electric vote recorder.

San Francisco, Oct. 21. Earthquake causes more than $3 million damage.

Philadelphia. Standard system of screw threads adopted by U.S. government.

California. John Muir arrives in Yosemite Valley to write and sketch nature.

Washington, D.C. Woman Suffrage Amendment is introduced in Congress for first time and defeated.

Hawaii. Some 150 Japanese immigrate to Hawaii to become plantation workers; [many eventually return home.]

Avery Island, Louisiana. Edmund McIlhenny, New Orleans banker and naturalist, begins selling Tabasco sauce.

United States. Bare-knuckles style boxing becoming increasingly popular sport.

Impeached, Johnson wins in Senate

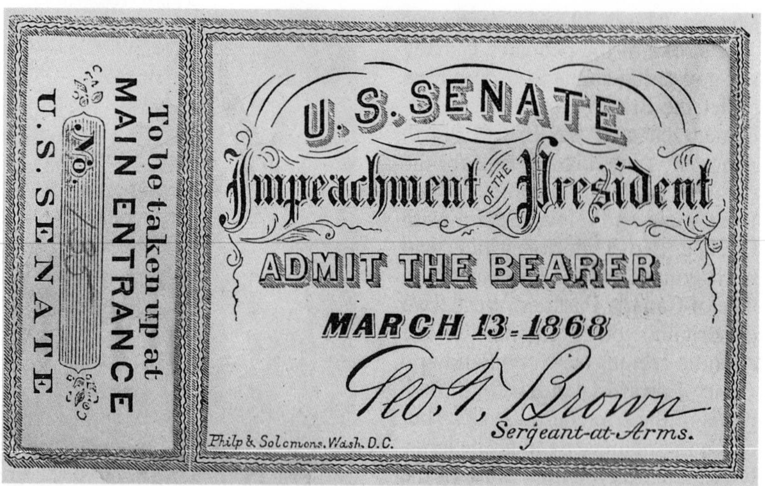

Many see the trial as does Secretary of the Navy Gideon Welles, who has remarked, "What a spectacle!" Only a ticket like the one above will get an observer into the Senate galleries for the impeachment proceedings.

Johnson, first President to undergo the ordeal of an impeachment trial.

Washington, D.C., May 26

One of the most dramatic trials in American history ended today when the Senate acquitted President Johnson of all the articles of impeachment that were brought against him earlier by the House of Representatives. The vote, 35 to 19, was just one short of the two-thirds required for conviction and removal from office.

The long ordeal for President Johnson began February 24, when the House of Representatives voted, 126 to 47, to impeach him for "high crimes and misdemeanors." One of the counts involved his effort to dismiss Secretary of War Edwin M. Stanton, in violation of the Tenure of Office Act passed earlier by the increasingly hostile Congress. The act, seeking to keep a tight rein on the President, forbade him to remove from office, without the consent of the Senate, any person who had been subject to Senate confirmation. The scene then shifted to the Senate when the trial opened in March, with Chief Justice Salmon P. Chase presiding. So many people tried to enter the galleries that admission tickets had to be issued, a different color for each day. President Johnson did not attend, but he conferred each day with his counsel.

Finally, on May 16, the moments of high drama arrived. Radicals had hoped their fellow Republican, Senator James W. Grimes of Iowa, who had suffered a stroke, would be too ill to attend. Instead, he was carried into the chamber by four men and, pale and shaking, voted not guilty.

Despite Grimes's defection from their ranks, the radicals thought they still had a chance. But their hopes were dashed when the Chief Justice asked Senator Edmund J. Ross, a young, first-term Iowa Republican, "How say you?" There was an eerie silence in the chamber as he rose and said: "Not guilty."

Today, 10 days later, the vote on the remaining counts was the same, just one short of the necessary two-thirds needed to remove President Johnson from office.

The gap between the sexes is being bridged on rinks all over the country. Americans are turning to ice skating in droves, perhaps because it is one of the few sports that bring men and women together. Lithograph by Currier.

Wells Fargo to take mail to California

Washington, D.C.

Wells Fargo, the stagecoach line founded in 1852, has been granted a subsidy by the government for daily mail service to California. The coming of the railroad, however, may spell an end to the run. In 1857, John Butterfield, Henry Wells and William Fargo contracted with the U.S. Post Office to carry mail twice a week to San Francisco. Transporting mail and passengers on a 2,700-mile run in 25 days required relay stations every 18 to 30 miles. The coaches, built to carry 15 passengers, travel at speeds of 3 to 12 miles an hour.

14th Amendment passes

Washington, D.C., July 28

Secretary of State William Seward today announced the ratification of the 14th Amendment. While the constitutional reform is perhaps the most complicated of all amendments, its essence is simple: Negroes are full citizens.

The amendment was proposed by a group of congressmen, the Joint Committee of 15, in 1866. The reform grew to encompass several issues, including representational apportionment and the status of those who fought with the South in the war. But at its core are the rights of newly freed slaves, and indirectly, their right to vote. As Horace Greeley argued in his *New York Tribune* on June 10, 1865, "If we give a Negro a bayonet, why can we not give him a ballot?"

The amendment includes apportionment of congressmen in accordance with each state's population, and it bans the holding of national office by anyone who took the constitutional oath but then fought against the union. Another plank states that Confederate debt will not be assumed by the nation or by any state, and will be invalid.

Congress passed the amendment and sent it to the states for the required three-fourths majority ratification. Many Southern states refused to ratify, until it was declared that passage is required for re-entry to Congress. This worked; the Constitution is expanded (→ Sept.).

Measure outfoxes Reconstruction foes

Reconstruction sheet music cover.

Washington, D.C., March 11

Congress passed the fourth Reconstruction Act today, outfoxing Southern congressmen. The act decrees that a simple majority is needed for passage of measures involving the Constitution. It foils the tactic employed by Southern politicians of boycotting the votes, thus denying passage of such legislation. The act, spearheaded by radical Reconstructionists, seems destined to pave the way for a much discussed law to enforce the rights of Negroes to vote. The act defies the struggling President Johnson, who vetoed the previous acts. As Congress did with those vetoes, it is likely to override his opposition to this one (→ July 28).

Sioux War ends; Indians get new land

Wyoming Territory, Nov. 6

An uneasy peace reigns in Wyoming today, following the signing of a treaty between the Oglala Sioux led by Chief Red Cloud and General William T. Sherman of the U.S. government at Fort Laramie. The pact ends two years of fighting that broke out over use of the Bozeman Trail in Wyoming. Miners claimed it was an essential route to gold fields in Montana. But the Sioux said it passed over sacred hunting grounds. The government forced the issue by building forts to protect travelers along the route.

Faces painted and feathers flying, the Oglala then started attacking wagon trains and forts along the trail. In 1866, 80 soldiers were lured from Fort Kearny and massacred as they rode to the aid of a group of pioneers. Fort Smith in Montana had been under constant siege since the fighting began.

Under the terms of the treaty, the United States has ceded part of northern Wyoming and a parcel of land in the Dakotas to the Sioux. But the treaty draws sharp boundaries around the Indians' lands and confines them to these reservations.

Survey shows 373 freed slaves slain

Two Klansmen seized in Alabama.

Washington, D.C., June

The Congressional Committee on Lawlessness and Violence has released statistics showing that, in the last two years, 373 freed slaves have been killed by whites, and that 10 whites have been killed by freedmen. Apart from these figures, it is widely believed that since the Civil War ended a group calling itself the Ku Klux Klan has killed thousands, not only Negroes, but also pro-abolition Republicans. Much of the violence has occurred this year in Florida and Louisiana. Although Governor Reed of Florida has asked the federal government for troops to help quell the killing, his requests have been ignored.

Elevator paves way for the skyscraper

New York City

Ever since Elisha Otis demonstrated his safety elevator in 1854, engineers have dreamed of buildings that could reach toward the sky. At a towering 130 feet, the new Equitable Life Assurance Society building will certainly realize that goal. Built by Arthur Gilman, Edward Kendall and George Post, it is the first building designed around Otis's device. When completed in 1870, the building's two steam-powered elevators will hoist passengers a full five stories. If the elevators prove successful, architects promise even taller buildings.

Sherman and the Sioux sign treaty outside Fort Laramie. Photo by Gardner.

San Antonio, home of ice cream soda

San Antonio, Texas

American ingenuity seems as easily applied to ice cream as to industry, with more new confections and soda fountain gadgets appearing every year. Here in San Antonio, where it can get very hot, people are cooling off with a new treat called the "ice cream soda." It was created by a German immigrant at the Harnisch & Baer Ice Cream Parlour. Harnisch's idea was to match the refreshing virtues of soda water with the sweet delight of ice cream, so he combined the two in a tall glass, offering his patrons both a straw and a spoon. ▷

Grant, Civil War General, is President

U.S. Grant by Samuel Bell Waugh.

Washington, D.C., Nov. 3

General Ulysses S. Grant was elected President of the United States today, easily defeating the Democrat Horatio Seymour of Indiana. Grant, a Republican, carried 26 states with 214 electoral votes; Seymour won eight states and 80 electoral votes. Chosen Vice President was Schuyler Colfax of Indiana. The 46-year-old President-elect, a native of Ohio, was ultimately in command of all Union armies during the Civil War. That war effectively ended when General Robert E. Lee surrendered on April 9, 1865, at Appomattox under terms laid down by Grant. Earlier, both Grant and Lee had served in the Mexican War (→ March 4, 1869).

Suffragists launch journal "Revolution"

New York City, Jan. 1

Suffragists are ringing in the New Year with a weekly journal titled *The Revolution*. Mrs. Elizabeth Cady Stanton is one of the editors, and Miss Susan B. Anthony is publisher and business manager. The backer of the expensive enterprise (it cost $600 to launch) is a rich noncomformist named George Train. This 16-page *Revolution* addresses suffrage and, of course, demands it. But it tackles other issues as well, such as equal pay for equal work, the church's position on women's issues, laws on divorce and the role of unions. And Mrs. Stanton, who has seven children, also gives tips on how to deal with crying babies (→ Dec. 10, 1869).

Susan B. Anthony, revolutionary.

Custer's Seventh Cavalry wipes out Indians at Battle of Washita

Indian Territory, Nov. 27

With bugles sounding "Charge" and the regimental band blaring the famous *Garryowen*, the 800-man Seventh Cavalry Regiment under Lieutenant Colonel (Brevet Major General) George A. Custer today struck a combined force of Arapaho and Cheyenne Indians led by Chief Black Kettle on the Washita River. The battle took place on the plains of the western Indian Territory, just east of the Texas Panhandle.

At the time the charge was sounded, the ground was covered by 12 inches of snow; by the time the battle was over, the blood of more than 100 dead Indians, including the 67-year-old Black Kettle and his wife, stained the snow. Custer's men dealt a severe blow to the Indians. Dozens of women and children were killed by the cavalrymen, who also reportedly scalped several Indians and shot 900 of their horses. One newspaper reporter says the battle scene looked like a slaughter pen, littered with the bodies of animals and Indians, covered with blood, lying on top of one another in holes and ditches. American casualties have been estimated at about 20 killed. One of the cavalrymen who died was the grandson of Alexander Hamilton, Captain Lewis M. Hamilton.

Custer believed he had good reason for his actions. Two months ago, more than 2,000 Indians from Kansas to Texas went on the warpath. Reliable sources indicate that 147 American settlers were killed, 57 wounded, 14 women raped and 426 women and children carried off to captivity. A total of 24 ranches had been destroyed, 11 stagecoaches attacked, and four wagon trains wiped out. The Washita affair was planned by Custer's commander, General Philip Sheridan, who was a scourge of the Confederate army during the Civil War.

In other actions this month, Chief Roman Nose was defeated by army scouts in Colorado; Indian resistance leader Leschi, convicted of murder, was hanged in Washington, and a treaty with the Crows opened 12 million acres of land in Montana to settlement (→ Jan. 1869).

Custer's Seventh Cavalry unleashes its grim surprise on a Cheyenne village.

Cavalry's Colonel George Armstrong Custer. The hero of Washita is skilled in battle, but not much in class, finishing last at West Point.

World's Almanac

New York City

In the heyday of Benjamin Franklin, almanacs were turned out for readers interested in being amused, or improved. They went for *Poor Richard's Almanac* and its pithy maxims, such as "A penny saved is a penny earned." But today's burgeoning entrepreneurs and would-be industrialists want hard facts. Do you need to know how much cotton Britain exported from its colony in India last year? Do you have to find out which of the states has the most railway mileage? Jam-packed with such data is the newly published *New York World's Almanac*. No more pithy maxims.

The latest in fashionable profiles: streamlined in the front, with a large pannier or bustle in back.

Pullman introduces railroad dining car

Palmyra, New York

A new degree of elegance and gentility rolled into the travel picture this year with the appearance of the world's first railroad dining car. Invented by George Mortimer Pullman of Palmyra, it has been placed on the Union Pacific Railroad and it is called the Delmonico, after the famed restaurant of that name in New York City. Now passengers who once might have subsisted on whatever meager fare was offered at railway stations can dine in a plush car offering all the amenities of a first-class restaurant – tables set with fine linens, a choice of a complete menu, wines and spirits, and professional cooks who prepare the food right on board and waiters who minister to any wish.

Wyoming is carved out of Dakota, Utah

Washington, D.C., July 25

President Johnson signed the Organic Act today, which officially creates the Territory of Wyoming. Made up primarily of parts of the old territories of Dakota and Utah, Wyoming is considered to be a political and economic product of the Union Pacific Railroad. There were no settlements of any real importance, with the exception of Fort Laramie, in the region until the arrival of the railroad last year. According to law, the federal Treasury will pay for the cost of the new territory's government. In addition, Washington expects to maintain land offices, military outposts and postal stations and it has disclosed plans to construct a system of territorial roads.

28 Negroes lose seats in Georgia house

Constitutional changes to give rights to Negroes are having mixed results.

Georgia, September

The Georgia legislature has expelled all 28 of its Negro members on the grounds that a Negro has a right to vote in Georgia but not to hold public office. Opponents of the move warned this could cost Georgia its place in the union.

Georgia was restored to statehood along with six other former states of the Confederacy in July. The seven states were re-admitted to the union after they adopted new constitutions and certified the 14th Amendment giving Negroes equal protection under the law. The first state to meet congressional demands was Tennessee, re-admitted in 1866. Arkansas then led a move toward re-admission in June. The states of North and South Carolina, Georgia, Florida, Alabama and Louisiana followed. Now the status of Georgia is in doubt. Mississippi, Texas and Virginia are the holdouts. In Louisiana, a convention made up of an equal number of white and Negro delegates revised the state constitution in March. That constitution gives Negroes the right to vote, prohibits any form of segregation in public places and provides for integrated schools. In June, Oscar J. Dunn, a runaway slave, was elected lieutenant governor (→ Feb. 27, 1869).

American inventors have fruitful year

Milwaukee, Wisconsin

A machine that prints type, letter by letter, on a sheet of paper is among this year's many new inventions. This typewriter was developed by three local men who have applied for a patent. Other new devices include an air brake to make trains safer and shock-absorbing springs to make them more comfortable. One young inventor, Thomas A. Edison, is seeking a patent for an electric vote-recording machine.

"Little Women" by Louisa May Alcott

Massachusetts

Four teen-age sisters – Meg, Jo, Beth, and Amy March – growing up in a Victorian New England village are the heroines of *Little Women*, a largely autobiographical novel for children that is setting sales records in many cities. Its author is Louisa May Alcott, aged 37 and previously best known for sketches about her experiences as a Civil War nurse and as the daughter of utopian reformer Bronson Alcott.

Kit Carson, nemesis of Indians, is dead

Colorado, May 24

Brigadier General Christopher "Kit" Carson is dead at 59. Considered by many Americans to be a national treasure, he passed away today at Boggsville. An original "mountain man," he was a friend and a longtime companion of both Jim Bridger and "The Pathfinder," General John Fremont. Known as "the eyes of the cavalry" in the Navajo War, Carson captured more than 10,000 Indians. Considering himself a "trapper" to the end, he was married to an heiress from New Mexico, where he owned vast lands.

Treaty opens doors to Chinese laborers

Washington, D.C., July 28

Under terms of a treaty signed here today by Secretary of State William Seward and Anson Burlingame, head of a diplomatic mission from China, the door is now open for unrestricted Chinese immigration into this country. Almost all the Chinese are likely to be laborers who will work at building railroads in the West. Burlingame, a former congressman, was named minister to China in 1861. He resigned last year and became the leading member of a three-man Chinese mission to Western countries (→ June 1870).

"Among the Sierra Nevada Mountains, California" (1868) by Albert Bierstadt. Fascinated with the frontier, Bierstadt first went west with a federal survey expedition in 1858. His gift for depicting the strange and fantastic in nature has earned him a very profitable popularity with the public.

1869

Grant

Washington, D.C., March 4. Ulysses S. Grant sworn in as 18th President; at 46, nation's youngest.

Washington, D.C., Apr. 10. Amendment to Judiciary Act raises number of Supreme Court justices from seven to nine.

Washington, D.C., Apr. 13. First annual meeting of National Grange held (→ March 23, 1874).

Texas, Apr. 15. Supreme Court rules in Texas v. White that Union is insoluble and secession is illegal and unconstitutional.

Washington, D.C., Apr. 16. Ebenezer Don Carlos Bassett, first Negro to join U.S. diplomatic corps, named consul general to Haiti.

Colorado, May 24. Major John Wesley Powell begins exploration of Grand Canyon (→ 1881).

Fossil Creek, Kansas, May 28. Band of Cheyenne Indians destroys section of Union Pacific railroad (→ Oct.).

Washington, D.C., June 8. Ives W. McGaffey granted patent for vacuum cleaner.

Kansas City, Missouri, July 4. Burlington Railroad officials open first railroad bridge to span Missouri River.

Avondale, Pennsylvania, July 6. Coal mine disaster kills 108.

San Francisco, July 13. Riots break out between whites and immigrant Chinese laborers.

New Hampshire, August. President Grant scales Mount Washington; he begins on foot, but must finish on horse.

United States, October. Train service begins on transcontinental railroad (→ July 24, 1870).

Washington, D.C., Dec. 12. Colored National Labor Union, first national Negro labor group, organized (→ Jan. 19, 1871).

Cambridge, Mass. Dean Shaler offers first summer course, in geology, at Harvard University.

United States. Approximately 100,000 Norwegians, seeking cheap land and social mobility, immigrated to the United States in last decade.

United States. Mark Twain publishes *The Innocents Abroad,* gaining national recognition.

Golden rail spike joins East to West

The Union Pacific and Central Pacific meet at Promontory Point, Utah.

With completion of the transcontinental railroad, a trip across the United States will take only eight days. The journey used to take three months.

Transcontinental railway disappears into the frontier, uniting the nation and opening the West to settlement and commerce. Lithograph by Currier and Ives.

Promontory Point, Utah, May 10

Above the thin hiss of steam engines facing across a final connecting track today, crowds in the arid valley here read a solemn prayer for the railroad that links the nation from coast to coast. Then president Leland Stanford of the Central Pacific Railroad stepped between the locomotives, the C.P.'s Jupiter and the Union Pacific's 119. To the east: 1,086 miles of U.P. track. To the west: 690 for the C.P. Stanford paused, then swung a silver hammer at a last golden spike. And missed. Amid much hilarity, vice president Thomas Durant of Union Pacific tried. He missed. Finally, the U.P.'s chief engineer, Grenville Dodge, slammed it home, and telegraphers sped the joyous message: "The Pacific railroad is done."

As champagne flowed, Indians eyed the revelers with foreboding. Across the nation, bells and cannons sounded as many paused to reflect on the vast undertaking. The rival companies had expanded furiously starting in 1863 – the U.P. from Omaha and the C.P. from Sacramento – with government subsidies and economic revenues for each mile gained over the other at stake. The Union Pacific overcame obstacles ranging from financial failings and logistical problems to Rocky Mountain peaks and the hostile Cheyenne and Sioux, embittered as white men thrust their iron trail through sacred hunting grounds. The Central Pacific spent well over $23 million blasting its way across the blizzard-swept Sierras and beyond, laying up to 10 miles of track a day. Each company commanded a virtual army of more than 12,000 men, the C.P. relying mostly on Chinese laborers and the U.P. on immigrants from Ireland.

With completion of the railway, a trip from New York to San Francisco has been cut from three months to eight days. As a Californian said of his state today: "She has become part of the great highway which is to unite her with her sister states of the Atlantic." Union Pacific chief engineer Dodge dared to look farther. Invoking Columbus's quest for a route to the Far East, he gazed down the Central Pacific tracks and said, "Gentlemen, *this* is the way to India" (→ 28).

Congress approves 15th Amendment

Washington, D.C., Feb. 27

Congress passed the 15th Amendment today, requiring all Southern states to allow Negroes to vote. While the 14th Amendment granted suffrage rights indirectly, the South circumvented its inference. The reform spells out the government's intentions: "The right of citizens of the United States to vote shall not be denied ... on account of race, color, or previous conditions of servitude." Despite the movement for woman suffrage, the word "sex" was deleted; reformers felt passage would be impossible with the inclusion of gender. The amendment now goes to the states for ratification (→ Feb. 25, 1870).

Manufacturers win increase in tariffs

Washington, D.C., Feb. 24

Rebuffing advocates of free trade, Congress has passed another tariff act that provides increased protection to a rising group of manufacturers. The guiding light of the new bill, as of every major tariff since 1861, is Senator Justin Morrill of Vermont, who inaugurated the policy of using high import duties not to increase revenue but to protect American industry from overseas competition. The first Morrill Tariff Act was passed in 1861 as a wartime measure to increase industrial production. Efforts to cut rates to their pre-war levels have come to naught because of effective resistance by the protected industries.

First pro team pays shortstop $1,400

Cincinnati Red Stockings.

Cincinnati, Apr. 7

Those innovative Red Stockings from Cincinnati have become the first salaried team in baseball. The captain-shortstop, George Wright, contracted for a salary of $1,400 for the season, which began March 15 and will end on November 15. Asa Brainard, the pitcher, will receive $1,200. The Red Stockings, while playing amateur ball last year, were the first club to perform in uniforms that featured shortened pants known as knickerbockers. While this seemed to amuse many of the team's fans, now other clubs are reportedly considering adoption of the new baseball fashion.

Harvard's top post is offered to Eliot

Cambridge, Mass., March 10

Charles Eliot, Harvard graduate and now a member of its board of overseers has been offered the position of president of the university to succeed Thomas Hill. Eliot, 35, was offered the presidency by the Rev. George Putnum, a fellow of the Harvard Corporation. The choice must, however, be approved by the overseers. Many members oppose Eliot's radical ideas on higher education. Eliot was graduated from Harvard second in his class, and has taught there and at M.I.T.

Act sets repayment of the debt in gold

Washington, D.C., March 18

Congress took a long step toward restoring the gold standard today by passing the Public Credit Act, which authorizes payment of the public debt in gold. The act leaves unresolved the issue of whether the $356 million in greenbacks, paper money issued to finance the Civil War, will be redeemable in gold. Financial interests are agitating for redemption in gold, but this is opposed by farmers and businessmen who fear trade will shrink if laws are too restrictive (→ May 1, 1871).

Is "only good Indian a dead Indian"?

Indian Territory, January. *Tochoway, a Comanche chief, entered Fort Cobb and introduced himself to General Philip Sheridan as "a good Indian." "The only good Indian is a dead Indian," was the reply. Two months ago, Black Kettle met with a similar attitude when he asked in vain for camping instructions. Soon after, his village on the Washita was wiped out by Colonel Custer. The land that was home to all American Indians is shrinking fast, bounded by rails and invaded by white fortune hunters.*

New national Negro rights group formed

The National Convention of Colored Men convenes in the nation's capital, with former slave and Negro rights leader Frederick Douglass presiding.

Washington, D.C., Jan. 12

An organization called the National Convention of Colored Men has been established with the distinguished Negro author, journalist and orator Frederick Douglass as its president. Douglass, a slave who escaped to freedom in 1838, was well known before the Civil War as an abolitionist and is now pursuing the cause of suffrage for Negroes. Suffrage as well as protection of Negro children are among the group's highest priorities.

Douglass serves in the Territorial Legislature of the District of Columbia and has been president of the New England Anti-Slavery Society. He has also been elected to serve as a delegate at a convention of Southern Loyalists and Northern Republicans to be held in September, although his attendance may result in controversy.

At meetings that were held in North and South Carolina last year, groups gathered to protest discriminatory legislation and called for proper wages and decent education for the former slaves.

Women's suffrage advocates split in two

Wyoming Territory, Dec. 10

Two decades ago, the Wyoming Territory's Governor witnessed one of the first women's rights conventions ever held. He never forgot it, and today he signed a law making the territory the first place to give women the vote. Yet American suffragists, who should be encouraged and cheering about this victory, find themselves dangerously divided on the question of whether this is the woman's "moment" or just the Negro's "hour." Back in January, the Equal Rights Association, which had fought for both Negro and woman's suffrage, voted to support the 15th Amendment to the Constitution, which allows male Negroes the vote. The Negro rights leader Frederick Douglass, who was once an ardent supporter of woman's suffrage, defended the move, insisting that "the government of this country loves women, but the Negro is loathed."

Mrs. Elizabeth Cady Stanton and Miss Susan B. Anthony demanded to know why they should back a Negro man's right to vote when he could not be trusted to support theirs. The two women formed an all-female organization, the National Woman Suffrage Association. Last month, Mrs. Lucy Stone began a less radical group, the American Woman Suffrage Association, with members of both sexes. Neither party seems strong enough to attain its goals soon (→Sept. 6, 1870).

College football begins, with a rebel yell

New Brunswick, N.J., Nov. 13

Soccer rules were in effect, but the game was called football when Rutgers and Princeton clashed for the first time. There were 25 men on each side as Rutgers scored a 6-4 victory on November 6. In today's return contest between the New Jersey rivals, the Princetons romped to an 8-0 victory with the help of a blood-curdling yell such as the Confederates used when they went into battle against the Union army. Princeton players had used the yell, which they called the "scarer," in the first meeting to no avail.

After the first game, the Princeton team decided that the rebel yell required too much breath, which the players needed for the game, so they taught it to some of their sideline spectators. In the second game, it was the student spectators who did the yelling.

Women mourn Gottschalk, musical idol

Rio de Janeiro, Dec. 18

With the death of Louis Moreau Gottschalk, 41, America has lost its leading matinee idol and one of its most original composers.

Gottschalk, the first American pianist to achieve recognition overseas.

Born in New Orleans of a French Creole mother and German father, he was trained in Paris and spent much of his life abroad. Gottschalk was a fine pianist and the first serious American composer to successfully incorporate native Negro and Creole rhythms in his works. Audiences filled theaters and concert halls to hear him play his own exotic music and many women were attracted by his dark good looks. After mesmerizing the country for four years, Gottschalk spent five years in Cuba. Upon his return, to San Francisco, he was treated like a king, only to be drummed out of town over a scandal involving a young woman at the Oakland Female Seminary. Branded a "bawdy miscreant" and threatened with violence, he returned to Latin America, leaving countless women to mourn his absence, and his death.

Horatio Alger publishes "Luck and Pluck"

New York City

A new assortment of unlikely heroes – destitute but earnest bootblacks, hard-working yet penniless newsboys, oppressed but virtuous scullery maids and orphaned yet optimistic factory hands – will travel the long and winding road from rags to riches in a new series of dime novels, called collectively *Luck and Pluck*, published by the most widely read practitioner of the genre, Horatio Alger. The success enjoyed by Alger, a 37-year-old defrocked Unitarian minister, rivals any enjoyed by the urchins turned entrepreneurs who serve as the protagonists of his wildly popular books. Perhaps the lasting moral to be drawn from Alger's story is that writing about fame and fortune is one way to achieve them. Profits from the sales of his earlier series, the *Ragged Dick* stories, enable Alger to live like a sultan, and there are few Americans who do not recognize the name of the prolific dime-novel laureate of the self-made man.

Alger's new inspirational work.

Gold traders cause panic

Black Friday stuns the traders inside New York City's Gold Room.

New York City, Sept. 24

A daring effort by two speculators, Jay Gould and Jim Fisk, to corner the gold market failed today when the government stepped in at the last minute. Dozens of Wall Street houses would have faced bankruptcy if the Treasury had not intervened by making gold available to them, ending the panic.

Gould and Fisk have made their fortunes by sometimes unscrupulous speculation in railroads. They recently have been involved in a major struggle with J. Pierpont Morgan for control of the Albany & Susquehanna Railway. In this latest effort, they turned their attention to the open market for gold as quoted in greenbacks on Wall Street. They hoped to gain control of the entire supply of gold, forcing dealers to pay any price to fill their contracts to supply the metal.

It appears that Gould and Fisk bribed men high in the Grant administration to make their scheme possible by stopping regular Treasury sales of gold. It is said that they even believed President Grant to be involved in their attempt. By quietly buying up as much gold as they could, they very nearly cornered the market The price of gold in greenbacks paid by desperate dealers rose as high as $162 an ounce today before the government acted, dumping $4 million in gold on the market and causing the corner to collapse. Grant was not involved, but he is being blamed for having allowed his name to be enmeshed in the scandal.

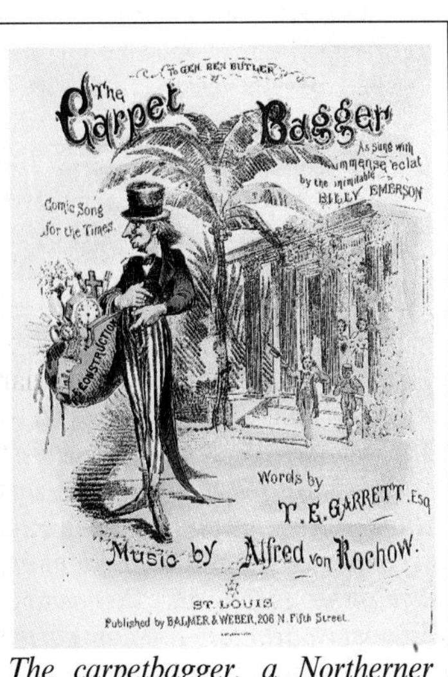

The carpetbagger, a Northerner who has invaded Southern politics, has now inspired a song.

Grandest concert celebrates peace

Boston, June 15

To one of Boston's critics, John Dwight, it seemed to reek of "claptrap." But the opening-day audience thrilled to the festival that was staged by "Musical Demonstrations." It was organized to herald the "Restoration of Peace." Held in the vast new Coliseum, built just for this purpose, the five-day event is featuring a chorus of more than 10,000 and an orchestra of 1,000. The effect has been truly staggering as the sound of the unprecedented chorus washes over the audience in echoing waves.

Knights of Labor founded for working men

Philadelphia, Dec. 9

Uriah S. Stephens, a garment cutter, has organized a secret society for laborers. Called the Noble Order of the Knights of Labor, it is designed to shape the labor movement into "something that will develop more of charity, less of selfishness," acording to members.

To give the society "honor," it refuses to admit anyone who earns a living making or selling liquor. It also bans from its ranks lawyers, gamblers, bankers, stockbrokers and others that it considers devious. To be admitted, one must be a hard-working wage-earner. While the order was started with just 11 Philadelphia tailors, Grand Master Workman Stephens plans to extend membership to other trades and beyond this City of Brotherly Love.

The Knights say their aim is "to uphold the dignity of labor, to affirm the nobility of all those who earn their bread through the sweat of their brows." It is expected that the society will work to mold public opinion in favor of the workers' struggle with management. Its motto extolls unity, saying that a perfect government is one in which "an injury to one is the concern of all."

Also this week in Washington, the first national organization of Negro workers is being formed by 214 delegates from 18 states. It is called the Colored National Labor Union and its president is Isaac Myers (→ 12).

Reformers focus on American kitchen

New York City

Two reformer-abolitionist educators, Catherine E. Beecher (who founded girls' schools in Hartford and Cincinnati) and Harriet Beecher Stowe (who wrote the revolutionary *Uncle Tom's Cabin*), are turning their attention to women's work in the home, with a new publication, *The American Women's Home.* Their views on how to organize a kitchen are particularly novel, calling for better lighting, maximum use of storage space, concepts of waste disposal and placement of the cooking range to cut heat and odors.

"Little Brown Jug" a temperance hit

United States, September

The newly formed Prohibition Party already has an official anthem – *Ten Nights in a Barroom* – but the anthem could just as well be this year's hit, *Little Brown Jug.* The latter's words spell out in detail the effects of John Barleycorn, which the party hopes to ban. Both the party and the song are products of the country's growing temperance movement. Other songs that carry a similar message include *The Gin Fiend*, the Hutchinson Family's *King Alcohol*, and *Father's a Drunkard and Mother is Dead.*

Since the first intercollegiate regatta in 1852, between Harvard and Yale, rowing has thrived. This year, Harvard won its eighth out of ten.

1870

Grant

Brooklyn, New York, Jan. 2. Construction begins on Brooklyn Bridge.

Piegen Camp, Montana, Jan. 23. U.S. cavalry under command of Eugene M. Baker slaughters 173 Indians, almost all women and children.

Washington, D.C., Feb. 25. The Rev. Hiram R. Revels, moderate Republican from Mississippi, is first Negro to be seated in Senate (→Dec. 12).

Helena, Montana, Apr. 27. J.L. Compton and Joseph Wilson, guilty of robbery and murder, are last to be executed from "Hangman's Tree."

Washington, D.C., June 22. Department of Justice established by act of Congress, illustrating attorney general's growing responsibilities.

Washington, D.C., June 30. In 28-28 tie, Senate rejects Secretary of State Hamilton Fish's plan to annex Dominican Republic (→March 9, 1871).

Wyoming, June. Union Pacific hires Chinese for $32.50 a month rather than pay whites $52 a month (→Oct. 24, 1871).

Washington, D.C., July 12. John and Isaiah Hyatt get patent for celluloid, discovered while seeking substitute for ivory used to make billiard balls.

Washington, D.C., Dec. 5. All states represented for first time since 1860, as 41st Congress convenes.

New England. Production of paper from pulpwood begins.

New Haven, Conn. Harvard and Yale organize first comprehensive programs of graduate study in country.

New York City. Thomas Edison starts "invention factory."

California. Legal precedent set as court rules in White v. Flood that Negro child may not attend white school.

Akron, Ohio. B.F. Goodrich begin manufacturing fire hose.

New York City. Literary magazine *Scribner's Monthly* begins publication.

New York City. Bret Harte's *The Luck of Roaring Camp and Other Sketches* published.

DEATH

Lexington, Virginia, Oct. 12. Robert E. Lee, Confederate general-in-chief (*Jan. 19, 1807).

Robert E. Lee wins Mississippi boat race

The Robert E. Lee and Natchez, neck and neck. Currier & Ives lithograph.

St. Louis, July 4

The banks of the Mississippi resounded with cannons and cheers as the Robert E. Lee docked here at 11:24 this morning, winning the great riverboat race with the Natchez. The powerful boat had completed a 1,100-mile trip up the Mississippi from New Orleans in three days 18 hours and 14 minutes. The Natchez arrived just before 6 p.m. to the not-quite-so-enthusiastic cheers of its backers. The Robert E. Lee's owner and captain, John W. Cannon, said on arriving that his engines, with 40-inch cylinders, are "the best in the world." The Natchez, with slightly less powerful engines, had been close, but lagging in the race since it left New Orleans June 30. The vessel's captain, the legendary Thomas P. Leathers of Natchez, claimed he would have come in first had he not been delayed in fog above Devil's Island. Leathers's Natchez came in fully six and a half hours behind the Robert E. Lee.

The historic race has galvanized the people of the Mississippi Valley. Hundreds of thousands lined the riverbanks from New Orleans all the way to St. Louis to cheer the boats on. Cannon and Leathers are longtime rivals. Leathers, whose Natchez was the early favorite, challenged Cannon to the race, a contest between the two greatest riverboats and the two most skillful captains on the Mississippi River.

Rockefeller forms Standard Oil Co.

Cleveland, Jan. 10

The Standard Oil Company was incorporated here today by John D. Rockefeller and his brother William. Standard Oil has a capitalization of $1 million. Its president, John D., is only 31 but already a commanding figure in the American oil industry. Rockefeller entered the oil business as a partner in Andrews, Clark and Company, the nucleus of the new corporation. He has been buying properties ever since, showing little mercy to competitors, and he is now in a position to extend his control of the industry even further (→Jan. 2, 1882).

Population surges

Washington, D.C.

The population of the United States has surged to 39.8 million, according to this year's census, with immigration more than making up for the lives lost in the Civil War. More than 2.3 million immigrants arrived in the 1860's. Although New York is still the most populous state with nearly 4.4 million residents, the continuing drive west is shown not only by entries of 9,000 residents in Arizona, 86,000 in Utah and 18,306 in Montana but also by a 2.5 percent decline in New Hampshire's population, the first drop in the history of that state.

Thomas Nast satirizes the influence wielded by Tammany Hall's "Boss" Tweed, the corrupt "power behind the throne" of New York Governor John B. Hoffman.

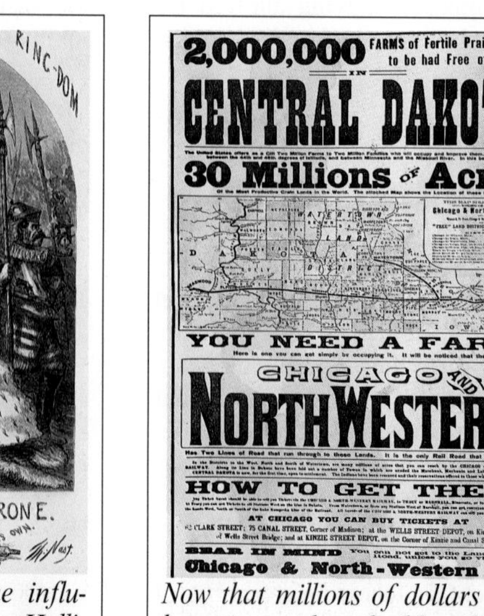

Now that millions of dollars have been invested to build rail lines across the land, the Chicago and Northwestern Railway wants to make sure that they will be used.

The Democratic Party, portrayed as a donkey for the first time by Thomas Nast, is busy kicking ex-Secretary of War Edwin Stanton even after his death. Democrats denounced Stanton, a fellow party member, because he supported the radical Republicans both during and after the Civil War.

First train from West arrives in New York

All aboard! "Through to the Pacific." Lithograph by Currier and Ives.

New York City, July 24

The first through train arrived from San Francisco today, completing a transcontinental route across the Central Pacific and Union Pacific lines and into the vast Eastern rail network to New York, a city served by rail links carrying 50,000 people daily. Alternate routes to the Far West are being planned. The Denver Pacific and Kansas Pacific have linked Missouri and Colorado; the companies now aim for Santa Fe. Northern Pacific, Southern Pacific and Atchison, Topeka & Santa Fe routes are also planned.

Great Atlantic & Pacific store is thriving

New York City

Prospering and growing from a small store opened in 1859 on Vesey Street here, the newly named Great Atlantic & Pacific Tea Company (in honor of the completion of the transcontinental railroad) continues making merchandising strides. George Huntington Hartford and George F. Gilman pioneered purchasing in large amounts from ships arriving in New York, thus cutting their costs and passing savings on to the customer. They now import right from the Orient, carrying exotic spices and staples.

First woman's vote cast

Laramie, Wyoming Terr., Sept. 6

Mrs. Louisa Swain today became the first woman in the nation to cast a legal ballot, voting under equal suffrage laws passed here last year. Some 1,000 other women in the territory also voted for the first time, and it appears the Republicans are headed for a sweeping victory.

Women in Wyoming, and out on the frontier generally, have always been highly respected, often performing the same arduous tasks as men. So it seemed only fitting when the territory's Governor signed the legislation giving women the right to vote last December 10.

Meanwhile in New York City, Victoria Woodhull, a self-styled clairvoyant and the editor of *Woodhull & Claflin's Weekly*, and her sister Tennessee Claflin have opened the first female-owned stock firm in the United States. The company is reportedly generating a healthy profit as well as lots of gossip on Wall Street. Mrs. Woodhull is a beautiful and outlandish woman, one who is divorced and advocates free love. And she seems to enjoy the spotlight. She plans to submit a petition to Congress next year, arguing that the 14th and 15th Amendments to the Constitution guarantee the franchise to all American citizens (→Feb. 1, 1871).

Two Negroes take seats in Congress

Washington, D.C., Dec. 12

Joseph H. Rainey of South Carolina today became the first Negro member of the House of Representatives and the second Negro to be seated in the United States Congress. The Rev. Hiram R. Revels of Mississippi was seated as a member of the Senate in February. The Negro minister will complete the term of former Mississippi Senator Jefferson Davis, who was president of the Confederacy. All Confederate states have now been restored to the union (→March 4, 1871).

The Red McIntosh, tasty to the core

Vermont

Of the many varieties of apples grown in the United States (though the apple is not a native American fruit), a new type called the Red McIntosh is becoming one of the most popular for its taste, aroma, juiciness and cross-breeding potential. The first seedling was planted in 1796 in Dundas County, Ontario, by John McIntosh. His wife kept the variety going (neighbors called it "granny's apple") and their son Allan conducts extensive propagation in New York and Vermont.

"The Barnyard" by A.E. Zeliff. With rail lines to transport livestock to the East, any cattleman can now produce meat for sale in distant markets.

New York City, August 8. *The Magic, under Captain Osgood, has defeated the British yacht Cambria to protect the America's Cup from its first challenger. The cup came to the New York Yacht Club from England after the America won it in a race around the Isle of Wight in 1851. It was first called the 100-guinea cup; today, its new name proved well-deserved.*

1871

Grant

Washington, D.C., Jan. 19. Colored National Labor Union petitions Congress for national system of educational and technical training.

Washington, D.C., Feb. 21. Territorial government instituted in District of Columbia.

Washington, D.C., March 9. President Grant forces Charles Sumner off Senate Foreign Relations Committee, retaliating for Sumner's opposition to Dominican annexation.

Cotton Gin Port, Mississippi, March 18. Ku Klux Klansmen force white schoolmarm Miss Sarah A. Allen to leave school for colored children.

Boston, Apr. 1. Alexander Graham Bell begins using his father's system of "visible speech" to teach deaf.

Springfield, Illinois, Apr. 7. Illinois Railroad Act passed, authorizing commission to fix maximum rates and curtail corporate monopolies.

Minneapolis, Minn., Apr. 12. Charles Pillsbury receives full title to flour mill, C.A. Pillsbury & Company.

Camp Grant, Arizona Territory, Apr. 30. Mob kills more than 100 Apaches, who are supposed to be under federal protection.

New York City, May 10. Equal Rights Party nominates Victoria Woodhull for president and Frederick Douglass for vice president.

New York City, July 12. Rioting between Scotch-Irish Presbyterians and Irish Catholics during Scotch-Irish parade leaves 31 civilians and two policemen dead.

New York City, July 30. William Marcy "Boss" Tweed asks defiantly, "As long as I count the votes, what are you going to do about it?" (→Nov. 19, 1872).

New Bedford, Massachusetts, August. United States Arctic whaling fleet trapped by earliest winter in memory; 32 of 39 vessels frozen in ice.

United States, Oct. 23. American yacht Columbia wins America's Cup.

Washington, D.C. National Rifle Association founded.

United States. *The Little Old Cabin in the Lane,* by Will S. Hays, published; it is lament for days of slavery.

"Boss" Tweed's corruption exposed; frauds total millions

New York City, July 8

The New York Times published a scathing expose this morning, charging William "Boss" Tweed with raiding the city treasury and lining his pockets with millions of tax dollars. Cartoonist Thomas Nast has long made the bloated face and torso of Tweed his target of caricature and ridicule in the pages of *Harper's Weekly*. Now *The Times* says it has the cold, hard facts on Tweed and his Tammany "Ring." If the newspaper and editor George Jones are correct, it is surprising that New York has any money left to pay its bills.

The Tammany Tiger loose. Thomas Nast's indictment of "Boss" Tweed.

Tweed has wielded virtually unchallenged political power in New York. He has handed out city jobs, selected nominees of the Democratic Party and, some charge, even counted the ballots. Tweed has also made millions by overcharging the city for services and drawing up leases for property that does not exist. "Thousands of dollars are paid for bare walls and unoccupied rooms," one headline says. James Ingersoll, nicknamed the "Chairmaker," is identified as Tweed's partner and president of an arms company who leases a non-existent armory. Other members of the ring are identified as Richard "Slippery Dick" Connolly, the city comptroller, Andrew Garvey, the "Prince of Plasterers," and John Keyser, the "Plumber." *The Times* says the ring has charged so much for floor coverings at City Hall that the building could have been carpeted three times over.

Tweed: "What are you laughing at? To the victor belong the spoils."

For cartoonist Nast, the porcine body, banana-like nose and beady eyes of Tweed have been easy targets. *The Times* has had to dig more deeply for the real goods on the Boss. Much of the paper's information has apparently been supplied by Matthew O'Rourke, who quit in May after serving five months as county bookkeeper. Supporters of Tweed say the Republican-inspired criticism of Tweed is designed to draw attention away from Democratic scandals in Washington (→ 30).

Grain exports show the nation's vigor

Chicago

Considered by many to be the chief indicator of economic welfare in the United States, grain crops have gained tremendously in volume and value. Exports alone total 50 million bushels of wheat and eight million of corn. A good part of this increase derives from the farming of recently opened land west of the Mississippi, with Minnesota, Iowa and California accounting for the bulk of it. The ability to bring the grain to market as an export results from new railroads in the West. The grain boom is so great that Illinois has passed a law to regulate grain elevators.

Victoria Woodhull's vote petition rejected

Washington, D.C., Feb. 1

The House Judiciary Committee has rejected the woman's suffrage petition that was submitted by Mrs. Victoria Woodhull on January 11. On that occasion, Mrs. Woodhull, a stockbroker and newspaper editor from New York, directly addressed the committee, an opportunity that no woman has ever been granted before. Mrs. Woodhull argued that the 14th and 15th Amendments to the Constitution implicitly guarantee the franchise to all people, white and Negro, men and women. In spite of the setback, Mrs. Woodhull, like the women's rights leader Miss Susan B. Anthony, will soon start a lecture tour to bring her message to the people (→ May 10).

Thomas Nast depicts Victoria Woodhull as an advocate of free love.

Act seeks to thwart racists in the South

Washington, D.C., Apr. 20

Intent on disciplining the South, Congress has passed still another so-called Force Act, aimed at ensuring Negro rights in that part of the nation. The new legislation, as well as two other bills enacted in recent months, seeks to stem efforts by the Ku Klux Klan and other racist groups that have sought to prevent registration, voting and jury service by Negroes. Because of terrorist activities by white supremacists, the bills have been called the Ku Klux Klan acts.

Leading the fight for the bill that passed today was Senator Ben Butler of New York, who served as attorney general in the Jackson administration. Under terms of the new law, the president would be authorized to use federal troops to enforce the Constitution's 14th Amendment, granting citizenship to anyone born or naturalized in the United States (→March 1872).

Civil Service body is created by Grant

Washington, D.C., March 3

Under political pressure for the corruption within his administration, President Grant today established the Civil Service Commission. It will be responsible for creating the means to hire candidates for federal jobs according to merit, not by the patronage system. Appointments will be made on the basis of competitive tests as in Britain.

Patronage appointments by the executive have always been subject to cronyism. But in the Grant administration, corruption has run rampant. The independent journal *The Nation* has accused Grant of making "some of the worst (appointments) ever made by a civilized Christian government." Republicans, who have seen Grant make several poor appointments and accept dubious political favors, promoted civil service reform.

Grant's reputation was sullied by involvement by association in the 1869 "Black Friday" scandal on Wall Street. No doubt, party chiefs are hoping to regain credibility before elections (→Sept. 4, 1872).

Indians become wards of United States

Since 1866, government grants to the railroads have been slicing parcels of land off the reservations. Now, with treaties replaced by even less authoritative "agreements," Indian lands can be enlarged or shrunk by executive order.

Washington, D.C., March 3

After the many decades of wrangling about the legal relationship of the American Indians to the American government, a decision has been reached that many people hope will last. Legislation was approved today that formally ends the tradition of treating the Indian Nations as European-like sovereign states, an old Anglo-American practice that began with the Treaty of Fort Stanwix back in 1768.

Under the new Indian Appropriations Bill, all Indians will be considered and treated as "individuals." And as such, they will be legally designated "wards" or charges of the government. One reason for the new approach to the Indian problem is this: Indians do not have the same concept of sovereignty as do Americans and Europeans. One chief may sign a treaty; but the extent of his authority is rarely agreed upon by his own people. So when Indians make treaties, neither they nor the United States government know for certain to whom the rules apply. Consequently, the American government has decided that it must be easier – and hopefully fairer to everyone concerned – to treat the Indians as "individual" people, and judge them on that legal basis.

"Max Schmitt in a Single Scull" (1871) by Thomas Eakins, 27, already a highly skilled realist. Eakins himself is depicted rowing in the background.

Southern power in Congress restored

Washington, D.C., March 4

The Georgia delegation returned to Congress today as the 42nd session gets under way with Southern strength restored. The return of the South follows close on the heels of Georgia's turnabout ratification of the 15th Amendment to the Constitution, which makes it illegal to deny the right to vote on racial grounds. The Georgia legislature, which had barred membership to Negroes but has now agreed to seat them, also voted to re-ratify the 14th Amendment, which guarantees equal protection. Both actions came after an earlier refusal to accept the 15th Amendment resulted in restoration of federal military rule in support of Governor Rufus Bullock. The 37-year-old Governor, who is an active supporter of the congressional plan of Reconstruction, has been accused of corruption. The charges against him include the sale of pardons (→Apr. 20).

Professionals form a baseball league

New York City

The Philadelphia Athletics were perched atop the new league as the first season of the National Association of Professional Baseball Players drew to a close. The Athletics won the championship with a record of 22 victories and seven losses, followed by Chicago. Boston was favored to win it all, but injuries destroyed its chances. Other clubs in the league are the Chicago White Stockings, the New York Mutuals, the Cleveland Forest Citys, the Fort Wayne Kekiongas, the Rockford City Citys, the Washington Nationals and the Washington Olympics.

The league was formed amid the noise and drinking of St. Patrick's Day at Colliers Cafe in downtown New York. James N. Kerns was elected president of the association. The Brooklyn Eckfords were supposed to join, but they felt the $10 entry fee was too risky. However, the Eckfords came in after the Kekionga franchise folded in August. The Eckfords' record was unremarkable; but the undaunted Brooklyns said: "Wait till next year."

Death toll is soaring in Chicago fire

Chicago, Oct. 8

As midnight approaches, one of America's greatest cities is shrouded in flames. Chicago has been afire for two and a half hours, and the conflagration grows fiercer by the minute. Already 100 people have been killed, and 1,000 are homeless. Damage so far is in the millions.

No one ever imagined this could happen; Lake Michigan and the Chicago River, flanking and dividing the city, seemed a natural defense against such a tragedy. And the fire department seemed fit to meet any emergency: only last night it efficiently put out a fire that had erupted in the West Division between Clinton and Canal Streets. But this is called the Windy City with good reason. Whenever the fire appears to be defeated, the wind whisks a flame yards away. The grass, parched from this summer's severe drought, feeds the flames and keeps them dangerously alive.

No one is sure how the fire started, but it is believed to have begun on the West Side of town at about 9:30. It headed northeast, and only moments ago it jumped the river at Adams Street. Flames are now driving out the inhabitants of Conley's Patch, a disreputable part of town. Gamblers and prostitutes are fleeing their places of business and the poorly constructed houses of clapboard pine crackle and snap before collapsing into embers.

At last report, many people were heading for the North Side, which may be out of the fire's path (→ 14).

The fire soars and spreads, now covering five square miles. Currier & Ives.

Blaze is out: 300 die, $200 million lost

Chicago, Oct. 14

Mayor Roswell Mason put his city in the care of the Chicago Relief and Aid Society today. The society, founded 11 years ago (an old institution for this young city), faces its greatest challenge. The Great Fire, as it is already being called, raged from October 8 through the 9th, leaving a path of destruction. As many as 300 people are believed dead, some 90,000 are without homes and the damage is estimated at nearly $200 million.

Rumors abound as to how the conflagration got started: the religious see it as God's judgment; the political see it as the work of Communists, and the common people blame a cow in Mrs. O'Leary's barn for knocking over a lantern. Mrs. O'Leary, who lives on De Koven Street on the West Side, says this is an out-and-out lie.

Fortunately, the fire missed both the stockyards and freight yards, and with food arriving from Cincinnati, Milwaukee and other cities, the people should be able to avert starvation. The society is drawing up plans to ration food and coal and to construct temporary housing. Meanwhile, the homeless are resolute: one man was seen displaying a sign that read: "All gone but wife and babes and pluck."

Near the river, a once-thriving business district laid waste by the fire.

The New-York Times.

NEW-YORK, TUESDAY, OCTOBER 10, 1871.

The Devastation of Chicago—Map of the Burned District as Far as Heard From.

The burned area includes the water and gas works and several rail depots.

Anti-Chinese riot causes 19 deaths

Los Angeles, Oct. 24

A mob of 400 stormed the center of the Chinese community at Arcadia and Los Angeles Streets today and murdered 19 Chinese. The outburst was the result of a feud between two secret Chinese organizations called tongs over the alleged abduction of a woman. The mob, which formed after an investigating policeman was shot, hanged any fleeing Chinese they caught, using the high frames of nearby prairie wagons as makeshift gallows. Resentment against the city's 200 Chinese is running high because the newcomers will work for low wages at a time when Los Angeles is still recovering from bankruptcy.

Staten Island ferry explodes, killing 72

New York City, July 30

A shattering blast on the Staten Island Ferry has turned a part of New York harbor into a pool of death. At 1:30 p.m., the Westfield sat in South Ferry, its unfortunate passengers crowded at the bay end of the vessel seeking relief from the sultry weather. Suddenly, just beneath them, in the bowels of the boat, the boiler exploded, splintering 75 feet of deck and scattering men, women and children like dolls. Park Hospital is a battlefield; 72 are dead and 135 more suffer from burns, lacerations and concussions.

Lumber town razed by fierce forest fire

Peshtigo, Wisconsin, Oct. 9

Yesterday at 9 p.m. there was a bustling lumber town of 2,000 here. At 10 there was a pile of ash. The fire came in gusts from the woods, blown in as though shot from a gun.

Before the fire died out, at least 1,100 people were dead, nearly all of whom had made their living from the very trees that killed them. Several farm families in clearings to the north and west of the blazing woods took their own lives rather than die in the fire storm.

Top court validates war-era greenbacks

Washington, D.C., May 1

The Supreme Court abruptly reversed itself today, upholding greenbacks. Officially called "Legal Tender Notes," $450 million worth were printed (the back was green) to help pay for the Civil War and they were not redeemable in gold. The new decision of the court means that it is legal to pay debts in greenbacks, which fluctuate in value, and have fallen to as low as 35 cents on the dollar. Similar Confederate currency is virtually worthless.

Only 15 months ago, the high court ruled the other way, holding the Legal Tender Act unconstitutional. The same day, President Grant filled two court vacancies. Four days later, the full body met and agreed to rehear the case. Today, with help from the latest Grant appointees, the greenbacks have a new lease on life (→ Jan. 14, 1875).

"Doctor Livingstone, I presume," says Henry Stanley in Africa

Stanley finds Dr. Livingstone alive near the shores of Lake Tanganyika.

Ujiji, Central Africa, Nov. 10

With the phrase "Dr. Livingstone, I presume," Henry Stanley, the world's most adventurous journalist, greeted the world's most famous and admired missionary, Dr. David Livingstone. The meeting occurred in this village on Lake Tanganyika, and was the culmination of a search that began two years ago when *New York Herald* owner James Gordon Bennett commissioned Stanley, a Welsh-born former Confederate soldier, to go to Central Africa to find Livingstone.

An explorer as well as a missionary, the Scottish-born Dr. Livingstone has spent some 30 years on the "dark continent." On his present journey, he has been searching for the sources of the Congo and Nile Rivers, as well as continuing his missionary work and fight against the slave trade; but his health is known to be poor and many thought that he had long been dead.

For Stanley this is by no means his first big "scoop." Four years ago, also on a *Herald* assignment, the journalist accompanied a British military expedition to Ethiopia and managed to get his account of the fall of Magdala back to London in advance of the official dispatches.

Brigham Young arrested for polygamy

Salt Lake City, Utah, Oct. 2

Federal officials today arrested the Mormon leader Brigham Young for "lewd and lascivious cohabitation" with 16 of his wives. Following his appearance before a federal judge, the 70-year-old Young was allowed to return home to await his trial. The arrest of Young seems to be part of an attempt by some of the federal authorities in the territory to destroy the power of the Latter Day Saints, as the Mormons call themselves. Several other Mormon leaders also were recently arrested for polygamy. Still others have been charged with murder as a result of the killings that occurred during the Mormon War of 1857.

The Mormons, ever mindful of the persecutions that they have endured, are afraid that if Young is jailed he will suffer the same fate as their founder, Joseph Smith, who was murdered by a mob while in a Carthage, Illinois, jail.

Barnum opens great traveling menagerie

Brooklyn, New York, Apr. 10

The wealthiest professional liar on earth has outdone himself again. Phineas T. Barnum, the self-proclaimed "Prince of Humbug," has opened the Great Travelling Museum, Menagerie, Caravan, and Hippodrome. Barnum seems unperturbed by the 1868 loss of his American Museum. Fire killed dozens of exotic animals that took years of effort to acquire. He merely turned his mind to getting more.

Attractions promised include Alaskan sea lions, an Italian goat on horseback and four Fiji cannibals, saved from the mouth of a royal captor. The show is a must, coming from the man who gave us the Fiji Mermaid, Siamese twins Chang and Eng, and Tom Thumb. As Barnum says, "This is a trading world, and men, women and children, who cannot live on gravity alone, need something to satisfy their gayer, lighter moods."

Domestic bliss: Brigham Young and his wives at home in Salt Lake City.

Barnum's is not the first traveling circus, but it may be the most glorious.

1872

Grant

New York City, Jan. 18. *Publishers Weekly* begins production in response to expansion of publishing industry.

Washington, D.C., Feb. 17. Senate rejects treaty with Samoan Islands, urging protective role for United States in area and construction of naval coaling station on Pago Pago.

Washington, D.C., Feb. 22. Congress passes resolution fixing date for congressional elections on Tuesday after first Monday in November, effective in 1876.

Indiana, March 23. *Indianapolis Sentinel* is first to describe anti-Blaine Republicans as "mugwumps."

South Carolina, March. Habeas corpus suspended; 500 Klansmen arrested and 55 of them are convicted (→ June 10).

New York City, Apr. 7. Western Electric Company founded by Anson Stager and Elisha Gray.

Nebraska, Apr. 10. Arbor Day celebrated for first time in United States.

Annapolis, Maryland, Oct. 21. John H. Conyers is first Negro to enter Naval Academy.

Washington, December. Serious earthquake splits mountain, causing rock slides that stop flow of Columbia River for several hours.

Washington, D.C. Luther Chicks Crowell invents machine to manufacture flat-bottomed paper bags.

Washington, D.C. Charlotte E. Ray becomes nation's first Negro woman attorney as well as first American woman to be graduated from law school.

Kansas. Town of Dodge City laid out, approximately five miles from Fort Dodge.

Omaha, Nebraska. "Buffalo Bill" elected to legislature.

Boston. *Boston Globe* begins publication.

United States. *The Courtship of Miles Standish* by Henry Wadsworth Longfellow published.

United States. *Roughing It* by Mark Twain published.

DEATH

New York, Nov. 11. Horace Greeley, newspaper publisher, editor and presidential candidate.

Betsy Ross flag story, fact or myth?

"Betsy Ross" by J.L.G. Ferris. Although there is no evidence that the Philadelphia seamstress and upholsterer made the first American flag, she did supply "ships colors," or flags, to the Pennsylvania State Navy Board in 1777.

Philadelphia

This city long ago gave way to Washington as the official home of the nation's flag, but it refuses to relinquish the flag's history. The latest account of the banner's origins, presented two years ago at the Pennsylvania Historical Society, is gaining currency now. According to William J. Canby, a Quaker seamstress named Betsy Ross gets the prize. In June of 1776, the story goes, Robert Morris and George Washington asked Betsy Ross for help. Using Washington's design, which some think drew its circle of stars from King Arthur's Round Table, she created the colonies' first symbol of nationhood.

Canby says his account is based on conversations with his grandmother in 1836. He was 11 then, and she 84. Though Ross did make naval flags for Pennsylvania, no good evidence supports her role as "mother" of the Stars and Stripes.

Other accounts are equally shaky. One traces the flag to the Washington family's Sulgrave Manor coat of arms, designed in 1539. The only claim actually stated at the time is that of Francis Hopkinson, a signer of the Declaration of Independence. He asked of Congress "a quarter cask of the public wine" for designing the flag, but his request was apparently denied.

An original American, "White Cloud, Head Chief of the Iowas," by George Catlin, frontier artist, who died on December 28.

An American original, Samuel F.B. Morse, a painter, the inventor of the telegraph and lately a philanthropist, died on April 2.

Violent earthquake strikes California

Lone Pine, California, March 26

The calm of a clear, moonlit night near the snow-capped Sierra Nevadas was shattered at 2:25 a.m. today by an earthquake that reduced all the adobe and stone buildings of this small community to rubble in a matter of minutes. Rescue crews clearing away the wreckage counted 27 dead and 60 injured out of Lone Pine's population of 300. The quake moved some fences as much as 18 feet, filled canyons with rubble piled as high as 100-foot redwood trees and created a depression that has become a lake. The Inyo County seat, nearby Independence, escaped without any loss of life, primarily because its buildings are made of wood.

James gang robs bank in Kentucky

Columbia, Kentucky, Apr. 29

The James gang has struck again! Witnesses say that a small group of bandits led by Jesse and Frank James robbed the Deposit Bank here today. They say that five gunmen rode into town separately and met at the town square. Three went into the bank, while two stood watch outside. Cashier R.A. Martin was shot to death. Unable to open the safe, the gang escaped on horseback with $200 found in the cash drawer (→ July 21, 1873).

It's a fad: Another roller rink opens

Cheyenne, Wyoming, February

From the chic types in Newport, Rhode Island, to poor, hardworking folks here in Cheyenne, Americans have found a new way to relax. It's called roller skating and most of the skating rinks aren't plush. Many charge 25 cents to rent a pair of the new mass-produced skates (far cheaper than the hand-made ones developed by Everett Plimpton in 1866). One rink pioneer here in Cheyenne calls the new pastime "a moral and exciting diversion." Now a few fancy rinks have come to downtown New York, too.

ienna's Strauss onducts in Boston

oston, June 17

Johann Strauss is the star of the Vorld's Peace Jubilee and Internationa Music Festival that began tonight, conducting his *Blue Danube* waltz with an orchestra of ,000 players. Strauss, who arrived une 13 from Austria on the steamhip Rhein, is one of Europe's most amous composers, best known for is waltzes. Ten concerts are being iven, ostensibly to celebrate the nd of the Franco-Prussian War. The massive event was organized y the famous American band leader P.S. Gilmore, who favors musical erformances with maximum instrumentation. He is also known s the composer of *When Johnny Comes Marching Home*. Eclectic nternational music is the theme of the jubilee. The hall where the oncerts are being performed seats housands of people, and Strauss is eing paid $1 per seat to conduct.

Bribery is exposed in Grant's regime

New York City, Sept. 4

Allegations of bribery rocked the re-election campaign of President Grant today, but it is unlikely that the charges of seedy financial manipulation will prevent the soldier-politician from serving another term in the White House. The damaging charges were published in Charles Anderson Dana's *New York Sun*. The paper reveals that top officials of the Union Pacific railroad firm have tried to head off a congressional investigation by paying off members of the Grant administration and Congress. The bribery scheme is outlined in a series of letters written by Oakes Ames, one of the founders of Credit Mobilier of America, to an associate, Henry McComb. The letters, obtained and published by the *Sun*, reveal that Ames planned to make stock available to certain congressmen at par, even though it was worth twice as much. In one of the letters, Ames wrote that giving stock to the congressmen made sense because that is "where it will produce the most good to us."

The Union Pacific, racing through a prairie fire, and now embroiled in scandal.

The *Sun* expose charges that Vice President Schuyler Colfax and Grant's new running mate, Henry Wilson, have both derived financial advantage from Credit Mobilier. The firm was established by investors who realized there is more money to be made in building a railroad than in running one. Ames and others established the construction firm so they could make contracts with themselves. They also made more than $20 million, profits that were extracted from the generous subsidies granted by Congress.

The Credit Mobilier affair is not the first scandal to touch the White House, and Grant's critics blame the President. They say he has a disturbing tendency to appoint unseasoned political cronies to top positions in his administration. He also associates with unscrupulous financiers. During his first term, Grant sided with fiscal conservatives and pledged to redeem for gold greenbacks issued during the war. His policy played into the hands of manipulators such as Jay Gould and James Fisk, who tried to corner the gold market. Grant stopped them but was embarrassed by reports that members of his administration had been bribed (→Nov. 5).

Congress allows Freedmen's Bureau to die

Vashington, D.C., June 10

The Freedmen's Bureau, threatened with extinction for years, has inally been allowed to lapse. The ureau was established in 1865 as a art of the War Department, with a commissioner to be appointed by he president. The commissioner ad power to "control all subjects elating to refugees and freedmen." The bureau was able to appropriate abandoned tracts of land and lease lots of up to 40 acres to freedmen, at low rent. It also founded schools, issued rations and clothing and spent millions for medical care. As a result, the death rate of freed slaves fell from 38 percent to a low of 2 percent. With the closing of the agency, Negroes now have little recourse if threatened with eviction from their land (→Dec. 7, 1874).

Freedmen, granted the right to vote, go to the polls in New Orleans.

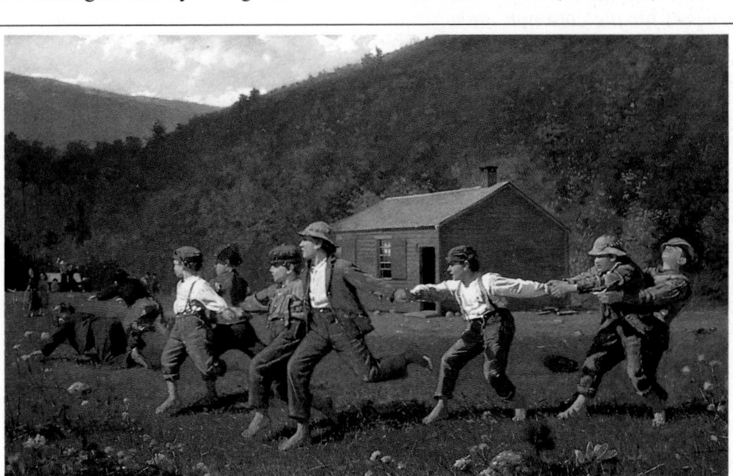

"Snap the Whip" (1872) by Winslow Homer. This depiction of carefree children playing in a meadow evokes the painter's own happy childhood in the rural New England village of Cambridge. Despite a trip to France in 1866, Homer's realistic portrayal of nature remains uniquely American.

Grant re-elected, beating Horace Greeley

Washington, D.C., Nov. 5

President Grant was elected to a second term today, defeating Horace Greeley, the noted but eccentric editor of the *New York Tribune*, as well as several lesser known candidates. While the President's first four years in office were marked by corruption on the part of some appointees and by Black Friday, in which an attempt by some financiers to corner the gold market ended in ruin for many investors, he scored a solid victory today, winning 3,597,132 votes and 29 states with 286 electoral votes. Greeley won 2,834,125 votes and carried six states with 66 electoral votes. Elected Vice President was Henry Wilson of Massachusetts, a successor to Schuyler Colfax of Indiana.

The campaign started with both major parties badly fractured. President Grant was the nominee of the Republican and Workingmen's Parties. Greeley, in turn, won the backing of Liberal Republicans, who broke away from the parent party, and he was endorsed by the Democratic Party. Others ran as candidates of the Prohibition and Revenue Reformer Parties.

Supporters of the major candidates exchanged heated barbs during the campaign. The Greeley partisans nicknamed Ulysses Grant "Useless Grant." The supporters of Grant, in turn, made fun of the way Greeley dressed, his long white duster and white hat, which matched his curly, white beard, often tucked into his collar. At one point in the heated campaign, Greeley wondered aloud whether he was running for the presidency or the penitentiary (→ 11).

A ticket for the common man.

Greeley: "Turn the rascals out!"

H.R. Revels (left), first Negro Senator and the first Negro representatives.

Tweed is jailed for fraud

Something that did blow over. Thomas Nast's view of "Boss" Tweed's downfall

New York City, Nov. 19

After a lengthy and controversial trial, William "Boss" Tweed was sentenced this morning on charges of graft and corruption. The jury found the former grand sachem of Tammany Hall guilty on 204 of 220 misdemeanor counts. Judge Davis ordered Tweed to serve 13 years and pay a fine of $12,500. The one-time Democratic boss winced and his face turned ashen when the foreman read the verdict. He was still pale when he was led away from the courtroom and dinner was brought to his lawyer's office from Delmonico's. Tweed was reportedly enraged upon learning that he will have to serve his term at the penitentiary rather than in the county jail.

A jury was unable to reach a verdict in an earlier case, where Tweed faced more serious felony charges. His lawyer, David Field, called the allegations politically motivated and exclaimed, "The father of these indictments should be in a pillory." Field was speaking specifically of District Attorney Garvin, but Samuel Tilden, the Democratic state chairman, is considered primarily responsible for bringing Tweed to trial. His power has increased as Tweed's has declined. Since his ouster in December, Tweed has devoted most of his energy to his defense (→ Dec. 4, 1875).

Colorado. *William Cody, on a card designed for viewing with a stereopticon. Cody received the Medal of Honor this year for invaluable service as a guide in the federal effort to wipe out Indian resistance. After serving in the Civil War, Cody went to Kansas, where he earned the nickname "Buffalo Bill" by killing 4,280 head of buffalo in eight months to feed rail crews. He was recently host to the Grand Duke Alexis of Russia on a buffalo hunting trip.*

Arbitrators rule in favor of U.S.

Geneva, Switzerland, Sept. 14

The acrimonious and protracted dispute between the United States and Britain about compensation for the damage done during the Civil War by the British-built raiders Alabama, Shenandoah and Florida was finally settled today with a ruling by an independent tribunal meeting here that the United States should be paid $15.5 million. The tribunal was set up as part of the Treaty of Washington that was negotiated last year by Secretary of State Hamilton Fish. Of the five arbitrators, two were nominated by the parties to the dispute and three were provided by Italy, Switzerland and Brazil. This is the first time that a major dispute has been submitted to international arbitration.

Mary Celeste adrift in a mystery at sea

Atlantic Ocean, Dec. 4

The Mary Celeste swayed in cold silence as a British ship sailed up to it today on the high seas. Captain David Morehouse discovered the American cargo ship floating aimlessly with no crew aboard. The abandoned Celeste has the maritime world utterly mystified. The Celeste, skippered by Captain Ben Briggs, left New York harbor for Italy last month, loaded with 1,700 barrels of alcohol. The last record of its course was a November 24 logbook entry; its fate after that remains unknown. One theory is that the crew broke into the cargo, got drunk, then, in a frenzy, killed the captain and escaped on a passing southbound vessel. The strange case is being investigated.

Boston center is consumed by fire

Boston, Nov. 11

The raging fire that occupied most of Boston's public resources for three days has finally abated after killing 14 people, ruining two churches and demolishing the city's dry goods industry. Starting in the engine room of a building occupied by Tebbets, Baldwin and Davis, the fire spread quickly to the heart of the business section. Even the solid granite of warehouses yielded to the withering heat of the blaze. Windows vomited smoke and flames and cries of "another Chicago" (which burned in October of last year) could be heard amid the constant tolling of fire bells. Not many have been left homeless, but with more than 1,000 firms reduced to ashes, thousands will be jobless.

Burbank breeds a better potato

Massachusetts

A superior potato, dubbed the "Idaho," may mean fame and fortune for 23-year-old Luther Burbank. A farm boy educated in the local schools, Burbank is greatly influenced by the Charles Darwin *Variation of Animals and Plants Under Domestication.* Two years ago, Burbank bought 17 acres of land here and began testing Darwin's ideas of natural selection, with an eye toward creating new commercial strains of domestic plants. The Idaho potato resulted from a simple experiment, growing plants from seeds rather than tubers. Acting as selection agent, Burbank discarded inferior spuds and replanted superior ones. Profits from his effort will go toward continued research.

Rockefeller corners Ohio oil refining

Cleveland

John D. Rockefeller, at 33, is sitting atop the nation's oil refining industry. His Standard Oil of Ohio now controls nearly all of the refineries here in the oil capital of the nation. Not content with easy access to Lake Erie shipping, however, Rockefeller is using the size of his firm to elicit rebates from railroads. The Pennsylvania Railroad this year reportedly signed a a secret contract with the oil titan's mysterious South Improvement Company.

Mail order business formed in Chicago

Chicago, August

The transcontinental railroad is only three years old and already it is spawning many new business techniques. The latest of these is a new mail-order house founded by Aaron Montgomery Ward. As a traveling salesman in rural Michigan, Ward sensed a growing hatred of profit-hungry middlemen. So he decided to start buying wholesale products for cash and selling them by mail. His first catalogue, issued this month, lists about 150 items available to consumers.

"Whistler's Mother" (1871-72) by James Abbott McNeill Whistler. Born in Lowell, Massachusetts, Whistler followed the artistic exodus to Paris in 1855 and never returned. Settling in London while the Civil War raged at home, he has chosen to exercise his gift for realism on the scenery around the Thames, and, of course, his mother.

1873

Grant

Hawaii, Jan. 8. Prince William Lunalilo becomes first elected monarch of Islands; he is crowned King Lunalilo.

Washington, D.C., Feb. 12. Coinage Act of 1873 passes Congress, ending use of silver in minting coins.

Washington, D.C., March 3. Congress doubles salary of president and Supreme Court justices, and its own by 50 percent (→Jan. 20, 1874).

Washington, D.C., March 4. Ulysses S. Grant sworn in for second term as president (→Dec. 5, 1876).

Washington, D.C., March 4. First issue of *Congressional Record* appears, reporting proceedings of Congress.

Washington, D.C., Apr. 14. In Slaughterhouse ruling Supreme Court holds that 14th Amendment does not protect civil rights granted by state constitutions.

Colfax, Louisiana, Apr. 14. Armed whites massacre most of Colfax, a predominantly Negro village.

United States, May 1. Penny postcards introduced.

Oregon, Aug. 2. "Great Fire" of Portland destroys 22 city blocks.

United States, Oct. 18. First football conference held to draft set of standard rules; Yale, Princeton, Rutgers and Columbia attend.

Cuba, Nov. 8. After seizing American steamer Virginius on October 31, Spanish authorities execute captain and 12 crew members; ship, flying U.S. flag, was transporting arms to rebels (→29).

Cuba, Nov. 29. After revelation that Virginius was under control of Cuban rebels, Spain offers to return ship and pay $80,000 to families of each American executed.

Denver, Colorado. Adolph Coors founds beer brewery.

South Carolina. Richard Greener, first Negro Harvard graduate, becomes professor of metaphysics at University of South Carolina.

United States. Children's magazine *St. Nicholas* begins publication; contributors include Louisa May Alcott, Mark Twain and Robert Louis Stevenson.

Vanderbilt thriving in midst of depression

Vanderbilt, commodore of rails.

New York City

Cornelius Vanderbilt, czar of the New York Central and Hudson River Railroads, is taking the depression in stride. In fact, he has begun an expansion that will allow trains to run from New York to Chicago solely on Vanderbilt track. In New York, as the jobless huddle around ashcan fires and in the parks, the Commodore is employing armies to install tracks for his Harlem Line. Obligingly, the city will pay half the $6.5 million bill for his elaborate elevated road bed. Living through crises in this manner seems to be one of the perks of running a family business worth $90 million. Four years ago, Vanderbilt consolidated the New York Central system and built Grand Central Depot, opened in 1871. New Yorkers held festivals to honor the 76-year-old industrialist. A statue of him in St. John's Park and a bronze relief on a Hudson Street warehouse will outlive the old man.

San Francisco gets its first cable car

San Francisco, Aug. 1

The city's first cable car climbed up Nob Hill through the 4 a.m. fog today. Andrew Hallidie, the 37-year-old British-born businessman who claims credit for much of the cable system's design, took control of the grip car himself on the 2,781-foot trial run to some 350 feet above the city's business district. The open first car, housing a device that grips a moving cable below the surface of the street, accommodates 10 passengers and pulls a covered car with room for 14 more. In the afternoon, some 60 San Franciscans, many hanging on the car's railing, participated in the Clay Street Hill Railroad's first public run.

A stockyard boom

Kansas City, Missouri, Autumn

A new business seems to be buoying the economy of this area. Cattle are brought up from Texas on the "long drive" to the railheads in central and western Kansas, then sent by train to the new stockyards here on the Kansas-Missouri border. Some are slaughtered here and the beef products are sold locally. Most of the cattle, however, are cut up in a rough fashion in Kansas City and then shipped on to the meatpacking houses in Chicago for finishing and distribution.

Free mail delivery

Washington, D.C.

In 1843, the *New England Journal* predicted, "Take away the high cost of postage, and all letters rush into the post office as naturally as water runs down a hill." Soon after, postage rates fell and letter-writing rose. This year, American cities with a population of 20,000 or more have begun receiving free delivery, resulting in even more mail. As the United States Post Office increases its outlets in rural areas, it hopes someday to provide free delivery in the country as well.

Honest John Kelly is Tammany chief

New York City

It would seem that this must be John Kelly's year in New York City. Kelly, 51, with a distinguished political career behind him, is now reshaping the once corrupt political system of the city. Prior to Kelly, William M. Tweed and his cohorts ran Tammany Hall, the city's Democratic organization. When their history of graft and extortion was finally revealed in *The New York Times*, Kelly rode the wave of political reform to the position of grand sachem of Tammany Hall.

Main Street, Salt Lake City, serves as a supply depot for pioneers in covered wagons on their way to California. And as mines and railroads develop, the city is becoming a major commercial center of the West.

"Patrick's Day Parade," by Harrigan and Hart, a bright young Irish singing comedy team.

,ouis Agassiz dies; ı titan of science

'gassiz, science's greatest promoter.

:ambridge, Mass., Dec. 14

One of the greatest proponents of cientific study, Louis Agassiz, has ied at the age of 66. While study- ıg for his medical degree in Mu- ich, the Swiss-born naturalist had ıe opportunity to work with a col- :ction of fish brought from the ımazon River. His classification ·f these species was published in 829. After receiving his degree in 830, Agassiz went to Paris to study /ith the French anatomist and pale- ntologist Georges Cuvier, and /ith scientific geographer Alex- ınder von Humboldt. Agassiz be- :an studying fossils, and though a taunch antievolutionist, his work aid a foundation for Charles Dar- /in's theories. Agassiz's work with ossils and glaciers led to a theory ·f an "ice age." He became a U.S. itizen in 1861 and went on to clas- ify the species of the New World.

With the war over, the North and South are eager to do business. An advertisement uses reconcilia- tion idea to sell "Love" tobacco.

Panic hits Wall Street

New York City, Sept. 20

The Stock Exchange has closed in panic, following a trail of ruined firms. After two days of turmoil starting with the failure of the government bond agent Jay Cooke & Co., backer of Northern Pacific Railroad construction, Wall Street was again the busiest (and unhappiest) place in town. Speculators rushed through the street looking "pale as ghosts," trying to unload their stocks at any price.

There were few buyers, except for Jay Gould, who helped check the turmoil by buying when everyone else was selling. By noon, however, after the suspension of the Union Trust Company, the governing committee of the Stock Exchange decided to close until accounts are put in order, at an as yet undetermined time. President Grant is expected to meet the Secretary of the Treasury tomorrow regarding emergency measures, although experts see no quick end to the financial debacle. They blame too little currency and too much speculation, with scores of firms ruined in just two days and with thousands more expected to fail.

Jesse James stages his first train heist

Adair, Iowa, July 21

Jesse James and his gang, long experienced in robbing banks, have now gone into the train-robbing business. At 8:30 this morning, the seven-man gang boarded a train belonging to the Chicago, Rock Island & Pacific Railway, and took more than $3,000 from the express delivery car's safe. The band also robbed the seven-car train's passengers of hundreds of dollars and some jewelry. The thieves did not injure any of the passengers, although the train's engineer was killed when the locomotive was derailed just before the robbery. James is about 26 years old, of medium height, and has blue eyes.

"Home On The Range"

Oh, give me a home, where the buffalo roam,
Where the deer and the antelope play,
Where seldom is heard a discouraging word,
And the skies are not cloudy all day,
Home, home on the range,
Where the deer and the antelope play,
Where seldom is heard a discouraging word,
And the skies are not cloudy all day.

Mails ban obscenity

Washington, D.C., Dec. 14

Acting under pressure from Anthony Comstock, the moral crusader, Congress has passed an act prohibiting "obscene" items from being sent through the mail. Comstock gained national attention during his recent campaign to stop the mailing of a written account of a scandal that involved the Rev. Henry Ward Beecher. The new Comstock Law, as it is being popularly called, not only bans erotic literature and pictures, but birth control instruction and information about abortion as well.

Resisting removal, Indians kill general

California Indians by Muybridge.

Tule Lake, California, Oct. 27

General E.R.S. Canby was shot and killed today by Modoc chief Captain Jack as he tried to arrange a peaceful settlement to what everyone hopes will be California's last Indian war. The fight began in November after the army tried to force Captain Jack and his people to return to their Klamath, Oregon, reservation from an area of Northern California near the Lost River they once inhabited. The Indians fled south to the Tule Lake lava beds, killing settlers on the way. Nine soldiers were killed and 30 wounded on January 17 in a disastrous effort to storm the Indians' natural fortress. There were no Indian losses.

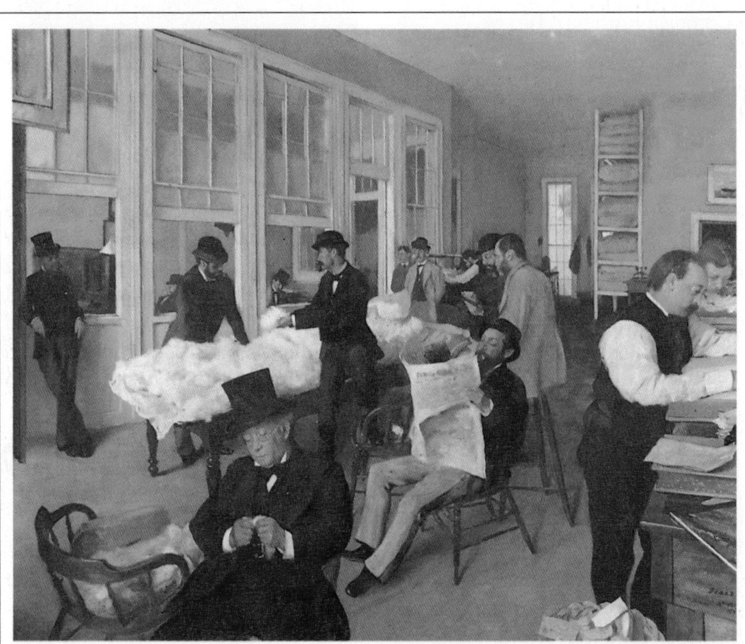
New Orleans, March. *French master Edgar Degas has left the United States after a five-month visit to relatives who work at the Cotton Exchange. "Le Bureau de Coton a Nouvelle Orleans" (above) is a product of his vacation.*

1874

Grant

New York City, Jan. 13. Unemployed riot in Tompkins Square Park.

Washington, D.C., Jan. 20. Congress, yielding to public pressure, repeals its own salary increase, while maintaining those for the president and Supreme Court justices.

Washington, D.C., Jan, 21. Senate confirms Morrison R. Waite to replace Salmon P. Chase as chief justice; Waite is President Grant's third choice to fill post.

Jackson, Mississippi, Feb. 3. Blanche K. Bruce, a Negro from Mississippi, elected to Senate.

Washington, D.C., Apr. 22. President Grant vetoes Legal Tender Act; it calls for $18 million more paper money.

Washington, D.C., May 4. Supreme Court, ruling in Bartemeyer v. Iowa, holds that 14th Amendment does not protect right to sell liquor.

Williamsburg, Massachusetts, May 16. Ashfield reservoir dam, on Mill River, collapses, killing more than 100 people and causing millions of dollars worth of property loss.

Berne, Switzerland, Sept. 15. First international postal conference held to standardize international mailing.

Kansas, September. Some 1,500 Mennonite immigrants from Russia introduce drought-resistant "Turkey Red" wheat.

Elizabeth Township, Pennsylvania, Nov. 29. First mass battle between strikers and strikebreakers, in "Battle of Buena Vista"; 12 workers killed.

Springfield, Massachusetts. Remington typewriter introduced.

Sioux City, Iowa. First Peavey "blind horse" grain elevator installed; operated by blinded horse walking around a wheel.

Colorado. Government surveyor and photographer W.H. Jackson discovers centuries-old Pueblo Indian "cliff dwellings" in Mancos River region.

Milwaukee, Wisconsin. Krug Brewery renamed Joseph Schlitz Brewing Company.

Philadelphia. Painter Thomas Eakins completes *John Biglan in a Single Scull*; it is inspired by his love of rowing.

Custer says there's gold in the Black Hills

General Custer (center) poses with a grizzly bear treated with a determination usually reserved for Indians.

Dakota Territory, Aug. 2

General George Custer has announced the discovery of gold in the Black Hills, a fact that has for years been known by the white prospectors living illegally on Sioux land. Custer left Fort Lincoln on the Missouri River on orders from Lieutenant General Philip Sheridan to reconnoiter the Dakota Territory and find a practical route to Fort Laramie. The 1868 treaty signed at Fort Laramie bars non-government whites from the sacred Black Hills, but generally the army has left the prospectors to their work. Many accompanied Custer (→ Nov. 1875).

Work hours for women, children limited

Bell time in a New England factory town. After a painting by Winslow Homer.

Boston, Massachusetts, May 8

Over the objections of conservative businessmen, this rapidly industrializing state passed into law today the Ten-Hour Act, limiting the amount of time women and children are permitted to spend working in factories. The law does not apply to farm workers or to work done at home. Nevertheless, to those seeking labor reform, it is a step in the right direction. And, unlike earlier laws, this measure has workable provisions for enforcement. Child laborers of 15 and under were first counted as a separate category in the census of 1870, when they numbered 750,000.

Chautauqua: Religion, education and fun

Lake Chautauqua, N.Y., August

Forty people have just finished the first two-week session of the Sunday School Teachers' Assembly here. The meetings, under the leadership of the Revs. John Heyl Vincent and Lewis Miller, are not at all like the camp meetings that preceded it. There is no room for extemporaneous speakers or sessions. Everthing is closely organized by the two founders. The content of the sessions is also different. Here at Chautauqua, the founders are trying to bring together Bible study and teacher-training classes, with musical entertainment, lectures and recreational activities.

Hawaii's King dies; succession stirs riot

Honolulu, Feb. 12

Rioting islanders who support Queen Emma's claim to the Hawaiian throne gutted the courthouse today and assaulted the legislators who elected Prince David Kalakaua as successor to King Lunalilo, who died on February 3. Lunalilo, who was affectionately called "lokomaikai" (merciful, generous one) by the people, died after a reign of only a year. A power struggle ensued between the factions backing popular Queen Emma, widow of King Kamehameha IV, and Prince David, whom Lunalilo had defeated in a bitter election for the crown a year earlier.

Three states order rail rate controls

Des Moines, Iowa, March 23

Railroad freight rates were regulated today in Iowa, following similar action in Illinois and Minnesota. Much to the dismay of railroad tycoons Cornelius Vanderbilt and Jay Gould, a set rate of return is abolished. The Granger Laws, so-called because the Grange is the chief force behind them, fix maximum rates for rail traffic in these states and provides elevators for farmers to store grain while awaiting shipment. The laws protect farmers and railroad managers, and insure quick delivery of market goods. Local Granges have 1.5 million members and are encouraged by today's reform (→ March 1, 1877).

Leaders of a rising agrarian revolt.

Carpetbagger power seen waning in South

Thomas Nast's carpetbagger.

Bullying Negro voters in the South.

Vicksburg, Mississippi, Dec. 7

Further evidence that the power of the Northern carpetbag Republicans is on the wane has come with yet another outbreak of racially motivated rioting. In this instance, some 75 Negroes are believed to have been killed when they attacked the courthouse here in an attempt to prevent the forcible ejection of a carpetbag sheriff. Similar disturbances have occurred elsewhere in the state, notably in Meridian and Clinton, prompted by the resentment of whites over the large number of Negroes in public office, including the lieutenant governor, A.K. Davis (→March 27, 1876).

Women establish new temperance group

Cleveland, Ohio, Nov. 18

Somewhere in this nation a child with a dime in his pocket is entering the side door of a saloon. He will leave without the dime but with a pint of raw whiskey to be delivered to the grasping hands of an adult. It is this kind of scenario that has led to formation of the national Women's Christian Temperance Union. Delegates from 17 states met today to elect Mrs. Annie Wittenmyer of Philadelphia president. Miss Frances E. Willard, formerly president of Chicago's temperance union, was voted corresponding secretary. Since the beginning of this year, the union has grown rapidly. In Chicago, Milwaukee and other major cities, Catholic and Protestant women have signed petitions protesting the opening of saloons on the Sabbath. Miss Willard came to general attention when she led women in public prayer and song to protest the Market Street saloon in Pittsburgh. She and Mrs. Wittenmyer believe that they will be able to achieve national temperance by holding many such demonstrations, and through education.

Women's holy war. Currier & Ives.

New game of tennis arrives via Bermuda

Staten Island, New York

Mary Ewing Outerbridge has introduced the English game of tennis to her neighbors on Staten Island, but not before she confused some customs officials. They couldn't decide whether she should pay duty on the strange collection of equipment she brought back from Bermuda and delayed her arrival home. They finally relented and Mrs. Outerbridge was able to demonstrate the sport that she saw British army officers playing on the island.

During the spring. a playing area called a court was laid out at the Staten Island Cricket and Base Ball Club and the game of tennis was launched here. There were some problems devising the regulations for the game, which was first played at a lawn party in the Welsh town of Nantclwyd a year earlier. Even the English have failed to reach an understanding about the rules or even how high the net should be.

Zoo in Philadelphia

Philadelphia

Hundreds of exotic animals are taking up residence in, of all places, a city. They have been doing so since the opening this year of the Philadelphia Zoological Gardens, America's first public zoo. The Zoological Society of Philadelphia was formed in 1859, and after the war it began obtaining bears, lions, tigers and other species. Now the animals are on a 143-acre Fairmount Park site designed after the London Zoo.

Apache chief dead

Arizona Territory, June 8

Cochise, Apache chief and leader of the fiercest resistance seen in the Southwest, is dead of natural causes. After witnessing the execution of five chiefs in 1861, Cochise turned on the whites. Apaches controlled Arizona that year until they were forced into the mountains with howitzers. From there, Cochise led a band of 200 in shrewd raids before surrendering to General George Crook in September 1871.

Henry Ward Beecher accused of adultery

The Rev. Beecher and sister Harriet.

Brooklyn, New York, Aug. 28

The minister of the Plymouth Church here, Henry Ward Beecher, has been upheld in a report issued by a church committee investigating charges of adultery brought against him by Timothy Tilton. Rumors of misconduct had been common since 1870, but not till June did Tilton accuse Beecher, the nation's most popular minister, of "improper advances" toward his wife, Elizabeth. The committee found in Beecher, who faces legal proceedings, nothing to impair the confidence of Plymouth Church in his "Christian character and integrity" (→Sept. 1876).

The Republican Party appears as an elephant for the first time in Thomas Nast's November 7 cartoon denying rumors of Grant seeking a third term.

Twain captures spirit of the "Gilded Age"

Thomas Nast's commentary on the "Brains" behind Tammany Hall.

New York City

Rampant greed, unchecked land speculation, fraudulent stock offerings and financial chicanery involving a United States senator. It all sounds like headlines from the newspapers. But instead, these are just a few gleanings from *The Gilded Age*, Mark Twain's caustic and hilarious view of what he sees as the unbridled materialism now loose in the land. Twain leaves little doubt that his portrait of charlatans and would-be financial tycoons is drawn from close observation; his work is subtitled *A Tale of Today*. But another contemporary observer, the popular lecturer and author John Fiske, implies in his recent *Outlines of Philosophy* that the bamboozled victims in Twain's novel got exactly what they deserve, and what society needs. Echoing the philosophy of Herbert Spencer, Fiske argues that society mimics nature in that it develops through a process of evolution. The strong survive and the weak perish.

Democrats regain dominance in the House

Washington, D.C., Nov. 3

In a dramatic shift of political power, the Democrats have regained control of the House of Representatives, prompted in large part by the economic depression that set in a year ago, and has continued, after the failure of Jay Cooke & Company, a major New York banking firm involved in railroad speculation. Voters appeared to be concerned, too, over suggestions of corruption in President Grant's administration. In the 43rd Congress just ending, the House Republicans outnumber the Democrats by 203 to 88. In the House just elected, Democrats will outnumber Republicans by 181 to 107. However, Republicans will keep control of the Senate.

Grasshopper swarm covers Great Plains

Kansas, Sept. 18

The Great Plains are suffering the worst grasshopper plague in history. Farmers say the insects fly in on the north wind in swarms a mile wide that literally blot out the midday sun. Blanketing the ground in a living mass over two inches deep, they eat everything: plants, clothes, trees and even mosquito netting. As one discouraged farmer put it, the grasshoppers leave nothing "but the mortgage." Little relief seems likely soon.

First truss bridge spans Mississippi

St. Louis, Missouri, July 4

Designed by Captain James Buchanan Eads, a bridge that many engineers thought impossible now spans the Mississippi River here. Congress had asked for spans so high and wide that Eads had to invent a new type of bridge, the steel truss, to meet the requirements. The 54-year-old Eads has many years of experience on the river, having salvaged wrecked ships as a young man and designed river gunboats for the Union army during the war. His project next year will be to clear the river mouth of mud and silt.

Commission to run District of Columbia

Washington, D.C., June 20

The District of Columbia is no longer a territory. From now on, the district will be run by a three-man commission to be named by the president. The move by Congress, signed into law today by President Grant, was prompted in large part by the soaring debt run up in the district in its years of territorial government. The district, in losing its territorial status, will no longer be entitled to a non-voting delegate in the House of Representatives.

Now a barbed wire to fence in cattle

Washington, D.C., Nov. 24

Settlers can now fence in their livestock cheaply and easily, thanks to Joseph Glidden. Today, the De Kalb, Illinois, farmer received a patent for his invention: barbed wire. With the scarcity of cheap timber on the Plains, ranchers were forced to let their herds roam. But the fencing, with its sharp barbs cut from sheet metal and fitted between twisted wires, could solve the problem. Animals are pricked by the barbs, deterring any desire to stray. Ranchers say the invention will mean more cattle raising on the Great Plains.

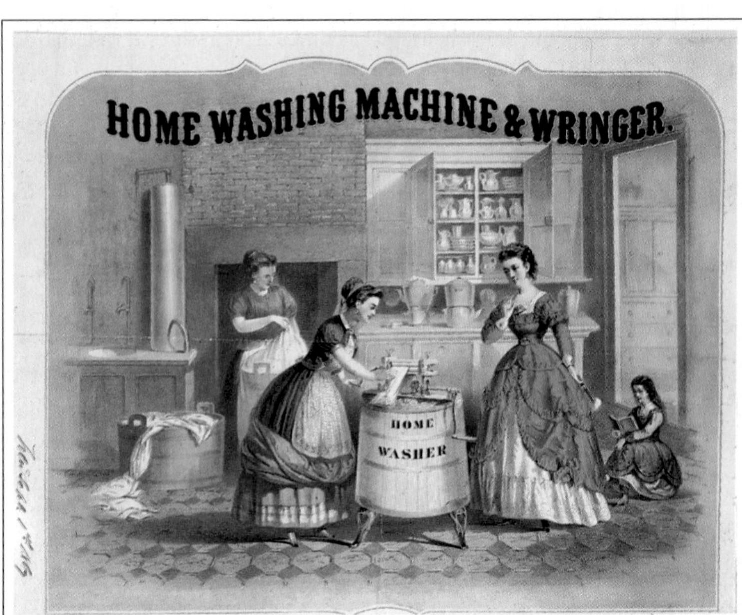

As the exodus from farm to city accelerates, women of sufficient means find themselves stripped of some old tasks. Butter and bread are bought, not churned and baked. And the wash is easily put through the wringer.

John Wesley Powell (left) lost an arm in the Civil War. But it did not keep the frontier geologist from a daring exploration of Grand Canyon five years ago. He is currently working on a book about the Colorado River.

1875

Grant

Washington, D.C., Jan. 14. Specie Resumption Act passed, allowing specie payments to resume in bid to compromise between West's desire for inflation and East's request for "sound" fiscal policy (→ Dec. 9, 1878).

Washington, D.C., Jan. 25. Despite questions over its constitutionality, Western farm relief is granted $30,000 by Congress.

Washington, D.C., March 1. Congress passes Civil Rights Act, guaranteeing equal rights in transportation, theaters, inns and on juries.

Laramie, Wyoming, March. Pattee Lottery swindle started by James Pattee, who floods country with circulars for nonexistent drawings.

Washington, D.C., May 3. United States joins General Postal Union, an international alliance of post offices.

New York City, Sept. 16. First Fast Mail train leaves Grand Central Station, an important mailing innovation.

Lynn, Massachusetts, Oct. 30. Mary Baker Eddy publishes *Science and Health with Key to the Scriptures,* setting down tenets of Church of Christ, Scientist.

New York City, Nov. 17. Helena Petrovna Blavatsky founds American branch of Theosophical Society, propounding reincarnation and world community.

Kalamazoo, Michigan. George F. Green patents dental drill.

Cambridge, Massachusetts. Harvard and Tufts are first teams to wear football uniforms in competition.

Boston. First baseman Charles G. Waite becomes first baseball player to use a glove; it is unpadded.

Portland, Maine. James A. Healy becomes first Negro Roman Catholic bishop in United States.

Rome. John McCloskey appointed first Catholic cardinal in United States.

Boston. Sculptor Daniel Chester French creates statue called *The Minuteman.*

Philadelphia. *The Gross Clinic,* painted by Thomas Eakins, realistically portrays a medical school class.

Whiskey Ring distillers cheating on taxes

Thomas Nast applauds the Treasury's crackdown on Whiskey Ring.

Washington, D.C., May 10

The Treasury Secretary Benjamin Bristow announced today that fumes from the Whiskey Ring scandal reach all the way to the White House. Bristow publicly implicated Orville Babcock, private secretary to President Grant, in the scandal. It is believed that Babcock was presented with expensive gifts from perpetrators of the fraud. Grant is still backing Babcock, however.

The Whiskey Ring conspiracy was hatched in St. Louis, but it was so profitable that it spread quickly to Wisconsin, Illinois, Ohio, Louisiana and the nation's capital. Under the scheme, distillers bribed government officials so they could retain the federal taxes they collected.

Those taxes increased sharply after the war. The officials used their spoils to finance political activities, hamper investigations and silence newspaper editors. Secretary Bristow was forced to use investigators outside of his department to uncover the scandal. The public began to learn of the dimensions of the Whiskey Ring earlier this month when the *St. Louis Democrat* published an expose.

"Hanging Judge"

Indian Territory, Autumn

The "Hanging Judge," Isaac Parker, is responsible for the execution of 60 of the last 79 criminals who have been hanged here. He selects hand-woven rope that is impregnated with pitch to prevent it from slipping. And on his gallows is the sign, "The Gates of Hell."

1st Kentucky Derby

Louisville, Kentucky, May 17

A horse race called the Kentucky Derby was run today at the new Churchill Downs course here. The winner was Aristides. Lewis, the jockey, earned for the horse's owner, H.P. McGrath, a purse of $2,850. Spectators are looking forward to next year's race.

Hawaiians to trade only with the U.S.

The two young giants, Ivan and Jonathan, reaching out for Asia.

Honolulu, March 18

Senate ratification of the Reciprocity Treaty means that Hawaii now is "off limits" to other foreign powers, observers said here today. King Kalakaua took the unusual step of going to Washington last year to oversee what no other ruler of the islands had done except under duress – grant an exclusive trading agreement to another country. However, the King took no direct part in the negotiations. Under the treaty, the United States admits almost all island products, including sugar and rice, free of duty. The United States sends its products and manufactured goods to the islands.

Pinkertons bomb James farm, but Jesse and Frank aren't home

Clay County, Missouri, Jan. 25

Operatives of the Pinkerton Detective Agency raided the farmhouse of the notorious outlaws Jesse and Frank James earlier this evening. According to witnesses, the Pinkerton men threw bombs made of balls of cotton soaked in kerosene and turpentine into the James home. Unfortunately for the law, the James brothers were not there. The attack did, however, kill their half-brother, Archie, and mangled their mother's arm, which will probably have to be amputated. While many people detest the James brothers as wanton murderers, local residents regard them as modern-day Robin Hoods, and children in the area view them as heroes. Before the day was out, these folks were calling the incident "the crime of the century" (→ Sept. 7, 1876)

Jesse and Frank James with their mother. Just mama's boys gone bad.

▷

Gold prospectors enrage Sioux, who refuse to give up ground

Prospector kills Indian in the battle for the West. "The Last Shot" by Maurer.

Revenge: scalping a white invader.

Dakota Territory, November

Conflict between white prospectors and Sioux Indians of the Black Hills has escalated to outright war as the United States government continues to ignore the terms of the Fort Laramie treaty protecting the Indians' land. Thousands of white prospectors and settlers have illegally infiltrated the once sacred Black Hills since gold was found there in the 1850's. The treaty of 1868, meant to keep all whites off these prosperous lands, has been consistently disregarded by the army forces stationed there to enforce it. To add insult to injury, on March 3, 1871, the government passed an act that disallowed any further treaties with the Sioux, and permitted only infrequent meetings to consider changing the existing ones.

Expeditions to "reconnoiter" the area verified rumors of gold, and last month the Indians of the Northern Plains were called together by the government in a futile attempt to gain legal access to the area, beyond the limits of the Fort Laramie treaty. The chiefs, including Red Cloud of the Teton Sioux, refused to give up ground, and pledged to continue enforcing the treaty themselves, protecting land considered hallowed ground, by force when necessary (→ June 25, 1876).

Member of Molly Maguires, radical miners, convicted of murder

Pennsylvania, Sept. 1

In what can be considered a personal victory for Franklin B. Gowen, president of the Reading Railroad, a verdict of guilty was brought in today against a member of the Molly Maguires accused of murder. The trial has come two years after Gowen, who is also head of the Philadelphia Coal and Iron Company, vowed to break the hold that he said the radical miners' organization had over Schuylkill, Carbon, Luzerne and other counties in the anthracite region of eastern Pennsylvania. Evidence given at the trial indicates that the secret group was infiltrated by an agent who was working for Gowen, but his identity has not been disclosed.

The Maguires, whose members are also known as the Buckshots, White Boys and Sleepers, are named after a group of anti-landlord agitators active in Ireland in the 1840's and led by a widow named Molly Maguire. The present group is composed mostly of Irish immigrant miners whose grievances include low pay, harsh working conditions, exploitation at company stores and anti-Catholic prejudice. Unlike the peaceful Ancient Order of Hibernians, the Maguires have often resorted to violence in fighting their "oppressors" (→ June 21, 1877).

Molly Maguires hold secret meeting during mine strike in Pennsylvania.

Swift opens large Chicago meat firm

Chicago

A tall stranger with a New England accent and a penchant for efficiency has moved his meat business to Chicago's stockyards. Gustavus Franklin Swift, a butcher's helper at 14, knows that Chicago is the place to be. The railroad hub of the nation has easy access to the fertile producing regions of the West, and to the voracious appetites of the urban East. Swift draws attention with his eccentric ways and exacting standards for quality. Legs dangling in the manure, he rides a Texas pony into the pens so he can feel cattle for excess fat, a defect that does not seem to trouble most vendors in this profitable business (→ 1885).

New Yorker makes gum with chicle

Brooklyn, New York

Americans have always liked a good chew of tobacco, paraffin wax or, as the Indians taught them, spruce resin. A few years ago, Thomas Adams of Brooklyn came up with a packaged gum made from chicle, a substance derived from the tropical evergreen tree. Adams says he got the idea when he noticed that General Santa Ana of Alamo infamy chewed chicle. Adams calls his product "Adams New York Gum – Snapping and Stretching," and his son is now selling the idea out West.

Carnegie mill uses Bessemer process

Braddock, Pennsylvania, Dec. 30

The only major steel plant in the country to employ the Bessemer process is now ending its first year of operation with production at record high levels. Brought from Europe by Andrew Carnegie, the Bessemer process uses the principle of oxidation to remove impurities by forcing air through the molten iron at a high temperature. The method was also developed independently by William Kelly of Eddyville, Kentucky, but Henry Bessemer was the first to obtain a patent.

›hotographers end ›urvey of the West

Coyotero Apache scout who served s a guide for an 1874 expedition. ›hotograph by Timothy O'Sullivan.

Vashington, D.C.

Mathew Brady is courting finan-ial disaster, but his proteges have ompleted a photographic record of ›e West that will live for years. erhaps the most interesting of Bra-y's students is Timothy O' Sul-van, who accompanied the master n the battlefield at Gettysburg. ›iven to wanderlust, O'Sullivan left › 1867 for a three-year tour of the Vest with a federal geographic sur-ey team. After a trip to Panama in 870, he returned to go out West gain, producing breathtaking nages of Rockies and "Big Sky" ountry. William Henry Jackson, ›lexander Gardner and others ave contributed with equal skill ›nd daring to the growing visual ecord of the frontier.

›evivals conducted ›y Dwight Moody

›rooklyn, New York, December

Recently returned from a suc-essful revival tour across Britain, ›wight Moody and his music direc-or, Ira Sankey, have begun a series f services in the Northeast. Since ›he first meeting in September, the rowds have poured into hear him. ›ere in Brooklyn, the transport ompany had to lay extra trolley ›racks to accommodate those flock-›g to hear Moody preach at the ›ink. Moody, a former shoe sales-›an who was never ordained, has ›uly found his calling in the pulpit.

Sound is sent over a telephone wire

Boston, June 3

While testing modifications on a device that enables deaf students to learn to speak, Alexander Graham Bell and his assistant Thomas A. Watson have made a discovery that may lead to the transmission of voice through telegraph equipment. When a transmitter spring on Bell's equipment became stuck, Watson began plucking it to free it. Bell, who was in the next room, burst in, shouting, "What did you do? Don't change anything ... " He had heard the plucking sound through the device. Bell holds the patent for a "harmonic telegraph" and, should such a voice transmission device be perfected, he would share rights to it with two other devel-opers, Thomas Sanders and Gar-diner Hubbard (→March 10, 1876).

"Boss" Tweed escapes, heads for Cuba

New York City, Dec. 4

Faced with a lengthy prison term for corruption and a civil suit for recovery of the public money he has stolen, William Marcy Tweed has escaped from the Ludlow Street Jail and is reportedly headed for Cuba.

As grand sachem of Tammany Hall, the 52-year-old "Boss" Tweed had complete control of Democratic politics in New York City. Members of the Tweed Ring, which included Mayor Oakey Hall and Comptroller Richard "Slippery Dick" Connolly, bought votes, cor-rupted judges and plundered the public treasury. When the County Courthouse was being built, costs were so padded they exceeded esti-mates tenfold, and then the build-ing was not completed. Such ex-cesses caused Tweed's downfall. Ridiculed by Thomas Nast's car-toons in *Harper's Weekly*, and ex-

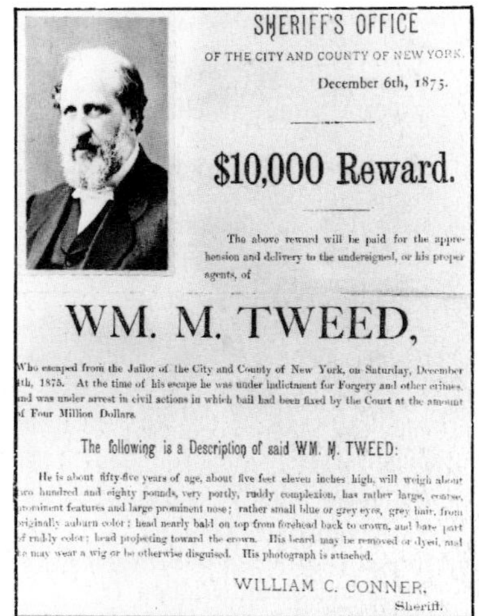

SHERIFF'S OFFICE
OF THE CITY AND COUNTY OF NEW YORK.
December 6th, 1875.

$10,000 Reward.

The above reward will be paid for the appre-hension and delivery to the undersigned, or his proper agents, of

WM. M. TWEED,

Who escaped from the Jailor of the City and County of New York, on Saturday, December 4th, 1875. At the time of his escape he was under indictment for Forgery and other crimes, and was under arrest in civil actions in which bail had been fixed by the Court at the amount of Four Million Dollars.

The following is a Description of said WM. M. TWEED:

He is about fifty-five years of age, about five feet eleven inches high, will weigh about two hundred and eighty pounds, very portly, ruddy complexion, has rather large, coarse, prominent features and large prominent nose; rather small blue or grey eyes, grey hair, from originally auburn color; head nearly bald on top from forehead back to crown, and bare part of ruddy color; head projecting toward the crown. His beard may be removed or dyed, and he may wear a wig or be otherwise disguised. His photograph is attached.

WILLIAM C. CONNER,
Sheriff.

"Boss" Tweed, fugitive from justice.

posed by *The New York Times*, Tweed was charged with a felony at the instigation of Samuel J. Tilden and the anti-Tammany Committee of 70, and was convicted.

Railroads criss-cross nation, transforming travel and transport

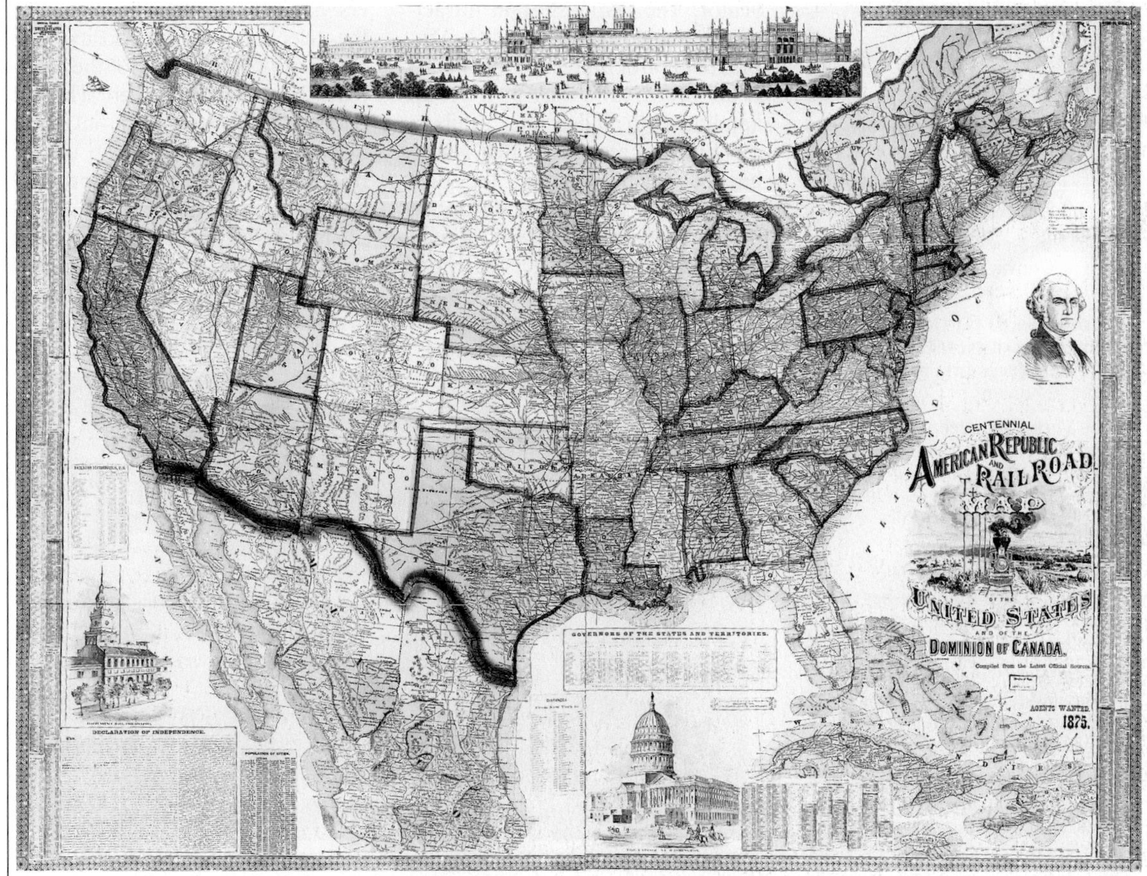

Ten years after the end of the Civil War and six years after the completion of the first intercontinental rail line, the railroad industry continues to transform the nation. Some 40,000 miles of track have been laid since war's end, more than doubling the previous total. Snaking through mountains and over plains, the rails unite the coun-try, bringing Easterners west, Westerners east and opening markets for products made hundreds of miles away.

1876

Grant

Washington, D.C., March 27. Supreme Court, in United States v. Cruikshank, restricts 14th Amendment to civil rights violations committed by states, not by individuals (→May 1, 1877).

Washington, D.C., Apr. 18. President Grant vetoes bill to cut presidential salary.

Indianapolis, May 10. Eli Lilly Co., pharmaceutical manufacturing firm, founded.

Cleveland, May 17. Prohibition Party nominates General Green Clay Smith of Kentucky for president and Gideon T. Smith for vice president.

United States, Aug. 12. U.S. yacht Madeleine wins America's Cup, beating Canada's Countess of Dufferin.

Dakota Territory, Sept. 8. Battle of Slim Buttes fought to stalemate between General George Crook and elements of Crazy Horse's band that had defeated Custer at Battle of Little Big Horn.

Bangor, Maine, Sept. 15. Two explosions jolt Warren Powder Company's mills; they are second and third in two days.

Brooklym, New York, September. Trial of the Rev. Beecher ends in hung jury.

New York City, November. Juliet Corson starts New York Cooking School, first in U.S.

Brooklyn, New York, Dec. 5. Fire at Conway's Theater kills almost 300 people.

Washington, D.C., Dec. 12. Henry Blair of New Hampshire introduces first prohibition amendment in Congress.

New York City, Dec. 25. Henry M. Robert publishes *Pocket Manual of Rules of Order for Deliberative Assemblies,* better known as *Robert's Rules of Order.*

Ashtabula, Ohio, Dec. 29. Pacific Express train crashes as bridge collapses, killing nearly 90 passengers.

Menlo Park, New Jersey. Thomas Edison invents carbon transmitter, making telephones commercially feasible.

New York City. Scientist John Draper is first to take photograph of solar spectrum.

Amherst, Massachusetts. Melvil Dewey creates Dewey Decimal System as means of classifying library books.

"Watson, come here, I need you"

Watson responds to Bell's call. The inventor's patent covers "the method of, and apparatus for, transmitting vocal or other sounds telegraphically . . . by causing electrical undulations, similar in form to the vibrations of the air."

Boston, March 10

The first electric transmissio[n] of the human voice by wire wa[s] achieved today by Alexander Graham Bell, a 29-year-old Canadia[n] who has been working for year[s] to develop such a device. Bell wa[s] in his home workshop with his assistant, Thomas Watson, when h[e] spilled battery acid on his leg. H[e] cried out, "Watson, come here, [I] need you." Watson, working o[n] another floor, heard the cry in hi[s] instrument and ran down to hel[p] Bell and tell him the good news.

The system that transmitted th[e] first message consists of a thin diaphragm that can be vibrated by th[e] voice, the center of which is attached to a conducting rod dippe[d] into a solution of water and acid. A flaring mouthpiece conduct[s] sounds to the transmitter, which i[s] connected to an electric battery an[d] through a wire to a receiver. Th[e] system transforms changes i[n] sounds into alterations in electrica[l] resistance; these are translated t[o] sounds at the other end of the wire.

A number of inventors have bee[n] racing to develop a sound transmission telephone system. Bell, a Boston University professor who work[s] with the deaf, appears to have wo[n] although others are questionin[g] that claim. He says that he plans t[o] apply for a patent, but other inventors say they intend to challeng[e] the Bell application (→June 25).

Bell shows off telephone, reciting Hamlet

Philadelphia, June 25

Visitors to the Centennial Exposition were fascinated here today by a demonstration of the telephone by Alexander Graham Bell, its inventor. The demonstration attracted few people at first, but it caught the attention of Emperor Dom Pedro II of Brazil, who was in a group appointed to judge the exhibits. The Emperor recognized Bell, whom he had recently met at the Boston School of the Deaf, and stopped the judging group. They listened in amazement as Bell recited Hamlet's soliloquy and Dom Pedro exclaimed in wonder, "It talks!"

Bell was urged to exhibit the telephone here by Gardiner Hubbard, his partner, who is trying to raise money from bankers to establish a telephone system. However, bankers have been cautious, regarding the telephone as a curiosity, and $100,000 contributed to the company by a third partner, Thomas Sanders, is starting run out. It is expected that the sensation caused by the exhibition will help produce financing. Bell plans to stimulate interest in the telephone by holding demonstrations in which he will appear in one theater and talk to Watson in another (→July 9, 1877).

"Breezing Up" (1876) by Winslow Homer. Leaving his New York studio behind every summer, America's premier nature painter spends the warm months hunting, fishing, camping and sketching in Pennsylvania, New England and the Hudson River Valley. Homer's recent use of watercolors to paint from direct observation has invigorated his more ambitious works.

Harvey Girls serve meals at rail depot

Topeka, Kansas, Spring

Until now, eating at an America[n] railroad station has been a hit-o[r] miss affair, with few facilities o[r] amenities for a good meal. No[w] Englishman Fred Harvey has decided to fill that void: He ha[s] opened a clean, well-appointe[d] dining room above the station o[n] the Atchison, Topeka & Santa F[e] line here. Orders are taken o[n] board and full-course meals ar[e] ready to be served on arrival at th[e] station by "Harvey Girls" in spotless uniforms that lend both a grac[e] and propriety to the enterprise. Harvey intends to put such dinin[g] rooms in stations all along the line.

uge exposition marks centennial of United States

On opening day, eager visitors flood the intersection of Elm and Belmont.

President Grant and the Brazilian Emperor Dom Pedro II start the Corliss Engine in Machinery Hall.

The torch of a huge statue, on display in Philadelphia. Just begun last year, it is intended as a gift from France.

Philadelphia, May 10

Thirteen giant bells swayed and chimed, 100 cannons fired a salute, 800 voices swelled the air with the *Hallelujah Chorus* from Handel's *Messiah*, and 4,000 foreign and American dignitaries gave a thunderous ovation. It was a stroke past noon today, and President Grant had declared the United States Centennial Exhibition open. This celebration of American know-how has been long in the making. In 1871, Congress called for "an International Exhibition of Arts, Manufactures, and Products of the Soil and Mine" to be held on the nation's 100th anniversary. Funds were slow to follow, but finally on July 4, 1874, the ground was broken at Fairmount Park. Now the City of Brotherly Love boasts a 284-acre park graced with exhibition halls extolling American advances in such areas as electricity, internal combustion and, of course, that modern miracle, steam power.

President Grant and the Emperor Don Pedro II of Brazil, the first reigning monarch to visit the United States, strode from the podium in front of the main building and proceeded directly to Machinery Hall. The crowds pressed in after them. A gasp of wonder went up at the sight of the largest steam engine ever created. Designed by George S. Corliss of Providence, Rhode Island, the Corliss Centennial Engine has a 56-ton flywheel that measures 30 feet in diameter. Praised for its graceful line and harmonious construction, the machine delivers 1,400 horsepower (a few engineers present privately noted that smaller engines already available offer the same amount of power, and that the high-speed six-horsepower engine operated by Miss Emma Allison at the Women's Pavilion achieves much better economy, relatively speaking). Other wonders in Machinery Hall include a hydrocarbon engine operating with a combustible liquid; an ice box using ammonia as a refrigerant, and a rotary printing press that prints, cuts and stacks two-sided sheets non-stop for an hour.

More inventions can be found in the exhibition halls of the 56 foreign nations and colonies participating in the exposition. Still, Americans may be forgiven if they linger at their own displays. Gazing at these immense achievements, they can dismiss the fact that America remains in an economic recession, enduring a negative balance of trade with overseas partners. This exhibition indicates that the handwriting is on the wall: The balance is on the verge of tipping in America's favor. And despite such problems as labor unrest, Indian wars and political corruption, the next 100 years promise to be even more glorious than the last.

The backbone of America. Centennial lithograph places the heartland farmer and his plow at the center of the republic's many and varied public servants.

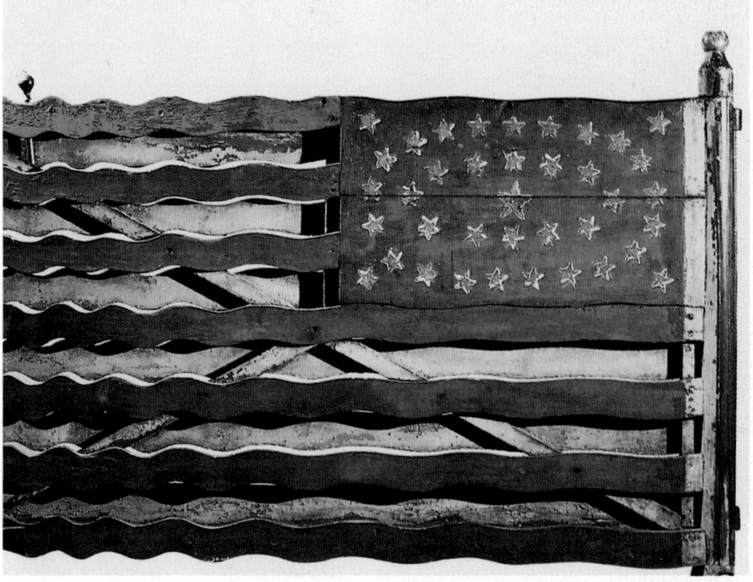

This sample of American folk art symbolizes the opening of the nation's second century. Flag Gate, c.1876, Darling Farm, Jefferson County, New York.

Custer's last stand at Little Big Horn

Pictograph by Amos Bad Heart Bull, an Oglala Sioux, portrays the Battle of Little Big Horn. Chief Crazy Horse, at center with spotted war paint, pursues the fight amid a crowd of fallen cavalrymen. The Oglala chieftain began his resistance in 1865, fighting the construction of a road to Montana's goldfields.

Curley, of the Crow tribe, served as a scout for Custer. Avenging losses in wars with the Blackfeet and Dakotas, the Crow often support whites.

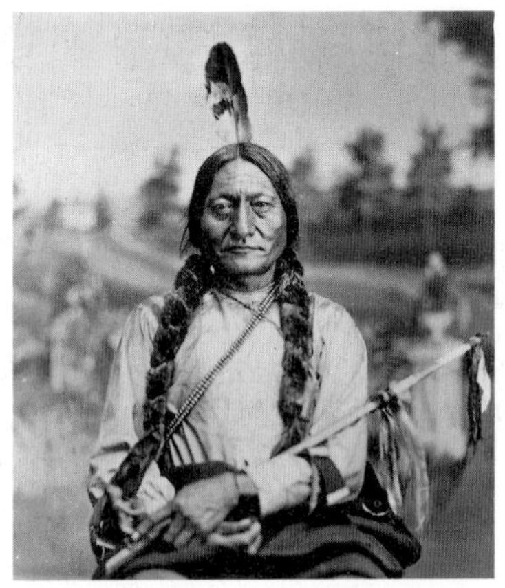

Only days before the battle, Sioux Chief Sitting Bull went into a trance and saw soldiers falling like grasshoppers from the sky into his camp.

The debacle at Little Big Horn. Colonel Custer, seeking out the Sioux who had left the reservation, was supposed to join up with General Alfred Terry. Instead of waiting, the overconfident Custer gave the fateful command to attack. Only a horse and a few hundred Sioux are still around to tell the story.

Dakota Territory, June 25

Custer is dead! The legendary general and 265 troopers of his famed Seventh Cavalry Regiment were attacked by Sioux and Cheyenne Indians today on the banks of the Little Big Horn River in the Dakota Territory. Reports indicate that Custer and every one of his men were killed by the estimated 2,500 Indians under Chiefs Sitting Bull and Crazy Horse. The body of Custer was found on the pinnacle of a hill, the Seventh Cavalry flag still flying over him and the corpses of his men all around him. After the battle, the only living remnant of the ill-fated regiment was Commanche, the faithful horse that belonged to Captain Miles Keough.

The Custer expedition was the key segment in a major campaign conducted by the army to force the Sioux and Cheyenne Indians to leave the Plains and return to their reservations.

Five days ago, Custer performed an impressive pass-in-review of his troops for his superiors, Generals Alfred Terry and John Gibbon. Then, to the stirring tune of the regimental march *Garryowen*, the buckskin-clad young general and his men left for the Little Big Horn. As the general approached the mouth of the river, he heard rifle shots. And as he had done so many times during the Civil War and in other fights against the Indians, he followed his tried-and-true strategy of "riding to the sound of the guns." When he got there, instead of a handful of Indians, there were thousands. Because of the presence of Indians to his rear, Custer's only choice was to launch a desperate "charge" into the massed enemy. After the charge, his outnumbered men shot their horses so they could be used as cover against the bullets and arrows of the Indians. The troopers arranged themselves in a square around their commander and took a heavy toll of the Indians. But in the face of odds of at least 10 to 1, they were overwhelmed.

George A. Custer finished at the bottom of his class at West Point in 1861. Nevertheless, two years later, he had become the youngest general in the history of the U. S. Army. At the time of his death, Custer was 37 years old (→ Sept. 8).

Colorado becomes 38th state in union

Washington, D.C., Aug. 1

The former territory of Colorado joined the union today as the 38th state. Its official nickname will be "the Centennial State," chosen because Colorado is being admitted 100 years after the Declaration of Independence was signed. The territory applied for admission several times before, but each of those applications was rejected for political or sectional reasons growing out of the Civil War. But with that conflict now well out of the way, admission has finally won approval. John L. Routt, who is a veteran of the Union army, will serve as Governor and the bustling little town of Denver has been designated as the capital.

Henry Heinz puts ketchup in bottle

Sharpsburg, Pennsylvania

The spicy, tomato-based condiment that Americans refer to as ketchup or catsup has always depended on long, careful cooking and stirring to give it its unique, tangy flavors. Now, Henry J. Heinz of Sharpsburg, Pennsylvania, has begun bottling a rich, thick tomato ketchup for sale that complements seafood, meats and poultry and requires no home cooking at all. Consumers seem to like the idea of a bottle that is made of clear glass.

Call is "Play Ball" for National League

Boston, Apr. 2

James "Orator Jim" O'Rourke has something to talk about today. O'Rourke whacked the first hit ever in the new National League and helped the Bostons beat the Philadelphias, 6-5. The loop was organized with eight teams on February 2, marking the official start of major league baseball. A Chicago businessman pirated four key Boston players from the National Association to form the basis of the new league and four association clubs defected. But two fell out for not completing schedules.

Tilden one vote short in presidential race

Fireworks illuminate the sky during New York torchlight parade for Tilden.

Washington, D.C., Nov. 7

Governor Samuel J. Tilden of New York came within one vote of winning the presidency today. Although he topped his principal rival, Governor Rutherford B. Hayes of Ohio, in popular and electoral votes, it is uncertain whether Tilden will be chosen as president. Election returns showed Tilden with 4,287,670 popular votes, to 4,035,924 for Hayes. The crucial vote, however, was for electors, with Tilden winning 184, one short of the 185 needed for a victory. Hayes won 165 electoral votes.

The outcome of this disputed election could rest with possible recounts in several states, most of them in the South, where some of the votes have been challenged.

Tilden, a millionaire lawyer serving his first term as Governor, is a Democrat who achieved fame as a result of his role in smashing the Tweed political ring of Tammany Hall. The Republican Hayes was a Civil War major general and had helped fugitive slaves win freedom during his years as a lawyer. A former congressman, he is in his third term as Governor (→ March 3, 1877).

Grant apologizes over corruption scandals

Washington, D.C., Dec. 5

President Grant responded directly to critics of the scandals in his administration as he delivered his eighth annual message to Congress today. "Mistakes have been made, as all can see and I admit," Grant said. He blamed the problems on his own inexperience, explaining, "It was my fortune, or misfortune, to be called to the office of Chief Executive without any previous political training." Grant also said his mistakes were "errors of judgment, but not intent."

Having addressed his critics, the President pointed to his accomplishments with pride. Grant said he has cut taxes by $300 million, reduced the national debt by $435 million and slashed "pork barrel" appropriations by Congress.

Grant begs from Lady Liberty.

Those accomplishments may be overlooked by history, however, with Grant's tenure being remembered for its scandals. In the last eight years, stories of stock manipulation, the Whiskey Ring and Credit Mobilier have left the White House floundering.

Jameses flee after bloody bank raid

Northfield, Minnesota, Sept. 7

The James and Younger gangs struck the Northfield bank today. They rode into this little town and ordered all the passers-by off the streets. Jesse James and Bob Younger went into the bank and ordered the cashier, J.L. Haywood, to open the safe. When he didn't comply, they roughed him up. The bold residents, most likely unaware of the deadly reputations of the gangsters, began to fire at them. Jesse James shot Haywood when the cashier drew a pistol. Jesse and the gang then ran into the street, blazing away with their revolvers. The robbers mounted their horses, but several were cut down. Gang members Bill Chadwell, Clell Miller and Charlie Pitts were killed. It is reported that while Bob, Cole and Jim Younger were captured, Jesse and Frank James made a getaway. Lawmen suspect they are headed back to Missouri (→ Apr. 3, 1882).

Mark Twain's mischievous "Tom Sawyer"

New York City

Mark Twain, social satirist and chronicler of the excesses of the Gilded Age, has now turned his corrosive wit to the mischievous adventures of youth in a sleepy Mississippi River town. Though young Tom Sawyer periodically vows to practice virtue, his high spirits keep interfering. Tom fakes his death, attends his own funeral, solves a murder and reconciles with his sweetheart, Becky Thatcher, in the process helping his reluctant friend, an adolescent river rat named Huckleberry Finn, to return to what Twain regards as the somewhat dubious benefits of "civilization."

A breakfast cereal to curb your sex drive

Battle Creek, Michigan

The new director of the Seventh Day Adventist Western Health Reform Institute, John Harvey Kellogg, has begun developing new types of flaked cereals. These, he claims, if included in a vegetarian diet, will help lower the sex drive of Americans. Kellogg also favors other kinds of abstinence, frowning on the use of alcohol, coffee, tea and tobacco. The Western Health Reform Institute provides surgical services, as well as help with "biologic living," including hydrotherapy, exercise and vegetarianism.

Hickok killed playing poker at Deadwood

Dakota Territory, Aug. 2

"Wild Bill" Hickok was slain today at a saloon in Deadwood. Born James Butler Hickok, he served as an army scout during the Civil War, later as the sheriff of Hays, Kansas, and most recently as a marshal in Abilene, where he carried two pistols, a sawed-off shotgun and a Bowie knife. About five years ago, "Wild Bill" retired, married and came to this territory to get into the gold-prospecting business. Today, while playing poker with some friends, he was shot in the back by a drunk named Jack McCall. A former buffalo hunter, McCall had been told that his reputation as a gunfighter would be assured if he killed Hickok. When he was shot, Hickok held a poker hand of two aces, two eights and another card – a hand that some are already calling "the dead man's hand."

"Wild Bill" by Henry H. Cross.

1877

Hayes

United States, April. Four dominant Eastern rail companies meet, agreeing to end rate war, raise rates and cut wages (→ Jan. 1880).

Yellowstone, May. Newspaper reports vandalism in park, including chipping away at geyser rims and rock formations and killing of birds.

New York City, June 14. Sculptor Augustus Saint-Gaudens and other artists found Society of American Artists.

Boston, July 9. Bell Telephone Company founded (→ Aug. 1).

Baltimore, July 20. State militia kill nine strikers, firing into crowd advancing on occupied rail station (→ 26).

United States, Oct. 9. First outdoor telephone transmission occurs.

Washington, D.C., Oct. 9. Over local objections, Southern Pacific Railroad is granted permission to expand into Arizona and New Mexico by presidential order.

Wyoming. Some 1,000 Arapaho Indians from Dakota Territory placed on Shoshone reservation despite traditional animosity between two tribes.

Kansas. Bat Masterson elected sheriff of Dodge City.

Alaska. United States troops withdraw from Alaska.

New York City. Walt Whitman publishes collection of 74 poems, *Passage to India.*

Washington, D.C. *Washington Post* founded.

New Hampshire. *Among the Clouds,* only newspaper in world printed on mountain top, established.

United States. John Ferguson Weir paints *Forging the Shaft, a Welding Heat.*

Philadelphia. Nudity in Thomas Eakins's *William Rush Carving The Allegorical Figure of the Schuylkill* leads to call for artist's resignation from Pennsylvania Academy of Art.

New York, City. Braham-Harrigan song, *Walking for Dat Cake,* billed as an "exquisite picture of Negro life and customs."

DEATH

Utah, Aug. 29. Brigham Young, Mormon leader (*June 1, 1801).

Hayes elected President

Washington, D.C., March 3

Rutherford B. Hayes of Ohio was declared winner of the contested race for President today, ending months of uncertainty over who would be the next resident of the White House. By picking up all 20 disputed electoral votes, Hayes barely edged out Samuel J. Tilden of New York to climax one of the most rancorous chapters in the nation's political history.

Tilden, a Democratic Governor, had led his Republican opponent in both popular and electoral votes when returns were counted last November 7. However, Tilden was one electoral vote short of the needed 185, while Hayes trailed with 165.

With 20 votes, most of them from Southern states, in dispute, a special electoral commission was established by Congress. It was made up of five men from the Senate, five from the House and five Supreme Court justices. The commission, dominated by Republicans, 8 to 7, assigned all 20 of the contested electoral votes to Hayes, the 54-year-old Governor of Ohio. This gave him the required 185 votes. Hayes and his vice presidential running mate, William A. Wheeler of New York, are scheduled to take the oath of office later this week.

Hayes (1884) by Daniel Huntington.

Court says states may regulate rates

Washington, D.C., March 1

Farmers 2, railroad tycoons 0. That's the score in a contest for regulation of rail grain shipping as decided by the Supreme Court.

In Munn v. Illinois, the court ruled today that states have the right to regulate intrastate rates in the transport of goods if it affects the public interest. According to the majority opinion, "Property does become clothed in public interest when used in a manner to make it of public consequence." And in another case, Peik v. Chicago and the Northwest Railroad Company, the court declared that states may even fix rail rates that may incidentally affect interstate charges. Dissenting justices argued that the states have no right to meddle in private corporate matters.

The decisions will serve as a restraint on rail magnates accused of sucking small businesses dry. Tonight, members of the Grange, a farmers' organization, are celebrating their victory (→ Apr.).

Last federal troops withdraw from South; Reconstruction ends

Washington, D.C., May 1

Making good on a promise issued on his behalf during the recent election deadlock, President Hayes has now withdrawn all federal troops from the South, thereby signaling an end to what has become known as Radical Reconstruction in the aftermath of the Civil War. The action comes scarcely two months after the new President took office, the declared winner in the hotly disputed contest with the Democrat Samuel J. Tilden of New York.

It was during the time that a special electoral commission was trying to determine a winner in the presidential election that Hayes supporters assured Southerners that if their man was elected, he would withdraw federal troops. This was viewed by many as tipping the scales in favor of Hayes, who was Governor of Ohio at the time.

Just what effect the troop withdrawal will have on the ravaged South is uncertain, though it may ease tensions that have built up steadily since the war's end. While called Reconstruction, the era was marked by destruction of the South as it had been. With the Negro slaves freed, old plantations were all but destroyed. Northern "carpetbaggers" teamed up with Southern "scalawags" to run the states, sometimes corruptly. Taxes rose and property values fell. And the era saw the birth of such terrorist groups as the Ku Klux Klan, the hooded marauders roaming the countryside, intent on preserving what they viewed as the Southern way of life by frightening, and, on some occasions lynching the freed Negroes and scaring off Yankee intruders and those Southerners whom the Klan saw as traitors.

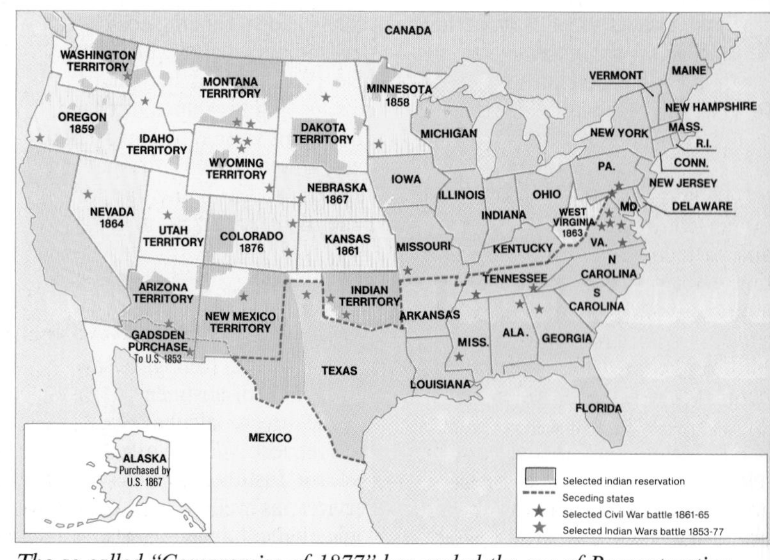

The so-called "Compromise of 1877" has ended the era of Reconstruction.

Crazy Horse gives up in Nebraska

Camp Robinson, Nebraska, May 6

The great Indian leader Chief Crazy Horse turned himself and several hundred of his warriors over to army officials today at Camp Robinson. Crazy Horse, who along with Sitting Bull, had masterminded the Custer massacre last year, surrendered after being assured by General George Crook that he and his Sioux followers could live in peace in the Powder River country. Witnesses say that the chief did not appear to be a broken man. Rather, he entered the army camp a seemingly proud man, at the head of 800 warriors in war paint and feathered headdress, brandishing weapons and chanting songs of war (→Oct.).

10 Molly Maguires hanged for murder

Pennsylvania, June 21

Convicted of capital crimes on the evidence of a Pinkerton agent who had infiltrated their ranks, 10 members of the Molly Maguires, a secret organization started by Irish-Americans to combat oppressive mining conditions, often by intimidation and killing, have been hanged for murder. At the trial, it was revealed that James McParlan is the name of the detective hired by the Reading Railroad to penetrate the organization.

Bell starts company with 778 phones

Boston, Aug. 1

The Bell Telephone Company was incorporated here today, with 5,000 shares of stock issued to Alexander Graham Bell, his family and partners. The firm has one full-time employee, Thomas Watson, and has exactly 778 telephones in service. The chief stockholder is Mrs. Mabel Bell, wife of the telephone's inventor, who has been given 1,497 shares of stock by her husband. Commercial prospects of the telephone company are questionable, and some shareholders are proposing the sale of Bell's patents to Western Union for $100,000.

First national strike against railroads

A new civil war? Sixth Maryland militia opens fire on strikers in Baltimore.

Chicago, July 26

Barely 12 days after workers on the Baltimore & Ohio Railroad went on strike to protest a cut in wages, work stoppages, often accompanied by violence, have spread from coast to coast, halting all through-line service. This first national strike has affected every industrial center, and the losses in life and property are rising daily. Here in Chicago, 19 people were killed today when the police, assisted by mounted troops, attacked a crowd of strikers. In Baltimore last week, nine men and boys were killed and many wounded when the Sixth Maryland Regiment opened fire on a crowd that was advancing on the railway station. Five days ago in Pittsburgh, a mob set fire to the Pennsylvania Railroad yards, destroying some 2,000 cars. Fires also were reported at the Union Depot, a grain elevator and in some sections of the city.

Rioting and violence also marked the outbreak of the strike at Martinsburg, West Virginia, on July 14. The immediate cause of the strike was a 10 percent cut in wages for workers on the B.&0. Railroad, where a brakeman's rate of pay for a 12-hour day is $1.75. The wage cut is the second in four years, and is in marked contrast with the high dividends that the railroads have been paying their stockholders.

Some conservative observers insist that the strike is the work of foreign agitators and tie it to what they call the spread of "communistic ideas." They have been especially worried by reports from Lebanon, Altoona and Harrisburg that units of the militia have openly sympathized with the strikers and refused to move against them.

Most of those involved in the strike appear, however, to have acted spontaneously. The Trainmen's Union represents a relatively small number of workers, and the railway brotherhoods – the Order of Railway Conductors, the Brotherhood of Locomotive Firemen and the Brotherhood of Engineers – have disavowed the strike.

Union membership certificate.

Are all four legs of a galloping horse momentarily off the ground at the same time? That is the question that Leland Stanford, ex-Governor of California, posed to photographer Eadweard Muybridge in 1872 in order to settle a bet with a friend. Through pictures in sequential frames, Muybridge proved Stanford correct: Once in every stride, a horse's legs are simultaneously in the air. The work took five years because it was interrupted while Muybridge was tried and acquitted for the murder of his wife's lover.

Combustion engine is planned for auto

Rochester, New York

George B. Selden, a local lawyer, has drawn up plans for an automobile to be powered by an internal combustion gasoline engine. Selden has not actually built the vehicle, but he plans to apply for a patent, believing that gasoline engines have great promise for propelling automobiles. Selden is inspired by the work of such inventors as Etienne Lenoir of France and Nicholas Otto and Eugen Langen of Germany, who have built internal combustion engines for automobiles. But gasoline engines must still prove that they are superior to steam power. ▷

Black Hills gold rush reaches its peak

Black Hills or bust, the only problem being convincing all parties concerned.

Deadwood, Dakota Terr., October

In the spring, George Hearst, 57, who owns mines in four states, purchased the Homestake Mining Company in nearby Lead. Moses Manuel, who sold him the mine for $105,000, came to the Black Hills to pan for gold in 1857. He hit upon the Homestake lode in April of last year, and the gold rush to the Black Hills was on. Now, with the rush at full tilt, there are mining districts at French Creek, Whitewood Gulch, Black Tail Gulch and Wolfe Mount, which turned out to be a hoax. Illegal white claims began as early as 1875 when the first mining district was set up at French Creek. When in September of 1875, the last great council of Northern Plains Indians failed to obtain the Black Hills from the United States government, the Fort Laramie Treaty of 1868 was broken. This made it legal to mine in the once-protected Black Hills.

Bass gang pulls off great train robbery

Big Spring, Nebraska, Sept. 18

In what is being called the biggest train robbery in history, Sam Bass and his band of desperadoes boarded a Union Pacific train today outside Big Spring and took its entire bounty – $60,000. Believed to operate out of Ogallala, the Bass gang is composed mainly of Texans. Sam Bass is said to live in or around Denton, Texas, where he was a cowboy before becoming active in his current occupation. Acquaintances say that Bass, aged about 25, is stocky and has a wide grin that flashes extremely white teeth.

Hires' Root Beer

Philadelphia

Birch bark, spikenard, sarsparilla and hops: These are a few of the 16 roots and spices that go into Charles Hires' root beer powder. He has offered the drink at his pharmacy here for seven years, but since it sold so well at the centennial exposition last year, he has started marketing it by mail. A 25-cent packet makes five gallons. Hires spent his honeymoon inventing the concoction in 1870.

Vanderbilt dies, leaves $100 million

New York City, Jan. 4

Cornelius Vanderbilt, who rose from poor agrarian roots to amass $100 million in shipping and railroads, has finally lost a fight – for his life. Irascible as ever at 83, he berated the journalists hovering outside his home. "I am not dying!" he bellowed. "Even if I was dying I should have vigor enough to knock this abuse down your lying throats and give the undertaker a job!"

Vanderbilt, who quit school at age 11, ran the first ferry service from Manhattan to Staten Island at 15. In the 1830's, as owner of a steamship firm, he cut fares with such vigor his competitors paid him to leave the Hudson Valley. Moving to the seaboard, the Commodore was a millionaire by 1846. In the 1850's, with profits from bringing gold seekers west, Vanderbilt turned to railroads. By 1873 he owned the Harlem, Hudson, New York Central, and Lake Shore and Michigan lines. Wall Street shook when the old man sneezed. Vanderbilt has left $90 million to his son William, $7.5 million to William's four sons and a paltry $2.5 million to his second wife, a Southerner in her 20's, and his eight daughters.

Chief Joseph, surrendering, says, "I will fight no more forever"

Bear Paw Mountains, Mont., Oct. 15

Nez Perce Chief Joseph rode up the hill accompanied by five warriors and offered his rifle to General O.O. Howard in a gesture of surrender after a five-day standoff with the army in a bitter snowstorm. The army took 418 prisoners. Only 87 were men, more than half of them wounded. The surrender ends the army's four-month pursuit of Chief Joseph that has cost the lives of 127 soldiers and 50 civilians.

Joseph, defeated chief of the Nez Perce: "My heart is sick and sad."

"I am tired of fighting," the 37-year-old Joseph told the remaining chiefs in the presence of an army emissary earlier in the day. "My heart is sick and sad. From where the sun now stands I will fight no more forever."

The conflict started when General Howard tried to enforce a 13-year-old treaty that requires the Nez Perce to relocate from their Wallowa Valley, Oregon, home to the Lapwai reservation in Idaho. Negotiations between the army and Nez Perce broke down June 13 after Indian bands killed 20 settlers in reprisals for outrages they felt had been committed against them.

Although General John Gibbon at Fort Shaw was in front of the chief and his forces, General Howard behind them and many detachments summoned by telegraph at their flank, Joseph's forces eluded the army over 1,000 miles through southwestern Montana, a corner of Idaho and the Yellowstone Park, hoping to escape to Canada. With fewer than 200 warriors and a large contingent of women and chidren, Joseph managed to defeat the army, most notably at Bird Canyon Idaho, on June 17 and Big Hole [Wisdom] River, Montana, on August 9, before being besieged August 30 just 30 miles short of the border by Colonel Nelson Miles. Even then, Joseph's skill did not fail him. He had trenches dug from which his small band defended their position against the army's 500 men until he realized the women and children would die of cold and starvation.

Gunfighter in Texas jailed for 25 years

Texas, August

The notorious gunfighter John Wesley Hardin, found guilty of murder, has been sentenced to the Texas State Prison in Huntsville for 25 years. The 24-year-old killer, who is said to have shot down at least 40 men, once warned in his Texas drawl that he would "take no sass but sasparilla." After killing Sheriff Charles Webb in Texas in May, he traveled throughout the South, and ended up in Pensacola, Florida, where he was seized by the police early this month. Hardin had boasted that he would never surrender to the police. He fought so fiercely before he was finally seized that the officer in charge of the operation said, "He's too brave to kill – the first man who shoots him – *I'll* kill!" If Hardin serves all his time, he will be released from prison in 1902.

Fishing dispute is finally settled

Washington, D.C., Nov. 23

The long-running fight between American fishermen and their British and Canadian counterparts over access to Northeast fishing grounds was finally settled today. After an arbitration process similar to the one that settled the claims five years ago involving Civil War damage done by British-built Confederate ships, it was agreed that while reciprocity will go on, the United States will pay $5.5 million in return for concessions made by Canada. Other disputes that the arbitration mechanism ended concern compensation for damage done by the Irish-American Fenian raids on Canada and the Puget Sound border dispute.

Desert land offered for 25 cents an acre

Washington, D.C., March 3

Legislation enacted today may prove a real boon to small farmers and ranchers, especially in the Great Plains and Midwest. The Desert Land Act is designed to help these operators obtain land holdings larger than the usual 160 acres in arid or barren regions where small ranches and farms are impractical. Under the new law, the government will sell land in 640-acre tracts at 25 cents per acre where the traditional homestead allotment of 160 acres is not deemed viable for farming and/or ranching. There is one catch: The cheap lands must be irrigated before the government will grant final title.

"The American," a tale by Henry James

London

New World naivete clashes with Old World sophistication in the second novel by Henry James, *The American*, a dark tale of a wealthy businessman set loose in the drawing rooms of Paris. Upon his arrival in the French capital, Christopher (as in Columbus) Newman (as in "new man") falls hard for a half-French, half-English widow, Claire de Cintre, and courts her strenuously – to the displeasure of her high-born family. Newman is out of his element but plunges into intrigues that lead to a tragic conclusion. James succeeds in contrasting his innocent American protagonist with a sophisticated, evil European antagonist, DeBellegardes.

This trans-Atlantic theme, enriched with handsome prose and penetrating insight, typifies the art of James, a New Yorker now living in London. At 34, he has spent many years abroad and has been welcomed by such literary lions as Flaubert and Turgenev. His *The Passionate Pilgrim and Other Stories* was published two years ago.

Edison seeks to patent his "phonograph"

Edison, haggard but successful, relaxes after working five days and five nights.

Menlo Park, New Jersey, Dec. 15

A patent application for a machine that reproduces the voice was filed today by its inventor, Thomas A. Edison, who calls it a "phonograph." Edison, already noted for inventing improved versions of the telegraph and telephone, started working on the phonograph as a means of recording telephone messages. The machine consists of a diaphragm attached to a stylus that etches grooves into a foil-covered cylinder, which is turned by a hand crank. A different kind of stylus is used to play back the message.

Edison first tried his machine on the night of November 29, singing the first verse of *Mary Had a Little Lamb* while his assistant, John Kreusi, turned the crank. Astounded when the phonograph played back the voice, Edison and his assistants stayed up all night playing with the device. Later, they took it to the New York editorial offices of the magazine *Scientific American* for a demonstration. Edison says the phonograph will be used primarily as a business tool and as a "speaking family album," recording the voices of loved ones. Others feel that it may some day be used to record music. The phonograph has made Edison famous, earning him an invitation to the White House.

Horse racing at the Brighton Beach Fair Grounds in Brooklyn, New York. As America's oldest sport – and highly popular since its beginnings on Long Island, New York, in the 18th century – it remains a strong favorite.

"Will Schuster and Blackman Going Shooting for Rail" (1876) by Thomas Eakins. With Reconstruction gone and Southerners seeking ways to restrict the Negro, even Eakins's image of uneasy friendship seems idealistic.

Yearning to Breathe Free 1878-1916

The United States is a nation of immigrants, a country inhabited by people whose ancestors all shared the painful experience of being uprooted from their native land to start a new life in a strange new world. From this common experience, America has earned a reputation as a land of opportunity for the world's oppressed and a "melting pot" where a variety of ethnic, religious and racial groups have mixed together to form a new culture. From 1870 to 1920, more immigrants – some 25 million – arrived in America than ever before. As they entered New York harbor, the Statue of Liberty beckoned: "Give me your tired, your poor, your huddled masses yearning to breathe free." One of the most obvious facts the newcomers faced was that the society they were joining was one undergoing a dramatic transformation.

In 1907, Henry Adams – historian, novelist, descendant of presidents – published his classic autobiography. In it, he reflected on the social and economic changes he had witnessed in his lifetime: the development of railroads and ocean liners and the telegraph; the rise of industry; the growth of cities; the explosion of technical and scientific knowledge. The world he observed around him in the last years of his life seemed so different from the one he had known as a child that he often felt himself a stranger in his own land, a relic soon to be consigned to oblivion by the forces of progress. "He could see," Adams wrote (referring to himself in the third person), "that the new American – the child of incalculable coal power, chemical power, electric power and radiating energy, as well as new forces yet undetermined – must be a sort of God compared with any former creation of nature. At the rate of progress since 1800, every American who lived into the year 2000 would know how to control unlimited power. He would think in complexities unimaginable to an earlier mind. He would deal with problems altogether beyond the range of earlier society."

The changes Adams described occurred over many decades. "With a stride that astonished statisticians," the historians Charles and Mary Beard wrote, "the conquering hosts of business enterprise swept over the continent; 25 years after the death of Lincoln, America had become, in the quantity and value of her products, the first manufacturing nation of the world. What England had accomplished in a hundred years, the United States had achieved in half the time." The Industrial Revolution had begun in America well before the Civil War; the nation's rise to economic greatness was not really as sudden as the Beards suggested. But it was true that the industrial accomplishments of the late 19th century overshadowed all earlier progress. And those accomplishments helped produce other profound changes as well. The United States was becoming not only an industrialized nation, but an urbanized one. It was changing from a fragmented and provincial society into a more centralized and consolidated one. It was moving from a position of relative unimportance in world affairs to that of a major power.

To many Americans, the dramatic changes of the age of industry were a cause for celebration and optimism. The titans of finance and industry, of course, rejoiced in their own success and in the previously unimagined fortunes they managed to accumulate. But the new affluence reached well beyond the ranks of the upper class: to the urban middle class, which grew rapidly in both size and wealth; to the agricultural world, where some farmers managed to accumulate great land holdings and establish themselves as rural "tycoons"; to the working class, where some laborers, at least, experienced slow but significant increases in their standards of living.

But the late 19th century was also a time of turbulence and crisis. For along with the undoubted benefits of economic growth came great costs. Cities were growing so rapidly that public services could not keep up with demand. Roads, sewers, transportation systems, housing, social services, government bureaucracies, public health systems: all were plunged into something approaching chaos as they strained to keep up with the changes around them. The political system, accustomed to the problems and the pace of an earlier and simpler time, reacted slowly and uncertainly to the new social problems of the new era; to many Americans, late 19th-century political life at every level was chiefly notable for its corruption. Major demographic changes – the arrival of the millions of new immigrants from Europe and Asia, the movement of rural Americans (including, for the first time, large numbers of blacks) from the country to the city – created social and economic tensions of their own. The agricultural economy, in the meantime, suffered both an absolute and a relative decline that left some American farmers wealthy and secure, but others desperate and resentful. Some workers enjoyed significant progress in good times, but all were vulnerable when times turned bad, as they often did.

These and other problems combined in the 1890's to produce a period of crisis more severe than any since the 1860's. Industrial workers rose up in a series of major, and at times violent, protests to challenge a labor system they believed oppressed them. Farmers in the West and South, both white and black, organized a great political movement known as populism to challenge economic and political institutions they considered exploitive and dangerous. Americans of all regions and classes suffered from the effects of the most severe economic depression in the nation's history up to that point – a panic that began in 1893, that lasted for over four years and that demonstrated how interdependent the new economy had become.

The crisis of the 1890's strengthened reform impulses that had already been growing in some sectors of society for years. A few Americans saw industrialization as a menace to the world they cherished and searched for ways to stop it or escape from it. Most, however, accepted, even welcomed economic progress and sought not to impede it but to curb the instability and injustice it had brought in its wake. Growth and progress could no longer be allowed to proceed without restraints, they believed. Society needed to take steps to impose order on the growing chaos and to find just solutions to glaring wrongs. The reform impulse gathered strength in the last years of the 19th century. By the early 20th, it had acquired a name: progressivism.

Neither at the time nor since was there agreement on what "progressivism" was, so various and even contradictory were the ideas and crusades the word came to describe. Many of the "reforms" that some Americans considered progressive at the time have come to seem to later generations highly reactionary: the imposition of legalized segregation on the American South in the 1890's and the early 20th century; the continuous effort to restrict immigration; the crusade to prohibit the sale of alcoholic beverages. But at the time, many "reformers" defended even these restrictive measures as part of the effort to bring order to a disordered world. Other efforts fit more comfortably into later notions of progressive reform: civil service reform, woman suffrage, direct election of senators, public supervision of railroads and trusts, restrictions on child labor, regulation of food, drugs and other commodities affecting public health. But whatever their intent and however much they varied, most "reforms" of the progressive era had at least a few things in common: their sense that government – local, state, and ultimately national – had to play a larger role in the life of society than it had in the past; their belief that the ideal of the autonomous, self-reliant individual, an ideal that had been at the heart of America's image of itself since the founding of the republic, must now compete with the reality of an increasingly interdependent society in which individual liberties would be balanced against public needs.

At the same time, the United States was finding itself propelled into a new relationship with the world – partly as a result of the same economic forces that were remaking politics at home. As a result of the brief, and some Americans believed "splendid," Spanish-American War of 1898, the nation joined the ranks of imperial powers, acquiring overseas possessions for the first time. America also joined other nations in developing commercial ties with Japan and China. It expanded its economic and, all too frequently, its military presence in Latin America. Under Presidents Theodore Roosevelt and Woodrow Wilson (in very different ways), it attempted to become a powerful moral force in international relations. And after 1914, it found itself drawn, despite strenuous efforts to avoid it, into the greatest armed conflict in world history up to that point: World War I, which was to propel America into still another relationship with other nations and into a period of dramatic new economic growth and social change.

◄ *"The Steerage" (1907), a photographic masterpiece by Alfred Stieglitz.*

1878

Hayes

Washington, D.C., Jan. 17. Congress ratifies treaty with Samoa, gaining harbor of Pago Pago as fueling station for American Navy.

New Haven, Conn. Feb. 21. First telephone directory issued.

Washington, D.C., Feb. 28. With currency values at lowest point since Civil War, Congress passes Bland-Allison Act over President's veto; compromise bill requires federal government to buy and mint $2 million to $4 million in silver each month.

United States, July 1. Rutherford B. Hayes writes in his diary, "Let all our dealings with the Red Man be characterized by justice and good faith . . ."

Saratoga, New York, Aug. 21. Attorneys meet to establish American Bar Association.

New York City, Oct. 15. Thomas A. Edison founds Edison Electric Light Company (→ Oct. 21, 1879).

Washington, D.C., Nov. 5. Democrats regain control of both houses of Congress for first time since 1858; 14 Greenback Labor candidates win seats (→ Dec. 9).

Springfield, Massachusetts. Remington adds shift key to typewriter.

Auburn, New York. First commercial milking machines produced.

Nashville, Tenn. Vanderbilt University ousts Professor Alexander Winchell for teaching scientific contradictions of biblical chronology.

Idaho. Band of 150 renegade Indians, called "sheepeaters" because of their diet, raid villages and steal horses (→ May 30, 1879).

Florida. During struggle for independence, Cubans flee to United States; numerous cigar makers arrive after Spanish destroy tobacco plantations.

Kansas. About 40,000 Negroes from former slave states, known as "Exodusters," settle in Kansas.

Deadwood, Dakota Territory. Calamity Jane aids victims of smallpox epidemic.

United States. James Freeman Clarke, comparative religion scholar, publishes *Ten Great Religions.*

Yellow fever takes 14,000 lives in South

New Orleans, November

The epidemic of the dreaded disease called "Yellow Jack" appears to be abating, but it has taken more than 14,000 lives in the South since it first struck in New Orleans back in May. This has been a time of death and horror for stricken communities in the Mississippi Valley and the Gulf Coast area. Here in New Orleans, yellow fever raged all through September and October, with a total of 27,000 cases and 4,046 deaths reported. There were also epidemics in Mississippi, Alabama and Tennessee. In New Orleans, wagons patrolled the city on a daily basis to collect bodies. There was no time for funerals. As one physician in Memphis commented, "Death was triumphant."

"By all means, don't let him in!"

Pulitzer purchases a St. Louis paper

St. Louis

Editor Joseph Pulitzer has purchased the *St. Louis Dispatch*. And, according to some observers, he has indicated that he would like to buy the *Evening Post* as well. Pulitzer, the son of a Hungarian Jewish father and an Austro-German mother, came to America from Hungary at age 17 in the early 1860's without a dime. He served in the Union army, and after his discharge in 1865 he soon began working on a German-language paper. He then began to buy and sell shares in local papers, building a base for this purchase. He paid $2,500 for the *Dispatch*, plus a lien of $30,000.

Hungarian-born Pulitzer.

120,000 Chinese migrate to U.S. in decade

In the San Francisco Custom House.

San Francisco

Boom times on the West Coast have brought at least 12,000 Chinese immigrants to America every year for the past 10 years. This Oriental influx got under way with the discovery of gold in California in 1849. Within three years, there were more than 25,0000 Chinese in America, and the number continued to grow. Most of the Chinese arriving here are men responding to the demand for cheap labor on the railroads. Low pay, long hours and racial prejudice make the lot of the Chinese an unhappy one.

Minstrel show sells lots of Sure Corn Killer

Newark, New Jersey

Patent medicines have been with us since the first colonists came to America and have proliferated to the point where their producers must find new and imaginative ways of reaching the clientele. The snake oil salesmen and flashy newspaper advertisements are making way for the newest popular medium, the minstrel show, which has already sold many bottles of Mennen's Sure Corn Killer. Patent cures and nostrums rarely have anything to do with the United States Patent Office; the name comes from the custom of British kings to grant "patents of royal favor" to tradesmen who served royalty.

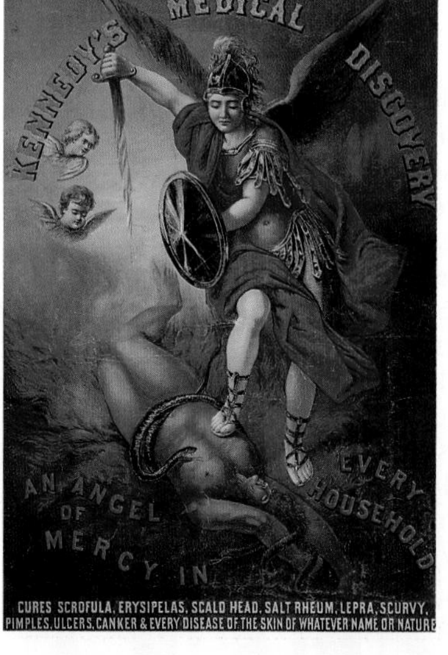

Procter & Gamble sells White Soap

Cincinnati

William Procter and James Gamble, who started a soap and candle business with $7,192 in 1837 and then single-handedly kept the Union Army clean during the war, may have hit on a winning product. Several years of trial and error in one of the country's few industrial research laboratories have produced an inexpensive hard white soap equal in quality to fine olive oil castille. The firm has named it P&G's White Soap, but Harley Procter, an enterprising young sales manager, thinks the name boring and is searching for a new one.

Court ruling gives segregation a boost

Washington, D.C., Jan. 14

The Supreme Court today ruled in Hall v. De Cuir, that states cannot forbid racial segregation on public transportation vehicles. The case came before the court when a Mississippi steamboat firm, abiding by a state statute banning separate compartments, offered only racially mixed accommodations for Negroes and whites. Many white passengers complained. The steamboat firm said the law interfered with business. Agreeing with that assessment, the court held that segregation is not a matter for states to decide and that it places a burden on interstate commerce. The ruling also applies to rails (→ May 1879).

Arthur dismissed as customs officer

Washington, D.C., July 11

In an effort to root out corruption, President Hayes has replaced Chester A. Arthur as port collector of customs in New York. In a recent investigation of the New York Custom House, officials found blatant disregard of President Hayes's demand for a nonpartisan civil service free of vice. Also being replaced is Alonzo C. Lornell, who was formerly the port naval officer and state chairman of the Republican Party.

Political murders charged in South

Washington, D.C., Dec. 2

Initial presidential election returns indicated no clear winner in 1876, with Democrat Samuel J. Tilden one electoral vote short. Congress gave the victory to Republican Rutherford B. Hayes in 1877. Ever since, accusations have flown in all directions. Now, the Attorney General says Southern Democrats stuffed ballot boxes and even committed political murders in South Carolina, Louisiana, Texas and Virginia in order to win. A Senate committee is being formed to study the situation. Still today, Tilden retains great popular support.

Whistler sues critic, wins one farthing

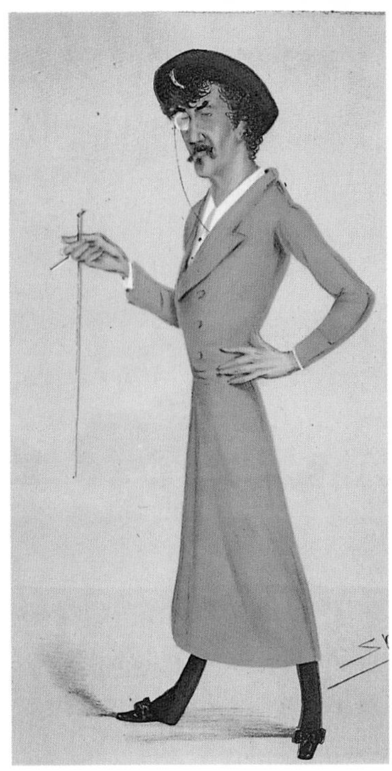

Whistler (1878) by Sir Leslie Ward.

Westminster, England, Nov. 26

Can a critic's judgment be construed as libel? The court has responded with a weak yes in the libel suit that the American expatriate painter James Whistler has filed against the English critic John Ruskin. Upon seeing *Nocturne in Black and Gold: The Falling Rocket*, Ruskin accused Whistler of "flinging a pot of paint in the public's face." "His ill-educated conceit," Ruskin added, "nearly approached imposture." The court battle was often farcical: The jury was shown the work upside-down, Whistler's star witness didn't testify because he was knighted the day he was to appear, and Ruskin was absent because of a mental condition. Whistler, a believer in "art for art's sake," is also responsible for painting the masterpiece known as *Portrait of the Artist's Mother*. The award – one farthing – was a moral victory but a financial disaster.

"Calamity" Jane aids victims of smallpox

Deadwood, Dakota Territory

Martha Jane Canary is an unlikely candidate for the role of savior. She drinks hard, runs with railroad gangs and "Wild Bill" Hickok, and serves frontier clientele as everything from show girl to bawd. But "Calamity" Jane is proving she values more than making herself a legend in her own time. Taking a respite from adventure, she has been nursing smallpox victims here in the plague-torn Dakotas. Always reinventing herself, Jane says she has spent recent years as a man. In 1875, the straight-shooting renegade concealed her gender to travel to the Black Hills with a geological expedition. The next year she claims to have spent tracking Indians with General George Crook and 1,300 male soldiers.

Uncle Sam riding a bicycle. Made for some child's amusement, this whirligig combines art and function, as is common in American folk culture.

Greenbacks finally reach face value

New York City, Dec. 9

Greenbacks, notes issued by the government to finance its Civil War debt, are now redeemable in gold at face value. Having bought bonds at depreciated values during the war, Eastern bankers stand to double their initial investment. A direct result of federal policy, the development antagonizes the farm-labor alliance whose Greenback Labor Party polled one million votes in this year's congressional elections. The alliance argues that the government should print more money, devaluing greenbacks and shoring up commodity prices; limit immigration to ease job competition and improve working conditions (→ Jan. 1, 1879).

Masked bandits get bank's $3.5 million

New York City, Oct. 27

Covered by dim morning light, a gang of masked thieves lifted $3.5 million from a vault in the Manhattan Savings Institution today. At 6 a.m., they accosted the janitor as he dressed in his home above the bank. Binding him and his wife and wrapping his mother-in-law in a sheet, they elicited the combination of the safe. Police have few clues, but Western George Leslie, said to have committed 75 percent of the nation's bank heists, is a suspect.

Factory shifts gears to turn out bicycles

Hartford, Connecticut

Should a successful businessman make gears for bicycles instead of sewing machines? Albert Pope thinks so. He changed his profitable sewing machine production firm into the nation's first bicycle factory today. James Starley was the first to patent the machine under the name "bicycle" in 1873. *The New York Times* predicted at the time that the bicycle would not become a valuable mode of transportation. But the cycling craze has proved that prediction wrong. Now the Pope Manufacturing Company is gearing up to pedal itself to a wheel of fortune.

1879

Hayes

Washington, D.C., Jan. 1. Under terms of 1875 Specie Resumption Act, government redeems greenbacks in coin (→March 3, 1884).

Washington, D.C., Jan. 25. Congress passes Arrears of Pensions Act, authorizing veterans to collect back pay from date of discharge to present.

England, January. William James publishes "Are We Automatons?" in *Mind* magazine, attacking "prevailing scientific materialism."

Washington, D.C., Feb. 15. President Hayes signs bill allowing female lawyers to argue cases before Supreme Court, provided they have practiced at state supreme court level for minimum of three years.

Washington, D.C., Apr. 29. Army appropriations bill vetoed by President Hayes, blocking rider barring President from sending federal troops to protect voting rights in congressional elections.

Boston, Apr. 30. First factory inspection law enacted, directing governor to appoint police to inspect factories and public buildings for safety violations.

Rochester, New York, May 8. Attorney George B. Seldon unsuccessfully applies for patent on idea for horseless carriage powered by an internal-combustion engine.

Grangeville, Idaho, May 30. Captain Reube Bernard and First Cavalry ordered to move against "sheepeater" Indians.

Mississippi, May. Southern whites threaten to sink all boats on the Mississippi River that carry Negroes; shipowners strand 1,500 Negroes along banks of river (→Oct. 15, 1883).

Pennsylvania, June 24. First Child's Cup rowing contest won by University of Pennsylvania.

England, July. William James publishes *The Future of Rationality*, dealing with "the motive which leads men to philosophize."

Idaho, October. Pacific Northwest Indian Wars end with capture of 388 Indians by Major Edward S. Farrow.

Detroit. Parke, Davis & Company introduces pharmaceuticals of standardized dosage.

Yellowstone is made first national park

Mammoth Hot Springs in Yellowstone National Park, the first such park.

Colorado, Spring

A vast area of land in Colorado and Wyoming has been officially designated Yellowstone National Park. The first such park to be established in the United States, Yellowstone is the result of the efforts of conservationists, nature lovers and assorted groups of people who want to preserve this area from the miners, timber-cutters and industrialists who they fear would despoil its natural resources and beauty. A rugged, mountainous region, it features a rich diversity of wildlife, flora and fauna. There is a huge hot-springs geyser that erupts several times a day. Yellowstone is also full of Indians, who were on the warpath just last year, until defeated by army troops under Generals O.O. Howard and Nelson Miles.

Now that Yellowstone has been established, efforts are under way to establish other national parks soon in the West.

Woolworth opens a "five-and-ten"

Lancaster, Pennsylvania, May

Frank W. Woolworth, a self-described "boob from the country," is making good in the urban retail trade. With backing from W.H. Moore, for whom he has clerked for several years, Woolworth has opened what he calls a "five-and-ten" store. The move is a bold one, considering the failure of his Great Five Cent Store, which opened on Washington's Birthday in Utica, New York. Moore and Woolworth are blaming its pitiful take of $2.50 a day on the location. They also hope the added variety of offering both five-cent and ten-cent items (on opposite sides of the store) will attract more customers.

The concept originated with the "five-cent counter," which Moore says gets people in the door to buy more expensive items. Woolworth, who was ineffective as a clerk but excels in the broader sphere of marketing strategy, wants to turn the idea into an empire. Born on a small farm in upstate New York, he understands the appeal of frugality. The future of merchandising, he believes, lies in selling large quantities of low-cost goods.

Jetties, levees and showboats bring new life to the Mississippi

New Orleans

James B. Eads has had his revenge. Many called the St. Louis engineer insane when he suggested deepening the channel at the mouth of the Mississippi by building jetties, or artificial walls leading into the Gulf of Mexico. The river, he said, would scour the channel to remove mudbars. The jetties were built, and today the channel at South Pass is 30 feet deep, enough for the largest ships to get through. No longer will the pass be blocked by ships stuck on the mudbars. Now, the port's future is assured. The Corps of Engineers also plans to strengthen the levee system.

One pride of the Mississippi that hasn't changed is the showboat, still the talk of the valley. Lavish steamers take circuses, museums and dramatic productions to towns from New Orleans up to Cairo, Illinois. Captain Augustus Byron French's New Sensation has a complete theater. The Floating Palace has a trained elephant, a giraffe and a museum with ancient relics from Greece and Egypt. The newest captain on the river is Callie French, wife of the New Sensation's owner and the first woman licensed as a pilot. She was once a high-wire performer.

Mississippi riverboats paddling downstream. Lithograph by Currier & Ives.

Edison succeeds with electric light

Menlo Park, N.J., Oct 21

Thomas A. Edison's determined quest for a long-lasting electric light bulb succeeded today with the production of a bulb that burned for more than 13 hours before being switched off. Edison tried literally thousands of materials to find one that would last long enough to be commercially practical. Success finally came with the test of a bulb filament made of carbonized cotton.

The bulb is just one element of an electric lighting system being developed in Edison's laboratory here. It includes a dynamo that can generate electricity reliably at low cost and a network of wiring that will carry electricity of the required voltage. While experts felt Edison was bound to fail, as so many others have, his fame is such that prices of shares in gas lighting firms plunged when he announced he would work on an electric lighting system.

Edison's most notable invention is the phonograph, but he has patents for dozens of other inventions, including a telephone that is said to be more effective than the one invented by Alexander Graham Bell and an improved telegraph that quadrupled the capacity of Western Union's lines. Perhaps his greatest invention is the laboratory at Menlo Park, the world's first facility established for the purpose of pursuing scientific developments methodically. It was the dedicated team of assistants that he assembled at Menlo Park that enabled Edison to create the revolutionary system of electric light (→Feb. 2, 1880).

Edison demonstrates his potentially profitable invention. But, he says, "I don't care so much for a fortune as I do for getting ahead of the other fellow."

Thomas Edison's vacuum tube, the foundation of the incandescent lamp.

Mrs. Eddy's friends organize a church

Lynn, Massachusetts, Apr. 12

At a meeting of the Christian Scientist Association tonight, the nine members present voted to organize a church to be called the Church of Christ under the leadership of Mary Baker [Patterson] Eddy. The goal is to restore primitive Christianity and its lost element of healing. Healing is a large part of Mrs. Eddy's teachings. She set these out fully in her 1875 book *Science and Health with Key to the Scriptures*. Mrs. Eddy argues that illness results from thinking that the objective world of the senses is real: once one realizes that pain and death are illusions, then healing begins.

Boarding school for Indians established

Carlisle, Pennsylvania, Nov. 1

On October 6, 84 Sioux children dressed in tribal garb arrived at the newly established Carlisle Indian School to begin learning English grammar school courses. Founded by Richard Henry Pratt, 39, the school is a first as it is not affiliated with any reservation. The goal of the school, now in full operation, is to offer Indian youth assimilation into white society. In 1878, Pratt organized the Indian branch of the Hampton Normal and Agricultural Institute in Virginia, and has spent the greater part of his life studying or fighting American Indian tribes like the Cheyenne and Kiowa.

George proposes a single tax on land

New York City

As a handful of land speculators get richer, most of their countrymen sink deeper into poverty, according to Henry George's economic treatise, *Progress and Poverty*. The culprit, according to the 40-year-old author, is private property, and the solution is a "single tax" on all land rents and no other taxes at all. George introduced this radical measure in his 1871 pamphlet, *Our Land and Land Policy*. He began his work during the depression of 1877.

America hears first Gilbert and Sullivan

New York City, Jan. 15

After conquering Boston, San Francisco and Philadelphia, Gilbert and Sullivan's operetta *H.M.S. Pinafore* steamed into New York today with predictable success. The team's first venture in America, *Pinafore* piles the preposterous on the absurd with fine effect and unrelenting wit. Such was the fast pace that many of the first nighters seemed themselves at sea sometimes as they laughed even during the more serious scenes.

Images of American Indians are used to sell Indian Corn Table Syrup.

1880

Hayes

New York City, Feb. 4. Steele MacKaye's *Hazel Kirke* opens at Madison Square Theater. Its portrayal of domestic issues marks shift away from romantic tradition in American theater.

Texas, Feb. 19. Gail Borden organizes *Houston Post* newspaper company.

Washington, D.C., March 1. In Strauder v. West Virginia, Supreme Court rules that 14th Amendment renders exclusion of Negroes from jury duty unconstitutional.

New York City, March 4. *New York Daily Graphic* becomes first newspaper to publish half-tone photographs.

Washington, D.C., March 8. President Hayes declares that United States will have jurisdiction over any canal built across Isthmus of Panama (→18).

Chicago, June 8. Republicans nominate James A. Garfield for president on 36th ballot; Ulysses S. Grant's name is put in nomination for third term, but he declines offer (→Nov. 2).

Chicago, June 8. Senator Blanche K. Bruce of Mississippi named temporary chairman by Republican Party, becoming the first Negro to head a major political convention.

Madrid, Spain, July 3. United States delegates meet with European envoys to organize support for Moroccan independence movement, attempting to keep out all foreign powers.

New York City, Dec. 20. One mile of Broadway is illuminated with arc-lamps (→Sept. 4, 1881).

United States. John Philip Sousa becomes 14th conductor of U.S. Marine Band.

United States. There are an estimated 93,000 miles of railroad track in the nation.

Alaska. Major gold strike made near Juneau.

United States. Sherwin-Williams manufactures first house paint from standard formulas.

United States. Margaret Sidney [Harriet Lothrop] publishes *Five Little Peppers and How They Grew* in magazine *Wide Awake*.

Immigrants push population to 50 million

The rural town. "After the Wedding in Warren, Pennsylvania," anonymous.

Washington, D.C.

Stimulated by a flood of immigrants, America's population grew by more than 11.5 million in the past decade to a total of 50 million, the 1880 census shows. And the nation, which up until now has been predominantly rural and populated with Northern and Western Europeans, is becoming increasingly heterogeneous and urban.

New York, landing place for most European immigrants, is the first state to top five million, with Pennsylvania close behind with 4.2 million residents.

Experts have detected a change in the pattern of immigration. Most of the new arrivals still come from the traditional sources, Scandinavia, Britain and Germany. But a growing percentage comes from Southern and Eastern Europe. Many Croats live in the Western states, as do the Volga Germans, Russians of German descent. Most of the latter have settled near Denver.

The nature of Jewish immigration also is changing. Most of America's 250,000 Jews are from Germany and have assimilated easily, dominating some trades. The newer Jewish immigrants tend to be from Russia and Poland. They are poorer, have fewer urban skills and their Western European brethren look askance at them.

Americans are still moving west, the census shows. California's population rose nearly 50 percent in the decade, to 864,000. Oregon's nearly doubled, to 175,000, and the population of the state of Washington more than tripled, to 75,000.

Americans are still moving out West. "Northwestern Town," anonymous.

U.S. illiteracy rate is cut to 17 percent

Washington, D.C.

The illiteracy rate in the United States has dropped to 17 percent, the 1880 census shows, and this despite a Negro literacy rate of only 30 percent. Even that is an improvement from 1870, when only 18.6 percent of Negroes were able to read. Credit is given to the system of free public schools and compulsory attendance established by such pioneers as Horace Mann in Massachusetts. Free public education has been opposed by the wealthy and by ethnic groups such as German immigrants, who fear its effect on their culture. But it now has the support of most of the public.

Jews control most of clothing trade

New York City

If you are buying retail clothing here, there is a good chance that the seller will be Jewish. Wholesale, the chances are greater still. There are 250,000 Jews living in America now compared to 50,000 in 1850. Central European Jews, fleeing oppression, are flocking to the United States and have made a cultural and economic home for themselves, especially in the clothing trade. Outside New York, Jewish clothing firms dominate 75 percent of the industry. Joseph Seligman's small shop here has blossomed into a multi-million dollar banking firm.

A women's "first": an American Ph.D.

Zurich, Switzerland, June

Miss Martha Carey has become the first American woman to receive a Ph.D. Because no American schools offer the degree to women students, Miss Carey studied overseas. Majoring in literature, she wrote her dissertation on Sir Gawain and the Green Knight and graduated summa cum laude. Miss Carey, 23 years old, was an undergraduate at Cornell University in Ithaca, New York. She says she would like to become a teacher at an American women's college.

Woman gets Supreme Court role for Negro

Belva Lockwood, through her own efforts, became the first woman to argue before the Supreme Court.

Washington, D.C., Feb. 2

Samuel R. Lowery today became the fifth Negro lawyer to win the right to practice before the United States Supreme Court. Lowery, who is president of the Industrial School for Colored People in Huntsville, Alabama, had previously argued before the U.S. Circuit Court and in Tennessee state courts. Anyone who has ever heard the fiery Belva Ann Bennett Lockwood will not be surprised that she had a hand in extending the scope of Lowery's practice. It was Lockwood, social reformer, suffragist, pacificist, temperance advocate and the first women ever to argue a case before the high court, who made the motion that won Lowery his privileges.

The Supreme Court ends railroad wars

Colorado, January

The Supreme Court has finally ended the violent "railroad wars" between the mammoth Santa Fe and the tiny Denver & Rio Grande Railroads for the right to build a line from Pueblo through the deep Royal Gorge, toward western Colorado and on to Salt Lake City. For many months, the two companies engaged in numerous lawsuits, while their construction crews battled with axes and hammers. Earlier this month, the high court ruled in favor of the locally owned Denver firm. It is expected to resume construction (→ Oct. 10, 1886).

The Salvation Army starts U.S. outpost

Pennsylvania, March 24

A British group of evangelists and philanthropists who wear military uniforms and call themselves the Salvation Army now has an outpost in the United States. Although the "army" is widespread and well entrenched in England, in America it consists of only one man and seven British women. Members of the organization believe that they are "saved to save" and pledge a vigilant "warfare against evil" that includes revival meetings, soup kitchens and other charitable work.

Product 300 times sweeter than sugar

Baltimore, Maryland, February

Ira Remsen has published an article describing his accidental discovery of saccharin, a substance that the scientist reports is 300 times sweeter than an equal amount of sugar. Saccharin is a white, crystalline, aromatic compound that apparently has no nutritive value as it passes through the body unchanged. But its developers say it may have great commercial value because it could prove quite useful for diabetics, for fat people and for others who are not allowed to use sugar. It's also special for those who like their food very sweet.

Wabash is first city to use electric light

Wabash, Indiana, Feb. 2

The world's first municipal electric street lighting system was inaugurated with great celebration in this city tonight. Thus far, it consists of a single light on the dome of the city courthouse, but there are plans to add four more lights, each of 4,000 candlepower, on a staff above the courthouse. The system is being built by the Brush Electric Light Company of Cleveland, which has received a payment of $100 and will get $1,800 more when the job is completed (→ Dec. 20).

Ads catch America's fancy and cash

Young Columbus and flag, enlisted to sell "the best" thread.

Trade cards try to identify their product with an image, for instance of a happy family wealthy enough to afford a servant.

The new mythmaker: Advertisement for silk portrays "a happy freedman."

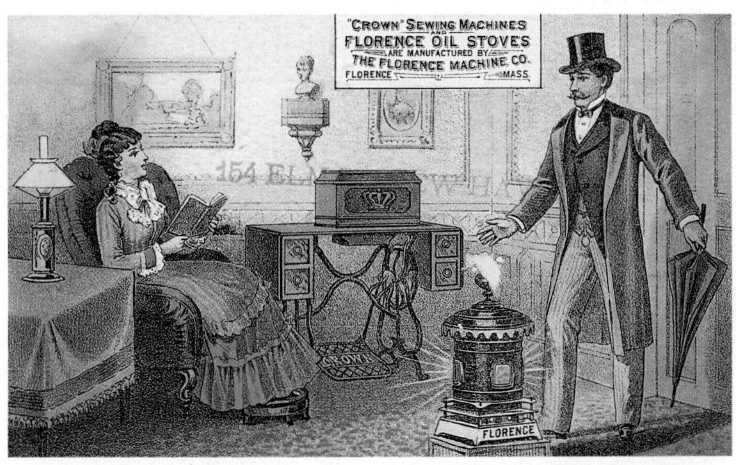

Sewing machines and stoves from the new diversified manufacturer.

Philadelphia

Since the Civil War, the volume of national expenditure on advertising has been growing by leaps and bounds. Five years ago, Francis W. Ayer, a former schoolteacher, and his father, founders of N.W. Ayer & Son, signed the first "open contract," with a firm of rose growers in Pennsylvania. For the first time, the advertising agent became solely the agent of the advertiser, offering him expert advice.

▷

National Farmers Alliance is established

The American farmer, dependent on the whims of nature, and now on the freight rates of railroad magnates. Painting by Arthur Burden Frost.

Chicago, April

The revolt growing in America's heartland has found fertile ground in the Midwest. Milton George, an editor with a penchant for sermons on agrarian virtue, has begun a group he calls the National Farmers Alliance. In fact, the organization's only real strength lies in Kansas and Nebraska. Its namesake in Texas dates to September 1877 and is more deserving of the title. But George pledges to "unite the farmers of America for their protection against class legislation, and the encroachments of concentrated capital and the tyranny of monopoly." If its leader can equal his rhetorical skills with organizational ones, the alliance may make headway in fighting falling prices, exorbitant freight rates and other agrarian ills.

"Divine Sarah" makes American debut

Bernhardt in the final scene of Dumas's "The Lady of the Camelias." The adored actress was born the illegitimate daughter of a Parisian courtesan.

New York City, Nov. 8

The excitement was palpable outside Booth's Theater on West 23rd Street, where Sarah Bernhardt was to make her American debut in the title role of "Adrienne Lecouvreur." By early evening, more than 1,000 spectators had gathered to purchase tickets from speculators who were selling them at up to three times their face value and to gawk as a Negro footman, bedecked in a high silk hat, plum vest and knee-breeches, opened the carriage doors for one elegant lady after another.

Theatergoers had to wait until the third scene of the second act for the appearance of "the Divine Sarah," as she is known to her fans. In the role of the starcrossed Adrienne, Bernhardt was passionate and tender, a woman deeply in love with the Comte de Saxe, whom she is destined to lose. Although her acting was far from flawless, her magnetism came through in the final scene, a blend of despair, hope and the agony of death.

Kansas becomes first state to "go dry"

Kansas

Not since Maine passed temporary prohibition laws in 1851 has the temperance movement shown such political might, with legislators being bombarded by calls for a prohibition law against the sale and consumption of alcohol. The National Women's Christian Temperance Union and the Prohibition party are lobbying with new fervor and their efforts are paying off. With W.C.T.U. support, Kansas Republican Governor John St. John has forced through a bill outlawing the sale of alcohol, after officials refused to shut down illegal saloons. With Kansas becoming the first state to "go dry," presaging a fight on the issue in every local, state and federal campaign, both proponents and foes are redoubling their efforts.

Chicago, June 8. *Tainted by the aura of corruption, Ulysses Grant declined a bid for the Republican presidential nomination. James Garfield won on the 36th ballot.*

Do-it-yourself with razor, basic camera

New York City

Two inventions that will make life simpler for millions of Americans have been placed on the market. One is a safety razor, made by the Kampfe Brothers company of New York. It consists of a hand-forged blade inserted in a frame designed to prevent accidental cuts. The second invention, marketed by the Eastman Kodak Company, is a camera that uses a photographic plate requiring no special preparation by the picture-taker. George Eastman, the founder of the company, is also working on a camera that uses rolls of treated celluloid to capture images. The owner will send the camera to the company, receiving a freshly loaded camera and the developed photos (→ 1884).

Panama canal said to have no French link

Washington, D.C., March 18

Seeking to allay fears of renewed European intervention in this hemisphere, the French promoter Ferdinand de Lesseps today assured a House committee that there is no connection between the government of France and the Interoceanic Canal Company, of which he is president. This assurance follows by 10 days the declaration by President Hayes that any canal built across the Panamanian isthmus will be under United States jurisdiction, a claim that will have to be reconciled with the Clayton-Bulwer Treaty of 1850, in which the United States and Britain agreed that neither party would try to obtain exclusive control if a canal were ever built.

De Lesseps, who completed the Suez Canal in 1869, is raising $60 million to build the sea-level canal across the isthmus. Work is expected to start early next year and, if all goes well, to be completed within eight years (→ Jan. 29, 1885).

Ferdinand de Lesseps, builder of the Suez Canal, towers over the isthmus.

Suffragettes barred from polling booth

Tenafly, New Jersey, Nov. 2

Long-time suffragettes Miss Susan B. Anthony and Mrs. Elizabeth Cady Stanton attempted to vote in the national election today, and when a polling booth inspector refused them the opportunity, Mrs. Stanton hurled a voting box in his direction. A gentleman of high standing in Tenafly had accompanied the women to the polling place and told the inspector he saw no reason why Mrs. Stanton, a resident of the town, should not "exercise this right of citizenship." The inspector placed his hand on the voting box slot and did not budge. It has been 30 years since Miss Anthony and Mrs. Stanton first sought the vote.

A New York Muffin is called English

New York City

An English baker named Samuel Bath Thomas is treating New Yorkers to a new muffin made from flour, yeast, malted barley, vinegar and farina. It is round, flat and baked on a griddle, with a distinctive taste and texture based on a recipe of Thomas's mother. The muffin is eaten with butter and jam. Thomas has dubbed the new cake an "English muffin."

Irish-American wins heavyweight crown

Colliers Station, W. Va. May 30

Paddy Ryan, a strapping Irish-American, stunned boxing fans today by knocking out Joe Goss, the world heavyweight champion from England, after 87 rounds of brutal bare-knuckle fighting. The Tipperary-born Ryan, 5 feet 11 inches tall and weighing 200 pounds, thus became the first American to hold the undisputed world title as he won his first recorded fight. Goss had come to the United States in search of fresh competition and won the title by beating his countryman, Tom Allen, in Kentucky in 1876. That triumph gave Goss the world title under London Ring Rules.

Garfield wins presidency; margin is 9,464

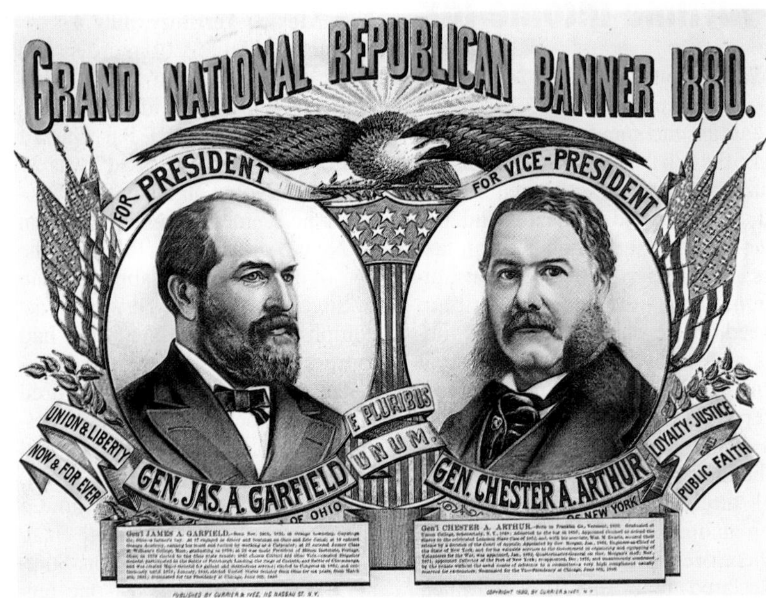

"Union and Liberty now and forever; Loyalty, Justice and Public Faith."

Washington, D.C., Nov. 2

James A. Garfield of Ohio has been elected President, winning a goodly majority of electoral votes but topping his Democratic opponent, Winfield Scott Hancock of Pennsylvania, by a mere 9,464 popular votes among more than nine million cast. Each man carried 19 states, thus shutting out their lesser known opponents, who represented the Prohibition, Greenback Labor and American Parties. Garfield received 214 electoral votes to 155 for Hancock.

Garfield, a Republican, is in the unique position of simultaneously being President-elect, senator-elect and a member of the House of Representatives. He will, of course, resign from the House before his inauguration in March and the seat that would have been his in the Senate will be filled by someone else to be chosen in Ohio.

The road to the White House was not an easy one for Garfield. He won the nomination on the 36th ballot at the June convention of the Republicans in Chicago. Chester A. Arthur of New York, elected Vice President on the winning ticket, initially backed President Grant for a third term (→ July 2, 1881).

"Blacksmith Shop" (1880) by Beckett. With the rise of factory production and interchangeable parts, the blacksmith appears to be a dying breed.

Treaty to restrict influx from China

Washington D.C., Nov. 17

In response to greater labor unrest and the swelling public sentiment against foreigners, a treaty was signed today with China that amends the Burlingame Treaty of 1868. The new Chinese Exclusion Treaty negotiated by James B. Angell, Minister to China, restricts the entrance and naturalization of immigrants from China. Academics, commercial traders and travelers, however, will not be affected. Under the new treaty, immigrant labor, which was once unlimited, will now be curbed. There was an attempt to alter the Burlingame Treaty last year, but that effort was thwarted when it was vetoed by President Hayes (→ May 6, 1882).

Caricatures of nativist laborers, all immigrants from Europe themselves, lynching Chinese worker.

Novel "Ben Hur" is a best-seller

United States

An eclectic trio stands out among this year's literary works. The melodramatic Lew Wallace novel *Ben Hur*, about the life of a Roman slave during the time of Jesus, has topped the best-seller lists since its release. *Ultima Thule*, a collection by Henry Wadsworth Longfellow, contains some of that 73-year-old bard's most moving reflections on mortality and the transience of life. And *Democracy*, published anonymously but known to be the work of Henry Adams, a grandson of John Quincy Adams, is a quintessential Washington insider's look at power politics.

1881

Garfield

Washington, D.C., March 3. Congress creates federal agency to register and protect business trademarks, signaling rise of national corporations.

California, March 4. Plant and produce quarantine legislation enacted as overseas trade expands.

Boston, March. "Story of a Great Monopoly," about John D. Rockefeller and Standard Oil's business tactics, published in the *Atlantic Monthly* (→ Jan. 2, 1882).

New Mexico, July. Railroad line from Durango, Colorado, to Chama, New Mexico, completed; cost to cross Rockies over $140,000 per mile.

Chicago, Aug. 8. With 36 delegates representing carpenters in 11 cities, Brotherhood of Carpenters and Joiners is organized.

Washington, D.C., Aug. 24. Lieutenant Adolphus W. Greely selected to lead expedition to establish scientific observation post in northern Greenland (→ May 15, 1882).

Philadelphia, Oct. 15. William C. Harris founds *American Angler,* first sport fishing journal in United States.

Boston, Oct. 22. Boston Symphony Orchestra gives its first concert.

Atlanta, Georgia, Nov. 18. First spike driven for Georgia Pacific Railroad, planned to link Atlanta with coal fields of Alabama.

Florida. Philadelphia industrialist Hamilton Disston buys four million acres of Everglades at 25 cents per acre, opening area for development.

Washington, D.C. Lewis Latimer patents first incandescent bulb.

Washington. Railroad laid from Tenino to Olympia is first in Northwest specifically constructed for hauling logs.

Brooklyn, New York. Coney Island becomes popular spot for rest and relaxation.

New York City. Henry James's *Washington Square* and *Portrait of a Lady* issued.

Boston. Publishers forced to withdraw new edition of Walt Whitman's *Leaves of Grass*, in response to charges of indecency.

High Court upholds wartime income tax

Washington, D.C., Jan. 24

The Supreme Court has ruled that an income tax imposed during the Civil War was constitutional. In Springer v. United States, the court decided the tax did not violate the ban on non-uniform taxes in Article II of the Constitution. During the war, the North, in need of revenue, successfully obtained it by passing the Federal Income Tax Law of 1862. Congress repealed the tax in 1870. Springer, a lawyer, filed suit, claiming that the legislation affected an individual directly, as opposed to a tax on manufacture or sales, and was therefore illegal. But the bench declared that "the tax of which the plaintiff in error complains is within the category of an excise."

Billy the Kid shot down by Sheriff Garrett

New Mexico Territory, July 4

After a lifetime of murder and years on the run from the law, William H. "Billy the Kid" Bonney is dead, slain by Sheriff Pat Garrett at Fort Sumner. The "Kid" was 21 years old. Not at all the native Westerner he seemed, Bonney was born in New York City in 1859. At the age of 12 he fatally stabbed a man in Silver City; by 18, he was an accomplished horse thief who had murdered 21 men, including an assassin sworn to kill him. Captured last December, Billy promptly escaped from jail. Since then, he had been trailed constantly by Garrett, an old drinking buddy and now a sworn peace officer. Garrett finally cornered him today in Fort Sumner. The sheriff fired just one bullet; Bonney fell dead, still clutching his six-shooter.

William H. Bonney, charged with 21 murders by the age of 18.

60 miles of elevated track cross New York

New York City

In 1874, with New York's streets a tangled mass of horse-drawn wagons and harried pedestrians, a newspaper heralded the elevated railway as the solution to "overcrowding which has imposed so many social, moral and political evils upon the city." At the time, a lone five-mile stretch of elevated track, built by Charles T. Harvey, ferried passengers along Ninth Avenue.

By 1875, however, the city's Rapid Transit Commission had awarded new contracts to Harvey's company and to another line that was planned by Dr. Rufus H. Gilbert, a Civil War surgeon turned engineer. Gilbert proposed a radical pneumatic tube design, but he settled for conventional steam locomotives. Despite an outcry and legal challenges from some residents who were opposed to the ungainly iron structures, construction proceeded until this year the lines traversed Manhattan with more than 60 miles of tracks high above Ninth, Eighth, Sixth and Third Avenues. The trip from the Battery to Harlem now takes 42 minutes, a fact sure to spur even faster city development.

New York's Third Avenue elevated railway, high above horse-drawn vehicles.

Alcohol outlawed at all military posts

Washington, D.C., Feb. 22

Responding to the growth of the temperance movement and, some say, to pressure from his teetotaling wife, President Rutherford B. Hayes has banned the sale of alcohol at military posts. Republicans fear even a small defection to the Prohibition Party may lose them the presidency. Hayes's wife, "Lemonade" Lucy, does not allow drinking in the White House, but the chef serves a sherbet with a potent secret ingredient.

"Jim Crow" rides trains of Tennessee

Tennessee

Railroad coaches in this state have been segregated by the passage of a "Jim Crow" law that provides separate first-class cars for Negroes. According to the law, railroad companies must provide a part of each train for Negroes that is equal in accommodation to the parts of the train reserved for whites. Formerly, Negroes were relegated to the second-class cars. Of course, Negroes will be forbidden from entering the white cars, just as in the past they could not enter first-class coaches.

Cattle "long drive" to Dodge City fades

Dodge City, Autumn

The era of "the long drive" appears to be coming to an end. Several thousand head of cattle arrived here from Texas earlier this summer, and the local people say it is likely to be the last. One reason is that farmers have begun enclosing their property with the new barbed wire fences. Also, the Plains states have passed laws that prohibit the driving of "foreign" cattle across their borders. Finally, local cattlemen have raised enough livestock on the Plains near the railheads to make the driving of cows all the way from Texas unprofitable. It is estimated that up to two million head of cattle have been driven up the Chisholm Trail and on to Dodge City in the past 15 years.

President Garfield shot

The President is shot down in the Washington railway station as Secretary of State James G. Blaine looks on in horror. The assassin, a disappointed office-seeker named Charles J. Guiteau, is said to be mentally unstable.

Washington, D.C., July 2

President Garfield was shot and critically wounded early today as he walked through the waiting room of the Baltimore and Potomac Railroad Station on his way to catch a train north. The two shots, one in the back and one in the arm, were fired by Charles J. Guiteau, a disappointed office-seeker from New York, who was quickly seized.

The President, who was rushed back to the White House, was heard to say as the shots were fired: "My God! What is this?" Bystanders also reported that after the man fired the gun the man shouted: "I am a Stalwart and now Arthur is President." Stalwarts are members of the conservative wing of the Republican Party. Vice President Chester A. Arthur, who earlier supported the Stalwart agenda, will succeed to the presidency should Garfield succumb.

The President took office only four months ago and recently was at odds with his Vice President, who protested the appointment of William H. Robertson as collector of the port of New York. At the time of today's shooting, Garfield was hurrying to catch a train to go to Williamstown, Massachusetts, where he was to deliver a commencement speech at Williams College, from which he graduated in 1856 with high honors (→ Sept. 20).

Red Cross granted neutrality status

Washington, D.C., May 21

A Red Cross constitution has been signed by a group of Americans in the home of Miss Clara Barton, acting head of the American branch of the worldwide organization. Yesterday, Miss Barton received a letter from a secretary to President Garfield stating that the President will favor adoption of the treaty. More than a dozen European countries have agreed to honor the Red Cross flag, which symbolizes the neutrality of the medical services of armed forces and civilians who volunteer humane treatment of the wounded. Miss Barton has advocated American signing of the treaty since the publication in 1878 of her pamphlet *The Red Cross of Geneva, What It Is.*

Dean of American anthropology dies

Rochester, New York, Dec. 17

Lewis Henry Morgan, lawyer, state congressman and founder of scientific anthropology, is dead at 63. He leaves a legacy of good books and good works. *Ancient Society,* a seminal work, charts social evolution "from Savagery through Barbarism to Civilization." It has earned the endorsement of Karl Marx. Morgan himself was firmly middle class. But his love for Indian culture made him a lifelong critic of white savagery on the frontier.

Finding better ways to deal with blazes

Chicago

Firefighters are finding imaginative ways to speed response times and save lives. In 1878, Chicago fireman David Kenyon devised a wooden pole that his cohorts could use to slide instantly from sleeping quarters to fire wagons. Other firehouses are adopting a brass pole first used in Worcester, Massachusetts, in 1880. In St. Joseph, Missouri, firemen invented a quick-hitch harness for horses, and some cities use telegraph alarm systems.

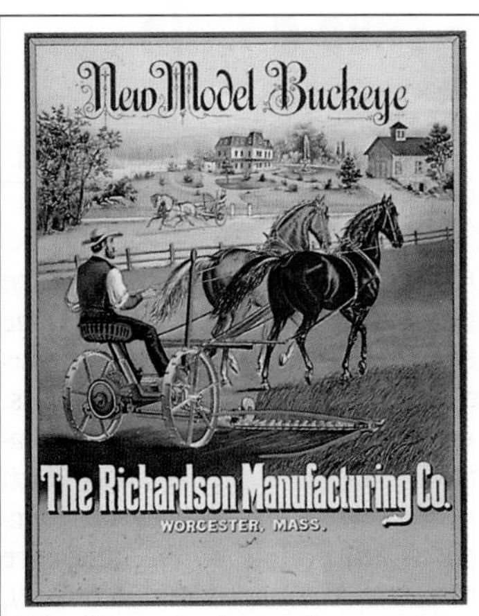

The latest in horse-drawn mowing technology, the New Model Buckeye Mowing Machine from Richardson Manufacturing Co.

Booker Washington heads Negro school

Tuskegee, Alabama, July 4

Tuskegee Institute, a training school for Negroes, opened today with Booker T. Washington as its principal. Washington, who was born a slave, was a faculty member at Virginia's Hampton Institute, one of the nation's outstanding schools for Negroes. He advocates industrial education rather than race mixing and political activity as the way to advance his people. Washington is a controversial figure among Negro leaders, but he remains steadfast in his views.

Sitting Bull, long in hiding, gives up

Fort Buford, Canada, July 20

A fugitive for the five years since he directed the massacre of General Custer and his troops at Little Big Horn, the Sioux Chief Sitting Bull surrendered to army authorities today. After insulting General Terry, the old Indian fighter, and proclaiming his "love" for Canada, Sitting Bull said he hoped that his children would grow up in Canada, not in the United States. As he surrendered, the Sioux chief chanted, "A warrior I have been; now it is over; a hard time I have."

New York, November. *The crowd calls for a touchdown, but to no avail as Yale and Princeton play to a 0-0 tie for third year in a row.*

Unions to cooperate on hours, benefits

Chicago, Aug. 8

Last week in Pittsburgh the Federation of Organized Trades and Labor Unions was established. The group, headed by Samuel Gompers, is bolstered by those dissatisfied with the Knights of Labor. And today in Chicago, 36 delegates, representing builders in 11 cities, organized the Brotherhood of Carpenters and Joiners. Its founder, Peter McGuire, will work with Gompers for an eight-hour day and the British system of sickness, unemployment and death benefits. Business has consistently spurned labor on the hours and benefits issues.

Garfield succumbs; Arthur succeeds him

James Garfield, the fourth President in nation's history to die in office.

Chester Arthur, a gentleman President. Paintings by O.P.H. Balling.

Washington, Sept. 20

Less than a day after the death of President Garfield, Chester Alan Arthur of New York became President in the early hours this morning. The new President took his oath of office at 2:05 a.m. in his New York City home at 123 Lexington Avenue and will lead the nation as it mourns the death of its leader.

The late President had been sinking since he was shot on July 2 at the Washington railroad station by Charles J. Guiteau, a disgruntled office-seeker. Death came at the seaside resort of Elberon, New Jersey, where he had been taken from the White House last month in hopes that the sea air might prove beneficial in curing the blood poisoning that set in after doctors used unsterile instruments to probe for the bullet in his back. David G. Swaim, his chief of staff, reported that the last words of the President were: "Oh, Swaim, there is pain here. Oh, oh, Swaim." A public memorial service is being planned.

The assassin Guiteau, who was seized at the time of the shooting, is in custody and will be tried for murder later this year.

The new President, a 51-year-old lawyer, was elected as Vice President on the Garfield ticket last year, but he had previously supported President Grant for a third term in the White House, a move pushed by the Stalwarts, the conservative wing of the Republican Party.

U.S. polar tragedy: Entire crew is lost

San Francisco, Oct. 30

Tragic word arrived today: Most of the Jeannette Expedition crew starved to death; the rest were lost. The team, led by U.S. Navy Lieutenant George W. De Long and sponsored by the *New York Herald*, left California July 8, 1879, for the Arctic to learn if there is a polar continent. De Long's diary says the Jeannette sank June 13, leaving its 34 men to make their way 600 miles to Siberia in three boats. One simply disappeared. Two made it to the Lena River delta, but the men died one by one of starvation. De Long's diary may be printed as a book.

Americans retain yachting trophy

New York City, Sept. 20

The Americans continue their mastery in international sailing. With J. Busk at the helm, the yacht Mischief defeated the Canadian challenger, Atalanta, today in the fifth United States defense of the America's Cup trophy, sailed over a 30-mile course in New York Bay. This was the second straight victory over Canada, the Madelaine having defeated the Countess of Duffer in 1876. The other America's Cup victories were against England, starting in 1851.

A couple of topers find gold in Alaska

Seattle, Washington

It appears that the Territory of Alaska is going to be earning its keep a lot sooner than anyone could have expected. News about a gold strike last year in the southeastern panhandle of the territory has caused a flurry of excitement in the Northwest. Discovered by Joe Juneau and Frank Harris, two miners of questionable sobriety, the gold strike may be large enough to support a town. Residents guffaw when they hear Joe Juneau insist the town be named in his honor.

Edison turns on lights in New York

New York City, Sept. 4

The Edison electric lighting system for this city went into operation today as a generator in a station at Pearl Street on the Lower East Side began supplying power for 85 paying customers who have a total of 400 lamps. Thomas A. Edison himself pulled the switch in the offices of Drexel, Morgan & Co., which is wired with 106 lamps. In contrast to the crowds that were drawn to Pearl Street during construction, there was little publicity today. More than $600,000 has been spent on the lighting system, and it must attract more customers before it is profitable (→Dec. 11, 1882).

Earps win a bloody gunfight at O.K Corral

Tombstone, Arizona, Oct. 26

After years of hard feelings between the Clanton brothers and the famous Earp brothers of Tombstone, things came to a showdown today on the corner of Fourth and Allen Streets, at the O.K. Corral. Deputy Marshall Wyatt Earp and his brothers, Virgil and Morgan, accompanied by the town dentist, "Doc" Holliday, gunned down their old nemeses in broad daylight. Just before Wyatt blazed away, he told the Clantons, "You S.O.B.'s, you've been looking for a fight and now you can have it." As they began to draw their guns, the two Clantons and their two cronies fell dead from the fire of the Earps' pistols and Holliday's shotgun.

Wyatt Earp, Tombstone lawman.

Girl risks her life to save a train

Boone County, Iowa, July 6

A 15-year-old girl saved a Northwestern train from disaster tonight. Kate Shelby, who lives east of the Des Moines River, heard a nearby bridge collapse in a flood, then heard a train crash. She found the engineer miraculously alive, clinging to a tree at riverside. Kate knew that another train was due. On her hands and knees, the rain and wind buffeting her, the girl crossed the damaged bridge 50 feet above the river. After a journey of a mile and a half, Kate reached the telegraph office in Moingona. The next train was warned to stop just in the nick of time.

"Century of Dishonor" tells Indians' story

A Hunkpapa Sioux in the Dakotas.

New York City

The relentless push of American settlers across the Western prairies and plains has left an ugly trail of broken promises, canceled treaties and bleached skulls. This bitter truth has been forced on Americans by *A Century of Dishonor*, a stinging indictment of the mistreatment of American Indians by the United States government. The volume's author, Helen Hunt Jackson, has raised eyebrows, but her claims rest on a bedrock of facts gathered during her painstaking hours of research at the Astor Library here.

Few readers would have predicted such a book would issue from the pen of the 51-year-old Amherst, Massachusetts, poet and storyteller whose previous books include *Verses by H.H.* (1870) – praised by Ralph Waldo Emerson – and *Mercy Philbrick's Choice* (1876), a novel based on the odd life of her reclusive neighbor and longtime friend, Emily Dickinson, who is herself rumored to be a writer.

Geological survey made of Grand Canyon

Washington, D.C.

Science is gaining a foothold in one of nature's most inscrutable wonders. Clarence E. Dutton, back from the first big geological survey of the Grand Canyon, says its endless chasms were chiseled by water over thousands of years. The Colorado (Spanish for "reddish") River, Dutton says, initially wound lazily to the ocean. When the land began to elevate, the river gained momentum, slicing downward as quickly as its banks rose. The Navajo, on the other hand, say the channel was carved to drain a great flood that endangered their ancestors. Whatever the cause, the result is a majestic work of art that has only recently proved hospitable to Europeans.

Its first white visitors, a Spanish party led by Don Lopez de Cardenas in 1540, never made it to the bottom. Missionaries returned in 1776 and named the canyon Bucareli Pass after the viceroy of New Spain. In the 1820's, fur traders found the big gap nothing but an obstacle. In 1857-58, Lieutenant Joseph Christmas Ives, in search of a supply route for Army troops fighting the Mormons in Utah, led the first true exploration. He found the region "valueless." But 11 years later, a one-armed Civil War veteran named John Wesley Powell entered the canyon with reverence. Braving the rapids with nine men in four tiny boats, he traveled 1,048 miles in 98 days to become the first to conquer the river. Powell, who is Dutton's mentor, observed with wonder: "Beds (of rock) hundreds of feet in thickness and hundreds of thousands of square miles in extent . . . have slowly yielded to the silent and unseen powers of the air, and crumbled into dust."

Monroe Doctrine is extended to Hawaii

Washington, D.C., Dec. 1

The Hawaiian Kingdom, which cemented relations with the United States by means of a reciprocity treaty in 1875, gained more support from America today with a reaffirmation of the Monroe Doctrine here. Secretary of State James Blaine declared that from now on the Hawaiian Islands are protected by the Monroe Doctrine, thus reasserting a vow made in 1842 by President John Tyler. Tyler told Congress that the United States recognized the islands as an independent state, thus extending the Monroe Doctrine to the Pacific. There is a feeling among Hawaiian Islanders that this latest American assurance will protect the kingdom from covetous foreign nations. The far-flung islands were targets of the French and also of the British at the middle of the century.

Uncle Remus's tales a delight to all ages

Atlanta, Georgia

Sometimes the master can learn from his servant – at least if the servant is Uncle Remus, the aged former slave who in *Uncle Remus: His Songs and His Sayings* delights the children of his employer with wise fables about Brer Rabbit, Brer Fox and other humorous characters. The anthology, a hit with children and adults alike, is the work of Joel Chandler Harris, who, since 1876, has been on the *Atlanta Constitution*, which ran the first Uncle Remus story in 1879. More tales, and verses, have appeared since then, all gathered by Harris on visits with Southern Negroes.

N.J. teacher builds practical submarine

New Jersey

A Catholic-school teacher, John P. Holland, has built a successful, cigar-shaped submarine that is powered by a petroleum engine and can be directed to dive and surface. The 41-year-old Holland, who migrated from Ireland in the 1870s, was motivated by his hatred of Britain, and he is hoping that his underwater vessel can be used to affix mines to the bottoms of British ships. The idea for this method of attack was inspired when Holland read Jules Verne's novel *Twenty Thousand Leagues Under the Sea*. Holland's work refines earlier vessels built by David Bushnell and Robert Fulton.

Grand Canyon, first viewed by the Spanish in 1540, now the subject of science.

1882

Arthur

Washington, D.C., Feb. 25. Reapportionment Act expands size of House of Representatives from 293 to 325 members.

New York City, Apr. 28. John Fox Slater incorporates John F. Slater Fund with a donation of $100,000; it is to be used for education of emancipated Negroes.

Ellesmere Island, Canada, May 15. Lieutenant Adolphus W. Greely leads Arctic expedition to within 600 miles of North Pole (→June 22, 1884).

Washington, D.C., May 22. United States signs treaty with Korea, recognizing Korean independence from China, Russia and Japan.

Pittsburgh, Penn., June. Amalgamated Association of Iron and Steel Workers launches nationwide strike.

Washington, D.C., Aug. 2. Congress passes River and Harbors Act, appropriating $18 million for public works.

Washington, D.C., Nov. 10. Canadian Alexander Graham Bell becomes U.S. citizen.

Boston, Dec. 11. Bijou Theater lit with 650 bulbs as Gilbert and Sullivan's operetta *Iolanthe* becomes first electrically illuminated theater production (→25).

New York City, Dec. 25. First electrically lit Christmas tree used (→June 2, 1883).

Hawaii, December. King Kalakaua, known as "Merry Monarch," builds Iolani Palace.

Appleton, Wisconsin. First hydroelectric plant in United States built.

New York City. Thomas Edison and Stephen Field form Electric Railway Company.

New York City. Theodore Roosevelt publishes *The Naval War of 1812.*

New York City. Mark Twain publishes *The Prince and the Pauper.*

DEATHS

Cambridge, Massachusetts, March 24. Henry Wadsworth Longfellow, poet, whose works include *The Song of Hiawatha* (*Feb. 27, 1807).

New England, Apr. 27. Ralph Waldo Emerson, essayist, poet and leading transcendentalist (*May 25, 1803).

Rockefeller oil firm becomes first "trust"

John D., the world in his hand.

New York City, Jan. 2

At the Pearl Street headquarters of oil baron John D. Rockefeller, a secret agreement has reportedly been signed, placing unprecedented command over the oil industry in the hands of nine men. Rockefeller's Standard Oil Company dominates the business already through a loose affiliation of refiners, transporters, wholesalers and retailers. Now the stockholders of 39 firms have transferred their shares "in trust" to Rockefeller, his brother William and seven others. The trustees have no legal status. But, from their lunch meetings here, "The Nine" will create and dissolve corporations in any state and allocate resources of $70 million.

At 42, the tall and stooping architect of the oil combine embodies the business trends of his age. Rockefeller's determination is legend, precluding friendship beyond the doors of his office. He is obsessed with detail, in one case personally chasing $2 in missing barrel stoppers. But the details are part of a grand design. Since going into oil in 1862, Rockefeller has sought expansion with a vengeance. Viewing the anarchic industry in 1870, he saw thousands of drillers and retailers, but only a few hundred refineries. First, he approached the railroads, gaining rebates by guaranteeing a steady flow of business. Then he went to refiners one by one, offering them lower freight rates if they would join his secretive South Improvement Company, and threatening ruinous competition if they refused. By 1878, 15 of the largest refiners had joined Rockefeller, who just last year finished the largest pipeline in the world.

John L. Sullivan wins title by K.O.

John L., the Boston strong boy.

Mississippi City, Miss., Feb. 7

Paddy Ryan's reign as king of the bare-knuckle fighters was short-lived. The Boston strong boy, John L. Sullivan, put away Ryan, the first undisputed American champion, in nine rounds. In addition to the purse, the 25-year-old Sullivan won a side bet for $5,000. The Bostonian may abandon the bare-knuckle fights because fan interest in them seems to be waning.

Thomas Moran's "Cliffs of the Upper Colorado River, Wyoming Territory" (1882) depicts the splendor of the American West in all its majesty. One of his paintings of the Grand Canyon helped establish Yellowstone as a national park.

Belle Starr is guilty of stealing horses

Oklahoma, Autumn

Belle Starr was recently tried and convicted on a charge of horse stealing. Taken before the famed "hanging judge," Isaac Parker, Belle was sentenced to prison for an indeterminate term. For years, she has had a reputation as a horse thief, a bandit queen and a lover. Her maiden name was Myra Belle Shirley. A resident of Dallas, she was once married to a bank robber and supposedly has been having torrid affairs with a variety of gangsters, including a former member of the Younger brothers gang.

Catholics establish social fraternity

New Haven, Connecticut, Feb. 2

The Roman Catholic Church announced today that it will permit the founding of the Knights of Columbus, an organization aimed at enhancing the lives of American Catholics. Founded by Father Michael McGivney, 30 years old, the group first met in a parish house on January 16 to discuss issues ranging from life insurance to education. McGivney is an 1877 graduate of St. Mary's Seminary in Baltimore.

Home sweatshops sanctioned by court

Washington, D.C.

They are called "sweatshops," small factories in New York tenements where whole families live and work for cigar manufacturers. Now the Supreme Court has ruled that these working conditions are not unconstitutional, striking down legislation that banned the making of cigars in tenements. The decision rebukes labor leader Samuel Gompers, who, repelled by the unsafe conditions, sought the law and New York Governor Grover Cleveland, who signed it. The court said: "It cannot be perceived how the cigar-maker is to be improved in his health or his morals by forcing him from his home and its hallowed associations and beneficent influences to ply his trade elsewhere."

Jesse James shot dead

Jesse in 1864, at the age of 17 . . .

St. Joseph, Missouri, Apr. 3

After more than 15 years of robbing banks and hijacking railroad trains, Jesse James has been killed – by his cousin, a member of the James gang. Townspeople say that James's kinsman, Bob Ford, had never liked Jesse, and that when a $10,000 reward was placed on the outlaw's head, Ford decided to go after it.

He supposedly asked James if he could join the band of outlaws for a robbery. This morning, the 19-year-old Ford, armed with a pistol, came up behind James's back as the outlaw was standing on a chair in his home dusting off a picture. Ford, firing from only a few feet away, shot James through the head and killed him instantly. The bullet is said to have entered James's skull at the base and to have gone out through his forehead.

The murder weapon, a silver mounted, pearl-handled Colt .45 revolver, had been given to Ford by Frank James a few days before. According to residents, Ford told Mrs. James that his gun had fired by accident. Mrs. James is reported to have replied, "Yes, I guess it went off – on purpose." Ford then fled, and authorities say that his whereabouts are still not known (→ Oct. 5).

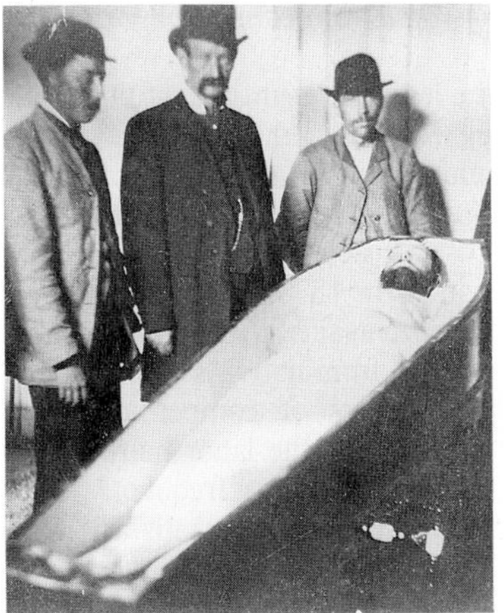

. . . and at the end, the 34-year-old desperado rests in peace in St. Louis.

Chinese immigrants halted for 10 years

Washington, D.C., May 6

With violence against Chinese nationals escalating across the country, Congress has passed the Chinese Exclusion Act prohibiting further Chinese immigration and naturalization for 10 years. The legislation is in conflict with the Burlingame Treaty of 1868, and when first presented to the President was vetoed. A small change in wording and a reduction of the moratorium from 20 to 10 years got the bill passed. The Workingman's Party of California led by Denis Kearney did much of the lobbying for the bill on the grounds that Chinese labor takes jobs away from Americans. Kearney, whose favorite slogan is, "The Chinese must go," is an Irish immigrant (→ Sept. 30, 1885).

Troops requested to fight "cowboys"

Washington, D.C., Apr. 26

President Arthur today ordered regular army troops into the Arizona Territory to combat the rising tide of violence that is sweeping across that Southwestern province. For months now, outlaws known as "cowboys" have been robbing and killing miners and rustling cattle in the territory. A brazen bunch, the desperadoes have also spread terror across the border into Mexico. Most of these outlaws are believed to be "outsiders" who have drifted in from the surrounding states.

Anaconda uncovers richest copper ore

Anaconda Range, Montana

Miners have struck the richest copper deposit so far in the world. Marcus Daly's crew dug the Anaconda mine shaft after 55 percent pure copper sulphate was unearthed at 300 feet. The brownish-red metal has been used to make tools since pre-historic times. But scientists have determined that copper ranks second only to silver in conductivity and the growing electricity markets have created a great demand for it.

The steam locomotive, shiny engine of progress in an Illinois Central poster. Since the end of the Civil War, ton-miles of freight carried by rail have risen six-fold; track mileage has quadrupled; and Henry Villard and the Northern Pacific are nearing completion of the second transcontinental line.

America bars paupers, criminals, insane

America is portrayed as a benign haven for the world's unfortunate in a cartoon by Joseph Keppler that opposes legislation restricting immigration.

Washington, D.C., Aug. 3

The federal government has taken decisive control over state immigration regulations today as Congress passed the Immigration Act. The measure authorizes the secretary of the treasury to contract with state agencies to monitor their own ports according to rules set out in the law. It states that if upon inspection there are found, "any convict, lunatic, idiot or any other person unable to take care of him or herself without becoming a public charge . . . such persons shall not be permitted to land." There will now be a 50-cent head tax on all arriving immigrants, and failure to follow the law will result in a $1,000 fine.

More than 100,000 Chinese have immigrated to America since 1868, along with countless Europeans. Possibly stemming from the depression of the 1870's, instances of mob violence against the foreigners have erupted from nativists who warn of the dangers of competition from foreigners in the labor market. Immigrant labor has frequently been used as a practical means of breaking a strike, and employers can often pay foreigners half the wages they generally pay Americans. According to the census of 1880, there are 6,600,000 immigrants now living in the United States.

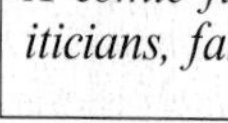

Puck's Pyrotechnics, free to all. A comic fireworks display of politicians, famous and infamous.

Frank James gives up without a fuss

Jefferson City, Missouri, Oct. 5

With little drama and absolutely no fanfare, Frank James, the vicious outlaw and popular folk hero, walked in and surrendered to Governor Crittenden today. Upon entering the office of the Governor, James turned over his Remington .44 revolver and commented: "I want to hand you that which no living man except myself has touched since 1861, and I am your prisoner." So only a half year after the death of his brother Jesse, the James gang is defunct. It is expected that Frank James will be sent to Independence, where he will be tried on at least one count of first-degree murder.

30,000 march in first Labor Day parade

The Knights of Labor lead the way through New York's Union Square.

New York City, Sept. 5

The workers of New York demonstrated peacefully yet undeniably today that labor is a force to be reckoned with. As many as 30,000 men and women took to the streets for this first Labor Day march in a show of unity that must have given pause to even the most imperious bosses and politicians.

The idea for a working class holiday was first proposed by Peter J. McGuire at a meeting of the Central Labor Union of New York on May 18. McGuire, a founder of the Social Democratic Party of North America and general secretary of the Brotherhood of Carpenters and Joiners, called for a "festive day to parade through the streets of the city." And festive it was. Virtually every working group in the area was represented, from bricklayers to seamstresses to cigarmakers, and as cheers and music filled the air they marched down Fifth Avenue to Union Square. Banners proudly proclaimed such messages as "Labor built this republic and labor shall rule it" and "Eight hours for a legal day's work."

The well-disciplined marchers conveyed the wishes of the parade's organizers that, despite a desire for change, their movement will abide by the law (→ June 28, 1894).

New York is seized by "Langtry fever"

New York City, Nov. 6

When Lillie Langtry stepped on an American stage for the first time tonight, she was preceded by a reputation for rare beauty and scandalous behavior. Although the Jersey Lily is better known for her violet eyes, flawless skin and loose ways – she has made no secret of her liaison with the Prince of Wales – than her acting, New York has been seized with "Langtry fever" for weeks. The drama of her appearance in Tom Taylor's *An Unequal Match* was heightened by the disastrous fire at Abbey's Park Theater just 48 hours before the opening. A glittering audience, including Vanderbilts and Goulds, was present at her debut, which was moved to Wallack's Theater on Broadway at 13th Street.

Emily Charlotte le Breton Langtry, the Jersey Lily, is one of Britain's first society types to step onto the stage.

American cowboys are passing into legend

The West

The success of the American Cattle Kingdom has depended on cowboys, most of whom are Civil War veterans, ex-slaves, Mexicans or Easterners in search of adventure. Their lot is not an easy one; for 18 hours a day, they ride the herd northward, round up stragglers and keep a lookout for Indians and rustlers. But afterwards comes payday ($25 a month), and the boys, armed with revolvers, ride into Abilene or Dodge City, "the wickedest city in the West," in wild celebration. Violence and lawlessness have been common in these cowtowns, where saloons are often scenes of reckless abandon. But now, the era of "the long drive" up the Chisholm Trail from Texas is fading, the victim of barbed wire, big business and new laws, and the cowboys are passing into legend. Speaking of Dodge City, one old cowhand said the only reason he's staying on is, he "has to play the organ twice a week in church."

1883

Arthur

Trenton, Feb. 14. New Jersey enacts first legislation in United States legalizing trade unions.

Atlanta, Apr. 11. Spellman College, dedicated to education of Negroes, founded in church basement.

Texas, Apr. 23. State buys historic Alamo from Catholic Church, placing it under authority of San Antonio city government.

Fort Wayne, Indiana, June 2. First baseball game played under electric lights.

Helena, Montana, July 4. Total of one million pounds of ore pulled from Gregory mine.

Tacoma, Washington, Sept. 3. Main line of Northern Pacific Railroad completed, extending from Minneapolis to Tacoma (→ 8).

Louisville, Kentucky, September. National Convention of Colored People refuses to endorse President Arthur's administration.

Washington, D.C., Dec. 3. The 48th Congress convenes, with two independents holding balance in Senate and Democrats firmly in control of House.

New York City, Dec. 4. Sons of American Revolution established.

New York City, Dec. 18. First boycott to attract national attention organized by Typographical Union No. 6 against *New York Tribune.*

New York City. George Westinghouse pioneers long-distance natural gas pipelines.

Chicago. National League and American Association agree to provide mutual protection for baseball players and post-season series.

Louisville, Kentucky. Kentucky Derby shortened to 1 and 1/4 miles.

United States. Thomas Eakins paints *The Swimming Hole.*

Missouri. Mark Twain publishes *Life on the Mississippi.*

United States. Humor magazine *Life* established.

Philadelphia. Cyrus H.K. Curtis begins publishing *Ladies Home Journal.*

Boston. Alexander Graham Bell founds *Science* magazine.

Buffalo Bill presents his Wild West Show

As it heads east, Buffalo Bill's Wild West Show is sure to shape the image of the cowboy into something unknown to those who actually were cow-punchers.

Omaha, Nebraska, May 17

The good people of Omaha were witness today to a whole new kind of entertainment. On the town's fairgrounds, William Frederick Cody, the one-time buffalo hunter who calls himself Buffalo Bill, presented something he calls a Wild West Show. He gathered a herd of buffalo, several cowboys, Indians and vaqueros (Spanish herdsmen) and had them play-act at holding up stagecoaches and rounding up cattle. While many spectators seemed to have a fine time, a few wondered out loud why if they pay money they should not see the real thing.

Cody has always made a living in and from the West. Born in Scott County, Iowa, in 1846, he rode for the Pony Express before he was 20. He served in the Seventh Kansas Cavalry during the Civil War and afterward hunted buffalo. Later, as a scout for the cavalry, he shot at unfriendly Indians in more than a dozen fights. His defeat of Yellow Hand made him famous – or rather the credit goes to his stirring description of the event in his 1879 autobiography. Cody has spent several seasons on the stage, acting in dramatizations about his life. But the work has proved less lucrative in recent years, so now Buffalo Bill will take his exhibition to Springfield, Illinois. In the East, his Wild West show may seem a bit wilder.

Vanderbilts throw nation's costliest party

New York City, March 26

Mrs. Alva Vanderbilt won sweet revenge tonight by throwing the world's most expensive party for the same high society that has snubbed her. The costume ball cost $75,000 for food and entertainment. Rumor has it that Mrs. Caroline Astor begged Mrs. Vanderbilt to allow her unmarried daughter Carrie to attend, even though neither Mrs. Astor nor her daughter had ever before set foot in the Vanderbilt residence. The Vanderbilt home, at 660 Fifth Avenue, is almost brand new. Its architect is Richard M. Hunt, who was the designer of the pedestal for the Statue of Liberty.

Half an hour before midnight, the guests began arriving at the mansion. There to greet them were William K. Vanderbilt, garbed as the Duc de Guise, and his wife arrayed as *The Power of Electricity.* A few of the 1,000 invited guests disdained masquerade attire, including the former President, Ulysses S. Grant. The entertainment included a series of dances performed for the partygoers. Miss Astor and seven other young ladies, wearing glittering stars on their heads, called themselves the Star Quadrille and performed a heavenly waltz. Champagne sparkled at supper, and two orchestras played following the dinner. The festivities ended too soon – at 4 a.m.

Congress creates U.S. Civil Service

Washington, D.C., Jan. 16

The House of Representatives voted the Pendleton Civil Service Act into law today. It requires candidates for civil service jobs to be judged on talent and merit rather than party affiliation. A bipartisan three-man commission will draft and administer examinations to fill civil service jobs. Senator George Pendleton of Ohio proposed the bill; the Senate passed it last month. It also forbids kickbacks to parties. It is intended to end a corrupt process that lived by the dictum: To the victor belongs the spoils. Such reform was attempted by President Grant, but proved to be only a veneer for political ends.

Ohio River flood peaks at 64 feet

Cincinnati, February

As the Ohio River continues on its rampage, sections of Cincinnati now lie under as much as 64 feet of water – the city's worst crisis ever. Thousands of families are living in their second-story rooms and many homes are completely under water. The city is down to one day's supply of oil. Those not flooded are without fuel or water and at night the town is dark. Telephone and telegraph lines are down. Nearby, a herd of 300 cattle drowned.

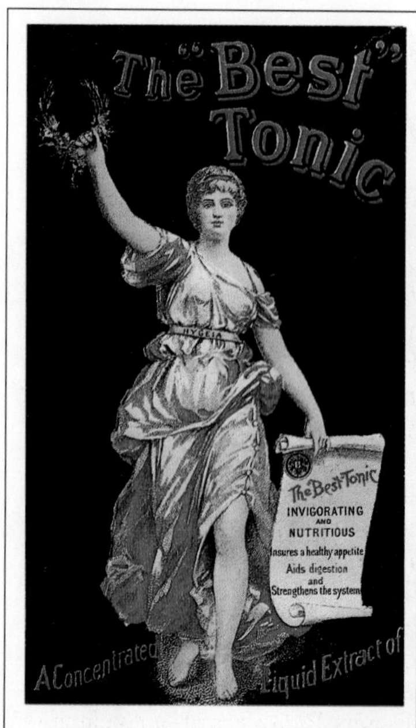

Coal mine flooded; 70 miners drown

Braidwood, Illinois, Feb. 16

At least 70 workers died today deep in the mines of the Wilmington Coal Field. The Diamond Company's No. 2 shaft, which has proved weak in the past, is the first to succumb to runaway flood waters that plague Western river basins. This little town of Braidwood is in shock. Women still kneel at the top of the mine praying as half-dead workers are pulled out. Some families have lost all male members to the tragedy. One woman saw her husband stagger into daylight with their dead son in his arms, only to tumble back down the shaft to his death. It may be several weeks before all the bodies are recovered.

Cowboys in Texas go out on strike

Texas, March 24

The techniques of the Northeastern workingman seem to have filtered down to the Texas Panhandle. A growing discontent and general unhappiness with skimpy pay, long hours and difficult working conditions are spreading among the cowboys of northwestern Texas. Taking their cue from the unionized industrial laborer, many cowpunchers have simply walked away from their jobs. So much for the traditions of the breed.

Pulitzer new owner of New York World

New York City, May 9

Joseph Pulitzer, owner of the *St. Louis Post-Dispatch*, bought the *New York World* today. Founded in 1860 as a churchgoers' paper, the *World* omitted news of lewd crime and scandal. Pulitzer will change that. Wealthy, with ambition and flair, he is expected to make the paper graphically exciting. The previous owner, Jay Gould, used the *World* to promote his business. Finally out of the red, he sold Pulitzer the paper for $346,000. A combination of stiff New York competition and meager circulation presents Pulitzer with a challenge.

Millions hail Brooklyn Bridge opening

Brooklyn, New York, May 25

When John A. Roebling proposed a bridge to unite Brooklyn and New York in 1867, he boldly envisioned it as "the great engineering work of this continent and of the age." Today, the German-born engineer's awesome steel-cable span, hailed as the "Eighth Wonder of the World," opened amid wildly enthusiastic celebrations, as millions waved their flags and cheered from streets, rooftops and riverboats, and dignitaries from President Arthur on down inaugurated the East River masterpiece under a brilliant, cloudless sky.

Before work began in 1869, skeptics wondered whether any bridge could accomplish the "flying leap from shore to shore over the masts of ships." But the Brooklyn Bridge, at 1,595 feet the world's longest by far, soars across the river with unparalleled grace. Its immense 276-foot stone towers and 16-inch-thick steel cables support a roadway in a gentle arch 135 feet over the river. Above the road is an elevated promenade on which, Roebling said, "people of leisure could enjoy the beautiful views."

This afternoon President Arthur led a formal procession over the walkway, while this evening crowds enjoyed an unrivaled view of fireworks. Tragically, Roebling himself was not present. The engineer who arrived in America in 1831 burning with genius and ambition died of lockjaw at 63 after a riverboat crushed his foot in 1869. His son Washington, only 32 at the time but himself a formidable talent, directed the operation through 14 years of untold hardships and engineering challenges.

To construct the foundations for the bridge, Washington Roebling designed a system to pump air into deep caissons under the riverbeds. But an underground fire nearly halted construction in 1870, and many workers suffered mysterious convulsions believed to be caused by changes in air pressure. Roebling himself suffered serious "caisson disease" in 1870 and after that brooded over construction from his home on the Brooklyn shore. His wife, Emily, tirelessly conveyed the Roebling orders to the site.

"I don't believe any man now living will cross that bridge," wrote one observer during a lag in construction. Indeed, the outcome at times seemed doubtful. As administrative scandals broke out, financial woes mounted and costs neared a staggering $16 million. Treacherous building conditions cost 26 lives. But the Roeblings' marvel stands as a monument to the daring and imagination of the era, and as one speaker said today from the walkway's dizzying heights, "it shows what multitudes democratically organized can do."

Fireworks mark the opening of "the great engineering work of the age."

Flanked by armed guards, President Arthur gives the bridge his blessing.

The Great East River Suspension Bridge spans 1,595 feet from Brooklyn to Manhattan, half again as much as any existing span. Currier and Ives.

Sherman-size fire razes Atlanta hotel

Atlanta, Georgia, Aug. 13

More than 1,000 guests escaped injury yesterday when Atlanta's finest hotel, the Kimball House, burned to the ground. Those watching the flames consume the luxury hotel agreed it was the worst blaze since General William Tecumseh Sherman left Atlanta in flames in 1864. An alert night watchman, William Flynn, first saw the hotel blaze and started evacuating the building. All guests escaped before flames enveloped the building. The fire is believed to have started when the owner of a fruit stand adjacent to the hotel left a cigarette near some tissues that are used for wrapping fruit on the stand.

Inventor patents "the Edison effect"

Menlo Park, New Jersey

Thomas A. Edison is patenting an odd discovery he made while trying to improve the electric light. Edison sealed a metal wire in the bulb near the filament, hoping to increase light output. To his surprise, he found that negative electricity flowed across the gap from the filament to the wire. The "Edison effect" has been reported in the technical literature, but Edison says he sees no practical use for it now. He is patenting the discovery in case future scientists and inventors should find some use for it.

First malted milk is made by Horlick

Racine, Wisconsin

James and William Horlick of Racine, Wisconsin, have begun selling a new milk supplement called Horlicks Malted Milk, designed to bolster the values of milk and to help infants sleep. William Horlick, a stonemason who migrated from England, formed the company in 1873 with his pharmacist brother, James, who came up with the new powder made from malted barley and wheat flour. When dissolved in milk, it gives the milk a delicious flavor.

Northern Pacific finishes 2nd line to coast

Spanning the country: wooden trestle in Idaho. Villard has given new meaning to mass construction by employing 25,000 workers, half of them Chinese.

Gold Creek, Montana, Sept. 8

"I have no golden spike, but an iron one," said Northern Pacific president Henry Villard to a huge crowd of dignitaries, workers and onlookers here today as they celebrated completion of the vast new railroad to the Pacific Northwest. And after 19 years of battling unforgiving terrain and near-ruinous financial upheavals, it seemed fitting that the final spike would be the same one used so long ago in Minnesota. First Villard and then former President Grant hammered the spike, as crowds cheered and cannons boomed from St. Paul to Portland, Oregon, across 1,222 miles of the new transcontinental line.

Signed into existence by President Lincoln in 1864, the Northern Pacific was plagued by economic troubles from its start, and construction was halted after the 1873 financial panic. Villard, a German immigrant and indefatigable financier, took over the ailing company in 1881 and was overseer in the final years of furious construction. The line's Chinese laborers from the West and Irish and Swedes from the East overcame staggering obstacles. One 130-mile stretch of the Rockies required unparalleled feats, including a 3,850-foot tunnel that had to be dug through solid granite, and an 1,800-foot trestle.

On the Northern Pacific, the round trip from the Mississippi to the Columbia River, which had taken Lewis and Clark 2 1/2 years, will take nine days (→Nov. 18).

Transient camps are abandoned and tons of wood devoured by railroad men.

First telegraph line to Brazil is opened

New York City, Sept. 21

The first message ever sent by telegraph nearly 40 years ago was "What hath God wrought!" Now, with the opening of the first telegraph line from the United States to Brazil, it seems that what God, or Samuel F.B. Morse, hath wrought is an unprecedented era of long-distance communication. What with two operating trans-Atlantic telegraph cables, laid in 1866, transcontinental lines between New York and San Francisco, and Alexander Graham Bell's recent invention of voice communication through telegraph lines, it seems the world is smaller and the network of wires around has grown quite formidable.

16-year-old creates new Banking game

Salem, Massachusetts

The very town where one could once be hanged for witchcraft has become a sort of national capital for fun and games. W. and S.B. Ives had the first big success with *The Mansion of Happiness* in 1843. This year, in the cellar of his home, a 16-year-old student named George S. Parker created a game he calls *Banking*. It is about making money, a subject Parker thinks is quite popular in America. The inventor is not averse to making some himself. He hopes to start a firm that will manufacture and market his ideas.

Hammerstein rolls cigars by machine

New York City, Feb. 27

His first love is the opera; his second love is a fat cigar. Now the German immigrant entrepreneur Oscar Hammerstein has put one passion in the service of the other with his invention of a rolling machine that turns out cigars said to be the equal of the hand-rolled kind. The machine is paying off handsomely, so much so that its proceeds will help finance the promotion of operas and opera houses as well as bring many of Europe's leading opera stars to America.

Court denies Negro equal accommodation

Washington, D.C., Oct. 15

The Supreme Court, in a nearly unanimous decision, struck down the Civil Rights Act of 1875, ruling that the 14th Amendment to the Constitution does not empower Congress to enact laws prohibiting discrimination in privately owned accommodations. The 8-to-1 decision was written by Associate Justice Joseph P. Bradley, while the lone dissent came from Associate Justice John Marshall Harlan.

The 1875 act, which was aproved in the aftermath of the Civil War, sought to end discrimination against the former Negro slaves, principally in the South. The law provided that hotels, railways, theaters and other privately owned concerns rendering public services be barred from discriminating on the basis of race or color. Today's decision marks a setback for those Negroes once held in slavery and is certain to increase turmoil between them and whites in the South.

The high court, in striking down the law, held that the Constitution empowers Congress to act only on discrimination by states and not on that by private citizens. The 14th Amendment, ratified by the states in 1868, grants citizenship to all born or naturalized in the United States and bars states from depriving all such persons of "life, liberty or property" without due process of law. It also extends voting rights to all male citizens 21 years and older, except those involved in rebellion or other crimes.

Opera moves uptown as new Met opens

New York City, Oct. 22

Musically, opening night at the new Metropolitan Opera House was less than a triumph. Italo Campanini in the title role of *Faust* has seen better days, the other singing rarely soared and the critics deplored the acoustics and sight lines in certain areas. The real star was the look of the hall, aglow in a gold and wine decor. It cost $1,750,000, including the land, and it can seat 1,989. In the eight private boxes repose the city's financial barons. With the encouragement of the Vanderbilts, millionaires who could not get private boxes at the old Academy of Music downtown financed the Met. For $6 here, you can get an orchestra seat up front. General admission is a dollar.

Charity ball for opera patrons.

A Southern lawyer addresses his argument to an integrated jury. However reluctantly, Negroes and whites in the South have been pushed together by the long arm of federal power. But with Radical Republicans out of favor in the North, the old Confederacy seems determined to turn back the clock.

Heavier-than-air glider makes first flight

San Diego, California, September

Through the ages, men from Leonardo da Vinci to the mythic character Daedalus have gazed into the heavens and longed to soar free of the earth like birds. Last month, a young science professor, John J. Montgomery, accomplished the feat with a strange winged contraption that he built after a lifetime of studying seagulls along the coast near his home here.

After abandoning earlier efforts to devise an orthopter, the 26-year-old teacher at Santa Clara College designed his graceful new glider to gain lift from the curved surfaces of its fixed, gull-shaped wings. With the help of a few cowboys from the area, he is said to have carted the vehicle to an isolated hill near his family's ranch at sunrise so as to avoid the ridicule of onlookers. As his brother James tugged a long rope connected to the nose of the craft, Montgomery clung to a metal bar connected to the main wings and actually soared into the wind for a distance of about 100 feet.

Continent divided into 4 time zones

Chicago, Nov. 18

A synchronization of clocks and watches across the continent was accomplished with apparent ease today as the nation was divided into four time zones relative to the prime meridian in Greenwich, England. A transcontinental railroad passenger will thus change only the hour hand of his timepiece as he travels through Atlantic, Central, Mountain and Pacific time belts. The new system will eliminate wide discrepancies in time standards that have existed across the nation.

U.S. won't compete with naval powers

Washington, D.C., Dec. 4

Declaring that "it is no part of our policy to create and maintain a navy able to cope with that of the other great powers of the world," President Arthur has sought to reassure Congress that his administration has no intention of joining the maritime arms race that is now heating up in Europe. The President's statement comes just nine months after Congress voted funds to build three steel cruisers and a dispatch boat, the first major additions to the navy since the Civil War.

Sumner's social theory: Survival of fittest

United States

The rich prosper because they are better equipped for survival than their competitors in the economic jungle. Although today's successful entrepreneurs bear scant resemblance to the sleek predators that are their counterparts at the top of the food chain in the world of nature, there are similarities, according to William Graham Sumner, a 43-year-old Yale professor. His recently released book, *What Social Classes Owe to Each Other*, argues that the same process of natural selection that Charles Darwin of England saw as governing survival in the natural world is at play in human society, a philosophy that has been dubbed Social Darwinism.

Thomas Nast's satirical stab at the theory of evolution. A gorilla, insulted by Darwin's claim on his genetic line, seeks redress from Henry Bergh, founder of the American Society for the Prevention of Cruelty to Animals.

1884

Arthur

Atlanta, Georgia, Feb. 9. Tornado sweeps South, killing some 700 people.

Cincinnati, Feb. 14. Ohio River peaks at 71 feet in new wave of flooding.

New York City, Feb. 14. Theodore Roosevelt's young wife, Alice, and his mother die within hours of each other (→ May 10).

Washington, D.C., March 3. Supreme Court rules that Congress has authority to print greenbacks, even in peacetime.

Washington, D.C., March 6. Some 100 suffragists, led by Susan B. Anthony, present President Arthur with demand that he voice public support for female suffrage.

Pocahontas, Virginia, March 13. Coal mine disaster kills 112 workers.

Louisville, Kentucky, May 16. Buchanan, a chronic loser, wins Kentucky Derby. The horse is trained by Negro William Bird and ridden by Negro jockey Isaac Murphy.

Chicago, June. Knights of Labor meet and call for national eight-hour work day, incorporation of labor unions and prohibition of work by children under the age of 14.

Washington, D.C., July 27. Department of Labor creates Bureau of Labor to gather information on workers and help "promote prosperity."

Newport, Rhode Island, Oct. 6. Naval War College founded.

New York City, Nov. 8. Samuel Sidney McClure establishes McClure's Syndicate, first newspaper syndicate.

Wyoming, December. Burlington Railroad lays 10 miles of track every two days.

Washington, D.C. Washington Monument completed (→ Feb. 21, 1885).

Utah. Polygamists prosecuted under 1882 Edmunds-Tucker Law.

Allegheny, Pennsylvania. Charles Taze Russell and six other Adventists charter International Bible Students Association [Jehovah's Witnesses].

United States. Winslow Homer paints *The Life Line* and wins fame.

Boston. *Ramona,* novel by Helen Hunt Jackson, exposes abuse of American Indians.

Mark Twain's "Huck Finn" a runaway hit

Missouri

What do you get when you put an orphan and a runaway slave together on a makeshift raft and send them down the Mississippi River? The answer is *The Adventures of Huckleberry Finn*, by Mark Twain, who has been working away at this sequel to *The Adventures of Tom Sawyer* since 1876.

In the new novel, Tom's sidekick, Huck, takes center stage for an epic escape from "sivilization," accompanied by Jim, a slave with a price on his head. On the way, the two meet a host of zany frontier folks, including a couple of con-men who style themselves the "Duke of Bridgewater" and the "Dauphin" and perpetrate a theatrical hoax that they call *The Royal Nonesuch.*

Huck Finn gone fishin'.

The laughs stop when Huck becomes embroiled in a murderous feud and when he catches his first glimpse of a lynch mob. Huck himself narrates the story in a style at once eloquent and unschooled. His grammar springs more than a few leaks, but his vivid phrases uncoil with the natural power of the mighty Mississippi itself.

Troops stop riots after 56 are killed

Cincinnati, March 30

After a final attack by the militia, rioters ended a 50-hour outburst of vigilantism today. Residents have been angry for months over lax law enforcement. The anger exploded into violence when a jury ruled manslaughter instead of murder in the case of William Berner, who killed his boss with a hammer to steal his money. A mass meeting on the demise of justice here the day after the verdict turned into a lynch mob 8,000 strong, converging on the jail with shouts of "Let's hang Berner." He was in Columbus. But no matter, the crowd launched into an orgy of lawlessness. Breaking into the jail, they beat the sheriff, besieged the fire house while the courthouse burned, and raided hardware stores, gun stores and pawnshops to get firearms. In all, 56 people were killed.

Baraboo is home of Ringling Bros. Circus

Baraboo, Wisconsin, May 19

All 600 seats were filled today for the opening of the Yankee Robinson and Ringling Bros. Great Double Show, Circus and Caravan. "This show," boomed Yankee Robinson to start the fun, "is destined to become the greatest circus on earth." For the moment, spectators will have to settle for a ring of red cloth and a 45- by 90-foot tent. The five mustachioed Ringlings, Al, Charles, Alf T., John and Otto, cut the poles and stakes and made the bleachers themselves. They have no animals and only $1,000 in capital. But their act hums with skillful juggling, contortioning, singing and joke telling. Al, who trained for years with Robinson's own circus, can stand a plow on his chin. The brothers, renting horses as they go, plan to take their nine-wagon show on the road.

CASTORIA
JUMBO FEEDS BABY CASTORIA
From peasant nurse to high born lady,
All mothers know what's good for baby.
While Jumbo, too, though not a lady,
Follows suit and feeds the great baby

Showman P.T. Barnum has outdone himself. On a recent overseas trip, he acquired Jumbo, an African elephant, from the London Zoological Society.

Eat at lunch wagon

Worcester, Massachusetts

An innovation in eating for the workingman has appeared on the streets of Worcester, Massachusetts, where an entrepreneur named Sam Jones has taken the idea of the lunch wagon – pioneered in 1872 in Providence, Rhode Island – and provided stools inside so that customers do not have to eat standing up or on the curb. Because it is moveable, Jones can set up pretty much wherever he wishes, bringing the dining room to customers, rather than the other way around.

103 are lost at sea

Martha's Vineyard, Mass., Jan. 18

The passenger ship City of Columbus ran aground early this morning off Martha's Vineyard, drowning at least 103 in freezing waters. Bound for Savannah from Boston, the vessel struck at Devil's Bridge, a reef sailors say deserves its name. The U.S. revenue cutter Dexter brought 21 to shore, most of whom were found clinging for life to the sinking ship's rigging. Two of them were frozen stiff and had to be pulled from their roost, only to expire on the way to shore.

arty of "Rum, Romanism, Rebellion"?

New York City, Oct. 29

With the presidential election only days away, Democrats have been labeled the party of "Rum, Romanism and Rebellion." The accusation was leveled by the Rev. Samuel Dickenson Burchard, pastor of a Presbyterian church here, during a visit that he and several hundred other New York ministers paid on James G. Blaine, the Republican candidate for president. The ministers had not dropped in casually. They came in response to a newspaper advertisement that Blaine and his supporters had run that day asking all clergymen interested in the campaign to come by and meet with him at the Fifth Avenue Hotel. As spokesman for the group, Burchard assured Blaine and his supporters: "We are Republicans and don't propose to leave our party and identify with the party whose antecedents are rum, Romanism and rebellion."

The remark, not even welcomed by the Blaine camp, apparently was prompted by the minister's feeling that Democrats are heavy drinkers, that many are Roman Catholics and that their party was on the rebellious side in the Civil War.

This attempt to sway the election was just the latest in a campaign marked by growing bitterness. Earlier this year, some Republicans, convinced that Blaine is corrupt, deserted their party and announced they would support Grover Cleveland, the candidate of the Democratic Party. They have been called "mugwumps," which means "big chiefs" in the Algonquin language.

As the campaign heats up, General William Tecumseh Sherman is no doubt glad he did not decide to run. Last summer, in refusing the Republican nomination for the presidency, General Sherman said: "I will not accept if nominated and will not serve if elected" (→Nov. 4).

Political piper. Blaine tries to lure disenchanted Republicans back to the fold.

Republicans: "Ma, Ma, where's my Pa?"

The political perils of personal problems. A Republican cartoon depicts Cleveland, the Democratic nominee, tormented by his illegitimate child.

Washington, D.C., Sept. 15

As the race for president continues to heat up, Republicans have coined a new campaign slogan: "Ma, Ma, where's my Pa?" It is designed to remind voters that the Democrat Grover Cleveland, a 47-year-old bachelor, allegedly fathered an illegitimate child, something that he has not denied.

Cleveland, the Governor of New York, will be opposed in the election by James Blaine of Maine, formerly speaker of the House of Representatives and later a senator. Nicknamed the "Plumed Knight" because of his magnetic personality and speaking ability, Blaine won the Republican nomination in June by defeating President Arthur.

Meanwhile, the two major parties are also being challenged by Benjamin Butler, running on the Anti-Monopoly and National Greenback Labor Party tickets.

While the paternity issue has begun to dominate the campaign, all has not gone smoothly for Blaine. Democrats have noted that Blaine was one of the House members given stock in a railroad holding company in the 1870's to influence legislation. Oakes Ames, a House member at the time, confessed he gave out stock "where it will produce the most good" (→Nov. 4).

Pen carries own ink

New York City

Finally, a fountain pen that does not leak, clog or spurt. Lewis E. Waterman has developed the first ink-storing pen successful enough to be manufactured, which is just what he plans to do through his new company, the Ideal Pen Company of New York. Waterman says that the ink-feeding device of his pen is the main improvement over other fountain pens. The ink, which is put in the pen by use of an eyedropper, will be welcomed by those tired of constant dipping.

Sweeney fans 19

Providence, R.I.

Charles Sweeney, a pitcher and part-time outfielder for Providence of the National League, has amazed the baseball world by striking out 19 batters in a nine-inning game. His teammate Old Horse Radbourne also helped Providence win the championship by pitching 60 victories while losing only 12 games. New rules allow a pitcher to throw overhand or side arm as well as underhand, which may have been a factor. Also, six balls, instead of eight, now give a batter first base.

In Sight of the Promised Land. Cleveland, as Moses, sights the Capitol.

Laws in place for District of Alaska

Washington, D.C., May 17

Law and order may have at long last come to Alaska. With so many gold seekers stampeding north, the United States Congress established the District of Alaska for legal purposes. In an attempt to bring a legal framework into existence for this new district as soon as possible, Congress also ordered that the laws of Oregon be used as the model for the District of Alaska. The only difference will be that wherever the statutes state "Oregon," the term "Alaska" will be inserted.

While everyone knows that a governor must be appointed by the President, no one knows whom President Arthur will choose. Inside sources say John M. Kinkead is the most likely choice and that the announcement of his appointment could be made by July 4.

There is also speculation that an operating civilian government will be in place in Juneau, the Alaskan district's capital, by year's end. This will finally bring a formalized civil service system to Juneau, which has been undergoing a boom since the opening of the Treadwell Mine.

Sargent causes a scandal with "Mme. X"

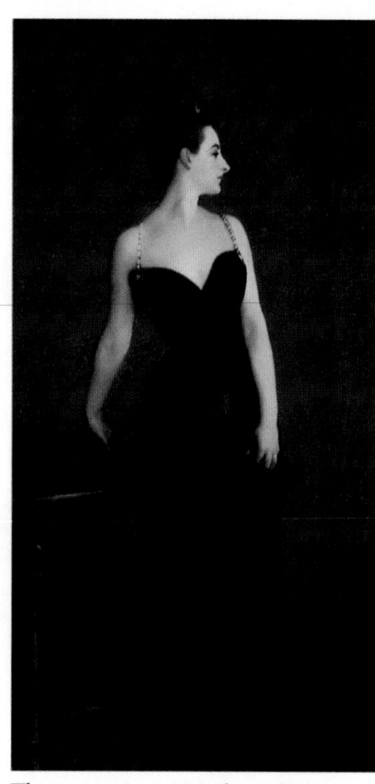

The mysterious "Madame X."

Paris, June

"Detestable! Boring! Curious! Monstrous!" These are some of the reactions provoked by John Singer Sargent's scandalous *Portrait de Mme.* ****, unveiled here last month. Sargent, the young expatriate painter, born in Florence of American parents, departs in this work from the decorous mien usually preferred by his aristocratic patrons in favor of the brash sensuality of this newcomer to the European social scene.

The subject of the painting, popularly known as "Mme. X," is the wife of an eminent Parisian banker, Mme. Gatreau. She is, in fact, an American whose rumored liaisons include Dr. Samuel Pozzi, one of the artist's closest friends and the subject of one of his best portraits. Such activities made Mme. Gatreau a subject of society gossip long before the first sketch for Sargent's picture. Salon visitors were titillated by the socialite's dramatic use of cosmetics, including lavender body powder, and the unusual stiffly formed and revealing black velvet gown. Mme. Gatreau's mother, on learning of the mocking crowds gathered before her daughter's likeness, told Sargent to remove it from view. The painter allowed the picture to remain on exhibit, but it may be some time before the portrait is shown again, for Sargent, perhaps driven by this "succes de scandal," has moved to England.

Electric streetcars start in Cleveland

Cleveland, Ohio, July 26

Since Thomas A. Edison's dramatic demonstration of an electric railway in 1880, many have toiled to apply the idea commercially. But it has taken Edward M. Bentley and Walter H. Knight of the East Cleveland Street Railway to solve the toughest problem: how to safely transfer electricity to the cars. Today their line, the first in the nation, opened. Self-propelled cars ferried riders with power from an underground, electrified third rail.

Bullfight in Kansas

Kansas, July 4

A Spanish-style bullfight was staged in Dodge City today. It is reportedly the first such event in the area and possibly in the United States. Local residents say that it seemed to be authentic, but then, they really have very little knowledge of what constitutes a traditional bullfight. Residents seemed to have mixed feelings about the event. It is said that the bullfight was arranged by itinerant cowboys from Texas and Mexico.

Survivors of 25-man Arctic team rescued

San Francisco, June 22

There was good news today for Adolphus Washington Greely and the six members of his team who are left alive: a rescue vessel finally reached them. Greely commanded one of two Arctic exploration teams that represented the United States as its contribution to the First International Circumpolar Year (1882-1883). Greely with a team of 22 army men and two Eskimo hunters spent the winter at Fort Conger on Ellesmere Island in the Arctic Ocean.

In from the cold: six of the survivors.

It was not a pleasant winter because their supply ship failed to get through before the ocean froze. The party did the best it could through that winter, and the next spring it abandoned Fort Conger and sailed south with what food remained. It took the team until October to make the 250 miles south to Cape Sabine. There, exhausted, the men spent another winter. Food ran low and, one by one, the men in the expedition starved to death. By the time the rescue ship arrived, only Greely and six of his contingent were alive.

There are rumors that Greely, now a lieutenant, will be promoted to head the Weather Service.

Maxim shows off murderous machine gun

London

The nightmarish imagery of the last war may soon pale beside the destructive potential of Hiram Maxim's deadly new machine gun. Maxim, an American electrician working here in London, designed the weapon to use its own recoil to eject, reload and fire rounds. Thus, a soldier need only squeeze the trigger to unleash a deadly hail of 600 bullets per minute. European military leaders have shown an intense interest in Maxim's demonstrations.

Maxim amuses himself with his deadly toy, the recoil-operated machine gun.

heodore Roosevelt s leaving Assembly

lew York City, May 10

The three-term "Cyclone Assemlyman" Theodore Roosevelt, a ugnacious 25-year-old legislator nown for his relentless attacks on overnment corruption and mahine politics, will not seek re-elecion this fall. Roosevelt, who reently lost both his wife and mother n the same day, plans to retire rom politics and hunt buffalo in he Dakotas. The boyish Republican received wide popular suport in his crusade for reform.

A Negro in majors

oledo, Ohio

A Negro player, the first in a "major" league, has been playing vith Toledo of the renegade American Association with good esults. Moses Fleetwood Walker batted an acceptable .241 in he 42 games he played. His broher, Welday Wilberforce Walker, vas also on the roster of the Toedo squad, but he played in only six ames. The American Association vas organized in 1882 as a rival to he National, which began in 1876.

"Gone to the White House, ha, ha, ha!"

"Grover the Good," the 22nd President. Eastman Johnson's painting.

Washington, D.C., Nov. 4

Just as his supporters had predicted, Grover Cleveland will be able to say in March that he has "Gone to the White House, ha, ha, ha!" Today's election returns showed that Cleveland, a 47-year-old bachelor, had defeated James G. Blaine of Maine after one of the most vicious presidential campaigns ever waged. Alluding to Cleveland's alleged paternity of an illegitimate child – a paternity that he never denied – Blaine's backers repeatedly taunted the Democratic candidate: "Ma, Ma, where's my Pa?" Cleveland's troops coined the reply: "Gone to the White House, ha, ha, ha!" (→March 4, 1885).

Cocaine introduced as an anesthetic

New York City

The surgeon William Stewart Halsted has achieved another major advance by developing a highly successful local anesthetic technique. Using injections of the drug cocaine, Halsted can desensitize the area to be operated on. Many in the profession expect the technique to be used widely. The drug, produced from a South American shrub, is sold by the Lehn & Fink Co. of Brooklyn. Cocaine is also said to have a euphoric side effect.

Eastman develops cheap, easy-to-use film

Rochester, New York

George Eastman has made the art of photography accessible to everyone with his invention of a process to coat flexible rolls of film with photographic emulsion. This type of film is inexpensive, easy to insert and remove from the camera and simple to develop once the pictures have been snapped. The 30-year-old Rochester man has already done quite a bit to promote photography as a hobby and to turn photographic equipment into an industry. Four years ago, Eastman made a major breakthrough with his invention of a process for making dry photographic plates. He has since come up with countless other inventions and improvements in both film and camera, and his operation in Rochester thrives (→1888).

Prime meridian set

Washington, D.C., October

Delegates at the International Prime Meridian Conference here have agreed to designate Greenwich, England, as the site of the earth's prime meridian, longitude 0. From now on, all longitudes and times will be described in terms of a line running through Greenwich, with time zones that extend 7 1/2 degrees in longitude and the time difference between adjacent zones exactly one hour. It is the world's first standard time system.

New Orleans Expo displays world of future

New Orleans, Dec. 16

The World's Industrial and Cotton Centennial Exposition opened today, displaying the world of the future. There was modern architecture, electric lights and the world's largest concentration of elevators. The exposition, aimed at boosting the economy of New Orleans as well as the "New South," is taking place in Audubon Park. The celebration is also marking the first shipment of cotton in 1784.

Edward A. Burke, director general, predicted the exposition would draw four million people and gross $5 miilion. The turnout today, however, was disappointing. The crowd was estimated at 14,000, far lower than Burke had predicted. The main building, said to be the largest edifice ever constructed, is complete. It covers a 33-acre site and has more elevators than exist in the rest of the world. An exhibition hall seats 3,000. The Horticultural Hall has a magnificent conservatory built of glass and wood in the shape of a cross. It is topped by a 90-foot glass tower illuminated by electric lights that make the tower visible 20 miles away.

From Washington, President Arthur opens the New Orleans Exposition with the flick of an electrical switch.

A steel "skyscraper" rises over Chicago

Chicago

As American cities are pressed to expand both outward and upward, architects are struggling with the problem of how to provide the structural strength needed for taller buildings. With the towering Home Life Insurance Building in Chicago, William LeBaron Jenney appears to have the answer.

Opened this year, the building is the same height as Chicago's other 10-story wonder, John W. Root's Montauk Building, completed in 1882. But the similarity ends there. To circumvent the strength limitations of masonry walls, Jenney designed an inner skeleton of wrought-iron and steel girders bolted together to support the structure, which also features an elevator. Though steel has been successfully employed in constructing bridges, Jenney's "skyscraper" is the first building to use the new material. Many engineers believe that such rigid steel inner frames will enable architects to construct buildings of previously unmanageable heights.

The Home Life Insurance Building in Chicago scrapes the sky.

1885

Cleveland

Oregon, Jan. 4. Ahantchuyuks Indians sign treaty with United States government, agreeing to relocate to reservation.

Washington, D.C., Jan. 29. Senate rejects 1884 treaty paving way for canal across Nicaragua.

Washington, D.C., Feb. 25. Congress prohibits barbed wire fencing of public lands in West.

Washington, D.C., March 3. Post Office inaugurates special delivery.

Washington, D.C., March 3. Congress establishes Board of Fortifications and Coast Defenses, to examine state of American defenses.

California, March 3. First state forest commission in United States authorized.

Washington, D.C., March 4. Grover Cleveland inaugurated as 22nd President, Thomas A. Hendricks as Vice President.

Washington, D.C., March 13. President Cleveland warns settlers to stay off Indian lands in Oklahoma (→Apr. 3).

New York City, June 19. Statue of Liberty arrives from France (→Oct. 28, 1886).

United States, Sept. 16. America's Puritan beats England's Genesta in America's Cup race.

United States, Dec. 20. Weightlifter William Curtis raises 3,239 pounds, "with harness."

Washington, D.C. Veterinarian Daniel Elmer Salmon describes salmonella bacteria, believed to cause food poisoning.

Fort Wayne, Indiana. Sylvanus Bowser begins operation of nation's first gasoline pump.

Camus, Washington Territory. First paper mill in Pacific Northwest to use ground wood established.

Alabama. Montgomery becomes first Southern city with streetcars.

United States. Westinghouse Electrical and Manufacturing Company founded.

New York City. Gilbert and Sullivan's *The Mikado* given American premiere, directed by Richard D'Oyly Carte.

New York City. Saloonkeeper purchases William Harnett's painting *After the Hunt*, after fascinating Parisians.

Highest tribute to Washington, at 585 ft.

The towering Washington Monument, "George Washington's finger pointing to the sky," rises 585 feet.

Washington, D.C., Feb. 21

The Washington Monument is complete. The world's tallest stone monument is considered perfect because of its strength and grace. British Ambassador Cecil Spring Rice said, "It is George Washington's finger pointing to the sky." The National Monument Society began raising funds in 1832, the 100th anniversary of Washington's birth. On July 4, 1848, the cornerstone was laid with the same trowel Washington used to lay the cornerstone of the Capitol. Red tape and the Civil War interrupted construction. But after 36 years and an expenditure of $1.3 million, it was finally dedicated today. The monument stands 585 feet high at the west end of The Mall and weighs 81,120 tons. An elevator in its shaft will allow visitors a spectacular view of the city when it opens to the public in three years.

Chicago leads Cincinnati in meat-packing

Chicago

"I like to turn bristles, blood and the inside and outside of pigs and bullocks into revenue," says Philip Armour with gusto. Judging by the mountains of meat that is packed and shipped each day in Chicago, Armour's colleagues share his idea of a good time. With joyful efficiency their cattle are run into winding paths, clobbered, dropped through trap doors, killed, hung from moving hooks and disassembled. Commercial meat-packing began in Cincinnati in 1818, but like everything else in the age of railroads, it is moving west. In Gustavus Swift's refrigerated car, in use since 1880, fresh meat can travel from Omaha to New York in the heat of summer. But Chicago, pierced with dozens of rail lines and graced by the services of Armour, Swift and Nelson Morris, handles most of the traffic.

With access to foreign markets by sea, New York is still a prime location.

A.T.&T. to develop interstate phoning

New York City, Feb. 28

The American Telephone & Telegraph Company was incorporated here today with a charter that authorizes it to build telephone lines "from any city in the state, to each and every other state." A.T.&T. is being established because local Bell companies cannot build intercity lines. Southern New England Bell, for example, has just abandoned a line between New York and Boston because of marginal earnings. The new company is headed by Theodore Vail, an experienced Bell executive. Its first project is a line from New York to Philadelphia.

Employers limited in importing labor

Washington, D.C., Feb. 26

At the urging of the Knights of Labor, Congress today passed the Foran Act prohibiting contract immigrant labor. Employers will no longer be able to pay for the passage of foreigners wishing to immigrate in exchange for indentured labor. Speaking for his bill, Ohio Republican Martin Foran denounced the "importing into this country large bodies of foreign labor to take the place of and crowd out American labor." Strike breaking has been the most common immigrant labor.

Appendix removal a success in Iowa

Davenport, Iowa, Jan. 4

Surgeons here have saved a life, and made medical history in the process, by successfully removing an inflamed appendix from a patient. Appendectomy may be the most effective way of treating appendicitis, a painful infection of the appendix that causes nausea, vomiting, fever, spasms and sometimes death. The appendix is a tiny tube that projects from the large intestine and is considered to serve no useful function. Appendicitis may occur when waste accumulates in the organ. If an infected appendix ruptures, the infection can spread.

Fishing rights pact with Canada ended

Washington, D.C., July 1
The United States today canceled an 1871 treaty with Canada, terminating reciprocal fishing rights in each other's waters. Washington's action was the climax of a 14-year-old dispute over fishing rights in the Atlantic. The Treaty of Washington had constituted the first formal recognition by United States authorities of Canada as an independent dominion under the British crown. The country's first Prime Minister, Sir John A. Macdonald, was among the participants when a combined British-Canadian team negotiated the treaty.

Dr. Pepper named for girlfriend's dad

Waco, Texas, Dec. 1
A new "tonic, brain food and exhilarant" is on sale at Wade Morrison's Old Corner Drug Store. Morrison came here from Virginia after his courtship with a Miss Pepper was ended by the girl's father, Kenneth, who also happened to be young Wade's boss. Lovesick and jobless, Morrison headed west and bought the pharmacy, where a clerk named Charles Alderton had concocted the new drink. Morrison named it after the most influential man in his past, Dr. Pepper.

Indians flee from Riel rebellion in Canada

Louis Riel (seated in wooden chair) poses with other Metis. As a leader of European-Indians in Canada, Riel led another revolt in Western Canada in 1869. Living in Montana since 1879, he became a U.S. citizen two years ago.

Helena, Montana, July
With the famous buffalo hunter Gabriel Dumont, a defeated force of Indian and Metis rebels from Canada's West has taken refuge in Montana. Their political-spiritual leader, Louis Riel, is in Canadian custody, awaiting trial for treason.

Dumont, of mixed French-Canadian and Indian blood, was instrumental in bringing Riel back from exile in the United States to lead the Saskatchewan Metis, a half-breed people, in claiming their political rights. Riel, himself of French, Irish and Indian ancestry, was banished in 1875 for his role in an earlier uprising in the Red River territory of Manitoba. While in exile, Riel became an American citizen and joined the Republican Party. But after arriving in Saskatchewan, he set up a provisional government and demanded the surrender of the Hudson's Bay Company fur trading post at Fort Carlton.

Canadian authorities promptly acted to crush the rebellion, and in the fighting that ensued Dumont took command of a tiny army of 300 Metis and Indian rebels. Despite their small numbers, they won several skirmishes with the Canadian forces. But after two months, the rebel headquarters at Batoche was overrun and captured. Riel surrendered and Dumont fled to the United States, where he joined the Buffalo Bill Wild West Show as an expert marksman.

U.S. will sell lands it seized for fraud

Washington, D.C., Apr. 3
Instituting President Cleveland's reform policy regarding Western lands, Land Commissioner W.A.J. Sparks has opened to settlers some 2.75 million acres taken fraudulently. The land in question was seized in a variety of underhanded ways by the railroads, cattlemen and individual claim-jumpers in the Dakotas, Kansas and Oklahoma. This legislation follows last month's warning to white settlers to stay off Indian lands in Oklahoma. These so-called "Boomers" have repeatedly been driven off the land by federal troops.

Machine is devised to record dictation

Massachusetts
Now you can record and play back your own voice. Charles Tainter, a scientist and instrument maker, has invented a machine called the graphophone with the aid of Alexander Graham Bell and his cousin Chichester A. Bell. The machine records, stores and reproduces sound using a rotating cardboard drum and mouthpiece similar to that on a telephone. The first sound recorded and played back was Tainter's voice reciting from Act I, Scene IV of *Hamlet*.

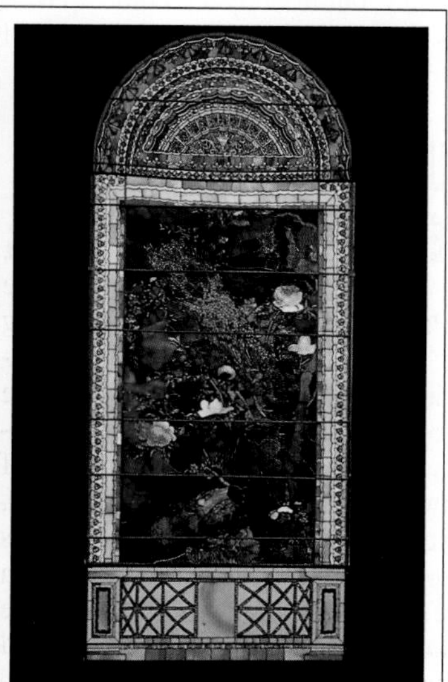

"Peacocks and Peony," c.1885, by John La Farge, who is reviving interest in stained glass windows.

Robert Odlum has come up with a new use for the Brooklyn Bridge. But he's not going to use it again.

The traveling phrenologist in the White Mountains: "Yes, Miss, you have a remarkable head."

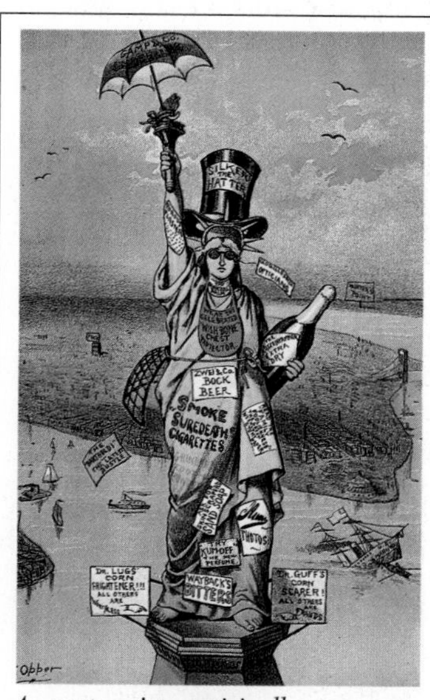

A cartoonist satirically suggests that the nation pay for the Statue of Liberty by pasting it with ads.

Railroad workers win strike against Gould

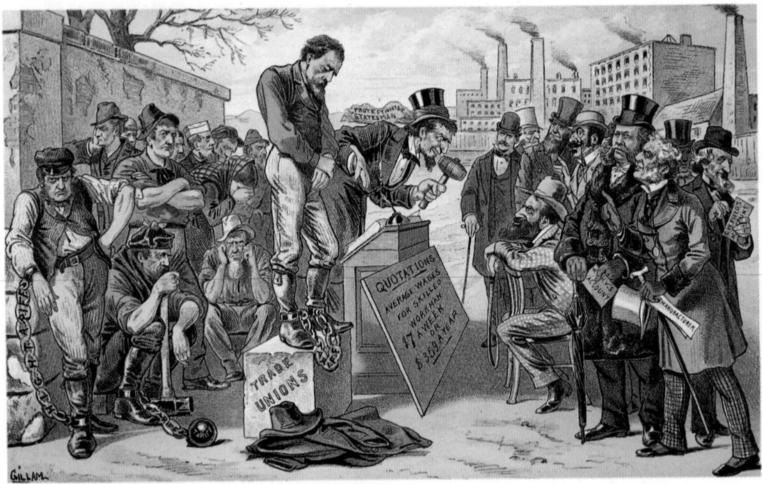

Today's Slave Market. Caricatures of capitalists, including W.H. Vanderbilt and Jay Gould, trying to underbid one another for labor's services.

Moberly, Missouri, September

Jay Gould, whose wizardry dominates Wall Street, has been brought to heel by striking workers for the second time this year. In March, after taking 10 percent pay cuts, workers on the trains supported shopmen in tying up 10,000 miles of track on three of Gould's Southwest lines. Cornered, the normally ruthless railway titan yielded, restoring pay cuts and rehiring strikers. In doing so, he released a flood of enthusiasm for the Knights of Labor, who gave $30,000 to the strike. To fight 30 new locals, the Wabash line began closing union shops and reopening them with scabs. Soon, faced with the prospect of a huge strike, Gould acquiesced again, promising that "no official shall discriminate against the Knights of Labor."

Young economists oppose laissez-faire

United States.

Amid the mounting squalor of industrial life, an intellectual revolt is emerging to challenge the gospel of laissez-faire economics. Founded this year around a core group of young economists, the American Economic Association is urging government to guide the course of industry to assure progress for all; unbridled competition is "unsafe in politics and unsound in morals." Founding members Henry Adams and Andrew Carnegie want to see workers aided in order to harmonize relations between the classes.

Life on the Mississippi. "The Levee – New Orleans" by Currier and Ives.

Attacks on Chinese soar

Wyoming Territory, Sept. 30

It has not been a good year for those Americans worried about the fate of the nation's minorities. Anti-Chinese sentiment appears to be running high everywhere.

Unfortunately, more than just ill will is being vented against the Chinese. Riots, beatings, destruction of property and killings are the order of the day. This anti-Chinese sentiment culminated in one of the most savage demonstrations of violence in Wyoming's history here today.

There has been a fierce resentment against the Chinese. And even though many of them have lived in Rock Springs for a decade, they have not organized into a cohesive body. What's more, they are willing to accept lower pay than white miners doing the same job. British and Swedish miners who have only recently migrated to the area took exception to the Chinese attitude and a fearsome riot developed. Before the smoke settled, 28 Chinese were dead and at least 15 wounded. Several hundred others were chased out of town.

Informed of the riots, Governor Francis E. Warren came to Rock Springs and judged the situation out of hand. Since the territory has no militia, he requested troops from President Grover Cleveland. Those troops will be needed not only to escort the frightened Chinese back to Rock Springs but also to insure law and order in the future.

Troubled residents, who are already calling this episode the "Rock Springs Massacre," feel that even with federal troops there is little hope of stemming the anti-Chinese sentiment.

Natives of Denver, mountain boom town, riot against the Chinese.

Riots elsewhere have produced similar results: violence and no indictments. Seattle, for example, had a race riot this month. In Tacoma, a white mob herded more than 700 Chinese into wagons and left them in the open all night. Two died and the rest were shipped to Portland.

Church and civic leaders worried by the situation wonder whether America has lost its sense of decency, but nobody has come up with a way to deal with the racial hatred (→ Feb. 7, 1886).

Furnaces used for garbage disposal

United States

The growth of city populations and the acceleration of industry has lifted garbage to the front of everyone's minds and yards. The most common solution to this age-old problem is incineration inside a furnace, as the use of pigs seems to poison the meat for later consumption. If garbage is not properly disposed of, it becomes a source of disease and vermin that thrive on human waste. Burning garbage is a pragmatic solution, and furnaces are being installed to do this.

U.S. vines destroy European vineyards

Paris

European vineyards are being devastated by the American plant louse phylloxera vasatrix, apparently brought in on American vines between 1858 and 1863. The louse destroys the roots of the vine, and its effects have crippled vineyards from France to Russia. Ironically, phylloxera, which originated in the Eastern United States, has now invaded the wine country of Northern California, and scientists on both sides of the Atlantic are at a loss as to how to stop the ravages of the plague.

Reform Jews state heir independence

ittsburgh, Pennsylvania, Nov. 19

At the end of a four-day meet-ng, delegates from the major re-ormed Hebrew congregations in he United States adopted a plat-orm outlining their views on reli-ion. This document, which Rabbi saac Mayer Wise called "the Jew-sh declaration of independence," ejects all parts of Mosaic law incon-istent with modern civilization and ecognizes in every religion an effort o grasp the "Infinite One." The latform also declares that its adher-nts expect "neither a return to alestine, nor sacrificial worship nder the sons of Aaron, nor the estoration of any laws concerning he Jewish State." Such statements eparate them from much of histor-cal Judaism, and objections from he more orthodox are expected.

Harvard cancels football for season

Cambridge, Massachusetts

Harvard University, whose Foot Ball Club brought rugby to the United States in 1874, has decided the game's American cousin is too dangerous for its own good and canceled this year's football season. Played on a 110-yard field, with no helmets or pads, the game rewards size and brute strength. Its bulky warriors are often referred to as "gorillas" on campus. Twice a week they play 45-minute halves with no rest. Players are only allowed off the field for injuries, and with only four substitutes, that excuse wears thin after a while. Linemen stand erect, toe to toe before entering into battle. To fill these positions, coaches generally look for sportsmen with plenty of boxing and wrestling experience.

Social activist role is urged on church

United States

Churches have an obligation to provide for more than just the spiritual needs of their own congregations, according to the Rev. Josiah Strong, a 38-year-old minister and author of the recent *Our Country*. Strong argues that despite the rampant materialism of the post-Civil War decades, capitalism and Anglo-Saxon civilization represent the pinnacle of human achievement, and he calls on the religious faithful to spread this "social gospel" throughout the world. Its triumph, he says, is inevitable: "Does it not look as if God were not only preparing in our Anglo-Saxon civilization the die with which to stamp the peoples of the earth, but as if he were massing behind that die the mighty power with which to stamp it?"

From Howells, story of a self-made man

Howells in Venice, where he served as the American consul during the Civil War, a post earned with his biography of Abraham Lincoln.

Boston

The self-made man, a fixture of this gaudy age, is portrayed in *The Rise of Silas Lapham*, the new novel by William Dean Howells. The hero, a Vermont farmer, parlays a paint business into wealth but runs up against the barriers of Boston society. He also hits bottom financially, but he "rises" ethically by snuffing a shady deal. The 48-year-old author has himself risen far, from poverty in Ohio to literary fame. His credits include a campaign biography of Lincoln and editing the *Atlantic Monthly*. Unlike his character, Howells has been welcomed by Boston's Brahmins.

Du Bois advocates ormation of elite

tlanta, Georgia

Dr. W.E.B. Du Bois, a new mem-er of the faculty of Atlanta Uni-ersity, has been asked to take over s director of the university's an-ual conferences on the advance-nent of the Negro race. Dr. Du Bois, who holds a Ph.D degree from Harvard, is one of the leading Ne-ro scholars in the United States. He has advocated the uplifting of he elite, a group that he defines s "the talented tenth."

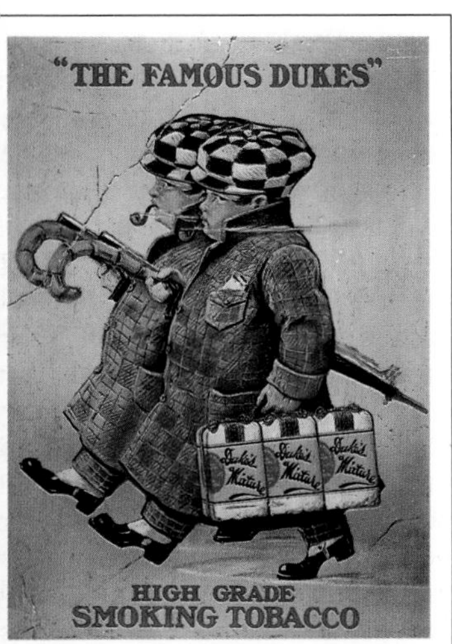

David and Benjamin Duke on an advertisement for their tobacco.

First hockey league started in Canada

Kingston, Ontario

The popularity of ice hockey has led to the formation of a four-team league with diverse membership. It is made up of the Royal Military College, Queen's University, the Kingston Athletics and the Kingston Hockey Club. Meanwhile, hockey has been gaining in the United States and a 17-year-old student at St. Paul's School in Concord, New Hampshire, has written the first set of rules for the American teams.

The latest fashion: bright and flouncy

New York City

Are you dressed for the "Moyen Age?" That's what *Harper's Bazaar* is calling the new fashion look. No longer dark and drab, fabric colors now almost jump off the clothing. Flounces in the skirt are also in. As *Harper's* noted, "there is a tendency to introduce orange and flame colors amid dark and quiet tints." Ten years ago, the magazine said, women out for a drive would be dressed in all black. Now, oranges, pinks, blues and lilacs with lace flounces are everywhere.

Memoirs finished, Grant dies at 63

Mount McGregor, N.Y., July 23

One of America's heroes, President Ulysses S. Grant, died here today at the age of 63, his luster tarnished only a little by the financial scandals that plagued his administration. Large crowds of well-wishers had been strolling past Grant's quaint cabin of late in hopes of catching a glimpse of the ailing former Union general. Grant, who had been at work completing his memoirs, died penniless.

"Rainy Day in Boston" (1885) by Childe Hassam. At 26, Hassam has not yet been to Europe. But his sensitivity to fine shades of light testifies to the number of American artists who have brought home the style of the French luminists. Hassam, trained in Boston, is going to France next year.

1886

Cleveland

Pasadena, California, Jan. 1. First Tournament of Roses held by Valley Hunt Club.

Maine, Jan. 30. State's coopers, shipowners and wharf owners, who have long suffered from foreign competition, call on Congress to tax all foreign shipping.

California, Feb. 14. First trainload of oranges leaves Los Angeles bound for East.

Seattle, Washington, March 22. Small steam plant, designed and built by Sidney Mitchell and Fred Sparling, powers electrification of city.

Great Barrington, Massachusetts, March. Alternating current system demonstrated by George Westinghouse and William Stanley.

United States, Sept. 11. U.S. retains America's Cup as Mayflower beats England's Galatea.

Tuxedo, New York, October. First recorded appearance of tuxedo, at Tuxedo Club.

Newark, New Jersey, Dec. 10. Mrs. Leonora Barry, general investigator for Knights of Labor, discovers corset factory where 10-cent fine is imposed on workers for eating, laughing, singing or talking.

Chicago. Dwight L. Moody founds Bible Institute for Home and Foreign Missions.

Florida. Henry M. Flagler buys a railroad to serve his new hotel in St. Augustine.

Rome, Italy. Augustus Toltan ordained as first Negro American priest, to minister to Negro American Catholics.

Redwood, Minnesota. Richard W. Sears begins selling watches by mail.

Wyoming. Some 15 percent of entire state's cattle die off due to blizzards, rain, cold and lack of drinking water.

New York City. Frances Hodgson Burnett's *Little Lord Fauntleroy* published.

New York City. Andrew Carnegie publishes *Triumphant Democracy,* in which he condemns monarchs.

DEATH

Niagara Falls, Canada, Apr. 13. John Humphrey Noyes, controversial religious leader who believed Second Coming of Christ had already occurred (*Sept. 13, 1811).

100,000 workers join national strike

Joseph Keppler cartoon pokes fun at Knights of Labor leader Terence Powderly's pledge that the Knights "extend the hand of fellowship to all mankind."

Chicago, May 1

In an impressive display of solidarity, more than 100,000 workers left jobs across the country today under the rallying cry, "Eight-hour day with no cut in pay." The Federation of Organized Trades and Labor Unions, which led the call for a general strike, says 240,000 more workers will show their support with strikes or slowdowns. Chicago, with 40,000 out and marching in the streets, is the center of the disruption. But across the country, the enclaves of industrialism have exploded like a steam boiler. Owners sense a purposeful hostility they have not felt since the railway strike of 1877. In the streets, red flags outnumber the red, white and blue. In Cincinnati, where German anarchists dominate unions, 400 Springfield rifles were carried in a march that opened the strike. Ever prepared, the Commercial Club of Chicago raised $2,000 to buy a machine gun for the business community.

The display of strength, from bakers in Baltimore to tinners in Texas, reaches across the broad spectrum of the working class. Since the depression of 1883, labor organizing has mushroomed, to the dismay of the conservatives. The Knights of Labor grew from 70,000 members to nearly 700,000 in the last two years, causing its leader, Terence Powderly, to suspend his ambitious organizers and call a 40-day halt to the start-up of new locals. This groundswell of new members, for the first time including the unskilled as well as elite workers, has forced the reluctant Knights to support the strike.

Inspiration came instead from the federation, which has staked its fortunes on the eight-hour day since 1884, and the anarchist Central Labor Union. Though often disagreeing, they share a distaste for politics and a taste for confrontation. After the repeated failure of legislative efforts, the federation resolved in December that, "Workmen, in their endeavor to reform the prevailing economic conditions must rely upon themselves and their own power exclusively" (→ 5).

Jay Gould, the pirate of Wall Street. Gould's concessions to rail strikers on the Southwest system last year gave workingmen a new feeling of power.

Seattle in chaos; Chinese driven out

Seattle, Washington, Feb. 7

This was one of the saddest days in the history of Seattle. Anti-Chinese mobs took to the streets, destroying sections of the city and forcing 200 Chinese aboard ships for San Francisco. After the rioting, the police reported that five people had been shot in the melee. Sentiment against the Chinese, who are usually willing to work for less pay than other workers, has been strong on the West Coast and this riot is not an isolated incident. Those who perpetrated this crime are promising to expel all the Chinese by next month. Many Seattle residents, however, are appalled at the violence and are worried about the future of their city.

resident proposes abor mediation

Vashington, D.C., Apr. 22

President Cleveland today pro-osed that Congress set up a special ommission to mediate labor dis-utes. His proposal comes at a time vhen the growing industrial system as brought about a revolutionary ibor movement in reaction to harsh onditions in the workplace. Many nce-docile workers have begun rotesting the 12-hour day and ack of plant safety, as well as the efusal of owners to engage in col-ective bargaining. The proposal is iewed as a relatively mild stance oward labor in view of the fact that Cleveland has few friends among vorkers and most of his friends are rom the employer ranks (→ May 1).

)rder of succession or presidency set

Vashington, D.C., Jan. 19

Congress today passed the Presi-lential Succession Act under which he secretary of state would take ver in the event that both the resident and the vice president ie, resign or are incapacitated. The new measure also provides a urther line of succession, based n the order of creation of other Cabinet posts. Next in line after he secretary of state would be he secretary of treasury, the sec-etary of war, the attorney gen-ral, the postmaster general and he secretary of the interior.

Bomb shatters Haymarket labor rally

Chicago, May 5

A bomb exploded in Haymarket Square yesterday, killing one policeman, wounding many and perhaps shattering at its peak the national labor movement for shorter hours. The attack appears to be the work of the Black International, an anarchist offshoot of Karl Marx's Socialist International. It came as 190,000 workers across the country were ending the fourth day of a vastly successful general strike. As the labor journalist John Swinton reported two days ago: "It is an eight-hour boom, and we are scoring victory after victory."

But the events of that day and the next make concessions won from Maine to Texas appear to be pyrrhic victories. While John Swinton was keeping score in the running battle between capital and labor, anarchist leader August Spies was addressing strikers at the McCormick Harvester Works. Since a February lockout, the Internationalists had taken up the cause of these workers. Now, emboldened by the May Day show of solidarity, the strikers attacked a group of scabs changing shifts at the factory. Police arrived and were met with stones. They answered with gunfire, killing four and wounding an untold number. Enraged, Spies returned to his office and issued a "revenge circular," urging workers to "rise in your might . . . To Arms! We call you to arms."

The next day, a crowd of 3,000 gathered in Haymarket Square to hear Spies and fellow Internationalists Albert Parsons and Samuel Fielden. By the time Fielden rose to speak, all but a few hundred stalwarts had fled an impending storm. As the British anarchist Fielden uttered the words, "In conclusion . . .," 180 Chicago police materialized under the ominous skies and ordered the area cleared. From the podium, Fielden insisted the meeting was peaceful. But as the captain turned to answer, a yellow flash erupted amidst a cluster of blue uniforms. As their fellow officers lay bleeding from the explosion, the police reformed ranks and fired into the retreating crowd, killing at least one.

The public seems to regard the police retaliation as small consolation. Cries of "Hang them first and try them afterward" ring through the streets of Chicago. A police dragnet is combing the offices of suspected anarchists, making arrests by the dozen. Yesterday, the public was regarding the strikers as soldiers in a just war for humane working conditions; today, they are common criminals. *The New York Times* called the bombing a "concerted, deliberately planned, and coolly executed murder." Unionism is in grave danger of becoming synonymous with anarchism.

Feeding off the ills of depression and the indifference of politicians, anarchism has taken solid root in the labor movement over the last two years. It finds fertile ground among laborers who identify themselves increasingly as working people rather than bakers, builders or bricklayers. As the failure of attempts to legislate shorter hours led many to consider violence, anarchists stepped in. The German Cigar Makers' Union, meeting in February 1884, declared, "The only means whereby the emancipation of mankind can be brought about is the open rebellion of the robbed class in all parts of the country against the existing economic and political institutions." Most Americans, however, do not seem to feel robbed enough to join in open class warfare. Labor solidarity is at an all-time high, but a bomb from the hand of one anarchist may have shaken the movement's foundation of public support (→ Aug. 20).

The bomb explodes amid a crowd of officers trying to police the labor rally.

Stragglers at the edge of the retreating crowd are felled by police bullets.

Atlanta druggist concocts Coca-Cola tonic

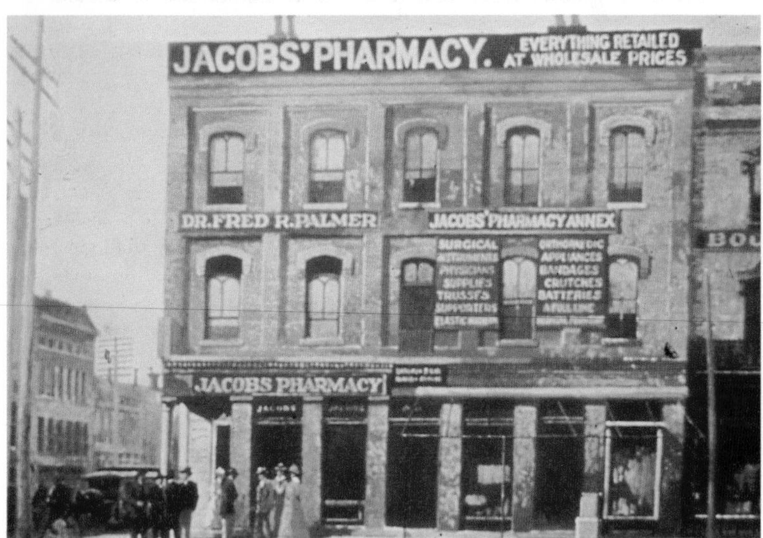

Jacob's Pharmacy at the corner of Marietta and Peachtree Streets in Atlanta, Georgia, is the site where a new drink called Coca-Cola is being dispensed.

Atlanta, Georgia, May

Sufferers of all kinds are finding consolation in a new coca-extract brew. Its inventor, John Styth Pemberton, calls it Coca-Cola. Billed as "the intellectual beverage and temperance drink," Coca-Cola is said to cure dyspepsia (upset stomach) and headaches. Pemberton claims it lifts the spirits as well.

Last year, the Atlanta pharmacist founded the Pemberton Chemical Company and registered a trademark for French Wine of Coca, an "Ideal Nerve Tonic and Stimulant." This year, to attract thirsty teetotalers, he took out the alcohol and added caffeine-rich kola nut extract. Dr. Joseph Jacob's Pharmacy sells only about 13 glasses a day, but Coca-Cola competes with products like Imperial Inca Cola, Coca-Coffee and Cocafeine. The original coca drink, Vin Mariani, has won prizes from committees all over Europe, one of which called it a "wine for athletes."

Experts say cocaine can cure everything from head colds to "the mental depression that accompanies hysteria in the female" to lack of energy. Pemberton, whose energy never seems to flag, has also invented Globe of Flower Cough Syrup, Indian Queen hair dye and Triplex Liver Pills (→May 1, 1889).

President weds ex-partner's daughter, 24

The happy First Couple.

Washington, D.C., June 3

Romantic history was made today as President Grover Cleveland became the first President to be married in the White House. The bride is 24-year-old Frances Folsom, who is 25 years the President's junior. The new Mrs. Cleveland is the daughter of the President's former law partner and fellow poker player, Oscar Folsom. Since Folsom died 11 years ago, Cleveland had served as the guardian for his friend's daughter. This is not the first time that President Cleveland's romantic activity has aroused interest. During the presidential election campaign, Cleveland did not deny that he was the father of an illegitimate child.

Corporations get rights of individual

Washington, D.C., May 10

A corporation must be considered a person with the protection of the 14th Amendment, according to today's landmark Supreme Court decision. In Santa Clara County v. Southern Pacific Railroad Company, the court stated in its majority opinion that no corporation can be denied profits or other rights without application of the due process clause. Some observers say the ruling gives companies citizenship without the ethical duties imposed on persons. It is another indication of the court's recent swing to judicial conservatism. The railroads hope it will lead to a reversal on state regulation of rates.

Law grants unions right to incorporate

Washington, D.C., June 29

Labor unions scored a major victory today as Congress voted to approve the incorporation of trade unions. Political pundits believe the new legislation demonstrates Congress's growing concern for the nation's industrial workers in the wake of last month's national strike and anarchist bombing in Chicago's Haymarket Square. Other observers say the new law is a way to compensate for the Supreme Court ruling last month that gives 14th Amendment protection to corporations. Labor leaders seem to care little about the act's motivation; they are happy to have gained some leverage with management.

Geronimo and Apaches surrender to army

Arizona, Sept. 4

After a decade of terrorizing and killing in an effort to discourage settlers in New Mexico and Arizona, the Apache leader Geronimo surrendered to General Nelson A. Miles today. The historic capitulation took place at Skeleton Canyon, which is about 65 miles southeast of Fort Bowie. General Miles's terms of surrender specified that Geronimo and his tribe are to be removed to Florida, there to be detained until final disposition has been determined by the President.

Geronimo was the scourge of the Southwest for more than 15 years. One of his warriors recently stated that of all the Apache leaders, Geronimo is "the most intelligent and resouceful as well as the most vigorous and farsighted. In times of danger, he is a man to be relied on." At the same time, Mexican peasants viewed the fierce Indian leader as a devil sent by God to punish them for their earthly sins. Most white Americans regard him as the personification and symbol of what they have come to regard as the primitive brutality of Apache barbarism.

Geronimo "surrendered" two years ago, but he promptly went back on the warpath. The army believes that by containing him, it will assure peace for Arizona.

Geronimo (first row, fourth from left) and other captive Apache warriors.

Eight anarchists guilty in bombing

Chicago, Aug. 20

After a trial heavily influenced by public rage, eight anarchists were convicted today of the bombing murder of seven policemen in Haymarket Square. Seven of them, including the three speakers at the May rally, are condemned to die. The prosecution never proved who threw the bomb. But Judge Joseph Gary told the jury that incitement "to sedition, tumult and riot" satisfies the conditions for guilt. The bombing shattered a May general strike. Workers settled for compromise reductions in hours, many of which have been rolled back. Union membership has hit one million for the first time. But employers are determined to fight. Lockouts, blacklists and iron-clad contracts are now the norm (→ Nov. 11, 1887).

Gompers will head merged labor body

Columbus, Ohio, Dec. 8

The nation's labor movement was strengthened today with creation of the American Federation of Labor out of the Federation of Trades and Labor Unions. Samuel Gompers, a leader of the Cigarmakers' International, and Adolph Strasser, the president of that union, organized the A.F.L. at a convention of local unions. Gompers will lead the new federation.

With the Knights of Labor's reputation tarnished, the A.F.L. may supplant it as the dominant power in American labor. The Knights shied away from strikes and boycotts, and became deeply involved in political ideology. The new group will adopt no political goals. Gompers told members, "Our labor movement has no system to crush." He also said the federation will use the strike as a weapon to improve working conditions nationally.

Another major difference between the A.F.L. and the Knights is the former's support of the creation of new local unions. Its constitution states: "We therefore declare ourselves in favor of the formation of a thorough federation, embracing every trade and labor organization in America."

Gigantic Statue of Liberty dedicated

New York City, Oct. 28

From 305 feet above the ground, sculptor Auguste Bartholdi gazed out upon New York harbor. Hundreds of vessels scudded about, their passengers eagerly awaiting the unveiling of Bartholdi's statue, *Liberty Enlightening the World,* a gift from France to the United States. Within the base of the figure's crown, Bartholdi was waiting for a signal to pull a cord that would show the world his creation. He was supposed to get the signal from a boy beside the statue's pedestal, but the wind and the distance drowned out all sound. In fact, he heard not a word of the orations of the dignitaries assembled on Bedloe's Island.

Suddenly, a ship drew near shore. All its passengers were women, 200 members of the New York Suffrage Association. They were watched by the almost all-male gathering on the island – the only females were Bartholdi's wife and the 8-year-old daughter of a French official. This is not unusual, since women are often excluded from public events. From the boat, a woman's voice echoed over the water: "We praise the embodiment of liberty as a woman. But is it not despicable that if liberty had life, she could vote neither in the United States nor in France?"

Suddenly a cannon was fired. Bartholdi took it as the long-awaited signal and released the cord. Liberty, at last, was unveiled.

As early as 1865, Bartholdi considered creating Lady Liberty. He and other Frenchmen thought the work could serve as an honor to America and a promise to France, which critics say only briefly enjoyed the "liberty, equality and fraternity" extolled during its 1789 revolution. In 1871, Bartholdi, then an obscure sculptor, visited America to see for himself whether freedom was a reality here. As his ship pulled into New York Bay, he saw Bedloe's Island and decided his statue would be built there. He toured the nation, admiring democracy at work but meeting no benefactors willing to finance his dream. Returning home, he learned that the Franco-American Union, a group of moderately republican businessmen, wanted to help. Eventually French people gave $450,000, including thousands of centimes donated by schoolchildren.

Bartholdi went to his Paris studio, where he started on the statue's arm and torch in hopes of having the lady raise her lamp at the start of the American bicentennial celebration in Philadelphia in 1876. The statue missed the opening, but the arm and torch arrived in time to become a major attraction.

Meanwhile, Bartholdi needed an engineer to design his statue's "skeleton"; though its copper skin was quite thin, it was clear Lady Liberty would eventually weigh tons. The artist took on railroad bridge designer Gustave Eiffel to build an iron framework. Eiffel arranged the framework so it could be easily taken apart to ship across the ocean.

As the statue neared completion in France, funds for its pedestal ran out. Publisher Joseph Pulitzer, himself a Hungarian immigrant, ran editorials in *The World* calling for help. The poor and middle class answered, and the $1 and $2 donations mounted. In all, Americans gave $350,000 for the pedestal.

Among those who helped were New York artists who organized an exhibition in 1883 and auctioned manuscripts by Brett Harte, Mark Twain and other writers. A poet named Emma Lazarus was asked to contribute a sonnet. She replied that she "could not write to order." But after seeing some Jewish immigrants who had fled a Russian pogrom, she wrote a poem titled *The New Colossus.* In the final lines, Liberty says: "Give me your tired, your poor, your huddled masses yearning to breathe free . . . I lift my lamp beside the golden door!"

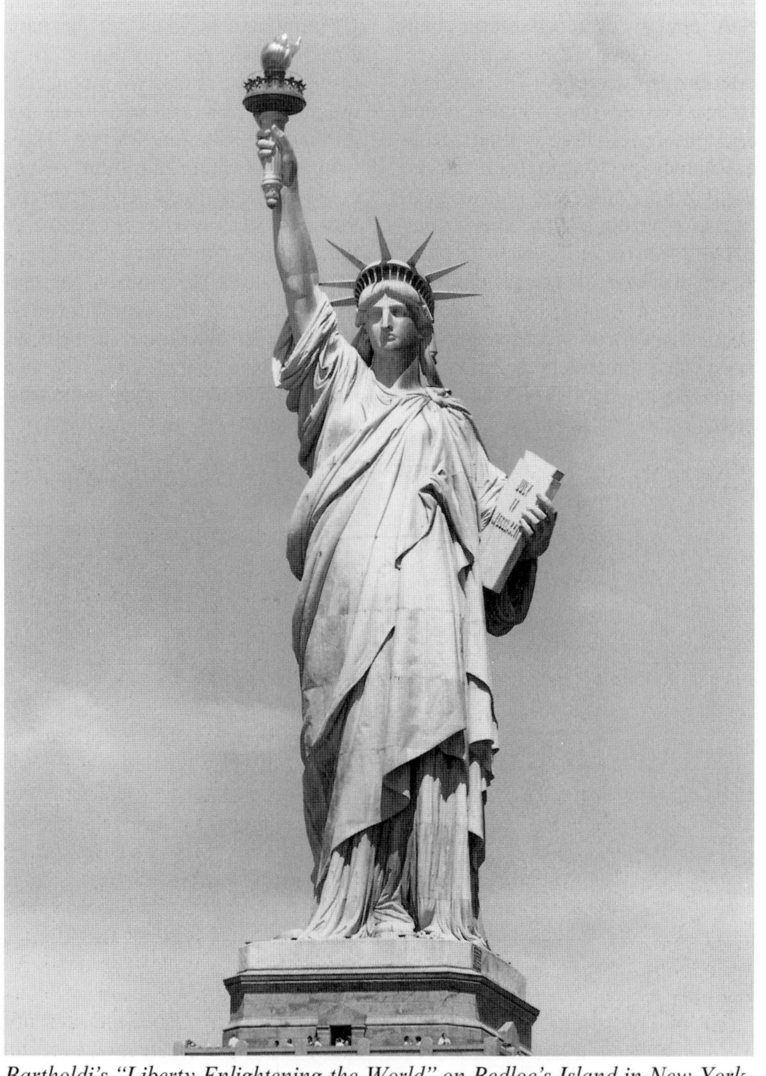

Bartholdi's "Liberty Enlightening the World" on Bedloe's Island in New York. ▷

U.S. Navy launches modernization plan

Washington, D.C., Aug. 3

The United States Navy, which only three years ago ranked 12th in the world and consisted for the most part of pre-Civil War wooden ships, is to be further strengthened by the construction of two ironclads. These constitute the second major addition to the fleet in three years and are part of Navy Secretary William C. Whitney's drive to upgrade the service. Two years ago, Whitney's predecessor, W.E. Chandler, established the Naval War College at Newport, Rhode Island, under Commodore Stephen B. Luce to train officers for higher command.

Court limits states' regulatory powers

Washington, D.C., Oct. 25

The Supreme Court today handed the railroads a sweet victory and the states a bitter defeat in Wabash, St. Louis and Pacific Railroad Company v. Illinois. It struck down its previous Granger rulings and said a state has no right to regulate interstate commerce even within its own borders. The earlier ruling, issued at the urging of the Grange farm group, gave the states regulatory rights and, in farm states, protection to farmers. Now, rail barons can set rates without interference. Rates do require national control, the court said. Congressional action is likely.

U.S. seizes ships of Canadian sealers

Washington, D.C., December

Government sources revealed today that the United States Navy had seized three Canadian seal-fishing ships earlier this year. The United States government is greatly disturbed about the great extent of seal hunting on the high seas, and believes that Canadian fisherman are primarily responsible. Therefore, it is staging a show of force to put an end to the illegal hunting. Marine biologists have warned that if the seal hunting continues at its current level, there will be no seals left by the end of this century.

U.S. meets British at polo, and loses

Newport, Rhode Island

American polo leaders, confident of their indoor game, decided to see whether they could match the British outdoors. They couldn't. The Americans invited a championship English squad this summer and were soundly beaten, 10-4 and 14-2, in this first American-British series. The British apologized for their "poor" showing in the first match, blaming their rocky Atlantic crossing. The Britons took home the International Challenge Cup, and the Americans went back to sharpening their outdoor play in preparation for a return engagement.

First ready-to-use bandage produced

New Brunswick, New Jersey

A newly developed sterile bandage may lead to a marked reduction in infections. The bandage is ready-made, individually sealed and antiseptic. Three brothers, Robert, James, and Mead Johnson, are going to manufacture the surgical dressing through their new company, Johnson & Johnson. Robert began working on the product last year after he heard the British surgeon Sir Joseph Lister speaking about cases in which the infections were the result of air-borne germs in the operating rooms.

Electrolysis is used to make aluminum

Pittsburgh, Penn., Feb. 23

Aluminum is likely to become cheaper and more available as a result of a recent discovery concerning the material. It was made by 22-year-old Charles Martin Hall, who found that aluminum oxide could be dissolved and reduced through electrolysis to produce aluminum. For consumers, that could be good news. Previously, the element could be isolated only through a more expensive process using sodium. Until now, the metal has sold for around $17 per pound, limiting its use to jewelry and novelties.

Steve Brodie leaps off Brooklyn Bridge

New York City, July 23

After boasting he could jump 140 feet off the Brooklyn Bridge, Steve Brodie finally did it. Or did he? Several friends say they witnessed the incident, but no one else was told when it would happen or saw it. Skeptics, including those who bet against the newsboy and former bootblack, believe a dummy was dropped from the bridge and that Brodie swam out from shore in time to be picked up by a passing barge. Regardless, he won't be jumping or pretending to jump for awhile: He was arrested for the leap.

Americans in love with magnitude

New York City, Nov. 19

Big things are for men who occupy big countries and big offices. Chester Arthur, who died yesterday, once mused after he left the White House, "there doesn't seem anything else for an ex-president to do but go into the country and raise big pumpkins." Says Teddy Roosevelt, whose only office is his North Dakota ranch after losing a mayoral bid in New York City, "Like all Americans, I like big things: big prairies, big forests and mountains, big wheatfields, railroads . . . and everything else."

Thomas Nast takes time out from political satire to depict a character loved by all. The Bavaria-born cartoonist has left his job at "Harper's Weekly," where he made a name for himself by firmly backing the Union cause during the war and later attacking the corruption of Tammany Hall's "Boss" Tweed.

1887

Cleveland

Washington, D.C., March 2. Hatch Act passed by Congress, providing for agricultural research centers to help reverse soil erosion and overuse.

Washington, D.C., March 3. Under pressure from President Cleveland, Congress repeals Tenure of Office Act, restoring chief executive's right to dismiss federal appointees.

Tacoma, Washington, March 4. Residents responsible for expulsion of Chinese in 1855 vindicated by grand jury.

Chicago, May 3. American Cattle Trust formed, in effort to monopolize cattle market.

Washington, D.C., June 15. Republican politicians and Union army veterans press President Cleveland into rescinding order to return all captured Confederate flags to South.

Honolulu, July 7. Revolution threatened after King Kalakaua is identified as ringleader in opium bribery case (→July 30, 1889).

Chatsworth, Illinois, Aug. 10. Burning bridge collapses, killing about 100 people on passenger train.

Santa Barbara, California, Aug. 19. First train enters city.

United States, Sept. 30. Volunteer beats England's Thistle to keep America's Cup.

Arkansas. Discovery of bauxite near Little Rock helps rejuvenate state's economy.

Florida. State enacts railroad segregation law based on Tennessee's 1881 law, with added proviso forbidding whites from annoying or insulting Negroes in Negro cars.

Utah. Under Edmunds-Tucker Act, federal government begins confiscating property belonging to polygamists.

United States. Photographer Eadweard Muybridge publishes *Animal Locomotion*; 781 groups of sequential frames.

Chicago. *Abraham Lincoln* statue by Saint-Gaudens completed.

San Francisco. William Randolph Hearst takes control of *San Francisco Examiner.*

New York City. Theodore Roosevelt publishes first volume of *The Winning of the West.*

American bicyclists race and banquet

Bicycles are available from the manufacturer, Colonel Albert Pope.

St. Louis, Missouri, May 20

Bicycle enthusiasts are elevating their vehicles of basic transportation to vehicles of pleasure and competition. The American Wheelmen, in their eighth annual convention here, pointed up the social aspects of cycling with races and a banquet. The sport was given a boost nine years ago by Colonel Albert Pope, a retired Union officer from Boston, who found that manufacturing sewing machines was no match for turning out bikes. So he began to build his own and found he could hardly keep up with the demand.

Hawaii grants U.S. use of Pearl Harbor

Honolulu, Jan. 20

A renewal of the Reciprocity Treaty between the Hawaiian Kingdom and the United States contains an amendment granting America exclusive rights to enter and maintain a coaling station at Pearl Harbor, according to word received today from Washington. King Lunalilo's government offered the United States Pearl Harbor during his short reign (1873-74), but few Americans were interested. Many Hawaiians opposed the idea. With little support, the proposal died. Observers here believe that the Americans will use the base to coal merchant ships.

Congress votes for rail rate regulation

Washington, D.C., Apr. 5

Five men met today to begin federal regulation of the railroads. Appointed by President Cleveland, their task is to interpret and apply the vague wording of the Interstate Commerce Act, signed on February 4. The bill calls for "just and equal" rates and limits "pooling," secret pacts by which railroads keep rates high. It also bans rebates given to large customers to the detriment of small merchants.

The most striking thing about the bill is its widespread support. The Senate passed it in January by a margin of 36 to 12, the House by 219 to 41. The initial impetus for regulation came from small merchants and farmers, who find that exorbitant freight and storage rates often make it cheaper to burn grain for fuel than pay to store it and ship it east. But the railroads have problems of their own. In five years, 27,000 new miles of track have been laid. Competing lines often build hundreds of miles of parallel track simply to drive each other out of the market. When one gives in, its line rusts. And despite pooling, freight rates have fallen 20 percent since 1882. It is no surprise then that John P. Green of the Pennsylvania Railroad told Congress his colleagues "would be very glad to come under the direct supervision and operation of the national government."

The commission seems less than threatening to the railroads. Its chairman, Thomas Cooley, is a theorist on the dangers of government action in the economy and was voted off the Michigan Supreme Court because of his ties to railroad interests. Already, farm spokesmen are calling the legislation a conservative sop to the railroads.

Indian lands made subject to private use

Washington, D.C., Feb. 8

President Cleveland today signed the Dawes Severalty Act, which permits the President to supersede Indian governments and to convert traditional, communally owned tribal lands to a private ownership system. More specifically, each Indian family head will receive 160 acres, with lesser amounts going to bachelors, women and children. In addition, under this law, each Indian who accepts a land grant will be given full United States citizenship. The law is a triumph for two rather divergent groups. One is made up of settlers who have hungered for the lands that they will now be able to obtain from the Indians in one way or another. The other is composed primarily of humanitarian groups in the East who would like the Indian tribes to have their own land, thus eventually assimilating them into a peaceful, biracial farming community.

Zuni village in New Mexico. The Dawes Act seeks to alter land ownership in order to subvert tribal authority and put the federal government in its place. ▷

Haymarket anarchists die by the noose

Chicago, Nov. 11

"Let me speak . . . let the voice of the people be heard!" shouted Albert Parsons, but the gallows door was sprung, dropping him to his death. August Spies was luckier. "There will come a time," he uttered from beneath his white hood, "when our silence will be more powerful than the voices you strangle today." Despite pleas for clemency, three fellow anarchists met the executioner today with Spies and Parsons. Two others had their sentences commuted to life. Another, Louis Lingg, cheated the hangman by exploding a dynamite cap in his mouth. Thus ends 18 months of furor over Haymarket, the bombing-murder of seven Chicago policemen that has excited public sentiment perhaps more than any event since the Civil War.

The loud cries for revenge have thrown organized labor into disarray. As reported by journalist John Swinton, the bombing is "a godsend to the enemies of the labor movement." Knights of Labor chief Terence Powderly rushed to denounce "the band of cowardly murderers, cutthroats and robbers." Ironically, the task of defending the radicals fell to Samuel Gompers and his conservative American Federation of Labor. Calling the executions "judicial murder," Gompers drew the support of many disillusioned Knights. But the bomb's biggest casualties are the eight-hour day, working conditions, wages and the image of labor in the public eye.

Strike by 10,000 Negroes ended; 20 slain

Thibodaux, Louisiana, Nov. 23

At least 20 Negro workers were killed by members of a sheriff's posse and state militiamen today as more violence erupted in the sugar cane workers strike. There are reports that the death toll may go as high as 30. The posse and militiamen fired into a mob in the Negro settlement here after two white men were shot early this morning. The two whites, who had been posted as guards, were shot by Negroes hiding in a cornfield. Cane field workers, organized by the Knights of Labor, have been striking for higher wages – $1.25 per day with all payments in cash. Some payments now are made in scrip that can be used only at plantation stores. The workers are being paid 65 cents a day on most plantations and are furnishe cabins or rooms as lodging.

Today's shooting may have ended the strike, which has involve some 10,000 workers on plantation in the Teche country of South Louisiana. Yesterday, two union men the Cox brothers, were taken fron jail and killed by whites. The brothers had been charged with makin incendiary speeches.

Governor S. D. McEnery sent the militia after the strike began Nov 1. In an earlier incident at Pattersonville, four Negroes arrested by a sheriff's posse were killed, reportedly when they tried to escape

A spokesman for the Knights o Labor says the union will plac the whole matter before Congres at its coming session.

Trusts proliferate, restricting supplies, raising prices and forming monopolies

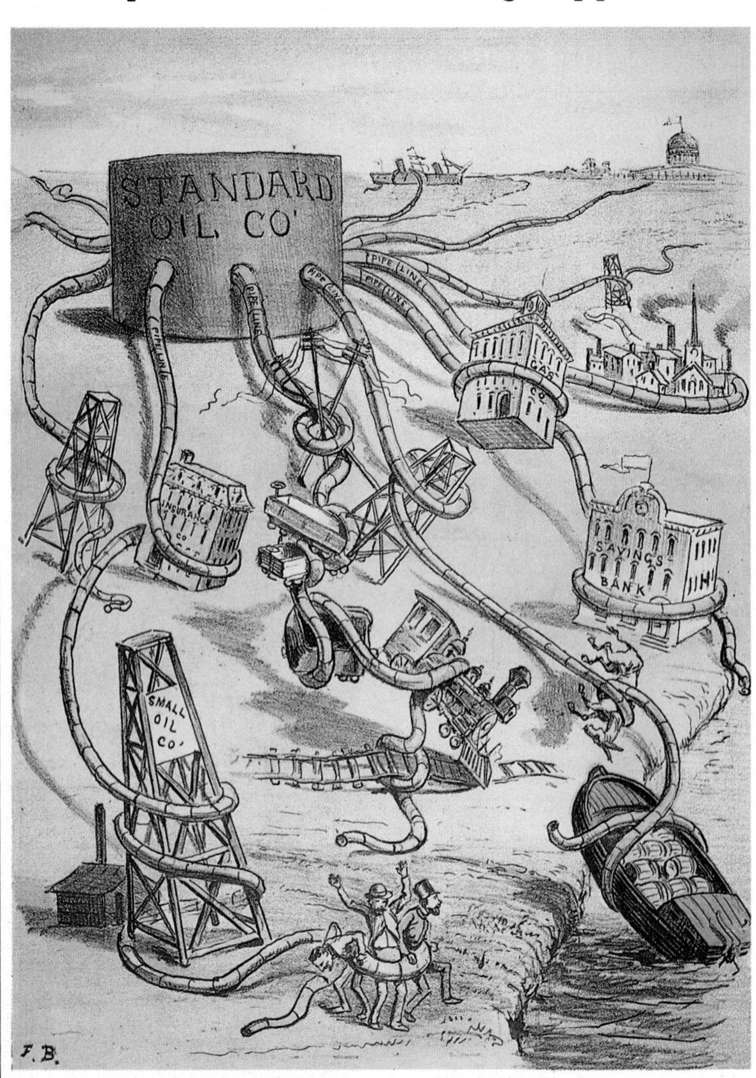

The monster monopoly, Rockefeller's Standard Oil, spreads its tentacles.

United States

"Like all Americans, I like big things," says Teddy Roosevelt. Unlike Founding Father Thomas Jefferson, who liked the small yeoman farmer, businessmen today agree with Roosevelt. As early as 1873, a congressional inquiry warned "the country is fast becoming filled with gigantic corporations wielding and controlling immense aggregations of money and thereby commanding great influence and power."

Congress was prophetic. Five years ago, John D. Rockefeller brought 39 oil firms under the control of nine men holding all the stock "in trust." Since then, the makers and distributers of cotton oil (1884), linseed oil (1885), sugar, whiskey and cattle (1887) have followed in Standard's footsteps.

Industrialists see in the trust a way to control the rabid competition that undercuts prices and destabilizes the business environment. For the titans of industry, business has been war. Said Daniel Drew, "Sphinx of the Stock Market," about Jay Gould, "Wizard of Wall Street," "His touch is death." But as corporations extend tentacles into all aspects of their business, control replaces competition. Steel firms acquire ore fields and shipping lines, assuring a steady, cheap supply to their finishing plants. The sugar trust, controlling 95 percent of the country's refineries, sets prices at will.

The new barons are often portrayed as heroes. Like Andrew Carnegie, who grew from a poor Scottish immigrant into a powerful steel magnate, many are rags-to-riches stories. And, as Abraham Lincoln said, "That some would be rich shows that others may become rich." But some believe the new self-made man gets rich on ruthlessness, not hard work. To this, Rockefeller responds in typical Darwinian language: "The growth of a large corporation is merely a survival of the fittest, the working out of a law of nature and a law of God." "Godliness," adds Episcopal Bishop William Lawrence, "is in league with riches."

The trusts' biggest enemies are state courts. But, if tried in New York, a firm simply moves to a tolerant climate in New Jersey. Meanwhile, the Senate defeats most bills to curb business, drawing charges it is beholden to "the interests." In the end, says Standard Oil lawyer and inventor of the trust, Samuel Dodd, "You might as well endeavor to stay the formation of the clouds, the falling of the rain, or the flowing of the streams."

ears wins U.S. tennis title 7 times in row

ennis, which has been spreading fast, came to the U.S. via Bermuda in 1874.

ewport, Rhode Island, September
Dick Sears, the undisputed king men's tennis, has extended his ign at the U.S. National Champi-nships by dispatching Henry Slo-ım, 6-1, 6-3, 6-2. Since his first title 1881, Sears dropped only three ts on the grass en route to seven raight singles crowns. In doubles, lost only the first year to Clar-ıce Clark and Fred Taylor, who nfounded Sears and his partner, r. James Dwight, by playing one net and one in the backcourt.

The game has come far since 875, the year Dwight and Dick's lder brother, Fred, played their rst game of "sphairistike," as the Greeks called the game, in a summer rain. Five years later, at the first interclub match, Staten Island-ers and Philadelphians argued over ball size and net height. The next year, spectators brought their own chairs to Newport's first national championships. The competitors, in knickerbockers, ties and striped blazers, played quite passively. Not till 1882 did they begin imitating Sears by rushing the net at every opportunity. But with no rest be-tween games, the strategy can be tir-ing. And Sears, always a step ahead, uses a looping shot he calls the lob, which drives net rushers back as quickly as they have advanced.

With the National League 11 years old, baseball is thriving. Batters get four strikes this year and will be allowed to take first base when hit by a pitch. In New Orleans, manager Abner Powell now offers "Ladies Day" to fans.

Iron ore discovered in Mesabi Range

Minnesota
Cassius, Alfred, Napoleon, Leo-nida and Louis Merritt may soon be extremely rich because brother Cassius fell flat on his face in the woods. While inspecting the tree-tops in the Mesabi Range for the family's lumber company, Cassius literally stumbled upon a tremen-dous chunk of iron ore on the forest bed. The area had previously been investigated by prospectors because the range lies amid so many iron deposits and mines. Although iron had never been found in the range itself, William Burt discovered some in the vicinity accidentally while on a government survey in 1844 when his compass deviated.

New men's clothiers

Chicago
The garment industry, which is now the city's fourth largest, has added yet another company. Hart, Schaffner and Marx will offer men's clothing for the well-to-do. The Hart stands for founders Harry and Max Hart. No gentleman today would be caught dead without a proper suit of clothes and such ac-cessories as fancy shirts, a silk hat, detachable collar and cuffs, and perhaps a pocketwatch and a cane. Modern clothiers aim to provide all of these and more.

Bertillon System

Boston
Measure the length of your head, feet and middle fingers, classify these as "small," "medium" and "large," then determine the length, breadth, height and span of your ear, the height of your bust and your eye color, subdividing the for-mer classifications by the latter. What you have got is a new method of criminal identification, imported from France courtesy of its invent-or, Alphonse Bertillon of the Paris police. The problem is getting a murderer to leave measurements at the scene of the crime. A more prac-tical means of identifying a scoun-drel has been developed by a British civil servant in India. It involves taking prints of one's fingertips.

Annie Oakley, 27, in Wild West Show

Annie Oakley, "Little Sure Shot."

London, June 20
"What a wonderful little girl!" pronounced Queen Victoria today as she accepted a handshake from Annie Oakley. The 27-year-old Miss Oakley is indeed little (just short of five feet) and wonderful. Her sharpshooting has made her the star attraction of Buffalo Bill's Wild West Show and the darling of America. At 30 paces, they say, "Little Sure Shot" can slice a play-ing card sideways. With a single bullet, she can shoot a cigarette out of a man's lips. And one day in a contest, she fired at 5,000 targets in nine hours, hitting 4,772 of them. In her early teens, Miss Oakley, born Phoebe Anne Oakley Mozee in Darke County, Ohio, shot rab-bits and quail to keep her fam-ily from starving. At 17, she met Frank Butler, a famous marksman who bet she could not outshoot him. When she did, he married her.

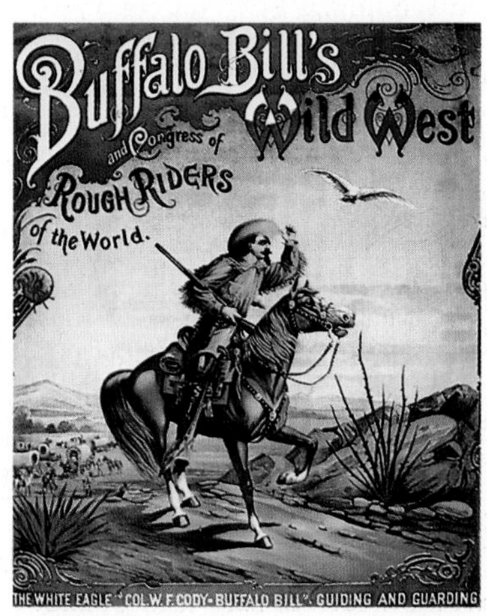

1888

Cleveland

Mount Vernon, Illinois, Feb. 19. Adding to rash of natural disasters plaguing Midwest, cyclone hits Mount Vernon, killing some 35 people.

Louisville, Kentucky, February. Secret ballot is adopted for first time in municipal election; it is referred to as "Kangaroo voting," after Australian voting system.

London, Apr. 24. Anglo-American Oil Company established, first foreign affiliate of Standard Oil.

Washington State, May 3. Mount Rainier tunnel completed as two work teams meet in middle of mountain.

Des Moines, Iowa, May 15. Equal Rights Party nominates Belva Ann Lockwood, first woman to argue case before Supreme Court, for president.

Oregon, July 10. Union Pacific Railroad opens first steel bridge on Pacific Coast to public.

Washington, D.C., July 13. Backed by Congress, Secretary of State Thomas F. Bayard invites Latin American nations to conference scheduled in Washington next year (→ Oct. 2, 1889).

Washington, D.C., Oct. 1. Arbitration commission set up to mediate disputes between railroad workers and management.

New York City, Oct. 21. Letter from British Ambassador Lord Sackville-West urging Americans to vote for President Cleveland galvanizes Irish vote against Cleveland (→ Nov. 6).

Pittsburgh, Nov. 25. First commercial aluminum made.

Washington, D.C. Negro-owned banks founded here and in Richmond, Virginia.

Washington State. Whooping cough, measles kill Indian children near Puget Sound.

Washington, D.C. John Philip Sousa, conducter of Marine Corps Band, composes *Semper Fidelis*.

United States. William Harnett paints study of musical instruments, *My Gems*.

New York City. Jacob Riis takes photograph of slum area called *Bandit's Roost*.

New York City. Theodore Roosevelt publishes *Ranch Life and the Hunting Trail.*

Worst blizzard in memory hits natio

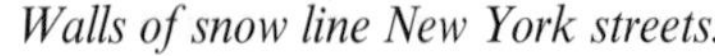

Walls of snow line New York streets.

Snowbound downtown Manhattan.

New Yorkers dig out following the worst snowstorm they can remember.

New England, March 14

By the calendar, spring is a wee away. But if there are any flower preparing to bloom, they will hav to do it under 50 inches of snow The worst blizzard in memory grip America as far south as Chesapeak Bay and as far north as Maine. Som 400 people have died since the storn began March 11. And although th Midwest is safe for now, earlier i was buffeted by high winds anc extreme cold. Hundreds of death were reported in Nebraska, th Dakotas, Minnesota, Montana an Wyoming. Future generations jus may call 1888 "The Year of th Great Blizzard."

Throughout New England, train have frozen to their tracks. Tele graphs lines have fallen, leavin small towns desperately isolated. I New Hampshire, snow drifts ar reported as high as 15 feet. Nev York City, where the blizzard wa its most vicious, reports $25 mil lion in property damage and 20 people dead. Most of the death have been attributed to exposure pneumonia and influenza. Mos people have had to stay indoors homeless men are sleeping on th floor of the 17th Precinct statio house and in other police faci ities. Streetcars are stalled on thei tracks. Telephone wires are dowr and the politicians now are prom ising that they will be routed ur derground once the snow is gone This may happen sooner than the think; tonight the sky seems clear a sign that New Englanders hav prayed for as much as Noah praye for a rainbow.

A yank in Louisiana

Baton Rouge, Louisiana, October

A medicine man in town is using a new come-on to sell his "cure-all" tonic. He pulls teeth free as a way of getting people to buy his extract, called Wild West Bitters. And "Dr." Frank Wallace not only pulls teeth, he also presents a vaudeville show that includes comedians and banjo players. Local dentists at first complained about Wallace's tooth-pulling. He has pacified them, however, by telling them that when he pulls teeth it gives the dentists the chance to replace them.

Care for a straw?

Washington, D.C., Jan. 3

Although Americans have long enjoyed sipping their summer lemonade through hollow stalks of rye, a new item should make the sipping even more enjoyable and sanitary. Marvin Chester Stone of Washington was issued a patent today for the manufacture of drinking straws that are made from manila paper coated with paraffin wax. Cheap enough to be disposed of after just one use, the new straws should be popular at ice cream parlors and wherever cool drinks are sold.

Watch your step!

New York City, Feb. 22

They walked softly and carrie big sticks. The sticks were calle golf clubs and the soft walking wa on a cow pasture in suburban Yonk ers. These Yonkers people, neigh bors of Scottish-born John Reid were learning how to play the gam of golf, invented in Scotland. Th sport was tried in Charleston, Sout Carolina, in the late 1700s and i some other American cities as we as in Canada, but the three-hol course in Yonkers seems to hav been the first where it took hold.

larrison wins despite loss in popular vote

'ictors: Thanks to Republican forefather and a friendly Electoral College.

/ashington, D.C., Nov. 6

Benjamin Harrison, grandson of former President, won his own key) the White House today by defeat-ıg the current chief of state, Grover 'leveland. Harrison lost to Cleve-.nd in the popular vote, 5,444,000) 5,540,000, in an eight-man race. lowever, he won 233 of the elector-l votes, far more than needed for lection. Cleveland was next with 68 electoral votes. Levi Morton of Jew York won the vice presidency.

The Harrison victory was viewed s something of a surprise, for just ıst year he lost his bid for re-.ection to the Senate. He took that efeat with good humor, remarking ı his presidential bid this year: "I m a dead statesman, but I am a living and rejuvenated Republican."

Harrison's grandfather, William Henry Harrison, was the ninth President, and the hero of the Battle of Tippecanoe. He died in 1841, a month after having taken office. The President-elect is a native of Ohio, but he moved to Indiana.

To a great extent, the campaign centered on the tariff question, with President Cleveland, a Democrat completing his first term in office, urging that the nation's tariffs be lowered, arguing that protectionism results in higher prices. Harrison, on the other hand, ran on a platform that advocated higher tariffs, a reflection of the heavy influence industrialists now have on the Republican Party (→ March 4, 1889).

Vriter sniffs Bacon ɔehind the Bard

Hamlet a hoax? Othello an im-ostor? Well, not really, but if the ɔrmer Minnesota congressman Ig-atius Donnelly is to be believed, ıe identity of their creator is open) question. In his newly published *'he Great Cryptogram*, Donnelly ɔins those who argue that Shake-peare, revered as perhaps the great-st writer ever, was no more than a ıodestly talented actor. The real ge-ius behind Hamlet, Othello and ıe others, says Donnelly in his ,000-page work, was Shakespeare's ɔntemporary, Francis Bacon.

Geographic Society planning magazine

Washington, D.C., Jan. 13

The Cosmos Club was the site of a meeting today of 33 distinguished men who have established "a society for the increase and diffusion of geographic knowledge." Known as the National Geographic Society, the fledgling organization hopes to sponsor expeditions and research projects, and to publish the *National Geographic Magazine*, an organ that will disseminate geographical information of popular interest. Graham Greene Hubbard has been named the society's first president.

"You push the button, we do the rest"

Rochester, New York

A new camera that makes photography simpler than ever before is being marketed by George Eastman. Weighing about two pounds, the camera uses film invented by Eastman. The owner snaps the pictures and sends the camera to Rochester, receiving the developed pictures and a newly loaded camera. "You push the button, we do the rest," is Eastman's triumphant slogan. He calls the camera a Kodak, a word he invented himself on the theory that the letter K is a lucky one. Eastman, who has dedicated his life to making photography an American habit, has now started work on an even more advanced system, with film that can be sent away for development, allowing the owner to take even more snapshots.

George Eastman, as photographed by Gaspard-Felix Tournachon, while on a tour of Europe.

"Looking Backward" on things to come

Boston

Rip Van Winkle dozed for 20 years and woke up to find things changed. But nodding off for 113 years is another story – the story, in fact, told by Edward Bellamy in *Looking Backward: 2000-1887*, which he terms a "fairy tale of social felicity." It takes place in Boston, though few of the city's current inhabitants will recognize the glittering metropolis Bellamy describes. Music is piped into the narrator's bedroom, and rain never reaches the pavement. The American Athens is not all that wears a new look. Something called "The Great Trust" keeps the national economy smoothly afloat, and common citizens attain a rare level of erudition. These advances astound Julian West, Bellamy's time traveler, but what really bowls him over is old-fashioned love. It appears in the person of Edith Leete, who happens to be related to the woman West had planned to marry back in 1887. The author, 38, has written four previous novels, none likely to be remembered in the year 2000. Not everyone this year is looking to the future: James Russell Lowell is offering collected gems from yesteryear in *Political Essays*.

"The Open Air Breakfast" (c.1888) by William Merritt Chase.

1889

Harrison

Oregon, Jan. 14. Anti-noise ordinance in Roseburg bans use of cowbells at night.

Chicago, Jan. 23. Provident Hospital incorporated, establishing first training school for Negro nurses.

Washington, D.C., Feb. 9. Department of Agriculture elevated to Cabinet status with Norman Colman as its first Secretary.

Washington, D.C., Feb. 20. Congress incorporates Maritime Canal Company of Nicaragua, with intention of building and operating canal across Central American isthmus (→ March 3, 1899).

Washington, D.C., March 4. Benjamin Harrison sworn in as 23rd President of United States, Levi P. Morton as Vice President.

Samoa, March 15. British, German and American warships collect menacingly in Apia harbor in attempt to influence negotiations on fate of Samoa; conflict is avoided as hurricane smashes all but British ship Calliope (→ June 14).

Washington, D.C., Apr. 29. Nationwide celebration commemorates centennial of George Washington's presidential inauguration.

Seattle, Washington, June 6. Fire caused by overturned gluepot levels entire 64 acres of business district.

Salem, Oregon, August. Grange, Farmers' Alliance, Knights of Labor and prohibitionists meet in convention to form progressive Union Party.

Milwaukee, Wisconsin, October. Negro wins judgment against Bijou Theater after it refuses to seat him.

Lynn, Masachusetts, Nov. 26. Some 80 acres in central business district gutted by fire that starts in engine room of wooden shoe factory.

Washington, D.C. Electric lights installed in White House, but President Harrison will not touch switches.

New York City. Jacob Riis's photograph, *Home of an Italian Ragpicker*, focuses attention on plight of immigrants.

DEATH

New Orleans, Dec. 6. Jefferson Davis, former President of the Confederate States of America (*June 3, 1808).

Indian Territory: Wildest land rush

A veritable floodgate is opened as homesteaders make a mad dash to stake their claims in a wild land.

Indian Territory, Apr. 22

What has become the largest, wildest land rush in American history symbolically "exploded" at noon today, when a government official's gunshot signaled the opening of the Indian Territory to settlers.

It is estimated that more than 200,000 land-hungry people along the northern border of Texas and the southern boundary of Kansas stampeded into the territory when the gun sounded. They swarmed across the borders in wagons, hacks and carriages, on bicycles, on horseback and on foot. According to reports received this evening, only 100 settlers have moved into Oklahoma City, while more than 12,000 people arrived in Guthrie. It is estimated that in the past nine hours, every one of the almost two million acres of the Oklahoma District has been claimed and settled.

The land boom was precipitated by an odd collection of forces – railroad executives, real estate people and other so-called "Boomers," along with simple farmers who jus wanted free land – putting pres sure on President Harrison to ope the once-protected territory tha had been home to 75,000 Indian from 22 tribes.

Local law enforcement officia have had a rough time. First the had to keep out the "Sooners," wh tried to sneak in sooner than wa permissible. Now they are har pressed to maintain order in a wil new society that more closely r sembles bedlam than civilization.

Kansas passes law to regulate trusts

Kansas City, March 2

A hotbed of rural rebellion, Kansas today became the first state to pass a law regulating trusts. Beset by drought for two years, people listen with rising interest to the National Farmers' Alliance's attacks on Eastern "money power." Spawned by Wall Street in growing numbers, trusts are combinations of firms ruled by a single directorate. To journalism's comic Mr. Dooley, and to the founts of folk wisdom out here, the trust is "somethin' for an honest, ploddin', uncombined manufacturer to sell out to" (→ May 9).

Jersey opens doors to big business

New Jersey, May 9

Hoping to draw businesses across the Hudson River from the nation's financial capital, New Jersey has passed a law enabling holding companies to obtain charters here. The move will provide big business with a haven from lawsuits in other states. Last year, however, President Cleveland hinted that the federal government may get involved in regulation. "Corporations, which should be carefully restrained creatures of the law and servants of the people," he proclaimed, "are fast becoming the people's masters."

Atlantan gets right to drink called Coke

Atlanta, Georgia, May 1.

Asa Briggs Candler of Atlant has bought the rights to a loc drink, Coca-Cola, derived from th kola nut. The bottled drink was fir made on May 8, 1886, as a syrup t help dyspepsia and headaches b John Styth Pemberton, who the mixed it with carbonated water a Dr. Joseph Jacob's Pharmacy an came up with the "Coke" everyon here began drinking. Pemberton' bookkeeper Frank Robinson inven ed Coca-Cola's name and logotyp which were used in its first adve tisement in today's *Atlanta Journa*

U.S. claims control over Bering Sea

Washington, D.C., March 2

Angered by the depredations of Canadian seal hunters, whose indiscriminate slaughter of female seals in the open waters of the Bering Sea has threatened the herd with extinction, Congress today proclaimed the entire sea to be under United States control. Supporters of the action cite the 1867 treaty with Russia that gave the Pribilof Islands to the United States, along with Alaska. Since these islands are the breeding ground for the migrating herds, it is argued that their ownership confers control of fur-sealing operations in the area. However, this claim to a "closed sea" is almost certain to be challenged by other maritime powers.

Johnstown hit by deluge

After two days of rain, a torrent sweeps away Johnstown and 2,000 lives after a dam broke and a reservoir emptied in just 45 minutes. Fires followed.

Johnstown, Pennsylvania, May 31

In one of the worst catastrophes of American history, Johnstown in south-central Pennsylvania was washed off the map today by a flood of awesome power. The disaster stemmed from the nearby South Fork Reservoir and its dam. Once part of the Pennsylvania canal system, the reservoir had become a private hunting and fishing club. Three miles long and said to be the largest in the country, the reservoir was in the hills several hundred feet higher than the town. The old dirt dam had had problems before. Though rebuilt, its central wall contained no masonry and it had neither discharge pipes nor a spillway. Confronted by the heavy rains of the past two days – which had already begun to flood the region – the strained dam gave way, dumping the waters on the town below.

The flood swept through the valley with the force of a tidal wave, swallowing up and sweeping away everything in its path – factories, houses and bridges. Witnesses tell of countless victims caught up in the swirling tide and drowned, and of hundreds of survivors clutching driftwood or clinging desperately to the roofs of their floating houses. Engineers at the dam had sent a warning, which some residents heeded. But the reservoir emptied in 45 minutes, and most of the people in the town were caught by surprise. Deaths are estimated at about 2,000. Only two roofs can still be seen.

Samoa put under Western protection

Berlin, June 14

Following an episode earlier this year in which American and German warships confronted each other in Apia harbor with guns loaded, the question of who will control the Samoan Islands appears to have been settled peacefully, at least for the time being. A conference held in the German capital and presided over by Prince Otto von Bismarck, has agreed that the United States, Britain and Germany will share in a protectorate of the islands, leaving King Malieota as nominal sovereign. American interest in Samoa dates back to 1872, when Commodore Meade negotiated with High Chief Mauga for a coaling station at Pago Pago (→ Dec. 2, 1899).

Pabst takes over Milwaukee brewery

Milwaukee, Wisconsin, March 18

In a move that could produce one of the largest breweries in the nation, Captain Frederick Pabst has reorganized the Philip Best Company into the Pabst Brewery Company. A former commander of the Great Lakes steamer Comet, the 53-year-old Pabst, who came to this country from Germany 41 years ago, is married to Best's daughter Marie. The newly named company now takes its place alongside other breweries owned by German-Americans such as Joseph Schlitz, Valentin Blatz and Frederick Miller.

Minnesota clinic opened by Mayos

Rochester, Minnesota

A new medical institution has been opened here by two famed physicians, William J. Mayo and Charles H. Mayo. Practicing at St. Mary's Hospital with their father, Dr. William W. Mayo, the brothers have achieved reputations that have spread far beyond this small town. At the new Mayo Clinic, Dr. William Mayo will be the chief administrator and Dr. Charles Mayo will continue his highly regarded work in surgery. Other physicians will join the brothers if the number of patients grows.

Law mandates English language in school

Parochial education: A choice between Americanization and Rome?

Wisconsin, Nov. 30

New legislation mandating the teaching of reading, writing and arithmetic in English to children between 7 and 14 years of age in all schools has been passed in the most recent Wisconsin State legislature session. Germans and Poles across the state usually teach in their native tongue in Catholic parochial schools. The law, which requires at least 12 weeks per year of instruction in English, provides no agencies for enforcement, and those opposed to it claim that the legislation is illegal.

With steel beams, skyscraper limit soars

Pittsburgh, Pennsylvania

The Jones & Laughlin Company has begun production of Bessemer steel I-beams for building construction. Use of the steel beams, as well as the elevator, will allow urban buildings to soar to unprecedented heights. Steel-frame structures such as the Home Life Insurance and the Tacoma Buildings already exist in Chicago. And while there are taller office towers elsewhere in the nation, in principle there is no limit to the height buildings constructed with steel frames can reach (→ 1891).

Steel being forged at Carnegie's Pennsylvania Iron and Steel Works. ▷

Jacob Riis shows America "How the Other Half Lives" in squalor

For one New York junkman, the American dream remains a distant hope.

The squalor and filth of the city's slums are harming even the most innocent.

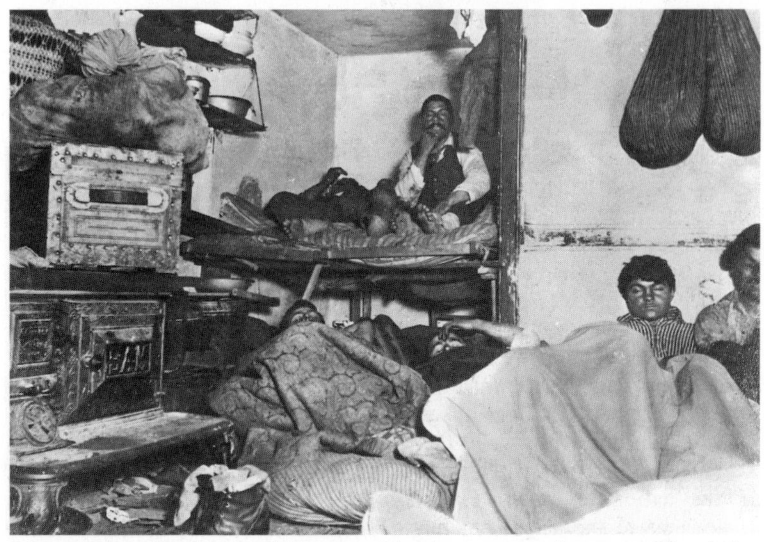
The photographs by Jacob Riis starkly demonstrate how a public shelter alone cannot alleviate the pain and dejection of one's lost expectations.

New York City, December

"The power of the fact is the mightiest lever of this or any day," says journalist Jacob Riis, who is using his trade to highlight the plight of the poor on New York's Lower East Side. His illustrated article *How the Other Half Lives*, published this month in *Scribner's*, paints a grim picture of the American slum. "In the tenements," Riis laments, "all influences make for evil." "Hotbeds of epidemics" and "nurseries of pauperism and crime," they breed "40,000 human wrecks" each year, "a round half million beggars" in the last eight years, and maintain "a standing army of ten thousand tramps." Riis's photos, many of them taken indoors with a newly invented flash powder, outline a world of dim hopes. Grimy sweatshops, ill-lit opium dens and squalid one-room flats make up the physical landscape. The human topography is littered with drunken rogues, street-tough ragamuffins, half-naked children huddled in concrete corners and dozens of craggy faces vacant with fatigue.

Riis, a Danish immigrant with a profound faith in American individualism, has harsh words for the lazy and the deceitful. But, bucking the rising tide of nativist feeling, Riis portrays the largely foreign-born slum dwellers as honest, hard-working heroes, "striving patiently against fearful odds and by their very courage coming off the victors in the battle with the tenement."

Personal courage is part of Riis's cure for urban ills. A police reporter for the *New York Tribune*, he has no radical agenda. For Riis, as for his friend Felix Adler, founder of the Ethical Culture Society, the critical thing is "deed not creed." He views the slums not as the inevitable outcome of capitalism, but as a creation of private greed, political corruption and ignorance.

But Riis, leading journalists in a movement for reform, offers more than just homilies on the work ethic. He wants to see better enforcement of housing laws; public funding for parks, flower gardens and children's camps; model tenements built at a low profit; lodging houses and compulsory work programs for the indigent, and clubs, settlement houses and better schools to help new arrivals adjust to America.

Jane Addams opens Chicago Hull House

Chicago, Sept. 14

Miss Jane Addams, a 30-year-old social worker, has rented part of an old mansion called Hull House and opened it to the needy. Miss Addams and her friend Miss Ellen Starr hope to educate the poor and their children – a kindergarten is planned – counsel couples on domestic problems and give shelter to the homeless. Hull House is situated on South Halstead Street in the city's 19th Ward, a lively if impecunious community that includes Polish and Russian Jews, Italians and French Canadians. Miss Addams comes from a wealthy Chicago family but says that a personal history of ill health has helped her understand suffering.

Social worker and peace advocate.

New clubs drawing women from home

New York City

After a recent trip to Philadelphia, British author Rudyard Kipling wrote, "The girls of America are clever – yea, it is said that they can think." One thing they have thought up is the General Federation of Women's Clubs, a group coordinating different clubs and promoting group activities for women. Women are looking outside the home for charity work and entertainment. Nor is physical culture neglected: Women have cycling clubs in Chicago, and here in New York tennis clubs are popular

4 Western states admitted to union

Washington, D.C., Nov. 11.
President Cleveland today signed a bill that puts an end to four years of political wrangling and clears the way for the territories of Washington, Montana and the Dakotas to become states. The Democratic majority in the House of Representatives had blocked the Republican strongholds of Washington and North and South Dakota from statehood since 1884. In turn, the Republicans, who hold sway in the Senate, had blocked admission of largely Democratic Montana. The Democrats had to concede defeat when the Republicans swept to a majority in both the Senate and the House during the elections this autumn.

Edison comes up with a Kinetoscope, putting pictures in motion

Menlo Park, New Jersey
The Wizard of Menlo Park, alias Thomas A. Edison, remains busy. "I am experimenting upon an instrument which does for the eye what the phonograph does for the ear," he says. No idle talk. He and his assistant, William Kennedy Laurie Dickson, noted for his zeal for all things photographic, have invented a Kinetoscope for viewing the strips of film they make with their Kinetograph, which they call a camera for moving pictures. It uses rolls of coated celluloid film, usually between 35 and 50 feet long, and takes series of photographs at the rate of 40 per second. The Kinetoscope is a rough cabinet device for peepshow viewing. While there seems to be no realistic future for all of this, the partly deaf, largely self-educated Edison displays his usual enthusiasm and claims it to be an educational tool.

"The first principle of education is to interest children," he says. "I will do that with moving pictures. The child will be so interested, he'll run to school. We shan't be able to keep him away. We'll teach children the alphabet – anything – because we will have their attention."

Edison has also asked Dickson to work on a Kinetophonograph, a voice-picture apparatus. At the laboratory here, researchers of different skills work in a team spirit. No "lone tinkerer" is the ever-curious Edison. He works closely with first-rate "earnest men," always open to new ideas in the "invention factory" that he started here back in 1876 (→Feb. 1, 1893).

Moving pictures for just one cent.

Bareknuckle finale

Richburg, Mississippi, July 23
The invincible John L. Sullivan put away Jake Kilrain today after 75 bruising rounds in what may be the last bareknuckle bout for the world title. In his future contests, Sullivan plans to wear gloves under the popular Marquess of Queensberry rules. "The Great John L." has been touring the country, sometimes fighting two and three opponents at each arena, alternating between bareknuckle contests and the Queensberry gloved battles.

"Gospel of Wealth"

New York City, June
When the steel magnate Andrew Carnegie talks about money, people listen, although they may not like what he has to say. Certainly his fellow tycoons are reeling from the impact of his essay, "The Gospel of Wealth," published this month in the *North American Review*. He argues that the free enterprise system has built in inequities and that those who profit from them are "trustees" of their wealth, obligated to wield it for the public good.

Hawaiian rebels die

Honolulu, July 30
Revolutionary zealot Robert W. Wilcox, leading about 150 soldiers, attacked Iolani Palace today but was repulsed with a loss of seven men. King Kalakaua was away at the time. The Cabinet's loyal forces repulsed the attack after skirmishing on the palace grounds. The insurrection was the result of resentment against the scandals in the King's administration, including an opium bribery case said to involve Kalakaua himself (→Jan. 29, 1891).

Please deposit coin

Hartford, Connecticut
The invention of the telephone 13 years ago promised easy communication over long distances. Now, with the latest invention, it will be even easier to spend your money on the telephone. A patent has been granted for a coin-operated telephone, a device that will be maintained in public places, and can be activated only by placing a coin in a slot. Pre-payment with more coins will give you an immediate link to many cities in the Northeast.

Will Indian Ghost Dance revive old ways?

Nevada, January
Following an eclipse of the sun on January 1, Wovoka, a Paiute Indian sometimes called Jack Wilson, has introduced a new religious movement among the local Indians. Friends of Wovoka, son of the Paiute shaman Tavibo, have long suspected him of having religious powers. Their suspicions seemed well-founded when he fell into a three-day trance. Many thought him dead and wanted to bury him. They would have, too, but for his wife, Mary, who insisted that he was still alive. Neither fire applied to the soles of his feet nor buckets of water splashed over him caused Wovoka to stir. Finally, on the third day, he emerged from the trance and ordered the people to meet the next evening at the ceremonial grounds.

At that meeting, Wovoka told of a vision he had experienced. In it, he had gone to heaven, seen all his ancestors and found everyone happy. He said there were no white people there, but that he had been told Jesus was upon the earth, moving as in a cloud. The Indians were not to harm any living thing, to drink no whiskey, and neither to fight nor hate the white man.

Wovoka then taught the Indians the Ghost Dance, saying that if they performed it, God would restore the earth to the way it was before the whites came and only Indians would inhabit the land again (→Dec. 29, 1890).

"Jingo Jim" Blaine gets his Latin parley

Washington, D.C., Oct. 2
A long-cherished dream of Secretary of State James Blaine has been realized with the opening here today of the First International Conference of American States. Except for the Dominican Republic, every independent country in the Western Hemisphere has sent representatives. The conference will address such topics as arbitration of disputes, adjustment of tariffs and the establishment of a commercial bureau. Blaine, whose vigorous style when dealing with European powers has earned him the nickname "Jingo Jim," has declared that he is seeking a Latin-American policy of solidarity that is based on "friendship, not force."

Although hailed as one of Secretary of State Blaine's greatest achievements, the commercial unity of the Americas may slowly be thwarted by the many high-tariff industrialists.

1890

Harrison

Chicago, Jan. 23. Atchison, Topeka and Santa Fe train sets American speed record of 78.1 miles per hour.

Washington, D.C., Feb. 14. New House rule requires roll call by head count rather than vocal response, ending tactic of remaining silent to force adjournment.

Washington, D.C., March 24. Supreme Court overturns lower court decision in Chicago, Milwaukee & St. Paul Railroad v. Minnesota, by ruling that states cannot set rail fees that obstruct "reasonable profit."

Philadelphia, May 1. Bank of America fails.

New York City, May 24. George Francis Train completes around-the-world balloon trip, setting record of 67 days 13 hours 3 minutes and 3 seconds.

Chicago, June 9. Reginald de Koven's *Robin Hood* opens; [play runs for more than 3,000 consecutive performances].

Washington, D.C., July 2. United States becomes signer of International Act for the Suppression of African Slave Trade.

Lawrence, Mass., July 26. Cyclone strikes southside tenement district, and within three minutes cuts swath nearly a mile long; eight are killed, 28 injured.

Washington, D.C., Sept. 25. Congress founds Yosemite Park.

Washington, D.C., Sept. 29. In effort to induce railroad construction, Congress decrees forfeiture of much undeveloped federal land to railroads.

Mississippi, Nov. 1. Clause adopted in state constitution withholding vote from those who cannot understand certain parts of U.S. Constitution; it is aimed at illiterate Negroes (→ May 6, 1896).

New York City. National Carbon Company markets first commercial dry cell battery under Ever Ready brand name.

New York City. Buffalo Bill brings 15 Georgian horseback riders from Russia to United States to join Wild West Show; they are first Georgian immigrants to United States.

Hawaii. E.W. Jordan imports macadamia nut from Australia to Hawaii for cultivation.

Oklahoma becomes white man's territory

Homesteaders seize the moment.

Washington, D.C., May 2

Congress today created the federal Territory of Oklahoma. Formerly known as the Indian Territory, the area that contains an estimated 100,000 Indians from many tribes possessed no formal federal territorial government until today. Instead, the vast region had been ruled, more or less, by the Indians themselves ever since passage of the Indian Intercourse Act of 1834. The Indian leaders usually were selected from what was known as the "Five Civilized Tribes," the Cherokees, Creeks, Choctaws, Seminoles and Chickashas.

Popular demand for the status of a federal territory became intense last year, when virtually the entire area was opened to American settlers for the first time. Since then, several hundred thousand people have moved into the Indian Territory. Local officials have recognized how desperate the need was for federal regulation in this lawless and often violent country. When the lands were first opened, local sheriffs did what they could to maintain law and order, but that has not been nearly enough.

Now that the Oklahoma Territory is a reality, many officials in Washington are estimating that statehood will be granted in a matter of a few years (→ Sept. 22, 1891).

Indians traveled to the capital, where they bargained away their land.

Top 1 percent owns a monopoly of wealth

United States

Recent estimates suggest more than half the nation's vast new wealth is owned by 1 percent of its population. In 1879, Henry George had already seen the irony in modern economics. "This association of poverty with progress," he wrote, "is the great enigma of our times." Today, the mystery remains. "Nature is rich," says George's fellow reformer Henry Demarest Lloyd, "but everywhere man, the heir of nature, is poor."

Technological progress has allowed man to exploit nature ever more efficiently. In 1830, a bushel of wheat took three hours to produce; with modern reapers, it takes less than 15 minutes. Yet farmers struggle to survive. One-quarter are tenants, while 90 percent in the South live on credit. Membership in the increasingly radical National Farmers' Alliance is up to 400,000. And cities now confront the existence of a permanent "dependent class" of wage laborers. The impersonality of the workplace, in the words of the Rev. Josiah Strong, renders it "vastly more difficult to rise from the condition of employee to that of an employer, thus separating the classes more widely." As yet, the state is unwilling to bridge the gap. Most elected officials believe, with Andrew Carnegie, that while unfettered competition in the marketplace "may be sometimes hard for the individual, it insures the survival of the fittest." Federal aid, says ex-President Grover Cleveland, "weakens the sturdiness of the national character."

Population of U.S. swells to 63 million

Washington, D.C.

The American population has grown to 63 million, a 25 percent increase in just a decade, the 1890 census shows. The total includes the 258,000 inhabitants of the newest territory, Oklahoma. New York again set a record as the most populous state, with more than six million residents, up one million since the last census. The least populous state is Nevada, but it, like other Western states, has shown steady growth. California topped one million for the first time and Washington's population leaped to 357,000.

Nellie Bly circles globe in 72 days

New York City, Jan. 25

It took Jules Verne's mythical Phileas Fogg 80 days to journey around the world, but Nellie Bly has proved he must have tarried. The intrepid reporter, best known for feigning insanity to expose conditions in the Blackwell Island asylum, took just 72 days, 6 hours and 11 minutes to circle the globe. Highlights of her journey, traveled mainly by train and steamship, included a visit with Jules Verne in India and Christmas in Hong Kong. Bly stepped off the Chicago Limited express here in New York almost two days ahead of schedule.

Nellie in a less adventurous moment.

Antitrust Law is enacted

Many hope that the Sherman Antitrust Law, aimed at the industrial monopolies, will restore the institutions of government to their rightful owners.

Washington, D.C., July 2

Just in time for the upcoming elections, Congress has responded to the growing clamor over monopolies and "the money power" by passing the Sherman Antitrust Act. The bill, which has barely survived four months of debate, offers guidelines for the punishment of "contracts and combinations in restraint of commerce among the several states or with foreign nations." One senator, referring to the ambiguous section defining a trust, says the act merely provides guidelines for those "seeking to evade the law."

The bill is meant to strengthen state attempts to regulate corporations whose reach extends beyond state lines. In the words of Ohio Senator John Sherman, whose name is attached to the act, the states are "unable to deal with the evil that now threatens us." But critics feel federal officials are unwilling to attack the trusts. Speaking for his bill in Congress, Sherman revealed the other "evil" the law is designed to confront. "You must heed (the people's) appeal," he warned, "or be ready for the socialist, the communist, the nihilist." In the words of Senator Orville Platt of Connecticut, the Senate has not sought a bill to "prohibit and punish," but one "with that title that we might go to the country with" (→ March 25, 1893).

Law mandates purchase of silver for coins

Washington, D.C., July 14

The Sherman Silver Purchase Act, which requires the Treasury to buy 4.5 million ounces of silver every month, just about every ounce that is being mined, today replaced the more moderate Bland-Allison Law of 1878. The new legislation, as well as being popular with silver-mining interests in the West for obvious reasons, has been supported by farmers, who believe that a big increase in the supply of silver coinage will inflate the currency, raising the price of farm products while at the same time reducing the real value of farm debts. The measure has also been backed by manufacturers in return for a promise of support for a higher tariff bill to be introduced soon (→ Nov. 1, 1893).

The silver sun of prosperity?

Duke is the "king" in world of tobacco

North Carolina, Jan. 31

James Duke has been crowned "king" of tobacco after combining five of the largest tobacco manufacturing companies in the United States to form the American Tobacco Company. Before this, farmers could auction their crop to the highest bidder. Now, the American Tobacco Company can virtually dictate the price of the crop. Duke rose to the top by investing millions in advertising and undercutting his competitor's prices.

Mine unions merge and join the A.F.L.

Columbus, Ohio, Jan. 23

Two mining organizations banded together today to found the United Mine Workers. The Order of the Knights of America and the World, and the National Federation had frequently clashed. But their leaders decided that greater bargaining power lay in solidarity, and the decision was made to combine amid cries of "Unity! Unity!" The newly merged organization will be affiliated with the American Federation of Labor.

Women unite to seek national suffrage

Elizabeth Cady Stanton (left) and Susan B. Anthony lead the struggle.

Washington, D.C., Feb. 18

Casting aside past differences to seek a common goal, the National Woman Suffrage Association and the American Woman Suffrage Association merged today to form the National American Woman Suffrage Association. Mrs. Elizabeth Cady Stanton, aged 73, was elected president. The new association acknowledges that progress has been achieved on the municipal and the state level toward gaining women's suffrage, but national voting rights have yet to be realized. Mrs. Stanton argues that "logically, our enfranchisement ought to have occurred in 1776, or at least in Reconstruction days" (→ Feb. 20, 1894).

Simplicity in a complex age. "Mahatango Valley Farm," anonymous.

Farmers organize, form People's Party

Indianapolis, Sept. 24

The new coalition People's Party was called to order today by a South Bend delegate who said he lost one leg freeing black slaves and pledged the other to free "white slaves." "I'm an oppressed man," John C. Maugherman told the Indiana amalgam of Union Labor, the Farmers' Alliance and Greenbackers "and I want relief from existing evils." The new Indiana coalition party is based on the declaration of principles set forth by the delegates to the Farmers' Alliance convention held in St. Louis last December. Throughout the country, state alliances are demanding increased coinage of silver to swell the money supply as a way out of farm mortgage debt. In an expression of the discontent of the nation's farmers, they also are calling for lower tariffs to widen farm markets and legislative efforts to curb banks and railroads (→ July 4, 1892).

Awakening a sleeping population.

George group for single tax on property

New York City, Sept. 2

At a meeting of the Single Tax National League held in Cooper Union, delegates from 30 states have adopted a platform based on the ideas of Henry George, the radical economist. George, who presided over the meeting, is the author of *Progress and Poverty*, published 11 years ago and a best seller in many countries. Four years ago, he ran for mayor of New York on a reform platform, and though he lost to the Tammany-sponsored Abram Hewitt, he won an impressive 67,000 votes – more than the Republican candidate, Theodore Roosevelt.

George's single tax proposal addresses what he has called "the great enigma of our time," which is that poverty has been increasing even faster than "the prodigious increase in wealth-producing power." He bases his solution on two fundamental beliefs. The first is that land and natural resources are the source of all wealth; and the second is that land and the wealth that results from its use rightfully belong to the community. Poverty, he maintains, is caused by permitting individual and corporate owners of the land to enrich themselves by charging rent; the solution is to tax rent and increased land value at 100 percent.

Supporters of the single tax on land believe that not only will it cure social ills caused by unequal distribution of wealth, but that it will also produce enough revenue to meet all the costs of government.

The attic muse: Dickinson's poems

Amherst, Massachusetts

Emily Dickinson must have been up to something all those years, or so Amherst folks had long suspected. The shy spinster, who died at the age of 56 in 1886, was a virtual recluse the last 25 years of her life. Now everyone – in Amherst and beyond – knows what kept her so busy: writing amazing poems, about 1,000 short lyrics in all, each an entry in her ongoing "letter to the world." She hid her talent even from her kin, but a rich sample of her secret scribblings has been published in *Poems*, and the gentle poet of Amherst is now posthumously the first lady of American verse.

Daguerreotype of the poet in 1848.

U.S. naval captain touts sea power

Washington, D.C.

To rule the seas is to rule the world. This is a proposition that, according to the acclaimed naval historian Captain Alfred Thayer Mahan, the United States can ignore only at its own peril. In his new work, *The Influence of Sea Power Upon History, 1660-1783*, a massive, meticulously researched study, Mahan posits the theory that national greatness is inextricably tied to control of the sea. Using the shifting balance of power among European nations as his example, Mahan says that if America aspires to a position of world power and influence, it must upgrade its navy.

McKinley Act raises tariffs to record level

McKinley makes ready for battle.

Washington, D.C., Oct. 1

A new tariff act sponsored by William McKinley, chairman of the House Ways and Means Committee, has increased duties on imported goods to an average of 48.4 percent, a level that is unprecedented in peacetime. The list of items affected is extensive. There are to be increased duties on hides and on farm produce such as wheat, potatoes and barley, while raw sugar will be on the free list. However, these concessions aren't much use to farmers, who face little competition from abroad but will have to pay more for a wide range of manufactured goods. Many domestic firms are already taking advantage of the new law to raise prices. And Democrats are already using the law as an issue in their campaigns against the Republicans they will oppose in next month's elections.

Navy sinks Army in first gridiron clash

West Point, New York, Nov. 29

The two service schools, the Naval Academy of Annapolis and the Military Academy of West Point, met for the first time on the football gridiron today and the middies sailed off with a 24-0 triumph. These players at least had their hair trimmed neatly, not like the Yale gridmen, who are wearing their hair extra long. But no one can argue with the Elis. They have dominated college football since 1883.

From William James, a psychology classic

Cambridge, Massachusetts

Novelist Henry James is not the only member of his family who has penetrating insights into the human mind. His older brother, William, a 48-year-old Harvard professor, has issued *The Principles of Psychology*, a major treatise 12 years in the making. This exhaustive work sheds new light on the complex interactions of the body, thoughts, emotions and behavior. One chapter, "What Is an Emotion?" was hailed as an instant classic when it appeared in the journal *Mind* in 1884.

The prolific, erudite William James.

Wyoming cowboys in statehood corral

Washington, D.C., July 10

Wyoming has become the 44th state in the union, despite the objections of many Democrats. Several of them in Congress claimed that Wyoming's population was too small – under 60,000 – and some of these legislators oppose women's suffrage – granted in Wyoming in 1869. Political observers charged that the Democratic opposition is really tied to the fact that Wyoming is a heavily Republican area. Territorial representative Joseph Carey helped turn the tide for Wyoming by proclaiming that the state had 12 million acres of "irrigable land" and that it was "one of nature's great storehouses of minerals."

New York institutes use of electric chair

New York, Aug. 6

New York State officals threw a switch and instituted a new type of capital punishment today – electrocution. After his lawyer failed to win an appeal against this unusual punishment, convicted ax murderer William Kemmler was strapped to an electric chair and hundreds of volts were sent surging through his body. Electrocution is intended to be a humane alternative to hanging, the official form of execution in the United States for the last 100 years. Kemmler, however, survived the first surge of electricity and had to be shocked several times before he died.

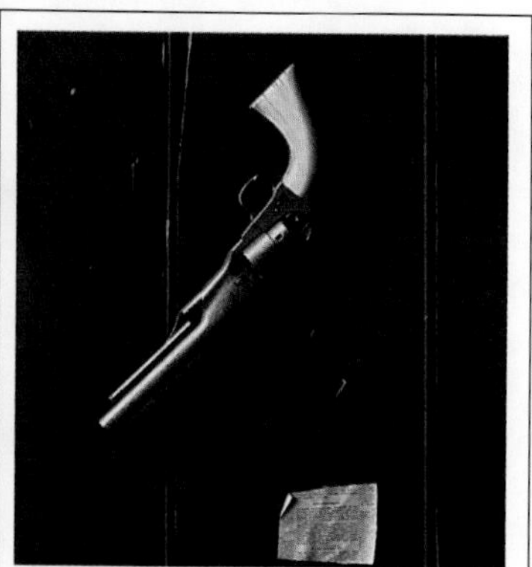

"The Faithful Colt" (1890) by William Michael Harnett. On the wild, often violent frontier, the revolver often keeps the peace.

Sioux slaughtered at Wounded Knee

South Dakota, Dec. 29

Those fallen braves, whom the Sioux in their Ghost Dance have urged to rise again, have only been joined by more dead. A terrible massacre is reported at Wounded Knee Creek on the Pine Ridge Reservation. The United States Seventh Cavalry has killed 153 Minneconjou Sioux, half of them women and children. The great leader Big Foot is among those slain. As tribes elsewhere in the nation learn the news, they pray with little conviction that this was the last battle.

Today's disaster can be traced to the fatal shooting of Sitting Bull two weeks ago. At the time, Sitting Bull, a Hunkpapa Sioux chief, was living with his people at Pine Ridge. He had become a believer in the Ghost Dance, a mystic rite born of a vision by a Paiute holy man named Wovoka. This holy man called upon Indians to gather, to fast and to dance in a circle around a sacred tree. After the ceremony, the dancers often had visions, dreams of good hunting grounds and visits with dead brothers who had once again risen. Some United States government officials were concerned about the development of the Ghost Dance, which seemed to be a binding force among tribes that had fought each other for decades. Last month, General Nelson Miles of the Seventh Cavalry had 5,000 troops monitor proceedings at the reservation. On the evening of December 15, he instructed a police force composed of Sioux loyal to the government to arrest Sitting Bull. A melee erupted, and Sitting Bull and several of the police force were killed.

When Hunkpapa Sioux Chief Big Foot heard of this, he feared reprisals, and so led 350 of his people to their old camp on the Cheyenne River. The weather was bitterly cold, there was little food and many of the tribe were ill. Still, the cavalry intercepted them and moved them to a camp on Wounded Knee Creek.

This morning, Colonel James Forsyth, leading 500 soldiers, entered the camp and asked for the Sioux's weapons. Tensions grew, and suddenly the parties were in hand-to-hand combat. Four cannons on a nearby hill slaughtered many of the women and children. Only 25 United States soldiers died.

Oglala Sioux perform the Ghost Dance. Begun about 1889 through the vision of Paiute Indian Wovoka, the Ghost Dance Cult loosely synthesizes Christian tenets and the ancient Indian beliefs. A last cry of desperation, the mystic rite promises the resurrection of dead ancestors and slain buffalo.

Frederic Remington's portrayal of the Battle of Wounded Knee merely hints at the extensive massacre that took place on the fateful day.

Sitting Bull, warrior chief of the Dakota Sioux, slain in a melee at his home when Sioux authorities under federal contract came to arrest him.

Big Foot, the Sioux chief, lies on the battlefield of Wounded Knee. The frozen, contorted corpse symbolizes not only a leader's death, but the loss of destiny. The fight over, the fate of the Indians is now in the hands of the whites.

▷

The end of a long trail of tears for a proud people

Sioux hunting buffalo, which, as frontier artist George Catlin remarked, "supplied the Indians with all the luxuries of life, as they knew of none other."

Either Babeshikit, a Kickapoo, or Meraparapa, a Mandan, in 1894.

Poison, a Cheyenne woman almost 100 years of age, in 1888.

Little Big Mouth, a medicine man.

White Bear, Oklahoma Kiowa chief.

On the trail of the white man. Painting is by Charles Russell, who, like George Catlin before him, was an artist who learned from the native American culture.

Eskimo mother and child in furs, in Nome, Alaska. By 1890, most remaining natives have been confined to reservations, where the generations continue.

After 400 years, Indians will fight no more forever

A Paiute brave aims his rifle, in southwestern Utah in 1873.

Milky Way, a Comanche, photographed by Alexander Gardner.

Black Cloud, a Cherokee chief, painted by George Catlin in 1836.

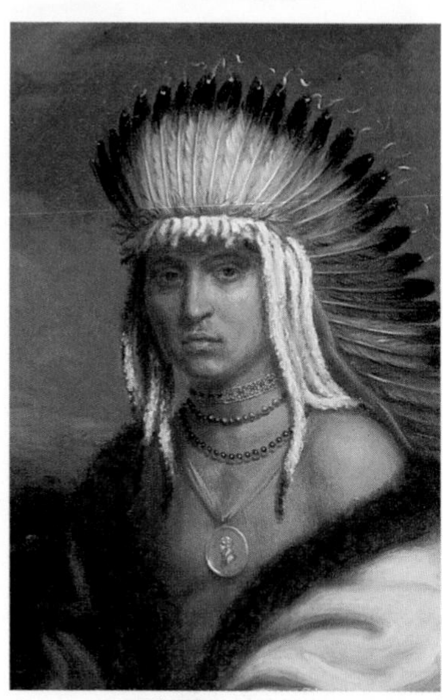

Generous Chief, a Pawnee, painted by Charles Bird King in 1822.

Rain-in-the-face, a Hunkpapa Sioux chief, wearing feathered headdress. With the defeat of the Sioux at Wounded Knee, Indian resistance has ended.

Sioux: Red Dog (left), Little Wound, Red Cloud, American Horse, Red Shirt.

Bison dance of the Mandan Indians in front of medicine lodge in 1844. Aquatint engraving after Karl Bodmer, a Swedish artist who also roamed the West.

1891

Harrison

Muscatine, Iowa, Jan. 26. German immigrant John Boepple starts first fresh-water-pearl button factory with mussels, in his basement.

Texas, Feb. 21. Texas legislature awards state pension to Andrea Candalaria, one of last survivors of the Battle of the Alamo.

Washington, D.C., March 3. Circuit Court of Appeals established by Congress to reduce Supreme Court's load.

Washington, D.C., March 3. Congress creates office of superintendent of immigration, to cope with growing influx of foreigners.→

Washington, D.C., March 4. Congress passes International Copyright Act, protecting foreign authors from piracy by American publishers.

New York City, May 5. Peter Ilyich Tchaikovsky conducts at opening of Music Hall on 57th Street.

United States, May 21. Negro Peter Jackson fights James Corbett to 61-round draw.

Arizona, June. Diamonds found in meteorites by Dr. George Koenig in Canon Diablo.

Bennington, Vermont, Aug. 19. President Harrison and New England governors dedicate Bennington battle monument.

Little Rock, Arkansas, Sept. 9. Negro cotton pickers, seeking $1 a day, stage and lose strikes in Arkansas and Georgia.

Washington, D.C., Sept. 22. President Harrison opens additional 900,000 acres of Oklahoma Indian land to white settlers (→Sept. 16, 1893).

United States. First picture of sun taken by George E. Hale, with spectroheliograph.

United States. Orello Cone's *Gospel Criticism and Historical Christianity* and Washington Gladden's *Who Wrote the Bible?* published.

Washington, D.C. Sculptor Augustus Saint-Gaudens finishes memorial to Mrs. Henry Adams, called *Grief* or *Death* or *Peace of God.*

DEATH

New York City. Herman Melville, author of *Moby-Dick* and other classic novels (*Aug. 1, 1819).

Hawaiian King dies; sister ascends throne

Honolulu, Jan. 29

Princess Liliuokalani, sister of King Kalakaua, was proclaimed Queen of Hawaii today in regal ceremonies at Iolani Palace. Liliuokalani had reigned as regent during Kalakaua's long illness. The King died in his suite at the Palace Hotel in San Francisco, where he had come to seek a cure, nine days ago. His body is being returned aboard the Charleston for royal burial here.

The new monarch was educated at the Royal School and she was among the royalty who attended the celebration of the Silver Jubilee of Queen Victoria in 1887. She is an accomplished author and has developed into a respected writer of songs, both in English and Hawaiian. Liliuokalani, an outspoken member of her sex, opposed ceding Pearl Harbor to the U.S. as a naval base. She believes in "Hawaii for the Hawaiians" (→Apr. 13, 1893).

Queen of the Hawaiian Islands.

President, on tour, dispenses wisdom

Salt Lake City, Utah, Aug. 28

With the election just a little over a year away, President Harrison is speaking more often, dispensing wisdom as he goes. In Mormon Salt Lake City, he glorified the American home "where one wife sits in single uncrowned glory." In San Antonio, he called wealth and commerce "timid creatures." In Vermont, he held out hope that prejudices of many generations might one day be rubbed away. In San Francisco, he called the nation's military might unexcelled but noted with satisfaction that Americans are "smitten by the love of peace." Here in Utah, he also spoke of a unity of feeling brought on by rich and poor children playing together.

President Harrison, nation's oracle.

Forest lands are set aside for public use

Washington, D.C., Oct. 16

In increasing amounts, public land is being set aside as forest reserves by President Harrison in keeping with the Forest Reserve Act signed into law on March 3. The act is actually a rider to the Sundry Civil Service Appropriation Act, and its success can be accredited to the diligent work of the American Forestry Association, which began petitioning for a new law in April of 1889, meeting with Harrison and one year later with Congress. The group then gained the support of the Secretary of the Interior, John W. Noble, convincing him to push Congress to include the rider. Noble approached the issue strongly, threatening to force a presidential veto if it was not included in the civil service bill.

Section 24 of the appropriation act states: "The President of the United States may from time to time set apart and reserve in any State or Territory having public land bearing forests . . . public reservations." The enactment of the legislation was followed on March 30 by the establishment of Yellowstone Timberland Reserve, a forest area of 1.2 million acres adjoining Yellowstone National Park.

Majestic Yosemite National Park, covering an area of 1,189 square miles.

Bored students toss balls into baskets

Springfield, Massachusetts

Campus life can get pretty dull in winter and students are easily bored by marching and even gymnastics. That's why the head of physical education here asked Dr. James Naismith at the Y.M.C.A.'s training school to come up with a solution. He did. After trying some children's pastimes, which all seemed a waste of time, he suspended some peach baskets from the balcony at the gym and had the students throw a large ball into the baskets. The game [basketball] is spreading.

ouisiana mob kills 11 reputed Mafiosi

Vativism is piqued as Uncle Sam is shown what immigration has brought.

Rome, Italy, March 31

The Italian government recalled its minister to the United States today to protest the murder of 11 Italian-Americans in Louisiana. A mob broke into the New Orleans parish prison March 14 and executed 11 reputed Mafia members suspected of having killed the city's police chief, David C. Hennessey. The mob hunted down 11 of 19 prisoners allegedly involved. Nine were shot and two were hanged. Hennessey was investigating Mafia links when he was assassinated last October 15. Of the 19 men who were indicted, nine were tried but found not guilty (→Apr. 12, 1892).

Gold rush at Cripple Creek; miners pour in

Colorado, Autumn

State officials say they cannot determine the exact number of gold seekers who have inundated the little settlements of Creede and Cripple Creek during the past year, but they must number in the thousands. While gold and silver miners have worked this state for years, renewed interest was sparked earlier this year when a cowboy, Bob Womack, accidentally discovered what appears to be a mammoth new gold field near Cripple Creek. With the government expected to retain the gold standard, experts are predicting that even more fortune seekers will be heading this way.

In mining boom towns like Creede, Colorado (pictured above), hotels, theaters, banks, saloons, jails, breweries and churches spring up almost overnight.

Finale for Edwin Booth in "Hamlet" role

Brooklyn, New York, Apr. 4

Edwin Booth, America's greatest actor, has brought down the curtain on his career in the role that made him famous, Hamlet, at the Brooklyn Academy of Music. Although this time his retirement is said to be definite, the 58-year-old actor had bowed out once before, in 1865, when he heard that his brother, John Wilkes Booth, had shot President Lincoln, one of the many tragedies in his unhappy life. Edwin's father died insane, both his wives died young and he has been plagued by financial and drinking problems. Publicly, he will be venerated for his sublime acting in a variety of roles, but especially his record-breaking 100 appearances as Hamlet in 1864.

Edwin Booth in his most famous role.

Bancroft, America's foremost historian

Washington, D.C., Jan. 17

At 90, the "father of American history" has finally passed into history himself. George Bancroft will live on in his 10-volume *History of the United States,* the nation's first comprehensive chronicle of its past. The Harvard scholar issued his first three volumes in the 1830s, but was forced by an active political career to stretch the rest over some 30 years. A Democrat who left the party in the 1850s over its pro-slavery stance, Bancroft had served as minister to England and Germany.

Leland Stanford's college opens doors

Palo Alto, California, Oct. 1

Opening ceremonies were held today to mark the founding of Leland Stanford Jr. University. Senator Stanford, who represents California in Congress and serves simultaneously as president of the Central Pacific Railroad, established and endowed the university as a memorial to his son, who died in 1884 at the age of 15. The university, situated 30 miles south of San Francisco, will be a coeducational institution for both graduate and undergraduate education.

The sport of football comes into its own as college rivals, such as Cornell and Rochester, take to the playing fields to match both skill and brawn.

American sailors assaulted in Chile

Valparaiso, Chile, Oct. 16

Two American sailors have been killed and 18 wounded when attacked by a mob while on shore leave from their ship, the cruiser Baltimore. The incident began with a fight in a saloon that got out of hand. The local police are said to have joined in the assault on the bluejackets. Anti-American feeling runs high here because of Washington's refusal to support the revolution against the authoritarian President Balmaceda (→Jan. 25, 1892).

Sullivan skyscraper goes up in St. Louis

St. Louis, Missouri

Architect Louis Sullivan has created a radical new building in St. Louis. Constructed around a steel skeleton, the Wainwright Building soars 10 stories into the Midwestern sky. Sullivan rejects the idea that the modern building should resemble a Greek temple or a medieval fortress. Instead, he believes that "form follows function." Sullivan's skyscraper was designed so that the steel grid of the structure is visible.

3rd Kentucky Derby victory for Murphy

Louisville, Kentucky, May 13

Isaac Murphy, the talented Negro jockey, has won his third Kentucky Derby. He rode Kingman to victory for a purse of $4,680. Murphy scored with Buchanan in 1884 and Riley last year. He has been one of Kentucky's top riders, many of whom have been Negroes since racing began because caring for horses has always been considered one of the chores of Negro farmhands. Some of these jockeys get only $5 for a winning ride.

Six-day bike race: Is it fun or cruelty?

New York City, Oct. 18

Round and round they went, for six grueling days at Madison Square Garden. Bicyclists from all over the world pedaled for cash and glory on their high wheelers. The spectators were seen betting on their favorite bikers during the many sprints, essentially little races within the big race, and the riders also won sprint purses. The grind, which was finally completed today, has been criticized by some people who look upon six-day racing as inhumane.

New slide fastener is called "zipper"

Chicago

Whitcomb L. Judson has been given a patent for a new invention that he calls a "zipper." It is a slide fastener that Judson believes will eventually replace buttons on many types of clothing. The new device involves two sets of interlocking teeth that are joined together by a slide. Move the slide up, and the garment is closed, move it down and it's open. The zipper can work well on all textiles and even on leather. If it works as Judson claims, and the pants or dress stay fastened, the zipper promises to be a profitable idea.

Burroughs hoping it will all add up

St. Louis

A patent has been granted to 36-year-old William Burroughs, who has created a device that will help bookkeepers keep up with the computational demands of a growing industry. Burroughs's invention is an "adding machine" that prints out each entry and then the final result of the calculation. Burroughs established the American Arithometer Company five years ago to develop and market the machine. His prototype was built when he was a young man in Auburn, New York, but at the time it was not commercially successful.

Farce "Chinatown" comes to Broadway

New York City, Nov. 9

After a year on the road, the musical *A Trip to Chinatown* has settled down on Broadway. Judging from its welcome, it promises to have a long run. The plot, set in San Francisco, is no stronger than it has to be, but the farce chugs along nicely with three characters named Welland Strong, Wilder Daly and Rashleigh Gay. The acclaimed librettist Charles Hoyt works his typical magic in the song *Reuben and Rachel* with the recurring lines, "Reuben, Reuben, I've been thinking." Another song, *The Bowery*, also has the sound of a hit.

Undertaker invents a dial telephone

Kansas City, Missouri

If you have a telephone and have had problems getting the right number, take heart; undertaker Almon B. Strowger may have the solution to your problem. No, Strowger has not decided to embalm the operator; what he has done is invented an electromechanical switching system that will enable callers to make their own connections. Strowger's new telephone has a dial on it that permits the caller to compose his or her own number, and in this way to eliminate the fallible human element at Central. What are the operators going to do now?

Advertisers target the purchasing power of the American woman.

Rainmaker draws a downpour of cash

Goodland, Kansas, Dec. 2

The fortunes of the "rainmaker" Frank Melbourne could rise with his fame. The Interstate Artificial Rain Corporation has been negotiating with the controversial Irishman for the sale of rights to his secret rainmaking process. Melbourne achieved hero status this August, when a half-inch of rain followed the application of his technique around drought-stricken Cheyenne, Wyoming. A week later, however, Melbourne's "rainmaking" failed to chase away the blue skies and sunny weather. Although this cast considerable doubt on Melbourne's ability, many still believe that he is capable of producing rain.

Kansas, November 7. *Comanche, the sole survivor of Custer's Last Stand at Little Big Horn in 1876, has died at Fort Riley at the age of 31.*

America has "more colors than any rainbow"

New York City

"A map of the city," writes reformer Jacob Riis of New York, "colored to designate nationalities, would show more stripes than on the skin of a zebra, and more colors than a rainbow." As the official port of entry for immigrants, New York symbolizes the nation's self-proclaimed role as haven for the world's "huddled masses." Its population is now 40 percent foreign-born, with Italians dominating the Lower East Side, Irish inhabiting the West, and Jews the center. High-growth cities like Brooklyn and Chicago have immigrant populations that equal their total population of a decade ago. Three million foreigners came to America in the previous decade. And they are coming from different places than in the past. In the 1850's, the British Isles, Germany and Scandinavia provided 95 percent of the flow. That figure has dropped to 60 percent. Italians, who have taken over New York's fruit trade, arrive at the rate of 30,000 per year. And Jews come by the droves to escape pogroms. As one writer laments, "The only hope for Jews in Russia is to become Jews out of Russia."

Most of the newcomers, short of money and eager to settle near their own kind, never leave the great urban melting pots. Relatively rich, Germans and Scandinavians have carved thriving farms out of the areas still open in the northern Midwest and Great Plains. The rest are forced to crowd into run-down sections of New York, Chicago, Boston and Philadelphia, becoming scapegoats for rising crime rates. According to a Wisconsin government report, the advocates of "socialism, confiscation, anarchy, disorder, violence and bomb-throwing, are the offspring of foreign countries." Calls for racial purity abound. According to one intolerant California doctor, "Castration is the supreme remedy for a diseased and bestialized race."

Immigration, however, has its economic rationale. Andrew Carnegie figures each immigrant is worth $1,500, as much as a slave before the Civil War. Each year, he says, America grows $1 billion richer. The Inman Steamship Co. sent 3,500 agents to sell passage across the Atlantic to European relatives of immigrants. Railroad baron J.J. Hill flooded Eastern Europe and China with stereopticon views of the Northwest. As surplus labor, new arrivals keep wages low, raising the ire of unions. Widespread use of Italians as scabs in the mines prompted one paper to call them "tools to victimize and oppress other workingmen." Friction is everywhere, but only a storm can produce a rainbow (→Jan. 1, 1892).

German immigrants leaving Chicago to settle in Colfax, Colorado. The German Colorado Company was organized in 1869 to help settle them.

An immigrant family doing garment piecework in their tenement home on New York City's Lower East Side. One such tenement might house 200 people, and as many as 4,000 immigrants might live on one block in the area.

One young immigrant wrote of her first day here: "I was craning my neck and standing on tiptoe to stare through the haze at the skyline. It was a day of breathtaking surprises . . . Anything might be true in this strange country."

1892

Harrison

Coeur d'Alene, Idaho, Jan. 16. As result of high freight costs and low silver prices, principal mines are shut down (→ July 23).

Washington, D.C., Jan. 25. President Harrison considers asking Congress to declare war on Chile in retaliation for violence against American sailors.

Washington, D.C., Feb. 12. Abraham Lincoln's birthday declared national holiday.

Washington, D.C., February. American and Canadian officials meet to discuss settlement of Alaskan boundary dispute.

Washington, D.C., Apr. 12. United States offers $25,000 in indemnity to Italian government for 1891 murder of Italian nationals in New Orleans.

Washington, D.C., May 5. Chinese Exclusion Act extended for 10 years, and expanded to require registration of all Chinese in United States (→ May 15, 1893).

Honolulu, May 20. Monarchy arrests Liberal leaders, charging treason in plot to overthrow government (→ Apr. 13, 1893).

Washington, D.C., Aug. 20. President Harrison orders canal keepers to collect tolls on Sault Ste. Marie Canal, in response to similar actions taken by Canada.

Washington, D.C., Aug. 30. Cholera reported carried into country on warship Moravia.

Montana, Oct. 15. Approximately 1.8 million acres of land belonging to Crow Indians opened to white settlers.

Baltimore, Maryland. William Painter invents bottle cap and capping machine.

New York City. Cuban national hero Jose Marti founds Cuban Revolutionary Party while in exile in United States.

United States. Central Conference of American Rabbis, at urging of Isaac Mayer Wise, unanimously condemns Zionism.

Brownville, Texas. First cotton boll weevil found; insect begins spreading to other cotton fields.

New York City. *Vogue* magazine begins publication.

State troops crush Homestead strike

Striking workers congregate on a hillside overlooking the mills of the Carnegie Steel Company. But how long will the halt in hostilities last?

Homestead, Penn., Nov. 20

With nine in their ranks dead and their union broke from fighting legal battles, 3,000 workers voted today to end a five-month strike at the Carnegie steel works. Despite vanquishing a 300-man Pinkerton force in July, they return defeated, as non-union men. Strike leaders, many of whom have faced exhausting trials for murder and treason, will find themselves blacklisted.

Trouble began in January, when Andrew Carnegie's deputy Henry Clay Frick, a union buster known as the "Coke King," demanded an 18 to 26 percent cut in the wages of the Amalgamated Association of Iron and Steel Workers. After finding himself hung in effigy, Frick shut the works in June. Some 3,000 unskilled workers joined the 800 Amalgamated men in a highly organized strike. All roads blocked, the rail depot guarded and the river patrolled, labor took over the town, closing saloons and passing laws. When the Pinkertons arrived via barge bearing Winchester repeaters, they were met by a crowd of thousands. Early on the morning of July 6, as the guards tried to debark, shots split the air. All day, strikers took potshots, lobbed dynamite at the barges, spread oil in the water and launched a flaming raft toward the intruders. Finally, with 20 hit and seven of them dead, the Pinkertons yielded. But the workers' rule did not last long. Six days later, an efficient state militia opened the plant to strikebreakers.

Pinkertons surrender as fires burn.

The failure of Amalgamated, the nation's strongest trade union, does not bode well for labor's future against the corporate giants that can weather strikes by transferring work to non-union plants.

Ellis Island opens as tide of immigration overflows old facilities

New York City, Jan. 1

Annie Moore from County Cork, Ireland, 15 years old, was the first immigrant to arrive at Ellis Island, opened today as the Federal Bureau of Immigration's new receiving station. Replacing the Barge Office in Battery Park, opened in 1890 to replace Castle Garden, Ellis Island is said to accommodate two ships at a time and up to 7,000 new arrivals per day. Castle Garden was closed in 1890 when the government dissolved its contract with New York's Commissioners of Emigration. A Treasury investigation in 1887 revealed massive overcrowding and corruption. Since 1882 it had processed over 3,500,000 immigrants, the last on April 18, 1890.

Hungry immigrants stop to eat in the dining hall at newly opened Ellis Island.

The bureau then opened the Barge Office to function temporarily while a new site was chosen. In 1891 the depot received 430,884 immigrants: 74,496 Germans, 52,022 Russians, 65,084 Italians, 35,951 Irish, 32,426 Swedes, and the list even includes 1 Arab. Meanwhile, the Joint Committee on Immigration had been scouring the harbor for a proper location. Ellis Island was chosen, and work began removing the old navy explosives stockpiled there and erecting the station itself on May 24, 1890. This first federal immigration depot is in keeping with the increase in government regulations controlling who can or cannot enter. Seven hundred people arrived at Ellis Island today, passengers of the Nevada, the City of Paris and the Victory, but only Annie got a $10 gold piece.

Mine strike broken by federal troops

Miners, who help fuel the nation, seek a better place in its economy.

Coeur d'Alene, Idaho, July 23

Proving its willingness to take an active role in the contest between labor and capital, the federal government has sent striking silver miners back to work without restoring a 15 percent wage cut. Troops were sent after martial law and a contingent of state militia failed to quell striker-scab violence. Trouble began on July 11, when miners clashed with guards at the Frisco mill. The striking miners blew up an old quartz mill and seized the strikebreakers, marching them as prisoners to the union hall. Federal authorities have replaced a popularly elected county sheriff and arrested dozens of strikers, placing them in stockades called "bull pens."

Populist Party convenes

Omaha, Nebraska, July 4

At its first national convention here today, the People's Party nominated James B. Weaver of Iowa as its candidate for president. The 59-year-old Weaver was the unsuccessful presidential candidate of the soft-money Greenback Party 12 years ago and helped form the Farmers' Alliance. He now represents a party of discontented farmers who want to increase the money supply by coining more silver to pay off crippling mortgage debt with cheaper dollars.

Weaver is running on a platform that declares the nation on "the verge of moral, political and material ruin." It charges that "the fruits of the toil of millions are boldly stolen to build up colossal fortunes for a few, unprecedented in the history of mankind." It says, "We breed two great classes, tramps and millionaires." Some 200 delegates gathered separately today to praise the ideas of Edward Bellamy, author of the popular *Looking Backward*, which promotes an imagined utopia under state socialism. An article on the Omaha convention appearing in *The New York Times* called the party's philosophy "socialism in disguise" (→ Nov. 1, 1893).

CONGRESSIONAL KITCHEN
THE POLITICAL POOR RELATION.—AN UNWELCOME GUEST

Seeking a rightful place at the political table, the long-suffering farmer arrives unwelcomed and derided by the moguls of commercial America.

America's poet, Walt Whitman, dies

The nation is mourning the loss of a great poet and benevolent sage.

New York City, March 26

Each of us inevitable
Each of us limitless

Walt Whitman wrote these words in praise of the singularity and potential of each person, but they seemed to apply to no individual as truly as to him. The bearded bard of Paumanok, as he referred to his native Long Island, died here today at 73. His sensual, exuberant poetry had once been deemed scandalous and been banned in certain cities. But in recent years Whitman had taken on the benign aura of a benevolent sage, and his work had come to seem the characteristic artistic expression of a young, self-confident and increasingly powerful republic as it steps onto the world stage.

Cartoonists delight in deflating pompous presidential rivals Harrison and Cleveland

Defeated for re-election in 1888 by Republican Benjamin Harrison (above left and second from left), former President Grover Cleveland (above right and second from right) is making an uncharacteristically lively bid to regain the White House from Harrison four years later. It is bountiful for the nation's political cartoonists as well. A legacy of high tariffs, record high budgets and the Silver Purchase Act have left Harrison and the Republicans particularly vulnerable. But Cleveland is by no means entering the race as a universally welcomed alternative. The Populist Party, which has emerged from rural America's sense of abandonment and bitterness, wants widespread reforms aimed at the moneyed class. Thus it is only through Populist presidential candidate James Weaver's strong showing in the general election that Cleveland, a Wall Street giant himself, can recapture the presidency for a second term.

Chicago fair marks 1492 discovery

"World's Columbian Exposition" (1894) by Theodore Robinson. The magnificence of the exposition testifies to the great progress made in the New World.

Among the mechanical marvels at the Columbian Exposition in Chicago is the Ferris wheel, a giant wheel 250 feet in diameter with 36 cars attached.

Chicago, Oct. 23

When Columbus sailed the ocean blue in 1492, he neglected to drop anchor in Lake Michigan. That fact has not deterred Chicago from making itself the site of the World Columbian Exposition, a celebration of the discovery of the New World 400 years ago. At this afternoon's dedication ceremony, Vice President Levi Morton announced to the 100,000 onlookers at Jackson Park, "I dedicate these buildings to humanity." And what buildings they are! Pristine white edifices of a classical design, they surround a beautiful man-made lake and fountain. From the Palace of Fine Art to the Fisheries Building, they represent a triumph in unified design Humankind showed less accord today; after the speech by the Vice President, free refreshments were served, and some people in the crowd resorted to fisticuffs to grab the limited number of sandwiches.

Two attractions at the fair seem especially popular. One is the Ferris wheel, the brainchild of inventor George W.G. Ferris. The device is a giant wheel, 250 feet in diameter with 36 boxes or cars attached. Dozens of passengers stand in each box as they are carried up and around the wheel. Another diversion is a dancer who calls herself "Little Egypt" and purports to be from Persia. She shocks women in the audience by wearing silk trousers and doing a "hoochee-coochee dance," which involves undulating movements as she waves a handkerchief in each hand. The ethnic dances at other foreign exhibition halls are not so provocative (→ May 1, 1893).

Sierra Club founded to lobby for nature

John Muir, conservationist, lobbyist and writer, in a reflective moment.

Yosemite Valley, California

Inspired by the dramatic beauty of California's Yosemite Valley and alarmed by the exploitation of the nation's natural beauty, Scottish-born naturalist John Muir has announced formation of the Sierra Club. The club has declared that its purpose is to "explore, enjoy, and protect the nation's scenic resources." Muir and other conservationists say the Sierra Club's first priority will be to fight lumbermen who continuously seek access to lands in the growing national park system. The club will also give Muir a platform from which to argue for more government control of forest land. Muir – writer, environmental lobbyist, and above all, man of the mountains – is already influential. In 1890, his efforts to preserve the sequoia trees prompted Congress to found Yosemite National Park.

It's General Electric

New York City

A bitter fight between two giants of the electrical industry has been ended with the merger of Edison General Electric, controlled by Thomas A. Edison, and Thomson-Houston Electric, controlled by George Westinghouse. The new company will be called General Electric. The merger was arranged by J. Pierpont Morgan to ensure rapid and profitable expansion of the industry. Edison is said to be bitter that the new company does not bear his name.

Duryeas give U.S. gas-powered motorcar

Springfield, Mass., Sept 22

A gasoline-powered motorcar designed and built by the Duryea brothers, Charles and Frank, made its first successful run here today. Propelled by a one-cylinder engine with electrical ignition mounted in a second-hand carriage, it is believed to be the first such vehicle to run in the United States. However, motorcars powered by an engine designed by Gottlieb Daimler of Germany already are being sold in Europe. Charles Duryea, 31, the older brother, is in the bicycle business. He got the idea for the new motorcar when he saw a gasoline engine displayed at the Ohio State Fair three years ago. He and Frank Duryea, who is just 23, built the machine in a rented loft in Springfield. The brothers are squabbling about credit for the achievement, each claiming he did the major part of the work. They have agreed, however, to produce more motorcars, which will be offered for sale to the public (→ Dec. 24, 1893).

Corbett takes title

New Orleans, Sept. 7

John L. Sullivan had the weight advantage, 212 pounds to 178, but Jim Corbett had more speed and finesse as he dethroned the world heavyweight champion from Boston in the 2lst round. "Gentleman Jim" scored a knockout over his favored opponent, who was clearly out of shape after touring the United States and Australia in a stage production. This was the first title won under Marquess of Queensberry rules, ending the bareknuckle era.

Grover Cleveland regains the presidency

It's President Cleveland . . . again.

Washington, D.C., Nov. 8

Grover Cleveland regained the presidency in today's election, defeating Benjamin Harrison, the Republican who ousted him from the White House four years ago. In one respect, the two elections were similar: neither Harrison in 1888 nor Cleveland this year won a majority of the popular vote. However, they won their respective races by piling up enough electoral votes. President-elect Cleveland, a Democrat, will be the first man in the nation's history to serve non-consecutive terms in the White House. His running mate for the vice presidency was Adlai Ewing Stevenson of Illinois. His earlier Vice President, Thomas Andrews Hendricks, died in office in 1885 (→ March 4, 1893).

Sousa, with new band, seeks a new sound

John Philip Sousa standing before the United States Marine Corps Band.

Plainfield, New Jersey, Sept. 26

Stillman Music Hall rang to the sound of a band unlike any ever before heard in this country. But could anyone be surprised that John Philip Sousa's new group is as fresh and exciting as his music? At 38, he has written some of the nation's most bracing marches. *The Washington Post* is world famous, while *The Gladiator* is near the million-copy mark. But then, marches are in his blood. Before stepping down as director of the United States Marine Corps Band, he led it to 12 years of musical glory.

In his own band, Sousa aims to "form a fresh combination" that will "cater for the millions rather than the few." From standard overtures to operatic favorites, the sound is clearly different. But people go to hear the "March King" for one main reason. Before the night is over they want to find themselves beating time to *The Thunderer*, *Semper Fidelis* and the bandmaster's other standbys.

I pledge allegiance to the flag . . .

Washington, D.C.

The headline above is the first six words of a new declaration of loyalty to the United States, as represented by the Stars and Stripes. The *Pledge to the Flag*, as the 29-word declamation is called, the brainchild of educators James B. Upham and Francis Bellamy, appeared on September 8 in the magazine *The Youth's Companion*. Congressional debates concerning the danger to the American way of life posed by unchecked immigration would seem to indicate that national pride is hardly in short supply, but many apparently feel that today's youth could benefit from an injection of patriotism in their daily routine.

Dalton boys killed while robbing bank

Coffeyville, Kansas, Oct. 5

The two Dalton brothers, Bob and Emmett, were shot to death today when they attempted to rob both the First National and the Condon Banks here. The Dalton brothers were well known in the area, having helped themselves to money in several banks and trains. At the time of his death, Bob Dalton had a price of $6,000 on his head, put up by the Southern Pacific Railroad Company, one of whose trains he had recently robbed. Neighbors say that the brothers came from a respectable family. Bob was said to have been both a chief of police and a marshal, but to have swapped his honor for a life of crime.

Does Coca-Cola cause cocaine addiction?

Atlanta

Asa Briggs Candler may have bought a little controversy along with his Coca-Cola, the rights to which he acquired in 1889. Sold as "the intellectual beverage and temperance drink" by inventor John Pemberton, the elixir relies on cocaine for its stimulating side-effects. Candler has a mystical faith in its powers and advertises it as a "sovereign remedy." Many scientists disagree. By 1890, 400 cases of acute suffering from cocaine abuse had been reported in medical journals. Physician Albrecht Erlenmeyer calls the drug "the third scourge on mankind," after morphine and alcohol. Its use is widespread, however. Parke Davis sells it in cigarettes, ointments, tablets and injections. Angelo Mariani, whose Vin Mariani was the drug's first commercial application, collected a list of users. It includes Thomas Edison and Sigmund Freud. Even Pope Leo XIII is said to keep a flask of Vin Mariani under his belt (→ 1906).

"Old Couple Looking" by Henry O. Tanner. The Negro artist spends most of his time in Europe.

"Old Models" (1892) by William Harnett. His paintings are so real, people are tempted to touch them.

1893

Cleveland

Washington, D.C., Jan. 4. In conciliatory move toward Mormon Church, government offers amnesty to all polygamists, provided they respect future laws against it.

Vatican City, Italy, Jan. 5. First apostolic delegate to United States sent by Pope Leo XIII.

United States, Feb. 24. Philadelphia and Reading Railroad files for bankruptcy, with debts exceeding $125 million.

Washington, D.C., March 1. Congress passes Diplomatic Appropriations Act, creating rank of ambassador for ministers posted in select countries.

Washington, D.C., March 4. Grover Cleveland, who was also 22nd President, inaugurated as 24th President.

New Orleans, Apr. 6. Longest bout in history of boxing, between Andy Bowen and Jack Burke, ended after seven hours 19 minutes with no winner.

Washington, D.C., May 15. Supreme Court rules Geary Exclusion Act, anti-Chinese immigration law, unconstitutional.

Chicago, June 20. American Railway Union, first industrial union of railroad workers, formed; Eugene Debs elected president (→July 6, 1894).

Chicago, June 26. At urging of Clarence Darrow and other reformers, Governor John P. Altgeld pardons three remaining defendants in prison for Haymarket Square Riot.

Minneapolis, Aug. 13. Massive fire drives 1,500 people from their homes and causes $2 million in property damage.

Oklahoma Territory, Sept. 16. Opening of six million acres of Cherokee land causes rush of over 100,000 white settlers (→Aug. 18, 1894).

United States, Oct. 13. Vigilant defeats England's Valkyrie to keep America's Cup in U.S.

Detroit, Dec. 24. Henry Ford, with wife Clara, starts and runs two-cylinder engine, using "theory of points" (→March 6, 1896).

New York City. L.C. Tiffany develops Favrile glass, with which he produces screens, lampshades and other objects.

United States. Stephen Crane, 21, publishes *Maggie: A Girl of the Streets*.

Antitrust Act used against union leaders

New Orleans, March 25

A United States attorney has for the first time persuaded a court to rule a strike illegal under the Sherman Antitrust Act. In the suit, leaders of the Workingmen's Amalgamated Council were convicted of conspiracy in leading a citywide general strike last year. "The evil ... consists in this," ruled District Judge Billings, "that (the defendants) endeavored to prevent, and did prevent, everybody from moving the commerce of the country."

The decision constitutes a sharp departure from precedent. Not since the early 19th century have unions been considered illegal combinations, and strikes have had general sanction since Commonwealth v. Hunt in 1842. The judge admitted that Congress intended the Sherman Act of 1890 to combat "the evils of massed capital." But the language of the bill is ambiguous, encompassing "every contract or combination in the form of a trust, *or otherwise* in restraint of trade or commerce." The decision appears to confirm the fears of one of Senator Sherman's colleagues, who warned that the law "would be a weapon in the hands of the rich against the poor" (→Jan. 21, 1895).

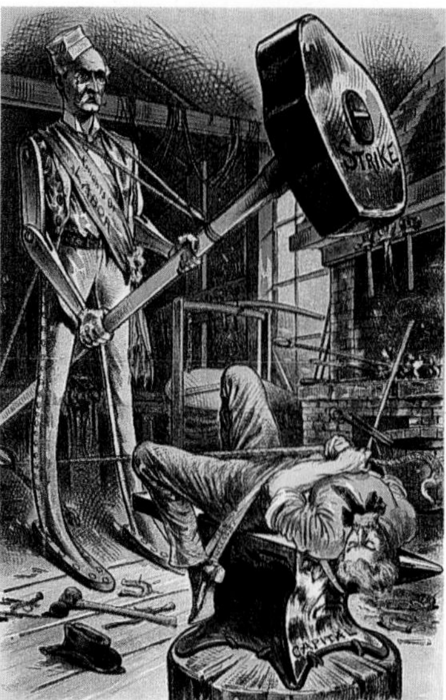

Caught between labor and capital.

Lord Stanley gives hockey cup to Montreal

Montreal

It only cost $48.67, but Lord Stanley of Preston decided to give hockey a going-away present as he ended his reign as Governor-General of Canada. He presented a trophy to the Montreal Amateur Athletic Association team with the understanding that it would be a challenge trophy. It was an aide to Lord Stanley, Lord Kilcoursie, who had become enthusiastic about the sport and urged that the Governor-General make the presentation.

The Montreal team was awarded the squat punch bowl-shaped trophy after it defeated the Ottawa Generals, 3-1, in the first cup game. The first goal ever scored in Stanley Cup play was by a Montreal player, Chauncey Kirby. Both the Montreal and Ottawa clubs are amateur. The Stanley Cup is expected to bring new life to hockey.

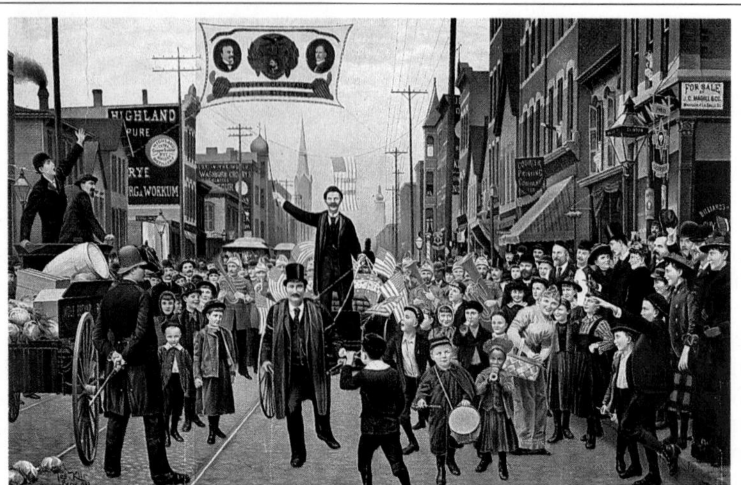

"The Lost Bet" (1893) commemorates the Cleveland-Harrison campaign.

J.J. Hill delivers Great Northern line

Everett, Washington, Sept. 18

Built without government assistance, the Great Northern Railway has become the northernmost transcontinental route operating between the Mississippi River and the Pacific Ocean. The last iron spike was driven today, without ceremony, and without even the presence of tycoon Jerome "J.J." Hill, who dreamed of, financed – and now has delivered – the new railway. Hill plans to run deluxe trains along the line, assuring the maximum of passenger comfort as well as fine food, and the line will connect with steamships bound for the Orient. The long stretch of track was completed in just three years.

Edison opens studio for motion pictures

West Orange, New Jersey, Feb. 1

William K.L. Dickson has designed what he and Thomas A. Edison call a film studio on the grounds of the Edison plant here. This laboratory is named Black Maria because it resembles a paddy wagon. It is a huge box, covered with black tar paper. Part of the roof can be removed to admit sunlight and the whole structure is mounted on a turntable to be able to follow the sun throughout the day. Vaudeville and circus artists have been invited to perform routines on stage. Annie Oakley and Buffalo Bill Cody have already done so (→Apr. 14, 1894).

At 112 m.p.h., train is world's fastest

Batavia, New York, May 10

Although some question remains about the exact speed, it can certainly be said that the New York Central & Hudson River Railroad locomotive No. 999 is the fastest vehicle on land or sea. Traveling down a slight grade, the locomotive, which pulled four cars and a tender, was clocked by the conductor at 112.5 m.p.h. This figure has been disputed by those who, working mathematically, say the engine is too small to attain such speed.

Bell achieves first long-distance call

Alexander Graham Bell receiving a long-distance call to Chicago.

Boston, March 27

The first long-distance call was made today with branch managers of the American Bell Telephone Company in Boston and New York exchanging remarks. "The words were heard as perfectly as though the speakers were standing close by, while no extra effort was needed at the other end of the line to accomplish the result," says an account in the *Boston Journal.* Many attempts have been made in the past few years to establish regular long-distance service, but they have failed because of poor revenues and equipment problems. Today's conversation across miles of line gives evidence of a new era in communications.

End of line at Bell?

Boston

Dozens of independent telephone companies are springing up across the country since the Bell monopoly ended with the expiration of the original telephone patent. Bell Telephone faced a similar challenge before, but it was able to beat back the competition by filing more than 600 successful suits based on its patents. Although Bell companies continue to dominate the industry, the new independents are growing faster, raising doubts about the future. While the number of Bell system telephones and exchanges continues to rise, the competition is starting to affect profits, which have begun to show some degree of decline.

U.S. ends coup in Hawaii

Honolulu, Apr. 13

President Cleveland's emissary, J. H. Blount, ordered United States troops to leave occupied Hawaiian soil today, ending a protectorate established four months ago. Men from the cruiser Boston poured ashore on January 15 "to protect American lives and property," according to United States Minister John L. Stevens. The action came a day before the committee of safety took possession of the government office building and abrogated the monarchy, forcing Queen Liliuokalani from her throne.

Judge Sanford B. Dole was appointed head of the provisional government with authority to negotiate for the annexation of Hawaii to the United States. A treaty was signed in Washington February 14, but the Senate refused to vote on it. On the advice of his Cabinet, newly inaugurated President Cleveland withdrew the treaty from the Senate and sent Commissioner Blount to the islands to find the reasons for the monarchy's overthrow. Blount informed Cleveland that Stevens had conspired with rebels to oust the Queen.

Cleveland then ordered the occupying forces to withdraw. He also sent a new minister, Albert S. Willis, to Hawaii to restore the monarchy and to attempt to make peace between the royalists and the American businessmen who are determined to achieve annexation with the United States (→ July 4, 1894).

Columbian Exposition: Opening Day again

Chicago, May 1

Millions of people have visited the World Columbian Exposition since last October, but that didn't stop President Cleveland from making this official opening day. Before a huge crowd at the fair grounds, the President pressed an electric key in a plush purple box: At once, a giant fountain gushed forth, the American flag ran up a mast and the drapery on a statue of Lady Liberty flew aside.

With the ceremonies over, the public can explore the White City, glistening buildings of classic Greek style. People admire the Daniel Chester French's sculpture *Republic*, symbolizing America, and *Modern Women*, Mary Cassatt's mural for the Woman's Building. Food and drink are also arts: Adolph Coors's prize-winning Golden Select beer is served, along with a treat of caramel popcorn and peanuts called Cracker Jack. Sadly, not all can take pride in the fair. Mrs. Ida Wells Barnett is handing out her pamphlet *The Reason Why the Colored American Is Not Represented in the World Columbian Exhibition* (→ Jan. 8, 1894).

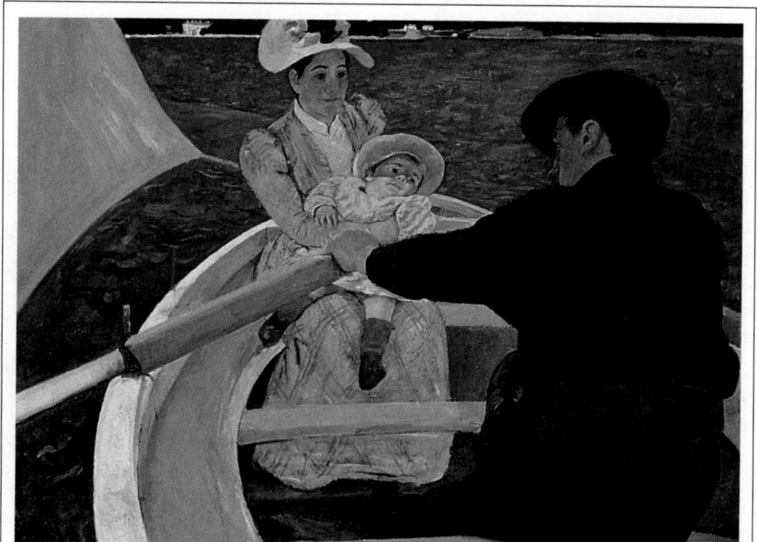

"The Boating Party" by Mary Cassatt. She urges her wealthy friends to buy Impressionist works, thus spreading the school's popularity across America.

Speculators unload stocks, rush to gold

Competing values of gold and silver make for a wobbly economy.

New York City, May 5

There was a wild rush to draw gold from the United States Treasury today as speculators unloaded stocks. Treasury gold is now below the $100 billion required by law. Paper currency is five times the required gold, and Treasury silver is valued at only 70 cents on the dollar. One result is the collapse this week of ventures such as S.V. White's National Cordage Trust, as speculators join the gold rush. It is the fourth failure by "Deacon" White, who tried to corner corn in 1891. Today's crowded exchange gallery included fashionable women elbowing each other for a better view of the battle below (→ June 27).

Self-service eatery

Chicago

Another new idea in restaurants has come out of the Midwest. It involves getting your own food. At Chicago's Columbian Exposition, there is a self-service restaurant in which customers move along a line, choose their food and carry it back to a table where they eat it. These new restaurants, which are being called "cafeterias," are fast, inexpensive and fun. And they save employers money because waitresses are not needed. Some patrons have nicknamed these places "conscience joints" because customers are on their honor to tally up their own bills. These restaurants are perfect for Americans on the move. ▷

Market crash leaves nation in panic

Panic on the Stock Exchange floor.

New York City, June 27
A stock market weakened by monetary uncertainty, dwindling gold stocks and business failures suffered additional setbacks today in the wake of the abandonment by India of silver coinage. The sudden switch to gold by the government that was the idol of free-silver men the world over promptly sent Western mining stocks and silver itself to new low price levels.

With the legal ratio of silver to gold in the United States at 15.98 to 1, the silver dollar is now worth only 60 to 61 cents, and it continues to drop.

Since the Secretary of the Treasury has refused comment, all eyes are on the special session of Congress President Cleveland has scheduled for August. The No. 1 subject will be the President's call for repeal of the Sherman silver law of 1890, under which the devalued silver certificates can be redeemed for a full measure of gold.

Until the drain of gold for silver ends, Eastern bankers believe that the financial panic will continue, although many farmers, laborers and other populists, along with the men who mine silver, see this as their long-awaited opportunity to impose the United States's bimetal gold-silver standard on the rest of the world. Silver, they believe, is the best way to get money back in circulation. They need money and they say that the best way to obtain it is by silver (→Dec. 31).

Ax murder trial jury frees Lizzie Borden

New Bedford, Mass., June 21
"Lizzie Borden took an ax and gave her mother 40 whacks . . ." The children's rhyme may last forever, but the accused murderer's trial ended today. After two weeks of testimony, Miss Borden has been acquitted of the killing of her father and stepmother. Last August 4, Miss Borden rushed into a neighbor's home and reported her parents dead, bloodily mutilated. There were no suspects in the small town of Fall River besides Lizzie, who at 32 is unmarried and stands to inherit her father's fortune. Yet who could think a shy, retiring woman was capable of committing such a heinous crime? Lizzie plans to live quietly with her sister.

Depression toll: 600 banks, 74 railroads

New York City, Dec. 31
As year-end figures pour into this financial capital, a grim picture is emerging. The silver dollar is worth less than 60 cents. Treasury gold reserves, which dropped below the legal floor of $100 million in April, have fallen further, to $80 million. The terrible toll for the year shows 600 banks have closed, 74 railroads have gone out of business and more than 15,000 commercial businesses have collapsed in the contraction that many observers are now calling the worst depression in the history of the country.

Biblical critics attack religious orthodoxy

New York City
Charles Briggs is the latest casualty in the war over church doctrine. A proponent of "biblical scholarship," Briggs has been suspended by the Presbyterian ministry for treating the gospel as a historical text. "The Bible," he says, "has no magical virtue in it, and there is no halo enclosing it. It will not stop a bullet." Inspired by German scholars, Briggs, Washington Gladden, Orello Cone and others question the authorship of the Bible, the biblical account of Creation and even the divinity of Jesus.

Congress rolls back Silver Purchase Act

Washington, D.C., Nov. 1
The great half-price gold sale is over, canceled today when the House voted 192-94 to join the Senate in repealing the Sherman silver law. Under that act of 1890, the Treasury had to buy 4.5 million ounces of silver a month, paying with paper redeemable "in gold or silver" at a ratio of 16 to 1. In theory, this meant that people could buy a dollar of gold for under 60 cents of silver. President Cleveland pushed for repeal as crucial in his drive to stop the run on Treasury gold and to end the panic. In a failed filibuster effort, populist silver congressmen were still touting silver as the key to higher farm prices and wages and prosperity. But the President followed the glitter of gold and signed the repeal measure within minutes of its passage (→Jan. 17, 1894).

Thundering herds of bison are all but silenced on Great Plains

Great Plains, Summer
It was estimated recently that there are probably fewer than 1,000 buffalo left in the United States. Naturalists say that there were as many as 20 million head roaming the Great Plains at the beginning of this century. According to old Indian storytellers, a man could ride his pony in a straight line all day and never come to the end of the herds. As late as 30 years ago, an estimated 13 million buffalo were still grazing the plains in two major herds, one northern and the other farther to the south.

The slaughter of the bison began in earnest during the transcontinental railroad construction boom that began in 1867. Professional hunters employed by the railroads to obtain meat for the thousands of workers killed millions of the animals. "Sportsmen" also took their toll, often shooting the bison from chairs that were mounted on moving trains. But the worst decimation took place when the market for buffalo leather became virtually insatiable.

The government has estimated that in 1873 more than three million buffalo were gunned down. By 1883, both major herds had been wiped out. One museum expedition out in search of specimens that year found fewer than 200 buffalo left. While their numbers have increased slightly since that time, the species still hovers near extinction.

As trains ply the prairies, buffalo fall for the amusement of restless sportsmen.

Storm kills 1,500 on Gulf Coast island

Cheniere, Louisiana, Oct. 1

Bodies were everywhere, even hanging from trees, on this island today after a hurricane raked the southern Gulf Coast. Deaths on the island were estimated at 1.500 while at least 500 were killed in coastal towns. At Cheniere Caminada, a resort area near Grand Isle, griefstricken survivors were the only ones available to bury relatives and friends. A gigantic tidal wave and roaring winds struck the island at about 1 p.m. yesterday. It was the worst disaster in these parts since an August storm killed nearly 1,000 in Georgia and the Carolinas.

Dvorak: New World

New York City, Dec. 16

To many Americans, the New World may no longer seem all that new, but it has inspired in visiting Czech composer Antonin Dvorak a work of exceptional beauty, his Symphony No. 9, *From the New World*. Dvorak, invited to be the director of a conservatory of music, completed the symphony several months after he arrived last year. In that short time, he had come under the sway of native American melodies and rhythms. Many listeners were struck by how the *New World* seems to allude to Negro spirituals and Indian dances.

Anarchist is held on incitement count

Philadelphia, Aug. 31

Miss Emma Goldman, the self-proclaimed anarchist, atheist and opponent of all laws and all forms of government, was arrested last night just moments before she was to address a throng of unemployed workers. As she walked into Buffalo Hall, where her speech was the stellar event, detectives charged her with inciting to riot in New York City. In the hall here, there was a terse announcement: "Miss Goldman has been arrested. Arouse." A mob raced for the doors but was quickly controlled by a cadre of police. Goldman was jailed and will be taken to New York tomorrow.

Frontier, major influence on American character, declared closed

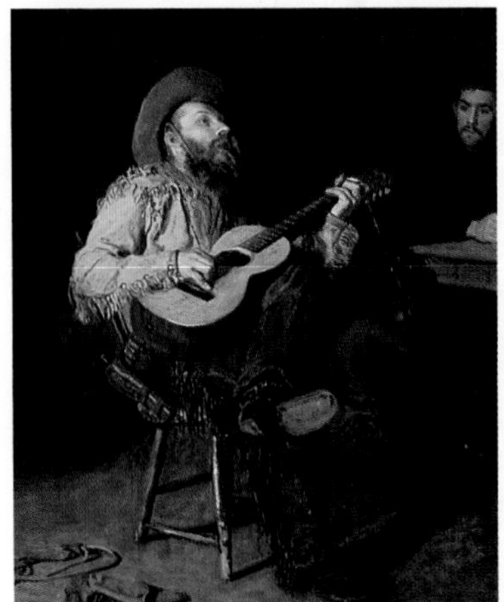

"Home Ranch" (1892) by Thomas Eakins. His works often capture a time remembered only in legend.

Chicago, July 12

"Since the days when the fleet of Columbus sailed into the waters of the New World, America has been another name for opportunity, and the people of the United States have taken their tone from the incessant expansion which has not only been open but has even been forced upon them . . . And now, four centuries from the discovery of America, at the end of a hundred years of life under the Constitution, the frontier has gone, and with it has closed the first period of American history." So concluded Wisconsinborn historian Frederick Jackson Turner today in an address at a meeting of the American Historical Association held in conjunction with the Workd Columbian Exposition.

In his paper, *The Significance of the Frontier in American History*, the 31-year-old instructor at the University of Wisconsin offered a novel interpretation of the American past. Rejecting the commonplace notion that institutions in the United States can be traced mainly to European origins, he pegged the nation's evolution to the continuous flow of Western colonization made possible by the abundance of free land. "The demand for land and the love of wilderness freedom," he explained, "drew the frontier ever onward."

Defined by the census as the margin of settlement which has a density of two or more to a square mile, this frontier ineluctably shaped the people of the United States, providing "a perennial rebirth", a "continuous touch with the simplicity of primitive society," and furnished "the forces dominating American character."

Pioneers building a home. Woodcut.

The historian went on to trace four stages in this evolution – the trader's frontier, the rancher's, the miner's and the farmer's. Each of these, he says, was won by a series of Indian wars and thus the frontier served as "a military training school, keeping alive the power of resistance to aggression, and developing the stalwart and rugged qualities of the frontiersman."

The frontier, Turner continued, particularly in the Midwest, decreased dependence on England and fused "a composite nationality for the American people, . . . a mixed race, English in neither nationality nor characteristics." Spurring a new nationalism and individualism, the "gate of escape" also led to "a laxity in regard to governmental affairs" and a "lack of a highly developed civic spirit."

"To the frontier," Turner maintains, "the American intellect owes its striking characteristics. That coarseness and strenght . . . acuteness and inquisitiveness, that practical, inventive turn of mind . . . restless, nervous energy . . . that byoyancy and exuberance which comes with freedom."

"Attack on an Emigrant Train" by Charles Wimar. From the time of the American Revolution, when the first Conestoga wagons crossed the Alleghenies, to 1830, when the first wagon train reached Oregon, to the prairie schooners of the mid-19th century, Americans have headed out West despite all danger.

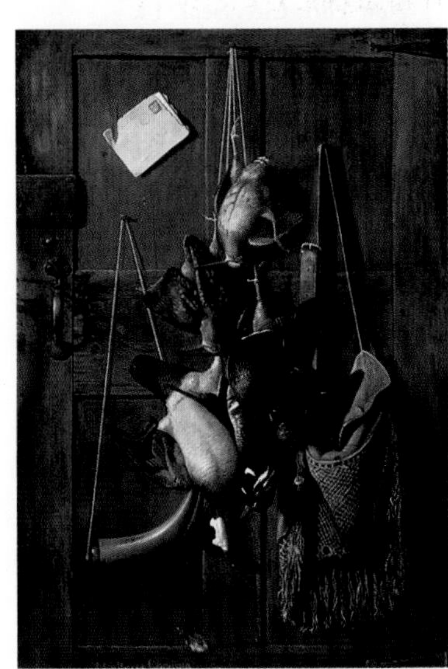

"Cabin Door Still Life" (c.1886) by Richard L. Goodwin. The door to an endless frontier is closing and the art world captures it one last time.

1894

Cleveland

Jackson, California, Jan. 11. St. Sava's Church consecrated as first Serbian Orthodox parish in United States.

Washington, D.C., Jan. 17. Federal bond issue of $50 million offered in attempt to shore up gold reserves that are declining despite repeal of Sherman Silver Purchase Act (March 30).

Washington, D.C., Feb. 8. Congress repeals Enforcement Act of 1871, leaving states in full control of elections.

New York City, February. Horse racing's Jockey Club founded, in part to win "favorable opinion of the public" for sport.

Oklahoma, March 14. Woodward railroad station held up by Doolin Gang; robbers leave with entire safe full of money.

Trenton, New Jersey, May 15. New Jersey becomes first state to prohibit employers from discriminating against union members in hiring.

New Haven, Conn., June 16. First squeeze play used in baseball game between Yale and Princeton.

Washington, D.C., Aug. 18. Congress passes Carey Act, granting one million acres of federal land to states provided it will be irrigated and given to settlers.

Hinckley, Minnesota, Sept. 1. Tornado and fire kill between 400 and 500 people and ravage more than 160,000 acres of forest land.

New York City, Sept. 14. Some 12,000 tailors strike to protest sweatshops.

Texas, Nov. 21. As result of West Texas feud between Jim Miller and Bud Frazier, Sheriff Royal is killed in Fort Stockton.

Washington, D.C., Nov. 22. Japan and United States sign treaty of commerce.

Boston, Nov. 25. *Boston Globe* distributes first color supplement on day of Harvard-Yale football game.

United States. One of first breakfast cereals appears on market; it is known as Cream of Wheat.

United States. The Rev. Howard Hyde Russell forms nationwide Anti-Saloon League.

New York City. Mark Twain's *Pudd'nhead Wilson* published.

Fire destroys exposition

Despite its destruction, the White City, a group of 150 buildings designed by Louis Sullivan and other leading architects, is sure to have lasting influence.

Chicago, Jan. 8

A fire destroyed most of the buildings in the World Columbian Exposition today, causing $2 million in damage. The beautiful White City, a showcase for American invention, is no more. Still, people will long remember the wonders of the fair: the replicas of Columbus's three ships, the giant Yerkes telescope (now being installed at the University of Chicago), the long-distance phone line that brought voices from New York, the automatic moving sidewalk and other wonders. The fair closed on October 30, but by then it had given Chicago $10.5 million in gate receipts and an inspiration to make the White City a reality.

Coal mines hit by strikes and accidents

Pennsylvania, June

Miners across the country have ended a bloody two-month wave of strikes called to protest falling wages. President McBride of the United Mine Workers boasted that there would not be "coal enough left in the general market to boil a tea kettle with." But anthracite production from unstruck mines here and in West Virginia kept supply high. At least 21 miners died in clashes with scabs or police. Mine accidents this year in Plymouth, Pennsylvania, and Franklin, Washington, have taken 50 more lives.

The coal miner's work is often risky. Aftermath of an explosion in the mines.

Cleveland vetoes silver bullion bill

Washington, D.C., March 30

President Cleveland sided with the gold bugs again today, vetoing a bill that favored silver coinage. The bill was the work of the Missouri Representative Richard Parks Bland, a mining camp veteran known by friend and foe alike as "Silver Dick." The Bland bill reached the President only four months after Congress dealt silver a blow by repealing the Sherman law. Reacting, "Silver Dick" Bland promised today's veto "will make silver the predominant feature in the coming election." William Jennings Bryan pledged a fight to end "Eastern domination and revive gold and silver coinage" (→ June 21).

For women's rights, a long, uphill fight

Washington, D.C., Feb. 20

Mrs. Isabella Beecher Hooker, Mrs. Elizabeth Cady Stanton and Miss Susan B. Anthony argued before a Senate committee today on behalf of women's suffrage. The women, who are in their 60s and 70s, will fight on regardless of the committee's decision. There has been some progress in women's rights: Last year Colorado granted women the vote, following in the steps of Wyoming and Utah. And a woman, Mrs. Estelle R. Myers, is being considered for the office of Wyoming's superintendent of public instruction (→ Nov. 16, 1907).

When will the Equality Bell ring?

Omaha hails Bryan in fight for silver

Omaha, Nebraska, June 21

High excitement swept through free-silver Democrats following today's forceful speech by Congressman William Jennings Bryan. Now running for the Senate, Bryan of Omaha brought 1,000 convention delegates to their feet cheering when he declared, "We need more money!" and again insisted that unlimited silver coinage is the way to get it. Last August, in the same vibrant voice, he tried, but failed to persuade Congress to keep the Sherman silver purchase law. But today, Bryan, 34, held the delegates spellbound and talking about a leading role for him in the campaign of 1896 (→Nov. 13).

Coxey's Army is crushed

Jacob Coxey and his army of malcontents chase elusive campaign promises.

Washington, D.C., May 1

The "resurrection of the nation," it appears, is not yet upon us. Jacob Coxey, who hoped to lift the country out of economic sin by leading a jobless army of 100,000 into the capital, has been arrested. His battalion of depression victims, which never equaled 1,000 even including a host of reporters, is dispersing.

Led by the Commonwealth of Christ Band, Coxey's Army left Massillon, Ohio, on Easter Sunday with heads held as high as their hopes. Their small, mild "general" prospers as a horse breeder and quarry owner. But success has only deepened his Christian devotion and his craving for utopian reform. The Treasury, Coxey says, should print currency to fund public projects that would provide thousands of jobs. His child, born during planning for the march, was dubbed Legal Tender, a crawling billboard for economic justice. The army, he says, is his "petition in boots."

After Coxey's ejection from the Capitol steps, a Populist legislator read his address to Congress. "Up these steps the lobbyists of trusts and corporations have passed unchallenged on their way to committee rooms, access to which we," he charged, "the representatives of the toiling wealth-producers, have been denied." Some 2,000 more foot soldiers of poverty are on their way from the West, but no doubt they will meet the same reception.

Dole, defying U.S., seizes Hawaii rule

Honolulu, July 4

Judge Sanford B. Dole and his supporters, defying Washington, instituted a new constitution today and proclaimed the Republic of Hawaii, after ousting the monarchy firmly and forcefully. The constitution makes Dole President through 1900 and imposes strict controls on voting and citizenship. Orientals are excluded unless they were born here. Deposed Queen Liliuokalani has appealed to London and Washington for help in ending the takeover, but her complaints have fallen on deaf ears. The same group that was involved in last year's revolution, headed by Dole and newsman Lorrin A. Thurston, is in charge.

Big bats battering baseball records

Boston

What's happening to baseball? All over the country, batters are reaching new heights with their base hits and home runs. Here in Boston, for example, Link Lowe became the first man to belt four homers in one game, getting two of them in one inning for the Boston Nationals. Another Bostonian, Hugh Duffy, batted a record .438. In addition, his Boston team collected 43 runs in a doubleheader against Cincinnati. Can it be that the ball is getting livelier?

Hershey to sweeten America's tooth

Lancaster, Pennsylvania

Declaring that "caramels are only a fad, chocolate is a permanent thing," candymaker Milton Hershey of Lancaster, Pennsylvania, has developed a chocolate product in the shape of a rectangular slab. The "bar" is priced cheaply enough so that chocolate can become an everyday sweet. The Hershey Milk Chocolate Bar, which will also come with almonds, is prepared with skimmed milk from Pennsylvania cows, and Hershey is planning to start mass production soon.

Periodic economic downswings have become a dreaded but accepted fact of the American business cycle. Thanks to the diversity and strength of American capitalism, however, full recovery never seems too far off.

Pullman workers launch rail strike

Ideal workers' town, no longer so ideal, as National Guardsmen open fire.

Chicago, July 6

The nation's railway capital is in chaos for the third day as troops armed with Winchesters and a federal injunction continue to battle armies of the unemployed and legions of rail workers striking in sympathy with laborers at the Pullman Palace Car Company. Not since the 1860s has the nation found its house so divided on Independence Day. On July 4, as the army entered Chicago, American Railway Union President Eugene Victor Debs warned, "The first shot fired by the regular soldiers at the mobs here will be the signal for a civil war." Since then, seven are dead and scores wounded. Today, at the Panhandle yards, 700 cars went up in flames and were joined by seven remaining buildings from the Columbian Exposition.

The conflict began in Pullman, Illinois, where George Pullman has built an entire town around his rail car works. Laborers eat company food, live in company housing and worship at company churches. Pullman fancies himself a benevolent father figure to his workers. But he has answered hard times like most employers, by cutting wages. At the same time, rents, which are deducted from paychecks, and prices at company stores have remained high. Union men say one of their fellows has a weekly check of two cents after expenses. Thus the *Chicago Times* is slightly more critical of Pullman than the industrialist is of himself: "He has a fat pudgy face . . . A pair of small piggish eyes gleam out from above puffed cheeks, and the glitter of avarice is plainly apparent in their depths."

After Pullman fired three members of a grievance committee on May 11, the local voted to strike. "We are working for less wages than will maintain ourselves and our families," said a union spokesman seeking arbitration. "There is nothing to arbitrate" came the reply. "A man should have the right to manage his own property."

Over a month later, on June 26, the A.R.U., an industry-wide union, began a boycott of Pullman cars. The move affects 24 lines and 41,000 miles of track, all controlled by the General Managers Association. In a week, transport out of Chicago was down 75 percent. By July 2, the G.M.A. admitted it had been "fought to a standstill." The next day, with only a touch of alarmism, the *Chicago Tribune* reported the struggle had attained "the dignity of an insurrection."

To this point, however, at the urging of the rail union leadership, the strike had been largely nonviolent. But President Cleveland was worried. "If it takes the entire army and navy of the United States to deliver a postal card in Chicago," he said, "that card will be delivered." Attorney General Richard Olney, former railroad lawyer and still a director of several lines, handled the legal issues. Declaring the strikers in restraint of trade under the Sherman Antitrust Act, he got an injunction from a judge who called his act a "Gatling gun on paper." Two days later, over the objections of Governor John Altgeld, soldiers flooded this city. Armed forces here total 14,000, including 3,600 Managers Association guards described by police as "thugs, thieves and exconvicts." As violence spreads, opinion turns against the strikers. But Debs hopes they will fight "until workingmen shall receive and enjoy all the fruits of their toil" (→ Dec. 14)

Under U.S. Cavalry escort, the first meat train leaves the Chicago stockyards.

Troops end strike; Debs will go to jail

Chicago, Dec. 14

Despite an impassioned defense by the young lawyer Clarence Darrow, Eugene Debs, president of the American Railway Union, has been sentenced to six months in jail for ignoring an injunction to end the Pullman railway strike. The rail union, broke, betrayed by the conservative trade unions and separated from its leaders by prison bars, ended the strike on August 3. Its effort was doomed by the federal government's decision to enter the fray in July, when troops invaded Chicago and ransacked union offices. Backed by federal officials and other employers, George Pullman has ignored an arbitration plea from 50 mayors, choosing to rehire strikers on a non-union basis.

Debs, king of American labor.

Resistance was strong in many places around the country. In Raton, New Mexico, hotel workers refused to serve federal marshals; even the 10th Infantry failed to open rail lines. In California, five companies of state militia backed the strikers. The Mayor of Hammond, Indiana, demanded to know "by what authority U.S. troops come in here and shoot up our citizens without the slightest warning." In Chicago, center of the storm, 13 were killed and 53 hurt.

Debs, who counseled peace during the strike, has come to symbolize violence in the public mind. Throughout the trial, he was optimistic. "They might as well try to stop Niagara with a feather," he said, "as to crush the spirit of organization in this country." Nonetheless, his conviction sets a precedent for the future (→ May 27, 1895).

Labor Day is made a national holiday

Washington, D.C., June 28

Hoping perhaps that the chaotic Pullman strike in Chicago would transform magically into a parade, President Cleveland today signed a bill declaring Labor Day a national holiday. Meanwhile, his Attorney General is seeking an injunction that will allow federal troops to legally put down the strike. Labor Day is already celebrated in 31 states on the first Monday in September. The idea was first proposed in 1882 by carpenters union founder Peter McGuire at a meeting of the New York Central Labor Union.

Moving pictures advancing with peep shows and bare ankles

New York City, Apr. 14

A Kinetoscope parlor in a converted shoe store at 1155 Broadway was opened today by a Mr. Howard. Ten machines, each loaded with a 55-foot film made by the Edison Kinetograph, offer viewings of *Barber Shop*, *Horseshoeing*, *Trapeze* and other titles for a nickel each.

Similar parlors have opened in Chicago, San Francisco and Atlantic City, among other places. In one parlor at a resort, however, Senator James Bradley of New Jersey was shocked and dismayed when he spotted a bare ankle in *Carmencita in Her Famous Butterfly Dance*. His complaint to the town's mayor resulted in an order for the peep show operator to discard the film clip or shut his shop.

In addition to the Kinetoscope Company, there is the Lambda Company, organized by Major Latham, who has worked out a way to expand the loading capacity of Edison's machine. And Jean Aime Le Roy, who has 20 years of experience in the field, has opened the Cinematograph Novelty Company with Eugene Lauste.

Reporters who viewed Edison's famed invention are greatly impressed. The views of three blacksmiths at an anvil and a boxing match were perfectly natural and lifelike. *Fred Ott's Sneeze*, with an Edison employee sporting a luxuriant mustache delivering a gigantic sneeze, was remarkable. From Edison's studio comes reports of a 30-second production, *Bucking Bronco*, featuring members of Buffalo Bill's Wild West Show. Another scheduled production is *Fun in a Chinese Laundry* (→ Autumn, 1896).

A Kinetoscope parlor in San Francisco, which opened just this year.

Government raises U.S. gold reserves

Washington, D.C., Nov. 13

The Treasury is going for gold again, offering a $50 million bond issue in one more effort to shore up the gold reserve. The dismal reception of an earlier issue in January surprised authorities because Congress had recently repealed the silver purchase law, removing weak silver from the monetary mix. President Cleveland thought that repeal would settle monetary unease and block the outflow of gold. But the run on gold has continued, and the silver crowd says, "We told you so! Silver coins are the only way back to prosperity" (→ March 3, 1895).

Populist Lloyd's book wants trusts busted

United States

Is the explosive economic growth in the United States, characterized by the concentration of vast amounts of capital and property in the hands of a few individuals, harmful to the well-being of the majority of the nation's citizens? "Never!" would be the answer thundered from the Olympian heights of affluence and privilege occupied by arch-capitalists such as the Standard Oil magnate John D. Rockefeller and banker J. Pierpont Morgan. But a different sentiment is being expressed by an expanding segment of the public.

As the title of Henry Demarest Lloyd's new *Wealth Against Commonwealth* indicates, the crusading journalist and labor lawyer stands squarely in the opposition camp. Lloyd, a founder of the Populist Party, believes that the economy would function more equitably for all Americans if huge trusts – in particular Rockefeller's Standard Oil – were broken up.

East side, west side all around the town

New York City

Walk along New York's 28th Street, music publishers' row, and the incessant clatter of upright pianos tells you why it's nicknamed "Tin Pan Alley." Two of the Alley's big hits this year are in the popular waltz-song style – *The Sidewalks of New York*, and *She May Have Seen Better Days*. Many songs continue to be tailored to New York's large Irish population.

Tariff Act passes; includes income tax

Washington, D.C., Aug. 27

President Cleveland has allowed the Wilson-Gorman Tariff Act to become law without his signature. The law uses an income tax to balance revenue losses the government has suffered. To a President dedicated to lower tariffs, the bill is bad, but better than none. He opposed modifications imposed by Senator A.P. Gorman, explaining, "There are provisions in this bill which are not in line with honest tariff reform, and it contains crudities which ought not to appear in laws of any kind. And yet, it presents vast improvement to existing conditions."

New York World prints color comics

New York City, Feb. 4

Readers of today's *New York World* are in for a surprise. When they turn to a comic strip by Walter McDougall and Mark Fenderson entitled *The Unfortunate Fate of a Well-Intentioned Dog,* they'll find the animal in question rendered in color! Intended to boost circulation, color has been attempted before by this and other newspapers. The leader was the *Chicago Inter-Ocean*, which published color cartoons and comic strips as a promotion during the 1892-93 Chicago World's Fair, including Charles Saalburg's popular *Ting-ling Kids*.

Minstrel shows remain a popular form of entertainment not only in the United States but also in Great Britain. Most shows feature whites in blackface parodying American Negro culture, but a few do employ Negroes.

1895

Cleveland

Portland, Oregon, Jan. 1. Water from Bull Run River begins flowing through household taps.

Butte, Montana, Jan. 5. Several people killed as Kenyon-Connell Company warehouse catches fire, blowing up 350 boxes of dynamite.

Washington, D.C., Feb. 11. Congress establishes Gettysburg National Military Park, a 2,400-acre tract including original battle site and national cemetery.

Washington, D.C., Feb. 20. Congress approves President Cleveland's offer to mediate in British-Venezuelan boundary dispute (→July 20).

Red Canyon, Wyoming, March 20. Explosion in coal mine kills 60 workers.

Washington, D.C., May 27. Supreme Court backs federal government's 1894 injunction against Eugene Debs as justifiable regulation of commerce.

California, Oct. 21. Southern California Fruit Exchange [Sunkist Growers] incorporated.

Washington, D.C., Nov. 5. George B. Selden receives patent, originally applied for in 1879, for clutch-operated car with carriage body.

Laramie, Wyoming, Nov. 18. Gaining social acceptance, cowboys play host to a public dance attended by several hundred people.

Illinois, November 28. First American motorcar race, from Chicago to Evanston in 7 hours 53 minutes, is won by a Duryea.

Kansas, Dec. 25. Natural gas discovered near Iola, in quantities sufficient for manufacturing purposes.

Hartford, Connecticut. First pneumatic tires in United States produced for bicycles.

Chicago. Sears, Roebuck & Company starts mail-order business.

Memphis, Tennessee. Negro woman Ida B. Wells compiles first statistical pamphlet on lynching, *The Red Record.*

United States. *Field and Stream* magazine first issued.

United States. Elizabeth Cady Stanton publishes *The Women's Bible*.

Queen of Hawaii is jailed for treason

Honolulu, Jan. 16

Former Queen Liliuokalani, who battled rebels for four years before being forced to give up her throne in 1892, was thrown into prison today and charged with treason. The Queen had been trying to win reinstatement through American mediators when she was seized. A spokesman for the Republic of Hawaii said Liliuokalani and her supporters were plotting a violent overthrow of the republic. About 200 royalists were arrested and some deaths have been reported in clashes in the city (→Aug. 12, 1898).

Frederick Douglass, activist to the end

Frederick Douglass, 1817-1895.

Anacostia Heights, D.C., Feb. 20

One of the great abolitionists, Frederick Douglass, died today at the age of 78. Dedicated to causes of freedom and equality right to the end, Douglass attended a women's suffrage meeting shortly before his death. Born a slave in Maryland, Douglass's long career included service as the United States Minister to Haiti, as a member of the Territorial Legislature of Washington, D.C., publisher of the *North Star* newspaper, and organizer of Negro regiments during the Civil War. He was also the central figure at many meetings of the New England Anti-Slavery Society.

Court rules income tax unconstitutional

Millionaires tearfully pay their taxes.

Washington, D.C., May 20

The Supreme Court today ruled that the income tax is unconstitutional. The $80,000 collected so far will be returned. In New York, collector John A. Sullivan said that he had received "between 4,000 and 5,000 returns, to fully 90 percent of which there were protests attached." And the president of the Fourth National Bank, J. Edward Simmons, said the decision "demonstrates that the Communistic and Populistic element cannot override the Constitution."

American beauty

Lillian, the one and only.

New York City

With a voluptuous figure, a natural voice and a flair for publicity, Lillian Russell is transforming herself into the darling of the American stage and fixture on the society pages. She has made her name as a sultry burlesque singer, as "The American Beauty" in Tony Pastor's casino and as "airy, fairy" Lillian in a host of comic operas. Raised in Chicago, Miss Russell developed her skills under the tutelage of the sisters of the Sacred Heart. By 17, she had outgrown their embrace and made her stage debut in *Time Tries All.* Then she moved to New York and left her fiance to join Edward Rice's Pinafore company. Since then, she has married and divorced twice, the second lasting only five months. Her liaison with financier "Diamond Jim" Brady is legendary. Her singing grabs almost as many headlines as her romantic life.

Morgan profits on government bailout

Washington, D.C., February

Eastern money men who stepped in to save the United States Treasury on February 8 are much richer as the month draws to a close. In a deal that has the populist silver backers crying "Foul!" colleagues sold $65 million worth of gold to the government in return for bonds worth 104 1/2, then quickly disposed of them in the market at 112 1/4. The deal was arranged the night before, at a White House meeting that included J. Pierpont Morgan and President Cleveland, under increasing pressure to stop the "endless chain" outflow of Treasury gold, already far below the level required to back the currency in circulation. Morgan, 57, has been a force in the world of finance ever since he defeated Jay Gould and Jim Fisk in their famous railroad battle. Morgan also broke Jay Cooke's government bond monopoly, contributing to the panic of 1873 (→Jan. 6, 1896).

J.P. Morgan, banker and financier.

igh court dilutes the Antitrust Act

Vashington, D.C., Jan. 21

In a ruling that severely restricts he scope of the Sherman Antitrust Act, the Supreme Court has decided to allow the American Sugar Refining Company to continue operaions. The trust controls 98 percent of the nation's sugar-making. But he justices drew a thin line between commerce, which the Sherman Act curbs, and manufacture, which it gnores. Years ago, a New York udge ruled that the sugar trust "can close every refinery at will" and control prices to "crush out" all opposition (→March 22, 1897).

Big business forms advocacy union

Cincinnati, Feb. 22

An editorial in a small Southern newspaper has sparked the formation of a business association that spans the United States. For the past two years, the country has been gripped by a serious depression. To stimulate the economy, the editor of the Dixie Manufacturer suggested that businessmen form a lobbying group. Today, close to 600 company presidents heeded his call and formed the National Association of Manufacturers. Their goal is to open new markets for their goods, both in and outside the U.S.

Bryan calls for 16-1 silver-to-gold ratio

President Cleveland holding the line against those calling for free silver.

Washington, D.C., March 3

Nebraska's young silver champion, William Jennings Bryan, is leaving Congress today to speak out across the nation for his beloved silver, at a ratio to gold of 16 to 1. In his final speeches as a congressman, the lawyer-turned-newspaper-editor continued his collision course with President Cleveland as the Democratic Party's split over silver widened. In one recent speech, the silver-tongued Bryan compared the President to "the trainman who has opened a switch and precipitated a wreck," referring to the President's preference for gold over silver as the way out of the depression. Bryan and Representative Richard P. "Silver Dick" Bland have signed a petition calling on free silverites to fight for control of the Democratic leadership before next year's convention (→July 9, 1896).

Lonely hearts find solace in news column

New Orleans, Dec. 8

A new columnist is offering advice to the lovelorn and defining a "new woman" for readers of the *Daily Picayune*. She is 26-year-old Elizabeth Meriwether Gilmer, whose pen name is Dorothy Dix. She has been on the staff of the *Picayune* since May 5. Today for the first time, the column in the Sunday paper was titled "Dorothy Dix Speaks." She responds to letters from the readers, offering common-sense advice on love, marriage and even divorce. Mrs. Gilmer was hired as a fledgling writer by Mrs. E.J. Nicholson, owner and manager of the *Picayune*.

Cleveland acts to cool fervor for rebels

Washington, D.C., June 12

In a move designed to avoid any direct involvement by the United States in the Cuban rebellion that broke out in February, President Cleveland today called on American citizens not to give aid to the insurgents. Sympathy for the rebels, already high, is being fanned by groups of exiled Cuban patriots living in this country as well as by William Randolph Hearst's *New York Journal* and Joseph Pulitzer's *New York World*. On the other hand, much of the business community favors the President's policy of neutrality and non-intervention (→May 22, 1896).

"Some Time in the Future" shows Uncle Sam courting a distraught Cuba.

The Pope challenges American secularism

Rome, Italy, Jan. 6

Pope Leo XIII today blessed the rapid growth of the Catholic Church in the United States – with some reservations. In a papal encyclical, he praised the freedom of religion found in the United States, but he opposed any "divorce" between church and state. The pontiff wrote that the church would "bring forth more abundant fruit" if it enjoyed the support of the state.

Bicycle sales rise; so do women's skirts

United States

They're called "silent steeds" and everyone seems to want one. Americans have fallen hard for the bicycle and salesmen report that they are all but flying out of the stores. But proper ladies, who frown at the divided skirt and wouldn't dare wear bloomers or trousers, have eschewed the two-wheeler in favor of the more dignified tricycle. Now that hems have risen several inches above the ankle, ensuring that a skirt will not become entangled in the spokes, more women can jump on the bandwagon – or the bicycle anyway. And with hems held down by lead, women need fear exposing only a bit of ankle.

"Bicycling in Riverside Park" (1895).

Negro leader would delay equality fight

Poster commemorates Atlanta Expo.

Atlanta, Sept. 18

In a speech titled *The Atlanta Compromise*, delivered at the Cotton States Exposition, the Negro leader Booker T. Washington today called on the Negroes of the South to renounce the aim of equality temporarily and accept a subordinate position in American society. Washington's emphasis is on education and the acquisition of vocational skills first, as the path to social and political equality. There are many Negroes who oppose such a compromise and hope for full equality immediately. Washington, who was born a slave in 1858, is now highly regarded, by Negroes and whites alike, as a speaker and educator and is accepted as the national leader of Negroes (→May 6, 1896).

U.S. intervenes in the Venezuelan crisis

Washington, D.C., July 20

Asserting that "the United States is practically sovereign on this continent, and its fiat is law upon the subjects to which it confines its interposition," Secretary of State Richard Olney today demanded that Britain submit its dispute with Venezuela over the Guiana boundary to arbitration. Refusal to do so, said Olney in a note to Lord Salisbury, would be tantamount to depriving Venezuela of "her free agency." Such an action, said the Secretary of State, would be construed as a violation of the Monroe Doctrine. The Guiana boundary dispute has been dragging on for the better part of a century, but it has been exacerbated by the discovery of gold in the area (→Jan. 1, 1896).

While British imperialism reasserts itself in Latin America, Cleveland's policy makers are shown as having forgotten the need for continued American vigilance in the world.

Struggle for Negro rights losing ground

Charleston, South Carolina

In the last 15 years, many of the rights given to Negroes when the war ended have, in one way or another, been abolished or curtailed. Difficult situations for Negroes exist not only in the South, but also across the nation. Many states have laws segregating transportation and accommodations. These "Jim Crow" laws often require railroads and other companies to provide separate facilities for Negroes that are of the same standard as those for whites. The term Jim Crow is from a minstrel show stereotyping Negroes as hapless and ignorant.

Jim Crow laws are only the tip of an oppressive iceberg. Lynchings have doubled since 1883 to over 100. Many states find ways around the 14th Amendment, thus depriving Negroes of the vote. Virginia did so with a complex ballot system; in South Carolina their vote was revoked by revising the Reconstruction charter. Literacy rules such as "grandfather clauses" may also block Negro voting. Last year, Congress held back funds for vote supervisors (→May 6, 1896).

"A Dog Swap" (1881) by Richard Brooke. Despite the oppressiveness of the nation's institutionalized discrimination, Negro life is often vibrant.

Alternating current from Niagara Falls

Niagara Falls, N.Y., Aug. 26

When he was still in kneepants, the Croatia-born Nikola Tesla became fascinated by a description he read of Niagara Falls. Now, three decades later, Tesla has become responsible for harnessing the fantastic force of the waterfall, creating electricity to run the trolleys and street lights of Buffalo, New York. The hydroelectric plant at Niagara, designed by Tesla and built by Westinghouse, is one of the first to make commercial use of alternating current, a system of producing electricity that was made practical by Tesla's invention of a rotating magnetic field.

U.S. successful defending America's Cup

New York City, Sept. 12

The Americans did it again today! Their Defender sailed to victory over the Valkyrie of England to keep the coveted America's Cup in the United States, where it has been since the first cup race was held in 1851. This was a rematch of the previous test in 1893, when Lord Dunraven entered his Valkyrie to challenge the Morgan-Iselin-owned Vigilant on the 30-mile course off New York Bay. The Defender, like its predecessor, did the job in a three-race series, the longest to date for the cup.

"Imaginary Regatta of America's Cup Winners" (c.1889), anonymous.

Over 300 motorcars now on U.S. roads

Detroit, Michigan

More than 300 motorcars have been built and sold in the United States, and companies are rushing into the business. Models being sold now include the King, made in this city, the Duryea, made in Massachusetts, and a steam automobile manufactured by the White Sewing Machine Company. The Studebaker Brothers, known for their horse-drawn carriages, are planning to build motorcars, as are George Pierce, a birdcage manufacturer, and Ransom E. Olds. The gasoline models account for only 20 percent of the market, with steam and electric vehicles splitting the remainder almost equally.

First Open won by a British ex-caddie

Newport, Rhode Island, Oct. 4

The first United States Golf Open was won by a British professional today. Horace Rawlins, only 19 years old, captured the inaugural event by defeating Willie Dunn. Rawlins, a former caddie in England, has been serving as assistant professional at the Newport Club here. The Open was established to sort out much of the confusion in the American golf picture. The American Golf Association was organized to put an end to the chaos and came up with the National Amateur as well as the U.S. Open as a solution. Charles MacDonald was the winner of the 1895 U.S. Amateur competition.

Player gets $10 for football game

Latrobe, Pennsylvania, Aug. 31

The competition among Pennsylvania's football teams has grown so intense that one club, the Latrobe Y.M.C.A., has actually paid $10 for a player's services. The player, John Brailler, was compensated for his duties as quarterback against a rival team from nearby Jeannette. There were reports that one W.W. "Pudge" Heffelfinger received $500 to play for the Duquesne Athletic Club in Pittsburgh two years ago, but his league didn't complete a full season. There were other reports of payment made by teams in Ohio and Western Pennsylvania, where outside players were hired to bolster local clubs.

Sheriff guns down outlaw John Hardin

El Paso, Texas, Aug. 19

John Wesley Hardin was gunned down today at the Acme Saloon in El Paso. According to witnesses, the infamous outlaw was having a drink and gambling when Sheriff John Selman entered the bar, came up behind Hardin and shot him three times. It is rumored that the sheriff's son, a policeman, had arrested Hardin's mistress for a public disturbance and for carrying a pistol. Because Hardin had said he was going to kill his son for making the arrest, the elder Selman apparently decided to kill Hardin before he carried out his threat. The fatal shot is said to have put a huge hole in the back of Hardin's hat.

The fabulous life styles of the rich and idle in the Gay Nineties

New York City

Being a millionaire these days is a full-time job. Never mind getting there: building railroads, making steel, refining oil and financing the whole lot of it. The real effort is staying in Ward McAllister's *Social Register,* which he says lists all the New Yorkers worth anything at a dinner party. There are, incidentally, only 400, exactly the capacity of Mrs. Astor's ballroom.

The richest of the new rich like to immortalize their wealth in castles that hold hundreds. "Keep it simple," said publisher Joseph Pulitzer to architect Stanford White. He got a ballroom and an indoor pool. In Newport, Rhode Island, summer mecca for the elite, such austerity is passe. Railroad heir William H. Vanderbilt, who understands the value of ostentation, spent $2 million on a marble "cottage" for his wife, Alva, and $9 million on furnishings. They will use it at least two months a year.

And oh, those months! Parties in Newport and New York are legend. Mrs. Bradley Martin's ball cost $360,000. It stimulates the economy, she says. Harry Lehr held a dinner for dogs. Mamie Fish, always seeking ways to enliven a party, once made all guests speak baby talk.

Entertaining is, of course, exhausting. The Pulitzers must supervise 19 servants in their New York mansion; Andrew Carnegie has 76. Anyone in the *Social Register* has at least a nanny, a cook, an upstairs and a downstairs maid, a butler and a coachman. If managing the staff taxes one's patience, there is always tennis at the Newport Casino, horse racing at Saratoga, or the New York Yacht Club regatta.

Despite all the "fuss and feathers," as Edward Harriman called it, there is insecurity in the drawing rooms of decadence. As novelist Henry James says, Americans have "their cash to pay," but no "intrenched prestige to work with." For status they look to Europe. Anna Gould brought Count Boni de Castellane to the altar with her father's millions; Alva Vanderbilt threatened her daughter's American lover to get young Consuelo to marry the Duke of Marlborough. Still, on a trip to London, the Vanderbilts fell into the gulf between the old and new rich. Their yacht outshone even the Queen's, yet the aristocracy snubbed them. But one paper gave voice to the deepest wishes of the American upper class, saying: "It is time that parvenu should be looked upon as a word of honor."

"The triumph of the title-hunting, money-bag Mama."

Millionaire William H. Vanderbilt and his daughter in Paris.

Cornelius Vanderbilt's "The Breakers," in Newport, R.I., cost $5 million.

1896

Cleveland

Washington, D.C., Jan. 6. After public outcry over deal with J.P. Morgan, President Cleveland authorizes fourth bond issue in public offering totaling $100 million.

Idaho, Feb. 20. Farmers drive out group of diggers from Boise Canal project.

Detroit, Mich., March 6. Charel Brady King is first to drive a motorcar on streets of Detroit; Henry Ford witnesses test of King's design (→Sept. 7).

Washington, D.C., March 16. Major boundary dispute between Oklahoma and Texas finally settled by Supreme Court.

Nicaragua, March 20. Revolution erupts, causing alarm in United States.

St. Louis, Missouri, May 27. Tornado kills 306 people and causes more than $13 million in damage.

Washington, D.C., June 11. Government turns house in which President Lincoln died into a national monument.

Martha's Vineyard, Massachusetts, Aug. 19. Waterspout appears off Oak Bluffs, 3,600 feet high and 140 feet at center.

Waco, Texas, Sept. 15. Stunt involving two trains colliding head on at 90 miles per hour results in two deaths.

San Francisco, Dec. 10. Ex-Queen Liliuokalani of Hawaiian Islands begins visit to United States.

New York City. Rabbi Isaac Elchanan Theological Seminary founded; first yeshiva in United States.

Washington, D.C. According to estimates, one-third of Americans own seven-eighths of country's wealth.

Washington, D.C. John Philip Sousa composes *The Stars and Stripes Forever.*

Cambridge, Massachusetts. Philosopher, poet and novelist George Santayana publishes *The Sense of Beauty.*

DEATHS

New York City, Jan. 16. Mathew Brady, pioneering photographer, who captured images of Civil War (*1823).

Hartford, Connecticut, July 1. Harriet Beecher Stowe, author, best known for *Uncle Tom's Cabin* (*June 11, 1811).

High court affirms "separate but equal"

Washington, D.C., May 6

Racial separatists are celebrating today's landmark Supreme Court decision that permits segregation. The court ruled in Plessy v. Ferguson that a law requiring restaurants, hotels, hospitals and other public places to have separate accommodations for Negroes is constitutional, provided those facilities are equal.

The case came before the high court after Homer Plessy refused to leave a "whites only" rail car in New Orleans. He was arrested for violating the Louisiana law that requires Negroes to ride in designated sections of trains. The statute is one of many "Jim Crow" segregation laws imposed on Negroes. Plessy lost his case in lower courts, and through appeal, it finally reached the Supreme Court.

The majority on the bench introduced the "separate but equal" doctrine, declaring that segregation has been "universally recognized as within the competency of states in the exercise of their police power."

Only Justice John Marshall Harlan, a former slaveholder, voiced a dissent. He wrote that the ruling "would stimulate aggressions, more or less brutal, upon the admitted rights of colored citizens." Negro blood is already staining the nation's soil, particularly in the South. An average of 180 lynchings has been reported every year since 1890, 82 percent of them in the segregated South (→Summer, 1900).

U.S. sets up commission on Venezuela

No longer in fear of the British lion, Cleveland employs new-found powers.

Washington, D.C., Jan. 1

In a quick response to President Cleveland's call for intervention in the long-simmering border dispute between Venezuela and British Guiana, Congress today voted $100,000 to fund a three-man commission that will help determine the correct boundary. The President, angered by Britain's rejection of the American demand that the issue be resolved by arbitration, has said that the United States "should resist by every means in its power" any move by the British to appropriate territory beyond the boundary line to be set by the commissioners.

The cause of the President's anger was the belated and condescending British reply to Secretary of State Richard Olney's July message. In a terse statement, the Prime Minister, Lord Salisbury, denied that the Monroe Doctrine had any validity under international law and dismissed Venezuelan claims to large areas of British Guiana as "exaggerated pretensions" that he refused to submit to arbitration.

Cleveland's strong stand against Britain has received widespread popular support. Despite England's naval superiority, war fever and anti-British sentiment are running high. This could work to the President's advantage in an election year. As one of his advisers has put it, "Turn this Venezuela question up or down, North, South, East or West, and it's a winner."

Spain rejects U.S. arbitration in Cuba

As Spain loses its international stature, far-flung colonies prove unruly.

Madrid, Spain, May 22

President Cleveland's offer to act as mediator in the bloody uprising that has been raging in Cuba for more than a year was rejected today by the Spanish government. The diplomatic snub is almost certain to increase American sympathy for the Cuban rebels, already fanned by press reports of atrocities committed by Spanish troops against the civilian population. Business interests, with investments of some $50 million in Cuban sugar plantations, have also been calling for the United States to take action, and only last month Congress passed a resolution to give the rights of belligerents to the insurgents, a move akin to granting them formal recognition. After today's rebuff, Cleveland's hands-off policy is clearly in jeopardy.

Montgomery Ward's latest fashion, an afternoon reception gown.

Bryan rails against "cross of gold"

Chicago, July 9

William Jennings Bryan, the silver-tongued orator from the Plains, won the Democratic nomination for President today, just a day after electrifying the convention with his dramatic "cross of gold" speech, advocating the free coinage of silver. The 36-year-old Nebraska lawyer and former congressman has become known as the "Great Commoner" because of his constant opposition to special privileges for the rich and powerful. He has often attacked the gold standard, but his speech this week was perhaps the most dramatic ever delivered at an American political convention.

"You shall not press down upon the brow of labor this crown of thorns," he told his rapt audience. "You shall not crucify mankind upon a cross of gold." When he finished, delegates broke into cheers. Bands played as the Democrats paraded through the convention hall, waving banners as they chanted: "Bryan! Bryan! Bryan!" Many urged an immediate vote on his nomination but Bryan advised against it, saying, "If the people want me nominated and that feeling could not endure overnight, it would perish before the campaign was a week old" (→Aug.)

William Jennings Bryan: "You shall not crucify mankind upon a cross of gold."

Gold is discovered on Klondike creek

Skagway, Alaska, Aug. 12

Whoever said success can't come before hard work hasn't met George Washington Carmack. Called lazy at best, Carmack and his Indian brothers-in-law discovered gold today while fishing on Rabbit Creek [Bonanza Creek], about 14 miles from Dawson City. The creek is a tributary of the Klondike River. Robert Henderson, who suggested to Carmack that he try this area in search of gold, could not be reached for comment and will probably miss out on the strike he inadvertently created (→July 17, 1897).

Light in your pocket

United States

Now you can carry a convenient supply of matches for your cigars or cigarettes. The Diamond Match Company, the nation's largest manufacturer of matches, has devised book matches – pocket-size cardboard folders carrying 20 paper matches with a pad on which to strike them. Diamond Match had some difficulty interesting the public in its new product until a brewery purchased 10 million books to advertise its company.

Utah joins union as the 45th state

Salt Lake City, Utah, Jan. 4

The news that Utah has finally become a state, the nation's 45th, arrived this morning at 8:03. When word was received that President Cleveland had signed the statehood bill, the town went wild. Fire alarms and whistles were sounded for hours, firecrackers were exploded, business was suspended and a flood of residents poured into the streets, dancing, causing mayhem and generally celebrating the biggest moment in the history of this region. With the controversial issue of Mormon polygamy seemingly settled, local officials expect that the transition to statehood will be smooth. Salt Lake City has been chosen as the state capital and Heber M. Wells will serve there as Utah's first Governor.

American is first Olympic champion

Athens, Greece, Summer

The Olympic Games, abolished in the year 394 after a 1,000-year history, have been resumed here and an American is the winner of the first gold medal. James B. Connolly, who left Harvard because the university wouldn't grant him leave to compete, placed first in the triple jump. In addition to the United States, nations participating with informal teams included Denmark, England, Germany, France, Hungary, Switzerland and the host, Greece. Most of the Americans taking part came from the Boston Athletic Association. The Olympics were revived by Baron Pierre de Coubertin, whose visit to the United States helped him shape his ideas about how athletics could become part of an education.

"What's the Matter With Kansas?"

Emporia, Kansas, August

Overnight, the weekly *Emporia Gazette* and its editor, William Allen White, have become as famous as the *New York World* and Joseph Pulitzer. An editorial, published August 15, did it. Titled "What's the Matter With Kansas?" it says that Populists who scare away wealth are what's the matter. Written by 28-year-old White, the editorial labels the Populist candidate for governor "an old mossback who howls because there is a bathtub in the State House." It calls the Populist running for chief justice a "shabby, wild-eyed rattlebrained fanatic who has said openly that the rights of the user are paramount to the rights of the owner." White didn't think it would go beyond Emporia, but it was picked up by a syndicate. Now anti-Bryan forces are spreading it across the country. Counterattacking, Emporia's Populist *Times* describes the White piece as "giddy, disgusting nonsense," adding, "No man who is well balanced would demean and deride the good name of his town and state in such style" (→Nov. 3)

Democratic nominee Bryan, with an anarchist and a Western Populist.

Post Office offers rural free delivery

Virginia, Oct. 1.
The Post Office Department inaugurated its new rural free delivery service across Virginia today. RFD, as it is called, will soon be available throughout the nation to farmers, ranchers and other folks who live out in the country and away from traditional city-oriented mail services. The concept of RFD has been pushed for several years by the Grange and other agrarian organizations, but the movement gathered both widespread popular support and the necessary congressional backing when it was recently taken up by Representative James O'Donnell of Michigan. It is expected that RFD will be a boon not only to rural dwellers, but also to mail-order companies such as Sears, Roebuck and Montgomery Ward that serve the farming community with shop-by-mail goods ranging from men's underwear to musical instruments, and from patent medicines to farming equipment. The government is expected to lose money on the RFD program this year and will continue to do so as the services expand.

McKinley defeats Bryan

A conservative man, McKinley holds fast to his belief in big business.

The new President's support for monopolies troubles many Americans.

Washington, D.C., Nov. 3
William McKinley, the former Governor of Ohio, was elected President today, defeating his Democratic opponent, William Jennings Bryan, after a heated campaign. With the aid of a big war chest assembled by Mark Hanna, a Cleveland industrialist, McKinley won 23 states with 271 electoral votes to Bryan's 22 states and 176 electoral votes. Garret A. Hobart of New Jersey won the vice presidency.

A principal dispute between the presidential candidates this year was over monetary policy. McKinley, a Republican, is in favor of retaining the gold standard, while Bryan called for the free coinage of silver in the now famous "cross of gold" speech that won him his nomination last July.

McKinley, a 53-year-old Civil War veteran, conducted much of the campaign from his home in Canton, with voters coming from near and far to hear his front-porch speeches (→March 14, 1900).

X-rays do wonders, but can be harmful

Chicago, Jan. 29
When the German scientist William Roentgen used the X-rays he discovered last year to photograph the bones within a human hand, the implications for medical science were immediately clear. But Emil H. Grubbe, a Chicago researcher, has discovered that the invisible radiation, originally considered harmless, can kill living cells if the doses are heavy. He made the finding when his hand was burned severely after exposure. Today, however, Grubbe aimed X-rays at the tumors of a breast cancer patient in hopes that the powerful new force would destroy the malignant cells.

Rio Grande sandbar is site of title bout

Rio Grande River, Feb. 21
On a sandbar in the Rio Grande River separating Texas from Mexico – the strangest site ever chosen for a heavyweight championship fight – Bob Fitzsimmons knocked out Peter Maher in 95 seconds today. Why the sandbar? Because the bout had been outlawed in every state of the union. The battle, staged 400 miles from El Paso, was orchestrated by Judge Roy Bean, an opportunist who dispenses both law and booze from his ginmill in Langtry. Technically, the wily judge reckoned, the bout was being held outside the United States.

Innovative American motorcars are being tested, raced and sold

Narragansett Park, R.I., Sept. 7
"Get a horse!" Such was the chant of bored spectators at America's first track race for motor wagons held here today. But in spite of the public's apathy, a handful of American engineers were unremitting this year in efforts to propel the nation into the Horseless Age.

Charles and Frank Duryea, who competed in this Narragansett competition, built their first gasoline-powered vehicle in 1892, and this year they began manufacturing it in Springfield, Massachusetts. The brothers have since completed 10 motorcars, which are being advertised as "the finest specimens of carriage makers' art ever produced for motor vehicles."

In February, the Duryeas made the first sale of an American-built motor vehicle, but others are right behind them. Ransom E. Olds has set up shop in Lansing, Michigan, while Alexander Winton of Cleveland has been building motorcars with tires specially designed by B.F. Goodrich. On March 6, Charles B. King sped along at seven miles per hour in Detroit's first demonstration of a gasoline-powered vehicle. Keeping a close watch was another Detroit machinist, Henry Ford, who by June 4 was tearing down a barn wall so he could get his own two-cylinder "Quadricycle" out on the street. Ford later sold that vehicle for $200 (→Aug. 5, 1899).

Inventor and craftsman Henry Ford prepares to test his horseless carriage.

2 New York teams join hockey league

New York City, Dec. 15
Hockey has spread southward from Canada and New England to metropolitan New York. A four-team league has been formed, with the St. Nicholas and Brooklyn skating clubs taking part in the first official game. The St. Nicholas team included three ranking American tennis players, who among them have won the United States singles title 14 times. A Yale player on the St. Nicholas squad, Malcolm Chace, was instrumental in starting the new league.

Audiences are flocking to the "flickers"

The Vitascope focuses starry-eyed audiences on a new era in entertainment.

New York City, Autumn

"Movies" or "flickers" are becoming one of the biggest things in the entertainment industry, largely as a result of inventions by the Lumiere brothers in France and Thomas A. Edison here. Edison, utilizing inventions by Thomas Armat and Francis Jenkins, has perfected a Vitascope projection system. A gala premiere was held April 23 at Koster and Bial's Music Hall. The program offered hand-tinted scenes, including an umbrella dance, a burlesque boxing bout, a comic allegory on the Monroe Doctrine and a marvelous view of waves breaking on a pier so realistic that spectators in the front feared they would get wet.

Lumiere Cinematograph made its film bow here at Keith's Union Square Theater in June, and in October came the American Biograph. Its program offered parts of the play *Rip Van Winkle*. Attracting wide interest is a so-called "tracking shot," taken from a moving train in Wales.

The tremendous success of these films seems to be making inroads in theaters throughout the country.

One-room schoolhouses, like Miss Blanche Lamonte's in Hecla, Montana, provide an education for millions of children living in small rural communities across the United States. Public school education did not take hold widely until the 1870's, but it is now common in states and territories alike.

"Red Badge of Courage" stirs excitement

United States

There's something for everyone in this year's books. Homebodies are gobbling up Fannie Merritt Farmer's *Boston Cooking-School Cook Book*, the first work of its kind to include weights, measures and instructions. On a higher plane, Charles M. Sheldon's *In His Steps* tells of a minister who models his life after Jesus. No less uplifting is *The Sense of Beauty*, a meditation on art by Harvard philosopher George Santayana. Three other volumes explore native themes. In *The Winning of the West*, Theodore Roosevelt wraps up his four-volume study of the frontier, a setting that proved inhospitable to the heroine of Hamlin Garland's *Rose of Dutcher's Coolly*, published last year.

Most remarkable of all is *The Red Badge of Courage*, the second novel by the 25-year-old Stephen Crane. This short work, published late last year, has stirred enthusiasm because of the author's unique rendering of the Civil War. All the action is perceived through the senses of one combatant, Henry Fleming, a wide-eyed youth about to test his mettle in his first battle. In Crane's haunting prose, he conjures up the sights, sounds and smells of war as he charts the progress of his hero, who "had dreamed of battles all his life," but learns to prefer "images of tranquil skies, fresh meadows, cool brooks – an existence of soft and eternal peace."

Ochs: "All the News That's Fit to Print"

New York City, Oct. 26

Adolph Ochs says that a sober, erudite newspaper can thrive in a city dominated by the lurid Hearst and Pulitzer scandal sheets. Today, the 38-year-old Chattanooga, Tennessee, publisher, himself deeply in debt, bought the failing *New York Times* with $75,000 borrowed from J.P. Morgan and others. *The Times* is now $300,000 in debt and its circulation is down to 9,000, as opposed to 600,000 for the Pulitzer *World*. But Ochs is determined to prove people will pay three cents for a paper that, as he put it, "won't spoil their breakfast linen." The revamped *Times* might not be the most exciting paper around, but Ochs promises the readers that he will provide "all the news that's fit to print" and "give the news without fear or favor, regardless of any party, sect or interest involved."

"The Yellow Kid" switches to Hearst

New York City, May 18

New York Journal publisher William Randolph Hearst recently raided rival publisher Joseph Pulitzer's *New York World* and walked off with a colorful prize, cartoonist R.F. Outcault's *Yellow Kid*. Previously labeled *Hogan's Alley*, Outcault's new version will take on the name of the bald tyke in the bright yellow nightshirt who brought the strip its fame. *The Yellow Kid* will run alongside the other comics in the *Journal's* American humor section. *World* fans of *Hogan's Alley* won't be disappointed, though. Pulitzer has hired the cartoonist George B. Luks to keep the panel running in the *World*. Those observing the bitter press rivalry have coined a new term for sensationalized newspaper reporting. They call it "yellow journalism" after the Kid's distinctive nightshirt.

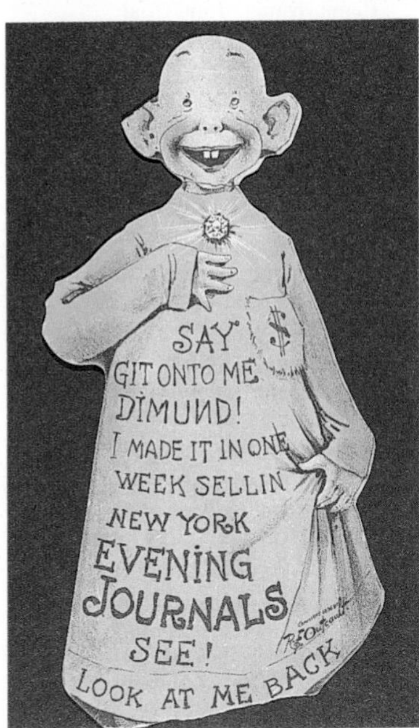

Cartoonist R.F. Outcault's creation symbolizes a new type of journalism.

1897

McKinley

Utah, Jan. 11. M.H. Cannon becomes first female state senator in nation.

Washington, D.C., March 15. Special session of 55th Congress convenes, with Republicans dominating both houses.

Washington, D.C., May 22. Congress allots $50,000 for relief of Americans in Cuba (→Nov. 25).

Newport, Rhode Island, May. In address at Naval War College, Theodore Roosevelt states, "No triumph of peace is quite so great as the supreme triumph of war."

London, June 2. Mark Twain cables New York newspaper, saying, "The reports of my death are greatly exaggerated" (→1899).

Washington, D.C., June 4. Congress authorizes commission to draft criminal codes for Alaska.

Chicago, June 15. Eugene Debs and Victor L. Berger preside over meeting at which Social Democracy of America is formed from various socialist groups (→July 29, 1901).

Portland, Oregon, June 20. Donald Macleay donates 107 acres to establish Macleay Park, largest contiguous park in United States.

Washington, D.C., July 7. Republican majority pushes Dingley Tariff Bill through Congress, raising tariffs to highest level in nation's history.

Pennsylvania, July. Coal miners launch major strike [it proves to be one of labor's first true successes].

New York City, Sept. 25. World's largest ship, Kaiser Wilhelm der Grosse, sails into harbor.

Chicago, Nov. 26. Marshall Field Company erects huge clock at corner of State and Washington Streets.

Washington, D.C.. "Patent War" begins, as scores of lawsuits over patent infringements are filed.

Kansas. Faculty of Kansas Agricultural College is dismissed, for failing to support political doctrines of populism.

New York City. Rudolph Dirk's *The Katzenjammer Kids*, printed in *New York Journal*, is first comic series to use speech balloons.

Rail lines convicted in fixing of rates

Washington, D.C., March 22

The Supreme Court today ruled that 18 railroad companies are violating the Sherman Antitrust Act by banding together to fix rates. Today's 5-4 decision, in United States v. Trans-Missouri Freight Association, reverses the court's path on rail regulation. The majority said the formation of rate bureaus is unconstitutional. The court went further by condemning trusts. Writing for the majority, Justice Rufus Peckman described how trusts forced independent dealers out of business and how those small businessmen were now subservient to big corporations with "no voice in shaping policy" and "bound to obey orders issued by others" (→Dec. 3, 1901)

McKinley sworn in, says war is last resort

McKinley delivers inaugural address after he is sworn in as 25th President.

Washington, D.C., March 4

William McKinley of Ohio was sworn in as President today, pledging to do everything in his power to keep the nation out of war. The 54-year-old Republican told the throng gathered near the east front of the Capitol: "We want no wars of conquest ... War should never be entered upon until every agency of peace has failed; peace is preferable to war in almost every contingency." He proposed the use of arbitration in efforts to settle international differences.

It was a clear day as the one-time member of Congress and ex-Governor took his oath of office, then began his speech, touching not only on keeping the peace but also on the need for monetary reform based on the gold standard (→May 22).

Literacy tests for immigrants vetoed

Washington, D.C., March 2

Calling it a "radical departure" from the "generous and free-handed policy" of the past, President Cleveland vetoed a bill today requiring literacy tests for immigrants. Strong support from the Immigration Restriction League helped push the bill's passage through both houses of Congress. There is concern that such a test would discriminate against new immigrants from Southern and Eastern Europe who have a high illiteracy rate. Cleveland believes a literacy requirement is unjustified and said it would not keep out "unruly agitators," who are only too adept at reading and writing.

New Orleans sets up area for prostitutes

New Orleans, Jan. 26

New Orleans Alderman Sidney Story says that if you can't eliminate prostitution, you can at least isolate it. Today, the Board of Aldermen adopted an ordinance that, in effect, legalizes prostitution in a district that centers around lower Basin Street, on the edge of the French Quarter. Jokesters are saying that the area will be called "Storyville" in honor of the congenial alderman. Open prostitution already exists in the area, where there are lavish bordellos that cater to the leading citizens and "cribs" or small rooms from which women beckon the not-so-leading citizens.

The newly inaugurated Niagara Falls Bridge links the United States with Canada, its neighbor to the north.

Klondike gold bugs swarm back to states

Seattle, Washington, July 17
The Seattle docks were abuzz today with news from the Canadian interior. There has been a major gold strike on a tributary of the Klondike River in the Yukon Territory. The news is more than just rumor. All 60 passengers on the steamer Portland were returning wealthy, the fruits of having been among the first to get to the gold field.

Hints of the Klondike gold strike first appeared in the San Francisco newspapers two days ago when a Seattle resident, Tom Lippy, disembarked from the steamer Excelsior with $50,000 in gold dust from his Klondike adventure. With the arrival of the Portland, the rumor of a strike was confirmed.

Now that the word is out, there are all the makings of a rush. Information about the Klondike, although sketchy, is being widely printed. The sale of staples and mining equipment is brisk and vessels offering passage north are being booked quickly.

A difficult time awaits those going north. Prospectors will dock in either Dyea or Skagway, the two towns in the territory that offer access to the Yukon interior. From there, these hardy souls will have to hike over the Chilkoot or White Pass and then ride through miles of white-water rapids and across lakes that are frozen half the year. It is not going to be an easy voyage but, if the rumors are true, the gravel banks of the Klondike River are chock-full of gold dust that is just waiting for the hardy prospector and his shovel and pan.

Argonaut to plumb depths of the ocean

Baltimore, Maryland
With his iron-wheeled Argonaut I creeping along the bottom of the harbor here, Simon Lake is transforming the visions of author Jules Verne into reality. The 36-foot-long submarine, launched in August, features double iron hulls, between which water is flooded for ballast, and runs on a 30-horsepower gasoline engine. Lake also designed a pressurized airlock for divers and glass portholes through which he has begun photographing fish. Unlike the submersible torpedo boat that rival designer John B. Holland is developing for the navy at the same dock, the Argonaut is made for peaceful research and salvage operations (→1900).

Busy Boston gets a streetcar subway

Boston, Sept. 1
Boston's 2,600 densely packed electric streetcars crawl to such a standstill each rush hour that irate workers claim they could get home faster by walking across the roofs of the cars. But today, the city took a step to ease such congestion when the Tremont Street line started service underground. Built at a cost of $4,350,000, the subway can handle up to 400 cars per hour along a distance of two miles from Allston to Cambridge. The subway was inspired by similar services in Budapest and London, where the song "Let's All Go Underground" is popular. Some 100 passengers took the song's advice today on the first ride (→Dec. 24, 1899).

Spain recalls brutal general from Cuba

Cuba, damsel in distress, protests.

Madrid, Spain, Nov. 25
Following the return to power of the Liberal Party statesman Praxedes Sagasta, the Madrid government today adopted a policy of conciliation in dealing with the Cuban insurgency. Among the new measures are a promise of partial self-government and the recall of General Valeriano Weyler, nicknamed "The Butcher." Weyler, who was installed as Governor-General of Cuba almost two years ago, earned a reputation for brutality by forcing the rural population into "reconcentration" camps in order to deprive the rebels of food and support. Many inmates, mainly women, children and the elderly, are said to have died of disease and starvation. Weyler held that such measures are the only way to combat the rebels' scorched-earth tactics and amount to no more than a policy of "salutary rigor" (→Feb. 16, 1898).

Since 1881, the two former circus rivals have dazzled and delighted young and old alike. Exotic beasts and human oddities make theirs a great show.

"Yes, Virginia . . ."

New York City, Sept. 21
It is now official! In today's editorial page of the *New York Sun*, writer Francis P. Church replied to a young girl, Virginia O'Hanlon, whose belief in Santa Claus was laughed at by her playmates. After an eloquent defense of old St. Nick, Church told the tyke, "The most real things in the world are those which neither children nor men can see . . . and yes, Virginia, there is a Santa Claus."

Title bout filmed

Carson City, Nevada, March 17
With three specially designed cameras clicking away at ringside today – the first time a fight has been filmed for screen projection – Bob Fitzsimmons demolished "Genleman Jim" Corbett in the 14th round and won the world heavyweight championship. A hard left under Corbett's heart ended the contest. Corbett was lifted clear off his feet by the impact and the cameras recorded it all.

Urban America near the close of the 19th century

"Pigeons" by John Sloan captures a familiar sight in the urban landscape.

Children play baseball, the national pastime, in the streets of San Francisco.

Calisthenics for the young in Seward Park on New York 's Lower East Side.

United States

A century ago, Thomas Jefferson and his followers envisioned an America full of freeholders, working their farms in small, self-governing communities. Today, little more than a third of the nation tills the land. With inexorable momentum, city skylines leap up across the country to render Jefferson's vision obsolete. Since the end of the Civil War, urban dwellers have risen from 16 to 30 percent of the population, and in the last 20 years, the number of cities with 100,000 or more residents has nearly doubled.

New York, Boston and Philadelphia, the main centers of urban life in early America, still lead the way. From their base in these three cities, bankers led by Jay Cooke and now J.P. Morgan financed the industrial boom that spawned the urban revolution. With the first transcontinental railroad in 1869 and the thousands of miles of track that followed, manufacturers gained access to markets never dreamed of before. Tons of fruit and grain traveled to feed armies of urban workers, and legions of new products made their way back.

Each new city has cut a niche for itself in the national economy. Pittsburgh, at the heart of a vast iron and coal reserve, grew up around the steel mills of Andrew Carnegie. Aided by Titusville oil and easy access to Lake Erie shipping, John D. Rockefeller has turned Cleveland into the world's oil refining capital. Chicago, with the help of Philip Armour and Gustavus Swift, takes livestock from the West and ships it to the East as packed meat. Minneapolis, using roller grinders to process a new hard-kernel strain of wheat, supplies the country with flour. Milwaukee, surrounded by plentiful hops farms, produces beer. New Orleans processes rice and sugar; Memphis produces cottonseed oil; Waterbury, Connecticut, works brass; Dayton, Ohio, makes cash registers, while Youngstown is turning out steel.

As urban industry grows to maturity, the social and physical landscape around it is left in gangling adolescence. Pressed by an immigration rate of nearly one million a year, many cities struggle with severe housing problems. In 1892, journalist Jacob Riis estimated New York held 1.2 million people in 37,000 tenements. Boston, Newark, Brooklyn, Chicago and Philadelphia also strain under the weight of overcrowding. Municipal services, particularly in immigrant ghettos, lag miserably behind demand. Only recently has poor water been linked to typhoid and dysentery, disposing taxpayers to demand underground pipelines for sewage removal. Baltimore as yet has some 90,000 backyard privies. Electric trolleys are only starting to expand city boundaries. Boston, which opened the nation's first subway this year, is one of the few cities that avoids overcrowding with "streetcar suburbs."

Some Americans view the urban masses with alarm. As early as 1871, poet Walt Whitman noted "cities, crowded with petty grotesques, malformations, phantoms, playing meaningless antics." As workers are thrust into the impersonal world of the large corporation, those with property to protect fear the rise of a permanent class of poor, hostile and desperate laborers. Since 1881, when immigration and urbanization began to take off, murders have increased six times faster than the population. Even municipal politicians hold the law in contempt. City bosses maintain an iron lock on power by taking bribes from contractors and distributing the spoils in exchange for votes. "Government," says New York City boss Dick Croker, "is nothing but a business."

Reform movements are rays of hope in the dark urban landscape. Jane Addams's Chicago Hull House, the Social Gospel preachings of Washington Gladden, the journalistic exposes of Jacob Riis, all of these are pleas for order in the anarchy of city life. Until now, however, few are listening. The White City at Chicago's World Columbian Exposition impressed visitors from all over the world, but budgets still ignore city planning. The dearth of paintings with urban subjects is testimony to the fact that there is little beauty in the new cities. Many seem to fear, with philosopher Josiah Royce, that an urban America will sink to "a dead level of harassed mediocrity."

Overcrowded industrial cities in search of order

A food stand, offering a hot dog for two cents, on the Bowery in New York.

Recreation in a tenement alley playground on New York's Lower East Side.

A military parade moves down the main street of Phoenix, Arizona, in 1888.

A horse-drawn carriage meets an electric trolley car in Philadelphia in 1897.

"Terminal" (1892) in New York City, by Hoboken-born Alfred Stieglitz.

Fashionable Fifth Avenue, N.Y.

State Street, Chicago, Illinois.

1898

McKinley

Washington, D.C., Jan. 7. Alexander Graham Bell appointed president of National Geographic Society.

Chicago, Feb. 8. Butter and Egg Board formed, in part, to grade butter and eggs.

Washington, D.C., Feb. 25. Assistant Secretary of Navy Theodore Roosevelt sends secret orders to Commodore George Dewey, in Hong Kong, to prepare for attack on Spanish fleet in Philippines (→ March 28).

Washington, D.C., Feb. 28. Supreme Court upholds Utah law limiting work day to eight hours, ruling that regulation is lawful when bargaining parties are of unequal strength.

Washington, D.C., March 28. Supreme Court rules in United States v. Wong Kim Ark that U.S. citizenship must be decided without regard for race or color.

Texas, March. Theodore Roosevelt's Rough Riders are recruited and trained in San Antonio (→ July 1).

Washington, D.C., Apr. 5. McKinley orders U.S. consuls back from Cuba (→ 24).

Cuba, May 12. American navy bombards San Juan (→ June 3).

Santiago Harbor, Cuba, June 3. Collier Merrimac destroyed as Lieutenant Richard P. Hobson attempts to block exit of Spanish ships by sinking his own vessel (→ 11).

Oyster Bay, Long Island, August. Theodore Roosevelt returns from Spanish-American War a hero, nicknamed "Teddy," to his annoyance.

Virden, Illinois, Oct. 12. Owners try to use Negro scabs to break coal strike; 13 killed.

New England, Nov. 26. Steamship Portland, ignoring storm warnings, leaves Boston on nightly run to Portland; all 163 aboard die in sinking.

Lake City, South Carolina. Appointment of Negro postmaster sparks riot; postmaster and family are killed.

New York City. *Origin of the Cake Walk*, written by Negroes and starring Negro minstrel Ernest Hogan, becomes first all-Negro show performed for white audiences.

New York City. Henry James publishes *The Turn of the Screw*.

Warship Maine blows up in Havana

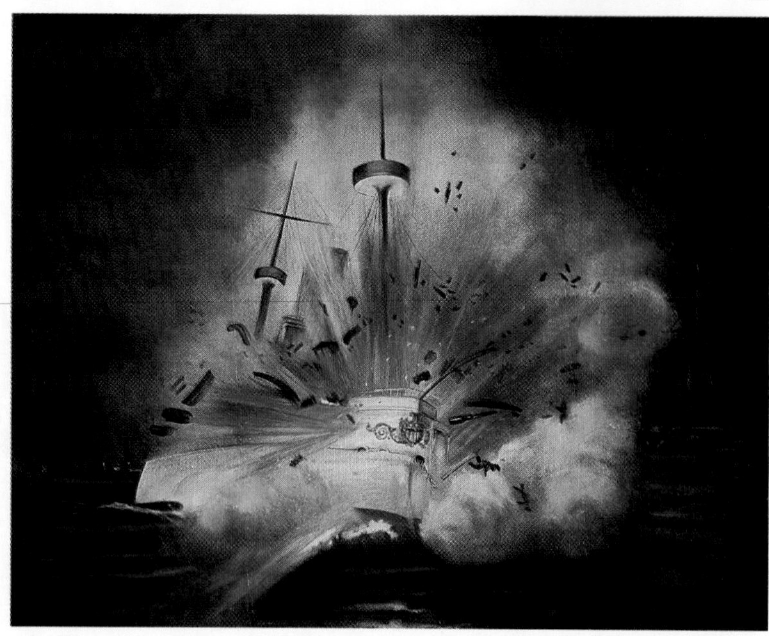

The disaster in Havana harbor inflames a nation eager for military conflict.

The American battleship Maine, now a twisted wreck in Havana harbor.

Havana, Cuba, Feb. 16

The battleship Maine was riding at anchor here last night when a terrific explosion blew out its bottom plates, sinking it almost immediately and taking the lives of 252 officers and men. Captain Charles Sigsbec and most executive officers survived the blast, which occurred at 9:40 p.m. on an otherwise peaceful evening. Most of the casualties were among sailors below decks. There had been no warning the ship would be attacked, and there are rumors it was the work of Spain. While these have not been proven, most Americans believe them.

All that remains of the battleship this morning are twisted sections of the mainmast and tangled remnants of the superstructure. Spectators in small boats have been moving about the harbor viewing the destruction.

Last month, President McKinley decided that an American warship should "show the colors" in Havana harbor as a sign of friendship with Spain despite recent articles in the popular press that have vilified the Madrid government for its treatment of Cuban insurgents who wish to break away from the mother country. While there were reports of Spanish anxiety over the presence of the warship in Cuban ports, it was noted that Madrid was going out of its way to receive the American gesture with courtesy. So, on the morning of January 25, the Maine sailed majestically past the guns of Morro Castle to a mooring that was to become its grave (→ 25).

Hearst: "You furnish the pictures and I'll furnish the war"

Havana, Cuba, March 28

Several months ago the editor and publisher of the *New York Journal*, William Randolph Hearst, sent the famous Western artist Frederic Remington to Cuba to wander about in the bush and to get sketches of the Cuban insurgents fighting for independence from Spain. Remington, unfortunately, found very little war to sketch and, after growing bored drawing pictures of burning sugar cane fields, sent a telegram to his boss that read: "Everything quiet, no trouble here. There will be no war. I wish to return. Remington." The artist is said to have received the following message in response: "Please remain. You furnish the pictures and I will furnish the war. Hearst."

Remington stayed and has been reinforced in Cuba by the presence of Richard Harding Davis, America's most famous war correspondent. Since the arrival of Davis, the two men have been traveling about Cuba aboard the mail steamer Olivette, luxuriating in boat travel after weeks spent on horseback and in decrepit Cuban trains, trying to get a fix on jungle fighters who, at least up to this point, appear to be nonexistent (→ Apr. 5).

The publisher also sits in Congress.

U.S. at war with Spain

Washington, D.C., Apr. 25

The firebrands and warhawks have finally had their way, plunging America into armed conflict with Spain over the fate of the island of Cuba. Congress today passed a joint resolution declaring the United States to be at war with Spain as of April 21.

This is the first major conflict for America since the end of the Civil War in 1865. President McKinley has ordered a blockade of the principal Cuban ports and called for 125,000 volunteers for the army. McKinley, a gentle, conservative Midwesterner, has been seen as a fence-straddler on the issue of war with Spain. But the sinking of the battleship Maine in Havana harbor two months ago finally pushed him to respond to the war fever that has been sweeping the country. This fever has been fanned in the pages of the popular press with the encouragement of such publishers as William Randolph Hearst, Joseph Pulitzer and James Gordon Bennett. These three probably have more to do with the current war than any hawkish senator or congressman, even more than the bellicose Under Secretary of the Navy, Theodore Roosevelt, who has called President McKinley a milquetoast for his attempts to prevent war with Spain. Men ready to do battle over Cuban freedom have begun to line up outside enlistment offices across the country (→ May 1).

War call-up swamps the recruiting offices

An American woman rallies men to battle in front of a recruiting station.

Washington, D.C., Apr. 24

The response to the congressional call for volunteers to fight in the war with Spain has been tremendous. Recruiting stations across the country have been swamped with young men rushing to join the colors. "We'll whip the dagos until they howl" was the typical cry of one young New York volunteer.

On March 9, the Senate passed an appropriations bill previously approved in the House that earmarked $50 million for the war. And on April 23 a call-up of 125,000 men was authorized. The nation's population stands at 60 million and, if you go downtown to the recruiting office in Anytown, U.S.A., it will seem that about half the men in the country want to drop whatever they are doing and go off to fight Spain so that the "insurrectos" can have Cuba. America will need all the fighting men it can get because in Cuba it is facing a battle-hardened Spanish army of 80,000 men under the tough Captain General Blanco.

At present, the American army is made up of 2,116 officers and 25,706 enlisted men. In addition, there is a partly trained militia that provides a reserve of 100,000 (→ 25).

Dewey demolishes fleet

The modern American navy proves its mettle as Commodore George Dewey's steel cruisers obliterate a tired and antiquated Spanish fleet in Manila Bay.

Manila, Philippines, May 1

In a lopsided battle that lasted seven hours, Admiral George Dewey destroyed the Spanish fleet riding at anchor in Manila Bay today. The admiral and his seven warships sailed for the Philippines on April 27 from Hong Kong, where he was asked to leave the neutral port by British officials. He was commanding a fleet considerably more powerful than that of his Spanish rival, Admiral Montogo, whose ships were relics compared to the American behemoths such as the flagship Olympia, boasting six- and eight-inch guns mounted on moving turrets that make these weapons fast as well as deadly.

At dawn, Admiral Dewey sailed into Manila Bay followed by his squadron. The ships were stretched out in a long line with 400 yards separating them. As soon as the Spanish batteries opened fire from Cavite Naval Base, the admiral prepared to respond. He turned to the captain who was his officer of the bridge and said, "You may fire when you are ready, Gridley." The Americans proceeded to annihilate the Spanish fleet, which had elected to fight in the harbor in the hope that the support it received from the fortified shore batteries might save the day (→ 12).

In Cuba: Naval daring and marine attack

Santiago, Cuba, June 11

In a courageous action today, Lieutenant Richard P. Hobson tried to keep the Spanish forces bottled up in Santiago by destroying a vessel to tie up the harbor. The plan was to scuttle an old collier, the Merrimac, under the noses of the Spaniards at Morro Castle, but they fired and the scuttled ship only partly blocked the channel. Hobson and his crew of seven volunteers were captured. Some 35 miles away, American marines landed at Guantanamo Bay, where they beat back a counterattack. Several marines were killed in the skirmish (→ 20).

Marines see action in Cuba.

U.S. Navy seizes Pacific isle of Guam

Guam, June 20

Lieutenant Guitterez was not aware that Spain was at war, so when the American warship began to shell the harbor he thought it was a salute. He rowed out to welcome the visitors. Captain Henry Glass of the cruiser Charleston invited the Spaniard aboard and brought him up to date with the world and with the fact that Guam was now part of the United States. The lieutenant's 60-man garrison was disarmed and the U.S. quietly acquired its first possession in the Pacific (→July 1).

Mr. Dooley offers his political wisdom

Chicago

If you're visiting this city, don't expect to find Martin Dooley behind the bar of a local Irish pub. Instead, look for the wit and wisdom of this working class philosopher in the pages of the *Chicago Journal*, and in a recently collected volume entitled *Mr. Dooley in Peace and War*. The popular creation of *Journal* editor Finley Peter Dunne, bartender Dooley delivers his caustic verbal assaults on politics and big business in a thick Irish brogue. Dooley on Americans as a great people: "We ar-re that. An' th' best iv it is we know we ar-re."

Warship influences U.S. foreign policy

Washington, D.C., May 24

The battleship Oregon is probably the most formidable warship afloat. The problem for the United States when the war broke out was that the Oregon was in the Pacific and the conflict was in the Caribbean. It took 67 days for the Oregon to make the voyage to Cuba. Followers of the political theories of Admiral Alfred Thayer Mahan, an advocate of sea power, say that the length of time it took to put that vessel to use proves an important point about American political policy overseas: a canal must be built across Panama and it must be done now.

Rough Riders overrun San Juan Hill

Bold, brash and committed to victory over Spain, Col. Theodore Roosevelt of the U.S. Army Volunteers.

Color Sergeant Wright is but one of a loyal band of Americans who make up Roosevelt's Rough Riders.

Men of the 16th Infantry take cover in San Juan Creek as Spanish fire rains down from the hill above. There is no choice but to take San Juan Hill.

Bugles, whoops and the thundering of hooves signal the charge up San Juan Hill as Colonel Theodore Roosevelt sees his Rough Riders through to total victory. Through his exploits, he makes himself a military hero in the process.

Santiago, Cuba, July 1

With a victorious bellow, Theodore Roosevelt and his Rough Riders, supported by Negro troopers of the 10th Cavalry, took the San Juan Heights overlooking Santiago today, but the victory was costly. After the battle, there were more than 1,000 Americans dead and wounded in the chapparal and cactus ravines below the heights. The Spanish, outnumbered ten to one, fought fiercely behind deep rifle pits and in concrete blockhouses. Their excellent defensive positions enabled them to inflict heavy damage on the advancing Americans, who had only jungle foliage for protection.

There wasn't any strategy to the battle for the heights defending Santiago, which consist of a series of small hills called the San Juan Heights. The American General Shafter feared malaria as much as the Spanish and decided not to wait for jungle fevers to decimate his troops the way they had the British when they tried to take the same city in the 18th century. The Americans went straight at the heights with 10,000 troops. The Spanish General Linares had only 1,000 men in front of the advancing Americans, but they were courageous fighters and were well dug in, factors that almost offset the numerical superiority of the Americans.

The battle began at dawn, when American soldiers of General J.F. Kent's First Division and the dismounted cavalry under General S.S. Sumner were ordered to take San Juan Hill and Kettle Hill in front of Santiago. First Lieutenant John J. Pershing, an officer in the 10th Cavalry, described the assault on San Juan as a "hellish business." "Fighting Joe" Wheeler, a former Confederate commander, kept his troops going by yelling "Keep moving! The damn Yankees can't stop us," apparently confusing his wars.

Roosevelt, leading his Rough Riders, galloped all over the battlefield on his horse, Little Texas. He was forced to dismount at a barbed wire fence, but that didn't stop him. "Follow me!" he yelled to his dismounted men and headed straight at the Spanish gunners, earning himself a reputation for bravery amounting to foolishness (→17).

U.S. captures Santiago

A juggernaut of United States naval might searches for Spanish quarry.

Santiago, Cuba, July 17

After lengthy negotiations, General Jose Toral today surrendered the besieged garrison of Santiago to the American army. This is fortunate for the Americans, because the wet season is beginning and rains have damaged military communications on the island. General Shafter is very anxious about the malaria rate, which continues to rise alarmingly. Witnesses said that General Shafter grunted with relief when the surrender was completed.

Santiago was doomed the minute the Spanish fleet was defeated on July 3. The Spanish garrison was completely surrounded, outmanned and outgunned, with the Americans holding the heights outside of town as well as the harbor itself. In an effort to make matters go better with the Americans, General Toral turned over Lieutenant Richard P. Hobson and the seven other Americans who, under the guns of Morro Castle, had scuttled the Merrimac in an attempt to tie up Santiago harbor. In this prisoner exchange, the Americans gave Toral 20 Spanish officers, knowing full well that they would be recaptured shortly.

The Cuban residents of Santiago are happy to see the Americans, whom they look upon as liberators. The Americans are pleased as well. According to Theodore Roosevelt, "It's a grand time to be alive. A bully time."

The biggest problems now confronting the army are yellow fever and malaria. Some 5,000 men of the Fifth Corps have been struck down by the two diseases (→ 28).

Americans seize Manila

Conquering Americans march victoriously through the streets of Manila.

Manila, Philippines, Aug. 13

Manila, capital of the Philippine archipelago, fell to the Americans today after a firefight that wasn't supposed to happen and under circumstances that resemble romantic fiction more than fact. The besieged Spaniards knew that the city was indefensible but they didn't want to surrender to Philippine insurgents under Commandante Emilio Aguinaldo for fear of reprisals after long years of abuse. Admiral George Dewey, commanding all United States forces in the area, knew this and had worked out a gentleman's agreement with the Spanish that they would surrender after a mock show of force and some shelling to satisfy "Pundonor," the Spanish code of military honor.

All well and good, but no one had told the troops involved that it was just a show, especially not the Filipino insurgents or the Spanish defenders. When the Astor battery, equipped and financed by John Jacob Astor and commanded by Colonel Payton March and soldiers of the 13th Minnesota, attacked Blockhouse No. 20, they faced a hailstorm of bullets. But after a brief fight, the city fell and is now in American hands. The insurgents are out as Admiral Dewey and General Jaudenes had planned. Details of the surrender were worked out the next day and strong guards were posted to prevent insurgents from entering the capital. None of the participants was aware that President McKinley had signed a peace protocol with Spain yesterday before the sham battle of Manila (→ Dec. 10).

Puerto Rico happily surrenders to U.S.

Ponce, Puerto Rico, July 28

The island of Puerto Rico has surrendered to the American army. In fact, the island of Puerto Rico has surrendered more than once. The inhabitants were so happy to see the "Yanquis" that every island official tried to surrender a hamlet or village. The village of Juana Diaz, for instance, was surrendered to the journalist Stephen Crane. Although there were 7,000 Spanish soldiers on the island, they had all heard about what happened at Santiago, so that no one wanted a fight and there wasn't one worth mentioning. As one officer said when the order to suspend hostilities was given, "There was nothing to suspend" (→ Aug. 13).

Reluctant Hawaiian islanders become part of United States

Honolulu, Aug. 12

Americans cheered and islanders wept as the sovereignty of the Republic of Hawaii was transferred to the United States today at Iolani Palace, ending hope of restoring the monarchy. Shore batteries joined with the cruiser Philadelphia in a 21-gun salute to the latest addition to the nation, although it may take up to two years to complete the annexation. Sanford Ballard Dole, former president of the republic and leader of the revolutionaries who overthrew the monarchy, became the first Governor of the territory-to-be when he was sworn into office. It was Dole, with the support of American businessmen and planters, who set up the coup against Queen Liliuokalani, sounding the death knell for the royal line.

With "our little brown brothers" safely under American protection, the Hawaiian Islands are now ripe for American investment. The bucolic and peaceful hills, valleys and shores of this Pacific paradise will offer many Americans a chance to get rich, particularly those who sell real estate.

Treaty of Paris concludes "a splendid little war"

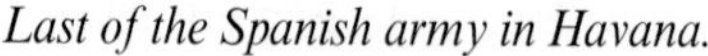

Last of the Spanish army in Havana.

American troops enjoying the peace.

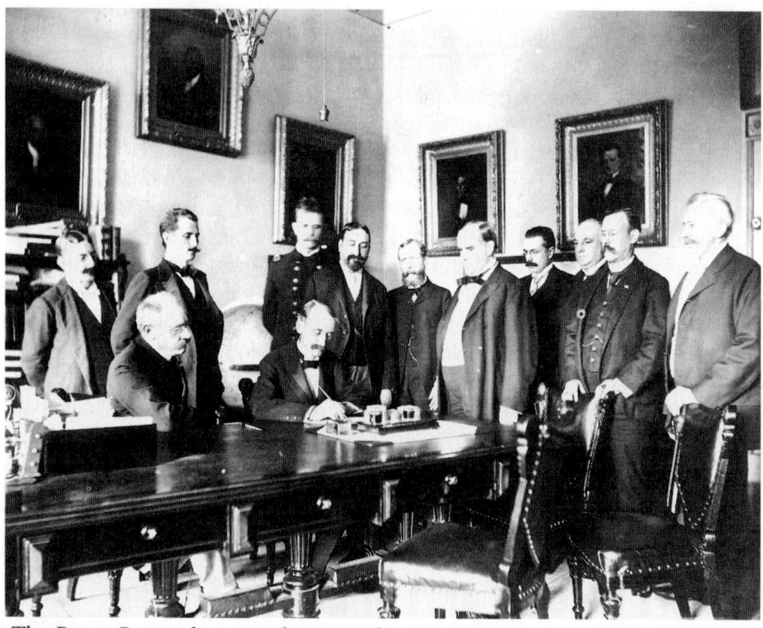

The Peace Protocol is signed as President McKinley looks on approvingly.

Paris, Dec. 10

At the French Foreign Ministry on the Quai d'Orsay, a treaty of peace was signed by American and Spanish ministers today in opulent Old World surroundings that were as far removed from the fever-ridden jungles where their war took place as could be imagined. The Spanish commissioners, who have developed procrastination into a fine art, had kept the discussions going since early autumn, well after the American and Spanish troops had gone home.

There was one real issue that the Spanish envoys fought over strenuously: the fate of the Philippines. From the beginning, the Madrid government thought it was possible to yield Cuba, Puerto Rico, Guam and, possibly, one Philippine island, such as Luzon, and keep the Philippines. But the American commissioners were tougher than the Spanish had expected; they wanted the works. This was, in part, due to the fact that they kept in constant touch with President McKinley, who was himself in touch with American expansionist interests.

Representative "Uncle Joe" Cannon of Missouri had publicly stated that McKinley's ears were so close to the ground that they were full of grasshoppers. The basic theme of the expansionists was simple: We won the war, didn't we? Then let's keep the spoils of war.

From the standpoint of strategy, there was more to it than that. While Admiral George Dewey and the American army were busy with the Spanish in the Philippines, they were constantly being shadowed by the fleet of the German Kaiser. It was clear to American politicians going against the current of isolationism so prevalent in American foreign policy that, if the aftermath of the war created a vacuum, then there were imperialist European powers, specifically Germany and France, who were quite willing to move into the void and gobble up whatever America chose to leave alone. Key Republicans such as Henry Cabot Lodge wanted the treaty ratified very badly and they worked as hard as possible to prevent America from budging an inch in the talks. Had Spain's commissioners known how fervently many Americans felt about their God-given expansionist prerogatives, they might just as well have signed the treaty in October and foregone the long diplomatic struggle.

The final result is that the United States gets the Philippines by paying Spain a $20 million indemnity.

In Cuba, General Maximo Gomez, the veteran insurgent leader, came aboard the Dellie, a ship carrying American "expeditionarios" home. His aide held an old Cuban battle flag, a relic of many battles. They raised the Cuban and American flags side by side in the breeze. What Secretary of State John Hay had called "a splendid little war" was over (→ Jan. 20, 1899).

Spanish-American War: 289 lives lost in battle, 4,000 to disease

Washington, D.C.

As wars go, it was a relatively bloodless affair. It did not last quite a year and there were plenty of opportunities for the young men who volunteered to perform acts of heroism, come home and get their honors. Only 289 lives were lost in battle, but the military has little to celebrate. Troops trained for the humid Cuban summer in wool winter uniforms. Hundreds succumbed to typhoid, yellow fever and "embalmed beef" before even reaching the battlefield, and the toll rose to 4,000 by war's end. Disembarking at Santiago, horses and mules were simply thrown overboard. And most of the campaigns, haphazardly planned and executed, would surely have faltered against a more worthy opponent.

Nonetheless, the United States has unfurled its colors in far away corners of the globe, much to the content of Manifest Destiny's spokesmen. As Henry Cabot Lodge boomed in the Senate chamber, it is high time the great republic entered the fight for the "waste places of the earth." The whole country, however, is in for an education. President McKinley needed a map to find the Philippines, admitting he "could not have told where those darned islands were within 2,000 miles!"

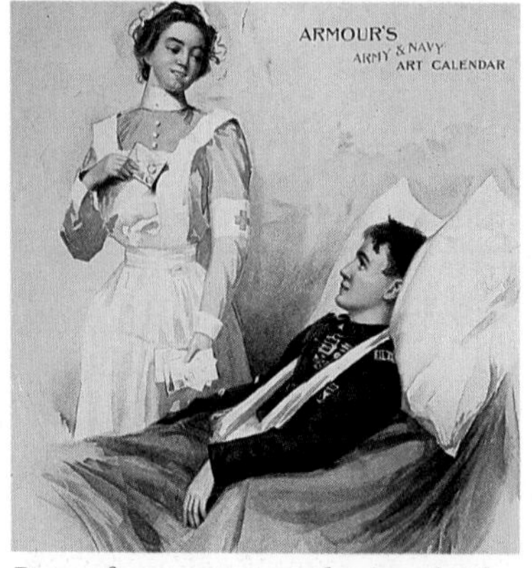

Pages from a meatpacker's calendar cannot hide the fact that hundreds of the country's soldiers have been killed by eating "embalmed beef."

From a misnomer, comes name Nome

Nome, Alaska Territory, Sept. 22

The city of Anvil on the coast of the Bering Sea got a rude shock today. The community will appear on all maps as "Nome." It seems that a British cartographer knew there was a strike on the cape where Anvil was situated but did not know the name of the city. Thus he wrote "Name ?" on the map. He forgot to answer his own question before he sent the map off to the printer. The printer thought that the "Name ?" was "Nome C." or Cape Nome. Thus, thousands of miles away, Nome was named.

Five boroughs form Greater New York

New York City, Jan. 1

New Yorkers suddenly found themselves living in the world's second largest city at noon today. Owing to a charter established last year, Brooklyn, Queens and Richmond joined with Manhattan and the Bronx to form one vast municipality, Greater New York. Mayor Robert Van Wyck, sworn in this afternoon at City Hall, thus is succeeding not one but several outgoing mayors. While the boroughs will share police, fire and health departments, they will retain some local government.

Evidence of Vikings found in Minnesota

Minnesota, Autumn

A farmer in west-central Minnesota has found a mysterious rock, covered with what appears to be runic writing that suggests the Vikings were here in 1362. The so-called "Kensington Rune Stone" was found by Olaf Ohman, an immigrant farmer from Sweden. Scholars are divided on the question of the rock's authenticity.

Painters come to Taos with artistic visions

"Pueblo of Taos" by Victor Higgins. Taos Art Colony gives birth to such works.

Taos, New Mexico, Sept. 5

Ernest L. Blumenschein arrived in Taos on horseback today carrying a broken wagon wheel. After outfitting in Denver, he and fellow painter Bert Phillips crossed La Veta Pass in a light wagon with two broncos, but their rear wheel broke 20 miles from Taos. With the toss of a coin, Blumenschein was assigned the task of getting the wheel to Taos. Muscles aching from exertion, he still did not fail to notice the stark beauty of the landscape, surpassing all the descriptions he had received from artist Joseph Sharp, who has lived in Taos for four years. If Phillips agrees, Blumenschein would like to end his wagon trip, settle in the Taos valley and devote himself to recording its unspoiled majesty on canvas.

Gatling's new gun is best killer yet

Cleveland, Ohio

Richard J. Gatling, creator of some of the world's most efficient killing machines since 1862, has topped all records with a gun that spews bullets at 3,000 rounds a minute. Previous Gatling weapons were all of the hand-cranked variety. But this latest, built by Otis Steel here, uses an electric motor to feed cartridges into the firing mechanism. The inventor was disappointed by the limited role his guns played in the Civil War, but all major powers now use them. This year they decimated Spanish infantry in Cuba.

Brad's drink, Pepsi, imitates Coca-Cola

New Bern, North Carolina

Coca-Cola's success has prompted imitation of the carbonated kola flavor. Caleb Bradham, a pharmacist here, has worked up a similar concoction that he hopes will compete with Coca-Cola. When he first made the drink, Bradham called the beverage "Brad's Drink." But he now calls it Pepsi-Cola and is bottling it to widen sales.

In use for a decade, the electric streetcar provides greater mobility in urban America. Cities expand as the outskirts become more accessible.

What's good for America is good for you. First used by foes of the War of 1812, Uncle Sam is now selling everything from soup to oranges.

1899

McKinley

New York City, Jan. 3. *The New York Times* refers to "automobile" in an editorial; first recognized use of word (→ Aug. 5).

Washington, D.C., Jan. 20. President McKinley names Philippine commission, headed by Jacob G. Schurman, with task of recommending how to administer islands (→ Feb. 6).

Washington, D.C., Feb. 6. Treaty of Paris ratified by United States Senate, by one vote (→ March 30).

Washington, D.C., Feb. 14. Congress authorizes states to use voting machines in federal elections.

Washington, D.C., March 3. Determined to construct canal across Central America, Congress forms Third Isthmian Canal Commission to investigate routes (→ Feb. 5, 1900).

Washington, D.C., March 3. Congress passes criminal codes for District of Alaska.

Philippines, Apr. 28. General Otis rejects Filipino request for peace terms, demanding unconditional surrender (→ Nov. 24).

The Hague, Netherlands, May 18. First Hague Peace Conference opens (→ July 29).

Long Island, New York, June 30. Charles Murphy rides bicycle behind train for a mile, in 57 and four-fifths seconds.

The Hague, Netherlands, July 29. International conference adjourns after appointing justices to form International Court of Arbitration.

Detroit, Mich., Aug. 5. Henry Ford forms Detroit Automobile Company (→ Oct. 14).

Washington, D.C., Oct. 14. President McKinley, riding in Stanley Steamer, becomes first President to use automobile.→

Alaska, November. Governor Brady calls for statehood.

Kansas. Record corn crop of 273 million bushels produced.

Kansas. Carry Nation starts anti-saloon drive in towns of Medicine Lodge and Kiowa.

United States. Song *My Wild Irish Rose* is popular.

Philadelphia. W.E.B. Du Bois publishes *The Philadelphia Negro*, a study based on historical and environmental rather than genetic or racial factors.

U.S. vs. Filipino rebels

American troops display fortitude as they vanquish the Filipino rebels.

Manila, Philippines, March 30

Without waiting for the military reinforcements voted by Congress earlier this month, General Arthur MacArthur has taken the initiative against the Filipino rebels and today drove them out of the city of Malolos, some 40 miles to the northwest of Manila. The rebels are now said to have moved north to the city of Tarlac. But military observers believe that in the months ahead they will avoid pitched battles and take advantage of the jungle terrain to wage guerrilla warfare.

It was in Malolos two months ago that the rebel leader, Emilio Aguinaldo, proclaimed an independent Philippine Republic. Fighting between the Americans and the Filipinos, who had been allies in the war against Spain, broke out here in Manila on February 4 and quickly escalated into a series of bitterly fought skirmishes that cost American forces 57 dead and 215 wounded. Casualties in the Malolos campaign are not yet known (→ Apr. 28).

War Secretary out after probe of army

Washington, D.C., July 19

Bowing to severe criticism of the way he conducted War Department affairs in the recent conflict with Spain, Secretary Russell Alger today tendered his resignation at the request of the President. Among the derelictions for which Alger has been held responsible are chaotic troop transportation, shortages of modern rifles, the provision of winter uniforms for a summer campaign in the Caribbean and sanitary conditions so inadequate that for every soldier killed in action, 13 died of disease.

"Peavy's Folly"

Minneapolis, Minnesota

Grain magnate Frank Peavy has again confounded his critics with a towering grain elevator that has yet to explode or crack as predicted. The 80-foot-tall "Peavy's Folly," on the outskirts of town, joins a network of Peavy's grain elevators. But this is the first such structure to be built of concrete. It will store millions of bushels of grain waiting to be shipped along rail and Great Lakes steamship lines also owned by Peavy.

Anti-Imperialist League formed as U.S. debates role overseas

United States

Since its acquisition of colonies, the nation has found itself embroiled in a heated debate over its role overseas. Partisans of empire are everywhere. Chief among them is Republican Senator Albert J. Beveridge, who in a speech entitled *The Republic That Never Retreats*, proclaimed, "Our institutions will follow our flag on the wings of our commerce. American civilization will plant itself on shores hitherto bloody and benighted."

American might crushing the rebellion in the Philippines.

But now, the Anti-Imperialist League, founded in Boston last year and claiming 30,000 members, is becoming equally vociferous. Reformers Jane Addams and Carl Schurz, novelist Mark Twain and philosopher William James, labor leader Samuel Gompers and industrialist Andrew Carnegie, all oppose the colonial mission, believing it will prove ruinous to the pursuit of American ideals at home.

The anti-imperialists draw inspiration from many sources, but perhaps none as eloquent as former President John Quincy Adams, who on July 4, 1821, counseled: "Wherever the standard of freedom and independence has been unfurled, there will America's heart, her benediction, and her prayers be. But she goes not abroad in search of monsters to destroy . . . She well knows that, by once enlisting under other banners than her own, she would involve herself . . . in all the wars of interest and . . . of avarice, which assume the color and usurp the standard of freedom. The fundamental maxims of her policy would insensibly change from liberty to force . . . She might become the dictatress of the world; she would no longer be the ruler of her own spirit."

With "Maple Leaf Rag," ragtime is hot

Sheet music cover for Joplin's hit.

Sedalia, Missouri, September

The incredible success of Scott Joplin's piano piece *Maple Leaf Rag* has made ragtime the newest rage. While the lurching rhythms of ragtime enlivened blackface minstrel shows, it came to public attention only in this decade with publication two years ago of the first so-called "rag," the *Mississippi Rag*. But this sudden popularity is belated, because Midwestern pianists have been playing ragtime for years.

Born in Arkansas of a violin-playing father and a banjo-playing mother, Joplin, who is now 31, took to the piano at an early age. He began playing in St. Louis nightspots in 1885, first at the Silver Dollar Saloon and then the famed Rosebud Cafe, a mecca for ragtime pianists. The itinerant Joplin now works out of Sedalia, where he often plays at the Maple Leaf Club. One music publisher, John Stark, lives in Sedalia, and was thus able to hear Joplin's music at first hand. He quickly signed the "ragtime king" to a contract.

U.S. urges nations to open doors to trade

Washington, D.C., Sept. 6

Alarmed at the prospect that the ailing Chinese Empire will be partitioned into exclusive spheres of economic and commercial influence by imperialistic European powers and Japan, Secretary of State John Hay today embarked on a diplomatic initiative that is becoming known as the Open Door policy. In identical notes sent out today to Germany, France, Britain, Italy, Russia and Japan, Secretary Hay urged them to declare that they will respect the territorial integrity of China and pursue a policy of free trade in their spheres of influence.

Hay's initiative, which is known to have the backing of Britain, is seen by some as a consequence of the American annexation of the Philippines, which has made the United States a player in Far East power politics (→ March 20, 1900).

John Hay, the Secretary of State, as seen by "Spy" Sir Leslie Ward.

Butch Cassidy gang robs train of $60,000

Wyoming, June 12

The "Wild Bunch" has struck again! Near the small railroad town of Wilcox Station, the band of outlaws stopped a Union Pacific train today and relieved its express car of $60,000, mostly in bank notes. While details of the robbery are sketchy, it has been confirmed that the holdup men were the gang led by Butch Cassidy and his pal, Harry Longabaugh, better know as "The Sundance Kid." Cassidy, about 30 years old, was pardoned by Governor Richards for a robbery just three years ago. Area informants say that Butch maintains his headquarters in or around the little towns of Dirty Devil Creek and Robbers' Roost Mesa. Feared by most law officers, Cassidy has acquired a large and loyal following among the more romantic people who live in this rugged region. In the meantime, a deputy sheriff with a large posse of cowboys are out looking for the gang and say that they are hot on its trail.

Horseless carriage: better than a bicycle?

Detroit, Michigan

Although the *Literary Digest* this year predicted that horseless carriages "will never come into as common use as the bicycle," more than 300 companies now manufacture them or their parts.

Some 4,000 motorcars are in use, with three-fourths using steam or electricity. Now the Stanley Steamer has confirmed its pre-eminence by climbing Mount Washington. Hydrocarbon or gasoline power is costly and unreliable, but young Henry Ford vows to change all that with his Detroit Automobile Company. The boom is spawning a separate industry – tires – with firms such as B.F. Goodrich and the Rubber Tire Wheel Company.

Meanwhile, *The New York Times* debates what to call the "noisy, odorous" contraptions. It deplores the "near indecent" French word "automobile," but it may be a losing battle: *Love in an Automobile* is now a popular song (→ Nov. 3, 1900).

Since 1895, Sears, Roebuck has provided goods through the mail.

Manilia Bay hero hailed in homecoming

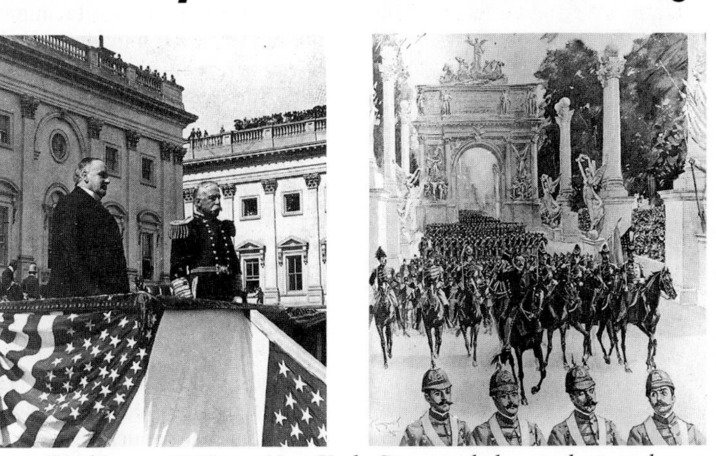

From Washington, D.C., to New York City, accolades are bestowed upon Admiral George Dewey for helping the United States win an island empire.

Achieving the buxom beauty of Miss Blossom with Ivory Soap.

Gibson Girl sets fashion trend for women

The Gibson Girl of Charles Dana Gibson represents the shape, grace and beauty of the ideal Edwardian lady to millions of American women.

Roxbury, Massachusetts

She may be just a drawing, but already her hair and clothes are setting the trend in fashion across the country. She is the Gibson Girl and she made her first appearance in a book of sketches by Charles Dana Gibson called *The Education of Mr. Pipp*. Gibson portrays this classic, dignified beauty in a well-fitted dress with a feminine, flowing skirt. Her long, dark hair is set neatly on top of her head. Now you can find women from one end of the country to the other who look as though they just walked off a page from the Gibson book. A staff artist and editor for *Life* magazine, Charles Gibson has become best known for his light, satirical drawings of society people. He says that he drew the Gibson Girl as his portrayal of the ideal woman.

Wireless reports America's Cup race

New York City, Oct. 20

The United States continued its dominance of America's Cup racing today and this time the American public didn't have to wait endless hours to hear results of the races. The *New York Herald* reported the progress of the boats with a wireless transmission from the steamship Ponce at 15 words a minute. Eager Americans learned that a Herreshoff boat owned by J. Pierpont Morgan and C.O. Iselin named the Columbia easily outsailed the English challenger Shamrock. The Columbia won the cup in three straight races. There was some sympathy among the Americans for the Shamrock's owner, Sir Thomas Lipton, who has won friends here with his grace, good humor and tea.

John Dewey advice is: Don't talk, Act

Chicago

Students should learn how to d things rather than how to talk abou them. So says the philosopher Joh Dewey, who has tested his theorie in experimental classrooms at th University of Chicago, where h heads the School of Education. Th 40-year-old Dewey explains his ap proach to teaching in his work *Th School and Society*, arguing tha since society has become democrat ic, urban and industrial, its school must adapt to reflect the change. H says traditional education, with stu dents memorizing facts under th steely gaze of an inflexible teacher must give way to a "new pedagogy" that encourages students to schoo themselves in the practical art o succeeding in the modern age.

Buddhist mission comes to San Francisco

San Francisco, July 10

Enlightenment, self-reliance, the concept of karma and actions in a former life that affect the present existence – these are some of the ideas that San Franciscans with a curiosity about religion will be hearing about now that Shuye Sonoda and Kakuryo Nishijima, the first two official missionaries of the Jodo Ching-T'u sect of Buddhism, have arrived here to found the North American Buddhist Mission.

Briefly, Buddhism is a religion and philosophy that was founded in India in the sixth to fifth century B.C. by Siddhartha Gautama, called the Buddha. The name means the "Enlightened One," or the "Awakened One." Basic doctrines include the "four noble truths": Existence is suffering; suffering has a cause, namely craving and attachment; there is a cessation of suffering; and a path to end suffering exists, meaning the "eightfold path" of right views, right resolve, right speech, right action, right livelihood, right effort, right mindfulness and right concentration. Reality is process and relation rather than entity and substance.

"The Gulf Stream" (1899) by Winslow Homer. For two decades, this great among American painters has captured the beauty, and terror, of the sea.

Roosevelt's advice to the weary: Exercise

Chicago, Jan. 15

Governor Theodore Roosevelt of New York has some advice to offer the nation's tired. Try a strenous life, he told an audience here today. He should know, for exercise has been his credo since the days when he was a sickly youth, subject to severe asthma attacks.

As a boy, he began a body-building program. Later, he took up big-game hunting. He operated a cattle ranch in the Dakota Territory for two years, once instructing a cow boy during a roundup: "Haste forward quickly there." The phras tickled pub patrons for years. An other time, Teddy and two friend built a raft in three days to pur sue and catch a thief who had stol en his boat. And as a colonel i the First Cavalry, the once-sick ly Roosevelt led the Rough Rid ers' heroic charge up San Jua Hill in the famous battle durin the Spanish-American War.

Twain calls for damnation of human race

United States

The country's favorite humorist doesn't seem too jolly these days. "I have been reading the morning paper," he wrote to William Dean Howells. "I do every morning well knowing that I shall find in it the usual depravities and . . . cruelties that make up civilization, and cause me to put in the rest of the day pleading for the damnation of the human race." Twain, at 64, is bitter over having squandered his fortune as publisher of the Ulysses Grant *Memoirs*. His comic sense hasn't completely deserted him, however. People are still chuckling about his reply in 1897 to rumors that he had died. "The reports of my death," he said, "are greatly exaggerated."

After a life spent studying huma nature, Mark Twain, in the twiligh of his life, seems bitter and pensive.

U.S. takes Luzon from Filipino guerrillas

Their long struggle over, rebels prepare to surrender to American authorities.

Manila, Philippines, Nov. 24

American troops under General Elwell S. Otis today completed the capture of Luzon, the largest island in the Philippines; but the fighting, now in its ninth month, is far from over. Although the United States has 56,000 troops here, the rebels have the advantage of being familiar with a countryside that favors guerrilla warfare.

Meanwhile, opposition to the annexation of the Philippines is growing. In Boston, one member of the Anti-Imperialist League, Andrew Carnegie, reacted to President McKinley's vow "to civilize and Christianize" Filipinos by saying, "About 8,000 of them have been completely civilized and sent to Heaven." The league says ruling people without their consent violates American principles (→Apr. 12, 1900).

Veblen analyzes conspicuous consumption

Nothing is understated in the Waldorf-Astoria's royal suite reception room.

Chicago

A new language has been invented by Thorstein Veblen, son of Norwegian immigrants who has written what some scholars call the first funny book about the "dismal science" of economics. In *The Theory of the Leisure Class*, the 42-year-old member of the University of Chicago faculty lampoons the vulgar values of America's well-to-do, whose creed is "conspicuous consumption," another way of saying: If you've got it spend it – or the neighbors won't be impressed. Not to be outdone, he writes, the neighbors will respond with "pecuniary emulation" and lay out even fatter sums. All this activity, Veblen believes, amounts to "waste because the expenditure does not serve human life or human well-being on the whole." Veblen's odd phrases mask a stinging attack on capitalism.

Three powers agree to carve up Samoa

Washington, D.C., Dec. 2

The Samoan Islands are to be divided between the United States and Germany, according to the terms of a treaty signed today by the United States, Germany and Britain. Germany will annex the western islands, some 1,100 square miles, and America will take the smaller eastern islands, about 75 square miles. Britain agreed to drop its claims to Samoa in view of its interests in the Solomon Islands and Tonga. The United States Navy, which has maintained a base at Pago Pago since an 1878 treaty with the Samoan kingdom, is expected to administer the new American possession in the Pacific. Samoa, a protectorate of the three powers for a decade, has been torn by wars between rival Polynesian chiefs.

A fond farewell for Boston's horsecars

Boston, Dec. 24

Though Boston's electric trolley system has revolutionized life in the city, a few stragglers from the days when horse-drawn cars ruled could still be heard clomping slowly down some streets. That is until today, when the last such vestige of a bygone era yielded to the wheels of progress. A decorative Back Bay car pulled by two handsome white horses made its last rounds as glum-looking bystanders watched along snowy Boylston Street. Although nearly everyone attests to the superiority of the electrics, the new cars are not without their drawbacks. In Boston, "off his trolley" is the new slang for eccentricity; it comes from the tendency of the cars to slip their overhead wires and, as a result, lose power.

"Devil Anse" Hatfield and clan during a lull in their feud with the neighboring McCoys of Kentucky. Trouble began in the 1880s when a Hatfield was accused of stealing a hog and murdering three McCoys. The McCoys raided the Hatfields' West Virginia home and arrested nine for trial. The Supreme Court ruled such action legal, and the Hatfields were convicted.

1900

McKinley

Tacoma, Washington, January. Lumberman Frederick Weyerhaeuser incorporates Weyerhaeuser Company.

Washington, D.C., Jan. 20. Negro Representative G.H. White of North Carolina introduces bill to make lynching a federal crime; it is defeated.

Washington, D.C., Jan. 25. Congressman-elect Brigham Henry Roberts of Utah unseated in House vote, on charges of polygamy.

Washington, D.C., Jan 26. Theodore Roosevelt tells friend, Henry Sprague, "Speak softly and carry a big stick and you will go far."

Chicago, Jan. 29. New baseball organization called American League formed; it fails to gain recognition from National League (→ Oct. 13, 1903).

New York City, March 5. New York University becomes site of Hall of Fame, for noted Americans.

Washington, D.C., March 20. Secretary of State John Hay announces that Germany, Russia, Britain, Italy and Japan have agreed upon Open Door policy in China (→ Aug. 14).

New Jersey, March 24. New Carnegie Steel Company incorporates, allegedly in violation of Sherman Antitrust Law (→ March 13, 1901).

New York City. Vanderbilts take control of Reading, Lehigh Valley and Erie Railroads.

New York City, Apr. 25. Cuba Company investment group allocates $8 million, to develop railroads in Cuba.

Oregon, May 22. Fire destroys 64 buildings in Lakeview.

Washington, D.C., May 22. Patent granted to Edwin S. Votey for "pneumatic piano attachment," or pianola.

New York City, June 15. Paderewski Fund of $10,000 started by virtuoso pianist Ignace Paderewski, to award American composers for best orchestral work.

Minnesota, Sept. 18. Direct primary held for coming elections; first in nation.

Boston, Oct. 15. Symphony Hall opens.

Boston. Booker T. Washington organizes National Negro Business League.

New arrivals swell U.S. population

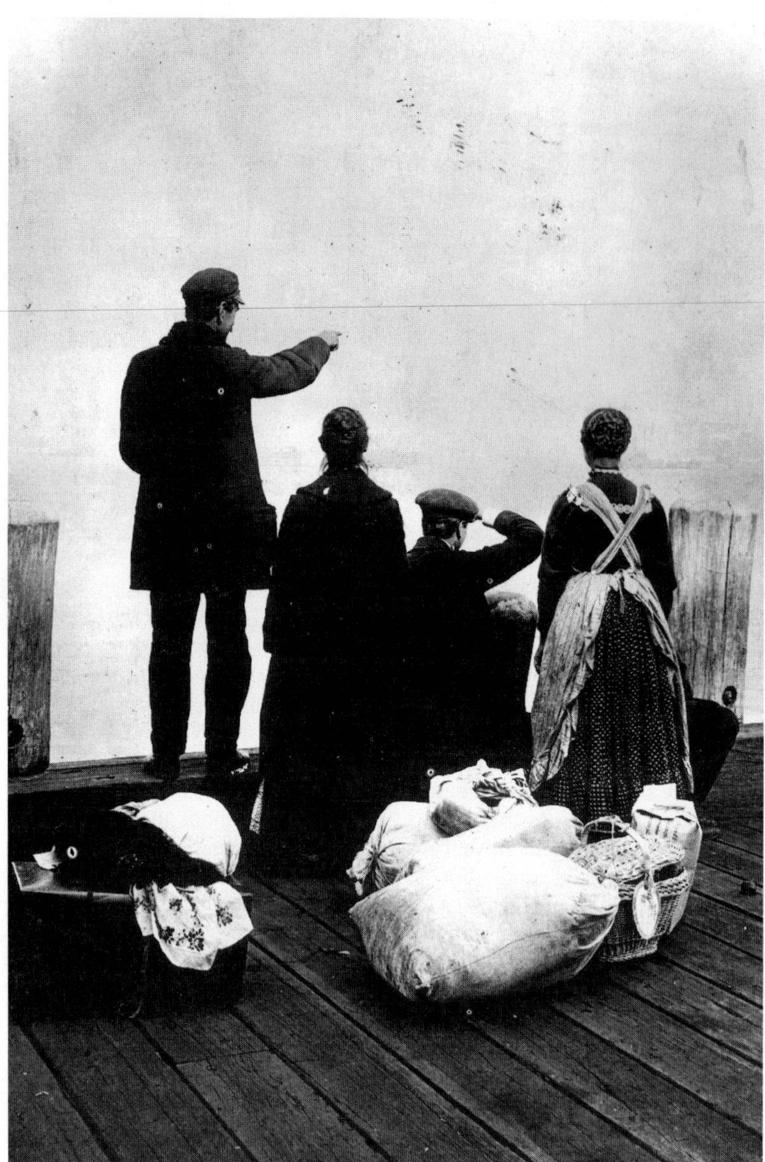

From an Ellis Island dock, an immigrant leads his family into the future.

Proud and determined, arrivals patiently await their chance at a new life.

United States

Bolstered by a flood of immigrants streaming through Ellis Island at a rate of 100 an hour, the population of the United States has jumped to 75.9 million, up from the 62.9 million counted in the last census 10 years ago. New York is still the largest city with 3.4 million inhabitants; Chicago follows with 1.6 million. Some 3.5 million immigrants arrived in the last decade, a flow that has increased steadily except for a lull during the depression years 1894 and 1895. Ellis Island's new facilities, rebuilt after being destroyed by fire three years ago, can handle 8,000 newcomers a day. To the dismay of nativists and many labor groups, the census reported 10 million foreign-born residents and 26 million second-generation Americans. But, as a share of the total population, the foreign-born have hovered at around 14 percent for the entire century.

In fact, it is less the sheer number than the changing character of immigration that leads people to call for restrictions. In 1896, for the first time, the huge trans-Atlantic steamboats carried more Southeastern Europeans than Northwestern Europeans. The foreign-born population still consists mostly of Germans, Irish, Canadians, Britons and Swedes, in that order. But Slavs, Poles and Italians, settling in New York, Pennsylvania and Illinois, will soon be in the majority at the present rate. The Italians alone accounted for 100,000 new arrivals this year, up from 12,000 in 1880.

The advocates of immigration reform argue that the "new immigrants" are unskilled and uneducated, poorly equipped to contribute to the economy or the political system. Prescott Hall of the Boston Immigration Restriction League calls them "historically downtrodden, atavistic and stagnant." Even reformer Jane Addams, who works closely with Eastern Europeans, says those in Chicago are "densely ignorant of civic duties." No proof exists, however, that the new wave is any less talented than the old. The biggest hurdles are more likely the squalid conditions of urban slums and the cultural gap between tight immigrant communities and the dominant Anglo-Saxon world.

8,000 automobiles, 4 billion cigarettes

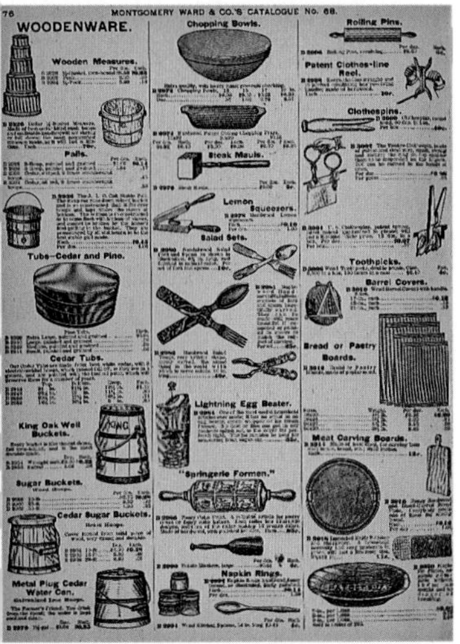

Americans can buy anything ...

New York City

The day when the average American can buy just about whatever he needs seems to have arrived – provided he has the money. Stores and mail-order houses stock an endless variety of goods. There are now at least 8,000 automobiles cruising the nation's roads. For some, the newfangled machines are too complicated; there are still an estimated 10 million bicycles and 18 million horses and mules in use. Businessmen, friends and relatives can call each other regularly on a telephone; there are at least 1,300,000 of them now in service. And for those who want to smoke but don't like to roll their own, tobacco makers produced over four billion cigarettes this year. Ah, democracy!

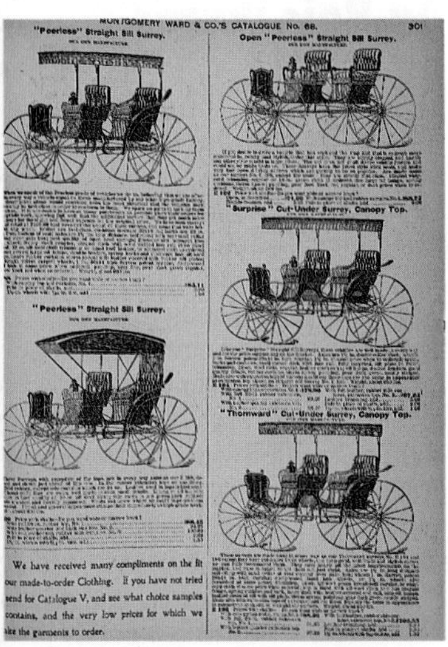

... from rolling pins to surreys from the Montgomery Ward catalogue.

U.S. finally goes on gold standard

Washington, D.C., March 14

Gold is the standard again. Using a new gold pen, President McKinley today signed the gold standard bill approved by the House, 166 to 120. Nine Democrats voted yea with the Republicans after the banking committee chairman closed debate, saying, "This is but one terrace in the height this nation is climbing to that position assured by manifest destiny." In opposition, the defeated free-silver forces charged "stealthy deceit, fraud and corruption," pledging that "the incorruptible, invincible William Jennings Bryan will drive the cohorts of corruption from power forever" in the next elections.

U.S. and Britain sign treaty for canal

Washington, D.C., Feb. 5

A major political obstacle to the construction of a canal across Central America has been removed with the signing here of a treaty with Britain that in effect abrogates the Clayton-Bulwer Treaty of 1850. Under the terms of that agreement, both nations promised not to claim exclusive control over any canal that might eventually be built between the oceans.

The new treaty, negotiated by Secretary of State John Hay and the British Ambassador Sir Julian Pauncefote, drops British claims to a share in the canal, which will now be built by the United States alone. It is, however, stipulated that the canal be unfortified and neutral, "free and open to the vessels of commerce and of war of all nations." Criticism of this clause is heard in the Senate, where the pact must be ratified (→ Dec. 16, 1901).

Canal will be an American project.

U.S. civil rule set for Puerto Ricans

Washington, D.C., Apr. 12

Under the terms of an act sponsored by Senator Joseph Foraker, military rule of Puerto Rico, which Spain ceded to the U.S. in the Treaty of Paris of 1898, is to be replaced by a civil government along the lines of a British crown colony. A single-chamber legislature will be popularly elected, but real power will rest in the hands of a governor and council appointed by the American president (→ Apr. 2, 1901).

70 dead as Hawaii is struck by plague

Honolulu, Apr. 30

Seventy people died and more than 4,000 are homeless as the result of the bubonic plague and intentionally set fires that devastated this city for four and one-half months. Health officials set the "controlled fires" after the outbreak began in December, hoping to kill the rats spreading the disease. Winds whipped the fires out of control, destroying Chinatown. Today, the plague was finally declared over.

Fifth Avenue buses begin regular run

New York City, Jan. 2

Some New Yorkers may have wondered whether the hangovers from their end-of-the-century parties were playing tricks on them when they saw a new contraption gliding down Fifth Avenue. It was the city's first autostage, or autobus. The vehicle runs quietly on electricity, carrying about a dozen passengers at a fare of five cents. Once refined, mechanics say, the bus will be a major mode of city transportation.

Trouble ahead: Casey Jones wrecks train, saves passengers

Memphis, Tennessee, Apr. 30

Train engineer Casey Jones set out on his route from Memphis to Canton, Mississippi, a little late today. Pressed to get back on schedule, he pumped the Cannon Ball express to its limit and slammed into another train at Vaughan, Mississippi. Jones died, but his brave and decisive maneuvering saved the lives of his passengers. Folks in the backwoods are calling Jones a hero. One resident said, "I've known Casey for years. He knew his locomotive and I'm sure he knew his time was up. He could've bailed out, but that would've killed a lot of passengers." Instead, Jones successfully fought to slow the speeding train and minimize the impact.

Casey Jones in the cab of Engine No. 638. Will he forget to watch his speed? ▷

U.S. forces help crush Boxer rebels

American troops march on the Temple of Agriculture grounds in Peking. They are among the 5,000 U.S. troops led by Brigadier General Adna Chaffee, and they are allied with British, French, Russian, Italian and Japanese forces.

A few of the Boxer rebels imprisoned by the allies after the lifting of the blockade by the expeditionary forces.

Upon entering the fallen city of Tientsin, expeditionary forces discover part of the toll paid by the Chinese.

An American cavalryman and Indian troops watch over Chinese dead.

Peking, China, Aug. 14

After two months under siege by Boxer and imperial army units, the foreign legations were rescued today by a force of 19,000 British, American, Russian, Japanese and French soldiers. The diplomats, along with other foreign residents of Peking and some 3,000 Chinese Christians, had barricaded themselves in the legation quarter on June 20, when they came under attack by the rabidly anti-foreign Boxer groups. That they were able to hold out until today is due in large part to the foresight of the first secretary of the American legation, Herbert G. Squiers, who stockpiled a plentiful supply of food.

The Boxers, a secret society officially known as I Ho Ch'uan (The Righteous and Harmonious Fists), are estimated to number 140,000. They are fiercely opposed to any kind of foreign influence. Though once banned, the society has been receiving tacit support from reactionary elements that now dominate the imperial court of the Dowager Empress T'zu Hsi.

The Boxers have not tried to conceal their goals. "The will of Heaven," they declared in a placard posted in Peking last spring, "is that the telegraph wires be first cut, the railways torn up and then shall the foreign devils be decapitated."

By May, Boxer gangs had already begun a campaign of terror against any Chinese suspected of being a Christian. On May 31, attacks on foreigners began with the killing of four French and Belgian railway engineers. This was followed by the murder here of Japanese Chancellor Sugiyama. Soon after, British Admiral Sir Edward Seymour gathered an international rescue force and set out for Peking. After heavy fighting, Tientsin was occupied on July 14. The relief column then regrouped and set out for the capital 10 days ago, making its way up the Pei Ho River. At daybreak this morning, Russian Cossacks took the lead in storming the walls of this city. Although the Boxers offered little resistance in the area of the legations, there are reports that heavy fighting was going on in other parts of the city. The Dowager Empress and her court have made their way to Sian (→Sept. 7, 1901).

Americans sweep Olympic Games

Paris, July 22

Americans made a virtual sweep of the second modern Olympics, although because of a misunderstanding some of the athletes thought they were actually taking part in the concurrent Universal Games. Winners received medals but didn't realize they were for their Olympic successes. The United States won 20 gold medals with a strong team of 55 athletes, headed by four-time winner Alvin Kraenzlein of Princeton. Most of the Americans balked at competing on a Sunday, but Kraenzlein raced and won his first gold medal on a program that was trimmed back by dropping swimming and other events.

Davis wins first tennis cup match

Longwood, Mass., Aug. 10

How appropriate it was that Dwight F. Davis should be a member of the American team that won the first International Lawn Tennis Trophy. It was Davis, a star college player, who put up the trophy. He and Holcombe Ward defeated the English pair of E.D. Black and H.R. Barrett in doubles today after each American won his singles match in the five-match series. With an insurmountable 3-0 lead, Davis was leading the fourth match when rain intervened, ending the competition.

Du Bois warns about "color line"

London, Summer

Addressing representatives to the Pan-African Conference, the noted American Negro leader W.E.B. Du Bois warned his audience that the biggest danger facing the peoples of the world in the new century is the continued existence of the "color line." Du Bois, the first Negro graduate of Harvard University, published *The Philadelphia Negro* last year. This sociological study argues that the Negro upper class, as stewards of their race, must provide the leadership necessary for liberation (→July 13, 1905).

[H]urricane in Texas [t]akes 8,000 lives

[G]alveston, Texas, Sept. 8

One of the worst hurricanes and [t]idal waves in American history [k]illed 8,000 people and destroyed [?],600 structures in this port city [t]oday. The hurricane's winds were [e]stimated at 120 miles per hour and [t]he tidal wave that swept across [G]alveston from one end to the oth[e]r was said to have been 14 feet [h]igh. With no place to bury the [v]ictims in this sea-level strand of a [c]ity, authorities are making plans to [p]lace the corpses in boats, haul [t]hem well out to sea and simply [d]ump them overboard. These offi[c]ials say that the total damage to [t]he city is expected to be more than [$]25 million.

[M]osquito transmits [y]ellow fever virus

[C]uba, September

Some of the sting has been taken [o]ut of yellow fever with the dis[c]overy by Army Surgeon Walter Reed that it is transmitted by mos[q]uito bite. Because the disease is [a] scourge of the tropics, Dr. Reed [h]as been conducting his research [i]n Cuba, where new epidemics have [j]ust broken out. He successfully pro[d]uced the fever in 22 human "guin[e]a pigs," thus proving a theory that [w]as first proposed in 1881 by Dr. Carlos Finlay of Havana. Fortu[n]ately, none of the subjects died.

Republican McKinley retains presidency

President McKinley begins a second term with the aid of Theodore Roosevelt.

Canton, Ohio, Nov. 7

William McKinley has been re-elected President, beating William Jennings Bryan. With the Nebraska results still in doubt, McKinley has 284 electoral votes, to Bryan's 155. The President's home was connected with Republican headquarters by telegraph, and the news passed quickly to the supporters who arrived from downtown with bands playing and rockets firing. He then appeared on the porch from which he had campaigned to thank them "for the very great compliment."

President McKinley, 57, carried with him New York Governor Theodore Roosevelt as his new Vice President, and retained Republican majorities in both houses of Congress. When the results reached Roosevelt's Sagamore Hill home from the railroad telegraph three miles away, the 42-year-old hero of the Rough Riders commented: "Isn't that fine. It shows what the American people are. It shows that they want the good times to continue, and are in favor of honest money and are for the flag." The new Vice President has alarmed some Republicans by urging tighter control of the big trusts, while McKinley enjoys the support of financiers who are pleased about the new gold standard he approved in March. Bryan, the 40-year-old "Boy Orator of the Platte," based his 24-state campaign on his opposition to American imperialism.

Olds and Firestone at first auto show

New York City, Nov. 3

Nearly 10,000 curious spectators jammed Madison Square Garden tonight for what some dubbed the "Horseless Horseshow." An exhibition staged by the Automobile Club of America, it featured the most up-to-date steam, electric and gasoline-powered vehicles. The Firestone Rubber Company and Goodyear Tire and Rubber Company also displayed the latest motorcar wheels. Particular notice was paid to Ransom E. Olds's new $1,250 Oldsmobile. A good horse and buggy costs just $400, but Detroit's Olds Motor Works hopes to sell all 400 curved-dashboard, gasoline-powered Oldsmobiles they finished this year.

$1 Brownie camera

Rochester, New York

George Eastman of the Eastman Kodak Company thinks Americans are ready for a new hobby and he's ready to help. The photography firm is manufacturing its new Brownie Box Camera and selling it for only $1. Eastman was the first to introduce transparent, flexible roll film in 1889. It now retails for 10 to 15 cents for a six-photo roll. The Brownie and inexpensive film will make it possible for thousands to become amateur photographers.

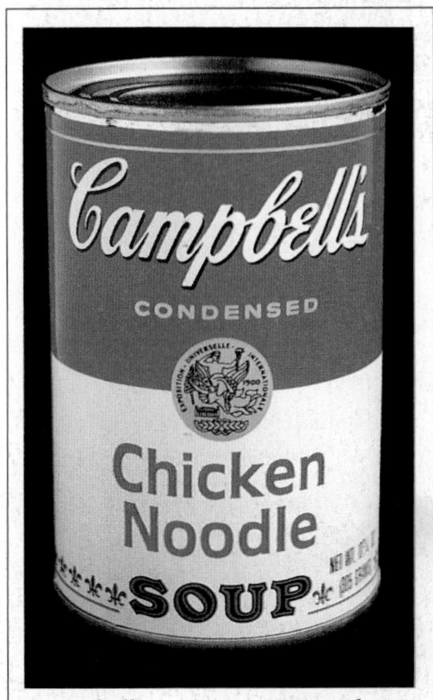

Campbell's Soup, served in American homes since 1897, won awards for quality this year.

The navy's newest: John P. Holland's revolutionary submarine is 53 feet long, powered by gasoline and electric engines and is stabilized by stern-mounted horizontal rudders. It is armed with one bow torpedo tube, one bow pneumatic dynamite gun and three short Whitehead torpedoes.

From Dorothy in Oz to Carrie in Chicago

United States

Two very different damsels in distress star in this year's fiction. Frank Baum's children's tale, *The Wonderful Wizard of Oz*, relates the adventures of Dorothy, a little girl who falls asleep in Kansas and wakes up in Oz, a magical land that she can escape from only with the help of its mysterious Wizard. The heroine of novelist Theodore Dreiser's *Sister Carrie* also leaves a rural life for an alien world, Chicago, where she boards with her sister and brother-in-law before becoming a married man's mistress.

1901

McKinley

Topeka, Kansas, Jan. 1. Agnes N. Ozman receives baptism of spirit and allegedly begins speaking in tongues; first modern instance of glossolalia.

New York City, Feb. 2. Puccini's opera *Tosca* has U.S. premiere at Metropolitan Opera.

New York City, March 12. New York public library system founded with $5.2 million grant from Andrew Carnegie.

Utah, March 14. Governor vetoes bill aimed at relaxing prosecution of polygamy cases.

Philippines, Apr. 2. Emilio Aguinaldo swears allegiance to United States; former rebel leader exhorts followers to submit to U.S. rule (→July 4).

Jacksonville, Florida, May 3. Fire destroys 2,300 buildings.

Springfield, Massachusetts, June 1. Newspapers announce public display of motorized bicycle, designed by Carl Hedstrom.

Washington, D.C., July 25. McKinley proclaims free-trade policy with Puerto Rico.

Peking, Sept. 7. Dozen nations, including United States, sign Boxer Protocol, in which Chinese agree to pay reparations for uprising; United States gets $24.5 million.

Dayton, Ohio, September. Orville Wright designs wind tunnel, with gas engine powering metal fan; it is used for flight-simulation experimentation (→Dec. 17, 1903).

United States, Oct. 4. Columbia beats Britain's Shamrock II to keep America's Cup here.

New York City, Nov. 16. New auto speed record for mile – 52 seconds – set by French driver Henri Fournier.

Washington, D.C., Nov. 27. In wake of criticism of army's performance during war with Spain, Secretary of War Elihu Root founds Army War College.

Alabama, Nov. 28. New state constitution disenfranchises Negroes by requiring property and literacy tests, and including grandfather clause (→Autumn, 1904).

New York City. Reformer Jacob Riis's autobiography, *The Making of an American*, published.

Morgan buys Carnegie's steel empir

Carnegie, handing the burden over.

New York City, March 13

Less than a month after J. Pierpont Morgan bought out Andrew Carnegie's steel enterprises for $250 million and created the U.S. Steel Corporation, Carnegie sailed for Scotland and his beloved golf links today. While Morgan worked out details on organization of what becomes the world's largest corporation, Carnegie declared at dockside that he has "just begun to give away money," and then turned to his thoughts of golf, calling it "one of the most bracing pastimes."

The 66-year-old self-made man, who rose from a poor youth to tycoon, has sold a complex that controls iron and steel processes from mine to mill. Carnegie is now pursuing a course he first laid out in an essay, "The Gospel of Wealth." He wrote that a rich man is but a "trustee" and that life is in two parts: first, acquiring capital, second, giving it away. In January, when Morgan agreed to meet his price, Carnegie told him, "Pierpont, I am now handing the burden over to you." The 64-year-old Morgan is credited with having stopped the run on Treasury gold in 189 when his syndicate provided $6 million worth at a profit som called exorbitant. His new U.S Steel trust is the largest in the tren toward gargantuan combinations.

Morgan, now at the top of the heap.

Black gold spews from Texas Spindletop

Beaumont, Texas, Jan. 10

Oil drillers have discovered what appears to be a huge petroleum deposit a few miles from this quiet town in northeastern Texas. While the Lone Star State has no developed oil fields, geologists have long suspected that this area sits on top of a vast reservoir of oil. For years, oil has seeped up from the ground, but no one has attempted to drill a well – until now. When the well, which the oil men are calling Spindletop, hit the gas deposits, the black gold spewed at least 200 feet into the air, covering every tree, animal and person for acres around. Latest reports say that the well is still blowing oil and is still out of control. The former mayor of Toledo, Samuel Jones, who witnessed the petroleum strike, says that "It is the greatest oil well ever discovered in the U.S. It means that liquid fuel is to be the fuel of the 20th century."

A gusher comes in at the Spindletop oil well, near Beaumont, Texas.

Leftists are united in Socialist Party

Indianapolis, July 29

Quieting their family quarrels fo now, the major socialist groups i America have united under one um brella. Eugene Debs, who was no present at the new Socialist Party' founding, calls the convention "monument above internal dissen sion and strife." Debs polled 98,00 votes in last year's presidential elec tion, leading a ticket backed by hi Chicago Social Democrats and faction of the Socialist Labor Party

Unity has been achieved, but th convention was less a monumen than a melting pot. Victor Berger the first Socialist congressman an a political intimate of Debs, led th fight for a moderate platform urgin election reform and public owner ship of utilities. "We are no longe a sect," he argued, "we are a poli tical party." A Springfield, Illinois group insisted on "only one im mediate demand, the complete sur render of the capitalist class." Th compromise includes demands fo reform, but only as necessary step toward revolution. Debs, publicl skeptical of unity, has vowed pri vately to "stick to the party through the gates of hell" (→Nov. 8, 1910).

Whitehead claims he flew 800 feet

Bridgeport, Conn., Aug. 15

An obscure Bavarian-born inventor today claimed victory in the quest to develop a motor-driven, heavier-than-air flying machine. He is Gustave Whitehead, who settled here in 1900, and he says he flew in his steam-powered, bat-winged craft for more than 800 feet over Long Island Sound yesterday. A local newspaper reported his flight along with a fanciful sketch of the event, but skeptics question the lack of photographic proof. Meanwhile, rival aviators work away. Dayton glider designers Orville and Wilbur Wright are testing aerodynamic shapes in a long wind tunnel they built, while Samuel Langley has flown an unmanned, gasoline-powered machine.

Panic hits Wall Street

New York City, May 9

The stock market collapsed today in a panic without parallel as the result of a corner in Northern Pacific Railroad shares. As crowds descended on Wall Street, the exchange closed its gallery for the first time in history. Thousands of messengers filled the streets, earning tips that were worth many times their $4-a-week salaries.

The panic erupted after Northern Pacific opened at 170 and jumped 200 or 300 points between sales, becoming scarce at even $1,000 because it had been cornered by forces of J. Pierpont Morgan on the one hand and E.H. Harriman on the other, in their titanic struggle for control. So fierce was their fight that they actually bought more Northern Pacific than exists. Much of it was from speculators who really didn't own it, but had sold it "short," betting that it would fall before they had to deliver. When it went up instead, the speculators were trapped in the position of having to deliver stock that they didn't own, and that they could neither buy nor borrow. Quickly, they had to sell their other holdings to make good their losses. Before noon, everyone was selling everything. Speculators and average investors alike were wiped out.

When the battling giants finally agreed under court order to break their corner and let their "short" victims off the hook at $150 a share, it was too late to undo damage that could be measured by a $100 million drop in the market value of U.S. Steel alone.

Supreme Court puts new lands in limbo

Washington, D.C., May 27

The troublesome question of the constitutional status of Puerto Rico and the Philippines was at last settled today by a Supreme Court decision in what is known as the Insular Cases. The former Spanish possessions, the court has ruled, are neither foreign countries nor integral parts of the United States; their inhabitants are American nationals but not American citizens; tariffs may be imposed on goods exported to the United States; their form of government will be whatever Congress decides. In short, the newcomers are to be treated as colonies – left, as one of the dissenting judges has put it, "in an indeterminate state of ambiguous existence for an indefinite period."

Cuban regime accepts Platt Amendment

Havana, Cuba, June 12

Relying on assurances that its sovereignty will not be affected, the constitutional convention that has been meeting here since November today voted to accept the Platt Amendment as part of Cuba's new constitution. The amendment, sponsored by Senator Orville Platt and passed by Congress three months ago, authorizes U.S. intervention in Cuba if it is needed "for the preservation of Cuban independence" and "the maintenance of a government adequate for the protection of life, property and individual liberty." Cuba is also required not to compromise its independence by a treaty with a foreign power, not to borrow beyond its resources and to grant America as yet unspecified naval and coaling bases (→ July 4).

U.S. sends Taft as Governor of Philippines

Manila, Philippines, July 4

United States military rule ended here today with the appointment of Judge William Howard Taft of Ohio as civil Governor. Taft, who arrived two months ago to head the American commission charged with setting up a government, has already won over many Filipinos with his friendly ways and encouragement of Filipino participation in the territorial government. While the guerrilla war against American rule goes on in isolated areas, the rebel cause was dealt a severe blow on March 23, when Emilio Aguinaldo was seized in his hideout by Brigadier General Frederick Funston. Aguinaldo is said to have been betrayed by pro-American scouts, then to have sworn allegiance to the United States (→ May 20, 1902).

King Camp Gillette has sparked a revolution in home grooming with the invention of his safety razor. It's a big help to American men on the go.

Aguinaldo, leader of the Philippine insurrection, arrives on board an American warship following his capture. The Philippines will remain in U.S. hands.

President McKinley shot by anarchist

President McKinley is shot by an anarchist at the Pan-American Exposition.

Buffalo, New York, Sept. 6

An anarchist shot President McKinley today, but the President's doctors say he is "rallying satisfactorily and resting comfortably."

McKinley was shot twice shortly after 4 p.m. by Leon Czolgosz of Cleveland during a reception at the Pan-American Exposition. The assassin had joined a crowd of well-wishers and came to within two feet of the President. At this close range, witnesses say, he raised a hand and fired twice, using a revolver concealed in a bandage or handkerchief. One bullet struck the breast bone and was removed. The other pierced the stomach and has not yet been found.

In the pandemonium, two Secret Service men and a bystander threw Czolgosz to the ground, disarmed him and rushed him away from the screaming crowd. Nearby, the 58-year-old President protested that he was "not badly hurt," until he saw the blood spreading over his white linen. He urged that extreme care be taken in telling his infirm wife about the shooting, and asked that his assailant not be harmed.

Czolgosz is an ordinary-looking man of medium height. He was plainly dressed in black, with nothing to mark him in a crowd. The police report that Czolgosz, who has seven brothers and sisters in Cleveland, has signed a six-page confession. He says that he is an anarchist in sympathy, and influenced by Emma Goldman, but that he is not part of an organization or plot. He says he bought the weapon three days ago because the country's form of government needs changing and he wanted to get the change started. Police are guarding him from a mob estimated at 30,000. They chanted "Lynch him! Hang him!" until they were driven back by a squad of police reserves.

Vice President Roosevelt is being rushed to Buffalo from Vermont by special train. At Isle La Motte, when informed of the shooting, he exclaimed, "My God!" and declared himself so "inexpressibly grieved, shocked and horrified that I can say nothing" (→ 14).

Second treaty gives U.S. canal rights

Washington, D.C., Dec. 16

As expected, the new and revised Hay-Pauncefote Treaty, negotiated last month by the Secretary of State with the British ambassador, has been ratified by the Senate without difficulty. The new accord confirms the abrogation of the Clayton-Bulwer Treaty of 1850 with the understanding that the United States will have the sole right to build and operate a canal across the isthmus of Panama, with equal transit rights for ships of all nations; but it deletes the earlier requirement that other countries join the treaty as well as the clause that forbids fortification (→ Jan. 4, 1902).

Teddy Roosevelt sworn in as President

At 42 the youngest man ever to become President, Theodore Roosevelt brings a fiery spirit to the office.

Buffalo, New York, Sept. 14

Theodore Roosevelt took the oath of office here this afternoon, becoming the youngest President in American history. At 42, he succeeds 58-year-old William McKinley, who died at 2:15 a.m., of an infection in one of the wounds inflicted eight days ago by the anarchist Leon Czolgosz. Roosevelt, the hero of the Spanish-American War and former Governor of New York, immediately promised "to continue unbroken the policy of President McKinley." He set aside September 19 as the funeral day.

Roosevelt was the object of an intensive search in the Adirondack Mountains most of yesterday, as McKinley's condition worsened. Finally located on top of Mount Marcy, he reached a nearby village at 5 a.m by horse and fast car, transferring to special trains and finally arriving in Buffalo at 1:30 p.m. An hour later, in a borrowed high hat that did not fit, Roosevelt arrived to view the body of the President he has succeeded. He looked shaken as he left for the nearby home of his friend Ansley Wilcox. In the low-ceilinged library of Wilcox's quaint vine-covered house, which is fronted by large colonial pillars, Roosevelt was sworn in as President shortly after 3 p.m.

Czolgosz will be indicted tomorrow, with a trial and sentencing reported likely within two weeks.

Mysterious Cardiff Giant at Buffalo Expo

Buffalo, New York

Thousands of people at the exposition here who have been paying to view the 10'4" Cardiff Giant weighing 2,990 pounds have now learned that it is a hoax. Known as the "Eighth Wonder of the World," the giant was the brainchild of George Hull, a tobacco farmer from Binghamton, N.Y., who bought a five-ton block of gypsum in Fort Dodge, Iowa, and hired two sculptors to carve the giant statue. Irritated by clergymen who were always quoting Genesis ("there were giants in the earth in those days"), Hull decided to ridicule them, making a giant man-like figure out of stone and promoting it as a petrified man. He shipped the statue to William Newell's farm in Broome County, N.Y., where it was buried. After workmen digging a well discovered the huge figure, Newell charged 50 cents a look, and it became the biggest tourist attraction in the state. Newell's partner Hull spent $2,200 and earned $35,000 when the giant was sold to five businessmen. P.T. Barnum built a replica and earned even more money from the hoax.

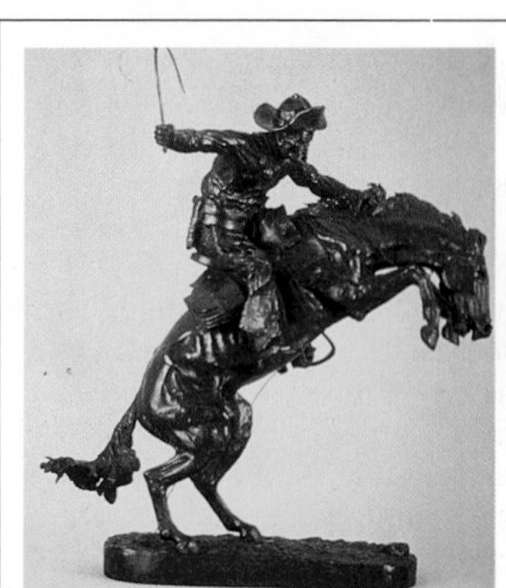

"Bronco Buster" (1895), by Frederic Remington, on display at this year's well-attended Pan-American Exposition in Buffalo, N.Y.

Booker T. Washington, White House guest

Booker T. Washington, the educator, serves as a voice for a seen but unheard part of American society.

Washington, D.C., Oct. 16

In an attempt to improve race relations and to get better acquainted with the nation's foremost Negro educator, President Roosevelt had Booker T. Washington to dinner tonight at the White House. In office less than a month, Roosevelt is apparently already in political hot water. After the invitation was made public, Southern reaction was fierce. Some called the invitation "a crime equal to treason." A Memphis newspaper remarked that "No Southern woman with proper self-respect would now accept an invitation to the White House." Washington is the author of the best-selling autobiography, *Up From Slavery*.

President Roosevelt warns of evil trusts

Washington, D.C., Dec. 3

In his first message to Congress, President Roosevelt today pointed to "real, grave evils" in rapidly spreading trusts. He called for federal supervision of interstate trusts "in the interest of the whole people" and for a Cabinet-level secretary of commerce. But the President warned that "the mechanism of modern business is so delicate that extreme care must be taken not to interfere with it in a spirit of rashness or ignorance." Discussing organized labor, he said the eight-hour day must be honored, and women and children protected in all jobs that involve government work. He also urged aid that "helps a man to help himself" (→ March 10, 1902).

The "Colossus" pulls the strings.

Planters in Georgia still holding slaves

Anderson County, Ga., Aug. 1

Thirty-six years after the Civil War came to an end, three of the most prominent planters in this state were charged by a grand jury today with practicing slavery. The plantation owners had confined to their stockades Negroes who had never been convicted of any legal offense. The grand jury, in its report, offered evidence that some of the Negroes had also been whipped and forced to submit to other acts of cruelty. A charge of false imprisonment was filed against the violators. Many residents are shocked by the revelations, but others say they are not surprised at all.

All Oklahoma Indians granted citizenship

Oklahoma Territory, March 3

Congress voted today to grant full American citizenship to all Indians living in the Oklahoma Territory – whether they want it or not. Although the ink is hardly dry on the paper, both Indians and whites in Oklahoma and Washington are already questioning the wisdom and the full implications of the law.

Most white Americans have assumed that the Oklahoma Indians, and indeed other tribe members, have always desired American citizenship. However, both white and Indian Oklahomans have pointed out that this is not necessarily so. Congress passed a little-known act in 1890 that allowed any member of an Indian tribe living in Indian Territory to apply to the United States Court at Muskogee for American citizenship. While this obviously well-intentioned move was designed to let Indians into the mainstream of American society, it was a dismal failure. Because of the Indians' pride in their traditional society and culture, the opinions of fellow Indians kept those who might desire citizenship from requesting it. In fact, only four Indians – three Cherokees and a Creek – out of the thousands who were eligible asked for citizenship. And the few who did so apparently became the object of scorn and suspicion on the part of other Indians. It would seem, therefore, that this well-intentioned act may have backfired.

Rockefeller's worth put at $200 million

New York City

Though a recent audit places the assets of John D. Rockefeller at $200 million, the world's richest man has made many times that. Following his own dictum that "A man should make all he can and give it away," the founder of the mighty Standard Oil trust has donated untold millions, including great sums to the University of Chicago and to the Rockefeller Institute for Medical Research, founded this year. But Rockefeller has also espoused the survival of the fittest, and his methods, as a result, have led more Americans to fear him than to admire him.

Adrenaline isolated

Baltimore, Maryland

Two chemists here have isolated adrenaline, the first pure hormone to be obtained from a natural source. The hormone, which is the active substance secreted by the medulla of the suprarenal glands in humans and some animals, has many therapeutic uses, including the easing of respiratory difficulties caused by asthma and allergies and the stimulation of the heart. Jokichi Takamine, a Japanese chemist, and John Jacob Abel, an American physician and physiological chemist, are credited with the discovery.

"Peskelechaco, Republican Pawnee" (c.1822) by Charles Bird King.

Red Tomahawk, an Indian who has adopted the dress of the white man.

Railroad Octopus

United States

As train lines reach out like tentacles across the continent, powerful railroad companies squeeze the life's blood out of all those who stand in their way. This is the theme of *The Octopus: A Story of California*, a gritty, realistic novel by Frank Norris. The first volume of a projected trilogy by the 31-yearold Chicagoan, *The Octopus* describes the epic battle in which a community of wheat farmers takes on wealthy railroad owners, who gain a stranglehold on the state government and newspapers.

1902

Roosevelt

Washington, D.C., Jan. 4. Panama Company lowers asking price for its holdings and franchises, from $103 million to $40 million (→ 18).

Washington, D.C., Jan. 18. Walker Commission recommends Panamanian route for proposed canal, given lowered price for Panama Company (→ June 28).

New York City, Jan. 25. Musical *Floradora* closes after record 505 performances.

Cuba, May 20. Tomas Estrada Palma becomes first president of Republic of Cuba; United States decides to withdraw (→ Jan. 4, 1904).

Oregon, June 2. State institutes general initiative and referendum so that public can override legislative action and initiate popular vote.

Washington, D.C., June 17. Congress passes Newlands Reclamation Act, providing for irrigation of arid lands in West through dam-building.

Washington, D.C., June 28. Congress passes Isthmian Canal Act, authorizing President to negotiate with French for right to build canal across Colombia (→ Nov. 2, 1903).

New York City, July 12. Twentieth Century Limited train sets new speed record, by traveling from New York to Chicago in 16 hours.

Detroit, Aug. 22 Automobile firm changes name to Cadillac, after French explorer.

Saratoga, New York, Aug. 31. Mrs. Adolph Ladenburg introduces split skirt for horseback riding, causing sensation.

Washington, September. "Yacolt Burn" is last of forest fires that have destroyed 12 billion feet of timber in state.

Washington, D.C., Dec. 19. United States persuades Britain, Germany and Italy to end blockade of five Venezuelan ports and enter arbitration.

United States. Song *In the Good Old Summertime* sells a million copies in first year.

United States. Saint-Gaudens completes *Victory*, winged bronze statuette of America.

DEATH

New York City, Oct. 26. Elizabeth Cady Stanton, woman's suffrage leader (*Nov. 12, 1815).

TR resolves mine strike

Washington, D.C., Oct. 16

Anthracite mine owners have finally agreed to the appointment of an arbitration panel, ending a five-month strike in the heart of America's coal country. The pact is a triumph for President Roosevelt, who stepped into the fray after local officials began to fear fuel riots. The presidency, says Roosevelt, ought to represent the third party in labor disputes, the public. News of the owners' acquiescence was brought to Washington by J. Pierpont Morgan, who appears to be enjoying his uncharacteristic role as benign statesman in the war between labor and capital. George Baer, head of the Reading Railroad, which controls many of the struck mines, was not so statesmanlike. At an October 3 meeting with Roosevelt and the United Mine Workers, Baer fumed, "The duty of the hour is not to waste time negotiating with the fomenters of anarchy" but to "reestablish order and peace at any cost." The President says John Mitchell, leader of the U.M.W., was the only gentlemanly presence at the meeting (→ March 21, 1903).

A certificate of union membership.

Government busts one railroad trust

Washington, D.C., March 10

In a drive to revitalize the Sherman Antitrust Act, Attorney General Philander Knox has filed suit against J. Pierpont Morgan's Northern Securities firm. A holding company of sorts, the corporation controls the Northern Pacific, Great Northern and Burlington Railroads. It was set up in November as a gentlemanly resolution of a power struggle among Morgan, J.J. Hill and associates, and Edward Harriman. Morgan is said to be irate over Knox, "that country lawyer," letting the case go to court. On a February 23 visit to the White House, he reportedly told President Roosevelt, "If we have done anything wrong, send your man to my man and they can fix it up." Roosevelt, a man of clear-cut moral convictions, merely told him, "That can't be done" (→ July 4).

"Here is an enormous force let loose upon mankind," Charles Francis Adams once said of the railroads, "Not many of those who fondly believe they control it, ever stop to think of it as the most tremendous and far-reaching engine of social change that has ever blessed or cursed mankind." Photo is Stieglitz's "Hand of Man."

TR says wealth is menace and danger

Pittsburgh, Penn., July 4

Half a million people turned out today to hear President Roosevelt blast the trusts again in a "preview" of his New England tour. On his first visit to this industrial center, they cheered when the President told them that wealth "becomes a menace and danger when not used right" and urged new laws in the public interest. He recently ordered Attorney General Philander Knox, who comes from Pittsburgh, to sue to dissolve the Northern Securities Company trust that evolved from last year's corner on Northern Pacific (→Feb. 19, 1903).

Business booming throughout America

New Jersey, Aug. 12

The economic upsurge that began two years ago shows no sign of waning.

Unemployment is at its lowest in 20 years. Industrial growth is reaching unforeseen heights. A major farm implement manufacturing company, International Harvester, was incorporated in this state today. Earlier this year, Gustavus Swift and J.O. Armour opened their huge National Packing Company plants in Chicago. And in Wyoming, J.C. Penney has announced the formation of nationwide retail clothing outlets that he calls "chain stores."

Helen Keller's "The Story of My Life"

In a reflective moment, a symbol of indomitable spirit over adversity.

Boston

Miracles happen daily in the life of Helen Keller. The 22-year-old native of Alabama, now a student at Radcliffe, lost her sight and hearing at the age of 19 months, yet, under the guidance of Miss Anne Sullivan, her teacher, she learned to read, write and, amazingly, to speak. Miss Keller relates these triumphs in *The Story of My Life*. A high point occurs when Sullivan places the hand of her 7-year-old pupil under the spout of a pump. "As the cool stream rushed over one hand," Miss Keller recalls, "my teacher spelled into the other the word water ... the mystery of language was revealed to me."

Jell-O, everybody!

New York City

Housewives bored with rich custard sweets are delighting in a new gelatin dessert called Jell-O. Children love it, and its nutritional values are being promoted as well. Originated by Pearl B. Wait, a Le Roy, New York, carpenter (his wife May coined the name), the rights to this shimmering, wobbly dessert were bought up by Orator Frank Woodward, who marketed it so well that sales this year may top $250,000.

"Automat" arrives

Philadelphia, June 9.

A new concept in self-service eating has opened on Chestnut Street – the "Automat." Patrons choose from rows of glass-fronted cases, drop in a coin or two, and out pops a freshly cooked dish. Opened by Joseph Horn and Frank Hardart, the Automat is called a great advance. Writes the *Evening Bulletin*, "The horseless carriage, the wireless telephone and the playerless piano have been surpassed ..."

The books are new, the religion old-time

United States

Charles Darwin may have cast a shadow over the Bible, but two up-to-date thinkers still espouse the old-time religion. William James, Harvard's "pragmatist" philosopher, argues in *The Varieties of Religious Experience* that belief in God is not only valuable but also practical because "the sense of union with the power beyond us is a sense of something, not merely apparently, but literally true."

Walter Rauschenbusch, a Baptist minister and professor of church history at Rochester Theological Seminary, sets forth the doctrine of Social Gospel in *Christianity and the Social Crisis*. This book holds that biblical lore can cure many of the ills created by industrialization. The liberal-minded author advocates social progress and calls upon the church to take an active role in a new holy struggle, that of bettering the lot of the working classes.

Hookworm afflicts poor whites in Dixie

Atlanta, Georgia, Feb. 10

Much of the South is poised for a drive to eradicate the hookworm, which, in the words of Dr. Charles Wardell Stiles, is the cause of "laziness" among its poor whites. While the existence of the hookworm dates back many centuries in other parts of the world, not until recently has it emerged in the American South, where it has been classified as Necator Americanus (New World hookworm). The parasitic worms, which thrive in warm and humid climates, can cause anemia, difficulty in breathing, weakness, dizziness, nausea, enlargement of the heart, abdominal pain, internal bleeding and other ailments, particularly in areas with poor sanitary conditions and among those who walk barefooted in moist soil.

Teddy averts death as carriage is hit

Pittsfield, Mass., Sept. 3

A streetcar hurtling along at 30 miles an hour came close to killing President Teddy Roosevelt and his fellow travelers today when it hit their landau. All but one of them were thrown free of the open carriage, receiving minor injuries. But Secret Service man William Craig was crushed under the car and killed instantly. The President had just delivered a speech at the park here. He was behind schedule and his driver, trying to make up time, didn't see the approaching streetcar as he spurred the four horses across the tracks. Roosevelt received a cut lip. The President, shocked by the Secret Service man's death, shook his fist at the motorman and roared, "This is the most damnable outrage I ever knew!"

Wister "Virginian" wins West again

United States

The West may already be won, but its legend survives in *The Virginian: A Horseman of the Plains*, a tale about rough-and-ready cowpunchers set in the Wyoming of the 1870s and '80s. The nameless protagonist, called simply "the Virginian," tall, brave and soft-spoken, is a model of Western valor. Readers are already repeating his retort to his nemesis, the ornery outlaw Trampus, who uses an unflattering epithet when addressing the Virginian. "When you call me that, smile!" says the hero, quickly winning his way into the heart of Molly Wood, a demure schoolteacher who has come out from Vermont to help civilize the frontier children. The author, Owen Wister, 42, is from a famous Philadelphia family.

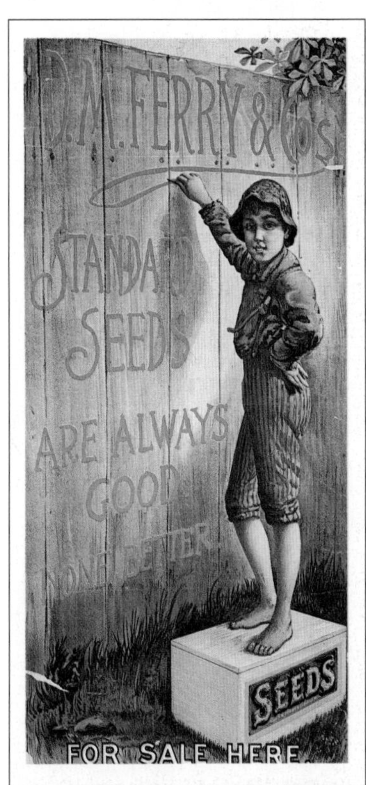

1903

Roosevelt

New York City, Jan. 20. *The Wizard of Oz* has premiere at Majestic Theater.

Washington, D.C., Feb. 14. Act of Congress, signed into law by President Roosevelt, creates Department of Commerce and Labor.

Washington, D.C., Feb. 14. Congress, at request of Secretary of War Elihu Root, establishes United States Army General Staff Corps to centralize military control.

Rochester, New York, Feb. 16. Suffragette Susan B. Anthony donates book collection to Library of Congress.

New York City, March 29. Regular news service opens between New York and London through use of Guglielmo Marconi's wireless system.

Nantucket, Mass., March. Limericks, published in newspapers, become popular.

Washington, D.C., July 4. President Roosevelt inaugurates first Pacific communications cable by sending message around world, to himself.

United States, Sept. 3. American yacht Reliance defeats Britain's Shamrock III for America's Cup.

Detroit, Michigan, Oct. 22. Electric Motor Vehicle Company files large suit against Ford Motor Company for patent violations.

Colon, Colombia, Nov. 2. President Roosevelt orders cruiser Nashville to drop anchor, ostensibly to protect "free and uninterrupted transit across the isthmus" (→6).

New York City, Dec. 27. Echo song *Sweet Adeline*, by Henry Armstrong, sung for first time at Pops Sunday Nights.

Chicago, Dec. 30. Fire in Iroquois Theater kills 588 people [public outrage leads to new theater codes across nation].

Chicago. John Dewey publishes *Studies in Logical Theory,* giving his definition of thought.

Chicago. Frank Norris publishes *The Pit*, novel about corrupt agricultural trading practices.

Atlanta, Georgia. W.E.B. Du Bois publishes *The Souls of Black Folk*, challenging views of Booker T. Washington.

Henry Ford sells first Model A, for $850

The very simplicity of Henry Ford's Model A defines a certain elegance.

Detroit, Michigan, July 23

Renowned for the success of his speedy "999" racer in the Detroit Challenge Cup auto race, Henry Ford formed a new company this year to produce the gasoline-powered "family horse," as he calls it. Today, his Ford Motor Company sold the first of these vehicles, called the Model A, for $850 to a Detroit physician.

Ford's philosophy is simply to build "more cars, better and cheaper." With financial backing mostly from local financier Alexander Malcolmson, the company set up shop here on Mack Avenue. Ford hired 10 workers at $1.50 per day and bought parts for 650 vehicles. The Model A, which was designed last year by Ford himself and chief engineer C.H. Wills, features a two-cylinder, eight-horsepower engine that can push it to 30 m.p.h. Advertisements are boasting that "the same genius which conceived the world's record holder – the '999' – has made possible the production of a thoroughly practical car at a moderate price."

Congress regulates railroads with law

Washington, D.C., Feb. 19

Congress moved to end the grip the nation's railroads have on commerce by enacting the Elkins Act today. The legislation will remove rebates on freight rates. Rebates worked like this: Shippers would pay regular rates to the railroads and, if they were in good favor, would receive money back. This cut into fair trade competition. Rebates have been known to breed corruption for years, but powerful rail lobbyists had worked to keep them legal. While many reformers are happy with the law, others, such as Senator La Follette of Wisconsin, feel the act does not go far enough in regulating rails (→Jan. 30, 1905).

Helium in Kansas

Dexter, Kansas

Kansas, known for its wheat and its cattle, now has a new resource – helium. A field of the natural gas has just been discovered at Dexter. The lightest gas after hydrogen, helium has been known to exist for some time but wasn't identified on earth until 1895. It is tasteless, colorless, odorless and will not burn, making its discovery all the more remarkable. Its uses are few.

Mother Jones leads children on strike

New York City, July

Labor leader Mother Jones, still tireless at 73, has led a small army of children into New York, many of them mutilated from accidents in the textile mills. She aims to disturb President Roosevelt at his summer home in Oyster Bay, Long Island. As the parade was leaving Philadelphia on July 4, Mother Jones announced the city's "mansions were built on the broken bones, the quivering hearts and drooping heads of these children." "Fifty years ago," she cried at Coney Island, "the black babies were sold C.O.D. Today the white baby is sold on the installment plan." In fact, some 1.5 million children now work nationwide for as little as 25 cents a day. The President has announced he will not receive Mother Jones and her children.

Clearly a woman to be reckoned with.

"Labor walks into House of Victory"

Washington, D.C., March 21

Ending hearings that have lasted nearly as long as last year's mine strike, the President's commission has granted most of the United Mine Workers' demands. Union recognition, however, was denied, prompting organizer Mother Jones to comment, "Labor walked into the House of Victory, through the back door." Nonetheless, the door is wide. Armed with the legal arguments of Clarence Darrow, John Mitchell's union now has a 10 percent raise for contract miners; an eight-hour day for engineers, firemen and pumpmen, and increased control over the weighing of coal. The panel may indicate a new federal willingness to stabilize the economy by arbitrating labor disputes.

Motorcar is first to cross continent

New York City, July 26

For the first time since its invention, an automobile has crossed the continent. H. Nelson Jackson, a physician from Burlington, Vermont, arrived here today after a coast-to-coast odyssey that began on May 23. He was accompanied by his chauffeur-companion, Sewall K. Crocker. Making the trip in a two-cylinder Winton, they were motivated by a $50 bet the doctor made that he could complete the grind. The car was designed and constructed by Alexander Winton, who gave up the bicycle business to produce cars. The machine has a six-horsepower, water-cooled engine that was mounted in the rear.

Herbert's "Babes in Toyland" is a hit

New York City, Oct. 13

After a troubled stint as conductor of the Pittsburgh Symphony, Victor Herbert has returned to what he loves best – writing musicals. The happy result, *Babes in Toyland*, is his first bona fide success. The book is about a couple of shipwrecked "Babes" washed up on the shores of a fabulous Toyland peopled by fairy-tale figures. From the martial *March of the Toys* to the poignant title song *Toyland*, Herbert taps a seemingly inexhaustible mine of melody.

Herbert's first bona fide success.

Boston upsets Pittsburgh, 5 games to 3, in first World Series

Huntington Avenue Ball Field in Boston is mobbed with fans as the Americans win the first World Series.

Boston, Oct. 13

The war of words between the National and American Leagues finally spilled over into the baseball field. The pennant winners of the two leagues met for a post-season showdown – though without league supervision – and Boston's Americans walked off today with an upset victory over the vaunted Pittsburgh Nationals. The upstart Bostons captured the series, five games to three, scoring a 3-0 triumph in the eighth and final game.

The Boston accomplishment convinced some critics that the American League was more than just a refuge for players who defected from the older circuit. The Nationals had outdrawn their rivals last year, but at the end of the season they made a gesture to establish peace. They and a minor league group banded into what they called Organized Baseball. National commissions will rule the leagues.

In the series, Cy Young pitched two of the Boston victories and lost once against the champions of his former league. The talents of Honus Wagner were not enough to save the Pittsburghers. The surehanded shortstop with the remarkably strong arm got six hits in the losing cause. Patrick Henry Dougherty proved to be a standout for Boston, hitting two homers in the second contest after the Pirates had won the opening game.

Northern border set in favor of the U.S.

Washington, D.C., Oct. 20

There is good news tonight for the United States, even though it involves land more than 3,000 miles away. The American-British commission studying the boundary between Alaska and Canada has made a decision that grants the United States much of the border area territory it had claimed. The decision was not unilateral; the British commissioner sided with the Americans. The commission, which started its work in January, has disbanded, leaving border matters settled (→Dec. 5, 1905).

Caruso debut at Met: notices fairly good

New York City, Nov. 23

The bravos still linger for soprano Marcella Sembrich's opening night *Rigoletto* at the Met. The baritone Antonio Scotti was also in excellent voice, but Sembrich as usual brought down the house. Of special interest was the debut of tenor Enrico Caruso. While he is fresh from a triumph in London and has great advance notices, critics here said he is sometimes betrayed by a rough voice and inept acting. Still, they said his singing was on the whole intelligent, passionate and generally good if never really overwhelming. He has a three-month contract and will soon sing in *Aida*.

Italian tenor Enrico Caruso.

U.S. recognizes Republic of Panama

President Roosevelt confidently shapes a new world role for the United States.

Washington, D.C., Nov. 6

Barely three days after the outbreak of a revolt against Colombian rule, the United States today recognized Panama as an independent state. The action comes as no surprise since it is an open secret that the uprising, which was largely engineered by Philippe Bunau-Varilla and other officers of the Panama Canal Company in conjunction with local dissidents, had the full backing of President Roosevelt. Indeed, it was the arrival of the cruiser Nashville in Panamanian waters, sent by the President ostensibly to protect "free and uninterrupted transit across the isthmus," that gave the signal for the outbreak of the revolt, just as it was the presence of the Nashville and other American warships that prevented the Colombians from suppressing it.

The American actions result from the rejection in August by Colombia's Senate of the Hay-Herran Treaty. Negotiations with the new Panama regime for a treaty permitting an American-controlled canal are to start soon (→ May 4, 1904).

Motion pictures get plot and narrative

New Jersey

This year, Edwin W. Porter, one of Thomas A. Edison's directors, first utilized narrative continuity, as opposed to filming skits, in *The Life of an American Fireman*, with firefighters racing to save a mother and child in a burning house. He also presented an epic nearly 12 minutes long called *The Great Train Robbery*, displaying a sense of time, space and logic. We follow each stage of the robbery, the escape and the capture of the robbers. Shot in New Jersey, the film draws long lines of avid spectators.

Chew your cheese thirty-two times

Chicago

Stuck in Chicago after being pushed out of his Buffalo, New York, cheese company by ungrateful partners, James Lewis Kraft has turned $65 into a thriving business. With a rented horse and wagon, he buys cheese from wholesalers and offers it to retail stores at a profit. Merchants are saved the trip and Kraft is saved from vagrancy. Out in San Francisco, food faddist Horace Fletcher wants to save people from a worse fate, gastronomic distress. Chew your food 32 times, he counsels.

The Olmsted legacy: parks for the people

Waverly, Massachusetts, Aug. 28

The 81-year-old park architect Frederick Olmsted died today, leaving behind acres of beautifully landscaped parks throughout the nation. After getting degrees in engineering and science, Olmsted trekked across the United States and Europe studying landscape gardening. His philosophy of using the natural landscapes in urban parks can be seen in his designs for Central Park in New York City, considered his masterpiece, and in parks that include Back Bay in Boston, and Washington and Jackson Parks in Chicago.

Toy boat lake, in New York's Central Park, Olmsted's greatest legacy of all.

Epidemic traced to "Typhoid Mary"

New York City

A typhoid fever epidemic has been traced to Mary Mallon, a cook who worked in an Oyster Bay summer house. Ten days after eating food prepared by "Typhoid Mary," several guests became sick and feverish from the highly contagious disease and were admitted to a New York hospital. After an extensive door-to-door search, Dr. George Soper of the N.Y. City Department of Health deduced that Miss Mallon was responsible. She changed jobs frequently and wherever she had worked, a case of typhoid was soon reported. Once cornered, she was told that she probably was the first known typhoid carrier in the nation. Insisting that she felt perfectly well, Miss Mallon refused to submit to a physical exam and chased Dr. Soper away with a rolling pin. A few years ago, German bacteriologists found that intestinal carriers such as "Typhoid Mary" were spreaders of the disease.

"Brown and Gold: Self-portrait" by James Abbott McNeill Whistler. The artist, an emotional and often cantankerous man, died in London on July 17 of this year.

Kate Wiggin novel, schoolgirl favorite

United States

"He who can, does," George Bernard Shaw has written. "He who cannot, teaches." One who can do both is Kate Douglas Wiggin. A Philadelphian, Miss Wiggin moved to San Francisco and in 1878 set up one of the nation's first kindergartens. She has since started writing children's books. Her latest is *Rebecca of Sunnybrook Farm*, and indications are that it will sell a million copies. The story of a precocious farmgirl and her six sisters, it has become a favorite among schoolgirls from coast to coast.

"Call of the Wild" heard by nation

San Francisco

A man's best friend is his dog, but is a dog's best friend ever a man? This question is posed in the latest adventure novel by Jack London, *The Call of the Wild*, a tale set in the rough-and-tumble world of the Klondike. The hero is Buck, a sled dog, part St. Bernard, part Scottish shepherd, who gives his all to his master, prospector John Thornton, helping him win a bet by hauling a 1,000-pound payload. But when Thornton is killed, the beastly ways of men disgust Buck, so he joins a wolfpack.

Jack London, who has been a sailor, a tramp and a gold miner, is now tasting success as a novelist.

Wright brothers' machine takes to air

Part machine and part bird, the Wright brothers' plane Flyer, lifts off the ground and onto the pages of history.

Kitty Hawk, N.C., Dec. 17

Almost everywhere, claims of motor-driven flight have aroused skepticism, especially since the spectacular failures that sent the Samuel Langley Aerodrome machine plunging into the Potomac River on two occasions this year. But the flights by Orville and Wilbur Wright today were seen by five witnesses, mostly from a nearby lifesaving station. Also, a photographer caught the Flyer just as it was leaving the ground.

Those who witnessed the tests said the Wright brothers, who have been building and flying their own gliders since 1900, hauled their 605-pound, gasoline-powered Flyer up the sandy Kill Devil Hill near Kitty Hawk this morning, and launched it four times into a freezing wind of about 20 miles per hour.

The brothers tossed a coin to determine which one would be the first to fly. The 32-year-old Orville won and climbed aboard the winged machine, dressed in his usual starched white shirt and necktie. A lightweight, 13-horsepower engine then came sputtering to life, setting the machine's two wooden propellers whirring noisily with bicycle chains.

With the 36-year-old Wilbur running alongside carrying a stopwatch, the Flyer accelerated down a 60-foot track. Finally, it took off at 10:35 on a flight that lasted 12 seconds over a distance of 120 feet. Single-minded and solitary, the Wrights rarely doubted that their machine would fly and spent little time on congratulations or, for that matter, reflecting on what could prove to be an epic achievement. Instead, they prepared for additional flights, each of which was longer than the one before it. On the fourth of the flights, Wilbur piloted the Flyer on a 59-second, 852-foot-long ascent. That "hop" came to an abrupt end when the machine nosed onto a nearby beach, crushing the frail spruce-and-muslin horizontal rudders.

Self-taught mathematicians and machinists from Dayton, Ohio, the bachelor brothers were drawn to the problems of human flight after reading about the German glider pilot Otto Lilienthal, who died in one of his unstable craft in 1896. Soon after, the Wrights began designing gliders in their bicycle shop. By 1900, they were flying them amid the favorable wind conditions at Kitty Hawk and testing new wing shapes in a wind tunnel; like nearly all their gear, including the Flyer's engine and propeller, the brothers built the tunnel themselves. They solved the stability problems that have plagued other aeronauts by coming up with a technique that is called wing warping, in which a taut cable bends the wings to help with lift and control.

Design and building expenses, including shipment to Kitty Hawk, amounted to just a little more than $1,000, compared to the $50,000 that was spent by Langley on just the launching mechanism for his Aerodrome, which was sponsored by the War Department.

The Wright brothers intend to withhold more detailed information about their machine until its innovations can be patented, and only time will tell the importance that history will accord today's claims from Kitty Hawk. But by any measure, the Flyer is a fantastic combination of craftsmanship, determination and vision.

1904

Roosevelt

Washington, D.C., Jan. 4. Supreme Court decision, in Gonzales v. Williams, rules that Puerto Ricans are not aliens and cannot be refused entry into United States (→ Dec. 6).

Michigan, Jan. 12. Henry Ford sets auto speed record of 91.37 miles per hour on frozen Lake St. Clair.

Baltimore, Maryland, Feb. 8. Two-day fire extinguished; it destroys 2,600 buildings, but there is no loss of life.

Washington, D.C., Feb. 20. United States sends circular note to belligerents in Russo-Japanese War, asking them to respect Open Door policy in Manchuria [it has no effect upon course of war] (→ Sept. 5, 1905).

New York City, Apr. 25. Will Rogers makes debut as entertainer at Madison Square Garden, appearing with Colonel Zack Mulhall's troupe.

St. Louis, Missouri, Apr. 30. Louisiana Purchase Centennial Exposition opens.→

Panama Canal Zone, May 4. Canal Zone legally becomes United States property (→ July 25, 1905).

New York City, May 20. Secretary of War Elihu Root reads letter from President Roosevelt, espousing Roosevelt Corollary to Monroe Doctrine (→ Dec. 6).

New York City, June 15. Excursion steamer General Slocum burns in East River, killing 1,030 people.

Kentucky, July 1. State legislature passes bill imposing $1,000 fine and $100-a-day penalty against institutions that admit both white and Negro students.

New York City, Nov. 19. Woodrow Wilson declares in a speech, "The Constitution was not made to fit us like a straightjacket. In its elasticity lies its chief greatness."

Albany, New York. First official road speed limits in nation set, at 10 m.p.h. in populated areas, 15 in villages and 20 on open country roads.

Washington, D.C. Deficiency Act bars Chinese laborers indefinitely; it is one of many such exlusionary laws passed.

United States. O'Henry publishes *Cabbages and Kings*.

Ice cream cones, iced tea at World's Fair

Festive Hall at the St. Louis World's Fair, held this year to mark the centennial of the Louisiana Purchase, Thomas Jefferson's big land deal with France.

St. Louis, Missouri

The World's Fair has proved to Americans that not every new invention has to be the result of long, difficult trial and error. Sweltering heat appears to be very much the mother of invention here. Take, for instance, concessionaire Richard Blechtynden, whose hot tea had not been selling too well. Blechtynden thought it might help if he put ice in his tea and, sure enough, sales took off, making iced tea one of the hits at the fair. Three ice cream vendors (of the 50 stationed at the fair) now claim to have come up with the idea for edible ice cream holders made from waffle pastry.

A Syrian immigrant, Ernest A. Hamwi, says that he first rolled a Persian pastry called zalabia into a cone-shaped holder when a colleague ran out of ice cream dishes. David Avayou, a Turkish vendor, insists that he took the idea from paper cones he had seen in France. And Abe Doumar claims his "cornucopias" were being sold first, at the "Old City of Jerusalem" section of the fair. Whoever was the first to sell ice cream in cones, the idea of licking one's ice cream and then eating the container that held it seems to be a delicious new treat as well as an excellent way to cut down on waste.

Chicago, May 1. *Indiana-born Eugene Victor Debs, leader of the American socialist movement, was renominated for president today on the Socialist Party ticket. He says, "I am for socialism because I am for humanity."*

U.S., Olympic host, wins 21 first places

St. Louis, Missouri, May 14

For the first time since their revival eight years ago, the Olympic Games have come to the United States. However, the hosts showed no mercy as they captured 21 first places on the 22-event program. The only foreigner to be awarded a gold medal was a Montreal policeman. The Olympic program has been expanded to include swimming, diving and water polo. But cycling and target shooting have been dropped from the competition. The turnout of both athletes and spectators was disappointing and club athletes continued to replace those from the colleges.

Duke firms become American Tobacco

North Carolina, Oct. 19

James Buchanan Duke has reshaped his conglomerate of tobacco companies into the American Tobacco Company. It will include all the snuff, plug and cigarette makers he has bought out over the years. Duke took over his competitors by slashing prices, using automatic cigarette-rolling machines and increasing advertising. As a boy at a Quaker academy, he prophesied his future: "I'm going to be a businessman and make a pile" (→ June 1911).

Carnegie sets up fund for heroes

New York City, Apr. 15

Life-saving deeds will no longer go unnoticed if the Carnegie Hero Fund has anything to say about it. Philanthropist Andrew Carnegie, who made his fortune in iron and steel, has donated $5 million to endow the fund, which will reward those who are injured in heroic lifesaving acts. Dependents of men and women who died while trying to save another's life will also be rewarded. The Hero Fund commission will investigate heroic acts, prepare reports and decide on compensation. Heroes will receive gold, silver or bronze medals, depending on the range of the heroism involved.

Steerage fare slashed; America affordable to all

New York City, May 23

The great Atlantic Ocean, once an endless sea of perils for the explorers of Renaissance Europe, has become a highway to heaven – bountiful America. A drastic cut in steerage rates goes into effect today that will allow Europeans to board a steamship with $10 in their pockets and arrive in Ellis Island less than a month later. If a decent job awaits them, they will earn the price of their passage in a week.

The new fare schedule is a result of European rivalries. Britain, Germany, Italy and France, vying for control of the seas, offer large subsidies to steamship lines. Hoping that volume will help control the routes, Inman, Cunard and the other big firms pass the savings along to passengers and use their grants to build monster ships. Inman's 11,000-ton City of Paris liner, queen of the seas since 1888, will be deposed by Cunard's 19,000-ton Caronia this year. Quarters are still cramped, but steam has mercifully cut travel time and regular schedules eliminate prolonged stopovers.

Attracting immigrants is a business for many Americans. Agents seeking laborers for American firms stand outside of Italian churches handing out leaflets and singing hymns to the Statue of Liberty's "golden door." But friends who have already made the voyage send home a more realistic picture. Half the new arrivals come with tickets paid for by contacts in the United States. They know better where to look for work and can seek out a number of government and private agencies that help channel newcomers into a niche in American society. And at the bottom line, despite a labor surplus, wages remain two to three times their levels in Europe (→ Dec. 5, 1905).

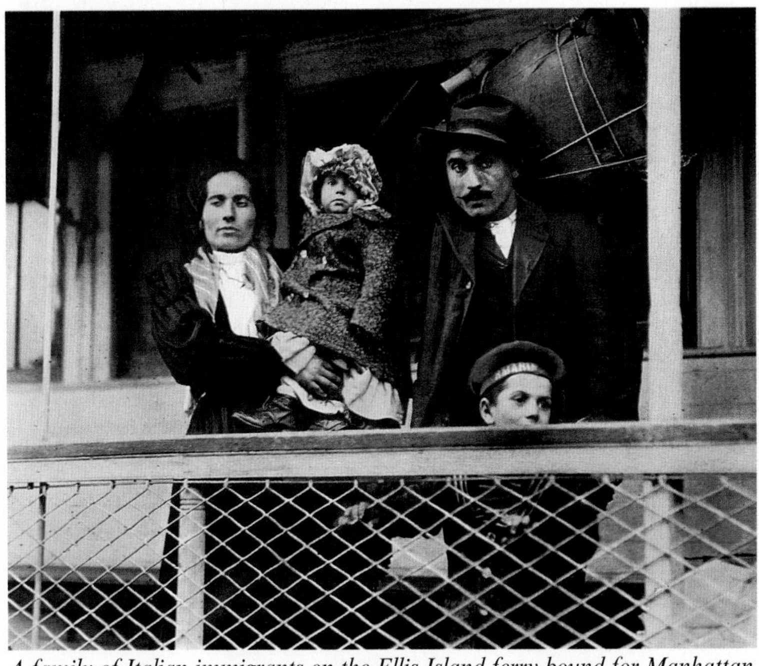

A family of Italian immigrants on the Ellis Island ferry bound for Manhattan. They, like millions of others, must still sacrifice to manage the lowered fare.

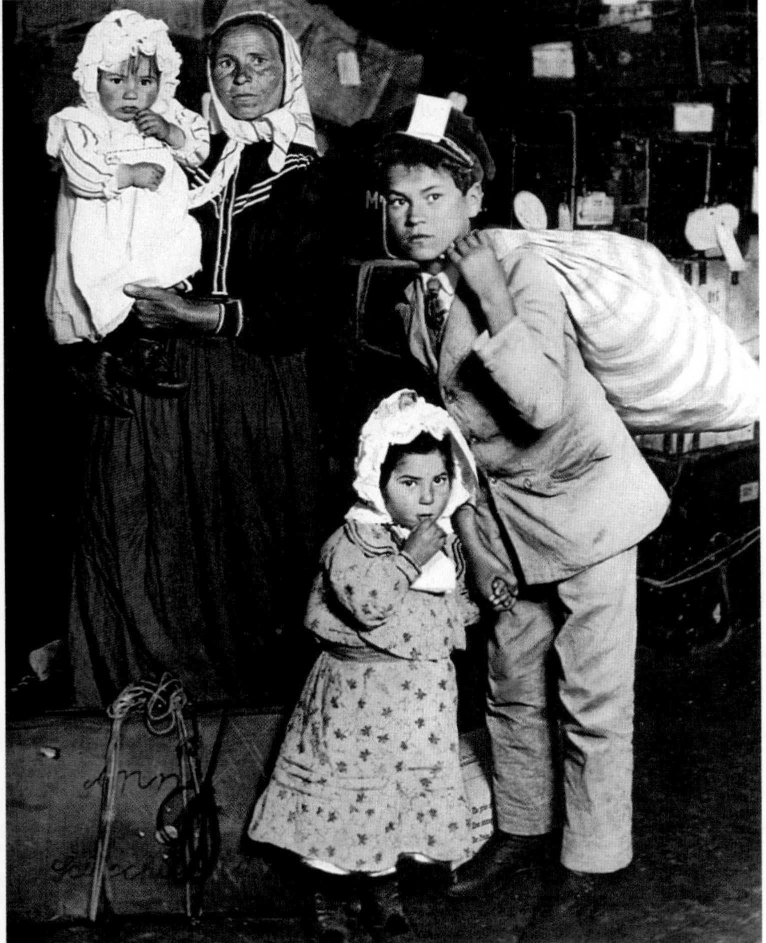

Italian mother and her three children upon arrival at Ellis Island after making the long voyage in steerage. Immigration from Italy has been growing steadily and at the present rate will lead the list with 220,000 arrivals this year.

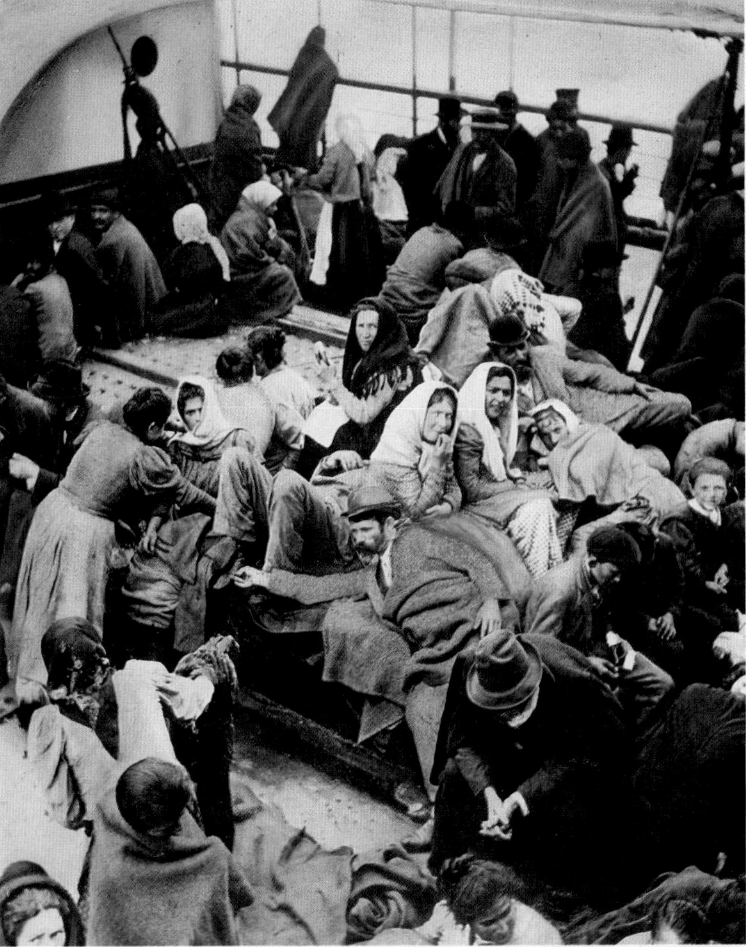

Crossing the Atlantic Ocean in steerage is a cramped, dirty and generally unpleasant experience. But for a majority, there is simply no alternative if they want to start over and begin a new life in the land of opportunity.

Roosevelt is elected to his own full term

Washington, D.C., Nov. 9

President Theodore Roosevelt won in his own right today. Nearly complete returns show the "Rough Rider" who succeeded to the White House on the assassination of President McKinley has been elected to a full term by an electoral vote of 336 for Roosevelt to 110 for the Democratic Party's Judge Alton B. Parker. When the Roosevelt victory became certain, the President issued a statement saying that he was "deeply sensible of the honor done me by the American people in thus expressing their confidence in what I have done and have tried to do." He concluded, however, by promising: "Under no circumstances will I be a candidate for or accept another nomination." Thus, the President has limited to only four more years his fight for such programs as his popular trust-busting campaign.

In March, the Supreme Court awarded him a resounding victory in his fight to regulate monopolistic big business that fails to operate in the public interest. By a vote of five to four, the court dissolved the Northern Securities Company railroad trust under the little-used Sherman Antitrust Act.

Promising a "square deal" for all if elected to a full term, Roosevelt ran in a campaign notable for the absence of William Jennings Bryan, the silver spokesman who lost the Democratic nomination to pro-gold Judge Parker of the party's Eastern wing (→March 4, 1905).

The President stands for his portrait. "Theodore Roosevelt" by J.S. Sargent.

Festival is tribute to Richard Strauss

New York City, March 21

A month-long Richard Strauss Festival marking the American debut of the famed German composer-conductor has been generally triumphant. Too bad, then, that it should end on a cool note with the world premiere of his *Symphonia Domestica* at Carnegie Hall. The music isn't as dramatic as his *Don Juan* or *Till Eulenspiegel*, and many deplore its autobiographical nature. Strauss has subtitled it, *A Day in the Life of My Family*. From here, Strauss will journey to Philadelphia for two concerts at Wanamaker's Department Store – for $1,000. "True art ennobles any building," the maestro explained.

Cy Young pitches a "perfect" game

Boston, May 5

Denton True "Cy" Young became the first major league pitcher to hurl a "perfect" game when he prevented any Philadelphia player from reaching first base today. The 37-year-old hurler for the Boston Americans, who switched from the St. Louis National club in 1901, amazed fans with his control as he surpassed his performance of last September 18, when he set down the Cincinnati team without a hit. Young, who started his career with Cleveland's Nationals in his home state of Ohio, won 33 games and lost only 10 in his first year at Boston and followed that with seasons of 32-11 and 28-9.

Woman in motorcar arrested for smoking

New York City, Sept. 28

Men, says the census, now outnumber women by about 1.5 million, and they exercise many privileges denied to the female of the species. In New York today, a woman was arrested for smoking in an open automobile. "You can't do that on Fifth Avenue," a policeman lectured. There is no law against the practice, but custom dictates otherwise. But what's a lady to do when the President's daughter Alice herself smokes, even in public and probably on Fifth Avenue if given the chance. In increasing numbers, it seems, women are defying convention. Clubs, saloons and tobacco shops, at least, still offer all-male havens.

Negroes in six cities boycott "Jim Crow"

Atlanta, Georgia, Fall

This has been a turbulent year for whites and Negroes alike. Following rioting, burning and lynchings, whites are increasingly turning to "Jim Crow" (segregationist) laws to isolate themselves from the Negro community. Kentucky has officially segregated both its public and private schools. In response, Negroes have become increasingly militant in combatting this form of second-class citizenship. During this past year, Negroes have protested Jim Crow laws by boycotting segregated streetcars in Atlanta, Augusta, Columbia, New Orleans, Mobile and Houston. The racial turmoil shows no signs of waning (→Sept. 24, 1906).

Tarbell exposes Rockefeller's Standard Oil

United States

No one is safe from the reformers, least of all a mighty financier. John D. Rockefeller is the latest to feel their wrath in *The History of the Standard Oil Company*, an expose by Ida Tarbell of *McClure's Magazine* about the powerful company and the ruthless methods it uses to ruin rivals, plunder the earth for crude oil and buy off politicians. The sensational findings, based on interviews with former Standard employees, first appeared last year in a *McClure's* series written by Miss Tarbell, a 47-year-old native of Pennsylvania. A graduate of Allegheny College, she taught briefly before moving to Paris, where she was hired 10 years ago by S.S. McClure, founder of the magazine bearing his name.

New York City gets shiny new subway

New York City, Oct. 27

"City Hall to Harlem in 15 minutes" has been the boast of the New York City subway since construction began in 1900. Today it lived up to the claim, as 150,000 cheering passengers jammed the gleaming, 25 m.p.h. electric cars. Chief Engineer John B. McDonald built the 15-mile line with financial backing from August Belmont. With congestion above ground growing, underground rapid transit has become a necessity. The first subway theft was also reported today. At 7:02 p.m., a passenger was relieved of a $500 diamond pin.

New steel company born in Bethlehem

Bethlehem, Penn., Dec. 10

Bethlehem Steel was incorporated today, 47 years after the nucleus of the company opened for business. Charles M. Schwab, a former U.S. Steel president, purchased an interest in the small Bethlehem Steel Company and merged it with the U.S. Shipbuilding Company last year. He will now preside over all Bethlehem Steel's activities. The firm will use the Bessemer process to manufacture steel in Pittsburgh.

Ashcan artist Robert Henri's "Young Woman in White" (1904).

Theodore Roosevelt wields Big Stick

Roosevelt, with navy in tow, turns the Caribbean into an American lake.

Washington, D.C., Dec. 6

The emergence of the United States as a world power with its own exclusive sphere of influence was highlighted today in the President's annual address to Congress in which he formulated an extension of the Monroe Doctrine that is being called the Roosevelt Corollary. Referring to recent events in Central America, the President declared that "chronic wrongdoing, or an impotence which results in a general loosening of the ties of civilized society . . . may force the United States, however reluctantly, in flagrant cases of such wrongdoing or impotence, to the exercise of an international police power."

Such police power is to be used to prevent a repetition of the 1902 incident when German, British and Italian warships blockaded Venezuela to force payment of debts on which that country had defaulted. But while deploring such armed intervention as a violation of the Monroe Doctrine, the President has shown no sympathy for countries that default. Therefore, as he put it to Secretary of War Elihu Root, "If we intend to say 'Hands off' . . . we must keep order ourselves." The newly formulated policy is likely to be applied early next year to the Dominican Republic, which recently reneged on debts that amount to some $32 million.

Despite America's acquisition of Puerto Rico and the Philippines, the President's policy is avowedly anticolonial. "I have about as much desire to annex it," he has said of the Dominican Republic, "as a gorged boa constrictor might have to swallow a porcupine wrong-end-to." Nor has Roosevelt shown any inclination to depart from the original Monroe Doctrine so far as it commits the United States not to interfere in Europe, where increasing hostility between the alliances of the great powers threatens to lead to a major war.

In automobile competition, gasoline power pulls way out ahead

Westbury, Long Island, Oct. 8

When George Heath's 90-horsepower Panhard racer whizzed past the finish line to win the first Vanderbilt Cup race today, it was new proof of the technical leaps taken by gasoline-powered cars. The race, sponsored by W.H. Vanderbilt Jr., covered a grueling 284-mile course starting in Westbury. Heath, an American, finished in 5 hours 26 minutes, as his low-slung, rakish French motorcar averaged over 50 m.p.h. At times, the speeds neared 70 m.p.h., and one vehicle, a Mercedes driven by George Arents, burst a tire and spun out of control, killing mechanic Carl Mensel.

This year, 22,130 automobiles were manufactured and sold from the Southeast to the Northwest. Steam and electric cars still abound, but as the race attests, gasoline power is unmatched for endurance and speed. In fact, New York has a new 20 m.p.h. open-road speed limit, and on September 3, an Oldsmobile driven by L.L. Whitman arrived in New York after leaving San Francisco just 33 days earlier. On August 10, St. Louis proclaimed "Automobile Day" when a 59-machine procession that left New York on July 25 crossed the Eads Bridge and entered the World's Fair grounds.

The 1904 Oldsmobile 7 is typical of the machines seen on the road. Its curved dashboard and buggy-style seat are reminiscent of the horse-drawn carriage.

1905

Roosevelt

Baltimore, Maryland, Jan. 5. B.&O. Railroad introduces electric freight locomotives, first in nation.

Washington, D.C., Jan. 20. President Roosevelt begins managing Dominican Republic's internal and foreign debts, without congressional approval (→ March 31).

New York City, Feb. 3. Polygamist Mary Arbogast jailed for bigamy.

Washington, D.C., Feb. 20. Supreme Court rules in Jacobson v. Massachusetts that states have right to enact laws requiring vaccination.

New York City, Apr. 12. Hippodrome arena opens, with seating capacity of 5,000.

Washington, D.C., Apr. 25. United States receives communication from Japan recognizing Open Door policy in Manchuria and pledging to restore that region to China.

New York City, June 7. Small parcel of land, 1250 square feet, on Wall Street sells for a record $700,000.

Washington, D.C., July 1. Congress passes Agricultural Appropriations Act, designating Bureau of Forestry as National Forest Service.

Washington, D.C., July 17. Supreme Court upholds decision forcing Oregon farmer Elias Hughes to relinquish claim to Willamette meteorite.

New York City, Oct. 1. Juilliard School of Music founded.

Dayton, Ohio, Oct. 5. Wilbur and Orville Wright solve equilibrium problem in circular flight of 24 miles.

New York City, Oct. 14. New York Giants defeat Philadelphia Athletics in second World Series, four games to one.

Washington, D.C., Dec. 5. President Roosevelt formally recommends to U.S. Congress that Alaska be granted an official congressional delegation (→ Dec. 3, 1906).

New York City. Thomas Dixon Jr.'s novel about Ku Klux Klan, *The Clansman*, published.

Cambridge, Mass. First part of philosopher George Santayana's five-volume *The Life of Reason* issued.

Boston. Edith Wharton's *The House of Mirth* is published.

Teddy mounts bully pulpit in Washington

With flags aflutter, Roosevelt takes the oath for first full term in office.

Washington, D.C., March 4

When Vice President Teddy Roosevelt moved into the Oval Office after the assassination of President McKinley in 1901, Senator Mark Hanna exclaimed, "Now that damned cowboy is President!" Last November, Teddy the Rough Rider silenced critics and was elected on his own. Today, he mounted the "bully pulpit" and delivered his presidential inaugural address.

In it, the popular, active President repeated a favorite theme: rights and duties. "We have duties to others and duties to ourselves; we can shirk neither," he exclaimed from the Capitol steps. He struck a rugged tone when he lauded America's "self-reliance and individual initiative" and, in progressive trust-busting words, he said that "accumulation of great wealth" has led to grave problems. TR ended his address with a reference to Abraham Lincoln: "We must show . . . devotion to a lofty ideal . . . which made great men who preserved this republic in the days of Abraham Lincoln." Roosevelt reveres Lincoln. Last night, Secretary of State John Hay gave Teddy a ring engraved with both "TR" and Lincoln's initials and a lock of his hair, snipped while he lay dying. After Roosevelt's speech, he watched the largest inaugural parade ever.

The President addresses the nation.

U.S. takes over Dominican finances

Dominican Republic, March 31

President Roosevelt today appointed a customs receiver for the Dominican Republic as part of his program to resolve the Caribbean country's financial problems. The republic has borrowed heavily from foreign sources and reportedly owes $32 million. Roosevelt decided strong measures were needed to prevent intervention by European powers. According to the agreement worked out with the Dominican government, the United States will control the country's customs house, its main source of income, and will allow the Dominican government 45 percent of the money collected for use domestically. The rest will be used to pay back foreign creditors. If estimates that 90 percent of customs revenues are pocketed by corrupt officials are accurate, the 45 percent allowance should not prove a hardship but a boon to the country's economy.

Roosevelt set the stage for today's action in his message to Congress last December when he stated that "in the Western Hemisphere adherence of the United States to the Monroe Doctrine may force the United States, however reluctantly, in flagrant cases of . . . wrongdoing or impotence, to the exercise of an international police power."

Supreme Court slaughters the beef trust

Washington, D.C., Jan. 30

The so-called "beef trust" was dealt a death blow today when the United States Supreme Court decided that Swift and Company was operating an illegal monopoly in violation of the Sherman Antitrust Act of 1890.

In ruling in favor of the government in Swift & Co. v. the United States, the high court held that the meat concern was acting in restraint of trade, that the effect of the company's action upon commerce among the states was not accidental.

The charge of the federal government was that "a dominant proportion" of the dealers in fresh meat throughout the country had not bid against one another in the livestock markets in order to fix prices and that they had restricted shipments of meat when that proved necessary. The government further accused the meat dealers of having sought to obtain less-than-lawful rates from the railroad companies.

The court's opinion, which was written by Justice Oliver Wendell Holmes, noted that "it is said this charge was too vague" and that it "does not set forth a case of commerce among the states." Actually, according to the Holmes opinion, when cattle are transported from one state to another and sold, interstate commerce is indeed taking place. Then, with tongue very much in cheek, Justice Holmes wrote: "It should be added that the cattle in the stockyard are not at rest" (→ March 12, 1906).

Today's less ornate and constrictive, simpler fashions are designed to meet the changing role of woman in American society.

President helps end Russo-Japanese War

The Old World powers respectfully submit to New World diplomacy.

Portsmouth, N.H., Sept. 5

President Roosevelt's energetic efforts to get the belligerents of the Russo-Japanese War to sit down together has borne fruit. Delegates to the peace negotiations here in Portsmouth have agreed on a treaty in which the Russians are conceding to the Japanese the superior position in Korea, the principal issue over which this war has been fought.

Although the Russian government also agreed to withdraw its troops from Manchuria and to hand over to Japan part of the island of Sakhalin, its position in Asia was not harmed. The worst damage is to the prestige of Czar Nicholas II, who is the first leader of a modern European power to lose a war to an Asian one. The breakthrough in the talks came when Roosevelt persuaded Japan to drop its demand for war reparations. He had accused the Japanese of continuing the fighting for the sake of money (→ Dec. 10, 1906).

Citing accord with U.S., Japan rules Korea

Tokyo, Dec. 21

Japan has declared Korea its protectorate, extending its control of that country into the one area that had eluded its grasp, foreign affairs. As justification for its action, Japan cited a memorandum negotiated this summer between American Secretary of War William Howard Taft and Prime Minister Taro Katsura, in which the United States recognized the Japanese control of Korea in return for Japan's pledge not to get involved in the Philippines. President Roosevelt has not protested Japan's interpretation of the Taft-Katsura memorandum, although at the time it was negotiated it was regarded as no more than a recognition of Japan's current position, not an endorsement of any future action.

Japan has been a major actor on the Korean political stage since 1895, when it overturned China's protectorate there. For a while, the Russian aspirations for Korea checked the Japanese, but Tokyo's victory in the Russo-Japanese War removed Russia as an obstacle.

Under the protectorate treaty imposed on the Korean Emperor, a Japanese regent-general will replace Korea's minister of foreign affairs and its foreign legations will be disbanded, destroying the last outpost of its already weak independence movement.

Americans get taste of pizza in Little Italy

New York City

Visitors to New York City's colorful neighborhood of Little Italy have become accustomed to sampling exotic specialties such as spaghetti and lasagna, and now a Spring Street restaurateur named Gennaro Lombardi has started to feature a new food item that the Italian immigrants here call a "pizza." This flat, yeast bread baked with oozing, melted cheese called mozzarella and tomatoes is served in wedgelike slices that may be eaten either with fork and knife or with the fingers. Said to be a specialty of Naples, the pizza has long been a favorite there, although it is apparently not much known in the other sections of Italy.

Scot wins U.S. Open for the fourth time

Pittsfield, Mass.

Willie Anderson, a dour, uncommunicative Scot who is considered the mystery man of golf, has astounded followers of the sport by winning the United States Open championship for the fourth time. He made it three in a row with a smashing victory over Alex Smith to take it this year. Anderson had beaten Smith in the 1901 Open final, taking the playoff by a stroke. He went on to win again in 1903, this time defeating David Brown. The next year, Anderson amazed his followers by outplaying Gil Nicholls with a score of 303. Before his breakthrough, Anderson was second in 1897, third in 1898, fifth in 1899 and 11th in 1900.

Hart captures title with 12th-round KO

Reno, Nevada, July 3

Marvin Hart captured the world heavyweight boxing championship today – well, sort of. One thing is certain: He knocked out Jack Root in the 12th round here. The promoter of the fight had declared that the winner would take over the title vacated by Jim Jeffries, who quit boxing because he could not find a suitable opponent to knock out. Jeffries had held the championship since he put away a badly overmatched Bob Fitzsimmons in 1899. Jeffries, by the way, was referee in the Hart-Root fight. While it took place, Tommy Burns of Canada has been in the background, saying he is the rightful heir to the title (→ March 23, 1906).

Meetings rotate; call them Rotarians

Chicago, Feb. 23

In an effort to promote high standards of practice and cooperation in business, Chicago lawyer Paul Percy Harris today founded a local organization that he calls the Rotary Club. The civilian service club will consist of at least one member from each local business or profession, without overrepresentation in any one area. Members are planning to meet at one another's offices in rotation, which explains how the organization got its name. The association said it hopes not only to foster fellowship and good will between members, but in the community as well.

States barred from setting work hours

Washington, D.C., Apr. 17

The Supreme Court ruled today that states cannot set the maximum number of hours any employee can work. By ruling so, the court overturned a New York law that sought to restrict bakery and confectionery employees to no more than 60 hours a week or an average of 10 hours a day. The state law, the court held, violated the Constitution in that it was illegal interference in the rights of both employers and employees. While conceding that such work is strenuous, the court also held there was no reasonable foundation for holding that the law in question was necessary to guard public health.

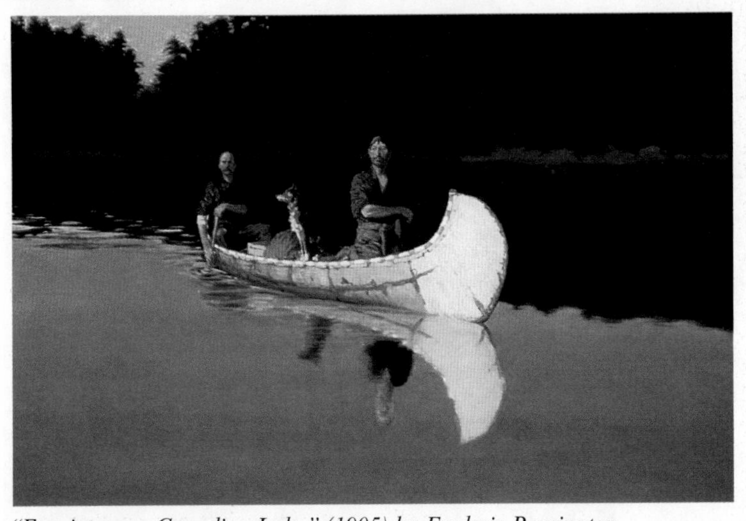

"Evening on a Canadian Lake" (1905) by Frederic Remington.

Du Bois movement urges racial equality

Fort Erie, Ontario, July 13
Responding to W.E.B. Du Bois's call for "organized determination and aggressive action," 29 Negroes from 14 states met today to formulate principles for the radical wing of the civil rights movement. Dr. Du Bois, a Harvard-educated sociologist and a reluctant entrant into politics, tells his race to "refuse to kiss the hands that smite us." The new "Niagara Movement" formalizes a split between Du Bois and educator Booker T. Washington. Washington, who runs a vocational school in Tuskegee, Alabama, says Negroes must stake a place in the industrial economy, and only then pursue political rights. Washington's followers have taken to calling Du Bois the "professor of hysterics." His "hysteria," apparently, is the belief that without full political equality, the Negro will always be shut out of a biased economy. The Niagara Movement thus seeks manhood suffrage, freedom of speech and criticism, abolition of all caste distinctions based simply on race or color and "recognition of the principle of human brotherhood as a practical present creed."

Panama canal construction is under way

Panama, July 25
John F. Stevens arrived here today to take charge of construction of a canal across Panama. Aware that a French attempt to dig a canal ended in bankruptcy because of the toll taken by tropical disease, the noted engineer is concentrating on good housing and sanitary facilities for workers. His design calls for locks through which vessels will travel across the isthmus. The effort is being spurred by the Roosevelt administration, which created the country of Panama and negotiated a canal treaty (→ June 29, 1906).

The jungle proves a deadly opponent.

Stieglitz promotes photography at gallery

New York City, Nov. 25
The latest innovations in the expanding field of art photography can be found in the Fifth Avenue brownstone of Alfred Stieglitz this month. An editor and founder of several photographic journals as well as a photographer, Stieglitz is the leading advocate of an esthetic rather than technical approach to photography. He brings this rather unexplored print medium closer to the status of full-fledged art by displaying in his three-room attic 100 works by members of the Photo-Secession Group, who claim to be "seceding from the acceptable idea of what constitutes a photograph."

Stieglitz's "Winter, Fifth Avenue," where the photographer's gallery is located.

Government opens insurance inquiry

Washington, D.C., Sept. 6
President Roosevelt began a comprehensive investigation today into alleged corruption among major life insurance companies. Charles Evans Hughes and William Armstrong will head the inquiry. The probe meets Roosevelt's campaign promises of last year to clean up American business. The first place the joint House and Senate committee will look is Wall Street. For years, there have been allegations that many prominent New York businessmen are tied to top-of-the-line insurance companies in defrauding the small-policy holder. The President has pledged that he won't stop here; corporations in other industries are next.

New Orleans acts to check epidemic

New Orleans, Nov. 1
City health authorities said today that aggressive measures to control mosquitoes have ended the yellow fever epidemic and held the death rate to a relatively low figure. Only 451 people died of the scourge in New Orleans compared to the more than 4,000 who died in the last epidemic in 1878. Health authorities urged citizens to oil and screen cisterns and other water containers, to place netting around beds and to apply pennyroyal or camphor to the skin. Street gutters were cleaned and oiled. Dr. Quitman Kohnke urged such measures five years ago, as soon as it was determined that mosquito bites caused yellow fever, but his pleas were ignored.

Put another nickel in the nickelodeon

United States
All across the land, in cities and small towns, storefronts are painted and embellished with colorful posters. A screen plus several rows of straight chairs and a piano are moved into a makeshift theater, an old storeroom or a new motion picture theater. The usual offerings are the 10-minute features, mainly vaudeville acts, but some film scenes as well, where larger-than-life images float across the screen, followed by an "illustrated song," sung by a soloist. And it's all for a nickel, hence the name "nickelodeons." It would seem that the "flickers" have established a firm hold on the affections of the urban working class. The cheap amusement appeals to the vast immigrant populations of New York, Chicago and Philadelphia. Pittsburgh has also put up its first nickelodeon. Reports indicate that the very first one was built in Los Angeles, the Electric Theater, in 1902. Wherever they are, they seem to be drawing crowds, all day, every day. It is not too expensive to become the proprietor of one of these and the motion pictures may be purchased outright from companies like Biograph for 12 cents per foot or rented from the film exchanges that are mushrooming everywhere.

Festival marks visit by Lewis and Clark

Portland, Oregon, Oct. 15

Today marks the end of the Lewis and Clark Exposition. The festival commemorates the 100th anniversary of the arrival of the Lewis and Clark Expedition on the Pacific Coast and honors the progress since then. Meriwether Lewis and William Clark, representatives of President Jefferson, had come out West to explore the newly acquired Louisiana Territory. They started up the Missouri River May 14, 1804, and sighted the Pacific on November 7, 1805. An interesting sidelight to the exposition was celebration of a Western Authors' Week to demonstrate the creative force of literature that was conceived and written in the Pacific Northwest generally and in Oregon specifically. The rise of literary magazines was cited as proof that this area's writers were as prolific and professional as those anywhere in the land.

Overland Limited gets electric lights

Chicago, Nov. 8

The Union Pacific Railroad today introduced electric lighting on its luxury passenger train, the Overland Limited, which runs between Chicago and San Francisco. Passengers now will be able to light up their compartments with the snap of a switch, instead of having to rely on gas lamps. Electricity for the compartments is provided by carrying steam from the engine to a forward section of a baggage car, where it drives a generator that provides power to the entire train. The Overland is not the first train to have electric power. As early as 1887, a generator was used to light up the Pennsylvania Limited on its run between Chicago and New York. But the adoption of electric power for the Overland is certain to set off competition among other railroads to provide similar luxuries for their passengers.

"Immigrants of the right kind" welcomed

Washington, D.C., Dec. 5

President Theodore Roosevelt told Congress in his annual message today that "there is no danger in having too many immigrants of the right kind." In the face of rising nativist sentiment in some sectors fo society, the President added that he "grows extremely indignant at the attitude of coarse hostility to the immigrant." The ideal of progressive immigration policy entails "Americanization." By immigrants "of the right kind," Roosevelt meant those of whatever ethnic origin willing to learn English, embrace the values and customs of the middle class, improve themselves through education, work hard in their profession and obey the law.

In fact, studies show that most of the newcomers, and particularly their children, do yearn to become part of the mainstream, and succeed in doing so, given a chance. Thus the President concluded, "I want to implant in the minds of our fellow Americans of foreign ancestry or birth the knowledge that they have just the same rights and opportunities as anyone else in this country" (→Feb. 26, 1907).

American family with roots in Bohemia; the children were born here.

Vice squad closes daring Shaw play

New York City, Oct. 31

Ticket-holders who didn't make it to the premiere of *Mrs. Warren's Profession* had better get a refund. Opening night was also closing night for the daring drama by the Irish playwright George Bernard Shaw, who wrote the work in 1898 but was prevented from staging it in London, where he has lived since 1876, because of England's tough censorship laws. Much the same happened in New York as police moved in after complaints by Anthony Comstock, head of the Society for the Prevention of Vice.

The controversial Shaw, whose previous works include *Man and Superman*, *Major Barbara*, and *The Devil's Disciple*, admits that *Mrs. Warren's Profession* is not pleasant stuff. The profession in question is prostitution. Shaw, though not an advocate of that line of work, is intent on exposing its "economic basis." This theme comes as no surprise to followers of Shaw's career. Since the Fabian Society was founded in 1884, he has been a leader of the London reform group, which favors the spread of socialism.

Western mine union, I.W.W. linked to murder of ex-Governor

Caldwell, Idaho, Dec. 31

Governor Frank Steunenberg's political career ended six years ago after he brutally suppressed a Western Federation of Miners strike in the Coeur d'Alene district. He never imagined he might be endangering his life. Yesterday, however, he was torn apart by a bomb that exploded at his front gate. The motive is apparently revenge and fingers are pointing to the Industrial Workers of the World, a radical spinoff of the miners federation.

The I.W.W. is the latest of "Big Bill" Haywood's attempts to broaden the base of the Western miners. After the failure of attempts to unite with the conservative American Federation of Labor, the rugged, heavy-drinking leader presided over a January conference of left-wing unionists and Socialists in Chicago. "Fellow workers!" he bellowed, "This is the Continental Congress of the working class." A formal convention on June 27, attended by Eugene Debs and Mother Jones, proclaimed the founding of "one great union for all."

Officials suspect Harry Orchard, a member of the I.W.W., killed Steunenberg (→July 28, 1907).

"Fabricating Steel" by Henry Bernstein. Industrialization spurs a new genre in painting, ennobling the workingman.

1906

Roosevelt

Washington, D.C., Feb. 24. United States receives note from Japanese government agreeing that Tokyo will not issue passports to workers trying to immigrate to United States.

Washington, D.C., March 12. Supreme Court, in Hale v. Henkel, holds that witnesses can be compelled to testify against their employers in antitrust suits (→June 29).

Los Angeles, March 23. Tommy Burns defeats Marvin Hart in 20th round to win world heavyweight boxing title.

Washington, D.C., May 8. Law is passed giving Alaska delegate to Congress.

New York City, May 26. Lewis Nixon announces invention of device giving submarines "eyes and ears" [sonar].

Washington, D.C., June 29. President Roosevelt signs act of Congress, providing for a lock-type canal in Panama (→Nov. 14).

Washington, D.C., July. *National Geographic* publishes George Shiras 3rd's unique photos of animals at night.

Brownsville, Georgia, Sept. 24. When Atlanta press urges disenfranchisement of Negroes and revival of Ku Klux Klan, violent rioting erupts.

San Francisco, Oct. 11. Board of education orders all schools to segregate Oriental and non-Oriental students (→15).

Chicago, Oct. 14. White Sox beat Cubs, four games to two, in all-Chicago World Series.

Tokyo, Oct. 15. Japanese government claims that segregation of schools in San Francisco violates treaty of 1894 (→Feb. 1907).

New York City, Nov. 23. Enrico Caruso found guilty of molesting a woman in Central Park Monkey House; he touched her left forearm with his right elbow.

Washington, D.C., Dec. 3. Alaska's first delegate to Congress is seated.

Atlanta. Coca-Cola Company, after threats of legal action, replaces cocaine in its soda with caffeine.

DEATH

Rochester, N.Y., March 13. Susan B. Anthony, leading suffragette (*Feb. 15, 1820).

Sinclair exposes meat-packing "Jungle"

Upton Sinclair, muckraker.

Chicago

It's no easy feat keeping your appetite after reading selected pages of *The Jungle*, a fictional glimpse of Chicago's meat-packing industry. Its 28-year-old author, Upton Sinclair, toured the city's stockyards as part of a team of investigators. What he saw has gripped – and shocked – the nation. At one point, Sinclair describes the remains of diseased cattle being processed into packaged food along with the bodies of workers who happen to fall into the mixing vats. "Sometimes they would be overlooked for days," the novelist wrote of these tragic men, "till all but the bones of them had gone out to the world as Durham's Pure Leaf Lard." This fact-based description has so outraged the public that an abashed Congress recently saved the pure food and drug bill from the edge of defeat. In addition, *The Jungle* has prompted a policy of federal meat inspection.

Sinclair, a prolific writer with half a dozen novels under his belt, welcomes the acclaim for his new book, but he feels that the purpose of his novel has been misunderstood. His true target was not the unsanitary conditions of the stockyards, he says, but the exploitation of immigrant laborers. As he commented after the passage in June by Congress of the Meat Inspection Act and Pure Food and Drug Acts: "I aimed at the public's heart and by accident hit it in the stomach."

In fact, *The Jungle* makes a direct plea for radical reform, a point made in Jack London's fiery introduction, which applauds the author's "proletarian" sympathies. Even conservative readers have been moved by the plight of Sinclair's hero, Jurgis Rudkus, a wide-eyed immigrant from Lithuania who is abused by his bosses, bilked by con men and mired in poverty. A string of setbacks causes him to quit his job and fall into criminality before he harkens to the call of socialism.

The author recently demonstrated his own commitment to the radical creed by investing his royalties in the Helicon Home Colony of Englewood, New Jersey, where 40 families, most headed by young writers, are now experimenting with communal living. Visitors to the compound have included John Dewey, William James and Emma Goldman (→March 1907).

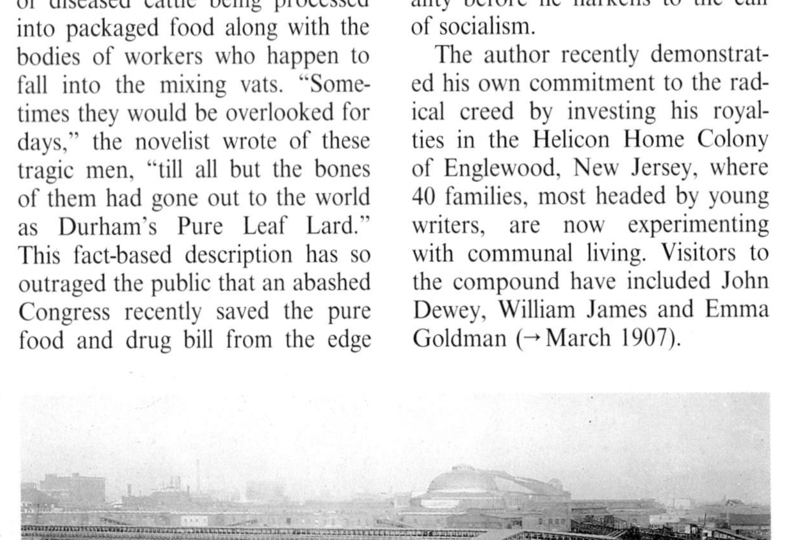

The stockyards in Chicago, the focus of Sinclair's expose of the meat-packing industry. He described diseased cattle being processed into packaged food.

Steffens reveals "Shame of Cities"

New York City

What have New York, Boston and Minneapolis in common? In these cities and many others, bad government reigns, with political bosses, greedy businessmen and crooked cops in charge. Since 1902, *McClure's* has been running a serial account of the nation's great cities and their woes. Its author, Lincoln Steffens, has now gathered them in a book, *The Shame of the Cities*. "No one class is at fault . . . nor any particular interest or group or party," writes Steffens. Who is the true culprit? Ordinary people, he says, a "shameless citizenship."

Lincoln Steffens, also a muckraker.

President criticizes muckraking writers

Washington, D.C., March 17

Too much printer's ink is being wasted on the subject of corruption, President Roosevelt complained tonight in a speech to journalists at the Gridiron Club. The President, who himself does not mince words, coined a tough phrase for the new breed of fault-finding writers – Ida Tarbell, Lincoln Steffens and others – whose work often appears in publications such as *McClure's*. The chief executive called them "muckrakers," an allusion to John Bunyan's *Pilgrim's Progress*, the classic Christian allegory that features a character so absorbed in the squalid task of raking muck that he can't see a heavenly crown when it's held over his head.

Amid quake ruins, Caruso in pajamas

San Francisco, Apr. 18

The Metropolitan Opera Company, with Madame Sembrich and Signor Caruso, performed a spirited *Carmen* at the San Francisco Opera House just hours before the quake hit. Minutes after the first shock, the famed Enrico Caruso sat, clad in pajamas, on his valise in the middle of the street outside the Palace Hotel this morning. Personal effects and costumes were lost, but no one in the company was hurt. The Naples-born Caruso feels the quake has "some relation to the eruption of Vesuvius." The catastrophe completely destroyed the Opera House.

Grain overcooked; now it's corn flakes

Battle Creek, Michigan

Breakfast cereal producers here were joined this year by W.K. Kellogg's Toasted Corn Flake Company, whose product was the result of an accident at the Battle Creek Sanitarium, run by Dr. John Harvey Kellogg, as cooks left some boiled grain unattended and then found it broke into crispy flakes. Now Kellogg will compete with C.W. Post, whose Postum cereal coffee and Grape Nuts have been successful.

Diamonds dug up in Arkansas field

Murfreesboro, Arkansas

John Huddleston was walking around his farm three miles from here not too long ago wondering why his land was growing such miserable crops. Kicking at the soil, he noticed two shiny objects. They were crystals. Taken to a Little Rock jeweler, they were identified as diamonds. Geologists sent to the site have discovered that Huddleston's land covers the "pipe" of an ancient volcano. Thus, they say, these diamonds may well have been spewed from the center of the planet. So far, the diamonds found have been brilliant and of an excellent luster, but most are small. The diamond mine is believed to be the only such deposit in the country.

San Francisco ravaged by earthquake

San Francisco, Apr. 18

Day had not yet dawned when, at 5:13 a.m., deep thunder rumbled from the earth's bowels. Then San Francisco shook like a maple leaf. Its highways cracked and split; the wharves warped and creaked; steel structures swayed, and many buildings split from cornice to foundation. There were six consecutive shocks, the third, at 8:45 a.m., bringing the worst destruction. Six hours of mortal dread and nameless terror ensued as the city was tossed upon seismic waves in the most disastrous earthquake in the history of America's West Coast.

Now confusion and helpless horror reign as countless dead lie in the morgues or under fallen walls. Some 1,000 lives are feared lost. Raging fires add to the disaster. Martial law has been declared, and this afternoon four thieves were shot for looting. Military units with orders to shoot looters on sight are allied with the police to keep things under control.

Thousands of panicked citizens are trying to leave the city, which looks as if the foot of a giant had crushed an anthill. Half the population is spending the night in public squares and parks, the living hunting for the dead or missing. Both the despair and the material loss are beyond any computation (→ 19).

Fire loss worse than quake damage

San Francisco, Apr. 19

Damage from the earthquake does not begin to compare with the loss from fire. Flames have destroyed the city's business district, and sweeping winds have carried the blaze to other areas of the devastated, terrified city. Eight square miles – several hundred city blocks – are totally burned out. Nearly 250,000 people are homeless today. Many small towns along the coast and within the earthquake area have been turned into scrapheaps. Everywhere there are smoldering ruins. The loss in San Francisco itself is estimated at $250 million; losses in San Jose are put at $5 million. Oakland and surrounding regions will add heavily to the total.

The devastation of the earthquake and subsequent fire leaves the people of San Francisco dazed, confused and with little else to do but watch the city crumble.

The aftermath of the San Francisco earthquake and subsequent fire, showing the ruins of Nob Hill and the Fairmont Hotel, with Chinatown in the foreground. Nearly 250,000 residents of the city are reported to be homeless.

President gives away his daughter Alice

French celebration of the marriage and the anniversary of Washington's birth.

Washington, D.C., Feb. 17

"I can do one of two things," President Theodore Roosevelt has said. "I can be President of the United States or I can control Alice. I cannot possibly do both." Today, the greater burden was lifted. His eldest daughter, who has puffed a cigarette in public and once raced about in an automobile in the company of three men, was wed today in a splendid White House ceremony. The groom is 35-year-old Nicholas Longworth, an Ohio congressman. Alice, 21, did not wear her favorite color, the blue-gray "Alice blue," but white – her mother's wedding dress.

U.S. puts Governor in charge in Cuba

Washington, D.C., Oct. 3

President Theodore Roosevelt has appointed a Nebraska lawyer, Charles Edward Magoon, Governor of Cuba, replacing the elected President, Tomas Estrada Palma. In August, Estrada Palma asked Roosevelt for help in putting down a rebellion led by Jose Miguel Gomez and Alfredo Zayas. In response, Roosevelt sent a contingent of United States troops under Secretary of War William Howard Taft. Authority for Magoon's appointment comes under the Platt Amendment, which permits Washington to intervene if necessary to maintain order and protect Cuba's independence. The United States was also involved in Cuba after the Spanish-American War, in order to protect the strategically situated island from European powers, especially Germany. When the Americans left Cuba in 1902, the terms of the Platt Amendment were incorporated in the Cuban constitution.

Devil's Tower made national monument

Wyoming, Sept. 24

President Roosevelt today announced the designation of Devil's Tower as a national monument. This spectacular rock formation is the first place of natural beauty to be so designated. By the provisions of the recently passed Preservation of American Antiques Act, the President will be authorized to protect distinctive American geologic formations, scenic locales and other national treasures for posterity.

Hepburn Act lets I.C.C. set rail rates

Washington, D.C., June 29

Swept along on a tide of reform, railroads have nestled further into the federal embrace. The Hepburn Act, signed today by President Roosevelt, empowers the Interstate Commerce Commission to investigate and set rates. Circumscribed by Nelson Aldrich's opposition in the Senate, the bill requires that inquiries be initiated by outside complaints, and subjects all decisions to judicial review. But it does put teeth in anti-rebate laws. Teddy touts the bill as a major victory against the "malefactors of great wealth" (→May 15, 1911)

Crime of passion: Architect is gunned down by jealous husband

New York City, June 25

The prominent architect Stanford White was brutally murdered tonight. White, a partner in McKim, Mead & White, was sitting in the Madison Square Garden Roof Theater, when a gunman came from behind and shot him in the head three times. The alleged murderer has been identified as the millionaire Harry K. Thaw. According to rumors long whispered in society, the 53-year-old White had been having an illicit love affair with Thaw's wife, Evelyn Nesbit, whom he helped put on the stage through his influence in the theater. Thaw had long suspected his wife of carrying on with White, who boasted of his passion for the lovely Miss Nesbit. A brilliant architect and a specialist in interior design, White created the furnishings for James Gordon Bennett's yacht as well as the covers of major magazines. His architectural works include Washington Arch, the Century Club and, ironically, the very building where he was slain. Thaw, charged with murder, is said to have a history of mental instability. He will be personally prosecuted by District Attorney William Travers Jerome.

The dashing looks and manner of prominent architect Stanford White (left) may have ultimately caused his death, since his affair with Evelyn Nesbit provoked a murderous rage in her millionaire husband, Harry K. Thaw (right).

Senate okays role in Moroccan crisis

Washington, D.C., Dec. 12

After bitter debate over the wisdom of American intervention in European affairs, the Senate reluctantly approved the Act of Algeciras today. The United States sent two envoys to the Algeciras Conference, which was called in January to help ease tensions that had developed between Germany and France in Morocco. According to the act, Morocco retains its territorial integrity, but France and Spain control the police force. And, the Open Door, assuring equal commercial opportunity, is to be maintained. While the Moroccan issue is a European matter, the Open Door principle also applies to the United States.

Sarah bids America a very fond adieu

The Alphonse Mucha portrayal of Sarah Bernhardt captures her grace.

New York City

Sarah Bernhardt, the dark-eyed, petite French actress who has bewitched audiences for more than 30 years, is making the final engagement of her "Farewell American Tour" at the Lyric Theater. Rivaled only by Duse as the world's greatest actress, Bernhardt is renowned for her voice, which has been likened to a "golden bell." Her Racine roles are legendary. In 1899, she appeared as Hamlet, to mixed reviews. The tour has been a grind – coast-to-coast in 62 cities – and the conditions not always the best. In some Southern cities she played in roller-skating rinks; in Texas, in tents. While in San Francisco, Madame Sarah, as she is called, gave a special recital for the prisoners of San Quentin – in French, as usual. Many Americans still hope that she can be lured back for an encore.

Pass made legal to cut football deaths

New York City, Jan. 12

Alarmed by the sharp rise in the number of deaths and injuries in college football, representatives of the Intercollegiate Athletic Association have carried out a series of rule changes, including the legalization of the forward pass. In the past, mass plays where brute strength and great weight were determining factors led to crippling injuries as well as fatalities, so much so that many college presidents have either banned the sport or threatened to do so. President Roosevelt said that the game must be made safer. As a result – in addition to the new forward pass rule – a neutral zone has been created between the offensive and defensive lines, and the offense will be required to have at least six players on the line of scrimmage before the ball can be snapped.

Welcome to Gary!

Gary, Indiana

Out of swamps and sand dunes, a steel town has been born. Gary, Indiana, named after the U.S. Steel chairman, Judge Elbert Gary, was chosen as a site for the corporation because of its good water supply and its rail transportation potential, vital ingredients for making steel.

The soaring atrium of Marshall Field's in Chicago symbolizes the range of the nation's prosperity.

TR, in Panama, is first President abroad

Astride a steam shovel at Culebra Cut, Roosevelt imbues a "can-do" spirit.

Panama, Nov. 14

President Roosevelt arrived in Panama today to inspect construction of the canal across the isthmus, establishing another precedent. Roosevelt is the first President to visit a foreign country while in office. Just four years ago, he pioneered by taking the first presidential ride in an automobile. Roosevelt sailed here from the United States on the steamer Louisiana. His Panama visit will last three days. He plans a short stay in Puerto Rico before returning to Washington.

The President finds that work on the canal is proceeding more slowly than had been hoped. Digging is disorganized, and some still oppose the decision to build a series of locks. Roosevelt views lock construction as the most effective way to deal with the difference in height between the Atlantic and Pacific sides of the isthmus. He is considering replacement of John Stevens, chief engineer, with Colonel George Goethals (→ 1910).

Nobel goes to Roosevelt for peace efforts

Oslo, Norway, Dec. 10

President Theodore Roosevelt, known more for his "big stick" than his diplomacy, was named winner of the Nobel Peace Prize today. Roosevelt, the first American to receive a Nobel, is being honored for his role as mediator in the Russo-Japanese War. Negotiations with the belligerents began in the spring of last year, and last August Roosevelt finally persuaded both Russia and Japan to have their diplomats sit down together at a peace conference in Portsmouth, New Hampshire. The Portsmouth Treaty was signed in September. Though ending a war between two countries with whom the United States has friendly relations was important, Roosevelt surely had other motives as well. Before the parley, he exacted assurances from the Japanese that they would retain the Open Door in Manchuria. While Japan won the war, it was in financial straits and there are those who speculate that without the peace conference the Japanese might have eventually been worn down by the Russians, who have made no promises about honoring the Open Door policy.

1907

Roosevelt

Oregon, Jan. 17. Citizens of Adams, desperate for fuel after a severe cold spell, hold up an Oregon and North train.

Chicago, Jan. 20. In a speech based on his book *Sex and Society*, Professor W.I. Thomas expounds on incapability of women to become scholars.

New York City, Jan. 22. Richard Strauss's opera *Salome*, based on an Oscar Wilde play, in U.S. premiere at Metropolitan Opera House.

Washington, D.C., Jan. 26. Congress, responding to public anger, bans corporate contributions to national campaigns.

New York City, Jan. 27. Metropolitan Opera House withdraws *Salome* after it is denounced as immoral.

Central America, Feb. 19. War erupts among Honduras, Nicaragua and El Salvador, further destabilizing region (→ Dec. 20).

Washington, D.C., February. In bid to stave off a crisis with Japanese over Oriental segregation in San Francisco, Roosevelt invites city's board of education to capital for talks (→ March 13).

San Francisco, March 13. School board rescinds its segregation orders following President's efforts to restrict Oriental immigration (→ 14).

Washington, D.C., March 14. President Roosevelt appoints Inland Waterways Commission to study the effects of increased technology on nation's lakes and rivers.

New York City, May. First fleet of metered taxicabs arrives from France.

Concord, New Hampshire, Aug. 14. Mary Baker Eddy, founder of Christian Science, is diagnosed as mentally fit.

Detroit, Mich., Oct. 12. Chicago Cubs win World Series, beating Detroit Tigers in four games. One game ended in a tie.

Jacobs Creek, Pennsylvania, Dec. 19. Coal mine explosion takes lives of 239 workers.

Washington, D.C., Dec. 20. In a treaty to which United States is not a signatory, a resolution is reached on Central American conflict.

New York City. Photographer Edward Curtis publishes illustrated *The North American Indian*.

Values on Wall Street take sharp drop

New York City, March 13

A wave of liquidation shook Wall Street today, sending stock prices tumbling in their worst one-day drop since the Northern Pacific panic of 1901. Large railroads led the declines, with the Reading, Great Northern, Northern Pacific and Union Pacific lines suffering losses of 10 to 11 points. Analysts link the crash to several banks with a heavy short-term need for cash. Trading was moderate at 2.2 million shares, never approaching the level of a general panic. But today's plunge follows a long period of declining prices that business leaders attribute to President Roosevelt's trust-busting efforts. Democratic leader William Jennings Bryan has a different view. He says the public is refusing to trade in watered stock. "Must the government," he asked today, "refuse to investigate rotten management for fear the mismanaged railroad no longer will be able to fool the public into buying inflated securities?" (→ Nov. 4).

Influx of unskilled labor causing concern

Sweatshops proliferate as poorly trained immigrants swell the nation's ranks.

Washington, D.C., Feb. 26

In response to a public outcry over the flood of "new" immigrants from Southern and Eastern Europe, Congress has allotted $600,000 to form a presidential panel on immigration. Labor groups have been the most vocal advocates of immigration reform. The foreign-born make up 14 percent of the nation's population, yet they provide half the labor force. And only 15 percent of these have experience in industry. "Cheap labor, ignorant labor, takes our jobs and cuts our wages," complains American Federation of Labor President Samuel Gompers. With subsistence pay at $745 a year, immigrant wages range from an average of $722 for Swedes to $400 for Southern Italians and Hungarians.

The "new" immigrants, few of them Anglo-Saxon or Protestant, have stirred the waters of racial and religious bias. Northern Europe now accounts for less than a quarter of Ellis Island's arrivals. Many are Slavs, Slovaks, Serbs, Croats, Bosnians and Herzegovinians. And many are Jewish or Catholic. The halls of academe ring with racial theories. According to zoologist H.F. Osborn, republican institutions can only be saved by facing our primary task, "the conservation and multiplication for our country of the best spiritual, moral, intellectual and physical forces of heredity." Reformers like Jane Addams, at least, have approached immigrant ghettoes with acceptance if not respect. Addams still believes America is Thomas Paine's "asylum for mankind." The foreign-born, she says, are but "accretions of simple people who carry in their hearts a desire for mere goodness" (→ March 26, 1910).

Coast issue settled by Immigration Act

March 14

Scene in a schoolroom:

Teacher: Who was the first man?

Pupil: "Washington!"

When reminded of a man called Adam, the pupil exclaims: "Yes, if you count foreigners!"

A lighthearted depiction, perhaps, but a telling one about American attitudes toward immigrants.

President Roosevelt today issued an executive order directing that Japanese or Korean laborers, skilled or not, who have received passports to go to Mexico, Hawaii or Canada, be refused permission to enter the continental territory of the United States. This is the final chapter, except for treaty negotiations with the Japanese, in the issue growing out of the conflict with Japan sparked by the San Francisco school board's order segregating Orientals. Authority to refuse permission to certain Orientals is part of the immigration law passed February 20. The Chinese are excluded unless they can prove they are not laborers. Japanese must be admitted unless they are laborers, the burden of proof being on the government. Still, the point is that any immigrant with a passport from a nation other than the United States may be barred from entry if it is deemed detrimental to U.S. labor conditions (→ Apr. 19, 1913).

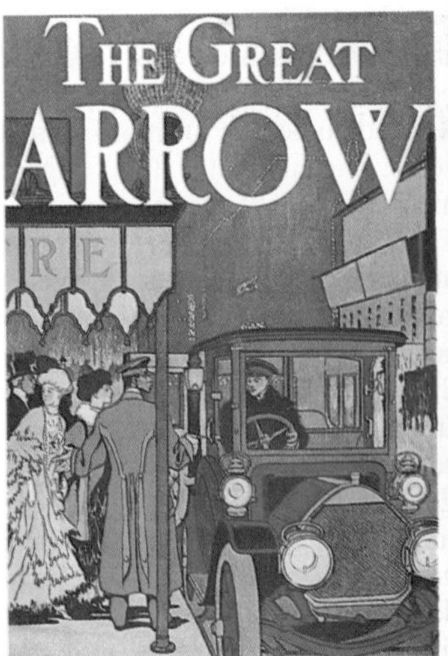

The Pierce-Arrow automobile is among the finest motorcars on the road. It is one of a class of machines designed specifically for a better class of consumer.

Good clean fight: Hurley vs. Maytag

Chicago

A washing machine operated by electricity rather than by hand has been marketed by the Hurley Machine Company here. Invented by Alva J. Fisher, the Hurley uses a small motor to spin a drum that holds clothes, water and soap. Its main competition is the Maytag Pastime, which is produced by an Iowa farm equipment manufacturer and is turned by a hand crank, like all washing machines that have been marketed since the first one appeared in the 1850's.

Hand-cranked washing machine by Maytag may get the job done, but Hurley's electric may get the buyers.

Verdict split in Idaho I.W.W. murder trial

Boise, Idaho, July 28

In a murder trial that attracted nationwide attention, William "Big Bill" Haywood was found not guilty today, while his colleague, Harry Orchard, was convicted of the murder of the former Governor of Idaho, Frank Steunenberg. Haywood was acquitted mainly because of lack of evidence associating him with the crime. Orchard, on the other hand, admitted that he had placed the bomb that killed the popular Steunenberg.

The 38-year-old Haywood has been a controversial labor personality ever since he helped found the often-violent Industrial Workers of the World in 1905. He has always opposed craft unionism, favoring instead a militant industrial-union philosophy. An avowed Socialist, Haywood is hated by conventional leaders of both industry and labor. There is about him, however, a strange romanticism that seems to attract unskilled workers.

Many people who attended the sensational trial felt that the brilliant defense by the rising young lawyer Clarence Darrow was mainly responsible for Haywood's acquittal. William Borah prosecuted the state's case.

"A. Mutt" appears six days a week

America's sidekicks Mutt and Jeff.

San Francisco, Nov. 15

Under the title *Mr. A. Mutt Starts In to Play the Races*, the *San Francisco Chronicle* today began a daring experiment. From now on, Bud Fisher's comic strip adventures of bettor (and born loser) A. Mutt will appear both daily and on Saturdays. This unprecedented step is a bid to boost circulation in the wake of the success of other popular strips such as Rudolph Dirks's *The Katzenjammer Kids* in the *New York Journal*, Lyonel Feininger's *The Kin-der Kids* and *Wee Willie Winkie's World* in the *Chicago Tribune*, Winsor McCay's *Dreams of the Rarebit Fiend* in the *New York Evening Telegram*, and his *Little Nemo in Slumberland* in the *New York Herald*.

Neiman-Marcus Co. opens in Dallas

Dallas, Texas, Autumn

A major new department store has opened its doors for business here. It is the Neiman-Marcus Company and the founders say that it is specifically designed for the discriminating customers who want the "best" in both contemporary and traditional fashions. Those who have visited the store report that prices are somewhat high, although there are bargains to be found. Neiman's seems to be exactly what the French writer Emile Zola meant when he said that department stores "democratized luxury."

"Three Weeks": It is banned in Boston

Boston

What is It? Every good Puritan with a young daughter knows. So does Elinor Glyn, the British novelist whose latest work, *Three Weeks*, refers to sex euphemistically as "It." A steamy tale about an adulterous Balkan queen who leads a younger man through a passionate three-week affair, the book has been banned in Boston. But Glyn, who is now touring the United States to adoring crowds, says "those who do look up beyond the material will understand the deep, pure love and the Soul in its all."

Rails can enforce racial segregation

Washington, D.C.

In a case concerning conflicting state and federal authority, the Supreme Court has supported segregation on interstate railway lines. Trains traveling across state lines, the court held, have no obligation to uphold state laws barring segregated cars. The ruling is the latest of many to validate state attacks on gains made during Reconstruction. Through "grandfather clauses" and literacy tests, Negroes have been disenfranchised in all Southern states except Tennessee, Kentucky and Maryland. Lynchings exceed 100 a year. And in all the South, high schools hold less than 8,000 Negro students (→Nov. 1910).

TR discharges 167 Negroes after riot

Washington, D.C., Jan. 15

President Roosevelt today ordered that the 167 Negro soldiers allegedly connected with a shooting spree in Brownsville, Texas, earlier this year be "discharged without honor" and "forever barred from re-enlistment." The shooting took place August 13, killing a bartender, wounding a policeman and causing pandemonium all over town. None of the soldiers, members of three army units stationed at Fort Brown there, has admitted knowing anything about the rioting. However, the President is said to be convinced that the soldiers have entered into a conspiracy of silence in order to protect the guilty.

"Stag at Sharkey's" (1907) by George Wesley Bellows. The artist, a rugged individual of the Ashcan School of painting, uses his brush to capture the toughness of urban life in America through its athletic outlets.

Oklahoma becomes 46th state in union

Oklahoma City, Nov. 16

The Indian Territory and Oklahoma Territory were formally merged and admitted to the union today as the state of Oklahoma. As a territory, Oklahoma has been enjoying a healthy economy and with it a steadily increasing population since the first massive influx of migrants during the "Boomer-Sooner" days of 1889. Although Oklahoma is predominantly rural and agricultural, the bustling, modern town of Tulsa boasts a population of more than 24,000, while this state capital now is home for over 50,000 people.

U.P. news agency formed by Scripps

Cleveland, Ohio

Following the trend of collective news gathering, the Scripps-McRae League of Newspapers has created the United Press news agency. The new U.P. is likely to contribute to a standardization of news, which has proven efficient and thorough, but, critics say, mechanical. Edward Scripps started his first paper, the *Cleveland Penny Press*, in 1878. Scripps-McRae was formed in 1885 by Scripps, his half-brother George and Milton McRae by merging four Midwest dailies.

Saint-Gaudens was best U.S. sculptor

Cornish, New Hampshire, Aug. 3

America's greatest sculptor, Augustus Saint-Gaudens, died here today. Born in Dublin in 1848, Saint-Gaudens was a cameo cutter and studied at New York's Cooper Union and in Paris before setting an American standard for sculptural excellence. The sculptor's early *Silence* depicts a mysterious shrouded figure. More civic-minded is the General William Tecumseh Sherman Memorial, at the southeast entrance to New York's Central Park. Most fascinating of his works, perhaps, is the abstract memorial designed for the wife of Henry Adams in 1891.

"... and the heavens have not fallen"

Business is business: a female secretary with her Remington typewriter.

The delicate Maude Adams is best known for her role as "Peter Pan."

United States, Nov. 16

In today's issue of the *Woman's Journal,* Mrs. Ellen Richards, one of America's first woman chemists, writes: "We may discount all the scare headlines about what will happen if women do thus and so. They have done nearly everything, and the heavens have not fallen." Indeed, women increasingly contribute to the arts and sciences, and the firmament seems firmly fixed.

The Impressionist painter Mary Cassatt has led the way for other women artists. Miss Maude Adams, nee Maude Kiskadden, is queen of the stage (though it should be noted that she plays boys as often as she does grown women: currently, she fills the title role in *Peter Pan*). Edith Wharton is but one of several female novelists receiving good notices; critics praised her 1905 novel about conformity, *The House of Mirth*. There are few women in the sciences, as Mrs. Richards would concede, but females are a key part of the new technological world, working in telephone offices and sitting long days before typewriters. Participation in sports, once held improper for women, is now encouraged, Wimbledon victor May Sutton setting an example. For all these advances, women cannot vote in national elections. British suffragists plan to join American women for a rally in New York next month and pass on their lobbying strategies. It might be interesting for them to meet Professor W.I. Thomas, whose book *Sex and Society* states that the female mind is weak. The heavens may fall on him!

Phone companies offer women one of the few jobs for which they are "suited."

Arson suspected in Sinclair co-op fire

Englewood, New Jersey, March

Local police authorities now believe that the fire that completely destroyed writer Upton Sinclair's co-operative community was deliberately set. He established the socialistic, workers' co-op in this small town only a few months ago. Sinclair, author of last year's best-selling and shocking expose of the meat-packing industry, entitled *The Jungle*, is a muckraking social critic and reformer who readily admits that he is not popular in all quarters. Apparently, his unpopularity has now focused on Englewood.

A better light bulb by General Electric

New York City

A light bulb with a tungsten filament is being marketed by General Electric, which says it gives better light and is more efficient than conventional carbon filament bulbs. Tungsten's high melting point allows it to glow at a higher temperature, emitting whiter light and using less electricity than old-style bulbs. The key to using tungsten in lamps was the development of a method of drawing it into fine wires, which General Electric has achieved after years of research.

L.A. is unlikely site for motion picture

Los Angeles

As winter descended on Lake Michigan, the director and the cameraman of the Chicago-based Selig Company, having already filmed parts of a one-reel version of *The Count of Monte Cristo*, went on a desperate search for the sun. They got off the train in Los Angeles and are now shooting the remaining scenes, with local actors, behind the Sing Loo laundry downtown and on the beach at La Jolla. Another "first": Reports from Cleveland tell of a film shot in color and with simultaneous sound, depicting a bullfight, a scene from an opera and a political speech.

An American credo outlined by James

Cambridge, Massachusetts

Americans always take pride in being practical, and now a noted philosopher has stepped forward to champion their point of view. He is William James, and his new book, *Pragmatism: A New Name for Some Old Ways of Thinking*, argues that "fixed principles, closed systems and pretended absolutes" will not do for pragmatic thinkers, who turn "toward concreteness and adequacy, toward facts, toward action, and toward power." James has opportunely turned to his Harvard colleague C. S. Peirce, the logician who invented the term pragmatism.

Morgan's intervention saves Wall St.

New York City, Nov. 4

J.Pierpont Morgan is not one to fool around with the nation's economic health. At midnight, with the city's biggest banks beset by runs that had gone on for three weeks, the No. 1 banker of them all locked the trust presidents into the West Room of his 36th Street office. By 5 a.m., they pledged $25 million to salvage the banks. Morgan did his part by buying Tennessee Coal and Iron, whose dying owner was about to tear Wall Street down by declaring bankruptcy.

Morgan sent his men to Washington to clear the purchase with President Roosevelt. Before the market opened, a call came through. "All is well," said Judge Elbert Gary. Morgan, who gains mineral reserves for U.S. Steel, agrees.

Trouble began back on October 16, when Charles W. Morse and F. Augustus Heinze tried to corner United Copper and failed, sparking a run on the Knickerbocker Trust Company and the Trust Company of America. Roosevelt, who spent much of the panic period hunting bear in Louisiana, has halted his attacks on the "malefactors of great wealth." Instead, he is praising "conservative and substantial businessmen" for acting with "wisdom and public spirit" (→ May 30, 1908).

It's rumored that Morgan plans to turn the whole world into a trust.

Henry Adams pens his autobiography

Boston

Some 100 handpicked readers have been given the opportunity to revisit the life of a pre-eminent man of his time. *The Education of Henry Adams*, issued privately, is the latest work by the grandson of John Quincy Adams and himself a sometime diplomat, historian, theorist, professor and novelist. At 69, Adams views himself not as a man but as "a manikin on which the toilet of education [was] draped." The "object of study," he adds, "is the garment, not the figure."

American awarded Nobel physics prize

Oslo, Norway, Dec. 10

Albert A. Michelson today became the first American to win a Nobel Prize in science. Michelson, 54, was given the physics prize for his studies of the properties of light. Perhaps his most important experiment, done with Edward Morley, was a series of tests showing that the speed of light is the same in all directions, which confounded existing theory. An explanation was offered two years ago by a German scientist, Albert Einstein, in what he calls his theory of relativity.

Milwaukee has first inter-urban electric

Milwaukee, Wis., Oct. 28

America's first inter-urban train powered by electricity began service today between Milwaukee and Cedarburg, Wisconsin, marking another milestone in railroad electrification. The Pennsylvania and New York Central Railroads are the leaders in electrification of their commuter lines, and New York City's elevated lines, which started with steam engines, have shifted completely to electricity, citing both increased efficiency and cleanliness for the change.

Nothing sucks it up like a Hoover

Cleveland, Ohio

A light, portable vacuum cleaner is being marketed by the Hoover Suction-Sweeper Company here. Designed by James M. Spangler, the machine uses an electric motor to run a fan that sucks dirt into a disposable dust bag. Spangler has sold his patent to the Hoover Company, which is offering the device to housewives. Previous vacuum cleaners have been too bulky and expensive for use in private homes, often being so large that women could not move them from room to room.

Company dissolved by Currier and Ives

New York City

The presses of America's best lithographer have taken their last turn with the dissolution of Currier and Ives. Nathaniel Currier founded the firm in 1834 and achieved his first success with a print of the sinking of the steamboat Lexington. The talented artist James Ives, a relation by marriage, was made partner in 1857. The firm flourished until both Currier and Ives died in the 1880's, having produced over 4,000 prints documenting American historical sites, sporting scenes and social customs. The last owner is disbanding the company due to ill health and competition from photography.

"Great White Fleet" begins world tour to show U.S. might

Hampton Roads, Va., Dec. 16

America's "Great White Fleet" weighed anchor here today and left for a globe-circling tour that is expected to take about 15 months. President Roosevelt was on hand for the historic departure. From the presidential yacht Mayflower, Roosevelt personally gave the fleet its orders to "proceed to duty assigned." The President has sent the fleet of 16 battleships on its mission to convince real as well as would-be enemies, especially Japan, that the U.S. Navy is so powerful that any attack on America would be foolish if not disastrous for the aggressor. The fleet is commanded by Commodore "Fighting Bob" Evans (→ Feb. 22, 1909).

The "Great White Fleet," including the Amphitrite, Puritan and Montgomery, proves an influential arm of American foreign policy. Without firing a shot, the fleet announces to the world that the United States has arrived.

1908

Roosevelt

New York City, Jan. 17. A wireless message from Puerto Rico is received at Times Tower.

Collingwood, Ohio, March 4. Schoolhouse blaze kills 175 children.

Chelsea, Massachusetts, Apr. 12. One-quarter of town is destroyed by fire; 19 deaths reported.

Chicago, May 10. Socialist National Convention nominates Eugene V. Debs of Indiana for president.

Washington, D.C., May 30. In response to last year's financial panic, Congress enacts Aldrich-Vreeland Act, establishing National Monetary Commission.

Washington, D.C., June 23. Diplomatic relations between United States and Venezuela are severed because of latter's unwillingness to compensate for injuries sustained by Americans during recent upheavals.

Rome, June 29. Pope Pius X issues encyclical *Sapienti Consilio,* declaring that United States is no longer a missionary area.

Springfield, Illinois, Aug. 15. When a white woman claims a Negro raped her, community of Negroes is attacked and some are lynched..

Yellowstone National Park, Aug. 24. On road between Old Faithful and Thumb, one man holds up 17 coaches in a day, assisted by a strategic bend in road.

Detroit, Mich., Oct. 14. Chicago Cubs defeat Detroit Tigers in World Series, four games to one.

Nyack, New York, Dec. 27. Followers of doomsday prophet Lee J. Spangler sit atop a mountain awaiting end of world dressed in white gowns, "specially made for occasion."

New York City. Ex-Lax Company founded by Max Kiss, who promotes his product with filmed advertisements in movie theaters.

Utah. Dinosaur bones discovered near Jensen.

California. Construction begins on Owens Valley Aqueduct, to bring water to Los Angeles.

Boston. Van Wyck Brooks's *The Wine of the Puritans* published.

Artists open "outlaw salon" in New York

New York City, February

A rebellious group of painters known as "The Eight" has dealt a blow to the stodgy arbiter of the art world, the National Academy of Design, with the opening of an independent display of paintings at the Macbeth Gallery. Frustrated by the outdated styles and restrictive exhibition policies favored by the academy, The Eight defied convention by arranging this presentation of 63 works to compete with the National Academy's spring show, the most prestigious art exhibition in the country.

The Eight are Robert Henri, the leader, William Glackens, Everett Shinn, John Sloan, George Luks, Ernest Lawson, Maurice Prendergast and Arthur B. Davies, and they offer an array of subjects and styles, from the urban urchins of Henri, to the seaside vistas of Prendergast, whose work one critic described as "a jumble of riotous pigment ... like an explosion in a color factory." A number of the artists also treat one subject deemed controversial – the cities of America, especially New York, as they are transformed by industrialization and swelling numbers of immigrants.

Though critical opinion on The Eight has been mixed, the artistically curious have thronged the gallery in crowds of 300 visitors per hour. Despite the reservations of the art establishment, the show tallied an impressive sales figure of $4,000. Gertrude Vanderbilt Whitney proved to be an adventurous collector, buying four paintings.

Those who cannot see the show in New York will get a chance to view the "outlaw salon" as it travels across the country, spreading its message of artistic anarchy. Next stop: the Pennsylvania Academy of Design in Philadelphia.

Artist John Sloane's scenes of urban America are noted for their realism.

Singer Building sets record: 47 stories

New York City

Construction has been completed on New York's tallest skyscraper, the Singer Building. With a record 47 stories, it towers to a height of 612 feet at the corner of Broadway and John Street, with a distinctive tapering spire designed by its architect, Ernest Flagg. The building is a tribute to the heights made possible by modern construction methods. It is not expected to retain its record for long, however. Plans for a 50-story building have already been drawn up, and Frank Woolworth is said to be considering construction of a 60-story skyscraper on a site in the City Hall area.

Iron, toaster help liberate housewife

New York City

The housewife's life has been made easier by introduction of two new electric appliances, an iron and a toaster. No longer does a woman need to labor next to a hot stove to iron the family's clothes or make toast, the advertisements say. Ironing can now be done in comfort on the veranda, the Westinghouse Company tells women, while its message to husbands is, "Why not kick that stove out and get a Westinghouse electric iron?"

Film producers told to clean up their act

New York City

Ever since Edison's *The Widow Jones*, with its 20-second kiss by a homely couple, provoked howls of indignation, the makers of films are being carefully watched. Now the Society for the Prevention of Crime has convinced Mayor McClellan to revoke the license of 550 theaters until they stop showing films on Sundays and stop showing immoral films at any time. The Chicago Police Department began enforcing local censorship ordinances last year. To avert further local actions, producers have established the National Board of Censorship for self-regulation.

.abor boycott ruled n restraint of trade

Vashington, D.C., Feb. 3

In a far-reaching opinion, the Su- preme Court ruled today that a abor boycott of industry violates he Sherman Antitrust Act by being conspiracy in restraint of trade. 'he opinion sustained a lower court ecision in the case of Loewe v. .awlor that granted treble damages o the employer as a result of a na- ionwide boycott organized by the atters union to further a strike for ecognition. The leader of the boy- ott, the hatters union, operates out f Danbury, Connecticut, which is ften called the "hat city of the vorld." Thus, the clash has been lubbed the Danbury Hatters Case.

'ou just drink up and toss cup away

Jnited States

The American paper industry al- vays seems to be coming up with ew uses for its products, uses that nake life easier and more efficient. 'irst there were paper bags, then lrinking straws. Now, the Interna- ional Paper Company has devel- ped a waxed drinking cup made ut of paper that is tough and non- orous. It's a sanitary way to take beverage, and it is so cheap that ou dispose of it after drinking. The roduct is named the Dixie Cup.

Journalism school opens in Missouri

Columbia, Missouri, April

A school of journalism has been established by the University of Mis- souri here and it will soon be accept- ng its first students. Considered to e the first professional institution f its kind in the nation, the jour- alism school is specifically de- igned to turn out the top quality vorking journalists and editors that he growing newspaper and maga- ine industries require. When Wil- iam Dean Howells was asked eight years ago what the educated upper- class Americans read, he replied, 'The newspapers." This school should help the reputation of the 'fourth estate."

Commission is formed to save the nation's natural resources

The Teton Range of the Rockies is a stunning example of America's beauty.

Washington, D.C., June 8

President Roosevelt today announced the establishment of a National Conservation Commission. Regarding the fate of the nation's endangered natural treasures, the President said, "We intend to use these resources, but to so use them as to conserve them."

This commission is actually the outgrowth of a conference of governors that was held here last month. At that time, the President brought together the governors of the states, as well as the "representatives of the people," who included such luminaries as the Democrats' perennial presidential candidate William Jennings Bryan, the steel giant Andrew Carnegie and the railroad magnate James J. Hill. At that session, this extraordinary gathering of leaders decided it was time to do something about the country's resources – for the present as well as the future.

Roosevelt has made available every tool of the government for this landmark commission. He has ordered "every department, bureau and government establishment" to cooperate fully with the commission in its efforts to establish a national conservation policy once and for all. It was quite a meeting, one that James J. Hill called "the directors' meeting of the corporation called the United States of America." In fact, the *Wall Street Journal* has described the mission of this gathering of corporate eagles as "a radical new departure in government." The commission already seems to have achieved some concrete results. For one thing, 41 states have pledged to create their own conservation commissions and the four others are sure to follow.

Country life: American farmers thriving in new age of prosperity

Washington, D.C., Aug. 10

President Roosevelt today announced the creation of the federal Country Life Commission. Its mission is to take a comprehensive look at American rural life as it exists today. While the commission's report has not yet been published, indications are strong that its conclusions will be optimistic.

For example, the average prices of farm products have increased almost 50 percent since 1900. During the same period, the average value of farm land has increased substantially, while the value of the average farm has risen from $5,471 to $6,444. At the same time, farm foreclosures have shown a marked drop, while new machinery has been purchased and additional lands put into cultivation. The average farmer has an amazing return, or profit, on his holdings of more than $540 per year.

Relative to the city dweller, the farmer's standard of living has risen dramatically. Mail-order firms such as Montgomery Ward and Sears, Roebuck have introduced the farmer to the bountiful appliances, clothes and luxuries of the city people at reasonable prices. And the Rural Free Delivery concept has brought affordable information to the farmer's doorstep. *Editor & Publisher* magazine recently said, "The daily newspapers have never seen such a boom in circulation as they have since RFD was established." Life on the farm is good – and it's getting better. ▷

Spring plowing in New England. American farmers are reaping lots of benefits.

General Motors formed

Detroit, Mich., Sept. 14

Henry Ford is said to be leaning toward producing just one versatile, low-priced car, but William C. Durant of the Buick Motor Company envisions turning out a wide range of motorcars. Today Durant formed General Motors, a base from which he hopes to build a vast conglomeration of automobile and parts manufacturers offering a line of machines to cover the entire spectrum of prices, styles and sizes. Thus, he reasons, under the protective wing of General Motors, no one company will be at the mercy of a changing marketplace that each year sends dozens of firms spiraling into bankruptcy.

Unlike most of Detroit's car magnates, Durant has little mechanical background. His forte is business, and his philosophy of conglomeration is not new. By 1900, he had built a national consortium of horse-drawn buggy companies into one massive Durant-Dort Carriage Company. In 1904, at the age of 42, Durant took over the ailing Buick firm. That year, the company produced just 31 cars. Now Buick is the nation's largest automobile maker, building 8,487 this year.

Durant is said to have his eye on about 12 companies. These include Oldsmobile, the well-known manufacturer that has fallen on hard times; Oakland, the company in Pontiac, Michigan, whose Model K is this year's hill-climbing champion, and Cadillac, a big moneymaker that produced 2,280 cars this year. Known for his persuasiveness, Durant will offer each of the companies huge stock holdings to join General Motors.

Ford builds the Model T

Detroit, Michigan, Oct. 1

"I will build a motorcar for the multitudes," Henry Ford has said. Today, his vision took a step toward reality, when the Ford Motor Company announced the arrival of its new Model T, a lightweight car with advanced features that will sell for $850.

The newest Ford won't win any awards for grace, but it boasts qualities not found in any automobile, much less in a low-priced model. Constructed of a tough but light vanadium steel alloy developed by Ford engineers, the Model T is built to last, with a new three-point suspension that is able to negotiate the rugged farm roads. For power, a four-cylinder, 20-horsepower engine, with a simple, easy-to-repair design, enables the car to cruise effortlessly at more than 25 miles per hour. Especially novel features are the magneto, which powers the sparkplugs while the engine runs, and the placement of the steering wheel on the left.

The first Model T was rolled out in late summer, and Ford himself took it for a triumphal test spin through the streets of Detroit. Back at the plant, he jumped from the car, slapped each of his engineers on the back and declared that he was "tickled to death" with its performance.

Ford is said to be feuding with the company's financial backers, who deplore his preoccupation with lower-priced cars. But the indomitable automaker is steadfast in his belief that the Model T is a winner. He told eager motorcar dealers recently that next year the company is planning to produce an incredible 25,000 machines.

General Motors plans to compete against Ford with sleek aerodynamic styling.

Home safe and sound, Henry Ford's first factory production Model T rests after carrying the manufacturer on an extensive hunting trip in September.

Washington, D.C., November 22. *The Postal Service bought automobiles today to facilitate rural delivery. Now the mail will always get through.*

An American family takes to the open road in their new Model T, specially designed to manage country byways. Their trip shouldn't be too bumpy.

Round-world race is won by U.S. auto

New York City, July 30

For a while, it seemed that the German team had won the great round-the-world automobile race, but in the end the honors went to the United States drivers. It seems that the Germans transported their car part of the way by rail after it was delayed by repairs en route. Their Protos was first to finish the grind in Paris, but they were penalized and the American Thomas car was ruled the winner. The Thomas received a 15-day allowance for changing its route after snow blocked its way in Alaska. The American winners were invited to visit President Roosevelt at the White House. Talking about his crossing of the United States, one German driver said: "I wish that America's roads were as nice as the people."

Ewry keeps winning gold at Olympics

Paris, July

Ray C. Ewry continues to dazzle the international track set, this time taking two gold medals in the Olympic Games. The New Yorker again won the standing high jump and the standing broad jump, as he had in the 1906 Games. Add those victories to his three each in the 1900 and 1904 Olympics for a total of 10, a figure that track experts say may never be surpassed. The number of participants, 2,082, more than doubled the 1906 turnout, but the acrimony more than doubled, too. The Finns marched flagless because they refused to carry the flag of the ruling Russians, the Irish were angry because they had to compete under the British flag, and widespread professionalism was charged. Besides, it rained a lot.

Taft and Republicans sweep national vote

Washington, D.C., Nov. 3

Republicans are singing sweet songs of success tonight as they waltz William Howard Taft of Ohio into the White House. Taft's victory over Democrat William Jennings Bryan coupled with the G.O.P.'s retention of both houses of Congress reflect the nation's satisfaction with the progressivism of Theodore Roosevelt. Teddy chose Taft as his successor. It is expected that Taft, at 300 pounds the biggest man ever to be President, will consult Roosevelt about key policy decisions. Congressman James Sherman of New York is the new Vice President. For Bryan, this is his third loss in a presidential election. He has already said it is his last. As they say in baseball, "Three strikes and you're out."

William H. Taft, 27th President.

Eugene Debs, the Socialist Party candidate, was joined by other third-party candidates, from the Prohibition National Party, the Socialist Labor Party and the Independence Party.

Johnson takes boxing title in 14 rounds

Sydney, Australia, Dec. 26

Jack Johnson finally caught up with Tommy Burns, flattened him in the 14th round and became the first Negro fighter to win the heavyweight championship of the world today. The self-styled "Li'l Arthur" (his name is John Arthur) with the bullet head and the gold-toothed grin had been challenging Burns ever since the Aussie won the title two years earlier. Burns finally agreed to take what he knew would be a terrible beating in exchange for the lion's share of the purse. Johnson was battering Burns so badly that the police finally stepped in to halt the mayhem. Johnson is also a great defensive fighter and he has tremendous strength in his 6-foot frame. Burns, on the other hand, was, at 5 foot 7, the smallest heavyweight champion ever. The challenger taunted him throughout the fight. "Hit here, Tahmy," Johnson would say. And when Burns would take his best shot at the indicated spot, Johnson would laugh.

November 30. *TR's reputation as "The World's Constable" grew today as his Secretary of War, Elihu Root, concluded the Root-Takahira Agreement, whereby the U.S and Japan will maintain the Open Door in China.*

Mahler and Toscanini make U.S. debuts

New York City, Nov. 16

Two brilliant European conductors, Arturo Toscanini and Gustav Mahler, made their American debuts this year, both at the Metropolitan Opera. Toscanini scored a triumph as he led a cast headed by Enrico Caruso in an *Aida* that older critics said was performed just as Verdi would have wanted to hear it. The year began auspiciously on January 1 when Mahler, reportedly ailing, all the more remarkably led a *Tristan und Isolde* that one critic described as unequaled in vitality and beauty. Mahler, who calls himself a weekend composer, has written seven symphonies. Though the Italian and the Czech take different tacks in conducting, the Met considers itself lucky this season to have two such giants on its podium.

Houdini, the master of the great escape

New York City

Harry Houdini's recent book, *The Unmasking of Robert-Houdin*, is not, as it would seem at first glance, an autobiography; it is a paean to a fellow magician, Frenchman Jean-Eugene Robert-Houdin. Still, each trick Houdini praises he does better himself and, like sleight of hand in reverse, it brings attention to his own feats. Houdini is thrilling crowds here and in Europe. After being handcuffed and locked in a box underwater, he emerges alive; he strolls through solid walls and frees himself from a straitjacket as he dangles high over the ground. Houdini was born Erich Weiss in 1874, the son of a Hungarian rabbi. Early on, he was a trapeze artist. Then, presto, he was a magician.

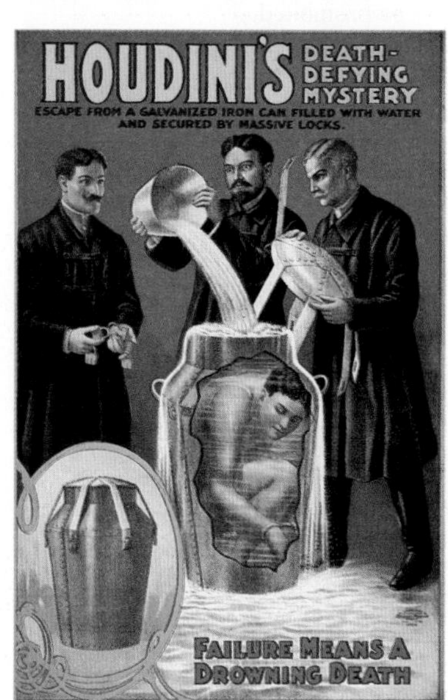

The great escape artist at his best.

1909

Taft

Virginia, Jan. 13. After army complains about an executive order demanding increased physical fitness for soldiers, President Roosevelt rides 100 miles across Virginia to make his point.

Washington, D.C., Jan. 27. United States and England submit a long-standing dispute over Newfoundland fisheries to international court of arbitration at The Hague (→ Sept. 7, 1910).

New Orleans, Feb. 8. Napoleon's death mask, lost during Civil War, is returned to Louisiana state museum.

Washington, D.C., May 22. President Taft opens 700,000 acres of land in Idaho, Washington and Montana to settlement.

Seattle, Washington, June 1. President Taft presses gold nugget which, by telegraph, opens Alaska-Yukon-Pacific Exposition [fair attracts 80,000 people].

Washington, D.C., July 15. Taft administration requests Chinese regent to permit participation of American bankers in international railway consortium operating in China.

Fort Myer, Virginia, Aug. 2. After repeated flight demonstrations, U.S. Army buys its first airplane, from Wrights.

Peru, Sept. 2. American Annie Smith Peck, 57, is first person to climb 21,000-foot Mount Huascaran, highest peak in Peru.

Dayton, Ohio, Sept. 24. Wilbur Wright states that importation of foreign aircraft should be prohibited.

Detroit, Mich., Oct. 16. Pittsburgh Pirates beat Detroit Tigers, four games to three, in World Series.

Northampton, Massachusetts, Nov. 11. Sergei Rachmaninoff makes his U.S. debut recital at Smith College.

Cherry, Illinois, Nov., 13. Explosion in Saint Paul Mine kills 259 miners.

Washington, D.C. Congress passes Weeks Act, authorizing government to acquire White Mountain region in New Hampshire as a national forest.

New York City. Photographer Lewis Hine delivers lecture entitled "Social Photography: How the Camera May Help the Social Uplift."

"Great White Fleet" home in triumph

"Great White Fleet," after more than a year at sea, heads home to America.

Hampton Roads, Va., Feb. 22

Almost 15 months after it set sail on a historic voyage around the world, the "Great White Fleet" arrived back home today to a tumultuous welcome at the naval installation here. Officers and men of the fleet were personally greeted by Theodore Roosevelt aboard the presidential yacht Mayflower. The armada left Hampton Roads on December 16, 1907. The mission had two objectives: to show good will toward the nation's friends and allies, and to demonstrate its vast naval might to any potential enemies. The fleet of 16 battleships was originally commanded by Rear Admiral Robert "Fighting Bob" Evans. After leaving Hampton Roads, the flotilla steamed around the tip of South America and up the American West Coast. Evans became seriously ill, and was succeeded by his second-in-command, Rear Admiral Charles Sperry. After crossing the Pacific Ocean, the fleet visited Australia and New Zealand.

The crew enjoyed a three-day stay in Japan in October. Enterprising Japanese merchants sold them Mitsuokia washing powder (which supposedly rids the body of blemishes). They were also presented with large, colorful posters that urged the continuation of peaceful Japanese-American relations. Many of the sailors report that they were startled by the sincere friendliness and Oriental hospitality offered by the Japanese.

Leaving Japan, the armada traversed the Indian Ocean, passed through the Suez Canal and the Mediterranean, then headed home across the North Atlantic. The cruise covered over 46,000 miles. American diplomats at home and in the countries the fleet visited call the historic mission a great success.

THE
PRUDENTIAL
HAS THE
STRENGTH OF
GIBRALTAR

Prudential Life claims it offers as much protection as the "Great White Fleet."

U.S. bans opium to curb addiction

Washington, D.C.

In a blow against the international trade in opium, Congress has voted to ban importation of the drug except for medical use. The action has been anticipated since passage of a law banning the opium trade in the Philippines two years ago. Despite American measures, trading in opium flourishes around the world. The Empress Dowager of China is trying to institute a ban in her country, but the drug is still widely available there. It is smuggled in quantities from India to most countries of Asia and Europe.

Terrier again wins Westminster title

New York City, Feb. 12

For the third year in a row, a fox terrier has won the coveted championship of the Westminster Kennel Club. There were 1,936 entrants. In fact, it was the same fox terrier, Ch. Warren Remedy, that was declared best in show for owner Winthrop Rutherford, as he was in 1907 and in 1908. The Westminster evolved from friendly competition among breeders and owners over the sleekness of their dogs. The show was first held in 1877 at Gilmore's Garden in Madison Square.

Cost of living up, family size down

Washington, D.C., Nov. 12

Government statistics show that the cost of living, which declined after the economic panic of 1907, has rebounded. Commodity prices are soaring, and there has been a 7.9 percent rise in the cost of living since the first of this year. Over the past three years, prices have risen 10.5 percent. Analysts think that the climbing cost of raw goods has pushed other prices higher, giving workers an incentive to demand higher wages. As prices go up, the number of children in families has been going down; federal census figures that were released in March showed many families have only two or three children.

Wobblies out West stage lumber strike

Kalispell, Montana, Autumn

The lumber business in Montana has almost been brought to a standstill by a series of strikes that have swept the state. Led by "Big Bill" Haywood's Industrial Workers of the World, most of the migratory workers and lumbermen have simply walked away from their jobs. The I.W.W. has also used more forceful tactics, such as strong-arming laborers who would otherwise remain at work. And there have been cases of union-sponsored arson and sabotage. The Wobblies' reliance on violence has appalled officials of the more conservative American Federation of Labor.

Peary gets to North Pole

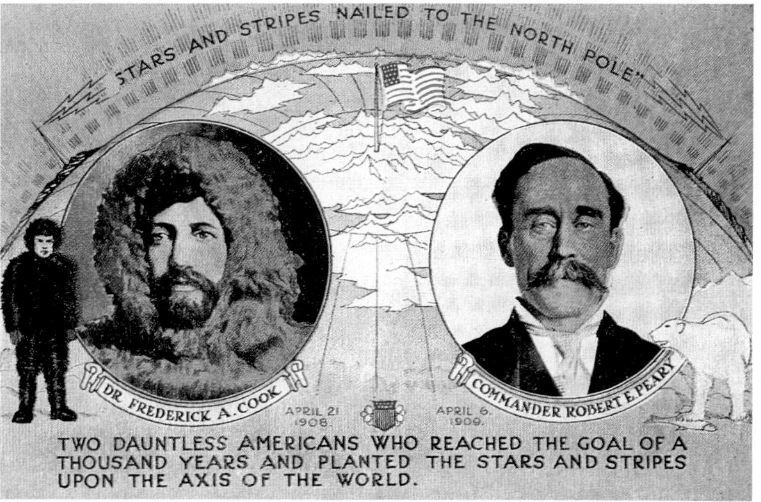

Postcard showing Peary as well as Cook, who claimed he reached Pole in 1908.

North Pole, Apr. 6

After more than a month on the ice, Robert Edwin Peary reportedly reached the North Pole today. At 10 a.m., Peary ordered what was left of his expedition to halt on the "roof of the world," 90 degrees north latitude. He had achieved his lifelong goal, to stand where all points on the compass were south.

But this accomplishment has not been without sacrifice. The expedition left on March 1 with 6 Americans, 17 Eskimos, 19 sleds and 133 dogs. Today, there was only one American beside Peary, Matthew Henson, a Negro who is an old hand at Arctic travel and speaks the Eskimo language fluently. Only 4 of the 17 Eskimos remain. Most were sent back; but one, Ross Marvin, died.

The temperature was mild by Arctic standards when Peary reached the North Pole, 15 degrees below zero and dead calm. After he unfurled a small American flag, a breeze rose "from nowhere," Henson reported, and Old Glory's colors stood out against the unending white of the Arctic icecap.

Immediately after raising the flag, Peary took photos of his men at the North Pole and buried a jar with two messages for posterity. One thanked the expedition's financial backers, the Peary Arctic Club of New York. The second stated that Peary had raised an American flag at the North Pole and had formally taken possession of the entire region and adjacent areas in the name of the President of the United States.

His quest for the pole over, Peary plans to head toward the United States at about 4 p.m. tomorrow.

Congress maintains protectionist tariff

Washington, D.C., Apr. 9

Ending a bitter fight with strong class overtones, President Taft today signed a healthy tariff increase into law. Senator Nelson Aldrich, speaking for the industrial interests of the Northeast, calls the Payne-Aldrich Act a victory for economic progress. Senator Robert La Follette of Wisconsin calls it a sell-out. Leading a block of insurgent Midwestern lawmakers, he blatantly attacked the Republican mainstream for aiding the growth of trusts. According to Henry Cabot Lodge, "the amount of ruthless selfishness that is exhibited on both sides surpasses anything I have seen."

A boom in Bakelite

Yonkers, New York

Manufacturers are finding more and more uses for Bakelite, a new plastic material marketed last year. Bakelite was invented here by a Belgian-born chemist, Leo H. Baekeland, who named it after himself. Made from phenol and formaldehyde, it starts as a liquid and hardens into any desired shape. It is water-resistant, can be cut with a knife and is easily machined. It is also an electrical insulator. Bakelite was developed as a substitute for shellac, a natural product with limited uses, but it already is being substituted for glass and wood in many products. Its success has stimulated research efforts to create other synthetic plastic materials.

Press gets wireless

Chicago, May 3

A revolution is taking place in the news industry. For the first time, a wireless telegraphic press message has been sent; it soared on the airwaves from New York to Chicago today. Such transmissions are soon expected to be commonplace and will no doubt transform the world into a place where communication is almost instantaneous. Guglielmo Marconi pioneered radio research, when he exhibited wireless transmission in 1895. In 1901, he sent the letter "s" across the Atlantic. Last month, music was broadcast from New York's Metropolitan Opera House to the home of Lee de Forest, inventor of the three-element tube that made radio possible.

Washington, D.C., March 4. *President Taft told his wife today: "Now I'm in the White House; I'm not going to be pushed around anymore."*

"Right and Left" (1909) by Winslow Homer. The painter received most of his artistic education as an apprentice to a lithographer in the 1850's.

Four women cross country in motorcar

San Francisco, Aug. 6

The use of the automobile for pleasure driving by women got a strong boost today when four adventurous drivers arrived on the West Coast after a two-month journey across the United States. The daring women were Alice Huyler Ramsey, president of the Women's Motoring Club of New York, and her companions, Nettie R. Powell, Margaret Atwood and Hermine Jahns. They left New York on June 9 and rolled into San Francisco with great fanfare. They drove a 30-horsepower open car, built by the Maxwell-Briscoe Company, which prices its two-cylinder runabouts at $500. A recent parade of 1,000 cars in Detroit also indicated that the automobile is here to stay.

Ford: Any color so long as it's black

Detroit, Mich., Autumn

Owing to a more specialized construction line, with workers concentrating on individual parts, the Ford Motor Company turned out an unprecedented 17,700 cars this year. Henry Ford has dropped his more expensive automobiles, and now produces just the Model T, the tough, low-priced car that won a transcontinental race this summer. The company hopes to get the Model T price below the current $850, and Ford stands by his goal of making a utilitarian car for the masses, ignoring the trends of rival auto makers, who seem to be bent on appealing only to the rich. "A customer can have a car painted any color so long as it is black," Ford said this year.

U.S. forces to shield rebels in Nicaragua

Washington, D.C., Nov. 18

The Taft Administration has sent troops to Nicaragua, after receiving reports that President Jose Santos Zelaya has executed 500 rebels, including two Americans. The rebellion against the government of Zelaya, a Liberal, is led by Conservatives Emiliano Chamorro and Juan Estrada, who reportedly have received financial support from American citizens living in Nicaragua. The U.S. troops will protect the rebel stronghold in Bluefields, a city on the Miskito coast that is also a center of American business interests. Zelaya seized power from the Conservatives in 1893 and wants to form a union of the five Central American countries, with himself as leader (→June 6, 1911).

Freud and Jung start American tour

Worcester, Mass., Sept. 10

Dr. Sigmund Freud, the noted Viennese neurologist, tonight began a series of five lectures at Clark University here. Freud is speaking on the subject of psychoanalysis at the invitation of Stanley Hall, the president of the university. The first lecture drew a large crowd, although Freud spoke in German, because of the controversial nature of the subject. One listener said that "Freud advocates free love, a removal of all restraints and a relapse into savagery." Freud is accompanied by Dr. Carl Jung, one of his most devoted disciples. The two plan to tour the East, visiting Niagara Falls and Lake Placid as well as Harvard University, before returning to Europe at the end of the month.

This year's print of "The Flatiron Building - Evening" (1905) by Edward Steichen shows the former painter has turned photography into high art.

Harriman is dead; a railroad tycoon

Arden, New York, Sept. 9

Edward H. Harriman, one of the greatest railway builders of his time, died at his home here today at the age of 61. From his start as a Wall Street office boy, he rose to become director of the Union Pacific and Southern Pacific Railroads. His battle for control of the Northern Pacific led to the 1901 panic. Ruthless in business, Harriman took pride in having founded the Tompkins Square Boys' Club for immigrants, the first of its kind. He was also quick to aid San Francisco's earthquake victims.

"Memphis Blues"

Memphis, Tennessee

Politics and music are unlikely bedfellows. But a song recently created by trumpeter W. C. Handy for Edward "Boss" Crump's election campaign has become this season's big hit in Memphis. The title was "Mr. Crump." Because of its popularity, Handy has notated it, with an eye to publication, and renamed it "Memphis Blues." While Negro musicians have been creating blues tunes for years, this is believed to be the first that was actually written down.

Equitable, banks bought by Morgan

New York City, Dec. 2

Financier J. Pierpont Morgan may not yet own everything in the country, but he moved closer today with the acquisition of the Equitable Life Assurance Company and its banks. This marks his biggest banking consolidation to date. Morgan's disclosed resources now approach $2 billion, but his real wealth is far greater. Through interlocking directorships, his company controls or influences more than 100 of the nation's top corporations and banks with total assets of well above $20 billion.

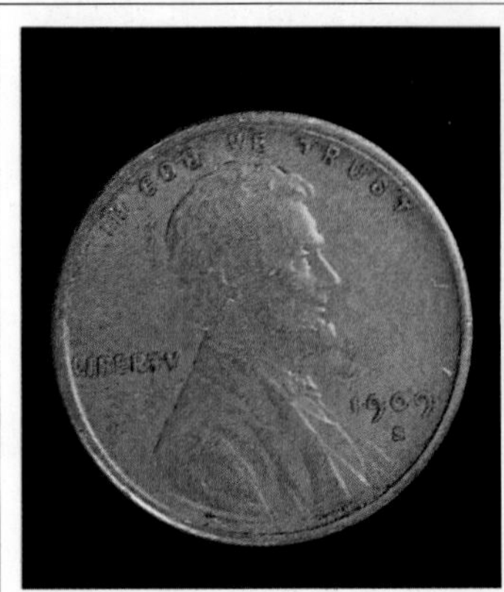

Philadelphia, August 2. *The Mint today issued a new penny to replace the Indian head penny.*

ational aviation industry is taking off

)rville Wright readies his airplane for an endurance flight test in July.

ew York City, December

About three dozen aeronauts, rom Florida to Nova Scotia to rance, are taking to the skies in owered machines. And, as spectaclar records are set almost monthy, a few look to a lucrative new inustry centered around airplanes.

Louis Bleriot's English Channel op notwithstanding, Orville and Vilbur Wright are still hailed by he world's press as the "kings of he air." Orville, recovered from a rash that killed a passenger last ear, dazzled the army at Fort Myer, Virginia, on July 20, when he et a duration record of one hour 20 ninutes. Thousands gasped while is plane Flyer swooped in figure ights 300 feet overhead. Duly impressed, the army bought a Wright lyer for $30,000 on August 2. On)ctober 26, Lieutenant Frank Humhreys, trained by the Wrights, became the army's first solo pilot.

Wilbur, meanwhile, electrified all New York on October 4, as the city was holding its gala Hudson-Fulton Celebration. Piloting a Flyer fitted with a red canoe in case of a water landing, Wilbur flew up the Hudson for 33 minutes.

The Wright brothers say they have retired from public flying, but on November 22 they announced that a new Wright Company, with $1 million in financing from August Belmont and other leading bankers, would sell airplanes to the public and the government. Rival aeronaut Glenn Curtiss, undaunted by patent suits filed by the Wrights, has started his own venture with Augustus Herring. The first Herring-Curtiss Company Golden Flier biplane has been sold to the Aeronautical Society of New York for $5,000.

A jaunty Frederic Remington. At the time of his death on December 26, the famous painter and sculptor stood as the undisputed illustrator of the Western frontier.

Chiricahua Apache Chief Geronimo, who died February 17, had in his later years taken up ranching, and appeared as a celebrity at the St. Louis World's Fair.

Innovative Wright builds the Robie House

Chicago

Frank Lloyd Wright's new Robie House is being acclaimed as the finest achievement of the brilliant young architect. Built on the South Side near the University of Chicago for the Robie family, the structure is the latest in Wright's "prairie house" style, featuring strong horizontal lines that create a sculptural effect. Critics particularly admire the way in which Wright has made maximum use of a small lot, putting the heating and other services on the ground floor and the living quarters on the two floors above.

The 41-year-old Wright attended college for only two years and began practicing his trade with the firm of Louis Sullivan, the acclaimed architect here. Wright split with Sullivan, who objected to his outside commissions, and designed a sensational series of buildings that won him immediate acclaim. Wright's avowed purpose is to develop a new architecture suited to the Midwest. He and others in the Prairie School use mass-produced materials and equipment. Their houses have plain walls and roomy family areas, combining comfort and convenience.

Wright also is designing innovative office buildings, most notably the Larkin Building, erected in 1904 in Buffalo, New York.

Wright's innovative Robie House, 5757 South Woodlawn Ave., Chicago, Ill.

"Chinese Restaurant" by John Sloan. One of "The Eight" of the Ashcan School of art, Sloan draws inspiration from the streets of New York City.

1910

Taft

Washington, D.C., March 26. Congress amends Immigration Act of 1907 to bar entry into United States of paupers, criminals, anarchists and diseased persons.

Spokane, Washington, June 19. Father's Day is first celebrated under guidance of Mrs. John B. Dodd.

Washington, D.C., June 24. Congress passes law requiring all American passenger ships to carry radio equipment.

The Arctic, July 2. American Oscar Tamm becomes first person to cross Arctic by automobile.

Columbus, Ohio, July 11. Phil Parmelee flies a plane with a string of silk, 500 yards long, attached to it, in order to promote a department store.

Atlantic City, New Jersey, July 12. To demonstrate future of military air attacks, Glenn Curtiss drops oranges from his plane onto a ship.

Osawatomie, Kansas, August. John Brown Memorial Park, named in honor of militant abolitionist, dedicated by Theodore Roosevelt.

Hammondsport, New York, Sept. 2. Blanche Stuart becomes first American woman to fly in an airplane.

The Hague, The Netherlands, Sept. 7. International court of arbitration extends American fishing rights in Newfoundland; starts commission to arbitrate individual grievances.

Chicago, Oct. 23. Philadelphia Athletics defeat Chicago Cubs in World Series, four games to one.

Ohio. Local elections result in 58 of state's 88 counties voting to outlaw liquor.

Baltimore. Report on medical education names Johns Hopkins University as only American equal of European institutions.

New York City. Artist John Sloan joins Socialist Party and runs for assemblyman, winning only 102 votes.

DEATHS

Redding, Connecticut, Apr. 21. Mark Twain, novelist and humorist (*Nov. 30, 1835).

Chocorua, New Hampshire, Aug. 26. William James, influential psychologist and philosopher (*Jan. 11, 1842).

Taft fires Pinchot, chief U.S. forester

Washington, D.C., Jan. 7

The chief of the United States Forest Service, Gifford Pinchot, a noted conservationist, alleged last year that the Secretary of the Interior, Richard Ballinger, was unfairly selling public lands to a Morgan-Guggenheim syndicate. After Congress conducted an investigation of these charges and determined that they were unfounded, President Taft, who had long regarded Pinchot as a "radical and a crank," removed him from office. Washington insiders say that the President's removal of Pinchot is certain to raise the anger of former President Roosevelt, who had been an early supporter of the deposed chief forester.

Opera is broadcast live from Met stage

New York City, Jan. 13

Wireless operators at sea were surprised to hear the golden voice of Enrico Caruso cut through the static. They were also apparently the main recipients of this second live broadcast from the Metropolitan Opera House. The first took place last April 3. Both were managed by Lee De Forest, who invented the three-element vacuum tube, and both offered brief excerpts from *I Pagliacci* and *Cavalleria Rusticana.* In one case, with the microphones placed as closely as possible, the Neapolitan tenor sang the prologue to *Cavalleria* from behind the curtain, as is normal. The microphones were then removed before the curtain was raised.

Ballerina Pavlova makes N.Y. debut

New York City, Feb. 28

Ballet enthusiasts here were treated to the graceful and inspired dancing of the Russian ballerina Anna Pavlova tonight. The 28-year-old Pavlova made her first American appearance at the Metropolitan Opera. Pavlova entered the Imperial Ballet School in 1895, when she was 10. She subsequently became a prima ballerina of the Marinsky Theater, to which the school was attached. Her elegant and skillful dancing has taken her all over the world, including Paris, where she performed with Sergei Diaghilev's Ballet Russe and with the renowned Nijinsky. She resigned from the Ballet Russe to begin her own company in London.

Population: 92 million; less than half have high school diploma

Washington, D.C.

The U.S. population now stands at 91.9 million according to the newly released 1910 census. Of these people, almost 50 million live in rural areas while some 42 million are urban dwellers. The farm population is put at 32 million. Of the total U.S. population, 8.7 percent have immigrated to America in the last decade. In the peak year of 1907, more than 1,285,000 arrived. Over two-thirds of these immigrants made the journey on tickets prepaid by friends, relatives or businesses in the United States.

The census reveals that the immigrants do not fit a single model at all. French immigrants have the best jobs and a higher standard of living. The Irish immigrants have the highest literacy rate (97 percent). Census figures indicate that over 35 percent of New Yorkers are foreign-born and, for the most part, poor. There are 340,000 Italians in New York City as well as 540,000 Jews, mainly from Eastern Europe. Some 2,600 Armenians now live in New York, 1,900 live in Providence and over 1,100 live in Boston. Detroit reports 400 Syrians living there.

The census indicates that Americans are not particularly well educated. Less than half of them over the age of 25 have high school diplomas, and only 4 percent have college degrees. They aren't wealthy either. The study found that the average American factory girl, for example, makes only $1.57 for a nine-hour day.

The federal census is compiled every 10 years.

"Local Industries" by John Ballator. The booming population helps fuel the growing diversity of American industry.

House revolt against "Uncle Joe" Cannon

The Speaker, a muted Cannon.

Washington, D.C., March 19

Once the most powerful Speaker in the history of the House, "Uncle Joe" Cannon is now the weakest, stripped of nearly all the controls by which he had held lawmakers hostage to all his wishes. A convivial man who loves to play poker with his colleagues, Cannon, nevertheless, was a czar who held a firm grasp on every aspect of House operations – that is, until now. A revolt led by Representatives George Norris of Nebraska and Champ Clark of Missouri has left him little more than a figurehead. He lost his membership on the powerful Rules Committee, was deprived of all authority to appoint committees of the House and he no longer has the power to decide who makes a speech or a motion.

N.A.A.C.P. is organized

New York City, November

Crisis, the journal of the new National Association for the Advancement of Colored People, made its debut this month. According to editor W.E.B. Du Bois, it will not only "show the danger of race prejudice," but also "stand for the rights of men, irrespective of color or race." The N.A.A.C.P., founded on May 1, is an inter-racial union of Negro radicals and liberal reformers that has grown out of the National Negro Committee, founded in June of last year. Du Bois is its only Negro officer. The group's white founders include reformers Jane Addams, John Dewey and John E. Milholland. Industrialist Andrew Carnegie is among its supporters (→Oct. 1, 1912).

William Edward Burghardt Du Bois of Great Barrington, Massachusetts.

Jews congregate on the Lower East Side

New York City, Autumn

New York has more people of Jewish ancestry than any other city in the United States – or in the world according to the latest census. Government figures indicate that 540,000 Jews now live in the city. The vast majority are concentrated in the shadow of the Brooklyn Bridge, on the Lower East Side.

Most of these Jews migrated to America from Central and Eastern Europe. Like most of the non-Jewish immigrants, they came for two reasons: hardship at home and the promise of a new life in America. These first-generation Jews talk freely about the "pogroms," anti-Semitic attacks, and anti-Jewish economic policies in the "old country" that literally force them to flee their "shetls," or ethnic villages. One Polish Jew says he decided to come to New York after he had seen a friend return to Poland "well dressed, with an overcoat, and a cigar in the mouth." Meanwhile, German Jews, who have been here longer, tend to look down on the new arrivals.

A mass of humanity brings the corner of Orchard and Hester Streets to life.

Teddy home after big-game trek in Africa

New York City, June 19

Colonel Teddy Roosevelt was given a hero's welcome today on his return from a year's trek in Africa hunting big game. As his 14-carriage parade proceeded from the Battery to 59th Street, crowds lining the five-mile route jubilantly waved hats and handkerchiefs. Teddy's reaction? "Bully!"

Roosevelt's safari actually ended in March. His party of six reported having bagged 13,000 specimens. Many were rare, such as the dik-dik, an antelope smaller than a jackrabbit. The more common game included lions, elephants, rhinos, leopards, cheetahs and waterbucks as well as other kinds of antelope. There was danger everywhere. On one occasion, the colonel shot and felled a bull elephant only to have its mate charge, brushing him with its trunk. But "Bwana Tumbo," as the expedition's gunbearers called him, emerged unscathed, typically stout and tanned. A journalist since he left the White House, Roosevelt has already begun working on a book about his African adventures.

The former President confidently takes the reins while on the sands of Egypt.

I.C.C. to rule over all communications

Washington, D.C., June 18

Congress passed the Mann-Elkins Act today, bringing telephone, telegraph, cable and wireless firms under the umbrella of the Interstate Commerce Commission. The bill is widely hailed by communications officials who fear the rapidly growing slate of intrusive state regulations. AT&T vice president E.K. Hall hopes the action will calm public hostility that could "crystallize at any time into adverse legislation." The new law also expands the I.C.C.'s authority over the railroads. Despite efforts by President Taft to weaken it, the bill allows the commission to revise rates on its own initiative, and bars railroads from acquiring competing lines.

Ezra Pound's prose

London

Europe continues to lure leading American writers. The latest emigre is Ezra Pound, a native of Idaho who grew up and studied on the East Coast before crossing the Atlantic. His first book of verse was published in Italy in 1908; since then, he has lived in London, where his next two collections met with acclaim. Only 25, Pound has now offered his quirky prose in *The Spirit of Romance*, essays that reveal his amazing knowledge of both classic tradition and popular folk forms.

Jack Johnson knocks out Jim Jeffries

The nation's two preeminent pugilists locked in combat before a sell-out crowd.

Reno, Nevada, July 4

Jack Johnson, the Negro heavyweight champion, knocked out Jim Jeffries today in the 15th round of a bout that set off a chain reaction of race riots across the country. Eight Negroes were reported killed in the aftermath of a bout that some had thought might provide "the great white hope." But Jeffries, who was overweight and out of shape, conceded after the fight, "I couldn't come back."

Johnson was not in top form either, but he didn't have to be against a foe who had come out of a five-year retirement because he needed the cash. The sickly Jeffries, dull of eye and rubbery in the legs, was hard put to keep from keeling over under Johnson's bludgeoning. But the former champion fought on, even after a cut was opened over his eye in the sixth round. "I thought this fellow could hit," Johnson was heard to say between rounds.

On a New Orleans trolley car, a Negro who jeeringly exulted over the Johnson victory was fatally slashed by a white man.

Mann Act restricts white slave traffic

Washington, D.C., June 25

Relying on federal authority over interstate trade, President Taft signed the Mann Act today, barring the transport of women across state lines for immoral purposes. Prostitution was vaulted into the public eye in 1907 when G.K. Turner published an article in *McClure's* claiming Chicago harbored a highly organized ring of 10,000 "ladies of illfame." That year, a Pittsburgh survey counted 200 "disorderly houses"; Portland, Oregon, found 113 full-time brothels. Ex-President Teddy Roosevelt led the fight for moral legislation. The family, he insisted, must be resurrected as a bulwark against the "race suicide" of declining birth rates.

Legends at the Met

New York City, Dec. 10

The world premiere of Giacomo Puccini's *The Girl of the Golden West* at the Metropolitan Opera House was the stuff of legends. The linking of the most popular opera composer and Arturo Toscanini, the greatest conductor of Italian opera, made tickets more precious than gold. Lucky patrons heard a fiery performance of Pucciniesque lyricism, followed by 52 frenzied curtain calls. When Puccini took a bow, Met manager Giulio Gatti-Casazza placed a silver crown on his head.

Halley's comet causes thousands to panic

Few can miss the nocturnal display.

Chicago, May 18

Comet pills are selling briskly as Halley's comet reaches its nearest point to earth. Sold as an antidote for the poisonous gas mistakenly thought to constitute its tail, the pills are symptomatic of a nation in panic. Chicagoans have boarded up their windows out of the same fear, while others expect the world to end in a shattering collision. Crying "Comet!" New Yorkers bolted from a trolley when it was struck on the roof by a most earthly object, later reported to be a brick. Con men prey on the frightened and suicide levels are up. Meanwhile, the more sophisticated have been throwing nightly "comet parties."

Boy Scouts, Camp Fire Girls founded

United States

Boys and girls now have a new way to learn about cooperation, service to others and work skills. The Boy Scouts of America was founded this year by William Boyce, a Chicago publisher, to train boys, to build character through a program stressing work, outdoor play and community duty. The group is modeled after the Canadian and British counterparts. The Camp Fire Girls was started by Dr. Luther Halsey Gulick, a leader in youth recreation, and his wife, Charlotte Vetter Gulick. The Gulicks base the program on the girls summer camp they run, where they emphasize work, health and love.

Scouts raise the Stars and Stripes.

Vhen labor strife jets out of hand

os Angeles

"In the name of labor, labor is enied," is the cry from *The Los ngeles Times*. On October 1, an xplosion ripped through the paer's plant, killing 21 people. Unnists point to a gas leak, but the aper blames the unions, saying 1at the cause was "dynamite by ssassins." Rewards are offered, ut no leads have been found. On 'hristmas Day, when a bomb hit 1e Llewellyn iron works, where a :rike is in progress, investigators ed the blast to the iron workers nion. In spite of Clarence Daryw's handling their defense, 38 on workers were convicted and nion president F. Ryan was senenced to seven years in prison.

ook on Hull House

'hicago

Two decades ago, a plucky 29ear-old named Jane Addams purhased a dilapidated house in South 'hicago's slums flanked by a funer- parlor and a saloon. Within a ear, 50,000 poor immigrants had assed through the doors of Hull Iouse, where a staff of volunteers ave them practical lessons in Engsh and other subjects. Miss Adams, a pioneer in the field of social ork, now writes of her famed "setement house" in *Twenty Years at Iull House*, a best-seller that is lled with humor as well as praccal advice for others who share the uthor's vision of a better society.

Eastman Kodak's easy-to-use portable cameras offer Americans a new way to enjoy their free time.

New football rules prohibit clipping

Chicago

Despite efforts to take the mayhem out of football, the number of injuries and fatalities has risen to the point where more changes are required. With 33 gridiron deaths recorded in 1909, the college athletic leaders have forbidden the flying tackle from behind (clipping). They have also banned the pushing or pulling of the ball carrier and interlocked interference. In addition, seven players are now required on the line of scrimmage. These changes follow others made over the past five years, first at the angry order of President Roosevelt and then by concerned college presidents who want the sport cleaned up or removed from school programs.

Socialist in House

Washington, D.C., Nov. 8

The Socialist Party of America continues to gain strength. Today, Victor Berger of Wisconsin became the first Socialist ever elected to Congress. Wisconsin is a beehive of progressive and socialist activity. In Milwaukee, Emile Seidel was elected mayor. The party was founded in 1900 and won 95,000 votes for its presidential candidate, Eugene Debs. In 1904, he pulled 400,000 votes, and in 1908, even more. Now the party is making legislative inroads (→Nov. 5, 1912).

Time is money!

Philadelphia

The methods of Frederick W. Taylor, who calls himself the "father of scientific management," are being hailed by industry and cursed by labor. Trained as an engineer, Taylor has increased the efficiency of many factories by close observation of individual workers with the idea of eliminating all wasted time and motion. Workers, naturally, object to having all their movements studied with a stopwatch, but companies such as Bethlehem Steel that have put Taylor's ideas into action say he has saved them millions of dollars. Taylor says scientific management can make the home and society more efficient, too.

Year of air records, but it wasn't all glory

Rarely pausing to rest, ex-President Roosevelt takes to the air in St. Louis.

Cape Hatteras, N.C.

Owing to what Commander Walter Wellman called "disastrous" wind shifts, the dirigible America failed in its attempt to cross the Atlantic. On October 18, the 228-foot airship foundered in the waves off Cape Hatteras after wandering off course and losing altitude. Luckily, a British steamer rescued the crew, which was at least consoled with a 71-hour, 1,000-mile duration record.

Elsewhere this year, airplane maker Glenn Curtiss, when he wasn't training America's first aviatrix, Blanche Stuart, or new navy fliers, was giving maritime strategists the jitters with "aerial bombing" of ships with oranges. A Curtiss biplane heralded another naval breakthrough on November 14, when Eugene Ely swept aloft from an 83-foot platform fitted to the cruiser Birmingham, then flew two miles to Hampton Roads, Virginia.

At the Boston-Harvard air meet on September 12, an Englishman, Claude Grahame-White, won the $10,000 prize in a 33-mile race. On the same day, Ralph Johnson set a duration record of more than three hours in a Bleriot monoplane. Then, on October 26, Johnson set an incredible altitude record of 9,714 feet, over Long Island.

Battling disease and almost impenetrable jungles, as many as 40,000 men are employed along the route of the Panama Canal at any one time. Chief engineer George Goethals has sped up the project (→March 23, 1911).

1911

Taft

San Diego, Jan. 26. Glenn Curtiss demonstrates feasibility of seaplanes by flying an airplane rigged with floats, as navy officials watch in awe.

New York City, Feb. 21. Gustav Mahler conducts New York Philharmonic [last time before his death].

Arizona, March 18. Theodore Roosevelt opens dam bearing his name; it spans Salt River.

Berkeley, Calif., March 23. Former President Roosevelt states in a speech, "I took the canal zone and let Congress debate, and while the debate goes on the canal does also" (→Aug. 24, 1912).

New York City, Apr. 11. Triangle Shirtwaist owners indicted on charges of first- and second-degree manslaughter.

Washington, D.C., May 1. In United States v. Grimaud, Supreme Court rules that federal government, not states, has control over forest reserves.

Cordova, Alaska, May 5. Irate townspeople shovel 350 tons of coal off ships in harbor, protesting government decision to close Alaska coal lands.

Indianapolis, May 30. Ray Harroun wins First 500-mile race here.

Washington, D.C., June 6. United States and Nicaragua conclude Knox-Castrillo Convention, giving United States official role in Nicaraguan internal affairs (→Aug. 14, 1912).

Washington, D.C., June 30. It is announced that President Taft has saved nation over $42 million in last fiscal year, by requiring that all government spending estimates be submitted to him personally.

Washington, D.C., July 7. In order to protect dwindling pelagic seal population, U.S., Britain, Russia, and Japan sign treaty barring hunting above 30th parallel for 15 years.

Europe, Aug. 3. United States signs treaties with Britain and France, pledging that signers will not fight a third nation with whom a general arbitration treaty is in force (→March 7, 1912).

Philadelphia, Oct. 26. Philadelphia Athletics defeat New York Giants in World Series, four games to two.

Triangle fire kills 146

New York City, March 25

A horrible fire this afternoon took the lives of 146 young women working at the Triangle Shirtwaist Company on Greene Street. The building was said to be fireproof, but there was no sprinkling system, and one of the two exits was bolted shut. The few employees who escaped alive said the door was kept locked to keep them from sneaking off with spools of thread. Many of the victims, mostly Italian and Jewish immigrant girls, leapt from the 10th floor to the pavement below, where some were found with their paychecks still grasped in their fists. The Women's Trade Union League places the blame squarely on the company owners. Triangle had been one of 13 firms to deny garment workers better conditions in a strike in February of last year. In fact, it is rumored that another reason the second escape door was locked was to keep out agitators (→Apr. 11).

The Triangle Shirtwaist Company fire kills 146 and draws national attention.

Negroes to get help from Urban League

New York City

In response to a growing numbe of Negroes moving to cities, the National League on Urban Condition Among Negroes has been founded. It aims to help migrants from the South find opportunities in industry and adjust to city living. Business religious and civic groups of both Negro and white races will work to improve housing and employment conditions for Negroes.

20,000 troops sent to Mexican border

Washington, D.C., March 7

The United States today ordered 20,000 troops to the Mexican border to protect American interests. A rebellion against Porfirio Diaz, who has ruled Mexico almost continuously since 1876, has been spreading rapidly. Many of the rebel leaders are in the state of Chihuahua, across from New Mexico and Texas. The rebellion began after the election last year in which Diaz claimed victory over his opponent, Francisco Madero. Madero, leader of a reform movement whom Diaz had kept in jail through much of the campaign fled to Texas. There he declared the elections void, named himself provisional president and urged a general uprising. Support for Madero has grown rapidly (→Nov. 24, 1913).

Indian who founded Peyote religion dies

Cache, Oklahoma, Feb. 23

Commanche Indian Chief Quanah Parker died today in this small town. Parker, the son of an Indian chief and a white woman, Cynthia Parker, first won fame as a capable adversary of the United States Army. After finally surrendering in 1875, he founded the Peyote religion, which embraced the hallucinogenic drug, derived from cactus, in conjunction with Christian belief and symbols. A cultural movement as well as a religion, popular among the Indians of the Southwest, it has become institutionalized as the Native American Church.

:adillac eliminating ıand-crank starter

'adillac's innovative electric starter ·ill liberate drivers from the strain ✓f hand-cranking their autos to life.

)etroit, Michigan

While countless Americans have rown to love their automobiles, ɛw look forward to the backbreak-ıg task of hand-cranking the en-ine to life, especially on a cold r rainy morning. Indeed, the hand-rank starter, which occasional-/ causes injuries when the crank naps back unpredictably, is the one actor that has limited the sale of asoline-powered vehicles to wom-n and older men.

But the models planned for next ear by the Cadillac division of Hen-y Leland's General Motors should hange all this. Leland has recruited young inventor named Charles Cettering, who had developed an lectric motor for cash registers hat provides short bursts of power. dapted to jolt Cadillac engines ıto action, the battery-powered tarter should send Cadillac's 1912 ales soaring past this year's im-ressive mark of 10,000.

Wrigley's lasts and lasts and lasts.

Rockefeller's Standard Oil broken up

Washington, D.C., May 15

John D. Rockefeller once called the growth of huge corporations "a survival of the fittest, the working out of a law of nature and a law of God." Unfortunately for the oil tycoon, the law of the United States held sway today over both the heavens and the earth. Ending an antitrust suit launched by President Roosevelt, the Supreme Court has ordered Rockefeller's Standard Oil Company of New Jersey to divest itself of holdings in 37 firms.

In sprawling, often impenetrable sentences, Chief Justice Edward White has allegedly clarified, and many say limited, the scope of the Sherman Antitrust Act. His "rule of reason" allows that some trusts may, in fact, serve the public interest – those that combine to create economies of scale, for instance. The court's decision merely codifies the policy of selective prosecution pursued by Presidents Roosevelt and Taft for 11 years. Roosevelt repeatedly distinguished between public spirited trusts and the "malefactors of great wealth." And Taft, addressing Congress in January, warned that an all-out war on trusts would "disturb the confidence of the business community," punishing "the innocent many for the faults of the guilty few."

Standard Oil, it appears, is one of the few. Roosevelt saw Rockefeller as the personification of industrial evil, "setting the pace in the race for wealth under illegal and improper conditions." A Bureau of Corporations inquiry opened by Roosevelt revealed heavy corporate intrigue.

By 1878, Standard had "bought out or frozen out refiners all over the country," controlling 80 percent of oil output. Rebates on rail freight rates helped Rockefeller ruin middlemen. Merchants who refused to buy from Standard found their freight rates had mysteriously doubled. Commercial spies were commonplace and owners of a Standard subsidiary in Buffalo, New York, sabotaged equipment in a competing refinery. It remains to be seen whether divestment will break Standard's hold on the oil industry.

Rockefeller sits for a Lamb portrait.

Bill Larned wins seventh tennis title

Newport, Rhode Island

William "Bill" Larned, who won his first title in 1901, capped a decade of tennis excellence by capturing the national tennis championship for the seventh time. His record was compared to the reign of Dick Sears, who won seven consecutive championships starting in 1881. Larned also performed well in Davis Cup play for the United States, but he has had little support against the mighty British and Australians, who have dominated cup play. While Larned was topping the men, Hazel Hotchkiss has won three straight women's titles.

American Tobacco Co. must reorganize

Washington, D.C., June

Complying with orders from the Supreme Court, the directors of the American Tobacco Company have agreed to split their firm into 14 allegedly separate units. Advocates of the plan say it will loosen founding owner James B. Duke's grip on the nation's tobacco business. Others remain skeptical. A Bureau of Corporations expert told Attorney General George Wickersham the new scheme "leaves very much to be desired if truly competitive conditions are to be reestablished."

The tobacco trust was launched in 1890 along with the Sherman Act, the instrument of its eventual destruction. Its secret was an ingenious cigarette-rolling machine, invented by Duke, and a tireless merger policy. Duke controlled 80 percent of American tobacco output and extended tentacles into Central America. But his purchase of Continental Tobacco in 1904 put him on President Teddy Roosevelt's list of "bad" trusts. Despite friendly offers of compromise, the Justice Department filed suit in 1907. The present conviction, and Standard Oil's in May, highlight President Taft's success in extending government regulation (→Sept. 26, 1914).

"Family Group" (1910-11) by William Glackens, renowned Ashcan artist.

End of the warpath for Carry Nation

Armed with Bible and hatchet.

Leavenworth, Kansas, June 9

Mrs. Carry Nation, a temperance reformer who had a lifelong ax – or hatchet – to grind, died today at her home at the age of 64. Mrs. Nation conducted a one-woman crusade to stamp out alcohol, wielding a sharp hatchet and using it to chop up liquor crates in saloons in Kansas and across the Midwest. Born Carry Amelia Moore in Garrard County, Kentucky, she married a doctor who proved to be an alcoholic. The 21-year-old Carry left him within half a year. In 1877, she wed a lawyer named David Nation. No temperance movement supported Mrs. Nation, who supplemented her income by giving lectures and selling souvenir hatchets.

Berlin's "Alexander's Ragtime Band"

New York City

The name Irving Berlin may be new to most, but his hit song *Alexander's Ragtime Band* promises to make it a household word. First sung this year in a Chicago vaudeville act, the song became a national craze after Sophie Tucker started belting it out. Born in Russia, the 23-year old Berlin learned his craft first-hand as a singing waiter and a song plugger in Tin Pan Alley. The author of a number of vaudeville songs, Berlin warbled two of his own numbers, *Sweet Italian Love* and *Oh, That Beautiful Rag*, in last year's revue, *Up and Down Broadway*. While this year's hit song is not strictly a "rag," it nevertheless keeps the toes tapping.

"Alexander's Ragtime Band. It' the best band in the land."

Biplane limps in, first to cross U.S.

Pasadena, California, Autumn

Aviation deaths reached 100 this year, but fliers are as cavalier as ever. On November 5, with the engine of his Wright biplane dying, Calbraith Rodgers landed to a wild welcome in Pasadena, California. It was the first cross-country flight, 3,220 miles from New York in 82 hours 4 minutes. Cromwell Dixon, 19, became the first man to fly over the Rockies on September 30; two days later, he died in a crash. Glenn Curtiss raised his hydroplane from San Diego harbor, and Eugene Ely landed a Curtiss plane on the battleship Pennsylvania. On Long Island, Earl Ovington made the first mail flight, and Harriet Quimby is now "the woman aviator in trousers."

Durant, Chevrolet start auto company

Detroit, Mich., Nov. 1

William C. Durant is hoping to rebound in the auto business by joining forces with Louis Chevrolet in a new company. Durant founded General Motors three years ago, but last year his whirlwind mergers overextended the firm's capital. A banking syndicate took over, ousted Durant and put Walter Chrysler and William C. Nash in charge. Chevrolet, a Swiss-born mechanic and race-car driver who worked for Buick, will design a low-priced car to compete with the Model T. But since Ford has built an empire around the "Tin Lizzie," producing 70,000 this year for the low price of $780, the new Chevrolet Motor Car Company faces a daunting task.

Krazy Kat beware!

New York City, July 1

Poor Krazy Kat won't be around long if Ignatz Mouse has anything to say about it. The rogue of a rodent is out to "bean" the aforementioned feline with whatever object is close at hand. Bricks are his weapon of choice in the *New York Journal* comic strip *Krazy Kat and Ignatz*, the brainchild of cartoonist George Herriman. But don't worry too much about Krazy. She's in love with Ignatz and interprets his brick-throwing as a sign of affection.

Cy Young, pitching great, has retired

United States

After 22 years as baseball's premier pitcher, Cy Young has retired. The tall (6 feet 2 inches) hurler from Gilmore, Ohio, who once hurled a perfect game, has hung up his spikes after a 1911 season plagued by illness. He also pitched two no-hit games, against Cincinnati in 1897 and the New York Americans in 1908. Young, who kept the Philadelphia Americans from reaching first base in a 1904 contest, had a fling as manager during the 1907 season with the Boston Red Sox, the team with which he spent eight years and helped to win a World Series in 1903. He ended his career with 509 victories, 316 losses and an ERA of 2.63.

Studio in Hollywood

Hollywood, California

The Nestor Company has rented the Blondeau Tavern, shut by temperance enthusiasts, at the Sunset and Gower intersection, as the first film studio here. Earlier, Colonel William N. Selig built a West Coast studio in nearby Edendale, and producer Thomas Ince hired a Wild West Show for the winter, using real cowboys, Indians, wild horses and buffalo in spectacular westerns. His "Inceville" in Santa Ynez Canyon covers 20,000 acres.

Foundation set up by Andrew Carnegie

New York City, Nov. 10

After years of generously donating his money to schools, public libraries and various funds, Andrew Carnegie has set up a foundation for distribution of his vast resources. The iron and steel manufacturer's foundation, endowed with $135 million, will work to promote knowledge through educational projects and governmental and international affairs programs for American citizens as well as some British dominions and colonies. Carnegie, who will serve as the foundation's president, is particularly interested in public libraries as a means of self-education.

The philanthropist and benefactor.

1912

Taft

New York City, Feb. 21. In declaring his intention to seek presidency again, Theodore Roosevelt is heard to exclaim, "My hat is in the ring."

Washington, D.C., March 7. Senate amends, then ratifies arbitration treaties signed with Britain and France.

Washington, D.C., March 14. Justice Department begins investigation into merger of Southern Pacific and Union Pacific Railroads.

Washington, D.C., May 1. In response to Titanic disaster, federal government orders all steamships to carry enough lifeboats for all passengers.

Washington, D.C., May 13. Senate refers to state proposal for a constitutional amendment to provide direct election of senators (→May 31, 1913).

Seattle, Washington, July 18. Sailors raid local office of Industrial Workers of the World, burning books and furniture in street.

Washington, D.C., Aug. 2. Senate passes resolution extending Monroe Doctrine to apply to non-European countries and private foreign companies.

Washington, D.C., Aug. 24. Congress passes Panama Canal Act, permitting toll-free passage of American ships through canal, provided they are engaged in coastwide trade (→Oct. 10, 1913).

Kentucky, Oct. 1. Lincoln Institute, dedicated to providing vocational training for Negroes, opens; Negro elite leaders such as W.E.B. Du Bois protest.

Boston, Oct. 16. Boston Red Sox defeat New York Giants to win World Series four games to three.

Chicago, Dec. 7. Dr. James B. Herrick makes first diagnosis of a heart attack in a living patient.

California. By 1912, over 5,000 Russian pacifists threatened with military service have fled to California.

DEATHS

Glen Echo, Maryland, Apr. 12. Clara Barton, founder of American Red Cross (*Dec. 25, 1821).

Dayton, Ohio, May 30. Wilbur Wright, co-inventor of airplane (*Apr. 16, 1867).

Lawrence textile strikers get pay hike

Lawrence, Mass., March 13

The *Internationale* rang out in a dozen languages today as strike leaders and workers celebrated victory and a pay raise in a heated struggle with textile mill owners. Two strikers were left dead and many injured. "Big Bill" Haywood, head of the radical Industrial Workers of the World, had warned employers they could not "weave cloth with bayonets." The last eight weeks have proved his point.

Trouble began when the first paychecks of the year showed wage cuts would accompany a two-hour reduction in the work week. The owners felt an average of $8.76 a week was too much for 54 hours. After a Polish group quit the looms on January 11, the flood gates opened. The next day, Italians at the American Woolen Company went from mill to mill on the Merrimack River and by evening, 10,000 workers had joined in; by month's end, 50,000. Fife-and-drum bands, parades and long speeches kept strikers busy. Pickets formed chains with thousands in human links circling some mills. Led by Mother Jones, women played a big role, inviting police intervention after sending their children to stay with sympathetic families in New York.

The strike, largely spontaneous, was run by the rank and file, encompassing 28 nationalities. Joseph Ettor of the I.W.W. oversaw the strike committee until he was arrested for murder after a striker was shot down during a demonstration. One labor spokesman charged that the I.W.W. seeks not a "treaty of industrial peace," but "the creation of a proletarian impulse which will eventually revolutionize society."

Businessmen, sporting flags in their buttonholes, have blamed foreign agitation for the unrest. One leading citizen is suspected of having planted dynamite in the strike district to discredit the workers. But police brutality played a bigger role in discrediting the forces of law and order. Company concessions will involve some 250,000 textile workers.

Union adds Arizona and New Mexico

Washington, D.C., Feb. 14

The Territory of Arizona today became the 48th state in the union. On January 6, New Mexico was also granted statehood. The admission of these two states has finally ended the bitter political wrangling that has been going on between the older states and the former territories over alleged special mining and land-holding groups that seemingly dominated Arizona and New Mexico for their exclusive welfare and profit. After the New Mexico bill was signed by President Taft, he said to its new citizens, "Well, it is all over; I am glad to give you life. I hope you will be healthy."

Sure! It's a cinch!

United States

Sure! You can learn to talk like young folks today. *It's a cinch!* For example, when someone treats you to something nice, like a *sundae,* say that it's just *peachy!* If somebody you know has donned stylish clothes, call the look *flossy!* Don't be *peeved* if English professors call you *lowbrow* and your new vocabulary *lousy.* Just *beat it* to a *movie* (what the old folks call a moving picture). Afterward, you can take a *joyride* in a rich friend's *speedy* automobile, and watch it being *serviced* at a garage. Easy? *Sure!*

Cherry trees, a gift from Japan to U.S.

Washington, D.C.

Japan has presented a gift of color and beauty to America. Viscountess Chinda, wife of the Japanese Ambassador, gave 2,000 tiny cherry trees to the First Lady, Mrs. Taft, as a token of friendship. The Japanese celebrate the dreamlike, flowering trees each spring. Mrs. Taft planted the first sapling during a quiet but elegant ceremony. The rest of the trees were planted along the Tidal Basin in Potomac Park. Washingtonians can expect delicate, brilliant pink blossoms each spring to accent their white marble city.

New York City, Jan. 9. *The growth of the metropolis brings with it unique perils. The Equitable Building burned today and is now encased in ice.*

Titanic goes down on maiden voyage

The mighty ship, said to be unsinkable, goes down off the Newfoundland coast.

Halifax, Nova Scotia, Apr. 15

Under a cloudless sky, the Titanic disappeared into the North Atlantic early today, leaving 1,517 people to die in freezing waters. The 700 survivors, who arrived here aboard the Cunard liner Carpathia, tell tales of a stark tragedy.

The White Star steamship, largest in the world, was four days out of Southampton, England, on its maiden voyage to New York. Its vast ballrooms and sprawling upper decks cradled the cream of high society, both London's and New York's. Some passengers paid well over $4,000 for this Atlantic crossing, while in the steerage area below it would have been difficult to find an annual income of $1,000.

The Titanic was believed to be as invincible as the Astors in their Fifth Avenue mansion. At 11:40 last night, however, even John Jacob Astor flinched when the great 46,000-ton hulk brushed an iceberg for a mere 10 seconds. It was barely enough of a touch to spill a glass of champagne, but the party was over. Thomas Andrews, the engineer who had overseen the building of the Titanic, rushed starboard to find that the hull was open to the sea along a 300-foot gash.

Within minutes, six distress signals had been issued by wireless. Passengers assembled quietly on deck, calm because of their implicit trust in the best technology known to man. Officers quickly tried to fit the 2,207 people into the lifeboats – where there was really only room for 1,178, while the ballroom band struck up a ragtime medley for encouragement. As the boat listed further starboard, the English hymn *Autumn* sounded a somber note:

God of mercy and compassion
Look with pity on my pain
Hold me up in mighty waters,
Keep my eyes on things above.

It seemed only moments later, from the lifeboats, that the lucky 700 in them watched the great Titanic's bow sink, sending the stern skyward. Gravity ripped away ventilators and stanchions with the screech of grinding metal. The aft compartments filled with water and the mighty vessel vanished, leaving only the tortured wail of hundreds of human beings freezing to death in the middle of nowhere (→ May 1).

Jim Thorpe stars at Stockholm Olympics

Stockholm, Sweden, Summer

Jim Thorpe, the amazing Indian out of Carlisle, Pennsylvania, was hailed as the "world's greatest athlete" following his smashing triumphs in the pentathlon and decathlon at this year's Olympics. He was also first in the 200-meter dash and the 1,500-meter run. The King of Sweden told him, "You are the greatest athlete in the world," and Russia's Czar Nicholas sent him a silver model of a Viking ship. [Since the Olympics are for amateurs, Thorpe was later stripped of his medals and returned the gift after admitting that he had played professional baseball in 1909 and 1910. Athletes who finished second to him were moved up to first]. These Games were also notable because they included women, though only in diving and swimming.

Jim Thorpe, all-American.

American athletes won 13 of a possible 28 gold medals, with sterling performances by Ralph Cook Craig in the sprints and Charley Reidpath at 400 meters, as well as in a sweep of the 110-meter hurdles (→ Oct. 13, 1982).

New on market: Life Savers, Oreos

United States

The American hunger for new products is being amply met every day in the marketplace: this year alone has seen the introduction of many tasty treats. One favorite is cranberry sauce – a sweetened, jellied condiment produced by Ocean Spray Cranberries, a Massachusetts growers cooperative. Richard Hellmann of New York has bottled his Blue Ribbon Mayonnaise, which is said to hold its texture and freshness almost indefinitely. A Cleveland confectioner has turned out a peppermint candy with a hole in it that he calls Life Savers, because it looks like a life preserver. And this spring a new cookie – two chocolate wafers sandwiching a cream filling – called the Oreo Biscuit is a winner for the National Biscuit Co.

"Flagler's Folly" chugs into Florida

Key West, Florida, Jan. 22

The first New York-Key West train arrived here at 10:43 today with the man who built the last section of the railroad aboard. Henry Flagler and his wife, Mary Lily, debarked to the noise of firecrackers, whistles and band music. Many here had never seen a train before. Critics called the 200-mile rail extension to this southernmost point in the United States "Flagler's Folly" because of the problems of building tracks from island to island, over water and through jungles. But Flagler, Florida's pioneer developer, persisted. Today, at the age of 82, he said, "Now I can die happy. My dream is fulfilled."

Expert links crime to low intelligence

Vineland, New Jersey

The director of research at the New Jersey Training School for Feeble-Minded Boys and Girls has stirred up a great deal of controversy over his study linking inherited low intelligence with crime. Henry Herbert Goddard's paper *The Kallikak Family: A Study in the Heredity of Feeble-Mindedness* traces the ancestry of a girl named Deborah Kallikak (a pseudonym Goddard devised, from the Greek meaning "good and bad"), and discloses an unbroken path of degeneracy. Goddard has coined the word "moron," from the Greek for "sluggish," to describe an adult with the intelligence of a child.

eddy rides Bull Moose into political fray

ıe former President hitches his hopes to a recognized symbol of tenacity.

hicago, Aug. 5

The Progressive Party has nomi-ıted Theodore Roosevelt as its esidential candidate. Adopting as ; symbol the bull moose (because oosevelt always likes to compare mself to this proud, ferocious an-ıal), the new third party offers the ›ters a broad range of progressive forms, including regulation of ısts, unemployment pay, old age pensions and female suffrage. The Bull Moose convention has been a wild spectacle, much like a religious revival. Roosevelt gave his enthusiastic supporters a "confession of faith," while they responded with loud choruses of "Onward Christian Soldiers" and "The Battle Hymn of the Republic." Look out, Republicans and Democrats – the Bull Moose is loose! (→Nov. 5).

Taft, Wilson nominated by major parties

Baltimore, Maryland, July 2

Woodrow Wilson has been nominated as the Democratic Party's presidential candidate today. After 46 ballots in which no candidate had a majority, the party turned to "dark horse" Wilson. A Virginian by birth, son of a Presbyterian minister and former president of Princeton University and Governor of New Jersey, the noted reformer recently said, "No one can worship God or love his neighbor on an empty stomach." Thomas R. Marshall, his running mate, is not so reform-minded. As he stated last month, "What this country needs is a good five-cent cigar."

Wilson will run against the Republican nominee, President Taft. Renominated by a wide margin at the G.O.P. convention in Chicago last month, he is expected to run on a pro-business platform. No political warrior, he said of the contest, "Even a rat in a corner will fight." Vice President James Sherman was also renominated (→Aug. 5).

Debs: "Every capitalist is your enemy"

Chicago

"Every capitalist is your enemy. Every workingman is your friend." Shouted from his "Red Special" campaign train, these words are helping Socialist Eugene Debs gain a lot of attention in the presidential election campaign this year. Debs, who was nominated for the third time by the Socialist Party in Indianapolis in May, has been emphasizing that elective office is only a step on the road to revolution. "Comrades," he proclaimed in Milwaukee with great optimism, "this is our year" (→Nov. 5).

lan jumps out of airplane with parachute

ew York City, Spring

On March 1, Lieutenant Albert ȝrry, strapped into a parachute, ımbed under the lower wing of an my biplane 1,500 feet above Kin-ch Field near St. Louis and flung mself free. The 33-year-old Berry, ho has made many jumps from ılloons, plunged for 500 harrow-g feet before the parachute bil-wed open. He repeated the feat ›on after, then said never again.

Other aeronauts press on. Bob Fowler completed the first West-to-East continental flight on March 5; it took four months. Fowler survived an early crash, but others were not so lucky. Julie Clark became the first female air fatality in a Springfield, Illinois, crash, and Harriet Quimby, the first aviatrix to cross the English Channel on April 17, was later jolted from her plane over Boston harbor. Cross-country flyer Cal Rodgers plunged into the ocean at Long Beach on April 3.

While the Socialists illustrate their contempt for the capitalist system, for most workers the prospect of climbing that pyramid is as strong as ever.

linimum wage law

›ston, June 4

Labor leaders are celebrating a ajor victory today as the Massa-ıusetts legislature passed the na-›n's first law assuring a minimum age for the state's lowest-paid orkers. The hourly wage has yet be established, but it will be t by July 1 of next year, when e law is to go into effect. It will event an employer from paying lave wages." Massachusetts has en a leader in the promotion of ›llective bargaining plans and orker protection laws. Labor aders will now campaign for simi-r legislation on the federal level.

A Dreiser tycoon

Chicago

You who dream of rising to the top, put away your morals and sharpen your claws – only the cruel survive. A survivor par excellence is Frank Cowperwood, cold-blooded hero of Theodore Dreiser's *The Financier*, who learns his life lessons by watching a lobster feast on a squid. Cowperwood becomes a human predator, devouring his foes in the business world. Dreiser admits a kinship between his hero and real-life tycoon Charles T. Yerkes; he, too, made his fortune in Philadelphia, then moved to Chicago, where the prey was more tempting.

Women get vote in three states

Washington, D.C., November

Arizona, Kansas and Oregon gave women the vote today, lifting the suffragists out of a 15-year period so dismal they refer to it as "the doldrums." From 1896 to 1910, suffrage made only six state referenda. Each lost by wide margins. For years activists have struggled for direction without a national headquarters. Elizabeth Cady Stanton's daughter Harriet stirred the waters when she returned from England in 1907 with a passion for massive parades. In California last year, the spark caught fire. Billboards, electric signs, essay contests, pageants and plays all helped a referendum win by 3,000 votes. But this month's victories give suffragists a total of only nine states. Liquor interests defeated referenda in Ohio and Wisconsin. Thinking they had Michigan won, women demanded a recount when officials claimed they lost by only 760 votes. The second total jumped magically to 100,000. To many, federal law looks like a better approach (→March 3, 1913).

Wilson elected, pledges New Freedon

Washington, D.C., Nov. 5

In a stunning victory, Woodrow Wilson was elected President today. When he said on the campaign trail that he "wanted to restore our politics to their full spiritual vigor again, and our national life . . . to its pristine strength and freedom," the voters listened – and they responded with an overwhelming endorsement of his "New Freedom" philosophy.

In an unusual, four-cornered contest, Democrat Wilson garnered 6,286,000 votes (41 percent). The Bull Moose candidate, Teddy Roosevelt, received 4,216,000 (27 percent). President Taft, the Republican candidate, got 3,483,000 votes (23 percent), and the Socialist Party nominee, Eugene V. Debs, received about 900,000 popular votes (6 percent). In the electoral vote, it was 435 for Wilson, 88 for Roosevelt and eight for Taft.

Political analysts are already conducting their post-mortems. They note that from the outset of the campaign, Wilson's "New Freedom" theme caught hold with the

The intellectual preaches a gospel of reform and democratic internationalisn

voters much quicker – and more effectively – than did Roosevelt's "New Nationalism" program.

Roosevelt said that big business, aided and abetted by big government, would help everybody. Early on, however, Wilson began to speak of the danger of an all-powerful national state, especially with r gard to the rights and freedoms the individual. Last month, Wilsc characterized this election as tl "second struggle for emancip tion." If Roosevelt were to win, said, then America "can have fre dom of no sort whatever."

Shot in the chest, the Bull Moose orates for 80 minutes

Milwaukee, Wis., Oct. 15

"I have a great deal to say," insisted Teddy Roosevelt after entering the presidential contest in February, "and I won't stand it for a moment" if "the discredited bosses and politicians decide against me." People wondered what creation of man *would* silence the presidential bluster. Yesterday, just after a gunman's bullet lodged in his chest, Roosevelt stood for 80 minutes to deliver the message of his Progressive "Bull Moose" Party. "Friends," he uttered upon reaching the podium, "I shall ask you to be as quiet as possible. I don't know whether you fully understand that I have been shot; but it takes more than that to kill a Bull Moose."

An intrepid hunter, Rough Rider and all-around sportsman, Roosevelt revels in public acts of bravery. From the charge up San Juan Hill to bear hunts in the Rockies to trust-busting on Wall Street, Teddy enjoys sharing danger with reporters. By his own admission, Roosevelt was "a sickly, delicate boy." But, "by acting as if I was not afraid," he says, "I . . . ceased to be afraid. Most men can have the same experience if they choose." Today, doctors say, Roosevelt is recovering, the bullet having been slowed by an overcoat, a glasses case and a folded manuscript of the speech. Would-be assassin John Chrank, an unbalanced man, is in custody.

Shot or not, Theodore Roosevelt campaigns with his characteristic dynamism.

Volcano eruption i Alaska buries town

Cordova, Alaska, June 12

One of the largest eruptions recorded history occurred today Katmai, on the southern tip of tl Alaskan Peninsula. Geologists a estimating that the eruption hurl vast amounts of volcanic matt into the atmosphere. The sm community of Kodiak, a good 1(miles from the site of the volcan has been buried under several fe of ash.

Giant clouds of the material we driven high into the atmospher and experts are now predicting th the Pacific Northwest will mc likely be affected by ash-laden ra for days. Interestingly, because the manner in which the volcar erupted, geologists are predicti that it may now implode, or c lapse into itself, and fill wi ash. If this does happen, there the possibility that the Katmai ar will become honeycombed wi vents and smoke for decades come.

A license required for radio operators

Washington, D.C., Aug. 13

A rapid growth in the number of individuals experimenting with the new medium of radio has spurred Congress to pass the Radio Act of 1912. The bill, which became law today, requires radio operators to obtain licenses from the Department of Commerce and Labor. The first known radio program in the nation was broadcast in 1906, when Reginald Fessenden of Brant Rock, Massachusetts, read a poem and played two musical selections over the air on Christmas Eve. Many experimenters since have been developing broadcast equipment, exchanging messages over great distances. As yet, no commercial use for radio broadcasting has emerged.

Boots by L.L. Bean

Freeport, Maine, Autumn

Leon Leonwood Bean and his brother officially went into the mail order business this year, selling their popular Maine hunting boots. The company, L.L. Bean, began selling shoes when Leon Bean, a hunter and fisherman, decided to attack the problem of wet feet. Bean sent out 100 of his rubber bottom-leather top boots last year. When 90 were returned because of a defect, Bean established his policy of refunding money for returned goods – no questions asked.

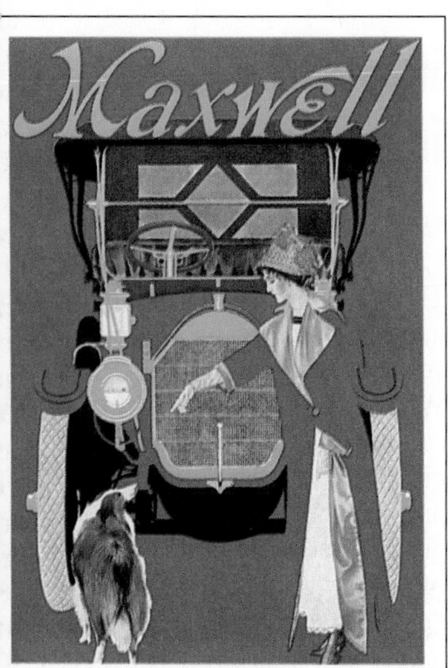

Competition among auto manufacturers remains fierce for the attention of a discerning public.

Journalism school set up at Columbia

New York City, July 2

The cornerstone of Columbia University's journalism school was laid by Mrs. Joseph Pulitzer today. The ceremony came nine years after editor and publisher Joseph Pulitzer announced that his will would provide for the endowment of the school. The advisory board will include prominent journalists from Pulitzer's own *New York World* and *St. Louis Post-Dispatch* as well as from other leading newspapers in the nation. Under president Nicholas Murray Butler, Columbia University has greatly expanded during the last 10 years, advancing its original philosophy of broadening education beyond the classic 18th-century subjects.

19 in row for Rube

New York City, July 8

The amazing pitching streak of Rube Marquard is over. The New York Giants hurler, who has defeated 19 consecutive opponents since opening day, was finally stopped by the Chicago Cubs, 7-2. The streak might have been put at 20 because Rube actually won a game in relief, but the rulebook says starter Jeff Tesreau gets credit for the victory because he pitched more innings. Three runners Tesreau put on base in the ninth scored, but the Giants won after Marquard came on.

Major French film imported by Zukor

Los Angeles

Movie maker Adolf Zukor has imported the acclaimed French film *Queen Elizabeth*, starring Sarah Bernhardt and Louis Mercanton, in an attempt to give motion pictures the prestige of legitimate theater and to kill what he sees as the "slum tradition" in movies. The film is released by Zukor's Famous Players Film Company, which also makes movies, often featuring the charming Mary Pickford. Other busy new producers out here are the brothers Warner, William Fox and the amalgamation known as Universal that Carl Laemmle heads.

Marines in Nicaragua to protect regime

The marines again prove useful in enforcing U.S. primacy in the Americas.

Washington, D.C., Aug. 14

United States Marines have been sent to help the government of Nicaragua, whose stability is threatened by civil war. Nicaragua's Conservative President Adolfo Diaz requested the troops to maintain order. In 1909, after the Senate rejected a plan to help Nicaragua financially, President Taft appointed an American customs collector by executive order, thus bypassing the Senate, and New York banks made loans, taking as collateral a controlling interest in both Nicaragua's railways and its national bank. The Liberals, who feel that Diaz and the Conservatives are allowing the U.S. too much influence, have led the revolt with the slogan "Down with Yankee imperialists." With anti-American feeling prevalent, it is not clear when the marines will be pulled out (→ Feb. 18, 1916).

Taft's "Dollar Diplomacy" causes a stir

Washington, D.C., Dec. 3

Departing President William Howard Taft, whose foreign policy rarely brings anything but approbation, told Congress today that diplomacy "is an effort frankly directed to an increase of American trade." This is hardly a new policy, but Taft's rivals have made political capital by attacking it as "dollar diplomacy." Treaties with Nicaragua and Honduras that protect U.S. bankers from revolution and embezzlement have been rejected by Congress. President-elect Wilson promises to replace money with morality as the basis of U.S. foreign relations (→ Oct. 27, 1913).

Dentist Grey rides "The Purple Sage"

Zanesville, Ohio

It's no surprise to hear of a man dreaming about the Old West while trapped in the dentist's chair. But an Ohio dentist whose thoughts stray to tumbleweed and sagebrush can cause real harm. Luckily, Zane Grey put away his drill after *Betty Zane* (1904) and kept out his pen. *The Last of the Plainsmen* (1908) won the hearts of frontier lovers, but now Grey, 37, has emerged as a two-fisted storyteller with his novel *Riders of the Purple Sage*, a big-time best-seller that may establish him as the heir of the dime novelists. It sure beats filling cavities.

June 1. *The latest pulp novel in a series, "Buffalo Bill and the Silk Lasso," continues the adventures of the legendary frontiersman.*

1913

Wilson

Washington, D.C., March 1. Congress passes Webb-Kenyon Interstate Liquor Act, banning shipments of liquor into states where its sale is forbidden (→Oct. 28, 1919).

Washington, D.C., March 18. President Wilson withdraws U.S. support from international industrial consortium in China, citing China's loss of "administrative independence."

Washington, D.C., Apr. 8. Woodrow Wilson becomes first President since John Adams to deliver State of Union address to Congress in person.

Washington, D.C., June 2. Department of Labor mediates first strike settlement, resolving dispute between Railway Clerks and New York, New Haven and Hartford Railroad.

Massachusetts, July 1. First state minimum wage law in effect.

Wimbledon, England, July 28. For first time since 1902, an American tennis team defeats British for Davis Cup.

Iowa, Aug. 26. Keokuk Dam, world's largest, at mouth of Des Moines River, inaugurated.

Panama, Oct. 10. Gamoa Dike explodes when President Wilson presses an electric button in White House intended to open Panama Canal to shipping (→Aug. 15, 1914).

New York, Oct. 11. Philadelphia Athletics defeat New York Giants, four games to one, in World Series.

Philippines, Oct. 16. Governor announces more Filipinos than Americans to be on Philippines Commission, islands' ruling body (→Aug. 29, 1916).

Mobile, Alabama, Oct. 27. President Wilson states in a speech that the United States "will never again seek one additional foot of territory by conquest."

United States. Julius Rosenwald, president of Sears, Roebuck, sets up fund providing scholarships for Negroes.

United States. Charles Beard publishes *Economic Interpretation of the Constitution.*

DEATHS

Auburn, New York, March 10. Harriet Tubman, fugitive slave and abolitionist (*1820).

Rome, Italy, March 31. John Pierpont Morgan, financier (*Apr. 17, 1837).

European art shocks the American public at the Armory Show

One critic called Duchamp's "Nude" "an explosion in a shingle factory."

Chicago, March 30

The Art Institute of Chicago this week opened an exhibition of either advanced artistic works or the insolent doodlings of lunatics, depending on one's view of modern art. The International Exhibition of Modern Art is popularly called the Armory Show after its original home at the 69th Infantry Regiment Armory in New York, where it had its premiere on February 17. Though the show was organized by the artist Walt Kuhn and the Association of American Painters and Sculptors, and a majority of its works are American, it highlights European trends, from older Post-Impressionists such as Gauguin, Cezanne and van Gogh to the new generation featuring Picasso, Matisse and Duchamp. Many Americans who prefer pleasantly realistic scenes are offended by the Cubists' geometric deformations and the strident colors of the fauvists (from fauves, or wild beasts), many of whose works are in America for the first time.

To citizens of a country that regards itself as dedicated to progress, the intentionally crude technique and unnatural colors of these "apostles of ugliness" represent the decadence and degeneration of Europe. Singled out for derision have been Duchamp's *Nude Descending a Staircase*, mocked by a contest to "find the nude," and Matisse's *Blue Nude*, burned in effigy here. The effects of the "topsy-turvyists" on American art remain to be seen.

Erector Set shown at U.S. Toy Fair

New York City

So you want to recreate the Eiffel Tower or the Brooklyn Bridge? Well, now you can with the Erector Set. A construction kit for kids, it was shown at this year's Toy Fair. Alfred C. Gilbert, the set's inventor, said: "If the idea appealed to me, I figured it would appeal to a lot of other kids." He got the idea for the set after seeing railroad power lines being constructed. Initially, he designed cardboard replicas of axles, pulleys, plates and girders. He now has what he calls, "the greatest construction toy for boys" – though some girls seem to like it, too.

Maggie and Jiggs get into the funnies

New York City

What would you do if you won the Irish Sweepstakes? For Jiggs, a former mason, the answer is simple. All he wants is to see his pals at Dinty Moore's tavern. Some corned beef and cabbage and a game of pinochle satisfy his every desire. His wife, Maggie, feels differently. She wants to forget her life as a washerwoman and enter high society ... and she's taking Jiggs with her, even if she has to clobber him with a rolling pin to keep him in line. George McManus's comic strip *Bringing Up Father* was introduced this year by the Hearst newspapers.

Hopeful Pollyanna is always cheerful

United States

Hope is always on the horizon. There's nothing new about this homily – except its source, an 11-year-old orphan named Pollyanna Whittier. She's the heroine of Eleanor Porter's *Pollyanna.* When the girl turns up at the door of her rich and crotchety Aunt Polly, she is given a bed in the attic. But instead of moping, Pollyanna plays the "glad game," searching for reasons to be cheerful. Soon her optimism infects everyone in Beldingsville, Vermont, even Aunt Polly. The author is playing a glad game of her own – tallying royalties.

16th Amendment allows income tax

Washington, D.C., Feb. 25

Following ratification by Delaware earlier this month, 38 states have approved the 16th Amendment to the United States Constitution, which takes effect today. The amendment, which allows Congress "to lay and collect taxes on income from whatever source derived," was necessitated by the Supreme Court decision of 1895 that declared a tax on income to be in violation of the "direct tax" clause of Article 1, Section 9, of the Constitution. No such challenge was raised to the first income tax, levied during the Civil War and lifted when peace came.

I.W.W. loses strike at New Jersey mill

Paterson, New Jersey, July

Silk workers are back at work after losing five strikers to police bullets, $4 million in wages and their bid for a halt to three-loom and four-loom shops. Spirits were lifted for a time by a pageant in Madison Square Garden. And when employers hung flags around town, strikers responded with the slogan, "We wove the flag. We dyed the flag. We won't scab under the flag." But mass arrests broke morale, sending 2,300 strikers to jail since the Industrial Workers of the World began the strike in February.

House report warns of oligarchy in U.S.

Washington, D.C., Feb. 28

A report issued today by the House Banking and Currency Committee, under the chairmanship of Louisiana Democrat Arsene Pujo, brings to a close the occasionally sensational investigation into the so-called "money trust." Among the highlights of the hearings was the dramatic questioning of J.P. Morgan by committee counsel Samuel Untermeyer, which helped prove the nation's money is controlled by a small number of financiers. The Pujo report's release is expected to help establish a federal banking system (→ Dec. 23).

Suffragettes: "Tell troubles to Woodrow"

Determined suffragettes take their cause to the main street of America.

Washington, D.C., March 3

A near-riot developed in the nation's capital today when rowdies attacked a parade of 5,000 women demanding the right to vote. Parading on the day before President-elect Woodrow Wilson's inauguration, the women carried banners reading, "Tell your troubles to Woodrow." Wilson found few well-wishers waiting to greet him.

All attention was on Pennsylvania Avenue, where angry men pushed, shoved and jeered at the suffragettes. The march was organized by Alice Paul and Lucy Burns, who had taken part in militant demonstrations led by Mrs. Emmeline Pankhurst in England.

The Misses Paul and Burns have come to the forefront of a movement that has had such leaders as Mrs. Lucretia Mott of Philadelphia, a Quaker matron; the fiery Susan B. Anthony, and Elizabeth Cady Stanton, a fine orator who was editor of *Revolution*, the militant woman's rights magazin. Mrs. Mott and Mrs. Stanton organized the landmark convention that first attracted attention to the women's rights cause in 1848. It was held at Seneca Falls, New York. Since then, victories for the movement have been few and far between. Nine states and territories have given women the right to vote. They are: Wyoming, 1838; Colorado, 1893; Idaho and Utah, 1896; Washington, 1910; California, 1911, and Arizona, Kansas and Oregon, 1912 (→ Oct. 15).

Making its debut this year: the Buffalo nickel, with an Indian head.

467 dead as floods hit in Ohio, Indiana

Dayton, Ohio, March 26

The Ohio River continued its rampage today in one of the worst floods in U.S. history. Latest reports on the five-day flood list 467 dead, 200,000 homeless and $180 million in damage. Ohio and Indiana have been devastated, with Dayton hit the hardest. Half the city is under 20 feet of water as people on roofs try to escape by sliding along telegraph lines. Houses floating away are a common sight. The National Guard has been called in and guard commanders have angrily denounced published reports that guardsmen are executing looters.

Georgia girl's death stirs anti-Semitism

Atlanta, Georgia, Aug. 26

As crowds outside the courtroom chanted "Kill the Jew," Leo Frank was sentenced to death today in the murder of Mary Phagan, a 13-year-old pencil factory worker. Frank was manager of the factory where the girl's battered body was found on April 27. She had gone to the factory on a weekend to get $1.20 due her for a day's work. Frank, who was from New York, had been president of Atlanta's B'nai B'rith, a Jewish fraternal organization. Jewish leaders say that anti-Semitism influenced the verdict.

Helen Keller urges suffrage, socialism

Philadelphia, May 5

Speaking through sign language today, Miss Helen Keller told reporters, "I am a militant suffragette because I believe suffrage will lead to socialism, and to me socialism is the real cause." An active member of the Socialist Party, Miss Keller has alienated a few Americans by her political statements, but everyone respects her accomplishments. Born healthy in 1880, she developed a fever at 19 months of age that left her deaf and blind. She has written a book, knows five languages and was graduated from Radcliffe College cum laude. ▷

Rockefeller sets up a fund for world aid

New York City, May 14

With the idea of promoting "the well-being of mankind throughout the world," John D. Rockefeller has initiated a foundation. The industrialist, oil businessman and philanthropist has set up a fund in New York to distribute his money on a worldwide basis. Among the areas Rockefeller and his foundation are concerned with are hunger, health care, education, resolution of international conflicts and cultural development. The name of Rockefeller, who was born in 1839, is now synonymous with Standard Oil and the petroleum industry in general. Though he has been a philanthropist most of his life, this is his first international effort.

Ladies' first flights

Los Angeles, June 21

In 1906, Mrs. Mary Miller was the first woman to be a passenger in an airship. In 1910, Mrs. Blanche Stuart Scott was the first woman to make a public solo flight. In 1911, Miss Harriet Quimby became the first woman to pass the admittance test of the Aeronautics Club of America. And today Miss Georgia "Tiny" Broadwick, 18, is the first woman to make a parachute jump. How time leaps and flies!

Ford assembly line open

On the assembly line: dropping the Ford engine into the Model T chassis.

Detroit, Michigan

"Time loves to be wasted," Henry Ford has philosophized. But on the new moving assembly lines of the Ford Motor Company, the "Speed-Up King" of the American autobile industry does not intend to give it much chance.

The Ford plant has been moving toward increased worker specialization over the years, but with the assembly line, this concept takes a great leap forward. Starting last spring, Ford and production manager Charles Sorensen devised a system to pull magneto coil frames past workers by rope, as they added parts along the way. It slashed the time of building a magneto from 20 minutes to 13. By summer, the entire Model T chassis was pulled by a windlass past workers along a 250-foot stretch of the factory. The process has reduced car assembly time from 13 hours to six.

Already the innovation is reaping dividends. Model T sales more than doubled this year, to 182,809, while the price dropped to just $440. Exclaimed Ford: "Every time I reduce the charge for our car by $1, I get 1,000 new buyers."

Election of senators by direct vote set

Washington, D.C., May 31

The Millionaires' Club, as its critics have long called the Senate, may well be getting some less affluent but more responsive members, thanks to the 17th Amendment, which was ratified today. Instead of being elected by the state legislatures, where vested interests are often well entrenched, from now on senators will have to put themselves before the voting citizens for direct election. The new legislation is a victory for reformers who are also pushing for introduction of such measures as the referendum, initiative, recall, presidential preferential primaries, the Australian, or secret, ballot and, of course, votes for women.

Cather's Nebraska

United States

"O you daughters of the West!" cried Walt Whitman in "Pioneers! O Pioneers!" He would have approved of one such daughter, the flinty heroine of Willa Cather's second novel, *O Pioneers!* Alexandra Bergson is the favorite child of a hard-working immigrant sodbuster. He passes the torch to Alexandra, who skillfully runs the family farm. Her personal life yields stingier harvests, especially when tragedy overtakes her beloved brother, but this daughter of the West meets the challenge. So does Cather, a published poet whose lyric gift ennobles her song of the Plains.

Woolworth Building now world's tallest

Four years and $13.5 million later.

New York City, Apr. 24, 1913

With the flick of a switch in Washington tonight, President Wilson lit up the Woolworth Building here as it claimed the title of the tallest building in the world. Designed by the architect Cass Gilbert, the Gothic skyscraper soars 55 stories, its concrete-and-steel structure rising 792 feet above Park Place in the City Hall area. At a cost of $13.5 million, the building was financed entirely by Frank W. Woolworth, the son of a poor farmer from Watertown, New York. Beginning as a country store clerk, he put together a national chain of five-and-ten-cent stores. "The business from which this building has grown began with a five-cent piece," Woolworth said tonight.

Suffragist showing her maternal side

Rockville Centre, L.I., Oct. 15

Mrs. Wilmer Kearns, a suffragist, announced today her plans to coordinate a series of baby shows to be held in various cities of Long Island. She said she hoped to have the approval and assistance of ministers and physicians in the communities, as the shows are to be of benefit to the babies; she reasons that mothers entering their children in the contests would naturally want them to have the glow of good health, and therefore would give them good food and care. Mrs. Kearns says she ardently hopes that her effort will help "overcome the notion that suffragists are not good mothers" (→ Sept. 8, 1916).

It is safe as well as convenient.

De Mille produces film in Hollywood barn

De Mille's rival D.W. Griffith has also made a film about an Indian.

Hollywood, California

Sent to Flagstaff to film *The Squaw Man*, Cecil B. De Mille took one look at the Arizona flatlands and went on to luxuriant California. For $75 a month, he rented a barn where he recorded the simple story of an Indian maiden who saves the life of an English aristocrat, bears his child and commits suicide.

De Mille's real-life adventures were more exciting. He was shot at twice. His first negative was sabotaged. He slept in the Vine Street barn, with the owner's horses, to protect the duplicate copy. The six-reel epic, budgeted for $15,450, ultimately cost $47,000. Its first showing was a disaster; the film was wrongly perforated. After corrective surgery in New York, the first full-scale Hollywood film was a hit.

Federal Reserve created

Washington, D.C., Dec. 23

Bowing to the President's threat to keep them in session through the Christmas season, Congress has ended debate and voted to pass the Federal Reserve Bank Act. The new measure, drafted by Representative Carter Glass of Virginia, provides a major restructuring of the nation's monetary and banking system.

Under the act, the country is to be divided into 12 districts, each with its own Federal Reserve bank. These banks are privately owned corporations and are authorized to issue banknotes backed by commercial paper. They will not deal with the public but will be the central banks for each district – "bankers' banks." The system is to be overseen by a Federal Reserve Board of seven members, each appointed by the President for 14 years. All national banks are required to join the system, and state banks may also join if they qualify.

An important feature of the new system is the power given to the Federal Reserve Board to control the supply of money and credit by raising or lowering the rediscount rate. It is hoped that this will both reduce the power of the Wall Street "money trust" and prevent any repetition of the financial panic of six years ago.

A radical change in the nation's banking system has long been a high priority for reform-minded Democrats, and has been pushed hard by President Wilson as part of his attack on the privileged.

Hop ranch workers strike in California

Wheatland, California

On the Durst hop ranch near Wheatland, some 2,800 workers live in unspeakable filth and discomforts, earning 78 cents to $1 a day. An Industrial Workers of the World local formed by about 30 men is demanding improved working and sanitary conditions as well as $1.24 per 100 hops, used to flavor beer. An attempted arrest of the I.W.W. leader Blackie Ford on August 3 led to a riot in which four people were killed and many hurt. Some workers have fled, while others continue a perilous but spreading strike.

New law reduces tariffs and implements graduated income tax

Washington, D.C., Oct. 3

After six months of debate and intensive behind-the-scenes campaigning by lobbyists acting on behalf of special interests, the Senate finally voted to pass the Underwood Tariff Bill today. The measure, which provides the first major reduction of tariffs since the Civil War, cuts rates on 958 items and puts more than 100 – including steel rails and raw wool – on the free list. Rates on a few luxury items have been raised, but the overall effect is to cut tariffs from an average of 41 percent to 27 percent.

To replace lost revenue, the law calls for a graduated tax on personal income, beginning at $3,000 for single people and $4,000 for married couples (→ Jan. 24, 1916).

Wilson threatens to bar aid and sympathy for Mexican dictator

Washington, D.C., Nov. 24

President Wilson informed Mexican President Victoriano Huerta today that the United States will not give either economic aid or sympathy to his regime. In fact, Wilson said, he will take any diplomatic action that is necessary to end the generalissimo's reign. Huerta, who has been described as a sadist, alcoholic and drug addict, had Francisco Madero, the father of the Mexican Revolution, murdered in February and seized the presidency. Meanwhile, the dictator is facing a rising tide of rebellion that is spreading throughout Mexico. The rebels are led in the south by Emiliano Zapata and in the north by Francisco "Pancho" Villa (→ July 15, 1914).

Alien rights curbed

California, Apr. 19

Anti-Japanese feeling in California persists and has led the legislature, over President Wilson's protest, to adopt the Webb Act, or Alien Land Law, which forbids aliens ineligible for citizenship to own farmland in the state or to lease such land for more than three years. Ostensibly, the measure applies to all aliens, but, in practical application, it is directed at the Japanese (two percent of the state's population). The national authorities fear that this measure will jeopardize cordial relations with Japan.

Equipped with high-speed automobiles and captured federalist artillery, Mexican rebels achieve striking victories.

1914

Wilson

Copperfield, Oregon, Jan. 1. In Copperfield affair, Governor Oswald West sends his secretary to administer this railroad boom town; she declares martial law and shuts all saloons within 80 minutes.

Washington, D.C., Jan. 13. Court decides litigation over airplane-balancing patent in favor of Wright brothers against Glenn Curtiss.

Wisconsin, Jan. 20. Circuit Court declares Wisconsin's marriage law, based on eugenic principles, unconstitutional.

New York City, Feb. 13. To improve copyright laws and protect members against infringements, American Society of Composers, Authors, and Publishers (ASCAP) organized.

New York City, March. First issue of Margaret Sanger's *The Woman Rebel* is sent to 2,000 subscribers (→ Oct. 20).

Washington, D.C., May 8. Congress passes Smith-Lever Act, providing federal aid for agricultural extension programs created by land-grant colleges and Agriculture Department, formalizing cooperative farm production.

New York City, May 22. Mother Jones declares, "Never mind if you are not ladylike, you are womanlike."

New York City, July 31. As news of London Stock Exchange's closing reaches New York, most of world's exchanges follow suit, including Wall Street, because of war (→ Aug. 19).

Boston, Oct. 13. Boston Braves sweep World Series against Philadelphia Athletics, 4 to 0.

United States, December. National Security League, to upgrade national defense, founded (→ 1915).

Detroit. Cadillac develops V-8 automobile engine.

United States. Poet Robert Frost publishes his first book of poems, *North of Boston.*

United States. *The New Republic* magazine founded by Herbert Croly.

DEATHS

Barre, Massachusetts, May 26. Jacob Riis, photographer and reformer (*May 3, 1849).

Los Angeles, California, Dec. 24. John Muir, explorer and naturalist (*Apr. 21, 1838).

To sell cars to the common man, Ford offers workers $5 a day

Detroit, Jan. 5

In a move that stunned rival automakers, Henry Ford today doubled the minimum wage of his workers, to an unprecedented $5 per day. The pay raise was announced by Ford's treasurer, James Couzens, along with a plan to share $10 million from last year's profits and the addition of an extra work shift. Instead of its two nine-hour shifts, the company's Highland Park factory will operate around the clock, with three eight-hour shifts.

Referring to profits of over $37 million last year, Couzens said, "We want those who have helped us to produce this great institution to share our prosperity." Ford is also said to believe that by pioneering higher wages for workers, he will help to create a vast new market for his own product, the ubiquitous Model T car.

Tonight, the Ford factory was so besieged with job applicants that the police had to disperse crowds with firehoses. While Ford is being called everything from a socialist to a spendthrift, some see the wage hike as a shrewd move to quell unrest and labor turnover among 26,000 workers who feel increasingly dehumanized by Ford's monotonous assembly line.

In 1909, a friend warned Ford that if everybody had a car, all the horses would be frightened. But Ford replied: "I'm not creating a problem at all. I am democratizing the automobile. The horses will disappear from our highways."

Florida gets first commercial airline

St. Petersburg, Fla., Spring

Those who have not yet booked passage on the St. Petersburg-Tampa Airboat Line need no longer apply. The three-month-old airline has quietly stopped the run. Started by Tony Jannus on January 1, it was the first regularly scheduled commercial airline between cities in America. Jannus is a pilot who got the idea of ferrying passengers on the 46-mile roundtrip between Tampa and St. Petersburg in a pair of flying boats. The pilot's idea quickly caught on with the tourist crowd and the Jannus business thrived. Soon he was winging his way over Tampa Bay with his plane full of wealthy thrill-seekers. But with the tourist season finished, Jannus is grounded – that is at least until next year, anyway.

A day is set aside to honor mothers

Washington, D.C., May 9

Was President Wilson thinking of his love for his mother today? He must have been, signing a joint resolution of Congress recommending that the executive departments of government recognize Mother's Day as an annual holiday. Congress proposes that the day be celebrated on the second Sunday in the month of May; this comes at the request of Miss Anna Jarvis, who wishes to honor the memory of her own mother, Mrs. Anna Reeves Jarvis, who died May 10, 1905. Miss Jarvis got the ball rolling when she petitioned Congress to create the holiday after marking her mother's passing yearly by wearing a white carnation and organizing special prayer sessions at Andrews Methodist Episcopal Church in her hometown of Grafton, West Virginia.

Tarzan of the Apes swings in America

California

Every youngster imagines his true parents are exotic strangers. And the hero of Edgar Rice Burroughs's *Tarzan of the Apes* shares this fantasy – with two big differences. First, the couple who raise him are hardly your ordinary Mom and Pop. In fact, they're apes, Kala and Tublat, who live in darkest Africa. Second, their son, Tarzan, though he thumps on his chest and swings on vines just like the other apes, isn't dreaming when he guesses he descends from different stock. His biological pater and mater – Sir John Greystoke and the Hon. Alice Rutherford – hardly envisioned a son who would wrestle gorillas. But then, who would have guessed a former light-bulb vendor and door-to-door book salesman would write a best-seller at the age of 39?

18 die in massacre at the Ludlow mine

Ludlow, Colorado, Apr. 20

National Guardsmen and security forces employed by the Colorado Fuel and Iron Company set fire to the tents occupied by striking mine workers today. When the tents went up in flames and the survivors fled, they were shot down by the guardsmen and security agents employed by the Rockfeller-owned mining company. Casualties resulting from the blaze and the subsequent shoot-out at the camp were three men, two women and 13 children.

Labor officials say the killing of the striking workers and their families by the guardsmen and hired guns was an act of cold-blooded murder. Company officials and National Guard spokesmen retort that they were simply trying to restore law and order in a situation that bordered on anarchy. They insist that if they hadn't acted, even more lives would have been lost. Residents say that this atmosphere of violence shows no signs of diminishing in the near future.

Unionism crushed in Butte mine fight

Butte, Montana, Nov. 13

Organized labor, a house divided in the copper region, has fallen after standing tall for 36 years in Butte. The state militia is gone today. But its two-and-a-half-month stay allowed mine officials to withdraw recognition from two competing unions and depose the town's Socialist mayor and sheriff.

The Western Federation of Miners local began to crumble in March of 1912 when it failed to challenge Anaconda Copper's firing of several hundred Socialist miners. In June of this year, 4,000 insurgents finally split with the miners federation, accusing it of stuffing ballot boxes and packing meeting halls with company men. The rebels blew up the old union hall and chased union president Charles Moyer out of town. But he met with Governor Stewart, and troops arrived soon after. Moyer insists he did not urge armed intervention. But the federation's leadership has shown its frontier activism is far from revolutionary.

U.S. troops depose Huerta in Mexico

Washington, D.C., July 15

Following a serio-comic invasion and much bizarre diplomacy, the United States finally suceeded in ridding Mexico – and itself – of Mexican President Victoriano Huerta. Five days ago, the Huerta forces in the federal garrison at Mexico City surrendered to the Constitutionalist General Alvaro Obregon, and Huerta capitulated. But most observers believe that the real reason for the downfall of "The Butcher" lies in the military efforts of the U.S. Navy and Marines.

After having failed to persuade Huerta to resign, President Wilson lifted the arms embargo on Mexico last February and all but gave his support to General Obregon, Huerta's rival in the Mexican Revolution. When that ploy didn't seem to topple Huerta quickly enough, Wilson decided that a military pretext would be found to hasten the Mexican's ouster. He found it in Vera Cruz. A motor whaleboat from the American warship Dolphin landed at this southern Mexican port on April 10. Its American crew was promptly arrested. Huerta's local commandant soon apologized for the inconvenience to the Americans, but Admiral Henry T. Mayo, with Wilson's enthusiastic backing, spurned the apology. A week later, Mayo told the Huerta forces they must either salute the American flag or face "the consequences." When the Mexicans did not respond, American sailors and marines swarmed ashore and took the city. American losses were listed as 19 killed and 71 wounded, while the Mexican toll was put at 126 killed and 195 wounded.

While Huerta's forces were being thrashed, he was threatening to invade Texas, to arm American Negroes and to attack Washington. Nothing came of his threats. In the meantime, the counterrevolutionary forces under Alvaro Obregon and Emiliano Zapata were scoring one success after another.

So finally, Huerta is deposed. But as one London editor said, "If war is to be made . . . by admirals and generals and if the government of the United States is to set the example for this return to medieval conditions, it will be a bad day for civilization" (→June 21, 1916).

The United States raises the flag and asserts its will in Vera Cruz, Mexico.

Mexican mountain guerrillas try but fail to defeat a superior American force.

U.S. sailors man an artillery piece in Vera Cruz, and use it with deadly effect. ▷

President Wilson pledges neutrality as war spreads in Europe

Determined to keep us out of war.

Washington, D.C., Aug. 19

In response to the growing European war, President Wilson today reiterated his statement of August 4 that the United States is taking a neutral stance. Citing the Declaration of London of 1901, the President said that the open seas are neutral territory and that, as a maritime nation, the United States will maintain its position and will not take sides in the European dispute. In a memorandum issued today, Wilson called on the American people "to be neutral in fact as well as in name . . . impartial in thought as well as in deed."

Since the assassination of the Austrian Archduke Ferdinand on July 28, pressure has been put on Wilson to support either the Central Powers – Germany and Austria – or the Allies – England, France and Russia. Pressure has also been put on the American people; since the day last month that proved so fateful, Americans of every European ethnic background have been urged to give support to the lands of their forefathers. Many influential newspapers, including *The New York Times*, have branded the Germans the aggressor and have demanded an American declaration of war against them. Other media giants have put the blame for the war on the Allied Powers.

The truth is that Wilson and the American people have been buffeted by the propaganda efforts of both sides. Those opposed to Germany say the war was caused by German imperialism and that Berlin's actions made the war inevitable. There have been reports that the Germans have committed atrocities during their invasion of Belgium (although American war correspondents serving with the German army say the reports are not true). At the same time, those of an anti-French-British-Russian persuasion argue that American interests will not be served by Anglo-French control of the postwar world economy. Wilson will have a tough time persuading most Americans that they should be neutral "in thought as well in deed," considering the Germans' violation of Belgian neutrality and their defiance of the moral conscience of the world (→Jan. 28, 1915).

Belgians attempt to repel the overwhelming might of the advancing Germans.

"Death" (1914) by Charles C. Buck. A face now well known.

1,500 women call for peace in Europe

New York City, Aug. 29

Some were dressed in white with black arm bands; others were clad in the darkest mourning. The 1,500 women who marched down Fifth Avenue this afternoon were there to call for peace in Europe, but they appeared to hold out little hope. The large crowds watching their progress from 58th Street to Union Square were solemnly respectful. The writer and lecturer Mrs. Charlotte Perkins Gilman was among the marchers, who carried white flags embroidered with the image of a dove and the word "Peace" in gold letters.

German-Americans divided in loyalties

Washington, D.C., Autumn

Ever since the outbreak of hostilities between the Central Powers and the Allies, German-Americans have faced a peculiar and pressing identity problem. Do they support an admitted militaristic autocrat, or do they back the prime sources of American political and cultural liberalism? While many Germans are openly promoting the Kaiser's cause, others are urging intervention on the side of the Allied Powers. Some reports say the German-Americans are backing their native land in the war, but others indicate they are pro-British "all the way."

Birth control leader said to flee arrest

New York City, Oct. 20

Mrs. Margaret Sanger, advoca[te] of birth control, is said to be on [a] train bound for Montreal, fleein[g] trial for violating the Comstoc[k] Law. The 35-year-old Mrs. Sang[er] has written and distributed a new[s]paper called *The Woman Rebe[l]* which makes assertions such as "[a] woman's body belongs to herse[lf] alone." While this paper was co[n]fiscated by the Post Office, Mr[s.] Sanger was not indicted until sh[e] tried to distribute *Family Limita[tion]*, a pamphlet outlining the us[e] of sponges, diaphragms and othe[r] birth control devices. If she ha[d] stood trial, she might have been sen[]tenced to 45 years (→Oct. 16, 1916[)].

Raggedy Ann doll

United States, Dec. 14

When 8-year-old Marcella Gru[]elle sadly approached her fathe[r] with a faceless rag doll that sh[e] had found in the attic, he put hi[s] creativity to work. John Gruelle[,] a political cartoonist, wanted t[o] please his terminally ill daughter[,] so he drew a face on the doll. The[n] his wife restuffed it and put a heart[-]shaped piece of candy with th[e] words "I love you" on its chest[.] The result is a cheery, soft, warm rag doll with a mop of red hair. Th[e] family has named the shabby bu[t] lovable doll Raggedy Ann.

Penrod has a knack for finding trouble

Indiana

It's not easy being 12 years ol[d] and at the mercy of cruel tyrant[s] such as parents and teachers. Bu[t] Penrod Schofield, the adolescen[t] hero of Booth Tarkington's lates[t] novel, isn't going down without [a] fight. Penrod is a city cousin t[o] another Midwesterner, Tom Saw[]yer. Like Tom, Penrod has an over[]active imagination that lands him i[n] some comical scrapes. And, lik[e] Tom, Penrod speaks for boys across the land, as his Indiana-born cre[]ator seems more at home in Amer[]ica than in England, where hi[s] "Monsieur Beaucaire" was set.

Canal open to commerce

The task completed, the Ancon officially inaugurates the Panama Canal.

Panama, Aug. 15

One of the greatest engineering feats in history was officially completed today with the opening of the Panama Canal. To mark the occasion, a shipload of officials on board the Ancon made the 40-mile journey from the Atlantic to the Pacific – a shortcut that will lessen the voyage between the west and east coasts of North America by some 7,000 miles.

Construction, begun in 1904, has required moving an estimated 240 million cubic yards of earth by a labor force that at times reached 40,000. Total costs so far have come to $366 million. Much of the credit for the successful management of the project must go to General George W. Goethals, who was appointed chief engineer by President Roosevelt in 1907.

Yellow fever and malaria took a heavy toll until they were brought under control by Gen. William Gorgas, chief sanitary engineer. Thanks to him, the death rate was cut from 39 per 1,000 in 1906 to 7 per 1,000 now. Even so, 6,000 workers died during the 10 years it took to build the canal (→ Feb. 20, 1915).

L.A. hates and loves the movie business

Los Angeles

Local residents find the growing number of movie people something of a bother; signs outside boarding houses proclaim: "No dogs, no actors." Young, tough movie makers, often disrespectful of private property, shoot in the streets, drawing in passers-by as needed. Still, the value of this new industry is inestimable. Since distribution of *The Squaw Man* early this year by the new Paramount company, the most notable new releases are: *Tillie's Punctured Romance* from Keystone, featuring Marie Dressler, "Fatty" Arbuckle, Charlie Chaplin and Mabel Normand; the serial *The Perils of Pauline*, starring Pearl White; Selig Company's *The Spoilers*, and D.W. Griffith's four-reel historic spectacle, *Judith of Bethulia*. Westerns are quite popular, and it seems that Bronco Billy Anderson may expect competition from William S. Hart at Ince's.

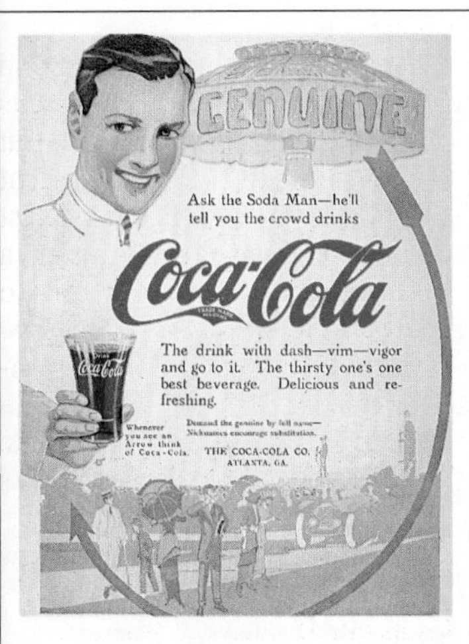

Clayton Act aids labor

Washington, D.C., Oct. 15

A major victory for labor was won today with the passage, after long and often bitter debate, of the Clayton Antitrust Act, a law that strengthens and clarifies the Sherman Antitrust Act of 1890.

Much of the act is concerned with outlawing such restrictive practices as price-cutting to force out competitors, interlocking directorates in large companies in the same line of business, intercorporate stockholdings, unfair rebates and contracts that prohibit the buyer from doing business with the seller's competitors. It also makes corporate officers personally responsible for antitrust violations.

But what has caused the unionist Samuel Gompers to hail the act as "the Magna Charta of American labor" are the provisions that exclude unions and agricultural cooperatives from laws against combinations in restraint of trade. This will prevent a repetition of the Danbury Hatters' Case of six years ago, when the High Court ruled against a union that had organized a nationwide boycott of a non-union manufacturer's products, and held the union liable for triple damages that amounted to a ruinous $250,000.

The act also limits the use of court injunctions against labor, except when there is a threat of "irreparable damage" to property, and legalizes peaceful boycotts, strikes and picketing (→ Jan. 3, 1921).

F.T.C. will enforce fair business practices

Washington, D.C., Sept. 26

Yet another reform measure that will use the power of the government to protect the interests of ordinary people was enacted today with passage of the Federal Trade Commission Act. The law replaces the Bureau of Corporations established by President Roosevelt and transfers its functions to a more powerful regulatory agency with broad powers to decide what business practices are unfair.

Abuses such as price-fixing, misleading advertising, false labeling, unfair competition and adulteration of products are expected to be among its targets. If the agency determines that a business is guilty of an unfair practice, it may issue a "cease and desist" order; if the order is violated, the offender may be punished by the courts. The courts may also, upon appeal, set aside an adverse finding.

The commission is to be made up of five members appointed by the president, subject to Senate confirmation, for seven-year terms. To ensure bipartisanship, no more than three members may belong to the same political party.

"Carolina Cotton Mill" (1908). For the last eight years, Lewis Hine has documented the shameful practice for the National Child Labor Committee.

1915

Wilson

Washington, D.C., Jan. 25. Supreme Court rules, in Coppage v. Kansas, that states do not have right to forbid employers from hiring because of union membership.

Washington, D.C., Jan. 28. President Wilson vetoes bill requiring immigrants to pass literacy test (→Feb. 5, 1917).

San Francisco, Feb. 20. San Francisco Panama-Pacific International Exposition, held to mark opening of Panama Canal, ends; 13 million attended.

Washington, D.C., May 1. German Embassy warns that Americans who travel into war zone around British Isles do so at their own risk.

Berlin, Germany, June 6. German government orders U-boat commanders not to sink passenger liners without warning, even those under enemy flags (→9).

Chicago, June 24. Steamer Eastland explodes and capsizes in Chicago River, killing more than 800 people.

Yellowstone National Park, July 31. Dr. and Mrs. Kingman Seiler's Model T Ford is first tourist car admitted into park.

Washington, D.C., September. President Wilson agrees to reverse his policy of resisting American loans to European belligerents (→Nov. 17).

Boston, Oct. 13. Boston Red Sox buy pitcher Babe Ruth's contract from Baltimore Orioles and put him in starting rotation; Red Sox beat Philadelphia, four games to one, in World Series.

New York City, Oct. 15. J.P. Morgan & Co. leads banking group in arranging $500 million loan to British and French governments.

Wilmington, Delaware, Nov. 30. An explosion rocks Du Pont munitions plant; sabotage is suspected.

Detroit, Mich., Dec. 10. Ford Motor Company produces one millionth automobile.

United States. *America's Coming of Age* by Van Wyck Brooks published.

DEATH

Tuskegee, Alabama, Nov. 14. Booker T. Washington, Negro leader and founder of Tuskegee Institute (*Apr. 5, 1856).

Comic masterpiece: Chaplin as "Tramp"

Charlie Chaplin's character, the Tramp, draws laughter, tears and applause.

Hollywood, California

America has fallen in love with an invincible vagabond with soulful eyes and a funny walk: "The Tramp," as created and portrayed by Charlie Chaplin. The son of music hall entertainers in London but soon fatherless and with a mother suffering a nervous breakdown, he and his brother were hungry street urchins, dancing on street corners and passing the hat for pennies until placed in an orphanage for destitute children. At 8, Charlie became a professional performer and at 17 joined a touring vaudeville company that came to the United States in 1910 and again in 1912.

Mack Sennett happened to see a performance, and in December 1913, Chaplin joined Keystone. His first film was *Making a Living*. Borrowing some clothes from "Fatty" Arbuckle, Chaplin began to develop a character in a bowler hat and baggy trousers, with a comic mustache and a cane. The Keystone Kops' roughhouse routines did not quite suit Chaplin's music hall comedy style, strongly based on pantomime. Having made 11 one- and two-reel films in three months, he began directing his own.

Now the 26-year-old Chaplin is making a new picture almost every week, and a trade paper proclaims him "the sensation of the year." Exhibitors find that they have only to put his picture on the sidewalk along with a sign, "He's here!" and they will enjoy sold-out houses.

Having just signed with Essanay for a staggering $1,250 a week (as compared to $175 a week at Keystone), Chaplin says he will make fewer films with increasing quality. He will write his own scripts about this shabby but fastidious little man, lonely and whimsical, with exquisite manners and a spirit that cannot be destroyed, just as in his new release, "The Tramp."

"Birth of Nation" condones the Klan

Hollywood, California

A "flagrant incitement to racial antagonism" or an epic? Both and more are said about D.W. Griffith's remarkable *Birth of a Nation*, the most expensive and longest film ever made, starring Lillian Gish, Mae Marsh, Robert Harron, Wallace Reid, Henry B. Walthall and Miriam Cooper. Controversy surrounded its March 3 premiere in New York and the National Association for the Advancement of Colored People has tried to bar the film, which is based on Thomas Dixon Jr.'s 1905 novel *The Clansman*, charging that it shows a distorted view of Negro history. In his passion to illustrate the Southern view of the Civil War and Reconstruction, Griffith has unwittingly sparked race riots and encouraged the revival of the Ku Klux Klan.

As a movie, *Birth of a Nation* has received critical acclaim. President Wilson calls it "writing history with lightning." The masterful Griffith, who began his film career as an actor and scenario writer in 1908 with the Biograph Company, has freed the movie screen from the restrictive methods of the stage. He moves the camera about, obtaining close-ups, distant views, fade-ins, fade-outs, angle shots and flashbacks. He rehearses scenes before shooting and takes great pains with lighting effects. Some call him "the poor man's Shakespeare," and many say the film is a landmark in cinema history as motion pictures will now be regarded as an art form.

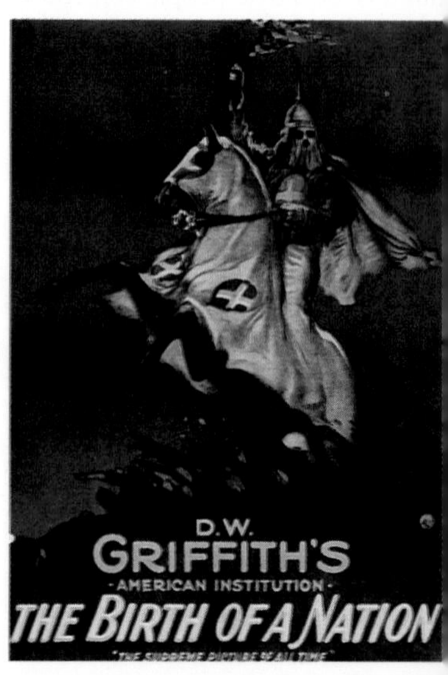

Coast Guard formed to protect shores

Washington, D.C., Jan. 28

The government announced today that a Coast Guard is being created and will be placed on duty "as soon as possible." The new service will be outwardly organized along traditional United States Navy lines. Its men will wear uniforms virtually identical with those of their navy counterparts and the system of ratings and ranks are also to be the same. But there the similarity ends. Not a "blue water" force, it will have the responsibility of protecting American coastal cities and waters from hostile attack. It will also be authorized to stop, search and arrest suspected smugglers and other unlawful intruders in American waters. The new service is to be placed under the peacetime command of the Treasury Department. During war, it will augment the navy (→ May 7).

U.S. "melting pot" isn't THAT melted

Washington, D.C., Apr. 19

"There is here a great melting pot," President Woodrow Wilson declared today, "in which we must compound a precious metal. That metal is the metal of nationality."

Wilson's metaphor comes from *The Melting Pot,* a 1908 play by Israel Zangwill. The newest contents of his "pot" come from Southern and Eastern Europe at a rate of one million a year. Its children, who fill a quarter of the nation's elementary schools, are soon singing of purple mountains' majesty. But many refuse to "melt." In 1913, 538 newspapers appeared in 29 foreign languages. New York Czechs meet in a five-story National Hall. And the Polish National Alliance has 800 branches. As reformer Emily Greene Balch says, "To many an immigrant the idea of nationality first becomes real after he has left his native country." So for many Americans, beset by war fever, "America first" is now a password for xenophobia. Thus the lyrics of the popular song *Don't Bite the Hand That's Feeding You:* "If you don't like your Uncle Sammy, then go back to your home over the sea."

America irate over Lusitania sinking

As the Lusitania falls prey to a German U-boat, Americans question how long they can maintain their neutrality.

Washington, D.C., May 7

The Lusitania has been sunk. Incomplete reports received today indicate that the great British Cunard liner, the largest passenger ship in the world, was torpedoed off the coaast of Ireland by a German submarine. Of the 1,800 passengers aboard, 1,200 were said to have drowned. The casualty toll is reported to include at least 128 American citizens. Reaction here in the capital ranged from shock to anger to sadness. When the news reached New York earlier today, commuters at the Hanover Station on Third Avenue Elevated began singing *In the Sweet Bye-and-Bye* as the hurdy-gurdy played the traditional lament. Not at all in a sentimental mood, former President Roosevelt, who has long advocated intervention by the United States on the side of the Allies, bluntly described the vessel's sinking as an act of "piracy" and international "murder."

Now everyone is asking one question: What will President Wilson's response be to this grave incident? Ever since the submarine issue and the question of American neutral rights came up earlier this year, the President has tried to maintain a strict but traditional interpretation and observance of international and maritime law regarding non-warring nations. This is, Wilson argues, that American and other neutral ships have the right of unhindered passage on the high seas. On February 10, the President told the German government that he would hold it to "strict accountability" if any American ships were lost to its submarines. But he didn't say what his position would be if American passengers on neutral or belligerent vessels were killed.

The Germans have attacked two American vessels this year and two lives were lost. Two British ships carrying American citizens have also been sunk by the Germans, with two more Americans killed. The German government apologized for both of those incidents.

The Lusitania sinking is greatly heightening tensions between Germany and the United States. It is apparent that the Kaiser's government has upped the ante in its attempt to strangle Britain's trade by means of the submarine blockade, even if this policy means killing neutral American citizens on ships of the Allies.

Most naval experts believe that the torpedoing of the Lusitania was planned in advance. Last week, the German government published a formal warning to American citizens against traveling on belligerent passenger ships. One of the ships mentioned in that warning was the Lusitania. Because the Lusitania was carrying tons of war materiel, including a reported 4,200 cases of rifle cartridges, perhaps the German government felt justified in its extreme action.

This drastic measure, however, is certain to poison relations between Germany and the United States, perhaps fatally. In the meantime, President Wilson and Secretary of State William Jennings Bryan are reportedly drafting a firm diplomatic letter of response to the German government (→ June 6).

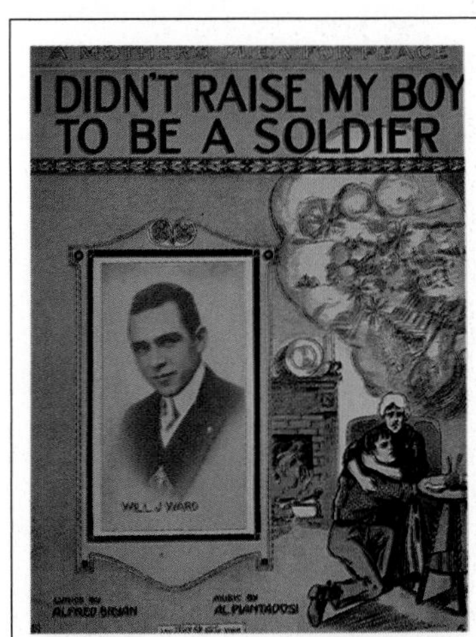

With war overseas threatening the United States, a song captures the feelings of every American mother.

Bryan quits Cabinet over U.S. war stance

"The Great Commoner" stands firm.

Washington, D.C., June 9

Secretary of State William Jennings Bryan submitted his resignation to President Wilson today. Citing irreconcilable philosophical differences with Wilson's increasingly aggressive stance toward Germany in the wake of the Lusitania sinking, Bryan said he had always advocated a pacifist, neutral position in the war and would continue to do so. The "Great Commoner" from Nebraska and former presidential candidate is expected to be succeeded as secretary by Robert Lansing, an expert in international law who shares the President's views on foreign policy (→ Sept.).

United States up in arms over naval war

Washington, D.C., Nov. 17

The Acona, an Italian merchant ship with at least 27 American passengers aboard, was sunk today and the United States is outraged. Since March, three major U-boat attacks on the high seas have convinced the United States that the Germans are a growing enemy – and one that means business. The worst affront occurred in May, when the liner Lusitania was sunk by U-boats. After that sinking, the German Ambassador, Count Johann Heinrich von Bernstorff, offered "condolences." And in response, President Wilson said that while "there is no such thing as a man being too proud to fight, there is such a thing as a nation being so right that it does not need to convince others by force that it is right."

Meanwhile, many people agree with the President's policy. Others are questioning his patience. Since the attack on the Lusitania, German U-boat commanders have been ordered to sink without warning all vessels that approach England. The Leelanaw was sunk off the coast of Scotland; the Arabic was sunk in the Atlantic. After months of what has developed into an undeclared naval war, German policy seems firm – and American resolve unsure (→ June 3, 1916).

Great White Hope wins in Havana

Havana, Cuba, Apr. 5

Jess Willard emerged today as the "Great White Hope." The 250-pound Kansas cowboy finished off the Negro heavyweight champion, Jack Johnson, in the 26th round, but there were cries of "fake" from many in the crowd of 15,000 in the Cuban capital. The fight was held in Havana because Johnson had jumped bail from his conviction for transporting a woman across state lines for immoral purposes. Did Johnson lose because he was promised amnesty if he would do so? For 20 rounds, he pounded Willard almost at will. Then he seemed to weaken. Willard caught the exiled champion with a wild right under the heart in the 25th round and finished him off in the next round with a jarring right to the jaw.

Whitney's filly wins the Kentucky Derby

Louisville, Ky., May 8.

In her first start of the 1915 season, Regret raced to victory for Harry Payne Whitney against a strong field in the Kentucky Derby. For the first time in years, powerful Eastern stables were represented in the derby. The Whitney filly, which had no trouble scoring a wire-to-wire victory, almost didn't make it to the race. It came just a day after the Lusitania was sunk off Ireland and Whitney's brother-in-law was one of the 1,198 passengers lost. But Regret was kept in the derby and became the first filly ever to win it. The Eastern stables returned to the derby because bookmakers, once barred, were allowed back to the Churchill Downs track. Star Eastern horses lured to the big race included Pebbles, the runner-up.

High court voids grandfather clause

Washington, D.C., May 15

The "grandfather clause" was declared unconstitutional today by the Supreme Court, which said that it was racially discriminatory. The court struck down Oklahoma and Maryland legislation that incorporated the clause. The case before the court concerned an amendment to the Oklahoma constitution that exempted some people from the literacy test for voters. This amendment was intended to permit whites to vote while disenfranchising Negroes. Such amendments usually exempted from literacy tests those men entitled to vote before 1867 and their lineal descendants, hence "grandfather clause." The whites could meet those conditions; Negroes could not because their slave grandfathers could not vote.

German's rampage ends with suicide

New York City, July 21

In a bizarre finish to an already incredible tale of violence, the man who bombed the Capitol in Washington and shot industrialist J. Pierpont Morgan committed suicide tonight by hurling himself headfirst from the top of a jail door.

Erich Muenter, also known as Frank Holt, died instantly in the Nassau County Jail, where he had been held for the bombing and shooting. His rampage began Saturday when a bomb wrecked a room in the Senate wing of the Capitol. During the same weekend, he invaded Morgan's Long Island home and wounded the Morgan heir in an attempt to kidnap Mrs. Morgan and their children. Muenter, a German professor, said he wanted to stop Morgan from exporting munitions.

Overland
$615
Roadster $595

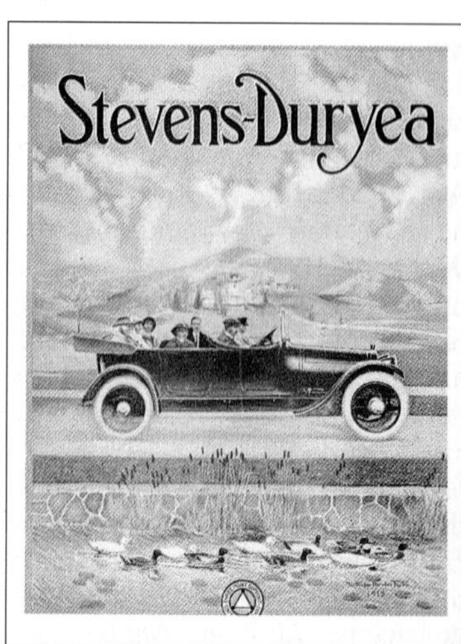

Marines in Haiti to impose order

Washington, D.C., Sept. 16

Seeking to regularize the presence of American troops in the Republic of Haiti, a treaty was signed today that in effect makes the country a protectorate of the United States. The troops will stay, to keep order and prevent any other country from interfering, and Washington will control finances, including customs. U.S. Marines landed in Port-au-Prince on July 28, a day after President Vilbrun Guillaume Sam was torn to pieces by a mob – the sixth president to meet a violent end in five years (→Aug. 6, 1934).

German sabotage plans are exposed

Washington, D.C., Dec. 1

As the result of a startling accidental discovery, the United States government has expelled two German military attaches, Captains Franz von Papen and Karl Boy-Ed. The German representatives were sent home after an attache case belonging to the Kaiser's propaganda minister was found purely by coincidence in a New York subway car. The briefcase contained detailed documentation on plans of the Germans to launch a series of sabotage strikes against American military installations.

Cobb rips up basepaths and record book

Detroit, Michigan, October

Ty Cobb, who has been scorching the basepaths for years, has become the greatest base-stealer in the history of the sport, with 96 thefts in a season. Cobb, who helped lead the Tigers to three pennants in a row starting in 1907, hit only .240 in 1905, his first year at Detroit. But he has not been under .300 since. The outfielder stole bases almost at will, turned singles into doubles and triples and even advanced two bases on a bunt. He has led the American League in hitting since 1907. His aggressive style on the bases – some call it dirty – intimidates the rival fielders.

Ty Cobb is not a nice guy. It's rumored he sharpens his spikes.

Just what can you get for a nickel?

Washington, D.C.

During a particularly tedious recent Senate debate, Vice President Thomas R. Marshall once more observed, "What this country really needs is a good five-cent cigar!" Usually, five cents goes a long way. For a nickel, you can see a Mack Sennett Keystone Kops short or buy a copy of *The Saturday Evening Post* or get a ride in a car from an enterprising owner of an automobile. Unfortunately, some folks don't have many nickels to spare. A third to a half of all laborers work up to seven days a week, 12 hours a day to earn $30 a month.

Wireless call spans the Atlantic Ocean

New York City, Oct. 21

This year has seen major advances in wireless communication around the world. Following a research push by American Telephone and Telegraph president Theodore Vail, a radiotelephone communication was sent out from Arlington, Virginia, today and was received at the Eiffel Tower in Paris. In January, the first transcontinental link was opened, with President Wilson in Washington, Alexander Graham Bell in New York, Thomas Watson in San Francisco and Vail at Jekyll Island, Georgia, taking part in a conversation.

40,000 in Chicago protest dry Sunday

Chicago, Nov. 7

Carrying signs such as "Some folks regard it a crime to be happy," a parade of 40,000 today registered displeasure at the state law closing saloons on Sunday. Under the aegis of United Societies for Local Self-Government, scores of ethnic organizations sported the colorful garb of their native lands, such as Lithuania, Bohemia, Croatia, Poland, Italy, Denmark, Austria and Hungary. Women also participated. Typical banners read "The Sabbath was made for man, not man for the Sabbath," and "Fanatical frenzy is the parent of the blue laws."

Joe Hill of I.W.W. is executed in Utah

Salt Lake City, Utah, Nov. 19

Joe Hill died today with all the world watching. For five years the Swedish-born minstrel of radicalism wrote songs for the Industrial Workers of the World. Though no witnesses identified him and no one can figure a motive, he was convicted of having slain a grocer. Despite Hill's objections, Wobbly president "Big Bill" Haywood turned his case into a cause celebre. President Wilson, besieged by pleas, sought to save Hill from execution, but to no avail. On Hill's last day alive, he resignedly wrote Haywood, "Don't waste time mourning. Organize!"

Atlantan resurrects the Ku Klux Klan

Atlanta, Georgia, Dec. 4

An Atlanta man today resurrected the defunct Ku Klux Klan, whose white-robed members once rode the Southern countryside, terrorizing freed blacks after the Civil War. William J. Simmons, a failed preacher and salesman, has incorporated the KKK as a "purely benevolent and eleemosynary" institution. But in a ceremony late last month outside Atlanta, he and a handful of supporters set up and burned a cross, symbol of the old night riders. The Klan's early history is outlined in the popular motion picture *Birth of a Nation*.

Edgar Lee Masters visits Spoon River

United States

Sometimes simple words speak the deepest truth. At least they do in *Spoon River Anthology*, by Edgar Lee Masters, a 46-year-old lawyer who has been publishing poetry since 1898. His new book takes the form of linked graveyard epitaphs that bare the sorrows and triumphs of fiddlers, philanderers and feisty old ladies – some 250 poems. Masters's burly free verse has spared him the fate of one of his forlorn souls, "Petit, The Poet," the local bard who penned "little iambics,/ While Homer and Whitman roared in the pines!"

Three new groups to prepare for war

United States

Most Americans still agree with the popular song *I Didn't Raise My Boy to Be a Soldier*. But militarism is gaining a growing constituency. The League to Enforce Peace, the American Defense Society and the American Rights Committee were each founded this year to promote preparation for war. According to Teddy Roosevelt, their most prominent advocate, "The man who believes in peace at any price ... should instantly move to China. If he stays here then more manly men will have to defend him, and he is not worth defending."

"Edith Wilson," as painted by Adolpho Muller-Ury. Marriage to the former Edith Galt brings Wilson peace in a troubled time.

1916

Wilson

United States, Jan. 17. Professional Golfers Association (P.G.A.) founded.

Washington, D.C., Jan. 24. Supreme Court rules, in Brushaber v. Union Pacific, that federal income tax is constitutional.

Washington, D.C., Jan. 28. Louis Brandeis is appointed to Supreme Court, becoming first Jewish associate justice.

Philadelphia, May 20. Norman Rockwell's first cover illustration for *Saturday Evening Post* appears.

Washington, June. William Boeing makes test flight in his first airplane (→July).

Washington, D.C., Aug. 29. Organic Act of Philippine Islands passed by Congress, reiterating American desire to give Philippines independence.

Washington, D.C., Aug. 29. Congress passes Army Appropriation Act, establishing Council of National Defense to coordinate national resources for defense.

Washington, D.C., Sept. 3. Adamson Act implemented, establishing eight-hour work day for all railway employees.

Boston, Oct. 12. Boston Red Sox top Brooklyn Dodgers, four games to one, in World Series; Babe Ruth hurls six-hit win.

Washington, D.C., Oct. 20. Congress allocates over $17 million to army to build 375 new airplanes.

Montana, Nov. 7. Jeannette Rankin becomes first woman elected to Congress.

Washington, D.C., Nov. 25. Commissioners from United States and Mexico sign joint agreement for equal but separate border surveillance.

New York City. Humorist Will Rogers, in Ziegfeld Follies, says, "All I know is what I read in the papers."

Stanford, California. Psychologist Lewis Madison Terman, developer of intelligence test, coins term "I.Q." for intelligence quotient.

DEATHS

London, Feb. 28. Henry James, internationally famous American author (*Apr. 15, 1843).

Glen Ellen, California, Nov. 22. Jack London, novelist, a suicide (*Jan. 12, 1876).

American troops killed searching for Villa

American soldiers striking a pose.

Washington, D.C., June 21

The War Department announced today that at least 18 American soldiers have been killed by Mexican forces at Carrizal, Mexico. The soldiers, members of General John J. Pershing's punitive foray against the Mexican rebel Pancho Villa, killed 29 enemy soldiers, including their commander, General Gomez. This incident comes just three days after President Wilson ordered 100,000 National Guardsmen to the Mexican border and several warships to patrol along both coasts of Mexico. Just yesterday, Secretary of State Robert Lansing warned the Mexican government that any further attacks on American forces would "lead to the gravest consequences." The killings at Carrizal earlier today have brought the United States and Mexico to the verge of war.

Animosity between the Mexicans and the Americans has been escalating steadily for six months. On January 16, Villa's men removed 16 American mining engineers from a train near Chihuahua City and shot them in cold blood. On March 9, Villa's soldiers crossed the border and sacked the tiny New Mexican town of Columbus, killing 19 Americans. The next week, President Wilson sent General Pershing with 12,000 soldiers to pursue Villa into the heart of Mexico. Because he had to bolster his sagging domestic influence, the Mexican President, Venustiano Carranza, recently informed Wilson that American forces would have to be withdrawn. Just as his note was received here on May 22, Villa's forces crossed the Texas border and killed three soldiers and a little boy in Glen Springs. As a result of this attack, members of Congress have begun calling for a full-fledged American intervention in Mexico, while the Texas Governor has asked for the military occupation of all of northern Mexico.

In the meantime, General Hugh Scott of the United States Army has reportedly requested that the War College begin drawing up contingency plans for a major invasion of Mexico. Rumors indicate that Carranza has ordered his commanders to prevent any American reinforcements from entering Mexico, and to attack Pershing's troops unless they retreat to United States territory. If a last-minute diplomatic solution cannot be found, it would appear that full-scale war is a virtual certainty.

Members of Company F, 26th Infantry, guard five captured Mexican bandits.

Treaty gives U.S. base in Nicaragua

Washington, D.C., Feb. 18

The Senate today ratified a treaty under which Nicaragua authorizes the United States to build a canal across Central America, and to build a naval base on the Gulf of Fonseca. In exchange, the United States will pay Nicaragua $3 million. Other Latin American nations such as Honduras, Costa Rica and El Salvador adamantly oppose the plan. The first two hold claims on the gulf, and all three resent what seems to be U.S. bullying.

Pasadena is site of football once again

Pasadena, Calif., Jan. 1.

In the first Tournament of Roses football game played since 1902, Washington State defeated Brown, 14-0. After that first Tournament of Roses game, football fell into disrepute and there was little interest among college presidents to continue the sport. Despite some changes, the death toll in football soared to 33 in 1909. With the legalization of the forward pass, the end of the flying wedge and other safety changes, football has been winning its way back into favor in the last few years.

Chicago is the city of the big shoulders

Chicago

Has Chicago become the nation's literary capital? Upton Sinclair, Theodore Dreiser and others have set novels there. And now the 36-year-old poet Carl Sandburg has announced himself as its bard in "Chicago," the title poem of a new collection that salutes the "city of big shoulders." Big as they are, they aren't able to support every writer. John Dewey, formerly of the University of Chicago, now philosophizes at Columbia University in New York City. His pet topic? It is still *Democracy and Education*, the title of his latest book. And Indiana's Booth Tarkington cozily depicts the life of a provincial lad in his latest work, *Seventeen*.

Wilson, urging readiness, is renominated

The climax of the Preparedness Day Parade in May was the greatest display of the American flag ever seen in New York, as depicted by Childe Hassam in "The Fourth of July" (1916). The Massachusetts-born Impressionist painter began as a wood engraver and studied at the Academie Julien in Paris.

St. Louis, Mo., June 14

The Democratic National Convention has nominated President Woodrow Wilson and Vice President Thomas R. Marshall for second terms. It is expected that Wilson will wage his re-election campaign, just as he did his nomination race, on the preparedness issue. Ever since the outbreak of the European war two years ago, most Republicans and even many Democrats have charged Wilson with being dangerously lax on the military preparedness question. The President has apparently realized the weakness of his position. In recent months, he has begun to speak out with increasing force on the twin issues of German aggression and the need for a strong American defense establishment. On February 1, he told an audience in Des Moines, Iowa, "There is a price which is too great to pay for peace, and that price can be put in one word. One cannot pay the price of self-respect." Three weeks later, he told the Senate Foreign Relations Committee that he would not tolerate any further German infringements on American neutral rights. Last month, Wilson used his presidential influence to ensure the passage of two bills that double the size of the army and fund a naval building program that he said would give us a navy "second to none." Idealism, it seems, has been replaced by hard-nosed reality (→Nov. 7).

Bomb disrupts Preparedness Day parade

San Francisco, July

While the war years seem to have brought about a strengthening of unions in Los Angeles, in Northern California new campaigns are being waged for the open shop, this time in the guise of a preparedness measure. That, in brief, was the setting on July 22, when 10 people were killed and 40 wounded by the explosion of a bomb thrown during the San Francisco Preparedness Day Parade. Arrested for the crime were Tom Mooney, a streetcar strike leader; his wife, a music teacher; Edward Nolan of the Machinists Union; Warren K. Billings of the Shoe Workers Union, and Israel Weinberg of the Jitney Bus Drivers.

There is an uproar in the land because many feel those arrested are not guilty of the bomb-throwing. At the request of several society women, Bourke Cockran, a New York attorney and ex-congressman, will defend without charge the five people indicted for murder. In New York, 15,000 A.F.L. members from all branches of industry, will march to show sympathy for the jailed strikers (→Jan. 7, 1939).

G.O.P. picks Hughes to run for president

Chicago, June 10

Charles Evans Hughes has been selected as the Republican presidential candidate. After pre-convention booms for Elihu Root and former Governor Herrick of Ohio, the Grand Old Party chose Hughes. An Associate Supreme Court Justice and a former two-term Governor of New York, Hughes is a respected liberal, a man of integrity and a bona fide intellectual. A philosophical rival of ex-President Roosevelt and his interventionist position, Hughes has criticized Wilson for weakness in foreign policy and pledges to defend U.S. rights "on land and sea." Roosevelt is not expected to give much support to the Hughes campaign (→June 14).

Wilson supports woman's suffrage, but ...

Atlantic City, N.J., Sept. 8

"I come not to fight for you, but with you!" So said President Wilson tonight at the annual convention of the National-American Woman's Party. However, his assertion that women would get the vote "in a little while" wasn't, as it seemed, his support for a woman's suffrage amendment to the Constitution. Carrie Chapman Catt, the party leader, failed to gain his approval of such legislation. Former party president and prohibition lecturer Dr. Anna Shaw told Wilson and the 4,000 delegates, "We have waited long enough to get the vote. We want it now" (→June 4, 1919).

Wilson's support of the suffragists earns him many new campaign workers.

Wilson wins; "He kept us out of war"

"Woodrow Wilson" by E.C. Tarbell.

Washington, D.C., Nov. 7

President Woodrow Wilson was elected to a second term today. He received nine million votes to about 8.5 million for his Republican challenger, Charles Evans Hughes. Already, political pundits are saying that Wilson's slogan, "He kept us out of war," (coined by Bob Wooley, a Democratic Party executive) was crucial in persuading thousands of erstwhile Republicans to cast their votes for him.

During the campaign, Hughes was associated with his party's extremists, who favor direct American intervention in both Mexico and Europe. The German ambassador, Count Johann Heinrich von Bernstorff, prophetically informed his superiors in Berlin earlier in the year that "If Hughes is defeated, he has Roosevelt to thank for it." The former President and his interventionists were recognized six months ago as an albatross around Hughes's political neck. Editor Oswald Garrison Villard said in July, "No other candidate for President within the memory of living man ever ran downhill so rapidly" (→Jan. 22, 1917).

Birth control clinic opens in Brooklyn

Brooklyn, New York, Oct. 16

There were 150 women on line in the chill autumn air today, restlessly awaiting the opening of Mrs. Margaret Sanger's first birth control clinic in the borough. The clinic, at 46 Amboy Street, was well publicized through the distribution of 5,000 leaflets printed in English, Italian and Yiddish. They read in part, "Mothers! Can you afford to have a large family? Do you want any more children? If not, why do you have them?" The women seeking answers to the last question will get assistance from Mrs. Sanger and two aides, who have stocked the clinic with models of birth control devices and various informational charts.

A defiant Margaret Sanger (left) on trial for her attempt to offer birth control to the women of America.

However, how long Mrs. Sanger will be allowed to disseminate her advice is another question. In 1914, when she was accused of distributing birth control literature, she was sentenced to one month in jail. She has spent the past year traveling in Europe to learn more about birth control methods, and came back extolling the advantages of limiting families through the use of condoms and pessaries.

Federal child labor law is finally passed

Washington, D.C., Sept. 1

After years of weak state efforts, the federal government has finally extended a hand to the nation's 1.8 million child laborers. The Keating-Owen Act, signed today, bans interstate commerce in products made by children under 14. It also shields children under 16 from mine work, night work and work days over eight hours. In 1906, the first federal child labor bill drew opposition even from the reformist National Child Labor Committee. This time, resistance was limited to the cotton-producing South, where mill owners argued that many children work out of necessity. Nonetheless, the bill carried 52-12 in the Senate and 337-46 in the House.

Some of America's children will no longer work in abysmal conditions.

Lumber man Boeing starts a plane factory

Seattle, Wash., July

From the moment he first beheld Puget Sound from the passenger seat of a Curtiss biplane in 1914, William E. Boeing has been hooked on flying. Soon after, the Seattle timber magnate purchased a Glenn Martin hydroplane, learned to fly, and began envisioning his own aircraft company. Not one to waste time dreaming, he built his first craft this year, a single-engine floatplane with a 52-foot wingspan, designed with the former navy engineer Conrad Westervelt. It has proven impressive in trials, and the new Boeing Airplane Company, with 21 employees, mostly carpenters and seamstresses, intends to build 50 Model C biplanes for the navy.

Catholics condemn doubtful morality

New York City, Aug. 21

"Alien radicalism" in the form of socialism could corrupt American youth. So says the National Committee on Public Morals of the American Federation of Catholic Societies as it scored those evils it says menace the nation. Regarding divorce, the group asked for a "national law so stringent" that "people of doubtful morality" could no longer take advantage of "pagan state laws" to separate "what God has joined together." The committee also denounced motion pictures for "foisting upon our women and children immoral" films and "insidious attacks on Christianity."

Industry booms as war rages overseas

New York City

Sparked by the war in Europe, the American economy has reached new heights as the nation completes its most prosperous year in history. Foreign trade soared this year to a record $8 billion, while domestic output hit a high of $45 billion. Feeding the vast need for capital overseas, America has carved its niche as the world's creditor nation. And the funds keep flowing. John D. Rockefeller became a billionaire in September. Prices are up, but so are wages. Indeed, the biggest problem is a labor shortage created by a jobless rate that remains enviably low.

Congress is doubling size of regular army

Washington, D.C., June 3

After months of bitter conflict between its pacifist and military preparedness wings, Congress has enacted a compromise army expansion bill. Signed into law today by President Wilson, the National Defense Act will more than double the size of the regular army over a five-year period, from 105,000 men to more than 220,000. In addition, the National Guard will be gradually brought up to a strength of over 450,000 citizen-soldiers and will be prepared for quick integration into the federal military establishment. The legislation also provides for establishing volunteer summer military camps at some colleges, where future officers are to be trained. The National Defense Act was approved partly in response to public demand for a better-prepared military establishment. A movie last year called *The Fall of a Nation* depicted an invasion of the United States by a Germanic-looking army. The movie, coupled with the sinking of the liner Lusitania by German U-boats, has resulted in a groundswell of support for a considerable American buildup of the armed forces. But it is going to require a large expenditure. As Congressman Claude Kitchin points out, when taxes have to be raised, "preparedness will not be so popular . . . as it is now" (→ 14).

U.S. military rules in Dominican Republic

Restoring order. American troops search huts for weapons in Santo Domingo.

Dominican Republic, Nov. 29

American military officials have declared martial law in the Dominican Republic in the wake of chaotic political and financial developments. The order, issued by Captain H.S. Knapp, included censorship of newspapers and the telegraph. Marines have been occupying Santo Domingo, the capital, since May. Unlike a similar occupation of Haiti a year ago, this one was not preceded by serious bloodshed or civil unrest. Rather, troops were sent after a series of dictators cound not avert the financial collapse of a nation heavily in debt to American and European concerns.

Lincoln Logs invented by architect's son

Chicago

While watching construction of a Tokyo hotel, John Wright, the son of Frank Lloyd Wright, decided it was something children could do – on a smaller scale. Wright has now invented Lincoln Logs, a construction toy of wood, so kids can make their own buildings. The younger Wright had accompanied his father on the construction of an earthquake-proof hotel, the Imperial.

Third of all cars sold this year were Fords

Detroit, Michigan

When the one millionth car rolled off the assembly line at the Ford plant last year, it was just the latest milestone of a revolution in auto manufacturing. This year, Ford's mass production techniques turned out almost 2,000 cars per day, with sales of 534,000 autos representing about one-third of the industry's 1,617,000. Americans own about 3.5 million autos, and Ford is as determined as ever to expand the market by making more cars at a lower cost per car – thus at lower prices. This year, the Model T price dropped from $440 to $360, but profits soared to $59 million.

On the road. Open-air Ford Model T and owner wearing a raccoon coat.

Wobblies battle authorities in Northwest

Everett, Washington, Nov. 5

In the heat of a six-month lumber strike, the Industrial Workers of the World are pressing their call for "One Big Union." The loudest answers so far have been bullets. Five days ago, a posse led by Everett's sheriff met a party of Wobblies and made them run a gauntlet that investigators say left "the roadway . . . stained with blood." Today, as union members arrived for a protest rally, their boat was riddled with bullets, killing five and wounding 31. Down in Seattle, authorities jailed 74 Wobblies for the murder of two deputies who were caught in the crossfire.

Talk of war sends stock prices soaring

Washington, D.C., Dec. 21

When Secretary of State Robert Lansing announced earlier today that the likelihood of American involvement in the European war was growing, stock market prices soared toward a 15-year high. Defense contractors and those in related industries apparently stand to gain by Lansing's announcement. It is obvious that investors support the warlike talk. Some of it could be tied to patriotic backing of a strong United States. But analysts suggest that one must not underestimate the attraction of wartime profit.

Americans are still entertained by the animals in the Barnum & Bailey circus, which this year is advertised by a ferocious tiger.

Progressive years restore promise of American life

Muckraking magazine, 1912, urging stronger enforcement of Pure Food and Drug Act – to halt drug abuse.

A confirmation class in La Crosse, Wisconsin, 1912. Scandinavian families predominate in the region, and the Lutheran Church plays a strong role. From 1900 to 1910, more than 190,000 Norwegians immigrated to the United States.

New York society women, members of the Woman Suffrage Party, join the parade for their right to vote.

Crusading photographer Jacob Riis, Danish immigrant, who documented "the foul core of New York's slums."

The man in the arena, Theodore Roosevelt, pictured here in 1912 after receiving news of his presidential nomination by the Progressive Party. More than any other American, the ebullient Teddy embodies the progressive era.

Senator Robert "Fighting Bob" La Follette of Wisconsin, one of the great progressive reformers in America.

American sheet music cover, c. 1908. These are years when the conservation of nature is coming into its own.

Armenians, Croats, Czechs, Hungarians, Italians, Poles, Russians, Ukrainians – they keep coming by the millions, irresistibly drawn by the promise of American life. Most are young men, who come to work and send money home.

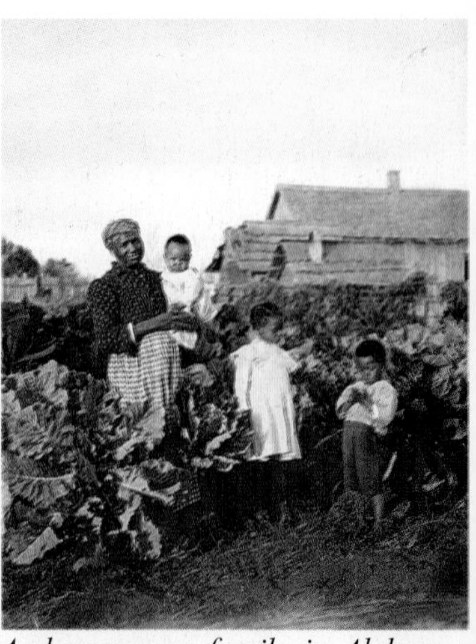

A sharecropper family in Alabama, 1902. Despite good intentions, progress has lagged in race relations.

A faster pace sets the tone for modern times

Policeman directing traffic in Chicago. In 1906, Woodrow Wilson said, "Nothing has spread socialistic feeling in this country more than the use of the automobile. To the countryman, they are a picture of the arrogance of wealth."

John Sloan's "McSorley's Bar" (1912) depicts the drama of urban nightlife.

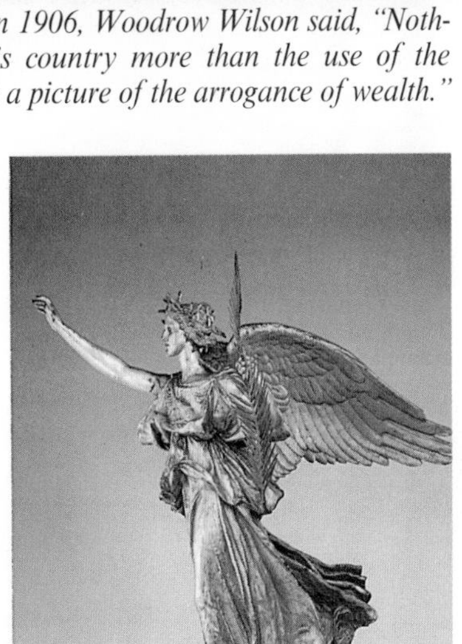

Movie poster of 1914. The popular serial always ends by asking, "Next time, will Pauline be saved again?"

"Victory" (1902), a bronze statuette symbolizing America, by Irish-born sculptor Augustus Saint-Gaudens.

"And down the stretch they come!" The finish of a race at a track in Lexington, Kentucky, breeding ground for many of the finest Thoroughbreds in America.

As the song goes: "You'd look sweet upon the seat of a bicycle built for two."

"Hold your horses!" Driving a 1900-vintage "devil wagon" can be dangerous.

Saving the Dream 1917-1945

To Europeans and Americans at the time, it was the "Great War," the largest and costliest conflict in the history of the old continent and the event that propelled the United States, at least for a time, into an international system from which it had long remained aloof. To President Woodrow Wilson and to those who shared his vision, it was "the war to end all wars," a cataclysm that would force the nations to construct a new world order free of the barbarism of the old. To historians, however, it is simply World War I, a terrible conflict that resolved few of the problems that had caused it and served as prelude to an even greater war a generation later.

The United States entered the conflict on April 6, 1917, amidst a burst of patriotic fervor. But there was never any real unity in the country's view of the war, never a universal belief in the correctness of America's role. A year and a half later, the war was over. And the United States, the only nation to emerge from the conflict stronger than when it had entered it, was now clearly the pre-eminent power in the world. The country's halting effort to come to terms with that pre-eminence was one of the principal forces that shaped American history over the next 40 years. But the rise of the United States to what some have called "globalism" was not the only great historical event of the years between the World Wars. Both economically and politically, American society experienced a series of profound and at times traumatic changes that permanently transformed the nation.

Beginning in 1921, the American economy began a period of unprecedented prosperity and expansion that continued almost uninterrupted for eight years. To observers from around the globe (many of whom traveled to the United States simply to witness its achievements), the American economy came to seem one of the wonders of the world. The nation's industrial capacity grew at an unparalleled rate. The income of its citizens soared. America's position in world trade became one of unrivaled supremacy. The corporate world, after having been on the defensive for many years, basked in a widespread popularity that transformed once-despised captains of finance and industry into national heroes.

Then, in the aftermath of a frightening stock market crash in October 1929 and a gradual weakening of the economy that had been in progress for many months before it, the imposing industrial edifice collapsed and the nation plunged into the severest and most prolonged economic crisis in its history. The "Great Depression," as it quickly became known, frustrated the optimistic tactics of business leaders. By 1932, the financial crisis had brought the nation's economy (and, some believed, its social and political systems) to the brink of total collapse.

Someone asked the British economist John Maynard Keynes in the 1930s whether he was aware of any historical era comparable to the Great Depression (which was affecting England and Europe as well as the United States). "Yes," Keynes replied. "It was called the Dark Ages, and it lasted 400 years." That was no doubt an exaggeration, both of the conditions of the 1930s and of the nature of the Middle Ages. But the misery of the Great Depression was indeed profound. More than a quarter of the work force was without jobs in 1932, the worst year of the crisis; and never in the 1930s did unemployment drop much below 15 percent. On American farms, economic problems that had been developing throughout the 1920s grew suddenly far worse. Hundreds of thousands of farmers lost their land and joined the growing numbers of citizens roaming the landscape looking for work – work that generally did not exist. Men and women accustomed to poverty experienced a marked deterioration in their conditions. Millions of families accustomed to security, even affluence, experienced deprivation and economic fear for the first time. In August 1928, President Herbert Hoover had proclaimed, "We in America today are nearer to the final triumph over poverty than ever before in the history of any land." A few years later, with Hoover discredited and poverty rampant in the land, those words seemed a tinny echo of a bygone era.

Politically, the contrast between the 1920s and 1930s was almost equally striking. The election of 1920 brought to office a Republican administration determined to restore to American life what the new President, Warren G. Harding, called "normalcy." In practice, that meant rejecting many of the progressive assumptions of the previous decades of reform. Throughout the 1920s, therefore, the policies of the federal government worked largely to promote the interests of the business world, sometimes conservatively, sometimes creatively. Taxes and federal spending were sharply reduced; new, collusive relationships between business and government, and among businesses themselves, were tolerated, even encouraged. The needs of workers, farmers, and the poor were, according to the conventional wisdom, best served by attending to the health of the corporate world.

The Great Depression discredited such notions and launched a new era of reform. The Democratic Party – the minority party for most of the previous 75 years – returned to power and achieved a dominance in both local and national politics that it would not relinquish for decades. A new President, Franklin Delano Roosevelt, quickly became one of the most important, and controversial, leaders in American history. Under Roosevelt, the federal government embarked on a series of initiatives and experiments – known collectively as the "New Deal" – that dramatically expanded and altered the role of the state in national life.

By the end of the 1930s, the Roosevelt administration had drawn the broad outlines of much of the political world Americans know today. It had built the beginnings of a modern welfare system. It had extended federal regulation over numerous areas of the economy. It had presided over, and provided important legal protections for, the birth of the modern labor movement. It had created an important government presence in the agricultural economy. And it had produced the beginnings of a new "liberal" ideology that would shape reform efforts for decades to come, an ideology that remains at the center of American political debate even 50 years later.

One thing the New Deal did not do, however, was to end the Great Depression. It helped stabilize the economy in the early, desperate months of 1933, and it kept things from getting worse. But by the end of 1939, unemployment remained almost as high as it had been five years earlier and the gross national product was no larger than it had been 10 years before. Politicians, economists and others despaired at times of ever finding a solution to the economic crisis. But in 1939, another World War erupted and created a new prosperity before which all previous eras of growth quickly paled.

For a time, Americans were as reluctant to become involved in World War II as they had been to intervene in World War I. Indeed, much of America's international behavior in the 1920s and 1930s had reflected a desire to insulate the United States from any possible future wars. In the end, however, the cautious, limited American internationalism of the inter-war years proved inadequate either to protect the interests of the United States or to encourage global stability. Throughout the 1920s and 1930s, the fragile world order established in the aftermath of World War I suffered a series of devastating economic, political and military blows. By the late 1930s, in the face of a new world crisis provoked by the expansionist aims of Germany and Japan, that order collapsed. Out of its ruins sprang the war that quickly engulfed the world.

The United States moved slowly even then – partly because the government itself was not certain how to act, partly because it was aware of how strongly much of the public opposed any involvement in international conflicts. But America was by then already deeply entangled in the affairs of the world despite its best efforts. Within a year, the United States was operating openly as an effective ally of Great Britain. A year later, it was actively, if unofficially, involved in hostilities. So the Japanese attack on Pearl Harbor on December 7, 1941, only confirmed what had been growing obvious for some time: that the United States was now so central to the affairs of the world that it could not remain isolated from its troubles. Four year later, with victory over Germany and Japan complete, it was clear to all that the United States of America was the greatest industrial and military power in history and had played the crucial role in saving the dream of democracy throughout the world.

◄ *"The Iwo Jima Memorial" at Arlington National Cemetery in Virginia.*

1917

Wilson

Washington, D.C., Jan. 22. In an address to Senate, President Wilson calls for "peace without victory" in Europe (→March 13).

Washington, D.C., March 2. Congress passes Organic Act for Puerto Rico, or Jones Act, organizing Puerto Rico as U.S. territory and granting its inhabitants rights of American citizens.

Washington, D.C., March 5. Word reaches United States that revolution in Russia has forced abdication of Czar Nicholas II (→Nov. 11).

Washington, D.C., March 13. Navy Department instructs merchant vessels sailing into war zones to act against German submarines if necessary (→20).

Washington, D.C., March 20. President Wilson's Cabinet unanimously advises him to ask Congress for a declaration of war against Germany.→

Speculator Mine, Montana, June 8. Disaster kills 164 men when a lamp ignites electrical insulation in a mine shaft.

France, June 14. American Expeditionary Force arrives under command of General John J. Pershing; its size is expected to swell to over one million within year (→July 4).

Paris, July 4. Appearing on behalf of General Pershing, Colonel Charles E. Stanton says, "Lafayette, we are here," at tomb of marquis (→Nov. 30).

Washington, D.C., Aug. 10. Food Administration is created; Wilson appoints Herbert Hoover as its chief.

New York City, Oct. 15. Chicago White Sox defeat New York Giants, four games to two, in World Series.

Montreal, Oct. 22. National Hockey Association disbanded; National Hockey League organized.

New York City, Oct. 27. Russian-born violinist Jascha Heifetz makes his American debut at age of 16.

Hollywood, Calif. By year's end, Charlie Chaplin has produced, directed or acted in more than 880 films.

DEATH

Denver, Colorado, Jan. 10. William F. "Buffalo Bill" Cody, founder of Wild West Show (*Feb. 26, 1846).

German U-boats cause rift with U.S.

A German U-boat crew cries out in victory as another ship lists and sinks.

Washington, D.C., March 20

Germany's submarine onslaught against American merchant shipping has brought the United States to the brink of war. At an imperial conference in January, the German military strategists decided to inaugurate a total U-boat war against all commerce, neutral as well as belligerent. On February 3, a German submarine sank the American liner Housatonic off the coast of Sicily, and President Wilson announced he was breaking off diplomatic relations with Germany.

Wilson addressed the Senate on January 22 and said, "Only a peace between equals can last" and that there must be "peace without victory." Despite the President's rhetoric about peace, he called upon Congress on February 26 to provide the means to achieve "an armed neutrality" to deal with the attacks on American shipping. In practical terms, this meant the arming of all American merchant vessels. But Congress still has a strong pacifist element and when the Armed Ship Bill was introduced into the Senate, filibuster resulted. Nevertheless, the measure won final approval on March 1.

The Germans now have some 120 submarines, and they can keep about two-thirds of them in operation at any one time. During the previous phase of unrestricted warfare, in 1915 and 1916, they sank about 120,000 tons of shipping a month and they accomplished that with only nine submarines operating at any given time.

But their U-boat strength is only half the story. The Germans are willing to play a card that can mean American entry into the war because they do not think the United States is much of a threat. Militarily, they rank the United States with Denmark, Holland and Chile. They are betting that the submarine campaign will bring Britain to its knees long before the Americans become involved and, should the United States finally get aroused, it is not likely to provide appreciable strength on the battlefield.

The latest U-boat effort began on February 1 and, by the end of the month, half a million tons of Allied shipping were on the bottom of the ocean. This month, the tonnage figure is approaching three-quarters of a million, and estimates for next month are more than a million. When shown the figures for lost shipping, one American admiral said, "But this means we are losing the war." His British counterpart replied, "That's right, and there's nothing we can do about it."

Actually, the British are taking measures. In an effort to restrict U-boat activity, they are attempting to seal the English Channel by creating a mine barrage across it. There are also plans to block the submarines in their bases at important ports such as Zeebrugge on the Belgian coast (→Apr. 6).

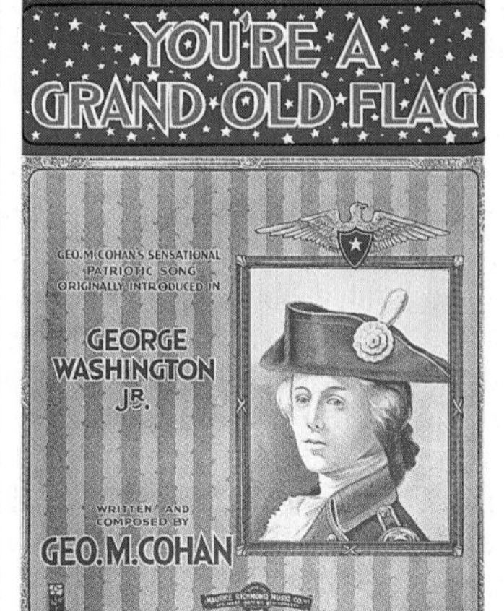

Composer George M. Cohan's "You're a Grand Old Flag" is one of the many songs urging Americans to rally round the flag.

Germany urges Mexico to invade U.S.

Washington, D.C., March 1

Since the United States broke relations with Germany in February, all that has stood between America and war has been President Wilson's statement to Congress that he would not believe Germany hostile to the U.S. "unless and until we are obliged to believe it."

The Germans have just provided some proof, in the form of an explosive telegram, published today by the Associated Press, in which Germany urges Mexico and Japan to make war on the United States. The telegram was sent on January 16 by German Foreign Minister Arthur Zimmermann and has been in Wilson's possession since February 24. In it, Zimmermann instructs the German Ambassador to Mexico to promise the Mexican government that in return for its allegiance in the event of a war between Germany and the United States, Germany will help it "to reconquer the lost territory in Texas, Arizona and New Mexico." As the final element in the so-called Prussian Invasion Plot, Zimmermann instructed the Mexicans to seek the assistance of the Japanese.

Mexico has been the chief trouble spot of Wilson's presidency and American troops have fought there three times in the last two years.

United States enters the war "to save democracy"

Washington, D.C., Apr. 6

At exactly 1:18 this afternoon, the United States announced that it was declaring war against Germany. Peace was the thing President Wilson wanted most, and in the end he couldn't have it because of Germany's decision, in January, to inaugurate total submarine warfare against all shipping, neutral as well as belligerent. On April 2, Wilson asked Congress to recognize that a state of war existed between the United States and the German Empire. The Senate passed a war resolution two days later by a vote of 90 to 6, and the House followed suit early this morning with a vote of 373 to 50 after 13 hours of emotional debate.

In his speech asking for a declaration of war, the President said that "the world must be made safe for democracy." He added that "it is a fearful thing to lead this great peaceful people into war, the most terrible of wars. But the right is more precious than the peace, and we shall fight for the things that we have always carried nearest our hearts . . . for democracy . . . for the rights and liberties of small nations, for a universal dominion of right by such a concert of free peoples as shall bring peace and safety to all nations and make the world itself at last free."

President Wilson asks Congress for a declaration of war, not in search of conquest, but to ensure universal rights.

Since the outbreak of a general European war in August of 1914, the United States, under Wilson's leadership, has struggled to maintain neutrality. Despite an avalanche of propaganda that came from the Central Powers as well as the Allies, the great majority of Americans has maintained a steadfast determination to avoid involvement. But this position was shaken on May 7, 1915, when the Germans sank an unarmed British liner, the Lusitania, killing more than 1,000 people, 128 of them Americans. There were difficulties with Britain as well, since it used its vast fleet to establish a blockade of Germany. This prevented the United States from exporting food and raw materials to Germany, and the State Department sent several notes of protest to London.

Despite the many declarations of strict neutrality by the United States, it evolved as the principal source of food, raw materials and munitions that fed the Allied war machine. Wilson also permitted the British and the French to borrow more than $2 billion in the United States to finance their war effort. The President resisted attempts by some German-Americans to institute an arms embargo against the Allies. Given these facts, it is not too difficult to understand Germany's rejection of the American claims of strict neutrality.

Naturally, Britain has praised America's entry into the war. Prime Minister Lloyd George said that "America has at one bound become a world power in a sense she never was before" (→June 14).

Virgin Islands sold to U.S. by Denmark

Washington, D.C., March 31

The Virgin Islands in the Caribbean Sea were transferred to the United States today, putting the final touch to the most expensive purchase of land the nation has ever made. The United States paid Denmark $25 million for the islands to make sure that Germany will never have them as a military base and to protect the Panama Canal. President Wilson signed the treaty with the Danish government in January. The three important islands in the group are St. Croix, St. John and St. Thomas.

Anti-war vote cast by Montana woman

Washington, D.C., Apr. 6

Montana Republican Miss Jeannette Rankin, the only woman ever elected to Congress, stood before her fellow legislators today and declared, "I want to stand by my country, but I cannot vote for war. I vote no." A tear ran down her face. Before she was elected last November, Miss Rankin was a social worker. She has expressed the belief that women gained the vote in Montana "because the spirit of pioneer days was still alive." Clearly, she believes pacifism is a part of that same spirit.

We won't be back till it's over over there

New York City

As the song goes, "The Yanks are coming!" Was ever a more stirring call-to-arms written than George M. Cohan's *Over There*? His inspiration was immediate, the song written on April 6, the very day the country declared war. Though this may become his biggest hit, *Yankee Doodle Boy* will never be far behind. Then there's his popular theme song, *Give My Regards to Broadway*. In all, the boy born in a trunk in Providence in 1878 to vaudeville troupers Jerry and Nellie Cohan has managed, with rare success, to give America something special to sing about.

George M. Cohan's inspirational hit.

Congress orders registration for war duty

Washington, D.C., May 18

On June 5, between the hours of 7 a.m. and 7 p.m., every American male between the ages of 21 and 30 will be expected to register for a manpower draft. The Selective Service Act that has mandated the registration was approved by congressional vote today to build up the country's armed services upon "the principle of universal liability to service."

Conscription will be supervised by civilian boards around the nation. More than 10 million men are expected to be registering and about a half million will be selected in the initial draft. The concept of the draft has been the subject of a heated debate for some three years, with those who favor it arguing that it constitutes the best way to strengthen the military of the United States. Opponents of the idea, on the other hand, particularly Democrats from the South and the West, have called a draft "un-American" and "another name for slavery."

Those who support the draft insist there is nothing humanitarian or patriotic about the opposition to it, that some of the draft's critics are motivated by a fear of large numbers of Negroes becoming members of the armed forces.

As late as February, President Wilson and Secretary of War Newton D. Baker said that their preference was a voluntary system. However, that month, the two men reversed their position and authorized the bill. The Selective Service System is to be headed by the provost marshal general, Enoch H. Crowder (→Nov. 30).

Over the past century, Uncle Sam has been used to symbolize the United States. And now artist James Montgomery Flagg, who sold his first drawing at age 12, has immortalized him – recruiting the manpower needed to win the war.

Two Liberty Loan drives fund war effort

Washington, D.C.

Some 9.5 million Americans are putting their money where their sentiments are, supporting the war effort to the tune of $4.6 billion in the second Liberty Loan drive. The Liberty Loan Act was approved by Congress on April 24. The second campaign began on October 1 and the target was $3 billion. To sell Liberty Bonds, Treasury Secretary William McAdoo enlisted famous people in many walks of life. Among them were such well-known artists as Charles Dana Gibson, James Montgomery Flagg and Howard Chandler Christy. Movie stars included Douglas Fairbanks and Mary Pickford. The Boy Scouts also lent a hand. The bonds, described as an alternative to explicit – and unpopular – taxing, pay 4 percent interest.

Anti-German feeling reaches a high pitch as officially sanctioned posters and unsubstantiated atrocity reports fan the fires of hatred in America.

Pulitzer Prizes

New York City

When newspaper tycoon Joseph Pulitzer died, he left Columbia University funds to honor the nation's best writers and the press annually. This was the first year of awards and, though the committee snubbed the novelists and playwrights, it honored biographers Laura Richards and Maude Elliott for *Julia Ward Howe* and historian J.J. Jusserand for *With Americans of Past and Present Days*. Other winners were *New York World* reporter Herbert Bayard Swope, and the *New York Tribune* for editorial writing.

Jasz, Jass, Jazz

New York City, March 17

No one spells it the same. But then, the Original Dixieland Jasz Band, now at Reisenweber's, is the first group ever to use the odd word. The advertisements for its first records, released today by Victor, call it "jass." The syncopated sounds are billed as "the First Sensational Amusement Novelty of 1917." Jazz is said to be the product of black musicians in New Orleans working from a ragout of ragtime, blues and other black musical forms. But some people fear the music may corrupt the young.

Wobbly offices raided throughout nation

Chicago, Sept. 18

After studying records seized in a nationwide raid two weeks ago, the Justice Department's raiders returned to the offices of the Industrial Workers of the World today with 166 warrants under the Espionage Act. Leading strikes this year in lumber fields and copper mines, the Wobblies have not been supportive of the war effort. The press has described them as "the waste material of creation" and advocated their elimination as the "first step in the whipping of Germany." I.W.W. is now translated as "I Won't Work," "I Want Whiskey," or "Imperial Wilhelm's Warriors."

President Wilson says they "certainly are worthy of being suppressed." The radical union has allegedly obstructed the draft. But Wobbly leader "Big Bill" Haywood has quieted the voices of discontent since the United States joined the war. Frank Little opposed Haywood, vowing to "face the firing squad rather than compromise," but somebody saved him the trouble. Little was found last month hanging from a trestle in Butte, Montana, wearing a note that read, "Others Take Notice. First and Last Warning" (→May 16, 1918).

Russian Revolution has U.S. troubled

Washington, D.C., Nov. 11.

Russia's role in the war is in doubt. Communist radicals, intent on peace, have seized control of the Russian government from Premier Alexander Kerensky. Washington fears that the Bolshevik government will pull Russia out of the alliance, freeing Germany to concentrate its forces on its Western Front with France and Italy. Many think the new regime's leaders, Vladimir Lenin and Leon Trotsky, are paid German agents.

President Wilson is reportedly dismayed by the overthrow of a regime he has described as "a fit partner for a league of honor." The United States has refused to recognize the new Bolshevik regime. By contrast, last March the United States was the first to recognize the legitimacy of Kerensky's provisional government when it took power following the forced abdication of Czar Nicholas II. Many hoped Russia's army would be rejuvenated once freed of the Czar's mismanagement. But Kerensky was no more able to win battles or end hunger than the Czar was, paving the way for the Bolsheviks' bloodless coup d'etat.

First on the Bolshevik agenda is an immediate cessation of war. "I shall issue a few proclamations and then shut up shop," said Trotsky, the new commissar of foreign affairs. The new regime has also announced a redistribution of land to the peasants (→Aug. 15, 1918).

American troops in France see action

Cambrai, France, Nov. 30

American troops today saw action in a major offensive for the first time since they began arriving here in June. These were Engineer Regiments who were supposed to serve only as support for British troops. But they were caught up in the combat. On November 2, the first Americans were killed near Bathelemont when German troops conducted a trench raid on the First Division.

The American Expeditionary Force, under the command of General John J. "Black Jack" Pershing, is eventually expected to total more than one million men. When American units landed in France this summer, Colonel Charles E. Stanton stood at the tomb of the French nobleman who had given so much to the American Revolution and said, "Lafayette, we are here."

At present, there are five American divisions on French soil. These include the 42nd, called the Rainbow Division because it is made up of National Guard units from almost every state; the First Division, made up of army regulars who were the first to arrive at St. Nazaire; the Second Division of marines and army regulars and the 41st Division from the American Northwest.

On October 20, the First Division entered the front lines near Luneville, a town that the army's regulars gave the nickname of Looneyville to the dismay of the local residents (→Jan. 8, 1918).

French Marshal Joseph Joffre stands with American General John J. Pershing.

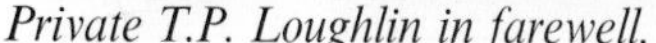

Private T.P. Loughlin in farewell.

They're off to fight the good fight.

Curbing war's foes

Washington, D.C., June 15

Stiff prison sentences and heavy fines await anyone who attempts to hinder the American war effort or help its enemies. Under the Espionage Act that won the approval of Congress today, violators can be fined as much as $10,000 and jailed for up to 20 years. Additionally, Postmaster General Albert Sidney Burleson has been given permission to bar from the mail any materials that are considered treasonous or seditious. Even before passage of the Espionage Act, the postmaster began banning publications turned out by the Socialists (→Sept. 18).

Immigrants limited

Washington, D.C., Feb. 5

Asian workers other than Japanese will be barred from the United States and all other immigrants must pass a literacy test under the terms of the Immigration Act of 1917 that was approved today by Congress. Specifically, the new legislation excludes vagrants, illiterates, alcoholics and persons seeking to enter the United States for "immoral purposes." When the measure was first passed, it was vetoed by President Wilson. But it became law when two-thirds of both houses voted to override the President's veto (→May 19, 1921).

Industries put under government control

Washington, D.C.

The war is rapidly coming home to America in a variety of ways, with preparations and supply affecting the day-to-day life of almost every citizen. There have been sweeping changes, and they include government controls over industry, railroading and food and fuel production; increases in the taxes on both personal income and corporations; jacked up postal rates, and even the censorship of certain kinds of mail.

After calling for "the organization and mobilization of all the material resources of the country" in April, President Wilson delegated responsibility for stepping up production and cutting down waste to the War Industries Board. He named a 41-year-old journalist, George Creel, to head the Commission on Public Information and a 43-year-old mining engineer, Herbert Hoover, to take over the Food Administration.

Other key personnel who will be in charge of regulating industry are the Treasury Secretary, William G. McAdoo, 54, who heads the Railroad Administration, and Harry A Garfield, 54, who is in charge of fuel administration.

Washington, D.C., Jan. 7. Supreme Court rules, in Arver v. United States, that wartime draft is constitutional.

New York City, Jan. 21. New York Philharmonic Society bars all works by living German composers.

New York City, Feb. 14. George Gershwin's *Swanee* sung publicly for first time.

Washington, D.C., Apr. 8. Frank P. Walsh and former President William Howard Taft co-chair National War Labor Board, which will be a court of labor arbitration.

Washington, D.C., May 19. Federal government appropriates $1 billion for maintenance of vital railways.

Mobile, Alabama, May 21. Fire in meat market spreads throughout city, destroying 40 blocks and 200 homes.

California, July, 25. Annette Adams begins term as first woman district attorney in United States.

Europe, Aug. 10. Allies agree to formation of an independent American force under General John J. Pershing (→27).

Washington, D.C., Aug. 12. Post Office Department takes over control of nation's airmail service from War Department.

Upton, New Jersey, Aug. 19. *Yip, Yip Yaphank*, musical by Irving Berlin, first performed.

Washington, D.C., Aug. 27. United States rejects Pope Benedict XV's peace proposal of August 1 on grounds that German government cannot be taken at its word (→Sept. 26).

Boston, Sept. 11. Babe Ruth's pitching helps Boston Red Sox beat Chicago Cubs in World Series, four games to two.

France, Oct. 29. Eddie Rickenbacker, leading American air ace, downs 26th enemy plane.

Washington, D.C., Nov. 5. Mid-term elections turn both houses of Congress over to Republican control.

New York City, Nov. 7. Newspapers erroneously report signing of an armistice, engendering premature public celebrations.

Brest, France, Dec. 13. President Wilson arrives for peace negotiations (→Feb. 14, 1919).

United States. Willa Cather publishes *My Antonia*.

Wilson proposes 14-point peace plan

Washington, D.C., Jan. 8

In a major speech to Congress today, President Wilson presented his vision and prescription for international peace and prosperity in the postwar world. Designed to bolster sagging Allied morale and to assure the Central Powers of a fair and just treatment after the war's end, Wilson's "14 Points" program defines a new and optimistic world order. As a preface to his proposals, the President said, "We demand that the world be made fit and safe to live in ... against force and selfish aggression. The program of the world's peace is our only program." In summary, the points of the Wilson plan are as follows

1. No secret diplomacy
2. Freedom of the seas during both peace and war
3. Removal of international trade barriers and the establishment of equal international trade conditions
4. Worldwide arms reductions
5. Impartial adjustment of all colonial claims
6. No foreign interference in Russian affairs
7. Full Belgian sovereignty
8. Return of Alsace-Lorraine to France
9. Redrawing Italian boundaries with equity for all internal nationalities
10. Free, autonomous development of all nationalities within Austro-Hungary
11. Restoration of the Balkan nations and Serbian access to the sea
12. Sovereignty for the Turkish parts of the Ottoman Empire
13. An independent Poland with access to the sea
14. Creation of an international body of arbitration (a League of Nations)

The 14 Points, President Wilson concluded, are the symbol of what he called "the moral climax of this final war for liberty" (→Apr. 14).

Activities of German-Americans are curtailed as suspicion rises

Washington, D.C., July 2

Congress voted today to repeal the charter of the National German-American Alliance. The mighty organization, boasting two million members four years ago, is silenced. Still, an uneasiness has settled across America. Are German-American neighbors loyal citizens or do they plot our government's fall? Rumors fly – spies on the Atlantic coast send messages to German U-boats. Agents incite strikes at arms plants. Even among Germans themselves, there is distrust; some recent immigrants are called "Hunnenfresser," Hun eaters, denigrators of their own people.

Yet just a few years ago, German-Americans were among the most respected of immigrants. German thinkers were widely admired, and German was taught in a fourth of the nation's high schools. When the war began, there was much empathy for the German cause. The $700,000 raised at a 1916 benefit at Madison Square Garden went to German war orphans. Opinions changed once the British cut the German telegraph cable; news went through the British service; it tells of atrocities, Huns butchering Belgian babies.

German-Americans either decry the tales or flee their identity. Muellers become Millers, Schmidts are Smiths. Their "purer" American neighbors eradicate all vestiges of German culture: sauerkraut is "liberty cabbage," hamburger is "liberty steak." Schubert and Bach performances are banned. Berlin, Iowa, is now Lincoln.

And as for the National German-American Alliance, what crime had it committed? It had urged American neutrality in the war. And rather than face the ignominy of a forced disbandment today, the group dissolved itself and donated all of its funds to the American Red Cross (→March 10, 1928).

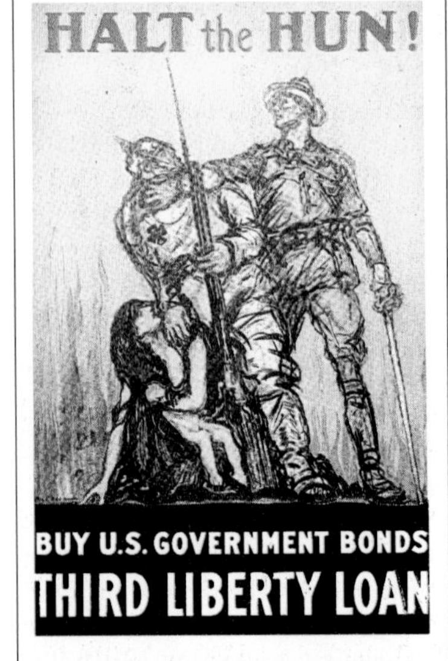

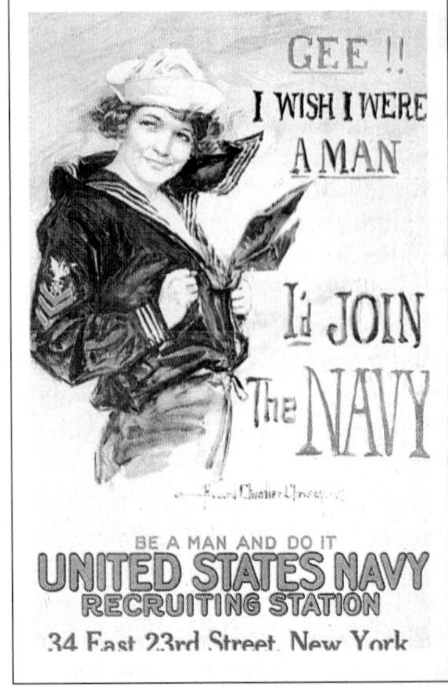

Foch given command of Pershing's troops

Pershing (right) agrees to accept the overall authority of Marshal Foch.

Western Front, Apr. 14

Ten months of bitter wrangling over who commands United States forces in France have been settled: The Americans will fight as one army under General John J. Pershing, but accept the overall strategic authority of Marshal Ferdinand Foch of France, the Allied supreme commander. When the Americans first arrived, they were larded in among the British and French forces, in piecemeal fashion when and where they seemed to be needed to plug holes or reinforce their beleaguered allies. They will campaign as a single army, although they will still lend individual units here and there (→30).

Americans on front lines

An American soldier is overcome by toxic mustard gas as U.S. troops advance.

France, Apr. 30

As the German spring offensive drives toward the Marne, it has run headlong into fresh American divisions thrown into the front lines. Most of the fighting for the American Expeditionary Force is taking place at a German bridgehead near Chateau-Thierry, although the First Division had been sent to the Somme to help stop Count Ludendorff's first drive. By March, there were 325,000 Americans on French soil with more arriving every week.

The veteran German troops are busily educating the Americans in the facts of war. The shock troops called "Stosstruppen" have been raiding behind the maze of trenches that the front has become, sometimes killing army mules and stealing sacks of mail to demoralize the green American troops. The inexperience of the Yanks is shown by a joke circulating among them: "How many Heinies do you think came at us this morning, Sergeant? Oh, not too many, I'd say about three saloons full."

The German drive, now that it has reached the Marne, is beginning to slow down. At this stage of the war, a 40-mile advance is almost impossible to sustain. The French and the British have finally recovered from their initial shock and they are beginning to stage fierce counterattacks.

Back in Washington, President Woodrow Wilson has responded to the latest offensive of the German military forces by saying that "Germany has once more said that force and force alone shall decide whether peace and justice shall reign ... " (→June 4).

Clock is set ahead to help war effort

Washington, D.C., March 31

Starting today, the sun will set at a later hour across the United States. This extension of daytime is not the result of some strange astronomical development, but a Daylight Savings Time measure that was signed by President Wilson today. Clocks are being moved forward one hour today and they will not be set back to standard time until the end of October. The change was instituted to help the war effort by cutting electricity needs. Nevertheless, it was vigorously opposed by farmers because their work day does not coincide with the new daylight hours.

Baruch takes over military industries

Washington, D.C., Apr. 5

While the War Industries Board under Bernard Baruch takes control of American industry, the War Finance Corporation, capitalized at $500 million, will be extending loans and selling bonds to assist with the war effort. The 48-year-old Baruch was given his post in May and was granted the broadest powers to make the United States function as if, from coast to coast, it were "a single factory." His responsibilities include creating and converting facilities for the war effort, setting production and delivery priorities and buying equipment for the Allied forces.

Laws limit freedom of speech in wartime

Washington, D.C., May 16

"Beware that no faction of disloyal intrigue break the harmony or embarrass the spirit of our people," President Wilson warned in his 1916 inaugural adress. A year into the war, and those words seem almost prophetic. Congress today added the Sedition Act to the federal government's arsenal, which already has the Espionage and Sabotage Acts. Now, dissenters can be put in jail for criticizing the flag, government, draft or arms production. The law protects these institutions from "profane, violent, scurrilous, contemptuous, slurring or abusive language."

More than 2,000 people are in jail for hindering the draft, including anarchist Emma Goldman, former congressman Victor Berger and reformer Kate O'Hare. But as John Dewey objects, "What shall it profit us to defeat the Prussians if we prussianize our own selves?" Says Max Eastman, editor of the banned *Masses,* "They give you 90 days for quoting the Declaration of Independence, six months for quoting the Bible, and pretty soon somebody is going to get a life sentence for quoting Woodrow Wilson in the wrong context" (→Sept. 14).

Donning French helmets, a Negro unit under a white officer holds the line. ▷

Americans win at Marne

American 14-inch guns pound a German troop and rail center 20 miles away.

Marne River, France, June 4
The doughboys of the First Division were to reinforce the French in the Picardy sector, not to drive the Germans back. But that is what happened. The American baptism of fire was terrible. The Yanks were heavily shelled and gassed, and lost two to four times as many men as the French units in the trenches on either side of them. Nevertheless, the Americans fought back to take the strategically important town of Cantigny, though 187 were killed and 636 wounded.

At Chateau-Thierry, a full American division was moved up to stop the German Seventh Army. The Second Division should have relieved the First at Cantigny, but it was used instead to plug the gap at Chateau-Thierry. The fighting was the worst for the Americans since the battle of Five Forks in the Civil War. The Fifth Marines had the worst of it in hand-to-hand fighting near the village of Bouresches, which they captured (→July 1).

Airmail is started but has a way to go

Washington, D.C., May 15
Perhaps airmail is an idea whose time has come, but on today's historic start of the service it came to an abrupt end in a farm field 20 miles southeast of where it began. Lieutenant George Leroy Boyle of the Army Signal Corps crashed his JN-6H "Jenny" in the Waldorf, Maryland, area not long after his tardy Washington send-off by President Wilson and a crowd of dignitaries. Boyle's plane, which initially wouldn't even start – someone forgot to fill the fuel tank – went off course after he followed the wrong set of railroad tracks and missed Philadelphia. But for airmail, all was not lost. Lieutenant Torrey Webb had a successful takeoff in New York and flew mail to Philadelphia. The new service has the President's strong backing.

Court strikes down child labor law

Washington, D.C., June 3
For a little less than two years, the ragged children of the factory had the federal government as their ally. Today, the Supreme Court broke that bond, striking down the Keating-Owen child labor law with the judgment that Congress cannot "control the states in their exercise of the police power over local trade and manufacture." Out of nearly two million working children, the law covered only the 20 percent or so who work in mines and factories. But it is there that conditions are worst. Kids in Southern mills get doused with cold water when they doze off during the night. Ten-year-old boys struggle to pick sharp slate off a speeding coal belt 14 hours a day. And these, says their radical advocate Mother Jones, are "to be the future citizens of the nation."

1.4 million women in wartime work force

Washington, D.C., March 29
Government statistics released today show that 1.4 million women have replaced men at their jobs since the United States entered the war last April. Women are doing everything from assembly-line work to delivering coal to steeplejacking, and over 10,000 women are performing secretarial duties as yeomen in the navy. Some are also serving without pay. Dr. Anna Shaw, erstwhile suffrage leader, chairs the Women's Committee of the Council of National Defense, which assists women in industry, aids overseas hospitals and performs a wide range of charitable acts. Even in the late hours at home, women are doing their part by knitting socks and sweaters for the boys over there.

The hilarious actor Charlie Chaplin sheds his tramp outfit for a doughboy's uniform in his latest movie, "Shoulder Arms."

New Orleans paper finds jazz a vice

New Orleans, June 20
Never mind that jazz, the musical craze sweeping the country, was born in New Orleans. The city's leading newspaper today carried a scorching editorial calling jazz, or "jass," as it is spelled in the *Times-Picayune*, "a musical vice." The newspaper urged that New Orleans "be the last to accept the atrocity in polite society . . . and make it a point of civic honor to suppress it." New Orleans has had a district of open prostitution, Storyville, but it was recently closed under pressure from the military authorities. Still, jazz thrives there in the form of ragtime piano music.

Out of the house and into the factory. American women weld bomb casings.

Meat, wheat, light curtailed by war

Washington, D.C., July 26

Housewives across the country will be combing through their cookbooks these days in search of ways to heed the call of Food Administrator Herbert Hoover today for one meatless, two wheatless and two porkless days each week. And these women and their families will have less time for evening reading, too, because Fuel Administrator Harry Garfield has proposed four lightless nights a week to conserve energy. Those with a craving for sweets will also have to sacrifice as the result of sugar rationing that has been put into effect by the United States Food Board. Under the new rationing, each person will be limited to two pounds a month.

U.S. severs ties with Bolsheviks

Washington, D.C., Aug. 15

Ambassador to Russia DeWitt C. Poole left Moscow today. His departure ends the very limited contacts the United States has with the Bolshevik regime, which it has never recognized. Poole's action was provoked by the arrest of his British and French counterparts and comes just days after the United States decided to join with Britain, France and Japan in sending troops to Russia. Although President Wilson pledged in his 14 Points address to leave Russia alone, he has decided to approve a limited military foray to stop Germany from seizing Russian supplies and to protect Czech troops marooned in Russia by the revolution (→June 1919).

343 die as luxury liner sinks off Alaska

Alaska, Oct. 27

Battered by two days of storms, the luxury steamer Princess Sophia sank yesterday with 343 passengers and crew aboard. The loss of the Canadian Pacific liner as it was swept across a reef in Alaska's Lynn Canal was the worst civilian maritime disaster of its kind in American history. The 2,320-ton ship had plied the Alaska-Vancouver run since it was built in 1912.

After boarding passengers at Skagway, the Princess Sophia ran into a snowstorm. The vessel issued distress signals that were answered by government and other craft and it weathered the storm. When a second storm blew up, the steamer was lifted out of the water and tossed against a reef. With lifeboats useless and rescue ships unable to approach the reef, the Sophia went to the bottom. This morning all that could be found were four empty lifeboats washed up on a nearby island, the body of a woman and the only known survivor – a dog.

Washington, D.C., June 27. *Secretary of War Newton D. Baker ceremoniously draws the first draft number. With congressional approval of the Selective Service Act, the United States has adopted a conscription policy for the first time since the Civil War. Local draft boards, administered by a federal agency, help to determine who will serve in the Great War.*

Yanks win Belleau Wood

Americans remain entrenched despite the German attempt to dislodge them.

Vaux, France, July 1

A brigade of Second Division American marines thought it would clear Belleau Wood of Germans in a few hours. Twenty days and 5,200 casualties later, the job was finally completed. One French officer described Belleau Wood as Verdun on a small scale. The Americans were slaughtered in a style that was more like the war of 1914 than 1918. The wood was a slight bulge in General Erich Ludendorff's line and the forest provided the Germans with an opportunity to hide machine-gun nests behind every boulder and fallen tree.

Militarily, the wood was useless, but the Germans had it and the Americans wanted it. The Yanks were determined to prove they were good enough to take it.

The American forces were rather pleased when a captured German officer told them that his men had fought Canadians, French and Australians, but that the American marines were the toughest. The marines also succeeded in recapturing the tiny hamlet of Vaux, just northwest of Chateau-Thierry.

In the meantime, the marines of the Third Division are holding all of the Marne crossings, with Ludendorff's drive beginning to lose steam. His attempts to capture the salient, or bulge, produced by a line running from the town of Montdidier to Noyen, appears to have failed. And this failure seems to have something special to say. The German command has lost more than 600,000 men in victories that are proving illusory (→Aug. 10).

School: It's the law

Jackson, Miss., Summer

Mississippi has finally passed a compulsory school attendance law, the last state in the union to do so. The measure was approved by the legislature this summer, but only after fierce debate. Opponents argued it would benefit Negroes who pay no taxes. Governor Theodore Bilbo, however, has advocated public education, as did his predecessor, James Vardaman, even though both men are segregationists. Vardaman once said educating a Negro "only spoils a good field hand."

Million American troops stem the tide

Doughboys establish a machine-gun nest during the Meuse-Argonne offensive.

St. Mihiel, France, Sept. 26

The St. Mihiel Salient, a bulge in the German lines near Verdun, which has been there since 1914, is no more, and the tide that threatened to put the Germans in Paris has turned and is sweeping back toward Germany instead. The operation against St. Mihiel is a portent of the future because it was basically American. The United States First Army was formally organized on August 10 with General John Pershing as its commander. The Americans immediately went into the line holding about 50 miles of the front from Verdun to Pont-a-Mousson. Supported by the French Second Colonial Corps, the Americans were ready by September 12 for Marshal Foch's counteroffensive against the territorial gains made by General Erich Ludendorff in his spring offensive. The Americans attacked in a heavy fog that cleared in time for them to receive help from an Allied air force, commanded by Colonel Billy Mitchell, which did a good job of breaking up German formations with machine-gun fire. Within 12 hours, the Germans were trying to get out of the pocket. But 15,000 didn't make it and were taken prisoner. In addition, some 250 guns were captured.

When General Pershing was planning his operation, he was presented with the French Eighth Army's plan, which was the size of the New York City telephone directory. Pershing came back with a plan just 14 pages long and left the rest to what he called "initiative" and "individual enterprise."

Marshal Foch, of course, had plans of his own that, when stripped of military jargon, meant that Pershing was supposed to give most of his Expeditionary Force of 999,602 to the French. In the end, Pershing was asked to launch two great attacks on battlefields 60 miles apart. The second of them would be in the Meuse-Argonne sector with Sedan as the objective. Difficult as the task seemed, with an absolutely green army and a Johnny-come-lately staff, General Pershing has succeeded in demoralizing the German forces completely and has been able to take back all the territory that the enemy had gained in 1918. The major remaining task for the Allied command now is achievement of the quick and final defeat of the Central Powers (→Nov. 4).

The all-Negro 15th Regiment parades up Fifth Avenue in New York City, en route to an army camp. The American armed forces are segregated.

Pacifist Debs gets 10 years in prison

Cleveland, Ohio, Sept. 14

Condemning those "who would strike the sword from the hand of this nation," a federal judge has sent Socialist leader Eugene Debs to prison for 10 years. Debs allegedly violated the Espionage Act in Canton in June, when he defended the I.W.W., the Bolshevik Revolution and pacifism. "The master class has always declared the wars," Debs asserted, "the subject class has always fought the battles." Refusing to contest the charges, Debs told the jury, "While there is a lower class, I am in it; while there is a criminal element, I am of it; while there is a soul in prison, I am not free" (→March 10, 1919).

Americans, Italians rout Austrian army

Vittorio Veneto, Italy, Nov. 4

The Austrian front has broken. What began as a retreat was turned into a rout as Austrian stragglers were harassed by cavalry and Allied planes. Back in July, the 32nd Regiment of the 83rd Division of the American Expeditionary Force was sent to Italy. Actually, the unit was sent for political and morale purposes; but the Americans ended up seeing combat when the Italians crossed the Piave River and went after the Austrians, who are sick, war-weary and under strength. The greatest resistance to the Allied offensive was the high, swift water of the Piave River and many soldiers drowned in it (→11).

Mae West shimmy

New York City

Actress Mae West appears in "Sometime" on Broadway, introducing her "shimmy" dance. A new fad? The 26-year-old daughter of a prizefighter, West can throw a few punches of her own in the form of double entendres such as "It's better to be looked over than overlooked" and "It's not the men in my life that count; it's the life in my men." An entertainer since she was 5, the former "Baby Vamp" writes most of her own salacious lines.

A record for Babe: 29 shutout innings

Boston, Sept. 11

Boston's Red Sox clinched the sixth and final game of the World Series today with a 2-1 victory over the Chicago Cubs, but fans are still talking about the remarkable pitching of Babe Ruth that highlighted the classic. When Chicago scored in the fourth game, Ruth's record of 29 2/3 shutout innings was ended. The Red Sox salvaged that game, but lost the next. They then came back to win the sixth game. In the opener, Ruth pitched a six-hitter as he shut out the Cubs. The Babe started his career with Baltimore in 1914 and was sold that same year to Providence, a farm club of Boston. He is also quite a hitter.

War is over in Europe: The joys and the sadness

Compiegne, France, Nov. 11

The Great War is over. The Germans signed an armistice agreement at 5 a.m. here and it went into effect at 11. Three days ago, a German armistice commission, led by Matthias Erzberger, head of the Catholic Centrists, arrived outside Allied Headquarters in the forest near Compiegne. The terms that were presented by Marshal Foch were such that it would be utterly impossible for the Germans to resume the war after the armistice has taken effect.

In the United States, there will be an opportunity to celebrate victory twice, since the United Press mistakenly reported an armistice four days ago. That report sent thousands of people pouring into the streets in celebration of an event that had not happened. President Wilson made it official this time when he informed both houses of Congress today that "the war thus comes to an end."

Under the terms of the armistice, the Germans must evacuate all the territory west of the Rhine and the Allies will establish three bridgeheads across the great river: the French around Mainz, the Americans at Coblenz and the British at Cologne. In addition to turning over hundreds of tons of war materiel to the Allies, the Germans must also surrender their holdings in East Africa, annul the treaties of Brest-Litovsk and Bucharest and continue to live under the blockade of the Allies.

The Germans obtained some mitigation of these terms by pleading the danger of Bolshevism in a nation that is on the verge of collapse. This is apparently a real danger for the Germans since the sailors' mutiny began at Kiel on October 29, and revolutionary organizations are now springing up in industrial centers throughout Germany.

The human cost of the war is unbelievable. The Allies mobilized more than 42 million men, and 5 million of them were killed, including 50,585 Americans. There were 21 million wounded combatants in all. The Central Powers mobilized 23 million men, of whom at least 3.4 million were killed. War expenditure figures differ widely, but the best guess for the Allied effort is $30 trillion; America contributed $32 billion to that total. And still, the figures do not tell the saddest story of all – the obliteration of a whole generation of young men on the Western Front. Who knows how many fine poems and scientific discoveries will never belong to humanity because the scientist and poet were destroyed in the bloom of their youth (→Feb. 14, 1919).

"Victory Won" (1919) by Childe Hassam. At last, an end to the carnage.

Spanish flu strikes one-quarter of nation

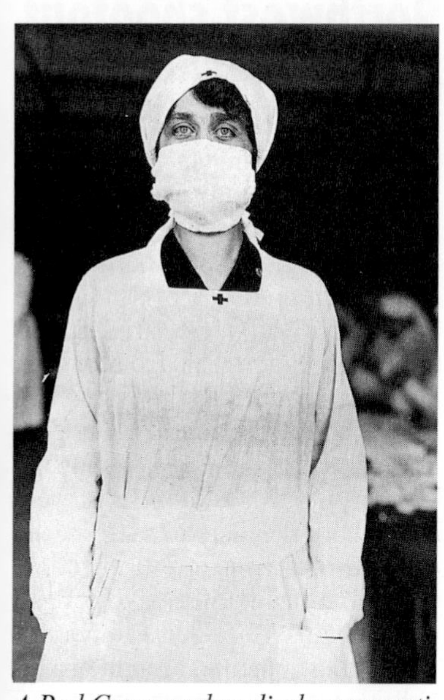

A Red Cross worker displays an anti-influenza mask she has prepared.

United States, September

One out of four people has come down with a life-threatening flu believed to have originated in Spain. Doctors have been unsuccessful in pinpointing a cure for the influenza, which is killing adults and children both here and in Europe. The Boston Stock Exchange and public buildings in several cities have been closed. In some cities, people are required to wear gauze masks in public. Philadelphia druggists are charging up to $52 for a gallon of whiskey, because it is popularly believed to be a cure for the flu. Other dubious remedies include applying onion paste to the chest and walking outdoors in the nude. In New York City alone, 400 children whose parents have died are in the care of city officials.

Wilson off to Europe for peace parley

December 4. *President Wilson boards the ship that will take him to the Versailles peace conference. Committed to the idea of making "the world safe for democracy," he sets out wholeheartedly believing that American blood has been spilled so that the world can live in peace. Under Secretary of the Navy Franklin D. Roosevelt, in top hat at center, in background* *(→ 13)*.

1919

Wilson

Washington, D.C., Jan. 29. 18th Amendment to Constitution, mandating Prohibition, is declared ratified by states.

Washington, D.C., March 2. A Republican group, led by Henry Cabot Lodge of Massachusetts, signs statement citing opposition of 37 senators and two senators-elect to proposed League of Nations (→ 4).

Seattle, Washington, March 3. Boeing flies first international airmail run, to Vancouver, Canada.

Washington, D.C., March 10. Supreme Court rules, in Schenck v. United States, that Espionage Act does not violate First Amendment (→ Dec. 21).

Hollywood, Apr. 17. Mary Pickford joins Charlie Chaplin, Douglas Fairbanks and D.W. Griffith in forming United Artists.

New York City, June 2. Poet Carl Sandburg is awarded a Pulitzer Prize for *Cornhuskers*; Booth Tarkington wins for *The Magnificent Ambersons*.

Washington, D.C., June 4. Congress approves 19th Amendment to Constitution, which would grant vote to women; it goes to states for ratification (→ Aug. 26, 1920).

Washington, D.C., July 14. State Department permits resumption of trade with Germany.

Chicago, Aug. 14. Court rules that *Chicago Tribune* libeled Henry Ford by calling him an anarchist.

Portland, Oregon, Sept. 1. About 20,000 union members in many trades march, urging adoption of Plumb Plan for joint ownership of railroads by workers, operators and federal government, and withdrawal of U.S. troops from Russia.

Chicago, Oct. 9. Cincinnati Reds defeat Chicago White Sox, five games to three, in World Series (→ 1920).

Tucson, Arizona, Nov. 20. First municipal airport opens.

DEATHS

Oyster Bay, New York, Jan. 6. Theodore Roosevelt, 26th President of United States (*Oct. 27, 1858).

Lenox, Massachusetts, Aug. 11. Andrew Carnegie, steel magnate and philanthropist (*Nov. 25, 1835).

Triumphant Wilson offers League of Nations plan to Europeans

Italy's Orlando, Britain's Lloyd George, France's Clemenceau and Wilson.

Paris, Feb. 14

President Wilson presented his final draft for a proposed League of Nations today. In Paris for a meeting of the victorious Allies, who will work out a final peace treaty with the Central Powers, the President outlined his concept of an international organization formed and dedicated to the preservation of global peace and prosperity. The league would consist of all the nations of the world, each having an equal vote. All members would agree to turn over to the league's Council all controversies among them that might lead to war. The Council, which would consist of five small nations and France, Britain, Italy, Japan and the United States, would then arbitrate the dispute and propose a peaceful and equitable solution. A member that refused the recommendations of the Council would be liable to economic sanctions and possible joint military action by the league. In essence, Wilson's proposed league is based on an international social contract. Peace, he explained, depends "upon one great force . . . the moral force of the public opinion of the world."

When Wilson arrived in France, he was met by hundreds of thousands of well-wishers who cried out, "Vive Wilson!" (→ March 2).

Senators attack League of Nations idea

Washington, D.C., March 4

Thirty-nine Republican senators led by Henry Cabot Lodge of Massachusetts announced their opposition to the President's League of Nations covenant today and said that they intend to prevent American approval of it. The Lodge faction argues that the covenant contains no procedures for a member to withdraw, does not explicitly recognize the Monroe Doctrine and allows the league to disregard the internal affairs of member nations when it makes decisions regarding those nations. President Wilson, when he heard of the Republicans' statement tonight, condemned their "selfishness" and "comprehensive ignorance of the state of the world." So the gauntlet has been thrown down – by both sides (→ June 28).

An American Legion

Paris, March 15

Delegates from 1,000 units of the American Expeditionary Force met in Paris this week to form an organization of veterans called the American Legion. Its purposes are: 1) to help with rehabilitation, 2) to promote national security, 3) to promote Americanism, and 4) to help with child welfare. Over a million Americans fought in the war.

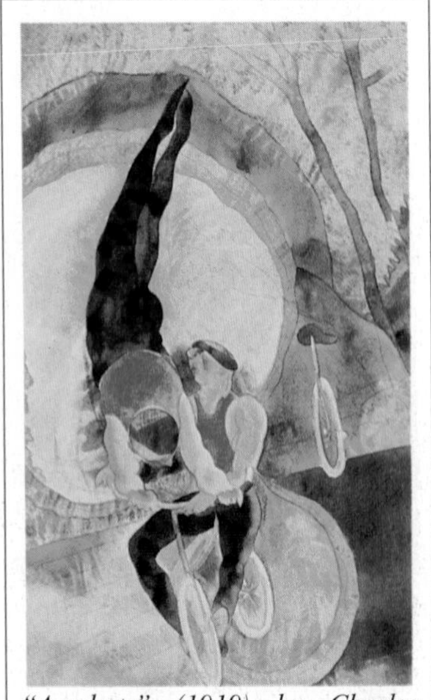

"Acrobats" (1919) by Charles Demuth, leader in Precisionism.

Molasses swamps Boston, killing 21

Boston, Jan. 15

The commercial district of Boston was mired in deadly molasses today after a 50-foot-high iron tank owned by the Purity Distilling Company exploded, killing 21 people and wounding 40. Shortly past noon, the tank, which is situated in the North End of Boston, poured forth a two-million-gallon tidal wave of molasses. The 15-foot-high surge swamped several small homes as well as a firehouse, burying and trapping many firemen. Further injuries were caused by flying sheets of metal. The surge of molasses also caused the death of a number of horses.

Northwest shootout against Wobblies

Centralia, Washington, Nov. 11

Armistice Day in Centralia does not apply to the war between capital and labor. A parade turned into a shootout today as the Industrial Workers of the World tried to defend their union hall from attack. The Wobblies, whose previous hall was demolished last year, say several men in the mob carried nooses. Three American Legionnaires were killed, and members of the Citizens Protective League are demanding justice. Tonight, after a blackout, the body of Wobbly Wesley Everest was found hanging, castrated and bullet-ridden. Other Wobblies survived, but are in jail (→ March 1920).

Versailles Treaty signed

Three of the "Big Four" in Paris.

Paris, June 28

The Great War was officially ended today as representatives of both the Allied and Central Powers formally accepted the Versailles Treaty. Meeting at the old royal palace near Paris, the signatory nations agreed to an accord that was originally inspired by the 14 Points program of President Wilson. But because of British-French opposition to many of these points and Wilson's subsequent acquiescence to the demands of the Allies, the final draft is hardly the idealistic and equitable document the President had once envisioned. The treaty brands the Germans as the specific aggressors who must bear full and final responsibility for the war. It also subjects them to backbreaking war reparations of $130 billion. It strips Germany of its colonial empire and essentially reduces it to the status of a small, powerless, agrarian nation. This Versailles Treaty unquestionably has flaws, but perhaps it will give the world an opportunity to get on with the business of living (→ Sept. 8).

2 West-East flights make it to Europe

Ireland, June 15

"The wonder is that we are here at all," said a dazed Captain John Alcock as he emerged from the wreckage of his Vickers-Vimy biplane today in an Irish bog. Together with American navigator Lieutenant Arthur W. Brown, the British pilot had just completed the first non-stop flight across a storm-tossed and fog-bound Atlantic, from Newfoundland to Clifton, Ireland, in 16 hours and 12 minutes. Back on May 27, all Lisbon cheered as a U.S. Navy NC-4 seaplane roared overhead, having just completed the first ocean crossing by air. Piloted by Lieutenant Commander A.C. Read, the big Curtiss biplane left New York on May 8 with two other planes. After engine failures and storms, and an Azores stopover, Read's plane had made it.

Boston Irish hail patriot De Valera

Boston, June 29

"The men who established your republic sought the aid of France; I seek the aid of America," said Irish nationalist Eamon De Valera today before an enthusiastic crowd of 40,000 at Fenway Park. The 36-year-old De Valera is one of the few surviving leaders of the failed Easter Rebellion of 1916. Like his compatriots, he was to be executed, but he was set free as public pressure mounted. De Valera was again arrested last year, but he escaped and went to America as a stowaway. Born in New York and raised in Ireland, the former mathematics professor aims to win support here for a unified, independent Ireland. Today, he said the Versailles Treaty must stress "the equality of right amongst nations, small no less than large," or it would be a "mockery."

First Triple Crown

New York City, June 29

Sir Barton swept to victory in the Belmont Stakes today and became the first horse to win the Triple Crown of racing. With Johnny Loftus in the irons, Sir Barton completed his sweep of the Kentucky Derby, the Preakness and the Belmont. It was the first time the feat has been achieved since 1875, when all three races were first run in one year. Ironically, Sir Barton almost didn't make it to the derby. A non-winner in six races, he had not competed in eight months. Also, he was 2 1/2 pounds overweight.

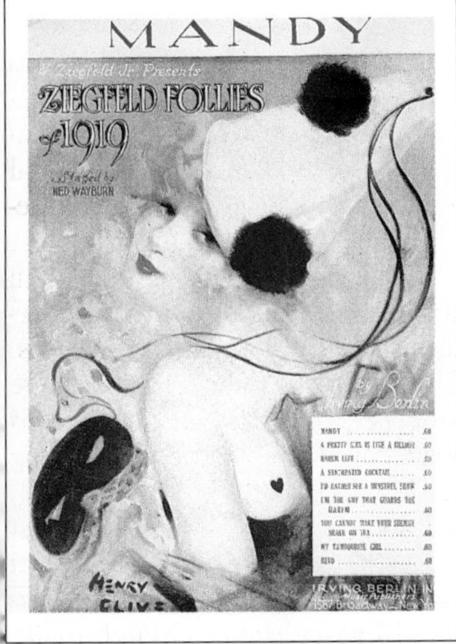

Idealist Wilson, on national tour, takes treaty to the people

Sioux Falls, S.D., Sept. 8

Faced with growing anti-League of Nations sentiment in the Senate, President Wilson has decided to take his case for ratification of the Versailles Treaty and its controversial league covenant directly to the people. Five days ago, the President launched an extensive tour of the Midwest and Far West. Advisers say that he will make about 35 major addresses during his three-week, 8,000-mile journey.

Today in Omaha, Nebraska, he said: "I can predict with absolute certainty that there will be another world war if the nations of the world do not concert the method by which to prevent it." In Sioux Falls tonight, he explained, "Some people call me an idealist. Well, that is the way I know I am an American. America is the only idealist nation in the world."

Even though his Republican adversaries in the Senate appear to be growing in strength, Wilson seems to have solid grass-roots backing among the people. Two-thirds of the state legislatures and governors have given the President their backing on the Versailles Treaty's League of Nations covenant.

A *Literary Digest* poll of newspaper editors that was taken in April suggests that the vast majority of these vital opinion-makers are in full support of the President's position. And even in the Senate, about two-thirds of the Republicans and an overwhelming number of Democrats have indicated that they favor some variation of league membership.

So even as Senator Henry Cabot Lodge and his small group of "irreconcilables" in the Senate thunder in opposition to the treaty, it would seem that President Wilson can still muster the required two-thirds majority to achieve its final approval. And the President's successful tour of the country appears to be galvanizing popular support toward that end (→ Nov. 19).

President Wilson hopes that by taking the treaty to the people, he will prevail.

Coolidge: End cop strike

National Guard restores order in Boston, endangered by strike of policemen.

Boston, Sept. 11

After stating that there is "no right to strike against the public safety by anybody, anywhere, anytime," Massachusetts Governor Calvin Coolidge today ordered the National Guard into Boston to help quell the city's police strike. The strike began two days ago when virtually all of the Boston police force refused to go to work. The mayor responded by firing the striking officers. Agreeing with the mayor, President Wilson called the strike "a crime against civilization."

With the cops off the streets, huge numbers of thugs and hooligans began roaming around. They assaulted passers-by, started fires, broke windows and looted stores. The violence did not subside until the National Guardsmen arrived late today. Spokesmen for the police say that their aims are not radical, and that their objectives are better wages and working conditions, and official recognition of their union.

Scores of Negroes die in rash of race riots

Washington, D.C., December

Federal and state leaders meeting in the nation's capital are at a loss to explain this year's racial violence – or to propose workable solutions to the growing crisis. Negroes are calling the latest outbreak of lynchings and riots the "Red Summer."

The racially inspired outbreaks began in Chicago late in July after fights erupted between Negroes and white youths at a Lake Michigan beach when a young Negro, adrift on a log and unable to swim, floated into an area that was marked "For Whites Only." The white men taunted him, then watched as he drowned. When the Chicago police refused to arrest any of the whites but did arrest a Negro, a riot ensued. Gangs of white youths invaded the Negro section of town, beat its inhabitants, looted stores and burned a number of buildings. In retaliation, Negro gangs went into the white areas of Chicago and committed the same kind of outrages. By the time the National Guard restored order two weeks later, 15 whites had been killed and 178 injured, and 23 Negroes killed and at least 342 hurt. Since then, there have been at least 24 additional race riots across the nation, and 76 Negroes have been lynched. With no solutions in sight, experts say the violence may continue into the new year (→May 31, 1921).

Vast steel strike is impressive, but it fails

Gary, Indiana, December

Demoralized by lack of funds, violence and martial law, the nation's striking steel workers are returning to their jobs in droves. Twenty people have died in the strike, 18 of them workers. In October, a clash between strikers and Negro scabs brought federal troops and martial law to Gary. Demands for union recognition, the eight-hour day and elimination of 24-hour shifts will not be met. And Judge Elbert Gary can stand by his vow that U.S. Steel "does not confer, negotiate with or combat labor unions as such." But the display of solidarity – 350,000 workers out for more than three months – rewards the effort of radical organizer William Z. Foster and proves that organized labor is returning to the steel industry.

Jack Dempsey takes world title with TKO

Toledo, Ohio, July 4

Jess Willard, the huge champion who regarded "little" Jack Dempsey as a joke, found the joke was on him today. In fact, Dempsey was all over him and battered the champion, 70 pounds heavier, into submission in three rounds. Willard was unable to answer the bell for the fourth round, unaware that Dempsey by then was also exhausted. Willard's idleness after taking the title from Jack Johnson, his lack of training and his age – 37 – all helped divest him of the title that he won in 1915.

U.S. withdraws troops from Soviet Russia

Washington, D.C., June

America's reluctant involvement in Soviet Russia's civil war is winding to a close. Having concluded that "the real thing with which to stop Bolshevism is food," President Wilson has ordered the unilateral withdrawal of 5,000 American troops now in northern Russia and has urged Britain, France and Japan to do likewise. The Allies have not succeeded in creating a democratic alternative to the Reds, which was perhaps inevitable given the disharmony that marked their intervention effort (→Nov. 16, 1933).

A stunned Jess Willard (right) watches Jack Dempsey as the title slips away.

Ostensibly deployed to aid the Czech Legion, U.S. troops parade in Vladivostok.

18th Amendment is enforced by new act

Washington, D.C., Oct. 28

A few months from now, America and non-medicinal alcohol part ways. Such is the gist of the Volstead Act, which will take effect January 16. After that, Americans may not legally make, sell or transport intoxicating liquors, which they like to call "hooch." The measure is designed to enforce the 18th Amendment, ratified January 29. It also prohibits the sale of liquor in restaurants, hotels and, of course, saloons. Though the bill was vetoed by President Wilson, his veto was overridden by the House and, today, by the Senate (→Jan. 16, 1920).

Wilson breaks down; League rejected

Washington, D.C., Nov. 19

Two months after President Wilson broke down on an 8,200-mile national tour through 14 states, the Senate today voted down the treaty that would have sanctioned a League of Nations. In three separate ballots on as many versions of the Versailles Treaty, the senators effectively denied the passage of any treaty.

The first vote concerned the treaty with reservations by Henry Cabot Lodge attached; it was defeated, 55 to 39. The second ballot offered a treaty that contained fewer Lodge reservations. It was defeated by a 51 to 41 vote. And finally, the Senate considered the full treaty, without any reservations attached. It also failed, by a vote of 53 to 38.

Although the treaty would now appear to be a dead issue, the struggle apparently continues. Wilsonian Democrats still desire a League of Nations, while Republicans, and the nation, need a treaty that will legally put an end to the war.

A major factor that led to today's Senate rejection of the Versailles Treaty was the absence of President Wilson's firm advocacy of the cause he has believed in for so long. While on a speaking tour in behalf of the treaty in Denver on September 25, he collapsed with a nervous breakdown that was aggravated by a recent attack of influenza. A week later, he suffered a cerebral hemorrhage that paralyzed his left side and almost killed him. Since his near-fatal stroke, he has been incapable of performing his presidential duties. His executive responsibilities are currently being carried out by his advisers. These, according to insiders, include his wife.

Had Wilson been in good health, his dream of a postwar world based on justice, peace and prosperity might have come true. But political reality is not based on "what ifs." Tragedy is (→March 19, 1920).

Left-wing Socialists establish own party

Chicago, Sept. 1

Battered by quarrels between reformers and revolutionaries, the Socialist Party has split. Its foreign-language leaders, ousted from the Socialist convention yesterday, have formed a Communist Party on the Bolshevik model. Another faction, led by John Reed, also advocates direct action and calls itself the Communist Labor Party. Many Socialists feel, with editor Max Eastman, that their leftist brethren seek a "Russian Bolshevik Church, with more interest in expelling heretics than winning converts."

Reed to Mencken to Winesburg, Ohio

New York City

It's a long way from Harvard's Crimson to Russia's Red revolution, but reporter John Reed, 32, made the journey in time to witness the 1917 Bolshevik coup. The Harvard grad's account of it, *Ten Days That Shook the World*, has jarred thousands of Americans. Just as fascinating is H.L. Mencken's *The American Language*, a monumental study of the evolution and special uses of the language on native shores. Also special is Sherwood Anderson's *Winesburg, Ohio*, tales that give voice to the "grotesques" inhabiting a quiet American town.

U.S., in crusading mood, deports 249 radicals to Soviet Russia

New York City, Dec. 21

"The seed of revolution is repression," counseled President Wilson earlier this month in his annual address to Congress. But no one in his Justice Department, or for that matter the nation, is listening. Today, they were too busy cheering the departure of the "Soviet Ark," which is carrying 249 aliens to the Soviet Union. Rounded up by Attorney General A. Mitchell Palmer in a series of raids last month, the 249 are considered dangerous enough to require 250 guards. But few have anything but radical beliefs to recommend their being sent out of the country.

Among the few with criminal records is Emma Goldman, who says she considers her place on the boat "an honor." Native radicals, however, are finding honor behind bars. More than 100 leaders of the Industrial Workers of the World, sentenced for sedition in August, languish in jail. Victor Berger, the first Socialist congressman, is out on appeal. Despite the resounding backing of Milwaukee voters, Congress refuses to seat him.

Economic decline and a blizzard of strikes have set the stage for the present mood. Since the end of the war, wheat prices have fallen from $2.20 to 60 cents, while a pound of cotton dropped from 40 cents to a nickel. Organized labor struck the railroad, coal, steel and construction industries. A general strike was called in Seattle that placed the city under the control of workers for several days in February. And more than 350,000 steel workers have been paralyzing the industry for the last three months.

The reaction, however, appears to far outweigh the stimulus. As journalist Walter Lippman wrote recently, "The people . . . are far more afraid of Lenin than they ever were of the Kaiser."

Funded by the American Defense Society, the National Security League and the National Civic League, a barrage of propaganda has hit the radicals. The *New York World* has charged that 10 to 15 million people have fallen under the influence of five million "Reds." Actually, membership in Bolshevik organizations is said to total less than 75,000 (→Jan. 2, 1920).

A creeping Bolshevik slithers under the American flag. Communist revolution abroad and a wave of radical activity at home incite a "Red Scare."

1920

Wilson

New York City, Jan. 5. Radio Corporation of America (RCA) formally founded, with capital of $20 million.

Washington, D.C., Feb. 28. Esch-Cummins Act approved by Congress, restoring private control of railroads and setting up Railway Labor Board.

Washington, D.C., May 20. Joint congressional resolution declares an end to state of war with Germany and Austro-Hungary [vetoed by President Wilson].

Washington, D.C., June 20. Congress passes Merchant Marine Act, to stimulate U.S. shipping by permitting government vessels to be sold to private shipping lines.

Chicago, June. Term "smokefilled room" coined to describe meeting place of party leaders who pick Warren G. Harding of Ohio to break Republican convention deadlock (→Nov. 2).

New York City, July 27. Resolute successfully defends America's Cup against British challenger Shamrock IV.

New York City, Sept. 8. First transcontinental airmail service, to San Francisco, begins.

Cleveland, Ohio, Oct. 12. Cleveland Indians defeat Brooklyn Dodgers in World Series, five games to two.

Provincetown, Mass., Nov. 3. Eugene O'Neill's play *Emperor Jones* opens, with Charlie Gilpin in title role.

Springfield, Ohio, Nov. 3. Judge F. W. Geiger, of common pleas court, erects courtroom "ankle curtain," requested by women jurors to hide their exposed ankles.

Cicero, Illinois, Nov. 20. Gangster Hymie Weiss fails in bid to invade Al Capone's fortified headquarters with an automobile convoy and troops [Weiss is murdered a few weeks later].

New York City, Nov. 27. Calvin Coolidge asserts in a speech that "civilization and profits go hand in hand."

United States, Dec. 10. President Woodrow Wilson wins Nobel Peace Prize for 1919 for work in bringing peace to Europe.

Chicago. Films *Mark of Zorro*, starring Douglas Fairbanks, and *Dr. Jekyl and Mr. Hyde*, starring John Barrymore, open.

Palmer raids net thousands of leftists

Washington, D.C., Jan. 2

In bowling alleys and pool halls, cafes, homes and offices, leaders of local radical groups across the nation were seized today. "The Department of Justice," said Attorney General A. Mitchell Palmer, "has undertaken to tear out the radical seeds that have entangled American ideas . . . the most radical socialists, the misguided anarchists . . . the moral perverts and the hysterical neurasthenic women who abound in communism."

Nearly all the 4,000 arrested are foreign-born. By the General Intelligence Office's estimate, aliens make up 90 percent of the American radical movement. And immigration rules allow deportation without trial. Wary of filing criminal suits against people whose only crime may be their political convictions, the Justice Department has left native suspects to local officials. Palmer and his deputy J. Edgar Hoover promise at least 2,700 deportations will result from this year's raid.

Attorney Gen. A. Mitchell Palmer.

A young, crusading J. Edgar Hoover.

Government officials have been zealous to say the least. In New Jersey, it took demolition experts to identify confiscated diagrams of a phonograph. In Massachusetts, 39 bakers were released after what was reportedly a "revolutionary caucus" proved to be a co-op bakery.

Prisoner treatment has not been above reproach. Captives in Boston were marched around in chains. In Detroit, 800 languish in a building with one toilet. But the *Washington Post*, its finger on the nation's pulse, says, "There is no time to waste on hair-splitting over infringement of liberty" (→Dec. 25, 1921).

City slickers now outnumber farm folk

Washington, D.C.

The census this year shows a population of 105,710,620, and a general urbanization of the nation. Less than half of those people live in the country, as the urban environment continues to seduce the rural population. The number of farm residents in America has fallen below 30 percent of the overall population. The change seems to be for the best, as the illiteracy rate has dropped to 6 percent, and since 1901 the average life expectancy of Americans has risen to 54 years from 49. The United States is producing two-thirds of the world's oil supply to help run the 15 million autos that are registered in the nation. More than 334,000 people now live in Arizona and over 960,000 people live in Florida.

Chicago's crowded streets are typical of the nation's growing urban centers.

Put your Baby Ruth in the Frigidaire

United States

What's cooking tonight – meat and potatoes? Naw! Americans are enjoying brand-new brand-name meals, featuring the likes of Underwood sardines, La Choy Chinese food, Maxwell House coffee (it's good to the last drop – Teddy Roosevelt once said so), Sunkist oranges, Campfire marshmallows, Kellogg's All-Bran cereal, Good Humor Ice Cream Suckers and Baby Ruth bars (named for the daughter of former President Cleveland). And to scour the pots and pans, folks are using Brillo.

Everything's easier nowadays. The ice chest is out and the Frigidaire is in. Silk stockings are out, and rayon hosiery from Du Pont Fibersilk Company is in. Still, it's tough deciding on an automobile. Do you want a Cadillac, a Chalmers-Franklin or a Chevrolet? A Maxwell, Mercedes or a Milburn Electric? A Packard, Peerless or Pierce-Arrow? A Salient, Stephens or Stutz? If you are health-minded, you might prefer a Ford Model T, because they say vibration from the "flivver" is good for the liver.

...ight get 25 years ...n I.W.W. killings

...eattle, Washington, March

Eight members of the Industrial ...Vorkers of the World were given ...5 to 40 years in prison today for ...nurders committed in defending ...heir union hall at Centralia last ...all. The jury urged leniency, but ...ressure for revenge won out. Since ...he killings, the county bar association has refused to defend Wob...lies, an advertisement advocated ...ynching and editors of a labor pa...er that counseled caution have ...een rewarded with indictments.

Prohibition begins: America goes dry

"The Spirit of Prohibition."

Washington, D.C., Jan. 16

At 12:01 this morning, the good ship America entered the dry dock of Prohibition. To the country's many jubilant temperance workers, it signaled heaven on earth, the Anti-Saloon League proclaiming it "dry America's first birthday." To those suddenly deprived of their "giggle-water," it was something else. The many big "farewell parties" so widely predicted were generally subdued mock funerals to better, wetter days, though New York's Hotel Vanderbilt responded in style. As a band played *Goodbye Forever*, patrons were served 100 cases of the best champagne. Elsewhere, many dealers saw their stocks seized as the country's new enforcement agents, 1,500 strong, put teeth in a temperance victory.

The temperance effort grew out of colonial Puritanism. The Rev. Cotton Mather, for one, felt liquor might drown out Christianity. The Rev. Lyman Beecher, who led the American Temperance Society early in the 19th century, said "drunkards no more than murderers shall inherit the kingdom of God." Led by fervent evangelists, temperance meetings became religious revivals. By 1835, all the Protestant churches were in the temperance camp.

With the post-Civil War founding of the Prohibition Party, the Women's Christian Temperance Union and the Anti-Saloon League, the movement took a legal tack and its arguments became more practical. Industry, it said, needed sober workers. As the legal crusade gathered steam, 26 states had prohibition laws by the time America entered the Great War. In fact, temperance leaders equated winning the war with national sobriety, and by December 18, 1917, Congress had enough votes to pass a Prohibition Amendment that was ratified on January 29, 1919.

Drink up while you can. Gentlemen in straw "skimmers" raise a final toast.

Wits for lunch

...New York City

Some of the bonnest of mots ...irculating among New York's in...siders can be traced to the Rose ...Room of the Algonquin Hotel, on ...Manhattan's 44th Street. A group ...of writers has been meeting there to ...rade gossip, barbs and putdowns. ...Regulars include journalists Alex...ander Woollcott, Heywood Broun ...and Franklin P. Adams; poet and ...fiction writer Dorothy Parker, and ...playwrights Russel Crouse, Robert ...Sherwood and George S. Kaufman. ...Now and again, a newcomer joins ...the group, but at serious risk to ...the ego. At the Algonquin Round ...Table, as the club is called, the ...wit is razor sharp.

At Plymouth Rock, ...myth with cement

Plymouth, Massachusetts

The granite boulder called Plymouth Rock has a new home. Although the Pilgrims' records do not mention the rock, Elder John Faunce identified it in 1741, more than 100 years later, as the place where the Pilgrims stepped off the Mayflower. Since then, the rock has become an American symbol. However, three years after its identification, the rock was split while being dragged in pre-Revolutionary agitation. It has been cemented together and this year the Society of Colonial Dames gave the rock a granite classical monument as a home. The structure is situated on the supposed Pilgrim landing site.

Negroes organize a baseball league

Chicago

In an effort to find a place for the nation's many talented Negro players, Andrew "Rube" Foster has organized the National Negro Baseball League. Foster, manager of the Chicago American Giants, assembled eight clubs, including the Kansas City Monarchs and the Kansas City Giants, Missouri's first Negro baseball teams. Some Negro players were included on otherwise all-white teams in the late 1800s, but by 1900 they were excluded from the organized sport, including the International League. In 1906, a league of two white and four Negro teams was formed, but it lasted just that one season.

Billy Sunday "buries" John Barleycorn

Norfolk, Virginia, Jan. 16

No sooner had Prohibition killed John Barleycorn than Billy Sunday performed the burial. With 10,000 of his followers gathered here, the noted evangelist met a special train from Milwaukee carrying Barleycorn's simulated coffin. Ever a consummate showman, Sunday sent off his nemesis with the words, "Goodbye, John. You were God's worst enemy, you were hell's best friend. I hate you with a perfect hatred." Sunday comes by the burial rites honestly: he was once assistant to an undertaker. After he was ordained a Presbyterian minister, he hit the "sawdust circuit" of evangelism with spectacular results, once converting 100,000 people at a New York revival.

Evangelist Billy Sunday strikes a pose while he brings his version of salvation to millions of Americans.

Senate spurns the Versailles Treaty

An isolationist Senate feels the wrath.

Washington, D.C., March 19

The Versailles Treaty is a dead issue after its final rejection by the Senate today. In spite of general support for the accord in the Senate and from the public, disagreement over "reservations" attached by Senator Henry Cabot Lodge, the Massachusetts Republican, were ultimately responsible for the defeat. Voting to approve the treaty were 49 senators, seven short of the two-thirds majority required. Ironically, the nay votes were made up of Republicans opposed to the treaty and Democratic supporters of the treaty who, at President Wilson's request, refused to vote for it with the attached reservations.

Senator Lodge is the leader of the opposition to the treaty and its League of Nations covenant. Last March, he introduced the Republican Round Robin, signed by 39 senators, stating their opposition to the proposed league. Lodge, as chairman of the Senate Foreign Relations Committee, used a variety of stalling tactics to give the anti-league forces time to try to sway public opinion, which has favored the treaty. Lodge spent two weeks reading the full treaty aloud to the committee before starting long and often irrelevant hearings. However, in spite of his opposition, Lodge would have accepted the treaty, if some reservations were included.

Another faction of Republicans, led by Senator William Borah of Idaho, were irreconcilably opposed to the treaty. Borah and the "irreconcilables" are proponents of the traditional American policy of isolation. The Senate voted several times on the treaty last November, and it was defeated both with the reservations and without. Strong public opinion in favor of the treaty forced the Senate's vote today.

It is possible that the Democrats, with the help of some Republican "reservationists," could have put together the votes to pass the treaty if Wilson had been willing to accept Lodge's reservations. Now, however, Wilson, who convinced the Allies at the Paris peace conference of the necessity of the League of Nations and who drafted the league covenant, is blamed for the Senate rejection of the pact and the league.

White Sox are blackened by charges they threw World Series

Chicago, Nov. 20

Can Judge Kenesaw Mountain Landis restore the tarnished image of baseball, blackened by the indictment of eight Chicago White Sox players on charges that they "threw" the 1919 World Series? Landis has been appointed baseball commissioner in an effort to win back the confidence of an American public shaken by the worst scandal in the history of the sport. In one of his first acts, he banned the eight indicted (though not convicted) athletes from organized baseball. They are Joe Jackson, Buck Weaver, Eddie Cicotte, Lefty Williams, Swede Risberg, Happy Felsch, Chick Gandil and Fred McMullin.

The eight were accused of conspiring to lose the World Series to the Cincinnati Reds in exchange for money from gambling interests. The National Commission, which was in charge of policing baseball, has been abolished and the austere Judge Landis given complete control over the game.

The most shocking indictment was that of Shoeless Joe Jackson, who had won public sympathy for his ability to rise above the background of a Southern cotton-picking family to rank with Ty Cobb and Tris Speaker as one of baseball's greatest hitters. As Jackson left the courtroom, a tearful boy reportedly pleaded, "Say it ain't so, Joe." Jackson, who received $5,000 of a promised $20,000 bribe, insisted that he had done his best in the series (he batted .375 but had some fielding lapses).

Rumors of a "fix" were widespread and bettors were putting huge amounts of money on the Reds even though the White Sox were clearly superior. Arnold Rothstein, the New York gambler, was one, knowing his group had bought off the White Sox in midseason. The signal that the "fix" was in occurred when the first Cincinnati batter was hit by a pitch. After Cicotte, a control pitcher, struck Morrie Rath in the first inning the big money poured in.

First commissioner Kenesaw Landis.

"Say it ain't so, Joe." But it is.

Garvey preaches Negro nationalism

Garvey at the helm of his movement

New York City, Aug. 1

Harlem's Liberty Hall today be came the site of a month-long meet ing of the Universal Negro Im provement Association. The na tional convention, initiated by Ne gro leader Marcus Garvey, will b attended by more than 3,000 dele gates from across the United State and will feature many speakers dis cussing the condition of Negroe around the world. On the agenda i a bill of rights for Negroes, the an nouncement of a national Negr holiday to be held annually on Au gust 31 and formation of a ship lin to help interested Negroes obtai passage to Africa. The 33-year-ol Garvey, a native of Jamaica, is bes known for his New York-base newspaper *The Negro World*, an for his "back to Africa" campaign.

Olympics resumed

Antwerp, Belgium, Aug. 24

The guns of World War I were hardly silenced before plans were made to resume the Olympics, last held in 1912. Antwerp won the honor and war-torn Belgium had only a year to build a stadium, but the Games resumed on time and the United States again carried off the lion's share of medals. There were three double winners, but none of them from America. The Finns and the Yanks each won eight golds, but the big U.S. team got many seconds and thirds. Charley Paddock won the 100-meter and Allan Woodring took the 200.

From Sinclair Lewis to Scott Fitzgerald

United States

Writers are having fun with the natives. *Main Street*, by Sinclair Lewis, laces into hometown U.S.A, in this case dubbed Gopher Prairie, Minnesota. Heroine Carol Kennicott urges her neighbors to open a book now and then, but they'll have none of her high-falutin' ways. The road from Main Street to Paradise does not pass through Princeton, at least not according to F. Scott Fitzgerald, an Ivy League dropout whose first effort, *This Side of Paradise*, reads: "Here was a new generation ... grown up to find all gods dead, all wars fought, all faiths in men shaken."

Weekly broadcasts over the air waves

Pittsburgh, Penn., Nov. 2

National radio broadcasting has begun with a bang, as well as a good deal of crackle and hiss. Station KDKA has started regular weekly broadcasts by announcing the presidential election results over the air. Although less than 1,000 receivers were tuned to the broadcast, KDKA has spurred national interest in radio and, probably, in buying radio sets. Sponsored by Westinghouse, the station featured the voice of radio hobbyist Frank Conrad, and his assistant, Donald Little. Westinghouse already has plans for several more stations.

"Babe" Ruth, bought by the New York Yankees this year, earned $20,000 and hit 54 home runs.

Suffrage succeeds: Women can vote

Washington, D.C., Aug. 26

They were denied admission to the ceremony at the home of Secretary of State Bainbridge Colby today; nevertheless, the representatives of the National Woman's Party had the last word. When Colby signed the papers certifying ratification of the 19th Amendment to the United States Constitution, he was granting half the nation's population, the women of America, the right to vote. Few of the great suffrage leaders lived to see this day. Mrs. Lucretia Mott, an abolitionist and a leader of the women's rights movement, only lived long enough to see women's suffrage in the territories of Wyoming and Utah. Mrs. Elizabeth Cady Stanton and Miss Susan B. Anthony, who each fought for suffrage for nearly 50 years, had the small satisfaction of witnessing the admission of Colorado and Idaho as woman suffrage states.

The torch was passed to today's leaders, and Miss Alice Paul and Mrs. Carrie Chapman Catt tirelessly lobbied the United States Senate to pass the federal amendment last year. The exhausting state-by-state ratification process ended a few days ago when Tennessee's legislature approved the amendment.

What is women's next step? Perhaps they will try to vote out of office some of the lawmakers who denied them the power to vote.

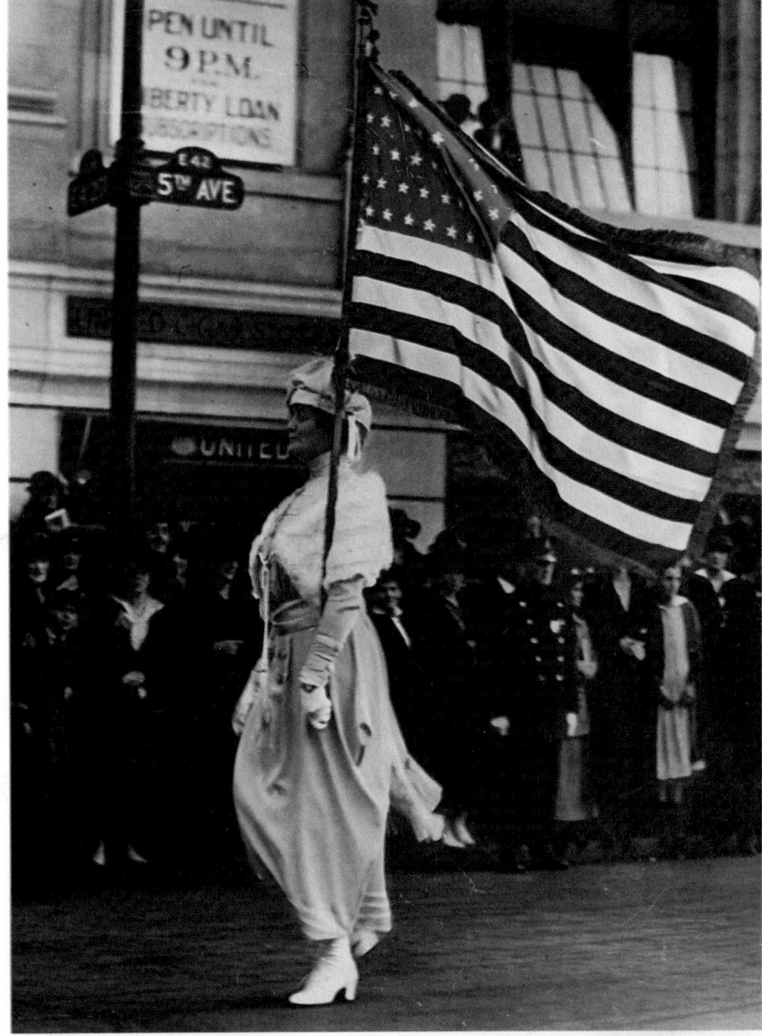

The efforts of Mrs. Herbert Carpenter, bearing the flag in a suffrage march, and scores of thousands like her, have finally led them to the voting booth.

Advocating return to normalcy, Harding and Republicans win big

Washington, D.C., Nov. 2

Warren Gamaliel Harding celebrated his 55th birthday today by winning the presidency. Republicans Harding and running mate Calvin Coolidge, Governor of Massachusetts, easily defeated Democrats James Cox for President and Franklin Roosevelt for Vice President. The party's majority in Congress also rose as voters opted for conservatism. "America's present need is not heroics but healing; not nostrums but normalcy," Harding has said. He was chosen, one pundit said, in "a smoke-filled room," after a deadlock in the convention. Socialist Party candidate Eugene Debs won 919,799 votes as he sat in jail for sedition.

After winning election, President-elect Harding strolls through the capital.

1921

Harding

Washington, D.C., Jan. 3. Supreme Court rules that trade unions are answerable to Sherman Antitrust Act, despite Clayton Act's specification that unions are not functioning in restraint of trade.

Washington, D.C., Jan. 13. Census Bureau report shows 51 percent of Americans live in towns of more than 2,500.

New York City, Feb. 23. Transcontinental airmail delivery record established: 33 hours 20 minutes.

Wichita, Kansas, March. Walter Anderson and Edgar Waldo Ingram open first White Castle hamburger stand.

Detroit, May 10. Ford Motor Company reports assets in excess of $345 million.

New York City. Edith Wharton wins Pulitzer Prize for *Age of Innocence*.

Pueblo, Colorado, June 3. About 200 are killed when a storm overflows Arkansas River.

Washington, D.C., June 20. Alice Robertson of Oklahoma becomes first woman to preside over House of Representatives; she does so for 30 minutes.

Washington, D.C., Aug. 9. Three agencies consolidate into Veteran's Bureau, to deal with all aspects of veteran relief.

Washington, D.C., Aug. 24. Congress passes Grain Futures Trading Act, guarding against manipulation and monopolies in market.

New York City, Oct. 13. World Series is "subway series" as New York Giants defeat New York Yankees, five games to three.

St. Louis, Missouri, Oct. 16. Court of Domestic Relations links increase in local divorce rate to growing economic independence of women.

Washington, D.C., Nov. 5. President Harding declares Armistice Day a legal holiday.

Moscow, Nov. 7. Isadora Duncan dances to *Internationale*, at Bolshoi Theater.

Washington, D.C., Dec. 13. Pacific Treaty, guaranteeing mutual rights to Pacific insular possessions, signed by United States, Britain, France, and Japan.

United States. Fashion-conscious women wear knee-length dresses and skirts.

Einstein tells U.S. that it's all relative

New York City

What would it be like to ride on a beam of light? Those who attended a recent lecture at Columbia University given by the theoretical physicist Albert Einstein may have had a glimpse of this. The German mathematician and scientist gained world fame last year when a total eclipse of the sun provided an opportunity to test his "general theory of relativity." His fame has been a long time coming, since his theories first saw publication in 1905 and 1910, while he was employed at the Swiss patent office.

In 1905, he published papers on the subjects of Brownian Movement (the tendency of molecules to jiggle about when heated), the Photoelectric Effect, and Special Relativity. This last paper, and one published in 1916 on General Relativity, resulted from his meditation on the course taken by a beam of light through space. Einstein's prediction that such a beam would be bent in proximity to the sun was proven true during last year's solar eclipse.

Quota system curbs flood of immigration

They made it to America in time.

Washington D.C., May 19

The government acted to curb the influx of European immigrants drastically today. Congress passed the Emergency Quota Act, which restricts entrance to only 3 percent of a given nationality's American population in the year 1910, and sets a new limit of 358,000 immigrants per year. Last year alone over 800,000 were admitted. The British, who made up 42 percent of the nation's population in 1910 will thus get 42 percent of all available visas, and Asian workers remain banned as a result of 1917 curbs. Some 40 percent of New York's 1910 population was foreign-born.

Jazz is banned in Zion (Illinois, that is)

Zion, Illinois, March 30

Along with the speakeasy and the hip flask, jazz has quickened America's postwar pulse. To some, such as temperance people, its genesis in Negro saloons and bordellos smacks of moral decadence. Therefore, the powers of Zion, Illinois, have banned its playing in public. Jazz does best in hothouses like Kansas City, where Benny Moten's Negro group plays. Moten is a protege of the ragtime composer Scott Joplin and some say his jazz is livelier than that of the all-white Original Dixieland Jazz Band. In New York, the immensely popular *Shuffle Along*, with music by pianist Eubie Blake, is building the demand for such Negro musicals.

Rx for all: whiskey

Chicago

Prohibition notwithstanding, one can still buy whiskey legally in some states of the union – whiskey prescribed by doctors for "medicinal purposes." Judging by the number of people who line up daily at the drug stores, whiskey is a popular remedy. It is now being dispensed at the rate of one million gallons a year.

Psychoanalyis is on everybody's mind

United States

When Sigmund Freud visited this country in 1909, he was amazed that "even in prudish America" his work was well known. Today, the descendants of Puritan repression are fixated on his theories. The young and wild welcome Freud as a scientific excuse for pursuing the pleasure principle. But even the generation that grew up with Queen Victoria is considering that sex may be more powerful than Shakespeare. To break down defense mechanisms, mass market therapy offers books like *Ten Thousand Dreams Interpreted* or *Sex Problems Solved.* Those who can afford it run off to Europe or corner psychiatrists at parties and ask for analysis as though it were a palm reading. Others pursue their own therapy, giving full reign to the libido at all-night petting parties and Theda Bara movies. Prudish America? Not anymore.

Business in schools

Chicago

Business is getting serious attention at major universities. Though the first business school opened in 1881, most of its subjects were academic, allowing little teaching in practical business experience. In recent years, Dartmouth, Chicago, Harvard and other major schools have been adding finance, banking and law to the curriculum.

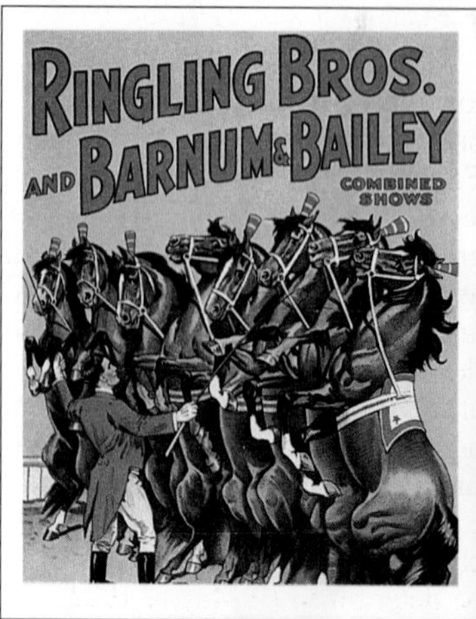

Gompers to lead A.F.L. for 40th time

Washington, D.C., June 25

Samuel Gompers was elected president of the American Federation of Labor today for the 40th time. Gompers, 71, gained prominence as head of a cigarmakers union in the 1870s, leading the fight to end sweatshop conditions in New York City. In 1886, he helped create the A.F.L., was soon elected its president and has since then been the labor movement's dominating force. Exercising what he calls "moral influence," a belief that collective persuasion befits reform better than rebellion, Gompers has led the fight for higher wages and safer conditions. The union now has 5 million members.

Gompers (right) with John L. Lewis.

Quiet Tulsa erupts; 79 die in race riots

Tulsa, Oklahoma, May 31

Residents of this small oilfield town in northeastern Oklahoma are breathing a lot easier this evening. Earlier in the day, a savage series of riots broke out, pitting Negroes against whites. The result: at least 79 people have been killed and scores wounded. Law and order were not restored until National Guardsmen sent by the Governor arrived this afternoon. Racial unrest has been plaguing this otherwise quiet town for weeks. The cause of today's violence has yet to be determined (→May 6, 1922).

Sacco and Vanzetti held guilty of murder

The defendants on their way to a trial that is provoking heated debate.

Dedham, Mass., July 14

In a most controversial decision, a jury has declared Nicola Sacco and Bartolomeo Vanzetti guilty of first-degree murder. The case concerned the slaying of a paymaster and his guard at a South Braintree, Massachusetts, shoe factory last year. Nearly $16,000 was stolen at the time, none of which has ever been found or traced to Sacco or Vanzetti. The month-long trial has attracted national attention, with many liberals and labor groups rallying to support the Italian-born defendants. Many claim that Sacco and Vanzetti were singled out for prosecution on political grounds, since they are known anarchists in an era when anti-radical sentiment is rampant in the United States.

The case against Sacco and Vanzetti began to be formed when witnesses claimed that the murderers and thieves were Italian. The defendants were arrested when they went with two other Italians to claim a car that had been linked to the crime. Both defendants were found to be carrying guns, and both made false statements upon arrest, though the defense says they did so in fear of deportation. The money was not found in their possession, neither had a criminal record, and further evidence has been scanty.

Judge Webster Thayer, criticized by many as having been unfair to the defense, has not yet sentenced the two men (→Aug. 23, 1927).

Taft dream comes true: He's Chief Justice

"William H. Taft" by MacCameron.

Washington, D.C., June 30

"Politics makes me sick," wrote William Howard Taft during his presidency. He always wanted to rise above politics and serve on the Supreme Court. Taft's dream came true today as President Harding named him Chief Justice. Taft brings conservatism and a respected reputation to the bench. While he advocates states' rights, many see him leaning to the liberal side on social issues. Major tasks will be to lighten the huge load of cases on the docket – the court is far behind schedule – and to unify the justices. Nearly a quarter of recent decisions have elicited strong dissents.

Troops and planes battle coal strikers

Logan County, W. Va., Sept. 5

Helped by 2,100 federal troops and cover from several planes, coal operators have warded off a retaliatory union attack. Five miners were slain earlier in labor strife here and 4,000 of their fellows were advancing on a wide front to avenge the deaths. The miners have now been halted, and 600 have surrendered to authorities. Violence has ruled coal country for two years as the United Mine Workers struggle to organize fields that are at least half non-union. Company guards patrol Logan County's borders keeping union men out. Last year in neighboring Mingo County, the labor war claimed 16 lives.

Ever new products to fit every need

United States

Drains clogged? Clean 'em fast with Drano! Rugs soiled? Vacuum 'em quick with Electrolux! No time to bake from scratch? Use Betty Crocker cake mix. No time to give your diet iodine? Add iodized salt! No time to write your grandma 3,000 miles away? Make a coast-to-coast telephone call. Too much time? Take up Ping Pong. Too much money? Buy a Lincoln! Is a meal too much? Eat a bag of Wise potato chips! Eat a Mounds bar! Eat an Eskimo Pie! Too good to be true? Buy some artificial or cultured pearls! Too much too soon? Perhaps.

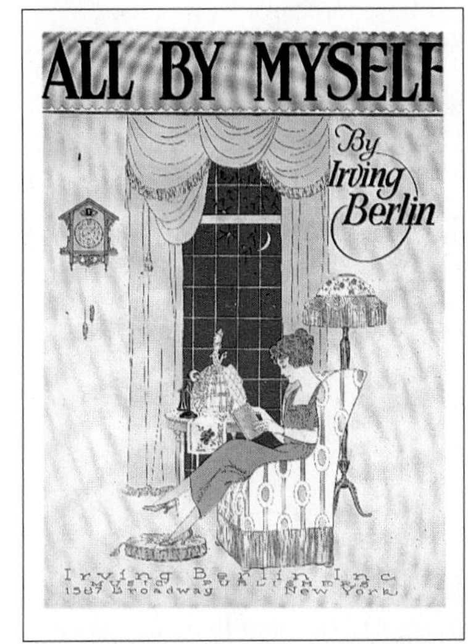

Depression hurting; Hoover has job plan

Washington, D.C., Sept. 26
The country remains mired in the grimmest economic depression since the stark pre-war slump of 1914. After the brief boom that began with the Armistice, the nation has slid steadily deeper into economic distress. The gross national product, for example, has fallen by a third since 1914. There have been more than 100,000 bankruptcies. It is estimated that the number of wage-earners in the manufacturing industries has been reduced by at least 25 percent in the last two years. Government statistics indicate that almost five million workers are now unemployed, their ranks swollen by the 453,000 farmers who have lost their homesteads and land.

Commerce Secretary Herbert Hoover, presiding over a national conference about the unemployment situation, announced today a desperate two-point program to deal with the depression. He is calling on manufacturers and industrialists to reduce their prices rather than their employees' wages. Secondly, he is proposing a sweeping, federally funded jobs program for the army of the unemployed. It remains to be seen whether the corporate executives will agree to such a novel – and voluntary – plan. And his demand that the government provide jobs makes him in the minds of many either a socialist or a communist. But everyone agrees that something has to be done – and soon.

Polio strikes FDR

Campobello, New Brunswick
Tragedy has crippled the rising political star Franklin Delano Roosevelt. The former vice presidential candidate has fallen ill with poliomyelitis and doctors say he may never walk again. He won a New York State Senate seat in 1910, gained national recognition as assistant navy secretary under President Wilson and has hinted at plans to run for governor of New York. Now, many speculate that his political aspirations may be scrapped.

Drive in, eat out

Dallas, Texas, September
With millions of cars on the roads, it's become good business to cater to mobile consumers. So a Dallas candy and tobacco wholesaler, J.G. Kirby, backed by Dr. Reuben Wright Jackson, a local physician, came up with a new roadside eating idea: It's the Pig Stand, and barbecued pork sandwiches are served to drivers who never leave their cars. "People with cars are so lazy," says Kirby, "that they don't want to get out of them to eat."

Miss America pageant held in Atlantic City

Margaret Gorman in all her glory.

Atlantic City, N.J., Sept. 7
Miss Margaret Gorman, a blue-eyed, blonde 16-year-old, has won the title "Miss America" in this resort city's first major beauty pageant. Miss Gorman stands 5 foot 1 and weighs 108 pounds; her measurements are 30-25-32. She won out over six girls, but there was a separate competition for women who fit the category of "professionals," actresses and shapely athletes. Atlantic City businessmen and reporters concocted the contest to encourage tourists to remain in town beyond the Labor Day weekend. While boosters say that the event offered the most beauteous maidens in the country, actually nobody in the competition came from farther west than Philadelphia.

Socialist Debs pardoned on Christmas Eve

"I either go out a man as I came in or I serve my term to the last day."

Washington, D.C., Dec. 25
Eugene Debs stopped in at the White House today on his way to freedom. "I either go out a man as I came in," the Socialist leader had written from the Atlanta Penitentiary, "or I serve my term to the last day." Pardoned unconditionally by President Harding, Debs leaves with his pride intact. Debs's sincerity impressed Harding during their brief meeting. The two agree on nothing politically, but they do share a passion for the cowboy film star Tom Mix.

Head of the American Railway Union in the 1890s, Debs read Karl Marx while jailed for his role in the 1894 Pullman strike. Upon his release, the tall, gaunt idealist turned to socialism. He was the par ty's perennial candidate, runnin for president in 1900 through 191 and last year, when he amasse 919,000 votes as convict No. 9653 A man who regards violence an hardball politics as abhorrent, Deb charms his following with integrit and faith. "Revolutions," he sai with total confidence at his trial "have a habit of succeeding whe the time comes for them." Now with radicalism torn by suppressio and wrangling, the need for chang that he expressed in prison echoe for all to hear: "If the earth and al it contains is not for the people . . then there is certainly a mighty mistake somewhere that needs th Almighty's correction."

Sports broadcasts

New York City
Americans no longer have to wait for morning newspapers to find out what's going on in sports. The Jack Dempsey-Georges Carpentier fight on July 2 in New Jersey was the first broadcast of a heavyweight title bout, and WJZ aired the play-by-play account of a World Series at the Yankee-Giant clash in New York. Dempsey was also involved in the first-ever prizefight broadcast, his easy victory over Billy Miske September 6 of last year. The first ringside description of a fight was broadcast on December 22, 1920, when Joe Lynch defeated Peter Herman in New York.

Enrico Caruso and Nellie Melba sing the praises of the Victrola.

1922

Harding

New York City, Feb. 5. *The Reader's Digest* begins publication in Greenwich Village.

Washington, D.C., Feb. 9. Congress authorizes a World War Foreign Debts Commission, to negotiate repayment agreements (→Jan. 10, 1923).

Hampton Roads, Va., Feb. 21. Of 45 men aboard dirigible Roma, 34 are killed as it strikes high-tension wires.

North Carolina, March 5. At Pinehurst Gun Club, Annie Oakley hits an astounding 98 out of 100 clay pigeons.

Blackstone, Virgina, May 12. A 500-square-foot hole created as 20-ton meteor falls to earth.

New York City, May 21. Pulitzer Prize goes to Booth Tarkington for *Alice Adams.*

Schenectady, N.Y., Aug. 3. First radio sound effect – two blocks of wood slapped together to simulate slamming door – produced on WGY.

Chicago, Sept. 13. Railway shopmen end two-month national strike.

Washington, D.C., Sept. 21. Congress passes Commodity Exchange Act, setting trade regulations on commodities.

New York City, September. Frank I. Cobb, in *New York World,* writes, "The forgotten man was never more forgotten than he is now."

Washington, D.C., Oct. 3. Rebecca Felton, 87, of Georgia, named nation's first woman senator, to fill vacant seat.

New York City, Oct. 8. New York Giants beat New York Yankees, four games to none, with one tie, in World Series.

Dayton, Ohio, Oct. 20. Harold Harris becomes first member of Caterpillar Club, as he parachutes safely from a crashing airplane.

New York City, Nov. 28. Jack Savage of Britain initiates skywriting in America.

Pittsburgh. *Pittsburgh Observer* reports "a change for the worse during the past year in feminine dress, dancing, manners and general moral standards."

New York City. Walter Lippmann's *Public Opinion* issued.

Teapot Dome lease spurs Senate probe

Washington, D.C., Apr. 16

The Senate, smelling a scandal in the making, has launched an investigation into charges that Secretary of the Interior Albert B. Fall has either improperly or illegally leased out the rich Teapot Dome oilfields of Wyoming that were reserved for the navy. Persistent rumors in Washington suggest that Fall took illegal loans from oilmen Edward L. Doheny and Harry Sinclair in return for favorable leases on the Wyoming reserves as well as on reserves in California. Asked about his Interior Secretary, President Harding said: "If Fall isn't an honest man, then I'm not fit to be President" (→March 4, 1923).

Film capital sweats under public lens

Hollywood, Calif., Feb. 6

William Desmond Taylor, one of Mary Pickford's directors, was shot to death in his Hollywood mansion the night of February 1. Mabel Normand and Mary Miles Minter had visited him that night. This latest scandal, just months after the Roscoe "Fatty" Arbuckle orgy, which left starlet Virginia Rappe dead after an alleged sexual assault by the 320-pound actor during one of his wild parties, has set tongues wagging and raised serious questions about the morals of filmland.

2 lynchings a week and legislation fails

Washington, D.C., May 6

There have been more than 50 lynchings of Negroes this year. In 30 of the cases, the Negroes were taken from the police by mobs. The most dramatic incident occurred in Kirvin, Texas, when 500 whites gathered to watch the burning of three Negroes. Meanwhile, the Dyer Anti-Lynching Bill failed in the Senate today following a long filibuster by Southerners. The bill, which called for the fining of law officers who allowed lynchings to take place, had been passed in the House (→Sept. 15, 1923).

5 powers sign naval pact in Washington

Washington, D.C., Feb. 6

The race to build a bigger navy has been halted, at least temporarily. The world's major naval powers signed a treaty today that places a 10-year moratorium on construction of battleships and cruisers. The treaty also limits the number of all warships and calls for the destruction of some existing ships. The five nations, the United States, Britain, Japan, France and Italy, agreed to maintain battleships in a ratio to one another of 5 to 5 to 3 to 1.7 to 1.7 respectively. In order to comply with the treaty, the United States will have to scuttle 30 warships, Britain 19 and Japan 17. Much of the credit for the success of this conference belongs to Secretary of State Charles Evans Hughes, who surprised the delegates and much of the world by proposing immediate disarmament in his opening talk. Hughes's proposals were eventually accepted with few changes. Japan accepted a smaller navy after the United States and Britain agreed not to build any further fortifications on their outposts in the region, which for the United States includes the Philippines, Guam and Wake Island, and for Britain, Hong Kong. Hughes had based the battleship ratio on current naval power, but France wanted it to reflect defensive needs. Strong public pressure finally forced France to accept the ratio, but as a concession, the treaty does not place a limit on smaller ships, including subs and destroyers (→July 21, 1930).

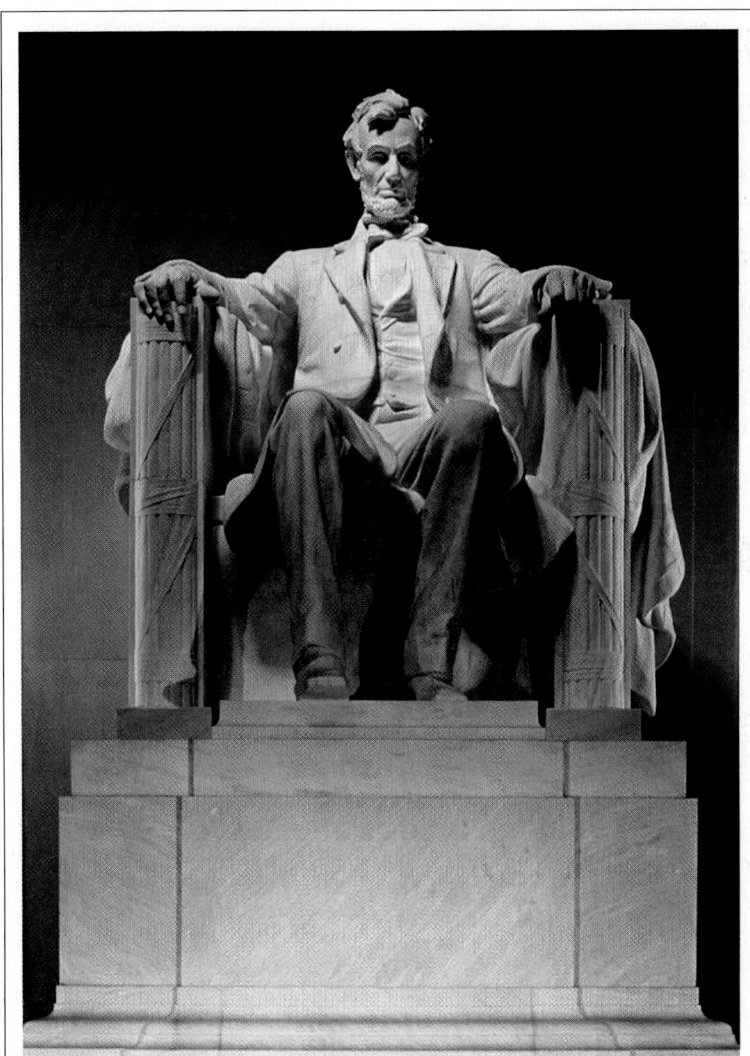

"Abraham Lincoln" designed by Daniel Chester French and carved by the Piccirilli brothers of New York. Dedicated May 30, the Lincoln Memorial, modeled after the Parthenon in Athens, honors both the 16th President and the virtues of tolerance, honesty, and constancy of the human spirit.

▷

"Tales of Jazz Age," from "Babbitt" to "The Waste Land"

Under the editorship of George Jean Nathan and H.L. Mencken, "The Smart Set" parodies the fast life.

United States

The dam has burst and – to the delight of some and the horror of others – has released a flood of new literature. Some say 1922 is a banner year in the history of Western art; others mutter prayers to the gods of decency.

Consider *Ulysses*, the epic novel by the wandering Dubliner James Joyce. Ezra Pound calls it a worthy successor to the Homer *Odyssey*, which it parallels. But censors, citing the author's use of four-letter words, think otherwise. The United States Post Office in New York set fire to 500 copies of the epic smuggled from overseas. Not that readers have found solace in the new poem by T.S. Eliot, of London by way of St. Louis and Harvard. His *The Waste Land* may be filled with high-brow allusions, but it reeks of S-E-X.

Even writers who have stayed put keep bringing up subjects that in pre-war days had no place in mixed company. F. Scott Fitzgerald, spokesman for "flappers and philosophers," relates their hangovers in his novel *The Beautiful and Damned*, and in *Tales of the Jazz Age*. And satirist Sinclair Lewis has surpassed his last smash hit, *Main Street*, in *Babbitt*, which roasts businessmen, boosters and bohemians. "His motorcar was poetry, tragedy, love and heroism," Lewis writes. From Baltimore, that sworn enemy of the "booboisie," H.L. Mencken, lights into the philistines with his *Defense of Women*.

With all that searching, is it any wonder that readers are buying up Emily Post's *Etiquette: The Blue Book of Social Usage*.

Boston puts ban on Isadora Duncan

The rebellious dancer in "Aulis."

Boston, Oct. 24

Mayor James Curley has banne Miss Isadora Duncan from furthe performances here after her pro Communist remarks and exposur of her person last night. The 24 year-old dancer had offered a pas sionate rendition of *Marche Sla* when she suddenly told her unre sponsive audience: "Life is not rea here!" Then she removed a red sash from her waist (at the same time ex posing herself) and held it aloft "This is red!" she said. "So am I It is the color of life and vigor!" She was booed off the stage.

The American-born dancer, a supporter of Bolshevism, began a dance school at a house in Moscow given her by Soviet leader Lenin She is married to Sergei Esenin, a Russian poet.

The "flapper" makes her daring debut

United States, May

The trade journal *American Hairdresser* reports that bobbed hair, worn by quite a few women this spring, will stay popular for the summer. But what right-thinking woman would have her long locks shorn, would abdicate her crown of femininity? She seems the same eccentric woman who binds her breasts to make them look smaller, who wears shapeless shirt dresses that show too much ankle. Who is this woman who drinks in speakeasies, wears rouge and lipstick, rejects cotton underwear for silk, uses shocking words like "damn," "hell" and "nerts" and puffs on cigarettes? *Vanity Fair* calls her a "flapper."

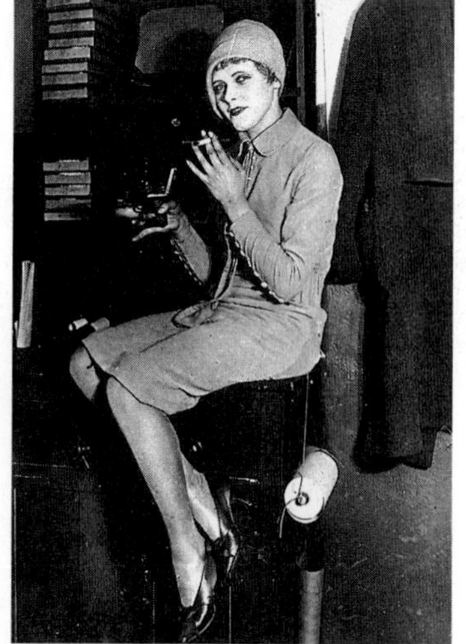

The flapper drinks and smokes.

"The Long and the Short of It."

Some adults think the girls are trying to catch the attention of today's restless, disenchanted men. These fellows don't like the responsibilities that come with wives or even girlfriends; they just want pals, so the females oblige. Some people think the opposite, that flappers neck too much to qualify as chums. In school, these girls learn all about Freud and are bent on proving his theories wrong . . . or right. Just so long as it's fun.

Mad for ads, fads

United States

Advertising proves an effective form of education. Americans now know more than ever before about halitosis, acid-stained teeth and body odor, and how these impede normal relationships. They know how to get "that school girl complexion" with Palmolive soap and how to guard the throat against excessive coughing by smoking Lucky Strikes. They have also learned it is wise to "eat more wheat," especially in the form of Gold Medal Flour. Economics is one popular course of study, as Americans begin to purchase appliances on the installment plan. "Buy now and pay later," gibberish a decade ago, now sells.

1923

Harding

Los Angeles, Jan. 1. Evangelist Aimee Semple McPherson opens her $1.5 million Angelus Temple.

Memphis, Tennessee, Feb. 16. Jazz singer Bessie Smith makes first recording, *Down-Hearted Blues*.

Washington, D.C., March 4. Agricultural Credits Act passed, making loans available to farmers.

Montana and Nevada, March 5. Legislatures enable qualifying people over 70 to draw pensions of up to $25, setting precedent.

Washington, D.C., Apr. 9. Supreme Court rules, in Adkins v. Children's Hospital, that District of Columbia's minimum wage for women and children is unconstitutional.

California, May 4. John Macready and Oakley Kelly are first to fly non-stop across continent, in 36 hours.

New York City, May 13. Pulitzer Prize awarded to Edna St. Vincent Millay for *A Few Figs from Thistles* and *The Ballad of the Harp-Weaver*.

Nenana, Alaska, July 15. President Harding hammers last spike, as Alaskan interior railroad is completed.

New York City, Oct. 15. New York Yankees beat New York Giants in World Series, four games to two.

Washington, D.C., Oct. 24. Department of Labor estimates nearly 500,000 Negroes have left South in past 12 months.

Washington, D.C., Nov. 6. Colonel Jacob Schick patents first electric shaver.

Washington, D.C., Dec. 25. First electrically lit White House Christmas tree appears.

New York City. Yankee Stadium opens; Babe Ruth celebrates with home run.

United States. Du Pont Corporation produces cellophane.

United States. Fifteen million automobiles are registered.

New York City. Photographer Edward Steichen signs contract with J. Walter Thompson agency; birth of commercial advertising photography.

New York City. Musical *Artists and Models*, with a bare-breasted chorus, stirs widespread public outrage.

Interior chief Fall quits in oil scandal

A hapless Secretary Albert B. Fall.

Washington, D.C., March 4

Secretary of the Interior Albert B. Fall submitted his resignation to President Harding early today. The embattled Fall has been the subject of a Senate investigation since last year because of suspected illegal dealings with executives of major oil companies and the unlawful leasing of government-owned oil properties. Now the cloud over Fall's head seems to be growing daily. He apparently can't explain how he was able to spend $170,000 for improvements on his ranch in New Mexico when his annual salary is only $12,000. President Harding can't believe the Interior Secretary is guilty and has said of Fall's misadventures, "I guess there'll be hell to pay" (→June 30, 1924).

U.S. pulling troops out of Germany

Washington, D.C., Jan. 10

President Harding today ordered American troops withdrawn from Germany to protest steps proposed by France and Belgium to enforce German reparations. The two Allies, angry at German failure to keep up reparations payments, have decided to occupy the Ruhr Valley in the industrial and coal-producing center of Germany. The British refuse to take part in any occupation, protesting that such a step is not sanctioned by the Versailles Treaty. Although the Allied Reparations Commission has determined that Germany owes $32 billion, no timetable was ever set to regulate payments (→Apr. 16, 1924).

Bryan defeated in bid to ban evolution

Indianapolis, May 22

After a tumultuous debate, the Presbyterian General Assembly has failed to support a motion by William Jennings Bryan to cut off financial support to any Presbyterian school "that teaches, or permits to be taught, as a proven fact either Darwinism or any other evolutionary hypothesis that links man in blood relationship with any other form of life." For years, Bryan has campaigned against evolution, saying "such a conception of man's origin would weaken the cause of democracy and strengthen class pride and the power of wealth." The former presidential nominee sees this crusade as part of his long struggle on behalf of the common people.

His battle against evolution is only part of Bryan's larger fight against modernism in religion as a whole. Bryan and the other fundamentalists reject what they see as modernism's attempts to water down the fundamentals of Christianity, especially the truth of the Bible, as well as the crucifixion and resurrection of Jesus. For them, the acceptance of evolution in place of the biblical story of creation is the first step toward destroying religious truth (→May 21, 1924).

Literary sex spawns Clean Books League

Washington, D.C.

"Foul!" is the cry reverberating through the land as steamy books roll off the presses and into the hands of eager readers. A group of outraged citizens, the Clean Books League, has fought back by mailing out leaflets that list untouchable titles such as Gertrude Atherton's *Black Oxen*, recently banned by the public library in Rochester, New York. The league, whose ranks include civic, church and law enforcement leaders, has been lobbying for the Clean Books Bill now being debated in Congress.

Dance marathons: a deadly passion

United States

"Of all the crazy competition ever invented," reports the *New York World*, "the dancing marathon wins by a considerable margin of lunacy." The madness reached its peak this year when Homer Morehouse's heart stopped beating in the 87th hour of a marathon. Homer died, but the diehards drove on, dancing to a record of 90 hours 10 minutes. Callous? Perhaps. But today's competitor will do anything for a record. Rivals have even been known to slip sleeping pills or laxatives in each other's water.

In a rare moment of rest, some of America's leaders gather. Among those seated are, from left, auto maker Henry Ford, inventor Thomas A. Edison, President Warren G. Harding and rubber magnate Harvey S. Firestone.

President Harding dies

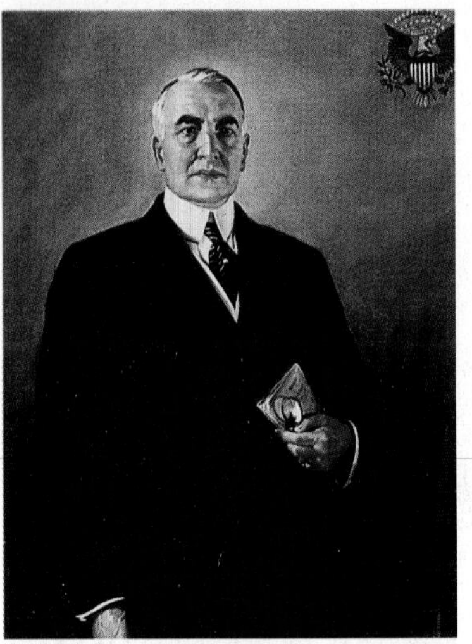
"Warren G. Harding" (1923) by Margaret L. Williams. Death may have spared him further humiliation.

Long on common sense and short on words, the new President from Vermont displays a bountiful catch.

San Francisco, Aug. 3

America grieves the death of its 29th President, Warren G. Harding. After a tiring transcontinental trip, he stopped here to rest. Yesterday, his wife was reading him a favorable article on his presidency, *A Calm Review of a Calm Man*, when he fell into his pillow, dead of apoplexy at 57. A likable man, Harding will probably be recalled as a hapless leader. Corruption surrounded him; the presidency overwhelmed him. He once said, "My God, this is a hell of a job! I have no trouble with my enemies ... my goddamn friends, they're the ones that keep me walking the floors nights." Today, Vice President Coolidge took the presidential oath (→ Dec. 6).

KKK terror spurs martial law in Oklahoma

Oklahoma City, Sept. 15

As the result of increasing racial violence, Governor J.C. Walton today activated the Oklahoma National Guard. Walton also issued an executive decree that placed the entire state under martial law. As he ordered more than 6,000 Oklahoma guardsmen to duty, he specifically blamed the rising tide of racial hatred on the Ku Klux Klan. Citing the Klan's leadership as being the primary cause of the current state of insurrection and rebellion, he proclaimed that any person found guilty of aiding the Klan's white supremacy programs would be declared an enemy of the state and subject to martial law.

The Klan is a powerful force in Oklahoma. Its members direct their philosophy of hate against not only Negroes, but also Indians, foreigners, Catholics, Jews and anyone who seems not to fit their particular concept of "American." For some years, Imperial Wizard Hiram Evans and Klan supersalesman Edward Clarke have been successful in promoting the growth of the Klan in Oklahoma, Texas and elsewhere in the Southwest. Memberships in the Klan reputedly sell for $10.

For opposing the Klan, Walton has received death threats, so his office is under 24-hour guard by state troopers. Pro-Klan state legislators have called for a special session so that impeachment proceedings can be introduced against the Governor. Walton has warned that he will jail legislators who attempt to remove him solely for his anti-Klan activities (→ March 14, 1925).

Imperial Wizard of the Ku Klux Klan rallies his followers around the flag.

U.S. Steel gives workers eight-hour day

New York City, Aug. 13

Bowing to pressure from Washington, U.S. Steel announced today that major steel firms will institute the eight-hour day. President Harding had been besieged by the clamor for reduced hours since a 1920 interchurch report detailed conditions in the steel industry. "Nothing will contribute so much to American industrial stability," said the President, "as the abolition of the 12-hour working day and the seven-day working week."

A bouquet of American beauties at the Miss America competition.

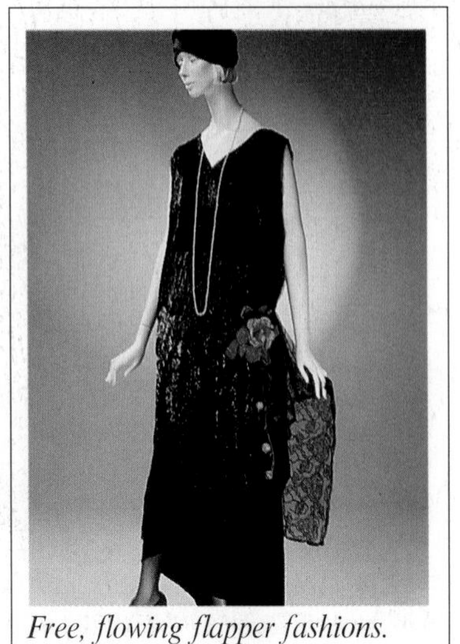
Free, flowing flapper fashions.

For the fun of it

United States

Dr. Emile Coue, a French psychologist who recently visited the United States, urges Americans to believe that "every day, in every way, they are getting better and better." They most certainly are getting better at amusing themselves, whether it be by playing contract bridge or the Chinese game of mah jongg or roller-skating or consulting ouija boards or sitting on flagpoles or taking raisin breaks instead of tea in the afternoons or yo-yoing a yoyo (the up-and-down toy invented in the Philippines).

Luce founds Time

New York City

In this age of the airplane and the radio, news happens so quickly that it's a struggle to keep up, especially if you've got your own row to hoe. At last, the busy can find time or, rather, *Time*, the first "newsmagazine" in the country. It's the brainchild of Henry A. Luce and Briton Hadden, recent graduates of Yale, where Luce edited the campus daily. *Time* is a slim weekly but it stretches across the whole world, condensing important and amusing events into capsule reports written in a distinctive style.

'ou may get a picture in your radio set

'ussian-born inventor Vladimir 'worykin. Though it is still in a ıdimentary phase, Zworykin's sys- 'm offers endless possibilities.

New York City, Dec. 23

Imagine a picture being transmitted through your radio set. It may someday be possible. Russian-born engineer Vladimir Zworykin has demonstrated his new invention, called the iconoscope, which may make possible widespread transmission of pictures, even moving pictures. The 34-year-old engineer has produced a crude but workable system, though a commercial application may be years away. Zworykin, who learned his craft in Russia and at college in France, came to the United States after the war, and studied at the University of Pittsburgh. His work has relied on earlier experiments by the English scientist Campbell Swinton, the Russian Boris Rosing, and on Albert Einstein's photoelectric theory.

Jation hears Silent Cal speak on airwaves

Vashington, D.C., Dec. 6

The man doesn't talk much, but 'hen he does, people listen. Thouands of Americans turned on their adios to hear taciturn President 'oolidge today as he delivered the rst official presidential message ver the airwaves. The speech was lso Coolidge's second to Congress nce entering the White House afer the death of President Warren ;. Harding in August.

Epitomizing his free enterprise philosophy, "Silent Cal" called for tax reductions in today's speech. He also reiterated his support for the World Court and repayment of war debts by the Allies, and declared his belief that America should distance itself from the League of Nations.

Coolidge, aware that he has a sober personality, once joked: "I think the American public wants a solemn ass as a President and I think I'll go along with them."

crowd listens carefully as Calvin Coolidge addresses Congress. Loudspeakers re set up so all can hear from a man who doesn't speak out all that much.

Warners to "Hunchback" to Rin Tin Tin

Hooray for Hollywood! As the movie industry grows, so too does its capital.

Hollywood, California

The film company Warner Bros. has been incorporated by Harry, Albert, Sam and Jack L. Warner, who started in the film business in 1903 with a nickelodeon in Newcastle, Pennsylvania. This year, Paramount has produced two of the biggest moneymakers ever, James Cruze's *The Covered Wagon* and Cecil B. De Mille's *The Ten Commandments*. The former chronicles the trek out West, using authentic locations and wagons, while the latter recreates Egypt in the California desert. From Universal comes *The Hunchback of Notre Dame* with Lon Chaney as Quasimodo – in an outfit that makes his suffering on screen rather genuine (it includes a 70-pound rubber lump on his back). The newest star in movies is Rin Tin Tin, a handsome German shepherd said to have been found in a trench during the World War. On the dark side, popular actor Wallace Reid has died of morphine addiction. Fame and sadness dwell in this place, which is now identified by a sign in the hills above that spells it out in letters three stories high: HOLLYWOOD.

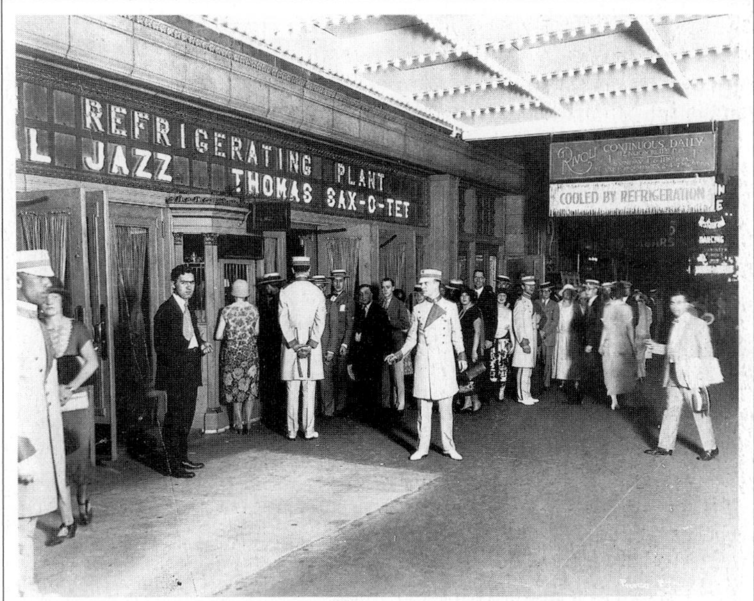

New Yorkers line up to hear the Thomas Sax-O-Tet at the Rivoli Theater. And no matter how hot the jazz may get, air-conditioning will keep it cool.

1924

Coolidge

New York City, Jan. 1. Radios in American homes now total 2.5 million; in 1920, there were only 2,000.

Washington, D.C., March 10. J. Edgar Hoover appointed acting director of Bureau of Investigation, vowing to administer it with "no politics and no outside influence."

Washington, D.C., March 31. Supreme Court rules, in Oregon Case, that states cannot compel children of school age to attend school.

New York City, May 11. Robert Frost wins Pulitzer Prize in poetry for *New Hampshire: A Poem with Notes and Grace Notes.*

San Antonio, Texas, May 21. Presbyterian General Assembly calls evolutionary theory untenable (→March 13, 1925).

Chicago, May 31. Nathan Leopold and Richard Loeb confess to "thrill murder" (→Jan. 1, 1925).

Lorain, Ohio, June 28. Tornado kills 75, injures 1,037 and causes $25 million in damages.

Tijuana, Mexico, July 4. American Cesar Cardini, owner of Caesar's Place restaurant, creates Caesar Salad.

New York City, July 9. Democrats nominate John W. Davis of West Virginia for President, on 103rd ballot.

New York City, Oct. 8. National Lutheran Conference bans use of jazz in churches.

Washington, D.C., Oct. 10. Senators beat Giants in World Series, four games to three.

New York City, Nov. 30. RCA transmits photographs from London by wireless.

New York City, November. Macy's department store holds first Thanksgiving Day Parade.

New York City. Clarence Birdseye introduces process for fish freezing, suitable for immediate oven cooking.

California. Walt Disney creates his first cartoon, *Alice's Wonderland.*

New York City. Herman Melville's *Billy Budd, Foretopman,* written in 1891, found in tin box and published.

DEATH

Washington, D.C., Feb. 3. Woodrow Wilson, 28th President (*Dec. 28, 1856).

Major debut for "Rhapsody in Blue"

New York City, Feb. 12

The soaring clarinet that opens *Rhapsody in Blue* fittingly heralds the arrival of its young composer, George Gershwin. A jazz-hungry crowd fought its way into Aeolian Hall tonight for the rhapsody's debut at a concert billed as "an Experiment in Modern Music." Once inside they heard the first piece of jazz ever written for the concert hall, with bandleader Paul Whiteman at the helm and Gershwin at the piano. When it was over, America had a new piece of music unlike any other, and the 25-year-old Gershwin had passed from a promising songsmith to a famous composer. While a few critics were cool, Deems Taylor spoke for most when he praised a "genuine melodic gift and a piquant and individual harmonic sense."

Master composer George Gershwin.

Born George Gershovitz on the Lower East Side, Gershwin took to the piano when he was 12. At 15, he dropped out of school to earn $15 a week as a song plugger in Tin Pan Alley and soon began writing songs. His first hit was *Swanee.* Recorded in 1920 by Al Jolson, it earned the composer $10,000 in royalties in that year alone. Gershwin is now teamed with brother Ira on a show to be mounted later this year – *Lady, Be Good!*

Senate override passes Army Bonus Bill

Washington, D.C., May 19

President Coolidge has lost the battle of the Soldiers' Bonus Bill. Today's Senate vote to override Coolidge's veto gives veterans the real victory, but Democrats also savor their triumph in this fight with the White House. The legislation allocates $2 billion in 20-year annuities for those Americans who served in the Great War. The Democratic Party has been in disarray of late. As comic Will Rogers puts it, "I am a member of no organized political party. I am a Democrat." But this time, party leaders united, swinging some liberal Republicans with them, to enact the bill.

"Summer, New England" (1912) by Maurice Prendergast. Despite his death on February 1, Prendergast's impact upon American art will continue to be felt. After studying in Paris (1891-94), the innovative painter returned home where he introduced Post-Impressionism to a responsive audience.

Watson's firm gets new name: I.B.M.

Endicott, New York, Feb. 14

The Computing-Tabulating-Recording Company, which produces machines that help compile such complex statistics as the United States Census, took a new name today: International Business Machines. Thomas J. Watson, president of the company, is successor to the company's founder, Herman Hollerith, who invented a method of making computations using a system of paper cards with holes punched in them. The I.B.M. machines are now used worldwide.

Crossword crazy

New York City, Nov. 24

The fans they chew their pencils,
The fans they beat their wives.
They look up words for dead birds,
They lead such puzzling lives!

So doggerel poet Gelett Burgess describes in the *New York World* today the behavior of crossword puzzle addicts. Mania struck in mid-April when a new publishing firm called Plaza, formed by partners named Richard Simon and M. Lincoln Schuster, put out the first book of crosswords. Right off the bat, the puzzles were stumpers: the clue to three across in crossword No. 1 was "albumin from castor-oil bean." Five letters. Starts with "r." Well . . . ?

An ode to excess

United States

Have you pondered on the wonders that our world has wrought this year? Inventions with intentions good have set earth on its ear.

We have dryers that spin clothes dry, deadbolt locks crooks fail to pry, celluwipes called Kleenex for the folks who sneeze or cry.

Machines now roll the cones that scoops of ice cream call home, and ones that put the plate on plated things of chrome, and spirals on notebooks so papers do not roam.

There are marriage courses on which the co-eds tend to rave, and gizmos that give hair a permanent wave. We've got Wheaties, and writing in the sky – to advertise more things than people ought to buy.

Immigration is cut back

Newcomers to America wait patiently in the reception hall at Ellis Island.

Washington, D.C., May 26

Congress has passed the Johnson-Reed Act establishing more severe limitations and regulation of immigration than the Emergency Quota Act of 1921. Quotas based on the population of each ethnic group present in 1890 cut the maximum number of European immigrants to 164,000 per year, half of what was allowed under the Quota Act of 1921. All new entry visas must now be obtained abroad, but the most controversial piece of the new legislation completely bars Asian immigration to the United States. Despite rumors that Japan's ambassador may resign, the bill passed through the House and the Senate by an overwhelming majority. Senator George is quoted as saying, "East is East and West is West . . . Japan will recognize the full wisdom of our choice."

The quota, based on 2 percent of the 1890 census, will particularly affect East European immigrants, who have recently increased in number but were not a large contingent in 1890.

Racists across the nation have been advocating the legislation, and among its most diligent supporters was the Ku Klux Klan. "The United States once admitted everybody," claimed one advocate of the act, "but we found out that we were becoming an insane asylum."

An immigrant mother at Ellis Island keeps her children close beside her.

Teapot Dome is boiling

Washington, D.C., June 30

After two years of congressional investigations and protracted legal and judicial proceedings, it would appear that the Teapot Dome scandal has reached the boiling point. A federal grand jury today indicted Secretary of the Interior Albert B. Fall and two major oil company executives, Harry Sinclair and Edward L. Doheny. Fall's indictment charges him with the misappropriation of federal lands and oil reserves in Wyoming and California, while Sinclair and Doheny stand accused of bribery and conspiracy.

President Coolidge is singularly determined that Secretary Fall and his colleagues be brought to justice. In a blistering comment to his Secretary of Commerce, Herbert Hoover, the President said: "There are only three purgatories to which people can be assigned: to be damned by one's fellows; to be damned by the courts; to be damned in the next world. I want these men to get all three – without probation."

And that may happen. All three of the principal characters in the Teapot Dome scandal are now scheduled to face both civil and criminal charges (→Nov. 1, 1929).

Justice blows the lid off the teapot.

Americans dominate Olympics in Paris

Paris, July 14

Paavo Nurmi, the Flying Finn, was the star of the show, but Americans won overall honors in the Olympic Games here. The United States scored 255 unofficial points to 166 for Finland, 85 for Britain, 31 for Sweden and 20 for France. After Charley Paddock was beaten at 100 meters by Harold Abrahams, a cigar-smoking, ale-drinking Briton in a major upset, America's field event stars took over and made up for some failures on the track. The coveted decathlon title went to an American, Harold Osborn, with Emerson Norton of Georgetown taking second place.

Before his death on December 13, American Federation of Labor president Samuel Gompers (right) met with Robert M. La Follette of Wisconsin, the presidential nominee of the League for Progressive Political Action. They have spent their lives fighting for the interests of the "common man."

Voters "Keep Cool With Coolidge"

"Calvin Coolidge" by J.E. Burgess.

Washington, D.C., Nov. 4
Since assuming the presidency when Harding died, Calvin Coolidge has won the hearts of many Americans with his wry wit and calm manner. Today, he won their votes for President with his laissez-faire policies and catchy campaign slogan, "Keep Cool With Coolidge." He and running mate Charles G. Dawes of Illinois scored a 382-136 electoral victory over Democratic challenger John Davis. Wisconsin Progressive Robert La Follette won six electoral votes.

Coolidge's radio address yesterday helped seal the triumph, as 30 million Americans listened. The election demonstrated the public's desire to let American business run its course with little government regulation. As Coolidge said when nominated, "America wouldn't be America if the people were shackled with government monopolies." The victory also represents the love affair the nation has with this man-of-midday-naps. Once, the President woke up from a snooze and asked, "Is the country still there?" Voters have chuckled over yarns like this: A White House guest once told Silent Cal she had a bet that she could make him say three words. "You lose," he told her.

For the first time, women won governors' races, Miriam "Ma" Ferguson in Texas and Nellie Taylor Ross in Wyoming.

Will Rogers displays wit and rope tricks

Elmira, New York, Oct. 1
Will Rogers, billed by his manager as America's Greatest Humorist, will be starting a six-month nationwide lecture tour here tonight. "If a smart man was going around the country doing this," he says, "it would be a lecture. If a politician was doing it, it would be a message." Rogers, 45, started out in the entertainment business doing rope tricks with Texas Jack's Wild West Circus. An Oklahoma native, he is proud of his Cherokee ancestry. "My folks didn't come on the Mayflower," he has said, "but they met the boat." Rogers ribs the government whenever possible, and insists that Congress has been writing his material for years.

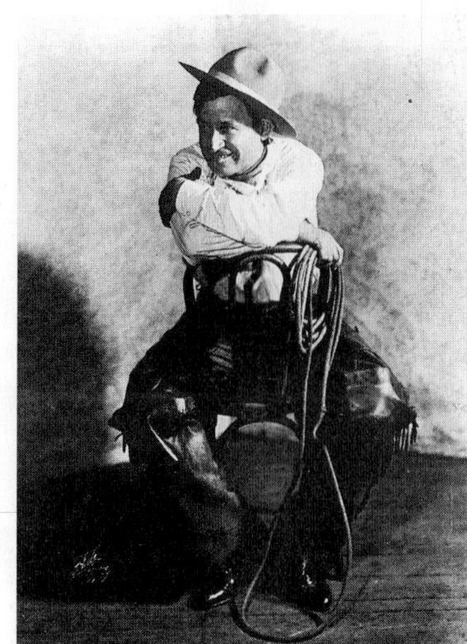
Humble and folksy, Rogers endears himself with a unique native humor.

"Orphan Annie" gets home at Daily News

New York City, Aug. 5
Look out! That feisty, curly-haired heroine of Harold Gray's new comic strip may be a little orphan, but nothing can stop Annie! With her two true friends – her dog, Sandy, and her doll, Emily Marie – she's more than capable of handling both bratty kids and bossy grown-ups! The blank-eyed *Little Orphan Annie* began today in the *New York Daily News.*

Dawes Plan for war reparations adopted

London, Apr. 16
The committee headed by Chicago banker Charles G. Dawes has agreed on a plan to stabilize the German economy and allow the resumption of reparations to the Allied nations. As part of the Dawes Plan, Allied troops will leave the Ruhr Valley, which they occupied last year to force the Germans to keep up their payments. The German Reichsbank will be reorganized and placed under Allied supervision. The plan also sets a schedule for annual reparations payments, which will start at one billion gold marks and rise over a five-year period to 2.5 billion (→June 7, 1929).

Moving pictures get new corporate image

Hollywood, California
As Hollywood steps up its export of manufactured fantasies five-fold and dominates the world's screens, the old "cottage industry" is evolving into a centralized and profitable product-marketing complex. Now Columbia Pictures, an outgrowth of the C.B.C./Film Sales Company, founded in 1920 by Harry and Jack Cohn with Joe Brandt, has incorporated. And Metro-Goldwyn-Mayer (M-G-M) has been established out of the Metro Corporation (formed in 1915), the Goldwyn Picture Corporation (1917) and Louis B. Mayer Pictures (1918) under the corporate control of Loew's, Inc.

President Coolidge throws out the first ball of the World Series. Once, during a nine-inning game, he uttered only four words: "What time is it?"

A TW-3 biplane, the first type to be produced by Consolidated Aircraft. Since the end of the war, innovations in aviation technology have enabled adventurous pilots to set many records, such as the one on September 28, when three army planes circled the globe in a flight time of 363 hours.

1925

Coolidge

Wyoming, Jan. 5. Mrs. Nellie Taylor Ross becomes first woman in nation to complete her late husband's term as Governor.

New York City, Jan. 8. Igor Stravinsky makes American debut, leading New York Philharmonic in program of his own works.

Chicago, Jan. 24. First total eclipse of sun in 300 years visible in Northeast and Great Lakes region.

Washington, D.C., Feb. 27. Glacier Bay National Monument, one of more accessible natural tourist attractions in Alaska, established by presidential proclamation.

Washington, D.C., March 3. House of Representatives approves resolution of adherence to World Court at The Hague.

Tennessee, March 13. Governor signs law forbidding teaching of theory of evolution in state's public school system, or any other theory denying creationism (→ July 26).

Greenwood, Mississippi, March 14. Local ministers and businessmen lead mob in lynching of two Negroes (→ Aug. 8).

Midcontinental United States, March 28. At least 800 people are killed by series of tornadoes.

New York City, Apr. 1. Dillon, Read & Co. acquires Dodge Brothers automobile company for $146 million, largest single cash transaction to date.

Osceola, Louisiana, Apr. 18. Minister, guilty of "preaching equality," is flogged and shot by mob.

New York City, Apr. 26. Pulitzer Prizes won by Edna Ferber for *So Big* and poet Edwin Arlington Robinson for *The Man Who Died Twice.*

Tallahassee, Florida, May 13. State legislature passes bill requiring daily Bible readings in all public schools.

Pittsburgh, Oct. 15. Pirates defeat Washington Senators in World Series, four games to three.

United States. Football great Red Grange quits college for pro football after signing contract with Chicago Bears.

New York City. Sinclair Lewis's *Arrowsmith* is published.

"The business of America is business"

Lucky Strike means fine tobacco.

Washington, D.C., Jan. 17

President Calvin Coolidge is a man for the times. "The business of America," he said today in a speech, "is business." And is anyone likely to disagree?

Since the 1921 recession, American industry has been humming along with the precision of a Swiss watch. Just ask Henry Ford, whose assembly lines churn out an automobile every 10 seconds. "Machinery," Ford has declared, "is the modern Messiah." But many people seem to be praying to the wizard of Detroit himself. Industrial scholars around the world are studying that special brand of scientific management that they call "Fordisimus." And the experts who run the modern factory pay attention, too, so they copy his system of high wages, low prices and an extensive division of labor. With 40 percent of American workers earning more than $2,000 a year, mass-produced commodities are provided with a ready-made mass market.

Two years ago, sociologists determined that half of the working class of "Middletown" America owned cars. Those who are still reluctant to purchase, even on credit, are subjected to an ever-growing swarm of salesmen. One-quarter of the way into the 20th century, advertisers are spending $1 billion a year trying to persuade Americans their social lives will collapse unless they use the latest deodorant, newest mouthwash, most fashionable soap or the trendiest cigarette that is being touted (→ Jan. 7, 1928).

Unbeaten "Irish" win at Rose Bowl

Rockne (left) with the team captain.

Pasadena, Calif., Jan. 1.

Knute Rockne, who lifted Notre Dame from obscurity to football greatness, saw his "Fighting Irish" win the biggest prize of all by upsetting Stanford, 27-10, in the Rose Bowl today. Rockne was a star player for Notre Dame before taking over the coaching job. His 1924 team went through the season without a defeat, helped by the forward pass, which he perfected.

Adman says Jesus was supersalesman

New York City

Advertising mogul Bruce Barton should have titled his book *The Man Nobody Will Recognize* instead of *The Man Nobody Knows.* The man is none other than Jesus Christ, though he's not the Son of God known to most readers. The author believes Jesus was a first-class salesman and offers a unique – or blasphemous – account of his life to prove it. According to Barton, Jesus should be seen as a go-getter who boldly "picked up 12 men from the bottom ranks of business and forged them into an organization that conquered the world." Moreover, this forerunner of today's modern hotshots charmed the pants off a world of skeptics who weren't buying his bill of goods, becoming the "most popular dinner guest in Jerusalem." How did he do it? Easy, says the adman author: by making headlines, Jesus "recognized the basic principle that all good advertising is news."

"Sheik With Sheba" magazine cover. With an increase in "petting parties," a judge has condemned the auto as "a house of prostitution on wheels."

Aimee turns up; says she was abducted

Aimee Semple McPherson saves souls with a flair found in few preachers.

Douglas, Arizona, June 24

Evangelist Aimee Semple McPherson stumbled into the Calumet Hospital yesterday, overjoyed to be free of the abductors whom she said held her prisoner for the past five weeks. Mrs. McPherson, founder of the Angelus Temple in Los Angeles and noted for her dramatic revival meetings, disappeared while on a beach outing May 18. Today she told a stirring tale, which she reenacted for photographers. The abductors bagged her in blankets, she said, hid her in a secluded home and bound her hand and foot. She said eventually she broke her bonds and leaped out a window. Reporters said her clothes were quite neat despite her travails (→ 1926).

Thrill killers Leopold, Loeb serve for life

Joliet, Illinois, Jan. 1

Richard Loeb and Nathan Leopold spent the first of all their remaining New Years behind the bars of Joliet prison where they were sentenced to life terms last September for the "thrill killing" of 14-year-old Bobby Franks. In a crime that shocked the world, the two wealthy University of Chicago students said they murdered Franks for "the sport" of it. They were defended by master lawyer Clarence Darrow. By citing the theories of Sigmund Freud, a legal "first," he saved their lives, persuasively arguing that they should not be held responsible because they were emotionally deranged at the time of the crime.

Thrill killers Richard Loeb (left) an Nathan Leopold, serving life term for what they say started as a lark.

Nine teams launch basketball league

New York City

It took a lot of compromise, but nine successful professional teams from the East and Midwest finally agreed to form the American Basketball League, the first circuit to go beyond regional limits. The two-hand dribble, which isn't used in the Midwest, was dropped. Only the Celtics, who are based in New York, failed to join the talented teams that signed up for the league. The Boston Whirlwinds dropped out early. Cleveland won the title.

Yale students toss Frisbie pie plates

New Haven, Connecticut

Has Yale University introduced a course in aeronautics? Not exactly, but undergraduates are enriching their lunches and dinners at the college cafeteria by spinning tin pie plates with stunning accuracy. The pie plates, which normally hold pies baked by the Frisbie Baking Company of Bridgeport, Connecticut, become flying objects when the young men send them sailing neatly across the dining hall tables.

Dogs save Nome after 650-mile trip

Nome, Alaska, Feb. 2

A stout-hearted team of Siberian huskies has won the "race of mercy," to deliver antitoxin to diphtheria-threatened Nome. Final relay driver Gunnar Kasson pushed through a blizzard so fierce that he often could not see the trail. "So I gave Balto, my lead dog, his head and trusted to him," Kasson said. "He never faltered. Balto led. The credit is his." The relay teams covered 650 miles, beating the nine-day record by three and a half days.

Chrysler founded; sells $1,500 car

Detroit, Mich., June 6

With its production of a six-cylin der $1,500 car, the new Chrysle Company has a job on its hands. O more than 1,000 would-be autc makers since 1905, only 15 survive While output is up since 1920, mos folks want a cheaper ride. But Wal ter Chrysler is not offering a Ford type Tin Lizzy. This former presi dent of Buick and vice president o General Motors has a class car. I remains to be seen if the public wil spend this kind of money.

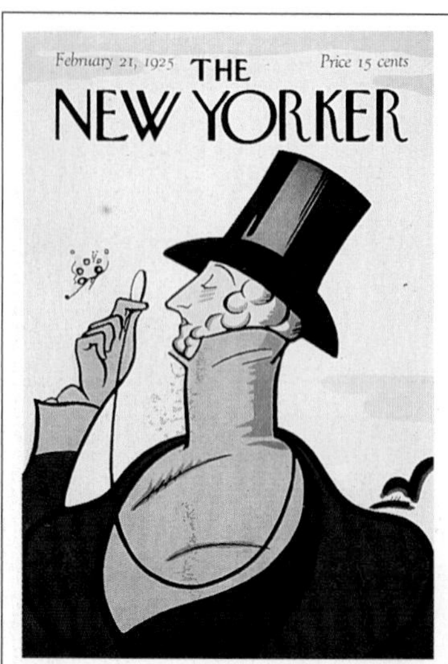

February 21. *First cover of "The New Yorker," by Rea Irvin, captures the intended level of sophistication of its writing and humor.*

At Nashville radio, the "Barn Dance"

Nashville, Tenn., Nov. 28

To some, it is country music; to others, it's hillbilly. Whatever it is, Nashville radio station WSM is now airing it on a weekly program, *Barn Dance*. Run by announcer-manager George Hay, the first hour-long effort featured "Uncle" Jimmy Thompson, an 80-year-old fiddler who protested at the end, "Shucks, a man don't get warmed up in an hour!" He says he knows 1,000 tunes and wants to play them all. Hay has been deluged with favorable mail. Aiming at down-to-earth sounds, he plans to put on groups like The Clod Hoppers and the Possum Hunters.

A frenzy of land-buying in sunny Florida

Coral Gables, Fla., August

Florida's land boom is at the frenzy stage with the offering by promoter George Merrick of a record $75 million worth of buildings, 1,000 of them, in French, Dutch, Venetian and Chinese styles, priced at $20,000 to $100,000. The sun craze has swollen Florida's population past a million and caused a housing shortage, with tourists as well as speculators camping out along hundreds of miles of roads. Citrus groves have been devoured to provide 20 million 50-foot building lots for sale in a gold-rush-style land hysteria. Some who sold one or two years ago are now buying back, sometimes at staggering multiples of what they paid.

The lure of Florida leaves a fev wealthy and too many the prouc owners of wet but worthless land.

Big Bill Tilden wins sixth straight title

New York City, Sept. 2.

"Big Bill" Tilden has done it again. The master tactician of tennis, with his cannonball serve, won the national championship for the sixth consecutive time today. In addition, he led the United States to the Davis Cup championship, also for a record sixth time. There were few who thought that Tilden, who won his first national title in 1920 at the age of 27, could come close to duplicating the perfection of his 1924 triumph, when he dispatched William Johnston in 58 minutes. Yet the sheer wizardry of Tilden's strokes remained constant through a smashing 1925 season.

The nattily dressed William Tilden.

Evolution on trial: Scopes convicted

Dayton, Tennessee, July 26

Five days after concluding his role in the prosecution at the trial of John Scopes for teaching the theory of evolution, William Jennings Bryan is dead of a cerebral hemorrhage. The so-called trial of the century was indeed that. Clarence Darrow led the defense. Bryan was asked to serve for the prosecution because of his crusade against evolution. The trial opened on July 10 in a carnival atmosphere. On July 16, people finally heard the oratory they expected. Bryan's first speech enthralled the crowd, which gave him a long ovation. Dudley Field Malone responded for the defense. Bryan even told Malone, "That was the greatest speech I ever heard."

The climax came when Bryan, "the Great Commoner," took the stand. Darrow called him as an expert witness on the Bible. It was not Bryan's best moment. Questioned by Darrow, he showed an ignorance of the biblical criticism he had so long been damning. The most shocking moments came as Bryan admitted to doubts that Joshua made the sun stand still – since the earth moves – and argued that the biblical creation in six days did not mean six 24-hour days. Scopes was convicted, but the Darrow grilling left Bryan a broken man. As a reporter said, "Darrow never spared him. It was masterful, but it was pitiful."

Bryan for the prosecution.

Darrow for the defense.

Clarence Darrow rests in the heat, but he remains riveted to the proceedings.

Fitzgerald, Dreiser expose social climbers

United States

If the year 1922 was a high point in world literature, 1925 belongs to the United States. Start with F. Scott Fitzgerald. Who would have guessed the glamor boy of American literature would ripen into the sure-handed artificer of *The Great Gatsby*, an utterly splendid work. Its hero, Jay Gatsby (born Gatz), has risen mysteriously, and probably illegally, from dull poverty to gleaming wealth. At his Long Island palace – it has "a marble swimming pool, and more than 40 acres of lawn and garden" – Gatsby gives parties that are costly pretexts for winning back the girl of his dreams, a Louisville belle whose brutish husband keeps low-class mistresses and a stable of polo ponies.

Social climbing is also the topic of Theodore Dreiser's new novel, *An American Tragedy*. Based on an actual homicide, it tells of a poor boy, Clyde Griffiths, poised on the brink of big money and love until a dark episode from his past threatens to ruin all. His dream concludes on the same note intoned this year by T.S. Eliot's poem, *The Hollow Men*:

This is the way the world ends
Not with a bang but a whimper.

There's also no room for sentimentality in the gibes of expatriate Gertrude Stein. In *The Making of Americans*, she declares: "A rose is a rose is a rose." So much for "a rose by any other name . . . "

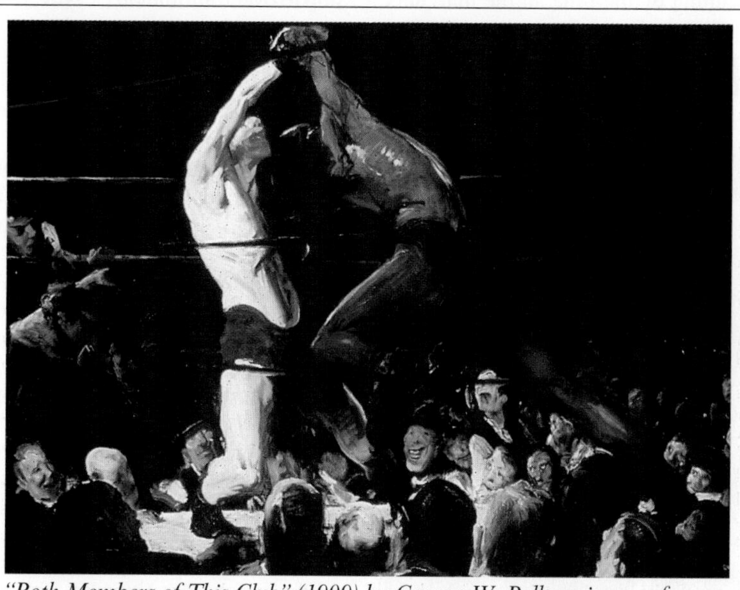

"Both Members of This Club" (1909) by George W. Bellows is one of many powerful works on boxing by the master realist, who died January 8.

Klan marches in capital

Members of the Ku Klux Klan assemble in a park in Washington, D.C.

Washington, D.C., Aug. 8

In white robes and conical caps, more than 40,000 members of the Ku Klux Klan marched through the streets of the capital today, many waving American flags. Over 200,000 spectators watched the gigantic parade, which ended at the foot of the Washington Monument. The klansmen evidently felt safety in numbers, since they did not wear the masks that they traditionally use to conceal their identities. Their costumes, however, may have provided them with some protection from the elements; it was dark and raining by the time all the marchers made it to the monument. The rain forced the white supremacist mob to cancel the massive ceremony it had planned, and to refrain from burning an 80-foot cross.

The Klan, founded in Tennessee in 1865, has carried on a reign of terror against Negroes ever since. For instance, before the 1868 election in Louisiana, it conducted "Negro hunts," murdered Republicans and left close to 500 dead. The Klan was investigated by Congress in 1871, but legislation passed against it did not last. A KKK revival that began in 1920 has swelled membership to over four million (→ Nov. 24).

Klan leader gets life term in rape death

A Grand Goblin in the night.

Noblesville, Ind., Nov. 24

D.C. Stephenson, Grand Dragon of the Indiana Realm of the Ku Klux Klan, was sentenced to life in prison today for the crimes of assault, rape and kidnapping. A sensational trial brought to light details of the capture of a young Indianapolis woman named Madge Oberholtzer, and her subsequent rape and beatings at the hands of Stephenson. Miss Oberholtzer lived just long enough to provide testimony against the Klan chief. While there has never been any evidence linking the group to the case, those who have observed the Klan don't think it is going to help the public's perception of it.

"Big Parade" brings biggest gross yet

An excited crowd packs the sidewalk in front of the Astor Theatre in New York City, awaiting show time for "The Big Parade," which has grossed $22 million.

Hollywood, California

Directed by King Vidor, *The Big Parade*, an impassioned portrait of the ordinary American caught up in war, is drawing immense audiences and has already become the biggest-grossing film ever, at $22 million. Its star, John Gilbert, has achieved worldwide popularity. M-G-M has imported a Swedish star, Greta Garbo, who came with her favorite director and mentor, Mauritz Stiller. Lon Chaney stars this year in *The Phantom of the Opera* and comedian Buster Keaton gets a lot of laughs in *Go West*. Joseph Schenck of United Artists (founded in 1919 by Charlie Chaplin, D.W. Griffith, Mary Pickford and Douglas Fairbanks) has hired a chorus girl named Lucille Le Sueur, who has been renamed Joan Crawford as a result of a fan magazine contest. An extra in *The Birth of a Nation* and a director since 1917, 30-year-old John Ford, who has transferred from Universal to Fox, shows great promise as a director. A favorite is *The Iron Horse*, which he turned out last year. William Fox has bought 450 acres on Pico Boulevard as a location ranch for Tom Mix westerns and other films, and he plans the world's largest stage with a powerhouse and generators providing enough power for a city of 60,000. Fox continues to speak out against censorship of motion pictures in the United States.

Billy Mitchell guilty

Washington, D.C., Dec. 17

Colonel William "Billy" Mitchell is guilty. In a tense courtroom, the 56-year-old champion of air power seemed relaxed as an army court-martial today suspended him for five years, finding him guilty of insubordination. The verdict follows his test sinkings of target battleships by airplanes. The colonel accused his superiors of "incompetency, criminal negligence and almost treasonable administration of national defense." But prosecuting officers branded him a "charlatan and demagogue."

Charlie Chaplin elicits laughs and tears as America's favorite little tramp in "The Gold Rush."

1926

Coolidge

Washington, D.C., Feb. 26. President Coolidge signs revenue act reducing income and inheritance taxes.

Washington, D.C., Apr. 29. United States and France sign agreement reducing French war debt.

New York City, May 5. Sinclair Lewis rejects Pulitzer Prize for *Arrowsmith*, declaring that such recognition undermines writing profession.

Washington, D.C., May 20. Congress passes Air Commerce Act, giving Commerce Department control over licensing of aircraft and pilots.

United States, July 4. On America's 150th birthday, Sherwood Anderson writes, "The machine (has caused) the herding of men into towns and cities ... Minds began to be standardized as were the clothes men wore."

Washington, D.C., July 5. Government report indicates that one in every six Americans owns an automobile.

Lackawanna, New York, July 26. Sanctuary of Our Lady of Victory Church is first Roman Catholic basilica in nation.

New York City, Aug. 27. Channel swimmer Gertrude Ederle almost crushed by well-wishers.

Chicago, Sept. 15. "Jelly Roll" Morton and "Red Hot Peppers" hold recording session for RCA.

New York City, Oct. 10. St. Louis Cardinals defeat New York Yankees in World Series, four games to three.

Washington, D.C., Oct. 25. Supreme Court, in Myers v. United States, declares 1867 Tenure of Office Act unconstitutional, giving presidents right to dismiss executive officers without senatorial consent.

United States. Aimee Semple McPherson's reputation suffers when it is suspected that her so-called kidnapping was a romantic interlude.

New York City. Book-of-the-Month Club founded.

New York City. H.L. Mencken's *Notes on Democracy* published.

New York City. *The Theory of the Gene*, published by Thomas Hunt Morgan, provides basis of genetic research.

Goddard launches first liquid fuel rocket

Robert Goddard beside the rocket he has fired into the atmosphere.

Auburn, Mass., March 16

Will it ever be possible for mankind to leave the planet Earth? A new invention of the Massachusetts physicist Robert H. Goddard has caused some to speculate in that direction. The 44-year-old professor at Clark University has developed a liquid fuel rocket that soared high into the atmosphere. Interested in high-altitude flight since he was a teenager, Goddard is the author of *A Method of Reaching Extreme Altitudes*, a report that chronicles the experiments he has conducted involving solid-propellant rocket motors. Goddard's efforts and the theories that he has developed have laid the groundwork for a whole new field of study, one that some scientists think could have great potential in two areas, transportation and warfare.

Mae West busted for moving navel

New York City, Apr. 26

Tantalizing, scintillating, sinful seductress. Ooo La La Lady of the Stage. Actress-playwright Mae West has been put under arrest. Her play, *Sex*, had the audiences squirming in their seats and the Society for the Suppression of Vice hot on her trail. The society's pressure got the police to close down the popular show and bust West for "corrupting the morals of youth." The play stars the author as a prostitute, swinging her hips and licking her lips. An undercover cop has said that the star "moved her navel up and down and from right to left" in a belly dance. His testimony may lead to her conviction and a jail sentence. No word as to whether she'd appeal (→Apr. 19, 1927).

Ford's work week: 40 hours, 5 days

Detroit, Michigan, Sept. 25

Some workers at the Ford factory are going on a 40-hour, five-day week, working less for the same pay than they received before. The plan, officially announced today, is based on ideas that Henry Ford outlined more than 10 years ago. The 40-hour week is going to help spread the work in these times of overproduction. The unions have praised it, but it's being condemned by some industrialists, who seem quite alarmed about Ford's pioneering pay of $6 a day.

Hall-Mills acquittal

New Jersey, Dec. 3

Mrs. Frances Hall was found not guilty today in the murder of her husband, the Rev. Edward Hall, and his paramour, Mrs. Eleanor Mills. Her two brothers were also absolved in New Jersey's longest, costliest trial. The crime took place at an abandoned farm four years ago, but Mrs. Hall was only recently accused after the *Daily Mirror* led a crusade against her. The public avidly followed the case, read the Hall-Mills love letters and was thrilled by the words of a dying pig farmer who implicated Mrs. Hall.

As the Roaring 20s roar on, the Charleston sets the style of the era. Developed in Charleston, South Carolina, the steps were first noted at an all-Negro review in New York in 1923. With turned-in toes, syncopated arms and flying legs, the dance even draws the older set, who do it in 4/4 time.

From Hemingway, "The Sun Also Rises"

Hemingway, expatriate in Paris.

New York City

Tales of Americans kicking up their heels in the bars and cafes of Europe have been confirmed in *The Sun Also Rises,* the first novel by Ernest Hemingway, 27. A native of Illinois who was wounded in Italy during the war, Hemingway has been in Paris since 1921 and writes for the *Toronto Star*. His *In Our Time*, a story collection, appeared last year. *The Sun*, narrated by a hard-boiled reporter wary of "all frank and simple people," stars some hell-raising young folks, mostly Yanks. Quoting Gertrude Stein in an epigraph, Hemingway writes of them, "You are all a lost generation."

Byrd and Bennett fly over North Pole

Kings Bay, Spitsbergen, May 9

Byrd and Bennett have reached the North Pole. The daring explorer Richard E. Byrd and his pilot, Floyd Bennett, returned here to an emotional reception today. Threatened by frozen fingers and engine oil leaks only 60 miles from their objective, the privately financed expedition circled the pole several times in brilliant sunlight on a flight that lasted 15 hours and 51 minutes. Their observations verify America's claim to the pole that was announced 17 years ago by Admiral Robert E. Peary and his Negro assistant, Matthew Henson.

U.S. woman swims the English Channel

Gertrude Ederle proves that neither gender nor age need be a hindrance.

Dover, England, Aug. 6

"It had to be done, and I did it," said Gertrude Ederle, the plucky little New Yorker, after she completed her swim across the English Channel today. She thus became the first woman to accomplish the feat and easily broke the best record made by any male cross-channel swimmer. Her time was 14 hours 31 minutes. The 19-year-old Miss Ederle twice ignored the advice of her coach to come out of the water, but her father and sister cheered her on. "I am doing it for Mommy," she told them. The channel was first crossed by a swimmer in 1911 (→ 27).

"You are all a lost generation?"

United States

Vanity Fair calls them "flaming youth." And Ernest Hemingway writes of a "lost generation." But are today's young Americans truly very different from those who have gone before? Yes – and no. No previous generation saw the kind of destruction this one saw in the Great War, an experience that can crush all innocence. No previous generation has seen a machine age that renders minds as "standardized as the clothes men wore," as Sherwood Anderson writes. What generation has seen so many of its parents brazenly break the law as they flout the Prohibition Amendment? And what generation has had such privileges, from the ownership of automobiles where lovemaking proceeds unseen, to pocketing so much spending money to afford so many dreams? These youths are celebrated in the art of John Held Jr. and the words of F. Scott Fitzgerald, who wrote this year, "The parties were bigger. The pace was faster . . . morals looser." But then, doesn't every generation feel it is somehow changing the world?

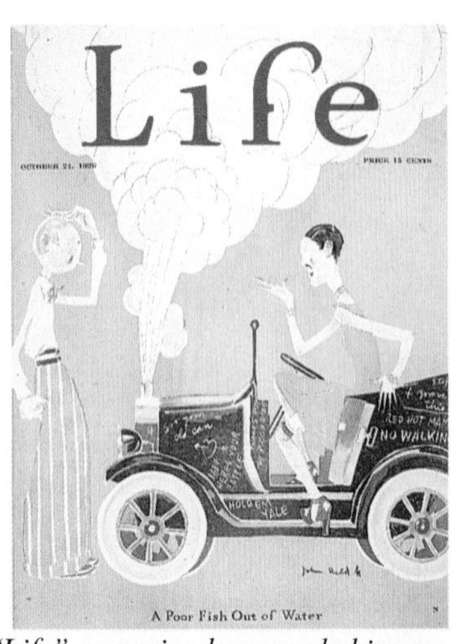

John Held Jr.'s cover illustrations for "Life" magazine have made him one of the most popular artists of the day. A full-time cartoonist since the age of 16, Held has achieved tremendous fame for his simple, lively portrayals of life in the Jazz Age. When not illustrating, the versatile artist draws newspaper comic strips, including, "Merely Margie, an Awfully Sweet Girl."

NBC is incorporated

New York City, Oct. 9

The National Broadcasting Company, the first radio chain in the United States and a subsidiary of the Radio Corporation of America, was incorporated today. David Sarnoff, the president of NBC, first impressed RCA directors with the possibilities of radio with his blow-by-blow coverage of the Dempsey-Carpentier fight in 1921. Sarnoff, a Russian immigrant who started at RCA as an office boy, has promoted the radio business for several years. He was largely responsible for the $83 million in radio set sales RCA chalked up from 1921 to 1924.

"Mother and Child" (1905) by Mary Cassatt. The Impressionist painter's career was prematurely ended in 1914 because of failing eyesight. She died on June 14.

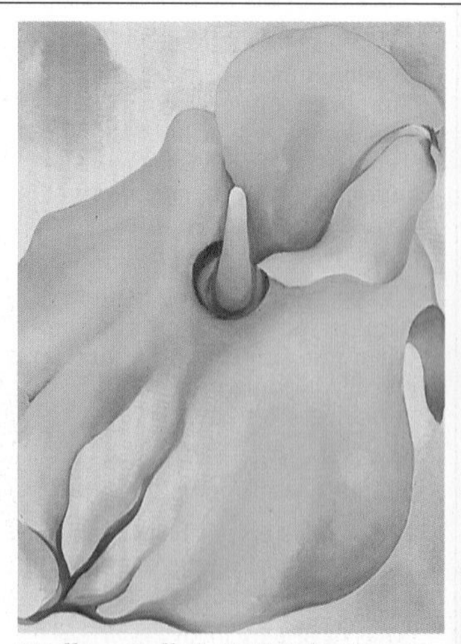
"Yellow Calla" (1926) by Georgia O'Keeffe. The Wisconsin artist's work with flowers and bones is hailed as unique for the variety of emotive responses that it evokes.

Valentino is dead; long live the Sheik

Valentino's striking good looks made him America's leading screen lover.

Hollywood, Calif., September

He died on August 23, at the age of 31, the darkly handsome Rudolph Valentino, who brought a sense of mysterious eroticism and fulfillment of dreams to the screen in movies such as *Blood and Sand*, *Monsieur Beaucaire*, *The Eagle*, and *The Son of the Sheik*. His sudden death, due to a perforated ulcer, caused mass hysteria among female fans. Thousands lined the streets at his funeral, where stars such as Pola Negri and Marion Kay broke down, sobbing loudly. A picture of Valentino meeting Caruso in heaven is being widely circulated.

"Ben Hur," "Don Juan" with musical sound, and Greta Garbo

Improved technology allows movie makers to leave the studio and create scenes such as the chariot race in M-G-M's "Ben Hur," featuring Ramon Novarro.

John Barrymore, starring in the big hit from Warner Bros., "Don Juan."

Hollywood, Calif., October

More than 14,500 movie houses show 400 films a year, with the movies becoming America's favorite entertainment, ever changing and developing. Ramon Novarro plays the title role in *Ben-Hur*, the most expensive film ever made. *The Black Pirate*, with Douglas Fairbanks, uses Technicolor film with great success. *Don Juan*, with John Barrymore, just opened and is the first motion picture with a synchronized musical score, produced by a phonograph. Warner Bros., which accomplished this in association with Vitaphone, talks of a "sound era." Fox has responded with Movietone, a sound-on-film process developed in association with General Electric. Stars are paid ever more money. M-G-M has raised Greta Garbo's salary from $550 to $5,000 a week, based on her first American film, *The Torrent*. Even football star Red Grange has been paid $300,000 for his role in *One Minute to Play*.

Interesting new releases include *Variety* from Paramount, starring Emil Jannings; *What Price Glory?* from Fox, starring Victor McLaglen and Edmund Lowe, and *The Strong Man*, with Harry Langdon playing the "dumb clown," directed by the inventive Frank Capra. Mary Pickford, still the "essence of America," is starring in *Sparrows*.

The personality cult growing up around the movies has reached immense proportions. Valentino was a good example of this. So is Garbo. Charlie Chaplin is mobbed if he so much as ventures into the street (last year's *The Gold Rush* is still enjoying great success). And coming next year, there's *It*, with newcomer Clara Bow, the "It Girl" who offers "the same as before but more of it showing" and "a little more available."

U.S. Marshal Matheus directs the destruction of some $300,000 worth of imported liquors and wines seized from a wholesale house in Philadelphia. Similar scenes are taking place from one end of the country to the other.

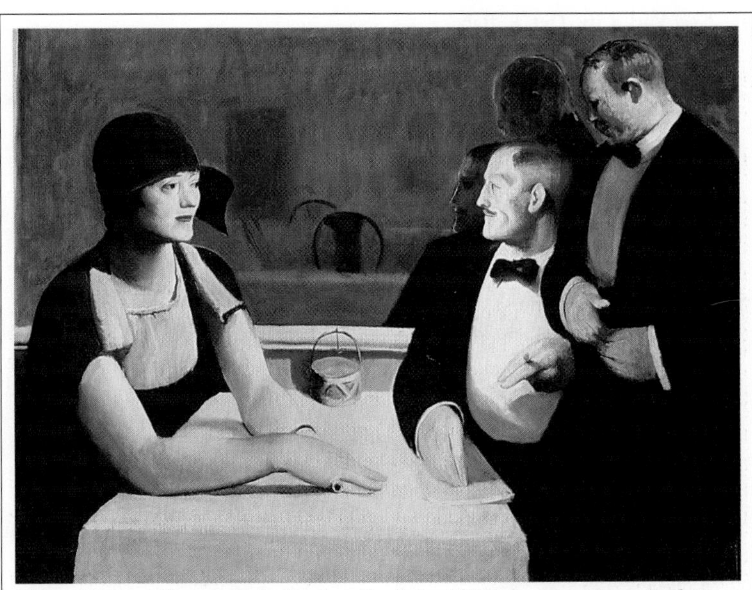

"Mr. & Mrs. Chester Dale Dining Out" (c. 1926) by Guy Pene Dubois, a Brooklyn-born painter of people of fashion who studied under Robert Henri.

1927

Coolidge

Washington, D.C., Jan. 5. *National Geographic* publishes first underwater photographs.

San Francisco, Jan. 15. Dumbarton Bridge opens, carrying first automobile traffic across San Francisco Bay.

Honolulu, Feb. 1. Royal Hawaiian Hotel, called "Pink Stucco Palace," opens at Waikiki Beach, with room for 1,200 guests.

Washington, D.C., Feb. 18. United States establishes diplomatic relations with Canada, independent of Britain.

New York City, Apr. 17. Alfred E. Smith, Democratic White House aspirant, denies Catholicism would influence his judgment as president.

New York City, Apr. 19. Mae West given 10-day sentence and fined $500 for her role in play *Sex*.

Mississippi Valley, May. Heavy rains cause Mississippi River and tributaries to overflow, drowning hundreds, leaving 675,000 homeless and creating a 30,000 square-mile lake in Louisiana.

Detroit, July 7. Henry Ford forced by court to retract published anti-Semitic remarks.

New York City, July 29. Drs. Philip Drinker and Louis A. Shaw operate an "iron lung," at Bellevue Hospital.

South Dakota, August. Gutzon Borglum begins work on carvings of Presidents' heads on Mount Rushmore (→ Nov. 1, 1941).

New York City, Oct. 8. Babe Ruth's three home runs help New York Yankees defeat Pittsburgh Pirates in World Series sweep.

New York City, Nov. 3. Musical *A Connecticut Yankee* opens, based on Mark Twain's story.

New York City, Nov. 13. Holland Tunnel under Hudson River opens; first such tunnel.

New York City, Dec. 4. Duke Ellington's band opens at Harlem's Cotton Club; [show will continue for four years].

New York City. Alexander Kerensky, head of overthrown Russian provisional government, settles here.

New York City. Willa Cather's *Death Comes for the Archbishop* published.

Television introduced to American public

New York City, Apr. 7

The first public demonstration in America of the new invention television has shown its potential not only as an entertainment medium, but as a political tool. The first image to appear in this demonstration was that of Secretary of Commerce Herbert Hoover. A speech that Hoover was delivering in Washington was seen by a group of bankers and investors here in New York. The demonstration was set up by American Telephone and Telegraph's president, Walter Gifford, to develop interest in the remarkable invention.

Television has developed from the work of several scientists and engineers, both here and abroad. The basis of the new device is something called a cathode ray tube, which uses a beam of electricity to illuminate a phosphorous-coated screen. A crude television system was built in 1923 by the Russian-American scientist Vladimir Zworykin, who based his experiments on the work of Campbell Swinton, a British scientist, the Russian scientist Boris Rosing, and the theories of the German Albert Einstein. The system was improved upon by Scottish inventor John L. Baird, who last year produced clear images on his tube. Baird predicts that television will become a household appliance.

Pan American wins Cuba airmail route

Key West, Florida, Oct. 19

The first airmail to Havana has gone through, just hours before the U.S. government contract deadline. A fledgling Pan American Airways, incorporated on March 8, did the job by flying seven mailbags from Key West in a floatplane rented from barnstorming pilot Cy Caldwell. Pan American president J.T. Trippe won the contract and control of Pan American because Cuban President Gerardo Machado gave him exclusive landing rights. Trippe, 28, is backed by Yale classmates, including Cornelius Vanderbilt and "Sonny" Whitney.

Hays code defines Hollywood do's, don'ts

Hollywood, California

Hollywood moguls created the Motion Pictures Producers and Distributors of America five years ago to improve the image of the industry after widely publicized scandals and pressure to create some form of film censorship. The organization, headed by Will H. Hays, is working out a code of "good taste." Regulations of the Hays Office include prohibition of "any licentious or suggestive nudity," "miscegenation," "ridicule of clergy," "inference of sexual perversion," "indecent or undue exposure" and "excessive and lustful kissing." The code urges care with themes such as "illegal drug traffic," and "justified revenge in modern times," but sex seems to be more dangerous than violence since "actual hangings or electrocutions . . . brutality and possibly gruesomenesss" may be shown "within the careful limits of good taste."

Many movie makers have found a way around the regulations: They give the public what it wants, namely sex, sin and corruption, but see to it that offenders are punished in the last 10 minutes of the movie. Cecil B. De Mille has become a master at this.

Paley founds CBS

New York City, Sept. 26

William S. Paley has taken over United Independent Broadcasters, a small, money-losing radio network, and renamed it the Columbia Broadcasting System. He paid $503,000 for 50.3 percent of the classical music network. The deal was closed yesterday and Paley became president today. A 28-year-old son of a Russian immigrant, Paley signed a radio advertising contract for his father's cigar business last year. Since then, he has been hankering to buy a small radio network. He reportedly spent half his savings on the company.

U.S. Postmaster Will Hays warns Hollywood that America will not accept any material that is considered licentious, sexually perverted or blasphemous.

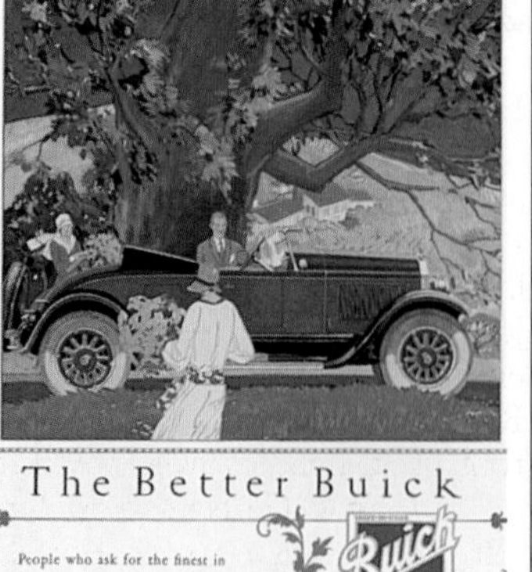

The Better Buick
People who ask for the finest in motor car design find it, at its most reasonable price, in the Better Buick.
Buick

The "Better Buick" is but one of a new breed of automobiles that stresses a combination of design, price and function in a market that is growing more competitive.

Al Capone makes fortune in rackets

Chicago
Education, hard work and a machine gun can work wonders. Take Al Capone. After an on-the-job stint with Brooklyn's Five Points Ring, he moved to Chicago, where he arrived with the family Bible in hand, and impressively blasted his way to the top of a 700-man organization. As a result, "Scarface" now controls most of the country's bootlegging. His profits this year alone amounted to $100 million in the liquor trade, $30 million in the protection business, $25 million in gambling, and $10 million in vice and sundry rackets (→ Feb. 14, 1929).

Marines sent south

Washington, D.C.
The United States has landed 2,000 marines in Nicaragua in an effort to bolster the government of Conservative Adolfo Diaz. Washington had withdrawn its troops in 1925, but it was forced to intervene again last year in response to a Liberal revolt led by General Augusto Cesar Sandino, a fervent foe of an American presence in Nicaragua. Sandino's insurrection quickly became a full-scale civil war. The Liberals, backed by Mexico, set up their own government, under Juan Sacasa, on the east coast (→ Jan. 2, 1932).

Strike up the brand

Dear John,
Can you pick us up a few things at the store? We need some Sanka, Pet milk, Libby's tomato soup, Milky Way candy bars, Welch's grape jelly, Popsicles, Borden's homogenized milk, Hostess cakes, B&M Brick Oven baked beans, A&W root beer, Lenders bagels, Wesson oil and some Gerber's baby food. Uh, sorry, forgot to tell you. I'm expecting. And keeping that in mind, since you'll be doing more of the cooking around here, can you pick up an electric eggbeater, an automatic potato peeler, a wall-mounted can opener, a G.E. refrigerator and a Conover electric dishwasher? Thanks, dear!
Love, Mary.

Lucky Lindy hops over the Atlantic

Paris, May 21
All Paris seemed fixed upon the sky tonight, as vast throngs at Le Bourget Field strained to hear the faint hum that would signal triumph for Charles A. Lindbergh. Then, just as hope was fading, the aviator's sleek, silver-gray monoplane, which had flown 3,600 miles from New York in 33 and a half hours, descended quietly, almost magically onto a distant runway at 10:24, setting off a hysterical rush by the cheering French. "Well, I made it," said the quiet Midwesterner as he was mobbed and carried off by the ecstatic crowd.

Lindbergh, just 25, barely got his plane off the ground early yesterday at Roosevelt Field, Long Island. The Spirit of St. Louis staggered down the runway with a huge fuel load, its engine snarling and its wings straining for lift. Once aloft, Lindy headed for Newfoundland, then out to sea, where he battled sleet, fog and exhaustion for 1,000 miles. Tonight, even Lindbergh, who navigated by dead reckoning, was astonished as he soared over the Irish coast, right on course.

The lanky flier will win a hotly contested $25,000 prize for the non-stop flight but seems surprised by the worldwide adulation his feat is generating. His main goal, he has said, is to further aviation.

Charles A. Lindbergh, son of a Minnesota congressman, developed his interest in flying during his years as a student at the University of Wisconsin. And after buying an old biplane, he began earning a living as a stunt-show pilot.

Lindbergh is hailed by adoring public

New York City
America has always loved its heroes, but nothing matches the adulation aimed at Charles Lindbergh this year. The aviator had hoped to explore Europe after reaching Paris, but President Coolidge would have none of it and sent a navy cruiser to fetch him. From a triumphant return to Washington to a parade down Broadway (featuring 1,800 tons of ticker tape) and on to a whirlwind 48-city tour in his Spirit of St. Louis, he has been feted by dignitaries and hounded by the press. "Lindbergh . . . has shown us that we are not rotten at the core," writes May B. Mullett in *American* magazine, "but morally sound and sweet and good."

Returning from Paris, the young, somewhat gawky pilot receives a hero's welcome in New York City. As tens of thousands line the streets of Manhattan for a glimpse of him, "Lindy" shows traces of the stoicism masking the dogged tenacity that helped carry him across the vast expanse of ocean.

Sacco and Vanzetti die

IL MARTELLO

Settimanale di battaglia diretto da CARLO TRESCA

5 SOLDI LA COPIA

LA TRAGEDIA E' TERMINATA

...Addio o mia compagna, o miei figli o miei amici! ...Addio mamma!... ...Viva l'Anarchia!...
N. SACCO

Desidero ripetere a voi che io sono innocente... Giammai mi macchiai di alcun delitto... Grazie a voi per tutto quello che avete fatto per me. Perdono a quegli uomini per cio' che in questo momento mi si fa...
B. VANZETTI

La statua della Liberta' nel Massachusetts

UNA PLUTOCRAZIA INFAME
UN GIUDICE ASSASSINO
UN POPOLO INCOSCIENTE
LI DANNARONO A MORIRE SULLA SEDIA ELETTRICA
REI SOLTANTO D'ESSERE ANARCHICI

MA IL LORO SANGUE E IL LORO MARTIRIO
LA FERMEZZA DEL CARATTERE
IL LORO SACRIFICIO
SONO AUREOLA DI LUCE SPLENDENTE
CH'E' LORO GLORIA E VITTORIA

O SACCO E VANZETTI
O FULGIDI MARTIRI
O COMPAGNI
L'ANARCHIA — VOSTRA VITA E VOSTRO CALVARIO —
E' VIVA E VIVRA'
ETERNAMENTE.

For the accused, the tragedy is over.

Dedham, Mass., Aug. 23

While sympathy demonstrations were being staged across the world, the switch was thrown here today, executing Nicola Sacco and Bartolomeo Vanzetti. The two Italian radicals were convicted in 1921 for the crimes of murder and theft in the 1920 robbery of a South Braintree, Massachusetts, shoe factory. The trial received national attention and many liberals and labor groups rallied to support the defendants. Many still believe that the evidence against Sacco and Vanzetti was slim and that the conviction and sentence were politically motivated. Both men were known as anarchists and draft evaders. Judge Webster Thayer, who presided at the trial, was recently quoted as saying of Vanzetti, "This man, although he may not actually have committed a crime . . . is . . . the enemy of our existing institutions . . . The defendant's ideals are cognate with crime."

Before his execution, Bartolomeo Vanzetti stated, "I am innocent. I am suffering because I am a radical . . . an Italian . . . "

The execution was put off while a committee named by the Governor investigated the trial. The committee upheld the court decision, saying that judicial procedure had been correct. A new trial was denied and the men were executed.

Babe swats 60th homer

The "Sultan of Swat" watches No. 60 as he sails into the record books.

New York City, Sept. 30.

The crack of the bat was audible throughout Yankee Stadium today and 10,000 fans there knew that the moment had arrived. As the ball headed for the rightfield bleachers, they were on their feet, screaming for their hero, George Herman Ruth. The Babe had fulfilled their earnest wish, smacking his 60th homer of the season, a feat never before accomplished. Who cares that some people deride Babe Ruth as a boozer and glutton. He is also the consummate batter and the name of Thomas Jonathan Walton Zachary of the Washington Senators will go down in history as the man who served up the historic pitch – fast, low and inside. Ruth's wallop, with one on and the score tied in the eighth, also enabled the Yanks to defeat the Washington Senators, 4 to 2.

Before he crossed the plate after walloping homer No. 60, the portly Yankee slugger jogged around the bases in almost regal style. And as he did, he carefully stomped on each sack, as if he were punctuating the feat officially.

The historic homer was a tribute to Colonel Jake Ruppert, Yankee owner, who had the foresight to buy Ruth from the financially troubled Boston Red Sox for $125,000. He transformed Ruth from a stellar pitcher – he once hurled 29 2/3 scoreless innings – into a slugging outfielder. In 1920, his first year with the Yanks, Ruth lofted 54 homers and was paid $20,000. He soon became a folk hero, hitting a record 59 homers in 1921. Although ill much of 1925, he still rapped out 25 homers.

Tunney retains title after long count

Chicago, Sept. 22

Jack Dempsey was hardly the fighting machine that he was when he first fought Gene Tunney a year ago and yet – despite easy living - he almost dethroned the former marine as heavyweight champion today. But the Manassa Mauler made a fundamental mistake: He ignored the rule that he should go to a neutral corner once Tunney was down in the seventh, and the extra five or six seconds of the count enabled Gene to recover. The 104,943 people jamming Soldiers Field were shocked into silence as Tunney's knees crumpled after Dempsey's crushing left to the jaw. No one knows just how many times Dempsey hit Tunney on the way down, but it was the first time Gene has been decked in his life.

Gene Tunney is downed by Jack Dempsey. As the ref's count begins, so too does a lingering controversy.

Both men had been warned that a boxer scoring a knockdown must retire to the farther neutral corner. Instead, Dempsey hovered over Tunney as he had with other floored rivals. The referee tried to tug Dempsey away, then started counting. After the "long count," Tunney recovered well enough to win the round on points. At the earlier title fight in Philadelphia, 120,757 people watched in the rain as Tunney took a 10-round decision. He battered Dempsey through every round and the beaten champ hardly looked like the young upstart who had pounded Jess Willard into a four-round defeat in 1919.

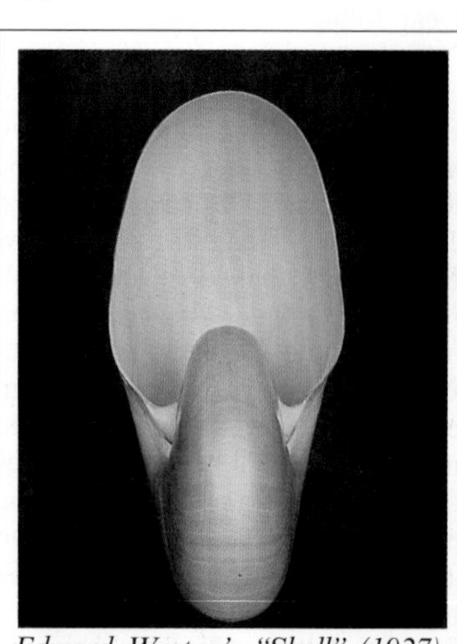

Edward Weston's "Shell" (1927), a study in detail and simplicity.

General Motors has largest dividend

Detroit, Mich., Nov. 10

General Motors announced today that it will distribute an extra $2.60 per share – the largest dividend in American history – making the total distribution to shareholders more than $65 million. The company has been offering a $1.25 regular quarterly dividend for each share of outstanding stock. Though the announcement came 20 minutes after the Stock Exchange closed, there were celebrations at several brokerage firms. The stock had traded heavily today. Analysts say that the distribution indicates that G.M. is not overly concerned about Ford's new Model A, and that G.M.'s Chevrolet is carrying its own weight in the automobile market (→ March 17, 1929).

Ain't heard nothin' yet

Al Jolson dons blackface, drops to one knee and croons to the nation.

Hollywood, California

The success of the second Vitaphone film, *The Jazz Singer*, enhanced by Al Jolson's songs and a few lines of improvised dialogue, is amazing. "Wait, you ain't heard nothin' yet," are Jolson's first quite audible words, and the response has been so great that Warner Bros. has announced there will be more "talkies." Other studios see this as a disruptive and unnecessary change and hope the fad will pass.

Meanwhile, major film makers have founded the Academy of Motion Picture Arts and Sciences to "improve the artistic quality of the film medium, provide a common forum for the various branches and crafts of the industry, foster cooperation in technical research and cultural progress, and pursue a variety of other stated objectives."

Cecil B. De Mille, a preacher's son, follows up on his formula of violence, sex and religion with another biblical epic, *King of Kings*, already a tremendous hit. It stars H.B. Warner as Jesus. The mammoth spectacle cost $2.5 million.

The last Model T; the first Model A

New York City, Dec. 1

Henry Ford has so stubbornly resisted changes in his beloved Model T over the years that he has been known to attack with a sledgehammer refined versions of the car presented to him by company engineers and his son Edsel. But after producing 15 million of the famous "Tin Lizzies," even Ford has had to admit that changing times have left the car behind, as rival cars like Chevrolet cut into its market. Today, though, Ford's answer to this trend, the Model A, caused a sensation when it was unveiled here. Thousands rushed to see the car, which features shock absorbers, a speedometer and more graceful lines than its utilitarian predecessor; orders already total 50,000.

"Showboat" sailing

New York City, Dec. 27

Broadway's new *Showboat* is likely to be a hit for all seasons, a real musical play with a serious plot and not just another musical comedy or operetta. And what musical wouldn't love to have just one of those sterling songs by Oscar Hammerstein II and Jerome Kern: *Ol' Man River*, *Make Believe*, *Why Do I Love You*, *Can't Help Lovin' Dat Man*, and *You Are Love*.

Holy hell exposed

United States

Nothing is sacred to novelist Sinclair Lewis. Early on, he lambasted small-town smugness; then it was boosters. Now he has "disrobed" a man of the cloth, although the best-selling satirist seems to think a cleric needs little help peeling off his collar if a lady gives the nod. Sex is just one sinful pastime enjoyed by the title character of *Elmer Gantry*, a holy heel who uses the pulpit for his own selfish ends. Churchgoers are steaming, and no one is betting that Lewis, who spurned last year's Pulitzer Prize, will get a chance to snub the committee again.

Bizarre auto death for Isadora Duncan

Nice, France, Sept. 14

Isadora Duncan, whose barefooted dances in sheer gowns and speeches on behalf of communism shocked the world, died a shocking death today. Miss Duncan, 47, was being chauffeured in an open car when her long red scarf, a characteristic part of her wardrobe, coiled around a spinning rear wheel. Her neck was snapped. It was the end of a tragic life, one that included several disastrous love affairs, the drowning deaths in 1913 of her two illegitimate children, Deirdre and Patrick, and the suicide by hanging of her psychotic husband, the Russian poet Sergei Esenin, in 1925.

Spearhead points to early era of man

Folsom, New Mexico

How long has civilization existed in North America? Since Jamestown? Since Columbus? Archeologists digging in stratified earth in New Mexico have uncovered a clue suggesting that Indians inhabited the area as far back as 8,000 B.C. A stone spearhead was found stuck in the ribs of an Ice Age bison skeleton. An estimate of the date is derived from knowledge of the species of bison, which existed during the Ice Age, and from the position of the skeleton in the layers of earth and rock. The spearhead suggests that there was a civilization advanced at least to the point of a Stone Age hunting culture.

A relativist theory of history put forth

United States

Historians are beginning to question the cult of science. As usual, Charles Beard is leading the way with a relativist theory of history. In the two-volume *Rise of American Civilization,* that he and his wife, Mary, wrote, the scholar's ability to unravel the "real" past is challenged. The value of historical knowledge, says Beard, lies in how useful it is, not how it corresponds to an objective reality. In 1913, Beard's *Economic Interpretation of the Constitution* shocked scholars by attributing cynical motives to the founding fathers. Four years later, Beard left Columbia to protest the firing of anti-war faculty.

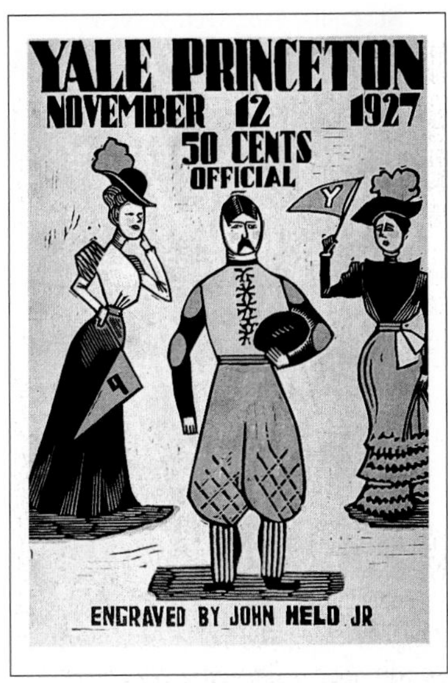

1928

Coolidge

New York City, Jan. 4. National Broadcasting Company links all 48 states to hear radio extravaganza with stars such as Will Rogers and Al Jolson.

Washington, D.C., March 10. President Coolidge signs order allocating $300 million to compensate German nationals and companies seized during Great War.

Santa Clara River Valley, California, March 13. Dam bursts 40 miles north of Los Angeles, killing 450 people as valley is flooded.

New York City, May 7. Pulitzer Prize in fiction awarded to Thornton Wilder for *The Bridge of San Luis Rey*.

New York City, May 9. *Blackbirds of 1928*, featuring an all-Negro cast, opens to popular acclaim.

Louisville, Ky., May 19. Reigh Count wins Kentucky Derby, as Shipwreck Kelly looks down from his 112-foot-high flagpole, where he has been perched for 100 hours.

Washington, D.C., May 22. Congress passes Jones-White Act, providing subsidies to American shipping industry.

Detroit, Mich., May 28. Chrysler and Dodge Motors unite in largest automotive industry merger in history.

Newfoundland, Canada, June 17. Passenger Amelia Earhardt becomes first female to cross Atlantic Ocean by plane.

Rochester, New York, July 30. George Eastman demonstrates color motion pictures.

Florida, Sept. 16. Hurricane strikes state, killing 2,000.

St. Louis, Mo., Oct. 9. New York Yankees sweep World Series, defeating Cardinals.

New York City, Nov. 6. *The New York Times* uses first moving electric bulletins to announce results of presidential election; called "zipper" because it wraps around building.

New York City. *Abie's Irish Rose* closes after record 2,400 performances on Broadway.

New York City. *The Man Who Knew Coolidge*, by Sinclair Lewis, published.

New York City. Margaret Mead, anthropologist, publishes *Coming of Age in Samoa*.

Coolidge's optimism excites Wall Street

President Coolidge remains unflappable in the face of an overheated economy.

Washington, D.C., Jan. 7

Enthusiasm kindled by President Coolidge inspired a huge volume on the booming New York Stock Exchange today. Trading was so heavy that abbreviated quotes were used, and the ticker was running 16 minutes behind transactions when the closing bell sounded. The latest surge in the soaring market follows publication of President Coolidge's assurance that he is not disturbed by unprecedented growth in loans that make it easier to buy stocks with less cash. Loans to brokers and dealers by New York Federal Reserve member banks have soared to $3.8 billion, the greatest amount in Federal Reserve history.

The President thinks that the surging loans represent a natural expansion of business in the securities market, and he sees nothing unfavorable in it. But The Nation reports that Wall Street is overflowing with "inexperienced suckers" attracted by "big, easy profits" in a "tremendous bull market" (→ Oct. 29, 1929).

Kellogg-Briand pact aims to outlaw war

Paris, Aug. 27

In a historic move designed to rid the world of war, 15 nations today signed a pact pledging to eschew the use of arms as a means of resolving international conflicts. The treaty calls on its signers to renounce war "as an instrument of national policy" and to resolve any differences peacefully. First proposed by the French Foreign Minister, Aristide Briand, as an alliance between the United States and France, the pact was broadened by the American Secretary of State, Frank B. Kellogg, to include all nations. The signers so far are France, England, Japan, Italy and the United States.

Hot Five records "West End Blues"

New York City, July 20

Judging from their recent release of *West End Blues*, Louis Armstrong's "Hot Five" get better and better. Since their first session in 1925, the group has cut some 50 records, including such gems as *Hotter Than That*, *Savoy Blues*, *Tiger Rag* and *Heebie Jeebie*, Armstrong's first recording as a "scat" singer, with vocal sounds that imitate an instrument. *West End Blues* is among the best. And for 75 cents, you can't go wrong.

Pioneering cartoon with mouse as star

New York City, Nov. 18

Steamboat Willie opened at the Colony Theater today and it did for the world of movie cartoons what *The Jazz Singer* has done for talkies. *Willie* is the first cartoon that features sound. The star of this short by Walt Disney, designed to showcase the new technology, is a mouse named Mickey, who turns the cargo of a riverboat – including the livestock aboard it – into an orchestra! Meanwhile, a replica of Otto Messmer's cartoon cat Felix is being used to monitor and to fine-tune a series of experiments with the brand new medium called television.

Mae West is "Diamond Lil" on Broadway

Mae West as "Diamond Lil." The buxom bombshell elevates the titillating to unprecedented dimensions.

New York City, Apr. 9

"When women go wrong, men go right after them." That is one of the gems that playwright-actress Mae West has given herself in *Diamond Lil.* As Lil, West unknowingly helps a Salvation Army captain knock out a white slavery ring involving a former lover. Her acting sparkles, but the writing is all rhinestone. The queen of the double entendre was last seen two years ago in *Sex*, which got her eight days in jail on a censorship charge. As she swaggered through *Lil's* opening night crowd, an admirer purred, "Your hands, your lips, your hair . . . " She responded, "Whataya doin', honey, makin' love or takin' inventory?"

Hoover wins, offering chicken in every pot

Washington, D.C., Nov. 6

Herbert Hoover swept into the White House today, defeating New York Governor Al Smith in a landslide. Hoover and his running mate, Charles Curtis, were elected with promises of prosperity, saying there will be "a chicken in every pot and a car in every garage" and that America is close to "triumph over poverty." A sardonic Calvin Coolidge offered Hoover this presidential advice: "You have to stand every day hours of visitors. Nine-tenths of them want something they ought not have." Socialist Norman Thomas and Workers' Party nominee William Foster each got a handful of votes. Republicans kept control of Congress.

"Herbert C. Hoover" by Douglas Chandor. The new President offers continuity in a time of prosperity.

Make a girl happy

United States

Guys, say you've got a wonderful girl – a pippin, a peach, a sweet patootie – and you want to show you care. If you've got the dough, get her a Plymouth or a De Soto. How about a quartz clock or a Philco radio? If you're a bit short on cash, enter a talkathon or a "noun and verb rodeo" (good for 80 hours or so of entertainment) or try tandem flagpole sitting. Or take her on an old-fashioned picnic with some new-fangled foods like Velveeta cheese, Nehi soda, Peter Pan peanut butter or Rice Krispies. Of course, if your girl's actually a pill, a pickle or a priss, leave her home.

U.S. wins Olympics

Amsterdam, Netherlands, Aug. 12

There were 22 track events on the Olympic agenda, but the United States could win only one of them. Even though the Americans were able to roll up enough points to win the unofficial title, there was much evidence, first shown in Antwerp, that their dominance may be over. With European critics accusing the Americans of overconfidence, overtraining and overeating, Ray Barbuti salvaged the 400 meters as the track phase was ending. Athletes in the field events saved the day for the United States, piling up 437 points, 60 more than the runner-up squad from Finland.

Poetry, fiction and all that jazz flower in Harlem Renaissance

Langston Hughes, poet.

Harlem, New York City

In the last 10 years, an important cultural movement has been spawned in the Negro ghettoes of the North. Generally referred to as the "Harlem Renaissance," the great flowering of literature, music and the arts has been stimulated by such societies as the National Association for the Advancement of Colored People and the Urban League. These groups, dedicated to the overall betterment of Negro life, along with such art-oriented societies as the Writers Guild in New York, the Black Opals in Philadelphia and the Saturday Evening Quill Club in Boston, have formed the core of a new Negro intelligentsia.

In 1925, a literary anthology titled *The New Negro*, edited by Alain Locke, included verse, fiction and nonfiction by Harlem writers. Locke's anthology, published at the peak of the Harlem Renaissance, was most influential in defining the content and direction of the movement. If Locke is Harlem's popularizer, James Weldon Johnson is its inspiration. After his pioneering novel *Autobiography of an Ex-Coloured Man* (1912), he acted as mentor to a generation of young Negro writers. Claude McKay's recent *Home to Harlem*, has proved popular with a general audience. And young Langston Hughes shows great promise in *The Weary Blues* (1926), his first volume of poetry. On stage, Negro playwrights Wallace Thurman and Garland Anderson have had productions in New York.

Jazz, of course, is popular everywhere. White people flock to the Cotton Club and Connie's Inn to hear the voices of Ethel Waters and Bill "Bojangles" Robinson, and the big-band sounds of Fletcher Henderson and especially Edward Kennedy "Duke" Ellington.

Duke Ellington and his band have played the Cotton Club for years.

The Roaring 20s: Fads, fashions and flappers

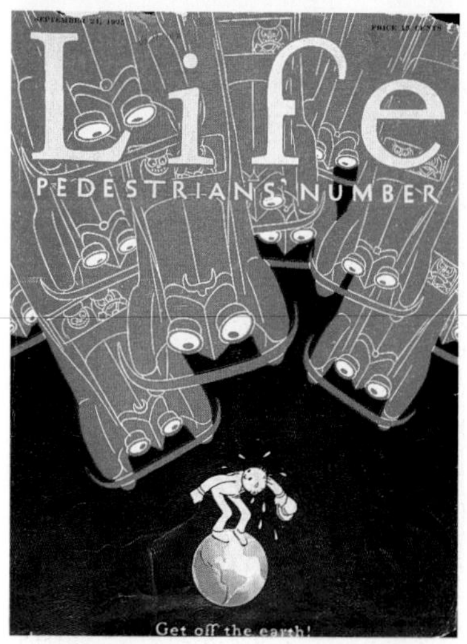

Some 78 percent of the world's autos – 24 million – are on U.S. roads.

Dancing at Tin Roof Cafe in New Orleans – no shimmying or drinking.

Police in Detroit inspect equipment found in a clandestine underground brewery. The Feds arrest 75,000 Americans a year for Prohibition violations.

Fashions of the times: The flapper dress, introduced in 1925, features a drop waist or no waist at all.

It takes two to tango. "Social dancing," says a female evangelist, "is the first and easiest step toward hell."

Tennis ace "Big Bill" Tilden, an idol of the era, learned to play at his wealthy parents' club in Philadelphia.

An American "sheba," sporting a cloche hat and knit sweater, emblems of freedom for women.

"They're desperadoes, these kids," says one writer, "the girls as well as the boys, maybe more than the boys."

The 21-horsepower Model 490 Chevrolet. "In the city of Zenith," wrote Sinclair Lewis, "a family's motor indicated its social rank and where Babbitt as a boy had aspired to the presidency, his son Ted aspired to a Packard Twin Six."

Six reels of joy! Chaplin's first real feature, made in 1921, launched Jackie Coogan as a major child star.

In the morning, in the evening, ain't we got fun!

"The Bersaglieri" by George Luks. The Great War is now just a memory.

F. Scott Fitzgerald and wife, Zelda.

A flapper doin' the Charleston.

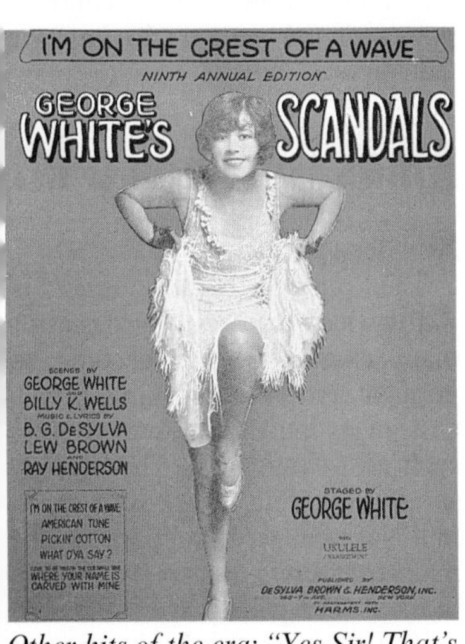

Other hits of the era: "Yes Sir! That's My Baby," "Where'd You Get Those Eyes?" and "Ain't We Got Fun."

Immigration was limited during the decade, but many newcomers have established themselves in all walks of life. They learned to speak English, served in the Great War, started their own businesses – and they have prospered.

Turn on the radio and hear "Amos 'n' Andy," "Roxy and His Gang" or "Jack Frost's Melody Moments."

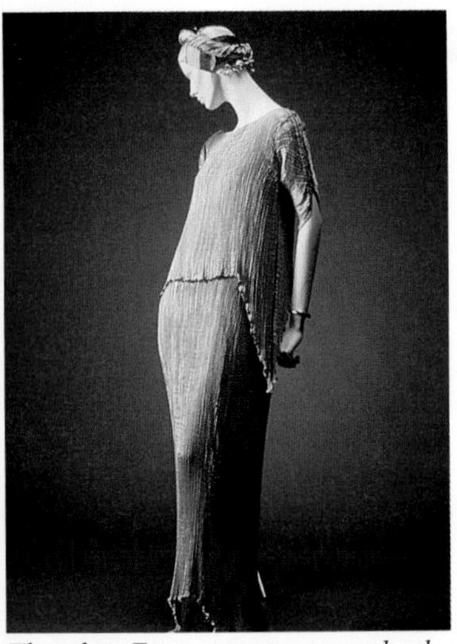

The chic Fortuny gown reveals the female body by caressing its surface with shimmering pleated silk satins.

Motorized taxis wait to take passengers from Union Station in Los Angeles. You need a car in this California metropolis; its 364 square miles in 1920 reflect a 13-fold expansion since the city's founding way back in 1781.

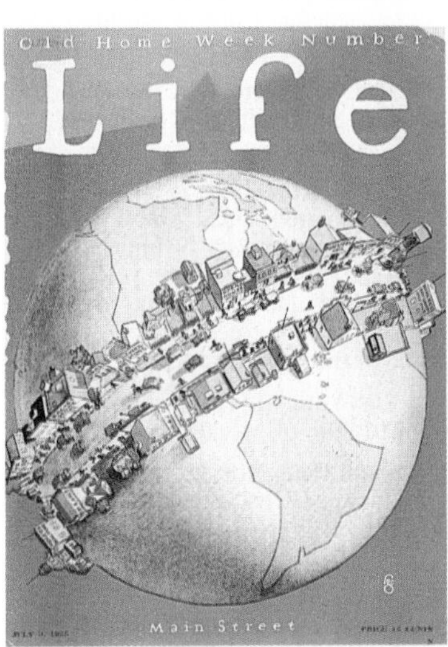

America projects itself around the world: Main Street has no end on this cover of the popular humor magazine.

1929

Hoover

Washington, D.C., Feb. 13. President signs bill authorizing construction of 15 10,000-ton cruisers.

Detroit, February. Henry Ford says, "Thinking is the hardest work there is, which is the probable reason why so few engage in it."

Detroit, March 17. General Motors announces purchase of Opel AG, largest German auto maker.

Atlantic Ocean, March 22. A 200-mile sea chase comes to an end, when Coast Guard sinks British schooner I'm Alone, suspected of carrying contraband, after its failure to obey a heave-to order.

New York City, May 12. Stephen Vincent Benet wins Pulitzer in poetry for *John Brown's Body*.

The Hague, May 13. Charles Evans Hughes appointed to World Court.

Louisville, Ky., May 18. Clem McCarthy announces during first worldwide radio hookup of Kentucky Derby.

Washington, D.C., May 29. Supreme Court rules that presidential pocket veto is unconstitutional.

New York City, June 20. *Hot Chocolates*, Negro musical revue by Fats Waller, opens.

New Jersey, Sept. 11. Fokker F-32, largest passenger plane of American design, unveiled.

Washington, D.C., September. Estimate is that 60 percent of U.S. population has an annual income of under $2,000.

Philadelphia, Oct. 14. Athletics defeat Cubs in World Series, four games to one.

St. Louis, October. C.L. Griggs markets Bib-Label Lithiated Lemon-Lime soda [7-Up].

Washington, D.C., Nov. 1 Former Secretary of Interior Albert B. Fall gets one-year sentence, fined $100,000 for taking bribe for lease of government oil lands.

New York City, Nov. 8. Museum of Modern Art opens.

South Pole, Nov. 29. U.S. Commander Richard Byrd is first to fly over pole, in round-trip lasting 19 hours.

New York City. Robert I. Ripley's *Believe It or Not* published.

Bloody Valentine's Day

Seven of "Bugs" Moran's men are dead after a quick and brutal execution.

Chicago, Feb. 14

The floor of a Windy City beer warehouse was stained with blood today as seven members of George "Bugs" Moran's gang were gunned down in a surprise attack. Police believe Moran's rival, "Scarface" Al Capone, may be responsible for what is being called the St. Valentine's Day Massacre.

The killers, wielding machine guns, were dressed in police uniforms. This outraged Police Commissioner William Russell, who declared war on such crime. "This is war to the finish," he said. "I've never known a challenge like this."

Capone has become the king of bootlegging and gambling. His annual income has skyrocketed to about $60 million since he moved here from New York in 1920. Two years ago, he defended his "job": "What's Al Capone done, then? He's supplied a legitimate demand. Some call it bootlegging. Some call it racketeering. I call it business. They say I violate the prohibition law. Who doesn't?" Considering the tolerance, even the glamorization of Capone, it does seem that Americans want their booze, and they don't seem to care whether it's legal or not (→Oct. 17, 1931).

Negro union gains charter from A.F.L.

Chicago, Feb. 23

The predominantly Negro Brotherhood of Sleeping Car Porters has been granted temporary admission to the American Federation of Labor. William Green, president of the federation, has been delivering a series of speeches that affirms the support of the A.F.L. for the porters brotherhood. Green hopes to help the union recruit 10,000 more members by September. He has also stressed that the A.F.L. will oppose any attempts by Pullman executives to form a company union. The brotherhood held its annual convention here this year and took up such issues as health and housing conditions of members and the mobilization of the economic power of the workers to improve their lives.

Amos 'n' Andy a hit

New Jersey

The radio program *Amos 'n' Andy*, which features Negroes as its main characters, has become so popular that it is regularly broadcast over loudspeakers at resorts such as Atlantic City. The comedy show uses white actors who speak in a Negro dialect, and portrays the main characters as hapless and humorous. The plots play on the stereotype of Negroes as being ignorant and, while millions like the show, many Negroes find it offensive.

Yale grad and crooner with a megaphone, Rudy Vallee appears in the film "Vagabond Lover."

The union blues in the age of business

United States

The union battle cry, muted by prosperity and hostility, has yielded to the hum of the well-oiled factory. Unions, recoiling from what H.L. Mencken calls "capital's vigorous and well-planned war of attrition," have lost three million members over the decade. And strikes have dropped from an average of 3,500 a year to fewer than 800.

Since the "Red Scare," labor has been saddled with the stigma of isms – communism, socialism, anarchism. The National Association of Manufacturers has named its drive for the open shop the "American Plan," and has tried to make unionism synonymous with Bolshevism. The American Federation of Labor has been accused of excluding the foreign-born and its leadership seems to be spending more time keeping leftists out than getting new workers in.

Many companies dangle the carrot as an alternative to the stick. With profit-sharing, grievance boards, recreational programs and insurance, management appears to be beating labor at its own benefits game.

Cascade Mountains get longest tunnel

Seattle, Washington, Jan. 12

Railroad president James J. Hill officially christened the new Cascade tunnel today. It is more than eight miles long and was dug through solid granite in the heart of the Cascade Mountains. Engineers with the Great Northern Railway say that it is the longest tunnel in North America. The longest railway tunnel in the world is the Simplon Tunnel in Switzerland, which is about 12.5 miles long. The construction of Hill's Cascade tunnel employed the latest civil engineering technology available. Rotary hydraulic rock drills were used to dig the tunnel, which lies several thousand feet beneath the summit of the mountain directly above it. Nitroglycerin was used for blasting out the rock.

Buck Rogers comics

United States, January

Awakening from a five-century-long sleep, a former air corps lieutenant finds himself in a devastated America overrun by Mongol invaders. *Buck Rogers*, a comic strip by Philip Nowlan and Dick Calkins, uses fantastic settings to tell stories of heroic adventure. Further heroism can be found in Hal Foster's *Tarzan* and in Elzie Segar's *Thimble Theater*, which has recently introduced a fighting sailor named Popeye.

"Soaring Steel" (1929) by Samuel Chamberlain. Photographers are finding heroism in the skyscrapers across the industrial landscape.

Academy honors movies

As movies grow so do women's roles.

Hollywood, Calif., May 17

"We want more respect," the film makers say. To focus attention on their achievements, they held a banquet last night at the Hollywood Roosevelt Hotel, where a couple of hundred movie people saw Douglas Fairbanks present artists and technicians with 15 golden statuettes, depicting a man with a crusader's sword standing on a reel of film. *Wings* won as best picture of 1927-1928, Janet Gaynor as best actress (for *Seventh Heaven*, *Street Angel* and *Sunrise*) while Emil Jannings took the prize as best actor (for *The Way of All Flesh* and *The Last Command*).

Movies are booming. Of the nation's 20,500 movie theaters, those with sound facilities have risen to 9,000, from 1,300. Musicals, such as *Broadway Melody*, *The Golddiggers of Broadway*, *Desert Song* and *The Singing Fool* are in vogue.

At the Roosevelt Hotel in New York, Guy Lombardo and His Royal Canadians are performing nightly, while Broadway has found a new favorite: handsome Britisher Archie Leach [Cary Grant], who appeared in the musical *A Wonderful Night* and then *Boom Boom*.

Young Plan eases German war debts

Paris, June 7

Thanks to a plan worked out by the Wall Street financier Owen D. Young, Germany will soon have some relief from its crippling burden of war reparations. The Young Plan reduces the total amount that the Germans must pay in reparations to $27 billion, down from the $33-billion figure that was fixed by the Allies in 1921, and allows 60 years for repayment. In spite of the loans from the United States under the U.S.-sponsored Dawes Plan, which was put into effect five years ago, Germany has been unable to meet its annual payments, due in large measure to the inflation that has devastated its economy. By ensuring that the Germans keep paying reparations, the new plan may enable the Allies to return to the United States some of the $10 billion they borrowed from it to carry on the war (→ June 20, 1931).

"Joe sent me": Speakeasies flourish under eye of Prohibition

United States

All it takes is the flash of a certain business card, a particular rhythm of knocks on a door or a whispered phrase like "Joe sent me." Nothing could be easier than slipping into a speakeasy. The estimates range from 32,000 to 100,000 illegal drinking joints in New York. A Chicago official estimated this year that there were just 10,000 in that city. To fit in the hordes who say they use them, those 10,000 would each have to be the size of a football field. Even towns in the Midwest, traditionally the driest of the dry spots, have "beer flats," "blind pigs" and "shock houses."

The clientele at the speakeasy is as varied as the drinks for sale, bricklayers and lawyers alike bellying up to the bar for potato-brewed whiskey and 60-day-old wine. Moving in among the men, and placing their orders just as loudly, are women who never would have been seen in a saloon. One of the famed speakeasy proprietors is Texas Guinan, who hails customers at her New York El Fay establishment with "Hello, sucker!" Miss Guinan has reason to be cheerful – profits are immense.

Admittedly, there are expenses, starting with installation of concealed drains where hooch can be poured in case of a raid, and the hook-up of electric switches that seal the doors when police try to drop in. There are also funds to be put aside for under-the-table distribution to federal agents and district attorneys. Some cops prefer to be paid in "liquid assets"; more than one place charges a paying customer 75 cents for a slug of gin, while an officer of the law imbibes for free. And, of course, you've got to have jack to spend on food and entertainment – people want hot jazz and cool cuisine. Meals are served at reasonable prices, because the profit margin on liquor is so high. The worst risk is indigestion. The booze is a real danger. Last year, known deaths in the nation from rotgut shot past the 1,000 mark.

Since last fall, police have increased their raids. Sometimes they are "jake foot," poorly or perfectly disguised in anything from a false mustache to a football uniform. They might make countless arrests, but the speakeasies just keep popping up. Last February, the Bar Association of New York threw in the towel, announcing opposition to Prohibition. Hearing the news, many upstanding citizens raise their shot glasses, mugs and teacups and declare, "I'll drink to that!"

At least the liquor is respectable.

Ambitious airlines invite American travelers to take to the air

AIR MAIL
is Socially Correct

Washington, D.C.

Has travel by airplane become accessible to all? A number of new American companies that provide air transport service would like the nation to think so. From the spectacle and thrill of barnstorming, air travel is apparently becoming a viable, growing industry.

Commercial service began before the war, with the huge German zeppelins flying scheduled routes in Europe. Heavier-than-air operators soon got the idea that they could make a buck with airplanes; the first scheduled passenger flights were made by the St. Petersburg-Tampa Air Boat Line, which provided twice-daily service across Florida's Tampa Bay. Its little airplane could carry only one passenger – so much for volume. The war provided a new variety of aircraft and trained pilots and mechanics. In 1918, the United States Post Office set up a regular air route between New York and Philadelphia, to speed mail delivery. At first, it used war-surplus Curtiss Jenny biplanes; but later, the Boeing company designed the B-l Mail Boat, a plywood biplane that could land on water. In 1921, the Martin MB-l bomber, developed for the army, was converted to a mail plane and a 12-seat passenger liner. More recently, the German Fokker company has opened a factory in New Jersey to produce its giant trimotor passenger craft. American manufacturers, including Henry Ford, have improved on the trimotor design. The all-metal Ford trimotor, known popularly as the "Tin Goose," is earning a reputation as the most durable plane in the air.

Companies such as Colonial Airlines and North West Airlines now ply regular routes between many cities. On July 7, the Transcontinental Air Transport company opened the first coast-to-coast passenger service. The trans-Atlantic hero Charles A. Lindbergh inaugurated the Pan American Airline by flying a cargo of mail to Panama on October 2. And Universal Air Line added entertainment to the flight plan when it showed a movie aboard a flight on February 17.

Lieutenant Jimmy Doolittle is the first pilot to rely solely on instrumentation.

American novelists prove their worth

New York City

The books are just about closed on the 1920s, but the decade hardly closed down on books, despite the efforts of the Clean Books League. This year, three novels stand out, each the work of a young writer. The trio's best-known member is Ernest Hemingway, 30, the master of the blue pencil. He has stripped every ounce of fat from his prose in *A Farewell to Arms*, set during the Great War. The tale, about love and combat, is told by an American youth posted on the Italian front, where he falls for a British nurse.

The year's other blockbusters are the work of Southerners. William Faulkner, 32, comes from Oxford, Mississippi, and the odor of Confederate decay seeps from his fourth novel, *The Sound and the Fury*, about the faded fortunes of the Compsons, privileged people who have plunged into debauchery. Tautly designed, the novel twines three tour de force monologues, including one spoken by an idiot.

Thomas Wolfe, born in 1900 in Asheville, North Carolina, exhibits none of the artistic control of his rivals. In fact, his literary debut, *Look Homeward Angel*, is a rambling monster of a novel. Its source material is Wolfe's own childhood and youth and his groping search for an identity in a large, chaotic family. The driving force of Wolfe's prose has excited many readers, who eagerly await the next installment in the life of Eugene Gant.

Sociologists study typical U.S. town

Muncie, Indiana

As Americans continue to leave the farm for the town, life in the towns continues to pique the curiosity of readers. Now the subject has been approached from a new angle by a Columbia University sociologist, Robert S. Lynd, and his wife, Helen, who asked Muncie's residents what was on their minds. The answers appear in *Middletown*, a study as haunting as a tale by Sherwood Anderson. One citizen says of the rest, "These people are afraid of something: what is it?"

Detroit makes 5.3 million cars; Ford hits millionth Model A

Detroit, Michigan

Are your windows rattling more than ever? Have you noticed that, even though there are more paved roads, they are more difficult to cross? The explanation, of course, comes from the automobile manufacturers here who have now turned out 5.3 million vehicles. Ford announces that it has just built its one-millionth Model A. Introduced in January of last year, the Model A is the successor to the popular Model T. The "A" is a low-priced general-purpose car that comes in a choice of four colors and 17 body styles. All these vehicles are competing for space on the nation's 695,000 miles of paved road and they are consuming about 16 billion gallons of gasoline a year. If you're still walking, look both ways when you cross the street.

One of the best. The Stutz Weymann-type 36-horsepower sports saloon.

Black Tuesday! Wall St. in chaos as stocks crash

New York City, Oct. 29

The stock market has collapsed in a "Black Tuesday" of violent trading that was the most disastrous in Wall Street history. It was the worst by three key measurements, total losses, total turnover and the number of speculators ruined. Frantic efforts to stabilize the market were met by "must sell" orders to liquidate at any price, accelerated by insistent brokers' calls for more cash to back the record loans behind the falling stocks. The selling storm was the most catastrophic of three that began last Thursday, "Black Thursday," and erupted again Monday. The only relief today was a smart upturn at the close, believed by some to mean that the end is not far away.

In Washington, the Federal Reserve met continuously, with no lunch break and no action. U.S. Steel and American Can, however, both declared $1 extra dividends as proof of prosperity. On the New York Stock Exchange, in today's session alone, it is estimated that the loss came to $9 billion. For the month, the total is $16 billion in 240 selected issues.

Because galleries overlooking the trading floor were barred to visitors, the public drama was concentrated in brokers' offices. There, huddled around glass-domed "tickers" that typed out the stock quotations, tense faces reflected the tragic news on the tape. There were no smiles, no tears. Just a sad camaraderie of shared losses.

In Providence, Rhode Island, 57-year-old David Korn dropped dead while watching the tape, though his holdings were in no special danger. And in Kansas City, Missouri, insurance man John Schwitzgebel unsuccessfully attempted suicide with two bullets in his chest, saying, "Tell the boys I can't pay them what I owe them."

On the brighter side, New York City Mayor Jimmy Walker urged a theater owners' meeting to "show pictures that will reinstate courage and hope in the hearts of the people." Chairman Julius Rosenwald of Sears, Roebuck & Company inspired hope in 40,000 employees by guaranteeing their stock market accounts. Assistant Secretary of Commerce Julius Klein went on a nationwide radio hookup to remind the nation that last Friday President Hoover said, "The fundamental business of the country, that is production and distribution of commodities, is on a sound and prosperous basis." And Dr. Klein told the nation, "There is no reason today to change a single word of this statement of the President." But the Democratic National Committee released a contrary opinion, charging that the crisis "belongs to the party in power" and that leaders who were talking "prosperity" a short time ago are now trying to find a "scapegoat in the face of a $15 billion loss in one week of American life" (→Dec. 31).

As the day wears on and panic grips the floor of the New York Stock Exchange, wild rumors spread through the financial district. Ambulances race to buildings where bankrupt investors are reportedly killing themselves. Whether these stories are true or not, the very spectacle of a market gone mad has drawn a crowd of thousands to the exchange building and 20 mounted officers have been rushed in to reinforce an overwhelmed police contingent. Among the desperate investors waiting to learn the fate of their life's savings, women, many of them stenographers on Wall Street, make up a sizable part of the multitude. Clearly, there is excitement in simply being near the scene. And even among those without a vested interest in the market, the chance to witness first-hand the collapse of Wall Street is just too great to resist.

Hoover tells shaky public economy is solid

Washington, D.C., Dec. 31

President Hoover exchanged New Year's wishes with reporters today, offering yet another profession of faith in America's economic future. Holiday retail receipts are running somewhat ahead of last year's totals. Earlier this month, the President told Congress that confidence in the nation's business affairs had been re-established, and the public seems to be nodding its assent. But then, according to Wall Street financier Thomas Lamont, the crash was just "a little distress selling on the Stock Exchange."

Despite the optimism of Wall Street and Washington, distress has spread quickly since October. Within two weeks of the crash, the nation had lost an estimated $30 billion. Hoover met separately with business and trade union leaders on November 21. But he has ignored voices that urge increased government spending to keep the economy from sagging along with stock prices. Instead, relying on the optimism of consumers, he has signed a tax cut of $160 million, hoping the excess funds will be pumped back into the economy rather than put away for a rainy day. "Any lack of confidence," implores the President, "in the .. basic strength of business in the United States is foolish."

Cartoonist Rollin Kirby depicts a worried investor in "Sold Out," published October 24, Black Thursday, the day the market crash began.

1930

Hoover

Chicago, Feb. 10. Federal grand jury indicts 31 corporations and 158 people on charges of operating a major bootlegging ring (→Jan. 19, 1931).

Flagstaff, Arizona, Feb. 18. Clyde William Tombaugh inadvertently discovers planet Pluto through examination of an earlier photograph.

New York City, May 4. Robert Frost wins Pulitzer Prize for poetry with *Collected Poems.*

New Hampshire, May 4. A major fire destroys most of Nashua, leaving 1,200 people homeless.

Chicago, May 11. Adler Planetarium opens in Grant Park.

Marion, Indiana, August. Two Negroes accused of killing two whites are dragged from jail and lynched by mob numbering in thousands.

Queens, New York, August. Harry Socoloff opens nation's first modern supermarket – King Kullen Grocery.

New Jersey, Sept. 3. Thomas A. Edison tests nation's first electric passenger train, from Hoboken to Montclair.

Newport, Rhode Island, Sept. 17. U.S. yacht Enterprise successfully defends America's Cup against British challenger Shamrock V.

Boston, Sept. 17. City celebrates 300th anniversary; 50,000 march through streets.

Philadelphia, Oct. 8. Athletics defeat St. Louis Cardinals, four games to two, in World Series.

Princeton, New Jersey. Institute for Advanced Study at Princeton University founded.

New York City. Elmer Davis writes in *Harper's*, "This year, when we all needed something to take our minds off our troubles, miniature golf did it . . . if we can't find bread, we are satisfied with the circus."

United States. Will Rogers says, "I never met a man I didn't like."

DEATHS

Washington, D.C., March 8. William Howard Taft, 27th President and former Chief Justice (*Sept. 15, 1857).

Silver Springs, Maryland, Mother Jones, reformer, union organizer (*May 1, 1830).

When Garbo talks, everbody watches

The sultry star in "Anna Christie."

Hollywood, California, March 15

"Gif me a viskey . . . and dawn't be stingy, baby." Those are Garbo's first spoken words on screen, in *Anna Christie*, causing the *New York Herald Tribune* today to rave about her "deep, husky, throaty contralto." One thing the elusive Garbo will not talk about is her romance with John Gilbert, her co-star in *Flesh and the Devil* and *Love*. Lewis Milestone has directed *All Quiet on the Western Front* for Universal, shooting it silent and dubbing the sound. Marie Dressler and Wallace Beery star in *Min and Bill*, which defies M-G-M's tradition of glamor. Paramount's newest star is Marlene Dietrich, who co-stars with Gary Cooper in *Morocco*.

Study sees crime getting out of hand

Washington, D.C., Jan. 10

As Prohibition reaches its 10th anniversary, President Hoover has issued a call to fight crime, much of which is related to bootlegging. His battle cry comes with the release today of the first report of a study by the Wickersham Commission that says crime is on the increase. The study, under former Attorney General George Wickersham, may result in tougher anti-crime laws, particularly in Prohibition enforcement. Forty percent of Americans favor repeal, but Hoover supports Prohibition, calling it an "experiment, noble in motive and far-reaching in purpose" (→Feb. 10).

New in Hoover era: the best and worst

United States

Signs of the times: new food – Wonder bread, Mott's applesauce; new airlines – United, TWA, American, Braniff; new inventions – windshield wipers, pinball machines; new fads – contract bridge, backgammon; new words – Hoover flags (pockets emptied and turned out), Hoover blankets (newspapers covering park bench indigents), Hoovervilles (shantytowns).

Blondie Boopadoop has beau Dagwood

Chicago, Sept. 15

In the first episode of *Blondie*, Chic Young's new comic strip, readers are introduced to the title character, a bird-brained flapper named Blondie Boopadoop. Her fondest admirer, Dagwood Bumstead, is a mild-mannered playboy and the son of a railroad tycoon. Readers suspect that they are going to become a couple, and that Dagwood's father will disinherit him.

Hi-yo, Silver, away!

New York City

Gather round the radio. There swells the William Tell Overture, and on "a fiery horse with the speed of light, a cloud of dust and a hearty 'Hi-yo, Silver,' the Lone Ranger rides again!" Or tune in to hear the Rev. Fulton J. Sheen on the *Catholic Hour*, broadcast by NBC. And already following on the heels of radio broadcasting, the first experimental television transmissions are being beamed from station W2XBS here.

Thomas Hart Benton's "Instruments of Power," one of the murals from his "America Today" (1930) series.

A flock of firsts for female flyers

Cheyenne, Wyoming, May 15

Miss Ellen Church stepped off a United Airlines plane today, having completed the country's first flight by a female steward. She still wore the cap and hip-length shawl she had donned for the chilly flight from San Francisco. Stewardship is but one of women's advances in aviation. Two years ago, Miss Amelia Earhart flew the Atlantic, the first woman passenger to do so. One young woman, Miss Lillian Boyer, makes her living as a stunt flyer, and Miss Laura Ingalls plans to set a women's loop-the-loop record the day after tomorrow in the skies over Oklahoma.

Hughes confirmed as Chief Justice

Washington, D.C., Feb. 13

Charles Evan Hughes survived a fierce Senate debate today to gain confirmation as the nation's Chief Justice by a 52-26 vote. The former New York Governor, United States Secretary of State and associate justice will succeed William Howard Taft, who retired earlier this month for health reasons. Hughes served on the high court from 1910 to 1916, resigning to run for president against Woodrow Wilson. He is expected to add to the court's conservative slant, but is known to hold that the Constitution is an active, flexible guide to jurisprudence.

Photographer Margaret Bourke-White atop the Chrysler Building.

Population hits 122 million; L.A. is fifth

Los Angeles, California, home of Universal Studios and other dream factories.

Washington, D.C., Dec. 31

The government has released the results of the 1930 federal census, and the facts are somewhat startling. Statistics put the nation's population at 122.7 million. This represents a dramatic increase, 30 million people over the 92 million counted in the 1920 census. While New York is still the largest city, the most spectacular growth occurred in the Far West. Los Angeles has become the fifth most populous metropolis. Among the states, Arizona has experienced the most rapid growth; more than 435,000 people now live there, an increase of about 100,000 in a decade. The only state in the union to have lost population is Montana.

The census also shows that while first-generation Irish and Jewish immigrants tended to settle in the poorest inner-city slums, the next generation is moving out to the more affluent suburbs. For example, the Irish population of St. Louis has dropped by half since 1900. The same phenomenon is taking place in Harlem, once the home of more than 177,000 Jews; now fewer than 5,000 live there.

Other statistics show that the current life expectancy of the typical American is 61 years, and that there are more than 26 million cars on America's roads.

One interesting change will be taking place in the 1940 census count. When that canvass takes place, housewives will be given the official job title of "homemaker," instead of being listed as having "no occupation," as in the past.

Schmeling gets title on Sharkey's foul

New York City, June 12

For the first time in history, a world heavyweight championship has been decided on a foul. Max Schmeling, the German giant, was awarded the title today because of a low blow by Jack Sharkey that left him writhing on the canvas. It happened with five seconds left in the fourth round. Schmeling was still on the floor when the bell rang for the fifth and the German was declared winner of the title vacated by Gene Tunney. Sharkey had been ahead from the start.

Gallant Fox wins the Triple Crown

New York City, June

With Earl Sande in the saddle, Gallant Fox sped to victory in the Belmont Stakes here to became the second colt ever to win racing's Triple Crown. Last month, he won the 56th Kentucky Derby in the view of the 17th Earl of Derby ("It's darby not durby," said his lordship). Sande, in a comeback after a stint as a trainer, got Gallant Fox out of the new-fangled mechanical starting gate slowly, edged into the lead in the backstretch and romped home by two lengths.

DeMar wins 7th Boston Marathon

Boston, Apr. 20

Most dedicated runners would be happy to win it once, and just finishing it is considered a personal triumph. But today, Clarence DeMar won the Boston Marathon for the seventh time. DeMar first captured the grueling run from suburban Hopkinton to Boston in 1911; a decade passed before he won again, in 1922. After that, the Melrose athlete was almost unstoppable, repeating his victory in 1923 as well as in 1924. Then, when no one thought it was possible, DeMar confounded track buffs by taking the marathon yet again in 1927, 1928 and, incredibly, this year.

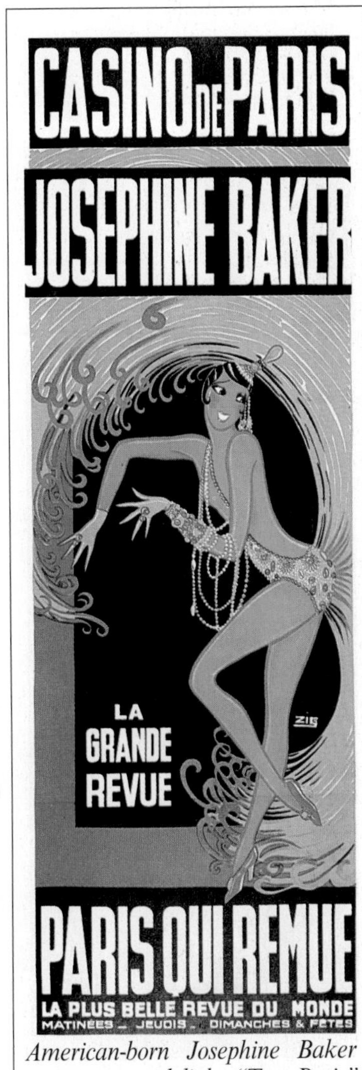

American-born Josephine Baker continues to delight "Tout-Paris" with her provocative dances. She may be best known for having appeared in nothing but a string of bananas in "La Revue Negre."

Disputed tariff is signed

Washington, D.C., June 17

President Hoover today placed the United States behind the highest tariff walls in the nation's history, with the help of six ceremonial pens. The President signed the tariff act and presented the pens to the six leaders who guided the measure on its stormy path through Congress. They included the bill's namesakes: Senator Reed Smoot of Utah, and Representative Willis Hawley of Oregon. The two had pressed for higher rates than the President wanted. It is believed he signed the bill mainly to calm Wall Street. On Monday, the market took a sharper drop than at any time since the November bottoming out of last year's crash.

London and Paris reacted with gloom, fearing a chill on international trade, while agricultural groups that fear higher prices for what the farmers buy moved to challenge the President, attacking the Smoot-Hawley tariff law even before the ink on it was dry.

"American Gothic," just plain farm folk

"American Gothic"(1930) by Grant Wood. In his attempt to depict the Iowa farmer, the artist has captured the spirit of rural America. The odd folks in the picture, modeled after his sister and his dentist, represent a protective father and spinster daughter. The dour couple proved popular with city as well as country folk: The Art Institute of Chicago bought the work for $300.

$116 million allocated to ease job crisis

Some 6,000 unemployed have been given surplus apples to sell for 5 cents.

Washington, D.C., Dec. 21

President Hoover today won approval of the emergency job program he wanted from Congress, and the lawmakers have adjourned for the holiday, after a session that lasted until five minutes past midnight. The measure appropriates $116 million to put the unemployed back to work on emergency construction projects. Major opponents were not so much against the idea of creating jobs in the wake of the crash as they were convinced that the President's emphasis on national voluntary community efforts is not enough. Senators Robert La Follette of Wisconsin and David I. Walsh of Massachusetts protested that 4.5 million are unemployed and that distress across the land is far worse than the President realizes. They argued against the "smallness" of the appropriation, and read into the record a number of unemployment reports they described as a "complete refutation of statements that the situation is well in hand." Senator La Follette said that he regarded the administration program as "totally inadequate." The senators left for home with La Follette's voice ringing in their ears: "I hope that when you return, you will be at least as generous as you were to corporations and income-tax payers last year" (→Jan. 7, 1931).

London naval pact ratified by Senate

Washington, D.C., July 21

The arms control effort took a step forward today as the Senate ratified the London Naval Treaty by a vote of 58 to 9. Signed in April by the United States, Britain and Japan, the pact supplements the five-power Washington Treaty of 1922, which limited the number of battleships each country could retain. The London Treaty sets ceilings for all types of warships, including cruisers, destroyers and submarines. The United States has won parity with Britain across the board, and Japan has been granted higher quotas in several categories, including submarines. Because of a dispute, however, neither France nor Italy signed the new treaty.

$45 million is voted for drought relief

Washington, D.C., Dec. 30

Relief is on the way. Congress today passed and sent to the President for his signature the first of his emergency programs. The bill appropriates $45 million to help farmers in areas that have been hard hit by either storms or drought. Calling for advances and loans to be used in farm production, including feed for livestock, it provoked a debate in which Senator James Heflin of Alabama argued: "Striking out human food and buying food for livestock puts hogs above humans and mules above men. Won't it be a glorious Christmas present to give a man money to buy food for his horse and hog and refuse it to him!" (→Jan. 4, 1931).

Sinclair Lewis wins Nobel literary prize

Oslo, Norway, Dec. 10

For the first time, the world's highest literary prize has gone to an American. Sinclair Lewis, who arrived in Stockholm aboard the liner Drottningholm, was awarded the Nobel Prize late today. The Nobel committee, which named Lewis on November 5, will gather two days from now to hear the famed satirist's acceptance speech. It should be an earful. Yesterday, Lewis sent a cable to his publisher, Alfred Harcourt, urging that he arrange for publication in full of his remarks. "Please try (to) get Sunday sections (of the) *Times* or *Herald Tribune*," the cable read in part. "Speech as it will be reported (by the) press (will) cause repercussions."

Golf Grand Slam enough for Bobby Jones

Premier golfer following through.

Georgia, Nov. 17

There are no more worlds for Bobby Jones to conquer. So with the Grand Slam of golf neatly tucked away among his laurels, Jones retired today from competition. He has run out of golfers to beat. At the age of 28, Robert Tyre Jones has won in a single year both the United States Open and Amateur and the British Open and Amateur. Jones, was especially pleased to capture the British Amateur, a new title for him. In a near gale, he won on the 19th hole. He took the United States Open in 100-degree heat with the help of his lily-pad shot, in which the ball skipped over a pond.

In all, this master of the amateurs has captured 13 championships in 14 years.

400,000 depositors find bank is closed

New York City, Dec. 11

Fearful crowds collected around the 60 branches of the Bank of United States this morning, anxious to withdraw their money, only to find the doors closed and mounted police on guard. The bank, with 400,000 depositors, blamed rumors for a run on cash, and said reopening would bring disorder. More than half its $160 million in deposits are in "thrift savings" of the lower classes. Others are concentrated in the garment industry. Many of its loans are in real estate, hard hit by the crash. To quiet fears overseas, Washington officials explained that in spite of the bank's name, there is no United States government connection with it (→21).

Painter Ferris dies

Philadelphia, March 18

Jean Leon Gerome Ferris, who dedicated his career in art to the depiction of American history, is dead. Ferris, son of the prolific portraitist Stephen Ferris, studied at the Pennsylvania Academy of Fine Arts and in Paris, where he was the pupil of the academic painter Jean-Leon Gerome, for whom he was named. Ferris was known for his humanizing depictions of famous Americans, whom he portrayed in both domestic and heroic scenes.

A mechanical brain

Cambridge, Massachusetts

A "differential analyzer" invented by Vannevar Bush at the Massachusetts Institute of Technology should be of great use to physicists and engineers, who can be helped by its approximations. This computer, actually an analog computing device, is a kind of mechanical brain. It does very quick, if not always very accurate, calculations. Those who need total accuracy in their figures are better off with the slower punch-card system.

Beards write "The American Leviathan"

United States

"Leviathan" means monstrous or enormous and applies in at least two ways to the new work by historian Charles A. Beard and his son William. *The American Leviathan* is, first of all, a monster of a book, with 824 fact-filled pages. And its subject is another sort of leviathan, the top-heavy ship of state that is the government of the United States. The Beards hold that the federal system has been totally transformed by modern scientific knowledge, which has created new "functions" and "has emphasized as never before the role of government as a stabilizer of civilization." The trouble, they claim, is that although technology has revamped the way the system works – in areas ranging from diplomacy to banking – it has added nothing to improve government. And it had better come up with something quick, because "historic morals and common sense" no longer suffice, as jobless millions know too well.

Harlow soars, Berkeley dazzles, Fox falls

Hollywood, California

Howard Hughes is converting his World War aviation saga, *Hell's Angels*, to sound. He began the film in 1927, but is reshooting with his 19-year-old discovery, platinum-blonde Jean Harlow, in the lead. Samuel Goldwyn has lured Busby Berkeley from Broadway to choreograph several Eddie Cantor vehicles. The trade is already talking about Busby's dizzying camera techniques for dance sequences, and Mary Pickford plans to try a musical with him. Though movie attendance is at a new high, William Fox, a top silent-era mogul, was wiped out by the Wall Street crash and had to sell his share of the Fox studio for $18 million.

Merger makes Pan Am No. 1; TWA formed

New York City, Oct. 10

Air travel is becoming more accessible as prices drop and more and larger airlines vie for business. The nation's biggest carrier is now Pan American Airlines. It became that August 21 by merging with smaller firms. A major competitor arose today with a merger of three smaller lines to form Transcontinental and Western Air (TWA). The fare from New York to the West Coast has dropped below $160. Meanwhile, new flight records are stimulating the growth of aviation. In January, Charles A. Lindbergh set a cross-country record of 14 hours 45 minutes, but in August, Frank Hawks beat that record by two hours and 20 minutes.

1931

Hoover

Noank, Connecticut, Feb. 7. New York publisher George Putnam and aviator Amelia Earhart marry, with stipulation that she may do as she pleases.

Boston, March 13. State legislature requests that Congress initiate proceedings necessary for repeal of 18th Amendment, which instituted Prohibition.

Chattanooga, Tennessee, Apr. 1. Jackie Mitchell, 19, becomes first professional woman pitcher, signed by Chattanooga.

New York City, May 5. *Atlanta Constitution* is awarded Pulitzer Prize; paper exposed graft in city government.

Kentucky, May 5. Two deputy sheriffs and 12 miners killed during strike of United Mine Workers of America.

Washington, D.C., June 20. President Hoover, hoping to ease Depression, proposes a one-year international moratorium on war reparation and debt payments (→Aug. 11).

Washington, D.C., July 26. Wickersham Commission recommends major reforms in nation's prison system.

Akron, Ohio, Aug. 8. Navy dirigible Akron, built by Goodyear, makes maiden voyage.

London, Aug. 11. Debt and reparations moratorium initiated by Hoover is accepted and signed by 18 countries.

Denver, Sept. 29. Episcopal Church eases its opposition to remarriage.

Washington, Oct. 5. Hugh Herndon and Clyde Pangborn make first non-stop trans-Pacific flight, from Japan to state of Washington.

St. Louis, Oct. 10. Cardinals defeat Philadelphia Athletics, four games to three, in World Series.

New York City, Nov. 13. Whitney Museum of American Art, first to show only American works, opens to public.

New York City. John Reed Clubs, named after Harvard-educated Communist journalist who died in Moscow in 1920, form across country.

United States. Will Rogers says, "We are the first nation . . . to go to the poorhouse in an automobile."

New York City. Irma S. Rombauer's *Joy of Cooking* published.

4 to 5 million jobless; social danger seen

"Down-and-outs" patiently wait outside New York's Doyers Street Mission.

Washington, D.C., Jan. 7

The number of unemployed in the United States now stands between four million and five million, representing a "social danger," according to the chairman of the President's Emergency Committee for Employment. Colonel Arthur Woods told the Senate Appropriations Committee today that the various construction programs across the country this year came to $2.5 billion, which he called "adequate." He testified that he agrees with Dr. Nicholas Murray Butler, president of Columbia University, that there is a danger to the social order, but not now, because "it has been foreseen." He told the committee there has been an "industrial evolution" since the days when industry met crises by firing everyone possible to cut costs. Today, he said, employers keep as many as possible on their payrolls. Asked what Congress can do to relieve the situation, Colonel Woods suggested that the senators cut the red tape that hinders conversion of appropriations into jobs.

Meanwhile, census authorities are moving apple-sellers from their lists of jobless to the category of "employed" because they say many people selling "unemployed apples" are earning a good living (→Oct. 7).

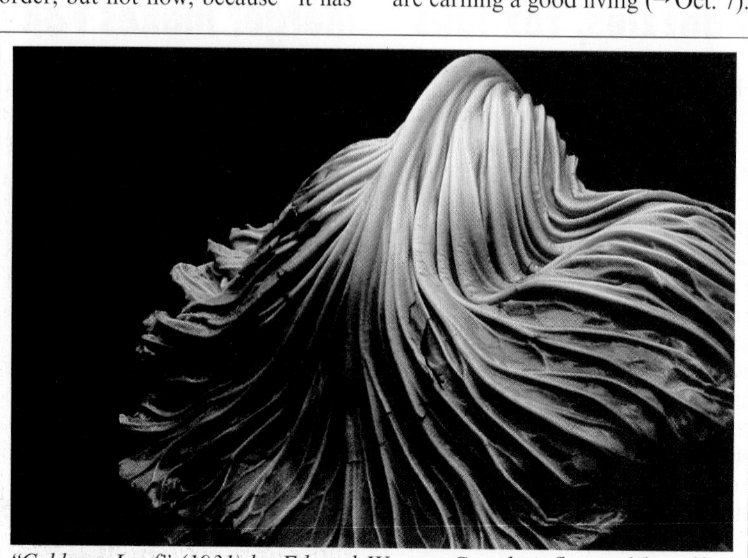

"Cabbage Leaf" (1931) by Edward Weston. Greatly influenced by Alfred Stieglitz and Paul Strand, Weston specializes in close-range photography.

"The Star-Spangled Banner" is anthem

Washington, D.C., March 3

After nearly 150 years, Americans finally have a song that they can call their own, officially. Congress today sent President Hoover a bill designating *The Star-Spangled Banner* as the national anthem. Ironically enough in these Prohibition days, what is now a patriotic tune began as a British drinking song in colonial times, an ode to Venus and Bacchus. It was taken up by Americans after the Revolution, with new patriotic words, but it was Francis Scott Key, in 1814, who penned the words used today. The song has been an unofficial anthem for a century, and, since the 1890s, in a John Philip Sousa arrangement, was used by the military whenever an anthem was needed.

Farmers need food

England, Arkansas, Jan. 4

Over 300 impoverished farmers shouting "We want food!" stormed into town today, threatening to loot the stores unless they got food for their children. The farmers, mostly white and some armed, arrived on horses, in buggies and on foot. The march started after Red Cross aides there to help in the economic crisis said they could dole out no food because they lacked food authorization forms that had to be filled out. Local merchants met and agreed to give food to all those demanding it.

U.S. chides Japan

Washington, D.C., Jan. 2

Reacting to Japan's invasion of Manchuria last September, Secretary of State Henry L. Stimson announced today that the United States would refuse to recognize any territorial acquisitions that violate American treaty rights. Since the Japanese seizure of Manchuria violates the Kellogg-Briand Treaty of 1928, which renounces aggression, as well as the nine-power Open Door pact of 1922, Stimson has in effect condemned Japan's action. However, since President Hoover opposes any further moves, Stimson's doctrine is likely to remain just a moral condemnation.

Scottsboro Boys sentenced to die for rape

Paint Rock, Alabama, Apr. 9

Demonstrations have erupted in 28 countries today to protest the conviction of the nine Scottsboro Boys for the rape of two white girls on March 25. Eight of the Negroes were sentenced to death; one received a life sentence.

The incident allegedly occurred aboard a freight train that was traveling from Chattanooga to Memphis. Near Stevenson, Alabama, a fight broke out between groups of Negro and white youths who had hitched a ride in the freight car. Five whites were thrown from the train. They told the townspeople of Stevenson their version of the story, adding that the Negro youths were traveling with two white girls. The Stevenson station master telegraphed down the line and a posse was formed to meet the train at Paint Rock. There were indeed two white girls on the train, Victoria Price and Nancy Bates, who claimed that they had been raped.

The Negro youths fled, but nine were captured: Andy Wright, Roy White, Haywood Patterson, Clarence Norris, Charley Weems, Ozzie Powell, Eugene Williams, who is only 13, Willy Roberson, who is crippled as the result of a venereal disease, and Olen Montgomery, who is blind. The Paint Rock jurors found the girls' testimony adequate and the nine youths were convicted.

Their defense has been taken up by a Communist group, the International Labor Defense, and by the National Association for the Advancement of Colored People. The groups are presently vying for the honor of defending the Scottsboro Boys on appeal (→Nov. 7, 1932).

Twinkies to Bahai

United States

New foods: Hotel Bar butter, Bisquick biscuit mix, Beech-Nut baby food, Hostess Twinkies, Toll House cookies. New products and inventions: Alka Seltzer, Breck shampoo, the air-conditioner, infra-red photography, Schick shavers, dry ice, coaxial cables, synthetic rubber. Also this year, the New School for Social Research opened, and the steel superstructure for the Bahai House of Worship, in Wilmette, Illinois, was completed after 21 years.

Debut of Dick Tracy

Chicago, Oct. 4

This is the town of Al Capone and Elliot Ness, of blazing machine guns and cold, hard justice. Now the innocent have another defender. Chester Gould's new comic strip, *Dick Tracy*, features an ordinary citizen who becomes a police officer after his sweetheart, Tess Trueheart, is kidnapped and her father murdered. Iron-jawed Tracy will pursue criminals relentlessly, dishing out justice daily and on Sundays in eye-for-an-eye fashion. Go get 'em, Dick!

Commission calls dry law unenforceable

Washington, D.C., Jan. 19

The Wickersham Commission report issued today left most people no wiser than before. Headed by former United States Attorney General George W. Wickersham and formally called the National Commission on Law Observance and Enforcement, the group was originally formed to study the problems of enforcing Prohibition. But it was hobbled by President Hoover's insistence that it study all national crime. The commission finds that Prohibition isn't working and can't be enforced because of general apathy, hostility and the iron grip of bootlegging. While the report suggests some mild modifications, it does not recommend repeal.

Many find the study little more than a farcical admission that problems indeed exist. As a possible remedy, the group ambiguously suggests that Congress either "adopt any system of effective control" or let the states decide Prohibition's future. This could lead to the repeal favored by the "wets," to whom the report otherwise smacks of pussyfooting and buck-passing. While the "drys" can claim it as an official victory, the report has ominous overtones for the temperance cause and portends a significant crack in their hitherto impregnable dike.

World's tallest building

New York City, May 1

A ceremony that included President Hoover and former New York Governor Alfred E. Smith today formally opened the Empire State Building, the tallest building in the world. Towering 1,245 feet over Manhattan, the Empire State has 86 floors of space, including ground floor shops and a restaurant, and above all a mooring mast for passenger dirigibles.

Officiating at the tape-cutting ceremony was the former Governor. The building's designer is the architectural firm of Shreve, Lamb and Harrison. After the ribbon was cut, President Hoover, in Washington, pushed a button that turned on the building's lights. Construction of the skyscraper is being hailed as a gesture of confidence during the Depression.

The site of the building, 34th Street and Fifth Avenue, was previously occupied by the Waldorf-Astoria Hotel and, before that, by John Jacob Astor's mansion. The skyscraper was planned during the boom years of the 1920s, but construction did not begin until 1930. The mighty structure required 400 tons of stainless steel, 10 million bricks and 6,400 windows. Constructed so it can withstand the worst storms conceivable, the top of the structure is often buffeted by winds of over 100 miles an hour.

The mooring mast surmounting the building will be available for the use of airships delivering passengers to New York City. Such facilities in the center of Manhattan, it is thought, will provide an enormous boost for the air transport industry, with the building offering a central terminal for dirigibles.

Experts say it is not likely that such an engineering feat will soon be surpassed or repeated, and the Empire State Building is likely to exist, along with the pyramids of Egypt, as a testimony to the building skills of the human race.

The 1,245-foot Empire State Building, tallest skyscraper of all, is a symbol of American confidence despite hard times. Much of the space remains vacant.

Around the world in eight and a half days

Long Island, N.Y., July 1

A world record was set today when pilot Wiley Post and navigator Harold Gatty landed their plane, the Winnie Mae, at Roosevelt Field after circumnavigating the globe in 8 days 15 hours 51 minutes. The previous record for around-the-world flight, set by the Graf Zeppelin, was 21 days. Traveling nearly 15,500 miles, the Winnie Mae made stops in England, Germany and Siberia, where it was delayed for 14 hours by bad weather, before returning via Alaska and Canada. The Winnie Mae, a Lockheed Vega high-wing monoplane belonging to Arkansas oil magnate F.C. Hall and named for his daughter, spent over 106 hours in the air.

Washington Bridge, the longest of its kind

New York City, Oct. 25

The George Washington Bridge, the longest suspension bridge in the world, was completed today, connecting Manhattan and New Jersey across the Hudson River for the first time. The bridge is 4,800 feet long and its towers rise 635 feet above the water. The four cables that support the roadway are each made up of 26,474 wires and measure 36 inches in diameter. Construction of the bridge was begun by the Port of New York Authority under the engineer Othmar Ammann in 1927. Eight spacious lanes are available, so the bridge will be a tremendous time-saver for those driving between New York and New Jersey.

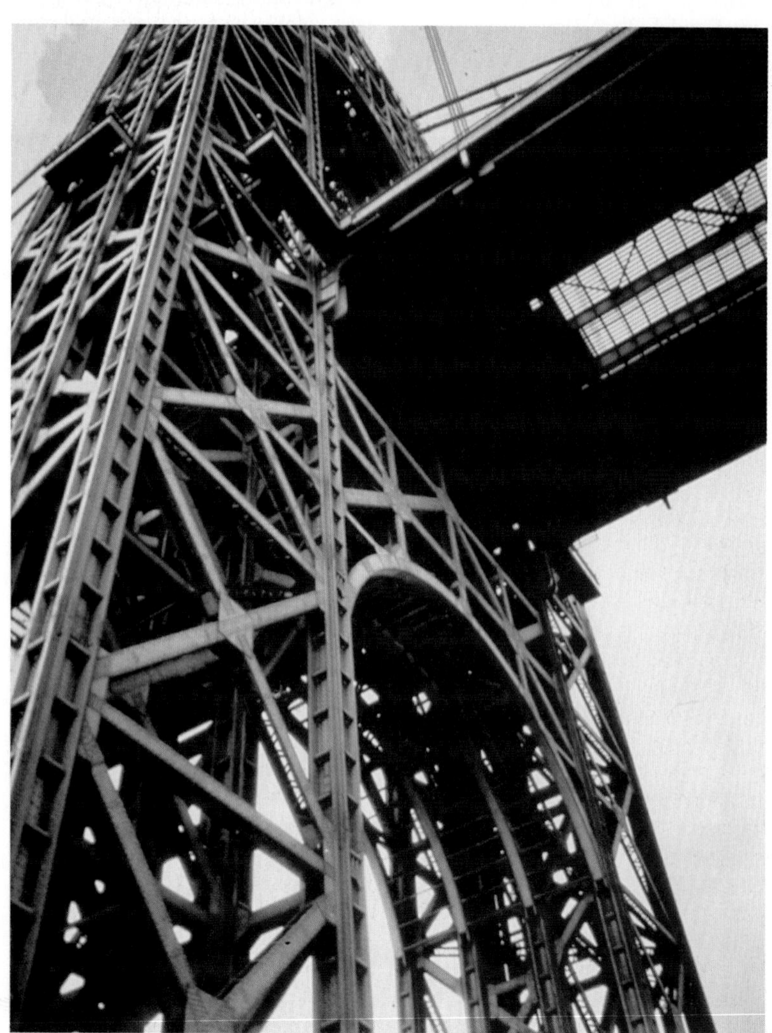

"George Washington Bridge" by Berenice Abbott. After studying sculpture in Berlin, Abbott moved to Paris to perfect her photographic skills. Returning to New York in 1929, she dedicated herself to capturing the city on film.

Facing the run on banks

Citizens gather in panic outside a bank, having lost access to their money.

Washington, D.C., Oct. 7

President Hoover acted at 20 minutes past midnight to end the run on banks, 800 of which have failed. After a secret meeting with congressmen, Hoover announced a plan to mobilize banking resources against hoarding and failure. It calls for more money to strengthen the farm loan system, a privately financed $500 million revolving pool to help ailing banks and a federal agency offering loans to industry. Flying from Texas to attend the meeting, Rep. John Nance Garner found that his wife had folded a scriptural quotation within his invitation: "The spirit of the Lord watches over you and keeps you in perfect safety. His spirit is guarding, protecting, inspiring and guiding you in all your ways." Said the congressman, "I was mighty glad to read it" (→ Dec. 8).

Capone finally imprisoned, as tax dodger

Chicago, Oct. 17

America's most notorious and elusive gangster, "Scarface" Al Capone, was sentenced today to an 11-year prison term for tax evasion. Authorities have been trying for years to corral the legendary bootlegger, racketeer and killer, (he was reportedly behind the St. Valentine's Day Massacre in 1929). But Capone always dodged prosecution. This time, they've nailed him, and hard; the sentence set by the Federal Court is the stiffest ever for income tax evasion. He must also pay $50,000 in fines along with $137,328 in back taxes. Capone grew up in Brooklyn, where he dropped out of school and joined various gangs. Once, as a nightclub bouncer, he was knifed in the cheek, gaining him his fabled nickname. Moving to Chicago in 1920, he quickly rose to the peak of criminal power. With today's conviction, "Scarface" has finally lost his grip on the Chicago underworld.

"Scarface" in "his favorite pose."

ane Addams wins Nobel Peace Prize

Oslo, Norway, Dec. 10

Miss Jane Addams, who angered many Americans during the Great War by espousing a pacifist philosophy, has become the first American woman to receive the Nobel Peace Prize. She shares the honors with Dr. Nicholas Murray Butler, founder of the Carnegie Endowment for International Peace and president of Columbia University. Twenty years ago, with the help of Mrs. Ellen Gates Starr, a college friend, Miss Addams began Chicago's Hull House. The settlement house became a model for urban betterment programs, helping the poor raise healthy families and gain self-reliance. Miss Addams, at 71 in poor health but unshakable spirit, now directs the Women's League for Peace and Freedom.

Hoover spurns dole but aids business

Washington, D.C., Dec. 8

President Hoover says business must be helped, but he opposes "any direct or indirect dole" for the needy, saying it would create more unemployment. In his State of the Union message, the President called for a $500 million emergency reconstruction program to aid business in general and railroads in particular. Speaking of the jobless, Hoover said, "The federal taxpayer is now contributing to the livelihood of 10 million of our citizens," indicating that was enough. He says that the Depression is caused by "an unjustified lack of confidence," saying that a first step toward recovery involves re-establishing confidence and thus restoring "the flow of credit which is the basis of our economic life" (→ Jan. 22, 1932).

Violent days: Cagney, Lugosi and Karloff

Hollywood, California

Movie theaters now show double features, providing the hordes of unemployed with a place to go and an affordable escape. Gangster and horror films have caught on. *Little Caesar, Public Enemy* (watch a snarling James Cagney smash a grapefruit into the face of Mae Clarke), *Dracula* with Bela Lugosi, and *Frankenstein* with Boris Karloff lead the pack. From Chaplin comes *City Lights*, a silent film except for sound effects and a musical score, composed and conducted by Chaplin himself. Silent-film extra Clark Gable, turned down by several studios because of his looks ("His ears are too big"), plays a secondary role to Leslie Howard in *A Free Soul* but delights audiences by slapping Norma Shearer around. Now he is this town's newest star, with leading ladies such as Garbo and Joan Crawford. Bing Crosby, a relaxed, engaging singer, croons his debut in Max Sennett shorts, and stage actress Bette Davis, 23, has been signed by Universal, despite having failed a screen test earlier. Carl Laemmle has reportedly said Miss Davis has "as much sex appeal as Slim Summerville," the gangling comic supporting actor.

Cagney is tough and outside the law.

Lugosi has the bite on horror films.

Lights turned out to honor Thomas Edison

The great inventor in his West Orange, New Jersey, laboratory. Although he had only three months' formal education, Edison changed the world.

West Orange, New Jersey, Oct. 18

Thomas Alva Edison, inventor, businessman and pioneer industrialist, died today at the age of 84. A colorful personality, Edison was renowned for many inventions that have changed the way Americans live, including electric lighting, the phonograph, a practical motion picture camera and a thousand other patented devices. These advances were the result of what was probably the inventor's greatest gift to American industry: organized commercial research.

Edison was born in Milan, Ohio, the son of a prosperous shingle manufacturer. A collapse of the family fortune when Thomas was 7 years old brought the family to Michigan and a frugal existence. Edison's childhood was characterized by an avid curiosity. He asked so many questions, and was so unable to adapt to the rote learning offered by public school, that his teacher decided he was "addled." He quit school and continued his education at home, taught by his mother, who was a former teacher.

At the age of 16, Edison got a job with the Western Union Telegraph Company in Boston, where he quickly earned a reputation as a rapid-fire telegrapher. At the same time, he studied Michael Faraday's writings on electricity and did experiments on his own.

He received his first patent in 1869, for an electric vote recorder. This was a commercial failure because politicians wanted to count their own votes. His first successful patent was an improved stock quotation ticker, which earned him $40,000 in 1870. This money allowed him to equip a laboratory in New Jersey, where he spent the rest of his life churning out inventions. In his memory, the lights of the nation are being turned off for one minute tonight.

1932

Hoover

Nicaragua, Jan. 2. Last U.S. Marines are withdrawn from Nicaragua.

Washington, D.C., Jan. 12. Justice Oliver Wendell Holmes resigns from Supreme Court, after almost 30 years on that bench.

Geneva, Switzerland, Feb. 2. Although not a member of League of Nations, United States sends delegates to World Disarmament Conference.

Dearborn, Michigan, March 7. As police and firemen try to quell rioters at Ford Motor Company plant, four are killed and many are injured.

Washington, D.C., March 14. Benjamin N. Cardozo appointed new associate justice of Supreme Court.

Southeastern United States, March 21. Tornado sweeps through five states, killing 365 people.

New Hampshire, April. Florence Clasr, 32, becomes first woman to drive a sled dog team to summit of Mount Washington, and back.

New York City, May 2. Pearl S. Buck wins Pulitzer Prize in fiction for *The Good Earth,* which examines life in China.

Washington, D.C., July 15. President Hoover announces that he is taking a 20 percent reduction in his salary.

Washington, D.C., July 24. Census reports that of 10 million women gainfully employed, 209 are in fishing industry and 87 are trappers, hunters and guides.

New York City, Nov. 7. *Buck Rogers* aired on CBS radio.

Arlington National Cemetery, Va., Nov. 11. Secretary of War Patrick J. Hurley dedicates Tomb of the Unknown Soldier.

New York City, Dec. 27. Radio City Music Hall, world's largest theater, opens in Rockefeller Center.

New York City. Two-a-day vaudeville closes on Broadway.

New York City. *Moral Man and Immoral Society,* by Rheinhold Niebuhr, published.

Missouri. Laura Ingalls Wilder issues first in series of books, titled *Little House.*

New York City. Erskine Caldwell's *Tobacco Road* published.

Lindy's baby found dead

Princeton, N.J., May 12

The search for the kidnapped son of Charles A. Lindbergh ended today in the worst way imaginable. The decomposed body of Charles Lindbergh Jr. was found in woods less than five miles from the family home. A truck driver discovered the naked form of the 20-month-old child in a shallow grave. It was taken to the county morgue in Trenton, where the child's nursemaid, Miss Betty Gow, identified the infant as the boy once called "the fat lamb." Mrs. Lindbergh, expecting another baby soon, will not be asked to confirm the grim findings; that burden will fall on her husband, who is expected in town tomorrow, having followed up on one of many dead-end leads. Since the child vanished on March 1, there have been no firm clues as to the identity of the kidnapper other than a poorly spelled ransom note and the delivery of the baby's pajamas by a man with a German accent who was heard but was not seen (→Apr. 3, 1936).

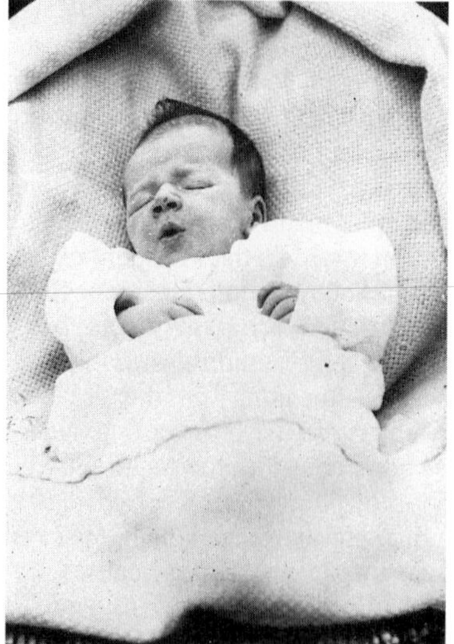

The child shortly before his death.

Hoover sets up new finance agency

Washington, D.C., Jan. 22

Only recently, President Herbert Hoover suggested that "a poem can do more than legislation" to fight the Depression. Today, he traded the idea of rhymes for the reality of legislation and signed a bill creating the Reconstruction Finance Corporation. Under the leadership of Charles Dawes, the R.F.C. will dispense $500 million in loans to failing firms, mostly banks and railroads. Its appearance signals the end of the National Credit Corp., a voluntary pool through which strong banks were expected to help weak competitors. Advocates of the plan hope the loans will halt bank failures, up from 659 in 1929 to 2,294 last year, and trickle down to the millions of jobless. But liberal critics, led by New York Rep. Fiorella La Guardia, call the R.F.C. a millionaire's dole (→July 22).

America's "descent from respectability"

United States

Statistics tell an ugly story these days. The jobless rate in some cities is over 50 percent; two million people wander the country as vagrants, and even Babe Ruth took a $10,000 salary cut. But numbers cannot tell the whole story. The enigma of suffering has sent people grasping for the less tangible dimension of our fate. John Dewey writes of "the breakdown of the particular romance known as business, . . . the revelation that the elated excitement of the romantic adventure has to be paid for with an equal depression." Writer Joseph Heffernan points to the "defeated, discouraged, hopeless men and women cringing and bowing as they come to ask for public aid." It is, he says, our "descent from respectability."

Once busy providers, the unemployed line up at a New York City soup kitchen.

Winter Olympics

Lake Placid, N.Y., Winter

After mediocre performances in the two previous Winter Olympics, American athletes came into their own when the Games took place in their own country. The weather was unseasonably warm, and some 80,000 spectators were on hand to watch Americans score in all four speed skating events. Americans also won both bobsledding events.

Pastor leads hungry on trek to capital

Washington, D.C., Jan. 6

The Rev. James R. Cox sees hungry Americans everywhere and he wants to do something about their plight. Today, the pastor and some 18,000 unemployed men from the Pittsburgh area concluded their visit to Washington by holding a meeting with several members of Congress and President Hoover, who in 1928 had promised "a chicken in every pot." The marchers are asking for relief measures for the growing numbers of destitute. It is expected that by year's end some 13 million will be jobless. Wages have fallen by 60 percent since 1929.

Earhart flies Atlantic

Safely down in Northern Ireland.

Londonderry, Ireland, May 21

A Lady Lindy has flown solo across the Atlantic Ocean, the first woman to meet the challenge. Amelia Earhart landed her gold and red Lockheed Vega in a cow pasture here this afternoon, having left St. John's, Newfoundland, 15 hours and 39 minutes earlier. The 34-year-old Kansas-born aviatrix first came to public attention in June 1928 when she became the first woman passenger on a trans-Atlantic flight. She expects to rendezvous in England with her husband-business manager George Putnam before sailing back to the United States (→ July 18, 1937).

Norris-La Guardia Act to protect workers

Washington, D.C., March 23

Continuing its search for effective answers to the Depression, Congress today approved the Norris-La Guardia Act, placing the force of law behind labor's struggle for union recognition. Under the new legislation, owners cannot legally require non-union pledges as a condition for employment. Injunctions are curbed and jury trials granted for contempt. But most importantly, the act acknowledges labor's right to "association (and) self-organization" as a counterweight to the power of management.

Labor leaders almost universally applaud the move, hoping it will reinvigorate legions of discouraged organizers. But the battle is still uphill. Trade union rolls have been cut nearly in half, from a peak of five million in 1920, while the American Federation of Labor has shrunk from four million members to 2.5 million. An atomized labor force has been hit hard by the crash. Wage payments fell from $50 billion in 1929 to an estimated $30 billion this year, and unemployment has soared to 11 million. The economists, who think greater consumption can end the Depression are some of the bill's most vociferous backers, hoping an emboldened labor movement will push wages up.

The Depression does not always discriminate in choosing victims.

4 from U.S. freed in Hawaiian's death

Honolulu, May 13

Four Americans convicted of killing a Hawaiian were freed today. The Hawaiian, who had been accused of raping the wife of U.S. Navy Lt. Thomas Massie, was kidnapped and killed by Lieutenant Massie, his mother-in-law and two sailors. Today, however, Hawaii Governor Judd reduced their 10-year sentences to an hour. A pardon for the four and an inquiry are being sought by U.S. senators and Clarence Darrow, the lawyer for the convicted group. Hawaiians are incensed, charging there are two sets of justice in Hawaii.

Bonus Army is dispersed

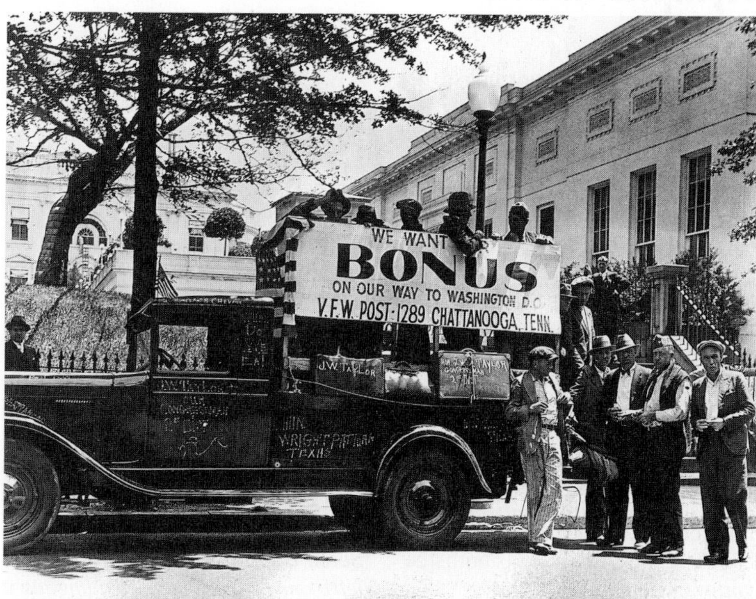

A group of bonus marchers from Tennessee finally arrive in Washington, D.C.

Washington, D.C., July 28

President Hoover today ordered that federal troops under the command of General Douglas MacArthur forcibly remove the "Bonus Army" from the nation's capital. Witnesses say that the army's treatment of the unemployed veterans was little short of barbaric. MacArthur, the army chief of staff, was called in earlier today after a clash between 800 Washington police and a gathering of 5,000 veterans led to the death of two of the veterans. Leading a massed force of four troops of cavalry and four companies of infantry supported by tanks, MacArthur and his soldiers, wielding sabers and throwing tear gas, assaulted the shacks set up by the Bonus Army. The troops then burned the entire temporary settlement and dispersed the estimated 9,000 former servicemen, some say brutally. MacArthur said that he "felt revolution in the air," and was forced to use violence. But his aide, Major Dwight D. Eisenhower, described the affair as "a pitiful scene" that should not have been permitted to happen.

The Bonus Army was led by a former navy man, Roy Robertson. The veterans of the Great War, mostly unemployed, planned to go to the White House and urge that the bonuses promised them for having served in the war be paid immediately, rather than in 1945 as Congress has provided.

Shacks, put up by the Bonus Army, burn after the battle with soldiers. President Hoover believed the bonus seekers had been infiltrated by Communists. ▷

Americans dominate Olympics in L.A.

Los Angeles, Aug. 14

The crowds were enormous, the weather was perfect and American performances were spectacular. What more was needed to make the Olympics a smashing success for the United States! No American team has ever achieved a greater haul of gold and in the unofficial points standings finished with 740.5, with runner-up Italy getting only 262.5. Despite dire predictions in a Depression year, record crowds turned out to see record performances. Eddie Tolan was the big star of the Games with two victories and his teammate, Bill Carr of Penn, took the 400 meters in 0:46.2, a time that broke both the world and Olympic marks.

Retrial for Scottsboro 9

Seven of Scottsboro Boys with Samuel Liebowitz of New York (second from left), one of the nation's leading lawyers, who was hired to defend them.

Washington, D.C., Nov. 7

The Supreme Court has ordered a retriai for the nine Scottsboro Boys, who were accused of raping two white girls on March 25 of last year and convicted of the crime on April 9. Eight of the Negro youths were sentenced to death; the ninth was given life imprisonment. The high court granted the new trial because it said there had been improper representation by counsel.

Since the trial in Paint Rock, Alabama, the defense of the Negroes has been taken over by the International Labor Defense, an organ of the Communist Party. The Labor Defense was chosen by the parents of the youths in preference to the National Association for the Advancement of Colored People, which had also offered its services. The I.L.D. stimulated demonstrations against the convictions in 28 countries, making the case an international cause. American embassies in Europe and Latin America have been stoned and picketed. The I.L.D. has hired Samuel Liebowitz of New York, a nationally prominent lawyer, to handle the case, and has raised over $1 million to help the youths (→ Apr. 1, 1935).

Hoover clears funds for relief, housing

Washington, D.C., July 22

The federal government has decided to help millions of the hungry and homeless. Yesterday, President Hoover gave the Reconstruction Finance Corporation power to lend $1.8 billion to the states for relief and public works. Until now, the R.F.C. has served only banks and businesses. Dwindling state relief agencies offer $5 a week at best. New Orleans has barred new applicants; St. Louis cut its rolls in half, and Dallas denies aid to Negroes and Hispanics. On the housing front, with foreclosures up to 25,000 a month, the Federal Home Loan Bank Act today formed 12 federal banks to make funds available for construction (→ Nov. 8).

"The Great I Am"

Los Angeles

The "I Am" movement founded by Guy and Edna Ballard two years ago now has over 300,000 followers. Guy Ballard claims to have received revelations from Saint Germain on Mount Shasta. Followers are called upon to visualize the "Great I Am Power" as violet light coming from heaven to surround them. They say the positive results of this will be wealth and power.

Rule by technocracy

New York City

Who should be the ruler of men? Plato said the philosopher; Marx said the proletariat; Rousseau said "the people." Howard Scott casts his vote for the engineer. An engineer himself, Scott leads the new Committee on Technocracy, started as a kind of temple to technology. He says technicians could govern above politics, guided by the imperatives of rationality. The technology-liberated masses would work sparingly and receive a secure living in "energy certificates."

Sultan of Swat calls shot; Series to Yanks

Babe Ruth in his most familiar pose.

Chicago, Oct. 2

Babe Ruth, stung by the taunting from the Cub bench, pointed to the spot in centerfield where he apparently planned to hit the ball – then put it there for a home run. It pointed up the consummate ease with which the Yanks were able to beat the Cubs in four straight World Series games, taking the finale by a whopping 13-6. The third game had turned out to be a home-run carnival in which Ruth and Lou Gehrig delivered two homers each, their back-to-back wallops in the fifth inning deciding a 7-5 game. In the final game, the Yanks overcame a 4-1 first-inning deficit when Tony Lazzeri hit two homers. Since 1920, the Yankees have built a dynasty, winning seven pennants and four World Series.

"Circus Elephants" (1932) by John Steuart Curry. A former magazine illustrator, Curry leads the regionalist school of American painters. He approaches all of his subjects with an absolute if not shocking realism.

New York Mayor quits in scandal

New York City, Sept. 1

He won't be leading parades anymore, or frequenting Manhattan's nightspots with the same style. The debonair and controversial Jimmy Walker resigned as Mayor today, following investigations and a hearing that disclosed evidence of improprieties. When he was questioned about a $26,000 stock gift, "Gentleman Jimmy" replied that he has "many kind friends." In fact, the Democrat was truly popular with New Yorkers, both prominent ones and average citizens, who were impressed by his creation of several excellent city services, including a comprehensive subway system and a good sanitation department.

Weston founds f-64

San Francisco

A show of photographs by the f-64 group at the M.H. de Young Museum in San Francisco marks the development of a new attitude toward photography. Unofficially led by Edward Weston, the group takes its name from the smallest lens opening on a camera, allowing for great precision and detail. The common concern of these photographers is a "straight" and unmanipulative approach to the image, as opposed to the contrived style of photography.

The Frito, the Zippo and boogie-woogie

United States

What's a hepcat like you sittin' 'round readin'? Get up and dance! Swing, do the jitterbug, the Susie-Q, the rumba, the conga, the shag, the Lindy Hop, the boogie-woogie, truckin' or the Big Apple (it's kinda like an old-fashioned square dance). Then let's catch a bite to eat – some new treat like Skippy peanut butter or Frito corn chips. Then let's light up a cigarette with a new Zippo lighter and scram, hop on America's grand new highway, Route 66, and hit the gas – 'cept there's a new tax on gasoline, isn't there?

Roosevelt elected, pledging new deal

Washington, D.C., Nov. 8

When Franklin D. Roosevelt exclaimed at the Democratic convention that he "pledged a new deal for the American people," they believed him – and took their beliefs to the polls. In an election that many experts consider the most crucial since Lincoln's victory more than 70 years ago, Roosevelt has been swept into the White House with an overwhelming plurality. The latest vote tally gives him almost 23 million to President Hoover's 15 million. Norman Thomas, the Socialist candidate, collected about 885,000 votes, while the Communist Party choice, William Foster, polled over 100,000 votes.

Just who is this 50-year old man who so soundly defeated an incumbent President who was himself overwhelmingly elected just four years ago? Roosevelt is descended from an old New York family of Dutch origin. A Harvard graduate and a lawyer, he is a fifth cousin of former Republican President Theodore Roosevelt. FDR, as his friends call him, served in the Wilson administration as assistant secretary of the navy and in 1920 he was his party's nominee for vice president. Just four years ago, he was elected Governor of New York. In 1921, he was stricken with polio and can walk only with heavy braces and additional support. Roosevelt married Anna Eleanor Roosevelt, who is a distant cousin, in 1905, and they have six children.

Taking hold of the reins of power.

During the campaign, Roosevelt championed such traditional progressive programs as government regulation of utilities and securities, and federal sponsorship of hydro-electric power programs. At the same time, he seems to contradict himself. At one point in the campaign, he proposed a 25 percent cut in government expenditures. Later, he said that he would consider deficit spending, if that was necessary. Contradictions notwithstanding, political experts say that his popularity stems from two primary strengths: his concern for the "forgotten man at the bottom of the economic pyramid," and his willingness to consider any economic or political program, regardless of its ideological origin. As he recently told an audience at Oglethorpe University: "The country needs . . . and . . . demands bold, persistent experimentation."

President Hoover has said that the Democrats are "exponents of a social philosophy different from the traditional American one." While this may or may not be so, the nation's voters have scuttled a Republican philosophy that wound up with the worst depression in the history of the modern world, and a President who seemed so sure of failure that, as the sculptor Gutzon Borglum remarked, "If you put a rose in Hoover's hand, it would wilt" (→March 4, 1933).

Garbo, Barrymore star in "Grand Hotel," Muni in "Scarface"

Hollywood, California

The Academy Awards offered a surprise this year as Fredric March (*Dr. Jekyll and Mr. Hyde*) and Wallace Beery (*The Champ*) shared the best actor award. Helen Hayes won as best actress for her first film, *The Sin of Madelon Claudet*, while *Grand Hotel*, teaming Garbo and the Great Profile, John Barrymore, took best picture. Aside from the Oscars, Ernst Lubitsch crowned a decade of sophisticated comedies, often satirical looks at sex and money, with *Trouble in Paradise*. Paul Muni, triumphant in *Scarface*, as a character loosely based on Al Capone, starred in *I Am a Fugitive From a Chain Gang*, Mervyn LeRoy's look at prison abuse. Audiences also flocked to Josef Von Sternberg's *Shanghai Express* with Marlene Dietrich, Frank Capra's *American Madness*, and Rouben Mamoulian's *Love Me Tonight*.

Garbo, Barrymore in a big embrace.

Gangsters make it to the big screen.

1933

Roosevelt

Daytona Beach, Florida, March 1. Clem Sohn parachutes from a plane with "bat wings" attached to his back, sparking a new fad.

Los Angeles, March 10. An earthquake kills 120 people and causes $40 million in property damage.

Washington, D.C., March 12. To alleviate anxiety across nation, President Roosevelt addresses the people over radio hookup in first "Fireside Chat."

Raiford, Florida, March 20. Giuseppe Zangara, who tried to assassinate President-elect Roosevelt on February 15, dies in electric chair.

Washington, D.C., March 22. Congress passes Beer-Wine Revenue Act, legalizing and taxing certain beverages according to alcoholic content.

Washington, D.C., Apr. 19. President Roosevelt issues proclamation, removing U.S. currency from gold standard (→June 15).

United States, May 1. A group of university professors issues "Humanist Manifesto," calling for a melding of religious and secular thought in response to perceived religious intolerance in United States.

New York City, May 4. Archibald MacLeish wins Pulitzer Prize for poetry with *Conquistador.*

New York City, May 7. New York Life insurance company refuses to issue new loans or policies, in an attempt to survive Depression.

New York City, June 29. Primo Carnera becomes new heavyweight champion by knocking out Jack Sharkey in sixth round.

Washington, D.C., Oct. 7. New York Giants defeat Washington Senators, four games to one, in World Series.

New York City. Mexican artist Diego Rivera dismissed from Rockefeller Center murals project for refusing to erase a picture of V.I. Lenin; the mural is destroyed.

Washington, D.C. Commission on Social Trends reports the automobile has "erased boundaries" between city and country life.

New York City. *Newsweek* and *Esquire* magazines begin publication.

"The only thing to fear is fear itself"

With the United States in desperate economic condition, President Franklin Delano Roosevelt takes charge.

Washington, D.C., March 4

As Franklin Delano Roosevelt took the presidential oath of office today, the weather matched the somber national mood: cold, rainy and gray. When Chief Justice Charles Evans Hughes began administering the oath, Roosevelt surprised the tens of thousands at the inauguration – and the millions of radio listeners at home – by carefully repeating each phrase, rather than the traditional "I do." After he was sworn in, Roosevelt turned to the crowd, not with his usual jaunty cheerfulness, but with an aura of gravity that somehow still radiated a feeling of confidence.

"First of all," began the new President, "let me assert my firm belief that the only thing we have to fear is fear itself – nameless, unreasoning, unjustified terror." With a voice beginning to show stark anger at the financiers and the bankers, Roosevelt pointed out that "the moneychangers have fled from their high seats in the temple of our civilization. We may now restore that temple to the highest truths."

Roosevelt is aware that the restoration process will be difficult, if not impossible. At present, more than one in four workers is unemployed. The steel industry is operating at about 12 percent of capacity. National income is less than half of what it was in 1930. Some 5,000 banks have collapsed, taking with them more than nine million savings accounts.

One Washington reporter describing the mood, wrote, "I come home from the Hill every night filled with gloom. I see on the streets filthy, ragged, desperate-looking men such as I have never seen before." One of the Roosevelt "brain trusters," Rexford Tugwell, said, "Never in modern times . . . has there been so widespread unemployment and such moving distress from sheer hunger and cold." Even former President Coolidge has said, "I now see nothing to give ground for hope."

The President concluded his inaugural address with a hint of his proposed course of action. If traditional executive-legislative measures do not bring an end to the Depression, Roosevelt said – almost shouting – he would ask Congress "for broad executive power to wage a war against the emergency, as great as the power that would be given to me if we were, in fact, invaded by a foreign foe."

After the customary ruffles-and-flourishes performed by cavalry bugles, the President headed for the White House (→Apr. 19).

'he first 100 days: FDR takes bold steps

Vashington, D.C., June 15

A weary Congress adjourned to-ay after three months of the most ntensive yet productive executive-egislative cooperation in Ameri-an history. During President Roo-evelt's first 100 days in office, the ew Chief Executive sent Congress 5 messages and personally pushed 5 major pieces of legislation into iw. At the same time, he gave 10 najor speeches and met with both ne press and Cabinet twice a week.

Roosevelt's first official act two ays after taking office on March 4 vas to issue an emergency execu-ive order that temporarily closed ll the nation's banks to stop the nassive "runs" that threatened to lestroy the entire banking system, nd to buy time for their reor-anization. Calling Congress in-o special session, he then pushed hrough numerous and significant - ome would say revolutionary – ieces of legislation. On March 31, Congress established the Civilian Conservation Corps. FDR had the egislators abandon the gold stand-rd on April 19. On May 12, he ressed Congress to enact the Fed-ral Emergency Relief Act, which et up a national relief system; he Agricultural Adjustment Act, which set a national farm policy, nd the Emergency Farm Mort-age Act, which enabled farmers to efinance their farms.

In another whirlwind of legisla-tive actions, Roosevelt and Con-gress enacted the Truth-in-Securi-ties Act, which called for full dis-closure in the issuance of new secur-ities, the National Industrial Recov-ery Act, which provided for indus-try codes guaranteeing fair labor practices, and the Glass-Steagall Act, which, among its other provi-sions, guaranteed bank deposits. And this was only the start!

Roosevelt remarked to reporters at his first press conference at the beginning of "the 100 days," "I am told that what I'm about to do will become impossible, but I am going to try it." He did, and even as traditional a conservative as Wil-liam Randolph Hearst told him, "I guess at your next election we'll make it unanimous."

In the meantime, the President began broadcasting weekly "Fire-side Chats" in which he described the problems he and the country were facing, and his proposed New Deal solutions. "Let us unite in banishing fear," he told his national audience on one of the broadcasts. "It is your problem no less than it is mine. Together we cannot fail."

Washington insiders are amazed at the energy of this polio-crip-pled President and his quick suc-cesses. Said Secretary of the Interi-or Harold Ickes: "It's more than a New Deal. It's a new world." Hap-py days may not be here yet, but they seem nearer (→ Aug. 5).

Roosevelt escapes assassin's bullet

Miami, Fla., Feb. 15

A short, wild-eyed man took aim, ired and nearly killed President-lect Roosevelt today. Chicago Mayor Anton Cermak was slain nd four people were wounded. The ssassin was identified as Giusep-e Zangara, a jobless bricklayer who said, "I don't hate Mr. Roose-elt personally ... I hate all offi-ials and everybody who is rich." ust last month, Roosevelt recalled liscussing assassination risks with iis cousin: "I remember TR saying o me 'The only real danger from an ssassin is from the one who does ot care whether he loses his own ife in the act or not. Most of the razy ones can be spotted first.'"

20th Amendment moves up inaugural

Washington, D.C., Feb. 6

The lame duck period for federal officials will be shortened with to-day's formal adoption of the 20th Amendment to the Constitution. The reform permits the president, vice president and members of Con-gress to take office in January in-stead of March. Senator George Norris of Nebraska deserves much of the credit for the law. He ar-gued for it for years. And the inabil-ity of lame duck President Hoover to act effectively in the economic crisis period of early this year spurred Congress to push for rati-fication. The new amendment will take effect after the congressional elections next year (→ Jan. 20, 1937).

"Century of Progress" expo in Chicago

The majesty of the Chicago Exposition belies the current American situation.

Chicago, May 27

In 1834, a visitor to the town of Chicago called it "one chaos of mud, rubbish and confusion." Lit-tle wonder that Chicagoans dub their World's Fair of technical ad-vancements a "Century of Prog-ress." The exposition, situated on two man-made parks off the shore of Lake Michigan, Burnham and Northerly Island, extends over 341 acres. The government did not pro-vide a penny; it is entirely a real-ization of the dreams of Chicago's businessmen. And what dreams!

At tonight's opening ceremony, the fair was instantly lit up by a unique electrical process triggered by a beam of light captured from the star Arcturus. *Skyride*, the "highest man-made structure west of Manhattan," carries visitors be-tween the parks in "rocket cars." One exhibit, the *Hall of the World a Million Years Ago*, boasts me-chanical dinosaurs that stomp and roar. General Motors has a super-swift assembly line to visit. Promo-tional materials laud the futuristic steel, glass and stucco buildings, but at least one visitor, architect Talbot Faulkner Hamlin, finds them "almost without meaning," lacking in "plan, material use and proportion." However, he has noth-ing unkind to say of Grant Wood's *American Gothic* or Leo Katz's Mexican-influenced murals.

What has the greatest exposure at this exposition? Sally Rand, a young woman who dances with fans and seemingly nothing else.

"Century of Progress" Exposition draws national attention, and America's manufacturers, such as Oldsmobile, are quick to associate themselves with it. ▷

N.R.A. Blue Eagle flies

Hopes for economic recovery ride on the wings of the N.R.A. Blue Eagle.

Washington, D.C., Aug. 5

Under the generalship of Hugh Johnson, the National Recovery Administration has sent its Blue Eagle into flight over cooperating businesses nationwide. The emblem, says President Roosevelt, is like the shiny night badge worn by soldiers "to be sure that comrades do not fire on comrades." New thinkers have been urging the government to bring peace to the economy since the 1880s. But it took the outbreak of a depression to turn theory into practice.

The National Industrial Recovery Act, signed June 16, forges an alliance between government and business. FDR called it "the most important and far-reaching legislation ever created" by Congress. It will, he said, assure "orderly, peaceful progress" and "wealth through cooperative action, wealth in which we can all share."

The law allows representatives of each industry to set prices, quotas, wages and hours under N.R.A. supervision. Labor spokesmen criticize the suspension of antitrust law provisions. But the act also includes a ringing endorsement of unionism and collective bargaining, and today set up a National Labor Board to hear grievances. Section 7a has been referred to as "Labor's Bill of Rights." And since June, organizers have been entering factories behind the slogan, "The President wants you to unionize."

Critics are reluctant to let the free market succumb. Senator Hugo Black said N.R.A. would give trade associations lawmaking powers not unlike those in the Italy of Benito Mussolini. Former President Hoover calls the act "fascism, pure fascism." To those who stand by laissez-faire, FDR responds: "If that philosophy hadn't proved to be bankrupt, Herbert Hoover would be sitting here right now" (→ 17).

U.S. recognizes U.S.S.R.

Washington, D.C., Nov. 16

In a move certain to stir bitter opposition from conservatives, President Roosevelt announced today that the United States was extending formal recognition to the Soviet Union. The bombshell announcement follows intensive secret negotiations conducted by Secretary of the Treasury Henry Morgenthau and Foreign Service official William Bullitt with Amtorg, the Russian trading company. In his visit here earlier this year, Maxim Litvinov, the Soviet Foreign Minister, is said to have made several pledges that laid the groundwork for the negotiations. Among other things, the Soviet Union said it would discontinue its propaganda in the United States and guarantee religious freedom at home.

Recognition, occurring 16 years after the Bolsheviks seized power, is expected to strengthen Russia as a bulwark against the increasingly expansionist Japanese. The prospect of a lucrative trade between America and the U.S.S.R. was another factor in Roosevelt's decision.

First American aircraft carrier is launched

Newport News, Va., Feb. 25

A bottle was smashed against the hull of the Ranger today, christening America's first true aircraft carrier, a ship from which planes can take off and land. There have been several previous experiments with operating planes from the decks of warships, including successful flights by Eugene Ely from a temporary wooden platform on the deck of the cruiser Pennsylvania in 1910 and 1911. In 1922, the United States Navy launched the Langley, a converted collier, as an experimental aircraft carrier. But the Ranger is the first American vessel that was designed and built from the start as a floating base for fighter planes.

Perkins announces rise in employment

Washington, D.C., Aug. 17

Good news from the capital. Secretary of Labor Frances Perkins, the first female Cabinet member in American history, says the hiring of one million workers since March has pushed the jobless rate down to its October 1931 level. Monthly industrial production nearly doubled from March to July; farm prices are up 60 percent, and stock values soared 85 percent. Still, experts fear industry is growing faster than the public's capacity to buy products. Wages, they say, must keep pace with production or the conditions that caused the Depression will continue (→ Feb. 15, 1934).

In a time of crisis, the unemployed turn to the federal government for help.

Hunger marchers in Washington, D.C. One in four Americans is out of work.

Kingfish promises to share the wealth

Senator Huey P. Long of Louisiana.

Washington, D.C., October

The Kingfish. That's what they call Senator Huey P. Long in his home state of Louisiana. Now the Senator and former Governor has a new title: author. Long has written a book in which he outlines his controversial plan for redistributing wealth in the United States. He recently denounced President Roosevelt as a "liar" for his failure to push Long's "share the wealth" plan, although Long said the President had given him a commitment. The book is titled *Every Man a King*. Roosevelt has reportedly told friends that Long is "one of the two most dangerous men in the country." The other, he said, was General Douglas MacArthur. Either, he said, could lead a revolution, Long from the left and MacArthur from the right.

Bears claw Giants

Chicago, Dec. 17

The Chicago Bears defeated the New York Giants, 23-21, today in the first championship playoff in National Football League history. The playoff became possible when the league was split into Eastern and Western Divisions. Bronco Nagurski paced the Bear attack with two touchdown passes. He was helped by a rule change that permits a forward pass to be thrown from any point behind the line of scrimmage. Thus, he could run toward the line and throw the ball as defenders left potential receivers unguarded to converge on him.

Prohibition law goes down the drain

New York City, Dec. 5

The "Noble Experiment" ended today, nearly 14 years after it began, when Utah became the 35th state to ratify the 21st Amendment repealing Prohibition. Given that both candidates in last year's presidential election – incumbent Herbert Hoover and winner Franklin Delano Roosevelt – favored repeal, its demise was a foregone conclusion for reasons long apparent.

When the Prince of Wales was asked during his 1925 visit to New York what he thought of Prohibition, he put his finger on the problem with the quip, "Great! When does it begin?" Not only didn't it work, but it also bred results contrary to its lofty aims. Saloons disappeared, but speakeasies quickly replaced them. And as crime flourished, money that might have gone into the federal Treasury ended up in the pockets of bootlegging gangsters. As it was, the government couldn't afford an all-out fight. Genuine enforcement would have necessitated a gargantuan national police force with vastly increased powers and with expenditures of $300 million a year compared with the current average of $10 million.

Finally, Prohibition was, to a great extent, an attempt by rural America to impose its moral standards on an increasingly urbanized citizenry for whom civilized living includes the right to drink. And with the United States in the lean time of Depression, even "drys" concede that the tax on alcohol may ease the unemployment crisis.

As Americans took to the streets, Prohibition had become a national farce.

"Invisible Man," "Duck Soup," "King Kong" and Fred Astaire

Hollywood, California

Actress Fay Wray was promised the tallest, darkest leading man in Hollywood by RKO. "I thought of Gable," she said. "When the script came, I was appalled and thought it a practical joke." Her co-star was the prehistoric gorilla, 50 times as strong as a man, known to movie audiences as King Kong of the picture of the same name. Playing the frightened girl carried to the top of the Empire State Building, Miss Wray proved that she could outscream anyone. *Invisible Man* introduces Claude Rains, who makes his non-presence felt in the H.G. Wells story. The Marx Brothers – Chico, Groucho, Harpo and even Zeppo – offer another insanely funny film with *Duck Soup*, briskly directed by Leo McCarey. Fred Astaire teams up with newcomer Ginger Rogers for his second film, *Flying Down to Rio*, offering flawlessly fluid dance numbers, while Charles Laughton and Robert Donat are both acclaimed for their roles in *The Private Life of Henry VIII*.

Meanwhile, labor organizing has come to Hollywood. Both a Screen Actors Guild and a Screen Writers Guild have been formed.

Folks may never look at the Empire State Building the same way again.

1934

Roosevelt

Washington, D.C., Jan. 8. Supreme Court upholds a Minnesota law that temporarily bans mortgage foreclosures.

Washington, D.C., Jan. 11. President Roosevelt orders cancellation of all federal mail contracts because of widespread corruption, assigning Army Air Corps to control airmail service instead.

Mississippi, March 10. State senate permits a private citizen to spring trap that hangs three Negroes convicted of raping his daughter.

Washington, D.C., March 27. Congress passes Vinson Naval Parity Act, authorizing naval buildup to level permitted by naval limitations treaties.

New York City, April. Ernest Hemingway, on returning from an African safari, writes *Green Hills of Africa.*

Washington, D.C., Apr. 20. Astronomers erroneously conclude that a 16,000-mile-wide sunspot will have a large effect on climate and weather.

Cuba, May 29. United States and Cuba sign treaty, releasing Cuba from requirements of Platt Amendment.

Washington, D.C., June 15. All former belligerents, except Finland, are officially in default of war debts stemming from Great War.

Bermuda, Aug. 15. William Beebe and Otis Barton navigate a bathysphere 3,028 feet below sea level, establishing new record.

New Jersey Coast, Sept. 8. Liner Morro Castle burns with loss of 120 lives.

Newport, Rhode Island, Sept. 25. U.S. yacht Rainbow retains America's Cup by defeating British challenger Endeavour.

New York City, Nov. 21. Musical *Anything Goes*, by Cole Porter, opens.

New York City, Dec. 9. Giants defeat Chicago Bears in National Football League championship, 30-13.

New York City. F. Scott Fitzgerald's *Tender is the Night* published.

New York City. Dashiell Hammett's *The Thin Man* issued.

Boston. Ornithologist Roger Tory Peterson publishes *A Field Guide to the Birds.*

Drought grips Midwest

Abandoned farms dot the landscape as the nation's food producers give up.

Omaha, Nebraska, Autumn

After nine months without rain, Midwest farmers are in a state of panic. The Department of Agriculture had predicted a severe drought this year. Not only did the forecast come true, but the drought has proved worse than expected. One member of President Roosevelt's "brain trust," Rexford Tugwell, reported recently that the usually lush wheat crop is so sparse that the few sprigs resemble "the stubble on an old man's chin." The wheat crop is so damaged by the months of deepening drought that the Agriculture Adjustment Administration has decided not to order excess wheat plowed back into the ground – because there isn't any. Farm prices have fallen more than 50 percent in the past four years and farmers are forcibly resisting foreclosures. As Edward O'Neal of the Farm Bureau Federation remarked in January, "Unless something is done for the American farmer, we will have revolution in the countryside in less than 12 months" (→Autumn, 1935).

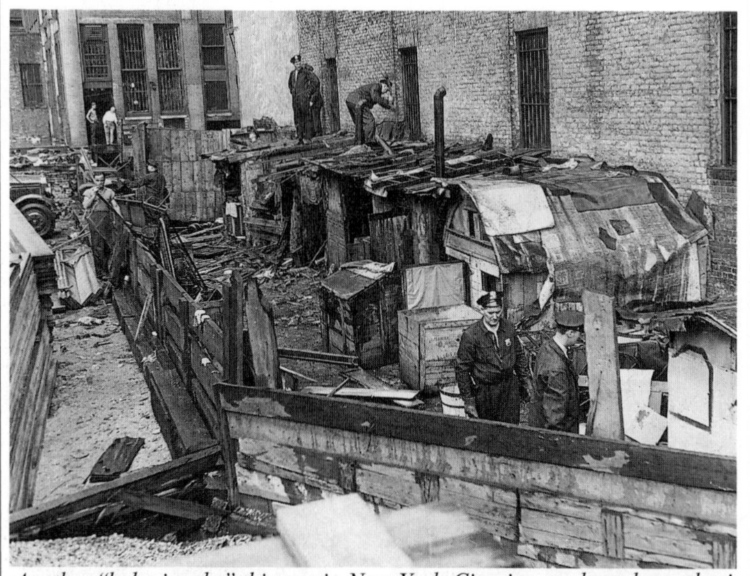

Another "hobo jungle," this one in New York City, is torn down by authorities who regard such "Hoovervilles" as unsafe, unsanitary and unsightly.

More job funding; help for the dollar

Washington, D.C., Feb. 15

Congress today gave Harry Hopkins's Civil Works Administration an infusion of $950 million. Founded in November, the C.W.A. has employed more than four million people through one of the harshest winters in memory. The administration's projects – endless miles of new roads, thousands of schools and hundreds of airfields, parks and playgrounds – have won acclaim even from conservatives. As *New Outlook* editor Al Smith says, "No sane local official ... is going to shoot Santa Claus just before a hard Christmas." The dollar got its own gift last month with passage of the Gold Reserve Act. It lets the President devalue the dollar 60 percent, using the $2 billion in proceeds for currency stabilization (→June 6).

Abner and Flash

New York City, Aug. 20

A new comic strip made its debut today, Al Capp's *Li'l Abner*, in which a hillbilly named Abner Yokum, dumb and muscular, lolls in a Kentucky mountain pool dreaming about his Mammy's cooking. Meanwhile, in the Alex Raymond *Flash Gordon* strip, Flash is struggling to defend the planet against Ming the Merciless. C'mon, Abner – lend Flash a hand!

Townsend has plan for pension to aged

Long Beach, Calif., January

A doctor who grew keenly aware of poverty issues in his general practice has proposed a pension plan for the elderly. Dr. Francis Townsend's plan includes $200 a month for all American citizens of 80 years or more. According to Townsend, the program would not only help the elderly, but would also stabilize the economy, because the law would require that recipients spend each month's allotment within the month. The money would be raised by taxes. Since Townsend proposed the plan in a local newspaper, it has received overwhelming support from the elderly.

Bonnie and Clyde killed

Bonnie Parker with pistol and cigar.

Clyde Barrow with a sizable arsenal.

Ruston, Louisiana, May 23

The Bonnie Parker-Clyde Barrow trail of terror and death ended abruptly today as lawmen gunned them down near this northern Louisiana town. Six officers armed with submachine guns riddled the couple's bodies as they sat in a car on a lonely dirt road. Bonnie and Clyde, both in their 20s, have been accused of murdering 12 people as they roamed the Mississippi Valley, robbing banks and gas stations and fleeing the law. Six of the dead were law officers. Frank Hammer, a former Texas Ranger hired to track them down, was with the group that shot them. Bonnie, a small woman with dyed red hair, was a Dallas waitress when she met Clyde Barrow, an ex-convict. They teamed up with Clyde's brother, Buck, and his wife, Blanche, and began their odyssey of crime. In Missouri, a town marshal told them they couldn't drink beer at a dance. Clyde killed the man. In January of last year, they narrowly escaped a police trap in Dallas and killed a sheriff's deputy. In April of last year, they shot two policemen, then crashed their car through a garage door and escaped arrest again. On one occasion, they eluded a 200-man posse that had surrounded the gang at a picnic ground near Dexter, Iowa. Another gangster, John Dillinger, once said of Bonnie and Clyde: "They're punks. They're giving bank-robbing a bad name."

G-men rub out Dillinger

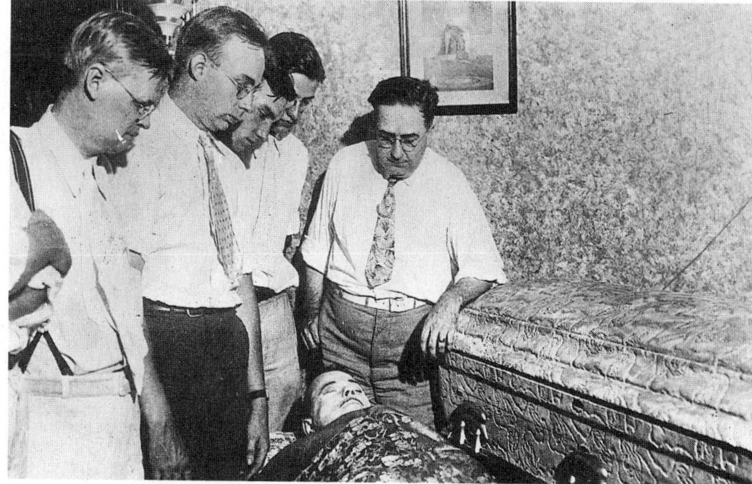

Even in death, the notorious bandit manages to fascinate the American public.

Chicago, July 22

J. Edgar Hoover's G-men shot and killed John Dillinger, the nation's Public Enemy No. 1, outside a Chicago movie house today. There were 20 armed agents of the Federal Bureau of Investigation waiting for the notorious bank robber as he left the theater at about 6 p.m. Fatally wounded, the gangster fell to the ground without having drawn his pistol. Dillinger's father said, "They shot him down in cold blood." A girlfriend of Dillinger's reportedly tipped off Hoover's F.B.I. that Dillinger would be at the movie.

In a major crime career of only 14 months, Dillinger captured the public imagination with his daring escapes from prisons and his Robin Hood approach to bank-robbing. During a Greencastle, Indiana, bank holdup last October, Dillinger spotted a farmer with $50 in his hand and asked, "Is that your money or the bank's?" When the farmer said it was his money, Dillinger said, "Keep it." Son of a prosperous grocer in a suburb of Indianapolis, Dillinger spent nine years in prison for a grocery holdup before beginning his bank-robbing career in June, 1933. Over the last 14 months, he took at least $265,000 from banks in Indiana, Ohio, Wisconsin and South Dakota.

Dillinger was the first criminal to be named Public Enemy No. 1 on Hoover's listed of wanted men.

"In the Barber Shop" (1934) by Ilya Bolotawsky. Shave and a haircut.

"Festival" (1934) by Celentano. The streets of Little Italy come alive.

S.E.C. is formed to regulate market

Washington, D.C., June 6

Stock exchanges now have someone to answer to – the Securities and Exchange Commission. Following his pledge to reform abuses in securities transactions in order to prevent another stock market collapse, President Roosevelt today signed a bill to create the commission. Its duties will be to administer the Federal Securities Act of 1933 and this year's Securities Exchange Act. The commission's main objective will be to provide full disclosure to the investing public and to protect the interests of the public and investors against malpractice in the securities market. If the commission succeeds, then the days of wild speculation and excessive credit may be numbered (→ May 6, 1935).

F.C.C. will regulate broadcast activities

Washington, D.C., June 19

President Roosevelt signed a bill to create the first communications regulation agency today. With a budget of $1,146,885 and a staff of 442, the Federal Communications Commission will oversee the development and the operation of broadcast services, and help the public get quick and efficient telephone and telegraph service at reasonable rates. In addition to reducing rates, Roosevelt is especially concerned about increasing services to rural areas and overseeing technical advances. The F.C.C., which is replacing and expanding upon the Federal Radio Commission, is being created as the result of congressional approval of the Federal Communications Act on May 31.

Waterfront and textile strikes are settled

Textile workers listen to speakers at a Rhode Island mass rally; 350,000 ha gone out on strike throughout the nation, fully aware of the tough days ahead

San Francisco, Oct. 12

In less than a month, the National Labor Relations Board has settled two brutal strikes, sending out utterly conflicting signals as to its position on the industrial battlefield. Longshoremen on the West Coast today won a shortened work week with a raise in pay, recognition of their union and increased control over hiring. But not without a struggle. From May to July, 15,000 dock workers and thousands of sympathy strikers clogged every port on the coast. Dock violence here led to a general strike orchestrated by Harry Bridges, Australian immigrant and an avowed Marxist. N.R.A. chief Hugh Johnson, none too fond of Bridges, helped set off a spree of vigilante raids by urgin the public to "wipe out this subversive element as you clean off a chalk mark on a blackboard with a we sponge." The labor board, however did not share its leader's feelings.

Textile workers were not so fortunate. On September 1, 350,00 struck the mills, charging owner with abrogating their liberal labo code. From Atlanta to Boston, National Guardsmen and strikers battled with guns and clubs. In thre weeks, the United Textile Worker were broken. They agreed to a federal settlement that offered no wag hikes, no union recognition and n job protection for strikers. The settlement also sanctioned a 100 per cent increase in the work load.

"Paper Workers" (1934) by Douglas Crockwell. "The machine has destroyed a whole age of art," writes one critic, "and is busy creating a new age."

Baby Face and Pretty Boy bite the dust

Barrington, Illinois, Nov. 28

George "Baby Face" Nelson, the trigger-happy bank robber, was killed in a gun battle with Federal Bureau of Investigation agents near here yesterday. Nelson killed two F.B.I. agents before he was mortally wounded. His wife, Helen, dumped her husband's naked body on a road and escaped in a car. Just last month, G-men killed Nelson's equally famous partner, Charles Arthur "Pretty Boy" Floyd, near East Liverpool, Ohio. Nelson and Floyd robbed banks with John Dillinger before Dillinger was shot down in July. In April, Nelson killed another F.B.I. agent while stealing his car near the Little Bohemia Lodge at Manitowish Waters, Wisconsin. Floyd, who, like Nelson, was known for killing law officers, got his nickname from a madam known as Mother Ash who ran a Kansas City bordello. She was once said to have approached Floyd and said, "I want you all to myself, pretty boy." Floyd hated the nickname, but it stuck. He became Public Enemy No. 1 after Dillinger's death. Like Dillinger, he was known as a Robin Hood type.

Radio priest attracts flock of five million

Father Coughlin combines radio and rhetoric to build a huge following.

Royal Oak, Michigan

Father Charles E. Coughlin has gained five million members for his National Union for Social Justice in the two months since it started. The radio priest has found a welcoming ear among many discouraged or destroyed by the Depression. He rails against big business. For Father Coughlin, the enemies are "godless capitalists, the Jews, the Communists, international bankers and plutocrats." The platform of his National Union demands the nationalization of public services, creation of a government-owned central bank and unionization of all workers. He supported Franklin Roosevelt in 1932, but Coughlin is increasingly critical of the President, and there are rumors that he will back a third party movement in the next presidential election.

"It Happened One Night" to Gable

Hollywood, California

Louis B. Mayer agreed to lend Columbia his star Clark Gable for a minor project: Frank Capra's *It Happened One Night.* Reluctantly, Gable accepted the part of the dashing reporter. Claudette Colbert did the same for her part as a madcap heiress. The film's success is overwhelming. Gable, a man's man and a woman's dream, has come to symbolize virility, and since he stripped to reveal a bare chest in one scene, the male underwear business has been losing its shirt!

Leadbelly's blues win him a pardon

Louisiana, Aug. 1

Huddie Ledbetter, that "sweet singer from the swamplands," has again sung his way to freedom. Better known as Leadbelly, the legendary blues singer, was released by Louisiana Governor O.K. Allen after Leadbelly wrote a song to him pleading for a pardon. No stranger to violence, the hard-living Leadbelly has been in and out of prison since 1918. In 1925, he similarly "sweet sung" Texas Governor Pat Neff into an early release from a 30-year sentence.

As Hollywood continues to thrive, a star system has evolved. This year, swashbuckler Douglas Fairbanks plays in "The Private Life of Don Juan."

Tigers choked by "Gas House Gang"

Detroit, Michigan, Oct. 9

They're a motley crew, they're the "Gas House Gang," they're the rowdy St. Louis Cardinals, and today they beat the Detroit Tigers to win the World Series in seven games. They star Pepper Martin, who rode freights to get to spring training, and 30-game winner Dizzy Dean. Great as he is, Diz was overshadowed in the All-Star Game by Carl Hubbell of the New York Giants, who fanned Babe Ruth, Lou Gehrig, Jimmy Foxx, Al Simmons and Joe Cronin in order.

Dizzy and Daffy Dean make a pitch.

American marines pull out of Haiti

Port-au-Prince, Haiti, Aug. 6

The United States withdrew its last marines from Haiti today, ending 19 years of military occupation. Although Washington will retain some control over Haiti's finances, today's action is the latest demonstration that President Roosevelt fully intends to carry out his inauguration pledge to be a "good neighbor" to Latin America, particularly by forgoing the interventionism of past decades. Last May, the United States negotiated a treaty abrogating the Platt Amendment that the Cubans hated. Forced on Cuba in 1901 as part of its constitution, this clause gave the United States the right to intervene to suppress disorder and restricted Cuba's right to make treaties and incur debts. The Americans will retain the naval base at Guantanamo Bay.

Sinclair loses race for coast governor

California, November

"The present depression is one of abundance, not of scarcity . . . The cause of the trouble is that a small class has the wealth, while the rest have the debts . . . The remedy is to give the workers access to the means of production, and let them produce for themselves, not for others . . . the American way." So wrote novelist Upton Sinclair in *The Nation.* The 56-year-old Sinclair, an ardent Socialist whose novel *The Jungle* related the brutal life of workers in Chicago's stockyards, has lost his race for governor of California. He was defeated by the cautious Frank Merriam, who had almost total press support. Sinclair, running as a Democrat, based his campaign on an End Poverty in California (EPIC) plan aimed at helping the jobless and the poor.

Donald Duck debut

Hollywood, California

Animator Walt Disney has given the nation a new character, Donald Duck, who makes his first appearance in the cartoon *Wise Little Hen.* This year, the 33-year-old Disney may realize a lifelong dream, a feature-length animated movie (he's talking about Snow White). Already, Oswald the Rabbit, Mickey Mouse and the Three Little Pigs have won American hearts, coming from the creative and perfectionist hand and mind of the former Red Cross ambulance driver who now heads a vast animation studio.

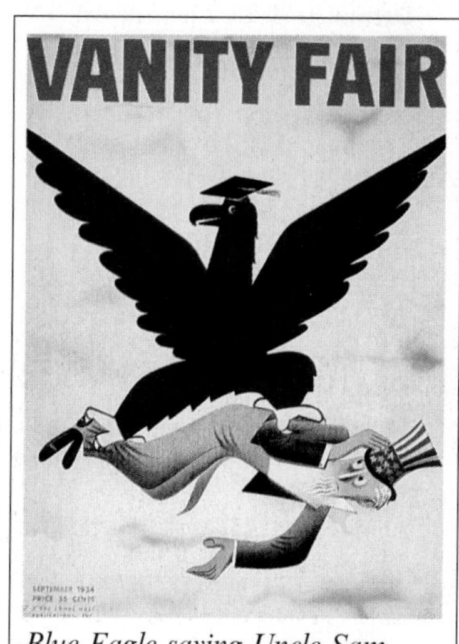

Blue Eagle saving Uncle Sam.

1935

Roosevelt

Pacific Ocean, Feb. 12. A strong gust of wind causes dirigible Macon to break up, killing two crew members.

New York City, March 7. In an effort to reduce street noise, city revokes licenses of all organ grinders.

New York City, March 19. Accusations of police brutality in case of a young Negro caught shoplifting touch off riots in which three people are killed and $200 million in damages result.

Kansas City, Mo., May 8. John Brock makes his 2,000th flight; he has flown everyday for five and a half years.

Orleans, Massachusetts, May 11. First restaurant under Howard Johnson franchise opens.

Boston, May 30. Babe Ruth's name appears in major league lineup for last time – with Boston Braves.

New York City, June 13. Jim Braddock defeats Max Baer in 15 rounds for heavyweight boxing title.

Washington, D.C., June 16. Herbert Hoover says in a speech, "Social security must be built on a cult of work, not a cult of leisure."

Detroit, Oct. 7. Tigers defeat Chicago Cubs, four games to two, in World Series.

New York City, Oct. 10. George Gershwin's musical *Porgy and Bess* opens.

Milwaukee, Nov. 9. Idzi Rutkowski, the "Mad Bomber of Milwaukee," is killed before city responds to his demands, when his dynamite cache explodes.

Detroit, Dec. 15. Lions defeat New York Giants, 26-7, in N.F.L. championship.

New York City. First Heisman Trophy awarded to Jay Berwanger, a halfback for the University of Chicago.

New York City. Clifford Odets publishes three plays: *Waiting for Lefty*, *Awake and Sing* and *Paradise Lost*.

DEATHS

Chicago, May 21. Jane Addams, social reformer (*Sept. 6, 1860).

Alaska, Aug. 15. Will Rogers, cowboy and humorist, in a plane crash (*Nov. 4, 1879).

N.I.R.A. is ruled illegal

Washington, D.C., May 27

The judicial branch has clamped down on the executive branch. The Supreme Court today voted unanimously that the National Industrial Recovery Act is unconstitutional. It is the first substantial act of the New Deal to be shot down. It had provided that industries be placed under codes of fair dealing that regulated wages, hours, working conditions and collective bargaining.

The court ruling came in Schecter Poultry Corporation v. United States. The court ruled that the wages and hours provisions of the codes exceeded the powers of Congress under the interstate commerce clause of the Constitution

President Roosevelt, stung by the defeat, said, "We have been relegated to the horse-and-buggy definition of interstate commerce." It is believed he will seek executive revenge for a decision that has destroyed one of his prize pieces of New Deal legislation.

Last week, the court ruled that Congress does not have the right to regulate the social welfare of workers, in declaring illegal the Railroad Retirement Act (→ Summer).

Court strikes down Scottsboro verdict

Washington, D.C., Apr. 1

Lawyer Samuel Liebowitz and his nine Negro clients, the Scottsboro Boys, accused of raping two white girls in 1931, took their case to the Supreme Court, and today the court reversed their convictions. The court held that the trial was unfair because Negroes had been excluded from the jury. Despite the ruling, the youths have not been freed and new warrants have been sworn out by one of the girls who first brought on the trial by charging she had been raped.

W.P.A. formed, biggest work program yet

W.P.A. projects around the nation may alleviate the burden of unemployment.

Washington, D.C., May 6

At a cost of $5 billion, the most extensive public works program yet has risen from the alphabet soup of the New Deal. The Work Progress Administration, set up today under the Emergency Relief Appropriations Act, will employ one-third of the nation's 11 million jobless, according to director Harry Hopkins.

The plan will return direct relief efforts to the states. "I am not willing," President Roosevelt told Congress in January, "that the vitality of our people be further sapped by the giving of cash, of market baskets, of a few hours' weekly work cutting grass, raking leaves, or picking up papers in public parks." One-quarter of American families now depend on direct relief. As W.P.A. officials see it, their task is "to help men keep their chins up and their hands in."

Adopted by a wide margin in the House, W.P.A. ran into fire in the Senate. Isolationists barred the use of funds for military projects. Democrats upset over FDR's non-partisan use of patronage got Senate control over appointments. Conservatives still denounce federal intrusion into the economy. To the Liberty League, W.P.A. signals the end "of the form of government under which we have lived." Liberals, on the other hand, want more of the same. Keynesians believe that $9 billion is necessary to fuel the economy. But to those the New Deal touches, it seems to instill pride. "There ain't no other nation in the world," says one North Carolina farmer, "that would have sense enough to think of W.P.A. and all the other A's" (→ 27).

Ma Barker killed in clash with F.B.I.

Lake Weir, Florida, Jan. 16

Kate "Ma" Barker, said to be the brains of the dreaded Barker gang, was killed in a gun battle with F.B.I. agents and local police here today. Her son Fred also was shot down. The two were hiding out in a cottage here. Ma Barker and her three sons, Fred, Herman and Arthur "Dock," working with other criminals, have been responsible for many bank robberies. Herman shot himself as police tried to arrest him in 1927. Arthur "Dock" Barker was sent to Alcatraz for life after a kidnapping conviction and he was shot trying to escape.

A movie about a French princess who runs off to America and falls in love with an Indian scout.

Dust storms hit again

)ubuque, Iowa, Autumn

At least half of this state's farm-rs are said to have lost their land ɔ the twin forces of depression nd drought. And with the increas-ıg severity of the dust storms that re skimming off the precious top-oil, agriculture experts say the ituation is becoming even worse. 'he dust storms began in earnest wo years ago in Texas and Okla-ıoma, and have gradually covered he Midwest. The biggest single ʋindstorm swept through the so-alled "Dust Bowl" this May. Tre-nendous clouds of dust obscured the sun as far east as the Appalachian Mountains. Here on the Plains, the dust drifts up against fences like snow in winter. And farmers report that many of their cattle eat so much dirt as they scratch for grass that they die from mudballs in their stomachs.

As one observer remarked, "The country seems to brood as though death were touching it."

Meanwhile, Congress has voted a Soil Conservation Act that should help. Sad to say, though, not even the New Deal can make the wind stop blowing.

'he life of a migrant cotton worker and his family is difficult. Thousands are naking their way to California via the Southwest to escape the "Dust Bowl."

C.C.C. employs 500,000

Forest Service men and C.C.C. youths lift seedlings from their beds in Oregon.

Washington, D.C., Summer

The Civilian Conservation Corps has announced that it plans to have at least half a million young men enrolled in its ranks by the end of the year. One of President Roosevelt's most popular relief programs, the C.C.C. was established in March 1933 as a way to put the growing army of unemployed youth to work and to help provide financial assistance to their families at the same time.

Under the charter of the corps, men between the ages of 18 and 25 whose families are on relief can be enrolled for a period of one year. They receive free room and board at federal camps. They are also paid a salary of $30 per month, $25 of which automatically goes to their families. The corps members are trained to work on a wide variety of projects, including reforestation, anti-soil erosion, national park construction and other public works projects.

The C.C.C. is being jointly administered by four governmental agencies. The Labor Department recruits the young men, the War Department operates the camps and the Agriculture and Interior Departments organize and supervise the work projects. While Congressmen William Green and Herbert Benjamin charge that the corps "smacks of fascism" and is little more than "a system of forced labor," most observers believe it has been a big success. The director of the corps is Robert Fechner, who was vice president of the American Machinists Union (→July 5).

Cincinnati is lit up for night games

Cincinnati, May 24

Baseball Commissioner Kenesaw Landis doesn't care much for the idea, but he did approve experimental night baseball and the first major league game was played here tonight between the Reds and Phillies. The Phillies won, 2-1, at flood-lit Crosley Field. The wary commissioner has given approval for seven night games. Others in the baseball establishment have also been slow to accept the nighttime concept because they feel the national pastime was meant to be played in sunlight, as God intended. Since teams travel by train, night games could snarl schedules.

Rural homes to get electric power

Washington, D.C., May 11

President Roosevelt announced today that he has established the Rural Electrification Administration. The R.E.A., as it is to be called, will make low-cost construction loans to private companies willing to construct electrical generating and delivery systems to rural areas that are not presently being supplied. While it is estimated that nine out of 10 farms in the nation do not have electricity now, government optimists predict that by 1941, more than 40 percent of them will be equipped to receive this miracle energy of the 20th century.

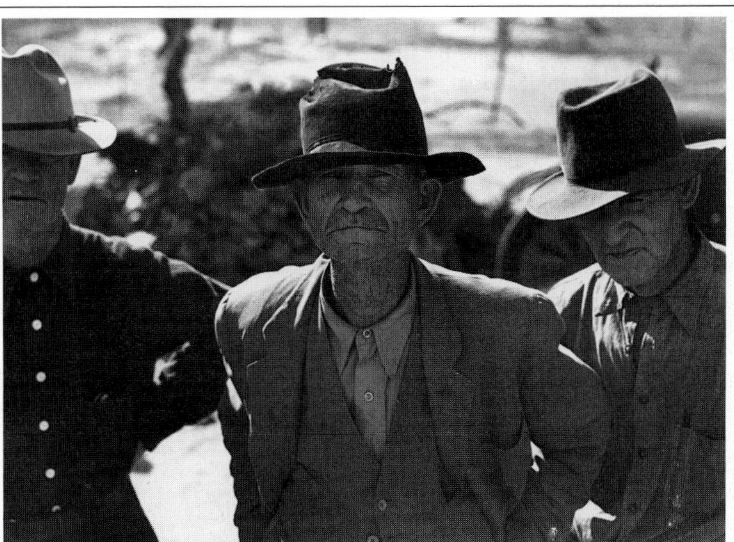

Washington, D.C., May 1. *The President today used new discretionary powers to set up the Resettlement Administration, to help farm owners and tenants, such as the men in this Dorothea Lange photo, move to better land.*

Wagner Act helps labor

Washington, D.C., July 5

According to advocates of the Wagner Labor Relations Act, management and labor have agreed to a permanent truce in the industrial war, with the federal government as the peacekeeper. Signed into law today, the bill outlaws company unions and gives a reconstituted National Labor Relations Board authority to punish employers for "unfair labor practices." The three-member board will also exercise control over union elections.

The Wagner Act offers a replacement for Section 7a of the National Industrial Recovery Act, struck down by the Supreme Court in May. Section 7a protected collective bargaining, but it was rarely enforced, leading unionists to translate N.R.A. as "National Run Around." New York Senator Robert Wagner, author of the bill, told the Senate N.R.A.'s failure to uphold labor's rights while allowing price-fixing and quotas had "driven a dagger close to the heart of" the recovery drive. Unemployment, he argued, is "as great as it was a year ago." Payrolls languish at 60 percent of 1926 levels, while corporate dividends and interest have soared 150 percent. He says the "failure to maintain a sane balance between wages and industrial returns" stifles every hint of recovery. The act, he insists, is the only way to "rely upon democratic self-help by industry and labor, instead of courting the pitfalls of an arbitrary or totalitarian state" (→Aug. 14).

Social Security is passed

As Americans grow older, they can now look forward to a brighter futu[re] thanks to Social Security. Photograph is "After Lunch" by Russell Lee.

Washington, D.C., Aug. 14

President Roosevelt signed into law today one of the most important pieces of legislation in American history, the Social Security Act. It provides a pension to Americans over the age of 65 (beginning in 1942), paid for by contributions from employee wages and matched by employers. It also gives assistance to the blind and disabled and to dependent children. At the same time, it establishes a system of unemployment compensation.

Glowing with pride because the act fulfills a campaign promise, the President called the legislation the "cornerstone" of the New Deal and a "supreme achievement." It diffe[rs] from welfare in that it is not funde[d] by taxes. However, liberal critics [of] the plan say the poor will pay a[n] inordinate amount of the burde[n]. Conservative critics say it is yet a[n]other measure pushed by the Pres[i]dent to "Sovietize America." Som[e] business owners are riled by the a[ct] because it cuts into their profits.

But a majority of Americans ha[il] it as a program that is long ove[r]due; other Western industrial na[tions] have had a system to care f[or] the elderly for years. The act ma[y] also allay what some see as a moo[d] of betrayal felt by the "forgotte[n] man" toward FDR (→Jan. 6, 1936).

Alcoholics uniting to help each other

Akron, Ohio, June 10

Bill W. and Dr. Bob S. are alcoholics. But they are facing up to their problems and hope to help others do the same through a group they have formed called Alcoholics Anonymous. The two men, one a New York stockbroker, the other a surgeon from Akron, Ohio, first began meeting last month to attack their drinking problem. Now, in a bold experiment, they hope to aid others through self-help and mutual support. For anonymity, members will be identified only by first name and last initial.

Omaha third horse to win Triple Crown

New York City, June 8

Omaha didn't do much as a 2-year-old, but Sunny Jim Fitzsimmons, his trainer, predicted that he would take the Kentucky Derby. Omaha not only won the derby but also the Preakness and Belmont, making him the third winner of the Triple Crown. The son of Gallant Fox (also a Triple Crown winner) had to wade through the Belmont mud to do it, but he beat Firethorn by a length and a half. He gave William Woodward the honor of being the only man to have bred and owned two Triple Crown winners.

Dancer and choreographer Martha Graham is rapidly becoming a major force in the development of modern dance. She has perfected a style that stresses sharp, angular movements through muscle release and contraction.

Dutch Schultz bumped off in New Jersey

Newark, New Jersey, Oct. 23

Dutch Schultz, who ran many of the underworld's bootleg whiskey operations during Prohibition, was shot down with three of his henchmen in a restaurant here today. Police said it was a gangland killing. Schultz was shot while eating at the Palace Chophouse. Some police say he was killed on orders from crime cartel boss Charles "Lucky" Luciano because he was planning to murder New York City District Attorney Thomas E. Dewey, arch enemy of the crime syndicate, an act that might have provoked a crackdown. Schultz, whose real name was Arthur Flegenheimer, also managed Harlem's numbers racket.

Dutch Schultz sits in the restaura[nt] where he was killed by rival thugs.

Huey Long assassinated

Baton Rouge, Louisiana, Sept. 10

Senator Huey P. Long of Louisiana died today, two days after being shot by an assassin as he walked through the halls of the state capitol. The Senator and former Governor, who has been called the first American dictator by his enemies and the champion of the little man by his friends, was walking toward the Governor's office when he was hit. His assailant was Dr. Carl A. Weiss, a Baton Rouge physician. Weiss fired at point-blank range. He was immediately shot down by Long's bodyguards. Weiss was the son-in-law of one of the Senator's political enemies, Judge Benjamin Pavy. Long was in the state capital for meetings with legislative leaders.

Elected Governor in 1928, Long attacked the "giant corporations" in populist syle. He also provided free schoolbooks for children and began a massive highway building program. He defeated an attempt to impeach him. As Senator since 1932, Long advocated a "share the wealth" program that he claimed would stave off a communist revolution.

C.I.O. is founded to reorganize labor

Atlantic City, N.J., Nov. 9

Craft unionism is "pretty small potatoes," said John L. Lewis at the American Federation of Labor convention before bloodying the nose of its main defenders. With his show of strength, the United Mine Workers boss has rallied dissatisfied A.F.L. members to the cause of industry-wide unions. Losing a vote on the issue by a 5 to 3 margin, Lewis, David Dubinsky and Sidney Hillman have formed the Committee for Industrial Organization to put pressure on the A.F.L. But the Federation mainstream sees industrial unionism as a first step to communism (→Nov. 18, 1938).

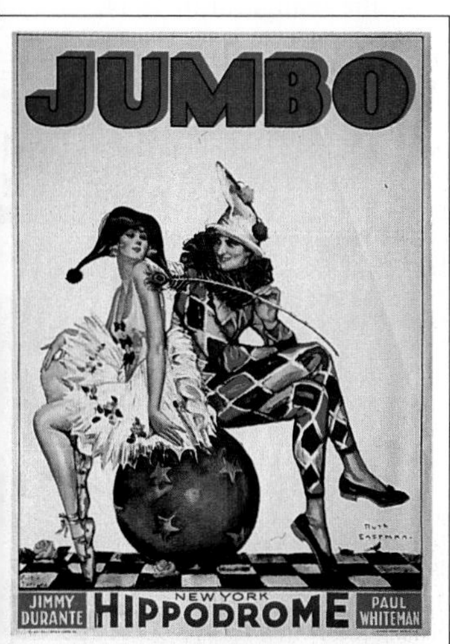

The Richard Rodgers production at New York's Hippodrome is one of several such musicals that are taking the U.S. stage by storm.

Monopoly, bingo and beer in cans

United States, December

Booming holiday sales of canned beer, bingo cards and the board game *Monopoly* reveal the mood in the land. A survey shows nearly a third of Americans drink beer at home. And nearly half of those asked said they prefer it in the newly introduced cans. *Monopoly*, a game for would-be wheeler-dealers in realty, is selling so fast its jobless inventor, Charles B. Darrow of Philadelphia, stopped looking for work. In the "O" game fad – Bingo! Keno! and Beano! – a woman undertaker was arrested in Michigan for running a 400-player Catholic Daughters of America game.

New 20th Century, old Fox in merger

Hollywood, California

The veteran Fox Company has merged with Twentieth Century, a production firm started two years ago by Joseph M. Schenck and Darryl F. Zanuck, the former production chief at Warner Bros. With Schenck as president and Zanuck as vice president in charge of production, the new 20th Century-Fox plans an ambitious production slate where technical polish and visual gloss will be emphasized. *Annie Oakley* is a current offering. At M-G-M, Rouben Mamoulian directed Hollywood's first full Technicolor feature, *Becky Sharp*.

American Airlines unveils its Douglas DC-3

Capable of carrying 21 passengers at 160 mph, the DC-3 is a major advance.

New York City, Dec. 21

American Airlines unveiled its new passenger plane, the Douglas DC-3, today. A comfortable craft, it can hold 14 sleeping berths, or 21 seated passengers, and fly at 160 miles per hour. American Airlines operates a popular coast-to-coast overnight sleeper route. Up to now, the route has been flown by Curtiss Condors, big biplanes that can accommodate sleeping berths. The new DC-3, with two big Wright Cyclone engines and a wing span of 95 feet, has a flight range of 1,500 miles, the longest of any commercial airliner. Douglas says its craft is built to last for years.

Artists and writers supported by W.P.A.

United States

Under the aegis of the Work Progress Administration, writers and artists are finding relief from the Depression. Federal Project No. 1, with a budget of $300 million, has employed 6,000 writers in collecting oral histories, researching guide books to the states and creating such useful resources as *Who's Who in the Zoo.* And artists are transforming the look of post offices and high schools by painting large murals. Critics call the program frivolous and unnecessary. But, as director Harry Hopkins points out, creative artists have "got to eat just like other people."

"Artists on W.P.A." (1935) by Moses Soyer, whose work captures a new spirit.

1936

Roosevelt

Washington, D.C., Jan. 25. Democrat Alfred E. Smith tells Liberty League that President Roosevelt is a socialist, trying to pattern United States in Soviet Union's image.

Washington, D.C., March 11. A District of Columbia court rules that a Senate committee used unreasonable methods to obtain copies of 1,000 telegrams sent to New Deal opponents by lobbyists.

New York City, March 14. Anti-German protests erupt against conductor Wilhelm Furtwängler's leading of New York Philharmonic.

New Hampshire, March. Floods leave hundreds of families homeless and destroy mills and factories.

New York City, May 24. Tony Lazzeri of New York Yankees hits two grand slam home runs in one game.

Dayton, Ohio, June 7. Henry Ford buys Wright brothers' old bicycle shop, to exhibit at his museum in Dearborn, Michigan.

Washington, D.C., June 29. Congress awards gold medal to George M. Cohan for his meritorious service as composer of patriotic songs during Great War.

New York City, July 11. Triboro Bridge opens, spanning two rivers to link three boroughs.

Copenhagen, Denmark, Aug. 11. At International Scientific Congress, Charles Lindbergh displays an artificial heart pump that he developed with Dr. Alexis Carrel.

New York, Sept. 30. New York Yankees defeat New York Giants, four games to two, in World Series.

United States, Nov. 12. American playwright Eugene O'Neill wins Nobel Prize in literature.

New York City, Dec. 13. Green Bay Packers defeat Boston Redskins, 21-6, for National Football League title.

New York City. In a speech attacking New Deal spending, Alfred E. Smith remarks, "Nobody shoots at Santa Claus."

United States. Margaret Mitchell's *Gone With the Wind* sells record one million copies in six months.

High court kills farm act

Washington, D.C., Jan. 6

The Supreme Court annulled the Roosevelt New Deal's farm program today by declaring the Agricultural Adjustment Act unconstitutional. The 1933 act was established to raise farm prices by lowering production. It did so because prices on agricultural products had plummeted, making rural Americans among the hardest hit by the Depression. It subsidized farmers who would take some acreage out of production, thereby creating artificial shortages. Government payments were financed by taxing the processing of food products. Critics balked at such a tax. *The New York Times* asked, "What will the great mass of consumers think of this form of sales tax, resting heavily on food?" Even President Roosevelt called it an "experiment." To a certain extent it has worked; farm prices have risen, but probably more as the result of poor harvests than from the act.

But in United States v. Butler, the high court declared by a 6-3 vote that the tax on processing unjustly benefits one group at another's expense. Dissenting opinions were strong. Justice Harlan Fiske Stone said the ruling contradicts constitutional provisions that give Congress the power "to levy taxes to provide for the general welfare."

It is believed that FDR is already working on a substitute plan to skirt today's ruling (→ Jan. 20, 1937).

Sarazen drives on in the world of golf

Sarazen's style sees him through.

Augusta, Georgia

Gene Sarazen is the country' premier golfer. In 1935, he won th Masters and became the only playe beside Bobby Jones to score victc ries in three major tournaments The others were the United State and British Opens, in 1932. Saraze also won the P.G.A. three times, i 1922, 1923 and 1933. In the fina round at the Masters, crowds wer awed by his double-eagle on th 15th hole. He tied Craig Wood a 282 and won the 36-hole playof the next day by five strokes. Sara zen began his career as a caddie an was only 20 years old when he wo the P.G.A. He is the second Mas ters victor, Horton Smith havin won the inaugural in 1934.

67% of Americans favor birth control

New York City, Nov. 30

The aim of the Comstock Law "was not to prevent the ... carriage by mail of things which might intelligently be employed by ... physicians for the purpose of saving life or promoting the well-being of their patients." Thus Judge Augustus Hand of the Circuit Court of Appeals today upheld an earlier ruling allowing a New York doctor to put pessaries in the mail. The judge echoes public opinion: A *Fortune* poll shows 67 percent of Americans favor birth control.

Hoover Dam opens; boon for Southwest

Arizona-Nevada border, October

What is 726 feet high, 1,244 feet long and holds more than 10 trillion gallons of water? The Hoover Dam on the Colorado River. Following three years of construction, the $120 million dam will provide the main source of low-cost hydroelectric energy to much of the Southwest, in addition to flood control for the immediate region. In backing up the Colorado River, the dam also creates the 115-mile Lake Mead, the largest man-made lake in the United States.

"Industrial" by Dacre F. Boulton. In the new machine age, artists find beauty in hard reality and even glorify concrete processes such as a construction crew erecting a building. Workers emerge as modern heroes.

"Years of Dust" poster by Ben Shahn, extolling the work of the Resettlement Administration.

FDR calls Americas ready for defense

Buenos Aires, Argentina, Dec. 1

Would-be aggressors will find the Western Hemisphere ready to take concerted action, President Roosevelt said today as he opened the Inter-American Conference for the Maintenance of Peace. FDR, who received an enthusiastic welcome from the Argentine people, spoke to delegates from 20 nations on the *Defense of Democracy*. He has been praised in Latin America for his "Good Neighbor Policy." Washington signed a treaty with Panama in March giving up America's right to intervene there. The pact also released the U.S. from the obligation to defend Panama's independence (→Apr. 22, 1937).

Muslims in Chicago

Chicago

To escape the disputes that broke out after the death of the movement's founder, W. D. Fard, two years ago, Elijah Muhammad has moved the headquarters of the Nation of Islam [Black Muslims] from Detroit to Chicago. This movement, an amalgam of Islam, the Bible and the writings of Fard, speaks out against the "blue-eyed devils," as whites are known, and suggests that Negroes separate from whites as much as possible until Allah ends white domination. It also seems to offer a message of dignity to some Negroes in cities like Chicago.

New naval ratio set

London, March 25

Hopes for keeping peace through disarmament took a turn for the worse today as the London Naval Conference came to an end. Although the United States, France and Britain were able to agree to some limitations on the size of their warships, the conference was virtually scuttled by Japan, which quit the proceedings early. Offended by the 5-5-3 ratio, the fives being for the United States and Britain, the three for Japan, the Japanese have already served notice that they will repudiate the Washington Naval Treaty of 1922. Italy also refused to participate.

Killer electrocuted in Lindbergh case

Trenton, N.J., Apr. 3

At 8:44 tonight, Bruno Hauptmann was strapped into the state prison's electric chair. Three and a half minutes later, he was dead. The illegal immigrant from Germany had been tried and convicted for the kidnapping and murder of Charles Lindbergh's infant son. The kidnapping took place March 1, 1932, but no one was found who was a witness to the crime; he was convicted on circumstantial evidence, including the discovery of Lindbergh's ransom money at his home. His prior arrest record and escape from a German prison certainly did not help his case. His wife still maintains his innocence.

Speed and luxury aboard Super Chief

Los Angeles, Calif., May

It will take you from Los Angeles to Chicago in record time, with air-conditioning and deluxe service. It's the Super Chief, a diesel-powered luxury passenger train. In just 39.75 hours, it crosses 2,225 miles of the Santa Fe rail route. That speed breaks the record set some three decades ago by almost six hours. There is also plenty for those who value their comfort more than speed, including Swiss stewards to serve the best in food and drink. Children will be not only well fed but entertained as well with an Indian chief in full regalia who will tell them all about the sights along the way.

"I'm trying to say something about the despised, the defeated ... about the last ditch," says photographer Dorothea Lange of her work for the Farm Security Administration. Her "Migrant Mother, Nipomo, California," was picked up by hundreds of newspapers throughout the country in March and told the story of an itinerant woman who feeds her children on stolen frozen vegetables and trapped birds. Meanwhile, photographer Walker Evans is in Alabama, also documenting the crisis in rural America, where drought has ruined crops in 336 counties and dust has denuded at least six states.

Ruth, Cobb named to Hall of Fame

New York City

Babe Ruth and Ty Cobb are among the first stars named by the writers' association to baseball's Hall of Fame. The others were Honus Wagner, the Pirate shortstop, and pitchers Walter Johnson of the Senators and Christy Mathewson of the Giants. All will be enshrined in a hall planned for Cooperstown, New York. Ruth won early fame as a Red Sox pitcher, but his real fame came with the Yankees as baseball's greatest slugger, with 714 career home runs and 60 homers in one season. Cobb spent most of his years as a Detroit outfielder, batting .300 or more for 23 consecutive seasons.

Coal county conflict

Harlan County, Kentucky

Despite the best efforts of the New Deal, "bloody" Harlan County is still a fortress against unionism. Organizers from the United Mine Workers are met regularly at the county line by two-gun deputies. Late this year, several unionists had their hotel rooms tear-gassed and their cars dynamited. Last year, 23 organizers were jailed for three days without charges. The county prosecutor is on the coal firm payrolls as a "labor adviser." His predecessor, who tried to enforce the law impartially, was blown up in broad daylight.

How to win friends

United States

In 1889, steel magnate Andrew Carnegie preached "The Gospel of Wealth." Now another Carnegie, author Dale, preaches the gospel of "getting along with people" in his best-seller *How to Win Friends and Influence People*. An outgrowth of lectures the 38-year-old Carnegie has been giving to men and women in business in New York since 1912, this simple introduction to applied psychology outlines *Six Ways to Make People Like You,* and *Twelve Ways to Win People to Your Way of Thinking*, as well as tactics used by President Roosevelt, Clark Gable, Guglielmo Marconi and others. ▷

Rightist, leftist candidates enter the race

Socialist Thomas on campaign trail.

Detroit, Mich., September

As the campaign for the presidency heats up, three minority parties are talking more about Roosevelt than about themselves. The Rev. Charles E. Coughlin, the Detroit radio priest, who backs South Dakota Representative William "Liberty Bill" Lemke on the Union Party ticket, has labeled Roosevelt anti-God. "As I was instrumental in removing Herbert Hoover from the White House, so help me God, I will be instrumental in taking a Communist from the chair once occupied by Washington," he said.

Socialist Norman Thomas, who won 2.2 percent of the vote in 1932, is waging an uphill fight to hold his ranks against the populist magic of the New Deal. Communist Party candidates Earl Browder and James Ford are in a "united front" campaign, embarrassing the President by taking it easy on his administration, blasting the Republican candidate, Governor Alf Landon of Kansas instead (→Nov. 4).

Americans watch rising tide of fascism

Washington, D.C., Aug. 7

Today's announcement that the United States will follow a policy of strict neutrality in the civil war that broke out in Spain on July 17 is dramatic proof of how powerful a hold isolationism has on both the nation's policymakers and its people. The war in Spain is not one between two sovereign states; rather, it is a civil war in which a democratically elected government is being challenged by a right-wing uprising led by Generalissimo Francisco Franco. His anti-government forces can be sure of getting troops, planes and supplies from the sympathetic regimes in Nazi Germany and Fascist Italy. But if the English and French follow the American policy of treating both sides equally, regardless of who is the aggressor, then the outlook for democracy in Spain is grim. Should the Loyalists lose, then Spain will be the third big European country to fall to totalitarianism.

Fascism, with its glorification of the state and its leader, its contempt for democracy and liberal institutions, its exaltation of the collective at the expense of the individual, and its love of military display and rash adventurism, first took root in Italy in 1922 when King Victor Emmanuel III appointed Benito Mussolini government leader after the "March on Rome" overthrew a weak parliamentary regime. A dozen years later, Adolf Hitler, after becoming German Chancellor, matched Mussolini's title of Il Duce by declaring himself Der Fuehrer. In both countries, freedom of the press, independent trade union and rival political parties have been abolished. National Socialism, or Nazism, seems more brutal and thorough than Italian Fascism and is also characterized by an official policy of anti-Semitism.

Parallel movements have arisen: in Norway, Vidkun Quisling's Nasjonal Samling party, in England, Sir Oswald Mosley's blackshirts. Austrian Chancellor Dollfuss was murdered largely because he resisted union – Anschluss – with Germany.

Before the Great War, most Americans opposed any role in Europe's conflicts. Results of the war brought disillusionment. Add to that preoccupation with economic ills and it becomes clear why Americans would like to believe that what happens in Europe is no concern of theirs.

Owens races to victory

Jesse Owens shatters records, showing what "non-Aryan" athletes can do.

Berlin, Germany, Aug. 16

There were 5,000 athletes from 53 countries on hand for the Olympic Games, the world was in turmoil and everyone concerned was expecting the worst. Instead, the crowds, the revenue and the performances all set records, and Jesse Owens emerged as the world's fastest athlete. He won both 100- and 200-meter dashes and the running broad jump, and was a member of the winning 400-meter relay team. The United States took eight other gold medals among the 23 track events, with notable victories being scored by Archie Williams in the 400 meters and John Woodruff in the 800 meters. Women competed in swimming, track and field and gymnastics events.

There was some embarrassme for the host country when it turne out that 10 Negroes (an alien rac Hitler had called them) were on th American team. Hitler reported snubbed Owens, but he apparent didn't greet any athletes other tha the Germans. The Americans crea ed their own problems. The Ame can committee head, Avery Bru dage, banned a star swimmer, El anor Holm, for breaking trainir (she sipped champagne!). And tw boxers were sent home for an u named infraction. But their absenc didn't dim the luster of the Ame can triumph. Even several unusu rule changes imposed by the Eur peans didn't keep the America from winning at basketball for th second Olympics in a row.

Adolf Hitler at the Berlin Games.

The Hindenburg over the Olympics

Auto factories hit y sitdown strikes

'lint, Michigan, Dec. 30

Workers on Midwest assembly ines are threatening to grind car roduction to a halt. With a cry of Shut the goddamn plant!", work-rs took over Fisher Body No. 2 to-lay after finding dies being shipped o non-union plants. And in Cleve-and two days ago, 7,000 sat down o protest delay of a long-awaited rievance meeting. In 45 days, the Jnited Auto Workers have won trikes at Bendix in South Bend, ndiana, and Kelsey-Hayes Wheel nd Midland Steel in Detroit. Flint nd Cleveland may open the way or all-out war on General Motors.

Promises of a new deal for labor ave induced a clamor for radical ction. "It seems to be a custom for nybody or any group to call a trike at will," observes the C.I.O.'s Adolph Germer. In the occupied actories, strikers maintain a fierce ndependence. Plans are made daily t general meetings. Liaison people ake off to organize "outside de-ense squads." Inside, the windows re covered in sheet metal; nuts nd bolts are collected as ammuni-ion. Strikers protect the machinery vith military discipline, while ad oc courts set up no-smoking and uiet zones. But at night, dancing nd story-telling take over. A scene hat looked like a prison seems like palace now (→March 12, 1937).

F.D.R. wins in landslide

Roosevelt portrait by Henry Hubbell.

New York City, Nov. 4

Overnight returns show Franklin Delano Roosevelt has won the biggest victory in election history, taking 523 electoral votes. Only Maine and Vermont went for Governor Alfred M Landon and Frank Knox. All this in the face of a *Literary Digest* poll that had predicted a Landon win. The formerly reliable *Digest* today announced it plans to change its polling method, declaring, "We may not have reached a representative cross-section of the population." The second-term victory by Roosevelt and John Nance Garner may also increase Democratic majorities in Congress.

In Topeka, Governor Landon said he was going to bed without conceding, but he congratulated President Roosevelt at 1:30 a.m. "The nation has spoken," he said. "Every American will accept the verdict and work for the common cause of the good of our country. That is the spirit of democracy. You have my sincere congratulations." A half hour later, the President wired history's worst-beaten aspirant: "I am confident that all of us Americans will now pull together for the common good. I send you every good wish."

Earlier, the Roosevelt family appeared on the porch of their Hyde Park estate, as a victory parade marched up, carrying torches and calcium flares and singing *Happy Days Are Here Again.* Laughing, the President refused radio microphones, saying, "This is just a home party." Then he happily urged photographers to hurry because, "I've got to get back and get the returns from California."

The Rev. Charles E. Coughlin's National Union for Social Justice, headed by North Dakota Representative William Lemke, polled negligible numbers. Father Coughlin himself was drubbed in his bid for a seat in the House of Representatives. The Detroit radio priest had promised he would deliver nine million votes to Lemke or retire forever from politics as well as from radio broadcasting.

At the new Automats, Americans get a meal just by inserting coins and turning knobs. A handful of change is all you need. Photo by Berenice Abbott.

New lease on Life

New York City, Nov. 23

A new magazine with a dramatic photograph on the cover and scads of pictures inside made its debut today. All readers need is a dime and they can buy *Life*, published by *Time* owner Henry Luce. He bought the moribund humor magazine of the same name because he wanted the title. Proving the adage that one picture is worth a thousand words, Luce's new magazine chronicles events in photographs. "Hundreds, perhaps thousands, of people contributed their photographic presence to the pages of this issue," the editors state. The cover was reserved for Margaret Bourke-White's image of Fort Peck Dam in Montana. She and other great photographers now have a new forum.

Shirley Temple, 8, a box-office queen

With a great smile, Shirley Temple has captured the hearts of America.

Hollywood, California

Today's biggest star is little Shirley Temple, 8 years old on April 23. The child with the curls was acting before she was 4 and was a star at 6, when her song-and-dance number *Baby Take a Bow* in the film *Stand Up and Cheer* led to a Fox contract and a special Academy Award. Her latest films are *Dimples* and *Stowaway*. Other top films are *The Story of Louis Pasteur* with Paul Muni, *Swingtime* with Fred Astaire and Ginger Rogers, Frank Capra's *Mr. Deeds Goes to Town* and *The Great Ziegfeld.* Also this year, Charlie Chaplin continues to defy convention. His *Modern Times*, with Paulette Goddard, is a silent film but still a big hit.

Chaplin and Goddard, married this year, walk off into the sunset.

1937

Roosevelt

Detroit, Jan. 18. Ford Motors makes 25 millionth automobile.

Cooperstown, New York, Jan. 20. Cy Young elected to Baseball Hall of Fame.

Washington, D.C., March 1. Congress passes Supreme Court Retirement Act, permitting justices to retire at age 70 with full pay (→July 22).

Raleigh, North Carolina, March 15. First state-run contraceptive clinic opens.

Chicago, March 17. Taxi drivers launch massive strike.

New London, Texas, March 18. Schoolhouse fire kills 294 students, faculty and staff.

Virgin Islands, March 26. William H. Hastie is first Negro federal judge in nation.

Washington, D.C., March 29. Supreme Court, in West Coast Hotel v. Parrish, upholds Washington state law, requiring minimum wage for women.

New York City, May 3. Pulitzer Prize in fiction awarded to Margaret Mitchell for *Gone With the Wind.*

New York City, May 12. British King George VI's coronation is first transoceanic radio broadcast.

Newport, Rhode Island, Aug. 5. Yacht Ranger successfully defends America's Cup, against Britain's Endeavour II.

Washington, D.C., Sept. 1. Congress passes National Housing Act, creating United States Housing Authority to make low-income housing more affordable.

New York City, Oct. 10. Yanks defeat Giants in World Series, four games to one.

Chicago, Dec. 9. Washington Redskins defeat Chicago Bears in National Football League championship, 28-21.

New York City, December. First NBC concert with Arturo Toscanini conducting.

Jersey City, New Jersey. Mayor Frank Hague proclaims, "I am the law."

Virginia. Restoration of colonial Williamsburg completed.

New York City. *Look* magazine begins publication.

DEATH

Hollywood, California, July 11. George Gershwin, composer (*Sept. 26, 1898).

FDR: "One-third of a nation ill-housed, ill-clad, ill-nourished"

President and Mrs. Roosevelt are undeterred as they ride into a second term.

Washington, D.C., Jan. 20

Franklin D. Roosevelt began his second term as President today in a cold rain on the Capitol steps. Before a sea of ruined top hats, he spoke of the job ahead. "In this nation," he cried over the drumming of rain on umbrellas, "... I see millions denied education, recreation, and the opportunity to better their lot and the lot of their children ... I see one-third of a nation ill-housed, ill-clad, ill-nourished."

Surely many citizens share the President's vision. "Despite all the recovery we have made," said one analyst at Cleveland Trust, "we are still in the Depression." And no one suffers more under its weight than the farmer. Crop output last year, cut by drought, hit its lowest level since the Great War, except for 1934. Studies show that over half the South's farmers are tenants or sharecroppers, as are a third in the North and a quarter in the West.

Yet the last few years offer hopeful, if uneven, signs of recovery. Six million more Americans had jobs last year than in 1932. National income rose from \$42.5 billion in 1933 to \$57.1 billion in 1935. Railroads languish at half their pre-Depression performance figures. But Detroit's assembly lines, before sitdown strikers halted them, began to turn out cars at a healthy rate. Christmas trade last month was 12 to 15 percent above the totals for 1935. And, for what it's worth, whiskey consumption hit a post-Prohibition high in November.

The flexing of the economic indices accounts for a lot of Roosevelt's landslide. But his New Deal is far from safe. Polls show an ideological chasm between rich and poor. Of the people listed in *Who's Who,* 69 percent oppose FDR, while among those on relief, 77 percent favor him. Republicans paint New Dealers as fanatics, fascists, "theorists and impractical experimenters." By the end of the election, only 15 percent of voters wanted the next administration to be "more liberal"; 50 percent hoped to see it grow "more conservative." Still, the benefits of federal policy are legion. The P.W.A. has built homes for 21,700 families in 36 cities. The R.E.A. extends power lines far into isolated areas. The W.P.A. employs over two million jobless and the N.Y.A., the youth organization, hires hundreds of thousands of students at \$5 to 30 a month.

So FDR ended his inaugural on a note of hope. "It is not in despair that I paint you that picture," he said of his earlier comments. "I paint it for you in hope ... We are determined to make every American citizen the subject of his country's interest and concern ... We will carry on" (→Apr. 12).

Billboards cannot mask the realities of Depression life with bread lines an all too common sight. "The Louisville Flood" (1937) by Margaret Bourke-White.

Arkansas Negroes to join land co-op

Helena, Arkansas, March

A group of Arkansas Negroes may soon be owning farms on land where their grandparents worked as slaves before the Civil War. The Farm Security Administration has purchased a 5,600-acre tract of plantation land at Lakeview and plans to form a cooperative colony for Negroes. The land has been divided into 95 farms that will be allotted to colonist families. The farmers may work on the land for a trial period before committing themselves to purchasing the farms. The cooperative is going to operate a general store, a cotton gin and community schools.

G.M. gives in to strikers

Strikers sit down, wait and read the papers at the Fisher body plant in Flint, Michigan, one of the G.M. factories that workers called home for 44 days.

Flint, Michigan, March 12

Behind a vast wave of sitdown strikes, the United Auto Workers have pushed their way into General Motors. Today, a month after giving in to arbitration, G.M. directors signed a pact with the union under the watchful eye of the National Labor Relations Board. The C.I.O. hailed the victory, which designates it as the sole bargaining agent in the G.M. talks. But line workers, including the many who struck spontaneously to fight work speedups, wonder what they have won. The pact gave management "full authority" over line speed and bars strikes without sanction of the union's national officers.

For 44 days, workers made the factories their home, supplied by outside networks with everything from food and first aid to song and dance. After the New Year, the movement spread from Flint to Anderson, Indiana; Janesville, Wisconsin; Norwood and Toledo, Ohio, and Detroit and Ternstedt, Michigan. In the final 10 days of the strike, only 151 cars left assembly lines. Police and vigilante attacks in Flint, Detroit, Saginaw and Anderson failed to clear the plants. An injunction foundered on the revelation that the judge held $219,000 in G.M. stock (→Feb. 27, 1939).

Union wins at U.S. Steel

Pittsburgh, Penn., March 2

Only last month, U.S. Steel's Benjamin Franklin Fairless reflected that his firm "has been the crouching lion in the pathway of labor." Today, lying down with the lamb, Fairless signed a pact giving bargaining rights to the C.I.O. Steel Workers Organizing Committee. The industry is in shock, its united front broken. Bethlehem, the other half of "Big Steel," has already fallen into line, with a 10 percent pay raise and a 40-hour week.

Why has Big Steel decided to deal? U.S. Steel chairman Myron Taylor, who met secretly with the C.I.O. president, John L. Lewis, has also visited the White House often of late. FDR says only that when friends get together, they naturally discuss the economy. The best answer is the steel union's 200,000 members, twice as many as enabled the United Auto Workers to bring General Motors to heel. With orders high, steel can't afford a walkout. And in a sellers' market, $100 million more in pay can be passed on in higher prices. In any case, the C.I.O. is jubilant. Said the negotiator Philip Murray, "This is unquestionably the greatest story in the history of the American Labor movement." With it, the C.I.O. steals the initiative from the A.F.L. With sitdowns threatened at Chrysler, Hudson and Firestone, Lewis had only one comment: "I have work to do" (→July).

Dock strike ends

San Francisco, Feb. 4

The country's costliest maritime strike ended today after paralyzing all Western and some Eastern ports for 98 days. The strike, which cost the shipping industry some $7 million per day in lost revenue, has won longshoremen's unions most of their demands for control of the hiring halls, an eight-hour day with overtime pay rather than comparable time off and union recognition. Said strike coordinator Harry Bridges: "Forty thousand men are grateful. I'm only one of them."

Floods hit Midwest

Cincinnati, Ohio, Feb. 1

As lines of W.P.A. workers pass sandbags, the worst floods since 1913 are receding, leaving in their wake a devastated Midwest. The flooding began a month ago when the Ohio, Mississippi and Allegheny Rivers spearheaded a deluge that swept away a half-million homes, left a million people homeless and killed nearly 1,000. Property damage has been placed at more than $400 million, and Congress has passed an emergency relief package of $790 million.

High court upholds Labor Relations Act

Washington, D.C., Apr. 12

The Supreme Court handed the administration a major victory today by upholding the National Labor Relations Act, the landmark legislation passed two years ago to benefit workers. Also known as the Wagner Act, bearing the name of its sponsor, Senator Robert F. Wagner of N.Y., the law supports the rights of workers to join unions and bargain collectively. It also prohibits employers from interfering with worker rights to join a union and authorizes investigation of unfair employment practices by a National Labor Relations Board that the law created (→Feb. 16, 1938).

Protesters pledge opposition to war

New York City, Apr. 22

The strength of anti-war feeling was dramatically evident here today as New Yorkers massed for the fourth annual Peace Demonstration. Drawing their largest crowd to date, the demonstrators emphasized their refusal to support American involvement in any war whatsoever. American pacifism has escalated following Senator Gerald Nye's hearings on the profits made by arms producers in the Great War. Books such as Walter Millis's best-selling *The Road to War* have also persuaded many that the only way to avoid war is to eschew any foreign involvement (→Oct. 5).

"White Tenements" by Niles Spencer. Hard times hit the nation's cities.

Hindenburg explodes; flames kill 36

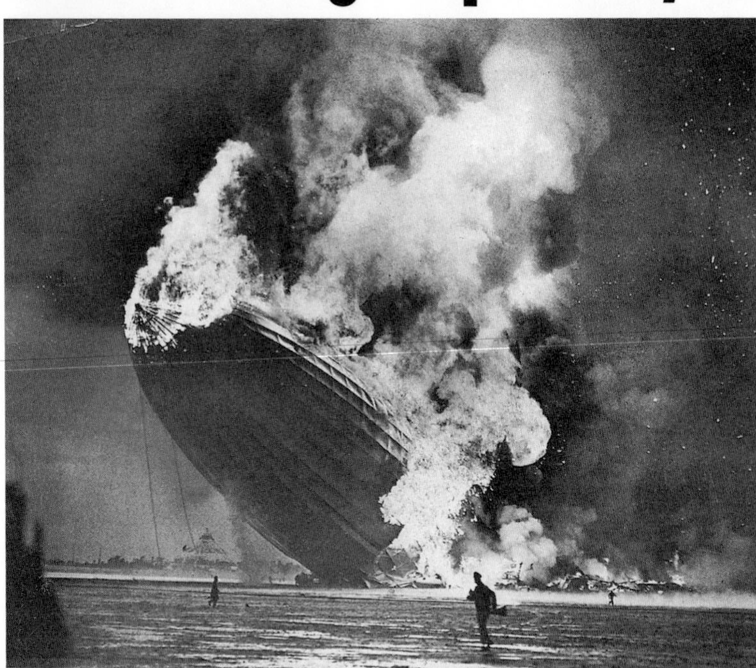
The Hindenburg's fiery end casts serious doubt on the future of dirigibles.

Lakehurst, N.J., May 6

"Oh, the humanity," cried radio broadcaster Herbert Morrison as he saw the dirigible Hindenburg erupt in flames that consumed it and killed 36 people. Morrison's anguished description of the disaster was heard across the country, on the nation's first coast-to-coast radio broadcast. Morrison, a 31-year-old announcer with WLS radio in Chicago, was assigned to cover the arrival of the Hindenburg on a trans-Atlantic trip. Listeners heard his smooth delivery suddenly turn to panic as the hydrogen in the Hindenburg caught fire.

"It burst into flames," he cried. "It's afire and it's crashing. It's crashing terrible ... It's burning, bursting into flames and it's falling on the mooring mast. This is one of the worst catastrophes in the world. Oh, the flames, 400 or 500 feet into the sky. It's a terrific crash ... the smoke and the flames now and the frame is crashing to the ground, not quite to the mooring mast. Oh, the humanity. And all the passengers."

The Hindenburg had inaugurated regular trans-Atlantic air service, making 10 round-trips between Germany and America in 1936. One-way passage cost $400. The craft began its first trip of 1937 in Hamburg on May 3, crossing the Atlantic in only 60 hours. The giant airship cruised slowly over Manhattan on its way to Lakehurst, passing over Times Square, where crowds gathered to watch for it. The Hindenburg ran into a thunderstorm over Staten Island and waited out the storm by cruising down the Jersey coast for an hour. It sailed back toward Lakehurst soon after 7 p.m. and began nosing toward the 75-foot mooring mast at the Lakehurst Naval Station.

At 7:25, when the motors had been switched off, there were two explosions just in front of the Nazi swastikas on the Hindenburg's tail. The ship was destroyed in less than a minute, as 35 of the 97 people aboard and one worker in the ground crew were killed. Heroic efforts by ground crew members saved many lives.

The disaster is a blow to the prestige of Nazi Germany, which used the Hindenburg for propaganda, as well as air service. The cause of the disaster is unknown, with speculation ranging from sabotage to static electricity that ignited hydrogen leaking from the craft.

Earhart disappears over South Pacific

Amelia christens a Ford airplane.

South Pacific, July 18

Sixteen days after the plane with Amelia Earhart and her co-pilot Frederick J. Noonan was reported lost on July 2, the navy today ended the search for the colorful aviation pioneer. The last words heard from the plane were "gas is low" and "we are flying on line of position," or on course. Earhart, 39, was the first woman to cross the Atlantic by plane, as a passenger in 1928, the first woman to make a solo flight across the Atlantic, in 1932, and the first person to fly alone from Honolulu to California, in 1935. She and Noonan were trying to circle the globe on this flight and were between New Guinea and Howland Island when the craft vanished.

John D. Rockefeller died on May 23, but he has left behind a multi-million dollar oil empire as well as a trail of shiny new dimes that he would give away to people.

Actress Jean Harlow, 26, died of uremic poisoning on June 7. Howard Hughes, her producer, set a new record this year by flying cross-country in nine hours.

Bessie Smith, the "empress of the blues," died tragically in an auto accident on September 26. She was refused admission to a segregated hospital in Memphis, Tenn.

Wallis Warfield Simpson of Baltimore became the Duchess of Windsor on June 6, when she wed the former King of England, who abdicated for "the woman I love."

Violence at River Rouge

River Rouge, Michigan, May 26

For decades, Henry Ford kept unions out of his auto empire with paternalism, high wages, profit-sharing and a host of company services. Today, he turned from the open hand to the closed fist. Richard Frankensteen, a cagey organizer for the United Auto Workers, had long sensed growing tension. Ford's 3,000-man "service department," a group of former cops and labor relations "experts" headed by Harry Bennett, has expanded espionage and agitation efforts against the union. Expecting trouble, Frankensteen invited prominent liberals to witness a leaflet drive. As the organizers and their guests lined up along an overpass here, men in felt hats approached with the greeting, "Get the hell off here; this is Ford property." Frankensteen turned to counter a blow, and was pinned by two men who pulled his coat over his head and knocked him flat, kicking him about the face and groin. Walter Reuther was bounced down the stairs, step by step. In 15 minutes, the area was cleared. Union spokesmen report 18 hurt, including four women. Bennett calls the attack a "frame-up" by the union. Frankensteen and Reuther, through bloodied teeth, disagree (→Apr. 11, 1941).

Memorial Day Massacre

Chicago, July

Eighteen strikers are dead, 10 of them shot down here on Memorial Day, thousands are streaming back to work, and still the steel union leaders refuse to admit defeat. But resolve on the picket lines has worn thin. A compromise offered July 1 at Inland Steel brought hungry strikers back to work without even a contract guarantee. And Republic, leader of the group of independents known as "Little Steel," has restarted four Cleveland plants – but without concessions.

Despite U.S. Steel's labor rapprochement in March, Little Steel violently defies compromise. "We'll go in the front door or not at all," vows Youngstown Sheet and Tube chief Frank Purcell. On May 30, a group of his guards fired on strikers from trucks, killing two and wounding dozens. On the same day, 400 miles away in South Chicago, 160 police confronted 1,500 pickets at a Republic plant. The strikers wielded car cranks, bolts and bricks; the police had guns. After the shooting, 10 strikers lay dead; of the 78 injured, five were police. The C.I.O. has criticized the White House for refusing to act against the steel firms. President Roosevelt's response: "A plague on both your houses."

Harry Bennett, chief of Ford security, among the victims of labor strife.

Golden Gate Bridge spans Frisco Bay

San Francisco, May 27

Some 200,000 people crossed the Golden Gate Bridge today to celebrate the opening of one of the 20th century's engineering marvels.

From 6 a.m. to 6 p.m., the longest suspension bridge in the world was a festival scene. At one point, as adults and schoolgirls sang such songs as *I Love You, California*, a man held up his hand and shouted "Be quiet, listen to the bridge!"

The crowd stopped and listened to an unearthly symphony of notes: a roar coming from below and high shrill sounds from the wires strung about them in four giant harps.

The festivities ended with a pageant and fireworks that bathed the bridge in a kaleidoscope of color.

The bridge, designed by engineers Joseph B. Strauss and Clifford Paine, took four years, four months and 22 days to complete. It measures 6,450 from anchorage to anchorage, with its main 4,200-foot span suspended on towers rising 746 feet above the surface of the bay. The bridge used up 100,000 tons of steel including 80,000 miles of wire cable. The construction, paid for by a $35 million bond issue, took 25 million man-hours and claimed the lives of 11 workers.

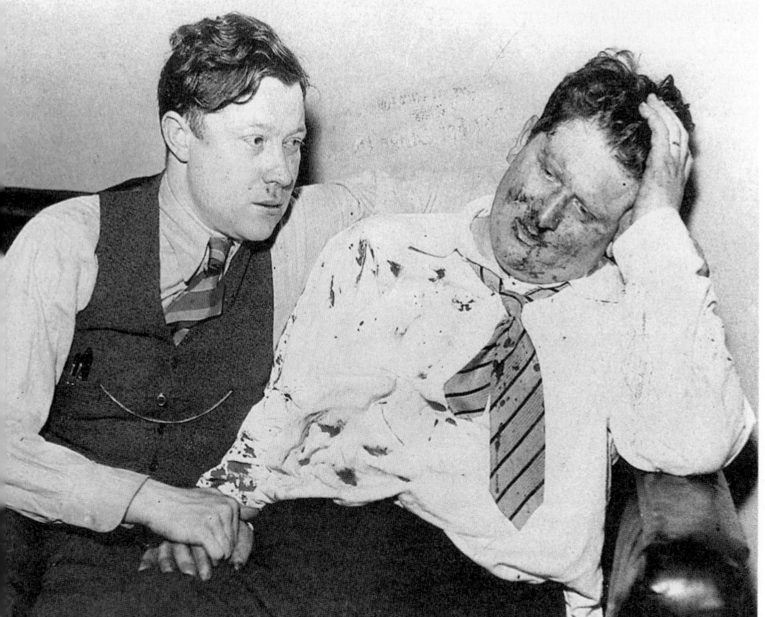

Richard Frankensteen, C.I.O. organizer, after being beaten by security men.

A spectacular accomplishment after more than four years and $35 million.

FDR loses in attempt to pack high court

Cartoonist J.H. "Ding" Darling draws the line between presidential leadership and abuse of power.

Washington, D.C., July 22

The Senate dealt President Roosevelt a severe blow today by decisively killing his plan to expand the Supreme Court. The vote was 70 to 20. Angered by the court's rulings against various New Deal programs, such as the National Recovery Act, the President had proposed that he be allowed to appoint as many as six additional justices if those 70 or older refused to retire. He argued that justices often remained on the court beyond their "physical and mental capacity." The court now has nine members, some of them older than 70.

The President's plan had been unveiled in March in a speech at a Democratic Victory Dinner. He said at that time that most of the justices were letting their personal economic ideas harm efforts by state and federal officials to deal with pressing problems. Critics, such as former President Hoover, called the plan "court packing," meant to assure court approval of questionable New Deal programs.

Hugo Black joins court despite link to KKK

Washington, D.C., Oct. 4

The nation's capital was abuzz today with the news that Associate Justice Hugo L. Black, the newest member of the Supreme Court, once belonged to the Ku Klux Klan in his native Alabama. He was appointed to the high court on August 12 by President Roosevelt and won easy confirmation a week later in the Senate, where he had served. Justice Black, now 51, joined the Klan in the early 1920s, but resigned in 1925 just before running for the Senate. He had earlier been a police court judge and then a county prosecuting attorney. It is said that the Klan, at the time he was a member, was considered to have populist leanings. Indeed, in his years in the Senate, Black was a leader of that chamber's liberals, playing a key role in New Deal legislation such as the bill to establish the Tennessee Valley Authority and a wages and hours law.

War Admiral is 4th Triple Crown victor

New York City, June 5

War Admiral won the Belmont Stakes in track record time today, the fourth horse ever to win the Triple Crown. Following up on their Preakness victory, Charlie Kurtsinger rode the son of Man o' War to a four-length triumph before a record Belmont crowd of 35,000. War Admiral missed taking the Kentucky Derby record by a second but made Governor Albert "Happy" Chandler, with $20 on his nose, a happier man. Sceneshifter, fifth to War Admiral at Louisville, was second in the Belmont. War Admiral, fractious at first, settled down to win handily.

Now shopping carts make buying easier

Oklahoma City, June

Standard Food Stores here are introducing carts that shoppers can put their purchases in. And what manner do those purchases take? They might be bottles of Aqua Velva after-shave, cans of Hormel soup, Alcoa Aluminum Foil, Niblet canned corn (with a Jolly Green Giant on the label), Pepperidge Farm bread or cans of Spam – all new this year. If the cart were wheeled outside, it might proceed to a liquor store. A recent study shows the United States is the world's largest consumer of spirits.

Joe Louis takes heavyweight crown

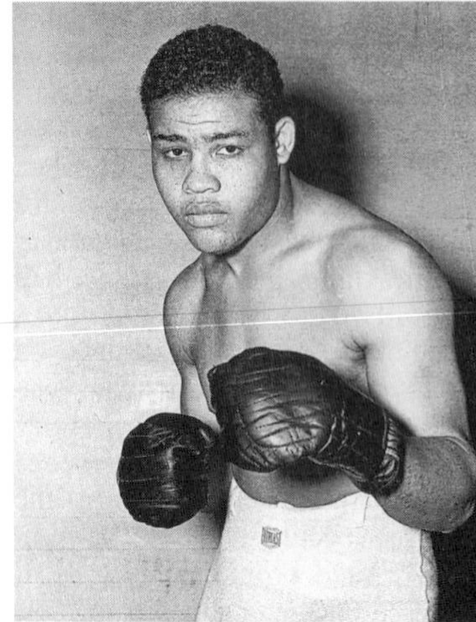

Joe Louis, the "Brown Bomber."

Chicago, June 22

Jim Braddock knocked Joe Louis to the canvas in the first round, and that may have been a mistake. In a cold fury, Louis battered the out-of-shape New Yorker for the next seven rounds before finishing him off a minute into the eighth. Louis thus became the first Negro to win the world heavyweight championship in 22 years. Braddock, eight years older than the 23-year-old challenger, was so badly beaten that the final head-jarring right left a blood stain on the canvas. Like other Negro boxers, Louis had trouble getting a title shot despite his record of 34 victories in 35 professional fights. His only defeat had been a 12th-round knockout by the German Max Schmeling.

"Bread line" by George Luks. The Ashcan artist died four years ago, but his work is immortal, here expressing the reality of the grim 30s.

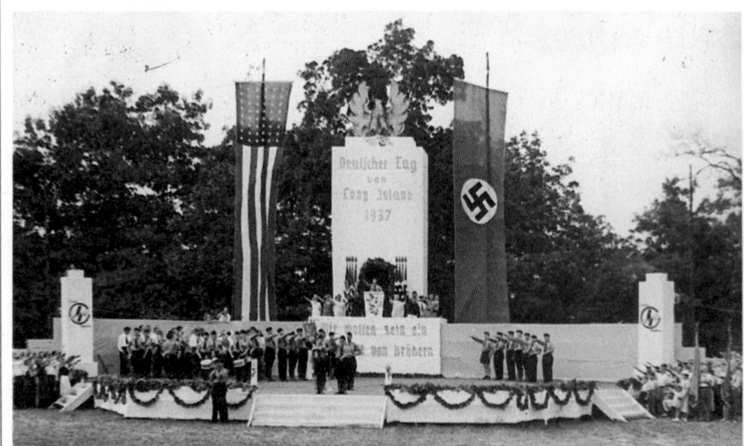

Some 20,000 American Nazis gather in Yaphank, Long Island, New York, to attend the second annual German Day celebration. With the Depression continuing to take a terrible toll, people turn to the extreme right in desperation. Fully 500 half-barrels of beer were consumed at the rally.

President urges quarantine of aggressors

Chicago, Oct. 5

President Roosevelt today called upon all "peace-loving nations" to "quarantine" aggressor states that are spreading an "epidemic of world lawlessness." Alluding to the Japanese war against China as well as to events in Ethiopia and Spain, the President condemned those nations "who are threatening a breakdown of all international order and law."

Speaking here in the capital of so-called isolationist America, FDR warned that "there is no escape through mere isolation or neutrality" from the "international anarchy" caused by aggressors. "War is contagion," FDR declared, that "can engulf peoples remote from the original scene of hostilities." And he predicted that unless concerted action is taken, the Western Hemisphere will also be attacked.

Despite the President's warnings, however, isolationist sentiment is strong. Last May, Congress passed its fourth Neutrality Law in two years. An arms embargo will be imposed on aggressor and victim states, despite Secretary of State Cordell Hull's plea for discretion in applying the law in order to deter aggression. Belligerent nations will be allowed to buy only certain non-military goods such as oil and scrap iron, and will have to do so on a "cash and carry" basis, the goods to be paid for in cash and to be transported in foreign ships (→ Dec. 25).

Japan apologizes for sinking U.S. gunboat

Washington, D.C., Dec. 25

The United States today accepted Japan's formal apology for sinking the gunboat Panay on December 12. The Japanese government, which denies ordering the bombing, will pay reparations that are likely to total more than $2 million.

In the incident, Japanese aircraft bombed the boat on the Yangtze River as it was rescuing war-stranded Americans near Nanking. The attack was carried out in broad daylight despite the boat's clearly displayed American flag. Two American sailors were killed and 30 wounded. Survivors report being strafed by machine-gun fire as they sought refuge on shore.

Americans in China have come under increasing attack by Japanese forces as the Nationalists continue to lose ground. Since July 7, the Japanese have seized Peking, Tientsin, Shanghai and Nanking. In the process, they have conducted devastating bombings raids, during which American hospitals, missions and schools, though clearly marked, have often been hit.

Japan's denial that it is at war with China has given the President an excuse not to invoke the provisions of the Neutrality Acts. This has enabled Americans to provide arms to China (→ March 13, 1938).

Lewis chides FDR

Washington, D.C., Sept. 3

John L. Lewis, head of the Committee for Industrial Organization, assaulted New Dealers in a Labor Day broadcast today. Angry with President Roosevelt for not backing the C.I.O. against Little Steel, Lewis spoke of betrayal. "It ill behooves one who has supped at labor's table," he scolded, ".. to curse with equal fervor and fine impartiality both labor and its adversaries when they become locked in deadly embrace." He said labor sought industrial peace. But in the absence of federal help, it will use "its own economic power" to bring employers to the bargaining table.

"U.S.A." finished

New York City

The story of the United States takes a lot of telling, but for now at least John Dos Passos has uttered the last word with *The Big Money*. This installment has completed *U.S.A*, a panoramic novel begun with *The 42nd Parallel* (1930) and *1919* (1932). Other writers till smaller fields. *The Red Pony* and *Of Mice and Men*, by John Steinbeck, are both slim books. John P. Marquand tackles one man's life in *The Late George Apley*. The *Golden Boy* in the Clifford Odets play is torn between his violin and boxing. He ought to read Karen Horney's *The Neurotic Personality of Our Time*.

Photographers document the Depression

All of the misery of the times is evident in the eyes of one hapless farmer.

Photographers for the Farm Security Administration – Berenice Abbott, Walker Evans, Dorothea Lange, Russell Lee and Arthur Rothstein – use their cameras as a social force, mobilizing the public to support New Deal programs. And Margaret Bourke-White is recording the plight of Southern blacks, publishing her pictures in a book, "You Have Seen Their Faces."

1938

Roosevelt

Ohio, Jan. 22. A guilty verdict is handed down to 16 oil companies and 30 executives, on charges of conspiring to fix gasoline prices.

Albany, New York, Apr. 12. New York becomes first state to pass law requiring medical tests for marriage licenses.

Atlanta, Apr. 22. Air ace Eddie Richenbacker assumes control of Eastern Airlines for $3.5 million.

New York City, May 2. John P. Marquand wins Pulitzer Prize in fiction for *The Late George Apley*.

Washington, D.C., May 11. President Roosevelt upholds Treasury Secretary Harold Ickes's decision to forbid sales of helium to Germany.

Washington, D.C., June 22. Congress amends Federal Bankruptcy Act with Chandler Act; persons or firms may settle with creditors while avoiding liquidation.

New York City, June 22. Joe Louis defeats Max Schmelling in one round at Yankee Stadium to retain world heavyweight championship.

Gettysburg, Pennsylvania, July 3. President Roosevelt dedicates monument, marking battle's 75th anniversary.

St. Lawrence River, Aug. 18. Thousand Islands Bridge, connecting United States and Canada, is dedicated by President Roosevelt.

New York City, Oct. 9. New York Yankees defeat Chicago Cubs in World Series sweep.

Queens, New York, Oct. 22. Chester Carlson creates first xerographic image.

Stockholm, Sweden, Nov. 10. Pearl S. Buck receives Nobel Prize for literature.

New York City, Dec. 12. Giants defeat Green Bay Packers, 23-17, in National Football League championship.

United States. Historian Charles Beard says, "The American people surely want to stay out of the next world war. It may cost us the blood of countless American boys."

Philadelphia. Jefferson-head nickel goes into circulation.

Delaware. Du Pont Company makes first nylon products.

New York City. *Our Town,* by Thornton Wilder, published.

The "King of Swing" at Carnegie Hall

New York City, Jan. 16

With Benny Goodman leading the charge, jazz has breached the august decorum of Carnegie Hall. Goodman headed an all-star band consisting of Harry James, Ziggy Elman, Lionel Hampton, Gene Krupa and Teddy Wilson, with soloists from the Count Basie and Duke Ellington bands sitting in. The result was electrifying. Goodman's star began to rise in 1935 when his band played Hollywood's Palomar Ballroom. Bored by standard dance music, he devoted the last set to the jazz he plays best – "swing." The audience went wild and the style swept the nation. A smash hit at the Paramount Theater last year enthroned the man with the stylish clarinet as "King of Swing." Goodman has been good for jazz. Because he is white, other white Americans have more readily accepted a music once deemed questionable. And his hiring of Negro musicians is the courageous act of a man whose convictions are as unique as his music.

Benny Goodman, "King of Swing."

Murrow airs Reich's seizure of Austria

Vienna, Austria, March 13

Nazi troops marched into Austria today, the CBS radio correspondent Edward R. Murrow reports. "It's 2:30 a.m., and young storm troopers are riding about the streets in trucks and vehicles of all sorts, singing and tossing oranges to the crowd," said Murrow in a live "news round-up" from Europe, the first of its kind on radio. The Austrians were to have voted in a plebiscite today to decide whether they wanted "Anschluss" – union with Germany. "We have yielded to force," said Chancellor Kurt von Schuschnigg, "since we are not prepared even at this terrible hour to shed blood." Schuschnigg resigned under pressure from Hitler and was replaced by Nazi Minister Arthur Seyss-Inquart (→Sept. 30).

New legislation lets farmers store surplus

Washington, D.C., Feb. 16

Congress passed the second Agricultural Adjustment Act today, two years after the first was shot down by the Supreme Court as unconstitutional. This act is expected to pass any judicial test, as it is funded not by a food processing tax – the downfall of its predecessor – but with general funds.

The A.A.A. of 1938 allows farmers to store excess grain and permits the federal government to lend farmers money based on their surplus. It should give stability to farm prices and incomes. In addition, it establishes the Federal Crop Insurance Corporation, which insures wheat crops against damage and loss by natural disaster.

The legislation is considered a political victory for President Roosevelt, who was frustrated by the 1936 ruling against the first act. Many observers believe that the act will help restore the American agricultural economy to where it was before the Depression (→June 25).

It's Superman!

New York City, June

Have you ever seen a man lift a car over his head? You can on the cover of Action Comics No. 1, where a figure in red and blue tights with a large "S" on his chest does just that! It's Superman, the brainchild of writer Jerry Siegel and artist Joe Shuster. Born on a distant planet, Superman is the possessor of powers and abilities far beyond those of mortal men. And what's more, he never has to call for a tow truck!

"Snow White and the Seven Dwarfs" opened in February across the country to the delight of young and old. Through this first feature-length cartoon film, Walt Disney raises animation, and his reputation, to new heights.

Mae West off radio

New York City, January

Mae West's saucy tongue has her in trouble again. In an appearance on the Edgar Bergen-Charlie McCarthy radio show, she shared some risque dialogue with actor Don Ameche during an *Adam and Eve* sketch that the Federal Communications Commission has ruled "vulgar" and "indecent." Though NBC quickly apologized, 130 stations have now banned even the mention of Mae West's name. Another upshot is that author Jane Storm is suing West, NBC and others for $10,000, charging the lines in question were pilfered from her dramatic oeuvre, *Love and Applesauce*.

Minimum wage law set

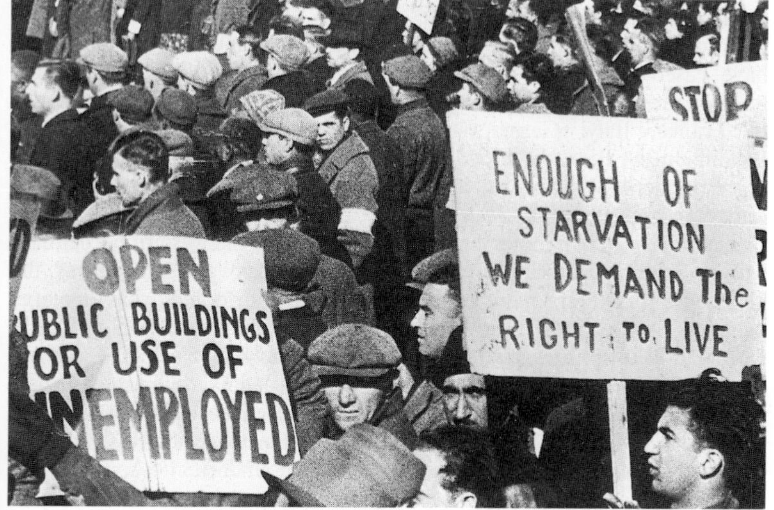

A minimum wage law could go a long way to ending scenes like this one.

Washington, D.C., June 25

America's work force got a hefty boost today when President Roosevelt signed into law the Fair Labor Standards Act, which sets a minimum wage and a mandatory ceiling on the number of work hours per week. The President, in signing the law at his home in Hyde Park, New York, predicted it would result in raising the national income to $60 billion a year, adding, "A few drops of rain have been coming from the heavens and probably will be followed by a much needed shower."

The law, which applies to most companies engaged in interstate commerce, sets the minimum wage at 25 cents an hour, eventually rising to 40 cents. It mandates a 44-hour work week, to be reduced to 40 hours over a period of time. It provides for time and a half for overtime, except in certain types of seasonal employment. It prohibits wage differentials based on age or sex. And, at last, it prohibits hiring those under 16 years of age.

Some labor leaders had opposed the bill, fearing a minimum wage would become a maximum in many jobs. But President Roosevelt hailed the law as perhaps the "most far-sighted program for the benefit of workers ever adopted in this or any other country" (→ Jan. 30, 1939).

FDR says South is top economic problem

Washington, D.C., July 4

President Roosevelt said today that the South is the nation's top economic problem, with conditions so severe that the entire nation is at risk. The President's remarks were made in a message to an economic conference here. It bore out many current statistics involving the South. Sickness and death rates far exceed those elsewhere in the nation. The South has 21 percent of America 's population, yet earns only 9 percent of the national income. The annual wage in the South is about $865, as compared to $1,291 nationally. Common laborers earn 16 cents an hour less than those elsewhere. And while the South has the most farms of any region, the average acreage there is also the smallest, thus producing less income.

All of this, President Roosevelt told the conference, has led to "an economic unbalance in the nation as a whole, due to this very condition in the South."

The South still waits for some relief.

"Wrong-way" Corrigan lands in Ireland

Dublin, Ireland, July 18

It was all a mistake, Douglas Corrigan said with a smile as he explained how he set out to fly from New York to California and ended up in Ireland. Corrigan, denied federal permission for a trans-Atlantic flight due to the rickety condition of his ancient Curtiss Robin J-6 monoplane, said he lost sight of the ground because of fog after taking off from New York's Floyd Bennett Field and made a wrong turn over Long Island. He says he misread his compass and didn't realize his error until he came out of the fog some 24 hours later. Corrigan, who had just set a California-to-New York speed record, said cheerfully, "I intended to fly to California but I got mixed up in the clouds and must have flown the wrong way."

Committee to study effects of the trusts

Washington, D.C., June 16

A panel of experts was created today to investigate the effects of monopolies on the nation's economy. The Temporary National Economic Committee, chaired by Wyoming Senator Joseph O'Mahoney, will study extensively a sector that President Roosevelt believes is stalling growth: trusts. Some feel the creation of the committee is a way to avoid adopting concrete guiding economic principles. But many feel that the concentration of wealth in America takes opportunity from the average man. One Tennessee man wrote the White House that Roosevelt's antitrust efforts bring forth hope that "burns anew."

Vander Meer, Feller blow away batters

Cincinnati, Ohio, Summer

They used to call Johnny Vander Meer the "Dutch Master." Now he will be known as "Double No-Hit Johnny." The Cincinnati pitcher held the Boston Braves hitless on June 11 and four days later totally blanked the Brooklyn Dodgers. In the American League, Bob Feller of the Cleveland Indians lived up to his nickname of "Rapid Robert" by striking out 18 Tigers in a nine-inning game, a modern record. Feller proved that he was fully recovered from the arm injury that held him to 26 games last year. Pinky Higgins of the Boston Red Sox turned in the batting exploit of the season with 12 straight hits.

Congress allots billions for works program

Washington, D.C., June 21

In the face of an unemployment figure reaching 10 million, President Roosevelt signed into law the Emergency Relief Appropriation Act today. The legislation allocates $3 billion in new funds, extending FDR's previous efforts to alleviate the recession of 1937. It will provide thousands of new work programs. Conservatives fought passage of the bill, but liberals in both houses pushed it through. In spite of the recent hard times, President Roosevelt says there is a renewed optimism in the American way of life. He said, "I sense a deep happiness that, despite the Depression, Americans are happy at surviving under a democratic form of government" (→ 25).

Artists strive to show Americans back at work. But with the Depression in its ninth year, this may be more impression than reality. "Days Without End" (1937) by Frank Cassara.

Budge is first to score a Grand Slam

Don Budge, Grand Slammer.

Forest Hills, N.Y., Sept. 24

With one last devastating cross-court backhand, Don Budge added the U.S. National title to victories in Australia, France and England, becoming the first tennis player ever to achieve a Grand Slam. In the final here, Budge attacked relentlessly to defeat his doubles partner, Gene Mako, 6-3, 6-8, 6-2, 6-1. Since winning the California boys' title in his first tournament, Budge has had a charmed career. In four years, he has compiled a 25 and 4 record in Davis Cup play and last year brought the cup to America for the first time since 1926. Budge is likely to turn pro next year.

"Clouds of war" are dispelled at Munich

Munich, Germany, Sept. 30

The crisis that has brought Europe to the brink of war appears to have eased greatly following yesterday's meeting here of the leaders of France, Italy, Germany and Britain. In a CBS radio broadcast, correspondent William L. Shirer said: "It took the Big Four just five hours and 25 minutes here at Munich to dispel the clouds of war and come to an agreement on the partition of Czechoslovakia. There is to be no European war after all." The present conference follows earlier unsuccessful meetings between Adolf Hitler and British Prime Minister Neville Chamberlain at Bad Godesberg and Berchtesgaden. Here they were joined by French Premier Edouard Daladier and Italian dictator Benito Mussolini, along with their foreign ministers. Soviet Russia was not invited, nor was the country most affected – Czechoslovakia. The accord calls for immediate German occupation of the western border area of Czechoslovakia known as the Sudetenland, which has a large German population. A plebiscite to decide the region's future was put off for a later date, but few expect it will ever be held. France and Britain have guaranteed Czechoslovakia's boundaries (→Apr. 1, 1939).

Air records set

New York City, Sept. 3

The adventurous Jackie Cochran and the daring Howard Hughes have proved that the world is shrinking. Winning the Bendix race, Miss Cochran flew a Seversky Pursuit 2,042 miles from Burbank, California, to Cleveland, Ohio, in 8 hours 10 minutes 31 seconds. She continued to New Jersey for a west-east cross-country mark of 10:07.10. Hughes and a crew of three circled the globe in a record 3 days 19 hours 17 minutes, but landed on the wrong runway here today.

Smoking harmful?

New York City, Oct. 19

Two New Orleans surgeons said here today that lung cancer is on the rise and that smoking may be the cause. Dr. Alton Ochsner, head of surgery at Tulane University, and Dr. Michael DeBakey, his former student, addressed the American College of Surgeons. They said lung cancer cases are up sharply at Charity Hospital in New Orleans. They link this to a rise in cigarette smoking since the war. Inhaling smoke over a long period, they said, irritates the bronchial tubes.

Open Door is shut

Washington, D.C., Nov. 18

Japan has put the United States on notice that it no longer recognizes the Open Door policy. Rejecting protests that American rights had been repeatedly violated, Tokyo asserted that the United States and other countries must recognize Japan's "New Order" for East Asia. The Japanese note comes in the wake of the State Department's July decision to impose a "moral embargo" on aircraft exports to Japan, which reportedly used American planes to bomb Canton last year.

Teflon, Fiberglas

New York City

Teflon and Fiberglas, two products of great potential, were introduced to the market this year. Teflon, discovered by Roy Plunkett, a research chemist at Du Pont, is a tough fluorocarbon resin that resists corrosion even at high temperatures. It is being proposed as a coating for cookwear. Fiberglas, manufactured by the Owens-Corning Fiberglas Corporation, consists of a mass of thin, flexible glass fibers whose uses range from insulation to structural parts.

President Roosevelt counts dimes with Basil O'Connor, his ex-law partner and new chief of the National Foundation for Infantile Paralysis. The campaign, led by the President, calls upon the American people to send in their dimes, a veritable "March of Dimes," as comedian Eddie Cantor says.

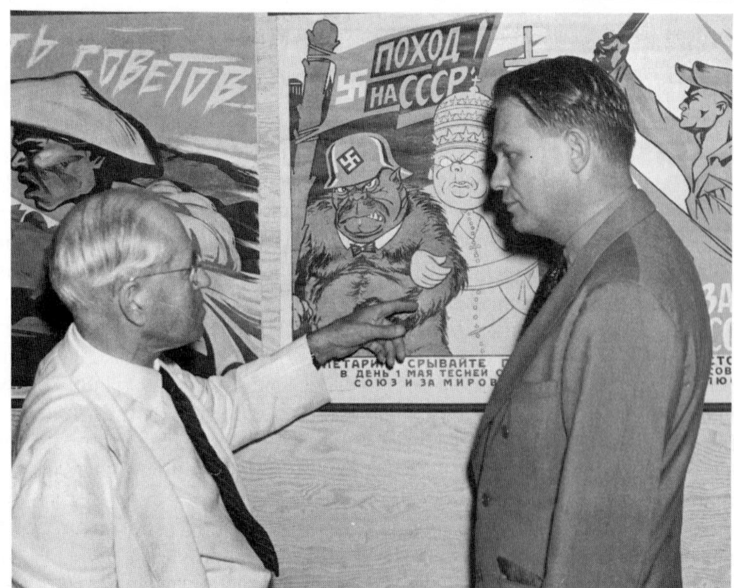

Washington, D.C., May 26. *The House Committee to Investigate Un-American Activities was established today under the chairmanship of Rep. Martin Dies (right), Democrat of Texas. Here, a labor union president shows him a Communist poster with Hitler and the Pope linked arm in arm.*

Radio Martian landing terrifies Americans

Welles broadcasts to a naive public.

New York City, Oct. 30

People were crying and praying, fleeing with bundled belongings to escape death from invading Martians intent on destroying the earth. Church services were interrupted by hysterics, traffic was jammed, communication systems clogged. All due to a one-hour CBS broadcast tonight in which Orson Welles and his Mercury Theater players let loose in Howard Koch's version of H.G. Wells's novel *War of the Worlds*. Welles says he had intended to entertain his audience with an incredible story appropriate for Halloween. But of six million listeners, more than a million were frightened by the too-realistic drama, starting with Welles's magnificent voice speaking: " ... Across an immense ethereal gulf, minds with vast intellects regarded this earth with envious eyes ... "

Dance music was interrupted by an announcer reporting gas explosions on Mars. More music, more bulletins: A flaming object, possibly a meteor, falling outside of Trenton, New Jersey. Thirty yards in diameter ... a humming sound ... something wriggling out ... "large as a bear and glistening like wet leather. Eyes ... gleaming like a serpent ... a V-shaped mouth with saliva dripping from rimless lips that seem to quiver and pulsate." Things got worse. "Poisonous black smoke ... death rays ... army wiped out ... people dropping like flies. Monstrous Martians landing all over the country ... people lying dead in the streets ... " Until the Martians themselves began to die, succumbing rapidly to disease germs ... Although there were four announcements over the hour that this was pure fiction, a tidal wave of panic swept the nation, as the rumor spread to those who did not have the radio on. At the end, Welles, now as himself, finished the make-believe ... "and if your doorbell rings and nobody's there, it was no Martian ... it's Halloween."

C.I.O. officially breaks away from A.F.L.

Pittsburgh, Penn., Nov. 18

The Committee for Industrial Organization, which has developed from an appendage of the American Federation of Labor to its chief rival in three years, has made the split official. Calling itself a Congress, the group named founder John L. Lewis as president. The C.I.O. already bans discrimination on the basis of "race, creed, color, and nationality." Radicals led by Harry Bridges tried unsuccessfully to add political beliefs to the list. Lewis, often caught defending his union against charges of communist influence, vowed privately to "lick" the leftists if they provoked a fight.

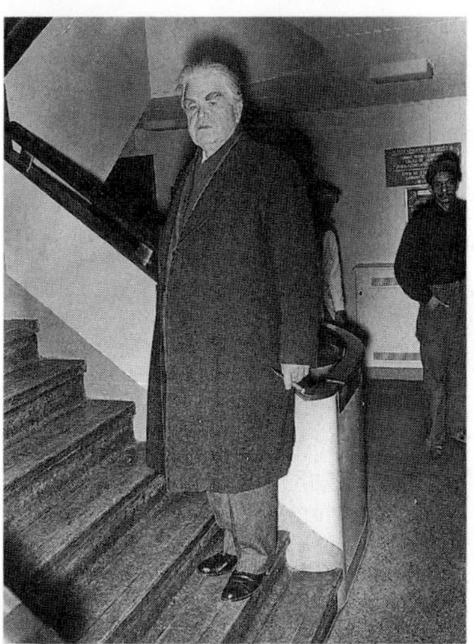

John L. Lewis, cigar in hand.

Debonair Grant and a dashing, sexy Flynn

Hollywood, California

Errol Flynn has had all kinds of real-life adventures. As a result, he has come to represent all kinds of heroes in one magnificent sexy, animal package. Currently, he and Olivia de Havilland are appearing in *The Adventures of Robin Hood*, about the socially conscious outlaw. Meanwhile, the debonair Cary Grant is showing a fine flair for screwball comedy in such vehicles as *Holiday* and *Bringing Up Baby*. The strong-minded and outspoken Katharine Hepburn sparkles in both these comedies, disproving beliefs that she is "box-office poison" and Dorothy Parker's quip that she "runs the gamut of emotions from A to B." A fine performance in *Boys' Town* with Spencer Tracy and his continuing role of cocky, wisecracking Andy Hardy, most recently in *Love Finds Andy Hardy*, are making Mickey Rooney a top juvenile star. Other top films are *Jezebel*, with Bette Davis and Henry Fonda, and Frank Capra's *You Can't Take It With You*, starring James Stewart.

'God Bless America'

United States, Nov. 11

Kate Smith, a home-spun singer if ever there was one, scored a coup on her radio show by offering a song that might well have been created with her in mind. Except that Irving Berlin wrote the tune, *God Bless America*, 20 years ago for his 1918 musical *Yip, Yip, Yaphank*. But it was withdrawn and never publicly sung until this *Kate Smith Hour*, marking the Great War's 20th Armistice Day. The words:

God bless America, land that I love.
Stand beside her, and guide her, through the night with a light from above.
From the mountains, to the prairies, to the oceans white with foam,
God bless America, my home, sweet home.
God bless America, my home, sweet home.

W.P.A. to aid music

United States, June 10

Very soon now, bands will be marching in the nation's struggle against the Depression. The Federal Music Project, one of the many arts projects of the W.P.A., will provide funds to hire more than 2,600 musicians for 38 bands and orchestras, But that's just a start – the numbers will grow. If all goes according to plan, next year should see more than 8,000 musicians performing in nearly 30 symphony orchestras, 90 small orchestras, 68 bands, 55 dance bands, 15 chamber music groups, 33 opera and choral groups and a small, special group of soloists. Governmental arts projects that are already in place include the Theater Project, which has commissioned a number of new plays, and the prolific Federal Arts Project.

Movie stars such as Cary Grant and Katharine Hepburn are part of a new breed of performers who are helping people to forget the troubles of the Depression for a few hours at a time.

Errol Flynn will always get his girl.

1939

Roosevelt

California, Jan. 7. Tom Mooney pardoned for Preparedness Day bombing in 1916.

St. Louis, Jan. 16. Major General Frank M. Andrews tells National Aeronautic Association that, with only slightly more than 400 fighter planes, United States is unprepared for war.

Madison, Wisconsin, Feb. 18. University of Wisconsin refuses a donation when donor specifies that it be used only for white students.

Washington, D.C., Feb. 27. In National Labor Relations Board v. Fansteel Metallurgical Corporation, Supreme Court rules sitdown strikes unconstitutional.

New York City, Apr. 30. President Roosevelt appears on television at New York World's Fair, becoming first President to do so.

New York City, May 1. Pulitzer Prize in fiction awarded to Marjorie Kinnan Rawlings for *The Yearling.*

New York City, June 12. King and Queen of England conclude five-day tour of United States, having bolstered Anglo-American relations.

Cincinnati, Oct. 8. New York Yankees overpower Cincinnati Reds four games to none, winning World Series for fourth year in a row.

Washington, D.C., Oct. 11. President Roosevelt receives report from Albert Einstein and other leading scientists, explaining possible military application of atomic power (→21).

New York City, Oct. 15. Mayor Fiorello La Guardia formally opens La Guardia Field, as 350,000 look on.

San Francisco, November. Gangster Al Capone paroled for good behavior, despite mental instability.

Milwaukee, Dec. 10. Green Bay Packers defeat New York Giants, 27-0, for National Football League title.

New York City. Gallup Poll indicates that 58 percent of Americans believe that United States will be drawn into war.

New York City. *The Milton Berle Show* in radio premiere.

New York City. Nathanael West's *Day of the Locust* published.

U.S. recognizes Franco Spain; Hitler takes over Czechoslovakia

Washington, D.C., Apr. 1

Nearly three months after President Roosevelt, in his annual message to Congress, warned of the threat to democracy posed by the rising tide of fascism, the United States has extended diplomatic recognition to the recently victorious Spanish government of General Francisco Franco. The move, however, is not viewed as an expression of approval of the regime, but an acceptance of the reality of the situation, along the same lines as the recognition of the Soviet government. Moreover, most observers say the Franco regime has neither the means nor the intention of spreading its brand of dictatorship beyond its own frontiers.

The same cannot be said for Nazi Germany, whose armies entered Prague three weeks ago, giving the lie to Hitler's repeated pledges that cession of the Sudetenland would satisfy German demands.

Czechoslovakia's destruction has been swift. Six months after the Munich agreement, Emil Hacha, who succeeded Eduard Benes as President of the country, was summoned to Berlin and forced to sign a treaty that in effect dismembered his country. Hitler has made himself the "Protector" of Bohemia and Moravia, and has agreed to "accept" a similar position for Slovakia. On March 15, the day the treaty was signed, German forces entered Prague, and Czechoslovakia ceased to exist. By contrast, the triumph of totalitarianism in Spain has come only after a long, bitter war. Rallying to the support of the Loyalists, volunteers came from all over the world – the Garibaldi Brigade from Italy, the Thaelmann Brigade from Germany, the Abraham Lincoln Brigade from the United States. But in the end, they were no match for Franco's regular army forces, who were also aided by warplanes and troops from Italy and Germany (→Sept. 4).

Court upholds Tennessee Valley Authority

Washington, D.C., Jan. 30

The Roosevelt New Deal, which has suffered setbacks at the hands of the Supreme Court, won a major victory today as the court upheld the constitutionality of the Tennessee Valley Authority's competition with private enterprise. The suit had been brought by the Tennessee Electric Power Company.

T.V.A. was created by Congress in 1933 during the first 100 days of the Roosevelt administration and has been under constant attack by private power sources, including a corporation headed by Wendell Willkie, a leading Wall Street attorney, who argued: "To take our market is to take our property."

In its ruling, the high court held that private utility companies have no legal right to protection from T.V.A. competition. The Tennessee authority was created by the federal government to improve the living standards in one of the nation's poorest sections, embracing seven Southern and Border states ranging from the Great Smoky Mountains to bleak hills and cotton country. By working with state and local governments, T.V.A. has promoted flood control, produced electric power and fostered the proper use of land and forests. At the outset of the project, only two of every 100 farms in the area had electric power. Many families lived on less than $100 a year. Floods often inundated farmlands, killing crops, and parts of the forests were being leveled by raging fires (→June 30).

"Storm Brewing" (1939) by Lyonel Feininger, New York-born Cubist.

D.A.R. fails to stop Marian Anderson

Miss Marian Anderson, owner of a voice that comes "once in 100 years."

Washington, D.C., Apr. 9

With the giant statue of Abraham Lincoln behind her and some 75,000 people before her, Marian Anderson sang today. The world-renowned contralto was to have appeared at Constitution Hall, but the Daughters of the American Revolution refused to allow her to perform there because she is a Negro. Subsequently, Mrs. Eleanor Roosevelt resigned her D.A.R. membership and arranged today's recital. Miss Anderson, who is 37 years old, sang with the New York Philharmonic in 1925, and in 1933 she toured Europe and South America. Conductor Arturo Toscanini once said that her kind of voice comes "once in 100 years."

$1.5 billion is voted for W.P.A. projects

Will unemployment lines ever end?

Washington, D.C., June 30

One of President Roosevelt's major New Deal agencies, the Work Projects Administration, received a congressional boost today with an allocation of $1.5 billion. Congress also voted to reduce wages and set an 18-month limit on W.P.A. jobs. The legislation has provided jobs to millions since its conception in 1935 (then called the Work Progress Administration.) Those employed have created roads, bridges, parks, post offices and even murals in public buildings. Critics contend today's allocation will speed inflation. But Roosevelt feels it is necessary to help employ the eight million Americans now out of work.

60 nations on display as FDR opens the New York World's Fair

New York City, Apr. 30

At 3:12 p.m., President Roosevelt announced that the New York World's Fair was "open to all mankind." But not all mankind is represented at *The World of Tomorrow*: The 60 nations exhibiting do not include Germany, Spain or China, and today's crowd was relatively meager. Officals said 600,000; others put the total at 150,000. Still, the throng cheered as Albert Einstein tried in a mere five minutes to explain how cosmic rays work before he hit a switch that made those rays light up the exposition.

Perhaps most striking of all the exhibits is the Trylon and Perisphere, a 700-foot triangular tower and a sphere housing Democracity, a view of life in the year 2036. Visitors ascend escalators in the Trylon, then descend to the sphere, where revolving platforms show them futuristic films. More popular, perhaps because it is free (the Trylon and Perisphere cost 25 cents), is the General Motors Futurama. Visitors on banquette cars wind through tunnels to view the autos and highways of 1960, and they watch a new three-dimensional film using polarized glasses. With huge color photos, the Kodak exhibit introduces a color film that is called Kodachrome. At the A.T.&T. building, some people win long distance calls. NBC shows off its experimental television.

"All those who come to the World's Fair," FDR said, "will find that the eyes of the United States are fixed on the future."

Washington against the Perisphere.

National Cash Register Pavilion.

The World's Fair aglow with illuminated water spouts and fireworks. The fair does more than simply display the latest of technological wonders. It presents a moment of brilliance and of hope for "The World of Tomorrow."

Dying Lou Gehrig is "luckiest man" alive

Big Lou, defying "a bad break."

New York City, July 4

There was a terrible sadness in the crowd of 61,808 fans today as Lou Gehrig, his voice echoing through Yankee Stadium, said: "I have been given a bad break, but I have an awful lot to live for; I consider myself the luckiest man on the face of the earth." Big Lou, wasting away from the fatal amyotrophic lateral sclerosis, was retiring after a 17-year career of 2,164 games. Incredibly, he appeared in 2,130 of them consecutively, a major league record. He drove in more than 100 runs in 13 of 14 seasons and had a lifetime batting average of .340.

Sub Squalus sinks

New Hampshire, May 23

Efforts have begun to rescue the 59 men aboard the submarine Squalus, which sank today in 240 feet of water off New Hampshire during a training cruise. The navy is rushing in a 10-ton rescue chamber, which can make repeated trips to the ocean floor. The chamber will be guided by divers, who have detected signs of life in the submarine's forward torpedo room. No sounds have been heard from the aft section of the submarine. Two civilian observers were aboard the sub when it failed to surface after making a routine dive.

Airliners to Europe

Lisbon, Portugal, June 28

The Pan American Airways flying boat Dixie Clipper landed here today after a flight of 23 hours and 52 minutes that inaugurated regular airline passenger service between the United States and Europe. Pan American's base in the United States is Manhasset Bay at Port Washington, Long Island. The service is the first over the Atlantic since Germany's dirigible flights were halted after the 1937 Hindenburg disaster. The Boeing Clipper, with four 750-horsepower motors, is the first plane designed specifically for transoceanic service.

U.S. neutral as war erupts in Europe

"I have seen war and I hate war ... I hope (we) will keep out of this war."

To Adolf Hitler and his Nazis, war is the supreme test of a people's will.

Washington, D.C., Sept. 4

Following Hitler's brutal and unprovoked attack on Poland three days ago, Britain and France have honored their treaty obligation to the Poles and declared war on Germany. Broadcasting from London, Prime Minister Neville Chamberlain announced: "This morning the British ambassador in Berlin handed to the German government a final note stating that unless we heard from them by 11 o'clock that they were prepared at once to withdraw their troops from Poland, a state of war would exist between us. I have to tell you now that no such undertaking has been received and that consequently this country is at war with Germany ..." Both the British and the French agreed to come to the aid of Poland in a treaty that was negotiated on March 31. Although the Soviet Union is also a guarantor of Poland, after Moscow's stunning non-aggression agreement with Nazi Germany last month, no help can be expected from that quarter. Italy's course is uncertain, although it is expected to be pro-German. Belgium has declared itself neutral.

Neutrality is also the policy of the United States. In a Fireside Chat on Labor Day, President Roosevelt told the American people: "I have said not once but many times that I have seen war and that I hate war. I say that again and again. I hope the United States will keep out of this war ... and I give you my assurance and reassurance that every effort of your government will be directed to that end" (→ Nov. 4).

Fritz Kuhn leads American Nazis

Fritz works for his Fuehrer.

New York City, Feb. 22

They sang the *Star Spangled Banner* and pledged allegiance to the American flag, but the German-Americans at a Bund rally in Madison Square Garden proclaimed a brand of patriotism foreign to most Americans. According to leader Fritz Kuhn, "The Nazi salute is the coming salute for the whole United States." He also preaches that the world Communist movement is run by Jews. His group, founded in 1932 as Friends of the New Germany, aims at spreading the Hitler theories to sympathetic German-Americans. Under Kuhn's anti-Semitic leadership, the Bund has built its own training camps, has its own uniformed storm troopers and follows the Nazi policies. Yet it isn't especially popular, with its membership probably not being much larger than the 22,000 who attended the rally.

Congress passes "cash and carry" law

Washington, D.C., Nov. 4

Congress today passed a law allowing warring nations to buy arms from the United States, if they pay in cash and carry the materiel in their own ships. This act will enable Washington to supply Britain and France with much-needed arms.

The vote is a victory for President Roosevelt, who called Congress into special session on September 21 to seek repeal of the arms embargo mandated by the Neutrality Acts of 1935-7. Roosevelt argued that the law forced the United States to give up its right to freedom of the seas. The measure passed both houses after prolonged debate. In the Senate, James F. Byrnes of South Carolina, backed by Secretary of State Cordell Hull, led the fight against isolationist Senators William Borah, Gerald Nye, Henry Cabot Lodge Jr. and Hiram Johnson. The public seems to support FDR. A Gallup Poll shows 62 percent favor American aid to France and Britain; 29 percent favor entering the war if Hitler seems on the verge of victory (→ May 10, 1940).

Presidential panel discusses atomic bomb

Washington, D.C., Oct 21

A newly appointed Advisory Committee on Uranium met here today to consider the possibility of building weapons of almost unlimited destructive power. The committee was created by President Roosevelt after he received a letter from Albert Einstein saying that "vast amounts of power" could be released by setting up nuclear chain reactions in a large mass of uranium. There are indications that German scientists already are working on such a uranium bomb, the Einstein letter warned.

The committee is headed by Lyman Briggs, director of the Bureau of Standards. Its meeting was attended by Leo Szilard, Edward Teller and Eugene Wigner, noted physicists who fled Europe to escape Nazism. Their fear that Germany would be the first to make a uranium bomb prompted Einstein to write to Roosevelt. The committee has decided to set up an expanded group to coordinate and accelerate the work being done on nuclear chain reactions by physicists at a number of American universities.

Sad Steinbeck tale: plight of the Okies

New York City

"It don't take no nerve to do sumpin' when there ain't nothin' else you can do" is the simple wisdom of the Joad family, whose travails are the subject of *The Grapes of Wrath*, John Steinbeck's new novel. For the Joads, doing something means loading their meager possessions into a $75 jalopy and leaving the Dust Bowl for California and its promise of plenty. This tale brims with real-life details of the 250,000 "Okies" who give up their farms to head out West – where nothing awaits them but the plight of the migrant laborer.

Gulping goldfish and wearing nylons

United States

What's to like about college? Extracurricular activities, that's what. You can swallow live goldfish or chew up phonograph records liberally sprinkled with salt and pepper, followed by a milk chaser. Then there are weekend dances, where you can do the boomps-a-daisy, the chestnut tree or the chicken scratch. If you're lucky, you can hear Gene Krupa beating his skins. If you're a co-ed, you might don skatarinas (bloomers and circular skirts) and nylon stockings. Back at the dorm, you can play Chinese checkers or swap some knock-knock gags – "Who's there?" "Alma mater." "Alma mater who?" "Alma mater does is nag!"

Sports on television

Brooklyn, N.Y., Aug. 26

There are only 400 sets on which to show it, but big league baseball arrived on television today. With Red Barber in the catbird seat, a ground-level camera near home plate and one in the upper deck, the first game of a Dodgers-Reds doubleheader was televised. It was put on by W2XBS, which learned some lessons by doing a May 17 baseball game between Princeton and Columbia. Bill Stern was the announcer for this first sports broadcast by NBC-TV's experimental station.

Hollywood gems: Southern melodrama and Midwestern fantasy

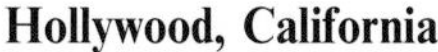

Maybe he does give a damn after all.

Hattie McDaniel gives Vivien Leigh a hand, and a little useful advice as well.

Hollywood, California

A year "of genius and glitter" has taken over Hollywood as the Depression seemed to fade away. *Gone With the Wind*, a Civil War epic with Vivien Leigh and Clark Gable, attracted more curiosity and acclaim than any other film. It had its premiere in Atlanta, of course, on December 15. And then there was that grand and glorious fantasy *The Wizard of Oz*, with a wide-eyed Judy Garland singing her way into the hearts of millions; John Ford's *Stagecoach*, which made stars of Monument Valley as well as John Wayne; the dark, gothic romance of *Wuthering Heights*; *Goodbye, Mr. Chips*, starring Robert Donat; *Dark Victory* with Bette Davis and George Brent; Jean Renoir's *Rules of the Game*; Disney's *Pinocchio*; the Frank Capra *Mr. Smith Goes to Washington*, making audiences cheer Jimmy Stewart's speech on liberty; adventure stories like *Gunga Din* with Cary Grant as a Cockney subaltern, then *Beau Geste*; sophisticated comedies such as *The Women*, *Idiot's Delight* and *Ninotchka*, in which Garbo laughs; historical dramas such as *Juarez*, *Union Pacific* and *The Story of Alexander Graham Bell*; *Intermezzo* with Ingrid Bergman; *The Cat and the Canary*, featuring Bob Hope; *Destry Rides Again*, *The Roaring Twenties*, W.C. Fields's *You Can't Cheat an Honest Man* ... the list goes on and on.

In all, 388 movies were issued this year, and the average American family spent an all-time high of $25 annually to go to see them.

McHugh, Cagney and Bogart looking for trouble in "The Roaring Twenties."

Yellow brick road. "We're off to see the wizard, the Wonderful Wizard of Oz."

Depression decade: Some sing and some dance

Hollywood enjoyed a boom during the decade. Seated on the "Shall We Dance" movie set are Fred Astaire, Ginger Rogers, and George Gershwin at piano; standing behind the famed composer is his brother, lyricist Ira Gershwin.

On a rain-soaked wharf in New York City, an unattended pushcart advertises "frankfurts" with sauerkraut or onions, ice-cold soft drinks and pies for five cents. Unfortunately, for many people, such a price for lunch is too high.

"Drummer" by Ira Becker of Federal Arts Project. Swing is the thing.

Hard times, even if you have a job. San Francisco General Strike, 1934.

A full house at the Metropolitan Opera in New York City in 1937. The sad songs heard inside do not even compare with the sadder songs on the streets.

Radio comes of age, with an average of 6.6 soap operas a day, including "Our Gal Sunday" and "Search For Tomorrow." Other popular shows are "Burns and Allen," "The Jack Benny Show," "The Shadow" and "Captain Midnight".

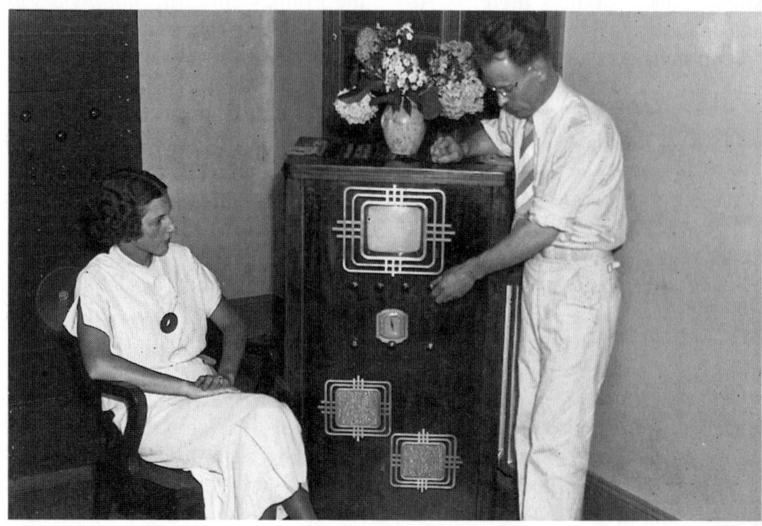

Television, the world of tomorrow. Prilo C. Farnsworth tunes in his version of the invention, which combines radio and a cathode ray tube. Others working in the new field include Vladimir Zworykin, and John L. Baird of Scotland.

Too many say, "Brother, can you spare a dime?"

"Cold drinks inside the Red Robin Cafe" by Russell Lee, a gregarious Texan.

Defying great heights and financial depths. Photograph is by Lewis Hine.

"Ask the man who owns one." Or find the man who can afford one!

Richard Rodgers and Lorenz Hart had four hit musicals in the 30s.

The soup kitchen, an all too familiar sight. Despite the best efforts of the federal government and American industry, the economy remains stagnant.

Streamlined locomotive, The Royal Blue, races into a better future. "As a result of the revolutionary changes brought about by modern methods of production," says one hopeful writer, "America may again become a new world."

The gorgeous gams of the Rockettes, who appear at the equally fabulous Radio City Music Hall. The world's largest indoor theater, with 6,000 seats, opened in New York City in 1932. Despite the lean years, Americans get their kicks.

1940

Roosevelt

Washington, D.C., Jan. 26. As 1911 trade treaty with Japan expires, United States declines to renew it.

Vermont, Jan. 31. Ida Fuller becomes first recipient of a monthly Social Security payment, receiving check number 000-00-001 for $22.54.

Washington, D.C., Feb. 26. To provide a coherent air defense plan for United States, Air Defense Command is created.

Hollywood, Feb. 29. Hattie McDaniel becomes first Negro woman to win an Oscar, for best supporting actress in *Gone With the Wind.*

Camden, New Jersey, Apr. 1. RCA laboratories demonstrate first electron microscope.

Washington, D.C., May 10. Following German invasions, President Roosevelt freezes all assets in United States of Belgium, the Netherlands and Luxembourg (→June 10).

New York City, May. Pulitzer Prizes are awarded to John Steinbeck for *Grapes of Wrath* and Carl Sandburg for *Abraham Lincoln: The War Years.*

Washington, D.C., June 28. Congress passes Alien Registration Act, requiring all foreigners to be registered and fingerprinted.

Chicago, July 4. In celebration of Emancipation Proclamation, American Negro Exposition is held.

Britain, September. American volunteer fighter pilots form Eagle Squadron in R.A.F.

Cincinnati, Oct. 8. Reds win their first World Series in 21 years, defeating Detroit Tigers, four games to three.

Washington, D.C., Dec. 8. Chicago Bears defeat Washington Redskins, by record score of 73-0, to win National Football League championship.

Hollywood, Calif. *My Little Chickadee*, starring Mae West and W.C. Fields, released.

New York City. *You Can't Go Home Again*, by Thomas Wolfe, published posthumously.

New York City. *Native Son* by Richard Wright is issued.

DEATH

Hollywood, California, Dec. 21. F. Scott Fitzgerald, novelist of "jazz age" (*Sept. 24, 1896).

Population 131.6 million; Oklahoma's off

"Manhattan Skyline" (1934) by John Cunning. Asphalt jungle on the horizon.

Washington, D.C.

The nation's population climbed to a new high of 131.6 million, and average life expectancy has reached 63 years, the 1940 census shows. Signs of progress include an illiteracy rate of only 4.2 percent, the 30 million American homes that have radios and the 33 percent of farms that now have electricity. But a bitter reminder of the dust bowl is the loss of population by hard-hit Oklahoma, down 60,000 since 1930, and by South Dakota, down 50,000. California is the new home of many former Oklahomans and Dakotans. Its population rose more than two million in the decade, to nearly 5.7 million, making it the fifth most populous state. The California climate clearly is the attraction, since Washington and Oregon experienced no such population surge.

New York is still the most populous state, with 13.5 million residents, including a large number of refugees from the war in Europe. Next in population come Pennsylvania, with 9.9 million, Illinois with 7.7 million and Texas with 6.4 million. Nevada has the lowest population, with just 110,000 residents.

Isolationists rally, urge America First

Chicago, Sept. 5

Peace or war? Which will you choose?
Should we fight for Britain?
Let's stop the rush toward war!

Those are among the slogans being voiced by the America First Committee. It is not alone. About a third of all Americans favor neutrality in the European war, and hundreds of isolationist groups are springing up this year. Most prominent are the "America Firsters," some 60,000 strong, who view President Roosevelt as a "warmonger" and his military aid to Britain as "interventionist." Their members include Charles A. Lindbergh.

Bugs Bunny debut

Hollywood, California, July 27

What's up, Doc? A new Warner Bros. Studio cartoon character, that's what! Bugs Bunny is the latest creation of cartoonist Tex Avery, whose previous characters have included Porky Pig and Daffy Duck. In the short film *A Wild Hare*, Avery comes up with another winner. According to film audiences, this rabbit's worth 24 carrots! We doubt that hunter Elmer Fudd would agree.

"Cowboy Dance" (1940), painted by Jenne Magafan for the Anson, Texas, Post Office is just one of the 1,125 murals that American artists have created in the last six years under the auspices of the Federal Arts Project.

irst U.S. helicopter shown by Sikorsky

Hartford, Conn., May 15

The first American helicopter, which can take off and land straight up and down, was shown here today by Igor Sikorsky, its Russian-born inventor. The Vought-Sikorsky VS-300 is lifted by a single rotating blade above its fuselage. Sikorsky has solved the major problem of direct-lift craft, the torque created by the rotor, by putting smaller rotors turning in opposite directions at the ends of the fuselage. Germany's Focke-Wulf FW-61 has counterrotating rotors on opposite sides of the fuselage to cancel the torque. Without some such device, the craft itself would rotate.

Batman in a book

United States, Spring

Batman, the costumed crime-fighter who made his first appearance less than a year ago in Detective Comics No. 27, has already been graduated to his own title. It is Batman Comics, and it will be drawn by Bob Kane and written by Bill Finger, who together created the character (and sidekick Robin) in response to the tremendous popularity of the first comic book hero, Superman.

State Dept. still limits Jewish entry

Washington, D.C.

Despite appeals from American Jewish organizations, the State Department has been slow to relax immigration laws that limit Jewish entry into the United States. The Johnson Act of 1924 restricts entry to 2 percent of the foreign-born of any nation. From 1933 to 1937, only 33,000 Jews were allowed into America. Now, with word reaching the United States of human rights abuses in Germany, American Jewish leaders are pressing for the admission of more refugees. But the State Department asserts it is limiting entry because the nation can't support all those who seek shelter. Recently, a ship carrying more than 900 European Jews was turned away at New York harbor.

As France falls, U.S. moves from neutrality to non-belligerency

Charlottesville, Va., June 10

In a speech at the University of Virginia that marks a shift away from a policy of strict neutrality to one of non-belligerency, President Roosevelt declared today, "We are convinced that military and naval victory for the gods of force and hate would endanger the institutions of democracy in the Western world, and that equally, therefore, the whole of our sympathies lie with those nations that are giving their life blood in combat against those forces."

Lending substance to the President's words are such recent actions as his sending to Congress a military supply measure that is to provide more than $1.3 billion to build up the armed forces, and his endorsement of an agreement with the British last week to sell large amounts of American surplus or outdated military equipment.

The latter arrangement comes in response to an urgent cable sent by British Prime Minister Winston Churchill in May. Britain desperately needs military supplies to replace the vast quantitites of ammunition, artillery, tanks and other weapons abandoned on the beaches of Dunkirk. Although the bulk of the British Expeditionary Force, 200,000 men, along with 140,000 French and Belgian troops, were evacuated over a nine-day period from May 26, few were able to bring even their weapons with them. Meanwhile, French resistance to the invasion by the Germans continues to be fragmented, half-hearted and ineffective. Although the French have an army of 800,000 combat troops as well as trained reserves of some 5,500,000, morale is quite poor and the military is short of power both in the air and on the ground.

These are areas where the German army excels. Flushed with the recent victories in Poland, Norway and the Netherlands, the invading forces are confident and bold. They have shown themselves to be masters of Blitzkrieg, literally, lightning war, where attacking forces move not at the traditional speed of the marching foot soldier but at that of motorized infantry, backed by columns of tanks and massive support in the air. And in fact, it was the dramatic attack by German General Ewald von Kleist through the supposedly impenetrable Ardennes region of forests, crags and ravines and his drive to the English Channel that very nearly annihilated the British forces.

To add to France's disastrous situation, Italy has just declared war and an army of 400,000 is starting to invade along the Riviera. Referring to these moves by the Italians in his speech today, President Roosevelt said, "The hand that held the dagger has struck it into the back of its neighbor" (→ July 20).

A sad day for Western Civilization. Nazi troops march through Paris.

Hemingway: For Whom the Bell Tolls

Havana, Cuba

From Lookout Farm, a little villa near Havana, Ernest Hemingway is enjoying the success of his new novel, *For Whom the Bell Tolls.* For the rugged author, both the moment of repose and the fact that people are buying his book in droves are unusual experiences. Hemingway is often indistinguishable from his hard-drinking, adventuresome heroes. He spent most of the Spanish Civil War reporting from the front lines and raising funds for republican Loyalists. It is not surprising then that his latest protagonist is an American volunteer in Spain engaged in a suicidal mission to blow up a bridge. Between respites in Havana, Hemingway has been covering the Japanese invasion of China.

Charlie Chaplin and Jack Oakie as the equivalents of Hitler and Mussolini in "The Great Dictator," proving comedy can be found even in tragedy.

FDR back for unprecedented 3rd term

Hyde Park, New York, Nov. 5.

President Roosevelt achieved a sweeping victory today, becoming the first man in history elected to a third term in the White House. The jubilant President, addressing a crowd outside his home here, promised to be "the same Franklin Roosevelt you have known." While he scored a decisive triumph over his Republican opponent, Wendell Willkie, carrying 38 states with 449 electoral votes, the margin was not of the landslide kind chalked up four years earlier over Alfred Landon. One reason, perhaps, was voter concern over the concept of a third term. Another may have been uneasiness over the possibility of American entry into the war now raging in Europe. FDR had less than solid support this year from organized labor, too, with John L. Lewis, president of the C.I.O., threatening to resign if Roosevelt was re-elected. But in the end, the voters signaled approval of the President's efforts to pull the nation out of the Great Depression with a monumental program of public works, relief programs, Social Security for older Americans, banking reforms, crop control and rural electrification. The Roosevelt charisma, too, was no doubt a major factor in this year's victory. While unable to walk unassisted and usually confined to a wheelchair, he has stayed close to the people by means of his Fireside Chats.

President radiates confidence as he prepares for another term.

A two-ocean navy, more planes OK'd

Washington, D.C., July 20

President Roosevelt asked for it and he got it: a powerful two-ocean navy. Congress passed a bill today to appropriate $4 billion for the building of more naval vessels for both the Atlantic and Pacific, answering the chief executive's request. Last month, funding was set aside for the construction of 50,000 fighter planes as the nation's armed services continue to stock their military arsenals. While FDR insists America has no intention of entering the European war, it is apparent he won't let the country get caught unprepared for battle (→Aug. 18).

U.S. plans defense of the hemisphere

Ogdensburg, N.Y., Aug. 18

President Roosevelt and Canadian Prime Minister Mackenzie King have agreed to establish a Permanent Joint Board of Defense to guard North America against possible attack by Germany or Japan. The move follows last month's Declaration of Havana, a mutual defense accord that was worked out by 21 members of the Pan American Union. The declaration provides for joint action to administer French, Dutch and Danish colonies and prevent them from falling under German control (→Sept. 3).

As Battle of Britain rages, U.S. agrees to provide old warships

Washington, D.C., Sept. 3

In an executive agreement made public today, the United States is to give Britain 50 over-age but still serviceable destroyers in return for 99-year, rent-free leases for naval and air bases in Newfoundland, Bermuda and six other sites ranging from the Bahamas to British Guiana. The deal, which has been widely discussed, is supported by 62 percent of the public, according to a Gallup Poll of August 17.

The destroyers, which date from World War I and are of the four-funnel class, are of no immediate use to the United States, but could prove vital to Britain in maintaining control of the seas in face of the German U-boat onslaught.

Also vital to England's survival is control of the skies, an issue that is still being fought out between the Royal Air Force and the Luftwaffe in what is becoming known as the Battle of Britain. The R.A.F. is said to have developed radar (radio detection and ranging) that can detect the position, speed and nature of enemy craft. And the R.A.F. has the advantage of fighting from home bases. Still, it is sorely outnumbered – 1,475 first-line craft against the Luftwaffe's 2,670.

The massive German air attacks, started less than a month ago by Field Marshal Hermann Goering, are aimed at exploiting the numerical edge and delivering a knockout blow to the R.A.F. If they succeed, the Germans will probably proceed to massive bombing raids on London and major industrial cities before invading across the English Channel. So far, however, the battle has not gone in Germany's favor. On the first day of the German attacks, R.A.F. pilots in Spitfires and Hurricanes downed 53 planes, and German losses since continue to be about double those of the British. In a tribute to the valor of the R.A.F., Prime Minister Churchill said in the House of Commons on August 20: "Never in the field of human conflict was so much owed by so many to so few" (→Dec. 29).

Japan is angered by oil, scrap bans

Washington, D.C., Sept. 12

Joseph C. Grew, American ambassador to Japan, said today that "further conciliatory measures" toward Japan "would be futile and unwise." The advice comes as relations between the countries continue to deteriorate. Japan has strongly protested President Roosevelt's July 25 ban on exports of oil and scrap metal, materials on which Japan is heavily dependent in its war with China. Tokyo also resents a U.S. warning against its putting pressure on the Vichy government to grant Japan further bases in the northern part of French Indochina.

Draft lottery starts; No. 158, you're in!

Washington, D.C., Oct. 29

As bands played and planes flew overhead, the nation's first peacetime military draft got under way today, with Secretary of War Henry L. Stimson drawing No.158 from a bowl of capsules. Other federal officials and members of Congress then took turns at picking numbers at random, as President Roosevelt watched. To date, 16 million Americans between the ages of 21 and 36 have registered for the draft. Those in each selective service area whose numbers correspond to those drawn today will be called up for a year's service in the army.

Roosevelt says U.S. must be "arsenal of democracy"

The formidable potential of American industry is waiting to be unleashed. "Auto Industry" by Marvin Beerbohm.

Washington, D.C., Dec. 29

As the first year of the decade comes to a close, America faces a perilous threat to its existence, President Roosevelt warned tonight in his Fireside Chat. The only way to prepare, the President said, is to provide an "arsenal of democracy" for those opposing the Axis powers.

Not since "Jamestown and Plymouth Rock has our American civilization been in such danger as now," Roosevelt declared. He vowed to send the Allies as many weapons as the United States can produce, saying no dictator would stop U.S. aid from reaching those who fight Nazi Germany. He said, "No nation can appease the Nazis. No man can tame a tiger into a kitten by stroking it." But he restated his pledge to do what he could to keep America out of the war.

Just how long American non-intervention will last is uncertain. But one thing is certain: the public wants to stay out of European conflicts. A recent poll showed that 39 percent of Americans think entering the Great War was a mistake. That sentiment holds true for this war as well.

Yet, Americans are behind the recent military buildup, approving of FDR's run around possible congressional roadblocks in exchanging 50 old-model destroyers for 99-year leases on eight British naval and air bases. The President called these "outposts of security" the most strategic addition to defense since the Louisiana Purchase. The people also agreed with November's deal to give half the nation's military production to England.

If any nation can supply the Allies with enough firepower to defeat fascism, it is America. The nation's industrial productivity now surpasses any in history. America is the leading producer of autos, radios and other high technology products, steel and other items essential for war. A shift in the focus of manufacturing, using the recent allocation of $18 million for rearmament, has transformed factories into high-intensity arms production plants. With the President setting the challenge, American industrial might will further flex its muscles, to provide the punch needed to win the war (→Jan. 6, 1941).

Everybody's kicking out to the Lindy

United States

Hey, hepcat. Get down to the malt shop. Everybody's in the groove there 'cause they just got a jukebox. It takes a nickel to spin a platter and you move to the sounds of Goodman, Shaw or Dorsey or just sit back and hear the melody of some canary. Fifty cents will get you 16 tunes. If some old long hair uses his nickel to shut off the swing, you can always find an open house. If it's Saturday night, you know there's an alligator somewhere in town that's got cats kicking out and doin' the Lindy Hop.

CBS demonstrates color TV technology

New York City, Aug 29

The press got a preview of color television today as the Columbia Broadcasting System demonstrated an apparatus invented by its chief engineer, Peter C. Goldmark. The pictures are transmitted by means of a system that uses rotating color disks placed in front of the television camera and a receiver tube to enable the audience to view the pictures in color. CBS plans to begin experimental color broadcasting soon over its New York television station, W2XAB, using a high-powered transmitter situated on top of the Chrysler Building.

Willys introduces jeep to Americans

Detroit, Michigan

A tough lightweight vehicle with the carrying power of a quarter-ton truck and the maneuverability of an auto has been introduced by the Willys Corporation. It weighs one and a quarter tons, is powered by a four-cylinder engine and has a high clearance and a four-wheel drive that allows it to operate on rough terrain. Top speed on good roads is 65 miles per hour. The army is interested in the military uses of the vehicle, which is nicknamed "jeep," from the first letters of "general purpose" and the lovable little animal in the *Popeye* cartoon.

Disney, Stokowski offer "Fantasia"

Hollywood, California

Fantasia is Walt Disney's ambitious attempt to marry animation with classical music in collaboration with conductor Leopold Stokowski. The film's "fantasound" gives a concert-hall effect. Other new and exciting films are *The Grapes of Wrath* with Henry Fonda, about the plight of the Okies, Chaplin's *The Great Dictator*, making fun of Hitler; Hitchcock's first American film, *Rebecca*, starring Joan Fontaine and Laurence Olivier, and *The Philadelphia Story* with Katharine Hepburn, James Stewart and Cary Grant.

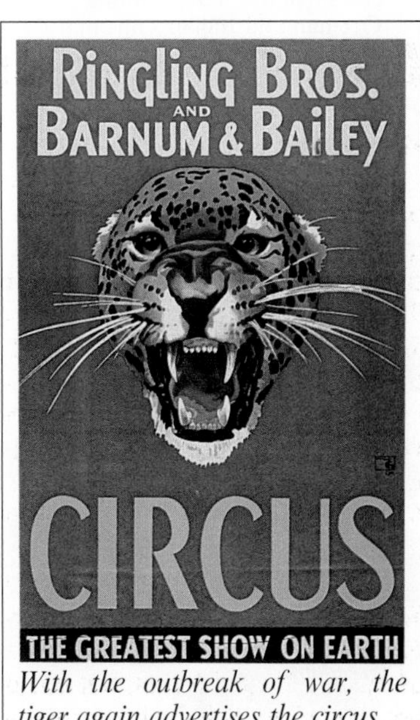

With the outbreak of war, the tiger again advertises the circus.

1941

Roosevelt

Washington, D.C., March 5. To provide for greater security of Panama Canal, Republic of Panama accepts U.S. air patrols beyond Canal Zone for duration of war.

Detroit, Apr. 18. General Motors now produces 50 percent of all American autos.

Washington, D.C., May 1. U.S. Defense Savings Bonds go on sale.

Washington, D.C., May 20. President Roosevelt moves Thanksgiving to last Thursday of November.

Washington, D.C., June 14. Roosevelt freezes all German and Italian assets in U.S.

Washington, D.C., June 16. American consulates in territories under German and Italian control ordered closed.

Washington, D.C., June 24. President Roosevelt pledges American aid to Soviet Union.

Washington, D.C., June 28. Office of Scientific Research and Development created by President Roosevelt.

Washington, D.C., July 26. All Japanese assets in United States frozen, in retaliation for Japanese occupation of French Indochina two days earlier.

New York City, Aug. 10. Dean Dixon, 26, leads New York Philharmonic, becoming first Negro to conduct a major American orchestra.

Washington, D.C., Sept. 11. President Roosevelt issues shoot-on-sight orders to naval commanders patrolling U.S. continental waters, warning German and Italian ships that they enter at their own risk.

New York City, Oct. 6. Yankees defeat Brooklyn Dodgers in World Series, four games to one.

Washington, D.C., Nov. 17. U.S. Ambassador to Japan Joseph Grew reports Japan may attempt surprise attack on some U.S. port (→ Dec. 6).

Chicago, Dec. 21. Bears defeat New York Giants, 37-9, in N.F.L. championship.

United States. Aerosol spray can is introduced.

New York City. *Let Us Now Praise Famous Men* by Walker Evans and James Agee issued.

New York City. Erich Fromm publishes *Escape from Freedom*.

Roosevelt calls for "Four Freedoms"

Washington, D.C., Jan. 6

President Roosevelt, citing what he called the "Four Freedoms," asked Congress today to approve a multimillion-dollar program of aid to the nations fighting the war against Nazi Germany. While still holding out hope that the United States would not be drawn into the war in Europe, the President called the proposed lend-lease program vital in promoting the defense of the nation.

"In the future days which we seek to make secure," the President told Congress, "we look forward to a world founded on four essential human freedoms: The first is freedom of speech and expression – everywhere in the world. The second is freedom of every person to worship God in his own way – everywhere in the world. The third is freedom from want – everywhere in the world. The fourth is freedom from fear – anywhere in the world."

As proposed by the President, the program would channel billions worth of weapons to Britain and its allies, the cost to be repaid within a reasonable time after the war in goods needed by the United States. The plan also would allow British warships to be repaired and refueled in American naval yards.

Preparing the nation for today's proposal, the President had said in a December Fireside Chat that he felt his re-election in November was a mandate for this country to become a great "arsenal of democracy." Although hopeful that America can stay out of war, he added: "If we are to be completely honest with ourselves, we must admit that there is risk in any course we take ... Never before since Jamestown and Plymouth Rock has our American civilization been in such danger ... If Great Britain goes down ... all of us ... would be living at the point of a gun."

The lend-lease proposal would permit the President to "sell, transfer title to, exchange, lease, lend or otherwise dispose of" ships, tanks, planes, guns, ammunition or other supplies to the Allied nations. FDR likened the plan to a man whose house is on fire and whose neighbor has lent him his garden hose. He warned of a "small group of selfish men who would clip the wings of the American eagle in order to feather their own nests" (→ March 27).

Mount Rushmore Memorial, a monument to American freedom

Mount Rushmore, S.D., Nov. 1

The faces of Washington, Jefferson, Theodore Roosevelt and Lincoln can look over the Black Hills unencumbered by scaffolding and laborers now that drilling is completed on America's latest monument, Mount Rushmore. Although workers were exhorted to "Rush More," the project was not finished before the death of its designer, John Gutzon de la Mothe Borglum, on March 6. Sculptor Borglum accepted the commission in 1925 while on the run from the state of Georgia and a memorial project he abandoned there. The Rushmore venture was not without problems. The reasons for honoring Washington, Lincoln, and Jefferson were obvious, but the choice of Roosevelt caused debate. TR's two years as a cowboy in the Dakota Territory led to his eventual acceptance.

Four faces from the past that helped shape the fortunes of the United States.

Funding was a constant struggle. The state of South Dakota spent only $2 million, and most of that on roads. Charles E. Rushmore, the New York lawyer for whom the mountain was named, gave $5,000, the largest individual contribution. Borglum also had difficulties with contemporary Presidents. Calvin Coolidge summered a few miles from the mountain and dedicated the first drilling. But he was angered when Borglum edited a historical text he had written to accompany the monument. From 1931 to 1938, construction proceeded during the drought and windstorms that raised clouds of black dust. In terms of manpower, the project was more fortunate: None of the 360 laborers was permanently injured or killed. Yet the granite proved a difficult medium (90 percent was removed with dynamite) and the drilling moved slowly as Borglum aged. In 1938, at 71, he named his son Lincoln to finish the project.

National art gallery opens in the capital

Washington, D.C., March 17

Thanks to the generosity of the late industrialist, banker and former Treasury Secretary Andrew W. Mellon, the United States can claim a federally owned collection of the highest quality art now that the National Gallery of Art has opened in Washington. Funds for the vast marble structure were provided by Mellon to house a collection to be built around the exceptional group of works he assembled over a lifetime. Highlights include paintings by Raphael, Van Eyck, Velazquez and Titian. Mellon's foresight and beneficence are especially remarkable in light of his lengthy tax battle with the federal government, which was resolved in his favor only after he died in 1937.

Watch on the Rhine

New York City, Apr. 1

Lillian Hellman has made no secret of her opinions, and her new drama may be her most forthright yet. She tackled homosexuality (*The Children's Hour*, 1934) and greed (*The Little Foxes*, 1939). Now she levels her sightsd on Nazism in *Watch on the Rhine*, which opened on Broadway tonight. The German anti-fascist hero is married to a rich American who joins him in the fight against Hitler. [The play won this year's Drama Critics' Circle Award for the best Broadway play, a first for Hellman.]

European allies to get lend-lease aid

Washington, D.C. March 27

The lend-lease bill, which President Roosevelt signed into law on March 12, has now been backed with an appropriation of $7 billion, most of which is expected to go to support a beleaguered Britain.

The program, which the President has compared to lending a hose to a neighbor whose house is on fire, with the understanding that the hose will eventually be returned, allows Roosevelt to lend or lease war material to "the government of any country whose defense the President deems vital for the defense of the United States." FDR has virtually complete discretion in administering the program.

Lend-lease will, in effect, put American industrial might at the disposition of those countries that are actually fighting the Axis powers, while it skirts the question of how such supplies are to be paid for. The financial reserves of Great Britain have disappeared almost entirely, and no one wants to see a repetition of the invidious war-debts issue that came up during the Great War and following it.

Rows of bombers await completion, and the opportunity to defend democracy.

To its critics, however, the program will go beyond making the United States the "arsenal of democracy" and inevitably is going to drag the country into the war itself. In the words of one isolationist Senator, Burton K. Wheeler, the bill is going to "plow under every fourth American boy." In contrast, Winston Churchill called it "an inspiring act of faith" and "a monument of generous and far-reaching statesmanship" (→ June 24).

Nation's auto makers cut production by 20% to aid war effort

Detroit, Mich., Apr. 17

America's automobile industry will shift gears beginning August 1, industry spokesmen reported yesterday. The major companies have agreed to slash production of civilian vehicles by one million units, or 20 percent, to redirect resources toward the war effort. And today, General Motors, supplier of 50 percent of American autos, announced it would make no changes in passenger-car models this year to focus on defense needs. The auto industry has churned out vehicles at an astounding rate since America was last at war. In 1916, there were 3.5 million autos in the nation. Last year, there were more than 31 million. Observers of American production are now able to see industry work like never before as it begins providing for the lend-lease program enacted last month.

Ford finally yields, signs pact with U.A.W.

Dearborn, Michigan, Apr. 11

Henry Ford, anti-union guardian of one of labor's last frontiers in the auto industry, opened his doors to the United Auto Workers today. Work on $158.7 million in defense contracts, he was happy to report, will continue. Ford's River Rouge plant has been shut tight since April 1, when plant managers fired three U.A.W. spokesmen just two months after a Supreme Court rebuke for discriminating against union members. Pickets blocked the 14 routes into the plant. And when a battle with Negro strikebreakers left about 200 injured, Ford gave up all attempts to open the plant.

The world's biggest industrial unit with 85,000 workers, River Rouge is the hand that feeds the Ford empire. Without its supply of parts, 34 plants closed in two days. Back orders piled up. The government warned that defense output was languishing at 13 percent of its projected level. So when Governor Murray Van Wagoner met Ford two days ago, the 77-year-old industrial wizard was resigned. All strikers will retain their jobs; grievance procedures will be restored and a federal board will mediate wage talks pending union elections.

400,000 striking miners get $1 more

Harlan County, Ky., Apr. 28

Some 400,000 miners will descend into the shafts tomorrow with the promise of a $1 raise. For the Northern miners, this means $7 a day. Despite the efforts of Dr. John R. Steelman, the Labor Department's crack negotiator, Southern operators are sticking by their 40-cent wage differential. The month-old strike, which tied up 85 percent of soft coal production, ends as shortages threatened defense output. Five graves dug after a gunfight in "bloody Harlan" County, a scene of violence in the 1930s, are a part of the walkout's legacy.

"The Miner" (1925) by George Luks. ▷

Freighter sunk; emergency declared

Washington, D.C., May 27

The tenuous neutrality between the United States and Germany in the Atlantic has been dealt a severe blow with the sinking of the Robin Moore by the German U-boat U-69. President Roosevelt is furious because he sees it as another in a series of unpreventable events that will force the United States into war regardless of how hard his government tries to avert it. The President's reaction to the sinking was quick and vehement. In a message to Congress, he proclaimed an unlimited national emergency and he spoke of the incident as an example of "the acts of an international outlaw." He also accused Germany of a "policy of frightfulness and intimidation," of "conquest based on lawlessness and terror on land and piracy on the sea."

The incident would never have happened if the U-boat captain, Just Metzler, had been obeying orders. Hitler does not want to provoke the Americans and he had therefore instructed his submarine chief, Admiral Karl Doenitz, to steer clear of American shipping at all costs. Nevertheless, the U-boat captain stopped the American vessel and had an officer sent on board to carry out a search. The inspecting officer came upon plane parts. Metzler then instructed the American crewmen to take to their lifeboats and ordered a torpedo fired into the freighter (→June 14).

FDR mandates an end to discrimination

Roosevelt's opposition to discrimination is vital to its eventual eradication.

Washington, D.C., June 25

Seeking to head off a threatened march on Washington by disgruntled Negroes, President Roosevelt today mandated an end to discrimination in defense contracts and government employment. He did so by issuing an executive order establishing the Fair Employment Practices Commission, which is authorized to investigate complaints of discrimination based on race, color, creed or national origin. The President acted at the urging of his wife, Eleanor, and of Negro civil rights leaders. A. Philip Randolph, president of the Brotherhood of Pullman Car Porters, had planned to lead a march on Washington to protest widespread discrimination against the hiring of Negroes by defense industries that are under government contracts to produce arms and other supplies for Britain and other European allies in the war against Germany. The committee, an independent body within the executive office of the President, will have the authority to study complaints, hold hearings and act to end discrimination in hiring and promotion. The panel also is authorized to order training programs for those seeking jobs in defense industries. If employers fail to comply with panel rulings, they will be subject to being cut off from all government defense contracts.

Yankee Clipper hits in 56 games in row

Cleveland, Ohio, July 17

It had to happen sometime. Joe DiMaggio's record streak of hitting safely in consecutive games was halted at 56 tonight by the Cleveland Indians before a record crowd of 67,468. "Jolting Joe," who was last held hitless two months ago, bounced into a double play with the bases loaded in the eighth, his last time at bat, but the Yankees pulled out a 4-3 victory. DiMag's streak was nipped by pitchers Al Smith and Jim Bagby.

Whirlaway is fifth Triple Crown victor

New York City, June

Whirlaway was a strong-willed, fractious animal, and people said that if someone could curb his temperament, the horse could win the Kentucky Derby. So trainer Ben Jones did just that and Whirlaway, with Eddie Arcaro aboard, won not only the Derby but the Preakness and Belmont as well to become the fifth Triple Crown winner. Whirlaway tended to run on the outside rail. Jones put a one-eyed blinker on him and the problem was solved.

"Palmerton, P.A., 1941" by Franz Kline, master of Abstract Expressionism.

CBS challenges NBC on commercial TV

New York City, July 1

Commercial television broadcasting has begun here, with NBC and CBS offering competing services. NBC was first in the field, starting with broadcasts of the opening ceremonies of the New York World's Fair two years ago. It was given its license for regular operation of station W2XBS from the Federal Communications Commission today. The license calls for four hours of broadcasting a week, but NBC says it will be on the air at least 15 hours. CBS quickly matched its rival with its own telecasts. Only a few households are equipped with sets to pick up the broadcasts.

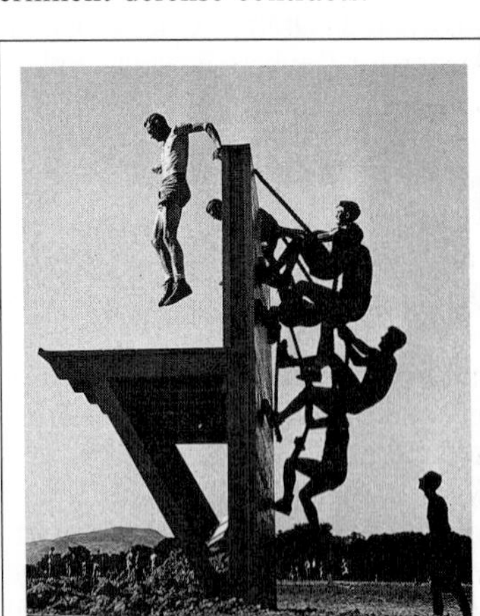

Navy pilot trainees master the quarter-mile obstacle course at pre-flight school. Although not in a state of war, the United States prepares for what may be the inevitable. The barriers of neutrality are very rapidly slipping away.

FDR and Churchill draft Atlantic Charter

Newfoundland, Aug. 12

A declaration of principles for which the war is being fought has been drawn up by President Roosevelt and Prime Minister Churchill after their secret meetings aboard the American cruiser Augusta and the British battleship Prince of Wales anchored here in Placentia Bay. The document, named the Atlantic Charter, sets forth "certain common principles" on which the two leaders "base their hopes for a better future for the world."

Among these principles are "the right of all peoples to choose the form of government under which they will live" and the outlawing of "territorial changes that do not accord with the freely expressed wishes of the peoples concerned." Also included are free international trade, full economic collaboration between all nations, freedom of the seas and "final destruction of Nazi tyranny" and a peace that will provide "freedom from fear and want."

Finally, the charter expresses the belief that "all the nations of the world, for realistic as well as spiritual reasons, must come to the abandonment of the use of force."

The charter is not an alliance or a treaty. Its significance lies in the fact that the United States of America, which is still technically neutral, has joined a belligerent nation in a statement of war aims (→ Dec. 22).

Germans sink more American vessels

Washington, D.C., Nov. 17

Relations between the United States and Germany are deteriorating by the day and the events in the Atlantic that resulted in Congress's amending the Neutrality Act seem to be propelling the country at an ever-quickening pace toward war.

October 17 saw the first American casualties in the war. Convoy SC-48 was 400 miles south of Iceland when it was attacked by a German wolf pack. Several ships were sunk. The warship Kearny took one torpedo through its bilge on that day, killing 11 men and wounding many. It remained afloat and made it to Iceland escorted by the Greer, which eluded German U-boats a month before. In response to the killings, Roosevelt told a huge audience at Washington's Mayflower Hotel, "We have wished to avoid shooting, but the shooting has started. And history has recorded who fired the first shot." Almost immediately, more Americans fell victim to the Germans. On October 31, the destroyer Reuben James, steaming 600 miles west of Ireland, took a torpedo in its port side. Of the ship's company of 160 men, only 45 were saved. All of the officers aboard were killed.

Following these events, Congress acted, on November 13, by amending the Neutrality Act, which permits the arming of all American merchantmen as well as granting them free passage to the war zones.

While Welles searches for Rosebud, Bogey hunts the Falcon

Hollywood, California

Citizen Kane marks the Hollywood debut of Orson Welles – as producer, imaginative director, co-writer and dynamic star. Its thinly disguised portrait of press tycoon William Randolph Hearst has provoked a boycott of RKO releases in the Hearst papers. But the rest of the world whispers "Rosebud," Kane's last word before his death, which prompts a reporter to try to unravel the meaning of the word. The world also hails the 26-year-old Welles as a genius. Another new director, John Huston, has guided Humphrey Bogart in a brilliant tour de force as private eye Sam Spade in *The Maltese Falcon*. Devastatingly charming Cary Grant ("I play myself to perfection") shines with Joan Fontaine in Hitchcock's *Suspicion*, while tall, handsome and laconic Gary Cooper draws audiences as the popular hero of the Great War in *Sergeant York*, which also stars Walter Brennan. *Dumbo*, about the elephant who could fly, is the year's offering from Disney and the two-faced *Dr. Jekyll and Mr. Hyde* leads his third screen life, this time with Spencer Tracy playing the title role and co-starring radiant Swedish-born Ingrid Bergman. Master director John Ford has turned his camera toward the miners of Wales in *How Green Was My Valley*, a compassionate movie about suffering and the brotherhood of man.

The treacherous Nazis are no match for the wit and cunning of Sam Spade.

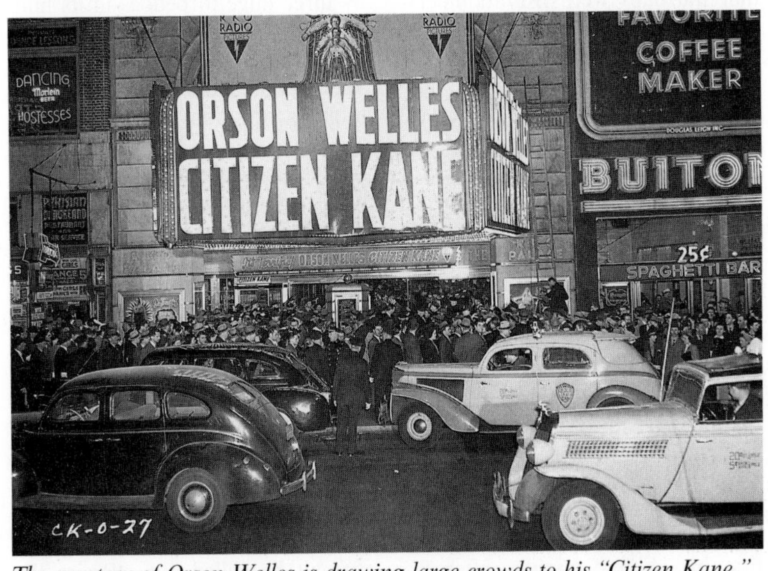

The mastery of Orson Welles is drawing large crowds to his "Citizen Kane."

Roosevelt appeals to Japan for peace

Washington, D.C., Dec. 6

Negotiations over the situation in the Far East appear to have reached an impasse and war in the Pacific seems not just possible but likely. Since October, President Roosevelt has contemplated writing directly to Emperor Hirohito, and today he instructed Ambassador Joseph Grew in Tokyo to deliver the letter he wrote earlier in the week.

This unprecedented personal appeal to the Emperor is a reflection of the extreme gravity of the situation. Diplomatic tensions between Japan and the United States have steadily worsened since Washington began an embargo of oil and rice to Japan and since the July freeze of all Japanese assets in the United States. In mid-October, Fuminaro Konoye and his Cabinet fell and were replaced by General Hideki Tojo, Konoye's war minister, and a Cabinet studded with military leaders. Since then, Ambassador Grew and Secretary of State Cordell Hull have failed to reach a modus vivendi with the Japanese.

Washington has demanded that Japan cease its military adventures in the Pacific. Meanwhile, Japan has been charging encirclement by the ABCD powers (American, British, Chinese, Dutch) a charge not unlike the encirclement accusations that have been made by Adolf Hitler in Europe (→ 7).

Japanese launch surprise attack on Pearl Harbor

As the warship Shaw is shattered, so too is the nation's complacency. The United States of America has been stung, and it is unlikely to forget Pearl Harbor.

Pearl Harbor, Hawaii, Dec. 7

"AIR RAID! PEARL HARBOR! THIS IS NO DRILL!"

Those words, broadcast at 7:58 on this peaceful Sunday morning by Admiral Patrick N.L. Bellinger, shattered the complacency of the United States military. By 8 a.m., two battleships had been dealt fatal blows and hundreds of American sailors had been killed. The Japanese Empire, using aircraft carriers within 300 miles of Pearl Harbor, launched wave after wave of torpedo bombers, dive bombers and fighters against soldiers, sailors and airmen who had just started into their Sunday morning routines. The surprise element was stunning. One radar operator got some blips indicating a massive movement of planes. He looked more closely, thought the radar was wrong or that the blips were B-17 bombers being shifted from Wake Island to Pearl Harbor and did nothing.

The first wave of Japanese aircraft, consisting of 49 high-level bombers, 51 dive bombers and 51 fighters, sighted the Oahu coastline at about 7:40 a.m. They deployed for Wheeler Field, Hickam Field and Battleship Row, which consisted of massive quays where 26 destroyers, five cruisers and eight battleships were moored. Most of the officers and men of the battleship Arizona were aboard when the first bombs and torpedoes began to rip it apart. Of its crew of 1,400, 1,103 men were killed. The Oklahoma, a 1916 dreadnought, was the next to last in line and probably the first hit. A few minutes after 8, it rolled completely over, destroyed by three huge torpedoes in its hull. Next in line were the battlewagons Tennessee and West Virginia. The West Virginia, outboard of the pair, took six or seven torpedoes, but it was saved from the Oklahoma's fate by an exceptionally alert and well-trained crew. By the time the sailors discovered what was happening, it was almost too late, but hundreds of men were brought topside and saved.

On other ships, long lines of ammunition handlers were organized to feed the guns, which began to fire back at the swarming Japanese Zeros. On the cruiser New Orleans, Chaplain Howell Fogey, a "sky pilot," was among the ammunition passers. When a Japanese plane was hit he called out, "Praise the Lord and pass the ammunition!"

Battleship Row tapered off at either end. The California was southernmost and the least prepared for war. It was considered completely unprepared for an admiral's inspection. Its magazine was hit and it rapidly settled into the mud.

Within two hours, the navy lost 2,000 men killed and 710 wounded, while the army and marines lost 327 killed and 433 wounded. Also killed were 70 civilians, mostly airfield workers, as were a few Honolulu residents.

By 9:45 a.m., the Japanese aircraft had returned to their carriers. But 29 did not make it back, which is a remarkable loss figure considering how completely the Americans had been surprised (→Jan. 26, 1942).

America declares war

Vashington, D.C., Dec. 11
Declaring Sunday, December 7, a date which will live in infamy," resident Roosevelt, on Monday, sked Congress to declare war on apan. Congress hastened to comly and war was declared six and ne-half minutes later. The Senate ote was unanimous. In the House f Representatives, there was one issenting vote, that of Representaive Jeannette Rankin of Montana, vho also voted against American ntry into the Great War.

Germany and Italy, in keeping vith the terms of their Tripartite 'act, declared war on the United tates today. And President Rooseelt has asked Congress to recogize that a state of war now exists.

The fact of war has come upon Americans with a bewildering suddenness, and the mood in the country is uneasy. In Washington's Tidal Basin, one overzealous patriot chopped down four Japanese cherry trees before he was arrested. Around the White House, crowds five deep pressed against the fence railings, hour after hour. On Monday, the America First Committee hastily called a membership meeting and disbanded, calling on all Americans to back the war effort.

The great white light that burned over the White House driveway is out now. One of the President's speech writers mentioned this to a colleague; "I wonder how long it will be before that light gets turned on again?" His friend answered, "I don't know, but until it does, the lights will stay turned off all over the world."

Britain, U.S. meet to map war strategy

Vashington, D.C., Dec. 22
Prime Minister Churchill and is military commanders met Presdent Roosevelt and his generals and admirals for the first time today in order to hammer out a strategy for the long-range conduct of the war. The Arcadia Conference is an idyllic sounding name for a parley of rancorous debate and some confusion, but that is to be expected in a situation as complex as this one. After stormy discussions and major disagreements, a degree of organization was achieved. Field Marshal Archibald Wavell, now in India, has been appointed commander-in-chief of all American, British, Dutch and Australian units in the Southwest Pacific. In addition to this so-called ABDA command, an outline for a combined British-American chiefs of staff organization was set down. The Arcadia conference is regarded by most participants as the beginning of sorting out one another's motives and objectives (→Jan. 1, 1942).

Japanese military overruns Pacific islands

Manila, Philippines, Dec. 26
The Japanese, following up on their surprise attack at Pearl Harbor, have continued to astonish the world with successful assaults all across the Western Pacific. In the early hours of December 8, Japanese naval and air forces struck almost simultaneously at Kota Bharu in British Malaya, Singora in Thailand, Guam, Hong Kong, Wake Island and the Philippines.

The blows from sea and air were immediately followed by land invasions, which were virtually unopposed. Many of the briefly trained Filipino "divisions" simply melted into the jungle when faced with the tough and disciplined veteran Japanese military units.

Elsewhere in the Pacific, British and American forces are beginning to fight back. In Kunming, China, a squadron of Colonel Claire Chennault's American volunteer group, the "Flying Tigers," shot down six Japanese raiders with no losses, and a combined force of Flying Tigers and the Royal Air Force in Rangoon, Burma, shot down several Japanese planes.

After successful Japanese landings at Luzon, Mindanao and Lingayen Gulf, American forces in the Philippines have retreated to the Bataan peninsula and to Corregidor, a tiny island at the entrance to Manila Bay (→Feb. 28, 1942).

"A date which will live in infamy"

Clouds of black smoke replace the Japanese Zeros that have returned to their carriers in triumph. Americans are reacting with shock and anger.

The twisted hulk of the warship Arizona rests on the bottom of Pearl Harbor. It is one of 18 ships that have been destroyed by the Japanese attack.

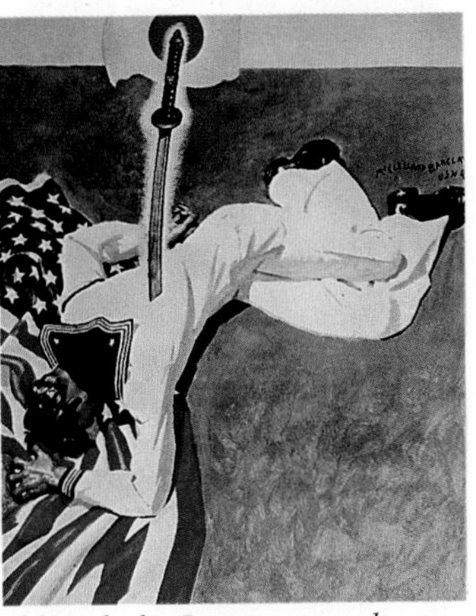

Although the Japanese attack was a military success, it has stirred a hatred that demands revenge.

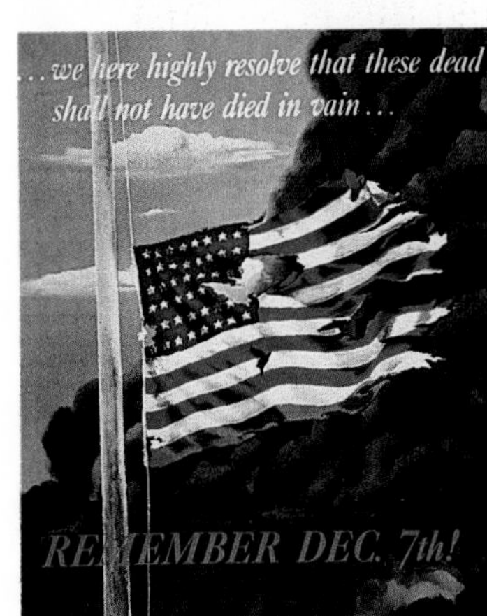

The loss of 2,397 Americans in the assault has aroused a nation that had shown no taste for war.

1942

Roosevelt

Washington, D.C., Jan. 1. Office of Production Management bans sales of new autos and trucks.

Washington, D.C., Jan. 1. United States joins 25 nations in signing Declaration of United Nations, binding them to uphold Atlantic Charter, work toward defeat of Axis and make no separate peace with enemy countries (→ June 24).

Washington, D.C., Jan. 26. Government commission finds General Walter C. Short and Admiral Husband E. Kimmel to have been derelict in their duties before and during bombing of Pearl Harbor.

Washington, D.C., Jan. 28. Office of Civilian Defense started to organize civilian assistance in national defense.

Washington, D.C., June 13. Office of War Information created to unify government's information activities.

Washington, D.C., June 17. Army-sponsored magazine *Yank* begins publication.

Chicago, June. Interracial group dedicated to non-violent action forms Congress of Racial Equality.

Florida, Aug. 8. After being put ashore by a submarine on June 17, four Germans are caught and executed as spies.

New York City, Oct. 5. St. Louis Cardinals beat New York Yankees, four games to one, to win World Series.

Washington, D.C., Oct. 7. On conclusion of war, it is decided that President Roosevelt will help establish a United Nations commission to investigate war crimes (→ March 21, 1944).

Washington, D.C., Oct. 9. United States and Britain announce renunciation of their extraterritorial rights in China.

Washington, D.C., Nov. 11. As U.S. troops invade French North Africa, President Roosevelt says, "We come among you to repulse the cruel invaders ... Vive La France eternelle" (→).

Boston, Nov. 28. Fire at Coconut Grove nightclub kills 487 people.

Washington, D.C., Dec. 4. Work Progress Administration terminated by Roosevelt.

Washington, D.C., Dec. 13. Redskins defeat Chicago Bears, 14-6, in N.F.L. championship.

Battle of Java Sea in South Pacific

Java Sea, Feb. 28

Although the United States has begun to hit back in the Pacific, the Japanese are still winning. Their latest victory was completed today in the Battle of the Java Sea. An incredibly confused tangle of ships maneuvering in the dark, the battle resulted in the loss of five Allied vessels while the Japanese suffered only one destroyer damaged.

Early in the year, the Allies put together a hastily conceived chain of command in the Pacific that was called Abdacom, which stood for American-British-Dutch-Australian Command. It was supposed to be a "Malay Barrier" to halt the Japanese octopus from spreading its tentacles into Java, Borneo and down the Malayan peninsula toward Singapore. But the "Malay Barrier" proved a myth and the Japanese hit the command area in coordinated attacks by carrier groups. Because of Japanese air superiority, the ABDA task force, under Dutch Admiral K.W.F.M. Doorman, could operate only at night. On February 4, he took four cruisers out of Surabaya in Java for a strike at Balikpapan. Japanese planes hit them and severely damaged the American warship Marblehead. Next, Doorman tried to prevent the Japanese from reaching Palembang, the great oil refinery on Sumatra. But Japanese planes did so much damage to his fleet he had to call off the attack. At this point, Doorman was replaced by Dutch Admiral Conrad Helfrich, who decided on a last-ditch battle to stop the Japanese advance. He gathered up all the rag-tag ABDA forces that he could find and set out for a fight. The result was the Battle of Java Sea.

American fighter plane sweeps by as Japanese stores are hit on Wake Island.

The Japanese, enjoying tactical control over the battle from its beginning, first hit the British cruiser Exeter. Four American destroyers used all their torpedoes defending it, but the British ship was badly damaged and had to leave the battle. Things only got worse for the Allies. Two Dutch cruisers, the Java and de Ruyter, were pounded by Japanese cruisers with full broadsides. De Ruyter, Helfrich's flagship, began to sink and the admiral ordered the American ship Houston and the Australian Perth to run. The Allies realized that the Malay Barrier had become a trap but it was too late. The Allied ships temporarily escaped into darkness but on the following day, the Exeter was sunk, leaving only the Perth and Houston, which then encountered a Japanese transport force. They waded into the enemy, but soon three Japanese cruisers and 10 destroyers showed up. The Perth took several torpedo hits and went down. The Houston fought until it was dead in the water and wouldn't respond to the wheel. The American vessel just lay there until the Japanese blew it to bits (→ Apr. 9).

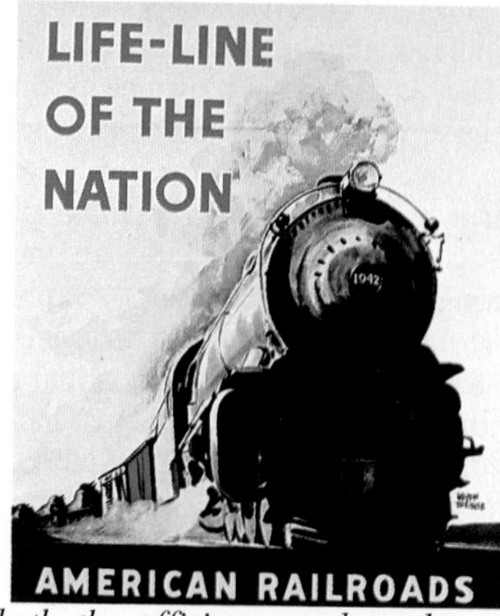

The speed with which the United States is mobilizing for war testifies to both the efficiency and resolve of the American people. Recruiting stations across the land are flooded with men, young and old, eager to sign up; the life plans of millions of families are being put on hold as sons and fathers become soldiers and leave for Europe and the Pacific. Americans have made a commitment and now they are uniting in the common cause.

Santa Barbara hit by Japanese sub

Santa Barbara, Calif., Feb. 23

A Japanese submarine shelled a Richfield Oil Company refinery at nearby Elmwood Field yesterday in the first such attack on the mainland. Most of the shells whistled harmlessly past derricks and tanks. The only damage: $500 worth of shattered wood on a pump-house roof. Southern California defense officals had rushed into action. Sirens wailed, broadcasts were halted and 30 miles of coast were blacked out. Tokyo hailed the sub's commander, Kizo Nishino, but oil officials think the raid was a personal vendetta. A few years ago, Nishino, then a tanker captain, fell on a cactus plant here, amusing the workers. The captain was heard to vow he would avenge his humiliation.

"G.I. Joe" reads Stars and Stripes

London, Apr. 17

Wherever American servicemen can be found, the newspaper *Stars and Stripes* is likely to be found as well. But most copies perform their duty in Europe, thanks to publication offices there and because the troops in the Pacific are scattered over dozens of islands. Today *Stars and Stripes* made a special contribution to the war effort by using the name "G.I. Joe." It's a term for the ordinary soldier – from Brooklyn or Boise – who bears the brunt of the fighting with no officer's clusters or bars, just a pair of dogtags and a snapshot of his girl or the family (→ June 17).

Sugar, gas rationed

Washington, D.C., May 14

The American people will start to feel the war in earnest and at home this month as many of the country's 131,669,275 inhabitants line up at schools to receive their War Ration Book No. 1, limiting each of them to one pound of sugar every two weeks. And today, some of the nation's 10 million motorists will also receive ration books. Gasoline limits of 25 to 30 gallons per motorist per month are expected.

American forces surrender on Bataan

Bataan, Philippines, Apr. 9

Quiet and modest Major General Edward P. King Jr., commander of the Luzon force under General Douglas MacArthur, has surrendered his army of 76,000 exhausted men to the Japanese. It is the greatest defeat for the American military to date. Since January, General King's mixed force of American soldiers, sailors, marines, civilians and Filipinos of all sorts had held out against an overwhelming force of Japanese under the command of Lieutenant General Homma Masahura. When King sent a flag of truce to the Japanese commander early today, he said that he felt like Lee at Appomattox. The comparison is an accurate one in that there remained only a single half ration of food in the quartermaster stores. Constant Japanese shelling, dwindling water supplies, heat and jungle humidity, and primitive or nonexistent medical supplies all had taken their toll.

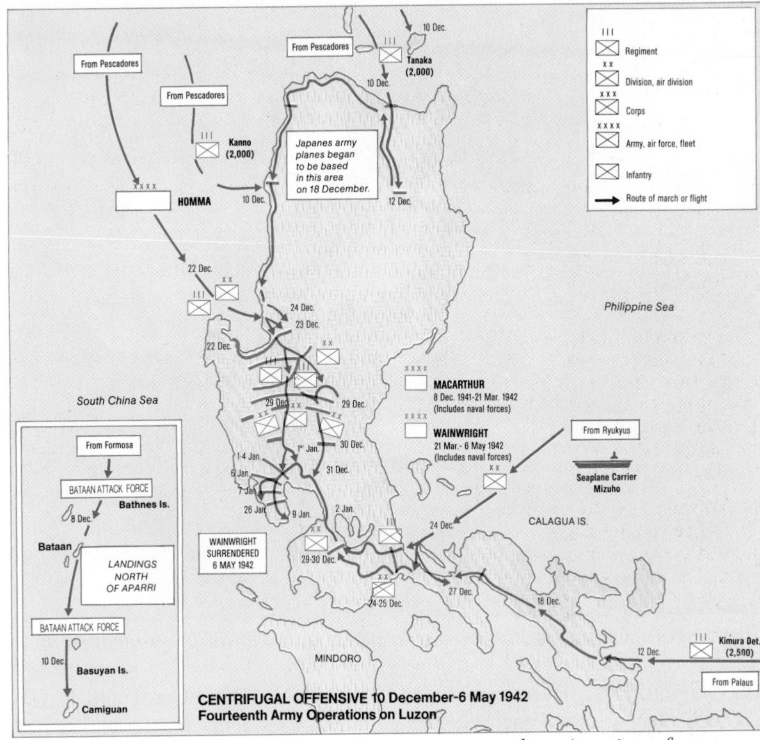

The speed of the invasion leaves little time to strengthen American forces.

The battle for the Bataan peninsula began for the defending Americans and Filipinos with the fall of Manila to the Japanese on January 2. Bataan lies due west of Manila and juts into Manila Bay. South of Bataan lies the two-square-mile island of Corregidor, shaped like a tadpole, where MacArthur's remaining troops are still holding out in the island fortress that is known as "The Rock."

While MacArthur was still on Bataan, a "main battle position" was drawn across the peninsula on a line that bisects Mount Natib. Below this position another battle line, a "reserve battle position," was created. The men of MacArthur and King have fought gallantly to maintain these defensive positions, giving ground slowly to the Japanese, who have been able to push the Americans back because they are willing to make sacrifices in battle. Upon his departure to Australia in March, General MacArthur vowed, "I shall return."

The defenders had many other things to worry about in addition to the fierce firefights on the jungle floor. At the beginning of the prolonged defensive battle, there was only enough food for a period ranging from 20 to 50 days, depending on how much the planners estimated each of the men would need to survive. In the end, the soldiers were fighting on about 2,000 calories a day – not nearly enough for troops who are waging a brutal war under terrible climatic conditions. The water was inadequate and, to make matters worse, the Japanese began to bomb and shell the peninsula from an assortment of positions that completely surround the defending Americans.

One officer put the situation this way: "Each day's combat, each day's output of physical energy, took its toll on the human body – a toll which could not be repaired . . . " He added that when this fact is understood, the story of Bataan is told. Despite the communiques that have been issued by General MacArthur's headquarters and the exaggerated press reports that somehow get back to America, there have been no great battles on Bataan (→ May 6).

Americans die on Bataan "death march"

The Philippines, June

After the fall of Bataan and Corregidor, the Japanese held 76,000 American and Filipino prisoners. They had expected only 25,000 captives and were short of provisions. This was bad enough but, since a Japanese warrior is expected to die rather than surrender, they had no respect for their prisoners. A captive was undeserving of honor or respect so the road to the P.O.W. camps became lined with American corpses that had been bayonetted, shot or beheaded. Some 3,000 to 10,000 men died this way while others succumbed to exhaustion, dysentery or malnutrition.

American prisoners on Bataan.

Japanese-Americans are imprisoned

Japanese-Americans, victims of war hysteria, arrive at an internment camp.

Washington, D.C., December

Swept by a post-Pearl Harbor hysteria that portrays every ethnic Japanese as a potential saboteur, the government has taken a step without precedent in American history: it has interned behind barbed wire 110,000 of its citizens, more than two-thirds born in the United States.

At the urging of politicians and the army to remove the large Japanese-American population settled on the West Coast and in Hawaii, President Roosevelt signed Executive Order 9066 on February 19 authorizing the War Department to remove "all persons" from designated military areas. Congress has made it a federal offense to defy the army and established the War Relocation Authority to oversee the transfer.

From March through May, all Japanese Americans, including persons with as little as one-sixteenth Japanese blood and foster children brought up in Caucasian families, were told to wind up their affairs in a week to 10 days and show up at an appointed time with bed rolls and no more baggage than they could carry. Many had to sell their property at a fraction of its value to bargain hunters and junk dealers.

The army moved the ethnic Japanese to assembly centers in converted livestock stalls and stadiums throughout the West. A bare room furnished only with cots, blankets and mattresses and separated from others by a thin partition made up a family apartment.

Throughout the summer the army moved the Japanese-Americans to 10 hastily prepared relocation centers in the interior of the country: Poston and Gila Bend, Arizona; Jerome and Rohwer, Arkansas; Minidoka, Idaho; Tule Lake and Manzana, California; Topaz, Utah; Granada, Colorado, and Heart Mountain, Wyoming.

There they will live in centers encircled by barbed wire and watch towers. Guards are instructed to shoot anyone who tries to leave. All of this is taking place despite the fact that there have been no criminal charges. As a Japanese-American asked at a congressional hearing: "Has the Gestapo come to America?" (→ May 20, 1959).

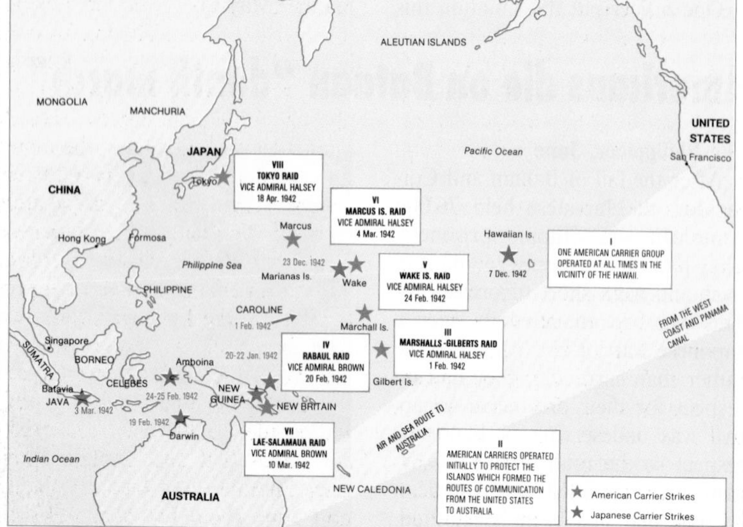

As the naval war in the Pacific expands, American military planners are relying heavily upon aircraft carriers. Originally employed to keep vital sea lanes open, they now form the backbone of the offensive strategy.

Armed services get record $42.8 billion

Washington, D.C., June 30

The Senate took just 34 minutes today to approve the largest military budget in American history – $42.8 billion. The appropriation – which represents more than the entire cost of World War I – will enable the nation to support an army of 4.5 million by the end of the the next fiscal year. And the cost of the war will hit Americans in their wallets, to the amount of $1.15 each per day. The bill was sent from the Senate to the House for final approval and was on its way to the White House for President Roosevelt's signature by mid-afternoon. The fiscal year ends today with the national debt at $76.6 billion and the deficit at $19.2 billion.

10,000 Nisei seek role in U.S. Army

Hawaii, June 5

Some 10,000 Americans of Japanese descent have volunteered for combat under the American flag, far exceeding the army's quota of 1,500 for the all-Nisei combat unit it is forming on the mainland. About 2,600 of these Nisei, American-born sons of Japanese immigrants, are to be sent to the mainland to train with the 442nd Combat Team. The number of volunteers seems to vindicate the policy toward the Japanese practiced by military governor Delos Emmons, who has been reluctant to carry out Washington's orders to deport Hawaii's Japanese. They make up 37 percent of the population.

Coughlin is curbed

Detroit, Mich., Apr. 14

The Shrine of the Little Flower has lost its bloom and the man in its pulpit has lost his right to publish. The man in question is the renowned radio priest, Father Charles E. Coughlin of Detroit, who has been haranguing the listening public since 1927 but who will no longer have a reading public. Under the 1917 Espionage Act, the government today banned his anti-Semitic weekly *Social Justice*.

FDR and Churchill meet on war again

Washington, D.C., June 24

Winston Churchill, accompanied by his top military chiefs, flew in from Scotland on June 17 to meet with Roosevelt and his war Cabinet. They discussed the war while traveling to and from Hyde Park, the President's residence on the Hudson River in New York. This is the second conference the two leaders have held in the United States. Chief subjects discussed have been the future Allied grand strategy as well as the deterioration of the Allied position in North Africa where German General Erwin Rommel has captured Tobruk. They also reportedly talked about the development of a new secret weapon (→ Jan. 24, 1943).

Doolittle bombs Tokyo

Colonel Doolittle's B-25 leaves the deck of the carrier Hornet bound for Tokyo.

Tokyo, Apr. 18

In a strike as surprising, though not nearly as devastating, as the Japanese attack on Pearl Harbor, Colonel James H. Doolittle and a squadron of B-25's today raided Tokyo, Nagoya, Osaka and Kobe. Completing the strike, all 16 of the American planes headed to China where they came down on darkened airfields. To prepare for the daring raid, Doolittle's men had practiced on airfields in Florida that were the size of an aircraft carrier. The pilots had to get to China because while it was possible to launch the big bombers from a carrier it was not possible to land them on one. The men flew 688 miles to Tokyo, then an additional 1,100 miles to the field in China.

Damage to Tokyo was slight, but the raid provided a great morale boost for Americans who have had only bad news for the past 19 weeks of war. Japanese authorities have no idea where the bombers came from. President Roosevelt told the American reporters that they came from "Shangri-la."

While B-25's can take off from aircraft carriers, they cannot yet land on them.

American forces give up at Corregidor

Corregidor, Philippines, May 6

"The Rock" has fallen. After months of bombardment from sea, land and air, and fierce hand-to-hand jungle fighting, Corregidor, "the Gibraltar of the East," has fallen into Japanese hands. General Jonathan M. "Skinny" Wainwright surrendered his 2,600-man force of soldiers, sailors and marines to Lieutenant General Homma Masahura following 27 days of brutal fighting.

The prolonged defense of the two-square-mile island was made possible, in part, by an intricate system of tunnels that allowed the defenders an underground retreat from the intense Japanese shelling that tore up almost every square foot of the island. No trees were left standing. The exact number of Americans killed may never be known, but in the final battle at least 40 lay dead in the wreckage and many times that number were wounded, filling the tunnel corridors in makeshift hospitals.

During the long siege, there were at least 1,800 casualties. Some 70 Filipinos were buried alive when a cliff collapsed, sealing their caves and dugouts. Marine officers said that Japanese casualties were at least five times as great because of their suicidal aggressiveness during the invasion of the island. At the moment of the surrender, Japanese tanks were just a few hundred yards from Malinta Tunnel, where General Wainwright's headquarters was situated (→8).

Battle of Coral Sea ends inconclusively

Internal explosions doomed the carrier Lexington after the Coral Sea battle.

Coral Sea, May 8

A most unusual naval battle in which the vessels of neither side could see each other ended today in the Coral Sea. The sea lies between the Equator and the Tropic of Capricorn, where the only previous conflicts have been between trading schooners and Melanesian war canoes. This battle has really been a series of events strung out over days and vast stretches of ocean, directed by leaders in huge aircraft carriers who had little or no idea where the enemy was. The result was a battle full of mistakes, some tragic and some comical. But two carriers were sunk, the Japanese Shoho and the American Lexington, which its crew had lovingly called "Lady Lex." On May 7, the light carrier Shoho was the first to go to the bottom when it accidentally encountered flyers from the Lexington and Yorktown. The Shoho sank in just 10 minutes and the Lexington's dive bomber commander exultantly radioed his ship to "scratch one flattop." A day later, the tables were turned when the two carrier groups finally came to grips after days of fumbling. The Japanese were shrouded in heavy overcast, but the Americans had no such protection and the Lexington took two torpedoes and two bomb hits. At the end of the battle, it seemed that the Lexington might still be saved. But suddenly, two internal explosions rocked it and Captain Frederick Sherman was forced to abandon ship. About 150 men were rescued by being lowered into motor whaleboats. The Yorktown was also hit, and lost 66 men, but it managed to survive the battle (→June 6). ▷

American navy turns tide at Midway

A Japanese bomber scores a direct hit on the American carrier Yorktown.

The Yorktown lists to starboard during the Battle of Midway. Its loss was a severe blow; nevertheless the American fleet achieved a smashing victory.

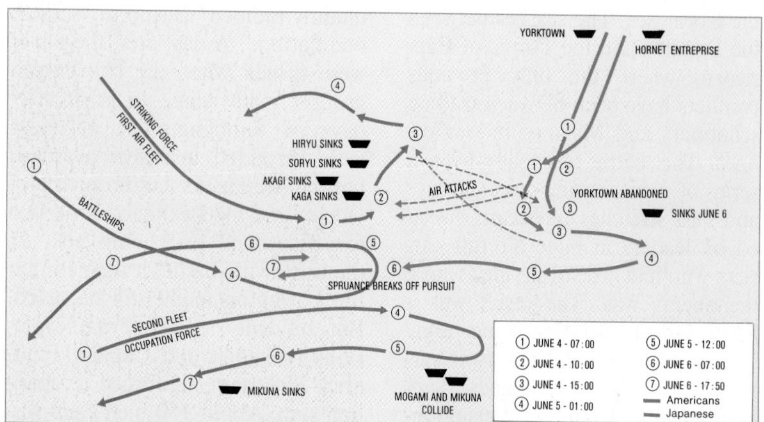

Knowledge of the Japanese command's strategy and intentions, thanks to U.S. intelligence, allows American naval forces not only to head off a major military disaster but to give chase to the retreating Japanese armada as well. Only a lack of fuel prevents the U.S. fleet from delivering one final, crushing blow.

Midway Island, June 6

Despite their overwhelming military superiority in the Pacific, the Japanese have suffered a crushing defeat in the Battle of Midway. They lost one heavy cruiser, four fleet carriers and 330 aircraft, most of which went down on their carriers. The Americans, on the other hand, lost only one carrier and about 150 aircraft.

The keys to the Japanese defeat were complacency and poor strategy. They had intended to invade both Midway Island, appropriately named because it is midway from just about anything in the Pacific, and the Aleutian chain off the coast of Alaska. Because of these fixed strategic objectives, the Americans had much greater flexibility and their admirals, Chester Nimitz and Raymond Spruance, used every bit of advantage they had. Nimitz was in overall command of the American force and Spruance commanded the carriers.

The Japanese fleet, which approached Midway Island in early June, was staggering in its size and complexity – 200 ships, including eight carriers, 11 battleships, 22 cruisers, 65 destroyers and 21 submarines. To meet this armada, the Americans had only three carriers with 233 planes, and no battleships. All the American battleships in the Pacific had been sunk or severely damaged at Pearl Harbor.

Admirals Yamamoto, who was in overall command, and Chuichi Nagumo, in command of carriers, believed that the United States fleet would not be at sea. The Americans had, therefore, the advantage of surprise. As the Japanese attacked Midway Island with dive bombers, the Americans attacked the Japanese fleet. Despite the surprise, the Americans lost the first round when 35 of the 41 torpedo bombers, relatively slow machines, were shot down. But moments later, 37 dive bombers from the Enterprise swept down on the Japanese from 19,000 feet and met almost no opposition. Three carriers were sunk in a period of just an hour.

Later in the same afternoon the carriers Yorktown and Hiryu slugged it out, and both ships were so badly damaged that they had to be abandoned (→Nov. 15).

Eisenhower is give command in Europe

New role for Dwight D. Eisenhower

Washington, D.C., June 25

A relatively obscure officer ha been named commander of Amer ican forces in the European theate of operations. He is Major Genera Dwight D. Eisenhower. He serve under two of the nation's foremos military leaders. He was senior aid to General Douglas A. MacArthu and, last month, General Georg C. Marshall assigned him to ex plore second-front possibilities i Britain. The 52-year-old Eisen hower, known as "Ike," was a foot ball star at West Point, ranking 61s in a class of 164 at the Militar Academy.

O.S.S. will gather secret information

Washington, D.C., June 13

America is officially in the spy business, as of today. An executive order created the Office of Strategic Services, to conduct covert operations and intelligence gathering overseas. Appointed head of the new agency is 59-year-old Colonel William J. "Wild Bill" Donovan, a World War I Congressional Medal of Honor winner who led "The Fighting 69th" Regiment. The United States has been the only major power without an intelligence service. Last July, President Roosevelt selected Colonel Donovan to be the coordinator of information, but his operation has been redesignated as the Office of Strategic Services (→July 26, 1947).

WAAC's and WAVES join the war effort

She's doing her part in the WAVES.

Washington, D.C., July 30

An act of Congress has created the Women Accepted for Volunteer Emergency Service (WAVES) on the heels of formation of the Women's Army Auxiliary Corps (WAAC) on May 14. Mildred McAfee, the president of Wellesley College, is expected to take a leadership role among the WAVES, who like their WAAC sisters will be doing noncombat duties at home and overseas. Several hundred of the WAAC women are already in training at Fort Des Moines, and their existence has met with controversy. Some women physicians refuse to serve with the the group because they have been denied admission to the all-male Medical Reserve Corps, which they feel performs more essential work.

28 seized by F.B.I. on sedition charges

Washington, D.C., July 23

As American forces battle the Axis powers overseas, the Federal Bureau of Investigation and the Attorney General are striking at domestic enemies. Today, 28 people – including writers and publishers – were arrested on sedition charges. A special grand jury, which heard some 150 witnesses, charged that the accused plotted to "interfere with, impair and influence the loyalty, morale and discipline" of the military. They allegedly worked through publications and organizations that included the Ku Klux Klan and the German-American Bund.

On the home front

United States

What's new on store shelves? Dannon Yogurt, Kellogg's Raisin Bran, Hunt's Foods. What's on people's minds? Daylight saving time, air raids and sirens, lights dimmed on Broadway, blackout drills and saving wastepaper (Boy Scouts salvaged 150,000 tons this year). What's on bookshelves? Not much; people are donating paperbacks to victory book rallies across the country. What's on women? Trousers. Sales of women's slacks are five times what they were last year, because of factory work. What's on windows? Service flags, some with eight stars representing eight million Americans overseas.

German targets bombed

As raids on German targets increase, the Boeing B-17, known as the "Flying Fortress," shows that it can do its job in spite of anti-aircraft defenses.

Rouen, France, Aug. 17

The American Army Air Force today conducted its first major bombing raid of the war. Compared to the 1,000-plane raids the Royal Air Force has conducted, the American strike was a modest beginning that involved only 18 heavy bombers. But it is a start. Protected by an R.A.F. Spitfire cover, four bombers made diversionary raids on the French coast while 12 American B-17's struck at the railroad marshalling yards at Rouen. Weather conditions were good, enemy opposition was negligible and the raid, led by General Ira Eaker, was considered a success.

This first raid is said to be a trial operation in what is intended to be a massive joint effort by the United States and Britain. The overall strategy of the two countries is not so much to defend Britain as to gain complete air supremacy over Europe. To accomplish this task the Americans will conduct daylight raids against Germany and occupied Europe while the Britons will do the same thing at night. This division of labor was set because the United States prefers daylight bombing, which it considers more accurate, while the British prefer the night because they have fewer losses to German fighters and anti-aircraft batteries.

This raid is considered important because the first British-American effort on July 4 was hardly a success. In a raid on the Netherlands, two U.S. planes were shot down and only two managed to bomb their targets (→ Dec. 31, 1943).

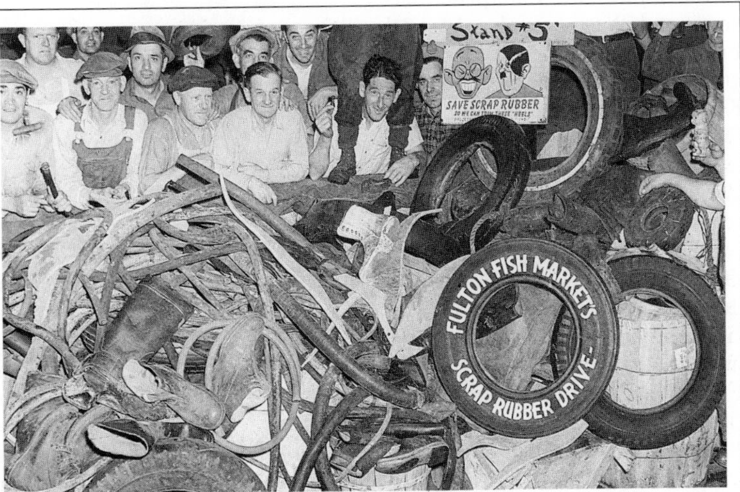

United States, June 30. *A scrap-rubber drive begun two weeks ago has ended; everything from tires to boots was donated to keep the war rolling.*

The bombs are taking their toll.

U.S. scores big victory in Solomons

Battle for Guadalcanal begins with amphibious assault by 10,000 marines.

Guadalcanal, Nov. 15

The Battle of Guadalcanal has been a long series of naval and land clashes for control of this key island in the Solomon chain and it appears that the United States has won a major victory here. The fierce engagements got under way with an amphibious assault by the marines that was almost unopposed. By evening, 10,000 men had come ashore and the Japanese decided to retire to tunnels and emplacements. Then, in a dangerous, tedious effort, they were blasted out by hand grenades and high explosives. Japanese help came by way of "The Slot," a sea passage opposite the northern edge of the island that saw so much traffic in the next few months that it became known as the Tokyo Express. Japanese commanders underestimated the island's marine force and sent in reinforcements piecemeal, enabling the marine forces to repulse steady attacks in places that they gave names such as "Bloody Ridge" and "Hell's Corner," as well as on the Henderson Field base. Japan wasted many men in kamikaze attacks – suicide missions – against well-defended positions, losing men in a ratio of as much as 10 to 1.

By October, the marines were so firmly entrenched on the island that attempts by the enemy to take it back proved futile. At sea, the final phase was the naval battle of Guadalcanal, in which the Japanese lost two destroyers and a battleship. The Americans suffered heavier losses, including the cruiser Juneau with 700 men killed, among them all five Sullivan brothers (→Feb. 9, 1943).

War rages on in the Pacific, but the tide seems to be turning

Solomon Islands

While Japanese and American land forces have been slugging it out for possession of Guadalcanal, both navies have engaged in a series of battles for possession of the surrounding waters. The results have been mixed, but the tide seems to have turned in favor of the United States.

Just north of Guadalcanal lies Savo, a small volcanic cone jutting up from the South Pacific. It is a piece of real estate neither side wanted but that neither side could afford to let the other have. The resulting battle was neither a decisive victory nor an unprofitable defeat. It was a bloody campaign for an unwanted island, and it cost the United States four heavy cruisers, one destroyer and 2,000 men dead.

On August 24, both navies geared up for a battle over the eastern Solomons, and this time the Americans scored a big victory. A strong carrier force – the Enterprise, Saratoga and Wasp – under Admiral Frank J. Fletcher defeated a carrier group under Admirals Nobutake Kondo and Chuichi Nagumo. In October, the Japanese again attempted to shake the marines off Guadalcanal and, when they sent reinforcements, a fierce battle was fought off Cape Esperance, north of the island. For a while, it seemed as though the Americans might lose Guadalcanal. The final engagement, called the Battle of the Santa Cruz Islands, led to the loss of the carrier Hornet, but the attrition of Japanese planes enabled the Americans to keep their grip on Guadalcanal and the surrounding waters and finally begin to turn the war against the Japanese.

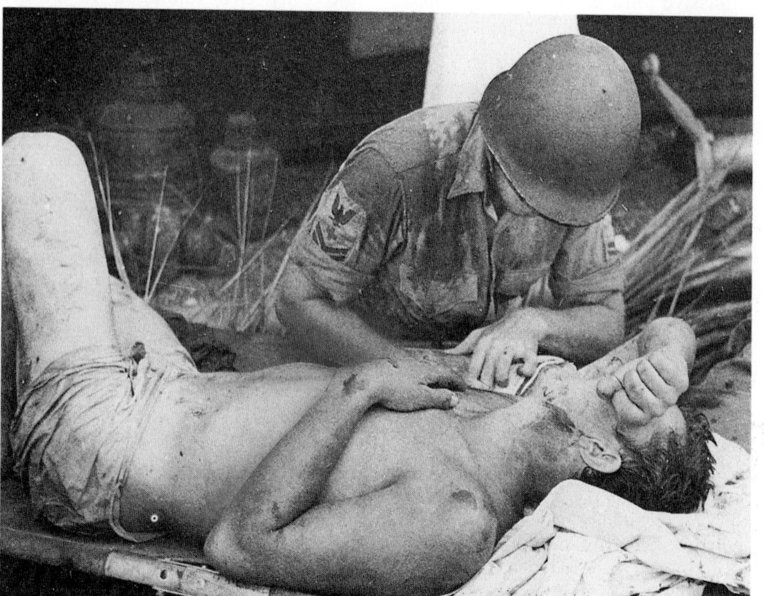

A lucky survivor of the warship Calhoun receives medical care in the Solomons.

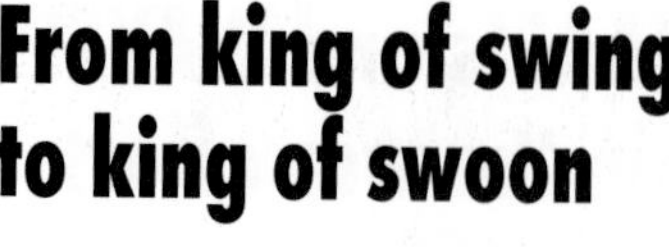

From king of swing to king of swoon

New York City, Dec. 30

The Paramount Theater is the Mount Olympus of American pop musicians. Benny Goodman was crowned king there in 1937, and now it seems to be Frank Sinatra's turn. Never has the hall seen quite such hysterical homage and swooning. The new king is an unlikely figure, described by his former boss, bandleader Harry James, as looking like a "wet rag." But to the thousands of squealing, fainting and entranced teenagers, the 27-year-old crooner with the wraith-like voice is the Pied Piper incarnate. And in the past few years his recordings of *White Christmas*, *Night and Day* and *Fools Rush In* have helped his claim to the throne.

Speaking of records, Glenn Miller's *Chattanooga Choo-Choo* has set a new mark of one million sales, making it the first "gold record." It's also been another good year for the Andrews Sisters, always at or near the top since their 1937 hit, *Bei Mir Bist Du Schon*. This year the trio triumphed with *Don't Sit Under the Apple Tree*.

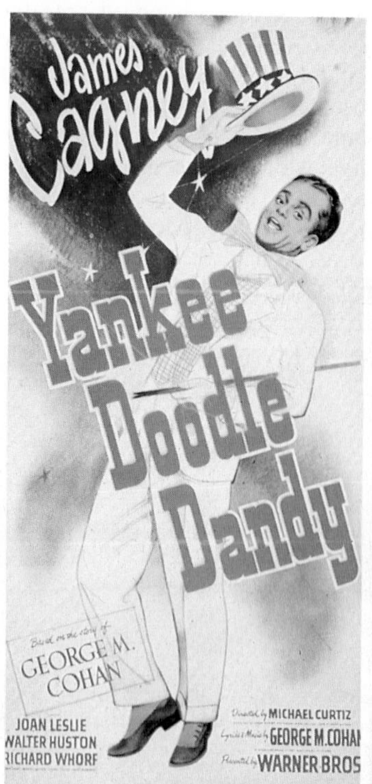

Composer George M. Cohan, who wrote "It's a Grand Old Flag" and other hits, died November 5, but his life is now on the big screen.

Atoms in chain reaction

Chicago, Dec. 2

The road to nuclear power was opened today when the world's first sustained nuclear chain reaction was achieved in a makeshift facility under the stands of Stagg Field at the University of Chicago. Though the amount of the energy released was small, it was energy from the atomic nucleus, a potentially unlimited source of power. Working in freezing conditions, a team of scientists under the direction of the brilliant Italian physicist Enrico Fermi built what they call an "atomic pile," consisting of blocks of graphite containing uranium. Fissioning of the uranium nucleus releases energy and neutrons that split other nuclei, in a potentially endless reaction. The chain reaction was kept under control by the use of rods of cadmium, which absorbs neutrons. Under Fermi's direction, the cadmium rods were slowly withdrawn from the pile. At exactly 3:45 p.m., the recorders showed that the reaction was self-sustaining, releasing enough neutrons to keep going forever.

Physicists say that the power in a few pounds of fissionable uranium could be fabulously productive, or destructive. The success today is a major step in America's growing effort to develop nuclear power.

Allies enter North Africa

Storming a beach in North Africa.

American soldiers prepare to fight.

Casablanca, Morocco, Nov. 11

The Allied invasion of North Africa called "Torch" is going well, but there has been more than token resistance by the French forces loyal to the government at Vichy in unoccupied France. The question of German collaboration was resolved when French batteries on Cap El Hawk, in Casablanca harbor, opened up on the British and American ships. The battleship Massachusetts, two cruisers and four destroyers were hit before the shore batteries were silenced. The unfinished French battleship Jean Bart also took part in the battle.

Before the landing operations, General George Patton gave one of his "blood and guts" speeches to the troops. "Never in history has the navy landed an army at the planned time and place," he said. "But if you land us anywhere within 50 miles of Fedala [Morocco] and within one week of D-day, I'll go ahead and win."

The landings in Algeria, at Oran, ran into even stiffer opposition than at Casablanca, but cooperation between the British and Americans got the troops ashore. The American First Division, under Major General Terry Allen, deceptively bypassed Oran in the dark, doubling back to the beaches where little opposition was met. However, at Oran harbor, big displays of American flags meant to discourage French resistance did not work. But after three days of fighting, the French gave up (→ Feb. 22, 1943).

"Casablanca" and a "Road to Morocco"

Hollywood, California

Adrift in a world at war, against a background of international intrigue, they meet, they love and they must part. The film is *Casablanca*, pairing Ingrid Bergman and Humphrey Bogart and offering witty, ironic twists. From the same country, this time with gags, the *Road to Morocco* proves a road to success for Bing Crosby, Bob Hope and Dorothy Lamour. *Now Voyager* with Bette Davis and Paul Henreid wins acclaim as does *Woman of the Year*, pairing Spencer Tracy and Katharine Hepburn for the first time. The big Academy Award winner is *Mrs. Miniver* with Greer Garson. James Cagney wins as best actor for *Yankee Doodle Dandy*. Disney's latest is *Bambi*, and Bing Crosby has recorded *White Christmas* from the movie *Holiday Inn*. Ronald Reagan, who was George Gipp in *Knute Rockne - All American* two years ago, tells his fans, "Mr. Norm is my alias. Nothing about me to make me stand out in the midway."

Clark Gable, whose wife, Carole Lombard, died in a plane crash in January while on a war bond drive, joined the armed forces, despite his age, 41. So have James Stewart, Cesar Romero, Spencer Tracy, Robert Stack and Douglas Fairbanks Jr.

Bogart and Bergman share a moment in "Casablanca" as Sam plays it again.

Muroc, California, October 1. *The XP-59, the first turbojet aircraft manufactured in the United States, was tested today by Robert Stanley, head pilot for the Bell Aircraft Corporation. Its future appears to be sound.*

1943

Roosevelt

Washington, D.C., Jan. 18. Supreme Court finds American Medical Association to be in violation of antitrust laws for attempting to block cooperative health groups.

Washington, D.C., Feb. 3. War Department declares state of prohibition on hard liquors at all army establishments.

Washington, D.C., Feb. 9. Journalist Clare Booth Luce tells House committee, "Much of what Mr. (Henry) Wallace calls his global thinking is, no matter how you slice it, still Globaloney."

Washington, D.C., Feb. 9. President Roosevelt mandates national 48-hour work week with overtime, effective immediately in areas where acute labor shortages occur.

New York City, Feb. 28. George Gershwin's musical *Porgy and Bess* revived on Broadway.

Honolulu, March 10. Martial law ends, but military retains control over criminal cases.

Washington, D.C., Apr. 8. By order of President, all wages and prices are frozen at present levels.

Washington, D.C., May 28. Supreme Court Justice James F. Brynes appointed head of Office of War Mobilization, created to coordinate activities of government agencies involved in civilian supply production and/or distribution.

Detroit, June 22. Riots, started June 20 by whites protesting employment of Negroes, put down by federal troops, with loss of 35 lives (→ Aug. 2).

St. Louis, Oct. 11. New York Yankees defeat St. Louis Cardinals, four games to one, in World Series.

Chicago, Oct. 16. City's first subway inaugurated.

Chicago, Dec. 26. Bears defeat Washington Redskins, 41-21, in National Football League championship.

United States. Shortage of tin for cans forces Campbell's Soup to stop sponsoring *Amos 'n' Andy*; show canceled after 4,000 performances and 15 years on radio.

United States. *One World*, by Wendell Willkie, published; it sells one million copies in two months.

U.S. defeats Japanese at Guadalcanal

American troops come ashore with Coast Guard manning the landing craft.

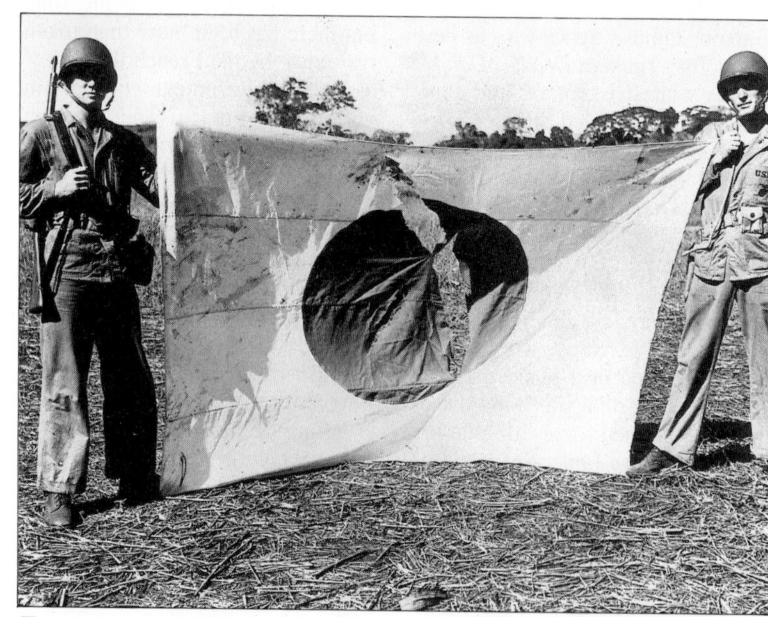

Two marines on Guadalcanal proudly exhibit a captured Japanese flag.

Guadalcanal, Feb. 9

Admiral William "Bull" Halsey received the following radio message from General Alexander Patch on Guadalcanal: "Total and complete defeat of Japanese forces on Guadalcanal effected today . . . Tokyo Express no longer has terminus on Guadalcanal." These words mark the first major offensive victory for the United States in the Pacific and the end of seven months of bitter and savage struggle for the navy and marines. The Americans now hold some 2,500 miles of swamp and jungle-covered volcanic mountains.

The battle for the island tipped toward the United States in October 1942, and by December the Japanese were starving. Their only relief came from submarines that would sneak close to the shore at night and place drums full of supplies in the tidal waters, hoping that a favorable current would get them to the beleaguered defenders. By January, the Americans had become aware that the Japanese were planning either an evacuation or a major reinforcement, because intelligence reports showed transports and freighters being assembled at Rabaul in New Guinea. The final evacuation began slowly toward the end of January, and on the nights of February 5 and 6, Japanese transports were able to slip past the vigilant Americans and remove about 11,000 men. The marines didn't realize what had happened until they began to explore the western end of the island and found not a living soul (→ March 4).

Allies, at Casablanca, agree on 2nd front

Casablanca, Morocco, Jan. 24

President Roosevelt and Prime Minister Churchill announced today that the war will not end until they have achieved the "unconditional surrender" of Germany, Italy and Japan. Roosevelt said he was determined to destroy the "philosophies in those countries which are based on conquest and the subjugation of other people." The two leaders agreed during 10 days of meetings here to open a southern front in June or July by attacking Sicily. An invasion of Sardinia was rejected. The attack will be led by General Dwight D. Eisenhower. Churchill also agreed to a "maximum" buildup of forces in Britain in preparation for a cross-English Channel invasion of France.

General Charles de Gaulle participated in most of the meetings in spite of Roosevelt's objections. After the conference broke up today, Roosevelt and Churchill drove together in a car to Marrakesh, where one dinner guest said they made "affectionate little speeches to each other, and Winston sang" (→ Dec. 6).

A new penicillin

Peoria, Illinois

The potent anti-bacterial agent penicillin, accidentally discovered in a moldy culture dish in 1928, has proven too scarce to play much of a medical role. But in a chance encounter, a researcher from a government laboratory here stumbled on a new type of penicillium mold this summer on a cantaloupe at a local market. Using new deep-fermentation techniques, the laboratory hopes to grow enough of the new strain to treat every wounded soldier or infected civilian needing it.

60,000 Americans are dead in battle

Washington, D.C., February

Figures released by the government on January 5 point up the terrible price that American families are paying as their sons go into the fighting. Some 60,000 American soldiers have been killed, and many more are certain to die before the war is over. Nevertheless, with every day that passes, the American resolve to win appears to toughen. As newspaper columnist Ernie Pyle wrote of the American troops after their Tunisian victory, "Even though they didn't do too well in the beginning, there was never at any time any question about the American bravery. It is a matter of being hardened and practiced by going through the flames."

Sub commander: "Take her down"

South Pacific, Feb. 7

The powerful American submarine Growler rammed a Japanese gunboat at 17 knots today, then was spattered with machine-gun fire. Many crewmen died, as did the courageous Commander Howard Gilmore. His last words ordered the crew to "Take her down," even though he remained on the sub's bridge, bleeding from enemy shrapnel. Any delay to get him in would have lost the time needed for the vessel to get away. His action saved most of the crew and a premier sub. Gilmore will be posthumously awarded a Medal of Honor.

Allies stop Rommel in North Africa

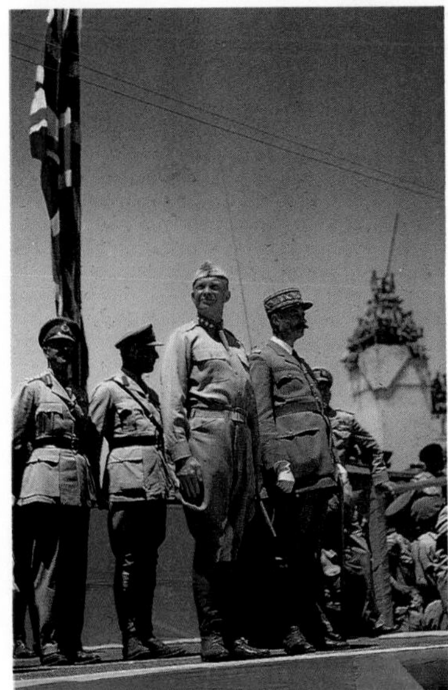

Ike and Allied leaders review forces.

An American advance observation post in the El Guettar Valley, Tunisia.

North Africa, Feb. 22

General Erwin Rommel and his Afrika Korps have introduced the newly arrived Americans to the very tough league of mechanized desert warfare, and the lesson has been a bloody one. The Americans, under Major General George S. Patton Jr., stopped Rommel at the Kasserine Pass in Tunisia on February 19, but suffered 6,000 casualties compared to Rommel's 1,000. Of greater significance was the fact that U.S. tanks did not hold up well against German armor. The American Stuarts could not dent the heavier German tanks and the armor on the Shermans was inadequate.

On the morning of February 14, the Germans under Rommel, who had retreated westward from Libya because of British pressure, began an assault against the Allies, hoping to buy time and to threaten their enormous supply base at Tebessa. Things might have gone better for Rommel, but he didn't have use of the 10th Panzer Division, which considerably weakened the attack. The Americans expected an assault, but they didn't anticipate its brute force. Rommel quickly cut off an infantry regiment and wiped it out. When the Americans counterattacked with an armored regiment, the Germans wiped that out as well. The Germans made steady progress for five days, breaking through the pass and advancing 70 miles into Allied territory. Rommel expected a counterattack as the advance slowed, but nothing serious developed, so he decided to pull back to the Kasserine Pass and prepare an eastward counterstroke against the British Eighth Army. At one point, the Germans used a clever ruse against the retreating British, who were fighting alongside the Americans, that resulted in the capture of 700 prisoners. They placed a captured British tank at the head of their column and followed closely behind the retreating soldiers, in the hope that the Allies would assume that the tank column was not really the enemy. The plan worked and the Germans burst into the Allied ranks, causing considerable destruction and confusion.

After their initial setback, the Americans regrouped and went on the attack. Yesterday, a week after the fighting began, the battle lines had returned to what they were at the start.

U.S. bombers prevail in Bismarck Sea

New Guinea, March 4

The American Fifth Air Force today delivered the most devastating air attack against the enemy since the start of the war with the Japanese attack on Pearl Harbor. Late in February, the Japanese attempted to reinforce their garrison at Lae, New Guinea, but the Fifth Air Force, commanded by Major General George Kenney, caught the convoy of ships in the Bismarck Sea and sank eight transports and four destroyers. The damage was caused by a change in American bomb fuses, which permitted a five-second delay. This allowed B-25's carrying 500-pound bombs to deliver them at sea level as a torpedo bomber would, and still escape.

Aided by Australia's Air Force, the Allies left Papua, New Guinea, with 207 bombers and 129 fighters. The Japanese had negligible air cover, and the Allies dropped 200 bombs on the hapless convoy. Because Japanese soldiers continued to fight back even if captured, many survivors were machine-gunned in the water (→ Dec. 26).

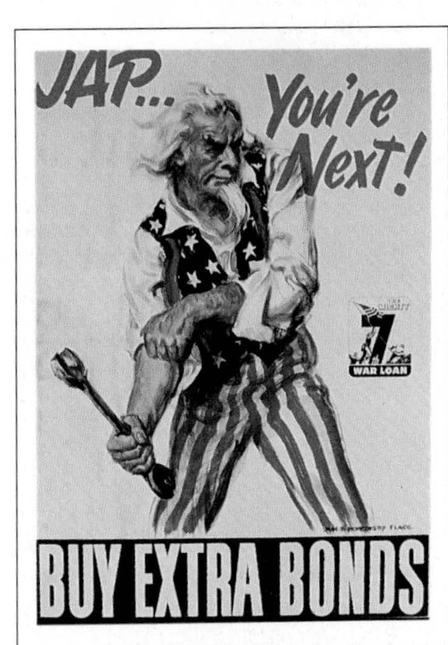

Coal strike halted by seizure threat

Washington, D.C., May 2

With a typical flair for drama, United Mine Workers chief John L. Lewis has ordered 500,000 miners back to work 20 minutes before President Roosevelt took to the radio to denounce his two-day strike. "Every idle miner ... is obstructing our war effort," FDR fumed after placing the mines under federal control yesterday. Labor closed ranks behind the miners, condemning a war policy that "freezes wages but permits, and indeed guarantees, a continued rise in the cost of living." Though forced to back off, Lewis has proved his skill and is likely to get his wage increase soon.

Churchill in capital: "V" and a pep talk

Washington, D.C., May 25

Prime Minister Churchill ended his visit to the capital today with another pep talk, and he was cheered after a press conference he held with President Roosevelt. Churchill stepped onto his chair and gave a "V" for Victory sign. Last Wednesday, the Prime Minister urged Congress to be steadfast and tenacious until the Axis powers are defeated. "We have surmounted many serious dangers," he said, but he warned that the most grave danger remaining is "the undue prolongation of the war." Churchill promised to continue in the war effort against Japan even after Germany and Italy are defeated.

Japanese forces are defeated in Aleutians

Armed with guns and tools for construction duty, Navy Seabees drill in Alaska.

Attu, Aleutian Islands, May 29

The Seventh Infantry Division has retaken the island of Attu from the Japanese, who have occupied it since 1941, but the cost has been high. The Americans landed on the treeless, bleak and mountainous island on May 11, and encountered stiff resistance. The burden of the battle settled upon the foot soldiers because the unpredictable weather made air and naval support virtually impossible.

After two weeks of fighting, the Japanese were left with only a flat area around the Chicagof harbor base, as the American troops closed in for the kill. They were met with a banzai attack by about 1,000 Japanese, of whom 500 were quickly killed. Most of the others committed suicide, either in the traditional hara-kiri ritual of disembowelment by sword, or by a rifle shot to the head. A few Japanese continued to hold on for about a day and a half, but those followed in their comrades' footsteps rather than be captured.

In the end, the American attack force of 11,000 men lost 600 in retaking the island. The Japanese death toll was 2,351, with only 28 men taken prisoner.

Count Fleet gallops to the Triple Crown

New York City, June 5

Count Fleet, a colt nobody wanted, even for $4,500, reached the peak of thoroughbred racing today. The Reigh Count colt won the Belmont Stakes, final leg of the Triple Crown after the Kentucky Derby and the Preakness. Count Fleet was a castoff when John Hertz bought him as a yearling and he was turned out to race when nobody would buy the horse. Because of the war, Churchill Downs has tried to discourage trips to the derby. Still, 65,000 fans showed up last month.

Court overturns law ordering flag salute

Washington, D.C., June 14

Some call it an irony. Some call it an act of respect for the First Amendment. But on this Flag Day, the Supreme Court has ruled that schoolchildren cannot be required by state law to salute the flag. In West Virginia Board of Education v. Barnette, the high court voted 5 to 4 in favor of the Jehovah's Witnesses, holding that a statute requiring such a salute is an abridgement of the freedom of religion and expression that is guaranteed in the Constitution.

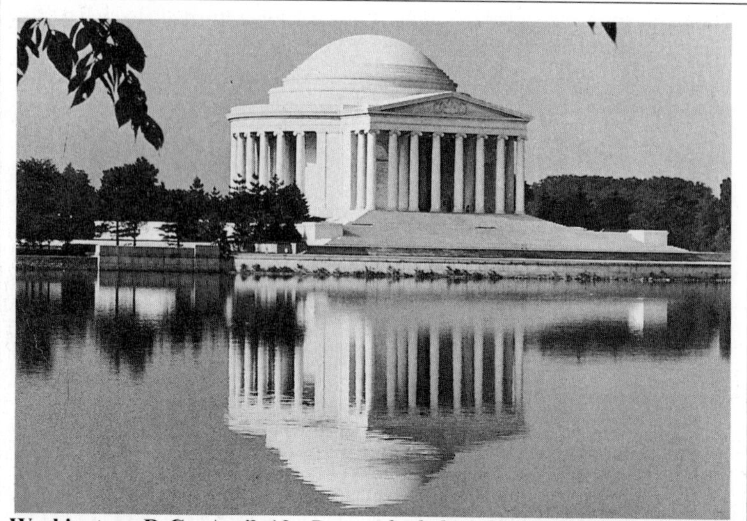

Washington, D.C., April 13. *Roosevelt dedicated the beautiful Jefferson Memorial today in honor of the third President of the United States.*

"Oklahoma!" wins raves from the press

New York City, March 31

The musical *Oklahoma!* has the critics groping for adjectives, which means it's in a class by itself. Reasons are easy to find with songs like *Oh, What a Beautiful Morning*, *The Surrey With the Fringe on Top*, *People Will Say We're in Love*, *Out of My Dreams* and, of course, the title song. A perfect cast is headed by Alfred Drake, Joan Roberts, Howard da Silva and Celeste Holm. Equally important, it seems that Americans yearn for a sentimental, nostalgic glimpse of an era when life was more direct, less complicated than in these war-torn days. Thus, more than the rural setting of an actual state, the Richard Rodgers-Oscar Hammerstein show mythologizes a vanished state of mind.

A singing and dancing "Oklahoma!"

"Use it up, wear it out, make it do, or do without"

United States

No one has lost a life wielding a hoe in a victory garden or lugging a tub of vegetable fat to the corner butcher's. Still, Americans on the homefront are doing their part, they hope, to help the boys overseas and bring the war to a swifter end. "Use it up, wear it out, make it do, or do without," is one version of a slogan going around, and so Americans are pitching in to conserve wartime materials. By year's end, however, few of the sacrifices are voluntary. Some food staples, such as butter (four ounces a week), cheese (four pounds a week), coffee and flour are rationed. Neighbors gather round a table where they once played bridge, now swapping their ration coupons. Tuesdays and Fridays are "meatless" days, and the weekly tuna casserole surprise surprises no one. What is news, however, is that, despite the 28-ounce-a-week allowance, meat consumption has actually gone up. Apparently, Americans are eating better when limits are thrust on them.

But their dress is not improved: designers have restrictions on the kind and amount of fabric they can use, and businessmen are doing without vests. Their "victory pants" lack cuffs. As for women, their dresses seem a bit on the drab side, and there is idle speculation that the hems will climb further as another sacrifice. Each American is allotted three pairs of leather shoes a year; sensible shoes are more sensible than ever.

Virtually all consumable goods have a second life, as tin and other metals, paper and nylon are recycled. Kitchen fat is processed for explosives. Rubber, found in inaccessible Asia, is one of the scarcest of commodities. Some municipalities try to ward off rubber thieves by having car owners record the serial numbers of their tires. With gas rationed and a 35 mph speed limit in effect, no one takes the car out of the garage much anyhow.

Everywhere there is delay. The trains, loaded with enlisted men or hauling war materiel, are late leaving and late arriving. Lines snake out of grocery stores, restaurants, and bars because there are too few employees waiting on customers.

Yet because manpower – and womanpower – are so much in demand, workers find themselves almost pampered. Factories have introduced coffee breaks and piped music, fringe benefits and awards for fine performance. Unfortunately, the sense of delay pervades the workplace: President Roosevelt ordered a freeze on all wages, prices and salaries, and the mandatory 48-hour week at the war plants is exhausting, coffee breaks or no. There is nothing like just going home at the end of a day, sitting in front of the old radio (factories aren't making new ones for civilians anymore) and gulping a small watered-down bottle of beer – not "sacrificing" a drop.

Norman Rockwell really hits home.

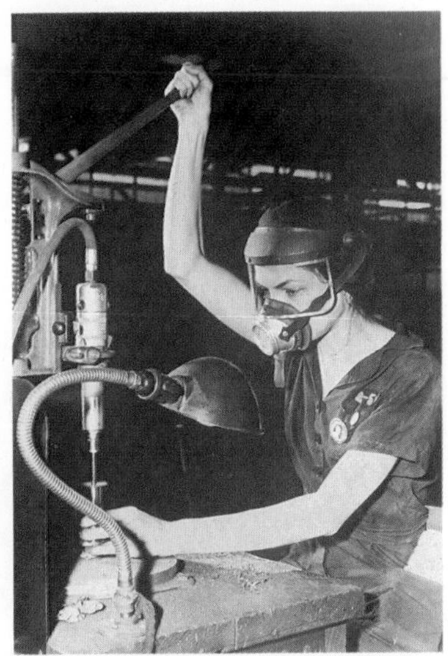

Women help fill the nation's arsenal.

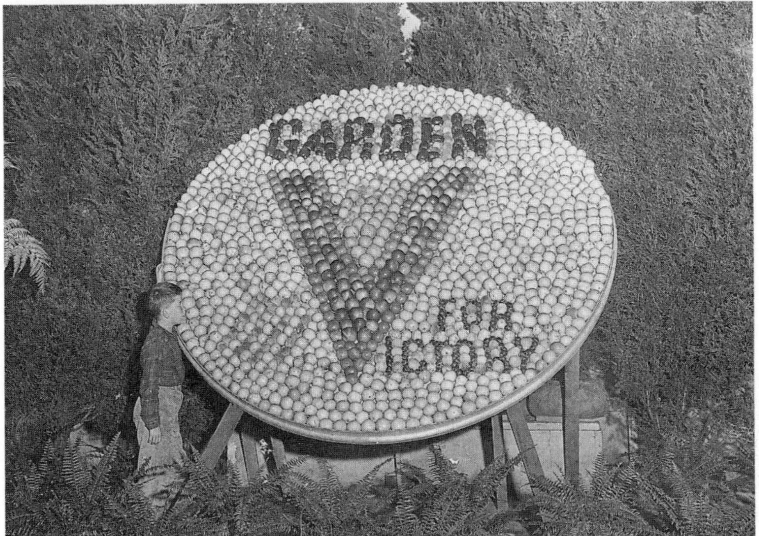

"Victory Gardens" ease a bit of the burden on the nation's food producers.

American war production is at its peak

Washington, D.C.

The new chief of the War Production Board, Donald Nelson, said, in January 1942, "We're going to have to rely on our great mass production industries for the bulk of our increase under the war program." This has led to a staggering growth in war production. The B-24 factory at Willow Run, Michigan, employs 100,000 workers and can disgorge planes at the rate of 500 a month. Some 47,000 were produced in 1942, but this year that rose to 86,000. From December 7, 1941, to the end of this year, more than 150,000 planes were built. The figures for shipbuilding are equally impressive: 1,949 built in 1943, 1,238 of them mass-produced, assembly-line Liberty Ships (there's a new one every four days). In two years of war, 27 million deadweight tons were produced, more than offsetting heavy losses to U-boats. Output of synthetic rubber is expected to hit 800,000 tons next year. These prodigious feats have led even Joseph Stalin to toast "American productivity without which this war would have been lost."

"Penn Station at Wartime" (1943) by Joseph Delaney. On the home front, there are constant delays. People come, people go and some never return.

Allies batter their way into Italy

American armor rolls through Palma, Sicily, on the way to mainland Italy.

Sicilian peasants gather sadly around a wounded soldier fighting for his life.

Naples, Italy, Oct. 3

The Allies, after three successful invasions of Italy, have conquered Sicily and worked their way up the "boot" to Naples and Foggia. The campaign began with the Sicilian invasion on July 10, when an armada of 3,000 ships unloaded 500,000 Allied soldiers along the southern beaches of the island. The Axis powers had 350,000 men to defend Italy, with six mobile German divisions at the core.

Although the landings were relatively easy, the Germans counterattacked on July 11. Armored strikes were beaten off and the British Eighth Army and the American Third began pushing north and west toward Messina. The Germans and Italians never intended to stay and fight in Sicily and they soon pulled most of their troops back to the Italian mainland. On August 17, the Allies pushed into the rubble that was Messina, and on September 21, the British began putting troops ashore on the mainland at Reggio Calabria. During this time, Italians were losing heart for the war and Mussolini's government began shaking apart, with defections to the Allies. Hitler said, disgustedly, that the Italians never managed to lose a war, no matter whose side they were on, because they were always on the winning side at the end. On September 9, Allied troops stormed ashore at Salerno, south of Naples, and continued to push north against tough German resistance (→ June 4, 1944).

600,000 flee Nazis and come to U.S.

Washington, D.C., Dec. 10

According to some of the testimony heard today by members of the House Foreign Affairs Committee, at least 600,000 people escaping persecution by the Nazis have been granted admission to the United States since 1933. Many of the refugees, such as Albert Einstein, who arrived in 1933, and composer Kurt Weill, who came two years later, are Jews. But others, such as the author Thomas Mann, who has lived in Princeton, New Jersey, since 1938, and Neils Bohr, the physicist who arrived this year, were persecuted for their secular beliefs.

U.S. agrees to join world relief body

Washington, D.C., Nov. 9

The United States has joined in a 44-nation agreement today to establish the United Nations Relief and Rehabilitation Administration. It is designed to help victims in Europe and the Far East who have suffered the most from the devastation of war. Former Governor Herbert Lehman of New York is to head the organization. The action was preceded by passage in the House of Representatives of the Fulbright Resolution, calling for an international peace organization. The Senate took up a similar proposal, the Connally Resolution.

Race rioting rocks N.Y., L.A. and Detroit

New York City, Aug. 2

As America fights a racist Hitler in Europe, racial hatred has set off riots at home. Today, a rumor of a murder in Harlem, then an argument between a Negro woman and a white policeman triggered widespread street violence, resulting in the death of five and injuries to 400.

In June, white servicemen in Los Angeles attacked blacks and Hispanics wearing "zoot" suits, the gaudy garb with long jackets and pegged pants. The assault fueled racial tension and rioting erupted. The military declared the city off-limits to servicemen before the battling was brought under control.

The worst violence erupted June 20 in Detroit, where 300,000 Southern whites and blacks have migrated to work in the war plants. In two days, 35 were killed, 600 wounded and thousands held. Thurgood Marshall of the National Association for the Advancement of Colored People said Detroit's police used "persuasion" on white rioters, but "ultimate force ... revolvers, riot guns and sub-machine guns" on Negroes. One report said of the police that they made mistakes, but "demonstrated courage, efficiency and ... good judgment."

Robeson as Othello

New York City

Last year, plans for a Broadway production of *Othello* starring Paul Robeson touched off intense debate. Will whites stand for a real-life black man as Shakespeare's Moor? Robeson opened in the title role on October 19 and the answer to the question was a record-breaking run and critical accolades – for Robeson and for co-stars Uta Hagen and Jose Ferrer. Broadway also saw a Negro cast this season in the long-awaited *Porgy and Bess*, George Gershwin's opera of 1935 about Negro life on Catfish Row in Charleston, South Carolina.

Railroads seized

Washington, D.C., Dec. 27

President Roosevelt acted firmly today in ordering the government to seize the railroads to avert a strike. Roosevelt had met for hours day after day with rail management and labor to mediate an end to the rift over a proposed wage hike. Fearing the threat to national security if workers struck, he took charge, directing the army to operate the railroads until the disputing parties reach a settlement. While a crisis has been temporarily avoided, the President will keep seeking an accord. A series of battles over salaries has raged since early spring.

Bombers ravaging German factories

Germany, Dec. 31

The German heartland is being saturated with bombs as the United States Army Air Force continues to step up the size of its daylight raids. In mid-October, the maximum number of bombers used was 400, but by this month that number has increased until three raids of 700 bombers each, per day, is not uncommon. The result is a rain of devastation on both the Rhine and the Ruhr industrial areas, and on such key cities as Regensburg, Hannover and Schweinfurt.

The principal targets are factories that are considered crucial to war production such as those manufacturing ball bearings, aircraft tires and latex rubber. But the cost to the Allies has been significant. In a raid on July 28, only 28 bombers, of a force of 120, made it to their targets. This attack was also notable for the fact that the Germans used a new weapon, an air-launched rocket that downed three B-17's (→March 6, 1944).

Allied chiefs meet in Quebec, Teheran and Cairo to map strategy

President Roosevelt and Prime Minister Churchill hold talks in Cairo with Generalissimo Chiang Kai-shek of China and his wife. The Allies hope that postwar China will be a friend of the West and a pillar of Asian stability.

Cairo, Egypt, Dec. 6

President Roosevelt sounded upbeat today as he spoke informally with a group of American soldiers near his villa. His series of meetings with the Allies have apparently made him more confident about winning the war. "This time when we clean out the enemy," Roosevelt pledged, "we are going to clean them out thoroughly, so that they can't start another war."

The Roosevelt declaration with Premier Stalin and Prime Minister Churchill on the recently concluded Teheran Conference is equally forceful. "No power on earth can prevent our destroying the German armies by land, their U-boats by sea and their war plants from the air," it said. The leaders agreed to open a second front in Western Europe, and Stalin pledged to join the war against Japan as soon as Hitler is defeated. Roosevelt has reportedly decided to put General Dwight D. Eisenhower in charge of the cross-English Channel invasion of France. "Operation Overlord" is tentatively set for next May.

The conference, which Churchill called "the greatest concentration of worldly power that had ever been seen in the history of mankind," marked the first time that all three leaders had met. Groundwork for it was carefully laid in Moscow at a foreign ministers' meeting and in Quebec, where Roosevelt and Churchill met. In Cairo, the two leaders and China's Generalissimo Chiang Kai-shek agreed that at war's end "Japan shall be stripped of all the islands in the Pacific which she has seized or occupied since the start of the first World War." They also pledged independence for Korea (→Feb. 11, 1945).

American forces advance on wide front in the Pacific theater

Solomon Islands, Dec. 26

Admiral William "Bull" Halsey's ability to keep the Japanese guessing and off balance has given the Americans several important victories. One reason for his success in some of the encounters was his ability to strike where he was not expected. For example, Halsey was intent on wresting the Solomons from the Japanese. Instead of hitting at Kolombangara, as would be expected, he landed on lightly defended Vella Lavella. He then returned to Kolombangara and has captured it as well.

The Solomon victories were less costly than at Tarawa, in the Gilbert Islands. There, in a direct assault, the marines took a bad hammering. They knew the tiny coral atoll would be formidable because it was defended by 3,000 troops who had built murderous beach obstacles. The marines went in against a deadly rain of fire, were caught behind sea walls, and could not advance or retreat. Some units had 50 percent casualties. Still, they took the atoll, then held it in the face of fierce counterattacks. But it cost them 3,000 men.

A B-25 strikes Japanese ships and positions at Rabaul harbor, New Britain.

They did better in other island engagements in regard to casualties, but the Japanese fought tenaciously for everything they had won. At Empress Augusta Bay in western Bougainville, there were few Japanese, but the landing vehicles ran up against uncharted reefs. In spite of air support, the marines lost 78 dead and 104 wounded. At Arawe, on Goodenough Island, the enemy used machine guns to deadly effect, sinking most of the rubber landing boats the men used. Destroyer fire finally took out the machine guns (→May 17, 1944).

"Bound for Glory"

United States

Most autobiographers are older than 31, but most have less living under their belts than does Woody Guthrie, the Okie troubadour who has hoboed from coast to coast with a guitar in hand and tunes in his head. His story, *Bound for Glory*, has made fans of high-brow critics.

Thomas Hart Benton's "July Hay."

1944

Roosevelt

Washington, D.C., Feb. 29. It is estimated that black market has earned about $1.2 billion over past year.

Washington, D.C., March 4. Because of Argentina's failure to cooperate fully with Allied war effort, Acting Secretary of State Edward Stettinius says United States has adopted policy of nonrecognition toward that nation.

Washington, D.C., Apr. 30. General Douglas MacArthur releases statement that he has no intention of seeking or accepting Republican presidential nomination.

New York City, May 1. Pulitzer Prize in poetry awarded to Stephen Vincent Benet for *Western Star.*

New York City, May 8. Nation's first eye bank formed through combined efforts of 20 city hospitals.

Washington, D.C., June 13. Americans receive word that Germans have launched robot bombs against targets as distant as London.

Hartford, Connecticut, July 6. Inept fire-eaters spark a blaze during performance of Ringling Brothers and Barnum & Bailey Circus, killing 167 people, mostly children.

Atlanta, July 12. Coca-Cola Company manufactures one billionth gallon of Coca-Cola syrup.

Port Chicago, California, July 17. Ammunition ship blows up, killing 300 people.

St. Louis, Oct. 8. St. Louis Cardinals defeat St. Louis Browns in World Series, four games to two.

Washington, D.C., Nov. 18. Statistical report shows cost of living has risen almost 30 percent in past 12 months.

New York City, Dec. 17. Green Bay Packers defeat New York Giants, 14-7, in National Football League championship.

Hood River, Oregon, December. American Legion removes names of JapaneseAmericans from its military service roll of honor.

Washington, D.C. Nearly half of steel, tin and paper needed for war effort provided by people salvaging goods.

United States. Tennessee Williams publishes play *The Glass Menagerie.*

Big night at Met, but sound is jazz

New York City, Jan. 18

Following jazz at Carnegie Hall, could Jazz at the Met be far behind? Billed as the *Esquire All-Stars*, the winners of the first critics' jazz poll in *Esquire* magazine scored another "first" by introducing that hallowed hall of opera to the primal sounds of jazz. It was a formidable group: Art Tatum, Louis Armstrong, Roy Eldridge, Coleman Hawkins, Oscar Pettiford, Sid Catlett, Barney Bigard, Red Norvo and Lionel Hampton, and singer Billie Holiday. But because the concert was arranged on short notice, the group had little rehearsal and seemed weak at the seams. And though some fine solos made the evening worthwhile, they did not include any by Armstrong, whose reputation as a singer has grown as his trumpet playing has declined. Over the years his lip has taken a beating and he's no longer at ease playing very high or very fast.

Bombers blast Berlin

A B-26 Marauder, armed with 26 100-pound bombs, drops its cargo.

London, March 6

In an all-out effort to destroy the Luftwaffe, the Allies have begun bombing raids on Berlin. American and British Air Force commanders know the Germans will throw everything they have at them to defend the city, the heartland of the Reich. They also know that the Germans can ill afford a war of attrition in aircraft production. The raids are a vote of confidence for the new P-51 fighter escorts, which because of their additional fuel tanks, can fly 850 miles into enemy territory to escort the bombers.

The first raid on March 4 did not do serious damage, but today the Americans sent over 660 bombers and delivered 1,626 tons of bombs. Their losses were great: 69 bombers and 11 fighters, but the figures for downed Luftwaffe aircraft were also high. American bomber crews claimed 97 kills, while the escort fighters shot down 82 planes. One sign of weakening air strength is that the Luftwaffe sent up night fighters against the Americans in a daytime raid. Of equal significance in the ground war is the fact that the Erkner ball bearing factory was knocked out, a loss that could cripple the production of German tanks.

Prizes in the Pacific: Kwajalein, Eniwetok, Hollandia and Wake

New Guinea, May 17

The grip of the Japanese Empire in the Far Pacific is slipping as American forces continue to capture some islands and isolate others. The marines learned a deadly lesson on Tarawa in the Gilberts, where they tried to take a strongly defended island and lost 3,000 marines in the process This time the commanders have hit the Japanese where they are weakest, Kwajalein, the key to the Marshall Islands and the world's largest coral atoll. Despite the fact that it was a command center, it was lightly defended, even after the fall of the adjacent islands of Roi and Namur. The Japanese never really had a chance against the huge armada – four carrier groups, with 12 carriers – that was sent against them. Admiral Chester Nimitz next moved against Eniwetok, the far western atoll in the Marshalls. After taking nearby tiny islands, the marines and army landed against stiff but brief opposition.

The U.S. high command decided to bypass Truk and invade Hollandia, on the north shore of Dutch New Guinea. The Americans had their largest force to date for the Hollandia-Aitape operation, some 84,000 men. Carrier groups sank two enemy destroyers and downed 300 aircraft in the softening up operations. By the time they went ashore, they had total sea and air control. Japanese losses were severe at Hollandia; 1,000 of their 11,000-man force survived. The Allies next hit Wake Island to the north because they view it as a promising air base. The Japanese responded fiercely soon after the Americans landed, but the marines held on and were starting their base even before the island was secured (→ Oct. 25).

American soldiers shielded by "Lucky Legs II" advance on Japanese positions.

[U].S. unveils plan for postwar peace

[W]ashington, D.C., March 21

Secretary of State Cordell Hull [c]alled for international cooperation [t]oday as he unveiled the postwar [g]oals of American foreign policy. [H]ull has been a strong supporter of [t]he emerging United Nations and [m]any of his goals reflect the spirit [o]f the international body, which is [y]et to be formed. Hull, who has [b]een a moderate voice in the Roo[s]evelt administration, has been urg[i]ng the President to formulate a [s]pecific policy for the governing of [G]ermany after the war. Roosevelt [i]s reluctant to proceed, and has [t]old Hull, "I dislike making de[t]ailed plans for a country which [w]e do not yet occupy." But Hull has [s]ucceeded in convincing FDR to [e]nd his support of the Morgenthau Plan, which envisages the dismem[b]erment of Germany into agrarian [s]tates. Hull and Secretary of War Henry Stimson have called the plan "blind vengeance" (→Oct. 7).

Meat rations end

Washington, D.C., May 3

Make that a double hamburger! The Office of Price Administration today ended national meat rationing (except for choice cuts of beef). Ironically, some Americans will now be less well nourished: The poor ate better with a weekly allowance of 28 ounces of meat than their usual income had permitted.

Allied forces enter Rome triumphant

Rome, June 4

Allied forces swept into Rome today, the first European capital liberated from the Nazis. Residents cheered the troops, who had advanced 15 miles in 24 hours, moving so swiftly that they seized 1,000 Nazi prisoners. While Rome is of little military value, the capture of the virtually undamaged city is a great morale booster. The takeover was the culmination of an offensive that broke the Gustav Line and the Hitler Line and created the Anzio breakout. Still, the German army, far from being destroyed, fights on tenaciously. After the invasions last summer, the Germans used the rugged southern half of Italy to great strategic advantage, holding on as long as they could, using rivers as defenses, then falling back to the next defendable position. The worst clash took place at the mountain stronghold of Monte Cassino, and the famous Benedictine Abbey above the town. To dislodge the Germans, the abbey was all but destroyed, a decision that caused much criticism. In the fight for Italy, the American Fifth Army worked its way up the west coast, while Britain's Eighth Army went up the Adriatic side. German resistance caused a near stalemate and, with the invasion of France near, the Allies decided on the May push with a huge cast: Americans, British, Indians, Canadians, Free French, South Africans, Poles and New Zealanders (→Apr. 30, 1945).

U.S. troops in Rome. Coliseum is backdrop for yet another triumphal march.

Residents of Rome welcome the liberating American forces with enthusiasm.

Merrill's Marauders march through Burma

Mules assist U.S. troops in Burma.

Burma, May 18

Merrill's Marauders, officially the 5307th Composite Unit (provisional), has been giving the Japanese fits in Burma. The volunteer group, named for its commanding officer, Colonel Frank D. Merrill, was trained in guerrilla and jungle tactics in India. It has helped General Joseph Stilwell's drive to retake northern Burma. The men marched over hundreds of miles of mountainous jungles to outflank and harass the enemy. They have seized the Myitkyina airfield and if the city falls, Stilwell will have access to deliveries by means of the Burma Road between India and China.

Army seizes firm

Chicago, Apr. 26

Sewell Avery, chairman of Montgomery Ward, has hated this administration since its inception. In 1942 it took a presidential threat to make him sign a closed shop contract mandated by the War Labor Board. He has refused to renew it, and today the President turned a threat into action. Declaring the merchandising firm a war industry, FDR ordered it placed under control of the army. A righteous Avery was carried out of his office in his own desk chair. Saving his most cherished epithet for Attorney General Francis Biddle, Avery yelled, "You New Dealer!"

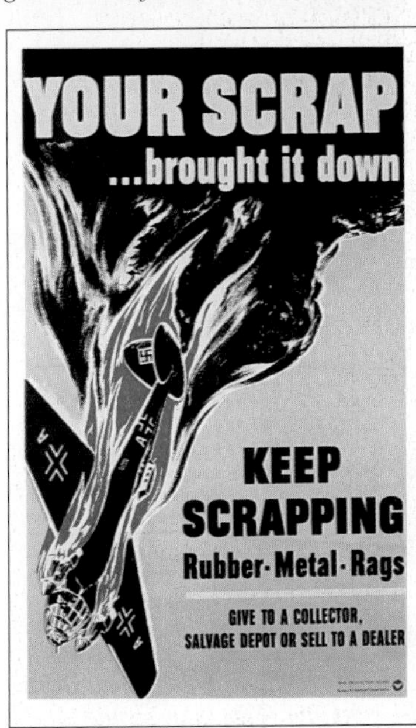

D-Day! Allied troops storm beaches at Normandy

American troops cross the English Channel en route to Normandy's beaches. Seasickness and foul weather complicate the task of the invading Yanks.

After their turbulent crossing, American forces take to the beaches of France. "Full victory," they were ordered by General Eisenhower, "Nothing else."

A small fraction of the Allied army wades ashore at Normandy. The size of the invading force is awesome, and so is the cost of liberating France.

Normandy, France, June 6

The Allies successfully landed about 150,000 men on the Normandy coast of France today, and Hitler's "Atlantic Wall" was breached. "Operation Overlord," the code name of the invasion of France across the English Channel, began at 6:30 a.m. and through the day – D-Day – thousands of men and tons of equipment were put ashore on five designated beaches.

The invasion began much earlier farther inland. Two divisions of Americans, the 82nd and 101st Airborne, left England at midnight and began dropping into their landing zones at about 1 a.m. High winds scattered the paratroopers and most put down far from their intended targets. Nevertheless, small groups were quickly formed and began to attack the Germans, causing more confusion and disarray than actual damage.

The resistance met at the landing beaches was less than had been anticipated because the Germans were taken almost completely by surprise. Considering the size of the invasion plan, eventually to involve almost three million soldiers, sailors and airmen, to be transported by 11,000 ships, it is amazing that the Germans did not learn the true location of the landing sites, making it the biggest secret ever kept. The nationalities of troops and the code names of the beaches, east to west, where they landed were: British troops at Sword, Canadians at Juno, British at Gold, and Americans at Omaha and Utah.

The British and Canadians went ashore against stiff opposition despite effective support from the offshore fleet. They were able to take and secure the beaches in spite of heavy losses. It was a mixed bag for American troops. There was little opposition at Utah Beach, but at Omaha the First Division faced German veterans of the 352nd Division, who held high bluffs commanding a wide view of the beach. They kept the Americans pinned down most of the day and could have pushed them back into the sea had they been better supported. The Americans finally realized that it would be wise to advance against the intense fire because staying put would get them killed. The move inland was sparked by Brigadier General Norman Cota, who calmly walked up and down Omaha Beach in withering fire, urging his troops to move farther ashore. This beach operation cost the Americans 2,000 casualties today.

The response of the Germans to the invasion was slow and confused. Hitler believed that it was only a feint. He expected the real invasion at the Pas de Calais and therefore withheld two Panzer divisions. By the time he released them late today, the Allies were safely ashore with secured beachheads. General Erwin Rommel, of Afrika Korps fame, had been designated by Hitler to stop the invasion. Rommel knew that for Germany this would be a fateful day, but Hitler had tied his hands.

By mid-day the beaches of Normandy swarmed with soldiers and tanks and the beautiful white sand was littered with bodies. Burning vehicles were everywhere and the air was heavy with pungent cordite. American Rangers stormed the Pointe du Hoc, a large protrusion used as a battery position for heavy guns. Offshore shelling had made the area around the guns look like "the craters of the moon" as one soldier described the scene, but when the emplacement was taken, the Rangers discovered that the guns were "Quakers," dummy pieces so named because they offer no resistance. As soon as the beaches were secured, the Allied command began unloading tons of equipment along with men onto "Mulberries," the huge, transportable docks or jetties (→ Aug. 25).

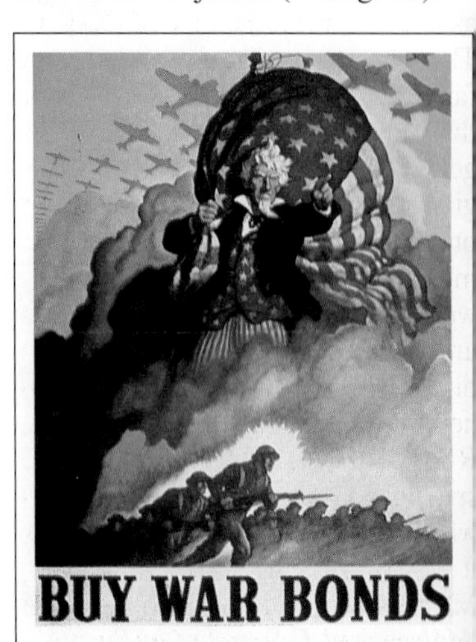

ʀoosevelt approves ;.I. Bill of Rights

ᐟashington, D.C., June 22

President Roosevelt, signing the ·.I. Bill of Rights today, said, "It ives emphatic notice to the men nd women in the armed forces that e American people do not intend) let them down." The Service-ıen's Readjustment Act (its offi-al name) will provide housing and ducational assistance for returning ar veterans. The bill is set in Jef-rsonian philosophy – that gov-rnment should promote educa-on. Money for a year's schooling ill be offered to all veterans, and) those with special skills, funds re available for three years (→ 1947).

ɩmericans invade rance from south

ɩijon, France, Sept. 11

The Allied army that invaded the outh of France on August 15 has riven up the Rhone Valley via the istoric Route Napoleon and linked p with units of General George 'atton Jr.'s Third Army. The Sixth ɩrmy Group, under General Ja-ob Devers, now becomes the right ɩank of an enormous Allied wedge imed at the heart of Germany.

Operation Anvil was renamed)peration Dragoon just before the ınding for security reasons, and he change is significant because it ymbolizes the overall squabbling hat plagued the high command in ɩlanning the operation. After more ɩf such squabbling, it was agreed hat three American divisions and even French divisions would go ɩshore on beaches east of Toulon. They met only light opposition, and arther inland, 25,000 members of he Free French underground ea-ɡerly rushed to join the invaders, ɡiving them detailed information ɩn German positions and troop ɩovements. The German defenses vere weak, consisting of reserves ɩnd second-line troops. These con-ɩitions allowed the combined Al-ied force to drive rapidly up the Rhone Valley. There was a brief, poradic German defense, but no-vhere was the fighting as fierce as t was in the north. By late August, Marseilles had fallen and the Allies ɩad reached Grenoble (→ Dec. 26).

Paris rejoices as Nazi grip is broken

Paris, Aug. 25

The great race for Paris is over and the liberation of the city has become a frenzied, tumultuous celebration. Originally, the Allies had intended to bypass the French capital because the Allied commander, General Dwight D. Eisenhower, did not want the problem of feeding several million people. But General Charles de Gaulle, who led the Free French forces, began acting on his own as soon as he arrived from Algeria and told General Philippe Leclerc of the Second Armored Division to go for Paris regardless of Eisenhower's wishes. After the collapse of the Falaise pocket, which resulted in the capture of 50,000 Germans and the death of 10,000 more, all roads to the Seine were open, precipitating a mad dash for the city.

The Third Army of General George S. Patton Jr. reached Mantes-la-Jolie, 30 miles from Paris, on August 19, the day the capital rose against its occupiers. Free French forces, Communists, Socialists and students began street uprisings against the Nazis. Hitler had planned to demolish Paris rather than allow it to fall into Allied hands, but the German demolition teams waited until it was too late and, before they could act, the streets were filled with French and American troops as de Gaulle marched down the Champs Elysees and went to mass at Notre Dame.

The American novelist Ernest Hemingway, who has lived in and loved Paris, arrived with the first group of liberators. He went to visit his old friend Pablo Picasso and gave him a large box as a present. "What's in the box, Ernest?" the painter asked. "Hand grenades," Hemingway replied.

As the Allies began entering the city, the French Resistance took over the main radio station and Parisians heard the following announcement: "Parisians, rejoice, we have come to tell you that the Leclerc division has reached Paris. We are mad with happiness." The announcer then quoted Victor Hugo: "Awake, be done with shame! Become again great France, become again great Paris." After five years of darkness, the City of Lights was reborn (→ Sept. 11).

An American military column stretching for miles rumbles past smashed German armor. Now all roads lead to the long-awaited liberation of Paris.

American paratroopers display a Nazi flag found while liberating a small French village. Allied strikes behind enemy lines help distract the already surprised and confused German troops.

With the Germans in retreat, American soldiers celebrate their victory at a makeshift Paris cafe. The city as well as their spirits have been liberated.

"I have returned," says MacArthur

The Philippines, Oct. 25

As the United States Sixth Army landed on the island of Leyte, General Douglas MacArthur, with film cameras rolling, announced, "People of the Philippines, I have returned." And as ground forces began to fight it out on the large island in the center of the Philippine archipelago, the Japanese prepared a counterattack called the "Sho plan" or Victory plan. The resulting series of naval engagements left the Americans in strategic control of the entire Pacific.

The Japanese knew that losing the Philippines would mean losing the war, so they threw everything they could into this effort. It was a complicated operation, consisting of several strike forces converging on the islands the Americans had just invaded. Vice Admiral Takeo Kurita's Central Force was intercepted while still in the South China Sea and, since the Japanese had little air cover, their ships were without effective defense. American flyers hit and sank the Musashi, the largest battleship in the world. But the Japanese drew blood when they sank the small aircraft carrier Princeton.

In Surigao Strait, the Japanese sailed into a trap baited with the ghosts of Pearl Harbor; battleships raised from the mud, rebuilt and out for revenge. The Japanese had to run a gauntlet that allowed the dreadnoughts to bring their enormous guns to bear and, within an hour, several ships were sunk and Vice Admiral Ahoji Nishimura was killed. Japan's losses were huge: 26 vessels, or 300,000 tons of combat shipping, lost. The American losses were minimal (→Nov. 24).

"People of the Philippines, I have returned," announced MacArthur, at left.

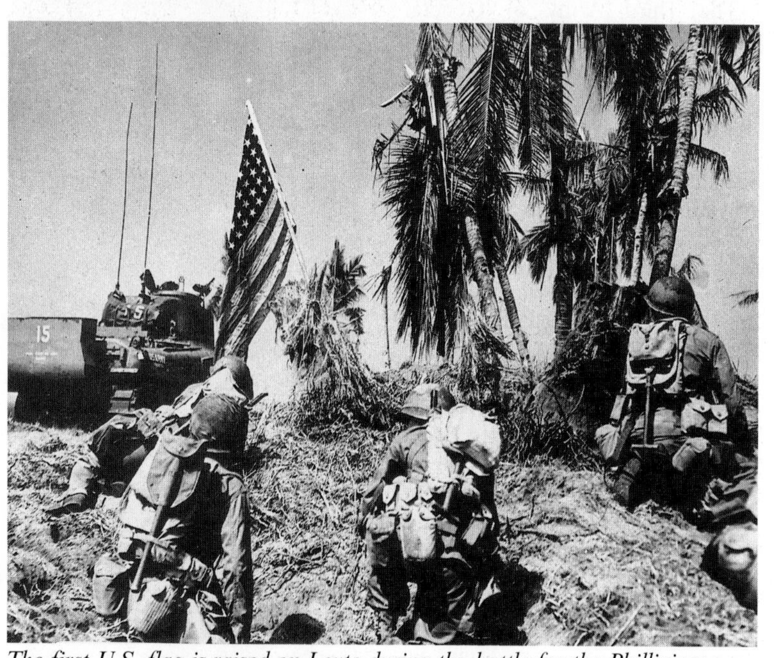

The first U.S. flag is raised on Leyte during the battle for the Phillipines.

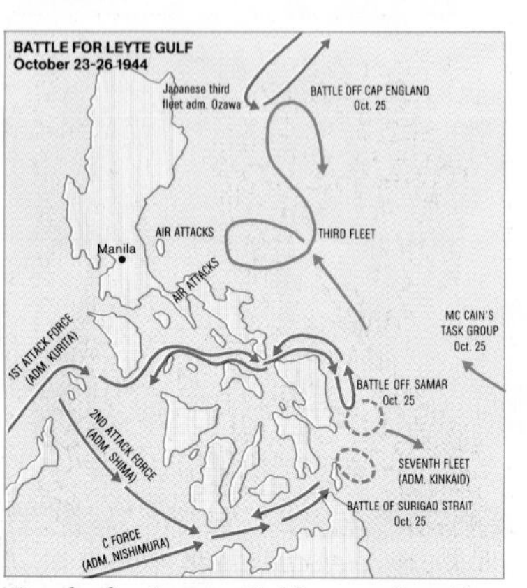

Battle for Leyte Gulf turns the tide.

FDR wins 4th term; Truman is new V.P.

Washington, D.C., Nov. 7

President Roosevelt rewrote th history books tonight as he won a unprecedented fourth term in o fice. Roosevelt, with his runnin mate Harry S. Truman, the feisty pragmatic Missouri Senator, de feated Governor Thomas E. Dewe of New York. Democrats also kep control of Congress. Reacting t attacks, FDR had said with mocl outrage: "Republican leaders ar not content with attacks (on me an my family); they now include m little dog, Fala. Unlike members o my family, he resents this." Roose velt won big in the electoral count but his popular vote margin wa smaller than before.

Lowbrow and high

New York City, Oct. 30

The Voice, sometimes called th King of Swoon, sometimes Frank Swoonatra, continues to mesmeriz teenaged girls. As 10,000 bobby soxers jostled for tickets and 70 cops tried to keep order, those wh got into the Paramount Theater o October 12 squealed as Sinatr crooned tunes in a tempo describe by *Life* magazine as invariabl "largo alla marcia funebre."

At the other end of the cultu ral scale is the composer Aaro Copland, whose ballet *Appalachia Spring* was given its premiere by th Martha Graham Dance Compan in Washington today. A rustic slic of Americana, it depicts a wedding in a Pennsylvania farm community Copland uses a tune borrowed fro the Shakers, *Simple Gifts*, to grea effect.

World leaders agree on postwar economic, political structure

Washington, D.C., Oct. 7

Positive steps have been taken to create a framework for a new world organization to be called the United Nations. Representatives of the United States, Britain, the Soviet Union and China attended a conference at the majestic Dumbarton Oaks estate here. The Allies agreed that the new organization will be divided into a General Assembly and a Security Council whose purpose would be "to take such action by air, naval or land forces to maintain or restore international peace and security."

The conferees failed to reach agreement on two key issues raised by Andrei A. Gromyko, the Soviet Ambassador to Washington. He insisted that all 16 Soviet republics be granted seats in the Assembly. Gromyko also demanded that the Great Powers all be empowered to exercise a veto over substantive matters before the Security Council. The conference highlighted a disagreement between Britain and the U.S. Roosevelt and Secretary of State Cordell Hull believe there should "no longer be any need for spheres of influence" that countries use "to safeguard their security or promote their interests." The British like the U.N., but they also like their empire (→Aug. 8, 1945).

As Guam falls, so does Tojo's regime

Guam, Nov. 24

The Japanese have lost Guam, and with it, the battle for the Marianas, a struggle that cost them 50,000 soldiers killed in action. The July invasion of the strategically important island was fiercely contested by the enemy, and some marine rifle companies suffered 50 to 55 percent casualties. The seizure of Guam has led to an unexpected result: the fall of Hideki Tojo's government in Tokyo. Elsewhere in the Pacific, in the air battle for Formosa [Taiwan], the Japanese Typhoon Attack Force was eliminated, and Admiral William Halsey reports the destruction of 500 enemy planes (→ Feb. 23, 1945).

Glenn Miller lost

Paris, Dec. 24

Americans have apparently lost one of their most beloved musicmakers – the band leader Glenn Miller, who left civilian life to play with the Air Force band. On December 16, Major Miller took a plane from England for Paris. The weather was bad, the plane never arrived and no traces have been found. Hopes that he might yet turn up were dimmed today when the 40-year-old Miller was officially listed as missing and presumed dead. The smoothly understated sound of Miller's music crystalized with the formation of his second band in 1939. His recordings of *In the Mood*, *Tuxedo Junction* and *Moonlight Serenade* have become classics. Despite Miller's absence, the band is still entertaining the Allied troops at a theater in Paris.

TV networks seen

New York City, March 1

"Television promises to be the greatest medium of mass communication yet evolved," said NBC president Niles Trammell today. He predicts a vast expansion in television operations right after the war, with the creation of regional and national networks. CBS, which halted its fledgling television news broadcasts after Pearl Harbor, is also preparing for expansion.

U.S. recoups losses in Battle of Bulge

German prisoners of war being marched out of Dutch town of Limbricht.

An American soldier views the shattered train station at Aachen, Germany.

Bastogne, Belgium, Dec. 26

It came to be called the Battle of the Bulge. In a gamble to stop the Allied advance into Germany and recapture the crucial Belgian supply port of Antwerp, Hitler secretly organized a desperate counterattack. It began on December 16, catching the Allies off guard, and punched a dangerous bulge into the American lines in Belgium. Now the Allies are hammering at the bulge and shrinking it.

The Germans had cannibalized their war machine to create two new Panzer armies under General Sepp Dietrich. They waited until bad weather had grounded Allied planes; then they hit hard.

A special English-speaking commando group, under Colonel Otto Skorzeny, the man who had rescued Mussolini, donned captured American uniforms and caused great confusion behind the American lines. When the word spread that Germans were impersonating Americans, anyone who looked suspicious was asked questions such as the names of the Brooklyn Dodgers or who married Betty Grable. The drive shattered two American divisions. The 101st Airborne was totally surrounded at Bastogne, a major junction in the Ardennes. The Germans sent word to Brigadier General Anthony McAuliffe demanding surrender, and were rebuffed with one word: "Nuts!"

The Germans' failure to take Bastogne deprived them of fuel they had hoped to capture at nearby dumps. As the Americans began retaking ground, they were horrified to find that some prisoners taken by the SS had been massacred (→ March 28, 1945).

"Kilroy was here," there and everywhere

United States

Nobody knows for certain who Kilroy is. But everyone knows his name gets around. One dictionary calls Kilroy a fictitious American created by G.I.'s who left the inscription "Kilroy was here" on surfaces all over the world. James Kilroy of Halifax, Massachusetts, says that as an inspector at a shipyard in Quincy he would chalk "Kilroy was here" on work he had inspected, and the slogan caught on.

In any case, G.I.'s and the name Kilroy have become linked, often evoking patriotic efforts back home. On assembly lines, workers are turning out cargo ships in 17 days, bombers in 13. In a year of salvage drives, the home folks collected seven million tons of wastepaper and 18 million tons of scrap metal to be made into war materiel. It's all to bring Kilroy back here.

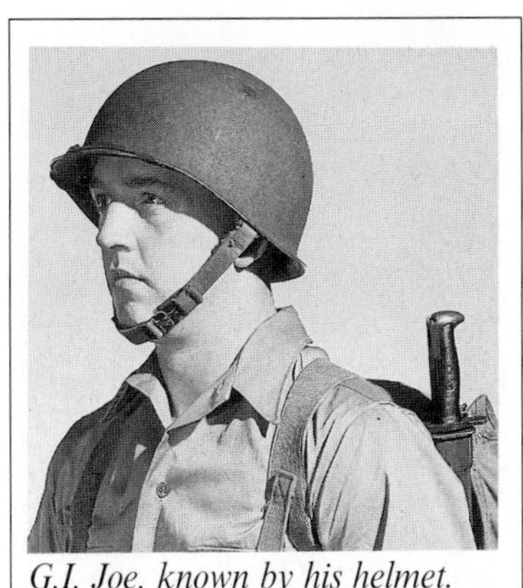

G.I. Joe, known by his helmet.

The Big War: Sixteen million Americans in uniform

Americans are urged to keep up their guard against enemy spies. "Loose lips sink ships" is a popular phrase.

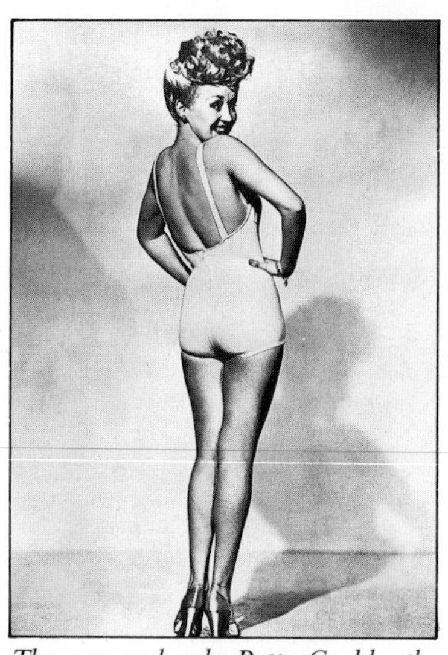

The one and only Betty Grable, the pin-up queen of the G.I.'s. This photo has made its way around the world.

On November 20, 1943, the entire crew of six that manned this gun, part o Battery F, 3rd Defense, on Bougainville, was killed by a Japanese bomb. Sur rounded by enemy fire on all sides, a G.I. never knows when his time has come

Infantry soldiers, the shock troops of the war, on the march. "Born to freedom, and believing in freedom," says FDR, Americans "are willing to fight to maintain freedom . . . We would rather die on our feet than live on our knees."

Robert W. Prescott with Curtiss P-40 of the American Volunteer Group, also known as the "Flying Tigers."

Brigadier General Benjamin Davis America's first Negro General, pic tured here in August of 1944.

The face of war. "Courage," said Mark Twain, "is resistance to fear, mastery of fear, not absence of fear."

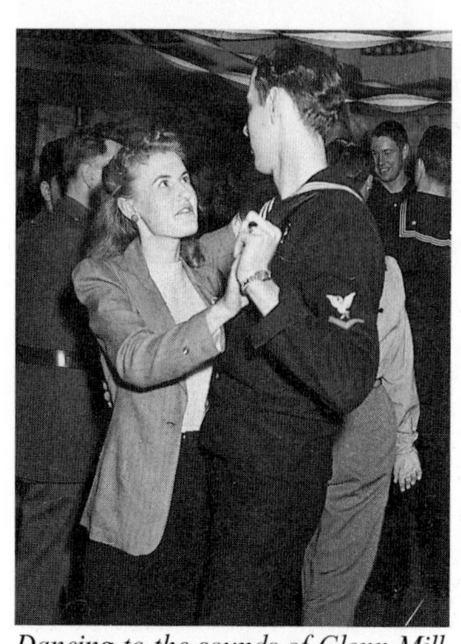

Dancing to the sounds of Glenn Miller, in a brief but cherished moment away from the front lines of battle.

Negro soldiers in training in Louisiana in September of 1941. While the Unite States fights against Adolf Hitler and his racist ideology, the American arme forces remain segregated. Such a contradiction will, perhaps, end someday.

A fierce fight to the finish for the world's freedom

rving Berlin wrote "This Is the Army," a show with an all-soldier cast, in 942. But the composer of "White Christmas" and "God Bless America" is est loved by soldiers for his "Oh, How I Hate to Get Up in the Morning."

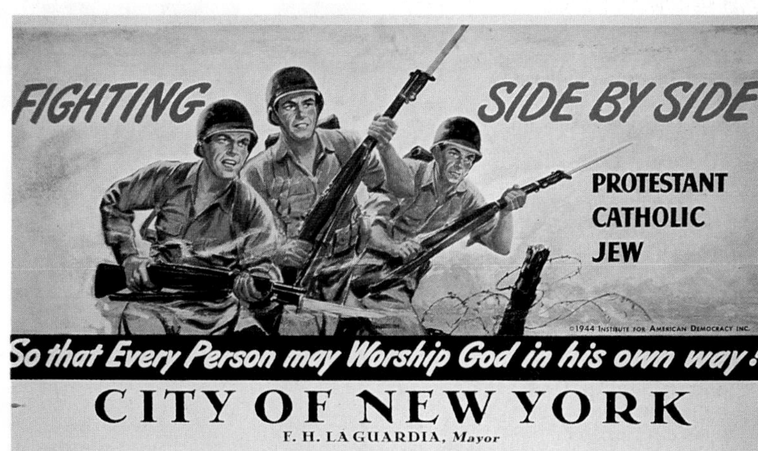

The United States went to war to fight for freedom and against fascism, a totalitarian philosophy that preaches hatred and religious persecution. In America, the Bill of Rights provides for freedom of religion. As President Franklin Roosevelt says, "We look forward to a world (founded on the) freedom of every person to worship God in his own way - everywhere in the world."

Vith their husbands, brothers and sons at war overseas, some 3.5 million American women have taken jobs on factory assembly lines, in stores and offices. For such working women, trousers have become a "badge of honor."

Waves of B-24's of the 15th Air Force fly over the Concordia Vega oil refinery in Ploesti, Rumania. After dropping their bomb loads on an oil cracking plant on May 31, 1944, they head for home base, unmindful of the bursting flak.

A kamikaze plane attack on the USS Missouri in 1945. Japanese pilots commit suicide for their country.

An aerial view of the southern tip of Manhattan. New York City is now the world's financial capital, replacing London, and its growth is symbolic of America's rise to global power and responsibilities in the wake of the war.

Bob Hope is off to entertain troops in a U.S.O. show. His theme song? "Thanks for the Memory."

1945

Truman

Washington, D.C., Jan. 3. House of Representatives votes to establish temporary Committee on Un-American Activities as permanent body.

Washington, D.C., Jan. 15. A "dim-out" ordered for entire United States to combat shortage of fuel.

New York City, May 7. John Hersey wins Pulitzer Prize in fiction for *A Bell for Adano.*

Washington, D.C., May 10. A point system will determine priority of military discharge, taking into consideration service record, length of service and parental status.

Washington, D.C., May 25. Federal government orders reduction in military aircraft production by 30 percent.

New York City, June 23. Eisenhower quoted as saying, "Morale is the single greatest factor" in winning wars.

Washington, D.C., July 6. Executive order establishes Medal of Freedom, to honor outstanding civilian achievement.

New York City, July 28. A B-25 bomber crashes into Empire State Building, killing 13 people and injuring 26.

Hiroshima, Japan, Aug. 5. Americans drop leaflets on city, warning, "Your city will be obliterated unless your government surrenders."

Gary, Indiana, Sept. 18. Almost 1,000 white students at Froebel School boycott classes, in effort to have their Negro classmates transferred to other schools.

Detroit, Sept. 21. Henry Ford resigns as president of Ford Motor Company, and grandson Henry Ford II is elected to replace him.

Chicago, Oct. 10. Detroit Tigers defeat Chicago Cubs in World Series, four games to three.

Washington, D.C., Nov. 27. President Truman announces appointment of Gen. George C. Marshall as special envoy to China, to mediate conflict between Nationalists and Communists (→ Jan. 7, 1947).

Cleveland, Dec. 16. Cleveland Rams edge Washington Redskins, 15-14, in National Football League championship.

New York City. *Cannery Row* by John Steinbeck published.

Big Three carve up world at Yalta

Churchill, Roosevelt and Stalin convene in order to create a new world order.

Yalta, U.S.S.R., Feb. 11

Premier Stalin was more than the host today as he bade farewell to his guests in the Crimea. As Prime Minister Churchill and President Roosevelt adjourned their difficult meeting at the Livadia Palace here, it seemed apparent that Stalin was also the victor. His stunning successes on the battlefield had strengthened his hand at the bargaining table, and Stalin got almost everything that he wanted.

The Western leaders reluctantly adopted Stalin's view that Germany be divided and punished harshly when the war is over. Reparations could run as high as $20 billion, and the Soviet Union will receive half the amount. Stalin did agree to allow France to be the fourth occupying power in Germany, but the French zone will be carved out of the territory controlled by the Americans and the British.

Poland was perhaps the thorniest issue, and Stalin didn't budge. "For the Russian people," he argued, "Poland is not only a question of honor but also a question of security. Throughout history, Poland has been the corridor through which the enemy has passed into Russia." Reluctantly, Roosevelt and Churchill allowed Stalin to move his border with Poland west to the Curzon Line. The Lublin Committee, a Russian puppet, was charged with forming a new regime, and the Polish government-in-exile in London was left out of negotiations.

Stalin's influence was also recognized in the Balkans, and Roosevelt made him new promises about the Far East. In exchange for joining the war against Japan, the Russians were promised the Kurile Islands, southern Sakhalin and railway rights in Manchuria.

Marines raise Old Glory over Iwo Jima

Iwo Jima, Feb. 23

Iwo Jima is a few square miles of volcanic ash and sand lying 700 miles south of Tokyo. Taking it from the Japanese has cost the lives of 6,800 men, and wounded 18,000 others. The U.S. high command was willing to pay the price because Iwo Jima is an ideal site for an air base from which to bomb the home island of Japan. The job of taking it went to the Fourth and Fifth Marine Divisions, under General Harry Schmidt. Battleships, cruisers and aircraft-carrier planes pounded the island relentlessly for three days before the marine landing, but the island, honeycombed with tunnels and concrete pillboxes, hid enough defenders to cause 3,000 American casualties the first day. It took four days, after the initial landing, to plant the American flag atop Mount Suribachi, where a photographer, Joe Rosenthal, caught the moment.

The flag rises on Mount Suribachi.

The battle for the rest of the island was just as tough because the enemy soldiers were dug in and had been ordered to fight to the death. The marines used satchel charges of dynamite and napalm to blast the fanatical defenders from their holes. In the end, only 200 Japanese soldiers were taken prisoner. All the others lay in the holes where they had died (→ March 4).

Enemy resistance ends in Manila

Manila, Philippines, March 4

General Douglas MacArthur had to blast the Japanese from the old walled city of Intramuros, in central Manila, with point-blank artillery fire, and most of the city is now in ruins. But that was the price that had to be paid to get it back. MacArthur's Eighth Army landed at Leyte Gulf on northern Luzon in mid-December and faced tough, often fanatical opposition to get back to the city he left in 1942. At that time, he declared Manila an open city, but the Japanese commander ignored such niceties, and the city was finally cleared in house-to-house fighting. The worst fighting occurred near the University of the Philippines, where the defenders had to be rooted out one by one. A big problem for MacArthur is the repatriation of thousands of American prisoners who suffered terribly in Japanese camps and looked like skeletons when released (→ June 22).

Patton leads U.S. troops across Rhine

General Patton leads the way.

The Rhine, March 28

A vital bridgehead across the Rhine has been secured by an armored spearhead of the U.S. 1st Army at Remagen. Once the bridgehead was secured Gen. Omar Bradley ordered all available forces to Remagen to take advantage of an incredible bit of American luck and daring. Gen. George S. Patton's troops have swept the west bank of German resistance and his troops began crossing the Rhine on pontoon bridges at Oppenheim, between Mainz and Mannheim.

On March 7, Patton's 3rd Army broke through weak German defenses at the Eifel plateau. Lt. Karl Timmerman, with an armored unit of the 1st Army, was amazed to find an intact bridge at Remagen, a small town halfway between Cologne and Coblentz. As Timmerman's men crossed the railroad bridge, explosions went off, but the bridge was not damaged (→ Apr. 25).

Collapsed bridge across the Rhine.

Beloved FDR dies; Truman steps in

Warm Springs, Georgia, Apr. 12

A shocked nation is in mourning tonight for Franklin Delano Roosevelt. The President died this afternoon at the "Little White House" in this small Georgia town. Vice President Harry S. Truman was on Capitol Hill when the President died. He was rushed to the White House, where he offered his condolences to Mrs. Roosevelt before he was sworn in as the 32nd President of the United States.

Doctors say Roosevelt passed away at 3:35 p.m., two hours after he suffered a cerebral hemorrhage. Grace Tully, his private secretary, said, "The shock was unexpected and the actuality of the event was outside belief." In recent days, Roosevelt appeared to be recuperating from the stresses of war and the Yalta Conference. His pulse was normal when Commander Howard Bruenn examined him this morning. In the afternoon, Roosevelt was sitting for a portrait by Elizabeth Shoumatoff, who had been introduced by his long-time friend, Lucy Mercer Rutherfurd. She was with Roosevelt when he slumped in his chair.

After Mrs. Roosevelt was informed of her husband's death, she said, "I am more sorry for the people of this country and of the world than I am for ourselves." When Truman asked the First Lady what he could do for her, she replied, "Is there anything we can do for you? You are the one in trouble now."

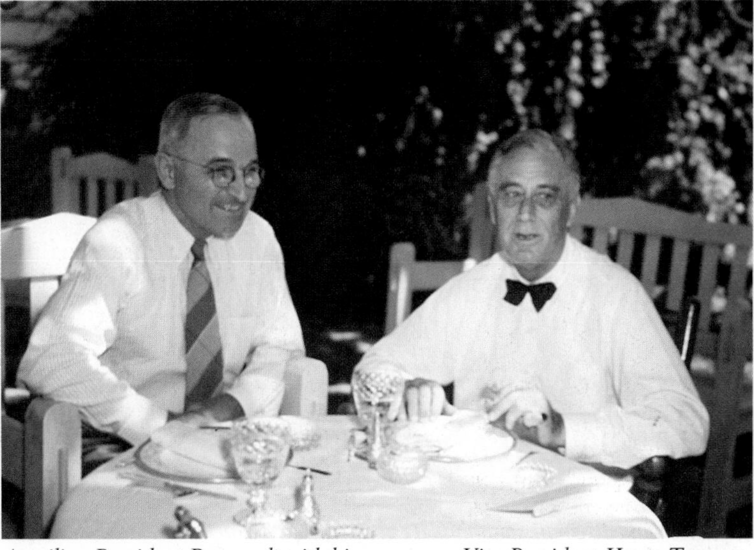

An ailing President Roosevelt with his successor, Vice President Harry Truman.

The President's casket makes its way toward Union Station and the trip home.

Ernie Pyle is killed

Iwo Jima, Apr. 18

His most recent book, published last year, was *Brave Men*. Its topic was the American soldiers, who considered Ernie Pyle one of their own. He was loved no less by readers; they studied his syndicated dispatches as intently as letters sent from a husband or son. But the beloved byline will appear no more. Today, Ernie Pyle became a casualty of the war he wrote about so eloquently. He died in the thick of the action, elbow to elbow with G.I.'s on Iwo Jima, the island taken by marines after ferocious fighting. A machine gun blast wrote the final word on Ernie Pyle. He was 45.

Marines vanquish Japanese on Okinawa

Okinawa, June 22

The beautiful island of Okinawa lies equidistant from Manila and Tokyo and it is strategically important because its fall would leave Formosa [Taiwan] isolated. The American commanders underestimated the number of defenders on the island as well as the existence of fortified defensive lines. The attackers had an easy time with landings on April 1, but then they ran up against the defensive lines. They hit the Machinato Line on April 7 and it took six days of fighting to get past it. The Japanese were, at the same time, sending massive air sorties against the surrounding fleet, using hundreds of suicide attacks. These kamikaze attacks, in which planes are deliberately crashed into their targets, caused the death of 5,000 American sailors and damaged many ships. On the island, the marines hit the Shuri Line next, causing it to collapse, then faced a last-ditch effort by the Japanese, now at the edge of the island. The two sides continued to pound each other until the Japanese defense crumbled. Rather than be taken prisoner, many Japanese soldiers leapt off cliffs to their deaths. The Americans suffered 50,000 casualties, and the Japanese 117,000, all but 7,000 of them killed (→ Aug. 2).

Americans and Russians meet at Elbe

American and Russian commanders greet each other at the Elbe River.

Allies-in-arms march through Torgau, Germany, as Third Reich collapses.

Torgau, Germany, Apr. 25
General Courtney H. Hodges of the United States First Army and Marshal Ivan Konev of the First Ukranian Army met at the Elbe River near Leipzig today and shook hands. The meeting symbolized the further collapse of the Third Reich, which has now been split in half by the conquering armies. After the Allies crossed the Rhine, the American Ninth Army and the First Army invaded the Ruhr industrial basin, encircling the Wehrmacht and trapping 300,000 men, two dozen generals and an admiral.

It is rumored that Field Marshal Walther Model committed suicide when the Ruhr pocket collapsed, though his body hasn't been found. Leaving several army corps to reduce the pocket and deal with the huge numbers of prisoners, the Americans headed for the Elbe.

About this time, General Dwight D. Eisenhower made a decision that has caused some controversy. Since the Americans and British were 200 miles from Berlin and the Russians only 35 miles, the Supreme Commander decided not to attempt to march on the city. This means that the German capital will fall into Russian hands, and Allied leaders, including Churchill, are concerned about the postwar political implications (→ May 7).

Tragedy unveiled: Death and life at Buchenwald and Dachau

Germany, April
Some American soldiers are learning in the grimmest way what they've been fighting for all these years. As they help free the survivors at the Buchenwald and Dachau death camps, they realize one purpose of the war: to end such atrocities. Many of the G.I.'s cannot bear to look at the Nazi legacy – lifeless bodies stacked in ovens, the emaciated living hovering near death. The Americans feel foolish offering their gifts; they brought books and papers, but some survivors don't have the strength to turn a page; their eyes are sunken, they hardly see. Still, they are grateful. One Dachau prisoner tells how he felt when he saw the tanks roll in: "We were free! We broke into weeping, kissed the tank. A Negro soldier gave us a tin of meat, bread and chocolate ... We sat down on the ground and ate up all the food together. The Negro watched us, tears in his eyes."

Eyes of the death camp inmates testify to man's inhumanity to man.

German military ousted from Italy

Milan, Italy, Apr. 30
The remainder of the Italian army surrendered to the Allies yesterday along with German forces under Colonel General Heinrich von Vietinghoff. On the day before, Mussolini's Salo Republic collapsed and Il Duce and his mistress Claretta Petacci, were executed by partisans who hung them upside down in Milan. The army's surrender was the culmination of an Allied drive to finish off Italy that was launched on April 2. The Germans held fast for a week, but the American Fifth Army then rolled into the Po Valley and entered Bologna and Modena.

Oregon "bombing"

Lakeview, Oregon, May 5
A woman and five children in a fishing party were killed by an explosion in the mountain country near here today. The only survivor was a Pastor Mitchell of the Christian Alliance Church. "Joan, 11, came and told us that there was an object nearby," he said. "We went to investigate. It blew up and killed them all." It is reported that the "object" was a Japanese bomb, but how it got there is a mystery. The children were 11 to 13 years old.

Nazi U-boat is sunk off of Block Island

Block Island, R.I., May 6
Despite the fact that the German military machine is collapsing, the deadly war between destroyers and U-boat packs continues, as evidenced by the sinking today of a U-boat off the coast of New England. A double screen of American warships was patrolling the Atlantic north of the Azores in an effort to crush the last-gasp attempt by Admiral Karl Doenitz to destroy Allied shipping with his new snorkel-equipped submarines. Destroyer sonar picked up a blip, and two warships, the Moseby and the Atherton, were quickly dispatched. After a chase, they ran their prey to ground and sank German U-853 with all its crew.

Victory in Europe: Germans surrender; Hitler dead

The fight in Europe is over and Americans delight in their hard-won triumph.

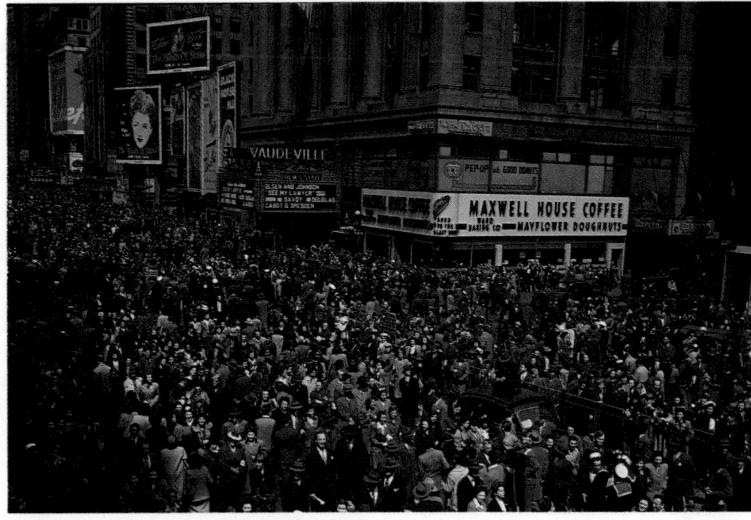

Victory in Europe, jubilation in New York: Whooping it up in Times Square.

Berlin, May 7

Adolf Hitler is dead, his Thousand Year Reich is destroyed, and the war in Europe is over. The beginning of the end for Germany was the Russian drive that began on April 16. Soviet troops reached Berlin by the 22nd and surrounded the city a few days later. Hitler and his mistress, Eva Braun, the Goebbels family and a few followers remained in an underground bunker where the Fuehrer played with nonexistent armies on a large war map. Above ground, the Russian army was blasting into rubble what Allied planes had failed to destroy. On May 1, as the last fanatical resistance was being eliminated, Hitler married Miss Braun and the two of them, followed by Joseph Goebbels and his family, committed suicide. SS troops burned their bodies with gasoline.

The next day, Russian soldiers hoisted the hammer and sickle flag atop the Brandenburg Gate. The leadership of the ruined Reich was turned over to Grand Admiral Karl Doenitz, who quickly moved to end the suffering of Germany. The Germans attempted to surrender to the Western Allies alone but the effort was spurned. Finally today, the new German leaders signed an unconditional surrender, thus making May 7 VE Day, to signify victory in Europe.

The cost of the war to the Germans proved horrendous. Unlike the Great War, which was fought on the soil of other countries, this war devastated the German homeland. Germany had mustered 20 million soldiers, half of whom were in uniform at a time. Some 3.25 million German men died from causes other than combat. A million more are listed as missing and the fate of these is not likely to be known, ever. Among the Allies, the British and the French each lost 250,000 in battle. More than six million Soviet soldiers died and the United States lost 400,000 men (→ Oct. 16, 1946).

Japan is ravaged by American bombers

Japan, August

Unlike the cities of Germany, which were well defended and built of masonry, the cities of Japan are completely undefended and built of highly flammable materials. The results have been catastrophic.

B-29 bombers set Japan's cities afire.

Early this year, General Curtis Lemay changed the bombing tactics. The B-29's began to bomb at night, descending to 7,000 feet for runs, and they used a far greater proportion of incendiary bombs. On March 9, Tokyo was hit by 200 Super Fortresses, a bigger version of the Flying Fortress, which delivered 1,600 tons of incendiaries. The city center, a 16-square-mile area, was destroyed. The bombers then began hitting Yokohama, Nagoya, Kobe and Osaka.

Japan's big cities have been virtually destroyed in two months of raids. And millions are homeless as the Army Air Force begins to hit the smaller cities. The United States wants to immobilize Japan's home islands before an invasion begins. Allied commanders believe such an invasion will cost over a million casualties.

Big Three demand surrender of Japan

Potsdam, Germany, Aug. 2

The mutuality of interests of the United States, Britain and the Soviet Union has disintegrated since the surrender of Germany, but at the Potsdam Conference here the Great Powers have come together to send a clear message to Tokyo. They have ordered the Japanese to follow Germany's example and surrender unconditionally. The alternative, they warn, is for Japan to "lay herself open to complete and utter destruction."

Of the three major leaders who participated in the conference at Yalta, only Premier Stalin has survived in power. President Roosevelt is dead and the British voters turned Prime Minister Churchill out of office. So at the conference here in Potsdam, Stalin was able to play a strong hand, and he played it forcefully. He has refused to move his troops eastward in Poland, he has described British accusations of repression in the Balkans as "fairy tales" and he has indicated that Soviet troops will continue to dismantle German factories and machinery (→ Aug. 10).

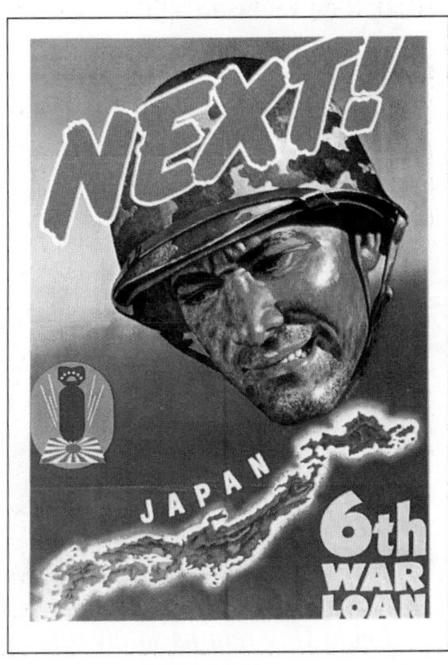

Atomic bombs unleashed on Hiroshima, Nagasaki

Japan, Aug. 10

The B-29 bomber Enola Gay, named after its commander's mother, dropped a single terrible weapon on the city of Hiroshima on August 6 and ushered in the Atomic Age. The bomb destroyed 80 percent of the buildings in Hiroshima and severely damaged the rest. At least 70,000 to 80,000 people were killed, many of them within a second of the explosion and its accompanying firestorm.

Sixteen hours after the bomb was dropped, President Truman called upon the Japanese government to surrender and thus avoid "a rain of ruin" from the air. Japan did not respond, and two days later Nagasaki suffered the same fate as Hiroshima. This time 35,000 people were killed, 60,000 were injured and more than 5,000 vanished. The entire city was flattened and, at ground zero, directly below the bomb's detonation, nothing at all remained standing.

During the summer of 1944, the 509th Bombardment Group began training under Colonel Paul W. Tibbets Jr., a pilot with an excellent record. Tibbets was the only member of the training group who knew the exact nature of the bomb: that it was made of fissionable material and that it would produce an explosion hundreds of times more deadly than any weapon ever known to man. The other pilots and men simply referred to their new weapon as "the gimmick." Before setting up its headquarters on Tinian Island in the Marianas, the group trained secretly at Wendover Field in Utah and in Cuba, always flying the same mock mission, which was to drop a single 500- or 1,000-pound bomb precisely on target.

For the mission on which the nuclear bomb would actually be dropped, seven B-29's were assigned. Involved was a single weapon with an explosive power equal to 20,000 tons of TNT. The first atomic bomb was successfully tested in New Mexico on July 16. On August 5, three weather planes left Tinian, followed the next day by three other Super Fortresses filled with civilian and military observers and scientific instruments. A seventh plane was in reserve. En route to Hiroshima, the crew began hearing the ominous word "atomic" for the first time and Colonel Tibbets told them to "watch your language this is being recorded for history."

At 8:05, the escort planes pulled away and the Enola Gay began its bomb run. As the T of the bomb sight on the B-29 moved over the Aioi Bridge, the bombardier let loose the 10,000-pound bomb from a height of 31,000 feet. Exactly 43 seconds later the plane filled with a bright light and the B-29 began to rock as if hit by flak. Below, there was "a fiery red core," then a huge mushroom cloud. In his mission book, the co-pilot, Robert Lewis, wrote, "My God, what have we done?"

At Hiroshima, the bomb exploded 1,850 feet above Shima Hospital, vaporizing the hospital and all its patients instantly. Of the people within 1,500 feet, 88 percent died in that first moment. Temperatures at the center reached 5,432 degrees Fahrenheit at once.

Near the hospital was the three-story Honkaua Elementary School. As Miss Horibe, a teacher, emerged from the basement, she saw another teacher, naked and covered with terrible burns. "Mother, Mother," the woman shouted to her, "this is hell on earth" (→ Sept. 2).

As the mushroom cloud rises, mankind embarks upon a new, uncharted age.

The Enola Gay returns safely after dropping the atomic bomb on Hiroshima.

The remains of Hiroshima shortly after the atomic bomb was exploded.

Japan surrenders: Peace settles over the world

Tokyo, Sept. 2

Aboard the new battleship Missouri today, two Japanese officials in formal morning dress and top hats surrendered to representatives of the Allied powers, led by General Douglas MacArthur, thus ending the worst war the world has ever seen. In a brief address, General MacArthur said that, with the signing, "men everywhere can walk upright in the sunlight." The end came quickly following the atomic destruction of Hiroshima and Nagasaki, and the Soviet declaration of war against Japan. The Japanese government ceased to be dominated by its military leaders and a new Cabinet went to the Emperor and persuaded him to call an imperial conference. In a deeply emotional scene, the Emperor gave his opinion that Japan must surrender. Capitulation messages were then sent to the Allies via diplomatic channels in Sweden and Switzerland.

Japan's surrender marks the end of a five-year period that has no precedent but that can only be compared with the Black Death in the 14th century, which killed a third of Europe's population and transformed the face of the continent. Not since that time have so many people been killed, wounded, displaced or had their lives so completely changed. In Asia, two huge nations, China and Japan, have been completely ruined and the colonial empires founded in the Pacific in the last century have been destroyed. China has probably suffered more than any other country. It has been at war since 1937 and has had more than two million combat deaths alone; there are no realistic figures for its civilian deaths. Many of its casualties could have been avoided if it had possessed modern medical facilities. Japan suffered about the same number of combat deaths as China but its civilian losses were far fewer.

As the war comes to an end, two superpowers dominate the globe: the United States and the Soviet Union. The Russians suffered by far the more grievous wounds. More than six million soldiers were killed and 14 million were wounded. If civilian deaths are counted, the Soviet Union probably lost 20 million lives during the war – though some say 30 million. More Russian soldiers were killed in the Battle of Stalingrad than the United States lost in the entire conflict.

The Americans probably have gained more from the war than any other country. With the exception of a raid by a single Japanese seaplane, no bombs fell on the continental United States. There were 16 million Americans in uniform during World War II, and of these 400,000 were killed and a half million were wounded. But there were significant results from America's role as the arsenal of democracy. Thousands of factories and hundreds of fortunes sprang up almost overnight and, by this year, Americans had a standard of living rivaled by no one on the planet (→ 8).

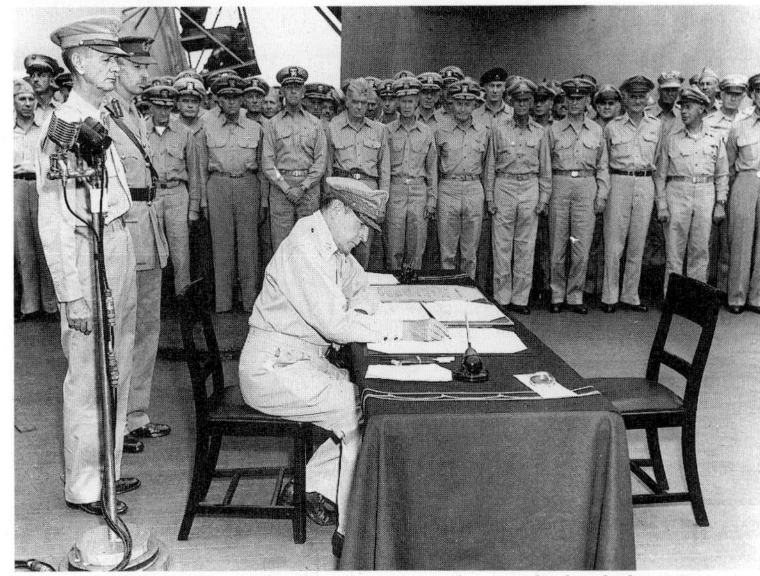
Supreme Allied Commander Douglas MacArthur on the battleship Missouri.

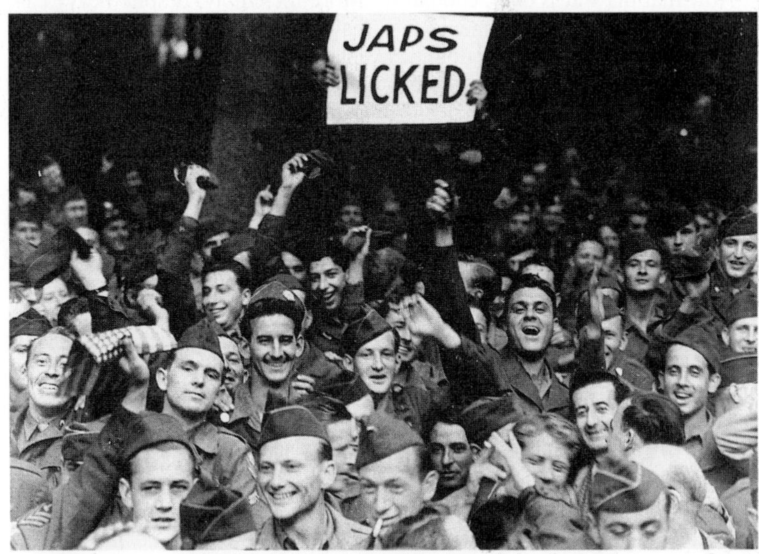

American troops in Paris celebrate after hearing of the Japanese surrender.

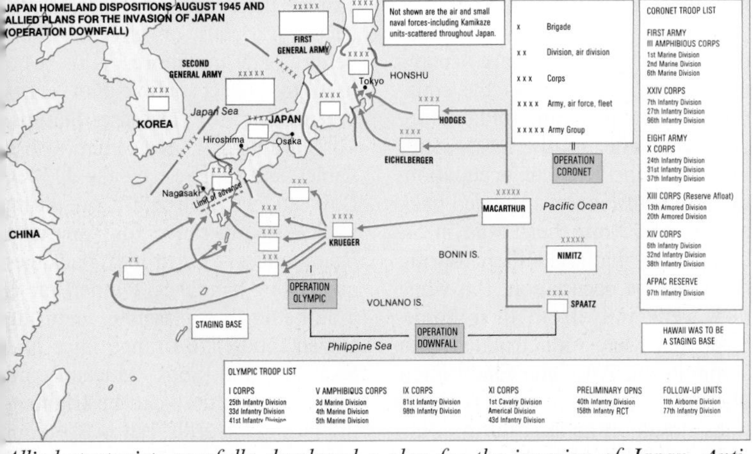

Allied strategists carefully developed a plan for the invasion of Japan. Anticipating fierce resistance and losses of one million men, Operation Downfall was intended to strike key military points, thus incapacitating enemy capabilities. With or without the atomic bomb, Japan was to be be vanquished.

Namoro Shigomitso signs the surrender documents as Allied officers look on. ▷

Japanese-American troops most honored

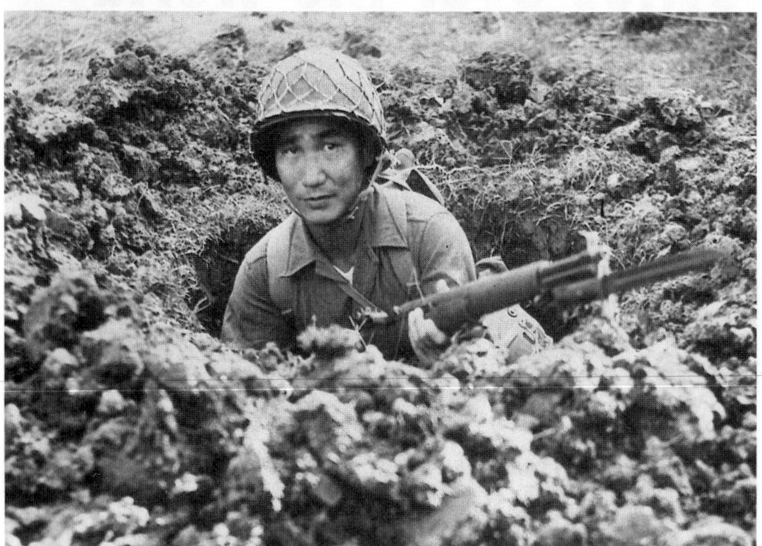

Japanese-Americans fought valiantly, in part to prove how loyal they were.

Washington, D.C.

Now that the war is over, combat statistics make the internment of Japanese-Americans seem doubly shameful. Nisei soldiers not only fought with great distinction, but the 33,000 men of the Nisei 442nd Regiment and the 100th Battalion also emerged as the most decorated men in American military history. For example, the 442nd in the Italian campaign was awarded 3,600 Purple Hearts, 810 Bronze Stars, 342 Silver Stars, 47 Distinguished Service Crosses, 17 Legion of Merits and numerous other citations. More incredibly, despite heavy casualties there were no known frontline Nisei desertions as against an overall service rate of about 15 percent. In all, some 8,000 Nisei joined the army after Secretary of War Henry L. Stimson announced in January 1943, that they could do so as volunteers in segregated units. As for ingenuity, Sergeant Kenny Yasui in Burma, passing as a Japanese colonel, ordered 13 Japanese soldiers to march back to his camp as his unsuspecting prisoners.

The Manhattan Project now comes to light

Washington, D.C., August

The atomic bombs that wrought destruction and carnage on Japan are the product of a titanic military and scientific effort. At the peak of this top-secret "Manhattan Project," 105,000 men and women labored to unleash the terrible power of the atom; and most had no knowledge of the awesome device they were helping create.

The Manhattan Project was born on October 9, 1941, when it got a go-ahead from President Roosevelt. After Pearl Harbor, the effort grew into a frantic race, as many top officials believed that the Nazis had an atomic program. Ironically, it was Hitler's pathological anti-Semitism that gave the United States a great edge. The best minds in atomic physics, including Leo Szilard, Hans Bethe, Enrico Fermi, Neils Bohr and Edward Teller, had fled to the West to escape Nazism.

To Dr. J. Robert Oppenheimer of the University of California fell the task of organizing this awesome array of talent, while Major General Leslie R. Groves had military control of the $2 billion operation. Though it involved three huge complexes, at Oak Ridge, Tennessee, Richland, Washington, and Los Alamos, New Mexico, it was shrouded in such secrecy that even Vice President Truman knew nothing of it until Roosevelt's death.

Oppenheimer and Groves examine the remains of the tower from which the first atomic bomb had dangled.

On July 16, a handful of scientists huddled on a New Mexico desert to test the first bomb. Some had doubts of its working; others feared it would ignite the atmosphere. But as a blinding flash cut the pre-dawn sky and a cauldron of radioactive dust and fire rose 40,000 feet, the lanky Oppenheimer, who once described the device as "technically sweet," recalled a line from Hindu scripture: "Now I am become death, the destroyer of worlds."

Fair Deal promised as war economy ends

Washington, D.C., Dec. 31

As President Truman moved to replace the War Labor Board with the Wage Stabilization Board today, he was bidding the year and the war a firm farewell. The rationing of shoes, tires and most foods has come to an end, and a demand for public housing and more jobs - peacetime concerns - has begun.

"Wartime Marketing" by Bache.

In August, Truman took the first steps in the journey to normalcy, ordering a full resumption of consumer production, free markets and collective bargaining. In September, he recommended to Congress a liberal, domestic 21-point economic recovery program, because, as he explained, "every segment of our population, and every individual, has a right to expect from his government a Fair Deal." This translates in most people's minds as jobs for the returning servicemen, white and Negro. But a few women auto workers in Detroit have marched in protest against the loss of their jobs, demanding that the Fair Deal apply also to the fair sex.

U.S. and U.S.S.R. split Korea in two

South Korea, Aug. 17

In an almost casual manner, and with the stroke of a pen, Korea has been divided in two at the 38th parallel. Russian troops are occupying the northern part of the country, while American soldiers are occupying the southern segment. Following the Russian occupation, thousands of Koreans flooded back into Korea from their exile in Siberia. They had fled there during the Japanese occupation. But while they were away from their homeland, they were indoctrinated with communism. After the repatriation of the Korean population, the Russians closed off an area north of the 38th parallel, making that division a political and economic barrier, not just a military convenience (→May 10, 1948).

Frozen orange juice, chicken and turkey

United States

It's tough to be a kid. Toys are scarce; there are no bikes, sleds, tricycles, skates or electric trains being made anymore. Kids who used to collect bubble-gum cards are settling for Defense Stamps. Girls are writing servicemen whose names are supplied by the U.S.O. Boys and girls alike are preparing CARE (Cooperative for American Remittances to Europe) packages and rolling bandages. Dinnertime is a bit better than playtime, featuring frozen foods like orange juice and Swanson and Sons' chicken and turkey. Schooltime can be frightening during air drills, but new school supplies such as ballpoint pens and wax pencils lend a sophisticated touch to the scrawl "Kilroy was here" in the margins of a textbook.

How MacArthur shapes a peacetime Japan

General Douglas MacArthur towers over Emperor Hirohito as the two awkwardly pose for photographers.

Tokyo, Sept. 8

A 29-year-old Japanese-American named Iva Togori D'Aquino is under arrest and charged with treason. Her real name means little to American servicemen. They knew her as Tokyo Rose, the broadcaster who taunted them daily with her propaganda program called "Zero Hour." She faces trial on charges that she gave wartime aid and comfort to the enemy.

General Douglas MacArthur, Supreme Commander of the Allied Powers in Japan, has pledged to bring all war criminals to trial. He has also promised to be compassionate, and President Truman has granted him a free hand. The President, mistrustful of the Russians since Potsdam, has rejected their demands to establish a "Big Four" control commission and give them a greater role in the occupation.

From his Dai Ichi Building office, MacArthur has set demobilization as his first goal. Seven million Japanese are still in uniform, at home and around the Pacific. The general's long-term goals are reconstruction and the introduction of democratic principles.

As supreme commander, he is aware that he needs the cooperation of Emperor Hirohito, and has rejected British and Russian demands that the Emperor be tried as a war criminal. "If the Emperor were indicted and perhaps hanged," he said, "military government would have to be instituted throughout all Japan, and guerrilla war would probably break out."

In a recent broadcast, MacArthur told Americans the problems in Japan must be resolved peacefully. "We have had our last chance," he said. "If we do not devise some greater and more equitable system, Armageddon will be at our door" (→ May 3, 1947).

United States joins the new United Nations

Following President Truman, Senator Arthur Vandenberg signs U.N. Charter.

Washington, D.C., Aug. 8

The United Nations, conceived in a time of war, now aims to be an instrument of peace. The organization is already a step ahead of the League of Nations, which began after the Great War. President Truman signed the U.N. Charter today, and the United States was officially a member. One reason the league failed was American refusal to join. "We had sponsored and helped establish the United Nations Organization," Truman wrote, "hoping to prevent again the too often recurring plague of humanity – war."

Sixty countries took part in the April United Nations conference at San Francisco to write the charter. It pledges to maintain world peace and security and to let the residents of colonial areas "gradually develop their free political institutions." The U.N. is divided into a General Assembly and a more powerful Security Council, where any initiative may be blocked by veto of just one of the five major powers, the United States, Britain, the Soviet Union, France and China (→ Oct. 23, 1946).

Around the world weekly: 151 hours

Washington, D.C., Sept. 28

An Army Air Transport Command plane lifted off the National Airport runway here today to inaugurate weekly round-the-world flights. The four-engine Douglas C-54 Skymaster, nicknamed the "Globester," headed for its first stop, the Azores, with about 3,000 pounds of mail and cargo and eight passengers, including photographers and reporters. The 23,000-mile trip will take the transports across North Africa, over Southern Asia and the Pacific, then across the United States and back to Washington. Each circumnavigation will involve about 12 changes in crews and three changes in planes. The complete circuit is expected to take about 151 hours, or from each Friday to the following Thursday.

Strike shuts G.M.; anti-labor bill due

Detroit, Mich., December

Beleaguered by a wave of peaceful but debilitating labor conflicts, President Truman has asked Congress for legislation to curb strikes. Montgomery Ward, Ford and Illinois Bell have been under siege recently. But the worst blow was a strike by 325,000 General Motors workers that began November 21. Asking a 30 percent pay raise and the opening of G.M.'s books to the public, the United Auto Workers shut 80 plants in 20 states. Parts output is hurt, threatening firms that G.M. supplies. The union, with a record 1.3 million members, says the company wants "an industrial economic dictatorship." Of the Truman anti-strike plan, union spokesman R.J. Thomas merely says: "I am opposed to it."

Priceless art is recovered from the Nazis

Bavaria, Germany, April

There is little room for aesthetics in war. But with fighting in Europe winding down, Generals Patton, Bradley and Eisenhower were treated this month to some of the most breathtaking sights in the history of Western art. In the Altausee salt mine and other caches in southern Bavaria, the U.S. Third Army uncovered thousands of art treasures, stolen by Nazis as spoils of war.

Some of the works were confiscated in Germany from Jewish patrons such as Rothschild, Kahn and Weil. But most of them come from France. Hitler returned many of these pieces as "loans," an act he considered a more powerful symbol of domination than outright seizure. Others were deemed too nationalistic to stay in an occupied country. These found their way to Germany, intended for a museum dedicated to Hitler's mother. The paintings, which include works by Rubens, Rembrandt, Holbein, Goya and others, are in good condition.

U.S. soldier guards a masterpiece.

The Eagle Ascendant 1946-1993

Early in 1945, as the Allied powers neared victory in Europe and the Pacific, Winston Churchill told the House of Commons, "America stands at this moment at the summit of the world." In an earlier time, such a pronouncement from a prime minister of Great Britain would have seemed extraordinary. But in 1945, it was simply a statement of the obvious. For the United States had emerged from World War II not just victorious, but supreme. As the columnist Walter Lippmann wrote that year: "What Rome was to the ancient world, what Great Britain has been to the modern world, America is to be to the world of tomorrow." In many respects, of course, the United States had been the world's most powerful nation for many years before World War II. But until the 1940s that power had not often been accompanied by a recognition of international responsibilities. The war produced a momentous change. In its wake, most Americans no longer viewed their power as a vehicle for insulating themselves from the problems of other nations; they considered it a mandate to become actively involved in trying to resolve those problems.

The nation did not, it soon became clear, have much choice in the matter. One reason was nuclear weapons, which America had brought into the world and of which it held (for a time) a virtual monopoly. Even more important was the new rivalry with the Soviet Union. That contest, eventually known as the Cold War, soon overshadowed every other consideration in international affairs and, to a great extent, in American domestic affairs.

The war also helped unleash another force, one that was at least equally important in determining the shape of postwar society: economic growth. For 10 years before the war, the United States had remained mired in a deep economic depression; some had come to believe that economic stagnation was now the norm to which the nation would have to adjust. But the war, and the massive public spending it required, not only ended the Depression, it also started the country on the road to a period of economic growth before which even the remarkable expansion of the 1920s paled. The vast new abundance this growth created affected virtually every area of American life. For members of the rapidly expanding middle class, it made possible a new level of affluence. For workers and farmers and others, it offered an escape from subsistence and poverty to a style of life previously reserved for a relative few. For those who remained economically marginal, it created new expectations and new demands.

At first, America's wealth and power seemed to insulate it from the usual frustrations of history. The Cold War was not won, certainly, but America retained a prestige and influence that the Soviet Union could not match. Social problems were not eliminated, of course, but there was widespread confidence that solutions lay within the nation's grasp. The presidency of Dwight D. Eisenhower, a genial leader who presided over a period of general calm, symbolized one side of this postwar confidence: a sense of general well-being. The presidency of John F. Kennedy, a glamorous leader who ran for office on the promise to "get America moving again," symbolized another side: the exuberance of a nation convinced that it could create a great future for itself if it only had the will and the energy to do so. When the United States first landed men on the moon in 1969, an important part of President Kennedy's vision seemed to have been fulfilled.

But the "American moment," as some have called it, did not long remain so untroubled. The assassination of President Kennedy in 1963, one of the most traumatic events in American history, came in retrospect to symbolize the beginning of a profound change in the nation's fortunes. Within two years of that tragedy, the United States was confronting powerful obstacles to both its international and domestic hopes.

The commitment to fighting communism throughout the world had led the country into a disastrous military venture in Vietnam – a conflict that continued inconclusively for more than a decade, eroding America's stature in the world and poisoning its political and social atmosphere at home.

At about the same time, a great mass movement in the American South was forcing the nation to confront the deepest national injustice of all: the oppression of America's black citizens. In the past, most white Americans had avoided confronting the problems of race, convinced that those problems were too intractable. Now, many white liberals embraced the civil rights movement, confident that the nation had the capacity to overcome even this great problem. The assault on racism produced important reforms and was responsible for improvements in the status of many black Americans. But like the war in Vietnam, it proved to be a far more difficult and costly commitment than most Americans had at first envisioned.

◀ *"That's How It Felt to Walk on the Moon" by astronaut Alan Bean.*

Finally, near the end of the 1960s, the American economy faltered. Economic growth had become the cornerstone of so many of the nation's hopes. Many Americans had come to believe the nation was now largely immune from inflation, stagnation and debilitating international competition. By the early 1970s, that confidence, too, was beginning to unravel.

Thus began the slow erosion of America's liberal euphoria – the belief that the nation had the resources and the will to do virtually everything, that it could (in President Lyndon Johnson's words) produce a "new world" and "bend it to our will." Instead, the United States entered a period of wrenching national turbulence. Urban ghettoes erupted in violence, as poor blacks struggled to draw attention to their grievances. College campuses became places of turmoil, as students raised a series of unsettling challenges to the conventions of the university and to the norms of middle class society. American women, drawing inspiration from the liberation efforts of other groups as well as from their own long history of struggle, transformed feminism from a largely intellectual stance into a powerful social movement that transformed society profoundly. Americans from almost all segments of society joined in a massive anti-war movement that shook national politics and created tremendous pressure on national leaders to end Vietnam war.

At the time, many Americans considered the turmoil of the 1960s and early 1970s the harbinger of something like a revolution. In fact, however, its principal political effect was to strengthen forces of conservatism committed to restoring order and stability to national life. The election of Richard Nixon to the presidency in 1968 (and the strong third-party presidential candidacy of George Wallace that same year) seemed to confirm the popular repudiation of liberal hopes and to express a yearning for a calmer, more familiar society. Yet America in the Nixon years did not experience stability and order. Instead, it witnessed new and even greater social and political crises: an escalation of domestic protest and social unrest, growing military frustration in Vietnam, a series of frightening economic problems, and a political scandal that forced the resignation of the President himself.

For a time in the 1970s, an uncharacteristic pessimism began to permeate America. Some spoke of the end of the "American Century," of the arrival of an "age of limits," of a future of more modest hopes and more restricted means. The humiliating end of the Vietnam War, the emergence of a prolonged energy crisis and the resurgence of Soviet military power: all contributed to a sense that America's ability to control world affairs was ebbing.

By the end of the 1970s, another vision emerged – one that combined a continued conservative retreat from the heady visions of the 1960s with a commitment to the idea of economic growth, international power and American destiny. The same belief in America's special virtues that had fueled the Cold War and the liberal crusades of the 1960s became the basis for the presidency of Ronald Reagan. For two terms, Reagan oversaw a tough foreign policy, while at home the budget deficit and unemployment grew. Reagan's unflinching pressure on the "Evil Empire" brought the Soviets to the negotiating table time and again. As the 1990s dawned, his successors, George Bush and then Bill Clinton, were faced with a challenge as great as any this century: the disintegration of the Soviet Union in 1991 meant that the United States was once again the only superpower. A superpower lacking a "supereconomy." Being the "global policeman," coping with crises in the Persian Gulf, in Somalia, or in the Balkans, is a costly business, as is coping with Japan's trade rivalry. Bill Clinton, the first Democrat to occupy the White House in 12 years, is also the first President to have been born after World War II. This may be what is needed in a world that bears little resemblance to that of 1946.

1946

Truman

Washington, D.C., Jan. 25. United Mine Workers readmitted to American Federation of Labor.

Washington, D.C., March 25. To dispose of surplus government property, an executive order establishes War Assets Administration.

New York City, May 6. Arthur Schlesinger's *Age of Jackson* awarded Pulitzer Prize in history.

New York City, May 9. Yankees become first baseball club to travel by air, signing contract with United Air Lines.

New York City, May 16. Irving Berlin's musical *Annie Get Your Gun*, starring Ethel Merman, opens.

Washington, D.C., June 3. Supreme Court rules, in Morgan v. Commonwealth, that seating must be provided on interstate buses regardless of race (→ Jan. 12, 1948).

Washington, D.C., June 4. Congress approves National School Lunch Act, helping states to develop non-profit lunch programs.

California, Aug. 26. Two unmanned B-17 bombers fly non-stop from Hawaii, controlled only by radio.

St. Louis, Oct. 15. Cardinals defeat Boston Red Sox in World Series, four games to three.

Washington, D.C., Nov. 5. Republicans make significant gains in national elections, taking control of both houses of Congress.

Germany, Dec. 2. United States and Britain agree to merge their zones of occupation.

New York City, Dec. 15. Chicago Bears defeat New York Giants, 24-14, in N.F.L. championship.

Washington, D.C., Dec. 31. President Truman formally proclaims an end to all hostilities in World War II.

Philadelphia. Roosevelt dime is issued by U.S. Mint.

Hollywood, California. Top films this year include *The Best Years of Our Lives, The Big Sleep, The Postman Always Rings Twice* and *Notorious.*

New York City. Eugene O'Neill's play *The Iceman Cometh* published.

Millions of American workers go on strike, but without strife

"Unemployed Rally" by Brodsky.

United States

As the nation readjusts to peace abroad, the reconverting economy finds itself plagued by war at home. Aided by tax breaks, industry enjoys healthy profits; and despite postwar layoffs, unemployment hovers below 5 percent. Still, 4.5 million workers struck this year, crippling the coal, auto, electric and steel industries and interrupting rail and maritime transport. Man-days lost to strikes mounted to 113 million. But strangely absent from the battlegrounds were the guns and clubs that have "arbitrated" labor disputes in the past. As suggested in *Fortune*, management and labor have been transformed into "calm, cool, even friendly warriors."

Led by Walter Reuther, Philip Murray and John L. Lewis, labor has marched eagerly to the bargaining table. At General Motors, Reuther insisted on access to corporate books. A 30 percent wage hike, he argued, could be absorbed without an increase in prices. Loath to give labor a role in corporate planning, G.M. refused. On March 13 the union settled for an 18.5-cent wage gain after 113 days on strike.

At U.S. Steel, Philip Murray was concerned with wages, not what steel would cost. So when 750,000 steel workers returned in February after a three-week strike, they, too, had an 18.5-cent raise. But the firms used the concession as a lever to lift price controls. Their $5-a-ton price rise should amount to a net gain of $250 million on the year.

Lewis added another element to the bargaining formula when the United Mine Workers walked out in April, asking health, welfare and safety benefits. After weathering federal seizure of the mines, he got retirement and medical benefits, a federal safety code and 18.5 cents in wages. But he paid a price that may draw the lines on labor's new power. Violating a no-strike pledge to punish operators for breaking the contract, the U.M.W. walked out again in November. In three days, a court fined Lewis $10,000 and his union $3.5 million, the stiffest penalty ever imposed on a union.

"Northern Minnesota Mine" by E. Dewey Albinson. A colorful landscape.

Computer manages 5,000 steps at once

Philadelphia, February

At 30 tons, the new ENIAC computer seems a far cry from the abacus or slide rule. Designed by J.P. Eckert and J.W. Mauchly of the University of Pennsylvania, the Electronic Numerical Integrator and Calculator has 18,000 vacuum tubes and adds, multiplies, divides and computes square roots, accomplishing 5,000 steps a second. The War Department will use ENIAC for artillery computations. International Business Machines plans a much less powerful calculator, the Model 603, for commercial use.

American rockets on fringe of space

White Sands, New Mexico

From a desolate base here, scientists are firing missiles to explore the fringes of space. A Corporal rocket reached an altitude of 43 miles last year, and this year American rocketeers, aided by German scientists, are launching captured V-2 rockets. The Nazi "Vengeance" weapon, which battered London, is now being put to peaceful research purposes. The rockets that haven't tumbled off course or been obliterated at ignition are probing the mysteries of the cosmos at heights above 100 miles.

Business is terrific, under the counter

United States

"Prices soar, Buyers Sore, Steers jump over the moon" a *New York Daily News* headline exclaims, putting in a nutshell the trouble with the economy. True, people are purchasing theater tickets and cars, but doing it too often "under the counter." Goods are available on store shelves, but they disappear in an instant. In vain, people try to get new Timex watches, Ecktachrome color film, Tide detergent, French's instant potatoes, Max Factor cosmetics or electric blankets. Luckily, ice cream is not deserting its fans.

Churchill: Iron Curtain has descended in Europe

Fulton, Missouri, March

"From Stettin in the Baltic to Trieste in the Adriatic, an 'iron curtain' has descended across the Continent," Winston Churchill proclaimed here on March 5. The former Prime Minister of Britain contended that those European countries that lie behind the "Iron Curtain" are subject to growing Soviet control and that they must be considered part of the Soviet sphere of influence. "Whatever conclusions may be drawn from these facts – and facts they are – this is certainly not the liberated Europe we fought to build up," Churchill said. "Nor is it one which contains the essentials of permanent peace."

The British Prime Minister issues a warning in the American heartland.

The British leader's incendiary remarks were delivered in a speech titled *The Sinews of Peace*, which he gave to an audience at Westminster College that included President Truman, and which was broadcast.

Warning his listeners that the Russians desire "the indefinite expansion of their power and doctrine," Churchill called on America to stand united with the British Commonwealth to discourage Russian hegemony. If the Western democracies are divided, he said, "catastrophe may overwhelm us all."

Reaction to the Fulton speech has been hostile, with many listeners considering Churchill's views unnecessarily grim, if not warlike. An editorial in the *Chicago Sun* said that Churchill's object was "world domination, through arms, by the United States and the British Empire." *The Nation* said that Churchill was adding a "sizable measure of poison to the already deteriorating relations between the Russians and the Western powers." The *Times of London* disagreed with the wartime Prime Minister's remarks about Russia, declaring that "while Western democracy and communism are in many respects opposed, they have much to learn from each other."

The metaphor of an iron curtain is not new. In 1914, Belgium's German-born Queen Elizabeth saw between Kaiser Wilhelm's Germany and her new land, "a bloody iron curtain which has descended forever." Shortly after the Russian Revolution, Vasili Rozanov wrote, "With a rumble and a roar, an iron curtain is descending on Russian history" (→March 12, 1947).

La Guardia: "Ticker tape ain't spaghetti"

Atlantic City, N.J., March 29

"People are hungry, and it is our responsibility to feed them," said Fiorello H. La Guardia today as he agreed to head the United Nations Relief and Rehabilitation Administration. In a passionate address here, he promised to take whatever actions are needed to feed a war-ravaged world.

The fiery former Mayor of New York implored Americans "not to overeat, not to waste," adding that "in my own city we waste enough food to feed a city of 350,000 ... I know, I picked up that garbage for 12 years." But he called Americans "kindly," saying they had "learned through a period of depression that ticker tape ain't spaghetti."

La Guardia said he intends to buy food wherever he can find it, for "wheat has no political complexion," and offered his "very personal greetings to Juan D. Peron" of grain-producing Argentina. The famed New York politician also warned that "our governments did not buy food in order to enrich a lot of black marketeers."

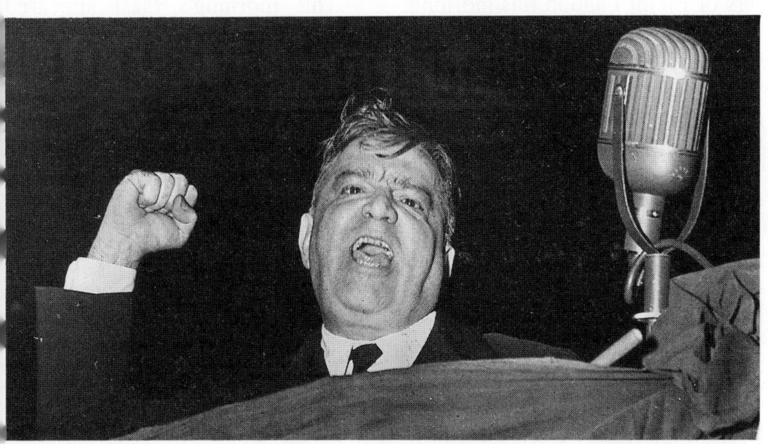

Fiorello La Guardia delivers fiery speech at an Italian-American labor rally.

Allies complete peace pacts with 4 ex-foes

Paris, July 1

The foreign ministers adjourned their peace conference here today after completing the treaties with Bulgaria, Hungary, Italy and Rumania. During much of the nine-week meeting, Secretary of State James Byrnes tried to improve the deteriorating relations with Moscow. He has little to show for his efforts. The Russians granted a few concessions on Trieste but showed little inclination to lift the "Iron Curtain" they have closed on Eastern Europe. By all accounts, the Russians have crushed all democratic resistance to their policies in East Germany, and Washington has halted all German reparations payments from its zone to Moscow.

"This is what makes America what it is"

Paris, July 27

Gertrude Stein is dead at 72. The American writer and patron of the arts moved in 1903 from Baltimore to Paris, where she lived with her lifetime companion Alice B. Toklas. Stein was a collector of Picasso and Matisse, then hostess of a literary salon that attracted expatriate writers, such as Hemingway and Fitzgerald, whom she called "The Lost Generation." Her 1933 autobiography was a best-seller. In 1934, she toured the United States, of which she wrote, "there is more space where nobody is than where anybody is. This is what makes America what it is."

"Gertrude Stein" by Pablo Picasso.

Philippines are free of American rule

Manila, Philippines, July 4

One of America's major ventures into colonialism came to an end today as President Truman granted the Philippines independence. The liberator of the Philippines, General Douglas MacArthur, attended the ceremonies in the nation's capital and said, "America buried imperialism here today." The United States bought the Philippines from Spain in 1898, then groomed it to be Asia's "showplace of democracy." In 1935, the Philippines became a self-governing commonwealth.

Mother Cabrini is first American saint

The Vatican, July 7

The late Mother Frances Xavier Cabrini has been canonized as a saint. She is the first American to be so honored, but countries around the world take pride in the event, for Mother Cabrini established convents and orphanages in Paris, Madrid, London, Turin and many cities in Latin America. Born July 15, 1850, in Lombardy, Italy, she became a naturalized American citizen in 1909. She died in 1917 after a long bout with malaria.

Baruch urges control of atomic weapons

Baruch in plea to U.N. commission.

New York City, July 24

"We are here to make a choice between the quick and the dead," Bernard M. Baruch, the United States representative to the United Nations Atomic Energy Commission, asserted on June 14. But hopes for the international agreement to avert the madness of a future atomic arms race that he proposed on that day now appear to be fading.

Baruch, at 75 an elder statesman of American diplomacy, challenged his listeners "to test if man can produce, through his will and faith, the miracle of peace, just as he has, through science and skill, the miracle of the atom." According to his proposal, the United States would surrender its monopoly on atomic weapons to an international authority backed by nations pledged by treaty never to develop or harness the power for military uses. Baruch insisted there could be no veto power for individual nations and called for an accord "with teeth in it," promising "swift, sure punishment for those who violate their solemn agreements."

Today, however, the Soviet delegate to the U.N., Andrei A. Gromyko, responded with a sharply worded rejection of the American proposal, which he said "could not be accepted in any way by the Soviet Union, either as a whole or in separate parts." Taking particular umbrage at the stipulation that no nation could wield veto power in a voting situation, Gromyko called it "dangerous and maybe fatal."

Little is known of the Soviet capacity to build a bomb, but most scientists and lawmakers believe the United States will retain a monopoly on its "winning weapon" for decades. Some observers feel the proposal's call for on-site inspections bothered the secretive Russians as much as the veto clause. Others questioned the wisdom of staging a dramatic demonstration of American atomic might at Bikini Atoll as the Russians were mulling over the Baruch plan (→26).

Fulbright program will help scholars

Washington, D.C., Aug. 1

Senator J. William Fulbright of Arkansas introduced a bill today to award academic grants to Americans for study and teaching abroad and to foreigners to study and teach here. The program will be funded by some of the proceeds from the sale of surplus federal property. Most observers believe Congress will pass this unique educational exchange plan. Fulbright is himself a Rhodes scholar and he has worked hard in Congress for the advancement of education.

"Clubfoot comet" Assault wins it all

New York City

They called Assault the "clubfoot comet" because of his strange gait, but he horse-laughed all the way to the bank after winning the Belmont to complete racing's Triple Crown. Assault was almost destroyed as a foal because of a foot injury, but he was saved for greater things, such as an eight-length victory in the Kentucky Derby, prior to his Preakness triumph. Assault's right forefoot never reached normal growth. Warren Mehrtens rides him.

July 13, 1946. *American physicists, including J. Robert Oppenheimer (second from right), inspect the new giant cyclotron at the University of California. Ions are introduced at the center of a circular magnetic field and accelerated. The wider the spiral orbit, the greater the energy produced.*

Bikini Atoll is American nuclear test site

Bikini Atoll, July 26

An atomic bomb believed to be the most powerful yet developed hurled a 9,000-foot-high column of steam and churning black smoke up from the normally placid waters of Bikini Lagoon this morning. The second explosion of Operation Crossroads, it was thought to be equal to about 50,000 tons of TNT, and cut a wide swath of destruction through a flotilla of abandoned warships anchored nearby.

The weapon was the fifth of its kind to be exploded and the first to be detonated under water. It quickly sank the old battleship Arkansas and left the aircraft carrier Saratoga and the Japanese battleship Nagato listing badly. Four submarines submerged in the lagoon were also believed to have been sunk. Scientists are still puzzled by the effects of radiation, which appear to have caused many deaths among Japanese bomb victims. Nevertheless, sailors were sent in to examine the damaged ships just hours after the explosion.

This morning's blast appeared considerably more destructive than the previous Operation Crossroads test on July 1. In that demonstration, a bomb exploded 500 feet over ships in the lagoon. It destroyed the carrier Independence, but there was little damage elsewhere, prompting an unimpressed Soviet observer to remark: "Pooh."

Today's test inspired a protest in New York against the military development of atomic energy, while the Russians charged it "fundamentally undermined the seriousness of American talk about atomic disarmament" (→Sept. 23, 1949).

Nazi leaders hanged for crimes against humanity

Nuremberg, Germany, Oct. 16

Nine of Hitler's Nazi henchmen were hanged early this morning for committing vicious war crimes. During their trial, the defendants claimed that they were only following orders, but they showed little remorse today. Julius Streicher, the editor who once wrote, "Jewish rabble will be exterminated like weeds and vermin," shouted "Heil Hitler" as the noose was fastened around his neck. Joachim von Ribbentrop, the foreign minister, said, "My last wish is that German unity be maintained."

The defendants were all accused of committing war crimes "so calculated, so malignant, and so devastating, that civilization cannot tolerate their being ignored because it cannot survive their being repeated." The evidence included sickening films of the mass executions in concentration camps. "After the bodies were removed" from the gas chambers, one witness testified, "our special commandos took off the rings and extracted the gold from the teeth of the corpses."

Hermann Goering escaped execution by swallowing poison in his cell. Second only to Hitler, Goering directed the secret mobilization of Germany, built up the Luftwaffe and founded the Gestapo, the dreaded secret police force. During his trial, he boasted to a doctor, "In 50 or 60 years, there will be statues of Hermann Goering all over Germany. Little statues, maybe, but one in every German house."

Former top Nazis follow the trial proceedings. The chief U.S. counsel at the Nuremberg War Crimes Tribunal is Supreme Court Justice Robert Jackson.

First pilot is ejected

Patterson Air Field, Ohio, Aug. 18

Larry Lambert, a heavy-drinking sergeant with a gap-toothed grin and a penchant for fibbing, was blasted from an Army P-61 at 7,800 feet yesterday to become the first American ejected from an airplane. Lambert, whose plane was called the Jack in the Box, exudes determination. He cut off a cast on a recently broken arm to avoid worrying the project directors, and it is rumored that he is suffering from a severe hangover today. On landing yesterday, Lambert was jubilant. "I never felt it a bit," he said, presumably meaning the ejection.

Hersey's Hiroshima

New York City, Aug. 31

If you read only one article in this week's *New Yorker*, you won't miss a thing – because there's only one article in it. *Hiroshima*, by John Hersey, takes up the entire issue. A year after the first atomic bomb leveled 90 percent of the Japanese city and took 130,000 lives, Hersey recreates the nightmarish event through the eyes of six people: a poor widow with three children, a clerk, the pastor of a Methodist church, a German missionary and two doctors. Hersey's chilling account, told in no-nonsense prose, lets the atom bomb speak for itself.

United Nations meets in New York City

Queens, New York City, Oct. 23

President Truman addressed the United Nations today as the General Assembly convened in Flushing, Queens. The Assembly met in London earlier this year, but it decided to seek a permanent home in the United States. It will presumably open its headquarters somewhere in New York City, but officials are still searching for the necessary funds and an appropriate site.

In his speech, Truman attempted to ease postwar concerns, but the United Nations is fast becoming the focal point of the escalating tensions between the Soviet Union and the United States. Washington has already used the Security Council effectively to put pressure on the Russians to leave Iran under the terms of the 1942 Tripartite Treaty. The U.S.S.R. was finally shamed into leaving in May, but not before it had whipped up nationalist sentiment in Azerbaijan and Kurdistan.

Truman has been a strong supporter of the U.N. and was hoping that it would become an international forum to promote peace. It is clear, however, that the President will use the world body to oppose what he calls a "surge of Communist tyranny" (→ Oct. 24, 1949).

From Dr. Spock, advice for new parents

Common sense from Dr. Spock.

New York City

A doctor named Benjamin McLane Spock has helped lots of fathers and mothers keep their original hair. Every time they feel ready to tear it out, they read Spock's *Common Sense Book of Baby and Child Care*, which offers flexible, easygoing solutions to the problems at hand. Spock has advice for pregnant mothers, babies and children up to age 12. The doctor realizes that life is not always rosy; he has hints for raising handicapped and adopted children, and tells working mothers and separated parents how to make the best use of their time.

President Truman addresses the General Assembly of the new United Nations.

1947

Truman

China, Jan. 7. General George Marshall's conciliation mission to China ends in failure (→8).

Washington, D.C., Jan. 8. President Truman appoints Marshall Secretary of State.

Washington, D.C., Feb. 10. Supreme Court upholds constitutionality of busing by public school systems of parochial school students.

New York City, Apr. 7. About 300,000 telephone employees walk off jobs in first national telephone strike.

Texas City, Texas, Apr. 16. A ship explosion kills 500 people and obliterates most of city.

New York City, May 5. Robert Penn Warren awarded Pulitzer Prize in fiction for *All the King's Men.*

Paris, July 12. Sixteen nations meet to draft proposal intended to avail themselves of economic recovery aid from United States offered under Marshall Plan.

Washington, D.C., July 18. Presidential Succession Act is passed by Congress, establishing official line of succession; it places Speaker of the House of Representatives after Vice President.

Washington, D.C., Oct. 5. Marking first time a president has addressed nation on television, Truman asks that all Americans conserve food to aid starving peoples of the world (→Jan. 20, 1949).

New Orleans, Dec. 3. *A Streetcar Named Desire*, by Tennessee Williams, has premiere here.

Chicago, Dec. 28. Cardinals defeat Philadelphia Eagles, 28-21, for N.F.L. title.

New York City. National Basketball League, American Basketball Assocation merge.

New York City. *Meet the Press* has television premiere.

New York City. Dwight D. Eisenhower's *Crusade in Europe* published.

DEATHS

Palm Island, Florida, Jan. 25. Al Capone, infamous gangster (*Jan. 17, 1899).

Dearborn, Michigan, Apr. 7. Henry Ford, inventor and founder of Ford Motor Company (*July 30, 1863).

Truman seeks anti-Communist funds

Washington, D.C., March 12

President Truman announced a new direction in American foreign policy today as he asked Congress for $400 million to support the governments of Greece and Turkey. Truman did not mention the Soviet Union by name, but the implication was that Soviet infiltration threatens freedom in both countries. "I believe that it must be the policy of the United States to support free peoples who are resisting attempted subjugation by armed minorities or by outside pressures," he said.

Truman sought bipartisan backing for the activist policy, and polls indicate that the American people generally favor his initiative. Senator Arthur Vandenberg, the Republican chairman of the Foreign Relations Committee, had urged Truman to give a strong speech that would "scare the hell out of the country." The speech did just that. Politicians on the left fear the new policy will bring war, and the right worries that it will cost too much.

Britain will pull out of Greece at the end of the month, and Truman fears that the Russians will move into the vacuum. The U.S. ambassador has warned repeatedly that Moscow is directing and funding the Communist guerrillas in Greece. Truman has also been advised that the Soviet Union will strangle the Middle East if it controls Greece and Turkey (→Apr. 16).

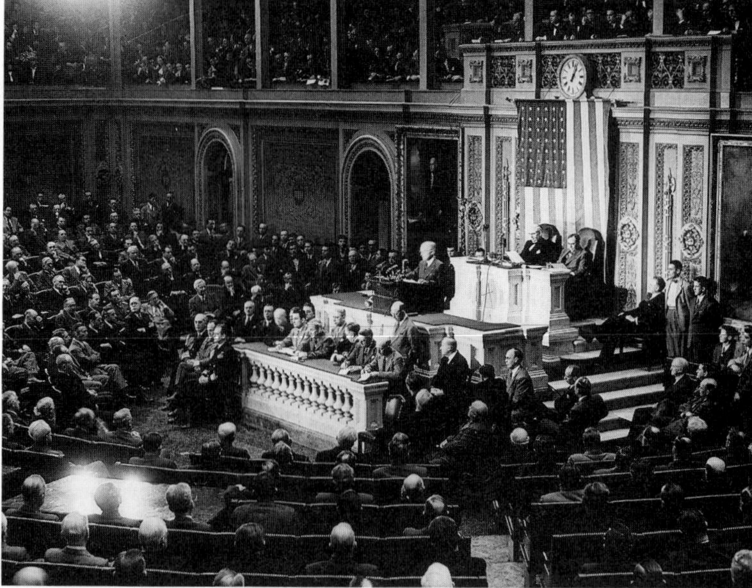

President Truman calls upon Congress to stop the spread of world communism and warns that Russian machinations are too great a threat to be ignored.

President Truman orders loyalty checks on federal employees

Washington, D.C., March 21

Only nine days after launching a new effort to contain communism overseas, President Truman has focused his attention on the home front. With $25 million at his disposal, the President has ordered all federal employees subjected to F.B.I. loyalty checks. Agency heads will be responsible for purging their departments of employees regarded as subversives. The Civil Service Commission will screen all new applicants. On seven occasions over the past eight years, a total of 1,429 people have been dismissed after they were charged as subversives, spies, Socialists, Communists and fellow travelers. But according to a presidential commission under A. Devitt Vanech, these types are still around. He says treason, sedition, sabotage, espionage and a variety of radicalisms must be pruned at once.

"Nude With Guitar" (1947) by Milton Avery, who is a leader of the Abstract Expressionist school.

Russians to tune in on Voice of America

Washington, D.C., Feb. 17

"One grain of truth dropped into Russia is like a spark landing in a barrel of powder," the 18th-century Frenchman, Comte de Custine, observed. The State Department, it would seem, agrees. Today, it began a Russian-language Voice of America broadcast aimed at countering what the Russians have been telling their people about the United States. Among other things, Russians are told America is a reactionary nation with slavery and cannibalism. There are a half million radios in Russia.

Truman's daughter in singing debut

Detroit, Mich., March 16

Most of the critics liked what they heard, a voice described as sweet and appealing, if inexperienced. The occasion: the singing debut of Margaret Truman on the *Hour of Music*, broadcast nationally from here with the Detroit Symphony. The soprano, performing without an audience, sang *Cielito Lindo, Charmant Oiseau* and, at her father's request, *The Last Rose of Summer*. The President phoned his praises from Key West, Florida. Miss Truman's public debut is in August at the Hollywood Bowl.

Baruch says nation is in a "cold war"

Columbia, S.C., Apr. 16
Bernard Baruch has added a new term to the lexicon of American-Soviet relations – "cold war." In an address before the South Carolina legislature today, Baruch said, "Let us not be deceived. We are today in the midst of a cold war. Our enemies are to be found abroad and at home." The financier used the phrase to describe the antagonism between the Communist East and the democracies of the West that has marked American-Soviet relations since the end of World War II. Baruch says the U.S. must prepare for the cold war as for any other war, by increasing expenditures on weapons and troops. To offset the inflation such an effort would cause, Baruch suggests extending the work week (→ June 5).

Marshall unveils plan to aid Europe

Secretary Marshall (front, third from left) at Harvard with fellow honorees.

Cambridge, Mass., June 5
Secretary of State George Marshall warned today that Europe's slow recovery from the war threatens international political stability, and he urged a massive American aid program to rebuild the continent. Marshall spoke this afternoon at Harvard after the university had granted him an honorary degree. "The remedy," Marshall said, "lies in breaking the vicious circle and restoring the confidence of the European people in the economic future of . . . Europe as a whole."

Marshall has been distressed by the sorry state of Europe, which Winston Churchill calls "a rubble heap, a charnel house, a breeding ground of pestilence and hate." In his recent visit to Moscow, Marshall witnessed appalling conditions. He also concluded that the Russians have no interest in the rebuilding of Western Europe, but his speech had less anti-Communist vitriol than President Truman's address to Congress. Marshall's speech was short on details, and he said the initiative for recovery must come from Europe itself (→ July).

Robinson breaks the color line in baseball

Brooklyn, N.Y., September
Some Southerners threatened to mutiny, at least two clubs threatened to strike and fans and bench jockeys rode him mercilessly, but there he was at first base, the first Negro to play in the major leagues.

Jackie Robinson was warned by Dodger president, Branch Rickey, that he had to have the courage to fight back against the bigots and he responded with his bat, hitting .295, scoring 125 runs and stealing 29 bases. Robinson was signed in 1945 to a contract with a Dodger farm club as pressure grew for the majors to hire Negroes. A football star at U.C.L.A., he went on to lead the International League in hitting and runs scored with Montreal. The Georgia-born son of a sharecropper and grandson of a slave opened the doors of integration on April 11, and in July the Cleveland Indians signed Larry Doby, the first Negro in the American League. There were some Negro players in pro ball in the late 1800s.

Jackie Robinson comes home in a triple steal against the Cincinnati Reds.

MacArthur constitution in effect in Japan

Tokyo, May 3
A historic new constitution went into effect in Japan today after it was approved by the Diet and was proclaimed the law of the land by Emperor Hirohito. The constitution greatly curtails the Emperor's power, introduces democratic principles and pledges that Japan will never again have military forces. The constitution says the Japanese people "renounce war . . . and the threat or use of force."

In a plebiscite on the constitution, Japanese women voted for the first time, and 75 percent of people eligible went to the polls. The constitution combines American and British principles. The prime minister serves four years, but is selected by the lower house of the Diet.

Much of the credit for the charter goes to the supreme commander, General Douglas MacArthur. He resisted pressure for an Allied-run military regime and pressured the Japanese to discard the ancient Meiji constitution (→ Dec. 23, 1948).

Taft-Hartley Act puts limits on big labor

Washington, D.C., June 23
Overriding a presidential veto and a barrage of invective from organized labor, Congress has passed legislation that rolls back many of the gains made by workers under the New Deal. The Taft-Hartley Act, proposed in response to a wave of postwar labor unrest, allows the President to obtain an 80-day injunction against any strike and appoint a board of inquiry to oversee collective bargaining. The act also bans the closed shop, allows states to void parts of the National Labor Relations Act and gives management greater latitude in fighting organizing drives.

Resistance to the bill was fierce. The A.F.L. described it as "conceived in a spirit of vindictiveness," the C.I.O. as "conceived in sin." A "veto caravan" of 1,450 protesters came from California to denounce the "slave labor bill." Besieged by 800,000 letters and 500,000 signatures, President Truman declared at the last minute that he would "blast hell out of the bill." It would, he charged, "reverse the basic direction of our national labor policy." His veto deepened the rift between the executive and the Republican Congress, but it may have saved the Democrats their working-class constituency.

X marks the spot to contain Russians

Washington, D.C., July

A mysterious author, X, has written an article in the current issue of *Foreign Affairs* saying the goal of United States policy toward the Soviet Union should be the "firm and vigilant containment of Russian expansionist tendencies." The author of *The Sources of Soviet Conduct* [later identified as George Kennan, a State Department Soviet expert], appears to be calling for a constant state of low-level warfare between the two superpowers.

According to the author's analysis, the Soviet Union is stubborn and intractable about its long-term objectives, yet flexible and cautious in the short-term. X compares the policy of the Communists to a fluid stream, flowing to fill all the openings available to it, yet changing direction whenever it finds a barrier in its path. He calls on the United States to stop the spread of communism by following a policy of containment and by confronting moves by "the Russians with unalterable counterforce at every point where they show signs of encroaching upon the interests of a peaceful and stable world."

Yeager breaks barrier

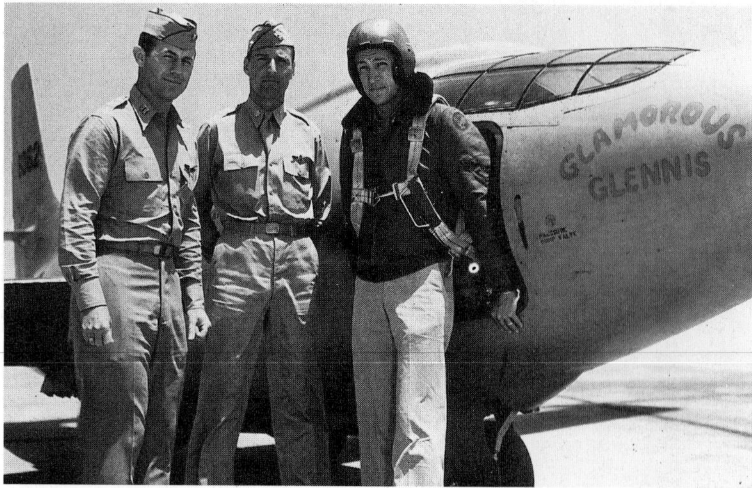

Captain Chuck Yeager (left) and other flight pioneers beside the rocket plane.

Muroc, Calif., Oct. 14

A sonic boom thundered across the desert here this morning, as Captain Chuck Yeager became the first man to shatter the sound barrier. Piloting a top-secret, bullet-shaped Bell X-1 rocket plane, Yeager hit a speed of 700 mph, or Mach 1.06, at an altitude of 43,000 feet.

The X-1, its fuel tanks loaded with explosive liquid oxygen, was carried aloft in the bomb bay of a B-29. As the four-engined bomber droned along at 20,000 feet, the bright orange X-1, nicknamed "Glamorous Glennis" after Yeager's wife, fell free then shot forward as the 6,000-pound thrust rockets were fired. Other planes suffer severe buffeting when approaching Mach speed, but the aerodynamically sleek X-1 sailed smoothly past the barrier.

Yeager, 24, was one of the army's hottest fighter pilots in Europe. But as the X-1 program is shrouded in secrecy, few people knew about his test-pilot activities.

U.S. armed services are now unified

Washington, D.C., July 26

President Truman today signed the National Security Act, uniting the armed services under one Department of Defense, to be headed by an official with Cabinet rank. James V. Forrestal, the current Secretary of the Navy, is slated to become the first Secretary of Defense.

The activities of the new National Military Establishment will be coordinated by a Joint Chiefs of Staff. A National Security Council will advise the president on military policy; a new information-gathering unit called the Central Intelligence Agency is established, and the Army Air Force becomes independent as the U.S. Air Force.

Both Congress and the State Department hope the new legislation will integrate domestic, foreign and military policy. Secretary of State George Marshall said last week that the weakened nations of Western Europe lie perilously near the brink of communism. The situation worsens daily, he said, and if economic aid fails, military efficiency may be at a premium. Said one State Department official: "It is later than you think."

Rosie abandons her rivets to raise babies

United States

"Hurry home, darling!" That's what women wrote their husbands overseas. And now that the men are back, the women are living happily ever after. Or are they? For some, the transition has been smooth:

While some women remain in the work force, most are finding that with the men returning the economy no longer has employment for them.

Men are now in school on the G.I. Bill, studying at the kitchen table while their wives cook dinner. Rosies have gladly abandoned riveting to raise babies. But many women are raising those babies alone.

Last year there were more divorces than ever recorded in American history, as the returning young men and waiting young women found themselves strangers. Some had not known each other well before they wed but had rushed to form a bond before death should prevent it. Other couples knew each other well before, but the war changed them. Men who were once carefree and boyish are now aloof and pessimistic; their wives hardly recognize them. As for the women, they had been holding down jobs and balancing checkbooks. All of a sudden the husband is taking charge and the woman is the inhabitant of a doll's house crammed with modern appliances.

4 million are taking advantage of G.I. Bill

Washington, D.C.

When the late President Roosevelt initiated the G.I. Bill in November 1942, he asked for quick congressional action. He got it and signed the bill into law a year and a half later. Now, more than four million veterans of the war are taking advantage of the housing, business and educational opportunities it has afforded. While a return from war is often difficult for service men and women, the bill has helped ease the adjustment to civilian life.

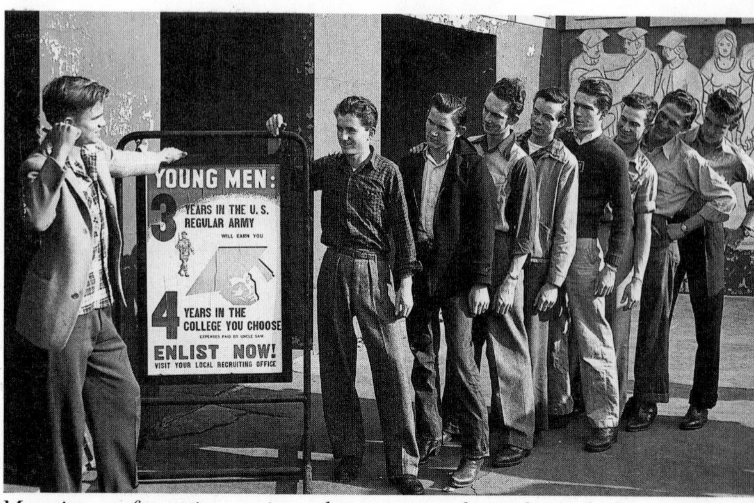

Men sign up for active service today to assure themselves a better tomorrow.

American nations sign defense pact

Rio de Janeiro, Brazil, Sept. 2

President Truman was on hand today to address the final session of the Rio de Janeiro Conference, where the United States and 19 Latin American nations signed the Inter-American Treaty of Reciprocal Assistance. The mutual defense pact stipulates that "an armed attack by any state shall be considered as an attack against all American states." In his speech, Truman said the treaty served as a warning to "any possible aggressor." In view of the current tensions in Europe, this appeared to be aimed at the Soviet Union (→ Apr. 30, 1948).

Record in U.S. aid to Europe's hungry

Washington, D.C., July 5

According to the Cabinet Committee on World Food Programs, over the last year the United States sent 18,443,000 tons of grain and other foodstuffs to Europe – the largest annual food shipment by any country. Commenting on the report, President Truman said that even such a record-breaking volume did not meet the "world's urgent postwar needs" and that millions of "still desperately hungry persons" need help. "We will continue to do our part to help other countries to help themselves," he said. The committee's report said that the shipments affected neither the American economy nor the nation's food supply (→ Oct. 5).

H.U.A.C. investigation into Hollywood ends with 10 blacklisted

Actors George Murphy and Ronald Reagan await their turns before H.U.A.C.

Washington, D.C., Nov. 25

An investigation into the alleged Communist infiltration of the movie industry was launched last month by the House Un-American Activities Committee. And today, in an unprecedented act of self-censorship, the film industry itself voted to bar 10 professionals who had been held in contempt of Congress.

One of the first people called before the panel was writer Ayn Rand, a friendly witness, who declared the movie *Song of Russia* propaganda. Another friendly witness, the actor Adolph Menjou, talked of anti-American pictures that should not have been made, such as *Mission to Moscow*. Robert Taylor stated that Communist activities were found mainly in the area of screenwriting, but he mentioned "party-line stuff" among actors and he named some names. Ronald Reagan, president of the Screen Actors Guild, testified that the guild is not controlled by Communists ("99 percent of us are well aware of what's going on") and spoke in favor of informed democracy. Gary Cooper said he had turned down a few scripts that were "tinged with Communist ideas."

Director Edward Dmytryk refused to answer some questions, citing his constitutional rights. And Emmet Lavery, president of the Screen Writers Guild, who other witnesses called a Communist, denied he was one and stated that his guild has no right to examine members on political or religious beliefs. Screenwriter John Howard Lawson said the committee was out to destroy the Bill of Rights and screenwriter Ring Lardner questioned the committee's right to question. The German playwright Bertolt Brecht spoke of the independent artist.

Charlie Chaplin sent the committee a telegram accepting an invitation to appear before them in Washington. "I understand that I am to be your guest at the expense of the taxpayers," he said, pointing out they could have seen him when they were in Hollywood "or even by means of a collect call ... While you are preparing your engraved subpoena, I will give you a hint on where I stand. I am not a Communist. I am a peace-monger" (→ Apr. 10, 1950).

"A Streetcar Named Desire" and "The Naked and the Dead"

New York City

It's hard to believe that only 20 years ago readers were scandalized by short skirts, bobbed hair and kids kissing in the front seat of a flivver. Today's writers go for stronger, often brutal stories. Take, for instance, the Tennessee Williams smash drama, *A Streetcar Named Desire*. Set in a sweltering New Orleans slum, it reaches a climax when the genteel heroine, a faded Southern belle, is crushed in the muscular embrace of a loud-mouthed galoot who also happens to be her brother-in-law. Some readers think the title of 24-year-old Norman Mailer's epic first novel about infantrymen in the Pacific *The Naked and the Dead*, ought to include *the Profane*.

Los Angeles, November 2. *Howard Hughes's Spruce Goose, made of wood and the world's largest plane, took to the air today, but flew only a mile.*

World Series on TV

New York City, Oct. 6

The Yanks and Dodgers served up a hair-tingling World Series that went down to seven games and provided superb fare for television viewers. An estimated 3.7 million saw the first telecast of the autum classic. Yankee relief ace Joe Page checked the Dodgers on one hit for the last five innings in the decisive game of this "subway" series today. The Bums had tied it at six-all yesterday in a game that saw a record 38 players in action. Bill Bevens missed a no-hitter by one out.

1948

Truman

Washington, D.C., Jan. 12. Supreme Court rules, in Sipeul v. Board of Regents of University of Oklahoma, that states may not use race as a criterion in judging law school applicants (→June 8, 1953).

Bogota, Colombia, Apr. 30. United States joins 21 nations in signing Organization of American States charter.

South Korea, May 10. Under aegis of United Nations Temporary Commission, elections are held in United States-occupied South Korea, but not in Soviet-occupied North (→Aug. 15).

Washington, D.C., May 19. Nixon-Mundt bill, requiring Communists to register with government, passed by House (→Oct. 21, 1949).

New York City, May. Pulitzer Prize awarded to James Michener for *Tales of the South Pacific.*

Washington, D.C., June 11. Senate adopts Vandenberg Resolution, permitting U.S. to be signatory to non-Western Hemispheric defense pacts.

Washington, D.C., Aug. 15. Word received of establishment in Seoul of Republic of South Korea; Syngman Rhee is president (→Sept. 9).

Washington, D.C., Sept. 9. U.S. learns of creation of Democratic People's Republic of Korea in Pyongyang; Kim Il Sung is president (→June 30, 1950).

New York City, October. Dwight D. Eisenhower inaugurated as president of Columbia University.

Cleveland, Oct. 11. Indians defeat Boston Braves, four games to two, in World Series.

Maine, Nov. 2. Republican Margaret Chase Smith is first elected woman senator.

Washington, D.C., Dec. 3. Colonel Mary Agnes Hallaren sworn in as first woman officer in regular army.

Philadelphia, Dec. 19. Eagles defeat Chicago Cardinals, 7-0, in N.F.L. championship.

DEATHS

Dayton, Ohio, Jan. 30. Orville Wright, co-inventor of airplane (*Aug. 19, 1871).

Hollywood, July 23. D.W. Griffith, pioneering movie director (*Jan. 22, 1875).

United States recognizes state of Israel

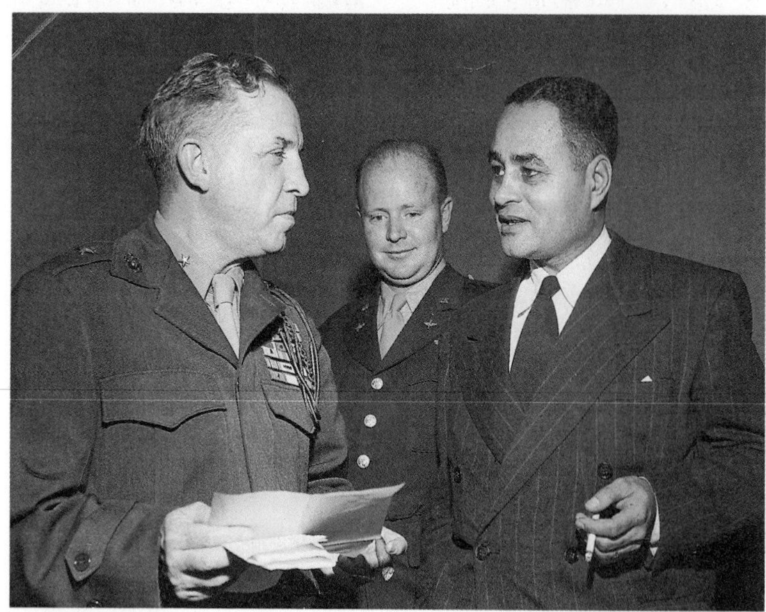

Ralph Bunche (right), acting U.S. mediator, oversees Israeli independence.

Jerusalem, May 14

As midnight struck in Palestine, Jewish leaders declared the independence of the new state of Israel. The announcement, timed to coincide with the end of Britain's control over Palestine, seemed certain to commit the new nation to a war with the Arab states, who are opposed to the partition of Palestine.

Although the United States had hoped that Israel would hold off until the United Nations agreed on a timetable for peaceful partition, President Truman waited only 11 minutes before pledging America's support to the new nation and granting its government recognition. The speed with which Truman acted took many in his own State Department by surprise.

The decision to divide Palestine into a Jewish and an Arab state, with Jerusalem under international control, was made by the U.N. General Assembly last November. But the world body was unable to get the Jews and the Arabs to agree to a plan. When Britain announced on December 3 that agreement or not, it would withdraw its troops from Palestine on May 15, hope faded for a peaceful reconciliation of Jewish and Arab claims.

Washington, D.C., April 3. *The Marshall Plan goes into effect as President Truman allocates $6 billion for overseas economic and military aid, keystones in the global struggle to contain the expansion of communism.*

Toscannini conducts NBC concert on TV

New York City, March 20

A local paper describes how the customers in a Greenwich Street bar got some Teutonic mythology mixed with their malt when the television set picked up the first telecast of the weekly NBC concerts. The indefatigable Arturo Toscanini, five days shy of his 81st birthday, led an all-Wagner program. Observed one patron, "He knows his onions, dat old boid. See the signals he got?" The program was also seen in Washington, Philadelphia, Schenectady and Buffalo. The "Old Man" maintains a youthful pace, with 16 NBC concerts a year. And in two weeks he can again be seen on television, conducting Beethoven's Ninth Symphony.

Millions can now watch the Maestro.

High court forbids prayer in schools

Washington, D.C., March 8

The Supreme Court added another brick to the "impregnable" wall separating church and state today. In McCollum v. Board of Education, the court ruled that a time set aside by public school districts at the start of each school day for prayer violates the Constitution. Lawyers for the state of Illinois argued that the First Amendment only forbids government preference of one religion over another. But, Justice Hugo Black held that "both religion and state can best work to achieve their lofty aims if each is left free from the other within its respective spheres."

Soviets blockade Berlin

Berlin, West Germany, June 26

Operation Vittles is under way. The West has launched a massive airlift of food to Berlin in response to the Soviet blockade of the Allied sections of the city. The blockade began two days ago when the Russians stopped all rail, road and barge traffic from the Western zone of Germany into Berlin, citing "technical difficulties" as the cause. A more likely reason is Soviet anger at the introduction by the Allies of a new currency into the Western zone to prevent the Russians from flooding it with counterfeit money, as they had been doing. According to an Allied estimate, 2,500 tons of food a day will have to be flown into Berlin to prevent the population from starving (→ May 12, 1949).

U.S. soldiers and German civilians unload coal during the Berlin airlift.

Armed forces integrated

Washington, D.C., July 30

President Truman issued an executive order today forbidding segregation in the nation's armed services. The President said that racial discrimination should end "as rapidly as possible." He also established the President's Committee on Equality of Treatment and Opportunity in the Armed Service to study the matter. The integration order is expected to create turmoil among Southerners. While nearly a million Negroes served in the military in World War II, most were confined to segregated and cheaper quarters. The President's campaign for racial equality took a major step four days ago when he ordered an end to discrimination in federal hiring.

The President rules Negroes may no longer be segregated in the military.

Rail strike blocked

Washington, D.C., May 10

Like his predecessor, President Truman has acted forcefully to end a strike threat by the nation's rail workers: He ordered the government to seize the railroads. Today's action averted a strike that union leaders had set. The army will operate the trains just as it did in 1943 when President Roosevelt seized them. Truman also intervened in a rail strike two years ago. It is hoped that mediation will end this dispute quickly, as it did in 1943 and 1946.

Citation triumphant

New York City, June

Citation has proved to be one of the few young colts that have lived up to their early promise. After a 27-for-29 record as a 2-year-old, he romped to victories in the Kentucky Derby and Preakness and wrapped it all up with a Triple Crown sweep by taking the Belmont Stakes. "He's the greatest I've ever seen," said jockey Eddie Arcaro, who in taking his fourth Derby surpassed a record shared by Earl Sande and Isaac Murphy.

Big lens dedicated

Mount Palomar, Calif., June 3

Amid a prevailing sense of gloom over science's role in the atomic age, astronomers dedicated a giant telescope here today to the peaceful pursuit of knowledge. With a 200-inch lens, the instrument will peer eight times deeper into space than any other telescope. Said one speaker: "Man spends his energies in fighting with his fellow man over issues which a single look through this telescope would show to be utterly inconsequential."

Draft is reinstated

Washington, D.C., June 24

President Truman signed the Selective Service Act today, reinstating a peacetime draft. It will require all men between the ages of 18 and 25 to register with the government for military duty, with all 19-year-olds eligible to be called up for 21 months of service. Between 200,000 and 250,000 men are expected to fill the ranks in the first year of conscription. Tension in both Europe and Southeast Asia is believed to have precipitated the legislation.

Eastern Europe falls into Soviet orbit

Washington, D.C.

Despite hope for a united Europe, an impenetrable barrier – an Iron Curtain – has riven East and West. Under the powerful arm of Soviet Premier Stalin, coalition governments have given way to Communist rule in Poland, Rumania, Hungary, Bulgaria and Czechoslovakia.

Poland, with a history of animosity toward the Russians, was the first to go. As Stalin insisted, "any freely elected government would be anti-Soviet and that we cannot permit." The Rumanians had helped the Nazis invade Russia, and the popular King Michael was ousted last December. Bulgaria, historically friendly to Russia, leaned easily to the left. King Simeon gave up his throne in 1946, and the Communists were soon ruling the Fatherland Front. In Hungary, control over farm policy gave the Communists popular appeal by means of land reform. The Czechs, victimized by a coup in February, had tried for middle ground, but to no avail. And in Yugoslavia, Marshal Tito firmly resisted, and was briskly expelled from the Soviet alliance this year. Hearing of Tito's "disloyalty," Stalin snarled, "I will shake my little finger and there will be no more Tito."

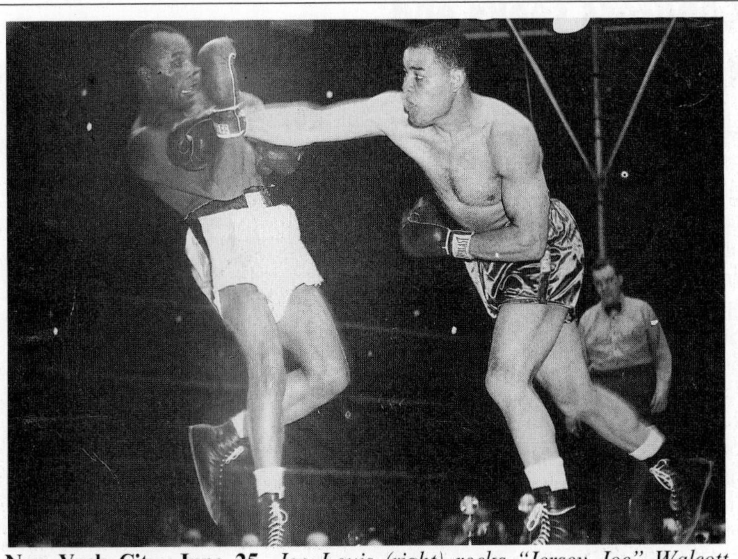

New York City, June 25. *Joe Louis (right) rocks "Jersey Joe" Walcott with a powerful right. Punching and jabbing, heavyweight champ Louis successfully defended his title by scoring an 11th round knockout.*

Alger Hiss indicted for perjury as Whittaker Chambers talks

Whittaker Chambers, an editor at "Time" magazine and former Soviet agent, is the principal witness in the government case against Alger Hiss.

New York City, Dec. 15

Whittaker Chambers led a group of investigators and reporters to a pumpkin patch on his Maryland farm earlier this month, where he produced evidence that has resulted in the grand jury indictment today of Alger Hiss for perjury. This sordid tale of espionage and backstabbing has Republicans excited and Democrats embarrassed.

The story starts in 1937, when Chambers, a Soviet agent at the time, is alleged to have received secret State Department documents from Hiss, then a department official. Chambers, now an editor at *Time* magazine, told the House Un-American Activities Committee that Hiss provided the documents and other strategic data that Chambers passed along to the Russians as part of a widespread pre-war Communist spy ring. Hiss, now president of the Carnegie Endowment for International Peace, denied the allegations before a federal grand jury and sued Chambers for libel. That denial is the basis for today's perjury charge.

California Rep. Richard M. Nixon has pursued the case, bringing it to national attention with the charge that the Truman administration is more interested in covering up the facts than in seeking out the truth. Truman, in showing support for Hiss, called the charges against him a "red herring." But, in a dramatic presentation, Chambers opened up a hollow pumpkin which he said served as a "drop," and pulled out three rolls of microfilm that contained secret State Department papers. The trial is expected to begin next year (→ 1949).

38 gold medals go to U.S. Olympians

London, Aug. 14

The postwar Olympics seemed to be the best-kept secret in this blitzed-out city, but once under way, they turned out to be a smashing success – especially for the United States. American athletes among the 6,000 competitors on hand rolled up 662 points, with 38 gold medals. Sweden was second best, scoring 353 points. One of the biggest American stars was 17-year-old Bob Mathias of California, who rolled up 7,139 points to win the grueling decathlon – on a rain-soaked track. The only political flap came up when some of the Czech and Hungarian athletes refused to return to their homeland behind the Iron Curtain and asked for asylum in the West.

Polaroid magic

United States

Push a button. Pull a tab. Wait a minute. And there you have an instant snapshot, developed and printed in the camera. That's the appeal of the $95, five-pound Polaroid Land Camera, designed by the inventor Edwin Land. It produces a black-and-white photo that can be removed from the back of the camera. Just coat it with a varnish to protect its surface.

Dixiecrats, Progressives offer alternatives

Washington, D.C.

This year's presidential election offers alternatives to the Democratic and Republican candidates. In July, two parties tossed candidates into the fray. The States' Rights Democratic ticket nominated South Carolina Governor Strom Thurmond at its convention. Known as "Dixiecrats," the party denigrates the civil rights campaign promoted by President Truman. Alabama's Governor Dixon delivered the keynote speech, saying Truman's policy "wants to reduce us to the status of a mongrel, inferior race, mixed in blood, our Anglo-Saxon heritage a mockery."

A few days later, the Progressive Party chose Henry Wallace, a Vice President under Roosevelt and recently fired as Truman's Secretary of Commerce. The parties are likely to splinter Truman's support.

McDonald's is open

San Bernardino, Calif., December

Taking their cue from self-service retail stores, Richard and Maurice McDonald have opened a hamburger drive-in with no carhops and no options on the burgers. Prewrapped with standard condiments ("Buy 'em by the bag," says McDonald's sign), they cost 15 cents; french fries are a dime, milk shakes 25. The idea has yet to attract a public that is used to car-side service.

Congress seeks end to rising inflation

Washington, D.C., Aug. 31

Back in November 1946, President Truman ended wage and price controls. It seemed like a good idea at the time. But today, an Anti-Inflation Act became law in response to skyrocketing inflation. Statistics show that a house costing $4,440 in 1939 costs $9,060 now. Clothing is up 129 percent, food 129 percent, home furnishings 93.6 percent. Only gas and electricity have had a cost decrease. In addition to the new anti-inflationary measures, the Federal Reserve has imposed limits on installment buying, hoping consumers will continue to pay for homes and other large items sooner than later.

New York City, August 16. *The Babe standing before a huge crowd celebrating the 25th anniversary of Yankee Stadium, "The House That Ruth Built," five days ago. Today, baseball's greatest slugger died of cancer.*

Quik, Dial, Honda: "brand" new world

United States

As new products arrive on the market, Americans wonder how they ever did without Honda motorcycles, Land Rovers, Michelin radial tires, Porsche sports cars, heat-conducting windshields, non-glare headlights, Nikon 35-mm. cameras, Salton Hottrays, color newsreels, Scrabble and Dial soap. How did they do without a Baskin-Robbins chain? Would they have wasted two quarters on what they now buy with a Franklin 50-cent piece? Would they have drunk tea instead of Nestle's Quik? And what would they have called bikinis if the island had not been bombed (maybe "next-to-nothing-atoll")?

Truman defeats Dewey

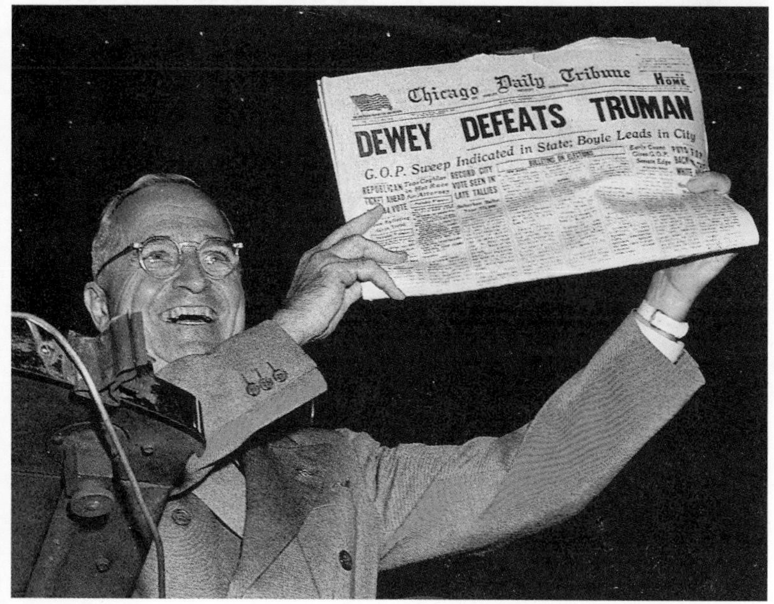

An exuberant Harry Truman mocks the skeptics who said it couldn't be done.

Washington, D.C., Nov. 3

The *Chicago Tribune's* headline screamed: "Dewey Defeats Truman." This early report was dead wrong as Harry S. Truman won a full term in the White House yesterday in one of the biggest political upsets in American history.

Give 'em Hell Harry and his running mate, Alben Barkley, defeated the heavily favored Thomas E. Dewey, Governor of New York, and his vice presidential nominee, Earl Warren, at dawn when the vote in Illinois pushed the Democrats over the top. Democrats also regained control of Congress, sweeping in on the President's coattails. Truman pulled out the election with his whistle-stop tour of the nation. On it, he was at his best. He described the Republicans as "bloodsuckers with offices on Wall Street, princes of privilege, plunderers." He tickled the electorate by saying that the polls predicting Dewey would win were like "pills designed to lull the voter into sleeping on Election Day. They ought to call them sleeping polls." The victory is even more remarkable in that the Progressive and Dixiecrat Parties each took over a million votes from the Democrats (→Jan. 20, 1949).

Japanese leaders hanged for war crimes

Tokyo, Dec. 23

Seven Japanese officials, including two former prime ministers, were hanged today following their convictions as war criminals. No photographs were allowed. Witnesses say none of the men expressed remorse. Each shouted "Banzai!" as he walked to the scaffold.

Former Prime Minister Hideki Tojo was in power for most of the war. He attempted suicide unsuccessfully to avoid trial. Koki Hirota was Prime Minister in 1936-37 and oversaw the signing of the Anti-Comintern Pact with Germany and Italy. An 11-judge civilian tribunal convicted the two of "crimes against peace." The supreme commander, General Douglas MacArthur, endorsed the verdicts, with little negative reaction.

MacArthur was severely criticized for refusing to block the executions of two Japanese generals in Manila in 1946. Military tribunals convicted Masaharu Homma, the leader for the Philippines invasion, and Tomoyuki Yamashita, the "Tiger of Manila," of war crimes. Evidence did not link either directly to the Bataan death march, where many Americans died on the way to war camps. Editor H.L. Mencken charged that MacArthur simply executed two men who beat him "in a fair fight" on the battlefield (→Sept. 8, 1951).

U.N. hails Mrs. Roosevelt's rights efforts

New York City, Dec. 10

People from around the world stood and applauded Mrs. Eleanor Roosevelt today for her efforts in winning passage of the United Nations Declaration of Human Rights. The President of the U.N. General Assembly, Dr. Herbert Evatt, said she "has raised a great name to an even greater honor." Mrs. Roosevelt thanked everyone in her usual self-effacing way. A U.N. delegate since 1945, the wife of the late President has long been active in humanitarian causes, with no issue too large or too small for her attention. In 1942, when wartime gas rationing began, Mrs. Roosevelt looked beyond the economic factors. She said that people on farms would have to stay home and "never see another soul for weeks and weeks." She cares.

The former First Lady never rests in the fight for humanitarian causes.

New on television

New York City

Television is rapidly becoming a permanent part of American lives. Shows that began this year include *Candid Camera*, *The Milton Berle Show*, *The Toast of the Town*, *Arthur Godfrey's Talent Scouts*, *Philco Television Playhouse* and *Studio One*. A Philco television set installed in a Capital airliner flying between Washington and Chicago works so well that video will be put on other flights. The Screen Actors Guild says that when a film is televised more than once in a locality, there must be "some additional payment for actors."

Kinsey sex report

Bloomington, Indiana

Dr. Alfred C. Kinsey specializes in insects. But his study of humans has made the University of Indiana professor a household name. It all began in 1938, when Kinsey started compiling dossiers about the sexual practices of American males. He eventually interviewed some 5,000 men, who related details about their preferences, habits and partners. At last, Kinsey's findings – long kept under lock and key – have been released in *Sexual Behavior in the Human Male*, a scholarly work with just enough spicy details to make it a runaway best-seller.

Tiny transistor may recast electronics

Murray Hill, N.J., July

It is only a minuscule metal disk with an even smaller germanium crystal soldered onto one face. But the Bell Labs physicists who displayed their creation this month say it will revolutionize electronics. The transistor, according to its inventor, Dr. William Shockley, amplifies electric current without a heated filament or other costly components. It may replace bulky vacuum tubes, making radios both smaller and more portable.

Celebrity endorsements are proving a lucrative marketing tool.

1949

Truman

Washington, D.C., Jan. 3. Supreme Court rules that the closed shop can be outlawed by individual states.

Washington, D.C., Jan. 3. Sam Rayburn of Texas elected Speaker of House of Representatives.

Washington, D.C., Jan. 21. Dean Acheson is sworn in as Secretary of State.

New York City, May 2. James Gould Cozzens awarded Pulitzer Prize in fiction for *Guard of Honor.*

Paris, June 20. Sixth session of Council of Foreign Ministers, with United States participation, closes, having failed yet again to reach accord on "German Question."

Washington, D.C., June 27. Supreme Court rules, in Wolf v. Colorado, that evidence gained through illegal search and seizure may be used by prosecutors.

Washington, D.C., July 15. President Truman signs Housing Act, extending federal assistance to nation's public housing.

United States, Oct. 1. Some 1,780 daily newspapers in nation reach 53 million in circulation.

New York City, Oct. 19. New York Yankees defeat Brooklyn Dodgers, four games to one, in World Series.

United States, Oct. 17. Northwest Airlines becomes first airline to serve alcohol on domestic flights.

Washington, D.C., Nov. 1. Total of 55 persons killed when an Eastern Airlines DC-4 collides with P-38 fighter plane.

Detroit, Nov. 7. General Motors announces that first three quarters of year have yielded a record profit of $500 million.

Los Angeles, Dec. 18. Philadelphia Eagles beat Rams, 14-0, for N.F.L. title.

Long Island, New York. William Levitt converts potato field into suburban community with houses selling for $7,990 [Levittown].

Rochester, N.Y. International Museum of Photography opens.

Hollywood, Calif. Film premieres include *All the King's Men* and *Gentlemen Prefer Blondes.*

Truman sworn in, offers poor nations aid

Washington, D.C., Jan. 20

Inaugurated as President today, Harry S. Truman offered "a bold new program" for underdeveloped areas and denounced communism as "a false philosophy." For the first time, television carried the inaugural as far west as Sedalia, in Truman's home state of Missouri. In all, 10 million people looked on, many times more than watched all previous inaugurations combined. The President outlined a four-point program, supporting the United Nations and world trade and denouncing communism. As Point Four, he said, we should "help the free peoples of the world lighten their burdens." The project will provide technological skills, knowledge and equipment to poor nations.

"President Harry S Truman," man from Missouri, by Greta Kempton.

Champ for 11 years, Louis calls it quits

United States, March 3

Joe Louis, boxing's popular and durable heavyweight champion, is hanging up his gloves. The "Brown Bomber," who limited his boxing to exhibition tours for the past eight months, said he is retiring after 11 years as champ. Since beating Billy Conn in a rematch that drew one of the richest gates in history, Louis knocked out Tami Mauriello in 1946 and defeated Joe Walcott twice, but he is obviously losing the blinding jab and lethal hook that won him world fame. The 35-year-old Louis, who is in dire need of money to pay back taxes, said he would box exhibition matches in an effort to pay his debts.

Lady wrestlers, roller derby and pizza

United States

Some nice things for women this year: prepared cake mixes, Pillsbury "Bake-offs," Revlon's "Fire and Ice," ripping needles for sewing machines, boned bras, decolletage bras, scented bras (by Love-E), mother-daughter matching playsuits and Gorgeous George, the wrestler. For men: roller derbies, pyramid clubs, Sara Lee cheesecake and lady wrestlers. Nice things for couples: LP record catalogues, canasta and the pizza pie. An article in the *Atlantic Monthly* says, "You eat it, usually sitting in a booth in a bare, plain restaurant, with a mural of Vesuvio on the wall, a jukebox, and a crowded bar. The customers are Italian families, Bohemians, lovers, and – if a college is nearby – students and faculty members." Some things kids like: Silly Putty and more pizza.

"Rose and Driftwood" (1932) by San Francisco-born Ansel Adams, who this year published "My Camera in Yosemite Valley." Originally trained as a pianist, Adams did not dedicate himself to photography until 1930. Since that time, as an ardent conservationist, he has focused on nature.

World-circling flight sets 94-hour record

Forth Worth, Tex. March 2

Another air record was set here at 10:31 a.m. today when Captain James Gallagher landed his Boeing B-50, Lucky Lady II, on the same runway at Carswell Air Force Base from which he had taken off 94 hours and 1 minute earlier. In the meantime, Captain Gallagher had completed the first non-stop round-the-world flight ever attempted.

Traveling eastward, Lucky Lady II was refueled in flight four times during the 23,452-mile journey: over the Azores, Saudi Arabia, the Philippines and Hawaii.

The feat is yet another triumph for American aviation, which has been breaking one record after another. On October 14, 1947, Captain Charles Yeager, flying a Bell X-I, became the first pilot to break the sound barrier. On January 5 of this year, Captain Yeager set a climbing speed record of 13,000 feet per minute. Then, on February 8 an Air Force XB-47 flew from Moses Lake, Washington, to Andrews Air Force Base in Maryland in 3 hours 46 minutes, setting a speed record of 607.2 miles per hour. And in a less dramatic technical development in this emerging nuclear era, the Air Force recently test-dropped a 42,000-pound bomb, the world's heaviest, from the bay of a B-36.

In "South Pacific," box office magic

New York City, Apr. 7

With their new musical, *South Pacific,* Richard Rodgers and Oscar Hammerstein are working at the same, high level as *Oklahoma!,* but in a palm-tree scene a world away. Based on stories by James Michener, the plot features the wartime romance of an American nurse and a French plantation owner. As Nellie Forbush and Emile de Becque, Mary Martin and Ezio Pinza are magical in songs like *A Cockeyed Optimist* and *Some Enchanted Evening.* With the largest advance sale in history, *South Pacific* should be around a long time. And with the advent of long-playing records, the financial reward may be staggering.

Snowy California

California, January

In Palm Springs and Santa Barbara, commonly known for semi-tropical weather, it's snowing. San Diego, on the Mexican border, got its first snow in its 99-year weather history. The virtually unprecedented snowfall, covering Los Angeles and coastal areas in depths up to one foot, is crippling traffic and menacing Southern California's fruit and vegetable farms.

Senate ratifies North Atlantic Treaty

American might assures NATO its necessary strength and credibility.

Washington, D.C., July 21

By a vote of 82 to 13, the Senate today ratified the North Atlantic Treaty which commits the United States to a mutual defense alliance with 11 other countries. This is the first time in its history that the United States has entered into such a treaty in peacetime, and is yet another milestone in the nation's assumption of the role of leader of the free world in the cold war.

The treaty, signed in Washington on April 4, includes Canada, Britain, France, Belgium, Italy, the Netherlands, Luxembourg, Norway, Sweden, Ireland and Iceland. Its principal purpose, as set forth in its preamble, is to "safeguard the freedom, common heritage, and civilization of their peoples, founded on the principles of democracy, individual liberty and the rule of law." To that end, "an armed attack against one or more of them in Europe or North America shall be considered an attack against them all." The pact is drawn up under Article 51 of the U.N. Charter, which provides for regional security arrangements.

Ratification, though opposed by a handful of diehard isolationists, was virtually a foregone conclusion after the passage last year by a 64-4 vote of Senator Arthur H. Vandenberg's resolution urging President Truman to encourage collective security arrangements. Public opinion also strongly backs the North Atlantic Treaty Organization (NATO) accord, with 67 percent approving. Not surprisingly, Communist opposition has been shrill. The *Daily Worker* called it "International Murder, Inc."

Western observers say that the need for strong measures to counter the aggressive policies of Russian-dominated communism has been made evident by recent events in Europe: the Communist coup in Czechoslovakia, the moves to subvert Greece and Turkey, and most glaringly, the blockade of Berlin.

By joining NATO, the United States has served notice that it does not intend to sit on the sidelines while aggression has its way and intervene only later, as happened in World War I and II. Instead, aggressors now know they will have to reckon with the full might of the United States from the outset. And this, it is hoped, will prevent World War III (→Sept. 1, 1951).

Year-long Allied air lift breaks Soviet Union's blockade of Berlin

Berlin, Germany, May 12

The Berlin Airlift, which for 321 days has brought food, clothes, fuel and other essential supplies to the beleaguered citizens of the Allied sectors of this city, is coming to an end. Thanks to an agreement worked out under United Nations auspices in New York, Soviet authorities have reopened the city to road, rail and canal communication with the West.

During the blockade, some 2.5 million tons of supplies were flown in by American and British planes at a cost estimated to exceed $200 million. Only three "air corridors" were available to the supply planes, which at times were landing at the rate of one a minute.

Much of the credit for the successful management of the operation is being given to General Lucius D. Clay, the autocratic 4-star general who is military governor of the United States occupation zone in Germany. From the start, he had a clear view of the strategic issues involved. "A retreat from Berlin," he said, "would have serious if not disastrous political consequences in Europe. I do not believe that the Soviets mean war. However, if they do, it seems to me that we might as well find out now as later."

Young Berliners cheer as an American airplane brings them more food.

Charles wins title that Louis vacated

Chicago, June 22

Ezzard Charles is the new heavyweight champion of the world. The quiet Georgian, who as a boy didn't even like prizefighting, outpointed Jersey Joe Walcott in a 15-round contest to gain the title vacated by Joe Louis. Charles found his talent for boxing at age 16 and went on to win 42 amateur fights in a row before turning pro at 18. He patterned his style after that of Joe Louis but said, "It didn't work out for me." Charles is an admittedly cautious fighter, which reduces him in the eyes of some critics, but he can box furiously when he is cornered. And though his knockout record is not notable, he walloped a lot harder than most of the experts expected.

Auto industry fueling postwar economy

"Graceful as a yacht," the ad says, "the smart car for young moderns."

Detroit, Michigan
The airlines may have stolen the spotlight for technological innovation, but it is the auto industry that provides the spark for postwar recovery. During the war, auto plants turned out one-fifth of the nation's military goods. Now Ford, Chrysler and General Motors have returned to the consumer market with a vengeance. A record six million cars rolled off American assembly lines this year, outstripping the rest of the world's output. G.M. reported profits of $500 million for the first three quarters, and offered dividends totaling an unprecedented $190 million. And with Detroit using steel, rubber and glass, prosperity spreads widely. Consumers glad to be rid of wartime rationing seem eager to buy.

Soviets detonate Bomb

Washington, D.C., Sept. 23
A major shift in the balance of power between the Soviet Union and the West was disclosed today with the announcement by President Truman that the Russians have succeeded in detonating a nuclear bomb. Though it was suspected that the Russians were working on an atomic weapon, it was generally believed that they were at least three years from their goal. The news means that the United States can no longer rely on its exclusive ownership of nuclear weapons to counterbalance the Soviet advantage in conventional weapons and land forces. The problem is not immediate, because the United States has a substantial stockpile of atomic weapons under the control of the Atomic Energy Commission, but its monopoly is now at an end.

While that monopoly lasted, the United States was widely praised for its offer to share its nuclear technology with the rest of the world, although under conditions that would prevent any country from using this knowledge for other than peaceful purposes. Since this would entail on-site inspection, the offer was turned down by the Russians on the grounds that such inspections would be used as an excuse for espionage. Now, however, it would seem that the reason for the Russians' refusal was a desire to conceal the fact that they were working on a bomb of their own.

Today's news will almost certainly lead to an acceleration of the arms race, with the emphasis on developing a hydrogen bomb. While technically more complicated than a fission bomb, a thermonuclear device would be 100 times more powerful (→ May 12, 1951).

U.N. cornerstone laid in New York City

New York City, Oct. 24
In an open-air plenary meeting of the General Assembly, the cornerstone of the United Nations building was laid today at a ceremony whose speakers included President Truman and Secretary-General Trygve Lie. The 18-acre site between 42nd and 48th Streets, bounded by First Avenue and the East River, was acquired in 1946 with an $8.5 million gift from John D. Rockefeller Jr. The American architect Wallace K. Harrison is heading an international team of architects working on plans for a 39-story Secretariat Building, domed General Assembly Hall and a long, low Conference Building.

The Secretariat Building is expected to be ready for at least partial occupancy late next year. In the meantime, the organization, after moving from temporary premises in London, then Hunter College in New York, is now in the Sperry Gyroscope building at Lake Success, Long Island (→ Oct. 14, 1952).

500,000 steel workers strike; get pension

Pittsburgh, Penn., Nov. 11
Even in the age of collective bargaining, the strike is labor's indispensable weapon. That was once again proved by United Steel Workers president Philip Murray, who has sent the last of 500,000 men back to work with pensions funded fully by the steel firms. For 77 days, Murray held off while federal mediator Cyrus Ching and a presidential fact-finding board did their work. He gave up on a wage raise, but insisted the firms pay for welfare and pensions. Company-funded welfare, retorted U.S. Steel, would "strike a blow at the principle of self-help and dignity." So in the age-old tradition of union self-help, 500,000 steel workers struck on October 1. Their action paid off.

Pound gets prize in mental institution

Washington, D.C., Feb. 19
From a hospital for the criminally insane, Ezra Pound today accepted the $1,000 Bollingen Prize for Poetry. The honored work, *The Pisan Cantos,* was finished in a U.S. Army prison in Italy, where the poet stood accused of making pro-Mussolini radio broadcasts during the war. Upon return, he was pronounced "insane and mentally unfit for trial." Pound has disavowed Fascism, but the judges still saw fit to defend their choice. "To permit other considerations," they stated, "than that of poetic achievement to sway the decision would destroy the significance of the award."

Communists take Peking as Americans ask who lost China

Peking, China, Oct. 1
With the proclamation here today of the People's Republic of China by the victorious 56-year old Mao Tse-tung, nearly one quarter of the world's population – some 500 million people – have come under the rule of a Communist government. To cold warriors, who view communism as a monolithic structure bent upon world conquest, it is a staggering blow, and the search for scapegoats is sure to start soon. American right-wing Republicans are already pointing the finger at the Democratic administration, which refused to intervene on behalf of the collapsing Nationalists. Secretary of State Dean Acheson is a key target, and there is already talk of Communist sympathizers entrenched in the upper reaches of the State Department.

However, the man who may be responsible is Chiang Kai-shek, the Nationalist generalissimo who has taken refuge along with the remnants of his army on the offshore island of Formosa [Taiwan], where he is protected by the American navy. Corrupt and inefficient, the Nationalists quite simply lost the support of the Chinese people, particularly the vast rural majority who were attracted by the Communists' promises of radical land reform. The Communists are also perceived to have taken a more active role in the wartime fighting against the Japanese (→ Dec. 8, 1950).

Peking falls to Communist forces.

11 Communists sentenced under Smith Act

New York City, Oct. 21

All but one of 11 leading Communists were sentenced today to five years in prison and a $10,000 fine for conspiracy to overthrow the United States government by force and violence. The 11th received only three years because of honorable military service during World War II. Judge Harold R. Medina set the sentence one week after the jury convicted all 11 men under the Smith Act of 1940. The charges stem from the activities of the Communist Political Association during an attempted reorganization in 1945. The men who received five years were Eugene Dennis, 44 years old and general secretary of the Communist Party of the United States; Gus Hall, 39, the Ohio chairman; John B. Williamson, 46, the party's national labor secretary; John Stachel, 49; Henry Winston, 35; John Gates, 36; Irving Potash, 47; Gilbert Green, 43; Carl Winters, 43, and Benjamin J. Davis Jr., 46, who is a New York City Councilman and chairman of the party's legislative committee. Robert Thompson, 34, New York State chairman, was sentenced to three years. Hundreds of demonstrators gathered in front of the courthouse on Foley Square protesting the convictions and sentences. In 1941, the Trotskyite Workers Party came under the scrutiny of the Smith Act; 12 members were convicted (→Sept 23, 1950).

Hiss testifies he was never a Communist

New York City

Alger Hiss, the former State Department official who has been accused of handing over government secrets to Soviet agent Whittaker Chambers in the 1930s, testified in June that he was never a Communist and that he never transmitted any department documents to anyone. The case has captured national attention with a series of dramatic circumstances: a secret drop for microfilm in a pumpkin patch; claims by Representative Richard Nixon that the Truman administration was hiding the truth about Hiss, as well as stories circulating widely that the State Department is a "Communist breeding ground" (→Jan. 25, 1950).

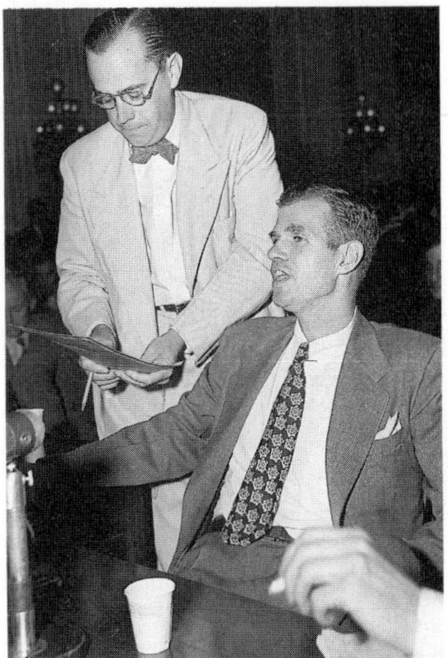

The defendant Alger Hiss (seated).

"Death of a Salesman" wins a Pulitzer

New York City

"A salesman has got to dream, boy. It comes with the territory." These words, from Arthur Miller's *Death of a Salesman,* could serve as the epitaph for every generation of Americans that lives from hope to hope, sure that someday its ship will come in. The dream is the American dream, and it goes sour in Miller's two act-drama. The loser is Willy Loman (that is, "low man"), an aging salesman "way out there in the blue, riding on a smile and a shoeshine." All his life, Willy has waited for better times, and now, as the wheel spins down, he's got no chips left, only a long-suffering wife and a pair of troubled sons who haven't grown up. Miller, 34, whose modern-day tragedy excited audiences and critics alike, has himself ridden off with something more substantial than "a smile and shoeshine" – the Pulitzer Prize.

A different prize is awarded in "The Lottery," the spooky title story of a collection by Shirley Jackson. It describes a ritual in a make-believe American town: Citizens draw lots with a bizarre prize for the "winner" – death by stoning.

No Flying Saucers, the Air Force insists

Dayton, Ohio, Dec. 28

Get the barbecues back out, because our skies were declared free of flying saucers by an Air Force report today. Project Sign, better known as project saucer, began on December 22, and investigated 244 sightings. These were explained as hallucinations, misinterpretations, hoaxes and natural phenomena, but for 23 percent of the cases the only answer was psychological malfunction. Major General L.C. Craigie headed the project.

Pogo and his pals back on comic page

New York City, May

Pogo is back! Walt Kelly's comic strip, last seen earlier this year in the *New York Sun,* now defunct, has been picked up for nationwide distribution by the Hall Syndicate and it is going to appear locally in the *New York Post.* Set in the Okefenokee Swamp, the strip describes the adventures of a mild-mannered little opossum named Pogo and his best friend, an outspoken, cigar-chomping alligator by the name of Albert.

C.I.O. throwing out Communist unions

Cleveland, Nov. 5

The Congress of Industrial Organizations is getting rid of its Communist albatross. Former president John L. Lewis's willingness to bring radicals into the C.I.O. has subjected the group to repeated attacks. This week at its annual convention, president Philip Murray seized the offensive. The United Electrical Workers and the Farm Equipment Workers, Murray insisted, were "diabolical apostles of hate" who "lied out of the pits of their dirty bellies." Both Communist-led unions were ousted. Panels were named today to investigate 10 other unions.

Burial mounds gain federal protection

McGregor, Iowa, Autumn

The Department of the Interior has announced that it will soon establish an Effigy Mounds National Monument about 15 miles from this small farming community in northeastern Iowa. Residents have long known and talked about the mysterious fortifications and burial mounds nearby. Anthropologists are of the belief that these earthen works were built in prehistoric times by American Indians. As a national monument, the rich archeological sites will be protected by the federal government from harm by careless visitors as well as looters.

TV firsts: Lone Ranger, Kukla, Quiz Kids

Hollywood, California

Now he is going to ride into our living rooms, that mysterious, masked stranger, as *The Lone Ranger* makes its debut on television along with *Quiz Kids, Original Amateur Hour, Captain Video and his Video Rangers, The Goldbergs*, and *Kukla, Fran and Ollie.* Milton Berle is the top-rated television entertainer and music lovers are hailing NBC for offering the Toscanini concerts. The Academy of Television Arts & Sciences handed out its first Emmy Awards at the Hollywood Athletic Club on January 25. Winners include a ventriloquist and her puppet, an adaptation of de Maupassant's *The Necklace* and *Pantomime Quiz Time.*

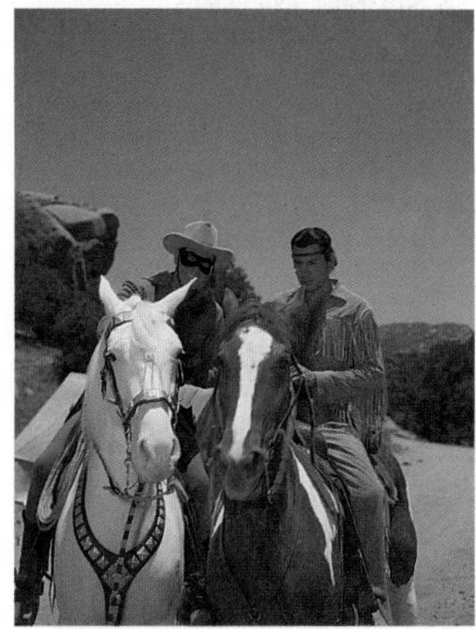

With Indian scout Tonto by his side, the Lone Ranger rides into the sunset and millions of American homes.

1950

Truman

New York City, Jan. 25. Alger Hiss sentenced to five years in jail on two counts of perjury.

Washington, D.C., Feb. 7. U.S. grants formal recognition to South Vietnamese regime of Bao Dai (→ May 8).

Washington, D.C., Feb. 20. Supreme Court rules, in U.S. v. Rabinowitz, that police may search, without a warrant, a limited area under control of an arrested suspect.

Washington, D.C., Apr. 10. By refusing to review contempt convictions of two film writers, Supreme Court upholds right of congressional committees to force witnesses to reveal their political affiliations.

Washington, D.C., April. In a speech to Newspaper Publishers Association, former President Herbert Hoover says, "I suggest the United Nations should be reorganized without the Communist nations in it."

New York City, May 1. Gwendolyn Brooks becomes first Negro woman poet to receive Pulitzer Prize, for her collection *Annie Allen.*

New York City, May 1. Richard Rodgers, Oscar Hammerstein and Joshua Logan win Pulitzer Prize for *South Pacific.*

Washington, D.C., July 7. Government implements use of draft, to increase size of military.

Washington, D.C., July 17. President Truman comments, "If you tell Congress everything about the world situation, they get hysterical. If you tell them nothing, they go fishing."

New York City, Oct. 7. Yankees sweep Philadelphia Phillies in World Series.

Washington, D.C., Dec. 8. President Truman imposes ban on trade with People's Republic of China (→ Feb. 2, 1953).

Brussels, Belgium, Dec. 19. North Atlantic Council names General Dwight Eisenhower Supreme Commander for Allied Powers, Europe.

Cleveland, Dec. 24. Browns defeat Los Angeles Rams, 30-28, for N.F.L. title.

New York City. Cartoonist Herblock coins terms "McCarthyism."

New York City. *The Betty Crocker Cookbook* published.

McCarthy flaunts "subversives" list

Washington, D.C., Feb. 22

"I have here in my hand," announced the junior Senator from Wisconsin, "a list of 205 . . . names that were known to the Secretary of State as being members of the Communist Party and who nevertheless are still working and shaping policy in the State Department." The ladies of the Wheeling, West Virginia, Republican Women's Club were shocked. Joe McCarthy barreled ahead. "The bright young men who are born with silver spoons in their mouths," he observed, "are . . . the worst," and they are led by Secretary of State Dean Acheson, a "pompous diplomat in striped pants with a phony British accent."

This was the scene on February 9. McCarthy had been chosen by Republicans to speak on Lincoln's Birthday. No one had expected a scandal. Until then, McCarthy's activities in Congress had gained scant attention. He was a tireless worker for a bottled drink firm, earning the nickname "Pepsi-Cola Kid." He had called a Wisconsin foe a "pinko," but never went beyond the usual cold war rhetoric.

"I have here in my hand a list of 205 names . . .," Senator McCarthy claims.

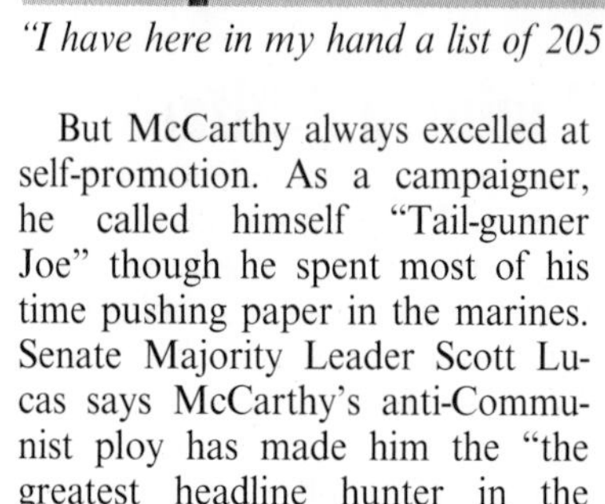

But McCarthy always excelled at self-promotion. As a campaigner, he called himself "Tail-gunner Joe" though he spent most of his time pushing paper in the marines. Senate Majority Leader Scott Lucas says McCarthy's anti-Communist ploy has made him the "the greatest headline hunter in the world." A week after McCarthy's speech, neither the news media nor Congress could ignore him. Two days ago, the Senate heard McCarthy discuss 81 anonymous cases. Today, the Foreign Relations Committee was assigned to investigate. State Department security chief John Peurifoy says anyone implicated will be fired "by sundown" (→ July 20).

Coplon convicted of spying for Soviets

New York City, March 7

A weak smile crossed the face of former Justice Department employee Judith Coplon and she paled as she heard a jury report a guilty verdict today on charges that she spied for the Russians. Her friend, Valentin Gubitchev, still listed as a member of the Soviet Foreign Ministry, was also found guilty. According to the jury, the two conspired to pass secret documents to the Russians at the height of the cold war. Both face stiff jail terms, to be determined on Thursday.

The convictions seem to mirror a mood among some government officials, a feeling that subversion is threatening America's national security. Prosecuting attorney Irving Saypol said after the trial, "We in the government are not oblivious to the sinister attempts to undermine us and we shall continue aggressively and forthrightly to vindicate our laws and protect our country."

Lewis wins nationwide truce in coal fields

Washington, D.C., March 6

After 10 months of fruitless talks and brutal work stoppages, there is coal peace and John L. Lewis has won his United Mine Workers their first industry-wide contract. The miners have been out for a month. An injunction had worried Lewis, who bears the scars of heavy fines. But his miners insisted, "No contract, no work." A judge cleared away the injunction and President Truman gave in, ordering the mines seized and a panel set up to rule on "just compensation," which means a raise and better welfare benefits.

John L. Lewis makes case for his miners before a committee of the Senate.

TWA changes its name and expands

New York City, Apr. 27

The dynamic world of American aviation is continuing its postwar expansion. Transcontinental and Western Air, Inc. (TWA) changed its name today; the company will henceforth be called Trans World Airlines. And the firm has placed a major order for a fleet of long-range, four-engine pressurized Constellation planes with Lockheed. In another recent aviation development, an Avro turbojet transport plane made the New York-Toronto flight in one hour last week; but experts predict that civilian jet transportation will not be commercially viable before the end of the decade.

U.S. to help French battle Indochinese

Paris, May 8

After conferring with French officials, Secretary of State Dean Acheson announced today that the United States is prepared to help the French defeat a rising Communist insurgency in Indochina. The French military has occupied the old colonial possession since the end of World War II, but Communist forces under Ho Chi Minh have announced their determination to liberate Cambodia, Laos and Vietnam from the French Union. Acheson is expected to offer France up to $10 million in economic and military aid (→ Apr. 7, 1954).

"Woman I" (1950) by Willem de Kooning, Abstract Expressionist.

U.S. backs South Korea against North

Washington, D.C., June 30

The United States will give all necessary military and economic aid to the Republic of Korea in the face of the Communist attack from North Korea, the State Department announced today. President Truman is steadily escalating the American response to the Communist moves. When the North Koreans crossed the 38th parallel five days ago, Truman simply said the United States supported its South Korean allies. But three days ago, the President authorized Douglas MacArthur, commanding general of American Far East forces in Tokyo, to provide the Republic of Korea troops with American naval and air power. And today, MacArthur reported that the Communist forces are so powerful that only the introduction of American ground forces can stop them. Accordingly, Truman has given MacArthur the authority to commit American infantry units as soon as possible. American intelligence sources report the North Korean army numbers about 89,000 men, supported by Russian-made T-34 tanks. The South Koreans' army consists of less than 38,000 soldiers, most of them poorly trained and without anti-tank weapons of any sort.

Three days ago, Truman explained America's position: "To return to the rule of force in international affairs would have far-reaching effects. The United States will continue to uphold the law" (→ July 7).

MacArthur says only American soldiers can stop powerful Communist forces.

U.S. troops, arriving in July, prepare a 75 mm recoilless gun on the front lines.

MacArthur to direct Korean campaign

Washington, D.C., July 7

President Truman has appointed General Douglas MacArthur to head the United Nations Command in Korea. Acting on a U.N. Security Council request today that he appoint a senior American general to direct all U.N. forces, the President immediately turned to MacArthur, conquerer of the Japanese in World War II and now head of the American Far East Command. MacArthur is expected to name a field commander in Korea but will lead the overall war effort from his Tokyo headquarters (→ Sept. 15).

Panel calls McCarthy charges a "Big Lie"

Washington, D.C., July 20

A majority on Senator Millard Tydings' panel has concluded that Senator Joseph McCarthy's "charges of Communist infiltration of and influence upon the State Department are false."

"A fraud had been perpetrated upon the Senate," the report asserts. McCarthy's "nefarious" plot, say committee Democrats, utilized the "technique of the Big Lie" for personal and political gain. Indeed, most of McCarthy's evidence was covered earlier by four House committees, none of which found cause for alarm. The F.B.I. and the Civil Service Commission have already purged from federal payrolls 2,000 people suspected of being radicals.

But the tempest is far from over. Senator Henry Cabot Lodge's dissenting report calls the inquiry "superficial and inconclusive." McCarthy sees it as "a green light for Reds" and charges that F.B.I. evidence had been "raped and rifled." The senator is now pursuing the case of Far East scholar Owen Lattimore, whom he calls "the top Russian espionage agent" in the United States. But his wrath embraces the "whole group of twisted-thinking New Dealers (who) have led America near to ruin at home and abroad" (→ March 26, 1952). ▷

U.S. troops swarm ashore at Inchon

U.S. infantrymen lay down fire and lob grenades as they overrun enemy lines.

American and South Korean troops search prisoners after the Inchon landing.

Guns of the North Carolina open fire on enemy installations at Inchon. Naval bombardment helps to make the difficult landing a little less so.

Korea, Sept. 15

The United Nations Command has announced that U.N. forces launched a major amphibious assault at Inchon this morning and operations are still being conducted. According to preliminary reports, the invasion was led by the United States First Marine Division and the Army's Seventh Infantry Division. The operation is being supported by an Allied naval armada of more than 200 ships and dozens of planes.

General Douglas MacArthur, chief architect of the daring plan, has command of the operation and is directing the invasion from the Seventh Fleet flagship, the Mount McKinley. The huge water-borne invasion has been expected for some time; the location comes as a surprise to many veteran military analysts. Because of its low tides and many mud flats, the harbor of Inchon is considered by amphibious warfare experts to be a nightmare. Others say that is precisely why MacArthur chose Inchon. His invasion forces achieved complete surprise and have suffered only minor casualties. While the objectives of the invasion of this port city on South Korea's west coast have not been announced, observers see the assault as designed to relieve the pressure on American units besieged to the south inside the "Pusan perimeter." MacArthur's men are likely to push eastward to the capital city of Seoul (→26).

Truman seizes rails as wartime action

Washington, D.C., Aug. 25

President Truman ordered the government to seize the railroad today to avert a strike. With the nation involved in the Korean conflict, it is feared that a work stoppage could threaten the stability of the country and the President is not willing to risk that. The rail union was offered an 18-cent per hour raise for yardmen, but management would not extend that increase to trainmen. In a show of solidarity, the union moved to strike, realizing that Truman might seize the lines as he did briefly in 1946 and again in 1948. The army will operate the rails until a settlement is reached.

62,000 reservists called up by army

Washington, D.C., Aug. 4

With the war in Korea heating up, President Truman today ordered the army to ready 62,000 reserves for military duty. The troop alert comes as part of the United Nations agreement to stop the Soviet-backed attack by North Korea against the South. Some see the conflict as a way to bolster the world organization's power. Political columnist Thomas Stokes has written, "Korea can be the beginning of a new era under a strengthened U.N., in which our leadership can be notable."

American invasion force liberates Seoul

Korea, Sept. 26

General Douglas MacArthur announced today that United Nations forces had recaptured Seoul. Spearheaded by elements of the United States First Marine Division and the Army's Seventh Infantry Division, the U.N. troops launched the attack on the capital four days ago.

The army troops, reinforced by the South Korean 17th Division, struck Seoul from the south, while the marines hit the North Koreans from the west. According to reliable estimates, the South Korean capital was occupied by 8,000 North Korean soldiers. American military sources say the Communist defense was formidable, with many reports of massed suicidal attacks against the advancing American forces. American losses have apparently been high. One marine company of 206 men suffered 176 casualties. On the plus side, Lieutenant Harry L. McCaffrey of the army's 32nd Infantry Regiment and his men killed 500 enemy soldiers, destroyed five tanks and captured 40 trucks. McCaffrey has been awarded the Silver Star. The struggle for Seoul has been ferocious. A British war correspondent, Reginald Thompson, said, "Few people can have suffered so terrible a liberation" (→Oct. 20).

First jet dogfight, and the U.S. wins it

Korea, Nov. 8

In history's first all-jet dogfight, Lieutenant Russell J. Brown of the United States Air Force shot down a Russian-built North Korean MIG-15 fighter today. Brown, piloting an F-80 Shooting Star, was flying escort for 70 B-29 bombers whose mission was to destroy bridges at Sinuiju, just south of the Yalu River on the North Korean-Chinese border. After evading heavy anti-aircraft fire, Lieutenant Brown and the other escorts were attacked by many MIG's at 18,000 feet. Air Force spokesmen report that all the American aircraft made it back to their bases (→ Dec. 5).

Security legislation to curb Communists

Washington, D.C., Sept. 23

Congress voted today to override President Truman's veto of the Internal Security Act. The law requires all Communist groups to report the identity of their officers and how they spend funds. It also bars any Communists from defense jobs. A Subversive Activities Board will enforce the law. Truman feels the act is unconstitutional and that it would drive Communists underground, thus hindering steps to contain them. Both houses of Congress collected the two-thirds majorities to override (→ Jan. 21, 1953).

Chinese flood across Yalu into Korea

Korea, Dec. 5

The massive Chinese military intervention in North Korea 10 days ago has broken the back of the advance by United Nations forces toward the Yalu River. Both the American and South Korean armies have suffered extremely heavy casualties and are engaged in a rapid but organized retreat. The American Eighth Army, the major fighting force in North Korea, has completely withdrawn to sites south of the 38th parallel. The other main American force, the 10th Corps, is engaged in a fighting retreat from northeastern Korea, near the Chosin Reservoir, toward the port city of Hungnam. Forward units of this battered group, mainly marines, and some army infantrymen, are being evacuated aboard a flotilla of navy ships standing by in the Hungnam harbor.

The Chinese Communists have been threatening to intervene in the war ever since September, when General Douglas MacArthur announced that he planned to carry the war to the Yalu River. The Chinese made good their warning on November 26, when an estimated 550,000 Chinese soldiers carried out a series of frontal attacks on American positions.

Last month, General MacArthur seemed on the verge of a brilliant military victory. With a degree of ironic understatement, he has acknowledged that "we face an entirely new war" (→ March 15, 1951).

U.S. troops pass through the carnage wrought by the Chinese as they retreat.

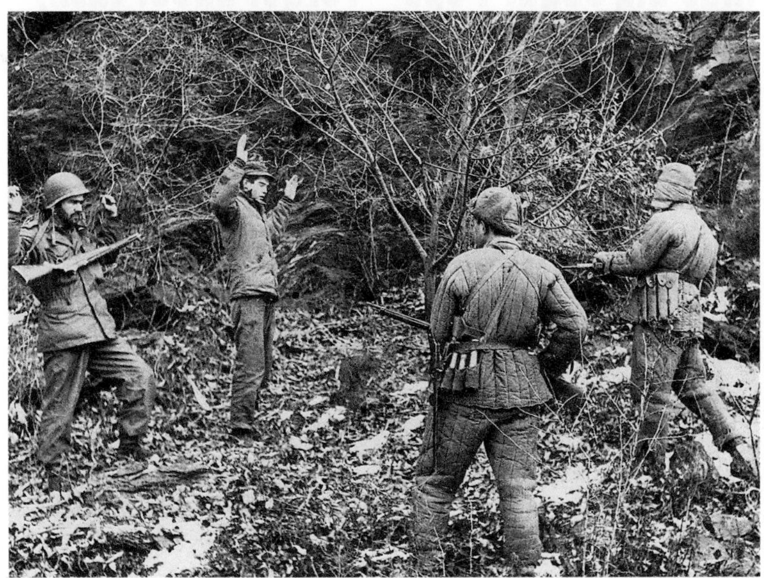

American soldiers surrender to members of the Chinese Communist Army.

North Korean capital seized by U.N. force

Korea, Oct. 20

With American troops in the lead, United Nations forces captured Pyongyang today. The United States Eighth Army under General Walton Walker crossed the 38th parallel into North Korea 11 days ago under direct orders from President Truman and the Joint Chiefs of Staff. Military observers here say that with South Korea cleared of Communist troops, the war is entering a new phase. Whereas the Americans entered the war in June only to defend their South Korean ally, the strategy is now to conquer North Korea and unify the two Koreas under a pro-Western government. General Douglas MacArthur reportedly informed the President of this plan on September 29. And when the General and the President met at Wake Island last week to discuss American war goals, Truman told reporters, "There is complete unity in the aims and conduct of our foreign policy." According to General MacArthur, the U.N. forces can conquer North Korea by Thanksgiving, and most American troops can be withdrawn to Japan by Christmas. When he was asked by Truman about the chances of Chinese or Soviet intervention in the war, MacArthur simply replied, "Very little" (→ Nov. 8)

From its encircled beachhead at Hungnam, the United States 10th Corps is successfully evacuated. The orderliness of the operation saved many lives.

Faulkner accepts Nobel, warns of timidity

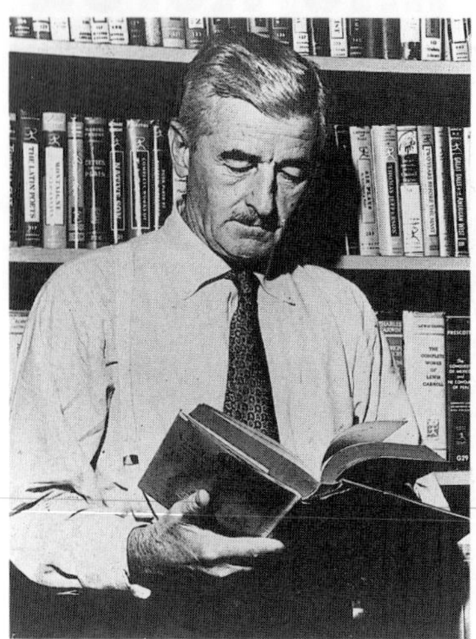

From William Faulkner, a warning.

Oslo, Norway, Dec. 10

For years he toiled in obscurity, his books out of print, his bills paid by Hollywood hackwork. But hard times are over for William Faulkner, this year's winner of the Nobel Prize for Literature. The dapper 53-year-old Mississippian delivered his acceptance speech here today and the world is likely to sit up and take notice. Referring to the atomic bomb and its impact on the modern mind, Faulkner accused younger writers of giving into fear and evading the eternal "problems of the spirit." He lamented that to some there is only the question: "When will I be blown up?"

Will TV create a "nation of morons?"

Boston

"If the television craze continues with the present level of programs," says Daniel Marsh, president of Boston University, "we are destined to have a nation of morons." A national survey shows children watch TV 27 hours a week, only 45 minutes less than their hours in school. New shows – no relation to the Marsh comments – include *Your Show of Shows, The Garry Moore Show, The Kate Smith Hour, The Steve Allen Show, What's My Line?, The George Burns and Gracie Allen Show* and *Truth or Consequences.* In March, RCA exhibited a tube to usher in the color era.

Garry Moore in a moronic moment.

Kids dig Sugar Pops and Smokey Bear

United States

How do you entertain kids today? Buy them toy guns, spurs, boots and other Hopalong Cassidy items. Serve them Sugar Pops for breakfast and take them to a lecture by Smokey Bear. Explain how nifty new inventions work: the Otis elevator with self-opening doors, phototransistors and Sony tape recorders. Teach the youngsters how to square dance or even do the mambo. Let them watch a Cinerama movie. Or take them out in search of Unidentified Flying Objects.

Forget about cash, join Diners Club

New York City, February

Frank MacNamara, head of a small commercial finance firm, was embarassed the other night. So he decided to launch a business venture. He had run up a formidable bill entertaining guests at a restaurant here before realizing his wallet was back home. This is never going to happen again, he vowed. MacNamara and a friend, Ralph Schneider, now offer a Diners Club card, allowing its 200 bearers to charge food and revelry. Made of cardboard, it lists the 28 participating establishments on the back.

Minneapolis Lakers win basketball title

Minneapolis, Minnesota

The nation's leading basketball teams finally got together in 1947 in one league – except for the Globetrotters – and this year, when the skirmishing ended, the Minneapolis Lakers were at the top of the heap. They won the championship of the National Basketball Association, an amalgam of the American Basketball Association and the National Basketball League. In the end, five teams fell by the wayside and 17 survived. George Mikan was outstanding for the Lakers as they defeated Syracuse for the title.

Ralph Bunche wins Nobel Peace Prize

Oslo, Norway, Dec. 10

The Nobel Peace Prize went to United Nations diplomat Ralph J. Bunche today for his work in mediating the conflict between Jews and Arabs in the Holy Land. Dr. Bunche is the first Negro American to win the Nobel Peace Prize. The grandson of a slave, the 46-year old Bunche graduated from the University of California and received his M.A. and Ph.D from Harvard. In 1946, after two years at the State Department, he joined the U.N. and became chief negotiator of its Palestine Commission in 1948.

The Fords – Benson, Henry II and William – with one of their models. The company thrives as Americans take to the road in record numbers.

Celeste Holm, Bette Davis and Hugh Marlowe take a ride in the film "All About Eve," which has won the Oscar for best picture of the year.

ruman declares state of emergency

Vashington, D.C., Dec. 16

Because of deepening strain on oth military and economic reources brought about by the Koran War, President Truman has delared a state of national emergeny. In a broadcast to the Amerian people last night, Truman said hat he needed extraordinary exective powers to overcome the great rises now facing the country. He romised that the United States would continue to fight to preserve he ideals of the United Nations – the principles of freedom and jusice," and to build up our armed orces and those of our allies. The President also said that "we will expand our economy and keep it on an even keel." He closed his dramatic speech with a somber request that every citizen "put aside his personal interests for the good of the country."

Analysts say Truman's emergency proclamation is a masterpiece of political strategy. It allows him the temporary authority to build up the nation's defense capabilities gradually rather than alarming both its allies and enemies by ordering a full-scale mobilization effort. The declaration also enables him to impose politically unpopular tax increases, wage and price controls and resource allocation measures.

wo Puerto Ricans ry to kill Truman

Vashington, D.C., Nov. 1

An attempt by two Puerto Rican ationalists to kill President Truan today ended in a gun battle n which one of the gunmen and police officer were killed. The unfight took place outside Blair House, where the President is staying during White House renovaions. The second gunman was arested. This week saw riots in Puero Rico over whether the territory hould be free. Truman supports a nove for independence. But the teritory is subordinate to the U.S. in offshore matters (→ July 24, 1952).

"Lonely Crowd"

Jnited States

Do Americans today differ from heir predecessors? Yes, say social cientists David Riesman, Nathan Glazer, and Reuel Denney, whose acerbic study, *The Lonely Crowd*, claims a new species of American is afoot. An urbanite, he tends to be 'other-directed," that is, he apes he behavior of others, from friends and acquaintances to "those with whom he is indirectly acquainted," chiefly through the mass media. The result? Conformity. For although "all people want and need to be liked by some of the people some of the time, it is only the modern other-directed types who make his their chief source of direction and chief area of sensitivity."

It's Charlie Brown, small-fry everyman

United States, Oct. 2

A new daily comic strip made its debut today. Charles Schulz's *Peanuts* is the work of a young cartoonist who wouldn't take no for an answer. Under the title *Li'l Folks*, the strip was rejected by a half-dozen major newspaper syndicates. But Schulz persisted, much like his central character, Charlie Brown, a hapless young everyman who waxes philosophical at each new defeat and who happens to share with his creator a first name, a barber father and a basic mistrust of adults.

Census: 150 million

Washington, D.C.

The first census since World War II shows the American population at 150.6 million people. Urbanites make up 64 percent of that figure while there are only 5.4 million family farmers. The nation's newest war effort, in Korea, has decreased the number of unemployed to fewer than two million, and on another economic note, the average weekly wage in industry has hit a new high of $60.53. Illiteracy has dropped to 3.2 percent, a new low, but a study at the University of Michigan shows that half the population does not read books anyway. Germans and Italians are the largest immigrant groups, and Arizona has the largest Indian population.

Faces from the front lines in the Far East

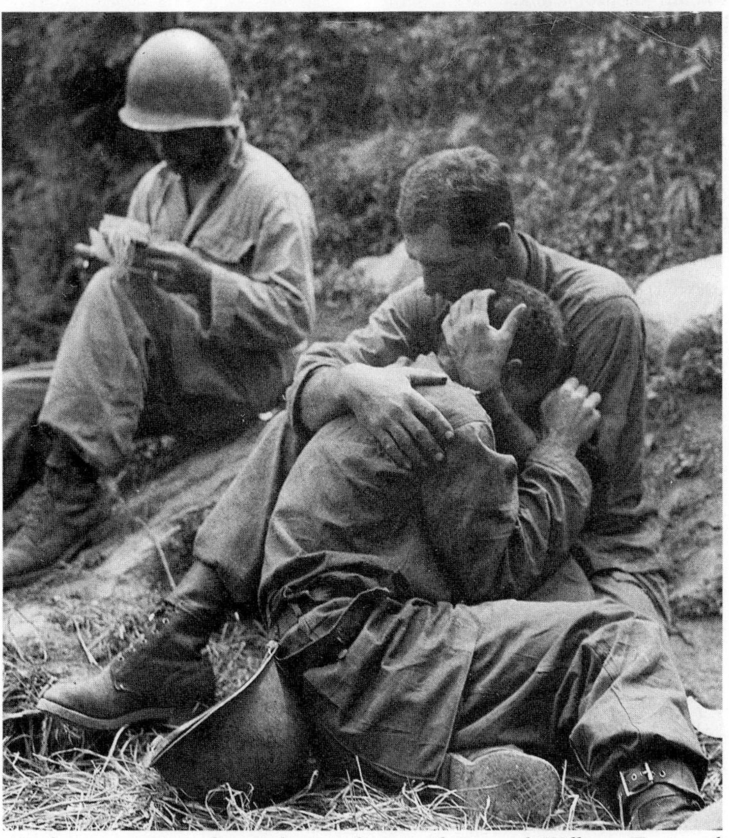

Another generation shares the conclusion of General William Tecumseh Sherman after the Civil War: "I am tired and sick of war. War is hell."

1951

Truman

Washington, D.C., Jan. 15. President Truman proposes $71.5 billion budget, over half of it to go to the military (→Jan. 21, 1952).

Washington, D.C., Jan. 26. Economic Stabilization Administration freezes most wages and mandates price ceilings for goods and services.

Washington, D.C., Apr. 16. In recalling General MacArthur, President Truman states, "In the simplest terms, what we are doing in Korea is this: We are trying to prevent a third world war" (→19).

Chapel Hill, North Carolina, Apr. 24. Univ. of North Carolina admits first Negro student.

Washington, D.C., Apr. 25. Servicemen's Indemnity Act signed into law by President Truman, providing sum of $10,000 to be paid to survivors of servicemen killed since beginning of Korean conflict, or any who die in future.

Rochester, New York, April. Rochester defeats New York Knicks, four games to two, in N.B.A. championship.

New York City, May. Pulitzer Prize awarded to Carl Sandburg for *Complete Poems.*

New Jersey, June 14. A human birth is shown on television for first time.

Illinois, July 12. Race riot, which erupted when a Negro family attempted to move into Chicago suburb of Cicero, prompts Governor Stevenson to call out National Guard.

Washington, D.C., Aug. 1. Tariff concessions to Eastern-bloc nations canceled by President Truman.

Korea, Sept. 3. Major Louis L. Sebille wins first Medal of Honor for air combat against ground artillery.

New York City, Oct. 10. Yanks defeat Giants in World Series, four games to two.

Englewood, New Jersey, Oct. 10. Transcontinental dial telephone service inaugurated.

Los Angeles, Dec. 23. Rams defeat Cleveland Browns 24-17 in N.F.L. championship game.

Hollywood, Calif. Films this year include *A Streetcar Named Desire, The African Queen* and *A Place in the Sun.*

New York City. *From Here to Eternity*, by James Jones, published.

Back on offensive, U.S. retakes Seoul

For the first time in military history, helicopters are used to ferry troops.

A tank of the U.S. First Division rumbles through devastated Chunchon.

Korea, March 15

American military authorities announced today that Seoul has been recaptured from Chinese and North Korean troops. The battle for Seoul began last week when General Matthew B. Ridgway, Eighth Army commander, launched Operation Ripper. His forces included nine divisions: six American and three South Korean. The offensive opened with a massive American artillery barrage and an infantry assault by the 25th Division against enemy positions on the Han River, 20 miles east of Seoul. After three days of bitter fighting, the Chinese began to withdraw. American military commanders report that their advance to Seoul was severely hampered by torrential spring rains and mudslides from hills surrounding the capital city. On most days, the Americans could advance only a mile or so. When they finally arrived in Seoul today, virtually all the Chinese and North Korean soldiers had been pulled out.

Army officials believe that the Communist evacuation is perhaps a ploy designed to draw the United Nations forces farther north, toward the 38th parallel, where the Chinese and North Korean troops can then launch a counterattack. But most military experts insist that Operation Ripper has been an unqualified success and that U.N. forces, with their superior aerial reconnaissance capabilities, will not be drawn into such a trap.

The capture of Seoul marks the fourth time in nine months the city has changed hands (→Apr. 11).

Rosenbergs are sentenced to death for selling atomic secrets

New York City, Apr. 5

Julius and Ethel Rosenberg, convicted of espionage last week, were sentenced today to die in the electric chair for revealing secrets of atomic weapons to the Soviet government. The law under which they were sentenced allows for the death penalty only if the act is committed during wartime, and though the Soviet Union was America's ally at the time, the Rosenberg crime occurred around June of 1944. Explaining his sentence today, Judge Irving R. Kaufman said, "The nature of Russian terrorism is now self-evident. Idealism as a rationale dissolves." Julius, who is 32, and Ethel, 35, are the parents of two young sons, and have stoically maintained their innocence during the proceedings, which began on March 6. Emanuel Bloch, who represented the Rosenbergs, described them today as "victims of political hysteria" and attributed their sentence to "extraneous political considerations having no legitimate or legal connection with the crime charged against them."

Bloch announced that he will file for an appeal with the Second Circuit Court and then with the United States Supreme Court should that fail. This will serve to stay the executions scheduled for May 21 at Sing Sing prison. Judge Kaufman, who during the trial often directly questioned Julius as to his Communist involvement, described the Rosenbergs as agents of a hostile totalitarian nation (→June 19, 1953).

ugar Ray captures niddleweight title

New York City, Feb. 14

Has there ever been a boxer so mooth and clever as Sugar Ray Robinson? Most experts say no. Their opinion was reinforced tonight as Robinson, for five years the world welterweight champion, added the middleweight title to his list by finishing off Jake LaMotta in the 3th round. Sugar Ray, who was born Walker Smith, has reigned as welterweight champion since he outfought Tom Bell in 15 rounds in 946. With no more welterweights o conquer, he opted to turn his boxing skills to the heavier division and pecked away at Jake LaMotta's brutal style.

22nd Amendment imits presidency

Washington, D.C., Feb. 26

The 22nd Amendment was ratified today, placing a limit of two elected terms on the presidency, with succession from the vice presidency with two years of service to count as a full term. Nevada was the 36th state to ratify, fulfilling the requirement of three-quarters of all states for passage. There has been no limit on how many terms a president could serve. Nobody before Franklin Roosevelt served more than two full terms. Foes of the reform say it cuts presidential accountability. But most say it appropriately limits presidential power.

Nevada atomic test

Las Vegas, Nevada, Feb. 6

The fifth and final detonation n a series of atomic bomb tests was carried out here today under the auspices of the Atomic Energy Commission. Shock waves from the explosion were felt in this resort town 45 miles from the test site, and the flash is reported to have been visible in San Francisco. Radioactive particles, resulting from earlier tests, have been found in snowfalls as far east as Rochester, New York, but the Atomic Energy Commission says the levels of radiation are far too low to have harmful effects (→ Oct. 10, 1963).

Truman fires a recalcitrant MacArthur

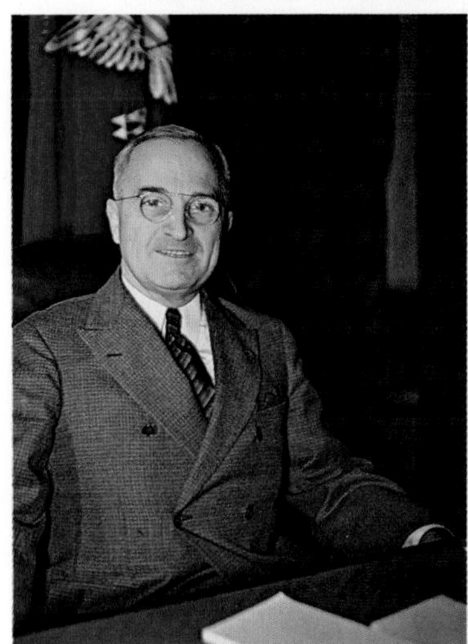

The buck stops here, not in Korea.

Washington, D.C., Apr. 11

In a momentous decision that came as a shock yet was not really that unexpected, the chief executive today formally relieved General of the Army Douglas MacArthur, the senior general in the United States Army, of all commands, including that of United Nations commander in Korea.

From the outset of the Korean War, personal and philosophical differences have plagued the Truman-MacArthur relationship. In July of last year, MacArthur conferred with President Chiang Kai-shek of Nationalist China without Truman's permission. A month later, the general sent the influential Veterans of Foreign Wars a scathing indictment of Truman's Formosa policy. In his message, the general blasted the President for supporting the argument of "those who advocate appeasement and defeatism in the Pacific." When the Chinese intervened in Korea, MacArthur lambasted the administration for not letting him bomb bases inside Chinese territory. And when Truman recently announced that a cease-fire was being considered, MacArthur said that if favorable terms for the United States couldn't be achieved, he would back the bombing of Chinese bases. Six days ago, Congressman Joseph Martin read before the House of Representatives a letter the general wrote him attacking Truman's policy of a limited Korean war. Suggesting a full-scale war against China and possibly the Soviet Union, he added that "... we must win. There is no substitute for victory."

When Truman received word of the letter, he conferred with the Joint Chiefs of Staff, who unanimously backed the President's decision to relieve MacArthur. In his announcement, Truman explained that "If I allowed him to defy the civil authority, I myself would be violating my oath to uphold and defend the Constitution."

President Truman has appointed Lieutenant General Matthew B. Ridgway to succeed MacArthur as commanding general of the United Nations forces in Korea (→ 16).

General Douglas MacArthur inspects the French battalion of the United Nations forces near the town of Wonju before beginning his journey home.

MacArthur: "Old soldiers never die; they just fade away"

Washington, D.C., Apr. 19

In an emotional address before both houses of Congress that was broadcast nationally on radio and television, General of the Army Douglas MacArthur gave his official farewell today to the American people. Fired last week by President Truman, the old warrior recounted his 52 years of military service in war and peace. Speaking eloquently and with intense sentiment, he closed his historic speech with a quote from a traditional British barrack-room ballad. "Old soldiers never die," he said, "they just fade away" (→ Nov. 27).

MacArthur, hero of the Asia campaigns, is cheered in New York on April 20. ▷

U.S. detonates H-bomb

Marshall Islands, May 12

The explosive equivalent of several million tons of TNT was released here today on the tiny atoll of Eniwetok as scientists of the Atomic Energy Commission detonated the world's first thermonuclear device – the H-bomb.

While most of the details concerning the bomb's design and construction are secret, scientists have long known of the tremendous energy that could be released if the nuclei of heavy hydrogen, deuterium, could be made to combine. This, after all, is the method by which many stars, including the sun, create their heat. But to make the nuclei react, temperatures of several million degrees would be required. The only way of achieving such heat on earth is by nuclear fission, using an atomic bomb of the kind dropped on Hiroshima as a trigger for the fusion bomb.

Much debate has surrounded the project; those opposing it included most of the members of the General Advisory Committee of the A.E.C. But news that the Russians had begun to test their own atomic weapons late in 1949 tipped the scale, and on January 31, 1950, President Truman approved the project.

Lady Senator, a quiet voice of conscience

Washington, D.C., August

Margaret Chase Smith has been tactful in opposing McCarthyism since her "Declaration of Conscience" last year. "I don't want to see the Republican Party," she had announced, "ride to victory on the four horsemen of calumny – fear, ignorance, bigotry and smear." Her honesty got her dropped from two G.O.P. posts and isolated in her own party. Smith, one of Washington's hardest workers, now speaks out through her votes. Liberals like her, but as the first woman elected to the Senate, she still contends with the patriarchs who have dubbed her "the girl scout with a mission."

Margaret Chase Smith of Maine.

UNIVAC, electronic computer, unveiled

Philadelphia, June 14

A powerful new electronic digital computer was unveiled here today by Remington Rand. It is UNIVAC (Universal Automatic Computer), the first such machine to be put on the market. The first customer will be the Census Bureau. The computer was designed by the physicist John W. Mauchly and the electronics engineer J. Presper Eckert, who developed the first large electronic digital computer, ENIAC, in 1945. UNIVAC includes revolutionary new features such as mercury delay lines for memory and magnetic tape for input instead of the punched paper used in the past.

Senator Kefauver airs U.S. crime problem

New York City, March 13

A reputed underworld "boss" upstaged the Senate Crime Investigating Committee's chairman, Estes Kefauver, today when Frank Costello took the stand and became television's first "headless star." After the bashful Costello protested that shots of his face jeopardized his privacy, the cameras trained on his hands, arms and chest instead. The effect mesmerized crowds gathered around the 2.5 million sets tuned in to the spectacle as the close-ups of his nervous hands conveyed intense emotion. Senator Kefauver is probing alleged links between the country's racketeers, its businessmen and public officials.

The United States is largest U.S. ship

Newport News, Va., June 23

Barely 15 months after its keel was laid, the United States was "floated out" today after a simple ceremony that was in marked contrast with the elaborate rituals that usually accompany launchings. Designed by William Francis Gibbs, the nation's leading marine architect, the ship was built at a cost of $77 million, three-quarters of which was paid by the government. At 990 feet, it is America's largest ship, and only 40 feet shorter than the Queen Elizabeth. After its fitting-out and sea trials, the United States is scheduled to sail on its maiden voyage next year, when it is hoped that it will capture the famed Blue Riband for the fastest trans-Atlantic crossing.

From bed vibrator to power steering

Detroit, Michigan

This is the year to start taking it easy. Buy yourself a Chrysler with power steering and cruise the new New Jersey Turnpike. Check into a hotel and nap on a vibrating mattress with foam pillows. When you get home, open the garage door with a push-button control in your car. Next, take a television course from Marquette University, collect trading stamps, try a Dacron suit (you won't like it). Quit worrying over cavities: chew sugarless gum. Don't let Dennis the Menace's antics upset you. And if your ulcer is acting up, remember this: research findings at Duke University show that burned toast, strong tea and milk of magnesia are antidotes for poisons of an unknown nature.

The heat is on, as the Kefauver crime committee hearings are televised.

The end may be in sight in Korea. As U.S. Marines fire rockets at Communist forces, the enemy's resistance is not nearly so stiff as had been expected.

Millions love Lucy, Roy and color TV

That zany redhead and sidekicks.

New York City
I Love Lucy, half an hour of fun with the Queen of Comedy, alias Lucille Ball, and her real-life husband, Desi Arnaz, is an instant success. Other television premieres include *The Roy Rogers Show*, *The Jack LaLanne Show* for fitness fans and the soap opera *Search for Tomorrow*. At this year's Emmy Awards, Imogene Coca and Sid Caesar took best acting awards and their program, *Your Show of Shows*, won the best variety show award. On May 2, the first live coast-to-coast hook-up was achieved, and the Radio Corporation of America is now broadcasting color programs from the Empire State Building. RCA has announced that it plans to give CBS the tri-color television tube for research to iron out current color problems. Last year, there were 3.8 million TV households (9 percent of all the homes in the country) and the number is constantly increasing.

Truce is forged in Korea

Troops of the U.S. 25th Infantry Division cross a narrow footbridge in Korea, as negotiators finally hammer out a truce in what was called "a police action."

Panmunjom, Korea, Nov. 27
After five months of haggling, United Nations and North Korean negotiators have finally taken the first concrete step that will, they hope, lead to the end of the war. After today's meeting, both sides announced that they will observe a truce along the entire battle line that stretches across the width of the Korean peninsula. If the negotiators fail to settle the other two major remaining items on their armistice agenda – specific provisions for enforcing the armistice, and the exchange of prisoners of war – it will expire in one month, on December 27.

Because of the inflexible positions taken on these two critical points by both the Americans and the North Koreans, the establishment of a final peace may prove exceedingly difficult. One of the negotiators, General Matthew B. Ridgway, the American commander of U.N. forces, has stated: "We have much to gain by standing firm. We have everything to lose through concession. With all my conscience, I urge we stand firm." With American casualties exceeding 22,000 since talks opened in July, Ridgway's tough stand may become impossible to maintain, either militarily or politically (→ Dec. 5, 1952).

U.S. joins alliance for Pacific defense

San Francisco, Sept. 1
With the signing here today of the Tripartite Security Treaty, generally known as the ANZUS pact, the United States has joined Australia and New Zealand in a mutual security agreement designed, at least in part, to counter the threat of Communist expansion in Southeast Asia. The treaty also sets up a Pacific Council composed of the three foreign ministers to coordinate mutual defense plans.

Pact gives Japan sovereignty again

San Francisco, Sept. 8
The restoration of full sovereign rights has been accorded Japan under terms of a treaty signed here today by the United States and 47 other nations. At the same time, a mutual security agreement has been signed by the United States and Japan; in return for military bases, U.S. forces will assume responsibility for the defense of Japan, whose constitution forbids it to maintain armed forces (→ Feb. 27, 1952).

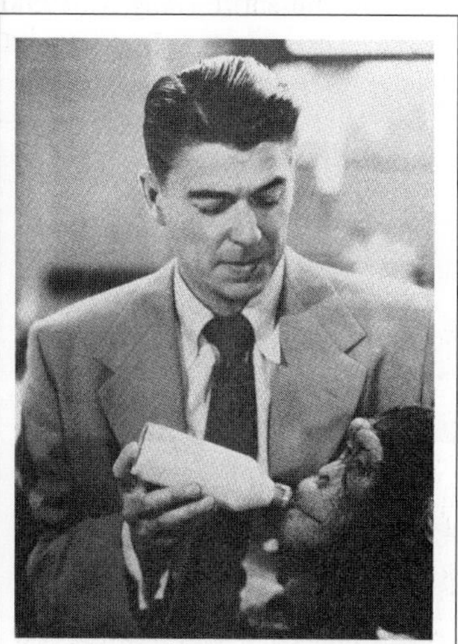
Actor Ronald Reagan offers his scene-stealing friend a snack in spoof called "Bedtime for Bozo."

"Catcher in Rye"

New York City
Young Americans have found a spokesman in 16-year-old Holden Caulfield, narrator of *The Catcher in the Rye*, the first novel by J.D. Salinger, 32, and a best-seller. Holden – tall, skinny, hapless and screamingly funny – deplores the "phonys" who rule the roost at Pencey, the high-tone prep school where he gets the boot. On impulse, he flees to New York City and checks into a flophouse. Holden has become a symbol of plain-talking to teens, but some bluenoses are crying "foul language." How would Holden respond? Probably with his pet expression: "That kills me."

As science and technology make giant strides, so does science fiction.

1952

Truman

New York City, Jan. 29. Herman Wouk wins Pulitzer Prize for *The Caine Mutiny.*

Washington, D.C., Feb. 27. Treaty concluded with Japan, allowing United States military bases on Japanese territory.

Washington, D.C., Apr. 2. Veteran diplomat George F. Kennan appointed U.S. ambassador to Soviet Union.

Minneapolis, Apr. 15. Lakers defeat New York Knicks in N.B.A. championship, four games to three.

Azores, Apr. 26. Destroyer Hobson and aircraft carrier Wasp collide in Atlantic, killing 176; Hobson sinks.

New York City, June 25. Journalist Edward R. Murrow inaugurates television news show *See It Now.*

London, July 7. Superliner United States wins Blue Riband.

Washington, D.C., July 24. Death sentence for Oscar Collazo, who tried to assassinate President Truman, commuted by President to life imprisonment.

New York City, July 31. General Douglas MacArthur is appointed chairman of board of Remington Rand Company.

Brooklyn, N.Y., Oct. 7. Yankees defeat Dodgers in World Series, four games to three.

Washington, D.C., Nov. 25. George Meany elected president of A.F.L., following death of William Green on Nov. 21.

Cleveland, Dec. 28. Detroit Lions defeat Browns, 17-7, for N.F.L. title.

Hollywood, Calif.. *The Jackie Gleason Show*, starring Gleason and Art Carney, has its premiere on television.

Washington, D.C. Republican vice presidential candidate Richard Nixon says, "Adlai [Stevenson] is the appeaser . . . who got his Ph.D. from Dean Acheson's College of Cowardly Communist Containment."

Springfield, Ill. Democratic presidential candidate Adlai Stevenson says, "Eggheads of the world unite. You have nothing to lose but your yolks!"

New York City. John Steinbeck's *East of Eden* issued.

New York City. Ralph Ellison publishes *The Invisible Man.*

Truman's budget allots 75% for arms

Washington, D.C., Jan. 21

Calling it a weapon in the fight for security and peace, President Truman has submitted to Congress the biggest peacetime budget in the nation's history. More than 75 percent of it is earmarked for major national security programs, with some $6 million for the expansion of atomic energy programs. The President's new budget would produce a deficit of more than $14 billion, but he says that this ought to be trimmed by means of higher taxes. Republicans oppose raising taxes and charge that Truman thinks spending solves all problems. The President calls Congress's tactic of percentage cuts unconstitutional.

Mad about comics

New York City, November

An entire generation of American children has gone Mad! *Mad Comics* No. 1 went on sale early this month and is a runaway hit. Published by E.C. Comics and edited by Harvey Kurtzman, *Mad* is the first humor comic book to parody every aspect of American culture, including comics, movies, television magazines and advertising. It follows on the heels of other successful E.C. titles, such as *Tales From the Crypt*, *The Vault of Horror*, *The Crypt of Terror*, *Weird Science*, *Weird Fantasy*, *Two-Fisted Tales*, *Incredible Science Fiction* and *Frontline Combat*.

Dinner by the TV

United States

It's the year to get off your duff! Dive into the Vinylite swimming pool, go bowling at an alley with automatic pinsetters, cut the grass with a motorized lawnmower. Do some flying saucer watching, race a hot rod, lead a panty raid, spin the propeller on top of your beanie and make like a whirlybird. Take up parachuting and break this year's record of 124 jumps in a day. Donate to a telethon, study psycholinguistics, down some No-Cal ginger ale and try to chew a Swanson TV dinner energetically – while watching television, of course.

McCarthy files libel suit

Senate colleagues have reacted bitterly to McCarthy's tactics and attacks.

Washington, D.C., March 26

Joseph McCarthy, for two years the storm center of the Senate, will take his tempest into court. Today, he filed a $2 million libel suit against Connecticut Democrat Senator William Benton. Since September, Benton has sought McCarthy's expulsion from the Senate. The Red-baiting Wisconsin lawmaker, he charges, accepted an illegal gratuity from the Lustron Corporation and perjured himself by telling Congress he implicated 57, not 205, officials in the February 1950 speech that set off a wave of national hysteria. Last week, Benton urged the Senate to vote on the issue, calling McCarthy's tactics Hitleresque.

The accused seems to revel in the martyr's role. His suit maintains that he "has been libeled, defamed held up to ridicule, disgrace, scorn and obloquy and has suffered injury to his good name and reputation."

McCarthy has achieved his reputation with such feats as persuading the Washington police to set up a unit "to investigate links between homosexuality and communism." Last week, he called fellow Republican Newbold Morris "either the biggest dupe or the biggest dope in all history." Morris denounced the inquiries of McCarthy and the Senate Permanent Investigations subcommittee as "mental brutality" and "ghastly distortion." "In the last three years," he roared, "you have created an atmosphere so vile the people have lost confidence in their government" (→Aug. 31, 1954)

April 15. *The Boeing YB-52 bomber on its maiden flight. Dubbed the Stratofortress, the Air Force's newest plane has eight engines and a 185-foot wing span that give it the capability of striking deep into enemy territory.*

igh court rules teel seizure illegal

Vashington, D.C., June 2

The Supreme Court dealt the na-ion's steelworkers a blow today, uling that President Truman over-tepped his powers when he nation-lized the mills April 8. As Jus-ice Hugo Black read the decision, ickets gathered at mills across the ountry. Truman intended to give he United Steelworkers a 26.5-ent wage and benefit increase and union shop, as proposed by the Vage Stabilization Board. This, the ourt ruled, infringed on the right f Congress to make law. Three dis-enting justices pointed to the Presi-lent's war powers, arguing that he noved "only to save the situation intil Congress could act."

U.S. first: A year without a lynching

Tuskegee, Alabama, Dec. 30

According to a report from the Tuskegee Institute, this has been the first year, since officials began keeping records 71 years ago, that no lynchings have been reported. Interestingly, the racially motivated violence seems to have declined without the benefit of Congress passing any of the anti-lynching legislation brought before it during this period. The absence of lynchings seems to parallel a recent decline in the membership and popularity experienced by the white supremacist Ku Klux Klan, an organization that has been responsible for many of the lynchings since the end of the Civil War.

Immigration quotas are set by Congress

Washington, D.C., June 27

The United States Senate today passed the Immigration and Naturalization Act over President Truman's veto, restricting and restructuring immigration into the country. The legislation establishes quotas based on national origin percentages as of 1920. Total immigration has been limited to 154,657 a year, and visas will be allotted with priority given to foreigners with "high education, technical training, specialized experience, or exceptional ability." In vetoing the bill, Truman said it would "intensify the repressive and inhumane aspects of our immigration procedures." The bill passed two days later.

U.S. stockholders number 6.5 million

Washington, D.C., June 30

More than 6.5 million Americans own a share in the nation's business, 76 percent of them earning less than $10,000 a year after taxes. These figures "clearly show that vast numbers of people have a direct stake in the ownership of business enterprise," according to the Brookings Institution, which conducted the study for the New York Stock Exchange. The 135-page survey released today shows that 28 percent bought stocks in the hope that they would go up, 22 percent for dividends, 10 percent because their brokers called them sound, and 8 percent because a family member worked for the company.

Republicans like Ike for presidency ...

He's commanding yet amiable, so what's not to like about Ike?

Chicago, July 11

It's Eisenhower and Nixon. The general won the Republican nomination for President on the first ballot today, and the senator got the vice presidential nomination by acclamation. Thus end the hopes of Ohio Senator Robert A. Taft, unsuccessful for the third time. As the second roll-call of the first ballot began, General Eisenhower was still nine votes short, with favorite sons such as California's Governor Earl Warren holding out in hopes that the general would fade in later rounds. But Minnesota's Harold Stassen delegation switched, providing the winning margin (→26).

Korea War G.I. Bill

Washington, D.C., July 16

President Truman signed into law today the Veterans' Readjustment Assistance Act, known as the G.I. Bill of Rights. The legislation will help veterans of the Korean War in much the same way as the G.I. bill served World War II vets. It provides those returning from military service in Korea with education benefits, housing, loan and business guarantees and other kinds of financial aid. The World War II program sent millions of veterans to college and was seen as a great success. Truman and an overwhelming majority in Congress expect this act will prove equally fruitful.

Bob Mathias stars

Helsinki, Finland, Aug 3

Led by star decathlete Bob Mathias, the United States has claimed victory in the 1952 Olympics, coming from behind to edge out the Soviet Union. Mathias, the one-man track team, pulled a muscle and still broke his own world record in the decathlon. Victories in the shot put, 400-meters, 100-meter hurdles, javelin and discus gave him a point total of 7,887. At 21, he says he may retire from the sport. Lifting the Americans past the Soviets on the last day were middleweight boxer Floyd Patterson and the U.S. basketball team, which defeated the Russians 36-25 for the gold.

...while Democrats go madly for Adlai

Stevenson, an admired intellectual.

Chicago, July 26

In a boisterous session that lasted past 2:30 a.m., the Democratic Party has nominated Illinois Governor Adlai E. Stevenson to run for President. After resting, they selected Alabama Senator John J. Sparkman as his running mate. Saluting Stevenson's victory, President Truman told the cheering throng, "I am going to take my coat off and help him win." Governor Stevenson told the delegates, "I have asked the merciful Father to let this cup pass from me. But, from such dread responsibility one does not shrink in fear" (→Nov. 5).

It is the envy of every American child. This top-of-the-line Schwinn comes equipped with whitewalls, light and, for that extra flair, tassled handlebars.

Ike wins: A general in the White House

The President-elect and Vice President-elect confer at Eisenhower's residence.

New York City, Nov. 5

General Dwight D. Eisenhower was elected 34th President of the United States today in a Republican landslide that carried both houses of Congress. Almost complete vote returns show nearly 34 million for Eisenhower, who campaigned against "Korea, Communism and Corruption," to 27.3 million for Adlai Stevenson, who said he tried to "talk sense to the American people." Taking the stump more actively than any other retiring chief executive, President Truman turned out to be a big issue himself. Republicans say the victory is a repudiation of the Truman Fair Deal. On communism, the role of the new Vice President, Richard M. Nixon, in the investigation of Alger Hiss was a major factor, and Eisenhower's pledge to go to Korea is believed to have been decisive. In the grand ballroom of the Commodore Hotel here, it was 2:05 a.m., when the President-elect, his wife, Mamie, at his side, said he will not give "short weight" to his job. Stevenson, in Springfield, said he "felt like a little boy who stubbed his toe in the dark. He was too old to cry, but it hurt too much to laugh" (→Jan. 20, 1953).

President-elect visits U.S. troops in Korea

G.I.'s hold their ground while next President holds to his promise to visit.

Seoul, Korea, Dec. 5

President-elect Eisenhower today secretly fulfilled his campaign promise: "I will go to Korea." Under a news blackout until one hour after he took off for home, the general's three-day visit ranged from the snow-covered front lines to a meeting with President Syngman Rhee. Eisenhower leaves convinced that achieving victory might require "enlarging the war." He believes Korea must have outside help "for a long time" to keep fighting Communists, and he promised the Western Allies will see it through together, in spite of differences. Eisenhower wore double-breasted civvies when he started in Washington, but he changed to army woolens with no insignia except that of his old European command. At the front, he was saluted by the unrehearsed thunder of rocket fire just as the First Marine Division band finished *Ruffles and Flourishes*. Surprised, the general asked, "What are they dropping in here?" One of the officers nearby explained to him that a pilot had attacked enemy positions somewhat farther away than it seemed, with sound carrying far and fast in the 8-degree temperature (→July 27, 1953).

Checkers speech helps Nixon cause

Wheeling, W. Va., Sept. 24

On a campaign stop here, General Dwight D. Eisenhower says his running mate "is completely vindicated as a man of honor," following Senator Richard Nixon's dramatic explanation on TV of his $18,235 "supplementary expense" fund. In Hollywood last night, the senator said he had never personally used any of his millionaire supporters' fund. Then he disclosed one gift. It was a little dog that their daughter Trisha had named Checkers. "We're gonna keep it!" Nixon said, adding he's "not quitting." Tonight, Ike read aloud a telegram from Nixon's mother and said her son is all right with him.

Lillian Hellman takes her stand

Washington, D.C., May 20

Lillian Hellman, the playwright and activist accused of Communist sympathies, today wrote John S. Wood, chairman of the House Un-American Activities Committee, concerning a subpoena calling for her appearance before the committee tomorrow. Miss Hellman wrote, "I am most willing to answer all questions about myself . . . But to hurt innocent people whom I knew many years ago in order to save myself is, to me, inhuman and indecent and dishonorable. I cannot and will not cut my conscience to fit this year's fashions." She may reluctantly take the Fifth Amendment.

New York City, October 14. *The United Nations today opened its first session in its new home, in America to ensure the organization's success.*

1953

Eisenhower

Washington, D.C., January. Charles E. Wilson says, "... for many years I thought what was good for our country was good for General Motors, and vice-versa."

Washington, D.C., Jan. 27. Secretary of State John Foster Dulles delivers radio speech promising that people held "captive" behind Iron Curtain can depend on United States.

Washington, D.C., Feb. 2. President Eisenhower, in State of the Union message, says Seventh Fleet will no longer prevent Nationalist attacks on Red China (→Jan. 28, 1955).

Washington, D.C., Feb. 5. U.S. steel production reaches 117.5 million short tons per year.

Washington, D.C., Feb. 6. Controls on wages and salaries lifted by Office of Price Stabilization.

New York City, Apr. 10. Minneapolis Lakers defeat New York Knicks, four games to one, for N.B.A. title.

New York City, May 4. Ernest Hemingway wins Pulitzer Prize in fiction for *The Old Man and the Sea.*

Washington, D.C., June 8. Supreme Court rules that restaurants in District of Columbia cannot refuse to serve Negroes (→23).

Washington, D.C., June 23. Dropping "separate but equal" theory, N.A.A.C.P. sets integration as goal (→May 7, 1954).

Washington, D.C., July 1. President Eisenhower tells reporters that United States will not militarily intervene in Eastern Europe.

Washington, D.C., Sept. 26. Spain agrees to establishment of American bases on its territory, in exchange for military and economic aid.

New York City, Oct. 5. Yankees win World Series for unprecedented fifth straight year, beating Brooklyn Dodgers, four games to two.

Washington, D.C., Oct. 12. United States reaches agreement with Greece, permitting U.S. military bases in Greece.

Oslo, Norway, Dec. 10. George Marshall awarded Nobel Peace Prize, for Marshall Plan providing economic aid to Europe.

Detroit, Dec. 27. Lions defeat Cleveland Browns, 17-16, for N.F.L. title.

Eisenhower takes the oath on television

As Vice President Richard Nixon looks on, Dwight D. Eisenhower takes the oath of office. He led Americans in war and now will lead them in peace.

Washington, D.C., Jan. 20

All America watched the biggest television hookup in history today as Dwight D. Eisenhower was sworn in as the 34th President of the United States. The New York Stock Exchange slowed to half its normal volume as millions left their usual pursuits to gather around TV sets and view the first inaugural ever telecast from coast to coast. Compared with the 10 million who watched four years ago on networks linked only as far west as Missouri, 21 million sets could receive 118 stations from New York to California today.

As many as 75 million people viewed the events in Washington, from schools and bars, offices, factories, homes and restaurants. At luncheon clubs, scheduled speakers were canceled in order that members would be able to watch history in the making, sometimes on several sets at once. The Astor Hotel used five screens in one room to give 300 luncheon guests close-up views denied to the 550,000 who crowded Washington curbs and elbowed for the best vantage points they could find. Radio was there, too, potentially reaching 98 percent of all the homes in America.

U.S. girl, 17, wins world skating title

Davos, Switzerland, Feb. 15

Tenley Albright, a 17-year-old from Boston, has become the first American to win the world figure-skating championship but she had to overcome dreaded poliomyeletis to do it. Miss Albright won all seven votes of a panel of judges today and completed a sweep of the skating events by Americans. Hayes Alan Jenkins of Ohio captured the men's championship. For Miss Albright, the victory capped a six-year comeback against the crippling disease, helped by skating exercises that she began at the age of 9. Miss Albright was runner-up in the 1952 Winter Olympics to Jeannette Altwegg of England.

McDonald's arches

Phoenix, Arizona, May

In search of an eye-catching look for their hamburger shops, Richard and Mac McDonald have discarded professional architects' ideas and decided on an oddly shaped building with a tilted roof, big windows, red-and-white tiles, a neon figure of a chef named "Speedee" and two sheet-metal parabolic "golden arches" with neon stripes that make the place look like a cross between an airport conning tower and a spaceship. It's quite a sight.

13 Reds convicted in conspiracy plot

New York City, Jan. 21

After a nine-month trial and a seven-day jury deliberation, a verdict was delivered today, convicting 13 Communists of conspiring to teach and advocate the overthrow of the United States government by force. Those facing sentencing next week include two founders of the Communist Party here, Alexander Bittelman and Alexander Trachtenberg. Judge Edward Dimock praised the jury's handling of the case. The foreman said, "We deliberated long and arduously and gave every possible consideration to each defendant. But after all was said and done, it was the only verdict we could reach" (→Aug. 24, 1954).

Wright, master builder, gets retrospective

New York City, November

The Solomon R. Guggenheim Museum is honoring the design and structural innovations of America's pre-eminent 20th-Century architect, Frank Lloyd Wright, with a retrospective exhibition of his work. Called *Sixty Years of Living Architecture*, it traces Wright's career, from the influential "prairie houses," which echo the horizontal lines of the Midwestern plains, through his latest skyscraper project. Wright, one of the first architects to work in concrete, made stunning use of the new technology in the Falling Water project: a house dramatically cantilevered over a waterfall. Wright is now working on a building for the Guggenheim that will feature spiral ramps.

Innovative architect Frank Lloyd Wright unveils his model of the Oklahoma skyscraper Price Tower.

Rosenbergs executed in electric chair

Ossining, New York, June 19

Julius and Ethel Rosenberg died in the electric chair tonight, convicted of selling atomic secrets to the Soviet government. They are the first civilians to be put to death under the General Espionage Act of 1917. The day was characterized by futile appeals to Judge Irving R. Kaufman, who sentenced them on April 5, 1951, judges of the Federal Circuit Court, the United States Supreme Court, and President Eisenhower, who refused executive clemency for a second time.

The trial opened on March 6, 1951, with an indictment charging the Rosenbergs with espionage dating back to June of 1944. Although the Espionage Act does allow for the death penalty during wartime, it has been noted that the Soviet Union was an ally of the United States, not an enemy, at the time of the crime. In every appeal, it was the serious nature of America's current relationship with Russia that served as justification for the sentence. Said President Eisenhower today, "I can only say that, by immeasurably increasing the chance of an atomic war, the Rosenbergs may have condemned to death tens of millions of innocent people all over the world."

In New York City, more than 5,000 people gathered on Union Square today to protest the execution. Representatives from the New York Clemency Committee of the National Committee to Secure Justice in the Rosenberg Case denounced Eisenhower, calling him "bloodthirsty." In another speech, the Rosenbergs were described as "freedom-loving people who were to die for world peace and American democracy." The implication that the Rosenbergs' conviction was part of a conspiracy involving Senator Joseph McCarthy was a key theme of the New York protest, but the appeals and speeches accomplished nothing.

At 8:04 p.m., Joseph Francel pulled the switch that sent Julius Rosenberg to his death, and seven minutes later Ethel joined her husband. On Union Square, the police ordered the sound system shut off and the crowd began to sing the spiritual *Go Down Moses*. In a letter Ethel wrote to the President on June 6, she asked "whether that sentence does not serve the ends of 'force and violence' rather than an enlightened justice."

For Ethel and Julius Rosenberg, appeals, protests and finally execution.

American aircraft fired on by MiGs

Alaska, March 14

The cold war has turned hot for American pilots. For the second time in four days, an American aircraft has come under attack by MiG fighters. A weather observation plane of the Strategic Air Command was fired upon today by one or two MiGs over international waters off Siberia. The Americans returned the fire, but no one was hit. On March 10, Czech Air Force MiGs shot down an American F-84 Thunderjet on routine patrol over the American zone in Germany. The pilot in that attack, which was the first on a United States plane since the start of the cold war, parachuted safely. He had not been wounded.

Miller's "Crucible"

New York City

Critics of Senator Joe McCarthy and of the House Committee on Un-American Activities often liken their proceedings to a witch hunt. Now Arthur Miller, himself a victim of the "Red Scare," explores the analogy in *The Crucible*, which recreates the 1692 Salem trials. The play focuses on the persecution of John Proctor, who was hounded to death for his beliefs.

Cochran surpasses the speed of sound

Edwards AFB, Calif., May 18

Attaining a speed of over 760 miles an hour as she flew her F-86 Saber jet over Rogers Dry Lake, Jacqueline Cochran today became the first woman to pilot a plane faster than the speed of sound. While she was about it, she also set a new international record of 652 mph for a 100-kilometer closed course. Miss Cochran was raised in a foster home and left school after third grade to work in a cotton mill. Receiving a pilot's license in 1932 after only three weeks of training, she became the second woman ever to win the Bendix transcontinental race and the first to ferry a bomber to England during World War II.

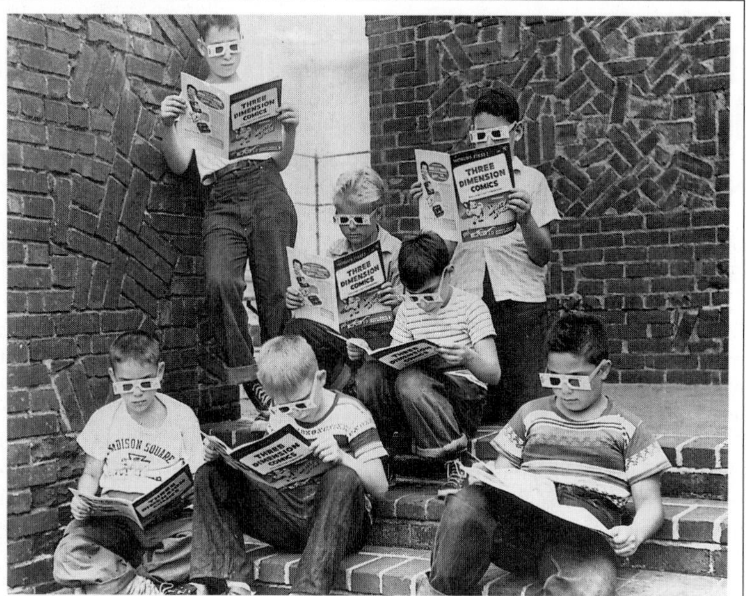

It's a country awash in fads, and these youngsters are enjoying one of the latest. With the aid of specially designed "glasses," you, too, can see the likes of Mighty Mouse jumping off a page of Three Dimension Comics.

"Little Mo" wins tennis Grand Slam

New York City, Sept. 7

"Little Mo" has done it! Maureen Connolly, who at the age of 16 won the United States singles title, proved her claim as the best woman tennis player in the world by scoring a Grand Slam. With her victory at Forest Hills today, she completed a sweep of all four major championships in a year, the first woman ever to do so. In addition to the United States title, she won Wimbledon and the French and Australian Opens. Miss Connolly began playing tennis when she was 10 years old after having won many prizes in the horse-show ring. She grew interested in tennis when her family moved near the city courts in Balboa, California.

Monroe and Hefner and a moon of blue

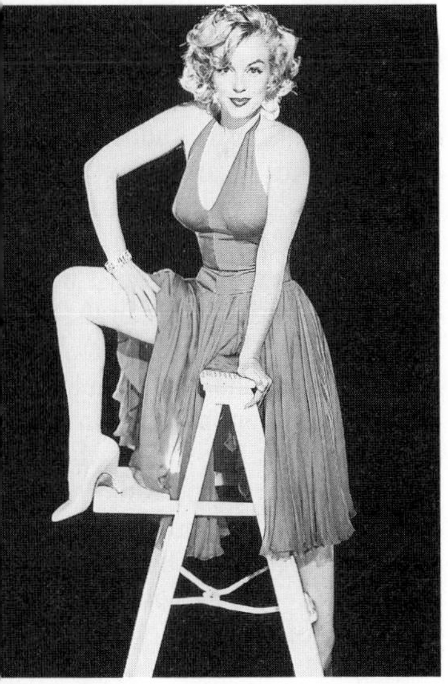

Some things speak for themselves.

Hollywood, California

Sexy is in! Marilyn Monroe is in three movies – *Niagara*, *Gentlemen Prefer Blondes* (with Jane Russell, too) and *How to Marry a Millionaire* – as well as on the cover and as a nude centerfold in the first issue of *Playboy*, a new magazine published by Chicago-born Hugh Hefner. Otto Preminger has released *The Moon is Blue* without the blessing of the Production Code. Other hit films include *Shane*, *From Here to Eternity*, *Roman Holiday* and *Julius Caesar*.

The new Massachusetts Senator John Kennedy, and his 24-year-old bride, Jacqueline, enjoy his family's home at Hyannisport.

War in Korea finally draws to a close

Panmunjom, Korea, July 27

Three years, one month and two days after it began, the Korean War has finally ended. Meeting this morning at 10 o'clock, senior Communist and United Nations delegates assembled, with few friendly gestures or kind words, for the ceremony. As dozens of journalists, photographers and military officials looked on, the senior representative of each side – General William K. Harrison for the United States and General Nam Il for North Korea – signed nine copies of the armistice agreement.

Actually, there was little to do when the representatives came together today, except to approve the armistice agreement formally. The three long-disputed obstacles to a peace agreement have already been resolved. The exchange of war prisoners has been started; the specific armistice details have been worked out, and the maverick President of South Korea, Syngman Rhee, who once violently opposed the agreement, has finally come around to supporting it.

The Korean War has been a costly conflict for limited objectives. Estimates put U.S. casualties at more than 55,000 dead and 102,000 wounded. But the count has not yet been completed (→Nov. 17, 1954).

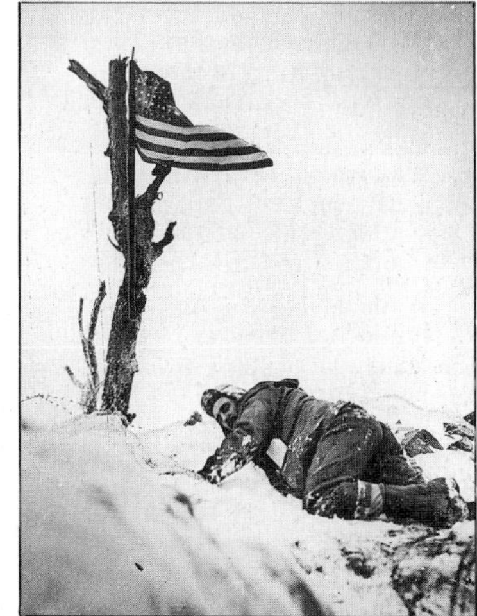

"... and our flag was still there."

Books: Science, fiction and science fiction

United States

The democratic experience has yielded a melting pot of books this year as three up-and-coming writers add spice to the native broth. One of these men is the son of a Harlem preacher; another is Jewish and ghetto-bred, and the third descends from venerable New England stock. James Baldwin, 29, is exploring the lives of inner-city churchgoers in *Go Tell It on the Mountain*, his first novel. The narrator of *The Adventures of Augie March*, the third novel by Saul Bellow, 38, exults in being "an American, Chicago born." John Cheever, 41, a prep-school dropout, flashes his verbal pedigree in a second set of stories, *The Enormous Radio*.

Other writers are peering past national borders. James Michener, 46, has gone Korean in *The Bridges of Toko Ri*. Science fiction writer Isaac Asimov, 33, resumes his galactic travels in *Second Foundation*, capping a trilogy. And some wags think B.F. Skinner has located a world all his own in *Science and Human Behavior*.

Scrabble, TV Guide

United States

Men: Is all you ever think about making it to first base? Or better yet, hitting a home run? Then maybe you're one of the 15 million people who attended major league ball games this year. Or maybe it means you like the new girlie magazine *Playboy*. Women: Do you prefer men who are the egghead type? Who like to play Scrabble? Who'd rather read *TV Guide*? Then join the 30 million people a year who attend performances of classical music and you'll probably find your man.

McCarthy acquiring foes in own party

Washington, D.C.

Senator Joseph McCarthy, that water-cannon of political assault, seems a bit nostalgic for old Democrats in high places. On November 24, he was still bashing former President Truman, insisting that his administration was "crawling" with Communists. Those are the old enemies. McCarthy, however, is not short on new foes, even in his own party. Most politicians are still cowed into silence, but President Eisenhower has assailed the senator's tactics, insisting that those attacked have a right to meet their accusers "face to face." Ike is angry over the rift in the Republican Party McCarthy has caused but does not want an ugly battle with him.

"42nd Street Nocturne" (1953), by Xavier J. Barile, shows a marquee with this year's controversial movie "The Moon Is Blue," a saucy comedy "spiced by more than a dash of sex" and in which the word "virgin" is used for the first time – to the shock of many an American moviegoer.

1954

Eisenhower

San Francisco, Jan. 14. Actress Marilyn Monroe marries New York Yankee baseball great Joe DiMaggio.

Washington, D.C., March 1. Senate confirms Earl Warren, as Chief Justice of Supreme Court.

Washington, D.C., Apr. 1. President Eisenhower signs bill establishing United States Air Force Academy in Colorado.

Minneapolis, Apr. 12. Lakers defeat Syracuse Nationals, four games to one, to win N.B.A. championship.

New York City, May 3. Charles A. Lindbergh wins Pulitzer Prize for *The Spirit of St. Louis.*

Atlantic City, New Jersey, Sept. 11. Miss America pageant, with Bert Parks as host, becomes first nationally televised beauty contest.

North America, Sept. 27. United States and Canada set up Distant Early Warning (D.E.W.) Line of radar north of common border.

Cleveland, Oct. 2. New York Giants win National League's first World Series victory since 1946, sweeping Cleveland Indians.

Hollywood, Oct. 3. *Father Knows Best* has TV premiere.

Washington, D.C., Oct. 25. Eisenhower holds first televised Cabinet meeting.

Washington, D.C., Nov. 2. Democrats regain both houses of Congress, in mid-term elections.

Washington, D.C., Nov. 17. Senate ratifies mutual defense pact with Republic of Korea.

New York City, Nov. 19. CBS public affairs program *Face the Nation* has TV premiere.

Cleveland, Dec. 26. Browns defeat Detroit Lions, 56-10, for N.F.L. championship.

Washington, D.C. Poll shows that 78 percent of Americans believe it important to report to F.B.I. relatives or acquaintances suspected of being Communists.

New York City. New York Stock Exchange has its best year since 1933, with 573,374,622 shares traded.

Hollywood, Calif. *On the Waterfront* released, starring Marlon Brando, Karl Malden and Eva Marie Saint.

Eisenhower explains: "You have a row of dominoes set up..."

President Eisenhower speaks out.

Washington, D.C., Apr. 7

Comparing the situation among Asian nations to a row of dominoes, President Eisenhower today expressed his concern that the conquest of Indochina by Communist forces could result in a disaster for the free world.

Noting that 450 million people are already living under Communist dictatorships in Asia, the President explained, "You have ... what you would call the 'falling domino' principle. You have a row of dominoes set up, you knock over the first one, and what will happen to the last one is the certainty that it will go over very quickly."

He pointed out that the entire island defense chain – meaning Japan, Formosa [Taiwan] and th Philippines – might be flanked which would threaten both Australia and New Zealand.

In its effort to combat the threa of communism in Indochina, th United States is also now mobilizing a multinational coalition.

The President says that stopping Communist expansion must be given high priority. Earlier in the year he called for a "New Look" in defense policy, one that would rel on atomic weapons and on strik forces to meet the threat whereve it might erupt. Speaking of thi evolving new defense policy, Secretary of Defense Charles E. Wilson described it as getting "a bigger bang for the buck" (→Oct. 23)

U.S. launches Nautilus, first atomic sub

Groton, Connecticut, Jan. 21

As an enthusiastic crowd of over 12,000 ship workers and spectators looked on, First Lady Mamie Eisenhower christened the nation's first nuclear-powered submarine, the Nautilus, today.

Named in honor of the submarine built by the inventor Robert Fulton in 1800, the vessel has a top speed of 30 knots and cost $55 million. Because its high-speed turbine engines are powered by an atomic reactor that needs no air, the submarine is expected to be able to circumnavigate the globe without having to surface.

Today's ceremony was a personal triumph for 54-year-old Rear Admiral Hyman Rickover, the outspoken Russian-born advocate of using nuclear energy to power submarines and other naval craft. As head of the naval reactors branch of the Atomic Energy Commission, and head of the nuclear power division of the navy, Admiral Rickover was the man responsible for directing the planning and construction of the Nautilus. A controversial figure because of his contempt for red tape and his unorthodox ways, Rickover was promoted to his present rank only after intense pressure was applied by Congress to a reluctant navy.

First Lady Eisenhower christens the submarine Nautilus as thousands watch.

Salk polio vaccine given to children

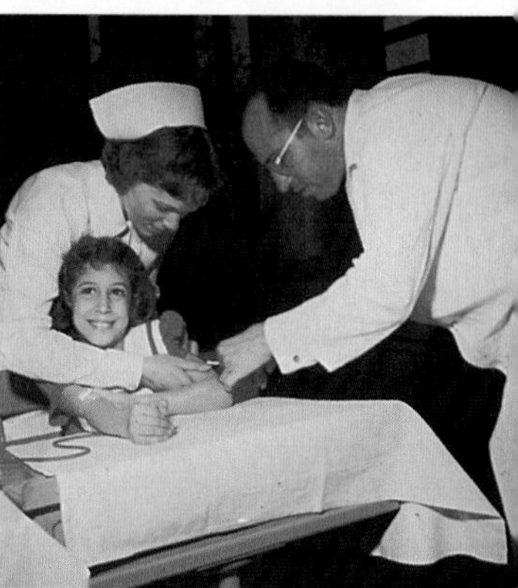

Dr. Jonas Salk administers his polio vaccine to a still-smiling recipient.

Pittsburgh, Penn., Apr. 12

The disease most feared by parents may soon be eradicated, following today's licensing of polio vaccines. The results of testing by virologist Dr. Jonas Salk of the University of Pittsburgh showed the vaccines to be safe and 70 percent effective. He tested 400,000 children with three vaccines: He and his colleagues had previously discovered that polio was caused by three viruses. The vaccines for each of the viruses were injected separately in every child. The government licensed the vaccines today, two hours after the results of the testing were made public. Scientists are hopeful that the vaccines will end the disease, which infected 21,000 individuals in 1952 alone.

:ommunist threat ·ops O.A.S. agenda

:aracas, Venezuela, March 1

Communist infiltration in Latin ·merica is at the top of the agenda ·s the Organization of American ·tates convenes here today – the ·irst time it has met since 1948. ·gainst the background of a Com-·munist-dominated government in ·juatemala, the United States will ·ecommend outlawing the Commu-·ist Party in the Western Hemi-·phere. While the United States ·elieves it is going to get broad ·upport, some members will be fo-·using on the "bread and butter" ·ssues, including the formation of a ·rade council that will deal with ·conomic matters.

'our Puerto Ricans ·pen fire in House

Vashington, D.C., March 1

Screaming "Viva Puerto Rico!" ·our Puerto Rican nationalists be-·an firing from the spectators' gal-·ery in the House of Representa-·ives, wounding five congressmen. ·ome 25 shots were fired before po-·ice officers entered. The governor ·f Puerto Rico says these national-·sts are part of a small faction. Ear-·ier this year, Puerto Rico rejected · resolution that would have meant ·ndependence for the territory.

Crewcuts are cool

Jnited States

What college girls are looking for ·n college boys: cool crew cuts, ·eat flattops and ducktails. Prefer-·bly, they have lots of bread and a ·lragster or a Mercedes 300 SL with ·uel injection. Nice if they're cadets ·t the new Air Force Academy who ·night someday fly the new super-·onic F-100 Supersaber. These ·uys should also be smart enough ·o remember Armistice Day is now ·eterans' Day. A plus if they look ·ike Audie Murphy. What the boys ·re looking for in girls: blondes (by ·Miss Clairol) wearing felt skirts ·vith poodle appliques. All right if ·hey have the "raccoon look" of ·eavy mascara, and hopefully, they ·an dance the cha-cha-cha. Grace ·Kelly lookalikes do fine.

Drama of Army-McCarthy hearings captivates American public

Washington, D.C., Aug. 31

In a distinct anticlimax to the marathon television spectacle of the Army-McCarthy hearings, the Senate Permanent Investigations subcommittee has mildly condemned both sides. According to the panel's Republican majority, Senator Joseph McCarthy allowed counsel Roy Cohn to attempt to put pressure on military officials to promote an aide named G. David Schine. Secretary of War Robert T. Stevens, the report said, vacillated in dealing with Cohn. Last year, Cohn and Schine virtually ran the investigations subcommittee, which McCarthy normally chairs. McCarthy had charged that Stevens held Schine "hostage" to halt a Senate inquiry into subversion in the army.

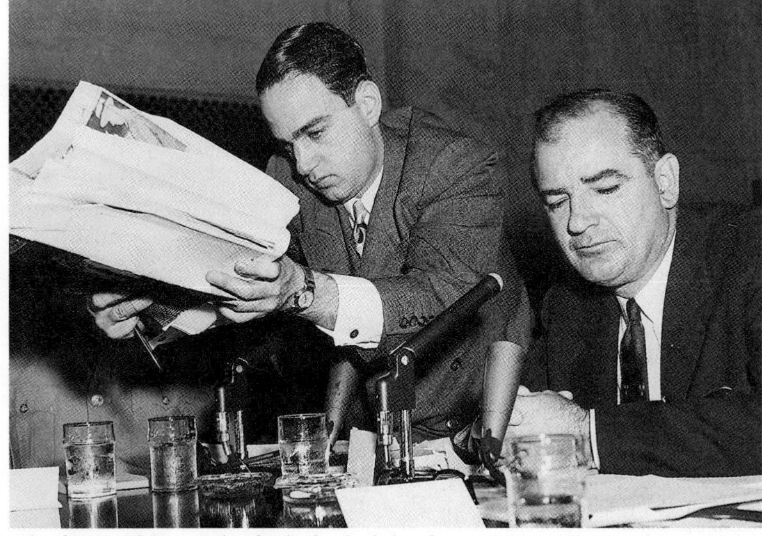

Chief counsel Roy Cohn feeds the fuel that keeps Senator McCarthy in action.

From late April through early June, however, the plot was secondary to the drama itself. Most Americans – sometimes 20 million at a time – were glued to the television set for at least a few of the 187 hours. Two million words of testimony poured forth, much of it screamed, shouted, squalled or sputtered through clenched teeth.

The proceedings opened with a speech by Karl Mundt, the rotund Republican who filled McCarthy's chair for the eight weeks. The hearings, he proclaimed, would be run with "dignity, fairness and thoroughness." It was there that the facade of parliamentary procedure ended. From the very first question, McCarthy imposed his own staccato pace. "Point of order, Mr. Chairman!" he interrupted, until schoolboys were imitating him in parks and playgrounds everywhere. Mundt was so obviously torn between his allegiance to McCarthy and his role as impartial moderator that one commentator labeled him the "tormented mushroom."

With everyone else abdicating, it was left to Army counsel Joseph Welch to supply the voice of reason. More than anyone, Welch was responsible for turning McCarthy's panel, his weapon of destruction for so long, into the vehicle of his own decline. With patience and humor, the long-faced Bostonian took Cohn apart, leaving him short-tempered and brutal before the cameras. But even Cohn flinched as McCarthy cast aspersions at a young aide on the Welch staff. Welch shed his lawyerly self-control completely. "Until this moment Senator," he cried, "I think I never really gauged your cruelty." And through watery eyes: "Have you no sense of decency, sir, at long last? Have you left no sense of decency?" In the solemn Senate Caucus Room, a burst of applause hinted that a cowering nation was having its long-awaited catharsis (→ Dec. 2).

G.E. hires Reagan

Schenectady, New York

General Electric has hired actor Ronald Reagan as host for its television anthology series, *The General Electric Theater*, and to tour its plants to speak on the virtues of free enterprise and the American way. Reagan has played rather square romantic leads in some 50 films, but his performances in *King's Row* (1942) and *The Hasty Heart* (1950) have won praise. Earlier, he was host of TV's *Death Valley Days* western series for three years.

The G.E. series, which began without a host in February of last year, will offer a wide range of material – from adventure to biblical drama, light comedy and melodrama. Reagan will also act in some of the presentations.

August 10. *Power Authority Chairman Robert Moses is the speaker at ceremonies inaugurating the St. Lawrence Power Project. Such joint ventures by the U.S. and Canada underscore the unique relationship between the two nations, which share an unguarded border almost 4,000 miles long.*

Supreme Court strikes down "separate but equal"

Washington, D.C., May 17

The case of Brown v. the Board of Education has culminated in a unanimous Supreme Court decision that overturns previous decisions permitting the segregation of public schools by race. The long-standing "separate but equal" policy was declared unconstitutional because "separate educational facilities are inherently unequal," as the opinion written by Chief Justice Earl Warren stated.

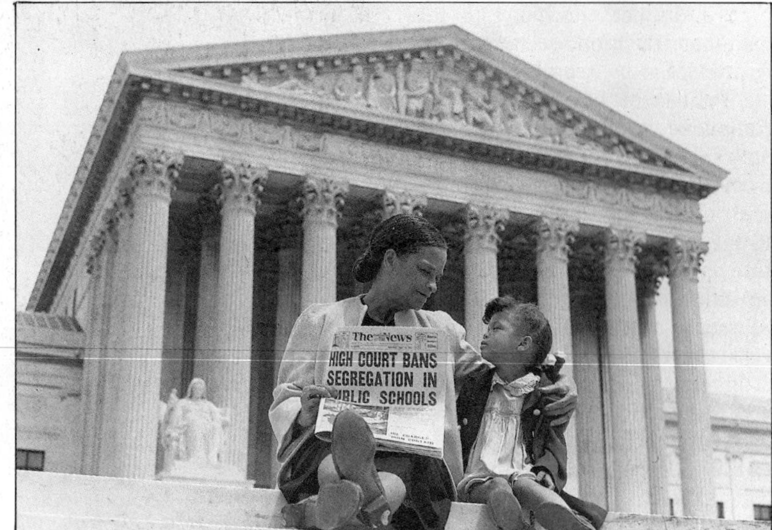

Mrs. Nettie Hunt explains to her daughter, Nikie, what the court ruling means.

The case began in 1950 when the National Association for the Advancement of Colored People decided to initiate a large-scale effort aimed at abolishing educational segregation. The N.A.A.C.P. put more than $100,000 into research and a campaign. A team of lawyers headed by Thurgood Marshall was assembled. Other members of the team included Robert L. Carter, Jack Greenberg, Louis Redding, James Nabrit, George E. C. Hayes, and Spotswood Robinson 3d. Many of the arguments presented by the N.A.A.C.P. were based on social and psychological research material gathered by Kenneth Clark. As a result of this campaign, in 1953 the Supreme Court ordered five school desegregation cases to be brought before it. The current decision, which began in a Topeka, Kansas, school district, sets a precedent that guides decisions in the other cases presently before the court, and in future cases.

The "separate but equal" doc trine had its roots in a preceden that was set by the Massachusett Supreme Court in 1849. A Negro Benjamin F. Roberts, sued the cit of Boston for damages when hi 5-year-old daughter was refuse admission to a white public school The case was argued with no suc cess and the supreme court of Mas sachusetts rejected the appeal. Th "separate but equal" doctrine wa further established by an 1896 cas that involved a New Orleans Negr who was arrested and convicted fo having attempted to ride in a whit railroad car. The defendant, Home Plessy, then appealed to the Su preme Court, but was rebuffed wit the ruling that the maintenance o "separate but equal" facilities wa a "reasonable" use of state polic funding and power. The court fur ther ruled it had not been the inten of the 14th Amendment to abolis segregation (→ May 31, 1955).

Ike promises more help to South Vietnam

Washington, D.C., Oct. 23

President Eisenhower wrote a letter to the President of South Vietnam early this month, promising more American support for that country, it was disclosed today. In his note to Ngo Dinh Diem, Eisenhower did not specifiy what type of assistance, military or economic, the United States is going to provide the Southeast Asian country in its struggle against a growing Communist insurgency. The President's position, however, is clear. He said in April that South Vietnam is like a domino among other dominoes, or nations, in that part of the world: if one of them falls to the Communists, then the rest of the democratic nations of Southeast Asia will inevitably be brought down too (→ Feb. 23, 1955).

Anti-Communists take over in Guatemala

Washington, D.C., Oct. 30

Guatemala's newly installed anti-Communist government, which came to power with the support of the United States Central Intelligence Agency, is going to receive $6,425,000 in United States aid. The road to the change in government began in June when rebels un der Colonel Carlos Castillo Arma invaded Guatemala. In 11 days they ousted the ruler, Jacobo Ar benz, replacing his Communist controlled regime with a military junta. Last month, Colonel Armas was installed as president.

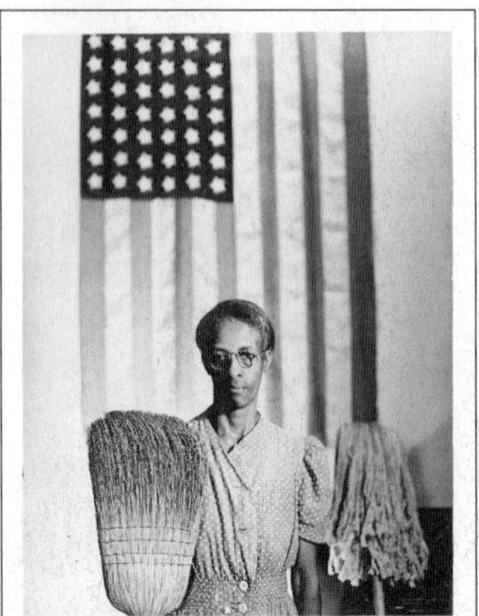

Can charwoman Ella Watson one day become a congresswoman? Why not? Photo by Gordon Parks.

Giant new carrier

Newport News, Va., Dec. 11

American naval power received a major boost here today with the launching of the aircraft carrier Forrestal, the first of a new class of carriers. With a length of more than 1,000 feet and a top speed of more than 30 knots, the new carrier is larger and faster than those of the Essex class, and at 59,650 tons it is the world's largest warship. Over the next 12 years, the navy expects to add at least seven more flattops of the Forrestal class. Plans are also in the works for an even larger carrier that will be driven by nuclear power.

Major new U.S. highway system planned

Washington, D.C., July 12

A major new road-building program that would cost $5 billion a year for the next 10 years was proposed today on behalf of the administration by Vice President Nixon. While the main emphasis would be on constructing a network of interstate and intercity highways, provisions would also be made to help local "farm-to-market" travel. The program comes at a time when the number of American families who own a car has risen to 70 percent. A blue ribbon panel, probably to be headed General Lucius Clay, will study methods of financing the program, which, if approved, will be the largest public works venture in American history.

As the number of Americans takin to the roads continues to increas dramatically, the highway system i being expanded to handle the load.

Congress puts curbs on U.S. Communists

Washington, D.C., Aug. 24

The Communist Party, caught in a game of political hardball, has been deprived of its rights under the law. Hurt by charges of softness on communism, Democrats led by Senator Hubert Humphrey proposed making party membership punishable by a $10,000 fine and five years in jail. Rushing in to take a public stand, the senators passed the proposal unanimously. Then the provision died in conference. But the bill that made it to the floor stripped the party of its rights and deprived Communist unions of National Labor Relations Board protection. Of 346 legislators present, just two voted nay.

A nation under God

Washington, D.C., June 14

President Eisenhower signed a congressional resolution today that alters the words of the Pledge of Allegiance. The resolution adds the words "under God," changing the phrase "one nation indivisible" to "one nation, under God, indivisible." At the signing, the President said that it served to rededicate the nation to its divine source and provided meaning to a world that recently experienced cruelty and violence and where a materialistic philosophy of life deadens millions.

Comics crackdown

New York City, October

Comic book publishers banded together this month to establish the Comics Code Authority, a self-regulating body created to assure parents of the wholesome content of their children's reading material. Code-approved comics will carry a seal similar to the Good Housekeeping Seal of Approval. The adverse impact of comic books on the emotional development of children was an issue first raised by psychiatrist Frederic Wertham in his book *Seduction of the Innocent* and later explored by Senator Estes Kefauver's subcommittee hearings on juvenile delinquency, which resulted in a public outcry against comic books.

McCarthy condemned for misconduct

Washington, D.C., Dec. 2

Casting off a yoke of fear, the Senate voted 67 to 22 today to condemn Senator Joseph McCarthy for abusing his colleagues. "We can probably get the sentence commuted to life in prison," quipped the senator from Wisconsin. But no amount of humor would dispel the consequences. The report avoided the term censure, but only three other senators in history have been so rebuked. Said Democrat Mike Monroney, McCarthy will be "buried back with the classified ads."

Sensing his demise, "Tail-Gunner Joe" lashed out at his attackers. Ralph Flanders had introduced the censure resolution, noting McCarthy's "habitual contempt for people." McCarthy called him "senile." He said the committee that recommended his censure, led by Mormon Senator Arthur Watkins, was a "lynch party." McCarthy's attacks on the Watkins panel and on an elections subcommittee were the immediate grounds for censure. But the rebuke stands as a condemnation of his four-year barrage of anti-Communist innuendo.

McCarthy supporters assemble at New York's Pennsylvania Station on their way to Washington to encourage him in his crusade against communism.

This Babe's a lady

United States

From a double Olympic track champ in 1932, Mildred "Babe" Didrikson has gone on to become winner of the U.S. Women's Open golf championship for the third time. The slim Texan became a pro after winning the women's national championship in 1946 and becoming the first American to take the British title in 1947. She also won the Open from 1948 through 1950.

Eight nations set up East Asian defense

Manila, Philippines, Sept. 8

A new weapon has been added to the arsenal being prepared in the effort to contain communism in Southeast Asia. It is an eight-nation defense alliance established here today. Known as the South East Asia Treaty Organization, it affirms the rights of Asian and Pacific people to self-determination and equality. Members of the new alliance, in addition to the United States, are Britain, France, Australia, New Zealand, the Philippines, Pakistan and Thailand. Unlike the North Atlantic Treaty Organization, the South East organization, to be known as SEATO, does not provide for a unified military command. Moreover, it does not obligate the United States or other members of the alliance to act militarily except in the event of a specific Communist danger.

G.M.'s 50 millionth

Flint, Michigan, Nov. 23

The 50 millionth General Motors car rolled off the assembly line here today, marking the start of a nationwide celebration. To commemorate the event, the custom-made Chevrolet sport coupe was gold-painted and manufactured with 60 gold-plated parts. General Motors was established in 1908, but it took 10 years to produce its first car. The company is now the largest auto maker in the nation, having turned out 2.8 million cars last year for a record-breaking sales figure of $10 billion. President Eisenhower said today that the anniversary epitomized "the industrial, scientific and creative genius of our people."

"Papa" Hemingway reels in Nobel Prize

Oslo, Norway, Dec. 10

His beard has grown grizzly and the lean body has gotten a mite soft in the middle, but Ernest Hemingway, 55, still reigns as the he-man of American letters. And today the outdoor athlete with the sinewy prose landed the biggest literary fish of them all, the Nobel Prize for literature. He had lately flopped with the critics, but his 1952 novella, *The Old Man and the Sea* (1952), the poignant story of an aging fisherman who won't accept defeat – even when sharks circle his battered skiff – has put "Papa" back on top. Now Hem can ease into old age without being reduced to telling fish stories – about, say, the prize that got away.

Ernest Hemingway with a swordfish he caught while on location for filming of "The Old Man and the Sea."

1955

Eisenhower

Washington, D.C., Jan. 4. United States awards $2 million in damages to 23 Japanese fishermen who sustained injuries as a result of hydrogen bomb testing on Bikini Atoll.

Washington, D.C., Jan. 19. President Eisenhower becomes first President to conduct a televised news conference.

Washington, D.C., Feb. 9. Senate ratifies U.S.-Nationalist China Mutual Security Pact.

Syracuse, N.Y., April. Syracuse Nationals win National Basketball Association title by beating Fort Wayne Pistons, four games to three.

Washington, D.C., May 19. According to Federal Trade Commission, business mergers have increased three-fold over a five-year period.

Detroit, June 6. Ford Motor Company signs agreement with United Auto Workers that, aside from providing a wage increase, also grants funds for laid-off workers.

Purchase, N.Y., July 13. First executive jet, Beech Paris, goes on display.

Anaheim, Calif., July 18. Illustrator Walt Disney opens Disneyland theme park.

Oceanside, N.Y., Aug. 2. Mrs. Sheldon Rubbins becomes first female cantor in history of Judaism.

Washington, D.C., Aug. 21. Department of Commerce estimates U.S. investments abroad total $26.6 billion.

New York City, Oct. 4. Brooklyn Dodgers defeat New York Yankees in World Series, four games to three.

Washington, D.C., Dec. 12. Upon opening national headquarters, evangelist Billy Graham comments, "I just want to lobby for God."

New York City, Dec. 12. Ford Foundation makes $500 million educational grant, largest in history.

Los Angeles, Dec. 26. Cleveland Browns defeat Rams, 38-14, for N.F.L. title.

New York City. *Family of Man* photo exhibit opens at Museum of Modern Art.

New York City. *Why Johnny Can't Read,* by Rudolph Flesch, published; examines American education.

President authorized to defend Formosa

Washington, D.C., Jan. 28

As the Formosa Straits crisis continues to heat up, President Eisenhower has received full authority from Congress to take whatever military action he deems necessary to repel a Chinese Communist assault on Generalissimo Chiang Kai-shek and his Nationalist army. The Nationalists have taken refuge on Formosa [Taiwan] and nearby islands. The resolution, which passed the House 410 to 3 and the Senate 83 to 3, is without precedent in the country's history. It was requested by President Eisenhower to avoid the criticism leveled at President Truman for entering the Korean conflict without congressional backing.

Just what steps should be taken in the present crisis is left to the President's discretion. On January 22, he ordered three aircraft carriers from Pearl Harbor to join the Seventh Fleet, which is patrolling the Formosa Straits. But it is not clear whether he intends to offer full protection to Quemoy and Matsu, two small islands close to the mainland that are heavily garrisoned by the Nationalists. Secretary of State John Foster Dulles favors a hard-line course, but the President seems to be following a policy of deliberate vagueness. "We do not believe in giving blueprints to the Communists of just what we will or will not do," he has said.

This is especially so in the case of nuclear weapons. At least five times last year he resisted advice to launch a nuclear attack against mainland China. "With modern weapons," he has said, "there can be no victory for anyone" (→Feb. 9).

U.S. sends military advisers to Vietnam

Washington, D.C., Feb. 23

Because of the increased success of the pro-Communist forces operating in South Vietnam, the United States will send a small force of military advisers to the Southeast Asian nation. The State Department said today an American Military Advisory Group is being formed and will be based in Saigon. The group will only give advice to officers and senior enlisted men in the South Vietnamese armed forces. According to State Department officials, the Americans will not be sent into active combat either as a unit or with the Vietnamese troops. President Eisenhower sent a group of 200 technicians to South Vietnam last year to assist the French before the Battle of Dienbienphu, but they were withdrawn soon after, and France was defeated (→Apr. 28, 1956).

"Downtown Kansas City in Winter" by Fred Bergere. Everything is up to date in the Midwest metropolis, including skyscrapers and shopping centers.

Einstein, citizen of the U.S., is dead

One of the world's greatest minds.

Princeton, N.J., Apr. 18

Albert Einstein, one of the grea[t] scientists of the world, died at hi[s] home here today. He was 76. In[-]trigued by the nature of light, th[e] German-born physicist lent ne[w] meaning to the concept of space an[d] time with his theories of relativity[,] for which he was awarded the No[-]bel Prize in 1921. Moving to th[e] United States, he became a citizen in 1941 and a popular figure, ad[-]mired for his warmth and commo[n] touch. When not working, he love[d] to play the violin and to sail.

Sanders, Landers and coonskin caps

United States

Disneyland has just opened i[n] Anaheim, California, but the coun[-]try seems to be one big amusemen[t] park. Where else are commercia[l] goods such a source of fun? Wher[e] else are there new food items suc[h] as the Kentucky Fried Chicken o[f] Colonel Sanders and the Special K of Kellogg? Where else roll-on de[-]odorants, a Texas-style departmen[t] store such as Neiman-Marcus, a[n] *Ann Landers Says* column, the con[-]servative William F. Buckley's *Na[-]tional Review* and the liberal *Villag[e] Voice?* And what land lavishes o[n] its kids Uncle Wiggley and Snake[s] and Ladders board games or Dav[y] Crockett coonskin caps?

chool integration: eliberate speed

Vashington, D.C., May 31

Following up on last year's deci-ion in Brown v. the Board of Edu-ation, the Supreme Court today nnounced its directives for school egregation on a national basis. The uidelines call for local boards to raw up their own plans for ending ne separation of white and Negro choolchildren "with all deliberate peed." This is a major disappoint-nent for the National Association or the Advancement of Colored eople, which had hoped the court vould announce a specific time mit. Under this plan desegrega-on is already proceeding in ma-y states, and, though not an easy rocess, it is expected that hun-reds of school districts will be in-egrated by year's end (→ Dec. 5).

$1 wage minimum

Vashington, D.C., Aug. 12

Minimum-wage workers will re-eive an extra 25 cents an hour be-inning next March 1. President isenhower signed an amendment ncreasing the minimum wage from 5 cents to $1 today. Under the air Labor Standards Act of 1938, sually called the Wages and Hours aw, the minimum wage was set at 0 cents an hour. Since then the law as been periodically amended.

Ike, at summit, proposes "open skies"

The plan would allow reconnaissance planes to take pictures for study.

Geneva, July 21

As Soviet Premier Nikolai Bulganin listened silently, President Eisenhower today unveiled a dramatic proposal to ease cold war tensions. Speaking at the summit conference here, Eisenhower said his plan would reduce the possibility of "surprise attack, thus lessening danger and relaxing tensions."

He suggested that the United States and Soviet Union exchange a "complete blueprint of our military establishments, from one end of our countries to the other." And he called for the two nations to open their skies and allow reconnaissance planes to "make all the pictures you choose and take them to your own country for study." He said the two nations "admittedly possess new and terrible weapons," and therefore urged that "we take a practical step, that we begin an arrangement very quickly, as between ourselves – immediately."

Britain and France like the plan. United Nations officials were said to be wary. The summit participants include Prime Minister Anthony Eden of Britain, Premier Edgar Faure of France and Soviet Communist Party First Secretary Nikita Khrushchev.

Number 1: "Rock Around the Clock"

United States, May

Bill Haley didn't know what to call his music when he first slipped a blazing rhythm and blues beat into his unique brand of country swing. But "rock 'n' roll" now suits him just fine. His new hit, *Rock Around the Clock,* fizzled on the charts last year, but it has jumped to No. 1 after it was included in the hit movie *Blackboard Jungle*. The film's marriage of rock 'n' roll and the juvenile delinquency theme proved irresistible to teenagers and it even sparked a riot or two. But as other rock 'n' rollers like Little Richard, Bo Diddley and Chuck Berry begin to crowd more sedate chart staples such as Perry Como, some critics have labeled the music "dirty, and as bad for kids as dope."

Enter I.B.M. 700's

New York City, Aug. 1

A major challenge to Remington Rand, whose UNIVAC computer has been considered the leader in the industry, has come with the introduction today of I.B.M.'s 700 line of computers. Masterminding the I.B.M. entry into the field is Thomas Watson Jr., who recently took over management of the international company from his legendary father.

Everybody is getting into the act. Senator Estes Kefauver, Tennessee Democrat, sports the coonskin cap that's been made famous by television's "Davy Crockett." No American boy and no presidential hopeful should be without one.

Television offers fantasy, facts and fun

United States

We have come a long way. In December 1945, 81 percent of respondents in a Gallup Poll had never seen a television set in operation. In 1946, there were 10,000 sets and six stations each programming 10 hours a week. By June 8, 1948, when NBC began *Texaco Star Theater* with Milton Berle's pie-in-the-face brand of comedy, movie theaters and restaurants took a beating, proving the power of the new medium.

Television personalizes the political process, as when Senator Richard Nixon, Republican candidate for Vice President, told a national audience about his personal and political finances in his "Checkers" speech on September 23, 1952. On January 19, 1953, all America went "aaah" as Lucille Ball's character on *I Love Lucy* gave birth to Little Ricky. Then the McCarthy hearings and the televised bus boycott in Montgomery, Alabama, took us right to the spot.

For children, there is *Captain Kangaroo* weekday mornings. New shows include *Davy Crockett*, with the Alamo hero and king of the wild frontier played by 6-foot 5-inch Texan Fess Parker, the thrilling anthology *Alfred Hitchcock Presents* and the soap opera *As the World Turns*. And film studios have even started producing films for TV and allowing theatrical releases to be shown.

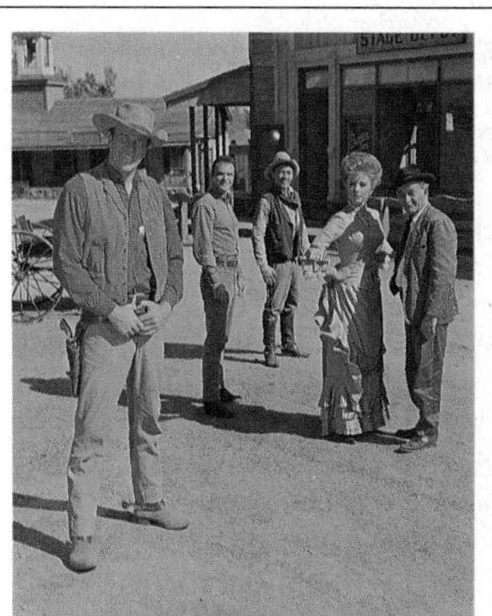

"Gunsmoke" is roaring across the television screens like a runaway stagecoach. Every week millions of Americans tune in to see plain folks go through the trials and tribulations of the Wild West – and even live to tell about it.

Dean lived too fast and died too young

Hollywood, Calif., Sept. 30

Driving his Porsche to Salinas to compete in a race, actor James Dean, 24, was killed in a highway crash today. Dean had a brief but spectacular screen career. In just a little over a year, his popularity soared and many regarded him as a personification of the alienated American youth of today. This year, he played a tender but rebellious boy in *East of Eden* and gives an equally outstanding performance as a restless teenager in *Rebel Without a Cause*, due for release next month. He had just finished the movie *Giant* with Elizabeth Taylor and Rock Hudson.

The rebel who ignited a generation.

Back of the bus no more

When Rosa Parks sat in the front of the bus, things really started moving.

Montgomery, Alabama, Dec. 5

When the Cleveland Avenue bus pulled up to a stop on December 1, 43-year-old Rosa Parks entered and took a seat at the front. That would not seem to be a particularly remarkable event, except that Rosa Parks is a Negro and, as such, has always been relegated to the rear seats. When Miss Parks refused to give up her seat to a white man, the bus stopped and she was arrested.

That evening, other Negro women from Montgomery gathered to call for a boycott of the city buses. Negro leaders met the next day to call for a widespread bus boycott today. The pastor of the Dexter Avenue Baptist Church, the Rev. Martin Luther King Jr., was chosen to head the publicity campaign and inform Montgomery's 50,000 Negroes of the boycott. He was then elected president of the Montgomery Improvement Association's boycott committee.

Normally, 75 percent of the bus passengers are Negro and today's boycott was effective. The demands of the Improvement Association do not include immediate desegregation, so it is not supported by the National Association for the Advancement of Colored People. But the boycott will go on until Negroes are treated as equals (→ March 1956).

A Monroe doctrine that's all about sex

Hollywood, California

She is Fox's biggest box-offic draw and Hollywood's newest se goddess: Marilyn Monroe, 29. Sh wiggles, she pouts, she speaks in husky, whispery voice and exudes both inviting and wholesome sensu ality with equal parts of reality an humor. She has proven to be a bi enough star to survive the disclo sure of nude photos ("I was hun gry") and that her mother is in a asylum. While at work on her ne movie, *The Seven-Year Itch*, sh divorced baseball hero Joe DiMag gio after a nine-month marriage The next movie she makes will b *Bus Stop*.

Marilyn in "The Seven-Year Itch."

Eisenhower suffers mild heart attack

Denver, Colorado, Sept. 26

President Eisenhower suffered a mild heart attack three days ago. While he is resting comfortably now, the pulse on Wall Street has slowed to an alarming pace. The New York Stock Exchange lost some $44 million, making today the market's worst in history. Financial experts say Ike's illness is the reason for the dramatic fall; investors shy away from activity in times of national crisis. And a serious illness to a popular president constitutes a crisis. Ike asked aides to be candid with the public about his condition. He feels the secrecy surrounding President Wilson's illness early this century was a mistake.

"Aspects of Suburban Life: Golf" by Paul Cadmus. In the 10 years since the end of World War II, the American middle class has developed its own way of life. Young couples marry, head for the suburbs, buy houses and start families. The nation's new role as world leader and its unprecedented prosperity have given its people the means to regain a life lost during 20 years of depression and war. For millions, the American dream is a reality.

A.F.L. and C.I.O. form single union

New York City, Dec. 5

In the cavernous 71st Regimen Armory, 16 million workers wer united today into one House of La bor. Ending their 20-year estrange ment, the American Federation o Labor and the Congress of Indus trial Organizations merged unde the leadership of the A.F.L. pres ident George Meany. Since the tim of C.I.O. founder John L. Lewis the craft-oriented A.F.L. has com around to accepting the C.I.O.'s in dustry-wide organizing methods The two labor giants have agree that recognition will be given t both craft and industrial unions and that both groups will stop raid ing sister unions for members.

1956

Eisenhower

Montgomery, Ala., Jan. 30. Home of the Rev. Martin Luther King Jr. is bombed.

Washington, D.C., March 12. In Florida ex. rel. Hawkins v. Board of Control, Supreme Court draws distinction between primary and secondary schools and professional programs, saying latter must integrate without delay (→Dec. 21).

Philadelphia, Apr. 7. Warriors defeat Fort Wayne Pistons, four games to one, in N.B.A. championship.

South Vietnam, Apr. 28. U.S. Military Advisory Group assumes responsibility for training of South Vietnamese army (→July 9, 1959).

New York City, May 7. Pulitzer Prize in fiction awarded to MacKinlay Kantor for *Andersonville.*

Washington, D.C., May 23. To reduce certain crop yields, Congress passes a measure providing $750 million per year, subsidizing farmers who reduce their production.

United States, July 16. Ringling Brothers and Barnum & Bailey Circus gives last performance under a tent.

Washington, D.C., July 19. Secretary of State John Foster Dulles withdraws American offer to help Egypt with construction of Aswan High Dam because Egypt has been dealing with Soviet Union (→Nov. 5).

Washington. D.C., Sept. 14. 63-year-old female patient at George Washington University Hospital is first person to undergo a lobotomy.

California, Nov. 6. D.S. Saund is elected to House of Representatives, becoming first Congressman of Asian ancestry.

New York City, Dec. 30. Giants defeat Chicago Bears, 47-7, for N.F.L. championship.

Hollywood, Calif. Top films this year include *Bus Stop, Giant, The Ten Commandments* and *Invasion of the Body Snatchers.*

New York City. Grace Metalious's *Peyton Place* is a best-seller.

New York City. William Whyte publishes *The Organization Man*, describing corporate pressure to conform.

Dulles: "If you are scared to go to the brink, you are lost."

Washington, D.C., Jan. 16

In a forceful defense of the Eisenhower administration's foreign policies, Secretary of State John Foster Dulles disclosed today that the United States has been on the "brink" of war on three occasions during the last three years.

In an article in *Life* magazine titled *How Dulles Averted War*, the 68-year-old secretary pointed to the conflicts in Korea and Indochina and the question of Formosa [Taiwan] as the three occasions when the United States was on "the verge of war."

In explaining his diplomatic policies, Dulles said: "You have to take chances for peace, just as you must take chances in war. Some say that we were brought to the verge of war. Of course we were brought to the verge of war. The ability to get to the verge without getting into the war is the necessary art. If you cannot master it, you inevitably get into war. If you try to run away from it, if you are scared to go to the brink, you are lost."

He added, "We walked to the brink and we looked it in the face. We took strong action."

Secretary Dulles, who had been a vigorous critic of former President Truman's policy of "containment" of communism, has long been an advocate of the use of the threat of massive nuclear retaliation as a deterrent to aggression by the Soviet Union.

Secretary John Foster Dulles believes U.S. must use its power to the fullest.

"My Fair Lady"

New York City, March 15

Eliza Doolittle has been reborn on Broadway in *My Fair Lady*, one of the wittiest musicals ever seen on the American stage. Except for the ending, this tuneful version is scrupulously faithful to George Bernard Shaw's *Pygmalion* as Julie Andrews's cockney Eliza is browbeaten by Rex Harrison's imperious Professor Higgins into learning the King's English. With this sparkling work, Alan Jay Lerner and Frederick Loewe fulfill the promise of their enchanting *Brigadoon*.

Will they bury us?

Moscow, November

The cold war is thriving in the freezing Moscow winter. Premier Nikita S. Khrushchev has gleefully offered Western diplomats here these chilling words. "Whether you like it or not, history is on our side. We will bury you." With less glee, one of the nuclear bomb inventors, J. Robert Oppenheimer, said America and Russia "are like two scorpions in a bottle, each capable of killing the other but only at the risk of his own life ... The atomic clock ticks faster and faster."

Drive-ins booming

United States

There are now 7,000 drive-ins across the country, more than triple the number in 1950. And because 11 percent of all cars sold are station wagons, the movies must often be kiddie fare. Regular movie theaters charge that drive-ins drive out their customers, and indeed, a drive-in can be just as comfy. In the winter some drive-ins supply heaters. But many people are staying home to watch TV, turned off by high theater admission prices ($2 in N.Y., $1.50 in Los Angeles).

U. of Alabama sued for banning Negro

Montgomery, Ala., March 1

A recent court order has allowed a Negro woman, Autherine Lucy, to enroll as a student at the University of Alabama. On February 7, only a day after her enrollment, the white student body rioted, leading the university to suspend Miss Lucy. Now, the National Association for the Advancement of Colored People has stepped in to help by filing a discrimination suit against the university. Although the Supreme Court ruled last year that public schools must desegregate, the ruling has not been applied in practice to colleges. In addition, the N.A.A.C.P. has not been effective in this Southern state (→12).

A B-57 light bomber equipped to test Boeing "Bomarc" supersonic interceptor missile components. Since the advent of the atomic bomb, planners of modern warfare have been relying more and more on technological advances. American planes are flying higher and faster, rockets are firing farther and more accurately and the possibilities brought on by the computer appear limitless. Man is slowly relinquishing the art of war to his machines.

Delinquency linked to absent parents

St. Louis, Missouri, June 6

Ellsworth Bunker, president of the American Red Cross, told its annual national convention today that "absentee parents" are the major cause of juvenile delinquency. While some might argue with that diagnosis, no one would dispute the prevalence of this social ill.

It is estimated that half the thieves arrested in New York are under 21, while in Los Angeles 20 percent of all crimes are committed by teenagers. The majority of auto thefts in larger cities are attributed to youths. A book this year by professors at Brooklyn College and the University of Chicago, *Delinquency: The Juvenile Offender in America Today,* looks hard for delinquency's causes. Everything from endocrine glands to comic books are said to be partly at fault; "broken homes" are frequently in the background of these offenders, but are not necessarily the primary factor. It says that the media and movies take their toll: James Dean in *Rebel Without a Cause* is as much a reflection of teenage angst as an instigator of crime. But psychologists say that rarely are these youths in leather jackets and slicked-back hair asked why they do what they do or what's on their minds. Which, the analysts feel, might be a reason in itself.

Elvis rocks America

Elvis has all of the right moves.

New York City

Elvis Presley is a phenomenon. Music critics call him "unspeakably untalented and vulgar," a clergyman branded him "a whirling dervish of sex" and business boomed for a Cincinnati car dealer who promised to smash 50 Presley records for each customer. But while adults recoil in horror from the 21-year-old's high-energy pelvic gyrations and defiant sneer, delirious teenage fans bought seven million copies of his records this year.

Two years ago, Presley was a Memphis truck driver making $35 a week and aching to sing. Sam Phillips of Sun Records, who felt that a white artist who could perform with the abandon of the best Negro stars would take the segregated pop charts by storm, was awed by Presley's raw talent and charisma. Local hits followed, and so did performances that sent female fans into such a frenzy that Presley was at times nearly mauled.

This year, Presley exploded onto the national charts with *Heartbreak Hotel, Don't Be Cruel* and *Blue Suede Shoes.* A brazen, high-voltage performance on a September 9 Ed Sullivan show grabbed a record TV audience of 54 million, but television censors have seen enough. His next appearance, in January, will show just his face.

American girls know what they like.

Pollock, Abstract Expressionist, dies

East Hampton, L.I., Aug. 11

A single-car crash today took the life of Jackson Pollock, a leading Abstract Expressionist painter. Pollock, who was born in Cody, Wyoming in 1912, studied at the Art Students' League in New York. Stimuli for his work of the 30s included the Social Realism of Thomas Hart Benton, his teacher, and the Mexican mural movement.

Pollock's discovery of an original signature style, the "drip" paintings dating from 1947, is recognized in avant-garde circles as a benchmark in modern art, though the public found it cryptic. "Jack the Dripper," as he was dubbed, would lay a huge canvas on the floor, then pour and drip house paints directly from the can onto its surface. The resultant work is not an image of an object, but rather an abstract "all over" organization of skeins of pigment that emphasizes the gestural component of painting. Extremes of ecstasy and anxiety are suggested, and Pollock's personal troubles have often been read into these paintings. Although he was painting figures once more in the early 50s, the drip works won Pollock privileged status among such Abstract Expressionists as Barnett Newman, Franz Kline, Clyfford Still, Mark Rothko and Willem de Kooning.

April 19. *The girl from Philadelphia has become a real princess with her marriage to Monaco's Prince Rainier. Grace Kelly's charm and beauty make her the perfect choice for the regal role.*

Andrea Doria sinks following collision

Nantucket, Mass., July 26

In a dense fog, two luxury liners collided just before midnight yesterday, killing 50 people. The Italian vessel Andrea Doria sank 11 hours after being struck by the Stockholm, a Swedish ship. The accident, which occurred 60 miles south of Nantucket, was reportedly caused by radar blindness. The Stockholm, a 40-foot hole in its bow, slowly made it to port. Some 1,650 people were rescued by four ships. Not all were so fortunate: one man said his wife vanished through a gaping hole in the Andrea Doria. Some passengers said the crew failed to sound an alarm or announce information about the rescue effort.

Girls: Wear his ring around your neck

United States

For the girl who has a steady: a gold necklace to put his ring on. Think Elvis Presley's the most? Buy an Elvis Presley key chain. And while you're in a buying mood, stock up on some of the new items on the market this year, such as Comet cleanser, Raid to do in bugs and Imperial margarine. Or just stay home and enjoy the TV commercials of Bert and Harry Piel, of Betty Furness and Westinghouse, of Julia Mead and Lincoln-Mercury. Should a young woman tire of men and materialism, consider the path of M.E. Tower, who has become the first woman ordained as a Presbyterian minister.

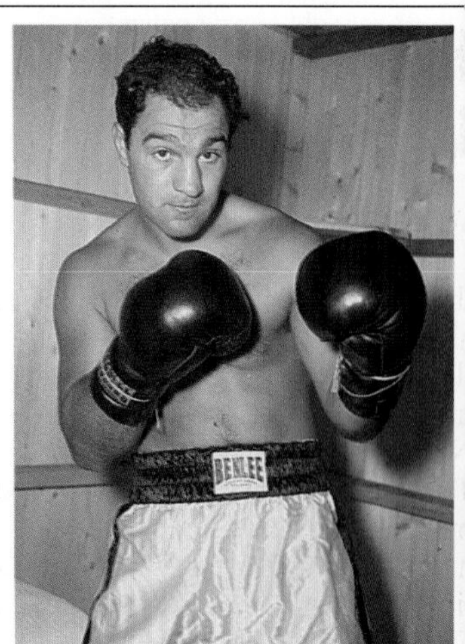

April 25. *As Rocky Marciano retires, he leaves behind an amazing record. He is the only heavyweight champ never to have lost a professional bout and won 43 of 49 fights by the knockout route.*

ke wins 2nd term vith landslide vote

Voters endorse Eisenhower's course.

Vashington, D.C., Nov. 6

Dwight D. Eisenhower was re-elected President today, scoring a andslide victory over Adlai E. Stevenson. The most impressive triumph since Franklin D. Roosevelt buried Alfred Landon, it makes Ike he first Republican in this century o win successive presidential elections. At 66, the World War II hero again carries the 43-year-old Vice President Richard Nixon into office with him. Voters backed the Republican contention that the nation needs Ike's experience, and rejected the Democrats' view that he s too old, a "part-time President" who delegated too much authority during his recent illnesses.

Hungarians revolt; U.S. won't act

Vashington, D.C., November

While Hungarian rebels battled he tanks and troops of the Soviet army, the United States offered little more than moral support, backing for a resolution at the United Nations and asylum for refugees. The Hungarian rebels, encouraged by Radio Free Europe broadcasts, had hoped for American intervention. But the response of the United States was tempered by fear of a possible land war in Europe or a nuclear showdown. Inspired by Polish riots earlier this year, the Hungarian uprising began on November 5. The rebels enjoyed five days of freedom before the Soviet army crushed them.

Bus segregation is unconstitutional

Montgomery, Alabama, Dec. 21

In a mass meeting, Montgomery's Negro citizens have agreed to end a year-long boycott of the city's bus system, a decision based on the city's announcement of compliance with a November 13 Supreme Court ruling that has declared segregation on buses unconstitutional. In offering an explanation of how this victory for Alabama Negroes was achieved, the Rev. Martin Luther King Jr., leader of the boycott, said, "Nonviolence is the most potent technique for oppressed people." King and 100 other Negroes had been arrested back in March for conducting an illegal boycott. Dr. King's case was settled with payment of a $500 fine. But it seemed a small price to pay because the case has led to desegregation in several Southern states (→Feb. 1957).

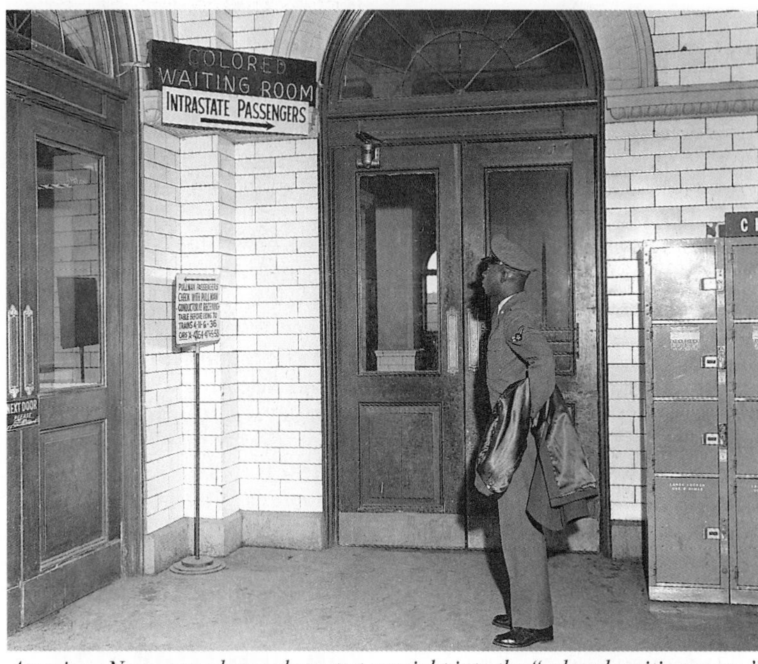

American Negroes no longer have to turn right into the "colored waiting room."

Larsen is perfect

Brooklyn, N.Y., Oct. 10

Don Larsen pitched a perfect game today, the first in the major leagues in 34 years. In setting down 27 batters in a row, he also turned in the first no-hitter in a World Series as the New York Yankees defeated the Brooklyn Dodgers, four games to three. Larsen uses a unique no-windup delivery.

U.S., Soviets agree in the Suez Crisis

Washington, D.C., Nov. 5

In one of their rare moments of accord, the United States and the Soviet Union today voted to support a United Nations call for an immediate cease-fire in Egypt as well as the withdrawal of French and British military units. Britain and France, America's usual allies, vetoed the resolution but the two are expected to comply. An invasion by English, French and Israeli forces was triggered by the Egyptian seizure of the Suez Canal in August. After the Russians threatened to intervene, the United States warned Britain, France and Israel that it did not intend to support them.

Russians trounce Americans at Olympics

Melbourne, Australia, Dec. 8

The United States took a drubbing from the Russians in the total Olympic standing but once again proved superior in track. The Soviet Union headed the standing, 722 to 593, using its own measure, or 622 to 497, using the European method. It also collected more medals than the Americans, 99 to 74, and more gold, 37 to 32. Bobby Morrow, 21-year-old sprinter from Abilene, Texas, proved to be the American star, winning both dashes with no trouble. Lee Calhoun and Glenn Davis accounted for hurdles victories, Charlie Jenkins took the 400 meters and Tom Courtney the 800. Bob Richards vaulted to an Olympic mark.

Arthur Miller and his new bride, Marilyn Monroe, meet Sir Laurence Olivier and Vivien Leigh. Both Miller and Monroe fans were surprised by the marriage of the playwright and the Hollywood goddess on June 29.

1957

Eisenhower

Washington, D.C., Jan. 28. Secretary of Defense Charles Wilson informs House Armed Services Committee that draft dodgers were harbored by Coast Guard during Korean conflict.

Washington, D.C., Feb. 25. Supreme Court, in Butler v. Michigan, holds that states do not have constitutional right to bar from sale materials that might be corrupting to minors.

Boston, Apr. 13. Boston Celtics defeat St. Louis Hawks, four games to three, in N.B.A. championship.

Greenville, South Carolina, Apr. 22. Stating that struggle is now against Communists and integration, Ku Klux Klan announces it is opening membership to Roman Catholics.

Bonn, West Germany, May 2. Secretary of State John Foster Dulles tells North American Council that United States will maintain its forces in Europe at current levels.

New York City, May 6. Diplomat and historian George F. Kennan wins both National Book Award and Pulitzer Prize for *Russia Leaves the War.*

New York City, May 6. Massachusetts Senator John F. Kennedy awarded Pulitzer Prize for *Profiles in Courage.*

Detroit, September. American Motors introduces nation's first compact car, the Rambler.

Nevada, Sept. 19. First United States underground nuclear tests begin.

New York City, Oct. 10. Milwaukee Braves beat New York Yankees, four games to three, to win World Series.

Cape Canaveral, Dec. 17. First Atlas I.C.B.M. tested by army.

Detroit, Dec. 29. Lions defeat Cleveland Browns, 59-14, for National Football League title.

Philadelphia. *American Bandstand* makes TV debut on ABC.

New York City. Dr. Seuss publishes *The Cat in the Hat* and *The Grinch Who Stole Christmas.*

New York City. *Atlas Shrugged* by Ayn Rand issued.

DEATH

Bethesda, Maryland, May 2. Joseph McCarthy, controversial U.S. Senator (*Nov. 14, 1908).

U.S. would respond to Mideast attack

Washington, D.C., Jan. 5

Any Communist aggression in the Middle East could result in American military intervention, according to President Eisenhower. Speaking before Congress today, the President asked the legislators for the power to use force to oppose any such aggression. He said that he would use American troops if requested by a nation that had come under attack, but only while he conducted "hour-by-hour" consultations with Congress and in accordance with the United Nations charter. The President also said he would seek $400 million for Mideast aid over two fiscal years.

Jasper Johns waves the American flag

New York City

Jasper Johns has said that he paints the American flag because he had a dream about doing so. *Flag on an Orange Field* joins the series of works on this theme begun in 1954 by the young painter from South Carolina. Little is known of Johns's work before that because he destroyed his youthful output. Done in encaustic, a technique combining paint and wax that is little used by contemporary artists, the flags, like the targets he paints, embody an alternative to Abstract Expressionism being developed by Johns and Robert Rauschenberg.

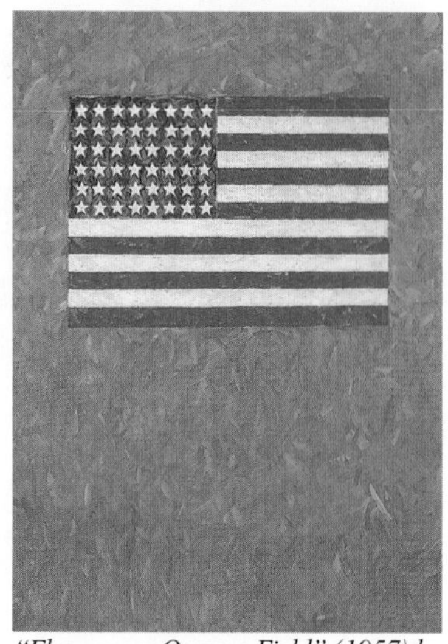

"Flag on an Orange Field" (1957) by Jasper Johns, who tests the limits.

King heads Southern Christian Leadership

The Rev. Martin Luther King Jr. has become a symbol of change in America

Atlanta, Georgia, February

With a popular base developed during last year's Montgomery, Alabama, bus boycott, Negro leaders from 10 states have organized the Southern Christian Leadership Conference. The Rev. Dr. Martin Luther King Jr., along with Bayard Rustin and Stanley Levinson have established the interracial society to coordinate the activities of nonviolent protest groups throughout the country. The goals of the Leadership Conference include full citizenship and "total integration" into American life for Negroes. Dr. King will head the new organization. Another key member of the group is Ella Baker, who was a field secretary for the National Association for the Advancement of Colored People and an organizer for the Urban League. Baker will organize mass meetings to win support for the S.C.L.C. And Dr. King plans a national tour on which he will speak in over 200 localities. He is becoming known as an excellent spokesman and dynamic organizer. He was ordained a minister in 1947 and led Montgomery's Dexter Ave Baptist Church. His role in the bus boycotts led to his jailing and the bombing of his house (→Aug. 29).

Communist Party in America in decline

New York City, December

The Communist Party, chained to Moscow and isolated from the American worker, is fading into obscurity. At a national committee meeting this month, the hard-line followers of William Z. Foster ousted reformer John Gates and deserted the "revisionist" *Daily Worker*, the party's official organ. At the party congress in February, Gates had the votes to force a break with Moscow, but backed off to save party unity. Since then, his faction has quit en masse. As one exiting New York leader complained, out of 160 members "a couple of dozen come to meetings; we sit around and argue about Hungary and Leninism. What the hell else is there to do?"

707 airliner crosses U.S. in record 3:48

Baltimore, Md., March 12

A National Airlines Boeing 707 broke a speed record for cross country passenger flight when it arrived here today non-stop from Seattle in just 3 hours and 48 minutes. The four-engine jet transport carried 42 passengers and a crew of 10 on the 2,330-mile trip. The Boeing Airplane Company, which was founded by William Edward Boeing in 1916, introduced the 707 model on July 15, 1954. Replacing the outmoded piston engine the 707 was the first American jet transport and on its maiden flight reached a cruising speed of 600 miles per hour. Built for intercontinental travel, it is capable of carrying 219 passengers.

Gibson first Negro to win Wimbledon

Wembley, England, July 6

Althea Gibson, born in a rundown cabin on a South Carolina cotton farm, has won the most coveted prize in tennis. She is the first Negro to win the All-England title at Wimbledon, in fact the first ever to take any major tennis tournament. Miss Gibson, who grew up on the streets of Harlem in New York, started by playing paddle tennis there and graduated to the bigger game. She won the New York State Negro girls' championship in 1945 and 1946 and the national title in 1948. In 1950, she broke the color line when she played at Forest Hills.

Sun-heated building

Albuquerque, N.M., Aug. 1

The nation's first totally sun-heated commercial building was dedicated today. The structure, appropriately named the Solar Building, uses the energy of the sun to generate heat during the day. Special battery-like collectors save the excess energy produced during the day, and it is then put to use heating the building at night. The innovative heating system was designed by Frank H. Bridgers and Donald Paxton.

Donning his trademark white bucks, now a nationwide fad, pop singer Pat Boone croons his way into the hearts of millions of Americans with such hits as "Love Letters in the Sand." Boone prides himself on his clean-cut image.

Basie band makes history, at Waldorf

New York City, June 15

The quick, breathless rhythms of the Count Basie Band are now making history at the Starlight Roof Room of the Waldorf-Astoria Hotel. It's the first Negro band ever to perform there. Ella Fitzgerald is also on hand. The Count's popular group seems to have played everywhere else, and pieces like *One O'clock Jump*, *Taxi War Dance* and *Jumpin' at the Woodside* are international favorites. After the Waldorf, the band heads for the Newport Jazz Festival. Later this year, the Count meets the Queen – or vice versa – in a Command Performance at London's Palladium.

Balloon 20 miles up

Forbes, North Dakota, Aug. 20

Paving the way for future space travelers, an Air Force balloonist has spent a record 32 hours suspended near the limits of Earth's atmosphere. Major David G. Simons landed near Forbes in his pressurized gondola after the flight took him to an altitude of 101,486 feet, nearly 20 miles up. An officer overseeing the test said it proved man can live in space. He said he would call for rapid development of manned rocket-powered vehicles.

Freed's radio show rocks 'n' rolls 'em

New York City, May 4

Alan Freed's old music teachers may be wondering just where they went wrong. The 35-year-old disk jockey has forsaken his classical roots to set an entire generation of teenagers rocking and rolling with his nightly radio show, which is now serving up the likes of Elvis Presley and Buddy Holly to a spellbound national network audience. Freed's live rock 'n' roll shows are also wowing young crowds, though a psychologist attending a recent extravaganza here warns the music could induce "medieval types of spontaneous lunacy," even "prehistoric rhythmic trances." But a 13-year-old fan begs to differ. She calls Freed "the mostest."

Rights act overcomes Thurmond filibuster

Civil rights movement continues as Negro students accompany whites to school.

Washington, D.C., Aug. 29

After much wrangling in the Senate, the Civil Rights Act finally won approval today. The major opposition came from Southern legislators, most notably from Senator Strom Thurmond of South Carolina, who broke all records by speaking for 24 hours and 18 minutes, making his performance the longest personal filibuster in history.

The Civil Rights Act was first proposed last year by President Eisenhower. The section of the bill that allows the Justice Department to bring suit on behalf of Negroes who are denied the right to vote was not included in the original draft, but was added later at the suggestion of Attorney General Herbert Brownell Jr. The bill was passed in the House and made its way to the Senate in June.

Title III of the bill, which would have allowed the Justice Department to sue to protect a civil right, was deleted from the act, partly because of Senator Richard Russell's argument that he doubted that the President actually understood the provision. The rest of the bill passed easily.

The Civil Rights Act establishes a commission to obtain facts, suggest further legislation, and amend the United States Code to affirm the right to vote or to sit on a jury regardless of race, color or previous condition of servitude. Opponents of the bill attached an amendment providing that, in cases of contempt arising under the act, a judge might impose a fine or sentence without jury trial (→ Sept. 25).

Britons and Yanks mark colonial events

Jamestown, Virginia, Oct. 16

This year has produced both British and American interest in commemorating two important colonial events. In a re-creation of the Mayflower's voyage of 1620, the 180-foot Mayflower II arrived in Plymouth, Massachusetts, on June 13, 54 days after having left Plymouth, England. A crowd of 25,000 people waited at the landing, while thousands watched the event on television. Today, Queen Elizabeth II paid a visit to Jamestown, Virginia, to commemorate the 350th anniversary of the first permanent English settlement in the New World.

A meeting on common ground.

▷

Troops help integrate in Little Rock

Negro student Johnny Gray strikes back during the integration of Little Rock.

Federal troops escort Negro students up the steps and through the front door.

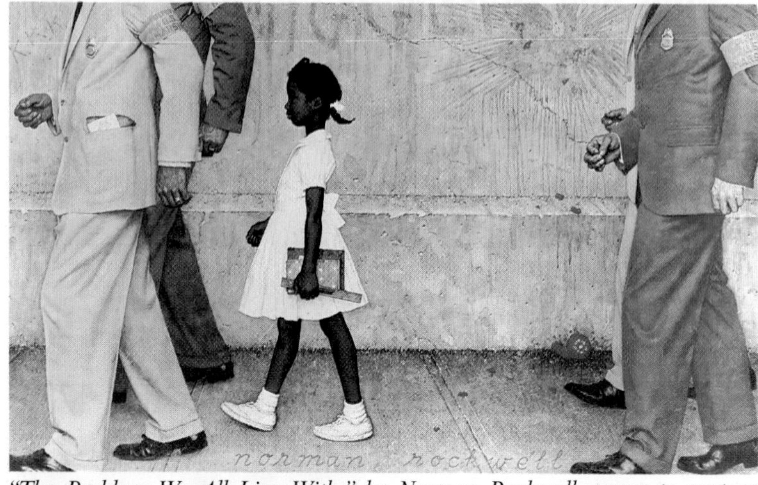

"The Problem We All Live With," by Norman Rockwell, seems to capture the quiet determination of one small child in the struggle for equality.

Little Rock, Ark., Sept. 25

Disputed and widely publicized for nearly a month, the integration of the Little Rock Central High School has finally taken place, with the help of 1,000 paratroopers and 10,000 Arkansas National Guardsmen ordered into federal service by President Eisenhower.

The election of Orval Faubus as Governor of Arkansas recently was hailed as a victory for liberals in Arkansas. The issue of race was never spoken of during the campaign. So it came as somewhat of a surprise when Faubus posted National Guardsmen outside Central High as a court-approved integration plan was to be implemented. As a first step toward total desegregation, nine Negro children were to attend the school. On September 5, the children were turned away when they attempted to attend their first classes at the school.

Commenting on the opposition of Governor Faubus to integration, the President said, "The federal Constitution will be upheld by me by every legal means at my command." On September 9, F.B.I. agents in Little Rock presented a 400-page report to a federal district judge who requested that the United States government enter the case. On September 20, after a hearing, the judge issued an injunction against Governor Faubus's attempts to impede integration.

On Monday, September 23, the guardsmen were gone and the children were able to enter the school. A mob of about 1,000 whites gathered outside it and there was talk of dragging the Negro children out of the school and lynching them. By noon, the order came from city authorities to take the children out. The N.A.A.C.P. said they would not attend school again without assurance that the President intends to protect them from the mob. The mob stayed at the school for two days. Today, the federal troops intervened and the Negro pupils entered Central High as the mob was dispersed. The paratroopers and guardsmen remain posted and may stay for the school year.

Eisenhower commented on the events by saying, "Mob rule cannot be allowed to override the decisions of our courts" (→Sept. 1959).

Sputnik prompts a frenzied failure

Cape Canaveral, Fla., Dec. 6

Its national prestigue shaken by the Soviet launchings of Sputnik I and II, the United States is racing to gain an equal footing on the high ground of space. Today, however, the American answer to Sputnik, the Navy Vanguard rocket bearing a 3 1/4-pound grapefruit-sized satellite lifted two feet off its Cape Canaveral, Florida, launching pad only to collapse in a raging inferno. The spectacular failure was blamed by some experts on the tremendous political pressure to rush the program along. But space scientists don't promise to slacken their pace as the Russians dazzle the world. More powerful Jupiter and Atlas rockets are being hurried for future satellite attempts (→July 29, 1958).

First atomic plant produces electricity

Shippingport, Penn., Dec. 18

The nation's first atomic power plant began generating electric energy today. The plant was opened by the Duquense Light Company in conjunction with the Atomic Energy Commission, as authorized by the Atomic Energy Act of 1954. This allows industry, with A.E.C. licensing, to use nuclear fuels to run atomic power plants. An A.E.C. report on nuclear accidents says that a worst-case scenario at a 200-megawatt reactor may kill 3,400 people within a 45-mile radius.

"West Side Story"

New York City, Sept. 26

West Side Story has exploded on the American stage like a bomb thrown at decades of conventional musical romance. True, it retells the Romeo and Juliet tale, but the warring gangs – the white Jets and the Puerto Rican Sharks – are right from the switchbladed streets of contemporary New York. The language thumbs its nose at the traditional gentility of the genre, and the hammering beat of Leonard Bernstein's music breaks like a new, overpowering wave. All in all, it's a revolutionary work.

1958

Eisenhower

Washington, D.C., March 3. President Eisenhower and Vice President Nixon reach an arrangement whereby, should chief executive become disabled, the Vice President would temporarily assume presidential duties.

New York City, March 11. Robert Penn Warren wins National Book Award and Pulitzer Prize for *Poems, 1954-1956.*

St. Louis, Apr. 12. St. Louis Hawks defeat Boston Celtics, four games to two, for N.B.A. title.

Moscow, Apr. 13. Texan Van Cliburn wins first prize in prestigious Tchaikovsky Piano Competition.

New York City, April. Ford Thunderbird unveiled, at International Automobile Show.

Arlington National Cemetery, Va., May 30. Burial ceremonies held for unknown soldiers of World War II and Korean conflict.

New York City, May. International News Service and United Press merge, to form United Press International.

Washington, D.C., June 16. Supreme Court rules in Kent v. Dulles that State Department has no right to refuse passports based upon political affiliations or views.

Washington, D.C., Aug. 6. President Eisenhower signs Defense Reorganization Act, giving defense secretary greater control over military.

United States, Sept. 26. Yacht Columbia successfully defends America's Cup against British challenger Sceptre.

Milwaukee, Oct. 9. Yankees win World Series, four games to three, over Braves.

New York City, Oct. 26. Pan American World Airways inaugurates first American jet service to Europe.

New York City, Dec. 28. Baltimore Colts defeat New York Giants, 23-17, for N.F.L. title.

New York City. American Express Company introduces credit card service; 500,000 use card by end of year.

United States. *Three Flags* painted by Jasper Johns.

Hollywood, Calif. *Vertigo*, starring James Stewart, released.

Vice President Nixon greeted by hostile crowds in Latin America

Washington, D.C., May 15

Vice President Richard Nixon returned to cheers today after a tumultuous 18-day Latin American tour that saw him besieged by violent mobs in Peru and Venezuela. The Vice President was welcomed home by an estimated 15,000 people at the airport and about 85,000 along his route to the White House.

His trip, which began with a visit to Argentina, grew violent May 8 when he reached Lima, Peru. Nixon had been scheduled to meet a student group at the University of San Marco. In a dramatic gesture, against the advice of his security staff, he ventured into a mob of demonstrators outside the university. He was spat upon, hit by a stone, shoved and booed. An hour later, he and his staff fought their way past 2,000 demonstrators outside his hotel. Similar violence beset him in Caracas, Venezuela.

Vice President Nixon meets with the President. Despite his violent reception in Latin America, Nixon is rapidly developing an expertise in foreign affairs.

President Eisenhower said in his welcoming address, "The occurrence of these incidents has in no way impaired the friendship between the United States and any other single one of our sister republics to the south."

Nixon said the Latin American masses support the United States, and that a "minority element" of Communists was to blame for the disturbances. He said Communist leaders stirred up crowds by exploiting local economic problems.

Millionth at I.B.M.

New York City

Less than a century since writing machines were invented, International Business Machines has produced its millionth electric typewriter. The first marketed typewriter, by E. Remington & Sons in 1874, only produced capital letters. Since I.B.M. introduced electrics in the 1920s, the company has made typing more popular and versatile.

Bums, Giants move

New York City

In Brooklyn, the Gowanus Canal was running high with the tears of the Faithful. In Manhattan, they were saying, "Say it ain't so, say it ain't so." The Dodgers, those beloved Bums, were moving to Los Angeles, and along with them the Giants were leaving the hallowed Polo Grounds and heading for San Francisco. It was all part of baseball's growing pains and the lure of gold out West. In 1954, the St. Louis Browns became the Baltimore Orioles and in 1955 the Philadelphia Athletics moved to Kansas City.

Michigan's Mackinac Bridge is dedicated

Mackinaw City, Mich., June 28

It is considered an engineering marvel, stretching about five miles to link upper and lower Michigan. Today, the Mackinac Bridge was formally dedicated. It is the world's longest suspension bridge, the suspension part of it measuring 8,614 feet, which is some 2,000 feet longer than the Golden Gate Bridge across San Francisco Bay. Altogether, the "Mack" spans 26,444 feet. It cost $100 million and took nearly four years to build, but it is soon to pay off because it will stimulate economic growth in northern Michigan. Governor G. Mennen Williams said it will be a "key link in America's system of modern arterial highways, as a gateway to the great outdoor vacationland of northern Michigan."

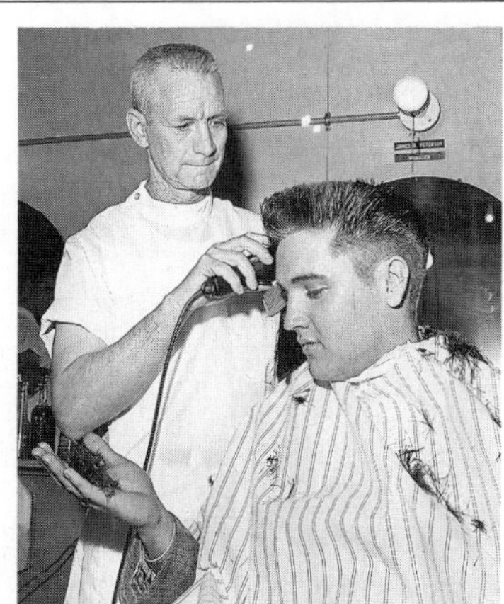

King Elvis loses his crown. Presley may rock America but he is ready and willing to serve it as well. When he was called up for duty in the army March 24, millions of his fans came out to catch a glimpse of their cropped idol.

▷

Marines go to Lebanon

Once again the United States Marines see action, this time in the Middle East.

Washington, D.C., July 15

President Eisenhower sent 5,000 marines to violence-torn Lebanon today to help preserve that country's government in the wake of internal revolts and a coup in neighboring Iraq. The troops, along with sea and air support, landed in Beirut and occupied its airport. The President said that the number of marines would be increased if necessary, but that they would be "withdrawn as rapidly as circumstances permit."

Their mission is to show support for President Camille Chamoun's government. Eisenhower said Chamoun sent an "urgent request" for help yesterday, after developments in Iraq. Chamoun said, "Without an immediate showing of United States support, the government of Lebanon would be unable to survive," Eisenhower reported.

Lebanon has been racked by an insurrection for two months, since violence broke out along the Syrian border. The crisis worsened yesterday after the Iraqi regime was ousted violently. Eisenhower says Syria and Egypt – which make up the United Arab Republic – are responsible for the trouble.

N.A.S.A. is to vie with Soviet in space

Washington, D.C., July 29

Congress feels that the United States must not be outdone by the Soviet Union in the space race. To compete with the Russians, the legislature passed a bill today allotting millions of dollars for the creation of the National Aeronautics and Space Agency to coordinate space technology research. Even many economic conservatives voted for the program, spurred into action by the successful launching last year of Sputnik, the first man-made satellite. America put up its first satellite, Explorer, January 31. But the Soviets are still ahead. N.A.S.A. is to start work on a manned space craft immediately (→Apr. 9, 1959).

Dr. King is stabbed

New York City, September

The Rev. Dr. Martin Luther King Jr., leader of the Southern Christian Leadership Conference, and a principal spokesman for the cause of civil rights, was stabbed by a Negro woman while in Harlem to promote his new book, *Stride to Freedom*. The woman is thought to be deranged. Dr. King is a Baptist minister and an eloquent advocate of non-violent protest as a means of gaining equality for Negroes. He is expected to recover from the injury.

U.S. acts to temper Chinese island spat

Washington, D.C., Oct. 1

Although President Eisenhower has committed the United States to protecting the Chinese Nationalist islands of Quemoy and Matsu – a move criticized by Senate leaders – the administration has also called for Taiwan to reduce its garrison there. A White House official said today if the Chinese Communists would stop bombing the islands from the mainland, talks could progress and the Nationalist force from Taiwan could be cut. The Communists have been shelling Quemoy since August. In September, the mainland Chinese extended their territorial limits to 12 miles, including the small islands.

"Affluent Society"

Cambridge, Massachusetts

Americans may not be as well off as they think, writes Harvard economist John Kenneth Galbraith in his new book, *The Affluent Society*. In such chapters as *The Theory of Social Balance*, *Security and Survival*, and *Labor, Leisure and the New Class*, Galbraith ties such ills as inflation and recession to a materialistic public and to the stale policies of timid leaders.

Americans go crazy for Hoola Hoops

United States

Last year's Frisbie fad has sailed off and this year the hoop-la is for the Hoola Hoop. The new hullabaloo began at about mid-year in Southern California when Arthur Melin and Richard Knerr decided to promote and sell a version of bamboo hoops that they had heard Australian schoolchildren used. With some chemists at a plastics factory, they designed a tubing of material called Grex (a form of polyethylene), which when stapled end to end formed a hoop. It was dubbed a Hoola Hoop, and now there are over 20 other manufacturers, calling it "Whoop De Do," "Hoop Zing" and other forgettable names. By this fall, 25 million have been sold at about $3 each. Millions of kids are delighted, and millions of adults have sore hips.

A new fad makes the rounds.

"Baltimore" by Palmer Hayden. In big cities and suburbs, American prosperity is unprecedented, symbolized by such features as fins on cars.

Nautilus under the ice

Reykjavik, Iceland, Aug. 8

In an achievement fraught with strategic implications, the world's first atomic-powered submarine, the Nautilus, has pioneered a new route beneath the frozen wastes of the Arctic. The feat, disclosed by the White House today, took the ship 1,830 miles under the polar ice cap from Point Barrow, Alaska, to the Atlantic near Spitsbergen, Norway, in just four days.

The Nautilus was designed and built under the direction of Rear Admiral Hyman G. Rickover and was commissioned on September 30, 1954. With just a few pounds of enriched uranium, the ship can "steam" for over 60,000 miles without refueling and can submerge for weeks while cruising at over 20 knots. "Operation Northwest Passage" began on July 23, when the 300-foot-long craft left Pearl Harbor with a crew of 116 led by Commander W.R. Anderson. The Nautilus passed directly beneath the North Pole on August 3 and reached Iceland yesterday.

On an ominous note, the Nautilus has proven that the fleet of Polaris submarines scheduled to be deployed starting in 1960 could hide under the polar ice cap while armed with thermonuclear missiles. Experts say the Russians have no atomic submarines, but they concede that, like most strategic advantages in the nuclear age, this one is not likely to last forever.

Ike adviser Adams ousted after scandal

President Eisenhower and White House aide Sherman Adams in happier times.

Washington, D.C., Sept. 22

President Eisenhower's chief of staff, Sherman Adams, reluctantly resigned his post today amid a storm of scandal. A congressional panel concluded that Adams received expensive gifts, an oriental rug and a vicuna coat, for using his influence at the Securities and Exchange Commission and the Federal Trade Commission to help Boston industrialist Bernard Goldfine.

The impropriety tarnishes the reputation of the President, who was once described by the diplomat George Kennan as "the nation's number one Boy Scout."

Adams quit to minimize the embarrassment to his boss and the Republican Party. He declared his innocence in a televised resignation speech, saying, "I have done no wrong." He blamed a Democratic "campaign of vilification" for his downfall. Eisenhower has supported Adams, saying, "How dreadful it is that cheap politicians can so pillory an honorable man."

The scandal seems to have contributed to a dramatic slump in Ike's popularity. In the first half of his second term, opinion polls show a drop in approval from 79 percent to 49 percent. Democrats say the decline will help them pick up seats in this year's congressional elections.

"Hang down your head, Tom Dooley"

United States

If parents were lucky this year, they might have heard the dulcet harmonies of the Kingston Trio wafting in from their kids' rooms. But the pounding beat and raucous shouts of Little Richard's high-powered rock 'n' roll stomp *Good Golly, Miss Molly* were the norm, as the new music continued to climb the charts.

The Kingston Trio emerged from the smoky folk clubs of San Francisco to move a huge, mostly college-aged audience with pensive folk ballads such as *Tom Dooley*. The Everly Brothers hit it big with the lilting country-tinged harmonies of *All I Have to Do Is Dream,* as did 17-year-old Ricky Nelson from TV's *Ozzie and Harriet* with *Poor Little Fool.*

Joining Little Richard among the rockers were Chuck Berry, whose ringing guitar and lyrics about cars and girls were pure poetry with kids on hits like *Johnny B. Goode*, Texas's Buddy Holly and the Crickets, with *Think it Over*, and J.P. *Big Bopper* Richardson.

American rocketry gets a big boost

Cape Canaveral, Fla., Nov. 28

The National Aeronautics and Space Administration reported the first successful launching of an Intercontinental Ballistic Missile today. The Atlas rocket hit its target in the South Atlantic, some 5,500 miles from its launching pad. The achievement helps restore confidence in space and defense technology after last month's semi-failure of the Pioneer. That satellite was launched to reach the moon's orbit, but it burned up and fell to Earth a third of the way to its destination. However, it did travel higher, 68,000 miles above the Earth, than any other space vehicle.

Effort is made to close education gap

Washington, D.C., Aug. 23

Is Johnny dimmer than Vladimir? Many observers of American education see students here falling behind their Soviet counterparts. A *Life* magazine editorial has commented, "The schools are in terrible shape ... the spartan Soviet system is producing many students better equipped with the technicalities of the Space Age." It blames poor curriculums, crowded classes and poorly paid teachers for the lag. Today, Congress acted to close the gap with the National Defense Education Act. It provides $1 billion, mostly in the form of student loans on the college and graduate level.

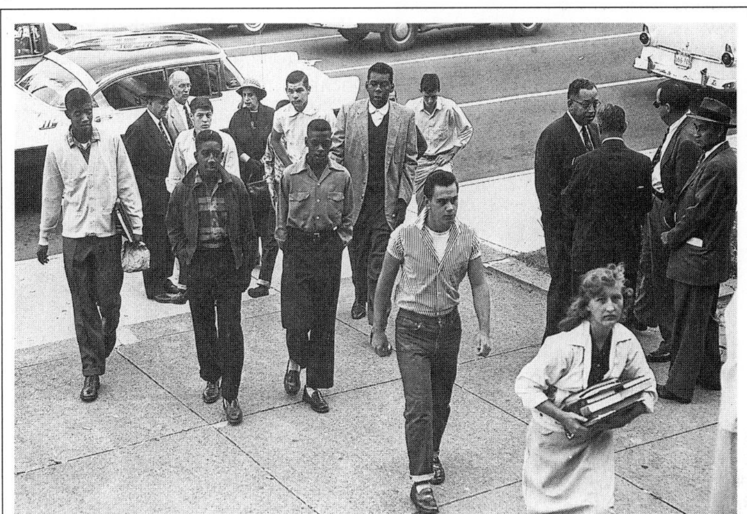

The national struggle goes on. In a rare moment of peaceful change, white and Negro students walk side by side on the first day of school integration in Louisville, Kentucky. This year alone, about one million student days were lost across the nation because of school closings to thwart integration.

1959

Eisenhower

Washington, D.C., Jan. 7. United States extends formal recognition to Cuban government of President Manuel Urrutia Lleo and military commander Fidel Castro (→Apr. 15).

Detroit, Feb. 26. General Motors recalls 4.9 million cars and trucks, largest recall yet.

New York City, March 11. Lorraine Hansberry's *A Raisin in the Sun* opens on Broadway.

Minneapolis, Apr. 9. Boston Celtics defeat Minneapolis Lakers, four games to none, in N.B.A. championship.

Washington, D.C., Apr. 9. NASA picks first seven candidates for space travel, known as astronauts (→July 21, 1961).

Moscow, May 1. Negro activist W.E.B. Du Bois is awarded Lenin Peace Prize.

Washington, D.C., May 20. President Eisenhower bestows nation's highest civilian decoration, Medal of Freedom, on former Secretary of State John Foster Dulles.

Washington, D.C., May 20. United States citizenship returned to 5,000 Japanese-Americans, who lost it during Second World War.

Washington, D.C., June 3. Radio signals reflected off moon allow President Eisenhower to send a message to Canadian Prime Minister John Diefenbaker.

Bienhoa, South Vietnam, July 9. Communist guerrillas kill two American soldiers (→May 11, 1961).

Washington, D.C., July 15. President Eisenhower signs Labor-Management Reporting and Disclosure Act, regulating internal practices of unions.

Washington, D.C., Sept. 7. United Council of Churches reports that 64% of Americans belong to an organized church.

Washington, D.C., Sept. 23. President Eisenhower signs six-year, $650 million urban renewal appropriation.

Chicago, Oct. 8. Los Angeles Dodgers defeat White Sox, four games to two, in World Series.

Baltimore, Dec. 27. Colts defeat New York Giants, 31-16, for N.F.L. title.

United States. Sociologist C. Wright Mills writes, "The immediate cause of World War III is the preparation of it."

New Cuban ruler pays a visit to the U.S.

Fidel Castro, Cuban revolutionary.

Washington, D.C., Apr. 15

Premier Fidel Castro of Cuba arrived in the United States today for what he termed a "truth operation," to counter "propaganda" against the Cuban Revolutionary Government. The 32-year-old former guerrilla leader, wearing his trademark green military fatigues, was greeted by 1,500 supporters, as well as State Department officials.

His visit grew from an invitation to address the American Society of Newspaper Editors, which has since been criticized for barring radio and television coverage of the event, scheduled for next Friday.

The United States recognized the new regime in January, a week after Castro's troops ousted dictator Fulgencio Batista. Many of Batista's forces have fled Cuba or been imprisoned or executed. The new government, nominally headed by President Manuel Urrutia Lleo, but in fact by Castro, has promised to hold free elections (→July 6, 1960).

Fly coast to coast with American Airlines

Los Angeles, Jan. 25

It was not very long ago that it took days to travel from coast to coast. Not any more. American Airlines announced today that it is opening same-day passenger service east-to-west as well as west-to-east between New York and Los Angeles on its Boeing 707 jets. The service is the first of its kind. Industry experts expect other airlines to be offering similar flights soon. Last month, Pan American World Airways inaugurated regular trans-Atlantic service on Boeing 707's from New York International Airport to Paris. It was the first American airline to offer the jet flight. It takes a third less time than on a propeller plane.

Sandburg addresses Congress on Lincoln

Washington, D.C., Feb. 12

Carl Sandburg accomplished two nearly impossible feats today: He pulled the nation's two parties together and, more remarkably, he reduced the members of Congress to silence. The occasion was the sesquicentennial of Abraham Lincoln's birth, and Sandburg, whose massive biography of "Honest Abe" won the Pulitzer Prize in 1939, sang Lincoln's praises on the floor of Congress. The usual yawns, snores, whispers and tapping pencils echoed through the hall as the white-haired bard strode to the podium. But Sandburg, unfazed, let his lyric cadences do their work, as he read his opening sentence. "Not often in the story of mankind does a man arrive on earth who is both steel and velvet, who is as hard as rock and as soft as drifting fog, who holds in his heart and mind the paradox of terrible storm and peace unspeakable ... " A hush fell over the congressmen, who seemed bewitched by Sandburg's address.

Sandburg sings Lincoln's praises.

Three rock stars die in plane crash

Buddy Holly, talented Texan.

Mason City, Iowa, Feb. 3

Rock 'n' roll fans were shocked today by the deaths in a small plane crash here of three top stars Buddy Holly, Richie Valens and J.P. "Big Bopper" Richardson. The plane, which plunged to earth after taking off in snowy conditions was to fly the singers to a show in Fargo, North Dakota. Holly, 22 was beloved for hits such as *Peggy Sue*, Valens, 17, for *La Bamba* and Richardson, 24, for *Chantilly Lace*. Teenage fans have "lost" other heroes as well lately, Elvis Presley to the United States Army, top disk jockey Alan Freed, done in by a payola scandal, and Little Richard whose searing hits included *Long Tall Sally* and *Lucille*, who has left rock 'n' roll in order "to make peace with Jesus."

Cranberry scare

Washington, D.C., Nov. 9

A weed-killer (ATZ) that has caused cancer in rats has contaminated some cranberry bogs in Oregon and Washington, the Department of Health, Education and Welfare said today. No contamination was found in the cranberry-growing states of New Jersey, Wisconsin and Massachusetts, but the scare caused stores and restaurants to avoid the fruit. The industry claims the contaminant is in so small an amount that it is harmless.

Able, Baker, Pioneer IV and Explorer IV

Cape Canaveral, Florida

The United States, lagging far behind the Soviet Union in the space race, succeeded in launching the first orbiting weather station on February 17. And since then, the new National Aeronautics and Space Administration has staged impressive otherworldly feats.

On May 29, two monkeys were rocketed 300 miles into space in the nose of a Jupiter rocket, then plucked safely from the Caribbean, 1,700 miles from the launching site here. The space travelers, a rhesus monkey named Able and a smaller squirrel monkey, Baker, were to show what effects weightlessness and high speed may have on mammals. NASA has now selected seven human astronauts and plans to send the first on a space trip within two years.

On March 13, a camera aboard a research rocket took ultraviolet pictures of the sun at an altitude of 123 miles, and on March 4, a gold-plated 13.4-pound Pioneer IV probe sped past the moon on its way to a perpetual orbit around the sun. Images of Earth transmitted from these satellites as well as from the 147-pound Explorer IV, launched on August 7, are forever altering the perspective of mankind.

St. Lawrence Seaway is officially opened

St. Lambert, Quebec, June 26

Queen Elizabeth and President Eisenhower today formally opened the St. Lawrence Seaway linking the Atlantic Ocean with the Great Lakes. The Canadian government, which bore 80 percent of the $750 million cost, was represented at the ceremonies by Prime Minister John Diefenbaker.

The seaway completion brought an end to years of controversy in both the United States and Canada regarding the desirability of the project. Washington was at first reluctant to participate, but changed its mind when Ottawa threatened to go ahead alone, building the entire seaway within its own territory.

More than 500 homes and 6,500 inhabitants along the Canadian shore had to be relocated to higher ground because of the flooding of Lake St. Lawrence. The 2,350-mile waterway allows bulk carriers of up to 730 feet long to pass through the system of canals, locks, rivers and lakes as far inland as Duluth, Minnesota. The seaway will have a major economic impact on both countries. It makes possible the exploitation of the iron ore deposits of Quebec and Labrador and it changes Canada from a net importer to an exporter of iron ore, mostly to the United States.

Sub with I.C.B.M. is launched by navy

Groton, Conn., June 9

Members of the United States Navy saluted the crew of the atomic submarine George Washington today as the vessel left its dock at the famous shipyard here. It is the first sub launched that carries and can fire intercontinental ballistic missiles, the powerful longrange Polaris rockets. The Joint Chiefs of Staff herald the George Washington as another advance to close the gap between Soviet and American weaponry. It is expected that the submarine will fire a test missile later this summer.

Ailing "Lady Day" finds peace at last

New York City, July 17

The melancholy song that was Billie Holiday's life ended in a hospital here today. She was 44. Before her death, she was arrested in her bed on a drug charge. The police confiscated her magazines, radio and Whitman's chocolates. "Lady Day" lived an unbelievably tough life, fed by the kind of bittersweet pride that can be heard in her recording of *Fine and Mellow*. As for the mysterious, haunting quality of her singing, someone said, "It ain't the blues. I don't know what it is, but you got to hear her."

"Lady Chatterley" still too hot for U.S.

Washington, D.C., July 21

Thirty-one years after it first appeared – in a private edition in Italy – D.H. Lawrence's *Lady Chatterley's Lover* is still too hot for American postal workers to handle. Today, Postmaster General Arthur Summerfield called the novel, about a torrid liaison between a married woman and her virile gamekeeper, "obscene and filthy" and banned it from the mails. This angered American fans of the English writer, who died in 1930. But they shouldn't feel cheated. The book is illegal in England, too.

Integrated schools open in Little Rock

Little Rock, Ark., September

Two high schools here have reopened this year with token integration – three Negro students at Hall High School and three at Central High. The presence of police is assuring the safety of the children. The mob violence and tension that characterized similar attempts in the past two years seem to be dissipating. This year's action is based on a decision by the newly elected Little Rock board of education and represents what some consider to be merely a first step in achieving equality for all (→Apr. 1960).

Upon his death on April 9, the architect Frank Lloyd Wright left behind an enduring legacy. Wright's innovative designs, from the "Falling Water" house to the Guggenheim Museum, have influenced an entire generation of architects and have set American design on a unique course.

Moscow kitchen debate

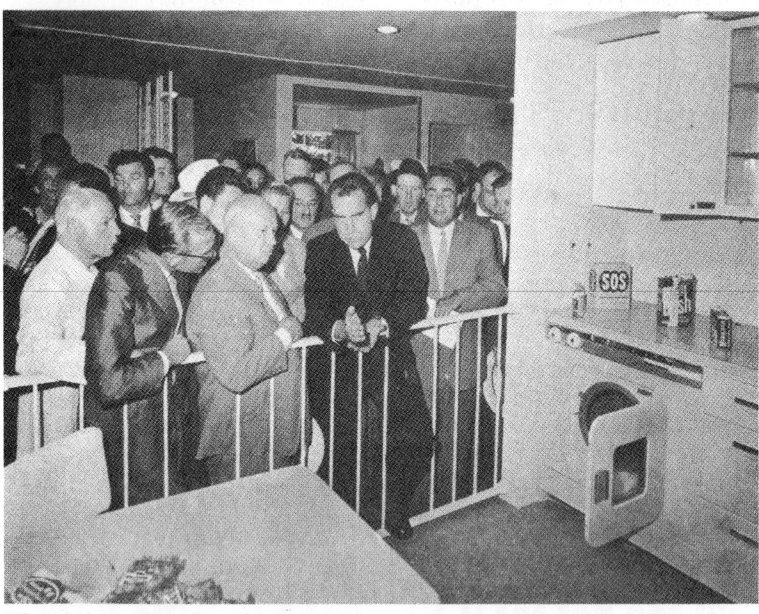

Khrushchev: "You don't know anything about communism except fear of it."

Moscow, July 24

Heated exchanges between Soviet Premier Nikita Khrushchev and Vice President Richard Nixon did not take place at the Kremlin. They began unexpectedly today in a model kitchen.

Khrushchev challenged the Vice President as Nixon was formally opening the United States National Exhibition before scores of reporters and television cameras. The show features a model American home equipped with all the latest domestic technology, including a washing machine and kitchen gadgets. It prompted the Soviet leader to say that "Americans should not think the Russian people will be astonished to see these things." Russian homes, he asserted, have modern conveniences.

The exchange between the two men reached a boiling point when it moved from a comparison of the standard of living in each country to war between the two nations over West Berlin.

Referring to the recent threats by Premier Khrushchev to "free" West Berlin from American control, Vice President Nixon said that neither country should be given the ultimatum to "accept dictation or fight," cautioning that "if war comes, we both lose" (→Sept. 27).

Alaska, Hawaii join USA

President Eisenhower unveils the new United States flag, resplendent with its 50 stars. The latest stars represent recently welcomed Alaska and Hawaii.

Honolulu, Hawaii, Aug. 21

Hawaii lost the race with Alaska to become the 49th state, but today, with a proclamation signed by President Eisenhower, it became the 50th star on the American flag.

Alaska became the 49th state on January 3, after Hawaii's non-voting delegate to Congress, John A. Burns, acceded to the Democratic leadership in Washington and agreed to a one-year delay. The nation's northernmost land had struggled for 42 years for the privilege of statehood. Its acceptance into the union was the first since 1912, when President Taft made Arizona the 48th state. Covering one-fifth the area of the rest of the United States, Alaska is the nation's largest but least populous state.

Hawaii has been ready for statehood for nearly a decade, having adopted a state constitution in 1950. The delay was marked by a long series of congressional hearings on the threat of communism in the islands. No proof of such a threat was established, but seven residents were convicted of conspiring to topple the government. The Supreme Court overturned their convictions. Still, the stigma prevailed to the moment Congress approved statehood, with most of the opposition coming from the South.

Detroit, November 19. *The Ford Edsel has a 120-inch wheel base, contour seats, self-adjusting brakes and a driver-operated lubrication system. But fewer than 100,000 were sold in two years, and today it was discontinued.*

TV quiz contestants admit role in rigging

Washington, D.C., Nov. 2

Charles Van Doren, a 33-year-old assistant professor of English at Columbia University, confessed today that he has lived a lie for three years. During 14 appearances on *Twenty-One*, he got the questions in advance, enabling him to win $129,000. Others have come forward telling tales of rigging: Hank Bloomgarden, who won $98,500 on the same program, and two $4,000 winners on *The $64,000 Challenge*, a clergyman and a salesman. As a result of the scandal, the Federal Trade Commission will try to rid television of deceptive practices (→Jan. 17, 1962).

Van Doren sweating for the cameras.

Khrushchev tours U.S.

Premier Khrushchev speaks following his arrival at Andrews Air Force Base.

New York City, Sept. 27

Soviet Premier Nikita Khrushchev was a happy man today as he sped to the airport after a 12-day tour of the United States, his first. "Let us have more and more use for the short American word, O.K.," Khrushchev said after he signed several accords with President Eisenhower at Camp David. The Premier had a fine time in Hollywood and on his visit to an Iowa farm, but, he was disappointed when he could not visit Disneyland for "security reasons." He spoke of world disarmament at the United Nations General Assembly, toured an I.B.M. plant in San Francisco and ate his first hot dog on his tour of the farm belt (→ May 17, 1960).

Americans are said to be status seekers

United States

It's open season on Americans. Readers have already been lambasted for being "other-directed" (David Riesman) and materialistic (John Kenneth Galbraith). Now, it seems, they are also hung up on what the neighbors think. So says Vance Packard, author of *The Status Seekers*, a withering look at the nation's class system; white- and blue-collar groups are being driven apart and the wedge is a college education. On the matter of status, ironically, Packard's critics dismiss him as *only* a journalist who has been encroaching on the exclusive turf of the sociologist.

Record steel strike, 116 days, is ended

Washington, D.C., Nov. 7

Under the Taft-Hartley Act, the Supreme Court has ordered an 80-day halt to the longest steel strike ever. And as union counsel Arthur Goldberg says, "From the Supreme Court, the only appeal is to God." So 500,000 workers returned to work after 116 days. President Eisenhower told both sides of their "obligation" to resolve all differences, the worst of which is the issue of labor's right to stop automation from eating up jobs. Most workers are happy to be back at work, but some resent the injunction. "How would Ike like it," said one striker, "if we told him he couldn't play golf for 80 days."

It's a gas! Get with it in a go-cart!

United States

If you think a go-cart is a gas, this is another year of great fads for you. Make the scene by parachute jumping. Get with it by trying some phone booth packing (the record to beat is 25 in a booth). Take up bowling or sailing. Become a member of the Chicago Buddhist Temple or Maharishi Mahesh Yogi's Spiritual Regeneration Foundation. But please, keep in mind the findings of a *Look* magazine poll on moral attitudes, which states that America's moral relativity is based on group acceptance. In other words, you should do whatever you want to do – as long as the neighbors are doing it too.

Films: "Ben Hur," "Some Like It Hot"

Hollywood, California

William Wyler's big-budget production of *Ben Hur*, with Charlton Heston, has been the year's top-grossing picture. Meanwhile, foreign films such as *La Dolce Vita*, *Breathless* and *The 400 Blows* were also successful. To combat the popularity of television, Hollywood went for the big laugh, and got it with Billy Wilder's brilliant farce *Some Like It Hot*, with Marilyn Monroe, Tony Curtis and Jack Lemmon. Monroe is proving to be a gifted comedienne with a hilarious innocence about her.

Doris Day and Rock Hudson entertain in *Pillow Talk*, Sandra Dee is a cute *Gidget*, while former child star Elizabeth Taylor confirms her versatility in the chilling *Suddenly, Last Summer*, with Katharine Hepburn and Montgomery Clift. Otto Preminger strains Production Code limits in *Anatomy of a Murder*, dealing with rape. And Alfred Hitchcock offered *North by Northwest*, a playful thriller with Cary Grant and Eva Marie Saint.

Independent film makers, unhampered by studio traditions, are experimenting, and some stars, such as Burt Lancaster, Marlon Brando, Richard Widmark, Kirk Douglas and William Holden, forgo star salaries for profit participation. Now location shooting and production of films at far-off studios are threatening the old Hollywood system.

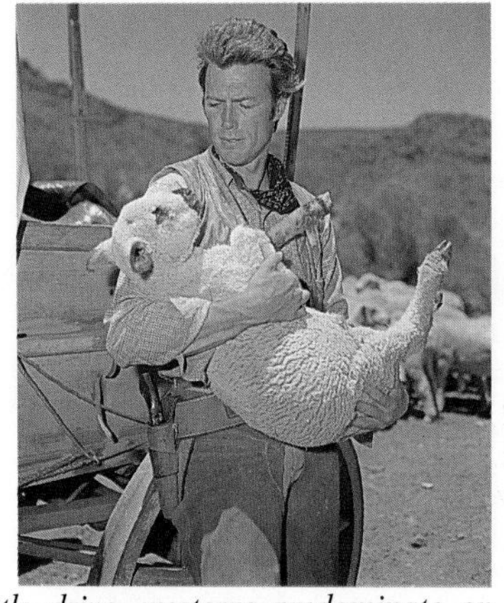

One hundred years after the first cattle drive, westerns predominate on television: Lorne Greene in "Bonanza" and Clint Eastwood in "Rawhide."

Charlton Heston plays "Ben Hur"

Curtis and Lemmon "Like It Hot."

The 1950s: A time of tranquility and prosperity

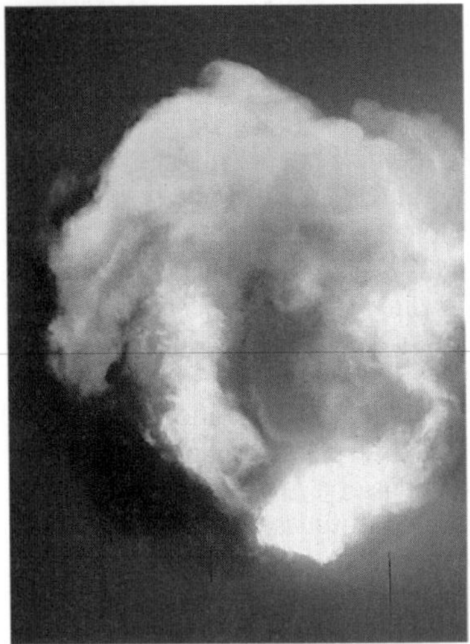

A nuclear test is conducted in the ongoing arms race with the Soviets. Lots of people worry about the Bomb.

The decade is filled with funny fads, from stuffing phone booths to coonskin caps to twirling hoola hoops.

President Eisenhower, affectionately known as Ike, presides over an era of seemingly endless tranquility, when the Yankees always seem to come in first and the United States of America always seems to be on top of the world.

The 50s are a time of mostly peaceful progress in civil rights – of integration – when Negroes in all walks of life register their grievances and stand up for the rights guaranteed, but too often denied them, by the Constitution.

A time when the nuclear family prospers, when everybody heads for the suburbs, when a convertible with whitewall tires is it, and when situation comedies on television, such as "Leave It to Beaver," actually seem to mirror real life.

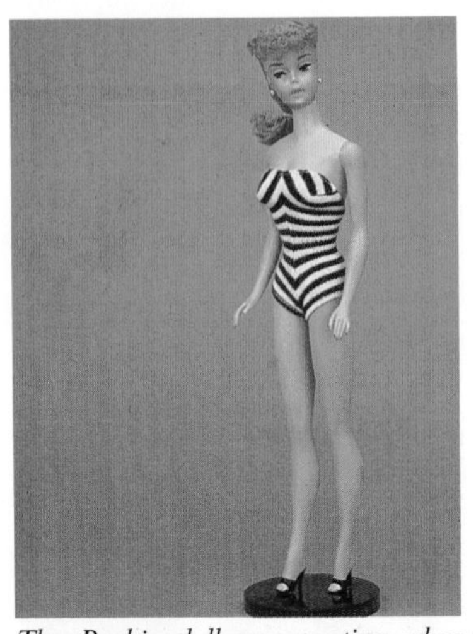

The Barbie doll, a sensation when introduced in 1959. Is she a symbol of the ideal woman of the future?

William Levitt converted a Long Island potato field into a prefabricated suburban community in 1949. In the next 10 years, his four-room $7,990 homes with outdoor barbecue, washing machine and built-in TV set sold fast.

In the wake of the suburban housing boom comes the baby boom, when America is a special land for kids.

When the United States of America leads the world

The only cloud on the horizon is Soviet Russia, the Communist enemy headed by Premier Nikita Khrushchev, the funny-looking little man who in 1956 said, "Whether you like it or not, history is on our side. We will bury you."

What the Barbie doll is to little girls, toy trucks are to little boys. In gravel driveways and on dirt mounds across the nation, future engineers spend hours digging and building an even better landscape than the one around them.

Elvis Presley, the man responsible for the emergence of rock 'n' roll. His "Hound Dog," "Don't Be Cruel" and "Love Me Tender" were instant hits.

The one and only Marilyn Monroe, the woman responsible for putting sex back in American life. "It's nice to be included in people's fantasies," she says.

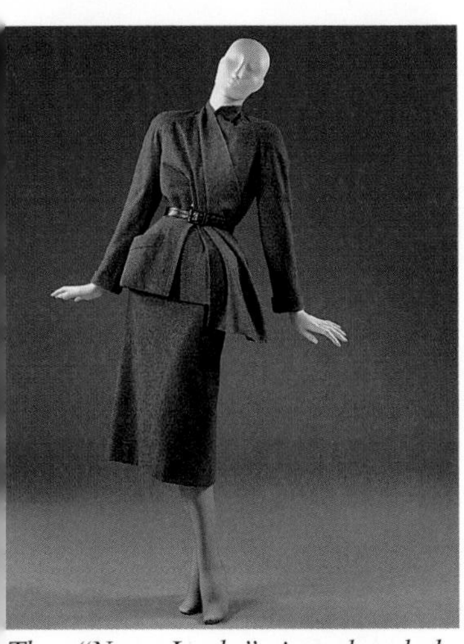

The "New Look," introduced by Christian Dior of Paris in 1947, has revolutionized women's fashion.

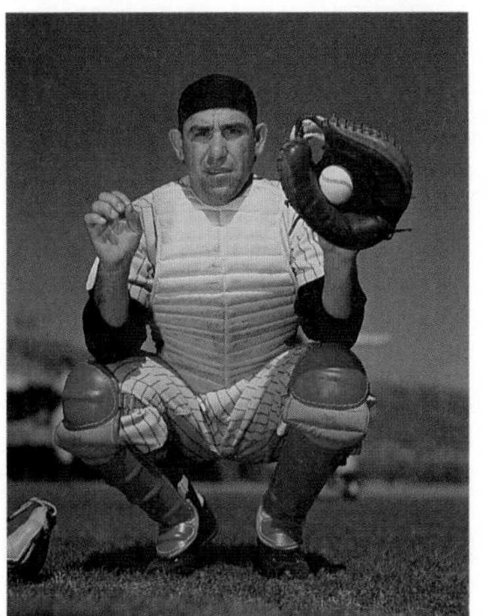

Baseball's dynasty lives happily ever after: New York Yankee slugger Mickey Mantle, catcher Yogi Berra and manager Casey Stengel, stars of a ball club that won eight pennants and six World Series victories in the 10 years from 1950-59. Mantle won the Triple Crown in 1956, and Berra was M.V.P. in 1951, 1954 and 1955.

1960

Eisenhower

Pacific Ocean, Jan. 7. Submarine Trieste descends 24,000 feet for new record.

Los Angeles, Feb. 11. Jack Paar, host of television's *Tonight Show*, walks off the set to protest censorship of one of his jokes.

Squaw Valley, California, Feb. 28. Eighth Winter Olympics closes.

Hollywood, Calif., Apr. 5. *Ben Hur* awarded record 10 Oscars.

Boston, Apr. 9. Celtics beat St. Louis Hawks, four games to three, for N.B.A. title.

West Virginia, Apr. 18. Presidential candidate John Kennedy, answering questions about his Roman Catholicism, says, "I don't think that my religion is anyone's business."

New York City, May 2. Pulitzer Prize in fiction awarded to Allen Drury for *Advise and Consent.*

Texas, May 7. Negro civil rights protester found hanging upside down from a tree, with "KKK" carved in his chest (→May 1961).

Washington, D.C., July 6. President Eisenhower orders 700,000-ton cut in sugar imported from Cuba (→9).

Washington, D.C., July 9. After Soviet warns that a U.S. invasion of Cuba would be met by Soviet missiles, President Eisenhower says United States will not permit a regime in Western Hemisphere controlled by "international communism" (→Jan. 3, 1961).

Los Angeles, July 13. Democratic convention nominates John F. Kennedy of Massachusetts for President (→27).

Chicago, July 27. Republican convention nominates Richard M. Nixon of California for President (→Oct. 22).

Spartanburg, South Carolina, Sept. 15. Senator Barry Goldwater says, "I fear Washington and centralized government more than I do Moscow."

Pittsburgh, Oct. 13. Pirates beat Yankees, four games to three, in World Series.

New York City, Dec. 3. Lerner-Loewe musical *Camelot* opens on Broadway.

Philadelphia, Dec. 26. Eagles beat Green Bay Packers, 17-13, for N.F.L. title.

Sit-ins, cutting edge in a war on bias

Greensboro, N.C., April

Throughout the South, Negroes have adopted a non-violent protest technique that has been dubbed the "sit-in," to combat discrimination at lunch counters, cafeterias, libraries, churches and beaches. The trend toward this type of protest got started on February 1, when four Negro college students refused to move from a Woolworth lunch counter in Greensboro, when they were denied service. The action quickly spread to lunch counters in more than 50 Southern towns. This led to wade-ins at all-white beaches, read-ins at libraries, and kneel-ins at racially segregated churches. Many Negro students have been arrested for the protests, and the National Association for the Advancement of Colored People has stepped in to defend quite a number of them. Among the highly respected people lending their assistance to provide lessons in non-violent protest for the students in Greensboro are the Rev. Dr. Martin Luther King Jr., head of the Southern Christian Leadership Conference, George Simpkins, the N.A.A.C.P. aide, and Len Holt of the Congress of Racial Equality.

Sit-ins at Nashville, Tennessee, led to 76 arrests, but they have forced politicians and businessmen to deal with the Negro community and a favorable resolution is believed to be near. There were 43 arrests at a Raleigh, North Carolina, sit-in. Race riots broke out after sit-ins and wade-ins at Chattanooga, Tennessee, and in Biloxi, Mississippi, where 10 Negroes were wounded by whites (→May 7).

Students of North Carolina A&T College stage a sit-in at Woolworth's lunch counter in Greensboro, N.C. A white woman refuses to sit with Negroes.

Sub Triton circles globe under water

Delaware, May 10

The American nuclear-powered submarine Triton poked its conning tower above the waves off Delaware just before dawn today, completing a record underwater circumnavigation of the globe. It took 84 days and covered 41,500 miles, retracing much of the route of the 16th-century explorer Ferdinand Magellan.

The 7,750-ton Triton is the largest and most powerful sub in the world. Captain Edward L. Beach, who is also the author of the best seller *Run Silent, Run Deep*, wrote in his log that "one can almost become lyrical thinking of the tremendous drive of the dual power plant of this great ship." The sub, with 183 aboard, left its Groton, Connecticut, base February 16. One aim was to test the endurance of humans deprived of sunlight and fresh air; a psychologist reported high morale, except when smoking was banned. The feat also raises the nuclear stakes: missile-carrying Polaris subs will soon roam the seas.

Basketball's Lakers move to Los Angeles

Los Angeles

Basketball has finally joined major league baseball and football in moving to California. Hit hard by the retirement of George Mikan, the Minneapolis Lakers have moved their National Basketball franchise to Los Angeles. The club had declined on the court and at the box office since Mikan's departure, but the outlook is changing. The Lakers now have Elgin Baylor, who scored 71 points in one game, and his partner, Jerry West, a rookie out of West Virginia. After a slow start, West quickly improved.

Golf is becoming the sport of choice among many Americans, thanks to the fact that it is favored by people like President Eisenhower, who spends a lot of time at it, and Arnold Palmer, who won the Masters again this year.

Population nearing 180 million mark

New York City

The national census report shows the population is now 179,323,175. This indicates that the annual average growth has been 18.5 percent since 1930. New York State, whose population increased by only 13.2 percent in the three decades, to 16,782,304, will lose two of its 43 seats in the House of Representatives because of a proportionate drop in relation to some states. California will gain eight seats, for a total of 38. The census shows large population gains in Nevada, Florida, Alaska and Arizona. Other statistics show the number of women over 14 who work is up, from 25 percent in 1940 to 34 percent now.

Will new computers slash work force?

Washington, D.C.

American industry is being seduced by the capabilities of computers. Last year, the first automated computerized control system was installed at a Texaco refinery, and for the first time banking is using MICR (Magnetic Ink Character Recognition). Languages such as FORTRAN are economically attractive because they allow computers to do the work of humans. Though 2,000 computers are in use, analysts point out that workers are always needed to run them.

Montreal captures its 5th straight cup

Montreal, Apr. 17

The Montreal Canadians have taken the Stanley Cup again, the first team ever to win it five straight times. They also won their third National Hockey League title in a row, beating Toronto by 13 points in the standings. In the playoffs, the Canadians went on to sweep Chicago, then Toronto, to win the cup in a minimum of eight games. The Montreal star was Jacques Plante, who excels despite 200 stitches in his face, a nose that has been broken four times, a fractured skull and two broken cheekbones.

Soviets down U-2; summit wrecked

Paris, May 17

The Big Four summit meeting here never got off the ground after the Russians downed an American U-2 spy plane over Soviet territory and captured its pilot, Francis Gary Powers, on May 1.

The talks stalled when President Eisenhower refused to meet a demand to "apologize for past acts of aggression" against the Soviet Union and to punish "those responsible" for the U-2 incident. He did agree to stop the spy flights over the Soviet Union. These were the conditions that Premier Nikita S. Khrushchev said must be met before he would participate in the Paris summit discussions with Eisenhower, Britain's Prime Minister Harold Macmillan and French President Charles de Gaulle that had been scheduled to get under way on May 15.

But today, the summit meeting that never really began ended officially. When the spy plane was first shot down, the State Department said it was a weather plane that had strayed from its course. But Moscow had the pilot as well as parts of the aircraft. Eisenhower admitted the truth (→Aug. 17).

Soviet citizens examine the wreckage of Gary Powers's downed U-2 spy plane.

"The Fantasticks"

New York City, May 3

This evening, 150 New Yorkers left the Sullivan Street Playhouse, a tiny theater in Greenwich Village, humming wistful bars from *Try to Remember*. The song is a highlight of *The Fantasticks*, a musical that opened tonight on a stage as bare as the one in *Waiting for Godot*. The show was written by two University of Texas graduates, Harvey Schmidt and Tom Jones.

Birth control pill is approved for market

Washington, D.C., May 9

The Food and Drug Administration today approved the use of a contraceptive pill. The hormonal tablets, which are said to be nearly 100 percent effective in preventing pregnancy, were tested over several years by women in Puerto Rico under Planned Parenthood supervision. One in five women reported nausea and/or a gain in weight. There have been no reports of tumors or unusual cysts; indeed, preliminary studies have shown a reduction in the expected numbers of uterine and breast cancer cases. The pills are to be placed on the market early next year under the brand names of Norlutin and Enovid, and one month's supply is expected to cost $10 to $15. Mrs. Margaret Sanger, the life-long advocate of birth control, is reportedly quite pleased with the news.

Eisenhower returns from Latin America

Puerto Rico, March 3

President Eisenhower returned to American soil today after a 10-day Latin American tour, which his aides said showed that backing of the United States there is at the highest level since World War II. Eisenhower's worst moments came on the flight home, when an engine of his plane lost power and it had to land in Suriname. The calm of his trip to Brazil, Argentina, Chile and Uruguay contrasted sharply with the violent demonstrations that erupted on Vice President Nixon's 1958 tour.

"People in the Sun" (1960) by Edward Hopper. A leader of the American realist school, Hopper uses a psychological approach. Whether painting people taking the sun or a lonely office worker, he always remains detached.

▷

Kennedy's image outshines Nixon's in series of TV debates

In the nation's first series of televised presidential debates, Senator John Kennedy and Vice President Richard Nixon square off on the major issues.

New York City, Oct. 22

The great presidential television debates have ended, and according to the Gallup Poll, Senator John F. Kennedy is the winner. Going into the series of four all-network programs, Gallup had Vice President Richard M. Nixon leading, 47 to 46, with 7 percent undecided. Coming out, it's Kennedy on top, 51 to 45, with 4 percent on the fence.

Political pundits and television critics alike believe that most of the shift came as early as the first of the four debates. They say both men handled themselves well, but they think Kennedy just looked better on the tube. On the radio, it sounded like a standoff, but on television, the senator from Massachusetts seemed healthy and vigorous, while the Vice President appeared haggard under a coat of pancake makeup intended to hide his heavy stubble. Only recently out of the hospital, where he lost weight recovering from a knee injury, Nixon also wore a shirt collar that was half a size too big. He regained his weight with milk shakes, but never won the sympathy that he did in 1952 with his emotional television chat about the Nixon family's finances and Trisha's dog Checkers.

Other factors aside, it is believed the series of four nationwide debates served to erase the Nixon advantage of being better known. Observers say the senator was able to come out "on top because he started far behind" (→ Nov. 9).

Wilma Rudolph, Cassius Clay and Russians star in the Olympics

Rome, September

The Soviet Union outpointed the United States again in the Olympics, but there were some shining performances in the losing cause. Wilma Rudolph captured the headlines with her three gold-medal performance in track, Americans scored a brilliant sweep of the hurdles and a brash young boxer from Louisville, Kentucky, Cassius Clay, took home the top prize for light heavyweights. The leggy Wilma ran the 100-meter final in 11 seconds for a record and ran a brilliant anchor in the 400 relay. An American, Rafer Johnson, set a decathlon record. Clay outboxed an experienced Polish Olympian in his final. Lee Calhoun paced the sweep of the 110-meter hurdles.

"The Library" (1960) by Jacob Lawrence, who uses art to study Negro life.

U-2 pilot Powers gets 10-year term

Moscow, Aug. 17

Francis Gary Powers, pilot of the American U-2 spy plane shot down near Sverdlovsk on May 1, showed no emotion in the crowded courtroom today as he was sentenced to 10 years in a Soviet prison and work farm for espionage against the Soviet Union. He is not permitted an appeal, but his family says that it will ask Premier Nikita Khrushchev for a reprieve. The pilot was not given the death penalty because, the court said, he expressed "sincere repentance and confession of his guilt." Powers said he was following orders from the C.I.A. (→ Feb. 10, 1962).

Patterson regains title, first to do so

New York City, June 20

For 359 days after his first loss to Ingemar Johansson, Floyd Patterson smoldered. His pride hurt, he was determined to defeat the young Swede in their rematch, and he did with a vengeance. Patterson caught Johansson with a knockout left hook in the fifth round and thereby became the first boxer ever to regain the world heavyweight title. The Swedish champion had been floored earlier by a hook, but he arose at the count of 9. For Johansson, it was his first defeat in 23 bouts; for Patterson it was the 36th victory in 38 fights. Such fighters as Joe Louis, Jack Dempsey and Jim Corbett were among those unable to recapture the title.

Biggest ship ever

Newport News, Va., Sept. 24

The Enterprise, the world's biggest ship and first nuclear-powered aircraft carrier, was launched today in the James River. Measuring 1,101 feet and displacing 83,350 tons, the ship is the largest vessel ever built. Its eight nuclear reactors drive four massive propellers, each as high as a two-story house. Capable of speeds above 30 knots, the vessel, built at an estimated cost of $365 million, could travel 20 times around the world non-stop.

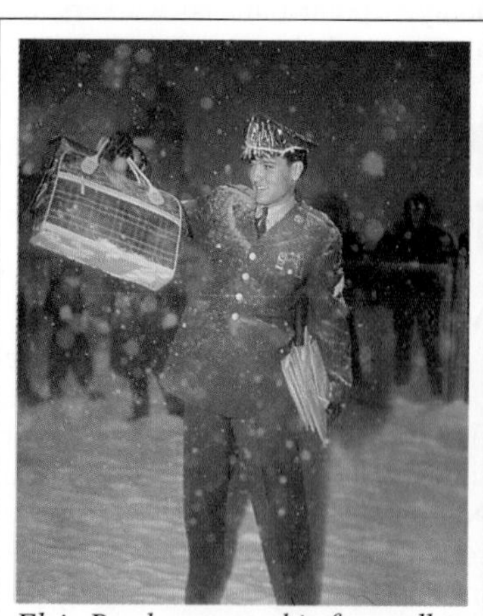

Elvis Presley waves his farewell to the army that drafted him in 1958 and his hello to the legions of his waiting fans. On returning from Germany, Elvis intends to pick up his career where he left it, with 14 million-selling records in a row.

Beehive: Whole lot of teasin' goin' on

United States

Things are looking up – literally. Rocket models are taking off, balloon satellites and cosmonauts are circling the globe, and people are craning their necks to view the tops of beehive hairdos. Figuratively, things are looking up too. Barbie doll has a new boyfriend, Ken. Sports nuts have the American Football League, and players have Astroturf. People want to laugh; sales of comedy records are soaring. People want racial equality: 70,000 Negroes and whites are staging sit-ins in more than 100 cities this year. And in California, where a law was just passed to reduce auto fumes, it may soon be possible to look up and see the sky.

Harvest of Shame

New York City, Nov. 25

In an uncompromising exposure of filth, despair and grinding poverty, Edward R. Murrow took us into the lives of millions of migratory farm workers tonight. We saw pickers stacked vertically in trucks while the picked products traveled in cool elegance. We met a mother of 14 children who worked 10 grueling hours for $1. *Harvest of Shame* on CBS was this year's *The Grapes of Wrath*, brilliantly and compassionately reported by Murrow.

"International Surface No. 1" (1960) by Stuart Davis. After studying under Robert Henri at the age of 16, Davis learned to apply his unique form of Cubism to the sights and the sounds of everyday life in modern America.

JFK wins presidency by close shave

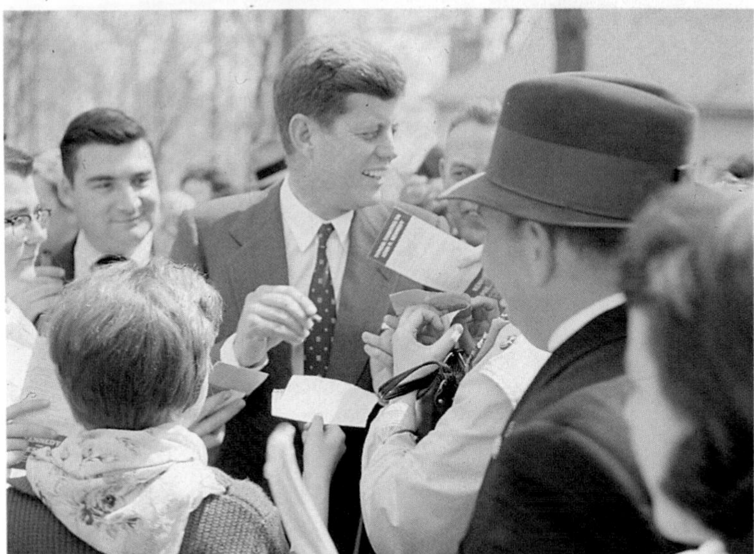

His looks and charm make the new President a natural in the television age.

Washington, D.C., Nov. 9

In one of the closest elections in American history, Senator John F. Kennedy has won the presidency by a plurality of less than half of 1 percent, or less than two votes per precinct. The outcome remained uncertain for long hours, and 52 electoral votes remain in doubt, but the Democratic candidate's total now amounts to 300 votes, or 31 more than required.

The popular vote was so close that the incumbent Vice President Richard M. Nixon stopped short of conceding at 3:20 this morning, though he told supporters at the Ambassador Hotel in Los Angeles that it looked as though Senator Kennedy had won, and he was going to bed. Instead, he stayed up, to see the Kennedy margin shrink to almost zero. Not until almost 1 in the afternoon, New York time, did he telegraph his formal concession, telling the President-elect, "I know that you will have the united support of all Americans as you lead the nation in the cause of peace and freedom." In reply, the President-elect congratulated the Vice President on "a fine race," and told him he knows the nation "can count on your unswerving loyalty."

"To all Americans," President-elect Kennedy said, "the election may have been a close one, but I think that there is general agreement that a supreme national effort will be needed in the years ahead to move this country safely through the 1960s. I ask your help, and I can assure you that every degree of mind and spirit that I possess will be devoted to the long-range interests of the United States and to the cause of freedom around the world. So now," he concluded, "my wife and I prepare for a new administration and for a new baby. Thank you."

At 43, the 6-foot 1-inch Kennedy enters the White House as the second youngest chief executive in American history (Theodore Roosevelt was 42), and as the first Catholic to hold the office. He defused the religious issue when he told the Houston Ministerial Association he believes in complete separation of church and state. If he could not resolve a conflict between conscience and his office, he said, he would resign. (→Jan. 20, 1961).

The King of Hollywood is dead but the realm continues to thrive

Hollywood, California

"The King" is dead. On November 16, Clark Gable, 59, died after a heart attack. Not only women loved him; his hulking frame and outspoken manner made him a working man's hero. His last role was in *The Misfits* with Marilyn Monroe and Mongomery Clift, written by Monroe's husband, playwright Arthur Miller, and directed by John Huston. At the Academy Awards, *The Apartment*, with Jack Lemmon and Shirley MacLaine, won top honors, while Elizabeth Taylor (*Butterfield 8*) and Burt Lancaster (*Elmer Gantry*) won the best acting awards. Kirk Douglas is star of the epic *Spartacus*, and *Psycho*, with Anthony Perkins and Janet Leigh, is scaring millions. Hitchcock says this is the last film he will shoot in black and white.

Arthur Miller (at top), Eli Wallach, John Huston, Montgomery Clift, Marilyn Monroe and Clark Gable (far right) on location while filming "The Misfits." For decades, Gable ruled the screen with his manly appearance and demeanor.

1961

Kennedy

Washington, D.C., Jan. 3. President Eisenhower orders diplomatic relations with Cuba broken off (→Apr. 12).

Boston, Apr. 11. Boston Celtics defeat St. Louis Hawks, four games to one, for N.B.A. championship.

Washington, D.C., Apr. 12. President Kennedy announces that United States will not militarily intervene in Cuba (→24).

New York City, May 1. Pulitzer Prize in fiction awarded to Harper Lee for *To Kill a Mockingbird.*

Mobile, Alabama, June 12. Mayor asks men of Mobile to grow beards marking city's 250th anniversary.

Freeport, Texas, June 21. President Kennedy activates nation's first salt water conversion plant, owned and operated by Dow Chemical Company.

Washington, D.C., Aug. 10. In response to spate of hijackings, President Kennedy announces federal agents will be placed on some flights (→Sept. 5).

Washington, D.C., Sept. 1. Word officially received of detonation of atomic bomb by Soviet Union, breaking 34-month silence (→5).

Washington, D.C., Sept. 5. President Kennedy orders atomic testing resumed.

Washington, D.C., Sept. 5. Congress makes hijacking a federal crime.

Cincinnati, Oct. 9. New York Yankees win World Series, four games to one, over Cincinnati Reds.

Washington, D.C., Oct. 26. President Kennedy sends note to South Vietnam's President Ngo Dinh Diem, pledging continued American assistance (→March 22, 1962).

Green Bay, Wisconsin, Dec. 31. Packers defeat New York Giants, 37-0, for N.F.L. title.

New York City. Jane Jacobs's *The Death and Life of American Cities* issued.

New York City. Theodore White's *The Making of the President, 1960,* published.

DEATH

Ketchum, Idaho, July 2. Ernest Hemingway, novelist, (*July 21, 1899).

President Kennedy: "Ask what you can do for your country"

President Kennedy exhorts the American people to join his New Frontier.

President Kennedy and the First Lady on their way to the inauguration.

Washington, D.C., Jan. 20

President Kennedy stirred the nation and the world today with an inaugural address that is being acclaimed by Democrats and Republicans alike as one of the best in memory. In a temperature of 22 degrees, the young President addressed a crowd that had braved an eight-inch overnight snowfall, telling them: "Ask not what your country can do for you. Ask what you can do for your country. Let the word go forth from this time and place, to friend and foe alike, that the torch has been passed to a new generation of Americans – born in this century, tempered by war, disciplined by a hard and bitter peace, proud of our ancient heritage – and unwilling to witness or permit the slow undoing of those human rights to which this nation has always been committed, and to which we are committed today at home and around the world."

The President declared that the United States was prepared to "pay any price, bear any burden, meet any hardship, support any friend, oppose any foe to assure the survival and the success of liberty."

President Kennedy spoke about new negotiations with the Soviet Union, and he issued this exhortation to the American people: "Let us begin anew. Let us never negotiate out of fear. But let us never fear to negotiate."

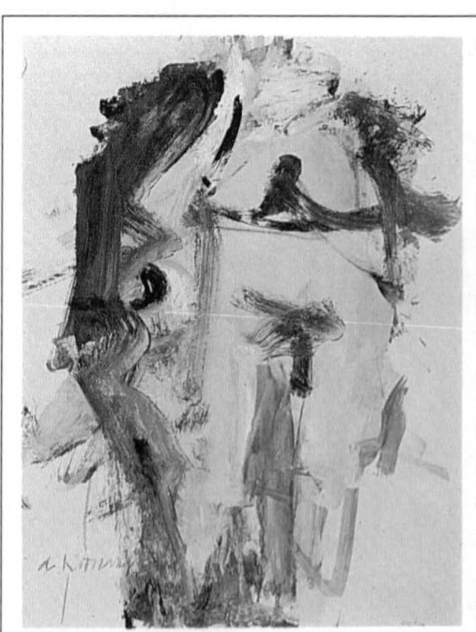

"Woman VIII" (1961) by Willem de Kooning. Born in Rotterdam, Holland, in 1904, de Kooning came to the United States in 1926. His technique in Abstract Expressionism has made him one foremost painters in the nation.

Military-industrial threat seen by Ike

Washington, D.C., Jan. 17

In a farewell address that has startled people in the capital, President Eisenhower tonight warned against "the acquisition of unwarranted influence by the military-industrial complex." National leaders had expected a soft and sentimental goodbye from the old soldier winding up 50 years of public service. Instead, his address bristled with warnings to America to guard its liberties from a "conjunction of an immense military establishment and a large arms industry." He concluded with a prayer that "all peoples will come together in peace guaranteed by mutual respect and love."

President's brother is Attorney General

Washington, D.C., Jan. 21

Just hours after his brother took the oath as the new Attorney General, President Kennedy was joking about it tonight. Speaking at the Alfalfa Club, a bigwigs' dining club, the President said that he doesn't see anything wrong with giving his brother a little legal experience "before Robert goes out to practice law." Robert Kennedy was sworn in with the rest of the new Cabinet on this first day of his brother's administration following mostly indulgent Senate hearings. The President is known to believe that the closeness with his brother outweighs considerably any lack of seasoning on Robert's part.

Peace Corps to aid those in poor lands

Washington, D.C., March 1

Beginning to develop his New Frontier, President Kennedy today signed an executive order to launch the Peace Corps, an organization to aid undeveloped countries. The program, directed by Kennedy's brother-in-law, R. Sargent Shriver, will train American volunteers to help "liberate independent nations from the bonds of hunger, ignorance and poverty," Kennedy said. The program will train people of all ages to teach skills such as agriculture and public health. Peace Corps workers will not be paid but will be given training, transport and living expenses.

The missile race

Washington, D.C.

Though fears of a "missile gap" have faded, America continues to build a huge arsenal of intercontinental ballistic missiles. The Russians are now said to have 50 missiles, while the United States can fire over 100 Atlas and Titan nuclear-tipped rockets. America plans to build 700 Minuteman missiles, which have been test-fired from impregnable underground silos. Powered by solid fuel, a Minutemen can be fired in seconds. Armageddon is as near as the pressing of a button.

23rd Amendment gives D.C. the vote

Washington, D.C., March 29

The 23rd Amendment was ratified today, granting residents of the District of Columbia the right to vote in presidential elections. It gives to the district "a number of electors of president and vice president equal to the number of senators and representatives in Congress to which the district would be entitled if it were a state, but in no event no more than the least populous state." Kansas became the 36th state to ratify the admendment. To some it seems incredible that the district had to push for such reform, charging racism to those who opposed it; the population is predominantly Negro.

Bay of Pigs invasion ends in disaster

Washington, D.C., Apr. 24

President Kennedy has accepted full responsibility for the failed Bay of Pigs invasion, even though the plan was hatched under the Eisenhower administration. As Kennedy noted, "There's an old saying that victory has a hundred fathers and defeat is an orphan."

The small force of anti-Castro Cubans, with the support of the United States Central Intelligence Agency, landed a week ago. Within days, Castro's troops had wiped out the rebel beachhead. At last count, 743 men had been captured.

The action has been condemned worldwide. In Congress, Senator Wayne Morse, Democat of Oregon, called the invasion "a colossal mistake." But for the most part, domestic criticism has been scant, pending a full investigation.

Tensions with Cuba had been mounting since the Castro government moved toward the Communist sphere. In January, Eisenhower broke diplomatic relations with the island nation.

Without proper back-up support, Cuban anti-Communist forces were doomed.

Officials say Eisenhower had been planning the invasion for months. Kennedy was faced with a decision: drop the effort, and possibly damage morale in the anti-Castro camp, or proceed with the risky venture. Proponents said the invasion had to take place swiftly, before Castro got enough Soviet arms to repulse any attack. Opponents said the time was not yet ripe (→Oct. 28, 1962).

400 Green Berets ordered to Vietnam

Washington, D.C., May 11

President Kennedy has ordered a contingent of 400 Special Forces soldiers and 100 military advisers to South Vietnam. Today's White House statement comes at a time when most unofficial estimates of the number of advisers there total about 2,000. The Special Forces troops are better known as "Green Berets" because of their distinctive headgear. Specially trained in jungle warfare and counter-insurgency tactics at Fort Bragg, North Carolina, these soldiers have the mission of training and advising an estimated 320,000 South Vietnamese troops in their war with the Communists. Aides close to Kennedy say the President believes that these additional forces will enable South Vietnam to win the war without the direct involvement of American fighting units. But Kennedy's chief military adviser, General Maxwell Taylor, argues that the U.S. will have to provide 8,000 additional soldiers (→Oct. 26).

Is television just "a vast wasteland"?

United States, May

One youngster calls television "chewing gum for the eyes" and the general mediocrity of the medium has prompted hard-hitting Newton N. Minow, 35, the New Frontier's chairman of the Federal Communications Commission, to put broadcasters on notice that station licenses won't be automatically renewed from now on. He says "performance" will be judged against "promises." What does he think of present performances? "A vast wasteland" of "game shows, violence, formula comedies about totally unbelievable families, blood and thunder, mayhem, violence, sadism, murder ... And most of all, boredom." The top networks, NBC and CBS, have been trying to produce more "blue ribbon programs," and Minow himself did praise *CBS Reports* and NBC's *Project 20.*

Familial bliss at its televised best.

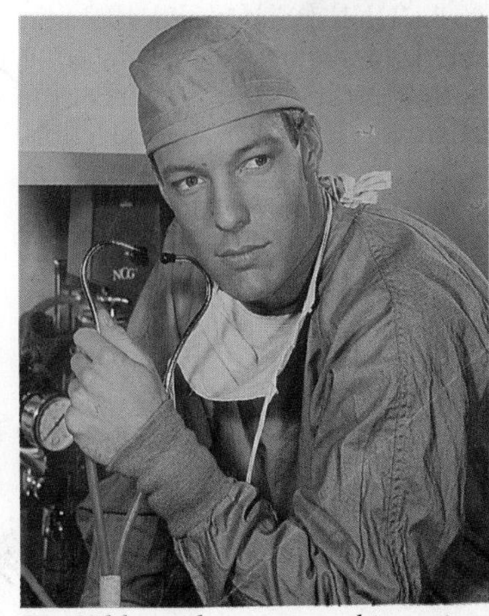

Dr. Kildare always saves his patient. ▷

"Freedom Riders" attacked in South

Segregationists block the path of buses that are about to leave the station.

Montgomery, Alabama, May

Organized by James Farmer of the Congress of Racial Equality (C.O.R.E) along with members of the Student Non-Violent Coordinating Committee, a Freedom Ride campaign has set out from Washington, D.C., on a bus tour of the South. This racially integrated collection of riders is testing Southern compliance with regulations for desegregation recently enacted by the Interstate Commerce Commission, and orders along similar lines from federal courts. Riders have been attacked, harassed and arrested along the route. Whites in Anniston, Alabama, attempted to burn their bus, and a Birmingham mob attacked and beat the demonstrators. A particularly violent attack in Montgomery prompted Attorney General Robert Kennedy to send out 600 federal marshals to restore order, while Alabama declared martial law and sent in the National Guard. At Jackson, Mississippi, 27 of the riders were arrested.

Farmer, of C.O.R.E., has long been involved with national anti-discrimination protests. He graduated from Wiley College with a divinity degree in 1941, but he has refused ordination on the grounds that congregations were segregated. Greatly influenced by the non-violence tactics of Gandhi in India, Farmer has stressed such non-violent protest, including the use of the sit-in and the Freedom Ride. Popular as a writer, radio commentator and speaker, Farmer donates his earnings to C.O.R.E.

The first of the Freedom Rides took place in April 1947, with a similarly integrated group touring the South, but the action did not receive nearly the attention of the ride this year. Non-violent sit-in protests have been widespread, resulting in the arrest of more than 3,600 Negro students, and the desegregation of churches, beaches, lunch counters and other public facilities in some 100 Southern cities. These activities have been aided by the Southern Christian Leadership Conference and the National Association for the Advancement of Colored People (→Oct. 1, 1962).

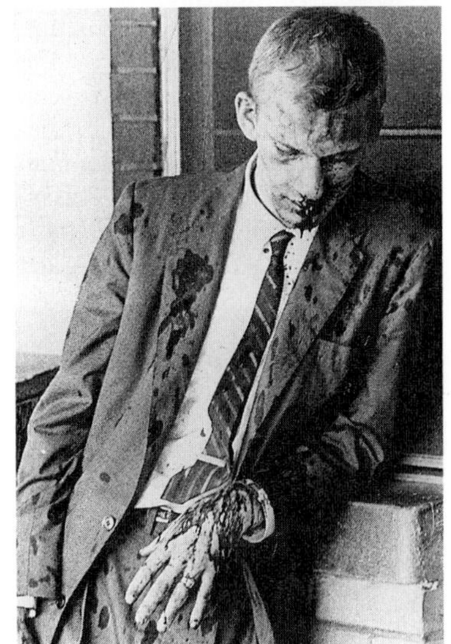

A beaten Freedom Rider awaits aid.

A young President encourages fitness

Washington, D.C., July 19

President Kennedy has called on the schools of the nation to seek out their underdeveloped pupils and work with them to improve their physical capacity. The President, in an unusual postscript to this morning's news conference, suggested that each school prepare a program of basic physical development, exercise and achievement. He urged the schools to adopt the recommendations that have been made by the National Council on Physical Fitness, which said such a program ought to encompass both boys and girls and ought to "use valid fitness tests" to evaluate the progress of the pupils.

X-15 at 4,070 mph

Edwards AFB, Calif., Nov. 9

Major Robert White streaked to a new speed record for winged craft today in a needle-nosed X-15 rocket plane. The plane dropped from a B-52 "mothership," then zoomed off to a speed of 4,070 mph, reaching a height of over 100,000 feet before gliding back to a desert landing here in California. The jet black X-15 suffered a cracked outer windshield from the tremendous heat and pressure, but Major White said that he was "never in danger." On October 12, White piloted the X-15 to a new record altitude of 215,000 feet.

The Alliance for Progress in Latin America

Punta del Este, Uruguay, Aug. 17

The United States and 19 Latin American nations today signed a charter creating the Alliance for Progress, a 10-year economic effort backed by $20 billion in long-term financing from the United States. Cuba cast the lone dissenting vote.

The alliance is aimed at providing not only economic betterment to the region, but accompanying gains in education, health, housing and agriculture. The United States representative, Treasury Secretary Douglas Dillon, then said that support under the program would be disbursed in relation to each nation's cooperation in furthering democracy and freedom.

Many of the delegates to the Inter-American Economic and Social Conference called the alliance "a turning point in the history of the Americas." But the Cuban envoy, Major Ernesto "Che" Guevara, bitterly denounced the plan as "an instrument of economic imperialism." Dillon replied that the United States has no intention of giving the Cuban regime funds so long as it remains "under the control" of the Soviet Union. Dillon will visit Venezuela before going home.

The long-range program of Latin American aid has the strong backing of President Kennedy.

"Come on, baby, let's do the twist"

PNew York City

From the moment Elvis Presley first gyrated across American television screens, teenagers have been caught in a feverish quest for new dance steps. But nothing compares with the full-blown craze being generated this year by Chubby Checker's *The Twist*. Checker, born Ernest Evans, recorded the Hank Ballard tune last year, but it didn't catch on until the 19-year-old did it on TV's *American Bandstand*. Overnight, the twist had replaced such crazes as the mashed potato at teen sock hops, and, unlike other dance sensations, it has been irresistible for many adults.

If proof is needed that we're out of the 1950s, here it is in the twist. The dance is sweeping the nation, a sure sign that society is loosening up.

Americans are in space

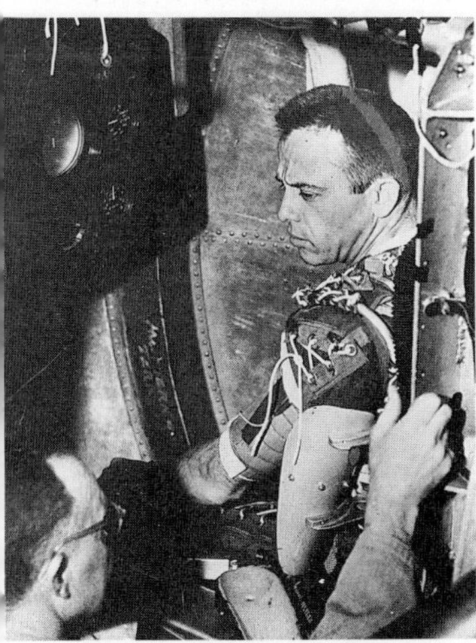

Astronaut Alan B. Shepard Jr., 37, America's first man in space. "What a beautiful view!" he exclaimed.

Cape Canaveral, Fla., July 21

"We are behind," said President Kennedy after Soviet cosmonaut Yuri Gagarin orbited the Earth in April, "and it will be some time before we catch up." But two Americans have since hurtled into space, and the President has expanded his New Frontier by pledging to put a man on the moon within 10 years.

On May 5, Navy Commander Alan B. Shepard Jr., 37, rocketed 115 miles into space via an Army Redstone missile trailing a yellow-orange tail of flames. Shepard, cramped into a tiny Mercury capsule, was weightless for just five minutes, barely long enough to peer down at the Caribbean and exclaim, "What a beautiful view!" As the capsule parachuted into the Atlantic just 15 minutes after liftoff from Cape Canaveral, the nation was both exultant and relieved.

Captain Virgil "Gus" Grissom, 35, duplicated the sub-orbital feat today, though the capsule sank after splashdown and the astronaut was barely saved from drowning.

American astronauts have yet to orbit the Earth, but on May 25, Kennedy said: "I believe this nation should commit itself to achieving the goal, before this decade is out, of landing a man on the moon and returning him safely to earth" (→Feb. 20, 1962).

Maris hits 61 home runs in 162 games

New York City, Oct. 1

Roger Maris has smashed the home-run record that some baseball experts said would stand forever. The Yankee slugger belted his 61st home run, one more than Babe Ruth, in the final game of the season. Of course, he needed a 162-game season to do it, eight more games than Ruth had in setting a mark that has stood for 34 years. Maris socked No. 61 off Tracy Stallard, a Boston rookie, and got the only run in the 1-0 Yankee victory. Maris also led the league in runs batted in with 142.

Wood, Newman and Tracy at the movies

Wood as the no-nonsense Maria.

Hollywood, California

Stimulating new films include *West Side Story*, combining Leonard Bernstein's music and Stephen Sondheim's lyrics, and starring Natalie Wood, George Chakiris and Rita Moreno in a New York gang war saga. Other standouts: *The Guns of Navarone*, with Gregory Peck and David Niven, *The Hustler*, with Paul Newman and George Scott, the Italian *Two Women*, with Sophia Loren, *Judgment at Nuremberg*, with Maximilian Schell and Spencer Tracy, *Breakfast at Tiffany's*, with Audrey Hepburn and George Peppard, and *A Raisin in the Sun*, with Sidney Poitier.

Kennedy at the summit

President Kennedy and Premier Khrushchev size each other up in Vienna.

Vienna, June 4

President Kennedy introduced himself at the start of his five-day summit tour of Europe as "the man who accompanied Jacqueline Kennedy to Paris." During the last two days in Vienna, the President introduced himself to Soviet Premier Nikita Khrushchev as a man able to cut through diplomatic red tape.

The fact that Kennedy managed to arrange a summit meeting with the Soviet leader was a victory in itself. The men held "frank and courteous" negotiations just a year after Khrushchev refused to meet with "cowardly, piratical" Americans in the doomed Big Four summit in Paris. The Russian already has kind words about Kennedy. "I don't agree with this man," he told an aide, "but I can talk with him." Actually, analysts say Khrushchev likes dealing with Kennedy because he is a diplomatic novice.

The two agreed that Laos should be neutral and independent and that there must be a cease-fire there. Their positions on Germany were restated: Kennedy warned Khrushchev the United States would go to war to defend Berlin. Khrushchev wants the city's status renegotiated and says he will sign a peace treaty with East Germany. On a nuclear test ban treaty, Khrushchev still wants three-man inspection teams with each man having a veto. In talks with France, the President pledged closer contacts on NATO.

President and Mrs. Kennedy visit with French President de Gaulle. "I am the man," quips Kennedy, "who accompanied Jacqueline Kennedy to Paris."

1962

Kennedy

New York City, Jan. 17. Television quiz show contestant Charles Van Doren and others convicted of game show fixing.

Cooperstown, New York, Jan. 23. Jackie Robinson elected to Baseball Hall of Fame.

Washington, D.C., Feb. 10. United States trades Soviet spy Rudolph Abel for captured U-2 pilot Gary Powers.

Boston, Apr. 18. Celtics defeat Los Angeles Lakers, four games to three, in N.B.A. championship.

Christmas Island, Australia, May 6. Nuclear submarine Ethan Allen tests first sub-launched atomic missile.

New York City, May 7. Theodore White wins Pulitzer Prize for *The Making of the President, 1960.*

Paris, June 3. Airline disaster takes lives of 111 prominent Atlanta citizens.

New Haven, Connecticut, June 12. Receiving honorary degree from Yale, President Kennedy comments, "It might be said now that I have the best of both worlds. A Harvard education and a Yale degree."

Newport, Rhode Island, Sept. 24. U.S. yacht Weatherly defeats Australian challenger Gretel for America's Cup.

Washington, D.C., Oct. 10. After revelation that thalidomide has caused birth defects in Europe, President Kennedy signs legislation banning use in United States.

United States, Oct. 14. Harry Truman comments, "If former President Eisenhower had understood the Monroe Doctrine, we would not have any trouble in Cuba today."

San Francisco, Oct. 16. New York Yankees defeat San Francisco Giants in World Series, four games to three.

California, November. Richard Nixon, defeated gubernatorial candidate, announces retirement from politics, stating, "You won't have Nixon to kick around any more."

New York City, Dec. 30. Green Bay Packers defeat New York Giants, 16-7, for N.F.L. title.

DEATH

New York City, Nov. 7. Eleanor Roosevelt, former First Lady (*Oct. 11, 1884).

Friendship 7 puts John Glenn in orbit

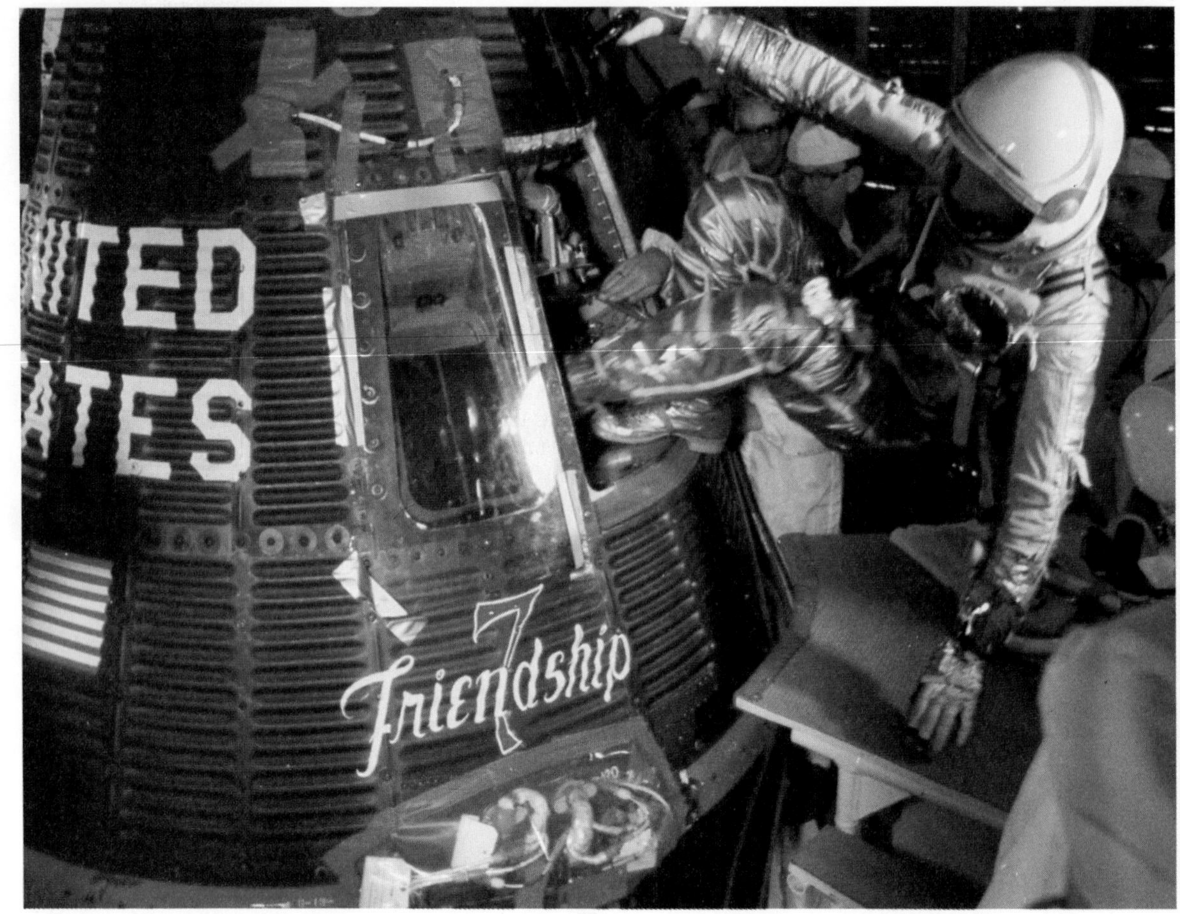

Astronaut John H. Glenn Jr. enters the spacecraft Friendship 7 as he prepares to lead his country into space.

Cape Canaveral, Fla., Feb. 20

John H. Glenn Jr. today became the first American to make an orbital flight, whirling around the Earth three times before splashing to a safe landing in the Atlantic at 2:43 p.m. The 40-year-old astronaut completed the flight despite a series of difficulties that at one time raised concern that his Mercury spacecraft might disintegrate as it attempted to return to Earth.

Glenn, a Marine Corps lieutenant colonel, waited a long time for the flight. It had been postponed 10 times since December because of bad weather or technical problems. Today, he was awakened at 2:20 a.m. and again entered the spacecraft, which has been named Friendship, about an hour later. The countdown proceeded smoothly, and Glenn was rocketed into orbit at 9:47 a.m., as some 100,000 spectators on the nearby beaches of Florida cheered and millions watched on television.

All went well at first, as Glenn reported frequently to ground stations around the globe that his condition was "fine." But a problem developed when the jets designed to maintain the spacecraft's orientation began to malfunction. They were guided by an automatic system that fired squirts of hydrogen peroxide from the jets to keep the craft at its designed attitude. Instead of firing the small control jets, the system began to fire larger jets for more radical corrections, raising the danger that all the fuel might be consumed. Glenn met the problem by shifting to a manual control system, called fly-by-wire.

A greater danger arose when instruments read at ground stations indicated that the spacecraft's heat shield had become detached from the main capsule body. Without the heat shield, Glenn and the spacecraft would have been consumed by the high temperatures generated as the capsule plunged back into the atmosphere. Worried that their instruments were giving a false reading, ground technicians changed the sequence of re-entry events to keep the heat shield in place even it it was detached. The changes retained the braking rockets that bring the capsule out of orbit, rather than jettisoning it early. Fears about the heat shield proved unwarranted.

While he was in orbit, Glenn received congratulations from President Kennedy by radio telephone and saw the lights of Perth, Australia, turned on in tribute as he flew over. "Oh, that view is tremendous," he exclaimed at one point. Glenn fired the braking rockets successfully and splashed into the Atlantic near Grand Turk Island in the Bahamas, 700 miles southwest of Cape Canaveral, where he was picked up by the destroyer Noa. His flight was two orbits more than flown last April by the Soviet cosmonaut Yuri Gagarin, the first man in space, but far short of the 17-orbit flight of Gherman Titov in August. But it is still a major step toward making the nation competitive in space and the most impressive achievement of the American space program to date (→ July 11).

Moving of peasants started in Vietnam

Saigon, South Vietnam, March 22

A special team of United States Army advisers and troops of the Army of South Vietnam (ARVN) have begun Operation Sunrise. The objective of Sunrise, a so-called "pacification" operation, is to transfer loyal South Vietnamese peasants from five hamlets in Binh Duong Province, a known refuge for Communist insurgents, to Bien Cat District, an area where the ARVN maintains control and the villagers can live in safety. The South Vietnamese will regard those remaining in the hamlets as Vietcong soldiers or sympathizers, and treat them accordingly – which means the "enemy" hamlet will probably be destroyed (→May 17).

A tour of the White House with Jackie

Washington, D.C., Feb. 14

Mrs. John F. Kennedy took millions of television viewers on a personal tour of the newly restored White House on a CBS News broadcast this evening. Accompanied by correspondent Charles Collingwood, Mrs. Kennedy related the history of the presidential mansion including the East Room, the Red Room and Lincoln's bedroom. The First Lady narrated the $100,000 production and the President discussed the renovations and the importance of history.

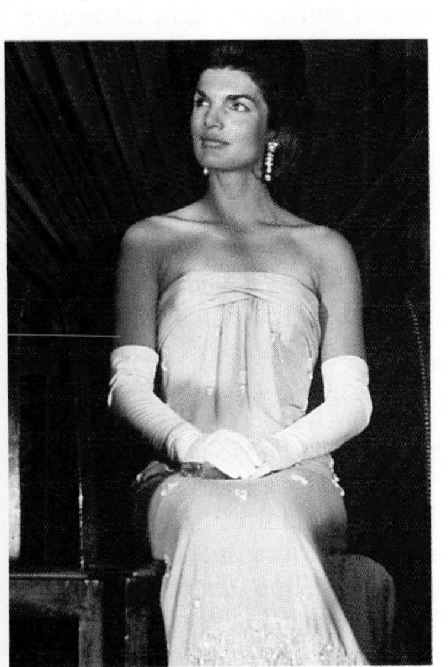

An elegant White House tour guide.

Steel yields to Kennedy

President Kennedy's resolve forces the steel industry to drop price increases.

Washington, D.C., Apr. 13

U.S. Steel officials have tested President Kennedy's mettle, only to find it as tough as their own. Today they rescinded price increases announced April 10 after the President, in excoriating terms, accused them of public irresponsibility in their "pursuit of private power and profit." Treating the planned increase as virtually traitorous at a time when he was asking unions to rein in their wage demands, Kennedy said it was unacceptable that "a tiny handful of steel executives could show such utter contempt" for the American people.

Seven firms in all had followed U.S. Steel's lead. When two of them, Inland Steel and Bethlehem Steel, changed their minds, U.S. Steel gave in. The possibility of collusion led Attorney General Robert Kennedy to order a grand jury investigation under the antitrust laws. And Albert Gore of Tennessee introduced three related bills in the Senate, one of which would amend the Sherman Antitrust Act so that courts could more easily break up monopoly practices.

Reaction in Congress was predictably split. The Republican leader, Everett Dirksen of Illinois, said Kennedy was "looking in the wrong place for the basic cause of inflation." Privately, the President said, "My father always told me that all businessmen were sons of bitches, but I never believed it till now."

No prayer in school

Washington, D.C., June 25

The Supreme Court today handed down its decision in the case of Engel v. Vitale, also known as the Regents' Prayer Case. By a vote of 6-1, the court held that the recitation of a prayer written by a state agency for use in the public schools violated the establishment clause of the First Amendment. In his opinion, Justice Hugo Black stated that no government has the "power to prescribe by law any particular form of prayer . . . to be used as an official prayer . . . " This decision is expected to result in a storm of protest.

S.D.S. issues credo

Port Huron, Michigan, July

The young activist group Students for a Democratic Society has issued a manifesto, *The Port Huron Statement*, seeking an "agenda for a generation" of radical politics. Tom Hayden drafted the credo at the group's convention here. In it, he calls for "participatory democracy" to overcome a sense of powerlessness in society. S.D.S. was started two summers ago in New York City by Al Haber and Hayden to support civil rights and to oppose militarism. "We may be the last generation in the experiment with living," said Hayden.

Force sent to Laos: "act of diplomacy"

Washington, D.C., May 17

The White House announced today that President Kennedy is ordering a small contingent of American naval and ground personnel to Laos. The message asserted that the United States recognizes the sovereignty of that nation and will work for the preservation of its neutrality under Prince Souvanna Phouma. Kennedy is convinced that both the Communist Pathet Lao and the North Vietnamese are out to undermine and ultimately overthrow the Laotian government. Since Kennedy does not want to appear to be sending troops into Laos for combat, he carefully called their introduction an "act of diplomacy" (→Nov. 2, 1963).

Chamberlain soars to 100-point game

Hershey, Penn., March 2

It was a night when Wilt Chamberlain could do nothing wrong. The new coach of the Philadelphia Warriors, Frank McGuire, wanted Wilt the Stilt to go to the basket as much as possible and the Big Dipper obliged with 100 points. He was virtually a one-man show in leading the Warriors to a 169-147 victory over the New York Knicks. Wilt got 36 baskets and 28 of 32 free throws. The performance evoked new complaints that his height, 7 feet 3 inches, was ruining the sport.

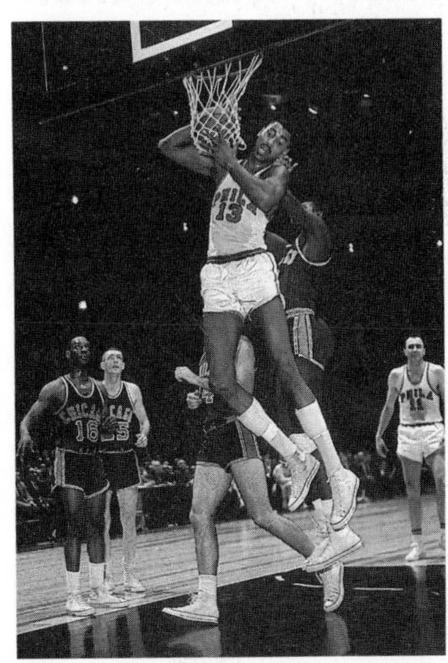

Basketball's Wilt the Stilt in action.

Marilyn Monroe is dead

Her sultry looks enticed millions but masked her warmth and intelligence.

Hollywood, Calif., August 5

The last of the love goddesses is gone. Marilyn Monroe (nee Norma Jean Baker) rose from a childhood of deprivation, foster homes and mistreatment, including rape, to become the whole world's symbol of the eternal female. She married at 16 to escape her surroundings. Working as a paint sprayer in a defense plant in 1944, she was discovered by an army photographer and became a pin-up girl and a model. In August of 1946, Fox signed her to a contract for $125 a week. From small parts as a dumb blonde, she moved on to starring roles in *Bus Stop*, *Some Like It Hot* and *Let's Make Love*. Director Joshua Logan called her "pure cinema ... the most authentic film actress since Garbo." But her health and confidence were stretched to the breaking point. In her last movie, *The Misfits*, Clark Gable looks at her and remarks, tenderly: "You're the saddest girl I ever saw." She divorced her third husband, playwright Arthur Miller (her second was baseball hero Joe DiMaggio) last year. In June, she began the movie *Something's Got to Give*, but was fired. This morning, the 36-year-old star was found lifeless in bed. The death was called a suicide, but questions have been raised.

Negro enrolls at Ol' Miss

Oxford, Mississippi, Oct. 1

Accompanied by federal marshals, James Meredith crossed a riot-torn campus today to become the first Negro student at the University of Mississippi. Burned-out cars, tear gas canisters and broken glass littered the campus where an angry mob of thousands gathered Sunday night to try to block Meredith's registration. Federal troops held the mob off with tear gas, but two people were killed and 28 marshals were wounded by gunfire in the melee. Those slain were a French reporter, Paul Guihard, and Ray Gunter, an Oxford resident. Over 200 people were arrested. Unknown to the crowd, Meredith had been installed in a dormitory room on campus at 6:30 p.m. Sunday.

While the riot raged on through the night, President Kennedy and his brother, Attorney General Robert Kennedy, directed federal operations from the White House. Mississippi Governor Ross Barnett, who had vowed he would go to jail to block integration, did not appear on campus. Both Kennedys talked with him by telephone during the day trying to reach a peaceful solution, but the negotiations broke down. The President then went on national television at 10 p.m. and appealed for order. "Americans are free ... to disagree with the law," he said, "but not to disobey it."

Meredith, 29, is a native Mississippian and a former sergeant in the air force (→May 13, 1963).

U.S. troops arrive on campus to ensure that the university will be integrated.

Telstar communications satellite in orbit

Communications in the space age.

Andover, Maine, July 11

Americans today watched the first transmission of television signals from Earth to a space satellite and back again. The revolutionary Telstar communications satellite, sent into orbit early this morning, received signals from an American Telephone & Telegraph ground station here for 17 minutes and flashed them back to be rebroadcast across the United States. Stations in England and France also received the signals, marking the start of an era of trans-Atlantic TV transmission. The first broadcasts from Europe to America via Telstar, a $50 million A.T.&T. project, will take place tomorrow (→Jan. 25, 1964).

Nobel for Steinbeck

Oslo, Norway, Dec. 10

It was no *Winter of Discontent* for John Steinbeck, who accepted the Nobel Prize today, but next season may become a *Silent Spring*, says Rachel Carson, who claims insecticides sneak 500 alien chemicals into our bodies. Other best-sellers this year: *Sex and the Single Girl* by Helen Gurley Brown; *Pale Fire* by Vladimir Nabokov; *The Guns of August* by Barbara Tuchman; *One Flew Over the Cuckoo's Nest* by Ken Kesey; *Fail Safe* by Eugene Burdick and Harvey Wheeler, and *Six Crises* by Richard M. Nixon.

Fine films featured

Hollywood, California

Movie-goers flock to see *Lawrence of Arabia* with Peter O'Toole, Anthony Quinn and Omar Sharif; Sean Connery as James Bond in *Dr. No;* Gregory Peck's brilliant acting in *To Kill a Mockingbird*; *The Miracle Worker* with Anne Bancroft and Patty Duke; *Days of Wine and Roses* with Jack Lemmon and Lee Remick; Bette Davis and Joan Crawford in *Whatever Happened to Baby Jane?*; *Long Day's Journey Into Night* with Katharine Hepburn, *How the West Was Won* and *The Manchurian Candidate*.

Missiles of October place the world at the brink

Washington, D.C., Oct. 28

A week of unprecedented worldwide tension that drove the United States and the Soviet Union to the brink of a thermonuclear confrontation ended today. Faced by an unwavering American President, Soviet Premier Nikita Khrushchev retreated, agreeing to remove from Cuba missiles that American military experts said could have wiped out the nation's defenses in 17 minutes. Khrushchev acted after getting a pledge from Kennedy not to invade Cuba. "I understand very well your anxiety and the anxiety of the people of the United States," Khrushchev said in a conciliatory letter to the President today.

Until yesterday, it was not clear that the crisis could be resolved peacefully. The Pentagon reported that a U-2 spy plane had been shot down over Cuba. Thousands of air force reservists were being called up. Florida looked like a D-Day invasion zone. Khrushchev was offering to withdraw his weapons, but only if Kennedy dismantled American missiles in Turkey.

"This is the first real, direct confrontation between the superpowers," said a United Nations aide, "and we all feel pretty powerless."

At the White House tonight, reaction to the diplomatic and military victory is restrained. The President will undoubtedly reap domestic political benefits, but administration insiders say that the global fallout is more important. "The need for a confrontation with the Soviets had been obvious for some time," one Kennedy adviser told *Newsweek*. "They were putting the pressure on us all around the world."

The President had been aware for weeks that the Soviet Union might be supplying Cuba with sophisticated new middle-range nuclear weapons. He received the evidence he needed to prove his case early on the morning of October 16. Aerial reconnaissance pictures showing a missile in Cuba were brought to Kennedy while he was still in bed.

During the next 48 hours, the White House inner circle considered an invasion of Cuba, but it was feared that Khrushchev would retaliate by seizing Berlin. On the afternoon of October 18, Kennedy asked Soviet Foreign Minister Andrei Gromyko about the missiles. Gromyko pulled a note from his pocket with the prepared answer. "Training by Soviet specialists of Cuban nationals in handling defensive armaments is by no means offensive," it asserted. Discussion was resumed at the White House after Gromyko's departure. It ended when Kennedy told his advisers, "The greatest danger of all is to do nothing." He used the same phrase four days later, when he addressed the nation on Monday the 22nd.

When he spoke to 50 million Americans on television, Kennedy was direct and determined. He accused Khrushchev of lying when he said the weapons were merely defensive, and he charged they could be launched against "most of the major cities in the Western Hemisphere." The President stated that an air and naval blockade would examine all ships approaching Cuba to determine whether they were carrying weapons. He demanded a withdrawal of all offensive weapons on the island and warned that the United States would retaliate if the weapons were fired at any country in the hemisphere. "Aggressive conduct, if allowed to go unchecked and unchallenged," Kennedy said, "ultimately leads to war."

In Cuba, the speech was interpreted as a declaration of war. Castro ordered a complete mobilization. In Europe, Kennedy's speech was applauded wholeheartedly.

By the middle of the week, Kennedy was receiving mixed signals from Khrushchev. He proposed a summit meeting at the same time that Soviet ships were voluntarily turning back from Cuba. But the Premier was also promising to retaliate for the blockade. On Thursday, he agreed to a U.N. proposal to stop sending missiles to Cuba if the United States ended the blockade. But on Friday, intelligence indicated that work was speeding up on Soviet bases in Cuba.

With the crisis finally ended, President Kennedy has seemingly won and Khrushchev has lost. But there could be a second dispute soon, possibly over Berlin. "The path we have chosen is full of hazards," Kennedy said. "The cost of freedom is always high, but Americans have always paid it."

Picture released by the Department of Defense showing Soviet ballistic missile installations at Sagua La Grande, Cuba. This and other intelligence photographs prove beyond any doubt that the Soviet Union has turned Cuba into a nuclear missile site a mere 90 miles off the coast of the United States.

President Kennedy (right) confers with his closest adviser, brother Robert.

1963

Kennedy

Denver, Colorado, May 5. Four cadets become first Negro graduates of United States Air Force Academy.

New York City, March 12. Leon Edel wins National Book Award and Pulitzer Prize, for Volumes II and III of his biography of Henry James.

Washington, D.C., March 18. In Gideon v. Wainwright, Supreme Court rules that all indigent defendants are entitled to court-appointed legal counsel in criminal cases.

Washington, D.C., Apr. 9. President Kennedy confers honorary United States citizenship upon Winston Churchill.

Los Angeles, Apr. 24. Boston Celtics defeat Los Angeles Lakers for N.B.A. title.

New York City, May 7. Pulitzer Prize in fiction awarded to William Faulkner.

New York City, May 14. Arthur Ashe becomes first Negro member of United States Davis Cup tennis team.

New York City, June 12. *Cleopatra*, produced at cost of $35 million, in premiere at Rivoli Theater.

Washington, D.C., July 1. Five-digit codes introduced by Post Office, called ZIP Codes (Zone Improvement Plan.)

Washington, D.C., July 4. Presidential Medal of Freedom awarded for first time to musicians; cellist Pablo Casals and pianist Rudolf Serkin honored.

Los Angeles, Oct. 6. Los Angeles Dodgers sweep World Series over New York Yankees.

Chicago, Dec. 4. Black Muslim leader Malcolm X censured by Islamic leaders for his reference to Kennedy's assassination as a case of "the chickens coming home to roost" (→ Feb. 21, 1965).

New York City, Dec. 24 Idlewild Airport renamed John F. Kennedy International Airport.

Chicago, Dec. 29. New York Giants lose National Football League championship, 14-10, to Chicago Bears.

Washington, D.C. Illegitimate births among American teenagers up 150 percent since 1940.

New York City. *The Fire Next Time,* by James Baldwin, published.

Integration in Alabama

Governor George Wallace confronts Deputy Attorney General Nicholas Katzenbach at "the schoolhouse door" of the University of Alabama.

Birmingham, Ala., June 11

Alabama Governor George Wallace vowed he would "stand in the schoolhouse door" to block integration. He did so today, but was brushed aside as National Guardsmen under federal orders escorted two Negro students, Vivian Malone and James Hood, into the University of Alabama's Foster Auditorium to register for classes.

The victory is the first for the Kennedy administration in its continuing struggle with Wallace. Attorney General Robert Kennedy met with the Governor in April, attempting to reach a peaceful resolution. He left in frustration, Wallace still vowing to defy federal integration orders. "It's like a foreign country," Kennedy complained. "There's no communication."

The struggle in Alabama is still far from its conclusion. Wallace insists he will continue to challenge the constitutionality of federal "interference" in the affairs of his state (→ 12).

King out of jail; protesters score gains

Birmingham, Ala., May 13

A relative calm has settled here after weeks of racial protest and violence. Federal troops are quartered at Fort McClellan, just 30 miles away. President Kennedy sent troops in after bombs exploded at the motel of the Rev. Martin Luther King Jr. and at the home of his brother. Rioting broke out after the bombing. Birmingham business leaders announced last week that they will desegregate lunch counters and hire Negroes for clerical and sales jobs. Dr. King told a crowd at a rally, "These things would not have been granted without your presenting your bodies and your very lives before the dogs and the tanks and the water hoses of this city!" Millions across the nation watched on television May 3 as officers directed by Birmingham public safety director Eugene "Bull" Connor turned fire hoses and snarling police dogs on children who were demonstrating.

Dr. King was jailed April 12 and, while held, wrote a 20-page message to clergymen. Called *Letter From the Birmingham Jail*, it explained his thoughts on civil disobedience: "I submit that an individual who breaks a law that conscience tells him is unjust, and who willingly accepts the penalty of imprisonment in order to arouse the conscience of the community over its injustice, is in reality expressing the highest respect for law" (→ June 11).

President requests $14 billion tax cut

Washington, D.C., Jan. 24

President Kennedy presented a tax bill to Congress today that would cut personal and business taxes by nearly $14 billion over the next three years. The bill is designed to stimulate the economy by giving the biggest breaks to low-income groups and small businesses. By 1965, the measure would reduce personal income taxes by 6 to 26 percent; corporate taxes and taxes withheld from paychecks would each drop 5 percent. On the other hand, the bill will not allow certain "loopholes" such as untaxed profits on stock option trades and deductions for minor casualties.

129 entombed as submarine sinks

Boston, Apr. 10

The nuclear submarine Thresher with 129 men aboard was lost today in stormy waters 220 miles east of Boston. The Thresher submerged at 9 a.m. in a test dive designed to reach its maximum depth of more than 1,400 feet. It never resurfaced. Searchers found an oil slick in the area of the dive, where the Atlantic is 8,400 feet deep. Admiral George Anderson, chief of naval operations, said the navy had no good theory to explain the disaster.

Birmingham, September 10. *Negro students Floyd and Dwight Armstrong enter an elementary school as integration proceeds.*

Evers of N.A.A.C.P. slain in Mississippi

Jackson, Mississippi, June 12

Medgar Evers was working late, but he called his wife, Myrlie, three times, each time saying, "I want you to know I love you." Just after midnight, a car door slammed and a shot rang out. Evers had been shot. He died soon after. A field aide in the National Association for the Advancement of Colored People, Evers was called "Mississippi's Martin Luther King." At a rally June 7, he said he would gladly die to make a better life for his family. [Byron de la Beckworth, a Greenwood, Mississippi, white, was tried twice for Evers's murder. Each trial ended in a hung jury] (→ 19).

California passes N.Y. in population

California, Autumn

There are more people in the state of Big Sur than in the state of the Big Apple. The official count is not complete, but population experts say California has surpassed New York as the nation's most populous state. At mid-year, New York had 17,708,000 and California had 17,590,000. But the traditional late summer migration to the West has put California ahead, and with the state's tendency to breed odd life styles, many feel, way out.

JFK: No "colored" signs on foxholes

Washington, D.C., June 19

While speaking to help the passage of his new equal rights bill, President Kennedy noted, "No one has been barred on account of his race from fighting or dying for America; there are no 'white' or 'colored' signs on the foxholes or graveyards of battle." Kennedy's bill, sent to Congress on the day of the funeral of Medgar Evers, a Negro leader who was shot to death, would guarantee equal rights in public facilities and give the attorney general power to sue for enforcement of the 14th and 15th Amendments. Kennedy holds that segregation is immoral (→ Aug. 18).

Kennedy at Berlin Wall

JFK at the Berlin Wall, near the Brandenburg Gate, where East meets West.

West Berlin, Germany, June 26

"All free men, wherever they may live, are citizens of Berlin. And therefore, as a free man, I take pride in the words, 'Ich bin ein Berliner'" ("I am a Berliner").

With this rousing declaration, President Kennedy today won thunderous applause from a crowd of about 150,000 West Berliners packed into the plaza facing the Rathaus, or city hall. Among those standing with the President on the balcony, which was draped with an enormous American flag, was West Berlin's popular mayor, Willy Brandt.

The President, who is on a 10-day visit to Europe, also took a look at the Berlin Wall as he visited Checkpoint Charlie. Although the wall has certainly succeeded in stemming the exodus of East Germans, who until two years ago were voting with their feet for freedom and prosperity, it has also served as a symbol to the rest of the world of Communist repression.

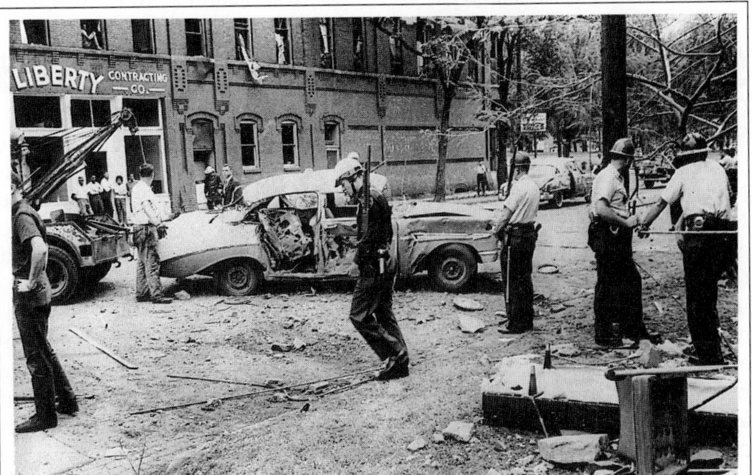

Birmingham, Alabama, September 15. *Police examine the wreckage left by a bomb that exploded at the 16th Street Baptist Church. Segregationists have gone beyond individual lynchings to widespread threats and murder in an effort to stop integration. In this case, four Negro children were killed and 17 were injured while they were attending Sunday school.*

Big powers agree to curb nuclear testing

Washington, D.C., Oct. 10

The Limited Nuclear Test Ban Treaty, which has been ratified by the Senate, signed by President Kennedy and agreed to by the Soviet Union and Britain, goes into effect today. Although only a modest step toward disarmament or even arms control, it constitutes an important victory for environmentalists: by allowing only underground testing, it will go far to curb the radioactive fallout that results from above-ground detonations. Many countries are expected to sign the treaty, with the notable exceptions of France and China (→ June 1, 1972).

Meredith graduates with class of whites

Oxford, Mississippi, Aug. 18

James Meredith, the first Negro to attend the University of Mississippi, became its first Negro graduate today. Mississippi Governor Ross Barnett tried to block Meredith's degree, but the state college board overruled him. The campus, where a riot erupted the day Meredith arrived to register in 1962, was quiet. Among those who looked on as Meredith was presented with his diploma was his father, "Cap" Meredith, the son of a slave (→ 28).

Newport sensation: a kid named Dylan

Newport, R.I., July 28

Some 47,000 fans of the booming East Coast folk music scene flocked here this weekend for a festival of tunes from Pete Seeger, Joan Baez, and Peter, Paul and Mary. Most hadn't bargained for a performance with the power to change lives. But Bob Dylan, a 22-year-old songwriter with the tattered appearance and social conscience of Woody Guthrie, the lyricism of Rimbaud and the defiance of James Dean, simply mesmerized the crowd with works like *Hard Rain*, *Talkin' John Birch Society Blues* and *Blowin' in the Wind*, an anti-war song that is stirring a generation.

King to 200,000: "I have a dream"

The Rev. Dr. Martin Luther King Jr. waves to thousands of his followers.

Washington, D.C., Aug. 28

In the largest civil rights demonstration ever, more than 200,000 non-violent protesters gathered at the foot of the Lincoln Memorial today to hear Dr. Martin Luther King Jr., president of the Southern Christian Leadership Conference, describe his vision of the future of race relations in the United States. "I still have a dream," Dr. King told the rapt audience. "It is a dream chiefly rooted in the American Dream. I have a dream that one day this nation will rise up and live out the true meaning of its creed: 'We hold these truths to be self-evident, that all men are created equal'." As the crowd cheered each repetition of his refrain, "I have a dream," King described a land where whites and Negroes would be brothers, and where his people would be "free at last, free at last, thank God Almighty, free at last."

Also at the rally to help speed the passage of civil rights legislation, were the folksingers Bob Dylan, Joan Baez and Peter, Paul and Mary, the legendary singer-dancer Josephine Baker and the baseball great, Jackie Robinson. The day also gave the Negro leaders a chance to meet President Kennedy.

King's speech turned the tone of the event from a party into a crusade. But though his words moved the hearts of a nation, it remains to be seen whether Congress will be moved to action (→ May 26, 1964).

U.S. gets hot line to Soviet Union

Washington, D.C., Aug. 30

With a simple exchange of routine test signals, the so-called "hot line" between the White House and the Kremlin has been put into service. The need for a direct link that can be used in the event of emergencies such as an accidental nuclear firing emerged during the Cuban missile crisis last year, when there were dangerous snags in communication between the Soviet and American governments. The system will use both a wire telegraph service and a radio telegraph service. For security reasons all messages will be encoded. The sender will use his own language for the messages, which will be sent and received by bilingual teleprinters at either end.

Art going pop

New York City

The Solomon R. Guggenheim Museum succumbed to pop art's appeal this year by staging a pop show of its own. Claes Oldenburg's soft sculptures, Andy Warhol's silk-screened portraits and the comic-strip canvases of Roy Lichtenstein have all angles covered: they satirize, laud and echo American values. Lichtenstein finds most modern fine art "despicable" and says that many artists could get away with "hanging a wet paint rag."

Friedan: Housewife isn't happy at all

United States

Mrs. Betty Friedan, a 42-year-old psychologist and housewife, has published *The Feminine Mystique,* a book that takes the boredom of housewives very seriously. After research and in-depth interviews, Friedan has concluded that women are unfulfilled and must develop their identities. She blames such forces as Freud, Margaret Mead and Madison Avenue for fooling women into thinking that cooking and cleaning should be satisfying enough. Her solution? A *New Life Plan for Women* that emphasizes work outside the home.

South Vietnamese Premier is assassinated as conflict worsens

Saigon, South Vietnam, Nov. 2

The South Vietnamese Premier, Ngo Dinh Diem, and his brother Nhu were murdered today by a group of military leaders headed by General Duong Van Minh. Trying to escape from the royal palace after Minh's coup d'etat, they were arrested and placed in an armored personnel carrier, where they were killed. Diem has been described by his detractors as an insufferable autocrat and a tyrant – but he was a fierce anti-Communist. A skilled leader, he had nevertheless alienated the Buddhists, the intellectuals and South Vietnam's urban middle class with his blatant corruption and oppression. Because Ambassador Henry Cabot Lodge and senior aides felt the war could not be won under a Diem regime, they were said to have encouraged Minh to plot his overthrow, probably with the administration's knowledge.

Meantime, more American soldiers are dying in the growing Indochinese conflict. In January, five American helicopters were downed and three crewmen killed. Dozens of G.I.'s have been killed this year.

Diem's murder has complicated the American position in South Vietnam. President Kennedy said the United States could play only a supporting role to Diem in what he felt would be a farce if it were not such a tragedy (→ Aug. 7, 1964).

A Buddhist monk who opposes the regime protests by self-immolation.

President Kennedy is slain by assassin in Dallas

Dallas, Texas, Nov. 22

President John F. Kennedy was killed today when a sniper fired three rifle shots at the presidential motorcade as it drove along Elm Street in downtown Dallas. Texas Governor John B. Connally, who rode in the President's car with his wife and Mrs. Kennedy, was seriously wounded in the attack. The Governor is at Parkland Memorial Hospital, where he is listed in serious condition. Mrs. Kennedy and Mrs. Connally were not wounded.

While the nation was still in shock at the loss of its elegant, dynamic and popular young President, the momentum of the government continued. Just 98 minutes after the death of President Kennedy, Lyndon Baines Johnson, the 55-year-old Vice President who had been in the motorcade several cars behind the President, took the 34-word oath of office aboard Air Force One and became the 36th President of the United States. Jacqueline Kennedy stood beside Johnson while he took the oath, her stockings and shocking pink skirt still spattered with her late husband's blood. She had just arrived in the hearse that carried Kennedy's casket to the plane to be taken to Washington for burial.

A few hours after the shooting, the Dallas police arrested Lee Harvey Oswald and later charged him with the murder. Oswald, 24, is a former marine who became a Soviet citizen in 1959 before returning to the United States in 1962. He was active in the Fair Play for Cuba Committee. He is believed to have fired at least three rifle shots at the President from the sixth floor of the Texas School Book Depository, where he had been employed as a clerk.

The shooting occurred at 12:35 p.m. just as the 12-car motorcade was nearing the end of its 10-mile tour and passing the textbook warehouse. As the shots rang out, the crowds scattered, people fell to the ground or ran for cover and some screamed and wept after the President took a lethal bullet in the back of his head. The first bullet to strike the 46-year-old President had hit him in the back below his collar bone.

"Oh no! Oh no!" Jacqueline Kennedy cried over and over, cradling his head in her lap as the limousine raced to the Parkland Memorial Hospital three miles away. At 1 p.m., John F. Kennedy, America's youngest elected President, was pronounced dead, a victim of what he had called a "dangerous and untidy world." At 2:41 p.m., Air Force One took off from Love Field carrying a new President and Kennedy's body home (→24).

President and Mrs. Kennedy join Texas Governor John B. Connally in a limousine for the ride to the Merchandise Mart. The day was so beautiful that the President had asked that the car's protective bubble be removed.

Oswald shot down as TV cameras roll

Dallas, Texas, November 24

Lee Harvey Oswald, the man accused of killing President Kennedy two days ago, was shot dead today in the basement of a jail as he was being moved to a tighter security prison. Jack Ruby, a Dallas nightclub owner, fired a revolver at point-blank range into Oswald's stomach. He died instantly, in view of 50 reporters, Oswald's police escort and millions of TV viewers. Oswald died without confessing to Kennedy's murder. There has been speculation that Ruby killed Oswald to keep him from testifying, but the vengeance motive is held more likely. Ruby could get the death penalty (→25).

Kennedy is buried and nation grieves

Washington, D.C., Nov. 25

President John F. Kennedy was buried today with full military honors in Arlington National Cemetery. A million mourners lined the streets of Washington and millions all over the world attended the ceremony through radio and television. Following the flag-draped casket drawn by six gray horses were 92 foreign leaders and the Kennedy family. The procession moved from the Capitol rotunda to the White House and then on to St. Matthew's Roman Catholic Cathedral for a short requiem mass before the burial at Arlington. His widow, Jacqueline Kennedy, lit the eternal flame at his grave (→Sept. 27, 1964).

John F. Kennedy Jr. snaps a salute as his father's casket passes. The boy's calm demeanor, the beauty of his innocence, touches his family and the entire nation as they mourn the President's loss. It was John-John's third birthday.

1964

Johnson

Washington, D.C., Jan. 17. Panama breaks diplomatic ties with United States (→Apr. 4).

California, Jan. 25. Echo 2, first American-Soviet communications satellite, launched, to relay radio signals worldwide (→July 31).

Washington, D.C., Feb. 29. President Johnson announces that Lockheed Corporation has produced a jet capable of speeds greater than 2,000 mph.

Washington, D.C., Apr. 4. United States concludes agreement with Panama, resuming diplomatic relations and negotiating settlement of grievances.

Boston, Apr. 26. Celtics beat San Francisco Warriors four games to one, for N.B.A. title.

Baltimore, Maryland, May 21. Baltimore Lighthouse becomes world's first nuclear-powered lighthouse.

Prince Edward Island, Virginia, May 26. Supreme Court rules county public schools, shut to avoid integration, must reopen and integrate (→July 3).

Alaska, May 27. "Good Friday Quake" strikes; 114 killed.

New Orleans, Louisiana, May 30. After 133 years, last streetcar runs on Canal Street.

Cape Canaveral, Florida, July 31. About 4,000 photographs of lunar surface received from Ranger 7 before it crashes on moon (→March 23, 1965).

Washington, D.C., Sept. 14. Theologian Reinhold Niebuhr receives Medal of Freedom.

Newport, Rhode Island, Sept. 21. Yacht Constellation successful in defense of America's Cup against British challenger Sovereign.

St., Louis, Oct. 15. Cardinals top Yankees, four games to three, in World Series.

New York City, Nov. 21. Verrazano-Narrows Bridge, world's longest suspension bridge, officially opens.

Cleveland, Dec. 27. Browns defeat Baltimore Colts, 27-0, for N.F.L. title.

Philadelphia. Kennedy half-dollar issued.

DEATH

Washington, D.C., Apr. 5. Douglas MacArthur, General of the Army (*Jan. 26, 1880).

Beatles invade America

John Lennon takes the lead as Britain's "Fab Four" rock 'n' roll America.

New York City, Feb. 10

"It's B-Day! It's 6:30 a.m.! The Beatles left London 30 minutes ago! Heading for New York!" It was all the kids awakening to transistor radios on February 7 needed, as thousands besieged Kennedy Airport to offer the Liverpool quartet a shrieking, frenzied welcome to America.

The Beatles – John Lennon, 23, Paul McCartney, 21, George Harrison, 21, and Ringo Starr, 23 – shaped their music and shaggy haircuts playing in rowdy Hamburg clubs. Returning to England, the prolific Lennon-McCartney writing team started churning out hits last year. They've sold six million records, and *I Want to Hold Your Hand* is now No. 1 here.

Pandemonium has followed the group everywhere this weekend, as obsessed fans even mobbed a befuddled cop, shouting "He touched a Beatle!" But if anyone doubted Beatlemania's impact, last night the group captured a record TV audience of 73 million on the Ed Sullivan Show, singing over the hysterical squeals of their fans. Said Ringo: "So this is America. They all seem out of their minds."

LBJ fights poverty; seeks $962 million

Washington, D.C., March 16

President Johnson sent a request to Congress today for $962 million to fight poverty. LBJ has given the destitute a high place on his presidential agenda. In his January State of the Union address, he lamented, "Unfortunately, many Americans live on the outskirts of hope – some because of their poverty, and some because of their color, and all too many because of both." He also said the administration is "declaring unconditional war against poverty." Congress is expected to approve the request. Johnson, a former majority leader of the Senate, is a great persuader among his old colleagues. He is also passionate about helping the poor, drawing from Michael Harrington's 1962 book on social injustice, *The Other America* (→Jan. 4, 1965).

"Times a changin'"

New York City, February

"Be-bop-a-lu-la, she's my baby" may have been poetry enough for an earlier generation of music fans, but as Bob Dylan sings on his new album, *The Times They Are a Changin'*. The enigmatic songwriter hitchhiked from Hibbing, Minnesota, to Greenwich Village two years ago and took the folk world by storm, giving a new depth to popular music with lyrics on social injustice and the horrors of war.

Surgeon General: Cigarettes cause cancer

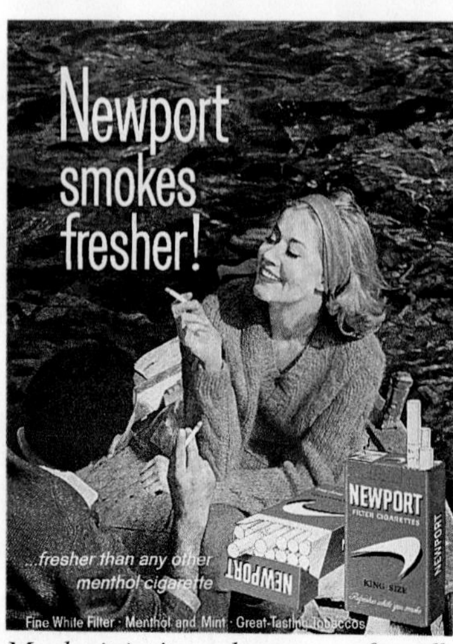

Maybe it isn't so glamorous after all.

Washington, D.C., Jan. 11

An expert committee appointed by the Surgeon General today declared cigarette smoking a "health hazard of sufficient importance to the United States to require remedial action." In a 150,000-word report, the 10-member panel said cigarettes are the leading cause of lung cancer and bronchitis and are involved in other forms of cancer, heart disease, ulcers and other diseases. Surgeon General Luther L. Terry called the report "the most comprehensive ... analysis ever undertaken" of the smoking-health controversy and said he would advise all smokers to stop.

Clay defeats Liston

Miami Beach, Fla., Feb. 25

Cassius Marcellus Clay is the new heavyweight champion of the world. Against all odds, he demolished the gargantuan Sonny Liston tonight with a seventh-round technical knockout. Some experts even wanted the fight called off because Liston might hurt "little" Cassius permanently. Instead, Clay buzzed Liston for three rounds and Sonny was so befuddled that he missed and missed again. This made him tired and angry. Some coagulant put on Liston's eye rubbed off on Clay in the fourth and blinded him, but Liston didn't follow up. He couldn't come out for the eighth.

Civil Rights Act passed

President Lyndon Johnson hands out pens used during the signing of the landmark Civil Rights Act. Attorney General Robert Kennedy (center) and the President appear to have put aside their personal differences for the day.

Washington, D.C., July 3

Providing many new measures and agencies to combat inequities based on race, sex, color, religion or national origin, the Civil Rights Act passed by Congress was signed into law today by President Johnson. He, as well as President Kennedy before him, lobbied intensively for the bill, which prohibits racial discrimination in public accommodations, employment, unions and federally funded programs. Passage of the bill required the Senate to impose cloture for the first time on a civil rights bill, to end a filibuster by Southern senators. The bill is the most sweeping civil rights legislation in American history and, as President Johnson said in a television address, it may help to "eliminate the last vestiges of injustice in America." The act will be of great benefit, it is hoped, to the country's 22 million Negroes.

President Johnson said he signed the legislation to "close the springs of racial poison." The measure codifies President Kennedy's policy of treating discrimination as a moral evil (→ July).

Race riots hit New York

Negro rioters flee from advancing policemen during the chaos that has gripped Harlem. The death of a Negro youth at the hands of an officer has released a sense of anger and frustration that is prevalent in most inner-city ghettos.

New York City, July

Riots in the state of New York have led to over 1,000 arrests, six deaths and the wounding of hundreds. Earlier this month, the first of the riots began when an off-duty police officer killed a 15-year-old Negro boy in Harlem. Negroes attacked police and white-owned stores with fire bombs. One person was killed, at least 140 injured and 500 arrests were made. The rioting spread from Harlem to predominantly Negro areas of Brooklyn, and raged for several days.

A similar riot exploded in Rochester on July 24 when police arrested a Negro man for allegedy molesting a Negro woman at a dance. It was rumored that the man was abused by police during the arrest. Five people died in the violence and 750 were arrested for looting, possession of illegal weapons and rioting. About 75 percent of those arrested were Negro. To restore order, the National Guard was called out by Governor Nelson Rockefeller. These riots constitute the first serious racially motivated mob violence in a Northern state since the 1940s (→ Aug. 4).

24th Amendment outlaws poll taxes

Washington, D.C., Jan. 23

The use of poll taxes in federal elections, a controversial symbol of racial discrimination in the South, became unconstitutional with the ratification of the 24th Amendment today. President Johnson called the act a "triumph of liberty over restriction." Five Southern states still require voting fees. Texas and Virginia have already set up a two-tiered registration that will preserve the poll tax in state and local elections. Ironically, the tax began as a democratic advance, replacing restrictive property qualifications.

Court rules malice is key in libel case

Washington, D.C., March 9

The Supreme Court today overturned a $500,000 judgment against *The New York Times* by an Alabama court in the case of The New York Times Co. v. Sullivan. Protecting freedom of speech, the high court ruled that in order for a government official to collect damages for libel against a publisher, the official must prove that the publisher showed "actual malice." *The Times* was sued by Montgomery city commissioner L.B. Sullivan for having printed an advertisement about racism in Alabama.

Hoffa found guilty of fraud, conspiracy

Chicago, July 24

For the second time in a year, James Hoffa, chief of the Teamsters union, has been convicted of serious crimes. Today, a federal jury found Hoffa guilty of mail fraud and conspiracy to abuse the union's pension fund. In March, a Tennessee jury convicted him of attempting to bribe a previous jury in a case that ended in mistrial. Tennessee Judge Frank Wilson told Hoffa, "You stand here convicted of seeking to corrupt the administration of justice . . . of having tampered with the very soul of this nation."

Congress irate at Tonkin Gulf attack

Washington, D.C., Aug. 7

After reports of two North Vietnamese attacks on American destroyers earlier this week in the Gulf of Tonkin, Congress has overwhelmingly backed President Johnson's request for broad emergency powers. By a unanimous vote in the House of Representatives and an 88 to 2 vote in the Senate, the Southeast Asia Resolution (which some legislators call the Gulf of Tonkin Resolution) has become law. The resolution, vaguely worded, says Johnson has full congressional authority "to take all necessary measures to repel any armed attack against the forces of the United States and to prevent further aggression." Thus Congress gave him virtually every power he needs to deal with this growing conflict – except a formal declaration of war.

American ships and aircraft carriers at sea. The reported attack by North Vietnamese vessels in the Gulf of Tonkin has led to firm U.S. retaliation.

The Gulf of Tonkin crisis erupted on August 2 when the navy destroyer Maddox reported having been attacked by North Vietnamese torpedo boats. The Maddox said it returned fire and called in fighter planes from the carrier Ticonderoga. The Americans sank two of the three boats and damaged the other. Two days later, the navy said, Communist boats attacked the Maddox and the destroyer Turner Joy, both in international waters. In response to the second attack, which Washington said was unprovoked, the President ordered a retaliatory attack by navy fighter-bombers on the North Vietnamese oil tanks and torpedo boat bases at Vinh. The next day, the President justified the attack, saying, "Aggression unchallenged is aggression unleashed."

After Johnson announced the strike at Vinh, he met with 18 congressional leaders from both parties seeking a statement of support for his overall policy in Southeast Asia. And he got it. Senator Frank Church said it was time to "rally 'round" the flag. And Senator Barry Goldwater warned, "We cannot allow the American flag to be shot at anywhere on earth if we are to retain our respect and prestige."

Senator Wayne Morse opposed the resolution, questioning both its purpose and the wisdom of open-ended commitments. Others doubted there had ever been an attack on the destroyers, and accused the President of over-reacting or seeking a pretext to expand his own powers (→ Nov. 1).

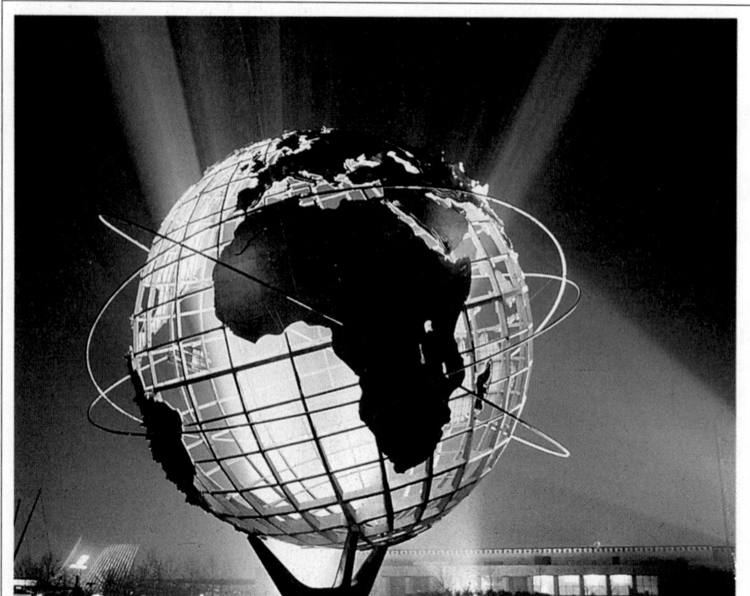

At the first New York World's Fair since 1940, which opened April 22, visitors view exhibits emphasizing "peace through understanding."

Reagan makes plea for Barry Goldwater

Sacramento, Calif., October

Governor Ronald Reagan of California is doing all he can to elect fellow conservative Barry M. Goldwater to the White House. Reagan made a televised speech this month, exalting the G.O.P. nominee's political savvy, intelligence, toughness and experience. Reagan has become a popular leader in the West, where Goldwater must win if he is to have a chance in the election. The plea should help bridge the gap in recent polls that show President Johnson leading Goldwater, who was nominated in July after a speech in which he said, "Extremism in the defense of liberty is no vice . . ." (→ Nov. 3).

F.B.I. finds bodies of 3 rights workers

Philadelphia, Mississippi, Aug. 4

The bodies of three civil rights workers, James Chaney, Andrew Goodman and Michael Schwerner, were discovered buried in an earthen dam near Philadelphia today. F.B.I. agents reportedly got a tip on the location. The three had been missing since June 21, when they were accused of speeding and taken to the Neshoba County jail. They had driven to Philadelphia to investigate the burning of a Negro church. Chaney, a Negro, was from nearby Meridian. Schwerner and Goodman were New Yorkers who had come to Mississippi for the summer to help register Negro voters. Fingers have been pointed at the county sheriff's office, but no arrests have been made yet (→ Dec. 10).

Mass in English

St. Louis, Mo., Aug. 24

This evening the Rev. Frederick R. McManus of Catholic University performed the Roman Catholic Mass in English for the first time ever. The event, part of the 25th anniversary meeting of the Liturgical Conference, is a result of the modernizing of the Roman Catholic Church at the Second Vatican Council. This English version was adopted by the American bishops last April, and next month the bishops will decide when to put it into general use in this country.

"William James, The Varieties of Religious Experience" by Boty.

ohnson retains presidency with landslide

Lyndon Johnson in the Oval Office.

Washington, D.C., Nov. 3

Lyndon Baines Johnson defeated Republican challenger Barry M. Goldwater by a lopsided margin in today's presidential election. Johnson called the victory for himself and his running mate Hubert Humphrey "a mandate for unity."

Political experts disagreed about whether the election is a "mandate." But it is clear that voters rejected Goldwater's conservatism, particularly on racial integration. In the campaign he said, "There's a freedom to associate and there's a freedom not to associate." Johnson used remarks like this to paint Goldwater in the colors of the radical right, saying, "Extremism in the pursuit of the presidency is an unpardonable vice." He also depicted the G.O.P. as nuclear hawks and the Democrats as peacekeepers: "There is no such thing as a conventional nuclear war." Democrats held on to both houses of Congress. And Robert Kennedy was elected a senator from New York.

Warren report says Oswald acted alone

Washington, D.C., Sept. 27

The Warren Commission investigating the assassination of President John F. Kennedy has found that Lee Harvey Oswald, the accused assassin, acted alone. The report states it did not find evidence of a conspiracy in the November 22 shooting. The commission, headed by Chief Justice Earl Warren, further states that Oswald fired three shots from the easternmost window on the sixth floor of the Texas School Book Depository building on Elm Street. The report also recommends that killing of a president or vice president be made a federal crime. The report reprimanded the F.B.I. for having failed to alert the Secret Service that Oswald was in the region during President Kennedy's visit.

Rebels hit air base of U.S. at Bien Hoa

Saigon, South Vietnam, Nov. 1

Vietcong guerrillas attacked the United States Air Force base at Bien Hoa today, killing four American servicemen and wounding 12. Five planes were destroyed and many were heavily damaged. According to officials at the base, the Communists launched a heavy mortar barrage. Then, as the shellfire lifted, enemy demolition units cut through the perimeter wire, exchanged fire with the American defenders and tossed explosive charges at the planes parked there. The base, which is about 10 miles northeast of Saigon, supports various types of combat aircraft, including the versatile B-57 Canberra light bombers that are used for ground support as well as aerial reconnaissance missions (→Feb. 7, 1965).

Olympics in Japan

Tokyo, Oct. 24

Don Schollander captured four swimming gold medals and American track stars swept 10 of 24 events in the Olympic Games that wound up today. Schollander set world records in the 100-meter and 400-meter free-style races and added gold medals in two relays. For the first time, an American won the 10,000 meters, Billy Mills breaking the Olympic record by cutting 50 seconds off his own best time. Bob Hayes tied the world mark of 10 seconds in the 100-meter sprint.

Protest at Berkeley

Berkeley, Calif., Nov. 12

The campus has been in turmoil since the University of California banned political activities here. The ban caused a 32-hour sit-in October 1 and 2 and unrest continues. President Clark Kerr says he will not allow "intimidation to replace reason" as the standard for school policy and denies the university is trying to prevent student participation in the civil rights movement. Led by Mario Savio, students have formed a Free Speech Movement to guard their constitutional rights.

King receives Nobel

Oslo, Norway, Dec. 10

The Rev. Martin Luther King Jr., who brought the concepts of non-violence to the American civil rights movement, won the Nobel Peace Prize today. He is, at 35, the youngest recipient of the award. The Baptist preacher first came to national attention when he led bus boycotts in Montgomery, Alabama. He later headed the Southern Christian Leadership Conference, a group that teaches the techniques of non-violent protest to civil rights activists (→Jan. 11, 1965).

"Dr. Strangelove"

Hollywood, California

The best movie around is *Dr. Strangelove or: How I Learned to Stop Worrying and Love the Bomb*, a black comedy on atomic annihilation with Peter Sellers and George Scott, followed by Julie Andrews's film debut in *Mary Poppins*; James Garner and Julie Andrews in *The Americanization of Emily*; a scary *Hush . . . Hush Sweet Charlotte* with Bette Davis and Olivia De Havilland; the Beatles romp, *A Hard Day's Night* and *The Pink Panther* with Peter Sellers and David Niven.

LBJ shows off his cattle-herding abilities during a luncheon with the press. The Texan has always retained close ties to the land of his birth.

October 25. *Another band out of Britain. The Rolling Stones, led by Mick Jagger (left), are introduced to Americans on "The Ed Sullivan Show."*

1965

Johnson

Arizona, Jan. 8. Lorna Elizabeth Lockwood is first woman named chief justice of a state supreme court.

New Orleans, Jan. 11. Negro players boycott American Football League's all-star game to protest racial bias in New Orleans (→ March 25).

Pleiku, Vietnam, Feb. 7. U.S. military advisers' compound struck; eight Americans die (→ March 17).

Cape Kennedy, Florida, March 23. Gemini III launched, orbiting Earth three times and splashing down in Atlantic (→ Apr. 6).

Cape Kennedy, Apr. 6. National Aeronautics and Space Administration launches first commercial satellite, Early Bird, designed to relay telephone and television signals (→ June 3).

Midwest, Apr. 11. Tornadoes strike seven states, killing 271 people and injuring 5,000.

Boston, April. Celtics defeat Los Angeles Lakers, four games to one, in N.B.A. championship.

Washington, D.C., June 7. Supreme Court rules that televised coverage of criminal trials violates due process.

Washington, D.C., Aug. 8. Congress passes Omnibus Housing Act, providing new funds for low-income housing.

Minnesota, Oct. 14. Los Angeles Dodgers defeat Minnesota Twins, four games to three, in World Series.

St. Louis, Oct. 28. World's tallest monument, 630-foot Gateway Arch designed by Eero Saarinen, completed.

East Coast, Nov. 10. Power restored following greatest electrical failure in history, which blacked out seven states and Ontario for two days.

Atlanta, Dec. 8. Delta Airlines puts first DC-9 jet into service.

Space, Dec. 16. Walter Schirra and Thomas Stafford, aboard Gemini 6, achieve first rendezvous of manned orbiting spacecraft when they maneuver within one foot of Gemini 7.

Berkeley, California. Term "Flower Power" coined by Allen Ginsberg, at anti-war rally.

Hollywood, Calif. Top films this year include *Dr. Zhivago*, *The Sound of Music*, *Help* and *The Pawnbroker*.

U.S. goes on the offensive in Vietnam

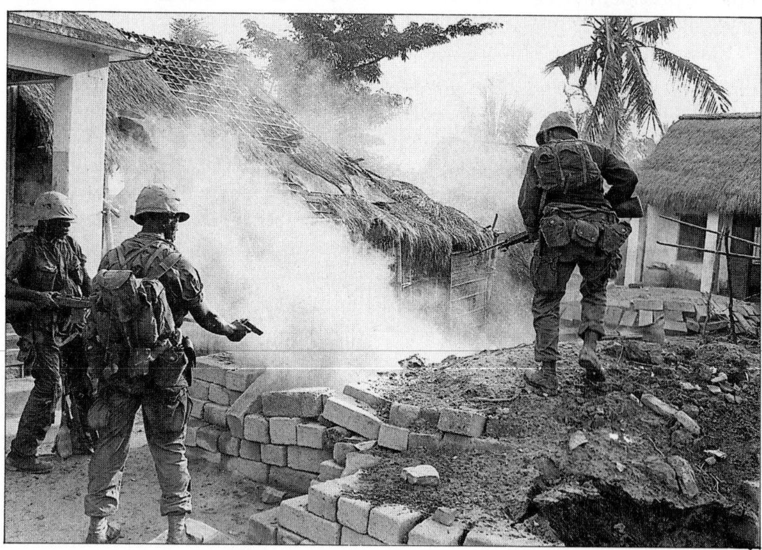

American marines patrol in a village suspected of harboring Vietcong soldiers.

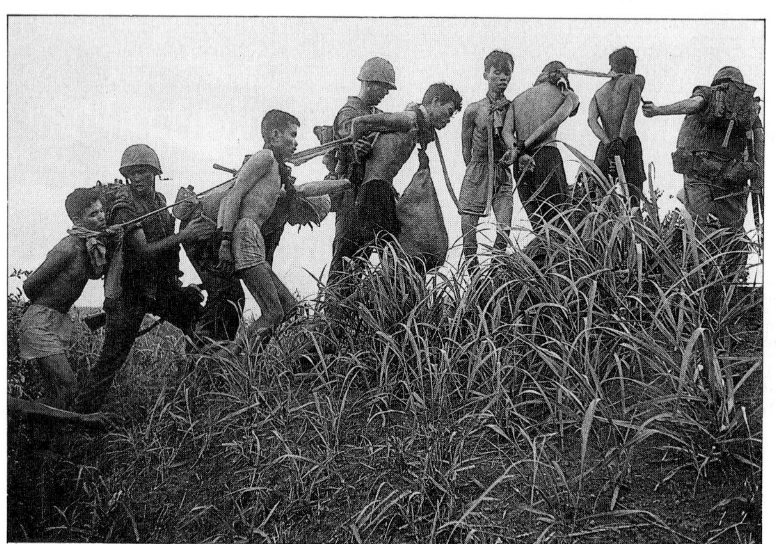

Captured Vietcong guerrillas, tethered to one another, are marched away.

Vietnam, December

When the history of the Vietnam War is written, 1965 will be remembered as the year the United States went from an advisory to a combat role and from a defensive strategy to a full-blown offensive one.

After American bases at Pleiku and Quinhon were attacked in February with significant casualties, President Johnson dramatically escalated the role of the air force. On February 13, he ordered the air force and navy to commence Operation Rolling Thunder, a vast bombing campaign directed against military targets in North Vietnam. He began a dramatic buildup of combat personnel in March when the first two battalions of marines landed at Danang. American troop strength at the end of 1964 was 23,000; it is now over 154,000.

By last August, the United States had begun regularly engaging the enemy in battalion-sized offensives. On August 21, marines destroyed a huge Vietcong force in Quangngai Province during Operation Star Light. By late November, the First Cavalry had sought out and soundly defeated thousands of enemy soldiers who gathered at Iadrang in the Central Highlands to cut South Vietnam in half. Although the troops of the cavalry achieved a decisive victory, both sides suffered tremendous casualties. The total of American combat deaths this year has passed the 1,500 mark (→ March 1966).

President Johnson pledges Great Society

Washington, D.C., Jan. 4

President Johnson outlined his domestic aims tonight in his State of the Union address, calling for the creation of a "Great Society." Although he conceived his program last May, tonight he expanded on it. Like the New Deal and Fair Deal before it, the Great Society is designed to help the politically and economically impoverished. It is founded on the premise that poverty and racial strife beleaguer the whole nation. As he has said, "The Great Society rests on abundance of liberty for all. It demands an end to poverty and racial injustice – to which we are totally committed."

He asked federal support for urban renewal, health care, education and the basic needs of the poor. The President hopes to capitalize on his huge electoral victory and a solid Democratic-controlled Congress to enact voting rights legislation. He appealed to the House and Senate tonight for such enactment. It is expected that by month's end he will also ask Congress to support a health care plan for the elderly and aid to education.

Many political experts believe Johnson has the potential to pass as many of his Great Society proposals as Franklin D. Roosevelt did his New Deal initiatives (→ July 30).

Woman immolates self over Vietnam

Detroit, Mich., March 17

In a ghastly scene more appropriate to a horror movie than day-to-day life, an elderly woman publicly burned herself alive today to protest the growing American involvement in Vietnam. Witnesses described how Mrs. Alice Hertz, aged 72, sat down in the street, doused herself with gasoline, and set fire to her clothes. By the time onlookers put out the flames, Mrs. Hertz was critically burned. She was rushed to a local hospital, where she died. No surviving family members have been found (→ Dec.).

Malcolm X silenced by assassin's bullets

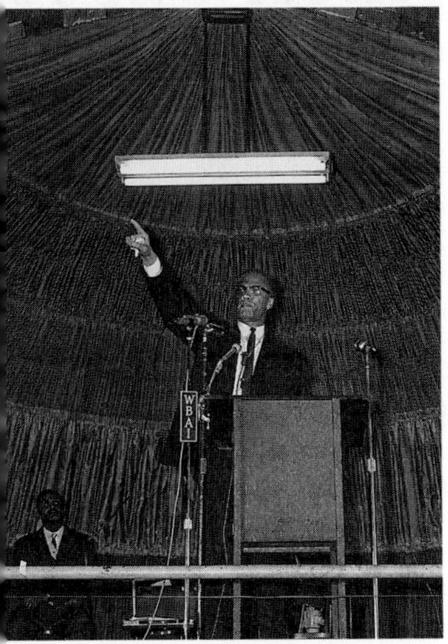

Malcolm X, the fiery Afro-American leader, addressing Muslim folowers shortly before he was assassinated.

New York City, Feb. 21

Black leader Malcolm X is dead today at the age of 39, shot by assassins as he was beginning to address an audience of 400. His death was apparently not caused by the white members of society he so often spoke against, but as the result of quarreling within the Black Muslim movement. Born Malcolm Little, he served 10 years in prison, beginning in 1946. While there, he became a convert to the Black Muslim organization that was led by Elijah Muhammad. Disagreements with Muhammad led Malcolm X to found his own group, the Organization for Afro-American Unity. The two sects continued to feud, ultimately resulting in the assassination.

March to Montgomery

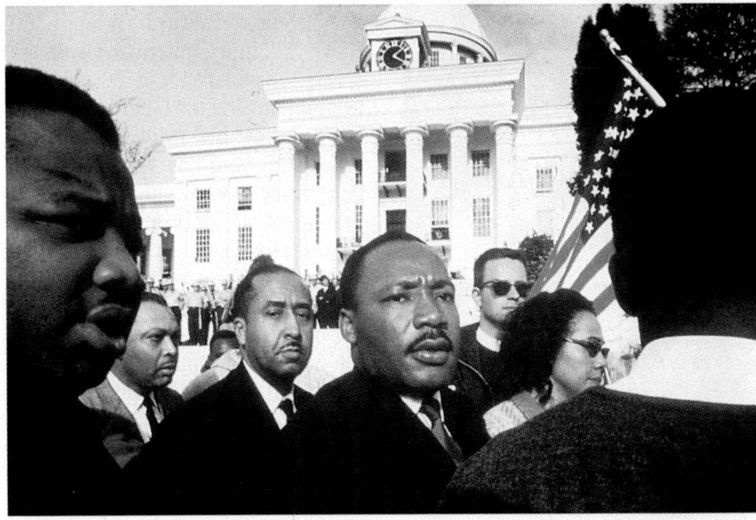

The Rev. Dr. Martin Luther King Jr. and other civil rights leaders at the head of the procession that marched from Selma to Montgomery, Alabama.

Montgomery, Alabama, March 25

Overcoming weeks of violence and intransigence, more than 25,000 people poured into Alabama's capitol today, affirming the right of Negroes to vote. With the protection of federal troops, Negroes accompanied by sympathetic whites marched 54 miles from Selma to the capitol building. The Rev. Dr. Martin Luther King Jr. addressed the crowd from the capitol steps with the flag of the Confederacy waving overhead.

The euphoria of the march soon ended. Viola Liuzzo, wife of a Detroit union official, was killed by whites who attacked her as she took groups of marchers back to Selma. The Selma march has been marked by violence from the beginning. On March 6, state troopers, some on horses, waded into a group of marchers at the Edmund Pettus Bridge near Selma. The sight on the television news of marchers being beaten and trampled has stunned the nation. After another march, a white Unitarian minister, the Rev. James Reeb, was clubbed, and died two days later. In February, Jimmy Lee Jackson, a 26-year-old black demonstrator, was beaten, and died seven days later (→Aug. 6).

Electric Bob booed

Newport, R.I., July 25

Bob Dylan seems determined to follow his own instincts as his music becomes more energized and his lyrics grow personal and imagistic. Tonight, however, he ran headlong into a backlash from folk purists as he took the stage here dressed in flamboyant clothes and armed with an electric guitar and high-wattage back-up band. As hundreds booed, an unperturbed Dylan offered searing versions of *Maggie's Farm* and *Like a Rolling Stone.*

Single life in L.A.

Los Angeles

The mating instinct often drives young people to the big cities in search of the Right One. There they find the usual singles meeting places, bars, clubs, dance halls. But most singles find this scene artificial and unpleasant. A Los Angeles realtor now has a possible solution. He has put up a "Singles Only" apartment project, a natural setting for people to get to know each other, with community rooms, pool, game rooms and planned parties.

Do your own thing, Krishna or Watusi

United States

Good vibes from overseas. The Beatles and James Bond toys were imports, as were the I Ching from the Orient, Krishna Consciousness from India and macrobiotic food. As for home-grown pleasures, there are computer dating, G.I. Joe, Allan and Midge dolls and body painting. Girls in go-go boots and mini paper dresses do the watusi, the frug and the swim. They're groupies or some guy's old lady. Everyone smokes, and if it's tobacco, don't blame Madison Avenue, because the F.T.C. has proposed warning messages on cigarette packs. In fact, don't listen to the bad vibes, just do your own thing!

Liston is flattened in two minutes by a taunting Cassius Clay

Lewiston, Maine, May 25

Cassius Clay knocked out Sonny Liston tonight for the second time as fans cried, "Fake! Fake! Fake!" They would have been even more upset if they had heard a taunting Clay say before the battle that he would win it in one minute 49 seconds of the first. One observer with a stopwatch reported Liston hit the canvas at 1:48 and, except for a timing mix-up, would have been counted out at 1:58. The official time was incorrectly set at a minute. The brash champion threw a short right hand that caught Sonny on the chin. Liston teetered like a huge redwood about to topple in the forest, then fell. He tried to get up, but his glazed eyes signaled his bewilderment. It was all over.

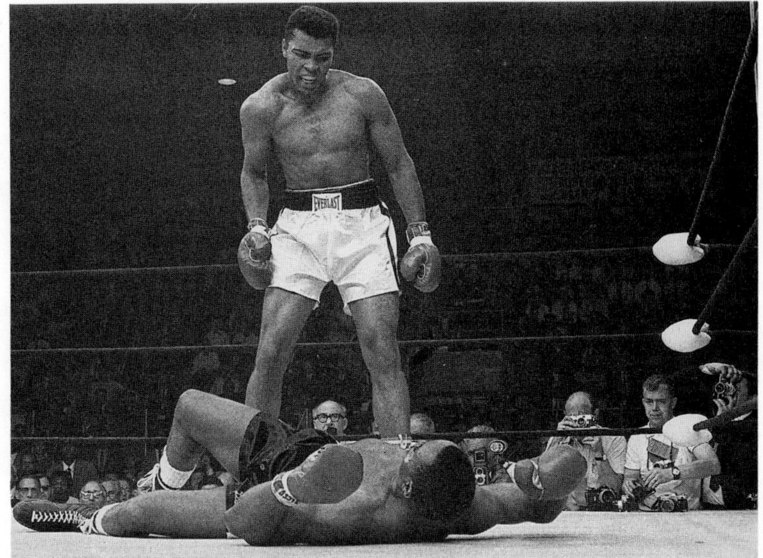

Champ Cassius Clay tells a floored Sonny Liston: "I told you I had a surprise." ▷

American astronaut takes a stroll in space

Edward White performing in space.

Houston, Texas, June 3

Astronaut Edward White 2nd took the first American walk in space today, spending 20 minutes floating outside his Gemini 4 spacecraft during the third orbit of its scheduled four-day flight. White and James McDivitt were lifted into space at 11:16 a.m. When the spacecraft was 150 miles above Australia, White opened its hatch, stood up and floated into space at the end of a 25-foot gold-plated nylon tether. He remained outside the spacecraft longer than planned, using all the fuel of a jet gas gun provided to propel himself. "This is the saddest moment of my life," White said ruefully as he had to return to the spacecraft (→ Dec. 1966).

Dominican turmoil eases

Santo Domingo, Aug. 31

The political turmoil that has plagued the Dominican Republic since the 31-year dictatorship of Rafael Trujillo ended with his assassination in May 1961 seems to be easing. A provisional government headed by 44-year-old Hector Garcia-Godoy has been formed with the backing of the United States and the Organization of American States. Since Garcia-Godoy is acceptable to the supporters of the deposed president, Juan Bosch, under whom he served as foreign minister, and to the right-wing of the army, hopes are high that the compromise will hold and the 22,000 American troops, here since April, will be able to return home.

Although the United States intervention was first justified as needed to protect American lives, it was obviously based on the fear that Santo Domingo under Juan Bosch might become another Cuba. However, the charge that he was a stalking horse for Communists has been vigorously denied by Bosch, the exiled professor who became president three years ago in the first free election since 1924. Washington's intervention is widely resented here as typical gringo imperialism. The O.A.S. has authorized an Inter-American Peace Force, but it consists almost entirely of the American forces already here.

Truman host to LBJ for Medicare signing

Independence, Missouri, July 30

It was a touching moment at the Harry S Truman Library here today when the Medicare Social Security Bill was signed into law by President Johnson.

The 81-year-old former President Truman was the first chief executive to recommend that a federal program be established to provide health insurance for the elderly under the auspices of the Social Security operations. And Truman was touched by the tribute that was bestowed upon him by President Johnson. Said LBJ, who was a congressman from Texas when the former Missouri senator was President, "The people of the United States loved and voted for Harry Truman, not because he gave them hell – but because he gave them hope."

The new Medicare legislation expands an existing insurance program by providing hospital care, nursing home care and out-patient diagnostic services for the senior citizens of the country. As it goes into effect, more than 19 million Americans will be eligible to receive the new assistance (→ Sept. 9).

New agency to run housing program

Washington, D.C., Sept. 9

Continuing his pledge to provide shelter for the poor, President Johnson today signed the Omnibus Housing Act, creating the Department of Housing and Urban Development. The new Cabinet-level office will administer the program for housing and urban renewal, which includes a plan to grant financial aid for low-income homes. Named by Johnson to head the department is Robert Weaver, the first Negro Cabinet member (→ Oct. 11, 1966).

Americans active in Vatican Council

Rome, Oct. 4

American bishops are playing a major role in the proceedings of the Vatican Council. Last month, the council adopted an American-written *Declaration on Religious Liberty*. The Americans have also been instrumental in drafting a document stating that the Jews are not to blame for Jesus's crucifixion. Today, Pope Paul VI is in New York City, where he celebrated an open-air mass in Yankee Stadium and later spoke at the United Nations.

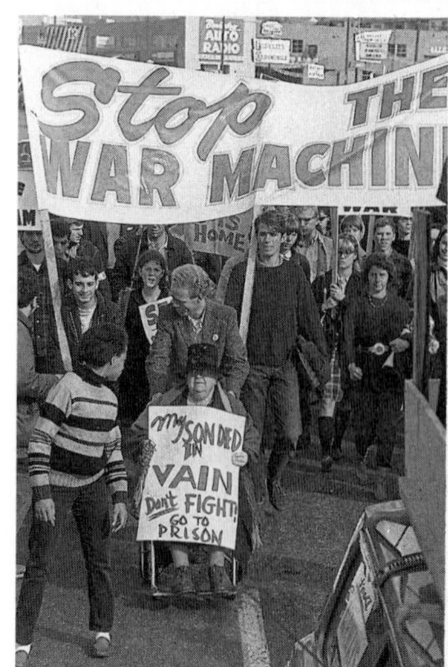

The war in Vietnam is beginning to polarize the nation. A growing number of Americans are questioning the role of the United States as casualties continue to mount. By the end of this year, the number of American servicemen in the small Southeast Asian nation passed the 150,000 mark. And as some young men of college age burn their draft cards in protest (left), even older citizens (right) join demonstrations to "stop the war machine."

Voting Rights Act guards Negro ballot

Washington, D.C., Aug. 6

The Voting Rights Act, which prohibits states from using poll taxes, literacy tests or other techniques to curtail voter registration among minorities, has been signed into law by President Johnson. Rigorously debated in Congress, the new legislation also makes it possible for federal examiners to insure compliance with the law in those states that have a history of voter discrimination. The Justice Department is expected, very soon, to announce a list of places where these examiners may be sent.

Signing the bill, President Johnson proclaimed that "three and a half centuries ago, the first Negroes arrived ... They came in darkness and ... in chains ... The story of our nation and of the American Negro are like two great rivers. Welling up from that tiny Jamestown spring they flow through the centuries along divided channels. ... When the Liberty Bell rang out in Philadelphia, it did not toll for the Negro. When Andrew Jackson threw open the doors of democracy, they did not open for the Negro. It was only at Appomattox, a century ago, that an American victory was also a Negro victory. And the two rivers, one shining with promise, the other dark-stained with oppression, began to move toward one another" (→16).

"Burn, baby, burn": Watts in chaos

Stores go up in smoke during rioting in the depressed area of Los Angeles.

Los Angeles, Aug. 16

The arrest of Marquette Frye, a 21-year-old Negro, was the spark that ignited five days of rioting in Watts, a Negro section of Los Angeles. His arrest for drunken driving, and subsequent allegations of police brutality, produced an explosion of racial tension that had been building throughout the nation for years.

The riot, which decimated the streets of Watts, was responsible for 34 deaths, over 1,000 injuries and 4,000 arrests. Some 200 businesses were destroyed, and 700 severely damaged. Property damage has been estimated at $40 million. Most of it was caused by Negroes who, outraged by the reports of police brutality, and by their impoverished and humiliating lives, attacked whites and police, fired guns and smashed and burned buildings. A witness to the violence said, "There were a lot of young hoods and agitators. But there were a lot of others who were just discontented and took advantage of the situation for emotional release."

It has been suggested that radical groups such as the Black Muslims helped to incite the riot by preaching violence against whites. A heat wave may also have served to raise tempers.

On August 13, it became clear that the police and riot control squads had little chance of quelling the violence. Therefore, 20,000 National Guardsmen were called out by California Governor Edmund Brown and a curfew from 8 p.m. to sunrise was established over a 35-mile area around the rioting. Still, it required more than two days for the soldiers to bring the area under control.

President Johnson said of the rioting: "It is not enough to simply decry disorder. We must also strike at the unjust conditions from which disorder largely flows." The President is now promoting legislation for restoration of the sacked ghetto, which has become a symbol for racial strife and urban deterioration across the nation. A commission of eight men, led by the former Director of Central Intelligence John A. McCone, will investigate the causes of the riot.

While Watts was in flames, similar rioting broke out in Chicago between August 12 and 14, after a Negro woman was killed by a fire engine driven by whites. It took 500 Chicago policemen to subdue more than 1,000 rioters. Some 80 people were injured and 140 arrested (→March 25, 1966).

Quotas lifted from immigration policy

Liberty Island, Oct. 3

The path to the American Dream became more accessible today as President Johnson signed the Immigration Bill at a ceremony in New York harbor. It ends most national origin curbs. It also raises the annual ceiling to 120,000 Western Hemisphere immigrants a year and 170,000 from the rest of the world, with a limit of 20,000 from any one nation. In encouraging refuge for those from oppressive regimes, LBJ said: "The future holds little hope for any government where the present holds no hope for the people." A ship of Cuban emigres is due here later this week.

Spirit of America races 600.601 mph

Bonneville Flats, November 15. *Craig Breedlove broke the world's record for ground speed today, traveling at 600.601 mph in his Spirit of America.*

Nader on bad cars; Leary on good trips

United States

Sixty years ago, Upton Sinclair's *The Jungle*, a novel about meat packing in Chicago, pushed the nation to the brink of vegetarianism. Now consumer advocate Ralph Nader, 31, has motorists pining for the days of the horse and buggy with his expose *Unsafe at Any Speed*, a high-octane indictment of auto safety standards. The good news is you can travel far without a car. So says Harvard's Dr. Timothy Leary, whose *Psychedelic Reader* plots another sort of trip that is available to those who taste the hallucinogenic nectar of LSD, or in Leary's words, who "tune in, turn on, drop out."

1966

Johnson

Wisconsin, Jan. 2. Green Bay Packers defeat Dallas Cowboys, 34-27, in N.F.L. championship.

Palomares, Spain, Jan. 17. After colliding with jet fueler, a B-52 bomber, armed with four hydrogen bombs, crashes.

New York City, March 15. Arthur Schlesinger Jr. wins both National Book Award and Pulitzer Prize, for Kennedy saga, *A Thousand Days.*

Washington, D.C., March 25. Supreme Court, in Harper v. Virginia Board of Elections, outlaws poll taxes, even in state elections (→ July 9).

Hernando, Mississippi, June 7. James Meredith, first Negro graduate of U. of Mississippi, shot in back while on civil rights march (→ July 30, 1967).

Chicago, Aug. 26. Mayor Richard Daley agrees to take measures to end de facto housing segregation (Sept. 11).

Grenada, Mississippi, Sept. 12. White mobs assault Negro children and their parents at newly integrated public schools while police stand by.

Baltimore, Oct. 9. Orioles sweep Los Angeles Dodgers in World Series.

Washington, D.C., Oct. 15. President Johnson signs bill establishing Cabinet-level Department of Transportation.

Chicago, Oct. 30. Anonymous caller informs police that recently stolen painting, Correggio's *Madonna, Child and St. John,* is in a Grant Park garbage can.

Washington, D.C., Nov. 3. President Johnson signs truth-in-packaging bill, prescribing standards in supermarket labeling.

California, Nov. 8. Ronald Reagan defeats Edmund Brown in race for Governor.

Edwards Air Force Base, California, Nov. 18. Major William J. Knight sets record air speed of 4,233 miles per hour, in X-15 jet.

Hollywood, Calif. Top films this year include *Blow-up, Who's Afraid of Virginia Woolf?* and *A Man for All Seasons.*

DEATH

Tucson, Arizona, Sept. 6. Margaret Sanger, pioneering birth control advocate (*Sept. 14, 1883).

American G.I.'s search and destroy in Mekong Delta

American troopers leap out of their helicopters and into the fray.

A wounded medic aids his fallen comrades as a rescue helicopter arrives.

South Vietnam, March

American forces have scored resounding victories in two recently completed search-and-destroy operations in the Mekong Delta region of South Vietnam. In Operation Marauder, which began the first week in January, troops of the 173rd Airborne Brigade engaged and destroyed an entire Vietcong battalion and the headquarters of a second battalion. Some 20,000 troops of the First Cavalry Division, aided by South Korean marines and South Vietnamese infantrymen, began another search-and-destroy campaign code-named Operation Masher/White Wing January 24. Military chiefs offered a "body count" of the enemy as a way of indicating the success of the effort. For the six weeks of the campaign against nine Communist battalions, they reported killing 1,342 enemy soldiers, capturing 633 and seizing 1,087 suspected Vietcong.

While the search-and-destroy operations have been militarily successful, they have been terrible for the civilians caught in the fighting. President Johnson and Prime Minister Nguyen Cao Ky agreed at their Honolulu talks February 8 that these operations must be accompanied by non-military efforts to "win the hearts and minds" of civilians. Otherwise, the war could easily be lost. The leaders pledged to improve medical care and education and to build a real political democracy in Vietnam (→ June 29).

Georgia House bars Bond for war stand

Atlanta, Georgia, Jan. 10

Julian Bond, the 25-year-old civil rights activist, was denied a seat in the Georgia legislature today because of his opposition to the Vietnam War. Legislators insisted Bond was disloyal to the United States because he said he admired draft-card burners. The vote barring him from a House seat was 184-12. Bond and seven other Negroes were the first of their race to be elected to Georgia's legislature since Reconstruction. Bond is a leader in the militant civil rights group, the Student National Coordinating Committee (S.N.C.C.) (→ May 15).

Seagren pole vaults to record 17 feet

Albuquerque, N.M., March 6

How high can man soar on his own power? For decades, the 17-foot pole vault, like the 4-minute mile, was considered unattainable. Today, Bob Seagren vaulted 17 feet 3/4 inch and set a world indoor record. The improvement in Seagren's performance has been remarkable considering the fact that last year he could do no better than 16 feet 4 inches outdoors. He seems certain to clinch an Olympic berth for 1968 and is expected to break records along the way. Another American, Fred Hansen, vaulted 17 feet 4 inches outdoors in 1964.

Celtics win eighth N.B.A. title in a row

Boston, April

The Boston Celtics have won their eighth straight National Basketball Association Championship – their ninth in 10 years – by defeating the Los Angeles Lakers in a seven-game series. However, the coach who presided over this dynasty, Red Auerbach, has announced that he is retiring. Bill Russell, the great shot-blocker, was named to replace him. The Celtics proved that as good as Bob Cousy was, they could win after his departure. Cousy, who left the Celtics in 1963, had made the All-N.B.A. first team for 10 years in a row.

Wave of anti-war protests sweeps country

Washington, D.C., May 15

Thousands of people marched and chanted in the nation's capital today to protest the deepening American involvement in Vietnam. They surrounded the White House and vowed to throw congressional supporters of the war out of office. Today's demonstration was the latest in a series of anti-Vietnam protests. At the University of Chicago, hundreds of students seized the administration building for three days. In New York, students shouted at the president of City College and sat on the floor outside his office.

The war seemed close to home yesterday as 400,000 students took the selective service qualification test. Those who score under 70 risk losing the 2-S deferment. Critics say the exam increases the war's burden on the poor and uneducated. Harlem lawmaker Adam Clayton Powell Jr. said the tests remind him of Nazism because they "weed out the intellectually deprived or socially undesirable by conscripting them for cannon fodder."

President Johnson called war critics "nervous Nellies," and stopped just short of branding them unpatriotic. He accused them of "turning on their leaders, their country and their fighting men." At Princeton, Johnson's admonition to critics to "cool it" was greeted with frigid silence. "This war is unconstitutional," the protesters' signs read. "Who are we to police the world?" (→Oct. 22, 1967).

B-52's hammer Hanoi

Wave upon wave of B-52 bombers strike at Hanoi with devastating effect.

Saigon, South Vietnam, June 29

For the first time in the war, North Vietnam's key cities of Hanoi and Haiphong have been blasted by waves of B-52 heavy bombers. The North Vietnamese capital and primary port cities had been considered off limits because Pentagon officials repeatedly have said that bombing strikes on these centers might provoke either Russian or Chinese intervention – or both.

The decision to bomb Hanoi and Haiphong is the latest step in the U.S. effort to destroy the North Vietnamese military machine in an undisguised campaign of attrition. On April 12, B-52's based on Guam bombed targets near the Laotian border. And last month, the big bombers hit enemy forces on the Cambodian side of the Caibac River in western South Vietnam.

The B-52's, originally designed to deliver nuclear weapons, carry a conventional bomb load of 58,000 pounds. Flying at a height of 50,000 feet, these giant bombers cannot be seen or heard – until each rains down its three dozen 2,000-pound block-busting bombs.

While the bombing of Hanoi and Haiphong is admittedly a strategic gamble, Pentagon officials believe this dramatic new phase in the air war will ultimately prove decisive in bringing about the defeat of North Vietnam (→Oct. 25).

H.E.W. offers birth control services

Washington, D.C., Apr. 1

The government has taken bold steps to provide contraceptives for those in need. The Department of Health, Education and Welfare is spending $3.1 million this year on family planning services. President Johnson says all families should have access to services which "allow freedom to choose the number and spacing of their children." Despite opposition from the Catholic Church federal funds for birth control will almost double yearly.

N.O.W. issues bold women's manifesto

Washington, D.C.

Calling for "true equality for all women in America," the National Organization for Women has promised to oppose vigorously any party or candidate who "ignores the principle of full equality between the sexes." N.O.W. leader Betty Friedan says women are "in relatively little position to influence or control major decisions." But N.O.W. plans to mobilize the women's vote and work on legislation to fight sex discrimination (→Aug. 26, 1970).

Masters & Johnson on human sexuality

United States

Human Sexual Response, the first book to utilize extensive experiments on human subjects to study sexual behavior, is based on an 11-year research program run by authors Dr. William Masters, a gynecologist, and Virginia Johnson, a psychologist. They studied and filmed the sexual activities of over 600 male and female volunteers ranging in age from 18 to 89. The book dispels old myths, providing detailed measurements of the sexual cycle, orgasms, and physiological patterns vital for treating sexual problems.

G.M. offers apology to crusader Nader

Washington, D.C., March 22

General Motors executives apologized publicly to safety crusader Ralph Nader today for having private detectives pry into his sex life and political beliefs. Company president James M. Roche and other officials admitted before a congressional committee that they ordered the investigation of Nader because of his book, *Unsafe at Any Speed,* which pointed out the safety flaws of the automobiles. Roche agreed with Senator Abraham Ribicoff that the snooping techniques used by detectives G.M. hired were "unworthy of American business."

American draftees are sworn into the army. The war in Vietnam keeps expanding, and the administration, determined to see it through to a successful conclusion, calls up ever-increasing numbers of young men.

Race riots inflame Atlanta, Chicago

Impelled by poverty, hunger and hopelessness in the midst of an affluent society, some ghetto dwellers loot local stores in full view of policemen.

Atlanta, Georgia, Sept. 11

Racial violence erupted again in Atlanta, where militant young Negroes shouting "Black Power" attacked cars and police vehicles with chunks of concrete last night. Atlanta police, who battled rioters with tear gas three days last week, worked to prevent another major outbreak. The Atlanta riots, which started after police shot a Negro suspect they said was fleeing, have dramatized the deep split between young militants and more moderate civil rights leaders. Atlanta Mayor Ivan Allen Jr. has blamed Stokely Carmichael, national chairman of the Student Non-Violent Coordinating Committee, for the rioting and Carmichael, who popularized the "Black Power" slogan, has been arrested and charged with inciting the violence. The Rev. Martin Luther King Jr. has criticized the rioting. Negro ministers and businessmen have gone door to door in Negro neighborhoods trying to bring order.

Dr. King left Atlanta for Chicago, where he has been leading marches to demand better housing for poor people. In early September, under the watchful eye of some 2,000 bayonet-wielding National Guardsmen, King led a march on Cicero, Illinois. Roving gangs of whites attacked the marchers with flying bottles and rocks, shouting "Kill 'em!" or "Tar and feather 'em!" The riots initially broke out in Chicago in mid-July only days after King launched his crusade. The National Guard was called in following three days of looting and burning (→ 12).

2 brutal killing sprees horrify nation

United States, Aug. 1

Two killing sprees have again stamped the country as a land of senseless violence. On July 19, Richard Speck, 26, was arrested in Chicago for the gruesome slaying of eight student nurses. He forced his way into their dormitory with a knife and gun, bound their hands with bedsheets, then strangled five and stabbed three. A ninth escaped by hiding under a bed. Today, in Austin, Texas, Charles Whitman mounted the 27-story University of Texas tower and opened fire on the people below, killing 16 and wounding 30. The 90-minute slaughter ended when he was killed by an off-duty policeman. Whitman had killed his wife and mother the night before. The 25-year-old honor student was a former marine.

As the war progresses, the introduction of new technologies such as the variable-sweep wing of the F-111B fighter increases American firepower.

Miranda case backs rights of suspects

Washington, D.C., June 13

"You have the right to remain silent. Anything you say may be used against you in a court of law." If an arresting police officer does not inform a suspect of these and other rights, the accused has been denied liberties, according to a Supreme Court decision today.

The court ruled in the controversial Miranda v. Arizona case. Weighing Fifth Amendment guarantees against self-incrimination, a 5-4 majority held that a confession obtained by police is invalid if the suspect is not told of his rights, including the right to have a lawyer present. The case came to the high court after convicted rapist Ernesto Miranda appealed, charging he had been denied his Fifth Amendment rights in confessing to his crime. Critics say that the decision will allow more criminals to go free on procedural technicalities. But proponents applaud the ruling as a victory for civil liberties and protection against police entrapment.

Black Power splits civil rights groups

Stokely Carmichael of S.N.C.C coined the term "Black Power."

United States, July 9

"Black Power." The Congress o Racial Equality has endorsed it The National Association for th Advancement of Colored People re jects it. Roy Wilkins, leader of th N.A.A.C.P., says his group "wi have none of this ... It is the rang ing of race against race on the irrelevant basis of skin color. It is the father of hatred and mother of violence." But C.O.R.E. says, "Black Power is not hatred. It is a means to bring Black Americans into the covenant of brotherhood, ... a unified Black voice reflecting racial pride in the tradition of our heterogeneous nation." Student Nonviolent Coordinating Committee chairman Stokely Carmichael gave birth to the phrase. He spoke of "Black Power" during a June Mississippi voter registration march (→ Aug. 26).

Mini-skirts a la mod

United States

Its a mod, mod, mod, mod world. Minis are bearing thighs for all the world to see, pushing Mom's morality further into the dark ages. Flower children are packing up and taking off to blow their minds on LSD. In the hippie havens of California, the Bible gives way to Tarot cards; the disco steps aside for the psychedelic Day-Glo dance hall, complete with strobe lights and electric Kool-Aid; and Elvis surrenders to the Stones and the Grateful Dead.

Child Nutrition Act gives food to kids

Washington, D.C., Oct. 11

"I know what it is like to teach children who are listless because they are hungry – and realize the difference a decent meal can make in lives and attitudes of school children." With those words, President Johnson signed the Child Nutrition Act today. It grants federal funds to feed impoverished students and is another Johnson initiative to help the nation's schools. Last year, he signed the Elementary and Secondary Education Bill. Many of the school supports come from recommendations by the LBJ-appointed task force on education, headed by John Gardner, president of the Carnegie Corporation (→Nov. 11).

Johnson, warned of failure, meets with Ky

Prime Minister Nguyen Cao Ky (left) is also an air force vice marshal.

Manila, Philippines, Oct. 25

Faced with a deteriorating political and military situation in South Vietnam, President Johnson began talks yesterday with South Vietnamese Prime Minister Nguyen Cao Ky and leaders of the other nations involved in the war. Warned 10 days ago by Secretary of Defense Robert McNamara that neither the heavy bombing campaigns nor the pacification programs have been effective enough to bring North Vietnam to the peace table, Johnson and the allies have issued a series of three statements designed to reassure the North Vietnamese of their limited war aims and thus hopefully speed up the peace process. The leaders announced today that while they remain dedicated to peace in Vietnam, they also promised to remove the allied troops from South Vietnam within six months after the war ends. In another statement, the Declaration of Peace, they said: "We do not threaten the sovereignty or territorial integrity of our neighbors, whatever their ideological alignment. We only ask that this be reciprocated."

In addition to President Johnson and Prime Minister Ky, those participating in the Manila talks include President Park Chung Hee of South Korea and President Ferdinand Marcos of the Philippines. Australia, New Zealand, and Thailand have also been participating in the conference (→Feb. 24, 1967).

$1 billion to rebuild 60 to 70 U.S. cities

Washington, D.C., Nov. 3

One might think of it as a War on Decay, urban decay. And with the signing today of the Demonstration Cities and Metropolitan Redevelopment Act, the first battle has been won. President Johnson, after signing the legislation, said, "I believe this law will be regarded as one of the major breakthroughs of the 1960s." The Model Cities Act, as it is called, provides nearly $1 billion in federal funds over two years for 60 to 70 "demonstration" cities for the reconstruction of their cores. It works with local arms of government and will be an experiment in inter-governmental administration.

Pop is growing up

United States

On the jacket of their innovative new album, *Revolver*, the Beatles gaze introspectively from behind dark glasses. The made-for-TV Monkees were a hit this year, but they were out of step with the new-found maturity of many pop musicians: Bob Dylan offered the far-ranging *Blonde on Blonde*, the Beach Boys, *Pet Sounds*. The Byrds soared with *Eight Miles High*, piloted by Jim McGuinn's shimmering guitar, but it was often banned for suspected drug allusions. More danceable but no less creative were Motown's Supremes and Miracles.

"In Cold Blood"

United States

What do you get when you fuse story-telling skills with dogged research? A "non-fiction novel." This is what Truman Capote calls his *In Cold Blood: A True Account of a Multiple Murder and Its Consequences*. A first printing of 100,000 sold out nearly overnight. The book is a blow-by-blow account of the brutal 1959 killing of a wealthy Kansas farm family, the Clutters. Capote reviews the lives of the victims, probes the minds of the cold-blooded murderers, Dick Hickok and Perry Smith, and follows them to Death Row and their execution.

Gemini: docking and walking in space

Houston, Texas, December

Project Gemini has paved the way for the landing of an American on the moon within this decade. With 10 two-man missions, the $1.35 billion program has pioneered long-duration flights, maneuvering, rendezvous and docking techniques and "walks" in space. These will be essential in the coming Apollo lunar missions.

In the first mission on March 23 last year, Gemini 3, the new capsule and a Titan 2 rocket were tested. In June astronaut Edward White was the first American to "walk" in space, spending 20 minutes swooping about with a gas-powered jet gun. Gemini 5 stayed up for the eight days required for a moon flight. And in December, Gemini 6 and 8 met in space after a 100,000-mile chase. Gemini 7 astronauts Frank Borman and James Lovell Jr. stayed in space a record 14 days.

This year, Gemini 8 completed the first space docking, with an Agena rocket on March 16. Pilot Neil Armstrong likened it to "parking a car," though a faulty rocket soon forced a premature end to the mission. On the final flight, Gemini 12, Edwin E. Aldrin Jr. spacewalked for 5 1/2 hours on November 15, after an Agena link-up (→Jan. 27, 1967).

Walt Disney dies; ruled empire of fantasy

Hollywood, Calif., Dec. 15

Walt Disney, who gave us Mickey Mouse, Donald Duck and many other fabulous characters, died of lung cancer today at the age of 65. But the empire he built with the help of his life-long collaborator, Ub Iwerk, a team of artists, ever-growing inventiveness and a great sense of fantasy, will live on. The Chicago-born animation pioneer became king of family entertainment through his fantasy park Disneyland in Anaheim, animated features such as *Snow White*, *Fantasia* and *Bambi*, nature films such as *The Living Desert* and regular films such as *Mary Poppins*.

The great showman at his zenith.

1967

Johnson

Washington, D.C., Jan. 10. Supreme Court, in United States v. Lamb, rules criminal charges may not be brought against Americans for visiting nations forbidden by State Department.

Cambridge, Mass., Jan. 18. Albert De Salvo, confessed "Boston Strangler," sentenced to life for armed robbery, assault and sex offenses.

South Vietnam, Feb. 24. U.S. forces shell targets inside North Vietnam for first time (→May 14).

Washington, D.C., March 16. Senate approves first bilateral treaty signed with Soviet Union since 1917, providing framework for greater diplomatic ties.

New York City, Apr. 21. Stalin's daughter, Svetlana Alliluyeva, arrives in U.S. after defecting in New Delhi, India.

New York City, May 1. Anne Sexton wins Pulitzer Prize in poetry, for *Live or Die.*

Washington, D.C., May 11. With installation of one millionth telephone, half of all world's telephones are in United States.

San Francisco, May 24. Philadelphia 76ers defeat San Francisco Warriors four games to two, for N.B.A. title.

Chicago, Aug. 15. Pablo Picasso's gift to city unveiled, steel sculpture weighing 163 tons and standing 50 feet high.

Washington, D.C., Aug. 30. Senate approves appointment of Thurgood Marshall to Supreme Court, first black to be seated on high court.

Newport, Rhode Island, Sept. 18. U.S. yacht Intrepid defeats Australian challenger Dame Pattie for America's Cup.

Boston, Oct. 12. St. Louis Cardinals defeat Red Sox in World Series, four games to three.

Mississippi, Oct. 20. Jury convicts 11 of 18 in 1964 slaying of three civil rights workers; deputy sheriff of Neshoba County among the guilty.

Stanford, California, Dec. 14. It is announced that Stanford University biochemists have successfully synthesized D.N.A.

Hollywood, Calif. Top films this year include *The Graduate*, *In the Heat of the Night* and *Bonnie and Clyde*.

Vince Lombardi's Packers defeat Kansas City in first Super Bowl

Lombardi at the halftime break in the Super Bowl, the new N.F.L. title game.

Los Angeles, Jan. 15

Winning was the only thing for Coach Vince Lombardi and the Green Bay Packers today when they went into the first Super Bowl and the Kansas City Chiefs were the victims of a 35-10 drubbing. The winning ingredient was pinpoint passing by Bart Starr; he completed 16 of 23 tosses. Jim Taylor's line-busting enabled the Packers to mix their attack sufficiently to keep the Chiefs off balance. Over the last seven years, a varied assault backed by a strong defense has built a Packer football dynasty, with a succession of Green Bay teams leading the league five times. Unfortunately, the stadium was only two-thirds full today.

3 astronauts burn to death on launching pad in Apollo tragedy

Cape Canaveral, Fla., Jan. 27

Astronauts Virgil Grissom, Edward White and Roger B. Chaffee died tonight when a flash fire swept through their Apollo capsule during a simulated countdown. The three astronauts, rehearsing for the first Apollo space flight, were consumed in a blaze made more intense by the 100 percent oxygen atmosphere of their spacecraft. They are the first astronauts to die in a spacecraft, after 16 successful Mercury and Gemini orbital space flights.

The countdown was only 10 minutes from the simulated liftoff that would have completed the test when the fire broke out. The launching crew was watching on closed-circuit television when there was a sudden flash on the monitor, then a torrent of smoke and fire. Smoke drove rescue crews back as they tried to enter the capsule. The cause of the fire is unknown, as is its effect on plans to reach the moon in this decade (→July 24, 1969).

Two major combat operations are launched north of Saigon

Washington, D.C., May 14

The Pentagon today announced the conclusion of the biggest combined American-South Vietnamese effort of the war. Operation Junction City, which was launched February 22, involved 22 American and four South Vietnamese battalions. In fierce fighting against veteran North Vietnamese forces in Tayninh Province north of Saigon on the Cambodian border, at least 282 Americans were killed and over 1,500 were wounded. The Communists did not list casualty figures.

This offensive follows the huge assault of January 8 to 26, Operation Cedar Falls, which was spearheaded by the American First and 25th Infantry Divisions and supported by South Vietnamese. In that attack, enemy headquarters and bases in the "Iron Triangle" area 25 miles north of Saigon were destroyed and a supply of rice seized that would feed 13,000 enemy soldiers for a year. Also seized were a half million pages of Communist military documents.

The latest escalation of the war began February 24 when marines shelled enemy positions in North Vietnam and United States aircraft mined rivers north of the demilitarized zone, both for the first time. In April, B-52 bombers were deployed to the U-Tapao airfield in Thailand for long-range strikes against North Vietnam (→Sept. 30).

Infantrymen leap from their "Huey." Though the helicopter was introduced into combat during the Korean War, its full impact is only now being realized.

ꞁli stripped of title ꞁor resisting draft

ꞁli, formerly Clay, formerly champ.

ꞁouston, Texas, Apr. 30
Muhammad Ali, who boxed his ꞁay to the top of the fistic heap as ꞁassius Clay, has been stripped of ꞁis world heavyweight championꞁhip for resisting the military draft. ꞁVhen Ali balked at taking the step ꞁhat would have put him in the serꞁice, the boxing association voted ꞁo take away his title. There is also ꞁ possibility of criminal prosecuꞁion. Ali, who claimed exemption ꞁs a Black Muslim minister, said, "I ꞁannot be true to my belief in my ꞁeligion" by joining the military. ꞁAli has fought twice this year, beatꞁng Ernie Terrell February 6 and ꞁcoring a six-round knockout of ꞁZora Folley March 22. He looked ꞁtale despite a busy 1966 in which ꞁe defeated five so-called Bums of ꞁhe Month (→June 28, 1971).

25th Amendment ꞁsets succession line

ꞁWashington, D.C., Feb. 10
The 25th Amendment to the ꞁConstitution was ratified today, asꞁuring clear lines of succession to ꞁhe presidency. "It's a happy day," ꞁaid Senator Birch Bayh of Indiana, ꞁ"A constitutional gap that has exꞁsted for centuries has finally been ꞁilled." The law provides for transꞁer of power to the Vice President ꞁf the President is incapacitated and ꞁllows the chief executive to name ꞁ Vice President if the spot is vacatꞁd. Previously, the position stayed ꞁacant until the next election.

Detroit race riot worst in U.S. history

Detroit, Mich., July 30
The worst race riot in the nation's history has ended here, leaving 38 people dead and sections of the city in charred ruins after four days of terror. Damage from the looting and fire-bombing has been estimated at $500 million. "It looks like Berlin in 1945," said Detroit's Mayor Jerome Cavanaugh.

The rioting in Detroit may have been the worst in deaths and destruction, but cities across the nation are being torn by racial violence. Forty have been hit in the past week alone. Since the July rioting in Newark, New Jersey, racial strife has erupted in some 70 cities, including Atlanta, Boston, Philadelphia, Birmingham, New York and Cincinnati.

After the Detroit riots, President Johnson commented: "We have endured a week such as no nation should live through: a time of violence and tragedy." A newspaper in Stockholm observed: "It threatens to become a revolution of the entire underclass of America."

The rhetoric was strong among many black groups. At a conference on black power in Newark last week, H. Rap Brown, new president of the Student Non-Violent Coordinating Committee, called on Negroes to "wage guerrilla war on the honkie white man," adding, "I love violence." Brown was arrested in July when fires broke out in Cambridge, Maryland, after he urged a crowd of 400 young blacks to "burn this town down."

The rioting in Detroit started after police officers raided an after-hours nightclub where black-power advocates often gather and arrested 75 blacks. Flames soon erupted over Detroit's West Side as arsonists tossed fire bombs into stores that had just been looted. In some neighborhoods where there was looting, a shocked Mayor Cavanaugh reported "a light-hearted abandon, a carnival spirit."

Offering reasons for the riots, sociologists have pointed to unemployment, poor housing and hopelessness in the ghettoes. Michigan's Republican Governor George Romney said Great Society programs had raised false hopes among Negroes. "They are bitter and frustrated," he said (→Feb. 29, 1968).

A group of Michigan National Guardsmen with bayonets fixed on their rifles advance toward rioters.

A guardsman stands ready while a section of Detroit burns around him.

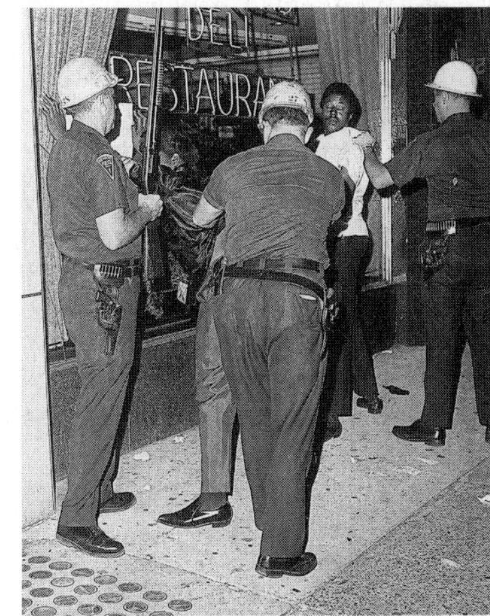

Police arrest black looters during race rioting in Newark, New Jersey.

Troops stand guard as residents return to view the wreckage after Detroit riots. ▷

Flower children flock to San Francisco for "Summer of Love"

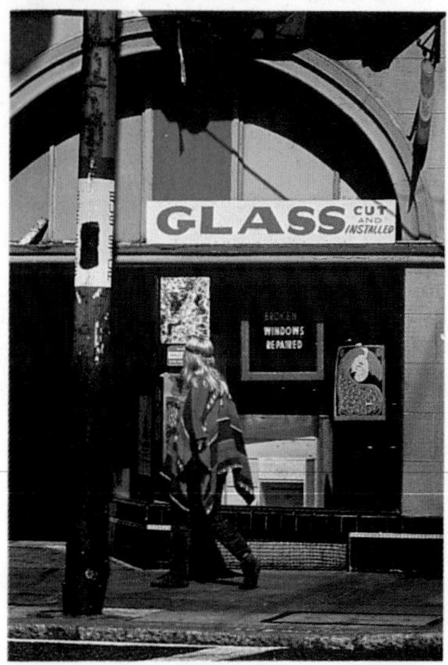

A colorfully bedecked and beaded hippie walks by a psychedelic glass shop on a street in San Francisco.

San Francisco, Summer

"We want the world, and we want it now," thundered Doors lead singer Jim Morrison this year. But many kids figured as long as society was ravaged by war, injustice and materialism, they would do just as well to heed drug guru Timothy Leary's advice and simply drop out. And what better place to do that than in San Francisco, where, as Scott McKenzie warbled in one hit song, everyone was sure to be wearing flowers.

The San Francisco "Summer of Love" began, more or less, in June at the Monterey Pop Festival. With the Beatles' masterpiece, *Sgt. Pepper's Lonely Hearts Club Band* as a beacon, the feeling that rock music had come into its own merged with a high-flying counterculture movement. About 50,000 kids, many with hair even longer than the Beatles' and dressed in a riot of colors, got high on everything from LSD to the communal vibes and grooved to a fantastic array of artists. There was the driving Memphis soul of Otis Redding, the cerebral ragas of Indian sitarist Ravi Shankar and a cavalcade of bands from California, including the Mamas and the Papas, Byrds, Jefferson Airplane, Grateful Dead and Buffalo Springfield. Newcomers like The Who and Janis Joplin were overpowering, while a young guitarist named Jimi Hendrix blew minds – and eardrums – with a brilliant display of stratospheric sounds and incandescent showmanship.

After the festival, the word had spread, and as the media declared San Francisco's Haight-Ashbury section a "Hippie Haven," thousands flocked here. Although the festival mood lingered all summer, as communes formed and acid rock bands played free concerts, the city soon felt the strain. Living space grew scarce, crime soared – and hard drugs wreaked havoc. One hippie called the Haight area "as bad as the squares say it is."

But the local music scene still thrives, with groups like the Airplane and Dead embarking on free-form psychedelic jams laced with lyrics of peace, love and flowers.

Making music and watching the world go by. A drummer takes in the sights and sounds of "the" summer.

Elsewhere, though, the groups couldn't help but reflect an outlook shaped by nightly violence on the TV news. "There's something happening here . . . There's a man with a gun over there," sang the Buffalo Springfield in *For What It's Worth*, a song about street fighting on the Sunset Strip in Los Angeles, while the Doors descended into a nightmare world of Oedipal psychosis and carnivalesque organ sounds on *The End*. The "Summer of Love" has some ominous overtones.

Glassboro summit is a cordial success

Glassboro, N.J., June 25

After conferring for 10 hour over a three-day period, Presiden Johnson and Soviet Premier Alek sei N. Kosygin have gone their sep arate ways. Their talks, which cov ered such topics as Vietnam, th Middle East and disarmament, al though officially described as cor dial, have clearly been inconclusive The meetings were held at Glass boro State College in southwes New Jersey. The site was selecte mainly for reasons of protocol: i is precisely half way between th White House and the United Na tions, where Kosygin has just ad dressed a special session of th General Assembly, called to discus the recent Arab-Israeli war.

Public broadcasting

Washington, D.C., Nov. 7

President Johnson has signed th Public Broadcasting Act of 1967. I establishes a 15-director corpora tion that will use public and pri vate funds to subsidize non-com mercial television and radio. News public events and cultural and ed ucational programs are to be of fered. Initial federal funding of thi "network of knowledge" is $9 mil lion. The Carnegie Corporation an CBS have pledged $1 million each the United Auto Workers $25,000.

Millions of Americans shedding hang-ups

Model Twiggy in minidress.

United States

To parents surveying the times through horn-rimmed glasses, the world of youth may look confusing. Colleges, which have doubled enrollment since 1960, are breeding a new hedonism. Co-ed dorms bring the sexes together. Mini-skirts, introduced last year, are now ubiquitous. Skin is bared and hang-ups shed at "Be-In's," psychedelic, dionysian attacks on the American success ethic. Far Eastern gurus offer spiritual guidance to a host of peaceniks. And San Francisco is host to 100,000 hippies. So confusion may be part of growing up, but to a new generation of iconoclasts looking at the times through shades, everything is beautiful.

Esalen Institute offers group gropes

San Francisco, September

Hugging, slapping and cuddling its way to success, the Esalen Institute, founded on the Big Sur, has now opened a branch at San Francisco's First Unitarian Society Church. Founded in 1962, the Esalen is dedicated to helping people redefine themselves and their relationships through the abandonment of words and the adoption of physical sensation. Everyone from the State Department officer to the housewife is enrolled in a weekend course. Resident fellows attend for two semesters, paying just $3,000 for the insights that fondling and tickling can bring.

A Ryun mile record two years running

Bakersfield, Calif., June 22

For the second year in a row, Jim Ryun has lowered the world record for the mile run. He deftly paced himself in the Amateur Athletic Union meet today, clipping two-tenths of a second off the mark of 3 minutes 51.3 seconds that he set last July at Berkeley. He posted a zippy 3:53.2 in the NCAA championships at Compton. Ryun, who at 16 was the youngest American to make the Olympic team, was ill for the Tokyo Games, but he quickly rebounded in 1965. Ryun recaptured the spotlight from foreign runners who have been shaving the mile mark for three decades.

.S. forces in war ising to 525,000

ashington, D.C., Sept. 30

President Johnson has signed a 70 billion defense appropriations ill – the largest money bill that ongress has passed in its 177-year istory. A huge part of the new inds – and the new 10 percent urcharge on the income tax pro-osed by LBJ in July – will be used o finance the military effort in ietnam. The President reported ix weeks ago that after conferring ith General William Westmore-and he had decided that 47,000 nore combat and support soldiers nust be sent to Vietnam. When nese troops have arrived there next une, the total of American military ersonnel in Vietnam will come to bout 525,000 (→ Jan. 21, 1968).

rainwashed?

etroit, Mich., Sept. 4

The *Detroit News* has withdrawn s endorsement of Michigan Gov-rnor George Romney for the Re-ublican presidential nomination. omney, who earlier endorsed the ietnam War, was asked today why e now calls the war a "tragic mis-ake." Romney said that on a 1965 ietnam visit he had been brain-vashed by generals and diplomats. he *News* says it now backs New ork Governor Nelson Rockefel-er, "who knows what he believes."

McNamara resigns as head of defense

ashington, D.C., Nov. 29

Defense Secretary Robert Mc-Namara sent shock waves through Washington today when he an-nounced he was resigning to be-come president of the World Bank. iberal historian Arthur M. Schle-inger Jr. called the resignation "ominous and scary." Critics of the ietnam War charged McNamara ad been forced out by Pentagon ardliners. The secretary has not een a dove on the war, but he has criticized the continued bombing of North Vietnam. Earlier this year, e said the bombing would not "seriously reduce the actual flow of nen and materiel to the south."

March on the Pentagon

With the march under way, a protester taunts military police at the Pentagon.

Arlington, Virginia, Oct. 22

Bonfires burned into the early hours today as demonstrators continued to jeer the helmeted military police protecting the Pentagon. The protest against the Vietnam War began yesterday afternoon as tens of thousands spilled across the Memorial Bridge from the Lincoln Memorial to the Pentagon. The demonstration started peacefully, and "Dump Johnson" banners outnumbered Vietcong flags. Many protesters were students who had been bused to Washington.

Tempers began to flare as radicals led by David Dellinger and Jerry Rubin confronted thousands of guards wielding rifles and tear gas grenades. The radicals' organization, the National Mobilization Committee to End the War in Vietnam, had vowed to shut down the Pentagon, and a small group did manage to break briefly into the fortress. They were quickly expelled, with more than a dozen protesters injured. Hundreds were arrested, including Dellinger and novelist Norman Mailer.

The march here capped a week of anti-war protests in San Francisco, Los Angeles, New York and Madison, Wisconsin (→ Nov. 11).

"Eve" (1967) by B.M. Jackson. As this realistic painting of a rural home adorned with the Stars and Stripes shows, many Americans still display an old-fashioned kind of patriotism. But others believe that the nation is in an illegal war that cannot be sanctified by wrapping it in a flag.

500 labor leaders meet to oppose war

Chicago, Nov. 11

Cracks appeared today in organized labor's support for President Johnson's conduct of the war in Vietnam. Some 500 officials from the A.F.L.-C.I.O. and independent unions met to urge an "immediate and unconditional end to the bombing of North Vietnam" and a negotiated settlement of the war. The declaration had little effect on the President, who is standing firm on Vietnam despite his decline in the polls. He still has many labor leaders in his corner, including George Meany. At a dinner for the A.F.L.-C.I.O. president, Johnson blasted critics of the war as "calamity howlers" and "forces of division" (→ Dec. 8).

Dr. Spock arrested

New York City, Dec. 8

Anti-war demonstrators were no match for the New York police this week as they tried to shut down the army induction center. More than 500 protesters were arrested. Baby doctor Benjamin Spock and poet Allen Ginsberg were among those taken into custody. So was Cathleen Fitt, daughter of the assistant secretary of defense for manpower. Her father is the man who decides how many men get drafted every month (→ March 6, 1968).

McCarthy will run anti-war campaign

Washington, D.C., Nov. 30

Senator Eugene McCarthy of Minnesota announced today that he will challenge President Johnson for the Democratic nomination in at least four primaries next spring. McCarthy, an outspoken critic of the Vietnam War, says the conflict has created a "moral crisis in America," while the administration has "set no limit to the price which it is willing to pay for a military victory." McCarthy's entry gives a new legitimacy to the anti-war movement, but few think he will stay in the race all the way. Many feel he is a "stalking horse" for Robert Kennedy (→ March 12, 1968).

1968

Johnson

Miami, Jan. 14. Green Bay Packers beat Oakland Raiders, 33-14, in Super Bowl II.

South Vietnam, Jan. 21. About 5,000 American marines are isolated and under attack by 20,000 North Vietnamese in Khesanh (→31).

Washington, D.C., Jan. 30. Clark Clifford confirmed by Senate as Defense Secretary.

Washington, D.C., March 16. Senator Robert Kennedy of New York announces intention of seeking Democratic presidential nomination (→31).

Saigon, South Vietnam, Apr. 8. About 100,000 American and South Vietnamese troops begin offensive against Communist forces in 11 provinces.

New York City, May 8. William Styron wins Pulitzer Prize for *The Confessions of Nat Turner.*

Lewisburg, Louisiana, May, 11. Seven Sisters Oak, with a diameter of 36 feet 10 inches, made president of Louisiana Live Oak Society.

Los Angeles, May. Boston Celtics defeat Los Angeles Lakers, four games to two, for N.B.A. title.

Saigon, South Vietnam, July 3. General Creighton Abrams replaces General William Westmoreland as U.S. commander in Vietnam.

Moscow, July 15. Aeroflot and Pan American World Airways open direct service between U.S. and Soviet Union.

St. Louis, Oct. 10. Detroit Tigers defeat St. Louis Cardinals in World Series, four games to three.

New York City, Nov. 5 Shirley Chisholm is first black woman to be elected to United States Congress.

United States. William Burroughs observes, "The youth rebellion is a worldwide phenomenon that has not been seen before in history."

United States. Books published this year include Tom Wolfe's *The Electric Kool-Aid Acid Test*, Eldridge Cleaver's *Soul on Ice*, Arthur Hailey's *Airport* and John Updike's *Couples.*

DEATH

Westport, Connecticut, June 1. Helen Keller, leader of the handicapped (*June 27, 1880).

Reds launch a massive Tet offensive

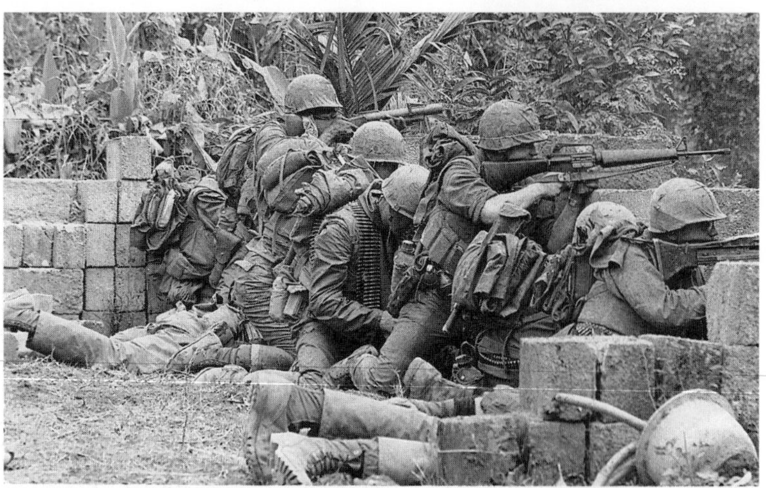

American troops fight back in the city of Hue. Much of the ancient capital was seized by North Vietnamese forces as they launched their Tet onslaught.

U.S. soldiers watch from behind a wall as an artillery shell explodes.

A wounded Vietnamese mother and her child, caught in the offensive.

Americans watch results of bombing against the North Vietnamese. The enemy has launched repeated assaults from the zone between the North and South.

Washington, D.C., Jan. 31

North Vietnamese and Vietcong forces have launched a massive offensive throughout South Vietnam, Washington confirmed today. The campaign began yesterday with a series of coordinated attacks aimed at American and South Vietnamese troops in the northern and central provinces. In the past 24 hours, an estimated 84,000 Communist combat troops – and an equal number of support forces – have struck at virtually all the provincial capitals and major cities in South Vietnam, incuding Saigon and Hue.

In Saigon, a North Vietnamese suicide squad blew a hole in the wall of the United States Embassy last night, killing two army military policemen. The North Vietnamese occupied the embassy yard for five hours, until they were all killed by other military policemen and marine guards at the embassy this morning. Fighting is continuing on the outskirts of Saigon.

Communist forces have also attacked and captured the port city of Hue. Early word indicates that civilian casualties are extremely high and there have been many reports of North Vietnamese atrocities.

The Tet offensive has been expected for some time by American military leaders. Their intelligence officials received word last week of the coming "decisive campaign," a contest that the Vietcong soldiers were being told would produce the "final victory." Last week President Johnson was informed by General William Westmoreland, the American commander in Vietnam, that he believed the Communist attack would come just before Tet, the Vietnamese lunar New Year – even though a truce between the two sides was in effect for the holiday period.

With the news that some 5,000 marines are besieged by at least 20,000 North Vietnamese soldiers at Khesanh and with the yearly cost of the war now approaching $25 billion, opposition to America's continuing commitment to the Saigon government is certain to increase. The Tet Offensive, if it is successful, may convince many American "doves" that the "light at the end of the tunnel" is dimmer than ever (→Feb. 24).

Johnson will step down

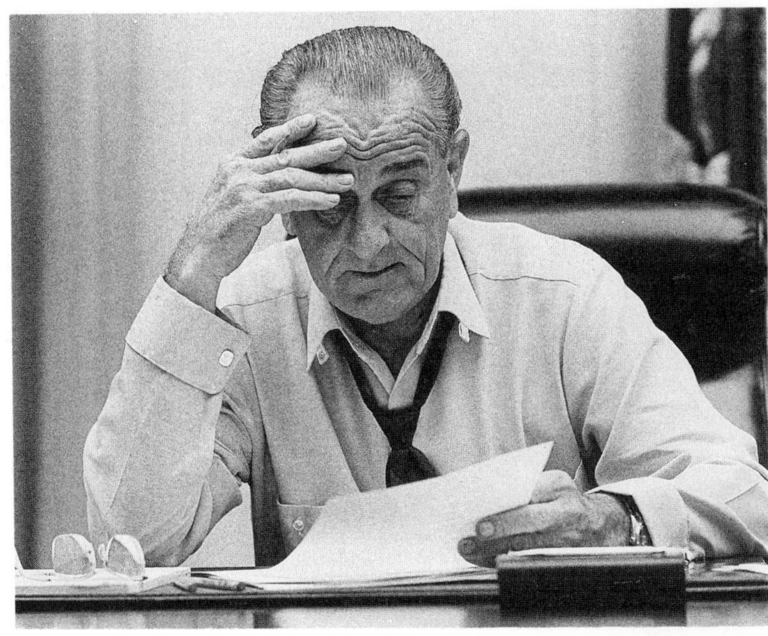

A weary, deeply concerned President Johnson at work on his historic speech.

Washington, D.C., March 31

President Johnson stunned the nation tonight when he announced unexpectedly on television that he does not intend to run for re-election. "I shall not seek and I will not accept the nomination of my party as your President," Johnson declared as he stared purposefully at a camera in the Oval Office.

The President's appearance tonight had been billed as an address to the country on the war in Vietnam. In his speech, he admitted that the conflict had created "division in the American house," and he went on to say that he would not "permit the presidency to become involved in the partisan divisions that are developing."

Johnson's conduct of the war has created deep divisions in the country and eroded his standing in the polls. The latest Gallup poll says only 26 percent of the people favor Johnson's handling of the war. An NBC poll released after the New Hampshire primary indicated half the Democrats were not even aware of Senator Eugene McCarthy's position on the war. Analysts concluded that much of McCarthy's support was as much anti-Johnson as it was anti-war (→ June 6).

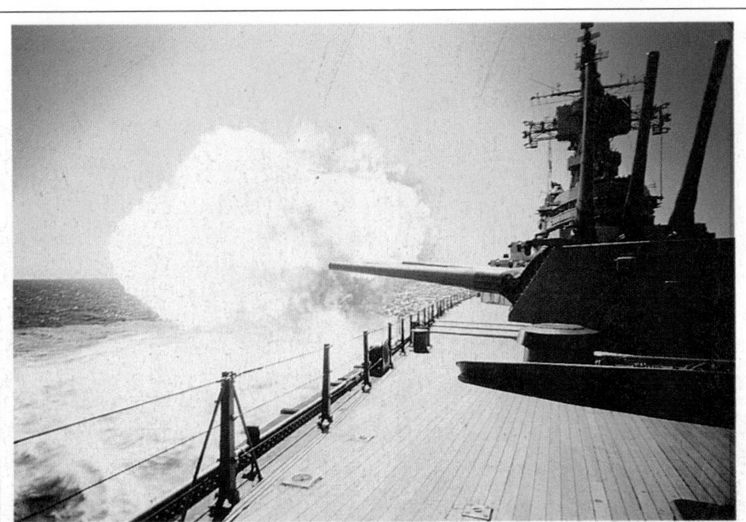

The New Jersey uses its 16-inch guns off North Vietnam. The firepower of the navy and air force is awesome, but the enemy keeps coming on.

Americans counter Vietcong offensive

Washington, D.C., Feb. 24

In the aftermath of the Communist Tet offensive, the United States is gearing up for a renewed military effort against the North Vietnamese and Vietcong. Pentagon officials say fighter-bomber planes from the nuclear-powered aircraft carrier Enterprise have begun major air strikes against the Communist capital of Hanoi. And General William Westmoreland, commander of United States forces in Vietnam, has again asked that more troops, 206,000 of them, be sent to reinforce his men in South Vietnam. Last month, 14,000 air force and navy reservists were called up to bolster the American position in Korea so that additional regular forces could be sent to Vietnam (→ May 10).

General William Westmoreland.

Cronkite joins cry against war effort

United States, March 6

Walter Cronkite, breaking a code of neutrality among major newscasters, has opposed the Vietnam War on national TV. Last night in a special report, Cronkite said a trip to Vietnam left him deeply disillusioned. He believes the war to be futile and immoral. "We have too often been disappointed by the optimism of the American leaders," he said, "to have faith any longer in the silver linings." Cronkite joins a growing group of prominent Americans who have publicly denounced the war effort (→ June 6, 1969).

McCarthy's surprise in New Hampshire

Concord, N.H., March 12

Senator Eugene McCarthy surprised the White House tonight by capturing 42 percent of the vote in the New Hampshire Democratic primary. McCarthy, who trailed President Johnson by just 7,000 votes, predicted that he will win the next race in Wisconsin. "I think I can get the nomination," McCarthy said. "I'm ahead now." After predicting that Johnson would "murder" McCarthy in the primary, the President's operatives were reduced to fighting from the gutter and talking of the senator as a "peace-at-any-price fuzzy thinker." McCarthy, who was helped by thousands of student volunteers here, says he owes it to them not to drop out of the race when Senator Robert Kennedy tosses his hat in the ring (→ 16).

"Come clean for Gene" McCarthy.

Panel warns nation on racial division

Washington, D.C., Feb. 29

The United States is "moving toward two societies, one black, one white, separate and unequal," says a report from the President's National Advisory Commission on Civil Disorders. The report ties recent widespread rioting to "white racism" and urges programs of job creation, bans on discriminatory practices and a reorganization of welfare systems. Headed by Illinois Governor Otto Kerner, the commission also recommended new riot-control and arrest-processing methods (→ Apr.).

Martin Luther King murdered; riots besiege nation

A photograph of the Rev. Dr. Martin Luther King Jr. that was taken shortly before the civil rights leader was felled by a sniper's bullet in Memphis.

Coretta Scott King mourns the loss of her husband with characteristic dignity.

Memphis, Tennessee, April

An assassin's bullet has put an end to the life of the Rev. Dr. Martin Luther King Jr., but apparently not to his influence. On April 4, the 39-year-old Baptist preacher and civil rights activist was leaning over a second-floor motel balcony, talking to fellow activist Jesse Jackson, when he was felled by a shot from a high-powered rifle. The assassin, who escaped, is thought to be a white man who was staying at a cheap boarding house less than 100 yards from the motel. Police think the man escaped in a white Mustang. The rifle was found about a block from the scene of the crime.

That night, Senator Robert Kennedy tried to console a crowd in Indianapolis. "What we need in the United States," he said, "is love and wisdom and compassion toward one another, and a feeling of justice toward those who still suffer within our own country, whether they be white or they be black."

Dr. King, who was in Memphis to help organize a strike by garbage collectors, was known as an advocate of non-violent protest to achieve racial justice. In spite of his stance, Bobby Kennedy's words and the efforts of black leaders to calm King's followers, rioting has broken out in Memphis and in 124 cities across the nation. More than 68,000 soldiers were called out to end the violence. At least 40 blacks and five whites are dead. Over $45 million in property was destroyed and more than 20,000 people were arrested. In the nation's capital alone, seven people were killed, more than 1,000 injured and over 7,000 arrested. It took more than 15,000 troops to stem the rampage. There were also major outbreaks in Baltimore, Chicago and Pittsburgh.

In the midst of the rioting, on April 9, Dr. King was buried in Atlanta, Georgia, after a nationally televised funeral march through the city. On April 11, President Johnson signed the Civil Rights Act of 1968, curbing discrimination in housing. He also signed a law making it a crime to cross state lines for the purpose of inciting a riot.

By April 15, much of the rioting had come to an end. In Chicago, however, continued violence led Mayor Richard Daley to tell police to "shoot to kill" anyone suspected of looting, rioting or arson.

King had been strangely unconcerned about threats on his life. The day before the assassination, he told a Memphis church congregation, "We've got some difficult days ahead. But it really doesn't matter with me now. Because I've been to the mountain top. Like anybody, I would like to live a long life, (but) I've seen the Promised Land. I may not get there with you, (but) we as a people will get (there) ... So I'm happy tonight. I'm not fearing any man. Mine eyes have seen the glory of the coming of the Lord."

Federal troops try to restore order in the nation's capital. The murder of Dr. King shattered black America at a time when it was making great strides.

A young black runs down a street in New York's Harlem as firemen attempt to put out a blaze. A night of chaos followed the assassination of Dr. King.

U.S., Vietnam open peace talks in Paris

Paris, France, May 10

After a successful series of military operations, the United States has started peace talks with the North Vietnamese. Last month, the army's First Cavalry Division finally rescued the 5,000 besieged marines at Khesanh. Other concurrent offensives have secured the areas around both Saigon and Hue. Now, apparently with a "carrot-and-stick" strategy in mind, American peace negotiators Cyrus Vance and Averell Harriman met today with North Vietnamese representative Ha Van Lau, to work out preliminary agendas and formats for subsequent discussions. After their initial meeting this afternoon, Vance said the first session was "cordial and businesslike." The talks resume tomorrow (→Oct. 31).

Broadway's "Hair"

New York City, Apr. 29

The most visible sign of the times – long tresses sported by men – is celebrated in the new "rock musical" *Hair*. The tale of a hippie's rebellion against "The Establishment" is untidy, but its fresh, contemporary sounds are a welcome infusion to mainstream fare. The song *Aquarius* limns the idealistic ethos with what a critic called its "harmony and understanding, sympathy and trust abounding."

King's heir leads poor to the capital

Washington, D.C., June 23

It was hot and humid in the nation's capital, but over 50,000 people marched a mile with the Rev. Ralph Abernathy in an effort to show legislators how many people live in abject poverty, burdened by discrimination. Abernathy is successor to the slain Rev. Martin Luther King Jr. as head of the Southern Christian Leadership Conference, and the march was originally conceived by King. Despite the non-violent techniques proclaimed by King and Abernathy, there have been instances of vandalism and violence among the marchers.

Robert Kennedy is killed in California

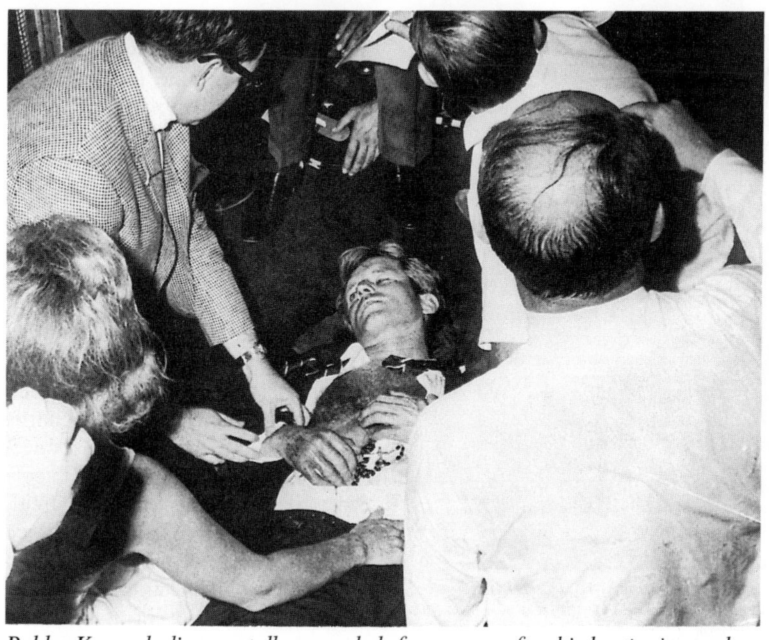

Bobby Kennedy lies mortally wounded, four years after his brother's murder.

Los Angeles, June 6

Life slipped away from Senator Robert Kennedy early this morning, 25 hours after he was shot by a gunman in a kitchen corridor of the Ambassador Hotel. The death of the vibrant senator is hard to explain to a land overrun by violence and a family numbed by tragedy. "All I can say is, good Lord, what is this all about?" lamented Richard Cardinal Cushing, a friend of the Kennedys. "We could continue our prayers that it would never happen again, but we did that before."

The accused assassin, Jerusalem-born Sirhan Sirhan, waited for Kennedy while the senator gave his California primary victory speech. Sirhan allegedly fired twice with a .22-caliber revolver that can be purchased easily for $32. Eight other people were wounded. The gunman was wrestled to the ground by eight Kennedy friends, including pro football star Roosevelt Grier, Olympic champion Rafer Johnson and author George Plimpton.

The murder, just two months after the assassination of the Rev. Martin Luther King Jr., fueled new conspiracy theories, but authorities said Sirhan acted alone. His diary shows him to be virulently anti-Jewish, and Kennedy was a strong supporter of Israel.

Kennedy had refused police protection in Los Angeles and his own bodyguard was unarmed. Congress is now moving to provide Secret Service protection to all major presidential candidates (→Aug. 29).

Radical students rule Columbia University campus for a week

New York City, Apr. 30

One of the decade's most publicized protests ended tonight when 1,000 police officers cracked down on the week-long student takeover of Columbia University. Some 700 people were arrested and 148 hurt in the confrontation as the police cleared five student-occupied buildings, including the ransacked office of university president Grayson Kirk. A school official admitted there were "breakdowns in the police action." Students countered the nightsticks by kicking, biting and hurling anything at hand.

About 5,000 students took part in the demonstrations, which were led by Mark Rudd, president of the Students for a Democratic Society, and joined by the Students' Afro-American Society and residents of Harlem. They protested the proposed erection of a university gym, and Columbia's ties with the Institute for Defense Analysis. The gym, to be built in an adjacent black area, was seen as a "racist" symbol of Columbia's disregard for black neighborhoods. The Defense Department project was scored as aiding the Vietnam War. The students also sought a restructuring of the university to give them greater participation. An emergency faculty committee agreed to drop the gym project but not the Defense Institute affiliation. During the week, acting dean Henry Coleman and two other officials were held captive for more than 24 hours. ▷

Students camp out in front of Low Memorial Library on the Columbia University campus, expressing frustrations felt by many Americans, as student activism reaches a level unprecedented in American academic history.

Chicago: The whole world's watching

Chicago policemen break up a demonstration at the Democratic convention.

Chicago, Aug. 29

A splintered Democratic Party nominated Hubert Humphrey as its presidential candidate on the first ballot tonight. Humphrey defeated Senator Eugene McCarthy by more than 1,100 votes, but the party he will lead against Richard M. Nixon is far from united. The convention was haunted by the ghost of the slain Robert Kennedy; a move to draft his young brother, Ted, nearly split the party, and the platform committee refused to embrace opponents of the Vietnam War.

All week Chicago was badly divided, and nowhere were the divisions more visible than in the blood-spattered streets near the convention Amphitheater. Ten thousand young people came to Chicago to protest the war, but flower power was no match for police power. "Kill 'em, kill 'em," the police shouted as they charged. "Pigs, pigs, oink, oink," the demonstrators screamed back. One witness heard an officer yell, "We'll kill all you bastards," as he clubbed a protester. And as news cameras rolled and clubs flew, the protesters chanted, "The whole world's watching! The whole world's watching!"

Some 700 demonstrators were hurt and 650 arrested. Police reported 80 of their men injured. Critics said the cops acted like Nazis, but Mayor Richard Daley backed the 20,000 police, National Guardsmen and soldiers. "How would you like to stand around all night," he said, "and be called names not even used in a brothel house?"

The worst violence unfolded tonight, as demonstrators tried to march south from Grant Park to the Amphitheater. Inside the convention hall, nervous security guards caught up in the violent scene scuffled with and clubbed some delegates and newsmen. Walter Cronkite, the normally reserved CBS anchorman, called the guards "thugs." At the podium, Connecticut's Senator Abraham Ribicoff stared at Daley and said, "With George McGovern as president, we wouldn't have Gestapo tactics in the streets of Chicago." The mayor's reply was not printable. McGovern of South Dakota had been in the running for the nomination.

Faced with anarchy in the party, Humphrey turned to Edmund Muskie of Maine, a quiet friend in the Senate, as his running mate. In his acceptance address, Humphrey urged his party to look to the future. "If there is any one lesson that we should have learned, it is that the policies of tomorrow need not be limited by the policies of yesterday," he said. But the platform committee defeated a bid to insert a plank urging a halt to bombing in Vietnam. For that reason, perhaps, many notables, including McCarthy and Ted Kennedy, did not join Humphrey at the podium (→ Dec. 1).

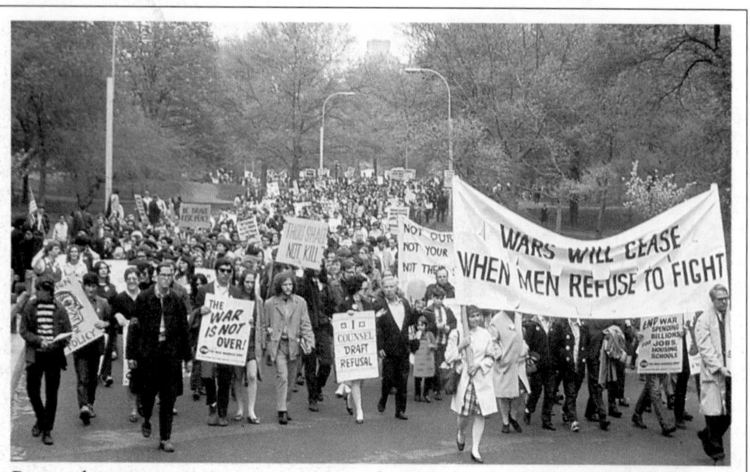

Peace demonstrations are attracting thousands of people from all walks of life. The conflict, which seems to roll on and on, has affected almost every American, whether through the loss of a loved one in Vietnam, or an increase in taxes. One thing that everyone now wants is a speedy end to the war.

Warhol wounded

New York City, June 3

Andy Warhol clings to life tonight, wounded in the chest under circumstances as weird as any of his avant-garde film plots. Valeria Solanis, 28, lesbian head of S.C.U.M. (Society for Cutting Up Men), was hired by Warhol to star in his film *I, a Man*. Today, when he refused to film a script she wrote, she shot him three times. Warhol won fame with silk-screen portraits of himself and Marilyn Monroe. He first attracted notice with realistic paintings of huge Campbell's soup cans. The fortyish Warhol had a successful career as an illustrator before making celebrity his profession.

James Ray seized in King's murder

London, June 8

James Earl Ray, the man accused of having assassinated the Rev. Dr. Martin Luther King Jr. on April 4, was arrested at the London airport today as he was disembarking from an airliner. Using a Canadian passport, Ray was traveling under the name Ramon George Sneyd. Ray has been accused of shooting the civil rights leader while King was in Memphis to help organize a strike among predominantly black sanitation workers. The murder was the last of several assassination attempts against King and inspired mass protests and rioting across the nation. Ray will be tried for the murder in a Memphis court (→ Oct. 27).

10% war surcharge

Washington, D.C., June 28

To help offset the expense of the Vietnam War, Congress passed a 10 percent surcharge on income taxes today. Critics say the tax exemplifies the high cost of the war and the great gains of arms contractors; corporate profits have soared since escalation of the American involvement in Vietnam. The Johnson administration recently turned down a proposal for an excess profits tax. When the surcharge was initiated, leaders of 13 major corporations sent wires to congressmen encouraging its passage.

Oct. 1. *Yippie leader Abbie Hoffman plays with a yo-yo after appearing before the House Un-American Activities Committee.*

U.S. ends bombing of North Vietnam

Washington, D.C., Oct. 31

President Johnson announced tonight that American aerial and naval bombing of North Vietnam will stop tomorrow in order to further the possibilities of a negotiated peace. He made it clear, however, that the end of the bombing does not mean that an end to the long war is at hand. As the President said, "There may well be very hard fighting ahead." Johnson's decision to halt the bombing was apparently approved in advance by the leaders of Congress. It is reported that the South Vietnamese government was opposed to a bombing halt that did not include equivalent concessions on the part of the North Vietnamese (→ Feb. 23, 1969).

Chicago cops chided

Washington, D.C., Dec. 1

The Chicago police force was severely criticized today for the attacks on demonstrators at the Democratic convention. A presidential panel, headed by Milton Eisenhower, concluded that the reaction of the officers could "only be called a riot." The report did accuse the protesters of having provoked the police with "obscene epithets ... rocks, sticks, bathroom tiles and even human feces." But the committee accused the police of having used "unrestrained and indiscriminate" violence (→ Feb. 18, 1970).

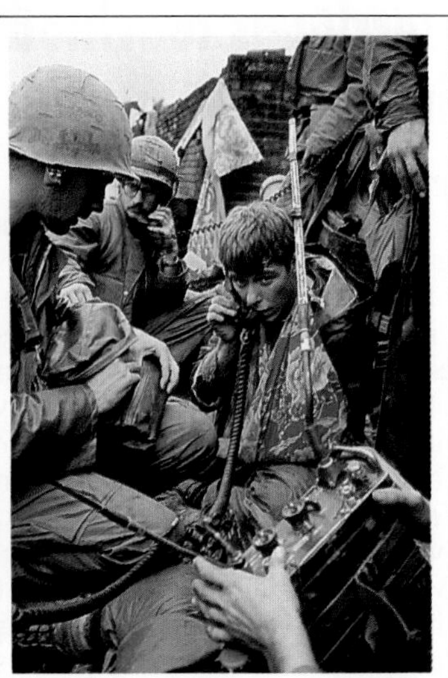

A wounded marine in Vietnam wears a "flower power" arm sling.

Nixon ekes out victory

The people hear his call for a restoration of "law and order" in the nation.

Washington, D.C., Nov. 5

Richard M. Nixon squeaked past Hubert H. Humphrey today to win the presidency in one of the closest votes in history. With 95 percent counted, Nixon appears to be a minority victor. As counting continues, he has 29,726,409 votes to Humphrey's 29,677,152, while the American Independent Party's law-and-order candidate George Wallace of Alabama nears the 10 million mark, apparently making good on his promise to deny the White House to the Democrats. Following a long, tense night, Nixon held off delivering his victory remarks until 11:35 a.m., when he thanked his tired but happy supporters. The President-elect described Vice President Humphrey's losing fight as "gallant and courageous," then went on to speak about a campaign incident in the little town of Deshler, Ohio. "I suppose five times the population was there in the dusk, almost impossible to see, but a teenager held up a sign, 'Bring us together.' And that will be the great objective of this administration at the outset, to bring the American people together".

Pueblo crew, held for a year, released

Panmunjom, Korea, Dec. 22

The 82-man crew of the Pueblo, led by its captain, Commander Lloyd M. Bucher, crossed the Bridge of No Return today, bringing along the body of a shipmate who was killed when the vessel was seized by North Korean patrol boats on January 23. Though full of sophisticated intelligence-gathering equipment, the ship carried only two machine guns and was not escorted at the time of its capture. Nevertheless, the prospect of a court-martial awaits Commander Bucher for having surrendered his ship without a fight and for having signed a confession that he was within North Korean territorial waters when seized (→ May 6, 1969).

Kubrick's "2001"

Hollywood, Calif.

Arthur C. Clarke wrote the short story *The Sentinel* 18 years ago. Now director Stanley Kubrick has transformed it into *2001: A Space Odyssey*, a $10 million science fiction film of dazzling imagery and visual splendor. With stunning special effects, it contrasts human frailty – in the conflict of earthlings and HAL, a computer that goes mad – with a mystical vision. Keir Dullea plays the astronaut.

Genesis in space

Space, Dec. 24

With their TV camera transmitting the first close-up images of the barren lunar surface, the Apollo 8 astronauts read a Christmas message to millions back on "the Good Earth" tonight. The space voyagers, Colonel Frank Borman, Captain James A. Lovell Jr. and Major William A. Anders, became the first men to orbit the moon at 4:59 a.m. Tonight, Borman described the moon as "a vast, lonely and forbidding sight," and Lovell called Earth "a grand oasis in the big vastness of space." The astronauts then took turns reading about Creation from the Book of Genesis. Borman concluded, saying "Merry Christmas. God bless all of you, all of you on the Good Earth."

Black militancy is displayed at Olympics

Mexico City, Oct. 27

Black athletes who were seeking a way to protest the treatment of blacks in the United States found their opportunity after Tommy Smith and John Carlos finished first and third in the Olympic 200-meter dash today. As medals were given out and the *Star-Spangled Banner* played, Smith and Carlos each held a dark-gloved fist aloft. Heads bowed, they defiantly refused to look at the flag. They were suspended from the Games and expelled from the Olympic Village. The demonstration was made in lieu of a Black Power boycott of the Games that never developed. With the help of Smith and Carlos, the U.S. team won 45 gold medals; the Soviets 30 (→ Dec. 6, 1969).

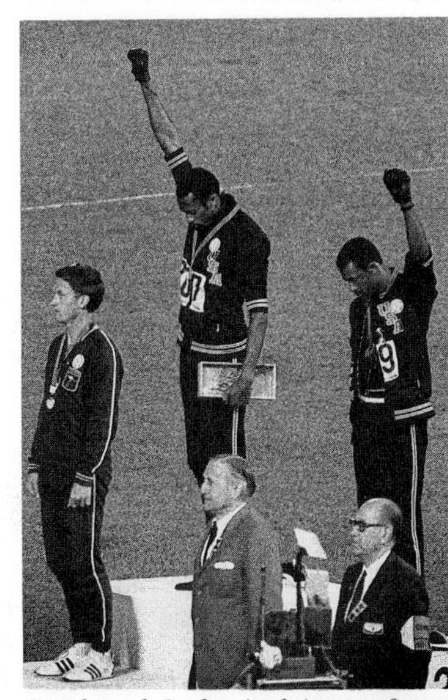

Smith and Carlos (right) raise fists.

1969

Nixon

Miami, Jan. 12. New York Jets defeat Baltimore Colts in Super Bowl III, 16-7.

New York City, Feb. 8. *Saturday Evening Post* prints final issue.

Vietnam, Feb. 23. North Vietnamese launch major offensive in 100 cities (→July 8).

Los Angeles, May 5. Boston Celtics defeat Los Angeles Lakers, four games to three, for N.B.A. title.

New York City, May 5. Norman Mailer wins Pulitzer Prize, National Book Award for *The Armies of the Night.*

Washington, D.C., May 6. Secretary of Navy bars disciplinary action against crew of Pueblo.

Dallas, May 17. Ira G. Korn buys one of 16 known copies of first printing of Declaration of Independence for $404,000.

Washington, D.C., June 9. Senate confirms Warren E. Burger as Chief Justice of Supreme Court.

Washington, D.C., Aug. 3. President Nixon returns from world tour on which he visited Rumania, becoming first President to visit a Communist nation since World War II.

New York City, Oct. 16. Mets beat Baltimore Orioles in World Series, four games to one.

Washington, D.C., Oct. 29. In Alexander v. Holmes Company, Supreme Court orders an immediate end to all school segregation.

Washington, D.C., Dec. 30. President Nixon signs tax reform act, reducing personal income taxes and removing nine million low-income people from tax rolls.

Washington, D.C. White House press secretary Ron Ziegler coins term "photo-opportunity."

Northeast. Formerly single sex colleges such as Williams, Trinity and Vassar become coeducational.

Hollywood, Calif. Top films include *Midnight Cowboy*, *Butch Cassidy and the Sundance Kid* and *Easy Rider.*

DEATH

Washington, D.C., March 28. Dwight D. Eisenhower, General and President (*Oct. 14, 1890).

Nixon begins "Vietnamization" plan

Wounded and weary U.S. troops.

Vietnam, literally a quagmire.

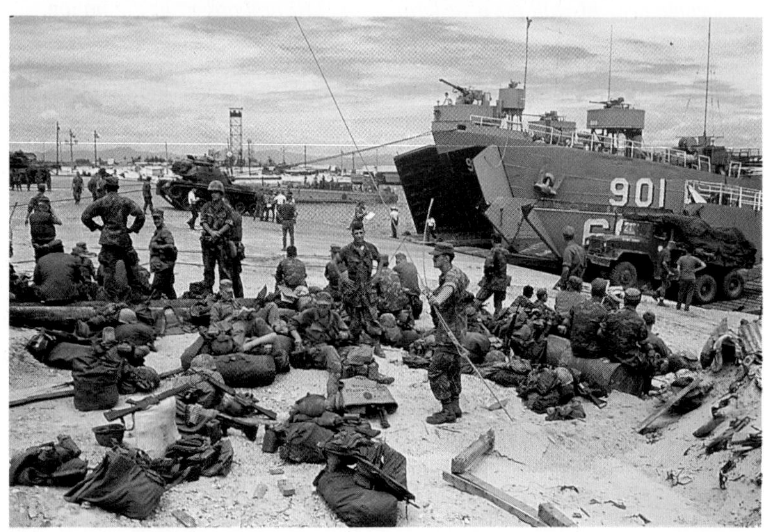

Due to recent policy changes, American troops are beginning to be withdrawn.

Washington, D.C., July 8

In accord with President Nixon's plans for a gradual disengagement from the Vietnam War and for turning over the burden of the fighting to the South Vietnamese military forces, the first American combat unit left Saigon today. A battalion of soldiers from the Ninth Infantry Division was flown out of Tan Son Nhut Airport for its permanent headquarters at Fort Lewis, Washington. The gradual withdrawal of American combat forces has been planned since June 8, when the President announced that 25,000 American troops would be sent home by the end of next month. Administration spokesmen say that even more American soldiers are going to be withdrawn if the South Vietnamese army shows it is capable of containing enemy military efforts.

The "Vietnamization" process began April 26 when the American 77th Field Artillery turned over its equipment to a South Vietnamese army artillery unit in the southern Mekong River region. In the same month, American military officials announced that all South Vietnamese units have been equipped with M-16 rifles along with most of the helicopters that will be needed for independent combat operations. It is expected that the South Vietnamese forces will be taking over the ground combat role completely by 1972 (→Nov. 16).

Oil leak smears Santa Barbara area

Santa Barbara, Calif., Feb. 9

"It's plugged." This brief comment from Union Oil signals victory in the 12-day fight to choke an undersea oilflow that has been going on since January 28. Some 231,000 gallons spilled into the Pacific, smearing 30 miles of beaches and killing waterbirds and marine life. But the trouble, caused by Union's Platform A, 5.5 miles off Santa Barbara, is not over. An oil slick covers 800 square miles. Governor Ronald Reagan has declared Southern California shores a disaster area, the clean-up goes on and so do protests against oil drilling.

Smothers Brothers get the ax at CBS

New York City, Apr. 4

"They're a little more topical than we anticipated," a CBS aide said a while ago about the Smothers Brothers, Tommy and Dick. "We're trying to make people aware of what's going on today," says Tommy. But CBS Program Practices, which the brothers call "Big Daddy Memo," has the final say on what goes out over CBS airways, and it seems to be in constant conflict with the comedy team over lines and skits about Vietnam, the administration and other "controversial" topics. Today, the conflict led to cancellation of *The Smothers Brothers Comedy Hour.*

Berrigans convicted in anti-draft action

Baltimore, Maryland, June 6

Fathers Daniel and Philip Berrigan, along with the other members of the Catonsville Nine, were convicted in state court today of charges stemming from the destruction of selective service records in May of last year. The Nine, who were found guilty on similar charges in federal court last November, burned the files of the Catonsville, Maryland, Draft Board to protest the Vietnam War. The Berrigans have orchestrated similar protests before and the two Roman Catholic priests have become heroes to antiwar activists (→Nov. 15).

Neil Armstrong on moon: "The eagle has landed"

"That's one small step for man, one giant leap for mankind," said astronaut Neil Armstrong from the "magnificent desolation" of the moon.

Houston, Texas, July 24

"Houston, Tranquility base here. The Eagle has landed." As these words crackled 238,000 miles through the blackness of space four days ago, humanity was awed by the news that two American astronauts, Neil A. Armstrong and Colonel Edwin E. Aldrin Jr., had landed on the moon. Soon after, Armstrong, 38, emerged from the spidery lunar lander. And as a television camera transmitted the otherworldly images to an audience of perhaps 600 million, the astronaut slipped softly onto the bleak, powdery lunar surface at 10:56 p.m., delivering the already immortal line, "That's one small step for man, one giant leap for mankind."

The mission, the culmination of a decade-long effort and an age-old dream, began on July 16, when Apollo XI blasted off from Pad 39-A at Cape Kennedy, Florida. With Lieutenant Colonel Michael Collins, 38, the astronauts thundered into Earth orbit atop a 363-foot-high Saturn V rocket, then fired for a trajectory to the moon. Four days later, Armstrong and Aldrin, 39, crawled from a narrow hatchway into the frail four-legged Lunar Module (LEM) and separated from Collins, who continued circling the moon in the Apollo capsule. "Eagle has wings," exclaimed Armstrong as he piloted the LEM into a descent of 200 feet per second. But 300 feet from the landing spot in the airless, waterless Sea of Tranquility, the astronauts were startled by a treacherous, boulder-strewn moonscape. Calmly, Armstrong detached the computer control and, as fuel ran low, guided the craft to a smooth plain, touching down at 4:17 p.m. "We're breathing again, thanks a lot," intoned a mission controller in Houston.

Within six hours, Armstrong had stepped into history; and 19 minutes later Aldrin joined him amid what he called the "magnificent desolation." The explorers wore 185-pound suits but they "kangaroo-hopped" over the low-gravity moonscape, which Armstrong said had "a stark beauty all its own." For over two hours, they collected samples and set up instruments and an American flag. From Washington, President Nixon told them that "for one priceless moment in the whole history of man the people of this Earth are truly one."

Indeed, Earth did seem united, as hundreds of millions from all political backgrounds thrilled to the feat. Tibet's Buddhist leader, the Dalai Lama, predicted, "Man's limited knowledge will acquire a new dimension of infinite scope," while Charles Lindbergh, the first man to solo across the Atlantic non-stop, spoke of "a flowering of civilization to the stars." But a black leader, the Rev. Jesse Jackson, wondered, "How can this nation swell and swagger with technological pride when it has a spiritual will so crippled?" Picasso dismissed the whole fuss, saying "I have no opinion about it, and I don't care."

On July 21, at 1:55 p.m., the Lunar Module lifted toward a rendezvous with Collins in his solitary orbit 69 miles above. Today, after a flawless return voyage, Apollo XI parachuted safely into the Pacific. It was the end of a week that Nixon, aboard the nearby carrier Hornet, called "the greatest in the history of the world since Creation" (→Apr. 17, 1970).

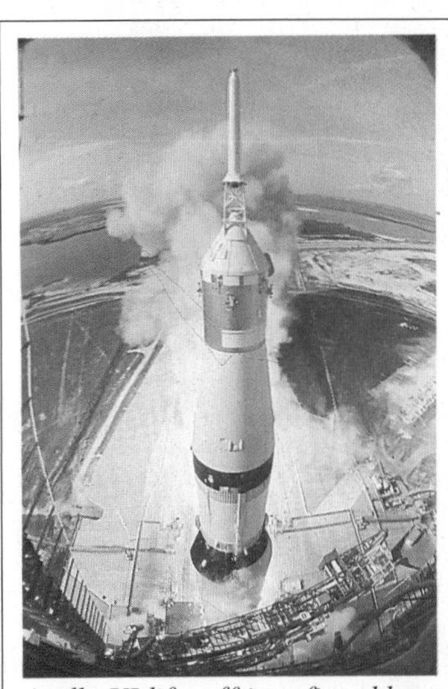

Apollo XI lifts off in a fiery blaze.

Woodstock: A coming together for rock, drugs, sex and peace

At Woodstock, Jimi Hendrix played a raucous "Star-Spangled Banner."

A young girl shows her sentiments up front as a friend paints her body.

Bethel, New York, Aug. 17

It is disbanded now, the Woodstock Nation of 400,000, a peaceful kingdom that for this one brief weekend was united by good vibrations. When farmer Max Yasgur turned over his 600-acre farm outside Woodstock to the agents of the Who, Jefferson Airplane and other groups, he had no idea of the eventual impact of the Aquarian Exposition. There were traffic jams, long exposures of nudity, acid trips (one person died of a bad one), casual sex and peace signs. One reporter estimated that 90 percent of the crowd was smoking marijuana. Despite all the anti-establishment trappings, it was one very peaceful event. Those within hearing distance of Jimi Hendrix, the Band, Janis Joplin et al cheered and waved, while those farther off just rocked to the bass beat that moved the ground beneath them.

On two nights, that ground was thick mud, churned up by downpours. People shared plastic bags for impromptu cover and they lent one another room in huts built of collapsible chairs. It was a time of coming together, and as cars roll out of Bethel tonight, there is a sense that they are all rolling in the same direction, revving to a common beat.

Ted Kennedy guilty in Kopechne case

Martha's Vineyard, Mass., July 25

Following the death of Mary Jo Kopechne that made Chappaquiddick a synonym for shame, Senator Edward M. Kennedy pleaded guilty today to a charge of leaving the scene of an accident. That accident happened a week ago, July 18, as Kennedy drove his companion away from a party of married men and younger women at Martha's Vineyard. At Chappaquiddick, the car plunged off a narrow bridge into a pond and Miss Kopechne drowned. Kennedy didn't report the accident until 10 hours later. He said he had "repeatedly dove" in rescue attempts, had been in "a state of shock," and did not realize what had happened until he awoke in his motel the following morning. Miss Kopechne, a 28-year-old Washington secretary, had once worked for Robert Kennedy.

Wiretapping of King and others revealed

Chicago, June 13

In testimony heard today in a federal court, it was alleged that the Justice Department has illegally eavesdropped on those suspected of subversion. Last week in Houston, Texas, witnesses testified that the F.B.I. set wiretapping devices on telephones of the Rev. Martin Luther King Jr. They were allegedly set after President Johnson had established limits on surveillance. It is no secret that F.B.I. chief J. Edgar Hoover disliked King, once calling the civil rights leader "the most notorious liar in the country." Formal charges are expected to be filed against those to blame for the taps.

Actress slain in Manson cult murder

Los Angeles, Aug. 10

The pre-dawn horror of August 9 left five people dead, with the words "HELTER SKELTER" and "PIGS" written in blood on the walls. The cultists, including young women from middle-class backgrounds and directed by Charles Manson, invaded the home of Sharon Tate and her husband, film director Roman Polanski (he was in London at the time). The band ritualistically slaughtered the beautiful actress, who was eight and a half months pregnant, three guests and a passer-by. Tonight, Manson's gang murdered a couple elsewhere in the city (→March 29, 1971).

"Buffalo Dancers" by Awa Tsireh. Native Americans, long relegated to second-class citizenship, are uniting to awaken the country to their needs.

2 Illinois Panthers slain in police raid

Chicago, Dec. 6

In a wild shoot-out on the west side of the city tonight, the police killed Fred Hampton, leader of the Illinois chapter of the Black Panthers, and Mark Clark, a party leader from Peoria. The killing, which took place during a police raid on the Panthers' Illinois headquarters, is only the latest in a series of confrontations between police and Chicago's black population. Several young blacks have been shot by the police under questionable circumstances, and some blacks have shot at policemen. In two years, confrontations with police have resulted in the deaths of 28 Panthers (→Apr. 20, 1971).

Stabbing incident mars rock concert

Tracy, Calif., Dec. 6

Believers in the Woodstock Nation were jolted awake tonight by a fatal stabbing at a rock festival headlined by the Rolling Stones. A crowd of 300,000 swamped the Altamont Speedway here for a show that also included the Jefferson Airplane and Grateful Dead, and there was violence right off the bat as Hell's Angels motorcycle gangs policed the stage. Jefferson Airplane singer Marty Balin was hurt trying to stop a fracas, and as the Stones began *Sympathy for the Devil* violence erupted with the stabbing of Meredith Hunter. Some link the violence to the hiring of Hell's Angels in exchange for free beer.

Massive anti-war rallies

Peace symbols come to Washington.

Washington, D.C., Nov. 15

The largest anti-war demonstration in the capital's history unfolded peacefully today as 250,000 people marched from the Capitol to the Washington Monument. Across the continent, nearly 200,000 people rallied in San Francisco's Golden Gate Park. "All we are asking is give peace a chance," they chanted.

The Washington protest was led by familiar faces in the movement, Senators Eugene McCarthy and George McGovern, Coretta King, wife of the slain civil rights leader, Benjamin Spock, author of the infant-care book, and folksinger Arlo Guthrie. "It takes little wisdom," Mrs. King said, "to realize that if it was unwise and inept to have gotten into this war in the first place; to stubbornly persist in staying in it becomes stupid and evil."

There were tense moments when counter-demonstrators clustered near 12 coffins containing names of American servicemen who have died in Vietnam. The situation was defused when they were allowed to add the names of civilians slaughtered by the Vietcong in the Tet offensive. Only one arrest was reported during the protest.

President Nixon, who vowed to ignore the demonstrations, spent much of the week solidifying support for his Vietnam policy. House members passed a resolution endorsing his "efforts to negotiate a just peace in Vietnam," and he made a dramatic appearance to thank them. "When the security of America is involved, when peace for America and the world is involved, and the lives of our young men are involved," Nixon said, "we are not Democrats, we are not Republicans, we are Americans." The President avoided the harsh language he used earlier to criticize campus revolt, discord and the violation of "old standards" and "old principles." Middle America, Nixon seems to believe, stands behind his efforts to end the war with honor (→Feb. 25, 1970).

Riot policemen plunge into a crowd of angry demonstrators in front of the instrumentation laboratory at the Massachusetts Institute of Technology in Cambridge on November 5. Many of the nation's research and development centers are targeted by protesters because of ties to the defense industry.

Massacre at My Lai

Washington, D.C., Nov. 16

Hundreds of Vietnamese civilians were massacred by American troops 18 months ago, Defense Department officials have disclosed, and senior officers of the Americal Division have allegedly been covering up the atrocity. On March 16 of last year, Task Force Barker, a battalion-sized unit of the Americal, launched a search-and-destroy operation against suspected Vietcong sympathizers in the hamlet of My Lai, part of the Song My village in Quangtri Province. The commander of Charlie Company apparently believed every Vietnamese in My Lai was either Vietcong or a sympathizer, and he ordered his men to burn and destroy the hamlet completely. No enemy forces were encountered in the attack. But the American soldiers swept through My Lai and killed every person in the hamlet – mainly old men, women and children. There were several sexual assaults on the women, including one gang-rape. The number of victims in the immediate vicinity of My Lai is estimated at 175 to 200. Army sources report that some 450 civilians were probably killed by troops of Task Force Barker in the overall Song My village complex. Murder charges are expected to be filed against some of the participants in the My Lai massacre (→Apr. 30, 1970).

"The Making of a Counterculture"

United States

Two new tracts are spreading the gospel of the New Left. Theodore Roszak takes an academic slant in *The Making of a Counterculture.* Scorning science and reason ("the myth of objective consciousness"), he laments "the final consolidation of a technocratic totalitarianism in which we shall find ourselves ingeniously adapted to an existence wholly estranged from anything that has ever made the life of man an interesting adventure." The only antidote is a "standard of truth" pegged to "illuminated personality."

Roszak's plan pales beside the visionary ramblings of Jerry Rubin, Chicago Seven defendant and co-founder, with Abbie Hoffman, of the Yippies. In *Do It*, Rubin predicts a "Youth International Revolution," staged by "tribes of long hairs, armed women, workers, peasants and students." The White House is slated to "become one big commune." Las Vegas has yet to lay odds on Rubin's assertion that the Pentagon "will be replaced with an LSD experimental farm."

Agnew: "Effete corps of impudent snobs"

Washington, D.C., Autumn

President Nixon has sent Vice President Spiro Agnew on a speaking tour of the nation – to brand the opposition and "divide on authentic lines." It has produced a barrage of heavy-handed, yet colorful, rhetoric hurled at the anti-war movement and the news media.

Agnew described war protesters as "anarchists and ideological eunuchs." Of the liberal news people, he said, "A spirit of national masochism prevails, encouraged by an effete corps of impudent snobs who characterize themselves as intellectuals." He also called journalists "nattering nabobs of negativism." Americans, he says, want "a cry of alarm to penetrate the cacophony of seditious drivel." Nonetheless, with dozens of lives lost weekly in Vietnam, "seditious drivel" sounds more and more like heartfelt compassion to a lot of Americans.

"Patriotic Boy" by Diane Arbus. As this photograph shows, there is continuity amid all of the change.

The Sixties: "There's something happening here"

President Kennedy claps along as daughter, Caroline, and son, John Jr., romp in the Oval Office. The First Family captured the hearts and imaginations of the American people and symbolized the vigor of a new generation.

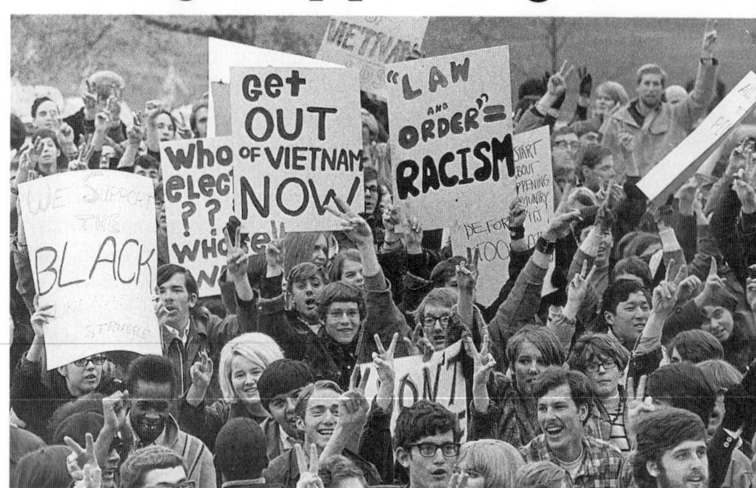

A decade of demonstrations. Students in Des Moines, Iowa, the heartland of America, like young people throughout the country, express their outrage at perceived injustice and war, appropriating the V for Victory sign for peace.

Smoking "grass" or "pot," one of the more prevalent practices of kids today. At least one-third of college students have tried marijuana, and some have used LSD, mescaline and other hard drugs in an effort to escape from reality.

1963 Corvette Sting Ray Coupe, one of the hottest cars on the road. Automobiles have taken on a longer, lower, leaner look, with the Ford Mustang and the GTO among the most popular in a mobile society that worships wheels.

A Mercury rocket poised on the launch pad. JFK's dream of putting a man on the moon has been realized.

Bob Dylan and Joan Baez. "You don't know what is happening," Dylan sings, "do you, Mr. Jones?"

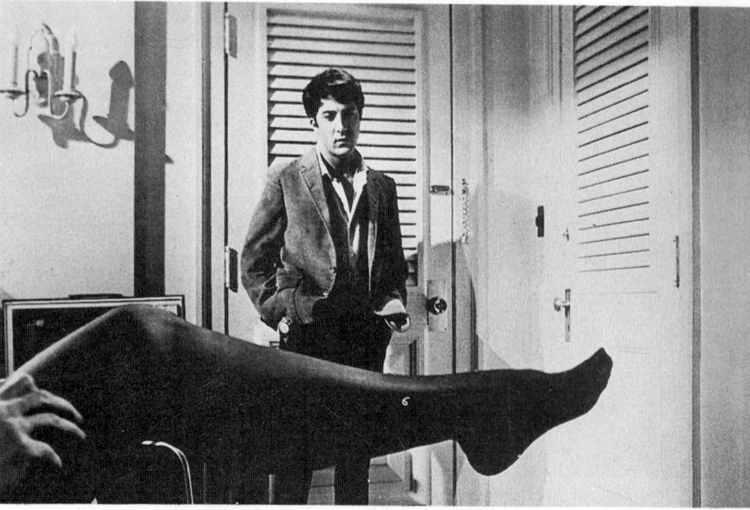

Dustin Hoffman pensively considers what Mrs. Robinson has to offer. The film "The Graduate" illustrates what many college graduates are now asking themselves: Is money and a comfortable suburban life style all there is?

"... There's a man with a gun over there ..."

A peace symbol – in the jungles of Vietnam. Perhaps no one wants an end to war more than the soldier.

While racial turmoil rages back home, the hardships of war continue to draw many Americans together.

On February 1, 1968, a South Vietnamese police chief executes a captured Vietcong officer with a single pistol shot to the head. This photo, by Eddie Adams of the Associated Press, has come to symbolize the horror of the war.

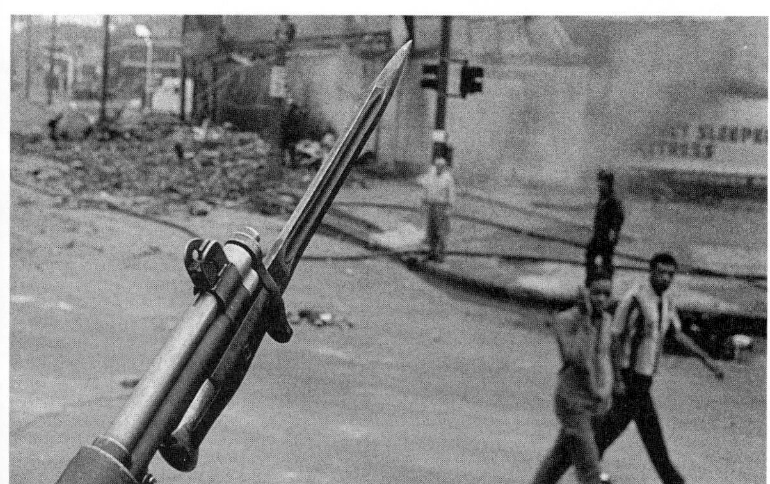

A fixed bayonet points out over the rubble-strewn, riot-torn West Side of Detroit in the long, hot summer of 1967. Tanks had to be used to restore order. Said Mayor James Cavanaugh of his city: "It looks like Berlin in 1945."

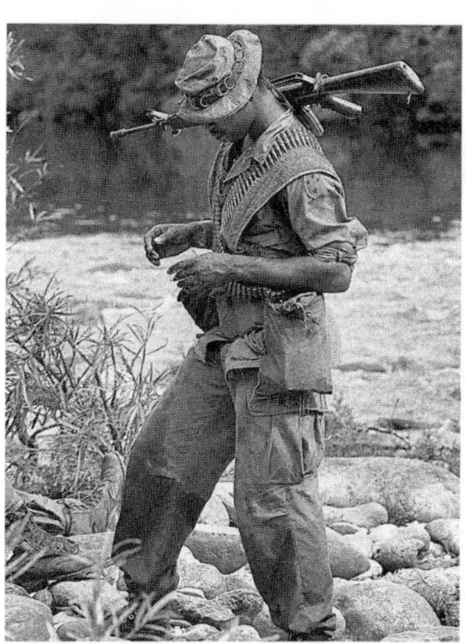

A G.I. crosses a stream while balancing his M-16 on his neck. Is there light at the end of the tunnel?

A major hugs his wife, clad in height of fashion, as he returns from Vietnam. There's no place like home.

National Guardsmen on patrol in Newark, New Jersey, one of 70 American cities torn by race riots in 1967. "We have endured a week such as no nation should live through," said President Johnson. "A time of violence and tragedy."

Purple smoke directs an evacuation chopper during the fierce battle for Ashua Valley. Although the United States has made a sizable military commitment to the defense of South Vietnam, final victory seems as elusive as ever.

1970

Nixon

New York City, Jan. 8. National Football League and American Football League form N.F.L. Players Association.

New Orleans, Jan. 11. Kansas City Chiefs defeat Minnesota Vikings, 23-7, in Super Bowl IV.

Vietnam, Jan. 26. Lieutenant Everett Alvarez sets record for longest time spent as prisoner of war by any American – 2,000 days.

Space, Apr. 17. Explosion of oxygen tank aboard service module prevents Apollo 13 from landing on moon (→ July 31, 1971).

Louisville, May 2. Diane Crump becomes first woman jockey in Kentucky Derby, finishing 12th on Fathom.

New York City, May 4. Jean Stafford wins Pulitzer Prize, for *Collected Stories.*

New York City, May 8. Knicks win N.B.A. title, four games to three, over Los Angeles Lakers.

Washington, D.C., June 15. Supreme Court, in Welsh v. United States, rules that moral conviction is equivalent to religious credo in qualifying for conscientious-objector status.

Chicago, June 26. American Medical Association votes to allow doctors to perform abortions for social and economic reasons (→ July 1).

Washington, D.C., Aug. 12. President Nixon signs Postal Reorganization Act, making postal service independent government corporation.

Newport, Rhode Island, Sept. 28. U.S. yacht Intrepid successfully defends America's Cup against Australian challenger Gretel II.

Baltimore, Oct. 15. Orioles defeat Cincinnati Reds in World Series, 4 games to 1.

Washington, D.C., Dec. 3. House subcommittee rejects an impeachment charge against Supreme Court Justice William O. Douglas by Michigan Representative Gerald R. Ford.

Washington, D.C., Dec. 29. President Nixon signs into law Occupational Safety and Health Act, establishing occupational standards.

Hollywood, Calif. Top films this year include *Patton, M*A*S*H** and *Woodstock.*

Chicago Seven hear fate

Jerry Rubin, Abbie Hoffman and Rennie Davis during a break in the trial.

Chicago, Feb. 18

In a trial that reached comic heights unparalleled in American jurisprudence, the "Chicago Seven" were found not guilty of conspiring to incite a riot. But five of the defendants – Rennie Davis, David Dellinger, Tom Hayden, Abbie Hoffman and Jerry Rubin – were convicted of crossing state lines with intent to cause a riot. Presiding Judge Julius Hoffman handed them five-vear sentences, the maximum term. The other two defendants, John Froines and Lee Weiner, were acquitted on both counts.

During the course of the trial, the five were also given contempt-of-court sentences, as were their lawyers, William Kunstler and William Weinglass. The trial was the result of the riots during the 1968 Democratic National Convention in Chicago. There were originally eight defendants. But Bobby Seale, leader of the Black Panthers, was granted a separate trial after having conducted a one-man war against the judge, who tagged him with 16 contempt-of-court charges. Their confrontation, which characterized the trial as a whole, bordered on Theater of the Absurd as Seale was ordered bound and gagged after having called Judge Hoffman a "racist," a "fascist" and a "pig." After the sentencing, the wife of defendant Abbie Hoffman was expelled for shouting at the judge, "We'll dance on your grave, Julie!"

Earth Day spotlights the environment

United States

Looking to the future and finding a picture clouded with exhaust fumes and sewage, Americans are mobilizing to protect their environment. On April 22, designated "Earth Day" by environmentalists, millions left their homes to participate in clean-ups, marches and teach-ins.

And perhaps none too soon. Demographics experts say the Earth's population may reach a saturation point of 3.6 billion by the year 2000. Americans alone pile up waste at the rate of 3.5 billion tons a year. Each of the 87 million cars driven in the United States emits 1.5 pounds of pollutants daily. And at least five percent of drinking water nationwide is contaminated.

The message is beginning to reach Washington. In November's elections, voters rejected six of the 12 lawmakers with the worst environmental records. In October, an Environmental Protection Agency was created with William Ruckelshaus as its director. And the Clean Air Act, passed in December, mandates pollution-free cars by 1975.

Anti-war protesters burn bank on coast

Santa Barbara, Calif., Feb. 25

Anti-war demonstrators set fire to a Bank of America branch in the troubled Isla Vista area near the University of California at Santa Barbara as rock- and bottle-throwing rampages continued for a second night. The crowd numbered over 1,000, but some were onlookers and objected to the violence as having little to do with issues. The climate around the campus has been tense since an "anti-establishment" instructor was dismissed, and the arrest of a student activist set off the "burn, baby, burn" and "death to corporations" rage. Police cars have been hit with rocks and one was set afire (→ May 4).

Joe Frazier wins heavyweight title

New York City, Feb. 16

Joe Frazier has solved the question of who will succeed Muhammad Ali now that the world heavyweight title has been vacated. The 26-year-old ex-Olympic champion thrashed every contender, topping off his streak today by putting away Jimmy Ellis in five rounds. Frazier provided some fun and money to the 200 Philadelphia "investors" who owned his contract. Frazier, though taller than Rocky Marciano, was compared to him in style and, like Rocky, he is undefeated.

Nation's population passes 203 million

Washington, D.C., Nov. 30

The 1970 census places the nation's population at 203,184,772, a 13.3 percent increase over 1960 and the smallest rise since the Depression 1930s. The biggest increase was in the South, eight million. California (20 million) passed New York (18.2 million) as the most populous state. The largest Asian group is the Japanese, with 597,000, followed by 435,106 Chinese. Of 1.5 million Puerto Ricans, 817,000 live in New York. There are five distinctly Byelorussian churches in the U.S.

U.S., Vietnam units sent into Cambodia

Washington, D.C., Apr. 30

President Nixon announced today that American and South Vietnamese forces have entered Cambodia. As he spoke, 40,000 cavalry and paratroopers were still crossing into the "Fish Hook" region just over the South Vietnamese-Cambodian border. On a map in his Oval Office, the President pointed out alleged Vietcong bases, shaded in red. The soldiers' objective, he claimed, is not to kill enemy forces, but merely to destroy supplies and drive the Communists from their sanctuaries. As such, he said, the operation is "not an invasion," but a necessary extension of the Vietnam War. "If, when the chips are down," Nixon said, "the world's most powerful nation, the United States of America, acts like a pitiful, helpless giant, the forces of totalitarianism and anarchy will threaten free nations and free institutions throughout the world."

Support for the President's war policy is down to 48 percent from a high of 65 percent in January, and the incursion will send it lower. But Nixon argues it is "indispensable" to the success of Vietnamization, the process by which the war is being turned over to the South Vietnamese. "I would rather be a one-term President and do what I believe is right," he said, "than to be a two-term President at the cost of seeing America become a second-rate power" (→ Feb. 8, 1971).

Kent State: Four are dead in Ohio

Kent, Ohio, May 4

Student dissent over the American invasion of Cambodia exploded in death at a university today. It did not happen at Berkeley. It happened at usually apathetic Kent State. Four unarmed students were killed by National Guardsmen.

Ohio Governor James Rhodes ordered the guard to the campus after bottles were thrown at police on Friday, May 1, and firebombs were thrown into the building of the Reserve Officer Training Corps (R.O.T.C.) on Saturday. Rhodes, who tied the violence to the "Communist element," vowed, "We are going to eradicate the problem."

The tired and nervous guardsmen moved in on a group of students who were holding an anti-war rally that Rhodes had banned. When the students refused to disperse, the guard fired tear gas. The students responded with rocks and cement. At 12:25 p.m., the unit commander says, his men heard a shot. They then unleashed a volley of gunfire at some students 25 yards away. Four were killed and 10 wounded.

Student leaders say the dead were all innocent bystanders, including 19-year-old William Schroeder, an R.O.T.C. member. Allison Krause, also 19, was with her boyfriend and had "just stopped to look around and see what was happening." Krause's shocked father wondered, "Is this dissent a crime? Is this a reason to kill her?" The Justice Department will investigate (→ May).

Ohio National Guardsmen fire tear gas as students congregate on campus.

A young coed grasps her head in horror as one of her fellow students lies dead in a pool of blood after National Guardsmen opened fire on protesters. Many of the guardsmen were no older than the students at whom they were firing.

Sympathy strike for peace at 451 colleges

Washington, D.C., May

The student protest against the war in Vietnam is gathering momentum all over the country. The large rallies this month here and in New York are attracting the biggest headlines, but the anti-war fervor is also felt in many small towns. The student strike center at Brandeis University says that protests have either shut down or curtailed activities at 451 colleges and universities.

This month, many students decided that megaphones alone will not end the war. They descended on the nation's capital to lobby congressmen against the war. A delegation from the University of Washington even managed to hand President Nixon an anti-war petition signed by 8,500 people. One student said, "The system can be worked within. We'll go back and tell the rock throwers." Attorney General John Mitchell is less sanguine. He is said to believe that "the students are abysmally ignorant of the facts they are complaining about."

The anti-war protest continues to spark violence. Police killed two students at Jackson State College in Mississippi. In New York, 70 people were hurt as construction workers backing the war fought with protesting students and secretaries on Wall Street (→ Oct.).

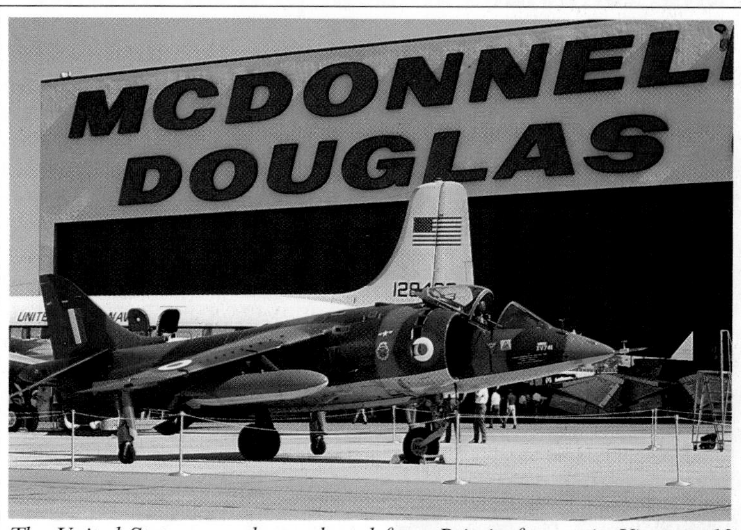

The United States recently purchased from Britain for use in Vietnam 12 V/STOL Harrier planes, which are able to take off and land vertically.

Women march in force for equality

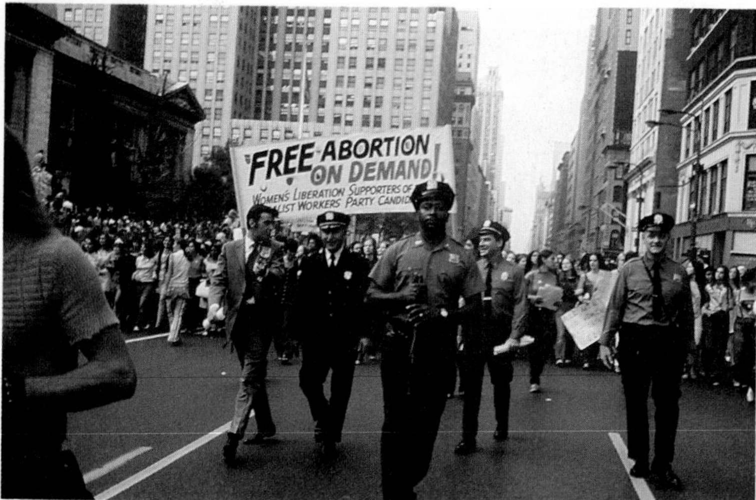

Thousands of women take to the streets to back the Equal Rights Amendment.

New York City, Aug. 26

American women across the nation celebrated 50 years of suffrage today by demanding equal rights under the law, guaranteed by a constitutional amendment. In some cities, women stayed off their jobs, which usually pay just 58.2 percent of a man's salary for equal work.

In New York, police estimated that 10,000 women marched up Fifth Avenue (the demonstrators put the number at 50,000). In Washington, D.C., the law forbids government workers to strike, but they marched with placards on their lunch hour. Some protesters ascended the Capitol steps and warned they would watch their senators closely when the Equal Rights Amendment is debated this fall. In Detroit, New Orleans, Indianapolis, San Francisco and Los Angeles, women took to the streets, some encountering hostile pushing and shoving from onlookers. In Boston, construction workers held counter-demonstrations, with signs reading "Hardhats for Soft Broads." But nothing stopped the women from demanding why they are forbidden to drink at some bars, why airline attendants lose their jobs when they have children, why there are so few women in Congress. Betty Friedan, author of *The Feminine Mystique* and organizer of the day's strike, said the turnout "exceeded" her "wildest dreams" (→March 22, 1972).

Strange case of the invisible billionaire

Paradise Island, December

It was Thanksgiving, well before dawn when the helicopter deposited Howard Hughes atop the Britannia Beach Hotel here in the Bahamas. Or did it? The 9th floor is sealed as tight as the resort workers' lips. Hughes, in seclusion since 1950, is fleeing a power struggle in his Las Vegas empire ($100 million in land and seven casinos). The 64-year-old billionaire was orphaned at 17 and took over his father's Hughes Tool Co. Since then he has produced films, piloted planes, bought and lost TWA and now disappeared. He is worth $2 billion.

New York adopts liberal abortion law

Albany, New York, July 1

Like Hawaii and Alaska, New York has adopted a liberal abortion law. It goes into effect today. More than 1,200 women here have applied for abortions, operations that will cost up to $500. The law is virtually "abortion on demand," with no questions asked regarding the circumstances of the pregnancy. In 16 other states, laws are also liberal, making concessions to a woman's mental and physical health. In the rest of the nation, however many women are still going to back-alley practitioners at the risk of losing their lives (→Jan. 22, 1973).

What's in, and out

United States

What's in: ergonomics, psychotechnology, encounter groups, sensitivity training, radical chic, Mickey Mouse watches, quadraphonic sound, safety tops on medicine vials, a woman jockey in the Kentucky Derby, women generals in the army and a woman in the air force who is also a nun. What's out: hassles, putdowns, preppies, hype, the blahs, blame in divorce (California has no-fault divorce) and blame in auto accidents (Massachusetts has no-fault auto insurance). And New York is out millions of dollars if someone wins its lottery.

Two rock stars fall

Los Angeles, Calif., Oct. 4

The excesses of stardom have taken two of rock's most talented and flamboyant performers, Jimi Hendrix and Janis Joplin. Hendrix, 27, was found dead of a sleeping pill overdose in London on September 18. A radically imaginative guitarist with the Experience, Hendrix changed the face of music with a fiery technique merging blues with electronics and a striking, sensuous stage show. Joplin, also 27, won fame singing in a raspy, passionate style with Big Brother and the Holding Co. Today in Los Angeles, she died of a heroin overdose.

Panel condemns student protest violence

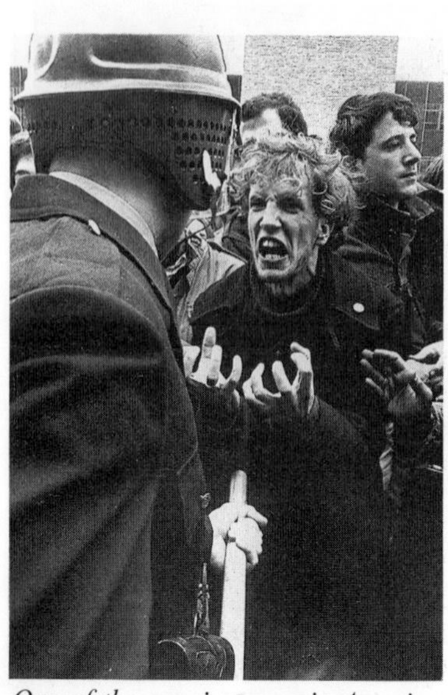
One of the angriest men in America.

Washington, D.C., October

A presidential commission has harsh words for students who use violence to protest the Vietnam war. "Students who bomb and burn are criminals," the panel concluded. President Nixon appointed the panel after the killings at Kent State and the deadly explosion at an army research center at the University of Wisconsin. The panel advised the President that he must solve a political crisis that "has no parallel in the history of the nation." Without singling out administration spokesmen like Vice President Spiro Agnew, the commission said divisive rhetoric must end. Otherwise, "the survival of the nation will be threatened" (→Nov. 3).

"Benign neglect"

Washington, D.C.

The last several years have seen the rise of a nationally active civil rights movement, the passage of Civil Rights Acts, the non-violent campaigns of the Rev. Martin Luther King Jr., the assassination of King and race riots across the nation. In the wake of controversy and headlines, Nixon aide Daniel Patrick Moynihan has been quoted as saying, "The issue of race has been too much talked about ... We may need a period in which Negro progress continues and racial rhetoric fades ... a policy of benign neglect." This is not the kind of policy that will sit well with radical groups such as the Black Panthers or Black Muslims.

"Silent Majority"

Washington, D.C., Nov. 3

President Nixon addressed "the great Silent Majority of my fellow Americans" tonight in a nationally televised speech, asking for support against anti-war "demonstrations in the streets." His message coined a new demographic category. Who are those in the Silent Majority? The President says they are the vast number of quiet, conformist citizens, living by traditional American values, not those responsible for "old standards violated, old values discarded," as he has said. The speech was intended to isolate dissenters. The Vietcong "cannot defeat or humiliate the United States." Nixon said. "Only Americans can do that" (→March 1, 1971).

1971

Nixon

Miami, Jan. 17. Baltimore Colts defeat Dallas Cowboys, 16-13, in Super Bowl V.

Hollywood, Calif., January. *All in the Family* has TV debut.

Laos, Feb. 8. Supported by American air power, Vietnamese army moves into Laos in effort to cut Communist supply lines (→ March 24).

New York City, March 4. James McGregor Burns wins National Book Award and Pulitzer Prize for *Roosevelt: the Soldier of Freedom.*

Washington, D.C., March 23. Citizens of District of Columbia elect first non-voting congressman since 1875, Walter E. Fauntroy.

Laos, March 24. In face of large losses, Vietnamese army ends efforts to cut Communist supply lines in Laos (→ 29).

Washington, D.C., Apr. 14. President Nixon announces end of trade embargo against People's Republic of China.

Washington, D.C., May 1. Amtrak, the National Railroad Passenger Corporation, begins operations.

Washington, D.C., May 25. Nixon signs bill halting U.S. production of Supersonic Transport jets (SST).

Milwaukee, May. Bucks win N.B.A. title, sweeping Baltimore Bullets.

Washington, D.C., June 28. Supreme Court finds state underwriting of nonreligious instruction in parochial schools unconstitutional.

Washington, D.C., June 28. Ex-champion Muhammad Ali cleared by Supreme Court of draft-dodging charges.

Washington, D.C., Sept. 21. Congress extends military draft for two years, with increased pay and benefits.

Orlando, Florida, Oct. 1. Disney World opens, at cost of $500 to $600 million.

Lake Havasu City, Arizona, Oct. 10. Relocated London Bridge reopens here.

Baltimore, Oct. 17. Pittsburgh Pirates defeat Baltimore Orioles, four games to three, in World Series.

Washington, D.C., Nov. 12. Senate adopts proposal making money paid for child care a deductible business expense.

A "new revolution" is urged by Nixon

Washington, D.C., Jan. 22

President Nixon today called upon Congress to help with "a new American revolution in which power is turned back to the people." In his State of the Union message, he called for revenue-sharing to "renew" state and local government. A Congress controlled by Democrats is cool to Nixon's "revolution," which *Time* magazine describes as "part flimflam." One correspondent says Nixon's revolution has been floated out there on "oratory, with no roots in the realities of Congress, labor unions, industry or Middle America."

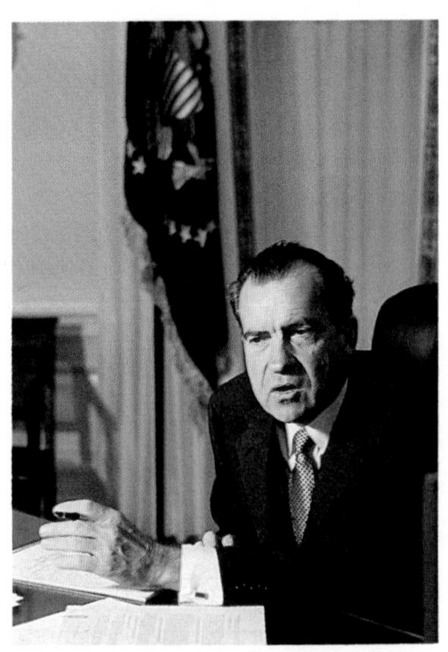

President Nixon in the Oval Office.

My Lai: Calley is guilty

Lieutenant William Calley leaves the courtroom shortly before the verdict.

Fort Benning, Georgia, March 29

In the most celebrated military court-martial of the Vietnam conflict, First Lieutenant William Calley was found guilty today. He was charged with the murder of 22 Vietnamese civilians in the My Lai massacre of March 1968. The prosecution argued that Calley had personally directed and participated in the brutal killing of unarmed innocent men, women and children in the hamlet of My Lai. Calley pleaded not guilty on the grounds that he was only following orders given by his company commander, Captain Ernest Medina. He will be sentenced later this week (→ Aug. 11).

Charles Manson is sentenced to death

Los Angeles, March 29

Charles Manson and the three women in his hippie "family" today were sentenced to death in the gas chamber following their January conviction for the gruesome murder of actress Sharon Tate and six others. Before their sentencing, the four were ejected for shouting at the judge. One of them, Susan Atkins, warned the court, "It's going to come down hard. Lock your doors. Protect your kids." The three women said that they had been high on LSD at the time of the murders, and insisted that Manson himself was innocent.

The eyes reflect the cultist's mind.

7,000 protesting war arrested in capital

Washington, D.C., May 3

Local police, the army, marines and guardsmen have stopped anti-war demonstrators from closing down the capital. But critics say the lawmen themselves broke the law by arresting everyone in sight, with total disregard for constitutional standards. More than 7,000 demonstrators were herded into the District of Columbia jail, a football field and the Coliseum. The crackdown had the full support of the President. "Short of killing people, Nixon had given Attorney General John Mitchell a blank check," one official said. He called it "overkill." Some anti-war leaders fretted that this protest by "crazies" threatened the real peace cause (→ June 30).

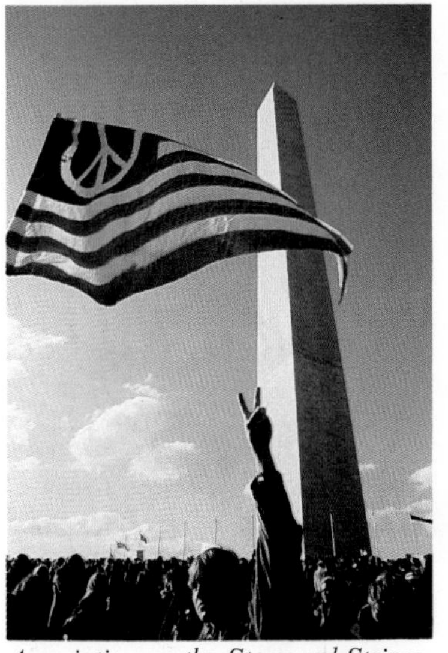

A variation on the Stars and Stripes.

Capitol is bombed

Washington, D.C., March 1

The Weather Underground today claimed responsibility for the bomb blast that destroyed a Senate bathroom at 1:32 a.m. The blast cracked walls, shattered windows and caused some $300,000 in damages. A telephone caller warned the Capitol switchboard earlier that a bomb would go off to protest "the Nixon involvement in Laos." The President called the bombing a "shocking act of violence." Senator George McGovern called it "barbaric," but noted it was prompted by the massive American bombing in Indochina (→ May 3).

N.Y. Times prints Pentagon Papers

Washington, D.C., June 30

The Supreme Court says *The New York Times* can resume publication of the top-secret *Pentagon Papers* about America's involvement in the Vietnam War. The court ruled today that the government has failed to show that its order to block news articles prior to publication is constitutional under the First Amendment. By a vote of 6 to 3, the justices thus upheld the right of *The Times* and other papers and ended the restraint imposed by the courts at the request of Attorney General John Mitchell, who claimed publication of the Pentagon study would cause "irreparable injury" to national defense. Today's decision apparently ends the spectacular battle between the Nixon White House and the press over the government's right to secrecy versus the public's right to know.

The source of the 40-volume leak is believed to be the former Defense Department analyst Daniel Ellsberg, who is said to have offered the files to *Times* reporter Neil Sheehan. Working in secrecy, 30 *Times* reporters and editors helped Sheehan process the huge study, which was commissioned by Defense Secretary Robert McNamara, who was increasingly upset by the course of the war.

The first installment on the front page of the Sunday, June 13, issue of *The Times* was drily headlined: "Vietnam Archive: Pentagon Study Traces 3 Decades of Growing U.S. Involvement." The six pages of documents and the two installments that followed drew little attention until the White House action forcing suspension of the series. *Times* publisher Arthur Sulzberger justifies the report as "a part of history that should have been made available a long time ago." *Times* managing editor A.M. Rosenthal believes, "the essence of journalism is to make information available. How could we say to our readers, 'We know, but you can't know'?" The articles, which have now been resumed, are based on 2.5 million words that are classified "secret, top secret or top secret-sensitive" (→July 12, 1974).

26th Amendment: 18-year-olds vote

Washington, D.C., July 25

President Nixon formally certified the states' ratification of the 26th Amendment to the Constitution today. The reform extends last year's law that gave 18-year-olds the right to vote in national elections, by granting them the vote in all elections. The Supreme Court struck down a provision of the 1970 act that gave 18-year-olds the vote in state and local balloting. The court held that Congress lacked authority to set age requirements in state elections, that it would have to be done through constitutional reform. A campaign for the 26th Amendment was started, and it won ratification easily.

High court O.K.'s busing for integration

Washington, D.C., Apr. 20

In its most important ruling on race relations since the Brown decision of 1954, the Supreme Court today unanimously upheld busing and redistricting as tools for integrating American schools. To the chagrin of many Southerners, the ruling curbs only "state-imposed segregation," thus largely exempting Northern states where barriers to integration are de facto, rooted in housing patterns rather than law.

Ironically, segregation is worse in the North than in the old slave states. Some 58 percent of Northern blacks attend schools that are 80 to 100 percent black, compared with 39 percent in the South. The N.A.A.C.P. will challenge courts to apply the ruling in the North. But last week Southern conservatives and Northern liberals killed a $20 billion desegregation plan offered by Connecticut Senator Abraham Ribicoff, who decried Northern "hypocrisy." "I do not see," he said, "how you can ever point your fingers at a Southern senator or a Southern school district and tell them that they are discriminating against black children when you are unwilling to desegregate schools in your own cities" (→Dec. 30, 1974).

U.S. turns over ground war to Vietnamese

Washington, D.C., Aug. 11

Secretary of Defense Melvin Laird says that as of today, ground operations in Vietnam will be conducted solely by the South Vietnamese Army (ARVN). These forces were reported to be doing quite well in their independent operations against the battle-hardened North Vietnamese regulars.

They conducted a highly successful attack on the Parrot's Beak region of Cambodia in February. Earlier this spring, they began a two-month campaign in eastern Laos to disrupt the Communist supply line along the Ho Chi Minh Trail, although the success of that effort was questionable. Ever since the Tet Offensive of 1968, South Vietnamese forces have improved dramatically. In the past two years, they have carried out three times as many operations as they did in 1966 and 1967, and suffered fewer casualties proportionately. One senior American officer says South Vietnam's forces "have demonstrated their ability to work without United States advisory assistance and have done remarkably well." He said that Vietnam's military ability is high and its success seems assured (→Apr. 16, 1972).

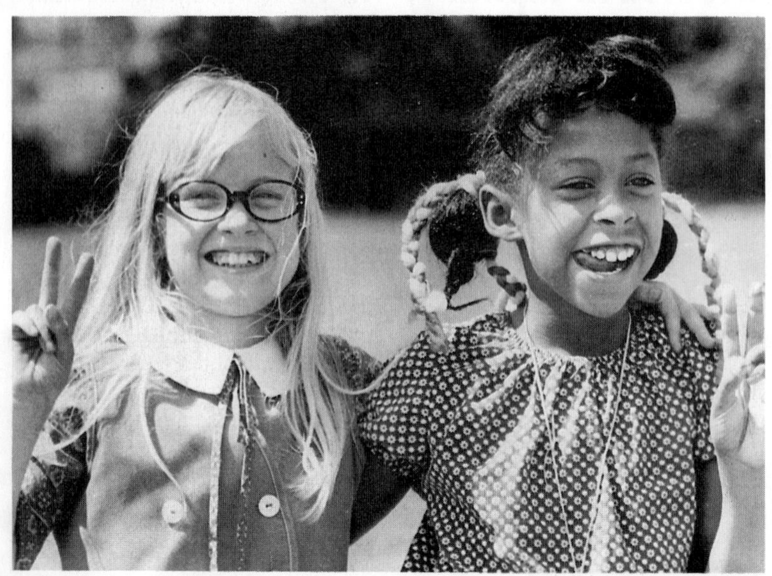

Robin Brosset (left) and Paula Moye seem to have overlooked the controversy.

A peace flag adorns American tank on the South Vietnam-Laos border.

Police attack ends Attica prison revolt

Attica, New York, Sept. 13

The Attica prison rebellion was crushed today when 1,500 state troopers stormed the facility, indiscriminately firing on both prisoners and hostages. A total of 31 prisoners and 9 hostages were killed in the attack, while 28 hostages were rescued unharmed. The uprising began when about 1,000 convicts seized control of the prison and took hostages. The assault, backed by Governor Nelson A. Rockefeller, came after four days of talks failed to produce a settlement. It also took place despite an injunction issued by a federal judge that met a prisoner demand that there would be no reprisals against them.

U.S. astronauts take a spin on the moon

The Lunar Rover allows the astronauts to examine a greater area of the moon.

The Moon, July 31

Shouting "Man, oh, man!" like a pair of teenagers with a hot rod, two astronauts set off for a drive across the desolate lunar surface today. They covered about five miles in the four-wheeled, electrically powered Lunar Rover for what astronaut David R. Scott called "exploration at its greatest."

Colonel Scott, 39, landed on the moon yesterday with his Apollo 15 colleague Lieutenant Colonel James B. Irwin, 41. They set their Lunar Module Falcon, down in the arid Sea of Rains, near the Hadley Rille and Apennine Mountains. As astronaut Major Alfred M. Worden, 39, piloted the Apollo 15 command ship Endeavor in a lunar orbit above, Scott and Irwin today became the sixth and seventh men to walk on the lunar surface. Scott stepped off the Falcon ladder at 9:26 a.m., followed by Irwin, who likened the surface to "soft-powdered snow," eight minutes later.

After unfolding the 10-foot-long Lunar Rover from Falcon's descent stage, the astronauts wheeled off at 5 mph for a "rock and roll" ride over the bumpy moonscape. They will spend two days on the moon before rejoining Worden. Because of budget constraints, just two more moon landings are planned, but scientists of the National Aeronautics and Space Administration still hope astronauts will be roving Mars in the late 1980s (→Jan. 5, 1972).

Wage-price limits are being relaxed

Washington, D.C., Nov. 14

Frozen prices and wages began to thaw today, as President Nixon's campaign against inflation entered Phase II. With the end of Nixon's three-month total wage-and-price freeze, the nation now enters one year of broad mandatory controls that will let both wages and prices rise again, but not by very much. Labor, which was denied retroactivity for wage increases delayed by the freeze, now appears ready to go along with an overall wage-ceiling guideline set at 6.6 percent per year. Prices will be permitted to go up enough to cover higher costs, but not enough to produce an increase in profits.

Jesus is superstar

New York City, Oct. 17

With the new *Jesus Christ, Superstar*, showbiz has conferred its ultimate if anticlimactic accolade. With melodies by Andrew Lloyd Webber, the rock musical is a surefire crowd-pleaser – tuneful, colorful and, with amplified sound, very loud. It also reverses the usual course of a musical by having first been a smash-hit rock album before ever having been staged. The show had inevitably sparked a reaction from certain Judeo-Christian critics. Some are grumbling about blasphemy, while others regard it as anti-Semitic.

Record G.M. recall

Detroit, Mich., Dec. 4

General Motors said today it will recall nearly 6.7 million cars – the largest recall in auto history – because of engine mount problems. The company acted after the government issued a safety bulletin warning owners of Chevrolets built between 1965 and 1969 that their cars could go out of control if the engine mounts broke. In a letter to the National Highway Traffic Safety Administration, G.M. denied any safety problems but said that it would recall the cars to install restraints to prevent engine runaways if the mounts break.

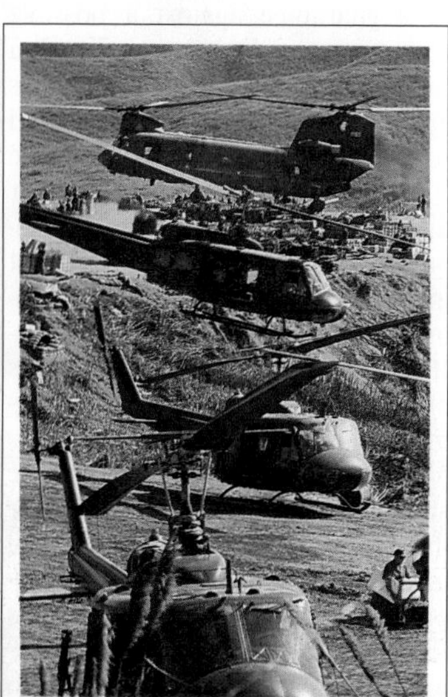

Helicopters move troops rapidly.

Some new ways, and yearning for the old

United States

The radical way of life of the late 1960s seems to be turning into the mainstream attitude of the early 70s. Many traditional barbers have gone out of business or become hair stylists in response to unisex hairdos. A Yankelovich poll indicates that 34 percent of the population believes marriage is obsolete, up 10 percent from 1969. Films seem geared only to youth, as polls reveal that three-fourths of all moviegoers are under 30 years old. A survey of women at a major Eastern college showed that 18 percent would stop working if they became mothers, compared with 59 percent in 1943. Smile buttons would have been frowned on a few years ago, and hot pants would have had their hems rolled down. Still, not everyone is into the up-front scene: 75 percent of the public polled opposed publication of the *Pentagon Papers,* and Senator George McGovern drew some harsh criticism when he said that every senator who backed the war in Vietnam is "partly responsible for sending 50,000 young Americans to an early grave." A lot of people are like Archie Bunker of TV's *All in the Family*, nostalgic for the days when we didn't have a welfare state and a meathead for a son-in-law. Right on!

The Nixon family at Christmas.

1972

Nixon

Washington, D.C., Jan. 2. Cigarette advertisements banned from airwaves.

Washington, D.C., Jan. 5. President Nixon approves $5.5 billion for NASA, to develop and build a reuseable space shuttle (→July 17, 1975).

New Orleans, Jan. 16. Dallas Cowboys 24-3 winners over Miami Dolphins in Super Bowl VI.

New York City, Jan. 20. Dr. Juanita Kreps elected first female governor of New York Stock Exchange.

Washington, D.C., March 22. Senate ratifies Equal Rights Amendment to Constitution (→July 15).

New York City, Apr. 13. Joseph Lash wins Pulitzer Prize, National Book Award for *Eleanor and Franklin.*

North Vietnam, Apr. 16. American planes bomb Hanoi and Haiphong for first time in four years (→May 8).

Hollywood, Calif., April. Charlie Chaplin given special Academy Award, for his "incalculable effect" on film.

Los Angeles, May 7. Lakers defeat New York Knicks for N.B.A. title, four games to one.

St. Louis, June 26. Air Force unveils F-15 jet fighter.

Reykjavik, Iceland, Sept. 1. Bobby Fischer becomes first American world chess champion by beating Boris Spassky of U.S.S.R. in 24-game match.

Washington, D.C., Sept. 14. Senate approves pact with Soviet Union, imposing freeze on offensive nuclear weapons.

Cincinnati, Oct. 23. Oakland A's defeat Cincinnati Reds, four games to three, in World Series.

Atlanta, Nov. 9. Andrew Young elected South's first black congressman since Reconstruction.

Hollywood, Calif. Movies out this year include, *The Godfather, Cabaret, Last Tango in Paris* and *Play it Again, Sam.*

DEATHS

Washington, D.C., May 1. J. Edgar Hoover, first F.B.I. director (*Jan. 1, 1895).

Kansas City, Missouri, Dec. 26. Harry S Truman, 33rd President of United States (*May 4, 1884).

Nixon pays historic visit to Red China

President Nixon, escorted by Chou En-lai, reviews a military honor guard.

The President and Mrs. Nixon atop the Great Wall. When asked his thoughts, Nixon said, "I think you would have to conclude that this is a great wall."

Shanghai, China, Feb. 28

The first visit ever made by a president of the United States to China ended today as Richard Nixon, accompanied by Mrs. Nixon, Secretary of State William Rogers, Henry Kissinger, the national security adviser, and a large entourage left this bustling city for home.

Before departing, the President and Premier Chou En-lai issued a joint statement, the Shanghai Communique, which summarizes the issues on which they have either come to an agreement or acknowledged their differing positions.

Foremost among these issues is Taiwan. The United States has abjured the "two-China" policy, recognized Taiwan as an integral part of China and agreed to "the ultimate objective of the withdrawal of all United States forces and military installations." The communique makes no mention of the 1955 defense treaty that binds the United States to the Nationalist regime, but it was reaffirmed yesterday by Kissinger during a news conference here. The Chinese leaders, for their part, have indicated that they are in no hurry to settle the Taiwan issue, and they understand that it would be politically impossible for President Nixon to abandon the Nationalists.

The Chinese are also understood to have promised that they will not intervene militarily in Vietnam, and have indicated that they regard American defense ties with Japan as a guarantee against a possible resurgence of Japanese militarism rather than as a threat. Both sides agreed to increased cultural and scientific contacts, but as yet there is to be no restoration of regular diplomatic ties. Implicit throughout has been the recognition that the countries share important common ground in their desire to restrain Soviet expansionism. This mutual interest has been the pragmatic basis of the whole venture.

The trip has been a diplomatic and public relations triumph for the President. Few who saw it will forget the sight of Nixon, the Republican President of the world's foremost capitalist country, shaking hands with the legendary Mao Tse-tung, the 79-year-old founder of the People's Republic of China.

U.S. to mine ports of North Vietnam

Washington, D.C., May 8

President Nixon has ordered the aerial mining of Haiphong and six other North Vietnamese harbors. In addition, he has sent air force and navy planes deep into North Vietnam to interdict all major sea and land routes used to transport enemy war supplies. Nixon's actions come as a direct response to the Communist Easter offensive, the largest such operation since the Tet offensive of 1968. The North Vietnamese army began the huge offensive on March 30, when it threw 14 divisions, supported by over 200 Russian-built tanks and 130-mm. guns, against outnumbered South Vietnamese forces in the country's northern provinces. In order to support the beleaguered South Vietnamese troops, on April 16, Nixon ordered the resumption of full-scale air and naval bombing of strategic North Vietnamese cities and military bases. Nevertheless, the Communist troops succeeded in capturing the key towns of Anloc, Dakto and Quangtri.

American military observers say Nixon's order to mine the North Vietnamese harbors will probably have little immediate effect on the fighting in the South. But the ever-confident American military predicts that the return of American air and naval power to North Vietnam will encourage the South Vietnamese forces to hold their ground and ultimately repel the Communist invaders (→ Dec. 30).

Nixon-Brezhnev summit

Nixon and Soviet General Secretary Leonid Brezhnev sign the arms treaty.

Washington, D.C., June 1

Declaring that "the foundation has been laid for a new relationship between the two most powerful nations in the world," President Nixon reported to a joint session of Congress today on his recent visit to Moscow, the first such visit by an American president. After landing at Andrews Air Force Base, Nixon flew by helicopter to Capitol Hill to address the joint session.

While at the summit meeting, where he conferred mostly with General Secretary Leonid Brezhnev, the President concluded talks for the SALT, or Strategic Arms Limitation Treaty. These are in fact two treaties, the ABM, or Anti-Ballistic Missile, Treaty and the Interim Offensive Weapons Agreement. The first allows each country to deploy only two anti-ballistic missile defense systems. Thus, each side is giving up attempts to achieve immunity, and the "balance of terror," with its promise of "mutual assured destruction," will remain as the principal guarantor of peace.

The offensive weapons pact freezes the number of intercontinental missiles for the United States at 1,764 and for the Soviet Union at 2,568. The Russians are allowed more because the American missiles are technologically superior.

Agreements on trade, technical and scientific cooperation, and a joint space effort were also signed. It is hoped that, along with SALT, these will help initiate an era of cooperation and detente.

But the President tempers optimism with caution. "Maintaining the strength, integrity and steadfastness of our free world alliances," Nixon says, "is the foundation on which all of our other initiatives for peace and security in the world must rest" (→ Nov. 24, 1974).

Gunman tries to kill candidate Wallace

Laurel, Maryland, May 15

The campaign of George Wallace has not ended, in spite of an assassination attempt that may relegate the Alabama Governor to a wheelchair for the rest of his life. While speaking at a campaign rally, Wallace was hit by bullets in the stomach, shoulders, arms and spine. The gunman, seized moments after he fired the shots, was identified as Arthur Bremer, who apparently had been following the Wallace campaign for some time, planning the assassination.

High court shelves the death penalty

Washington, D.C., June 29

In setting aside the death sentences of two men for murder, and one for rape, the Supreme Court ruled by a 5-4 vote today that the death penalty as usually enforced represents cruel and unusual punishment and is thus unconstitutional. But the separate majority opinions differed in their reasoning, hinting that the ruling might have been different if state death penalties had met certain, non-discriminatory standards. The defendants were represented by the National Association for the Advancement of Colored People, which has led a national campaign against the death penalty. The last execution was in June 1967 (→ July 2, 1976).

Burned children from Trang Ban, South Vietnam, flee after napalm struck their school during a raid.

Jury in California clears Angela Davis

San Jose, Calif., June 4

Angela Davis, the black activist, was found not guilty of murder, kidnapping and conspiracy charges today. It took the white jury 13 hours to reach the verdict. The charges were filed when guns used in a San Rafael court-escape murder case were traced to her. The 28-year-old Miss Davis first won national attention when she was dismissed from a teaching position for being a Communist. When the jury announced the not-guilty verdict today, Davis broke into sobs.

Liberated women start Ms. magazine

New York City, July 15

The second issue of *Ms.*, the feminist magazine created by journalists Gloria Steinem and Letty Cottin Pogrebin, is in the mail. For $1, the August issue offers articles on Marilyn Monroe, vaginal self-examination, essays by Kate Millett and Angela Davis, a short story by Alice Walker and articles on how television, film and theater misrepresent women. Of course, there are advertisements, too, such as the one showing an A.T.&T. phone operator with sideburns (→ Nov. 21, 1977).

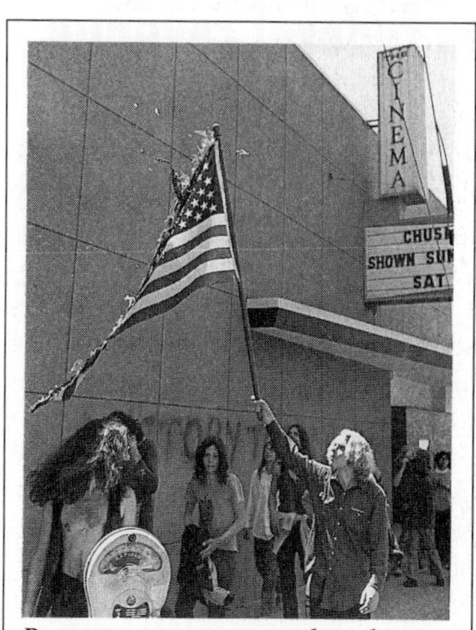

Demonstrators opposed to the war in Vietnam burn the flag as an act of protest in Berkeley, California.

Nixon is re-elected in landslide victory

Washington, D.C., Nov. 7

Richard M. Nixon was re-elected President today with the highest percentage ever amassed by a Republican: 60.7 percent of the vote. Nixon's triumph resembles the landslide victories of Presidents Franklin D. Roosevelt and Lyndon B. Johnson.

His success comes 10 years to the day after Edmund Brown beat him in the race for governor of California. After that loss, he told reporters, "You won't have Nixon to kick around any more, because, gentlemen, this is my last press conference." Often dogged by questions about his campaign financing, Nixon entered the White House after the narrowest of victories over Vice President Hubert Humphrey four years ago, and now caps his career with an enormous personal achievement, winning in every state but Massachusetts. George McGovern conceded shortly before midnight in a telegram pledging support for the President's goals of "peace abroad and justice at home." In two televised statements from the White House, President Nixon, who will turn 60 just before his second term begins, called on the nation "to get on with the great tasks that lie before us." He promised that there would be "a peace with honor in Vietnam" and "a new era of peace throughout the world."

Watergate break-in: Where will it lead?

Was President Nixon involved?

Washington, D.C., June 20

The break-in at Democratic National Committee offices in the Watergate complex last week has become the basis of a million-dollar lawsuit against the Republican Committee to Re-elect the President. Democratic Chairman Lawrence F. O'Brien announced the suit today, calling the break-in "a blatant act of political espionage." Meanwhile, the F.B.I. has subpoenaed records of the hotel where the alleged burglars were registered. They are anti-Castro Cuban exiles who conferred recently with E. Howard Hunt, a C.I.A. retiree who worked as a White House consultant. Hunt refuses to cooperate with the F.B.I. White House press secretary Ronald Ziegler says Hunt was recommended by Charles W. Colson, special counsel to the President, who has "assured me that he has in no way been involved in this matter." Also today, former Attorney General John Mitchell, who now heads the Committee to Re-elect the President, said, "This committee did not authorize and does not condone the alleged actions of the five men apprehended" (→March 23, 1973).

Bombing off again; is peace at hand?

Washington, D.C., Dec. 30

After four confusing, contradictory and painful months of bombing-then-talking and talking-then-bombing, the United States is again calling a halt to the bombing of North Vietnam.

The last American combat force was withdrawn from South Vietnam on August 12. After discussions with North Vietnamese representatives in Paris, national security adviser Henry Kissinger announced October 26 that "peace is at hand." The next day, President Nixon halted the bombardment of Hanoi and Haiphong.

But since then, American B-52 bombers have conducted the largest aerial attack of the entire war. Dozens of the giant planes carried out a massive, around-the-clock "carpet bombing" campaign. On television, Senator George McGovern has described it as "the most murderous aerial bombardment in the history of the world." And it has been costly. The American air force has lost about 20 B-52's to anti-aircraft fire as well as surface-to-air missiles.

But once again, the Communist negotiators in Paris have shown a willingness to hold peace talks. And the President has again called a halt to the bombing. So, does all this mean that peace is now really close at hand? (→Jan 27, 1973).

Porno films, acupuncture, Jesus freaks

United States

Problems? This year has solutions. Under the weather? Try health food or acupuncture. Having a crisis of faith? Talk to a Jesus freak or a believer in Transcendental Meditation. Trouble with your libido? Join the millions watching pornographic films. Trouble with a spouse? Take her (him) out to dine, perhaps at one of the thousands of new fast-food chains. Home robbed too often? Buy a plasticcard-operated lock-and-key system. Tired of taking out the garbage? Give it to Union Electric, St. Louis, which uses trash as boiler fuel. Burn, baby, burn!

States will share in federal revenue

Philadelphia, Oct. 20

President Nixon flew to Independence Hall by helicopter today to sign the $30.2 billion revenue-sharing bill during his only Pennsylvania campaign appearance, described as "official" business. The idea of signing at the historic location was that of Philadelphia Mayor Frank Rizzo, the former police chief, who has campaigned energetically for Nixon, though a Democrat himself. The President proposed revenue-sharing in his 1971 "new American revolution" State of the Union message. State and local governments are to benefit for five years.

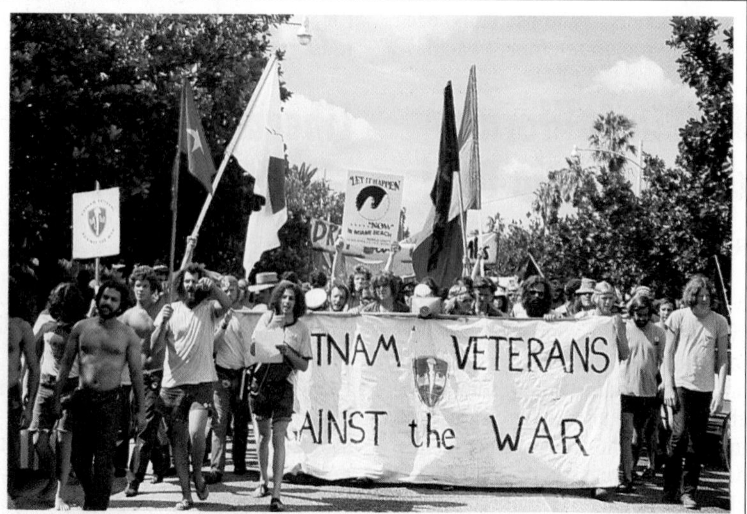

Opposition to the war in Vietnam has come from virtually every sector of American society, but now that veterans of the conflict have joined in the protests, the peace movement is taking on a new dimension. If those who were in the war are criticizing U.S. involvement, something must be amiss.

Spitz Olympic king with 7 gold medals

Munich, West Germany, Sept. 4

Mark Spitz finally lived up to his promise in the Olympics here. A big disappointment in 1968, when as a brash youngstser he was expected to make a gigantic splash in Olympic diving, he came of age at Munich by taking seven gold medals. Spitz even splashed to a world mark in the 200-meter butterfly, an event in which he finished last at Mexico City. Tragedy overshadowed these Games when Arab terrorists scaled the fence of the Olympic Village and stormed the compound of the Israeli athletes. In the shootout, 11 Israelis were murdered.

1973

Nixon

New Orleans, Jan. 8. Sniper atop Howard Johnson motel kills one police official and seven other people.

Washington, D.C., Feb. 15. United States and Cuba conclude five-year extradition treaty (→June 3, 1977).

Washington, D.C., Apr. 2. I.T.T. admits having offered C.I.A. funds in 1970 to oppose Chile's Marxist President Salvador Allende (→Dec. 4, 1975).

Chicago, Apr. 26. Chicago Board of Options Exchange, first of its kind, opens.

New York City, May 7. Pulitzer Prize awarded to Frances Fitzgerald for *Fire in the Lake.*

Los Angeles, May 10. New York Knicks defeat Lakers, four games to three, for N.B.A. title.

Los Angeles, May 29. Run-off election makes Thomas Bradley city's first black mayor.

Washington, D.C., June 27. Clarence Kelley appointed director of F.B.I.

Washington, D.C., July 1. President Nixon signs law ending all U.S. military activity in Indochina (→Apr. 30, 1975).

Washington, D.C., Sept. 21. Senate confirms Henry Kissinger as Secretary of State.

Boston, Oct. 3. Six blacks burn a white woman to death.

Oakland, California, Oct. 21. A's defeat N.Y. Mets, four games to three, in World Series.

Washington, D.C., Oct. 25. President Nixon puts military on worldwide alert in anticipation of Soviet Union's intervening in Mideast.

New York City, Nov. 6. First coast-to-coast hot air balloon flight completed by Malcolm S. Forbes.

Oslo, Norway, Dec. 10. Henry Kissinger shares Nobel Peace prize with North Vietnam's Le Duc Tho.

Washington, D.C. Pentagon reports 45,997 Americans were killed in combat and 10,928 died from other causes since 1961 in Vietnam.

DEATH

San Antonio, Texas, Jan. 22. Lyndon B. Johnson, 36th President of United States (*Aug 27, 1908).

U.S. role in Vietnam War is ended

Paris, France, Jan. 27

The official cease-fire agreement that effectively ends the American combat role in the Vietnam War was signed here today. According to the statement agreed to by Henry Kissinger and North Vietnamese negotiator Le Duc Tho, the cease-fire order will take effect at 8 a.m. tomorrow (Saigon time). The agreement also stipulates that the North Vietnamese will release all American prisoners of war and that all American troops will be removed from South Vietnam. In addition, it calls for the end to foreign military intervention in Laos and Cambodia, and for the establishment of an international force to supervise the truce itself.

After the controversial, devastating American bombing of Hanoi and Haiphong last month, President Nixon ordered air and naval operations against North Vietnam to cease as of January 15. Four days ago, Kissinger and Le Duc Tho formally announced that the cease-fire accord had been reached and that it would be officially implemented today.

The American response to the cease-fire has been more of a feeling of relief than celebration. When he announced the agreement earlier today, President Nixon never used the word "victory" to describe the termination of America's role in the war. Rather, he continuously referred to the cease-fire as having achieved "peace with honor" for the United States (→July 1).

Secretary of State William Rogers signs the accords ending U.S. combat role.

Captain Michael S. Kerr returns to his family after six years as a P.O.W.

As war role ends, so does U.S. draft

Washington, D.C., Jan. 27

On the same day that President Nixon announced that the Paris peace accords have finally ended the Vietnam War, Secretary of Defense Melvin Laird has also called an end to the military draft. He told the press this afternoon that because the conclusion of the war would result in a reduction of military manpower requirements, the draft will no longer be needed. Secretary Laird says that the postwar military forces will consist entirely of volunteers.

January 14. *Quarterback Bob Griese of the Miami Dolphins in the Super Bowl against the Washington Redskins. Miami won the championship by a score of 14-7, finishing the season with an unprecedented 17-0 record.*

Watergate men sentenced; one may talk

Washington, D.C., March 23

James McCord, the Watergate conspirator, seems ready to talk. Judge John Sirica today delayed McCord's sentencing and agreed to hear him next week. Also today, the judge sentenced G. Gordon Liddy to prison for up to 20 years in a case that is increasingly embarrassing the Nixon administration. Five other men who pleaded guilty to a charge of second-degree burglary at the Democratic national headquarters were sentenced "provisionally" to 35 to 40 years. McCord, Nixon's political chief of security, told Judge Sirica he is under "political pressure to plead guilty and remain silent." He was arrested at the Watergate complex on June 17, with Bernard Parker, Frank Sturgis, Eugenio Martinez and Virgilio Gonzalez, all involved earlier in clandestine work against Cuba's Premier Fidel Castro. Liddy, of President Nixon's re-election staff, was arrested outside.

Today's sentencing is the latest Watergate development casting a shadow on the White House. Judge Sirica has complained that much about the intrigue remains shrouded in secrecy. Though McCord appears ready to talk, he says that members of his family have expressed "fear for my life if I disclose knowledge of the facts," either publicly or privately.

Larry O'Brien, Democratic Party national chairman, has gone to court charging that the burglaries are "political espionage" (→ July 30).

Sioux Indians ousted from Wounded Knee

Wounded Knee, S.D., May 8

In what has been called the "Second Battle of Wounded Knee," the 120 remaining occupiers of that Indian hamlet have surrendered to federal agents under an agreement reached by the two sides. Only about half the occupiers were Indians. The battle of 1890 was the last major conflict between Indians and white Americans. Unlike that one, which saw nearly 200 Indians killed, this one was relatively bloodless. Nevertheless, two Indians were killed and several injured during the 70-day skirmish with some 250 officers. Wounded Knee is on the Oglala Sioux reservation.

The confrontation began when some 200 supporters of the militant American Indian Movement, led by Dennis Banks and Russell Means, took over the hamlet and presented the government with a list of grievances that included broken treaties and violations of civil rights. The government has agreed to look into the charges. During the siege, federal agents arrested about 300 people trying to enter or leave the village, including four members of a television crew who were charged with "aiding a civil disorder." Wounded Knee itself was virtually burned down, with damages put at $240,000.

Sioux Indians camp out at Wounded Knee during their occupation of the area.

2 top Nixon aides testify

Dean testifies before the committee.

Senator Sam Ervin leads the panel.

Washington, D.C., July 30

Former top Nixon aides John D. Ehrlichman and H.R. Haldeman again ringingly denied guilt in testimony before the Senate Watergate Committee today. Winding up five days of testimony, Ehrlichman repeatedly challenged former Nixon counsel John Dean, who has implicated his ex-associates. Ehrlichman, who left his job as chief White House domestic adviser to prepare for his appearance, said, "I do not apologize for my loyalty to the President." Then, taking Ehrlichman's place at the witness table, former White House chief of staff H.R. Haldeman joined in the attack on Dean. Haldeman invoked still-secret White House tape recordings as proof that Dean "did not keep us fully and accurately informed on Watergate." The committee has no way to check on the matter because the President refuses to release the tapes, the existence of which was casually revealed July 16 by surprise witness John Butterfield, another former White House aide. The committee asked for the tapes on July 17, but the White House said they were presidential papers. Commenting on today's testimony, House Republican leader Gerald Ford said, "I personally respect John Ehrlichman. I think it premature to form conclusions." But Ohio Democrat Wayne Hays said, "Ehrlichman acts like a Nazi. Part of the Nazi program was to tell a big lie, over and over until it was believed" (→ Nov. 17).

High court allows abortion in Roe v. Wade

Washington, D.C., Jan. 22

The "right of privacy ... is broad enough to encompass a woman's decision whether or not to terminate her pregnancy." Having stated its position, the Supreme Court today overturned all state laws that restrict or deny a woman's right to obtain an abortion during the first trimester of pregnancy. A Texas case, Roe v. Wade, brought the explosive issue to the court. A state law had permitted abortions only to preserve a woman's life, but the court has ruled that "the unborn have never been recognized in the law as persons in the whole sense."

Anti-abortion forces led by the Catholic Church are appalled by the decision; they argue that a fetus is a human being from the moment of conception and must be protected from murder. Feminists hail the ruling, rejoicing that no more will women die of abortions botched by back-alley practitioners.

A few questions still linger: Will abortions be affordable to the poor? How are states going to interpret their right to "protect a woman's health" and regulate second-trimester abortions? And will pregnant teens need parental permission for the procedure? (→ Dec. 7, 1977).

Nixon: I'm not a crook

Disney World, Florida, Nov. 17

President Nixon took the Watergate offensive today, assuring the 400 editors at the Associated Press Managing Editors convention that he is no crook. "I welcome this kind of examination," he said, "because people have got to know whether or not their President is a crook. Well, I'm not a crook. I've earned everything I've got."

Near the monorail to the Magic Kingdom, the beleaguered President denied all charges and told editors from 43 states that he will not resign. Shifting his counter-offensive into high gear, the President answered a dozen questions about the latest Watergate events. The editors' questions ranged from recent revelations that White House tape recordings containing key conversations are missing, to the famous "Saturday Night Massacre." On that night, October 20, Attorney General Eliot Richardson resigned rather than follow the White House orders to fire the Watergate special prosecutor, and his deputy was also fired for refusing. The prosecutor was discharged anyway.

At Disney World today, President Nixon said the reason "there are difficulties in hearing" some of the White House tapes is that "this is no Apollo system." It cost only $2,500, he told the editors, and "I found it was a Sony, a little Sony" with "these little lapel mikes in my desks" (→March 1, 1974).

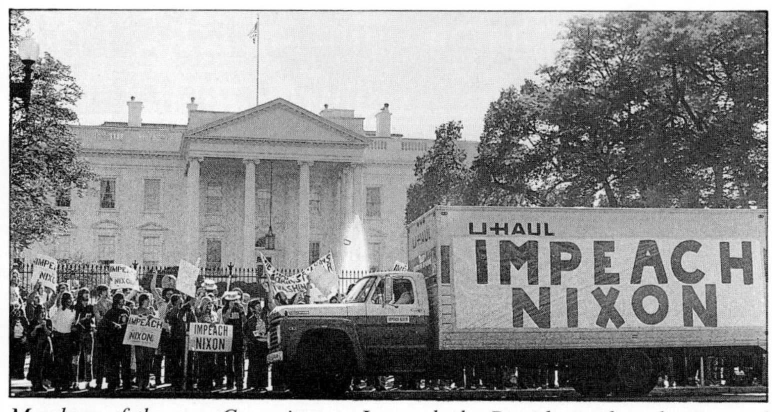

Members of the new Committee to Impeach the President take advantage of a federal court's decision to permit marches in the White House area.

President sees oil embargo causing crisis

The embargo of Arab oil-exporting nations is causing chaos at gas stations across America, where motorists wait hours for their turn at the pumps.

Washington, D.C., Nov. 7

Against a background of rapidly rising fuel prices and long lines at gas stations, President Nixon went on television this evening to warn Americans of "the stark fact" that they are facing the worst energy crisis since World War II.

The basic cause of the shortage is last month's oil embargo by the Organization of Petroleum Exporting Countries to punish those who backed Israel in the Middle East war. But Nixon also sees the crisis as part of a long-term problem: With only 6 percent of the world's population, America consumes one-third of its energy output. So while Nixon favors increasing energy supplies by constructing more nuclear plants, deregulating natural gas prices and building the Alaskan pipeline, he feels equal importance must be given to conservation.

To meet the crisis, he favors emergency measures such as year-round daylight saving and a national speed limit of 50 mph. For the long term, there is Project Independence, to make the nation self-sufficient in energy terms by 1980 (→Apr. 18, 1974).

Secretariat is a Triple Crown winner

New York City, June 9

Even longtime racing fans could hardly believe their eyes. Here was Secretariat, with Ron Turcotte in the saddle, winning the Belmont Stakes, the test of champions, by an amazing 31 lengths. Some were calling him the fastest thoroughbred that ever lived. He clinched the first Triple Crown in 25 years after setting a track record in the Kentucky Derby and winning, but not in record time, the Preakness. The Belmont gave Secretariat a 12-for-15 record, but in one race he was disqualified from first. The large Virginia-bred chestnut thoroughbred, with earnings totaling well over $1 million, will be put to stud at the end of the year.

President restricted by War Powers Act

Washington, D.C., Nov. 7

Congress handed President Nixon his worst legislative defeat today by overriding his veto of the War Powers Act limiting his authority to send armed forces into overseas combat. In a crushing blow to presidential power. the House overrode the veto by a margin of four votes, the Senate by a margin of 13. A total of 111 Republicans sided with the Nixon opponents. In his veto, the President, whose stature is being eroded by Watergate developments, said the measure is "clearly unconstitutional." He said that it would "seriously undermine this nation's ability to act decisively and convincingly in times of international crisis."

Gerald Ford is V.P. as Agnew resigns

Washington, D.C., Dec. 6

Gerald R. Ford has taken the oath as 40th Vice President of the United States, replacing Spiro T. Agnew, who resigned in disgrace before pleading no contest to a charge of income tax evasion. Ford was sworn in with his wife, Betty, their children and President Nixon at his side. He was the first chosen under a new constitutional procedure for replacing a vice president. Sixty years old and a veteran of 25 years in Congress, Vice President Ford has been House minority leader since 1965. Today, he inspired friendly laughter when he said, "a funny thing happened to me on the way to becoming Speaker of the House of Representatives."

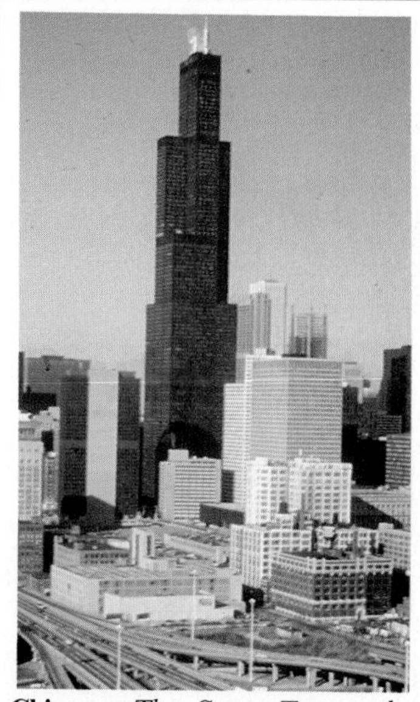
Chicago. *The Sears Tower, the world's tallest building at 110 stories or 1,450 feet, 104 feet higher than N.Y.'s World Trade Center.*

1974

Nixon

Washington, D.C., Jan. 3. President Nixon signs amendments to Social Security Act providing automatic cost-of-living allowance.

Houston, Jan. 13. Miami Dolphins beat Minnesota Vikings, 24-7, in Super Bowl VIII.

Washington, D.C., Jan. 31. Congress passes Child Abuse Prevention and Treatment Act.

United States, January. *Happy Days* premieres on ABC-TV.

New York City, May 7. Poet Robert Lowell awarded Pulitzer Prize for *The Dolphin.*

Milwaukee, May 12. Boston Celtics beat Bucks, four games to three, for N.B.A. title.

Cincinnati, June 14. Dr. Henry Heimlich announces new technique for saving life of a person choking on food.

North Philadelphia, Penn. July 29. Four bishops ordain 11 women to Episcopal priesthood in defiance of church law (→Sept. 16, 1976).

Washington, D.C., Sept. 4. United States establishes formal diplomatic ties with (East) German Democratic Republic.

United States, Sept. 17. Yacht Courageous defeats Australian challenger Southern Cross, for America's Cup.

Washington, D.C., Oct. 8. President Ford offers economic reform program, dubbed Whip Inflation Now (W.I.N.).

Oakland, California, Oct. 17. A's beat Dodgers, four games to one, in World Series.

Hartford, Connecticut, Nov. 5. Ella Grasso becomes nation's first female state Governor elected in her own right.

Fullerton, California, Nov. 13. Graduates of Monterey Institute of Frisbee Dog Studies compete in first all-dog Frisbee competition.

Hollywood, Calif. Top films this year include *Godfather, Part II* and *Chinatown.*

DEATHS

New York City, May 24. Edward Kennedy "Duke" Ellington, jazz composer and musician (*Apr. 29, 1899).

Washington, D.C., July 9. Earl Warren, ex-Chief Justice of United States (*March 19, 1891).

Hawaii, Aug. 26. Charles A. Lindbergh, aviation pioneer (*Feb. 4, 1902).

Patty Hearst, kidnapped heiress, helps radical captors rob bank

Patty Hearst, now calling herself "Tania," as she appeared before bank cameras during the robbery.

San Francisco, Apr. 15

Patty Hearst, missing since her abduction by Symbionese Liberation Army members two months ago, showed up for three minutes during an armed bank robbery this morning, then disappeared again as the bandits got away.

Surveillance cameras photographed Patricia Campbell Hearst, the 20-year-old daughter of millionaire newspaper publisher Randolph Hearst, as she entered the Sunset District branch of San Francisco's Hibernia Bank with four of her captors. She pointed a .30-caliber carbine as the army's leader, "Cinque" Donald DeFreeze, shouted, "This is a holdup. This is the S.L.A. This is Tania Hearst." During the holdup, Patty "Tania" Hearst screamed at the small startled group of employees and patrons, "Keep down or we'll shoot your f— heads off," according to a 66-year-old bank guard, Edward E. Shea. During the getaway with $10,960, DeFreeze shattered the bank's glass doors with a spray of bullets and left two people lying wounded on the street.

Patricia Hearst's part in the robbery and her relationshp with her captors are not clear. Her April 3 taped message said she had "converted" to their cause, but photos taken by the bank camera show she may be an unwilling accomplice. Miss Hearst is seen under the gun of at least one other bandit throughout the robbery (→Sept. 18, 1975).

Court says schools must teach English

Washington, D.C., Jan. 21

The Supreme Court ruled today that public schools must teach English to foreign-speaking students. The case involves a San Francisco school system that did not provide English instruction to some 1,800 Chinese-speaking pupils. To neglect them, the court maintains, is racial discrimination. Justice William Brennan, author of the majority opinion, wrote that "students who do not understand English are effectively foreclosed from any meaningful education."

OPEC lifts embargo on oil sales to U.S.

Vienna, Austria, Apr. 18

Except for Libya and Syria, the Arab members of the Organization of Petroleum Exporting Countries today voted to resume exports to the United States and most other countries embargoed last year for supporting Israel in its war against the Arabs. There will, however, be no rollback in prices, which have risen from an average of $4 a barrel before the crisis to $12 now. The news cheered Americans who have been coping with long lines and limited sales at gas stations (→May 2).

Jury orders 5 tried in Watergate case

Washington, D.C., March 1

A grand jury dealt President Nixon two staggering blows today; first, by issuing criminal indictments against his top aides, John Ehrlichman and four others; second by giving Judge John J. Sirica sealed evidence for delivery to the House panel considering impeachment of the President himself. Today's proceedings took just 13 minutes in a courtroom that is too small to handle the huge number of people who want to attend the proceedings (→Aug. 8).

Evel Knievel fails in daring cycle leap

Twin Falls, Idaho, Sept. 8

With a guarantee of $6 million hanging in the balance, Evel Knievel failed in his effort to rocket 1,600 feet across Snake River Canyon in a motorcycle-like vehicle today. Instead, the daredevil made a nose-first crash-landing on the rocks of the river bank. His only injuries were some superficial cuts and bruises. The failure was caused by a tail parachute that opened prematurely on takeoff. The big crowd on the rim of the canyon worried that the wind might blow Evel's rocket in its direction.

Winnebago Indians dancing during a tribal powwow. Native Americans have struggled to preserve their heritage in the face of a changing world.

Amid energy crisis, oil profits surge

Washington, D.C., May 2

While the energy crisis continues to strangle consumers of gas and oil, the only clear winners seem to be the oil firms. As demand outruns supply, prices have skyrocketed, and taken profits along. In the last quarter of 1973, Exxon profits rose 59 percent, and in the first quarter of this year, Occidental Petroleum's soared 748 percent. In response to oil profiteering and the ongoing shortages, Congress, prodded by President Nixon, has approved creation of a Federal Energy Administration to develop conservation measures, advise on foreign trade, administer gas rationing and curb windfall profits (→ Apr. 18, 1977).

Kissinger shuttle scores in Mideast

Geneva, Switzerland, May 31

After 32 days of commuting between Jerusalem and Damascus, Secretary of State Henry Kissinger took another step toward peace with his "shuttle diplomacy" today, this time persuading the anti-Zionist President of Syria, Hafez al-Assad, to agree to a troop disengagement in the Golan Heights. Back in January, after a week of shuttling between Egyptian President Anwar el-Sadat and Israeli Premier Golda Meir, Kissinger arranged a similar Egyptian-Israeli disengagement.

A note of concern over nuclear energy

Morris, Illinois

They open to the sky like ominous vats and many think they are the panacea for America's energy woes. Nuclear cooling cones are popping up in great numbers; 42 plants are now operating. The Atomic Energy Commission says by 1980 the U.S. will have 100, generating 102,000 megawatts of power. But some people are wary. In Morris, site of Dresden, one of the nation's first plants, a citizen said : "Dresden is also the name of a city leveled by fire-bombing in World War II. I hope that's not an omen."

Aaron blasts his 715th

Aaron swings into history. He started with the all-black Indianapolis Clowns.

Atlanta, Georgia, Apr. 8

With a towering drive over the fence in left-center field 385 feet away, Hank Aaron hit his 715th homer today to became the leading home-run hitter in baseball history. He erased Babe Ruth's 39-year-old record, one that he tied four days earlier. Aaron, a 40-year-old Atlanta Braves outfielder, hit his fourth-inning home run off Al Downing, enabling the Braves to beat the Dodgers, 7-4. Hank's reaction? "All I could think about was that I wanted to touch all the bases."

A big baseball fan, Georgia Governor Jimmy Carter presented Aaron with a license plate marking the epic homer. It read "HLA715" for Henry Louis Aaron. Hank, who was born in Mobile, Alabama, began his career with the Indianapolis Clowns of the Negro American League.

The Hammer, as Aaron is called, came up to the majors with Milwaukee, which became the Atlanta Braves. When newly acquired Bobby Thomson broke an ankle in 1954, Aaron stepped into the lineup and hit .280 as a rookie. He has been named to every National League All-Star team since, and was named the most valuable player in the loop in 1957, when he led the Braves to victory in the World Series. Some experts have called him the greatest natural right-handed hitter of all time.

"Old Faithful" keeps visitors entertained faithfully. The most famous of the 200 geysers in Yellowstone National Park erupts about every 65 minutes.

Ehrlichman is guilty in Ellsberg break-in

Washington, D.C., July 12

President Nixon's former chief domestic adviser, John D. Ehrlichman, became the highest aide to be convicted in the web of Watergate cases today. A jury of six men and six women found Ehrlichman and three members of the White House "plumbers" unit, which staged the Watergate break-in, guilty in a bizarre aspect of the *Pentagon Papers* case that involved the secret papers that were made public by Daniel Ellsberg. The jury decided that Ehrlichman conspired with the others in the break-in at the office of Ellsberg's former psychiatrist, in an effort to find papers that would discredit Dr. Ellsberg.

Nixon in Mideast and Soviet Union

Moscow, July 3

Concluding his third summit meeting with General Secretary Leonid Brezhnev, President Nixon left Moscow for home today. Although there was no major arms-control breakthrough, the summit furthered the general process of detente and the two leaders agreed to meet again before the end of the year. The Nixon trip follows last month's six-day tour of the Mideast, designed to firm up the recent peace settlement, which was largely the result of American diplomacy.

Baring bottoms and feminist power

Nukes no ! Nudes yes ! Thousands of college students, some in Nixon masks, tennis shoes and nothing else, are baring their buttocks in this year's streaking fad. Women also are making waves, such as Massachusetts state representative Elaine Nobel, who admitted she was a lesbian before being elected, and Janet Hayes, who came to power in San Jose, California, as the first woman mayor of a major city. Girls play Little League baseball and 11 women are now Episcopal priests. Is it a coincidence that businesses catering to singles net $40 billion a year? ▷

Nixon, cornered, resigns as President

Washington, D.C., Aug. 8

Snarled in Watergate and prodded by the threat of impeachment, President Richard M. Nixon has resigned the presidency as of noon tomorrow. In effect, he named his own replacement when he nominated Gerald R. Ford 10 months ago as successor to Vice President Spiro T. Agnew, who quit in disgrace. Speaking from the Oval Office tonight, the 61-year-old Nixon was delivering his second farewell in 12 years. After losing a gubernatorial race in California in 1962, he told reporters, "You won't have Nixon to kick around any more." Tonight, seemingly calm in an anguish-laden White House, he said he would have preferred to "stay on and fight as my family unanimously urged. I have never been a quitter." His remarks recalled to many the famous television appearance in 1952 in which he fought off charges of irregular finances with help from the family dog, Checkers.

"To leave office before my term is completed is opposed to every instinct in my body," Nixon said tonight. "But as President I must put the interests of America first. By taking this action, I hope that I will have hastened the start of that process of healing so desperately needed in America." The departing President then expressed his deep regrets for "any injury that may have been done. I would say only that if some of my judgments were wrong – and some were wrong – they were made in what I believed at the time to be the best interests of the nation."

As the first President in history to resign, Nixon removes himself from the threat of impeachment, but not from the onrushing wave of Watergate, because he appears to lack immunity, and the incoming President Ford says that he has made "no deals" (→9).

Farewell to a disillusioned nation.

Nixon, in a TV address on April 30, released edited transcripts of the tapes.

Parents seek ban on "vulgar" books

West Virginia, Sept. 3

Holden Caulfield doesn't have many friends in West Virginia. The J.D. Salinger novel *Catcher in the Rye*, where Holden "lives," is one of many books being deemed "vulgar" by parents of schoolchildren in this state. Hundreds of angry parents, led by fundamentalist ministers, picketed the opening of the school year today with a call to bar texts that they feel are obscene and blasphemous. The protesters are to meet with the school board to negotiate an end to the dispute.

Rockefeller sworn in as Vice President

Washington, D.C., Dec. 19

After four months of investigation by 300 F.B.I. agents, Nelson Aldrich Rockefeller was sworn in today as 41st Vice President of the United States. "There is nothing wrong with America that Americans cannot right," the new Vice President said. Rockefeller, whose family is worth about $1.3 billion, becomes the second Vice President in little more than a year to attain the office under the recent 25th Amendment, which authorizes a president to fill a vice presidential vacancy without an election, although the consent of Congress is required.

Rocky, scion of a wealthy family. "There is nothing wrong with America that Americans cannot right."

Ford is President, declaring "long national nightmare is over"

Washington, D.C., Aug. 9

Emotions were high today as the resigning President Richard Nixon said tearful farewells and Gerald R. Ford took the oath to succeed him, declaring, "Our long national nightmare is over." Ford, who was elected Vice President on Nixon's nomination, offered some emotional parting remarks to the President, whose letter of resignation was received by Secretary of State Henry Kissinger at 11:35 a.m. It read: "Dear Mr. Secretary: I hereby resign the office of President of the United States. Sincerely, Richard Nixon."

Tears streaked Nixon's face as he told his staff, "Others may hate you. But those who hate you don't win unless you hate them – and then you destroy yourself." As the Nixon family left for California, President Ford urged the nation to pray for them. "May our former President, who brought peace to millions, find it for himself," said the new President. Ford, 61, is an ex-college football hero and a 25-year veteran of the House (→Sept. 8).

Chief Justice Warren Burger administers the oath of office to President Ford.

ongress lifts ban on record access

Vashington, D.C., Nov. 21

Congress voted today to override President Ford's veto of the Freedom of Information Act of 1974. As a response to former President Nixon's abuse of "executive privilege," the amendments to the 1966 Act prohibit the government from "arbitrarily or capriciously" denying access to offical documents. It puts the burden on the government to justify the classification of documents. And it forces federal agencies to act quickly on requests for information. The reform is regarded by some as a defeat for presidential power. Others believe it is only the beginning of congressional curbs on the executive branch in the wake of Watergate.

Nixon pardoned by Ford

Washington, D.C., Sept. 8

President Ford has pardoned former President Nixon – the man whose actions made Ford chief executive. The pardon is unconditional for all crimes Nixon may have committed in the White House. The pardon's timing surprised many because it came without warning on a Sunday morning and because it is a sharp reversal from the position his aides ascribed to him when Ford became President. Press secretary J.F. terHorst resigned today in protest, but Leon Jaworski's office said the Watergate special prosecutor believes the pardon is lawful and "accepts the decision."

In his announcement, President Ford said he issued the pardon because "the tranquility to which this nation has been restored by the events of recent weeks could be irreparably lost" by the year or more it would take to conduct a trial.

The pardon was flown out to Nixon in California by a White House lawyer who said that "a pardon has to be accepted after it is offered." Ten minutes later, the former President released a statement that said, "No words can describe the depths of my regret and pain at the anguish my mistakes over Watergate have caused the nation and the presidency." Nixon added that those events are "still in my mind a confusing maze of events, decisions, pressures, and personalities ... which grew from a political scandal into a national tragedy" (→Feb. 21, 1975).

Summit yields arms pact with U.S.S.R.

Vladivostok, U.S.S.R., Nov. 24

The momentum that led to three Nixon-Brezhnev summits in two years continues as President Ford ends two days of talks here with Soviet leader Leonid Brezhnev. Planned only as a get-acquainted meeting, the talks have produced an arms pact that extends the 1972 SALT treaties limiting strategic arms. Details haven't been issued, but it is known that both sides agreed to limit the number of MIRVs (multiple independently targetable re-entry vehicles) and to resume SALT talks in January. Secretary of State Henry Kissinger, who laid the basis for the pact, said a cap has been put on the arms race for 10 years (→June 18, 1979).

Violence erupts as busing starts in Boston

Boston, Dec. 30

Three months of often-violent protests over court-ordered busing resulted in punitive action today against three Boston school officials for their failure to enforce integration measures.

Trouble began on September 12, when students opposed to desegregation in Boston schools rioted. Many white pupils boycotted classes and attacked black students. Police escorted buses to South Boston High School, and tried to defuse tension. On October 15, fighting reached a peak. Seven students were hurt and police were called out after a white girl was assaulted by 20 blacks, igniting gang wars.

Governor Francis Sargeant requested help from the National Guard. But President Ford said federal troops "should be used only as a last resort." His stance prompted criticism from civil rights leaders.

Rioting has subsided. But opposition to busing continues, despite court insistence that it is necessary to attain equality in education (→March 11, 1975).

Ali KO's Foreman in Zaire to regain title

Kinshasa, Zaire, Oct. 29

Muhammad Ali became the second heavyweight in boxing history to regain the world championship today when he knocked out George Foreman midway through their title fight in this exotic African setting. Only Floyd Patterson, in 1960, had won back a lost heavyweight title. The 32-year-old Ali knocked out 25-year-old Foreman in the eighth round of a 15-rounder to the chant of "Ali kill him" from most of the fans at the predawn (for TV transmission) fight.

The Louisville slugger, after taking the best Foreman had to offer, sent his rival to the canvas with a one-two combination that convinced those cynics who thought Ali could not get back into fighting shape. Foreman, who had flattened three earlier challengers in less than five minutes each, was a 3-1 favorite. In a reversal of his usual strategy, Ali dropped his tricky dancing tactic and let Foreman flail away at his body. When Foreman tired, Ali let loose with bursts of left and rights.

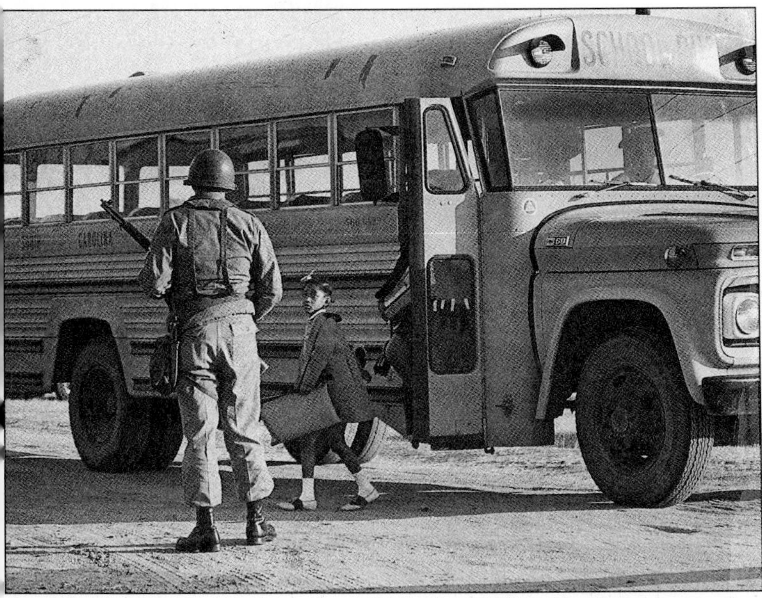

Bewilderment marks the face of a child in the middle of busing controversy.

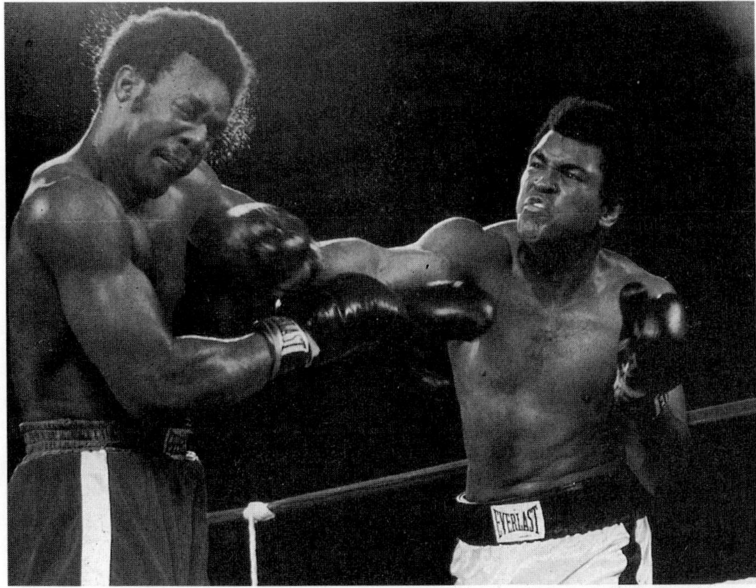

Ali rocks Foreman with a hard right to the head in the fight of the year.

1975

Ford

New Orleans, Jan. 12. Pittsburgh Steelers defeat Minnesota Vikings, 16-6, in Super Bowl IX.

Detroit, Jan. 20. To stimulate sales, major auto makers offer rebates to customers purchasing new cars.

Minnesota, Jan. 26. U.S. Geological Survey announces discovery of oldest known scientifically dated rock, some 3,800 million years old.

Washington, D.C., Feb. 14. In nation's first acquisition of territory in almost 60 years, Northern Mariana Islands become U.S. commonwealth.

Saigon, South Vietnam, Apr. 4. Air Force C-5 transport plane, carrying 300 Vietnamese children and their caretakers to United States, crashes, killing over 200 people.

New York City, Apr. 16. Dumas Malone wins Pulitzer Prize for biography *Thomas Jefferson and His Times.*

Phnom Penh, Cambodia, Apr. 17. Cambodian government toppled by Communist Khmer Rouge rebels (→Apr. 30).

Alaska, May 27. State Supreme Court legalizes marijuana use in the home.

Oregon, June 16. State is first to ban sale and use of aerosols containing chlorofluorocarbons.

Washington, D.C., June 30. Supreme Court holds that criminal defendants have right to conduct own defense rather than accept court-appointed counsel.

Orange, New Jersey, Aug. 21. Renee Richards, former navy officer who underwent surgical sex-change, wins first tennis match as woman athlete.

Boston, Oct. 22. Cincinnati Reds beat Red Sox, four games to three, in World Series.

Washington, D.C., Oct. 25. Soviet-American grain pact concluded, binding Russians to buy six million to eight million tons of American grain a year, beginning in 1976.

Washington, D.C., Nov. 29. President Ford signs legislation requiring states to provide free education for handicapped between ages of 3 and 21, effective within five years.

Hollywood, Calif. Top films include *Jaws, One Flew Over the Cuckoo's Nest, Nashville.*

Watergate principals get prison sentences

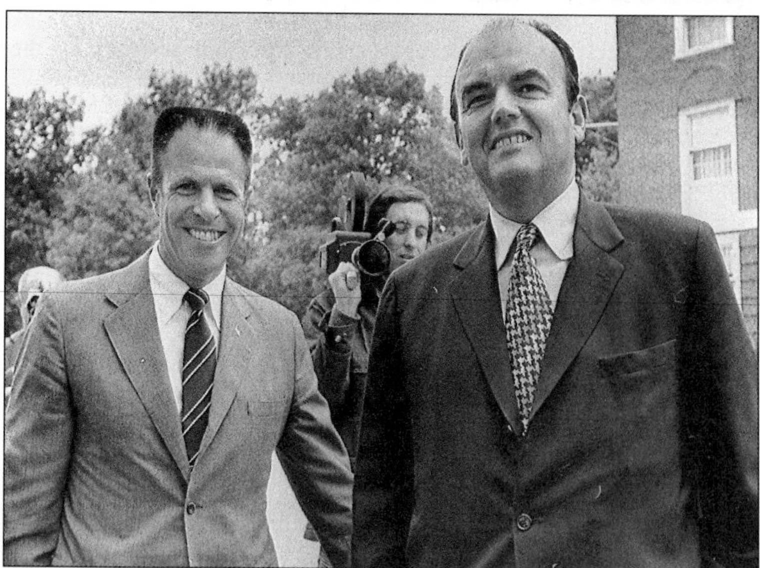

Co-conspirators Haldeman and Ehrlichman could serve up to eight years.

Washington, D.C., Feb. 21

The three most powerful men in the Nixon administration have been sentenced to prison terms that range from two and a half to eight years for their Watergate cover-up crimes: former Attorney General John Mitchell, former White House chief of staff H.R. Haldeman and former chief domestic adviser John Ehrlichman, along with former Assistant Attorney General Robert Mardian, who drew a lesser sentence. Federal Judge John Sirica denied Ehrlichman's request to do his time on an Indian reservation instead of in prison. Haldeman's attorney brought up the recent presidential pardon, protesting, "whatever Bob Haldeman did, so did Richard Nixon." Judge Sirica offered no comment. Neither did Nixon, now golfing behind the walls of Walter Annenberg's estate in Palm Desert, California.

Mitchell saved his remarks for reporters: "It could have been a hell of a lot worse. They could have sentenced me to spend the rest of my life with Martha." A judge in New York today denied Mrs. Mitchell's request for a quick divorce trial, stating that her husband's sentence was no excuse for bypassing the normal six-month waiting period (→July 8, 1976).

"Trail Riders" by Thomas Hart Benton of Missouri. With his death on January 15, the American art world lost one of its best regional painters.

F.B.I. abused data on political figures

Washington, D.C., Feb. 27

J. Edgar Hoover, the late director of the Federal Bureau of Investigation, made improper use of files that he collected on political activists, a House of Representatives subcommittee was told today. Attorney General Edward Levi said that Hoover, who died in 1972, kept documents with derogatory information on presidents, on congressmen and on a variety of prominent people. The Attorney General's testimony indicated that at least three Presidents – John Kennedy, Lyndon Johnson and Richard Nixon – had data collected regarding congressmen and senators who opposed them (→May 19, 1976).

Clemency is over

Washington, D.C., March 31

President Ford's clemency program for Vietnam-era military deserters and draft evaders ended today. A total of 22,500 men of a possible 124,400 applied for an opportunity to "earn a return" to American society under the program. Charles E. Goodell, chairman of the Presidential Clemency Board, described most of the applicants as "unfortunate orphans" of a system that favored those who were "educated, clever, articulate and sophisticated" (→Jan. 21, 1977).

Segregation debate is shifting to North

Washington, D.C., March 11

The Commission on Civil Rights issued a report today, indicating that Southern schools are more integrated than their Northern counterparts. The study underlines a changing trend: resistance to racial mixing is stiffer in the North, as evidenced by the recent violence in Boston, Detroit and Denver over school busing. Opponents of busing won a major victory last year when the Supreme Court ruled in Milliken v. Bradley that Detroit's program was unconstitutional. But civil rights leaders are still striving for school integration, including support for busing (→June 28, 1978).

Americans evacuate as Saigon falls to Communists

Emergency evacuation by helicopter.

Saigon, South Vietnam, Apr. 30
The Vietnam War ended today with the unconditional surrender of South Vietnamese forces to the Communist Vietcong. Though the event took place thousands of miles from Washington, many Americans feel the Vietcong have handed the United States its first military defeat in 200 years as a nation. The 1,000 Americans remaining in Vietnam were evacuated by military helicopters, as were thousands of Vietnamese who feared for their lives under Communist rule. Secretary of State Henry Kissinger estimated the number of Vietnamese refugees evacuated at 56,000. Some 22,000 more fled by boat and were picked up by United States Navy ships in the South China Sea.

The number of Americans killed in 10 years of fighting exceeded 46,000, with 10,000 more dying of related causes; more than 300,000 were wounded. South Vietnamese losses topped 184,000. North Vietnam released no figures. The American troop strength in Vietnam peaked at 543,400 in 1969 before President Nixon began withdrawal.

American losses in Vietnam far exceeded those suffered in Korea. They were substantially lower, however, than the 291,557 American battle deaths recorded in World War II or the 50,585 of World War I. Nor did they approach the level of total losses on both sides in the Civil War – 360,000 on the Union side, 258,000 for the Confederacy.

Nevertheless, the long conflict in Asia was one of the bleakest episodes in the nation's history. The war caused grievous wounds in society that may take a generation or more to heal. To avoid conscription, thousands of American young men fled to Canada and other countries, vowing that they would never return to the land of their birth. Riots and demonstrations were common on college campuses, and the unpopularity of the war was a major influence on the course of American politics and relations with the other powers of the world.

Although serious involvement in Vietnam began under two Democratic Presidents, John Kennedy and Lyndon Johnson, it reached its greatest intensity during the Republican administration of President Nixon. In spite of Nixon's repeated attempts to achieve a peaceful solution, it became a contributing factor in the President's eventual resignation at a time when he was under threat of impeachment.

President Ford, who succeeded Nixon, said that with the end of the fighting in Vietnam it was time to "look ahead to the many goals we share and to work together on the great tasks that remain to be accomplished" (→ May 7).

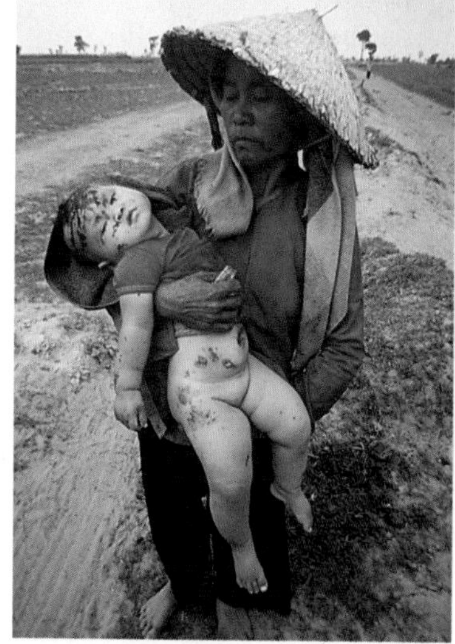
Victims of the Communist advance.

As the withdrawal continues, South Vietnamese desperately seek any way out.

Alexander Calder, after 40 years, is still at work creating mobiles.

Ford declares turbulent Vietnam era over

Washington, D.C., May 7
President Ford has declared the end "of the Vietnam Era" in a speech announcing the termination of veterans' benefits. The fall of Saigon, he said, "closes a chapter in the American experience. I ask all Americans to close ranks, to avoid recrimination about the past."

But old wounds were opened as the North Vietnamese drove into Saigon. Two years after the embarrassment of withdrawal, it seemed the United States had lost again. Conservatives decried a half-hearted effort. "We failed," said General William Westmoreland. "We let an ally down," said Ronald Reagan, blaming "the most irresponsible Congress in history." Liberals gave cautious advice. "What we've learned is that there aren't American answers for every problem in the world," said Senator Hubert Humphrey. Radicals cheered as Tom Hayden, founder of Students for a Democratic Society, called the fall of Saigon "the rise of Indochina."

Amid the torrent of words, a few stark facts elude argument. Hundreds of thousands of Americans were killed or maimed; 7 million tons of bombs fell and $141 billion was spent. Figures endure as does the pain they represent. At least one veteran abhors Ford's plea for what he called national amnesia. Said Thomas Hyland, "My brother-in-law wakes up every day without his legs. How can he forget?"

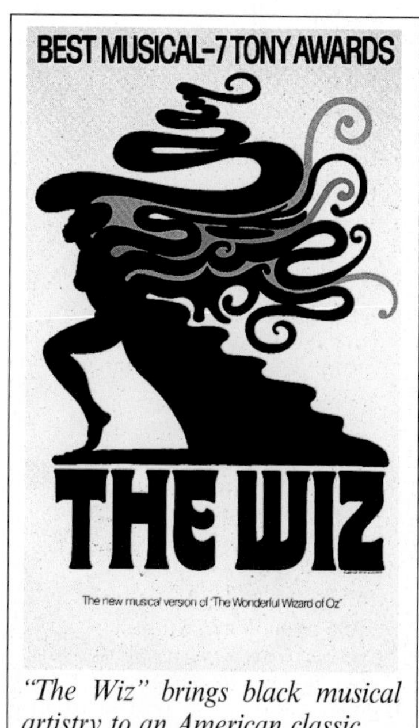

BEST MUSICAL-7 TONY AWARDS
THE WIZ
The new musical version of 'The Wonderful Wizard of Oz'

"The Wiz" brings black musical artistry to an American classic.

C.I.A. is accused of domestic spying

Washington, D.C., June 10

The Central Intelligence Agency, whose charter bans "internal security functions," systematically spied on alleged radicals during the administrations of Presidents Johnson and Nixon. According to the report of an eight-man panel headed by Vice President Nelson Rockefeller, the agency amassed 13,000 files on domestic dissidents by illegally scrutinizing mail from the Soviet Union. It used wiretaps and break-ins to police its own employees and held a defector in solitary confinement for three years. But the panel blames the Presidents, not the C.I.A. Johnson, for one, insisted that foreign money was behind the student anti-war effort. Rockefeller says the violations were "not major." But Senator Frank Church, who is investigating the C.I.A. on foreign assassinations, disagrees. "Ours is not a wicked country," he said, "and we cannot abide a wicked government" (→May 19, 1976).

Apollo and Soyuz reach detente in space

The link-up in space proves Americans and Russians can work together.

Houston, Texas, July 17

Astronaut Thomas Stafford and cosmonaut Aleksei Leonov shook hands today as the Apollo 18 and Soyuz 19 docked in the first joint American-Soviet space mission. The rendezvous occurred four days after Apollo was orbited from Cape Canaveral, Florida, and Soyuz was launched from the Tyurtam space center. Apollo and Soyuz will remain docked for two days, while the six American and Soviet crew members exchange visits and perform experiments together before returning to Earth (→Apr. 14, 1981).

35 nations sign accord in Helsinki

Helsinki, Finland, Aug. 1

After 22 months of negotiations, leaders of the 35 member nations of the Conference on Security and Cooperation in Europe gathered here today to sign the Final Act, a statement of principles "guiding their mutual relations." Among these are recognition of all national boundaries as they were at the end of World War II, settlement of disputes by peaceful means, non-intervention, and a commitment to "take positive action" to promote personal liberties. President Ford praised the pact for its "moral commitments aimed at lessening tensions," but critics charge that it has sold out the Baltic states and East Germany to the Soviet Union. They also question the commitment of the Soviet Union to personal liberties and they point to its invasion of Hungary in 1956 and Czechoslovakia in 1968 as examples of how the Russians interpret the principle of non-intervention.

Cambodians seize U.S. merchant ship

Phnom Penh, Cambodia, May 14

American air, sea and ground forces attacked Tang Island in the Gulf of Siam today in retaliation for the Cambodian seizure two days ago of the United States merchant ship Mayaguez and its 39-man crew. The ship and crew were released before the American attack took place. Three Cambodian gunboats were destroyed by American jet fighters in the course of the attack, and the Communist defense shot down three United States helicopters. American losses included one marine killed in the fighting on the island and the 14 crewmen in the downed helicopters.

Aircraft from carrier Coral Sea rescue marines under Cambodian attack.

Sony VCR's invade the United States

United States

The nation's dance crazes, which include the bump, the hustle and the robot, have a mechanical air about them. And why not? America has gone techno-illogical, loving gizmos never sold at five-and-tencent stores (which have been replaced by 69-cent discount stores). Digital records and Sony videocassette recorders (VCR's) move into our homes; word processors electrify our offices and computers zip us through the supermarket checkout. Only skateboards and mood rings don't need motors. Pet rocks, while not requiring remote control, may need to be kept on a leash.

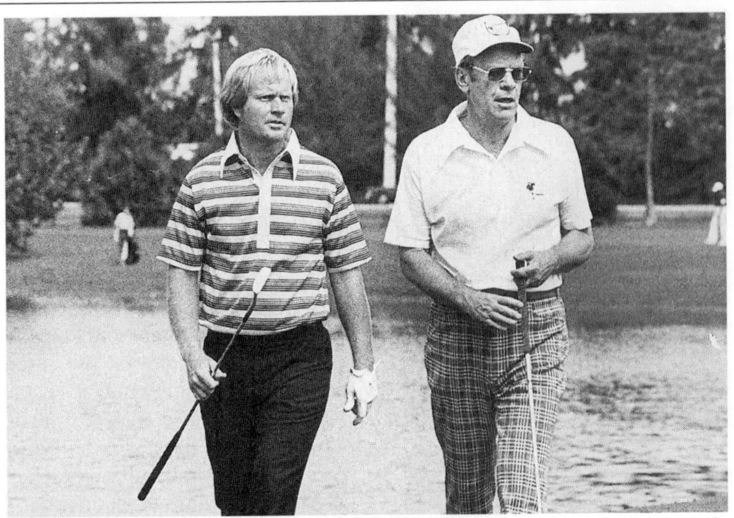

President Ford teams up with pro golfer Jack Nicklaus, who has won the Masters five times, the PGA four times, and the U.S. Open three times.

Ford survives pair of attempts on his life

San Francisco, Sept. 22

An attempt to assassinate President Ford was foiled September 5 as Lynette "Squeaky" Fromme, a follower of mass murderer Charles Manson, stepped from a crowd on a Sacramento sidewalk and aimed a loaded .45-caliber automatic pistol at the President from point-blank range. Miss Fromme, 27, wearing a long red dress and red turban, was wrestled to the ground by a Secret Service agent, Larry Buendorf, as she screamed repeatedly, "It didn't go off!" Experts determined that the pistol's loading mechanism had not been operated properly. None of the four live rounds in the clip had been loaded into the firing chamber.

Today, the second attempt on the chief executive's life occurred here in San Francisco when Sara Jane Moore, a 45-year-old part-time police informer and sometimes radical, pulled a .38-caliber revolver from her purse while standing in a crowd across the street from the Hotel St. Francis and fired a single shot at the President from a distance of about 40 feet. A bystander, Oliver "Bill" Sipple, slapped Mrs. Moore's arm, causing the bullet to go astray. The slug, a flat-nosed projectile designed to cause a massive wound, smashed into a planter box near where the President stood, ricocheted off the pavement and, finally spent, struck a nearby cab driver.

U.S. saves New York City from bankruptcy

Washington, D.C., Dec. 9

Two days before New York City would have defaulted on its loans, President Ford today signed legislation authorizing the Treasury to lend the financially strapped city \$2.3 billion annually until June 30, 1978. The loans will have to be repaid at the end of each city fiscal year (June 30) at an interest rate one percentage point higher than the current Treasury borrowing rate. Opponents of the bill said it would drain the American taxpayer, create more federal control over local government and encourage fiscal irresponsibility in local governments. Proponents felt the loan would not be enough to keep the city from bankruptcy.

The twin towers on shaky ground.

Patty Hearst seized in raid by the F.B.I.

San Francisco, Sept. 18

After a 19-month search, F.B.I. agents caught up with Patty Hearst today. They arrested the 21-year-old publishing heiress who was kidnapped February 1 of last year by Symbionese Liberation Army members and later joined their cause. Patricia Campbell Hearst gave up meekly to the F.B.I. at her apartment in the Mission District. She faces bank robbery and other charges. The F.B.I. believes that with today's arrest of Miss Hearst and three friends they have rounded up the last of the S.L.A. members.

C.I.A. linked to assassinations, Chile coup

Washington, D.C., Dec. 4

The Central Intelligence Agency, according to two congressional panels, encouraged coups in several countries and sought the assassination of at least two world leaders. Today's report concluded that the United States spent \$13.5 million to keep Chilean Marxist Salvador Allende out of office. After his election, the C.I.A. financed an anti-Allende newspaper and encouraged the 1973 coup in which the leftist leader was killed.

Last month, Frank Church's Senate panel revealed that the C.I.A. plotted to kill Premier Patrice Lumumba of the Congo (now Zaire) and Premier Fidel Castro of Cuba. American officials "encouraged or were privy to" coups that killed Vietnamese President Ngo Dinh Diem, Chilean General Rene Schneider and dictator Rafael Trujillo of the Dominican Republic. In 1963, on the day President Kennedy was killed, the C.I.A. was reported to be equipping a Cuban dissident with a poison-tipped pen designed to kill Castro. According to the panel, the agency also hired Mafiosi to kill the Cuban leader. The Church report is the first official indication that the United States employed assassination as an instrument of foreign policy (→May 19, 1976).

Seton is canonized; first U.S.-born saint

Vatican City, Sept. 14

Elizabeth Bayley Seton today became the first person born in the United States to be cannonized as a Roman Catholic saint. Mother Seton, who was the founder of the Sisters of Charity of Emmitsburg, Maryland, converted to Catholicism shortly after the death of her husband and was active in aiding the small American Catholic community of the early 1800s in attaining some organizational structure. In addition to founding the order, she was responsible for building schools, orphanages and hospitals.

Deng Hsiao-ping shows the President how it's done. The renewal of ties between the United States and China has altered international politics.

Doctorow goes from Ragtime to riches

New York City

The ragtime music craze crested in the early 1900s, but the form has found new life, thanks to *Ragtime*, the best-seller by E.L. Doctorow. The novel examines the country before World War I and finds it to be a familiar place – fraught with racism and hatred, laced with scandal, money and sex. Doctorow's prose rhythms give his story a bright syncopated beat, and he adds a medley of real-life celebrities, including Henry Ford, Houdini, anarchist Emma Goldman, and Scott Joplin, the king of ragtime.

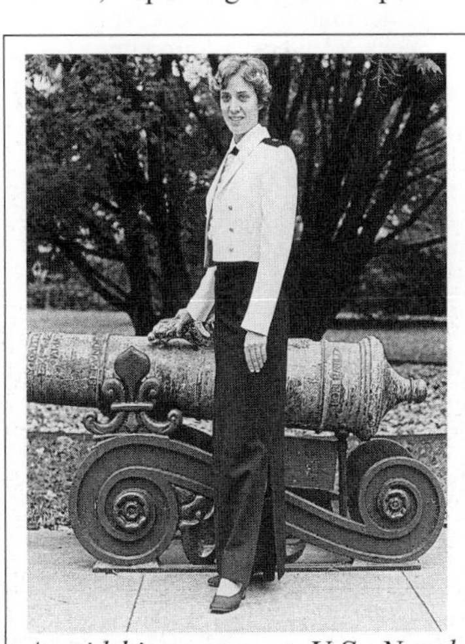

A midshipwoman at U.S. Naval Academy. Admission of women to the military academies is turning traditions upside-down.

1976

Ford

Miami, Jan. 18. Pittsburgh Steelers beat Dallas Cowboys, 21-17, in Super Bowl X.

Washington, D.C., Jan. 31. Supreme Court, in Buckley v. Valeo, rejects limits on political campaign spending.

Washington, D.C., Apr. 13. Secretary of State Kissinger warns that Communist success in any West European country will adversely affect U.S. policy toward that country.

New York City, May 3. Saul Bellow wins Pulitzer Prize, for *Humboldt's Gift.*

Washington, D.C., May 24. First commercial supersonic transport, Anglo-French Concorde, lands at Dulles International Airport.

Snake River Valley, Idaho, June 5. Teton River Dam bursts, releasing 80 billion gallons of water, which causes about $1 billion in damage.

Phoenix, Arizona, June 8. Boston Celtics beat Suns, 4 games to 3, for N.B.A. title.

New York, July 8. For his obstruction of justice during Watergate, ex-President Nixon is disbarred in New York.

Minneapolis, Sept. 16. Episcopal Church approves ordination of women to priesthood (→Sept. 16, 1977).

West Point, New York, September. Some 700 cadets at Military Academy suspended for violating honor code.

Washington, D.C., Oct. 4. Sec. of Agriculture Earl Butz resigns over racist comment.

New York City, Oct. 21. Cincinnati Reds defeat New York Yankees in four-game sweep of World Series.

Alabama, Oct. 25. Governor George Wallace pardons Clarence Norris, last surviving Scottsboro Boy.

Plains, Georgia, Nov. 14. President-elect Carter's church is integrated.

Chicago. In *Playboy* interview, Jimmy Carter says, "I've committed adultery in my heart many times."

Hollywood, Calif. Hit films this year include *Rocky* and *Network.*

DEATH

Houston, Texas, Apr. 5. Howard Hughes, eccentric billionaire (*Dec. 24, 1905).

Americans migrate south to the Sun Belt

"Storm over Taos" by John Marin. Warmth and beauty attract Northerners.

Washington, D.C., Feb. 7

"Go West, young man," was the old adage. Well, the direction has changed. Northern city dwellers are moving south at an unparalleled rate, according to a new Census Bureau report. Spurred by a number of developments, not the least of which is air-conditioning, the Sun Belt grew twice as fast as the North over the last 25 years. Florida has doubled its population since 1960; and Arizona shows a growth rate of 25 percent over the last five years, the highest in the nation.

The migrants, it seems, bring prosperity with them. Businesses, attracted by low wage scales and tax bills, are relocating in warmer climes. Lear Jet moved to Tucson, Greyhound to Phoenix and Shell to Houston. From 1967 to 1972, manufacturing employment increased 7 percent in the Sun Belt, while dropping 12 percent in the North. Professionals are escaping the rat race of New York and Chicago in packs. And the growth of Sun Belt universities has been causing a "brain drain" on the North.

Southerners also benefit from a $13 billion net gain in federal funds after taxes; Northerners lose $20 billion. And with the lion's share of defense contracting centered in the Sun Belt, Northerners will certainly think twice before reprising the Civil War.

Agency to oversee intelligence units

Washington, D.C., May 19

Closing a three-year battle between Congress and the intelligence community, the Senate has set up a 15-member agency with broad powers to oversee the nation's intelligence activities. Observers had been worried that a recent spate of congressional leaks would jeopardize attempts to police the C.I.A. and the F.B.I. In February, the Pike Committee report showed up in the pages of the *Village Voice*. It placed C.I.A. spending at $10 billion (three times the announced figure) and blasted Secretary of State Henry Kissinger's "passion for secrecy." Kissinger calls the panel "a new version of McCarthyism."

An Apple with byte

Mountain View, Calif., Apr. 1

A company called Apple that intends to make and sell small computers for personal use has been started by two young engineers, Steven Jobs and Stephen Wozniak, who have a total of $1,300 in capital and plan to assemble their computer in a garage. Both men work for established electronic companies but see great possibilities in personal computers. They originally planned to sell 100 computers for $50 each to make a quick profit, but local stores already have placed orders for four times that number.

High court, in shift, OK's death penalty

Washington, D.C., July 2

In a series of companion cases, the Supreme Court ruled today that laws in Florida, Georgia and Texas permitting imposition of the death penalty are constitutional. In Jurek v. Texas, the court voted 7-2 to reverse its 1972 decision outlawing capital punishment. Texas officials hailed the decision, hoping the high cost of violent crime will be a deterrent. Justices Thurgood Marshall and William Brennan dissented, adhering to the 1972 view that the death penalty violates the Eighth Amendment protection against "cruel and unusual punishment."

U.S. Olympic stars: Jenner, swimmers

Montreal, Canada, July 8

The image of Bruce Jenner waving a small American flag on his victory lap in the decathlon provided a poignant memory of the 1976 Olympics. The flag had been handed to him by a small boy after his race. The swimmers from America made the greatest impact in the unofficial point standings, by winning 12 of 13 events. John Naber was the individual star with records in both backstroke events. The United States had threatened to withdraw from the Games over a Canadian ban on the flag of Communist China, but relented.

State law barring gay sex is upheld

Washington, D.C., March 29

The Supreme Court ruled today that states have the right to enforce laws banning homosexual acts. The decision upholds a ruling of a Virginia court that prohibited such activities, even between consenting adults in the privacy of their own homes. The high court's ruling is a reversal of its record of the last 10 years, which had expanded guarantees of privacy. Civil liberties groups and gay activists are outraged over the decision and are planning to protest it. But social conservatives believe it appropriately curbs "abnormal behavior."

National revelry marks 200 years of independence

Jnited States, July 4

A bicentennial is worth two cen-ennials, and then some. The frol-s of 1876 were no match for the estivities of 1976; the first cen-ennial was mostly celebrated by eding from a simple picnic basket r watching an amateur marching and perform without the benefit of ousa. The year 1976, however, of-ered a splendid show of 225 tall-nasted ships, the opening of a great viation museum, a 10-mile-long nternational parade and, briefly, he largest American flag ever, a anner boasting stars as big as bath-ubs. As for meaningfulness, there nay be segments of the population nhappy with the current state of ocial and political affairs, but 1976 lelivers more of the promises of 776 than 1876, 100 times over.

Today, New York played host to Operation Sail, as the ships of 30 nations were elegantly navigated hrough New York harbor. Visit-ors crowded the wharves and New Yorkers found perches in sky-crapers to get a glorious view. One hing they did not get to see was the mmense flag along the side of the Verrazano-Narrows Bridge that had been sewn by volunteers hail-ng from Marblehead, Massachu-etts. Because planners failed to provide vents to let the high winds hough, the flag was quickly torn to shreds. In Washington, D.C., thou-sands of visitors were welcomed to he Smithsonian Institution's new National Air and Space Museum and 33.5 tons of fireworks were sent up near the normally sedate Lincoln Memorial. The Boston Pops Orchestra played the *1812 Overture,* punctuated by harmonious howitzers. President Ford rang the Liberty Bell in Philadelphia, Chicago swore in 1,776 citizens, and in Los Angeles an *All Nations, All Peoples* conga line swayed to the Pacific. New Orleans retired to a jazz marathon last night; San Antonio rose to a balloon race this morning. Small-town U.S.A. did its duties, too, with pie-eating, baton twirling and greasedpole shinnying contests.

People who thought hard about what *independence* means enjoyed the holiday less. The July 4th Coalition held a mostly peaceful protest in Philadelphia, drawing attention to the fact that its members (blacks, Indians, gays and feminists) were all created equal but lost ground the instant they stepped into society. Others who reviewed America's democratic traditions felt its people weren't so badly off: true, a President just resigned in disgrace, but that isn't bad for nearly 200 years of chief executives. One writer noted how content people seem with the new President, and wondered if they would have liked him any less if they had voted him into office. But most Americans focused on the revelry at hand. Will the tricentennial outdo it?

Americans remember those patriots who fought and died to win liberty.

Independence Hall in Philadelphia is carefully preserved as a symbol.

The British are coming! Across the country, Americans are staging re-enactments to commemorate the pitched battles of the War for Independence.

"Old Ironsides" sails again. The warship Constitution is back in the water, this time as a symbol of America's strength and dedication to freedom.

The colonial Minuteman is best remembered for his heroic convictions.

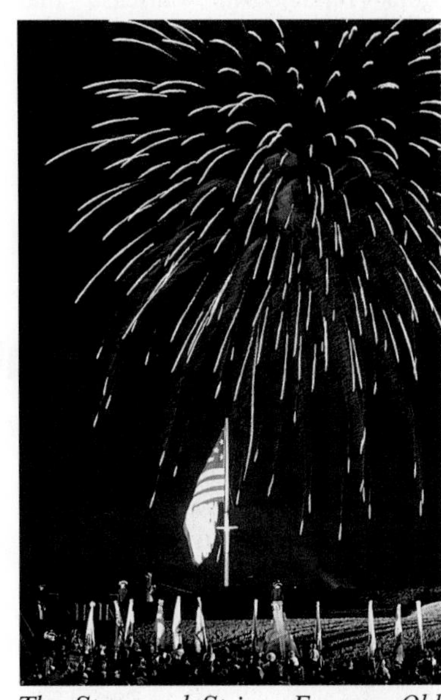

The Stars and Stripes Forever. Old Glory, illuminated in all its majesty.

Slowdown gives economic issue to Carter

Washington, D.C., October

The stagnating economic recovery that experts keep trying to predict away is stubbornly hanging on to poison Republican fortunes in next month's election. The rate of expansion slowed from 9.2 percent in the first quarter to 4.5 percent in the second. Leading economic indicators dropped in August for the first time in a year and a half. Unemployment did fall from 7.9 to 7.8 percent in September, but only after rising three months in a row. And according to the Census Bureau, 25.9 million Americans are poor, the highest number since 1970.

With the figures bared to the public eye, the first presidential debate, on September 23, quickly became a nationally televised forum on economic policy. President Ford, defending his record, spoke of a glass half full. He took credit for creating four million jobs and bringing the total number of employed Americans to 88 million, "the most in the history of the country." Jimmy Carter insisted that Ford's tenure has seen a 50-percent increase in unemployment. Both are correct. A 14-percent rise in the cost of living has sent women and teens flocking into the labor force faster than the economy can produce new jobs.

The two candidates also clashed on taxes. Ford offered a $28 billion cut, while Carter argued that most of the benefits would go to corporations and "special interests."

Ford trips on Soviet issue in Carter debate

Ford's uncertainty about Soviet sway over the East bloc is troubling voters.

San Francisco, Oct. 6

President Ford declared tonight, "There is no Soviet domination in Eastern Europe." The President made the statement in the second of two televised campaign debates with the Democratic presidential nominee, Jimmy Carter, broadcast from the San Francisco Palace of Fine Arts.

Carter said he would like to see Ford convince Americans of Polish, Czech and Hungarian descent that their ancestral homelands are not under the "domination and supervision of the Soviet Union behind the Iron Curtain."

Ford accused Carter of "looking with sympathy" toward the idea of having a Communist government in the North Atlantic Treaty Organization, which he said would destroy the alliance. Carter denied that he had ever advocated such a course for Italy, saying it would be a "ridiculous thing for anyone to do who wanted to be President of this country" (→ Nov. 2).

15 percent of adults functionally illiterate

Washington, D.C.

Tfgrx pj kuuyl mxstqv, lpqw. To you, the above collection of letters holds no meaning. To millions of Americans, this "sentence" means as much as any other; it is a cluster of symbols that cause embarrassment, frustration, harm. According to a Census Bureau report, 15 percent of all American adults are functionally illiterate, living blindly in a world of written words. The impact of illiteracy on the individual is clear: a parent can't read to his child, can't decipher antidote instructions on a bottle of roach poison in an emergency. When a whole society is involved, the problem multiplies. In the face of these figures, literacy foundations have been pushing harder for the government to provide some assistance.

Mysterious "Legionnaires" flu kills 28

Philadelphia, Aug. 26

The death toll from the mysterious influenza-like disease that struck the Pennsylvania American Legion convention here last month now stands at 28, and epidemiologists say they have no clues to its cause. The outbreak was first spotted by Dr. William Campbell, a family doctor who noted similar symptoms in three of his patients who attended the convention. Studies found 180 cases across the state. Patients have an unusual pneumonia with high fever and a persistent cough. The largest force of federal investigators ever assembled combed the Bellevue-Stratford Hotel, the convention site, in vain. Speculation on the cause ranges from an unidentified toxic substance to a new kind of bacteria.

California asserts patient's right to die

Sacramento, Calif., Sept. 30

Governor Jerry Brown signed into law today California's Natural Death Act, dubbed the "right-to-die" law, the first of its kind in the nation. Its application, however, is limited. A patient's natural-death directive must be witnessed by two persons, neither of whom is related to the patient nor involved in his medical treatment. At least two physicians must certify to the patient's imminent terminal condition as well as to his or her mental competence to make the decision. The patient can cancel the directive at any time. The controversial statute contains a strong statement that this in no way condones mercy killing or euthanasia.

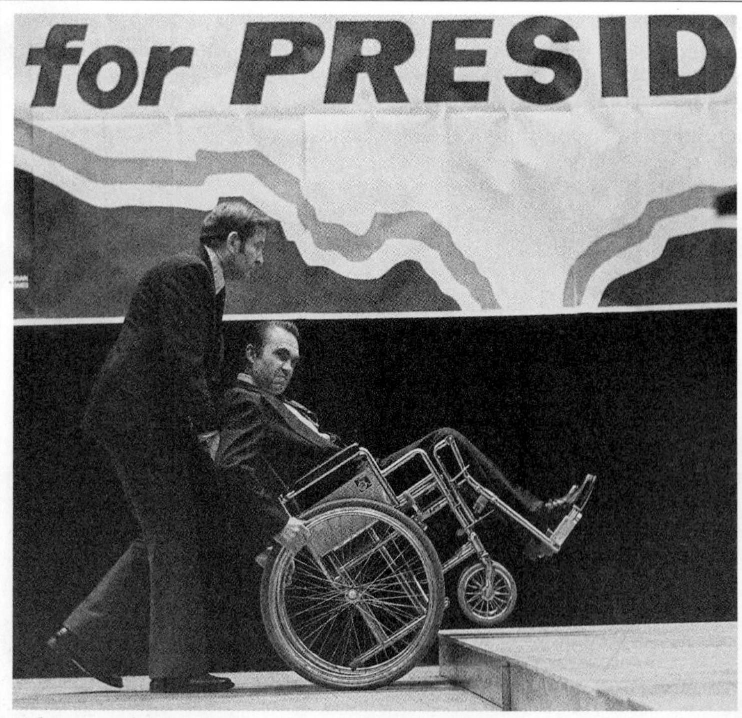

Taking to the hustings with a little help. Permanently paralyzed by a would-be assassin in 1972, George Wallace runs again for the White House.

Americans win all Nobels but Peace

Stockholm, Sweden, Dec. 10

Americans have scored a near sweep of the 1976 Nobel Prizes. The literature winner was Saul Bellow, the Canadian-born novelist who lives in Chicago. Conservative economist Milton Friedman won the economics prize and William Lipscomb Jr. was the chemistry winner for his work on compounds called boranes. Baruch Blumberg and Daniel Carleton Gajdusek shared medicine honors for virus research, and Burton Richter and Samuel Ting won for discovering a subatomic particle. Mairead Corrigan and Betty Williams of Northern Ireland won the Peace Prize.

U.S. to name firms in boycott of Israel

Washington, D.C., Oct. 8

The Commerce Department announced today that it will publish the names of all American firms that are asked to join the Arab boycott against Israel, and whether or not they do. The announcement was in compliance with a pledge made on television by President Ford during his debate with Jimmy Carter, who denounced American acquiescence in the embargo as "a national disgrace." A Commerce Department report of September 30 found that 94 percent of American firms went along with the boycott.

Bermuda Triangle claims another ship

Bermuda, Oct. 15

A 590-foot cargo ship with a crew of 37 is missing in the Bermuda Triangle, the ocean area between Bermuda, Puerto Rico and Norfolk, Virginia, where over the years hundreds of men, ships and planes have reportedly vanished without explanation. The Panamanian-registered Sylvia L. Ossa, was bound from Brazil to Philadelphia with a cargo of iron ore. It had radioed that its arrival would be delayed because of gale winds and high seas. Then it fell silent. Coast Guard planes are searching the area.

Carter retakes White House for Democrats

Jimmy Carter goes to Washington.

Washington, D.C., Nov. 2

In one of the closest elections of the century, Democratic Party nominee Jimmy Carter was elected President of the United States today, defeating the Republican incumbent, Gerald Ford.

The outcome split the nation on East-West lines. Carter won the South and a number of key states including New York, Pennsylvania, Texas, Ohio, two states in the upper Midwest and Hawaii. Ford won most of the Midwestern stastes and all of the West except Hawaii. Although Ford won 27 states to Carter's 23 and the District of Columbia, Carter obtained 279 electoral votes to Ford's 241.

It was the eighth time in the nation's history that a sitting president had been defeated. The last previous occasion was the Franklin D. Roosevelt triumph over Herbert Hoover in 1932. Carter was the first candidate from the "Deep" South to be elected since the Civil War, although another Southerner, Texan Lyndon Johnson won in 1964.

Tom Wolfe proclaims the "Me Decade"

New York City

Writing in *New York* magazine, satirist Tom Wolfe has called this the "Me Decade." Chronologically, 1976 is smack in the middle of "meness," and there are some statistics to bear Wolfe out. One report reveals three out of five marriages end in divorce, and one out of five children lives in a one-parent home. Is it a coincidence that the teenage SAT scores are so low? What were parents doing while their children's average scores dropped to 472 in math and 453 in English (from 501 and 480 in 1968)? Perhaps they were joining the Me generation, filling up on bran to live longer (bran cereal sales climbed 20 percent this year), or worrying more about the numbers on their paychecks than those on their kids' tests. No longer, it seems, are people willing to risk life and limb to march for peace, harmony and civil rights. Unless, of course, the price is right.

Cadillac Eldorado is last convertible

Detroit, Mich., Apr. 22

The last assembly-line convertible built in the United States, a white Cadillac Eldorado, rolled out of the factory today. Doomed by auto air-conditioners and freeway speeds, convertibles have steadily lost market share since 1965, the peak year, when more than 500,000 were sold. Chrysler, Ford and other General Motors divisions stopped convertible production earlier, but Cadillac kept making them until its last supplier of convertible soft tops went out of business. This model is likely to become a collectors' item.

A Watergate movie on whistle blowers

Carl and Bob bask in the glory.

Washington, D.C.

What's happening in the news can be tomorrow's successful film, as demonstrated by *All the President's Men*, in which Robert Redford and Dustin Hoffman portray Bob Woodward and Carl Bernstein, the *Washington Post* reporters who broke the news of the Watergate scandal in 1972. The picture was actually considered before the book was written and published in 1974. Redford, irate over the abuse of public trust, got in touch with Woodward and Bernstein and grew fascinated by the story. The two reporters have written a second best-seller, *The Final Days*. Also a best-seller is *Blind Ambition: The White House Years*, by John Dean, former White House counsel.

For John Beasley, 20, repainting the house plain old green didn't seem to fit the bicentennial spirit. So, with brush in hand, he created a patriotic masterpiece. He says dad thinks it's "kind of cool," but mom is not amused.

1977

Carter

Pasadena, California, Jan. 9. Oakland Raiders defeat Minnesota Vikings, 32-14, in Super Bowl XI.

Beverly Hills, California, March 1. Bette Davis becomes first female film performer to win American Film Institute's Life Achievement Award.

Canary Islands, March 27. In worst commercial aviation accident in history, 561 people die as Pan Am jet from Los Angeles and two KLM 747's collide on runway at Tenerife.

New York City, Apr. 29. Alex Haley receives special Pulitzer Prize for *Roots*.

New York City, May 20. In TV interview with David Frost, ex-President Nixon asserts, "When the President does it, that means it is not illegal."

Washington, D.C., June 3. United States and Cuba conclude pact, trading diplomatic missions (→ Sept. 26, 1980).

Portland, Oregon, June 5. Trail Blazers defeat Philadelphia 76ers, four games to two, for N.B.A. title.

Biloxi. Mississippi, June 6. Joseph Lason installed as city's Roman Catholic bishop, becoming first black American bishop since 19th century.

Washington, D.C., June 6. United States charges Soviet Union with violating Helsinki accords.

Washington, D.C., June 30. President Carter cancels development project for B-1 bomber in favor of cruise missile.

North Korea, July 13. North Koreans shoot down U.S. military helicopter after it strays into N. Korean airspace, killing three and wounding one.

Mojave Desert, California, Aug. 12. Space shuttle Enterprise makes first test flight.

New York City, Oct. 18. Yankees defeat Los Angeles Dodgers, four games to two, in World Series.

United States. Over 400,000 teenage abortions performed worldwide, third of them in U.S.

United States. John McPhee's *Coming into the Country* published.

DEATH

Switzerland, Dec. 25. Charlie Chaplin, silent film star (*Apr. 16, 1889).

Carter calls energy crisis battle "the moral equivalent of war"

Washington, D.C., Apr. 18

The nation must wage "the moral equivalent of war" to overcome an energy crisis that could lead to "national catastrophe," President Carter told the nation in a televised address from the Oval Office tonight. Unless the United States reduces energy consumption, Carter said, its spending on imported oil could rise from the current $36 billion a year to $550 billion by 1985, an increase he said, that "will threaten our free institutions." The energy goals he set for 1985 include a cut in the annual energy growth rate to 2 percent from today's 4 percent and a reduction of 10 percent in gasoline consumption.

Public opinion polls show half the public believes there is no energy crisis or that it is artificially created. To counter that skepticism, the President released a Central Intelligence Agency report predicting sharp oil price increases unless a major conservation program is begun. Carter did not give details of his plan, but he said it would depend on financial sacrifices and changes in living habits. "With the exception of preventing war, this is the greatest challenge that our country will face in our lifetimes," he said somberly. "The energy crisis has not yet overwhelmed us, but it will if we do not act quickly" (→ Sept. 13)

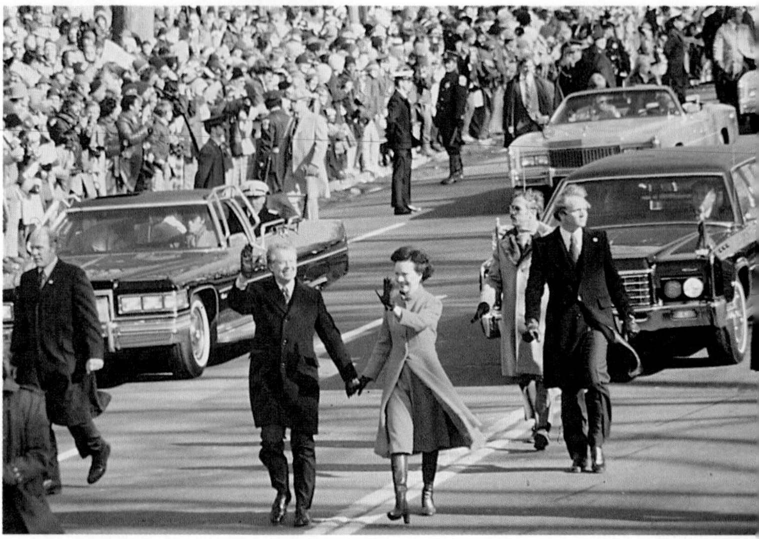

President Jimmy Carter and First Lady Rosalynn broke convention by walking a part of the way to the White House on Inauguration Day, January 20.

"Roots," TV event

New York City, Feb. 1

Alex Haley's *Roots* began with a birth in an African village in 1750 and ended seven generations later at a black professor's funeral in Arkansas. Haley is that professor's son. The ABC series ran an unprecedented eight consecutive nights with more than 51 percent of all television sets tuned in each night. The nightly audience of 80 million was the biggest ever for a TV show.

Carter pardons all Vietnam draft evaders

Washington, D.C., Jan. 21

Acting promptly to fulfill a campaign pledge, President Carter today granted a full pardon to all Vietnam-era draft evaders, providing they had not engaged in violent acts. The amnesty was not extended to those who entered the forces and then deserted, but an immediate study was promised to consider upgrading discharges that were less than honorable.

The presidential pardon was criticized by some who thought it went too far, and by others who felt it did not go far enough. Senator Barry Goldwater, the 1964 Republican presidential nominee, called it "the most disgraceful thing that a President has ever done." But Democratic Senator Edward Kennedy called his action "a major, impressive and compassionate step toward healing the wounds of Vietnam".

Gilmore executed; first in a decade

Utah, Jan. 17

Gary Gilmore's death wish came true tonight when the killer of two men was executed by a firing squad at the Utah State Prison. It was the first time the death penalty has been carried out in the nation since 1967. Gilmore, who twice tried to commit suicide in prison, became highly publicized because of his demand that he be executed. After a last-minute challenge to the death penalty by the American Civil Liberties Union, the Supreme Court refused to grant a stay of execution.

February 18. *The space shuttle Enterprise, scheduled to make orbital space flights in 1979, got its first test run today on the back of a Boeing 747.*

U.S. to reduce aid for rights violators

Washington, D.C., Feb. 24

Following through on President Carter's campaign pledge to make human rights a top priority, Secretary of State Cyrus Vance today announced cutbacks in foreign aid to three offenders, Argentina, Ethiopia and Uruguay. Strategically important countries such as South Korea, where civil rights are also abused, do not face aid cutoffs now, but there will be more American pressure for better conditions. The step comes a week after Carter wrote Andrei Sakharov, the dissident scientist, pledging to urge broader human rights in the Soviet Union (→March 22, 1981).

Vast pipeline will bring oil from Alaska

A project of epic proportions, the Alaska pipeline carries oil over 800 miles.

Valdez, Alaska, July 28

After more than a month of delays, spills and false alarms, the first barrel of North Slope oil has arrived in Valdez. This year-round, ice-free port on Prince William Sound will be the southern terminus of the TransAlaska Pipeline System, known as TAPS.

Completed on May 30 at a cost of $8 billion, TAPS will channel two million barrels of petroleum a day from the Prudhoe Bay oilfield on the shore of the Arctic Ocean. The 800-mile trail of 48-inch pipe is considered by many to be the technological wonder of the age. With 78,000-above ground supports, TAPS crossed more than 800 rivers, the longest being the Yukon, where a 2,290-foot bridge had to be built for both pipeline and road traffic. Although laying the pipeline was expensive, it will more than pay for its cost when the estimated seven billion recoverable barrels of oil are extracted.

Though Prudhoe is the largest oilfield on the North American continent, it is modest when compared to the oilfields of the Middle East. Nevertheless, economists estimate that, on the basis of current needs, Alaskan oil from this one field will enable the United States to reduce its imports from the Middle East and elsewhere by more than 15 percent.

2,000 at Seabrook besiege atom plant

Seabrook, N.H., May 2

Sponsored by a group called the Clamshell Alliance, a demonstration to halt the planned nuclear reactor at Seabrook drew a crowd of 2,000 today. The protesters occupied the site, saying they would remain until plans for the atomic plant were abandoned. About 1,400 of the demonstrators were arrested, loaded into buses and brought to court. A similar, but smaller demonstration occurred last August, when more than 100 were arrested. "If they keep building, we'll come back with 18,000," said an alliance leader. Use of nuclear energy has raised environmental concerns.

Spanking held legal

Washington, D.C., Apr. 19

"Spare the rod, spoil the child" is the old adage, and the Supreme Court seems to agree. Today, in a 5-4 decision, the court ruled that spanking schoolchildren does not violate Eighth Amendment protection against "cruel and unusual punishment." But the court did say that school officials who use "excessive" force in disciplining students are subject to criminal penalties. It also said sufficient protection against such abuse exists. In dissent, Justice Byron White called spanking a "barbaric" punishment.

It's Seattle Slew

New York City, June 11

He was not the kind to win any beauty contest for horses and, in fact, was sold at auction for a very modest $17,000. But races aren't won by looks or money and today Seattle Slew accomplished the toughest task in horse racing as he swept to the Triple Crown. He did this by taking the Belmont Stakes, where he was the 2-5 favorite as a result of his victories in the Kentucky Derby and the Preakness. The undefeated colt outraced Run Dusty Run, who also chased him in the first two legs.

Ray is recaptured

Tennessee, June 13

James Earl Ray and six other convicts were found today, three days after their escape from Brushy Mountain State Prison. They got away with the help of a bogus fight staged by fellow inmates. Ray is serving a 99-year sentence for the murder of the Rev. Dr. Martin Luther King Jr., and the escape fueled national skepticism. Despite the finding that Ray acted alone, many believe he was involved in a conspiracy and regarded the escape as an engineered effort to silence the one man who might air the truth. Governor Ray Blanton, citing the cost and security problems, has asked the federal government to take charge of Ray.

"Moonies" held to be brainwashed, given back to parents

California, March 24

California Superior Court Judge S. Lee Vauris ordered a group of five adult members of the Unification Church placed in the temporary custody of their parents today. In issuing his order, Judge Vauris said it would appear that the Rev. Sun Myung Moon's Unification Church (Moonies) exerted a brainwashing influence on the young adults, making it impossible for them to consciously choose to remain with or leave the church. The Unification Church has acquired great notoriety in this country and many feel that this case is directed against the church itself and would not have been heard had it involved one of the regular denominations.

Critics question how the Rev. Sun Myung Moon controls his young followers. ▷

New diesel cars need 40% less fuel

Detroit, Mich., Sept. 13

Reacting to the energy crisis, General Motors today introduced a new line of diesel cars whose major selling point is a claimed 40 percent mileage advantage over gasoline-powered autos. This diesel, available first in full-size Oldsmobiles, is a modification of G.M.'s 350-cubic inch gasoline engine and will be built in a new $500 million plant near Lansing. General Motors acknowledges that its diesel has the traditional faults of such engines, including greasy exhaust fumes, noise and slow starting on cold days, as well as a price $1,000 higher than conventional models, but it is counting on the low cost of diesel fuel and the new energy consciousness of American drivers.

Foreign cars pour in

Detroit, Michigan

Auto imports hit a new high this year, with foreign car makers expected to sell 2.1 million vehicles, capturing nearly 20 percent of the American market. Imports, mostly Japanese, account for 40 percent of all sales in some Western states. American auto companies are fighting back by reducing prices of their small cars, which have suffered the greatest sales decline, and introducing new models designed to compete directly with the most popular Japanese subcompacts.

Farrakhan leads separatist Muslims

Chicago, December

Louis Farrakhan, formerly Malcolm X's successor at Temple No. 7 in Harlem, has led a group of followers out of the World Community of al-Islam in the West. The separatists dislike the drift toward orthodox Islam and away from racial separatism that has marked the Black Muslim movement since Elijah Muhammad died. Farrakhan has reorganized the old Nation of Islam (Black Muslims) along the strict separatist and racial lines that distinguished the movement at its start.

Elvis, king of rock, gone

By the time of his death, Elvis had gained weight and given in to drug abuse.

Memphis, Tennessee, Aug. 16

Elvis Presley died at his Graceland mansion today. He was 42. Rock 'n' roll might still be an innocuous hillbilly genre had Elvis Aaron Presley not shown up. Born in Tupelo, Mississippi, to working-class parents, Presley had a voice brushed with a shade of Southern blues. When parents heard his first hit, *Heartbreak Hotel*, in January 1956, they knew they didn't want their teenagers to hear it, and when they saw him gyrating on the Ed Sullivan Show in September of the same year, they didn't want him seen, either. But his songs *Hound Dog*, *Don't Be Cruel*, *Love Me Tender* and *Blue Suede Shoes*, and his films, including *Viva Las Vegas* and *Jailhouse Rock*, had an irresistible appeal to a generation longing to seem a little more dangerous than it really was.

Elvis lived on the edge: He took up karate and earned a black belt, stayed up at night and slept by day and had several lovers after his five-year marriage to Priscilla Beaulieu. Though a near teetotaler, he took amphetamines and barbiturates, and though physicians have blamed his death on a "cardiac arythmia," rumors are that he succumbed to a drug overdose, a king who sadly dethroned himself.

Serving an energy-hungry America. The Indian Point nuclear plant in New York State is one of several such facilities providing the new source of power.

Episcopalians split over women priests

St. Louis, Mo., Sept. 16

In a reaction to the ordination of women to the Episcopal priesthood, several conservative Episcopalians have left the Protestant Episcopal Church of America to organize a new denomination, the Anglican Church in North America. At a three-day meeting, the 1,700 dissidents adopted a charter for the new denomination and declared themselves to be true heirs to the Anglican tradition. The dissidents view the ordination of women as contrary to the historical doctrines of Anglicanism and say it puts the Americans at odds with Anglican churches in other nations. While women's ordination was the catalyst for the separation, the split had been long in the making.

$2.65 wage floor

Washington, D.C, Nov. 1

President Carter signed legislation today to raise the minimum wage for workers to $2.65 an hour. The bill also mandates a rise in the hourly minimum to $3.35 in 1981. Unions wanted this year's increase to be $3. Some union leaders feel the President did little to help their cause. *Congressional Quarterly* reported, "Only after months of negotiations did labor succeed in gaining administration support (for the bill.)" Low wage-earners see it as a step in the right direction.

Divorced Catholics allowed to remarry

Washington, D.C., Nov. 10

At their annual meeting, Roman Catholic bishops announced today that Pope Paul VI has ended the automatic excommunication imposed on divorced American Catholics who remarry. It was last year that the bishops asked the Pope to lift the excommunication first imposed by the Plenary Council of Baltimore in 1884. The bishops said the aim of this step was to extend reconciliation to divorced and remarried Catholics and to encourage them to regularize the status of their marriages.

Irate farmers: "No dough, no grow!"

Washington, D.C., Dec. 10

Thousands of tractors rumbled into Washington, Atlanta, Denver and some 30 other state capitals today to demand increased crop support from the government. The farmers are planning their first national strike since 1932, and one sign reads "No Dough, No Sow, No Grow." Critics doubt that the farmers, traditionally hard to organize, can be mobilized. But, said Bill Schroeder of Colorado, "If I work, I lose money. If I sit on my rear, I lose money. What would you do?" Since 1973, farmers have suffered a drop in net annual income from $9,950 to $5,300, while costs continue to climb. Protesters say a bushel of wheat worth $2.70 on the market costs $5.06 to produce.

Abortion funds cut

Washington, D.C., Dec. 9

Congress has placed strict curbs on the use of federal Medicaid financing of abortions. Previously, Medicaid covered all abortions considered "medically necessary." But now they are limited to those for physically ill women and the victims of incest and rape. Abortion rights activists fear that poor women will again become victims of dangerous "back-alley" abortions.

U.S. signs away canal

The end of a U.S. monopoly. President Carter could not have chosen a more polarizing issue to tackle. Built with United States money, know-how and muscle, the Panama Canal represents to many America at its industrious best.

Washington, D.C., Sept. 7

The leaders of the United States and Panama agreed today that the Panama Canal shall be Panama's canal by the year 2000 – if the American Senate ratifies the treaty. President Carter and Brigadier General Omar Torrijos signed accords that would revoke the treaty of 1903 under which the United States built and controls the canal.

The Senate must approve the new accord by a two-thirds majority before it can take effect. Under its terms, American control of the canal will expire on the last day of 1999, but the United States will still be authorized to "counter any threat to the canal's neutrality." A bitter fight is likely in the Senate, because of American pride in the canal and strong feelings about its importance to national security.

Torrijos urged Senate "statesmen" to approve the new treaty. He pointed out that the original one was not signed by a Panamanian, but by a Frenchman acting on the behalf of a small nation that had recently seceded from Colombia.

Of discos, muscles and "Star Wars"

Hollywood, California

Disco seems to be contagious after *Saturday Night Fever*, a new film in which John Travolta puts his best foot forward as the intense and moody Brooklyn youth who yearns for glory and finds it as king of the discos. The latest media trend king, Travolta has inspired vast numbers of inner-city dancers. Clad in silk shirts and skin-tight pants, they are flocking to discos across the country and writhing under multi-colored strobe lights to the sounds of the Bee Gees and Donna Summer.

Elsewhere in the world of film, Woody Allen presents another personal picture, witty *Annie Hall*, with himself and Diane Keaton. Arnold Schwarzenegger muscles his way to stardom via *Pumping Iron*. Good and evil fight in George Lucas's forceful *Star Wars*, a fantasy inspired by the work of mythology scholar Joseph Campbell. It's loaded with spectacular effects, and people return to see it again and again. Steven Spielberg alienates no fans with his huge hit, *Close Encounters of the Third Kind*. In *Julia*, Jane Fonda is playing Lillian Hellman, Vanessa Redgrave is her brave friend and Jason Robards is Dashiell Hammett. Liza Minnelli and Robert De Niro make music in Martin Scorsese's big band-era musical *New York, New York*. And the movies refight World War II in Richard Attenborough's $25-million *A Bridge Too Far*.

National Women's Conference meets to plan feminist future

Two ladies of liberty. Ardent feminists from around the country express their hopes and dreams for an America without sex disctimination.

Houston, Texas, Nov. 21

On November 18, at the start of the four-day First National Women's Conference, a flaming torch led a phalanx of marchers through Houston. The torch had traveled 2,500 miles from Seneca Falls, New York, site of the first women's convention in 1849, and one woman runner after another had carried the flame on the trek across the country. Now marching behind it were 2,000 delegates, led by tennis star Billie Jean King, politician Bella Abzug and the N.O.W. founder Betty Friedan, all holding hands and linked by womanhood. Later, First Lady Rosalynn Carter stood shoulder to shoulder with former First Ladies Betty Ford and Lady Bird Johnson.

Clearly, the conference at Houston has had form. Has it had function? Its resolutions are many: It calls upon Congress to establish full employment, thus making more jobs available to would-be working women. It seeks sex education at all school levels, including the elementary grades. It urges voluntary, flexible-hour child care. It demands enforcement of the Federal Equal Credit Opportunity Act of 1974. And minorities in the women's movement have not been forgotten: special attention is demanded for disabled women, Hispanics, blacks, Indians and the elderly of all races. So much for demands. As delegates disperse, they know the hard part is ahead: working to get the demands met (→ June 30, 1982).

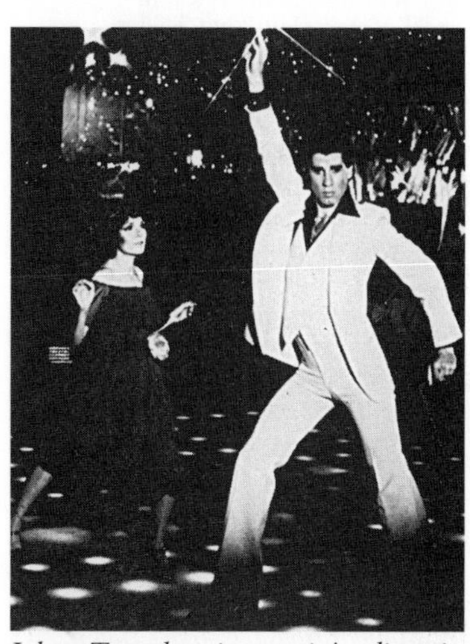

John Travolta is stayin' alive in "Saturday Night Fever," a film that celebrates the latest fad – disco dancing – sweeping the nation.

1978

Carter

New York City, Jan. 11. Walter Jackson Bate wins National Book Critics Circle Award, National Book Award and Pulitzer Prize, for biography *Samuel Johnson.*

New Orleans, Jan. 15. Dallas Cowboys beat Denver Broncos, 27-10, in Super Bowl XII.

Boston, Jan. 20. Blizzard drops 23 inches of snow on Boston in one day.

Washington, D.C., Jan. 31. Secretary of Agriculture Robert Bergland announces hog cholera has been eradicated from American agriculture.

Washington, D.C., Feb. 1. Postage stamp issued bearing likeness of abolitionist Harriet Tubman, first in honor of a black woman.

Chicago, March 4. *Chicago Daily News*, 15-time Pulitzer Prize winner, stops publication.

New York City, Apr. 17. Stock Exchange sets trading record of 63.5 million shares.

New York City, Apr. 17. Carl Sagan awarded Pulitzer Prize, for *The Dragons of Eden.*

Washington, D.C., Apr. 19. Supreme Court, in McDaniel v. Paty, overturns Missouri law banning clergy from holding public office.

Seattle, June 7. Baltimore Bullets defeat Seattle Supersonics, four games to three, for N.B.A. title.

Jordan, June 15. Elizabeth Halaby, 26-year-old American, marries King Hussein, becoming Queen of Jordan.

Washington, D.C., June 15. Supreme Court rules, in T.V.A. v. Hill, that Tellico Dam may not be completed, as area is only known habitat of endangered snail darter.

Atlanta, Aug. 10. State Senator Julian Bond files suit to end use of word "nigger" on radio and television.

Chicago, Oct. 6. University of Chicago inaugurates Hannah Gray first woman president of an American university.

United States. Books published include John Irving's *The World According to Garp* and Herman Wouk's *War and Remembrance*.

Hollywood, Calif. Hit films include *National Lampoon's Animal House, Coming Home* and *The Deer Hunter.*

160,000 miners end longest strike

Washington, D.C., March 24

Keeping the United Mine Workers and the coal operators at the bargaining table, says Labor Secretary Ray Marshall, is like "trying to corral quicksilver." But today the efforts paid off. After a record 16 weeks on strike, 160,000 miners approved a pact to raise wages from $7.80 to $10.20 an hour over three years. The union, however, is broke and torn by dissension. Nearly half the rank-and-file opposed the contract, which requires annual contributions to a health plan. According to one West Virginia union official, strikers voted yea "just because they (were) hungry."

Sneaker sales soar

Chicago

Some call them tennies or tractor treads. Some call them felony flyers, gumshoes, plimsolls, pussyfooters, perpetrator boots or simply gym shoes or sneaks. Basically, they are sneakers and basically they account for 50 percent of all shoe sales. In a country where 30 million people play tennis, other millions play racquetball and one person in nine runs almost daily, their feet have gone to their head.

U.S. and Japan discuss economic malaise

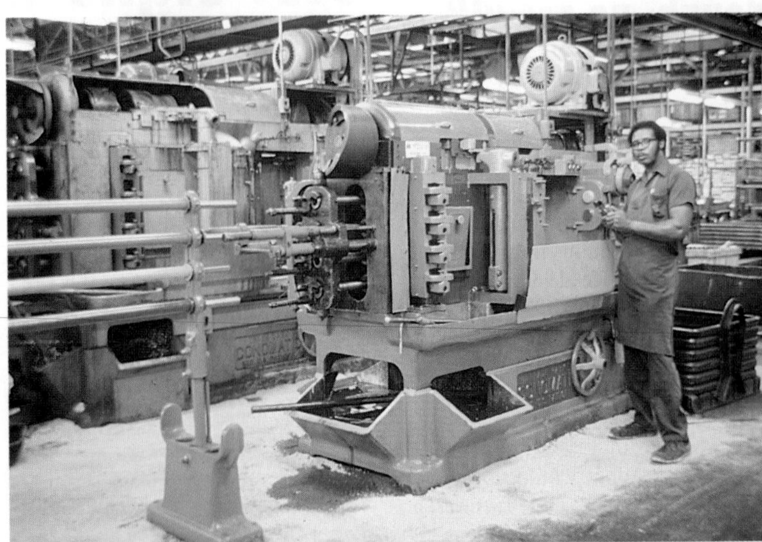

International Harvester uses color as an inducement to increase productivity.

Washington, D.C., May 3

Accompanied by Foreign Minister Sunno Sonoda, and Minister for External Economic Affairs Nobuhiko Ushiba, Premier Takeo Fukuda met today with congressional leaders to discuss Japan's troubled economic relationship with the United States. The meeting was arranged by former Senate majority leader Mike Mansfield, now ambassador to Tokyo, in hopes of heading off protectionist laws aimed at halting the loss of American jobs to Japan. There is a vast surplus of Japanese exports over imports. Last year, there was an $8.9 billion trade imbalance with the United States.

Fukuda has come ready to make concessions. Exports of Japanese cars to America, which totaled 1.9 million last year, are to be cut back to 1977 levels; steel exports will be pared 10 to 20 percent, and color TV sets to 30 percent below 1976 levels. Fukuda has also promised to stimulate domestic consumption by $7 billion to $10 billion a year, thus creating opportunities for American exports, but he has resisted suggestions that Japan spend more on defense (→ Dec. 17, 1987).

U.S. acts to curb nuke proliferation

Washington, D.C., March 10

President Carter today signed the Nuclear Non-Proliferation Act, placing strict curbs on the export of fissionable materials. The law requires the renegotiation of all agreements with recipient nations. The United States seeks to gain veto power over re-export and over the reprocessing of spent fuels into material capable of producing weapons. Western Europeans, who rely on the United States for over half their nuclear fuel, have already expressed grave reservations. Sources say West German Chancellor Helmut Schmidt, who is scheduled to meet with Soviet leader Leonid Brezhnev next month, may seek to buy more uranium from the Russians.

New law raises age of retirement to 70

Washington, D.C., Apr. 6

As President Carter signed a law to raise the mandatory retirement age for most Americans from 65 to 70, Representative Claude Pepper beamed with pride. The senior congressman from Florida, who lobbied hard for the bill, called this "a happy day for millions of American elderly." Opponents of the change say it will disturb employment practices, taking jobs from women, the young and minorities. But Labor Department studies indicate it will have no long-term effects on the economy and, in fact, may even result in a saving from undistributed Social Security payments. Senior citizen groups applauded the legislation as a morale booster for older people.

Carter will hold off on a neutron bomb

Washington, D.C., Apr. 7

President Carter today indefinitely "deferred production" of the neutron bomb. This "enhanced radiation weapon" has caused much public debate because of its effectiveness against human beings, and the fact that it does relatively little damage to buildings. This makes it more likely to be used, its opponents argue. Ultimately, the President said, the decision on developing the weapon would be influenced "by the degree to which the Soviet Union shows restraint in its conventional and nuclear arms programs." The Defense Department, in the meantime, will modernize the missiles and artillery delivery systems to be used if Carter should change his mind.

Californians vote vast cut in property tax

Sacramento, Calif., June 6

After a hard and often rancorous campaign, in which there was as much mud-slinging as debate, Proposition 13 has been approved by an overwhelming majority of the California voters.

The proposition, which restricts property taxes to no more than 1 percent of assessed valuation, got under way as part of a campaign to put a limit on the powers of the state's legislature. But California politics aside, the vote appears to have turned into the starting gun for a nationwide effort to roll back what many property owners all over the country feel are exorbitant property taxes.

The California property owners have long felt that their representatives in Sacramento were overtaxing them to support social programs from which they did not benefit. Noting the overwhelming vote of support, Howard Jarvis, father of the tax reform movement, said today that it was a clear indication of the end of the days of "spend, spend, spend."

Property tax reform organizations throughout the nation have been keeping a close eye on the kind of reception Proposition 13 would receive. A victory by a wide margin in California, many of their leaders believe, may carry the message that there is also sentiment for federal tax reform in California as well as other states.

Bakke wins reverse discrimination ruling

Washington, D.C., June 28

In what many call the most widely anticipated ruling of the decade, the Supreme Court decided today that fixed racial quotas are unconstitutional. In a case brought by Allan P. Bakke against the University of California Medical School at Davis, the justices ruled that Bakke was a victim of reverse discrimination. While public educational institutions had to recognize the need for minority students, the court ruled that no school could set fixed quotas. Many jurists are not sure what the ruling means. All that has been outlawed are fixed racial quotas. The ruling does not do anything about any other form of discrimination (→Feb. 13, 1979).

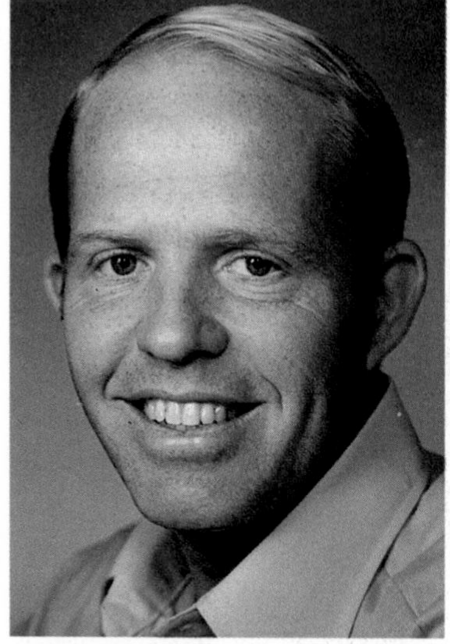

Challenging the "social engineers."

The star who made women's tennis shine

Forest Hills, New York

Equal pay for equal play, Billie Jean King insisted, and she made it work. She became the leading force in putting women's tennis on a par with men's and along the way reigned as the nation's foremost female player. Billie Jean, short of legs but stout of heart, became in 1971 the first woman to win more than $100,000, and by 1975, Chris Evert was earning $300,000 a year. King nurtured the Virginia Slims circuit, a separate tour which brought women greater attention. She helped equalize United States Open prize money for men and women. And it was her passion and intensity that got World Team Tennis off the ground. Meanwhile, she won four U.S. Open singles titles and rushed to more Wimbledon crowns than any other player.

Her most public triumph came in September of 1973 when she beat "male chauvinist pig" Bobby Riggs. She called this the "culmination of 19 years of tennis." Before a Houston crowd of 30,492 and with millions watching on TV, she won, 6-4, 6-3, 6-3. Breaking gender boundaries in sports, a traditionally male enclave, King has become a source of inspiration for the women's movement in a way that transcends her contribution to tennis.

Harvard introduces new core curriculum

Cambridge, Mass., May 2

"Changing undergraduate education," says Harvard president Derek Bok, "is like trying to move a graveyard." But his faculty did just that today by approving a core curriculum. A backlash against the 60s, the plan requires students to take 10 courses in five basic areas. Dean Henry Rosovsky says it will ensure "literacy in the major forms of intellectual discourse." But many criticize the program's European bias. One student called it "a step back ... to the old English idea of spoon-feeding students."

Mormon priesthood is opened to blacks

Salt Lake City, Utah, June 9

Spencer W. Kimball, president of the Church of Jesus Christ of Latter Day Saints (Mormons), announced today that the church had received a revelation allowing black males to be admitted to the Mormon priesthood. The letter announcing the revelation states that "all worthy male members of the church may be ordained to the priesthood without regard for race or color." The church has never offered an explanation for the exclusion of blacks except that there "were reasons known only to God."

Billie Jean shows her stuff. Aside from her amazing record of 21 American titles, King has been pivotal in achieving recognition for women's tennis.

The Ford Fairmont is one of the American automotive industry's latest attempts to combine ample passenger room with increased fuel economy.

Ali wins title third time

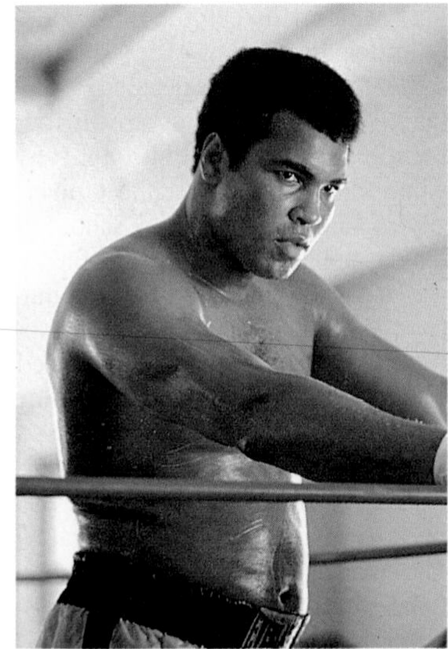
A little older, but again the greatest.

Spinks, no match for Ali tonight.

New Orleans, La., Sept. 17

It was vintage Ali. He floated like a butterfly and stung like a bee. And in the end, Leon Spinks was no longer the world heavyweight champion. Ali was champ, for the third time, a feat never achieved in boxing. He outfought Spinks, who said after tonight's bout, "My head wasn't in it." His head was in it long enough to be jarred by stinging left jabs from the 36-year-old Ali. Spinks had taken the title away from Ali in February on a decision, when Ali's rope-a-dope and peek-a-boo strategy – bobbing up and down, weaving in and out – wasn't working. Ali said after that bout, "I want to be the first man to win the championship back for a third time."

After the fight, its promoter, Bob Arum, offered some clues to the reverse in fortunes that led to Ali's victory. "Leon was out every night, disco dancing," said Arum. "He was running around. He didn't deserve to win." Even his manager walked away from Spinks's corner after the fifth round, leaving the Superdome before the bout ended. "Ali wasn't tougher than last time," Spinks said, "but my mind wasn't ready." As for Ali and the earlier fight, Arum said "he didn't move in Las Vegas because he didn't train. Now he moved." Questioned later about retirement, Ali was evasive.

American balloon is 1st to cross Atlantic

Paris, Aug. 17

They missed the Eiffel Tower by about 60 miles, but three natives of Albuquerque, New Mexico, have become the first human beings ever to cross the Atlantic Ocean by balloon. Ben Abruzzo, Max Anderson and Larry Newman piloted the Double Eagle for 138 hours and six minutes, a record for balloon flight. They will return to the United States next week by some faster, more secure means of transport. A reception at the White House will be one of the first stops. Then, not yet satisfied with a mere hop across the ocean, the three travelers are planning a 30-day balloon trip around the world.

Ethics law signed

Washington, D.C., Oct. 26

Some may question President Carter's economic policy or his ability to lead. But none question his ethical integrity. So it is fitting that he signed the comprehensive Government Ethics Law today. It requires United States legislators, judges and members of the executive branch to make financial disclosures, and it changes the guidelines for federal employees returning to the private sector. It also sets procedures for picking special prosecutors to examine charges of impropriety in the executive branch.

Carter announces anti-inflation plan

Washington, D.C., Oct. 24

In a nationwide address on television this evening, President Carter unveiled a voluntary program that he said would put a rein on the country's inflation by means of wage and price standards, inflation "insurance" for workers and continued deregulation of government-controlled industries. "Of all our weapons ... competition is the most powerful," the President said, referring to his plans for deregulating the surface transportation industry, as the airlines industry has been. Carter said that the recommendations would result in a reduction of inflation by between 1 and 2 percentage points.

Rockwell is dead

Stockbridge, Mass., Nov. 8

America's best-loved illustrator, Norman Rockwell, died today at the age of 84. Rockwell, who first studied at the Art Students' League in New York, gained fame for his magazine covers. From 1916 to 1963, Rockwell did 322 covers for the *Saturday Evening Post*. In designs like *Girl With Black Eye* and the *Look* cover that featured John F. Kennedy and the Peace Corps, Rockwell succeeded in portraying Americans as they wished to be seen, with patriotism, kindness and a gentle humor.

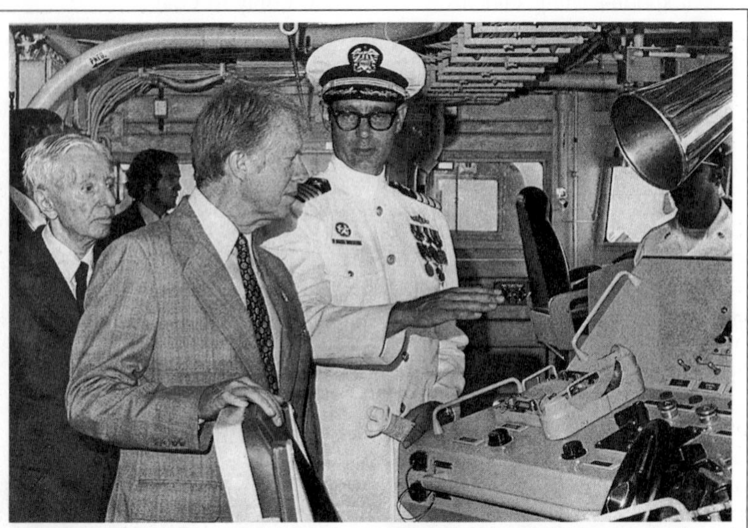
President Carter is joined by retired Admiral Hyman Rickover (left) and Captain Peter Hekman on a visit to the nuclear-powered missile cruiser Mississippi, during its commissioning at the base in Norfolk, Virginia.

Las Vegas, Nevada. *This city has changed enormously since the Mormons first settled here in 1855 and left two years later. Since 1931, when gambling was legalized, "The Strip" has always proved a good bet for high rollers.*

Cleveland defaults; first city since 30s

Cleveland, Ohio, Dec. 16

Cleveland today won the dubious distinction of becoming the first American city since the Depression to go into default. The city owes $14 million to six local banks, which have yet to take court action to collect. A major part of the problem is a political battle between Mayor Dennis Kucinich and the City Council. According to a report in the *Wall Street Journal*, Cleveland "has the financial capacity to get out of the predicament, if only its leaders can work in harmony." In fact, Cleveland bonds are now in brisk demand. One of the city's resources is a fairly low tax base.

Affirmed wins it all

New York City, June 10

It took a photo-finish camera to rule that Affirmed had won the Belmont Stakes in one of the most dramatic finishes ever in this third leg of the Triple Crown. The photo showed Affirmed had a margin of a head over Alydar, who also ran second to Affirmed in the first two legs of the series, the Kentucky Derby and Preakness. Affirmed and Alydar ran head and head for the last half-mile of the mile-and-a-half grind but the Harbor View colt bobbed his head just at the finish. Steve Cauthen rode Affirmed.

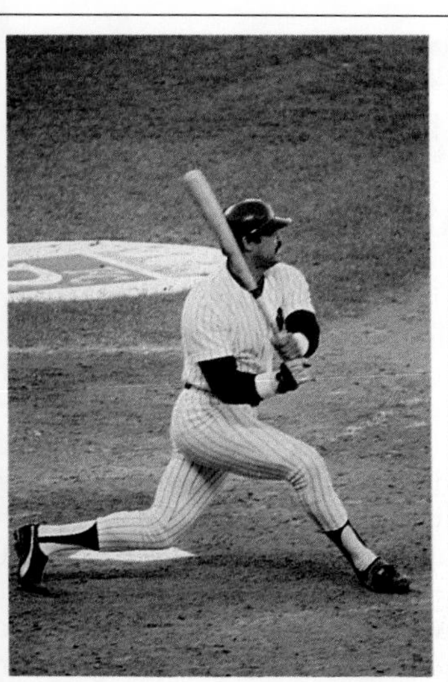

Reggie Jackson, "Mr. October," leads the Yankees to World Series win over Dodgers, 4 games to 2.

Tragedy at Jonestown

A scene of indescribable horror. The mass suicide in Guyana brings into focus the power a cult leader, Jim Jones in this case, can have over his followers.

Jonestown, Guyana, Nov. 18

Representative Leo J. Ryan was killed today and hundreds more are reported dead in a bizarre murder and mass suicide at an American religious cult community in this South American country. Ryan, 53, was reportedly killed by followers of the Rev. Jim Jones, a controversial California religious figure. Some 900 of Jones's followers then committed mass suicide.

The congressman had gone to Guyana to investigate reports that members of the Jones community were being held prisoner. Ryan and several aides and reporters with him were fired upon by some of Jones's associates after leaving the community and trying to board a plane bound for the United States.

Reports from the area indicate that hundreds of the cultists then swallowed a concoction of Kool-Aid and cyanide – at Jones's direction – and that Jones himself also committed suicide. Hundreds of bodies, adults and children, have been found in the Guyana jungle around Jonestown. There were no marks of violence. Not one living person was found in the camp.

Jones moved his San Francisco-based People's Temple to a 27,000-acre land grant in Guyana four years ago. His followers included blacks and whites who believed in his vision of racial harmony.

Gay Frisco official and Mayor killed

San Francisco, Nov. 27

Former Supervisor Dan White, 32, walked into City Hall today in a rage. He shot and killed Mayor George Moscone, 49, a father of four, then Supervisor Harvey Milk, 48. Why? The Mayor had not reinstated White, who had quit his job November 10 but changed his mind a week later. Milk was a different case. White, a self-proclaimed defender of family and morals, hated homosexuals, and Milk, a leader in gay politics, was the first openly gay city official. Dianne Feinstein, board president, was sworn in as temporary mayor.

More Indochinese refugees accepted

Washington, D.C., Nov. 28

The United States plans to admit 21,875 more Indochinese refugees in addition to the current quota of 25,000 a year. They would include both Cambodians and Vietnamese. Attorney General Griffin Bell, who formulated the plan, said today that he would proceed unless Congress balked. He also said that Congress should consider a broader admissions policy. The majority of the new refugees would be "boat people" such as the 2,500 aboard the Hai Hong, who were accepted on November 17 after Malaysia had denied them permission to land.

Kennedy and King conspiracy victims?

Washington, D.C., Dec. 30

President John F. Kennedy and the civil rights leader, the Rev. Dr. Martin Luther King Jr., were not killed by gunmen working alone, contrary to previous evidence, the House Select Committee on Assassinations asserted today. Based on reports from acoustical experts, the committee believes President Kennedy was shot at from a grassy knoll in Dealey Plaza as well as from the Texas School Book Depository in 1963. The committee said there was a "likelihood" that Dr. King's convicted killer, James Earl Ray, worked with his two brothers or for a businessman who offered $50,000 for King's death.

Dallas all the rage

Dallas, Texas

CBS has brought soap opera to prime time in the form of *Dallas*, a series about the complicated lives of a wealthy Texas oil family, the Ewings. Head of the family is J.R., a crooked-wheeling and dirty-dealing villainous hero, who gets what he wants any way he can. The part is played by Larry Hagman, himself born in Texas. While the series *Dallas* is growing in popularity, so is the real city. Attracted by seemingly unlimited job and housing possibilities, more than 1,000 families move to Dallas each month.

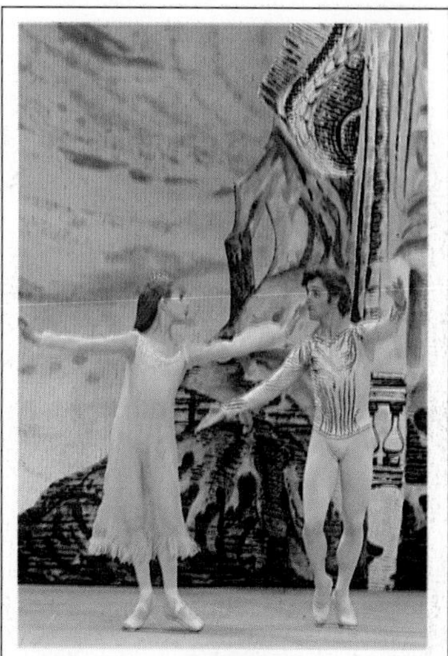

Mikhail Baryshnikov, who defected from the U.S.S.R. in 1974, dances in the "Nutcracker Suite."

1979

Carter

New York City, Jan. 15. *The Stories of John Cheever* earns Cheever both National Book Critics Circle Award and Pulitzer Prize.

Miami, Jan. 21. Pittsburgh Steelers defeat Dallas Cowboys, 35-31, in Super Bowl XIII.

Texas, January. William P. Clements is first Republican elected Governor of Texas since Reconstruction.

New York City, Feb. 9. Nelson Rockefeller's will leaves $13.5 million worth of art to Museum of Modern Art and Metropolitan Museum of Art.

Washington, D.C., Apr. 6. Because of Pakistan's attempts to build a uranium-enrichment facility, all United States aid is terminated.

Seattle, Washington, June. Seattle Supersonics defeat Washington Bullets, four games to one, for N.B.A. title.

Washington, D.C., July 25. President Carter appoints Paul Volcker chairman of Federal Reserve Board.

Detroit, July 31. Chrysler Corporation reports second quarter losses of more than $207 million (→ Dec. 20).

Washington, D.C., Aug. 31. Government reveals that Soviet Union maintains combat-ready contingent of 2,000 to 3,000 troops on Cuba.

Washington, D.C., Oct. 17. Special prosecutor clears President Carter and brother Billy of wrongdoing related to business loans obtained through banker Bert Lance.

Baltimore, Oct. 17. Pittsburgh Pirates defeat Baltimore Orioles, four games tó three, in World Series.

Cincinnati, Dec. 3. Eleven fans die of asphyxiation trying to get into rock concert by The Who.

Washington, D.C., Dec. 13. A suit brought by conservative congressmen to block termination of Taiwan treaty dismissed by Supreme Court.

United States. Ronald Reagan says, "For the average American, the message is clear. Liberalism is no longer the answer. It is the problem."

United States. Books published include, Tom Wolfe's *The Right Stuff* and Norman Mailer's *The Executioner's Song*.

Carter: Peace has come

A diplomatic miracle: Jimmy Carter links Egypt's Sadat and Israel's Begin.

Washington, D.C., March 26

Building on the success of last year's Camp David accords, which set the framework for a settlement in the Middle East, President Anwar el-Sadat of Egypt and Prime Minister Menachem Begin of Israel signed a peace treaty this evening in a ceremony held in a huge tent on the south lawn of the White House. Clasping hands with the two leaders, who shared the Nobel Peace Prize last December, a jubilant President Carter proclaimed, "Peace has come."

But, as the President was careful to point out, the treaty is only "a first step on a long and difficult road." No other Arab country, not even Jordan or Saudi Arabia, the two that are friendliest to the United States, has taken part in the settlement. The status of Jerusalem is vague and it will be many months before Israeli troops withdraw from the Sinai Peninsula. The future of the Israeli-occupied West Bank of the Jordan River is also unclear, and a likely source of future contention. And both leaders can expect to pay a heavy political price – Begin at the hands of right-wing Israelis who are reluctant to give up Sinai settlements, and Sadat at the hands of other Arab states, which are already treating him as a pariah and will almost certainly end their oil-financed subsidies.

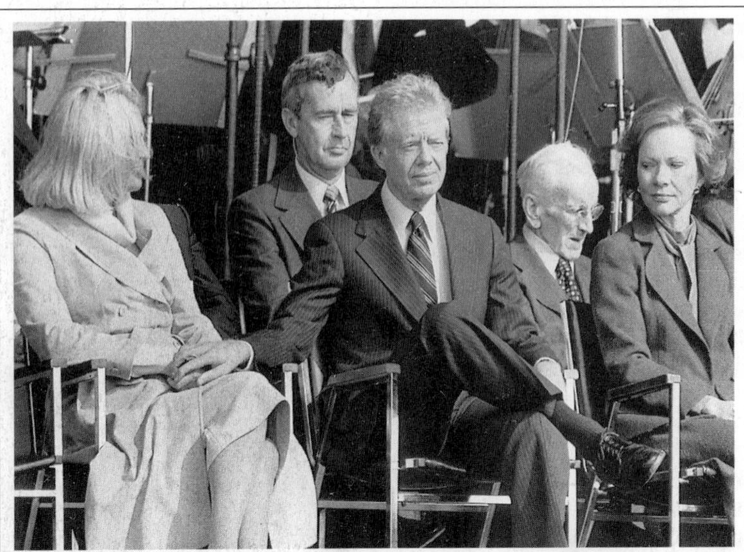

President Carter comforts Joan Kennedy, Senator Edward Kennedy's wife, during dedication ceremony of the Kennedy Library in Cambridge, Mass.

46% in U.S. attend segregated schools

Washington, D.C., Feb. 13

A report from the Civil Rights Commission disclosed today that 46 percent of the nation's minority students still attend segregated schools. This is in spite of a national desegregation effort that began with the Supreme Court's 1954 ruling in Brown v. the Board of Education that "separate educational facilities are inherently unequal." The court followed this decision with a directive for school boards to integrate "with all deliberate speed." It has also been suggested that many schools in traditionally segregated areas have enacted only token desegregation to comply with the directives (→ Nov. 2, 1983).

Marking past victories and failures.

Divorce rate soars 69% over a decade

United States

Sociologists say clothes with designer labels, bumper stickers and T-shirts with slogans like "Kiss me, I don't smoke" express a wish for connection with other people. If there were ever a disconnected time, this is it. The divorce rate is up 69 percent since 1968. The average marriage lasts 6.6 years, and 40 percent of children born this decade will spend some of their youth in a one-parent home. Backgammon may be popular now, but it takes two to play; electronic games like Chess Challenger may have lasting appeal for our solitary society.

)PEC oil price up; J.S. to curb imports

Vashington, D.C., July 15

Since the Organization of Petro-·um Exporting Countries (OPEC) as set the average price of a barrel f oil at $23.50 – a rise of over $7 1 the past three months alone – 'resident Carter today announced n energy program that in 10 years /ould bring oil imports down to 977 levels. Conservation and de-elopment of new energy sources, 1cluding nuclear power, are ma-)r features in the program, which /ould cost $140 billion. At last 1onth's Tokyo "energy summit" 1eeting of the seven major indus-rialized democracies, the United ·tates agreed to hold oil imports to .5 million barrels a day.

;ilkwood avenged

)klahoma City, May 18

A jury has awarded $10.5 million ɔ the Karen Silkwood estate in suit against the Kerr-McGee plu-onium plant for negligence in radi-tion poisoning. Silkwood, an ex-mployee, was poisoned in 1974 by ·lutonium in her apartment. No one nows how it got there, and the lamage it did fortified the judge's ontention that the material was so 1herently dangerous that Kerr-/IcGee could be liable. Silkwood /as killed in a car crash before her ase was decided and there have een rumors of foul play.

MX missile system 'o cost $30 billion

Vashington, D.C., June 7

President Carter today an-·ounced plans to build the MX mo-·ile intercontinental ballistic mis-ile for $30 billion. The MX, which tands for "missile experimental," /ill entail the production of 200 ehicles, each weighing 120,000 ·ounds and carrying as many as 10 /arheads. Each of the warheads ·as the explosive power of 335 kilo-ɔns, 22 times the power of the ·omb dropped on Hiroshima. The /IX will replace the Minuteman-3 nissile currently deployed in under-,round silos in the Western part of he country.

Nuclear disaster at Three Mile Island

Harrisburg, Penn., March 31

A faulty cooling system at the Three Mile Island nuclear power plant has caused the worst nuclear accident in the history of the United States. Two days ago, a combination of human error and stuck valves allowed the fissioning core of the reactor, normally submerged in water, to become exposed to air. The highly radioactive fuel rods that make up the core began to melt, releasing radioactive gases. Although officials say that it is unlikely, the danger remains that a bubble of radioactive hydrogen within the containment vessel might explode, which would cause a greater release of radiation. It is also still possible that a complete meltdown might occur, allowing the entire molten contents of the core to be released into the environment. Only a small amount of radiation has actually escaped so far, federal officials say, but the inside of the reactor is highly contaminated and it is still considered too hot to approach.

The cooling towers of the Three Mile Island nuclear power plant jut into the Pennsylvania sky. While the damage from this accident may well prove to be slight, it raises serious doubts about the feasibility of nuclear energy.

Governor Richard Thornburgh of Pennsylvania has advised the evacuation of children and pregnant women from within a five-mile radius of the damaged plant. A general evacuation, he has said, will not be necessary. President Carter, who holds an advanced degree in nuclear physics, has announced that he plans to make an inspection of the accident site.

Anti-nuclear protesters are planning to stage a demonstration tomorrow at the state capitol. The failure of the Three Mile Island reactor may serve to confirm what anti-nuclear protesters have been predicting for several years now. There have been protests to halt the construction of new atomic plants at several sites, including Seabrook, New Hampshire.

U.S. and Soviet agree on SALT II treaty to set missile limits

Washington, D.C., June 18

Right after signing SALT II, a new agreement with Soviet leader Leonid I. Brezhnev in Vienna to limit strategic arms, President Carter returned home to address a joint session of Congress today and to deliver a strong plea for treaty approval. The pact, the result of tough bargaining between Secretary of State Cyrus Vance and Soviet Foreign Minister Andrei Gromyko, limits each country to 2,250 missile launchers. No more than 1,320 of them may be equipped with multiple warheads (MIRV's), with further restrictions on bombers that can use long-range cruise missiles.

Prospects for Senate ratification are uncertain. Carter points out that with this treaty the Russians will have a third fewer missile launchers and bombers by 1985 than they would have had if they kept on building at the present rate. And he stresses that the treaty allows the United States to keep developing its MX missile.

Senator Henry Jackson and other hard-liners call the terms too favorable to Moscow and say the deal smacks of "appeasement." But liberals like Senators William Proxmire and George McGovern say the pact does not do enough to limit nuclear arsenals (→ Dec. 8, 1987).

President Carter and Leonid Brezhnev agree to a problematic arms treaty.

Carter says a crisis of confidence threatens America's future

The President senses a "crisis of confidence" and appeals to self-reliance.

Washington, D.C., July 15

President Carter said today that the United States faces a "crisis of confidence" at least as serious as the energy crisis, and called for measures to stem both problems. In a nationally televised speech, Carter outlined a six-point program of energy initiatives that he said would save 4.5 million barrels of oil a day by 1990.

During his 33-minute address, Carter said the nation has spiraled downward into self-doubt since the assassination of President Jonn F. Kennedy, the Vietnam War years, the Watergate scandal and the current inflation and energy crises. He called for Americans to recapture their old spirit of self-reliance.

Carter's energy plan would limit oil imports, require utilities to cut their oil use, allow the President to ration gasoline and establish or strengthen government boards that regulate energy consumption.

House Speaker Thomas "Tip" O'Neill Jr. described the speech as "one of the strongest and best the President has made." But some Republican leaders expressed the view that it showed an indecisive President. John B. Connally, a Republican presidential hopeful, said, "The crisis of confidence is one of the President's own making." And George Bush, the former Director of Central Intelligence, said that the speech raised questions about "how much follow-through, courage and leadership the President will have in his own country."

Congress bails out struggling Chrysler

Washington, D.C., Dec. 20

Is the bastion of capitalism adop ing socialism for corporations? I the biggest bailout ever by the Ur ited States government, Congres has approved a $1.5 billion loan t the ailing Chrysler Corporation The firm gets the matching-typ loan if it can raise $5 billion pr vately. Part of the loan deal woul be a three-year wage freeze for th unionized workers. All this has le Senator William Proxmire of Wis consin to ask, "Are we going t guarantee businessmen agains their own incompetence?" But a some people in industry say, a Detroit goes, so goes the nation. O does it? (→ May 13, 1980).

Inflation soaring; interest rates fluctuate

Washington, D.C., Oct. 10

With the consumer price index up by 13.3 percent, the largest rise in 33 years, the balloon of inflation continues to expand. Countermeasures by Federal Reserve Chairman Paul Volcker created fears among the nation's money managers when he announced that the Fed would curb the money supply. This is a significant departure from past practice, though the result is the same. When money is made scarce, interest rates are driven up. But with no benchmark to go by, rates fluctuated wildly. Said one trader, "They're going up and down like a roller coaster." In one day alone the federal funds rate rose to 15 percent, then dropped to 7 percent. Bonds plummeted by record amounts as investors sought better long-term returns.

Wall Street reacted like a yo-yo. After setting a year high of 897.61 the day before Volcker's move, the Dow Jones fell 40 points in the next two days. Heavy trading included today's volume of 81.6 million, the largest in history. Many investors, caught in a "margin squeeze," sold at a loss. But the dollar seemed to gain strength – one of Volcker's aims (→ Apr. 16, 1980).

Young sees P.L.O., is out of U.N. job

New York City, Aug. 15

Andrew Young, the first black American delegate to the United Nations, has resigned over his controversial talk with the Palestine Liberation Organization's U.N. observer. He said the meeting was unplanned, but he was chided by Secretary of State Cyrus Vance for breaching American policy, which bars such contacts. Young favors recognition of the P.L.O., a stance the Israelis oppose. He said the Israeli government decided to make the meeting a public issue.

Four are shot dead opposing the Klan

Greensboro, N.C., Nov. 3

Four demonstrators opposin the Ku Klux Klan were killed to day when Klan sympathizers op ened fire on them with automati weapons and shotguns. The four and a fifth person who was wound ed, were members of the Commu nist Workers Party, conducting "Death to the Klan" march. Th assailants tried to flee in two veh cles but were seized near the scen by the police. All 12 were charge with murder and conspiracy t commit murder (→ Nov. 17, 1980).

Righteous indignation: Women protest over pornography. During the past decade the proliferation of sexually explicit material has shocked many.

Beirut, October 4. *Civil rights leader Jesse Jackson turns to world affairs as he meets with the P.L.O.'s Yasir Arafat to talk about the Mideast.*

Ailing U.S. Steel shuts 10 factories

Pittsburgh, Penn., Nov. 27

Citing unfairly priced imports and excessive environmental spending, U.S. Steel is closing 10 plants, shutting parts of six others and laying off 13,000 workers. It will also trim its product line and raise its prices. The nation's biggest steel producer blames the government for its predicament, particularly the $1.8 billion it must put out by 1983 to comply with clean-air standards. Analysts reply that the company deliberately delayed meeting the requirements. They also claim that the steel industry, but especially U.S. Steel, has been slow to modernize and thus to respond to foreign competition (→ July 1986).

99% now own TV, but 41% like it less

Washington, D.C., March 1

More Americans have TV sets than ever before, but is television any better? In a *Washington Post* poll today, 99 percent said they owned a set. But only 17 percent said the shows were better now than five years ago, and 41 percent said they were worse. The *Post* found TV watching has declined, with 54 percent watching less than they did five years ago. More than a third said they would pay a small fee to get rid of commercials, which they found too long, loud and untrue.

Haves to have-nots

Washington, D.C., Dec. 31

It isn't what it used to be, $1 million, so more people are making it. U.S. Trust reports that 520,000 Americans are millionaires, or one in every 424 of us. On the other side of that coin, the Commerce Department says that about 25 million people, 11.6 percent of the population, earned less in 1979 than the official poverty level of $7,412 (for a non-farm family of four). The 1979 median family income, $19,684, was up 11.6% from a year ago but inflation took all but three-tenths of 1 percent of it. The 1979 median incomes: white families, $20,520; Hispanic, $14,320; black, $11,651.

Iranian militants seize U.S. Embassy

Angry Iranian students burn the American flag and shout "Death to America!"

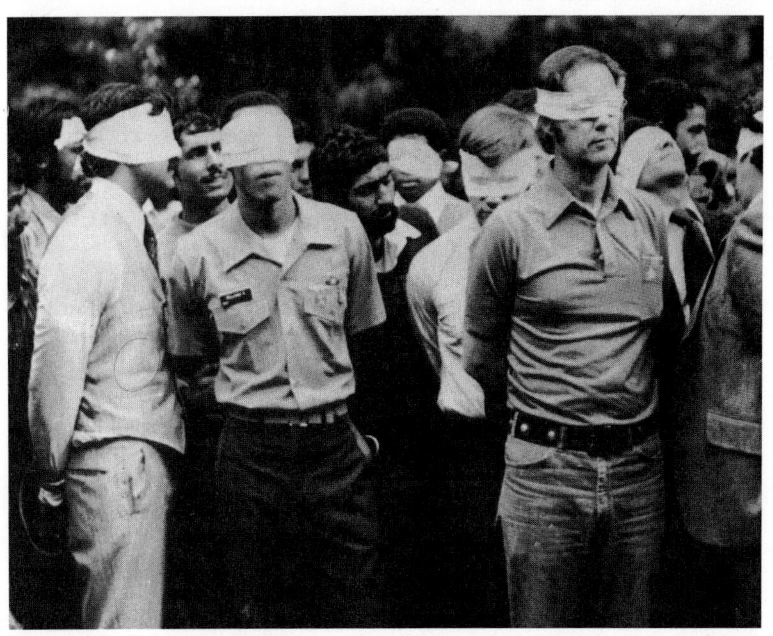

Some of the hostages seized by Iranian militants who raided the U.S. Embassy.

Teheran, Iran, Nov. 20

A mob of 500 Iranian students seized the United States Embassy here on November 4, taking 90 hostages. The takeover has turned into a diplomatic nightmare and the situation continues to deteriorate as President Carter begins to hit back. Carter's latest actions have been to freeze all of the considerable Iranian assets in the United States and to send a naval task force to the Indian Ocean, where carrier-based jets and helicopters would be within easy striking range of Iran.

Meanwhile, American television audiences have been shocked to see blindfolded members of the United States Marines embassy guard, with their hands tied behind their backs, as they were paraded before TV cameras while students chanted "Death to America, Death to Carter, Death to the Shah." Effigies of Uncle Sam and Carter were burned and scores of American flags were spat upon, trampled and burned in the street.

The United States immediately sent mediators to Iran to seek the release of the hostages, but they have met with little success. The students, who have the support of Ayatollah Khomeini's government, continue to take a hard line even though a trickle of hostages, mainly women and blacks, have gained their freedom. There are still 52 Americans in captivity.

The deposed Shah is hospitalized in the United States. His arrival set off the embassy attack and the students are demanding his return to Iran (→ Apr. 25, 1980).

End of a decade in Hollywood: Down memory lane at the movies

Hollywood, California

Kramer vs. Kramer was the big winner at this year's Academy Awards. Dustin Hoffman took the prize as best actor while Sally Field won for *Norma Rae*. Among other films audiences have applauded lately are *All That Jazz*; Woody Allen's *Manhattan*; *Star Trek – the Motion Picture*; *Being There* with Peter Sellers; *Apocalypse Now*, and *The China Syndrome*. The 70s offered a wide variety of films, starting in 1970 with George C. Scott as *Patton* and James Earl Jones as the first black heavyweight champion in *The Great White Hope*. *Love Story* sold a lot of handkerchiefs. In 1971, *Carnal Knowledge* and *Klute* won respect for Ann-Margret and Jane Fonda, respectively. William Friedkin's *The French Connection* and Stanley Kubrick's *Clockwork Orange* were stand-outs. In 1972, Diana Ross played Billie Holiday in *Lady Sings the Blues* and Liza Minnelli dazzled us in *Cabaret*. Marlon Brando was a double sensation in Bertolucci's *Last Tango in Paris* and *The Godfather*. In 1973 Jack Lemmon in *Save the Tiger* and Tatum O'Neal in *Paper Moon* were noteworthy, as were *The Sting* and *The Exorcist*. With 1974 came *Chinatown* and in 1975 everyone was talking about *One Flew Over the Cuckoo's Nest* and Steven Spielberg-directed *Jaws*. The bicentennial year sent conflicting signals with *All the President's Men*, *Bound for Glory*, *Network*, *Rocky* and *Taxi Driver*. In 1977, there were *The Turning Point* and *Julia*. And last year Bette Midler acted her heart out in *The Rose*.

1980

Carter

Pasadena, California, Jan. 20. Pittsburgh Steelers defeat Los Angeles Rams, 31-19, in Super Bowl XIV.

Philadelphia, Jan. 26. Mary Decker becomes first woman to run a mile in under four and one-half minutes.

New York City, Feb. 15. Anchorman Walter Cronkite announces he will retire from CBS Evening News.

Iowa, March 20. Linda Eaton, 27, Iowa City's first female firefighter, awarded $28,400 in damages and lawyer's fees by Iowa Civil Rights Commission, after legal battle over her right to breast feed her baby at firehouse.

New York City, Apr. 14. Edmund Morris wins Pulitzer Prize and new American Book Award for *The Rise of Theodore Roosevelt.*

Washington, D.C., Apr. 29. Senator Edmund S. Muskie named Secretary of State.

Tampa Bay, Fla., May 9 The *Summit Venture*, a freighter piloted by John Lerro, slams into the Skyway Bridge, knocking a bus and cars into the bay; 35 people are killed.

Los Angeles, June. Lakers defeat Philadelphia 76ers, four games to two, for N.B.A. title.

Detroit, July 16. Republican National Convention chooses Ronald Reagan of California as presidential nominee and George Bush of Texas as running mate (→Nov. 4).

United States, Sept. 25. Yacht Freedom defeats Australian challenger Australia to keep America's Cup.

Washington, D.C., Oct. 17. President Carter signs Foreign Service Act, creating Senior Foreign Service and upgrading diplomatic corps in general.

Philadelphia, Oct. 21. Phillies defeat Kansas City Royals, four games to two, in World Series.

Washington, D.C., Dec. 2. President Carter signs law to preserve huge tracts of land in Alaska.

Hollywood, Calif. Top movies include *Raging Bull* and *Coal Miner's Daughter.*

DEATH

Los Angeles, Nov. 22. Mae West, actress and sex symbol (*Aug. 17, 1892).

Carter bans grain sales to Soviet Union after Afghan invasion

Washington, D.C., Jan. 4

President Carter intends to back up his tough talk concerning the recent Soviet invasion of Afghanistan. He has halted delivery of 17 million metric tons of grain that had been earmarked by the Russians for their livestock herds. The eight million tons that were ordered in 1976, however, will be delivered.

In a television address to the nation, Carter described the Soviet invasion as "an extremely serious threat to peace" and added that an Afghanistan ruled by Moscow is a threat to both Iran and Pakistan. In addition to the grain embargo, Carter intends to suspend sales of high technology, such as advanced computers and oil drilling equipment, until further notice. Soviet fishing in American waters will be curtailed, leading to the loss of 350,000 tons of fish this year. And all new cultural and economic exchanges have been canceled. The President is also considering pulling the United States out of the Olympics Games that are to be held in Moscow this summer.

To prevent losses to farmers, the government plans to buy the grain intended for the Soviet Union at current market prices and store it.

The Russians have responded by calling Carter "wicked and malicious." They claim their action in Afghanistan is not an invasion but a move to support a legitimate government in Kabul (→Apr. 24, 1981).

Afghani students demonstrate against the December 1979 Soviet invasion of their nation. They attacked the Soviet Embassy and lowered the Soviet flag.

Windfall oil tax

Washington, D.C., Apr. 2

Thanks to the decontrol of oil prices, American oil tycoons stand to earn an extra $1 trillion by 1990. But because of the Windfall Profit Tax Act signed today by President Carter, $227 billion of it will go to the Internal Revenue Service. Real profits should be about $221 billion, which the tax does not cover. It's after the new, higher profits.

U.S. captures hockey title at Olympics

Lake Placid, N.Y., Feb. 2

An American team made up of itinerant players and a few collegians accomplished the seemingly impossible feat of winning the hockey gold medal at the Olympic Games today. The United States six scored a 4-2 victory over Finland, and earlier had upset the mighty Soviet team. The dramatic finish set off a joyous demonstration here that reverberated across the United States. The result of the game was announced at a matinee in New York's Radio City Music Hall, and the audience cheered, then sang the *Star-Spangled Banner*. The result of the Olympic series was a vindication of what is known as American hockey, in which players utilize more of the ice for passing and use harder body checks.

Silver market crash corners the Hunts

New York City, March 27

A $5-per-ounce plunge in the price of silver today to $10.80 may wipe out the Texas billionaire brothers Nelson and Bunker Hunt. Their activity last year drove the price up from $6 to its January peak of over $50. But when they began to issue silver bonds, their evident need for cash steadily drove the market down for a record 15 consecutive days, wreaking havoc on Wall Street. As a result, the Hunts have been left holding the silver-lined bag.

Going for gold! The U.S. hockey team won the Olympics as America cheered.

Carter admits U.S. is hit by recession

Washington, D.C., Apr. 16

With unemployment up and personal bankruptcies the highest in five years, President Carter today conceded what everyone else is saying. The economy, he observed, "has slowed down and probably entered a recession." He said it will be "mild and short" but that the arch-enemy, inflation, would rise for several more months. Most economic indicators are bad. February-March production was down and housing starts fell 21.8 percent to their lowest rate since 1975. The Federal Reserve has increased farm loans and Carter said he favored a congressional expansion of federally backed mortgages (→Dec. 19).

Computer's alarm almost starts war

Washington, D.C., June 6

A false alarm reporting a Soviet missile attack put American nuclear strike forces on alert today, defense officials say. They attribute the mistake to a malfunction of a computer at North American Defense Command headquarters in Cheyenne Mountain, Colorado. It took only three minutes to discover the mistake, but the alert, which resulted in 100 bomber crews armed with nuclear weapons starting their engines, lasted 20 minutes. It is the second such alarm in three days. The cause is being investigated.

Mt. St. Helens blast shocks Northwest

Mount St. Helens, Wash., May 18

In one of the most spectacular displays Mother Nature has offered the Northwest this century, Mount St. Helens erupted at 8:32 a.m. today. With a rumble that registered 4.1 on the Richter scale, the volcano hurled almost a cubic mile of earth and ash into the atmosphere. Destruction is widespread, with hundreds of square miles of trees flattened by the blast and Spirit Lake clogged with ash. Naturalists say it will take a decade for the Washington area to recover.

Disaster in Iran's desert

The rescue attempt was a complete fiasco, as this helicopter wreckage shows.

Washington, D.C., Apr. 25

A United States military expedition to free the hostages held by Iran met with disaster today after a helicopter collided with a transport plane at a staging area in the Iranian desert. Eight Americans were killed and several more were injured in the fiasco. After an early morning report at the White House on the failed mission, a stony-faced and haggard President Carter appeared on national television to tell the nation what happened. He gave few details, but said he had "ordered the cancellation of an operation in Iran that was under way to prepare for a rescue of our hostages. The mission was terminated because of equipment failure. During the subsequent withdrawal, there was a collision between aircraft on the ground at a remote desert location."

None of the casualties resulted from military action. The President said that the mission was not motivated by hostility toward Iran or the Iranian people and that there were no Iranian casualties. The operation involved helicopters, C-130 Hercules transport planes and 100 men and it took place 200 miles southeast of Teheran.

The Iranians celebrated the failure of the rescue mission at a rally that was staged in front of the occupied American Embassy, and a broadcast from Teheran announced that the Iranians "had inflicted defeat and flight upon Americans and their mercenaries" (→Jan. 21, 1981).

Jimmy Carter, a peanut farmer, with brother, Billy, and Ronald Reagan, chopper of wood. Reagan's ideological outlook has turned the presidential race into more than just a referendum on the Carter administration.

Labor leader to sit on Chrysler board

Rockford, Illinois, May 13

Trying to insure labor support for its recovery program, the beleaguered Chrysler management has placed United Auto Workers president Douglas Fraser on its board of directors. Fraser, who used to work on a Chrysler assembly line, is the first union leader ever elected to the board of an American company. Nearly 500,000 shares were voted against him. Several stockholders took the floor to argue that a labor spokesman would not pursue the interests of the firm. But Chrysler president Lee A. Iacocca, unwilling to jeopardize a $1.5 billion government loan approved last week, gave Fraser his support (→Feb. 27, 1981).

Patents permitted on living organisms

Washington, D.C., June 16

Living organisms can be patented, the Supreme Court ruled today in a case that takes on added significance in the era of genetic engineering. In the case of Diamond v. Chakrabarty, the court ruled in favor of General Electric, which filed for a patent on an oil-eating bacteria created by research scientist Ananda Chakrabarty. Scores of patent applications for organisms produced by genetic engineering already have been filed, and the court's decision will give a major boost to the fledgling biotechnology industry.

18 people are dead in Miami race riots

Miami, Florida, May 19

National Guardsmen armed with shotguns are patrolling Miami's streets today after rioting that has cost 18 lives and more than $100 million in damage. Officials say it is the worst race riot since the Newark and Detroit outbreaks of 1967. Crowds of enraged blacks surged into the streets Saturday night after a white jury in Tampa acquitted four white policemen in the death of a black businessman. The policemen were accused of having beaten the man to death. ▷

U.S. 226 million: Latins, Asians, Bosnians, Acadians and Manx

Washington, D.C.

There are 226,504,825 people in the United States, according to the latest census. A majority of Americans come from somewhere else, and more keep coming. While Los Angeles is acknowledged as a melting pot – it has become the first city in the nation where the bulk of the population is made up of Latin Americans and Asians – the rest of the country is also an exotic mixture with some 70,000 Albanians, 820,000 Acadians (bringing Mardi Gras to New Orleans), 80,000-plus Amish, up to 100,000 Basques, 600,000 Carpatho-Rusyns, about 750,000 Croatians, four million Dutch or people of Dutch descent, 2,500 Afghans, 1,100 Georgians, 435,000 Greeks, 21,000 Icelanders, 10,000 Indonesians, more than a million Lithuanians, up to 30,000 Macedonians, 50,000 Manx (from the Isle of Man), over five million Poles and their descendants, up to 30,000 Serbs, 30,000 South Africans, 20,000 Thais, over 487,000 Ukrainians, 3,500 Bangladeshi, 300,000 Dominicans and so on. About 500 Burmese arrive annually, as do 2,000 Armenians. In Detroit live 70,000 Arabs. Boston was and remains the center for Albanian Americans. Most Cossack (Ukrainian) groups are based in New Jersey. Chicago is the center for Bosnian Muslims. Miami has the largest concentration of Cubans and is officially a bilingual city. Bulgarian periodicals have a circulation of 7,000. More than a million people have migrated from Central and South America since 1820. And since then, over 500,000 West Indians, descendants of slaves, have arrived. There are presently six Hindu temples serving Indians in New York City. Over 1.5 million Scots, 740,000 French and five million Italians have immigrated to the United States. In Hawaii, Chinese make up 7 percent of the population (the biggest concentration of Chinese in America) and have an average income 40 percnt higher than Chinese on the American mainland.

Hispanic residents in Miami take the oath of citizenship at a naturalization ceremony. Despite its problems, America remains a beacon of hope and light.

After Gamal Abdel Nasser took power in Egypt and turned his land toward Islam, many Coptic Christians migrated; up to 85,000 have come to America since 1966. Since the founding of Israel, over 300,000 Jews have arrived; about half settled in New York. The three cities with the largest Greek populations are New York, Chicago and Washington, D.C. In North Dakota and Montana live about 6,000 Hutterites, teaching their children German and practicing Christian communal living. The number of illegal aliens in America is estimated at 3.5 million to 6 million (about half from Mexico) (→June 22, 1981).

Games in U.S.S.R.; U.S. leads boycott

Moscow, August

The United States and 50 other nations were missing from the competition, but the Soviet Union held the Summer Olympics as scheduled and they turned out to be quite successful. A total of 36 world records were set despite the absence of talented athletes from countries that joined in the boycott to protest the Soviet invasion of Afghanistan. However, the security was so strict that the athletes had to forgo the traditional victory laps. The Soviets accounted for 80 gold medals, but such athletes as eight-medal winner Aleksandr Dityatin might not have done nearly so well against the world's best.

Cuban boatlift ends

Miami, Florida, Sept. 26

Fidel Castro abruptly ended a sealift that poured 125,000 Cuban refugees into the United States. On Friday, Cuban soldiers forced more than 100 boats from the United States out of Mariel harbor without passengers. Castro offered no explanation for closing the open door he gave some Cubans five months ago. Miami Mayor Maurice Ferre said Castro opened prison doors to some of Cuba's worst criminals. "He flushed his toilets," said Ferre (→Apr. 19, 1982).

Larry Holmes foils comeback bid by Ali

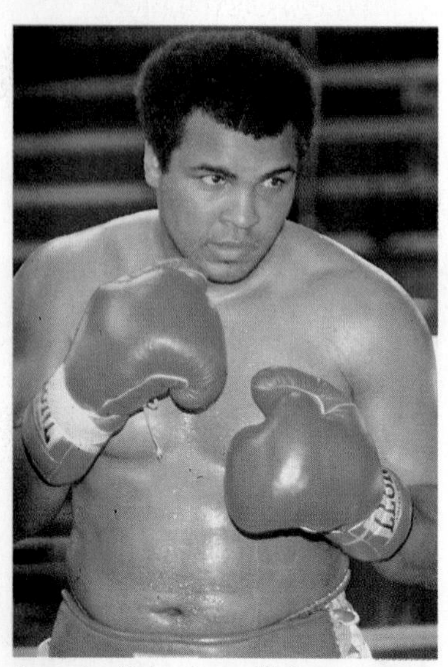

Lost the fight, but still the greatest.

Las Vegas, Nevada, Oct. 2

It's all over for Muhammad Ali. The former heavyweight champion, in his effort to win the title for a fourth time, ended his career at the age of 38 tonight, sitting weary and beaten on a stool, unable to come out for the 11th round of what was to have been a 15-round fight. He was no match for his former sparring partner, Larry Holmes, the 30-year-old undefeated champion. It was Ali's manager, Herbert Muhammad, who put an end to the one-sided contest in which the former Cassius Clay could land no more than 10 blows in 10 rounds. Many in the crowd wept at the defeat of one of boxing's greatest champions.

Falwell: "Get in step" with conservatism

Trenton, N.J., Nov. 10

The Rev. Jerry Falwell held a revival meeting on the steps of the New Jersey State House today. Or was it a political rally? Falwell, who reaches an audience of 18 million with his television ministry, founded the Moral Majority two years ago to spread the church's conservative agenda. This year, the group spent $3 million opposing liberal Senate candidates. Today, he told liberals to "get in step with conservative values or be prepared to be unemployed." Falwell's group supports family values and a strong defense and opposes abortion, pornography and homosexuality. "God created Adam and Eve," says Falwell, "not Adam and Steve."

Crossing the line between church and state? Jerry Falwell wants to restore morality through political channels.

NATO warns Russia on role in Poland

Brussels, Belgium, Dec. 12

Nine days after President Carter warned that Soviet military intervention in Poland would have "most negative consequences," the ministers of the NATO countries, prodded by Secretary of State Edmund Muskie, have issued a statement that intervention would mean the end of detente and would "fundamentally alter the entire international situation." Strikes and political unrest are in their sixth month in Poland. Despite reassurances by First Secretary Stanislaw Kania that his country's commitment to the Warsaw Pact remains firm, the Kremlin leaders are concentrating troops on the Polish border.

Reagan in a landslide

He's proud to be an American. Ronald Reagan pledges to revive national spirit.

Washington, D.C., Nov. 4

Ronald Wilson Reagan, a former movie star and television personality, was elected President today, toppling Jimmy Carter, the Democratic incumbent. At age 69, the one-time California Governor is the oldest man ever elected to the nation's highest office.

Returns showed a surprisingly strong Reagan victory, sweeping the East, Middle West and even what had been President Carter's stronghold in the South just four years earlier. Reagan received 489 electoral votes, almost twice the 270 needed to win, while Carter took just 49. George H.W. Bush was elected Vice President.

The outgoing President is the first elected incumbent to lose since Franklin D. Roosevelt ousted Herbert Hoover in 1932 early in the Depression. Gerald R. Ford, an incumbent, was defeated four years ago by Carter. But Ford was never elected to the office. He was serving the unexpired term of Richard M. Nixon, who resigned under threat of impeachment.

Prime rate zooms to 21.5 percent

New York City, Dec. 19

As of yet, no bright rays have dispelled the fog of recession. On the contrary, the nation's prime lending rate – the minimum charge on corporate loans – has just hit 21.5 percent after rising over 4 percentage points in the past month. This is the highest since April, when it began to fall. The Federal Reserve has also raised the discount rate. Banks link the rate rise to an increased demand from corporations. They say that they have also been hit by a rise in the federal funds rate to nearly 19 percent. This is the amount those in the financial circle charge one another for an overnight "quick-fix."

Who shot J.R.?

Hollywood, Calif., Nov. 21

Last season's final episode of the television series *Dallas* left J.R. Ewing shot by an unidentified assailant. Tonight, in the first episode of the fall season and after five months of ballyhoo and speculation, it was revealed that Kristin Shephard, played by Mary Crosby, did it. The show had the highest ratings ever for a regular television series: 88.6 million viewers.

Record loss for Ford

Detroit, Mich., Dec. 31

Chrysler isn't the only auto company running on empty. Ford has suffered a third-quarter loss of $595 million, a record for American corporations. Ford's 1981 deficit could thus hit $1.5 billion. Factors cited are the recession, high interest rates and Japanese competition. Rumors are spreading of G.M. rebates next year similar to those now offered by Chrysler.

All-white jury clears Klansmen of murder

Fanning the flames of hatred. It is not so prominent today, but the Ku Klux Klan is still an insidious force.

Greensboro, N.C., Nov. 17

Six supporters of the Ku Klux Klan were acquitted today of murder charges by an all-white jury in the 1979 killings of five anti-Klan demonstrators in Greensboro. After a week of deliberations, some jurors said they believed the defendants acted in self-defense. The charges stemmed from a November 3, 1979, "Death to the Klan" march by the Communist Workers Party in this textile city. Four marchers were killed when two carloads of white men opened fire on them and a fifth died later of wounds from the shooting. Five other men are also facing murder charges, but have yet to be tried. Signe Waller, the widow of one of the slain marchers, said, "I was so outraged I could hardly talk," after hearing the verdict.

Imagine . . . music without John Lennon

New York City, Dec. 8

John Lennon, musical icon and passionate spokesman for pacifism, died a victim of violence today. The former Beatle was returning home after a night of recording with wife, Yoko Ono, when a man stepped out of the shadows and fired four bullets into his back. When police arrived, they found an unemployed amateur guitarist named David Chapman thumbing through J.D. Salinger's *Catcher in the Rye* as he awaited arrest. Until today, Lennon was enjoying an emotional comeback after several years of seclusion. He was, as the title of his new single proclaims, *Starting Over*. By midnight, hundreds of mourners had gathered by candlelight outside the Dakota apartments where he lived, singing, "All you need is love. Love is all you need."

"Some say I'm a dreamer," John Lennon sang plaintively. Now, for the ex-Beatle, "the dream is over."

1981

Reagan

Washington, D.C., Jan. 5. Congress convenes, with House controlled by Democrats and Senate by Republicans.

New Orleans, Jan. 25. Oakland Raiders whip Philadelphia Eagles, 27-10, in Super Bowl XV.

Washington, D.C., March 13. President Reagan allots $1.5 million for inquiry on slain black children in Atlanta (→June 21).

Boston, May 14. Celtics defeat Houston Rockets, four games to two, for N.B.A. title.

Washington, D.C., June 25. Census finds large numbers of blacks living in suburbs.

Kansas City, July 17. Two suspended walkways collapse at Hyatt Regency Hotel, killing 111 people.

United States, Oct. 4. After a British writer raises doubts, body in grave marked "Lee Harvey Oswald" is exhumed and identified as man who assassinated John F. Kennedy.

Washington, D.C., Oct. 16. Walter Polovchak, 12-year-old who stayed in United States in 1980 after his parents returned to Soviet Union, is granted political asylum.

New York, Oct. 21. L.A. Dodgers beat Yankees, four games to two, in World Series.

Washington, D.C., Nov. 6. President Reagan states that he no longer believes a balanced budget by fiscal 1984 is attainable.

Cape Canaveral, Fla., Nov. 12. Space shuttle Columbia is first spacecraft to be used a second time.

Washington, D.C., Dec. 4. President Reagan expands powers of C.I.A., to engage in "pertinent" domestic intelligence gathering.

Washington, D.C., Dec. 29. Charging that Soviet Union is largely responsible for Polish repression, President Reagan reduces ties with Russians.

United States. Auto production reaches 20-year low of 6.2 million cars built.

Hollywood, Calif. Films include *Chariots of Fire*, *Reds* and *Raiders of the Lost Ark*.

DEATH

Las Vegas, Apr. 12. Joe Louis, former heavyweight champion (*May 13, 1914).

Hostages freed as Reagan takes over

Washington, D.C., Jan. 21

A few minutes after Ronald Reagan was sworn in yesterday as 40th President of the United States, the 52 American hostages in Iran were boarding a plane in Teheran, bound for West Germany and freedom after 444 days of captivity. Former President Carter had hoped the Iranian affair would end on his watch, but it was not to be.

Reagan made no mention of the hostages in his brief inauguration speech. He urged the nation to "begin an era of national renewal" and said that our new priority is to curb government. "Government is not the solution to our problem, government is the problem," the new President said. His first official act will be to freeze federal hiring. After his speech, the President, wearing a charcoal-gray suit, accompanied First Lady Nancy Reagan, wearing a bright red coat, down Pennsylvania Avenue in an open limousine while they waved to enthusiastic crowds lining the way.

Ronald Reagan talks of a nation reborn, one rededicated to preserving liberty.

The hostages could have been freed earlier, but there was a last minute snag. The Iranians challenged the appendix to the formal financial agreement that allowed the return of $8 billion in Iranian assets that had been frozen by the U.S. government after the takeover of the American Embassy by militant Iranian students on November 4, 1977. Executive State Minister Behzad Nabavi, Iran's chief negotiator, said the appendix was a surprise and that, upon examination, he discovered that the change of one word meant a potential loss of $900 million to Iran. The dispute was settled, however, by Deputy Secretary of State Warren Christopher and Algerian intermediaries. As soon as the hostages were released, President Reagan disclosed that "some 30 minutes ago the Algerian planes bearing our prisoners left Iranian air space and they are now free of Iran."

Former President Jimmy Carter flew to Wiesbaden, West Germany, to greet the hostages on behalf of President Reagan.

Following an hour-long meeting with the hostages at the United States Air Force Hospital, Carter charged that many of the hostages had been mistreated by their Iranian captors. "Our Americans were mistreated much worse than was previously believed," he said. "The acts of barbarism which were perpetrated on our people by Iran can never be condoned." According to former White House aides of Carter, the hostages had been subjected to "mock firing squads," to games of Russian roulette and to other forms of mental as well as physical torture. One marine sergeant, John McKeel Jr., told his mother that his captors had informed him that she was dead and that they would let him come home to attend her funeral if he told them what they wanted to know. Iran had denied that it was responsible for any abuse of the American captives (→27).

President welcomes the hostages home

Washington, D.C., Jan. 27

Two days after setting foot on American soil, the American hostages released by Iran were honored at a reception in the White House. President Reagan greeted the 52 Americans on the South Lawn of the White House after a motorcade through Washington where a crowd of 200,000 people cheered them. The reception was attended by hostages and their families, as well as the families of the eight soldiers who died in the aborted rescue attempt last April.

Welcome home. The Ayatollah drove a final stake into the Carter presidency.

President seeks cut in budget and taxes

Washington, D.C., Feb. 18

Warning that the United States is fast approaching "a day of reckoning," President Reagan today proposed a sweeping economic plan that would cut the budget as well as reduce certain taxes. His proposal, in a televised speech to Congress, calls for spending $695.5 billion in the coming fiscal year, $41.4 billion below the amount sought by former President Carter. The new plan would trim individual and business taxes by $53.9 billion. While raising military spending by $7.2 billion, it would slash such domestic programs as student loans, public service jobs, food stamps, welfare payments and free school lunches.

U.S. lends Chrysler $400 million more

Detroit, Mich., Feb. 27

In a deeper hole than previously estimated, Chrysler may yet roll again. The corporation will be given $400 million more by the Congressional Loan Board after having met several conditions. One is that its United Auto Workers employees approve a $644 million wage-benefit cut. Another concerns Canada, which will lend the company about $170 million. Chrysler is to repay it by investing some $850 million in Canada this year. Last year Chrysler broke an American corporation record by losing $1.71 billion.

Reagan survives attack

President Reagan waves to the crowd moments before his assailant strikes.

Washington, D.C., March 30

President Reagan was shot and gravely wounded today as he was leaving the Washington Hilton Hotel after addressing a labor convention. Also wounded were his press secretary, James Brady, and two security officers.

The President was reported to be in "stable" condition tonight after two hours of surgery at George Washington University Hospital, just blocks from the White House. "The prognosis is excellent," Dr. Dennis S. O'Leary reported. "He is alert and should be able to make decisions by tomorrow."

Just minutes after the shooting, officers arrested John W. Hinckley Jr., 25, a resident of Colorado, and charged him with having attempted to assassinate the President. He is being held without bond.

When he arrived at the hospital, the 70-year-old President attempted to reassure his wife and friends that he was fine. "Honey," he told his wife, Nancy, "I forgot to duck." The President then winked at his chief of staff, James A. Baker 3rd. After that, he next turned to Edwin Meese 3rd, his chief White House counselor, and quipped: "Who's minding the store?" Later, in the operating room, the President remarked to his surgeons with a chuckle: "Please tell me you're Republicans."

Most seriously wounded in the shooting spree was Jim Brady, the press secretary, who suffered severe head wounds (→June 21, 1982).

U.S. will act to cut influence of Soviets

Washington, D.C., March 22

In a reversal of the human rights policies of the Carter administration, Secretary of State Alexander M. Haig Jr. told Congress today that the major concern of the Reagan White House will be to contain and turn back Soviet influence in the developing world. "It does no good to pretend in our policies or our proclamations that (Soviet activity) is not the most serious threat to world peace we're facing today," Secretary Haig said this week in his public testimony on Capitol Hill. He said such Carter era concerns as human rights and South African apartheid would be subordinate to dealing with the Soviet Union.

El Salvador to get more U.S. support

Washington, D.C., March 2

The State Department today announced plans to expand military assistance to El Salvador, and White House sources are saying that the Reagan administration is considering even greater support for the Salvadoran economy. The military package will total $25 million and the economic aid will come to as much as $225 million. El Salvador's military has been severely criticized by human rights groups for alleged terrorism, including the murders of three Catholic nuns and a lay worker in December 1980.

North Dakota tops Kansas wheat total

Bismarck, North Dakota

Leadership in the nation's wheat production has unexpectedly shifted. Harvesting 338 million bushels this year, North Dakota passed Kansas as the leading producer. Frost kept Kansas from sharing in a national increase of 10 percent over last year's record-setting volume. But, in one of the economy's many ironies, healthy harvests can mean hard times. With the market glutted, grain prices are plummeting, and Washington has ordered a 15 percent cut in planting.

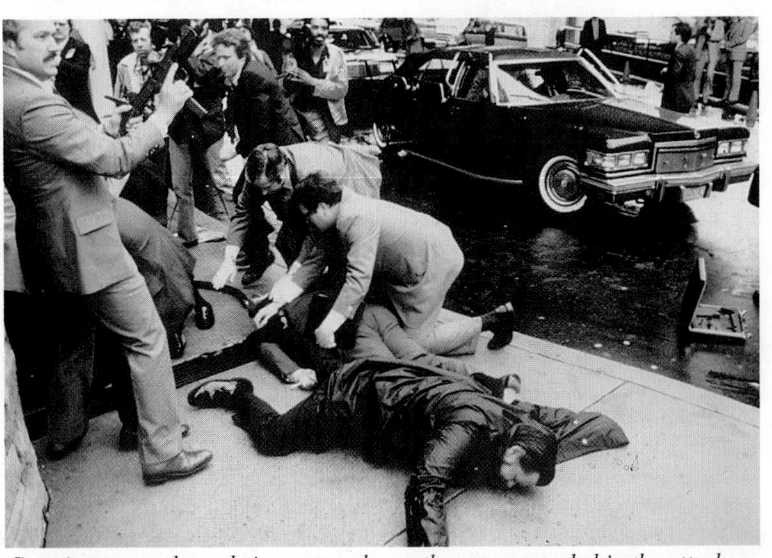

Security agents draw their guns as three others are wounded in the attack.

Honolulu at the top of living-cost list

Honolulu, Hawaii

Fueled by a heavy influx of Japanese money and wealthy tourists, prices in Honolulu have risen to give the city the highest cost of living rate in the country. All over Hawaii, residents are organizing to oppose rampant development. Here, however, the tourist trade is too lucrative to resist, and hawkers abound, offering "freebies" as lead-ins to land and condominium sales pitches. "A $32.50 show for $10," says one. "Jim Nabors. He does a half-hour of Gomer Pyle." ▷

First Columbia shuttle flight orbits Earth

Want a lift? The success of the shuttle marks a new era in space exploration.

Edwards AFB, Calif., Apr. 14
The Columbia, the world's first reusable spacecraft, has touched down gracefully in the California desert, completing the first flight of America's proposed fleet of space shuttles. Riding atop a spectacular plume of smoke and fire, the shuttle was piloted into orbit two days ago by astronauts John W. Young and Robert L. Crippen. The winged orbiter circled the Earth 36 times during a flight of 54 hours 22 minutes. The flight provided the opportunity to deploy a variety of scientific equipment, as well as to run general tests of all systems aboard the new spacecraft. The only potential trouble spot came when the orbiter lost a few of the ceramic tiles from its heat shield, apparently during the launching. The damage was relatively minor and did not interfere with the flight schedule. Designing and constructing the ceramic tile shield was one of the greatest difficulties to be overcome in the production of the shuttle. National Aeronautics and Space Administration officials say that the Columbia could be ready for its next flight within six months. Three additional orbiters are being built to meet the space agency's rigorous schedule of one flight every two weeks (→June 13, 1983).

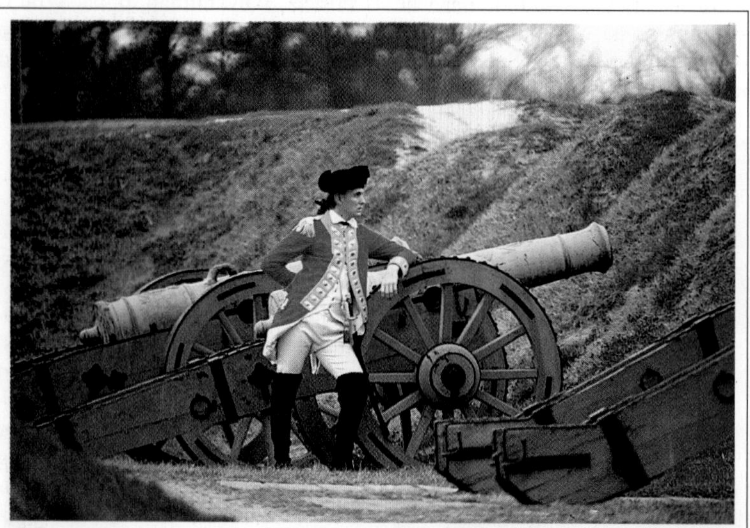
Celebrating the triumph of liberty. Americans mark the 200th anniversary of the Battle of Yorktown with a re-enactment of the Revolutionary War's decisive military encounter. In October 1781, a French-American force of 17,000 cornered a smaller British force under General Cornwallis at Yorktown, Va., forcing their surrender and securing American independence.

Reagan fires striking air traffic workers

Washington, D.C., Aug. 12
The 15,000-member Professional Air Traffic Controllers Organization has challenged Ronald Reagan head on, and lost. Rejecting an annual raise of 11.4 percent, the union struck on August 2. In three days, the President had fired 2,000 of them for refusing to return to work. "Dammit," he exclaimed, "the law is the law, and the law says they cannot strike." Within a week, the union was fighting for its life, with fewer than 5,000 members left. Its president, Robert Poli, who had backed Reagan in the election campaign, blasted the administration's "scorched earth" policy; but a Gallup poll showed he had only 29 percent of the public behind him.

Of the other 71 percent, many were angry that safety worries had forced them to desert the airports. The Federal Aviation Administration got traffic back to 75 percent of normal using non-strikers and 500 military controllers. But, feeding the flames, Poli has announced that "chaos" prevails inside the control towers. Airlines put losses since the strike crisis at $35 million.

When the smoke clears, Reagan may be the big winner. With widespread public approval, he has projected a tough image both at home and overseas. In the words of one aide, "He wanted to jut his jaw out." Asked if he felt bad about firing so many workers, he replied, "You bet. But the law is the law."

Air traffic control union strikers challenged the new President, and lost.

President resumes Soviet grain sales

Washington, D.C., Apr. 24
President Reagan fulfilled his campaign pledge to resume grain sales to the Soviet Union today by lifting the embargo Jimmy Carter imposed after the Russian invasion of Afghanistan in 1979. This was the President's first major political decision since he was wounded on March 30. The embargo had denied 13 billion metric tons of grain as well as phosphate fertilizers, which were later included in the ban. Sales of soybeans, meat and other non-grain products will also resume, but restrictions on high-technology products and permission to fish in American waters are still in effect.

Williams conviction ends Abscam trials

Washington, D.C., May 1
Senator Harrison A. Williams has been convicted on nine charges related to the "Abscam" operation. He is the last of eight legislators to be sentenced. All were found guilty. "Abscam," short for "Arab Scam," began when F.B.I. agents posing as Arab sheiks offered several politicians bribes in exchange for political favors. Williams, a New Jersey Democrat, and seven men in the House of Representatives were named as having accepted bribes. Williams is the third American senator ever convicted on criminal charges while in office, and the first since 1905. He faces up to 18 years in prison and Senate expulsion.

Atlanta has suspect after 28 blacks die

Atlanta, Georgia, June 21

A 21-year old black photographer was charged today with the murder of one of 28 black children and young adults slain in Atlanta over the last two years. Wayne B. Williams was charged after tests linked fibers found on the victim with evidence taken from his home. He was implicated in the death of Nathaniel Cater, 27, whose body was found May 24 in the Chatahoochee River. Williams, who proclaims his innocence, is the first person officially accused in any of the killings of 23 children and five adults since they began in the city (→ Feb. 27, 1982).

Supreme Court gets first woman justice

Washington, D.C., Sept. 25

Chief Justice Warren Burger today swore in the 102nd Supreme Court justice, who is also the first woman on the court: Mrs. Sandra Day O'Connor. On July 7, President Reagan nominated her to fill the vacated seat of Associate Justice Potter Stewart, and confirmation was swift. Mrs. O'Connor, 51, has a firm Republican record, favoring the death penalty and urging balanced budgets. However, she has backed the right of women to choose abortions and supports most civil rights legislation. She, her lawyer husband and three adult sons live in Paradise Valley, Arizona.

President wants $180 billion for arms

Washington, D.C., Nov. 18

President Reagan has proposed a weapons package that will cost $180 billion over six years as a "strategic program which America can afford." The program calls for cancellation of the mobile basing system proposed by President Carter in favor of "super-hardened" silos for MX missiles. It also calls for 100 B-1 long-range bombers to replace the aging B-52's, a program that was cut by Carter, and the radar-evading "Stealth" bomber. At a time when many domestic programs have been cut, Reagan's plan actually costs less than many had expected. The response to his plan in Congress has generally been favorable.

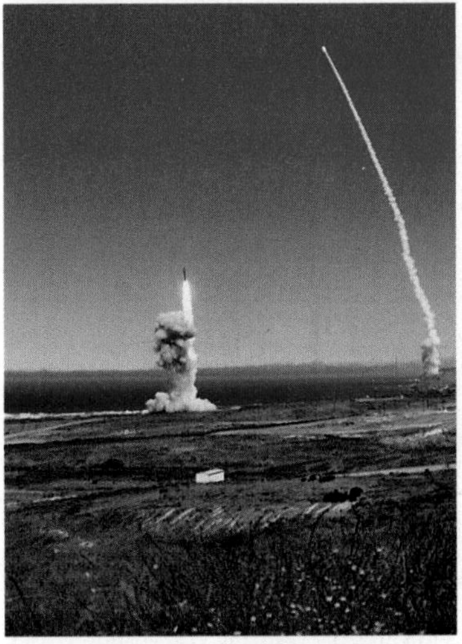

Launching the buildup. Two unarmed Minuteman III's are tested.

9,700 become citizens in mass ceremony

Los Angeles, Calif., June 22

Memorial Stadium was a shrine of nationality today as 9,700 immigrants became citizens in the biggest naturalization ceremony the country has ever held. The mass swearing-in dramatizes a surge in immigration that brought 808,000 new arrivals in the last year. Most are from Asia and the Pacific. They represent the fastest growing ethnic group in the country, one that has swelled from 1.5 million to 3.5 million during the 1970's. Optimism dominated the ceremony. Said one Vietnamese, "It is great to be an American. There is so much opportunity here" (→ June 23, 1982).

Reagan responds to Libyan terror threat

Washington, D.C., Dec. 10

The White House acknowledged today having receiving detailed intelligence reports that a Libyan-trained terrorist squad has entered the United States with the intention of killing President Reagan and other officials. Reagan commented to reporters: "I think in view of the record you can't dismiss them out of hand. On the other hand, they're not going to change my life much." He declined to comment further on security moves. F.B.I. sources say that the reported assassination plan, which appeared in a *Newsweek* article this month, was exaggerated (→ Apr. 16, 1986).

I.B.M. personal computer promises to revolutionize the office

New York City, August

International Business Machines has introduced its long-awaited version of the personal computer, a move experts say will give new impetus to the revolution in office automation. A first evaluation is that I.B.M.'s P.C. is no great advance over presently available personal computers, but that its arrival is significant in several major ways.

For millions of people, the fact that I.B.M. has put its name on a personal computer means that the machine is more than a fad. Purchasing agents who have been reluctant to buy personal computers now can say they're going with a P.C. made by the company that dominates the industry. For I.B.M., introduction of the P.C. is a revolutionary move. The strength of the company has been in large mainframe computers, which offer centralized data processing. Personal computers, which make for office decentralization, could cut mainframe sales. But the P.C. success of firms such as Apple Computer could not be ignored.

One advantage of the I.B.M. computer is that it offers more memory than most personal computers. Other key factors include its choice of an operating system, the set of basic instructions that runs a computer. I.B.M.'s choice promises to become the standard in an unstandardized field. Small companies reportedly already are busily copying the P.C. of I.B.M.

Will it byte? Americans now face the task of learning to use the computer.

Immune deficiency disease identified

Washington, D.C.

A disease that has caused a number of deaths within the nation's homosexual community and among Haitian immigrants to the United States has been identified by doctors in America and in France. Called human lymphotropic virus-III (HLTV-III) at the National Cancer Institute, the ailment has been given the name AIDS, for Acquired Immune Deficiency Syndrome. It is spread by the exchange of bodily fluids through sexual contact, use of contaminated hypodermic needles or blood transfusions. The virus destroys T lymphocytes, white blood cells that help defend the body against disease. AIDS deaths usually occur from massive systemic infections or cancer. Known cases of the disease have been limited to homosexual men, but the potential for epidemics exists (→ Oct. 22, 1986).

1982

Reagan

Pontiac, Mich., Jan. 24. San Francisco 49ers edge Cincinnati Bengals, 26-21, in Super Bowl XVI.

New York City, Jan. 28. John Updike wins National Book Critics Circle Award, American Book Award and Pulitzer Prize, for *Rabbit Is Rich.*

Atlanta, Georgia, Feb. 27. Wayne Williams convicted of murder and sentenced to life imprisonment.

New York City, March 12. Sylvia Plath awarded Pulitzer Prize, for *The Collected Poems.*

Washington, D.C., Apr. 19. U.S. bars private travel to Cuba, permitting entry only to government officials, reporters, academic researchers and private citizens visiting members of their families (→Dec. 15, 1984).

Washington, D.C., June 1. Supreme Court rules "probable cause" is sufficient for police to search a car without first obtaining a warrant.

Los Angeles, June 8. Lakers defeat Philadelphia 76ers, four games to two, for N.B.A. title.

Washington, D.C., June 15. Supreme Court rules that children of illegal aliens have a right to tuition-free public education.

Washington, D.C., June 21. By reason of insanity, John W. Hinckley Jr., would-be assassin of President Reagan, is found not guilty.

United States, Oct. 13. Jim Thorpe has Olympic gold medals restored posthumously.

Los Angeles, Oct. 19. Independent auto maker John De-Lorean arrested for possession of cocaine.

St. Louis, Oct. 20. Cardinals beat Milwaukee Brewers, four games to three, in World Series.

Alabama, Nov. 3. George Wallace wins fourth term as Governor, with widespread support of blacks.

Washington, D.C., Dec. 8. Police kill nuclear arms protester who threatened to blow up Washington Monument.

California, December. Apple Computer becomes first personal computer firm to reach $1 billion annual sales.

Hollywood, Calif. Hit films include *E.T. the Extra-Terrestrial, Tootsie* and *First Blood.*

New Reagan budget shows a huge deficit

Promises kept. President Reagan's call for cuts in social programs and a rise in funds for arms shows he meant what he said in the election campaign.

Washington, D.C., Feb. 6

President Reagan asked Congress today for an unprecedented shrinkage of domestic spending. However, even if such cuts were approved, the deficit would still stand at a startling $91.5 billion in the coming fiscal year.

"We are putting the false prosperity of overspending, easy credit, depreciating money and financial excess behind us," Reagan said in his budget message. "Our task is to persevere, to stay the course, to shun retreat, to weather the temporary dislocations and pressures that must inevitably accompany the restoration of national economic, fiscal and military health."

While proposing deep slashes in domestic spending, the President called for an expansion of the nation's military strength, despite the huge overall budget deficit. His proposal was greeted with deep skepticism in both political parties. The Democrats called it "unfair" and "unworkable," while several members of the President's own party expressed shock at the size of the deficit. The President attributed the size of the deficit to the heavy spending policies of earlier administrations (→Dec. 10, 1985).

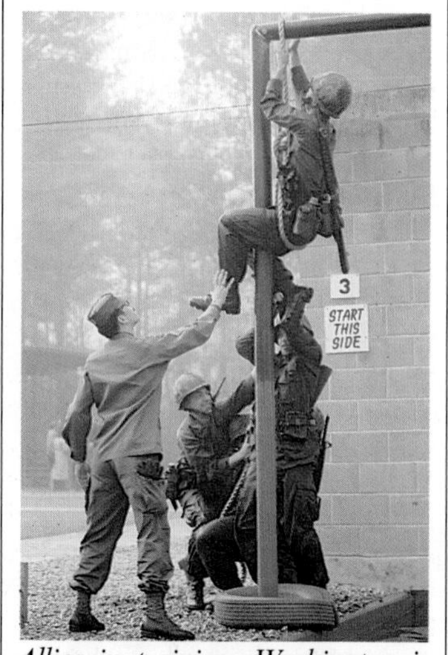

Allies in training. Washington is committed to keeping El Salvador out of the hands of Communists and believes that a competent military force is the way to do it.

U.A.W. trades a cut in pay for security

Detroit, Mich., Feb. 28

For the first time in the history of the recession-torn auto industry, workers have taken wage and benefit cuts in exchange for job security. Ford chairman Philip Caldwell hailed the "cooperation and trust" displayed in negotiations, but fear played as large a role. Some 55,000 United Auto Workers were laid off at Ford, and in a month, General Motors closed seven plants. The new contract pledges Ford to share profits, support laid off workers with 15 years' seniority, and avoid closing their plants by shifting work to outside suppliers. In return, the union gives up regular pay raises and defers cost-of-living increases.

Antitrust suit ends the Bell monopoly

Washington, D.C., Jan. 8

American Telephone & Telegraph has agreed to sell two-thirds of its assets, ending a seven-year antitrust suit that cost the communications monolith $360 million. A grim Charles Brown, the A.T.&T. chairman, said, "It's exactly what the government wanted." And Justice Department officials seemed to be pleased. But Ma Bell loses only its 22 local phone operations, the sluggish sector of its business. Left with long-distance service, Bell Laboratories research and Western Electric manufacturing, a lean A.T.&T. is now free to explore the new frontiers of the communications revolution.

TV ads deregulated

Washington, D.C., Nov. 23

Broadcasters and the Justice Department agreed today to end restraints on the length and frequency of television commercials, now at a maximum of eight and a half minute an hour. The Federal Communications Commission chief wants TV ads totally deregulated, making owners as free to operate as newspapers, with no limit on contents or amounts. Networks have their own ad guidelines and claim some are stiffer than the old code.

Getty is the envy of other museums

Malibu, Calif., November

While other museums struggle to mantain operations, the J. Paul Getty Museum is required by law to spend at least $51 million every year in order to maintain its status as a private foundation. Getty left virtually his entire estate, valued at $1.1 billion, to the art museum that he founded in 1953. Museum officials were surprised to learn that the money, amassed from the vast Getty oil operations, was bequeathed with no strings attached. The museum, which is now housed in a building copied after the Villa dei Papiri in ancient Herculaneum, has drawn up plans to expand into three facilities.

Anti-nuclear rally in N.Y. biggest ever

New York City, June 12

An army of 550,000 protesters, the biggest America has seen, flooded New York today to appeal to the United Nations Special Session on Disarmament. "One, two, three, four," they sang, "we don't want a nuclear war. Five, six, seven, eight, we don't want to radiate." Spurred to action by President Reagan's hard line, the peace drive is at its apex. But with wars raging in the Falklands and Lebanon, U.N. Secretary General Javier Perez de Cuellar said peace hopes "are further from our reach now than they were four years ago." Of protests, Reagan said American foreign policy will "not be set in the streets."

Handguns banned by San Francisco

San Francisco, June 28

Legislation banning private possession of handguns was signed into law here today by Mayor Dianne Feinstein. She said it is the "first time a large city has spoken out and said we have had enough of the death, dismemberment and desecration of our society from the handgun." The statistics convinced her: In 1979, handguns killed eight people in Britain, 48 in Japan, 34 in Switzerland, 52 in Canada, 58 in Israel, 21 in Sweden, 42 in West Germany and 10,728 in the United States. The board of supervisors approved the ordinance 6 to 4.

Hope for E.R.A. expires

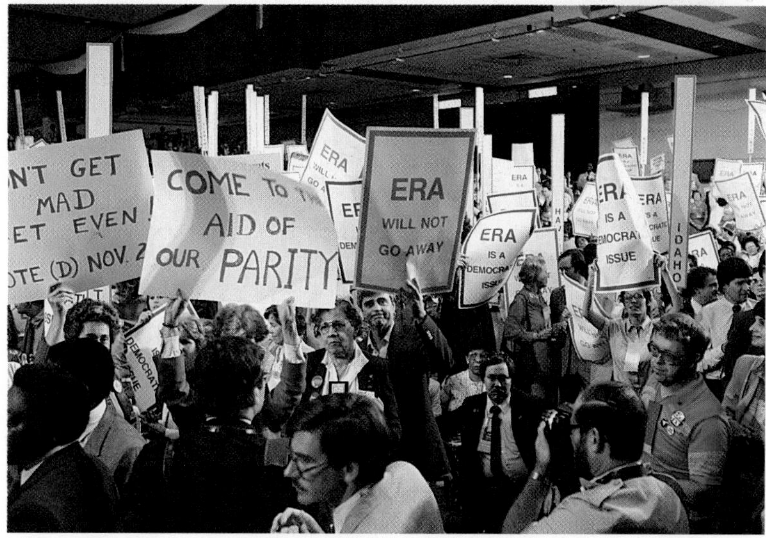

Proponents of E.R.A. fell three states short in their campaign for change.

Washington, D.C., June 30

Millions of women feel that "We the people" is an empty phrase because the Equal Rights Amendment failed to become a reality today. The amendment, which would have been the Constitution's 27th, fell three states short of ratification. Humorist Erma Bombeck once said of the proposed law that its words have never been so misunderstood since the four words "one size fits all." For Representative Martha Griffiths, who sponsored it, and the National Organization of Women that fought for it, the amendment would have prevented the denying or abridging of rights on account of sex; equal work would have received equal pay, and equal opportunity would have been guaranteed, regardless of the whims of individual state legislatures.

For one homemaker, Phyllis Schlafly, who will be enjoying a victory ball tonight celebrating the triumph over the amendment, it would have meant that her daughters could be drafted in case of a war. Countless times she stressed that women already have special societal privileges and that equal rights would threaten them. Foes of Mrs. Schlafly see irony in the idea of a woman campaigning for an issue – in effect acting as politician, promoter and activist – with the goal of insisting that the only place she belongs is in the home.

Smugglers of illegal aliens are indicted

Albuquerque, N.M., June 23

A federal judge today handed down indictments charging 38 people with smuggling some 24,000 illegal aliens a year into the United States. For 11 months, undercover immigration agents posing as drivers watched the ring from the inside. Their reports detail a huge business, grossing over $24 million annually. Clients were shipped out of six hotels in Mexico, mainly to Chicago, but also to sites in California, Michigan and New York. In a related Supreme Court ruling arrived at earlier this month, children of illegal aliens were given the right to tuition-free education in public schools (→Sept. 26, 1983).

Presbyterians unite

Hartford, Conn., June 29

The General Assembly of the United Presbyterian Church today voted to merge with the Presbyterian Church, U.S.A. The latter group approved the accord June 15. The merger, which heals a division caused by the Civil War, has been years in the making. If approved by the presbyteries, it will make the denomination the fourth largest in the country and leave the Southern Baptist and American Baptist Conventions as the only remaining denominational division from the Civil War period.

Survival of the fittest. Braniff, the nation's eighth largest airline, filed for bankruptcy May 13 as the industry restructures under deregulation.

Knoxville plays host to World's Fair

Knoxville, Tenn., May 1

The 1982 World's Fair opened its gates today, beginning a scheduled 184-day run in which millions of visitors will see a complex of exhibitions geared to the energy crisis of the 1970s. Opening ceremonies were attended by President and Mrs. Reagan, scores of dignitaries and thousands of tourists. Nearly two million advance oneand two-day tickets have already been sold to the Southeast's first World's Fair ever. Although a few exhibitions were not entirely ready by today's deadline, all but one of them were open. Some critics say the fair's theme, "Energy Turns the World," is already outdated.

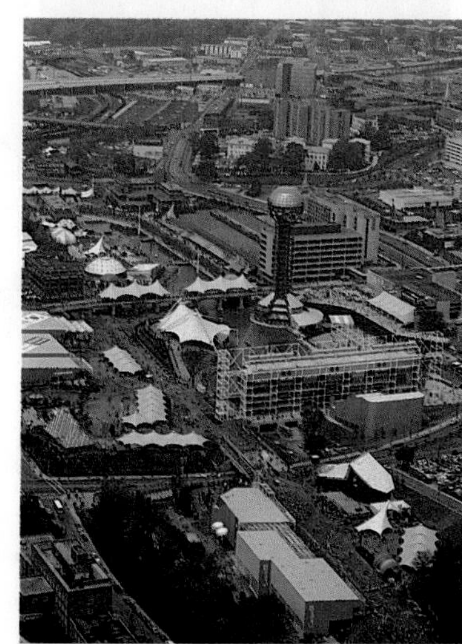
World's Fair finally comes to Dixie

U.S. poverty level highest since 1967

Washington, D.C., July 19

After 12 months of recession and 18 of the Reagan presidency, more Americans are poor than at any time in the last 15 years. A new Census Bureau report places the current poverty rate at 14 percent, up from 11.1 percent in 1973. Last year saw the annual incomes of 2.2 million people fall below the official poverty line, set at $9,287 for a family of four. Blacks, many of whom say they have suffered disproportionately under Reagan's budget cuts, sustained the largest income drop. Their poverty rate is 34.2 percent, compared to 26.2 percent for Hispanics and 11.1 percent for whites. Median family income fell 3.5 percent to $22,390 (→ Dec.).

Marines join multi-national force in Beirut

U.S. Marines try to bring peace to Lebanon, a troubled land in the Mideast.

Beirut, Lebanon, Sept. 19

Marines of the 32nd Amphibious Unit landed in Beirut on August 25, taking up positions in the port area recently abandoned by the French. President Reagan announced on August 20 that he was ordering 800 marines to Beirut as part of a multi-national group supervising the withdrawal of Palestinian and Syrian fighters from the beleagured city. The deployment of marines is part of a plan negotiated by American envoy Philip Habib and accepted by the Lebanese, the Palestinians and the Israelis. Reagan said that the marines would stay in Lebanon no longer than 30 days and would perform "a carefully limited non-combat role." He said they would be withdrawn if any party in the dispute attempted to draw them into the fighting.

Removal of the Palestine Liberation Organization fighters was proceeding as the marines were landing. Almost 400 Palestinian guerrillas left by ship on August 21 for Cyprus and then were flown to Iraq and Jordan. The next day, King Hussein of Jordan greeted the soldiers and told them that they had "held the flag high and fought well for (their) rights" (→ Apr. 18, 1983).

Reagan gets $98 billion tax hike

Washington, D.C., Aug. 19

Responding to heavy lobbying by President Reagan, Congress has approved a bill to increase taxes and reduce spending in the coming fiscal year. Overall, the measure would increase taxes by $98.3 billion and cut federal outlays by $17.5 billion in order to trim the deficit during the current recession. Much of the tax increase would affect businesses by speeding the collection of corporate payments as well as by limiting tax breaks for some firms. A lesser amount of the increase would come from individual taxpayers, mainly by improving collections. The bill had strong support from House Speaker Thomas P. "Tip" O'Neill.

USA Today in color

Virginia, Sept. 15

A new national newspaper published by the Gannett Company, USA Today, made its debut today. The full-color paper carries lots of national news, comprehensive sports, entertainment and business sections and eye-popping graphics. Gannett president Allen Neuharth hopes to appeal to a wide audience. "I think it will sell," he said. So do the firm's shareholders: A reported $30 million was invested just to get it off the ground.

It's the Cats' meow

New York City, Oct. 7

Critics took like catnip tonight to the new British musical, *Cats*. The spectacle, based on T.S. Eliot's *Old Possum's Book of Practical Cats*, presents a fantasy world of larger-than-life felines in an equally large junkyard as they vie to get into Cat Heaven. Andrew Lloyd Webber's music is mostly clawless, but it purrs along nicely and the audience seems to find their never-never world a pleasant change – indeed the cat's pajamas.

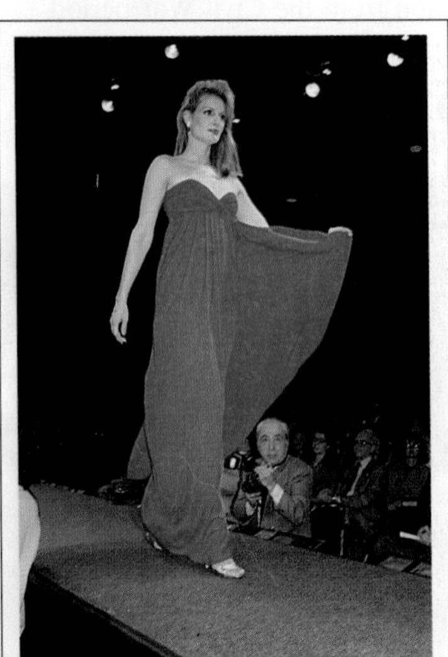

Red and stunning. Bill Blass introduces his latest line of evening wear, reflecting America's return to style, elegance and formality.

Washington, D.C., October 13. *Preparing for America's future today. President Reagan is joined by job trainees as he signs the Job Training Partnership Act. Despite his professed distaste for government intervention, Reagan feels business and government can cooperate to promote growth.*

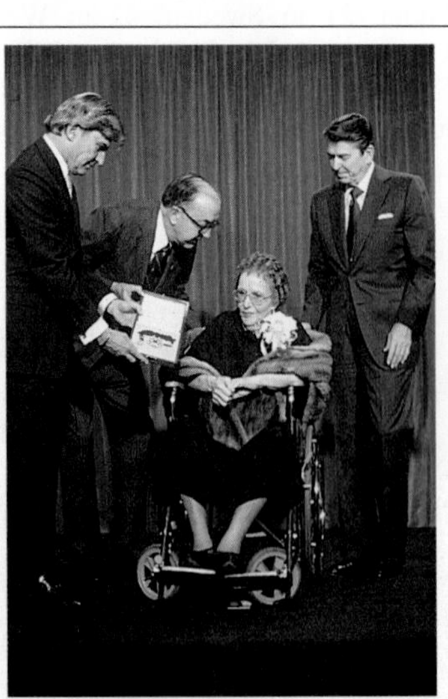

Singer Kate Smith receives the Medal of Freedom. Generations of Americans recall her thrilling version of "God Bless America."

Tylenol laced with cyanide kills seven

Chicago, Oct. 5

Seven people are dead in Chicago after using a Tylenol pain reliever in capsules laced with cyanide, and a man in California has been stricken after swallowing Tylenol capsules that had been contaminated with strychnine. Today, Johnson & Johnson, the manufacturer of the aspirin substitute, recalled all Extra Strength Tylenol. The contamination was apparently the result of deliberate tampering with the product, although the perpetrator has not been identified and the motive remains unclear. It is also not clear whether there is any connection between the incidents in Chicago and California. Federal authorities announced they are going to meet with the drug companies to work out new regulations that could protect the public against further tampering with over-the-counter products.

Recession takes over; industry grinds to lowest level in 34 years

Washington, D.C., December

As the economy sputters into its 18th month of recession, experts are still looking for signs of recovery. A third of the industrial capacity lies idle. Interest rates stay stubbornly high. The jobless rate hit 10.8 percent last month, putting more people on unemployment benefit lines than at any time since the Great Depression. In the view of Harvard economist Otto Eckstein, "The economy is probably in the worst shape that it has been in nearly half a century."

As in the 1930s, the condition extends worldwide. Western Europe suffers from 10.3-percent unemployment. And the nations of the third world languish under a $626 billion debt burden.

At home, record deficits seem to suffocate the recovery. Housing starts and car sales are up. Renegade members of the Organization of Petroleum Exporting Countries are cracking the production quotas to lower oil prices. And conservatives hope Reagan's 10 percent income tax cut and 7 percent rise in defense spending will generate both demand and supply. But with a deficit of $110.7 billion, neither tax cuts nor increased spending are likely to win long-term support.

An idled oil rig symbolizes the recession that is gripping the nation. Jobless figures have soared, but the President says good economic times lie ahead.

EPCOT, world of tomorrow, opens today

Florida, Oct. 1

If you are about as old as former Mouseketeer Annette Funicello (40), the Experimental Prototype Community of Tomorrow may be just right for you. Walt Disney World's EPCOT, opening today, promises educational fun for adults. Covering 260 acres and entered through an 18-story geodesic dome called Spaceship Earth, it offers among its many exhibits Journey into Imagination, a Kodak-sponsored video and music festival, and the Universe of Energy, an Exxon-supported show that somehow makes sense of solar-heating displays and odiferous lava flows.

The Experimental Prototype Community of Tomorrow Center at Lake Buena Vista, Florida, is a companion park to nearby Disney World, in Orlando, opened in 1971. Disneyland amusement park in Anaheim, California, opened its gates in 1955. All three provide fun and education to all visitors.

Barney Clark is first to get artificial heart

Salt Lake City, Utah, Dec. 22

His own defective heart replaced by a plastic and metal artificial one on December 2, retired dentist Barney Clark has recovered enough to take his first steps since the operation was performed. The 61-year-old patient was close to death from heart failure before the operation. The mechanical heart, named the Jarvik-7 after its inventor, Robert Jarvik, was placed in Clark's chest by a surgical team headed by Dr. William C. DeVries at the University of Utah Medical Center. The device has been implanted successfully in animals, but this is the first human application.

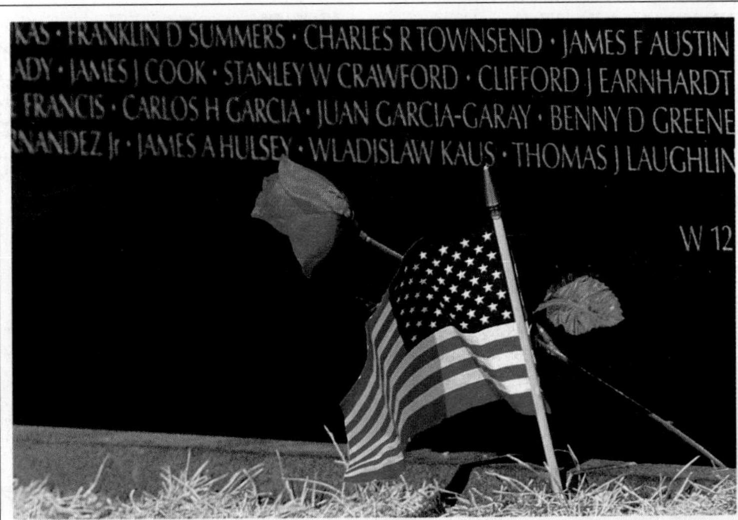

Tribute to the fallen. Designed by Yale University architecture student Maya Yang Lin, the Vietnam Veterans Memorial in Washington was dedicated on November 13. The names of more than 58,000 dead inscribed in the black granite testify to the terrible cost of the war in Vietnam.

1983

Reagan

Washington, D.C., Jan. 7. Reagan administration lifts arms embargo against Guatemala, citing significant human rights improvements.

Pasadena, Calif., Jan. 30. Washington Redskins beat Miami Dolphins, 27-17, in Super Bowl XVII.

Medina, N.D., Feb. 13. Gordon Kahl, extremist foe of federal income tax, and his son kill ~~two U.S.~~ marshals, who stopped them at roadblock.

New York City, Apr. 18. Alice Walker wins Pulitzer Prize and American Book Award for *The Color Purple.*

Montgomery, Ala., May 24. Jesse Jackson is first black man to address legislature here.

Philadelphia, May 31. The 76ers defeat L.A. Lakers, 115-108, for N.B.A. title.

Space, June 13. Pioneer 10 becomes first spacecraft to leave solar system; it has been aloft for 11 years (→18).

Washington, D.C., June 21. First giant panda offspring born in United States dies three hours after being delivered by Ling-Ling.

Cape Canaveral, Fla., Sept. 30. Shuttle Challenger, first spacecraft launched at night, carries into orbit first black astronaut, Guion Bluford (→Feb. 7, 1984).

Hollywood, Fla., Oct. 5. Delegates to A.F.L.-C.I.O. convention endorse Walter Mondale as Democratic presidential nominee; first such labor endorsement of a candidate for presidential nomination (→Nov. 3).

Philadelphia, Oct. 16. Baltimore Orioles defeat Philadelphia Phillies, four games to one, in World Series.

Beirut, Lebanon, Dec. 4. Eight American marines killed at airport by Syrian troops, as U.S. planes attack Syrian bases in Lebanon (→Feb. 24, 1954).

United States. Estimated 4.1 million VCR's are sold in America this year.

United States. Automobile production up by 10.2%; personal income rises by 6.3%, and new home construction is up 60%.

Hollywood, Calif. Top films of year include *Terms of Endearment, Tender Mercies.*

First black elected Mayor of Chicago

Washington, breaking the barriers.

Chicago, Apr. 13

The first black man to be elected Mayor of Chicago, Harold Washington, won by a narrow margin in one of the fiercest races the city has known. Some 82 percent of Chicago's 1.6 million registered voters went to the polls, a record turnout for the city. Washington received 51 percent of the vote, and his white opponent, Bernard Epton, got 48 percent. Though most blacks voted for Washington, and most whites voted for Epton, as expected, there were more whites voting for Washington than there were blacks voting for Epton. Washington said, "We have kept faith."

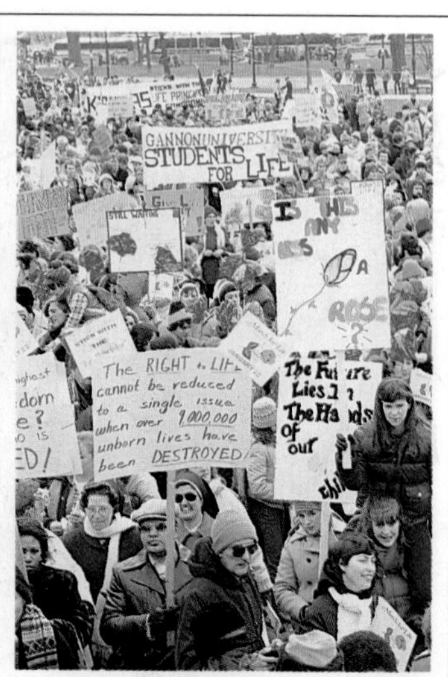

Demonstrators against abortion march in Washington, D.C. No single issue since the Vietnam War has so divided Americans.

Reagan aims high with space shield idea

Washington, D.C., March 23

President Reagan has proposed construction of an anti-ballistic missile (ABM) system that would render nuclear missiles "impotent and obsolete" and that would hold out "the promise of changing the course of human history." Using charts and graphs to illustrate the growing Soviet effort to build a worldwide offensive military force, Reagan today urged American scientists to "turn their great talents" to developing a system that would destroy Soviet missiles before they reached their targets. He sees the project as a first step in an "intensive effort to define a long-term research and development program to begin to achieve our ultimate goal of eliminating the threat posed by stategic nuclear missiles."

If this program is approved, it would signal a fundamental shift in the nuclear strategy of the United States, which for 35 years has been based on massive retaliation to deter an attack. The new Reagan system would employ a wide range of sophisticated technology, including lasers, microwave devices, particle beams and projectile beams, and would be based both on land and in space.

Some critics have argued that the President's proposals would be in violation of the 1972 ABM treaty with the Soviet Union. But administration aides have denied this. Their position is that deployment of such a system was barred but not research and development of one.

Reagan declares Soviet "evil empire"

Orlando, Florida, March 8

Describing the Soviet Union as an "evil empire," President Reagan called upon a group of Protestant evangelicals to oppose a nuclear arms freeze and to return to a political philosophy based on "respect for the rule of law under God." The President described himself as being out of step with modern secular ideas that have discarded "the time-tested values upon which our very civilization is based." In addition, he told his audience it must not rest until abortion on demand has been outlawed.

Reagan also renewed his plea for a constitutional amendment that would permit prayer in public schools. He defended the administration's policy of notifying the parents when a clinic provides a birth control drug or devices to a minor. This so-called "squeal rule" has come under attack as violating a student's right to privacy. The President maintains that the parents' rights supersede those of "Washington-based bureaucrats and social engineers."

Jailing of Japanese held grave injustice

Washington, D.C., Feb. 24.

Citing "racial prejudice, war hysteria and failure of political leadership," a congressional committee today formally condemned the internment of Japanese-Americans during World War II. The report of the Commission on Wartime Relocation and Internment of Civilians described the relocation as "unique" and blamed President Roosevelt in particular. According to the report, Roosevelt agreed to release inmates only after the 1944 elections, thus avoiding any political backlash. The commission may recommend financial compensation for surviving victims.

American doctors call for boxing ban

Chicago, Jan. 13

The *American Medical Association Journal* has reported new evidence suggesting that chronic brain damage is prevalent among prizefighters. An editorial in the journal called for the banning of the sport. If the sport is to continue, the editorial went on, steps should be taken to improve monitoring a boxer's condition before, during and after a fight. In the study of 38 boxers that led the AMA to call for the ban, more than half showed some brain tissue loss or atrophy. A fighter in this condition is commonly referred to as being "punch drunk."

Beirut embassy bombed

Terrorists strike again. Americans and Lebanese search rubble for survivors.

Beirut, Lebanon, Apr. 18

The United States Embassy in Lebanon was demolished today by a car bomb containing 300 pounds of TNT and driven by a man who perished in the suicide attack. Dozens of people are feared dead and over 100 wounded. The exact number of casualties will not be known until rescue workers, digging round the clock, complete their grim task of pulling bodies out of the twisted ruins. The central part of the horseshoe-shaped building collapsed, leaving only shattered masonry, all that remained of offices and balconies. The dead and wounded are primarily American embassy staff, marine guards and Lebanese clerical workers. Civilians who were at the embassy applying for visas were also among the casualties.

A group calling itself Islamic Jihad (Holy War) claimed responsibility for the blast, telephoning a news office immediately after the explosion. In a departure from usual practice, the Central Intelligence Agency acknowledged that its top Middle East analyst, Robert Clayton Ames, had been killed. Most of the C.I.A.'s Beirut staff was reportedly wiped out. Witnesses said they saw a large van force an entrance through the driveway of the embassy (→ Oct. 23).

Report on education: "A Nation at Risk"

Washington, D.C., Apr. 26

The country's educational standards, according to a bipartisan commission, "are . . . being eroded by a rising tide of mediocrity that threatens our very future as a nation and as a people." The panel, formed two years ago by Education Secretary T.H. Bell, surveyed research, commissioned studies and held hearings across the country. Its report, *A Nation at Risk*, says that "if an unfriendly power had attempted to impose on America the mediocre educational performance that exists today, we might well have viewed it as an act of war."

The panel recommended a tightening of high school requirements and college admissions standards; extended school days and years; "far more homework"; higher pay for teachers, and "master teachers" to train new instructors.

The panel avoided controversy, but its report has become a political football. Carl Perkins, head of the House Education and Labor Committee, praised the call for more educational funding, but noted it followed "three years of administration efforts to cut back." President Reagan, however, lauded the "call for an end to federal intrusion" and vowed to continue working for "tuition tax credits . . . voluntary school prayer and abolishing the Department of Education." One thing is sure: The findings will get a response from Washington. As the panel so ominously warned, "History is not kind to idlers."

Williamsburg is host to economic summit

Williamsburg, Va., May 30

The annual summit meeting of the seven industrialized nations came to a close today, leaving several divisive issues unresolved. The leaders of the United States, Canada, England, France, West Germany, Italy and Japan met in this uniquely American setting ostensibly to discuss the recent global recession and such specifics as the ballooning American budget deficit and how open the Japanese markets are or are not. Despite President Reagan's declaration that "recovery is what this summit is all about," America's allies came here principally hoping to gauge Reagan's anti-Soviet stance. The President's support for such controversial measures as East Bloc trade restrictions and the deployment of American missiles in Western Europe continues to strain the Western alliance. In a pre-summit concession, the administration agreed to resume talks on long-term grain sales to the Russians, but the move did little to turn the meeting into more than a telegenic success.

Sally rides shuttle, a woman in space

Cape Canaveral, Florida, June 18

Expressing regret that it has taken the United States so long, Dr. Sally Ride shot up into space on the shuttle Challenger today. She is the first American woman to do so. As the shuttle rose, watchers chanted, "Ride, Sally, ride." Dr. Ride, 32, is a woman for all seasons: a fine tennis and rugby player, a physicist and a Shakespeare scholar. In graduate studies at Stanford University, she studied the behavior of free electron lasers. Noted for her calm under pressure, she faces the task of using a robotic arm to maneuver an errant satellite into the shuttle's cargo bay (→ Sept. 30).

Ex-newscaster wins in sex bias case

Kansas City, Mo., Aug. 8

"Too old, unattractive and not deferential enough to men," 38-year-old Christine Craft was nevertheless smart enough to sue her employer, Metromedia, for unlawful demotion. A jury awarded her $500,000 in damages this afternoon. When hired as a co-anchor at KMBC-TV in 1981, she said she had no intention of being "made over" as a stereotypically fashionable anchorwoman. Eight months later she was demoted to reporter status. Television executives say the court ruling sets a bad precedent. It also happens to curb their authority (→ Jan. 13, 1984).

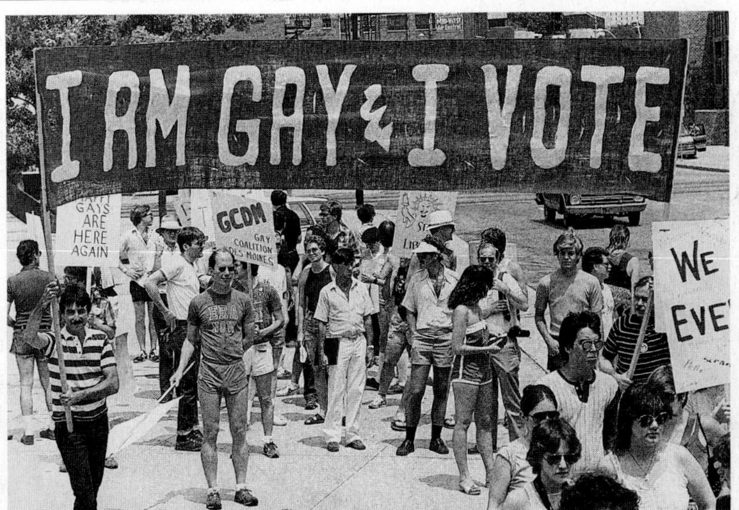

Marching in the heartland of America. Representatives from around the nation kick off National Gay and Lesbian Pride Week with a parade through Des Moines, Iowa. Always on the periphery of American society, many homosexuals say that only through activism can they win equal rights.

Bomb rips Marine compound in Beirut

As American marines search for bodies of their comrades in Beirut, at home officials are asking what went wrong with security and who was to blame.

Beirut, Lebanon, Oct. 23

Shortly after dawn today a TNT-laden truck was driven into the United States Marines' headquarters building and detonated. The resulting explosion killed more than 200 sleeping marines and completely destroyed the building. Two minutes later, a second truck blew up a French paratrooper barracks about two miles away, killing 47 French soldiers and wounding 15. The marine death toll exceeds the number of casualties in any single day of the Vietnam War.

Pentagon officials say that a big Mercedes truck filled with 2,500 pounds of TNT breached a barbed wire fence surrounding the marine compound, swerved between two sentry posts, crashed through a chain-link gate and drove into the lobby of the four-story cinder block building where it was detonated by the driver. A sentry reported that the driver was smiling as he entered the lobby. The force of the blast created a crater 30 feet deep and 40 feet wide and hurled bodies 50 feet into the air. Surviving marines and Lebanese firemen struggled to unearth the dead and injured from the enormous pile of rubble that had been the headquarters. They managed to extinguish a fire before it could reach a load of ammunition that had been stored in the basement.

President Reagan expressed outrage over the "vicious, cowardly and ruthless" attack and asserted that the United States was determined to remain in Lebanon. This blast, occurring six months after a car bomb attack on the American embassy in Beirut, has raised serious questions about marine security precautions (→ Dec. 4).

Sailing cup leaves America first time

Newport, R.I., Sept. 26

For the first time in its 132-year history, the America's Cup will be leaving the United States. The symbol of yachting supremacy the world over was won today by an Australian boat that came from behind in all four races of the series. "It was pretty frustrating," said H.C. Herreshoff, who was navigator of the losing Liberty. "Everyone worked very hard and yet we were losing," he said of the critical fifth leg, when the Australia II again overtook the Liberty. "We were all doing everything we could to hold them off." Herreshoff added, "It hurts pretty bad. It will hurt for a long time."

Liberty (foreground) sails to defeat.

U.S. irate after Soviets down Korean airliner, killing 269

New York City, Sept. 1

The Soviet Union's destruction of a South Korean airliner flying from New York to Seoul has produced a cry of outrage from the international community. The Boeing 747 evidently strayed off course and was shot down by missiles from a Soviet fighter.

According to Korean Airlines, among the 269 passengers and crew who died were 81 South Koreans, 61 Americans, 28 Japanese, 16 Filipinos, 10 Canadians, six Thais and four Australians. One of the American passengers was Representative Larry P. McDonald, head of the ultraconservative John Birch Society.

There is much speculation as to why Flight 007 strayed off course and flew directly over the Kamchatka Peninsula and Sakhalin Island where strategic Soviet bases are situated. Navigational equipment had been installed after a 1978 incident in which a Soviet plane fired on a South Korean jetliner, killing two passengers and forcing it to land on a frozen lake near Murmansk. The Soviet news agency Tass said that an intruder plane, which did not respond to signals or warnings, had been shot down.

President Reagan condemned the downing of flight 007 as a "horrifying act of violence." Secretary of State George Shultz said, "The world is waiting for the Soviet Union to tell the truth." The plane was fitted with three separate navigational computers and it is considered extremely unlikely that all three would have failed at the same time.

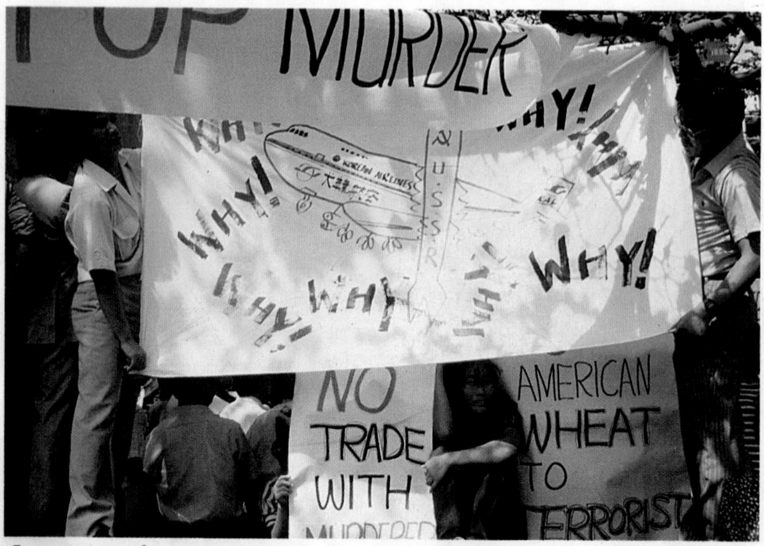

Outpouring of anger against the Russians spreads quickly around the world.

Million are caught crossing border

Washington, D.C., Sept. 26

Spokesmen for the Immigration and Naturalization Service say that so far this year it has caught more than one million illegal aliens trying to slip into the United States. The vast majority of them are Hispanic, fleeing either the poverty of Mexico or the political instability and poverty of Central America. According to the immigration service, most of them cross the long and difficult-to-guard border along the Rio Grande River in southern and far-western Texas.

Dr. King's birthday is national holiday

Washington, D.C., Nov. 2

President Reagan today signed legislation that will make the birthday of the Rev. Dr. Martin Luther King Jr. a national holiday. According to the holiday provisions, the celebration, including the closing of schools and public facilities, will take place on the third Monday in January. The bill will take effect in January of 1986. Dr. King, who was born in 1929 and assassinated in 1968, is being honored because of his work in bringing the techniques of non-violent protest to the civil rights movement. The Baptist leader preached a doctrine of harmony and equality among all people (→ Dec. 2).

Jesse Jackson plans to seek presidency

Washington, D.C., Nov. 3

Black civil rights activist Jesse Jackson announced today that he will toss his hat into the ring as a Democratic candidate for President. The 42-year-old Baptist minister worked closely with the late Rev. Martin Luther King Jr. and has been active in such civil rights organizations as the Congress of Racial Equality and the Southern Christian Leadership Conference. Before he announced his bid for the nomination, Jackson had begun a major voter-registration drive among blacks (→ July 20, 1984).

Anti-war TV fare drawing millions

Hollywood, Calif., Nov. 20

After 251 episodes and 14 Emmy Awards, the television screen went dark March 2 on the TV series *M*A*S*H*. Over 125 million people watched the antics of Hawkeye and the rest for the last time – the biggest TV audience ever for a non-sports program. Tonight, a film on the horrors of nuclear war, *The Day After*, drew over 100 million viewers. As the town of Lawrence, Kansas, was devastated, the point was made that nuclear war is neither "winnable" nor "survivable."

Americans take Grenada

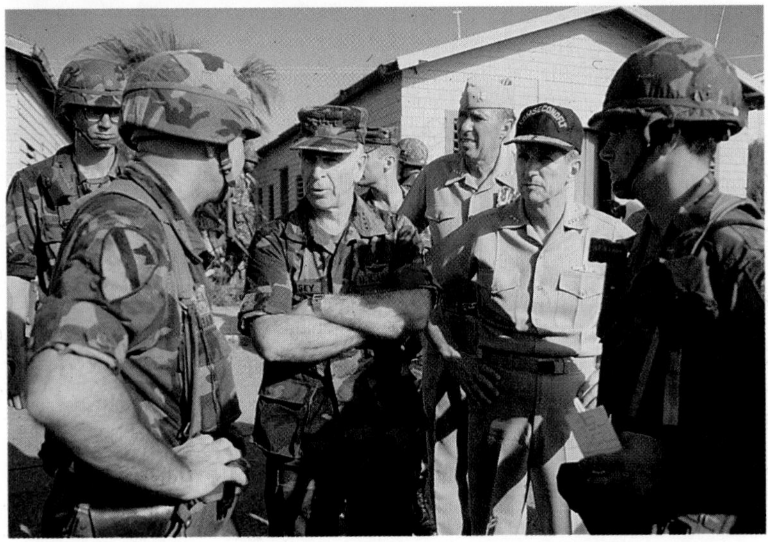

General George Vessey (center) confers with marines during the invasion.

Grenada, Oct. 25

A force of American marines and rangers today invaded the tiny island of Grenada, where the United States says a "brutal group of leftist thugs violently seized power." President Reagan said he ordered the attack because he is concerned about the welfare of some 1,100 American citizens on the island. The world press and many Democratic members of Congress reacted negatively to the invasion, which is the first military intervention in this hemisphere by the United States since the 1965 invasion of the Dominican Republic.

In defending his actions, Reagan said he responded to a formal request from the Organization of Eastern Caribbean States to restore order in the region. Washington agreed to become part of a multinational effort with contingents provided by Antigua, Barbados, Dominica, Jamaica, St. Lucia and St. Vincent.

In the fighting, against inferior Cuban troops, 16 Americans died and 77 were injured. The death toll of the Cubans is not known, but 630 were taken prisoner. An English journalist reported 47 mental patients killed when the United States bombed a hospital by mistake.

Before the invasion, Prime Minister Maurice Bishop of Grenada had been placed under arrest by military commander General Hudson Austin and Deputy Prime Minister Bernard Coard, both Marxists with strong Soviet and Cuban ties.

Objective achieved. American troops guard captured Cubans and Grenadans.

G.M., Toyota agree to joint car venture

Washington, D.C., Dec. 20

The Federal Trade Commission has given approval to a joint venture between the Japanese Toyota company and General Motors, America's biggest auto maker. The two will build and operate a factory in Fremont, California, where they will be able to produce up to 250,000 East-West hybrid cars. Although American auto production was up this year, Japanese and other foreign cars have recently taken a big bite out of the American market. New car buyers have been buying smaller, more efficient imports in preference to larger American models. This move may regain some of the market for G.M.

Washington to end racial hiring quotas

Washington, D.C., Dec. 2

The Reagan administration has announced its intent to end hiring quotas for blacks set by the Equal Employment Opportunity Commission. The commission was created by the Civil Rights Act of 1964 to end discrimination in employment that might be based on race, color, religion, sex or national origin. Minority hiring quotas have been one of its tools to achieve integrated hiring practices. The agency also promotes voluntary programs by employers and unions to end discrimination (→ Jan. 17, 1984).

America is wired for cable television

New York City

The networks are aware of a steady loss of viewers as more and more people turn to cable television. The number of subscribers to the 20 basic services and 10 extra-pay services now totals 25 million. Basic cable averages a 16.4 percent share of the audience from 9 a.m. to 11 p.m. However, the Entertainment Channel, devoted to cultural events, is ending service because of heavy losses. But HBO, Showtime, Playboy, Disney and the Movie Channel are doing well.

1984

Reagan

Missouri, Jan. 13. A federal jury awards newswoman Christine Craft $325,000 in damages against KMBC-TV of Kansas City, which was accused of firing her because of her age and appearance.

Washington, D.C., Jan. 17. Commission on Civil Rights votes to discontinue use of numerical quotas, in employment promotion of blacks.

Tampa, Florida, Jan. 22. Los Angeles Raiders beat Washington Redskins, 38-9, in Super Bowl XVIII.

Lebanon, Feb. 24. Last of U.S. Marines are withdrawn.

New York City, Feb. 25. *Ironweed* by William Kennedy wins Pulitzer Prize in fiction.

Boston, June 12. Celtics defeat Los Angeles Lakers, four games to three, for N.B.A. title.

Hollywood, Calif., June 19. Motion Picture Association of America creates PG-13 film rating, meaning "some material may be inappropriate for children under 13."

Orlando, Florida, June. Donald Duck's 50th anniversary celebration held, at Walt Disney World.

Washington, D.C., July 3. Supreme Court, in Gomez Bethe v. U.S. Jaycees, rules that Jaycees cannot exclude women from full membership.

Albany, New York, July 11. New York becomes first state to institute compulsory seat belt law.

Mississippi, July 13. A 48-page collection of unpublished poems by William Faulkner given to University of Mississippi.

New York City, Oct. 1. Olympic ceremonies organizer Peter V. Ueberroth named commissioner of baseball.

Detroit, Oct. 14. Tigers defeat San Diego Padres, four games to one, in World Series.

New Jersey, Dec. 20. Bell Labs invents megabyte chip, capable of storing four times as much data as any other.

Hollywood, Calif. Top films include *Amadeus, Beverly Hills Cop* and *Ghostbusters*.

DEATH

Martha's Vineyard, Mass., June 30. Lillian Hellman, playwright and screenwriter (*June 20, 1907).

Kissinger study suggests $8 billion in aid for Central America

Washington, D.C., Jan. 12

A committee headed by former Secretary of State Henry Kissinger named to investigate alternatives for improving the situation in Central America today finally issued its recommendations. They include an $8 billion economic aid program and a substantial increase in military aid to the government of El Salvador. The National Bipartisan Commission on Central America was created by President Reagan in 1983 to develop recommendations on American policy in the region. The report is largely in agreement with the administration's current Latin America policy. The only major change involves linking aid to El Salvador to gains in human rights.

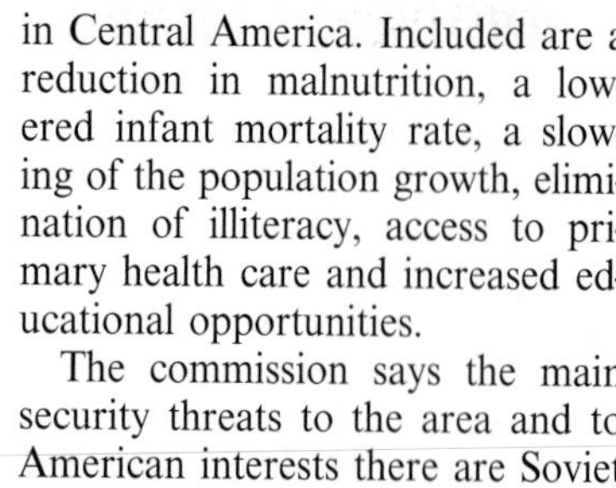

Kissinger, still shaping policy.

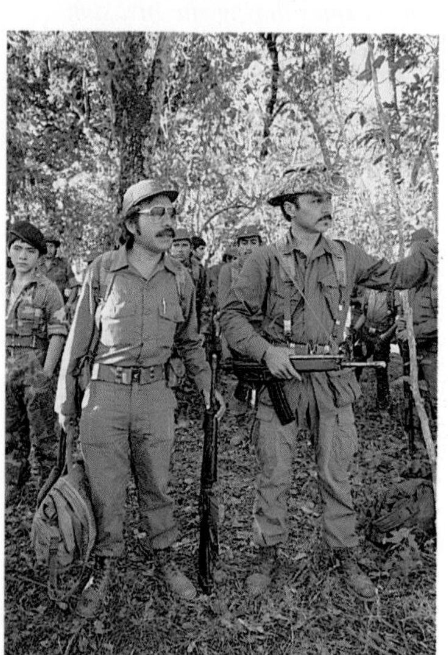

Salvadoran guerrillas on the march.

The five-year economic aid package doubles current levels of assistance provided by the United States.

The report proposes that American aid form the basis for long-term programs of reconstruction and development that would include the elimination of violence and the development of stable democratic institutions. Efforts to improve social conditions and a more equitable distribution of wealth were also recommended. The panel urged that all barriers to Central American imports be removed and that other nations extend duty-free trade to the region. Both long-term and short-term stabilization programs called for "realistic objectives" to improve living conditions in Central America. Included are a reduction in malnutrition, a lowered infant mortality rate, a slowing of the population growth, elimination of illiteracy, access to primary health care and increased educational opportunities.

The commission says the main security threats to the area and to American interests there are Soviet and Cuban activity in Nicaragua.

Reprentative Michael D. Barens, Democrat of Maryland, one of the eight congressional advisers to the commission, was sharply critical of the report. "Our real objective in the region is peace," he said, "and the whole thrust of the report is that the way to achieve peace is by sending more guns."

Marxist Nicaragua: A Soviet proxy?

Reagan tells U.S. it now stands tall

Washington, D.C., Jan. 25

President Reagan said today that "America is back – standing tall, looking to the 80s with courage, confidence and hope." The President's State of the Union address was upbeat and optimistic, but he mentioned problems such as the huge increase in the federal deficit. He proposed a bipartisan approach to the deficit with the goal of a $100 billion reduction over three years. The administration is going to study a plan that calls for simplification of the entire tax code as well as a plan to construct a permanent space station.

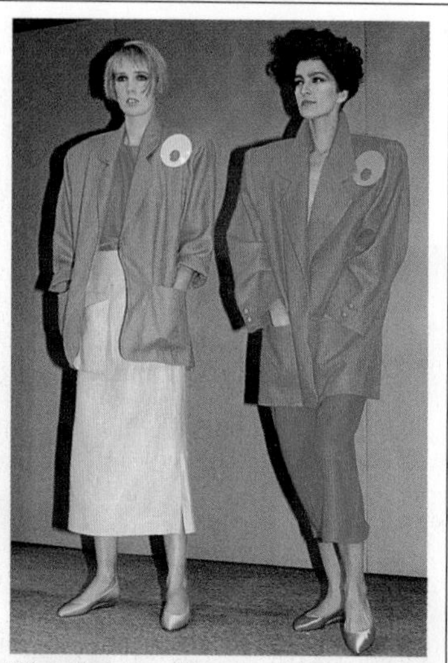

The fashion designs of Oscar de La Renta utilize bold colors and simple lines to accent the woman.

2 astronauts trip the light fantastic

Space, Feb. 7

In a balletic display 170 miles above the Earth, two astronauts flew through space today totally free of their Challenger shuttle. "That may have been one small step for Neil, but it was a heck of a giant leap for me," joked Captain Bruce McCandless 2nd, paraphrasing Armstrong's famous line when he set foot on the moon. The astronaut, along with Lieutenant Colonel Robert L. Stewart, maneuvered with a jet backpack worthy of Buck Rogers. The walks were a happy note on a troublesome mission that included two wayward satellites.

Texas O.K.'s study of evolution as fact

El Paso, Texas, Apr. 14

The Texas board of education today repealed a decade-old rule requiring textbooks used by Texas schools to teach evolution "as only one of several explanations of human origins" and to present it as a theory and not as fact. The rule had come under indirect attack by the governor's select committee on education, which blamed the board for the state's weakness in science teaching. The repeal also was hastened by a decision of the state attorney general that it was unconstitutional and that he would not defend the board against lawsuits filed as a result of it.

Socal acquires Gulf in record merger

New York City, June 15

Stockholders of the Gulf Corporation have approved what will be the largest corporate merger in history. Pending approval by the Federal Trade Commission, Standard Oil of California will acquire Gulf for $13.2 billion, or $80 a share. With the stroke of a pen, Socal would enlarge its oil and gas reserves by 1.97 billion barrels, more than any firm could hope to gain through exploration in a decade. The new conglomerate would be the third largest oil firm in the country, behind Exxon and Mobil, but lawyers claim antitrust legislation poses no barrier.

Democrats pick woman for Vice President

Geraldine Ferraro breaks a barrier.

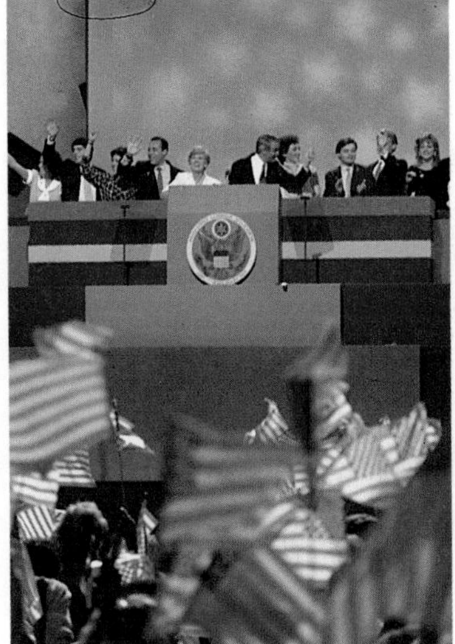

Mondale-Ferraro, that's the ticket.

San Francisco, July 20

Representative Geraldine Ferraro of New York became the first woman in American history to be chosen as a nominee for Vice President on a major party ticket. The 48-year-old legislator was hand picked as his running mate by Walter F. Mondale, the Democratic nominee for President, and was approved for the slot today by delegates to the party's convention in San Francisco. "She's a woman, she's ethnic, she's Catholic," said one Mondale aide in explaining why she was chosen for the ticket. "We have broken the barrier."

Mrs. Ferraro is slim and attractive and a shrewd politician. A lawyer, she was an assistant district attorney in Queens County before her 1978 election to Congress. The daughter of an Italian immigrant, she is married to a Manhattan real estate developer, John Zaccaro, and they have three children. She, like many women, has kept her maiden name for professional purposes.

Some strategists view her selection as an effort by the presidential nominee to fire up the party's seemingly hopeless effort to topple President Reagan, the Republican incumbent, by attracting women voters. Others feel it is a gamble. However, Mrs. Ferraro has the support of many top party leaders, including Governor Mario Cuomo of New York and House Speaker Thomas P. "Tip" O'Neill (→ Nov. 6).

Reagan, in China, promotes wider trade

Peking, China, Apr. 30

The United States, which is now China's third largest trading partner, will play an even larger role in its economic growth as a result of agreements signed here today by President Reagan. American investments, which already exceed $700 million, will increase as tax law changes and bureaucratic streamlining clear the way for joint ventures in offshore oil exploration and the development of electric power systems. Reagan has also agreed to sell nuclear reactors and technology for peaceful uses, despite the fact that China has not signed the 1968 Nuclear Non-Proliferation Treaty.

Trade with China has boomed in the 12 years since President Nixon made his historic visit to China, rising from $4.9 million in 1971 to $5.5 billion in 1981. A major boost came in 1979 when China won most-favored-nation status, qualifying it for U.S. Export-Import Bank financing. Last year, China canceled a 4.4-million-ton grain purchase in retaliation for American textile quotas. But a January visit to Washington by Premier Zhao Ziyang smoothed matters and cleared the way for today's accords.

Preparedness and peace. President Reagan reviews American troops in Honolulu before he flies to Peking.

The Reagans atop the Great Wall. Since 1972, relations between China and U.S. have been on firm ground.

Agent Orange fight wins fund for vets

New York City, May 7

A huge class-action suit filed by Vietnam veterans against seven chemical companies was settled out of court today just hours before jury selection was to begin in the trial. The companies agreed to pay $180 million as compensation if the veterans drop all claims against the companies. Veterans assert that exposure to Agent Orange, a herbicide used in Vietnam, led to high rates of cancer, nerve, skin and liver damage. While the companies deny any link between Agent Orange and the medical problems, they are ready to pay.

Court tightens law on political asylum

Washington, D.C., June 5

The Supreme Court ruled today that the alien who seeks refuge in America must prove he faces "a clear probability" of persecution in his native country to avoid deportation. The decision is less lenient than a lower court's, which allowed refuge if an alien showed a "well-founded fear" of persecution. The ruling was unanimous but, to the surprise of many, its lack of breadth fails to define a distinct standard for political asylum. John Paul Stevens, who wrote the majority opinion, said, "That issue is not presented in this case" (→ May 2, 1986). ▷

L.A. Olympics open with celebration and close with U.S. gold

Greeting an adoring crowd. Team members Edwin Moses and Sharon Weber lead the other members of the American squad in a march around the track at the Los Angeles Coliseum, where the Olympics are being held this year.

Los Angeles, July
In an appropriate Hollywood setting, not far from the heart of Tinseltown, the 1984 Olympic Games got off to a glitzy start, staged a star-spangled finish, and crammed lots of excitement in between. When the Olympic flame flickered and died, the United States was in possession of 83 gold medals, 81 silver and 30 bronze. It would not have been that easy had the Soviet team not stayed home in retaliation for the boycott of its 1980 Games by 50 nations. This year, West Germany was second in medal production with 59. Even without the Communist bloc nations, 7,000 athletes from 140 countries took part, making it the largest national representation in Olympic history.

The opening ceremony included thousands of pigeons, a 1,000-voice choir, a 100-piece orchestra, gospel singers, break dancers, square dancers, a 750-member marching band and 84 pianists playing *Rhapsody in Blue*. The closing program had fireworks, a laser show, a simulated flying saucer suspended from a helicopter and singing and dancing on a 23,000-square-foot stage.

Among America's leading individual stars was Greg Louganis of Mission Viejo, California, who won both platform and springboard diving events.

Feds bail out bank with $4.5 billion

Chicago, July 26
Offering a shot in the arm to the ailing banking industry, the Federal Deposit Insurance Corporation announced today it would give Continental Illinois an infusion of $4.5 billion to cover bad loans. The aid package is one of the biggest ever offered to a private business. It gives the government an 80 percent stake in the bank and leaves federal regulators in charge of policy. Experts say Continental's new managers will steer the bank away from large corporate clients, but keep its role as an international lender.

Bankers fear the action will slow deregulation. But, plagued by the 1982 recession and a host of bad investment decisions, many of them may have no choice. "This isn't the go-it-alone path we aspired to," said departing Continental chief David Taylor, "but it was the best course open to us."

Sullivan first U.S. woman to walk in space

Space, Oct. 11
Dr. Kathryn Sullivan had a fine view of Cape Cod and the rest of planet Earth during the first space walk by an American woman this morning. Following in the "steps" of 38 American men and one Soviet woman before her, Dr. Sullivan, 32, started her jaunt at 11:46 a.m. Working with Commander David Leestma, she completed a difficult refueling operation, monitored a set of 10 tools and snapped several photographs of Leestma and Earth. As the three-hour round neared completion, a safety cap for a valve on the airlock's hatch fell off and wandered out of sight. After a brief search the astronauts recovered it and reboarded (→Jan. 28, 1986).

Most American bank failures since 1938

Washington, D.C.
Despite the continuing economic recovery, 79 banks failed this year, more than in any other year since 1938. The figure pales in comparison to the 4,000 that went under in 1933 without federal insurance to back deposits. But the Federal Deposit Insurance Corporation lists a record 817 banks as problem cases. Many are burdened by loans to the troubled agriculture, energy or real estate sectors of the economy. Others, like Jake Butcher's United American Bank of Knoxville, Tennessee, seem to be victims of widespread fraud. Whatever the cause, the failures have put pressure on banks to raise reserves, which some warn could slow economic growth.

Indian rights leader gives himself up

Rapid City, S.D., Sept. 13
Indian leader Dennis Banks has surrendered to legal authorities. A fugitive for nine years, he was sentenced last month to three years in prison for his part in the Custer County Courthouse riot of 1973. An Oglala Sioux, he is a founder of the American Indian Movement (AIM), established in Minneapolis in 1968. Banks and fellow AIM leader Russell Means have been demanding that the federal government return to native Americans tribal lands ceded to them at a time in the 19th century when Indians were being ousted from prime land.

American balloonist first across Atlantic

Savona, Italy, Sept. 18
An American making the first solo balloon flight across the Atlantic crash-landed in Italy today and walked away with a record. Actually, he was flown by helicopter from the landing area to a hospital in Nice, suffering from a broken ankle. Joe W. Kittinger reached Savona with rain and strong winds lashing his 10-story-tall balloon. The flight from Maine covered 3,535 miles and lasted 84 hours. Kittinger, 56, said he had been hoping to set down in Moscow. The previous record distance for a solo balloon flight was 2,475 miles.

Quincy Jones bestows yet another honor on the reclusive and eccentric Michael Jackson at the Grammy Awards. Jackson's distinct sound and fancy footwork have made his "Thriller" the best-selling album in history.

Reagan romps to victory

A winning team. President Reagan has won the heart of America's voters.

Washington, D.C., Nov. 6

President Ronald Reagan was re-elected today, soundly defeating Democrat Walter F. Mondale by carrying 49 of the 50 states. The President, the oldest man ever to occupy the White House, had campaigned on the slogan, "It's morning again in America," and, indeed, his landslide victory seems to indicate that America's voters approved of his performance over the past four years. Vice President George Bush also was re-elected.

Mondale, Vice President under Jimmy Carter, had taken a risk by conceding during recent months that he would propose a tax increase to reduce the country's enormous deficit. The President, on the other hand, declared that only "over my dead body" would there be any increase in taxes.

As a band played *Hail to the Chief*, the President entered a ballroom in Los Angeles to greet his supporters as they chanted: "Four more years." The smiling President said: "I think that's just been arranged." Promising to extend the economic and military policies of his first term, Reagan added: "You ain't seen nothing yet."

The Democratic campaign had been hampered by disclosures involving the tangled financial problems of the vice presidential candidate, Geraldine Ferraro.

U.S. bishops issue critique of capitalism

United States, Nov. 11

America has failed to provide its people with a just economic system. That is the thrust of a draft *Pastoral Letter on Catholic Social Teaching and the Economy* presented at the the annual meeting of the National Conference of Catholic Bishops today. The 120-page document is to be discussed during the coming year before the final draft is issued next year. The letter recognizes the positive impact capitalism has had in providing a high level of production but states that the tremendous inequality that continues to pervade the country is immoral. Homelessness and hunger in a country as wealthy as the United States are only two examples the letter uses to illustrate the failure of society and individuals to create an equitable economic system. The bishops said: "We believe that the level of inequality in income and wealth in our society and even more the inequality on the world scale today must be judged morally unacceptable." They argue that the federal government should be playing a greater role in overcoming this inequality.

The issuance of the letter seems to be a victory for the those bishops who argued for a spectrum of approaches to contemporary moral and social problems over those who preferred a concerted effort against abortion. The three issues upon which the bishops have chosen to center are economics, abortion and nuclear weapons.

Fair at New Orleans closes with lawsuits

New Orleans, Nov. 11

The New Orleans World's Fair closed today as a financial fiasco and a national flop, but with thousands of local residents mourning its closing. While contractors and others who lost money on the fair were planning lawsuits, visitors to the New Orleans area crowded onto the fairgrounds for one final, fabulous fling. One couple said they had used their season tickets to attend the fair 145 times since its opening on May 12.

The failure of the fair was attributed to inadequate financing, poor marketing, the city's location and a negative reception from the nation's press. Some experts said such an exposition is "a tired idea" and the New Orleans fair may be the last such show. Fair officials expected 11 to 12 million visitors, but only 7 million came. The fair emphasized New Orleans jazz and Louisiana's Cajun culture.

Cuba takes back criminal refugees

Washington, D.C., Dec. 15

The United States and Cuba have agreed that Cuba will accept the return of 2,746 criminals and mental patients who entered the United States during the Mariel boatlift in 1980. President Fidel Castro announced the decision Friday night, but he denied that those who will return were criminal or mentally ill when they left Cuba. The Cubans being returned were among some 129,000 refugees who arrived in the United States in boats from the port of Mariel. Thousands of them are still confined to refugee camps and prisons.

Pro-abortion nuns facing expulsion

Vatican City, Dec. 18

A Vatican spokesman today confirmed that 24 American nuns who signed a statement supporting a woman's right to choose an abortion have been threatened with expulsion. The statement, which appeared in a full page advertisement in *The New York Times* October 7, was signed by several prominent Roman Catholics. It affirmed their belief in a woman's right to choose an abortion. The Vatican said that the Sacred Congregation for Religious and Secular Institutes had written letters demanding that the nuns retract their statement.

Bruce Springsteen is "Born in the U.S.A."

United States

Singing about hard-luck cases yearning for hope against a fading American dream, Bruce Springsteen stirred millions this year with *Born in the U.S.A.* From the opening strains of the album's title song, about forsaken Vietnam vets, to the melancholy *My Hometown*, the album presented a grim view of American society, yet one tinged with a tough-minded compassion and wary optimism. Even President Reagan jumped on the bandwagon this summer, invoking the name of the New Jersey singer while campaigning. But "The Boss" would have none of it. Countering Reagan's *Morning in America* theme, Bruce said that he had seen places where "It's midnight, and like, there's a bad moon risin'."

One of the hardest driving rock stars in America, "The Boss" has breathed new life into old-time rock 'n' roll.

1985

Reagan

New Orleans, Jan. 3. Rotating blackouts instituted across southeast Louisiana leave 70,000 people without electrical power.

Palo Alto, California, Jan. 20. San Francisco 49ers defeat Miami Dolphins, 38-16, in Super Bowl XIX.

New Orleans, Apr. 4. Tulane University cancels school's basketball season, after allegations of point shaving and illegal payments.

New York City, Apr. 24. Pulitzer Prizes awarded to Alison Lurie, for *Foreign Affairs*, and Studs Terkel, for *The Good War: An Oral History of World War II.*

Pittsburgh, May 2. Heads of U.S. Steel, LTV Steel, Bethlehem Steel, Inland Steel, Armco dissolve their 30-year-old coordinated bargaining committee.

Boston, June 9. Los Angeles Lakers defeat Boston Celtics, four games to two, for N.B.A. title.

Washington, D.C., July 1. Supreme Court rules that public school teachers may not enter parochial school classrooms, to provide remedial or enrichment instruction.

Mississippi, Aug. 15. Tourists flock to Tupelo, Elvis Presley's birthplace, to mark eighth anniversary of his death.

Maine, Aug. 25. Bar Harbor Airlines plane crashes, killing 13-year-old Samantha Smith, who had visited Soviet Union upon invitation from Soviet government.

Kansas City, Oct. 27. Royals defeat St. Louis Cardinals, four games to three, in World Series.

New York City, Nov. 26. Random House will pay $3 million for rights to official biography of President Reagan by Edmund Morris.

Texas, Dec. 11. State court upholds $11 billion damage award Texaco must pay Pennzoil for undermining its bid to acquire Getty.

St. Louis, Missouri. Anheuser-Busch sells 68 million barrels of beer this year, greatest volume ever.

Hollywood, Calif. Hit movies this year include *Out of Africa, Prizzi's Honor* and *Kiss of the Spider Woman.*

Westmoreland ends suit against CBS

New York City, Feb. 17

In a surprise move, General William C. Westmoreland dropped his libel suit against CBS today, as the case was within days of going to jury. The retired general agreed to an out-of-court settlement in which no money changed hands. Westmoreland filed his $120 million suit after a CBS documentary, *The Uncounted Enemy: A Vietnam Deception*, implied that Westmoreland deceived the government and the public about the troop strength of the Vietnamese enemy. A joint statement makes it appear that CBS is standing by its broadcast and that Westmoreland construes the CBS statement as an apology.

Capital Cities buys ABC for $3.5 billion

New York City, March 17

Capital Cities Communications and the American Broadcasting Company shook hands today on a deal by which Capital Cities bought ABC for over $3.5 billion, provided stockholders, the Department of Justice and the Federal Communications Commission approve. The surprise deal is the largest ever in the entertainment industry. To keep off "unfriendly suitors" until the merger is final, Capital Cities put down a $53 million option to buy 5.3 million shares of ABC common stock at $118 a share. ABC has 214 affiliated stations; Capital Cities owns newspapers, magazines and cable TV systems.

Union Carbide sued over India disaster

New York City, Apr. 8

The Indian government filed suit against Union Carbide Corporation in Manhattan District Court today for unspecified damages arising from the December 1984 gas leak at the company's plant in Bhopal. The suit stated that 1,700 people died and 200,000 were injured in the lethal leak. India seeks compensatory damages for the victims as well as punitive damages "in an amount sufficient to deter Union Carbide ... from the willful, malicious and wanton disregard of the rights and safety of the citizens of those countries in which they do business." It is reported that India might settle out of court.

Chavez trying to revive Farm Workers

Tehachapi Mountains, Calif.

High in the Sierra headquarters of the United Farm Workers, isolated from the rank and file, Cesar Chavez is trying to rekindle the energy he rode to national prominence in the 1960s and '70s. Some 42 percent of Californians have joined his new grape boycott, a tactic that once forced dozens of growers to bargain with the U.F.W.

Chavez began the union in 1962 when migrant workers, ignored by the New Deal, had no bargaining power. A long strike in 1965 had pickets chanting "Viva la Huelga" ("Long Live the Strike") on national television. Liberals and clergy flocked to support Chavez, and by 1975, he had 50 contracts in the grape industry alone. Now he has three. Chavez drifted into meditation, holistic health and encounter groups. Union officials deserted in droves, calling him a dictator. But Chavez remains committed. "The workers," he says, "will ask me to leave when they are ready."

San Francisco. *Invented by Andrew Hallidie, a British-born businessman, in 1867, charming, efficient cable cars have been running here since 1873.*

Supreme Court bars moment of silence

Washington, D.C., June 4

In a 6-3 ruling today, the Supreme Court struck down an Alabama law that required a moment of silent meditation at the beginning of each school day. In another chapter of the school prayer debate that has agitated the country off and on since the court's 1962 decision in Engel v. Vitale, the court stated that a moment of silence was not in itself unconstitutional if used for some purpose such as bringing order to a classroom at the beginning of the day. In the Alabama case, the court found that the intent of the law was explicitly to promote religion and thereby violated the First Amendment of the Constitution as applied to the states by the 14th Amendment.

The school prayer issue, however, does not seem destined to go away soon. President Reagan has called for a constitutional amendment allowing required prayer in schools, and bills are regularly introduced into Congress with that intent. The Rev. Jerry Falwell of the Moral Majority has made it a major element in the agenda of that political organization, in spite of the fact that board meetings of Moral Majority itself do not begin with a prayer because of the possibility that any particular prayer would offend some members.

Reagan stirs uproar by visiting Bitburg

Bitburg, West Germany, May 5

President Reagan's short visit to a military cemetery in Bitburg today in the midst of the annual Western economic summit meeting drew protests from American and European Jews. The protests, aides to the President said, marred the summit aspects of the trip.

Reagan delivered an eloquent speech after visiting the cemetery where 2,500 German soldiers, 49 of them SS men, are buried. He condemned Nazi atrocities and hailed the 40 years of German-American friendship. Despite the President's sentiments and an earlier visit to the Bergen-Belsen camp, holocaust survivor and scholar Elie Wiesel said of the Bitburg visit, "We have been wounded ..." Jews in Europe and the United States had urged Reagan not to go to Bitburg. Hundreds turned up to protest.

T.W.A. hijack drama comes to an end

Damascus, Syria, June 30

The 39 American hostages on the T.W.A. flight hijacked by Arab terrorists 17 days ago are free. A spectacular convoy sped them to Damascus from the Beirut slum where they were held captive after removal from the aircraft. Also today, two of the hijackers still guarding the plane strode into an airport lounge and bragged to reporters about "the ability of the oppressed to control America." Hooded in pillow cases, the pair concluded with the slogan: "America is the great Satan." The freed hostages said they will never forget the screams of fellow passenger Robert Stethem, a navy diver, before he was murdered. The passengers hailed purser Uli Derickson for her brave calm. So far, the Shiite terrorists have failed in their demand that the Israelis free Palestinians, as the price for today's release.

Hijackers talked with journalists and labeled America "the great Satan."

On television, President Reagan told terrorists that America "will fight back against your cowardly attacks." Reporters also heard the President declare in a microphone test, "Boy, I'm glad I saw *Rambo*, last night. Now I know what to do next time."

Treasure hunter unearths Spanish galleon

Key West, Fla., July 21

"It's the mother lode! We're sitting on silver bars!" cried diver Andy Matroci as he splashed to the surface. So ends Mel Fisher's obsessive 16-year search for the Nuestra Senora de Atocha, a treasure-laden Spanish galleon that last saw sky in 1622. To the archeologists with Fisher's Treasure Salvors Inc., the ship is a "virgin time capsule." To the trip's 700 investors, it is 60 pounds of gold and 47 tons of silver worth close to $400 million. For Fisher, it may be a small consolation for the loss of his son and daughter-in-law, who drowned in the search for the Atocha.

Live-Aid concert for African famine relief

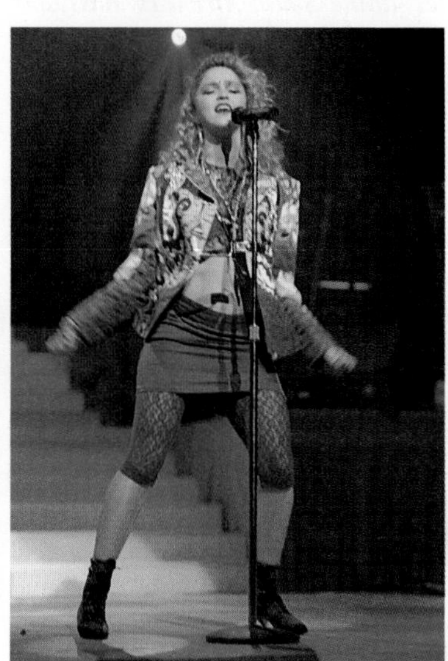

At the Live-Aid benefit, Madonna shows her navel for a good cause.

Philadelphia, July 13

"To me this is not a pop concert, to me this is not a TV show," said Irish singer Bob Geldof of today's Live-Aid extravaganza, "to me this is simply a means of keeping people alive." The all-star intercontinental rock fete was organized by Geldof to raise money for African famine relief. Centered at Wembley Stadium in England and Philadelphia's JFK Stadium, the shows included Sting, Paul McCartney, U2, Dire Straits, The Who, Madonna, Crosby, Stills, Nash & Young, Bob Dylan and Led Zeppelin. Geldof hopes the shows, TV broadcasts to 152 nations and phone pledges will raise $50 million. As Woodstock alumnus Neil Young said, "This time you know it's going to help."

Growing homeless ranks face bitter winter

Washington, D.C., December

As the winter winds begin to howl through the streets of the urban North, a legion of homeless people once again faces the perennial challenge of survival. Unemployment may be the lowest in five years, but homelessness is worse than at any time since the Depression. No one really knows how bad; estimates range from 350,000 to 3 million. But the facilities are inadequate for handling even the best-case scenario. Only 91,000 shelter beds exist in the whole country. A public outcry has forced higher expenditures in some states. But corporate contributions to health and human services are down. And the Reagan administration has slashed spending on low-income housing. As one Department of Health and Human Services official explained, "We think it is a local problem."

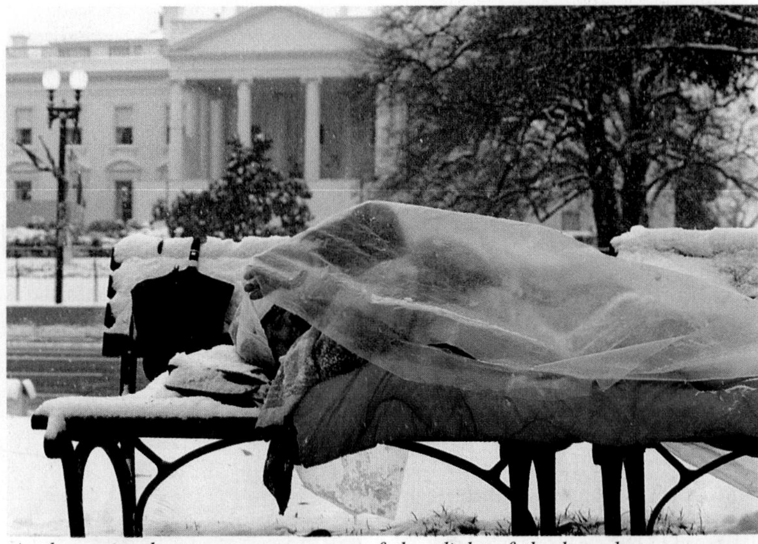

As the nation becomes more aware of the plight of the homeless, many are blaming the government for not doing enough to alleviate the awful situation. ▷

Pete Rose breaks Ty Cobb's record

Cincinnati, Ohio, Sept. 11

One of baseball's most enduring records, held by Ty Cobb since 1928, has gone the way of most "unbreakable" marks. Pete Rose of the Cincinnati Reds got a line single for the 4,192nd hit of his 23-year career, surpassing the Cobb record, and followed that six innings later with a triple for No. 4,193. The feat of the 44-year-old Cincinnati hero touched off a seven-minute standing ovation and a fireworks display. There were tears in Pete's eyes. "The only other time I remember crying was when my father died," he noted after belting out his record hit off Eric Show of the San Diego Padres.

Smashing performance. Pete Rose gets a single and jogs into history.

U.S. now debtor nation

Washington, D.C., Sept. 16

In a few years, the United States has fallen from its lofty position as the world's largest lender, to a shaky place in the debt cellar. According to figures issued today by the Commerce Department, the nation will accumulate a current accounts deficit of $130 billion this year, the largest in the world. It will be the first time since 1914 that the United States has owed foreigners more than they have owed to this country. At 3 percent of the gross national product, the figure doubles the previous high of 1.5 percent, reached during the 1870s, when the developing West absorbed huge quantities of foreign capital.

Not surprisingly, economists disagree on the effects of the historic shift. Borrowing appears to have few intrinsic pitfalls as long as the capital is used for productive investment. Certainly America developed on foreign money throughout the 19th century. But industrial production has been stagnant for a year under a flood of imports. And the future promises an even greater drain on investment capital. The debt may hit $1 trillion by 1990, with interest and dividend alone equaling the 1985 total deficit. Dependence on foreign money also opens America further to international fluctuations. As an official at the Institute for International Economics put it, "If there was a run on the dollar tomorrow, we'd be hurt."

Reagan's new revolution: tax revision

Washington, D.C., May 28

Labeling it a "second American Revolution for hope and opportunity," President Reagan has proposed a far-reaching plan to reshape the federal income tax system. The losers, he said in a message to Congress, would be "those individuals and corporations who are not paying their fair share or, for that matter, any share."

The plan would replace individual tax rates, now ranging from 11 to 50 percent, with three new rates of 15, 25 and 35 percent. Families of four with incomes of about $12,000 or less would pay no taxes. And the top corporate tax rate would drop from 46 to 33 percent.

The plan would retain deductions for charitable contributions as well as interest payments on all primary residences, but it would eliminate many other tax breaks, including deductions to help offset state and local tax payments. It also would limit deductions for interest payments on second homes.

Reaction to the plan was mixed on Capitol Hill. Dan Rostenkowski, chairman of the House Ways and Means Committee, said "the battle for reform will be long and tough." He predicted some changes would be made, that the Congress would not rubber-stamp the plan.

Going to the people. President Reagan unveils his tax program on television.

U.S. curbing trade with South Africans

Washington, D.C., Sept. 9

President Reagan announced today that the administration will impose economic sanctions against South Africa. In a policy reversal, Reagan said he would prohibit most loans, computer sales and nuclear technology deals with the Pretoria government in an effort to end its policy of apartheid against South African blacks. Critics of the President refuse to give him much credit for the action, saying it comes only after a public outcry, both here and abroad, against South Africa's program of oppression. It is expected that other Western nations will follow Reagan's lead with economic sanctions of their own.

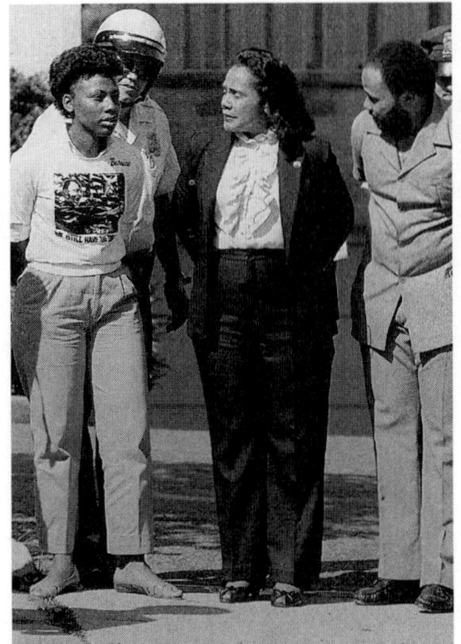

Coretta King and children join a protest at the South Africa Embassy.

Rebuffed by CBS, Turner eyes MGM

Atlanta, Georgia, Aug. 7

Broadcaster Ted Turner is determined to become a media mogul. Rebuffed in his "hostile" takeover bid for CBS, he is going for the MGM/UA Entertainment Company for about $1.5 billion ($29 a share). He would kick back UA to major stockholder Kirk Kerkorian for $470 million ($9 a share). If Turner can raise the money, he will run a major Hollywood theatrical, TV and home video supplier and own a library of 2,200 films, 600 of them silents, many classics.

Montgomery Ward dropping catalogue

Chicago, Aug. 2

After 113 years of mailing catalogues and merchandise to customers, Montgomery Ward is going out of the mail-order business. The company will send its final issue in December. Montgomery Ward was founded in 1872 in a livery stable loft with $2,400 in capital and a single-sheet brochure listing a few dry goods items. It began catalogue sales before its nearest competitor, Sears, Roebuck & Co. Now officials say the catalogue business is losing money.

Law intends to end U.S. deficit by 1991

Washington, D.C., Dec. 10

President Reagan today signed into law a radical revision of the budgeting procedures, requiring an end to the federal deficit by 1991. The President praised it as "an important step toward putting our fiscal house in order." The new law was sponsored by Representative Phil Gramm of Texas and Senators Warren B. Rudman of New Hampshire and Ernest F. Hollings of South Carolina, and bears their names. To achieve gradual elimination of the monumental national debt, the new law would require cuts in many programs if Congress fails to agree to reductions in the deficit (→June 6, 1986).

Superpower summit

The Communist and the Cold Warrior set course for an era of cooperation.

Geneva, Switzerland, Nov. 21

In the latest of the 10 summit meetings held since World War II between the leaders of the United States and the Soviet Union, President Reagan today opened discussions on a wide range of topics with General Secretary Mikhail Gorbachev. Meeting at the Chateau Fleur d'Eau outside Geneva, the President greeted Gorbachev with a firm ceremonial handshake. The two men strolled in the wintry Swiss wind, then adjourned to a warm fireplace with their advisers to begin tough negotiations on arms control and human rights. According to reliable sources, Gorbachev quickly told Reagan he must abandon his touted "Star Wars" space defense program. And the President, just as quickly, refused to do so. While this event might have ruined other summit meetings right from the start, insiders say that in spite of their differences, Reagan and Gorbachev did seem to hit it off personally and that agreements on their broad agenda still may be reached.

While the President is debating "Star Wars" with the Soviet leader, Nancy Reagan is engaged in "style wars" with Raisa Gorbachev. But the First Lady is keeping a sense of perspective about their alleged fashion rivalry. Says she, "I think that's a little silly. I mean there are very important things being discussed here, and what somebody wears or doesn't wear really isn't terribly important."

President signs costliest farm bill

Washington, D.C., Dec. 23

With quick strokes of his pen, President Reagan today signed into law the most expensive federal farm bill in American history. The $169 billion expenditure includes a huge fund reserved for crop insurance and long-term, low-interest loans to the economically distressed farming sector. This law comes after a year of farm protests. In January, 10,000 people held a rally in St. Paul, Minnesota, to protest low farm prices and high interest rates. The next month, a crowd of more than 14,000 gathered at Iowa State University in Ames to demand immediate federally funded farm credits.

Frank Zappa zaps plan to censor rock

Washington, D.C., Sept. 19

From Presley to Prince, rock music has always exploited shock value. But Tipper Gore, wife of Senator Albert Gore and founder of the Parents' Music Resources Center, has seen enough. At a congressional hearing today she urged warning labels on "offensive" albums. Folksinger John Denver and heavy metal icon Dee Snider disagree. And rock's daring experimenter Frank Zappa likened the center's demands to "some sinister kind of toilet training program to housebreak all composers and performers."

The President and the First Lady, reviving frontier spirit of the West.

Chris Evert at 30 just keeps winning

New York City

Chris Evert, once the darling of women's tennis, is now perhaps the most consistently dominating figure in the sport's history. In 1971, at 16, her backcourt patience and trademark two-handed backhand took her to the U.S. Open semifinals. For five straight years in the '70s, she held the No. 1 spot, streaking to 125 straight clay court wins. For 11 years she made the semifinals of every Grand Slam event she entered. And this year, at 30, Evert won in Paris, still unwilling to give ground to the young and eager.

Youth from Russia to be U.S. citizen

Los Angeles, Oct. 3

Walter Polovchak, the Ukrainian youth who ran away from his parents five years ago rather than return to the Soviet Union, won the right to seek United States citizenship today. He became an adult. The Chicago youth celebrated his 18th birthday on a television program here. Polovchak came to the United States with his parents six years ago, but refused to go back to the Soviet Union with them a year later. "I'm celebrating my freedom today." said Polovchak.

Largest atom lab opens in Illinois

Batavia, Illinois, Oct. 13

The Fermi National Accelerator Laboratory is the home of the world's largest atom smasher, a huge accelerator that measures four miles in diameter. Switched on for the first time today, the enormous device has produced energy levels three times higher than any previously achieved. The accelerator is expected to help the United States regain the lead in high-energy physics that was lost to a European consortium in the 1970s. As a research tool, the device is unequaled.

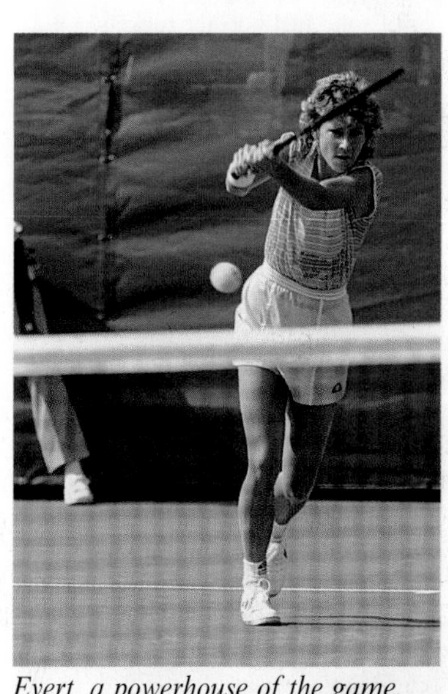

Evert, a powerhouse of the game.

1986

Reagan

New Orleans, Jan. 7. Chicago Bears defeat New England Patriots, 46-10, in Super Bowl XX.

Hanover, New Hampshire, January. Group of Dartmouth students opposed to college's divestment of funds in South Africa stage midnight sledgehammer attack on campus protesters' shanties.

New York City, Feb. 26. Robert Penn Warren named first official poet laureate of United States by Librarian of Congress Daniel Boorstin.

Florida, March 6. Divers recover Challenger crew compartment, containing remains of astronauts (→June 9).

New York City, Apr. 17. Pulitzer Prizes awarded to J. Anthony Lukas, for *Common Ground* and Larry McMurtry, for *Lonesome Dove.*

Washington, D.C., Apr. 23. House of Representatives approves Garrison Diversion Project in North Dakota, though project is scaled back from 250,000 to 131,000 acres.

New York City, Apr. 27. A video pirate transmits protest over cost of pay television to millions watching Home Box Office television.

Detroit, Apr. 28. General Motors becomes biggest U.S. company, replacing Exxon.

Tuscon, Arizona, May 1. Eight Christian activists convicted, of smuggling and harboring illegal aliens (→Nov. 7).

Washington, D.C., June 9. President's commission on Challenger disaster pinpoints fault on a defective "o-ring" seal on one of solid fuel booster rockets (→Sept. 29, 1988).

Philadelphia, June 18. Academy of Fine Arts acquires 1,000 works by Thomas Eakins.

Washington, D.C., June 23. President Reagan states: "The one thing that I do seek are judges that will interpret the law and not write the law."

Atlanta, Oct. 1. Ex-President Carter officially opens Carter Presidential Center.

New York City, Oct. 27. Mets beat Boston Red Sox, 4 games to 3, in World Series.

Las Vegas, Nov. 22. Mike Tyson knocks out Trevor Berbick in second round, for World Boxing Council title.

Shuttle Challenger explodes; 7 killed

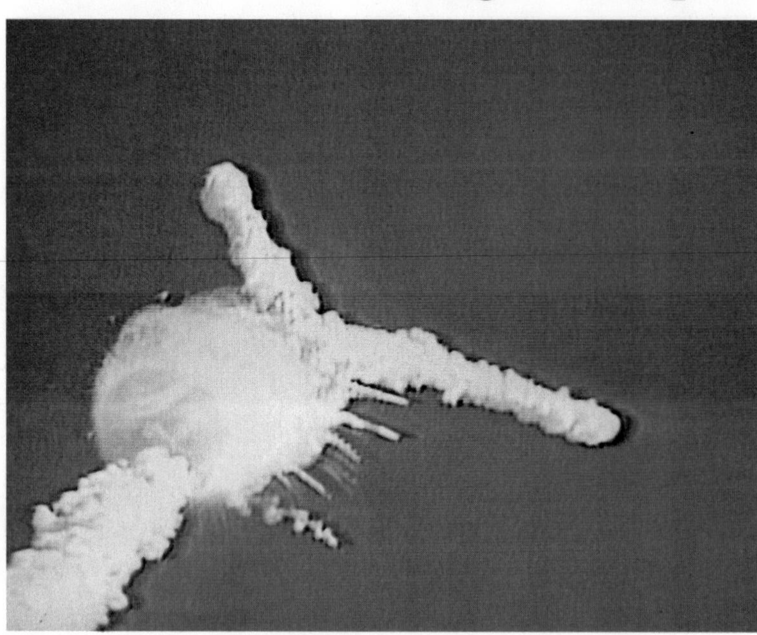

Tragedy in the sky. Booster rockets careen away from the space shuttle.

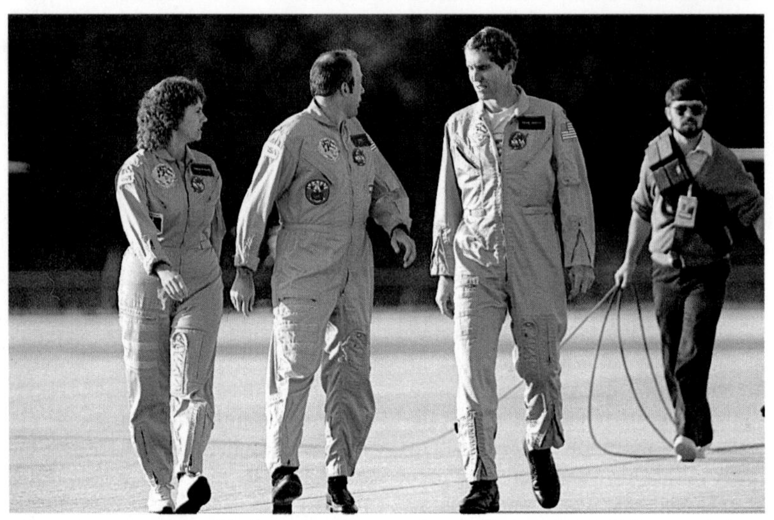

A quiet moment for Challenger crew members. Christa McAuliffe is at left.

Cape Canaveral, Fla., Jan. 28

The space shuttle Challenger exploded into a massive orange fireball today 73 seconds after liftoff, killing all seven astronauts aboard. The shocking scene was witnessed by thousands of spectators here, while millions who were watching their televison screens stared in disbelief. The worst catastrophe in the history of American space exploration, the tragedy has closed down the country's space shuttle program indefinitely.

The winged spacecraft lifted off flawlessly at 11:38 a.m., after delays related to unusually cold temperatures. Many in the crowd of spectators were students, cheering for Christa McAuliffe of Concord, New Hampshire, who was to have been the first schoolteacher in space. As Challenger soared to a height of nine miles and a speed of 2,900 feet per second, Commander Francis "Dick" Scobee said, "Roger, go with throttle up, up," signaling a power increase. But the craft was suddenly engulfed by a massive eruption of its liquid hydrogen tank at 11:39; its two solid fuel boosters continued to fire, leaving two smoke trails across the cloudless sky. Thousands of pieces of debris fell into the Atlantic.

The other members of the Challenger crew were Commander Michael J. Smith, Dr. Judith A. Resnik, Dr. Ronald E. McNair, Lieutenant Colonel Ellison S. Onizuka and Gregory B. Jarvis. Space officials have not determined the cause of the tragedy (→March 6).

Scientology guru writes kinky novel

New York City, Jan 24

Once upon a time, L(afayette). Ron Hubbard wrote science fiction. Then he gave it up to found the Church of Scientology, a religion whose main goal, say skeptics, is lining Hubbard's pockets. In any case, Hubbard's back in sci-fi and is at work on a 10-volume work ("dekalogy" in Hubbardese) titled *Invader's Planet*. The maiden novel, *Mission Earth*, came out today. It is weak in the science and fiction areas, but it has lots of kinky sex.

AIDS silence ends; condom use urged

Washington, D.C., Oct. 22

"The silence must end." That was the message of Surgeon General C. Everett Koop's report on acquired immune deficiency syndrome today. The study urged education for schoolchildren on the causes of the disease and condom use by adults not in "mutually faithful monogamous relationships." Teenagers should abstain from sex, according to the report, which also tries to allay fears that AIDS is spread through casual contact.

Wall Street plagued by insider trading

New York City, Nov. 18

In the midst of its greatest boom in history, Wall Street has been shaken to its foundations by scandal. Ivan Boesky, one of the nation's richest arbitrageurs, has pleaded guilty to buying and selling stocks based on illegal information. He will pay $100 million as penalty for his involvement in the insider trading game. Half of that total represents illegal profits, half is a civil penalty. He will also be barred from the securities industry for life.

U.S. bombs Libya for terrorist attacks

Terrorism gets punished. Libya is hit hard by the American reprisal raid.

Washington, D.C., Apr. 16

Last night's surprise American raid on Tripoli has taken the lives of Colonel Muammar el-Khadafy's 15-month-old adopted daughter and two American pilots. President Reagan told a meeting of businessmen here today, "We would prefer not to have to repeat the events of last night. What is required is for Libya to end its pursuit of terror for political goals." The President ordered the attack in retaliation for Libya's "direct" role in the April 5 bombing of a West Berlin discotheque popular with American servicemen. Sounds of bombs and guns in Tripoli were heard clearly by Americans listening to radio broadcasts live from the scene. The 18 bombers striking from a base in England were hampered by Paris's refusal to let them cross French air space. An additional 15 planes took off from American aircraft carriers in the Mediterranean just before the White House began a briefing for some key congressmen.

Republican Senator Richard Lugar said today that the briefing began early enough so that the raid "could have been called off" if the legislators had insisted. But the Democratic Senate leader Robert Byrd, who was present at the briefing, strongly dissented. "We were not consulted," he said. "We were notified of a decision that had already been made."

Ad agencies merge into world's largest

New York City, Apr. 27

Three major advertising agencies today agreed to merge and create the largest agency in the world. The agencies – BBDO International, the Doyle Dane Bernbach Group and Needham Harper Worldwide – bring in some $6 billion a year in billings. "We want to be nothing less than advertising's global creative superpower," according to Allen G. Rosenshine, chairman and chief executive officer of BBDO. He added that the merger will offer extra resources for major clients and diversity for restless, creative-talent employees. Advertising has grown increasingly important as products become more alike and rely on extra "hype" to distinguish themselves.

Oil prices plummet; Southwest hurting

Houston, Texas

When oil hit a low of $10.77 a barrel this year, most Americans applauded. A Merrill Lynch analyst viewed it as "a huge tax break." Experts said drivers would save $23 billion, heating consumers $12.5 billion, truckers $7.7 billion and farmers $1.1 billion. But the Southwest is not smiling. Oil output is off 800,000 barrels a day; profits are off 50 percent; foreclosures, bankruptcy and unemployment are endemic, and bank failures in Texas are up 119 percent.

Boston Celtics win 16th N.B.A. title

Boston, June 8

The Boston Celtics won their 16th National Basketball Association title today, but the score could have read Bird 114, Houston 97. It was Larry Bird at his best, doing all and playing all but two minutes in the decisive sixth game in the best-of-seven series. He got 29 points even though he was double- and triple-teamed. He broke up Rocket plays and forced 11 first-quarter turnovers. He even untangled the net for the officials.

U.S. to recognize new Philippine regime

Washington, D.C., Feb. 27

The Reagan administration announced today that it will give full diplomatic recognition to the new Philippine government headed by Corazon C. Aquino. The decision by Washington to recognize Mrs. Aquino as the legal head of the new Philippine government is a severe blow to former President Ferdinand Marcos, who still claims to have won the presidential election three weeks ago.

For years, Marcos headed a regime that was known for its corruption and its indifference to a 20 percent unemployment rate, with two-thirds of the Filipino people living in poverty. The Marcos government also had been implicated in the political assassination of many enemies, including Mrs. Aquino's husband, opposition leader Benigno Aquino.

Incoming: New Philippine President, Corazon Aquino, greets the people.

Outgoing: Ferdinand Marcos, ousted Philippine leader, reaches Hawaii.

What Asian influx may mean for U.S.

Los Angeles, June 29

As the number of European newcomers to the United States steadily declines, Asians are flocking to America's shores. And these Asians now account for half of all legally admitted foreigners. And as Thais, Indians and others pursue the American dream, experts are beginning a serious examination of the long-term effects on American society.

The sights and sounds of the East are enveloping entire communities. Surgeons, entrepreneurs and laborers are creating urban microcosms of their homelands; their children are excelling in school, and Asians often economically surpass other Americans and minorities. In short, most are succeeding.

But many experts warn that self-supporting socio-economic enclaves are rapidly supplanting the need for assimilation. Economic success can now be achieved with only a marginal understanding of American life. But there are some who believe that should the current trend continue, future national unity might be endangered. ▷

National debt passes the $2 trillion mark

Washington, D.C., June 6

The omnipresent federal budget deficit, long the talk of economic pessimists, has now reached such absurd proportions – $2 trillion – that it can no longer be ignored. According to Keynesian economic theory, a moderate federal debt is no cause for concern so long as sustained growth keeps pace with it. It is a fact, however, that the deficit has doubled over the past five years, and this has experts on both the left and the right deeply worried.

Much of the American debt has been incurred by what many call a spending-happy Congress, but consumer debt, business debt and foreign debt have significantly added to the problem. Spending far more than it takes in, the United States has created what some consider to be an artificial prosperity. True or not, no nation can continue amassing huge debts without a day of reckoning. Should foreign financial institutions call in their United States loans, the effects could be extreme. In the final analysis, Americans must find a long-term, programmatic solution, lest that day of reckoning be worse than need be.

Star Wars system wrecks Iceland summit

Reykjavik, Iceland, Oct. 13

The once-promising arms meeting between President Reagan and Soviet leader Mikhail Gorbachev broke up late yesterday. According to administration spokesmen, the talks ended because of the continuing U.S.-U.S.S.R. impasse over Reagan's refusal to drop the "Star Wars" space defense program. The Russians offered to make major cuts in their medium- and long-range nuclear weapons system, but only if the Americans would agree to stop both the testing and deployment of space-based weapons envisioned in the President's so-called "Strategic Defensive Initiative." Reagan apparently said he would not do so, and the talks came to an abrupt and confused end.

Observers say that when the talks suddenly stalled, Reagan and Gorbachev were on the verge of a comprehensive agreement that would have severely cut back the deployment of both intermediate and long-range nuclear weapons systems. It is expected that discussions on arms control will resume next year when experts of both countries meet at Geneva (→Dec. 8, 1987).

Steel in crisis as imports flood America

Washington, D.C., July

The steel crisis hit a new level this month as LTV, the nation's second largest steel firm, filed for bankruptcy. Since 1982, the rusted industry has lost $7 billion under the pressure of heavy imports, which have seized a 25 percent share of the market, up from 14 percent 10 years ago. And the market itself is shrinking; cars are smaller, plastics are on the rise and computers are replacing heavy equipment.

Some analysts blame the high cost of labor. LTV supports two pensioners for every worker on the payroll. But unionists have grown compliant in the face of mass layoffs that have thinned the ranks of steelworkers from 450,000 to 200,000 since 1979.

Labor has led the call for federal help. Says union president Lynn Williams: "The steel industry – and industrial America in general – will continue to disintegrate if vigorous action is not taken." But the administration will not impose import quotas and hurt consumers. Says the Commerce Department, "It's a fact of life that changes in technology and demand affect an industry's ability to compete. Some people win, some people lose." Most analysts say the losers will be the big, integrated firms. Decentralization, it appears, is steel's key to survival.

Industry gives way to service sector

Washington, D.C.

"This nation is becoming a nation of hamburger stands," said the A.F.L.-C.I.O. in 1974, "a country stripped of industrial capacity and meaningful work, ... a service economy ... busily buying and selling cheeseburgers and root beer floats."

The intervening years have in fact witnessed what is called the "hollowing of American industry." Beset by competition from abroad, American firms shift output to low-wage nations, or they import products, becoming marketers and distributors for foreign firms. Since 1953, manufacturing fell from 30 to 21 percent of gross national product.

Service industries have taken over, creating 10 million jobs in seven years, while 1.5 million were lost in manufacturing. A few economists see the shift as a healthy adaptation to international competition that will allow America to specialize in high-tech services. But most of the new jobs offer low pay and low productivity growth. "The McDonald's counter jobs will offset the McKinsey consultant jobs," says one expert. And industries like trucking, banking and computers rely directly on manufacturing for demand. As a Japanese Toyota director said bluntly, "You can't survive with just a service industry."

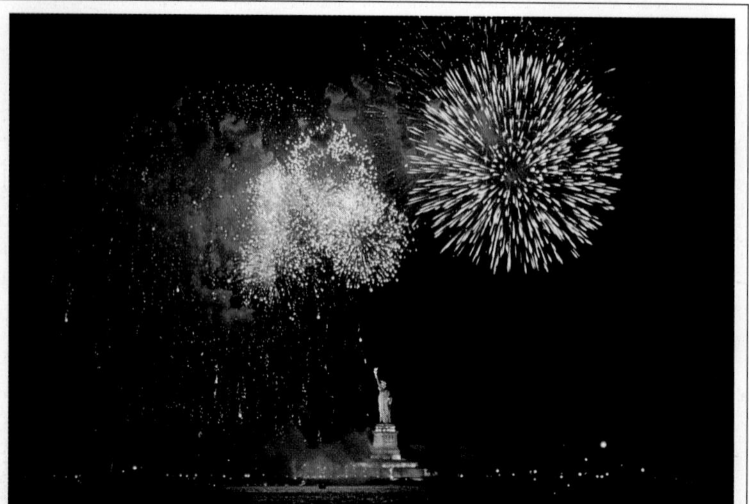

New York City, July 4. *Fireworks light up the Statue of Liberty as America marks the lady's 100th birthday. Thanks to careful restoration, this gift of the French people will stand for another century as a symbol of freedom.*

The United States Bullion Depository at Fort Knox, Kentucky, has held the nation's gold reserves since 1936. It is the gold here that the currency is based on and it is against these reserves that Congress is able to borrow.

High court upholds affirmative action

Washington, D.C., July 2

The Supreme Court today approved the practice of affirmative action to remedy past discrimination against minorities. The 6-3 decision is a blow to the Reagan administration, which has fought to remove employment preference on account of race, color or gender. Assistant Attorney General William Reynolds, speaking for President Reagan, called the ruling "disappointing." But Benjamin Hooks, head of the National Association for the Advancement of Colored People, called it a "significant rebuke to the Reagan administration's pernicious efforts to destroy affirmative action."

Workers hash out beef with Hormel

Austin, Minn., Sept. 12

The P-9 local of the United Food and Commercial Workers Union wearily voted to end a bitter yearlong strike at the Hormel meatpacking plant here today. The new contract restores hourly wages to the levels of the early 1980s, before they were cut from $10.60 to $8.25. The strikers, who have weathered the National Guard and condemnation of their national union leaders, received no guarantees that they will be rehired.

Law offers amnesty to illegal migrants

Washington, D.C., Nov. 7

President Reagan today signed a landmark immigration bill that bans the hiring of illegal aliens. It also offers legal status to immigrants who can prove that they have lived here continuously since January 1, 1982. There are an estimated three million illegal aliens in the United States. The bill imposes fines ranging from $250 to $10,000 on employers who violate its provisions. The President insists it will remove "the incentive for illegal immigration by eliminating the job opportunities." He added, "Future generations of Americans will be thankful for our efforts to humanely regain control of our borders."

"How the Reagan Revolution Failed"

Washington, D.C.

In 1980, David Stockman was, at 34, the wunderkind of the Reagan team, point man on the-slash-and-trim attack. Four and a half years later, the savant of supply-side economics quit his job as budget director and got a job on Wall Street. Now he's back in the news with *The Triumph of Politics: How the Reagan Revolution Failed*, a memoir that depicts the President as a muddle-headed leader who'd rather tell anecdotes than face tough issues.

Iran arms deal revealed

Washington, D.C., Nov. 13

The Reagan administration has confirmed a flood of worldwide reports that it indeed has been sending Iran weapons – against both United States law and official policy – for some time. The bizarre story began to break last week when a pro-Syrian Beirut newspaper, *Al Shirra*, ran a story that said the United States had sent Iran spare parts and ammunition for jet fighters. The newspaper also reported that the United States had airlifted weapons from the Philippines to Iran in four C-130 cargo planes.

Al Shirra also said that White House assistant Robert McFarlane had met in September with Iranian officials in Teheran, who asked for military equipment. About the same time, a spokesman for a Danish maritime union reported that Danish ships had carried at least five loads of arms and ammunition for the United States from Israel to Iran.

By shipping arms to Iran, the Reagan administration has violated the spirit if not the letter of a long string of federal laws that are designed to stop any arms transfers, direct or indirect, to Iran. In addition, the arms sales run totally counter to the administration's worldwide campaign to embargo the sale of all military weaponry to Iran.

Despite a flurry of official "no comments" along with "off-the-record" responses, most observers say that the objective of the arms sales was to win the release of the American hostages now held in the Mideast, and to establish some degree of relations with the government of the Ayatollah Khomeini.

The arms deal was reportedly organized and carried out by a "crisis management" group within the 46-member National Security Council staff. In addition to McFarlane, a prominent member of the team is marine Lieutenant Colonel Oliver North, a decorated Vietnam veteran and deputy director for political-military affairs at the Security Council. He helped plan the 1983 invasion of Grenada and the April bombing of Libya (→ July 1987).

President faces the nation's press.

Americans do it again. The experimental airplane Voyager becomes the first to circumnavigate the globe non-stop without refueling on December 23. The 25,012-mile trip took nine days three minutes 44 seconds. Piloted by Richard Rutan and Jeana Yeager, Voyager holds 1,500 gallons of fuel.

The Presidential Palace, better known as the White House for obvious reasons, has become the symbol of the American presidency. Home to the nation's chief executives since 1800, the three-story, 100-room mansion has endured the British torch, three expansions and total reconstruction.

1987

Reagan

New York City, Jan. 13. *Today* show celebrates 35th anniversary on television.

Pasadena, California, Jan. 25. New York Giants defeat Denver Broncos, 39-20, in Super Bowl XXI.

South Pacific, Feb. 4. Yacht Liberty regains America's Cup by defeating Australian challenger Australia II.

Washington, D.C., March 18. Congress votes to raise rural highway speed limit from 55 miles per hour to 65.

Los Angeles, June 14. Lakers defeat Boston Celtics for N.B.A. title.

Los Angeles, July. Motorists on freeways use guns to vent traffic frustrations.

New York City, Sept. 11. Anchorman Dan Rather walks off set during *CBS Evening News* over disagreement with management; screen goes blank for five minutes.

Los Angeles, Oct. 1. Host Johnny Carson celebrates 25th anniversary of television's *Tonight Show*.

Washington, D.C., Oct. 23. Senate rejects President Reagan's nomination of Robert Bork for Supreme Court associate justice.

Minnesota, Oct. 25. Twins defeat St. Louis Cardinals in World Series, four games to three.

New York City, Nov. 11. Vincent Van Gogh's painting *Irises* sells for $53.9 million, highest price ever for an auctioned painting.

Washington, D.C., Nov. 15. Mr. Potato Head vows to Surgeon General C. Everett Koop that he is giving up his 35-year-old pipe smoking habit, as part of American Cancer Society's anti-smoking campaign.

New York City, Nov. 17. Columbia University loses 40th straight football game, setting an all-time record.

Chicago, Nov. 23. Mayor Harold Washington's sudden death precipitates a heated power struggle among city's black and white aldermen.

Hollywood, Calif. Top films this year include *Platoon, Wall Street, Broadcast News, The Untouchables, The Last Emperor* and *Empire of the Sun.*

Evangelist Bakker toppled in sex scandal

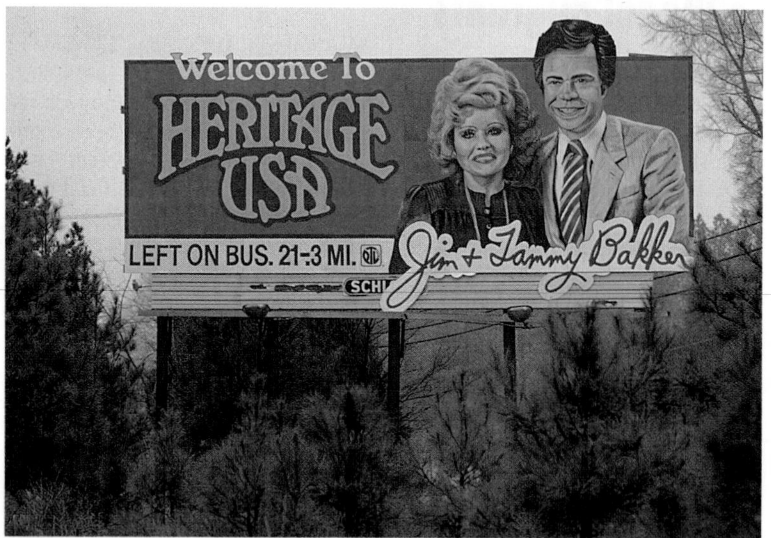

Smiling down from on high, though there doesn't seem much to smile about.

Springfield, Missouri, May 6

The governing board of the Assemblies of God voted today to strip Jim Bakker of his ordination. Bakker has been in the midst of a sex and money scandal since early this year. The founder of the tremendously successful PTL Club television ministry has admitted to a "sexual encounter" in December of 1980 and claims to have been blackmailed as a result. Since news of Bakker's indiscretion became public, donations to PTL (Praise the Lord, People That Love), which previously received over $100 million a year from viewers, have fallen sharply (as have donations to other television ministries).

When Bakker resigned as head of PTL March 20, the new governing board of the ministry was headed by Jerry Falwell, the founder of the Moral Majority and host of the *Old Time Gospel Hour*. This was an unusual development since Falwell has been outspoken in his opposition to the Pentecostal movement. Still, it points to important contact between various elements within the so-called religious right.

The scandal over Jim Bakker's sexual liaison with Jessica Hahn has been titillating the country for months. Stories about Bakker and his wife and partner Tammy Faye have been widely reported. Their luxurious style of life, Tammy's heavy use of makeup and their seeming unawareness of public opinion have also been material for satire and humor.

Marvel or albatross? Scrapped by President Carter but salvaged by President Reagan, the B-1 bomber is intended to replace the aging B-52. Many Americans, however, question whether it's worth $283 million per plane.

Andy Warhol, guru of Pop Art, is dead

New York City, Feb. 21

After surviving the excessive life style of his acolytes and an assassination attempt by the lone member of S.C.U.M. (Society for Cutting Up Men), Andy Warhol died today of complications resulting from surgery. After working in commercial illustration, Warhol initiated the Pop Art movement with his deadpan representations of banal objects, from Campbell's Soup cans to dollar bills and celebrities such as Elvis Presley and Marilyn Monroe. Warhol manufactured his own stars, from the people who were associated with his studio, The Factory, and his films.

Andy Warhol took art to its extremes, creating a new genre in the process.

Robot at sea finds Civil War's Monitor

Hatteras, N.C., July 23

A deep-sea robot descended 220 feet to survey the Monitor, a warship that sank 125 years ago. The small armored ship, built for the Union navy in the Civil War, fought only one battle against the Confederate enemy before it went down with a crew of 20 in a storm off Cape Hatteras. The navy and other organizations are leading a 10-day survey using electronic devices to learn whether the ship is salvageable. The Monitor was equipped with many "firsts," including armor plating and a flush toilet.

G.E. divests itself of electronics unit

Fairfield, Conn., July 22

General Electric announced today that it is selling its $3 billion-a-year consumer electronics operations to Thomson S.A., the electronics company run by the French government. The G.E. move stunned the electronics industry, with Zenith now the only major American manufacturer of videocassettes and TV sets. John Welch, chairman of General Electric, said consumer electronics has been a company "stepchild." In light of Japanese competition, the Americans have increasingly been bowing out of the price-cutting wars.

General Electric's TV, VCR, radio, telephone and tape recorder units will all go to Thomson, one of the world's largest electronics companies, in exchange for $800 million and Thomson's medical equipment business, a sector where G.E. is expanding. Some 31,000 employees will transfer to Thomson.

Colonel Oliver North takes the stand

Washington, D.C., July

After seven months of invoking the Fifth Amendment's protection against self-incrimination, Lieutenant Colonel Oliver North has finally told his version of the Iran-contra affair and his role in it. Testifying before Senate and House investigating committees under a grant of limited immunity, North spent six full days artfully defending his actions in the illegal arms-for-hostages deal, saying that "I assumed that the President was aware of what I was doing and had, through my superiors, approved." He claimed that he had sent five memoranda to the President through Admiral John Poindexter, Reagan's national security adviser, requesting permission to divert money from the Iranian arms sales to the contras. North's hard-hitting testimony left the impression that the late director of the Central Intelligence Agency, William J. Casey, had masterminded the financing of the contras with profits from the Iranian arms sales. North said that Casey referred to this operation as "the ultimate irony, the ultimate covert operation."

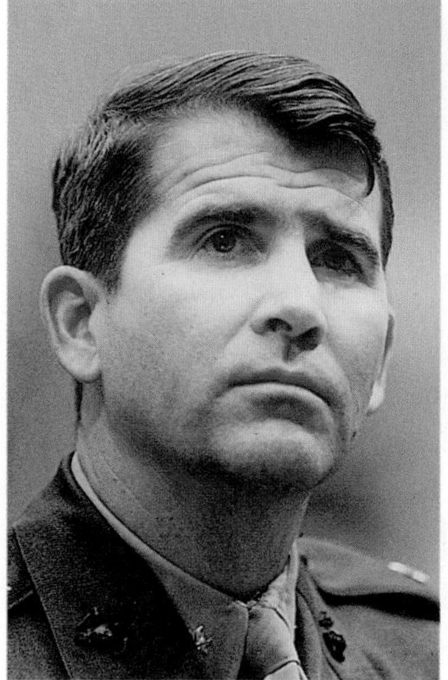

North: American hero or villain?

Referring to Casey as his "personal friend and adviser," North said that he had "never disagreed with any of the things I was doing."

North's testimony has evoked mixed reactions. Democratic Senator Daniel Inouye, presiding over the hearings, said that the Iran-contra arms-for-hostages operation was a naked attempt to create a "secret government within our government." In a *Time* magazine poll conducted two weeks ago, 60 percent of the respondents said they sympathized with the 43-year-old marine officer, but only 51 percent saw him as totally truthful. Still, 69 percent felt he should not go to jail for his Iran-contra activities.

North was described by Neil Livingstone, a former counter-terrorist colleague, as a man who came "into the N.S.C. as an easel carrier and ended up as the world's most powerful lieutenant colonel." He has also emerged as a loose cannon, or an American hero (→Nov. 19).

America faces up to Japanese challenge

Washington, D.C.

Launching a new attempt to fight off Japan's economic challenge, Congress barred Japanese construction firms from public works projects on December 17. On the high-tech battleground, President Reagan imposed high duties on Japanese electronics in March. And in January, a Pentagon-C.I.A. study convinced semiconductor firms to cooperate in order to keep America ahead in the silicon chip race.

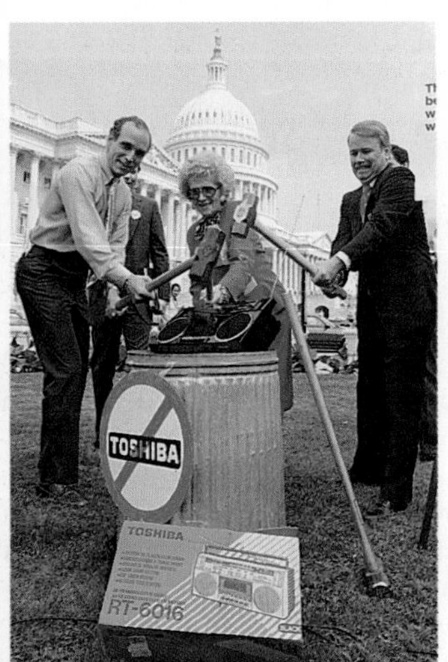

Japan-bashing: U.S. legislators smash a Toshiba radio with zeal.

Why such an uproar? Soaring exports in automobiles, textiles, televisions and computer chips have given Japan bigger trading profits than any other nation. As the world's biggest creditor, the small Pacific nation spreads its capital far and wide. In 1985, the Japanese bought $6 billion worth of American real estate. Mazda, Mitsubishi, Honda and Fuji-Isuzu are opening plants in the Midwest. And American industry appears to be abdicating in the face of the onslaught. Says economist Nestor Terleckyj, "If Ford ... can make money by making loans, it will become a bank and let the Japanese make more and more of its cars." But with the American corporations providing services instead of making things, and the balance of payments going in their competitors' favor, the American role in the world economy may soon be far different from what it was in an earlier time.

Black American middle class is growing

New York City, August

The total of middle-class blacks in America has more than doubled between 1969 and 1984, according to an article in *Ebony* magazine. The report defines "middle class" as taxpayers with an income between $20,000 and $50,000. While nearly half of all white families are middle class, the article says, only about 30 percent of black families fall into the category. Two-fifths of middle-class blacks, *Ebony* reports, have some college education, while one-fourth have completed four years of advanced schooling. Although these statistics show some gains for blacks, a report from the National Urban League says that Reagan policies have hurt them.

In the wake of the Iran-contra affair, President Reagan assembles the National Security Council staff to outline its new system of operation.

▷

Stock market tumbles by 508 points

Panic! The New York Stock Exchange goes wild as millions of dollars are lost.

New York City, Oct. 19

The stock market plunged 508 points today. The debacle was described by the New York Stock Exchange chairman as "the nearest thing to a meltdown that I ever want to see." The rout was the worst day in history, wiping out more than $500 billion in stock equity. It came on an awesome volume of 604 million shares, almost double the previous record set last Friday, when stocks plunged 108.35 points. After topping out at a record 2,722.42 on August 25, the Dow Jones industrial average has plummeted 1,000 points, or 36 percent – nearly three times the calamitous decline that ushered in the Great Depression.

With the tape running two hours late, desperate stockholders flooded phone lines in vain. It seemed everyone who owned mutual fund shares wanted to switch to any other kind, all at once, so that almost no one could get through with an order. One official at Kemper Financial Services said, "We've just seen a genuine panic." Fidelity, which increased its 24-hour telephone staff by 20 percent over the weekend, expects 200,000 calls tomorrow, up from 115,000 today. In a business that loves a laugh, the head of Drexel Burnham's equity desk said, "This is not a laughing matter." At Shearson Lehman Brothers, traders tacked up a sign: "To the lifeboats!"

The White House tried to buoy spirits with news that President Reagan was watching the collapse "with concern," and that he remains certain "that the underlying economy is sound." But the stockholders wanted more, studying tickers and television in search of answers that they failed to find. One New York actor said that he was being battered, but couldn't get through to his broker so he could sell out. Others were holding firm. "The only way for people to stop something like this," one of them advised "is to stop the panic and hold their stock" (→ Feb. 2, 1988).

Fairness Doctrine abolished by F.C.C.

Washington, D.C., Aug. 4

The Federal Communications Commission, in a historic action expected to fuel a war with Congress, today scrapped a 38-year-old policy requiring broadcasters to air all sides of controversial issues. In a unanimous vote, the F.C.C. said the Fairness Doctrine is unnecessary because of the number of radio and television stations serving the nation and may be unconstitutional since it gives the government editorial control over broadcasters. A storm of protest comes from citizen groups and Congress. The F.C.C. said the ruling did not affect "equal time," "reasonable access" or "issue-responsive programming."

Pope says Catholics must not dissent

Detroit, Mich., Sept. 19

Pope John Paul II, in a statement issued today, ignored the request of American bishops that he affirm his belief in freedom of speech. Instead, the Pope declared that dissent from the Magisterium was incompatible with being a Catholic. This statement is destined to fuel the continuing controversy over dissent in the Roman Catholic Church in America. All during his trip to the United States the pontiff praised its Constitution but reminded Catholics that the church is not a democracy.

Pope, in the U.S., is firm on dissent.

United States retaliates against Iran for attacks in Persian Gulf

The long arm of America. U.S. makes Iran pay for attack in Kuwaiti waters.

Washington, D.C., Oct. 19

The navy reported today that two of its warships have shelled an Iranian oil platform in the Persian Gulf. According to Pentagon sources, the two destroyers approached the platform, announced their intention to attack, and called for the workmen to abandon it. After the Iranians had climbed down from the platform, the American warships threw salvo after salvo of 5-inch cannon fire at the rig, leaving it ablaze.

The strike retaliates for an Iranian missile attack, on October 16, on a U.S.-flagged tanker off Kuwait. In May, an Iraqi missile hit the U.S. frigate Stark, killing 37 sailors. (→ July 1988).

Superpowers sign first missile reduction treaty

Washington, D.C., Dec. 8

The United States and the Soviet Union formally agreed to the first comprehensive arms control treaty in the nuclear age today. Coming after the serious breakdown in their arms limitations talks in Reykjavik, Iceland, President Reagan and General Secretary Gorbachev announced the terms of the far-reaching Intermediate Nuclear Forces (I.N.F.) treaty, which will go into effect as soon as the legislatures of both nations complete the ratification process.

The treaty calls for the elimination of ballistic and Cruise missiles that have striking ranges of up to 3,500 miles. Under the terms of the treaty, the United States is to dismantle and destroy its 102 Pershing-2 missiles now based in West Germany and its 256 ground-launched Cruise missiles currently in place in Britain, West Germany, Italy and Belgium. In turn, the Russians have agreed to destroy 132 SS-4 and SS-12's as well as 441 SS-20 missiles, each of which carries three warheads. The treaty means the Russians have agreed to destroy more than four times as many nuclear warheads (1,500) as the Americans (350). Elimination of the intermediate-range missiles will result in the reduction of the combined American-Soviet inventory of nuclear warheads by about 4 percent.

Thousands of warheads still exist, but the world can rest a little easier.

To insure that both sides comply with the I.N.F. treaty, a comprehensive set of verification procedures will be implemented. Observers from the United States will be stationed in the Soviet Union. In turn, Soviet inspectors will be posted in America. Each team of observers will carry out 20 scheduled inspections during the first three years of the treaty. Other "surprise" inspections will be conducted if either team regards it as necessary. The first team of Soviet inspectors is to be stationed at Magna, Utah, while its American counterpart will be stationed in Votkinsk, about 600 miles from Moscow (→ May 31, 1988).

Iran-contra report blames the President

Washington, D.C., Nov. 19

The House and Senate committees investigating the Reagan administration's handling of the Iran-contra affair have concluded that "the common ingredients of the Iran and contra policies were secrecy, deception, and disdain for the law." The 690-page congressional report states, "The ultimate responsibility for the events in the Iran-contra affair must rest with the President ... If the President did not know what his national security advisers were doing, he should have." The minority reports of the committees took issue with the majority position, which it termed a bunch of "hysterical conclusions."

Riots by Cubans rock 2 Southern prisons

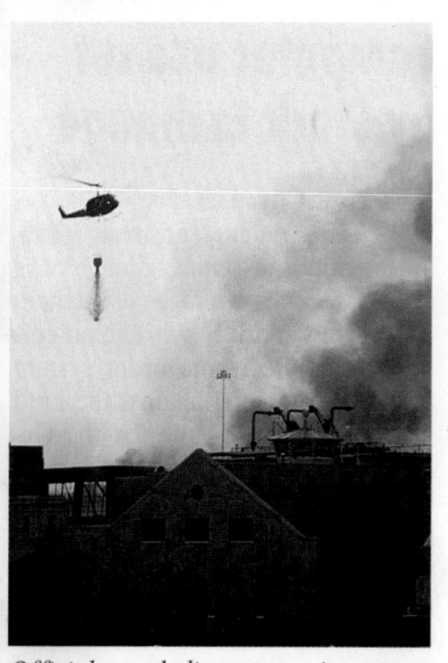

Officials use helicopter at riot scene.

Atlanta, Georgia, Dec. 4

Cuban inmates at the federal prison here released 89 hostages today, ending the 11-day riot over plans to return the prisoners to Cuba. Riots here and at a detention center at Oakdale, Louisiana, left one man dead and more than 20 injured. The Oakdale center is a charred ruin and the Atlanta prison severely damaged. The Oakdale riot ended November 29. The riots began after President Reagan announced a plan to deport the inmates, who arrived in the 1980 boatlift from the Cuban port of Mariel. Most committed crimes in the United States and were awaiting deportation. Cuba has agreed to accept the inmates.

Amerasian children find home in America

Bangkok, Thailand, Dec. 31

They were greeted with gifts of American flags and picture books titled *This Is America* when they arrived in Bangkok today. A group of 65 of the many Vietnamese fathered by Americans during the Vietnam War are headed to the land of their fathers – the United States. They left Vietnam, some with family members, under the renewal of a resettlement program stalled for two years. The program, which began in 1979, has resettled 4,000 Vietnamese-Americans in the states. At least 10,000 are still in Vietnam. The process was halted by Hanoi in 1986, because of the complexity of screening procedures; the United States has since simplified the process. Most of these Amerasians, whose average age is 18, expressed a desire to see their fathers. Many noted the pain of growing up with a Western face in Vietnam, and hoped for a new acceptance.

15 billion photos

Rochester, N.Y., January

The photographic exposure took up to eight hours when first invented, but now, 150 years after the debut of photography, the snapshot rules. Americans click their shutters 15 billion times a year, taking an average of 155 photos per household. Some 400 million rolls of film are purchased by the 95 percent of American families who own cameras. What would Louis Daguerre, who published the first photography manual 150 years ago this month, have to say about the new Fujicolor Quick Snap, the first throwaway camera?

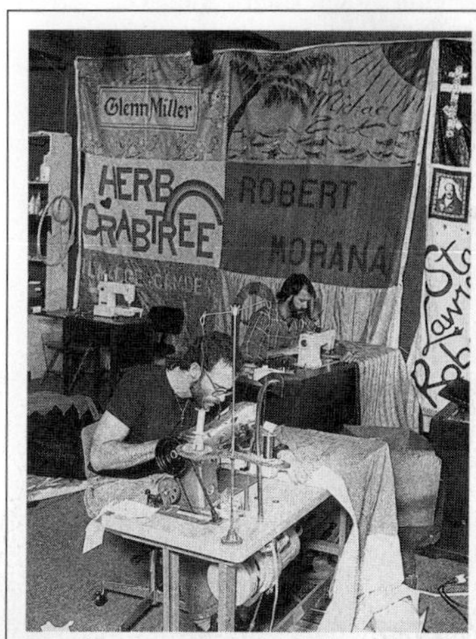

Workers stitch a quilt bearing the names of AIDS victims to be displayed in the capital in November.

1988

Reagan

New Orleans, Jan. 31. Washington Redskins defeat Denver Broncos, 42-10, in Super Bowl XXII.

Los Angeles, Jan. 21. Lakers defeat Detroit Pistons, four games to three, for N.B.A. title.

Washington, D.C., Feb. 5. United States indicts Panama's General Manuel Noriega, on drug smuggling charges.

Washington, D.C., Feb. 18. Anthony Kennedy is sworn in as Associate Justice of Supreme Court.

Washington, D.C., March 13. I. King Jordan becomes president of Gallaudet University, institute of higher learning for deaf, following series of protests by students opposing earlier appointment of president who can hear.

New York City, March 31. Pulitzer Prize awarded to Toni Morrison for *Beloved.*

Phoenix, Arizona, Apr. 4. Governor Evan Mecham removed from office by state legislature, because of campaign fund diversions.

Atlanta, May 5. Eugene Antonio Marino installed as archbishop of Atlanta, becoming nation's first black Roman Catholic archbishop.

Washington, D.C., June 14. White House chief of staff Howard Baker resigns post after having restored order to White House in wake of Iran-contra affair.

Atlanta, July 21. Michael Dukakis of Massachusetts nominated for President (→Aug. 17).

Hollywood, Calif., Aug. 12. Film *Last Temptation of Christ* released, sparking protests across nation.

New Orleans, Aug. 17. George Bush nominated for President (→Nov. 8).

San Diego, California, Sept. 9. Catamaran Stars & Stripes defeats challenger New Zealand, for America's Cup.

Gulf of Mexico, Sept. 17. Hurricane Gilbert batters Texas coast with 218 mph winds, worst in state history.

Los Angeles, Oct. 20. Dodgers defeat Oakland A's, four games to one, in World Series.

Hollywood, Calif. Movies this year include *Bull Durham, Big* and *Working Girl.*

Evangelist Swaggart falls from grace

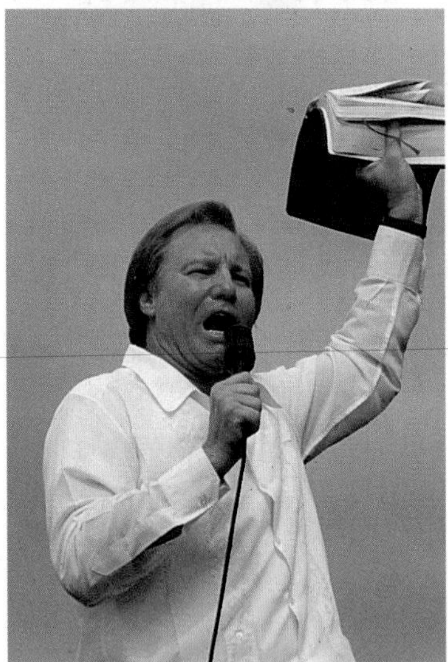

Jimmy Swaggart of the Bible belt.

Baton Rouge, Louisiana, Feb. 21

In yet another installment of religion and sex, the television evangelist Jimmy Swaggart has admitted to visiting a prostitute. "I have sinned against you, and I beg your forgiveness," said Swaggart in a tear-flooded confession to his congregation. Swaggart, a flamboyant preacher, was among the most virulent in denouncing Jim Bakker last year when a sex scandal rocked the latter's ministry. Swaggart, who called Bakker a "cancer on the body of Christ," was forced to humble himself after church officials were shown photographs of Swaggart's visit to a prostitute.

The Bakker and Swaggart scandals have brought television ministers under greater public scrutiny. This will increase in the future as Pat Robertson's campaign for the presidency develops. Robertson, founder of the 700 Club television ministry, is an outspoken representative of fundamentalist Christianity and political conservatism. It remains to be seen whether these scandals will affect the Robertson campaign.

Sandinistas reach truce with contras

Washington, D.C., March 24

News received from Nicaragua today confirms that the pro-Communist Sandinista government has signed a temporary cease-fire agreement with the contra rebels. At a news conference in Managua, President Daniel Ortega reportedly said to his old foes, "We are here together determined to bury the ax of war and raise the olive branch of peace." In response, contra leader Alfonse Calero noted, "Today we have taken a first and firm step to end this fratricidal war."

The terms of the cease-fire require that the Sandinista government release its 3,000 contra prisoners; in return, the contras have promised to recognize the Ortega regime as being the legitimate government of Nicaragua and to refuse further military assistance from foreign governments.

Troops in Honduras to warn Sandinistas

Washington, D.C., March 19

The State Department said today that 3,000 soldiers of the 82nd Airborne Division are being airlifted to bases in Honduras. They will serve as reinforcememts for the 3,000 troops that have moved to the area over the past several months. Secretary of State George Shultz says that the American forces will not actively participate in any Honduran military action against Sandinista troops. The Nicaraguan soldiers have reportedly been crossing the border into Honduras in "hot pursuit" of contra forces taking refuge in that country. Honduran jet fighters have bombed Sandinista troops twice this week after they chased contra soldiers into Honduras.

State Department officials said the administration believes that the reinforcememt of American forces will serve to inhibit the Sandinistas while giving a psychological boost to the contra troops (→24).

The 82nd hits the ground during Golden Pheasant operation in Honduras.

Farmers better off

Washington, D.C., Feb 15

America's farmers seem to be more prosperous now than at any time in this decade. While at least 10 percent of farmers are in debt, their cash income has reached $58 billion, up from, $37 billion in 1983. Farm debt has dropped more than 28 percent since 1983. The continuing drought in the South and Midwest, however, is expected to take a heavy toll on agriculture later in the year.

Computer use cut by Stock Exchange

New York City, Feb. 2

Big-time traders who make a killing buying and selling giant blocks in split seconds won't have the help of the New York Stock Exchange's Super Dot electronic order system any more. Moving against the kind of trading some blame for the October crash, Big Board directors have decided that during big swings the system will be barred to giant traders who program their computers to take advantage of small differences between the prices of stocks and stock index futures.

Income disparities growing in nation

Washington, D.C., Apr. 30

According to the Census Bureau, the economic separation between the upper-income and lower-income Americans keeps growing. A sampling of some 60,000 American homes showed incomes averaging $36,300. And while the annual income for the top 5 percent rose by over $6,000 during the 1980s, average income for the poor decreased by more than $7,000.

The study illustrates the uneven success of the economic boom of the mid-1980s. The growth of a service economy and the premium placed on technological know-how have left many less educated workers, particularly those formerly employed in heavy industries, with few opportunities. The need for temporary employees has risen, but such jobs rarely provide adequate family-supporting income.

America in decline?

United States

As the American Century nears an end, some fear the nation's glory days will end "not with a bang but a whimper." One gloomy seer is Paul Kennedy, author of *The Rise and Fall of the Great Powers: Economic Change and Military Conflict From 1500 to 2000.* The Yale professor says the United States, now a victim of "imperial overstretch," will sink under global commitments while other nations grow stronger.

Pentagon unveils Stealth bomber

Washington, D.C., Apr. 20

The U.S. Air Force today released pictures of the B-2 or Stealth bomber, a project it has kept secret for 10 years. The artist's rendering shows a tailless, multiple-engine boomerang-shaped craft that resembles the YB-49 Flying Wing developed by Northrop in the late 1940s. The plane is built from materials that make it virtually invisible to radar. The air force would not provide information regarding the bomber's dimensions, size of crew and payload.

Reagan visits changing Soviet Union

Ronald Reagan in the heart of what he once called "the evil empire."

Moscow, May 31

President Reagan's trip to the Soviet Union has had mixed results so far. According to Howard Baker, White House chief of staff, Reagan and Soviet leader Mikhail Gorbachev collided almost immediately after they met formally. Sparks flew as Reagan assailed the Soviet Union's human rights record. One Russian spokesman said flatly, "We don't like it when someone from the outside is teaching us how to live, and that is only natural." So far, the two leaders have produced no significant agreements. But they recognized the need of continuing the thaw in the cold war and of maintaining a dialogue on the crucial issues of disarmament and the resolution of regional conflicts.

While Reagan has had his problems with Gorbachev, he apparently is well-liked by the Soviet people. Today, he met with 600 students and intellectuals at Moscow State University and was welcomed with enthusiasm. Explaining why the President is so popular with the Russian people, a Soviet editor said, "Reagan is a simple man. He likes astrology, and he was an actor."

In spite of his initial conflict with Gorbachev, it seems that Reagan has begun to realize that the "evil empire" he spoke about in earlier years is perhaps no longer all that evil, and that the era of "perestroika," or economic restructuring, and "glasnost," or openness, represents a new and positive phase in the U.S.-Soviet relationship (→Dec. 7).

After four decades, the cold war just may be finally ending

New York City

The year 1988 will pass into history as the year the cold war ended, say those who think Mikhail Gorbachev means what he said at the United Nations December 7. Though the Russian Revolution "radically changed the course of world development," the Soviet leader said, "today we face a different world, for which we must seek a different road to the future." He said "closed" societies are impossible, because "the world economy is becoming a single organism." He also spoke out for individual rights, calling freedom of choice "mandatory." The Gorbachev remarks came four decades after the term "cold war" first came into use, a time when Stalin called on the Soviet Union to defend itself because there would be wars as long as there were capitalist nations. Moscow swallowed neighbors, dropped an Iron Curtain around them and entered an arms race. Gorbachev told the U.N. to "let historians argue who is to blame for it," and proceeded to proclaim the cold war over, saying he will reduce Soviet arms, use capitalist economic techniques and allow political freedom. So powerful is his message that he is winning such unlikely allies as British Prime Minister Margaret Thatcher. She feels the cold war is indeed over and "it is in the Western interest" for Gorbachev to succeed But many in Washington still hold back, causing some to think they mean "nyet" when they say "not yet." Gorbachev is waiting for a sign from Vice President Bush.

▷

Yellowstone National Park is burning

Forest fires ravage Yellowstone.

Yellowstone Park, Wyo. July 27

The oldest national park in the nation is ablaze and firefighters said today that they haven't been able to control the 12 separate wildfires. One experienced park official called it "the worst inferno I've seen in 17 years." The fires have consumed more than 88,000 acres of lush timber land and are threatening to isolate the famed geyser Old Faithful. Fortunately, the park is so large - 2.2 million acres – that the animals can stay out of the path of the fires and still have plenty of room to roam. Authorities at the park say that the fires are not likely to be completely extinguished until the extended drought is broken by some good rains.

While the fire has blackened the mountains this year, experts say that no permanent harm has been done. The fire releases nutrients in the form of burned trees and other vegetation, which is an excellent form of natural fertilizer. Also, as the heat from the fire warms the pine cones, they open and drop the seeds that one day will grow into a new generation of trees. As one of the park officials put it, "Life and geysers go on."

Americans return to space with Discovery

Cape Canaveral, Fla., Sept. 29

The shuttle Discovery blasted flawlessly into orbit today, heralding a long-awaited comeback for the beleaguered American space program. An unspoken tension surrounded the launching, at 11:37 a.m., reaching a peak as the Discovery, riding the familiar billowing white smoke trail, passed the 73-second mark, the point at which the Challenger exploded, plunging NASA into a somber 32 months of redesign of the shuttle fleet and reassessment of the nation's space goals. Six hours later the craft's five-man crew launched a $100 million communications satellite. Said one official: "We're back in business, and it hasn't been easy."

Age of Discovery begins anew.

Crack and other drugs plague inner cities

United States

"Our children are hooked on drugs that have come straight from the pit of hell," a Brooklyn minister said recently. Indeed, the inner cities of America are being ravaged by crack, an inexpensive, mind-numbingly addictive form of cocaine. In the ghettos, where the family barely exists as a social unit, almost a whole generation is being swept into a netherworld of drug addiction and violent street gangs, armed with semi-automatic weapons, who kill to keep control of drug-selling zones. Older addicts, more likely to use narcotics such as heroin, face the added danger of AIDS, which is spread by shared hypodermic needles. The older addicts are often the parents of crack users, completing a cycle of despair.

Gulf war ends; U.S. downs Iran airliner

Washington, D.C., July

The "on again, off again" war between Iran and Iraq drew to a close this month in spite of a deadly error by an American destroyer that many had feared would prolong the conflict. Only 16 days after an American ship shot down an Iranian airliner with 290 passengers aboard, Iran's Ayatollah Khomeini on July 20 agreed to the United Nations cease-fire plan. On Teheran radio, Khomeini recalled he "had promised to fight to the last drop of my blood and my last breath." Changing this decision, he said, "was more deadly than taking poison." But he said he decided to end the war "based only on the interest of the Islamic republic."

One frightening aspect of the airliner tragedy was that the destroyer Vincennes mistakenly identified the big airliner as a hostile fighter plane and downed it only days after the speaker of the Iranian Parliament, Hojatolislam Hashemi Rafsanjani, had stated that Teheran was willing to accept an immediate cease-fire. After the plane was downed, Washington apologized for the loss of life and tried during its inquiry to calm the troubled waters.

The war caused a million casualties and involved the United States as defender of oil routes in the gulf.

Drugs are no stranger to the streets, but crack, a cocaine derivative, is particularly heinous, leaving violence in its wake. Mural by Keith Haring.

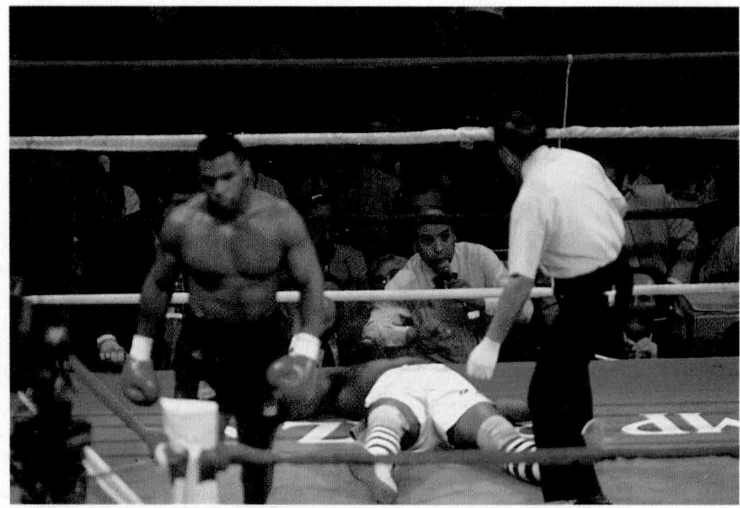
Atlantic City, N.J., June 27. *Mike Tyson walks away from a floored Michael Spinks; he earns $200,000 a second and retains his heavyweight title.*

Gorbachev, at the U.N., offers troop cuts

New York City, Dec. 7

Mikhail Gorbachev announced today that he is willing to make major troop and weapon reductions in Eastern Europe. Speaking before the United Nations General Assembly, the Soviet leader said that he would reduce the Red Army in Europe by at least 500,000 soldiers and 10,000 tanks. These proposed cuts would shrink Soviet military personnel by 10 percent and armor strength by 25 percent. Although the Gorbachev offer has startled some Western observers, his plans to shift the Soviet military strategy from an offensive to a defensive posture has been under discussion for some time. Over the past three years, the Russians have stated that a large-scale conventional war in Europe would be almost as catastrophic in its results as would a nuclear war. Their military leadership has now been instructed to make the prevention of war, rather than victory in one, their principal objective.

Although the proposed Soviet reductions are significant, the Warsaw Pact forces will still have a decided superiority over NATO in manpower, tanks and artillery. Nevertheless, President Reagan expressed satisfaction with the Gorbachev offer, saying, "I heartily approve" of the plan. President-elect George Bush, echoing "the Gipper," stated simply, "I support what the President says."

U.S. talks to P.L.O.

Carthage, Tunisia, Dec. 16

The United States and the Palestine Liberation Organization began formal talks here today, ending Washington's 13-year ban on contacts with the P.L.O. Resumption follows by just two days P.L.O. chairman Yasir Arafat's acceptance of three American conditions. In an about-face, Arafat now says he recognizes Israel, renounces terrorism and accepts United Nations Security Council Resolutions 242 and 338 as the basis for Middle East peace. Today's historic 90-minute meeting is seen by many observers as a potential breakthrough in the conflict.

Selling out America

United States

The latest economic crisis to hit the nation is the apparent "selling out" of major industries and assets to foreigners, particularly the British, Japanese, Canadians and Dutch. Foreign investment in the United States, now running at $200 billion a year, has increased six times since 1974. Some states are even competing to attract the business. The phenomenon has three main causes: the cheap dollar, strong consumer markets here and a huge capital surplus overseas. At the current rate, however, all reducible assets (that is, those except land) in the country will be sold in 50 years.

U.S.-Canada pact

Ottawa, Canada, Dec. 24

Overcoming fears that Canada might lose its economic independence, the House of Commons today "chose an instrument that promises more jobs and more wealth for future generations of Canadians." In a 141-111 vote, Canada's legislative body approved a major free-trade agreement between Canada and the United States. Designed to increase the gross national product of the two nations and counter the economic integration of Western Europe that is set for 1992, the pact provides for the elimination of all tariffs and trade barriers between the world's largest trading partners.

Is America happy?

New York City, Dec. 24

The Fordham Institute for Innovation in Social Policy reported today that problems in America, from the growing income gap to the teenage suicide rate, are getting steadily worse. How, then, explain a Gallup poll showing 56 percent of the public content with "the way things are going." Maybe facts are no match for feeling, reality a puny rival of dreams. Despite homelessness, joblessness, drugs, AIDS and a rising cost of living, many look back on the nation's history with a sense of gradual gains for all, saying that life, liberty and happiness have come in their own sweet time.

George Bush sweeps to 40-state victory

Washington, D.C., Nov. 8

George Herbert Walker Bush, a decorated hero of World War II, was elected President of the United States today, winning 40 of the 50 states to defeat Governor Michael Dukakis of Massachusetts, his Democratic challenger. The final tally showed Bush with 426 electoral votes to 112 for Dukakis. He will take office January 20, succeeding Ronald Reagan, whom he served as Vice President for eight years.

Bush: Assuming Reagan's mantle.

Bush, a New Englander who made his fortune in the oil fields of Texas, is the first sitting Vice President elected to the nation's highest office since Martin Van Buren in 1836. The Bush running mate, Senator Dan Quayle of Indiana, was elected Vice President.

This year's campaign was viewed by many voters as one of the most negative in the nation's history. Bush repeatedly attacked Governor Dukakis on such issues as a dirty Boston harbor, prison furloughs for felons and the death penalty, accusing him of being too liberal. During their nationally televised debates, as well as in stump speeches, Bush often avoided taking firm stands on critical issues. But he did slam the door on any rise in taxes, despite the soaring national debt. The next President's stand on this crucial issue is almost certain to lead to an intense political struggle with Congress, which stays in control of the Democrats in spite of the Dukakis defeat.

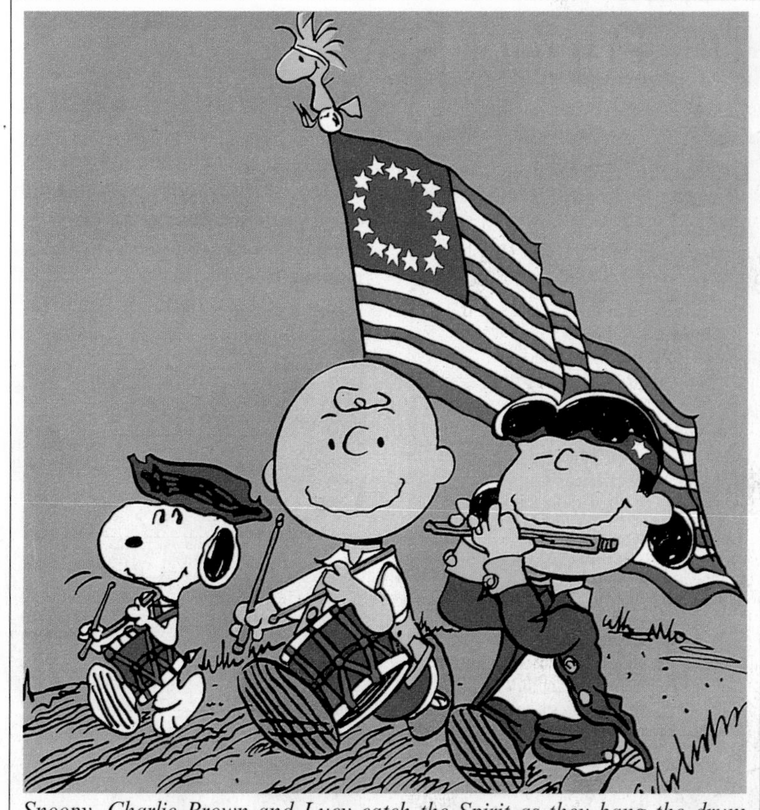

Snoopy, Charlie Brown and Lucy catch the Spirit as they bang the drum for Old Glory. The Peanuts gang typifies the way we like to think American kids grow up in an average community, happy, secure and above all, free.

1989

Bush

Stockton, Calif., Jan. 17.
A crazed gunman opens fire in an elementary school, killing five children before committing suicide.

Miami, Jan. 18.
Two days of race riots leave a total of six people shot and 250 arrested.

Miami, Jan. 22.
San Francisco 49ers defeat Cincinnati Bengals, 20-16, to win Super Bowl XXIII.

Starke, Florida, Jan. 24.
Serial killer Ted Bundy is executed.

New York City, Feb. 3.
Former first baseman Bill White becomes the first black president of the National League.

Washington, D.C., Feb. 8.
The Rand Corporation reports that women currently earn only 65 percent of men's wages.

Las Vegas, Nevada, Feb. 25.
Mike Tyson retains world heavyweight title after stopping Britain's Frank Bruno in 5th round.

Washington, D.C., March 9
The Senate rejects President Bush's appointment of John Tower as secretary of defense.

Washington, D.C., April 9
An estimated 450,000 people demonstrate in favor of the right to abortion (→ May 23, 1991).

Washington, D.C., May 31.
House Speaker Jim Wright resigns after denying financial improprieties.

Rochester, N.Y., June 18
American golfer Curtis Strange wins U.S. Open.

Sioux City, July 19
A United Airlines DC-10 crashes on landing, killing 148 people.

San Francisco, Oct. 28.
The Oakland A's beat the San Francisco Giants, 9-6, and sweep the World Series.

Los Angeles, Oct. 31.
Sony Corp. buys the stock of Columbia Pictures for $3.4 billion.

Malta, Dec. 3.
After a summit meeting, President Bush and Soviet leader Mikhail Gorbachev hail the end of Cold War.

Hollywood, Calif.
Top movies this year include *Rain Man, Indiana Jones and the Last Crusade* and *Batman.*

Huge oil spill in Alaska

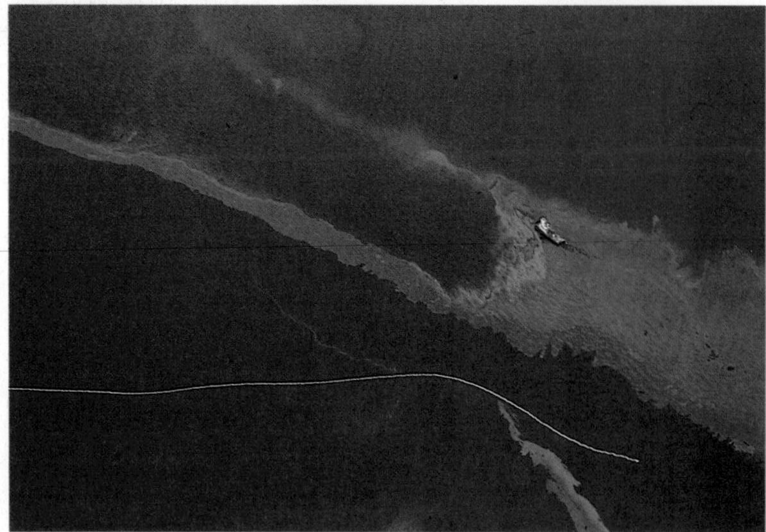

A massive operation to clean up crude oil spilt by the Exxon Valdez.

Alaska, March 30
President Bush today called the spill of 11 million gallons of crude oil a "major tragedy." A week after the 987-foot supertanker Exxon Valdez ran aground on a reef soon after sailing from Valdez, shocked experts estimate that oil has spread over 500 square miles of Alaskan waters and coated hundreds of miles of coastline. The millions of gallons of crude have poured into Prince William Sound, an area rich in marine wildlife and economically crucial to local fishing communities. Angry environmentalists say the clean-up will take years and cost millions. Federal authorities are questioning the ship's captain, Joseph Hazelwood, who is reported to have been in his cabin at the time of the accident.

George Bush sworn in as 41st president

Washington, D.C., Jan. 20
George Bush today took the oath of office to become the nation's 41st president. He thanked President Ronald Reagan for "the wonderful things you have done for America," but implied that his administration would not be a carbon copy of his predecessor's. In what is perhaps a comparison with the Reagan presidency, Bush vowed "to celebrate the quieter, deeper successes that are made not of gold and silk, but of better hearts and finer souls."

Bush is flanked by his wife, Barbara, and predecessor Ronald Reagan.

Two Libyan fighters shot down by U.S.

The U.S. presents its case at U.N.

Washington, D.C., Jan. 5
The Reagan administration has firmly rejected Libyan claims that yesterday's downing of two Libyan fighters by U.S. Navy aircraft was unprovoked.

Defense Secretary Frank C. Carlucci said two F-14 Tomcats, on combat air patrol from the carrier USS John F. Kennedy, fired their missiles defensively. The Libyan planes, two MiG-23 Floggers, approached in a hostile manner and the F-14s opened fire when the MiGs were just 14 miles away, Carlucci added. Both Libyan pilots parachuted into the sea.

This was the second time U.S. and Libyan warplanes have clashed during the Reagan administration. In 1981, Navy fighters downed two Libyan jets over the Gulf of Sidra.

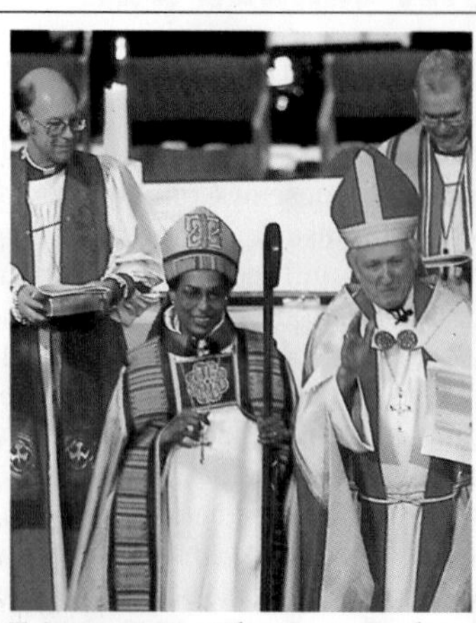

February 11. *The Rev. Barbara Clement becomes the Episcopal Church's first woman bishop.*

Colonel North convicted

Washington, D.C., May 4

The long-running Iran-contra affair at last reached a conclusion of sorts today.

Marine Lieutenant Colonel Oliver North was convicted in federal court on three of 12 counts against him. The jury found that North, a National Security Council aide during the Reagan administration, destroyed and falsified documents, used public funds to pay for a personal security system and aided the obstruction of Congress. But he was acquitted of the most serious charges, one of which was lying to Congress. U.S. District Court Justice Gerhard Gesell fined North $150,000, gave him a three-year suspended sentence and ordered him to perform 1,200 hours of community service. Gesell said North should be viewed as a "low-ranking subordinate working to carry out the initiatives of a few cynical superiors." The trial disclosed much about secret arms sales to Iran and the diversion of funds to Nicaraguan contras. The administration's refusal to release classified documents permitted only circumstantial light to be shed on the roles played by Reagan and then Vice President Bush (→June 11, 1990).

Blast kills 47 seamen aboard USS Iowa

The battleship's huge 16-inch guns explode during training mission.

Atlantic Ocean, April 19

A 16-inch gun turret – the world's largest naval guns – blew up today on the U.S. battleship Iowa. These awesome guns can fire a shell weighing one ton up to 23 miles. The explosion killed 27 sailors who were inside the 17-inch-thick hardened-steel walls of the turret, and a fire tore through the interior to the deck, killing 20 more. The blast occurred as the ship fired a broadside during exercises in the Atlantic, 300 miles northeast of Puerto Rico.

The 58,000-ton warship, built in 1943, is one of the biggest as well as the oldest battleships afloat. She is one of four World War II Iowa-class battleships taken out of mothballs by President Reagan in his drive to give the United States a 600-ship navy. The Iowa was outfitted to carry Tomahawk sea-launched cruise missiles with nuclear warheads.

Today's mystery blast was the first in a U.S. warship's gun turret since 1972, when 20 were killed and 36 injured on a heavy cruiser off Vietnam. The last main-gun explosion on a U.S. battleship took 43 lives aboard the Mississippi during World War II.

Lucille Ball dies; all America loved Lucy

The zany comic was a TV delight.

Los Angeles, April 26

Lucille Ball, perhaps America's best known comic, died today of an aortal rupture at the age of 77. She is best known for her portrayal of the accident-prone hatcher of ridiculous schemes on the television show "I Love Lucy," which ran from 1951 to 1957, with more than 1,000 episodes. The show, which also starred her husband, Desi Arnaz, was the first to be filmed rather than broadcast live, and was also the first to be filmed before a live audience. "I Love Lucy" won five Emmys and continues to delight TV viewers in syndication.

U.S. sanctions after Beijing massacre

Washington, D.C., June 5

Barely 24 hours after Communist Chinese troops killed more than 2,500 pro-democracy students in Beijing, President Bush today suspended all U.S. arms sales to China for an indefinite time.

The White House, however, rejected calls to impose economic sanctions or break diplomatic relations with China. Outraged politicians on Capitol Hill are calling for a firmer U.S. response to the brutal crushing of anti-Communist demonstrations on Tiananmen Square. Live television coverage of the events brought the full horror of the massacre into millions of American homes.

Flag burning is free speech, says Court

Washington, D.C., June 21

In a controversial decision, the Supreme Court has ruled that burning the American flag is "expressive conduct," and therefore a constitutionally protected form of free speech. The case, Texas v. Johnson, dates from 1984, when protesters at the Republican Convention in Dallas burned the flag, chanting "America, the red, white and blue, we spit on you." Gregory Johnson, one of the protesters, was found guilty of violating a Texas law proscribing flag desecration and was sentenced to a year in prison. The issue cropped up in the 1988 presidential race; President Bush came out in favor of anti-desecration laws.

June. *Tim Burton's magnificent "Batman," with Jack Nicholson playing the deliciously evil Joker and Michael Keaton in the role of the Caped Crusader, is a mega-hit nationwide immediately after its release.*

Muslim extremists execute U.S. hostage

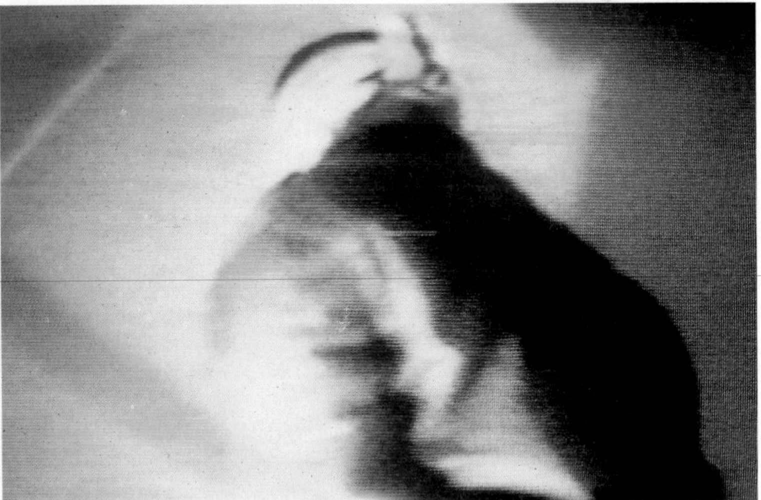

Body of Lt. Col. William R. Higgins, videotaped by his Shiite captors.

Beirut, July 31

A pro-Iranian terrorist group claims to have hanged a senior U.S. military officer, Lieutenant Colonel William R. Higgins. The killing was apparently carried out by a group called the Organization of the Oppressed of the Earth. According to President Bush, Americans "were shocked right to the core" to see a shadowy half-minute videotape showing Higgins hanging by a noose. The American officer had been attached to a U.N. observer force in Lebanon until his abduction on February 17, 1988. Higgins's Shiite captors said the execution was in retaliation for the Israeli kidnapping of Sheik Abdul Karim Obeid, a leader of the pro-Iranian Party of God. Israeli commandos seized the sheik in southern Lebanon three days ago.

Pete Rose banned from game for life

New York City, Aug. 24

Pete Rose has been banned from baseball for life, but continues to deny allegations that he placed bets on ball games. In March it was revealed that Peter Ueberroth, then commissioner of baseball, was investigating "serious allegations" against Rose involving gambling. Commissioner A. Bartlett Giamatti's decision today to ban Rose from the game was the result of a deal in which Rose signed a statement stating that the commissioner had a "factual basis" for banning him, while Giamatti agreed not to make "formal findings or declarations" on the charges.

July 22. *American racer Greg LeMond wins the Tour de France by just eight seconds as France celebrates the bicentennial of its Revolution.*

Hurricane Hugo lashes shores of Carolinas

East Coast, Sept. 21

Hurricane Hugo, the most destructive storm to hit the U.S. in two decades, struck Georgia and the Carolinas after midnight last night. Coastal areas of the Carolinas were wracked by 135-mph winds, and 17-foot walls of water crashed over homes. Damage is expected to climb into the millions. Puerto Rico and the Virgin Islands were the first to feel Hugo's destructive force. The storm left at least 25 dead, hundreds injured and 100,000 homeless in a matter of hours after the storm reached the islands on the 17th. Widespread looting was reported from the Virgin Islands, and 1,000 military police were flown in to restore order.

Wrecked pleasure boats litter the coast of the Carolinas in Hugo's wake.

Bush commits billions to drugs crusade

Washington, D.C., Sept. 5

In a televised address to the nation, President George Bush tonight launched a major offensive against drugs. Showing viewers a bag of crack, Bush urged Americans to work together and said: "Drugs are sapping our strength as a nation. Let there be no mistake, this stuff is poison." The $7.86-billion plan is aimed at reducing both supply and consumption of drugs in the U.S. by 10 percent by 1992 and by 50 percent by the end of the century. Money will also be spent on more prisons and for more police to control what has become a $110-billion industry.

Hotel queen Leona guilty in tax case

New York City, Aug. 30

"Only the little people pay taxes," said Leona Helmsley, but that remark has come back to haunt her. Mrs. Helmsley, president of Helmsley Hotels, Inc., the company founded by her husband, was tried on charges of defrauding the government by claiming personal expenditures as business deductions. Today she was convicted on 33 counts of tax evasion. The bill for back taxes from the years 1983-85 comes to a total of $1.2 million (→Apr. 15, 1992).

September 22. *America's songwriter, Irving Berlin, dies.*

San Francisco devastated by earthquake

A house lists like a sinking ship while ruins smolder in San Francisco.

San Francisco, Oct. 19

At exactly 5:04 p.m. two days ago, an earthquake measuring 6.9 on the Richter scale struck the Bay area. More than 200 people are feared dead. From its epicenter northeast of Santa Cruz on the San Andreas fault, tremors reached north to Sacramento and south to Los Angeles. There was severe damage on the Bay Bridge, where a span collapsed, on Interstate 880, where a half-mile upper section of the highway fell onto the lower one, killing 42, and in the Marina district, where older, less "earthquake-safe" buildings were demolished and a ruptured gas main sparked an inferno. Baseball fans at Candlestick Park held their breath as the stadium swayed, halting the third game of the World Series.

A collapsed part of Bay Bridge.

Evangelist Bakker gets 45-year term

Charlotte, N.C., Oct. 24

Jim Bakker, wearing stone-washed jeans and handcuffs, was led out of a Charlotte courthouse today after being sentenced to 45 years in prison and a $100,000 fine. He had been convicted on October 5 of fleecing followers of his now-bankrupt PTL (Praise the Lord, People That Love) ministries to the tune of $158 million. The 24 counts of fraud and conspiracy are related to the Heritage USA Christian theme park and PTL, both of which he founded.

Judge Robert "Maximum Bob" Potter, who heard the case, stated: "Those of us who do have religion are sick of being saps for money-grubbing preachers and priests." Lawyers for Bakker said that he will appeal the verdict.

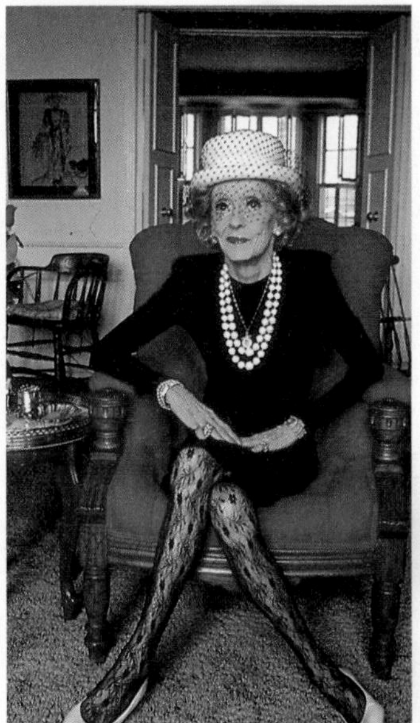

October 6. *The inimitable Bette Davis, star of such classics as "All About Eve" and "Jezebel," died in a Paris hospital today of breast cancer at the age of 81.*

U.S. forces launch invasion of Panama

Panama City, Dec. 20

An estimated 24,000 U.S. troops swept into Panama early today as the Bush administration moved to topple the country's corrupt dictator, General Manuel Antonio Noriega.

Noriega has gone into hiding and is being hunted by U.S. forces. Panama's strongman has already been replaced by Guillermo Endara, who had been elected president by the Panamanian people in a contest voided by Noriega. The U.S. operation, code-named "Just Cause," began with three simultaneous attacks against pro-Noriega strongholds in the capital. U.S. forces quickly took control of much of the area, although they are being harassed by snipers belonging to Noriega's fiercely loyal Dignity Battalions. About 200 civilians, and 19 U.S. and 59 Panamanian soldiers are reported dead. President Bush wants Noriega to stand trial in the U.S. on drug-trafficking charges, and has offered a $1-million reward for information leading to his capture (→ Jan. 4, 1990).

West rejoices over fall of Berlin Wall

United States, Nov. 10

America and its NATO allies are elated today following the dismantling of the world's most visible symbol of Communist oppression. The Berlin Wall, a 28-mile-long concrete and barbed-wire barrier that had divided Berlin ever since August 1961, has fallen at last. East Germans can now freely travel to the West.

Yesterday's historic event came 26 years after President John F. Kennedy stood by the Wall and declared: *"Ich bin ein Berliner."*

Big Apple elects its first black mayor

New York City, Nov. 7

David Dinkins, former Manhattan borough president, has been elected mayor of New York City. The 62-year-old Democrat beat Edward Koch, the outgoing mayor, in the primaries, and then his Republican opponent, former federal prosecutor Rudolph Giuliani. Dinkins won with a majority of the black vote and about 30 percent of the white vote. He inherits a city burdened with a massive budget deficit, AIDS and drugs problems, and more than 50,000 homeless.

U.S. troops stop and search suspected partisans of General Noriega.

1990

Bush

New York City, Jan. 10. Time Inc. acquires Warner Communications Inc. for $14.1 billion.

Cove Neck, N.Y., Jan. 25. A Colombian Boeing 707 crashes on approach to Kennedy Airport, killing 73.

Moscow, Jan. 31. McDonald's opens its first restaurant in the U.S.S.R.

Tokyo, Feb. 11. James "Buster" Douglas flattens fellow American Mike Tyson to win world heavyweight title.

Hollywood, Calif., March 26. Bruce Beresford's *Driving Miss Daisy* wins four Oscars.

Augusta, Georgia, April 9. Briton Nick Faldo edges out U.S. golfer Ray Floyd to win U.S. Masters.

Ohio, June 14. Flash floods caused by violent thunderstorms leave 33 dead.

Philippines, June 27. All 260 Peace Corps volunteers told to leave country due to fears for their safety.

Channelview, Texas, July 5. A blast at a chemical plant kills 17 workers.

Plainfield, Illinois, Aug. 28. A tornado leaves 29 people dead and 297 injured.

Helsinki, Finland, Sept. 9. Presidents Bush and Gorbachev agree that Iraqi troops must withdraw from Kuwait.

Washington, D.C., Oct. 9. Judge David H. Souter joins the U.S. Supreme Court following the retirement in July of Justice William J. Brennan.

Oakland, Calif., Oct. 20. Cincinnati Reds defeat Oakland A's to sweep World Series.

Washington, D.C., Oct. 26. Mayor Barry is sentenced to six months in jail for possession of cocaine.

Washington, D.C., Dec. 31. Census Bureau puts population of the U.S. at 248,709,873, or 10.2 percent more than in 1980.

Hollywood, Calif. Top fims include *Pretty Woman, Dances With Wolves, Home Alone* and *Total Recall.*

DEATH

New York City, Apr. 15. Greta Garbo, American actress (*Sept. 18, 1905).

Gen. Noriega faces drug charges in Miami

En route from Panama to Miami.

Miami, Jan. 4

Panama's fallen strongman, General Manuel Noriega, stood in a U.S. courtroom today charged with drug trafficking. "Pineapple face," as his opponents call him, was arrested when he left the Vatican embassy in Panama City, where he took sanctuary 10 days ago following the U.S. invasion of Panama. If found guilty, Noriega faces a jail term of up to 145 years and over $1.5 million in fines on today's charges. More criminal charges are likely. Noriega's alleged links to the C.I.A. are sure to figure in his defense and may prove an embarrassment to President Bush, a former C.I.A. director (→July 10, 1992).

F.B.I. sting nabs Washington's mayor

Washington, D.C., January 19

Marion Barry, one of America's best-known black politicians, was secretly videotaped smoking a pipeful of crack, a highly addictive form of cocaine, the F.B.I. said today. The filming took place shortly after the mayor of the nation's capital had been lured to a hotel room in the city by an ex-girlfriend. F.B.I. agents arrested Mayor Barry as he lit the pipe.

The popular 53-year-old mayor, who strongly denies any wrongdoing, now faces a possible prison sentence (→Oct. 26).

Eighty-seven die in New York disco fire

New York City, March 25

The Happy Land Social Club, a Bronx discotheque, became a nightmarish inferno tonight. Firefighters from a neighboring station managed to put out the blaze quickly, but that was not enough to avert tragedy. When they entered the small, windowless club, they found the dance floor littered with bodies. All but one of the 88 people in the club when the fire broke out died from smoke inhalation. "It was so tightly packed that all the oxygen was consumed by the fire within seconds," said a policeman. Police have arrested a suspect on charges of arson.

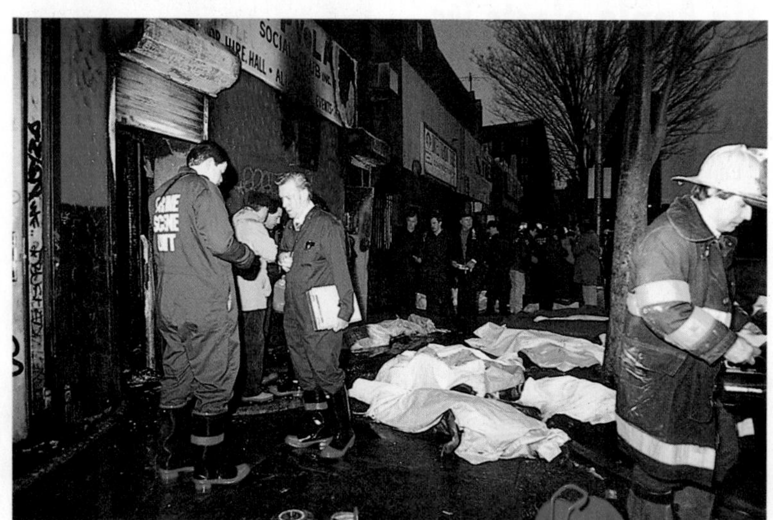
Rescue teams work through the night to retrieve the dead and injured.

January 25. *Hollywood's sultry beauty, Ava Gardner, dies at 68.*

U.S. Perrier scare

United States, Feb. 14

Yuppies will be deprived, temporarily at least, of one of their favorite thirst quenchers.

Traces of benzene, a carcinogen, have been discovered in sparkling mineral water bottled by Perrier. The French company has recalled its entire stock of 160 million bottles from the world market. The chemical was originally found in bottles examined in the U.S., but has since been found in supplies exported to Denmark, Japan and Britain as well. Perrier says the problem was apparently caused by dirty filters at its plant in Vergeze, in southern France.

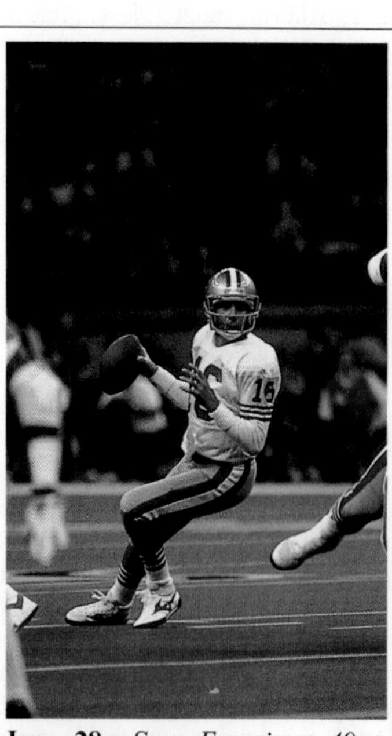
Jan. 28. *San Francisco 49ers quarterback Joe Montana stars in Super Bowl XXIV, in New Orleans. The 49ers defeated the Denver Broncos 55-10.*

[wo American hostages freed in Beirut

.ebanon, Apr. 30

Frank Reed, the American col-
:ge administrator held hostage
y the pro-Iranian Islamic Jihad
roup since September 1986, was
eleased into Syrian custody in Bei-
ut today. His freeing, following
hat of another U.S. hostage, Rob-
rt Polhill, eight days ago, gives
ope that all Western hostages may
oon be out. The Iranians are ma-
ing it clear that much depends on
resident Bush's response to their
atest "gesture of goodwill." The
White House has thanked Syria's
resident Assad for facilitating the
elease of the two hostages.

When Reed appeared on tele-
ision this evening, the effects of his
ong ordeal were only too apparent.
Ie said he had been blindfolded for
nuch of his captivity.

Bob Polhill was held for 1,183 days.

Bush makes U-turn on campaign tax vow

Washington, D.C., June 26

Today's presidential about-face could not have come at a worse time for George Bush. As Republican leaders are gearing up for November's mid-term elections, Bush has admitted he can no longer stick to the most memorable pledge of his 1988 presidential campaign: "Read my lips: no new taxes."

The president's embarrassing reversal was motivated by the urgency of the budget crisis. In a memo, Bush coyly refers to "tax revenue increases" as a means of attempting to deal with the spiraling deficit. Republicans and Democrats alike are anxious to cut the deficit, and so far there has been little sniping at Bush's U-turn. Rises are most likely in indirect taxes rather than income tax.

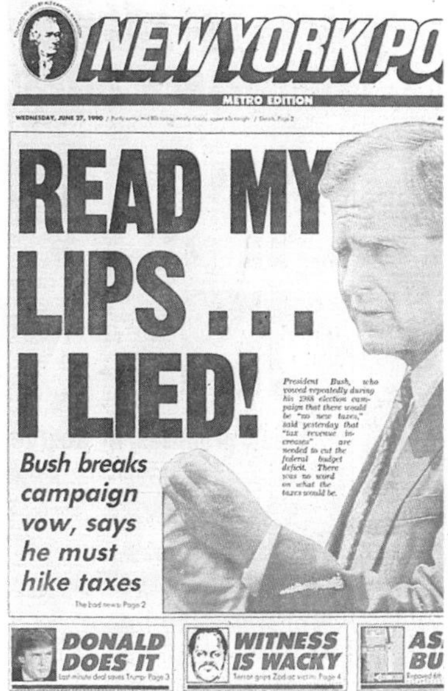

NEW YORK PO

METRO EDITION

READ MY LIPS . . . I LIED!

Bush breaks campaign vow, says he must hike taxes

DONALD DOES IT

WITNESS IS WACKY

AS BU

How the New York Post saw it.

Major flaw found in NASA space telescope

Houston, June 27

The Hubble Space Telescope, which was launched in April from the shuttle Discovery, is myopic. One, if not both, of the $1.5-billion telescope's mirrors, which focus images so that pictures can be taken, has an incorrect curvature. This results in a condition that NASA scientists compare to nearsightedness. The space agency had high hopes for the Hubble telescope; pictures taken from space would provide more profound detail and be intensely clearer than those made from earth. The defects could have been detected during pre-launch tests, but the tests were not performed because of constraints of time and money.

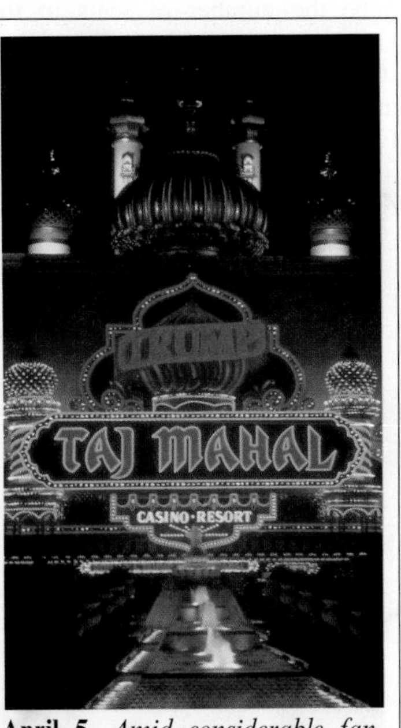

April 5. *Amid considerable fanfare, Donald Trump's giant new casino venture, the extravagant Trump Taj Mahal, opens in Atlantic City, New Jersey.*

Former N.S.C. head sentenced to jail

Washington, D.C., June 11

Retired Admiral John Poindexter today became the seventh former Reagan administration official to be found guilty of wrongdoing in the Iran-contra affair.

Poindexter, who served as the President's national security adviser for a year, was convicted on April 7 on five felony counts of conspiracy, obstructing Congress and making false statements to legistators about his role in the plot. Today, a federal judge sentenced Poindexter to six months in jail for his involvement in secret arms sales to Iran and the diversion of profits to Nicaragua's contra rebels despite a congressional ban. None of the other defendants already tried and found guilty have been sent to jail (→Sept. 16, 1991).

Brando's son Chris arrested for murder

Los Angeles, May 16

Marlon Brando's 32-year-old son, Christian, was arrested today and charged with the murder of his half-sister's French companion, Dag Drollet.

Police believe that Christian shot Drollet at the Brando residence here during a violent argument, apparently because he was opposed to the young Frenchman's relationship with Cheyenne, Christian's half-sister (→Feb. 28, 1991).

Superpower discord on united Germany

Washington, D.C., June 3

There was a time when U.S.-Soviet summits were headline-grabbers. Now that superpower relations are warmer, they seem mostly routine.

At the core of the second Bush-Gorbachev meeting was the Soviet leader's attempt to convince the U.S. President that when East and West Germany reunify on October 3, the new nation should not be a NATO member. Gorbachev even suggested that a united Germany could be a member of both NATO and the Warsaw Pact. Bush rejected both Soviet proposals.

Show biz mourns Sammy Davis Jr.

Los Angeles, May 16

Sammy Davis Jr. could do it all: He was a singer, dancer, actor, musician and mime. He began his career at the age of 3 in a vaudeville act with his father and uncle. A star of the Las Vegas nightclub scene, he ran with the Rat Pack, which included his pals Dean Martin and Frank Sinatra. In 1956 he debuted on Broadway in *Mr. Wonderful* and on the screen in *The Benny Goodman Story*. Hard living led to ill health – kidney, heart and liver problems – in the latter part of his life. He died today after a long battle with throat cancer.

Sammy Davis Jr. was just 64.

Bush draws 'line in sand' for Saddam

Thousands of American troops are being airlifted to Saudi Arabian bases.

Washington, D.C., Aug. 8

Just six days after Iraqi forces swept into Kuwait, the first contingent of U.S. troops landed at Dhahran today. The forces being deployed in Saudi Arabia include units of the 82nd Airborne Division, of the Marine Corps as well as U.S. Navy and Air Force assets.

As Iraqi armor was massing on Saudi Arabia's northern borders, President Bush went on nationwide television this evening to denounce Iraq's "naked aggression" and explain his objectives in the first major crisis of the post-Cold War world. Bush told Americans that the troops being airlifted into the region had drawn "a line in the sand." If President Saddam Hussein crossed it, there would be war. He added that chief among U.S. aims was the unconditional withdrawal of Iraqi forces from Kuwait. Bush also expressed concern for the safety of the hundreds of Americans and other Westerners taken to Baghdad after being seized in Kuwait. Saddam, who formally annexed the oil-rich emirate today, has warned that their lives will be in danger if their countries take military action against Iraq. Bush is calling on NATO allies and Arab states to join a multinational coalition to oppose Iraq (→ Nov. 29).

Ready for "Mother of all Battles".

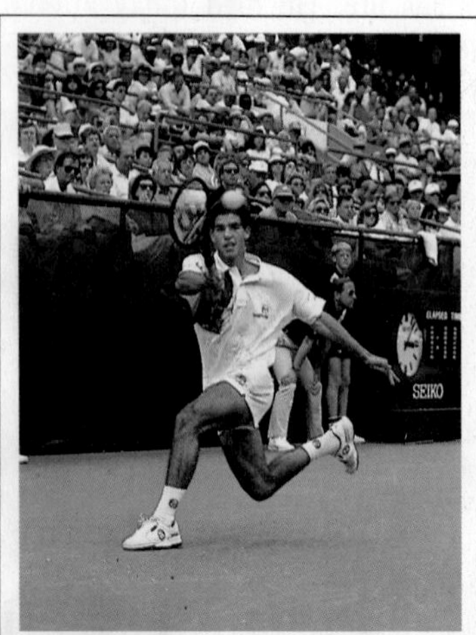

Sept. 9 *Pete Sampras, 19, the youngest to win U.S. Open, beats Andre Agassi 6-4, 6-3, 6-2.*

Neil Bush involved in S & L scandal

Denver, Colorado, July 10

The savings and loan scandal that has rocked the administration and banking circles became a personal crisis today for President George Bush.

Neil Bush, one of the President's five children, has been implicated in the collapse of Denver's Silverado Banking, Savings and Loan Association. The collapse of the institution, of which Neil Bush was a director, has resulted in a $1-billion loss to the federal government.

Although it seems highly unlikely that he will be prosecuted, the President's son has been accused by federal regulators of conflicts of interest as a result of his financial dealings with the bank and several of its chief borrowers. The bailout of the hundreds of insolvent S & Ls will probably cost the federal government $500 billion over the next 40 years.

Atlanta wins battle for 1996 Olympics

Tokyo, Sept. 18

Six cities had battled for the honor of hosting the 1996 Olympic Games. Manchester, Melbourne, Belgrade and Toronto were early casualties of the voting today.

That left Athens, the sentimental favorite and birthplace of the modern Olympics in 1896, and Atlanta. By a comfortable 51 votes to 35 the International Olympic Committee meeting in Tokyo awarded the Games to Atlanta. The Atlanta delegations's carefully costed proposals and the prospect of lucrative television contracts won the day.

Census controversy as results come in

Washington, D.C., July 1

The U.S. Census Bureau estimated the population at 251,394,000 today. This estimate is higher than the actual count: Early results put the number at just under 246 million, but the final total, to be reported in December, is likely to be higher. Six years of planning and $2.5 billion went into the census.

This year's census had many firsts. Computers were used more than ever before, and a computerized map that showed the nation block by block was developed to help in enumeration. New questions were designed to take into account the evolution of family groups, including gay households. Only 26 percent of households with children under 18 included a married couple. For the first time an attempt was made to count the nation's homeless population.

One in four Americans is a member of a minority group. Asians and Pacific Islanders, the fastest growing group, accounted for 2.9 percent of the population. Hispanics made up 9 percent of the population, and blacks 12.1 percent.

Despite a bid to increase accuracy, there are charges of undercounting. Results are used to determine the number of seats in the House of Representatives for each state, as well as for the apportionment of federal and state funds. Even broadcast advertising rates for different regions are determined by census figures (→ Dec 31).

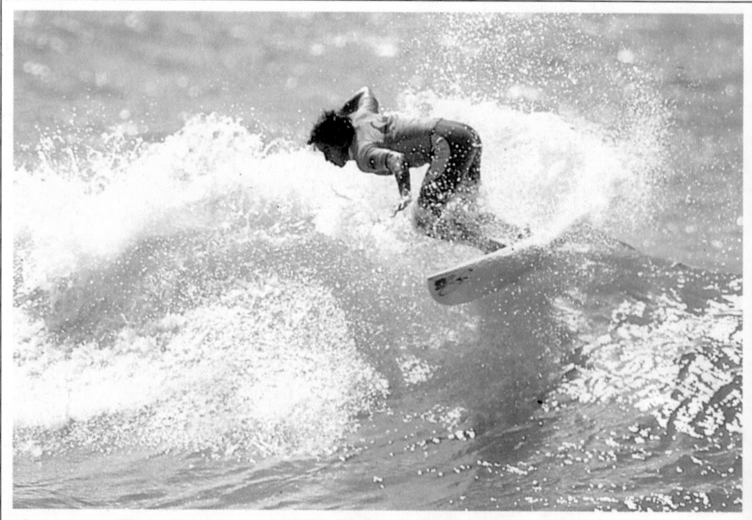

American Tom Curren wins World Surf Championship in France.

JDL founder Kahane shot in Manhattan

New York City, Nov. 5

Rabbi Meir Kahane, the U.S.-born Israeli politician who founded the Jewish Defense League in 1968, was shot to death in a Manhattan hotel tonight. Kahane was hit by two bullets reportedly fired by an American of Egyptian descent as the rabbi was leaving a meeting with his supporters. The suspect was arrested. Kahane had spent a year in a U.S. jail for plotting to make bombs before moving to Israel in 1971. There he founded the extremist and anti-Arab Kach political party. In 1988, he lost his seat in the Knesset, or parliament, after Israel banned Kach for its "Nazi-like," anti-democratic policies.

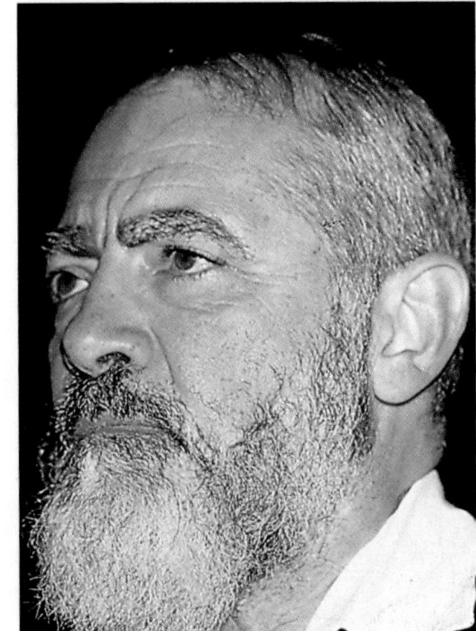

Rabbi Kahane, a militant Zionist

Italian mogul buys slice of Hollywood

Hollywood, Calif., Nov. 1

Promising to restore the studios to their former greatness, Italian entrepreneur Giancarlo Parretti has won a hard-fought battle to buy MGM-United Artists for $1.3 billion.

Dubbed the "mystery mogul" by the press, Parretti's ever-growing media empire now spans the Atlantic. Parretti, a farmer's son, launched his Hollywood takeover bid after purchasing the French Pathé Cinéma group. However, French authorities are already asking whether Parretti has the full support of his financial backers (→ Dec. 30, 1991).

Republican setback in mid-term voting

United States, Nov. 6

As is often the case in mid-term elections, voters tend to favor the party that failed to win the White House two years earlier. Today's voting results run true to form, with the Democrats picking up eight seats in the House of Representatives and gaining one in the Senate. Democrats now control 56 seats to the G.O.P.'s 44, while they have 268 House seats to the Republicans' 167.

Politicians and media commentators are attributing today's Republican losses to President Bush's June 26 backdown on his 1988 campaign promise not to increase taxes to cut the budget deficit.

$600-million fine for junk-bond king

New York City, Nov. 21

Former Drexel Burnham Lambert whiz kid Michael Milken, who made a colossal fortune on Wall Street during the 1980s trading in so-called "junk" bonds, was today sentenced to a 10-year jail term, three years on probation and $600 million in fines.

The 44-year-old bond trader, who earned $550 million in 1987 alone – the highest paycheck in history – had pleaded guilty to securities violations and helping to file false income tax returns. He had persuaded investors to buy high-risk, high-yield "junk" bonds used in corporate takeovers.

U.N. backing for war to free Kuwait

New York City, Nov. 29

President Bush, who says he has "had it" with Saddam Hussein's intransigence, has won a crucial battle at the United Nations.

The Security Council voted today to approve use of military force against Iraq if Iraqi troops do not withdraw from Kuwait by January 15. Cuba and Yemen were the only nations to vote against the resolution, while China abstained. The U.N. ultimatum, which also calls on Iraq to free all hostages, gives the U.S. and its Desert Shield allies in the Gulf about six weeks to bolster their military presence in the region (→ Jan. 1991).

Aid to Soviet Union announced by Bush

Washington, D.C., Dec. 12

In a bid to alleviate the looming threat of famine and civil strife, President Bush today agreed to send an aid package to the Soviet Union.

The wide-ranging package includes emergency medical supplies, credits to buy $1 billion worth of U.S. grain and long-term assistance to improve the country's infrastructure. Overturning previous administration policy, which made aid conditional on the Soviets relaxing emigration laws, Bush explained that he wanted to help the Soviet people "stay the course of democratization" (→ July 17, 1991).

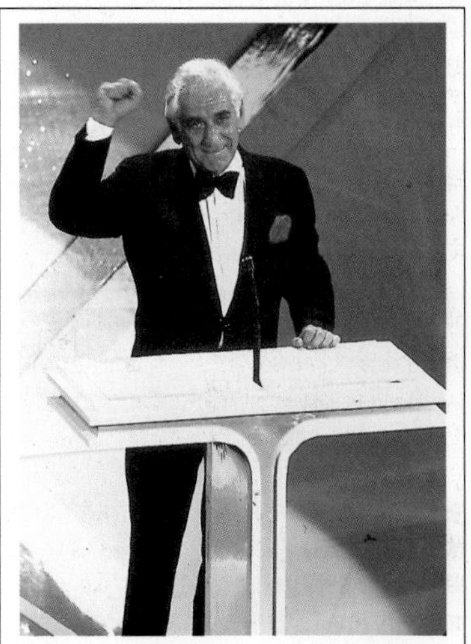

October 14. *Leonard Bernstein, composer of "West Side Story," dies at the age of 72.*

Nov. 22 *President Bush and his wife, Barbara, are in Saudi Arabia to spend Thanksgiving Day with the soldiers of Operation Desert Shield.*

Political Correctness: How's that again?

United States

Mao once asked, "Where do correct ideas come from?" While that puzzler may go unanswered, most would agree that ideas, correct or not, are transmitted by language. The modifier "politically correct," or PC, was originally used by those on the left, somewhat ironically, to describe a range of progressive thought. To spread PC ideas, PC lingo was needed. The proponents of PC speech say that they are battling racism and sexism. Critics say that they are massacring English with Orwellian newspeak.

Here are some examples of the Brave New English:

Differently abled: disabled
Temporarily abled: not disabled
Enslaved person: PC for slave, preferable because it emphasizes the personhood of the oppressed
Eurocentrism: the belief that Western culture is superior
Herstory, hystery: feminist replacements for history
Human animal: non-speciesist replacement for human
Longer-living: old
Mutant albino genetic-recessive global minority: white people

1991

Bush

Tampa, Fla., Jan. 27.
The New York Giants win Super Bowl XXV by defeating the Buffalo Bills, 20-19.

Los Angeles, Feb. 28.
Marlon Brando's son, Christian, is jailed for 10 years for the killing of his half-sister's lover.

California, June 16.
Former President Reagan denies having delayed the release of U.S. hostages in Iran to win the 1980 election.

Washington, D.C., July 10.
President Bush lifts economic sanctions imposed on South Africa in 1986.

Washington, D.C., July 24.
The government announces that no further space shuttles will be built.

Washington, D.C., Sept. 16.
A federal judge orders all Iran-contra charges against Oliver North dropped (→Dec. 24, 1992).

Indianapolis, Sept. 16.
U.S. gymnast Kim Zmeskal, aged 15, wins a gold medal at the world championship.

Minneapolis, Oct 27.
The Minnesota Twins beat Atlanta Braves to take World Series, four games to three.

Las Vegas, Nevada, Dec. 15.
Rodeo star Ty Murray of Texas wins the title of world champion all-round cowboy.

Moscow, Dec. 25.
The U.S.S.R. disintegrates as President Gorbachev resigns.

Los Angeles, Dec. 30.
Control of MGM-Pathé is awarded to Crédit Lyonnais, a French bank, after the arrest for tax fraud of studio owner Giancarlo Parretti.

Hollywood, Calif.
Top films of the year include *Thelma and Louise*, *Robin Hood: Prince of Thieves* and *Terminator 2*.

DEATHS

La Jolla, Calif., Sept 24.
Theodor S. Geisel (Dr. Seuss), author (*March 2, 1904).

Santa Monica, Calif., Sept 28.
Miles Davis, jazz trumpeter (*May 25, 1926).

Santa Monica, Calif., Nov. 5.
Fred MacMurray, actor (*Aug. 30, 1908).

Canary Islands, Nov. 5.
Robert Maxwell, British publisher, owner of *New York Daily News* (*June 10, 1923).

Operation Desert Storm frees Kuwait

The U.S. carrier Theodore Roosevelt launches its aircraft against Baghdad.

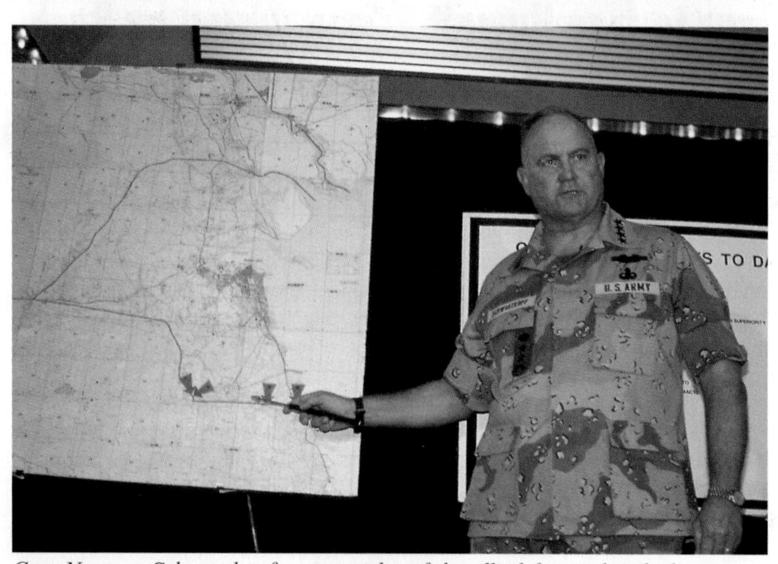

Gen. Norman Schwarzkopf, commander of the allied forces, briefs the press.

U.S. armor slices through battered Iraqi defenses on Kuwait's border.

Persian Gulf, January

The U.S. went to war at dawn on the 17th. Operation Desert Storm, placed under the overall command of General Norman Schwarzkopf, began with waves of high-tech bombing raids on Baghdad. The Iraqi capital was hit by dozens of laser-guided "smart bombs" dropped by USAF F-117 Stealth aircraft. Over the next days, U.S. and allied planes launched thousands of raids over Iraq and Iraqi-occupied Kuwait. While President Saddam Hussein's forces hunkered down in bunkers, Iraq retaliated by launching Scud missiles at Israeli cities, killing at least four Israeli civilians. U.S. bases in Saudi Arabia were also targeted by Scuds.

Ground troops went into action on January 29 after a column of Iraqi armor and infantry crossed the Kuwaiti border and seized the Saudi town of Khafji. Three days of fighting forced an Iraqi retreat, but left 12 Marines dead.

Feb. 28

The Gulf war is over. President Bush went on nationwide television yesterday at 9 p.m. to announce: "Kuwait is liberated. At midnight tonight, exactly 100 hours since ground operations began, all coalition and United States forces will suspend offensive combat operations." This morning, the people of Kuwait City, who have endured six months and 25 days of Iraqi occupation, are celebrating their new-found freedom. Their country is in ruins. Before withdrawing, the defeated Iraqi troops set fire to hundreds of Kuwaiti oil wells, and a thick pall of smoke hangs over the emirate. In Saudi Arabia, allied commanders are counting the cost of the short, brutal war. A total of 148 U.S. servicemen were killed in action, and 472 were wounded. The allies estimate that 150,000 Iraqis were killed. Tens of thousands were captured or surrendered. The turning point in what Saddam Hussein called the "mother of all battles" came two days ago when the U.S. 82nd and 101st Airborne Divisions and the 7th Corps reached the Euphrates River in southern Iraq. Supported by British and French units, the U.S. forces trapped six divisions of Iraq's elite Republican Guard (→Apr. 19).

S. mounts aid operation to save Kurds

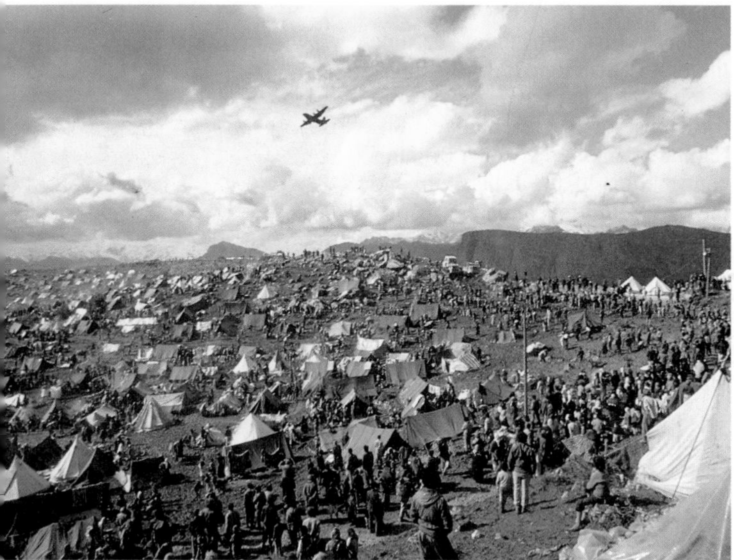

AF aircraft drop supplies to refugees who wait in makeshift camps.

, Apr. 19
everal thousand U.S. troops are ving into northern Iraq to set up ps for the 500,000 Kurdish re- es struggling to survive near Turkish border. U.S., British French aircraft are dropping d and medicine to the starving gees, who fled to the area to pe from Iraqi troops.
ollowing the failure of a Kurd- revolt against Saddam Hussein, sident Bush decided to create a haven for the Kurds. Lieute- t General John Shalikashvili, U.S. commander in the area, told Baghdad that the U.S. will tolerate overflight of the safe en by Iraqi military aircraft.

arch 20. *Sony Corp. signs a -billion multi-year contract with p star Michael Jackson.*

Book's salacious details ruffle Reagans

California, Apr. 9
An angry Ronald Reagan struck back at Kitty Kelley, the author of an unauthorized biography of his wife, Nancy, dismissing the book's salacious claims as "flagrant and absurd falsehoods" that went beyond "the bounds of decency." The book includes allegations of adultery, marijuana use and child abuse, and characterizes the former first lady as mean, greedy, deceitful and manipulative.

Kelley countered: "Everything is documented ... I spent four years doing this book and talked with 1,000 people." The book is a tremendous success, and Simon & Schuster, the publishers, have ordered 150,000 extra copies to add to the 600,000 already in print.

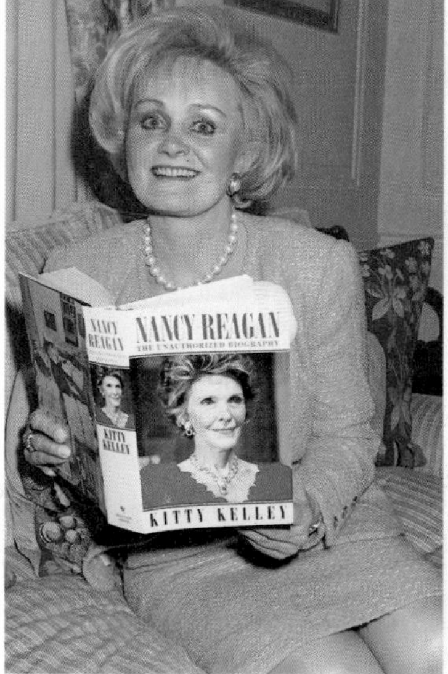

Kitty Kelley: controversial author.

Court upholds curb on family planners

Washington, D.C., May 23
In a 5-4 ruling, the Supreme Court today upheld regulations issued under the Reagan administration which forbid family planning clinics to "encourage, promote or advocate abortion," or to hand out written material on the subject. Judge David Souter, the only justice appointed by President Bush, voted with the majority, despite his earlier observation that the regulations "may preclude professional speech" (→June 29, 1992).

Ivana Trump gets large settlement

New York City, March 20
The 13-month public feud between Donald Trump and his ex-wife Ivana has been resolved with an agreement to settle the affair out of court.

The divorce agreement, which was announced by the millionaire real estate developer today, gives the former model $10 million, their mansion in Connecticut and their apartment on the East Side of Manhattan. "I'm very happy that it worked out so well," he said.

Ex-Senator Tower dies in plane crash

Brunswick, Georgia, Apr. 5
This afternoon a twin-engine turboprop dove into the woods and crashed, just two miles from its destination here. Among the 23 people killed in the crash was John Tower, the former Texas senator. Tower, whose nomination by President Bush for defense secretary was rejected by the Senate in 1989, had recently published a book of memoirs, *Consequences*, in which he struck back at his critics, especially Georgia Senator Sam Nunn.

Video of beating in L.A. causes outcry

Los Angeles, March 15
Four Los Angeles police officers were indicted today following the March 3 beating of a black motorist, 25-year-old Rodney King.

The incident was taped by a bystander trying out a new video camera. The tape shows four officers repeatedly clubbing King as he lay on the ground. The videotape has been shown on television news programs across the country, and has led to a nationwide outcry against police brutality. There have also been calls for the resignation of Los Angeles Police Chief Daryl Gates (→May 2, 1992).

Minimum wage is $4.25 per hour

Washington, D.C., Apr. 1
The national minimum wage has been raised to $4.25 per hour. This increase, from the previous minimum of $3.80 set in April 1990, comes as a result of legislation passed by Congress and signed into law by President Bush in November 1989. Critics of the increase claim that it will cause hardships for small businesses and increase unemployment.

A lower training wage of $3.61 was set for workers 16 to 19 years old in the first six months of their first job. This training wage will expire on March 31, 1993.

March 25. *Kevin Costner's film, "Dances With Wolves," receives no less than six Oscars.*

Bush taken to hospital for heart problem

Bush reassures reporters.

Bethesda, Maryland, May 6
A smiling President Bush left the National Naval Medical Center today, apparently eager to get back to work after spending two days in the hospital.

He had been rushed to Bethesda after suffering from irregular heart rhythms while jogging at the Camp David, Maryland, presidential retreat. It seems the President's busy schedule was at least partly responsible for the trouble. Bush, aged 66, was given two heart-regulating drugs after his doctors decided against an electric shock procedure to stabilize his heart rhythm. This avoided the need for sedation, a move that would have required a temporary transfer of power to Vice President Dan Quayle.

Historic address by Queen Elizabeth II

Washington, D.C., May 16
Queen Elizabeth today became the first British monarch to address a joint session of the Senate and the House of Representatives. She reminded Congress of Britain's contribution to the Gulf War and the two countries' alliances in previous wars, but also joked about her height. "I do hope you can see me today," she said. When she had spoken earlier at the White House she was almost invisible behind the microphones. The high points of the Queen's trip were the speech to Congress and a visit to a poor neighborhood, where she was embraced by an admirer. The Queen is not accustomed to such American familiarity: Touching the monarch is against royal protocol.

Congress applauds the Queen.

Texas picks fast French train system

Austin, Texas, May 28
By 1998 Texans should be able to travel by rail between Houston, Dallas and San Antonio at speeds of up to 185 miles per hour. Passengers will be whisked from downtown Houston to central Dallas in just 90 minutes.

The Texas High Speed Rail Authority today awarded the franchise for the triangular 600-mile route to a group using existing French *Train à Grande Vitesse*, or TGV, technology. This was chosen over Germany's ICE system. The cost of the privately financed project has been set at $5.7 billion.

June 10. *Cheering New Yorkers give a rousing ticker-tape welcome to veterans of Operation Desert Storm at a victory parade on Broadway.*

Thurgood Marshall retires from Court

Washington, D.C., June 27
Thurgood Marshall, the fi black ever to serve on the U Supreme Court, retired today af 24 years of distinguished but oft stormy service. The 84-year- justice cited failing health but sa he will remain on the bench u his successor has been confirmed the Senate. Justice Marshall, w came to the Supreme Court on O ober 2, 1967, has been a staun liberal and ardent defender of ci rights. His greatest legal vict came in 1954, when the court b ned segregation in "separate equal" public schools (→Oct. 15

New financial woes hit New York City

New York City, May 10
Mayor David Dinkins today presented the New York City Council with his "doomsday budget," a plan developed in response to the city's worst fiscal crisis in a generation.

The proposed budget calls for cuts of $1.5 billion in municipal services. The Central Park Zoo would be closed, more than 29,000 employees, including 2,800 teachers, laid off and a quarter of the city's 295,000 street lights turned off. The cutback plan would affect every agency except the police and jails. It calls for the elimination of many educational, sanitation and preventive health programs. In addition, Dinkins has asked for $1 billion in tax increases to help eliminate a deficit that could reach $3.4 billion for the fiscal year beginning July 1. By law, the city must begin the fiscal year with a balanced budget. "No adjectives can explain the consequences of cuts so large," said the mayor. "For unless our friends in labor, in the legislature, in the governor's office, in the Municipal Assistance Corporation and in the City Council step forward and help out, the unthinkable will become the unavoidable."

June 9. *U.S. tennis star Ji Courier wins the French Open.*

U.S. to sign vital Antarctic protection pact

Washington, D.C., July 4

President Bush announced today that, despite lingering doubts about some aspects of the pact, the United States will sign a tough international agreement to ban mining and oil exploration in the Antarctic for at least 50 years.

The new accord is aimed at protecting Antarctica's fragile environment and wildlife and promoting scientific research there. The pact, which will not come into force until it is ratified by its signatories, is to be added to the 1961 Antarctic Treaty. That 30-year-old accord strictly prohibits weapons testing and the dumping of nuclear waste in the Antarctic.

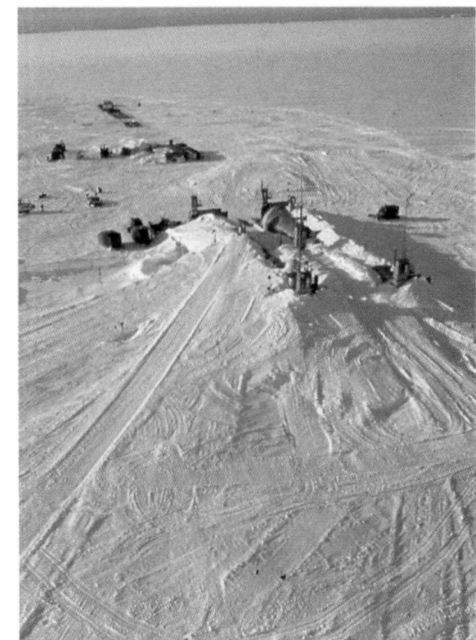

A 50-year respite for Antarctica.

Bush refuses blank check for Gorbachev

London, July 17

President Mikhail Gorbachev will be returning to the Kremlin practically empty-handed.

It was the first time that a Soviet leader had been invited to attend a Western economic summit. Gorbachev had come here in the hope of persuading President Bush and the leaders of the world's six other wealthiest nations, known as the Group of Seven, to agree to a massive Western aid package. However, Bush and John Major, the British Prime Minister, argued that Gorbachev's latest economic reform proposals were not radical enough to create a viable free-market economy. Despite this rebuff, the G7 leaders agreed to share their nations' technical know-how so that the Soviets can press ahead with their efforts to modernize their economy (→ March 11, 1992).

As George Bush meets leaders, Barbara visits HIV patients with Lady Diana.

Sprinter Lewis sets sensational record

U.S. runner delights the crowds.

Tokyo, Aug. 25

"This is the best race of all time, the best sprinters in the best race," exulted Carl Lewis, who set the world record for the 100-meter sprint today at the World Track and Field Championships, an event rivalled in importance only by the Olympics. Lewis finished at 9.86 seconds, followed by two fellow Philadelphia natives. Kenny Burrell, who had set the previous record in June at 9.90, led the race until the final 10 meters and finished at 9.88, and Dennis Mitchell came in third at 9.91 seconds.

Lewis was world champion in 1983 and 1987 and won gold medals in the 1984 and 1988 Olympics, but this is his first individual world record.

Brooklyn race riots sparked by accident

Brooklyn, New York, Aug. 22

A measure of calm has returned to Crown Heights after four days of rioting. Tension between the Jewish and black communities here flared into violence after a tragic car accident three days ago. A car in a motorcade of the Lubavitcher sect's grand rabbi hit two black children, killing one of them. An ambulance regularly used by the Lubavitcher community did not pick up the injured child. Angry crowds of blacks quickly formed, chanting anti-Semitic slogans. Just hours later, a Jewish scholar from Australia was stabbed to death by a group of young blacks. Rioting ensued, and 84 police and at least 25 civilians were injured in the next three days.

July 1. *Actor Michael Landon, aged 54, dies of cancer.*

West hails failure of Soviet coup bid

Washington, D.C., Aug. 23

White House officials breathed a sigh of relief today. Four days ago a group of Soviet hardliners, including senior K.G.B. and military officers, announced that they had taken control of the Soviet government. When the dramatic coup attempt unraveled, President Bush was one of the first Western leaders to telephone Gorbachev and express his support. Gorbachev survived the coup, but his authority has been badly shaken (→ Dec. 25).

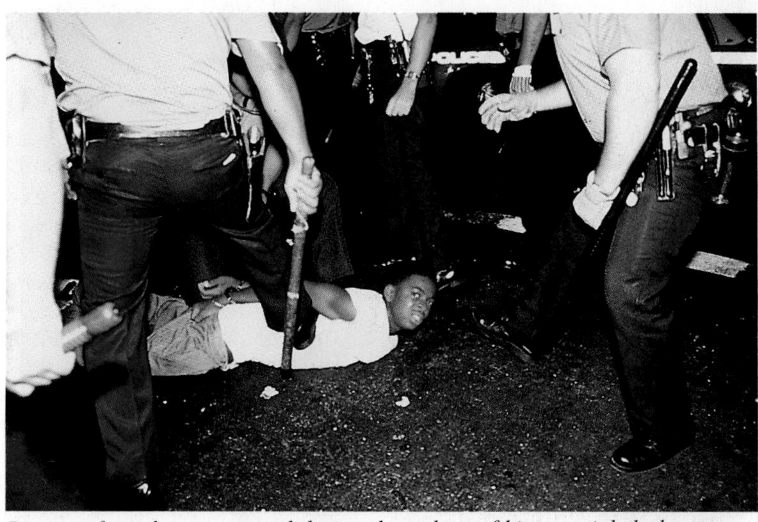

Dozens of youths are arrested during three days of bitter racial clashes.

Navratilova palimony case ends in deal

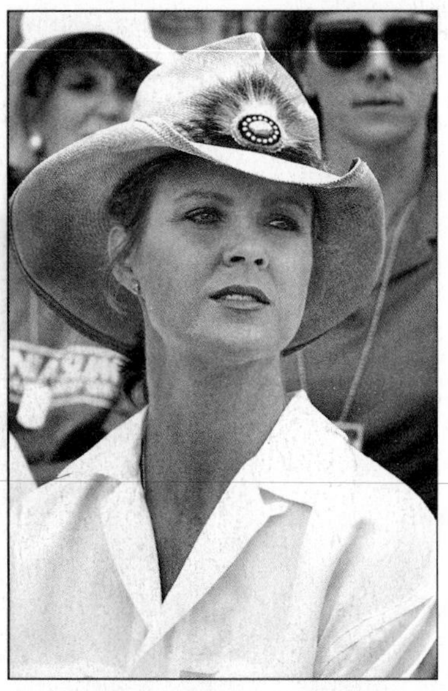
Judy Nelson settled out of court.

Texas, Sept. 11

Tennis star Martina Navratilova and her former lover, Judy Nelson, have made a tentative financial deal to settle the palimony claim brought by Nelson in June. Nevertheless, their relationship is still far from love-all.

Nelson will receive an undisclosed sum, but still claims that she and Navratilova had an agreement entitling her to half of Navratilova's earnings, estimated at $5 million to $9 million over the seven years during which they had a relationship. Navratilova says she was defrauded and disputes the validity of the cohabitation agreement. Nelson says she is not just after the money: "It's about Martina honoring a contract."

Tough U.S. refuses Israel a vital loan

Washington, D.C., Sept. 13

Israel is enraged at President Bush because he has refused a loan guarantee of $10 billion to build housing for Soviet immigrants in Israel. Bush has said that in order to "give peace a break" in the Middle East he would ask Congress to defer consideration of the Israeli request. He also said the loans cannot be used to build housing in the Occupied Territories. The glitch in U.S.-Israeli relations comes as Washington is trying to organize Mid-East peace talks (→Oct. 30).

Computer giants to share technology

New York City, Oct. 2

I.B.M. and Apple, fierce rivals ever since Apple was founded in the 1970s, have agreed to form an alliance which they hope will boost lagging sales.

The two computer giants announced plans to make their products compatible and develop a family of powerful new microprocessors. I.B.M. and Apple have also decided to create "open" systems which will allow consumers to mix and match as they buy hardware and software.

Oct. 23. *Fires rage for three days through Oakland and Berkeley, Calif., leaving at least 24 dead, and damage is estimated at over $1.5 billion.*

Senators focus on sexual harassment

Clarence Thomas is confirmed despite allegations by Anita Hill.

Washington, D.C., Oct. 15

Senate hearings that have thrust sexual harassment to the forefront of American debate ended today. Clarence Thomas, a federal appeals court judge, was confirmed as a Supreme Court justice by a vote of 52-48. Thomas was accused of sexual harassment by Anita Hill, a law professor who had worked for him. Hill said that the judge made lewd suggestions to her, boasted of the size of his penis, and described pornographic movies he had seen, mentioning in particular one starring "Long Dong Silver."

Judge Thomas denies all the charges. Accuser and accused are both black, both graduates of Yale law school, and one of them is lying. Thomas is passionate, eloquent, outraged that anyone should question him. Hill is calm, deliberate and restrained. The hearings were televised live, and more people watched them than tuned into the daytime soap operas.

Thomas is a conservative, and President Bush nominated him in order to cement the conservative majority on the court. Liberals tried to stop him, and Hill's allegations were leaked to the media, changing the focus of the hearings from judicial philosophy to questions of sexism and abuse of power.

Loner kills 22 in a Texas gun rampage

Killeen, Texas, Oct. 16

A man crashed his pick-up truck through the window of a restaurant and pulled out a semi-automatic pistol and slaughtered 22 people before killing himself.

Gregory Kennard, 35, jumped out of his truck and cried, "This is what Bell County has done to me!" Then he opened fire on people waiting in line in the cafeteria. Customers hid under tables as the gunman walked through the restaurant shooting and reloading his gun with 17-round magazines. After the killer was hit by police gunfire, he shot and killed himself. At least 20 people were wounded, and they were taken to three different hospitals in the area. Many of them are in critical condition.

U.S. backs Mid-East peace conference

Madrid, Oct. 30

President George Bush, flanked by Soviet leader Mikhail Gorbachev and U.S. Secretary of State James Baker, today attended the opening of crucial Mid-East peace talks.

As Bush and Gorbachev made their opening remarks, Yitzhak Shamir, Israel's premier, sat impassively at the huge table, facing the Palestinian delegation. The conference, sponsored by the U.S. and the Soviet Union, marks the beginning of the first direct negotiations between Israelis and Palestinians. All sides at the talks stress that today's meeting is just a start, adding that the road to peace in the Middle East will be long and tortuous (→Aug. 11, 1992).

Magic Johnson is HIV-positive, will retire

Los Angeles, Nov. 8
America is shocked by the revelation that one of its top sports stars, the L.A. Laker forward Earvin "Magic" Johnson, has tested positive for the virus that causes AIDS. The star – described today by President Bush as a "hero" – made the announcement himself yesterday. The item dominated TV news bulletins for two reasons: first, because Johnson is hugely popular, and second, because he says he contracted the disease through heterosexual sex. Johnson, who is 32, intends to retire from basketball and devote his time to campaigning for greater awareness of AIDS among heterosexuals. Until now, most Americans had linked the disease with homosexuals and drug users.

Basketball legend to fight AIDS.

End of an era as Pan Am ceases flying

Miami, Dec. 4
The end of the road came today for one of America's greatest commercial aviation pioneers.

Pan American World Airways, the 64-year-old airline founded by Juan Trippe, ceased operations, a victim of deregulation and a deep recession in the industry.

Pan Am, burdened by huge losses and operating under court protection from its creditors since January, is the third major U.S. airline to fold this year. The carrier's demise comes after a decision by Delta Air Lines to withdraw from a deal that would have helped Pan Am emerge from bankruptcy. Delta announced yesterday that it would not put up any more money to keep Pan Am flying.

Last Pan Am flight lands in Miami.

Last U.S. hostages freed from Lebanon

Free at last: Joseph Cicippio, Terry Anderson and Alann Steen.

Damascus, Syria, Dec. 5
Associated Press correspondent Terry Anderson, the last of the 17 U.S. citizens who have been taken hostage in Lebanon since 1984, is free. Anderson, who was held for a total of 2,455 days – more than any other American hostage – will now be flying to Germany to join two other U.S. hostages, Alann Steen and Joseph Cicippio. They were released earlier this week. Shortly after Anderson was freed, he was reunited in Damascus with his fiancee, Madeleine, and their 6-year-old daughter Sulome – whom he had never seen. The release of the three Americans leaves two Germans as the only Western hostages held in Beirut.

Tragic Kimberly dies of AIDS

Florida, Dec. 8
Kimberly Bergalis, 23, who was infected with the AIDS virus after being treated by a dentist with HIV, died today. Doctors reacted with skepticism when Bergalis insisted in September, 1990, after the dentist died of AIDS, that she had not contracted the disease through sexual intercourse, intravenous drug injections or a blood transfusion. But the Centers for Disease Control established that the strain of HIV with which she was infected was identical to that of her dentist.

William Kennedy Smith acquitted of rape

Senator Ted Kennedy's nephew is cheered as he leaves the courtroom.

Rate cut boosts ailing economy

United States, Dec. 30
The economic year is ending on an upbeat note. Experts claim the end of the recession is in sight. Traders on Wall Street have been on a buying spree since the Federal Reserve cut the discount rate 10 days ago, from 4.5 to 3.5 percent, its lowest level since 1964. The Dow Jones industrial average rose 8.6 percent in 10 days, ending the year at a record high of 3,168.83. The annual inflation rate stands at just 2.9 percent, compared with 6.1 percent last year.

West Palm Beach, Fla., Dec. 11
The jury took just 80 minutes to acquit William Kennedy Smith of raping a 30-year-old woman at the Kennedy family's Florida estate last March. The trial had been televised throughout the country and sharpened the debate about "date rape" and the difficulty of proving sexual assault. Smith admitted that he had had sex with the woman, but claimed that she had consented. In the end, it was his word against hers, and the jury found that there was insufficient evidence to prove the charges. Senator Edward Kennedy, Smith's uncle, was among those who gave evidence, saying that he had heard no screams on the night of the alleged assault.

1992

Bush

Louisville, Apr. 15.
Leona Helmsley, president of Helmsley Hotels Inc., begins serving a four-year jail term for tax evasion.

New York City, May 18.
Doctors who autopsied President John F. Kennedy say they are sure he was shot from behind, as the Warren Commission concluded in 1964 (→Aug 23, 1993).

Indianapolis, May 24.
Al Unser Jr. wins Indy 500.

New York City, June 23.
Mafia boss John Gotti gets life in prison for murder.

Washington, D.C., June 24.
The Supreme Court rules that cigarette manufacturers cannot claim protection from damages simply because their packages carry health warnings.

Miami, July 10.
General Noriega, former leader of Panama, gets 40 years in prison for drug trafficking.

Kennebunkport, Me., Aug. 11.
President Bush agrees to an Israeli request for guarantees on $10 billion in loans.

Boston, Aug. 18.
Basketball star Larry Bird retires from the Boston Celtics.

Washington, D.C., Sept 4.
The Census Bureau reports that the number of poor people increased in 1991 by nearly two million, to 35.7 million, the highest since 1964.

Washington, D.C., Dec. 10.
Senator Bob Packwood of Oregon apologizes for making unwelcome sexual advances to female employees.

Washington, D.C., Dec. 24.
President Bush pardons six officials, including former Defense Secretary Caspar Weinberger, who are charged with or convicted of misleading Congress in the Iran-Contra investigations.

Iraq, Dec. 27.
A U.S. fighter downs an Iraqi MIG-25 which had violated the U.N.-backed "no-fly" zone over southern Iraq (→June 26, 1993).

Hollywood, Calif.
The year's top films include *Basic Instinct, Wayne's World* and *Batman Returns*.

DEATH

Paris, France, May 6.
Marlene Dietrich, actress and singer (*Dec. 27, 1901).

Bush is taken ill at state dinner in Tokyo

Aides and agents rush to assist the President as he keels over and vomits.

Tokyo, Jan. 8
President Bush's misfortune tonight will surely be remembered as the most public case of an intestinal flu attack ever. As video cameras taped the formal state dinner, the President turned white as steamed rice, flopped backward in his chair, vomited on the Japanese Prime Minister and hit the floor as Secret Service agents scrambled to assist him. Bush's visit was focused on "jobs, jobs, jobs." He was accompanied by the heads of the Big Three U.S. automakers, but met stiff resistance from Japanese officials reluctant to open their markets to U.S. trade.

Silicone breast implants cause scare

Hemlock, Michigan, January 14
Dow Corning Co. plants here and in Arlington, Tennessee, which make silicone breast implants, have been shut down, at least temporarily. On January 6, the Food and Drug Administration called for a 45-day moratorium on the use of the implants and asked producers to halt distribution. New information on the safety of implants, including the possibilty that silicone in the body may lead to inflammatory autoimmune disease, will be examined by an advisory panel. Officials of Dow Corning say they are sure the implants are safe, and have scientific tests which prove it, but stopped production in compliance with the FDA's request.

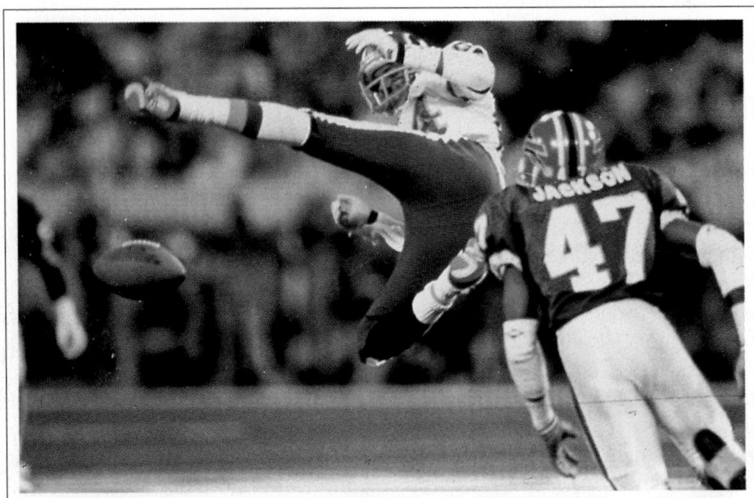

Jan. 26. *Another disappointing year for the Buffalo Bills, defeated in Super Bowl XXVI by the Washington Redskins, 37-24, in Minneapolis.*

Danger signs for American economy

United States, Feb. 24
To say the least, the economic signs are worrisome. The unemployment level reported on January 10 was the highest since 1987, at 7.1 percent. A week later, I.B.M. announced its first ever annual loss, $564 million for 1991. On January 30, TWA, with a debt of nearly $2 billion, was added to the long list of airlines seeking Chapter 11 protection against creditors. Today General Motors announced its largest loss ever, $4.5 billion for 1991, preceded earlier this month by Ford's posting of a record annual loss, at $2.3 billion.

Serial killer gets life for 15 murders

Milwaukee, Feb. 17
One of the most gruesome criminal cases in U.S. history ended today with the sentencing of Jeffrey Dahmer to 15 consecutive terms of life in prison. There is no possibility of parole.

Last month Dahmer, 31, pleaded guilty to the murder, mutilation and dismemberment of 15 men and youths, most of them black gays. He also confessed to acts of cannibalism and necrophilia during a killing spree that lasted several years. Dahmer then pleaded not guilty by reason of insanity. The jury of seven men, one of them black, and five women rejected the insanity plea two days ago, ruling that the accused was not suffering from a mental disease at the time of the killings.

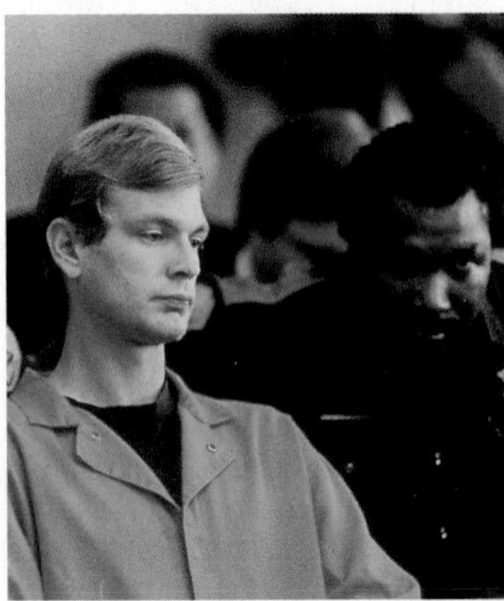

Jeffrey Dahmer listens to verdict.

Tyson given six-year term for rape

Indianapolis, March 26

The boxing career of the world's youngest heavyweight champion came to a jarring halt today. Five years after he won the world title, 25-year-old Mike Tyson was sentenced to 10 years in prison, four of them suspended, after being found guilty of one count of rape and two counts of criminal deviant conduct. Tyson was convicted for the rape of a Miss Black America contestant, Desiree Washington, in his Indianapolis hotel room last year. The ex-champ was led off to prison after the verdict was announced and will have to serve at least three years of his term (→ March 25, 1995).

Former heavyweight boxing champion is driven to court to hear the verdict.

Nixon slams Bush policy on Russia

Washington, D.C., March 11

Former President Richard M. Nixon is back in the limelight. His charges that the Bush administration has provided "pathetically" inadequate aid to Russia have stung the White House.

Today, Nixon stressed there was no rift between him and Bush, but reiterated his call for stronger U.S. support for democratic reform in Russia. Nixon has warned that if Russian President Boris Yeltsin were to be overthrown by hardliners, Bush and his administration would have to face the question of "who lost Russia."

Disney exports Magic Kingdom to Europe

The $4-billion Euro Disney theme park opens just outside Paris.

April 10. *Former tennis champ Arthur Ashe announces that he is HIV-positive (→ Feb. 6, 1993).*

Marne-la-Vallée, France, Apr. 12

Euro Disneyland opened its gates to the public today in the suburbs east of Paris. The opening of the $4-billion complex was celebrated last night with a show featuring stars of film, stage and song that was seen on television by 100 million people around the world.

Euro Disney can handle an estimated 50,000 to 60,000 guests a day, and six hotels decorated in different American themes with 5,200 rooms have been built on the grounds to accommodate them. To staff the enormous complex, the largest hiring campaign ever seen in France was launched. Euro Disney has hired 14,000 "cast members," efficient, smiling and clean-cut, *à l'américaine.*

Wal-Mart founder dies of cancer at 74

Little Rock, Arkansas, Apr. 5

Sam Walton, one of the richest men in the country, died of cancer today at the age of 74. Walton was the founder and chairman of Wal-Mart, a chain of discount stores which sells everything from jeans to popcorn to car stereos. There are 1,735 Wal-Mart stores, with an average floor space of more than 86,000 square feet, situated in rural areas and small towns in 42 states. Since Walton opened the first Wal-Mart Discount City in 1962, the company has become the largest and most successful retailer in the United States.

NASA bird peers into cosmic past

Washington, D.C., Apr. 23

Scientists believe that they have finally found the Holy Grail of cosmology. A NASA satellite, the Cosmic Background Explorer, or COBE, has found evidence of huge, wispy clouds of matter near what could be "the edge" of the universe. These clouds explain how galaxies were produced after the Big Bang, the cosmic explosion scientists say created the universe. The clouds date back 15 billion years, just 300,000 years after the Big Bang. COBE's findings were announced here today at a meeting of the American Physical Society.

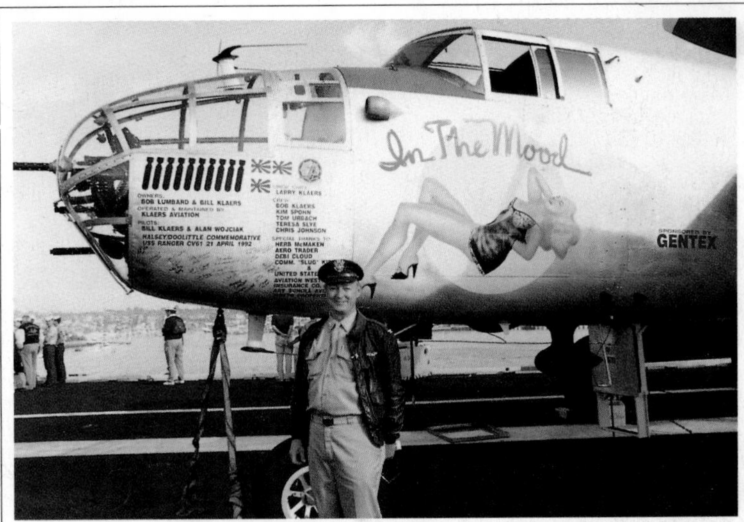

April. *Vintage B-25s are launched from a carrier off San Diego to mark 50th anniversary of General Doolittle's historic bombing raid on Tokyo.*

Rioters ravage Los Angeles after King verdict

Resentment flares into violence, looting and arson in South Central area, as police struggle to restore order.

Los Angeles, May 2

An uneasy calm has returned to this battered city, where the death toll of three days of rioting stands at 37. National Guard troops and federal law-enforcement officers are patrolling South Central, the area where the worst of the rioting took place. The White House has placed 5,000 soldiers and Marines on standby outside the city.

The rioting erupted soon after the acquittal of four white Los Angeles police officers who had been charged with beating a black motorist, Rodney King. The jury at the trial in Simi Valley did not include a black. As police watched helplessly, violence and looting quickly spread from the predominantly black South Central area to adjoining communities. More than 1,500 people have been injured, dozens of them critically, and property damage is estimated at $600 million.(→Apr.17,1993).

U.S. Navy rocked by Tailhook sex scandal

Washington, D.C., June 26

At last year's convention of the Tailhook Association, a private group of active-duty and retired naval pilots, drunken male Navy and Marine Corps aviators made women run a gauntlet along a hallway in a Las Vegas hotel, touching and grabbing them in a sexually aggressive manner, according to the 26 women, half of them naval officers, who claim to be the victims. Today the Defense Department suspended the investigation into the sexual harassment scandal, saying that the naval officers who were conducting it might be suspects themselves.

May 16. *Billionaire Bill Koch, skipper of America³, sails to victory in the America's Cup, ahead of the Italian entry, Il Moro di Venezia.*

Supreme Court upholds abortion rights

Washington, D.C., June 29

In a politically explosive decision destined to figure prominently in the presidential election campaign, the conservative-dominated Supreme Court today upheld a ruling giving states the power to restrict the right to have an abortion. The court stopped short of overturning its own historic 1973 ruling in the case of Roe v. Wade, which enshrined abortion as a constitutional right. The vote was 5-4. The decision satisfies neither side in the bitter abortion fight, which has divided America for nearly 20 years.

The battle involves both President Bush and his likely opponent, Bill Clinton. The President said he is pleased with the court's decision to uphold "reasonable restrictions on abortion." The Arkansas Governor warned that a woman's right to an abortion was now "hanging by a thread," and only a Democratic victory would preserve that right.

Johnny Carson ends 30-year run on NBC

Burbank, Calif., May 22

A chapter of television history closed with Johnny Carson's last "Tonight Show." With tears in his eyes, the legendary 66-year-old entertainer told millions of viewers and the invited audience of friends, family and staff members: "It has been an honor and a privilege to come into your home all these years and entertain you." Carson, who took over the show from Jack Paar in 1962, was the highest-paid personality in the history of television, earning an estimated $2,380 per minute of airtime.

"Tonight Show" host retires.

Florida reels in wake of Hurricane Andrew

Life must go on despite massive destruction of property in the Miami area.

Florida, Aug. 25

After devastating much of Dade County south of Miami, Hurricane Andrew is crossing the Gulf of Mexico, on its way to the Louisiana coast. At least 15 people have been killed, and damage estimates range from $15 to $20 billion, more than for any other natural disaster in the history of the U.S. Andrew wrenched trees from the ground, mowed down houses and picked up boats, car and planes, flinging them into the air. Miami and Coconut Grove were virtually under martial law, as riot-equipped police and 15,000 National Guard troops went on patrol to prevent looting.

U.S. sends troops to aid starving Somalia

Mogadishu, Dec. 9

U.S. Marines and Navy frogmen stormed ashore at dawn today ready to do battle with the Somali gunmen who have been holding their famine-stricken country to ransom. The troops were confronted not by bandits, but by the press, tipped off by U.S. officials. The plan is to secure the airport and harbor areas before moving out to get food and medicine to Somalis in the hinterland, where thousands have died of starvation. Followers of rival warlords Mohammed Farah Aidid and Mohammed Ali Mahdi have pulled out of the capital under a U.S.-brokered agreement (→Oct. 3, 1993).

U.S. marines hit Somalia's beaches at dawn in a huge relief operation.

Bill Clinton beats Bush

At 46, Governor Clinton is the first baby-boomer to reach the White House.

United States, Nov. 4

The results of yesterday's voting are in. Americans have chosen their 42nd president, Arkansas Governor Bill Clinton. The 46-year-old Democrat will be the first U.S. president of a post-World War II generation.

The first candidate from his party to be elected president since Jimmy Carter in 1976, Clinton campaigned as a "New Democrat," combining traditionally Democratic liberal social themes with calls for greater fiscal responsibilty and closer cooperation with business.

Clinton received 43 percent of the popular vote, well ahead of President George Bush, who received 38 percent, and pulled in 370 electoral votes, much more than the 270 needed to win. A third party candidate, the Texas billionaire Ross Perot, won an unprecedented 19 percent of the popular vote. Perot, who ran on a deficit-reduction platform, may have lost some of his support when he abandoned the race after the Democratic Convention in July, only to jump back in in October.

The President-elect has begun to outline the priorities of his presidency. Creating new jobs, reducing the deficit and reforming the health-care system will be the primary domestic goals. Clinton also revealed his foreign policy objectives: he wants to move forward in global trade talks and peace talks between Israel and its Arab neighbors, complete arms agreements with Russia, aid the famine victims in Somalia and work toward an end to the civil war in the former republics of Yugoslavia (→Jan. 20, 1993).

Aug. 9. *Michael Jordan, Magic Johnson and fellow Dream Team members celebrate their Olympic victory in Barcelona. U.S. athletes won 108 medals, including 37 gold and 34 silver, to the former U.S.S.R.'s total of 112.*

1993

Clinton

Pasadena, Jan. 31.
The Dallas Cowboys defeat the Buffalo Bills 52-17 in Super Bowl XXVII.

Waco, Texas, Feb. 28.
Four federal agents are killed in a shoot-out with the Branch Davidians, an apocalyptic cult (→Apr. 19).

Pensacola, Florida, March 11.
A doctor who performed abortions is murdered outside a clinic by an anti-abortion activist (→May 12, 1994).

Washington, D.C., April 22.
The Holocaust Museum opens.

Washington, D.C., April 28.
The armed forces ban on women combat pilots ends.

Washington, D.C., June 7.
Congress hears testimony of mysterious ailments afflicting thousands of Gulf War vets.

Phoenix, June 20.
The Chicago Bulls defeat the Phoenix Suns to win their third straight N.B.A. championship.

New York, June 24.
The F.B.I. arrests eight men on charges of plotting to blow up the U.N. building.

Iraq, June 26.
The U.S. launches a missile attack on Iraqi intelligence headquarters in retaliation for a plot to assassinate former President Bush.

Washington, D.C., July 20.
White House aide Vincent Foster commits suicide (→June 30, 1994).

Washington, D.C., Aug. 23.
The National Archives opens nearly all files relating to the assassination of President John F. Kennedy.

Somalia, Oct. 3.
Twelve U.S. soldiers are killed in a failed raid to capture leaders of Mohammed Farah Aidid's militia.

Atlanta, Oct. 23.
The Toronto Blue Jays beat the Philadelphia Phillies to win the World Series.

Manassas, Virginia, Nov. 10.
John Wayne Bobbitt is acquitted of marital sexual assault; his wife claimed she cut off his penis because he had raped her (→Jan. 21, 1994).

Houston, Dec. 10.
NASA astronauts repair the faulty Hubble Space Telescope.

Hollywood, Calif.
Top films of the year include *The Fugitive*, *The Firm*, *Sleepless in Seattle* and *Aladdin*.

Clinton is inaugurated

Bill Clinton, the nation's third-youngest President, takes the oath of office.

Washington, D.C., Jan. 20
William Jefferson Clinton took the oath of presidential office from Chief Justice William H. Rehnquist today, swearing to "preserve, protect and defend the Constitution" on his grandmother's King James Bible. Tens of thousands of spectators turned up on the Mall on this bright, chilly day to witness the inauguration on the steps of the Capitol. The ceremony included a prayer led by the Reverend Billy Graham and a poem read by Maya Angelou. The new President's inaugural speech took "renewal" as its theme, and he challenged Americans to "answer the call" to service and sacrifice in order to "reinvent America."

Tennis champion Arthur Ashe dies of AIDS

New York, Feb. 6
Arthur Ashe, one of America's most loved and respected athletes, has died at the age of 49 of pneumonia brought on by AIDS. Ashe was not only a tennis champion, but also a human-rights and AIDS activist, *Washington Post* columnist, TV sports commentator and author of a history of America's black athletes. He was the first black athlete to win a Grand Slam event, in the first U.S. Open in 1968, and the first to win the Wimbledon men's title, in 1975.

Jan. 6. *Dizzy Gillespie, the innovative trumpeter who helped create the bebop style and introduced Cuban rhythms into jazz, dies of cancer at 75.*

Bomb attack under World Trade Center

New York City, Feb. 26
A bomb exploded in an underground parking garage between the 110-floor twin towers of the World Trade Center at lunchtime today. Five people were killed, and hundreds were treated for smoke-related injuries. A fire raged for two hours, sending smoke billowing into the streets and up to the 96th floor of the towers. Fire fighters worked into the night to get people out of the buildings. Some people were rescued by helicopter from the roof, but workers and visitors managed their own evacuation for the most part. The towers accommodate 55,000 workers and 80,000 visitors each day (→June 24).

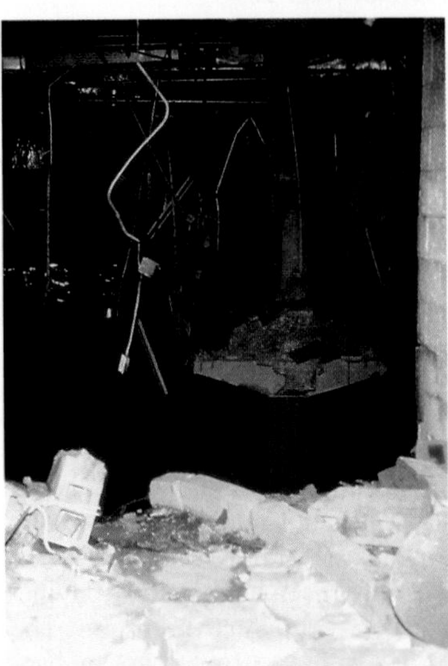

A huge hole was opened between the garage and commuter train station.

March 15. *One of the worst winter storms this century lashes the eastern U.S. from Atlanta to Boston, leaving at least 93 people dead.*

Rodney King verdict eases tensions in LA

Los Angeles, April 17

Los Angeles has been a tense city for the last week. The jury in the civil-rights trial of four policemen accused in the beating of Rodney King went into deliberations last weekend. Gun sales were up and the National Guard standing by in anticipation of a repeat of last year's riots. The tension was lifted today when the jury came in with its verdict. Sgt. Stacy Koon, the ranking officer present at the beating, was found guilty of allowing excessive force to restrain King. Officer Laurence Powell, who was seen to strike most of the blows against King in the video of the beating made by a bystander, was convicted of using excessive force. The other officers, Theodore Briseno and Timothy Wind, were acquitted.

Waco standoff ends in fiery tragedy

Waco, Texas, April 19

Ranch Apocalypse, as the headquarters of the Branch Davidian cult has been nicknamed, burned today after an armored-vehicle assault by federal agents.

The F.B.I. has been in a standoff with the cult since February 28, when four federal agents were killed in a failed surprise raid on the compound. The heavily armed cult was led by the charismatic David Koresh, who told his followers that the end of the world was nigh. The F.B.I. alternated tactics of negotiation and harrassment, at one point playing Tibetan chants to drive out the Davidians.

Early this morning a negotiator warned the cult that tear gas would be injected into the compound to force them to give themselves up. Warnings broadcast on loudspeakers were ignored, and the F.B.I. began their assault. F.B.I. snipers say they saw two people setting fires about noon. The blaze spread rapidly, engulfing the buildings as police and reporters watched helplessly. About 90 adults are believed to have been inside; nine escaped from the self-inflicted inferno. Among the dead are at least 17 children.

The assault ends a 51-day siege of the cult headquarters by U.S. federal agents.

Last call for laughs on tap at Cheers bar

Boston, May 20

The cast of the hit show *Cheers* gathered here at the Bull & Finch, the bar that served as a model for Sam's watering hole, to watch the final episode. Advertisers are betting that huge numbers of Americans will join them: They're paying $650,000 for each 30-second spot aired during the special 98-minute show. *Cheers*, which debuted on September 30, 1982, was a critical as well as a popular success. The show won 26 Emmy awards and was nominated for 111, and it was seen in 38 countries around the world.

A grand total of 275 episodes.

Mystery illness hits Navajo reservation

Navajo Reservation, May 31

A mysterious illness researchers are calling "unexplained adult respiratory distress syndrome" has killed 12 people here on the Navajo reservation that is located at the meeting point of the states of Arizona, New Mexico, Colorado and Utah. The victims, not exclusively Navajo, first notice mild flu-like symptoms, then hours or days later suddenly die from respiratory failure. Navajo nation President Peterson Zah is encouraging residents of the reservation to collaborate with the medical authorities.

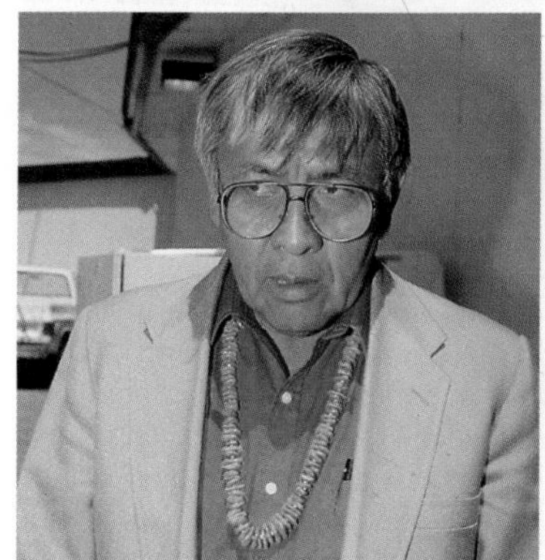

Navajo President Peterson Zah urged cooperation with U.S. authorities.

Spielberg's Jurassic dinos invade theaters

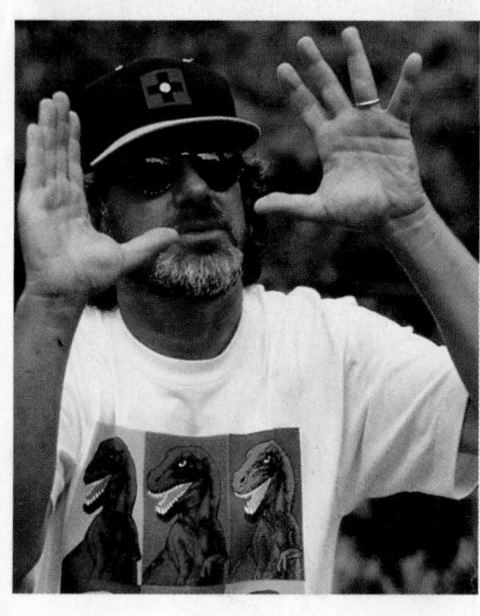

United States, June 10

Steven Spielberg's heavily hyped new movie, *Jurassic Park*, roared into theaters across the country today. The stars are, of course, the dinos, and their development began more than two years ago. New computer graphics software – more than 200 programs – and robotic technologies, including a life-size T-rex using flight simulator machinery, were designed to bring them to life. The movie's marketing campaign is bronto-sized, including T-shirts, toys and a new *Jurassic* ride to be built at Universal Studios' theme park.

June 12. *More than 60,000 easy riders gather in Milwaukee, Wisconsin, to celebrate the 90th anniversary of the creation of Harley-Davidson "hogs."*

Pentagon can't ask, gays mustn't tell

Washington, D.C., July 19

President Clinton and the Joint Chiefs of Staff have reached a compromise on gays in the armed forces. "Don't ask, don't tell, don't pursue" is the new rule. "Don't ask" means that although the ban on homosexual conduct is not removed, the military may not ask recruits if they are gay. "Don't tell" means that gays cannot declare their homosexuality, because showing "propensity or intent" to engage in homosexual acts is forbidden. "Don't pursue" means that only "credible" evidence of homosexual acts is cause for dismissal. Going to gay bars or reading gay magazines would not suffice to launch an investigation, for example.

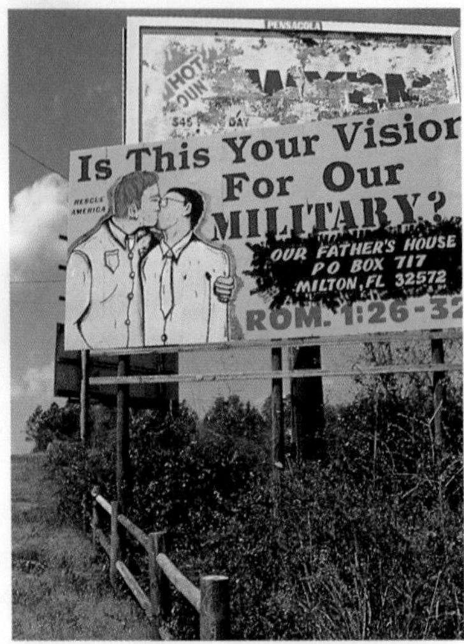

The new policy is controversial.

Midwest is drowned in record floods

The Mississippi has been above flood stage since June 27, and 20 million acres of farmland have been inundated.

Midwest, Aug. 1

The United States has seen the worst flooding in recorded history. The Father of Waters, as Native American tribes called the Mississippi River, and its tributaries overflowed their banks and the walls and levees built to protect Midwest farms and towns.

The first of many crests was recorded near Saint Paul on June 26. The upper Mississippi became unnavigable, with trees, dead animals and other detritus being rapidly swept along by the current, and a 500-mile stretch of the river was closed to shipping. Since June 27, the Mississippi has been above flood stage. Mid-July brought hope in the form of blue skies, but those hopes were dashed as new rains, and with them new record crests, came. The Midwest now resembled a great lake. Its raging rivers were a muddy brown, and the standing water stank and was dangerous, polluted with fertilizer, sewage, diesel fuel and other contaminants.

The end of July saw the climax of the flooding. The Missouri and Kansas rivers, at their convergence near Kansas City, both set records on July 27. The Kansas reached 55 feet, and the Missouri reached 49 feet. The Mississippi's largest crest came today, when it reached 49.5 feet at Saint Louis.

The flood's toll is monumental. The homes of 38,000 families have been damaged, and 20 million acres of farmland are underwater. At least 50 people died due to the catastrophe, and 70,000 were driven from their homes. The damage is estimated at $12 billion.

The Great Flood of 1993 seems to have come to an end, but much work remains to be done. It will take weeks for the river to recede to its normal levels, and the massive cleanup will last several months.

Aug. 12. *The pope was diplomatic, avoiding direct references to abortion when he met with Clinton on his arrival in Denver for World Youth Day.*

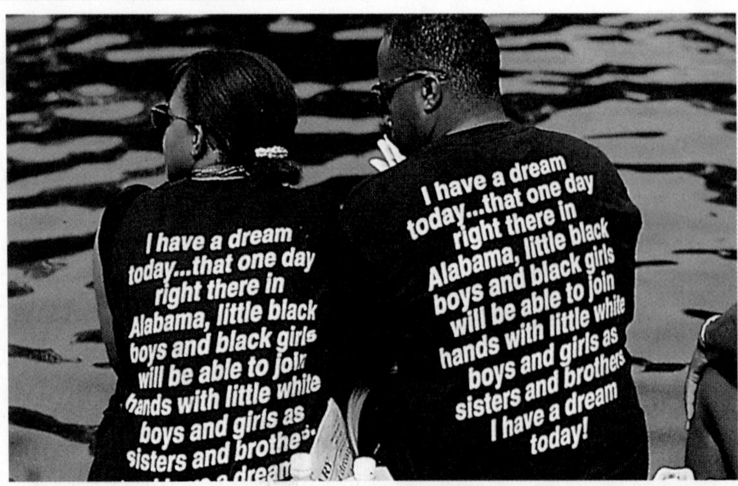

Aug. 28. *Thousands gather in Washington, D.C., to mark the 30th anniversary of Martin Luther King's historic "I have a dream" speech.*

Deficit-reduction plan barely passes

Washington, D.C., Aug. 6

Bill Clinton's deficit-reduction plan has scraped through Congress after much heated debate and presidential arm-twisting. No Republicans voted for the plan, and the President had to work the phones all week to get enough Democrats to back his budget. The House passed the bill yesterday with a vote of 218 to 216, and tonight Vice President Al Gore cast the tie-breaking vote in the Senate. The plan combines higher taxes, never a vote-getter in Congress, with a freeze of discretionary spending at 1993 levels. Increases hit incomes above $115,000, and a higher percentage of Social Security benefits for individuals who make more than $34,000 are taxable.

Rabin and Arafat sign historic accord

Recognition and Palestinian autonomy are the first steps to a lasting peace.

Washington, D.C., Sept. 13

History was made today on the White House South Lawn when two bitter enemies shook hands. It was Yasir Arafat, chairman of the P.L.O., who extended his hand to Israeli Prime Minister Yitzhak Rabin, who briefly hesitated, then took it, to seal an agreement on Palestinian self-rule. President Clinton praised the two leaders and thanked Norway's government, which brokered the secret talks that led to the accord. The agreement gives Palestinians a measure of self-rule immediately in Gaza, Jericho and parts of the West Bank. Much more work will be necessary to reach the ultimate objective of today's accord – a country shared by Jews and Arabs in peace.

Hillary presents her health plan on Hill

Washington, D.C., Sept. 29

First Lady Hillary Clinton has dazzled Congress with her performance as the White House's chief representative for its health-care reform plan. She said that the White House was open to compromise on methods for reform but insisted that the end result be a guarantee for every Amerian of "a comprehensive package of benefits that can never be taken away." It remains to be seen if the momentum of this early success will hold up through the legislative process to become law.

'Air' Jordan says goodbye to Bulls

Deerfield, Illinois, Oct. 6

The world's greatest basketball player and perhaps its most famous sportsman announced his retirement from the game here today. "I have no more challenges," explained Michael Jordan. "I had achieved everything in basketball I could." Jordan has led the Chicago Bulls to three straight championships, being named MVP in all three series. He has the game's highest scoring average in the regular season, 32.3 points a game, and in the playoffs, 34.6 points (→March 19, 1995).

Brady bill regulates handgun purchases

Washington, D.C., Nov. 24

Concern about violent crime has reached a point where the influence of the powerful National Rifle Association could no longer prevent passage of gun-control legislation. The Senate today enacted a bill imposing a five-day waiting period during which background checks will be made on handgun purchasers.

"How sweet it is," said James Brady, the Reagan aide who was wounded in a 1981 assassination attempt on the President and for whom the bill was named.

'I'm innocent' says Jackson live on TV

Santa Ynez, Calif., Dec. 22

Michael Jackson, fighting back tears in a four-minute speech broadcast live on TV, denied that he had sexually molested a 13-year-old boy. He called an examination of his genitals by criminal investigators a "horrifying nightmare." The results could be used to verify the boy's description of discoloring spots on the singer's skin. Jackson decried the treatment of the story "terrible mass media" and said, "I ask all of you to wait to hear the truth before you label or condemn me."

Aug. 16. *Cancer claims the life of movie star Stewart Granger, 80.*

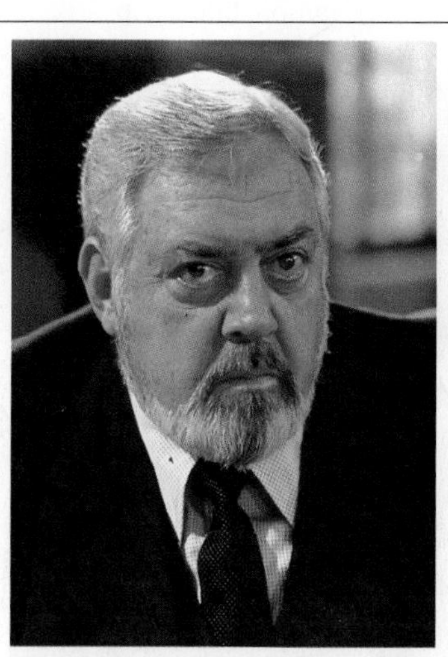

Sept. 12. *Raymond Burr, TV's Perry Mason, dies of cancer at 76.*

Oct. 7. *Princeton's Toni Morrison wins the Nobel Prize for literature.*

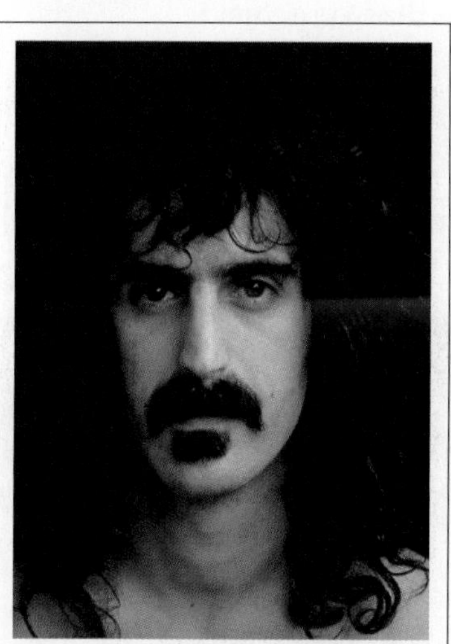

Dec. 4. *Rocker Frank Zappa dies just before his 53rd birthday.*

1994

Clinton

Detroit, Jan. 6.
Figure skater Nancy Kerrigan's knee is badly bruised by crowbar-wielding assailant (→ Feb. 27).

Manassas, Virginia, Jan. 21.
Lorena Bobbitt, who cut off part of her husband's penis, is found not guilty by reason of insanity of malicious wounding.

Atlanta, Jan. 30.
The Buffalo Bills lose an unprecedented fourth straight Super Bowl to the Dallas Cowboys, 30-13.

Seattle, April 8.
Rock star Kurt Cobain, 27, of the group Nirvana, kills himself with a shotgun.

Alexandria, Virginia, April 28.
C.I.A. agent Aldrich Ames is sentenced to life in prison for spying for the Soviet Union.

Singapore, May 5.
An American teenager, Michael Fay, receives four strokes of a cane for vandalism.

Washington, D.C., May 12.
Congress passes a bill banning violence, blockades and threats against abortion clinics.

Houston, June 22.
The Houston Rockets defeat the New York Knicks to win the N.B.A. championship.

Washington, D.C., Aug. 25.
Congress passes Clinton's crime bill, which budgets for more police on the streets, crime-prevention programs and the building of prisons and bans assault weapons.

Los Angeles, Oct. 12.
Steven Spielberg, David Geffen and Jeffrey Katzenberg announce the creation of a new movie studio.

Las Vegas, Nov. 5.
George Foreman, 45, beats Michael Moorer, 27, to retake the world heavyweight title.

Hollywood, Calif.
Top films included *Pulp Fiction, Schindler's List, Four Weddings and a Funeral, The Lion King* and *Forrest Gump*.

DEATHS

Big Sur, California, Aug. 19.
Linus Pauling (*Feb. 28, 1901), who won Nobel prizes for Peace and Chemistry.

Connecticut, Sept. 11.
Stage and screen actress Jessica Tandy (*June 6, 1909).

Delaware, Nov. 18.
Big Band leader Cab Calloway (*Dec. 25, 1907).

Major earthquake jolts Los Angeles

The earthquake hit just before dawn, spreading mayhem and killing dozens.

Los Angeles, Jan. 18
Aftershocks measuring 4.7 on the Richter scale added further damage to the devastation caused by a 6.6-Richter-scale earthquake which struck here yesterday at 4:31 a.m. local time.

The tremor was the strongest to have hit the city this century. Freeways crumbled, water mains burst and fires spread from the area where the quake was centered, in the suburban San Fernando Valley at the city's northern edge. Property damage has been estimated in excess of $7 billion, and 34 people have died. It could take this urban region with a population of 9 million – tens of thousands of whom are now homeless – more than a year to repair the damage.

Winter Olympics a hit despite media frenzy over Tonya and Nancy

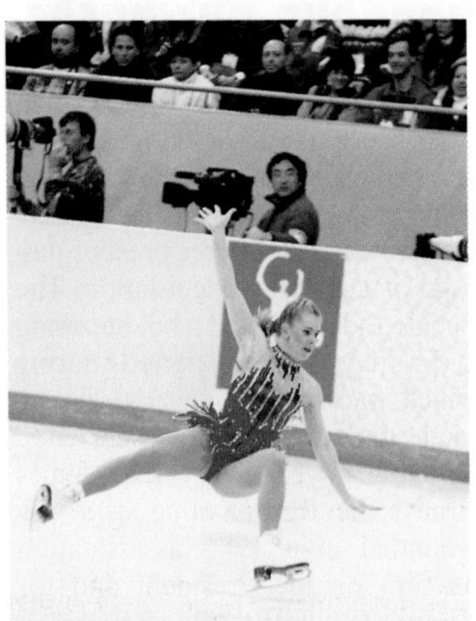

Not a good day for Tonya Harding.

Lillehammer, Norway, Feb. 27
The two million visitors to this year's Winter Olympics nearly unanimously proclaimed them the best ever. They certainly were for the U.S.; the team won more medals here, 13, than in any other Winter Games. Skiers Tommy Moe and Diann Roffe-Steinrotter and speed skater Dan Jansen won golds.

Unfortunately the intensive press coverage of the tension between figure skaters Tonya Harding and Nancy Kerrigan somewhat overshadowed Kerrigan's winning a silver medal. Harding denies charges of being involved in a bizarre attack on Kerrigan on January 6.

Silver, not gold, for Nancy Kerrigan.

Jan. 22. *Telly "Kojak" Savalas, who turned 70 yesterday, dies of cancer.*

We don't spike our smokes, say CEOS

Washington, D.C., April 14
Six chairmen from the biggest American cigarette companies appeared before Congress today to deny claims by the Food and Drug Administration that they spike smokes with extra nicotine to keep their customers hooked. Phillip Morris took ABC to court last month over a TV documentary making the same accusation. If the F.D.A. decides that the companies do add nicotine, cigarettes could be prohibited like cocaine and heroin.

Death claims two American icons: Nixon and Jackie

Nixon worked hard in his later years to reclaim his place as a great U.S. leader.

Jacqueline Kennedy Onassis was a role model for many American women.

New York, April 22

Richard M. Nixon, who died today at 81, was probably America's most controversial politician. His presidency came at a time when the country was divided, and it remains split in its view of the man. Nixon's successful 1946 and 1950 California campaigns for the Senate won him the nickname "Tricky Dicky" because of his tactics of accusing his opponents of being communist sympathizers. As Vice President to Dwight Eisenhower, he developed the foreign policy expertise which would serve him well later. He won m[illegible]itchen debate" with Soviet leader Nikita Krushchev over the relative merits of capitalism and communism. Elected President in 1968 by a narrow margin in the popular vote, his 1972 re-election was a landslide. The Watergate scandal led to his resignation and deepened his reputation as a devious, vengeful and even paranoid politician. But his foreign policy triumphs, especially the opening up of relations with China and initiating detente with the Soviet Union, have been widely praised. In recent years his legacy has undergone revision, and he has taken a role of grey eminence to U.S. preside[illegible]

New York, May 19

Jacqueline Kennedy Onassis was loved and admired by Americans and around the world. Her struggle against lymphatic cancer was revealed earlier this year; she died today at the age of 64.

Jacqueline Bouvier was born on July 28, 1929, to a rich Republican family whose French ancestors fought with the Americans in the Revolutionary War. She was dubbed "Queen Deb of the Year" when she came out in New York society in 1946. Working as a photojournalist she interviewed the young Massachusetts Senator John F. Kennedy, whom she had previously met at a Washington party. Her beauty and sophistication helped create the Camelot myth of her husband's presidency. When he died, her courage was lauded, and she gave strength to a nation in mourning. Her later marriage to an older Greek shipping tycoon, Aristotle Onassis, at first caused some controversy in the U.S. For many, she would always be Jackie Kennedy, but for others, she became a symbol of international high society – Jackie O. For the last few years, she epitomized the successful businesswoman, working as an editor for Viking and Doubleday.

Whitewater findings favor White House

Washington, D.C., June 30

No White House officials will be charged with breaking laws in connection with their receiving briefings on an investigation into Whitewater said Robert Fiske, the special counsel appointed to look into the matter, in his first findings.

The Whitewater affair takes its name from an Arkansas real estate development in which President Clinton invested while governor of the state. James McDougal, who was a partner in Whitewater with Clinton, ran Madison Guaranty Savings and Loan, which later went bankrupt. The investigation centers on the question of whether money was diverted from the S&L to pay Clinton's 1984 gubernatorial campaign debt or to the coffers of the Whitewater Development Corp.

Today's findings concern the Washington phase, or the question of whether the White House was illegally briefed about an earlier investigation by the Resolution Trust Corp. into whether funds had been diverted. Fiske is now turning to the Arkansas phase: his investigation of the Whitewater real-estate company dealings themselves.

Fiske had also looked into the death last year of a close friend and aide of Clinton's, Vincent Foster. He found that Foster did indeed commit suicide and that there was no evidence that concern over the Whitewater affair contributed to his severe state of depression.

Millions watch fall of American hero O.J. Simpson

Los Angeles, June 17

A white Ford Bronco led a group of California Highway Patrol cars and a fleet of television news helicopters across the freeways of Los Angeles County as thousands of people stared and millions more watched on TV. In the Bronco was movie star, corporate spokesman and former football hero O.J. Simpson. Simpson led the pack to his home and then gave himself up. Earlier today, he had failed to appear for an agreed-upon arraignment on charges of murdering his former wife and another man.

Nicole Simpson, 35, and Ron Goldman, 25, a waiter at a restaurant that she frequented, were found dead from multiple stab wounds on Monday the 13th. Police found blood stains on Simpson's vehicle and in his driveway. Simpson, who had flown to Chicago the night of the murder, was asked to return for questioning.

After the police announced that Simpson had disappeared, his lawyer, Robert Shapiro, described him as suicidal and released a note he had written. "Please think of the real O.J., not this lost person," he wrote. Police located the Bronco in Orange County by tracing cellular phone calls. The 40-m.p.h. chase began at 6:25 p.m., ending when Simpson led the convoy to his home at 8:50 p.m. (→ Jan. 27, 1995)

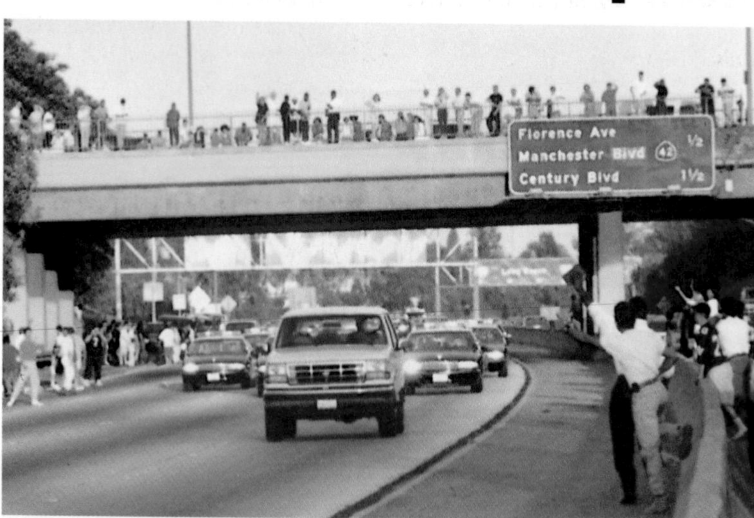

Fans waved "Go Juice" signs as the former football star was chased by police.

First World Cup U.S.A. is won by Brazil in a penalty shootout

Brazil's fourth soccer world championship came after 120 scoreless minutes.

Pasadena, July 17

After two hours of unadventurous and goalless play on both sides which emphasized defense over fancy footwork, Brazil won the penalty shootout which gave them the victory over Italy in the final game of the World Cup.

The first soccer championship to be held in the U.S. saw the host team ousted by Brazil 1-0 in the second round. A smashing success, World Cup U.S.A. drew more spectators than any before. Total attendance in the sweltering heat was 3,567,415 – [illegible]ore than 68,000 per match – compa[illegible] million who tu[illegible] ou[illegible]

Castro threatens a flood of emigrants

Guantanamo Bay, Aug. 24

Cubans are taking to the Strait of Florida by the thousands in rickety boats, rafts and even inner tubes to head for the U.S. Fidel Castro, angered by a huge demonstration in Havana earlier this month and by the U.S. policy of automatically granting asylum to Cubans who flee the country, has threatened to stop blocking their exit. President Bill Clinton ended this policy last week, and today ordered the expansion of the U.S. [illegible] here [illegible]

Aug. 1. *Graceland meets Neverland: Lisa-Marie Presley, Elvis's daughter, says that the rumors that she had married Michael Jackson in May are true.*

Race, IQ and class debate rages in U.S.

United States, Oct. 19
The United States is currently embroiled in a controversy over the relationship of intelligence to race and class. The debate, which has often raged in the U.S., has been rekindled by three new books: *Race, Evolution and Behavior: A Life History Perspective* by J. Phillipe Rushton, *The Decline of Intelligence in America: A Strategy for National Renewal* by Seymour W. Itzkoff and especially *The Bell Curve: Intelligence and Class Structure in American Life*, which has attracted most of the media's attention, by Charles Murray and Richard Herrnstein, who died last month.

All three books assert that IQ is a real and accurate indicator of intelligence and that it is correlated to job success and rates of crime and other social pathologies. The authors say that a low-IQ underclass is reproducing more quickly than what Murray and Herrnstein have called the "cognitive elite," lowering the intelligence of the country. They also point out that blacks make up a large proportion of this underclass and that blacks as a group score lower on IQ tests than whites.

While some people say the books spell out a hard truth that the country must face, others discount them as unscientific and racist. Many scientists reject the value of IQ tests, and there is little if any agreement on how much of a person's intelligence is inherited.

U.S. invades Haiti

Haiti, Sept. 19
American soldiers seized Haiti today and did not fire a shot. As the announcements from loudspeakers in army helicopters flying over Port-au-Prince put it: "We're not at war. We're here to restore democracy and supply humanitarian aid." The United Nations Security Council had approved a U.S.-led invasion to drive out the military government and restore the president they had forced into exile, Jean-Bertrand Aristide. An 11th-hour agreement brokered by Jimmy Carter, which calls for junta leader Raoul Cédras to step down, circumvented a bloody battle with his forces.

Strike cancels Series

New York City, Sept. 14
"Nineteen ninety-four – the season that struck itself out," is how former baseball commissioner Peter Ueberroth defined the cancellation of the season and the World Series by major league owners. The players strike that led to the decision began August 12, when the players rejected a proposal by the owners calling for a 50-50 split of industry revenues and a salary cap. Bud Selig, the acting commissioner, announced the cancellation by a fax in which he said: "This is a sad day. Nobody wanted this to happen, but the continuing player strike leaves us no choice but to take this action." The owners voted last night; all but two, Peter Angelos of Baltimore and Marge Schott of Cincinatti, signed the resolution to kill the Series. Angelos agreed with the decision but wanted to change the wording; Schott, however, wanted to continue the season with replacements. "Let's see the real players instead of the million-dollar babies," she said.

President Clinton has said that perhaps baseball's anti-trust exemption should be reviewed. A bill modifying the status failed in the Senate last night, but Congress is still considering a repeal (→April 2, 1995).

Republicans take the Hill in elections

Washington, D.C., Nov. 9
Republicans won control of both houses of Congress, for the first time in 40 years, in yesterday's elections. In the Senate, 53 of the 100 seats are now Republican, and in the House there are now 230 Republicans and 204 Democrats. Voters turned out Democratic governors as well, including New York's Mario Cuomo, defeated by George Pataki; a majority of the statehouses are now Republican. Republicans say the results are a rebuke by voters to Bill Clinton, who said today, "They sent us a clear message – I got it."

Cooperation between the White House and the new majority will be difficult. Although Bob Dole, the Senate's Republican leader, seems willing to make deals with the president, Jesse Helms, likely to head the powerful Senate Foreign Relations Committee, and Newt Gingrich, expected to be the next House Speaker, are more combatitive. Both these right-wing Southerners have built reputations as "bomb throwers" and have blasted Bill Clinton at every opportunity. The Grand Old Party is now preparing to capitalize on their electoral momentum and vote on the points – such as a balanced-budget amendment and tax cuts – of the "Contract With America," their campaign platform, in the first 100 days of their new majority (→Jan. 24, 1995).

Gingrich is expected to be Speaker.

"Forrest Gump" is the surprise hit of the summer, having taken in $222 million. Disney's "The Lion King," at $257 million, is at the top of the heap.

Oct. 20. *Hollywood's humane tough guy, Burt Lancaster, shown here with Deborah Kerr in "From Here to Eternity," dies of a heart attack at 80.*

1995

Clinton

Washington, D.C., Jan. 2.
Marion Barry, who spent six months in prison for a 1990 drug conviction, returns as the capital's mayor.

Wyoming, Jan. 13.
Gray wolves are reintroduced to Yellowstone National Park after a 20-year debate.

Miami, Jan. 29.
The San Francisco 49ers beat the San Diego Chargers, 49-26, to win Super Bowl XXIX.

Washington, D.C., Jan. 31
President Clinton says he will create a $20 billion line of credit to Mexico to help save the peso.

Paris, Feb. 22.
France accuses five Americans, including four diplomats, of "economic espionage."

New York City, Feb. 23.
The Dow Jones industrial average rises above 4,000 points for the first time.

United States, Feb. 24.
Diver Greg Louganis, who won gold medals in the 1984 and 1988 Olympics, announces he has AIDS.

Beijing, Feb. 26.
The signing of an accord on the protection of intellectual property averts a U.S.-China trade war.

Washington, D.C., March 11.
President Clinton chooses John M. Deutch, the Pentagon's second-ranking official, to head the C.I.A.

New York City, March 14.
The *New York Times*, first published on Sept. 18, 1851, prints its 50,000th issue.

Washington, D.C., March 17.
President Clinton welcomes Sinn Fein leader Gerry Adams to the White House.

San Francisco, April 18.
Thousands of fans cheer Kansas City Chiefs quarterback Joe Montana after he announces his retirement from the N.F.L.

DEATHS

Locarno, Switzerland, Feb. 4.
Mystery writer Patricia Highsmith (*Jan. 19, 1921).

Washington, D.C., Feb. 9.
J. William Fulbright, former Democratic Senator from Arkansas who inspired Fulbright scholarships (*April 9, 1905).

Anacortes, Wash., April 14.
Folksinger and actor Burl Ives (*June 14, 1909).

Clinton's agenda fails to sway Republicans

Washington, D.C., Jan. 24

House Speaker Newt Gingrich jumped up to applaud Bill Clinton's call, in his State of the Union speech for "leaner, not meaner" government, but for most of his 82-minute address, the new Republican majority remained stonily silent. Bob Dole, the Senate majority leader, said that the President was "going to run into reality pretty quick." The reality is that the Republicans are preparing an offensive on the way Washington now works. They plan to dismantle many welfare programs, pass a balanced-budget amendment, repeal last year's assault-weapons ban and decrease U.S. contributions to the U.N., all projects opposed, at least in part, by the President.

President's State of the Union speech.

Big Blue gives green light for blue jeans

Armonk, N.Y., Feb. 3

I.B.M., the home of the dark conservative suit and no-nonsense tie, has lightened up its unwritten, but nonetheless strict, dress code. Employees will now be able to wear whatever they think is appropriate to the office.

Big Blue has joined a large number of American companies that are relaxing dress codes. Many have instituted "Dress-down Fridays," a day when employees can drop their stuffy three-pieces and dresses for jeans and loafers. Law firms and banks, even "The Company," the C.I.A., have gone casual for the entry to the weekend.

O.J. Simpson's defense slams 'rush to judgement' by prosecutors

Los Angeles, Jan. 27

Americans, shocked at the brutal slaying of Nicole Simpson and Ronald Goodman, have been waiting for this moment for seven months. How would football hero O.J. Simpson respond to the charges that he killed his former wife and her friend? Today, Simpson takes his case into bookstores with *I Want to Tell You.* "How can anybody say I killed this woman," he writes in his new book. "Don't they understand I'd jump in front of a bullet for Nicole?"

Prosecutors presented a different Simpson in their opening arguments this week. They portrayed an abusive man bent on controlling his ex-wife. State attorneys said O.J.'s motive was simple, "If he couldn't have her, nobody else could." They presented a trail of blood and hair linking the victims to Simpson by way of a bloody glove found at his home.

The defense, which wound up its first arguments yesterday, said the prosecution condemned Simpson in a "rush to judgement at any cost," which ignored other suspects and leads. Sloppy police work was magnified by racism, they said, focusing on Detective Mark Fuhrman, who found the notorious bloody glove. He planted it, they insist.

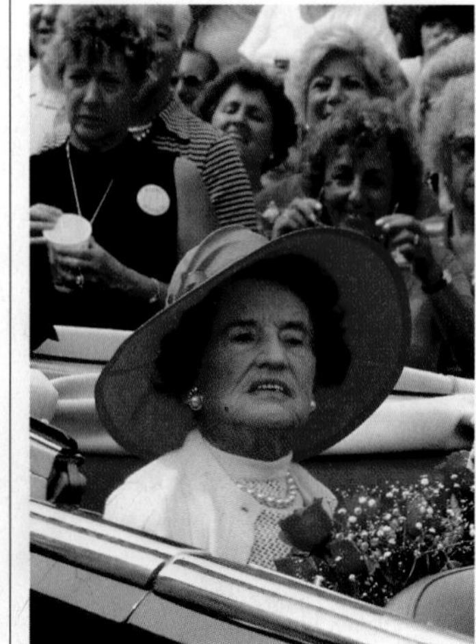

Jan. 22. *Rose Fitzgerald Kennedy (*July 22, 1890), the mother of the 35th President of the United States, dies of pneumonia at 104.*

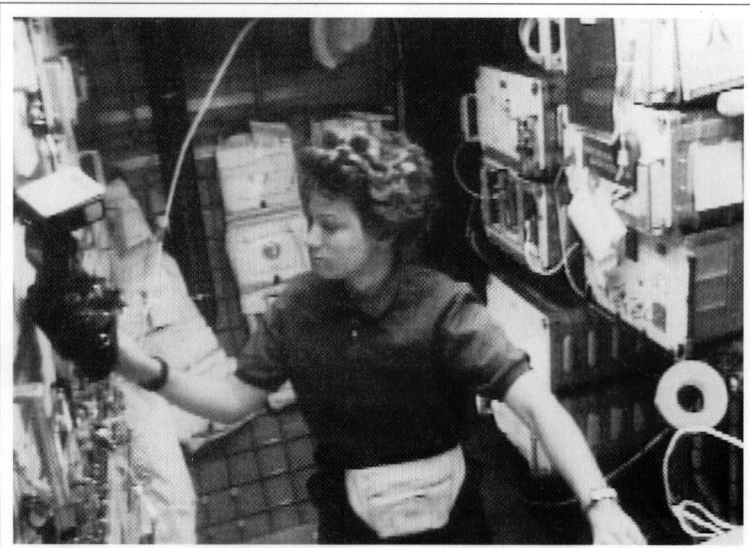

Feb. 6. *Lieutenant Colonel Eileen Collins, 38, NASA's first female shuttle pilot, prepares for Discovery's rendezvous with Russia's Mir space station.*

Hoops king Air Jordan reclaims his throne

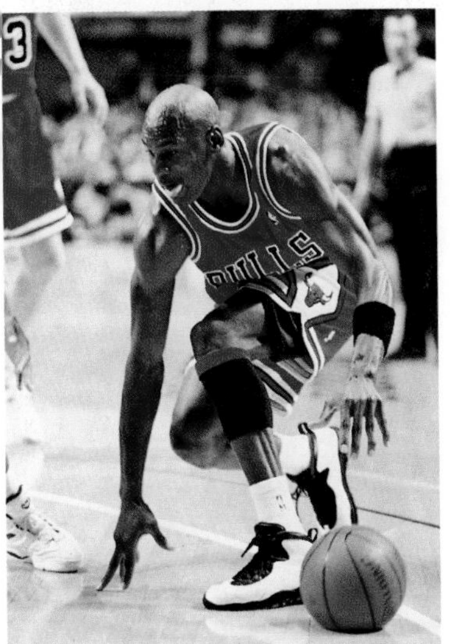
He's back after a 21-month absence.

Indianapolis, March 19

"I'm back" was all Michael Jordan's press release said, and that was enough. For two weeks, since the three-time National Champion and MVP announced he was quitting baseball and started working out with his old club, the Bulls, basketball fans have been waiting for those two words.

Tonight, His Airness graced the court once again, only to lose his comeback game against the Indiana Pacers in overtime, 103-96. Jordan took 16 minutes to sink the first of only 7 of 28 shots from the field, but that didn't matter. The important thing is – as Pacers coach Larry Brown put it – "The Beatles and Elvis are back."

Tyson released after 1,095 days in prison

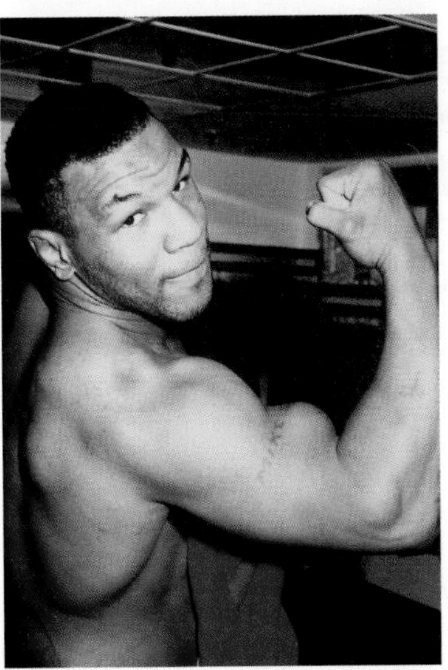
The former heavyweight champion.

Southington, Ohio, March 25

Mike Tyson, one of the most promising heavyweight boxers the world has ever seen, returned to his palatial mansion here today. The former champ, wearing an Islamic prayer cap and saying nothing to reporters and fans, had earlier left the prison near Indianapolis where he has spent the last three years. Tyson was convicted in 1992 of the rape of a Miss Black America contestant, Desiree Washington. The big question now is what the future holds in store for the man who became the world's youngest heavyweight champ. Experts say he could make $50 million from his first fight, and millions more if he tries to recapture the world crown.

Major league strike ends after 234 days

Chicago, April 2

The 234-day strike by major league baseball players has come to an end. After a four-hour meeting here today, team owners accepted the players' offer to return to the diamond. Two days ago, a federal judge ordered owners to restore free-agent bidding, salary arbitration and the anti-collusion provisions of baseball's expired collective bargaining agreement, fulfilling the players' conditions for ending the strike. The owners only alternative would have been to institute a lockout.

Greenback plunges to new record lows

New York City, April 10

The U.S. dollar's steady downward spiral over the past weeks got worse today, when the greenback hit a new postwar low of 80.15 yen.

Germany and Japan have been buying dollars to prop up the U.S. currency but complain that the U.S. Federal Reserve is not doing enough to stop the fall. They blame the Fed's policy of "benign neglect" for the drop and say the U.S. has an obligation to support its currency because of the dollar's status as the world's reserve currency.

Terrorism hits Oklahoma

Oklahoma City, April 19

A car bomb tore a nine-story hole in the Alfred Murrah federal building here at 9:00 this morning. The massive blast could be heard as far as 30 miles away, and the bomb is estimated to have been 1,000 to 1,200 pounds.

As many as 100 people have died in the attack, but rescue workers are still searching the rubble for victims. Nearly half of the 550 people who work in the office building are still unaccounted for, and it is feared that many of them have perished. The building housed offices of the Drug Enforcement Administration and the Bureau of Alcohol, Tobacco and Firearms and other federal workers as well as a childcare center.

Theories on the responsibility for the bombing range from Middle Eastern terrorists to Colombian drug cartels to parties seeking revenge for the federal raid two years ago on the Waco headquarters of the Branch Davidians religious cult, in which some 80 people died. President Clinton, speaking just hours after the attack, vowed to swiftly bring to justice the "evil cowards" who perpetrated the attack.

March 13. *Flooding due to heavy rain has turned 39 of California's 58 counties into disaster zones, killing 12 people and devastating farmland.*

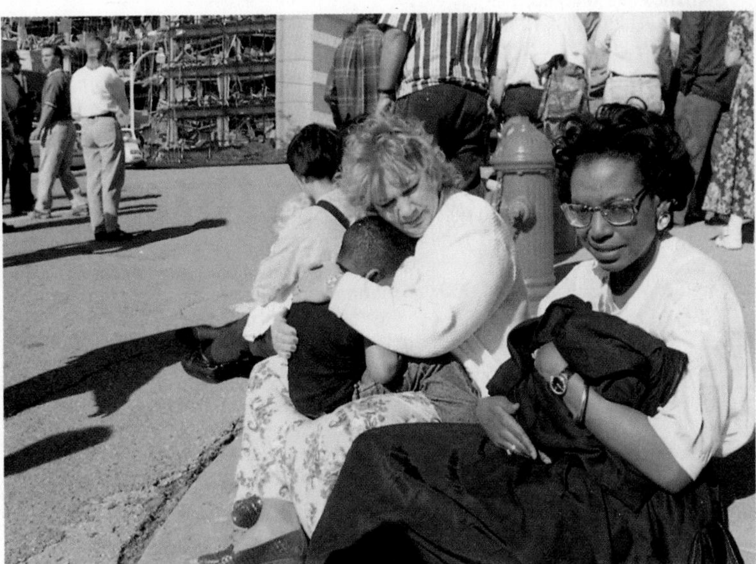
The bombing of the Murrah building in Oklahoma City comes on the second anniversary of the federal raid on the Branch Davidian compound in Waco.

IMMIGRATION TO THE

NO RELIABLE IMMIGRATION STATISTICS ARE AVAILABLE FOR THE PERIOD PRIOR TO 1820

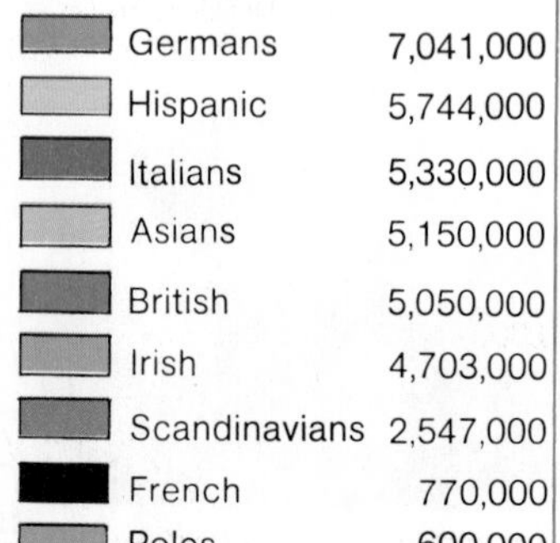

DISTRIBUTION OF IMMIGRANTS

Group	Number
Germans	7,041,000
Hispanic	5,744,000
Italians	5,330,000
Asians	5,150,000
British	5,050,000
Irish	4,703,000
Scandinavians	2,547,000
French	770,000
Poles	600,000

AMERICA: LAND OF OPPORTUNITY FOR THE WORLD'S OPPRESSED

The United States is, above all, a nation of immigrants, of men and women who came in search of freedom, happiness and fortune. Many were fleeing religious or political persecution, war or intolerable socio-economic conditions at home.

America's history has been marked by great waves of immigration. Between 1820 and 1990, more than 56.9 million people immigrated to the United States.

For decades, these millions of immigrants found a welcome in the New World. They were able to build a new life for themselves, becoming part of the "melting pot" of American society. Many immigrants played key roles in their adopted country's economic and political life.

Gradually, however, this began to change. Doors that had been wide open began to close. There was growing talk of the problems posed by immigrants. The U.S. government began to restrict immigration on the basis of national origin in 1882, when the Chinese Exclusion Act barred Chinese laborers. Later legislation excluded most Asians. The national origins quota system was abolished in 1965.

The arrival of many thousands of often illegal immigrants caused tensions in many communities during the early 1980s. The Immigration Act of 1990 set an annual cap of 714,000 on immigration, not including refugees. The cap drops to 675,000 in 1995. The lure of the New World remains strong: A visa lottery in 1991 attracted 15 million applications for 40,000 visas.

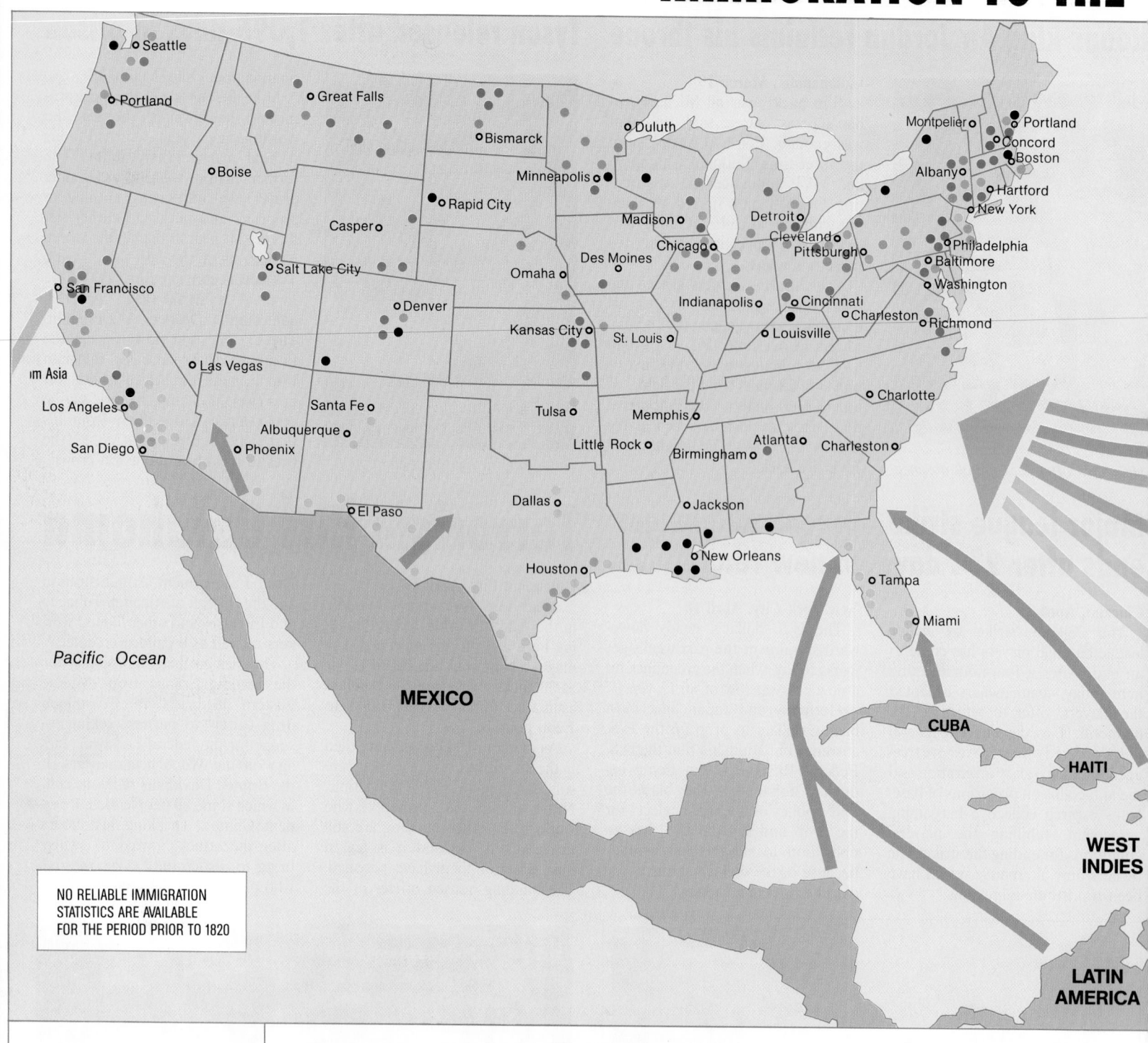

UNITED STATES FROM 1820

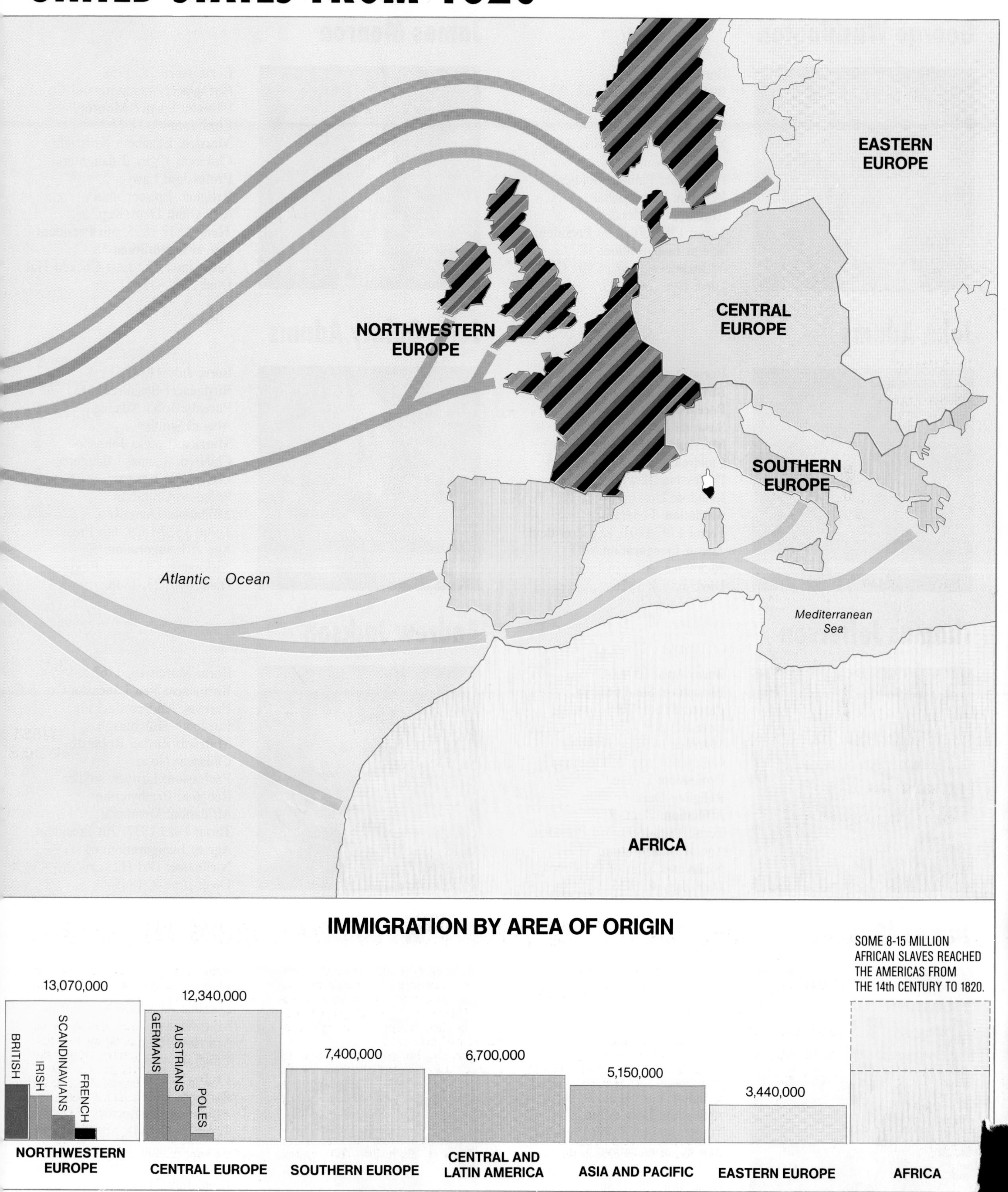
EASTERN
EUROPE
CENTRAL
EUROPE
NORTHWESTERN
EUROPE
SOUTHERN
EUROPE
Atlantic Ocean
Mediterranean
Sea
AFRICA
IMMIGRATION BY AREA OF ORIGIN
SOME 8-15 MILLION
AFRICAN SLAVES REACHED
THE AMERICAS FROM
THE 14th CENTURY TO 1820.
13,070,000
BRITISH
IRISH
SCANDINAVIANS
FRENCH
12,340,000
GERMANS
AUSTRIANS
POLES
7,400,000
6,700,000
5,150,000
3,440,000
NORTHWESTERN
EUROPE
CENTRAL EUROPE
SOUTHERN EUROPE
CENTRAL AND
LATIN AMERICA
ASIA AND PACIFIC
EASTERN EUROPE
AFRICA

George Washington

Born: Feb. 22, 1732
Birthplace: Pope's Creek, Va.
Parents: Augustine Washington, Mary Ball
Married: Martha Custis
Children: None
Profession: Planter, Soldier
Religion: Episcopalian
Affiliation: Federalist
Term: 1789-1797, 1st President
Age at Inauguration: 57
Nickname: Father of His Country
Died: Dec. 14, 1799

John Adams

Born: Oct. 30, 1735
Birthplace: Braintree, Mass.
Parents: John Adams, Susanna Boylston
Married: Abigail Smith
Children: 2 sons, 3 daughters
Profession: Lawyer
Religion: Unitarian
Affiliation: Federalist
Term: 1797-1801, 2nd President
Age at Inauguration: 61
Nickname: Atlas of Independence
Died: July 4, 1826

Thomas Jefferson

Born: April 13, 1743
Birthplace: Shadwell, Va.
Parents: Peter Jefferson, Jane Randolph
Married: Martha Skelton
Children: 1 son, 5 daughters
Profession: Lawyer
Religion: Deist
Affiliation: Dem.-Rep.
Term: 1801-1809, 3rd President
Age at Inauguration: 57
Nickname: Man of the People
Died: July 4, 1826

James Madison

Born: March 16, 1751
Birthplace: Port Conway, Va.
Parents: James Madison, Eleanor Conway
Married: Dorothea "Dolley" Todd
Children: None
Profession: Lawyer
Religion: Episcopalian
Affiliation: Dem.-Rep.
Term: 1809-1817, 4th President
Age at Inauguration: 57
Nickname: Father of Constitution
Died: June 28, 1836

James Monroe

Born: April 28, 1758
Birthplace: Westmoreland Co., Va.
Parents: Spence Monroe, Eliza Jones
Married: Elizabeth Kortright
Children: 1 son, 2 daughters
Profession: Lawyer
Religion: Episcopalian
Affiliation: Dem.-Rep.
Term: 1817-1825, 5th President
Age at inaguration: 58
Nickname: The Last Cocked Hat
Died: July 4, 1831

John Quincy Adams

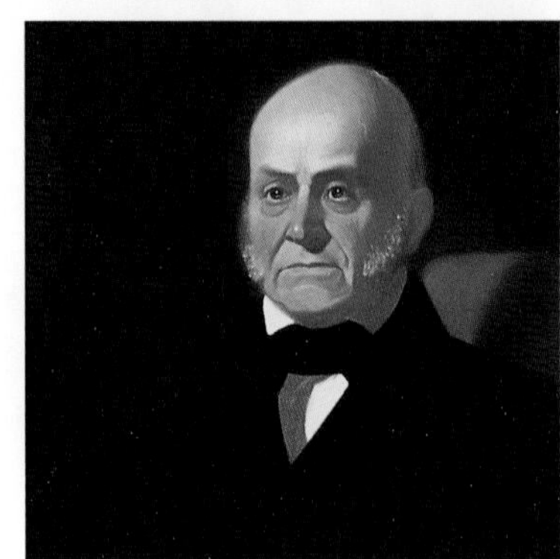

Born: July 11, 1767
Birthplace: Braintree, Ma.
Parents: John Adams, Abigail Smith
Married: Louisa Johnson
Children: 3 sons, 1 daughter
Profession: Lawyer
Religion: Unitarian
Affiliation: Dem.-Rep.
Term: 1825-1829, 6th President
Age at Inauguration: 57
Nickname: Old Man Eloquent
Died: Feb. 23, 1848

Andrew Jackson

Born: March 15, 1767
Birthplace: New Lancaster Co., S.C.
Parents: Andrew Jackson, Elizabeth Hutchinson
Married: Rachel Robards
Children: None
Profession: Lawyer, soldier
Religion: Presbyterian
Affiliation: Democrat
Term: 1829-1837, 7th President,
Age at Inauguration: 61
Nickname: Old Hickory
Died: June 8, 1845

Martin Van Buren

Born: Dec. 5, 1782
Birthplace: Kinderhook, N.Y.
Parents: Abraham Van Buren, Mary Hoes
Married: Hannah Hoes
Children: 4 sons
Profession: Lawyer
Religion: Dutch Reformed
Affiliation: Democrat
Term: 1837-1841, 8th President
Age at inauguration: 54
Nickname: The Little Magician
Died: July 24, 1862

William Henry Harrison

Born: Feb. 9, 1773
Birthplace: Berkeley, Va.
Parents: Benjamin Harrison, Elizabeth Bassett
Married: Anna Tuthill Symmes
Children: 6 sons, 4 daughters
Profession: Public official, soldier
Religion: Episcopalian
Affiliation: Whig
Term: 1841, 9th President
Age at Inauguration: 68
Nickname: Old Tippecanoe
Died: April 4, 1841

John Tyler

Born: March 29, 1790
Birthplace: Greenway, Va.
Parents: John Tyler, Mary Armistead
Married: L. Christian, J. Gardiner
Children: 8 sons, 7 daughters
Profession: Lawyer
Religion: Episcopalian
Affiliation: Independent Whig
Term: 1841-1845, 10th President
Age at Inauguration: 51
Nickname: Accidental President
Died: Jan. 18, 1862

James Knox Polk

Born: Nov. 2, 1795
Birthplace: Mecklenburg County, N.C.
Parents: Samuel Polk, Jane Knox
Married: Sara Childress
Children: None
Profession: Lawyer
Religion: Presbyterian
Affiliation: Democrat
Term: 1845-1849, 11th President
Age at Inauguration: 49
Nickname: Young Hickory
Died: June 15, 1849

Zachary Taylor

Born: Nov. 24, 1784
Birthplace: Orange Co., Va.
Parents: Richard Taylor, Sarah Strother
Married: Margaret Smith
Children: 1 son, 5 daughters
Profession: Soldier
Religion: Episcopalian
Affiliation: Whig
Term: 1849-1850, 12th President
Age at Inauguration: 64
Nickname: Old Rough and Ready
Died: July 9, 1850

Millard Fillmore

Born: Jan 7, 1800
Birthplace: Summerhill, N.Y.
Parents: Nathaniel Fillmore, Phoebe Millard
Married: A. Powers, C. McIntosh
Children: 2 daughters
Profession: Teacher, lawyer
Religion: Unitarian
Affiliation: Whig
Term: 1850-1853, 13th President
Age at Inauguration: 50
Nickname: Am. Louis Philippe
Died: March 8, 1874

Franklin Pierce

Born: Nov. 23, 1804
Birthplace: Hillsboro, N.H.
Parents: B. Pierce, A. Kendrick
Married: Jane Appleton
Children: 3 sons
Profession: Lawyer, Public Official
Religion: Episcopalian
Affiliation: Democrat
Term: 1853-1857, 14th President
Age at Inauguration: 48
Nickname: Young Hickory of the Granite Hills
Died: Oct. 8, 1869

James Buchanan

Born: April 23, 1791
Birthplace: Stony Batter, Pa.
Parents: James Buchanan, Elizabeth Speer
Married: Never married
Children: None
Profession: Lawyer
Religion: Presbyterian
Affiliation: Democrat
Term: 1857-1861, 15th President
Age at Inauguration: 65
Nickname: Old Buck
Died: June 1, 1868

Abraham Lincoln

Born: Feb. 12, 1809
Birthplace: Hardin Co., Ky.
Parents: Thomas Lincoln, Nancy Hanks
Married: Mary Todd
Children: 4 sons
Profession: Lawyer
Religion: not affiliated
Affiliation: Republican
Term: 1861-1865, 16th President
Age at Inauguration: 52
Nickname: Honest Abe
Died: April 15, 1865

Andrew Johnson

Born: Dec. 29, 1808
Birthplace: Raleigh, N.C.
Parents: Jacob Johnson, Mary McDonough
Married: Eliza McCardle
Children: 3 sons, 2 daughters
Profession: Public Official
Religion: Not affiliated
Affiliation: Democrat; Unionist
Term: 1865-1869, 17th President
Age at Inauguration: 56
Nickname: None
Died: July 31, 1875

Ulysses Simpson Grant

Born: April 27, 1822
Birthplace: Point Pleasant, Oh.
Parents: Jesse Grant, Hannah Simpson
Married: Julia Dent
Children: 3 sons, 1 daughter
Profession: Soldier
Religion: Methodist
Affiliation: Republican
Term: 1869-1877, 18th President
Age at Inauguration: 46
Nickname: Hero of Appomattox
Died: July 23, 1885

Rutherford Birchard Hayes

Born: Oct. 4, 1822
Birthplace: Delaware, Oh.
Parents: Rutherford Hayes, Sophia Birchard
Married: Lucy Webb
Children: 7 sons, 1 daughter
Profession: Lawyer
Religion: Methodist
Affiliation: Republican
Term: 1877-1881, 19th President
Age at Inauguration: 54
Nickname: Dark-Horse President
Died: Jan. 17, 1893

James Abram Garfield

Born: Nov. 19, 1831
Birthplace: Orange, Oh.
Parents: Abram Garfield, Eliza Ballou
Married: Lucretia Rudolph
Children: 5 sons, 2 daughters
Profession: Public Official
Religion: Disciples of Christ
Affiliation: Republican
Term: 1881, 20th President
Age at Inauguration: 49
Nickname: None
Died: Sept. 19, 1881

Chester Alan Arthur

Born: Oct. 5, 1830
Birthplace: Fairfield, Vt.
Parents: William Arthur, Malvina Stone
Married: Ellen Lewis Herndon
Children: 2 sons, 1 daughter
Profession: Lawyer
Religion: Episcopalian
Affiliation: Republican
Term: 1881-1885, 21st President
Age at Inauguration: 50
Nickname: The Gentleman Boss
Died: Nov. 18, 1886

Grover Cleveland

Born: March 18, 1837
Birthplace: Caldwell, N.J.
Parents: Richard Cleveland, Ann Neale
Married: Frances Folsom
Children: 2 sons, 3 daughters
Profession: Lawyer
Religion: Presbyterian
Affiliation: Democrat
Term: 1885-1889, 1893-1897, 22nd and 24th President
Age at Inauguration: 47, 55
Died: June 24, 1908

Benjamin Harrison

Born: Aug. 20, 1833
Birthplace: North Bend, Oh.
Parents: John Harrison, Elizabeth Irwin
Married: C. Scott, M. Dimmick
Children: 1 son, 2 daughters
Profession: Lawyer
Religion: Presbyterian
Affiliation: Republican
Term: 1889-1893, 23rd President
Age at Inauguration: 55
Nickname: Kid Gloves Harrison
Died: March 13, 1901

William McKinley

Born: Jan. 29, 1843
Birthplace: Niles, Oh.
Parents: William McKinley, Nancy Allison
Married: Ida Saxton
Children: 2 daughters
Profession: Lawyer
Religion: Methodist
Affiliation: Republican
Term: 1897-1901, 25th President
Age at Inauguration: 54
Nickname: Idol of Ohio
Died: Sept. 14, 1901

Theodore Roosevelt

Born: Oct. 27, 1858
Birthplace: New York City, N.Y.
Parents: Theodore Roosevelt, Martha Bulloch
Married: A. Lee, E. Carow
Children: 4 sons, 2 daughters
Profession: Lawyer
Religion: Dutch Reformed
Affiliation: Republican
Term: 1901-1909, 26th President
Age at Inauguration: 42
Nickname: TR, Trust Buster
Died: Jan. 6, 1919

William Howard Taft

Born: Sept. 15, 1857
Birthplace: Cincinnati, Oh.
Parents: Alphonso Taft, Louisa Torrey
Married: Helen Herron
Children: 2 sons, 1 daughter
Profession: Lawyer
Religion: Unitarian
Affiliation: Republican
Term: 1909-1913, 27th President
Age at Inauguration: 51
Nickname: None
Died: March 8, 1930

Woodrow Wilson

Born: Dec. 28, 1856
Birthplace: Staunton, Va.
Parents: Joseph Wilson, Janet Woodrow
Married: E. Axson, E. Galt
Children: 3 daughters
Profession: Professor
Religion: Presbyterian
Affiliation: Democrat
Term: 1913-1921, 28th President
Age at Inauguration: 56
Nickname: Schoolmaster in politics
Died: Feb. 3, 1924

Warren Gamaliel Harding

Born: Nov. 2, 1865
Birthplace: Corsica, Oh.
Parents: George Harding, Phoebe Dickerson
Married: Florence De Wolfe
Children: None
Profession: Publisher
Religion: Baptist
Affiliation: Republican
Term: 1921-1923, 29th President
Age at Inauguration: 55
Nickname: None
Died: Aug. 2, 1923

Calvin Coolidge

Born: July 4, 1872
Birthplace: Plymouth, Vt.
Parents: John Coolidge, Victoria Moor
Married: Grace Goodhue
Children: 2 sons
Profession: Lawyer
Religion: Congregationalist
Affiliation: Republican
Term: 1923-1929, 30th President
Age at Inauguration: 51
Nickname: Silent Cal
Died: Jan. 5, 1933

Herbert Clark Hoover

Born: Aug. 10, 1874
Birthplace: West Branch, Ia.
Parents: Jesse Hoover, Hulda Minthorn
Married: Lou Henry
Children: 2 sons
Profession: Engineer
Religion: Society of Friends
Affiliation: Republican
Term: 1929-1933, 31st President
Age at Inauguration: 54
Nickname: None
Died: Oct. 20, 1964

Franklin Delano Roosevelt

Born: Jan. 30, 1882
Birthplace: Hyde Park, N.Y.
Parents: James Roosevelt, Sara Delano
Married: Eleanor Roosevelt
Children: 5 sons, 1 daughter
Profession: Lawyer
Religion: Episcopalian
Affiliation: Democrat
Term: 1933-1945, 32nd President
Age at Inauguration: 51
Nickname: FDR
Died: April 12, 1945

Harry Truman

Born: May 8, 1884
Birthplace: Lamar, Mo.
Parents: John Truman, Martha Young
Married: Bess Wallace
Children: 1 daughter, Margaret
Profession: Public Official
Religion: Baptist
Affiliation: Democrat
Term: 1945-1953, 33rd President
Age at Inauguration: 60
Nickname: Give 'Em Hell Harry
Died: Dec. 26, 1972

Dwight David Eisenhower

Born: Oct. 14, 1890
Birthplace: Denison, Tex.
Parents: David Jacob Eisenhower, Ida Stover
Married: Mamie Doud
Children: 2 sons
Profession: Soldier
Religion: Presbyterian
Affiliation: Republican
Term: 1953-1961, 34th President
Age at Inauguration: 62
Nickname: Ike
Died: March 28, 1969

John Fitzgerald Kennedy

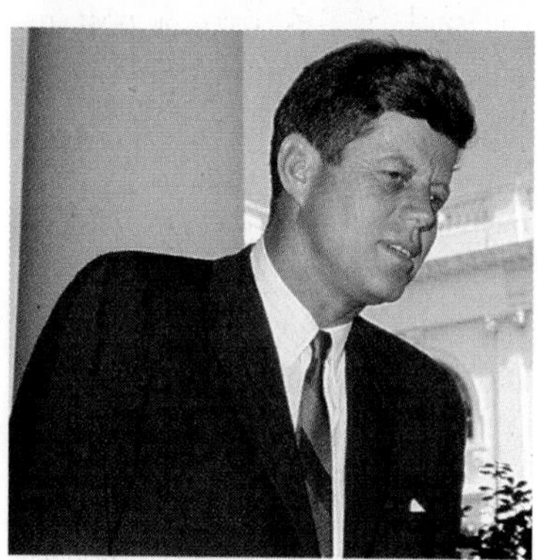

Born: May 29, 1917
Birthplace: Brookline, Mass.
Parents: Joseph Kennedy, Rose Fitzgerald
Married: Jacqueline Bouvier
Children: 2 sons, 1 daughter
Profession: Public Official
Religion: Roman Catholic
Affiliation: Democrat
Term: 1961-1963, 35th President
Age at Inauguration: 43
Nickname: JFK, Jack
Died: Nov. 22, 1963

Lyndon Baines Johnson

Born: Aug. 27, 1908
Birthplace: near Stonewall, Tex.
Parents: Sam Johnson, Rebekah Baines
Married: Claudia "Lady Bird" Alta
Children: 2 daughters
Profession: Public Official
Religion: Disciples of Christ
Affiliation: Democrat
Term: 1963-1969, 36th President
Age at Inauguration: 55
Nickname: LBJ
Died: Jan. 22, 1973

Richard Milhous Nixon

Born: Jan. 9, 1913
Birthplace: Yorba Linda, Calif.
Parents: Francis Nixon, Hannah Milhous
Married: Thelma Ryan
Children: 2 daughters
Profession: Lawyer, Public Official
Religion: Society of Friends
Affiliation: Republican
Term: 1969-1974, 37th President
Age at Inauguration: 56
Nickname: Dick
Died: April 22, 1994

Gerald Rudolph Ford

Born: July 14, 1913
Birthplace: Omaha, Neb.
Parents: Leslie King, Dorothy Gardner
Married: Elizabeth "Betty" Bloomer
Children: 3 sons, 1 daughter
Profession: Lawyer
Religion: Episcopalian
Affiliation: Republican
Term: 1974-1977, 38th President
Age at Inauguration: 61
Nickname: Jerry
Died: –

James Earl Carter

Born: Oct. 1, 1924
Birthplace: Plains, Ga.
Parents: James Carter, Lilian Gordy
Married: Rosalynn Smith
Children: 3 sons, 1 daughter
Profession: Farmer, public official
Religion: Baptist
Affiliation: Democrat
Term: 1977-1981, 39th President
Age at Inauguration: 52
Nickname: Jimmy
Died: –

Ronald Wilson Reagan

Born: Feb. 6, 1911
Birthplace: Tampico, Ill.
Parents: John Reagan, Nellie Wilson
Married: J. Wyman, N. Davis
Children: 2 sons, 2 daughters
Profession: Actor, Public Official
Religion: Presbyterian
Affiliation: Republican
Term: 1981-1989, 40th President
Age at Inauguration: 69
Nickname: Dutch
Died: –

George Herbert Walker Bush

Born: June 12, 1924
Birthplace: Milton, Mass.
Parents: Prescott Bush, Dorothy Walker
Married: Barbara Pierce
Children: 4 sons, 2 daughters
Profession: Public Official
Religion: Episcopalian
Affiliation: Republican
Term: 1989-1993, 41st President
Age at Inauguration: 64
Nickname: Poppy
Died: –

William Jefferson Clinton

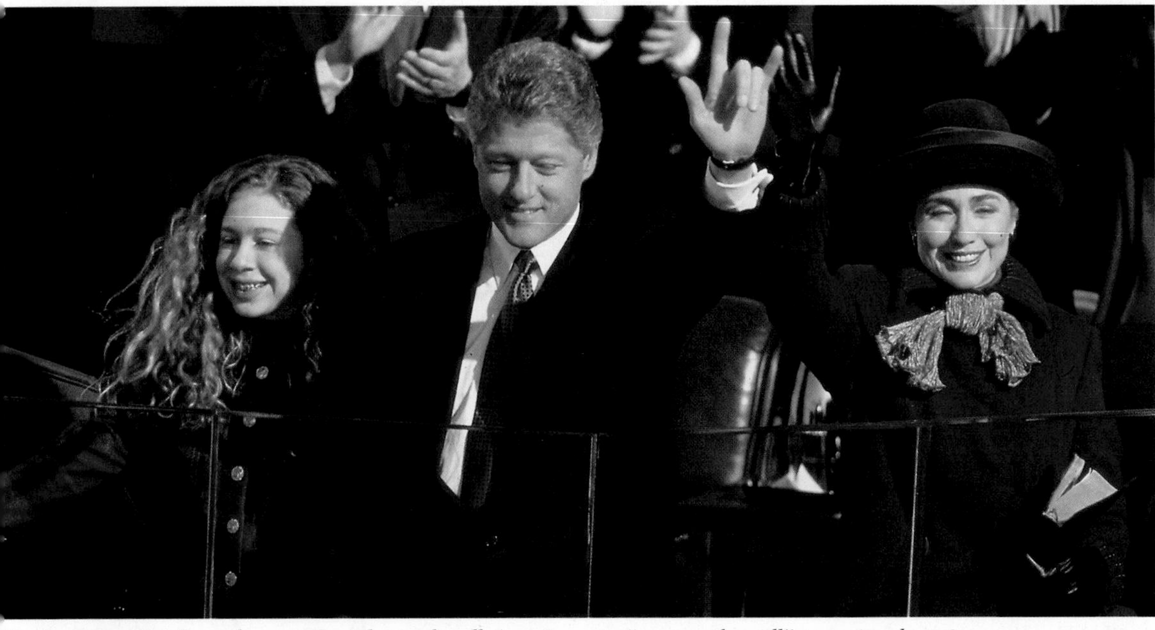

On Inauguration Day, the new President asks all Americans to "answer the call" to national service.

The nation's 42nd President was born Billy Blythe on August 19, 1946. Four months later, his father was killed in a car crash. Young Billy was raised by his storekeeper grandparents in Hope, Arkansas. At the age of 15, he took his stepfather's name, becoming Bill Clinton. He studied at Georgetown University, in Washington, D.C., England's Oxford University and Yale. He first ran for office, unsuccessfully, in Arkansas in 1974, a year before marrying Hillary Rodham. The couple have one daughter, Chelsea. In 1978, he was elected Governor of Arkansas, a post he held for all but two years until December 1992. He announced his presidential candidacy in late 1991. Bill Clinton is the third youngest man to be reach the White House, and the first "baby-boomer."

Alabama

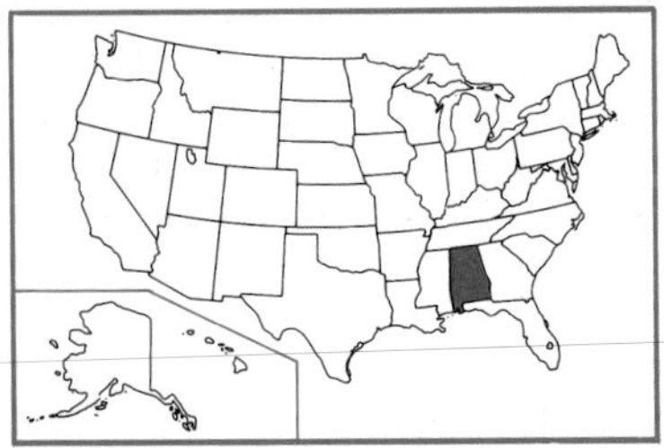

Capital: Montgomery
Entered Union: Dec. 14, 1819
22nd state
Nickname: Heart of Dixie
Population: 4,186,806
Rank by population: 22nd
Total area: 51,705 sq. mi.
Rank by area: 29th
Largest cities: Birmingham, Mobile, Montgomery, Huntsville
State bird: Yellowhammer
State flower: Camellia

The first Spanish explorers are said to have landed at Mobile Bay in the early 16th century. It was the French who in 1702 founded the first permanent European settlement in Alabama, at Fort Louis. Britain gained control of the area in 1763, but had to cede most of the region to the U.S. after the American Revolution. Andrew Jackson defeated the Creeks in 1814, and they were forced to relocate to Oklahoma. In 1861, the Confederacy was founded at Montgomery.

Alabama was the site of several landmark civil rights actions in the 1950s and '60s, most notably the Montgomery bus boycott and the "Freedom March" to Selma.

Alabama produces cast iron, steel and textiles, as well as electronics, chemicals, pulp and paper.

Alaska

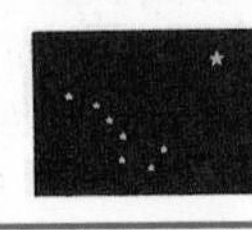

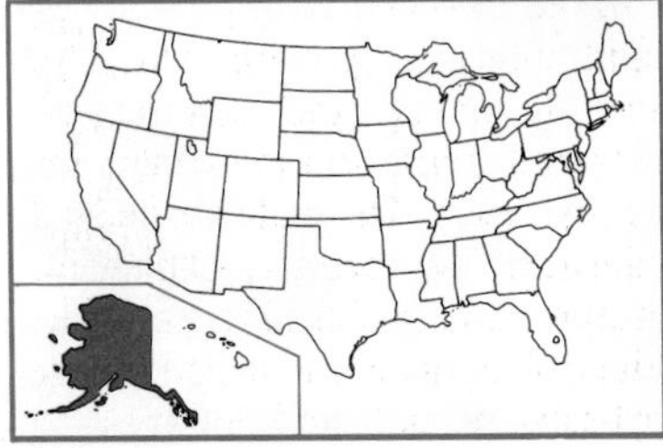

Capital: Juneau
Entered Union: Jan. 3, 1959
49th state
Nickname: The Last Frontier
Population: 599,151
Rank by population: 48th
Total area: 591,000 sq. mi.
Rank by area: 1st
Largest cities: Anchorage, Fairbanks, Juneau
State bird: Willow ptarmigan
State flower: Forget-me-not

Alaska and the Aleutian Islands were discovered in 1741 by Vitus Bering, a Dane working for the Russians. Most of this vast territory was unexplored in 1867 when Secretary of State William Seward arranged for its purchase from the Russians for $7.2 million, a cost of some two cents per acre. This deal was ridiculed as "Seward's Folly."

In the late 19th century, the Gold Rush led to a massive influx of people. The 1890 census showed a total of only 32,052 Alaskans; the 1900 census counted 63,592.

A huge reservoir of oil and gas was discovered near Prudhoe Bay, on the Arctic Coast, in 1968. Crude oil is conducted by the Trans-Alaska pipeline, completed in 1977, to the port of Valdez. Tourism, furs, wood and fisheries are other industries important to Alaska's economy.

Arizona

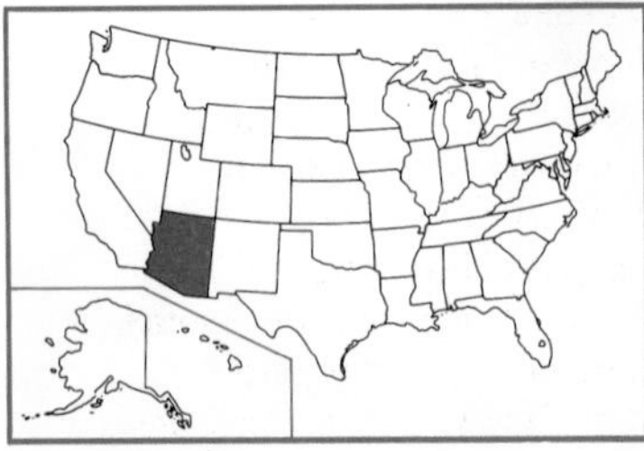

Capital: Phoenix
Entered Union: Feb. 14, 1912
48th state
Nickname: Grand Canyon State
Population: 3,936,142
Rank by population: 23th
Total area: 114,000 sq. mi.
Rank by area: 6th
Largest cities: Phoenix, Tucson, Mesa, Tempe, Glendale, Scottsdale
State bird: Cactus wren
State flower: Flower of the Saguaro cactus

Arizona's name derives from the Indian word "arizonac" or "little spring." Marcos de Niza, a Spanish friar, was the first European to explore the territory, arriving in the late 1530s in search of the fabled Seven Cities of Gold. Fort Tucson was founded by the Spanish in 1776. Most of the territory became part of the U.S. after the Mexican War, and the southern part of the territory was added by the Gadsden Purchase of 1853. It was in Arizona that such Indian chiefs as Geronimo and Cochise fought against frontiersmen, and the state has one of the nation's largest Indian populations.

Arizona's chief industries include aeronautical, electrical and communications equipment. The state produces much of the nation's copper. Tourists also flock to visit the Grand Canyon.

Arkansas

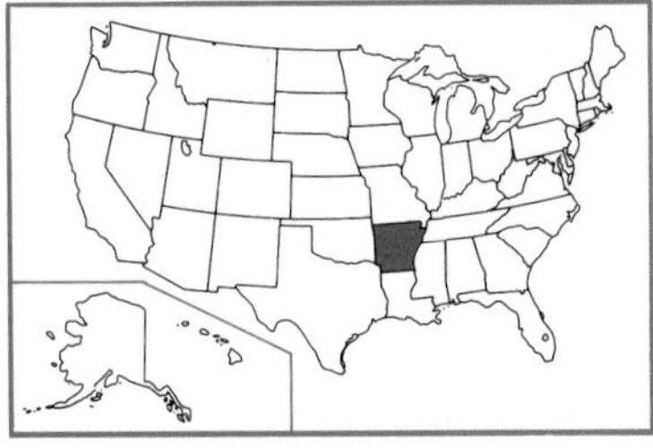

Capital: Little Rock
Entered Union: June 15, 1836
25th state
Nickname: Land of Opportunity
Population: 2,424,418
Rank by population: 33rd
Total area: 53,187 sq. mi.
Rank by area: 27th
Largest cities: Little Rock, Fort Smith, North Little Rock
State bird: Mockingbird
State flower: Apple blossom

The first permanent European settlement in the region, the Arkansas Post, was founded in the late 17th century by a Frenchman, Henri de Tonti. The state's name comes from the French variant of the name of the Quapaw Indians.

The area had previously been visited by European explorers, including de Soto, who traveled there in 1541. By the early 1720s, the Arkansas Post had become one of the chief administrative centers of the Louisiana Territory. The area was acquired by the U.S. as part of the Louisiana Purchase.

Today, the principal products of Arkansas are food, chemicals, lumber and wood products. The state is also a leading producer of soybeans, rice and cotton. It is rich in ores, and in 1989 led the nation in production of nonfuel minerals, principally copper, gold, sand and gravel.

California

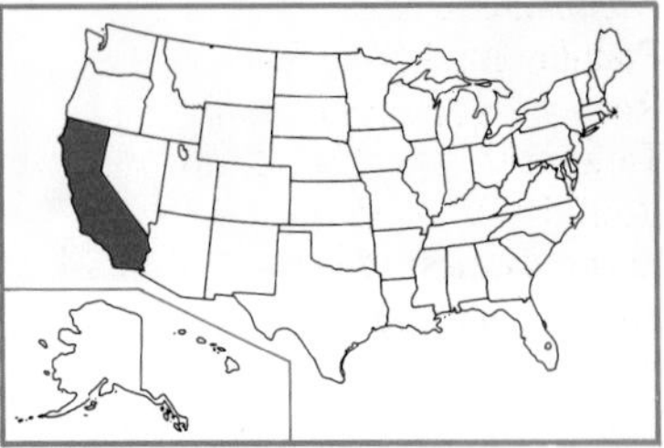

Capital: Sacramento
Entered Union: Sept. 9, 1850
31st state
Nickname: Golden State
Population: 31,210,750
Rank by population: 1st
Total area: 158,706 sq. mi.
Rank by area: 3rd
Largest cities: Los Angeles, San Diego, San Jose, San Francisco
State bird: California valley quail
State flower: Golden poppy

The Conquistadors named California after the island paradise in a book written by Garcia Ordonez de Montalvo in 1510. Although California was sighted by Spanish navigator Juan Rodriguez Cabrillo in the early 1540s, its first Spanish mission was not established until the late 1760s. It became a U.S. territory in 1848 when Mexico surrendered it to John Fremont.

That same year, James Marshall discovered gold at Sutter's Mill, starting the California Gold Rush. The next year 80,000 prospectors came to the region. In 1964, California became the most populous state, surpassing New York.

California's leading industries include manufacturing (electronics and transportation equipment, machinery), agriculture, tourism and film-making. The chief natural resources include petroleum, cement and natural gas.

Colorado

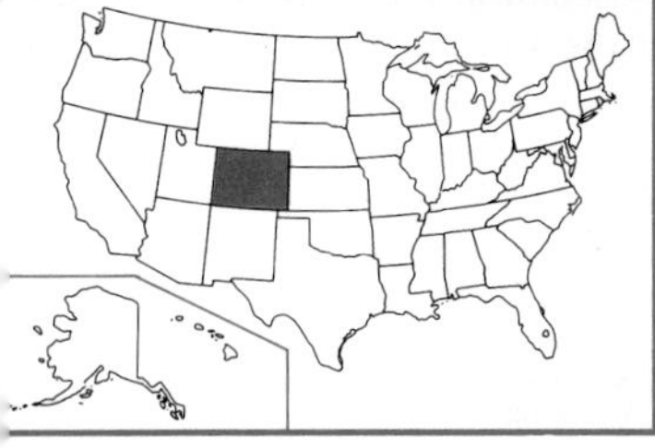

Capital: Denver
Entered Union: Aug. 1, 1876
38th state
Nickname: Centennial State
Population: 3,565,959
Rank by population: 26th
Total area: 104,091 sq. mi.
Rank by area: 8th
Largest cities: Denver, Colorado Springs, Aurora, Lakewood
State bird: Lark bunting
State flower: Rocky Mountain Columbine

Colorado, from the Spanish word meaning "red," was first visited by Spanish explorers in the 1500s. The territory was claimed for Spain in the early 1700s. Eastern Colorado was acquired by the U.S. as part of the Louisiana Purchase in 1803, while the central part was obtained in 1845 with the admission of Texas as a state. The remaining western portion was acquired in 1848 as a result of the Mexican War.

The first discovery of gold near present-day Denver came in 1858. Colorado has the world's largest molybdenum mine, and produces uranium, lead, tin and zinc as well. Denver is a leading electronics center. The Rocky Mountains, with 54 peaks towering above 14,000 feet, attract many tourists.

Connecticut

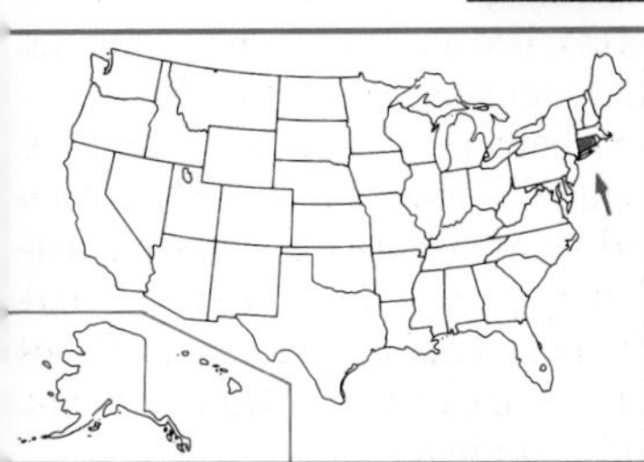

Capital: Hartford
Entered Union: Jan. 9, 1788
5th state
Nickname: Nutmeg State
Population: 3,277,316
Rank by population: 27th
Total area: 5,108 sq. mi.
Rank by area: 48th
Largest cities: Bridgeport, Hartford, New Haven, Waterbury
State bird: Robin
State flower: Mountain laurel

The region, whose name derives from an Indian word meaning "beside the long tidal river," was first explored in 1614 by the Dutch navigator Adriaen Block. In the late 1630s, English settlements in the area united to form the Connecticut Colony. They adopted the *Fundamental Orders*, the first constitution written in the Americas. Connecticut played a major role in the Revolutionary War, supplying much of the Continental Army.

Connecticut quickly became one of the most industrialized states in the nation. It now produces jet engines, submarines, weapons, sewing machines and helicopters. The first nuclear-powered submarine can be seen at the U.S.S. Nautilus Memorial in Groton. Retail trade is an important industry, and Hartford has become the insurance capital of the nation.

Delaware

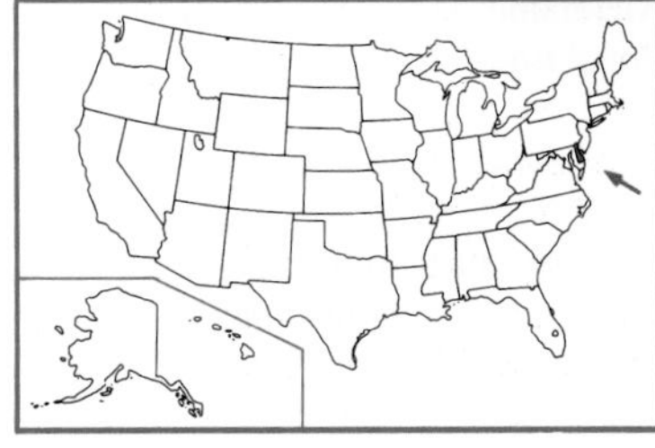

Capital: Dover
Entered Union: Dec. 7, 1787
1st state
Nickname: First State
Population: 700,269
Rank by population: 46th
Total area: 2,045 sq. mi.
Rank by area: 49th.
Largest cities: Wilmington, Newark, Dover, Brookside, Pike Creek
State bird: Blue hen chicken
State flower: Peach blossom

The state's name is derived from that of the Englishman Lord De La Warr. Delaware is believed to have been discovered by Henry Hudson. A Dutch settlement was established in 1631, and Swedish colonization began in 1638, but New Sweden fell to the Dutch in 1655.

The area was taken over by England within a decade. It was then transferred to William Penn in the early 1680s. Delaware fought as a separate state in the American Revolution and was the first state to ratify the Constitution in 1787. Although it was a slave state, Delaware did not secede from the Union during the Civil War.

A Frenchman, Eleuthère Irénée du Pont, set up a gunpowder mill near Wilmington in the early 19th century, thus laying the foundation for the state's huge chemical industry.

Florida

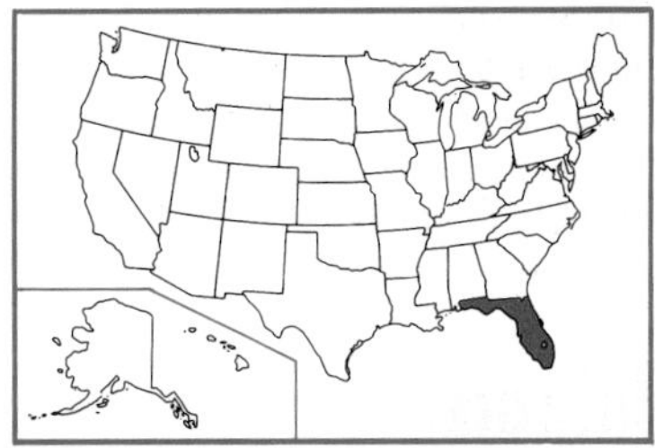

Capital: Tallahassee
Entered Union: March 3, 1845
27th state
Nickname: Sunshine State
Population: 13,678,914
Rank by population: 4th
Total area: 58,664 sq. mi.
Rank by area: 22nd
Largest cities: Jacksonville, Miami, Tampa, St. Petersburg
State bird: Mockingbird
State flower: Orange blossom

Florida, meaning "Easter of flowers," was discovered and named by Juan Ponce de Leon, who claimed it for Spain in 1513. A French colony, Fort Caroline, was established in the territory in 1564. The oldest city in the nation, St. Augustine, was founded in 1565. Florida, for a time held by England, was ceded to the United States by Spain in 1819.

Fighting with the Seminole Indian tribe marked the first half of the 19th century, the Seminole War ended in 1842, and the Indians were forced to relocate to Oklahoma.

Florida is one of the fastest-growing states, with a population that has jumped from 6.8 million in 1970 to nearly 13 million in 1990. Tourism remains the linchpin of its economy, although the state also plays a key role in the U.S. space program, with the Cape Canaveral space center. Crops include citrus fruits and strawberries.

Georgia

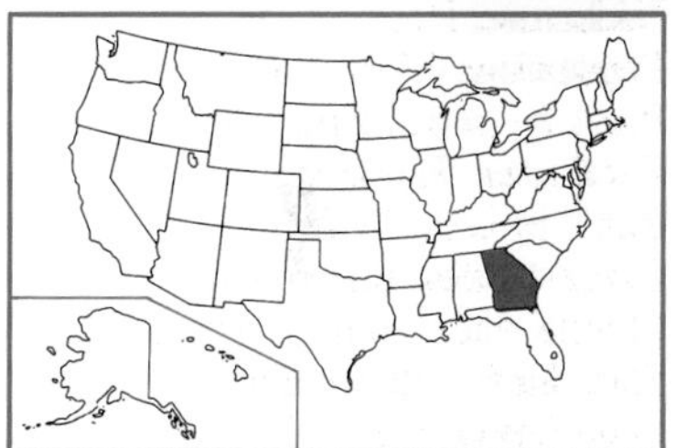

Capital: Atlanta
Entered Union: Jan. 2, 1788
4th state
Nickname: Peach State
Population: 6,917,140
Rank by population: 11th
Total area: 58,910 sq. mi.
Rank by area: 21st
Largest cities: Atlanta, Columbus, Savannah, Macon, Albany
State bird: Brown thrasher
State flower: Cherokee rose

Named in honor of King George II of England, Georgia was first explored by the Spaniard Hernando de Soto in 1540. A Briton, General James Oglethorpe, established the first permanent settlement in Georgia in 1733. General Oglethorpe defeated Spanish invaders at Battle of Bloody Marsh in 1742.

During the Civil War, Georgia, a Confederate stronghold, saw a great deal of fighting. Atlanta was burned by Union General William Tecumseh Sherman, who cut a 60-mile swath to the coast where he seized the city of Savannah.

In recent years, Georgia has seen rapid industrial growth, with Atlanta becoming the communications and transportation center for the Southeast. The state's principal industries are forestry, chemicals, printing and publishing, and its principal agricultural products are soybeans, peanuts and poultry.

Hawaii

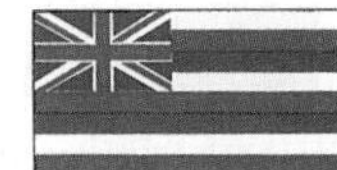

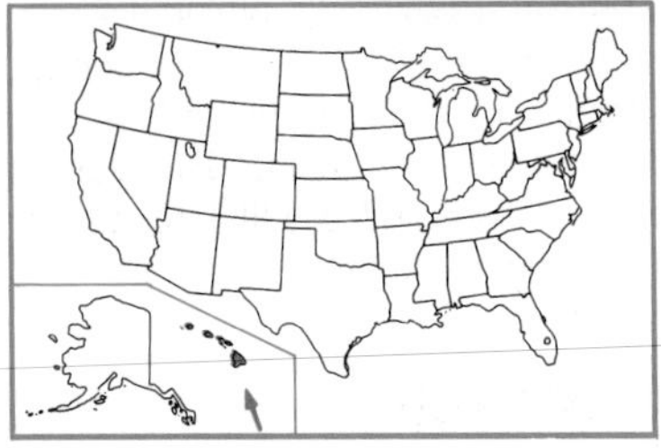

Capital: Honolulu
Entered Union: Aug. 21, 1959
50th state
Nickname: Aloha State
Population: 1,171,592
Rank by population: 40th
Total area: 6,471 sq. mi.
Rank by area: 47th
Largest cities: Honolulu, Pearl City, Kailua, Hilo
State bird: Hawaiian goose
State flower: Yellow hibiscus

Hawaii was first settled in the 6th century by Polynesians. In 1778, Captain James Cook of England landed there and named the group the Sandwich Islands. During most of the 19th century, the islands remained a native kingdom. Queen Liliuokalani was deposed in 1893 and the Republic of Hawaii was established. Following its annexation, Hawaii became a U.S. territory in 1898.

The attack by Japanese forces on the naval base at Pearl Harbor, on December 7, 1941, led to the U.S. entry into World War II.

Hawaii is a chain of volcanic and coral islands nearly 1,600 miles long. Most of these are tiny, while the eight main ones are Hawaii, Maui, Oahu, Lanai, Kauai, Niihau, Kahoolawe and Molokai.

Idaho

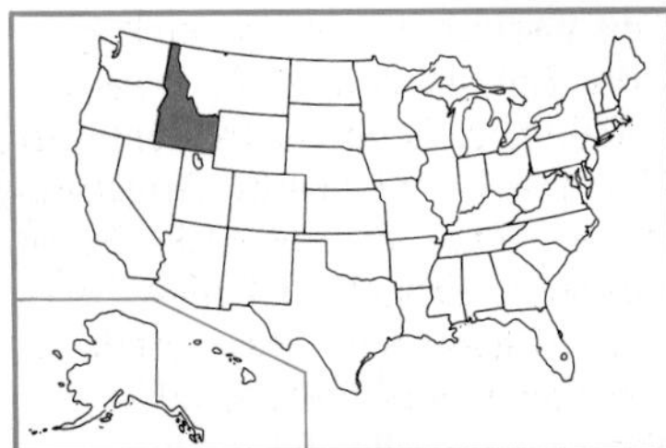

Capital: Boise
Entered Union: July 3, 1890
43rd state
Nickname: Gem State
Population: 1,099,096
Rank by population: 42nd
Total area: 83,564 sq. mi.
Rank by area: 13th
Largest cities: Boise, Pocatello, Idaho Falls
State bird: Mountain bluebird
State flower: Syringa

Idaho was widely explored by the expedition of Meriwether Lewis and William Clark in 1805-1806. Fur trappers and missionaries followed. The Oregon Treaty put an end to boundary disputes with Britain in 1846. Mormons established the first permanent U.S. settlement in Idaho at Franklin in 1860. Idaho became a U.S. territory in 1863.

The arrival of settlers on Indian lands in the 1870s led to a series of clashes between U.S. troops and warriors of the Nez Perce, Bannock and Sheepeater tribes.

World War II's military needs made the processing of agricultural products a major industry in Idaho, in particular the freezing of potatoes. Idaho, also known as the Spud State, produces about one-quarter of the nation's potato crop, as well as beets, wheat and corn.

Illinois

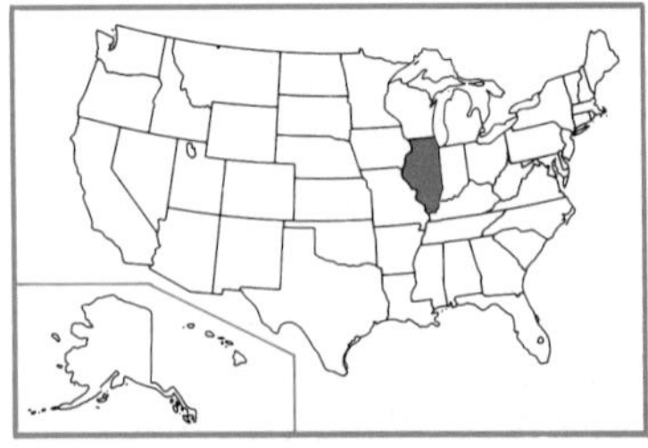

Capital: Springfield
Entered Union: Dec. 3, 1818
21st state
Nickname: Prairie State
Population: 11,697,336
Rank by population: 6th
Total area: 56,345 sq. mi.
Rank by area: 24th
Largest cities: Chicago, Rockford, Peoria, Springfield, Aurora, Naperville, Decatur
State bird: Cardinal
State flower: Violet

Illinois, from an Indian word meaning "tribe of superior men," was first explored by the Frenchmen Marquette and Joliet in 1673, followed by La Salle. The French established settlements at Fort St. Louis in 1692 and at Kaskaskia in 1700. At the end of the French and Indian War in 1763, Britain obtained the region.

The state figured prominently in frontier struggles during the Revolution. After the Erie Canal was completed in 1825, many settlers migrated to Illinois from the east. During the early 19th century, the region saw a series of Indian wars.

Illinois has since become a leader in the export of agricultural products, manufacturing, coal, mining and oil production. Today, Chicago is a major iron and steel producer, and grain exchange, as well as a railroad and meat-packing center.

Indiana

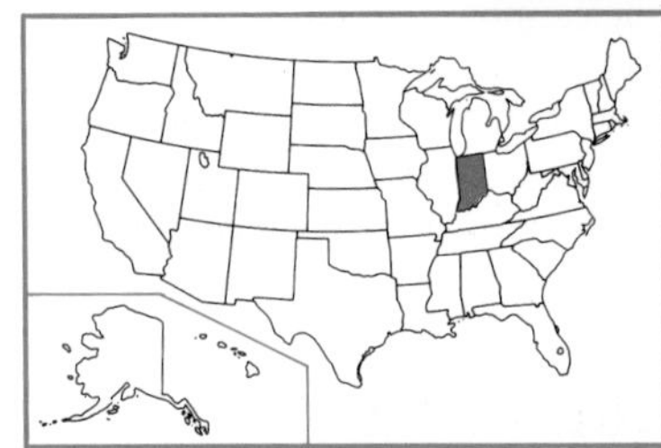

Capital: Indianapolis
Entered Union: Dec. 11, 1816
19th state
Nickname: Hoosier State
Population: 5,712,799
Rank by population: 14th
Total area: 36,185 sq. mi.
Rank by area: 38th
Largest cities: Indianapolis, Fort Wayne, Gary, Evansville
State bird: Cardinal
State flower: Peony

Indiana was first explored by the Frenchman La Salle in 1679 and later figured in the struggle for North America between France and England. This culminated in a British victory in 1763. During the Revolutionary War, George Rogers Clark led American forces against the British in the region.

Indiana saw repeated Indian uprisings until the victory of General William Henry Harrison at Tippecanoe in 1811.

The Lake Michigan region of Indiana has become an important industrial center, manufacturing aircraft engines, automobile and truck parts, mobile homes and farm machinery. The state also has a large agricultural output, which includes soybeans, hogs, wheat, tomatoes, oats, onions, rye and poultry. As well as producing coal, Indiana provides much of the building limestone used in the U.S.

Iowa

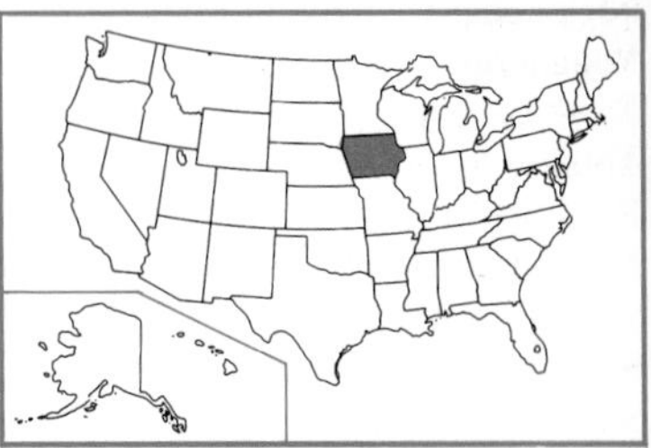

Capital: Des Moines
Entered Union: Dec. 28, 1846
29th state
Nickname: Hawkeye State
Population: 2,814,064
Rank by population: 30th
Total area: 56,275 sq. mi.
Rank by area: 25th
Largest cities: Des Moines, Cedar Rapids, Davenport, Sioux City
State bird: Eastern goldfinch
State flower: Wild rose

French explorers Louis Joliet and Jacques Marquette were the first Europeans to visit Iowa. The name is believed to come from an Indian word meaning "the beautiful land." In 1803, the U.S. acquired control of the area as part of the Louisiana Purchase. There was bloody fighting between Indians and white settlers during the first half of the 19th century. The Indians lost their lands after the Black Hawk War in 1832.

When Iowa achieved statehood, in 1846, its capital was Iowa City. However, the more centrally located Des Moines became its capital 11 years later, when the state's present boundaries were drawn.

Iowa is one of the nation's foremost agricultural states, leading the nation in acres harvested. The state produces corn, soybeans, oats and hay. One of its principal manufactured products is farm machinery.

Kansas

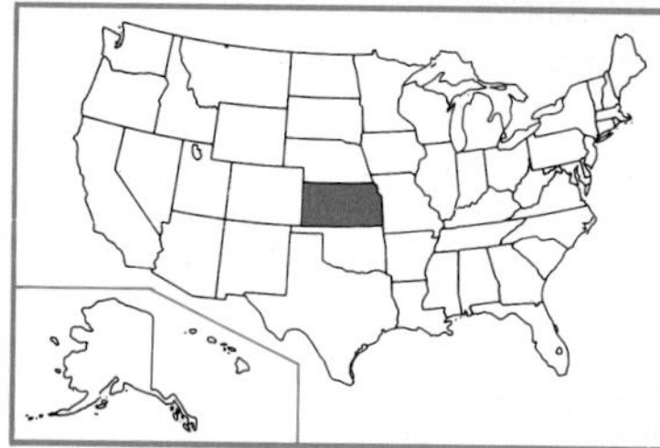

Capital: Topeka
Entered Union: Jan. 29, 1861
34th state
Nickname: Sunflower State
Population: 2,530,746
Rank by population: 32nd
Total area: 82,277 sq. mi.
Rank by area: 14th
Largest cities: Wichita, Kansas City, Topeka, Overland Park
State bird: Western meadowlark
State flower: Sunflower

The Spanish explorer Francisco de Coronado is believed to have been the first European to visit Kansas, the name of which is derived from a Sioux word meaning "the people of the south wind." Kansas was ceded to Spain by France in 1763, but the territory reverted to France in 1800. It was sold to the U.S. as part of the Louisiana Purchase of 1803.

Kansas was the scene of violent struggles between pro- and anti-slavery groups before the Civil War. The Kansas-Nebraska Act of 1854, which made it a U.S. territory, left the decision about slavery to the popular vote of the territories. Kansas is a leading wheat growing state. Wichita has become one of the nation's chief aircraft manufacturing centers.

Kentucky

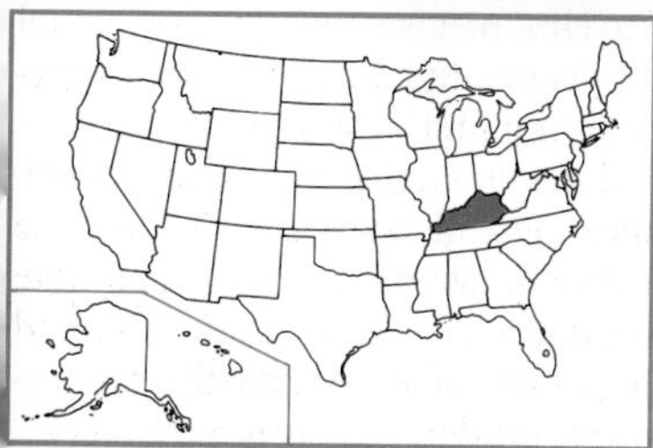

Capital: Frankfort
Entered Union: June 1, 1792
15th state
Nickname: Bluegrass State
Population: 3,788,808
Rank by population: 24th
Total area: 40,410 sq. mi.
Rank by area: 37th
Largest cities: Louisville, Lexington, Fayette, Owensboro
State bird: Cardinal
State flower: Goldenrod

Kentucky, from an Indian word which has been translated as "great meadow" and "land of tomorrow," was the first region west of the Alleghenies to be settled by American pioneers. The first permanent settlement was established at Harrodsburg in 1774. The following year Daniel Boone blazed the Wilderness Trail and founded Boonesborough. Kentucky, a slaveholding state with a large abolitionist population, supplied troops to both Confederate and Union forces during the Civil War.

Kentucky produces outstanding horses, whiskey and tobacco. The Bluegrass region near Lexington is the center of some of the world's finest stud farms, while Louisville is famed for the Kentucky Derby and its whiskey distilleries. Agriculture and mining, chiefly for coal, remain vital to the state's economy.

Louisiana

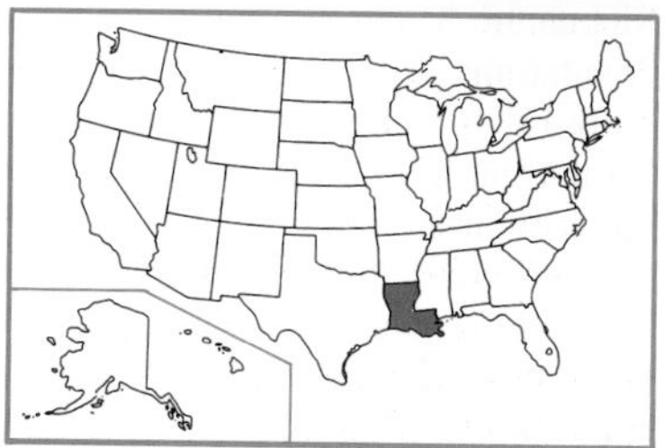

Capital: Baton Rouge
Entered Union: April 30, 1812
18th state
Nickname: Pelican State
Population: 4,295,477
Rank by population: 21st
Total area: 47,752 sq. mi.
Rank by area: 31st
Largest cities: New Orleans, Baton Rouge, Shreveport, Lafayette, Lake Charles, Monroe
State bird: Eastern Brown Pelican
State flower: Magnolia

The area was explored in the first half of the 16th century by the Spanish. In 1682, La Salle reached the mouth of the Mississippi and claimed the land drained by it and its tributaries for France, naming it Lousiana in honor of his king, Louis XIV.

The territory became a colony of the French crown, before being ceded to Spain in 1762, returned to France in 1800 and sold to the U.S. by Napoleon as part of the Louisiana Purchase. In 1815, General Andrew Jackson defeated a British army in the Battle of New Orleans. During the Civil War, the state fought for the Confederacy.

Louisiana is now a leading producer of petroleum and gas. New Orleans, founded in 1717, attracts many tourists to the state with its jazz festivals and the French Quarter.

Maine

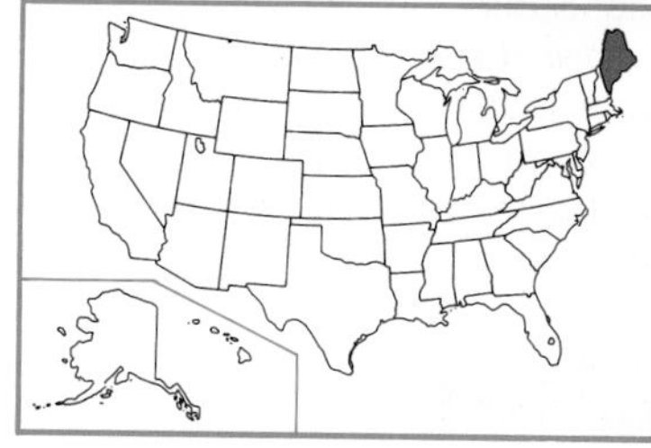

Capital: Augusta
Entered Union: March 15, 1820
23rd state
Nickname: Pine Tree State
Population: 1,239,448
Rank by population: 39th
Total area: 33,265 sq. mi.
Rank by area: 39th
Largest cities: Portland, Lewiston, Bangor, Auburn
State bird: Chickadee
State flower: White pine cone

Maine may have been visited by the Vikings in the ninth century, and John Cabot is said to have visited the Maine coast in the late 15th century. The first permanent English settlements were not established until 1623. The first naval action of the Revolutionary War took place in 1775 when colonials seized an English sloop off the coast of Maine. Falmouth (now Portland) was burned by the British in the same year.

Maine became part of Massachusetts in 1761, but broke off to become a separate state in 1820 as part of the Missouri Compromise.

Maine, with more than 80% of its area forested, is one of the world's chief pulp-paper producers and is a leader in shoe manufacturing. Lobster fishing is another major activity. The state's 2,500 lakes and 5,000 streams attract many tourists.

Maryland

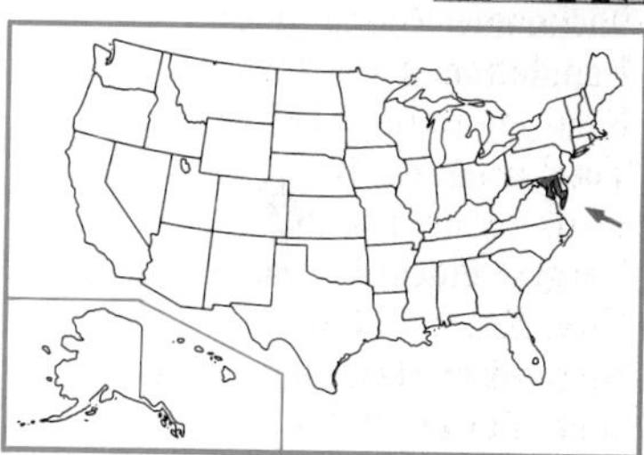

Capital: Annapolis
Entered Union: April 28, 1788
7th state
Nickname: Free State
Population: 4,964,898
Rank by population: 19th
Total area: 10,460 sq. mi.
Rank by area: 42nd
Largest cities: Baltimore, Dundalk, Bethesda, Silver Spring
State bird: Baltimore oriole
State flower: Black-eyed susan

Chesapeake Bay in Maryland, named in honor of Henrietta Maria, wife of Charles I, was explored by Captain John Smith in 1608. Charles granted a royal charter to Lord Baltimore in 1632. Soon after, Roman Catholics from England landed on St. Clement's (now Blakistone) Island. A Puritan revolt in 1654-58 put an end to religious freedom granted to Christians by the Toleration Act passed by the Maryland Assembly in 1649.

A British attempt to capture Baltimore in 1814 was marked by the bombardment of Fort McHenry. This inspired Francis Scott Key to write *The Star-Spangled Banner*.

Baltimore is one of the foremost U.S. ports, and nearby Annapolis is the home of the U.S. Naval Academy. Despite pollution problems, Chesapeake Bay produces vast amounts of oysters, crabs and clams.

Massachusetts

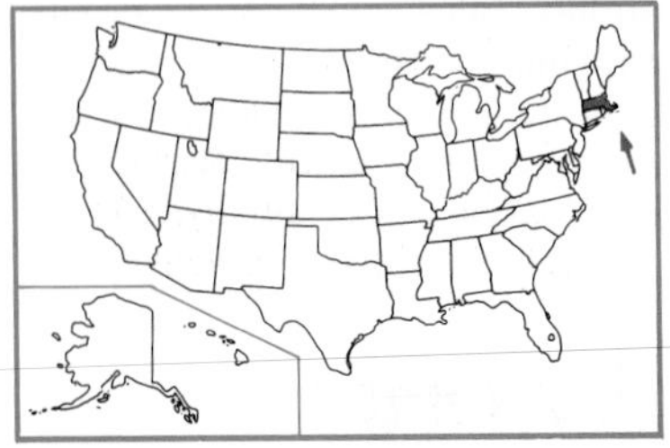

Capital: Boston
Entered Union: Feb. 6, 1788
6th state
Nickname: Bay State
Population: 6,012,268
Rank by population: 13th
Total area: 8,284 sq. mi.
Rank by area: 45th
Largest cities: Boston, Worcester, Springfield, New Bedford
State bird: Chickadee
State flower: Mayflower

Massachusetts, from two Indian words meaning "large hill place," became one of the most important of the 13 colonies. The Pilgrims founded Plymouth Colony in 1620. Massachusetts played a leading role in resistance to British oppression, and in 1773 the Boston Tea Party marked a turning point in the protest against unjust taxation. In 1775, the Minutemen sparked off the American Revolution by resisting British troops at Lexington and Concord.

For Massachusetts, the 19th century was a time of expanding shipping, commercial fishing and manufacturing. The state was a pioneer in the manufacture of shoes and textiles, but now these industries have given way to communications equipment and electronics.

Michigan

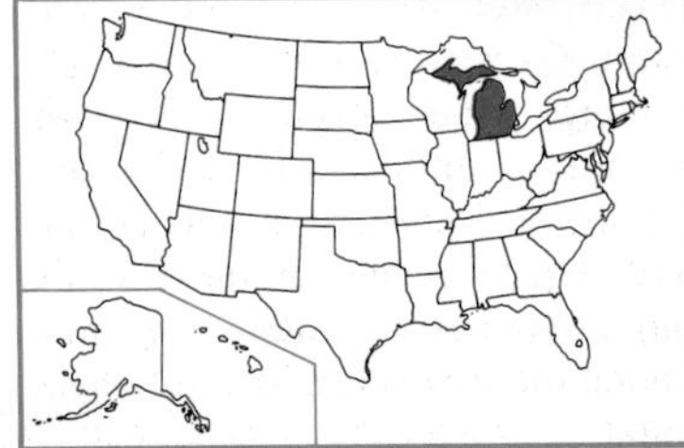

Capital: Lansing
Entered Union: Jan. 26, 1837
26th state
Nickname: Wolverine State
Population: 9,477,545
Rank by population: 8th
Total area: 58,527 sq. mi.
Rank by area: 23rd
Largest cities: Detroit, Grand Rapids, Warren, Flint, Lansing
State bird: Robin
State flower: Apple blossom

Etienne Brulé of France became in 1618 the first European to travel to Michigan, a name taken from the Indian words meaning "great lake." He was followed by other French explorers, including Joliet, La Salle and Marquette. In 1668, the first permanent settlement was established at Sault Ste. Marie. Britain ousted France from the territory in 1763. Following the Revolutionary War, the U.S. obtained most of the region, which was the scene of constant conflict between British and U.S. forces and their respective Indian allies.

Michigan borders on four of the five Great Lakes and is divided by the Straits of Mackinac, linking Lakes Huron and Michigan. The state is the nation's foremost producer of motor vehicles and is a leader in the manufacture of airplane parts and machine tools.

Minnesota

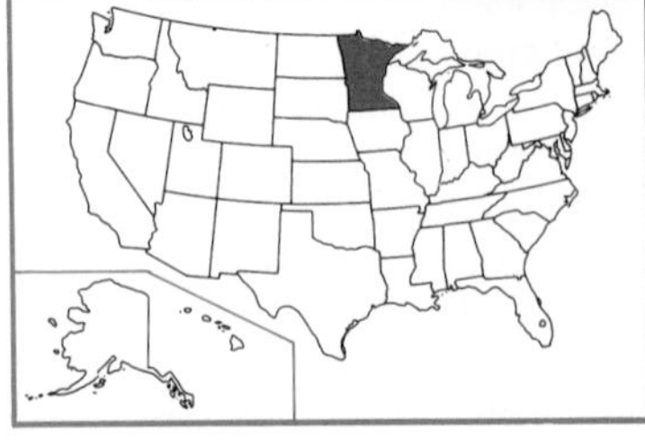

Capital: St. Paul
Entered Union: May 11, 1858
32nd state
Nickname: North Star State
Population: 4,517,416
Rank by population: 20th
Total area: 84,402 sq. mi.
Rank by area: 12th
Largest cities: Minneapolis, St. Paul, Duluth, Bloomington, Rochester, Edina
State bird: Common loon
State flower: Lady's slipper

Minnesota, whose name was derived from a Dakota Sioux word meaning "sky-tinted water," was explored by Frenchmen Pierre Radisson and Sieur Des Groseillers in the 1650s. They were followed by Joliet, Marquette, La Salle and other explorers, missionaries and fur traders. After the Revolution, the U.S. acquired eastern Minnesota from Britain and later acquired the western part from France in the Louisiana Purchase. In 1818, Britain ceded the northern part of the region to the U.S.

The state is rich in natural resources, notably iron ore. Minneapolis has become the trading center of the region, while nearby St. Paul is the nation's biggest publisher of calendars and law books. An internationally famous medical center, the Mayo Clinic, is based in Rochester.

Mississippi

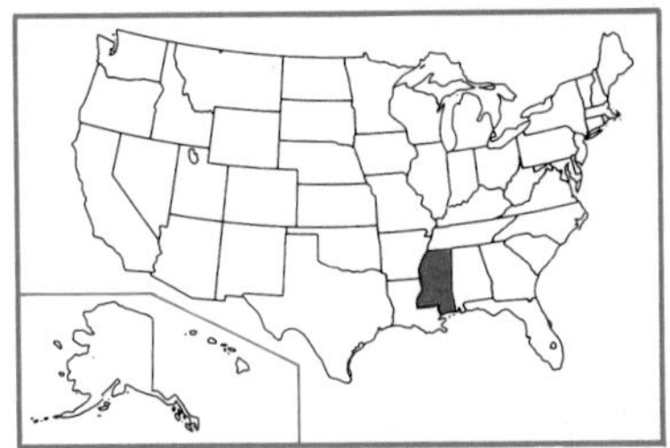

Capital: Jackson
Entered Union: Dec. 10, 1817
20th state
Nickname: Magnolia State
Population: 2,642,748
Rank by population: 31st
Total area: 47,689 sq. mi.
Rank by area: 32nd
Largest cities: Jackson, Biloxi, Hattiesburg, Greenville, Gulfport
State bird: Mockingbird
State flower: Magnolia

Mississippi, from an Indian word meaning "father of waters," was first explored for Spain by Hernando de Soto, who discovered the Mississippi River in 1540. The region was later claimed by France and in 1699 a French group led by Sieur d'Iberville established the first permanent settlement near present-day Biloxi. Following the French and Indian War, Britain took over the area, ceding it to the U.S. after the Revolution. Spain relinquished its claims in 1798, and in 1810 the U.S. annexed West Florida from Spain, including what is now southern Mississippi.

Until an industrialization program was launched in the 1970s, Mississippi was one of the least industrialized states, with more than 50% of its population making a living from the soil. The state is one of the nation's top producers of cotton, rice, sorghum and soybeans.

Missouri

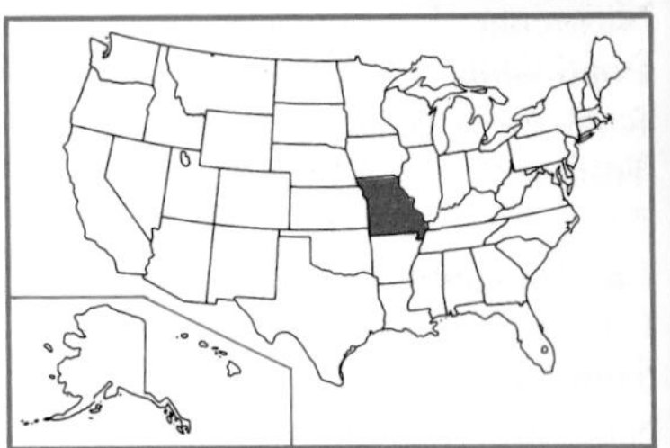

Capital: Jefferson City
Entered Union: Aug. 10, 1821
24th state
Nickname: Show Me State
Population: 5,233,849
Rank by population: 16th
Total area: 69,697 sq. mi.
Rank by area: 19th
Largest cities: St. Louis, Kansas City, Springfield, Independence
State bird: Bluebird
State flower: Hawthorn

Missouri means "muddy water," and the name was applied to an Indian tribe and to the Missouri River before it became the territory's name. France's claim to the region was based on La Salle's travels there. French fur traders established Ste. Genevieve in 1735. Acquired from France as part of the Louisiana Purchase in 1803, it became a state following the Missouri Compromise of 1820.

The state remained in the Union during the Civil War, although it supplied troops to both the Confederacy and the Union. Missouri also played a major role as a gateway to the West. St. Joseph became the starting point of the Pony Express and the Oregon and Santa Fe Trails began in Independence.

Manufacturing, especially for the aerospace industry, is the state's chief economic activity. Missouri is also a leading beer producer.

Montana

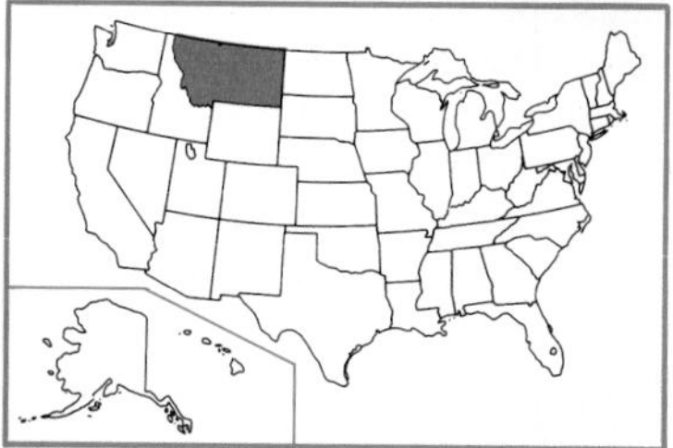

Capital: Helena
Entered Union: Nov. 8, 1889
41st state
Nickname: Treasure State
Population: 839,422
Rank by population: 44th
Total area: 147,046 sq. mi.
Rank by area: 4th
Largest cities: Billings, Great Falls, Butte-Silver Bow, Missoula
State bird: Western meadowlark
State flower: Bitterroot

French fur trappers were among the first Europeans to visit the region, also explored by François and Louis-Joseph Verendrye of France in the early 1740s. In 1803, much of the territory was acquired from France as part of the Louisiana Purchase. Western Montana was obtained from Great Britain in the Oregon Treaty, although American forts and trading posts had been established in the area before then.

Montana was the scene of some major clashes during the 1867-77 Indian wars, including the Battle of Little Big Horn, also known as "Custer's Last Stand."

Mining for coal, copper, lead, zinc and silver has figured prominently in Montana's history. The state is also famous for its hunting and dude ranches.

Nebraska

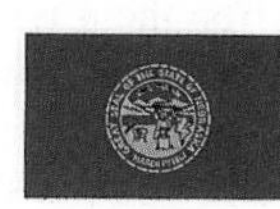

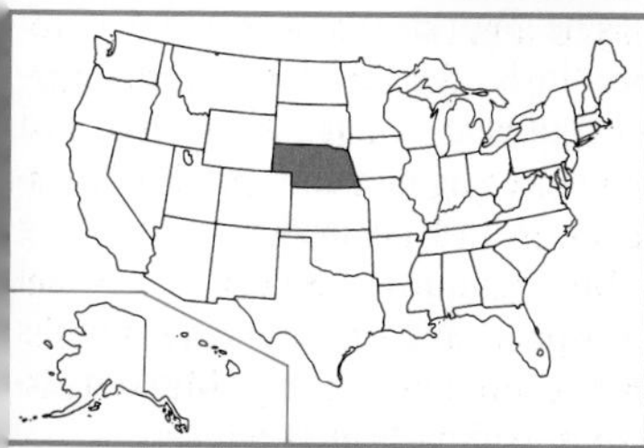

Capital: Lincoln
Entered Union: March 1, 1867
37th state
Nickname: Cornhusker State
Population: 1,607,199
Rank by population: 37th
Total area: 77,355 sq. mi.
Rank by area: 15th
Largest cities: Omaha, Lincoln, Grand Island, Bellevue
State bird: Western meadowlark
State flower: Goldenrod

Nebraska, from an Omaha or Oto Indian word meaning "flat water," was visited by French fur traders in the early 1700s. Following the Louisiana Purchase, the territory was explored by Lewis and Clark. Before the first permanent settlement was established at Bellevue in 1823, the Oregon Trail was opened across Nebraska by Robert Stuart. The western part of the region was acquired after the Mexican War. The Union Pacific began its transcontinental railroad at Omaha in 1865.

Nebraska became in 1937 the only state in the union to have a unicameral legislature, to which members are elected without party designation.

Nebraska is a leading producer of rye, corn and wheat. Omaha is a meat-packing center and has a large cattle market.

Nevada

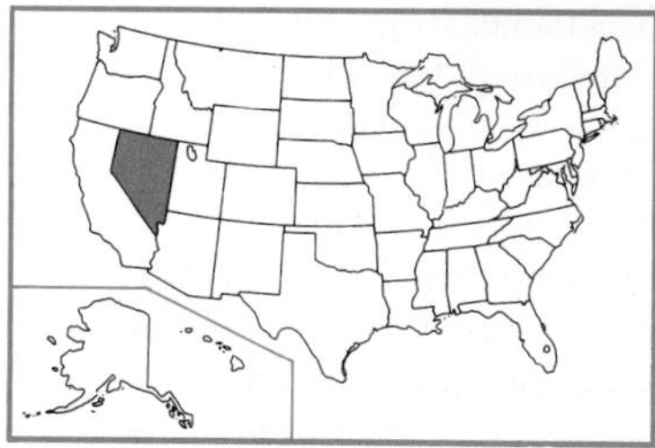

Capital: Carson City
Entered Union: Oct. 31, 1864
36th state
Nickname: Silver State
Population: 1,388,910
Rank by population: 38th
Total area: 110,561 sq. mi.
Rank by area: 7th
Largest cities: Las Vegas, Reno, Paradise, Sunrise Manor, Henderson
State bird: Mountain bluebird
State flower: Sagebrush

The Spanish were the first European explorers in Nevada, in 1775. The name comes from the Spanish word meaning "snowy." Trappers from the Hudson's Bay Company explored the north and central regions in the 1820s. The Sierra Nevada and Great Basin were explored by Kit Carson and John Fremont in the mid 1840s. The U.S. acquired the region in 1848, after the Mexican War.

Nevada, the most arid state in the nation with an average rainfall of only 4.19 inches, remains sparsely populated outside of the large cities .

Since 1931, when Nevada created two industries, gambling and divorce, the state has become the entertainment and gambling capital of the U.S. It has several resorts, including Lake Tahoe, Reno, Lake Mead and Pyramid Lake.

New Hampshire

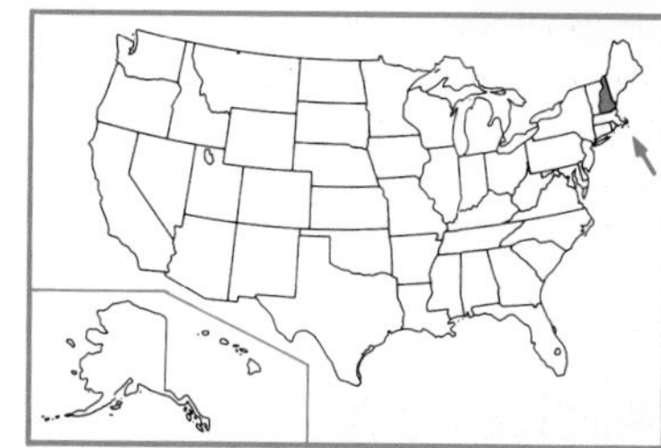

Capital: Concord
Entered Union: June 21, 1788
9th state
Nickname: Granite State
Population: 1,125,310
Rank by population: 41st
Total area: 9,279 sq. mi.
Rank by area: 44th
Largest cities: Manchester, Nashua, Concord
State bird: Purple finch
State flower: Purple lilac

New Hampshire was named by Captain John Mason after his home county of Hampshire, England, in 1630. In 1623, Captain John Smith had sent settlers to set up a fishing colony at the mouth of the Piscataqua River, near present-day Rye. New Hampshire was made a separate royal colony in 1679, after a 38-year union with Massachusetts.

As leaders in the revolutionary cause, New Hampshire delegates received the honor of being the first to vote for the Declaration of Independence on July 4, 1776. New Hampshire is also the only state ever to have hosted the formal conclusion of a foreign war. This occurred in 1905 when the treaty ending the Russo-Japanese War was signed at Portsmouth.

New Hampshire soon became an industrial state, chiefly because of its abundant water supply. Manufacturing is still its chief activity.

New Jersey

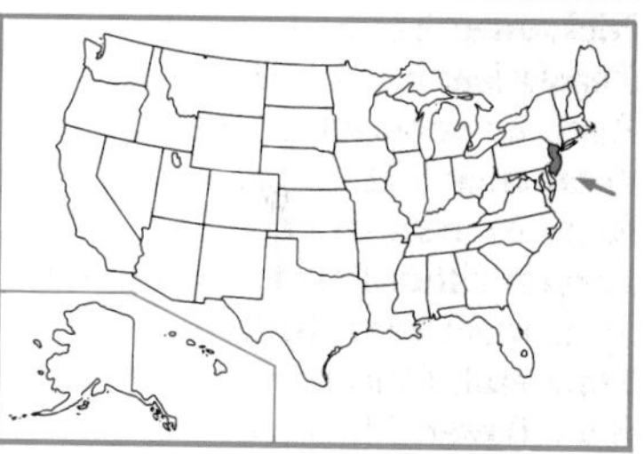

Capital: Trenton
Entered Union: Dec. 18, 1787
3rd state
Nickname: Garden State
Population: 7,879,164
Rank by population: 9th
Total area: 7,787 sq. mi.
Rank by area: 46th
Largest cities: Newark, Jersey City, Paterson, Elizabeth
State bird: Eastern goldfinch
State flower: Purple violet

The Dutch were the first Europeans to settle in the region. When the British took over in 1664, it was named for the island of Jersey, one of the Channel Islands, and Jersey was organized as an English colony under Governor Philip Carteret. In the late 17th century, the colony was divided between Carteret and William Penn. In 1776, Trenton, on the eastern shore of the Delaware River, was the site of Washington's first decisive victory of the American Revolution. During the Civil War, much of New Jersey's population supported the Southern cause.

The state saw rapid industrialization during the 19th century, attracting large corporations with permissive antitrust laws. Today, the chief industry is chemicals. New Jersey is one of the world's major research centers. It was among the first states to enact legislation to protect the environment.

New Mexico

Capital: Santa Fe
Entered Union: Jan. 6, 1912
47th state
Nickname: Land of Enchantment
Population: 1,616,483
Rank by population: 36th
Total area: 121,593 sq. mi.
Rank by area: 5th
Largest cities: Albuquerque, Santa Fe, Las Cruces, Roswell
State bird: Roadrunner
State flower: Yucca

Indians first lived in New Mexico about 10,000 years ago. The first European to visit the region is believed to have been Alvar Nunez Cabeza de Vaca. In 1598, the first Spanish settlement was established on the Rio Grande River. Much later, in the early 1820s, New Mexico became a province of Mexico. Most of the territory was acquired by the U.S. as a result of the Mexican War. During the Civil War, Confederate forces captured much of the area.

New Mexico became effectively linked to the rest of the U.S. in 1881, on completion of the southern trans-continental railroad.

Since 1945, when the first atomic bomb was tested at Trinity Site, New Mexico has been a leader in energy research.

New York

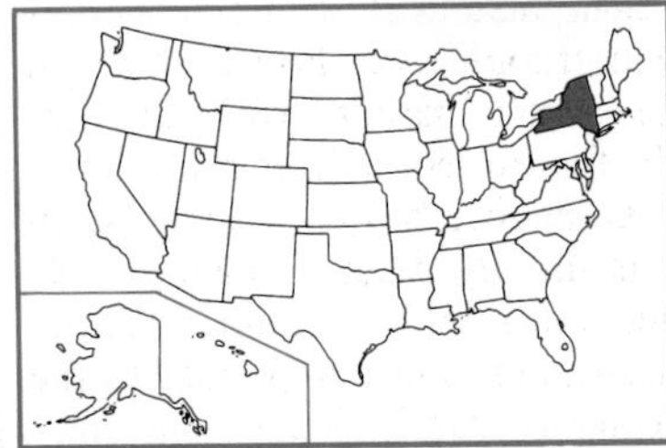

Capital: Albany
Entered Union: July 26, 1788
11th state
Nickname: Empire State
Population: 18,197,154
Rank by population: 2nd
Total area: 49,108 sq. mi.
Rank by area: 30th
Largest cities: New York, Buffalo, Rochester, Yonkers, Syracuse
State bird: Bluebird
State flower: Rose

The area, named after the Duke of York, was visited in 1524 by the navigator Giovanni da Verrazano. The Dutch arrived 100 years later and established settlements at Fort Orange (now Albany) and on the island of Manhattan.

For a short time, New York City was the U.S. capital and George Washington was inaugurated there as first President in 1789. New York was also the capital of New York State until 1796.

During the 19th century, millions of European immigrants arrived annually, many of them staying in the New York area. This helped build New York City into the great metropolis it is today. The city has become a leader in foreign trade, manufacturing, commercial and financial transactions, fashion, broadcasting, publishing and theatrical production.

North Carolina

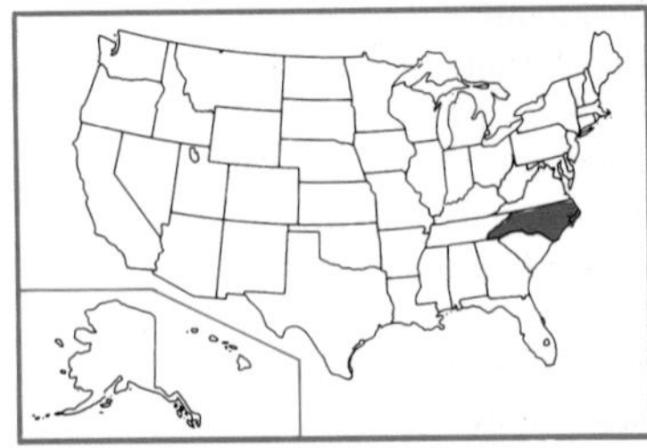

Capital: Raleigh
Entered Union: Nov. 21, 1789
12th state
Nickname: Tar Heel State
Population: 6,945,180
Rank by population: 10th
Total area: 52,669 sq. mi.
Rank by area: 28th
Largest cities: Charlotte, Raleigh, Greensboro, Winston-Salem, Durham, High Point, Asheville
State bird: Cardinal
State flower: Dogwood

Although human settlement in North Carolina is traced to 8,000 B.C., the first Europeans to visit the area were French explorers led by Giovanni da Verrazano in 1521. The first settlements were established on Roanoke Island by English colonists who named the region after their King, Charles I. The first group, in 1585, returned to England, and the second, in 1587, disappeared mysteriously.

During the Civil War, North Carolina joined the Confederacy despite considerable pro-Union sentiment.

The state's industrialization began in 1880. World War I boosted the economy and led to the establishment of major military bases. During the 1930s North Carolina was severely hit by the Depression. Today, it is the nation's largest tobacco and textile producer.

North Dakota

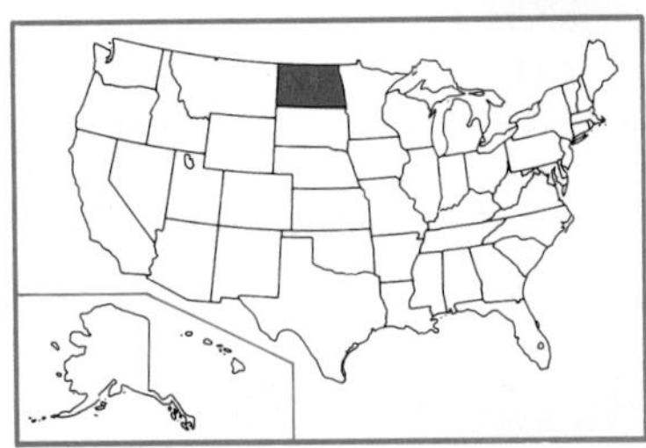

Capital: Bismarck
Entered Union: Nov. 2, 1889
39th state
Nickname: Peace Garden State
Population: 634,935
Rank by population: 47th
Total area: 70,702 sq. mi.
Rank by area: 17th
Largest cities: Fargo, Bismarck, Grand Forks, Minot, Jamestown
State bird: Western meadowlark
State flower: Wild prairie rose

The first Europeans to visit the area were the Verendryes, French fur trappers from Canada. However, a hunting society inhabited the region thousands of years ago. The name Dakota is from a Sioux Indian word meaning "ally." At the time of the Louisiana Purchase, the U.S. acquired half of North Dakota. Scottish and Irish families began to settle the region in 1812 while it was still in dispute between Britain and the U.S.

Agriculture grew dramatically after World War II and North Dakota, a large state with a small population, remains one of the most rural states, with 40 million acres of farmland in 1990. Manufacturing industries have grown in recent years. The strategic importance of the state was enhanced in the 1960s by the establishment of several major air bases and intercontinental ballistic missile sites.

Ohio

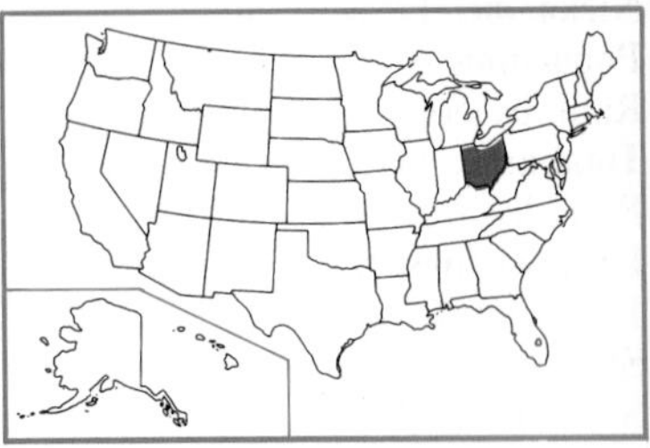

Capital: Columbus
Entered Union: March 1, 1803
17th state
Nickname: Buckeye State
Population: 11,091,301
Rank by population: 7th
Total area: 41,330 sq. mi.
Rank by area: 35th
Largest cities: Cleveland, Columbus, Cincinnati, Toledo
State bird: Cardinal
State flower: Scarlet carnation

Ohio, named after an Iroquois word meaning "fine river," became a U.S. territory after the Revolutionary War. Fighting with the Indians ended with the U.S. victory at Fallen Timbers in 1794. In the War of 1812, Commodore Oliver Perry defeated the English in the Battle of Lake Erie.

Ohio's early years were marked by dramatic population increases and political and military turmoil. After the Civil War, Ohio became a political power on the national level. Seven U.S. presidents were born in the state.

The World Wars and the conflicts in Korea and Vietnam triggered massive industrialization, and the state has become one of the nation's industrial leaders, producing transportation equipment, metal products and machinery. Ohio's thousands of factories almost overshadow its agriculture.

Oklahoma

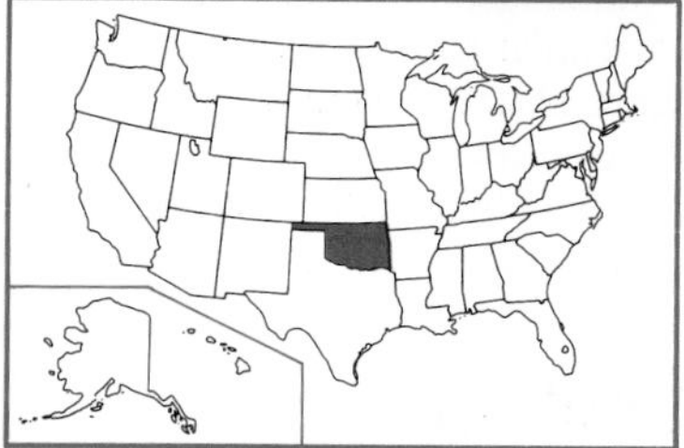

Capital: Oklahoma City
Entered Union: Nov. 16, 1907
46th state
Nickname: Sooner State
Population: 3,231,464
Rank by population: 28th
Total area: 69,919 sq. mi.
Rank by area: 18th
Largest cities: Oklahoma City, Tulsa, Lawton, Norman
State bird: Scissor-tail flycatcher
State flower: Mistletoe

Oklahoma, a name derived from two Choctaw Indian words meaning "red people," has been nicknamed the Sooner State for the homesteaders who tried to enter the area and claim land sooner than it was legal to do so. The Spanish were the first Europeans to explore Oklahoma in 1541. Since Oklahoma achieved statehood, it has changed from a rural to an urban state, from an agricultural economy to one based on industry. Its population increased until the times of the Dust Bowl and the Depression. Massive emigration ensued, and the population did not begin to grow again until the 1950s.

Oil has made Oklahoma a rich state. It is a major center for military activities and its plains produce bumper wheat crops.

Oregon

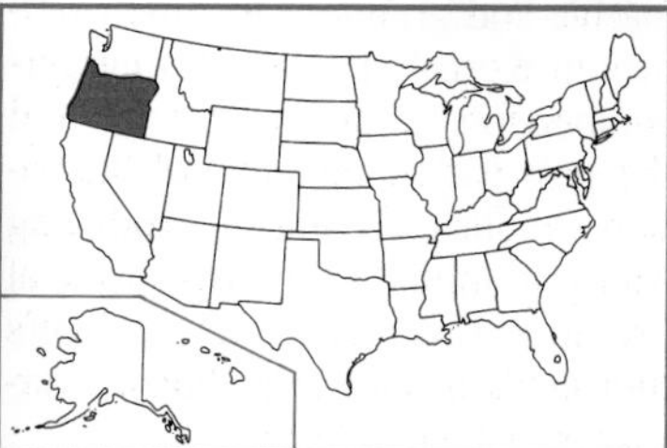

Capital: Salem
Entered Union: Feb. 14, 1859
33rd state
Nickname: Beaver State
Population: 3,031,867
Rank by population: 29th
Total area: 97,073 sq. mi.
Rank by area: 10th
Largest cities: Portland, Eugene, Salem, Gresham
State bird: Western meadowlark
State flower: Oregon grape

Indians came to Oregon at least 10,000 years ago, but the origin of its name is uncertain. Spanish and English sailors are believed to have sighted the coast of Oregon in the 1500s and 1600s. Captain James Cook charted some of the coastline in 1778 while seeking the Northwest Passage.

Lengthy disputes for control of Oregon between American settlers and the Hudson's Bay Company were finally resolved by the 1846 Oregon Treaty in which Britain gave up claims to the region. The Columbia River was the end of the line of the Oregan Trail, which brought thousands to the territory in the 1840s.

Oregon has a large wood processing industry and its salmon fishing industry is one of the world's largest. Oregon has also developed steadily as a manufacturing state.

Pennsylvania

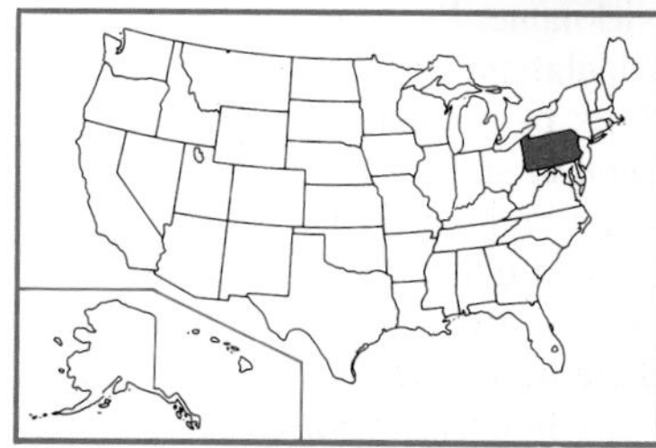

Capital: Harrisburg
Entered Union: Dec. 12, 1787
2nd state
Nickname: Keystone State
Population: 12,048,271
Rank by population: 5th
Total area: 45,308 sq. mi.
Rank by area: 33rd
Largest cities: Philadelphia, Pittsburgh, Erie, Allentown, Scranton, Reading, Bethlehem
State bird: Ruffed grouse
State flower: Mountain laurel

Pennsylvania is known as the Keystone State because of its location along the arch of the original 13 states. Pennsylvania, or "Penn's Woods," was named by King Charles II in honor of Admiral William Penn, the father of William Penn, founder of the colony.

The state has played a leading role in the nation's development. The first Continental Congress met in Philadelphia and the Declaration of Independence was signed there. Valley Forge, of Revolutionary War fame, and Gettysburg, the turning-point of the Civil War, are both in Pennsylvania.

After the Civil War, there was tremendous industrial expansion in the state based on the increased use of metals. Pittsburgh is the nation's steel capital, and the manufacture of fabricated metal products is a leading industry in Pennsylvania.

Rhode Island

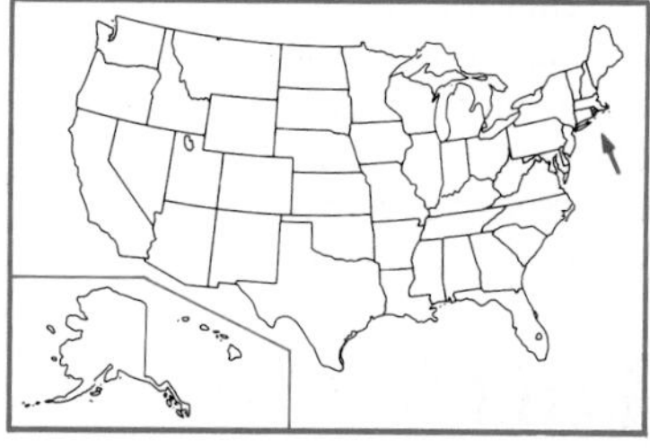

Capital: Providence
Entered Union: May 29, 1790
13th state
Nickname: Ocean State
Population: 1,000,012
Rank by population: 43rd
Total area: 1,212 sq. mi.
Rank by area: 50th
Largest cities: Providence, Warwick, Cranston, Pawtucket
State bird: Rhode Island Red
State flower: Violet

Rhode Island may have got its name from a mention in Verrazano's notes of an island the size of the Greek island of Rhodes. Despite its size – Rhode Island is by far the smallest state in area – it has played a prominent role in U.S. history. It was the first colony to declare its independence from Britain. From the start, Rhode Island has been distinguished by its support for freedom of conscience. It provided a haven for Quakers and for Jews from Holland in the 1650s. Rhode Island's rebellious, defiant nature was demonstrated by the burning of the British revenue cutters *Liberty* and *Gaspee* prior to the Revolution and by its refusal to participate in the War of 1812.

Rhode Island is densely populated and highly industrialized. The state pioneered in the manufacture of jewelry and silverware and still leads the nation in these crafts.

South Carolina

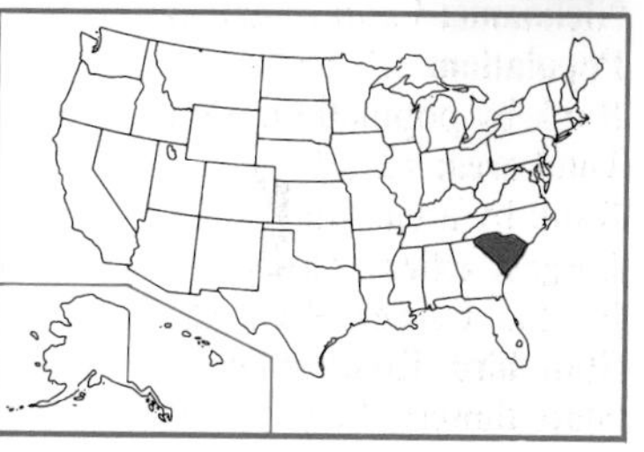

Capital: Columbia
Entered Union: May 23, 1788
8th state
Nickname: Palmetto State
Population: 3,642,718
Rank by population: 25th
Total area: 31,113 sq. mi.
Rank by area: 40th
Largest cities: Columbia, Charleston, North Charleston
State bird: Carolina wren
State flower: Yellow jessamine

The coastal regions of South Carolina, named in honor of Charles I of England, were first explored in 1521 by Francisco de Gordillo. Following this, the Spanish tried unsuccessfully to establish a colony near present-day Georgetown and the French also failed to colonize Parris Island in 1562. The first English settlement was established in 1670 at Albermarle Point, but poor conditions drove the settlers to the site of Charleston in 1680.

South Carolina saw much military action during the Revolution and during the Civil War, which began there in 1861 as South Carolina troops took Fort Sumter in Charleston harbor. The state was the first to secede from the Union.

Once mostly agricultural, South Carolina has built so many textile and other mills that today its industries are more important to the economy than its farms.

South Dakota

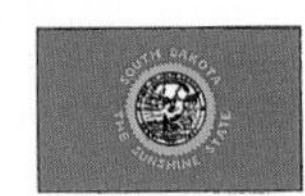

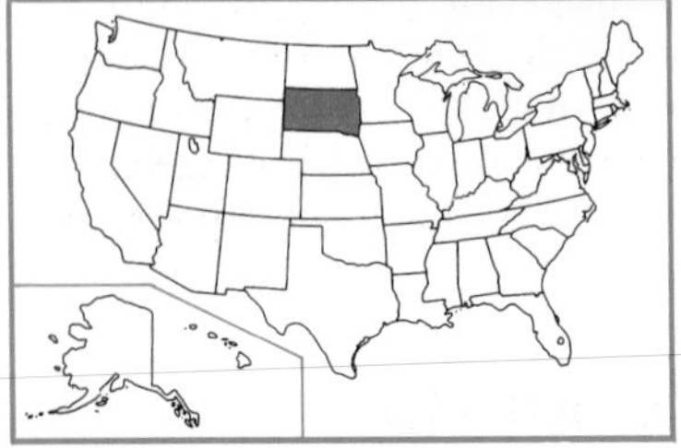

Capital: Pierre
Entered Union: Nov. 2, 1889
40th state
Nickname: Coyote State
Population: 715,392
Rank by population: 45th
Total area: 77,116 sq. mi.
Rank by area: 16th
Largest cities: Sioux Falls, Rapid City, Aberdeen, Watertown
State bird: Ring-necked pheasant
State flower: Pasque flower

As early as 1250, Dakota, a Sioux word meaning "ally," was inhabited by a tribe capable of constructing fortresses with a capacity of up to 5,000 people. Exploration of the area in earnest began in 1743 when Louis-Joseph and François Verendrye came from France to search for a route to the Pacific. The first permanent white settlement, Fort Pierre, was established in 1817. Gold was discovered in the Black Hills area of the Sioux Reservation in the 1870s, leading to an influx of settlers. This intensified conflicts with the Sioux, culminating in 1890 with the massacre of Indians at Wounded Knee.

South Dakota is essentially an agricultural state, and produces corn, oats and wheat. Gold mining is another important activity.

Tennessee

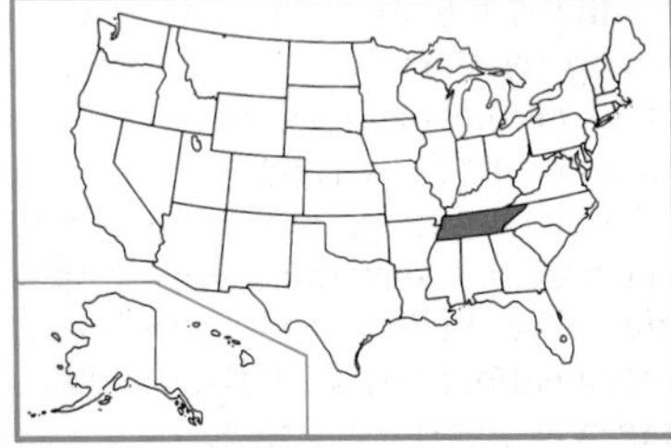

Capital: Nashville
Entered Union: June 1, 1796
16th state
Nickname: Volunteer State
Population: 5,098,798
Rank by population: 17th
Total area: 42,144 sq. mi.
Rank by area: 34th
Largest cities: Memphis, Nashville, Knoxville, Chattanooga
State bird: Mockingbird
State flower: Iris

Tennessee gained its nickname, the Volunteer State, from the large numbers of soldiers it sent to the Revolutionary War, the War of 1812, the Mexican War and the Civil War. Although Tennessee joined the Confederacy during the Civil War, there was considerable pro-Union sentiment in the state, the last Southern state to secede, and it was the scene of extensive military action.

The Tennessee Valley Authority, created in 1933 under Franklin Roosevelt's administration, was formed to promote flood control, produce electricity, and to help the Southern states economically.

Tennessee, particularly the eastern part of the state, is now predominantly industrial. Chemicals, machinery, electric and electronic equipment and textiles are among the principal manufactured goods.

Texas

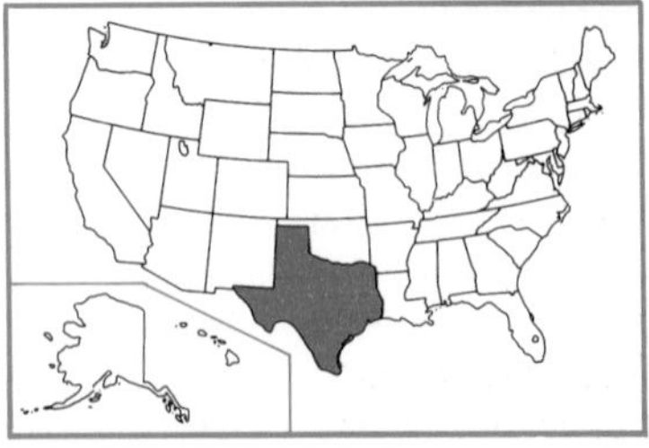

Capital: Austin
Entered Union: Dec. 29, 1845
28th state
Nickname: Lone Star State
Population: 18,031,484
Rank by population: 3rd
Total area: 266,807 sq. mi.
Rank by area: 2nd
Largest cities: Houston, Dallas, San Antonio, El Paso, Fort Worth, Austin
State bird: Mockingbird
State flower: Bluebonnet

Spanish explorers, including Coronado and Cabeza de Vaca, were the first to visit the region in the 16th century. In 1682 the Spanish established the first European settlement at Yselta, near present-day El Paso. In 1836, after a short war between American settlers and the Mexican government, famous for the battle at the Alamo, the Republic of Texas, from an Indian word meaning "friends," was proclaimed with Sam Houston as its president.

At the start of the 20th century, Texas had only three million inhabitants, but the discovery of vast oil reserves has turned the state into an industrial giant. Today, Texas, second only to Alaska in land area, leads all other states in such categories as oil, livestock and cotton. Tourism has also become a major industry: In 1990 visitors spent nearly $20 billion in the state.

Utah

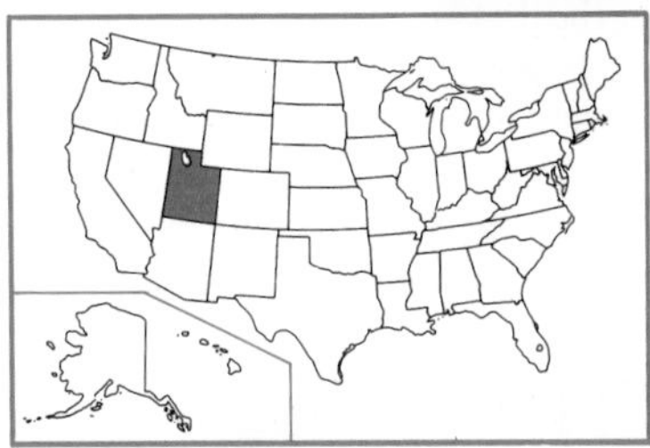

Capital: Salt Lake City
Entered Union: Jan. 4, 1896
45th state
Nickname: Beehive State
Population: 1,859,582
Rank by population: 34th
Total area: 84,899 sq. mi.
Rank by area: 11th
Largest cities: Salt Lake City, Provo, Ogden, Orem, Sandy City
State bird: Seagull
State flower: Sego lily

Utah derives its name from the Ute Indians, meaning "people of the mountains." It was first explored for Spain by Franciscan friars in 1776. Permanent settlement by whites began in 1847, when Mormons, fleeing religious persecution in the East, reached the Great Salt Lake and began to build Salt Lake City. Difficulties between Mormons and the federal government over polygamy continued until the Mormon Church abandoned the practice six years before Utah achieved statehood. The completion of the first transcontinental railroad in 1869 was marked by the driving of a golden spike at Promontory Point.

Manufacturing has become the chief industry in Utah over recent years, ahead of mining, tourism and agriculture. The state has also become an important aerospace research center.

Vermont

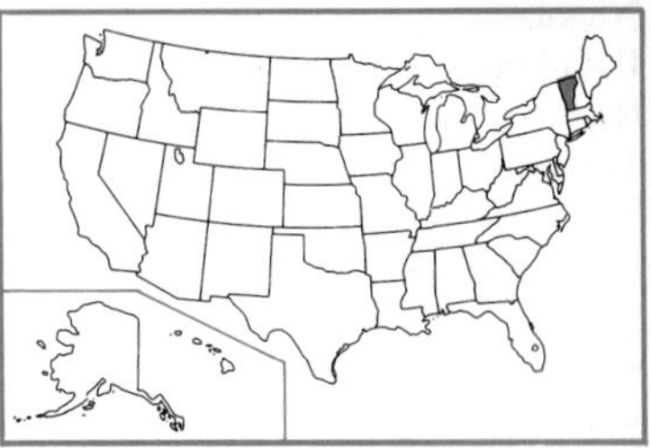

Capital: Montpelier
Entered Union: March 4, 1791
14th state
Nickname: Green Mountain State
Population: 575,691
Rank by population: 49th
Total area: 9,614 sq. mi.
Rank by area: 43rd
Largest cities: Burlington, Rutland, Bennington, Essex
State bird: Hermit thrush
State flower: Red clover

Vermont, which derives its name from the French "verts monts," meaning "green mountains," was explored and claimed for France by Samuel de Champlain in 1609. England gained control over the area after the French and Indian War. Vermont adopted its first constitution in 1777, abolishing slavery and providing for universal male suffrage without property qualifications. In 1791, Vermont became the first state after the original 13 to join the union.

The state is famous for its maple syrup, and is a top producer of marble and granite. Machine tools, furniture, scales, books, computer components and fishing rods are the principal manufactured goods. Tourism has become a major industry. Outdoor sports, such as hiking and camping, are especially popular, and Vermont has more than 56 ski areas.

Virginia

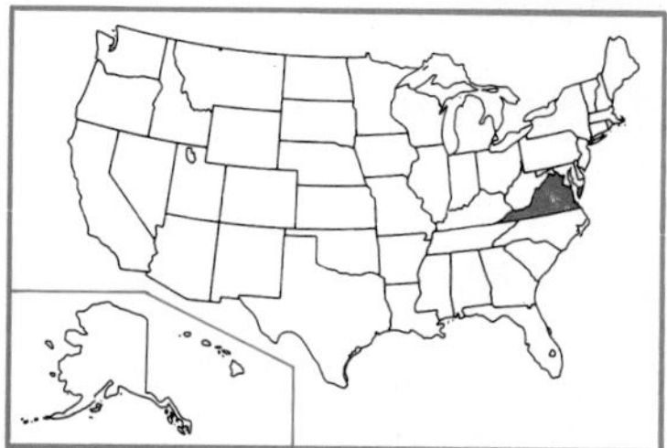

Capital: Richmond
Entered Union: June 25, 1788
10th state
Nickname: Old Dominion
Population: 6,490,634
Rank by population: 12th
Total area: 40,767 sq. mi.
Rank by area: 36th
Largest cities: Norfolk, Virginia Beach, Richmond
State bird: Cardinal
State flower: Dogwood

Named for Elizabeth I of England, the "Virgin Queen," Virginia has played a central role in American history. Jamestown, founded in 1607, was the first permanent English settlement in North America, and the first African laborers, indentured servants, entered the colonies there in 1619. The surrenders ending the American Revolution (Yorktown) and the Civil War (Appomattox) occurred in Virginia.

Virginia came into conflict with the federal government over racial integration in the 1950s. Today, the state ranks among the nation's leaders in tobacco, apples and sweet potatoes. Virginia, which has a large dairy industry, is also famous for and Smithfield hams. Virginia is the birthplace of more Presidents than any other state – eight.

Washington

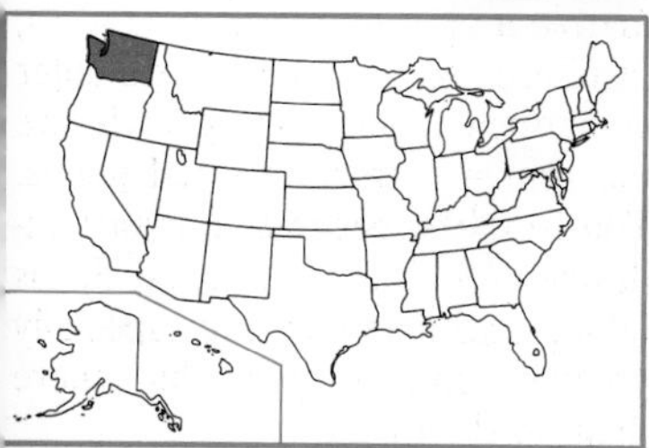

Capital: Olympia
Entered Union: Nov. 11, 1889
42nd state
Nickname: Evergreen State
Population: 5,255,276
Rank by population: 15th
Total area: 68,139 sq. mi.
Rank by area: 20th
Largest cities: Seattle, Spokane, Tacoma, Bellevue, Everett
State bird: Willow goldfinch
State flower: Rhododendron

Washington territory, as part of the vast Oregon Country, was visited by French, Spanish, British and American explorers in the late 18th and early 19th centuries. The fur trade was Washington's first major industry. The dispute over the northern boundary of the U.S., the 49th parallel, was settled with Britain in 1846. From the mid-19th century, lumber operations sprang up along Puget Sound. The state is still a leading lumber producer, with rich stands of Douglas fir, hemlock, spruce, larch, and white and ponderosa pine. Commercial fishing and canning of salmon and halibut are leading industries, as are shipbuilding and the manufacture of aircraft.

Washington's Columbia River is harnessed by the Grand Coulee Dam, the world's third largest in hydroelectric capacity.

West Virginia

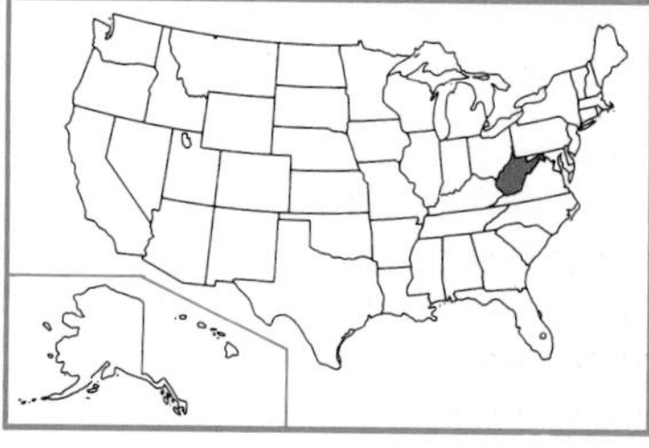

Capital: Charleston
Entered Union: June 20, 1863
35th state
Nickname: Mountain State
Population: 1,820,137
Rank by population: 35th
Total area: 24,232 sq. mi.
Rank by area: 41st
Largest cities: Charleston, Huntington, Wheeling, Parkersburg, Morgantown
State bird: Cardinal
State flower: Big Rhododendron

West Virginia, the state with the most rugged terrain east of the Mississippi, largely shared its 17th, 18th and early 19th century history with Virginia, of which it was a part until Virginia seceded from the Union in 1861. At that time, the delegates of 40 western counties formed their own separate government, which was granted statehood in 1863.

Although coal was discovered near Racine in the 1740s, it was not until after the Civil War that industrialization on a large scale began. Frequent strikes in the early 20th century led to clashes between miners and company guards, sometimes backed by federal troops.

Today, the state ranks high in bituminous coal production. Tourism has become increasingly popular in West Virginia, 75% of which is covered with forests.

Wisconsin

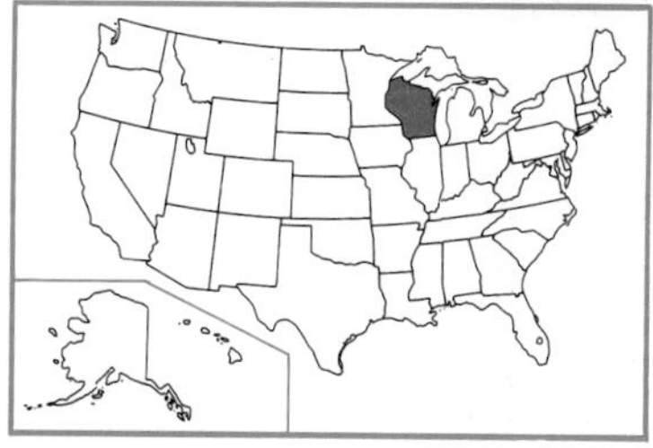

Capital: Madison
Entered Union: May 29, 1848
30th state
Nickname: Badger State
Population: 5,037,928
Rank by population: 18th
Total area: 56,153 sq. mi.
Rank by area: 26th
Largest cities: Milwaukee, Madison, Green Bay, Racine
State bird: Robin
State flower: Wood violet

Wisconsin's name derives from a Chippewa Indian word thought to mean "grassy place." The French were the first Europeans explorers in the region, but the British took over in 1763. The U.S. had nominal control after the Revolution, but the British did not leave until after the War of 1812. Wisconsin's nickname, the Badger State, comes not from the animal of that name but from the nickname given to lead miners in the 1830s.

Wisconsin was a pioneer in social legislation in the early 20th century. By 1925, it provided pensions for the blind, aid to dependent children and old-age assistance. The state was the first to enact an unemployment compensation law.

Today, Wisconsin is a leader in milk and cheese production. Its many lakes, of which Winnebago is the largest, and water sports have become popular.

Wyoming

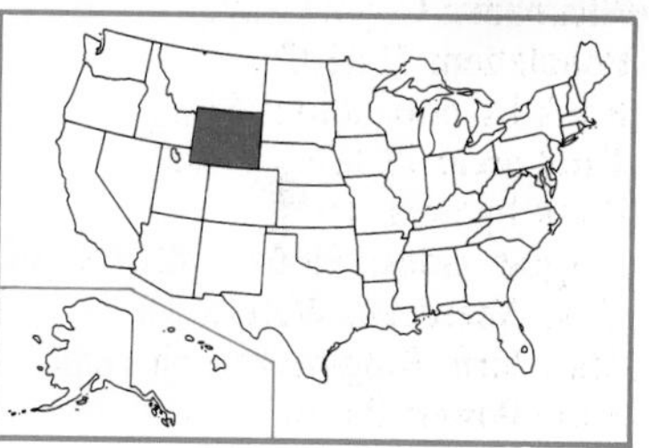

Capital: Cheyenne
Entered Union: July 10, 1890
44th state
Nickname: Equality State
Population: 470,242
Rank by population: 50th
Total area: 97,809 sq. mi.
Rank by area: 9th
Largest cities: Cheyenne, Casper, Laramie, Rock Springs, Gillette
State bird: Meadowlark
State flower: Indian paintbrush

Wyoming, which competes with Alaska for the rank of least populated state, derives its name from an Algonquin Indian term meaning "large prairie place." Its nickname was earned in 1869 when Wyoming became the first state in the union to grant women the right to vote. In 1924, Nellie Tayloe Ross was elected the first woman governor in the United States.

The Verendrye brothers were the first Europeans to explore the region, in 1743. The eastern part of what is now Wyoming was acquired by the U.S. in 1803 as part of the Louisiana Purchase. Wyoming territory was carved out of parts of the old territories of Dakota and Utah in 1868.

Today, mining, oil and natural gas are the most important industries. The Yellowstone and Grand Teton national parks make the state a prime tourist attraction.

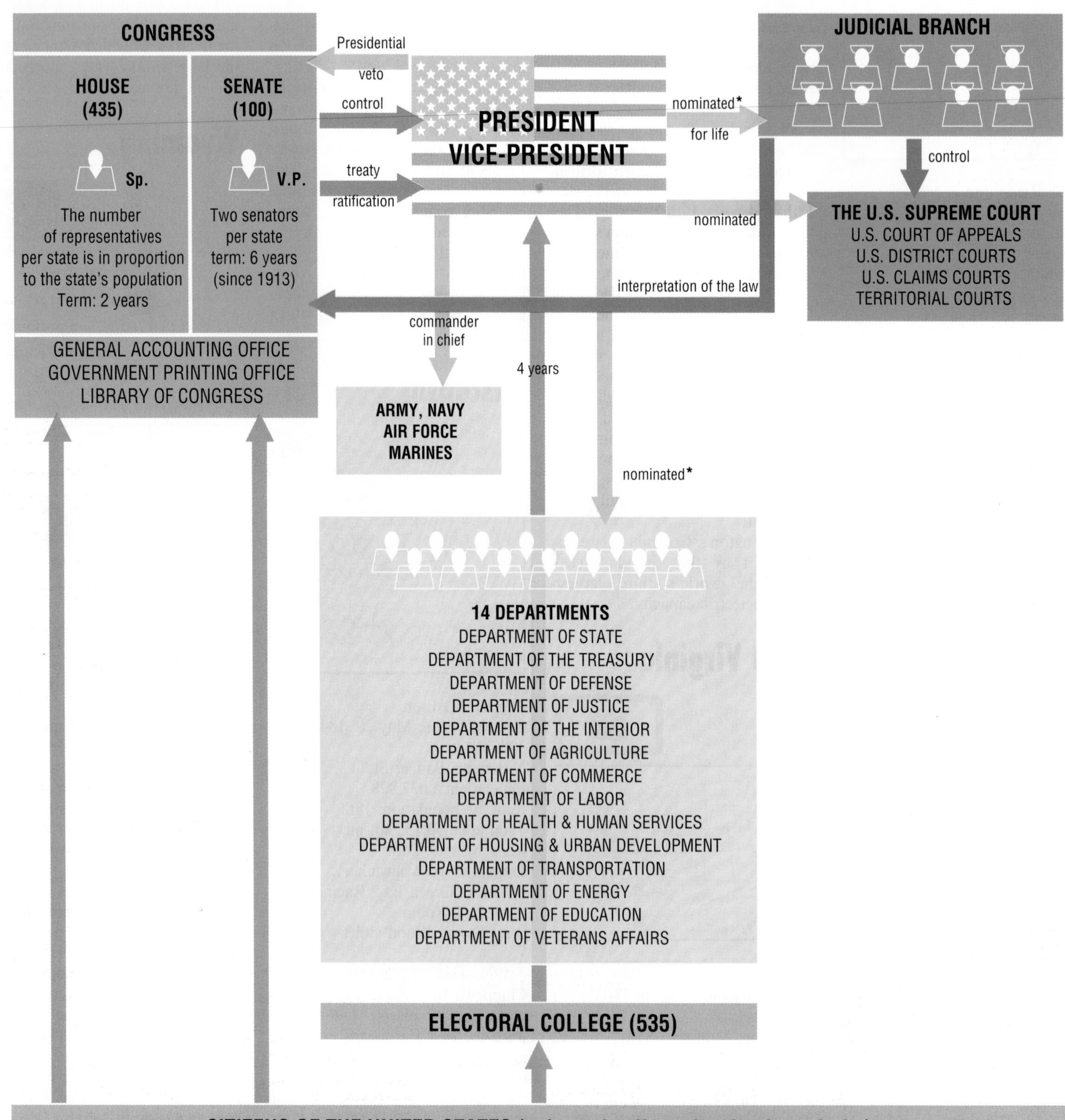

Apart from some local differences due to custom and necessity, the governments of the 50 states are organized along the same general lines as the federal government.

V.P.: Vice-President
Sp.: Speaker

* Confirmation by the senate

General Index

This index provides rapid access to the information you seek. Each entry is followed by a page number and a letter indicating the column in which the article begins (a, b, c or d). Page numbers in italic refer to the chronology panels.

A

B

D

G

H

J

K

N

P

Q

R

S

U

V

XYZ

Picture credits

Some agency names have been abbreviated in this index. The list below provides full names of pictures agencies:

Am. Railroads: Association of American Railroads
AMNH, Smithsonian: American Museum of Natural History, Smithsonian Institution
Appomattox: "Surrender at Appomattox" by Tom Lovell, © 1988 The Greenwich Workshop, Inc., Trumbull, CT, 800/243-4246
Ass. Press: Associated Press
Becker: Becker Collection
Bettmann: The Bettmann Archive, New York
Bourke-White, Time-Life: Courtesy of Margaret Bourke-White, Time-Life Magazine
Brown: Courtesy of the John Carter Brown Library at Brown University (John Carter Brown Library)
Can. Railways: Canadian National Railways
Chrysler: Chrysler Museum
CHS: Courtesy, Colorado Historical Society
Cinematheque: Cinemateque de Paris
Cleveland Museum of Art: The Cleveland Museum of Art, Hinman B. Hurlbut Collection
Coca-Cola: Courtesy of The Coca-Cola Company
DeSomma: DeSomma, Vincent
Eastman: International Museum of Photography at George Eastman House
Equitable Life: Courtesy of the Equitable Life Assurance Society of the U.S.
Ferris: J.L.G. Ferris, Estate of
Gables: Photo Courtesy of the House of Seven Gables Settlement Association
Granger: Granger Collection, New York
Kendall Whaling Museum: The Kendall Whaling Museum, Sharon, Massachusetts, USA
Kirshon: Kirshon, John
Mary Evans: Mary Evans Picture Library
National Portrait Gallery, Smithsonian: National Portrait Gallery, Smithsonian Institution
Metropolitan: Metropolitan Museum of Art
Modern Art: Museum of Modern Art, New York
NJHS: From the Collection of the New Jersey Historical Society
NMAA, Smithsonian: National Museum of American Art, Smithsonian Institution
NYPL: New York Public Library
NMAH, Smithsonian: National Museum of American History, Smithsonian Institution
NYHS: Courtesy of the New York Historical Society, New York
NYPL, Map Division: New York Public Library, Map Division
Paramount: Paramount Pictures
Reuters/Bettmann: Reuters/Bettmann Newsphotos
Sears: Sears Archive
Sipa: Sipa Press, New York
Smithsonian: Smithsonian Institution
Seaver: Seaver Center for Western History Research, Natural History Museum of Los Angeles Coun
Teich: Lake County (IL) Museum, Curt Teich Collection
UPI/Bettman: UPI/Bettmann Newsphotos
Vicksburg: "The Union Fleet Passing Vicksburg" by Tom Lovell, © 1989 The Greenwich Workshop, Inc., Trumbull, CT, 800/243-4246
Walt Disney: © The Walt Disney Company

Whilst every effort has been made to trace the Copyright of the photographs and illustrations used in this publication, there may be a possibility where an inadvertent error has been made in the picture credit. If this is the case, we apologize for the mistake and ask the copyright holder to contact the publisher so that it can be rectified.

The position of the pictures is indicated by two letters: B: bottom, T: top, M: middle, L: left, R: right, X: middle left, Y: middle right, SP: spread

Credits are given for pages 932 to 937 from left top to bottom and right top to bottom

4 SP: Courtesy of White House
6 SP: Granger
8 TL: JL International – **BL:** NMAA, Smithsonian
9 TL, TR: Granger – **BR:** Smithsonian
10 TL: Smithsonian – **BL:** National Park Service – **MR:** AMNH, Smithsonian
11 BL: Granger – **TR, BR:** Smithsonian
12 TL: Architect of the Capital – **ML:** Signal Hill N.H.P.
13 TL: Granger – **MR:** Bettmann
14 TX: Granger – **MR, BL:** Bettmann
15 TL, BR: Granger – **TR:** JL International
16 All pictures from Granger
17 TR: Granger – **BR:** NYPL, Map Division
18 TM: Library of Congress – **BX:** JL International
19 TL, BL: Granger – **TR:** Bettmann
20 TM: Granger – **MM:** NYPL, Map Division – **BX:** Bettmann
21 TR: Library of Congress – **TL, BR:** Granger
22 TR, BX: Granger – **BR:** Bettmann
23 TR, BL, BR: Granger – **BX:** Bettmann
24, 25 All pictures from Granger
26 TM: New York Power Authority
27 TL: NYPL – **MR, BR:** Granger
28 TR: Architect of the Capital – **MR:** NYPL – **BR:** Granger
29 TR: Granger – **BR:** Brown
30 TM: Brown – **MR, BX:** Granger
31, 32, 33, 34 All pictures from Granger
35 TR, ML, MX: Granger – **BL:** NYPL
36 to 40 All pictures from Granger
41 All pictures from Pierpont Morgan Library
42 TM: Granger – **BR:** Bettmann
43 TR: NMAA, Smithsonian – **TL:** Ferris – **BL:** Granger – **BR:** Brown
44 SP: Ferris
46 TM: Library of Congress – **BM:** Bettmann – **MM:** Granger
47 TR, BL: NYPL – BR: Library of Congress
48 TX, MR: Granger – **BM:** New Mexico, State of
49 ML, MR: Ferris – **BR:** Architect of the Capital
50 TM: Virginia State Library – **BM:** Granger
51 TR, TL, MX: Granger – **BL:** NYPL
52 TM: Architect of the Capital – **MR:** Granger – **BM:** Ferris
53 TL, TR: Granger – **BM:** Museum of the City of New York
54 TR: Ferris – **MX, BR:** Granger
55 TR, BR: Ferris – **MR:** Bettmann
56 All pictures from Granger
57 MR: Granger – **BR, TR:** Bettmann
58 TM: Bettmann – **BX:** Granger
59 TR: Maryland Historical Society, Baltimore – **BL:** Wisconsin Historical Society – **TL:** Granger
60 TM: Granger – **MM:** NYPL
61 BR: Bettmann – **TY:** Granger – **BL:** Courtesy, Vermont Historical Society
62 TL: The Permanent Collection of the University of Delaware
63 TR: Bettmann – **BR, BL:** Granger
64 TR: Granger – **MX, BM:** Bettmann
65 All pictures from Bettmann
6 6 TM: Bettmann – **BX:** Granger – **BR:** Pilgrim Society
67 TM, BL: Granger – **BR:** Brown
68 TM, MR: Granger – **BM:** Bettmann
69 All pictures from Granger
70 TR: Ferris – **BY:** Granger
71 All pictures from Granger
72 TR: Granger – **BR:** Trotters Hall of Fame
73 All pictures from Bettmann
74 TM: Granger – **MR:** Bettmann
75 TM, BL: Granger – **BR:** National Gallery of Art
76 TY: Granger – **TR:** Bettmann – **BR:** New York Power Authority
77 TY, BR: Granger – **ML:** Ferris
78 TM: Ferris – **BM:** Bettmann
79 TM: National Gallery of Art – **BR:** Bettmann – **BL:** Granger
80 TR, BX: Granger – **MM:** Bettmann
81 All pictures from Granger
82 TM: Ferris – **MM:** Granger – **BM:** Bettmann
83 TL: Schenectady County Historical Society – **BR, BL:** Granger
84 TM: Ferris
85 TL: Cape Code Chamber of Commerce – **TR:** Maryland Historical Society, Baltimore – **ML:** Bettmann – **MM:** Granger – **MR:** Chrysler – **BL:** Philipsburg Manor – **BR:** Gables
86 All pictures from Granger
87 TR: Bettmann – **BR:** Smithsonian
88 TR: Granger – **BM:** Bettmann
89 TR: Granger – **BR:** Peabody Museum of Salem
90 TX: Brown – **BX:** Bettmann – **BR:** Ferris
91 TM: Granger – **BM:** Ferris
92 TM: Ferris – **BX:** Granger – **BR:** Bettmann
93 TR, TX: Granger – **BR:** Kendall Whaling Museum
94 All pictures from Granger
95 TR, BL: Granger – **BR:** Texas Department of Commerce
96 All pictures from Granger
97 TR: National Gallery of Art – **BR:** Maryland Historical Society, Baltimore
98 TR, MR: Granger – **BX:** Bettmann
99 TR, BL, BR: Granger – **TX:** Bettmann
100, 101 All pictures from Granger
102 TM: JL International – **MR:** Granger – **BM:** Ferris
103 TL, BR: Granger – **BY:** Ferris – **MR:** Bettmann
104 TM: NYPL – **BM:** Granger – **BR:** Texas Department of Commerce
105 All pictures from Bettmann
106 TM: Ferris – **BM:** National Gallery of Art
107 TL: Granger – **BR:** JL International
108 TL, TR: Winterthur Museum – **BL, MR, BR:** Granger
109 TL: Granger – **BL, TR, BR:** Winterthur Museum
110 All pictures from Granger
111 TR, ML: Granger – **MR:** Chicago Historical Society
112 TM: Granger – **BR:** Bettmann
113 TR: Granger – **TL:** Bettmann – **BM:** Ferris
114 MM, BR: Ferris – **TR:** Bettmann
115 TM: Granger – **MM:** Bettmann
116, 117 All pictures from Granger
118 TY, TR: JL International – **MR:** Brown
119 TX: Granger – **MR, BR:** Bettmann – **BX:** Touro Synagogue
120 SP: Granger
122 MM, BX: Granger – **TR:** Missouri Historical Society
123 TR, ML: Granger – **BR:** Hartford Courant
124 TY, TR, MR, BY: Granger – **BR:** Bettmann
125 TX, BX: Granger – **BR:** Brown
126 to 129 All pictures from Granger
130 TX, MR: Granger – **BY:** Bettmann
131, 132 All pictures from Granger
133 TL, TR: Bettmann – **BL:** Granger
134 TR: Library of Congress – **BX:** Bettmann
135 TR, MX, BR: Granger – **BL:** National Gallery of Art
136 All pictures from Granger
137 TM, BM: Granger – **BR:** Bettmann
138 MR: Granger
139 TR: Library of Congress – **BY, BR, BL:** Granger
140 TR: The Historical Society of Pennsylvania
141 All pictures from Bettmann
142 TM, BX: Bettmann – **MR:** Granger
143 TR, BL: Bettmann – **BR:** Granger
144 TL: Granger
145 TM: Bettmann – **MM, BL, BR:** Granger
146 TL: National Gallery of Art – **BR:** Granger
147 TR: National Gallery of Art – **MR:** Brown – **BR:** Bettmann
148 TL: Granger – **MR, BL:** Bettmann
149 TR: Bettmann – **BR, MX:** Granger
150 TY: Granger – **TR:** National Gallery of Art – **BX:** Bettmann

151 **TR:** Bettmann – **BR, ML:** Granger
152 **BL:** Ferris
153 **TL, MR:** Bettmann – **BL:** Granger
154 **TL:** Granger – **BL:** Architect of the Capital
156 **BL:** Granger – **BR:** Bettmann
157 **TM, BL:** Granger – **BR:** Bettmann
158 **TL, MM:** Granger – **BL:** National Gallery of Art
159 **BB:** Bettmann
160 All pictures from Bettmann
161 **MY, BX:** Bettmann – **MR, TL:** Granger – **BL:** Cincinnati Art Museum
162 **TL, BL:** Granger – **BR:** Bettmann
163 All pictures from Granger
164 **TR:** Architect of the Capital
165 **TR:** National Gallery of Art – **BR:** Ferris – **BL:** Granger
166 **TX, BM:** Bettmann – **MR:** Granger
167 **TL, MR:** Bettmann – **BL:** Granger
168 **TL, BR:** Granger – **BL, TR, BY:** Bettmann
169, 170 All pictures from Granger
171 **TM:** Ferris – **MR:** Bettmann – **BL:** Granger
172 All pictures from Granger
173 **ML, MX, BR:** Granger – **TR:** Bettmann
174 **TL, ML, BL, BX:** Bettmann – **BR:** Granger
175 **TX:** Bettmann – **TY:** Granger – **BR:** Ferris – **BL:** Brown
176 All pictures from Granger
177 **TL:** Granger – **TR, BR:** Bettmann
178 **BR, BL:** Granger – **TL:** Bettmann
179 **TT:** Architect of the Capital
180 **TM:** Winterthur Museum – **MR:** Bettmann – **BX:** Granger
181 **TM:** Architect of the Capital – **BR:** National Gallery of Art – **BL:** Granger
182 **TM:** Granger
183 **TR:** Granger – **BR:** Architect of the Capital – **BL:** Bettmann
184 All pictures from Bettmann
185 **TM:** Granger – **BM:** NJHS
186 **MM:** Ferris
187 **TM, BR:** Granger – **BL:** Smithsonian
188 **TM, BM:** Granger – **MR:** Bettmann
189 **TX:** Granger – **MR:** Bettmann
190 All pictures from Granger
191 **TR, ML:** Granger – **BR:** JL International
192 **MM:** National Gallery of Art – **TT:** Granger
193 **TT:** Architect of the Capital
197 **TL, TR, ML, MR, BL, BR:** Granger – **MM:** Ass. Press
198 All pictures from Granger
199 **TR, BR:** Granger – **ML:** Brown
200 **SP:** Ferris
202 All pictures from Granger
203 **TR:** Granger – **BL:** Brown
204 **TR:** Daughters of the American Revolution – **BX:** Smithsonian
205 **BR, TR:** Granger – **TX:** Bettmann
206 **TR:** Bettmann – **BM:** Granger
207 **TM, MM, BM:** Winterthur Museum – **BR:** NMAH, Smithsonian
208 **TR:** Architect of the Capital – **BX:** Granger
209 All pictures from Granger
210 **TM:** Granger – **MR:** Bettmann – **BM:** Ferris
211 **TM:** Bettmann – **BL, BM:** Granger – **BR:** National Gallery of Art
212 **TM, MR:** Granger – **BM:** National Gallery of Art
213 **TL, BR:** Granger – **TR:** Bettmann
214 **TX:** Granger – **TR:** National Gallery of Art – **BM:** Ferris
215 All pictures from Granger
216 **BX:** Art Resource
217 **BR:** Architect of the Capital – **TL:** NMAA, Smithsonian
218 **TX, TR:** Bettmann – **BM:** Granger
219 **TR:** Granger – **BR:** Ferris – **BL:** NMAH, Smithsonian
220 **TR:** Granger – **BX:** NMAH, Smithsonian
221 **TR, BR:** Granger – **MR:** Bettmann
222 **TM:** Granger – **MR, BR:** Bettmann
223 **MY:** Bettmann – **TR:** Winterthur Museum – **BL:** Brown
224 **TM:** Granger – **BX:** Bettmann
225 **BL, TR:** Granger – **BR:** Brown
226 **TX:** Bettmann – **TY, MR:** Granger
227 **TR:** Bettmann – **ML:** Peale Museum – **BR:** Granger
228 **MY:** NYHS – **BR:** Granger
229 **TR, MM:** Granger – **BL:** Bettmann
230 All pictures from Granger
231 **TR:** Granger – **BR:** JL International
232 **TM:** Granger – **BX:** Bettmann
233 **TX:** Bettmann – **TR, BR, BL:** Granger
234 All pictures from Bettmann
235 **TM:** Amon Carter Museum, Fort Worth – **MM:** Missouri Historical Society – **BM:** Bettmann
236 **MM:** Granger – **BX:** Missouri Historical Society
237 **TM, BL:** Bettmann – **BR:** Granger
238 **TM:** Bettmann – **BX:** Granger
239 **TL:** Granger – **TR, BR:** Bettmann
240 **TX, BR:** Bettmann – **MX:** Granger
241 **TL:** Granger – **BR:** NMAA, Smithsonian
242 **TM:** Granger – **BX, MR:** Bettmann – **BR:** National Gallery of Art
243, 244 All pictures from Granger
245 **ML, TR:** Bettmann – **BR:** National Gallery of Art
246 **TX:** Bettmann – **MM:** Granger
247 **MR, BR:** Granger – **TR:** Bettmann
248 **TR:** Bettmann – **BX, BY:** Granger
249 **TR:** Bettmann – **BL:** Granger – **BR:** NMAA, Smithsonian
250 All pictures from Granger
251 **TL, TR:** Bettmann – **BL:** The Historical Society of Pennsylvania – **BR:** Granger
252 **MM:** Granger
253 **TR, BR:** Bettmann – **ML:** Granger
254 All pictures from Granger
255 All pictures from Bettmann
256, 257 All pictures from Granger
258 **TL, ML:** Bettmann – **BL:** Granger
259 **TR, BY, BR:** Granger – **MR:** Bettmann
260 **TL:** NMAA, Smithsonian – **BL:** Granger
261 **TL:** Chicago Historical Society – **ML:** Bettmann – **BL, MR:** Granger
262 All pictures from Granger
263 **TX:** Bettmann – **BR:** Granger
264 **BM:** National Gallery of Art
265 **TL:** Bettmann – **TR, BR:** Granger
266 **TX:** Architect of the Capital – **BM:** Bettmann
267, 268 All pictures from Granger
269 **TL:** Architect of the Capital – **TR, BM:** Bettmann
270 All pictures from Granger
271 **TR, BL:** National Gallery of Art – **BR:** Bettmann
272 **BR:** NMAA, Smithsonian
273 **TL, TR:** Bettmann – **BR:** Granger
274, 275 All pictures from Granger
276 **TM:** Granger – **BX:** Bettmann
277 **TR:** Bettmann – **BL:** National Gallery of Art – **BR:** Granger
278 All pictures from Granger
279 **MR:** Bettmann – **TL, BR:** Granger
280 **TX, TR, BM:** Granger – **BR:** NYHS
281 **TM:** Bettmann – **BM:** Library of Congress
282 **TX:** Granger – **TY, BM:** Bettmann
283 **TX, ML:** Granger – **MR:** Bettmann
284 All pictures from Granger
285 **TL:** Granger – **BR:** Bettmann
286 **TM, MR:** Granger – **BX:** Bettmann
287 **TM:** National Gallery of Art – **BL, BR:** Granger
288 **TM:** Bettmann – **MM, BM:** Granger
289 **TL, TR:** Bettmann – **BM:** NMAA, Smithsonian
290 **TX:** Bettmann – **BM:** Granger
291 to 293 All pictures from Granger
294 **TM, BX:** Granger – **BR:** NMAA, Smithsonian
295 **TL, BR:** Granger – **BL:** Bettmann
296 **TM:** Granger – **BX:** Bettmann
297 **TM:** Granger – **BM:** National Gallery of Art
298 All pictures from Bettmann
299 **TR:** NMAA, Smithsonian – **BR:** Granger
300 **TM:** Granger – **BM:** Bettmann
301 **TL, MR:** Granger – **TR, BR:** National Gallery of Art
302 **TX:** Granger – **TY:** Bettmann – **BM:** NYPL
303 **TL, TR:** Bettmann – **BR:** NMAA, Smithsonian
304 **TL, BL:** Granger – **TR:** Bettmann
305 **BM:** Granger
306 **TL, TR:** Granger – **MM:** NMAA, Smithsonian
307 **TL, BL:** Granger – **BR:** NMAA, Smithsonian
308, 309 All pictures from Granger
310 **TX, BR:** Granger – **BX:** Bettmann
311 **TR, BL, BX:** Bettmann – **BR:** Granger
312 All pictures from Granger
313 **TR, BL:** Granger – **TL:** NMAA, Smithsonian – **BR:** Bettmann
314 **TM, MM:** Granger – **BY:** Bettmann
315 **TM:** Granger – **BR, BL:** Bettmann
316 **TM:** Granger – **BM:** Bettmann
317 **BL:** Bettmann – **BR:** National Gallery of Art
318 **TY, MR:** Granger – **BY, MX:** Bettmann
319 **BM:** Bettmann
320 All pictures from Granger
321 **TL:** Granger – **TR, BR:** Bettmann
322 **TR:** Architect of the Capital – **BR:** Granger
323 **BR:** Granger
324 **TR:** Granger – **MM, BM:** Bettmann
325 **TL, BL:** Bettmann – **TR, BR:** Granger
326 **TL:** Bettmann – **BR:** Granger
327 All pictures from Granger
328 All pictures from Bettmann
329 **TL, BL, BM, BR:** Granger – **TR:** Bettmann
330 **TL, ML:** Bettmann – **BL, BR:** Granger
331 **TX, TR:** Bettmann – **BR:** Ferris
332 **TR:** JL International – **BR:** Granger – **BX:** Bettmann
333 **TR, ML:** Granger – **BR:** National Gallery of Art
334 **TM, MY, BM:** Granger – **MX:** Seaver
335 All pictures from Granger
336 **SP:** Ferris
338 **TX, TR:** Bettmann – **BM:** Granger
339 All pictures from Granger
340 **MM:** Bettmann – **TR, BR:** Granger
341 **TR:** Bettmann – **BL, MM:** Granger
342 All pictures from Granger
343 **TR:** Granger – **BL, BR:** NMAA, Smithsonian
344 **TX, BR:** Granger – **MR:** Levi Strauss & Co.
345 **TR:** Bettmann – **BR:** Granger
346 All pictures from Granger
347 **TL, BR:** Granger – **BL:** Bettmann
348 **TM:** Granger – **BM:** National Gallery of Art – **BR:** Bettmann
349 **TR, TL:** Granger – **BR:** National Gallery of Art
350 **MX:** Bettmann – **TR, BR:** Granger
351 **TL, MR:** Bettmann – **TX, BL:** Granger
352 **TM:** Bettmann – **BB:** Granger
353 All pictures from Granger
354 **TY:** Granger – **BM:** National Gallery of Art
355 All pictures from Granger
356 **TR, BX:** Granger – **BR:** Bettmann
357, 358 All pictures from Granger
359 **TR:** Brown
360 **TM, BM:** Granger – **MR:** Bettmann
361 **TL, BL:** Granger – **BR:** Bettmann
362 All pictures from Granger
363 **TM, BR:** Bettmann – **TR:** Granger
364 **TX, TR:** Bettmann – **BX:** Library of Congress – **BR:** Granger
365 **TR, MR:** Granger – **BR:** JL International
366 **TM:** National Gallery of Art – **MX:** Granger – **BL:** Bettmann – **BR:** Ferris
367 **TR:** National Archives – **MR, BL:** Bettmann – **BR:** Granger
368 **TM:** National Gallery of Art – **BM:** Granger
369 **TR:** Granger – **MR:** JL International – **BL:** National Gallery of Art
370 **TL, TM, BR:** Bettmann – **BL:** Granger
371, 372 All pictures from Bettmann
373 **TR, MR:** Bettmann – **BR:** JL International – **BL:** Granger
374 **BX:** Bettmann
375 **TM:** Granger – **TR:** National Gallery of Art – **BR, BL:** Bettmann
376 **TL:** Granger – **ML:** Bettmann – **BX:** JL International – **BL:** JL International
377 **TR:** Granger – **MR:** Bettmann – **BR:** JL International – **BL:** National Archives
378 **TL:** Vicksburg – **TY:** JL International – **BL:** Granger
379 **MY, MR, TL:** Granger – **BL, BM, BR:** Bettmann
380 **TL, TR, BR:** Granger – **BL:** Bettmann
381 **TR:** Bettmann – **BR:** Ferris
382 **TR, BR:** Granger – **BX:** JL International
383 **TL, BL:** Bettmann – **BR:** Joslyn Art Museum
384 **ML, TR:** Bettmann – **BR:** Granger
385 **TL:** Granger – **MR, BL:** Bettmann
386 **TL, ML, BL:** Bettmann – **TR:** JL International
387 All pictures from Bettmann
388 **TL, BY:** Granger – **MX:** Ferris – **BR:** Bettmann
389 **TR, MR:** JL International – **MR** – **MM:** Granger – **TL, TX, TY, ML, BL, BX, BY, BR:** National Archives
390 All pictures from Bettmann
391 **TT:** Appomattox
392 **ML:** JL International – **TL, TX, BL, BR:** Bettmann
393 All pictures from Bettmann
394 **TL:** Granger – **BL, BR:** JL International
395 **MX:** National Archives – **BM:** Granger
396 **TL:** National Archives – **TR, BR:** Granger – **BL:** Metropolitan
397 **TM:** National Gallery of Art – **BL:** Bettmann – **BR:** NMAA, Smithsonian
398 **TM, MR:** Granger – **BM:** Bettmann
399 **TL, MR:** Granger – **BL:** Bettmann
400 **TL, BL:** Bettmann – **TR:** National Archives
401 **TR:** Bettmann – **BR:** NMAA, Smithsonian
402 All pictures from Granger
403 **BR:** Granger – **TL:** Bettmann
404 **TL, MM:** Granger – **BR:** Bettmann
405 All pictures from Bettmann
406 **TM, BM:** Granger – **TR:** Bettmann
407 **TL, TR:** Granger – **BM:** National Archives
408 **TL, TR:** Bettmann – **BL:** JL International – **MM:** Granger – **BR:** Cincinnati Art Museum
409 **TR:** Granger – **BR:** NMAA, Smithsonian
410 **TM, MM:** Bettmann – **BM:** Granger
411 **ML:** Bettmann – **RR:** Granger
412 **TL, BY:** Granger – **BL:** Bettmann
413, 414 All pictures from Granger
415 **TL, BR:** Granger – **BL:** National Gallery of Art
416, 417 All pictures from Granger
418 **TM:** Granger – **BL:** UPI/Bettmann – **BY:** Bettmann
419 **TM, BL:** Granger – **BR:** Bettmann
420 **TM:** Ferris – **BX:** National Gallery of Art – **BY:** Bettmann
421 **TR:** Bettmann – **BL, BR:** Granger
422 **TR, ML, MX, BL:** Granger – **BR:** Bettmann
423 **BR:** Bettmann
424 **TX, BM:** Bettmann – **BR:** Granger
425 **TR, TL:** Bettmann – **BL, BR:** Granger
426 **TX:** Bettmann – **MM, BR:** Granger
427 **TL, TX, TR, BR:** Granger – **BL:** Bettmann
428 **TL, BR:** Bettmann – **BL:** Granger
429 **TX, TR:** Granger – **BR:** Bettmann
430 **TL, TY:** Bettmann – **BL:** Granger
431 **TR:** Bettmann – **TL:** National Archives – **BR:** Library of Congress
432 **TM:** Bettmann – **BM:** Granger
433 **TL, ML, BL:** Granger – **MX:** Bettmann – **BR:** Museum of American Folk Art
434 **TL, BL:** Granger – **ML:** National Archives – **MX:** Bettmann
435 **TL, BR:** Granger – **TR:** Bettmann
436 **TY:** Granger – **BR:** JL International
437 **TM, MR:** Granger – **BM:** Eastman
438 **BL:** National Archives – **TL:** Granger
439 **TR:** Bettmann – **BR, BL:** Granger
440 **SP:** Eastman
442 **TY:** AMNH, Smithsonian – **MR, MX, BY:** Granger
443 **TX:** Granger – **BM:** Museum of American Folk Art
444 **TM:** National Park Service – **BR:** Granger
445 **TR:** Granger – **MR:** Bettmann – **BR:** JL International
446 All pictures from National Gallery of Art
447 **TL:** Bettmann – **TY, TR, MR, BR:** Granger
448 **TL, BL:** Granger – **TR, BR:** Bettmann
449 **TM:** Granger – **MR:** Bettmann – **BM:** National Gallery of Art
450 All pictures from Granger
451 **TM:** Bettmann – **BL, BR:** Granger
452 **TX, BY:** Bettmann – **TY:** Granger
453 **BR:** Tom Bean – **TL:** National Archives
454 **TX, TR:** Bettmann – **BR:** NMAA, Smithsonian
455 **TX, MY:** Bettmann – **BR:** Granger
456 **TL, TR:** Granger – **BR, BL:** Bettmann
457 **TL, TR, MR, BL, BR:** Bettmann – **ML:** Granger
458 All pictures from Granger
459 **TR:** Bettmann – **BX, BR:** Granger
460 **TM:** Am. Railroads – **BM:** Paramount
461, 462 All pictures from Granger
463 **TR, BR:** Bettmann – **ML:** Granger
464 **TX:** Granger – **BL, BR:** Bettmann
465 **TX, BX:** Granger – **BR:** Chicago Historical Society
466 **TX:** Bettmann – **BM:** Granger
467 **TM, BY:** Bettmann – **BL:** NMAA, Smithsonian – **BR:** Granger – **BX:** JL International
468 **TR:** Bettmann – **TL, BL:** Granger
469 **TR:** Bettmann – **BR, BL:** Granger
470 All pictures from Granger
471 **TR:** Bettmann – **BR, BL:** Granger
472 **TL:** Coca-Cola – **BL:** Granger – **BR:** National Archives
473 **BR:** Statue of Liberty
474 All pictures from Granger
475 **BR:** National Archives – **TX:** Granger
476 **BL:** Granger
477 **TR:** Bettmann – **BR:** NYPL – **TL, BL:** Granger
478 **TX:** Granger – **TY, MM:** Bettmann
479 **TL, BR:** Granger – **TR:** UPI/Bettmann
480, 481 All pictures from Granger
482 All pictures from Bettmann
483 **TR:** Granger – **BR:** Bettmann
484 **TX:** Granger – **MY:** National Archives – **BR:** Bettmann
485 **TL, TR:** Granger – **BL:** Bettmann – **BR:** National Gallery of Art
486 **TX, BL:** Granger – **MY, BR:** Bettmann
487 **TR, MY, BL:** Granger – **MR:** National Archives – **BR:** Bettmann
488 **TL:** Granger – **TY, TR, ML, MX, BR:** National Archives – **BL:** Bettmann
489 **TY, TR, BR:** Granger – **TL, TX, BL, MR:** National Archives
490 **TY, MR:** Granger – **BM:** National Park Service
491 **TL, BR, TR:** Granger – **BL:** CHS
492 **BL:** Granger – **BR:** Bettmann
493 **TR, BL:** Granger – **BR:** Bettmann
494 **TX:** Bettmann – **TR, BM:** Granger
495 **MM, TR, BR:** Granger – **TL:** Levi Strauss & Co. – **BL, BY, BX:** Bettmann
496 **TL, TR:** Granger – **ML:** Bettmann
497 **TL, TR:** Bettmann – **BY:** NMAA, Smithsonian – **BR:** Granger
498 All pictures from Granger
499 **TR:** Bettmann – **TL:** Granger – **BM:** National Gallery of Art
500 All pictures from Granger
501 **TX:** Granger – **MY, MM:** Bettmann – **BR:** NMAA, Smithsonian
502 **TM:** Bettmann – **BM, BR:** Granger
503 to 505 All pictures from Granger
506 **TY:** National Archives – **MX, MR:** Granger – **BY:** Bettmann
507 All pictures from Granger
508 **TL, TR:** Granger – **BR:** National Gallery of Art – **BL:** NMAA, Smithsonian
509 **MY:** Granger – **MR, BR:** Bettmann
510 **MM, TR:** Granger – **BR:** Bettmann
511 All pictures from Granger
512 **TX:** Bettmann – **TY, BL:** Granger
513 **TL:** Library of Congress – **BR, BL:** Granger
514 **TR:** Bettmann – **BR:** Can. Railways
515 All pictures from Granger
516 **TL:** Bettmann – **ML:** National Archives – **BL:** Granger
517 **TL, TR, BR:** Granger – **ML, MR, BL, BY:** National Archives
518 **TM:** Granger – **MM, BR:** Bettmann
519 **TR:** Granger – **BR, ML:** Bettmann
520 **TX, BM:** Granger – **TY, MM:** Bettmann
521 **TL, TR:** Bettmann – **BR:** Granger
522 **TL, TX, ML:** Bettmann – **BY:** Granger
523 **TM:** Houston Museum of Fine Art – **BL:** Bettmann – **BR:** JL International
524 All pictures from Bettmann
525 **TL, TR:** Granger – **BL:** Sears – **BY, BR, BX:** Bettmann
526 **TL, BR:** Bettmann – **BL:** Granger
527 All pictures from Bettmann
528 **TM:** Bettmann – **BM:** Granger
529 **TL, BL, TR:** Granger – **BR:** Bettmann
530 All pictures from Bettmann
531 **TM:** Granger – **BL:** General Dynamics Corporation – **BR:** JL International
532 **TX, TR:** Bettmann – **BM:** Granger
533 **BR:** Bettmann – **BL:** Gillette
534 **TL:** Granger – **MY:** Bettmann – **BR:** Houston Museum of Fine Art
535 **TL:** Bettmann – **TR, BX:** Granger – **BY:** National Archives
536 **TY:** Granger – **BR:** Georgia O'Keefe, Estate of
537 **TY:** Bettmann – **BR:** Granger
538 All pictures from Bettmann
539 **TR:** UPI/Bettmann – **BL:** Granger – **BR:** Bettmann
540 **TL:** Granger – **BL:** Bettmann – **BR:** National Gallery of Art
541 **TR:** Granger – **BL:** Bettmann
542 **TM:** Bettmann – **BM:** Granger
543 **TR, BR:** Granger – **BL:** Bettmann
544 **BL:** Bettmann
545 **TM, BR:** Granger – **BL:** National Gallery of Art
546 All pictures from Bettmann
547 **TL:** Bettmann – **BR:** Granger
548 **TR:** Granger – **BL:** Georgia O'Keefe, Estate of
549 **BR:** NMAA, Smithsonian – **TR:** Kirshon
550 **BM:** Bettmann – **TX, MR:** UPI/Bettmann
551 All pictures from Granger
552 All pictures from Bettmann
553 **TR, TL:** Granger – **BX:** Marshall Fields
554 **MM:** Granger – **BR:** JL International
555 **ML:** Maytag Corporation – **TR:** Granger – **BR:** Cleveland Museum of Art
556 **TX, BM:** Granger – **TY:** Bettmann
557 **TR:** Granger – **BR:** Bettmann
558 **BM:** National Archives
559 **TM:** U.S. Department of the Interior – **BM:** Granger
560 **MR, BR:** Bettmann – **ML:** Granger – **BL:** U.S. Postal Service
561 **TR:** Becker – **BR, BL:** Granger
562 **TM:** Bettmann – **BM:** Granger
563 **TM, BR:** Granger – **BL:** Bettmann
564 **TL:** JL International – **BL:** Eastman – **BR:** The Creators
565 **TL, BL:** Bettmann – **MR:** Office of Alumni Relations, University of Chicago – **BX, BR:** National Archives
566 **BR:** NMAA, Smithsonian
567 **BL, TR:** Granger – **BR:** Bettmann – **TL:** Architect of the Capital
568 **TM, BR:** Bettmann – **BL:** Granger
569 **TR, BL:** Bettmann – **BR:** Granger
570 **BM:** Bettmann
571 **TR, TL:** Bettmann – **BR:** National Gallery of Art – **BL:** Wrigley's Company
572 **TL:** Bettmann – **TR, BR:** Granger – **BL:** JL International

Picture credits

573 **BR:** NYHS
574 **TL:** Mary Evans – **BL:** Bettmann – **BR:** Granger
575 **TL:** Bettmann – **BR:** Granger
576 **TR:** Bettmann – **BL:** Granger
577 **TR, BR:** Bettmann – **BL:** JL International
578 **TM:** JWT Archives
579 **TM:** Bettmann – **BM:** Granger
580 **TM, BL:** Bettmann – **BR:** Granger
581 **TL:** Granger – **BR:** Bettmann
582 **TR:** Granger
583 All pictures from Bettmann
584 **TL, MM:** Bettmann – **BL:** NMAA, Smithsonian
585 **TL:** Bettmann – **BR:** Eastman – **BL:** Granger
586 **TM:** NYPL – **BR:** Granger
587 **TR:** Ferris – **BR:** Bettmann
588 **TL:** Bettmann – **BL, BX, BY, BR:** Granger
589 All pictures from Granger
590 **TX:** Bettmann – **MM:** UPI/Bettmann
591 **TL:** National Gallery of Art – **BR:** Bettmann
592 **TL, BL:** Granger – **TR:** Bettmann
593 **TR, BL:** Bettmann – **BR:** Granger
594 **TM:** Olson, Dr. Richard F. – **TR, ML, MR:** Bettmann – **MM, BL, BR, TL:** Granger – **BM:** UPI/Bettmann
595 **TR:** Bettmann – **MM:** JL International – **MR, ML:** Granger – **BL, BR, TL:** National Archives
596 **FP:** Granger
598 **TM:** Bettmann – **BX:** Granger
599 All pictures from Bettmann
600 All pictures from Granger
601 **TR:** UPI/Bettmann – **MY, MR:** Bettmann
602 All pictures from Granger
603 All pictures from Bettmann
604 **TL:** Bettmann – **BR:** Granger – **BL:** NYPL
605 **TR, BR:** Granger – **BL:** Bettmann
606 All pictures from Bettmann
607 **TR:** National Gallery of Art – **BL, BR:** Bettmann
608 **TM:** Granger – **BX:** Modern Art
609 **TL, BL:** Bettmann – **BR:** Bettmann
610 **TL, BR:** Bettmann – **BL:** Granger
611 **BR:** Granger
612 **TY, TR:** Bettmann – **BM:** Granger
613 **TX:** Granger – **MR, BR:** Bettmann
614 **TL, BX:** Granger – **BL, TR:** Bettmann
615 All pictures from Bettmann
616 **TY:** Migdail-Smith, Shari – **BX:** JL International – **BR:** Granger
617 **TM, ML:** UPI/Bettmann – **BX, BR:** Granger
618 **TR:** Bettmann – **BL, BR:** Granger
619 **BR:** Granger
620 **TL:** Granger – **TR, BR, MX:** Bettmann – **BL:** JL International
621 All pictures from Bettmann
622 **TL, MR:** Granger – **TX, BL:** Bettmann – **BX:** Houston Museum of Fine Art
623 **TR, BL:** UPI/Bettmann – **TL:** Bettmann – **BR:** Rivoli Theater, New York
624 **TY:** UPI/Bettmann – **BM:** NMAA, Smithsonian
625 **TL, BL:** Granger – **TR:** Bettmann – **BR:** UPI/Bettmann
626 **TL, TR:** Granger – **BL:** Bettmann – **BR:** General Dynamics Corporation
627 **TX:** JL International – **TR, BR:** Granger
628 **TL, BR:** Granger – **TR:** Bettmann – **BL:** New Yorker Magazine, Inc.
629 **TY, TR, MR:** Bettmann – **ML:** UPI/Bettmann – **BR:** National Gallery of Art
630 **TL, TR, BR:** Granger – **BL:** Bettmann
631 All pictures from Granger
632 **TL, BL, BX:** Granger – **TR:** Bettmann – **BY:** National Gallery of Art – **BR:** NMAA, Smithsonian
633 **TL, TR, BR:** Granger – **TM:** Bettmann – **BL:** UPI/Bettmann
634 **BM:** Bettmann – **BR:** JL International
635 All pictures from Granger
636 **TL, BL:** Granger – **TR:** UPI/Bettmann – **BR:** National Archives
637 All pictures from Granger
638 **TM:** Bettmann – **BM:** JL International
639 **TR, TL, BR:** Granger – **MX:** Bettmann
640 **TL, TX, BM, BL, BR:** Granger – **TR:** National Archives – **ML, MX, MR, MY:** Bettmann
641 **TL:** National Gallery of Art – **TY:** Bettmann – **TR, ML, MR, BR:** Granger – **MM:** DeSomma – **BL:** Cincinnati Art Museum – **BM:** National Archives
642 **TM:** Bettmann – **BY:** Granger
643 **TX:** Granger – **BR:** Bettmann – **BL:** NMAA, Smithsonian
644 **MM:** Bettmann – **TL:** JL International – **BR:** Granger
645 **TR:** UPI/Bettmann – **BY, BR:** Granger
646 **TX:** Granger – **BR:** Equitable Life
647 **TM:** JL International – **BR:** Granger – **BL:** Bourke-White, Time-Life
648 All pictures from Bettmann
649 **TX:** Bettmann – **BL, BR:** Granger
650 **TM:** UPI/Bettmann – **BM:** Metropolitan
651 **BR:** Bettmann
652 **TR, BR:** Bettmann – **BL:** NMAA, Smithsonian
653 All pictures from Granger
654 **TY:** Bettmann – **BM:** Granger
655 **TR:** Bettmann – **BR:** National Archives – **TL, BL:** Granger
656 **TM, BL:** Bettmann – **BR:** National Gallery of Art
657 All pictures from Granger
658 **TM:** UPI/Bettmann
659 **TR:** Bettmann – **BR:** Teich
660 All pictures from Bettmann
661 **TR, BM:** Bettmann – **TL:** UPI/Bettmann – **BR:** Granger
662 All pictures from Bettmann
663 **TL, TX, TR:** Bettmann – **BL, BR:** NMAA, Smithsonian
664 **TR:** UPI/Bettmann – **BL:** NMAA, Smithsonian
665 **TR, TL, BR:** Granger – **BL:** Bettmann
666 All pictures from Bettmann
667 **ML:** Bettmann – **TR:** UPI/Bettmann – **BR:** Library of Congress
668 **TR:** Library of Congress – **BR:** UPI/Bettmann – **BL:** Granger
669 **TR, BL:** Granger – **BR:** NMAA, Smithsonian
670 **TR:** Bettmann – **BM:** NMAA, Smithsonian – **BR:** Granger
671 **BM:** Bettmann
672 **TR, BR:** Bettmann – **BY, TL:** UPI/Bettmann
673 **TX:** Bettmann – **TR, BR:** Granger – **BL:** JL International
674 **TM:** Bettmann – **BM:** Bourke-White, Time-Life
675 **TL:** UPI/Bettmann – **BR:** Bettmann
676 **TL:** Granger – **TR, BX, BY, BR:** Bettmann – **BL:** UPI/Bettmann
677 **ML, BL:** UPI/Bettmann – **BR:** Bettmann
678 **TL, BL, BR:** Bettmann – **TR:** Granger
679 All pictures from Granger
680 **TY:** Bettmann – **BM:** Cinemateque
681 **TL, TR:** Bettmann – **BR:** NMAA, Smithsonian
682 **TL:** UPI/Bettmann – **BL:** March of Dimes Birth Defects Foundation – **BR:** Bettmann
683 **TR, TL:** Bettmann – **BY, BR:** Granger
684 **MR:** UPI/Bettmann – **BM:** National Gallery of Art
685 All pictures from Bettmann
686 **TL:** Granger – **ML:** UPI/Bettmann – **TR:** Bettmann
687 **TX, TR, MR:** Granger – **BR:** Bettmann
688 **TL:** Granger – **ML:** NMAA, Smithsonian – **MX, MR, TR:** National Archives – **BL:** National Portrait Gallery, Smithsonian – **BR:** UPI/Bettmann
689 **TL:** Library of Congress – **TR:** National Archives – **MX, BR:** Granger – **MR, ML:** Bettmann – **BL:** Am. Railroads
690 All pictures from NMAA, Smithsonian
691 **TR:** UPI/Bettmann – **BR:** Granger
692 **TM:** Bettmann
693 **TR:** NMAA, Smithsonian – **BR:** Granger
694 **BM:** Granger
695 **TR:** Bettmann – **BR:** National Gallery of Art
696 **TR:** UPI/Bettmann – **BL:** NMAA, Smithsonian – **BR:** Bettmann
697 All pictures from Granger
698 **T:** UPI/Bettmann
699 **TR, BY, BR:** Granger – **MR:** Bettmann
700 **TR, BX, BR:** Bettmann – **BY:** UPI/Bettmann
701 **TR:** JL International – **BR:** UPI/Bettmann
702 **TL:** Bettmann – **BL:** JL International
703 **TL:** UPI/Bettmann – **BL, MR:** Bettmann
704 **TL, ML, TR:** Bettmann – **BL:** JL International
705 **TR:** Granger – **BY, BR, TL, BL:** Bettmann
706 **TL:** Bettmann – **BL, BR:** Granger
707 **TY, TR:** Bettmann – **BL, BR:** Granger
708 All pictures from Bettmann
709 **TX, TR:** UPI/Bettmann – **BY, BR:** Bettmann
710 **TR, BL:** Bettmann – **BR:** Granger
711 **TY:** JL International – **TR, MR:** Bettmann – **BR:** NMAA, Smithsonian
712 **TL:** Bettmann – **ML:** UPI/Bettmann
713 **TM:** UPI/Bettmann – **BL, BR:** Bettmann
714 **TY:** UPI/Bettmann – **BM:** Granger
715 **TR, BL, BR:** Bettmann – **MR:** UPI/Bettmann
716 **TL, ML, BL:** Granger – **BR:** JL International
717 **TR, MR:** Bettmann – **BR:** Granger
718 **TM, MM:** Bettmann – **BL:** JL International
719 **TM, BR:** Bettmann – **MM:** UPI/Bettmann
720 **BX, BR, TL, TX, TR, ML, MY, BL:** Bettmann – **MR:** UPI/Bettmann
721 **TL, BL:** Granger – **TR, MR:** Bettmann – **BM:** National Archives – **BR, ML:** UPI/Bettmann
722 **TM:** UPI/Bettmann – **BX:** Bettmann
723 **TR, MR, BL:** UPI/Bettmann – **TL:** Bettmann
724 **TL, BX:** Bettmann – **ML, BL:** UPI/Bettmann
725 **TL:** Bettmann – **TR, BR:** Granger – **BL:** UPI/Bettmann
726 **TM:** Bettmann – **BL, BR:** Granger
727 **TR, MR, BR:** Bettmann – **BL:** JL International
728 **TL:** Bettmann – **TR:** UPI/Bettmann – **BL:** NMAA, Smithsonian
729 **TL:** Bettmann – **TR, BR:** UPI/Bettmann
730 **FP:** America's Team–We're No. 1 by Alan Bean
732 All pictures from NMAA, Smithsonian
733 **TM:** UPI/Bettmann – **BL:** Bettmann – **BR:** Granger
734 **TX:** Bettmann – **BL:** UPI/Bettmann
735 **TR:** Granger – **BR:** UPI/Bettmann – **BL:** Bettmann
736 **TR:** UPI/Bettmann – **BX:** NMAA, Smithsonian
737 All pictures from UPI/Bettmann
738 **TM:** UPI/Bettmann – **BR:** Bettmann – **BL:** Granger
739 **TM:** JL International – **BR:** Granger – **BL:** UPI/Bettmann
740 **TM, MR:** Bettmann – **BM:** UPI/Bettmann
741 **TX:** UPI/Bettmann – **TR, BR:** Bettmann
742 **TL:** Bettmann – **BM:** UPI/Bettmann
743 **TL:** UPI/Bettmann – **TR:** Bettmann – **BR:** Granger
744 **TY:** Bettmann – **BM:** High Museum of Art, Atlanta
745 **TM:** Bettmann – **BM:** UPI/Bettmann
746 **BR:** Granger – **TL:** Bettmann
747 **TR:** UPI/Bettmann – **BR:** Bettmann
748 All pictures from UPI/Bettmann
749 **TR:** Bettmann – **MR:** UPI/Bettmann – **BL:** NMAA, Smithsonian
750 **TL:** UPI/Bettmann – **ML, BL:** Bettmann
751 All pictures from UPI/Bettmann
752 **TL, TR, BR:** Bettmann – **BL:** UPI/Bettmann
753 **TY, MR, BR:** Bettmann – **TR:** Granger – **MY:** UPI/Bettmann
754 **TM:** UPI/Bettmann – **MM:** Granger
755 **TX:** UPI/Bettmann – **MR, BR:** Bettmann
756 All pictures from UPI/Bettmann
757 **TR:** UPI/Bettmann – **TL, BR:** Bettmann – **BL:** JL International
758 **TR:** Bettmann – **BR:** Granger
759 **ML, BL:** Bettmann – **BR:** Smithsonian
760 **TL:** Bettmann – **TR:** UPI/Bettmann – **BR:** Granger
761 All pictures from UPI/Bettmann
762 **TM:** Bettmann – **BM:** UPI/Bettmann
763 **TR, BL:** UPI/Bettmann – **TL:** Granger – **BR:** NMAA, Smithsonian
764 **TX, MR:** UPI/Bettmann – **BM:** Bettmann
765 **TR:** UPI/Bettmann – **BR:** Bettmann
766 **TM:** UPI/Bettmann – **BR:** National Archives – **BL:** Library of Congress
767 All pictures from Bettmann
768 **TR:** UPI/Bettmann – **BM:** NMAA, Smithsonian
769 **TM:** Granger – **BL:** UPI/Bettmann – **BR:** Bettmann
770 **TM:** UPI/Bettmann – **ML, MR:** Granger – **BM:** NMAA, Smithsonian
771 **TR:** Bettmann – **BR:** Granger
772 All pictures from UPI/Bettmann
773 **TR, TL:** UPI/Bettmann – **BR:** Bettmann
774 **TR:** UPI/Bettmann – **BX:** JL International
775 **TR, BR:** UPI/Bettmann – **BL:** Granger
776 **TL, ML:** UPI/Bettmann – **BL:** National Archives
777 **TR, BR:** UPI/Bettmann – **BY:** Granger
778 **TM, BR:** UPI/Bettmann – **BL:** National Archives
779 **TR:** UPI/Bettmann – **BR:** Bettmann
780 **TX, TR:** UPI/Bettmann – **BX:** Bettmann
781 All pictures from Bettmann
782 **TL:** Bettmann – **TR, BR, BL:** UPI/Bettmann
783 **TL:** UPI/Bettmann – **BY, BR, BL, BX:** Bettmann
784 **TL, TR, TX, ML, BM:** UPI/Bettmann – **MR:** Bettmann – **BL:** Mattel Toys – **BR:** Jeanette Hall
785 **TL:** Bettmann – **TR:** Tonka Corporation – **ML, MR:** Granger – **BL:** Cincinnati Art Museum – **BX, BR, BY:** UPI/Bettmann
786 **TR, BR:** UPI/Bettmann – **BX:** Bettmann
787 **TR:** UPI/Bettmann – **BR:** NMAA, Smithsonian
788 **TL, BR:** UPI/Bettmann – **BL:** NMAA, Smithsonian
789 **TM:** UPI/Bettmann – **BR:** Granger – **BL:** NMAA, Smithsonian
790 **TM, MM:** UPI/Bettmann – **BR:** NMAA, Smithsonian
791 **TR, BR:** UPI/Bettmann – **BY:** Bettmann
792 All pictures from UPI/Bettmann
793 **TR, BR:** UPI/Bettmann – **TL:** Bettmann – **BL:** Granger
794, 795 All pictures from UPI/Bettmann
796 **TL:** Granger – **MR, BL:** UPI/Bettmann
797 All pictures from UPI/Bettmann
798 **TM:** National Archives – **BR:** UPI/Bettmann
799, 800, 801 All pictures from UPI/Bettmann
802 **TM:** UPI/Bettmann – **BX:** Granger
803 **TL, TR:** UPI/Bettmann – **BR:** Granger
804 **TM, BL:** UPI/Bettmann – **BR:** NMAA, Smithsonian
805, 806, 807 All pictures from UPI/Bettmann
808 **TL:** Granger – **BL, BR:** UPI/Bettmann – **BM:** Bettmann
809, 810, 811, 812 All pictures from UPI/Bettmann
813 **TM:** Bettmann – **BR:** Granger
814, 815, 816 All pictures from UPI/Bettmann
817 **TM:** UPI/Bettmann – **BM:** National Gallery of Art
818 to 825 All pictures from UPI/Bettmann
826 **TL, TX:** UPI/Bettmann – **BL:** NMAA, Smithsonian
827 **TL:** Keystone – **BL:** UPI/Bettmann – **BR:** NMAA, Smithsonian
828 **BR, TL, MR:** Bettmann – **TR, ML, BL, BX:** UPI/Bettmann
829 **TL:** Granger – **TX:** Bettmann – **TR:** Wide World Photos – **ML, MY, MR, BR, BL:** UPI/Bettmann
830 **TM:** UPI/Bettmann
831 to 842 All pictures from UPI/Bettmann
843 **TM:** UPI/Bettmann – **BM:** National Park Service
844, 845 All pictures from UPI/Bettmann
846 **TM:** UPI/Bettmann – **BM:** National Gallery of Art
847 **TL, TR, MM, BL:** UPI/Bettmann – **BR:** Granger
848 All pictures from UPI/Bettmann
849 **TR:** Kirshon – **BL:** UPI/Bettmann – **BR:** Bettmann
850 **TM:** National Gallery of Art
851 All pictures from National Park Service
852 to 855 All pictures from UPI/Bettmann
856 **TM:** Sipa – **BM:** UPI/Bettmann
857 **TM, BL:** UPI/Bettmann – **BR:** JL International
858, 859 All pictures from UPI/Bettmann
860 **TX, TY, BL:** UPI/Bettmann – **BR:** Bettmann
861 to 864 All pictures from UPI/Bettmann
865 **TM:** Sipa – **MM:** UPI/Bettmann
866 All pictures from UPI/Bettmann
867 **TM:** Sipa – **BX, BY:** UPI/Bettmann
868 to 871 All pictures from UPI/Bettmann
872 **MR, TL:** UPI/Bettmann – **BL:** National Park Service
873 **TR:** UPI/Bettmann – **BM:** International Business Machines
874, 875, 876 All pictures from UPI/Bettmann
877 **TR, BR:** UPI/Bettmann – **BL:** Walt Disney
878 All pictures from UPI/Bettmann
879 **TL:** Sipa – **BR:** UPI/Bettmann
880 to 885 All pictures from UPI/Bettmann
886 **BM:** Bettmann
887 to 890 All pictures from UPI/Bettmann
891 **TM, BY:** Sipa – **BX:** Reuters/Bettmann
892 All pictures from UPI/Bettmann
893 **TR, BL:** UPI/Bettmann – **BR:** Granger
894 **TM, MR:** Sipa – **BM:** UPI/Bettmann
895 All pictures from UPI/Bettmann
896 **TL:** UPI/Bettmann – **BR:** Sipa – **BL:** Reuters/Bettmann
897 **TM, BR:** Reuters/Bettmann – **BL:** Sipa
898 **TX:** Sipa – **BM:** Bettmann
899 **TM:** Reuters/Bettmann
900 **TL, BR:** Sipa – **TR:** UPI/Bettmann – **BL:** Kirshon
901 **TR:** Sipa – **BR:** JL International
902 **TL:** Orth/Sipa Press – **TR:** Savino/Sipa Press – **BR:** Sobol/Sipa Press – **BL:** Trippett/Sipa Press
903 **BR:** Suu/Joffet/Sipa Press – **ML:** Trippett/Sipa Press – **TR:** US Navy/Sipa Press
904 **BL:** Allsport – **TL:** Bermann/Sipa Press – **MR:** Bob McNelly/Sipa Press – **BR:** Sipa Press
905 **BR:** DOD/Sipa Press – **M:** Joffet/Sipa Press – **TR:** Lehr/Sipa Press – **TL:** Rex Features
906 **BL:** Rex Features – **TL:** Sipa Press – **TR:** Sunshine/Sipa Press – **BR:** Win McNamee/Sipa Sport
907 **TR:** New York Post – **BR:** Popperfoto – **TL:** Robert Polhill/Sipa Press – **BL:** Savino/Sipa Press
908 **TM:** Gromik/Sipa Sport – **BL:** Savino/Sipa Press – **TL:** Topham Associated Press – **BR:** Topham Picture Library
909 **MR:** Emerson/Maras/Sipa Press – **TL:** Sipa Press – **BL:** Witt/Sipa Press
910 **TM:** Halley/Sipa Press – **BM:** Sipa Press – **M:** Witt/Sipa Press
911 **BR:** Joffrey/Aslan/Barthélemy/Sipa Press – **BL:** Morris/Sipa Press – **TR:** Press Association/Topham – **TL:** Rex Features
912 **BL:** Chesnot/Sipa Press – **BR:** Colin/Sipa Sport – **M:** Rex Features – **TL:** Rex Features – **TR:** Rex Features
913 **TR:** Rex Features – **BR:** Savino/Sipa Press – **BL:** Sipa Press – **ML:** Sipa Press – **TL:** Sipa Press
914 **BL:** B. Ward/San Francisco Chronicle/Sipa Press – **TL:** Popperfoto – **TM:** Popperfoto – **TR:** Rex Features
915 **ML:** Associated Press – **TR:** Joe Rimkus/Miami Herald – **MR:** Rex Features – **TL:** Sipa Sport
916 **TL:** Akihiro Mishimura/Sipa Press – **BR:** Orton/Mil. Jour/Sipa Press – **BL:** Star Tribune/Sipa Press
917 **ML:** Boulat/Sipa Press – **BR:** Courtesy of Mark Pyle – **BL:** Nina Bermann/Sipa Press – **TM:** Nina Bermann/Sipa Press
918 **BL:** Klein/Sipa Sport – **TL:** Lee Celano/Sipa Press – **BR:** Rex Features/Sipa Press
919 **TL:** Christopher Brown/Sipa Press – **BR:** Jean-Michel Psaila/Sport+/Sipa Sport – **TR:** Sobol/Sipa Press – **BL:** Malanca/Sipa Press
920 **T:** Bob Strong/Sipa Press – **M, BR:** John Mantel/Sipa Press – **BL:** Luc Delahaye/Sipa Press
921 **T:** Ft Worth Star Telegraph/Sipa Press – **ML, BL:** Sipa Press – **BR:** Schlabowske/Sipa Press – **MR:** Groshong/Sipa Press
922 **TR:** Mac Bride/Sipa Press – **TL:** Chavez/Sipa Press - - **BR:** Abramson/Sipa Press – **BL:** Stanley/Denver Post/Sipa Press
923 **TM:** Villard/Sipa Press – **BL:** Sunshine/Sipa Press – **BX:** Boutefeux/Sipa Press – **BY:** Mantel/Sipa Press – **BR:** Rudling/Sipa Press
924 **TM:** Taylor/Mooney/Sipa Press – **ML, MR:** Razliki/Sipa Press – **BM:** Sipa Press
925 **TL:** Tripett/Sipa Press – **TR:** Hulton Deutsch/Sipa Press – **BL:** Boulat/Sipa Press
926 **TR:** Hartog/The Outlook/Sipa Press – **ML:** Walsh/Action Images/Sipa Press – **BL:** Nivière/Sichov/Sipa Press – **BR:** Strong/Sipa Press
927 **MR:** Tripett/Sipa Press – **BR:** Rex/Sipa Press – **BL:** Sipa Press
928 **TM:** Tripett/Sipa Press – **BL:** RPN/Sipa Press – **BR:** NASA/Sipa Press – **M:** Sipa Press
929 **TR:** Lash/Don King Productions/Sipa Press – **TL:** Smith/Sipa Press – **BR:** Edmund Evening News/Sipa Press – **BL:** Stevens/Sipa Press
930-931 JL International
932 Bettmann; NMAA, Smithsonian; Granger; National Gallery of Art; Bettmann; Granger; Architect of the Capital; Granger
933 Library of Congress/Sipa Press; Bettmann; Granger; Granger; Granger; Granger; Bettmann; Granger
934 Bettmann, JL International, Granger, Granger, Bettmann, Granger, Library of Congress/Sipa Press, Library of Congress/Sipa Press
935 Granger; Granger; Bettmann; Library of Congress/Sipa Press; Bettmann; Granger; Granger; UPI/Bettmann
936 Bettmann; Sipa Press, Paris; UPI/Bettmann; UPI/Bettmann; Topham Picture Library; UPI/Bettmann; UPI/Bettmann; Bettmann Archive, New York
937 **B:** Abecasis/Sipa Press – **TL:** Bob Strong/Sipa Press
948 JL International (Catherine Jambois)